The American Republic Since 1877

Features and Benefits

Dynamic Instructional Structure

. . . presents a clear and comprehensive coverage of American history.
- Each engaging section introduction includes a Main Idea, Key Terms and Names, a Reading Strategy, Reading Objectives, a Section Theme, a Preview of Events, and an American Story feature. *(see p. 12)*
- The Chapter Summaries offer concise synopses of important chapter topics. *(see p. 38)*
- The Skillbuilders features teach students the skills they need to be successful in their study of history. *(see p. 29)*

A Strong Reading Strand

. . . encourages active reading and learning for students of all reading levels.
- The Reading Skills Handbook provides students with vital strategies to improve their reading comprehension. *(see p. RH1)*
- The American Literature features ask students to analyze poems, biographies, and American fiction. *(see p. 17)*
- Reading Checks help students check their reading comprehension. *(see p. 13)*

Differentiated Instruction

. . . makes *The American Republic Since 1877* accessible to students of all learning levels.
- Differentiated Instruction activities and strategies are designed for students of varying ability levels and learning styles. *(see p. 14)*
- A variety of question types and strategies provide students of differing ability levels and learning styles with a variety of assessment activities that cater to their strengths. *(see p. 16)*

Standardized Test Preparation

. . . gives students the opportunity to practice for state and national exams.
- A Standardized Test Practice question at the end of each chapter provides a variety of forms of standardized test practice, including multiple choice questions, open-ended short response, and open-ended extended response. *(see p. 39)*
- Test-Taking Tips help students learn how to approach test questions successfully. *(see p. 39)*

A Variety of Activities and Features

. . . are essential for student success and to get students excited about history.
- Different Viewpoints features challenge students to interpret opposing views on events in history. *(see p. 113)*
- The Primary Sources Library provides students with examples of sources vital to understanding American history. *(see p. 928)*
- Geography and History features show students how geography has affected key events in American history. *(see p. 36)*

Teacher Resources

. . . provide convenient strategies to help new and experienced teachers.
- Unit and Chapter resources provide background and extension material to help in lesson preparation.
- Reading and Study Skills Foldables help students organize and process key concepts as they read.
- The Active Reading Note-Taking Guide prepares students for assessment using a system based on the Cornell Note-Taking system.
- The Reading Essentials and Study Guide helps reluctant readers understand key concepts.

Technology

. . . provides time-saving software products to help you reduce preparation time and engage students creatively.
- The *American Republic Since 1877* Video Programs offer interesting and diverse content extension.
- *TeacherWorks*™ and *ExamView*® *Assessment Suite* make lesson preparation and assessment easier.
- *StudentWorks*™ includes an electronic version of the Student Edition, along with a full audio read.
- History Online at tarvol2.glencoe.com provides resources and activities designed for your book.
- *Study Central*™ is an Internet homework helper that makes more content, skills practice, and vocabulary development available.
- *Study-to-Go*™ provides content and vocabulary review activities for portable electronic devices.

Improving Active Reading and Study Skills

Dinah Zike's

FOLDABLES™

Foldables are easy-to-make, three-dimensional, interactive graphic organizers that students create out of simple sheets of paper. The Teacher Classroom Resources include *Dinah Zike's High School American History Reading and Study Skills.* This booklet provides you with step-by-step instructions for using Foldables in your classroom. Each Foldable is designed to be used as a study guide for the main ideas and key points presented in a chapter. Foldables can also be used for a more in-depth investigation of a concept, idea, opinion, or event, or people or places studied in a chapter. These unique hands-on tools for study and review were created exclusively for Glencoe by education specialist Dinah Zike.

Why Use Foldables in Social Studies?

Because they:

- organize, display, and arrange information, making it easier for students to grasp social studies concepts, theories, facts, opinions, questions, research, and ideas.

- are student-made study guides that students themselves create as they listen for main ideas, read their textbook, or conduct research.

- provide a multitude of creative formats in which students can present projects, research, interviews, and inquiry-based reports.

- replace teacher-generated writing or photocopied sheets with student-generated print.

- incorporate the use of such skills as comparing and contrasting, recognizing cause-and-effect relationships, and understanding similarities and differences.

- reinforce previously learned vocabulary, concepts, information, generalizations, ideas, and theories, providing students with a strong foundation that they can build upon with new observations, concepts, and knowledge.

- can be used by students or teachers to easily communicate data through graphs, tables, charts, models, and diagrams, including Venn diagrams.

- allow students to make their own journals for recording observations, information, primary and secondary source data, surveys, and so on.

- can be used as alternative assessment tools by teachers to evaluate student progress or by students to evaluate their own progress.

- integrate language arts, the sciences, and mathematics into the study of social studies.

- provide a sense of student ownership or investment in the social studies curriculum.

Teacher Wraparound Edition

The American Republic

Since 1877

Joyce Appleby, Ph.D.

Alan Brinkley, Ph.D.

Albert S. Broussard, Ph.D.

James M. McPherson, Ph.D.

Donald A. Ritchie, Ph.D.

NATIONAL GEOGRAPHIC

 McGraw Hill Glencoe

New York, New York   Columbus, Ohio   Chicago, Illinois   Peoria, Illinois   Woodland Hills, California

Authors

Joyce Appleby, Ph.D., is Professor of History at UCLA. Dr. Appleby's published works include *Inheriting the Revolution: The First Generation of Americans; Capitalism and a New Social Order: The Jeffersonian Vision of the 1790s;* and *Ideology and Economic Thought in Seventeenth-Century England,* which won the Berkshire Prize. She served as president of both the Organization of American Historians and the American Historical Association, and chaired the Council of the Institute of Early American History and Culture at Williamsburg. Dr. Appleby has been elected to the American Philosophical Society and the American Academy of Arts and Sciences, and is a Corresponding Fellow of the British Academy.

Alan Brinkley, Ph.D., is Allan Nevins Professor of American History at Columbia University. His published works include *Voices of Protest: Huey Long, Father Coughlin, and the Great Depression,* which won the 1983 National Book Award; *The End of Reform: New Deal Liberalism in Recession and War; The Unfinished Nation: A Concise History of the American People;* and *Liberalism and its Discontents.* He received the Levenson Memorial Teaching Prize at Harvard University.

Albert S. Broussard, Ph.D., is Professor of History and Graduate Coordinator at Texas A&M University. Before joining the Texas A&M faculty, Dr. Broussard was Assistant Professor of History and Director of the African American Studies Program at Southern Methodist University. Among his publications are the books *Black San Francisco: The Struggle for Racial Equality in the West, 1900–1954* and *African American Odyssey: The Stewarts, 1853–1963.* Dr. Broussard has also served as president of the Oral History Association.

James M. McPherson, Ph.D., is George Henry Davis Professor of American History at Princeton University. Dr. McPherson is the author of 11 books about the Civil War era. These include *Battle Cry of Freedom: The Civil War Era,* for which he won the Pulitzer Prize in 1989, and *For Cause and Comrades: Why Men Fought in the Civil War,* for which he won the 1998 Lincoln Prize. He is a member of many professional historical associations, including the Civil War Preservation Trust.

Donald A. Ritchie, Ph.D., is Associate Historian of the United States Senate Historical Office. Dr. Ritchie received his doctorate in American history from the University of Maryland after service in the U.S. Marine Corps. He has taught American history at various levels, from high school to university. He edits the Historical Series of the Senate Foreign Relations Committee and is the author of several books, including *Doing Oral History, The Oxford Guide to the United States Government,* and *Press Gallery: Congress and the Washington Correspondents,* which received the Organization of American Historians Richard W. Leopold Prize. Dr. Ritchie has served as president of the Oral History Association and as a council member of the American Historical Association.

The National Geographic Society, founded in 1888 for the increase and diffusion of geographic knowledge, is the world's largest nonprofit scientific and educational organization. Since its earliest days, the Society has used sophisticated communication technologies, from color photography to holography, to convey knowledge to its worldwide membership. The School Publishing Division supports the Society's mission by developing innovative educational programs—ranging from traditional print materials to multimedia programs including CD-ROMs, videodiscs, and software. "National Geographic Geography & History," featured in each unit of this textbook, and "National Geographic Moment in Time," featured in chapters 8–29 of this textbook, were designed and developed by the National Geographic Society's School Publishing Division.

About the Cover The background image on the cover shows immigrants on a ship bound for the United States. The smaller images, from left to right, are: immigrants in New York harbor; army recruiting poster; astronaut on the moon; Martin Luther King, Jr.; and firefighters raising the flag amid the ruins of the World Trade Center in New York City.

Glencoe

The **McGraw·Hill** Companies

Send all inquiries to: Glencoe/McGraw-Hill, 8787 Orion Place, Columbus, OH 43240-4027

ISBN-13: 978-0-07-874359-7 (Student Edition)
ISBN-10: 0-07-874359-1 (Student Edition)

ISBN-13: 978-0-07-874360-3 (Teacher Wraparound Edition)
ISBN-10: 0-07-874360-5 (Teacher Wraparound Edition)

Printed in the United States of America.

3 4 5 6 7 8 9 10 027/055 10 09 08 07

Academic Consultants

Richard G. Boehm
Professor of Geography
Southwest Texas State University
San Marcos, Texas

Gloria Contreras
Professor, Department of Teacher Education
and Administration
University of North Texas
Denton, Texas

Frank de Varona
Visiting Associate Professor
Department of Curriculum and Instruction
Florida International University
Miami, Florida

Larry Elowitz
Carl Vinson Professor of Political Science
Georgia College and State University
Milledgeville, Georgia

Susan Hartmann
Professor of American Women's History
The Ohio State University
Columbus, Ohio

Cole C. Kingseed
Professor of Military History
United States Military Academy
at West Point
West Point, New York

David E. Maas
Professor of History
Wheaton College
Wheaton, Illinois

William E. Nelson, Jr.
Research Professor of Black Studies and
Professor of Political Science
The Ohio State University
Columbus, Ohio

Bernard Reich
Professor of Political Science and
International Affairs
George Washington University
Washington, D.C.

Calbert A. Seciwa
Director, American Indian Institute
Arizona State University
Tempe, Arizona

Athan Theoharis
Professor of History
Marquette University
Milwaukee, Wisconsin

Mark Van Ells
Professor of History
Queensborough Community College
New York, New York

Teacher Reviewers

Ann T. Ackerman
Teacher
Nashua High School
Nashua, New Hampshire

Edward Brickner
Social Studies Teacher
Woodbury High School
Prescott, Wisconsin

P. Nathan Collins
Social Studies Teacher
Buffalo Gap High School
Swoope, Virginia

Carmen Crosse
Teacher and Department Head
Socorro High School
Socorro Independent School District
El Paso, Texas

Bruce L. Eddy
Teacher, History and Social Science
Department
Evanston Township High School
Evanston, Illinois

Debra B. Elarbee
Social Studies Teacher and Chairperson
Central High School
Carrollton, Georgia

Bette Gilmore
Campus Instructional Specialist
Killeen Independent School District
Killeen, Texas

George W. Henry, Jr.
History Teacher
Rowland Hall St. Mark's School
Salt Lake City, Utah

Marjorie B. Hollowell
Social Studies Teacher
John A. Holmes High School
Edenton, North Carolina

Pat Jordan
Social Studies Curriculum Consultant
Lubbock ISDR Education Service Center
Region 17
Lubbock, Texas

Merle Knight
Emeritus Social Studies Teacher and
Coordinator of Social Studies
Department
Lewis S. Mills High School
Torrington, Connecticut

Tom Laichas
History Teacher
Crossroads School
Santa Monica, California

Elizabeth Pederson
Teacher
Grand Prairie High School
Grand Prairie Independent School District
Grand Prairie, Texas

Holly C. Sharpe
Secondary Social Studies Coordinator
Plano Independent School District
Plano, Texas

Denny Shillings
Social Studies Teacher
Homewood Flossmoor High School
Flossmoor, Illinois

Julia Ann Stodghill
Social Studies Teacher
Troup County Comprehensive High School
Lagrange, Georgia

Steve Swett
History Teacher
Hingham High School
Hingham, Massachusetts

James Wolfe
History Teacher and Department Chair
Suitland High School
Forrestville, Maryland

Contents

Contents

Contents

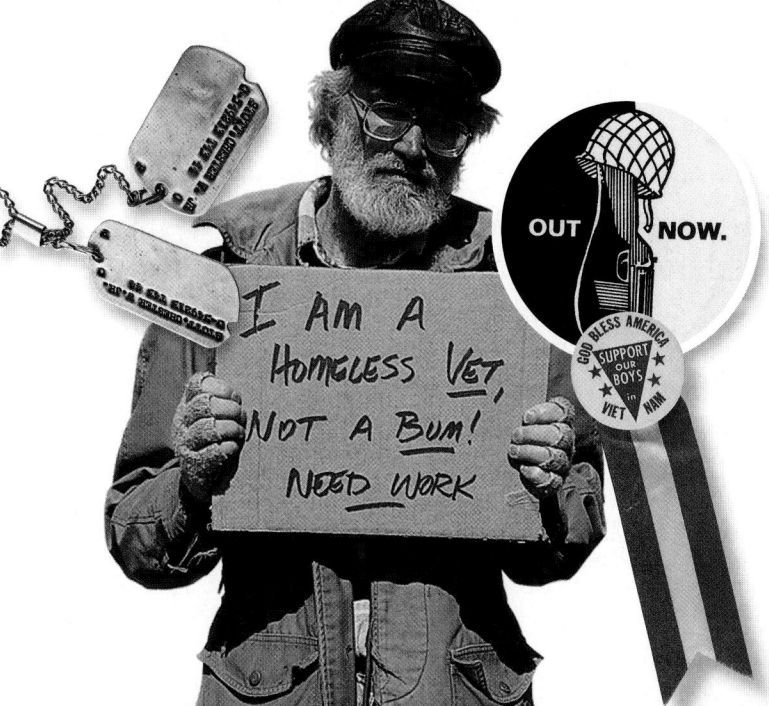

Features

NATIONAL GEOGRAPHIC MOMENT in HISTORY

What Life Was Like...

World History Connection

NATIONAL GEOGRAPHIC Geography & History

World Geography Connection

What If...

Looking Back...

Features

Profiles IN HISTORY

Fact | Fiction | Folklore

Causes and Effects

Primary Source Quotes

A variety of quotations and excerpts throughout the text express the thoughts, feelings, and life experiences of people, past and present.

Primary Source Quotes

Primary Source Quotes

Primary Source Quotes

NATIONAL GEOGRAPHIC Maps

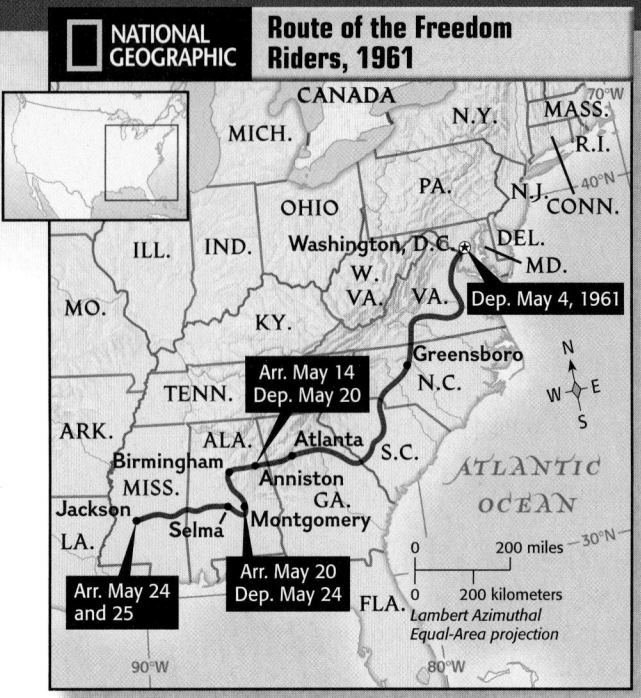

NATIONAL GEOGRAPHIC Route of the Freedom Riders, 1961

CANADA
MICH. N.Y. MASS. 70°W
R.I.
PA. N.J. 40°N
OHIO CONN.
ILL. IND. Washington, D.C. DEL.
W. MD.
MO. VA. VA. Dep. May 4, 1961
KY.
Greensboro N.C.
Arr. May 14 / Dep. May 20
TENN.
ARK. ALA. Atlanta S.C.
Birmingham
MISS. Anniston GA.
Jackson Montgomery
LA. Selma ATLANTIC OCEAN
Arr. May 24 and 25 Arr. May 20 / Dep. May 24 FLA.
0 200 miles 30°N
0 200 kilometers
Lambert Azimuthal Equal-Area projection
90°W 80°W

NATIONAL GEOGRAPHIC

War in the Persian Gulf, 1991

In Motion

TURKEY

50°E

Mosul

Irbil

SYRIA

Tigris R.

IRAQ

Beirut
LEBANON · Damascus
Haifa
Euphrates R.
Baghdad
Tel Aviv-Yafo
ISRAEL · Amman
Jerusalem

IRAN

❷ Operation *Desert Storm* begins, January 16, 1991

An Nasiriyah

❸ Allied ground war against Iraqi troops, February 23–26, 1991

EGYPT   JORDAN

As Samawah

As Salman

Basra

30°N

❶ Buildup of Allied troops begins along Saudi Arabia/Iraq border, August 1990–February 1991

Kuwait City

KUWAIT

❹ Cease-fire declared by President Bush, February 27, 1991

Persian Gulf

Red Sea

BAHRAIN · Manama
Dhahran

QATAR · Doha

0   400 miles
0   400 kilometers
Lambert Azimuthal Equal-Area projection

SAUDI ARABIA   Riyadh

U.A.E.

Legend:
- Iraq and occupied territory
- Allied against Iraq
- Neutral countries
- Iraqi SCUD attacks
- Allied air attacks
- ▲ Iraqi troop placements
- ■ Allied troop buildup
- ◄ Allied troop movement
- Major oil fields

In Motion

Maps, charts, and graphs labeled with the In Motion icon have been specially enhanced in the StudentWorks™ Plus CD-ROM and the Presentation Plus! CD-ROM. These In Motion graphics allow students to interact with layers of displayed data and listen to audio components.

Charts & Graphs

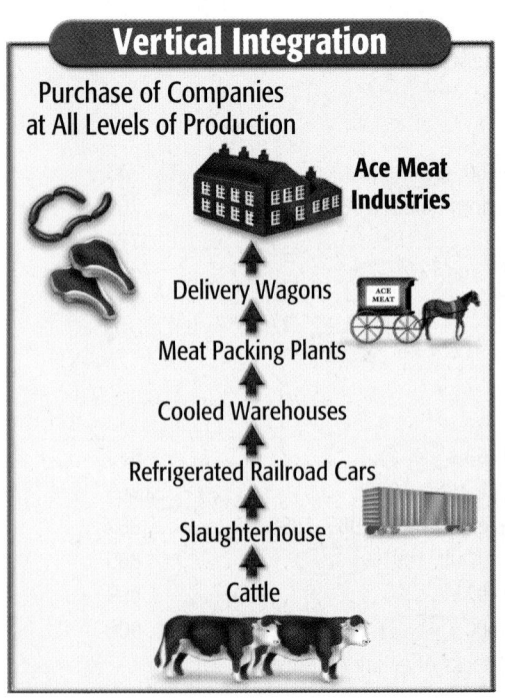

Vertical Integration

Purchase of Companies at All Levels of Production

Ace Meat Industries

Delivery Wagons

Meat Packing Plants

Cooled Warehouses

Refrigerated Railroad Cars

Slaughterhouse

Cattle

Horizontal Integration

Purchase of Competing Companies in Same Industry

U.S. Oil Company

Independent Oil Refineries

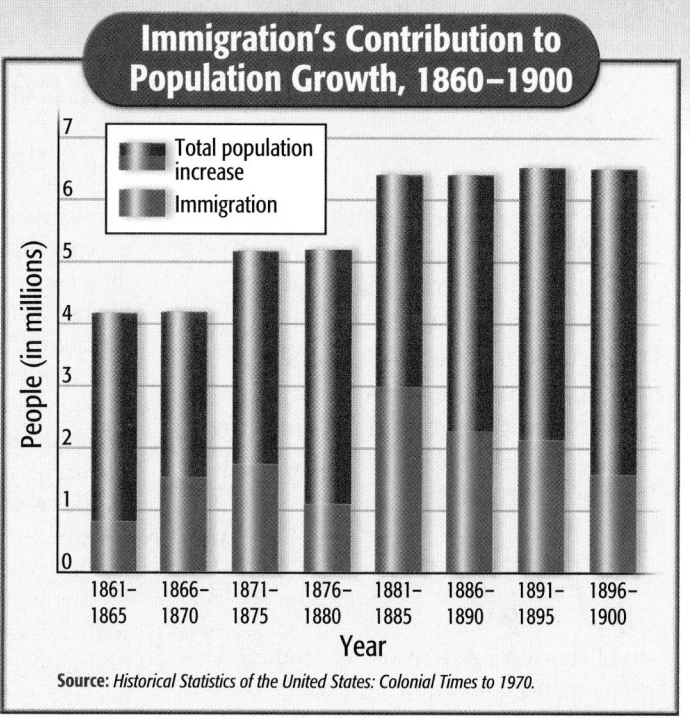

Immigration's Contribution to Population Growth, 1860–1900

People (in millions) vs. Year

Legend:
- Total population increase
- Immigration

Years: 1861–1865, 1866–1870, 1871–1875, 1876–1880, 1881–1885, 1886–1890, 1891–1895, 1896–1900

Source: *Historical Statistics of the United States: Colonial Times to 1970.*

Unit 8

One-Stop Internet Resources

This textbook contains one-stop Internet resources for teachers, students, and parents. Log on to tarvol2.glencoe.com for more information. Online study tools include Study Central™, Study-to-Go™, Chapter Overviews, ePuzzles and Games, Self-Check Quizzes, Vocabulary eFlashcards, and Multi-Language Glossaries. Online research tools include Student Web Activities, Beyond the Textbook Features, Current Events, Web Resources, and State Resources. The interactive online student edition includes the complete Interactive Student Edition. Especially for teachers, Glencoe offers an online Teacher Forum, Web Activity Lesson Plans, and Literature Connections.

Project CRISS

How Can I Teach My Students How to Learn Social Studies?

by Carol M. Santa, Ph.D.

We all know that teaching social studies involves far more than teaching just course content. We understand that students need to become engaged, confident learners. Achieving that goal means helping them to understand, organize, and retain information.

Teaching Both Content and Skills

In other words, we want our students to have the skills and confidence to be life-long learners. With its rich content, social studies offer an ideal arena for teaching both content and skills.

✔ **A Dual Responsibility** Let's take a moment to consider why the dual responsibility of teaching both content and skills is so important. Think back to your own middle and high school years. What do you remember about the content

you learned? If I recall my experiences, I find I remember remarkably little content. What did I learn in biology or history? What did my textbooks look like? As the years go by, I don't even remember the names of most of my teachers.

✔ **An Inspiring Teacher** Yet I have vivid memories of my eighth-grade social studies teacher, who came out of retirement to fill in for a history teacher who left on maternity leave. I remember how fascinated I became with ancient history; I recall giving oral reports and how she helped me become comfortable speaking before a group. In fact, I remember more from her class than any other I took during high school.

✔ **Teach How to Learn** More important, I now understand that she taught me how to learn to learn. She showed me how to underline, how to organize information using different note-taking formats, and how to write coherent

answers on essay tests. She taught me the need to test myself on what I knew. And during that vulnerable, adolescent year, I went from being a mediocre student to being an excellent one.

This inspirational teacher did something else for me. At some point during that eighth-grade year, I decided to become a teacher. Later I realized that she had launched me on my professional mission—to spread her wisdom to others. Eventually this led to Project CRISS.

What is CRISS?

CRISS stands for **CR**eating **I**ndependence through **S**tudent-owned **S**trategies. It is a staff development program that I created in collaboration with middle and high school teachers in Kalispell, Montana.

✔ **Origin of CRISS** CRISS had its start 20 years ago in a lunchtime conversation in a teacher's lounge. One of the social studies teachers said, "My students aren't doing a good job of answering chapter questions. In fact, I don't think they even read my assignments. My reading assignments are becoming a waste of time!" His words struck a chord. "My students don't know how to study, and they don't write very well either," another teacher lamented.

✔ **Evolving Strategies** Supported by a state grant, we started working together to find practical ways to help students read, write, and learn content. We met in teams, read professional literature, and designed studies to test classroom strategies. From these efforts, we evolved a project to help students become better readers, writers, and learners. Once the project took shape, we shared our discoveries with other teachers by offering a two- or three-day CRISS workshop to schools and districts in the state.

✔ **Constant Growth** Over the last two decades, Project CRISS has spread from teacher to teacher across this country, into Canada, and to several European countries. The project seems to sell itself. Teachers who use CRISS principles and strategies find that their students attain a deeper understanding of course content and become better readers, writers, and learners at the same time. In fact, data from numerous quantitative studies shows that using CRISS strategies improves student learning. (For the most recent data and for information on CRISS workshops, see www.projectcriss.com.)

CRISS Strategies in the Teacher Edition

When the editors of Glencoe/McGraw-Hill asked me and my colleagues to help them integrate CRISS strategies into their social studies texts, we welcomed the opportunity. In this teacher wraparound edition, we offer many references to CRISS strategies. We have packed the pages with strategies that help students gain a deeper understanding of specific content.

CRISS Training

We have one word of caution, however: the integration of CRISS strategies within this teacher wraparound edition does not take the place of a Project CRISS workshop, which provides an in-depth knowledge of CRISS. So, if you haven't yet participated in a CRISS workshop, we encourage you to do so. During a workshop, CRISS trainers take you step-by-step through the philosophy and instructional strategies. Participants are actively involved in all aspects of the program—practicing, adapting, and applying strategies to meet teaching needs.

Long-lasting change occurs when teachers and administrators work together to share, extend ideas, and problem solve. The most effective implementations occur when the initial workshop is supported by follow-up sessions, including a specific follow-up day. At this session, teachers bring examples of strategies they have used since the initial training. Part of this time may be spent in review and in learning new strategies. The rest of the time is for sharing applications. Additional on-going support can occur in teacher planning periods.

In any case, for those of you unfamiliar with Project CRISS, let's begin with a little background knowledge. In this way you will have some context for the various activities suggested throughout the teacher wraparound edition.

The CRISS Philosophy

The first thing to know is that Project CRISS is more than a collection of learning strategies. Its underlying power rests not on the individual strategies but on the teaching philosophy behind them. This philosophy integrates work from cognitive psychology, social learning theory, and neurological research about how the brain learns. It includes these overlapping principles:

✔ background knowledge and purposeful reading
✔ author's craft
✔ active involvement
✔ discussion
✔ organization
✔ writing
✔ teacher modeling

Let's look at each of these principles in more detail, along with examples of instructional strategies that illustrate them.

Background knowledge and purposeful reading are powerful determinants of reading comprehension.

Teachers involved in Project CRISS often talk about the importance of background knowledge. Readers are

(Continued on next page)

Using CRISS to Set a Purpose

Advice from Malla S. Kolhoff
Palm Harbor University High School
International Baccalaureate Program
Palm Harbor, Florida

As educators, it is our responsibility to set a purpose for historical reading. Students often must struggle to connect history with their own lives. To compare and contrast, establish cause and effect, and sequence events in chronological order presents a challenge for even the best reader. CRISS strategies allow students to move beyond words to the real significance for their society. With CRISS, my students are able to become engaged in the learning process through:

a. background knowledge
b. active reading, listening, and learning
c. discussion

d. metacognition
e. writing
f. organization
g. understanding

I have found that these strategies help my students attain a higher level of historical thinking and understanding.

Project CRISS

far more likely to learn new information when they have some previous knowledge and have a purpose in mind before they read or listen.

✔ **More Than Simply Reading** We warn students not to simply begin reading. We ask them, *"What might you already know about the topic? What questions do you have about the topic?"* We also remind them to preview the assignment and think about their goals for reading. We often have to be very explicit about the goals. For example, we might tell students, *"After reading this selection, you should be able to . . . ,"* or, *"After viewing the video, you should be able to identify. . . ."*

✔ **KWLH** In the teaching strategies included for each chapter in this book, we offer ideas for helping students tap into their background knowledge. For example, we suggest that students preview their reading assignment and consider what they already know about a topic. Or, we might develop a whole class **KWLH** chart (**K**now, **W**ant to learn, **L**earned, **H**ow to learn more), where students work on this task together. They can generate questions about what they want to learn, and then, after completing the assignment, they can list the new information they have learned and how they can learn more.

K	W	L	H
What I **Know**	What I **Want** to Find Out	What I **Learned**	**How** I Can Learn More

✔ **Reading Goals** We also suggest ways to make sure your students have clear goals for their reading. Each section opener lists reading strategies and main ideas that outline reading goals. Most students will skip over this material and simply start reading. Teachers need to help students understand that the reading goals are important tools for understanding. We tell students, *"Don't ignore your purposes for reading. Take time to think about them before delving into your reading."* Project CRISS also provides hints about how to get students to use these purpose statements to evaluate whether they have understood their reading.

Good readers have an intuitive understanding of the author's craft.

When students know how authors craft their writing, they can more readily understand and remember what they read.

✔ **Pay Attention** Good readers and writers know that paying attention to how text is organized—its headings and paragraphs, for example—makes it easier to comprehend its content. Good readers will analyze the author's style of presentation as they read. They might ask themselves, *"What is this author doing to help me learn key concepts? How does the writer lead me from one idea to the next?"* When students become aware of what the author is doing to impart content, they have a clearer idea of what the author is saying.

✔ **The Walk Through** In the sample lesson on pages T26–T27, we offer advice about "walking through" the text to discover the author's style of presentation. Our suggestions go beyond examining the surface structure (headings, bold print, color coding of topical headings, italicized words) to analyzing how the author elaborates on key topics.

Effective learners are actively involved when they listen and read.

We learn best when we act on the information presented. We can do this by using a variety of organizing activities that require us to write, talk, and transform the information we are absorbing. None of us learns much from reading alone—it's far too passive.

CRISS strategies encourage active engagement in learning. We might ask students to read a section and describe what they are learning to a partner, or we might be more elaborate and have students develop concept maps or write summaries.

Students need many opportunities to talk with one another about what they are learning.

Discussion is critical to learning. The discussions we advocate are different from those in which the teacher remains the authority figure, with students simply reciting answers to

(Continued on next page)

Jose L. Pelaez/CORBIS STOCK MARKET

questions. If discussion becomes mere recitation and there is little interaction among students, little learning occurs. Thus we focus on how to get students to lead their own discussions about a topic. We want them to understand that it is their discussing, their oral grappling with meaning—not ours—that leads to deeper understanding.

Competent readers know several ways to organize information for learning.

Learning depends on organization. We show students different ways to organize information. They can take notes, underline selectively, develop concept maps, and summarize ideas in charts. Once we have taught students these techniques, we tell them, *"You have to do more than just read this assignment. How are you going to organize the information from this assignment? You have to change it, to transform it so that it becomes your own."*

For each chapter of this text, we offer ideas for assisting students in organizing information. Once students have learned a variety of organizing systems, we suggest ways to help them apply these structures independently.

Students deserve opportunities to write about what they are learning.

Writing is an integral part of the CRISS project. Writing lets us figure out what we know and what we still need to know. We cannot write about something we do not understand. While we teach students how to write expository papers and essay exams, we also encourage students to write more informally by questioning, speculating, and writing explanations in learning logs. We make sure that students are writing continually about what they are learning.

For each chapter of this text, we offer ideas for assisting students in organizing information. Once students have learned a variety of organizing systems, we suggest ways to help them apply these structures independently.

Teaching involves explanation and modeling.

Our final principle has to do with our own teaching. Students learn to think strategically when we use these processes as part of our instruction. Our demonstrations are especially critical for struggling readers. Most have never been taught how to learn.

We have to show them how.

✔ **Take Center Stage** When you introduce a new strategy, you should take the center stage: showing, telling, modeling, demonstrating, and explaining not only the content but the process of active reading. As students learn, gradually release responsibility to them. Strategy instruction involves two overlapping steps. First we explain what the strategy is and why students should use it. If students do not know why they are performing an activity, they will rarely use the activity on their own. Next, we demonstrate and talk about procedures for carrying out the strategy. We discuss, demonstrate, and think aloud while modeling. Then, students practice under our guidance and feedback.

✔ **A Systematic Approach** Project CRISS is a valuable basis for instruction. It provides a systematic approach for using what we now know about teaching and learning. The following chart lists questions we need to continually ask ourselves while we are teaching. Use this chart to monitor your efforts to incorporate CRISS principles into your teaching.

CRISS Principles	The CRISS Philosophy	Yes	No	Somewhat
Background knowledge:	Did I assist students in thinking about what they already knew about the topic before beginning the unit? Did I develop necessary concepts before students read?			
Purpose setting:	Did my students have a clear purpose about what they were going to learn before beginning the lesson?			
Author's craft:	Can my students use the author's style of presentation to facilitate their understanding?			
Active involvement:	Were my students engaged in the topic? Did I help students become actively involved in their learning?			
Discussion:	Did my students have opportunities to talk about what they were learning?			
Organization:	Did my students organize information in a variety of ways?			
Writing:	Did my students write about what they were learning?			
Teacher modeling:	Did I do enough teacher modeling of learning strategies so that students could begin doing them on their own?			

Project CRISS

How Do I Use Project CRISS to Teach The American Republic Since 1877?

When students know how authors structure their writing, they can better understand and remember what they read. For the first several chapters of this book, show students how to analyze the author's craft by "walking through" the chapter. Then show students how to use the author's organization to develop two-column notes.

To demonstrate these strategies, make transparencies of pages 10–17 of Chapter 1, *Converging Cultures*. Then organize students into small groups to complete the following activities.

Introducing the Chapter

Place the transparencies of pages 10–11 on the overhead and begin modeling.

Tell students: *"Before reading a text, I take time to figure out how the author has presented the information. The authors of this book have a consistent plan for organizing and presenting information. Let's discover what it is."*

Ask students to turn to pages 10 and 11 of their textbooks. Then say: *"In your small groups, read through these two pages and discuss the following questions:*
✔ *What type of information have the authors included?*

Ohio Historical Society

✔ *How might you use this information (Why It Matters, The Impact Today, and the time line) to understand the content of this chapter?*
✔ *How do these pages help you gain an overview of what you will learn?*
✔ *How might you use the reference to History Online to expand your understanding of the chapter content? Be prepared to share what you have discovered with the whole class."*

Introducing the Section

Guide to Reading

Place a transparency of page 12 on the overhead and ask students to turn to that page in their textbooks. *"Notice how this page is organized. Let's take a moment and talk about how these features might help you."* (It begins with a Guide to Reading that includes a Main Idea, Key Terms and Names, a Reading Strategy, Reading Objectives, a Section Theme, and a Preview of Events.)

Main Idea

"Why have the authors included the main idea at the beginning of the chapter?" (to let readers know what they are going to learn, help them think about what they might already know about the topic, and help them set goals.)

Key Terms and Names

"Now look at the list of key terms and names (Ice Age, glacier, nomad, Mesoamerica, etc.) and skim the first several pages of the chapter. What do you notice about how the key terms are sequenced and highlighted in this chapter?" (Key terms are highlighted in blue and key names in black bold print. All key terms and names are presented in the same order as they appeared in the chapter.)

Reading Strategy

"Notice the reading strategy suggested for this chapter. How could you use it to organize the information for learning?" (The graphic organizer helps readers organize the information in the section.)

Reading Objectives

"How might you use the reading objectives while you read?" (They help readers identify what they should learn in the section.)

Section Theme

"Why have the authors included a section theme?" (to identify the main theme, or idea, of the section)

Preview of Events

"How might the time line help you comprehend the information in this section?" (provides an overview of the time period for this section and helps to organize information)

An American Story

Ask students to read this excerpt. *"An American Story opens the section. What do you think is the purpose of this story?"* (to provide background knowledge and generate interest in reading the section)

Walking Through the Narrative

As you talk aloud about the narrative, point out each of the features on the chapter transparencies of pages 12–17. *"Now let's see how the authors have helped us figure out the main topics covered in this chapter. Notice the bold-print heading. The main topics are printed in larger blue print, and the subtopics are printed in smaller red print. This organization and color coding should help me figure out what is important.*

At the end of each subsection, I notice a Reading Check. The Reading Check questions will help me know if I have comprehended each subsection. When I come to a Reading Check, I will stop and try to answer the question. If I can't, I will reread the subsection. I should also read through these questions before I begin reading a section. In this way, I will know what I am supposed to get out of this section.

As I continue my walk-through of the chapter, I skim the inserts like the Picturing History photos and captions on pages 13 and 16 and the map on page 14. I also read the American Literature feature on page 17 that immediately follows the section. I realize that these inserts and features contain important information for understanding the content. I should never just skip over them.

There are also assessments at the end of each section (page 16). The questions in this assessment will help me make sure that I understand everything I have read and that I can identify the Main Idea, Reading Objectives, and Section Theme outlined in the Guide to Reading."

Reading the Chapter

Ask students to read the first section of the chapter. Tell them to keep in mind the Reading Check questions for the section as they read.

Main Idea-Detail Notes

Ask students to divide their notebook paper into two columns to create a graphic organizer similar to the one on the right. Explain that they will record key points in the left column and details about the key points in the right column. Main points should be questions or key words. Students then use their notes as a study guide. They can use the key words or questions to quiz themselves.

✔ Demonstrate how to use the author's clues (headings, bold-print vocabulary) to develop main idea-detail notes. On a blank transparency, develop two-column notes

about the first section of the chapter while students write down their own notes at their desks. In the left column, model how to include main topics and vocabulary essential to understanding the content. In the right column, record details that elaborate on the main points. Talk about being brief and using your own words. Explain why making the author's message your own ensures better comprehension and retention.

✔ Continue modeling notes on the rest of this section. Then ask students to work in pairs or small groups to develop two-column notes about the remaining chapter. Ask students to share their notes in a class discussion.

✔ Demonstrate how to use the notes to test themselves. Show students how you cover the right column with a sheet of paper and recite what you can remember. Talk about why testing yourself is important for learning. *"You are the only one who knows if you know. Testing yourself is an excellent way to learn and to check your understanding."*

✔ Take time for reflection. After students have completed their notes, allow time for discussion about reading and learning strategies. Ask students to write and then talk about how analyzing the author's craft and developing two-column notes helped them read and learn content, and how they might use these strategies in the future.

SAMPLE ORGANIZER

Main Ideas	Details
When did first Americans appear?	Not sure—maybe between 15,000-30,000 yrs ago
Origins of ancient people?	DNA studies—earliest people probably Asian
How old?	Determined by radiocarbon dating
How did they get to America?	New land bridge—developed during Ice Age, much of earth's water froze into glaciers, ocean level dropped, land bridge formed
nomads	Moved from place to place, migrations continued until 10,000 years ago, rising seawater submerged bridge
agricultural revolution	planting and raising crops; 9,000–10,000 years ago in Mesoamerica; pumpkins, peppers, squash, beans and maize
How did civilizations develop?	agriculture led to villages, complex forms of government and specialized skills developed
the first civilizations in Mesoamerica	Olmec—began 1500–1200 B.C. to 300 B.C., in southern Mexico, temple complexes and pyramids Teotihuacán—built by another people, first large city, near present-day Mexico City Maya—Yucatán Peninsula and Central America, engineering and mathematics, temple pyramids Aztec—Tenochtitlán, built empire, by 1500 ruled about 5 million people

Colonial Williamsburg

Reading in the Content Areas

How Can I Use Jamestown Education Products to Help Struggling Readers?

For over 30 years, Jamestown Education has made its primary focus helping older readers become better readers. The Jamestown products shown on this page support the basic elements of reading cited by the National Reading Panel. Each of them can help your struggling readers become better readers.

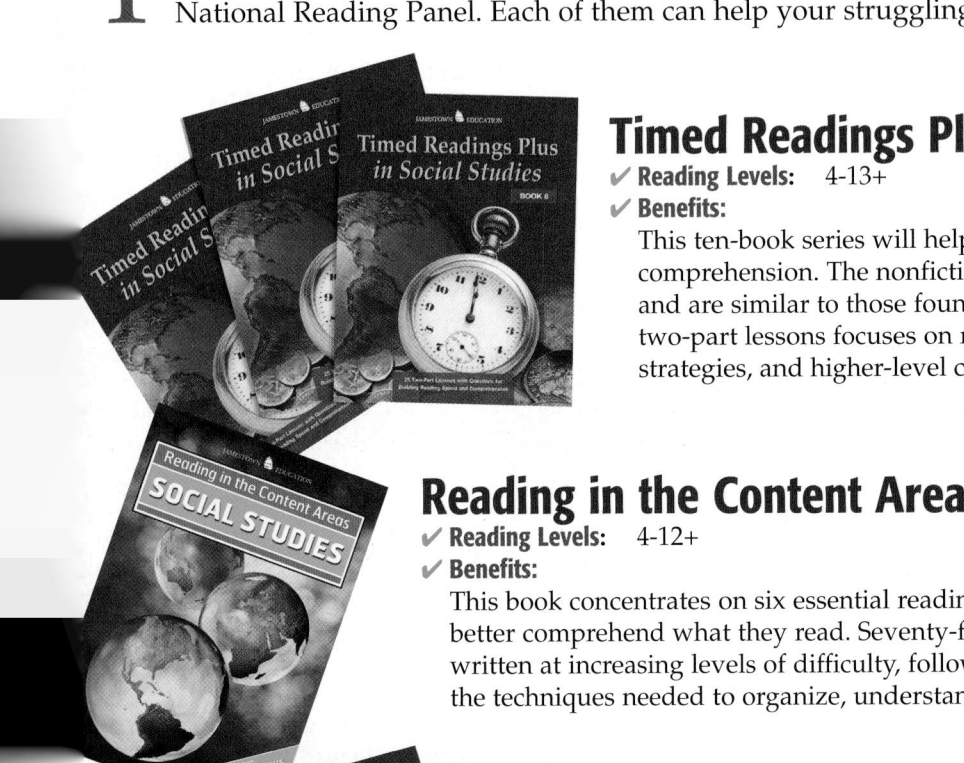

Timed Readings Plus in Social Studies
✔ **Reading Levels:** 4-13+
✔ **Benefits:**
This ten-book series will help your students increase both reading rate and comprehension. The nonfiction passages cover current social studies topics and are similar to those found on both state and national tests. Each of the two-part lessons focuses on reading rate, factual recall, comprehension strategies, and higher-level critical thinking skills.

Reading in the Content Areas: Social Studies
✔ **Reading Levels:** 4-12+
✔ **Benefits:**
This book concentrates on six essential reading skills that will help your students better comprehend what they read. Seventy-five high-interest nonfiction passages written at increasing levels of difficulty, followed by consistent, targeted skills, teach the techniques needed to organize, understand, and apply information.

Reading Fluency
✔ **Reading Levels:** 1-10
✔ **Benefits:**
This seven-book series will help your students read smoothly, accurately and expressively. Students work in pairs to provide immediate feedback and self-assessment. Author Camille Blachowicz states that "the ability to read fluently is highly correlated with many other measures of reading competence."

Jamestown's Reading Improvement
✔ **Reading Levels** 4-10
✔ **Benefits:**
Authored by renowned reading expert Edward Fry, this eight-book series focuses on helping build your students' comprehension, vocabulary, and skimming and scanning skills. Repeated practice with targeted exercises ensures mastery of valuable reading skills.

Critical Reading Series

✔ **Reading Levels:** 2-8

✔ **Benefits:**

This twenty-four book high-interest series, written at three reading spans, encourages your reluctant readers to build a love for nonfiction while focusing on critical reading skills. Topics ranging from Fateful Journeys to Weird Science to Heroes draw students in, while giving students ample opportunities to master important skills found on both state and national tests.

To order Jamestown products, call 1-800-334-7344

In addition to the Project CRISS Reading Strategies, you may find it effective to implement some of the following instructional methods. They help *your* struggling students take increasing ownership of the reading process.

Reciprocal Teaching

Reciprocal teaching is characterized by a dialogue between you and your student, and ultimately among students in a group, in which students take the role of dialogue reader. Construction of meaning is built upon four reading strategies:

✔ **Summarizing** Readers identify the most important information in a segment of text and state that information in their own words. Summarizing involves students in recognizing and communicating the significant ideas in a text.

✔ **Questioning** Readers ask themselves questions about the text segment. Self-questioning aids comprehension by helping students identify where their understanding of the text has broken down and what they still need to know in order to understand what they have read.

✔ **Clarifying** Readers try to find answers to the question they have raised and to make sense of parts of the text that have caused confusion. They seek clarification by rereading, reading ahead or by seeking outside help, such as through a peer or a reference source.

✔ **Predicting** Readers tell what they think will happen next, basing their predictions on evidence from the text they have already read.

Modeling

An important element of strategic instruction is teacher modeling. As a part of the modeling process, think aloud as you apply a strategy to solve a reading problem, putting words to the inner voice that successful readers have with text and demonstrating the strategy used for understanding. To construct a "think-aloud," read aloud a passage, stopping at pertinent points to talk about what you are thinking. A think-aloud demonstrates the cognitive process and allows students to observe how a proficient reader approaches a problem with reading.

"Fix-Up" Strategies

Explain that readers perform certain tasks. Guide them through these following steps:

✔ **Stop** Tell students to stop and fix the problem when they do not understand.

✔ **Identify the Problem** Have students ask themselves when they stopped understanding and what they don't understand.

✔ **Apply a Fix-up Strategy** Encourage students to try these strategies:

✔ **Reread**

✔ **Read ahead**

✔ **Alter** the pace or voice

✔ **Ask** for help

CRISS and the Jamestown Reader

Advice from Dr. Sara Wartenberg
Palm Harbor University High School
International Baccalaureate Program
Palm Harbor, Florida

Help your students achieve testing success by combining CRISS strategies with the Jamestown Readers. The stories appeal to students of all reading levels. The stories are interesting and informative for students and teachers alike. Implementing CRISS strategies as students read the selections will help them respond with greater success to the questions that accompany each selection. Students will gain confidence and thus work for greater skill in reading comprehension and critical thinking.

Test-Taking Strategies

How Can I Help My Students Succeed on Tests?

It's not enough for students to learn social studies facts and concepts—they must be able to show what they know in a variety of test-taking situations.

How Can I Help My Students Do Well On Objective Tests?

Objective tests may include multiple choice, true/false, and matching questions. Applying the following strategies can help students do their best on objective tests.

Multiple Choice Questions

✔ Students should read the directions carefully to learn what answer the test requires—the best answer or the right answer. This is especially important when answer choices include "all of the above" or "none of the above."

✔ Advise students to watch for negative words in the questions, such as *not, except, unless,* and *never.* If the question contains a negative, the correct answer choice is the one that does not fit.

✔ Students should try to mentally answer the question before reading the answer choices.

✔ Students should read all the answer choices and cross out those that are obviously wrong. Then they should choose an answer from those that remain.

True/False Questions

✔ It is important that students read the entire question before answering. For an answer to be true, the entire statement must be true. If one part of a statement is false, the answer should be marked *False.*

✔ Remind students to watch for words like *all, never, every,* and *always.* Statements containing these words are often false.

Matching Questions

✔ Students should read through both lists before they mark any answers.

✔ Unless an answer can be used more than once, students should cross out each choice as they use it.

✔ Using what they know about grammar can help students find the right answer. When matching a word with its definition, the definition is often the same part of speech (noun or verb, for example) as the word.

How Can I Help My Students Do Well On Essay Tests?

Essay tests require students to write a thorough and well-organized answer to a question or questions. Help students use the following strategies on essay tests.

Analyze:	To **analyze** means to systematically and critically examine all parts of an issue or event.
Classify or Categorize:	To **classify** or **categorize** means to put people, things, or ideas into groups, based on a common set of characteristics.
Compare and Contrast:	To **compare** is to show how things are similar, or alike. To **contrast** is to show how things are different.
Describe:	To **describe** means to present a sketch or impression. Rich details, especially details that appeal to the senses, flesh out a description.
Discuss:	To **discuss** means to systematically write about all sides of an issue or event.
Evaluate:	To **evaluate** means to make a judgment and support it with evidence.
Explain:	To **explain** means to clarify or make plain.
Illustrate:	To **illustrate** means to provide examples or to show with a picture or other graphic.
Infer:	To **infer** means to read between the lines or to use knowledge and experience to draw conclusions, make a generalization, or form a prediction.
Justify:	To **justify** means to prove or to support a position with specific facts and reasons.
Predict:	To **predict** means to tell what will happen in the future, based on an understanding of prior events and behaviors.
State:	To **state** means to briefly and concisely present information.
Summarize:	To **summarize** means to give a brief overview of the main points of an issue or event.
Trace:	To **trace** means to present the steps or stages in a process or event in sequential or chronological order.

Read the Question

The key to writing successful essays lies in reading and interpreting questions correctly. Teach students to identify and underline key words in the questions, and to use these words to guide them in understanding what the question asks. Help students understand the meaning of some of the most common key words, listed in the chart on page T24.

Plan and Write the Essay

After students understand the question, they should follow the steps below to develop and write their essays.

1. Map out an answer. Make lists, webs, or an outline to plan the response.

2. Decide on an order in which to present the main points.

3. Write an opening statement that directly responds to the essay question.

4. Write the essay. Expand on the opening statement. Support key points with specific facts, details, and reasons.

5. Write a closing statement that brings the main points together.

6. Proofread to check for spelling, grammar, and punctuation.

How Can I Help My Students Prepare for Standardized Tests?

Students can follow the steps below to prepare for a test.

✔ **Read About the Test** Students can familiarize themselves with the format of the test, the types of questions that will be asked, and the amount of time they will have to complete the test.

✔ **Review the Content** Consistent study throughout the school year will help students build social studies knowledge and understanding. If there are specific objectives or standards that are tested on the exam, help students review these facts or skills to be sure they are proficient.

✔ **Practice** Provide practice, ideally with released tests, to build students' familiarity with the content, format, and timing of the actual exam. Students should practice all the types of questions they will encounter on the test—multiple choice, short answer, and extended response.

✔ **Analyze Practice Results** Help students improve test-taking performance by analyzing their test-taking strengths and weaknesses. Spend time discussing students' completed practice tests, explaining why particular answers are right or wrong. Help students identify what kinds of questions they had the most difficulty with. Look for patterns in errors and then tailor your instruction to the appropriate skills or social studies content.✦

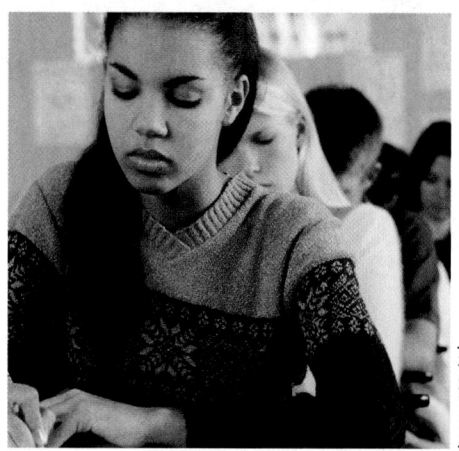

Image 100, Ltd.

Help Students Learn by Reviewing Graded Tests

Advice from Tara Musslewhite
Humble Independent School District
Humble, Texas

Frequently reviewing graded tests is a great way for students to assess their test-taking skills. It also gives teachers the opportunity to teach test-taking strategies and review content. As the class re-reads each test question, guide students to think logically about their answer choices. Show students how to:

1. Read each question carefully to determine its meaning.
2. Look for key words in the question to support their answers.
3. Recognize synonyms in the answer choices that may match phrases in the question.
4. Narrow down answer choices by eliminating ones that don't make sense.
5. Anticipate the answer before looking at the answer choices.
6. Circle questions of which they are unsure and go back to them later. Sometimes a clue will be found in another question on the test.

Alternative Assessment Strategies

How Can I Go Beyond Tests to Assess Students' Understanding of Social Studies Facts and Concepts?

In response to the growing demand for accountability in the classroom, educators must use multiple assessment measures to accurately gauge student performance. In addition to quizzes, tests, essay exams, and standardized tests, assessment today uses a variety of performance-based measures and portfolio opportunities.

What Are Some Typical Performance-Based Assessments?

There are many kinds of performance-based assessments. They all share one common characteristic: they challenge students to create written or oral reports that demonstrate what they know. One good way to present a performance assessment is in the form of an open-ended question.

Writing

Performance-based writing assessments challenge students to apply their knowledge of social studies concepts and information in various ways. Writing activities are most often completed by one student, rather than by a group.

✔ **Journals** Students write from the perspective of a historical character or a citizen of a particular historical era.

✔ **Letters** Students write a letter from one historical figure to another or from a historical figure to a family member or other audience.

✔ **Position Paper or Editorial** Students explain a controversial issue and present their own opinion and recommendations, supported with strong evidence and convincing reasons.

✔ **Newspaper** Students write a variety of stories from the perspective of a reporter living in a particular time period.

✔ **Biographies and Autobiographies** Students write about historical figures either from the third person point of view (biography) or from the first person (autobiography).

✔ **Creative Stories** Students integrate historical events into a piece of fiction, reflecting the customs, language, and geography of the period.

✔ **Poems and Songs** Students follow the conventions of a particular type of song or poem as they tell about a historical event or person.

✔ **Research Reports** Students synthesize information from a variety of sources into a well-developed report.

Oral Presentations

Oral presentations allow students to demonstrate their social studies literacy before an audience. Oral presentations are often group efforts, although this need not be the case.

✔ **Simulations** Students hold simulations, or reenactments, of actual events, such as trials, acts of civil disobedience, battles, speeches, and so forth.

✔ **Debates** Students debate two or more sides to a historical policy or issue. Students can debate from a contemporary perspective or through role-playing, from the viewpoint of a historical character.

✔ **Interview** Students conduct a mock interview of a historical character or bystander.

✔ **Oral Reports** Students present the results of research efforts in an oral report.

✔ **Skits and Plays** Students use historical events as the basis for a play or skit. Details should accurately reflect the customs, language, and the setting of the period.

Visual Presentations

Visual presentations allow students to demonstrate their social studies understandings in a variety of visual formats. Visual presentations can be either group or individual projects.

✔ **Model** Students make a model to demonstrate or represent a process, place, event, battle, artifact, or custom.

✔ **Museum Exhibit** Students create a rich display of materials around a topic. Typical displays might include models, illustrations, photographs, videos, writings, and audiotaped presentations.

✔ **Graph or Chart** Students analyze and represent historical data in a line graph, bar graph, table, or other chart format.

✔ **Drawing** Students represent or interpret a historical event or period through illustration, including political cartoons.

✔ **Posters and Murals** Posters and murals may include maps, time lines, diagrams, illustrations, photographs, and text that reflect students' understandings of historical information.

- **Quilt** Students sew or draw a design for a patchwork quilt that shows a variety of perspectives, events, or issues related to a key topic.
- **Videotapes** Students film a video to show historical fiction or to preserve a simulation of a historical event.
- **Multimedia Presentation or Slide Show** Students create a computer-generated multimedia presentation containing historical information and analysis.

How Are Performance Assessments Scored?

There are a variety of means used to evaluate performance tasks. Some or all of the following methods may be used.

- **Scoring Rubrics** A scoring rubric is a set of guidelines for assessing the quality of a process and/or product. It sets out criteria used to distinguish acceptable responses from unacceptable ones, generally along a scale from excellent to poor.
- **Models of Excellent Work** Teacher-selected models of excellent work give a concrete illustration of what is expected and help students set goals for their own projects.
- **Student Self-Assessment** Common methods of self-assessment include ranking work in relation to the model, using a scoring rubric, and writing their own goals and then evaluating how well they have met these goals. Regardless of the method or methods students use, they should be encouraged to evaluate their behaviors, processes, and the finished product.
- **Peer or Audience Assessment** Many of the performance tasks target an audience other than the classroom teacher. If possible, the audience of peers should give the student feedback. Have the class create rubrics for specific projects together.

- **Observation** As students carry out their performance tasks, you may want to formally observe students at work. Start by developing a checklist, identifying the specific behaviors and knowledge you expect students to demonstrate. Then observe students as they carry out performance tasks and check off these items on your checklist as you observe them.
- **Interviews** As a form of ongoing assessment, you may want to conduct interviews with students, asking them to analyze, explain, and assess their participation in performance tasks. When projects take place over an extended period of time, you can hold periodic interviews as well as exit interviews. In this way you can gauge the status of the project and guide students' efforts along the way.♦

Targeting Multiple Intelligences

Advice from John Cartaina
Consultant, New Jersey Council of Social Studies

Authentic performance assessment provides students with different learning styles opportunities to demonstrate their successful learning. The table below lists types of learning styles.

Learning Style	Characteristics of Students
Linguistic	Read regularly, write clearly, and easily understand the written word
Logical-Mathematical	Use numbers, logic, and critical thinking skills
Visual-Spatial	Think in terms of pictures and images
Auditory-Musical	Remember spoken words and produce rhythms and melodies
Kinesthetic	Learn from touch, movement, and manipulating objects
Interpersonal	Understand and work well with other people
Intrapersonal	Have a realistic understanding of their strengths and weaknesses
Naturalist	Can distinguish among, classify, and use features of the environment

You may want to assign activities to students that accommodate their strongest learning styles, but frequently ask them to use their weakest learning styles.

Primary Source Strategies

How Do I Use Primary Sources in My Classroom?

A primary source is direct evidence of an event, idea, period, or development. It is an oral or written account obtained from actual participants in an event. Examples of primary sources include the following:

- ✔ official documents (records, statistics)
- ✔ political declarations, laws, and rules for governance
- ✔ speeches and interviews
- ✔ diaries, memoirs, and oral histories
- ✔ autobiographies
- ✔ songs and audio recordings
- ✔ advertisements and posters
- ✔ letters

Physical objects, such as tools and dishes, can be primary sources; so can visual evidence in the form of fine art, photographs, maps, films, and videotapes.

Why Use Primary Sources in Your Classroom?

Using primary sources to teach transforms the study of social studies from a passive process to an active one. Students become investigators—finding clues, formulating hypotheses and drawing inferences, making judgments, and reaching conclusions. Bringing primary sources into the classroom stimulates students to think critically about events, issues, and concepts rather than simply memorizing dates, names, and generalizations reached by others.

Choosing Primary Sources

- ✔ Provide exposure to a variety of source types, including historic photographs, folk or popular music, financial records or household accounts, as well as letters, journals, and historic documents.
- ✔ When choosing print sources, consider the interests and reading levels of your students. Many texts contain challenging vocabulary and unfamiliar sentence structure. You may need to create a reader's guide that defines key vocabulary and paraphrases the main points of the reading.
- ✔ Some documents may be too long. Decide whether using an excerpt will provide enough information for students to draw conclusions.
- ✔ Depending upon the topic and your instructional objectives, you may need to provide several different primary sources to expose students to a variety of perspectives.
- ✔ Decide how students will access the primary sources: through the Internet, the library, a museum, or other print resources. Consider the possibility of an Internet virtual field trip for students.

Moving from URL to URL, students can visit museum sites and other Web pages to view artifacts, interpret economic or census data, and read journals, letters, and official documents.

How Do I Introduce Students to Primary Sources?

Carefully explain the nature of primary sources when you introduce them to students. Although primary sources contain valuable clues, be sure to alert students that primary sources contain biases and prejudices, and must be approached with caution. Every primary source reflects the creator's point of view to some degree.

Using Primary Sources in the Classroom

Primary sources provide a rich source of inspiration for a variety of instructional strategies. They can be used to spark interest in a new topic, foster deeper exploration into a historical era, or assess students' understanding of social studies concepts and facts.

- ✔ **Pre-Reading Activities** Present a primary source for students to study at the beginning of a new chapter or topic. Have students analyze the source, using the questions and guidelines presented on the next page. Then have students make predictions about what they might learn in the upcoming lessons.

Anthony Redpath/CORBIS STOCK MARKET

Aaron Haupt

PhotoL

Interpreting a Primary Source

Before students interpret a primary source, they need to know its context. Then they can use questions and guidelines, such as those below, to help them analyze and interpret the primary source.

Print Sources

- Who created the source, and what was the purpose for doing so?
- Did the writer personally experience or witness the event(s)?
- At what point did the writer record the information—as it happened or afterward? How long after?
- Who was the intended audience?
- Was the writer trying to record facts, express an opinion, or persuade others to take action?
- What is the author's main message?
- What values does the document convey?
- What bias does it reflect?
- What information about the topic can you gather from this document?
- Compare this document with what you know about the topic. Does it confirm those ideas or introduce a new perspective?
- How might other accounts about this topic support or modify the message this source delivers?

Visual Sources

- Who created the source, and what was the purpose for doing so?
- What does the image show?
- What mood does the image convey?
- Who or what dominates the image or catches your eye?
- How does the view impact the message?
- What details can you learn from the image?
- What is excluded from view?
- What bias does the visual reflect?
- What information about the topic can you gather from this visual?
- How might other visuals about this topic support or modify the message this one delivers?

Audio Sources

- Who created the source? What was the purpose for creating this source?
- What is the main idea of the audio?
- What mood does the recorder's voice convey?
- What bias does the audio text reflect?
- What information about the topic can you gather from this audio source?
- Compare the information in this source with what you already know about the topic. Does it confirm those ideas or introduce a new perspective?
- How might other sources about this topic support or modify the message that this one delivers?

✔ **Exploring Information** Provide a variety of primary sources related to a topic or time period. Have students compare and contrast the items, analyzing the information, making inferences, and drawing conclusions about the period.

✔ **Evaluation Activities** Have students evaluate a primary source and tell how it supports or refutes what they learned in the textbook. Students can also read a primary source document that provides one perspective on a topic, and then write their own account with another perspective.✦

How to Use the Declaration of Independence in Your Classroom

Advice from Susan Hirsch
East Wake High School
Wendell, North Carolina

Divide students into groups of three or four. Tell students that it is 1777, and one member of their group has been arrested for joining the revolutionary struggle against Great Britain. This person will be sent to London to be tried on charges of treason. Hanging is the punishment for those found guilty of treason. Each group must prepare a defense using only one source—the Declaration of Independence. One person from each group will speak to the class, acting as either the defendant or the defendant's attorney. After all the presentations, the class will vote to determine which person did the best job of defending himself or herself or the client.

Addressing the Needs of Special Students

How Can I Help ALL my Students Learn Social Studies?

Today's classroom contains students from a variety of backgrounds and with a variety of learning styles, strengths, and challenges. With careful planning, you can address the needs of all students in the social studies classroom. The following tips for instruction can support your efforts to help all students reach their maximum potential.

✔ Survey students to discover their individual differences. Use interest inventories of their unique talents so you can encourage contributions in the classroom.

✔ Be a model for respecting others. Adolescents crave social acceptance. The student with learning differences is especially sensitive to correction and criticism, particularly when it comes from a teacher. Your behavior will set the tone for how students treat one another.

✔ Expand opportunities for success. Provide a variety of instructional activities that reinforce skills and concepts.

✔ Establish measurable objectives and decide how you can best help students meet them.

✔ Celebrate successes and praise "work in progress."

✔ Keep it simple. Point out problem areas if doing so can help a student effect change. Avoid overwhelming students with too many goals at one time.

✔ Assign cooperative group projects that challenge all students to contribute to solving a problem or creating a product.

How Do I Reach Students with Learning Disabilities?

✔ Provide support and structure. Clearly specify rules, assignments, and responsibilities.

✔ Practice skills frequently. Use games and drills to help maintain student interest.

✔ Incorporate many modalities into the learning process. Provide opportunities to say, hear, write, read, and act out important concepts and information.

✔ Link new skills and concepts to those already mastered.

✔ Allow students to record answers on audiotape.

✔ Allow extra time to complete tests and assignments.

✔ Let students demonstrate proficiency with alternative presentations, including oral reports, role plays, art projects, and musical presentations.

✔ Provide outlines, notes, or tape recordings of lecture material.

✔ Pair students with peer helpers, and provide class time for pair interaction.

How Do I Reach Students with Behavioral Disorders?

✔ Provide a structured environment with clear-cut schedules, rules, seat assignments, and safety procedures.

✔ Reinforce appropriate behavior and model it for students.

✔ Cue distracted students back to the task through verbal signals and teacher proximity.

✔ Set very small goals that can be achieved in the short term. Work for long-term improvement in the big areas.

How Do I Reach Students with Physical Challenges?

✔ Openly discuss with the student any uncertainties you have about when to offer aid.

✔ Ask parents or therapists and students what special devices or procedures are needed, and whether any special safety precautions need to be taken.

✔ Welcome students with physical challenges into all activities, including field trips, special events, and projects.

Michael Newman/PhotoEdit

✔ Try to incorporate the students' cultural experience into your instruction. The help of a bilingual aide may be effective.
✔ Avoid cultural stereotypes.
✔ Pre-teach important vocabulary and concepts.
✔ Encourage students to preview text before they begin reading, noting headings, graphic organizers, photographs, and maps.

How Do I Reach Gifted Students?

✔ Make arrangements for students to take selected subjects early and to work on independent projects.
✔ Ask "what if" questions to develop high-level thinking skills. Establish an environment safe for risk taking.
✔ Emphasize concepts, theories, ideas, relationships, and generalizations.
✔ Promote interest in the past by inviting students to make connections to the present.
✔ Let students express themselves in alternate ways, such as creative writing, acting, debate, simulations, drawing, or music.
✔ Provide students with a catalog of helpful resources, listing such things as agencies that provide free and inexpensive materials, appropriate community services and programs, and community experts.
✔ Assign extension projects that allow students to solve real-life problems related to their communities. ✦

✔ Provide information to help able-bodied students and adults understand other students' physical challenges.

How Do I Reach Students with Visual Impairments?

✔ Facilitate independence. Modify assignments as needed.
✔ Teach classmates how and when to serve as guides.
✔ Limit unnecessary noise in the classroom if it distracts the student with visual impairments.
✔ Provide tactile models whenever possible.
✔ Foster a spirit of inclusion. Describe people and events as they occur in the classroom. Remind classmates that the student with visual impairments cannot interpret gestures and other forms of nonverbal communication.
✔ Provide taped lectures and reading assignments.
✔ Team the student with a sighted peer for written work.

How Do I Reach Students with Hearing Impairments?

✔ Seat students where they can see your lip movements easily and where they can avoid visual distractions.

✔ Avoid standing with your back to the window or light source.
✔ Use an overhead projector to maintain eye contact while writing.
✔ Seat students where they can see speakers.
✔ Write all assignments on the board, or hand out written instructions.
✔ If the student has a manual interpreter, allow both student and interpreter to select the most favorable seating arrangements.
✔ Teach students to look directly at each other when they speak.

How Do I Reach English Language Learners?

✔ Remember, students' ability to speak English does not reflect their academic abilities.

Customize Your Classroom!

Advice from Marilyn Gerken
Pickerington Local Schools
Pickerington, Ohio

Provide individualized activities and assignments for a variety of student ability levels. Develop learning packets for chapters and units of study with varying formats, levels, and types of assignments. Assign points and contract students based on their selection of activities to be completed. The activities in the Student Edition can be used for many of the learning activities and assignments.

NCSS Ten Thematic Strands

In *Curriculum Standards for Social Studies: Expectations of Excellence*, the National Council for the Social Studies (NCSS) identified 10 themes that serve as organizing strands for the social studies curriculum at every school level. These themes are interrelated and draw from all of the social science disciplines. Each theme provides student performance expectations in the areas of knowledge, processes, and attitudes. The 10 NCSS themes were the basis for the themes used in the *American Republic Since 1877*.

Theme and Performance Expectations	Student Pages
I. Culture	
The study of culture helps students understand similarities and differences within groups of people. By studying a culture's beliefs, values, and traditions, students begin to gain a perspective that helps them relate to different groups. In high school, students can understand and use complex cultural concepts such as adaptation, assimilation and acculturation to explain how culture and cultural systems function.	
The *American Republic Since 1877* Related Theme: Culture and Traditions	
A. Analyze and explain the ways groups, societies, and cultures address human needs and concerns.	48–52, 348–352, 492–495, 535–539, 618–623, 698–703, 850–854
B. Predict how data and experiences may be interpreted by people from diverse cultural perspectives and frames of reference.	48–52, 490–491, 618–623, 628
C. Apply an understanding of culture as an integrated whole that explains the functions and interactions of language, literature, the arts, traditions, beliefs and values, and behavior patterns.	348–352, 492–495, 535–539, 649, 698–703, 850–854, 874–879, 887
D. Compare and analyze societal patterns for preserving and transmitting culture while adapting to environmental or social change.	48–52, 61, 346–347, 618–623, 303, 887
E. Demonstrate the value of cultural diversity, as well as cohesion, within and across groups.	626, 850–854, 874–879
F. Interpret patterns of behavior reflecting values and attitudes that contribute or pose obstacles to cross-cultural understanding.	346-347, 490-491, 595-600, 628, 649
G. Construct reasoned judgments about specific cultural responses to persistent human issues.	13-16, 194-201, 746-766
H. Explain and apply ideas, theories, and modes of inquiry drawn from anthropology and sociology in the examination of persistent issues and social problems.	12-13, 194-201, 348-352, 353-358
II. Time, Continuity, and Change	
Understanding time, continuity, and change involves being knowledgeable about what things were like in the past and how things change and develop over time. Knowing how to read and reconstruct the past helps students gain a historical perspective. In high school, students examine the past's relationship with the present while extrapolating into the future. They also integrate individual stories about people, events, and situations to form a more complete conception, in which continuity and change persist in time and across cultures. Students will use their knowledge of history to make informed choices and decisions in the present.	
The *American Republic Since 1877* Related Theme: Continuity and Change	
A. Demonstrate that historical knowledge and the concept of time are socially influenced constructions that lead historians to be selective in the questions they seek to answer and the evidence they use.	364-369, 471-475
B. Apply key concepts such as time, chronology, causality, change, conflict, and complexity to explain, analyze, and show connections among patterns of historical change and continuity.	53-56, 74-79, 202-209, 364-369, 408-413, 434-437, 448-455, 471-475, 482-488, 589-594, 625-630, 706-710
C. Identify and describe significant historical periods and patterns of change within and across cultures, such as the development of ancient cultures and civilizations, the rise of nation-states, and social, economic, and political revolutions.	24-28, 53-56, 170-173, 202-209, 238-239, 408-413, 434-437, 448-455, 482-488, 496-497, 570-571, 589-594, 625-630, 666-667, 692-697, 740-741, 800-805, 918-919
D. Systematically employ processes of critical historical inquiry to reconstruct and reinterpret the past, such as using a variety of sources and checking their credibility, validating and weighing evidence for claims, and searching for causality.	80-81, 113, 202-209, 276, 338, 364-369, 406-407, 408-413, 460, 490-491, 543, 646-647, 664, 778-779, 782-783, 866

Theme and Performance Expectations	Student Pages
E. Investigate, interpret, and analyze multiple historical and contemporary viewpoints within and across cultures related to important events, recurring dilemmas, and persistent issues, while employing empathy, skepticism, and critical judgement.	24-28, 80-81, 238-239, 324-325, 406-407, 471-475, 482-488, 490-491, 496-497, 570-571, 666-667, 692-697, 706-710, 740-741, 782-783, 918-919
F. Apply ideas, theories, and modes of historical inquiry to analyze historical and contemporary developments, and to inform and evaluate actions concerning public policy issues.	24-28, 53-56, 434-437, 448-455, 482-488, 625-630

III. *People, Places, & Environments*

The study of people, places, and environments will help students as they create their spatial views and geographic perspectives of the world. Students begin to make informed and critical decisions about the relationship between humans and their environment. In high school, geographic concepts become central to student's comprehension of global connections as they expand their knowledge of diverse cultures, both historical and contemporary.

The *American Republic Since 1877* Related Theme: Geography and History

A.	Refine mental maps of locales, regions, and the world that demonstrate understanding of relative locations, direction, size, and shape.	58-64, 292-295, 631-637
B.	Create, interpret, use, and synthesize information from various representations of the earth, such as maps, globes, and photographs.	RA2-RA18, 2, 3, 14, 43, 57, 63, 249-255, 257-263, 291, 292-295, 336-340, 337, 415, 466, 477, 485, 627, 882, 914, 921
C.	Use appropriate resources, data sources, and geographic tools such as aerial photographs, satellite images, geographic information systems (GIS), map projections, and cartography to generate, manipulate, and interpret information such as atlases, data bases, grid systems, charts, graphs, and maps.	336-340, 872-873
D.	Calculate distance, scale, area, and density, and distinguish spatial distribution patterns.	346-347, 627, 872-873
E.	Describe, differentiate, and explain the relationships among various regional and global patterns of geographic phenomena such as landforms, soils, climate, vegetation, natural resources, and population.	249-255, 257-263
F.	Use knowledge of physical system changes such as seasons, climate and weather, and the water cycle to explain geographic phenomena.	58-64, 631-637
G.	Describe and compare how people create places that reflect culture, human needs, government policy, and current values and ideals as they design and build specialized buildings, neighborhoods, shopping centers, urban centers, industrial parks, and the like.	62, 218-224
H.	Examine, interpret, and analyze physical and cultural patterns and their interactions, such as land use, settlement patterns, cultural transmission of customs and ideas, and ecosystem changes.	58-64, 218-224, 336-340, 631-637
I.	Describe and assess ways that historical events have been influenced by, and have influenced, physical and human geographic factors in local, regional, national, and global settings.	36–37, 168–169, 218–224, 249–255, 257–263, 264–265, 336–340, 346–347, 432–433, 540–541, 634–635, 638–639, 824–825, 872–873
J.	Analyze and evaluate social and economic effects of environmental changes and crises resulting from phenomena such as floods, storms, and drought.	293–295, 420–421
K.	Propose, compare, and evaluate alternative policies for the use of land and other resources in communities, regions, nations, and the world.	430–433, 822, 900–901, 904–905

Theme and Performance Expectations	Student Pages
IV. Individual Development and Identity	
People and culture influence a person's identity. Examining the different forms of human behavior improves one's understanding of social relationships and the development of personal identity. The study of human behavior helps students become aware of how social processes influence a person's identity. In high school, students use methods from the behavioral sciences to examine individuals, societies, and cultures.	
The *American Republic Since 1877* Related Theme: Individual Action	
A. Articulate personal connections to time, place, and social/cultural system.	237, 326–331, 353–358, 380–384, 464–469, 601–606
B. Identify, describe, and express appreciation for the influence of various historical and contemporary cultures on an individual's daily life.	18–23, 36–37, 197, 237, 353–358, 422, 626, 628
C. Describe the ways family, religion, gender, ethnicity, nationality, socioeconomic status, and other group and cultural influences contribute to the development of a sense of self.	185, 197, 237, 303, 326–331, 353–358, 380–384, 422, 601–606, 626, 628, 800–805, 860–864
D. Apply concepts, methods, and theories about the study of human growth and development, such as physical endowment, learning, motivation, behavior, perception, and personality.	353–358, 464–469, 552–555
E. Examine the interaction of ethnic, national, or cultural influences in specific situations or events.	12–16, 36–37, 164, 297–302, 303, 338, 380–384, 427–431, 461, 464–469, 473–475, 626, 628, 668–673, 800–805, 860–864, 881–886
F. Analyze the role of perceptions, attitudes, values, and beliefs in the development of personal identity.	12–16, 33, 36–37, 185, 197, 303, 380–384, 427–431, 443, 552–555, 601–606, 628, 800–805, 860–864
G. Compare and evaluate the impact of stereotyping, conformity, acts of altruism, and other behaviors on individuals and groups.	18–23, 297–302, 314–318, 628
H. Work independently and cooperatively within groups and institutions to accomplish goals.	552–555
I. Examine factors that contribute to and damage one's mental health and analyze issues related to mental health and behavioral disorders in contemporary society.	194–201, 424–425
V. Individuals, Groups, and Institutions	
Institutions, such as schools, governments, and churches, influence people and often reflect a society's values. Because of the vital role that institutions play in people's lives, it is important that students know how institutions develop, what controls and influences them, and how humans react to them. High school students must understand the traditions and theories that support social and political traditions.	
The *American Republic Since 1877* Related Theme: Groups and Institutions	
A. Apply concepts such as role, status and social class in describing the connections and interactions of individuals, groups, and institutions in society.	194–201, 266–271, 326–331, 572–577
B. Analyze group and institutional influences on people, events, and elements of culture in both historical and contemporary settings.	42–47, 100–106, 194–201, 226–231, 244–248, 266–271, 326–331, 498–502, 542–546, 556–562, 572–577, 612–617, 819–823
C. Describe the various forms institutions take, and explain how they develop and change over time.	226–231, 227, 244–248, 266–271, 498–502, 542–546, 556–562
D. Identify and analyze examples of tensions between expressions of individuality and efforts used to promote social conformity by groups and institutions.	42–47, 194–201, 244–248, 612–617, 800–805
E. Describe and examine belief systems basic to specific traditions and laws in contemporary and historical movements.	42–47, 100–106, 194–201, 238–239, 496–497, 498–502, 570–571, 572–577, 612–617, 666–667, 740–741, 819–823, 860–864, 918–919
F. Evaluate the role of institutions in furthering both continuity and change.	100–106, 194–201, 226–231, 227, 266–271, 498–502, 542–546, 556–562, 819–823
G. Analyze the extent to which groups and institutions meet individual needs and promote the common good in contemporary and historical settings.	100–106, 194–201, 227, 266–271, 542–546, 556–562, 819–823
H. Explain and apply ideas and modes of inquiry drawn from behavioral science and social theory in the examination of persistent issues and social problems.	348–352, 353–358

Theme and Performance Expectations	Student Pages

VI. Power, Authority, and Governance

Studying structures of power, authority, and governance and their functions in the United States and around the world is important for developing a notion of civic responsibility. Students will identify the purpose and characteristics of various types of government and how people try to resolve conflicts. Students will also examine the relationship between individual rights and responsibilities. High school students study the various systems that have been developed over time to allocate and employ power and authority in the governing process.

The *American Republic Since 1877* Related Theme: Government and Democracy

A.	Examine persistent issues involving the rights, roles, and status of the individual in relation to the general welfare.	187–193, 238–239, 418–425, 438–442, 460, 496–497, 564–569, 570–571, 628, 640–648, 666–667, 732–738, 740–741, 746–752, 800–805, 918–919
B.	Explain the purpose of government and analyze how its powers are acquired, used, and justified.	90–93, 108–115, 120–149, 161–167, 187–193, 227, 238–239, 341–345, 399–405, 418–425, 420–421, 456–461, 496–497, 510–513, 543, 564–569, 570–571, 666–667, 732–738, 740–741, 772–775, 790–794, 838–842, 906–909, 918–919
C.	Analyze and explain ideas and mechanisms to meet needs and wants of citizens, regulate territory, manage conflict, establish order and security, and balance competing conceptions of a just society.	108–115, 120–149, 161–167, 187–193, 227, 341–345, 420–421, 456–461, 564–569, 732–738, 746–752, 772–775, 790–794, 838–842, 860–864, 906–909
D.	Compare and analyze the ways nations and organizations respond to conflicts between forces of unity and forces of diversity.	226–231, 227, 456–461, 628, 746–752, 800–805, 860–864
E.	Compare different political systems (their ideologies, structure, institutions, processes, and political cultures) with that of the United States, and identify representative political leaders from selected historical and contemporary settings.	108–115, 161–167, 187–193, 238–239, 496–497, 510–513, 570–571, 666–667, 740–741, 838–842, 906–909, 918–919
F.	Analyze and evaluate conditions, actions, and motivations that contribute to conflict and cooperation within and among nations.	94–99, 187–193, 399–405, 438–442, 640–648, 746–752, 772–775, 790–794, 800–805, 838–842
G.	Evaluate the role of technology in communications, transportation, information-processing, weapons development, or other areas as it contributes to or helps resolve conflicts.	94–99, 399–405, 892–895, 906–909
H.	Explain and apply ideas, theories, and modes of inquiry drawn from political science to the examination of persistent ideas and social problems.	341–345, 564–569, 732–738, 746–752, 800–805
I.	Evaluate the extent to which governments achieve their stated ideals and policies at home and abroad.	187–193, 399–405, 418–425, 438–442, 456–461, 564–569, 628, 732–738, 746–752, 772–775
J.	Prepare a public policy paper and present and defend it before an appropriate forum in school or community.	827, 857

VII. Production, Distribution, and Consumption

Societies try to meet people's needs and wants by trying to answer the basic economic questions: What is to be produced? How should goods be produced? How should goods and services be distributed? How should land, labor, capital, and management be allocated? By studying how needs and wants are met, students learn how trade and government economic policies develop. In high school students develop economic perspectives and a deeper understanding of key economic concepts and processes.

The *American Republic Since 1877* Related Theme: Economic Factors

A.	Explain how the scarcity of productive resources (human, capital, technological, and natural) requires the development of economic systems to make decisions about how goods and services are to be produced and distributed.	65–69, 308–312, 319–323, 521–524, 530–534, 686–691, 843–849, 865–871, 896–901
B.	Analyze the role that supply and demand, prices, incentives, and profits play in determining what is produced and distributed in a competitive market system.	286–291, 308–312, 319–323, 372–379, 530–534, 686–691, 843–849, 865–871
C.	Consider the costs and benefits to society of allocating goods and services through private and public sectors.	324–325, 865–871, 896–901
D.	Describe the relationships among the various economic institutions that comprise economic systems such as households, business firms, banks, government agencies, labor unions, and corporations.	319–323, 521–524, 530–534, 686–691, 865–871, 892–895

Theme and Performance Expectations	Student Pages
E. Analyze the role of specialization and exchange in economic processes.	319–323
F. Compare how values and beliefs influence economic decisions in different societies.	65–69, 286–291, 521–524, 686–691, 860–864, 881–886, 892–895, 896–901
G. Compare basic economic systems according to how rules and procedures deal with demand, supply, prices, the role of government, banks, labor and labor unions, savings and investments, and capital.	324–325, 372–379, 865–871
H. Apply economic concepts and reasoning when evaluating historical and contemporary social developments and issues.	324–325
I. Distinguish between the domestic and global economic systems, and explain how the two interact.	286–291, 372–379
J. Apply knowledge of production, distribution, and consumption in the analysis of a public issue such as the allocation of health care or the consumption of energy, and devise an economic plan for accomplishing a socially desirable outcome related to that issue.	735–737, 822, 896–901, 902–905
K. Distinguish between economics as a field of inquiry and the economy.	521–522, 572–577, 867–868

VIII. Science, Technology, and Society

The study of science, technology, and society is ever changing. It raises questions about who will benefit from it and how fundamental values and beliefs can be preserved in a technology-driven society. In high school students will confront issues that balance the benefits of science and technology against the accompanying social consequences.

The *American Republic Since 1877* Related Theme: Science and Technology

A. Identify and describe both current and historical examples of the interaction and interdependence of science, technology, and society in a variety of cultural settings.	20–21, 178–185, 182, 259, 272–277, 287, 342, 514–520, 558–559, 724–729, 753–760, 776–781, 874–879, 892–895
B. Make judgments about how science and technology have transformed the physical world and human society and our understanding of time, space, place, and human-environment interactions.	26–27, 178–185, 182, 259, 287, 342, 410–411, 514–520, 540–541, 675–680, 695, 724–729, 753–760, 874–879, 892–895
C. Analyze how science and technology influence the core values, beliefs, and attitudes of society, and how core values, beliefs, and attitudes of society shape scientific and technological change.	20–21, 178–185, 182, 514–520, 668–674, 675–680, 724–729, 753–760, 776–781
D. Evaluate various policies that have been proposed as ways of dealing with social changes resulting from new technologies, such as genetically engineered plants and animals.	272–277, 410–411, 892–895
E. Recognize and interpret varied perspectives about human societies and the physical world using scientific knowledge, ethical standards, and technologies from diverse world cultures.	20–21
F. Formulate strategies and develop policies for influencing public discussions associated with technology-society issues, such as the greenhouse effect.	819–823, 904–905

IX. Global Connections

As countries grow more interdependent, understanding global connections among world societies becomes important. Students will analyze emerging global issues in many different fields. They will also investigate relationships among the different cultures of the world. High school students will address critical issues such as peace, human rights, trade, and global ecology.

The *American Republic Since 1877* Related Theme: Global Connections

A. Explain how language, art, music, belief systems, and other cultural elements can facilitate global understanding or cause misunderstanding.	152–159, 675–680, 911–917
B. Explain conditions and motivations that contribute to conflict, cooperation, and interdependence among groups, societies, and nations.	30–35, 36–37, 152–159, 392–397, 584–588, 654–658, 659–665, 675–680, 832–837, 864–871, 902–905, 911–917

Theme and Performance Expectations	Student Pages
C. Analyze and evaluate the effects of changing technologies on the global community.	30–35, 392–397, 406–407, 410–411, 412, 659–665, 675–680, 865–871, 881–886, 892–895, 902–905
D. Analyze the causes, consequences, and possible solutions to persistent, contemporary, and emerging global issues, such as health, security, resource allocation, economic development, and environmental quality.	30–35, 392–397, 654–658, 659–665, 832–837, 865–871, 902–905, 911–917
E. Analyze the relationships and tensions between national sovereignty and global interests, in such matters as territory, economic development, nuclear and other weapons, use of natural resources, and human rights concerns.	30–35, 152–159, 410–411, 584–588, 654–658, 659–665, 675–680, 881–886, 900–901, 902–905
F. Analyze or formulate policy statements demonstrating an understanding of concerns, standards, issues, and conflicts related to universal human rights.	584–588
G. Describe and evaluate the role of international and multinational organizations in the global arena.	654–658, 659–665, 900–901, 911–917
H. Illustrate how individual behaviors and decisions connect with global systems.	900–901, 911–917

X. Civic Ideals and Practices

Understanding civic ideals and practices is crucial to complete participation in society and is the main purpose of social studies. Students will learn about civic participation and the role of the citizen within his or her community, country, and world. High school students learn, through experience, to identify social needs, setting directions for public policy, and working to support both individual dignity and the common good.

The *American Republic Since 1877* Related Theme: Civic Rights and Responsibilities

A. Explain the origins and interpret the continuing influence of key ideals of the democratic republican form of government, such as individual human dignity, liberty, justice, equality, and the rule of law.	82–89, 90–93, 120–149, 238–239, 268–269, 496–497, 570–571, 666–667, 718–723, 740–741, 761–766, 806–810, 812–817, 918–919
B. Identify, analyze, interpret, and evaluate sources and examples of citizens' rights and responsibilities.	82–89, 90–93, 120–149, 232–236, 238–239, 496–497, 570–571, 595–600, 666–667, 668–674, 740–741, 918–919
C. Locate, access, analyze, organize, synthesize, evaluate, and apply information about selected public issues—identifying, describing, and evaluating multiple points of view.	232–236, 668–674, 718–723, 761–766, 784–789
D. Practice forms of civic discussion and participation consistent with the ideals of citizens in a democratic republic.	784–789, 806–810, 812–817
E. Analyze and evaluate the influence of various forms of citizen action on public policy.	82–89, 232–236, 670–671, 761–766, 784–789, 806–810, 812–817
F. Analyze a variety of public policies and issues from the perspective of formal and informal political actors.	82–89, 113, 595–600, 718–723, 761–766, 784–789, 806–810, 812–817
G. Evaluate the effectiveness of public opinion in influencing and shaping public policy developments and decision-making.	461, 473–475, 595–600, 668–673, 761–766, 784–789, 806–810, 812–817
H. Evaluate the degree to which public policies and citizen behaviors reflect or foster the stated ideals of a democratic republican form of government.	88–89, 238–239, 268–269, 461, 473–475, 496–497, 570–571, 628, 666–667, 668–674, 670–671, 740–741, 784–789, 918–919
I. Construct a policy statement and an action plan to achieve one or more goals related to an issue of public concern.	806–810, 812–817
J. Participate in activities to strengthen the "common good," based upon careful evaluation of possible options for citizen action.	232–236, 595–600, 761–766

Scope and Sequence

Themes and Concepts

Each section of the *American Republic Since 1877* focuses on one central theme, although related themes also appear in each section. The section numbers highlighted here in **red** indicate the central theme that is key to that section. Related themes are listed in black.

	1	2	3	4	5	
Culture and Traditions	Section 4	Sections 2, 4, 5				
Continuity and Change		Section 1		Section 3	Section 4	
Geography and History	Section 1	Section 1	Section 4		Sections 1, 3	
Individual Action	Section 4		Sections 1, 2	Section 2		
Groups and Institutions		Section 4		Section 3	Section 3	
Government and Democracy		Section 2	Sections 2, 4, 5	Sections 1, 2	Section 2	
Economic Factors	Section 3	Section 3			Section 1	
Science and Technology	Section 2				Section 1	
Global Connections	Sections 1, 2, 3	Section 3	Section 3	Section 1		
Civic Rights and Responsibilities		Section 5	Sections 1, 3, 5		Section 3	

Skills

These skills are taught in the Chapter SKILLBUILDERS and reinforced in the Chapter Assessment Activities, **Reinforcing Skills Activities** in the Unit Resource books, and **Glencoe's Skillbuilder Interactive Workbook CD-ROM**.

	1	2	3	4	5	
Skill Category	*Social Studies Skill*	*Social Studies Skill*	*Critical Thinking Skill*	*Social Studies Skill*	*Social Studies Skill*	
Specific Skill	Reading a Time Line	Understanding the Parts of a Map	Making Comparisons	Reading a Flowchart	Reading a Line Graph	

6	7	8	9	10	11	12	13
Section 1		Sections 1, 3		Sections 1, 3			Section 1
Section 2					Section 1	Section 3	Section 3
Section 1	Sections 2, 3	Section 2	Section 2	Section 1			
	Sections 1, 3	Section 3	Sections 2, 4	Section 4	Sections 2, 3	Section 2	Section 2
Section 2	Sections 1, 4		Section 4		Section 1		
				Section 2	Section 2	Section 2	Sections 1, 4
	Section 5	Section 1	Sections 1, 3		Section 2	Section 1	
	Section 1	Section 2	Sections 1, 2				
						Sections 1, 2, 3	
Sections 1, 3			Section 4	Section 4	Section 3		Section 1
Critical Thinking Skill	*Technology Skill*	*Social Studies Skill*	*Critical Thinking Skill*	*Critical Thinking Skill*	*Critical Thinking Skill*	*Technology Skill*	*Study and Writing Skill*
Predicting Consequences	Evaluating a Web Site	Interpreting Statistics	Making Inferences	Hypothesizing	Interpreting Points of View	Using an Electronic Spreadsheet	Taking Notes

Chapter	14	15	16	17	18	19	20	
Themes and Concepts								
Culture and Traditions	Section 1	Section 1, 2		Section 2				
Continuity and Change	Sections 1, 4	Section 1				Section 2		
Geography and History							Section 4	
Individual Action	Section 3				Section 1	Section 4	Sections 1, 2	
Groups and Institutions		Section 3	Section 1	Section 3	Sections 1, 2, 4		Section 5	
Government and Democracy	Section 2		Section 1	Section 3	Section 3		Section 5	
Economic Factors	Section 2		Sections 2, 3	Sections 1, 2, 3	Sections 2, 3			
Science and Technology			Section 2					
Global Connections	Sections 1, 3, 4					Sections 1, 2, 3, 4	Sections 1, 2, 3, 4, 5	
Civic Rights and Responsibilities		Section 3				Section 3	Sections 1, 3	
Skills								
Skill Category	*Critical Thinking Skill*	*Critical Thinking Skill*	*Critical Thinking Skill*	*Technology Skill*	*Study and Writing Skill*	*Critical Thinking Skill*	*Social Studies Skill*	
Specific Skill	Analyzing Information	Synthesizing Information	Distinguishing Fact From Opinion	Building a Database	Outlining	Making Generalizations	Reading a Thematic Map	

21	22	23	24	25	26	27	28	29
Section 3	Section 3		Section 1		Sections 2, 3	Section 4	Section 3	
	Sections 2, 4		Section 2		Section 1			Sections 2, 3
				Section 1				
	Section 1		Section 1	Section 2			Section 4	Section 5
		Sections 1, 3		Section 4	Section 4	Section 2		
Section 4		Section 3	Section 1	Sections 1, 4	Section 1	Sections 1, 2, 3	Section 1	Section 4
	Sections 1, 2				Section 4	Section 3	Sections 1, 4	Sections 1, 2
Section 4	Section 3	Section 2	Section 2	Section 2			Section 3	
Sections 1, 2		Section 2				Section 1	Section 2	Sections 3, 5
Section 3	Section 4	Section 1	Sections 1, 2, 3	Section 3	Sections 2, 3			
Critical Thinking Skill	*Social Studies Skill*	*Critical Thinking Skill*	*Study and Writing Skill*	*Social Studies Skill*	*Critical Thinking Skill*	*Critical Thinking Skill*	*Critical Thinking Skill*	*Social Studies Skill*
Making Decisions	Writing a Journal	Problem Solving	Preparing a Bibliography	Conducting an Interview	Analyzing Primary Sources	Analyzing Secondary Sources	Analyzing News Media	Reading a Cartogram

Previewing Your Textbook

Your textbook has been organized to help you learn about the significant events and people that make up American history. Before you start reading, though, here is a road map to help you understand what you will encounter in the pages of this textbook. Follow this road map before you read so that you can understand how this textbook works.

Units

Your textbook is divided into 8 units. Each unit begins with two pages of information to help you start your study of the topics.

WHY IT MATTERS

Each unit begins with *Why It Matters.* This is a short summary about the important topics and what you will study in the unit.

QUOTATION

A short quotation gives a glimpse of the ideas of a key figure from the unit's era.

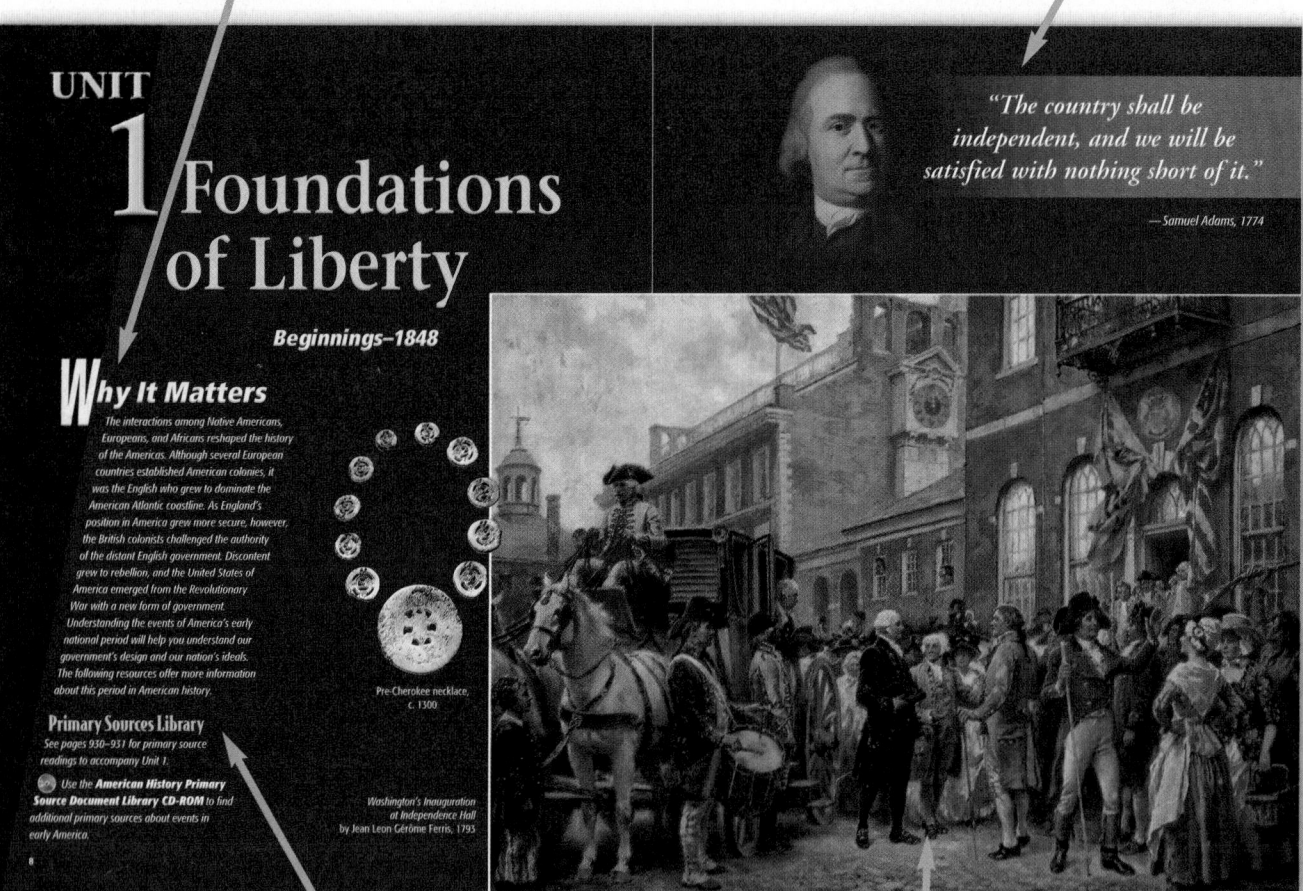

UNIT

1 Foundations of Liberty

Beginnings–1848

Why It Matters

The interactions among Native Americans, Europeans, and Africans reshaped the history of the Americas. Although several European countries established American colonies, it was the English who grew to dominate the American Atlantic coastline. As England's position in America grew more secure, however, the British colonists challenged the authority of the distant English government. Discontent grew to rebellion, and the United States of America emerged from the Revolutionary War with a new form of government. Understanding the events of America's early national period will help you understand our government's design and our nation's ideals. The following resources offer more information about this period in American history.

Primary Sources Library

See pages 930–931 for primary source readings to accompany Unit 1.

Use the **American History Primary Source Document Library CD-ROM** to find additional primary sources about events in early America.

Pre-Cherokee necklace, c. 1300

Washington's Inauguration at Independence Hall by Jean Leon Gérôme Ferris, 1793

"The country shall be independent, and we will be satisfied with nothing short of it."

—Samuel Adams, 1774

PRIMARY SOURCES LIBRARY

This tells you where to find the *Primary Sources Library* readings that accompany the unit.

VISUALS

A photograph or painting shows you what life was like during the time period of the unit.

Chapters

Each unit in *The American Republic Since 1877* is made up of chapters. Each chapter starts by providing you with background information to help you get the most out of the chapter.

CHAPTER TITLE
The chapter title tells you the main topic you will be reading about.

WHY IT MATTERS
Why It Matters tells you why the events you will study are important.

THE IMPACT TODAY
The Impact Today explains how these events changed the way we live today.

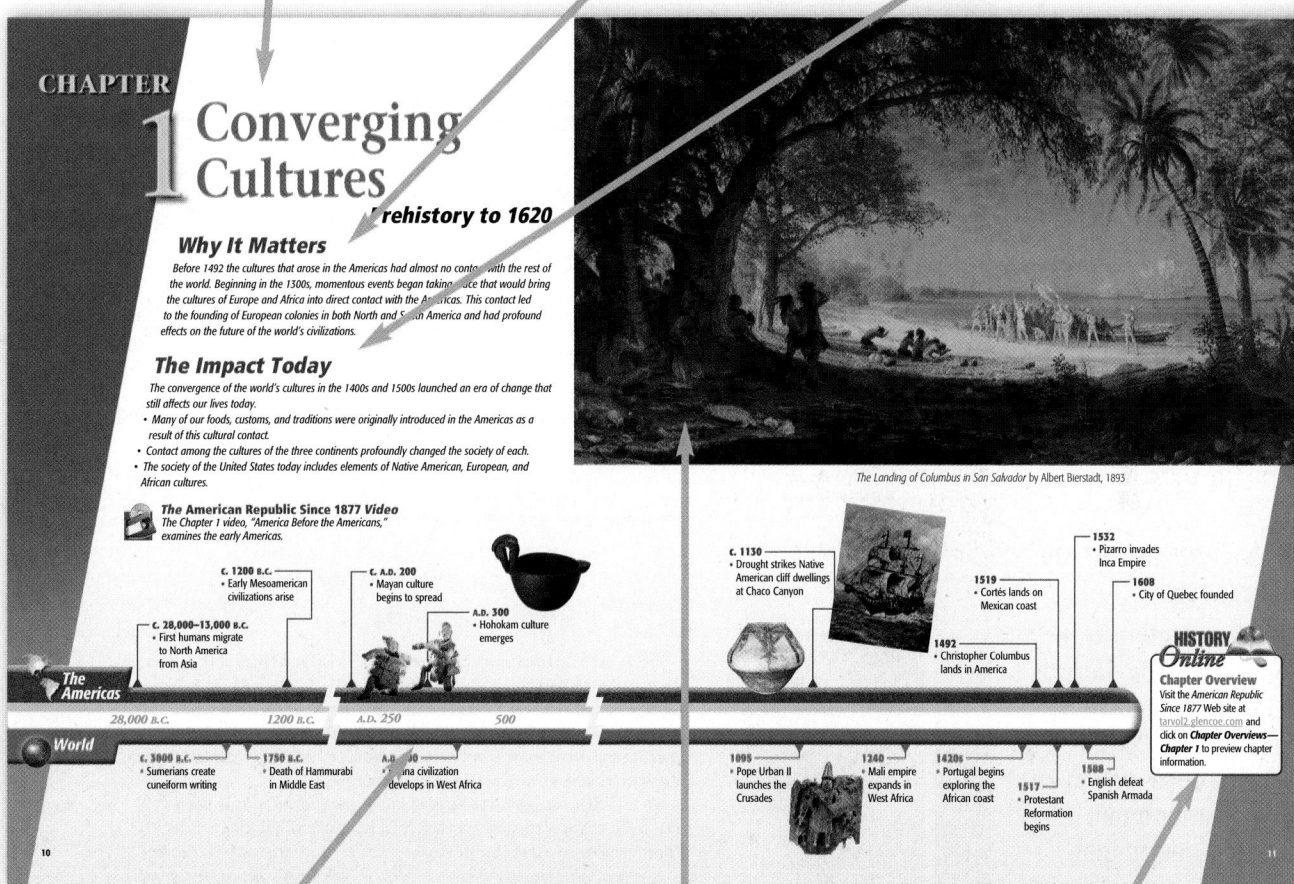

TIME LINE
The time line shows you when and where events happened during the period of time covered in the chapter.

VISUALS
A photograph or painting depicts a scene from the chapter's era.

WEB SITE
History Online directs you to the Internet, where you can find activities and quizzes, along with more information about the chapter's topic.

Previewing Your Textbook

Sections

A section is a division, or part, of the chapter. The first page of the section, the section opener, helps you set a purpose for reading.

READING STRATEGY

Completing the *Reading Strategy* activity will help you organize the information as you read the section.

READING OBJECTIVES

Keep the *Reading Objectives* statements in mind as you read the section.

SECTION THEMES

Your textbook organizes the events of your nation's past and present around themes. You can read about the themes on pages xxx–xxxi (T56–T57).

MAIN IDEA

The *Main Idea* of this section is introduced here. Below it are important terms you will encounter as you read.

TIME LINE

The time line identifies important events you will study in the section.

AN AMERICAN STORY

Think of *An American Story* as a moment in time. It introduces you to an important event that you will read about.

SECTION 1 **The Migration to America**

Guide to Reading

Main Idea
Many diverse Native American groups inhabited Mesoamerica and North America by the 1500s. They were descendants of Asians who probably migrated 15,000 to 30,000 years ago.

Key Terms and Names
Ice Age, glacier, nomad, Mesoamerica, civilization, pueblo, Cahokia, kachina, slash-and-burn agriculture, longhouse

Reading Strategy
Categorizing As you read about early American peoples, complete a graphic organizer by filling in the names of Native American groups who lived in each region.

Regions	Native American Groups
Mesoamerica	
Eastern Woodlands	
Southwest	
Great Plains	

Reading Objectives
• **Explain** why scientists believe that the earliest Americans migrated from Asia.
• **Describe** the early civilizations of Mesoamerica.

Section Theme
Geography and History Scientists theorize that Asian nomads began settling North America between 15,000 and 30,000 years ago.

Preview of Events

♦30,000	♦15,000	♦0	♦A.D. 1500

c. 28,000–13,000 B.C.
First humans migrate to North America

c. A.D. 850
Chaco Canyon pueblos are built

c. A.D. 1300
Cahokia collapses

Late 1500s
Iroquois League created

★ *An American Story* ★

Folsom point, lying between animal bones

In 1925 an African American cowboy named George McJunkin was riding along a gully near the town of Folsom, New Mexico, when he noticed something gleaming in the dirt. He began digging and found a bone and a flint arrowhead. J.D. Figgins of the Colorado Museum of Natural History knew the bone belonged to a type of bison that had been extinct for 10,000 years. The arrowhead's proximity to the bones implied that human beings had been in America at least 10,000 years, which no one had believed at that time.

The following year, Figgins found another arrowhead embedded in similar bones. In 1927 he led a group of scientists to the find. Anthropologist Frank H.H. Roberts, Jr., wrote, "There was no question but that here was the evidence. . . . The point was still embedded . . . between two of the ribs of the animal skeleton." Further digs turned up more arrowheads, now called Folsom points. Roberts later noted: "The Folsom find was accepted as a reliable indication that man was present in the Southwest at an earlier period than was previously supposed."

—adapted from *The First American: A Story of North American Archaeology*

The Asian Migration to America

No one knows exactly when the first people arrived in America. The Folsom discoveries proved that people were here at least 10,000 years ago, but more recent research suggests that humans may have arrived much earlier—between 15,000 and 30,000 years ago.

Reading Roadmap

You will get more out of your textbook if you recognize the different elements that help you understand what you read.

MAPS

Easy-to-read maps link geography and history. In Motion icons on some maps indicate interactive information located on the StudentWorks™ Plus CD-ROM and the Presentation Plus! CD-ROM.

PHOTOGRAPHS

Photographs show you important people, places, and events of the time. Questions help you interpret the photographs and relate them to content.

READING CHECKS

Reading Checks allow you to stop and check your understanding of the main ideas.

OUTLINE

Think of the headings as forming an outline. The blue titles are the main headings. The red titles that follow are the subheadings.

VOCABULARY

The words in blue are the section's key terms. They are defined within the text.

SECTION ASSESSMENT

The *Section Assessment* is the last item in every section. Completing the assessment can help you evaluate your comprehension of section material.

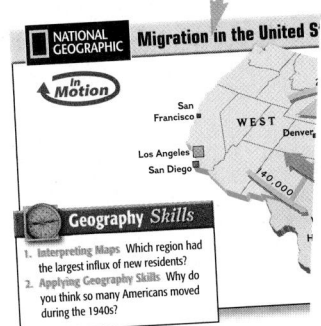

NATIONAL GEOGRAPHIC Migration in the United States

In Motion

San Francisco
Los Angeles
San Diego
WEST
Denver

Total Population Increase 1940–1950
400,000 and over

Geography Skills

1. **Interpreting Maps** Which region had the largest influx of new residents?
2. **Applying Geography Skills** Why do you think so many Americans moved during the 1940s?

fruit and vegetables in the Southwest. Many also helped to build and maintain railroads. The Bracero Program continued until 1964. Migrant farmworkers became an important part of the Southwest's agricultural system.

✓ Reading Check **Describing** How did mobilizing the economy help end the Depression?

A Nation on the Move

The wartime economy created millions of new jobs, but the Americans who wanted these jobs did not always live nearby. To get to the jobs, 15 million Americans moved during the war. Although the assembly plants of the Midwest and the shipyards of the Northeast attracted many workers, most Americans headed west and south in search of jobs.

Taken together, the growth of southern California and the expansion of cities in the Deep South created a new industrial region—the Sunbelt. For the first time since the Industrial Revolution began in the United States, the South and West led the way in manufacturing and urbanization.

The Housing Crisis Perhaps the most difficult facing cities with war industries was deciding where to put the thousands of new workers. Many people had to live in tents and tiny trailers. To help solve the housing crisis, the federal government allocated $1.2 billion to build public housing, schools community centers during the war.

Although prefabricated government housing had tiny rooms, thin walls, poor heating

---

Not all Japanese Americans accepted the relocation without protest. Fred Korematsu argued that his rights had been violated and took his case to the Supreme Court. In December 1944, in *Koremastu v. the United States,* the Supreme Court ruled that the relocation was constitutional because it was based not on race, but on "military urgency." Shortly afterward, the Court did rule in *Ex Parte Endo* that loyal American citizens could not be held against their will. In early 1945, therefore, the government began to release the Japanese Americans from the camps. *(See page 963 for more information on Koremastu v. the United States.)*

Despite the fears and rumors, no Japanese American was ever tried for espionage or sabotage. Japanese Americans served as translators for the army during the war in the Pacific. The all-Japanese 100th Battalion, later integrated into the **442nd Regimental Combat Team,** was the most highly decorated unit in World War II.

After the war, the **Japanese American Citizens League** (JACL) tried to help Japanese Americans who had lost property during the relocation. In 1988 President Reagan apologized to Japanese Americans on behalf of the U.S. government and signed legislation granting $20,000 to each surviving Japanese American who had been interned.

✓ Reading Check **Comparing** Why did racism lead to violence in Detroit and Los Angeles in 1943?

Daily Life in Wartime America

Housing problems and racial tensions were serious difficulties during the war, but mobilization strained society in many other ways as well. Prices rose, materials were in short supply, and the question of how to pay for it all loomed ominously over the entire war effort.

ECONOMICS

Wage and Price Controls As the economy mobilized, the president worried about inflation. Both wages and prices began to rise quickly during the war because of the high demand for workers and raw materials. To stabilize both wages and prices, Roosevelt created the **Office of Price Administration** (OPA) and the Office of Economic Stabilization (OES). The OES regulated wages and the price of farm products. The OPA regulated all other prices. Despite some problems with labor unions, the OPA and OES were able to keep inflation under control.

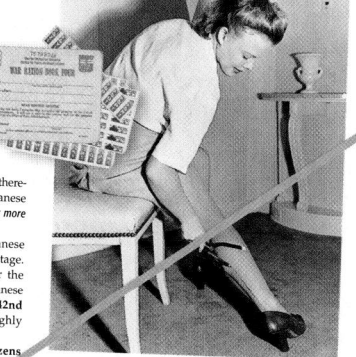

Picturing History

Rationing Products War rationing affected everyone. Women painted seams on their legs to make it appear they were wearing stockings because silk was needed to make parachutes instead of stockings. Why was rationing so vital to the war effort?

While the OPA and OES worked to control inflation, the War Labor Board (WLB) tried to prevent strikes that might endanger the war effort. In support, most American unions issued a no strike pledge," and instead of striking, asked the WLB to serve as a mediator in wage disputes. By the end of the war, the WLB had helped to settle over 17,000 disputes involving more than 12 million workers.

Blue Points, Red Points The demand for raw materials and supplies created shortages. The OPA began rationing, or limiting the availability of, many products to make sure enough were available for military use. Meat and sugar were rationed to provide enough for the army. To save gasoline and rubber, gasoline was rationed, driving was restricted, and the speed limit was set at 35 miles per hour.

Every month each household would pick up a book of ration coupons. Blue coupons, called blue points, controlled processed foods. Red coupons, or red points, controlled meats, fats, and oils. Other coupons controlled items such as coffee and sugar. When people bought food, they also had to give enough coupon points to cover their purchases.

CHAPTER 20 America and World War II **629**

---

planes into American ships, killing ... also inflicting severe damage. Luckily for the Americans, just as their situation was becoming

✓ Reading Check **Describing** What strategy did the United States Navy use to advance across the Pacific?

HISTORY Online **Study Central**™ To review this section, go to **tarvol2.glencoe.com** and click on **Study Central**™.

SECTION 4 ASSESSMENT

Checking for Understanding

1. **Define:** amphtrac, kamikaze.
2. **Identify:** Casablanca Conference, Operation Overlord, D-Day, Omar Bradley, Guadalcanal.
3. **Explain** why D-Day's success was so vital to an Allied victory.

Reviewing Themes

4. **Geography and History** How did the geography of the Pacific affect American strategy?

Critical Thinking

5. **Analyzing** What made the invasion of Normandy so important?
6. **Organizing** Use a graphic organizer to explain the significance of each leader listed below.

Leader	Significance
Dwight Eisenhower	
George Patton	
George Marshall	
Omar Bradley	
Douglas MacArthur	

Analyzing Visuals

7. **Examining Photographs** Study the photograph on this page. What effect do you think MacArthur's return had on Philippine morale?

Writing About History

8. **Expository Writing** Using library or Internet resources, find more information on one of the battles discussed in this section. Use the information to write a report detailing the importance of the battle. Share your report with the class.

CHAPTER 20 America and World War II **637**

Previewing Your Textbook

Special Features

A variety of special features will help you as you study *The American Republic Since 1877.*

PROFILES IN HISTORY

Profiles in History tell you the stories of individuals who have influenced American history.

SKILLBUILDERS

Skillbuilders teach valuable skills that will be useful throughout the book.

DIFFERENT VIEWPOINTS

Different Viewpoints compare the opposing viewpoints of two historic figures on a particular issue.

AMERICAN LITERATURE

American Literature analyzes poems and excerpts from biographies, American fiction, and other writings, and describes the excerpts' historical lessons.

Cold War rival. Less than four months later, on January 31, 1958, the United States launched its own satellite from Cape Canaveral, Florida. Reporter Milton Bracker described the jubilant scene:

Profiles IN HISTORY

Dr. Jonas Salk
1914–1995

The man who developed the vaccine for one of the nation's most feared diseases almost did not go into medicine. Jonas Salk enrolled in college as a pre-law student but soon changed his mind. "My mother didn't think I would make a very good lawyer," Salk said, "probably because I could never win an argument with her." Salk switched his major to premed and went on to become a research scientist.

Salk initially directed the search for a cure to the dreaded ailment of polio at

...can remember how the staff used to kid Dr. Salk—kidding in earnest—telling him to hurry up and do something."

Salk became famous for his break-

❝As the firing command neared, a deadly silence fell on those who were watching. In the glare of the search-lights, a stream of liquid oxygen could be seen venting like a lavender cloud from the side of the seventy-foot rocket. . . . At fourteen and one-half seconds after time zero, after the priming fuel had ignited almost invisi-

---

Social Studies SKILLBUILDER

Understanding the Parts of

Why Learn This Skill?

Maps can direct you down the street or around the world. There are as many different kinds of maps as there are uses for them. Being able to read a map begins with learning about its parts.

Learning the Skill

NATIONAL GEOGRAPHIC

---

it killed civilians indiscriminately. He believed that an economic blockade and conventional bombing would convince Japan to surrender. Secretary of War Henry Stimson wanted to warn the Japanese about the bomb while at the same time telling them that they could keep the emperor if they surrendered. Secretary of State James Byrnes, however, wanted to drop the bomb without any warning to shock Japan into surrendering.

President Truman later wrote that he "regarded the bomb as a military weapon and never had any doubts that it should be used." His advisers had warned him to expect massive casualties if the United States invaded Japan. Truman believed it was his duty as president to use every weapon available to save American lives.

The Allies threatened Japan with "prompt and utter destruction" if the nation did not surrender unconditionally, but the Japanese did not reply. Truman then ordered the military to drop the bomb. On August 6, 1945, a B-29 bomber named the *Enola Gay* dropped an atomic bomb, code-named "Little

Boy," on Hiroshima, an [...] bomb was dropped at 8 [...] later, it exploded. Heat [...] shock wave slammed in [...]

The bomb destroyed [...] percent of the city. Son [...] 120,000 people died in [...] died later from bur [...] Everywhere, as witne [...] were "horrific scenes":

❝The center of the c [...] like live charcoal. Roof [...] numerous war dead w [...] We found five or six h [...] Inside were piles of c [...] smoke. . . . A young r [...] tucked under her bre [...] wax dolls than humar [...]

Different Viewpoints

Dropping the Atomic Bomb: Was It the Right Decision?

More than half a century later, people continue to debate what some historians have called the most important event of the twentieth century—President Truman's order to drop the atomic bomb on Japan. Did his momentous decision shorten the war and save lives on both sides, or was it prompted by Truman's fear that the Soviet Union, poised to invade, would gain control of Japan after the war?

A historian opposes Truman'[...]

Historian Gar Alperovitz ma[...] alternatives to the atomic bomb[...] in order to force Japan's surren[...] could mount an invasion and [...] territory.

"Quite simply, it is not true [...] because it was the only way t[...] sands' or 'millions' of lives as [...] readily available options were [...] and/or await the shock of the [...]

Perhaps it is [...] confront our ow[...] questions—for [...] most inflated e[...] atomic bomb, [...] of violent dest[...] tions of noncombatants.

—quoted in *The Decision to Use the Atomic Bomb, and the Architecture of an American Myth*

Hiroshima in the aftermath of the atomic bomb

American LITERATURE

Selected Poems by Langston Hughes

Langston Hughes was born in Joplin, Missouri, in 1902. After high school Hughes went on to Columbia University to study engineering, but he soon dropped out to pursue his first love—poetry. Hughes eventually became known as the "Poet Laureate of Harlem." The following poems are representative of Hughes's work. In "I, Too" he describes the disenfranchisement many African Americans felt in the United States in the 1920s, and their willingness to stand up and take pride in their heritage. In "The Negro Speaks of Rivers," Hughes reveals a profound love of his heritage.

Read to Discover
What is Hughes's perception of the place of African Americans in society at the time he wrote these poems?

Reader's Dictionary

Euphrates: River in the Middle East

Congo and **Nile:** Rivers in Africa

lulled: calmed; soothed

The Negro Speaks of Rivers

I've known rivers:
I've known rivers ancient as the
   world and older than the
   flow of human blood in human veins.

My soul has grown deep like the
   rivers.

I bathed in the Euphrates when
   dawns were young.
I built my hut near the Congo and it
   lulled me to sleep.
I looked upon the Nile and raised
   the pyramids above it.
I heard the singing of the Mississippi
   when Abe Lincoln went down to
   New Orleans, and I've seen its
   muddy bosom turn all golden in
   the sunset.

I've known rivers:
Ancient, dusky rivers.

My soul has grown deep like the
   rivers.

I, Too

I, too, sing America.

I am the darker brother.
They send me to eat in the kitchen
   When company comes,
   But I laugh,
   And eat well,
   And grow strong.

Tomorrow,
I'll be at the table
When company comes.
Nobody'll dare
   Say to me,
"Eat in the kitchen,"
   Then.

Besides,
They'll see how beautiful I am
And be ashamed—

I, too, am America.

Analyzing Literature

1. **Recall and Interpret** How do you think Hughes's use of punctuation and line breaks helps convey his point?
2. **Evaluate and Connect** Do you think these poems convey a positive message or a negative one? Why?

Interdisciplinary Activity

Response Writing The poem "I, Too" is a response to Walt Whitman's poem, "I Hear America Singing." Using the Internet or other resources, find and read Whitman's poem. In small groups, try to figure out how Hughes's poem ties in to Whitman's. Then write your own response poem to "I Hear America Singing."

1. Whic[...] do you think is the most valid? Why?
2. Using the Internet or other resources, find an account of the bombing from the point of a Japanese citizen. How does it differ from the accounts above, and why?

Scavenger Hunt

The American Republic Since 1877 contains a wealth of information. The trick is to know where to look to access all the information in the book. If you go through this scavenger hunt, either alone or with your teacher or parents, you will quickly learn how the textbook is organized and how to get the most out of your reading and study time. Let's get started!

1 How many units and chapters are in the book?
8 units and 29 chapters

2 Where do you find the glossary? appendix

3 Most sections of a chapter open with a primary source—a document or other testimony dating from the period. Where else can you find primary sources in the textbook?
Primary Sources Library in the appendix

4 In what special feature can you find the definition of a physical map, a political map, and a special-purpose map? Geography Handbook

5 If you want to quickly find all the maps, charts, and graphs about World War II, where in the front do you look? Table of Contents

6 How can you find information about William Penn's colonization of Pennsylvania? look in the index

7 Where can you find a graphic organizer that summarizes the major events of the Civil War discussed in Chapter 7?
Chapter Summary

8 Where and how do you find the key terms and names for Chapter 15, Section 3? listed in Guide to Reading and Section Assessment, boldfaced in text (terms are also in blue)

9 The Web site for the book is listed three times in Chapter 24. After finding all three, list how the Web site can help you.
provides overviews, practice tests, and additional activities and resources

10 Which of the book's main features will give you strategies for improving your studying and writing skills?
Skillbuilders

Reading for Information

Think of your textbook as a tool that helps you learn more about the world around you. It is an example of nonfiction writing—it describes real-life events, people, ideas, and places. Here is a menu of reading strategies that will help you become a better textbook reader. As you come to passages in your textbook that you don't understand, refer to these reading strategies for help.

✓ Before You Read

Set a purpose
- Why are you reading the textbook?
- How does the subject relate to your life?
- How might you be able to use what you learn in your own life?

Preview
- Read the chapter title to find what the topic will be.
- Read the subtitles to see what you will learn about the topic.
- Skim the photos, charts, graphs, or maps. How do they support the topic?
- Look for vocabulary words that are boldfaced. What are their definitions?

Draw From Your Own Background
- What have you read or heard concerning new information on the topic?
- How is the new information different from what you already know?
- How will the information that you already know help you understand the new information?

Question

■ What is the main idea?

■ How do the photos, charts, graphs, and maps support the main idea?

Connect

■ Think about people, places, and events in your own life. Are there any similarities with those in your textbook?

■ Can you relate the textbook information to other areas of your life?

Predict

■ Predict events or outcomes by using clues and information that you already know.

■ Change your predictions as you read and gather new information.

Visualize

■ Pay careful attention to details and descriptions.

■ Create graphic organizers to show relationships that you find in the information.

Look For Clues As You Read

Comparison and Contrast Sentences

■ Look for clue words and phrases that signal comparison, such as *similarly, just as, both, in common, also,* and *too.*

■ Look for clue words and phrases that signal contrast, such as *on the other hand, in contrast to, however, different, instead of, rather than, but,* and *unlike.*

Cause-and-Effect Sentences

■ Look for clue words and phrases such as *because, as a result, therefore, that is why, since, so, for this reason,* and *consequently.*

Chronological Sentences

■ Look for clue words and phrases such as *after, before, first, next, last, during, finally, earlier, later, since,* and *then.*

✓ After You Read

Summarize

■ Describe the main idea and how the details support it.

■ Use your own words to explain what you have read.

Assess

■ What was the main idea?

■ Did the text clearly support the main idea?

■ Did you learn anything new from the material?

■ Can you use this new information in other school subjects or at home?

■ What other sources could you use to find more information about the topic?

How Do I Study History?

As you read *The American Republic Since 1877*, you will be given help in sorting out all the information you encounter. This textbook organizes the events of your nation's past and present around 10 themes. A theme is a concept, or main idea that happens again and again throughout history. By recognizing these themes, you will better understand events of the past and how they affect you today.

Themes in *The American Republic Since 1877*

Culture and Traditions
Being aware of cultural differences helps us understand ourselves and others. People from around the world for generations have sung of the "land of the Pilgrims' pride, land where our fathers died," even though their ancestors arrived on these shores long after these events occurred.

Continuity and Change
Recognizing our historic roots helps us understand why things are the way they are today. This theme includes political, social, religious, and economic changes that have influenced the way Americans think and act.

Geography and History
Understanding geography helps us understand how humans interact with their environment. The United States succeeded in part because of its rich natural resources and its vast open spaces. In many regions, the people changed the natural landscape to fulfill their wants and needs.

Individual Action

Responsible individuals have often stepped forward to help lead the nation. Americans' strong values helped create such individuals. These values spring in part from earlier times when the home was the center of many activities, including work, education, and spending time with one's family.

Groups and Institutions

Identifying how political and social groups and institutions operate helps us work together. From the beginning, Americans formed groups and institutions to act in support of their economic, political, social, and religious beliefs.

Government and Democracy

Understanding the workings of government helps us become better citizens. Abraham Lincoln explained the meaning of democracy as "government of the people, by the people, for the people." Democracy, at its best, is "among" the people.

Science and Technology

Americans have always been quick to adopt innovations. The nation was settled and built by people who blended their old ways with new ways. Americans' lives are deeply influenced by technology, the use of science, and machines. Perhaps no machine has so shaped modern life as the automobile. Understanding the role of science and technology helps us see their impact on our society and the roles they will play in the future.

Economic Factors

The free enterprise economy of the United States is consistent with the nation's history of rights and freedoms. Freedom of choice in economic decisions supports other freedoms. Understanding the concept of free enterprise is basic to studying American history.

Global Connections

Being aware of global interdependence helps us make decisions and deal with the difficult issues we will encounter.

Civic Rights and Responsibilities

For a democratic system to survive, its citizens must take an active role in government. The foundation of democracy is the right of every person to take part in government and to voice one's views on issues. An appreciation for the struggle to preserve these freedoms is vital to the understanding of democracy.

Using the Themes

You will find Section Themes at the beginning of every section of your text. You are asked questions that help you put it all together to better understand how ideas and themes are connected across time—and to see why history is important to you today.

The Early American History Review Test is designed to help you decide which of the first seven chapters of the textbook to focus on as you help your students review American history, prehistory to 1877. The review test provides information and questions representative of the content covered in the study of early American history.

1. B
Test-Taking Strategy: Encourage students to read the question carefully. Overlooking words like NOT or EXCEPT in a question is a common error. Students are looking for the answer choice that does NOT fit with the question.
Content can be found in **Chapter 1, pp. 30–35**

2. J
Test-Taking Strategy: Before students answer this question, review with them what a valid generalization is. It is a general statement based on the available facts. Ask students to eliminate incorrect answer choices, keeping this definition in mind. Students should remember that Columbus's arrival produced both positive and negative effects, the colonization of the Americas was not the goal of all European explorers, and Vasco da Gama completed an eastern sea route to Asia.
Content can be found in **Chapter 1, pp. 20–21**

3. D
Content can be found in **Chapter 1, pp. 27–28**

4. H
Content can be found in **Chapter 1, p. 16**

Early American History
Review Test

The following pages contain questions to review your knowledge of American history from the beginnings to 1877. Taking this test will help you and your teacher decide which of the first seven chapters of this textbook you need to study to refresh your memory of events that happened during the early years of the Republic.

Directions: Choose the best answer to each of the following multiple choice questions. If you have trouble answering a question, use the process of elimination to narrow your choices. Write your answers on a separate sheet of paper.

1. Rivalry between European countries in the Americas in the mid-1500s was caused by all of the following EXCEPT

   A competition over wealth and power.

   B disagreements over slavery.

   C the desire for new trade routes and gold.

   D competition for trade.

2. Which of the statements below is a valid generalization?

   F Christopher Columbus's arrival in the Americas produced only positive effects for humankind.

   G All European explorers wanted to colonize the Americas.

   H Vasco da Gama's plan was to find a western sea route to Asia.

   J Advances in technology made European voyages of exploration possible.

3. All of the following statements about the Columbian Exchange are true EXCEPT

   A food products were traded between the continents.

   B enslaved Africans were brought to the Americas.

   C Europeans introduced diseases to Native Americans.

   D Native Americans introduced Europeans to domestic animals such as cattle and horses.

4. The Iroquois League was important because it

   F protected the Aztec from the Spanish.

   G was created by Hiawatha.

   H was an early American form of democratic assemblies.

   J was copied by the Mayans.

Use the information in the box below and your knowledge of social studies to answer question 5.

> Roger Williams—Rhode Island
> Thomas Hooker—Connecticut
> John Smith—Virginia
> James Oglethorpe—Georgia

5. An appropriate title for the information above would be

   A Early European Explorers of the Americas.

   B Missionaries to North America.

   C Leaders of the American Revolution.

   D Leaders or Founders of the American Colonies.

6. In 1620 a group of people drew up a document in which they pledged their loyalty to England and declared their intention of forming "a civil body politic, for our better ordering and preservation." The excerpt above can be found in which American document?

   F the Magna Carta

   G the Mayflower Compact

   H *The Federalist,* No. 10

   J the Declaration of Independence

5. D
Test-Taking Strategy: To answer this question, students must decide what all of the items in the box have in common. Encourage students to compare the answer choices against the information presented. Then delete answer choices one by one, and decide the best answer from the answers remaining.
Content can be found in **Chapter 2, pp. 45, 50, 51, 56**

6. G
Test-Taking Strategy: If students do not recognize the answer immediately, they can use clues from the question to infer the answer. Clues include the following: 1620, "they pledged their loyalty to England," and "a civil body politic." **Ask:** Which historical document fits all three of these clues?
Content can be found in **Chapter 2, p. 48**

Use the cartoon below and your knowledge of social studies to answer question 7.

JOIN, or DIE.

7. In the early 1770s, this cartoon would have most likely appeared in a

A British journal. C Royal Army comic strip.

B Loyalist pamphlet. D colonial newspaper.

8. Which important American document was written and ratified between the signing of the Declaration of Independence and the ratification of the U.S. Constitution?

F The Wealth of Nations

G the Bill of Rights

H the Articles of Confederation

J The Federalist

9. Which First Amendment right protects citizens who are staging a protest outside a government building?

A freedom of speech C freedom of assembly

B freedom of the press D freedom of religion

10. According to the Declaration of Independence, an unalienable right

F cannot be taken away by the government.

G belongs only to citizens of the United States.

H is granted to people by state governments.

J exists only in wartime.

Use the chart below and your knowledge of social studies to answer the question that follows.

11. The principle of checks and balances was put in place because

A delegates realized that the U.S. Constitution might need to be changed over time.

B delegates feared that one branch of the federal government might become too powerful.

C the newly independent colonies needed a central government.

D the states began to act as independent countries.

Problem	Solution
The newly independent colonies needed a central government.	The Articles of Confederation were adopted as the country's first constitution.
The weak central government created by the Articles led to diplomatic problems with other nations. The states began to act as independent countries to protect their trade rights.	Delegates at the Constitutional Convention adopted the Virginia Plan, which proposed the creation of a new federal government.
Opponents of the proposed new federal government feared that it would become too powerful.	The Constitution divided power between the federal government and the state governments and established three branches of power in the federal government.
Constitutional delegates feared that one branch of the federal government would become too powerful.	The Constitution gave each branch of the federal government the ability to limit the power of the other branches.
Delegates realized that the Constitution might need to be changed over time.	A system for making amendments was added, and the Constitution was ratified.

Review Test xxxiii

9. C
Test-Taking Strategy: Remind students of the basic freedoms guaranteed by the First Amendment–freedom of speech, freedom of religion, freedom of the press, freedom of assembly, and the right to petition. To answer the question, students need only to define the rights listed in the answer choices.
Content can be found in the Constitution Handbook, p. 124

10. F
Test-Taking Strategy: Students must define unalienable right to correctly answer this question. This phrase is defined in the Declaration of Independence with the words, "We hold these truths to be self-evident, that all men are created equal, that they are endowed by their Creator with certain unalienable Rights, that among these are Life, Liberty, and the pursuit of Happiness. . . ."
Content can be found in Chapter 3, p. 90

11. B
Test-Taking Strategy: Students must interpret information from the problem-solution chart to answer this question. Tell students to identify what the question is asking (the question gives a solution and is asking students to identify the problem). Also tell students to make sure the answer they select is supported by information on the chart.
Content can be found in Chapter 3, p. 101, and the Constitution Handbook, pp. 123–124

7. D
Test-Taking Strategy: Encourage students to look for clues in the question to support their answers. What was happening in the colonies in the 1770s? Students should make note of important words in the possible answers and eliminate those that don't make sense. A Loyalist was a colonist who supported the British government during the American Revolution.
Content can be found in Chapter 3, pp. 82–89

8. H
Test-Taking Strategy: To help jog students' memories, ask students to try to sequence the answer choices by date of adoption or formation. Remind students that the Articles of Confederation was adopted in November 1777. It was America's first constitution.
Content can be found in Chapter 3, p. 103

T59

12. F

Test-Taking Strategy: To correctly answer this question, students must realize that Article II of the U.S. Constitution established the executive branch, headed by the president. After these guidelines were set, Washington was selected as the nation's first president.
Content can be found in **Chapter 3, p. 115**

13. B

Test-Taking Strategy: Students must know the definition of *federalism* to correctly answer this question. If they are having trouble remembering it, advise them to try to eliminate answer choices. For example, power shared between the three branches of government is the system of checks and balances, not federalism.
Content can be found in the **Constitution Handbook, pp. 122–123**

14. H

Test-Taking Strategy: In order to determine relative location, students must look for a compass rose on the map.
Ask students to determine where San Jacinto is in relation to San Antonio.
Content can be found in **Chapter 5, pp. 205–207**

15. D

Test-Taking Strategy: This question requires students to read a special purpose map and sequence battles of the Texas war for independence. Extend students' understanding by asking what the various symbols on the map mean. Also ask students to explain why the battle at the Alamo was significant.
Content can be found in **Chapter 5, pp. 205–207**

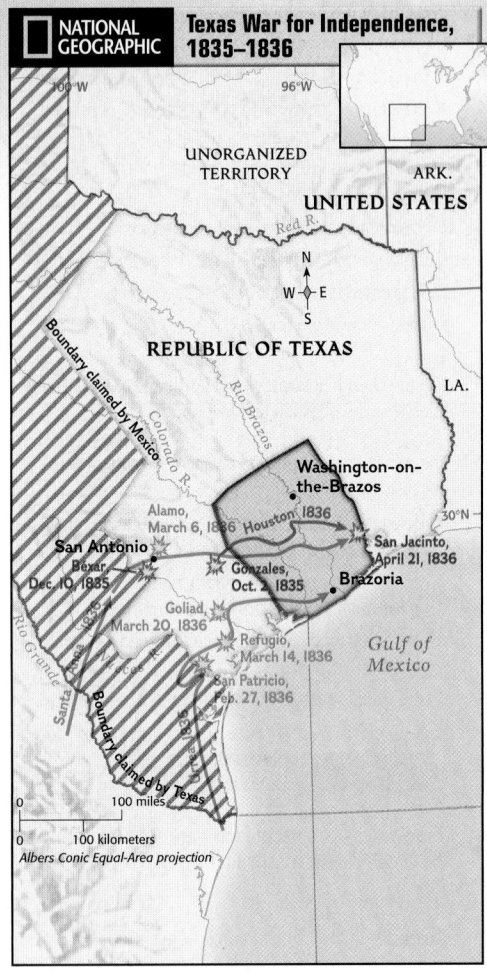

Texas War for Independence, 1835–1836

Use the map to the left and your knowledge of social studies to answer questions 14 and 15.

14. San Jacinto is located _____ of San Antonio.

F west
G south
H east
J north

15. According to the map, what is the correct chronological sequence of battles?

A Gonzales, San Jacinto, the Alamo
B Goliad, the Alamo, Gonzales
C Refugio, the Alamo, Goliad
D Gonzales, the Alamo, San Jacinto

16. The United States doubled in size in 1803 with the acquisition of

F Texas.
G Florida.
H the Oregon Territory.
J the Louisiana Purchase.

17. Those who supported ratification of the U.S. Constitution were called

A Liberals.
B Antifederalists.
C Whigs.
D Federalists.

18. The signing of the Treaty of Paris in 1783 was a victory for the United States because

F France agreed to provide military aid to the United States.
G Great Britain recognized the United States as an independent nation.
H France agreed to sell the Louisiana Territory to the United States.
J it dissolved most of the Spanish Empire.

19. Frederick Douglass is best known for his contributions to the _____ movement.

A abolitionist
B temperance
C woman suffrage
D Antifederalist

20. The principle of judicial review was established by the Supreme Court's ruling in

F *Plessy* v. *Ferguson.*
G *Marbury* v. *Madison.*
H *Dred Scott* v. *Sandford.*
J *McCulloch* v. *Maryland.*

12. George Washington became president under which plan of government?

F the U.S. Constitution
G the Magna Carta
H the Articles of Confederation
J the Declaration of Independence

13. Under federalism, power is shared between

A the three branches of government.
B the national and state governments.
C the two houses of Congress.
D the justices of the Supreme Court.

16. J
Content can be found in **Chapter 4, p. 163**

17. D
Content can be found in **Chapter 3, pp. 112–115**

18. G

Test-Taking Strategy: Tell students to carefully read the question, eliminating answers that don't make sense. If students note the date—1783—they may realize that this treaty occurred after the Revolutionary War. Students may also recall that a Treaty of Paris did dissolve much of the Spanish Empire, but this treaty occurred in 1898.
Content can be found in **Chapter 3, p. 99**

21. Which of the following people would most likely have been a member of the Democratic-Republican political party in the 1790s?

A a wealthy merchant living in New York

B a Southern cotton farmer

C a factory owner in the North

D a rich banker

22. Which of these events occurred first?

F The Northwest Ordinance was passed.

G Gold was discovered in California.

H A treaty setting the northern border of Oregon was signed.

J The Louisiana Territory was purchased.

Use the graph below and your knowledge of social studies to answer questions 23 and 24.

23. In which decade did the United States's urban population see the most growth?

A 1860s   C 1820s

B 1840s   D 1810s

24. In which year was there the widest gap between the urban and rural populations?

F 1810   H 1860

G 1840   J 1850

25. The phrase "We, the people . . ." is found in the

A U.S. Constitution.

B Articles of Confederation.

C Declaration of Independence.

D First Amendment.

Use the quotation below and your knowledge of social studies to answer questions 26 and 27.

"I wish to speak today, not as a Massachusetts man, nor as a Northern man, but as an American. . . . I speak today for the preservation of the Union. . . . Peaceable secession is an utter impossibility. . . . I see as plainly as I see the sun in heaven that disruption itself must produce; I see that it must produce war, and such a war as I will not describe."

—Daniel Webster, 1850

26. The quotation is an example of a

F secondary source.   H compromise.

G referendum.   J primary source.

27. The war Webster was predicting was the

A war with Mexico.   C American Revolution.

B Civil War.   D War of 1812.

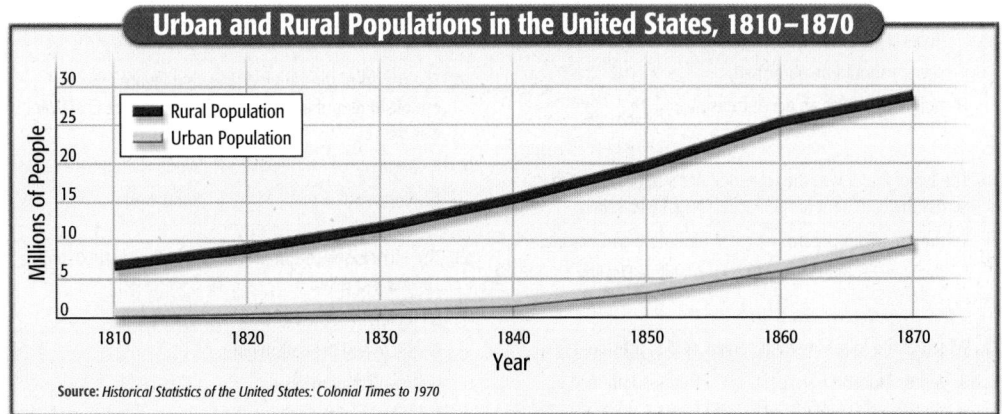

Urban and Rural Populations in the United States, 1810–1870

Rural Population
Urban Population

Millions of People

30
25
20
15
10
5
0

1810   1820   1830   1840   1850   1860   1870

Year

Source: *Historical Statistics of the United States: Colonial Times to 1970*

23. A
Test-Taking Strategy: Make sure that students carefully examine the labels on the line graph to determine what they symbolize. Point out the key words used in the question—*urban population* and *the most growth.*
Content can be found in **Chapter 5, p. 186**

24. H
Content can be found in **Chapter 5, p. 186**

25. A
Content can be found in the **Constitution Handbook, p. 131**

26. J
Test-Taking Strategy: To answer this question, students must first conclude that this excerpt does not reflect a referendum or a compromise. (Have students look up these terms in the dictionary or glossary.) Students must also be able to recognize a primary source and distinguish it from a secondary source.
Content can be found in **Chapter 6, p. 221,** *and* **Chapter 26, p. 818**

27. B
Content can be found in **Chapter 6, p. 221**

19. A
Content can be found in **Chapter 5, p. 184**

20. G
Test-Taking Strategy: This question asks students to recall which Supreme Court ruling reflects the principle of judicial review. If students don't know the answer, have them eliminate answer choices they know are wrong.
Content can be found in **Chapter 4, p. 162**

21. B
Content can be found in **Chapter 4, p. 155**

22. F
Content can be found in **Chapter 3, pp. 104–105**

28. F
***Content can be found in* Chapter 3, pp. 88, 89**

29. B
Test-Taking Strategy: If students know two key terms in the question, they could answer correctly. *Nullify* means to cancel. *States' rights* is the idea that the states have many rights and powers that are independent of the federal government. During the Nullification Crisis, South Carolina threatened to secede from the Union in anger over the so-called Tariff of Abominations.
***Content can be found in* Chapter 5, pp. 190, 191**

30. J
***Content can be found in* Chapter 5, pp. 202, 203**

31. C
Test-Taking Strategy: This question requires students to properly sequence presidential administrations. If students are having trouble, encourage them to narrow down the choices by thinking of events associated with each president and sequencing the events instead.
***Content can be found in* Chapter 4, pp. 161, 162**

32. J
Test-Taking Strategy: Students are asked to make an inference. To help students, ask them what was "king" in the South. What product transformed the Southern economy into a prosperous, robust economy?
***Content can be found in* Chapter 5, pp. 182, 183, Chapter 7, p. 245**

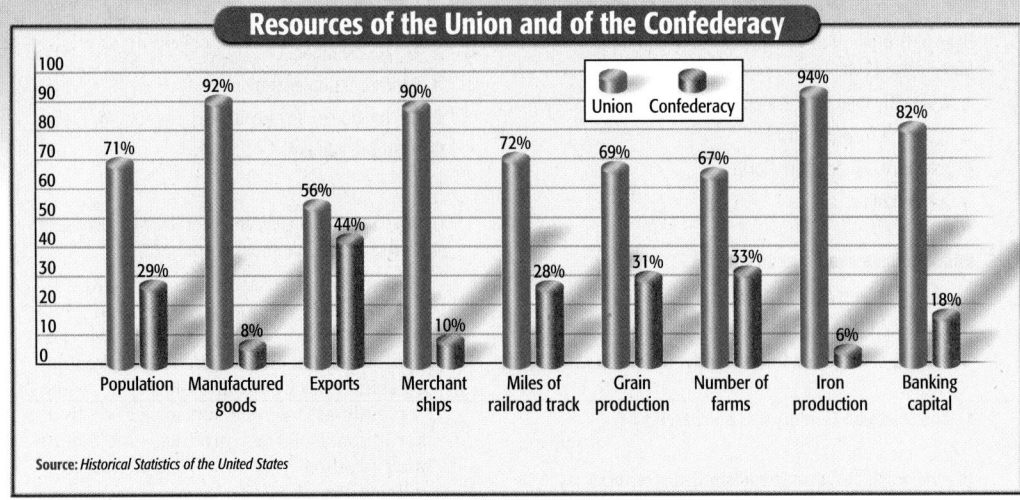

Resources of the Union and of the Confederacy

Source: *Historical Statistics of the United States*

28. One of Thomas Paine's major contributions to the Patriot cause was
   F a pamphlet entitled *Common Sense*.
   G the founding of the Sons of Liberty.
   H his fiery speech in the Virginia House of Burgesses.
   J his leadership at Lexington and Concord.

29. Supporters of states' rights felt that states had the right to nullify a tariff passed by Congress in 1828. They argued that
   A the Union must be preserved.
   B states had powers and rights independent of the federal government.
   C slavery should be abolished.
   D nullification was an act of treason.

30. The belief that it was the United States's right to spread across the continent to the Pacific Ocean was called
   F the American Dream.   H the Monroe Doctrine.
   G the New Frontier.   J Manifest Destiny.

31. Which of the following men served as U.S. president first?
   A James Monroe   C Thomas Jefferson
   B Abraham Lincoln   D Andrew Jackson

Use the graph above and your knowledge of social studies to answer questions 32 and 33.

32. The graph shows that the amount of resources of the Union and the Confederacy were the closest in the area of exports. What good was the South's chief export?
   F indigo   H rice
   G tobacco   J cotton

33. The Union's advantage in miles of railroad track is related to what other resource?
   A population   C merchant ships
   B iron production   D banking capital

34. The region of the United States that favored the establishment of protective tariffs before the Civil War was the
   F South.   H West.
   G Northeast.   J Southwest.

35. The increase in cotton production between 1800 and 1860 was a result of
   A factories in the North.
   B the use of the cotton gin.
   C the plantation system.
   D the lack of factories in the South.

33. B
Test-Taking Strategy: Students must draw on background information to make a correct inference. Encourage students to read through all of the answer choices before coming to a final decision. Which of the resources listed in the answer choices relates to the construction of railroad track?
***Content can be found in* Chapter 7, pp. 245, 246**

34. G
Test-Taking Strategy: This question deals with the economy of the nation prior to the Civil War. First, students should recognize that *prior* means "before." Then students should recall which part of the nation at the time would welcome taxes paid by merchants who imported goods. Northeasterners welcomed tariffs because they made European goods more expensive, cutting competition for the goods made in the Northeast.
***Content can be found in* Chapter 4, p. 171, Chapter 5, pp. 190, 191**

Read the passage below, and then answer questions 36 and 37.

"With malice toward none, with charity for all . . . let us strive to finish the work we are in, to bind up the nation's wounds . . . to do all which may achieve and cherish a just and lasting peace among ourselves and with all nations."

36. This passage would most likely be

F a paragraph from a textbook.

G a quotation by Abraham Lincoln.

H a quotation by King George III during the American Revolution.

J a letter to the editor in a current newspaper.

37. How would you summarize the tone of this passage?

A full of bitterness and opposition

B inspiring reconciliation

C encouraging action and sacrifice

D proud, delighting in victory

38. One purpose of the Thirteenth Amendment was to

F change the method of electing the vice president.

G prevent quartering of soldiers in private homes.

H establish a consistent definition of citizenship.

J abolish slavery.

1. Battle of Gettysburg
2. First Battle of Bull Run
3. Firing on Fort Sumter
4. Meeting at Appomattox Courthouse

39. The correct chronological order for the events listed above is

A 1, 3, 4, 2.   C 4, 1, 3, 2.

B 3, 2, 1, 4.   D 2, 3, 1, 4.

40. One of the purposes of the Fourteenth Amendment was to

F abolish slavery.

G guarantee freedom of religion.

H protect the right of African American men to vote.

J define citizenship.

41. "[G]overnment of the people, by the people, and for the people, shall not perish from the earth" was the conclusion to a speech given by _____ after the Battle of Gettysburg.

A Abraham Lincoln   C Robert E. Lee

B Jefferson Davis   D George Meade

Use the quotation below and your knowledge of Social Studies to answer question 42.

"What, to the American slave, is your Fourth of July? I answer: A day that reveals to him, more than all other days in the year, the gross injustice and cruelty to which he is the constant victim. . . ."

—Frederick Douglass, 1852

42. To which of the following documents does Douglass indirectly refer in the passage above?

F U.S. Constitution

G Mayflower Compact

H Declaration of Sentiments

J Declaration of Independence

Use the circle graph below and your knowledge of social studies to answer question 43.

43. The greatest number of deaths in American wars took place during the

A 1900s.   C 1800s.

B 1600s.   D 1700s.

American War Deaths
(approximate figures)

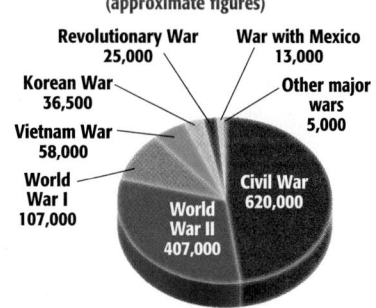

Revolutionary War 25,000
War with Mexico 13,000
Korean War 36,500
Other major wars 5,000
Vietnam War 58,000
World War I 107,000
Civil War 620,000
World War II 407,000

Source: United States Civil War Center; *For the Common Defense*

37. B
Content can be found in **Chapter 7, pp. 266, 267**

38. J
Test-Taking Strategy: Students often confuse the amendments to the U.S. Constitution, so it may be helpful for students to think about *when* the Thirteenth Amendment was passed. It was ratified in 1865, and approved by states loyal to the Union.
Content can be found in **Chapter 7, pp. 262, 263**

39. B
Content can be found in **Chapter 6, p. 235, Chapter 7, pp. 249, 258, 263**

40. J
Content can be found in **Chapter 7, pp. 269–270**

41. A
Content can be found in **Chapter 7, p. 259**

42. J
Content can be found in **Chapter 3, p. 89**

43. C
Content can be found in **Chapter 7, p. 260**

35. B
Content can be found in **Chapter 5, p. 182**

36. G
Test-Taking Strategy: Before students answer, remind them to consider the differences between primary and secondary sources. If they correctly conclude that the passage is a primary source, they have narrowed down the answer choices, and then may select the most logical one.
Content can be found in **Chapter 7, pp. 266, 267**

Why Should I Teach Reading to My Social Studies Students?

For many social studies teachers, helping students develop reading skills is a low priority—nice to do if there's time, but not necessary. After all, there is scarcely time to meet many of the state-mandated subject-area learning objectives. Why add reading instruction to the list? The answer is that reading skills are essential to the learning of subjects. In the social studies, students must read to learn. Struggling readers risk learning less than those who are proficient in reading.

Teachers who infuse literacy strategies with social studies content actively engage students in learning. Once students internalize reading strategies such as visualizing, predicting, and making connections, they inevitably become better social studies students.

READING TO LEARN

This handbook focuses on skills and strategies that can help you understand the words you read. The strategies you use to understand whole texts depend on the kind of text you are reading. In other words, you don't read a textbook the way you read a novel. You read a textbook mainly for information; you read a novel mainly for fun. To get the most out of your reading, you need to choose the right strategy to fit the reason you're reading.

USE THIS HANDBOOK TO HELP YOU LEARN

- how to identify new words and build your vocabulary
- how to adjust the way you read to fit your reason for reading
- how to use specific reading strategies to better understand what you read
- how to use critical thinking strategies to think more deeply about what you read

You will also learn about

- text structures
- reading for research

TABLE OF CONTENTS

Professional Development: Teaching Reading

The following sources will help you teach reading skills:

- *Subjects Matter: Every Teacher's Guide to Content-Area Reading,* by Harvey Daniels and Steven Zemelman. Portsmouth, NH: Heineman, 2004.
- *When Kids Can't Read, What Teachers Can Do: A Guide for Teachers, 6–12,* by G. Kylene Beers. Portsmouth, NH: Heinemann, 2003.
- *I Read It But I Don't Get It: Comprehension Strategies for Adolescent Readers,* by Cris Tovani. Portland, ME: Stenhouse Publishers, 2000.
- *Teaching Reading in the Middle School,* by Laura Robb. New York, NY: Scholastic Professional Books, 2000.

Reading Skills Handbook

Identifying Words and Building Vocabulary

What do you do when you come across a word you do not know as you read? Do you skip over the word and keep reading? If you are reading for fun or entertainment, you might. But if you are reading for information, an unfamiliar word may get in the way of your understanding. When that happens, try the following strategies to figure out how to say the word and what the word means.

Reading Unfamiliar Words

Sounding out the word One way to figure out how to say a new word is to sound it out, syllable by syllable. Look carefully at the word's beginning, middle, and ending. Inside the word, do you see a word you already know how to pronounce? What vowels are in the syllables? Use the following tips when sounding out new words.

- **Roots and base words** The main part of a word is called its root. When the root is a complete word, it may be called the base word. When you come across a new word, check whether you recognize its root or base word. It can help you pronounce the word and figure out the word's meaning.

ASK YOURSELF

- What letters make up the beginning sound or beginning syllable of the word?
  Example: In the word *coagulate*, *co* rhymes with *so*.
- What sounds do the letters in the middle part of the word make?
  Example: In the word *coagulate*, the syllable *ag* has the same sound as the

 ag in *bag*, and the syllable *u* is pronounced like the letter *u*.
- What letters make up the ending sound or syllable?
  Example: In the word *coagulate*, *late* is a familiar word you already know how to pronounce.
- Now try pronouncing the whole word: *co ag u late*.

- **Prefixes** A prefix is a word part that can be added to the beginning of a root or base word. For example, the prefix *pre-* means "before," so *prehistory* means "before history." Prefixes can change, or even reverse, the meaning of a word. For example, *un-* means "not," so *unconstitutional* means "not constitutional."

- **Suffixes** A suffix is a word part that can be added to the end of a root or base word to change the word's meaning. Adding a suffix to a word can also change that word from one part of speech to another. For example, the word *joy,* which is a noun, becomes an adjective when the suffix *-ful* (meaning "full of") is added. *Joyful* means "full of joy."

Determining a Word's Meaning

Using syntax Like all languages, the English language has rules and patterns for the way words are arranged in sentences. The way a sentence is organized is called the **syntax** of the sentence. If English is your first language, you have known this pattern since you started talking in sentences. If you're learning English now, you may find the syntax is different from the patterns you know in your first language.

Reading Skills Handbook   **RH1**

Reading Skills Handbook

Identifying Words and Building Vocabulary

Why It's Important
Research documents the relationship between a strong vocabulary and the ability to read and write proficiently. Vocabulary may be the most important factor in comprehension, showing that ongoing, specific vocabulary instruction must be an integral part of every lesson.

Before Reading
Activating Prior Knowledge
Distribute index cards with a key word from the chapter written on each card. Organize students into groups of four, and give them time to discuss their words. After the group discussion, ask each group to write what they think the word means on the back of the card. Then have groups present the words to the class by writing their words and definitions on the board. Other students should help confirm or revise the definitions. Use pictures or graphs to enhance or correct the students' definitions.

Differentiated Instruction

Meeting Special Needs: Less-Proficient Readers One way to help students increase their vocabularies is to have them play word games before they read the chapter. Give students a word from the chapter that they do not know, and allow them to ask questions about its definition. When a student correctly guesses its meaning, he or she can then be "it," choosing a new word for the class to question. This type of game demonstrates that there are often many definitions for a word, and it allows students to learn from each other.

Reading Skills Handbook

During Reading

Learning Vocabulary Post a chart on the wall listing the steps for learning new vocabulary. Students may refer to the chart as they read. Steps include: sound out the word; look at prefixes, suffixes, and roots; look at how the word is used in the sentence; use context clues in surrounding sentences; use reference materials such as dictionaries and thesauruses; ask someone the meaning of the word. Encourage students to experiment with different steps to find the one that works best for them.

After Reading

Reinforcing Vocabulary

Students should use graphic organizers and web diagrams to explain the definition of a word. Have students write the word in the center of a sheet of notebook paper. Then have them write *What it is* at the top left of the page, *What it is like* at the top right, *Examples of its meaning* at the bottom left of the page, and *What it is not* at the bottom right. Have students write the appropriate information under each head.

In a simple sentence in English, someone or something (the *subject*) does something (the *predicate* or *verb*) to or with another person or thing (the *object*): The *soldiers attacked* the *enemy*.

Sometimes adjectives, adverbs, and phrases are added to add details to the sentence: The *courageous young* soldiers *fearlessly* attacked the *well-entrenched* enemy *shortly after dawn*.

CHECK IT OUT

Knowing about syntax can help you figure out the meaning of an unfamiliar word. Just look at how syntax can help you figure out the following nonsense sentence.

The blizzy kwarkles sminched the flerky fleans.

Your experience with English syntax tells you that the action word, or verb, in this sentence is *sminched*. Who did the *sminching?* The *kwarkles*. What kind of kwarkles were they? *Blizzy*. Whom did they *sminch?* The *fleans*. What kind of fleans were they? *Flerky*. Even though you don't know the meaning of the words in the nonsense sentence, you can make some sense of the entire sentence by studying its syntax.

Using context clues You can often figure out the meaning of an unfamiliar word by looking at its context, the words and sentences that surround it. To learn new words as you read, follow these steps for using context clues.

1. Look before and after the unfamiliar word for:
   - a definition or a synonym, another word that means the same as the unfamiliar word.
   - a general topic associated with the word.
   - a clue to what the word is similar to or different from.
   - an action or a description that has something to do with the word.
2. Connect what you already know with what the author has written.
3. Predict a possible meaning.
4. Use the meaning in the sentence.
5. Try again if your guess does not make sense.

Using reference materials Dictionaries and other reference sources can help you learn new words. Check out these reference sources:

- A **dictionary** gives the pronunciation and the meaning or meanings of words. Some dictionaries also give other forms of words, their parts of speech, and synonyms. You might also find the historical background of a word, such as its Greek, Latin, or Anglo-Saxon origins.

- A **glossary** is a word list that appears at the end—or Appendix—of a book or other written work and includes only words that are in that work. Like dictionaries, glossaries have the pronunciation and definitions of words.

- A **thesaurus** lists groups of words that have the same, or almost the same, meaning. Words with similar meanings are called *synonyms*. Seeing the synonyms of words can help you build your vocabulary.

More About the Reading Strategy

How can teachers help students understand word concepts instead of just learning simple definitions? One way is to use words often and in a variety of ways. Teams of teachers can choose common vocabulary words which they will present in various content area classes. Teachers should provide opportunities for integrating the words into meaningful contexts. The goal is for students to develop full knowledge of the words so that they become fixed parts of their vocabularies.

Recognizing Word Meanings Across Subjects

Have you ever learned a new word in one class and then noticed it in your reading for other subjects? The word probably will not mean exactly the same thing in each class. But you can use what you know about the word's meaning to help you understand what it means in a different subject area.

CHECK IT OUT

Look at the following example from three subjects:

Social studies: One major **product** manufactured in the South is cotton cloth.

Math: After you multiply those two numbers, explain how you arrived at the **product.**

Science: One **product** of photosynthesis is oxygen.

Reading for a Reason

Why are you reading that paperback mystery? What do you hope to get from your geography textbook? And are you going to read either of these books in the same way that you read a restaurant menu? The point is, you read for different reasons. The reason you are reading something helps you decide on the reading strategies you use with a text. In other words, how you read will depend on **why** you're reading.

Knowing Your Reason for Reading

In school and in life, you will have many reasons for reading, and those reasons will lead you to a wide range of materials. For example,

- **to learn and understand new information,** you might read news magazines, textbooks, news on the Internet, books about your favorite pastime, encyclopedia articles, primary and secondary sources for a school report, instructions on how to use a calling card, or directions for a standardized test.

- **to find specific information,** you might look at the sports section for the score of last night's game, a notice on where to register for a field trip, weather reports, bank statements, or television listings.

- **to be entertained,** you might read your favorite magazine, e-mails or letters from friends, the Sunday comics, or even novels, short stories, plays, or poems!

Adjusting How Fast You Read

How quickly or how carefully you should read a text depends on your purpose for reading it. Because there are many reasons and ways to read, think about your purpose and choose a strategy that works best. Try out these strategies:

- **Scanning** means quickly running your eyes over the material, looking for *key words or phrases* that point to the information you're looking for. Scan when you need to find a particular piece or type of information. For example, you might scan a newspaper for movie show times.

Reading Skills Handbook

Reading for a Reason

Why It's Important

When students have a reason or purpose for reading, the task becomes relevant and meaningful, both of which are necessary for comprehension. Good readers inherently set purposes for themselves, but less-proficient readers might need help finding a reason for reading.

Before Reading

Skimming Help students establish a reason for reading by skimming the text. Point out section headings, illustrations, and boldfaced words. Tell students that these text features can help establish a purpose for reading.

During Reading

Identifying a Reason for Reading Give students a specific task to perform while they read, such as looking for a specific piece of information, summarizing content, finding details to support a position, or writing a response to what they have read.

Differentiated Instruction

Meeting Special Needs: Less-Proficient Readers Students need practice with establishing a reason for reading. Encourage students to read news magazines, newspapers, historical novels, nonfiction books, or Internet articles. Before reading, have students write a rationale for why they have chosen that type of reading. Students should describe what they will do after they read, such as present an oral report.

Reading Skills Handbook

After Reading

Paraphrasing When students finish reading, have them work with a partner to paraphrase what they have read. Encourage them to reread sections of text or share notes and answers to questions in order to clarify the reading.

Understanding What You Read

Why It's Important

Students who read but don't "get it" or who simply will not read at all cannot adequately master the content of their courses. Helping students learn to use a variety of reading strategies as tools for comprehension will lead to long-term benefits in school and everyday life.

Before Reading

Making Predictions On index cards, write important words from the chapter—one word per card. Place the cards on various desks around the room. Allow students to move from desk to desk until they find a word that they think they may know something about. Have students use the word to make predictions about what they will learn in the chapter.

- **Skimming** means quickly reading a piece of writing *to find its main idea* or to *get a general overview* of it. For example, you might skim the sports section of the daily newspaper to find out how your favorite teams are doing. Or you might skim a chapter in your textbook to prepare for a test.

- **Careful reading** involves *reading slowly and paying attention* with a purpose in mind. Read carefully when you're learning new concepts, following complicated directions, or preparing to explain information to someone else.

Understanding What You Read

Reading without understanding is like trying to drive a car on an empty gas tank. Fortunately, there are techniques you can use to help you concentrate on and understand what you read. Skilled readers adopt a number of strategies before, during, and after reading to make sure they understand what they read.

Previewing

If you were making a preview for a movie, you would want to let your audience know what the movie is like. When you preview a piece of writing, you are trying to get an idea about that piece of writing. If you know what to expect before reading, you will have an easier time understanding ideas and relationships. Follow these steps to preview your reading assignments.

DO IT!

1. Look at the title and any illustrations that are included.
2. Read the headings, subheadings, and anything in bold letters.
3. Skim over the passage to see how it is organized. Is it divided into many parts?

Is it a long poem or short story? Don't forget to look at the graphics—pictures, maps, or diagrams.

4. Set a purpose for your reading. Are you reading to learn something new? Are you reading to find specific information?

Using What You Know

Believe it or not, you already know quite a bit about what you are going to read. You bring knowledge and personal experience to a selection. Drawing on your own background is called *activating prior knowledge,* and it can help you create meaning in what you read. Ask yourself, *What do I already know about this topic?*

Predicting

You do not need any special knowledge to make *predictions* when you read. The predictions do not even have to be accurate. Take educated guesses before and during your reading about what might happen in the story or article you are reading.

Visualizing

Creating pictures in your mind as you read—called *visualizing*—is a powerful aid to understanding. As you read, set up a movie theater in your imagination. Picture the setting—city streets, the desert, or the surface of the moon. If you can visualize what you read, selections will be more vivid, and you will recall them better later on.

More About the Reading Strategy

What does it mean to read? What do we know about how the brain processes the written word? Consider forming a study group with other teachers interested in learning more about the process of reading. There are books available through several educational presses that focus on new research about the learning process and comprehension.

Identifying Sequence

When you discover the logical order of events or ideas, you are identifying *sequence.* Do you need to understand step-by-step directions? Are you reading a persuasive speech with the reasons listed in order of importance? Look for clues and signal words that will help you find the way information is organized.

Determining the Main Idea

When you look for the *main idea* of a selection, you look for the most important idea. The examples, reasons, and details that further explain the main idea are called *supporting details.* Some main ideas are clearly stated within a passage—often in the first sentence of a paragraph, or sometimes in the last sentence of a passage. Other times, an author does not directly state the main idea but provides details that help readers figure out what the main idea is.

ASK YOURSELF

- What is each sentence about?
- Is there one sentence that tells about the whole passage or that is more important than any of the other sentences?
- What main idea do the supporting details point out?

Questioning

Keep up a conversation with yourself as you read by *asking questions* about the text. Ask about the importance of the information you are reading. Ask how one event relates to another. Ask yourself if you understand what you just read. As you answer your questions, you are making sure that you understand what is going on.

Clarifying

Clear up, or *clarify,* confusing or difficult passages as you read. When you realize you do not understand something, try these techniques to help you clarify the ideas.
- *Reread* the confusing parts slowly and carefully.
- *Look up* unfamiliar words.
- Simply *"talk out"* the part to yourself.

Reread the passage. The second time is often easier and more informative.

Reviewing

You probably *review* in school what you learned the day before so the ideas are firm in your mind. Reviewing when you read does the same thing. Take time now and then to pause and review what you have read. Think about the main ideas and reorganize them for yourself so you can recall them later. Filling in study aids such as graphic organizers, notes, or outlines can help you review.

Monitoring Your Comprehension

As you read, check your understanding by using the following strategies.

- **Summarize** what you read by pausing from time to time and telling yourself the main ideas of what you have just read. Answer the questions *Who? What?*

During Reading

Engaging With the Text
Encourage students to write questions or mark confusing parts of the text with a sticky note as they read. Organize students into groups and allow them to discuss the comments they made on their notes. Have a member of the group record common difficulties. Discuss as a class the sections of the reading that were difficult or confusing, and help clarify the material for the students.

After Reading

Reviewing Remind students to use the following strategies after each section or chapter to ensure greater comprehension:
- Readers should summarize the most important parts of the text in their own words.
- Readers should clarify confusing content by rereading, asking questions, or seeking outside help.
- Readers should predict what might happen next.

Differentiated Instruction

Meeting Special Needs: Less-Proficient Readers Prediction guides (often called anticipation guides) are an effective way of setting a purpose for reading, engaging students during reading, and monitoring comprehension after reading. Create statements related to the upcoming section or chapter. Write some statements that are true, some that are false, and some that are outrageous or funny. Have students write *True* or *False* beside each statement. Students should then check and make corrections to their predictions as they read.

Thinking About Your Reading

Why It's Important

While many students are capable of reading the text and answering specific comprehension questions about what they have read, understanding subtleties of meaning or thinking critically may be more difficult. Students become better readers, writers, and thinkers when they know how to use critical thinking skills.

Before Reading

Modeling When teaching critical thinking skills, it is best to focus on teaching only one or two skills prior to reading. Explain the skill, and model how you, as a reader, use it to comprehend the reading.

During Reading

Thinking Critically Students who interact with the text will have a better chance of thinking more critically about it. Organize students into small groups, and assign a section of text for each group to read. Have students discuss questions such as, "Why did the stock market fall at this particular time?" or "Is the reason why this event occurred based on fact or opinion?" Encourage students to examine the questions from different perspectives. Have students share their discussions with the class.

Where? When? Why? and *How?* Summarizing tests your comprehension by encouraging you to clarify key points in your own words.

- **Paraphrase** Sometimes you read something that you "sort of" understand, but not quite. Use paraphrasing as a test to see whether you really got the point. *Paraphrasing* is retelling something in your own words. So shut the book and try putting what you have just read into your own words. If you cannot explain it clearly, you should probably have another look at the text.

Thinking About Your Reading

Sometimes it is important to think more deeply about what you have read so you can get the most out of what the author says. These critical thinking skills will help you go beyond what the words say and get at the important messages of your reading.

Interpreting

When you listen to your best friend talk, you do not just hear the words he or she says. You also watch your friend, listen to the tone of voice, and use what you already know about that person to put meaning to the words. In doing so, you are interpreting what your friend says. Readers do the same thing when they interpret as they read. *Interpreting* is asking yourself, *What is the writer really saying here?* and then using what you know about the world to help answer that question.

Inferring

You may not realize it, but you infer, or make inferences, every day. Here is an example: You run to the bus stop a little later than usual. There is no one there. "I have missed the bus," you say to yourself. You may be wrong, but that is the way our minds work. You look at the evidence (you are late; no one is there) and come to a conclusion (you have missed the bus).

When you read, you go though exactly the same process because writers don't always directly state what they want you to understand. By providing clues and interesting details, they suggest certain information. Whenever you combine those clues with your own background and knowledge, you are making an inference.

An *inference* involves using your thinking and experience to come up with an idea based on what an author implies or suggests. In reading, you *infer* when you use context clues and your own knowledge to figure out the author's meaning.

Drawing Conclusions

Skillful readers are always *drawing conclusions,* or figuring out much more than an author says directly. The process is like a detective solving a mystery. You combine information and evidence that the author provides to come up with a statement about the topic. Drawing conclusions helps you find connections between ideas and events and gives you a better understanding of what you are reading.

Analyzing

Analyzing, or looking at separate parts of something to understand the entire piece, is a way to think critically about written work.

- In analyzing persuasive *nonfiction,* you might look at the writer's reasons to see if they actually support the main point of the argument.

More About the Reading Strategy

Have students evaluate their proficiency with using different types of critical thinking skills. Draw a continuum on the board for each skill, with 0 representing great difficulty using the skill and 10 indicating mastery of it. Have students rate their abilities by answering questions such as: Am I usually able to infer and understand what the author is suggesting, even if it is not stated? Can I usually draw conclusions when I read? Can I easily tell facts from opinions?

- In analyzing *informational text,* you might look at how the ideas are organized to see what is most important.

Distinguishing Fact From Opinion

Distinguishing between fact and opinion is one of the most important reading skills you can learn. A *fact* is a statement that can be proved with supporting information. An *opinion,* on the other hand, is what a writer believes, on the basis of his or her personal viewpoint. Writers can support their opinions with facts, but an opinion is something that cannot be proved.

FOR EXAMPLE

Look at the following examples of fact and opinion.

Fact: George III was the British king during the American Revolution.

Opinion: King George III was an evil despot.

You could prove that George III was king during that period. It's a fact. However, not everyone might see that King George III was a despot. That's someone's opinion.

As you examine information, always ask yourself, "Is this a fact or an opinion?" Don't think that opinions are always bad. Very often they are just what you want. You read editorials and essays for their authors' opinions. Reviews of books, movies, plays, and CDs can help you decide whether to spend your time and money on something. It's when opinions are based on faulty reasoning or prejudice or when they are stated as facts that they become troublesome.

Evaluating

When you form an opinion or make a judgment about something you are reading, you are *evaluating.* If you are reading informational texts or something on the Internet, it is important to evaluate how qualified the author is to be writing about the topic and how reliable the information is that is presented. Ask yourself whether the author seems biased, whether the information is one-sided, and whether the argument presented is logical.

Synthesizing

When you *synthesize,* you combine ideas (maybe even from different sources) to come up with something new. It may be a new understanding of an important idea or a new way of combining and presenting information. For example, you might read a manual on coaching soccer, combine that information with your own experiences playing soccer, and come up with a winning plan for coaching your sister's team this spring.

Understanding Text Structure

Good writers do not just put together sentences and paragraphs in any order. They structure each piece of their writing in a specific way for a specific purpose. That pattern of organization is called *text structure.* When you know the text structure

After Reading

Writing Questions Tell students that after they read, they will write one question that reflects each type of the thinking skills described in the *Reading Skills Handbook.* For example, "What conclusion can you make about Rosa Parks' refusal to give up her seat on the bus?" Knowing that they will have to write questions about the text will help students think more about it as they read.

Understanding Text Structure

Why It's Important

Students who begin reading without understanding text structures may have difficulty with comprehension and retention. Students can categorize information better and make sense of the text more easily when they learn how authors organize the text.

Before Reading

Skimming Before students read the chapter, walk them through it. For each page, note photos, charts, diagrams, maps, headings, and boldfaced words. Ask students questions such as: Why did the author choose this particular photograph to illustrate this topic? How does this map relate to the topic described in the title? What do you think the author intends for you to learn in this section?

Differentiated Instruction

Meeting Special Needs: Less-Proficient Readers When students find connections to their own lives in the text, their ability to comprehend it improves. Offer projects that build upon these connections. Projects may include: debating issues presented in the text; writing articles for the school or local paper; conducting interviews with others who have knowledge of the subject; role playing; finding relevant poetry, art, or music to share with the class; and reading and reporting on books or magazine articles related to the subject.

Reading Skills Handbook

During Reading

Identifying Text Structure

Organize students into groups of four, and assign different sections of the text to each group. Have groups choose a facilitator, a reader, a recorder, and a reporter. As the reader reads a section aloud, have the recorder note all the signal words. The facilitator will help the group identify the section's text structure based on the categories listed in the *Reading Skills Handbook.* The reporter will describe to the class the signal words and the text structure that the group identified.

After Reading

Organizing Information

Graphic organizers help students organize and comprehend ideas and events. Have a variety of blank graphic organizers available for students to choose from to help them organize text information, including flow charts, time lines, and Venn diagrams.

Reading for Research

Why It's Important

There are vast amounts of information available to students today. It is important for students to know how to access, evaluate, and use it.

---

of a selection, you will find it easier to locate and recall an author's ideas. Here are four ways that writers organize text.

Comparison and Contrast

Comparison-and-contrast structure shows the similarities and differences between people, things, and ideas. Maybe you have overheard someone at school say something like "He is better at throwing the football, but I can run faster than he can." This student is using comparison-and-contrast structure. When writers use comparison-and-contrast structure, often they want to show you *how things that seem alike are different, or how things that seem different are alike.*

- **Signal words and phrases:** *similarly, on the one hand, on the other hand, in contrast to, but, however*

Cause and Effect

Just about everything that happens in life is the cause or the effect of some other event or action. Sometimes what happens is pretty minor: You do not look when you are pouring milk *(cause);* you spill milk on the table *(effect).* Sometimes it is a little more serious: You do not look at your math book before the big test *(cause);* you mess up on the test *(effect).*

Writers use cause-and-effect structure to explore the reasons for something happening and to examine the results of previous events. This structure helps answer the question that everybody is always asking: *Why?* A historian might tell us why an empire rose and fell. Cause-and-effect structure is all about explaining things.

- **Signal words and phrases:** *so, because, as a result, therefore, for the following reasons*

Problem and Solution

How did scientists overcome the difficulty of getting a person to the moon? How will I brush my teeth when I have forgotten my toothpaste? These questions may be very different in importance, but they have one thing in common: Each identifies a problem and asks how to solve it. *Problems* and *solutions* are part of what makes life interesting. Problems and solutions also occur in fiction and nonfiction writing.

- **Signal words and phrases:** *how, help, problem, obstruction, difficulty, need, attempt, have to, must*

Sequence

Take a look at three common forms of sequencing, *the order in which thoughts are arranged.*

- **Chronological order** refers to the order in which events take place. First you wake up; next you have breakfast; then you go to school. Those events don't make much sense in any other order.

  Signal words: *first, next, then, later,* and *finally.*

- **Spatial order** tells you the order in which to look at objects. For example, take a look at this description of an ice cream sundae: *At the bottom of the dish are two scoops of vanilla. The scoops are covered with fudge and topped with whipped cream and a cherry.* Your eyes follow the sundae from the bottom to the top. Spatial order is important in descriptive writing because it helps you as a reader to see an image the way the author does.

More About the Reading Strategy

Why should students understand the different types of text structure? Knowledge about the different types of text structure helps students remember content. It also helps students make sense out of unfamiliar text. Students who internalize the process of cause and effect or problem and solution are developing thinking processes that will serve them for the rest of their lives.

Signal words: *above, below, behind,* and *next to.*

- **Order of importance** is going from most important to least important or the other way around. For example, a typical news article has a most-to-least-important structure.

  Signal words: *principal, central, important,* and *fundamental.*

CHECK IT OUT

- **Tables of contents** Look at the table of contents first to see whether a resource offers information you need.
- **Indexes** An index is an alphabetical listing of significant topics covered in a book. It is found in the back of a book.
- **Headings and subheadings** Headings often tell you what information is going to follow in the text you're reading. Subheadings allow you to narrow your search for information even further.
- **Graphic features** Photos, diagrams, maps, charts, graphs, and other graphic features can communicate large amounts of information at a glance.

Reading for Research

An important part of doing research is knowing how to get information from a wide variety of sources. The following skills will help you when you have a research assignment for a class or when you want information about a topic outside of school.

Reading Text Features

Researching a topic is not only about asking questions; it is about finding answers. Textbooks, references, magazines, and other sources provide a variety of text features to help you find those answers quickly and efficiently.

Organizing Information

When researching a topic, you have to make sense of that information, organize it, and put it all together in ways that will help you explain it to someone else. Here are some ways of doing just that.

- **Record** information from your research and keep track of your resources on note cards.

- **Interpret graphic aids** carefully. These could include charts, graphs, maps and photographs.

- **Summarize** information before you write it on a note card. That way you will have the main ideas in your own words.

- **Outline** ideas so you can see how subtopics and supporting information will fit under the main ideas.

- **Make a table or graph** to compare items or categories of information.

Before Reading

Writing a Research Plan
Help students create a research plan for organizing information. The plan should include: a topic question to research; a list of related subtopics; sources for finding information; forms that show how to cite bibliographic information; and a time line for the completion of the research project.

During Reading

Organizing Information
Have students divide a piece of notebook paper into three columns to help them organize research information. The first column should list the main ideas found in the source. The second column should identify supporting details, and the last column should include an exact quote from the article, book, or Web site that supports the research.

After Reading

Evaluating Sources Discuss as a class the Web sites that were the most helpful for researching topics. Students should identify Web sites and search engines that were easy to use, and they should share them with the class.

Differentiated Instruction

Meeting Special Needs: Less-Proficient Readers Remind students to evaluate the sources that they cite in their research before they use them. Evaluating requires making a judgment or forming an opinion. Students should remember that the author should be qualified to write about the topic. Students should also evaluate the information for biases or opinions.

REFERENCE ATLAS

NATIONAL GEOGRAPHIC

ATLAS KEY

Tundra

Evergreen forest

Mixed forest

Mountains

Grassland

Ice cap

Oceans

Seas

Desert

SYMBOL KEY

⌐⌐⌐ Canal	∘ Depression	⊂⊃ Below sea level	⟆ Lava
·········· Claimed boundary	+ Elevation	⊂⊃ Dry salt lake	⟆ Sand
▓▓▓ International boundary	⊛ National capital	⬭ Lake	⊏⊐ Swamp
	• • ● Towns	⪡ Rivers	

UNITED
STATES
POLITICAL

0 mi   600
0 km   600

OBLIQUE AZIMUTHAL EQUIDISTANT PROJECTION

NATIONAL
GEOGRAPHIC

GREENLAND
(KALAALLIT NUNAAT)
Den.

ARCTIC CIRCLE

C A N A D A

MONTANA
Helena
Billings

NORTH
DAKOTA
Bismarck

MINNESOTA

Lake Superior

MICHIGAN

Lake Huron

MAINE
Augusta
Montpelier
Portland
Concord, N.H.
Boston, MASS.
NEW
YORK
Albany
Providence, R.I.
Hartford, CONN.

SOUTH
DAKOTA
Pierre

WYOMING
Casper
Cheyenne

Minneapolis St. Paul
WISCONSIN
Milwaukee Lansing
Madison

Lake
Ontario
L. Erie
Detroit Buffalo
Cleveland PA.
New York City
Trenton, N.J.
Philadelphia

Sioux City
IOWA
Des Moines

Chicago
ILLINOIS IND.
Toledo
Columbus
OHIO

Pittsburgh
Harrisburg
Dover, DEL.

COLORADO
Denver

NEBRASKA
Lincoln Omaha

Indianapolis
Springfield
Cincinnati
Dayton W. VA.
Baltimore
Annapolis, MD.
Washington, D.C.

Kansas City
MISSOURI
Topeka
Jefferson City
KANSAS

St. Louis
Frankfort
Louisville
KENTUCKY

Charleston
Richmond
VIRGINIA
Virginia Beach

Santa Fe
Albuquerque
NEW
MEXICO
El Paso

Tulsa
Oklahoma City
OKLAHOMA

Nashville
TENNESSEE

Raleigh
NORTH CAROLINA
Charlotte
SOUTH
CAROLINA
Columbia

Little Rock
ARKANSAS
Memphis

Atlanta
Charleston

Birmingham
MISS. ALABAMA
Montgomery
GEORGIA
Savannah

Fort
Worth Dallas
TEXAS

LOUISIANA
Jackson

Tallahassee
Jacksonville

Austin
San Antonio

Baton Rouge
New Orleans

FLORIDA

Houston

Tampa

Miami

Gulf of
Mexico

M E X I C O

Bermuda Is.
U.K.

A T L A N T I C   O C E A N

BAHAMAS

Straits of Florida

CUBA

Caribbean
Sea   JAMAICA

HAITI
DOMINICAN
REPUBLIC

San Juan
PUERTO
RICO
U.S.

ANTIGUA
& BARBUDA
ST. KITTS
& NEVIS

DOMINICA

Rio Grande

Arkansas

Missouri

Mississippi

ROCKY   MOUNTAINS

APPALACHIAN   MTS.

1 | **2** | **3** | **4** | **5** | **6** | **7** | **8**

A

C A N

Cape Flattery
Mt. Olympus
7,965 ft
2,428 m
Seattle

Columbia

Missouri

B

Blue Mts.
Clearwater
Mts.

Bitterroot Range

Absaroka Range

Bighorn Mts.

Black
Hills

Great Sandy
Desert

Salmon
River
Mts.

Snake

Snake River
Plain

Shoshone
Falls

Wind River Range

Laramie Mts.

N. Platte

Missouri

C

Cape Mendocino

Great Salt
Lake

Wasatch Range

Uinta Mts.

Sand Hills

Platte

D

P A C I F I C

O C E A N

Lake
Tahoe

Central Valley

GREAT
BASIN

San Francisco

Colorado

Denver

14,433 ft
4,399 m +Mt. Elbert

Arkansas

E

Mt. Whitney
+14,494 ft
4,418 m

Death Valley
-282 ft, -86 m

Lake
Mead

Lake
Powell

Colorado

San Juan Mts

Sangre de Cristo Mts.

Point Conception

Mojave
Desert

Grand
Canyon

Colorado
Plateau

Red

F

Los Angeles

Channel
Islands

Salton
Sea

San Diego

Colorado

Phoenix

Sonoran
Desert

Sacramento Mts.

Llano
Estacado

Dallas

Brazos

G

ARCTIC OCEAN

Point Barrow

Beaufort
Sea

115°W

Edwards
Plateau

O

Chukchi
Sea

North Slope
Brooks Range

CANADA

RUSSIA

Bering
Strait

ARCTIC CIRCLE

ALASKA

H

Seward
Pen.

Yukon

Kuskokwim

St. Lawrence
Island

Tanana

Alaska Range
+Mt. McKinley (Denali)
20,320 ft, 6,194 m
Anchorage

Rio Grande

C

Nunivak
Island

J

Bering
Sea

Bristol
Bay

Gulf of
Alaska

Alexander
Archipelago

M E X I C O

TROPIC OF CANCER

Alaska Peninsula

Kodiak I.

K

ALASKA

0 mi   300
0 km   300

P A C I F I C
O C E A N

Rio Grande

1 | **2** | **3** | **4** | **5** | **6** | **7** | **8**

UNITED STATES

PHYSICAL

0 mi   300
0 km   300
ALBERS CONIC EQUAL-AREA PROJECTION

NATIONAL GEOGRAPHIC

CANADA

N

Lake of the Woods

Isle Royale
Lake Superior

Upper Peninsula

Minneapolis

Lake Huron

Lower Peninsula

Lake Michigan

Milwaukee

Chicago

CENTRAL

LOWLAND

Mississippi

Detroit

Lake Erie

Cleveland

Pittsburgh

Lake Ontario

Niagara
Falls

Lake
Champlain

Adirondack
Mts.

APPALACHIAN MOUNTAINS

White
Mts.

Green Mts.

Connecticut

Gulf of
Maine

Boston

Cape Cod

Hudson

Long Island

New York City

Philadelphia

Baltimore

Delaware Bay

Washington

Chesapeake Bay

ATLANTIC

OCEAN

Indianapolis

Ohio

St. Louis

Wabash

Flint
Hills

Ozark Plateau

Boston Mts.

Memphis

Ouachita Mts.

Mississippi

Tennessee

Red

Black Belt

Cumberland

Appalachian Plateau

Cumberland Plateau

Allegheny Mts.

Blue Ridge

APPALACHIAN

Piedmont

Mt. Mitchell
6,684 ft
2,037 m

Atlanta

Savannah

Cape Hatteras

COASTAL

PLAIN

Jacksonville

Cape Canaveral

Houston

New Orleans

Mississippi
River Delta

Gulf of Mexico

Lake
Okeechobee

The
Everglades

Miami

Florida Keys

Straits of Florida

TROPIC OF CANCER

CUBA

PACIFIC
OCEAN

Niihau

Kauai

Oahu

Honolulu

Molokai

Lanai

Kahoolawe

Maui — 21°N

Hawaii

Mauna Kea
13,796 ft
4,205 m

PRINCIPAL HAWAIIAN
ISLANDS

0 mi   100
0 km   100

Grid coordinates (top):
1 — 130°W — 50°N — 120°W — 110°W — 100°W (columns 1–8)

A

C A N

B

WASHINGTON
9

Seattle
Olympia ⊙
Columbia

Portland ·
Salem ⊙

Eugene ·

OREGON
5

I D A H O

Boise ⊙

Snake

M O N T A N A
1

Helena ⊙

Missouri

NORTH
DAKOTA
1
Bismarck ⊙

C

SOUTH
DAKOTA
1
Pierre ⊙
Sioux Falls ·

40°N

CALIFORNIA

Sacramento ·
San Francisco ·
San Jose ·

Carson City ⊙

NEVADA
3

Salt Lake ⊙
City

WYOMING
1

N. Platte

Cheyenne ⊙

NEBRASKA
3
Lincoln ⊙

D

UTAH
3

COLORADO
7

Denver ⊙

Colorado
Springs ·

KANSAS
4

E

53

Las
Vegas ·

Arkansas

Wichita ·

PACIFIC
OCEAN

Los Angeles ·

San Diego ·

120°W

Colorado

ARIZONA
8

Phoenix ⊙

Tucson ·

Santa Fe ⊙

Albuquerque ·

NEW MEXICO
3

Amarillo ·

Oklahoma
City ⊙

OKLAHOMA
5

Red

F

ARCTIC OCEAN

68°N
180°

RUSSIA   ARCTIC CIRCLE

Yukon

CANADA

68°N

110°W

30°N

El Paso ·

Rio Grande

Dallas ·
Fort
Worth ·

32

T E X A S

Austin ⊙

G

172°W
60°N

ALASKA
1

Anchorage ·

60°N

M E X I C O

San
Antonio ·

H

Bering
Sea

Juneau ⊙

Corpus
Christi ·

J

State gaining 2 seats
State gaining 1 seat
No change
State losing 1 seat
State losing 2 seats

ALASKA

52°N 0 mi.   300
       0 km   300

52°N

*Numerals in each state indicate
number of representatives the
state sends to the House of
Representatives

PACIFIC
OCEAN

164°W   156°W   148°W   140°W   132°W

K

UNITED STATES
2000 CONGRESSIONAL REAPPORTIONMENT

0 mi.   300
0 km   300
ALBERS CONIC EQUAL-AREA PROJECTION

NATIONAL GEOGRAPHIC

MINNESOTA
8
Minneapolis St. Paul

WISCONSIN
8
Milwaukee
Madison

MICHIGAN
15
Lansing
Detroit

Lake Superior
Lake Huron
Lake Michigan
Lake Ontario
Lake Erie

MAINE
2
Augusta

Montpelier
VT.
1
N.H.
2
Concord

NEW YORK
29
Albany
Buffalo

MASS.
10
Boston
Hartford Providence
CONN. RHODE ISLAND
5   2

IOWA
5
Des Moines
Omaha

ILLINOIS
19
Springfield
Chicago
Fort Wayne

INDIANA
9
Indianapolis

OHIO
18
Cleveland
Columbus
Cincinnati

PENNSYLVANIA
19
Harrisburg
Pittsburgh

N.J.
13
Trenton
New York City

Philadelphia
Dover
DELAWARE
1

MARYLAND
8
Washington,
D.C.
Annapolis

WEST
VIRGINIA
3
Charleston

VIRGINIA
11
Richmond
Virginia Beach

Kansas
City
Topeka
Jefferson
City
St.
Louis

MISSOURI
9

KENTUCKY
6
Louisville
Frankfort

Ohio

Tulsa

ARKANSAS
4
Little
Rock

TENNESSEE
9
Memphis
Nashville

Tennessee

NORTH CAROLINA
13
Raleigh
Charlotte

SOUTH
CAROLINA
6
Columbia

ATLANTIC
OCEAN

MISSISSIPPI
4
Jackson

ALABAMA
7
Birmingham
Montgomery

GEORGIA
13
Atlanta
Savannah

Savannah

LOUISIANA
7
Baton Rouge
New Orleans

Mobile
Tallahassee

FLORIDA
25
Jacksonville
Tampa
Miami

Houston

Gulf of Mexico

N

70°W

30°N

90°W

80°W

PRINCIPAL HAWAIIAN ISLANDS

Niihau
Kauai
159°W
156°W
Oahu
Honolulu
Molokai
Lanai Maui 21°N
Kahoolawe

Hawaii
2

PACIFIC
OCEAN

0 mi.   100
0 km   100

156°W

TROPIC OF CANCER

CUBA

20°N

80°W

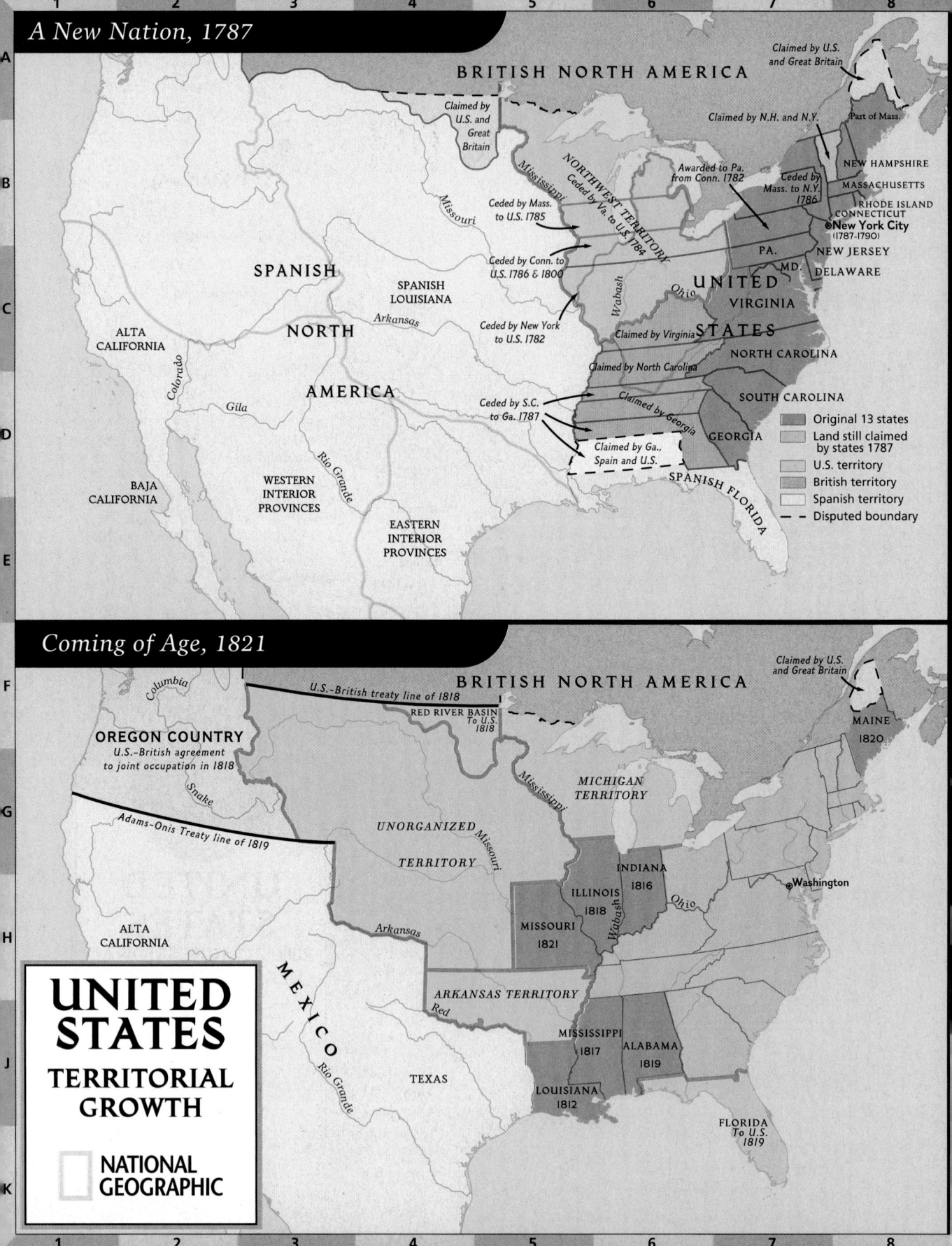

A New Nation, 1787

BRITISH NORTH AMERICA

Claimed by U.S.
and Great Britain

Claimed by
U.S. and
Great
Britain

NORTHWEST TERRITORY
Ceded by Va. to U.S. 1784

Claimed by N.H. and N.Y.

Part of Mass.

Mississippi

Missouri

Ceded by Mass.
to U.S. 1785

Awarded to Pa.
from Conn. 1782

Ceded by
Mass. to N.Y.
1786

NEW HAMPSHIRE

MASSACHUSETTS

RHODE ISLAND

CONNECTICUT

New York City
(1787-1790)

SPANISH

SPANISH
LOUISIANA

Arkansas

Ceded by Conn. to
U.S. 1786 & 1800

Wabash

Ohio

PA.

MD.

NEW JERSEY

DELAWARE

UNITED

NORTH

Colorado

Gila

Ceded by New York
to U.S. 1782

Claimed by Virginia

VIRGINIA

STATES

AMERICA

Claimed by North Carolina

NORTH CAROLINA

ALTA
CALIFORNIA

Ceded by S.C.
to Ga. 1787

Claimed by Georgia

SOUTH CAROLINA

GEORGIA

Rio
Grande

BAJA
CALIFORNIA

WESTERN
INTERIOR
PROVINCES

Claimed by Ga.,
Spain and U.S.

SPANISH FLORIDA

Original 13 states

Land still claimed
by states 1787

U.S. territory

British territory

Spanish territory

Disputed boundary

EASTERN
INTERIOR
PROVINCES

Coming of Age, 1821

Columbia

U.S.-British treaty line of 1818

BRITISH NORTH AMERICA

Claimed by U.S.
and Great Britain

RED RIVER BASIN
To U.S.
1818

MAINE
1820

OREGON COUNTRY

U.S.-British agreement
to joint occupation in 1818

Snake

MICHIGAN
TERRITORY

Mississippi

Adams-Onis Treaty line of 1819

UNORGANIZED

Missouri

INDIANA
1816

Washington

TERRITORY

ILLINOIS
1818

Ohio

ALTA
CALIFORNIA

Arkansas

MISSOURI
1821

Wabash

M
E
X
I
C
O

ARKANSAS TERRITORY

Red

MISSISSIPPI
1817

ALABAMA
1819

Rio
Grande

TEXAS

LOUISIANA
1812

FLORIDA
To U.S.
1819

UNITED
STATES

TERRITORIAL
GROWTH

NATIONAL
GEOGRAPHIC

Expanding West of the Mississippi, 1803

BRITISH NORTH AMERICA

Claimed by U.S. and Great Britain

OREGON COUNTRY
Claimed by Great Britain, Russia, Spain, and United States

Claimed by U.S. and Great Britain

Mississippi

INDIANA

VERMONT 1791

LOUISIANA PURCHASE
Purchased by U.S. in 1803 from France

Missouri

TERRITORY

OHIO 1803

Ohio

Philadelphia (1790-1800)

Washington (new capital 1800)

NEW SPAIN (SPANISH MEXICO)

Arkansas

KENTUCKY 1792

TENNESSEE 1796

Red

Ceded by Georgia to U.S. 1802

Rio Grande

Claimed by U.S. and Spain

MISSISSIPPI TERR.

SPANISH FLORIDA

Claimed by U.S. and Spain

BAJA CALIFORNIA

Claimed by U.S. and Spain

□ States previously in the Union
■ States newly admitted

Coast to Coast, 1850 and beyond

BRITISH NORTH AMERICA

Treaty line of 1846

Treaty line of 1842

Treaty line of 1842

WASHINGTON 1889

OREGON TERRITORY
Added to U.S. in 1846

OREGON 1859

Snake

MONTANA 1889

NORTH DAKOTA 1889

MINNESOTA 1858

MINNESOTA TERRITORY

MICHIGAN 1837

IDAHO 1890

WYOMING 1890

SOUTH DAKOTA 1889

WISCONSIN 1848

NEVADA 1864

UNORGANIZED

NEBRASKA 1867

Missouri

IOWA 1846

UTAH TERRITORY

TERRITORY

UTAH 1896

COLORADO 1876

KANSAS 1861

Wabash

Ohio

W. VA. 1863

Washington

CALIFORNIA 1850

Arkansas

ARIZONA 1912

Colorado

Gila

NEW MEXICO TERRITORY

OKLAHOMA 1907

Red

ARKANSAS 1836

Mississippi

GADSDEN PURCHASE
To U.S. 1853

NEW MEXICO 1912

Rio Grande

TEXAS 1845

RUSSIA

ALASKA 1959
Purchased by U.S. 1867

MEXICO

FLORIDA 1845

········ States admitted after 1850

HAWAII 1959
Annexed by U.S. 1898

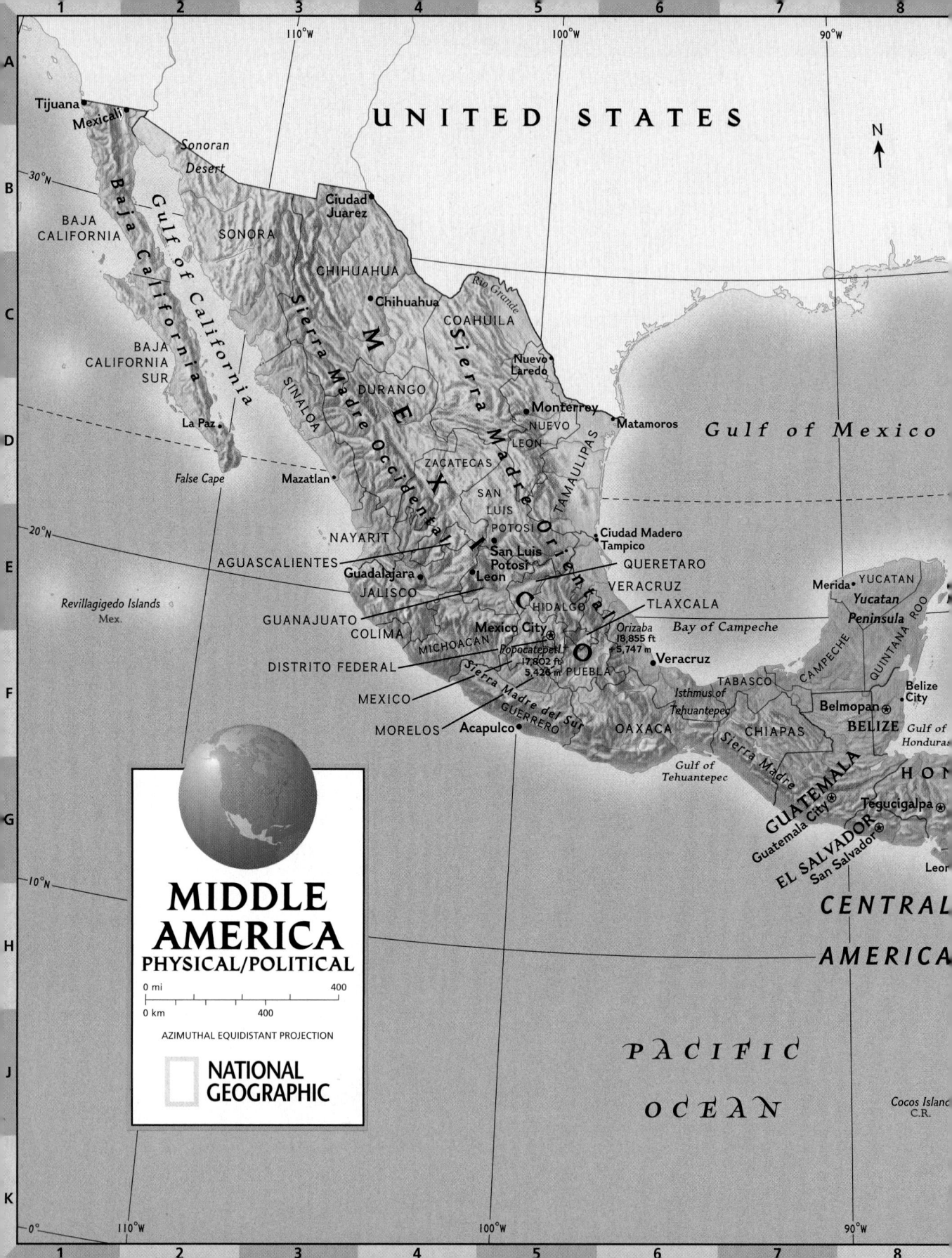

UNITED STATES

Tijuana
Mexicali

Sonoran
Desert

30°N

BAJA
CALIFORNIA

SONORA

Ciudad
Juarez

CHIHUAHUA

Chihuahua

COAHUILA

Rio Grande

Gulf of Mexico

Gulf of California

BAJA
CALIFORNIA
SUR

Baja California

La Paz

SINALOA

DURANGO

Sierra Madre Occidental

Nuevo
Laredo

Monterrey

NUEVO
LEON

Matamoros

False Cape

Mazatlan

ZACATECAS

M E X I C O

Sierra Madre Oriental

TAMAULIPAS

20°N

NAYARIT

AGUASCALIENTES

Guadalajara

JALISCO

SAN
LUIS
POTOSI

San Luis
Potosi

Leon

Ciudad Madero
Tampico

QUERETARO

VERACRUZ

Revillagigedo Islands
Mex.

GUANAJUATO

COLIMA

MICHOACAN

DISTRITO FEDERAL

MEXICO

MORELOS

Acapulco

Sierra Madre del Sur

GUERRERO

HIDALGO

Mexico City

Popocatepetl
17,802 ft
5,426 m

TLAXCALA

PUEBLA

Orizaba
18,855 ft
5,747 m

Veracruz

Bay of Campeche

Merida

YUCATAN

Yucatan
Peninsula

QUINTANA ROO

CAMPECHE

TABASCO

Isthmus of
Tehuantepec

OAXACA

CHIAPAS

Sierra Madre

Gulf of
Tehuantepec

Belmopan

Belize
City

BELIZE

Gulf of
Honduras

GUATEMALA

Guatemala City

EL SALVADOR

San Salvador

Tegucigalpa

HON

Leor

CENTRAL

AMERICA

**MIDDLE
AMERICA**
PHYSICAL/POLITICAL

0 mi   400

0 km   400

AZIMUTHAL EQUIDISTANT PROJECTION

**NATIONAL
GEOGRAPHIC**

10°N

PACIFIC

OCEAN

Cocos Island
C.R.

0°

110°W

100°W

90°W

ATLANTIC

OCEAN

TROPIC OF CANCER

20°N

30°N

BAHAMAS

Freeport

Nassau

Andros
Island

Straits of Florida

Turks &
Caicos Islands
U.K.

W   E   S   T   I   N   D   I   E   S

ST. KITTS & NEVIS

ANTIGUA &
BARBUDA

Havana

CUBA

Camaguey

Holguin

Santiago
de Cuba

Santiago

Hispaniola

Santo
Domingo

San Juan

Virgin
Islands
U.S. & U.K.

Isle of Youth

Cayman
Islands
U.K.

umel
nd

G   r   e   a   t   e   r

HAITI

Port-au-
Prince

DOMINICAN
REPUBLIC

Puerto
Rico
U.S.

Guadeloupe
Fr.

DOMINICA

Montego
Bay

JAMAICA

Kingston

A   n   t   i   l   l   e   s

Bird I.
Venez.

Martinique
Fr.

ST. LUCIA

L
e
s
s
e
r

A
n
t
i
l
l
e
s

BARBADOS

ST. VINCENT &
THE GRENADINES

GRENADA

C   a   r   i   b   b   e   a   n   S   e   a

Neth.
Curacao
Bonaire

TRINIDAD & TOBAGO

Tobago

10°N

Aruba
Neth.

Lesser Antilles

Port-of-Spain

Trinidad

60°W

DURAS

Coco

Mosquito Coast

NICARAGUA

Managua

Lake
Nicaragua

COSTA

Puerto
Limon

Gulf of
Mosquitos

Isthmus of Panama

Panama City

SOUTH

San Jose

RICA

PANAMA

David

Gulf of
Panama

AMERICA

EQUATOR

0°

70°W

80°W

RUSSIA

ARCTIC OCEAN

Queen

North Magnetic Pole +

Elizabeth

Prince
Patrick I.

Islands

Melville
Island

Bathurst
Island

ARCTIC CIRCLE

Beaufort
Sea

Banks
Island

Somerset
Island

Prince of
Wales I.

ALASKA
U.S.

Inuvik

Victoria
Island

Boothia
Peninsula

YUKON
TERRITORY

Mackenzie Mts.

Mackenzie

Great
Bear Lake

Mt. Logan
19,551 ft
+ 5,959 m

Yukon
Plateau

NORTHWEST
TERRITORIES

N U N

Whitehorse

Coast Mo

ROCKY

Virginia Falls

Yellowknife

Great
Slave Lake

C A N A D I A N

Slave

Peace

Queen
Charlotte
Islands

BRITISH

COLUMBIA

Fraser
Plateau

Prince George

Lake
Athabasca

ALBERTA

Athabasca

Churchill

Nelson

Churchill

MANITOBA

PACIFIC

Fraser

Columbia Mts.

MOUNTAINS

Edmonton

GREAT

SASKATCHEWAN

Saskatchewan

Lake
Winnipeg

OCEAN

Vancouver
Island

Calgary

P L A I N S

Saskatoon

Lake
Winnipegosis

Vancouver
Victoria

Regina

Winnipeg

Lake of
the Woods

UNITED STATES

CANADA
PHYSICAL/POLITICAL

0 mi — 400
0 km — 400

AZIMUTHAL EQUIDISTANT PROJECTION

NATIONAL GEOGRAPHIC

Ellesmere

Island

Devon Island

Baffin
Bay

GREENLAND
(KALAALLIT NUNAAT)
Den.

ICELAND

Melville
Peninsula

Foxe
Basin

Baffin Island

Davis Strait

A V U T

Southampton
Island

⊙ Iqaluit

Hudson Strait

Labrador
Sea

Ungava
Bay

Hudson

Bay

Belcher
Islands

NEWFOUNDLAND

Cartwright

Schefferville

Happy Valley-
Goose Bay

Smallwood
Reservoir

"Churchill Falls

AND LABRADOR

Island of
Newfoundland

James Bay

QUEBEC

SHIELD

Manicouagan
Reservoir
Sept-Iles

Anticosti I.

St. John's
Avalon
Peninsula

St.-Pierre & Miquelon
Fr.

ONTARIO

Lake
Nipigon

Gulf of
St. Lawrence

Gaspe
Pen.

PRINCE
EDWARD
ISLAND

Cape Breton I.

Thunder
Bay

Lake
Superior

Chicoutimi

Rouyn-Noranda

Quebec
City ⊙

St. Lawrence

NEW
BRUNSWICK

⊙ Charlottetown

NOVA
SCOTIA

ATLANTIC

Sudbury

Montreal

Fredericton

Saint John

Bay of Fundy

⊙ Halifax

OCEAN

Ottawa ⊛

Lake
Huron

Toronto ⊙

L. Ontario

Niagara Falls

London

L. Erie

Lake Michigan

United States Facts

Washington, D.C.
Population: 572,059
Land area: 61 sq. mi.

U.S. Territories

Puerto Rico
Population: 3,808,610
Land area: 3,425 sq. mi.

Guam
Population: 155,000 (est.)
Land area: 209 sq. mi.

U.S. Virgin Islands
Population: 121,000 (est.)
Land area: 134 sq. mi.

American Samoa
Population: 65,000 (est.)
Land area: 77 sq. mi.

The states are listed in the order they were admitted to the Union.

Population figures are based on U.S. Bureau of the Census for 2000. House of Representatives figures are from the Clerk of the House of Representatives. States are not drawn to scale.

1 Delaware
Year Admitted: 1787
Population: 783,600
Land area: 1,955 sq. mi.
Representatives: 1
★ Dover

2 Pennsylvania
Year Admitted: 1787
Population: 12,281,054
Land area: 44,820 sq. mi.
Representatives: 19
Harrisburg ★

3 New Jersey
Year Admitted: 1787
Population: 8,414,350
Land area: 7,419 sq. mi.
Representatives: 13
Trenton ★

9 New Hampshire
Year Admitted: 1788
Population: 1,235,786
Land area: 8,969 sq. mi.
Representatives: 2
Concord ★

10 Virginia
Year Admitted: 1788
Population: 7,078,515
Land area: 39,598 sq. mi.
Representatives: 11
Richmond ★

11 New York
Year Admitted: 1788
Population: 18,976,457
Land area: 47,224 sq. mi.
Representatives: 29
★ Albany

17 Ohio
Year Admitted: 1803
Population: 11,353,140
Land area: 40,953 sq. mi.
Representatives: 18
★ Columbus

18 Louisiana
Year Admitted: 1812
Population: 4,468,976
Land area: 43,566 sq. mi.
Representatives: 7
★ Baton Rouge

19 Indiana
Year Admitted: 1816
Population: 6,080,485
Land area: 35,870 sq. mi.
Representatives: 9
Indianapolis ★

25 Arkansas
Year Admitted: 1836
Population: 2,673,400
Land area: 52,075 sq. mi.
Representatives: 4
Little Rock ★

26 Michigan
Year Admitted: 1837
Population: 9,938,444
Land area: 56,809 sq. mi.
Representatives: 15
Lansing ★

27 Florida
Year Admitted: 1845
Population: 15,982,378
Land area: 53,997 sq. mi.
Representatives: 25
★ Tallahassee

33 Oregon
Year Admitted: 1859
Population: 3,421,399
Land area: 96,003 sq. mi.
Representatives: 5
★ Salem

34 Kansas
Year Admitted: 1861
Population: 2,688,418
Land area: 81,823 sq. mi.
Representatives: 4
Topeka ★

35 West Virginia
Year Admitted: 1863
Population: 1,808,344
Land area: 24,087 sq. mi.
Representatives: 3
★ Charleston

36 Nevada
Year Admitted: 1864
Population: 1,998,257
Land area: 109,806 sq. mi.
Representatives: 3
★ Carson City

42 Washington
Year Admitted: 1889
Population: 5,894,121
Land area: 66,582 sq. mi.
Representatives: 9
★ Olympia

43 Idaho
Year Admitted: 1890
Population: 1,293,953
Land area: 82,751 sq. mi.
Representatives: 2
★ Boise

44 Wyoming
Year Admitted: 1890
Population: 493,782
Land area: 97,105 sq. mi.
Representatives: 1
Cheyenne ★

45 Utah
Year Admitted: 1896
Population: 2,233,169
Land area: 82,168 sq. mi.
Representatives: 3
★ Salt Lake City

4 Georgia
Year Admitted: 1788
Population: 8,186,453
Land area: 57,919 sq. mi.
Representatives: 13
★ Atlanta

5 Connecticut
Year Admitted: 1788
Population: 3,405,565
Land area: 4,845 sq. mi.
Representatives: 5
★ Hartford

6 Massachusetts
Year Admitted: 1788
Population: 6,349,097
Land area: 7,838 sq. mi.
Representatives: 10
Boston ★

7 Maryland
Year Admitted: 1788
Population: 5,296,486
Land area: 9,775 sq. mi.
Representatives: 8
Annapolis ★

8 South Carolina
Year Admitted: 1788
Population: 4,012,012
Land area: 30,111 sq. mi.
Representatives: 6
Columbia ★

12 North Carolina
Year Admitted: 1789
Population: 8,049,313
Land area: 48,718 sq. mi.
Representatives: 13
Raleigh ★

13 Rhode Island
Year Admitted: 1790
Population: 1,048,319
Land area: 1,045 sq. mi.
Representatives: 2
★ Providence

14 Vermont
Year Admitted: 1791
Population: 608,827
Land area: 9,249 sq. mi.
Representatives: 1
★ Montpelier

15 Kentucky
Year Admitted: 1792
Population: 4,041,769
Land area: 39,732 sq. mi.
Representatives: 6
Frankfort ★

16 Tennessee
Year Admitted: 1796
Population: 5,689,283
Land area: 41,220 sq. mi.
Representatives: 9
★ Nashville

20 Mississippi
Year Admitted: 1817
Population: 2,844,658
Land area: 46,914 sq. mi.
Representatives: 4
★ Jackson

21 Illinois
Year Admitted: 1818
Population: 12,419,293
Land area: 55,593 sq. mi.
Representatives: 19
★ Springfield

22 Alabama
Year Admitted: 1819
Population: 4,447,100
Land area: 50,750 sq. mi.
Representatives: 7
Montgomery ★

23 Maine
Year Admitted: 1820
Population: 1,274,923
Land area: 30,865 sq. mi.
Representatives: 2
★ Augusta

24 Missouri
Year Admitted: 1821
Population: 5,595,211
Land area: 68,898 sq. mi.
Representatives: 9
Jefferson City ★

28 Texas
Year Admitted: 1845
Population: 20,851,820
Land area: 261,914 sq. mi.
Representatives: 32
Austin ★

29 Iowa
Year Admitted: 1846
Population: 2,926,324
Land area: 55,875 sq. mi.
Representatives: 5
Des Moines ★

30 Wisconsin
Year Admitted: 1848
Population: 5,363,675
Land area: 54,314 sq. mi.
Representatives: 8
Madison ★

31 California
Year Admitted: 1850
Population: 33,871,648
Land area: 155,973 sq. mi.
Representatives: 53
★ Sacramento

32 Minnesota
Year Admitted: 1858
Population: 4,919,479
Land area: 79,617 sq. mi.
Representatives: 8
Saint Paul ★

37 Nebraska
Year Admitted: 1867
Population: 1,711,263
Land area: 76,878 sq. mi.
Representatives: 3
Lincoln ★

38 Colorado
Year Admitted: 1876
Population: 4,301,261
Land area: 103,730 sq. mi.
Representatives: 7
Denver ★

39 North Dakota
Year Admitted: 1889
Population: 642,200
Land area: 68,994 sq. mi.
Representatives: 1
Bismarck ★

40 South Dakota
Year Admitted: 1889
Population: 754,844
Land area: 75,898 sq. mi.
Representatives: 1
Pierre ★

41 Montana
Year Admitted: 1889
Population: 902,195
Land area: 145,556 sq. mi.
Representatives: 1
★ Helena

46 Oklahoma
Year Admitted: 1907
Population: 3,450,654
Land area: 68,679 sq. mi.
Representatives: 5
Oklahoma City ★

47 New Mexico
Year Admitted: 1912
Population: 1,819,046
Land area: 121,365 sq. mi.
Representatives: 3
★ Santa Fe

48 Arizona
Year Admitted: 1912
Population: 5,130,632
Land area: 113,642 sq. mi.
Representatives: 8
Phoenix ★

49 Alaska
Year Admitted: 1959
Population: 626,932
Land area: 570,374 sq. mi.
Representatives: 1
Juneau ★

50 Hawaii
Year Admitted: 1959
Population: 1,211,537
Land area: 6,432 sq. mi.
Representatives: 2
Honolulu ★

NATIONAL GEOGRAPHIC

1 FOCUS

BELLRINGER
Motivational Activity

Ask students to think of descriptive, colorful terms, such as those in the song "America the Beautiful," that describe their region of the country.

FYI

The early Inuit labeled distances on their maps with the time it took to travel rather than with miles. A map would show the distance between what is now Nome and Point Barrow (both in Alaska) as 10 days rather than 525 miles (845 km).

Geography Handbook

The story of the United States begins with geography—the study of the earth in all of its variety. Geography describes the earth's land, water, and plant and animal life. It is the study of places and the complex relationships between people and their environments.

The United States is a land of startling physical differences. Within the borders of the United States is a rich variety of landscapes—dense forests, hot deserts, rolling grasslands, and snow-capped mountains. It is also a nation of diverse groups of people. With a total land area of 3,537,441 square miles (9,161,930 sq. km)—the United States is the world's fourth largest country in size. Only Russia, Canada, and China are larger. Because of its size and diversity, the United States has offered people from Europe, Africa, Asia, and other parts of the Americas many opportunities. Today more than 287 million people make the United States their home.

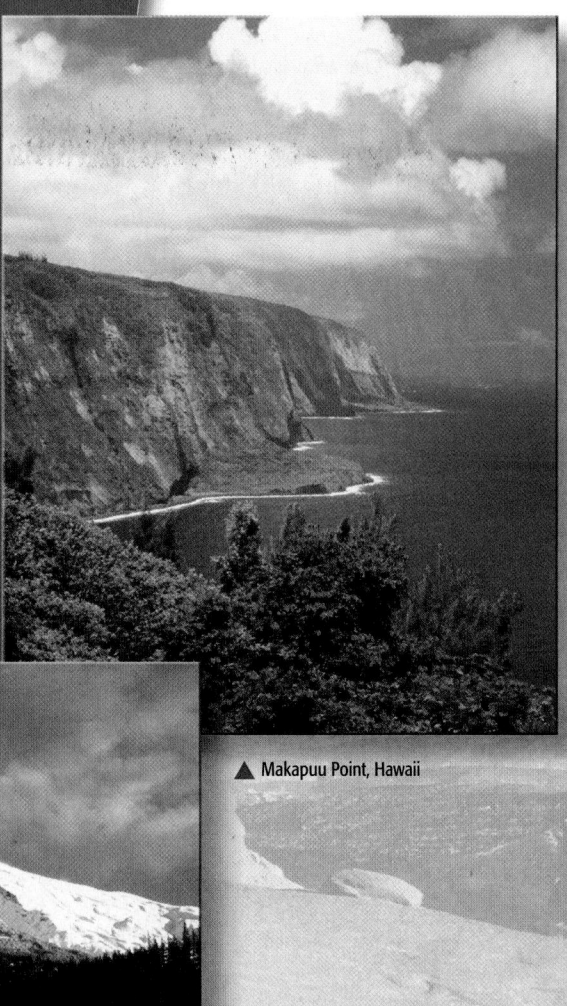

▲ Makapuu Point, Hawaii

◀ Mount Hood, Oregon

EXTENDING THE CONTENT

Careers in Geography Geographers work for the federal government in the Defense Mapping Agency, United States Geologic Survey, Central Intelligence Agency, Army Corps of Engineers, National Science Foundation, Smithsonian Institution, and Office of the Geographer in the Department of State. State environmental and transportation agencies hire geographers as analysts, planners, and cartographers. Some states even have an Office of the State Geographer. In the private sector, geographers work as professors, researchers, and cartographers.

Globes and Maps

Globes

Photographs from space show the earth in its true form—a great ball spinning around the sun. The most accurate way to depict the earth is as a globe, or a round form. A globe gives a true picture of the earth's relative size and the shape of its landmasses and bodies of water. Globes are proportionally correct, thus showing the true distances and directions between places.

Maps

A map is a flat drawing of the earth's surface. People use maps to locate places, plot routes, and judge distances. Maps can also display useful information about the nation's peoples, such as political boundaries, population densities, or even voting results by city and state.

What advantages does a map have over a globe? Unlike a globe, a map allows you to see all areas of the world at the same time. Maps also show much more detail and can be folded and more easily carried.

Types of Maps

This text uses many different kinds of maps to help you see the connection between geography and the history of the United States.

General-Purpose Maps Maps that show a wide range of general information about a particular area are called **general-purpose maps.** Two of the most common general-purpose maps are physical maps and political maps. **Physical maps** show the location and the shape, or **topography,** of the earth's physical features. **Political maps** show the boundaries between different countries.

Special-Purpose Maps Special-purpose maps, also called **thematic maps,** show information on specific topics, such as climate, land use, or vegetation. Human activities, such as exploration routes, territorial expansion, or battle sites, also appear on special-purpose maps. Colors and map key symbols are very important on these maps.

LANDSAT Maps LANDSAT maps are made from photographs taken by camera-carrying LANDSAT satellites in space. The cameras record millions of energy waves invisible to the human eye. Computers then change this information into pictures of the earth's surface. With LANDSAT images, scientists can study whole mountain ranges, oceans, and geographic regions. Changes to the earth's environment can also be tracked using the satellite information.

◀ Special-purpose map

▲ LANDSAT map

Geography Handbook **1**

Using Geographic Terms
Survey students' knowledge of geographic terms. Create three columns on the board with the following headings: *Landforms, Bodies of Water,* and *Climates.* List one term that fits each column, such as *canyon, bay,* and *tropical.* Ask students to volunteer as many other terms for each column as they can. Have students turn to pages 6–7 and read the **Geographic Dictionary.** Then have them close their books and continue suggesting terms for each column on the board. **L1**

National Boundaries National boundaries run to the center of the earth and to the top of the atmosphere. Because of this, an airplane pilot needs a country's permission to fly into its air space.

COOPERATIVE LEARNING ACTIVITY

Identifying Place Organize students into groups of four. Have them draw a large outline map of their state on poster board. Then have them research the state's plants, animals, and major economic products, and list these items on the back of the poster. Distribute magazines (gardening, wildlife, and local) and tell students to find and cut out pictures of the items listed on the backs of their posters. Finally, direct students to glue the photos in the appropriate locations on the outline map, creating a montage of distinctive characteristics of the state. 👆

Use the rubric for a cooperative group management plan on pages 71–72 in the ***Performance Assessment Activities and Rubrics.***

1

Using Maps

Demonstrating Ideas Write the words *Distance* and *Direction* on the chalkboard. **Ask: How do maps show distance and direction?** *(scales and compass roses)* Then, give students practice in determining distance by showing them how to mark a map scale on the edge of a piece of paper. Have students practice measuring the distance between cities on the map on page 2. Give students practice in determining direction by having volunteers identify the direction from one city or country to another. **L2**

CURRICULUM CONNECTION

History Until the 1700s, sailors seldom knew exactly where they were because they only had lines of latitude to guide them. John Harrison, an English instrument maker, invented a clock that could keep accurate time at sea. A navigator could determine longitude by figuring the difference between Greenwich Mean Time and the time at the ship's location.

Map Projections Maps, however, do have their limitations. As you can imagine, drawing a round object on a flat surface is very difficult. **Cartographers,** or mapmakers, have drawn many projections, or kinds of maps. Each map projection is a different way of showing the round earth on a flat map. Different map projections include the Winkel Tripel, Robinson, Goode's Interrupted Equal-Area, and Mercator projections. It is impossible to accurately represent the round earth on a flat surface without distorting some part of the earth. Thus, map projections typically distort distance, direction, shape, or area.

Winkel Tripel Projection

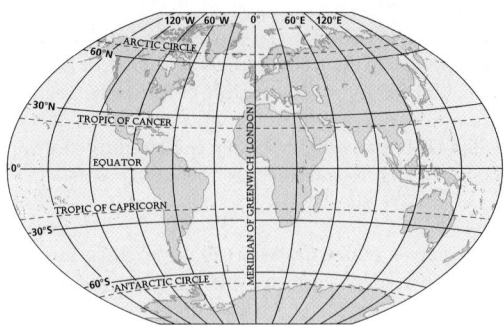

▲ Most general reference maps use the Winkel Tripel projection. Adopted by the National Geographic Society in 1998, this projection provides a better balance between the size and shape of land areas as they are shown on the map.

Reading a Map

Maps include several important tools to help you interpret the information contained on a particular map. Learning to use these map tools will help you read the symbolic language of maps more easily.

Compass Rose A compass rose is a marker that indicates directions. The four cardinal directions—north, south, east, and west—are usually indicated with arrows or points of a star. Sometimes a compass rose may indicate only one direction, because the other directions can be determined in relation to the one given. The compass rose on this map indicates all four cardinal directions.

Key Cartographers use a variety of symbols to represent map information. Because these symbols are graphic and commonly used, most maps can be read and understood by people around the world. To be sure that the symbols are clear, however, every map contains a key—a list that explains what the symbols represent. This key shows symbols used for a battle map in this text. It indicates troop movements, supply lines, and U.S. bases.

2 Geography Handbook

DIFFERENTIATED INSTRUCTION

Visual/Spatial To help students remember the several different categories and examples of maps discussed in this section, guide them in creating a graphic organizer entitled "Types of Maps." Branching from this main head should be three boxes labeled "Political," "Physical," and "Special-Purpose." Have students complete the organizer by taking notes on each of the different types of maps. **L1**

Refer to *Inclusion for the High School Social Studies Classroom Strategies and Activities* in the TCR.

Robinson Projection

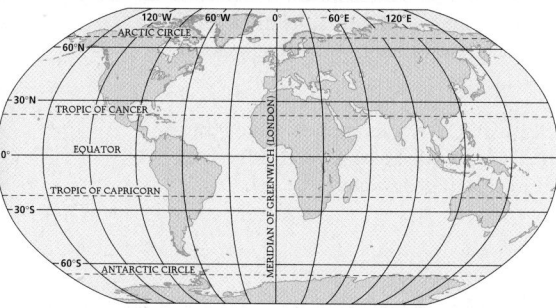

▲ The Robinson projection has minor distortions. The sizes and shapes near the eastern and western edges of the map are accurate, and the outlines of the continents appear much as they do on the globe. The shapes of the polar areas, however, are somewhat flat.

Goode's Interrupted Equal-Area Projection

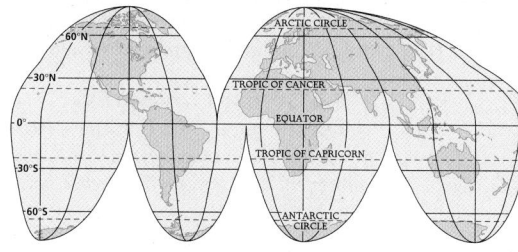

▲ An interrupted projection looks something like a globe that has been cut apart and laid flat. Goode's Interrupted Equal-Area projection shows the true size and shape of the earth's landmasses, but distances are distorted.

Relative Location Relative location is the location of one place in relation to another, while absolute location indicates the exact position of a place on the earth's surface. On this map, the relative location of where the Vietnam War took place is given in relation to the rest of Asia.

Cities and Capitals Cities are symbolized by a solid circle. Sometimes the relative sizes of cities are shown with circles of different sizes. Capitals are represented by a star within a circle.

Boundary Lines On political maps of large areas, boundary lines highlight the borders between different countries, states, or counties.

Scale Bar Every map is a representation of a part of the earth. The scale bar shows the relationship between map measurements and actual distance. Scale can be measured with a ruler to calculate actual distances in standard or metric measurements. On this map, 5/8 inch represents 150 miles (241 km).

Mercator Projection

▲ The Mercator projection increasingly distorts size and distance as it moves away from the Equator. However, Mercator projections accurately show true directions and the shapes of the landmasses.

Geography Handbook **3**

Using a Map Key On slips of paper, write the page number of a map from the textbook and a question that requires the use of the map key. Ask volunteers to select slips and answer the questions. L1

Using Special-Purpose Maps Ask volunteers to bring to class special-purpose maps. As an example, explain that the subject of these maps may include hiking trails, ocean currents, energy use, and bus routes. Allow time for volunteers to show and explain their maps. Display selected maps on the wall. L1 ELL

Classifying Maps Have students work in groups to scan the textbook and classify the maps according to type: physical, political, or special-purpose. Give each group the task of listing page numbers for maps of one type. L1 ELL

COOPERATIVE LEARNING ACTIVITY

Using Absolute Location Organize the class into teams. Have each team record the absolute location (in degrees of latitude and longitude) of 20 named places on the globe (cities, natural features, and so on). Then have teams challenge each other in a round-robin Absolute Location Tournament. In each round, one team will state the latitude and longitude of five places, then time how long it takes the other team to locate the places on a globe. The teams will then switch roles. The team with the better time wins the round.

Use the rubric for a cooperative group management plan on pages 71–72 in the **Performance Assessment Activities and Rubrics.**

The Elements of Geography

To understand how our world is connected, some geographers have broken down the study of geography into five themes. The **Five Themes of Geography** are (1) location, (2) place, (3) human/environment interaction, (4) movement, and (5) regions.

Six Essential Elements

Recently, as suggested in the **Geography Skills for Life,** geographers have broken down the study of geography into **Six Essential Elements.** Being aware of these elements will help you sort out what you are learning about geography.

Understanding the Six Essential Elements Have students complete the following activities to learn more about the Six Essential Elements of Geography.

Element 1: The World in Spatial Terms Have students create a map that shows the route they travel from their home to school. Students should identify major roads and human-made landmarks on their maps. Display the maps on the class bulletin board. **L2**

Element 2: Places and Regions Explain that physical characteristics play a part in shaping human characteristics in a given place. For example, Native Americans in Alaska and Native Americans in Florida had widely differing clothing, economic pursuits, architecture, and lifestyles because of the physical characteristics of their regions. Ask students to describe a favorite city, state, or country. Ask them how the physical characteristics in the place might influence characteristics or customs of the inhabitants. **L1**

Element 3: Physical Systems Ask students to think of ways that physical systems affect their lives and cultures. Have students explain how events such as hurricanes influence a region's population and economy. **L2**

Element 1

The World in Spatial Terms Geographers first look at where a place is located. **Location** serves as a starting point by asking, "Where is it?" Knowing the location of places helps you develop an awareness of the world around you. For example, the surrender of Confederate General Robert E. Lee took place at Appomattox Courthouse, located in Virginia.

Element 2

Place and Regions **Place** has a special meaning in geography. It means more than where an area is located. It also describes what features a place includes. These features may be physical characteristics, such as landforms, climate, and plant or animal life. They may also be human characteristics, including language and way of life. For example, the English settlement of Jamestown was located in a swampy area with mosquitoes and high humidity. This made the way of life difficult for the new settlers.

To help them organize their study, geographers often group places into regions. **Regions** are united by one or more common characteristics. The original thirteen colonies, for instance, were divided into three regions—New England Colonies, Middle Colonies, and Southern Colonies.

4   Geography Handbook

DIFFERENTIATED INSTRUCTION

At-Risk Students Students who have trouble understanding the material found on pages 4–5 should use graphic organizers to help them organize the information. Students should create three-column tables with the labels *Element, Theme,* and *Description.* As they read each element, they should complete their tables. **L1**

📂 Refer to ***Inclusion for the High School Social Studies Classroom Strategies and Activities*** in the TCR.

Element 3

Physical Systems When studying places and regions, geographers analyze the ways in which **physical systems**—such as hurricanes, volcanoes, and glaciers—shape the earth's surface. They also look at communities of plants and animals that depend upon one another and their surroundings for survival. Glaciers are an example of a physical system. Near the end of the Ice Age, glaciers melted, raising ocean levels and covering a land bridge that once connected Asia and North America.

Element 4

Human Systems Geographers also examine an area's **human systems,** or how people have shaped our world. They look at how boundary lines are determined and analyze why people settle in certain places and not in others. A key theme in geography is the continual **movement** of people, ideas, and goods. An example of such movement occurred in the 1820s, when Stephen F. Austin organized a group of Americans to settle in the Mexican territory of Texas.

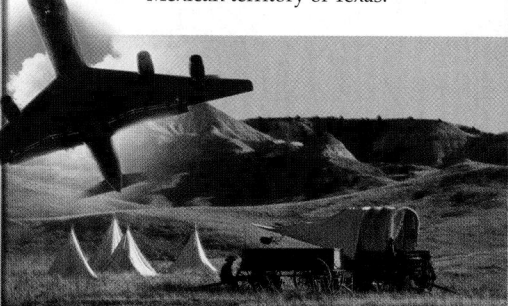

Element 5

Environment and Society "How does the relationship between people and their natural surroundings influence the way people live?" This is one of the questions that the geographic element of **environment and society** answers. This element also shows how people use the environment and how their actions affect it. One example was when some people in the South established large plantations to take advantage of the warm climate and fertile soil.

Element 6

The Uses of Geography Knowledge of geography helps people understand the relationships between people, places, and environment over time. Understanding geography and knowing how to use the tools and technology available to study it prepares you for life in our modern society. Early European explorers, for example, relied on their knowledge of geography to discover lands never seen before by Europeans.

Element 4: Human Systems Call on volunteers to name places from which their family or ancestors moved. Students may describe a move within the United States or a migration from another country. Discuss the reasons that people move to different places. **L1** ELL

Element 5: Environment and Society Give examples of ways that humans use and modify the environment in places they live. For example, people convert fields and forests into towns and irrigate arid land to support farming. Call on students to give examples of the ways people have modified the environment where they live in both positive and negative ways. **L2**

Element 6: The Uses of Geography Have students give examples of ways businesses use geography. Have students explain how various geographic conditions influence where businesses such as gas stations and shopping malls are built. **L2**

EXTENDING THE CONTENT

Regions Geographers organize regions into three types: formal regions, functional regions, and perceptual regions. A common human property (for example, language, religion, nationality, and political identity) or common physical property (for example, climate, landforms, and vegetation cover) characterizes formal regions. Functional regions are organized around a node or focal point with surrounding areas linked to that node through transportation or communication systems or economic associations. Perceptual regions reflect human feelings or attitudes and are defined by subjective images of the area (for example, New England and the Corn Belt).

Constructing a Model Have students use clay to make a model landscape with the features mentioned on pages 6–7. Suggest that students paint the model after the clay dries to make it look more realistic. **L1**

you don't say...

Foreign Geography Terms The terms geographers use to describe the earth come from many different languages. To illustrate this, have students locate the term *mesa* on page 7. Point out that geographers use this word, which means "table" in Spanish, to describe flat-topped, steep-sided hills. Other foreign terms American geographers use include *tsunami,* a Japanese word meaning "overflowing wave," and *fjord,* a Norwegian word meaning "long, narrow bay."

Geographic Dictionary

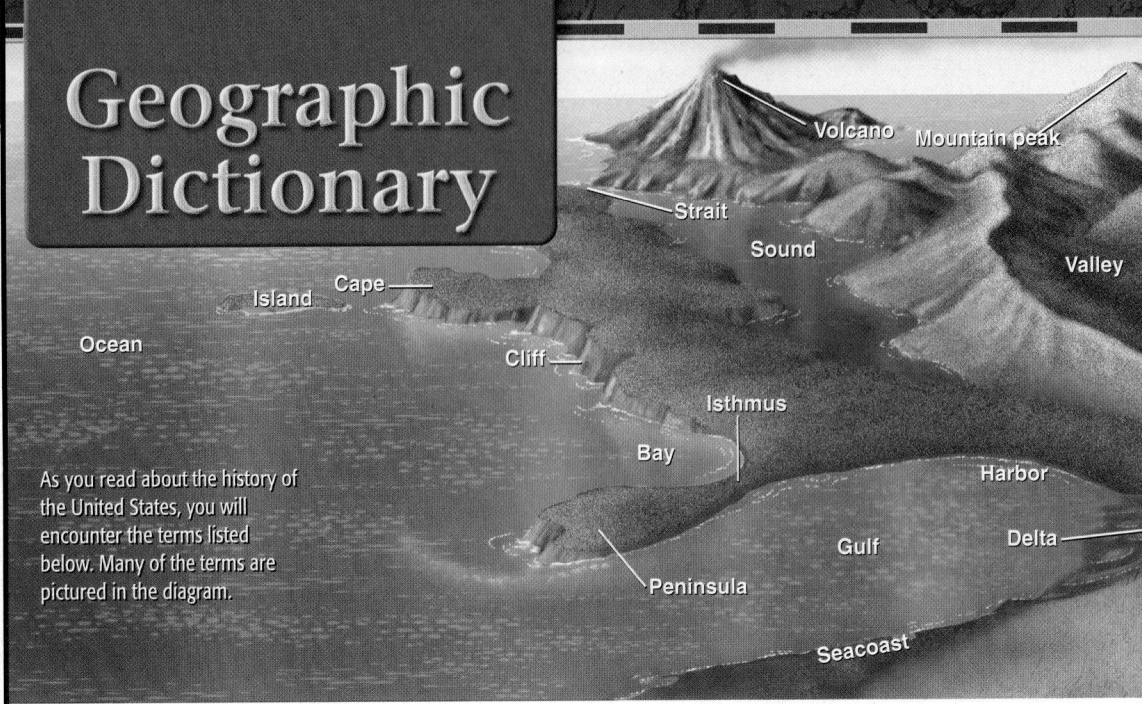

As you read about the history of the United States, you will encounter the terms listed below. Many of the terms are pictured in the diagram.

absolute location exact location of a place on the earth described by global coordinates

basin area of land drained by a given river and its branches; area of land surrounded by lands of higher elevations

bay part of a large body of water that extends into a shoreline, generally smaller than a gulf

canyon deep and narrow valley with steep walls

cape point of land that extends into a river, lake, or ocean

channel wide strait or waterway between two landmasses that lie close to each other; deep part of a river or other waterway

cliff steep, high wall of rock, earth, or ice

continent one of the seven large landmasses on the earth

cultural feature characteristic that humans have created in a place, such as language, religion, housing, and settlement pattern

delta flat, low-lying land built up from soil carried downstream by a river and deposited at its mouth

divide stretch of high land that separates river systems

downstream direction in which a river or stream flows from its source to its mouth

elevation height of land above sea level

Equator imaginary line that runs around the earth halfway between the North and South Poles; used as the starting point to measure degrees of north and south latitude

glacier large, thick body of slowly moving ice

gulf part of a large body of water that extends into a shoreline, generally larger and more deeply indented than a bay

harbor a sheltered place along a shoreline where ships can anchor safely

highland elevated land area such as a hill, mountain, or plateau

hill elevated land with sloping sides and rounded summit; generally smaller than a mountain

island land area, smaller than a continent, completely surrounded by water

isthmus narrow stretch of land connecting two larger land areas

lake a large inland body of water

latitude distance north or south of the Equator, measured in degrees

longitude distance east or west of the Prime Meridian, measured in degrees

lowland land, usually level, at a low elevation

map drawing of the earth shown on a flat surface

meridian one of many lines on the global grid running from the North Pole to the South Pole; used to measure degrees of longitude

6 Geography Handbook

COOPERATIVE LEARNING ACTIVITY

Analyzing Maps Organize the class into two teams. Provide one team with a United States map and the other team with a map of your state. Assign each team the following task: Locate every major body of water in your assigned area. Record your findings, including: (1) the name of each major body of water; (2) its relative and/or absolute location; and (3) the type of feature it is— lake, river, bay, and so on. When teams have completed their tasks, have them create a map quiz based on their work. The teams should then trade maps and challenge one another with their quizzes.

Use the rubric for a cooperative group management plan on pages 71–72 in the **Performance Assessment Activities and Rubrics.**

Mountain range
Source of river
Channel
Glacier
Highland
Lake
Plateau
Hills
Mouth of river
Canyon
Dese...
River
Upstream
Downstream
Plain
Lowland
Basin
Tributary

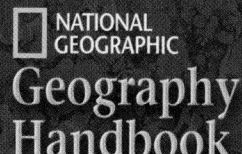

NATIONAL GEOGRAPHIC

Geography Handbook

3 ASSESS

Provide students with an outline map of the United States and colored pencils. Have students use a different color to label each of the following: Appalachian Mountains, Great Lakes, Mississippi River, Atlantic Ocean, Pacific Ocean, Rocky Mountains, Great Plains, and Gulf of Mexico. Have students think about how these features might affect European settlement patterns in North America.

4 CLOSE

Have students describe how a region's physical geography influences its economic development.

---

mesa broad, flat-topped landform with steep sides; smaller than a plateau

mountain land with steep sides that rises sharply (1,000 feet or more) from surrounding land; generally larger and more rugged than a hill

mountain peak pointed top of a mountain

mountain range a series of connected mountains

mouth (of a river) place where a stream or river flows into a larger body of water

ocean one of the four major bodies of salt water that surround the continents

ocean current stream of either cold or warm water that moves in a definite direction through an ocean

parallel one of many lines on the global grid that circle the earth north or south of the Equator; used to measure degrees of latitude

peninsula body of land jutting into a lake or ocean, surrounded on three sides by water

physical feature characteristic of a place occurring naturally, such as a landform, body of water, climate pattern, or resource

plain area of level land, usually at a low elevation and often covered with grasses

plateau large area of flat or rolling land at a high elevation, about 300–3,000 feet high

Prime Meridian line of the global grid running from the North Pole to the South Pole at Greenwich, England; starting point for measuring degrees of east and west longitude

relief changes in elevation over a given area of land

river large natural stream of water that runs through the land

sea large body of water completely or partly surrounded by land

seacoast land lying next to a sea or ocean

sea level position on land level with surface of nearby ocean or sea

sound body of water between a coastline and one or more islands off the coast

source (of a river) place where a river or stream begins, often in highlands

strait narrow stretch of water joining two larger bodies of water

tributary small river or stream that flows into a larger river or stream; a branch of the river

upstream direction opposite the flow of a river; toward the source of a river or stream

valley area of low land between hills or mountains

volcano mountain created as ash or liquid rock erupts from inside the earth

Geography Handbook   **7**

CRITICAL THINKING ACTIVITY

Analyzing Information Have students use atlases and other resources to plan a cross-country trip through the United States. Have them choose a starting point and destination, then plot the route between the two points. Have them calculate the approximate distance of the journey and how long the journey might take, then list points of interest along the way. Allow time for students to share their itineraries. L2

SUGGESTED PACING CHART

Unit 1 (1 Day)	Chapter 1 (5 Days)	Chapter 2 (6 Days)	Chapter 3 (6 Days)	Chapter 4 (4 Days)	Chapter 5 (5 Days)	Unit 1 (2 Days)
Day 1 Introduction	**Day 1** Chapter 1 Intro, Section 1 **Day 2** Section 2 **Day 3** Section 3 **Day 4** Section 4 **Day 5** Chapter 1 Assessment	**Day 1** Chapter 2 Intro, Section 1 **Day 2** Section 2 **Day 3** Section 3 **Day 4** Section 4 **Day 5** Section 5 **Day 6** Chapter 2 Assessment	**Day 1** Chapter 3 Intro, Section 1 **Day 2** Section 2 **Day 3** Section 3 **Day 4** Section 4 **Day 5** Section 5 **Day 6** Chapter 3 Assessment	**Day 1** Chapter 4 Intro, Section 1 **Day 2** Section 2 **Day 3** Section 3 **Day 4** Chapter 4 Assessment	**Day 1** Chapter 5 Intro, Section 1 **Day 2** Section 2 **Day 3** Section 3 **Day 4** Section 4 **Day 5** Chapter 5 Assessment	**Day 1** Wrap-Up/Project **Day 2** Unit 1 Assessment

GLENCOE'S ASSESSMENT ADVANTAGE

Use the following tools to easily assess student learning in a variety of ways:

- Performance Assessment Activities and Rubrics
- Chapter and Unit Tests
- Section Quizzes
- Standardized Test Practice Workbook

- tarvol2.glencoe.com
- Interactive Tutor Self-Assessment CD-ROM
- MindJogger Videoquiz
- ExamView® Pro Testmaker CD-ROM
- SAT I/II Test Practice

TEACHING TRANSPARENCIES

Unit 1 Map Overlay Transparencies L2

Cause-and-Effect Transparency 1 L2

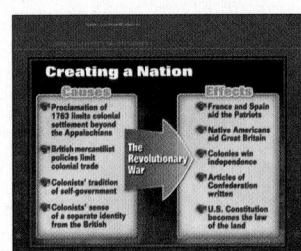

KEY TO ABILITY LEVELS

Teaching strategies have been coded.

L1   BASIC activities for all students

L2   AVERAGE activities for average to above-average students

L3   CHALLENGING activities for above-average students

ELL   ENGLISH LANGUAGE LEARNER activities

READING SUPPORT FROM JAMESTOWN EDUCATION

- **Timed Readings Plus in Social Studies** help students increase their reading rate and fluency while maintaining comprehension. The 400-word passages are similar to those found on state and national assessments.

- **Reading in the Content Area: Social Studies** concentrates on six essential reading skills that help students better comprehend what they read. The book includes 75 high-interest nonfiction passages written at increasing levels of difficulty.

- **Reading Fluency** helps students read smoothly, accurately, and expressively.

- **Jamestown's Reading Improvement,** by renowned reading expert Edward Fry, focuses on helping build your students' comprehension, vocabulary, and skimming and scanning skills.

- **Critical Reading Series** provides high-interest books, each written at three reading levels.

For more information about these products, see the Jamestown Education materials in the Classroom Solutions in the front of this Teacher Wraparound Edition. To order these products, call Glencoe at 1-800-334-7344.

Unit 1 Pretests L2

Unit 1 Posttests L2

American Biography 1 L2

History Simulation and Problem Solving 1 L1

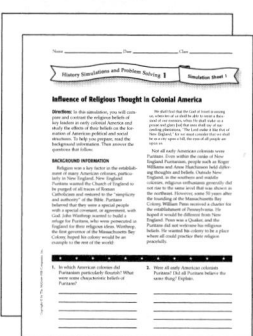

Geography and History Activity 1 L2

American Literature Reading 1 L2

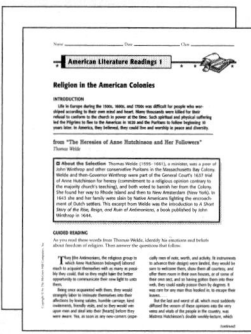

Economics and History Activity 1 L2

Team-Teaching Interdisciplinary Strategies and Activities 1 L2

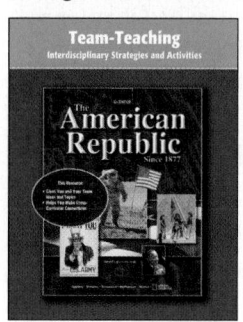

Reading List Generator CD-ROM

GLENCOE BOOKLINK

The Glencoe BookLink CD-ROM is a database that allows you to search more than 15,000 titles to create a customized reading list for your students.

■ Reading lists can be organized by students' reading level, author, genre, theme, or area of interest.

■ The database provides Degrees of Reading Power™ (DRP) and Lexile™ readability scores for all selections.

■ A brief summary of each selection is included.

Leveled reading suggestions for this unit:

For students at a Grade 8 reading level:

■ *Native Americans,* by James Wilson.

For students at a Grade 9 reading level:

■ *The American Revolutionaries,* by Milton Meltzer.

For students at a Grade 10 reading level:

■ *The Eagle and the Raven,* by James A. Michener.

Extending the Content

Readings for the Teacher

■ *The American Revolution: Writings from the War of Independence,* edited by John Rhodehamel. Library of America, 2001.

Multimedia Resources

■ *Mexico Before Cortez.* Social Studies School Service. VHS. (14 minutes)

0:00 **Out of Time?**

If time does not permit teaching each chapter in this unit, you may want to use the **Reading Essentials and Study Guide** summaries.

Unit Overview

Unit 1 presents the foundations of liberty from the variety of cultural influences that shaped America to the struggle to form a free nation. **Chapter 1** discusses the converging cultures from prehistory to 1620. **Chapter 2** focuses on the English arrival in America from 1607 to 1763. **Chapter 3** explores the American Revolution from 1754 to 1789. **Chapter 4** introduces the fundamental workings of government from 1789 to 1820. **Chapter 5** addresses the growth of the nation from 1816 to 1848.

Unit Objectives

After studying this unit, students will be able to:
1. Describe the early civilizations of Mesoamerica.
2. Explain the religious and economic reasons why England became interested in America.
3. Summarize the reasons for colonial discontent.
4. Describe the growing divisions between the nation's political parties.
5. Discuss why cotton dominated the Southern economy.

Why It Matters Activity

Discuss how the events of America's early period shaped its form of government. Compare and contrast the American form of government with other forms of government around the world.

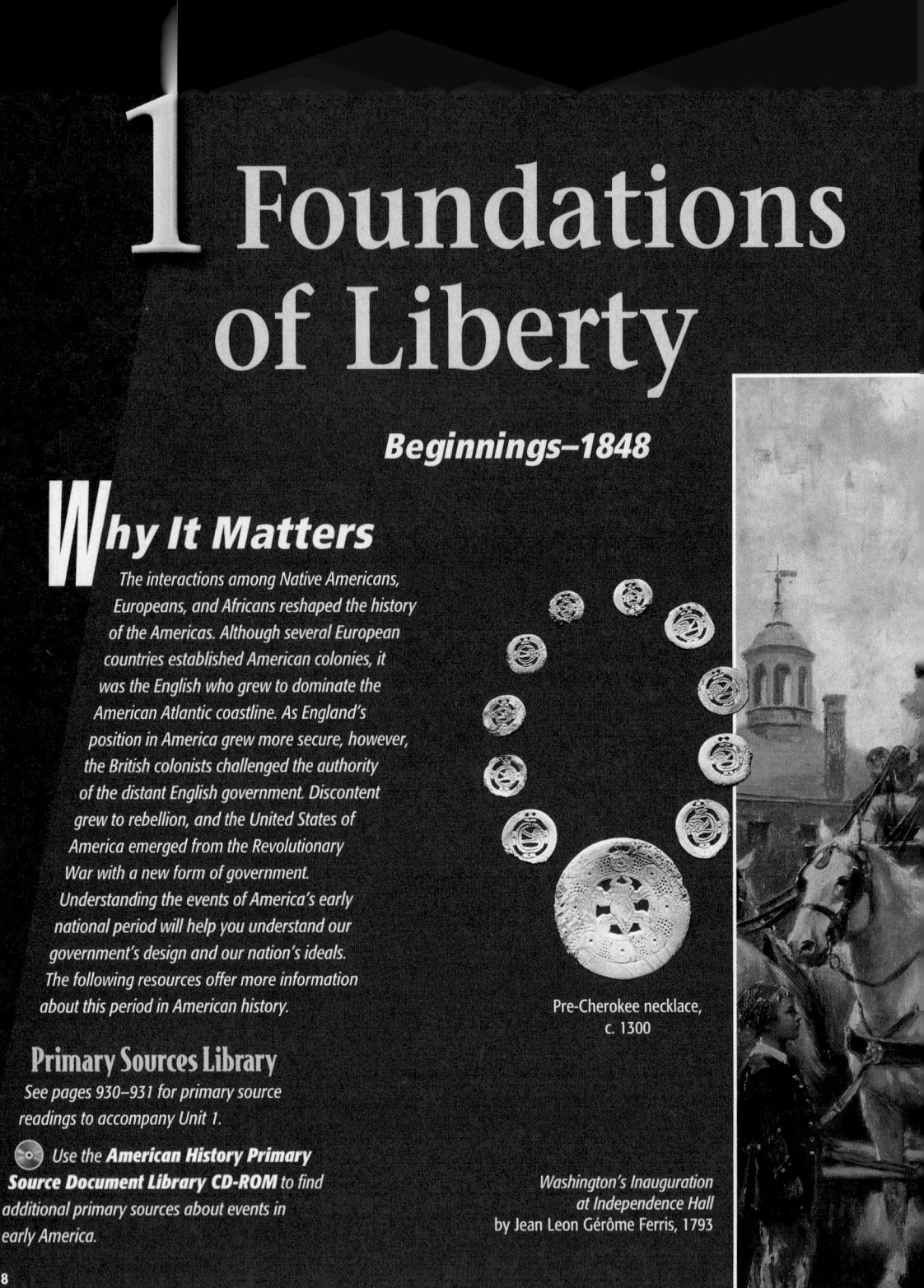

1 Foundations of Liberty

Beginnings–1848

Why It Matters

The interactions among Native Americans, Europeans, and Africans reshaped the history of the Americas. Although several European countries established American colonies, it was the English who grew to dominate the American Atlantic coastline. As England's position in America grew more secure, however, the British colonists challenged the authority of the distant English government. Discontent grew to rebellion, and the United States of America emerged from the Revolutionary War with a new form of government. Understanding the events of America's early national period will help you understand our government's design and our nation's ideals. The following resources offer more information about this period in American history.

Primary Sources Library

See pages 930–931 for primary source readings to accompany Unit 1.

Use the **American History Primary Source Document Library CD-ROM** to find additional primary sources about events in early America.

Pre-Cherokee necklace, c. 1300

Washington's Inauguration at Independence Hall by Jean Leon Gérôme Ferris, 1793

8

TEAM TEACHING ACTIVITY

Geography Tell students that the world in the 1400s looked very different from the way it looks today. In the 1400s the eastern part of North America was covered by thick forests. Marshland stretched along much of Europe's Mediterranean coast and covered vast areas of northern Germany and Russia. Have interested students research the environment of each continent in the 1400s. Based on their research, have them create a world vegetation map. Have them discuss their findings with the class. 🔲

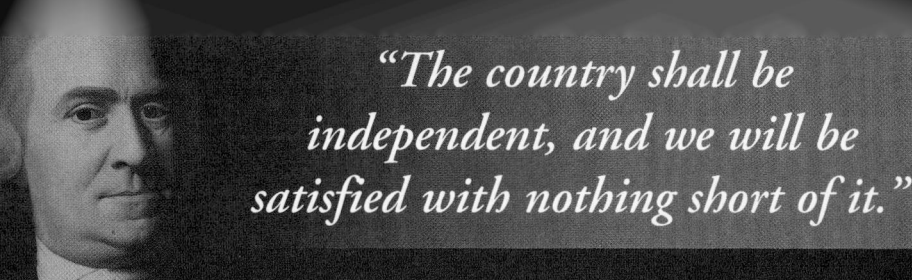

"The country shall be independent, and we will be satisfied with nothing short of it."

—Samuel Adams, 1774

GLENCOE TECHNOLOGY

CD-ROM
American History Primary Source Document Library CD-ROM
Use the **American History Primary Source Document Library CD-ROM** to access primary source documents related to this period in history.

More About the Art

Washington's first inauguration took place in New York City on the balcony of Federal Hall. The second inauguration occurred at Congress Hall in Philadelphia, Pennsylvania. The cupola of Congress Hall can be seen on the far left side of the painting. Philadelphia served as the nation's capital from 1790 to 1800.

Glencoe Literature Library

The following books from the *High School American History Literature Library* may be used to enrich the study of this unit:
- *The Autobiography of Benjamin Franklin* by Benjamin Franklin
- *The Scarlet Letter* by Nathaniel Hawthorne

SERVICE-LEARNING PROJECT

Organize students into small groups. Have each group research some aspect of your local community's history. Based on their research, have each group contribute to one large display featuring the history of your community. Have students select an appropriate title for the display. If possible, arrange for the display to be placed in a public building such as a library or town hall where it can be seen by the community at large.

Refer to ***Building Bridges: Connecting Classroom and Community through Service-Learning in Social Studies*** from the National Council for the Social Studies for information about service-learning.

Timesaving Tools

TeacherWorks™ All-In-One Planner and Resource Center

● **Interactive Teacher Edition** Access your Teacher Wraparound Edition and your classroom resources with a few easy clicks.

● **Interactive Lesson Planner** Planning has never been easier! Organize your week, month, semester, or year with all the lesson helps you need to make teaching creative, timely, and relevant.

Use Glencoe's **Presentation Plus!** multimedia teacher tool to easily present dynamic lessons that visually excite your students. Using Microsoft PowerPoint® you can customize the presentations to create your own personalized lessons.

TEACHING TRANSPARENCIES

Graphic Organizer 1 L2

Why It Matters Chapter Transparency 1 L2

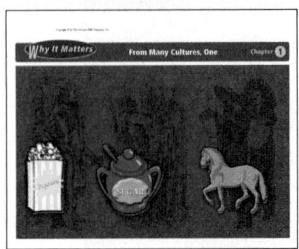

APPLICATION AND ENRICHMENT

Linking Past and Present Activity 1 L2

Enrichment Activity 1 L3

Primary Source Reading 1 L2

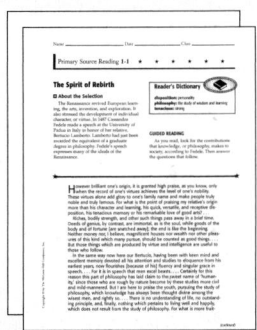

REVIEW AND REINFORCEMENT

Reteaching Activity 1 L1

Vocabulary Activity 1 L1

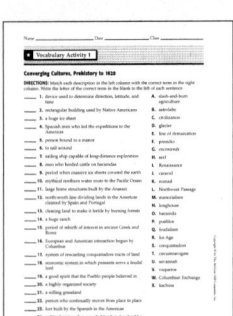

Time Line Activity 1 L2

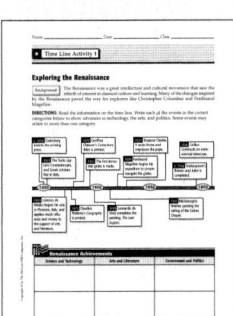

Critical Thinking Skills Activity 1 L2

Meeting NCSS Standards

Local Standards

The following standards are covered in Chapter 1:

Section 1 IV Individual Development and Identity: E, F
Section 2 V Individuals, Groups, and Institutions: B, G
Section 3 II Time, Continuity, and Change: C, E, F
Section 4 IX Global Connections: B, C, D, E

Chapter 1 Resources

ASSESSMENT AND EVALUATION

GLENCOE'S ASSESSMENT ADVANTAGE

Chapter 1 Test Form A L2

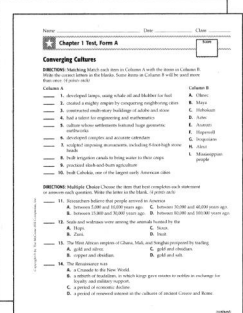

Chapter 1 Test Form B L2

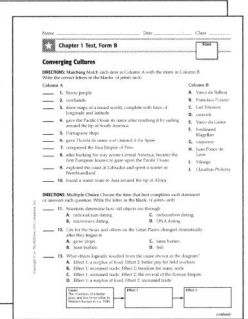

Standardized Test Practice Workbook Activity 1 L2

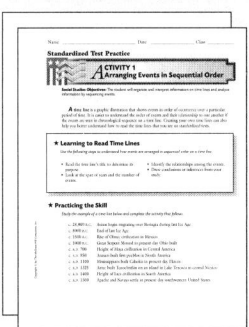

Performance Assessment Activities and Rubrics 1 L1/ELL

ExamView® Pro Testmaker CD-ROM

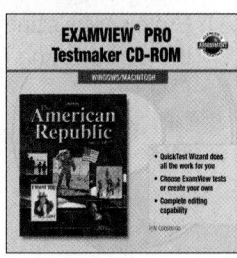

EXAMVIEW® PRO Testmaker CD-ROM

WINDOWS/MACINTOSH

American Republic

- QuickTest Wizard does all the work for you
- Choose ExamView tests or create your own
- Complete editing capability

MULTIMEDIA

- Vocabulary PuzzleMaker CD-ROM
- Interactive Tutor Self-Assessment CD-ROM
- ExamView® Pro Testmaker CD-ROM
- Audio Program
- American History Primary Source Documents Library CD-ROM
- MindJogger Videoquiz
- Presentation Plus! CD-ROM
- TeacherWorks™ CD-ROM
- Interactive Student Edition CD-ROM
- Glencoe Skillbuilder Interactive Workbook CD-ROM, Level 2
- The *American Republic Since 1877* Video Program
- American Music: Hits Through History
- American Music: Cultural Traditions

A&E HOME VIDEO — Biography® — THE HISTORY CHANNEL®

The following videotape programs are available from Glencoe as supplements to Chapter 1:

- **The Secret Mounds of Prehistoric America** (ISBN 1-56-501681-5)
- **The Aztec Empire** (ISBN 0-76-700542-2)
- **Leif Ericsson: Voyages of a Viking** (ISBN 1-56-501673-4)
- **Ponce de Leon: The First Conquistador** (ISBN 1-56-501669-6)

To order, call Glencoe at 1-800-334-7344. To find classroom resources to accompany many of these videos, check the following home pages:
A&E Television: www.aande.com
The History Channel: www.historychannel.com

SPANISH RESOURCES

The following Spanish language materials are available:

- Spanish Reading Essentials and Study Guide
- Spanish Guided Reading Activities
- Spanish Reteaching Activities
- Spanish Quizzes and Tests
- Spanish Vocabulary Activities
- Spanish Summaries
- The Declaration of Independence and United States Constitution Spanish Translation

HISTORY Online

Use our Web site for additional resources. All essential content is covered in the Student Edition.

You and your students can visit tarvol2.glencoe.com, the Web site companion to the *American Republic Since 1877*. This innovative integration of electronic and print media offers your students a wealth of opportunities. The student text directs students to the Web site for the following options:

- **Chapter Overviews**
- **Student Web Activities**
- **Self-Check Quizzes**
- **Textbook Updates**

Answers to the student Web activities are provided for you in the **Web Activity Lesson Plans.** Additional Web resources and Interactive Tutor Puzzles are also available.

Chapter 1 Resources

SECTION RESOURCES

Daily Objectives	Reproducible Resources	Multimedia Resources
SECTION 1 **The Migration to America** 1. Explain why scientists believe that the earliest Americans migrated from Asia. 2. Describe the early civilizations of Mesoamerica.	◻ Reproducible Lesson Plan 1–1 ◻ Daily Lecture and Discussion Notes 1–1 ◻ Guided Reading Activity 1–1* ◻ Section Quiz 1–1* ◻ Reading Essentials and Study Guide 1–1* ◻ Performance Assessment Activities and Rubrics	◻ Daily Focus Skills Transparency 1–1 ◻ American Art & Architecture ◻ Interactive Tutor Self-Assessment CD-ROM ◻ ExamView® Pro Testmaker CD-ROM* ◻ Presentation Plus! CD-ROM ◻ TeacherWorks™ CD-ROM ◻ Audio Program ◻ American Music: Hits Through History ◻ American Music: Cultural Traditions ◻ ABCNews Interactive™ Historic America Electronic Field Trips
SECTION 2 **Europe and Africa** 1. Analyze the impact of the Renaissance on European exploration. 2. Describe the culture of early West African kingdoms.	◻ Reproducible Lesson Plan 1–2 ◻ Daily Lecture and Discussion Notes 1–2 ◻ Guided Reading Activity 1–2* ◻ Section Quiz 1–2* ◻ Reading Essentials and Study Guide 1–2* ◻ Performance Assessment Activities and Rubrics	◻ Daily Focus Skills Transparency 1–2 ◻ Interactive Tutor Self-Assessment CD-ROM ◻ ExamView® Pro Testmaker CD-ROM* ◻ Presentation Plus! CD-ROM ◻ TeacherWorks™ CD-ROM ◻ Audio Program ◻ American Music: Cultural Traditions
SECTION 3 **Europe Encounters America** 1. Describe Columbus's journeys and their impact on Native Americans and Europeans. 2. Evaluate the workings and impact of the Columbian Exchange.	◻ Reproducible Lesson Plan 1–3 ◻ Daily Lecture and Discussion Notes 1–3 ◻ Guided Reading Activity 1–3* ◻ Section Quiz 1–3* ◻ Reading Essentials and Study Guide 1–3* ◻ Performance Assessment Activities and Rubrics ◻ Interpreting Political Cartoons	◻ Daily Focus Skills Transparency 1–3 ◻ Interactive Tutor Self-Assessment CD-ROM ◻ ExamView® Pro Testmaker CD-ROM* ◻ Presentation Plus! CD-ROM ◻ Skillbuilder Interactive Workbook, Level 2 ◻ TeacherWorks™ CD-ROM ◻ Audio Program
SECTION 4 **Spain and France Build Empires** 1. Describe the early Spanish settlement of North America. 2. Explain how New France was founded and settled.	◻ Reproducible Lesson Plan 1–4 ◻ Daily Lecture and Discussion Notes 1–4 ◻ Guided Reading Activity 1–4* ◻ Section Quiz 1–4* ◻ Reading Essentials and Study Guide 1–4* ◻ Performance Assessment Activities and Rubrics	◻ Daily Focus Skills Transparency 1–4 ◻ American Art & Architecture ◻ Interactive Tutor Self-Assessment CD-ROM ◻ ExamView® Pro Testmaker CD-ROM* ◻ Presentation Plus! CD-ROM ◻ TeacherWorks™ CD-ROM ◻ Vocabulary PuzzleMaker CD-ROM ◻ Audio Program ◻ American Music: Cultural Traditions ◻ ABCNews Interactive™ Historic America Electronic Field Trips

0:00 OUT OF TIME?
Assign the Chapter 1 **Reading Essentials and Study Guide.** ◻

*Also Available in Spanish

 Printed Materials　 Transparency　 CD-ROM　 DVD

 Poster　 Music Program　 Audio Program　 Videocassette

NATIONAL GEOGRAPHIC Teacher's Corner

INDEX TO NATIONAL GEOGRAPHIC MAGAZINE

The following articles relate to this chapter.

- "1491: America Before Columbus," October 1991
- "The Anasazi," April 1996
- "Cherokee," May 1995
- "Dawn of Humans: The First Americans," December 2000
- "Living Iroquois Confederacy," September 1987
- "Pueblo Ancestors Return Home," November 2000

NATIONAL GEOGRAPHIC SOCIETY PRODUCTS

To order the following, call National Geographic at 1-800-368-2728:

- *American Indians: A Brief History* (Video)

NGS ONLINE

Access National Geographic's Web site for current events, atlas updates, activities, links, interactive features, and archives.
www.nationalgeographic.com

From the Classroom of...

Karen O'Connor
San Diego Unified School District
San Diego, CA

The Influence of the East on the West

The Crusades brought Europeans into contact with Muslim and Byzantine civilizations in the Middle East. Traders followed the European armies eastward and brought back spices and silk. They also brought back the concept of paying with money instead of trading goods.

Gather students into small groups and ask them to research other areas where the contact between the East and West during this time period influenced European culture. Assign each group one of the following areas: architecture, art, literature, science, or language.

Give them one week to prepare an oral presentation. Their written reports are due one week later.

MEETING SPECIAL NEEDS

In addition to the Differentiated Instruction strategies found in each section, the following resources are also suitable for your special needs students:

- *ExamView® Pro Testmaker CD-ROM* allows teachers to tailor tests by reducing answer choices.
- The *Audio Program* includes the entire narrative of the student edition so that less-proficient readers can listen to the words as they read them.
- The *Reading Essentials and Study Guide* provides the same content as the student edition but is written two grade levels below the textbook.

ADDITIONAL RESOURCES FROM GLENCOE

- American Music: Cultural Traditions
- American Art & Architecture
- Outline Map Resource Book
- U.S. Desk Map
- Building Geography Skills for Life
- Inclusion for the High School Social Studies Classroom Strategies and Activities
- Teaching Strategies for the American History Classroom (Including Block Scheduling Pacing Guides)
- Dinah Zike's High School American History Reading and Study Skills Foldables

KEY TO ABILITY LEVELS

Teaching strategies have been coded.

L1 BASIC activities for all students
L2 AVERAGE activities for average to above-average students
L3 CHALLENGING activities for above-average students
ELL ENGLISH LANGUAGE LEARNER activities

Block Schedule

Activities that are suited to use within the block scheduling framework are identified by:

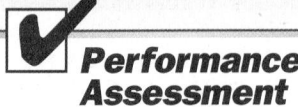

Performance Assessment

Refer to Activity 1 in the Performance Assessment Activities and Rubrics booklet.

Why It Matters Activity

On the board, create a list with three columns labeled Native American, European, and African. Under each column have students contribute ideas of foods, cultural traditions, and holiday celebrations that are part of American culture today.

GLENCOE
TECHNOLOGY

The *American Republic Since 1877* **Video Program**
To learn more about America before 1620, have students view the Chapter 1 video, "America Before the Americans," from the *American Republic Since 1877* **Video Program.**

MindJogger Videoquiz
Use the **MindJogger Videoquiz** to preview Chapter 1 content.

Both programs available in DVD

CHAPTER

1 Converging Cultures

Prehistory to 1620

Why It Matters

Before 1492 the cultures that arose in the Americas had almost no contact with the rest of the world. Beginning in the 1300s, momentous events began taking place that would bring the cultures of Europe and Africa into direct contact with the Americas. This contact led to the founding of European colonies in both North and South America and had profound effects on the future of the world's civilizations.

The Impact Today

The convergence of the world's cultures in the 1400s and 1500s launched an era of change that still affects our lives today.
• Many of our foods, customs, and traditions were originally introduced in the Americas as a result of this cultural contact.
• Contact among the cultures of the three continents profoundly changed the society of each.
• The society of the United States today includes elements of Native American, European, and African cultures.

The American Republic Since 1877 *Video*
The Chapter 1 video, "America Before the Americans," examines the early Americas.

c. 1200 B.C.
• Early Mesoamerican civilizations arise

C. A.D. 200
• Mayan culture begins to spread

A.D. 300
• Hohokam culture emerges

C. 28,000–13,000 B.C.
• First humans migrate to North America from Asia

The Americas

| 28,000 B.C. | 1200 B.C. | A.D. 250 | 500 |

World

c. 3000 B.C.
• Sumerians create cuneiform writing

1750 B.C.
• Death of Hammurabi in Middle East

A.D. 400
• Ghana civilization develops in West Africa

10

Reading Strategy — PURPOSE FOR READING

Pre-reading Organizers Students can use a pre-reading organizer to help them connect their prior knowledge with the information in this chapter. Ask students to create a two-column chart on a piece of paper. They should write "Event" on the top of the left column and "What I already Know or Think I Know" on top of the right column. Have students write in the left column two or three historical events prior to 1400 from the time line on pages 10 and 11. Then, have them complete the right columns with what they know or think they know about this event. **L1**

Refer to *Inclusion for the High School Social Studies Classroom Strategies and Activities* in the TCR.

The Landing of Columbus in San Salvador by Albert Bierstadt, 1893

Introduce students to chapter content and key terms by having them access the **Chapter 1 Overview** at tarvol2.glencoe.com.

More About the Art

Ask: What techniques does the painter use to convey his opinion of the landing party? *(Answers may vary. Students will note that the native peoples are bowing to the landing party. They should also note that the focus of the light is on the landing party, while the land itself is shrouded in darkness. Both convey a sense of superiority and dominance of the landing party.)*

c. 1130
• Drought strikes Native American cliff dwellings at Chaco Canyon

1519
• Cortés lands on Mexican coast

1532
• Pizarro invades Inca Empire

1608
• City of Quebec founded

1492
• Christopher Columbus lands in America

HISTORY Online

Chapter Overview
Visit the *American Republic Since 1877* Web site at tarvol2.glencoe.com and click on *Chapter Overviews— Chapter 1* to preview chapter information.

1095
• Pope Urban II launches the Crusades

1240
• Mali empire expands in West Africa

1420s
• Portugal begins exploring the African coast

1517
• Protestant Reformation begins

1588
• English defeat Spanish Armada

TIME LINE
ACTIVITY

Have students use a globe or world map to identify the approximate location where the events shown on the time line occurred. Encourage students to use library and Internet resources to determine the present-day names of locations. For example, Sumer, home of the Sumerians, was located in the area that is now southern Iraq.

FOLDABLES
Study Organizer

Dinah Zike's Foldables are three-dimensional, interactive graphic organizers that help students practice basic writing skills, review key vocabulary terms, and identify main ideas. Have students complete the foldable activity in the *Dinah Zike's Reading and Study Skills Foldables* booklet.

GRAPHIC ORGANIZER ACTIVITY

Organizing Information Have students outline Chapter 1, using the format shown below.

I. The Migration to America
  A. The Asian Migration to America
  B. Early Civilizations in America
    1. Mesoamerica
    2. The American Southwest
    3. Mound Builders
  C. Native American Cultural Diversity

II. Europe and Africa
III. Europe Encounters America
IV. Spain and France Build Empires

11

1 FOCUS

Section Overview

This section explores the Native American groups that inhabited Mesoamerica and North America by the 1500s.

BELLRINGER
Skillbuilder Activity

Project transparency and have students answer the question.

Daily Focus Skills Transparency 1–1

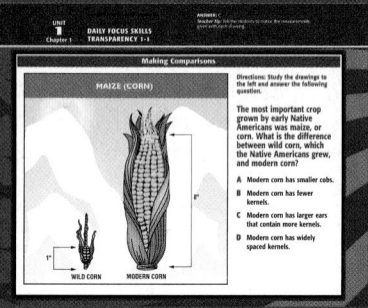

Reading Preview

Answers to Graphic: Mesoamerica: *Olmec, Mayan, Aztec cultures* Eastern Woodlands: *Hopewell culture* Southwest: *Hohokam and Anasazi cultures* Great Plains: *Mississippian culture*

Preteaching Vocabulary
Have students write a paragraph using at least three of the Key Terms and Names.

SECTION 1 — The Migration to America

Guide to Reading

Main Idea
Many diverse Native American groups inhabited Mesoamerica and North America by the 1500s. They were descendants of Asians who probably migrated 15,000 to 30,000 years ago.

Key Terms and Names
Ice Age, glacier, nomad, Mesoamerica, civilization, pueblo, Cahokia, kachina, slash-and-burn agriculture, longhouse

Reading Strategy
Categorizing As you read about early American peoples, complete a graphic organizer by filling in the names of Native American groups who lived in each region.

Regions	Native American Groups
Mesoamerica	
Eastern Woodlands	
Southwest	
Great Plains	

Reading Objectives
- **Explain** why scientists believe that the earliest Americans migrated from Asia.
- **Describe** the early civilizations of Mesoamerica.

Section Theme
Geography and History Scientists theorize that Asian nomads began settling North America between 15,000 and 30,000 years ago.

Preview of Events

♦30,000   ♦15,000   ♦0   ♦A.D. 1500

c. 28,000–13,000 B.C. First humans migrate to North America

c. A.D. 850 Chaco Canyon pueblos are built

c. A.D. 1300 Cahokia collapses

Late 1500s Iroquois League created

★ An American Story ★

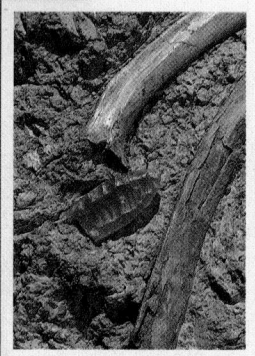

Folsom point, lying between animal bones

In 1925 an African American cowboy named George McJunkin was riding along a gully near the town of Folsom, New Mexico, when he noticed something gleaming in the dirt. He began digging and found a bone and a flint arrowhead. J.D. Figgins of the Colorado Museum of Natural History knew the bone belonged to a type of bison that had been extinct for 10,000 years. The arrowhead's proximity to the bones implied that human beings had been in America at least 10,000 years, which no one had believed at that time.

The following year, Figgins found another arrowhead embedded in similar bones. In 1927 he led a group of scientists to the find. Anthropologist Frank H.H. Roberts, Jr., wrote, "There was no question but that here was the evidence. . . . The point was still embedded . . . between two of the ribs of the animal skeleton." Further digs turned up more arrowheads, now called Folsom points. Roberts later noted: "The Folsom find was accepted as a reliable indication that man was present in the Southwest at an earlier period than was previously supposed."

—adapted from *The First American: A Story of North American Archaeology*

The Asian Migration to America

No one knows exactly when the first people arrived in America. The Folsom discoveries proved that people were here at least 10,000 years ago, but more recent research suggests that humans may have arrived much earlier—between 15,000 and 30,000 years ago.

SECTION RESOURCES

📂 Reproducible Masters
- Reproducible Lesson Plan 1–1
- Daily Lecture and Discussion Notes 1–1
- Guided Reading Activity 1–1
- Section Quiz 1–1
- Reading Essentials and Study Guide 1–1

🖥 Transparencies
- Daily Focus Skills Transparency 1–1

Multimedia
- Interactive Tutor Self-Assessment CD-ROM
- ExamView® Pro Testmaker CD-ROM
- Presentation Plus! CD-ROM
- TeacherWorks™ CD-ROM
- Audio Program
- American Music: Hits Through History
- American Music: Cultural Traditions

To learn the origins of ancient peoples, scientists study their skulls, bones, and teeth and analyze their DNA (deoxyribonucleic acid, the basic chemical building material of all life). Such evidence indicates that the earliest Americans probably came from Asia. Radiocarbon dating provides even more information. By measuring the radioactivity of the carbon 14 molecules left in ancient material and knowing how fast carbon 14 loses its radioactivity, scientists can calculate the age of the material.

Geology offers other clues. About 100,000 years ago, the earth began to cool, gradually entering the period known as the Ice Age. Much of the earth's water froze into huge ice sheets, or glaciers. The dropping water levels in the oceans eventually exposed a stretch of seafloor that connected Asia to what is now Alaska. Scientists think that about 15,000 years ago, or even earlier, people from Asia began trekking east across this land bridge to America.

These early arrivals were probably nomads, people who continually move from place to place. These early peoples did not come all at once. Their migrations probably continued until about 10,000 years ago, when rising seawater once again submerged the land bridge. This created a waterway now called the Bering Strait.

Reading Check **Explaining** How do scientists learn the origins of ancient peoples?

Early Civilizations in America

As time passed, Native Americans learned how to plant and raise crops. This **agricultural revolution** occurred between 9,000 and 10,000 years ago in the region anthropologists call **Mesoamerica.** This area includes what is now central and southern Mexico and Central America.

The first crops grown in America included pumpkins, peppers, squash, and beans. Most important was **maize,** or corn, which could be ground into flour for bread or dried for future use. The shift to agriculture forced people to stay in one place to tend their crops. Thus, the cultivation of crops led to the first permanent villages and also to new building methods.

As more and more people began to live in one place, more complex forms of government arose, as did social classes. People developed specialized skills and traded their products for food and other goods.

As these village societies became more complex, America's first civilizations emerged. A civilization is a highly organized society marked by advanced knowledge of trade, government, the arts, science, and, often, written language.

Mesoamerica Anthropologists think the first people to build a civilization in America were the Olmec, beginning between 1500 and 1200 B.C. in what is today southern Mexico. The Olmec built large villages, temple complexes, and pyramids. They also sculpted imposing monuments, including 8-foot-high stone heads. Olmec culture lasted until approximately 300 B.C.

About that same time, another people constructed the first large city in America, Teotihuacán, close to what is now Mexico City. Teotihuacán became a center of trade and greatly influenced the development of Mesoamerica until about A.D. 650, when enemies destroyed the city.

Meanwhile, around A.D. 200, the Mayan culture emerged in present-day Mexico's Yucatán Peninsula and spread into Central America. The Maya had a talent for engineering and mathematics. They developed accurate calendars and built cities such as Tikal and Chichén Itzá with great temple pyramids.

The Maya in the Yucatán thrived until the A.D. 900s, when they abandoned their cities for unknown reasons. Some anthropologists believe they fled from northern invaders. Others think overfarming may have exhausted the soil, leading to famine and riots. Mayan cities in the highlands of what is today Guatemala flourished for several more centuries, but by the 1500s, they too were in decline.

Picturing **History**

Mesoamerican Civilizations Archaeological evidence such as this Mayan pyramid and these Toltec statues demonstrate that early Americans had developed a complex way of life. Why did many nomadic peoples stop wandering and settle down to create permanent civilizations?

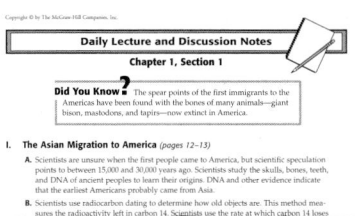

CHAPTER 1
Section 1, 12–16

2 TEACH

Daily Lecture and Discussion Notes 1–1

Picturing **History**

Answer: The agricultural revolution caused people to settle in one place. **Ask:** How do you think the buildings in the picture show an organized civilization? *(Possible answers include permanent structures built for specific purposes and the specialized skills needed to construct such dwellings.)*

Reading Check

Answer: Scientists study the bones and DNA of ancient peoples to trace their ethnic history and use radiocarbon dating to determine the age of objects. Scientists also study geology to understand peoples' geographic origins.

 History *and the* **Humanities**

- American Music: Hits Through History: "Iroquois Round Dance"
- American Music: Cultural Traditions: "Rain Dance"
- American Art & Architecture: Serpent Mound, Cliff Palace, Quilled Buckskin Robe

Reading Strategy **READING THE TEXT**

Previewing Have students preview the text's structure before they begin reading. Text structures include time order, compare-contrast, description, cause and effect, and problem-solution. Noticing how ideas are organized will prepare students for the types of information they will receive. L1

Refer to *Inclusion for the High School Social Studies Classroom Strategies and Activities* in the TCR.

L1/ELL
Guided Reading Activity 1-1

Name _____ Date _____ Class _____

★ Guided Reading Activity 1-1

DIRECTIONS: Filling in the Blanks In the space provided, write the word or words that best complete the sentence. Refer to your textbook to fill in the blanks.

1. To determine how old objects are, scientists rely on _____
2. About 100,000 years ago much of the earth's water froze into huge ice sheets, or _____
3. The region called _____ was located in what is now central and southern _____ and Central America.
4. _____ are people who continually move from place to place.
5. The first crops grown in America included _____, _____, and _____
6. _____ was important because it could be ground into flour to make bread and could be dried for later use.

Discussing a Topic Ask students to discuss how members of the early civilizations of Mesoamerica might have spent their time on a typical day. Discuss what people might have eaten, and what different roles people might have had in these early societies. **L2**

ABCNEWS INTERACTIVE™

VIDEOCASSETTE
Historic America Electronic Field Trips

View **Tape 1, Chapter 3:** "Cahokia Mounds."

Geography Skills

Answers:
1. fish
2. The land was too dry to farm, so they hunted migrating buffalo herds.

Geography Skills Practice
Ask: What type of culture do you think each picture represents?
(Southwest pueblo: agricultural; Northeastern longhouse: agricultural)

NATIONAL GEOGRAPHIC
Native American Cultures, Including Mesoamerica, 500 B.C.–A.D. 1500

In Motion

Legend:
- Agriculture
- Fishing
- Hunting
- Hunting-Gathering
- Uninhabited

Northeastern longhouse

Southwest pueblo

Geography Skills

1. **Interpreting Maps** What was the main food source for the Northwest?
2. **Applying Geography Skills** Why were Great Plains peoples nomadic?

Around that time in what is now central Mexico, the Aztec civilization emerged. About 1325 the **Aztec** established the city of Tenochtitlán (tay·NAWCH·teet·LAHN), where Mexico City now stands. They created a mighty empire by conquering neighboring cities, demanding tribute from them, and controlling trade in the region. By the 1500s, roughly five million people lived under Aztec rule.

Many anthropologists think that the agricultural technology of Mesoamerica spread north into the American Southwest and beyond.

There it transformed many of the scattered hunter-gatherers of North America into farmers.

The American Southwest Beginning about A.D. 300, a group called the **Hohokam** began farming in what is now south-central Arizona. They devised irrigation canals to bring water from the Gila and Salt Rivers to their corn, cotton, and bean fields hundreds of miles away. In the 1300s, the Hohokam began to abandon their lands, probably because of floods, and by 1500 their culture had vanished.

14 CHAPTER 1 Converging Cultures

DIFFERENTIATED INSTRUCTION

English Learners Have students select one portion of Section 1 to teach to another student. Ask students to read the passage and then to teach it to a partner. Have the student doing the teaching ask questions about what has been taught. Direct the student/teacher to review any concepts that the student/learner did not understand. **L1 ELL**

☞ Refer to *Inclusion for the High School Social Studies Classroom Strategies and Activities* in the TCR.

Farther north, in the Four Corners area where Utah, Colorado, Arizona, and New Mexico now meet, the **Anasazi** civilization arose between roughly A.D. 700 and 900. The Anasazi farmed in the harsh desert by building basins and ditches to collect rainwater. Sometime between 850 and 1100, the Anasazi in Chaco Canyon in what is now northwest New Mexico began constructing pueblos—large multi-story buildings of adobe and stone. Beginning around 1130, Chaco Canyon suffered at least 50 years of drought, probably driving out the Anasazi. Attacks by hunter-gatherers or epidemics may also have contributed to the collapse of Anasazi civilization.

Mound Builders About the time that the Olmec civilization began in Mesoamerica, the people in North America's eastern woodlands were developing their own cultures. These people buried their dead under massive dome-shaped earthen mounds. Between 200 and 100 B.C., a new culture known as the Hopewell arose. The Hopewell built huge geometric earthworks that served as ceremonial centers, observatories, and burial places.

Between A.D. 700 and 900, another new culture emerged, this time in the Mississippi River valley. The Mississippian people created **Cahokia,** one of the largest cities early Americans ever built. Located near present-day St. Louis, Cahokia was home to an estimated 16,000 people at its peak. The city collapsed around A.D. 1300, perhaps because of an epidemic, an attack by other Native Americans, or overpopulation and famine.

✓ Reading Check **Examining** How did the shift to agriculture allow early peoples to advance beyond mere subsistence?

Native American Cultural Diversity

Mississippian culture spread widely across the Southeast, but after its decline, the Native Americans there were fragmented into many smaller groups. That had long been the case elsewhere in North America.

The Far North Two different groups made the Far North their home. The Inuit inhabited the lands from what is now Alaska to Greenland; the Aleut settled present-day Alaska's Aleutian Islands. Both groups hunted seals, walruses, whales, polar bears, and caribou. They invented ingenious devices to cope with the harsh environment, including the harpoon, kayak, and dogsled. They also were the only Native Americans to develop lamps, using whale oil and blubber for fuel.

The Pacific Many groups of fishing peoples, including the Kwakiutls and Chinook, lived along the Pacific Coast from what is now southeastern Alaska to Washington state. Although not farmers, they made permanent settlements because the coastal waters and nearby rivers teemed with salmon and other fish.

Farther inland, between the Cascade Range and the Rocky Mountains, the Nez Perce, Yakima, and other groups fished, hunted deer, and gathered roots and berries. To the south, the Ute and Shoshone roamed the dry terrain between the Sierra Nevada and Rocky Mountains. In what is now central California, groups such as the Pomo enjoyed abundant wildlife and a mild climate.

The Southwest The Zuni, Hopi, and other Pueblo peoples of the Southwest were descendants of the Anasazi and Hohokam. They continued their ancestors' farming tradition.

Like most Native Americans, these groups believed in a spirit world. When men married, they joined the kachina cult, wearing masks and dancing to summon the kachinas, or good spirits.

Around the 1500s two other peoples—the Apache and the Navajo—came to the region from the far northwest. Although many of the Apache remained primarily nomadic hunters, the Navajo learned farming and settled in widely dispersed villages.

The Great Plains The inhabitants of the Great Plains practiced agriculture until about 1500, when they abandoned their villages, possibly because of war or drought. They became nomadic hunters, following migrating buffalo herds on foot. Life for the Great Plains people changed dramatically after they began taming the wild descendants of horses brought to North America by the Spanish. They became expert riders, hunters, and warriors.

GOVERNMENT

The Eastern Woodlands
East of the Mississippi River and south of the Great Lakes lay almost a million square

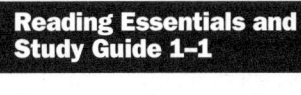

HISTORY Online

Student Web Activity Visit the *American Republic Since 1877* Web site at tarvol2.glencoe.com and click on *Student Web Activities— Chapter 1* for an activity on America's prehistory.

✓ Reading Check

Answer: The shift to agriculture allowed people to stay in one place to tend their crops and store their harvest. Because people stayed in one place, permanent villages were established. Village life led to specialized skills and complex societies.

HISTORY Online

Objectives and answers to the student activity can be found in the **Web Activity Lesson Plan** at tarvol2.glencoe.com.

3 ASSESS

Assign Section 1 Assessment as homework or as an in-class activity.

🖥 Have students use the **Interactive Tutor Self-Assessment CD-ROM.**

L1/ELL

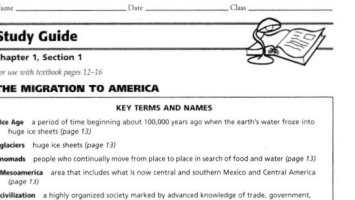

Reading Essentials and Study Guide 1–1

Name _____ Date _____ Class _____

Study Guide

Chapter 1, Section 1
For use with textbook pages 12–16

THE MIGRATION TO AMERICA

KEY TERMS AND NAMES

Ice Age a period of time beginning about 100,000 years ago when the earth's water froze into huge ice sheets (*page 13*)

glaciers huge ice sheets (*page 13*)

nomads people who continually move from place to place in search of food and water (*page 13*)

Mesoamerica area that includes what is now central and southern Mexico and Central America (*page 13*)

civilization a highly organized society marked by advanced knowledge of trade, government, the arts, science, and, often, a written language (*page 13*)

pueblos large multistory buildings of adobe and stone (*page 15*)

INTERDISCIPLINARY CONNECTIONS ACTIVITY

Visual Arts Have students conduct research about pre-Columbian art using library, museum, and Internet resources. Ask students to focus their research on one of the cultures addressed in this section. Using their findings, have students prepare a short oral presentation. Encourage students to bring books with photographs and illustrations to pass around during their presentation. **L2**

L2

Section Quiz 1–1

Name _____ Date _____ Class _____

★ Chapter 1   Score [ ]

Section Quiz 1-1

DIRECTIONS: Matching Match each item in Column A with the items in Column B.
Write the correct letters in the blanks. *(10 points each)*

Column A   Column B
____ 1. method used to calculate the age of material   A. Chaco Canyon
____ 2. Anasazi lived here   B. kachinas
____ 3. large Mississippian city   C. Cahokia
____ 4. good spirits   D. radiocarbon dating
____ 5. built a system of irrigation canals   E. Hohokam

DIRECTIONS: Multiple Choice In the blank at the left, write the letter of the choice that
best completes the statement or answers the question. *(10 points each)*

Picturing History

Answer: ceremonial centers, observatories, and burial places
Ask: What cultural facts can scientists learn from the copper falcon?
(The Hopewell knew how to mine, refine, and work with metals; they used animal symbols in their culture.)

✓ Reading Check

Answer: determined hunting, fishing, and agricultural practices; influenced tool invention and animal domestication

Reteach

Have students trace a map of North America and mark key locations with the names and dates of the cultures.

Enrich

Have students research and write a report about the ways members of one of the cultures in this section communicated with other Native American groups.

HISTORY Online

Study Central™ provides summaries, interactive games, and online graphic organizers to help students review section content.

4 CLOSE

Ask students to explain why people from Asia migrated to America and why they ended up in Mesoamerica.

16

---

miles of woodlands rich in plant and animal life. Most Native Americans in the Eastern Woodlands combined hunting and fishing with farming. They planted corn, beans, and squash and hunted the plentiful deer for meat and hides.

The Iroquois of New York, like many groups in the Northeast, practiced **slash-and-burn agriculture.** They cut down forests, burned the cleared land, and used the nitrogen-rich ashes to make the soil more fertile. They surrounded their villages with wooden stockades and built large rectangular **longhouses** that housed up to 10 families. These kinship groups, or extended families, were headed by the elder women of each clan.

Despite their similar cultures, war often erupted among the Iroquois groups. In the late 1500s, five groups in western New York—the Seneca, Cayuga, Onondaga, Oneida, and Mohawk—formed an alliance to maintain peace. The Great Binding Law defined how this Iroquois League worked.

Although the ruling council was all male, the women who headed the kinship groups selected its members and could remove appointees they disagreed with. Thus Iroquois women enjoyed considerable political influence.

Like the Iroquois in the Northeast, the people in the Southeast generally lived in towns enclosed by

Picturing History

Adena and Hopewell Culture The Great Serpent Mound in southern Ohio (above) is an example of the earthen mounds built by the Adena culture. The copper falcon (right) is a Hopewell design. These artifacts help scientists learn more about the culture of ancient civilizations. *For what did Native Americans use their earthen mounds?*

stockades. Houses built of grass, mud, or thatch stood around a central plaza. Women did most of the farming, while the men hunted deer, bear, and even alligator.

By the 1500s, Native Americans had established a wide array of cultures and languages. They had also developed economies and lifestyles suited to their particular environments.

✓ Reading Check
Explaining How did climate and food sources help shape Native American lifestyles?

HISTORY Online | **Study Central**™ To review this section, go to **tarvol2.glencoe.com** and click on **Study Central**™.

SECTION 1 ASSESSMENT

Checking for Understanding

1. **Define:** Ice Age, glacier, nomad, civilization, pueblo, kachina, slash-and-burn agriculture, longhouse.
2. **Identify:** Mesoamerica, Cahokia.
3. **Explain** how the agricultural revolution led to the growth of permanent settlements.

Reviewing Themes

4. **Geography and History** How did geography and climate influence the settlement of America?

Critical Thinking

5. **Evaluating** Choose an early culture group in Mesoamerica or North America. What kind of civilization did this group develop?
6. **Categorizing** Use a graphic organizer similar to the one below to list North American regions and the ways Native Americans in each region obtained food.

Region	Ways of Getting Food

Analyzing Visuals

7. **Examining Photographs** Study the photographs of the Great Serpent Mound and the copper falcon on this page. How did the Native Americans in this region adapt to their environment?

Writing About History

8. **Descriptive Writing** Take on the role of an early Native American teenager. Write a journal entry describing a typical day in your life. Remember to consider how your life might be different if you are a male or female Native American.

16   CHAPTER 1   Converging Cultures

SECTION 1 ASSESSMENT ANSWERS

1. Terms are in blue.
2. Mesoamerica *(p. 13)*, Cahokia *(p. 15)*
3. It forced people to stay in one place to tend to their crops.
4. Asians, searching for food, crossed a land bridge that once connected Asia and Alaska.
5. Possible choices–Olmec, Aztec, Hohokam, Anasazi
6. Far North: hunting; Pacific: fishing; Southwest: farming; Great Plains: farming, hunting, and hunting-gathering; Eastern Woodlands: hunting, fishing, and farming.
7. Answers may vary. For example, Native Americans used natural resources such as metal ores to create objects.
8. Students' reports will vary. Entries should focus on typical daily activities such as getting food and clothing, socializing with friends, and finding shelter.

American LITERATURE

 Block Schedule

Team Teaching This selection from *The Constitution of the Five Nations* can be presented in a team teaching context, in conjunction with English or Language Arts.

from *The Constitution of the Five Nations*

Among the Native American groups with the richest oral literary traditions are the Iroquois. The Iroquois lived in what is today New York state. For a long time they were a mighty and warlike people given to fighting amongst themselves. During the 1500s a shaman, or tribal elder, named Dekanawidah urged the Iroquois to stop fighting and unite to protect themselves from their common enemies. Dekanawidah's ideas led to the formation of the Iroquois Confederation of the Five Nations, commonly known as the Iroquois League.

Read to Discover
How did the Iroquois Confederation organize the Confederate Council?

Reader's Dictionary
foundation: basis
unanimous: in complete agreement
render: make; provide

I am Dekanawidah and with the Five Nations' Confederate Lords I plant the Tree of Great Peace. . . .

The Mohawk Lords are the foundation of the Great Peace and it shall, therefore, be against the Great Binding Law [the constitution] to pass measures in the Confederate Council after the Mohawk Lords have protested against them.

All the business of the Five Nations Confederate Council shall be conducted by the two combined bodies of Confederate Lords. . . . In all cases the procedure must be as follows: when the Mohawk and Seneca Lords have unanimously agreed upon a question, they shall report their decision to the Cayuga and Oneida Lords who shall deliberate upon the question and report a unanimous decision to the Mohawk Lords. The Mohawk Lords will then report the standing of the case to the Firekeepers [the Onondaga], who shall render a decision as they see fit in case of a disagreement by the two bodies. . . .

There shall be one War Chief for each Nation and their duties shall be to carry messages for their Lords and to take up the arms of war in case of emergency. They shall not participate in . . . the Confederate Council.

Whenever a very important matter or a great emergency is presented

before the Confederate Council [that] affects the entire body of the Five Nations . . . the Lords of the Confederacy must submit the matter to the decision of their people and the decision of the people shall affect the decision of the Confederate Council.

Analyzing Literature

1. **Recall and Interpret** Which of the Five Nations settles a dispute within the Confederate Council?
2. **Evaluate and Connect** Which Nation seems to have the most individual power?

Interdisciplinary Activity
Government Imagine that you and several classmates are leaders of five small nations that are going to join together as one. In small groups, develop a new constitution under which all members of the new nation will live.

Read to Discover
Answer: They organized it into two bodies of Lords.

Reinforcing Vocabulary
Have students take turns using one of the terms in a sentence that they speak aloud.

Historical Connection
The portion of *The Constitution of the Five Nations* that appears in the text is only a small part of the complete document, which contains more than 12,000 words.

Portfolio Writing Activity
Ask students to find and read the entire document *The Constitution of the Five Nations* and write a summary of the key elements. The document is available at most libraries and on the Internet.

HISTORY Online

Refer to tarvol2.glencoe.com for additional Glencoe Literature titles, lesson plans, and study guides related to this unit.

Answers to Analyzing Literature

1. The Onondaga can settle disputes.
2. It appears that the Mohawk nation has the most power since binding laws cannot be passed if the Mohawk Lords have objected to them.

Interdisciplinary Activity
Constitutions will vary. At a minimum, students should deal with how to live at peace as a group, how to resolve differences in the group, and how to handle attacks from enemies. To make this activity more realistic, have students name and describe their nations.

1 FOCUS

Section Overview

This section explores the inter-action between Europeans and Africans during the period of European exploration.

BELLRINGER
Skillbuilder Activity

 Project transparency and have students answer the question.

Daily Focus Skills Transparency 1–2

Reading Preview

Answers to Graphic: Possible time line entries are 600s and 700s, Islam grew throughout the Middle East and Africa; A.D. 1000, economy of western Europe improves; A.D. 1095, the Crusades begin at the urging of Pope Urban II; 1200s, Mongol empire expands; 1300s, emergence of strong states in Europe.

Preteaching Vocabulary

Have students use index cards and write the Key Term or Name on one side and the definition or description on the other side. Encourage students to use their cards as study tools.

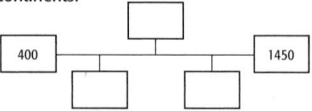

Guide to Reading

Main Idea
As Europeans began exploring the world, they interacted with Africans who had developed diverse cultures of their own.

Key Terms and Names
Middle Ages, feudalism, manorialism, serf, Urban II, Crusades, Renaissance, astrolabe, caravel, Sahara, savannah

Reading Strategy
Sequencing As you read about European and African life, complete a time line like the one below by filling in key events in the development of both continents.

400 ⎯⎯⎯⎯⎯⎯⎯ 1450

Reading Objectives
• **Analyze** the impact of the Renaissance on European exploration.
• **Describe** the culture of early West African kingdoms.

Section Theme
Global Connections European exploration of the globe set in motion events that decisively shaped North American history.

Preview of Events

♦A.D. 400	♦750	♦1100	♦1450

600s
Ideas of Islam begin spreading across Middle East and Africa

1095
Pope launches first Crusade to free Holy Land from Muslim control

1300s
Renaissance begins in Italy

1420s
Portugal begins exploring African coast

Mansa Musa

★ An American Story ★

In 1324 Mansa Musa, ruler of the Mali empire, made a pilgrimage to the Arabian city of Makkah (Mecca), a place holy to his religion, Islam.

Musa had encouraged scholarship and trade in his realm, establishing his empire's leading city, Timbuktu, as a great center of learning. A man named Mahmoud Kati, a native of the city, wrote a book praising Timbuktu for "the solidity of its institutions, its political liberties, the purity of its morals, the security of persons, its consideration and compassion toward foreigners, its courtesy toward students and men of learning and the financial assistance which it provided for the latter. . . ."

Musa was not the first African king to visit Makkah, but no one there or along his route had ever seen anything as dazzling as his traveling party. With him came 60,000 men, 12,000 of them personal servants he had enslaved. All were lavishly dressed. His vast caravan included 80 camels carrying 300 pounds of gold each.

Along the route, Musa's generous spending brought prosperity to the towns he passed and made his name famous. More importantly, the unmistakable wealth of his empire opened the eyes of North Africans, Arabs, and Europeans to the greatness of the Mali civilization.

—adapted from *Wonders of the African World*

European Society

Europe's interest in Africa came only after a long period of isolation. For centuries the Roman Empire had dominated much of Europe. By A.D. 500, however, the Roman political and economic systems had collapsed, isolating western Europe from the rest of the world.

SECTION RESOURCES

📁 Reproducible Masters
• Reproducible Lesson Plan 1–2
• Daily Lecture and Discussion Notes 1–2
• Guided Reading Activity 1–2
• Section Quiz 1–2
• Reading Essentials and Study Guide 1–2

Transparencies
• Daily Focus Skills Transparency 1–2

Multimedia
🔵 Interactive Tutor Self-Assessment CD-ROM
🔵 ExamView® Pro Testmaker CD-ROM
🔵 Presentation Plus! CD-ROM
🔵 TeacherWorks™ CD-ROM
🔵 Audio Program
🔵 American Music: Cultural Traditions

Trade declined, cities and roads fell into disrepair, law and order vanished, and money was no longer used. During the **Middle Ages,** as the period from about 500 to 1400 is called, most people knew nothing of life beyond the tiny villages where they were born.

Feudalism With the weakening of central government, feudalism developed in western Europe. Under this political system, a king would give estates to nobles in exchange for their military support. The nobles swore loyalty to the king and provided knights, or mounted warriors, for the royal army. In return, the nobles could raise their own armies, dispense justice, and mint their own coins. Most built fortified castles for defense.

Peasants who could not secure their own land or protection worked for the feudal lords and lived on their estates, or manors. These ranged in size from several hundred to several hundred thousand acres and were largely self-sufficient, with livestock pastures, fields for crops, and a peasant village. While feudalism describes the political relationships between nobles, manorialism describes the economic ties between nobles and peasants.

In return for protection, peasants farmed the lord's land and made payments of various goods. They worked long and hard and rarely left the manor. Most were serfs, people who were bound to the manor and the lord's will. They were not considered enslaved, however, since they could not be sold. Serfs typically lived in tiny, one-room houses with dirt floors, a hole in the roof for a chimney, and one or two pieces of crude furniture. They ate bread, porridge, and a few types of vegetables, and they slept huddled together for warmth.

Expanding Horizons The economy of western Europe, devastated since the fall of Rome, began to improve around A.D. 1000. The invention of the horse collar and better plows enabled farmers to grow more. The ability of many villages to produce a surplus of food helped revive trade in Europe. At the same time, some rulers succeeded in building strong central governments, thereby discouraging warfare and bandit raids. Roads soon filled with traders, and the number of western European towns grew tremendously between 1000 and 1200.

The Roman Catholic Church also promoted stability and order. With its laws addressing doctrine, marriage, and morals and its severe penalties for disobedience to Church teachings, it became a force uniting western Europeans.

Meanwhile, the religion known as **Islam** swept across the Middle East and Africa during the 600s and 700s. The followers of Islam, known as **Muslims,** steadily won converts both by making armed conquests and by instilling a sense of brotherhood.

As Muslim power grew, European Christians became fearful of losing access to the Holy Land, the birthplace of Christianity, in what is now Israel. In 1095 Pope **Urban II,** the head of the Roman Catholic Church, urged Christians to take up arms to regain their sacred sites. He spoke before a huge crowd, saying that Jerusalem "is now held captive by . . . enemies. . . . It looks and hopes for freedom; it begs unceasingly that you will come to its aid."

The pope's speech launched at least nine expeditions, called **Crusades,** over the next two centuries. The Crusades changed western European society in several ways. First, they helped break down feudalism and increased the authority of kings. As kings levied

History *Through Art*

The Middle Ages The Bayeaux tapestry (right) and this prayer book (below) show art styles in Europe in the Middle Ages. What aspect of life in the Middle Ages does the tapestry depict?

2 TEACH

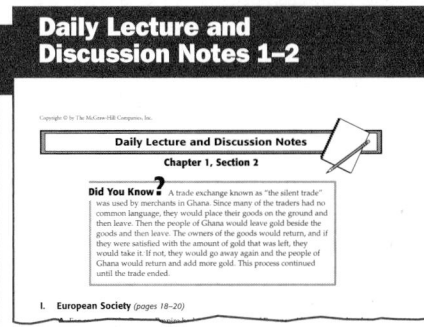

Writing a Job Description Have students write a job description for a serf. Use employment ads from newspapers and the Internet for examples of job descriptions. **L1**

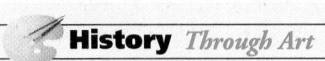

History *Through Art*

Answer: a medieval feast
Ask: What barriers do you think manorialism created? *(Possible answers—It created a barrier between classes in society and it created barriers to trade.)*

History *and the* Humanities

🎵 American Music: Cultural Traditions: "Yarum Praise Songs"

COOPERATIVE LEARNING ACTIVITY

Building a Model Have students work in small groups to build a model of a typical lord's manor and peasant village from the 1100s. Encourage students to supplement the information provided in the text with library and Internet research. Arrange for students' models to be displayed for classmates. 💻

Use the rubric for a cooperative group management plan on pages 71–72 in the *Performance Assessment Activities and Rubrics.*

L1/ELL

Guided Reading Activity 1–2

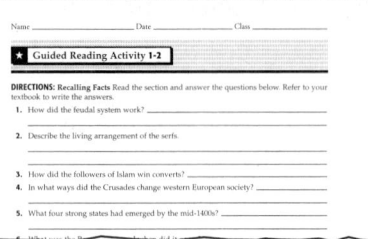

Name _____ Date _____ Class _____

★ Guided Reading Activity 1-2

DIRECTIONS: Recalling Facts Read the section and answer the questions below. Refer to your textbook to write the answers.

1. How did the feudal system work? _____

2. Describe the living arrangement of the serfs. _____

3. How did the followers of Islam win converts? _____

4. In what ways did the Crusades change western European society? _____

5. What four strong states had emerged by the mid-1400s? _____

Graphic Organizer → Skills

Answer: Advances in technology allowed long-distance travel

Graphic Organizer Skills Practice
Ask: What parts of the world were affected by European exploration? *(Europe, Asia, Africa, the Americas)*

✓ Reading Check

Answer: They helped break down feudalism, increased the power of kings, brought Europeans into contact with other civilizations, increased the desire for trade, created a need for an economy based on money and gold.

Creating a Graphic Organizer

Have students create a cause-and-effect graphic organizer for the following cause: Monarchs began centralizing power. Encourage students to identify several effects. **L2**

📁 Use the rubric for creating a map, display, or chart on pages 65–66 in the *Performance Assessment Activities and Rubrics.*

Causes and Effects of European Exploration

Causes

- The Crusades broadened European horizons and stimulated interest in luxury goods.
- Monarchs of new states wanted to acquire gold to strengthen their rule.
- The Renaissance promoted a scientific and practical view of the world.
- New technology like the compass and astrolabe made exploration possible.

Effects

- An exchange of goods and ideas between Europe and the Americas began.
- European diseases devastated Native American populations; American diseases spread to Europe.
- Europeans became increasingly involved in the West African slave trade.

Graphic Organizer → Skills

European explorations brought profound cultural changes to many parts of the world.

Evaluating How did technology play a role in exploration?

---

taxes and raised armies, nobles joining the Crusades sold their lands and freed their serfs. Second, the Crusades brought Europeans into contact with the Muslim and Byzantine civilizations of the Middle East. Europeans began demanding spices, sugar, silk, and other goods from the East. Chinese and Indian traders sold these items to Arab merchants, who then moved them overland to the Mediterranean coast. Arab merchants then sold the goods to Italian merchants for huge profits.

The expanding trade with the Middle East and Asia changed Europe's economic system as well. As trade increased, merchants found bartering impractical, and many Arab traders insisted on monetary payments. This led to the rise of an economy based on money and to greater demand for gold to make coins.

The development of the Mongol Empire in the 1200s also facilitated the flow of goods from the East. Mongol horsemen emerged from central Asia in the early 1200s

---

and built one of the largest empires in world history. The Mongol conquest integrated much of Asia's economy by breaking down trade barriers, opening borders, and securing the roads against bandits.

By the 1300s, Europe was importing vast quantities of luxury goods from Asia. However, when the Mongol Empire collapsed in the 1300s, Asia again split into dozens of independent kingdoms. The flow of Asian goods declined, and the price of spices soared. Many Europeans began to look for a route to Asia that would bypass the Muslim traders. Perhaps, they thought, they could reach China by sea.

✓ Reading Check **Summarizing** How did the Crusades change Europe?

New States, New Technology

By the 1300s, western Europeans had the motive but not the means to seek a direct water route to Asia. Feudalism and frequent warfare had kept rulers and merchants from amassing the wealth necessary to finance exploration and overseas trade. Europeans also lacked the technology to attempt a long-distance voyage by sea.

GOVERNMENT

The Emergence of Strong States Things began changing in the 1300s. The feudal system was in decline, weakened by the Crusades and trade with Asia. The rise of towns and merchants had provided kings and queens with a new source of wealth they could tax. They used their armies to open up and protect trade routes and to enforce trade laws and a common currency within their kingdoms.

Revenue from trade and loans from merchants, who also stood to benefit from increased commerce, made western European rulers less dependent on the nobility for support. Monarchs began centralizing power, and by the mid-1400s, four strong states—Portugal, Spain, England, and France—had emerged. All four started financing exploration in the hope of expanding their trade and national power.

Scientific Advances At about the same time that European kingdoms were unifying, an intellectual revolution known as the Renaissance began. Lasting from about 1350 to 1600, the Renaissance marked an artistic flowering and a rebirth of interest in the cultures of ancient Greece and Rome. European scholars rediscovered the works of Greek and Roman philosophers, geographers, and mathematicians. In their quest for learning, they also read the teachings of Arab scholars.

DIFFERENTIATED INSTRUCTION

Reading Support Have students find maps showing common overland and sea trade routes from Europe to China. Using the map scales, have them calculate the approximate distance of common routes. Ask students to prepare a chart comparing these distances. As an extension, you could ask students to research the approximate time required to make a complete trip using each route. Add that information to the charts. **L2**

📁 Refer to *Inclusion for the High School Social Studies Classroom Strategies and Activities* in the TCR.

By the 1400s, western Europeans had acquired knowledge of a key navigational instrument, the astrolabe, from Arab texts. An astrolabe uses the position of the sun to determine direction, latitude, and local time. Europeans also acquired the compass, a Chinese invention that reliably shows the direction of magnetic north.

Navigational tools were vital to exploring the world, but the most important requirements were ships capable of long-distance travel. Late in the 1400s, Europeans began building ships with redesigned sails, multiple masts, and repositioned rudders. These improvements made ships much faster.

Prince Henry the Navigator

Portuguese explorers, outfitted with ships called caravels that incorporated the latest technology, were the first Europeans to search for a sea route to Asia. In 1419 Prince Henry of Portugal, known as Henry the Navigator, set up a coastal center for astronomical and geographical studies. Mapmakers, astronomers, and shipbuilders from throughout the Mediterranean went there to study and plan voyages of exploration.

In 1420 Portuguese captains began mapping Africa's west coast. They discovered the Azores, the Madeira Islands, and Cape Verde. In 1488 a Portuguese ship commanded by **Bartolomeu Dias** reached the southern tip of Africa, later named the Cape of Good Hope. A little over nine years later, four ships commanded by **Vasco da Gama** sailed from Portugal, rounded Africa, and then landed on the southwest coast of India. A water route to eastern Asia had been found.

During the decades that Portuguese ships were exploring the African coast, they began trading with West African merchants. European goods were exchanged for gold, ivory, pepper, and palm oil. The Portuguese also began purchasing enslaved Africans to work on Portuguese sugar plantations.

✓ **Reading Check Examining** What political and technological developments made it possible for Europeans to begin exploring the world?

West African Civilization

Long before the arrival of the Portuguese, trade had been a central feature of West African civilization. The three great empires that arose in this region between the 400s and 1400s—Ghana, Mali, and Songhai—gained much of their prosperity by trading in two precious commodities: gold and salt.

The Lay of the Land West Africa is an immense bulge of territory bordered on the north by the Mediterranean Sea and on the west and south by the Atlantic Ocean. Its northern and southern perimeters are well watered and fertile, but between them lies a vast desert, the **Sahara.**

The Niger River, which cuts through West Africa, long served as its major pathway for east-west trade. Important trade routes across the Sahara did not develop until camels arrived from Arabia between the A.D. 200s and 400s. Camels could carry more weight and walk for longer periods than oxen or horses. Most important, camels could go without water for over a week and could withstand the desert's scorching days and cold nights.

Merchants began using camels to transport gold, ivory, ostrich feathers, and furs from regions south of the Sahara to North Africa. As demand for these goods increased, large trading settlements developed around the northern and southern boundaries of the Sahara.

Ideas as well as goods traveled along the African trade routes. The Muslim nomads who controlled the caravans in the Sahara carried Islam into the heart of West Africa. There, many people in the cities and market towns embraced the religion.

The Lure of Gold West Africa prospered primarily because of the gold trade. The Muslim conquest of North Africa led to a much greater demand for gold

World History Connection

The Compass

While the Europeans made numerous advances in navigation, it was the Chinese who invented one of the more important seafaring tools: the compass. Evidence of this includes a Chinese document from 1086 that talks of sea captains relying on a "south-pointing needle" to help them find their way in foggy weather. The date on the document is more than 100 years earlier than the first recorded use of the compass in Europe. *What other inventions aided European exploration?*

Early compasses

Salt Salt has been used throughout the ages to season and preserve food. It has also been used in religious ceremonies and as a medium of exchange. The word *salary* is derived from the Latin word *salarium* referring to the ration of salt issued to soldiers.

Determining Word Origins To illustrate the impact of the Arab world on Europe, give the following list of words derived from Arabic to students: apricot, cotton, damask, lemon, muslin, and orange. Have students look up these words in an etymological dictionary. Then ask students to suggest how these words came into the English language. *(They were names of unfamiliar products brought to Europe by traders.)* L2

✓ **Reading Check**

Answer: political–rise of strong, wealthy states; technological–astrolabe, compass, caravels

World History Connection

The Chinese also invented movable type used in printing in the 1000s. The first characters used in movable type were made from fired clay. By the 1300s, both metal and wood were used to make movable type.

INTERDISCIPLINARY CONNECTIONS ACTIVITY

Government List on the board various empires that have ruled vast territories for some period of time such as the Ghana, Mali, Songhai, Greek, Roman, Chinese, Japanese, Spanish, and British. Tell students that none of these empires has been able to remain in power indefinitely. Have students research to find out what factors contributed to the decline of each of these empires. L2

Geography Skills

Background: The Almoravid Empire of the Berber Muslims existed during the 1000s and 1100s. They founded the city of Marrakech in 1062 to serve as their capital. The city remains one of the major cities in Morocco.

Answers:
1. Songhai
2. access to water and fertile soil, and proximity to trade routes or resources such as gold or salt

3 ASSESS

Assign Section 2 Assessment as homework or as an in-class activity.

🖑 Have students use the **Interactive Tutor Self-Assessment CD-ROM.**

L1/ELL

Reading Essentials and Study Guide 1–2

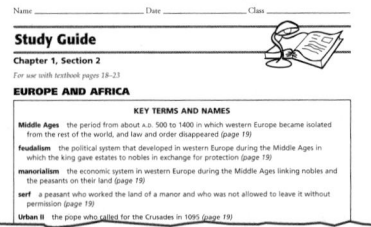

L2

Section Quiz 1–2

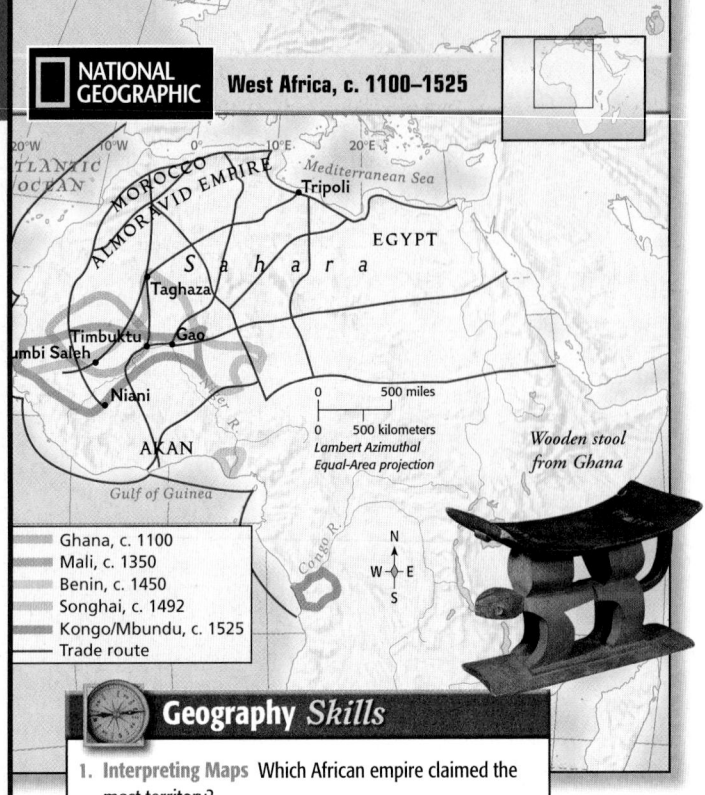

NATIONAL GEOGRAPHIC **West Africa, c. 1100–1525**

	Ghana, c. 1100
	Mali, c. 1350
	Benin, c. 1450
	Songhai, c. 1492
	Kongo/Mbundu, c. 1525
	Trade route

Wooden stool from Ghana

Geography Skills

1. **Interpreting Maps** Which African empire claimed the most territory?
2. **Applying Geography Skills** What natural feature determined the location of these empires?

---

in the 800s and 900s because the new Muslim states of the region used gold coins. Later, in the 1200s, European rulers shifted from using silver and copper coins to using gold coins, and they too sought gold from Africa.

The African people who lived on the southern edge of the Sahara were perfectly positioned to benefit from the growing trade in gold. With access to both gold from the south and salt and other goods from the north, they were able to amass wealth and power and build large empires.

Ghana The earliest African empire to emerge was Ghana in the A.D. 400s. The **Soninke** people settled between the gold mines of Bambuk (just east of present-day Senegal) and the salt mines of Taghaza in the Sahara, where they controlled the region's trade. After the Muslims conquered North Africa and the Sahara, Ghana's merchants grew rich by trafficking in gold and salt. Ghana's ruler taxed the trade and gained great wealth as well. Most people, however, were farmers and herders.

Ghana became a Muslim kingdom in the 1100s, but frequent wars with the Muslims of the Sahara took their toll. Equally damaging was a change in the environment that left Ghana's land exhausted and its farmers unable to feed its people. At the same time, new gold mines opened in Bure to the east. Trade routes to these mines bypassed Ghana, depriving its rulers of the wealth they needed to maintain their empire. By the early 1200s, the empire of Ghana had collapsed.

Mali East of Ghana, the **Malinke** people controlled the upper Niger valley and thus the gold trade from Bure. With their newfound wealth and power, the Malinke conquered Ghana and built the empire of Mali. By the mid-1300s, Mali stretched east past the city of Timbuktu and west to the Atlantic Ocean.

The emperor of Mali, called the *mansa,* was based in the capital. In outlying towns, traditional rulers managed local affairs, collected tribute from the farmers, and sent a portion to the capital. To enforce this system, the *mansa* relied on a large army. Although Mali's rulers and traders adopted Islam, many people—especially the farmers—clung to their traditional belief in "spirits of the land."

The empire of Mali reached its peak in the 1300s under the leadership of Mansa Musa and his brother Mansa Sulayman. By that time, the opening of new gold mines had shifted the trade routes farther east and helped make Timbuktu a great center of trade and Muslim scholarship.

Songhai The **Sorko** people who lived along the middle Niger, east of Mali, built the Songhai empire. The Sorko fished for a living and controlled trade along the river. This gave them wealth and power, and by the 800s they had created the kingdom of Songhai.

When Mali began to decline, the ruler of Songhai, Sonni Ali, seized Timbuktu in 1468. He then pushed north to the Taghazi salt mines and expanded southward about 200 miles down the Niger. According to legend, Sonni Ali's army never lost a battle.

Songhai's next great leader, Askiya Muhammad, was a devout Muslim. He revived Timbuktu as a great

---

Reading Strategy READING THE TEXT

Synthesizing Information Using a blank outline map of Africa that includes the present-day country borders, have students create a thematic map showing the land areas controlled by the Ghana, Mali, Songhai, Ife, Benin and Kongo kingdoms. Tell students to assign a different color to each kingdom and use the color to shade the area of land controlled by each. Have students create a legend for the kingdoms that includes their approximate dates of existence. Tell students that some areas will overlap. **L1 ELL**

📂 Refer to *Inclusion for the High School Social Studies Classroom Strategies and Activities* in the TCR.

center of learning, encouraged more trade across the Sahara, and centralized power in the capital, Gao. Songhai remained a powerful and wealthy empire until 1591, when Moroccan troops shattered its army.

Benin The sprawling empires of Ghana, Mali, and Songhai arose on West Africa's expansive savannah, a kind of rolling grassland. In the dense, almost impenetrable forests of West Africa's southern coast, an area called Guinea, smaller kingdoms such as Benin developed.

The Edo people of Benin were a mix of hunters, farmers, and traders living in small village communities. They developed Benin as a city-state in the 1000s or 1100s. By the mid-1400s, Benin had become an empire stretching from the Niger delta west to about where the city of Lagos, Nigeria, is located today. When the Portuguese reached Benin, the Edo sold them ivory, pepper, gum, and cotton. They also traded Africans they had captured and enslaved as they expanded their territory.

✓ **Reading Check** **Examining** Why were the West African kingdoms in Guinea smaller than those in the savannah area?

Slavery and Sugar

Slavery had existed in Africa and other parts of the world for centuries. At first, most African slaves were war captives who were eventually ransomed back to their people or absorbed into their captors' culture. West African slavery began to change with the arrival of Arab traders, who exchanged horses, cotton, and other goods for slaves. The gold trade also increased the demand for slaves. In the early 1400s, the Akan people began mining gold and trading it to the Mali empire. To boost their production, the Akan people acquired enslaved Africans from Mali traders for use in clearing the land and mining the gold.

Sugar growers from Spain and Portugal sought African slaves as well. Until about 1100, the people of western Europe had generally used honey and fruit juices to sweeten their foods. During the Crusades, they learned about sugarcane from the Muslims, and the demand for sugar rose steadily.

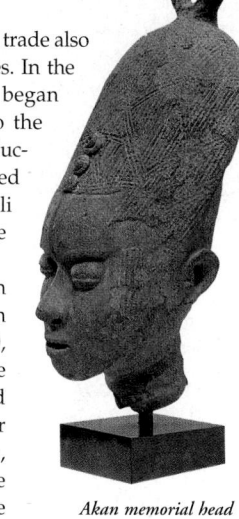
Akan memorial head

In the 1400s, Spain and Portugal established sugarcane plantations on the Canary and Madeira Islands off the west coast of Africa. There, unlike most of Europe, the climate and soil were favorable for growing sugarcane. Chopping the tough cane and producing sugar required heavy manual labor, though, and plantation owners brought in enslaved Africans for that purpose.

Because Europeans had a limited amount of land available for sugarcane, their participation in the slave trade remained modest during the 1400s. This would change dramatically after Christopher Columbus landed in America.

✓ **Reading Check** **Analyzing** Why did Europeans want slaves?

HISTORY Online **Study Central™** To review this section, go to **tarvol2.glencoe.com** and click on **Study Central™**.

SECTION 2 ASSESSMENT

Checking for Understanding

1. **Define:** feudalism, manorialism, serf, Renaissance, astrolabe, caravel, savannah.
2. **Identify:** Middle Ages, Muslim, Urban II, Crusades, Sahara.
3. **Explain** why Songhai became a great empire.

Reviewing Themes

4. **Global Connections** How did slavery change as trade between Africa and Europe flourished in the 1400s?

Critical Thinking

5. **Comparing** How were West African societies different from European societies?
6. **Contrasting** How were the West African empires of Ghana, Mali, and Songhai similar to one another?
7. **Categorizing** Use a graphic organizer similar to the one below to list the effects of the Crusades.

Analyzing Visuals

8. **Examining Artifacts** Study the West African artifacts on pages 22 and 23. The craftsmanship of these items indicates a society able to devote time to artistic pursuits instead of simple survival. What two commodities were essential to the prosperity of West Africa?

Writing About History

9. **Descriptive Writing** Imagine you are a Portuguese explorer in West Africa. Write a journal entry describing a West African civilization.

CHAPTER 1 Converging Cultures **23**

SECTION 2 ASSESSMENT ANSWERS

1. Terms are in blue.
2. Middle Ages (p. 19), Muslim (p. 19), Urban II (p. 19), Crusades (p. 19), Sahara (p. 21)
3. The Songhai controlled trade along the Niger River.
4. Enslaved Africans were taken from Africa and could not escape slavery.

5. different religions; Western Africans enslaved their own people
6. All three traded in salt and gold.
7. weakened feudalism, strengthened kings, increased European contact with Middle East, created an economy based on trading and money
8. salt and gold

9. Students' journal entries will vary. Journal entries should include details about daily activities, food, and clothing.

Creating a Model Have interested students create a model showing the process of growing and harvesting sugarcane. Encourage students to clearly label the model so that a person observing the model can appreciate how difficult the labor is. **L2**

✓ **Reading Check**

Answer: The thick vegetation made large empires difficult to achieve.

Reteach
Have students explain the importance of trade on the development of African cultures.

Enrich
Have students use library or Internet resources to research slavery in Africa prior to the 1400s. Have students write a research report of their findings.

✓ **Reading Check**

Answer: to work on sugarcane plantations

HISTORY Online

Study Central™ provides summaries, interactive games, and online graphic organizers to help students review section content.

4 CLOSE

Remind students that trading between West African and European cultures changed both cultures and had a dramatic influence on American history. Have students create a list of what each culture gained from the other culture.

23

1 FOCUS

Section Overview

This section explains how Columbus encountered islands in North America.

Reading Preview

Answers to Graphic: Vikings, no permanent settlements or ongoing relationship; Columbus, began exploration of the Americas; Vespucci, continued exploration of the Americas which are named for him; Balboa, first European to reach the Pacific coast of America; Magellan, named the Pacific Ocean and led the crew that was first to circumnavigate the globe

Preteaching Vocabulary
Have students classify the Key Terms and Names as persons, places, or things.

Guide to Reading

Main Idea
Columbus sought a sea route to Asia. Instead, he encountered several outlying islands of North America.

Key Terms and Names
Leif Ericsson, Claudius Ptolemy, San Salvador Island, line of demarcation, Treaty of Tordesillas, Ferdinand Magellan, circumnavigate, Columbian Exchange

Reading Strategy
Organizing As you read about Europe's exploration of the Americas, complete a chart like the one below by filling in the outcome of each exploration listed.

Exploration	Outcome
Vikings	
Columbus	
Vespucci	
Balboa	
Magellan	

Reading Objectives
- **Describe** Columbus's journeys and their impact on Native Americans and Europeans.
- **Evaluate** the workings and impact of the Columbian Exchange.

Section Theme
Global Connections The Treaty of Tordesillas helped determine that Spain would be the first strong European power in the Americas.

Preview of Events

♦1490   ♦1510   ♦1530

1492
Christopher Columbus lands in America

1494
Treaty of Tordesillas

1513
Vasco de Balboa sees the Pacific Ocean

1522
Ferdinand Magellan's expedition completes first trip around the world

---

A replica of a Spanish caravel at sea

★ An American Story ★

In 1492 Christopher Columbus led 87 sailors on a voyage into the unknown. On September 9 Columbus noted in his log: "This day we completely lost sight of land, and many men sighed and wept for fear they would not see it again for a long time." As the voyage dragged on, the sailors grew nervous and began plotting mutiny. Columbus wrote:

❝All day long and all night long those who are awake and able to get together never cease to talk to each other in circles, complaining that they will never be able to return home. . . . I am told . . . that if I persist in going onward, the best course of action will be to throw me into the sea some night.❞

Then, on the morning of October 12, the *Pinta's* lookout, Rodrigo de Triana, let out a joyous cry—"Tierra! Tierra!" ("Land! Land!"). At dawn a relieved and triumphant Columbus went ashore. He believed he had arrived in the Indies—islands located southeast of China.

—adapted from *The Log of Christopher Columbus*

The Vikings Arrive in America

Although his historic journey set the stage for permanent European settlement in the Americas, Christopher Columbus was not the first European to arrive there. Strong archaeological evidence credits that accomplishment to the Norse, or **Vikings,** a people who came from Scandinavia.

SECTION RESOURCES

📖 Reproducible Masters
- Reproducible Lesson Plan 1–3
- Daily Lecture and Discussion Notes 1–3
- Guided Reading Activity 1–3
- Section Quiz 1–3
- Reading Essentials and Study Guide 1–3
- Performance Assessment Activities and Rubrics
- Interpreting Political Cartoons

📽 Transparencies
- Daily Focus Skills Transparency 1–3

Multimedia
- 💿 Interactive Tutor Self-Assessment CD-ROM
- 💿 ExamView® Pro Testmaker CD-ROM
- 💿 Presentation Plus! CD-ROM
- 💿 TeacherWorks™ CD-ROM
- 🎧 Audio Program

Beginning in the late 700s, Viking ships, called longboats, began to venture from their homeland. Around A.D. 1000, **Leif Ericsson** and 35 Vikings explored the coast of Labrador and may have stayed the winter in what is now Newfoundland. Although the Vikings later tried to found colonies in the region, their attempts failed, largely because they were outnumbered by hostile Native Americans.

✓ **Reading Check** **Examining** How do we know that Columbus was not the first European in the Americas?

Columbus's Plan

During the Renaissance, the scientific works of scholars like **Claudius Ptolemy** were rediscovered. In the A.D. 100s, he had drawn maps of a round world projected onto a flat surface, complete with lines of longitude and latitude. Nonetheless, Ptolemy had seriously underestimated the distance that each degree of longitude represented, making the earth seem much smaller than it actually was.

Basing his calculations on Ptolemy's, an Italian navigator named Christopher Columbus reckoned Japan to be only 2,760 miles (4,441 km) west of Spain. In reality it was five times farther. Columbus was also unaware that a large landmass lay in the Atlantic between Europe and Asia.

Columbus needed financial backing to make a voyage across the Atlantic to Asia. For six years Columbus tried to persuade the rulers of Portugal, England, France, and Spain to fund his expedition. He promised Spain's King Ferdinand and Queen Isabella that his scheme would bring them wealth, empire, and converts to Catholicism. Finally, in 1492, after it became clear that Portugal was about to reach Asia by going east around Africa, the Spanish rulers agreed to finance his venture.

✓ **Reading Check** **Explaining** Why did the rulers of Spain agree to support Columbus's voyage to Asia?

Columbus's Explorations

In all, Columbus made four expeditions to the Americas. His first ended in glory and the promise of future riches. Each succeeding journey, however, brought him no closer to fulfilling that promise or finding the expected sea route to Asia.

TURNING POINT

The First Voyage Columbus and his three ships finally left Spain in August 1492, embarking on the harrowing westward voyage across the Atlantic and reaching what is today the Bahamas in October. He probably landed on present-day **San Salvador Island.** Columbus called the people he encountered *Indians,* thinking he had reached the fabled Indies.

Columbus headed deeper into the Caribbean searching for gold. He found the island of Cuba and then the island of Hispaniola, which the countries of Haiti and the Dominican Republic now share. Columbus mistakenly concluded that Cuba was the coast of China and that Hispaniola was Japan.

The islanders Columbus met must have been curious about the white-skinned, bearded Spanish. Columbus described their meeting this way:

> ❝The people kept coming down to the beach, calling to us and giving thanks to God. Some brought us water, some food; others, seeing that I did not wish to go ashore, swam out to us. . . . [They] kept shouting, 'Come and see the men who have come from Heaven; bring them food and drink.'❞

—quoted in *The Voyage of Christopher Columbus*

🖌 **History** *Through Art*

Archaeological Evidence This carving of a European figure (left), and Viking calendar (above) prove that the Vikings arrived in North America before Columbus. Why were Vikings unable to colonize successfully?

CHAPTER 1 Converging Cultures **25**

2 TEACH

Daily Lecture and Discussion Notes 1–3

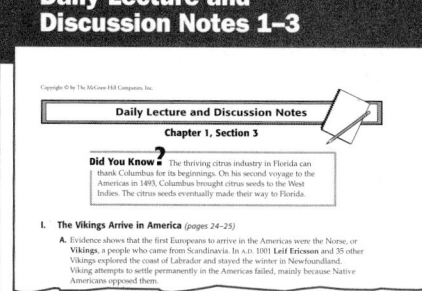

Copyright © by The McGraw-Hill Companies, Inc.

Daily Lecture and Discussion Notes
Chapter 1, Section 3

Did You Know? The thriving citrus industry in Florida can thank Columbus for its beginnings. On his second voyage to the Americas in 1493, Columbus brought citrus seeds to the West Indies. The citrus seeds eventually made their way to Florida.

I. The Vikings Arrive in America *(pages 24–25)*

  A. Evidence shows that the first Europeans to arrive in the Americas were the Norse, or **Vikings**, a people who came from Scandinavia. In A.D. 1001 **Leif Ericsson** and 35 other Vikings explored the coast of Labrador and stayed the winter in Newfoundland. Viking attempts to settle permanently in the Americas failed, mainly because Native Americans opposed them.

✓ **Reading Check**

Answer: archeological evidence of the Vikings in America

Creating a Display Have students create a display of the food component of the Columbian Exchange. Have students use actual food samples or pictures of the food that represent both sides of the exchange. **L1** ELL

📁 Use the rubric for creating a map, display, or chart on pages 65–66 in the *Performance Assessment Activities and Rubrics.*

✓ **Reading Check**

Answer: They were concerned that Portugal could monopolize trade with Asia.

🖌 **History** *Through Art*

Answer: They were outnumbered by hostile Native Americans.
Ask: About how long before Columbus's voyage did Leif Ericsson make his voyage? *(about 500 years)*

📜 **Reading Strategy** **READING THE TEXT**

Varying Reading Rate Students will learn that some text is more difficult to read than others, and they must make adjustments to their reading rate. Remind students to slow down when they encounter difficult concepts, connections to previous ideas, new vocabulary, or text that contains a great deal of information. **L1**

📁 Refer to *Inclusion for the High School Social Studies Classroom Strategies and Activities* in the TCR.

Guided Reading Activity 1–3

Name _____ Date _____ Class _____

★ Guided Reading Activity 1-3

DIRECTIONS: Identifying Supporting Details Read each main idea. Use your textbook to supply the details that support each main idea.

☐ **Main Idea:** Archaeological evidence shows that the Norse, or Vikings, were the first Europeans to arrive in the Americas.

1. **Detail:** In A.D. 1001, _____ and 35 Vikings explored the coast of Labrador.

2. **Detail:** The Vikings' attempts to found colonies in the Newfoundland region failed because they were outnumbered by hostile _____.

☐ **Main Idea:** During the Renaissance, the Europeans rediscovered the scientific works of scholars like Claudius Ptolemy.

3. **Detail:** Ptolemy's calculations and maps were inaccurate because they made the earth seem much _____ than it was.

📁 Use *Interpreting Political Cartoons,* Cartoon 2.

Why It Matters

Food production increased on both sides of the ocean as a direct result of the exchange of cultivated plants and livestock. Increased food production led to population growth in Europe and among European colonists in America.

One of the reasons food production increased in Europe, and later in Asia, was the introduction of crops from America that flourished where traditional European crops could not. For example, the climate, topography, and soil conditions in Ireland were not conducive to growing wheat or rice, but white potatoes from America thrived.

The introduction of livestock and poultry from Europe, Africa, and Asia provided new sources of nourishment for Native Americans and colonists living in America.

Reading Check

Answer: to establish who had the right to control new lands and trade routes

Why It Matters

The Columbian Exchange

European contact with the Americas marked the start of an extensive exchange of plants and animals between the two areas of the world. Dramatic changes resulted from the exchange of plant life, leading to a revolution in the diets of peoples in both hemispheres.

Maize (corn), potatoes, many kinds of beans, tomatoes, and pumpkins were among the products the Eastern Hemisphere received from the Americas. Meanwhile, the Eastern Hemisphere introduced rice, wheat, barley, oats, melons, coffee, bananas, and many other plants to the Western Hemisphere.

▲ **Animals**
The Spanish reintroduced horses to the Americas. Horses native to the Americas had died out during the Ice Age. Their reintroduction transformed Native American societies.

◄ **Plants**
By about 1600, American maize and sweet potatoes were staple crops in China. They contributed to a worldwide population explosion beginning in this period.

On Christmas Eve, Columbus's flagship, the *Santa María,* struck a reef off Hispaniola and broke apart. Columbus built a small fort called **La Navidad** on the island and left about 40 crew members to search for gold while he headed home with his remaining ships.

In March 1493 Columbus made a triumphant return to Spain, bringing back gold, parrots, spices, and Native Americans. The king and queen awarded him the titles "Admiral of the Ocean Sea" and "Viceroy and Governor of the Indies." Ferdinand and Isabella listened closely as Columbus promised spices, cotton, and "as much gold as they want if their Highnesses will render me a little help."

The Treaty of Tordesillas Although pleased with Columbus's findings, Ferdinand and Isabella were concerned about claiming the new lands. Portugal, after all, had claimed the right to control the Atlantic route to Asia. To resolve the issue, the two Catholic nations appealed to the pope. In 1493 Pope **Alexander VI** established a line of demarcation, an imaginary north-to-south line running down the middle of the Atlantic. Spain was to control everything west of the line, while Portugal would control everything to the east.

In 1494, with the **Treaty of Tordesillas,** a line was approved by both nations. The treaty confirmed

Portugal's right to control the route around Africa to India. It also confirmed Spain's claim to most of the newly discovered lands of America.

Columbus's Later Voyages Columbus made three more voyages from Spain in 1493, 1498, and 1502. He explored the Caribbean islands of Hispaniola, Cuba, and Jamaica, and he sailed along the coasts of Central America and northern South America. Columbus claimed the new lands for Spain and established settlements, but he did not satisfy his dreams.

Reading Check **Analyzing** Why did Spain and Portugal sign the Treaty of Tordesillas?

Continuing Expeditions

Later explorations made it clear that Columbus had not reached Asia but a part of the globe unknown to Europeans, Asians, and Africans. In the following years, the Spanish explored most of the Caribbean region, paving the way for the Spanish Empire in the Americas.

Naming America In 1499 an Italian named **Amerigo Vespucci,** sailing under the Spanish flag, repeated Columbus's attempt to sail west to Asia.

DIFFERENTIATED INSTRUCTION

At-Risk Students To help visual learners remember the various navigators and trips discussed in the section, have them trace and label the voyages of Christopher Columbus, Amerigo Vespucci, Juan Ponce de Leon, Vasco de Balboa, and Ferdinand Magellan on a map of the world. **L1**

📁 Refer to *Inclusion for the High School Social Studies Classroom Strategies and Activities* in the TCR.

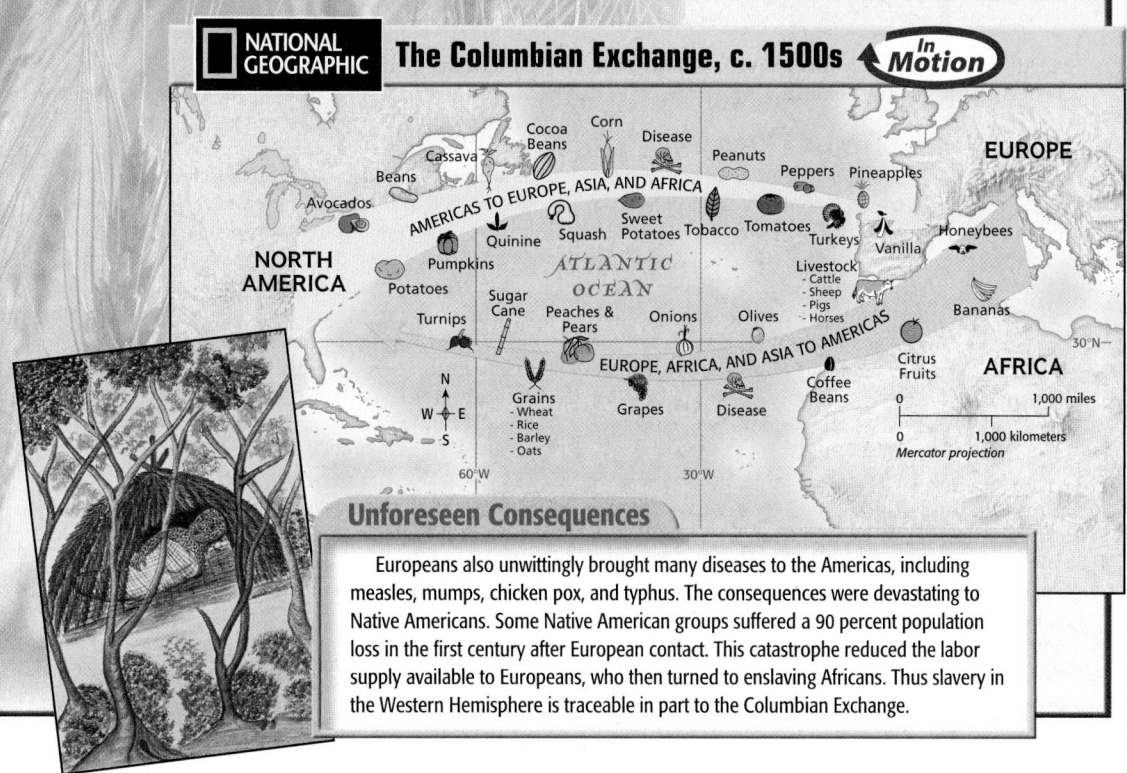

NATIONAL GEOGRAPHIC — The Columbian Exchange, c. 1500s — In Motion

Cocoa Beans, Corn, Disease, Peanuts, Peppers, Pineapples — EUROPE

Beans, Cassava, Avocados — AMERICAS TO EUROPE, ASIA, AND AFRICA

Quinine, Squash, Sweet Potatoes, Tobacco, Tomatoes, Turkeys, Vanilla, Honeybees

NORTH AMERICA — Pumpkins, ATLANTIC OCEAN

Potatoes, Sugar Cane, Peaches & Pears, Onions, Olives — Livestock: Cattle, Sheep, Pigs, Horses — Bananas

Turnips — EUROPE, AFRICA, AND ASIA TO AMERICAS — 30°N

Grains: Wheat, Rice, Barley, Oats — Grapes — Disease — Coffee Beans — Citrus Fruits — AFRICA

0 — 1,000 miles
0 — 1,000 kilometers
Mercator projection

60°W — 30°W

Unforeseen Consequences

Europeans also unwittingly brought many diseases to the Americas, including measles, mumps, chicken pox, and typhus. The consequences were devastating to Native Americans. Some Native American groups suffered a 90 percent population loss in the first century after European contact. This catastrophe reduced the labor supply available to Europeans, who then turned to enslaving Africans. Thus slavery in the Western Hemisphere is traceable in part to the Columbian Exchange.

Exploring the coast of South America, Vespucci, like Columbus, assumed he had reached outermost Asia.

Vespucci made his next voyage in 1501, this time representing Portugal. After sailing far south along the coast of South America, he realized that this large landmass could not be part of Asia. Vespucci's descriptions of America were published and widely read in Europe. In 1507 a German scholar, Martin Waldseemüller, proposed that the new continent be named America for "Amerigo the discoverer."

GEOGRAPHY

Spanish Explorations In 1513 the Spanish governor of Puerto Rico, **Juan Ponce de Leon,** sailed north. Legend has it that he was searching for a wondrous fountain that could magically restore youth. Whether or not this was his motive, Ponce de Leon did discover a land full of blooming wildflowers and fragrant plants. He claimed the area for Spain and named it **Florida,** which means "land of flowers."

In 1510 **Vasco de Balboa,** an indebted planter from Hispaniola, stowed away on a ship heading west to the American mainland. He and a group of followers founded a colony on the Isthmus of Panama. There Balboa heard tales from Native Americans of a

"south sea" that led to an empire of gold. Avid for the treasure, he hacked his way across steamy, disease-ridden jungles and swamps until he reached the opposite coast. There, in 1513, Balboa became the first European known to gaze upon the wide ocean that actually does lead to China and India.

In 1520 **Ferdinand Magellan,** a Portuguese mariner working for Spain, discovered the strait later named for him at the southernmost tip of South America. After navigating its stormy narrows, he sailed into the ocean Balboa had seen. Its waters seemed so peaceful—or *pacific,* in Portuguese—that Magellan gave the new ocean that name. Although Magellan died in the Philippine Islands on the way home to Spain, his expedition returned in 1522. Magellan is credited as the first person to circumnavigate, or sail completely around, the globe.

☑ **Reading Check** **Synthesizing** Why was Magellan's expedition significant?

The Columbian Exchange

The arrival of European colonists in the Americas set in motion a series of complex interactions between peoples and ecologies. These interactions,

3 ASSESS

Assign Section 3 Assessment as homework or as an in-class activity.

🔘 Have students use the **Interactive Tutor Self-Assessment CD-ROM.**

L1/ELL

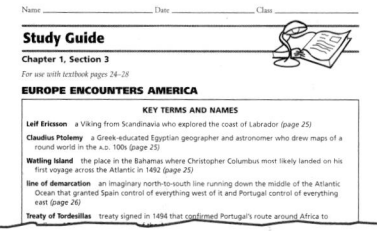

Reading Essentials and Study Guide 1–3

Study Guide
Chapter 1, Section 3
For use with textbook pages 24–28
EUROPE ENCOUNTERS AMERICA
KEY TERMS AND NAMES

L2

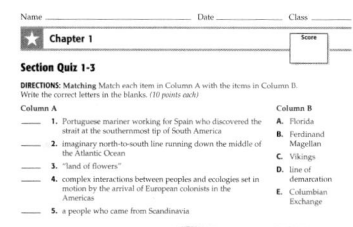

Section Quiz 1–3

Chapter 1
Section Quiz 1-3

☑ **Reading Check**

Answer: It was the first to circumnavigate the earth.

CURRICULUM CONNECTION

Mathematics Greek geographer Eratosthenes, who lived from c. 276 to c. 194 B.C., came close to accurately calculating the circumference of the earth at about 25,000 miles. He determined the size by measuring the angles of the sun at two separate points. One point was a well in Syene (now Aswan). The other point was in Alexandria, Egypt where he lived and worked in the great library. Although Eratosthenes' information was available to Columbus, he chose to ignore it in favor of more modern estimates that underestimated the circumference of the earth by about one half.

Reteach

Have students create a time line of events mentioned in this section starting with A.D. 1001.

Enrich

Have students write a descriptive essay on the long-term impact of the line of demarcation established by Pope Alexander VI and the Treaty of Tordesillas.

Reading Check

Answer: They contracted diseases and were killed by European troops.

HISTORY Online

Study Central™ provides summaries, interactive games, and online graphic organizers to help students review section content.

4 CLOSE

As a class discuss the following question: **Did humanity, as a whole, benefit or suffer from the Columbian Exchange?**

28

---

called the Columbian Exchange, would bring change to almost every culture in the world.

From America to Europe Native Americans introduced the Europeans to new farming methods and crops. Corn, which colonists soon made a staple, traveled back to Spain with Columbus and then spread to the rest of Europe. Other American foods, such as squash, pumpkins, beans, sweet potatoes, tomatoes, chili peppers, peanuts, chocolate, and potatoes, also made their way to Europe, as did tobacco and chewing gum. Europeans also adopted many Native American inventions, including canoes, snowshoes, hammocks, ponchos, and toboggans.

One of the most important discoveries for Europeans was the potato. European farmers learned that land planted with potatoes instead of rye could support about four times as many people. Potatoes had another key advantage. Because grain had to be harvested all at one time and then stored, families risked losing an entire year's supply to pillagers. Potatoes, by contrast, could be left in the ground all winter and dug up only when needed for eating.

From Europe to America The Europeans introduced Native Americans to many new sources of food, including wheat, oats, barley, rye, rice, coffee, onions, bananas, oranges, and other new citrus fruits. Europeans also brought over domestic livestock such as chickens, cattle, pigs, sheep, and horses. In addition, they introduced Native Americans to new technologies, including new metalworking and shipbuilding methods, as well as firearms and other new weapons.

Offsetting these beneficial imports, however, was a deadly and invisible one—the bacteria and viruses that caused influenza, measles, chicken pox, mumps, typhus, and smallpox. Europeans carried some resistance to these diseases, but Native Americans had never experienced them and therefore had no immunity. Exposure led to epidemics in which millions died. The movement of disease was not one way—Europeans may have also brought Native American diseases back to Europe. Those illnesses, however, did not lead to a catastrophic collapse of the European population.

Within 50 years after contact with Europeans, groups living in parts of the Caribbean had become extinct. On Hispaniola, the native population plummeted from about 1 million to about 500. In Mayan Mexico, an estimated 95 percent of the local people died.

No one should discount the negative effects of the exchange Columbus initiated: the tragic epidemics and military conquests that devastated Native Americans and, later, the introduction of slavery. Yet Columbus's explorations led ultimately to the founding of the United States and the building of a nation that honors individualism and protects human rights and freedoms. This too is part of Columbus's legacy.

Reading Check
Describing Why did millions of Native Americans die as a result of contact with Europeans?

HISTORY Online
Study Central™ To review this section, go to tarvol2.glencoe.com and click on **Study Central™**.

SECTION 3 ASSESSMENT

Checking for Understanding

1. **Define:** line of demarcation, circumnavigate, Columbian Exchange.
2. **Identify:** Leif Ericsson, Claudius Ptolemy, San Salvador Island, Treaty of Tordesillas, Ferdinand Magellan.
3. **Explain** why the Vikings did not settle in Canada.

Reviewing Themes

4. **Global Connections** How did the maps drawn by Ptolemy revolutionize European sea exploration?

Critical Thinking

5. **Analyzing** Why did Spain's rulers agree to Columbus's second voyage?
6. **Categorizing** Use a graphic organizer similar to the one below to list the exchanges between the Native Americans and the Europeans in the Columbian Exchange.

Columbian Exchange

Europeans Received	Native Americans Received

Analyzing Visuals

7. **Examining Images** Study the images on page 26 and 27 illustrating the importance of the Columbian Exchange. Do you think the positive effects of the exchange outweigh the negative effects? Explain your answer.

Writing About History

8. **Descriptive Writing** Take the role of a sailor on Columbus's first voyage to the Americas. Write a journal entry about the Caribbean islands you have discovered.

28   CHAPTER 1   Converging Cultures

SECTION 3 ASSESSMENT ANSWERS

1. Terms are in blue.
2. Leif Ericsson *(p. 25)*, Claudius Ptolemy *(p. 25)*, Watling Island *(p. 25)*, Treaty of Tordesillas *(p. 26)*, Ferdinand Magellan *(p. 27)*
3. They encountered a large, hostile Native American population.
4. They indicated that the earth was round and made the earth seem much smaller than it actually is.
5. They hoped to gain gold and spices and extend their empire.
6. Europeans: Native American food and inventions. Native Americans: European food, livestock, technologies, and deadly bacteria and viruses
7. Answers will vary. Students should support their point of view with reasoned arguments.
8. Students' journal entries will vary. Entries should contain detailed descriptions of what the student/explorer observes and feels.

SKILLBUILDER

Reading a Time Line

c. 1000
Vikings arrive

1270s
Drought forces Anasazi
to abandon pueblos

c. 1300
Cahokia collapses

1492
Columbus arrives

The Americas

| 1000–1100s | 1200s | 1300s | 1400s |

The World

1095
Pope Urban II
launches Crusades

1271
Marco Polo journeys
to China

1324
Mansa Musa makes
pilgrimage to Makkah

c. 1475
Ptolemy's *Geography*
is republished

Why Learn This Skill?

When you read a time line, you see not only when an event took place but also what events took place before and after it. A time line can help you develop the skill of **chronological thinking.** Developing a strong sense of chronology—when events took place and in what order they took place—will help you examine relationships among the events. It will also help you understand what events caused or were the result of other events.

Learning the Skill

A time line is a chart that lists events that occurred between specific dates. The number of years between dates is the **time span.** A time line that begins in 1490 and ends in 1500 has a 10-year time span. Some time lines are divided into centuries. The twentieth century includes the 1900s, the nineteenth century includes the 1800s, and so on.

Time lines are usually divided into smaller segments, or **time intervals.** If you look at the two time lines below, you will see that the first time line has a 30-year time span divided into 10-year time intervals, and the second time line has a 6-year time span divided into 2-year time intervals.

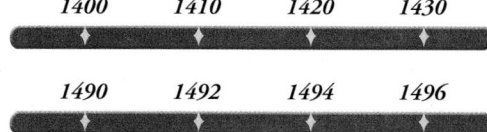

| 1400 | 1410 | 1420 | 1430 |

| 1490 | 1492 | 1494 | 1496 |

Practicing the Skill

Sometimes a time line shows events that occurred during the same time period but in two different parts of the world. The time line above shows some events in the Americas and in the rest of the world during the same time span. Study the time line, and then answer the questions.

❶ What time span and intervals appear on this time line?

❷ What important event took place around A.D. 1300 in North America?

❸ How many years before Ptolemy's *Geography* was published did the Vikings reach North America?

❹ When did Pope Urban II begin the Crusades?

Skills Assessment

Complete the Practicing Skills questions on page 39 and the Chapter 1 Skill Reinforcement Activity to assess your mastery of this skill.

Applying the Skill

Reading a Time Line Extend the time line on this page to include at least five additional events that took place in North America between A.D. 500 and 1000.

 Glencoe's **Skillbuilder Interactive Workbook CD-ROM, Level 2,** provides instruction and practice in key social studies skills.

29

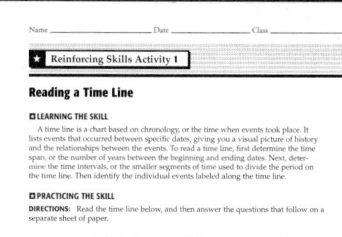

ANSWERS TO PRACTICING THE SKILL

❶ A.D. 1000 to A.D. 1500; 100-year intervals

❷ Cahokia collapses

❸ about 474 years

❹ 1095

Applying the Skill
Students' answers will vary. Ask students to provide a page reference for each selected event.

1 FOCUS

Section Overview

This section describes the Spanish and French colonies that were established in the Americas.

BELLRINGER
Skillbuilder Activity

Project transparency and have students answer the question.

Daily Focus Skills Transparency 1–4

Reading Preview

Answers to Graphic:
I. The Conquest of Mexico
   A. The Spanish Meet the Aztec
   B. The Aztec Are Defeated
II. New Spain Expands
   A. Conquering the Inca
   B. Searching for Cities of Gold
   C. Settling the Southwest

Students should complete the outline by including all heads in the section.

Preteaching Vocabulary
Have students look up the pronunciation and practice the Key Terms that are derived from Spanish.

SECTION 4 Spain and France Build Empires

Guide to Reading

Main Idea
The Spanish and French colonies in America reflected the values of European society and the geography of the regions in which they settled.

Key Terms and Names
Hernán Cortés, conquistador, Francisco Pizarro, Hernando de Soto, presidio, hacienda, vaquero, *encomienda,* Quebec, Northwest Passage

Reading Strategy
Taking Notes As you read about the Spanish and French colonies in North America, use the major headings of the section to create an outline similar to the one below.

Spain and France Build Empires
I. The Conquest of Mexico
   A.
   B.
II.
   A.
   B.

Reading Objectives
• **Describe** the early Spanish settlement of North America.
• **Explain** how New France was founded and settled.

Section Theme
Culture and Traditions Native American religious beliefs helped the Spanish overcome the resistance of central and South American cultures.

Preview of Events

♦1500   **♦1550**   **♦1600**   **♦1650**

1519
Cortés lands on Mexican coast

1532
Pizarro invades Inca empire

1565
St. Augustine, Florida, established

1608
City of Quebec founded

1609–1610
Santa Fe, New Mexico, founded

Aztec depiction of Montezuma viewing ominous signs of invaders

★ An American Story ★

In the spring of 1519, a courier arrived in Tenochtitlán, capital of the Aztec empire. He had news for the emperor, Montezuma II. Bearded white men bearing crosses were encamped on the eastern shores of the emperor's realm.

Montezuma was worried. For several years he had heard reports of strange men with "very light skin" operating in the Caribbean. His subjects had also seen "towers or small mountains floating on the waves of the sea." Now these strange white men had come to his lands, and Montezuma did not know what to do.

The men on the coast were Spanish soldiers. As they watched the soldiers, the people of eastern Mexico felt both fear and awe. One Aztec later recalled:

❝They came in battle array, as conquerors . . . their spears glinted in the sun, and their pennons fluttered like bats. They made a loud clamor as they marched, for their coats of mail and their weapons clashed and rattled. . . . They terrified everyone who saw them.❞

—**quoted in *The Broken Spears: The Aztec Account of the Conquest of Mexico***

The Conquest of Mexico

Leading the Spanish march into the Aztec Empire was 34-year-old **Hernán Cortés.** He had sailed from Cuba with two aims: to find Native Americans to toil for the Spanish in Cuba, and to investigate reports of a wealthy civilization on the Yucatán Peninsula.

SECTION RESOURCES

📁 Reproducible Masters
• Reproducible Lesson Plan 1–4
• Daily Lecture and Discussion Notes 1–4
• Guided Reading Activity 1–4
• Section Quiz 1–4
• Reading Essentials and Study Guide 1–4

📖 Transparencies
• Daily Focus Skills Transparency 1–4

Multimedia
• Interactive Tutor Self-Assessment CD-ROM
• ExamView® Pro Testmaker CD-ROM
• Presentation Plus! CD-ROM
• TeacherWorks™ CD-ROM
• Vocabulary PuzzleMaker CD-ROM
• Audio Program
• American Music: Cultural Traditions

Cortés landed in the Yucatán with 11 ships, 550 men, and 16 horses. Soon after, thousands of Native Americans attacked. Although outnumbered, the Spanish had superior weapons. Their swords, crossbows, guns, and cannons quickly killed more than 200 warriors. As a peace offering, the Native Americans gave Cortés 20 young women. One was **Malinche,** who helped translate for Cortés as he continued up the coast. Malinche became one of Cortés's closest advisers. He had her baptized and gave her the name Doña Marina.

The Spanish Meet the Aztec From local rulers, Cortés learned that the Aztec had conquered many people in the region and were at war with others, including the powerful Tlaxcalan people. He decided to make allies of the Tlaxcalans by impressing them with his army's might. The local people had never seen horses before. Their foaming muzzles and the glistening coats of armor they wore were astonishing and terrifying. When they charged, it seemed to one Aztec chronicler "as if stones were raining on the earth." Equally terrifying were the "shooting sparks" of the Spanish cannons. After several displays of Spanish power, the Tlaxcalans agreed to join with Cortés against the Aztec.

Two hundred miles away, Montezuma fretted. He believed an old prophecy foretelling that Quetzalcóatl—a fair-skinned, bearded deity—would someday return to conquer the Aztec. Montezuma did not know if Cortés was Quetzalcóatl. To be safe, he sent envoys promising a yearly payment to the king of Spain if Cortés halted his advance. As further appeasement, the envoys sacrificed several captives and gave their blood to the Spanish to drink. This act horrified the Spanish and alarmed Montezuma, who knew that Quetzalcóatl hated human sacrifice.

With a joint Spanish-Tlaxcalan force heading toward him, Montezuma decided to ambush Cortés at the city of Cholula. Warned in advance by Doña Marina, the Spanish struck first, killing over 6,000 Cholulans. Montezuma now believed Cortés was unstoppable. On November 8, 1519, Spanish troops peacefully entered the Aztec capital of Tenochtitlán.

The Aztec Are Defeated Sitting on an island in the center of a lake, Tenochtitlán astonished the Spanish. It was larger than most European cities and featured stone canals that people traveled by canoe. The central plaza had an enormous double pyramid and a huge rack displaying thousands of human skulls—a sight that repelled the Spanish.

Surrounded by thousands of Aztec, Cortés decided to take Montezuma hostage. Montezuma did not resist. Following orders from Cortés, he stopped all human sacrifice and had the statues of the Aztec gods replaced with Christian crosses and images of the Virgin Mary. The Aztec priests were furious and organized a rebellion in the spring of 1520. The battle raged for days before the Spanish, realizing they would be overrun, retreated. Over 450 Spaniards died, as did more than 4,000 Aztec, including Montezuma.

Cortés and his men took refuge with the Tlaxcalans and began building boats to attack the Aztec capital by

2 TEACH

Daily Lecture and Discussion Notes 1–4

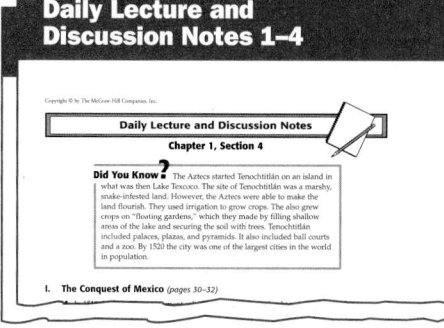

Copyright © by The McGraw-Hill Companies, Inc.

Daily Lecture and Discussion Notes

Chapter 1, Section 4

Did You Know? The Aztecs started Tenochtitlán on an island in what was then Lake Texcoco. The site of Tenochtitlán was a marshy, snake-infested land. However, the Aztecs were able to make the land flourish. They used irrigation to grow crops. The also grew crops on "floating gardens," which they made by filling shallow areas of the lake and securing the soil with trees. Tenochtitlán included palaces, plazas, and pyramids. It also included ball courts and a zoo. By 1520 the city was one of the largest cities in the world in population.

I. **The Conquest of Mexico** (pages 30–32)

ABCNEWS INTERACTIVE™

VIDEOCASSETTE
Historic America Electronic Field Trips

View **Tape 1, Chapter 4:** "St. Augustine."

✎ **History** *Through Art*

Background: The piece of art is one of many remaining codices that have allowed archeologists to learn a great deal about the Aztec culture. The codices were recorded on animal skins or pieces of bark from fig trees.
Answer: Cortés formed an alliance with the Tlaxcalan people against the Aztec.
Ask: Why did Montezuma fear Cortés? (He believed that Cortés was the fulfillment of an old prophecy that a fair-haired deity would defeat the Aztec.)

✎ **History** *Through Art*

Aztec Defeated Hernán Cortés led the Spanish attack on the Aztec people. Though the Aztec killed many Spanish, their weapons were no match for Spanish cannons and guns. The Aztec depiction of one of the battles (left) shows the uneven match. What other circumstances gave the Spanish an advantage?

Spanish sword

Aztec war club

📖 **Reading Strategy** ▶ **READING THE TEXT**

Using Word Parts The *root* is the part of a word that contains its basic meaning. Unlike a base word, a root is not a word by itself. Many roots come from Greek or Latin. For example, *bio* means "life" (biology, biography); *tele* means "distant" (television, telescope); *dent* means "tooth" (dentist, trident). Have students find root words in their study of the section, particularly in the Spanish vocabulary, and find their meanings using a dictionary. **L1**

🗂 Refer to *Inclusion for the High School Social Studies Classroom Strategies and Activities* in the TCR.

Guided Reading Activity 1–4

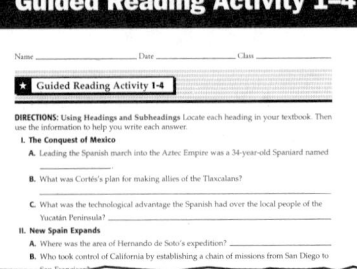

Name _____ Date _____ Class _____

★ **Guided Reading Activity 1-4**

DIRECTIONS: Using Headings and Subheadings Locate each heading in your textbook. Then use the information to help you write each answer.

I. The Conquest of Mexico

A. Leading the Spanish march into the Aztec Empire was a 34-year-old Spaniard named

B. What was Cortés's plan for making allies of the Tlaxcalans?

C. What was the technological advantage the Spanish had over the local people of the Yucatán Peninsula?

II. New Spain Expands

A. Where was the area of Hernando de Soto's expedition?

B. Who took control of California by establishing a chain of missions from San Diego to

✓ Reading Check

Answer: to find people to work the farms and mines the Spanish had built in Cuba and to investigate reports of a wealthy civilization

Fact	Fiction	Folklore

Today the state flag of Spain contains a coat of arms that includes the castle and lion symbols. The coat of arms represents the current reigning monarch who is a descendant of the French Bourbon kings. The Latin motto entwined on the columns reads PLVS VLTRA, which means "more beyond," and refers to the former Spanish lands in the Americas.

Creating a Map Have students create a map that illustrates the extent of the Inca Empire in 1500, the cities of Cajamarca and Cuzco, and present-day country borders of South America. The map should include appropriate labels. **L2**

📁 Use the rubric for creating a map, display, or chart on pages 65–66 in the *Performance Assessment Activities and Rubrics.*

---

water. At the same time, smallpox erupted in the region, devastating the defenders of Tenochtitlán. As one Aztec recounted, "We were covered with agonizing sores from head to foot. The illness was so dreadful that no one could walk or move." In May 1521, Cortés again attacked the greatly weakened Aztec forces. By August he had won.

✓ Reading Check
Examining What was the purpose of Hernán Cortés's expedition to Mexico?

New Spain Expands

On the ruins of Tenochtitlán, the Spanish built the city of Mexico, which became the capital of the colony of New Spain. Cortés then sent several expeditions to conquer the rest of Central America. The men who led these expeditions became known as conquistadors, or "conquerors."

Conquering the Inca Spain also sent adventurers to South America. In 1526 **Francisco Pizarro** found the Inca Empire in Peru. He returned to conquer the Inca in 1532 with a small force of infantry and cavalry. Pizarro stationed his troops in the town of Cajamarca and invited the Inca ruler, Atahualpa, to meet him there. The emperor arrived with some 6,000 followers. When Atahualpa rejected the Bible a Spanish priest handed him, Pizarro ordered the cannons to fire and the cavalry to charge. He and 20 soldiers then took the emperor prisoner.

Pizarro tried to rule Peru by keeping Atahualpa as a hostage. Less than a year later, however, he executed Atahualpa and installed a series of figurehead emperors who had to follow his orders. Although many people accepted the new system, others fled to the mountains and continued to fight the Spanish until 1572.

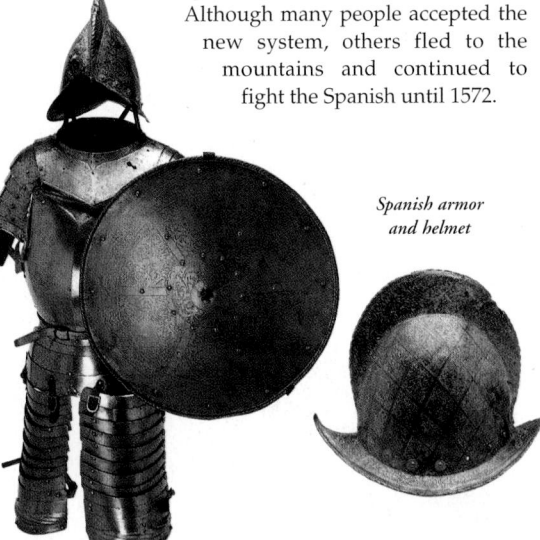

Spanish armor and helmet

Fact	Fiction	Folklore

Spain, 1492 Christopher Columbus proudly carried the Spanish banner of Castile and León to the shores of the Bahamas. The flag's castle represented Queen Isabella. The lion symbolized her husband, King Ferdinand.

Searching for Cities of Gold The riches Pizarro found in Peru fueled rumors of other wealthy cities. In 1528 Pánfilo de Narváez vainly searched northern Florida for a fabled city of gold. Then he and his men built rafts and tried to sail to Mexico. They made it to present-day Texas, although most of the men, including Narváez, died in the attempt. The survivors, led by Álvar Núñez Cabeza de Vaca and an enslaved man named Estéban, wandered across what is now Texas and New Mexico before reaching New Spain in 1536.

Many conquistadors had also heard of the Seven Golden Cities of Cibola north of New Spain. Hoping to find Cibola, in 1540 Francisco Vásquez de Coronado headed into what is now the American Southwest. Members of his expedition traveled west to the Colorado River and east into present-day Kansas. Finding nothing but windswept plains and strange "shaggy cows" (buffalo), Coronado returned to Mexico.

Meanwhile, **Hernando de Soto** took an expedition north of Florida. They searched the region for several years, killing many Native Americans and stealing supplies from them. They were the first Europeans to see the Mississippi River. After de Soto died, his men buried him in the Mississippi and returned home.

Settling the Southwest The failure of explorers to find gold or other wealth north of New Spain slowed Spanish settlement of the region. It was not until 1598 that settlers, led by Juan de Oñate's expedition, migrated north of the Rio Grande, almost perishing while crossing northern Mexico. When they finally reached the Rio Grande, the survivors organized a feast to give thanks to God. This "Spanish Thanksgiving" is now celebrated each April in El Paso, Texas.

The Spanish gave the name **New Mexico** to the territory north of New Spain. Pedro de Peralta, the first governor of New Mexico, founded the capital city of Santa Fe in 1609 or 1610. The Spanish built forts called presidios throughout the region to protect settlers and to serve as trading posts. Despite these efforts,

---

DIFFERENTIATED INSTRUCTION

At-Risk Students Have students create a pyramid-shaped diagram to help them understand the structure of society in New Spain. The diagram should be divided into sections to illustrate the hierarchy of the societal groups. Ask students to label the diagram using the appropriate Spanish words along with a brief description of what kind of people were included in each group. **L1** ELL

📁 Refer to *Inclusion for the High School Social Studies Classroom Strategies and Activities* in the TCR.

few Spaniards migrated to the harsh region. Instead, the Catholic Church became the primary force for colonizing the southwestern part of America.

Throughout the 1600s and 1700s, Spanish priests built missions and spread the Christian faith among the Navajo and Pueblo peoples of New Mexico. Beginning in 1769, Spanish missionaries led by the Franciscan priest Junipero Serra took control of California by establishing a chain of missions from present-day San Diego to San Francisco. A road called **El Camino Real**—the Royal Highway—linked the missions together.

The priests and missionaries in California and those in New Mexico took different approaches to their work. In California they forced the mostly nomadic Native Americans to live in villages near the missions. In New Mexico, on the other hand, the priests and missionaries adapted their efforts to fit into the lifestyle of the Pueblo people. They built churches near where the Pueblo people lived and farmed and tried to teach them Catholic ideas and European culture.

The Spanish priests tried to end traditional Native American religious practices that conflicted with Catholic beliefs. Some priests beat and whipped those who defied them. In response, a Native American religious leader named Popé organized an uprising against the Spanish in 1680. Some 17,000 warriors destroyed most of the missions in New Mexico. It took the Spanish more than a decade to regain control of the region.

✓ Reading Check **Identifying** Where did most people who colonized the southwest part of North America come from?

Spanish American Society

The conquistadors were adventurers who had come to America seeking wealth and prestige. The society they built in New Spain reflected those goals.

Mining, Ranching, and the *Encomienda* When the Spanish realized that most Native American cities did not have much gold, they built mines. Ultimately, it was not gold that enriched Spain, but

Profiles IN HISTORY

Bartolomé de Las Casas
1474–1566

In the years following the Spanish conquest, many people began to protest against the abuses of the *encomienda* system. One prominent advocate for the Native Americans was Bartolomé de Las Casas, Bishop of Chiapas. As a young man, Las Casas traveled to Hispaniola in 1502. He soon became horrified by what he saw. The Spanish settlers tortured, burned, and cut off the hands and noses of Native Americans to force them to obey.

Las Casas maintained that the Church and the king had a duty to protect Native Americans. In this view, he had the support of the pope. "The said Indians," declared Pope Paul III, "are by no means to be deprived of their liberty or the possessions of their property . . . nor should they in any way be enslaved."

Las Casas published several books describing the destruction of the Native Americans. His books were read throughout Europe, creating pressure on the Spanish to change their policies.

In response, the Spanish government stopped granting *encomiendas* and banned Native American slavery. Slowly, as *encomenderos* died without heirs, the *encomienda* system came to an end. Las Casas died in 1566, still outraged at the treatment of the Native Americans. "Surely," he wrote in his will, "God will wreak his fury and anger against Spain some day for the unjust wars waged against the American Indians."

silver. The Spanish discovered huge deposits of silver ore in the 1540s and set up mining camps all across northern Mexico, transforming the economy. The work in the dark, damp mineshafts was very difficult. Many miners were killed by explosions and cave-ins. Others died from exhaustion.

To feed the miners in this arid region, Spaniards created large cattle ranches called haciendas. The land could not grow crops but it could feed vast herds of cattle and sheep. The vaqueros who worked with the cattle later influenced cowhands in the United States.

Another feature of Spanish colonial society was the *encomienda,* a system that granted control of Native American towns to Spanish *encomenderos.* The villagers paid their *encomendero* a share of what they harvested or produced and also worked part-time for him for free. The *encomendero,* in return, was supposed to protect the villagers and try to convert them to Christianity. Sadly, many abused their power and worked the Native Americans to death.

A Class-Based Society The people of Spain's colonies in the Americas formed a highly structured society based on birth, income, and education. At

Profiles IN HISTORY

Have students explain how the *encomienda* system led to abuse of Native Americans and why the Spanish government felt that discontinuation of the system would reduce or eliminate the abuse.

✓ Reading Check

Answer: Spain

FYI

Twenty-one missions were established along the El Camino Real between 1769 and 1823. Junipero Serra founded seven of the first nine missions. The 21 missions in order of their founding are: (1) San Diego de Alcalá, (2) San Carlos Borromeo de Carmelo, (3) San Antonio de Padua, (4) San Gabriel Arcángel, (5) San Luis Obispo de Tolosa, (6) San Francisco de Asís (Mission Delores), (7) San Juan Capistrano, (8) Santa Clara de Asís, (9) San Buenaventura, (10) Santa Bárbara, (11) La Purísima Concepción, (12) Santa Cruz, (13) Nuestra Señora de la Soledad, (14) San José, (15) San Juan Bautista, (16) San Miguel Arcángel, (17) San Fernando Rey de España, (18) San Luis Rey de Francia, (19) Santa Inés, (20) San Rafael Arcángel, and (21) San Francisco Solano.

 History *and the* Humanities

🎵 American Music: Cultural Traditions: "Ay como flecha"
🏛 American Art & Architecture: Mission San Xavier del Bac

INTERDISCIPLINARY CONNECTIONS ACTIVITY

Sociology Tell students that conflicts between cultures and religions have lead to wars and atrocities. Have students compare the treatment of the Native Americans by the Spanish priests to ethnic, religious, or cultural conflicts that occur in the world today. Have students present their findings in an appropriate graphic organizer. **L2**

☑ Reading Check

Answer: They set up mines to obtain gold and silver. They set up cattle ranches to provide food for the laborers, since the land was not suitable for farming.

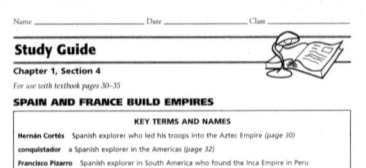

Linking Past & Present

Ask students to share their personal knowledge about a person or group of persons involved in refugee immigration. Encourage students to talk about the immigration of their own families, their ancestors, acquaintances, or ancestors of acquaintances. Ask students to explain the reason why these people fled their homeland and came to America. *(Students' answers will vary. Encourage students to think about the reasons behind the immigration.)*

3 ASSESS

Assign Section 4 Assessment as homework or as an in-class activity.

🌐 Have students use the **Interactive Tutor Self-Assessment CD-ROM.**

L1/ELL

Reading Essentials and Study Guide 1–4

Name _____ Date _____ Class _____

Study Guide

Chapter 1, Section 4
For use with textbook pages 30–35

SPAIN AND FRANCE BUILD EMPIRES

KEY TERMS AND NAMES

Hernán Cortés   Spanish explorer who led his troops into the Aztec Empire *(page 30)*
conquistador   a Spanish explorer in the Americas *(page 32)*
Francisco Pizarro   Spanish explorer in South America who found the Inca Empire in Peru *(page 32)*
Hernando de Soto   Spanish explorer in the area north of Florida *(page 32)*
presidio   a Spanish fort *(page 32)*
hacienda   a huge cattle ranch in New Spain *(page 33)*
vaquero   Spanish cowhand *(page 33)*

---

the top were *peninsulares*—people who had been born in Spain. They held most of the high government and church positions. Below the *peninsulares* were *criollos*—those born in the colonies to Spanish parents. Many *criollos* were wealthy, but they held slightly lesser positions. Next came the numerous *mestizos*, people of Spanish and Native American parents, whose social status varied greatly. A few were part of the upper class. Others worked as artisans, merchants, and shopkeepers. Most, however, were poor and relegated to the lowest class, along with Native Americans, Africans, and people of African and Spanish or African and Native American descent. These people provided most of the labor for New Spain's farms, mines, and ranches.

To govern this vast, diverse empire in America, the Spanish king divided it into regions called

Linking Past & Present

Refugee Migration to America

Past: The Huguenots
French Protestants, known as Huguenots, migrated to America in large numbers during the late 1600s. Violent persecutions under King Louis XIV caused around one million people to leave France. Many settled in South Carolina, while others found sanctuary in Rhode Island, New York, and Virginia.

Present: Jewish Immigration
Following the tragic events of World War II, thousands of homeless European Jews came to the United States. Many Eastern Jews, particularly from Iran and Syria, soon followed. With the collapse of the Soviet Union in 1991, many Russian Jews migrated to America. Unlike the Russian immigrants of the 1800s, these Jews had little opportunity to maintain Jewish customs or to study Hebrew.

---

viceroyalties, each ruled by a viceroy. The king also created the Council of the Indies to advise him. The Council advised the king and watched over all colonial activities. To manage local affairs, the king created a special court in Mexico known as the *audiencia*. The *audiencia's* members were not only judges but also administrators and lawmakers.

☑ Reading Check **Describing** Why did the Spanish set up mines and cattle ranches in northern Mexico?

The French Empire in America

In 1524, three years after Cortés conquered the Aztec, King Francis I of France sent Giovanni da Verrazano to map North America's coastline. Verrazano wanted to find the Northwest Passage—a northern water route through North America to the Pacific Ocean. He traveled from what is today North Carolina to Newfoundland but found no sign of the passage.

Ten years later, realizing that Spain was growing wealthy from its empire, Francis sent another explorer named Jacques Cartier. Cartier made three trips to North America, discovering and mapping the St. Lawrence River. In the decades after his last voyage in 1541, fighting between Catholics and Protestants tore France apart. For the next 60 years, the French largely ignored North America.

New France Is Founded In 1602, with the religious wars over, King Henry IV of France authorized a colonization effort by a group of French merchants. The merchants, who hoped to build a profitable fur trade with Native Americans, hired Samuel de Champlain to help them. In 1608 Champlain founded the trading post of **Quebec,** which became the capital of the colony of New France.

Instead of having settlers clear the land and build farms, the backers of New France sought profits from fur. As a result, the colony grew slowly. By 1666 it had just over 3,000 people. Most of the fur traders did not even live there, preferring to make their homes among the Native Americans with whom they traded. Jesuit missionaries, known as "black robes," likewise lived in the woods with the local people.

France's Empire Expands In 1663 France's King Louis XIV made New France a royal colony and focused on increasing its population. The government paid the shipping costs for over 4,000 immigrants, and it sent some 900 young women to provide wives for the

---

CRITICAL THINKING ACTIVITY

Synthesizing Have students work in groups to research one of the 21 missions or four presidios linked by El Camino Real. Encourage students to use a variety of resources including books, magazines, travel brochures, and the Internet to collect facts, figures, illustrations, and photographs. Using the results of their research, have students create a multimedia presentation about the mission or presidio they selected. **L2**

many single men in the colony. It also gave couples financial incentives to marry young and have many children. By the 1670s New France's population was nearly 7,000, and by 1760 it was over 60,000.

In addition, the French began exploring North America. In 1673 a fur trader named Louis Joliet and a Jesuit priest named Jacques Marquette began searching for a waterway the Algonquian people called the "big river." The two men finally found it—the Mississippi. In 1682 René-Robert Cavalier de La Salle followed the Mississippi all the way to the Gulf of Mexico, becoming the first European to do so. He claimed the region for France and named the territory Louisiana in honor of Louis XIV.

GEOGRAPHY
Settling Louisiana

The geography of the lower Mississippi hindered settlement. The coastline had no good harbors, and shifting sandbars made navigation dangerous. The oppressive heat caused food to spoil quickly, and mosquito-filled swamps made the climate unhealthy. The French did not establish a permanent settlement in the region until 1698, when Lord d'Iberville founded Biloxi. Mobile, New Orleans, and several forts followed over the next few decades.

The French settlers in southern Louisiana realized that the crops that could be grown there, such as sugar, rice, tobacco, and indigo, required hard labor that few settlers were willing to do. As a result, the French began importing enslaved Africans to work on their plantations.

Fact | Fiction | Folklore

Flag of New France Settlers in New France often flew this flag of the French Royal Navy. They also flew the French Royal Banner, which was blue instead of white.

Rivalry With Spain The Spanish had always been concerned about the French in North America. Indeed, they had founded St. Augustine, Florida, in 1565 to counter French settlement attempts to the north. St. Augustine prospered and became the first permanent town established by Europeans in what is today the United States.

The arrival of the French at the mouth of the Mississippi River spurred the Spanish to action once again. In 1690 the Spanish built their first mission in what is today eastern Texas. In 1716 Spanish settlers arrived to secure Spain's claim and to block French expansion into the region. The French and Spanish empires in North America now bordered each other. Neither, however, posed a serious threat to the other. The real challengers for domination of North America were the rapidly growing English colonies along the Atlantic coast.

✓**Reading Check** **Explaining** How did making New France a royal colony help the colony?

SECTION 4 ASSESSMENT

HISTORY Online **Study Central™** To review this section, go to tarvol2.glencoe.com and click on **Study Central™**.

Checking for Understanding
1. **Define:** conquistador, presidio, hacienda, vaquero, *encomienda*, Northwest Passage.
2. **Identify:** Hernán Cortés, Francisco Pizarro, Hernando de Soto, Quebec.
3. **Explain** how the fur trade contributed to the slow growth of New France.

Reviewing Themes
4. **Culture and Tradition** How did Mesoamerican culture aid Spain's efforts to conquer the resistance of native peoples?

Critical Thinking
5. **Synthesizing** How did competition between France and Spain affect their colonization of North America?
6. **Categorizing** Use a graphic organizer similar to the one below to list the social classes that developed in New Spain.

Highest _____
_____
Lowest _____

Analyzing Visuals
7. **Analyzing Art** Study the Aztec image on page 31 of the Spanish conquest of the Aztec capital city of Tenochtitlán. What elements of the image give you clues that the two sides were unevenly matched?

Writing About History
8. **Persuasive Writing** Write an advertisement for a French newspaper to encourage people to settle in New France.

SECTION 4 ASSESSMENT ANSWERS

1. Terms are in blue.
2. Hernán Cortés *(p. 30)*; Francisco Pizarro *(p. 32)*, Hernando de Soto *(p. 32)*, Quebec *(p. 34)*
3. Fur trading did not require large settlements so fewer people were needed.
4. They believed Cortés was the fulfillment of prophecy.

5. Both wanted to claim large territories and they needed colonists to enforce these claims. Both encouraged people to move to the colonies.
6. *peninsulares, criollos, mestizos,* all others including Africans, Native Americans
7. Answers may vary but should

mention the difference in armor and weaponry.
8. Students' advertisements will vary. They should be descriptive and make promises such as wealth or adventure.

Section Quiz 1–4

Name _____ Date _____ Class _____

⭐ **Chapter 1** | Score

Section Quiz 1-4

DIRECTIONS: Matching Match each item in Column A with the items in Column B. Write the correct letters in the blanks. *(10 points each)*

Column A
_____ 1. founded the trading post of Quebec
_____ 2. Native American woman who became one of Cortés's closest advisers
_____ 3. a northern water route through North America to the Pacific Ocean
_____ 4. the men who led the expeditions to conquer Central America
_____ 5. a road that linked missions from San Diego to San Francisco

Column B
A. Northwest Passage
B. Malinche
C. El Camino Real
D. conquistadors
E. Samuel de Champlain

Fact | Fiction | Folklore

Today the flag of France consists of three vertical panels of equal size. The left panel is blue, the center panel is white, and the right panel is red. The French flag has remained the same since 1848.

Reteach
Have students review the time line on page 30 and explain the significance of the events shown.

Enrich
Have students research one of the individuals mentioned in this section and prepare a short biography of the person.

✓**Reading Check**

Answer: It encouraged French people to move there and settle the land.

HISTORY Online

Study Central™ provides summaries, interactive games, and online graphic organizers to help students review section content.

---

4 CLOSE

Ask students how their lives might be different if Europeans had not colonized America. Have them speculate how colonization by people from Africa, the Middle East, or Asia might have shaped America.

1 FOCUS

As students study the layout of a typical mission, have them determine how the following areas/groups helped the mission to be self-sufficient: the tannery, the granary, the cemetery, the workshop, the pottery makers, the church, the stable, the priests, and the soldiers.

2 TEACH

Tracing a Route Have students practice their map skills by planning a trip to visit several of the missions. Tell students they will travel from Loreto to San Francisco. Have them count the number of missions that they would pass on the trip. Then have them write down the names, in order, of the missions on their journey that are labeled by name on the map. Ask students to speculate on why the route passes so many missions. *(Routes developed to connect the missions. In many places, the missions were placed a day's journey apart so that travelers could sleep in the safety of the mission walls.)* **L1**

L2

Geography and History Activity 1a

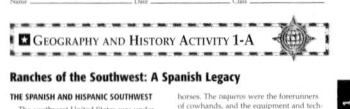

☐ GEOGRAPHY AND HISTORY ACTIVITY 1-A

Ranches of the Southwest: A Spanish Legacy

THE SPANISH AND HISPANIC SOUTHWEST
The southwest United States was under Spanish and Hispanic rule from the time of Coronado's explorations in 1540 until the end of the Mexican-American War in 1848. During Spain's rule, the area was divided into three provinces: New Mexico, California, and Tejas (Texas). The vast province of New Mexico included what is now the state of New Mexico, most of Colorado and Arizona, and parts of Utah, Wyoming, Kansas, Oklahoma, and Texas.

horses. The *riqueros* were the forerunners of cowhands, and the equipment and techniques they used were well suited to the open-range style of ranching. The clothing worn by cowhands, the gear for their horses, and the techniques for roping and herding cattle all originated with the Spanish.

SHEEP IN NEW MEXICO
Santa Fe, New Mexico, was founded in 1609 or 1610. It was the first permanent settlement west of the Mississippi River.

UNIT 1

Spanish Missions

The Spanish settlers who came to the American Southwest had two aims: to claim the land and to convert the Native Americans to Catholicism. To achieve these aims, the Spaniards set up fortified religious settlements known as missions.

The missions reflected both the culture of Spain and the demands of life in an arid land. By the late eighteenth century, the missions were thriving, self-contained communities.

Arranged in a quadrangle around a central courtyard, the complex was a bustling world of workshops, storage areas, gardens, and living quarters. Its location was often determined by the availability of wood, water, and fields for raising crops and grazing the livestock that the Spanish brought to the Americas. The form of the mission was dictated by the building materials available. The thick walls of the one-story buildings were usually made of stone or sun-dried mud bricks known as adobe.

For security, most of the mission's residences were connected, and all windows faced inward. The entrances were locked at night. A covered arcade, or outdoor hallway, ran along the inner walls of the residences. The complex was usually dominated by a large church. Thousands of Native Americans were attracted to the missions by gifts and by the prospect of finding safety and food. They were instructed in Catholicism and Spanish. Women wove cloth and cooked; men labored at handicrafts or in the fields. In addition to the native beans and corn, the converts planted crops introduced by the Spaniards such as wheat, oats, oranges, olives, and grapes.

Some of the missions would not allow the Native Americans to leave without permission once they had entered the community. Making this transition to a regimented life was difficult, and escapes were common. To enforce order and hunt down runaways, many missions had a small detachment of soldiers. The soldiers rode on horses, which the Spaniards brought to the Southwest.

The Spaniards also brought measles and smallpox—devastating diseases against which the Indians had no natural immunity. Mission cemeteries often held the bones of thousands of Native Americans who died of these European diseases.

Crops

Priests' quarters

Soldiers' barracks

Stable

Watering trough

LEARNING FROM GEOGRAPHY

1. What factors determined the selection of a mission site?

2. Why did the Spanish station troops at missions?

36 CHAPTER 1 Converging Cultures

Spanish Missions, 1776

✝ Mission	⋯⋯ Present–day boundary
✝ Mission & Presidio	Road
■ Presidio	Migration

0 ——— 200 miles
0 ——— 200 kilometers

San Francisco
San Juan
SanLuis Obispo
San Juan Capistrano
San Diego
Tubac
Tucson
Fronteras
Horcasitas
Loreto
Monterrey
Santa Fe
Tomé
Socorro
El Paso
San Antonio
San José y San Miguel de Aguayo

EXTENDING THE CONTENT

Presidio of San Francisco In 1776 the Presidio of San Francisco began as the northernmost military outpost of the Spanish in North America. From 1822 to 1848, the Mexican flag flew over the presidio. When Mexico ceded California to the United States in 1848, the presidio became a U.S. Army post. During World War II, it served as the headquarters of the Western Defense Command and foxholes were dug along nearby beaches in preparation for troops to defend against attack.

The Virgin of Guadalupe adorns the church at the mission of San José y San Miguel de Aguayo.

Fruit trees

Living quarters

Gate

Oven

Workshop

Well

Pottery makers

Livestock corral

Nut trees

Garden

Fruit trees

Catholic church

Cemetery and garden

Granary

Tannery and workshops

Entrance

Soldiers

Years before the English unfurled their flag at Jamestown, Spanish missionaries and colonists from New Spain, as Mexico was known, were settling in the Southwest. The map shows their major migration routes into present-day New Mexico, Texas, and California, as well as the location of their missions and presidios, or garrisoned forts.

The Spanish built the church of San José y San Miguel de Aguayo in San Antonio, Texas, in the 1720s. Such churches were only part of much larger mission complexes. The art above shows the layout of a typical mission.

Making a Drawing Have students reread the feature. Then have them make a drawing from the perspective of a Native American or the perspective of a Franciscan monk about what life was like at the mission. Have volunteers share their drawings with the class. Use the drawings to discuss the different points of view of the purpose and reality of life in the mission. **L2**

you don't say...

Presidio The term *presidio* means *fort* or *military post.*

3 ASSESS

Have students answer the Learning from Geography questions.

4 CLOSE

Ask students to describe what lasting influences the Spanish mission system has had on the Southwestern United States.

NGS ONLINE

Access National Geographic's Web site for current events, atlas updates, activities, links, interactive features, and archives at www.nationalgeographic.com.

ANSWERS TO LEARNING FROM GEOGRAPHY

1. The availability of wood, water, and grazing lands determined the location of the missions.

2. The Spanish used troops to enforce order and to capture Native Americans who entered the community and then escaped.

CHAPTER 1 ASSESSMENT and ACTIVITIES

GLENCOE
TECHNOLOGY

MindJogger Videoquiz

Use the **MindJogger Videoquiz** to review Chapter 1 content.

 Available in DVD

Reviewing Key Terms

Students' answers will vary. The pages where the words appear in the text are shown in parentheses.

1. **Ice Age** *(p. 13)*
2. **glacier** *(p. 13)*
3. **nomad** *(p. 13)*
4. **civilization** *(p. 13)*
5. **pueblo** *(p. 15)*
6. **kachina** *(p. 15)*
7. **slash-and-burn agriculture** *(p. 16)*
8. **longhouse** *(p. 16)*
9. **feudalism** *(p. 19)*
10. **manorialism** *(p. 19)*
11. **serf** *(p. 19)*
12. **Renaissance** *(p. 20)*
13. **astrolabe** *(p. 21)*
14. **caravel** *(p. 21)*
15. **savannah** *(p. 23)*
16. **line of demarcation** *(p. 26)*
17. **circumnavigate** *(p. 27)*
18. **Columbian Exchange** *(p. 28)*
19. **conquistador** *(p. 32)*
20. **presidio** *(p. 32)*
21. **hacienda** *(p. 33)*
22. **vaquero** *(p. 33)*
23. *encomienda* *(p. 33)*
24. **Northwest Passage** *(p. 34)*

Reviewing Key Facts

25. Mesoamerica *(p. 13)*, Cahokia *(p. 15)*, Crusades *(p. 19)*, Sahara *(p. 21)*, San Salvador Island *(p. 25)*, Treaty of Tordesillas *(p. 26)*, Francisco Pizarro *(p. 32)*, Quebec *(p. 34)*

26. Asians came to America by crossing the land bridge, an area now submerged and known as the Bering Strait, on foot.

38

Reviewing Key Terms

On a sheet of paper, use each of these terms in a sentence.

1. Ice Age
2. glacier
3. nomad
4. civilization
5. pueblo
6. kachina
7. slash-and-burn agriculture
8. longhouse
9. feudalism
10. manorialism
11. serf
12. Renaissance
13. astrolabe
14. caravel
15. savannah
16. line of demarcation
17. circumnavigate
18. Columbian Exchange
19. conquistador
20. presidio
21. hacienda
22. vaquero
23. *encomienda*
24. Northwest Passage

Reviewing Key Facts

25. **Identify:** Mesoamerica, Cahokia, Crusades, Sahara, San Salvador Island, Treaty of Tordesillas, Francisco Pizarro, Quebec.
26. How did Asians migrate to the Americas during the Ice Age?
27. How were slave labor and the cultivation of sugarcane related to one another?
28. What major factors encouraged European exploration in the 1400s and 1500s?
29. Why were Europeans searching for a sea route to Asia?
30. Why were the Spanish able to defeat the Aztec and the Inca?
31. How were the missionary practices of the Spanish different in California than in the Southwest?
32. What factors determined a person's social class in Spanish colonial society?
33. What was the purpose of the Council of the Indies?

Chapter Summary

Europe

- **A.D. 1095—late 1400s:** The Crusades, the emergence of strong states, the Renaissance, and new technology lead to European exploration of Africa and North America.
- **1400s:** European explorers map the west coast of Africa and begin using enslaved Africans on sugarcane plantations.
- **Late 1400s:** Europeans arrive in the Americas, explore the region, and begin to establish colonies.

North America

- **Between 15,000 and 30,000 years ago:** Asians begin migrating to North America.
- **Between 9,000 and 10,000 years ago:** Agricultural revolution begins.
- **A.D. 200—late 1500s:** Various Native American culture groups shaped by the environment develop.
- **1500s:** Native American groups begin to be affected by European diseases and military conquests.
- **1565—early 1600s:** Spanish and French establish towns in St. Augustine, Quebec, and Santa Fe.

Africa

- **A.D. 400—1450:** Various African groups with different cultures shaped by the environment developed in West, Central, and Southern Africa.
- **1400s:** The arrival of Europeans leads to an expansion of the slave trade; many cultures are destroyed as the demand for enslaved Africans increases.

27. Slaves were needed to perform the difficult labor required to cultivate and harvest sugarcane.

28. the Renaissance, new technology, desire for luxury goods from Asia, and advances in geography

29. The collapse of the Mongol empire resulted in reduced trade with Asia while the demand for Asian luxury goods remained high. Europeans thought a sea route to Asia would increase trade.

30. They had technologically superior weapons.

31. In California, they forced the nomadic Native Americans to settle in villages near the missions. In New Mexico, the missionaries adapted their efforts to fit the lifestyle of the Pueblo people.

32. birth, income, and education

33. The Council of the Indies was created to help the king of Spain govern his vast empire.

Critical Thinking

34. In dry areas the Native Americans found crops that would grow in the dry soil or they moved from place

HISTORY Online

Self-Check Quiz
Visit the *American Republic Since 1877* Web site at tarvol2.glencoe.com and click on *Self-Check Quizzes—Chapter 1* to assess your knowledge of chapter content.

Critical Thinking

34. Analyzing Themes: Cultures and Traditions How did environment, climate, and food supplies influence the lifestyles of early peoples in the Americas?

35. Forming an Opinion If you had been King Ferdinand or Queen Isabella, would you have agreed to support Christopher Columbus's voyages to the Americas? Why or why not?

36. Categorizing Use a graphic organizer similar to the one below to list how the relationships between Native Americans and the Spanish differed from those between Native Americans and the French.

Native American relations with the Spanish	Native American relations with the French

Practicing Skills

37. Reading a Time Line Refer to the time line on page 29. Then answer the following questions.
   a. What is the time span on this time line?
   b. How much time elapsed between the republication of Ptolemy's *Geography* and Columbus's landing in America?

Chapter Activities

38. Technology Activity: Using a Database Search a library or the Internet to find information about the early civilizations in the Americas and Africa that were discussed in this chapter. Build a database collecting information about the cultures of these early civilizations. Include information about religious customs and traditions, ways of making a living, government, and housing. Include a map showing the locations of these civilizations.

39. American History Primary Source Document Library CD-ROM Read "Letter From Christopher Columbus" under *Exploring the Americas.* Work with a few of your classmates to describe how Columbus mapped the region he visited.

Writing Activity

40. Portfolio Writing: Script for a Documentary Choose an early civilization described in the chapter. Write a script for a scene in a documentary featuring this civilization. Describe

The Crusades, 1095–1204

☐	Christian world
☐	Islamic world
←	1st Crusade
←	2nd Crusade
⟵	3rd Crusade
←	4th Crusade

Azimuthal Equidistant projection

the setting of the scene, and explain what the people in the scene would be doing. Place the script in your portfolio.

Geography and History

41. The map above shows the routes of the Crusades. Study the map and answer the questions below.
   a. Interpreting Maps Which Crusade ended at Constantinople?
   b. Applying Geography Skills Which Crusade traveled almost exclusively by land?

Standardized Test Practice

Directions: Choose the best answer to the following question.

The Treaty of Tordesillas resolved differences between

A Spain and France.

B Spain and Portugal.

C Portugal and England.

D France and Portugal.

Test-Taking Tip: In addition to thinking about what the purpose of the Treaty of Tordesillas was, you can use the process of elimination to help answer this question. Which country listed in the answer choices was not discussed in this chapter?

CHAPTER 1 Converging Cultures **39**

HISTORY Online

Have students visit the Web site at tarvol2.glencoe.com to review Chapter 1 and take the Self-Check Quiz.

39. Have several groups share their findings with the class and discuss ways that maps are made today.

Writing Activity

40. Provide samples of scripts for students to review. Have students share their scripts with a classmate for critique. Encourage students to make revisions based on the feedback they receive.

Geography and History

41. a. 4th Crusade, **b.** 1st Crusade

Standardized Test Practice

Answer: B
Test-Taking Tip: Help students use the process of elimination to answer this question. If students remember that at the time of the Treaty of Tordesillas England was not yet involved in the colonization of America, they will be able to eliminate answer C.

---

to place looking for food. In the damp coastal areas that did not support farming, the Native Americans became expert fishers. In mild climates, they hunted and trapped wildlife.

35. Student opinions will vary. Students should be able to clearly defend their position.

36. The relationship between Native Americans and the Spanish was antagonistic while the relationship between the Native Americans and the French was cooperative.

Practicing Skills

37. a. 500 years, **b.** 17 years

Chapter Activities

38. Encourage students to create fields for each category of information such as religious customs and ways of making a living. Have students use their databases as a study tool.

Bonus Question ?

Ask: What is the name of the flint arrowhead that led scientists to conclude that humans inhabited the Southwest earlier than had previously been believed? *(Folsom points)*

Chapter 2 Resources

Timesaving Tools

TeacherWorks™ All-In-One Planner and Resource Center

- **Interactive Teacher Edition** Access your Teacher Wraparound Edition and your classroom resources with a few easy clicks.
- **Interactive Lesson Planner** Planning has never been easier! Organize your week, month, semester, or year with all the lesson helps you need to make teaching creative, timely, and relevant.

Use Glencoe's **Presentation Plus!** multimedia teacher tool to easily present dynamic lessons that visually excite your students. Using Microsoft PowerPoint® you can customize the presentations to create your own personalized lessons.

TEACHING TRANSPARENCIES

Graphic Organizer 2 L2

Why It Matters Chapter Transparency 2 L2

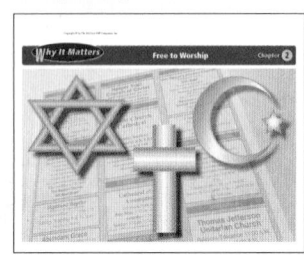

APPLICATION AND ENRICHMENT

Linking Past and Present Activity 2 L2

Enrichment Activity 2 L3

Primary Source Reading 2 L2

REVIEW AND REINFORCEMENT

Reteaching Activity 2 L1

Vocabulary Activity 2 L1

Time Line Activity 2 L2

Critical Thinking Skills Activity 2 L2

Meeting NCSS Standards

The following standards are covered in Chapter 2:

Section 1	V	Individuals, Groups, and Institutions: B, D, E
Section 2	I	Culture: A, B, D
Section 3	II	Time, Continuity, and Change: B, C, F
Section 4	III	People, Places, and Environments: A, F, H
Section 5	VII	Production, Distribution, and Consumption: A, F

Local Standards

_____

_____

_____

_____

_____

ASSESSMENT AND EVALUATION

GLENCOE'S
ASSESSMENT
ADVANTAGE

Chapter 2 Test Form A L2

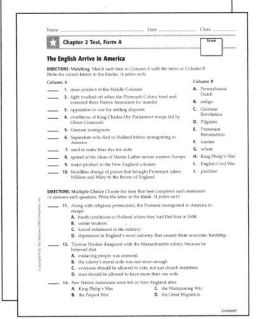

Chapter 2 Test Form B L2

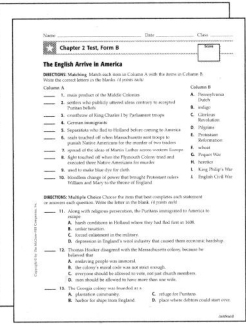

Standardized Test Practice Workbook Activity 2 L2

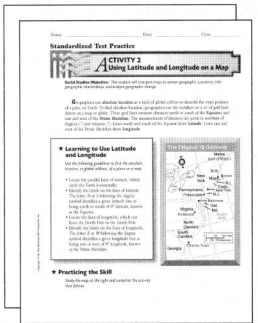

Performance Assessment Activities and Rubrics 2 L1/ELL

ExamView® Pro Testmaker CD-ROM

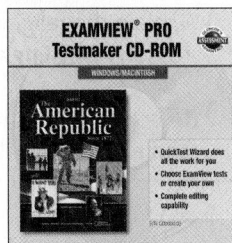

EXAMVIEW® PRO
Testmaker CD-ROM
WINDOWS/MACINTOSH

American Republic

- QuickTest Wizard does all the work for you
- Choose ExamView tests or create your own
- Complete editing capability

MULTIMEDIA

- Vocabulary PuzzleMaker CD-ROM
- Interactive Tutor Self-Assessment CD-ROM
- ExamView® Pro Testmaker CD-ROM
- Audio Program
- American History Primary Source Documents Library CD-ROM
- MindJogger Videoquiz
- Presentation Plus! CD-ROM
- TeacherWorks™ CD-ROM
- Interactive Student Edition CD-ROM
- Glencoe Skillbuilder Interactive Workbook CD-ROM, Level 2
- The *American Republic Since 1877* Video Program
- American Music: Hits Through History
- American Music: Cultural Traditions

Biography

THE HISTORY CHANNEL®

The following videotape program is available from Glencoe as a supplement to Chapter 2:

- **Pocahontas: Her True Story** (ISBN 1-56-501555-X)

To order, call Glencoe at 1-800-334-7344. To find classroom resources to accompany many of these videos, check the following home pages:
A&E Television: www.aande.com
The History Channel: www.historychannel.com

SPANISH RESOURCES

The following Spanish language materials are available:

- Spanish Reading Essentials and Study Guide
- Spanish Guided Reading Activities
- Spanish Reteaching Activities
- Spanish Quizzes and Tests
- Spanish Vocabulary Activities
- Spanish Summaries
- The Declaration of Independence and United States Constitution Spanish Translation

HISTORY
Online

Use our Web site for additional resources. All essential content is covered in the Student Edition.

You and your students can visit tarvol2.glencoe.com, the Web site companion to the *American Republic Since 1877*. This innovative integration of electronic and print media offers your students a wealth of opportunities. The student text directs students to the Web site for the following options:

- Chapter Overviews
- Self-Check Quizzes
- Student Web Activities
- Textbook Updates

Answers to the student Web activities are provided for you in the **Web Activity Lesson Plans**. Additional Web resources and Interactive Tutor Puzzles are also available.

Chapter 2 Resources

SECTION RESOURCES

Daily Objectives	Reproducible Resources	Multimedia Resources
SECTION 1 **England's First Colonies** 1. Explain the religious and economic reasons why England became interested in America. 2. Describe the founding of Jamestown and explain why it succeeded.	Reproducible Lesson Plan 2–1 Daily Lecture and Discussion Notes 2–1 Guided Reading Activity 2–1* Section Quiz 2–1* Reading Essentials and Study Guide 2–1* Performance Assessment Activities and Rubrics American History in Graphic Novel	Daily Focus Skills Transparency 2–1 Interactive Tutor Self-Assessment CD-ROM ExamView® Pro Testmaker CD-ROM* Presentation Plus! CD-ROM TeacherWorks™ CD-ROM Audio Program
SECTION 2 **The New England Colonies** 1. Explain why the Pilgrims moved to America and why Plymouth Colony succeeded. 2. Discuss why King Philip's War began and describe its results.	Reproducible Lesson Plan 2–2 Daily Lecture and Discussion Notes 2–2 Guided Reading Activity 2–2* Section Quiz 2–2* Reading Essentials and Study Guide 2–2* Performance Assessment Activities and Rubrics	Daily Focus Skills Transparency 2–2 American Art & Architecture Interactive Tutor Self-Assessment CD-ROM ExamView® Pro Testmaker CD-ROM* Presentation Plus! CD-ROM TeacherWorks™ CD-ROM American Music: Cultural Traditions
SECTION 3 **The Middle and Southern Colonies** 1. Explain the effect of the English Civil War on the American colonies. 2. Summarize why the English colonies succeeded.	Reproducible Lesson Plan 2–3 Daily Lecture and Discussion Notes 2–3 Guided Reading Activity 2–3* Section Quiz 2–3* Reading Essentials and Study Guide 2–3* Performance Assessment Activities and Rubrics Interpreting Political Cartoons	Daily Focus Skills Transparency 2–3 American Art & Architecture Interactive Tutor Self-Assessment CD-ROM ExamView® Pro Testmaker CD-ROM* TeacherWorks™ CD-ROM Skillbuilder Interactive Workbook, Level 2 Audio Program American Music: Hits Through History
SECTION 4 **Colonial Ways of Life** 1. Describe the Southern economy and the plantation system. 2. List the geographical conditions that determined the New England Colonies' economy.	Reproducible Lesson Plan 2–4 Daily Lecture and Discussion Notes 2–4 Guided Reading Activity 2–4* Section Quiz 2–4* Reading Essentials and Study Guide 2–4* Performance Assessment Activities and Rubrics	Daily Focus Skills Transparency 2–4 Interactive Tutor Self-Assessment CD-ROM ExamView® Pro Testmaker CD-ROM* Presentation Plus! CD-ROM TeacherWorks™ CD-ROM American Music: Hits Through History
SECTION 5 **A Diverse Society** 1. Describe mercantilism's effect on the colonial attitude to England. 2. Outline patterns of immigration in colonial America.	Reproducible Lesson Plan 2–5 Daily Lecture and Discussion Notes 2–5 Guided Reading Activity 2–5* Section Quiz 2–5* Reading Essentials and Study Guide 2–5* Performance Assessment Activities and Rubrics	Daily Focus Skills Transparency 2–5 Interactive Tutor Self-Assessment CD-ROM ExamView® Pro Testmaker CD-ROM* Presentation Plus! CD-ROM TeacherWorks™ CD-ROM Audio Program

`0:00` OUT OF TIME?
Assign the Chapter 2 **Reading Essentials and Study Guide.**

*Also Available in Spanish

Printed Materials   Transparency   CD-ROM   DVD

Poster   Music Program   Audio Program

NATIONAL GEOGRAPHIC Teacher's Corner

INDEX TO NATIONAL GEOGRAPHIC MAGAZINE

The following articles relate to this chapter.

- "The Cajuns: Still Loving Life," October 1990
- "La Salle's Last Voyage," May 1997
- "The Millennium Series Exploration," February 1998
- "New Face for a Desert Mission," December 1995
- "Pizarro, Conqueror of the Inca," February 1992
- "Search for Columbus," January 1992
- "Search for Columbus's Lost Colony," November 1987

NATIONAL GEOGRAPHIC SOCIETY PRODUCTS

To order the following, call National Geographic at 1-800-368-2728:

- *Historical Atlas of the United States*
- *Millennium in Maps Series: Colonization and Trade in the Americas*
- *Millennium in Maps Series: Exploration*

NGS ONLINE

Access National Geographic's Web site for current events, atlas updates, activities, links, interactive features, and archives.
www.nationalgeographic.com

MEETING SPECIAL NEEDS

In addition to the Differentiated Instruction strategies found in each section, the following resources are also suitable for your special needs students:

- **ExamView® Pro Testmaker CD-ROM** allows teachers to tailor tests by reducing answer choices.
- The **Audio Program** includes the entire narrative of the student edition so that less-proficient readers can listen to the words as they read them.

KEY TO ABILITY LEVELS

Teaching strategies have been coded.

L1 BASIC activities for all students
L2 AVERAGE activities for average to above-average students
L3 CHALLENGING activities for above-average students
ELL ENGLISH LANGUAGE LEARNER activities

From the Classroom of...

Erin Barrett
Lexington High School
Lexington, MA

Enlightenment Thinkers

Ask students to brainstorm a list of grievances about the school. With the students, weed out any illegal issues or silly grievances. Combine similar complaints into one.

Then ask the class to agree on one issue that needs to be changed. Allow for ample time for them to debate and discuss together. Tell them that the issue they agree on must be within the control of the principal to change. Once they agree on an issue, work through the process of their choosing a representative to take the issue to the school principal.

Then create a scenario in which the student representatives present their issue calmly and thoroughly, but the principal disdainfully dismisses their complaints. Explain that their feelings of being unfairly dismissed stem from their living in a country that is built on Enlightenment principles. Discuss those principles.

ADDITIONAL RESOURCES FROM GLENCOE

- American Music: Cultural Traditions
- American Art & Architecture
- Outline Map Resource Book
- U.S. Desk Map
- Building Geography Skills for Life
- Inclusion for the High School Social Studies Classroom Strategies and Activities
- Teaching Strategies for the American History Classroom (Including Block Scheduling Pacing Guides)
- Dinah Zike's High School American History Reading and Study Skills Foldables

Block Schedule

Activities that are suited to use within the block scheduling framework are identified by:

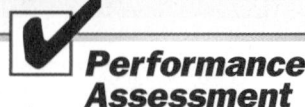
**Performance
Assessment**

Refer to Activity 2 in the
Performance Assessment
Activities and Rubrics
booklet.

Why It Matters Activity

Ask students to name some of the core
values that they believe all Americans
share and explain how they think
colonists shaped these values. Students
should evaluate their answers after they
have completed the chapter.

GLENCOE
TECHNOLOGY

**The *American Republic
Since 1877* Video Program**
To learn more about America from
1607 to 1763, have students view the
Chapter 2 video, "Early Explorers,"
from the *American Republic Since
1877* Video Program.

MindJogger Videoquiz
Use the **MindJogger Videoquiz** to
preview Chapter 2 content.

  Both programs available in
DVD

CHAPTER

2 The English Arrive in America
1607–1763

Why It Matters

*English settlers traveled to America seeking land and an escape from religious persecution. By
the early 1700s, 13 colonies had been founded along the Atlantic coast of North America. The
Southern Colonies grew labor-intensive cash crops on large plantations using indentured and
enslaved labor. Small farms and towns based on congregations developed in the Northern
Colonies. Small farms in the Middle Colonies produced grain and other cash crops. Cities based
on fishing, trade, and commerce also developed in the Northern and Middle Colonies.*

The Impact Today

Several developments of the early colonial period still affect the nation today.
• *Religious conflicts in Europe influenced the colonists' ideas of religious tolerance.*
• *The northern United States is still more urban than much of the South.*
• *The United States remains a nation made up of immigrants from many countries.*

The *American Republic Since 1877* Video
*The Chapter 2 video, "Early Explorers," chronicles the
voyages of some of the early European explorers.*

The Americas

— **1587**
• Roanoke Colony
is founded

— **1607**
• Jamestown Colony
is founded

— **1619**
• Virginia House of Burgesses
meets for first time

— **1630**
• Massachusetts Bay
Colony is established

— **1639**
• Fundamental Orders
of Connecticut
adopted

1580   *1620*   *1660*

World

1600 —
• Tokugawa period of feudal
rule begins in Japan

1642 —
• English Civil War begins

1660 —
• Charles II becomes
king of England

40

Reading Strategy ▶ **PURPOSE FOR READING**

Think/Write–Pair–Share Before reading the subject matter, engage students through discussion.
Give students the topic "Colonial Life in America." Ask them to think silently about this topic and
write down what they know or already have learned about what it was like to live in the American
colonies. After writing, students should pair with a partner and share ideas and thoughts. Conclude
with a class discussion. **L1**

📁 Refer to ***Inclusion for the High School Social Studies Classroom Strategies and Activities***
in the TCR.

This painting by Dutch artist Adam Willaerts is believed to depict the Plymouth Colony.

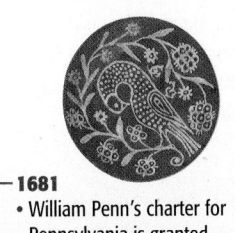

1681
• William Penn's charter for Pennsylvania is granted

1686
• Dominion of New England is established as royal colony

1692
• Salem witchcraft trials begin

1721
• Cotton Mather promotes inoculation

c. 1740
• Great Awakening religious revival peaks

1689
• English Bill of Rights issued

1725
• Russian czar Peter the Great dies

1742
• Handel's "Messiah" debuts in Dublin, Ireland

1700   *1740*

HISTORY Online

Chapter Overview
Visit the *American Republic Since 1877* Web site at tarvol2.glencoe.com and click on *Chapter Overviews— Chapter 2* to preview chapter information.

41

More About the Art

Ask: What seems to be the reaction of the colonists to the arrival of the sailing ships? *(They appear to be running toward the ships, indicating they were excited or anxious about their arrival.)*

TIME LINE
ACTIVITY

Have students select a world event that is shown on the time line and learn more about it. From their research have them write a brief description of the impact the event had on American history.

FOLDABLES
Study Organizer

Dinah Zike's Foldables are three-dimensional, interactive graphic organizers that help students practice basic writing skills, review key vocabulary terms, and identify main ideas. Have students complete the foldable activity in the *Dinah Zike's Reading and Study Skills Foldables* booklet.

GRAPHIC ORGANIZER ACTIVITY

Organizing Information Have students use a graphic organizer similar to the one at right to identify world events and movements that contributed to the development of the American colonies.

A. The Enlightenment
B. European population explosion (wheat boom)
C. Glorious Revolution
D. Great Awakening
E. Mercantilism
F. Religious intolerance

Contribution to Development of American Colonies

A B C D E F

41

1 FOCUS

Section Overview

This section explores the religious, economic, and political changes in England that caused England to establish colonies in North America.

BELLRINGER
Skillbuilder Activity

 Project transparency and have students answer the question.

Daily Focus Skills Transparency 2–1

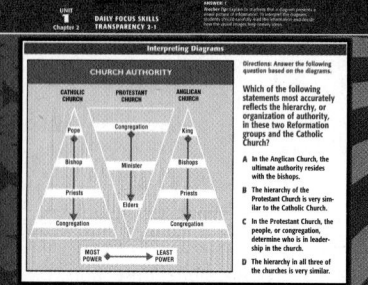

Reading Preview

Answers to Graphic: Jamestown's troubles included: (1) colonists who did not know how to hunt, fish, or farm, (2) gentlemen who refused to do manual labor, (3) a governing council that argued constantly and could not make decisions, (4) food shortages, and (5) weak leadership.

Preteaching Vocabulary
Have students classify each term into one of the following headings: Religious, Economic, or Political.

SECTION 1 England's First Colonies

Guide to Reading

Main Idea
Religious, economic, and political changes in England caused the English to begin establishing colonies along the eastern coast of North America.

Key Terms and Names
Puritan, enclosure movement, joint-stock company, privateer, John Smith, Chief Powhatan, burgesses, headright, Lord Baltimore, proprietary colony

Reading Strategy
Organizing As you read about the early troubles of the Jamestown colony, complete a graphic organizer similar to the one below by listing the problems that faced the colonists.

Jamestown's Troubles ◁

Reading Objectives
• **Explain** the religious and economic reasons why England became interested in America.
• **Describe** the founding of Jamestown and explain why it succeeded.

Section Theme
Geography and History England's rivalry with Spain encouraged Queen Elizabeth to seek bases for naval operations in North America.

Preview of Events

♦1500	♦1540	♦1580	♦1620

1497
John Cabot explores North America's coastline for England

1517
Protestant Reformation begins

1587
Roanoke colony is founded

1607
Jamestown is founded

1619
House of Burgesses meets for the first time

★ An American Story ★

Virginia House of Burgesses

On July 30, 1619, delegates gathered from the communities surrounding the main settlement of the English colony of Jamestown, Virginia. This meeting marked the first assembly of an elected legislature of representatives in the English colonies. The first session of the governing body, known as the House of Burgesses, met in the choir of the Jamestown church—"the most convenient place we could find to sit," said one representative.

Governor Sir George Yeardley had organized the idea of the legislative body soon after his arrival in April 1619. Here, he lays out the basic idea of the assembly, as specified in "A Brief Declaration of the Plantation of Virginia":

❝[So that the colonists] might have a hand in the governing of themselves; it was granted that a general assembly should be held yearly once, whereat were to be present the governor and council and two burgesses from each plantation freely to be elected by the inhabitants thereof.❞

—quoted in *Jamestown, 1544–1699*

England Takes Interest in America

In 1619 Jamestown was only 12 years old, although England had begun exploring the American continent more than a century earlier. In 1497 John Cabot had sailed to present-day Nova Scotia, hoping to discover a sea route through North America to China. Cabot and his crew of 18 traveled south along the coast without finding any trace of the fabled Northwest Passage.

SECTION RESOURCES

📂 Reproducible Masters
• Reproducible Lesson Plan 2–1
• Daily Lecture and Discussion Notes 2–1
• Guided Reading Activity 2–1
• Section Quiz 2–1
• Reading Essentials and Study Guide 2–1
• Performance Assessment Activities and Rubrics

🖺 Transparencies
• Daily Focus Skills Transparency 2–1

Multimedia
🔘 Interactive Tutor Self-Assessment CD-ROM
🔘 ExamView® Pro Testmaker CD-ROM
🔘 Presentation Plus! CD-ROM
🔘 TeacherWorks™ CD-ROM
🎧 Audio Program

For the next 80 years, the English made no effort to colonize America. The English government had little money, and Cabot had found no wealth to spur migration. Furthermore, the Spanish had claimed America, and in 1497 Spain and England were allies. During the late 1500s, however, religious, economic, and political changes led to the founding of the first English colonies in North America.

TURNING POINT

The Reformation At the time Cabot sailed to America, most of western Europe was Catholic and acknowledged the pope as the head of the Catholic Church. This unity began to break apart in 1517, when

a German monk named Martin Luther published an attack on the Church, accusing it of corruption.

Luther's attack marked the beginning of the **Protestant Reformation.** In 1520 Luther was expelled from the Catholic Church, but his ideas continued to spread across western Europe. Luther himself went on to found the German Protestant Church, now called the Lutheran Church.

In England the rebellion against Catholicism began in 1527, when Henry VIII asked the pope to annul his marriage to Catherine of Aragon. The pope resisted because he did not want to anger the king of Spain, Catherine's nephew. Infuriated, Henry broke with the Church, declared himself the head of England's

2 TEACH

Daily Lecture and Discussion Notes 2–1

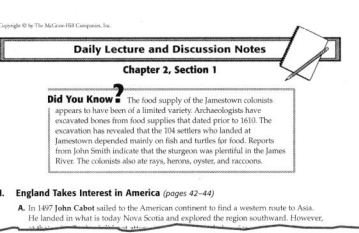

Copyright © by The McGraw-Hill Companies, Inc.

Daily Lecture and Discussion Notes

Chapter 2, Section 1

Did You Know ? The food supply of the Jamestown colonists appears to have been of a limited variety. Archaeologists have excavated bones from food supplies that dated prior to 1610. The excavation has revealed that the 104 settlers who landed at Jamestown depended mainly on fish and turtles for food. Reports from John Smith indicate that the sturgeon was plentiful in the James River. The colonists also ate rays, herons, oyster, and raccoons.

I. England Takes Interest in America *(pages 42–44)*

   A. In 1497 **John Cabot** sailed to the American continent to find a western route to Asia. He landed in what is today Nova Scotia and explored a region southward. However,

Creating a Chart Have students create a chart showing English explorations and settlements of North America between 1497 and 1682. The chart should include names, locations, and dates, along with the main purpose of the exploration or settlement. **L1** ELL

📁 Use the rubric for creating a map, display, or chart on pages 65–66 in the *Performance Assessment Activities and Rubrics.*

Geography *Skills*

Answers:
1. England
2. They concentrated their efforts in present-day Canada, near its eastern shores and down the St. Lawrence River and Great Lakes.

Geography Skills Practice

Ask: Which explorers used the Mississippi River to explore parts of North America? *(Marquette and Joliet and La Salle)* When did this exploration take place? *(Marquette and Joliet in 1673; La Salle in 1679–1682)*

NATIONAL GEOGRAPHIC **European Explorations and Settlements, 1497–1682**

Map legend:
- English exploration
- French exploration
- Spanish exploration
- Dutch exploration

AFRICA

NORTH AMERICA

Hudson 1610
Hudson 1609
Cabot 1497
Cartier 1534–42
Champlain 1603–15

Missouri R.
Hudson Bay
Quebec
Montreal
Marquette and Joliet 1673
Plymouth
Cabrillo 1542–43
Colorado R.
Coronado 1540–42
La Salle 1679–82
Jamestown
Santa Fe
De Soto 1539–42
Cabeza de Vaca 1528–36
Mississippi R.
Ohio R.
St. Augustine
Verrazano 1524
Rio Grande
Narváez 1528
Ponce De León 1513
Narváez 1527–28
ATLANTIC OCEAN
PACIFIC OCEAN
Tenochtitlán (Mexico City)
Cortés 1519
Gulf of Mexico
Caribbean Sea
EQUATOR
Balboa 1513
Amazon R.
SOUTH AMERICA
Pizarro 1531–33
Lima
Cuzco

0   1,000 miles
0   1,000 kilometers
Azimuthal Equidistant projection

180° 170°W 160°W 150°W 140°W 110°W 100°W 90°W 80°W 40°W 30°
80°N 70°N 60°N 50°N 40°N 30°N 20°N 10°N 10°S 20°S 30°S

N W E S

Geography *Skills*

1. **Interpreting Maps** According to the map, what nation first explored North America?
2. **Applying Geography Skills** In what areas did French explorers Champlain and Cartier concentrate their efforts?

Reading Strategy   READING THE TEXT

Activating Prior Knowledge Before students begin to take in any new knowledge, prepare them by bringing to mind what they already know. Use the key concepts and boldfaced terms in the text to frame general questions that encourage students to think about the topic and to share ideas. Then provide specific information that will enhance their understanding of the subject. **L1**

📁 Refer to *Inclusion for the High School Social Studies Classroom Strategies and Activities* in the TCR.

Guided Reading Activity 2-1

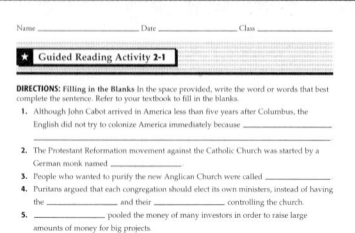

✔ Reading Check

Answer: They were willing to leave to purify their church of the influences of the king and to elect their own ministers.

Creating a Diagram Have students create a diagram for the English monarchy starting with Henry VIII and continuing through the reign of James I. The diagram should include information about spouses and the political motivation of the marriages. **L2**

📁 Use the rubric for creating a map, display, or chart on pages 65–66 in the *Performance Assessment Activities and Rubrics.*

Picturing History

Answer: Answers will vary, but students may mention that England was able to sail the seas and colonize unhindered by the Spanish.
Ask: Why do you think governments licensed privateers? *(Answers will vary. Most governments wanted to profit from what the privateers took and to weaken enemy governments.)*

---

church, and arranged his own divorce. The new church, the Anglican Church, was Protestant, although its organization and rituals were mostly Catholic.

Some English people supported the new church, but others did not. Puritans wanted to purify the Anglican Church of any remaining Catholic elements. They especially hated the fact that monarchs and their appointed bishops controlled the church. In their view, every congregation should elect its own ministers to run the church.

When James I became king in 1603, the Puritan cause was set back. He refused to tolerate Puritan reform ideas since they would lessen his power. As a result, many Puritans became more interested in leaving England.

ECONOMICS

Economic Changes in England A revolution in trade and agriculture was also changing English society at this time. Traditionally English nobles owned large estates and rented their land to tenant farmers. In the 1500s, however, a large market for wool developed, and landowners decided they could make more money by converting their estates into sheep farms. During the enclosure movement, they fenced in their lands and evicted thousands of tenant farmers. Continuing economic turmoil in England later encouraged many people to immigrate to America.

The wool market had another impact on American settlement. When wool prices fell, many wool merchants organized joint-stock companies to find new markets. A joint-stock company pooled money to support big projects. Many merchants could now better afford to trade with and colonize other parts of the world.

✔ Reading Check
Explaining Why were some Puritans willing to leave England for America?

England Returns to America

The quest for new markets convinced English merchants to resume the search for a northern water route to Asia. Between 1576 and 1578, Martin Frobisher made three trips to America to look for a northwest passage. He never found one, but his explorations were still significant. For the first time since Cabot's voyage in 1497, England had returned to America.

England's new interest in America contributed to its growing rivalry with Spain, which dated from the Reformation. The Reformation had changed Europe's balance of power. England had become the leading Protestant power, Spain the leading Catholic power.

44 CHAPTER 2 The English Arrive in America

Religion also brought England into a new alliance with the Dutch, who were then part of the Spanish empire. By the 1560s, most of the Dutch had become Protestants, and they rebelled when the Spanish government tried to suppress their faith.

To help the Dutch against Spain, Queen Elizabeth allowed attacks on Spanish ships by English privateers—privately owned ships licensed by the government to attack the merchant ships of other countries. English privateers found it difficult to strike at Spanish ships in the Caribbean because England had no bases there. This led Queen Elizabeth to seek outposts in America.

The first attempts at colonization were not promising. In 1578 and 1583, Sir Humphrey Gilbert, a well-known English soldier, tried to create a colony in America, but both attempts failed. After Gilbert was lost at sea, his half-brother, Walter Raleigh, sent two ships to scout the American coastline. Along the outer banks of what is today North Carolina, the ships found an island the Native Americans called **Roanoke.**

Picturing History

Warring Empires In 1588 the Spanish Armada set out with about 130 ships to settle scores with the English, Spain's rival in religion and empire. In the decisive battle, English fireships outmaneuvered the Spanish fleet, setting some of their galleons on fire. A "Protestant wind," as the English called it, did the rest. If Spain had won, Catholicism might have been reestablished in England. Why do you think the defeat of the Spanish Armada is important to American history?

DIFFERENTIATED INSTRUCTION

Reading Support Have students prepare a speech that a recruiter working in an English town could use to recruit women for life in one of the American colonies. The speech should incorporate details about life in America, including information about the geography and climate. **L2**

📁 Refer to *Inclusion for the High School Social Studies Classroom Strategies and Activities* in the TCR.

Impressed by the discovery, Queen Elizabeth knighted Raleigh, and he in turn named the land Virginia—in honor of Elizabeth, "the Virgin Queen."

Raleigh sent settlers to Roanoke Island twice, once in 1585 and again in 1587. The first group returned to England after a difficult winter. The fate of the second group is unknown. War between England and Spain kept supplies from reaching them on time. When English ships arrived in 1590, the colony had vanished, leaving only the word "Croatoan" carved on a post. The Croatoan were Native Americans who lived nearby. The fate of the "Lost Colony" remains a mystery.

Reading Check **Summarizing** Why did England want to establish outposts in America?

Jamestown Is Founded

In 1606 King James I granted the English investors of the Virginia Company a charter to plant colonies in Virginia. The investors sent three small ships and 144 men to Virginia on December 20, 1606. After a difficult trip, the ships arrived off the coast of North America. In May 1607, the colonists founded a settlement they named **Jamestown** in honor of their king.

Unfortunately, the colonists had chosen a site too close to the sea, on low, swampy land swarming with malaria-carrying mosquitoes. Poor location, however, was just the beginning of Jamestown's problems.

Early Troubles Most of Jamestown's colonists were townspeople who knew little about living in the woods. They could not make use of the area's abundant fish and game, nor could they raise livestock or cultivate crops. Furthermore, the upper-class "gentlemen" among them refused to do manual labor. To make matters worse, Jamestown's governing council argued constantly and could not make decisions. Lawlessness, sickness, and food shortages were the result. Although 190 new settlers arrived in 1608, only 53 colonists were alive by the end of the year. Everyone might have died, in fact, had it not been for Captain John Smith and Chief Powhatan.

Captain **John Smith,** a member of the colony's governing council, emerged as Jamestown's only strong leader. In late 1607, with winter approaching and the colony short of food, Smith explored the region around Jamestown and began trading goods for food with the local Native Americans—a group called the Powhatan Confederacy, led by **Chief Powhatan.** This trade helped the colony survive its first two winters.

Frustrated by the events in Jamestown, the Virginia Company appointed a new governor, Thomas West, Lord De La Warr, and gave him absolute authority. To entice settlers, the company offered free land to anyone who worked for the colony for seven years. The offer produced results, for in August 1609, 400 new settlers arrived in Jamestown.

The newcomers created a crisis in the colony. There was not enough food to feed everyone, nor could enough be grown before winter. Lord De La Warr had not accompanied the new settlers, and John Smith had suffered a gunpowder burn and returned to England. Without strong leadership, the situation in Jamestown rapidly deteriorated. As winter approached, the settlers began to steal food from the Native Americans. In response, warriors attacked the settlers.

The winter of 1609 to 1610 became known as the "starving time." The colonists at Jamestown ate "dogs, rats, snakes, toadstools, [and] horsehides," and a few even engaged in cannibalism, digging up corpses from their graves and eating them.

By the spring of 1610, only 60 settlers were still alive. They abandoned Jamestown and headed downriver. On the way, they met three English ships bringing supplies, 150 more settlers, and the colony's governor. Lord De La Warr convinced the settlers to stay. His deputy, Thomas Dale, then drafted a harsh code of laws. Settlers were organized into work gangs and required to work at least six hours per day. The death penalty was imposed for many crimes, including rape, adultery, desertion, mutiny, theft, lying, swearing, and derision of the Bible.

CHAPTER 2   The English Arrive in America   **45**

Reading Check

Answer: They wanted to give privateers a base of operations.

Writing a Letter Have students assume the role of a Puritan and write a letter to a friend or relative explaining his or her decision to move to America. **L1**

Use the rubric for a diary, short story, memorandum, or letter on pages 69–70 in the *Performance Assessment Activities and Rubrics.*

FYI

Among the artifacts found in Jamestown is a goffering iron. These tapered cylinders were used to crimp or frill the neck ruff that was fashionable for English gentlemen to wear. The gentleman used starch to add stiffness to the ruff. Then he heated the goffering iron by putting a smaller, hot iron inside the tube. The man shaped his ruff with the hot goffering iron.

Burgess In the 1600s, burgess was the term used by the English for a member of Parliament who represented a town or borough.

INTERDISCIPLINARY CONNECTIONS ACTIVITY

Visual Arts Have students create a set of fashion sketches for the typical wardrobe of the Puritans. The sketches should include an ensemble for a woman and one for a man. Encourage students to use library and Internet resources to learn more about clothing and fashion in colonial times. **L2**

Picturing History

Answer: Possible answer: It was easier to build and defend three sides than four.

Ask: The fort is constructed of what material? *(wood)*

3 ASSESS

Assign Section 1 Assessment as homework or as an in-class activity.

🔹 Have students use the **Interactive Tutor Self-Assessment CD-ROM.**

L1/ELL

Reading Essentials and Study Guide 2–1

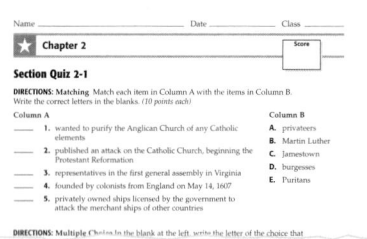

Name _____ Date _____ Class _____

Study Guide

Chapter 2, Section 1
For use with textbook pages 42-47

ENGLAND'S FIRST COLONIES

KEY TERMS AND NAMES

Puritans people who wanted to purify the Anglican Church of all Catholic elements *(page 44)*

enclosure movement English landowners fenced in their lands and evicted thousands of tenant farmers *(page 44)*

joint-stock company company that pooled the money of many investors for big projects *(page 44)*

privateer privately owned ships licensed by the government to attack merchant ships of other countries *(page 44)*

John Smith leader of the Jamestown colony *(page 45)*

Chief Powhatan Native American leader that lived in the area of Jamestown *(page 45)*

L2

Section Quiz 2–1

Name _____ Date _____ Class _____

⭐ **Chapter 2** Score ____

Section Quiz 2-1

DIRECTIONS: Matching Match each item in Column A with the items in Column B. Write the correct letters in the blanks. *(10 points each)*

Column A	Column B
___ 1. wanted to purify the Anglican Church of any Catholic elements	A. privateers
___ 2. published an attack on the Catholic Church, beginning the Protestant Reformation	B. Martin Luther
___ 3. representatives in the first general assembly in Virginia	C. Jamestown
___ 4. founded by colonists from England on May 14, 1607	D. burgesses
___ 5. privately owned ships licensed by the government to attack the merchant ships of other countries	E. Puritans

DIRECTIONS: Multiple Choice In the blank at the left, write the letter of the choice that

---

Picturing History

Critical Leadership Captain John Smith helped save early Jamestown by trading with local Native Americans. Sidney King painted its fort as it might have appeared around 1607. *Why do you think the fort was set up with only three sides?*

Dale's code imposed the discipline necessary to save the colony, but it still did not thrive. In 1614 Dale decided to permit private cultivation of land. Settlers could acquire 3 acres of land if they gave the colony a month of work and 2½ barrels of corn. Whatever else they produced, they could keep for themselves. According to one colonist, Ralph Hamor, the new system increased production:

> 66When our people were fed out of the common store and labored jointly in the manuring of the ground and planting corn, glad was the man that could slip from his labor . . . presuming that howsoever the harvest prospered, the general store must maintain them, by which means we reaped not so much corn for the labors of 30 men, as three men have done for themselves.99
>
> —quoted in *Colonial America*

Tobacco Saves the Colony Although the new policy increased productivity and ensured Jamestown's survival, the colony still had to find something it could produce that could be sold in England for a profit. The solution was a product King James had already condemned as a "vile weed [of] black stinking fumes [that were] baleful to the nose, harmful to the brain, and dangerous to the lungs"—tobacco.

Well before the founding of Jamestown, the Spanish had begun shipping tobacco from their Caribbean colonies to Europe. Smoking tobacco

became very popular in Europe in the early 1600s. The Jamestown settlers had tried growing tobacco, but the local variety was too bitter.

A colonist named **John Rolfe** continued to experiment, using tobacco seeds imported from Trinidad. Rolfe also developed a new method for curing tobacco, and in 1614 he shipped about 2,600 pounds to England. Rolfe's tobacco was inferior to Spanish tobacco, but it sold for a good price, and the settlers soon began planting large quantities of it.

GOVERNMENT

Luring Settlers In 1618 the new head of the Virginia Company, Edwin Sandys, introduced several major reforms to attract more settlers. The first reform gave the colony the right to elect its own lawmaking body. Virginia's first general assembly met in the Jamestown church on July 30, 1619. The new government included a governor, 6 councillors, and 20 representatives, 2 from each of the colony's 10 towns. The representatives were called burgesses, and the assembly was called the House of Burgesses.

The Virginia Company also introduced the system of headrights. New settlers who bought a share in the company or paid for their passage were granted 50 acres of land. They were granted 50 more acres for each family member over 15 years of age and for each servant they transported to Virginia.

In addition, the Virginia Company realized that it needed to provide more marriage opportunities for the many single men in the colony. In 1619 it sent about 90 women to Jamestown. A bachelor could purchase a bride for 120 pounds of tobacco, roughly what it cost the company to bring each woman to America.

The same year the women arrived, the first Africans were brought to Virginia as well. A Dutch slave ship stopped to trade for supplies, and the Jamestown settlers purchased 20 African men as "Christian servants," not slaves. The Africans had been baptized, and at that time English law said that Christians could not be enslaved.

Virginia Becomes a Royal Colony The policies introduced by the Virginia Company in 1619 triggered a wave of new immigration to the colony. By 1622 more than 4,500 settlers had arrived in Virginia. The dramatic increase in colonists alarmed the Native Americans, who attacked Jamestown in March 1622. They burned homes, destroyed food supplies, and killed nearly 350 settlers.

The settlers eventually put an end to the uprising, but the colony was devastated. After blaming the

46 CHAPTER 2   The English Arrive in America

CRITICAL THINKING ACTIVITY

Evaluating Decisions Have students write a report evaluating the decisions that were made in the settlement of Jamestown. The report should be addressed to the Virginia Company and should include a list of suggestions for future attempts to set up a colony. Suggestions for duplicating successes and avoiding mistakes should be included on the list. **L2**

Virginia Company for the colony's high death rate, an English court revoked the company's charter. Virginia became a royal colony run by a governor who was appointed by the king.

☑ **Reading Check** **Describing** How did Captain John Smith and the Powhatan Confederacy save Jamestown?

Maryland Is Founded

The next colony in America was founded not by another joint-stock company but by one man, George Calvert, also known as **Lord Baltimore.** Lord Baltimore had been a member of the English Parliament until he converted to Catholicism. This decision ruined his career, but he remained a good friend of King James and his son, Charles.

Catholics were persecuted in England for much the same reason as Puritans. Catholics did not accept the king as head of the Church, nor did they accept the authority of Anglican bishops and priests. As a result, they were viewed as potential traitors who might help Catholic countries overthrow the English king. Consequently, they were forbidden to practice law or teach school. They were also fined for not attending Anglican services.

Seeing the persecution of his fellow Catholics, Lord Baltimore decided to found a colony in America where Catholics could practice their religion freely. In 1632 King Charles granted him a large area of land northeast of Virginia. Baltimore named the new colony Maryland, to honor either the king's wife, Queen Henrietta Maria, or the Virgin Mary.

Lord Baltimore owned Maryland, making it England's first proprietary colony. The proprietor, or

Fact | Fiction | Folklore

English Flag This flag flew over the English settlements throughout the colonial period. First used in 1606, the flag displays the red cross of England (cross of St. George) superimposed on the white cross of Scotland (cross of St. Andrew), on the blue background field of Scotland. This "Union Flag," as it was called, remained in use until January 1, 1801.

owner, could govern the colony any way that he wanted. He could appoint government officials, coin money, impose taxes, establish courts, regulate trade, grant lands, create towns, and raise an army.

Lord Baltimore died shortly before settlers arrived in his colony. His son Cecil became the new Lord Baltimore. In 1634, 20 gentlemen, mostly Catholic, and 200 servants and artisans, mostly Protestant, arrived in Maryland. Despite Baltimore's hope that Maryland would become a Catholic refuge, Protestants remained in the majority. The government officials and most of the large estate owners were Catholic, however. To reduce friction between the two groups, Maryland passed the Toleration Act in 1649, granting religious toleration to all Christians in the colony.

☑ **Reading Check** **Analyzing** Why was Maryland founded?

HISTORY Online **Study Central™** To review this section, go to tarvol2.glencoe.com and click on **Study Central™**.

CHAPTER 2
Section 1, 42–47

☑ **Reading Check**

Answer: They established trade between the colony and the Native Americans that supplied the food the colonists needed to survive.

Fact | Fiction | Folklore

Saint George is the patron saint of England. It is believed that George was a Roman citizen who was beheaded by Diocletian for protesting the emperor's persecution of Christians. Saint Andrew is the patron saint of Scotland. He was one of Jesus's original followers and Christian tradition says he was crucified by the Romans.

Reteach
Have students describe the difficulties that colonists faced when they arrived in North America.

Enrich
Have students use library and Internet resources to research one of the colonies mentioned in this section and write a report about colonial life.

☑ **Reading Check**

Answer: to allow Catholics to freely practice their religion

Study Central™ provides summaries, interactive games, and online graphic organizers to help students review section content.

SECTION **1** ASSESSMENT

Checking for Understanding
1. **Define:** Puritan, enclosure movement, joint-stock company, privateer, burgesses, headright, proprietary colony.
2. **Identify:** John Smith, Chief Powhatan, Lord Baltimore.
3. **Explain** how tobacco saved the Jamestown colony.

Reviewing Themes
4. **Geography and History** How did the enclosure movement change English society?

Critical Thinking
5. **Interpreting** What caused friction in the Maryland colony?
6. **Categorizing** Use a graphic organizer similar to the one below to list three ways the Virginia Company tried to attract settlers to the Jamestown colony.

Ways to Attract Settlers

Analyzing Visuals
7. **Examining Paintings** Study the painting of the conflict between the British navy and the Spanish Armada on pages 44 and 45. How has the artist shown the importance of the conflict depicted?

Writing About History
8. **Descriptive Writing** Imagine you are a colonist at Jamestown. Write a journal entry describing the first winter in the colony. Describe the weather as well as the problems that colonists faced during that time.

CHAPTER 2 The English Arrive in America **47**

SECTION **1** ASSESSMENT ANSWERS

1. Terms are in blue.
2. John Smith *(p. 45)*, Chief Powhatan *(p. 45)*, Lord Baltimore *(p. 47)*
3. Tobacco gave the colonists something to trade with England.
4. It evicted thousands of farmers from the land.
5. Lord Baltimore, the government

officials, and the large estate owners were Catholic, but most of the settlers were Protestant.
6. They gave the colony the right to elect its own general assembly to propose laws; they introduced the system of headrights; and they provided opportunities for marriage.

7. The Spanish ships are huge. The English victory is thus stunning.
8. Journal entries should discuss the extreme hardships suffered that winter.

4 CLOSE

Ask students to explain the roles religion and economics played in the colonists' decisions to move to America.

1 FOCUS

Section Overview
This section explores the colonies founded in New England by English Puritans.

BELLRINGER
Skillbuilder Activity

Project transparency and have students answer the question.

Daily Focus Skills Transparency 2–2

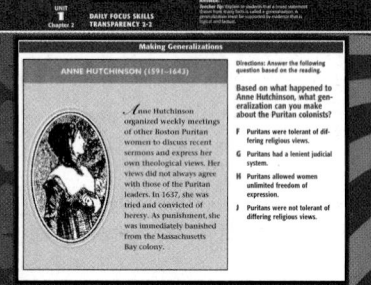

Reading Preview

Answers to Graphic: The main causes of King Philip's War were: (1) the decline in fur trade minimized need for settlers to get along with Native Americans, (2) the colonial government's demand that Native Americans follow English law and customs threatened the Native American way of life, (3) the arrest and execution of three Wampanoag on murder charges.

Preteaching Vocabulary
Have students select two of the words that are in some way related. Have them use the words in a sentence to explain the relationship.

SECTION 2 The New England Colonies

Guide to Reading

Main Idea
In the 1600s, English Puritans fleeing religious persecution and economic difficulties founded several colonies in New England.

Key Terms and Names
Separatist, Pilgrim, Squanto, Great Migration, heretic, Anne Hutchinson

Reading Strategy
Organizing As you read about the founding of colonies in New England, complete a graphic organizer similar to the one below listing the reasons for King Philip's War.

Causes of King Philip's War

Reading Objectives
- **Explain** why the Pilgrims moved to America and why Plymouth Colony succeeded.
- **Discuss** why King Philip's War began and describe its results.

Section Theme
Culture and Traditions Puritan beliefs and organization provided the basis for some of the nation's oldest traditions of government and community.

Preview of Events

✦1620	✦1640	✦1660	✦1680

1620	1630	1636	1639	1675
Pilgrims arrive at Plymouth	Massachusetts Bay Colony established	Roger Williams founds Providence	Fundamental Orders of Connecticut adopted	King Philip's War

✦ An American Story ✦

The Mayflower, anchored in Plymouth harbor

On a bleak November day in 1620, a tiny three-masted English ship named the *Mayflower* dropped anchor off the coast of Cape Cod. The eyes of all those aboard focused on the low strip of land before them. They were not where they were supposed to be. They had a patent for land in Virginia, but the land bobbing on the horizon was clearly not Virginia. If they went ashore, they would be on land to which they had no title, in a territory where no English government existed.

On November 11, 1620, 41 adult men met in the ship's cabin to sign a document later known as the Mayflower Compact. In it they declared their intention to create a government and obey its laws. They agreed to "solemnly and mutually in the presence of God and one of another, covenant and combine ourselves together in a civil body politic, for our better ordering and preservation," and to "frame such just and equal laws, ordinances, acts, constitutions and officers, from time to time, as shall be thought most meet and convenient for the general good of the Colony, unto which we promise all due submission and obedience."

—adapted from *Basic Documents in American History*

The Pilgrims Found Plymouth Colony

The events that led to the arrival of the *Mayflower* off the New England coast began several years earlier in England. A group of Puritans, called Separatists, began separating from the Anglican Church to form their own congregations. King James I responded

48 CHAPTER 2 The English Arrive in America

SECTION RESOURCES

📁 **Reproducible Masters**
- Reproducible Lesson Plan 2–2
- Daily Lecture and Discussion Notes 2–2
- Guided Reading Activity 2–2
- Section Quiz 2–2
- Reading Essentials and Study Guide 2–2

🖥 **Transparencies**
- Daily Focus Skills Transparency 2–2

- American Art & Architecture

Multimedia
- 💿 Interactive Tutor Self-Assessment CD-ROM
- 💿 ExamView® Pro Testmaker CD-ROM
- 💿 Presentation Plus! CD-ROM
- 💿 TeacherWorks™ CD-ROM
- 🎧 Audio Program
- 🎵 American Music: Cultural Traditions

to this challenge to his authority as head of the Church with severe persecution, including imprisonment of Separatist leaders. To escape this persecution, a group of Separatists fled to Holland in 1608. These Separatists, who came to be known as the Pilgrims, found it hard to live in Holland. They also worried that their children were losing their English heritage. In early 1617, the congregation decided to leave Holland and immigrate to America.

Before crossing the Atlantic, the Pilgrims returned to England, where they joined another group of Puritans aboard the *Mayflower.* On September 16, 1620, 102 passengers set off for Virginia. The trip took 65 days. Most of the food ran out, many passengers became ill, and one died. Making matters worse, a severe storm blew the small ship far north of its course. Finally, in November, the Pilgrims sighted Cape Cod and tried to follow the coastline south. After encountering rough weather, they turned back.

Although they were not where they expected, the Pilgrims were not completely lost. In 1614 the Virginia Company had hired Captain John Smith to explore the region. The Pilgrims had a copy of John Smith's "Map of New England," and they decided to settle in the area labeled "Plymouth."

According to William Bradford, one of the colony's leaders, the Pilgrims went to work building homes as soon as they arrived at Plymouth. After constructing a "common house," the settlers built modest homes of frame construction and thatched roofs. Soon, however, a plague swept through the colony, sparing only 50 settlers.

Even the surviving Pilgrims might have perished were it not for the help of **Squanto,** a Native American man who taught them about their new environment. Bradford wrote that Squanto "directed them how to set their corn, where to take fish and [how] to procure other commodities." Squanto also helped the Pilgrims negotiate a peace treaty with the Wampanoag people who lived nearby. The following autumn, the Pilgrims joined with the Wampanoag in a three-day festival to celebrate the harvest and give thanks to God for their good fortune. This celebration later became the basis for the Thanksgiving holiday.

Reading Check **Summarizing** How did Squanto help the Pilgrims?

The Puritans Found Massachusetts

Less than five years after the Pilgrims left England, King Charles took the throne, and persecution of the Puritans mounted. At the same time, a depression struck England's wool industry. The depression caused high unemployment, particularly in the southeastern counties where large numbers of Puritans lived.

As he watched his fellow Puritans suffering both religious and economic hardships, **John Winthrop,** an attorney, grew concerned. Winthrop and several other wealthy Puritans were stockholders in the Massachusetts Bay Company. The company had already received a charter from King Charles to create a colony in New England. Convinced that Puritans no longer had a future in England, Winthrop decided to change what had been a business investment into something more: a refuge for Puritans in America.

Other Puritans embraced the idea, and in March 1630, 11 ships carrying about 900 settlers set sail. En route, in a sermon titled "A Model of Christian Charity," John Winthrop boasted that the new colony would be an example to the world: "The Lord will make our name a praise and glory. . . . We shall be like a City upon a Hill; the eyes of all people are on us."

John Winthrop

History *Through Art*

Solemn Signing Tompkins Matteson painted his vision of the Mayflower Compact signing. By signing this document, the Pilgrims wanted to set up a legal basis for their colony. How did the artist try to suggest the seriousness of the occasion? 📖 *(See page 943 for an excerpt from the Mayflower Compact.)*

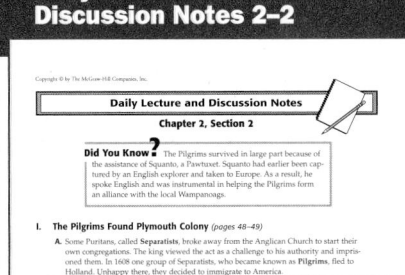

Daily Lecture and Discussion Notes 2–2

2 TEACH

Daily Lecture and Discussion Notes 2–2

Copyright © by The McGraw-Hill Companies, Inc.

Daily Lecture and Discussion Notes

Chapter 2, Section 2

Did You Know? The Pilgrims survived in large part because of the assistance of Squanto, a Pawtuxet. Squanto had earlier been captured by an English explorer and taken to Europe. As a result, he spoke English and was instrumental in helping the Pilgrims form an alliance with the local Wampanoags.

I. The Pilgrims Found Plymouth Colony *(pages 48–49)*

    A. Some Puritans, called Separatists, broke away from the Anglican Church to start their own congregations. The king viewed the act as a challenge to his authority and imprisoned them. In 1608 one group of Separatists, who became known as Pilgrims, fled to Holland. Unhappy there, they decided to immigrate to America.

Creating a Thematic Map Have students use a blank map showing the outline of the New England states to locate and label the colonies presented in this section. **L1**

📁 Use the rubric for creating a map, display, or chart on pages 65–66 in the *Performance Assessment Activities and Rubrics.*

✔Reading Check

Answer: Squanto helped the Pilgrims with farming, fishing, hunting, and gathering. He also helped them negotiate peace with the Wampanoag.

🎨 History *Through Art*

Answer: dark clothing and surroundings except for the Compact; faces are serious and intent on the speaker
Ask: How does the portrait of John Winthrop indicate his status in the community? *(possible answer: His more formal dress and well groomed hair and beard show that he is wealthy.)*

Reading Strategy   READING THE TEXT

Summarizing Information Summarizing information teaches students to reduce information to the main points and to rethink what they have read. Have students read the paragraphs under "The Puritans Found Massachusetts" and then summarize what they have read. Remind them that they should include only the main ideas in a summary. Tell students that to determine whether they have included all the main ideas in the summary, they should ask themselves: Can my summary be easily understood by someone who has not read the selection? **L1**

📁 Refer to *Inclusion for the High School Social Studies Classroom Strategies and Activities* in the TCR.

L1/ELL
Guided Reading Activity 2-2

[Worksheet: Guided Reading Activity 2-2]

Name _____ Date _____ Class _____

★ **Guided Reading Activity 2-2**

DIRECTIONS: Recalling Facts Read the section and answer the questions below. Refer to your textbook to write the answers.

1. Who were the Separatists? _____
2. What was one reason the Separatists did not like living in Holland? _____
3. Using John Smith's "Map of New England," where did the Pilgrims finally land? _____
4. Who helped the Pilgrims survive at Plymouth, and what did he teach them? _____
5. Who increased the persecution of the Puritans in England in 1625? _____

Profiles IN HISTORY

Have students use library and Internet resources to learn more about Anne Bradstreet and her poetry. Then have them compose a short poem describing some aspect of their own lives.

you don't say...

Women in the Colonies Husbands in colonial society controlled the property of their wives. If a woman worked for money she was either single or a widow carrying on her husband's business.

✓ Reading Check

Answer: His Puritan beliefs eventually led to the same sort of religious intolerance by the government of Massachusetts that had caused the Puritans to found the colony in North America.

History *and the* Humanities

🎵 American Music: Cultural Traditions: "Ainsworth Psalm 100," "Standish"

🪑 American Art & Architecture: Brewster Chair

Rapid Growth By the end of the year, 17 ships had brought another 1,000 settlers, and Massachusetts rapidly expanded. Several towns were founded, including Boston, which became the colony's capital. As conditions in England worsened, large numbers of people began to leave the country in what was later called the **Great Migration.** By 1643 an estimated 20,000 settlers had arrived in New England.

GOVERNMENT

Church and State The charter of the Massachusetts Bay Company defined the colony's government. People who owned stock in the company were called "freemen." All of the freemen together were called the **General Court.** The General Court was to make the laws and elect the governor.

John Winthrop had been chosen as governor. He ignored the charter, however, and told the settlers that only he and his assistants could make laws for the colony. No one knew that this violated the charter, because Winthrop kept it locked in a chest.

Winthrop stayed in power for four years, but the settlers eventually grew frustrated with how little voice they had in governing. In 1634 each town sent two representatives to Boston and demanded to see the charter. Winthrop had no basis to refuse the request. As they read the charter, the representatives realized that the General Court, not the governor, was supposed to make the laws. When the General Court assembled in May 1634, they reorganized the government. The General Court became a representative assembly, with the freemen from each town electing up to three deputies to send to the Court each year.

As for government's role in religion, John Winthrop believed that each congregation should control its own church but that the government should support religion. Laws were passed requiring everyone to attend church. The government also collected taxes to support the church and regulated moral behavior. Gambling, blasphemy, adultery, and drunkenness were all illegal and punished severely.

The government also discouraged new and different religious ideas. Heretics—people whose religious beliefs differ from the majority—were considered a

Profiles IN HISTORY

Anne Bradstreet
c. 1612–1672

Anne Dudley was born about 1612 in Northampton, England. At the age of 16 she married Simon Bradstreet, and two years later she accompanied her husband to America. The Bradstreets, traveling with John Winthrop's party, were among the first settlers of the Massachusetts Bay Colony.

In America Anne Bradstreet faced the difficult task of building a home in the wilderness. Despite the hard work of raising eight children, she found time to write poetry. In 1650 the first edition of her poetry was published in England as *The Tenth Muse Lately Sprung Up in America.* Bradstreet had not anticipated this recognition. Her brother-in-law had secretly taken a copy of her manuscript to a London publisher.

Anne Bradstreet was a devoted supporter of her husband, who became a leading political figure in Massachusetts, serving two terms as governor. During the period of the Dominion of New England, he spoke out against the harsh rule of Edmund Andros. In a poem, *To My Dear Loving Husband,* published after her death, Anne described their relationship:

If ever two were one, then surely we.
If ever man were loved by wife, then thee;
If ever wife was happy in a man,
Compare with me ye women if you can.

threat to the community. Settlers who publicly uttered ideas contrary to accepted Puritan beliefs could be charged with heresy and banished.

Puritan efforts to suppress other religious beliefs inevitably sparked conflict. Eventually, just as Anglican intolerance of the Puritans had led to the founding of Massachusetts, Puritan intolerance led to the founding of other colonies in New England.

✓ Reading Check
Synthesizing How did John Winthrop's beliefs affect the government of Massachusetts?

The Founding of Rhode Island

In 1631 a young minister named **Roger Williams** arrived in Massachusetts. Williams was a strict Separatist who believed Puritans corrupted themselves by staying part of the Anglican Church. His continuing condemnation of the Puritan churches angered many people, and for a time he moved to Plymouth Colony. There Williams declared that the land belonged to the Native Americans and that the king had no right to give it away.

Williams's ideas greatly alarmed John Winthrop. If the king heard that Puritan colonists were denying his authority, he might revoke Massachusetts's charter and impose a royal government. If that happened, the Puritans would lose control of their churches.

DIFFERENTIATED INSTRUCTION

Logical/Mathematical Have students use a map to locate two points: the original destination of the *Mayflower* and the area where the *Mayflower* actually docked. Students should identify the latitude and longitude of these two locations, and calculate the approximate distance between the two. **L1** ELL

📁 Refer to *Inclusion for the High School Social Studies Classroom Strategies and Activities* in the TCR.

When Williams returned to Massachusetts in 1633, he continued to challenge Puritan authority. In October 1635, the General Court ordered him to leave the colony. With five friends, Williams headed south to establish his own colony. He purchased land from the Narragansett people and founded the town of Providence in 1636. In Providence, the government had no authority in religious matters. Different religious beliefs were tolerated rather than suppressed.

In the midst of the uproar over Roger Williams, a devout Puritan named **Anne Hutchinson** began causing a stir in Boston. Hutchinson held prayer meetings in her home to discuss sermons and compare ministers. She soon began claiming to know which ministers had salvation from God and which did not. Puritan leaders understood that Hutchinson was attacking the authority of ministers. In late 1637, the General Court charged her with heresy.

When questioned, Hutchinson vigorously defended herself. Then she made a mistake. When asked how God let her know "which was the clear [correct] ministry and which the wrong," she explained that God spoke to her directly. In so doing, Hutchinson flatly contradicted the Puritan belief that God spoke only through the Bible. The General Court immediately banished her for heresy. Hutchinson and a few followers headed south and founded the town of Portsmouth.

Over the next few years, Massachusetts banished other dissenting Puritans. They too headed south and founded Newport in 1639 and Warwick in 1643. In 1644 these two towns joined Portsmouth and Providence to become the colony of Rhode Island and Providence Plantations. Religious freedom was a key part of the colony's charter.

✓ **Reading Check** **Explaining** Why were Roger Williams and Anne Hutchinson banished from Massachusetts?

The River Towns of Connecticut

In 1636 the Reverend Thomas Hooker asked the General Court of Massachusetts for permission to move his entire congregation to the Connecticut River valley. His congregation wanted to relocate because they did not have enough land to raise cattle. Hooker, moreover, was frustrated by the Massachusetts political system. He thought that everyone should be allowed to vote, not just church members. Hooker argued that "the foundation of authority is laid in the consent of the governed."

The General Court granted Hooker's request. A few months later, some 100 settlers headed to the

Connecticut River and founded the town of Hartford. Hooker's congregation joined two others in the area that had established Windsor and Wethersfield. In 1637 the towns joined together to create their own General Court. Two years later, they adopted the **Fundamental Orders of Connecticut,** a constitution which allowed all adult men, not just church members, to vote and serve in government. 📖 *(See page 944 for more on the Fundamental Orders of Connecticut.)*

East of the Connecticut River lived the **Pequot** people. At first the Pequot chief Sassacus, who ruled both the Pequot and the Mohegan people, tolerated the English settlers because he needed allies against the Narraganset people in Rhode Island. In 1636, however, two Massachusetts traders were killed in Pequot territory. When Massachusetts sent troops to punish the Pequot, war erupted, and the Pequot began raiding towns along the Connecticut River.

In April 1637, the Pequot surprised the town of Wethersfield and killed nine people. Furious, the Connecticut settlers assembled an army under the command of Captain John Mason. Seizing the opportunity to free themselves, the Mohegan rebelled against the Pequot and sent warriors to

NATIONAL GEOGRAPHIC New England Colonies, c. 1700

NEW FRANCE

St. Lawrence R.

MAINE (Part of MASS.)

Lake Champlain

N.H.

Portsmouth, 1623

N.Y.

Salem, 1626

MASS.

Massachusetts Bay

Boston, 1630

Plymouth, 1620

Hartford, 1636

Providence, 1636

New Haven, 1638

CONN.

R.I.

Long Island

ATLANTIC OCEAN

N.J.

45°N

40°N

75°W   70°W

0   100 miles
0   100 kilometers
Albers Conic Equal-Area projection

 Geography *Skills*

1. **Interpreting Maps** How long after the establishment of Plymouth Colony was Boston founded?
2. **Applying Geography Skills** Which English settlement was not located directly on the coast?

✓ **Reading Check**

Answer: Williams was banished for trying to completely separate the Puritans from the Anglican Church. Hutchinson was banished for the heresy of saying that God spoke directly to her. The Puritans believed that God spoke only through the Bible.

Geography *Skills*

Answers:
1. 10 years
2. Hartford

Geography Skills Practice
Ask: What body of water was Hartford built on? *(Connecticut River)* Why was it important to be close to a body of water? *(for drinking water and as a source of transportation)*

3 ASSESS

Assign Section 2 Assessment as homework or as an in-class activity.

🔘 Have students use the **Interactive Tutor Self-Assessment CD-ROM.**

L1/ELL

Reading Essentials and Study Guide 2–2

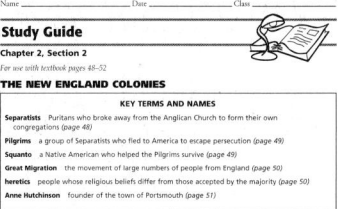

Name _____ Date _____ Class _____

Study Guide

Chapter 2, Section 2
For use with textbook pages 48–52

THE NEW ENGLAND COLONIES

KEY TERMS AND NAMES

Separatists Puritans who broke away from the Anglican Church to form their own congregations (page 48)

Pilgrims a group of Separatists who fled to America to escape persecution (page 49)

Squanto a Native American who helped the Pilgrims survive (page 49)

Great Migration the movement of large numbers of people from England (page 50)

heretics people whose religious beliefs differ from those accepted by the majority (page 50)

Anne Hutchinson founder of the town of Portsmouth (page 51)

INTERDISCIPLINARY CONNECTIONS ACTIVITY

Science Invite someone from a historical society or museum to visit your class to talk about the importance of preserving historical documents. Ask the speaker to give a short history on how documents have been preserved in the past and to explain the scientific innovations that are currently used in preservation. Encourage students to ask questions at the end of the presentation to learn more about the role that science plays in preserving important historical documents. **L2**

L2

Section Quiz 2-2

✓ Reading Check

Answer: All men, not just church members, were able to vote and serve in the government.

✓ Reading Check

Answer: New Hampshire and Maine

Reteach

Ask students to name the historical figures mentioned in this section and explain the role each played in colonizing America.

Enrich

Have students write a one-page description of what life in the colonies would have been like if the settlers and Native Americans had cooperated.

✓ Reading Check

Answer: By the war's end, there were few Native Americans left in New England.

Study Central™ provides summaries, interactive games, and online graphic organizers to help students review section content.

4 CLOSE

Ask students to discuss the challenges the New England colonies faced.

52

---

fight alongside Mason's troops. The Pequots' bitter rivals, the Narraganset, also joined in the attack.

Mason took his force up the coast by ship and attacked the Pequot from the east. He and his Native American allies surrounded the main Pequot fort near Mystic Harbor and set it on fire. When the Pequot tried to surrender, the Connecticut troops opened fire, killing about 400 people, including women and children. The Connecticut General Court then put a bounty on the surviving Pequot. Many who were captured or surrendered were sold into slavery, while others were given to the Narraganset and Mohegan as war prizes. The Pequot were treated so poorly by the other Native Americans that in 1655, the Connecticut government resettled the survivors in two villages near the Mystic River.

✓ Reading Check **Contrasting** How did Connecticut's constitution differ from that of Massachusetts?

New Hampshire and Maine

Not all of the settlers who left Massachusetts headed for Rhode Island or Connecticut. Although Anne Hutchinson had moved south, 36 of her followers headed north and founded the town of Exeter. During the 1640s, several other towns were also established north of Massachusetts. Many of the settlers in these towns were fishers and fur traders.

Much of the territory north of Massachusetts had been granted to two men, Sir Fernando Gorges and Captain John Mason. The pair split their holdings, with Mason taking the southern part and naming it New Hampshire, and Gorges taking the territory in the north, which he called Maine. The government of Massachusetts, however, challenged the claims of both men. In 1677 an English court ruled against Massachusetts. Two years later, New Hampshire became a royal colony. Meanwhile, Massachusetts bought Maine from Gorges's heirs, and Maine remained part of Massachusetts until 1820.

✓ Reading Check **Identifying** What two colonies were established north of Massachusetts?

King Philip's War

For almost 40 years after the Pequot War, the settlers and Native Americans of New England had good relations. The fur trade helped keep the peace because it enabled Native Americans to acquire tools, guns, and other European goods, while the settlers acquired furs. By the 1670s, however, the fur trade was in decline, and colonial governments were demanding that Native Americans follow English laws and customs. Native Americans felt that the English were trying to destroy their way of life.

Tensions peaked in 1675 when Plymouth Colony arrested, tried, and executed three Wampanoag for a murder. This touched off what came to be called **King Philip's War,** named after the Wampanoag leader Metacomet, whom the settlers called King Philip. After the colonists won the war in 1678, very few Native Americans were left in New England. New England now belonged to the English settlers.

✓ Reading Check **Analyzing** In what way was King Philip's War a turning point for Native Americans?

HISTORY Online **Study Central™** To review this section, go to **tarvol2.glencoe.com** and click on **Study Central™**.

SECTION 2 ASSESSMENT

Checking for Understanding

1. **Define:** Separatist, Pilgrim, heretic.
2. **Identify:** Squanto, Great Migration, Anne Hutchinson.
3. **Explain** why the Pilgrims and the Puritans migrated to America.

Reviewing Themes

4. **Culture and Traditions** How did Thomas Hooker's beliefs promote the idea of separation of church and state?

Critical Thinking

5. **Comparing** In what ways were the causes and effects of the Pequot War and King Philip's War similar?
6. **Categorizing** Use a graphic organizer similar to the one below to list the New England colonies and the reasons for their founding.

Colony	Reasons Founded

Analyzing Visuals

7. **Examining Art** Study the painting of the signing of the Mayflower Compact on page 49. Do you think the artist's depiction of the people and the ship is accurate, considering that they have just completed a long journey? Why or why not?

Writing About History

8. **Descriptive Writing** Imagine you are a Pilgrim in the Plymouth colony. Write a letter to your friends in Europe describing your first few weeks in the new land.

SECTION 2 ASSESSMENT ANSWERS

1. Terms are in blue.
2. Squanto (p. 49), Great Migration (p. 50), Anne Hutchinson (p. 51)
3. They sought religious freedom.
4. He thought that church membership was not necessary to participate in government.
5. Both started because of supposed murders by Native Americans; both resulted in a decline in Native American population.
6. Massachusetts: to escape Anglican intolerance; Rhode Island: to escape Puritan intolerance; Connecticut: to obtain more land and establish a political system separating church and state; New Hampshire and Maine: Gorges and Mason split their grants
7. Answers will vary, but should discuss how a long voyage would affect passengers.
8. Students' letters will vary. The letters should include plausible details about colonial life.

The Middle and Southern Colonies

Guide to Reading

Main Idea
After the English Civil War, economic, strategic, and religious factors led to the founding of seven new English colonies along the Atlantic seaboard.

Key Terms and Names
English Civil War, William Penn, pacifism, James Oglethorpe, debtor

Reading Objectives
Organizing As you read about the growth of the Middle and Southern Colonies, complete a graphic organizer listing ways that colonies attracted settlers.

Ways to Attract Settlers

Reading Objectives
• **Explain** the effect of the English Civil War on the American colonies.
• **Summarize** why the English colonies succeeded.

Section Theme
Global Connections The end of the English Civil War marked a renewal of British colonization in America.

Preview of Events

| ◆1640 | ◆1670 | ◆1700 | ◆1730 |

1642
English Civil War begins

1660
English monarchy restored

1664
English capture New Amsterdam

1681
William Penn receives charter for Pennsylvania

1733
First English settlers arrive in Georgia

1 FOCUS

Section Overview
This section describes the factors that led to the founding of seven new English colonies.

BELLRINGER
Skillbuilder Activity

Project transparency and have students answer the question.

Daily Focus Skills Transparency 2–3

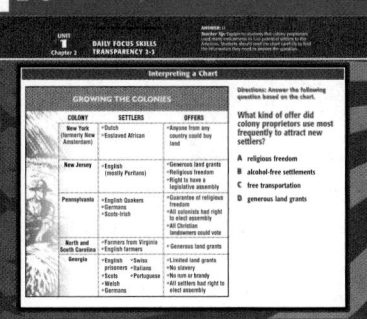

Reading Preview

Answers to Graphic: The proprietors of the Middle and Southern Colonies attracted people to settle in the colonies by offering generous land grants, religious freedom, the right to elect a legislative assembly, and by helping the poor start over.

Preteaching Vocabulary
Have students make a two-column list. Instruct them to write the Key Terms and Names in the left column and in the right column write the name of the colony most closely associated with the term or name.

Peter Stuyvesant

★ An American Story ★

On August 26, 1664, an English fleet arrived near the Dutch town of New Amsterdam. Its commander sent a note to Governor Peter Stuyvesant of New Netherland, demanding the town surrender. Stuyvesant bellowed that he would rather "be carried out dead in his coffin." Badly outnumbered, however, leading Dutch citizens petitioned the governor to surrender:

❝We, your sorrowful community and subjects, beg to represent, with all humility, that we cannot conscientiously foresee that anything else is to be expected . . . than misery, sorrow, conflagration, the dishonor of women . . . and, in a word, the absolute ruin and destruction of about fifteen hundred innocent souls, only two hundred and fifty of whom are capable of bearing arms. . . .❞

Two days later, Stuyvesant watched two English warships approach. Beside him stood a gunner, ready to fire. The minister at New Amsterdam talked to the governor, then led him away. On September 8, the Dutch surrendered, and New Amsterdam became New York.

—adapted from *A New World* and *Colonial New York*

The English Civil War and the Colonies

The fall of New Amsterdam and the founding of New York in 1664 marked the beginning of a new wave of English colonization in America. For more than 20 years, colonization had been at a standstill because of the violent struggle between the Puritans

CHAPTER 2   The English Arrive in America   **53**

SECTION RESOURCES

📁 **Reproducible Masters**
• Reproducible Lesson Plan 2–3
• Daily Lecture and Discussion Notes 2–3
• Guided Reading Activity 2–3
• Section Quiz 2–3
• Reading Essentials and Study Guide 2–3

📖 **Transparencies**
• Daily Focus Skills Transparency 2–3

• American Art & Architecture

Multimedia
🔘 Interactive Tutor Self-Assessment CD-ROM
🔘 ExamView® Pro Testmaker CD-ROM
🔘 Presentation Plus! CD-ROM
🔘 TeacherWorks™ CD-ROM
🎧 Audio Program

2 TEACH

Daily Lecture and Discussion Notes 2–3

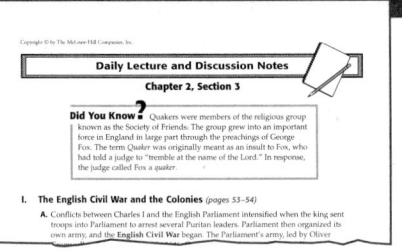

Copyright © by The McGraw-Hill Companies, Inc.

Daily Lecture and Discussion Notes
Chapter 2, Section 3

Did You Know? Quakers were members of the religious group known as the Society of Friends. The group grew into an important force in England in large part through the preachings of George Fox. The term Quaker was originally meant as an insult to Fox, who had told a judge to "tremble at the name of the Lord." In response, the judge called Fox a quaker.

I. The English Civil War and the Colonies (pages 53–54)
   A. Conflicts between Charles I and the English Parliament intensified when the king sent troops into Parliament to arrest several Puritan leaders. Parliament then organized its own army, and the **English Civil War** began. The Parliament's army, led by Oliver

✓ Reading Check

Answer: Colonies were vital sources of raw materials and markets for English goods.

Creating a Flyer Have students choose one colony and create a flyer advertising the benefits of migrating to the colony. **L1**

📁 Use *Interpreting Political Cartoons,* Cartoon 2.

Chart *Skills*

Answer: English: traded and farmed; French: exported furs; Spanish: mined and ranched

L1/ELL

Guided Reading Activity 2–3

Name _____ Date _____ Class _____

★ Guided Reading Activity **2-3**

DIRECTIONS: Outlining Read the section and complete the outline below. Refer to your textbook to fill in the blanks.
I. The English Civil War and the Colonies
   A. The _____ began in 1642, when King Charles I sent troops into the English Parliament to arrest several _____ leaders.
   B. _____, the commander of Parliament's army, dissolved Parliament and seized power as the military dictator of England.
   C. In 1660 English leaders began to view the American colonies as vital sources of _____ and as _____.
II. New York and New Jersey
   A. The Dutch located their major settlement, New Amsterdam, on today's

---

and the English king. The war was also political. Many English people felt the king was ruling as an absolute ruler and failing to consult Parliament.

The **English Civil War** began in 1642 when King Charles I sent troops into Parliament, which was dominated by Puritans, to arrest Puritan leaders. In response, Parliament organized an army. Parliament's forces defeated the king's troops, and in 1649 the king was put to death. A few years later, Oliver Cromwell, the commander of Parliament's army, seized power and became dictator of England.

By the time of Cromwell's death in 1658, England's leaders longed for stability. The army returned Parliament to power, and King Charles's son, Charles II, took the throne in 1660. With the monarchy restored, the English government began enthusiastically backing a new round of colonization in America. Colonies were no longer seen as risky business ventures, but as vital sources of raw materials and as markets for English goods.

✓ **Reading Check** **Examining** Why were the English enthusiastic about colonization after the English Civil War?

New York and New Jersey

King Charles II was especially interested in the land between Maryland and Connecticut, which was controlled by the Dutch. If he could control this region, it would link Virginia and Maryland to New England.

In 1609 navigator Henry Hudson explored the Hudson River valley for a group of Dutch merchants. The Dutch claimed the region, calling it New Netherland, and established their main settlement at New Amsterdam on Manhattan Island.

The colony grew slowly, partly because the fur trade was the focus of activity. To increase the population, the Dutch allowed anyone from any country to buy land. This strategy worked, and by 1664 the colony had more than 10,000 people. The need for labor also brought unwilling immigrants, as the Dutch first brought enslaved Africans in the 1620s.

By 1660 the Dutch and the English had become commercial rivals. The Dutch often defied English laws meant to control colonial trade, as when they helped English colonists smuggle tobacco to Europe.

Comparing European Colonies in the Americas, c. 1700

Colony	Early Settlement	Population	Areas Where Concentrated	Political and Economic Organization	Economic Focus
Spanish					
	1490s–early 1500s	Between 5–7 million (including conquered Native Americans)	Mexico, Florida, Texas, Central America, the Caribbean, California, New Mexico, north and west coast of South America	Governors with strong links to Spain; large bureaucracy; *encomiendas* and haciendas	Gold, silver mining; ranching
English					
	1490s–early explorers; early 1600s–permanent settlements	250,000	Eastern seaboard of North America	Governors with weak links to English Crown; elected assemblies; small farms; plantations; private merchants	Trade and farming
French					
	1535–early explorers; 1670s–permanent settlements	15,000	St. Lawrence River; Louisiana territory; outposts on Great Lakes and Mississippi River	Strong governors; large estates	Exporting furs

Chart *Skills*

England's quest for colonies brought it into direct conflict with Spain and France.

Making Generalizations How did the economic activity of the English colonies differ from the Spanish and French?

54 CHAPTER 2 The English Arrive in America

📖 Reading Strategy ▶ READING THE TEXT

Monitoring Comprehension One of the most important reading strategies students can learn is that they must monitor their reading comprehension. As they read, students should note when they don't understand a word or concept. They can monitor comprehension by questioning themselves as they read. If they do not understand an important idea, they need to reread, review, or read on to clarify what is unclear. As they read, have students practice this strategy by writing down anything they don't understand and adding explanations after completing the reading. **L1**

📁 Refer to *Inclusion for the High School Social Studies Classroom Strategies and Activities* in the TCR.

In 1664 King Charles decided to take **New Netherland** from the Dutch. After he had done so, Charles granted the land to his brother, James, the Duke of York. The colony was renamed New York, in James's honor. James also received land between Delaware Bay and the Connecticut River.

James later granted some of this land to two of the king's advisers and named it New Jersey. To attract settlers, New Jersey offered generous land grants, religious freedom, and the right to have a legislative assembly. Such good terms attracted many settlers, including a number of Puritans.

✓ **Reading Check** **Summarizing** Why did King Charles II want to seize New Netherland from the Dutch?

Pennsylvania and Delaware

William Penn was another of King Charles's beneficiaries. The king owed a debt to Penn's dead father and repaid it even though Penn was a member of the Quakers, a religious group the king had banned. The Quakers viewed religion as a personal experience. They saw no need for ministers and viewed the Bible as less important than each person's "inner light" from God. Because of their beliefs, Quakers often objected to political laws, for example, those requiring tax payment. They specifically advocated pacifism—opposition to war as a means of settling disputes.

In 1681 the king followed through on his promise and granted Penn land that lay across the Delaware River from New Jersey. Penn wanted his new colony of Pennsylvania to be a refuge for the persecuted of all nations—the colony would be a "holy experiment." Penn also tried to treat Native Americans fairly. He signed a treaty with a local group in 1682, bringing many years of peace to the people of Pennsylvania.

Penn named the capital Philadelphia, from the Greek meaning "city of brotherly love." The colony's government provided for an elected assembly and a guarantee of religious freedom. The right to vote was limited, however, to people with 50 acres of land and who professed Christianity.

The availability of land attracted English and Welsh Quakers, but German and Scotch-Irish settlers came as well. By 1684 Pennsylvania had more than 7,000 residents, and by 1700 Philadelphia rivaled Boston and New York as a center of trade and commerce. In 1682 Penn bought three counties south of Pennsylvania from the Duke of York. These "lower counties" became the colony of Delaware.

✓ **Reading Check** **Evaluating** Why did William Penn regard Pennsylvania as a "holy experiment"?

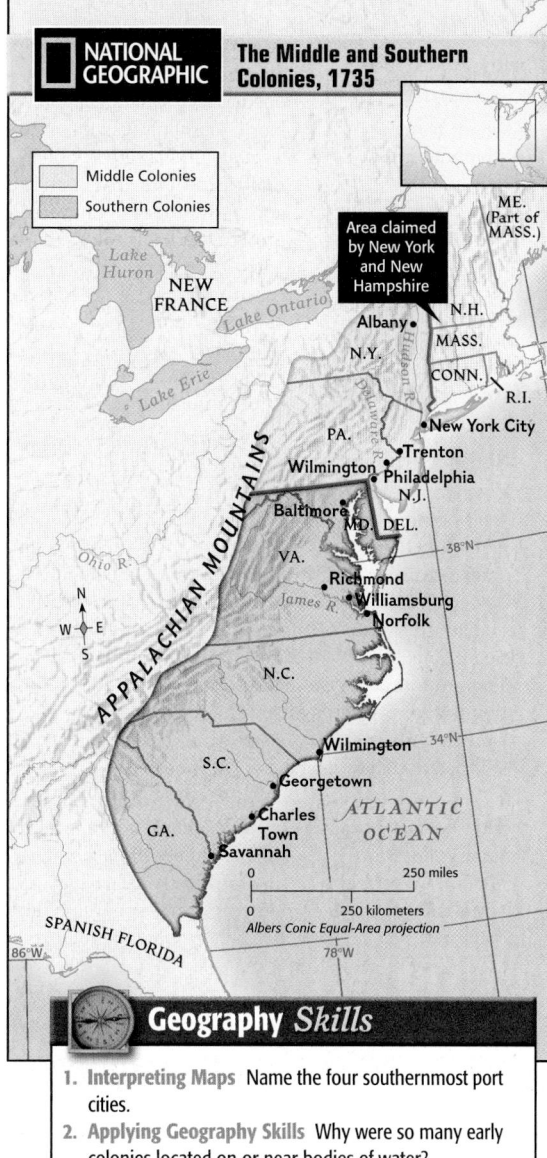

NATIONAL GEOGRAPHIC The Middle and Southern Colonies, 1735

Middle Colonies
Southern Colonies

Area claimed by New York and New Hampshire

ME. (Part of MASS.)

NEW FRANCE

Lake Huron
Lake Ontario
Lake Erie

N.H.
Albany • MASS.
N.Y. CONN.
R.I.
• New York City
PA. • Trenton
Wilmington • Philadelphia
N.J.
Baltimore • MD. DEL.
VA. 38°N
• Richmond
• Williamsburg
Norfolk

APPALACHIAN MOUNTAINS

Ohio R.
James R.

N.C.

• Wilmington 34°N
S.C.
• Georgetown
• Charles Town
GA. ATLANTIC OCEAN
• Savannah

0   250 miles
0   250 kilometers
Albers Conic Equal-Area projection

SPANISH FLORIDA
86°W   78°W

✓ **Geography** *Skills*

1. **Interpreting Maps** Name the four southernmost port cities.
2. **Applying Geography Skills** Why were so many early colonies located on or near bodies of water?

New Southern Colonies

While King Charles encouraged colonization between the Chesapeake Bay region and New England, he also took a keen interest in the unsettled land between Virginia and Spanish Florida. The year before he granted New York to his brother, Charles had awarded a vast territory south of Virginia to eight friends and political allies. The land was named Carolina, from the Latin for "Charles."

✓ **Reading Check**

Answer: to link Virginia and Maryland to New England

✓ **Reading Check**

Answer: He wanted to create a safe haven for the persecuted.

Geography *Skills*

Answers:
1. Savannah, Charles Town, Georgetown, Wilmington
2. for drinking water and transportation

3 ASSESS

Assign Section 3 Assessment as homework or as an in-class activity.

🖳 Have students use the **Interactive Tutor Self-Assessment CD-ROM.**
L1/ELL

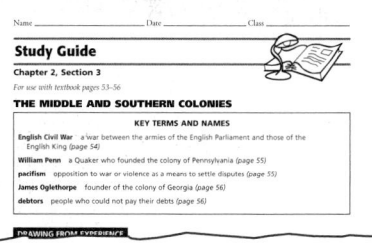

Reading Essentials and Study Guide 2–3

Name _____ Date _____ Class _____

Study Guide

Chapter 2, Section 3
For use with textbook pages 53–56

THE MIDDLE AND SOUTHERN COLONIES

KEY TERMS AND NAMES

English Civil War a war between the armies of the English Parliament and those of the English King (page 54)
William Penn a Quaker who founded the colony of Pennsylvania (page 55)
pacifism opposition to war or violence as a means to settle disputes (page 55)
James Oglethorpe founder of the colony of Georgia (page 56)
debtors people who could not pay their debts (page 56)

DRAWING FROM EXPERIENCE

L2

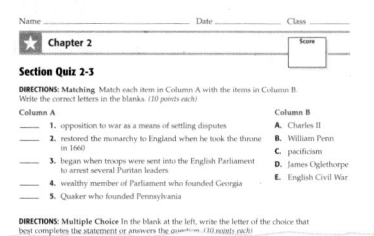

Section Quiz 2–3

Name _____ Date _____ Class _____

★ Chapter 2   Score

Section Quiz 2-3

DIRECTIONS: Matching Match each item in Column A with the items in Column B. Write the correct letters in the blanks. *(10 points each)*

Column A   Column B

___ 1. opposition to war as a means of settling disputes   A. Charles II
___ 2. restored the monarchy to England when he took the throne in 1660   B. William Penn
___ 3. began when troops were sent into the English Parliament to arrest several Puritan leaders   C. pacifism
___ 4. wealthy member of Parliament who founded Georgia   D. James Oglethorpe
___ 5. Quaker who founded Pennsylvania   E. English Civil War

DIRECTIONS: Multiple Choice In the blank at the left, write the letter of the choice that best completes the statement or answers the question. *(10 points each)*

DIFFERENTIATED INSTRUCTION

Kinesthetic Divide the textbook section into smaller parts using the headings in the text. Organize the class into small groups and assign one of the parts to each group. Have the groups read the part and prepare a short reenactment of the events described. Have the groups present their reenactments to the rest of the class. **L2**

📁 Refer to *Inclusion for the High School Social Studies Classroom Strategies and Activities* in the TCR.

HISTORY
Online

Objectives and answers to the student activity can be found in the **Web Activity Lesson Plan** at tarvol2.glencoe.com.

Reading Check

Answer: It allowed colonies to experiment with new types of worship, land ownership, and government.

Reteach

Ask students to identify the seven new colonies established after the English Civil War.

Enrich

Have students prepare a two-minute oral presentation about the founders of one of the colonies discussed in this section.

HISTORY
Online

Study Central™ provides summaries, interactive games, and online graphic organizers to help students review section content.

4 CLOSE

Have students summarize the reasons that the English colonies succeeded.

History *and the* **Humanities**

American Art & Architecture: *Penn's Treaty with the Indians*

HISTORY *Online*

Student Web Activity Visit the *American Republic Since 1877* Web site at tarvol2.glencoe.com and click on *Student Web Activities— Chapter 2* for an activity on English settlers in America.

North Carolina From the beginning, Carolina developed as two separate regions. North Carolina was home to a small and scattered population of farmers. The lack of good harbors hindered growth, and the colony had only 3,000 people by 1700. Eventually, the farmers began growing tobacco for sale. They also used native pine to make and export shipbuilding supplies.

South Carolina The proprietors of Carolina were always far more interested in the southern half of their holdings, where they hoped to cultivate sugarcane. In 1670 three ships brought settlers from England to South Carolina. They named their first settlement, Charles Town, after the king.

The first years of the new colony were difficult. Sugarcane, as it turned out, did not grow well. The first product exported in large quantity was deerskin, popular for English leather. The colony also began to capture and enslave Native Americans, who were shipped to plantations in the Caribbean.

The Georgia Experiment In the 1720s, General **James Oglethorpe,** a wealthy member of Parliament, began investigating English prisons. He was appalled to find so many debtors—people who could not pay their debts—behind bars. Oglethorpe

asked King George II for a colony south of South Carolina where the poor could start over.

The English government saw several advantages to a new southern colony. It would help England's poor and provide a strategic buffer to keep Spain from expanding north. King George granted Oglethorpe and his friends permission to settle between the Savannah and Altamaha Rivers. The new colony was named Georgia, in honor of the king, and the first settlers arrived in 1733.

Oglethorpe and his fellow trustees banned slavery, rum, and brandy in Georgia, and they limited the size of land grants. Still, the colony attracted settlers from all over Europe, including Scotch-Irish, Welsh, Germans, Swiss, and Italians. Increasingly, the settlers objected to the colony's strict rules. In the 1740s, the trustees lifted the restrictions on brandy, rum, and slavery, and in 1750, they granted the settlers their own elected assembly. The next year, the trustees gave control back to the king, and Georgia became a royal colony.

By 1775 roughly 2.5 million people lived in England's American colonies. Despite the stumbling start in Jamestown, the English had succeeded in building a large and prosperous society on the east coast of North America.

England's success, however, would prove its undoing. By permitting new patterns of land ownership and new types of worship and government in its colonies, the English government had planted the seeds of rebellion.

Reading Check **Summarizing** In what ways was England permissive with its American colonies?

HISTORY *Online* | **Study Central**™ To review this section, go to tarvol2.glencoe.com and click on **Study Central**™.

SECTION 3 ASSESSMENT

Checking for Understanding

1. **Define:** pacifism, debtor.
2. **Identify:** English Civil War, William Penn, James Oglethorpe.
3. **Summarize** how the Quakers came to have a colony of their own.

Reviewing Themes

4. **Global Connections** After Charles II became king, why did the English government openly work to promote colonization in North America?

Critical Thinking

5. **Analyzing** Why did England regard the Dutch and Spanish presence in North America as a threat, and how did England respond?
6. **Categorizing** Use a graphic organizer similar to the one below to list the reasons that the listed colonies were founded.

Colony	Reasons Founded
New York	
New Jersey	
Pennsylvania	

Analyzing Visuals

7. **Analyzing Charts** Study the chart on page 54 on Spanish, English, and French colonization. In political organization, what was a trait of the English colonies that the French and Spanish colonies did not share?

Writing About History

8. **Persuasive Writing** Imagine you have been hired by the proprietors of New Jersey to persuade settlers to come to their colony. Write an editorial for a newspaper in England to convince people to settle in New Jersey.

SECTION 3 ASSESSMENT ANSWERS

1. Terms are in blue.
2. English Civil War *(p. 54),* William Penn *(p. 55),* James Oglethorpe *(p. 56)*
3. The king repaid a debt to Penn's father by granting him a colony.
4. The colonies were seen as a vital source of raw materials and a market for English goods.

5. The Dutch helped colonists smuggle goods. The English took their colonial lands. To stop Spanish growth the English founded Georgia.
6. New York/New Jersey: sources of raw materials, markets for English goods; Pennsylvania: to repay a debt to Penn's father, and create a

Quaker colony
7. The English allowed colonists to form assemblies with broad governmental powers.
8. Students' editorials should express favorable opinions of New Jersey.

Understanding the Parts of a Map

 In Motion

Why Learn This Skill?

Maps can direct you down the street or around the world. There are as many different kinds of maps as there are uses for them. Being able to read a map begins with learning about its parts.

Learning the Skill

Maps usually include a key, a compass rose, and a scale bar. The map key explains the meaning of special colors, symbols, and lines used on the map. On a road map, for example, the key tells what map lines stand for paved roads, dirt roads, and interstate highways.

After reading the map key, look for the compass rose. It is the direction marker that shows the cardinal directions of north, south, east, and west. A measuring line, often called a scale bar, helps you estimate distance on a map. The map's scale tells you what distance on the earth is represented by the measurement on the scale bar. For example, 1 inch (2.54 cm) on the map may represent 100 miles (160.9 km) on the earth. Knowing the scale allows you to visualize the extent of an area and to measure distances.

Practicing the Skill

The map on this page shows the early English colonization of the eastern coast of North America. Look at the parts of the map, and then answer the questions.

❶ What information is given in the key?

❷ What body of water serves as the eastern border for the colonies?

❸ What color represents the Middle Colonies?

❹ What is the approximate distance, in miles, between the settlements of Charles Town and Jamestown?

❺ What is the approximate distance, in kilometers, between the northernmost and southernmost settlements shown on the map?

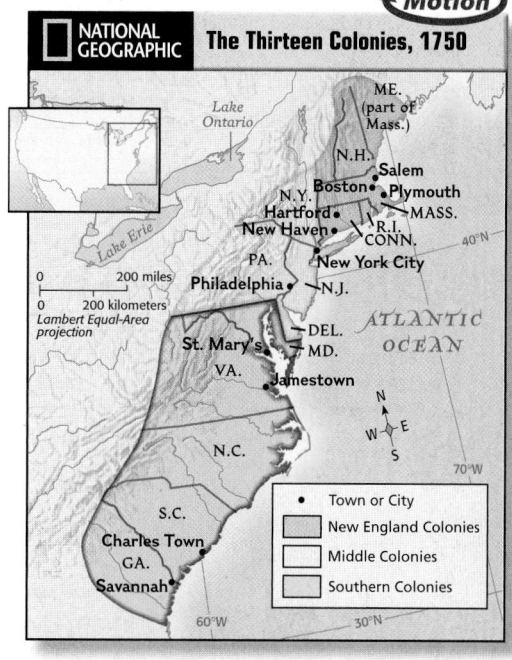

NATIONAL GEOGRAPHIC **The Thirteen Colonies, 1750**

Skills Assessment

Complete the Practicing Skills questions on page 71 and the Chapter 2 Skill Reinforcement Activity to assess your mastery of this skill.

Applying the Skill

Understanding the Parts of a Map Study the map of European Explorations and Settlements on page 43. Use the map to answer the following questions.

1. When did Marquette and Joliet explore the Mississippi River?

2. What English explorer arrived in North America at the end of the 1400s?

3. Which explorer traveled the farthest north?

 Glencoe's **Skillbuilder Interactive Workbook CD-ROM, Level 2,** provides instruction and practice in key social studies skills.

57

ANSWERS TO PRACTICING THE SKILL

❶ meanings of symbols and colors
❷ Atlantic Ocean
❸ yellow
❹ 400 miles
❺ 1,600 kilometers

Applying the Skill

1. 1673

2. Cabot

3. Hudson

1 FOCUS

Section Overview

This section explains the different economies developed by the Southern, New England, and Middle Colonies.

Reading Preview

Answers to Graphic: Southern: geography: rich, wet soil; economy: based on labor-intensive crops. **New England:** geography: thin, rocky soil, plentiful forests, and waterfalls; economy: shipbuilding, lumber, and fishing. **Middle:** geography: fertile land, good river system; economy: trade and cash crops such as wheat

Preteaching Vocabulary
Have students write a paragraph using at least four of the Key Terms and Names.

Guide to Reading

Main Idea
The Southern Colonies developed agricultural economies, while the New England and Middle Colonies developed commercial economies.

Key Terms and Names
cash crop, indentured servant, subsistence farming, Nathaniel Bacon, slave code, entrepreneur, capitalist, triangular trade

Reading Strategy
Organizing As you read about life in the Southern, New England, and Middle Colonies, complete a graphic organizer similar to the one below describing how the geography of each region affected its economic development.

Region	Geography	Economic Activities

Reading Objectives
• **Describe** the Southern economy and the plantation system.
• **List** the geographical conditions that determined the New England Colonies' economy.

Section Theme
Culture and Traditions At first, slavery was not used in the colonies, but by the late 1600s, it was in widespread use in the Southern Colonies.

Preview of Events

♦1620	♦1660	♦1720	♦1760

1619 First Africans arrive in North America

1676 Bacon's Rebellion

1692 Salem witchcraft trials begin

1705 Virginia slave code introduced

1740s Indigo first cultivated in South Carolina

★ An American Story ★

William Byrd's Westover plantation

William Byrd II, a wealthy Virginia planter in the 1700s, played a central role in his colony's government. In addition to serving as colonel of the county militia and as a member of the House of Burgesses, Byrd founded the city of Richmond and experimented with a variety of crops on his plantation. His wealth gave him the leisure to pursue cultural interests, and he amassed over 4,000 books—the biggest private library in the colonies. He left behind several diaries detailing life on Southern plantations. On January 27, 1711, he noted:

❝I rose at 5 o'clock and read two chapters in Hebrew and some Greek in Lucian. I said my prayers and ate boiled milk for breakfast. . . . I settled several accounts; then I read some English which gave me great light into the nature of spirit. . . . In the afternoon my wife and I took a little walk and then danced together. Then I read some more English. At night I read some Italian and then played at piquet [a card game] with my wife. . . . I said my prayers and had good health, good thoughts, and good humor, thank God Almighty.❞

—quoted in *The Growth of the American Republic*

Southern Society

In the Southern Colonies, wealthy planters like William Byrd stood on society's top rung. They were sharply divided from enslaved Africans at the bottom and small farmers in the middle. What linked all groups, however, was an economy based on agriculture.

SECTION RESOURCES

📁 **Reproducible Masters**
• Reproducible Lesson Plan 2–4
• Daily Lecture and Discussion Notes 2–4
• Guided Reading Activity 2–4
• Section Quiz 2–4
• Reading Essentials and Study Guide 2–4

📊 **Transparencies**
• Daily Focus Skills Transparency 2–4

Multimedia
🔵 Interactive Tutor Self-Assessment CD-ROM
🔵 ExamView® Pro Testmaker CD-ROM
🔵 Presentation Plus! CD-ROM
🔵 TeacherWorks™ CD-ROM
🎵 Audio Program
🎵 American Music: Hits Through History

Tobacco, Rice, and Indigo The Jamestown colony made tobacco the South's first successful cash crop, or crop grown primarily for market. Tobacco took off in Virginia and Maryland and, to a lesser extent, in North Carolina.

In early colonial days, there was plenty of land for tobacco farmers, but not enough labor to work it. England had the opposite problem. The English enclosure movement had forced many peasants off the land. Many of them, hoping to acquire their own land in America, became indentured servants. They made labor contracts with colonists, agreeing to work for a set term, usually four years. In return, the colonist would pay for a servant's passage and provide food, clothing, and shelter until the contract expired.

For many years, indentured servitude benefited tobacco planters. By 1760 they were producing more than 80 million pounds of tobacco per year. Unfortunately, close to half of the indentured servants who came to Virginia and Maryland in the 1600s died before earning their freedom. Of those who did become free, less than half acquired their own land.

In South Carolina, meanwhile, after trying unsuccessfully to grow sugarcane, settlers turned to rice. This too failed at first, but in the 1690s, a new variety was introduced, and enslaved Africans were imported to cultivate it. Rice rapidly became a major cash crop in both South Carolina and Georgia.

In the early 1740s, South Carolina began to develop another cash crop called indigo, used to make blue dye for cloth. Indigo was a good second crop for rice farmers and it could be planted where rice could not. A 17-year-old named Eliza Lucas had discovered that indigo needed high ground and sandy soil, not the wetlands that suited rice.

Disparities in Wealth Tobacco and rice farming required difficult and tedious manual labor. Planters who could afford to bring in many slaves or indentured servants received extra land under the headright system. With a large labor force and acreage, these planters could produce a much larger crop, multiply their earnings, and build expansive estates.

The wealthy plantation owners, sometimes referred to as the Southern gentry or the planter elite, were few in number, but they enjoyed enormous economic and political influence. They served in the governing councils and assemblies, commanded the local militias, and became county judges. With few towns or roads in the region, their plantations functioned as self-contained communities. In addition to the planter's large house, the workers' cabins, and stables and barns, large plantations often had a school, a chapel, and

workshops for blacksmiths, carpenters, weavers, coopers (barrel makers), and leatherworkers.

The majority of landowners in the colonial South, however, were small farmers living inland. These "backcountry" farmers worked small plots of land and lived in tiny houses. Although they grew some tobacco, they largely practiced subsistence farming, raising only enough to feed their families.

Landless tenant farmers made up another group in the South. Although land itself was easy to acquire, many settlers could not afford the costs of the deed, land survey, tools, seed, and livestock. Instead they worked land that they rented from the planter elite. Tenant farmers usually led difficult lives but had higher social status than indentured servants or slaves.

✓ **Reading Check** **Discussing** What led to the rise of the planter elite in colonial Southern society?

Bacon's Rebellion

By the 1660s, Virginia's government was dominated by wealthy planters led by the governor, Sir William Berkeley. Berkeley arranged to restrict voting to property owners, cutting the number of voters in half. Berkeley also exempted himself and his councilors from taxation. These actions angered the backcountry farmers and tenant farmers. Ultimately, however, it was the governor's policies toward Native American lands that led to a rebellion.

Crisis Over Land The most important issue for most colonists was to acquire land. Many indentured servants and tenant farmers wanted to own farms eventually. Backcountry farmers wanted to expand their holdings. By the 1670s, most land left was in areas claimed by Native Americans in the Piedmont, the region of rolling hills between the coastal plains and the Appalachians.

Most wealthy planters lived near the coast in the region known as the Tidewater. They had no interest in the backcountry and did not want to endanger their plantations by risking war with the Native Americans. Therefore, they opposed expanding Virginia's territory into Native American lands.

In 1675 war broke out between settlers and a Susquehannock group. When Governor Berkeley refused to support further military action, backcountry farmers were outraged. In April 1676, a group of them met to discuss the situation. **Nathaniel Bacon,** a well-to-do but sympathetic planter, took up their cause. Bacon organized his own militia and attacked the Native Americans. He then ran for office and won

CHAPTER 2 The English Arrive in America **59**

---

2 TEACH

Daily Lecture and Discussion Notes 2–4

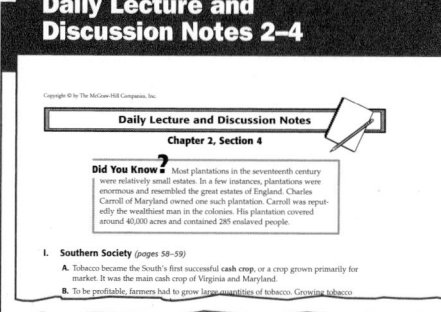

Copyright © by The McGraw-Hill Companies, Inc.

Daily Lecture and Discussion Notes

Chapter 2, Section 4

Did You Know ? Most plantations in the seventeenth century were relatively small estates. In a few instances, plantations were enormous and resembled the great estates of England. Charles Carroll of Maryland owned one such plantation. Carroll was reputedly the wealthiest man in the colonies. His plantation covered around 40,000 acres and contained 285 enslaved people.

I. Southern Society (pages 58–59)

A. Tobacco became the South's first successful **cash crop**, or a crop grown primarily for market. It was the main cash crop of Virginia and Maryland.

B. To be profitable, farmers had to grow large quantities of tobacco. Growing tobacco

✓ **Reading Check**

Answer: Land was granted to people under the headright system. As planters hired more indentured servants or bought enslaved persons, they were granted more land.

Writing an Advertisement Have students write an advertisement for recruiting indentured servants. The advertisement should include information about what the landowner is willing to provide, what the servant must agree to do, and the length of service required. **L1**

📁 Use the rubric for creating a magazine/newspaper/Web site article or help-wanted ad on pages 75–76 in the *Performance Assessment Activities and Rubrics.*

Making Contracts The contract of an indentured servant was indented (folded) and torn along the indenture. Each party to the contract kept half.

Reading Strategy | READING THE TEXT

Using Context Clues Provide students with these tips to use context to determine meaning; look before, at, and after the unfamiliar word for a context clue; connect with what you already know with what the author has written; predict a possible meaning; apply the meaning in the sentence; decide if the meaning makes sense; if the meaning does not make sense, try again. **L1**

📁 Refer to *Inclusion for the High School Social Studies Classroom Strategies and Activities* in the TCR.

L1/ELL
Guided Reading Activity 2–4

Name _____ Date _____ Class _____

★ **Guided Reading Activity 2-4**

DIRECTIONS: Recording Who, What, When, Where, Why, and How Answer the questions below. Refer to your textbook to write the answers.
1. What is a cash crop? _____
2. Who were indentured servants? _____
3. What were the main cash crops of South Carolina by the early 1740s? _____
4. Who was Eliza Lucas? _____
5. What is subsistence farming? _____
6. How did Governor Berkeley's policies favor his supporters? _____

Picturing **History**

Background: William Berkeley and Nathaniel Bacon were cousins. Nathaniel Bacon had been sent to the colonies in hopes that he would mature. Berkeley, as governor, gave Bacon a large land grant. However, Bacon's reputation as a troublemaker and schemer accompanied him to the colonies.
Answer: He appears clean-shaven and better dressed, so students may conclude that he was a member of the gentry.
Ask: What sorts of emotions and ideas does the image evoke? *(possible answer: Bacon looks like a great commander, his soldiers with musket and drum look hardened and ready. They inspire support because they will be victorious.)*

Reading Check

Answer: The government's refusal to support military action against the Native Americans caused the backcountry farmers to rebel.

Picturing **History**

Bacon's Rebellion This uprising led by Nathaniel Bacon pitted backcountry farmers against Virginia's ruling gentry. From Bacon's dress, do you think he himself was a backcountry farmer or a member of the gentry?

a seat in the House of Burgesses. The assembly immediately authorized another attack on the Native Americans. It also restored the right to vote to all free men and took away the tax exemptions Berkeley had granted to his supporters.

These reforms did not satisfy Bacon, however. He marched to Jamestown in July 1676 with several hundred armed men and charged Berkeley with corruption. Berkeley fled to raise his own army, and a civil war erupted. The two sides battled for control of Jamestown until September 1676, when the town burned down. **Bacon's Rebellion** ended abruptly the next month, when Bacon, hiding in a swamp, became sick and died. Without his leadership, his army rapidly disintegrated, and Berkeley returned to power.

Slavery Increases in Virginia Bacon's Rebellion convinced many wealthy planters that land should be made available to backcountry farmers. From the 1680s onward, Virginia's government generally supported expanding the colony westward, regardless of the impact on Native Americans.

Bacon's Rebellion also helped accelerate an existing trend in Virginia. By the 1670s, many planters had begun using enslaved Africans instead of indentured servants to work their plantations. In the 1680s, after the rebellion, the number of Africans brought to the colony rose dramatically.

Planters began to switch to enslaved Africans for several reasons. Enslaved workers, unlike indentured servants, did not have to be freed and therefore would never need their own land. In addition, when cheap land became available in the 1680s in the new colony of Pennsylvania, fewer English settlers were willing to become indentured servants.

At the same time, the English government adopted policies that encouraged slavery. English law limited trade between the English colonies and other countries. Prior to the 1670s, settlers who wanted to acquire enslaved Africans had to buy them from the Dutch or Portuguese, which was difficult to arrange. In 1672, however, King Charles II granted a charter to the Royal African Company to engage in the slave trade. With an English company in the slave trade, it was much easier to acquire enslaved people. Planters also discovered another economic advantage to slavery. Because enslaved Africans, unlike indentured servants, were considered property, planters could use them as collateral to borrow money and expand their plantations.

Reading Check **Identifying** What government policies caused backcountry farmers to rebel?

Slavery in the Colonies

For enslaved Africans, the voyage to America usually began with a forced march to the West African coast, where they were traded to Europeans, branded, and crammed onto ships. Chained together in the ships' filthy holds for more than a month, the Africans could hardly sit or stand. They were given minimal food and drink, and those who died or became sick were thrown overboard. Olaudah Equiano, a West African shipped to America in the 1760s, later wrote about the terrible journey across the Atlantic, known to Europeans as the **Middle Passage:**

❝We were all put under deck. . . . The closeness of the place, and heat of the climate . . . almost suffocated us. . . . The shrieks of the women, and the groans of the dying, rendered the whole a scene of horror almost inconceivable. ❞

—from *The Interesting Narrative of the Life of Olaudah Equiano, or Gustavus Vassa the African*

DIFFERENTIATED INSTRUCTION

Reading Support Divide this section of the chapter into six parts using the primary headings as a guide. Assign each section to at least one student. Have students read their section and become familiar with the content. Invite students to present an oral summary of their section to the class.
L1

📁 Refer to *Inclusion for the High School Social Studies Classroom Strategies and Activities* in the TCR.

Historians estimate that between 10 and 12 million Africans were enslaved and sent to the Americas between 1450 and 1870. On the way, roughly 2 million died at sea. Of the 8 to 10 million Africans who reached the Americas, approximately 3.6 million went to Brazil, and another 1.5 million went to the Spanish colonies. The British, French, and Dutch colonies in the Caribbean imported nearly 3.7 million others to work on their plantations. Approximately 427,000 Africans were transported to British North America.

When the first Africans arrived in Virginia in 1619, they were treated much like indentured servants. English law did not recognize **chattel slavery**—the actual ownership of one human being by another.

Many English settlers, however, found it acceptable to enslave Africans if they were not Christians. Over time, the number of enslaved Africans increased in the colonies, particularly in the South, where they became the backbone of the labor force.

Beginning in the 1660s, new laws gradually lowered the status of all Africans, regardless of their religion, and made slavery a hereditary system based on race. In 1705 Virginia created a slave code—a set of laws defining the relationship between enslaved Africans and free people. Other colonies followed suit. Africans could not own property, testify against a white person in court, move about freely, or assemble in large numbers. By the early 1700s, slavery had become generally accepted in colonial society.

✓ **Reading Check** **Explaining** How did the relationship between English settlers and Africans change over time?

Life in New England

While the Southern Colonies depended on agriculture, many New Englanders earned a living from maritime activities or lumber. With such enterprises and Puritan beliefs drawing colonists together, towns became the heart of New England society.

GEOGRAPHY

A Diverse Economy New England's thin and rocky soil was ill suited to cash crops and the development of large plantations. Instead, on small farms from Connecticut to Maine, New England colonists practiced subsistence farming. The main crop was corn, but farmers grew other grains, vegetables, and berries as well. They also tended apple orchards and raised dairy cattle, sheep, and pigs.

More than any other industry, fishing brought prosperity to New England. Nearby lay the Grand Banks, a shallow area in the Atlantic Ocean that teemed with cod, mackerel, halibut, and herring. In addition, New England had good harbors and plenty of timber for building fishing boats. Colonists found markets for their fish in the colonies, southern Europe, and the Caribbean.

Whaling also played a major role in New England's economy. Whale blubber was used for making candles and lamp oil, and whale bones were used to fashion buttons, combs, and other items.

New England developed a thriving lumber industry, too. Maine and New Hampshire had many waterfalls near the coast that could power sawmills.

Writing an Article Have students imagine that they are reporters for a British magazine. Ask them to write an informative article for the magazine explaining the causes and results of Bacon's Rebellion. Tell them to be sure to include enough information that readers in England will clearly understand the situation in Virginia. Encourage students to share their articles with the rest of the class. **L2**

✓ **Reading Check**

Answer: The relationship changed from one similar to indentured servitude, to enslavement of non-Christians, to enslavement by race based on a hereditary system, and finally to a slave code that defined the relationship between enslaved Africans and free people.

FYI

Before Nathaniel Bacon's sudden death, he burned the estates of his rivals and controlled most of Virginia.

History and the Humanities

American Music: Hits Through History: "Love in a Village/Love Forever," "Rufty Tufty," "Reel de Dennis McGee"

African Culture Crosses the Ocean: A Woman's Song

On a steamy March day in 1997, in the tiny town of Senehun Ngola in Sierra Leone, West Africa, Mary Moran, an African American from Georgia, first met Baindu Jabati, a Sierra Leonean. The two women had something amazing in common: a song each woman had known all her life.

In an emotional meeting, Moran and Jabati shared the song that the female ancestors of each of them had passed down for more than 200 years. Although the melody of the American version had changed, the words of this song in the Mende language of Sierra Leone probably came to America's South on the slave ships that sailed from West Africa in the 1700s.

The women in Mary Moran's family had passed the song down through the generations. Over time, the true origin of the song was lost. Although she had sung the song all her life, Moran never knew what its words meant. She imagined that it was an old African song.

Wanting to trace her family's history, Moran consulted with ethnomusicologists, who study folk music. Moran discovered that her family's song came from southern Sierra Leone and that it was traditionally sung at funerals. Jabati, who had inherited the traditional duty to sing at funerals, said that meeting Moran would have been better only if her ancestors could have been there also for the joyous occasion.

Elmira Castle in Ghana, a former outpost of the Portuguese slave trade

Mary Moran at left, with glasses

INTERDISCIPLINARY CONNECTIONS ACTIVITY

Music Have the music teacher discuss various musical traditions related to ethnic groups or to specific cultures. If possible, the teacher should include samples of various musical styles and where the style originated. Have students work in small groups to select one of these styles and write a song about what life was like on a plantation using the chosen style. **L2**

Creating a Thematic Map
Provide students a blank outline map of the New England, Middle, and Southern Colonies. Have students label the colonies. Then have them use symbols for each of the various crops and industries present in each group of colonies. Remind students to create a key showing what the various symbols represent.

📁 Use the rubric for creating a map, display, or chart on pages 65–66 in the *Performance Assessment Activities and Rubrics.*

✓Reading Check

Answer: They gave colonists experience and desire to govern themselves.

📷*Picturing* History

Background: New England settlers not only lived together in close-knit communities, but also sometimes traveled to America together. There are records showing that some whole communities crossed the Atlantic as a group.
Answer: The town proprietors distributed farmland based on family size, wealth, and other social factors.
Ask: What building serves as a central point for the community shown? *(the meetinghouse, which also serves as the community church)*

Lumber cut at these mills could easily be transported downriver to the coast and shipped to other colonies or to England. Demand for lumber never waned. It was needed for furniture, building materials, and other products such as barrels, which were used to store and ship almost everything in the colonial era.

The lumber industry made possible another important business in New England: shipbuilding. With forests and sawmills close to the coast, ships could be built quickly and cheaply, for 30 to 50 percent less than in England. By the 1770s, one out of every three English ships had been built in America.

If self-sufficient plantations defined the social unit in the South, New England's social life centered on the town. Puritans believed that Christians should form groups united by a **church covenant**—a voluntary agreement to worship together. The commitment to a church covenant encouraged the development of small towns surrounded by farms.

Life in these small communities of farmers centered around a **"town common,"** or open public area. Adjoining the common were the marketplace, school, and "meetinghouse," or church. Each family had a home lot where they could build a house and storage buildings and plant a garden.

📷*Picturing* History

Sudbury, Massachusetts The town was the basic unit of community life in New England in the 1600s. Houses were laid out around a central pasture called a common. In this map, the holdings of one man, John Goodnow, are highlighted in purple to show the way each person's land holdings could be scattered about the town. Who decided how much land each person received?

Local Government In the early days of colonial New England, the General Court appointed town officials and managed the town's affairs. Over time, however, townspeople began discussing local problems and issues at **town meetings.** These developed into the local government, with landowners holding the right to vote and pass laws. They elected selectmen to oversee town matters and appoint clerks, constables, and other officials. Any resident, however, could attend a town meeting and express an opinion.

Because the settlers in New England, unlike English peasants, were allowed to participate directly in local government, they developed a strong belief in their right to govern themselves. Town meetings thus helped set the stage for the American Revolution and the emergence of democratic government.

Puritan Society New England Puritans valued religious devotion, hard work, and obedience to strict rules regulating daily life. Card playing and gambling were banned, and "Stage-Players" and "Mixed Dancing" were frowned upon. Watching over one's neighbors' behavior, or "Holy Watching," was elevated to a religious duty. The Puritans did not lead pleasureless lives, however. They drank rum, enjoyed music, and wore brightly colored clothing.

✓Reading Check **Synthesizing** How did New England town meetings prepare the colonists for the future?

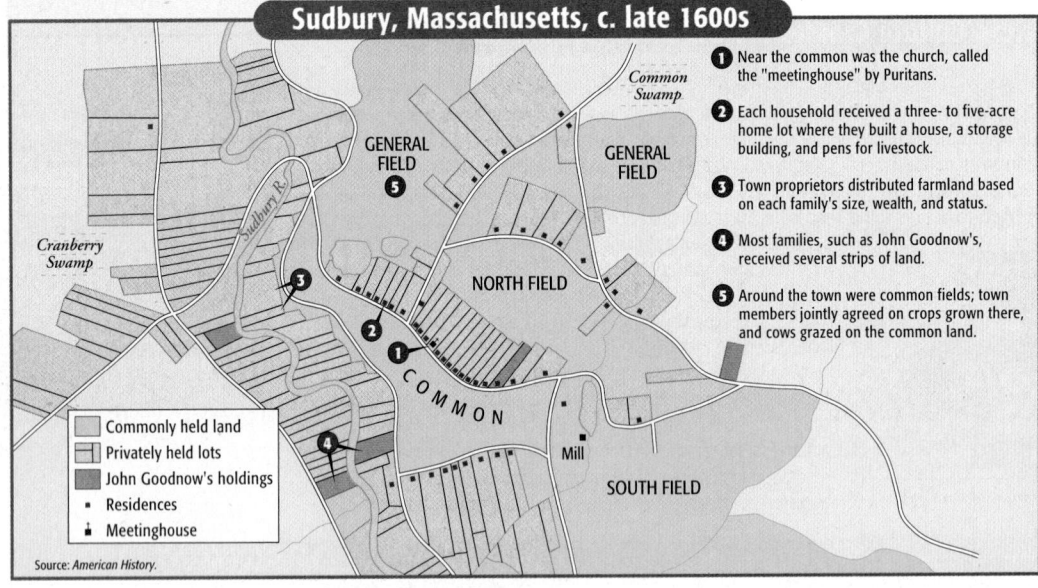

Sudbury, Massachusetts, c. late 1600s

1 Near the common was the church, called the "meetinghouse" by Puritans.

2 Each household received a three- to five-acre home lot where they built a house, a storage building, and pens for livestock.

3 Town proprietors distributed farmland based on each family's size, wealth, and status.

4 Most families, such as John Goodnow's, received several strips of land.

5 Around the town were common fields; town members jointly agreed on crops grown there, and cows grazed on the common land.

GENERAL FIELD 5

GENERAL FIELD

Common Swamp

Cranberry Swamp

Sudbury R.

3

2 1

NORTH FIELD

C O M M O N

4

Mill

SOUTH FIELD

☐ Commonly held land
⊟ Privately held lots
▦ John Goodnow's holdings
▪ Residences
🏠 Meetinghouse

Source: *American History.*

CRITICAL THINKING ACTIVITY

Comparing To help students understand the significance of geography and economics in history, have them focus their attention on agriculture in the Southern Colonies. Have students create a table to compare and contrast commercial agriculture and subsistence farming. The table should include information about crops, land use, transportation, and labor. **L2**

Triangular Trade, 1750

NATIONAL GEOGRAPHIC

In Motion

Geography *Skills*

1. **Interpreting Maps** Which commodities were both British colonial exports and intercolonial trade items?
2. **Applying Geography Skills** What products did the colonies import from Britain? Why did they need these products?

Life in the Middle Colonies

The Middle Colonies—Pennsylvania, New York, New Jersey, and Delaware—were blessed with fertile land and a long growing season. Farmers produced bumper crops of rye, oats, barley, and potatoes. Most important, however, was wheat, which rapidly became the region's main cash crop.

As merchants in the Middle Colonies began selling wheat and flour to colonies in the Caribbean, they benefited from the region's geography. Three wide rivers—the Hudson, the Delaware, and the Susquehanna—ran deep into the interior, making it easy for farmers to ship their crops to the coast and on to more distant markets. At the same time, thousands of wagons moved goods overland from interior farms to river towns.

In the early and mid-1700s, the demand for wheat soared, thanks to a population explosion in Europe triggered by the decline of disease. Between 1720 and 1770, wheat prices more than doubled in the Middle Colonies, bringing a surge of prosperity. Europe's population growth also brought a new wave of

immigration to America, particularly to the Middle Colonies where land was still available.

Some farmers grew rich by hiring poor immigrants to work on their farms to increase their wheat production. Other colonists became entrepreneurs, businesspeople who risk their money, by buying land, equipment, and supplies and selling them to immigrants for a profit.

The wheat boom created a new group of wealthy capitalists who had money to invest in new businesses. Although industry did not develop on a large scale during the colonial era, these early capitalists did build many large gristmills near New York and Philadelphia that produced vast quantities of flour for export. Other early capitalists in the Middle Colonies established glass and pottery works.

✓ **Reading Check** **Identifying** What crop was most important to farmers in the Middle Colonies?

Trade and the Rise of Cities

In the early colonial era, settlers lacked money to invest in local industry. As a result, they had to import most manufactured goods from England. Unfortunately, they produced few goods that England wanted in return.

CHAPTER 2 The English Arrive in America **63**

Geography *Skills*

Answers:
1. molasses, sugar, and fish
2. manufactured goods, clothes, furniture, luxuries; the colonies had very little industry

Geography Skills Practice
Ask: What exports to Great Britain were returned in a different form to the colonies? *(possible answer: lumber and furs, returned as furniture and clothing)*

✓ **Reading Check**

Answer: wheat

3 ASSESS

Assign Section 4 Assessment as homework or as an in-class activity.

🖥 Have students use the **Interactive Tutor Self-Assessment CD-ROM.**

L1/ELL

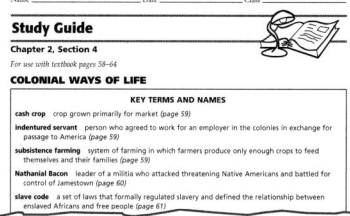

Reading Essentials and Study Guide 2–4

Name _____ Date _____ Class _____

Study Guide

Chapter 2, Section 4
For use with textbook pages 58–64

COLONIAL WAYS OF LIFE

KEY TERMS AND NAMES

cash crop crop grown primarily for market (page 59)

indentured servant person who agreed to work for an employer in the colonies in exchange for passage to America (page 59)

subsistence farming system of farming in which farmers produce only enough crops to feed themselves and their families (page 59)

Nathanial Bacon leader of a militia who attacked threatening Native Americans and battled for control of Jamestown (page 60)

slave code a set of laws that formally regulated slavery and defined the relationship between enslaved Africans and free people (page 61)

EXTENDING THE CONTENT

Indentured Servants In 1750, Gottlieb Mittelberger traveled to Pennsylvania as an indentured servant. He later wrote about his experiences in an essay entitled *On the Misfortune of Indentured Servants.* He notes that if a child's parents died during the voyage, the child had to serve long enough to pay for both his or her voyage, as well as the parents' voyage. When they finally paid off their voyages and finished their term of service, an indentured servant was to be given a new suit of clothes. Depending on the terms of service, some male servants also received a horse, while female servants received a cow.

L2

Section Quiz 2–4

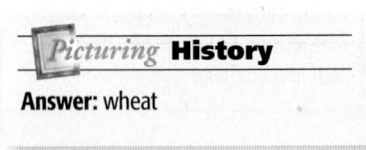

Answer: wheat

Reteach

Have students create a sentence outline of the section based on the section's headings.

Enrich

Have students use library and Internet resources to read and then summarize *The Interesting Life of Olaudah Equiano, or Gustav Vassa the African.*

Answer: wealthy merchants

Study Central™ provides summaries, interactive games, and online graphic organizers to help students review section content.

---

4 CLOSE

Ask students to describe why the status of Africans brought to Virginia and Maryland gradually changed from indentured servants to enslaved peoples.

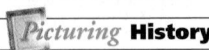 **History**

Bethlehem, Pennsylvania Laid out along a river with farmsteads on the village outskirts, this town is typical of many in the Middle Colonies. What was the region's main cash crop?

Triangular Trade Instead of trading directly with England, colonial merchants developed systems of triangular trade involving a three-way exchange of goods. New England merchants, for example, sold fish, lumber, and meat to Caribbean sugar planters. As payment, they accepted raw sugar or **bills of exchange,** which were credit slips from English merchants. New England merchants would then trade the bills and sugar to English merchants for hardware, linens, and other English goods.

Trade with the Caribbean sugar plantations enriched many New England merchants. With their new wealth, they built factories to refine raw sugar and distilleries to turn molasses into rum. They also traded with the Southern Colonies, exchanging fish, rum, and grain for rice, tobacco, and indigo.

A New Urban Society The rise of trade in the colonies caused several Northern ports to grow rapidly into cities. By 1760 Philadelphia had nearly 24,000 people, making it the largest colonial city. New York City had about 18,000 and Boston had more than 15,000. Charles Town, South Carolina, with a population of 8,000, was the largest city in the South. In these cities and others, a new society with distinct social classes developed.

At the top of the social structure were wealthy merchants who controlled the city's trade. They patterned themselves after the British upper class, wearing elegant imported clothing, building luxurious mansions, and riding in fancy carriages. These rich merchants, however, were a tiny minority. Skilled artisans and their families made up nearly half of the urban colonial population. They included carpenters, silversmiths, glassmakers, coopers, bakers, masons, seamstresses, and shoemakers. Alongside the artisans in social status were innkeepers and retailers who owned their own businesses.

At the bottom of urban colonial society were the people without skills or property. Many of these people loaded and serviced ships at the harbor. Others worked as servants, washing clothes, grooming horses, cleaning houses, and sweeping streets. These people made up about 30 percent of urban society. Below them in status were indentured servants and enslaved Africans. Although relatively few enslaved people lived in the North, most dwelled in the cities there, making up 10 to 20 percent of the urban population.

The rapid development of cities created many problems, including overcrowding, crime, pollution, and epidemics. In response, city governments established constables' offices and fire departments, and charities arose to help the poor.

Reading Check **Examining** What occupation made up the majority of the wealthiest class in colonial society?

HISTORY Online **Study Central™** To review this section, go to **tarvol2.glencoe.com** and click on **Study Central™**.

SECTION 4 ASSESSMENT

Checking for Understanding

1. **Define:** cash crop, indentured servant, subsistence farming, slave code, entrepreneur, capitalist, triangular trade.
2. **Identify:** Nathaniel Bacon.
3. **Describe** how Europe's population explosion in the 1700s affected the Middle Colonies.

Reviewing Themes

4. **Culture and Traditions** Why did slavery become so important to the Southern Colonies?

Critical Thinking

5. **Analyzing** How did the slave trade develop in the Americas?
6. **Organizing** Complete a chart like the one below listing the causes and consequences of Bacon's Rebellion.

Causes	Consequences

Analyzing Visuals

7. **Examining Art** Study the painting on page 60 depicting Bacon's Rebellion. What motivated Nathaniel Bacon to lead his rebellion against the Virginia gentry?

Writing About History

8. **Descriptive Writing** Imagine you are an artisan in a Northern city in 1760. Write a letter to a friend in England, describing your daily life and urban society.

64 CHAPTER 2 The English Arrive in America

SECTION 4 ASSESSMENT ANSWERS

1. Terms are in blue.
2. Nathaniel Bacon (p. 59)
3. It led to a growing demand for wheat, which was the main cash crop of the Middle Colonies.
4. Enslaved persons became the primary labor force on plantations.
5. Enslaved persons were originally like indentured servants. Then they were increasingly restricted until slave codes removed all freedoms.
6. Causes: restrictions on voting rights, tax exemptions for the wealthy, desire to take land from Native Americans; Consequences: restrictions on voting rights removed, expansion westward supported by colonial governments, increase in use of enslaved persons
7. Answers will vary, but should discuss Bacon's role in the rebellion.
8. Answers will vary, but should discuss challenges and benefits of urban life.

SECTION 5 A Diverse Society

Guide to Reading

Main Idea
In the mid-1600s, England adopted measures to make trade with the colonies more profitable. With population growth, a colonial spirit of individualism emerged.

Key Terms and Names
mercantilism, John Locke, Enlightenment, revival, Great Awakening

Reading Strategy
Classifying As you read about colonial society in America in the 1700s, complete a graphic organizer similar to the one below identifying the reasons why various immigrant groups settled in the colonies.

Group	Where They Settled	Reasons for Immigrating
Germans		
Scotch-Irish		
Jews		

Reading Objectives
- **Describe** mercantilism's effect on the colonial attitude to England.
- **Outline** patterns of immigration in colonial America.

Section Theme
Culture and Traditions With economic and political stability, the colonies developed their own identity.

Preview of Events

◆1680   ◆1700   ◆1720   ◆1740

1686
Dominion of New England established

1688
Glorious Revolution takes place in England

1690
Two Treatises of Government published

1721
Cotton Mather promotes inoculations

c. 1740
Great Awakening peaks

★ An American Story ★

Benjamin Franklin

In the second half of the 1600s and the early 1700s, the British Parliament passed a series of laws that restricted and controlled colonial manufacturing. One of these laws affected the hat industry and another affected the iron industry. These laws annoyed many colonists, including Benjamin Franklin, who argued:

❝The hatters of England have prevailed to obtain an act in their own favor restraining that manufacture in America. . . . In the same manner have a few nail makers and a still smaller body of steelmakers (perhaps there are not half a dozen of these in England) prevailed totally to forbid by an act of Parliament the erecting of slitting mills or steel furnaces in America; that Americans may be obliged to take all their nails for their buildings and steel for their tools from these artificers [craft workers].❞

—**quoted in *The Rise of American Civilization***

Mercantilism

Mercantilism is a set of ideas about the world economy and how it works. These ideas were popular in the 1600s and 1700s. Mercantilists believed that to become wealthy and powerful, a country had to accumulate gold and silver. A country could do this by selling more goods to other countries than it bought from them. This would cause more gold and silver to flow into the country than flowed out to pay for products from other countries.

Mercantilists also argued that a country should be self-sufficient in raw materials. If it had to buy raw materials from another country, gold and silver would flow out to pay for them. Thus to be self sufficient, a country needed colonies where raw materials were

CHAPTER 2   The English Arrive in America   **65**

---

1 FOCUS

Section Overview
This section describes the growth of the economy, population, and spirit of individualism that arose in the colonies.

BELLRINGER
Skillbuilder Activity

Project transparency and have students answer the question.

Daily Focus Skills Transparency 2–5

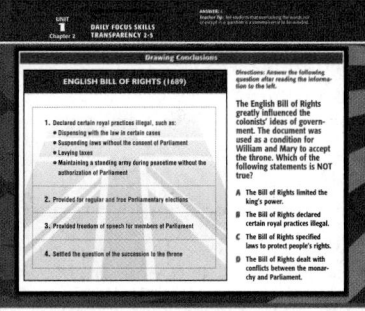

Reading Preview

Answers to Graphic: Germans settled in Pennsylvania to pursue religious freedom and escape religious wars. Scotch-Irish settled in Pennsylvania to escape rising taxes, poor harvests, and religious discrimination. Jews settled in New York, Philadelphia, Charleston, Savannah, and Newport to pursue religious freedom.

Preteaching Vocabulary
Assign students one of the Key Terms and Names. Have them prepare a 30-second oral presentation describing the term, event, or the person.

SECTION RESOURCES

📂 Reproducible Masters
- Reproducible Lesson Plan 2–5
- Daily Lecture and Discussion Notes 2–5
- Guided Reading Activity 2–5
- Section Quiz 2–5
- Reading Essentials and Study Guide 2–5
- Performance Assessment Activities and Rubrics

🖋 Transparencies
- Daily Focus Skills Transparency 2–5

Multimedia
- ⬤ Interactive Tutor Self-Assessment CD-ROM
- ⬤ ExamView® Pro Testmaker CD-ROM
- ⬤ Presentation Plus! CD-ROM
- ⬤ TeacherWorks™ CD-ROM
- ⬤ Audio Program

2 TEACH

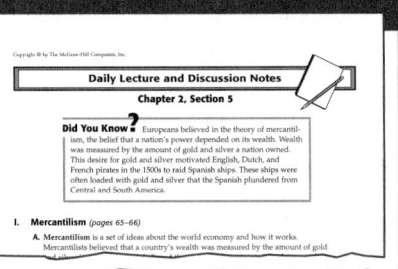

✓ Reading Check

Answer: They made raw materials from the colonies more expensive and encouraged illegal activities such as smuggling.

Creating a Bar Graph Have students use the population data on page 67 to create a bar graph showing the number of immigrants from each of the groups. Remind students to give the graph a title and to properly label the axes. **L1**

 Use the rubric for creating a map, display, or chart on pages 65–66 in the *Performance Assessment Activities and Rubrics.*

FYI

Sybilla Masters, wife of a Philadelphia merchant, invented a corn mill for producing hominy meal from Indian maize. As a woman, she could not own a patent; therefore she filed the patent application for her mill under her husband's name.

---

available. The home country would then buy raw materials from its colonies and sell them manufactured goods in return.

Mercantilism did provide some benefits to colonies. It gave them a reliable market for some of their raw materials and an eager supplier of manufactured goods. Mercantilism also had drawbacks, however. It prevented colonies from selling goods to other nations, even if they could get a better price. Furthermore, if a colony produced nothing the home country needed, it could not acquire gold or silver to buy manufactured goods. This was a serious problem in New England, and it partly explains why merchants there turned to triangular trade and smuggling. These methods were the only ways to get the gold and silver their colonies needed.

The Navigation Acts When Charles II assumed the throne in 1660, he and his advisers were determined to generate wealth for England in America. Charles asked Parliament to pass the Navigation Act of 1660, requiring that all goods shipped to and from the colonies be carried on English ships. Under this act, specific products could be sold only to England or other English colonies, including sugar, tobacco, lumber, cotton, wool, and indigo—the major products that earned money for the colonies.

Three years later, in 1663, Parliament passed another navigation act, the Staple Act. It required all colonial imports to come through England. Merchants bringing foreign goods to the colonies had to stop in England, pay taxes, and then ship the goods out again on English ships. This increased the price of the goods in the colonies.

Frustration with the **Navigation Acts** encouraged colonial merchants to break the new laws. New England merchants routinely smuggled goods to Europe, the Caribbean, and Africa. For the next few years, Massachusetts, especially, continued its defiance. Finally, in 1684, Charles II deprived Massachusetts of its charter and declared it a royal colony.

The Dominion of New England James II, who succeeded his brother Charles on the English throne in 1685, went even further in punishing New England merchants. In 1686 the English government merged Massachusetts, Plymouth, and Rhode Island together to create a new royal province called the **Dominion of New England.** The following year Connecticut and New Jersey were forced to join the Dominion, and by the spring of 1688, New York had been added as well.

King James II appointed Sir Edmund Andros to be the Dominion's first governor-general. Andros quickly made himself unpopular by levying new taxes and rigorously enforcing the Navigation Acts. Equally disturbing to Puritans were Andros's efforts to undermine their congregations. For example, Andros declared that only marriages performed in Anglican churches were legal.

✓ **Reading Check** **Examining** In what ways did the Navigation Acts affect trade in the colonies?

The Glorious Revolution of 1688

While Andros was angering New England colonists, King James II was losing support in England. He offended many by disregarding Parliament, revoking the charters of many English towns, and converting to Catholicism.

The birth of James's son in 1688 triggered protests against a Catholic heir. To prevent a Catholic dynasty, Parliament invited James's Protestant daughter Mary and her Dutch husband, William of Orange, to claim the throne. James fled, and William and Mary became the new rulers. This bloodless change of power is known as the **Glorious Revolution.**

Before assuming the throne, William and Mary had to swear their acceptance of the English Bill of Rights. This document, written in 1689, said monarchs could not suspend Parliament's laws or create their own courts, nor could they impose taxes or raise an army without Parliament's consent. The Bill of Rights also guaranteed freedom of speech within Parliament, banned excessive bail and cruel and unusual punishments, and guaranteed every English subject the right to an impartial jury in legal cases. 📖 *(See page 945 for an excerpt from the English Bill of Rights.)*

Consequences in America The English Bill of Rights later influenced American government. Almost immediately Boston colonists ousted Governor-General Andros. William and Mary then permitted Rhode Island and Connecticut to resume their previous forms of government, and they issued a new charter for Massachusetts in 1691.

The new charter combined Massachusetts Bay Colony, Plymouth Colony, and Maine into the royal colony of Massachusetts. The king retained the power to appoint a governor, but he restored the colonists' right to elect an assembly. Voters no longer had to belong to a Puritan congregation, and Anglicans there were granted freedom of worship.

▌▌ Reading Strategy ◀ READING THE TEXT

Identifying the Main Idea Students should identify main ideas as they read. Text features, such as headings, subheadings, boldfaced terms, and graphics, are good indicators of main or key ideas. As students read, have them make a list of ideas by creating an outline or drawing a graphic organizer. **L1**

 Refer to *Inclusion for the High School Social Studies Classroom Strategies and Activities* in the TCR.

GOVERNMENT

John Locke's Political Theories The Glorious Revolution of 1688 had another important legacy. It suggested there were times when revolution was justified. In 1690, **John Locke's** *Two Treatises of Government* was published on this subject. 📖 *(See page 946 for an excerpt from the* Two Treatises.*)*

Locke argued that a monarch's right to rule came from the people. All people, he said, were born with certain natural rights, including the right to life, liberty, and property. Because their rights were not safe in the state of nature in which people originally lived, people had come together to create a government. In effect, they had made a contract—they agreed to obey the government's laws, and the government agreed to uphold their rights. If a ruler violated those rights, the people were justified in rebelling.

Locke's ideas struck a chord with American colonists. When Thomas Jefferson drafted the Declaration of Independence in 1776, he relied upon the words and ideas of John Locke. The colonists understood Locke's "natural rights" to be the specific rights Englishmen had developed over the centuries and that were referred to in documents such as the Magna Carta and the English Bill of Rights. 📖 *(See page 942 for an excerpt from the Magna Carta.)*

✓ **Reading Check** **Summarizing** What actions did William and Mary take upon becoming the British monarchs?

America's Population Grows

After 1688 the American colonies grew quickly. People were having large families, and immigrants were flooding in from Europe and Africa.

Health Conditions American colonists in the 1700s married young and had numerous children. Between 1640 and 1700, the colonial population increased from 25,000 to more than 250,000. In the 1750s, the population surpassed 1 million.

An important factor in population growth was improved housing and sanitation. Although women often died in childbirth, many adults lived into their early sixties. Contagious diseases, however, such as typhoid fever, tuberculosis, cholera, diphtheria, and scarlet fever, remained a threat. In 1721 Puritan minister **Cotton Mather** promoted a novel practice "to prevent and abate the Dangers of the Small-Pox." His approach, inoculation, saved many lives.

Immigrants Immigration also contributed to population growth. Some 300,000 white immigrants arrived between 1700 and 1775. Most settled in the Middle Colonies, especially Pennsylvania. As early as 1683, German Mennonites had come to Pennsylvania to escape religious wars at home. By 1775 more than 100,000 Germans lived in the colony, making up about one-third of the population. Known as the **Pennsylvania Dutch** from their own word *Deutsch,* for German, these settlers often became prosperous farmers.

The Scotch-Irish also flocked to Pennsylvania. Burdened by rising taxes, poor harvests, and religious discrimination in Ireland, an estimated 150,000 Scotch-Irish came to the American colonies between 1717 and 1776.

Jews also found religious tolerance in America. In 1654 a small group of Portuguese Jews had arrived in New York, then New Amsterdam. By 1776 approximately 1,500 Jews lived in the colonies, mainly in New York, Philadelphia, Charles Town, Savannah, and Newport. They were allowed to worship freely, but could not vote or hold public office.

Women Like Jews, women did not receive equal rights in colonial America. At first, married women could not legally own property or make contracts or wills. Husbands were the sole guardians of the children and were allowed to physically discipline both them and their wives. Single women and widows, however, had more rights. They could own property, file lawsuits, and run businesses. In the 1700s, the status of married women improved. Despite legal limitations, many women worked outside their homes.

Port of Boston As one of the main cities in the colonies, Boston was a center of activity in colonial America. It was a central point for the anger over the creation of the Dominion of New England.

L1/ELL

Guided Reading Activity 2–5

Name _____ Date _____ Class _____

★ Guided Reading Activity 2-5

DIRECTIONS: Using Headings and Subheadings Locate each heading below in your textbook. Then use the information under the correct subheading to help you write each answer.

I. Mercantilism

A. According to the mercantilists, what did a country need to do in order to become wealthy and powerful?

B. What did New England merchants resort to in order to obtain the gold and silver they needed?

C. What were the requirements of the Navigation Act of 1660 and the Staple Act of 1663?

D. What was Massachusetts' punishment for smuggling?

II. The Glorious Revolution of 1688

✓ **Reading Check**

Answer: They signed the English Bill of Rights. They also permitted Rhode Island and Connecticut to resume their previous forms of government and issued a new charter for Massachusetts that combined the Massachusetts Bay Colony, Plymouth Colony, and Maine into one royal colony. The colony of Massachusetts was allowed to elect an assembly and worship freely.

More About the Art

Ask: Why did Massachusetts resist the Navigation Acts more strongly than the other colonies? *(They suffered the most since they had many of the major ports.)*

DIFFERENTIATED INSTRUCTION

Gifted and Talented Tell students that some people strongly objected to the idea of inoculations. Have students list possible objections that Cotton Mather may have encountered as he tried to convince his fellow citizens in Boston to be inoculated against smallpox. Using the list of objections, have students write a speech that Cotton Mather could have given to convince friends and fellow citizens to be inoculated. **L3**

📂 Refer to *Inclusion for the High School Social Studies Classroom Strategies and Activities* in the TCR.

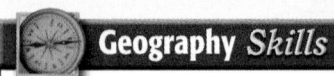

Geography *Skills*

Answers:

1. German, Scotch-Irish, and English
2. They followed the Hudson River up from New York, which used to be New Amsterdam.

Geography Skills Practice

Ask: Were most of the major cities located north or south of 35°N?

(Four of the five were north of 35°N.)

✓ Reading Check

Answer: Some escaped to the North, some refused to work, lost their tools, or rebelled.

3 ASSESS

Assign Section 5 Assessment as homework or as an in-class activity.

🌐 Have students use the **Interactive Tutor Self-Assessment CD-ROM.**

L1/ELL

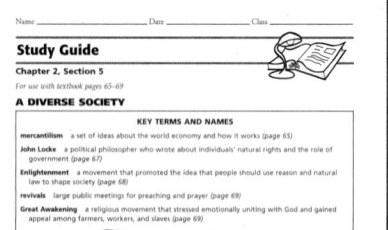

Reading Essentials and Study Guide 2–5

Name _____ Date _____ Class _____

Study Guide

Chapter 2, Section 5
For use with textbook pages 65–69

A DIVERSE SOCIETY

KEY TERMS AND NAMES

mercantilism a set of ideas about the world economy and how it works (page 65)

John Locke a political philosopher who wrote about individuals' natural rights and the role of government (page 67)

Enlightenment a movement that promoted the idea that people should use reason and natural law to shape society (page 68)

revivals large public meetings for preaching and prayer (page 69)

Great Awakening a religious movement that stressed emotionally uniting with God and gained appeal among farmers, workers, and slaves (page 69)

NATIONAL GEOGRAPHIC — Ethnic Diversity in Colonial America, 1760

0 ——— 200 miles
0 ——— 200 kilometers
Albers Conic Equal-Area projection

MAINE
(Part of MASS.)

N.H.
Boston
MASS.
N.Y.
CONN. Newport
R.I.
New York City 40°N
N.J.
PA.
Philadelphia
MD.
DEL.
VA.
ATLANTIC OCEAN
35°N
N.C.
S.C.
Charles Town
GA.

APPALACHIAN MTS.

Legend:
- African
- Dutch
- English
- German
- Scottish
- Scotch-Irish
- English, German & Scotch-Irish
- ---- Proclamation line

Major Cities, c. 1760

Population (in thousands)

- Boston: 15,631
- New York City: 18,000
- Charles Town: 8,000
- Newport: 7,500
- Philadelphia: 23,750

Source: *Colonial America to 1763.*

Geography *Skills*

1. **Interpreting Maps** What ethnic groups settled inland in the Pennsylvania area?
2. **Applying Geography Skills** Why did the Dutch settle in a narrow region north of New York?

Africans No group in the American colonies endured lower status or more hardship than enslaved Africans. By about 1775, these unwilling immigrants and their descendants numbered about 540,000, roughly 20 percent of the colonial population.

Most lived on Southern plantations, where they worked long days and were subjected to beatings and brandings by planters. Planters also controlled enslaved Africans by threatening to sell them away from their families.

Family and religion helped enslaved Africans maintain their dignity. Some resisted by escaping to the North; others refused to work hard or lost their tools. In 1739 a group of Africans who lived near the Stono River in South Carolina rebelled against their white overseers and raced south toward Spanish Florida. The

militia quickly ended the **Stono Rebellion,** which took the lives of 21 whites and 44 Africans.

✓ Reading Check   **Summarizing** In what ways did Africans resist their enslavement?

The Enlightenment and the Great Awakening

During the 1700s, America came under the influence of two great cultural movements. One championed human reason, while the other stressed an intense, personal relationship with God. Both challenged traditional views of the social order.

During the 1700s in Europe, a period known as the **Enlightenment,** thinkers believed that people should

---

INTERDISCIPLINARY CONNECTIONS ACTIVITY

Government Ask the government teacher to discuss why the English Bill of Rights was developed and what fundamental rights were granted under the bill. Have the teacher also explain the influence that John Locke had on the political thinking of his time. Ask students to list the rights they believe all Americans should have today. Then have them identify which items on the list relate to items that are found in the English Bill of Rights or in the theories of John Locke. 📦

use reason and natural law to shape society. John Locke's contract theory of government is an example of Enlightenment thinking. Locke also developed an influential view of human nature. He argued that people were not born sinful. Instead their minds were blank slates that would be shaped by experience and education. These ideas became very influential in American society.

While some Americans turned away from a religious worldview in the 1700s, others renewed their Christian faith. Throughout the colonies, ministers held revivals—large public meetings for preaching and prayer—where they stressed piety and being "born again," or emotionally uniting with God. This widespread resurgence of religious fervor is known as the Great Awakening.

The Great Awakening reached its height around 1740 with the fiery preaching of **Jonathan Edwards** and **George Whitefield**. Churches soon split into factions. Those that embraced the new ideas—including Baptists, Presbyterians, and Methodists—won many converts, while older, more traditional churches lost members.

In the South, the Baptists gained a strong following among poor farmers. Baptists also welcomed Africans at their revivals and condemned slavery. Despite violent attempts by planters to break up Baptist meetings, about 20 percent of Virginia's whites and thousands of enslaved Africans had become Baptists by 1775. The Enlightenment and the

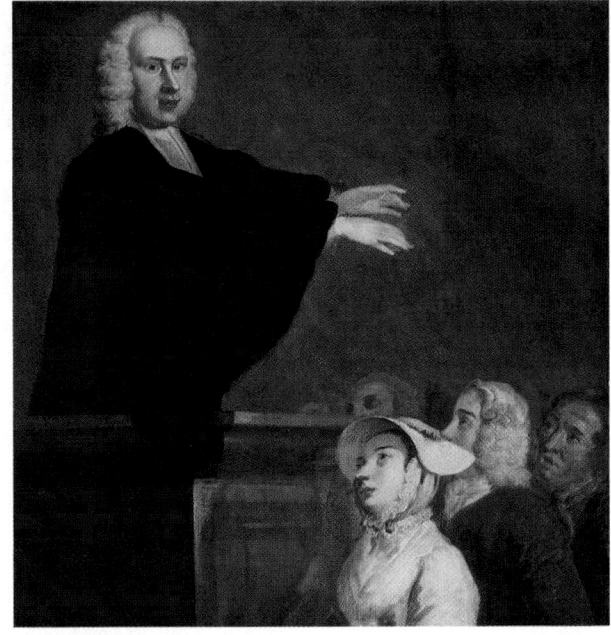

History *Through Art*

The Great Awakening George Whitefield, pictured here standing, was one of the most famous ministers of the colonial religious revival. Which religious denominations saw their memberships grow during the Great Awakening, and why?

Great Awakening had different origins, but both emphasized an individualism that inclined American colonists toward political independence.

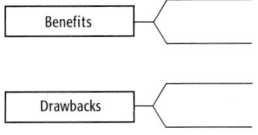 **Reading Check** **Determining Cause and Effect**
How did the Great Awakening affect the established order?

HISTORY Online **Study Central™** To review this section, go to tarvol2.glencoe.com and click on **Study Central™**.

SECTION 5 ASSESSMENT

Checking for Understanding
1. **Define:** mercantilism, Enlightenment, revival, Great Awakening.
2. **Identify:** John Locke.
3. **Explain** why the population of the American colonies increased dramatically in the 1700s.

Reviewing Themes
4. **Culture and Traditions** In what ways did the Enlightenment and the Great Awakening contribute to the independent spirit of American colonists?

Critical Thinking
5. **Analyzing** How did England's Glorious Revolution influence the American colonies?
6. **Categorizing** Use a graphic organizer similar to the one below to explain the benefits and drawbacks of mercantilism for both England and the colonies.

Benefits

Drawbacks

Analyzing Visuals
7. **Analyzing Maps** Study the map of ethnic diversity in colonial America on page 68. In what areas were African immigrants most concentrated in the mid-1700s? Why do you suppose this concentration occurred?

Writing About History
8. **Descriptive Writing** Imagine you are a teenager living in the colonies around 1750. Keep a journal of your daily activities for one week.

CHAPTER 2 The English Arrive in America **69**

SECTION 5 ASSESSMENT ANSWERS

1. Terms are in blue.
2. John Locke (p. 67)
3. large families, many immigrants, better health conditions
4. The Enlightenment stressed human reason and support for education. The Great Awakening emphasized an individual Christian experience and encouraged individualism.
5. It offered a justification to stage a revolt against Andros, and led to the English Bill of Rights.
6. Benefits to England: source of raw materials and market for goods. Benefits to American colonies: market for raw materials and a source for manufactured goods.
7. South Carolina and Virginia because of labor needs on plantations.
8. Students' journal entries will vary, but should match the place they have chosen to live. For example, life on a plantation would be considerably different from life in Boston.

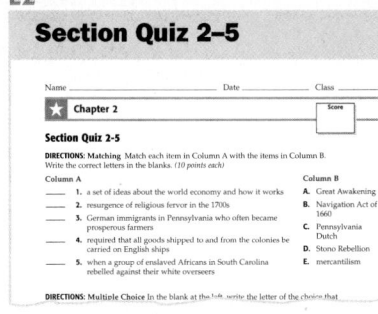

History *Through Art*
Answer: Baptists, Presbyterians, and Methodists, because they embraced new ideas

Reteach
Have students compose a review question for each page of this section. Ask students to take turns asking their questions until the important points of the section are covered.

Enrich
Have students select a person, an event, or a movement from this section and write an essay about the continuing influence of the person, event, or movement.

Reading Check
Answer: It split churches into various factions with some factions openly condemning slavery. It also reinforced the concept of individualism.

HISTORY Online
Study Central™ provides summaries, interactive games, and online graphic organizers to help students review section content.

4 CLOSE
Have students compare and contrast the Enlightenment and the Great Awakening.

CHAPTER 2 ASSESSMENT and ACTIVITIES

ASSESSMENT and ACTIVITIES

GLENCOE TECHNOLOGY

MindJogger Videoquiz
Use the **MindJogger Videoquiz** to review Chapter 2 content.

 Available in DVD

Reviewing Key Terms
Students' answers will vary. The pages where the words appear in the text are shown in parentheses.

1. Puritan *(p. 44)*; **2. enclosure movement** *(p. 44)*; **3. joint-stock company** *(p. 44)*; **4. privateer** *(p. 44)*; **5. burgesses** *(p. 46)*; **6. headright** *(p. 46)*; **7. proprietary colony** *(p. 47)*; **8. Separatists** *(p. 48)*; **9. Pilgrim** *(p. 49)*; **10. heretic** *(p. 50)*; **11. pacifism** *(p. 55)*; **12. debtor** *(p. 56)*; **13. cash crop** *(p. 59)*; **14. indentured servants** *(p. 59)*; **15. subsistence farming** *(p. 59)*; **16. slave code** *(p. 61)*; **17. entrepreneur** *(p. 63)*; **18. capitalist** *(p. 63)*; **19. triangular trade** *(p. 64)*; **20. mercantilism** *(p. 65)*; **21. Enlightenment** *(p. 68)*; **22. revival** *(p. 69)*; **23. Great Awakening** *(p. 69)*

Reviewing Key Facts
24. John Smith *(p. 45)*, William Penn *(p. 55)*, Nathaniel Bacon *(p. 59)*, John Locke *(p. 67)*

25. Joint-stock companies pooled the money of multiple investors in order to raise large sums of money for large projects. This meant that English merchants could afford to trade with and colonize other parts of the world without government financing.

26. Roger Williams left Massachusetts because he believed the Puritans were corrupting themselves by continuing to be part of the Anglican Church.

27. The English wanted to expand their colonial interests in America. They decided to seize New Netherlands because it would connect their existing colonies.

Reviewing Key Terms
On a sheet of paper, use each of these terms in a sentence.

1. Puritan
2. enclosure movement
3. joint-stock company
4. privateer
5. burgesses
6. headright
7. proprietary colony
8. Separatist
9. Pilgrim
10. heretic
11. pacifism
12. debtor
13. cash crop
14. indentured servant
15. subsistence farming
16. slave code
17. entrepreneur
18. capitalist
19. triangular trade
20. mercantilism
21. Enlightenment
22. revival
23. Great Awakening

Reviewing Key Facts
24. **Identify:** John Smith, William Penn, Nathaniel Bacon, John Locke.
25. How did joint-stock companies help colonize North America?
26. What caused Roger Williams to leave Massachusetts and found the town of Providence?
27. Why did the English government seize New Netherland from the Dutch?
28. Why did Southern planters come to depend on enslaved labor?
29. Why did England pass the Navigation Acts?

Critical Thinking
30. **Analyzing Themes: Global Connections** How did events in Europe contribute to the development of the American colonies?

Chapter Summary

The American Colonies

Region	Geography	Economy	People and Society
New England Colonies	Coastal areas with good natural harbors; inland areas with dense forests; poor rocky soil and short growing season	Small farms, lumber mills, fishing, shipbuilding, and trade flourished; cities developed along coast.	Most people organized as congregations lived on farms; in the cities merchants controlled trade, artisans made goods, unskilled workers and enslaved Africans provided labor.
Middle Colonies	Fertile soil and long growing season; rivers ran into backcountry	Colonies grew large amounts of rye, oats, barley, potatoes, and wheat as cash crops to sell; cities developed on the coast.	Wealthiest people owned large farms and other businesses. Most farmers produced a small surplus. Tenant farmers rented land from large landowners or worked for wages.
Southern Colonies	Favorable climate and soil for agriculture; wide rivers made cities unnecessary	Tobacco, rice, and indigo grown on large plantations emerged as cash crops.	Wealthy elite controlled most of the land. Cash crops required a large amount of labor, which was supplied on large farms by indentured servants and enslaved Africans.

28. The crops grown in the Southern Colonies required intense manual labor. Southern planters could not afford to pay wages to workers, but with slave labor they could make a living from their agricultural endeavors.

29. The Navigation Acts were passed to support England's mercantilist policy of encouraging English exports and restricting imports. Mercantilism also emphasized the use of colonies as sources of raw materials and markets for manufactured goods.

Critical Thinking
30. Colonization in the Americas was affected by England's foreign policy and internal crises. For example, it founded Georgia as a buffer against Spain and took New Amsterdam from the Dutch to found New York. Colonization came to a standstill during the English Civil War, but resumed in earnest afterwards. Also, changes in English policy regarding slavery helped plantations develop.

HISTORY Online

31. Identifying Cause and Effect How did the English Civil War affect the English colonies in North America?

32. Forming an Opinion Do you think slavery would have become entrenched in the South if the region's economy had not depended on cash crops and a large labor force? Why or why not?

Practicing Skills

33. Understanding the Parts of a Map Study the map of the Triangular Trade on page 63. Then use the skills described in the SkillBuilder on page 57 to answer the following questions.
   a. What information is included on the green lines?
   b. What do the arrows on the map indicate?

Geography and History

34. The map on this page shows colonization and exports in the Americas in 1750. Study the map and answer the questions below.
   a. Interpreting Maps Which region produced diamonds?
   b. Applying Geography Skills Which export products involved the use of enslaved persons? Why?

Chapter Activity

35. Technology Activity: Using the Internet Search the Internet for places to visit that provide insight into colonial life in America in the 1700s. Use the information to create a travel brochure titled "Visit Colonial America." Display the brochures in your classroom.

36. American History Primary Source Document Library CD-ROM Read John Winthrop's article "Views on Liberty" under *Colonial America.* Answer the Guided Reading questions with your classmates. Do you think Winthrop's comparison of the relationship of citizens and their officials to that of husbands and wives would be accepted in the United States today? Why or why not?

Writing Activity

37. Portfolio Writing New governments in the English colonies often offered incentives for settlers. Pretend you have decided to move to America. In which colony would you choose to settle? Write a letter to your family explaining your choice. Place the letter in your portfolio.

NATIONAL GEOGRAPHIC
Colonization and Exports in the Americas, 1750

FRENCH NORTH AMERICA

NEW SPAIN

Whale products, fish, furs, grain, tobacco, rice, and naval stores

THIRTEEN COLONIES (BRITISH)

Sugar, tobacco

Silver

Skins

ATLANTIC OCEAN

Cochineal, gold

Gold

Tobacco, cocoa beans, hides

GUIANA

NEW GRANADA

Rare plants

BRAZIL

Dyewoods, tobacco, sugar, cotton, gold, diamonds

PACIFIC OCEAN

PERU

Beef

Hides, silver

0   1,000 miles
0   1,000 kilometers
Azimuthal Equal-Area projection

- ☐ British
- ☐ Dutch
- ☐ French
- ☐ Portuguese
- ☐ Spanish

Standardized Test Practice

Directions: Choose the best answer to the following question.

Which of the following is true about the early colonies of Jamestown AND Plymouth?

A Both colonies were started by people interested in establishing a new nation.

B Both colonies suffered severe loss of life.

C The primary source of income for both colonies was tobacco.

D Both colonies were started by religious separatists.

Test-Taking Tip: The important word in the question is *and.* Look for an answer that applies to *both* colonies. For example, while it is true that the Pilgrims founded the Plymouth colony for religious reasons, the Jamestown founders were primarily looking for gold and adventure.

HISTORY Online

36. Students' answers will vary. Their responses will likely indicate that the roles of husbands and wives and citizens and officials have changed in some respects over time. Some may point out similarities. Students should be able to defend their points of view.

Writing Activity

37. Student's answers will vary, but should include specific geographic, economic, or other reasons for the choice.

Standardized Test Practice

Answer: B

Test-Taking Tip: Suggest that students look for an answer that applies to both colonies. The primary source of income for Jamestown was tobacco, but there is no evidence that the Pilgrims grew tobacco. Therefore, students can rule out C. Religious separatists started Plymouth while the Jamestown founders were looking for gold and adventure, not a new nation. Therefore, students can rule out both A and D.

---

31. The English Civil War forced the colonies to choose sides between the King and Parliament. The war limited trade and all but stopped the immigration of new settlers. The end of the war and the Restoration brought renewed efforts to colonize America.

32. Students' answers will vary. Their stated reasons should support their point of view.

Practicing Skills

33. a. intercolonial trade; **b.** the flow of goods

Geography and History

34. a. Brazil; **b.** sugar and tobacco, because these were labor-intensive crops

Chapter Activities

35. Displays will vary. Encourage students to keep proper documentation of the sites they referenced, including the date on which the information was retrieved.

Bonus Question ?

Ask: What is the name of the Puritan group that separated from the Anglican Church and fled to Holland? *(Pilgrims)*

Chapter 3 Resources

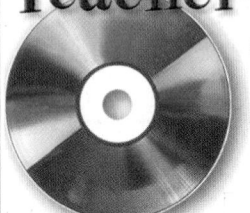

TeacherWorks™ All-In-One Planner and Resource Center

- **Interactive Teacher Edition** Access your Teacher Wraparound Edition and your classroom resources with a few easy clicks.
- **Interactive Lesson Planner** Planning has never been easier! Organize your week, month, semester, or year with all the lesson helps you need to make teaching creative, timely, and relevant.

Use Glencoe's **Presentation Plus!** multimedia teacher tool to easily present dynamic lessons that visually excite your students. Using Microsoft PowerPoint® you can customize the presentations to create your own personalized lessons.

TEACHING TRANSPARENCIES

Graphic Organizer 3 L2

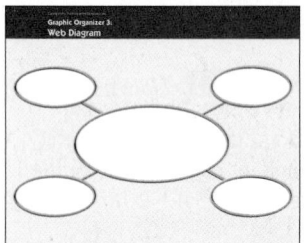

Why It Matters Chapter Transparency 3 L2

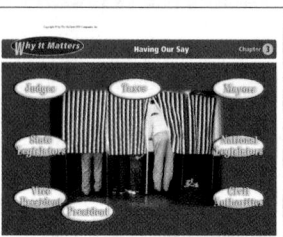

APPLICATION AND ENRICHMENT

Linking Past and Present Activity 3 L2

Enrichment Activity 3 L3

Primary Source Reading 3 L2

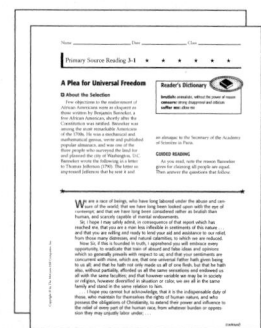

REVIEW AND REINFORCEMENT

Reteaching Activity 3 L1

Vocabulary Activity 3 L1

Time Line Activity 3 L2

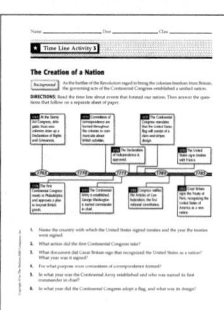

Critical Thinking Skills Activity 3 L2

Meeting NCSS Standards

Local Standards

The following standards are covered in Chapter 3:

Section 1	II	Time, Continuity, and Change: B
Section 2	X	Civic Ideals and Practices: A, B, E, F
Section 3	VI	Power, Authority, and Governance: F, G
Section 4	V	Individuals, Groups, and Institutions: B, E, F, G
Section 5	VI	Power, Authority, and Governance: B, C, E

Chapter 3 Resources

ASSESSMENT AND EVALUATION

**Chapter 3 Test
Form A L2**

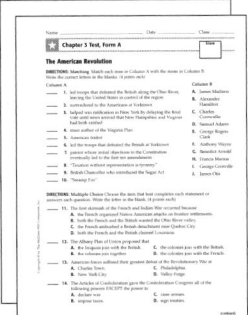

**Chapter 3 Test
Form B L2**

**Standardized Test Practice
Workbook Activity 3 L2**

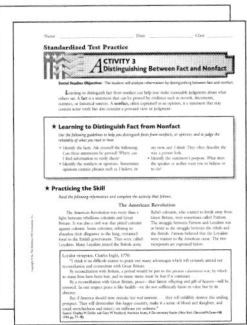

**Performance Assessment
Activities and Rubrics 3 L1/ELL**

**ExamView® Pro
Testmaker CD-ROM**

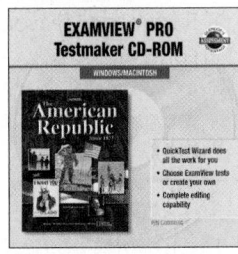

MULTIMEDIA

- 💿 **Vocabulary PuzzleMaker CD-ROM**
- 💿 **Interactive Tutor Self-Assessment CD-ROM**
- 💿 **ExamView® Pro Testmaker CD-ROM**
- 🎧 **Audio Program**
- 💿 **American History Primary Source Documents Library CD-ROM**
- 💿 **MindJogger Videoquiz**
- 💿 **Presentation Plus! CD-ROM**
- 💿 **TeacherWorks™ CD-ROM**
- 💿 **Interactive Student Edition CD-ROM**
- 💿 **Glencoe Skillbuilder Interactive Workbook CD-ROM, Level 2**
- 💿 **The *American Republic Since 1877* Video Program**
- 🎵 **American Music: Hits Through History**
- 🎵 **American Music: Cultural Traditions**

SPANISH RESOURCES

The following Spanish language materials are available:

- **Spanish Reading Essentials and Study Guide**
- **Spanish Guided Reading Activities**
- **Spanish Reteaching Activities**
- **Spanish Quizzes and Tests**
- **Spanish Vocabulary Activities**
- **Spanish Summaries**
- **The Declaration of Independence and United States Constitution Spanish Translation**

The following videotape programs are available from Glencoe as supplements to Chapter 3:

- **George Washington: Founding Father** (ISBN 1-56-501377-8)
- **Benjamin Franklin: Citizen of the World** (ISBN 1-56-501426-X)
- **Thomas Jefferson: Philosopher of Freedom** (ISBN 1-56-501502-9)
- **The American Revolution** (Six Video Set) (ISBN 1-56-501436-7)

To order, call Glencoe at 1-800-334-7344. To find classroom resources to accompany many of these videos, check the following home pages:
A&E Television: www.aande.com
The History Channel: www.historychannel.com

Use our Web site for additional resources. All essential content is covered in the Student Edition.

You and your students can visit tarvol2.glencoe.com, the Web site companion to the ***American Republic Since 1877***. This innovative integration of electronic and print media offers your students a wealth of opportunities. The student text directs students to the Web site for the following options:

- **Chapter Overviews**
- **Self-Check Quizzes**
- **Student Web Activities**
- **Textbook Updates**

Answers to the student Web activities are provided for you in the **Web Activity Lesson Plans.** Additional Web resources and Interactive Tutor Puzzles are also available.

Chapter 3 Resources

SECTION RESOURCES

Daily Objectives	Reproducible Resources	Multimedia Resources
SECTION 1 **The Colonies Fight for Their Rights** 1. Summarize reasons for colonial discontent. 2. Explain how the Stamp Act affected the relationship between Britain and the colonies.	Reproducible Lesson Plan 3–1 Daily Lecture and Discussion Notes 3–1 Guided Reading Activity 3–1* Section Quiz 3–1* Reading Essentials and Study Guide 3–1* Performance Assessment Activities and Rubrics	Daily Focus Skills Transparency 3–1 Interactive Tutor Self-Assessment CD-ROM ExamView® Pro Testmaker CD-ROM* Presentation Plus! CD-ROM American Music: Cultural Traditions
SECTION 2 **The Revolution Begins** 1. Summarize the first battles between Britain and the colonies. 2. Explain the circumstances under which the colonies declared their independence.	Reproducible Lesson Plan 3–2 Daily Lecture and Discussion Notes 3–2 Guided Reading Activity 3–2* Section Quiz 3–2* Reading Essentials and Study Guide 3–2* Performance Assessment Activities and Rubrics American History in Graphic Novel	Daily Focus Skills Transparency 3–2 American Art & Architecture Interactive Tutor Self-Assessment CD-ROM ExamView® Pro Testmaker CD-ROM* Presentation Plus! CD-ROM ABCNews Interactive™ Historic America Electronic Field Trips
SECTION 3 **The War for Independence** 1. List the advantages and disadvantages of each side at the beginning of the war. 2. Discuss the roles of France and Spain in the war, and explain how the war ended.	Reproducible Lesson Plan 3–3 Daily Lecture and Discussion Notes 3–3 Guided Reading Activity 3–3* Section Quiz 3–3* Reading Essentials and Study Guide 3–3* Performance Assessment Activities and Rubrics Interpreting Political Cartoons	Daily Focus Skills Transparency 3–3 American Art & Architecture Interactive Tutor Self-Assessment CD-ROM ExamView® Pro Testmaker CD-ROM* Presentation Plus! CD-ROM American Music: Hits Through History American Music: Cultural Traditions
SECTION 4 **The Confederation** 1. Discuss the new political ideas that prevailed following the war. 2. Examine the strengths and weaknesses of the newly formed Confederation Congress.	Reproducible Lesson Plan 3–4 Daily Lecture and Discussion Notes 3–4 Guided Reading Activity 3–4* Section Quiz 3–4* Reading Essentials and Study Guide 3–4* Performance Assessment Activities and Rubrics	Daily Focus Skills Transparency 3–4 Interactive Tutor Self-Assessment CD-ROM ExamView® Pro Testmaker CD-ROM* Presentation Plus! CD-ROM Skillbuilder Interactive Workbook, Level 2
SECTION 5 **A New Constitution** 1. Outline the framework for the new federal government. 2. Summarize the main points in the debate between Federalists and Antifederalists.	Reproducible Lesson Plan 3–5 Daily Lecture and Discussion Notes 3–5 Guided Reading Activity 3–5* Section Quiz 3–5* Reading Essentials and Study Guide 3–5* Performance Assessment Activities and Rubrics	Daily Focus Skills Transparency 3–5 Interactive Tutor Self-Assessment CD-ROM ExamView® Pro Testmaker CD-ROM* Presentation Plus! CD-ROM Vocabulary PuzzleMaker CD-ROM

`0:00` **OUT OF TIME?**
Assign the Chapter 3 **Reading Essentials and Study Guide.**

*Also Available in Spanish

 Printed Materials   Transparency   CD-ROM   DVD

 Poster   Music Program   Audio Program   Videocassette

NATIONAL GEOGRAPHIC Teacher's Corner

INDEX TO NATIONAL GEOGRAPHIC MAGAZINE

The following articles relate to this chapter.

- "Phips's Fleet," August 2000
- "Thomas Jefferson: Architect of Freedom," February 1976
- "Two Revolutions," July 1989
- "Yorktown Shipwreck," June 1988

NATIONAL GEOGRAPHIC SOCIETY PRODUCTS

To order the following, call National Geographic at 1-800-368-2728:

- *Branches of Government Series* (Video)
- *The Complete National Geographic: 109 Years of National Geographic Magazine* (CD-ROM)
- *Democratic Government Series, "The United States"* (Video)
- *Historical Atlas of the United States*

NGS ONLINE

Access National Geographic's Web site for current events, atlas updates, activities, links, interactive features, and archives.

www.nationalgeographic.com

MEETING SPECIAL NEEDS

In addition to the Differentiated Instruction strategies found in each section, the following resources are also suitable for your special needs students:

- *ExamView® Pro Testmaker CD-ROM* allows teachers to tailor tests by reducing answer choices.
- The *Audio Program* includes the entire narrative of the student edition so that less-proficient readers can listen to the words as they read them.
- The *Reading Essentials and Study Guide* provides the same content as the student edition but is written two grade levels below the textbook.

KEY TO ABILITY LEVELS

Teaching strategies have been coded.

L1   BASIC activities for all students
L2   AVERAGE activities for average to above-average students
L3   CHALLENGING activities for above-average students
ELL   ENGLISH LANGUAGE LEARNER activities

From the Classroom of...

Mike Midler
Elsik High School
Houston, TX

King Eggbert of Eggtonia

King Eggbert is an absolute monarch in the Kingdom of Eggtonia. Many subjects wish to see major changes. Some of the more radical subjects want to secede entirely and start a new country.

Create a list of ten restrictive rules, such as: an 8 P.M. curfew; the king assigns all jobs; all subjects must belong to the Eggtonian Church; no more than three people can gather together at once; tax rate of 75%; no one may leave Eggtonia; and all subjects must carry ID papers to present to authorities on demand. Present the list to the students.

Each student role-plays one of King Eggbert's subjects who wants to bring reform or start a new nation. They write a one-page letter to the king discussing five specific grievances they have and justifying their solutions.

Students must decorate a cover sheet to depict what King Eggbert or his kingdom might look like based on their grievances. (Use a sheet of 12 × 18 paper folded over with the art on the cover and the letter pasted inside.)

ADDITIONAL RESOURCES FROM GLENCOE

- American Music: Cultural Traditions
- American Art & Architecture
- Outline Map Resource Book
- U.S. Desk Map
- Building Geography Skills for Life
- Inclusion for the High School Social Studies Classroom Strategies and Activities
- Teaching Strategies for the American History Classroom (Including Block Scheduling Pacing Guides)
- Dinah Zike's High School American History Reading and Study Skills Foldables

 Block Schedule

Activities that are suited to use within the block scheduling framework are identified by:

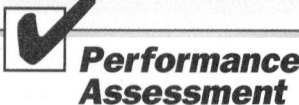

Performance Assessment

Refer to Activity 3 in the Performance Assessment Activities and Rubrics booklet. 📇

Why It Matters Activity

Ask students what the colonists were fighting for during the American Revolution. Students should evaluate their answers after they have completed the chapter.

GLENCOE
TECHNOLOGY

The *American Republic Since 1877* Video Program
To learn more about America from 1754 to 1789, have students view the Chapter 3 video, "The Power of the Constitution," from the *American Republic Since 1877* Video Program.

MindJogger Videoquiz
Use the **MindJogger Videoquiz** to preview Chapter 3 content.

💿 Both programs available in DVD

CHAPTER
3 The American Revolution *1754–1789*

Why It Matters

In the early colonial period, colonists grew accustomed to running their own affairs. When Britain tried to reestablish control, tensions mounted over taxes and basic rights. In 1775 these tensions led to battle, and in 1776 the colonists declared their independence. With the help of France and Spain, the colonists defeated the British in 1781; the conflict formally ended with the Treaty of Paris in 1783. After the war, the new nation drew up a plan of government that balanced the power of a central government against the powers of the states.

The Impact Today

The American Revolution and the country's early experiences had lasting results.
• Americans value and protect local liberties and the right to representation in government.
• The Constitution remains a model for representative government.

💿 **The American Republic Since 1877 *Video***
The Chapter 3 video, "The Power of the Constitution," discusses one of the nation's most important documents.

1770
• British troops fire on colonists in Boston Massacre

1754
• French and Indian War for control of eastern North America begins

1765
• Parliament passes the Stamp Act, triggering protests throughout the colonies

United States
PRESIDENTS

1750   *1760*   *1770*

World

1748
• Montesquieu's *Spirit of the Laws* published

1755
• Samuel Johnson's *Dictionary of the English Language* published

1751
• Chinese invade Tibet and control succession to the throne

1769
• Steam engine patented by James Watt

72

📖 Reading Strategy ▸ **PURPOSE FOR READING**

Hypothesis-Proof Notes This strategy is integral to teaching the research process by analyzing written materials according to theoretical assumptions. Have students create a two-column chart. In the first column, titled "Hypothesis," they should write a hypothesis about why the colonists declared their independence from Britain and list three reasons. Students should complete the right column, titled "Proof," as they read the chapter, verifying the hypothesis statement and reasons. **L2**

📂 Refer to *Inclusion for the High School Social Studies Classroom Strategies and Activities* in the TCR.

Washington Crossing the Delaware by Emanuel Gottlieb Leutze, 1851

1775
- The first shots of the Revolutionary War fired at Lexington and Concord in Massachusetts

1776
- Declaration of Independence signed

1781
- Cornwallis surrenders at Yorktown
- Articles of Confederation ratified

1783
- Treaty of Paris signed, officially ending war

1786
- Shays's Rebellion begins

1787
- Constitutional Convention begins in Philadelphia

1789
- George Washington becomes first president under the Constitution

Washington 1789–1797

1780

1790

1776
- Adam Smith's treatise on mercantilism, *The Wealth of Nations,* published

1778
- James Cook lands on Hawaii

1787
- Freed Africans found colony in Sierra Leone

1789
- French Revolution begins

Chapter Overview
Visit the *American Republic Since 1877* Web site at tarvol2.glencoe.com and click on *Chapter Overviews—Chapter 3* to preview chapter information.

73

HISTORY Online

Introduce students to chapter content and key terms by having them access the **Chapter 3 Overview** at tarvol2.glencoe.com.

More About the Art

Ask: What techniques does the artist use to communicate the season? *(possible answers: ice floating on the water, the flag is being held against a strong wind, people are bundled up)*

TIME LINE ACTIVITY

Have students use the chapter and section time lines to create a single time line that incorporates all of the significant dates related to the American Revolution.

FOLDABLES™ Study Organizer

Dinah Zike's Foldables are three-dimensional, interactive graphic organizers that help students practice basic writing skills, review key vocabulary terms, and identify main ideas. Have students complete the foldable activity in the *Dinah Zike's Reading and Study Skills Foldables* booklet.

GRAPHIC ORGANIZER ACTIVITY

Organizing Information Have students create a chapter time line in which they list all the significant British acts above the time line and all the battles below the time line.

(Students' time lines will vary but should include all the relevant British acts and all the battles. Encourage students to use the time line as they study for chapter and unit assessments.)

1 FOCUS

Section Overview

This section focuses on Britain's attempts to control the American colonies and the colonists' growing discontent.

BELLRINGER
Skillbuilder Activity

Project transparency and have students answer the question.

Daily Focus Skills Transparency 3–1

Reading Preview

Answers to Graphic: dispute over control of the Ohio River valley, building of French forts from Lake Ontario to the Ohio River

Preteaching Vocabulary
Have students skim the section to preview each of the Key Terms and Names.

SECTION 1 The Colonies Fight for Their Rights

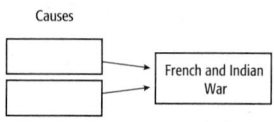

Guide to Reading

Main Idea
Tensions grew as British leaders sought greater control over the American colonies.

Key Terms and Names
Albany Plan of Union, French and Indian War, Royal Proclamation of 1763, customs duty, Sons of Liberty, Stamp Act Congress, nonimportation agreement, writs of assistance

Reading Strategy
Organizing As you read about the growing tensions between Britain and the American colonies, complete a graphic organizer like the one below by listing the causes of the French and Indian War.

Causes

→ French and Indian War

Reading Objectives
• **Summarize** reasons for colonial discontent.
• **Explain** how the Stamp Act affected the relationship between Britain and the colonies.

Section Theme
Civic Rights and Responsibilities The colonists' belief that they had the same rights as English citizens led to a struggle against Parliament and the king.

Preview of Events

| ♦1754 | ♦1760 | ♦1766 | ♦1772 |

1754
French and Indian War begins; Albany Conference meets

1763
Treaty of Paris ends French and Indian War

1765
Stamp Act passed

1767
Townshend Acts passed

1770
Boston Massacre

★ An American Story ★

British revenue stamp

At first, Pennsylvania colonist John Hughes was delighted when his friend Ben Franklin helped him to get the position of stamp tax collector. By September 1765, however, he feared his job might cost him his life. Anti-tax protests had grown so strong that Hughes barricaded himself inside his house to avoid being attacked. He wrote frantically to Franklin in London:

❝You are now from Letter to Letter to suppose each may be the last you will receive from your old Friend, as the Spirit of . . . Rebellion is to a high Pitch. . . . Madness has got hold of the people. . . . I fancy some Lives will be lost before this Fire is put out. . . .❞

Just a few years earlier, British soldiers and American colonists had fought side by side in a successful war against France. After the war ended, tensions between Britain and its colonies grew. Britain wanted the colonies to help pay for the war, while the colonists questioned Britain's authority to make them do so. Misunderstanding and distrust slowly turned many colonists against the British, creating situations that would eventually lead to revolution.

—adapted from *What They Didn't Teach You About the American Revolution*

The French and Indian War

The French and English had been vying for dominance in Europe since the late 1600s, fighting three major wars between 1689 and 1748. Most of the action took place in Europe, but when France and England were at war, their colonies were at war as well. In 1754 a new struggle began.

SECTION RESOURCES

📂 Reproducible Masters
• Reproducible Lesson Plan 3–1
• Daily Lecture and Discussion Notes 3–1
• Guided Reading Activity 3–1
• Section Quiz 3–1
• Reading Essentials and Study Guide 3–1

📖 Transparencies
• Daily Focus Skills Transparency 3–1

Multimedia
🖥 Interactive Tutor Self-Assessment CD-ROM
🖥 ExamView® Pro Testmaker CD-ROM
🖥 Presentation Plus! CD-ROM
🖥 TeacherWorks™ CD-ROM
🔊 Audio Program
🎵 American Music: Cultural Traditions

The First Skirmish In the 1740s, the British and French both became interested in the Ohio River valley. By crossing from Lake Ontario to the Ohio River and following the river south to the Mississippi, the French could travel from New France to Louisiana easily. Meanwhile, British fur traders were entering the Ohio region, and British land speculators began eyeing the land to sell to settlers.

To block British claims in the region, the French built a chain of forts from Lake Ontario to the Ohio River. The British decided to counter with a fort of their own in western Pennsylvania. Before they could complete it, however, the French seized it and built **Fort Duquesne** on the site.

In an attempt to expel the French, a young Virginian, **George Washington,** led troops toward the Ohio River in the spring of 1754. After a brief battle with a small French force, Washington retreated to a hastily built stockade, **Fort Necessity.** A little over a month later, a large French force arrived and forced Washington to surrender. Ownership of the Ohio River valley was far from settled, however. Within a few years, the conflict would grow into a worldwide war involving several European powers.

The Albany Conference Even before the fighting started, the British government anticipated hostilities. It urged the colonies to work together to prepare for war and to negotiate an alliance with the Iroquois. The Iroquois controlled western New York, territory the French had to pass through to reach the Ohio River. Accordingly, in June 1754, delegates from seven colonies met with 150 Iroquois leaders at Albany, New York.

This meeting, known as the Albany Conference, achieved several things. Although the Iroquois refused an alliance with the British, they did agree to remain neutral. The colonies also agreed that Britain should appoint one supreme commander of all troops in the colonies. Finally, Benjamin Franklin and others at the conference developed the **Albany Plan of Union,** which proposed that the colonies unite to form a federal government.

Although the colonies rejected the plan, it showed that many colonial leaders had begun to think about joining together for defense.

The British Triumph In 1755 the new British commander in chief, General **Edward Braddock,** arrived in Virginia with 1,400 troops. He linked up with 450 local militia troops and appointed Lieutenant Colonel George Washington to serve as his aide. Braddock then headed west, intending to attack Fort Duquesne. The general disregarded warnings about the Native American allies of the French. "These savages may indeed be a formidable enemy to your raw American militia," he told Benjamin Franklin. "Upon the King's regular and disciplined troops, it is impossible they should make any impression."

Braddock's comments later came back to haunt him. Seven miles from Fort Duquesne, French and Native American forces ambushed the British. Braddock was shot and later died. His inexperienced soldiers panicked, and only Washington's leadership saved them from disaster. As enemy shots whizzed past him—leaving four holes in his hat and clothes—Washington rallied the troops and organized a retreat.

The ambush emboldened the Delaware people of western Pennsylvania to begin attacking British settlers on their land. For the next two years, the **French and Indian War,** as it was called, raged along the

History *Through Art*

Fatal Meeting The Battle of Quebec in 1759 was one of Britain's most dramatic victories over the French during the French and Indian War. Both commanding generals, the French Montcalm and the British Wolfe, were killed on the Plains of Abraham, the bluffs above the St. Lawrence River. *From studying the painting, why do you think it was difficult for the British to invade Quebec?*

CHAPTER 3   The American Revolution   **75**

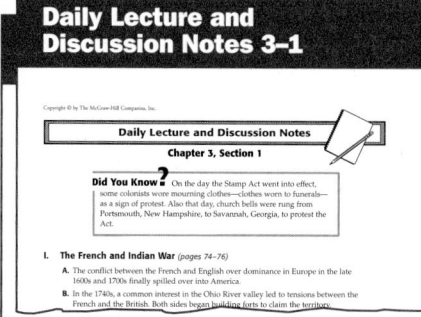

CHAPTER 3
Section 1, 74–79

2 *TEACH*

Daily Lecture and Discussion Notes 3–1

Copyright © by The McGraw-Hill Companies, Inc.

Daily Lecture and Discussion Notes
Chapter 3, Section 1

Did You Know? On the day the Stamp Act went into effect, some colonists wore mourning clothes—clothes worn to funerals—as a sign of protest. Also that day, church bells were rung from Portsmouth, New Hampshire, to Savannah, Georgia, to protest the Act.

I. **The French and Indian War** *(pages 74–76)*

  A. The conflict between the French and English over dominance in Europe in the late 1600s and 1700s finally spilled over into America.

  B. In the 1740s, a common interest in the Ohio River valley led to tensions between the French and the British. Both sides began building forts to claim the territory.

Discussing a Topic As a class, discuss the advantages and disadvantages of the Albany Plan of Union. Then extend the discussion to encourage students to consider how United States history might have been different if the colonies had adopted the plan. **L1**

History *Through Art*

Answer: The steep bank to the river made the city easy to defend against attackers from the river. The hills behind the city also gave a measure of protection to the city.

Ask: Why do you think control of the river was of such importance? *(Most supplies traveled by boat. Control of the river meant control of the supply lines.)*

Reading Strategy   READING THE TEXT

Identifying Cause and Effect Identifying causes for events and evaluating their effects helps students understand these events in their historical context. As students read through the section, have them note on a piece of paper the various British actions and the colonists' responses. They should note the events that evoked reactions, the types and levels of responses, and whether any of the reactions involved violence. Have students review the reactions to see if any pattern is visible. **L1**

☞ Refer to **Inclusion for the High School Social Studies Classroom Strategies and Activities** in the TCR.

Guided Reading Activity 3–1

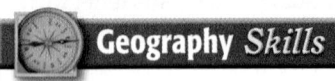

★ **Guided Reading Activity 3-1**

DIRECTIONS: Filling in the Blanks In the space provided, write the word or words that best complete each sentence. Refer to your textbook to fill in the blanks.

1. In the 1740s, the British and French both became interested in the _____
2. The _____ controlled western New York, which the French had to pass through to reach the Ohio River.
3. The _____ was a meeting in 1754 of colonial representatives and Iroquois leaders wherein the Iroquois agreed to remain neutral.
4. The Albany Plan of Union proposed that the colonies unite to form a _____
5. The defeat of the British troops by the French and Native Americans inspired the _____ people of western Pennsylvania to attack British settlers in their territory.
6. The British victory _____

✓ Reading Check

Answer: The French used the Ohio River to travel from the region of Lake Ontario to the Mississippi River. The Ohio River thus helped to connect New France to Louisiana. The British were interested in the Ohio River valley for fur trade and land speculation.

🧭 Geography *Skills*

Answers:
1. Appalachian Mountains
2. possible answers—to have more land for farming, to trap furs for trading

Geography Skills Practice
Ask: How was most of the British territory west of the Proclamation Line used? *(as an Indian reserve)*

Creating a Thematic Map Have students create a thematic map showing the area controlled by France in 1754 and after the Treaty of Paris was signed in 1763. Remind students to include an appropriate title and legend for the map. **L2**

📁 Use the rubric for creating a map, display, or chart on pages 65–66 in the *Performance Assessment Activities and Rubrics.*

---

frontier. In 1756 the fighting between Britain and France spread to Europe, where it became known as The Seven Years' War. Other countries entered the fray, and battles were waged around the globe.

In North America, the British fleet quickly cut off the flow of supplies and reinforcements from France. The Iroquois, realizing the tide had turned in favor of the British, pressured the Delaware to end their attacks. With their Native American allies giving up, the French found themselves badly outnumbered.

In 1759 a British fleet commanded by General James Wolfe sailed to Quebec City in New France. There the British defeated the French troops of General Louis Joseph Montcalm. The battle cost both Wolfe and Montcalm their lives, but Britain's victory was the war's turning point in North America.

Elsewhere in the world, the fighting continued. Spain joined forces with France in 1761, but the British ultimately triumphed. Under the terms of the

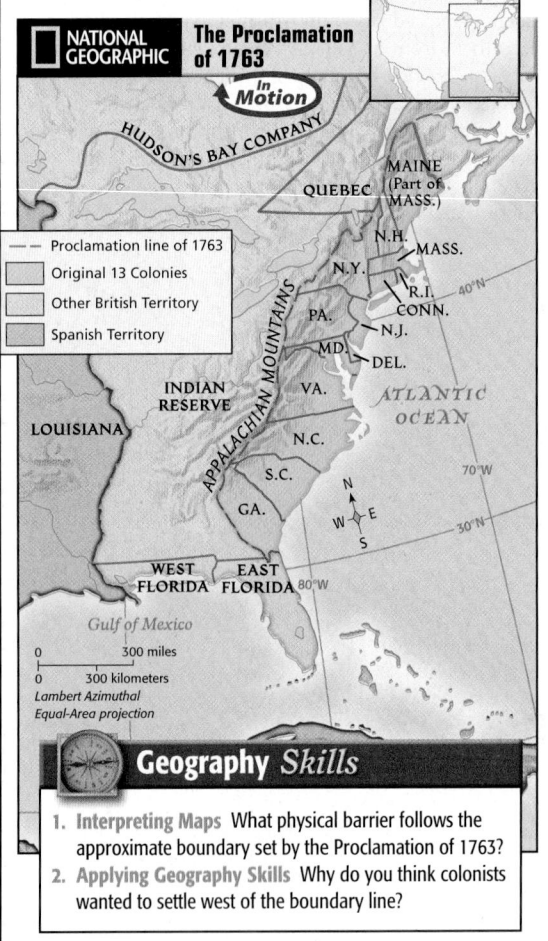

🗺️ **NATIONAL GEOGRAPHIC**
The Proclamation of 1763
In Motion

HUDSON'S BAY COMPANY

MAINE (Part of MASS.)
QUEBEC
N.H.
MASS.
N.Y.
R.I.
CONN.
PA.
N.J.
MD.
DEL.
VA.
ATLANTIC OCEAN
N.C.
S.C.
GA.
APPALACHIAN MOUNTAINS
INDIAN RESERVE
LOUISIANA
WEST FLORIDA
EAST FLORIDA
Gulf of Mexico

40°N
70°W
30°N
80°W

- - - Proclamation line of 1763
☐ Original 13 Colonies
☐ Other British Territory
☐ Spanish Territory

0 _____ 300 miles
0 _____ 300 kilometers
Lambert Azimuthal Equal-Area projection

🧭 Geography *Skills*

1. **Interpreting Maps** What physical barrier follows the approximate boundary set by the Proclamation of 1763?
2. **Applying Geography Skills** Why do you think colonists wanted to settle west of the boundary line?

76 CHAPTER 3 The American Revolution

Treaty of Paris in 1763, France lost all claims to mainland North America. Ownership of New France and most of Louisiana east of the Mississippi went to Britain. Spain lost Florida but retained Cuba and the Philippines. As compensation for the loss of Florida, the Spanish gained New Orleans and western Louisiana.

✓ Reading Check
Examining Why were the French and the British interested in the Ohio River valley?

The Colonies Grow Discontented

Great Britain's victory in 1763 left the country deeply in debt. It had to pay not only the cost of the war, but also the cost of governing and defending its new territories. Many British leaders thought that the colonies should share in the costs, especially the cost of stationing troops in the colonies. As the British government adopted new policies to solve its financial problems, colonial resentment grew.

The Proclamation Act of 1763 In the spring of 1763, **Pontiac,** the chief of the Ottawa people, decided to go to war against the British. After uniting several Native American groups, including the Ottawa, Delaware, Shawnee, and Seneca peoples, Pontiac's forces attacked several forts and towns along the frontier before British troops were able to stop them. Pontiac's war did not surprise British officials. They had been expecting trouble since 1758, when reports first indicated that settlers were moving into western Pennsylvania in defiance of the colony's treaty with the region's Native Americans.

British officials did not want to bear the cost of another war. Many officials also owned shares in fur trading companies operating in the region, and they knew that a war would disrupt trade. They decided that the best solution was to limit western settlement until new treaties could be negotiated.

When news of Pontiac's raids reached Britain in the summer of 1763, officials hurried to complete their plans. In early October, King George III issued the **Royal Proclamation of 1763.** The Proclamation drew a line from north to south along the Appalachian Mountains and declared that colonists could not settle any land west of the line without the British government's permission. This enraged many farmers and land speculators.

Customs Reform and New Taxes At the same time the Proclamation Act was angering western farmers, eastern merchants were objecting to new tax policies. In 1763 **George Grenville** became the prime

---

DIFFERENTIATED INSTRUCTION

Reading Support Have students identify examples of Britain's mercantile policies described in the section. Ask them to write a paragraph explaining why colonists might oppose these policies. Ask students to discuss what policies the British might have employed that would not have led to war. **L2**

📁 Refer to *Inclusion for the High School Social Studies Classroom Strategies and Activities* in the TCR.

minister and first lord of the Treasury. Grenville had to find a way to reduce Britain's debt and pay for the 10,000 British troops now stationed in North America.

Grenville discovered that merchants were smuggling goods into and out of the colonies without paying customs duties—taxes on imports and exports. Grenville pushed for a law allowing smugglers to be tried in a new vice-admiralty court in Halifax, Nova Scotia. Unlike colonial courts, where juries often sympathized with smugglers, vice-admiralty courts were run by naval officers and had no juries, a violation of the traditional English right to a jury of one's peers. Sending colonists to distant Nova Scotia also violated their right to a speedy public trial.

Among those tried under the new system was **John Hancock** of Massachusetts. Hancock had made a fortune in the sugar trade, smuggling molasses from French colonies in the Caribbean. Defending Hancock was a young lawyer named **John Adams.** Adams argued that the use of vice-admiralty courts denied colonists their rights as British citizens.

George Grenville

In addition to tightening customs control, Grenville introduced the American Revenue Act of 1764, better known as the **Sugar Act.** The act changed the tax rates on imports of raw sugar and molasses. It also placed new taxes on silk, wine, coffee, and indigo.

Merchants throughout the colonies complained to Parliament that the Sugar Act hurt trade. Many were also furious that the act violated several traditional English rights. Merchants accused of smuggling were presumed guilty unless proven innocent. The act also let officials seize goods without **due process,** or proper court procedures, in some circumstances, and prevented lawsuits by merchants whose goods had been improperly seized.

In many colonial cities, pamphlets circulated condemning the Sugar Act. In one pamphlet, James Otis argued that taxes could be levied to regulate trade, but those designed to raise money were unjust because the colonists had no representatives in Parliament. Otis wrote, "No parts of His Majesty's dominions can be taxed without their consent. . . ." His words gave rise to the popular expression, "No taxation without representation."

Parliament soon passed another unpopular measure, the **Currency Act of 1764.** This act banned the use of paper money in the colonies because it tended to lose its value very quickly. Colonial farmers and artisans liked paper money for precisely that reason. They could take out loans and easily repay them later with paper money that was worth less than when they originally borrowed.

✓ **Reading Check** **Summarizing** How did Britain hope to solve its financial problems after the French and Indian War?

The Stamp Act Crisis

Although the Sugar Act had begun to generate money for Britain, Grenville did not believe it would cover all of the government's expenses in America. To raise more money, he persuaded Parliament to pass the **Stamp Act** in March 1765.

The Stamp Act required stamps to be bought and placed on most printed materials, including newspapers, pamphlets, posters, wills, mortgages, deeds, licenses, bonds, and even diplomas, dice, and playing cards. Unlike previous taxes, which had always been imposed on trade, the stamp tax was a direct tax—the first Britain had ever placed on the colonists. Parliament then passed one more law. The **Quartering Act** was intended to make the colonies pay more for their own defense. The act required colonists to provide barracks for British troops or pay to house them in taverns, inns, vacant buildings, and barns.

It was the Stamp Act, however, that triggered a reaction. Editorials, pamphlets, and speeches poured out against the impending tax. The Virginia House of Burgesses, roused by Patrick Henry's speeches, passed resolutions declaring that Virginians were entitled to the rights of British people and could be taxed only by their own representatives. Newspapers in other colonies reprinted the resolutions, and other assemblies passed similar statements. By the summer of 1765, groups calling themselves the **Sons of Liberty** were organizing meetings and protests and trying to intimidate stamp distributors. 📖 *(See page 930 for more on one of Patrick Henry's speeches.)*

In October 1765, representatives from nine of the colonies met for what became known as the **Stamp Act Congress.** Together, they issued the Declaration

Drawing a Political Cartoon
Have students select an event in this section and draw a political cartoon that expresses a strongly held opinion of the day. **L2**

✓ **Reading Check**

Answer: by strictly enforcing custom duties, raising taxes on sugar and molasses, and placing new taxes on silk, wine, coffee, pimento, and indigo.

Discussing a Topic Ask students to identify the rights that the various laws enacted by the British denied colonists. Then explain how the denial of rights to colonists led to independence for the colonies. **L1**

The Sugar Act of 1764 replaced the Molasses Act of 1733, which was about to expire. In addition to sugar and other products imported into the colonies, the act also regulated the export of lumber and iron.

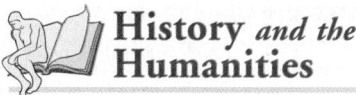
History *and the* Humanities

💾 American Music: Cultural Traditions: "Junto Song," "British Grenadiers"

INTERDISCIPLINARY CONNECTIONS ACTIVITY

Civics Ask students to consider how the British government and the colonists viewed the concept of representation. Then have them create a diagram that shows the similarities and differences in their points of view. Ask volunteers to share their diagrams with the entire class. **L3**

✓ **Reading Check**

Answer: They ignored it and boy-cotted British goods.

Graphic Organizer → Skills

Answer: Most students will likely express their support for colonists' actions as the best ways to get Britain to respond to their demands for representation.

Graphic Organizer Skills Practice

Ask: How did the Boston Tea Party boost colonists' confidence in their cause? *(Their actions showed that they could successfully stand up to the British.)*

3 ASSESS

Assign Section 1 Assessment as homework or as an in-class activity.

🌐 Have students use the **Interactive Tutor Self-Assessment CD-ROM.**

L1/ELL

Reading Essentials and Study Guide 3–1

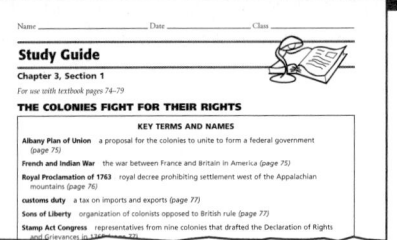

Name _____ Date _____ Class _____

Study Guide

Chapter 3, Section 1
For use with textbook pages 74–79

THE COLONIES FIGHT FOR THEIR RIGHTS

KEY TERMS AND NAMES
Albany Plan of Union a proposal for the colonies to unite to form a federal government (page 75)
French and Indian War the war between France and Britain in America (page 75)
Royal Proclamation of 1763 royal decree prohibiting settlement west of the Appalachian mountains (page 76)
customs duty a tax on imports and exports (page 77)
Sons of Liberty organization of colonists opposed to British rule (page 77)
Stamp Act Congress representatives from nine colonies that drafted the Declaration of Rights and Grievances in 1765 (page 78)

---

of Rights and Grievances. Drafted by a wealthy Pennsylvania farmer and lawyer named John Dickinson, the declaration argued that only the colonists' political representatives, and not Parliament, had the right to tax them. The congress then petitioned King George for relief and asked Parliament to repeal the Stamp Act.

When the Stamp Act took effect on November 1, the colonists ignored it. They began to boycott all goods made in Britain. In New York, 200 merchants signed a nonimportation agreement, pledging not to buy any British goods until Parliament repealed the Stamp Act.

The boycott had a powerful effect on England. Thousands of workers lost their jobs as orders from the colonies were cancelled. British merchants could not collect money the colonies owed them.

With protests mounting in both England and America, British lawmakers repealed the Stamp Act in 1766. To demonstrate its authority over the colonies, however, Parliament also passed the **Declaratory Act.** This asserted that the colonies were subordinate to the British Parliament, and that Parliament had the power to make laws for the colonies.

✓ **Reading Check** **Summarizing** What actions did colonists take in response to the Stamp Act?

The Townshend Acts

During the Stamp Act crisis, Britain's financial problems had worsened. Protests in England had forced Parliament to lower property taxes there, yet somehow the government had to pay for its troops in America. In 1767 Charles Townshend, the new Chancellor of the Exchequer, introduced new measures to raise money from the colonies. These came to be called the **Townshend Acts.**

One measure, the Revenue Act of 1767, put new customs duties on glass, lead, paper, paint, and tea imported into the colonies. Violators of the Revenue Act could be tried in vice-admiralty courts, where they were presumed guilty and had to prove their innocence. The Townshend Acts, like the Sugar Act, also allowed officials to seize private property under certain circumstances without following due process.

To help customs officers arrest smugglers, the Revenue Act legalized the use of writs of assistance. These were general search warrants that enabled customs officers to enter any location during the day to look for evidence of smuggling. Writs had been used before, but in 1760 James Otis had challenged them in court. The issue remained unresolved until the Revenue Act of 1767 declared writs of assistance to be legal.

Action and Reaction The Townshend Acts infuriated many colonists. During the winter of 1767 to 1768, John Dickinson published his *Letters from a Pennsylvania Farmer* in colonial newspapers. In these essays, Dickinson reasserted that only assemblies elected by the colonists had the right to tax them. In addition, he called on the colonies to become "firmly bound together" to "form one body politic" to resist the Townshend Acts.

Less than a month after Dickinson's first letter appeared, the Massachusetts assembly began organizing against Britain. Among the leaders of this resistance was **Sam Adams** of Massachusetts, cousin of John Adams. In February 1768, Sam Adams, with the help of James Otis, drafted a "circular letter" for the Massachusetts assembly to pass and circulate to other colonies. The letter expressed opposition to the Townshend Acts, and British officials ordered the Massachusetts assembly to withdraw it. When the assembly refused, the British government

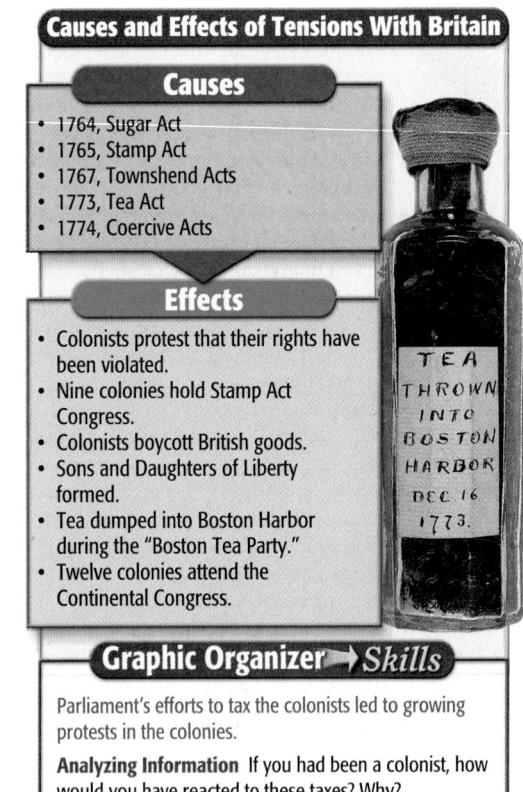

Causes and Effects of Tensions With Britain

Causes

- 1764, Sugar Act
- 1765, Stamp Act
- 1767, Townshend Acts
- 1773, Tea Act
- 1774, Coercive Acts

Effects

- Colonists protest that their rights have been violated.
- Nine colonies hold Stamp Act Congress.
- Colonists boycott British goods.
- Sons and Daughters of Liberty formed.
- Tea dumped into Boston Harbor during the "Boston Tea Party."
- Twelve colonies attend the Continental Congress.

TEA THROWN INTO BOSTON HARBOR DEC. 16 1773.

Graphic Organizer → Skills

Parliament's efforts to tax the colonists led to growing protests in the colonies.

Analyzing Information If you had been a colonist, how would you have reacted to these taxes? Why?

78 CHAPTER 3 The American Revolution

CRITICAL THINKING ACTIVITY

Comparing Remind students that General Braddock underestimated the fighting ability of his enemy, the Native Americans. Ask students to give examples of other times in history when underestimating the enemy has led to dire consequences. *(Answers will vary. Students may suggest that Saddam Hussein underestimated the abilities of the United Nations forces in the Persian Gulf War, or that the Japanese underestimated the resolve of the Americans when attacking Pearl Harbor.)*
L2

ordered the body dissolved. In August 1768, the merchants of Boston and New York responded by signing nonimportation agreements. Philadelphia's merchants joined the boycott in March 1769.

In May 1769, Virginia's House of Burgesses passed the **Virginia Resolves,** which stated that only the House could tax Virginians. When Britain ordered the House dissolved, its leaders—including George Washington, Patrick Henry, and Thomas Jefferson—immediately called the members to a convention. This convention then passed a nonimportation law that blocked the sale of British goods in Virginia.

As the boycott spread, the colonists again stopped drinking British tea and buying British cloth. Women's groups known as the **Daughters of Liberty** began spinning their own rough cloth, called "homespun." Wearing homespun rather than British cloth became a sign of patriotism. Throughout the colonies, the Sons of Liberty encouraged people to support the boycotts. In 1769 colonial imports from Britain declined sharply from what they had been in 1768.

The Boston Massacre In the fall of 1768, as violence against customs officers in Boston increased, Britain dispatched roughly 1,000 soldiers to the city to maintain order. Bostonians heckled and harassed these troops, referring to them as "lobster backs" because of the red coats they wore. On March 5, 1770, a crowd of colonists began taunting and throwing snowballs at a British soldier guarding a customs house. His call for help brought Captain Thomas Preston and a squad of soldiers. Preston described what happened next:

❝The mob still increased and were more outrageous, striking their clubs and bludgeons one against another, and calling out, 'Come on you rascals, you bloody backs, you lobster scoundrels, fire if you dare . . . we know you dare not.' . . . They advanced to the points of the bayonets, struck some of them and even the muzzles of the pieces, and seemed to be endeavoring to [fight] with the soldiers.❞

—quoted in *American Voices, American Lives*

In the midst of the tumult, one soldier was knocked down. He rose angrily and fired his weapon into the crowd. This triggered a volley of shots from the rest of the troops, who thought they were under attack. When the smoke cleared, three colonists lay dead, two more would die later, and six more were wounded. According to accounts, the first person to die was a part African, part Native American man known as both Michael Johnson and Crispus Attucks.

The incident became known as the **Boston Massacre.** Colonial newspapers portrayed the British as tyrants who were willing to kill people who stood up for their rights. Further violence might have ensued, had not news arrived a few weeks later that the British had repealed almost all of the Townshend Acts. Parliament kept one tax—on tea—to uphold its right to tax the colonies. At the same time, it allowed the colonial assemblies to resume meeting. Peace and stability returned to the colonies, but only temporarily.

✓**Reading Check** **Identifying** Who led resistance to British taxation in Massachusetts? In Virginia?

SECTION 1 ASSESSMENT

Study Central™ To review this section, go to tarvol2.glencoe.com and click on **Study Central**™.

Checking for Understanding

1. **Define:** customs duty, nonimportation agreement, writs of assistance.
2. **Identify:** Albany Plan of Union, French and Indian War, Royal Proclamation of 1763, Sons of Liberty, Stamp Act Congress.
3. **Summarize** the causes of the French and Indian War.

Reviewing Themes

4. **Civic Rights and Responsibilities** What argument did the colonists use to protest the Stamp Act?

Critical Thinking

5. **Evaluating** Was it reasonable for Great Britain to expect the colonists to help pay for the French and Indian War and for their own defense? Why or why not?
6. **Categorizing** Use a graphic organizer to describe the acts Parliament passed after the French and Indian War.

Act	Year	Key Features

Analyzing Visuals

7. **Analyzing Charts** Study the chart on page 78 of causes and effects of tensions with Britain. Then make your own similar chart. Use the causes listed in the chart you studied as the effects in your own chart. The causes in your chart should reflect the reasons Britain passed these acts.

Writing About History

8. **Persuasive Writing** Imagine you are a member of the Sons or Daughters of Liberty. Write a pamphlet explaining what your group does and urging fellow colonists to join.

CHAPTER 3 The American Revolution **79**

SECTION 1 ASSESSMENT ANSWERS

1. Terms are in blue.
2. Albany Plan of Union (p. 75), French and Indian War (p. 75), Royal Proclamation of 1763 (p. 76), Sons of Liberty (p. 77), Stamp Act Congress (p. 77)
3. dispute over the Ohio River valley, building of French forts

4. that only their own representatives had the right to tax them
5. Answers may vary, but should discuss both British and colonial viewpoints.
6. The graphic organizer should be completed based on acts discussed in the text.

7. The effects should be linked logically to the results Britain hoped to achieve.
8. Students' pamphlets will vary, but should include information about the activities of the group and a call for colonists to join the group.

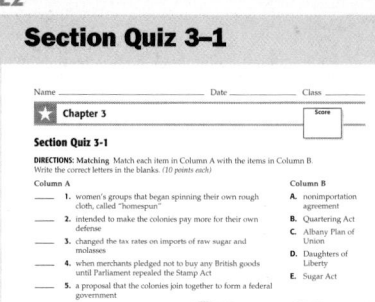

L2

Section Quiz 3–1

Reteach
Ask students to summarize the events that fueled colonial discontent.

Enrich
Have students identify a law with which they disagree. Have them write an essay expressing the reasons for their disagreement and arguing for their point of view.

✓**Reading Check**

Answer: Massachusetts, Sam Adams; Virginia, George Washington, Patrick Henry, and Thomas Jefferson

HISTORY Online

Study Central™ provides summaries, interactive games, and online graphic organizers to help students review section content.

4 CLOSE

Ask students to explain how the Stamp Act affected the relationship between Britain and the colonists.

1 FOCUS

Remind students that historians believe that the first clash between Americans and British troops was sparked by about 50 men and boys taunting British soldiers. When the crowd threw sticks and snowballs, the soldiers panicked and opened fire. Five Americans were killed, and as news of the event spread, it became known as the Boston Massacre.

2 TEACH

Evaluating Eyewitness Accounts Organize the class into two groups. Place all the students who witnessed a particular incident or event in one group. Each person in this group will write an account of the event. The other group, students who did not witness the event, will read the various accounts. Have the second group meet to discuss discrepancies in the accounts and present an oral account of the event or incident based on the written accounts. As a class, discuss why the accounts vary. **L2**

FYI

Despite the rising hostility of the colonists against the British, John Adams, a lawyer, took on the task of defending the soldiers who stood trial for the Boston Massacre.

You're the Historian

Comparing Accounts of the Boston Massacre

The Bloody Massacre,
engraving by Paul Revere, 1770

On the night of March 5, 1770, Captain Thomas Preston sent British troops to protect the Customs House in Boston from a group of colonists who had gathered nearby. Twenty minutes later, the troops had killed or wounded 11 people. The tragedy became known as the Boston Massacre. What happened that night? You're the historian.

Read the two accounts of the Boston Massacre below. One is Captain Preston's report of the event. The other is a colonist's account that quotes eyewitness Samuel Drowne. After reading the accounts, answer the questions and complete the activities that follow.

From Captain Thomas Preston's account

On Monday night . . . about 9 some of the guards came to and informed me the town inhabitants were assembling to attack the troops. . . . In a few minutes after I reached the guard, about 100 people passed it and went towards the custom house where the king's money is lodged. They immediately surrounded the sentry posted there, and with clubs and other weapons threatened to execute their vengeance on him. . . .

I immediately sent a noncommissioned officer and 12 men to protect both the sentry and the king's money, and very soon followed myself to prevent, if possible, all disorder, fearing lest the officer and soldiers, by the insults and provocations of the rioters, should be thrown off their guard and commit some rash act. . . .

Nay, so far was I from intending the death of any person that I suffered the troops to go . . . without any loading in their [guns]; nor did I ever give orders for loading them. . . .

The mob still increased and were more outrageous, striking their clubs or bludgeons one against another, and calling out come on you rascals, you bloody backs, you lobster scoundrels, fire if you dare. . . .

At this time I was between the soldiers and the mob . . . endeavoring all in my power to persuade them to retire peaceably, but to no purpose. They advanced to the points of the bayonets, [and] struck some of them. . . . A general attack was made on the men by a great number of heavy clubs and snowballs being thrown at them, by which

all our lives were in imminent danger, some persons at the same time from behind calling out, damn you bloods—why don't you fire. Instantly three or four of the soldiers fired, one after another, and directly after three more in the same confusion and hurry. . . .

The whole of the melancholy affair was transacted in almost twenty minutes. On my asking the soldiers why they fired without orders, they said that they heard the word fire and supposed it came from me. This might be the case as many of the mob called out fire, fire, but I assured the men that I gave no such order; that my words were, don't fire, stop your firing. In short, it was scarcely possible for the soldiers to know who said fire, or don't fire, or stop your firing.

80 CHAPTER 3 The American Revolution

EXTENDING THE CONTENT

Resistance Merchants and wealthy planters opposed the British Parliament's efforts to tax Americans. Other opponents of Britain's policies included shopkeepers, clerks, and laborers. These colonists were instrumental in the resistance efforts, using tactics such as boycotts. They were also responsible for some violence. It is likely that the British soldiers suspected any group of colonists as potential troublemakers.

Crispus Attucks, the first colonist to die in the Boston Massacre

From the colonist's account

Samuel Drowne [a witness] declares that, about nine o'clock of the evening of the fifth of March current, standing at his own door in Cornhill, he saw about fourteen or fifteen soldiers. . . . [The soldiers] came upon the inhabitants of the town, then standing or walking in Cornhill, and abused some, and violently assaulted others as they met them; most of them were without so much of a stick in their hand to defend themselves, as he clearly could discern, it being moonlight, and himself being one of the assaulted persons.

All or most of the said soldiers he saw go into King Street (some of them through Royal Exchange Land), and there followed them, and soon discovered them to be quarreling and fighting with the people whom they saw there, which he thinks were not more than a dozen. . . .

The outrageous behavior and the threats of the said party occasioned the ringing of the meeting house bell . . . which bell . . . presently brought out a number of the inhabitants, who . . . were naturally led to King Street, where [the British] had made a stop but a little while before, and where their stopping had drawn together a number of boys, round the sentry at the Custom House. . . .

There was much foul language between them, and some of them, in consequence of his pushing at them with his bayonet, threw snowballs at him, which occasioned him to knock hastily at the door of the Custom House. . . .

The officer on guard was Captain Preston, who with seven or eight soldiers, with firearms and charged bayonets, issued from the guardhouse, and in great haste posted himself and his soldiers in front of the Custom House, near the corner aforesaid. In passing to this station the soldiers pushed several persons with their bayonets, driving through the people in disturbance. This occasioned some snowballs to be thrown at them, which seems to be the only provocation that was given. . . .

Captain Preston is said to have ordered them to fire, and to have repeated the order. One gun was fired first; then others in succession, and with deliberation, till ten or a dozen guns were fired; or till that number of discharges were made from the guns that were fired. By which means eleven persons were killed or wounded.

The site of the Boston Massacre in present-day Boston

Understanding the Issue

1. On what events of the night of March 5, 1770, do the two accounts excerpted here agree?
2. On what descriptions of the events do the two accounts differ?
3. As the historian, how do you assess the credibility of the two accounts?

Activities

1. **Investigate** What happened to Captain Preston after the events of March 5? What were the immediate results of the Boston Massacre? Check other sources, including those available on the Internet.
2. **Mock Trial** Role play a mock trial of the Boston Massacre. Include witnesses, a prosecutor, a defense attorney, a judge, and a jury.

PORTFOLIO ACTIVITY

Newspaper Story Ask students to write a 300-word newspaper article regarding the events of March 5, 1770. Have them imagine that they interviewed two eyewitnesses—Preston and Drowne. Tell students to consider the printed accounts as transcripts of what Preston and Drowne told them when they asked what happened. Remind students to report both sides of the story. **L2**

1 FOCUS

Section Overview

This section focuses on the tensions immediately preceding the Revolutionary War and the beginning of the war.

BELLRINGER
Skillbuilder Activity

Project transparency and have students answer the question.

Daily Focus Skills Transparency 3–2

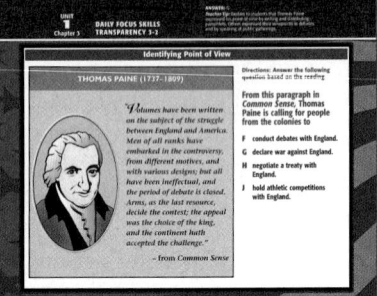

Reading Preview

Answers to Graphic:
I. Massachusetts Defies Britain
  A. The *Gaspee* Affair
  B. The Boston Tea Party
  C. The Coercive Acts
  D. The First Continental Congress
II. The Revolution Begins
  A. Loyalists and Patriots
Students should complete the outline by using all the heads in the section.

Preteaching Vocabulary

Have students create a database of the Key Terms and Names. Instruct students to define them as they read the section.

Guide to Reading

Main Idea
After years of escalating tensions and outbreaks of fighting, the colonists declared their independence from Britain on July 4, 1776.

Key Terms and Names
committee of correspondence, Boston Tea Party, Intolerable Acts, Suffolk Resolves, minuteman, Loyalist, Patriot, Olive Branch Petition, *Common Sense*

Reading Strategy
Taking Notes As you read about the escalating tensions between the colonists and Britain and about the colonists' declaration of independence, use the major headings of the section to create an outline similar to the one below.

The Revolution Begins
I. Massachusetts Defies Britain
  A.
  B.

Reading Objectives
• **Summarize** the first battles between Britain and the colonies.
• **Explain** the circumstances under which the colonies declared their independence.

Section Theme
Government and Democracy As tensions between Britain and the colonies escalated, the colonial leaders began to act like an independent government.

Preview of Events

◆1773	◆1774	◆1775	◆1776
1773 Boston Tea Party	**1774** First Continental Congress	**1775** Battles of Lexington and Concord; Second Continental Congress	**1776** Declaration of Independence drafted and signed

★ An American Story ★

Tea chest

On the night of December 17, 1773, a group of men secretly assembled along a Boston dock to strike a blow against Britain. One of the men was George Hewes, a struggling Boston shoemaker, who had grown to despise the British. Initially, Hewes had taken offense when British soldiers stopped and questioned him on the street and when they refused to pay him for shoes. After the Boston Massacre, which Hewes witnessed, his hatred grew more political.

So, after he "daubed his face and hands with coal dust, in the shop of a blacksmith," he gladly joined the other volunteers on that cold December night as they prepared to sneak aboard several British ships anchored in Boston Harbor and destroy the tea stored on board:

❝When we arrived at the wharf . . . they divided us into three parties for the purpose of boarding the three ships which contained the tea. . . . We then were ordered by our commander to open the hatches and take out all the chests of tea and throw them overboard, and we immediately proceeded to execute his orders, first cutting and splitting the chests with our tomahawks, so as thoroughly to expose them to the effects of the water. . . . In about three hours . . . we had thus broken and thrown overboard every tea chest . . . in the ship.❞

—quoted in *The Spirit of 'Seventy-Six*

Massachusetts Defies Britain

For more than two years after the Boston Massacre, the repeal of the Townshend Acts had brought calm. Then, in the spring of 1772, a new crisis began. Britain introduced several policies that again ignited the flames of rebellion in the American colonies. This time, the fire could not be put out.

SECTION RESOURCES

📁 Reproducible Masters
• Reproducible Lesson Plan 3–2
• Daily Lecture and Discussion Notes 3–2
• Guided Reading Activity 3–2
• Section Quiz 3–2
• Reading Essentials and Study Guide 3–2
• Interpreting Political Cartoons

🕯 Transparencies
• Daily Focus Skills Transparency 3–2

Multimedia
⊙ Interactive Tutor Self-Assessment CD-ROM
⊙ ExamView® Pro Testmaker CD-ROM
⊙ Presentation Plus! CD-ROM
⊙ TeacherWorks™ CD-ROM
🎧 Audio Program

The *Gaspee* Affair After the Townshend Acts were repealed, trade with England had resumed, and so had smuggling. To intercept smugglers, the British sent customs ships to patrol North American waters. One such ship was the *Gaspee,* stationed off the coast of Rhode Island. Many Rhode Islanders hated the commander of the *Gaspee* because he often searched ships without a warrant, and he sent his crew ashore to seize food without paying for it. In June 1772, when the *Gaspee* ran aground near Providence, some 150 colonists seized and burned the ship.

The incident outraged the British. They sent a commission to investigate and gave it authority to bring suspects back to England for trial. This angered the colonists, who believed it violated their right to a trial by a jury of their peers. Rhode Island's assembly sent a letter to the other colonies asking for help.

In March 1773, the Virginia House of Burgesses received the letter. Thomas Jefferson suggested that each colony create a committee of correspondence to communicate with the other colonies about British activities. The committees of correspondence helped unify the colonies and shape public opinion. They also helped colonial leaders coordinate strategies for resisting the British.

The Boston Tea Party In May 1773, Britain's new prime minister, Lord North, made a serious mistake. He decided to help the struggling British East India Company. Corrupt management and costly wars in India had put the company deeply in debt. At the same time, British taxes on tea had encouraged colonial merchants to smuggle in cheaper Dutch tea. As a result, the company had over 17 million pounds of tea in its warehouses that it needed to sell quickly to stay in business.

To help the company, Parliament passed the Tea Act of 1773. The **Tea Act** refunded four-fifths of the taxes the company had to pay to ship tea to the colonies, leaving only the Townshend tax. East India Company tea could now be sold at lower prices than smuggled Dutch tea. The act also allowed the East India Company to sell directly to shopkeepers, bypassing colonial merchants who normally distributed the tea. The Tea Act enraged these merchants, who feared it was the first step by the British to squeeze them out of business.

In October 1773, the East India Company shipped 1,253 chests of tea to Boston, New York, Philadelphia, and Charles Town. The committees of correspondence decided that the tea must not be allowed to land. When the first shipments arrived in New York

and Philadelphia, the colonists forced the agents for the East India Company to return home with their cargo. In South Carolina, the ships sat in the harbor until customs officers seized the tea and stored it in a local warehouse, where it remained unsold.

The most dramatic showdown occurred in December 1773, when the tea ships arrived in Boston Harbor. On the night before customs officials planned to unload the tea, approximately 150 men boarded the ships. They dumped 342 chests of tea overboard, as several thousand people on shore cheered. Although the men were disguised as Native Americans, many Bostonians knew who they were. A witness later testified that Sam Adams and John Hancock were among the protesters. The raid came to be called the **Boston Tea Party.**

Picturing History

Tea Tantrum In December 1773, colonists in Boston took matters into their own hands and dumped hated British tea into Boston Harbor. *Why did Boston tea merchants object so much to the Tea Act?*

CHAPTER 3 The American Revolution **83**

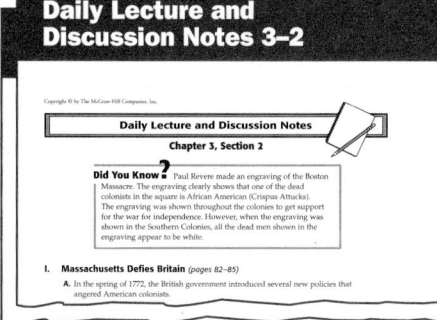

2 TEACH

Daily Lecture and Discussion Notes 3–2

Copyright © by The McGraw-Hill Companies, Inc.

Daily Lecture and Discussion Notes
Chapter 3, Section 2

Did You Know? Paul Revere made an engraving of the Boston Massacre. The engraving clearly shows that one of the dead colonists in the square is African American (Crispus Attucks). The engraving was shown throughout the colonies to get support for the war for independence. However, when the engraving was shown in the Southern Colonies, all the dead men shown in the engraving appear to be white.

I. Massachusetts Defies Britain (pages 82–85)
  A. In the spring of 1772, the British government introduced several new policies that angered American colonists.

Working in a Committee
Assign students to groups representing one of the colonies. Tell the groups that they are part of the committee of correspondence representing their designated colony. Have groups research events that occurred in their colony in 1773. Then have groups compose a letter addressed to Thomas Jefferson stating events that are happening in their colony and expressing an opinion about what to do next. **L1**

Picturing History

Background: The East India Company held a seven-year tea surplus at the time and faced financial ruin if the tea was not sold.
Answer: It took away their business.
Ask: What tactics did the colonists in other places use to prevent the East India Company from selling tea in the colonies? *(In New York and Philadelphia, colonists forced agents to return home with their tea. In Charles Town customs officers seized tea and locked it up so that it could not be sold.)*

Reading Strategy ▶ READING THE TEXT

Synthesizing Information When students synthesize, they combine ideas to come up with a new understanding of an important idea or a new way of combining and presenting information. As students read through this section, have them indentify individual events and their effects. Ask students if they think that at any point reconciliation would have been possible between the British and the colonists. Students should identify the event and what would have been required of each party. **L1**

📂 Refer to *Inclusion for the High School Social Studies Classroom Strategies and Activities* in the TCR.

L1/ELL

Guided Reading Activity 3–2

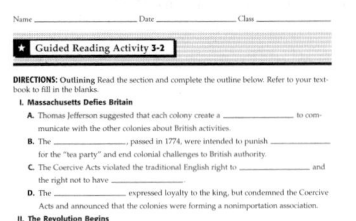

Name _____ Date _____ Class _____

★ **Guided Reading Activity 3-2**

DIRECTIONS: Outlining Read the section and complete the outline below. Refer to your textbook to fill in the blanks.

I. **Massachusetts Defies Britain**
   A. Thomas Jefferson suggested that each colony create a _____ to communicate with the other colonies about British activities.
   B. The _____, passed in 1774, were intended to punish _____ for the "tea party" and colonial challenges to British authority.
   C. The Coercive Acts violated the traditional English right to _____ and the right not to have _____.
   D. The _____ expressed loyalty to the king, but condemned the Coercive Acts and announced that the colonies were forming a nonimportation association.

II. **The Revolution Begins**

Organizing Information Have students use a graphic organizer similar to the one shown below to describe the purpose of the Coercive Acts. **L1**

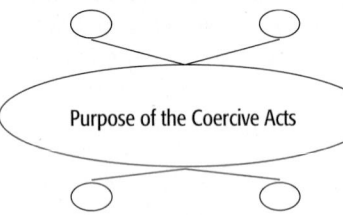

Purpose of the Coercive Acts

📁 Use the rubric for creating a map, display, or chart on pages 65–66 in the *Performance Assessment Activities and Rubrics.*

Graphic Organizer ➜ *Skills*

Answer: It made the continual intrusion by the British into affairs of the colonial governments intolerable. Also, it gave colonists some experience in organizing and rallying around a cause.

**Graphic Organizer Skills Practice
Ask:** When do you think the world should recognize the independence of a country? *(possible answers--after its defeated enemy recognizes it, when it forms a legitimate government, or when it seeks to participate as a member of the world community as a separate entity)*

The Coercive Acts The Boston Tea Party was the last straw for the British. King George concluded that concessions were not working. "The time has come for compulsion," the king told Lord North. In the spring of 1774, Parliament passed four new laws that came to be known as the **Coercive Acts.** These laws applied only to Massachusetts, but they were meant to dissuade other colonies from also challenging British authority.

The first act was the Boston Port Act, which shut down Boston's port until the city paid for the tea that had been destroyed. The second act was the Massachusetts Government Act. Under this law, all council members, judges, and sheriffs were appointed by the colony's governor instead of being elected. This act also banned most town meetings. The third act, the Administration of Justice Act, allowed the governor to transfer trials of British soldiers and officials to England to protect them from American juries. The final act was a new quartering act. It required local officials to provide lodging for British soldiers, in private homes if necessary. To enforce the acts, the British moved several thousand troops to New England and appointed General **Thomas Gage** as the new governor of Massachusetts.

The Coercive Acts violated several traditional English rights, including the right to trial by a jury of one's peers and the right not to have troops quartered in one's home. The king was also not supposed to maintain a standing army in peacetime without Parliament's consent. Although the British Parliament had authorized the troops, colonists believed their local assemblies had to give their consent, too.

In July 1774, a month after the last Coercive Act became law, the British introduced the **Quebec Act.** This law had no connection to events in the American colonies, but it also angered the colonists nonetheless.

The Quebec Act stated that officials appointed by the king would govern Quebec. The act also extended Quebec's boundaries to include much of what is today Ohio, Illinois, Michigan, Indiana, and Wisconsin. If colonists moved west into that territory, they would have no elected assembly. The Quebec Act, coming so soon after the Coercive Acts, seemed to signal Britain's desire to seize control of colonial governments.

The First Continental Congress As other colonies learned of the harsh measures imposed on Massachusetts, they reacted with sympathy and outrage. The Coercive Acts and the Quebec Act together became known as the **Intolerable Acts.**

In May 1774, the Virginia House of Burgesses declared the arrival of British troops in Boston a "military invasion" and called for a day of fasting and prayer. When Virginia's governor dissolved the House of Burgesses for its actions, its members adjourned to a nearby tavern and issued a resolution urging all colonies to suspend trade with Britain. They also called on the colonies to send delegates to a colonial congress to discuss what to do next.

In New York and Rhode Island, similar calls for a congress had already been made. The committees of correspondence rapidly coordinated the different proposals, and in June 1774, the Massachusetts assembly formally invited the other colonies to a meeting of the First Continental Congress.

The Continental Congress met for the first time on September 5, 1774, in Philadelphia. The 55 delegates represented 12 of Britain's North American colonies. (Florida, Georgia, Nova Scotia, and Quebec did not attend.) They also represented a wide range of opinion. Moderate delegates opposed the Intolerable Acts but believed a compromise could

Causes and Effects of the American Revolution

Causes	Effects
• Colonists' tradition of self-government • Americans' sense of a separate identity from Britain • Proclamation of 1763 • British policies toward the colonies after 1763	• United States declares independence • A long war with Great Britain • World recognition of American independence

Graphic Organizer ➜ *Skills*

The conflict between Britain and America grew worse after the passage of the Intolerable Acts of 1774.

Analyzing Information Why do you think the tradition of self-government played a role in the colonists' decision to declare independence?

84 CHAPTER 3 The American Revolution

DIFFERENTIATED INSTRUCTION

English Learners This section is especially adaptable to role-playing, which can greatly aid students whose reading skills are weak. Organize students into two groups. Have one group play the role of members of the British Parliament and the other group play the role of American colonial leaders. Have each group present its case on imposing taxes on the colonies. **L1** **ELL**

📁 Refer to *Inclusion for the High School Social Studies Classroom Strategies and Activities* in the TCR.

be worked out. More radical delegates felt the time had come for the colonies to fight for their rights.

The Congress's first order of business was to endorse the **Suffolk Resolves.** These resolutions, prepared by Bostonians and other residents of Suffolk County, Massachusetts, urged colonists not to obey the Coercive Acts. They also called on the people of Suffolk County to arm themselves against the British and to stop buying British goods.

The Continental Congress then began to debate a plan put forward by Joseph Galloway of Pennsylvania. Galloway proposed that the colonies remain part of the British Empire but develop a federal government similar to the one outlined in the Albany Plan of Union. After the radicals argued that Galloway's plan would not protect American rights, the colonies voted to put off consideration of the plan.

Shortly afterward, the Congress learned that the British had suspended the Massachusetts assembly. In response, the Congress issued the Declaration of Rights and Grievances. The declaration expressed loyalty to the king, but it also condemned the Coercive Acts and stated that the colonies would enter into a nonimportation association. Several days later, the delegates approved the Continental Association, a plan for every county and town to form committees to enforce a boycott of British goods. The delegates then agreed to hold a second Continental Congress in May 1775 if the crisis had not been resolved.

✓ **Reading Check** **Examining** How did the British react to the Boston Tea Party?

The Revolution Begins

In October 1774, while the Continental Congress was still meeting, the members of the suspended Massachusetts assembly gathered and organized the Massachusetts Provincial Congress. They then formed the Committee of Safety and chose John Hancock to lead it, giving him the power to call up the militia. In effect, the Provincial Congress had made Hancock a rival governor to General Gage.

A full-scale rebellion against authority was now under way. The Massachusetts militia began to drill in formation and practice shooting. The town of Concord created a special unit of men trained and ready to "stand at a minute's warning in case of alarm." These were the famous *minutemen.* All through the summer and fall of 1774, colonists created provincial congresses, and militias raided military depots for ammunition and gunpowder. These rebellious acts further infuriated British officials.

Loyalists and Patriots British officials were not alone in their anger. Although many colonists disagreed with Parliament's policies, some still felt a strong sense of loyalty to the king and believed British law should be upheld. Americans who backed Britain came to be known as *Loyalists,* or Tories.

Loyalists came from all parts of American society. Many were government officials or Anglican ministers. Others were prominent merchants and landowners. Quite a few backcountry farmers on the frontier remained loyal as well, because they regarded the king as their protector against the planters and merchants who controlled the local governments. Historians estimate that about 20 percent of the adult white population remained Loyalist after the Revolution began.

On the other side were those who believed the British had become tyrants. These people were known as *Patriots,* or Whigs. Patriots also represented a wide cross section of society. They were artisans, farmers, merchants, planters, lawyers, and urban workers. Historians think that 30 to 40 percent of Americans supported the Patriots once the Revolution began. Before then, Patriot groups brutally enforced the boycott of British goods. They tarred and feathered Loyalists who tried to stop the boycotts, and they broke up Loyalist gatherings. Loyalists fought back, but they were outnumbered and not as well organized.

The Patriots were strong in New England and Virginia, while most Loyalists lived in Georgia, the Carolinas, and New York. Everywhere, however, communities were divided. Even families were split. The American Revolution would not be a war solely between the Americans and the British. It would also be a civil war between Patriots and Loyalists. Caught in the middle were many Americans, possibly a majority, who did not support either side. These people simply wanted to get on with their lives.

Lexington and Concord In April 1775, General Gage received secret orders from Britain to arrest the members of the Massachusetts Provincial Congress. Gage did not know where the Congress met, so he decided to seize the militia's supply depot at Concord instead. On April 18, 700 British troops set out for Concord on a road that took them past the town of Lexington.

Patriot leaders heard about the plan and sent two men, **Paul Revere** and **William Dawes,** to spread the alarm. Revere reached Lexington by midnight and warned the people there that the British were coming.

CHAPTER 3   The American Revolution   **85**

Creating Pamphlets Tell students that they may choose to be a Loyalist or a Patriot. Encourage them to research both their chosen position and the opposing position. Have students create pamphlets that express their point of view and urge readers to join their cause. Have students share their pamphlets with the class. **L2**

✓ **Reading Check**

Answer: They enacted the Coercive Acts.

 VIDEOCASSETTE
Historic America Electronic Field Trips

View **Tape 1, Chapter 6:** "Lexington and Concord."

 FYI

Trained by his father as a silversmith, Paul Revere became one of America's great artists. In addition to his work in silver, Revere engraved copper plates. One of his most famous engravings, which depicts the Boston Massacre, appears on page 80.

History *and the* **Humanities**

American Art & Architecture: Independence Hall; *The Declaration of Independence, July 4, 1776*

INTERDISCIPLINARY CONNECTIONS ACTIVITY

Literature Invite students to locate and read the poem *Paul Revere's Ride* by Henry Wadsworth Longfellow. Have students compare the content of the poem with the scenario presented on page 86. Ask students to notice differences between the poem and the events recorded on the map. Ask them why they think there are differences and what effect these differences may have on our understanding of the events. **L2**

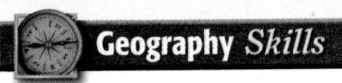

Geography Skills

Answers:
1. The British
2. 15 miles

Geography Skills Practice

Ask: From what city did Paul Revere begin his journey? *(He left from Charlestown.)* Which direction were Revere, Dawes, and Prescott traveling when they left Lexington and headed for Concord? *(They were traveling west.)*

Determining Cause and Effect

Ask students to create a cause-and-effect chart. The causes should be a list of the rights that were denied colonists by the various laws enacted by the British. The effects should indicate how these laws affect our laws today. **L2**

CURRICULUM CONNECTION

Role of Religion in Declaring Independence The Revolutionary War effort drew powerful support from the Congregational, Presbyterian, and other Christian churches whose clergy had no official ties with England. In contrast, the Anglican Church in America opposed the Revolution. The Anglican clergy saw opposition to British rule as a danger to all authority. Their support of Britain drew widespread acceptance among colonial aristocracy, particularly in the Southern Colonies.

NATIONAL GEOGRAPHIC — **Battles of Lexington and Concord, April 1775**

In Motion

❸ Colonial militia inflict 14 casualties on British at Concord's North Bridge.

❹ In retreat to Boston, British suffer over 250 casualties and Americans suffer 95.

North Bridge — Minutemen — Prescott — Minutemen — Lexington April 19, 1775

Concord April 19, 1775 — Gage

❷ Revere captured; Dawes turned back.

❶ April 19, 1775, fighting begins on Lexington Common: eight Americans die, 10 wounded.

Medford — Menotomy (Arlington) — Charlestown — Cambridge — Boston — Boston Harbor — DORCHESTER HEIGHTS

Mystic River — Sudbury River — Charles River — Revere — Dawes

MASSACHUSETTS

0 ——— 5 miles
0 ——— 5 kilometers
Lambert Equal-Area projection

← Colonial troops
← Colonial messengers
← British troops
✳ American victory
✳ British victory

Geography Skills

1. **Interpreting Maps** Which side suffered the most casualties at Lexington and Concord?
2. **Applying Geography Skills** About how far was Lexington from Boston?

Revere, Dawes, and a third man, Dr. Samuel Prescott, then set out for Concord. A British patrol stopped Revere and Dawes, but Prescott got through in time to warn Concord.

On April 19, British troops arrived in **Lexington** and spotted 70 minutemen lined up on the village green. The British troops marched onto the field and ordered them to disperse. The minutemen had begun to back away when a shot was fired, no one is sure by whom. The British soldiers, already nervous, fired into the line of minutemen, killing 8 and wounding 10.

The British then headed to **Concord,** only to find that most of the military supplies had already been removed. When they tried to cross the North Bridge on the far side of town, they ran into 400 colonial militia. A fight broke out, forcing the British to retreat.

Having completed their mission, the British decided to return to Boston. Along the way, militia and farmers fired at them from behind trees, stone walls, barns, and houses. By the time the British reached Boston, 73 of their men had been killed, and another 174 were wounded. The colonists had 49 men dead and 46 wounded. As news of the fighting spread, militia raced from all over New England to help. By May 1775, militia troops had surrounded Boston, trapping the British inside.

86 CHAPTER 3 The American Revolution

The Second Continental Congress Three weeks after the battles at Lexington and Concord, the **Second Continental Congress** met in Philadelphia. The first issue under discussion was defense. The Congress voted to "adopt" the militia army surrounding Boston, and they named it the Continental Army. On June 15, 1775, the Congress appointed George Washington as general and commander in chief of the new army.

Before Washington could get to his troops, however, the British landed reinforcements in Boston. Determined to gain control of the area, the British decided to seize the hills north of the city. Warned in advance, the militia acted first. On June 16, 1775, they dug in on Breed's Hill near Bunker Hill and began building an earthen fort at the top.

The following day, General Gage sent 2,200 troops to take the hill. His soldiers, wearing heavy packs and woolen uniforms, launched an uphill, frontal attack in blistering heat. According to legend, an American commander named William Prescott told his troops, "Don't fire until you see the whites of their eyes." When the British closed to within 50 yards, the Americans took aim and fired.

CRITICAL THINKING ACTIVITY

Synthesizing Write the events listed below on large cards and ask students to arrange the cards using relative chronology. Consider asking volunteers to hold the cards up in front of the class and ask them to move around until the class is satisfied that the cards are in the correct order. **L2**

Battle of Bunker Hill	French and Indian War
Boston Massacre	*Gaspee* Affair
Boston Tea Party	Paul Revere's ride
Declaration of Independence	Lexington and Concord
First Continental Congress	*Common Sense* published

They turned back two British advances before they ran out of ammunition and had to retreat.

The **Battle of Bunker Hill,** as it came to be called, helped build American confidence. It showed that the largely untrained colonial militia could stand up to one of the world's most feared armies. The British suffered more than 1,000 casualties in the fighting. Shortly afterward, General Gage resigned and was replaced by General **William Howe.** The situation then returned to a stalemate, with the British trapped in Boston, surrounded by militia.

✓ **Reading Check** **Interpreting** Why was the Battle of Bunker Hill important to the Americans?

The Decision for Independence

Despite the onset of fighting, in the summer of 1775 many colonists were not prepared to break away from Great Britain. Most members of the Second Continental Congress wanted the right to govern themselves, but they did not want to leave the British Empire. The tide of opinion turned, however, when Britain refused to compromise.

Efforts at Peace In July 1775, as the siege of Boston continued, the Continental Congress sent a document known as the **Olive Branch Petition** to King George. Written by John Dickinson, the petition asserted the colonists' loyalty to the king and asked him to call off hostilities until the situation could be worked out peacefully.

In the meantime, radical delegates convinced the Congress to order an attack on the British troops based in Quebec. They hoped their action would inspire the French in Quebec to join in fighting the British. The American forces captured the city of Montreal, but the French did not rebel. Moreover, the attack convinced British officials that there was no hope of reconciliation. When the Olive Branch Petition arrived in England, King George refused to look at it. Declaring the colonies to be "open and avowed enemies," he issued a proclamation ordering the military to suppress the rebellion in America.

With no compromise likely, the Continental Congress increasingly began to act like an independent government. It sent people to

negotiate with the Native Americans, and it established a postal system, a Continental Navy, and a Marine Corps. By March 1776, the Continental Navy had raided the Bahamas and begun seizing British merchant ships.

The Fighting Spreads With fighting under way, Lord Dunmore, governor of Virginia, organized two Loyalist armies to assist the British troops in Virginia—one composed of white Loyalists, and the other of enslaved Africans. Dunmore proclaimed that Africans enslaved by rebels would be freed if they fought for the Loyalists. The announcement convinced many Southern planters that the colonies had to declare independence. Otherwise, the planters might lose their labor force.

🎨 **History** *Through Art*

Colonial Confidence Artist Alonzo Chappel painted *The Battle of Bunker Hill.* The battle showed the colonists that they could win against the British. How does the artist portray the colonists' courage?

CHAPTER 3   The American Revolution   **87**

✓ **Reading Check**

Answer: It helped build American confidence by showing that a largely untrained colonial militia could stand up to the British army.

Interpreting Art Have students locate a picture of Percy Moran's *Battle of Bunker Hill* or John Trumbull's *Battle of Bunker's* [sic] *Hill.* Direct students to compare and contrast the piece of art they selected with Alonzo Chappel's work that appears on page 87. **L2**

Many citizens of Boston had a bird's-eye view of the Battle of Bunker Hill. Some climbed onto rooftops and church steeples to watch the fighting.

🎨 **History** *Through Art*

Background: Alonzo Chappel combined his artistic talent and his love of history into a career of painting and drawing famous moments in American history. Although not an eyewitness to most of the events he painted, Chappel based his portrayals on his study of history.
Answer: They look determined, fighting with whatever they can, even the wounded fight.
Ask: Why did the colonists finally retreat from Bunker Hill? *(They ran out of ammunition.)*

📁 Use *Interpreting Political Cartoons,* Cartoon 3.

EXTENDING THE CONTENT

The American Navy At the beginning of the Revolutionary War, the colonists had no navy, so they began to commission private ships to attack British vessels. Owners of these ships could keep half the cargo of any captured enemy vessels. This arrangement greatly aided the American cause by cutting deeply into British supply routes. One ingenious American captain, Jonathan Haraden, instructed his crew to cover the ship's gun ports with canvas to make the vessel look like a vulnerable merchant ship. However, when an unsuspecting British ship neared, it was met with gunfire from the disguised gun ports.

What If...

HISTORY Online

Objectives and answers to the student activity can be found in the **Web Activity Lesson Plan** at tarvol2.glencoe.com.

3 ASSESS

Assign Section 2 Assessment as homework or as an in-class activity.

⊕ Have students use the **Interactive Tutor Self-Assessment CD-ROM.**

What If...

The Declaration of Independence Had Condemned Slavery?

In 1776 the Continental Congress chose a committee to draft the Declaration of Independence. The committee included Thomas Jefferson, John Adams, Roger Sherman, Benjamin Franklin, and Robert Livingston. Jefferson later recalled the following in his memoirs: "[The committee members] unanimously pressed on myself alone to undertake the draught. I consented; I drew it; but before I reported it to the committee I communicated it separately to Dr. Franklin and Mr. Adams requesting their corrections. . . ."

Franklin and Adams urged Jefferson to delete his condemnation of King George's support of slavery. The two realized that the revolution needed support from all the colonies to succeed, and condemning slavery would alienate pro-slavery colonists and force them to support the king. Jefferson modified the draft accordingly. If the Declaration of Independence had included Jefferson's condemnation of slavery, which is excerpted below, the history of the United States might have been very different.

❝He [King George] has waged cruel war against human nature itself, violating its most sacred rights of life and liberty in the persons of a distant people who never offended him, captivating and carrying them into slavery in another hemisphere, or to incur miserable death in their transportation thither. . . . He has [stopped] every legislative attempt to prohibit or to restrain this execrable commerce determining to keep open a market where [people] should be bought and sold. . . .❞

Southern Patriots increased their efforts to raise a large army. In December 1775, their troops attacked and defeated Dunmore's forces near Norfolk, Virginia. The British then pulled their soldiers out of Virginia, leaving the Patriots in control. In February 1776, Patriots in North Carolina dispersed a Loyalist force of backcountry farmers at the Battle of Moore's Creek. In South Carolina, the local militia prevented British troops from capturing Charles Town.

Meanwhile, in the North, Washington's troops seized the hills south of Boston. From that vantage point, they intended to bombard the British with cannons. The British troops fled Boston by ship, however, leaving the Patriots in control.

Everywhere, the British seemed to be on the run. Nonetheless, despite their defeats, it was clear that they were not backing down. In December 1775, the king issued the Prohibitory Act, ending all trade with the colonies and ordering the British navy to blockade the coast. The British government also began expanding its army by recruiting mercenaries—paid foreign soldiers. By the spring of 1776, the British had hired 30,000 Germans, mostly men from the region of Hesse, or Hessians.

The Colonies Declare Independence As the war dragged on, more Patriots began to think the time had come to formally break with Britain although they feared that most colonists were still loyal to the king. Even radicals in the Continental Congress worried that a declaration of independence might cost them public support.

Things began to change in January 1776, when Thomas Paine published a lively and persuasive pamphlet called *Common Sense*. Until then, everyone had regarded Parliament, not the king, as the enemy. Paine attacked the monarchy instead. King George III, he said, was responsible

HISTORY Online

Student Web Activity Visit the *American Republic Since 1877* Web site at tarvol2.glencoe.com and click on **Student Web Activities— Chapter 3** for an activity on the American Revolution.

88 CHAPTER 3   The American Revolution

CRITICAL THINKING ACTIVITY

Comparing In the 1900s, the world witnessed violent protests against totalitarian governments such as the Tiananmen Square massacre in China. It has also seen the successful use of nonviolent action in the drive for independence in India and in the American civil rights movement. The American colonists used both violent and nonviolent protest in the period preceding the Revolutionary War. Ask students to list two examples of each type of protest and their outcomes. Then ask students which form of protest, in their opinion, was more successful. Encourage them to explain their reasoning. **L3**

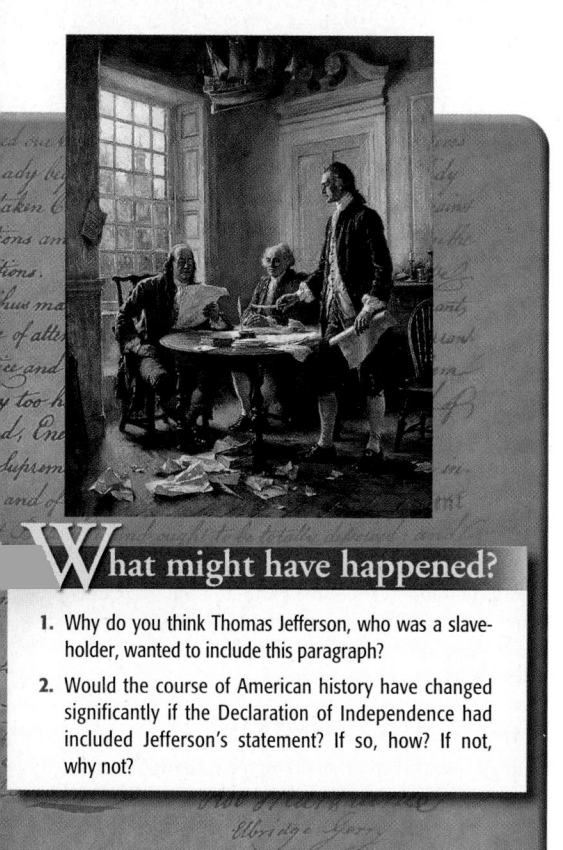

by seizing power from the people. George III was a tyrant, he proclaimed, and it was time to declare independence:

Everything that is right or reasonable pleads for separation. The blood of the slain, the weeping voice of nature cries, 'Tis Time To Part. . . . Every spot of the old world is overrun with oppression. Freedom hath been hunted round the globe . . . [and] England hath given her warning to depart.99

—from *Common Sense*

Within three months, *Common Sense* had sold over 150,000 copies. George Washington wrote, "*Common Sense* is working a powerful change in the minds of men." One by one, provincial congresses and assemblies told their representatives at the Continental Congress to vote for independence.

In early July, a committee composed of John Adams, Benjamin Franklin, Roger Sherman, Robert Livingston, and Thomas Jefferson submitted a landmark document Jefferson had drafted, in which the colonies declared themselves to be independent. On July 4, 1776, the full Continental Congress then issued this **Declaration of Independence.** The colonies had now become the United States of America, and the American Revolution had begun.

What might have happened?

1. Why do you think Thomas Jefferson, who was a slave-holder, wanted to include this paragraph?

2. Would the course of American history have changed significantly if the Declaration of Independence had included Jefferson's statement? If so, how? If not, why not?

for British actions against the colonies. Parliament did nothing without the king's approval. Paine argued that monarchies had been established

✓ **Reading Check** **Analyzing** How did Thomas Paine help persuade colonists to declare independence?

HISTORY Online **Study Central™** To review this section, go to **tarvol2.glencoe.com** and click on **Study Central™.**

SECTION 2 ASSESSMENT

Checking for Understanding

1. **Define:** committee of correspondence, minuteman, Loyalist, Patriot.

2. **Identify:** Boston Tea Party, Intolerable Acts, Suffolk Resolves, Olive Branch Petition, *Common Sense.*

3. **Explain** why the First Continental Congress met.

Reviewing Themes

4. **Government and Democracy** After King George III refused to consider the Olive Branch Petition, in what ways did the Continental Congress begin to act like an independent government?

Critical Thinking

5. **Synthesizing** What role did the committees of correspondence play in the colonists' move toward independence?

6. **Organizing** Use a graphic organizer similar to the one below to indicate ways in which colonists defied Britain after the repeal of the Townshend Acts.

Colonists' Acts of Defiance

Analyzing Visuals

7. **Analyzing Art** Study Chappel's painting, *The Battle of Bunker Hill,* on page 87. What elements of the painting show that the artist was sympathetic to the American cause?

Writing About History

8. **Descriptive Writing** Imagine that you were a member of the Sons of Liberty and a participant in the Boston Tea Party. Write a diary entry describing the event. Be certain to use correct spelling, grammar, and punctuation.

CHAPTER 3 The American Revolution **89**

SECTION 2 ASSESSMENT ANSWERS

1. Terms are in blue.
2. Boston Tea Party (p. 83), Intolerable Acts (p. 84), Suffolk Resolves (p. 85), Olive Branch Petition (p. 87), *Common Sense* (p. 88)
3. to discuss issues related to the problems with England and to decide what steps to take to

respond to the issues
4. It sent negotiators to the Native Americans, established a postal system, a navy, and a marine corps.
5. By communicating with other colonies about British activities, the committee helped unify colonies and shape public opinion.
6. Boston Tea Party, boycotts, burning

of the *Gaspee,* formed committees of correspondence
7. Americans willing to fight against superior forces
8. Diary entries should be written as if students were participants.

L1/ELL

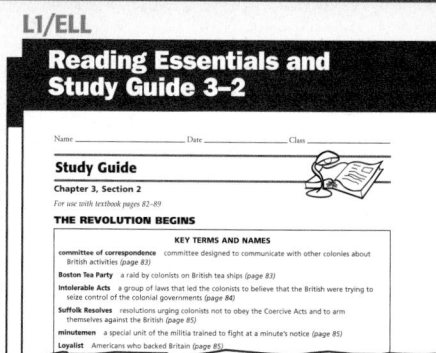

Reading Essentials and Study Guide 3–2

L2

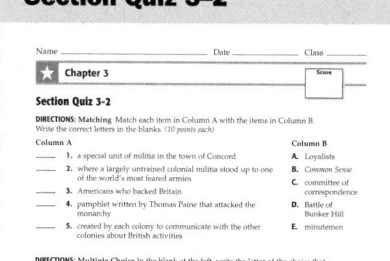

Section Quiz 3–2

Reteach

Ask students to summarize the events that fueled colonial discontent.

Enrich

Invite students to read Thomas Paine's *Common Sense* and write a summary of the main ideas.

 Reading Check

Answer: by publishing *Common Sense*

Study Central™ provides summaries, interactive games, and online graphic organizers to help students review section content.

4 CLOSE

Ask students to explain the events that led up to the actions taken by the Second Continental Congress.

The Declaration of Independence

The Declaration
of Independence

1 FOCUS

Analyzing Concepts Ask students if they would risk their lives for an idea and, if so, for what idea. Remind students that the American Revolution involved great risks for the people who fought it.

Ask what ideas were being fought for in the American Revolution. *(self-government, freedom, representation, equality)* Direct students to read the first paragraph of the Declaration of Independence on page 90. Ask the following questions:

- What is the tone of the document? *(possible answers: forceful, sober, respectful)*
- To whom is the document addressed? *(to the colonists to obtain the support of all Americans, especially those who were uncommitted; to foreign nations to gain their support; indirectly to King George III and the English Parliament)*

2 TEACH

Paraphrasing Choose a student to read aloud the first paragraph under "Declaration of Natural Rights" on page 90. Discuss with students any unfamiliar terms such as *self-evident* and *inalienable*. Then have students close their textbooks and write a paraphrase of the first paragraph. **L1** ELL

In Congress, July 4, 1776. The unanimous Declaration of the thirteen united States of America,

What It Means

The Preamble The Declaration of Independence has four parts. The Preamble explains why the Continental Congress drew up the Declaration.

impel *force*

[Preamble]

When in the Course of human events, it becomes necessary for one people to dissolve the political bands which have connected them with another, and to assume among the Powers of the earth, the separate and equal station to which the Laws of Nature and of Nature's God entitle them, a decent respect to the opinions of mankind requires that they should declare the causes which **impel** them to the separation.

What It Means

Natural Rights The second part, the Declaration of Natural Rights, states that people have certain basic rights and that government should protect those rights. John Locke's ideas strongly influenced this part. In 1690 Locke wrote that government was based on the consent of the people and that people had the right to rebel if the government did not uphold their right to life, liberty, and property. The Declaration calls these rights *unalienable rights.* Unalienable means nontransferable. An unalienable right cannot be surrendered.

endowed *provided*
despotism *unlimited power*

[Declaration of Natural Rights]

We hold these truths to be self-evident, that all men are created equal, that they are **endowed** by their Creator with certain unalienable Rights, that among these are Life, Liberty, and the pursuit of Happiness.

That to secure these rights, Governments are instituted among Men, deriving their just powers from the consent of the governed,

That whenever any Form of Government becomes destructive of these ends, it is the Right of the People to alter or to abolish it, and to institute new Government, laying its foundation on such principles and organizing its powers in such form, as to them shall seem most likely to effect their Safety and Happiness. Prudence, indeed, will dictate that Governments long established should not be changed for light and transient causes; and accordingly all experience hath shown, that mankind are more disposed to suffer, while evils are sufferable, than to right themselves by abolishing the forms to which they are accustomed. But when a long train of abuses and usurpations, pursuing invariably the same Object evinces a design to reduce them under absolute **Despotism,** it is their right, it is their duty, to throw off such Government, and to provide new Guards for their future security.

What It Means

List of Grievances The third part of the Declaration lists the colonists' complaints against the British government. Notice that King George III is singled out for blame.

usurpations *unjust uses of power*

[List of Grievances]

Such has been the patient sufferance of these Colonies; and such is now the necessity which constrains them to alter their former Systems of Government. The history of the present King of Great Britain is a history of repeated injuries and **usurpations,** all having in direct object the establishment of an absolute Tyranny over these States. To prove this, let Facts be submitted to a candid world.

He has refused his Assent to Laws, the most wholesome and necessary for the public good.

90 The Declaration of Independence

EXTENDING THE CONTENT

Real Title Strictly speaking, the title of this famous document is not the "Declaration of Independence" but rather "The Unanimous Declaration of the Thirteen United States of America." The document was not the act by which independence was declared. That had been done on July 2, when the Continental Congress adopted Lee's resolution.

He has forbidden his Governors to pass Laws of immediate and pressing importance, unless suspended in their operation till his Assent should be obtained; and when so suspended, he has utterly neglected to attend to them.

He has refused to pass other Laws for the accommodation of large districts of people, unless those people would **relinquish** the right of Representation in the Legislature, a right **inestimable** to them and formidable to tyrants only.

He has called together legislative bodies at places unusual, uncomfortable, and distant from the depository of their Public Records, for the sole purpose of fatiguing them into compliance with his measures.

He has dissolved Representative Houses repeatedly, for opposing with manly firmness his invasions on the rights of the people.

He has refused for a long time, after such dissolutions, to cause others to be elected; whereby the Legislative Powers, incapable of **Annihilation,** have returned to the People at large for their exercise; the State remaining in the mean time exposed to all the dangers of invasion from without, and **convulsions** within.

He has endeavoured to prevent the population of these States; for that purpose obstructing the Laws for **Naturalization of Foreigners;** refusing to pass others to encourage their migrations hither, and raising the conditions of new Appropriations of Lands.

He has obstructed the Administration of Justice, by refusing his Assent to Laws for establishing Judiciary Powers.

He has made Judges dependent on his Will alone, for the **tenure** of their offices, and the amount and payment of their salaries.

He has erected a multitude of New Offices, and sent hither swarms of Officers to harass our people, and eat out their substance.

relinquish *give up*
inestimable *priceless*

annihilation *destruction*

convulsions *violent disturbances*

Naturalization of Foreigners *process by which foreign-born persons become citizens*

tenure *term*

The Declaration of Independence **91**

Identifying Central Issues
Refer students to the painting on this page. Mention that the painting includes many of the delegates who also signed the Constitution. Discuss differences and similarities between this group and the current members of the United States Congress. The discussion can include observations about numbers, gender, ethnicity, age, style of dress, and so on. Conclude by pointing out that the calmness of the setting obscures the desperation of this step. In the eyes of the British government, each of these representatives was guilty of treason. For some time after, the names of the signers were kept secret, presumably to protect them from British reprisal. **L1**

Synthesizing Information
Organize students into small groups. Assign groups one or two of the grievances listed in the Declaration of Independence. Have the groups find specific events, acts, or statements made by the king or Parliament that relate to the grievance. Have the groups read aloud the grievances that they were assigned and state the information that relates to the grievance. **L2**

FYI

The Continental Congress cut about one quarter of the original document, most notably a scathing attack on slaveholding and the slave trade.

COOPERATIVE LEARNING ACTIVITY

Making Oral Presentations Tell students that the Declaration of Independence had significant influence on other independence movements. Organize the class into groups of four. Assign each group one of the following: the French Revolution, Latin American independence movements, Tiananmen Square demonstrations, the breakup of the Soviet Union. Have the groups use library and Internet resources to learn about their assigned movement and the effects that the Declaration of Independence had on the movement. Have the groups prepare an oral report on their findings. **L2**

Use the rubric for a cooperative group management plan on pages 71–72 in the **Performance Assessment Activities and Rubrics.**

Determining Cause and Effect

Ask students to think about the impact of the Declaration on the colonists. Have them list as many different effects as they can resulting from news that the Congress had issued the Declaration. *(Answers will vary, but might include the following: The time for indecision was over. It forced colonists to decide whether they supported independence or the king. It rallied support and boosted morale. It also raised the conflict above the level of discontent over economic issues.)* **L2**

Researching

Organize students into groups of four. Point out that the Declaration has been a force for change in the United States. People have used its words and ideas to promote such measures as the abolition of slavery and equal rights for women. Have each group do research to find three examples in which an individual or a group used the words and ideas expressed in the Declaration to promote change or reform. **L2**

 VIDEOCASSETTE
Historic America Electronic Field Trips

View **Tape 1, Chapter 7**: "Independence Hall."

He has kept among us, in times of peace, Standing Armies without the Consent of our legislature.

He has affected to render the Military independent of and superior to the Civil Power.

He has combined with others to subject us to a jurisdiction foreign to our constitution, and unacknowledged by our laws; giving his Assent to their acts of pretended legislation:

For **quartering** large bodies of troops among us:

For protecting them, by a mock Trial, from Punishment for any Murders which they should commit on the Inhabitants of these States:

For cutting off our Trade with all parts of the world:

For imposing taxes on us without our Consent:

For depriving us in many cases, of the benefits of Trial by Jury:

For transporting us beyond Seas to be tried for pretended offences:

For abolishing the free System of English Laws in a neighbouring Province, establishing therein an Arbitrary government, and enlarging its Boundaries so as to **render** it at once an example and fit instrument for introducing the same absolute rule into these Colonies:

For taking away our Charters, abolishing our most valuable Laws, and altering fundamentally the Forms of our Governments:

For suspending our own Legislature, and declaring themselves invested with Power to legislate for us in all cases whatsoever.

He has **abdicated** Government here, by declaring us out of his Protection and waging War against us.

He has plundered our seas, ravaged our Coasts, burnt our towns, and destroyed the lives of our people.

He is at this time transporting large armies of foreign mercenaries to compleat the works of death, desolation and tyranny, already begun with circumstances of Cruelty & **perfidy** scarcely paralleled in the most barbarous ages, and totally unworthy the Head of a civilized nation.

He has constrained our fellow Citizens taken Captive on the high Seas to bear Arms against their Country, to become the executioners of their friends and Brethren, or to fall themselves by their Hands.

He has excited domestic **insurrections** amongst us, and has endeavoured to bring on the inhabitants of our frontiers, the merciless Indian Savages, whose known rule of warfare, is an undistinguished destruction of all ages, sexes and conditions.

In every stage of these Oppressions We have **Petitioned for Redress** in the most humble terms: Our repeated Petitions have been answered only by repeated injury. A Prince, whose character is thus marked by every act which may define a Tyrant, is unfit to be the ruler of a free People.

Nor have We been wanting in attention to our British brethren. We have warned them from time to time of attempts by their legislature to extend an **unwarrantable jurisdiction** over us. We have reminded them of the circumstances of our emigration and settlement here. We have appealed to their native justice and magnanimity, and we have conjured them by the ties of our common kindred to disavow these usurpations, which, would inevitably interrupt our connections and correspondence. They too have been deaf to the voice of justice and of **consanguinity**. We must, therefore, acquiesce in the necessity, which denounces our Separation, and hold them, as we hold the rest of mankind, Enemies in War, in Peace Friends.

Glossary

quartering *lodging*

render *make*

abdicated *given up*

perfidy *violation of trust*

insurrections *rebellions*

petitioned for redress *asked formally for a correction of wrongs*

unwarrantable jurisdiction *unjustified authority*

consanguinity *originating from the same ancestor*

92 The Declaration of Independence

DIFFERENTIATED INSTRUCTION

Auditory/Musical Have interested students listen to the soundtrack of the Broadway play *1776*. Ask students to select one song to share with the class. Have them explain who sang the song, the historic events being portrayed, and how the lyrics and music convey the ideas of the Continental Congress. Also encourage students to point out any historical inaccuracies that they find in the song. **L2**

Refer to **Inclusion for the High School Social Studies Classroom Strategies and Activities** in the TCR.

[Resolution of Independence by the United States]

We, therefore, the Representatives of the united States of America, in General Congress, Assembled, appealing to the Supreme Judge of the world for the **rectitude** of our intentions, do, in the Name, and by Authority of the good People of these Colonies, solemnly publish and declare, That these United Colonies are, and of Right ought to be Free and Independent States; that they are Absolved from all Allegiance to the British Crown, and that all political connection between them and the State of Great Britain, is and ought to be totally dissolved; and that as Free and Independent States, they have full Power to levy War, conclude Peace, contract Alliances, establish Commerce, and to do all other Acts and Things which Independent States may of right do.

And for the support of this Declaration, with a firm reliance on the Protection of Divine Providence, we mutually pledge to each other our Lives, our Fortunes and our sacred Honor.

John Hancock
   President from
   Massachusetts

Georgia
Button Gwinnett
Lyman Hall
George Walton

North Carolina
William Hooper
Joseph Hewes
John Penn

South Carolina
Edward Rutledge
Thomas Heyward, Jr.
Thomas Lynch, Jr.
Arthur Middleton

Maryland
Samuel Chase
William Paca
Thomas Stone
Charles Carroll
   of Carrollton

Virginia
George Wythe
Richard Henry Lee
Thomas Jefferson
Benjamin Harrison
Thomas Nelson, Jr.
Francis Lightfoot Lee
Carter Braxton

Pennsylvania
Robert Morris
Benjamin Rush
Benjamin Franklin
John Morton
George Clymer
James Smith
George Taylor
James Wilson
George Ross

Delaware
Caesar Rodney
George Read
Thomas McKean

New York
William Floyd
Philip Livingston
Francis Lewis
Lewis Morris

New Jersey
Richard Stockton
John Witherspoon
Francis Hopkinson
John Hart
Abraham Clark

New Hampshire
Josiah Bartlett
William Whipple
Matthew Thornton

Massachusetts
Samuel Adams
John Adams
Robert Treat Paine
Elbridge Gerry

Rhode Island
Stephen Hopkins
William Ellery

Connecticut
Samuel Huntington
William Williams
Oliver Wolcott
Roger Sherman

> **What It Means**
> **Resolution of Independence**
> The Final section declares that the colonies are "Free and Independent States" with the full power to make war, to form alliances, and to trade with other countries.

rectitude *rightness*

> **What It Means**
> **Signers of the Declaration** The signers, as representatives of the American people, declared the colonies independent from Great Britain. Most members signed the document on August 2, 1776.

The Declaration of Independence **93**

FYI

Roger Sherman was the only person who signed all three of the most important documents of the United States: the Declaration of Independence, the Articles of Confederation, and the Constitution.

3 ASSESS

Reteach
Ask students to identify the most important points in the Declaration of Natural Rights.

Enrich
Ask students to write a paragraph stating which idea expressed in the Declaration they think is the most important one and explaining their choice.

4 CLOSE

Have students list the powers that the new Free and Independent states planned to claim.

PORTFOLIO ACTIVITY

Writing an Editorial Tell students that they should write an editorial reacting to the Declaration of Independence for an influential newspaper in Boston. Tell students that they must first decide if their newspaper supports the Loyalists or the Patriots. Explain that their editorials should support the position of the newspaper. **L2**

1 FOCUS

Section Overview

This section focuses on the War for Independence.

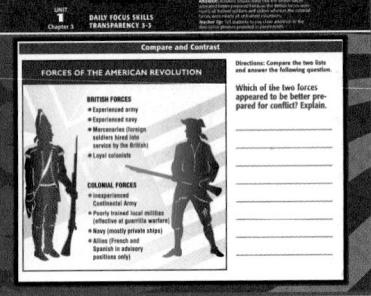
Reading Preview

Answers to Graphic:
Students should include battles for each year from 1776 to 1781. Make sure students discuss the importance and outcome of each battle.

Preteaching Vocabulary
Have students pose questions that can be answered by using the Key Terms and Names.

The War for Independence

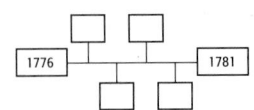

Guide to Reading

Main Idea
After a war lasting several years, Americans finally won their independence from Britain.

Key Terms and Names
Robert Morris, guerrilla warfare, John Burgoyne, letter of marque, Charles Cornwallis, Nathaniel Greene, Francis Marion, Benedict Arnold

Reading Strategy
Sequencing As you read about the war for independence, complete a time line similar to the one below to record the major battles and their outcomes.

1776 — 1781

Reading Objectives
• **List** the advantages and disadvantages of each side at the beginning of the war.
• **Discuss** the roles of France and Spain in the war, and explain how the war ended.

Section Theme
Global Connections Hostility between the French and British caused France to support the colonies.

Preview of Events

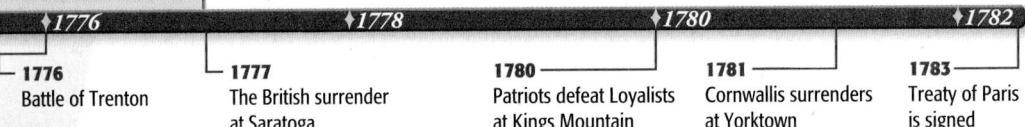

♦1776   ♦1778   ♦1780   ♦1782

1776
Battle of Trenton

1777
The British surrender at Saratoga

1780
Patriots defeat Loyalists at Kings Mountain

1781
Cornwallis surrenders at Yorktown

1783
Treaty of Paris is signed

★ An American Story ★

Colonel Henry Beckman Livingston could only watch helplessly the suffering around him. A veteran of several military campaigns, Livingston huddled with the rest of George Washington's army at its winter quarters at Valley Forge, Pennsylvania. The winter of 1777 to 1778 was brutally cold, and the army lacked food, clothing, and other supplies. Huddled in small huts, soldiers wrapped themselves in blankets and survived on the smallest of rations. Livingston described the army's plight in a letter to his brother, Robert:

❝Our troops are in general almost naked and very often in a starveing condition. All my men except 18 are unfit for duty for want of shoes, stockings, and shirts. . . . Poor Jack has been necessitated to make up his blanket into a vest and breeches. If I did not fear starveing with cold I should be tempted to do the same.❞

—adapted from *A Salute to Courage*

Troops at Valley Forge

The Opposing Sides

The struggle at Valley Forge was a dark hour for the patriots. No one knew if they were strong enough to defeat the powerful British Empire. On the same day the Continental Congress voted for independence, British troops, called "redcoats" because of their uniforms, began landing in New York. By mid-August, an estimated 32,000 men had assembled under the command of General William Howe. This was an enormous force

---

The Opposing Sides

Colonial Advantages	British Advantages
Fighting on home ground	Well-trained, well-supplied army and navy
Good decisions by generals	Wealth of resources
Fighting for their rights and freedoms	Strong central government
French alliance: loans, navy, troops	
Colonial Disadvantages	**British Disadvantages**
Untrained soldiers; small army	Fighting in unfamiliar, hostile territory
Food and ammunition shortages	Fighting far away from Britain and resources
Weak and divided central government	Troops indifferent; halfhearted support at home

Chart *Skills*

1. **Interpreting Charts** Why was fighting for their rights and freedoms an advantage for the colonists?
2. **Analyzing** In what ways would a weak government be a disadvantage in wartime?

in the 1700s, and the troops were disciplined, well trained, and well equipped. Given their strength, the British did not expect the rebellion to last very long.

The Continental army was comparatively inexperienced and poorly equipped. Although more than 230,000 men served in the Continental army, they rarely numbered more than 20,000 at any one time. Many soldiers deserted or refused to reenlist when their terms were up. Others left their posts to return to their farms at planting or harvest time.

Paying for the war was another challenge. Lacking the power to tax, the Continental Congress issued paper money. These "Continentals" were not backed by gold or silver and quickly became almost worthless. Fortunately, **Robert Morris,** a wealthy Pennsylvania merchant and banker, personally pledged large sums for the war effort and arranged for foreign loans.

In addition to the Continental army, the British also had to fight the local militias in every state. The militias were untrained, but they were adept at sneak attacks and hit-and-run ambushes. These guerrilla warfare tactics proved to be very effective against the British.

Another problem for the British was disunity at home. Many merchants and members of Parliament opposed the war. If Britain did not win quickly and cheaply, support for the war effort would erode. Therefore, the United States simply had to survive until the British tired of the economic strain and surrendered.

The European balance of power also hampered the British. The French, Dutch, and Spanish were all eager to exploit Britain's problems, which made these countries potential allies for the United States. To defend

against other threats to its empire, Britain had to station much of its military elsewhere in the world.

✓ **Reading Check** **Identifying** What three major disadvantages did the British face in the American Revolution?

The Northern Campaign

The British knew that a quick victory depended on convincing Americans that British military superiority made their cause hopeless, and that they could safely surrender without being hanged for treason. General Howe's strategy, therefore, had two parts. He placed many troops in New York to intimidate the Americans and to capture New York City. He also invited delegates from the Continental Congress to a peace conference, promising that those who surrendered and swore loyalty to the king would be pardoned.

When the Americans realized that Howe had no authority to negotiate a compromise, they refused to talk further. Although Howe's peace offer was rejected, his military strategy was initially successful. Washington's Continental army was unable to prevent the British from capturing New York City in the summer of 1776. In the fall of that year, Washington moved most of his troops from the northern end of Manhattan Island to White Plains, New York.

CHAPTER 3   The American Revolution   95

2 TEACH

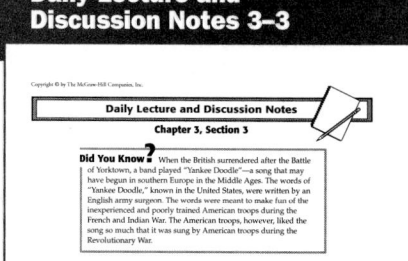

Daily Lecture and Discussion Notes 3–3

Chart *Skills*

Answers:
1. It gave them a very personal, sustaining reason to fight.
2. It would not be able to formulate a central policy.

Chart Skills Practice
Ask: How do you think fighting for a cause that you believe in strongly affects the outcome of battles?
(possible answers: will fight to the end and despite all odds)

Discussing an Idea Ask students to explain why the Continental army did not need to defeat the British in order to win independence. *(Many in England did not support a long, costly war.)* **L1**

✓ **Reading Check**

Answer: guerrilla warfare, opposition at home, and the European balance of power

Reading Strategy   READING THE TEXT

Previewing Students can quickly gain an understanding of what the text will be about by looking over features such as headings and subheadings, charted information, illustrations, captions, and graphics. Students should preview the section by looking at these elements before they begin reading so they know what they will be reading about. **L1** **ELL**

☞ Refer to *Inclusion for the High School Social Studies Classroom Strategies and Activities* in the TCR.

L1/ELL

Guided Reading Activity 3–3

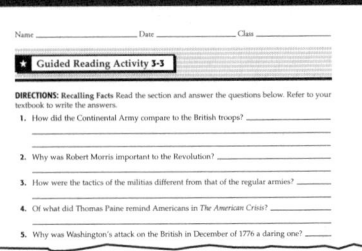

Name _____ Date _____ Class _____

★ **Guided Reading Activity 3-3**

DIRECTIONS: Recalling Facts Read the section and answer the questions below. Refer to your textbook to write the answers.

1. How did the Continental Army compare to the British troops? _____

2. Why was Robert Morris important to the Revolution? _____

3. How were the tactics of the militias different from that of the regular armies? _____

4. Of what did Thomas Paine remind Americans in *The American Crisis*? _____

5. Why was Washington's attack on the British in December of 1776 a daring one? _____

Geography *Skills*

Answers:
1. Trenton and Princeton
2. transporting troops and equipment

Geography Skills Practice

Ask: What British victory was farthest south? *(Savannah)*

Synthesizing Information Have students view copies of paintings of the crossing of the Delaware by artists George Caleb Bingham and Thomas Sully. Ask them which one seems closest to historical accounts. **L2**

History *and the* Humanities

🎵 American Music: Hits Through History: "General Scott's March," "The World Turned Upside Down"

🎵 American Music: Cultural Traditions: "Tunes from Colonial America," "The President's March"

🖌 American Art & Architecture: *Washington Crossing the Delaware*

NATIONAL GEOGRAPHIC — The Revolutionary War, 1776–1781 *In Motion*

→ British forces
→ American and allied forces
✺ British victory
✺ American victory
✺ Indecisive battle

❸ Burgoyne surrenders at Saratoga, 1777

❶ British capture New York City, 1776

❷ Americans attack British at Trenton and Princeton, 1776

❼ Washington and Rochambeau rush toward Virginia, August, 1781

❹ Howe captures Philadelphia, 1777

❾ Cornwallis is trapped; the British surrender at Yorktown, 1781

❽ French Admiral De Grasse keeps British ships away

❻ British capture Charles Town and win the battle of Camden, but are defeated at Kings Mountain in 1780 and at Cowpens in 1781

❺ British capture Savannah, 1778

0   200 miles
0   200 kilometers
Albers Conic Equal-Area projection

Geography *Skills*

1. **Interpreting Maps** Name two sites of colonial victories in New Jersey.
2. **Applying Geography Skills** What was the role of the British navy in the war?

Crossing the Delaware After Howe managed to push Washington's troops back from New York City, he moved his forces toward Philadelphia, where the Continental Congress was meeting. Caught by surprise, the Continental army had to move quickly to get in front of Howe's forces before they reached Philadelphia.

By the time Washington's troops reached Pennsylvania, the weather had turned cold. Both armies halted the campaign and set up winter camps to conserve food supplies. Attempting to bolster morale, Washington had Thomas Paine's latest pamphlet read to the troops. Paine's words reminded all that "the harder the conflict, the more glorious the triumph":

❝These are the times that try men's souls. The summer soldier and the sunshine patriot will in this crisis shrink from the service of their country; but he that stands it now deserves the love and thanks of man and woman.❞

—from *The American Crisis*

At this point, Washington decided to launch a daring and unexpected winter attack. On the night of December 25, 1776, he and some 2,400 men crossed the icy Delaware River from Pennsylvania to New

96 CHAPTER 3 The American Revolution

DIFFERENTIATED INSTRUCTION

Gifted and Talented Have students consider what it would have been like to be one of the following people involved in the Revolutionary War: a Continental soldier, a Hessian mercenary, a wife waiting for news of her husband, a merchant smuggling supplies to the troops, or a woman serving as a spy for the Continental army. Have students write a letter about the dangers they faced and the reasons for their commitment to the cause. **L3**

👉 Refer to *Inclusion for the High School Social Studies Classroom Strategies and Activities* in the TCR.

History *Through Art*

A Savage Winter William B.T. Trego's painting, *The March to Valley Forge*, depicts the difficult conditions that led to almost 2,500 deaths during the winter encampment of 1777 to1778. Why did the British and Continental armies stop fighting to camp during the winter months?

Jersey. They then marched about nine miles and, during a sleet storm, defeated a group of Hessian mercenaries at Trenton. Several days later, the Patriot army overcame three British regiments at Princeton. After these small victories, the Continental army camped in the hills of northern New Jersey for the winter.

Philadelphia Falls In March 1777, British General **John Burgoyne** had devised a plan to combine his troops with General Howe's and isolate New England from the other American states. Unfortunately, Burgoyne did not coordinate this with Howe, who was launching his own plan.

Howe sent about 13,000 men to launch a surprise attack on Philadelphia. He believed that capturing Philadelphia and the Continental Congress would cripple the Revolution and convince Loyalists in Pennsylvania to rise up and take control of the state.

Howe's action was a military success but a political failure. He defeated Washington at the Battle of Brandywine Creek and captured Philadelphia, but the Continental Congress escaped. Furthermore, no Loyalist uprising occurred.

TURNING POINT

The Battle of Saratoga Unaware of Howe's movement to Philadelphia, Burgoyne continued with his plan. In June 1777, he led an estimated 8,000 troops from Quebec south into New York, believing Howe was marching north to meet him. Burgoyne's forces easily seized Fort Ticonderoga, but American forces blocked their path by felling trees, and they removed crops and cattle to deprive the British of food.

Burgoyne eventually retreated to Saratoga, only to be surrounded by an American army nearly three times the size of his own. On October 17, 1777, he surrendered to General **Horatio Gates.** Over 5,000 British troops were taken prisoner. This was an unexpected turning point in the war. It not only dramatically improved American morale but also convinced the French to commit troops to the American cause.

The Alliance with France Although both France and Spain had been secretly aiding the Americans well before Saratoga, that battle's outcome convinced

France that the Americans could win the war. On February 6, 1778, the United States signed two treaties with France that officially recognized the new nation and committed France to fight alongside the United States until Britain was forced to recognize American independence.

In 1779 Spain allied with France but not with the United States. These countries provided vital military and financial aid to the United States. Their attacks also forced the British to divert troops and ships from their campaigns along the Atlantic coast.

Reading Check **Summarizing** What was General Howe's two-part strategy to win the war quickly?

Other Fronts

Not all of the fighting in the Revolutionary War took place in the East. Patriots also rallied to the cause on the western frontier, out at sea, and in the South.

The West In 1778, **George Rogers Clark** took 175 Patriots down the Ohio River and captured several towns. Although the British temporarily retook one of the towns, they eventually surrendered to Clark in February 1779. The United States now had control of the West. American troops soon secured control of western New York as well. In the summer of 1779, they defeated the British and the Iroquois, their Native American allies in the region. The Iroquois had allied with the British, hoping that a British victory would keep American settlers off Iroquois land.

The War at Sea In addition to the war on land, Americans also fought the British at sea. Although the Congress assembled a Continental navy, no one expected it to defeat the huge British fleet in battle. Instead, the United States sent its warships to attack British merchant ships. In addition, Congress issued letters of marque, or licenses, to about 2,000 privateers. By the end of the war, millions of dollars' worth of cargo had been seized from British merchant ships, seriously harming Britain's trade and economy.

CHAPTER 3 The American Revolution **97**

INTERDISCIPLINARY CONNECTIONS ACTIVITY

Visual Arts Invite an art teacher or artist to speak to your class about the artwork related to the War of Independence. Ask the speaker to give examples of works that inspired patriotism during the war and works that illustrate historical events. Encourage the speaker to talk about how artists learned about the historical events they depicted. Have students draw their own Revolutionary War scenes based on the information they have learned. **L2**

✓ **Reading Check**

Answer: They attacked British merchant ships and hired privateers to disrupt British trade and hurt the economy.

Profiles IN HISTORY

Background: During the summer of 1786, while charting the coastline of the Gulf of Mexico, Jose de Evia named Galveston Bay for Bernardo de Gálvez, the Spanish colonial governor. Gálvez died later that year having never seen the area.

Ask: What did Bernardo de Gálvez do to help the U.S. war effort before Spain declared war on Britain? *(He allowed French, Spanish, and American ships to use the Mississippi to smuggle arms to American troops.)*

3 ASSESS

Assign Section 3 Assessment as homework or as an in-class activity.

🔹 Have students use the **Interactive Tutor Self-Assessment CD-ROM.**

L1/ELL

Reading Essentials and Study Guide 3–3

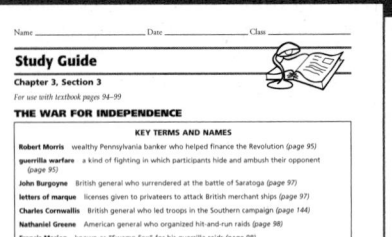

Name _____ Date _____ Class _____

Study Guide

Chapter 3, Section 3

For use with textbook pages 94–99

THE WAR FOR INDEPENDENCE

KEY TERMS AND NAMES

Robert Morris wealthy Pennsylvania banker who helped finance the Revolution (page 95)

guerrilla warfare a kind of fighting in which participants hide and ambush their opponent (page 95)

John Burgoyne British general who surrendered at the battle of Saratoga (page 97)

letters of marque licenses given to privateers to attack British merchant ships (page 97)

Charles Cornwallis British general who led troops in the Southern campaign (page 144)

Nathaniel Greene American general who organized hit-and-run raids (page 98)

Francis Marion known as "Swamp Fox" for his guerrilla raids (page 98)

Perhaps the most famous naval battle of the war involved **John Paul Jones,** American commander of the *Bonhomme Richard.* While sailing near Britain in September 1779, Jones encountered a group of British merchant ships protected by two warships. Jones attacked one of them, the *Serapis,* but the heavier guns of the British ship nearly sank the *Bonhomme Richard.* When the British commander called on Jones to surrender, he replied, "I have not yet begun to fight." He lashed his ship to the *Serapis* so it could not sink and then boarded the British ship. After more than three hours of battle, the British surrendered.

The Southern Campaign After the British defeat at Saratoga in 1777, General Howe had resigned. His replacement, Sir Henry Clinton, began a campaign in the South, where the British believed they had the strongest Loyalist support. British officials hoped that even if they lost the Northern states, they might still keep control of the South, which produced valuable tobacco and rice.

In December 1778, 3,500 British troops captured Savannah, Georgia. They seized control of Georgia's backcountry, while American troops retreated to Charles Town, South Carolina. Soon afterward General Clinton attacked Charles Town. Nearly 14,000 British troops surrounded the city, trapping the American forces. On May 12, 1780, the Americans surrendered. Nearly 5,500 American troops were taken prisoner, the greatest American defeat in the war. Clinton returned to New York, leaving General **Charles Cornwallis** in command.

Patriots Rally Cornwallis moved next to Camden, South Carolina, where he stopped a Patriot force from destroying a British supply base. After winning the Battle of Camden, the British found the tide turning against them in the South. Although many Southerners sympathized with Britain, they objected to the brutal tactics of some Loyalist forces in the region.

One such group, led by a British cavalry officer named Patrick Ferguson, finally went too far in trying to subdue the people living in the Appalachian Mountains. A band of overmountain men, as they were known, assembled a militia force. They intercepted

Ferguson at Kings Mountain on October 7, 1780, and destroyed his army. The Battle of Kings Mountain was a turning point in the South. Southern farmers, furious with British treatment, began to organize their own militias.

The new commander of American forces in the region, General **Nathaniel Greene,** organized the militias into small units to carry out hit-and-run raids against British camps and supply wagons. The most famous of these guerrilla units was led by **Francis Marion,** who was known as the "Swamp Fox." General Greene hoped that while militia destroyed enemy supplies, the regular army could wear down the British in a series of battles.

Greene's strategy worked. In 1781 the Americans engaged the British at Cowpens and Guilford Court House, and both battles resulted in hundreds of British casualties. By late 1781, the British controlled very little territory in the South except for the cities of Savannah, Charles Town, and Wilmington.

✓ **Reading Check** **Explaining** What was the American strategy for attacking the British at sea?

The War Is Won

In the spring of 1781, General Cornwallis decided to invade Virginia. If he could take control there, he could stop new supplies and troop reinforcements from reaching American forces in the South.

Profiles IN HISTORY

Bernardo de Gálvez
1746–1786

Bernardo de Gálvez was born in Málaga, Spain, in 1746. Following family tradition, he joined the military. At age 18, he traveled to America with his uncle, who had been sent by the government to inspect New Spain. In 1769 Gálvez was placed in command of Spanish forces on New Spain's northern frontier. During the next two years, he led his forces in battle against the Apache people in what is today west Texas. In 1777 he was appointed governor of Louisiana.

Even before Spain entered the Revolutionary War, Gálvez took steps to aid the United States. He exchanged letters with Patrick Henry and Thomas Jefferson. He also used his authority as governor to secure the Mississippi against the British, while allowing French, Spanish, and American ships to use the river to smuggle arms to the American forces. When Spain declared war on Britain, Gálvez raised an army, fought British troops near Baton Rouge and Natchez, and captured British forts at Mobile and Pensacola. His campaigns were important to the U.S. victory because they tied down British troops that might otherwise have been used against the Americans farther north. The city of Galveston, Texas, is named in his honor.

98 CHAPTER 3 The American Revolution

CRITICAL THINKING ACTIVITY

Predicting Outcomes Have students select one of the major battles of the American Revolution. Tell them to consider what would have happened if the other side had won. Have them consider what advantage the winning side would gain and what their next likely move would be. Have students share their predictions as part of a class discussion. **L2**

The Battle of Yorktown In May 1781, Cornwallis arrived in Virginia, where he joined with forces led by **Benedict Arnold.** Arnold had been an American commander but had later sold military information to the British. When his treason was discovered, Arnold fled to British-controlled New York City, where he was put in charge of British troops and ordered south.

Arnold's and Cornwallis's forces began to conquer the state together. They encountered little resistance at first and almost captured Virginia's governor, Thomas Jefferson. George Washington quickly dispatched troops led by the Marquis de Lafayette and General Anthony Wayne to defend Virginia. As the American forces increased, General Clinton ordered Cornwallis to secure a naval base on the coast. Following orders, Cornwallis headed to the coastal town of Yorktown.

Cornwallis's move created an opportunity for the Americans and their French allies. George Washington and a French commander, Jean Baptiste Rochambeau, led a joint force south to Yorktown. Meanwhile, the French navy, under the command of Admiral François de Grasse, moved into Chesapeake Bay, preventing Cornwallis from escaping by sea or receiving supplies. On September 28, 1781, American and French forces surrounded Yorktown and began to bombard the British. On October 14, Washington's aide, Alexander Hamilton, led an attack that captured key British defenses. Three days later, Cornwallis began negotiations to surrender, and on October 19, 1781, approximately 8,000 British troops marched out of Yorktown and laid down their weapons.

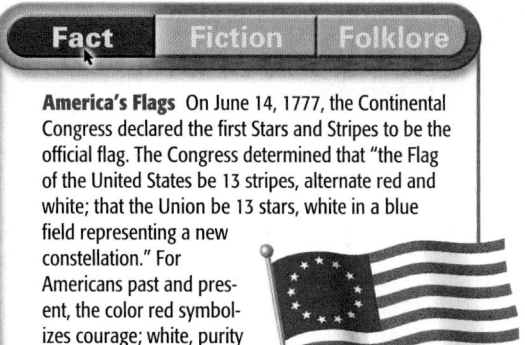

Fact | Fiction | Folklore

America's Flags On June 14, 1777, the Continental Congress declared the first Stars and Stripes to be the official flag. The Congress determined that "the Flag of the United States be 13 stripes, alternate red and white; that the Union be 13 stars, white in a blue field representing a new constellation." For Americans past and present, the color red symbolizes courage; white, purity of ideals; and blue, strength and unity of the states.

The Treaty of Paris After learning of the surrender at Yorktown, Parliament voted to end the war. Peace talks began in Paris in early April 1782.

The final settlement, the **Treaty of Paris,** was signed on September 3, 1783. In this treaty, Britain recognized the United States of America as a new nation with the Mississippi River as its western border. The British kept Canada, but in a separate treaty they gave Florida back to Spain and returned to the French certain colonies they had seized from them in Africa and the Caribbean.

On November 24, 1783, the last British troops left New York City. The Revolutionary War was over, and the creation of a new nation was about to begin.

Reading Check **Describing** How was the war won at Yorktown?

SECTION 3 ASSESSMENT

HISTORY Online | **Study Central™** To review this section, go to tarvol2.glencoe.com and click on **Study Central™.**

Checking for Understanding

1. **Define:** guerrilla warfare, letter of marque.
2. **Identify:** Robert Morris, John Burgoyne, Charles Cornwallis, Nathaniel Greene, Francis Marion, Benedict Arnold.
3. **List** the terms of the Treaty of Paris.

Reviewing Themes

4. **Identifying Cause and Effect** How did the Battle of Saratoga influence the outcome of the American Revolution?

Critical Thinking

5. **Evaluating** How did European countries aid the Americans in the war for independence?
6. **Categorizing** Use a graphic organizer similar to the one below to list the advantages and disadvantages of each side in the American Revolution.

	Advantages	Disadvantages
Britain		
United States		

Analyzing Visuals

7. **Analyzing Maps** Study the map of the Revolutionary War on page 96. How many British victories, American victories, and indecisive battles are depicted? Although both sides won about the same number of battles, the Americans won the war. Why?

Writing About History

8. **Persuasive Writing** Imagine that you are a colonist fighting in the American Revolution. Write a letter to convince European nations to support the Americans in the war.

SECTION 3 ASSESSMENT ANSWERS

1. Terms are in blue.
2. Robert Morris (p. 95), John Burgoyne (p. 97), Charles Cornwallis (p. 98), Nathaniel Greene (p. 98), Francis Marion (p. 98), Benedict Arnold (p. 99)
3. Britain recognized the United States as a new nation, gave Florida back to Spain, and gave France colonies in Africa and the Caribbean.
4. It improved American morale and gained French support.
5. secretly sent arms and supplies
6. Students' organizers should include information from the chart on page 95, and from the text on pages 94–95.
7. 7 British, 8 American, and 1 indecisive. Americans surrounded Yorktown and cut off supply lines.
8. Letters might include unfair British treatment and desire not to see England grow stronger.

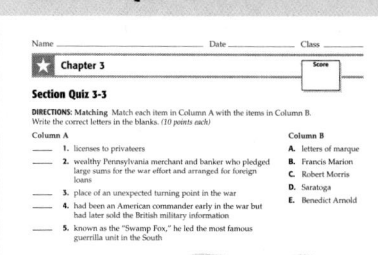
Fact | Fiction | Folklore

Francis Hopkinson is credited with the actual design of the first Stars and Stripes. Historians agree that Betsy Ross made flags for the Pennsylvania navy. She may have made the first national flag.

Reteach

Ask students to describe the strategies behind the Northern Campaign.

Enrich

Invite students to locate the words and music for the song "The World Turn'd Upside Down." Ask them if the song was a good choice for the occasion.

Reading Check

Answer: American and French forces surrounded Yorktown and cut off Cornwallis's access to the sea.

HISTORY Online

Study Central™ provides summaries, interactive games, and online graphic organizers to help students review section content.

4 CLOSE

Ask students to explain the terms of the Treaty of Paris.

1 FOCUS

Section Overview

This section addresses the impact of the War for Independence on American society.

BELLRINGER
Skillbuilder Activity

Project transparency and have students answer the question.

Daily Focus Skills Transparency 3–4

Reading Preview

Answers to Graphic: Achievements: Northwest Ordinance gave people in new territories basic rights, did not allow slavery, negotiated several trade treaties
Weaknesses: could not effectively raise money to pay debts and finance its operation, could not regulate commerce, lacked authority to enforce Treaty of Paris, could not settle dispute with Spain (see chart, p. 105)

Preteaching Vocabulary
Have students write a sentence explaining the significance of each of these Key Terms and Names.

SECTION 4 The Confederation

Guide to Reading

Main Idea
After the war, the 13 states were loosely united under the Articles of Confederation.

Key Terms and Names
republic, Virginia Statute for Religious Freedom, manumission, ratification, Northwest Ordinance, recession, inflation

Reading Strategy
Organizing As you read about the new government created by the Articles of Confederation, complete a graphic organizer similar to the one below to identify the strengths and weaknesses of the Confederation Congress.

Confederation Congress	
Achievements	Weaknesses

Reading Objectives
• **Discuss** the new political ideas that prevailed following the war.
• **Examine** the strengths and weaknesses of the newly formed Confederation Congress.

Section Theme
Geography and History While the weak Confederation government ultimately failed, it created the system by which new states became part of the new nation.

Preview of Events

♦1775   ♦1779   ♦1783   ♦1787

1776
Virginia creates Declaration of Rights

1781
Articles of Confederation ratified

1786
Virginia's Statute for Religious Freedom is passed

1787
Northwest Ordinance becomes law

Wooden statue of an African American breaking his chains

★ An American Story ★

In the late 1700s, an enslaved Massachusetts man named Quock Walker took an extraordinary step: He took legal action against a white man who had assaulted him. Given the times, this was a bold step, but Walker believed he had the law on his side. Massachusetts's new constitution referred to the "inherent liberty" of all men. The judge, William Cushing, agreed:

66Our Constitution [of Massachusetts] sets out with declaring that all men are born free and equal—and that every subject is entitled to liberty, and to have guarded by the laws, as well as life and property—and in short is totally repugnant to the idea of being born slaves. This being the case, I think the idea of slavery is inconsistent with our own conduct and Constitution.99

While the Quock Walker case did not abolish slavery, it demonstrated that the Massachusetts courts would not support the institution. As a result of this ruling and various antislavery efforts, slavery ceased to exist in Massachusetts.

—adapted from *Founding the Republic*

New Political Ideas

When American leaders declared independence and founded the United States of America, they were very much aware that they were creating something new. By breaking away from the king, they had established a republic. A **republic** is a form of government where power resides with a body of citizens entitled to vote. This power is exercised by elected officials who are responsible to the citizens and who must govern according to laws or a constitution.

100   CHAPTER 3   The American Revolution

SECTION RESOURCES

📖 Reproducible Masters
• Reproducible Lesson Plan 3–4
• Daily Lecture and Discussion Notes 3–4
• Guided Reading Activity 3–4
• Section Quiz 3–4
• Reading Essentials and Study Guide 3–4
• Performance Assessment Activities and Rubrics

🖥 Transparencies
• Daily Focus Skills Transparency 3–4

Multimedia
🔘 Interactive Tutor Self-Assessment CD-ROM
🔘 ExamView® Pro Testmaker CD-ROM
🔘 Presentation Plus! CD-ROM
🔘 TeacherWorks™ CD-ROM
🔘 Audio Program

While many Europeans viewed a republic as radical and dangerous, Americans saw its benefits. In an ideal republic, all citizens are equal under the law, regardless of their wealth or social position. This conflicted with existing ideas, including beliefs about slavery, about women not being allowed to vote or own property, and about wealthy people being "better" than people in poorer classes. Despite these contradictions, republican ideas began to change American society.

New State Constitutions American leaders believed that the best form of government was a constitutional republic. At the same time, many, including John Adams, worried that a true democracy would lead to tyranny by the majority. For example, the poor might vote to seize all property from the rich. Adams argued that government needed "checks and balances" to prevent any group in society from becoming too strong and taking away the rights of the minority.

Adams favored a "mixed government" with a separation of powers. The executive, legislative, and judicial branches would be independent of one another. Adams also argued that the legislature should have two houses: a senate to represent people with property and an assembly to protect the rights of the common people. Adams's ideas influenced several states as they drafted new constitutions during the Revolution. Virginia's constitution of 1776 and Massachusetts's constitution of 1780 established an elected governor, senate, and assembly. By the 1790s, most of the other states had similar documents.

Many states attached a bill of rights to their constitutions as well. This began in 1776, when George Mason drafted Virginia's **Declaration of Rights.** This document guaranteed to all Virginians freedom of speech, freedom of religion, the right to bear arms, the right to trial by jury, and freedom from unreasonable search and seizure of property.

Several state constitutions also provided for government-funded universities. American leaders considered an educated public to be critical to the republic's success. Jefferson called it the "keystone of our arch of

government." In 1795 the University of North Carolina was the first state university to open.

Voting Rights Expand The experience of fighting side by side during the Revolution with people from every social class and region increased Americans' belief in equality. If all men were risking their lives for the same cause, then all deserved a say in choosing their leaders. In almost every state, the new constitutions made it easier for men to gain the right to vote. Many states allowed any white male who paid taxes to vote, whether or not he owned property.

People still had to own a certain amount of property to hold elective office, although usually much less than before the Revolution. The practice of giving veterans land grants as payment for their military service also increased the number of people eligible to hold office. Before the Revolution, over 80 percent of elected officials in the North came from the upper class. Ten years after the war began, a little more than one-third did. In the South, higher property qualifications kept the wealthy planters in power, although their numbers dropped from almost 90 percent of those holding office to about 70 percent.

Freedom of Religion The new concern with rights included opposition to "ecclesiastical tyranny"—the power of a church, backed by the government, to

Picturing History

New State Constitutions From 1776 to 1807, the New Jersey state constitution allowed "all inhabitants . . . who are worth fifty pounds" to vote. This decree allowed women to vote, as seen in this painting of women at a polling place. How else did voting rights change following the Revolutionary War?

CHAPTER 3   The American Revolution   **101**

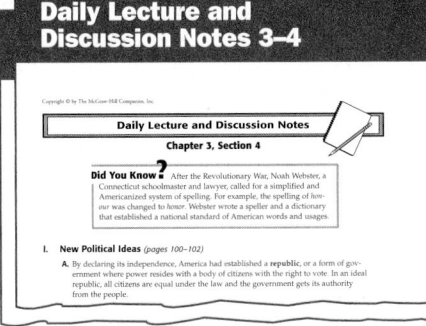

Daily Lecture and Discussion Notes
Chapter 3, Section 4

Did You Know? After the Revolutionary War, Noah Webster, a Connecticut schoolmaster and lawyer, called for a simplified and Americanized system of spelling. For example, the spelling of honour was changed to honor. Webster wrote a speller and a dictionary that established a national standard of American words and usages.

I. New Political Ideas (pages 100–102)

A. By declaring its independence, America had established a **republic**, or a form of government where power resides with a body of citizens with the right to vote. In an ideal republic, all citizens are equal under the law and the government gets its authority from the people.

Creating a List Write the words *Monarchy* and *Republic* on the board. Have students list words that describe each of these forms of government. Review the lists and ask students to identify pairs of opposite words. **L1** ELL

you don't say...

Right to Vote *Suffrage* is another term for the right to vote. For example, you can say that suffrage was extended to more citizens after the revolution.

Picturing **History**

Answer: Many states allowed all white men who paid taxes, not just property owners, to vote.
Ask: Who was allowed to hold elected offices? *(In most states only landowners could hold an elected office.)*

COOPERATIVE LEARNING ACTIVITY

Comparing and Contrasting Organize the students into groups of four or five. Assign each group a state close to your own state. Have groups use library and Internet resources to learn about the constitution of their assigned state. Have the groups learn when the constitution was ratified and identify its basic provisions. Conduct a class discussion comparing and contrasting the various constitutions with each other and with the United States Constitution.

Use the rubric for a cooperative group management plan on pages 71–72 in the ***Performance Assessment Activities and Rubrics.***

L1/ELL

Guided Reading Activity 3-4

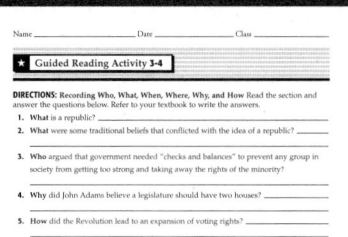

✓ **Reading Check**

Answer: freedom of speech, freedom of religion, right to bear arms, right to trial by jury, and freedom from unreasonable search and seizure

Margaret Cochran Corbin fought earlier in the defense of Fort Washington. She was wounded in the battle and was the first woman to receive a pension from the United States government as a disabled soldier.

FYI

While her husband, future president John Adams, served in the Continental Congress, Abigail Adams remained at home, running the farm and raising their children. The two wrote each other often. Abigail was a keen observer of current affairs and a strong advocate for the rights of women. In her most famous letter, she urged her husband to "remember the ladies" in the laws for the new country. "Do not put such unlimited power into the hands of husbands. Remember, all men would be tyrants if they could."

make people worship in a certain way. In Virginia, Baptists led a movement to abolish tax funding for the Anglican Church. Governor Thomas Jefferson wrote the **Virginia Statute for Religious Freedom,** passed in 1786. The statute declared that Virginia no longer had an official church, and that the state could not collect taxes for churches. It further declared:

❝[O]ur civil rights have no dependence on our religious opinions, any more than our opinions in physics or geometry . . . therefore . . . proscribing any citizen as unworthy of the public confidence . . . unless he profess or renounce this or that religion opinion, is depriving him injuriously of those privileges and advantages to which in common with his fellow citizens he has a natural right.❞

—quoted in *Founding the Republic*

The idea that the government should not fund churches spread slowly. Massachusetts, for example, permitted Quakers and Baptists to assign their tax money to their churches instead of to the Congregational churches—the successors to Puritan congregations—but it did not abolish religious taxes entirely until 1833. 📖 *(See page 947 for the text of the Virginia Statute for Religious Freedom.)*

✓ **Reading Check** **Identifying** Which freedoms did Virginia's constitution guarantee in its bill of rights?

The Revolution Changes Society

The postwar notions of greater equality and liberty, as noble as they were, were not widely applied to women or African Americans. Both groups did, however, find their lives changed by the Revolution, as did the Loyalists who had supported Britain. The war also helped Americans develop a national identity.

Women Women played a vital role during the Revolution, contributing on both the home front and the battlefront. With their husbands, brothers, and sons at war, some women took over running the family farm. Others traveled with the army—cooking, washing, and nursing the wounded. Women also served as spies and couriers, and a few even joined the fighting. Mary Ludwig Hays, known as **Molly Pitcher,** carried water to Patriot gunners during the Battle of Monmouth. Margaret Corbin accompanied her husband to battle, and after his death she took his place at his cannon until the battle ended.

After the war, as Americans began to think about what their revolutionary ideals implied, women made

some advances. They could more easily obtain a divorce, and they gained greater access to education.

African Americans Several thousand enslaved Africans obtained their freedom during the Revolution. Although the British seized numerous enslaved people and shipped them to British plantations in the Caribbean, they also freed many others in exchange for military service. Many planters offered freedom to slaves who would fight the British. General Washington permitted African Americans to join the Continental Army, and he urged state militias to do likewise. In all, about 5,000 African Americans served with the Patriot forces.

After the Revolution, many Americans realized that enslaving people did not fit with the new language of liberty and equality. Opposition to slavery had been growing steadily even before the Revolution, especially in the northern and middle states. After the war began, Northern governments took steps to end slavery entirely. Vermont banned the practice in 1777. In 1780 Pennsylvania freed all children born enslaved when they reached age 28. Rhode Island decreed in 1784 that enslaved men born thereafter would be free when they turned 21 and women when they turned 18. In 1799 New York freed enslaved men born that year or later when they reached age 28 and women when they reached age 25. The ending of slavery in the North was thus a gradual process that took several decades.

The story was different in the South. The South relied heavily on enslaved labor to sustain its agricultural economy. As a result, Southern leaders showed little interest in abolishing slavery. Only Virginia took steps in this direction. In 1782 the state passed a law encouraging manumission, or the voluntary freeing of enslaved persons, especially for those who had fought in the Revolution. Through this law, about 10,000 slaves obtained their freedom, but the vast majority remained in bondage.

Loyalist Flight For many Loyalists, the end of the war changed everything. Former friends often shunned them, and state governments sometimes seized their property. Unwilling to live under the new government and often afraid for their lives, approximately 100,000 Loyalists fled the United States after the war. Some went to England or the British West Indies, but most moved to Canada.

Americans grappled over what to do with the property of Loyalists. In North Carolina and New York, Patriots confiscated Loyalist lands. Public officials elsewhere, however, opposed such actions. The

---

DIFFERENTIATED INSTRUCTION

Gifted and Talented Tell students that Josiah Tucker, an English clergyman, claimed that once the British government was gone, "the Americans will have no center of union among them, and no common interest to pursue." Ask students if they think Tucker was accurate in his description of Americans in the 1780s. Have students create an original story based on historical facts that demonstrates how difficult it was to form a union. **L3**

☞ Refer to *Inclusion for the High School Social Studies Classroom Strategies and Activities* in the TCR.

Massachusetts Constitution of 1780, for example, extended the rights of "life, liberty, and property" to Loyalists, and the relatives and agents of departing Loyalists were often able to claim the land they left behind.

An Emerging American Culture The victory over the British united Americans and created powerful nationalist feelings. The Revolutionary War gave Americans a common enemy and a shared sense of purpose as they fought side by side in each other's states. The Revolution also gave rise to patriotic symbols and folklore about wartime deeds and heroes, which helped Americans think of themselves as belonging to the same group.

In addition, the Revolution sparked the creativity of American artists whose work helped shape a national identity. **John Trumbull,** for example, stirred nationalist pride with his depictions of battles and other events in the Revolution. **Charles Willson Peale** painted inspiring portraits of Washington and other Patriot leaders.

Education also became American-centered. Schools tossed out British textbooks and began teaching republican ideas and the history of the struggle for independence.

✓ **Reading Check** Describing How did the civil rights of African Americans change after the Revolutionary War?

The Achievements of the Confederation

As the American people began to build a national identity, leaders of the United States turned their attention to creating a government that could hold the new nation together. Even before independence was declared, Patriot leaders had realized that the colonies needed to be united under some type of central government. In November 1777, the Continental Congress adopted the **Articles of Confederation and Perpetual Union**—a plan for a loose union of the states under the authority of the Congress. To go into effect, the plan required the ratification, or approval, of all the states. Most of the states quickly ratified the articles, but Maryland held out.

The main reason for delay was that a number of states claimed ownership of great tracts

of land west of the Appalachian Mountains. Maryland, which had no land claims, led five other states in proposing that the Congress assume control of all western territories. They argued that all 13 states had jointly won the territories by fighting for American independence. The states already claiming land in the west resisted this proposal. Finally, in 1780, New York and Connecticut agreed to give up most of their claims. Virginia followed in early 1781, which convinced Maryland that the remaining states with land claims would eventually give them up. In February 1781, Maryland ratified the Articles of Confederation, and on March 2, they went into effect. The United States now had its first constitution.

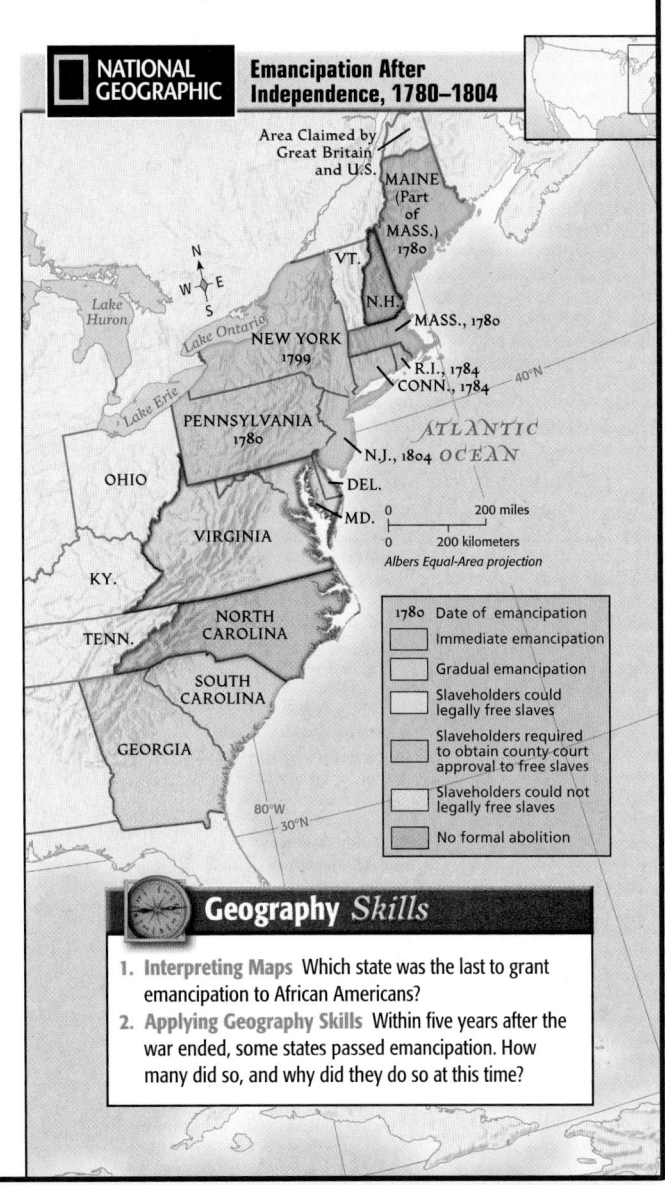

NATIONAL GEOGRAPHIC
Emancipation After Independence, 1780–1804

Area Claimed by Great Britain and U.S.

1780	Date of emancipation
	Immediate emancipation
	Gradual emancipation
	Slaveholders could legally free slaves
	Slaveholders required to obtain county court approval to free slaves
	Slaveholders could not legally free slaves
	No formal abolition

Geography *Skills*

1. **Interpreting Maps** Which state was the last to grant emancipation to African Americans?
2. **Applying Geography Skills** Within five years after the war ended, some states passed emancipation. How many did so, and why did they do so at this time?

✓ **Reading Check**

Answer: Many were freed after the war, and Northern states began to ban slavery. In the South, only Virginia enacted legislation that led to freeing slaves.

Creating Circle Graphs Provide the data shown below. Ask students to select one of the states and create three circle graphs, one for each year, showing the number of slaves as a segment of the total population. **L2**

Number of Slaves

	1790	1800	1810
New York	21,193	20,613	15,017
Pennsylvania	3,707	1,706	795
Rhode Island	958	380	108

Total Population

	1790	1800	1810
New York	340,241	586,182	959,049
Pennsylvania	433,611	602,365	810,019
Rhode Island	69,112	69,122	76,931

Use the rubric for creating a map, display, or chart on pages 65–66 in the *Performance Assessment Activities and Rubrics.*

Geography *Skills*

Answers:
1. New Jersey in 1804
2. two states—Connecticut and Rhode Island; republican ideals of liberty and equality for all

Geography Skills Practice
Ask: How many states did not permit freeing slaves? *(2)*

INTERDISCIPLINARY CONNECTIONS ACTIVITY

Mathematics Present the data at right to illustrate the effects of Virginia's law encouraging manumission. Ask students to create a bar chart that illustrates the relationship between the number of slaves and the total population between 1790 and 1830. Ask students if they think the law was effective. **L2**

Virginia Population Data

	Total Population	Number of Enslaved Persons
1790	747,550	292,627
1800	885,171	346,671
1810	974,622	392,518
1820	1,065,379	425,153
1830	1,211,405	469,757

Geography *Skills*

Answers:
1. townships
2. By creating slave-free territories, it continued the division of slave-holding and non-slave-holding states in the South and North.

Geography Skills Practice

Ask: Examine the order the states entered the Union. What geographic features may have influenced the order? *(Students should note that proximity to the original colonies and access to the states by the Ohio River played a part in getting enough people to move to the areas to apply for statehood.)*

Creating an Advertising Campaign Have students review the part titled Western Policies. Have students assume that they are working for the governor of the territory to help in getting people to move to the territory. Tell students to design an advertising campaign using media available in the late 1700s. Have students display the campaign plans and media pieces they have created. **L3**

FYI

The neat squared-off patterns of farms that is seen in much of the Midwest dates to the system of land survey adopted in the Land Ordinance of 1785.

NATIONAL GEOGRAPHIC **Northwest Territory, 1780s**

British North America

TOWNSHIP
Base Line
6 miles

36	30	24	18	12	6
35	29	23	17	11	5
34	28	22	16	10	4
33	27	21	15	9	3
32	26	20	14	8	2
31	25	■	13	7	1

Range Line — 6 miles

Section 19

Half section
320 Acres

Quarter section
160 Acres

1 mile — 1 mile

WISCONSIN 1848

MICHIGAN 1837

The Seven Ranges

OHIO 1803

ILLINOIS 1818

INDIANA 1816

Ohio River

Northwest Territory
Present-day state boundaries
1818 Date state admitted to Union

0 — 200 miles
0 — 200 kilometers
Albers Equal-Area projection

Geography *Skills*

1. **Interpreting Maps** The Land Ordinance of 1785 provided that the territory be divided into areas of 36 square miles. What were these areas called?
2. **Applying Geography Skills** Why was the prohibition of slavery in this territory significant?

The Articles of Confederation The Articles of Confederation established a very weak central government. The states had spent several years fighting for independence from Britain. They did not want to give up that independence to a new central government that might become tyrannical.

Under the Articles, each state would select a delegation once per year to send to the **Confederation Congress.** The Congress was the entire government. It had the right to declare war and raise armies. It also could negotiate with other nations and sign treaties, including trade treaties. It could not, however, regulate trade, nor could it impose taxes.

GEOGRAPHY

Western Policies Lacking the power to tax or regulate trade, the only way for the Confederation Congress to raise money to pay its debts and finance its operations was to sell the land it controlled west of the Appalachian Mountains. To attract buyers, the Congress had to establish systems for dividing up and selling the land and for governing the new settlements.

The Land Ordinance of 1785 set up a scheme for dividing the land into square townships, which were then subdivided into smaller sections and sold at auction. The **Northwest Ordinance** of 1787 provided the basis for governing western lands and developing them into states. The law created a single territory bounded roughly by Pennsylvania on the east, the Ohio River on the south, the Mississippi River on the west, and the Great Lakes on the north. Initially the Congress would choose a governor, a secretary, and three judges for the territory. When 5,000 adult male citizens had settled in a district, they could elect an assembly. When the population reached 60,000, the district could apply to become a state "on an equal footing with the original states." Between three and five states could be formed from the territory.

The Northwest Ordinance also guaranteed certain rights to people living in the territory. These included freedom of religion, property rights, and the right to

104 CHAPTER 3 The American Revolution

Reading Strategy ❘ READING THE TEXT

Making Inferences When students make inferences, they use their reason and their experience to make educated guesses about what might have been an individual's or group's motivation. Ask students to make inferences about where state leaders got their ideas about which rights to incorporate in their state's bill of rights. *(Students' answers should reflect their knowledge of what rights were denied colonists under Britain's rule. They might also mention the English Bill of Rights. It is important that they understand that the U.S. Constitution and Bill of Rights had not yet been formulated.)* **L1**

trial by jury. The ordinance further stated that "there [would] be neither slavery nor involuntary servitude in the said territory." The exclusion of slavery from the Northwest Territory did not affect Southern territories. Like the original states, the frontier would be divided between Southern slave-holding states and Northern free states.

Success in Trade The Confederation Congress also tried to promote foreign trade. After the Revolutionary War, the British government sharply restricted American access to British markets. As a result, the Congress negotiated several trade treaties with other countries, including Holland, Prussia, and Sweden. American merchants also sold goods to France and its Caribbean colonies. By 1790 the trade of the United States was greater than the prewar trade of the American colonies.

✔ **Reading Check** **Explaining** What were the provisions of the Land Ordinance of 1785 and the Northwest Ordinance of 1787?

Weaknesses of the Congress

Despite the Confederation Congress's success in signing commercial treaties, trade problems beset the young nation. The Congress also faced other challenges that it could not easily solve.

Problems With Trade During the boycotts of the 1760s and the Revolutionary War, American artisans and manufacturers had prospered. After the war, the British flooded the United States with low-cost goods, putting thousands of Americans out of work.

The states fought back by restricting British imports. Unfortunately, the states did not all impose the same duties and restrictions. Because the Confederation Congress was not allowed to regulate commerce, the states began setting up customs posts on their borders to prevent the British from exploiting the different trade laws. They also began to levy taxes on each other's goods to raise revenue for themselves. New York, for example, taxed cabbage from New Jersey, which retaliated by charging New York for a lighthouse on the New Jersey side of the Hudson River. In effect, each state was beginning to act as a totally independent country.

Problems in Diplomacy In other areas of foreign policy, the Congress showed weakness. The first problems surfaced over the Congress's inability to enforce all the terms of the Treaty of Paris.

Before the war, many American merchants and planters had borrowed money from British lenders. In the peace treaty, the United States had agreed that British creditors should be allowed to recover their debts. They also agreed that states would return property confiscated from Loyalists during the war. In neither case, however, was the Congress able to compel the states to cooperate with these treaty provisions. In retaliation, the British refused to leave some American frontier posts. The Congress had no way to resolve these problems. Without the power to legally compel individuals, state legislatures, or state courts to comply with the terms of the peace treaty, Congress appeared weak and ineffective.

The Confederation Congress felt similarly helpless to settle a dispute with Spain over the boundary between Spanish territory and the state of Georgia. The Spanish then stopped Americans from depositing their goods in Spanish territory at the mouth of the Mississippi River. This effectively closed the Mississippi to farmers who used the river to ship their goods to market. Once more, the

Some Weaknesses of the Articles of Confederation

Provision	Problem Created
Congress has no power to tax	Weak currency and growing debt
	Inability to pay army leads to threats of mutiny
Congress has no power to enforce treaties	Foreign countries angry when treaties are not honored; for example, Britain keeps troops on American soil
Every state, despite size, has one vote	Populous states not equally represented
Congress has no power to regulate commerce	Trade hindered by states imposing high tariffs on each other
Amendment requires unanimous vote of states	Difficult to adapt articles to changing needs

Chart *Skills*

1. **Interpreting Charts** What was the problem with requiring a unanimous vote of the states to create changes in the Articles of Confederation?
2. **Analyzing** Why did the states approve a government with so many weaknesses?

✔ **Reading Check**

Answer: Land Ordinance of 1785—set up scheme for dividing the land into square townships, which were then subdivided and auctioned; Northwest Ordinance of 1787—created a new territory north of the Ohio River and east of the Mississippi; provided a plan for territorial legislature and application for statehood; guaranteed certain rights; banned slavery from the territory

Chart *Skills*

Answers:
1. It was virtually impossible to adapt the articles to changing needs.
2. Possible answer: They wanted to retain power.

3 ASSESS

Assign Section 4 Assessment as homework or as an in-class activity.

🌐 Have students use the **Interactive Tutor Self-Assessment CD-ROM.**

L1/ELL

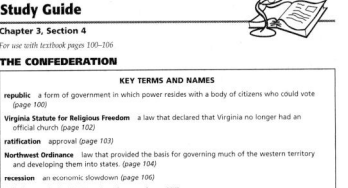

Reading Essentials and Study Guide 3–4

Name _____ Date _____ Class _____

Study Guide

Chapter 3, Section 4
For use with textbook pages 100–106

THE CONFEDERATION

KEY TERMS AND NAMES

republic a form of government in which power resides with a body of citizens who could vote *(page 100)*

Virginia Statute for Religious Freedom a law that declared that Virginia no longer had an official church *(page 102)*

ratification approval *(page 103)*

Northwest Ordinance law that provided the basis for governing much of the western territory and developing them into states *(page 104)*

recession an economic slowdown *(page 106)*

inflation a decline in the value of money *(page 1*

EXTENDING THE CONTENT

Food A French visitor to the United States was horrified at the meals Americans consumed. They were, he said, "calculated to injure the stomach, the teeth, and the health in general." For dinner, he continued, "they have boiled pastes under the name of puddings, . . . all their sauces, even for roast beef, are melted butter." In fact, early Americans did not eat well-balanced meals. Settlers on the frontier mostly ate meat—wild turkey, duck, rabbit, deer, and bear meat.

L2

Section Quiz 3–4

Name	Date	Class
★ **Chapter 3**		Score

Section Quiz 3–4

DIRECTIONS: Matching Match each item in Column A with the items in Column B.
Write the correct letters in the blanks. *(10 points each)*

Column A		Column B
_____	1. better known as Molly Pitcher, she took her husband's place in the Battle of Monmouth when he was killed	A. ratification
_____	2. painted inspiring portraits of Washington and other Patriot leaders	B. inflation
_____	3. the power of a church, backed by the government, to make people worship in a certain way	C. "ecclesiastical tyranny"
_____	4. approval	D. Mary Ludwig Hays
_____	5. decline in the value of money	E. Charles Wilson Peale

DIRECTIONS: Multiple Choice In the blank at the left, write the letter of the choice that

Reteach

Have students create a sentence outline for this section. Suggest that they use the headings in the textbook as a guide.

Enrich

Have students review the problems that the Confederation Congress experienced. Have them select one of the problems and suggest a potential solution. Have students present their proposals to the class, while the class plays the role of the Confederation Congress.

✓ Reading Check

Answer: could not control national trade or commerce, could not enforce treaties

HISTORY Online

Study Central™ provides summaries, interactive games, and online graphic organizers to help students review section content.

4 CLOSE

Have students describe the major changes in American society following the War for Independence.

---

limited power of the Confederation Congress presented a diplomatic solution from being found.

Problems With Debt While the Confederation Congress struggled with foreign affairs, many Americans struggled economically. Wartime debts and the British trade imbalance plunged the nation into a severe *recession,* or economic slowdown.

Farmers were badly hit by the recession. They were not earning as much money as they once did, and they had to keep borrowing in order to plant their next crop. Many also had mortgages to pay. The cost of the Revolution also left individual states and the Congress in debt.

To pay off their debts, the states could raise taxes, but farmers and others urged that the state governments begin issuing paper money instead. Paper money would not be backed by gold and silver, so people would not trust it. As a result, *inflation*—a decline in the value of money—would begin. Debtors would be able to pay their debts using paper money that was worth less than the value printed on it. This would let them pay off their debts more easily.

Not surprisingly, merchants, importers, and lenders strongly opposed paper currency because they would not be receiving the true amount they were owed. Nonetheless, starting in 1785, seven states began issuing paper money.

In Rhode Island, the paper money eventually became so worthless that some creditors insisted on being repaid only with gold or silver. After an angry mob rioted in 1786 against merchants who refused to take paper money, Rhode Island passed a law

forcing people to accept the currency at its stated value. Those who refused could be arrested and fined.

Shays's Rebellion A more serious disturbance erupted that same year in Massachusetts. Known as **Shays's Rebellion,** it started when the Massachusetts government raised taxes to pay off its debts instead of issuing paper money. The taxes fell most heavily on poor farmers in the western part of the state. Many farmers found themselves facing the loss of their farms.

In late August, armed mobs closed down several county courthouses to prevent farm foreclosures. Daniel Shays, a bankrupt farmer and former army captain, emerged as one of the rebellion's leaders. In January 1787, Shays and about 1,200 followers advanced on the arsenal at Springfield, Massachusetts, to seize weapons before marching on Boston. In response, the governor sent more than 4,000 volunteers to defend the armory. This militia quickly ended the rebellion.

Many wealthy Americans worried that uprisings like those in Rhode Island and Massachusetts might occur in other states. "What is to afford our security against the violence of lawless men?" asked General Henry Knox, a close aide to George Washington. "Our government must be braced, changed, or altered to secure our lives and property."

The Confederation Congress's continuing problems in trade and diplomacy underscored its powerlessness. By 1787 many people had begun to argue for a stronger central government.

✓ Reading Check **Summarizing** In what ways was the Confederation Congress ineffective?

HISTORY Online
Study Central™ To review this section, go to tarvol2.glencoe.com and click on **Study Central™**.

SECTION 4 ASSESSMENT

Checking for Understanding

1. **Define:** republic, manumission, ratification, recession, inflation.
2. **Identify:** Virginia Statute for Religious Freedom, Northwest Ordinance.
3. **Summarize** the conditions that led to Shays's Rebellion.

Reviewing Themes

4. **Geography and History** How did the Confederation Congress provide for the division, sale, and eventual statehood of western lands?

Critical Thinking

5. **Analyzing** How did fear of tyranny shape new state constitutions and the Articles of Confederation?
6. **Categorizing** Use a graphic organizer similar to the one below to identify how revolutionary ideas affected American life.

	Effects
Political Ideas	
Social and Cultural Ideas	
Economic Ideas	

Analyzing Visuals

7. **Studying Maps** Examine the map of the Northwest Ordinance on page 104. What significant provision of the ordinance do the dates on the map signify?

Writing About History

8. **Expository Writing** Imagine you are on a committee to write a new constitution for your state. List the freedoms you want attached to your state's constitution. Explain why you feel it is important to guarantee these rights.

SECTION 4 ASSESSMENT ANSWERS

1. Terms are in blue.
2. Virginia Statute for Religious Freedom (p. 102), Northwest Ordinance (p. 104)
3. Raising taxes on poor farmers forced farm foreclosures.
4. Land was divided into townships, sections, and parcels, then sold at auction. Rights to self-government grew with the population. They could apply for statehood with 60,000 residents.
5. They provided many individual freedoms to prevent tyranny.
6. political: more people could vote; social/cultural: patriotic symbols gave sense of unity; economic: trade problems, recessions, increased taxes
7. the date each territory achieved statehood
8. Each item should have an explanation of its importance.

Critical Thinking

Making Comparisons

Why Learn This Skill?

Suppose you want to buy a portable compact disc (CD) player, and you must choose among three models. You would probably compare characteristics of the three models, such as price, sound quality, and size to figure out which model is best for you. In the study of American history, you often compare people or events from one time period with those from a different time period.

Learning the Skill

When making comparisons, you examine two or more groups, situations, events, or documents. Then you identify any similarities and differences. For example, the chart on this page compares two documents with regard to the powers they gave the central government. The Articles of Confederation were passed and implemented before the United States Constitution, which took their place. The chart includes a check mark in each column that applies. For example, the entry *Protect copyrights* does not have a check under *Articles of Confederation.* This shows that the government under the Articles lacked that power. The entry is checked under *United States Constitution,* showing that the government under the Constitution does have that power.

When making comparisons, you first decide what items will be compared and determine which characteristics you will use to compare them. Then you identify similarities and differences in these characteristics.

Practicing the Skill

Analyze the information on the chart on this page. Then answer the questions.

❶ What items are being compared? How are they being compared?

❷ What are the similarities and differences of the documents?

❸ Which document had the most power regarding legal matters? How can you tell?

The Articles of Confederation and the United States Constitution

Powers of the Central Government	Articles of Confederation	United States Constitution
Declare war; make peace	✔	✔
Coin money	✔	✔
Manage foreign affairs	✔	✔
Establish a postal system	✔	✔
Impose taxes		✔
Regulate trade		✔
Organize a court system		✔
Call state militia for service		✔
Protect copyrights		✔
Take other necessary actions to run the federal government		✔

❹ Which document had the most power in dealing with other nations? How can you tell?

Skills Assessment

Complete the Practicing Skills questions on page 119 and the Chapter 3 Skill Reinforcement Activity to assess your mastery of this skill.

Applying the Skill

Making Comparisons On the editorial page of your local newspaper, read two columns that express different viewpoints on the same issue. Identify the similarities and differences between the two points of view.

 Glencoe's **Skillbuilder Interactive Workbook CD-ROM, Level 2,** provides instruction and practice in key social studies skills.

TEACH

Making Comparisons Making comparisons is an important life skill that can be applied to many different situations. It is particularly helpful when trying to make choices. Hold up a pen and a pencil and ask a student volunteer to use the chalkboard to create a simple table comparing the two items. Point out that a table is a valuable tool when you are making comparisons, regardless of the topic.

Additional Practice
L1

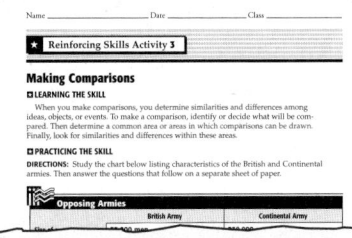

Reinforcing Skills Activity 3

Name _____ Date _____ Class _____

★ Reinforcing Skills Activity 3

Making Comparisons

☐ LEARNING THE SKILL

When you make comparisons, you determine similarities and differences among ideas, objects, or events. To make a comparison, identify or decide what will be compared. Then determine a common area or areas in which comparisons can be drawn. Finally, look for similarities and differences within these areas.

☐ PRACTICING THE SKILL

DIRECTIONS: Study the chart below listing characteristics of the British and Continental armies. Then answer the questions that follow on a separate sheet of paper.

Opposing Armies	British Army	Continental Army

GLENCOE
TECHNOLOGY

 CD-ROM
Glencoe Skillbuilder
Interactive Workbook
CD-ROM, Level 2

This interactive CD-ROM reinforces student mastery of essential social studies skills.

ANSWERS TO PRACTICING THE SKILL

❶ the powers of the federal government in the Articles of Confederation and the Constitution

❷ Answers should match the chart.

❸ The Constitution: organized a court system

❹ The Constitution: In addition to powers both documents provided, the Constitution granted the power to regulate trade.

Applying the Skill
Students' answers will vary. Answers should be presented in a table.

1 FOCUS

Section Overview
This section focuses on the creation of the Constitution.

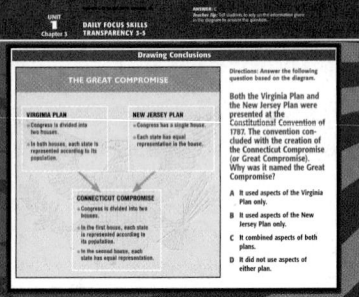
Reading Preview

Answers to Graphic: Federalists–Source of Support: large landowners, merchants, artisans, farmers who exported goods; Goals: create a strong central government that could regulate trade and impose taxes Antifederalists–Source of Support: western farmers; Goals: wanted the state governments to have more power than the national government

Preteaching Vocabulary
Organize students into groups and assign each group one of the Key Terms and Names. Have each group create and present a visual that explains the term or name.

SECTION 5 | A New Constitution

Guide to Reading

Main Idea
In Philadelphia in 1787, members of the Constitutional Convention created a stronger central government.

Key Terms and Names
Virginia Plan, New Jersey Plan, Great Compromise, Three-Fifths Compromise, popular sovereignty, federalism, separation of powers, checks and balances, veto, impeach, amendment

Reading Strategy
Categorizing As you read about the efforts to ratify the Constitution, complete a graphic organizer similar to the one below by listing the supporters and goals of the Federalists and Antifederalists.

	Federalists	Antifederalists
Source of Support		
Goals		

Reading Objectives
• **Outline** the framework for the new federal government.
• **Summarize** the main points in the debate between Federalists and Antifederalists.

Section Theme
Government and Democracy The new Constitution tried to uphold the principle of state authority while providing needed national authority.

Preview of Events

◆April 1787	◆June 1787	◆August 1787	◆October 1787
May 14 Constitutional Convention opens in Philadelphia	**May 29** Virginia Plan introduced	**June 15** New Jersey Plan introduced	**July 2** Franklin's committee begins to seek compromise	**September 17** Final draft of Constitution signed

★ An American Story ★

Washington's chair at the Constitutional Convention

As Benjamin Franklin arrived at the Pennsylvania statehouse on September 17, 1787, he rejoiced with his colleagues about the freshness of the morning air. All summer the 81-year-old Franklin had made the short journey from his home just off Market Street to the statehouse. There, delegates to the Constitutional Convention had exhaustively debated the future of the nation. Today, they would have a chance to sign a draft plan for the nation's new constitution.

When it came Franklin's turn to sign, the elderly leader had to be helped forward in order to write his name on the parchment. Tears streamed down his face as he signed. When the remaining delegates had finished signing, a solemn silence enveloped the hall. Franklin relieved the tension with a few well-chosen words. Pointing to the half-sun painted in gold on the back of George Washington's chair, he observed:

❝I have often . . . looked at that [sun] behind the President [of the Convention] without being able to tell whether it was rising or setting; but now, at length, I have the happiness to know it is a rising, and not a setting, Sun.❞

—quoted in *An Outline of American History*

The Constitutional Convention

For some time, the weakness of the Confederation Congress had worried many Americans. They believed that the United States would not survive without a strong central government. People who wanted to strengthen the central government became known as nationalists.

SECTION RESOURCES

Reproducible Masters
• Reproducible Lesson Plan 3–5
• Daily Lecture and Discussion Notes 3–5
• Guided Reading Activity 3–5
• Section Quiz 3–5
• Reading Essentials and Study Guide 3–5
• Performance Assessment Activities and Rubrics

Transparencies
• Daily Focus Skills Transparency 3–5

Multimedia
🖥 Interactive Tutor Self-Assessment CD-ROM
🖥 ExamView® Pro Testmaker CD-ROM
🖥 Presentation Plus! CD-ROM
🖥 TeacherWorks™ CD-ROM
🎧 Audio Program

One of the most influential nationalists was **James Madison,** a member of the Virginia Assembly. In 1786 Madison convinced Virginia's assembly to call a convention of all the states to discuss trade and taxation problems. Delegates were to meet in Annapolis, Maryland, in September. When the convention began, however, representatives from only five states were present—too few to reach any final decisions. In spite of this, the delegates did discuss the weaknesses of the Articles of Confederation, and many expressed interest in modifying them.

Alexander Hamilton, a delegate from New York, recommended that the Congress itself call for another convention to be held in Philadelphia in May 1787. The Congress hesitated at first, but news of Shays's Rebellion and reports of unrest elsewhere finally convinced it to act. In late February 1787, the Congress invited the states to meet "for the sole purpose of revising the Articles of Confederation."

Every state except Rhode Island sent representatives to what became known as the Constitutional Convention. The delegates faced a daunting task: to balance the rights and aspirations of the states with the need for a stronger national government.

The Founders The 55 men who gathered in May at the Pennsylvania statehouse included some of the most shrewd and distinguished leaders in the United States. The majority were lawyers, and most of the others were planters and merchants. Most had experience in colonial, state, or national government. Seven had served as state governors, 39 had been members of the Confederation Congress, and 8 had signed the Declaration of Independence.

The delegates chose George Washington of Virginia, hero of the American Revolution, as presiding officer. Benjamin Franklin was a delegate from Pennsylvania. Now 81 years old, he tired easily and had other state delegates read his speeches for him. He provided assistance to many of his younger colleagues, and his experience and good humor helped smooth the debates.

Other notable delegates included New York's Alexander Hamilton and Connecticut's **Roger Sherman.** Virginia sent a well-prepared delegation, including the scholarly James Madison, who kept a record of the debates. Madison's notes provide the best account of the convention. The meetings themselves were closed to the public in order to promote honest, open discussion and minimize outside political pressures.

The Virginia and New Jersey Plans The Virginia delegation arrived at the convention with a detailed plan—mostly the work of James Madison—for a new national government. The so-called **Virginia Plan** proposed scrapping the Articles of Confederation entirely and creating a new central government with power divided among legislative, executive, and judicial branches. This government would have the power to raise its own money through taxes and to make laws binding upon the states.

The Virginia Plan also proposed that Congress be divided into two houses. The voters in each state would elect members of the first house, who would then elect members of the second house. In both

Profiles IN HISTORY

James Madison
1751–1836

Although many individuals contributed to the framing of the United States Constitution, the master builder was James Madison. An avid reader, the 36-year-old Virginia planter spent the better part of the year preceding the Philadelphia Convention with his nose in books. Madison read volume after volume on governments throughout history. He scoured the records of ancient Greece and Rome and delved into the administrations of Italian city-states such as Florence and Venice. He even looked at the systems used by federal alliances like Switzerland and the Netherlands. "From a spirit of industry and application," said one colleague, Madison was "the best-informed man on any point in debate."

Bringing together his research and his experience in helping to draft Virginia's constitution, Madison created the Virginia Plan. His proposal strongly influenced the final document. Perhaps Madison's greatest achievement was in defining the true source of political power. He argued that all power, at all levels of government, flowed ultimately from the people.

At the Constitutional Convention, Madison served his nation well. The ordeal, he later said, "almost killed" him. In the years to come, though, the nation would call on him again. In 1801 he became President Thomas Jefferson's secretary of state. In 1808 he was elected the fourth president of the United States.

CHAPTER 3 The American Revolution **109**

2 TEACH

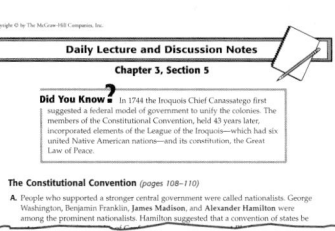

Daily Lecture and Discussion Notes 3–5

Copyright © by The McGraw-Hill Companies, Inc.

Daily Lecture and Discussion Notes
Chapter 3, Section 5

Did You Know? In 1744 the Iroquois Chief Canassatego first suggested a federal model of government to unify the colonies. The members of the Constitutional Convention, held 43 years later, incorporated elements of the League of the Iroquois—which had six united Native American nations—and its constitution, the Great Law of Peace.

I. **The Constitutional Convention** *(pages 108–110)*

A. People who supported a stronger central government were called nationalists. George Washington, Benjamin Franklin, James Madison, and Alexander Hamilton were among the prominent nationalists. Hamilton suggested that a convention of states be

Writing a Newspaper Article
Have students choose a date from the time line on page 108 and write a newspaper article about the event. **L1**

📁 Use the rubric for writing a magazine/newspaper/Web site article or help-wanted ad on pages 75–76 in the *Performance Assessment Activities and Rubrics.*

Profiles IN HISTORY

Have students review the profile of James Madison and write down three questions about Madison's life that cannot be answered by reading the passage. Instruct students to use library and Internet resources to find the answers. Use these questions and answers as a basis for a classroom discussion about James Madison.

Although 55 delegates attended the Constitutional Convention, each state had only one vote.

Reading Strategy READING THE TEXT

Using Graphic Organizers Venn diagrams are ways for students to compare and/or contrast two or more items. Have students draw two overlapping circles on their papers. Label one circle "New Jersey Plan," one circle "Virginia Plan," and the overlapping area "Constitution." Ask students to list the main components of each plan in the appropriate area. Students should list the parts of each plan that were incorporated into the Constitution in the overlapping area. **L1 ELL**

📁 Refer to *Inclusion for the High School Social Studies Classroom Strategies and Activities* in the TCR.

History *Through Art*

Answer: to promote open, honest discussion and minimize outside political pressures

Ask: Why was George Washington chosen to be the presiding officer? *(He was a widely respected war hero.)*

✓ Reading Check

Answer: Smaller states feared larger states would outvote them if representation were based on population.

Making Comparisons Have students create a table to compare and contrast the basis for representation in the Virginia Plan, the New Jersey Plan, and the Connecticut Compromise. **L2**

📁 Use the rubric for creating a map, display, or chart on pages 65–66 in the *Performance Assessment Activities and Rubrics.*

FYI

Thomas Jefferson did not attend the Constitutional Convention. He was representing the United States in France at the time.

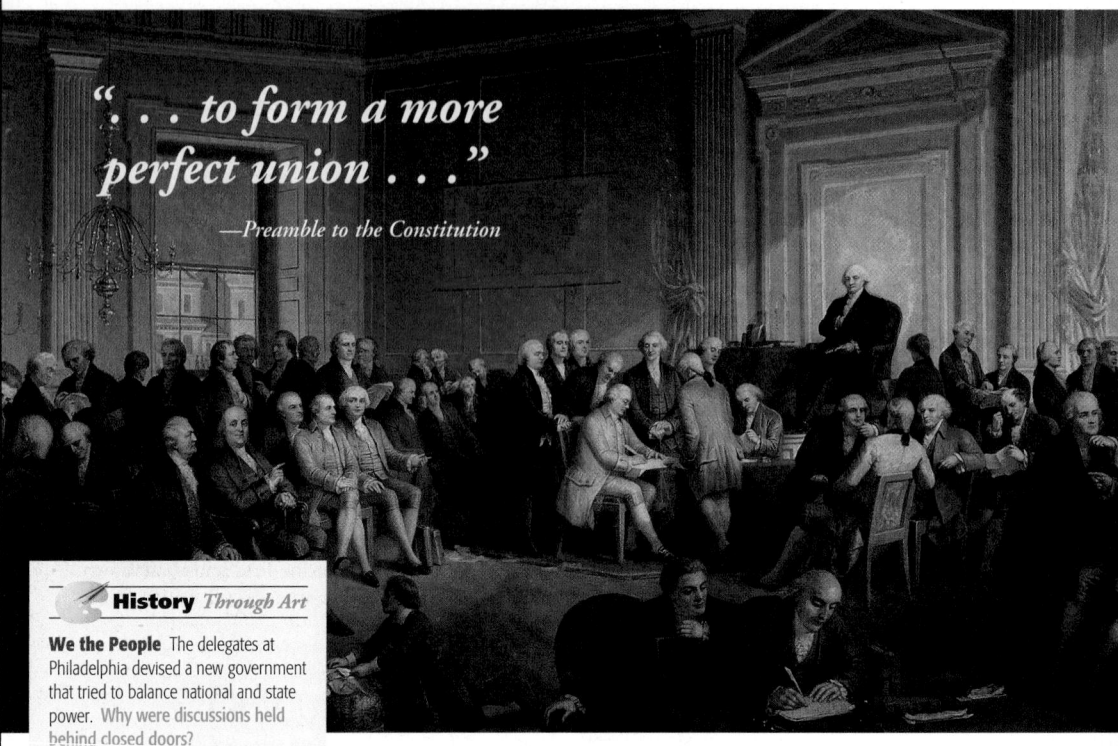

"... to form a more perfect union ..."
—Preamble to the Constitution

History *Through Art*

We the People The delegates at Philadelphia devised a new government that tried to balance national and state power. Why were discussions held behind closed doors?

houses, the number of representatives for each state would reflect that state's population. The Virginia Plan, therefore, would benefit large states like Virginia, New York, and Massachusetts, who would have more votes than the smaller states.

The Virginia Plan drew sharp reactions. The delegates accepted the idea of dividing the government into executive, legislative, and judicial branches, but the smaller states strongly opposed any changes that would decrease their influence by basing representation on population. They feared that the larger states would outvote them.

On June 15, the **New Jersey Plan** was offered as a counterproposal. It did not scrap the Articles of Confederation but proposed modifying them to make the central government stronger. Under the plan, Congress would still have a single house where each state was equally represented, but it would also have the power to raise taxes and regulate trade.

Intense discussion of the two plans followed. After a long debate, on June 19 the convention voted to use the Virginia Plan as the basis of its discussion. With this decision, the convention delegates agreed to go beyond their original purpose of revising the Articles

of Confederation. Instead, the Convention began to work on a new constitution for the United States.

✓ Reading Check
Explaining Why did small states oppose the Virginia Plan?

A Union Built on Compromise

As the delegates began to hammer out the details of the new constitution, they found themselves divided geographically. Those from small states demanded changes that would protect them against the voting power of the big states. At the same time, Northerners and Southerners disagreed on how to address slavery in the new constitution.

TURNING POINT

The Connecticut Compromise Tempers flared as the impasse dragged on in the summer heat. Delegates from the small states insisted that each state had to have an equal vote in Congress. Angry and frustrated delegates from the larger states threatened to walk out.

110 CHAPTER 3 The American Revolution

DIFFERENTIATED INSTRUCTION

Reading Support Have students write and perform a song that will help them remember the details of one of the following: the Virginia and New Jersey Plans, the Connecticut Compromise, the system of checks and balances built into the Constitution, or the process for amending the Constitution. Encourage students to learn more about the topic to help them compose their song. **L2**

📁 Refer to *Inclusion for the High School Social Studies Classroom Strategies and Activities* in the TCR.

In an attempt to find a solution, the convention appointed a special committee to find a compromise. Ben Franklin, one of the committee members, had a calming influence. The delegates took to heart his warning about what would happen if they failed to agree:

❝[You will] become a reproach and by-word down to future ages. And what is worse, mankind may hereafter, from this unfortunate instance, despair of establishing governments by human wisdom, and leave it to chance, war, and conquest.❞

—quoted in *American History*

The committee's solution, variously known as the **Connecticut Compromise** or the **Great Compromise,** was based on a suggestion by Roger Sherman of Connecticut. The committee proposed that in one house of Congress, the House of Representatives, the states would be represented according to the size of their populations, with one House member for every 40,000 people. In the other house, the Senate, each state would have equal representation. The eligible voters in each state would elect members to serve in the House of Representatives, but the state legislatures would choose senators.

Other Compromises The Great Compromise sparked fresh controversy. Southern delegates wanted to count enslaved people when determining how many representatives they could elect to the House. Northern delegates objected, pointing out that enslaved people were considered property, not people. They also suggested that if slaves were going to be counted for purposes of representation in government, they should be counted for purposes of taxation as well. The matter was settled by the **Three-Fifths Compromise.** Every five enslaved people in a state would count as three free persons for determining both representation and taxes.

Southern delegates also feared giving Congress the power to regulate trade. If Congress decided to tax exports of tobacco, rice, and indigo, or to ban the import of enslaved Africans, the Southern economy would be crippled. Northern delegates, on the other hand, knew that Northern merchants and artisans needed a government capable of controlling foreign imports into the United States.

In another compromise, the delegates agreed that the new Congress could not tax exports. They also agreed that it could not ban the slave trade until 1808 or impose high taxes on the import of enslaved persons.

The Great Compromise and the subsequent compromises on slavery and trade matters ended most of the major disputes among the state delegations. The convention then focused on the details of how the new government would operate.

✓ **Reading Check** **Summarizing** What did the Three-Fifths Compromise accomplish?

A Framework for Limited Government

The new Constitution the delegates crafted was based on the principle of popular sovereignty (SAH·vuhrn·tee), or rule by the people. Rather than a direct democracy, it created a representative system of government in which elected officials speak for the people.

To strengthen the central government but still preserve the rights of the states, the Constitution created a system known as federalism. Under federalism, power is divided between the federal, or national, government and the state governments.

The Constitution also provided for a separation of powers among the three branches of the federal government. The two houses of Congress made up the legislative branch of the government. They would make the laws. The executive branch, headed by a president, would implement and enforce the laws passed by Congress. The president would perform other duties as well, such as serving as commander in chief of the armed forces. The judicial branch—a system of federal courts—would interpret federal laws and render judgment in cases involving those laws. To keep the branches separate, no one serving in one branch could serve in either of the other branches at the same time.

Roger Sherman

Checks and Balances In addition to giving each of the three branches of government separate powers, the framers of the Constitution created a system of

CHAPTER 3   The American Revolution   **111**

INTERDISCIPLINARY CONNECTIONS ACTIVITY

Mathematics Write the approximate population of the states in 1790 on the board: Connecticut, 238,000; Delaware, 59,000; Georgia, 83,000; Maryland, 320,000; Massachusetts, 379,000; New Hampshire, 142,000; New Jersey, 184,000; New York, 340,000; North Carolina, 395,000; Pennsylvania, 434,000; Rhode Island, 69,000; South Carolina, 249,000; Virginia, 750,000. Ask students to determine if it was possible for the Constitution to have been ratified by nine states with a combined population of less than half of the people living in the 13 colonies. *(Yes, because the total of the nine smallest colonies is less than half the total population.)*

Creating a Political Cartoon
After students have reviewed the positions of the Federalists and Antifederalists, have them create a political cartoon that expresses the views of one side of the debate. Remind students that effective political cartoons express an opinion in creative, sometimes subtle ways. Label one wall or area in your classroom as Federalists and another as Antifederalists. Have students post their cartoons in the appropriate area. Encourage students to read and react to each other's cartoons. **L2**

 Use the rubric for creating a political cartoon, pamphlet, or handbill on pages 77–78 in the *Performance Assessment Activities and Rubrics.*

✓ Reading Check

Answer: Power is divided between the federal government, also known as the national government, and state governments.

FYI

Until 1998 Andrew Johnson, the seventeenth president of the United States, had the distinction of being the only U.S. president to be impeached. This changed when President Bill Clinton was impeached for perjury and obstruction of justice.

---

checks and balances—a means for each branch to monitor and limit the power of the other two.

For example, the president could check Congress by deciding to veto, or reject, a proposed law. The legislature, however, could override a veto with a two-thirds vote in both houses. The Senate also had the power to approve or reject presidential appointees to the executive branch and treaties the president negotiated. Furthermore, Congress could impeach the president and other high-ranking officials in the executive or judicial branch; that is, Congress could formally accuse such officials of misconduct. If the officials were convicted during trial, they would be removed from office.

Members of the judicial branch of government could hear all cases arising under federal laws and the Constitution. The powers of the judiciary were counterbalanced by the other two branches. The president would nominate judges, including a chief justice of the Supreme Court, but the Senate had to confirm or reject such nominations. Once appointed, however, federal judges, including a chief justice of the Supreme Court, would serve for life, thus ensuring their independence from both the executive and the legislative branches.

Amending the Constitution The delegates in Philadelphia recognized that the Constitution they wrote in the summer of 1787 might need to be revised over time. To ensure this could happen, they created a clear system for making amendments, or changes, to the Constitution. To prevent frivolous changes, however, they made the process difficult.

Amending the Constitution would require two steps: proposal and ratification. An amendment could be proposed by a vote of two-thirds of the members of both houses of Congress. Alternatively, two-thirds of the states could call a constitutional convention to propose new amendments. To become effective, the proposed amendment would then have to be ratified by three-fourths of the state legislatures or by conventions in three-fourths of the states.

✓ Reading Check
Explaining How is power divided under the system of federalism?

Debating the Constitution

By mid-September, the convention had completed its task. On September 17, 39 delegates signed the new Constitution. No one came away entirely satisfied, but most believed it was a vast improvement over the Articles of Confederation. The creation of a flexible framework for government that reflected the states' many different viewpoints was, in Washington's words, "little short of a miracle." The convention, John Adams declared, was "the single greatest effort of national deliberation that the world has ever seen."

On September 20, the delegates sent the Constitution to the Confederation Congress for approval. Eight days later, the Congress voted to submit it to the states. Now the struggle to craft a new government moved into another phase. Each state would hold a convention to vote on the new Constitution. Nine of the thirteen states had to ratify the Constitution before it could take effect.

Federalists and Antifederalists As soon as Americans learned about the new Constitution, they began to argue over whether it should be ratified. The debate took place in state legislatures, mass meetings, newspaper columns, and everyday conversations.

Supporters of the Constitution called themselves **Federalists** to emphasize that the Constitution would create a federal system, with power divided between a central government and the state governments. Federalists hoped the name would remind those Americans who feared a central government that the states would retain considerable power.

Many Federalists were large landowners who wanted the property protection that a strong central government could provide. Supporters also included merchants and artisans in large coastal cities. The inability of the Confederation Congress to regulate foreign trade had hit these citizens hard. They believed that an effective federal government that could impose taxes on foreign goods would help their businesses.

Farmers who lived near the coast or along rivers that led to the coast also tended to support the Constitution, as did farmers who shipped goods across state borders. These farmers depended on trade for their livelihood and had been frustrated by the different tariffs and duties the states imposed. They wanted a federal government that could regulate interstate trade consistently.

Opponents of the Constitution were called **Antifederalists.** This was a somewhat misleading name, as they were not truly against federalism. Antifederalists accepted the need for a national government. The real issue, in their minds, was whether the national government or the state governments would be supreme.

Leading Antifederalists included John Hancock, Patrick Henry, Sam Adams, Richard Henry Lee of

112 CHAPTER 3 The American Revolution

CRITICAL THINKING ACTIVITY

Analyzing Asks students why they think both the Northern states and the Southern states agreed to the Three-Fifths Compromise. *(Answers should reflect the idea that both sides benefited from the compromise. The Northern states benefited because enslaved people would be counted for purposes of taxation, thus generating more revenue for the country. The Southern states benefited because five enslaved people would be counted as three people when collecting population data to be used to calculate representation. This method of calculation would increase the population figures and result in additional representation.)* **L2**

Different Viewpoints

Should the Majority Rule?

James Madison argued persuasively for the Constitution's ratification. In *The Federalist #10*, Madison explained that the Constitution would prevent the effects of *faction*—the self-seeking party spirit of a democracy. In contrast, Thomas Jefferson argued that the will of the majority would thwart the tyranny of oppressive government.

James Madison opposes majority rule:

"When a majority is included in a faction, the form of popular government . . . enables it to sacrifice to its ruling passion or interest both the public good and the rights of other citizens.

. . . [A] pure democracy . . . can admit of no cure for the mischiefs of faction [and has always] been found incompatible with personal security or the rights of property. . . .

A republic, by which I mean a government in which the scheme of representation takes place . . . promises the cure for which we are seeking. . . . The effect of [a republic] is, on the one hand, to refine and enlarge the public views, by passing them through the medium of a chosen body of citizens, whose wisdom may best discern the true interest of their country, and whose patriotism and love of justice will be least likely to sacrifice it to temporary or partial considerations."

Thomas Jefferson defends majority rule:

"I own I am not a friend to a very energetic government. It is always oppressive. The late rebellion in Massachusetts has given more alarm than I think it should have done. Calculate that one rebellion in 13 states in the course of 11 years, is but one for each state in a century & a half. No country should be long without one.

. . . After all, it is my principle that the will of the Majority should always prevail. If they approve the proposed [Constitution] in all its parts, I shall concur in it chearfully, in hopes that they will amend it whenever they shall find it works wrong. . . . Above all things I hope the education of the common people will be attended to; convinced that on their good sense we may rely with the most security for the preservation of a due degree of liberty."

Learning From History

1. What were the "mischiefs" that Madison believed republican government could prevent?
2. Was Jefferson correct in believing the voice of the common people would preserve liberty? Explain.

Virginia, and George Clinton, governor of New York. Two prominent members of the Constitutional Convention, Edmund Randolph and George Mason, were also Antifederalists because they believed the new Constitution needed a bill of rights.

Antifederalists drew support from western farmers living far from the coast. These people considered themselves self-sufficient and distrusted the wealthy and powerful. Many of them were also deeply in debt and suspected that the new Constitution was simply a way for wealthy creditors to get rid of paper money and foreclose on their farms. As one western farmer, Amos Singletary, wrote:

> ❝These lawyers and men of learning, and moneyed men, that talk so finely, and gloss over matters so smoothly, to make us poor, illiterate people swallow down the pill, expect to get into Congress themselves; they expect to be managers of this Constitution, and get all the power and all the money into their own hands, and then they will swallow up all us little folks, like the great Leviathan, Mr. President; yes, just like the whale swallowed up Jonah.❞
>
> —quoted in the *Massachusetts Gazette*

GOVERNMENT

The Federalist Although many influential American leaders opposed the new Constitution, several factors worked against them. First of all, the Antifederalist campaign was a negative one. The Federalists had presented a definite program to meet the difficulties facing the nation. Although the Antifederalists

---

EXTENDING THE CONTENT

Completing the Constitution With the resolution of the major issues, the delegates moved slowly toward completing the Constitution. By the fall of 1787, they had shaped a document that became the foundation for the government of the United States. Despite mixed feelings regarding some aspects of the Constitution, most delegates were hopeful about the future. Benjamin Franklin expressed the feelings of many present when he called for the unanimous endorsement of the document despite his confession "that there are several parts of this constitution which I do not at present approve."

Answer: Delaware

Ask: Which states followed Delaware? *(Pennsylvania, New Jersey, Georgia, Connecticut, Massachusetts, Maryland, South Carolina, New Hampshire)*

✓ **Reading Check**

Answer: large landowners, merchants, artisans, and farmers who exported crops

3 ASSESS

Assign Section 5 Assessment as homework or as an in-class activity.

◉ Have students use the **Interactive Tutor Self-Assessment CD-ROM.**

L1/ELL

Reading Essentials and Study Guide 3–5

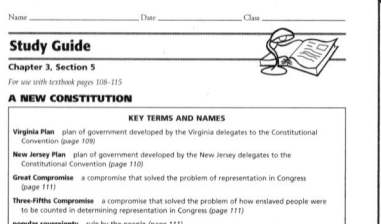

Name _____ Date _____ Class _____

Study Guide

Chapter 3, Section 5

For use with textbook pages 108–115

A NEW CONSTITUTION

KEY TERMS AND NAMES

Virginia Plan plan of government developed by the Virginia delegates to the Constitutional Convention *(page 109)*

New Jersey Plan plan of government developed by the New Jersey delegates to the Constitutional Convention *(page 110)*

Great Compromise a compromise that solved the problem of representation in Congress *(page 111)*

Three-Fifths Compromise a compromise that solved the problem of how enslaved people were to be counted in determining representation in Congress *(page 111)*

popular sovereignty rule by the people *(page 111)*

---

complained that the Constitution failed to protect basic rights such as the freedoms of speech and religion, they had nothing to offer in its place.

The Federalists were also better organized than their opponents. Most of the nation's newspapers supported them. The Federalists were able to present a very convincing case in their speeches, pamphlets, and debates at the state conventions.

The arguments for ratification were summarized in *The Federalist,* a collection of 85 essays written by James Madison, Alexander Hamilton, and John Jay. Under the joint pen name of Publius, the three men had originally published most of the essays in New York newspapers in late 1787 and early 1788. They were hoping to sway the vote in New York, where Antifederalist sentiment was strong.

The essays explained how the new Constitution worked and why it was needed. They were extremely influential. Even today, judges, lawyers, legislators, and historians rely upon *The Federalist* papers to help them interpret the Constitution and understand what the original framers of the document intended. 📖 *(See page 948 for an excerpt from Federalist Paper No. 10.)*

✓ **Reading Check** **Summarizing** Which groups of people tended to support the new Constitution?

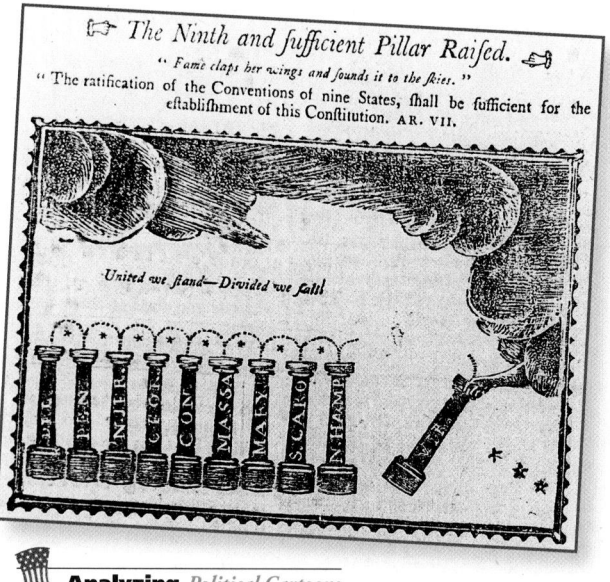

☞ *The Ninth and sufficient Pillar Raised.* ☜

" *Fame claps her wings and sounds it to the skies.* "

" The ratification of the Conventions of nine States, shall be sufficient for the establishment of this Constitution. AR. VII.

United we stand—Divided we fall!

Analyzing *Political Cartoons*

Support for Ratification A pro-Federalist cartoon celebrates New Hampshire becoming the ninth state to ratify the Constitution in 1788. Based on the cartoon's imagery, which state was the first to ratify the Constitution?

114 CHAPTER 3 The American Revolution

The Fight for Ratification

As the ratifying conventions began to gather, the Federalists knew they had clear majorities in some states. In others, however, including the large and important states of Massachusetts, Virginia, and New York, the vote was going to be much closer.

Delaware became the first state to ratify the Constitution, on December 7, 1787. Pennsylvania, New Jersey, Georgia, and Connecticut quickly followed suit. The most important battles, however, still lay ahead.

Ratification in Massachusetts When the Massachusetts convention met in January 1788, opponents of the proposed Constitution held a clear majority. They included the great patriot Samuel Adams, who had signed the Declaration of Independence. Adams strongly believed the Constitution endangered the independence of the states and failed to safeguard Americans' rights.

Federalists moved quickly to address Adams's objections. They promised to attach a bill of rights to the Constitution once it was ratified. They also agreed to support an amendment that would reserve for the states all powers not specifically granted to the federal government. These promises eventually led to the first ten amendments to the Constitution, which came to be known as the Bill of Rights. In combination with the fact that most artisans sided with the Federalists, the promises persuaded Adams to vote for ratification. In the final vote, 187 members of the Massachusetts convention voted in favor of the Constitution while 168 voted against it.

Maryland easily ratified the Constitution in April 1788, followed by South Carolina in May. On June 21, New Hampshire became the ninth state to ratify the Constitution. The Federalists had now reached the minimum number of states required to put the new Constitution into effect. Virginia and New York, however, still had not ratified. Together, Virginia and New York represented almost 30 percent of the nation's population. Without the support of these states, many feared the new government would not succeed.

Virginia and New York At the Virginia convention in June, George Washington and James Madison presented strong arguments for ratification. Patrick Henry, Richard

---

DIFFERENTIATED INSTRUCTION

Reading Support Have students review the arguments of the Federalists and Antifederalists about the Constitution. Then, ask them to write a newspaper editorial that might have been published during that time, either supporting or opposing the Constitution. Students can write their editorials from the viewpoint of one of the colonists, such as a western farmer, a merchant in a coastal city, or a large landowner. **L1**

Henry Lee, and other Antifederalists argued against it. On the day of the final debate, as thunderclaps rang out and lightning forked across the sky, Patrick Henry took aim at the framers of the Constitution. "Who authorized them," he demanded, "to speak the language of We, the People, instead of We, the States?"

Henry was a former governor of Virginia. Before the American Revolution, he had stirred many with his passionate cry, "Give me liberty, or give me death." This time, however, his fiery oratory would not sway enough of his fellow Virginians. Madison's promise to add a bill of rights won the day for the Federalists—but barely. The Virginia convention voted 89 in favor of the Constitution and 79 against.

In New York, two-thirds of the members elected to the state convention, including Governor George Clinton, were Antifederalists. The Federalists, led by Alexander Hamilton and John Jay, managed to delay the final vote until news arrived that New Hampshire and Virginia had both voted to ratify the Constitution and that the new federal government was now in effect. If New York refused to ratify, it would be in a very awkward position. It would have to operate independently of all of the surrounding states that had accepted the Constitution. This argument convinced enough Antifederalists to change sides. The vote was very close, 30 to 27, but the Federalists won.

By July 1788, all the states except Rhode Island and North Carolina had ratified the Constitution. Because ratification by nine states was all that the Constitution required, the new government could be launched without them. The members of the Confederation Congress prepared to proceed without them. In mid-September 1788, they established a timetable for electing the new government. The new Congress would hold its first meeting on March 4, 1789.

The two states that had held out finally ratified the Constitution after the new government was in place. North Carolina waited until a bill of rights had actually been proposed and then voted to ratify the Constitution in November 1789. Rhode Island, still nervous about losing its independence, did not ratify the Constitution until May 1790. Even then, the margin of victory was only two votes—34 to 32.

The United States now had a new government, but no one knew if the Constitution would work any better than the Articles of Confederation. With both anticipation and nervousness, the American people waited to see their new government in action. Many expressed great confidence, however, because George Washington had been chosen as the first president under the new Constitution.

Reading Check **Examining** Why was it important for Virginia and New York to ratify the Constitution, even after the required nine states had done so?

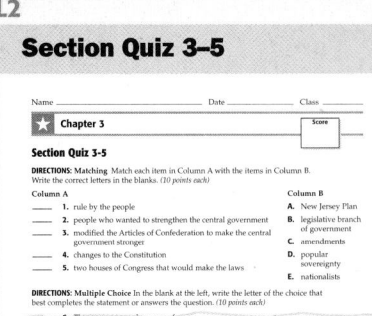

L2

Section Quiz 3–5

Reteach
Have students review the timeline on page 108 and explain the significance of each event.

Enrich
Have students create a diagram that shows the powers granted to each branch of government and how each branch can limit the power of the other two branches.

HISTORY Online **Study Central**™ To review this section, go to tarvol2.glencoe.com and click on **Study Central**™.

SECTION 5 ASSESSMENT

Checking for Understanding
1. **Define:** popular sovereignty, federalism, separation of powers, checks and balances, veto, impeach, amendment.
2. **Identify:** Virginia Plan, New Jersey Plan, Great Compromise, Three-Fifths Compromise.
3. **Summarize** the factors that worked against the Antifederalists.

Reviewing Themes
4. **Government and Democracy** In many ways, the delegates to the Constitutional Convention were not representative of the American public. Should a broader cross section of people have been involved in shaping the new government? Why or why not?

Critical Thinking
5. **Analyzing** Do you think the Founders were right to make the amendment process difficult? Why or why not?
6. **Organizing** Use a graphic organizer similar to the one below to list the compromises the Founders reached at the Constitutional Convention.

Compromises Reached

Analyzing Visuals
7. **Analyzing Paintings** Examine the painting of the Constitutional Convention on page 110. How does the tone of the painting compare with the text's description of differences and difficulties at the convention? What purpose do you think the artist had that might account for any difference?

Writing About History
8. **Descriptive Writing** Take on the role of an observer at the Constitutional Convention. Write a journal entry describing what you witnessed. Be sure to record the arguments you heard from each side of the issues discussed, and relate your own opinion on the issues.

CHAPTER 3 The American Revolution **115**

HISTORY Online

Study Central™ provides summaries, interactive games, and online graphic organizers to help students review section content.

4 CLOSE
Ask students to explain the heading on page 110, "A Union Built on Compromise," with specific examples of compromises made during the Constitutional Convention.

SECTION 5 ASSESSMENT ANSWERS

1. Terms are in blue.
2. Virginia Plan *(p. 109),* New Jersey Plan *(p. 110),* Great Compromise *(p. 111),* Three-Fifths Compromise *(p. 111)*
3. The campaign was negative, had no better plan to introduce, and lacked organization and financing.
4. Answers should be supported by a logical explanation.
5. Answers should be supported by a logical explanation.
6. Great Compromise, Three-Fifths Compromise, compromise on trade issues, compromise on the slave trade
7. The painting does not really show

division, tension, and the difficult working conditions. The artist may have wanted us to picture these important men at their best.
8. Entries should focus on the feelings related to actual events.

115

TIME NOTEBOOK

TEACH

Verbatim

Have students review the quotes in the Verbatim section and discuss each item as it relates to the people and themes found in their textbooks. Have students research a current political, economic, or social issue. Have them create a list of quotations about the issue along with a brief statement explaining the quote, identifying the person quoted, and describing how the quote relates to the issue. Ask students to share their lists in a class discussion.

Profile

Have students read the list of rules of civil behavior. Have students state these rules in modern language. Ask volunteers to share their versions. **Ask: Which of these rules may still be widely observed today?** *(Possible answers: to not put your hands on any part of the body that is usually covered; to stay awake while people are speaking; to not show yourself glad at another's misfortune; think before you speak; and so on)* **Why do you think some rules of civil behavior change little over time, while others change significantly?** *(Customs and manners tend to follow trends. Today's more casual society lives by different rules, but some behaviors, such as thinking before you speak, will always apply.)*

Visit the **TIME** Web site at www.time.com for up-to-date news, weekly magazine articles, editorials, online polls, and an archive of past magazine and Web articles.

Profile

HULTON GETTY

GEORGE WASHINGTON *At the age of 16, George Washington carefully transcribed in his own hand the* Rules of Civility and Decent Behaviour in Company and Conversation. *Among the rules our first president lived by:*

- Every action done in company ought to be with some sign of respect to those that are present.

- When in company, put not your hands to any part of the body, not usually [un]covered.

- Put not off your clothes in the presence of others, nor go out your chamber half dressed.

- Sleep not when others speak.

- Spit not in the fire, nor stoop low before it. Neither put your hands into the flames to warm them, nor set your feet upon the fire, especially if there is meat before it.

- Shake not the head, feet or legs. Roll not the eyes. Lift not one eyebrow higher than the other. Wry not the mouth, and bedew no man's face with your spittle, by approaching too near him when you speak.

- Show not yourself glad at the misfortune of another though he were your enemy.

- Be not hasty to believe flying reports to the disparagement of any.

- Think before you speak.

- Cleanse not your teeth with the Table Cloth.

VERBATIM
WAR'S END

"I hope you will not consider yourself as commander-in-chief of your own house, but be convinced, that there is such a thing as equal command."

> **LUCY FLUCKER KNOX,**
> *to her husband Henry Knox, upon his return as a hero from the Revolutionary War*

"The American war is over, but this is far from being the case with the American Revolution. Nothing but the first act of the drama is closed."

> **BENJAMIN RUSH,**
> *signer of the Declaration of Independence and member of the Constitutional Convention*

"You could not have found a person to whom your schemes were more disagreeable."

> **GEORGE WASHINGTON,**
> *to Colonel Lewis Nicola, in response to his letter urging Washington to seize power and proclaim himself king*

"It appears to me, then, little short of a miracle that the delegates from so many states . . . should unite in forming a system of national government."

> **GEORGE WASHINGTON,**
> *in a letter to the Marquis de Lafayette at the close of the Constitutional Convention*

"It astonishes me to find this system approaching to near perfection as it does; and I think it will astonish our enemies."

LEONARD de SELVA/CORBIS

> **BENJAMIN FRANKLIN,**
> *remarking on the structure of the new United States government*

COOPERATIVE LEARNING ACTIVITY

Creating a Magazine Spread Organize the class into small groups. Assign each group one of the decades in the 1700s and ask them to create their own two-page magazine spread for the decade. Encourage students to use elements similar to those that appear in the Time Notebook but to be creative as they select information that is of particular interest. Students should look at current magazines and books for ideas about page design. This activity can be completed using desktop publishing software or the more traditional cut-and-paste method.

Use the rubric for a cooperative group management plan on pages 71–72 in the ***Performance Assessment Activities and Rubrics.***

Annual Salaries

Annual federal employee salaries, 1789

President (he refused it)	$25,000
Vice President	$5,000
Secretary of State	$3,500
Chief Justice	$4,000
Senator	$6 per day
Representative	$6 per day
Army Captain	$420
Army Private	$48

CORBIS

Milestones

SETTLED, 1781. LOS ANGELES, by a group of 46 men and women, most of whom are of Native American and African descent.

CALLED, 1785. LEMUEL HAYNES, as minister to a church in Torrington, Connecticut. Haynes, a veteran of the Revolutionary War who fought in Lexington, is the first African American to minister to a white congregation. A parishioner insulted Haynes by refusing to remove his hat in church, but minutes into the sermon, the parishioner was so moved that the hat came off. He is now a prayerful and loyal member of the congregation.

BETTMANN/CORBIS

PUBLISHED, 1788. THE *ELEMENTARY SPELLING BOOK*, by Noah Webster, a 25-year-old teacher from Goshen, N.Y. The book standardizes American spelling and usage that differs from the British.

NUMBERS

5 Number of years younger in age of average American brides compared to their European counterparts

6 Average number of children per family to survive to adulthood

7 Average number of children born per family

8 Number of Daniel Boone's surviving children

68 Number of Daniel Boone's grandchildren

$5 Average monthly wage for male agricultural laborer, 1784

$3 Average monthly wage for female agricultural laborer, 1784

PIX/FPG

Portfolio Writing Project

Have students research one of the following people: George Washington, Benjamin Rush, Benjamin Franklin, Lemuel Haynes, Noah Webster, or Lucy and Henry Knox. Ask students to write a one-page essay about the person's contribution to history.

Comparing and Contrasting

Have students research to find how the salary of the president and vice president have changed over time. Based on the information, have students create a line chart that shows the growth in salary. Ask students if they think today's salaries for these offices reflect the importance of the job. Encourage students to explain their reasoning.

CLOSE

Have students create a matching game for popular items of clothing. If possible, have older adults see if they can make the correct matches.

1780s WORD PLAY
Dressing the "Little Pudding Heads"

Can you match these common items of Early American clothing with their descriptions?

1. clout

2. stays

3. surcingle

4. pilch

5. pudding cap

a. a band of strong fabric wrapped around a baby to suppress the navel

b. a diaper

c. the wool cover worn over a diaper

d. a head covering for a child learning to walk to protect its brain from falls

e. a garment worn by children to foster good posture, made from linen and wood or baleen splints

answers: 1. b; 2. e; 3. a; 4. c; 5. d

EXTENDING THE CONTENT

American Spelling Book Noah Webster's *Elementary Spelling Book* was used by schoolchildren for nearly a century. It had a blue-green cover and was nicknamed "the blue-backed speller." The book contains a large collection of maxims, proverbs, fables, and some very stern views of how children should behave, including the following quote: "As for those boys and girls that mind not their books, and love not the church and school, but play with such as tell tales, tell lies, curse, swear, and steal, they will come to some bad end, and must be whipt till they mend their ways."

CHAPTER

3 ASSESSMENT and ACTIVITIES

Reviewing Key Terms

Students' answers will vary. The pages where the words appear in the text appear below.

1. customs duty *(p. 77)*;
2. nonimportation agreement *(p. 78)*;
3. writ of assistance *(p. 78)*;
4. committee of correspondence *(p. 83)*; **5. minutemen** *(p. 85)*;
6. Loyalist *(p. 85)*; **7. Patriot** *(p. 85)*;
8. guerrilla warfare *(p. 95)*; **9. letter of marque** *(p. 97)*; **10. republic** *(p. 100)*;
11. ratification *(p. 103)*; **12. recession** *(p. 106)*; **13. inflation** *(p. 106)*;
14. popular sovereignty *(p. 111)*;
15. federalism *(p. 111)*; **16. separation of powers** *(p. 111)*; **17. checks and balances** *(p. 112)*; **18. veto** *(p. 112)*;
19. impeach *(p. 112)*; **20. amendment** *(p. 112)*

Reviewing Key Facts

21. Albany Plan of Union (p. 75), Sons of Liberty (p. 77), Stamp Act Congress (p. 77), Boston Tea Party (p. 83), Intolerable Acts (p. 84), Suffolk Resolves (p. 85), Olive Branch Petition (p. 87), John Burgoyne (p. 97), Charles Cornwallis (p. 98), Francis Marion (p. 98), Northwest Ordinance (p. 104), Great Compromise (p. 111), Three-Fifths Compromise (p. 111)

22. access to land and control of waterways west of the Appalachian Mountains

23. to prevent war with Native Americans over the settlement of the land west of the Appalachian Mountains

24. King George III issued the Coercive Acts; the colonists gained confidence.

Reviewing Key Terms

On a sheet of paper, use each of these terms in a sentence.

1. customs duty
2. nonimportation agreement
3. writs of assistance
4. committee of correspondence
5. minuteman
6. Loyalist
7. Patriot
8. guerrilla warfare
9. letter of marque
10. republic
11. manumission
12. ratification
13. recession
14. inflation
15. popular sovereignty
16. federalism
17. separation of powers
18. checks and balances
19. veto
20. impeach
21. amendment

Chapter Summary

- **1760**
- **1763** French and Indian War ends, leaving Britain in debt
- **1765** Stamp Act passed
- **1765**
- **1767** Townshend Acts passed
- **1768–1769** Colonists boycott British imports to protest Townshend Acts
- **1770** Boston Massacre
- **1770**
- **1773** Tea Act passed; Boston Tea Party held in protest
- **1775** Battles of Lexington and Concord
- **1775**
- **1776** Declaration of Independence signed
- **1781** General Cornwallis surrenders at Yorktown
- **1780**
- **1783** Treaty of Paris officially ends Revolutionary War
- **1787** Constitutional Convention drafts a new plan of government
- **1785**
- **1788** New Hampshire becomes ninth state to ratify the Constitution, putting it into effect

Reviewing Key Facts

22. **Identify:** Albany Plan of Union, Sons of Liberty, Stamp Act Congress, Boston Tea Party, Intolerable Acts, Suffolk Resolves, Olive Branch Petition, John Burgoyne, Charles Cornwallis, Francis Marion, Northwest Ordinance, Great Compromise, Three-Fifths Compromise.

23. What caused the French and Indian War?

24. Why did King George III issue the Proclamation of 1763?

25. What were the effects of the Boston Tea Party?

26. Why was the Battle of Saratoga a turning point in the Revolutionary War?

27. How did Shays's Rebellion indicate the need for a stronger national government?

28. In what city did delegates gather to consider revising the Articles of Confederation?

29. What were the two competing plans for a basic framework for a new constitution?

30. How did the Founders provide for a separation of powers in the federal government?

Critical Thinking

31. **Analyzing Themes: Civic Rights and Responsibilities** What rights did the colonists want from Britain?

32. **Evaluating** In the colonies, Thomas Paine's *Common Sense* influenced public opinion on the issue of declaring independence. Why do you think this happened?

33. **Analyzing Themes: Government and Democracy** What do you think was the most serious flaw of the Articles of Confederation? Why do you think so?

34. **Evaluating** What do you think would have happened if New York and Virginia had not ratified the Constitution?

35. **Categorizing** Use a graphic organizer similar to the one below to list events that led to the War for Independence.

Events Leading to the War for Independence

25. It improved American morale and convinced the French to join the Americans against the British.

26. It indicated a need for a unified government to control trade and stabilize the economy.

27. Philadelphia

28. the Virginia Plan and the New Jersey Plan

29. They specified three branches—executive, legislative, and judicial—each with specific powers. The legislative branch would make laws; the executive branch would implement and enforce laws; and the judicial branch

would interpret laws. No one is allowed to serve in more than one branch at the same time.

Critical Thinking

30. right to tax themselves, trial by jury, protection against home searches without a warrant, and government seizing property without court proceedings

31. because it spoke against the monarchy in principle, roused feeling

HISTORY
Online

Self-Check Quiz
Visit the *American Republic Since 1877* Web site at tarvol2.glencoe.com and click on *Self-Check Quizzes—Chapter 3* to assess your knowledge of chapter content.

Geography and History

36. The map at right shows the land claims in North America as a result of the 1783 Treaty of Paris. Study the map and answer the questions below.

   a. **Interpreting Maps** What were the borders for the United States after the war for independence?

   b. **Applying Geography Skills** Which countries shared a border with the United States?

Practicing Skills

37. **Making Comparisons** Reread the passage about the Virginia and New Jersey Plans from Chapter 3, Section 5, on pages 109–110. Then answer the following questions.

   a. Which plan gave more power to the states?

   b. What new power did the New Jersey plan grant to Congress?

Chapter Activities

38. **Research Project** Research some popular American painters of the post-Revolutionary War period, such as John Trumbull and Charles Willson Peale. Find and study examples of their paintings. Then write a report explaining how the themes in their paintings helped build an American identity. Share the paintings and your report with your class.

39. **American History Primary Source Document Library CD-ROM** Read "On Liberty" by John Adams, under *Nation Building.* Assuming the role of a Patriot or a Loyalist, write a letter to the editor of the *Boston Gazette* in reaction to the article by Adams.

40. **Internet Research** Use the Internet to research the lives of one Federalist and one Antifederalist discussed on pages 112 and 113. Write a short report comparing the two men and their positions on the proposed Constitution. Use standard grammar, spelling, sentence structure, and punctuation.

Writing Activity

41. **Descriptive Writing** Take on the role of an American at the time the Constitution was ratified. Write a letter to a friend in Britain describing to him or her the kind of government provided for by the Constitution. Explain why you support or oppose ratification and what you think life will be like under the new government.

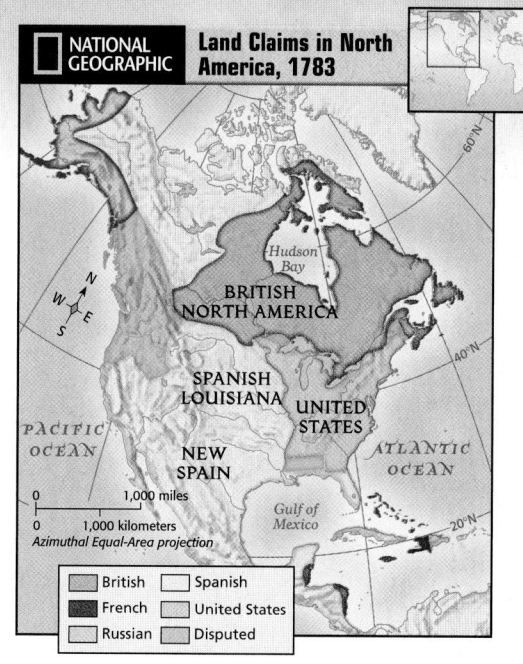

NATIONAL GEOGRAPHIC
Land Claims in North America, 1783

Hudson Bay

BRITISH NORTH AMERICA

SPANISH LOUISIANA

UNITED STATES

PACIFIC OCEAN

NEW SPAIN

ATLANTIC OCEAN

Gulf of Mexico

0   1,000 miles
0   1,000 kilometers
Azimuthal Equal-Area projection

- British
- French
- Russian
- Spanish
- United States
- Disputed

Standardized Test Practice

Directions: Choose the best answer to the following question.

Although the Coercive Acts were meant to punish Massachusetts for the Boston Tea Party, what impact did they have on the rest of the colonies?

A The acts caused trade in other harbors to suffer as well.

B The acts caused the other colonies to fear standing up to the king.

C The acts were so harsh that other colonies wanted to fight back against the king.

D The acts caused the colonies to respond with their own laws, called the Intolerable Acts.

Test-Taking Tip: Eliminate answers that don't make sense. For example, the colonies were subject to the laws of the British government, not the other way around, so choice D is unlikely. (You may also remember that "Intolerable Acts" was the nickname the colonists gave to the Coercive Acts.)

CHAPTER 3   The American Revolution   **119**

HISTORY
Online

Have students visit the Web site at tarvol2.glencoe.com to review Chapter 3 and take the Self-Check Quiz.

Chapter Activities

37. Encourage students to consider how these paintings affect patriotism.

38. Letters should reflect a strongly held opinion that is concisely stated and adequately defended.

39. Reports should consider the viewpoints of the people chosen. Check for proper grammatical usage.

Writing Activity

40. Remind students that the person receiving the letter will not be familiar with the American form of government.

Standardized Test Practice

Answer: C
Test-Taking Tip: B and C express opposite ideas. Remind students that if they can rule out other answers, they can narrow their focus to the opposites and decide between them.

Bonus Question ?

Ask: What is the system by which the Constitution can be revised? *(The delegates provided for changes to the Constitution through the amendment process.)*

---

32. Answers should focus on actual flaws, such as no power to impose taxes, regulate trade, or to force states to abide by the peace treaty.

33. They would have joined later, formed a separate union, or union would have crumbled.

34. Proclamation Act of 1763, Sugar Act, Currency Act of 1764, Stamp Act, Quartering Act, Declaratory Act, Townshend Acts, Tea Act of 1773, Intolerable Acts (Coercive Acts and Quebec Act)

Geography and History

35. **a.** Mississippi River to the west, Canada to the north, and original colonies in the East; **b.** British-owned Canada, Spanish-owned Spanish Louisiana and New Spain

Practicing Skills

36. **a.** the New Jersey Plan; **b.** power to raise taxes and regulate trade

The Constitution Handbook

Beginning the Handbook

Inform students that when members of the first Congress gathered in New York in 1789, a bill of rights had not been added to the Constitution. These amendments were important because a number of states made their ratification conditional on such an addition. Other states had threatened to revoke their ratification if the bill of rights proved too radical. Have students speculate why Congress moved so quickly to inaugurate the new government. *(The country was eager for a new government. Congress perhaps felt that if the process of government had begun, it would be harder for wavering states to leave the Union.)*

FYI

Constitutions vary from country to country. For example, Article XXIII of Japan's constitution guarantees academic freedom. During the era of communism, the constitutions of Communist countries emphasized economic and social rights such as the right to work, the right to choose an occupation, and the right to leisure.

EXTENDING THE CONTENT

Constitutions The United States has the oldest written national constitution still in effect. Compared to other written constitutions, it might be characterized as succinct. The average federal constitution contains about 26,500 words, whereas the United States Constitution with its 27 amendments has fewer than 7,500 words.

Guide to Reading

Main Idea
The Constitution was designed to provide the United States with a stronger national government while remaining flexible enough to meet the changing circumstances of the growing nation.

Key Terms and Names
popular sovereignty, federalism, enumerated powers, reserved powers, concurrent powers, override, appropriate, impeach, constituent, bill, standing committee, select committee, joint committee, conference committee, cabinet, judicial review, due process

Reading Strategy
Taking Notes As you read about the Constitution, use the major headings of the handbook to fill in an outline similar to the one below.

I. Major Principles
  A.
  B.
  C.
  D.
  E.
  F.
  G.
II.

Reading Objectives:
• **Identify** the branches of the federal government and their separate areas of power.
• **Understand** and describe the responsibilities that American citizens share.

Section Theme
Civic Rights and Responsibilities The success of the American system of government depends on citizens being informed. An understanding of the Constitution is key to understanding how the American government operates.

Preview of Events

♦1786	♦1787	♦1788	♦1789	♦1790	♦1791	♦1792

September 1786
Annapolis Convention begins

May 1787
Constitutional Convention begins

September 1787
Constitution signed and Convention adjourns

June 1788
New Hampshire ratifies Constitution, making it the new form of government

December 1791
The Bill of Rights becomes part of the Constitution

Daniel Webster and George Bush

★ An American Story ★

In 1987 the United States began a four-year celebration commemorating the Constitution's bicentennial. In a series of ceremonies that lasted to 1991, the nation reflected on the writing and ratifying of the document providing the country's foundation of government. Proclaiming the creation of Citizenship Day and Constitution Week in August 1990, President George Bush quoted the words of Daniel Webster:

66 'We may be tossed upon an ocean where we can see no land—nor, perhaps, the sun or stars. But there is a chart and a compass for us to study, to consult, and to obey. That chart is the Constitution.' 99

Serving as the framework of national government and the source of American citizens' basic rights, the Constitution is the United States's most important document. As President Bush reminded the nation in his proclamation: "[I]f we are to continue to enjoy the blessings of freedom and self-government, each of us must understand our rights and responsibilities as citizens."

—adapted from the Citizenship Day and Constitution Week Proclamation

The Constitution Handbook **121**

EXTENDING THE CONTENT

Historic Building The red brick building in which the Framers met to draw up the Constitution is now known as Independence Hall. Several important events took place there, including the meetings of the First and Second Continental Congresses and Jefferson's reading of the Declaration of Independence.

2 TEACH

Discussing Precedents Have groups of students recall aspects of self-government with which American colonists had experimented. *(Answers include the Mayflower Compact, the Articles of Confederation, and organizations such as the Virginia House of Burgesses and the Continental Congress.)* Explain that this handbook will help them see how those experiments helped shape the American system of government **L1** ELL

Picturing History

Answer: the authority of the people
Ask: How is the concept of limited government a reflection of popular sovereignty? *(The central government is not all powerful, it is limited. The people give consent to be governed.)*

FYI

The power to award titles of nobility is denied to Congress. This clause was written into the Constitution to prevent the development of a noble class in the United States.

Major Principles

The principles outlined in the Constitution were the Framers' solution to the complex problems of a representative government. The Constitution rests on seven major principles of government: (1) popular sovereignty, (2) republicanism, (3) limited government, (4) federalism, (5) separation of powers, (6) checks and balances, and (7) individual rights.

Popular Sovereignty The opening words of the Constitution, "We the people," reinforce the idea of popular sovereignty, or "authority of the people." In the Constitution, the people consent to be governed and specify the powers and rules by which they shall be governed.

The Articles of Confederation form of government had few powers, and it was unable to cope with the many challenges facing the nation. The new constitutional government had greater powers and influence, but it also had specific limitations. A system of interlocking responsibilities kept any one branch of government from becoming too powerful.

Republicanism Voters hold sovereign power in a republican system. The people elect representatives and give them the responsibility to make laws and conduct government. For most Americans today, the terms *republic* and *representative democracy* mean the same thing: a system of limited government where the people are the final source of authority.

Limited Government Although the Framers agreed that the nation needed a stronger central authority, they feared misuse of power. They wanted to prevent the government from using its power to give one group special advantages or to deprive another group of its rights. By creating a limited government, they restricted the government's authority to specific powers granted by the people.

The Federal System

Enumerated Powers	Concurrent Powers	Reserved Powers
Powers *enumerated* to national government; for example, declaring war	Powers *concurrent* to national and state governments; for example, the power to tax	Powers *reserved* for state governments; for example, setting up educational system

122   The Constitution Handbook

The Right to Vote The voting booth is a symbol of one of the Constitution's major principles—popular sovereignty. What does popular sovereignty mean?

The members of the Constitutional Convention wished to list the range of powers granted to the new government as specifically as possible. Their decision to write down the governmental outline also served as a clear record of what they intended. Article I of the Constitution states the powers that the government has and does not have. Other limits on government appear in the Bill of Rights, which guarantees certain rights and liberties to the people.

Federalism In establishing a strong central government, the Framers did not deprive states of all authority. The states would give up some powers to the national government while retaining others. States could no longer print their own money or tax items imported from other states, but mostly, each state continued to govern itself much as it had in the past.

This principle of shared power is federalism. Our federal government allows the people of each state to deal with their needs in their own way. At the same time, it lets the states act together to deal with matters that affect all Americans.

The Constitution defines three types of government powers. Certain powers belong only to the

Reading Strategy   READING THE TEXT

Exploring Key Concepts Have students read through and define in their own words each of the Constitution's underlying principles described in these pages: popular sovereignty, limited government, federalism, and separation of powers. Students should then locate at least one part of the constitution that addresses that principle. Ask students which principle they think affects their lives the most today. **L1**

Refer to ***Inclusion for the High School Social Studies Classroom Strategies and Activities*** in the TCR.

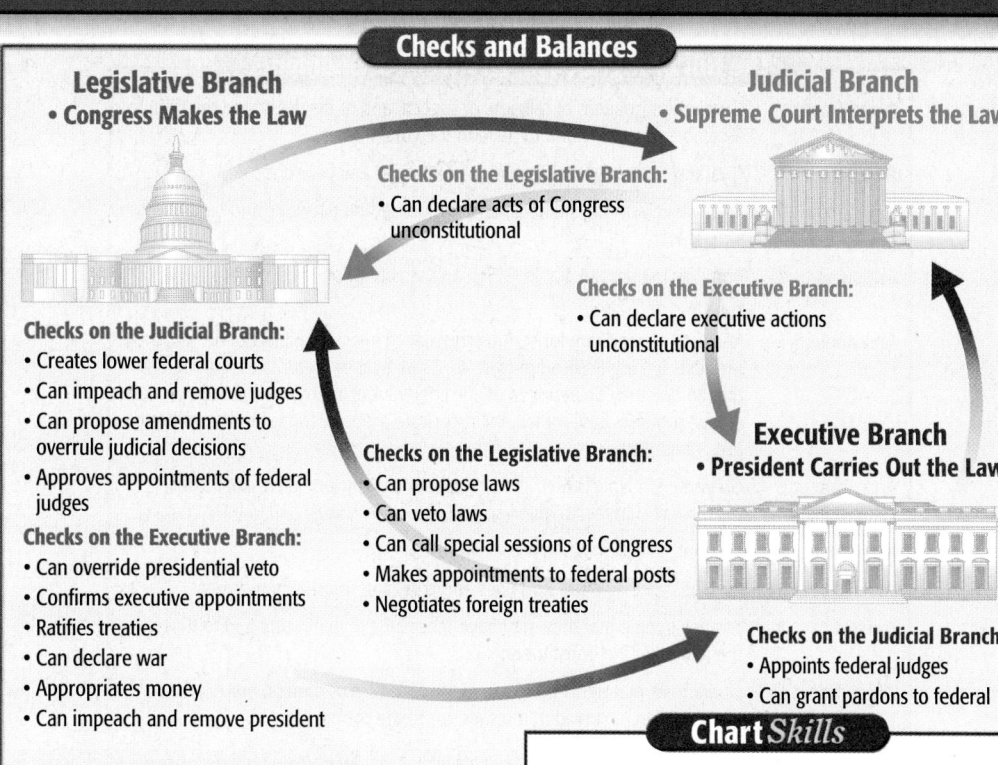

Checks and Balances

Legislative Branch
• Congress Makes the Law

Judicial Branch
• Supreme Court Interprets the Law

Checks on the Legislative Branch:
• Can declare acts of Congress unconstitutional

Checks on the Executive Branch:
• Can declare executive actions unconstitutional

Checks on the Judicial Branch:
• Creates lower federal courts
• Can impeach and remove judges
• Can propose amendments to overrule judicial decisions
• Approves appointments of federal judges

Checks on the Executive Branch:
• Can override presidential veto
• Confirms executive appointments
• Ratifies treaties
• Can declare war
• Appropriates money
• Can impeach and remove president

Checks on the Legislative Branch:
• Can propose laws
• Can veto laws
• Can call special sessions of Congress
• Makes appointments to federal posts
• Negotiates foreign treaties

Executive Branch
• President Carries Out the Law

Checks on the Judicial Branch:
• Appoints federal judges
• Can grant pardons to federal

Chart *Skills*

Each branch can limit the others' power.

Analyzing Information How can the president help control the judiciary?

you don't say...

Check The term *check* comes from Persian and is related to the royal title *shah.* It is also a sports term, relating to a blocking action in hockey.

FYI

Students may hear so much grumbling about governmental issues today that they may wonder why we say that the government is empowered by popular sovereignty. Point out that *popular* comes from the Latin word *populus,* meaning "the people." The same Latin word also gives us *population* and *populate.*

federal government. These enumerated powers include the power to coin money, regulate interstate and foreign trade, maintain the armed forces, and create federal courts (Article I, Section 8).

The second kind of powers are those retained by the states, known as reserved powers, including the power to establish schools, pass marriage and divorce laws, and regulate trade within a state. Although specific reserved powers are not listed in the Constitution, the Tenth Amendment says that all powers not specifically granted to the federal government "are reserved to the States."

The third set of powers defined by the Constitution are concurrent powers—powers the state and federal governments share. They include the right to raise taxes, borrow money, provide for public welfare, and administer criminal justice.

Conflicts between state law and federal law must be settled in a federal court. The Constitution declares that it is "the supreme Law of the Land."

Separation of Powers To prevent any single group or institution in government from gaining too much authority, the Framers divided the federal government into three branches: legislative, executive, and judicial. Each branch has its own functions

and powers. The legislative branch, Congress, makes the laws. The executive branch, headed by the president, carries out the laws. The judicial branch, consisting of the Supreme Court and other federal courts, interprets and applies the laws.

In addition to giving separate responsibility to separate branches, the membership of each branch is chosen in different ways. The president nominates federal judges and the Senate confirms the appointments. People vote for members of Congress. Voters cast ballots for president, but the method of election is indirect. On Election Day the votes in each state are counted. Whatever candidate receives a majority receives that state's electoral votes, which total the number of senators and representatives the state has in Congress. Electors from all states meet in December after the November election to formally elect a president. A candidate must receive at least 270 of 538 electoral votes to win.

Checks and Balances The Framers also established a system of checks and balances in which each branch of government can check, or limit, the

The Constitution Handbook **123**

DIFFERENTIATED INSTRUCTION

Gifted and Talented Committing the Preamble of the Constitution to memory provides a useful language model for students' spoken language development. To aid in this memory task, structure the activity by asking students to write the words *who, why,* and *what* in their notebooks. Have students write the various phrases of the Preamble under the words to which they are most closely related. **L3**

☞ Refer to *Inclusion for the High School Social Studies Classroom Strategies and Activities* in the TCR.

Constitution Handbook

The Bill of Rights: The First Ten Amendments

Amendment 1	Guarantees freedom of religion, of speech, and of the press, and the right to assemble peaceably and to petition the government
Amendment 2	Guarantees the right to organize state militias and bear arms
Amendment 3	Prohibits quartering soldiers in private homes in peacetime and limits it in time of war
Amendment 4	Prohibits the unreasonable search and seizure of persons and property without a valid warrant
Amendment 5	Requires a grand jury for serious criminal charges; prohibits double jeopardy; prohibits forcing accused persons to testify against themselves; guarantees that no one may be deprived of life, liberty, or property, without due process of law; prohibits government taking private property for public use without just compensation
Amendment 6	Guarantees suspects the right to a speedy trial by jury in criminal cases; to know all charges; to question and obtain witnesses; and to have counsel
Amendment 7	Guarantees a jury trial in most civil cases
Amendment 8	Prohibits excessive bail and fines and cruel and unusual punishment
Amendment 9	Assures people that they may have other basic rights in addition to those mentioned in the Constitution
Amendment 10	Guarantees that rights not given to the federal government, nor denied to the states, are reserved to the states or to the people

Chart Skills

Answer: to protect individual rights by limiting the powers of the police

Chart Skills Practice
Ask: Why do you think a higher degree of approval is needed to ratify an amendment than to propose one? (Students may suggest that this is one way in which the Framers sought to discourage minor or frequent changes to the Constitution.)

Constitution A *filibuster* is an attempt to delay for as long as possible or stop altogether the passage of a bill through the Senate. A filibuster exploits the long-held tradition in the Senate of not limiting debate. A senator can hold the floor as long as he or she wants to, as long as he or she remains talking. The Senate can halt a filibuster by passing a vote of cloture to force a vote.

Chart Skills

Antifederalists demanded a specific list of individual rights and freedoms.

Analyzing Information Why did the Framers include Amendment 4, prohibiting unreasonable searches?

power of the other branches. This system helps balance the power of the three branches. For example, imagine that Congress passes a law. Then the president can reject the law by vetoing it. However, Congress can override, or reverse, the president's veto if two-thirds of the members of both the Senate and the House of Representatives vote again to approve the law.

Individual Rights The Bill of Rights became part of the Constitution in 1791. These first 10 amendments protect basic liberties and rights that some Americans may take for granted—including freedom of speech, freedom of the press, freedom of assembly, freedom of religion, and the right to a trial by jury.

The 17 amendments that follow the Bill of Rights expand the rights of Americans and adjust certain provisions of the Constitution. Included among them are amendments that abolish slavery, define citizenship, guarantee voting rights, authorize an income tax, and set a two-term limit on the presidency.

The Legislative Branch

The legislative branch includes the two houses of Congress: the House of Representatives and the Senate. Congress's two primary roles are to make the nation's laws and to control federal spending.

The Role of Congress The government cannot spend any money unless Congress appropriates, or sets aside, funds. All tax and spending bills must originate in the House of Representatives and gain approval in both the House and the Senate before moving on to the president for signature.

Congress also monitors the executive branch and investigates possible abuses of power. The House of Representatives can impeach, or bring formal charges against, any federal official it suspects of wrongdoing or misconduct. If an official is impeached, the Senate acts as a court and tries the accused official. Officials who are found guilty may be removed from office.

INTERDISCIPLINARY CONNECTIONS ACTIVITY

Civics Federalism can be graphically illustrated in many ways. After reading the section on federalism, ask students to graphically represent federalism. Encourage them to reflect shared powers as well as independent powers in their graphics. **L1**

The Senate also holds certain special powers. Only the Senate can ratify treaties made by the president and confirm presidential appointments of federal officials such as department heads, ambassadors, and federal judges.

All members of Congress have the responsibility of representing their constituents, the people of their home states and districts. As a constituent, you can expect your senators and representative to promote national and state interests.

Congress at Work Thousands of bills—proposed laws—are introduced in Congress every year. Because individual members of Congress cannot possibly study all these bills carefully, both houses use committees of selected members to evaluate proposed legislation.

Standing committees are permanent committees in both the House and the Senate that specialize in a particular topic, such as agriculture, commerce, or veterans' affairs. These committees are usually divided into subcommittees that focus on a particular aspect of an issue.

The House and the Senate sometimes form temporary select committees to deal with issues requiring special attention. These committees meet only until they complete their task.

Occasionally the House and the Senate form joint committees with members from both houses. These committees meet to consider specific issues, such as the system of federal taxation. One type of joint committee, a conference committee, has a special function. If the House and the Senate pass different versions of the same bill, a conference committee tries to work out a compromise bill acceptable to both houses.

Once a committee in either house of Congress approves a bill, it is sent to the full Senate or House for debate. After debate the bill may be passed, rejected, or returned to the committee for further changes.

When both houses pass a bill, it goes to the president. If the president approves the bill and signs it, the bill becomes law. If the president vetoes the bill, it does not become law unless Congress overrides the veto.

The Executive Branch

The executive branch of government includes the president, the vice president, and various executive offices, departments, and agencies. The executive branch carries out the laws that Congress passes. The president plays a number of different roles in government, each of which has specific powers and responsibilities. These roles include the nation's

How a Bill Becomes Law

1. A legislator introduces a bill in the House or Senate, where it is referred to a committee for review.

2. After review, the committee decides whether to shelve it or to send it back to the House or Senate with or without revisions.

3. The House or Senate then debates the bill, making revisions if desired. If the bill is passed, it is sent to the other house.

4. If the House and Senate pass different versions of the bill, the houses must meet in a conference committee to decide on a compromise version.

5. The compromise bill is then sent to both houses.

6. If both houses pass the bill, it is sent to the president to sign.

7. If the president signs the bill, it becomes law.

8. The president may veto the bill, but if two-thirds of the House and Senate vote to approve it, it becomes law without the president's approval.

Chart *Skills*

The legislative process is complex.

Analyzing Information What is the role of a conference committee?

The Constitution Handbook **125**

CRITICAL THINKING ACTIVITY

Analyzing Information More than 9,000 amendments to the Constitution have been proposed, but only 27 have become part of the Constitution. Using this numerical information, ask students to calculate the odds of a proposed amendment being approved. Ask them to discuss the wisdom of making the amendment process so difficult. **L3**

Researching Amendments The Constitution states that either Congress or a national convention requested by two-thirds of the states may propose changes to the Constitution. Tell students that of the 27 amendments to the Constitution, all were proposed by Congress; not a single ratified amendment to the Constitution has come via the states requesting a national convention. Tell students to research the amendment process and come up with at least two reasons why Congress has proposed all of the amendments. **L3**

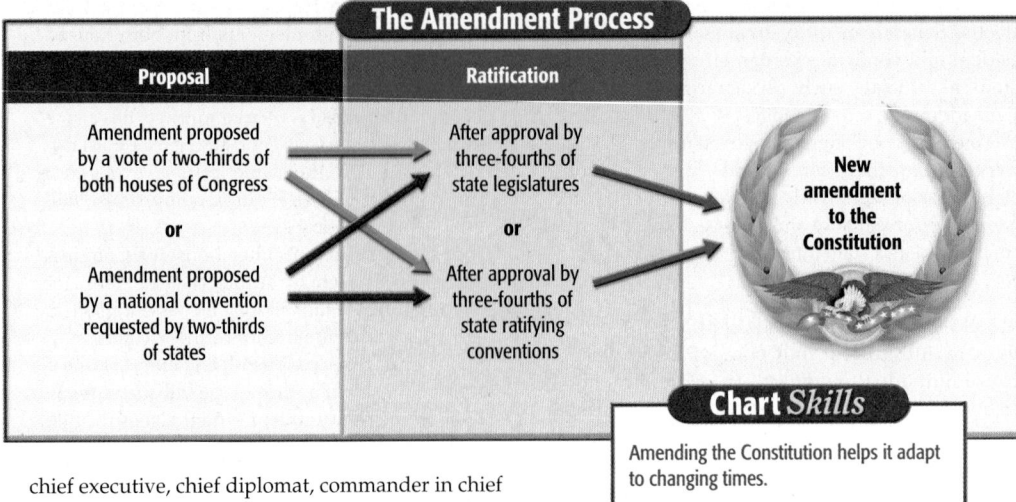

The Amendment Process

Proposal	Ratification
Amendment proposed by a vote of two-thirds of both houses of Congress	After approval by three-fourths of state legislatures
or	**or**
Amendment proposed by a national convention requested by two-thirds of states	After approval by three-fourths of state ratifying conventions

New amendment to the Constitution

chief executive, chief diplomat, commander in chief of the military, chief of state, and legislative leader.

The President's Roles

- **Chief Executive and Chief Diplomat** As chief executive, the president is responsible for carrying out the nation's laws. As chief diplomat, the president directs foreign policy, appoints ambassadors, and negotiates treaties with other nations.
- **Commander in Chief** As commander in chief of the armed forces, the president can use the military to intervene or offer assistance in crises at home and around the world. The president cannot declare war; only Congress holds this power. The president can send troops to other parts of the world for up to 60 days but must notify Congress when doing so. The troops may remain longer only if Congress gives its approval or declares war.
- **Chief of State** As chief of state, the president serves a symbolic role as the representative of all Americans. The president fulfills this role when receiving foreign ambassadors or heads of state, visiting foreign nations, or honoring Americans.
- **Legislative Leader** The president serves as a legislative leader by proposing laws to Congress and working to see that they are passed. In the annual State of the Union address, the president presents goals for legislation.

The Executive Branch at Work Many executive offices, departments, and independent agencies help the president carry out and enforce the nation's laws. The Executive Office of the President (EOP) is made up of individuals and agencies that directly assist the president. Presidents rely heavily

on the EOP for advice and for gathering information needed for decision making.

The executive branch also includes 15 executive departments, each responsible for a different area of government. For example, the Department of State plans and carries out foreign policy, and the Department of the Interior manages and protects the nation's public lands and natural resources. The heads of these departments, who have the title of secretary, are members of the president's cabinet. This group helps the president make decisions and set government policy.

The Judicial Branch

Article III of the Constitution calls for the creation of a Supreme Court and "such inferior [lower] courts as Congress may from time to time ordain and establish." Today the judicial branch consists of three main categories of courts, including:

- **District Courts** United States district courts are the lowest level of the federal court system. These courts consider criminal and civil cases that come under federal authority, including such criminal offenses as kidnapping and federal tax evasion. Civil cases cover claims against the federal government and cases involving constitutional rights, such as free speech. There are 91 district courts, with at least one in every state.
- **Appellate Courts** The appellate courts, or appeals courts, consider district court decisions in which the losing side has asked for a review of the

---

EXTENDING THE CONTENT

Ambassadors As part of the duties as chief diplomat for the United States, the president appoints ambassadors who carry the title *Ambassador Extraordinary and Plenipotentiary* to foreign posts. As official representatives of the United States, ambassadors protect the political, economic, and social interests of the United States government.

verdict. If an appeals court disagrees with the lower court's decision, it can either overturn the verdict or order a retrial. There are 14 appeals courts in the United States, one for each of the 12 federal districts, a military appeals court, and an appellate court for the federal circuit.

- **The Supreme Court** The Supreme Court, the final authority in the federal court system, consists of a chief justice and eight associate justices. Most of the Supreme Court's cases come from appeals of lower court decisions. Only cases involving foreign ambassadors or disputes between states can begin in the Supreme Court.

Supreme Court Independence The Supreme Court is the least public of the government's branches. The president appoints the Court's justices for life, and the Senate confirms the appointments. The public has no input. The Framers hoped that because judges were appointed rather than elected, they would be free to evaluate the law with no consideration of pleasing a group of electors.

Judicial Review The role of the judicial branch is not described in very much detail in the Constitution, but the role of the courts has grown as powers implied in the Constitution have been put into practice. In 1803 Chief Justice John Marshall expanded the powers of the Supreme Court by striking down an act of Congress in the case of *Marbury* v. *Madison.* Although not mentioned in the Constitution, judicial review has become a major power of the judicial branch. Judicial review gives the Supreme Court the ultimate authority to interpret the meaning of constitutional provisions and explain how the words of this 200-year-old document apply to our modern nation. *(See page 963 for more information on* Marbury v. Madison.*)*

The Rights of American Citizens

The rights of Americans fall into three broad categories: the right to be protected from unfair actions of the government, to receive equal treatment under the law, and to retain basic freedoms.

Protection from Unfair Actions Parts of the Constitution and the Bill of Rights protect all Americans from unfair treatment by the government or the law. Among these rights are the right to a lawyer when accused of a crime and the right to trial by jury when charged with a crime. In addition, the Fourth Amendment protects us from unreasonable searches and seizures. This provision requires police to have a court order before searching a person's home for criminal evidence. To obtain this, the police must have a very strong reason to suspect the person of committing a crime.

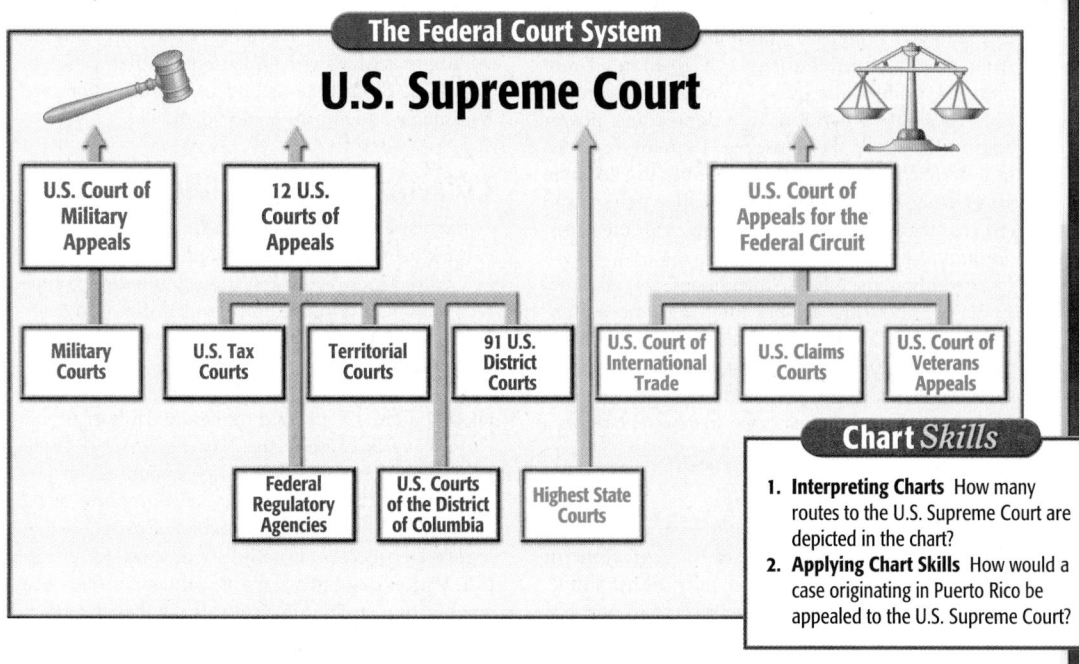

The Federal Court System

U.S. Supreme Court

- U.S. Court of Military Appeals
- 12 U.S. Courts of Appeals
- U.S. Court of Appeals for the Federal Circuit

- Military Courts
- U.S. Tax Courts
- Territorial Courts
- 91 U.S. District Courts
- U.S. Court of International Trade
- U.S. Claims Courts
- U.S. Court of Veterans Appeals

- Federal Regulatory Agencies
- U.S. Courts of the District of Columbia
- Highest State Courts

Chart *Skills*

1. **Interpreting Charts** How many routes to the U.S. Supreme Court are depicted in the chart?
2. **Applying Chart Skills** How would a case originating in Puerto Rico be appealed to the U.S. Supreme Court?

CRITICAL THINKING ACTIVITY

Analyzing Information Ask students to create a chart with the following presidents in the headings: Franklin D. Roosevelt, Richard M. Nixon, Harry S Truman, Ulysses S. Grant, and Ronald Reagan. Have students research the following information for each president: the total number of vetoes, the number of overturned vetoes, and the number of "pocket" vetoes. Then have students compare each president's acts and offer suggestions for them. **L2**

Discussing the Limits of Rights
The First Amendment guarantees an individual's right to free speech. The First Amendment does not, however, give individuals the right to shout "fire" in a crowded theater. Have students discuss the government's need to balance an individual's constitutional rights with society's need for order and safety. **L2**

The Eighteenth Amendment, ratified in 1919, prohibited the "manufacture, sale, or transportation of intoxicating liquors," and began what is commonly known as the era of Prohibition. The Twenty-first Amendment, ratified in 1933, repealed the Eighteenth Amendment. This is the only constitutional amendment that has been repealed.

Democracy in Action Town meetings in New England give local residents the chance to express their views. It is a responsibility of American citizens to remain informed about the actions of their local, state, and national government.

Equal Treatment All Americans, regardless of race, religion, or political beliefs, have the right to be treated the same under the law. The Fifth Amendment states that no person shall "be deprived of life, liberty, or property, without due process of law." Due process means that the government must follow procedures established by law and guaranteed by the Constitution, treating all people equally. The Fourteenth Amendment requires every state to grant its citizens "equal protection of the laws."

Basic Freedoms The basic freedoms involve the fundamental liberties outlined in the First Amendment—freedom of speech, freedom of religion, freedom of the press, freedom of assembly, and the right to petition. In a democracy, power rests in the hands of the people. Therefore, citizens in a democratic society must be able to exchange ideas freely. The First Amendment allows citizens to criticize the government, in speech or in the press, without fear of punishment.

In addition, the Ninth Amendment states that the rights of Americans are not limited to those mentioned in the Constitution. This has allowed basic freedoms to expand over the years through the passage of other amendments and laws. The Twenty-sixth Amendment, for example, extends the right to vote to American citizens who are at least 18 years of age.

Limits on Rights The rights of Americans have certain limitations, based on the principle of respecting everyone's rights equally. For example, many cities and towns require groups to obtain a permit to march on city streets. While such a law does limit free speech, it also protects the community by allowing the police to make provisions so that the march will not disturb the lives of other people. However, a law banning all marches would be unreasonable and would violate the First Amendment rights of free speech and assembly. Similarly, a law preventing only certain groups from marching would be unfair because it would not apply equally to everyone.

In this and other cases, the government balances an individual's rights, the rights of others, and the community's health and safety. Most Americans are willing to accept some limitations on their rights to gain these protections as long as the restrictions are reasonable and apply equally to all.

Citizens' Responsibilities

Participation in a democratic society involves certain duties and responsibilities. Duties are actions required by law. Responsibilities are voluntary actions. Fulfilling both your duties and your responsibilities helps ensure good government and protects your rights.

Duties One of the fundamental duties of all Americans is to obey the law. Laws serve three important functions. They help maintain order; they protect the health, safety, and property of all citizens; and they make it possible for people to live together peacefully. If you disobey laws, for example, you endanger others and interfere with the smooth functioning of society. If you believe a law

COOPERATIVE LEARNING ACTIVITY

Debating Rights Organize the class into five groups, one for each of the five rights incorporated in the First Amendment. Tell students they will have 10 minutes to prepare an outline about the right assigned to their group. Also tell them they will have five minutes to persuade the class that the right they represent is more important than the other four. Tell them to include as many factual details and real-life scenarios as possible. After each group has presented, have the class vote on which right they think is most important.

Use the rubric for a cooperative group management plan on pages 71–72 in the **Performance Assessment Activities and Rubrics.**

needs to be changed, you can work through your electoral representatives to improve it.

Americans also have a duty to pay taxes. The government uses tax money to defend the nation, provide health insurance for people over 65, and build roads and bridges. Americans benefit from services provided by the government.

Another duty of citizens is to defend the nation. All males aged 18 and older must register with the government in case the nation needs to call on them for military service. Military service is not automatic, but a war could make it necessary.

The Constitution guarantees all Americans the right to a trial by a jury of their equals. For this reason, you should be prepared for jury duty when you become eligible at the age of 18. Having a large group of jurors on hand is necessary to guarantee the right to a fair and speedy trial. You also have a duty to serve as a trial witness if called to do so.

Most states require you to attend school until a certain age. School is where you gain the knowledge and skills needed to be a good citizen. In school you learn to think more clearly, to express your opinions more accurately, and to analyze the statements and ideas of others. These skills will help you make informed choices when you vote.

Responsibilities The responsibilities of citizens are not as clear-cut as their duties. Responsibilities are as important as duties, however, because they help maintain the quality of government and society.

One important responsibility is to become well informed. You need to know what is happening in your community, your state, your country, and the world. Knowing what your government representatives are doing and expressing your feelings about their actions can help keep the government responsive to the wishes of the people.

You also need to be informed about your rights and to exercise them when necessary. Knowing your rights helps preserve them. Other responsibilities include respecting diversity, accepting responsibility for your actions, and supporting your family.

Vote, Vote, Vote! Perhaps your most important responsibility as an American citizen will be to vote when you reach the age of 18. Voting allows you to participate in government and guide its direction. When you vote for people to represent you in government, you will be exercising your right of self-government. If you disapprove of the job your representatives are doing, it will be your responsibility to help elect other people in the next election. You can also let your representatives know how you feel about issues through letters, telephone calls, and petitions and by taking part in public meetings or political rallies.

To enjoy your rights to the fullest, you must be prepared to respect the rights of others. Respecting the rights of others also means respecting the rights of people with whom you disagree. Respecting and accepting others regardless of race, religion, beliefs, or other differences is essential in a democracy.

3 ASSESS

Assign the Constitution Handbook Assessment as homework or as an in-class activity.

HISTORY Online

Study Central™ provides summaries, interactive games, and online graphic organizers to help students review section content.

4 CLOSE

Have students offer one-sentence definitions of the terms *legislative, executive, judicial, checks and balances,* and *amendments.*

Citizenship Handbook Assessment

Checking for Understanding

1. **Define:** popular sovereignty, federalism, enumerated powers, reserved powers, concurrent powers, override, appropriate, impeach, constituent, bill, standing committee, select committee, joint committee, conference committee, cabinet, judicial review, due process.
2. **Summarize** the provisions of the First Amendment.

Reviewing Themes

3. **Civic Rights and Responsibilities** What is the difference between a duty and a responsibility?

Critical Thinking

4. **Comparing** Some people want a limit on the number of terms one can serve in the legislature. What are some of the advantages of the present system, which does not limit the number of terms? What are some of the disadvantages? How would one make term limits an official part of the Constitution?
5. **Organizing** Use a graphic organizer like the one below to list reasons why the Framers of the Constitution provided for separation of powers.

Separation of Powers

Analyzing Visuals

6. **Analyzing Photographs** Study the photograph on page 122. How does the democratic voting process reflect our national identity?

Writing About History

7. **History and Government** Working with a partner, choose one of the constitutional rights listed below. Write a report that traces the right's historical development, from the time the Constitution was ratified to the present.
   suffrage
   freedom of speech
   freedom of religion
   equal protection of law

Constitution Handbook — ASSESSMENT ANSWERS

1. Terms are in blue.
2. freedom of speech, religion, and the press; right of assembly; and the right to petition
3. Duties are actions required by law; responsibilities are voluntary.
4. advantages: system functions more smoothly and efficiently with more experienced legislators; disadvantages: cronyism, willingness to stick to status quo, fewer fresh ideas; through the amendment process
5. to prevent one branch of government from becoming too powerful; to provide a system for each branch of government to check and balance the others; to protect individual rights
6. Answers will vary but should note that the ability to vote is a right shared by all citizens.
7. Reports will vary but must include the historical development of the right.

BELLRINGER
Motivational Activity

Ask students to read the Preamble to the Constitution. Have them identify which purpose of the Constitution is most important to them personally.

FYI

The members of the Committee of Style—William Samuel Johnson, Alexander Hamilton, Gouverneur Morris, James Madison, and Rufus King—wrote the final draft of the Constitution.

Constitution The word *constitution* has various definitions. It can refer to the system of laws and principles that defines the right to rule and distribute power, or it can refer to the document on which those laws and principles are actually written.

The Constitution of the United States

The Constitution of the United States is a truly remarkable document. It was one of the first written constitutions in modern history. The entire text of the Constitution and its amendments follow. For easier study, those passages that have been set aside or changed by the adoption of amendments are printed in blue. Also included are explanatory notes that will help clarify the meaning of important ideas presented in the Constitution.

A burst of fireworks celebrating the 200-year anniversary of the Constitution highlights Independence Hall in Philadelphia.

Preamble

We the People of the United States, in Order to form a more perfect Union, establish Justice, insure domestic Tranquility, provide for the common defence, promote the general Welfare, and secure the Blessings of Liberty to ourselves and our Posterity, do ordain and establish this Constitution for the United States of America.

Article I

Section 1

All legislative Powers herein granted shall be vested in a Congress of the United States, which shall consist of a Senate and House of Representatives.

Section 2

[1.] The House of Representatives shall be composed of Members chosen every second Year by the People of the several States, and the Electors in each State shall have the Qualifications requisite for Electors of the most numerous Branch of the State Legislature.

[2.] No person shall be a Representative who shall not have attained to the Age of twenty five Years, and been seven Years a Citizen of the United States, and who shall not, when elected, be an Inhabitant of that State in which he shall be chosen.

[3.] Representatives and direct Taxes shall be apportioned among the several States which may be included within this Union, according to their respective Numbers, which shall be determined by adding to the whole Number of free Persons, including those bound to Service for a Term of Years, and excluding Indians not taxed, three fifths of all other Persons. The actual Enumeration shall be made within three Years after the first Meeting of the Congress of the United States, and within every subsequent Term of ten Years, in such Manner as they shall by Law direct. The Number of Representatives shall not exceed one for every thirty Thousand, but each State shall have at Least one Representative; and until such enumeration shall be made, the State of New Hampshire shall be entitled to chuse three; Massachusetts eight, Rhode-Island and Providence Plantations one, Connecticut five, New-York six, New Jersey four, Pennsylvania eight, Delaware one, Maryland six, Virginia ten, North Carolina five, South Carolina five, and Georgia three.

[4.] When vacancies happen in the Representation from any State, the Executive Authority thereof shall issue Writs of Election to fill such Vacancies.

[5.] The House of Representatives shall chuse their Speaker and other Officers; and shall have the sole Power of Impeachment.

The Preamble introduces the Constitution and sets forth the general purposes for which the government was established. The Preamble also declares that the power of the government comes from the people.

The printed text of the document shows the spelling and punctuation of the parchment original.

Article I. The Legislative Branch

The Constitution contains seven divisions called articles. Each article covers a general topic. For example, Articles I, II, and III create the three branches of the national government—the legislative, executive, and judicial branches. Most of the articles are divided into sections.

Section 1. Congress

Lawmaking The power to make laws is given to a Congress made up of two chambers to represent different interests: the Senate to represent the states and the House to be more responsive to the people's will.

Section 2. House of Representatives

Division of Representatives Among the States The number of representatives from each state is based on the size of the state's population. Each state is entitled to at least one representative. The Constitution states that each state may specify who can vote, but the Fifteenth, Nineteenth, Twenty-fourth, and Twenty-sixth Amendments have established guidelines that all states must follow regarding the right to vote. *What are the qualifications for members of the House of Representatives?*

Vocabulary

preamble: *introduction*
constitution: *principles and laws of a nation*
enumeration: *census or population count*
impeachment: *bringing charges against an official*

The Constitution Handbook **131**

TEACH

Analyzing Information Have students research data from the 1990 and 2000 censuses. Students should create a chart that identifies the populations of each state and the number of representatives each state had in 1990. Then students should list the populations each state had in 2000 and whether or not that state lost or gained representation in the House of Representatives. Have students identify which states gained the most seats and speculate as to why those states are gaining populations. **L2**

Answer: A member of the House of Representatives must be at least 25 years old, be a United States citizen for at least seven years, and be an inhabitant of the state from which he or she was elected.

ABCNEWS INTERACTIVE™

 VIDEOCASSETTE
Historic America Electronic Field Trips

View **Tape 1, Chapter 7:** "Independence Hall."

EXTENDING THE CONTENT

Sergeants-at-Arms House and Senate sergeants-at-arms are the police officers of Congress. They enforce the rules and maintain order. When they walk down the aisle of the legislature, carrying a ceremonial staff called a mace, Congress must be orderly. Any member of Congress who persists in disorderly conduct is guilty of contempt. The sergeants-at-arms also maintain security within the Capitol and associated buildings and supervise the Capitol police force. Sometimes the sergeants-at-arms round up members for floor votes, personally escorting any member who refuses to attend.

United States Constitution

Analyzing Information Write on the chalkboard the following, which George Washington supposedly said to Thomas Jefferson in defense of the Senate: "We pour legislation into the senatorial saucer to cool it." Have students speculate on what Washington meant by this. (*The Senate was seen as the more deliberative of the two houses of Congress.*) **L1**

Answer: The Senate has the power to remove impeached officials from office and disqualify them from holding office in the future.

Experience, Not Age The title Senior Senator refers to the senator from each state who has more experience as a senator. A senior senator may actually be younger than the other senator from his or her state.

Section 3. The Senate

Voting Procedure Originally, senators were chosen by the legislators of their own states. The Seventeenth Amendment changed this, so that senators are now elected by their state's people. There are 100 senators, 2 from each state.

What Might Have Been

Electing Senators South Carolina delegate Charles Pinckney suggested during the Convention that the members of the Senate come from four equally proportioned districts within the United States and that the legislature elect the executive every seven years.

Section 3. The Senate

Trial of Impeachments One of Congress's powers is the power to impeach—to accuse government officials of wrongdoing, put them on trial, and, if necessary, remove them from office. The House decides if the offense is impeachable. The Senate acts as a jury and, when the president is impeached, the Chief Justice of the United States serves as the judge. A two-thirds vote of the members present is needed to convict impeached officials. *What punishment can the Senate give if an impeached official is convicted?*

Vocabulary

president pro tempore: *presiding officer of Senate who serves when the vice president is absent*
quorum: *minimum number of members that must be present to conduct sessions*

Section 3

[1.] The Senate of the United States shall be composed of two Senators from each State, chosen by the Legislature thereof, for six Years; and each Senator shall have one Vote.

[2.] Immediately after they shall be assembled in Consequence of the first Election, they shall be divided as equally as may be into three Classes. The Seats of the Senators of the first Class shall be vacated at the Expiration of the second Year, of the second Class at the Expiration of the fourth Year, and of the third Class at the Expiration of the sixth Year, so that one third may be chosen every second Year; and if Vacancies happen by Resignation, or otherwise, during the Recess of the Legislature of any State, the Executive thereof may make temporary Appointments until the next Meeting of the Legislature, which shall then fill such Vacancies.

[3.] No Person shall be a Senator who shall not have attained to the Age of thirty Years, and been nine Years a Citizen of the United States, and who shall not, when elected, be an Inhabitant of that State for which he shall be chosen.

[4.] The Vice President of the United States shall be President of the Senate, but shall have no Vote, unless they be equally divided.

[5.] The Senate shall chuse their other Officers, and also a President pro tempore, in the Absence of the Vice-President, or when he shall exercise the Office of the President of the United States.

[6.] The Senate shall have the sole Power to try all Impeachments. When sitting for that Purpose, they shall be on Oath or Affirmation. When the President of the United States is tried, the Chief Justice shall preside: And no Person shall be convicted without the Concurrence of two thirds of the Members present.

[7.] Judgment in Cases of Impeachment shall not extend further than to removal from Office, and disqualification to hold and enjoy any Office of honor, Trust or Profit under the United States: but the Party convicted shall nevertheless be liable and subject to Indictment, Trial, Judgment and Punishment, according to Law.

Section 4

[1.] The Times, Places and Manner of holding Elections for Senators and Representatives, shall be prescribed in each State by the Legislature thereof; but the Congress may at any time by Law make or alter such Regulations, except as to the Places of chusing Senators.

[2.] The Congress shall assemble at least once in every Year, and such Meeting shall be on the first Monday in December, unless they shall by Law appoint a different Day.

Section 5

[1.] Each House shall be the Judge of the Elections, Returns and Qualifications of its own Members, and a Majority of each shall constitute a Quorum to do

---

CRITICAL THINKING ACTIVITY

Analyzing Information Remind students that representation in the House of Representatives is based on each state's population. Then have students ascertain the number of members in the House currently representing their state, and also the number in 1990 and 1980. This information is readily available in many almanacs. Ask students to discuss how a change in the number of House seats might affect a state. **L2**

Business; but a smaller Number may adjourn from day to day, and may be authorized to compel the Attendance of absent Members, in such Manner, and under such Penalties as each House may provide.

[2.] Each House may determine the Rules of its Proceedings, punish its Members for disorderly Behaviour, and, with the Concurrence of two thirds, expel a Member.

[3.] Each House shall keep a Journal of its Proceedings, and from time to time publish the same, excepting such Parts as may in their Judgment require Secrecy; and the Yeas and Nays of the Members of either House on any question shall, at the Desire of one fifth of those Present, be entered on the Journal.

[4.] Neither House, during the Session of Congress, shall, without the Consent of the other, adjourn for more than three days, nor to any other Place than that in which the two Houses shall be sitting.

Section 6

[1.] The Senators and Representatives shall receive a Compensation for their Services, to be ascertained by Law, and paid out of the Treasury of the United States. They shall in all Cases, except Treason, Felony and Breach of the Peace, be privileged from Arrest during their Attendance at the Session of their respective Houses, and in going to and returning from the same; and for any Speech or Debate in either House, they shall not be questioned in any other Place.

[2.] No Senator or Representative shall, during the Time for which he was elected, be appointed to any civil Office under the Authority of the United States, which shall have been created, or the Emoluments whereof shall have been encreased during such time; and no Person holding any Office under the United States, shall be a Member of either House during his Continuance in Office.

Section 7

[1.] All Bills for raising Revenue shall originate in the House of Representatives; but the Senate may propose or concur with Amendments as on other Bills.

[2.] Every Bill which shall have passed the House of Representatives and the Senate, shall, before it become a Law, be presented to the President of the United States; If he approve he shall sign it, but if not he shall return it, with his Objections to that House in which it shall have originated, who shall enter the Objections at large on their Journal, and proceed to reconsider it. If after such Reconsideration two thirds of that House shall agree to pass the Bill, it shall be sent, together with the Objections, to the other House, by which it shall likewise be reconsidered, and if approved by two thirds of that House, it shall become a Law. But in all such Cases the Votes of both Houses shall be determined by yeas and Nays, and the Names of the Persons voting for and against the Bill shall be entered on the Journal of each House respectively. If any Bill shall not be returned by the President within ten Days (Sundays excepted) after it

Vocabulary

adjourn: *to suspend a session*
concurrence: *agreement*
emoluments: *salaries*
revenue: *income raised by government*
bill: *draft of a proposed law*

Section 6. Privileges and Restrictions

Pay and Privileges To strengthen the federal government, the Founders set congressional salaries to be paid by the United States Treasury rather than by members' respective states. Originally, members were paid $6 per day. In 2002, all members of Congress received a base salary of $150,000.

Section 7. Passing Laws

Revenue Bill All tax laws must originate in the House of Representatives. This ensures that the branch of Congress that is elected by the people every two years has the major role in determining taxes.

Section 7. Passing Laws

How Bills Become Laws A bill may become a law only by passing both houses of Congress and by being signed by the president. The president can check Congress by rejecting—vetoing—its legislation. *How can Congress override the president's veto?*

Constructing a Chart Have students construct a chart categorizing the legislative powers of Congress. Suggest that they list the powers under the following categories: *Monetary, Commerce, Regulatory, Judicial, War, Implied.* L1

FYI

Republican and pacifist Jeannette Rankin of Montana was the first woman elected to the House of Representatives in 1916. In 1917, along with 49 House colleagues, Rankin voted against the United States entering World War I. On December 8, 1941, the day after the bombing of Pearl Harbor, she was the only member of Congress to vote against declaring war on Japan.

Answer: A bill can become law, despite not being signed by the president, if two-thirds of the House of Representatives and two-thirds of the Senate approve the bill.

The Constitution Handbook **133**

COOPERATIVE LEARNING ACTIVITY

Understanding Ideas Organize students into groups of five to consider one of the expressed powers of Congress: taxing and spending; regulating commerce, foreign policy, and national defense; and providing for the nation's growth. Have each group discuss why the power it selected was delegated to Congress rather than to the executive branch.

Use the rubric for a cooperative group management plan on pages 71–72 in the **Performance Assessment Activities and Rubrics.**

United States Constitution

FYI

When the first Congress was called to assemble in New York City in 1789, it took nearly a month for enough members to arrive to make a quorum.

Answer: Article 1, Section 8, Clause 11

Writing Letters Point out that because of the heavy volume of legislation, both houses of Congress have committees that do much of the work in preparing bills. Each committee deals with a particular issue, such as banking, foreign affairs, or natural resources. Encourage students to write letters asking representatives and senators from your state about the committees on which they serve. Invite volunteers to share the replies they receive. **L1**

Section 8. Powers Granted to Congress

Expressed Powers Expressed powers are those powers directly stated in the Constitution. Most of the expressed powers of Congress are itemized in Article I, Section 8. These powers are also called enumerated powers because they are numbered 1 to18. *Which clause gives Congress the power to declare war?*

Though Congress has many specific powers, the people have the right of protest.

Vocabulary

resolution: *legislature's formal expression of opinion*

naturalization: *procedure by which a citizen of a foreign nation becomes a citizen of the United States.*

134 The Constitution Handbook

---

shall have been presented to him, the Same shall be a Law, in like Manner as if he had signed it, unless the Congress by their Adjournment prevent its Return, in which Case it shall not be a Law.

[3.] Every Order, Resolution, or Vote to which the Concurrence of the Senate and House of Representatives may be necessary (except on a question of Adjournment) shall be presented to the President of the United States; and before the Same shall take Effect, shall be approved by him, or being disapproved by him, shall be repassed by two thirds of the Senate and House of Representatives, according to the Rules and Limitations prescribed in the Case of a Bill.

Section 8

[1.] The Congress shall have the Power to lay and collect Taxes, Duties, Imposts and Excises, to pay the Debts and provide for the common Defence and general Welfare of the United States; but all Duties, Imposts and Excises shall be uniform throughout the United States;

[2.] To borrow Money on the credit of the United States;

[3.] To regulate Commerce with foreign Nations, and among the several States, and with the Indian Tribes;

[4.] To establish an uniform Rule of Naturalization, and uniform Laws on the subject of Bankruptcies throughout the United States;

[5.] To coin Money, regulate the Value thereof, and of foreign Coin, and fix the Standard of Weights and Measures;

[6.] To provide for the Punishment of counterfeiting the Securities and current Coin of the United States;

[7.] To establish Post Offices and post Roads;

[8.] To promote the Progress of Science and useful Arts, by securing for limited Times to Authors and Inventors the exclusive Right to their respective Writings and Discoveries;

[9.] To constitute Tribunals inferior to the supreme Court;

[10.] To define and punish Piracies and Felonies committed on the high Seas, and Offences against the Law of Nations;

[11.] To declare War, grant Letters of Marque and Reprisal, and make Rules concerning Captures on Land and Water;

[12.] To raise and support Armies, but no Appropriation of Money to that Use shall be for a longer Term than two Years;

[13.] To provide and maintain a Navy;

[14.] To make Rules for the Government and Regulation of the land and naval Forces;

[15.] To provide for calling forth the Militia to execute the Laws of the Union, suppress Insurrections and repel Invasions;

[16.] To provide for organizing, arming, and disciplining, the Militia, and for governing such Part of them as may be employed in the Service of the United States, reserving to the States respectively, the Appointment of the Officers, and the Authority of training the Militia according to the discipline prescribed by Congress;

CRITICAL THINKING ACTIVITY

Synthesizing Information Call on students to list the qualifications for serving in Congress as set forth in the Constitution. Then ask students what other qualifications, if any, they think should be applied to members of Congress. Discuss with students whether they would like to serve in Congress. **L1**

[17.] To exercise exclusive Legislation in all Cases whatsoever, over such District (not exceeding ten Miles square) as may, by Cession of particular States, and the Acceptance of Congress, become the Seat of Government of the United States, and to exercise like Authority over all Places purchased by the Consent of the Legislature of the State in which the Same shall be, for the Erection of Forts, Magazines, Arsenals, dock-Yards, and other needful Buildings; And

[18.] To make all Laws which shall be necessary and proper for carrying into Execution the foregoing Powers, and all other Powers vested by this Constitution in the Government of the United States, or in any Department or Officer thereof.

Section 9

[1.] The Migration or Importation of such Persons as any of the States now existing shall think proper to admit, shall not be prohibited by the Congress prior to the Year one thousand eight hundred and eight, but a Tax or duty may be imposed on such Importation, not exceeding ten dollars for each Person.

[2.] The Privilege of the Writ of Habeas Corpus shall not be suspended, unless when in Cases of Rebellion or Invasion the public Safety may require it.

[3.] No Bill of Attainder or ex post facto Law shall be passed.

[4.] No Capitation, or other direct, Tax shall be laid, unless in Proportion to the Census or Enumeration herein before directed to be taken.

[5.] No Tax or Duty shall be laid on Articles exported from any State.

[6.] No Preference shall be given by any Regulation of Commerce or Revenue to the Ports of one State over those of another: nor shall Vessels bound to, or from, one State, be obliged to enter, clear, or pay Duties in another.

[7.] No Money shall be drawn from the Treasury, but in Consequence of Appropriations made by Law; and a regular Statement and Account of the Receipts and Expenditures of all public Money shall be published from time to time.

[8.] No Title of Nobility shall be granted by the United States: And no Person holding any Office of Profit or Trust under them, shall, without the Consent of the Congress, accept of any present, Emolument, Office, or Title, of any kind whatever, from any King, Prince, or foreign State.

Section 10

[1.] No State shall enter into any Treaty, Alliance, or Confederation; grant Letters of Marque and Reprisal; coin Money; emit Bills of Credit; make any Thing but gold and silver Coin a Tender in Payment of Debts; pass any Bill of Attainder, ex post facto Law, or Law impairing the Obligation of Contracts, or grant any Title of Nobility.

[2.] No State shall, without the Consent of the Congress, lay any Imposts or Duties on Imports or Exports, except

Section 8. Powers Granted to Congress

Elastic Clause The final enumerated power is often called the "elastic clause." This clause gives Congress the right to make all laws "necessary and proper" to carry out the powers expressed in the other clauses of Article I. It is called the elastic clause because it lets Congress "stretch" its powers to meet situations the Founders could not have anticipated.

What does the phrase "necessary and proper" in the elastic clause mean? It was a subject of dispute from the beginning. The issue was whether a strict or a broad interpretation of the Constitution should be applied. The dispute was first addressed in 1819, in the case of *McCulloch v. Maryland,* when the Supreme Court ruled in favor of a broad interpretation. The Court stated that the elastic clause allowed Congress to use its powers in any way that was not specifically prohibited by the Constitution.

Section 9. Powers Denied to the Federal Government

Original Rights A writ of habeas corpus issued by a judge requires a law official to bring a prisoner to court and show cause for holding the prisoner. A bill of attainder is a bill that punishes a person without a jury trial. An "ex post facto" law is one that makes an act a crime after the act has been committed. *What does the Constitution say about bills of attainder?*

Section 10. Powers Denied to the States

Limitations on Powers Section 10 lists limits on the states. These restrictions were designed, in part, to prevent an overlapping in functions and authority with the federal government.

Evaluating Issues Article I, Section 9, prohibits the suspension of the writ of habeas corpus. Discuss with students the protection this offers. Ask students if they think this is an outdated principle today or still necessary to the Constitution. *(Most students will see this as a major principle of our legal system.)* **L2**

Answer: No bills of attainder shall be passed.

CURRICULUM CONNECTION

Civics On many occasions when the United States has intervened militarily, Congress has not issued a declaration of war. These "undeclared wars" of the 1900s and 2000s include the conflicts in Korea and Vietnam and the war against terrorism. All three wars were fought on the president's authority to support governments against external aggression.

EXTENDING THE CONTENT

The Capitol The interior of the Capitol is a combination of new and old. Many of the furnishings and works of art date from the mid-1800s. However, signs of modern technology are everywhere. Roll-call votes are counted electronically. In addition, members of both houses have access to computers and other electronic information services. There are even electric subways connecting many of the office buildings on Capitol Hill.

United States Constitution

FOCUS

BELLRINGER
Motivational Activity

Point out that one of the difficult questions for the Framers of the Constitution concerned the Chief Executive—exactly how much power should the president have? Have students discuss why the Framers set up an office of president with limited powers. *(Discussion should focus on the Framers' fear of a single leader with uncontrolled powers.)*

FYI

One of the most important traditional measures of public opinion of the president's performance is the Gallup presidential approval survey, or poll. Since 1945 the Gallup Organization has polled members of the public monthly—and sometimes more often—about whether they approve or disapprove of the president's handling of the job.

Article II. The Executive Branch

Article II creates an executive branch to carry out laws passed by Congress. Article II lists the powers and duties of the president, describes qualifications for office and procedures for electing the president, and provides for a vice president.

What Might Have Been

Term of Office Alexander Hamilton also provided his own governmental outline at the Constitutional Convention. Some of its most distinctive elements were that both the executive and the members of the Senate were "elected to serve during good behaviour," meaning there was no specified limit on their time in office.

Section 1. President and Vice President

Former Method of Election In the election of 1800, the top two candidates received the same number of electoral votes, making it necessary for the House of Representatives to decide the election. To eliminate this problem, the Twelfth Amendment, added in 1804, changed the method of electing the president stated in Article II, Section 3. The Twelfth Amendment requires that the electors cast separate ballots for president and vice president.

---

what may be absolutely necessary for executing it's inspection Laws: and the net Produce of all Duties and Imposts, laid by any State on Imports and Exports, shall be for the Use of the Treasury of the United States; and all such Laws shall be subject to the Revision and Controul of the Congress.

[3.] No State shall, without the Consent of Congress, lay any Duty of Tonnage, keep Troops, or Ships of War in time of Peace, enter into any Agreement or Compact with another State, or with a foreign Power, or engage in War, unless actually invaded, or in such imminent Danger as will not admit of delay.

Article II

Section 1

[1.] The executive Power shall be vested in a President of the United States of America. He shall hold his Office during the Term of four Years, and, together with the Vice-President, chosen for the same Term, be elected, as follows

[2.] Each State shall appoint, in such Manner as the Legislature thereof may direct, a Number of Electors, equal to the whole Number of Senators and Representatives to which the State may be entitled in the Congress: but no Senator or Representative, or Person holding an Office of Trust or Profit under the United States, shall be appointed an Elector.

[3.] The Electors shall meet in their respective States, and vote by Ballot for two Persons, of whom one at least shall not be an Inhabitant of the same State with themselves. And they shall make a List of all the Persons voted for, and of the Number of Votes for each; which List they shall sign and certify, and transmit sealed to the Seat of the Government of the United States, directed to the President of the Senate. The President of the Senate shall, in the Presence of the Senate and House of Representatives, open all the Certificates, and the Votes shall then be counted. The Person having the greatest Number of Votes shall be the President, if such Number be a Majority of the whole Number of Electors appointed; and if there be more than one who have such Majority, and have an equal Number of Votes, then the House of Representatives shall immediately chuse by Ballot one of them for President; and if no person have a Majority, then from the five highest on the List the said House shall in like Manner chuse the president. But in chusing the President, the Votes shall be taken by States, the Representation from each State having one Vote; A quorum for this Purpose shall consist of a Member or Members from two thirds of the States, and a Majority of all the States shall be necessary to a Choice. In every Case, after the Choice of the President, the Person having the greatest Number of Votes of the Electors shall be the Vice-President. But if there should remain two or more who have equal Votes, the Senate shall chuse from them by Ballot the Vice President.

EXTENDING THE CONTENT

Two-term Limits The Constitution originally did not limit the number of terms the president could serve. George Washington set a precedent by serving only two terms. Until FDR, no president had served more than two terms. Many people opposed Roosevelt's four terms in office. This opposition eventually led to the ratification of the Twenty-second Amendment in 1951, which limited presidents to two terms.

[4.] The Congress may determine the Time of chusing the Electors, and the Day on which they shall give their Votes; which Day shall be the same throughout the United States.

[5.] No Person except a natural born Citizen, or a Citizen of the United States, at the time of the Adoption of this Constitution, shall be eligible to the Office of President; neither shall any Person be eligible to that Office who shall not have attained to the Age of thirty five Years, and been fourteen Years a Resident within the United States.

[6.] In Case of the Removal of the President from Office, or of his Death, Resignation, or Inability to discharge the Powers and Duties of the said Office, the Same shall devolve on the Vice-President, and the Congress may by Law provide for the Case of Removal, Death, Resignation or Inability, both of the President and Vice-President, declaring what Officer shall then act as President, and such Officer shall act accordingly, until the Disability be removed, or a President shall be elected.

[7.] The President shall, at stated Times, receive for his Services, a Compensation, which shall neither be increased nor diminished during the Period for which he shall have been elected, and he shall not receive within that Period any other Emolument from the United States, or any of them.

[8.] Before he enter on the Execution of his Office, he shall take the following Oath or Affirmation—"I do solemnly swear (or affirm) that I will faithfully execute the Office of President of the United States, and will to the best of my Ability, preserve, protect and defend the Constitution of the United States."

Section 2

[1.] The President shall be Commander in Chief of the Army and Navy of the United States, and of the Militia of the several States, when called into the actual Service of the United States; he may require the Opinion, in writing, of the principal Officer in each of the executive Departments, upon any Subject relating to the Duties of their respective Offices, and he shall have Power to grant Reprieves and Pardons for Offences against the United States, except in Cases of Impeachment.

[2.] He shall have Power, by and with the Advice and Consent of the Senate, to make Treaties, provided two thirds of the Senators present concur; and he shall nominate, and by and with the Advice and Consent of the Senate, shall appoint Ambassadors, other public Ministers and Consuls, Judges of the supreme Court, and all other Officers of the United States, whose Appointments are not herein otherwise provided for, and which shall be established by Law: but the Congress may by Law vest the Appointment of such inferior Officers, as they think proper, in the President alone, in the Courts of Law, or in the Heads of Departments.

Section 1. President and Vice President
Qualifications The president must be a citizen of the United States by birth, at least 35 years of age, and a resident of the United States for 14 years.

What Might Have Been
Qualifications At the Constitutional Convention, the New Jersey Amendments, sponsored by the smaller states, raised the possibility of making the executive a committee of people rather than a single individual. Also, executives were not allowed to run for a second term of office under this plan.

Section 1. President and Vice President
Vacancies If the president dies, resigns, is removed from office by impeachment, or is unable to carry out the duties of the office, the vice president becomes president.

Section 1. President and Vice President
Salary Originally, the president's salary was $25,000 per year. The president's current salary is $400,000 plus a $50,000 nontaxable expense account per year. The president also receives living accommodations in two residences—the White House and Camp David.

Section 2. Powers of the President
Cabinet Mention of "the principal officer in each of the executive departments" is the only suggestion of the president's cabinet to be found in the Constitution. The cabinet is an advisory body, and its power depends on the president. Section 2, Clause 1 also makes the president the head of the armed forces. This established the principle of civilian control of the military.

Section 2. Powers of the President
Treaties With Foreign Nations The president is responsible for the conduct of relations with foreign countries. *What role does the Senate have in approving treaties?*

The Constitution Handbook **137**

Classifying Information Have students read Article II to find the powers of the president. Suggest that they classify these powers under the headings *Executive, Legislative, Diplomatic, Military,* and *Judicial.* L1

Making Judgments Ask students to discuss why the Framers of the Constitution made the president commander in chief of the armed forces and any state militias called to serve the United States. (*The Framers wanted to ensure civilian control of the military.*) L2

FYI

The electors in the Electoral College almost always vote as expected. Exceptions are rare: there have been only a small number of "faithless electors" among the more than 17,000 electors chosen since 1789. For example, in 1988 Democratic nominee Michael Dukakis was denied one of his 112 electoral votes when a West Virginia elector cast her ballot for Dukakis's running mate, Lloyd Bentsen. She gave her vice presidential vote to Dukakis.

Answer: Two-thirds of the Senators present must concur in order for a treaty to be approved.

CRITICAL THINKING ACTIVITY

Determining Cause and Effect Discuss examples showing the increase in presidential power during this century. For example, increasing globalization has expanded the president's foreign relations responsibilities, such as negotiating international treaties, military policing interventions, and waging "undeclared wars." Write the following statement on the chalkboard: "The increase in presidential power during this century has been largely related to crises, whether domestic or foreign."
Ask: Do you think this is the true cause of the increase in presidential power? Why or why not? If not, what do you think caused the increase? L3

United States Constitution

FOCUS

Ask students to consider the meaning of the phrase "respect for the law." Guide their discussion by asking the following questions: What is the law? How can the law affect individuals and society? Why is respect for the law necessary to good government?

FYI

In the first election, the American people had no problem selecting a president. George Washington was the unanimous choice, winning all of the 69 electoral votes that were cast in the 1789 election. No other president has matched that feat, although Franklin D. Roosevelt came close in 1936 with 98.5 percent of the electoral vote. Most other presidential elections have been more competitive, sometimes creating issues the Founders did not foresee.

Section 3. Duties of the President

Executive Orders An important presidential power is the ability to issue executive orders. An executive order is a rule or command the president issues that has the force of law. Only Congress can make laws under the Constitution, but executive orders are considered part of the president's duty to "take care that the laws be faithfully executed." This power is often used during emergencies. During the Civil War, for example, President Lincoln issued an order suspending writs of habeas corpus. Over time the scope of executive orders has expanded, increasing the president's power. Decisions by federal agencies and departments are also considered to be executive orders.

Section 4. Impeachment

Reasons for Removal From Office This section states the reasons for which the president and vice president may be impeached and removed from office. Only Andrew Johnson and Bill Clinton have been impeached by the House. Richard Nixon resigned before the House could vote on possible impeachment.

Article III. The Judicial Branch

The term *judicial* refers to courts. The Constitution set up only the Supreme Court but provided for the establishment of other federal courts. The judiciary of the United States has two different systems of courts. One system consists of the federal courts, whose powers derive from the Constitution and federal laws. The other includes the courts of each of the 50 states, whose powers derive from state constitutions and laws.

Section 2. Jurisdiction

General Jurisdiction Federal courts deal mostly with "statute law," or laws passed by Congress, treaties, and cases involving the Constitution itself.

Vocabulary

original jurisdiction: *authority to be the first court to hear a case*

appellate jurisdiction: *authority to hear cases that have been appealed from lower courts*

Section 2. Jurisdiction

The Supreme Court A court with "original jurisdiction" has the authority to be the first court to hear a case. The Supreme Court generally has "appellate jurisdiction" in that it mostly hears cases appealed from lower courts.

[3.] The President shall have Power to fill up all Vacancies that may happen during the Recess of the Senate, by granting Commissions which shall expire at the End of their next Session.

Section 3

He shall from time to time give to the Congress Information of the State of the Union, and recommend to their Consideration such Measures as he shall judge necessary and expedient; he may, on extraordinary Occasions, convene both Houses, or either of them, and in Case of Disagreement between them, with Respect to the Time of Adjournment, he may adjourn them to such Time as he shall think proper; he shall receive Ambassadors and other public Ministers; he shall take Care that the Laws be faithfully executed, and shall Commission all the Officers of the United States.

Section 4

The President, Vice-President and all civil Officers of the United States, shall be removed from Office on Impeachment for, and Conviction of, Treason, Bribery, or other high Crimes and Misdemeanors.

Article III

Section 1

The judicial Power of the United States, shall be vested in one supreme Court, and in such inferior Courts as the Congress may from time to time ordain and establish. The Judges, both of the supreme and inferior Courts, shall hold their Offices during good Behaviour, and shall, at stated Times, receive for their Services, a Compensation, which shall not be diminished during their Continuance in Office.

Section 2

[1.] The judicial Power shall extend to all Cases, in Law and Equity, arising under this Constitution, the Laws of the United States, and Treaties made, or which shall be made, under their Authority;—to all Cases affecting Ambassadors, other public Ministers and Consuls;—to all Cases of admiralty and maritime Jurisdiction;—to Controversies to which the United States shall be a Party;—to Controversies between two or more States; —between a State and Citizens of another State;— between Citizens of different States,—between Citizens of the same State claiming Lands under Grants of different States, and between a State, or the Citizens thereof, and foreign States, Citizens or Subjects.

[2.] In all Cases affecting Ambassadors, other public Ministers and Consuls, and those in which a State shall be Party, the supreme Court shall have original Jurisdiction. In all the other Cases before mentioned, the supreme Court shall have appellate Jurisdiction, both as to Law and Fact, with such Exceptions, and under such Regulations as the Congress shall make.

EXTENDING THE CONTENT

Minorities and the Supreme Court The first African American Supreme Court justice, Thurgood Marshall, was named to the Court by President Lyndon Johnson in 1967. President Ronald Reagan nominated the first woman justice, Sandra Day O'Connor, in 1981.

[3.] The Trial of all Crimes, except in Cases of Impeachment, shall be by Jury; and such Trial shall be held in the State where the said Crimes shall have been committed; but when not committed within any State, the Trial shall be at such Place or Places as the Congress may by Law have directed.

Section 3
[1.] Treason against the United States, shall consist only in levying War against them, or in adhering to their Enemies, giving them Aid and Comfort. No Person shall be convicted of Treason unless on the Testimony of two Witnesses to the same overt Act, or on Confession in open Court.
[2.] The Congress shall have Power to declare the Punishment of Treason, but no Attainder of Treason shall work Corruption of Blood, or Forfeiture except during the Life of the Person attainted.

Article IV

Section 1
Full Faith and Credit shall be given in each State to the public Acts, Records, and judicial Proceedings of every other State. And the Congress may by general Laws prescribe the Manner in which such Acts, Records and Proceedings shall be proved, and the Effect thereof.

Section 2
[1.] The Citizens of each State shall be entitled to all Privileges and Immunities of Citizens in the several States.
[2.] A Person charged in any State with Treason, Felony, or other Crime, who shall flee from Justice, and be found in another State, shall on Demand of the executive Authority of the State from which he fled, be delivered up, to be removed to the State having Jurisdiction of the Crime.
[3.] No Person held to Service of Labour in one State, under the Laws thereof, escaping into another, shall, in Consequence of any Law or Regulation therein, be discharged from such Service or Labour, but shall be delivered up on Claim of the Party to whom such Service or Labour may be due.

Section 3
[1.] New States may be admitted by the Congress into this Union; but no new State shall be formed or erected within the Jurisdiction of any other State; nor any State be formed by the Junction of two or more States, or Parts of States, without the Consent of the Legislatures of the States concerned as well as of the Congress.
[2.] The Congress shall have Power to dispose of and make all needful Rules and Regulations respecting the Territory or other Property belonging to the United States; and nothing in this Constitution shall be so construed as to Prejudice any Claims of the United States, or of any particular State.

Section 2. Jurisdiction
Jury Trial Except in cases of impeachment, anyone accused of a crime has the right to a trial by jury. The trial must be held in the state where the crime was committed. Jury trial guarantees were strengthened in the Sixth, Seventh, Eighth, and Ninth Amendments.

Article IV. Relations Among the States

Article IV explains the relationship of the states to one another and to the national government. This article requires each state to give citizens of other states the same rights as its own citizens, addresses the admission of new states, and guarantees that the national government will protect the states.

Section 1. Official Acts
Recognition by States This provision ensures that each state recognizes the laws, court decisions, and records of all other states. For example, a marriage license issued by one state must be accepted by all states.

Vocabulary

treason: *violation of the allegiance owed by a person to his or her own country, for example, by aiding an enemy*

Section 3. New States and Territories
New States Congress has the power to admit new states. It also determines the basic guidelines for applying for statehood. Two states, Maine and West Virginia, were created within the boundaries of another state. In the case of West Virginia, President Lincoln recognized the West Virginia government as the legal government of Virginia during the Civil War. This allowed West Virginia to secede from Virginia without obtaining approval from the Virginia legislature.

TEACH

Analyzing Ideas Point out that federal judges are appointed for life and can be removed only by their death, resignation, or impeachment. Ask students why they think the Framers of the Constitution made judgeships lifetime appointments. *(The Framers believed that judges who felt secure in their positions would be more likely to make correct decisions, uninfluenced by public opinion.)* **L2**

Writing Reports Encourage students to listen to excerpts from "May It Please the Court," recordings of the Supreme Court in session. Have them write a brief report on the case or cases they listened to. **L2**

CURRICULUM CONNECTION

Civics The judiciary is only briefly described in the Constitution. The federal court system was established by the Judiciary Act of 1789.

CRITICAL THINKING ACTIVITY

Predicting Outcomes Have students discuss the pros and cons of federal judges being elected rather than appointed. Direct them to list the possible outcomes they foresee if the federal judiciary was subject to the electoral process. Encourage students to share and compare their lists. **L3**

United States Constitution

FOCUS

Inform students that one political scientist has called the supremacy clause (Article VI, Section 2) "the most important single provision of the Constitution." Ask students to think about why this might be so. *(This clause made it clear that the national Constitution and laws are supreme over state constitutions.)*

TEACH

Expressing Viewpoints Have students speculate about why the Framers of the Constitution established the amendment process as they did. *(The Framers wanted to make the Constitution flexible, but not so easy to amend that it would not be respected.)*

Ask: Should the amendment process be made easier? Why or why not?

Vocabulary

amendment: *a change to the Constitution*
ratification: *process by which an amendment is approved*

Article V. The Amendment Process

Article V explains how the Constitution can be amended, or changed. All of the 27 amendments were proposed by a two-thirds vote of both houses of Congress. Only the Twenty-first Amendment was ratified by constitutional conventions of the states. All other amendments have been ratified by state legislatures. *What is an amendment?*

Article VI. Constitutional Supremacy

Article VI contains the "supremacy clause." This clause establishes that the Constitution, laws passed by Congress, and treaties of the United States "shall be the supreme Law of the Land." The "supremacy clause" recognizes the Constitution and federal laws that conform to the Constitution as supreme when in conflict with those of the states.

Article VII. Ratification

Article VII addresses ratification and states that, unlike the Articles of Confederation, which required approval of all thirteen states for adoption, the Constitution would take effect after it was ratified by nine states.

Section 4
The United States shall guarantee to every State in this Union a Republican Form of Government, and shall protect each of them against Invasion; and on Application of the Legislature, or of the Executive (when the Legislature cannot be convened) against domestic Violence.

Article V

The Congress, whenever two thirds of both Houses shall deem it necessary, shall propose Amendments to this Constitution, or, on the Application of the Legislatures of two thirds of the several States, shall call a Convention for proposing Amendments, which, in either Case, shall be valid to all Intents and Purposes, as Part of this Constitution, when ratified by the Legislatures of three fourths of the several States, or by Conventions in three fourths thereof, as the one or the other Mode of Ratification may be proposed by the Congress; Provided that no Amendment which may be made prior to the Year One thousand eight hundred and eight shall in any Manner affect the first and fourth Clauses in the Ninth Section of the first Article; and that no State, without its Consent, shall be deprived of its equal Suffrage in the Senate.

Article VI

[1.] All Debts contracted and Engagements entered into, before the Adoption of this Constitution, shall be as valid against the United States under this Constitution, as under the Confederation.
[2.] This Constitution, and the Laws of the United States which shall be made in Pursuance thereof; and all Treaties made, or which shall be made, under the Authority of the United States, shall be the supreme Law of the Land; and the Judges in every State shall be bound thereby, any Thing in the Constitution or Laws of any State to the Contrary notwithstanding.
[3.] The Senators and Representatives before mentioned, and the Members of the several State Legislatures, and all executive and judicial Officers, both of the United States and of the several States, shall be bound by Oath or Affirmation, to support this Constitution; but no religious Test shall ever be required as a Qualification to any Office or public Trust under the United States.

Article VII

The Ratification of the Conventions of nine States, shall be sufficient for the Establishment of this Constitution between the States so ratifying the same.
Done in Convention by the Unanimous Consent of the States present the Seventeenth Day of September in the Year of our Lord one thousand seven hundred and Eighty seven and of the Independence of the United States of America the Twelfth. In witness whereof We have hereunto subscribed our Names,

---

COOPERATIVE LEARNING ACTIVITY

Writing Reports Organize students into four groups and assign to each group one of the four sections of Article 1 (sections 2, 3, 4, and 9) that has been modified by amendment. Have each group research how, why, and when the amendment to its assigned section was made. Encourage groups to present their findings to the rest of the class in brief written reports.

Use the rubric for a cooperative group management plan on pages 71–72 in the *Performance Assessment Activities and Rubrics.*

Signers

George Washington,
President and Deputy
from Virginia

New Hampshire
John Langdon
Nicholas Gilman

Massachusetts
Nathaniel Gorham
Rufus King

Connecticut
William Samuel Johnson
Roger Sherman

New York
Alexander Hamilton

New Jersey
William Livingston
David Brearley
William Paterson
Jonathan Dayton

Pennsylvania
Benjamin Franklin
Thomas Mifflin
Robert Morris
George Clymer
Thomas FitzSimons
Jared Ingersoll
James Wilson
Gouverneur Morris

Delaware
George Read
Gunning Bedford, Jr.
John Dickinson
Richard Bassett
Jacob Broom

Maryland
James McHenry
Daniel of St. Thomas
Jenifer
Daniel Carroll

Virginia
John Blair
James Madison, Jr.

North Carolina
William Blount
Richard Dobbs Spaight
Hugh Williamson

South Carolina
John Rutledge
Charles Cotesworth
Pinckney
Charles Pinckney
Pierce Butler

Georgia
William Few
Abraham Baldwin

Attest:
William Jackson,
Secretary

Amendment I

Congress shall make no law respecting an establishment of religion, or prohibiting the free exercise thereof; or abridging the freedom of speech, or of the press; or the right of the people peaceably to assemble, and to petition the Government for a redress of grievances.

Amendment II

A well regulated Militia, being necessary to the security of a free State, the right of the people to keep and bear Arms, shall not be infringed.

Amendment III

No Soldier shall, in time of peace be quartered in any house, without the consent of the Owner, nor in time of war, but in a manner to be prescribed by law.

Amendment IV

The right of the people to be secure in their persons, houses, papers, and effects, against unreasonable searches and seizures, shall not be violated, and no Warrants shall issue, but upon probable cause, supported by Oath or affirmation, and particularly describing the place to be searched, and the persons or things to be seized.

Amendment V

No person shall be held to answer for a capital, or otherwise infamous crime, unless on a presentment or indictment of a Grand Jury, except in cases arising in the

The Bill of Rights

The first 10 amendments are known as the Bill of Rights (1791). These amendments limit the powers of the federal government. The First Amendment protects the civil liberties of individuals in the United States. The amendment freedoms are not absolute, however. They are limited by the rights of other individuals. *What freedoms does the First Amendment protect?*

Amendment 2

Bearing Arms This amendment is often debated. Originally it was intended to prevent the national government from repeating the actions of the British, who tried to take weapons away from the colonial militia, or armed forces of citizens. This amendment seems to support the right of citizens to own firearms, but the Supreme Court has ruled that it does not prevent Congress from regulating the interstate sale of weapons.

Vocabulary

quarter: *to provide living accommodations*
warrant: *document that gives police particular rights or powers*
probable cause: *police must have a reasonable basis to believe a person is linked to a crime*

The Constitution Handbook **141**

FOCUS

TEACH

Writing Biographical Sketches
Ask students to research and write brief biographical sketches of one of the signers of the Constitution. Suggest that students focus on such factors as background, education, or family life, that might reveal the person's motivation in taking part in the Constitutional Convention.

Answer: freedom of religion, freedom of speech, freedom of the press, freedom to peaceably assemble, and freedom to petition the government for a redress of grievances

FYI

The first five states to ratify the Constitution—Delaware, Pennsylvania, New Jersey, Georgia, and Connecticut—did so quickly and by large majorities.

EXTENDING THE CONTENT

Signers of the Constitution Of the 55 delegates who attended the Constitutional Convention, only 38 signed the document. A thirty-ninth signature—that of John Dickinson—was written by George Read at Dickinson's request. Elbridge Gerry of Massachusetts and Edmund Randolph and George Mason of Virginia refused to sign, while 13 other delegates left the Convention early.

United States Constitution

Answer: The Grand Jury evaluates whether there is enough evidence to bring the accused person to trial.

Answer: The requirement of a "speedy" trial ensures that an accused person will not be held in jail for a lengthy period as a means of punishing the accused without a trial.

Researching the Constitution

Encourage volunteers to research the number of amendments to the California state constitution, a relatively easy constitution to amend. Have them report to the class, using California as an example of what happens when a constitution is easily amended. Encourage students to discuss whether they think the national Constitution would work better if it were easier to amend. **L3**

Amendment 5

Rights of the Accused This amendment contains important protections for people accused of crimes. One of the protections is that government may not deprive any person of life, liberty, or property without due process of law. This means that the government must follow proper constitutional procedures in trials and in other actions it takes against individuals. *According to Amendment V, what is the function of a grand jury?*

Amendment 6

Right to Speedy and Fair Trial A basic protection is the right to a speedy, public trial. The jury must hear witnesses and evidence on both sides before deciding the guilt or innocence of a person charged with a crime. This amendment also provides that legal counsel must be provided to a defendant. In 1963, in *Gideon* v. *Wainwright*, the Supreme Court ruled that if a defendant cannot afford a lawyer, the government must provide one to defend him or her. *Why is the right to a "speedy" trial important?*

Vocabulary

common law: *law established by previous court decisions*

bail: *money that an accused person provides to the court as a guarantee that he or she will be present for a trial*

Amendment 9

Powers Reserved to the People This amendment prevents government from claiming that the only rights people have are those listed in the Bill of Rights.

Amendment 10

Powers Reserved to the States This amendment protects the states and the people from the federal government. It establishes that powers not given to the national government and not denied to the states by the Constitution belong to the states or to the people. These are checks on the "necessary and proper" power of the federal government, which is provided for in Article I, Section 8, Clause 18.

Amendment 11

Suits Against States The Eleventh Amendment (1795) provides that a lawsuit brought by a citizen of the United States or a foreign nation against a state must be tried in a state court, not in a federal court. The Supreme Court had ruled in *Chisholm* v. *Georgia* (1793) that a federal court could try a lawsuit brought by citizens of South Carolina against a citizen of Georgia.

land or naval forces, or in the Militia, when in actual service in time of War or public danger; nor shall any person be subject for the same offence to be twice put in jeopardy of life or limb; nor shall be compelled in any criminal case to be a witness against himself, nor be deprived of life, liberty, or property, without due process of law; nor shall private property be taken for public use without just compensation.

Amendment VI

In all criminal prosecutions, the accused shall enjoy the right to a speedy and public trial, by an impartial jury of the State and district wherein the crime shall have been committed, which district shall have been previously ascertained by law, and to be informed of the nature and cause of the accusation; to be confronted with the witnesses against him; to have compulsory process for obtaining Witnesses in his favor, and to have the assistance of counsel for his defence.

Amendment VII

In Suits at common law, where the value in controversy shall exceed twenty dollars, the right of trial by jury shall be preserved, and no fact tried by a jury, shall be otherwise reexamined in any Court of the United States, than according to the rules of common law.

Amendment VIII

Excessive bail shall not be required, nor excessive fines imposed, nor cruel and unusual punishments inflicted.

Amendment IX

The enumeration in the Constitution, of certain rights, shall not be construed to deny or disparage others retained by the people.

Amendment X

The powers not delegated to the United States by the Constitution, nor prohibited by it to the States, are reserved to the States respectively, or to the people.

Amendment XI

The Judicial power of the United States shall not be construed to extend to any suit in law or equity, commenced or prosecuted against one of the United States by Citizens of another State, or by Citizens or Subjects of any Foreign State.

EXTENDING THE CONTENT

The Bill of Rights Critics of the Constitution felt that it did not go far enough in protecting individual rights and liberties. To answer these objections, supporters of the Constitution promised to introduce a series of amendments listing the rights of individuals. On June 8, 1789, James Madison kept this promise by proposing 12 amendments to the Constitution, 10 of which were adopted and are now known as the Bill of Rights. One amendment not adopted concerned pay raises for members of Congress. It eventually became part of the Constitution as the Twenty-seventh Amendment.

Amendment XII

The electors shall meet in their respective states and vote by ballot for President and Vice-President, one of whom, at least, shall not be an inhabitant of the same state with themselves; they shall name in their ballots the person voted for as President, and in distinct ballots the person voted for as Vice-President, and they shall make distinct lists of all persons voted for as President, and of all persons voted for as Vice-President, and of the number of votes for each, which lists they shall sign and certify, and transmit sealed to the seat of the government of the United States, directed to the President of the Senate;—The President of the Senate shall, in the presence of the Senate and House of Representatives, open all the certificates and the votes shall then be counted;—The person having the greatest number of votes for President, shall be the President, if such number be a majority of the whole number of Electors appointed; and if no person have such majority, then from the persons having the highest numbers not exceeding three on the list of those voted for as President, the House of Representatives shall choose immediately, by ballot, the President. But in choosing the President, the votes shall be taken by states, the representation from each state having one vote; a quorum for this purpose shall consist of a member or members from two-thirds of the states, and a majority of all the states shall be necessary to a choice. And if the House of Representatives shall not choose a President whenever the right of choice shall devolve upon them, before the fourth day of March next following, then the Vice-President shall act as President, as in the case of the death or other constitutional disability of the President. The person having the greatest number of votes as Vice-President, shall be the Vice-President, if such number be a majority of the whole number of Electors appointed, and if no person have a majority, then from the two highest numbers on the list, the Senate shall choose the Vice-President; a quorum for the purpose shall consist of two-thirds of the whole number of Senators, and a majority of the whole number shall be necessary to a choice. But no person constitutionally ineligible to the office of President shall be eligible to that of Vice-President of the United States.

Amendment XIII

Section 1

Neither slavery nor involuntary servitude, except as a punishment for crime whereof the party shall have been duly convicted, shall exist within the United States, or any place subject to their jurisdiction.

Amendment 12
Election of President and Vice President The Twelfth Amendment (1804) corrects a problem that had arisen in the method of electing the president and vice president, which is described in Article II, Section 1, Clause 3. This amendment provides for the Electoral College to use separate ballots in voting for president and vice president. *If no candidate receives a majority of the electoral votes, who elects the president?*

Answer: the House of Representatives

Vocabulary

majority: *more than half*

Amendment 13
Abolition of Slavery Amendments Thirteen (1865), Fourteen, and Fifteen often are called the Civil War amendments because they grew out of that conflict. The Thirteenth Amendment outlaws slavery.

The Constitution Handbook **143**

CURRICULUM CONNECTION

Civics Some lawyers maintain that the mass media threaten a defendant's Sixth Amendment rights. Extensive coverage of a crime on television and in the newspapers, these lawyers argue, makes it difficult to find jurors who are truly impartial.

Analyzing Ideas Ask students to identify areas of concern that they would like to see addressed by a constitutional amendment. Write suggestions on the board and have students discuss each in terms of the following questions: Why is an amendment needed? Would it be better for Congress to pass laws or the courts to establish precedents on this issue? **L2**

CRITICAL THINKING ACTIVITY

Expressing Problems Clearly point out that the Fifth Amendment protects the right of people charged with crimes to remain silent. In some countries, however, silence is equated with an admittance of guilt. Ask students to write a paragraph that supports or challenges the following statement: The Fifth Amendment is little more than a shield for the guilty. **L3**

United States Constitution

Identifying Alternatives Point out that the Electoral College has been criticized as being obsolete, and various reforms have been suggested for changing it or abolishing it altogether. Lead a discussion about the 2000 presidential election that continued the debate over the role of the Electoral College. Ask students to research, discuss, and assess alternatives to the Electoral College. **L2**

Names of Political Parties The nickname of the Republican Party is the GOP, which stands for the Grand Old Party. The term began to be used around the time of the 1880 Republican convention. Prime Minister William Gladstone of Great Britain was fondly referred to as the Grand Old Man, and some Republican admirers of the prime minister applied the same term of affection to their political party. Ironically, the Grand Old Party is several decades younger than the Democratic Party.

Answer: Former slaveholders could not collect compensation for the loss of their slaves.

Amendment 14
Rights of Citizens The Fourteenth Amendment (1868) originally was intended to protect the legal rights of the freed slaves. Its interpretation has been extended to protect the rights of citizenship in general by prohibiting a state from depriving any person of life, liberty, or property without "due process of law." In addition, it states that all citizens have the right to equal protection of the laws in all states.

Amendment 14. Section 2
Representation in Congress This section reduced the number of members a state had in the House of Representatives if it denied its citizens the right to vote. Later civil rights laws and the Twenty-fourth Amendment guaranteed the vote to African Americans.

Vocabulary

abridge: *to reduce*
insurrection: *rebellion against the government*

Amendment 14. Section 3
Penalty for Engaging in Insurrection The leaders of the Confederacy were barred from state or federal offices unless Congress agreed to remove this ban. By the end of Reconstruction, all but a few Confederate leaders were allowed to return to public service.

Amendment 14. Section 4
Public Debt The public debt acquired by the federal government during the Civil War was valid and could not be questioned by the South. However, the debts of the Confederacy were declared to be illegal. *Could former slaveholders collect payment for the loss of their slaves?*

Section 2
Congress shall have power to enforce this article by appropriate legislation.

Amendment XIV

Section 1
All persons born or naturalized in the United States, and subject to the jurisdiction thereof, are citizens of the United States and of the State wherein they reside. No State shall make or enforce any law which shall abridge the privileges or immunities of citizens of the United States; nor shall any State deprive any person of life, liberty, or property, without due process of law; nor deny to any person within its jurisdiction the equal protection of the laws.

Section 2
Representatives shall be apportioned among the several States according to their respective numbers, counting the whole number of persons in each State, excluding Indians not taxed. But when the right to vote at any election for the choice of electors for President and Vice-President of the United States, Representatives in Congress, the Executive and Judicial officers of a State, or the members of the Legislature thereof, is denied to any of the male inhabitants of such State, being twenty-one years of age, and citizens of the United States, or in any way abridged, except for participation in rebellion, or other crime, the basis of representation therein shall be reduced in the proportion which the number of such male citizens shall bear to the whole number of male citizens twenty-one years of age in such State.

Section 3
No person shall be a Senator or Representative in Congress, or elector of President and Vice-President, or hold any office, civil or military, under the United States, or under any State, who, having previously taken an oath, as a member of Congress, or as an officer of the United States, or as a member of any State legislature, or as an executive or judicial officer of any State, to support the Constitution of the United States, shall have engaged in insurrection or rebellion against the same, or given aid or comfort to the enemies thereof. But Congress may by a vote of two-thirds of each House, remove such disability.

Section 4
The validity of the public debt of the United States, authorized by law, including debts incurred for payment of pensions and bounties for service, in suppressing insurrection or rebellion, shall not be questioned. But neither the United States nor any State shall assume or pay any debt or obligation incurred in aid of insurrection or rebellion against the United States, or any

---

EXTENDING THE CONTENT

Racial Discrimination and the Constitution The Thirteenth, Fourteenth, and Fifteenth Amendments represent attempts to use the Constitution to end slavery, to extend citizenship to formerly enslaved persons, and to guarantee male African Americans the right to vote. Literacy tests, poll taxes, and grandfather clauses, however, continued to keep large numbers of African Americans from voting in many Southern states after Reconstruction.

claim for the loss or emancipation of any slave; but all such debts, obligations and claims shall be held illegal and void.

Section 5

The Congress shall have power to enforce, by appropriate legislation, the provisions of this article.

Amendment XV

Section 1

The right of citizens of the United States to vote shall not be denied or abridged by the United States or by any State on account of race, color, or previous condition of servitude.

Section 2

The Congress shall have power to enforce this article by appropriate legislation.

Amendment XVI

The Congress shall have power to lay and collect taxes on incomes, from whatever source derived, without apportionment among the several States and without regard to any census or enumeration.

Amendment XVII

Section 1

The Senate of the United States shall be composed of two Senators from each State, elected by the people thereof, for six years; and each Senator shall have one vote. The electors in each State shall have the qualifications requisite for electors of the most numerous branch of the State legislatures.

Section 2

When vacancies happen in the representation of any State in the Senate, the executive authority of such State shall issue writs of election to fill such vacancies: *Provided,* That the legislature of any State may empower the executive thereof to make temporary appointments until the people fill the vacancies by election as the legislature may direct.

Section 3

This amendment shall not be so construed as to affect the election or term of any Senator chosen before it becomes valid as part of the Constitution.

Amendment XVIII

Section 1

After one year from ratification of this article, the manufacture, sale, or transportation of intoxicating liquors within, the importation thereof into, or the

---

Amendment 15

Voting Rights The Fifteenth Amendment (1870) prohibits the government from denying a person's right to vote on the basis of race. Despite the law, many states denied African Americans the right to vote by such means as poll taxes, literacy tests, and white primaries.

Amendment 16

Income Tax The origins of the Sixteenth Amendment (1913) date back to 1895, when the Supreme Court declared a federal income tax unconstitutional. To overturn this decision, this amendment authorizes an income tax that is levied on a direct basis.

Amendment 17

Direct Election of Senators The Seventeenth Amendment (1913) states that the people, instead of state legislatures, elect United States senators. *How many years are in a Senate term?*

Vocabulary

apportionment: *distribution of seats in House based on population*
vacancy: *an office or position that is unfilled or unoccupied*

Amendment 18

Prohibition The Eighteenth Amendment (1919) prohibited the production, sale, or transportation of alcoholic beverages in the United States. Prohibition proved to be difficult to enforce. This amendment was later repealed by the Twenty-first Amendment.

Time Lines Have students make a time line that includes each of the amendments, the year of ratification, and significant concurrent political, economic, and social events. Encourage students to display and compare their time lines. **L2**

Answer: 6 years

CURRICULUM CONNECTION

Civics Section 1 of the Fourteenth Amendment sets out two of the three alternative requirements of American citizenship: birth on American soil and naturalization. The third possible requirement is birth to a parent who is an American citizen.

EXTENDING THE CONTENT

Due Process of Law References to due process of law are made in the Fifth and Fourteenth Amendments. As a result of Supreme Court rulings, two types of due process have developed. Procedural due process requires that the government use fair procedures in enforcing the law. Substantive due process requires that the laws under which the government acts be fair.

United States Constitution

exportation thereof from the United States and all territory subject to the jurisdiction thereof for beverage purposes is hereby prohibited.

Section 2
The Congress and the several States shall have concurrent power to enforce this article by appropriate legislation.

Section 3
This article shall be inoperative unless it shall have been ratified as an amendment to the Constitution by the legislatures of the several States, as provided in the Constitution, within seven years from the date of the submission hereof to the States by the Congress.

Making Reasoned Judgments
Inform students that, at times, the constitutional provisions protecting personal liberties have been tested. One such test occurred during World War II, when more than 100,000 Japanese Americans were put into relocation camps. Ask students: In times of crisis, is the government justified in suspending personal liberties? Why or why not? **L2**

Answer: January 20

FYI

Direct election of senators was one of the many political reforms advanced by the Progressive movement.

Amendment 19
Woman Suffrage The Nineteenth Amendment (1920) guaranteed women the right to vote. By then women had already won the right to vote in many state elections, but the amendment made their right to vote in all state and national elections constitutional.

Amendment 20
"Lame Duck" The Twentieth Amendment (1933) sets new dates for Congress to begin its term and for the inauguration of the president and vice president. Under the original Constitution, elected officials who retired or who had been defeated remained in office for several months. For the outgoing president, this period ran from November until March. Such outgoing officials, referred to as "lame ducks," could accomplish little. *What date was fixed as Inauguration Day?*

Amendment 20. Section 3
Succession of President and Vice President This section provides that if the president-elect dies before taking office, the vice president-elect becomes president.

Vocabulary

president-elect: *individual who is elected president but has not yet begun serving his or her term*

146   The Constitution Handbook

Amendment XIX

Section 1
The right of citizens of the United States to vote shall not be denied or abridged by the United States or by any state on account of sex.

Section 2
Congress shall have power by appropriate legislation to enforce the provisions of this article.

Amendment XX

Section 1
The terms of the President and Vice President shall end at noon on the 20th day of January, and the terms of the Senators and Representatives at noon on the 3rd day of January, of the years in which such terms would have ended if this article had not been ratified; and the terms of their successors shall then begin.

Section 2
The Congress shall assemble at least once in every year, and such meeting shall begin at noon on the 3rd day of January, unless they shall by law appoint a different day.

Section 3
If, at the time fixed for the beginning of the term of the President, the President elect shall have died, the Vice President elect shall become President. If a President shall not have been chosen before the time fixed for the beginning of his term, or if the President elect shall have failed to qualify, then the Vice President elect shall act as President until a President shall have qualified; and the Congress may by law provide for the case wherein neither a President elect nor a Vice President elect shall have qualified, declaring who shall then act as President, or the manner in which one who is to act shall be selected, and such person shall act accordingly until a President or Vice President shall have qualified.

EXTENDING THE CONTENT

The Poll Tax After the Civil War, poll taxes were levied in many Southern states. Although the poll tax kept many low-income white males from voting, its major purpose was to keep African Americans away from the polls. Not until the 1960s did Congress take firm action to enforce the Fifteenth Amendment to end this kind of racial discrimination.

Section 4

The Congress may by law provide for the case of the death of any of the persons from whom the House of Representatives may choose a President whenever the right of choice shall have devolved upon them, and for the case of the death of any of the persons from whom the Senate may choose a Vice President whenever the right of choice shall have devolved upon them.

Section 5

Sections 1 and 2 shall take effect on the 15th day of October following the ratification of this article.

Section 6

This article shall be inoperative unless it shall have been ratified as an amendment to the Constitution by the legislatures of three-fourths of the several States within seven years from the date of its submission.

Amendment XXI

Section 1

The eighteenth article of amendment to the Constitution of the United States is hereby repealed.

Section 2

The transportation or importation into any State, Territory, or possession of the United States for delivery or use therein of intoxicating liquors, in violation of the laws thereof, is hereby prohibited.

Section 3

This article shall be inoperative unless it shall have been ratified as an amendment to the Constitution by conventions in the several States, as provided in the Constitution, within seven years from the date of the submission hereof to the States by the Congress.

Amendment XXII

Section 1

No person shall be elected to the office of the President more than twice, and no person who had held the office of President, or acted as President, for more than two years of a term to which some other person was elected President shall be elected to the office of the President more than once. But this Article shall not apply to any person holding the office of President when this Article was proposed by the Congress, and shall not prevent any person who may be holding the office of President, or acting as President, during the term within which this Article becomes operative from holding the office of President or acting as President during the remainder of such term.

Amendment 21
Repeal of Prohibition The Twenty-first Amendment (1933) repeals the Eighteenth Amendment. It is the only amendment ever passed to overturn an earlier amendment. It is also the only amendment ratified by special state conventions instead of state legislatures.

Amendment 22
Presidential Term Limit The Twenty-second Amendment (1951) limits presidents to a maximum of two elected terms. The amendment wrote into the Constitution a custom started by George Washington. It was passed largely as a reaction to Franklin D. Roosevelt's election to four terms between 1933 and 1945. It also provides that anyone who succeeds to the presidency and serves for more than two years of the term may not be elected more than one more time.

Writing Reports Point out that a number of states preceded the national government in giving women the vote. Encourage students to research the fight for woman suffrage in these states. Ask them to present their findings in written reports. **L2**

CURRICULUM CONNECTION

Health Although Prohibition caused many problems, it did succeed in reducing the consumption of alcohol in the United States, thus decreasing the number of alcohol-related deaths and accidents.

The Constitution Handbook **147**

CRITICAL THINKING ACTIVITY

Analyzing Information Make sure students understand the "lame-duck" issue by reminding them that lame ducks are presidents and members of Congress waiting to leave office after retiring or failing to gain reelection. Since lame ducks often were members of the defeated party, they were in a position to affect legislation even though they no longer spoke for the majority of voters. Ask students to note how the Twentieth Amendment addressed this problem. *(It shortened the waiting period between Election Day and the beginning of a new term.)* **L1**

United States Constitution

Categorizing Information Have students categorize on a chart the amendments according to the following headings: *Personal Freedoms, Relations Among States, Process of Government,* and *Citizenship.* They should keep in mind the substance of the amendment and its effect on American life. Remind students that some amendments might fit in more than one category. **L1**

FYI

Gerald R. Ford became the thirty-eighth president of the United States in 1974. He was the only president who was not elected either president or vice president. He replaced Spiro T. Agnew when Agnew resigned as vice president, then replaced President Richard Nixon who resigned on August 9, 1974.

you don't say...

Incapacitated Presidents The United States has had a disabled president several times in its history. In the 1880s James Garfield remained bedridden for 79 days before dying from injuries sustained by an assassin's bullet. Woodrow Wilson had a stroke and was incapacitated for the last several months of his presidency.

Answer: the president pro tempore of the Senate (the vice president) and the Speaker of the House of Representatives

Vocabulary

District of Columbia: *site of nation's capital occupying an area between Maryland and Virginia*

Amendment 23
D.C. Electors The Twenty-third Amendment (1961) allows citizens living in Washington, D.C., to vote for president and vice president, a right previously denied residents of the nation's capital. The District of Columbia now has three presidential electors, the number to which it would be entitled if it were a state.

Amendment 24
Abolition of the Poll Tax The Twenty-fourth Amendment (1964) prohibits poll taxes in federal elections. Prior to the passage of this amendment, some states had used such taxes to keep low-income African Americans from voting. In 1966 the Supreme Court banned poll taxes in state elections as well.

Amendment 25
Presidential Disability and Succession The Twenty-fifth Amendment (1967) established a process for the vice president to take over leadership of the nation when a president is disabled. It also set procedures for filling a vacancy in the office of vice president.

This amendment was used in 1973, when Vice President Spiro Agnew resigned from office after being charged with accepting bribes. President Richard Nixon then appointed Gerald R. Ford as vice president in accordance with the provisions of the Twenty-fifth Amendment. A year later, President Nixon resigned during the Watergate scandal, and Ford became president. President Ford then had to fill the vice presidency, which he had left vacant upon assuming the presidency. He named Nelson A. Rockefeller as vice president. Thus individuals who had not been elected held both the presidency and the vice presidency. *Who does the president inform if he or she cannot carry out the duties of the office?*

Section 2
This article shall be inoperative unless it shall have been ratified as an amendment to the Constitution by the legislatures of three-fourths of the several States within seven years from the date of its submission to the States by the Congress.

Amendment XXIII
Section 1
The District constituting the seat of Government of the United States shall appoint in such manner as the Congress may direct:

A number of electors of President and Vice President equal to the whole number of Senators and Representatives in Congress to which the District would be entitled if it were a State, but in no event more than the least populous State; they shall be in addition to those appointed by the States, but they shall be considered, for the purposes of the election of President and Vice President, to be electors appointed by a State; and they shall meet in the District and perform such duties as provided by the twelfth article of amendment.

Section 2
The Congress shall have power to enforce this article by appropriate legislation.

Amendment XXIV
Section 1
The right of citizens of the United States to vote in any primary or other election for President or Vice President, for electors for President or Vice President, or for Senator or Representative in Congress, shall not be denied or abridged by the United States or any State by reason of failure to pay any poll tax or other tax.

Section 2
The Congress shall have power to enforce this article by appropriate legislation.

Amendment XXV
Section 1
In case of the removal of the President from office or his death or resignation, the Vice President shall become President.

Section 2
Whenever there is a vacancy in the office of the Vice President, the President shall nominate a Vice President who shall take the office upon confirmation by a majority vote of both Houses of Congress.

Section 3
Whenever the President transmits to the President pro tempore of the Senate and the Speaker of the House of

COOPERATIVE LEARNING ACTIVITY

Discussing a Concept Organize students into groups to present either the pros or cons of Prohibition. Give groups time to prepare their arguments and encourage group members to be responsible for different parts of the research. As each group presents its arguments, note major points on the chalkboard. When groups have presented their arguments, lead the class in a discussion of the following question: **Is Prohibition an issue that should have been addressed in a constitutional amendment? Why or why not?**

Use the rubric for a cooperative group management plan on pages 71–72 in the *Performance Assessment Activities and Rubrics.*

Representatives his written declaration that he is unable to discharge the powers and duties of his office, and until he transmits to them a written declaration to the contrary, such powers and duties shall be discharged by the Vice President as Acting President.

Section 4
Whenever the Vice President and a majority of either the principal officers of the executive departments or of such other body as Congress may by law provide, transmit to the President pro tempore of the Senate and the Speaker of the House of Representatives their written declaration that the President is unable to discharge the powers and duties of his office, the Vice President shall immediately assume the power and duties of the office of Acting President.

Thereafter, when the President transmits to the President pro tempore of the Senate and the Speaker of the House of Representatives his written declaration that no inability exists, he shall resume the powers and duties of his office unless the Vice President and a majority of either the principal officers of the executive department or of such other body as Congress may by law provide, transmit within four days to the President pro tempore of the Senate and the Speaker of the House of Representatives their written declaration that the President is unable to discharge the powers and duties of his office. Thereupon Congress shall decide the issue, assembling within forty-eight hours for that purpose if not in session. If the Congress, within twenty-one days after receipt of the latter written declaration, or, if Congress is not in session, within twenty-one days after Congress is required to assemble, determines by two-thirds vote of both Houses that the President is unable to discharge the powers and duties of his office, the Vice President shall continue to discharge the same as Acting President; otherwise, the President shall resume the power and duties of his office.

Amendment XXVI
Section 1
The right of citizens of the United States, who are eighteen years of age or older, to vote shall not be denied or abridged by the United States or by any State on account of age.

Section 2
The Congress shall have power to enforce this article by appropriate legislation.

Amendment XXVII
No law, varying the compensation for the services of Senators and Representatives, shall take effect, until an election of representatives shall have intervened.

Amendment 26
Voting Age of 18 The Twenty-sixth Amendment (1971) lowered the voting age in both federal and state elections to 18.

Amendment 27
Congressional Salary Restraints The Twenty-seventh Amendment (1992) makes congressional pay raises effective during the term following their passage. James Madison offered the amendment in 1789, but it was never adopted. In 1982 Gregory Watson, then a student at the University of Texas, discovered the forgotten amendment while doing research for a school paper. Watson made the amendment's passage his crusade.

The Constitution Handbook **149**

Expressing Viewpoints Write the following statement on the board: "That the people of Washington, D.C., have no representation in Congress is a violation of their democratic rights." Call on volunteers to express their views on this statement. **L2**

you don't say...

The Twenty-sixth Amendment Many people used the Vietnam War to justify the adoption of the Twenty-sixth Amendment. These people argued that those old enough to fight and die for their country were also old enough to vote.

CURRICULUM CONNECTION

Geography Why do states such as Maine and Minnesota consistently turn out 60 percent of their voters in presidential elections when the national average is about 50 percent? Some states make it easy for voters to get on the election rolls. Maine, Minnesota, and Wisconsin permit registration at the voting place on Election Day. North Dakota permits citizens to vote without registering.

CRITICAL THINKING ACTIVITY

Evaluating Information Have students list the advantages and disadvantages of the two-term limit for presidents. Ask volunteers to present and defend their lists. Then have students discuss the following: Should there be presidential term limits? If so, how many terms should the president be limited to? Should members of Congress have term limits? Why or why not? **L2**

Chapter 4 Resources

TeacherWorks™ All-In-One Planner and Resource Center

- **Interactive Teacher Edition** Access your Teacher Wraparound Edition and your classroom resources with a few easy clicks.
- **Interactive Lesson Planner** Planning has never been easier! Organize your week, month, semester, or year with all the lesson helps you need to make teaching creative, timely, and relevant.

Use Glencoe's **Presentation Plus!** multimedia teacher tool to easily present dynamic lessons that visually excite your students. Using Microsoft PowerPoint® you can customize the presentations to create your own personalized lessons.

TEACHING TRANSPARENCIES

Graphic Organizer 4 L2

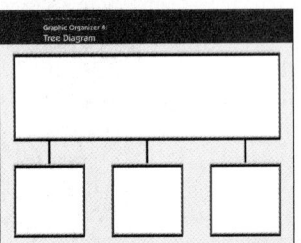

Why It Matters Chapter Transparency 4 L2

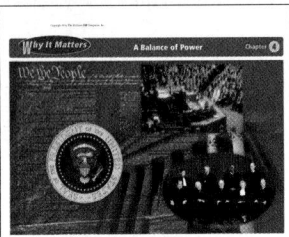

APPLICATION AND ENRICHMENT

Linking Past and Present Activity 4 L2

Enrichment Activity 4 L3

Primary Source Reading 4 L2

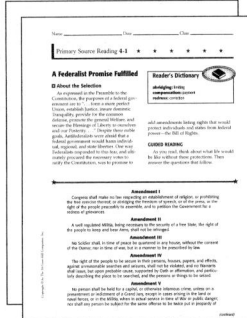

REVIEW AND REINFORCEMENT

Reteaching Activity 4 L1

Vocabulary Activity 4 L1

Time Line Activity 4 L2

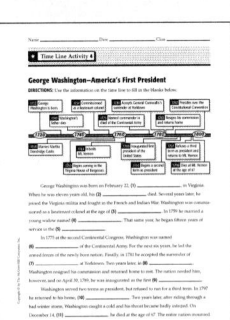

Critical Thinking Skills Activity 4 L2

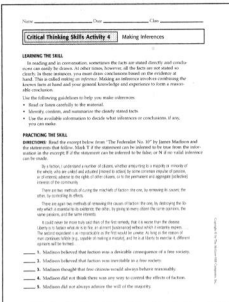

🌐 Meeting NCSS Standards

Local Standards

The following standards are covered in Chapter 4:

Section 1	IX	Global Connections: A, B, E
Section 2	VI	Power, Authority, and Governance: B, C, E
Section 3	II	Time, Continuity, and Change: C

Chapter 4 Resources

ASSESSMENT AND EVALUATION

Chapter 4 Test Form A L2

Chapter 4 Test Form B L2

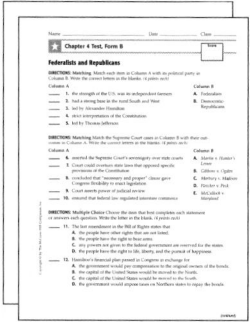

Standardized Test Practice Workbook Activity 4 L2

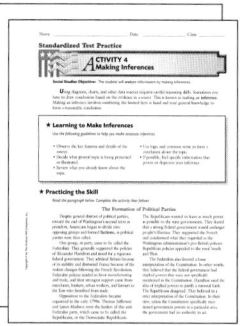

Performance Assessment Activities and Rubrics 4 L1/ELL

ExamView® Pro Testmaker CD-ROM

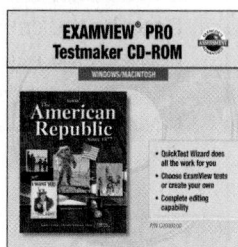

MULTIMEDIA

- Vocabulary PuzzleMaker CD-ROM
- Interactive Tutor Self-Assessment CD-ROM
- ExamView® Pro Testmaker CD-ROM
- Audio Program
- American History Primary Source Documents Library CD-ROM
- MindJogger Videoquiz
- Presentation Plus! CD-ROM
- TeacherWorks™ CD-ROM
- Interactive Student Edition CD-ROM
- Glencoe Skillbuilder Interactive Workbook CD-ROM, Level 2
- The *American Republic Since 1877* Video Program
- American Music: Hits Through History
- American Music: Cultural Traditions

SPANISH RESOURCES

The following Spanish language materials are available:

- Spanish Reading Essentials and Study Guide
- Spanish Guided Reading Activities
- Spanish Reteaching Activities
- Spanish Quizzes and Tests
- Spanish Vocabulary Activities
- Spanish Summaries
- The Declaration of Independence and United States Constitution Spanish Translation

THE HISTORY CHANNEL®

The following videotape programs are available from Glencoe as supplements to Chapter 4:

- **Thomas Jefferson: Philosopher of Freedom** (ISBN 1-56-501806-0)
- **Lewis and Clark** (ISBN 1-56-501592-4)

To order, call Glencoe at 1-800-334-7344. To find classroom resources to accompany many of these videos, check the following home pages:
A&E Television: www.aande.com
The History Channel: www.historychannel.com

HISTORY Online

Use our Web site for additional resources. All essential content is covered in the Student Edition.

You and your students can visit tarvol2.glencoe.com, the Web site companion to the *American Republic Since 1877.* This innovative integration of electronic and print media offers your students a wealth of opportunities. The student text directs students to the Web site for the following options:

- **Chapter Overviews**
- **Self-Check Quizzes**
- **Student Web Activities**
- **Textbook Updates**

Answers to the student Web activities are provided for you in the **Web Activity Lesson Plans.** Additional Web resources and Interactive Tutor Puzzles are also available.

Chapter 4 Resources

SECTION RESOURCES

Daily Objectives	Reproducible Resources	Multimedia Resources
SECTION 1 **The Federalist Era** 1. Describe the growing divisions between the nation's political parties. 2. Discuss the major foreign policy developments during the Washington and Adams administrations.	Reproducible Lesson Plan 4–1 Daily Lecture and Discussion Notes 4–1 Guided Reading Activity 4–1* Section Quiz 4–1* Reading Essentials and Study Guide 4–1* Performance Assessment Activities and Rubrics	Daily Focus Skills Transparency 4–1 Interactive Tutor Self-Assessment CD-ROM ExamView® Pro Testmaker CD-ROM* Presentation Plus! CD-ROM Skillbuilder Interactive Workbook, Level 2 TeacherWorks™ CD-ROM Audio Program
SECTION 2 **The Republicans Take Power** 1. Summarize the changes Thomas Jefferson brought to the federal government. 2. Describe the causes and the outcome of the War of 1812.	Reproducible Lesson Plan 4–2 Daily Lecture and Discussion Notes 4–2 Guided Reading Activity 4–2* Section Quiz 4–2* Reading Essentials and Study Guide 4–2* Performance Assessment Activities and Rubrics Interpreting Political Cartoons Supreme Court Case Studies	Daily Focus Skills Transparency 4–2 American Art & Architecture Interactive Tutor Self-Assessment CD-ROM ExamView® Pro Testmaker CD-ROM* Presentation Plus! CD-ROM TeacherWorks™ CD-ROM Audio Program
SECTION 3 **The Growth of American Nationalism** 1. Analyze how John Marshall strengthened the Supreme Court. 2. Evaluate how nationalism affected American foreign policy after the War of 1812.	Reproducible Lesson Plan 4–3 Daily Lecture and Discussion Notes 4–3 Guided Reading Activity 4–3* Section Quiz 4–3* Reading Essentials and Study Guide 4–3* Performance Assessment Activities and Rubrics Supreme Court Case Studies	Daily Focus Skills Transparency 4–3 Interactive Tutor Self-Assessment CD-ROM ExamView® Pro Testmaker CD-ROM* Presentation Plus! CD-ROM TeacherWorks™ CD-ROM Vocabulary PuzzleMaker CD-ROM Audio Program American Music: Hits Through History

`0:00` **OUT OF TIME?**
Assign the Chapter 4 **Reading Essentials and Study Guide.**

*Also Available in Spanish

 Printed Materials   Transparency   CD-ROM   DVD

Poster   Music Program   Audio Program

NATIONAL GEOGRAPHIC
Teacher's Corner

INDEX TO NATIONAL GEOGRAPHIC MAGAZINE

The following articles relate to this chapter.

- "Ghost Ships from the War of 1812: Hamilton and Scourge," March 1983
- "L'Enfant's Washington," August 1991
- "Lewis and Clark," October 1998
- "Old Ironsides," June 1997

NATIONAL GEOGRAPHIC SOCIETY PRODUCTS

To order the following, call National Geographic at 1-800-368-2728:

- *1600 Pennsylvania Avenue: The White House* (Book and Video Set)
- *Wall Maps: Laminated North America Political*
- *Washington, DC* (Video)

NGS ONLINE

Access National Geographic's Web site for current events, atlas updates, activities, links, interactive features, and archives.

www.nationalgeographic.com

MEETING SPECIAL NEEDS

In addition to the Differentiated Instruction strategies found in each section, the following resources are also suitable for your special needs students:

- *ExamView® Pro Testmaker CD-ROM* allows teachers to tailor tests by reducing answer choices.
- The *Audio Program* includes the entire narrative of the student edition so that less-proficient readers can listen to the words as they read them.
- The *Reading Essentials and Study Guide* provides the same content as the student edition but is written two grade levels below the textbook.

KEY TO ABILITY LEVELS

Teaching strategies have been coded.

- **L1** BASIC activities for all students
- **L2** AVERAGE activities for average to above-average students
- **L3** CHALLENGING activities for above-average students
- **ELL** ENGLISH LANGUAGE LEARNER activities

From the Classroom of...

Vince Pompo
Vernon Verona Sherrill
High School
Verona, NY

Influence of the American Revolution on the French Revolution: A Slideshow

This activity requires students to create a PowerPoint® slideshow that demonstrates the connection between the American and French Revolutions. The students must draw upon information from several primary sources and insert images taken from clip art, the Internet, or scanned pictures. Students can also create and insert charts, graphs, and tables.

I give them the following outline as a guide:

- 1st slide: Title slide
- 5–8 slides on causes of the French Revolution
- 4–6 slides on influence of American Revolution
- 2–4 slides on similarities and differences between revolutions
- Last slide: Summary

As a way to recognize exemplary work, I award prizes for Most Accurate Slide Show, Best Use of Images, and Most Original Design.

ADDITIONAL RESOURCES FROM GLENCOE

- American Music: Cultural Traditions
- American Art & Architecture
- Outline Map Resource Book
- U.S. Desk Map
- Building Geography Skills for Life
- Inclusion for the High School Social Studies Classroom Strategies and Activities
- Teaching Strategies for the American History Classroom (Including Block Scheduling Pacing Guides)
- Dinah Zike's High School American History Reading and Study Skills Foldables

Block Schedule

Activities that are suited to use within the block scheduling framework are identified by:

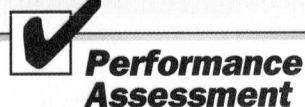

Performance Assessment

Refer to Activity 4 in the Performance Assessment Activities and Rubrics booklet.

Why It Matters Activity

Have students look at the time line on pages 150 and 151 and choose the event that they think is most significant. Students should evaluate their answers after they have completed the chapter.

GLENCOE
TECHNOLOGY

The *American Republic Since 1877* Video Program

To learn more about America from 1789 to 1820, have students view the Chapter 4 video, "Federalists and Republicans," from the *American Republic Since 1877* Video Program.

MindJogger Videoquiz

Use the **MindJogger Videoquiz** to preview Chapter 4 content.

 Both programs available in DVD

4 Federalists and Republicans *1789–1820*

Why It Matters

In the nation's new constitutional government, important new institutions included the cabinet, a system of federal courts, and a national bank. Political parties gradually developed from the different views of citizens in the Northeast, South, and West. The new government faced special challenges in foreign affairs, including the War of 1812 with Great Britain. After the war, a spirit of nationalism took hold in American society. A new national bank was chartered, and Supreme Court decisions strengthened the power of the federal government.

The Impact Today

Policies and attitudes that developed at this time have helped shape the nation.
- *Important precedents were set for the relations between the federal and state governments.*
- *Washington's caution against foreign involvement has powerfully influenced American foreign policy.*
- *Many Americans have a strong sense of national loyalty.*

The American Republic Since 1877 *Video*
The Chapter 4 video, "The Battle of New Orleans," chronicles the events of this pivotal battle of the War of 1812.

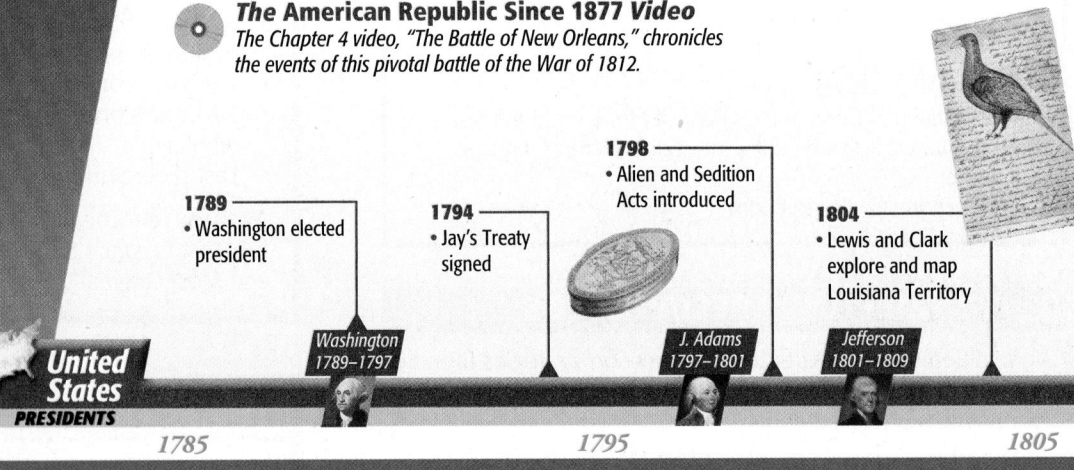

1789
- Washington elected president

1794
- Jay's Treaty signed

1798
- Alien and Sedition Acts introduced

1804
- Lewis and Clark explore and map Louisiana Territory

Washington 1789–1797
J. Adams 1797–1801
Jefferson 1801–1809

United States
PRESIDENTS

1785   *1795*   *1805*

World

1793
- Louis XVI guillotined during French Revolution

1794
- Polish rebellion suppressed by Russians

1799
- Beethoven writes Symphony no. 1

1805
- British navy wins Battle of Trafalgar

150

Reading Strategy | PURPOSE FOR READING

K-W-L Chart Students can use this tool to determine their background knowledge and generate interest before, during, and after studying a section or chapter. Ask students to share what they **K**now about the first four presidents of the United States. Four students, one for each president, should record the answers using markers on large sheets of paper that can be displayed in the classroom. Then ask students to determine what else they **W**ant to learn about these presidents. Finally, as they read, have students add to the lists what they **L**earn. **L1**

Refer to *Inclusion for the High School Social Studies Classroom Strategies and Activities* in the TCR.

Painter and President by J.L.G. Ferris

1808
• Congress bans international slave trade

1811
• Battle of Tippecanoe fought against Tecumseh's Shawnee confederacy

1812
• United States declares war on Great Britain

1819
• Spain cedes Florida to the United States; Supreme Court decides *McCulloch* v. *Maryland* case

1823
• Monroe Doctrine declared

Madison 1809–1817

Monroe 1817–1825

1815

1825

1812
• Napoleon's invasion and retreat from Russia

1815
• Napoleon defeated at the Battle of Waterloo

1821
• Mexico achieves independence from Spain
• Greek independence declared

HISTORY Online

Chapter Overview
Visit the *American Republic Since 1877* Web site at tarvol2.glencoe.com and click on *Chapter Overviews—Chapter 4* to preview chapter information.

151

More About the Art

Images of George Washington abound. Early paintings and sculptures tended to make him a regal, unapproachable figure. As time progressed, his image was used commercially and by the mid-1800s, artists had made Washington a more human figure. Artists in the late 1800s and early 1900s returned Washington to a lofty pedestal during the Colonial Revival Movement. Artists included in the Colonial Revival Movement include J.L.G. Ferris (1863–1930), Norman Rockwell, and N.C. Wyeth.

TIME LINE ACTIVITY

Have students select an event from the time lines on pages 150–151, 152, 161, and 170. Ask students to read the corresponding portion of the chapter to identify the cause(s) and effect(s) of the events. Students should then create a new time line to reflect six events they view as most important.

FOLDABLES
Study Organizer

Dinah Zike's Foldables are three-dimensional, interactive graphic organizers that help students practice basic writing skills, review key vocabulary terms, and identify main ideas. Have students complete the foldable activity in the *Dinah Zike's Reading and Study Skills Foldables* booklet.

GRAPHIC ORGANIZER ACTIVITY

Organizing Information Have students create a graphic organizer similar to the one shown below to explain strategies employed by the United States and Britain during the War of 1812. *(A. Invade Canada. B. Raid coastal cities. C. Isolate New England. D. Seize New Orleans)*

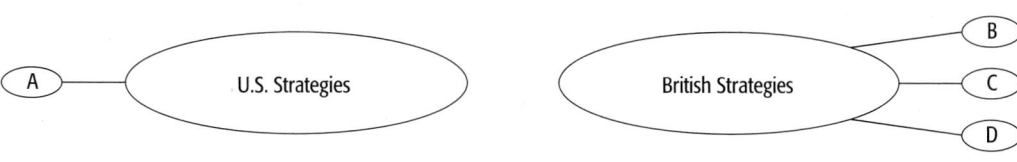

A — U.S. Strategies

British Strategies — B, C, D

151

1 FOCUS

Section Overview

This section focuses on the economic, political, and foreign policy challenges faced by Washington and Adams.

BELLRINGER
Skillbuilder Activity

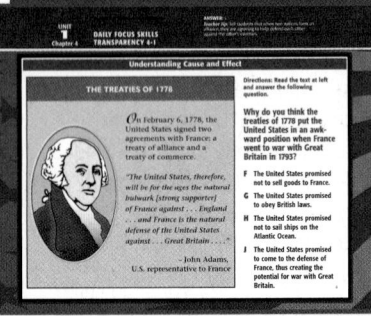

Project transparency and have students answer the question.

Daily Focus Skills Transparency 4–1

Reading Preview

Answers to Graphic: Tasks of Congress: organized government by creating departments; organized judicial branch, adopted the Bill of Rights; financed government by imposing tariff and tonnage; created national bank; accepted debt of Confederation Congress at face value to establish ability to borrow money

Preteaching Vocabulary
Have students skim Section 1 to glean the meaning or significance of each of the Key Terms and Names.

SECTION 1 The Federalist Era

Guide to Reading

Main Idea
President Washington had to tackle economic and foreign policy challenges. President Adams continued to guide the country through troubled times.

Key Terms and Names
cabinet, enumerated powers, implied powers, excise tax, most-favored nation, XYZ Affair, alien, interposition, nullification

Reading Strategy
Organizing As you read about how the United States established a central government, complete a graphic organizer similar to the one below by indicating the tasks completed by Congress.

Tasks of Congress

Reading Objectives
• **Describe** the growing divisions between the nation's political parties.
• **Discuss** the major foreign policy developments during the Washington and Adams administrations.

Section Theme
Global Connections The United States settled its differences with Britain and Spain but then faced the threat of war with France.

Preview of Events

♦1790	♦1794	♦1798	♦1802
1789 Washington elected president	**1794** Whiskey Rebellion quelled	**1798** XYZ Affair; Alien and Sedition Acts passed	**1800** Convention of 1800 ends Quasi-War

---

★ An American Story ★

George Washington

On April 6, 1789, the ballots of the presidential electors were officially counted in the new United States Senate. As expected, George Washington became the first president of the United States under the new Constitution. Americans everywhere greeted the news with great joy, but Washington remained unexcited. Calling his election "the event which I have long dreaded," Washington described his feelings as "not unlike those of a culprit who is going to the place of his execution."

Although Washington had high hopes for the new Constitution, he did not know if it would work as intended. "I am . . . [bringing] the voice of the people and a good name of my own on this voyage; but what returns will be made of them, Heaven alone can foretell." Despite his doubts and frustrations with the "ten thousand embarrassments, perplexities and troubles of the presidency," the new president retained his faith in the American people. He explained that "nothing but harmony, honesty, industry and frugality are necessary to make us a great and happy people. . . . We are surrounded by the blessings of nature."

—adapted from *Washington: The Indispensable Man*

Creating a New Government

When Washington and the newly elected Congress took office, one of the first tasks they faced was organizing the government itself. In the summer of 1789, Congress created three executive departments: the Department of State, which focused on foreign affairs, the Department of the Treasury, and the Department of War. Congress also created the Office of the Attorney General to advise the government on legal matters.

152 CHAPTER 4 Federalists and Republicans

SECTION RESOURCES

📂 Reproducible Masters
• Reproducible Lesson Plan 4–1
• Daily Lecture and Discussion Notes 4–1
• Guided Reading Activity 4–1
• Section Quiz 4–1
• Reading Essentials and Study Guide 4–1
• Performance Assessment Activities and Rubrics

📽 Transparencies
• Daily Focus Skills Transparency 4–1

Multimedia
⊙ Interactive Tutor Self-Assessment CD-ROM
⊙ ExamView® Pro Testmaker CD-ROM
⊙ Presentation Plus! CD-ROM
⊙ TeacherWorks™ CD-ROM
⊙ Audio Program

To head these departments, Washington wanted men who were "disposed to measure matters on a Continental Scale" instead of thinking about their own states. He chose Thomas Jefferson to serve as secretary of state, Alexander Hamilton to lead the Treasury Department, General Henry Knox as secretary of war, and Edmund Randolph as attorney general. During his presidency, Washington regularly met with these officials. Over time, the department heads came to be known as the cabinet, a group of advisers to the president.

In addition to creating the executive departments, Congress also organized the judicial branch. The **Judiciary Act of 1789** established 13 federal district courts and three circuit courts of appeal. Washington, with the consent of the Senate, then selected the first federal judges. The Judiciary Act also stated that the Supreme Court would have six justices, and Washington chose John Jay as the first chief justice of the United States.

One of the most important acts of Congress during its first session in 1789 was passing the **Bill of Rights.** During the campaign to ratify the Constitution, the Federalists had promised on several occasions to add a bill detailing the rights of American citizens. James Madison, who emerged as one of the key leaders in Congress, made the passage of such a bill top priority. He hoped it would demonstrate the good faith of federal leaders and build support for the new government.

In late September 1789, after many debates, Congress sent 12 constitutional amendments to the states for ratification. Ten were approved and went into effect in 1791. They are generally referred to as the Bill of Rights, although only the first eight offer safeguards to protect the rights of individuals against the government. The Ninth Amendment states that the people have other rights that are not listed in the Constitution. The Tenth Amendment states that any powers not specifically given to the federal government are reserved for the states. At the time, Madison tried to word the Bill of Rights to apply to the state governments as well, but Congress rejected that idea. Not until after the adoption of the Fourteenth Amendment after the Civil War would the Supreme Court begin to apply the Bill of Rights to the states.

✓ **Reading Check** **Identifying** What executive departments did Congress establish?

Hamilton's Financial Program

By the end of 1789, the new federal government was up and running. Now its most pressing concerns were economic.

ECONOMICS

Repaying the National Debt The federal government had inherited a huge debt from the Continental Congress. To fund the Revolutionary War, the Congress had issued bonds—paper notes promising to repay money after a certain length of time. By 1789 the new United States owed roughly $40 million to American citizens and another $11.7 million to France, Spain, and the Netherlands.

Alexander Hamilton believed the only way for the new federal government to establish its credit was to make good on these debts. If it called in the old bonds and exchanged them at full value for new, interest-bearing ones, then the wealthy creditors, bankers,

Picturing **History**

New Government The cabinet and the Congress, which met in New York's Federal Hall (left), included some of the new elements of Washington's first administration. What departments did the four cabinet members head?

2 TEACH

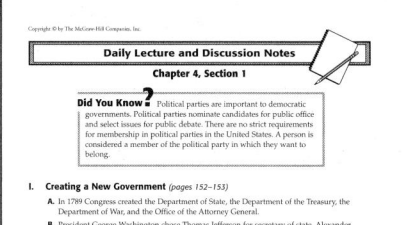

Daily Lecture and Discussion Notes 4–1

Copyright © by The McGraw-Hill Companies, Inc.

Daily Lecture and Discussion Notes
Chapter 4, Section 1

Did You Know? Political parties are important to democratic governments. Political parties nominate candidates for public office and select issues for public debate. There are no strict requirements for membership in political parties in the United States. A person is considered a member of the political party in which they want to belong.

I. Creating a New Government (pages 152–153)
   A. In 1789 Congress created the Department of State, the Department of the Treasury, the Department of War, and the Office of the Attorney General.
   B. President George Washington chose Thomas Jefferson for secretary of state, Alexander

✓ **Reading Check**

Answer: Department of State, Department of the Treasury, Department of War, Office of the Attorney General

FYI

Of the 12 amendments Congress sent to the states, the first 2 were not ratified. The first proposed amendment outlined a plan for proportional representation for the House of Representatives. The second proposed amendment dealt with compensation for senators and representatives. Amendments 3 through 12 were renumbered 1 through 10.

Picturing **History**

Answer: Thomas Jefferson, Secretary of State; Alexander Hamilton, Secretary of the Treasury; General Henry Knox, Secretary of War; Edmund Randolph, Attorney General
Ask: Why was Thomas Jefferson a logical choice for Secretary of State? (He had represented the nation in France after the War for Independence.)

COOPERATIVE LEARNING ACTIVITY

Preparing an Oral Presentation Organize the class into 10 groups. Assign each group one of the amendments included in the Bill of Rights. Have each group research their amendment and create an oral presentation answering the following question: Why was this amendment important to citizens of the United States in 1789?

Use the rubric for a cooperative group management plan on pages 71–72 in the *Performance Assessment Activities and Rubrics.*

Guided Reading Activity 4–1

Name _____ Date _____ Class _____

★ **Guided Reading Activity 4-1**

DIRECTIONS: Outlining Read the section and complete the outline below. Refer to your text-book to fill in the blanks.

I. Creating a New Government

  A. One of the first tasks George Washington and the new Congress faced was organizing the _____

  B. _____ was chosen as the first secretary of state.

  C. The _____ states that the people have other rights than those listed in the Constitution.

II. Hamilton's Financial Program

  A. The federal government had inherited _____ from the Confederation Congress.

  B. Alexander Hamilton asked Congress to create a _____ to manage the country's debt _____

Writing a Job Description Have students write a job description for the position of President of the United States in 1789. The job descriptions should include a list of duties and qualifications. Encourage students to use help wanted ads in local newspapers or on the Internet as references. **L2**

History *Through Art*

Answer: the high excise tax imposed on whiskey

Ask: What artistic device does the illustration use to show the importance of George Washington? *(places him in foreground and riding a horse; he appears to tower over the troops in the background)*

The founding of the Bank of the United States did not end the controversy surrounding the national bank issue. In 1811 its 20-year charter was not renewed.

---

and merchants who held the bonds would have a stake in the federal government's success. In his First Report on Public Credit, issued in January 1790, Hamilton proposed funding the Confederation's debts in this way. He also proposed that the federal government take over the states' debts from the war.

Led by Madison, critics attacked Hamilton's proposals. During the 1780s, many original bond purchasers such as farmers and Revolutionary War veterans had been forced to sell their bonds at a discount to speculators, people willing to take a business risk in hopes of financial gain in the future. Madison was outraged that Northern speculators who had paid as little as $10 for a $100 bond would now receive full value, while the original buyers received nothing. Furthermore, Northerners now owned roughly 80 percent of the bonds, but much of the tax money that would be used to pay off the bonds would come from the South.

Madison objected to taking over state debts for similar reasons. Most Southern states had already paid their debts. They did not want their taxes used to pay the debts of the Northern states.

The congressional debate over Hamilton's proposals raged for months. Finally, in July 1790, Hamilton struck a deal with Madison and Jefferson. The latter two would use their influence to convince Southerners in Congress to vote for Hamilton's plan. In return, the capital of the United States

History *Through Art*

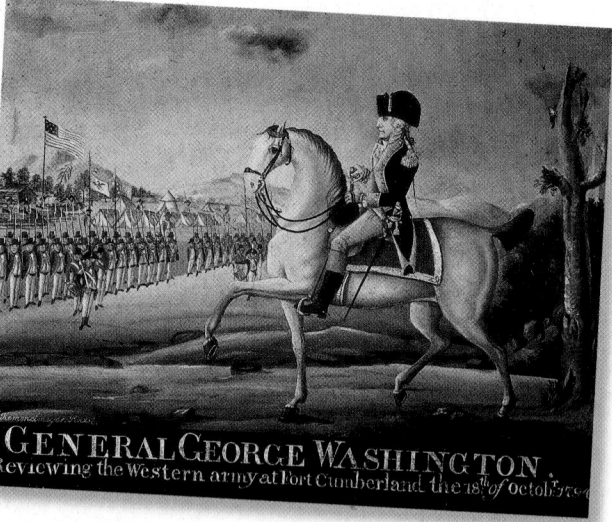

Commander in Chief This illustration shows the president reviewing troops at the time of the Whiskey Rebellion. What triggered the rebellion?

GENERAL GEORGE WASHINGTON, Reviewing the Western army at Fort Cumberland the 18th of October 1794

would eventually be moved from New York to a location along the Potomac River. Southerners believed that having the capital in the South would help to offset the strength of the Northern states in Congress. To get the last few votes he needed, Hamilton also agreed that the federal government would compensate the states that had already paid off their debts.

The Bank of the United States With his system of public credit finally in place, Hamilton asked Congress to create a national bank to manage the country's debts and interest payments. Under Hamilton's plan, the **Bank of the United States** would also have the power to make loans to the government and to private individuals. Most importantly, the bank would be allowed to issue paper money, providing a national currency that would stimulate trade, investment, and economic growth.

Hamilton's proposal for a national bank immediately encountered opposition. Southerners pointed out that Northern merchants would own most of the bank's stock because only they could afford it. At the same time, Madison argued that Congress had no power to establish a bank because that was not among its enumerated powers, or powers specifically mentioned in the Constitution.

Despite Madison's objections, Congress passed the bank bill and sent it to the president. Unsure whether to sign or veto the bill, Washington consulted Attorney General Randolph and Secretary of State Jefferson. Both opposed the bill, arguing that the Constitution did not authorize the government to create a bank. Washington then asked Hamilton for his opinion.

Hamilton pointed out that Article I, Section 8, of the Constitution gave the federal government the power "to make all laws which shall be necessary and proper" to execute its responsibilities. The "necessary and proper" clause created implied powers—powers not explicitly listed in the Constitution but necessary for the government to do its job. A national bank, Hamilton argued, was necessary to collect taxes, regulate trade, and provide for the common defense. Jefferson agreed the implied powers existed, but he believed "necessary and proper" meant absolutely necessary and not simply convenient. Hamilton's logic persuaded Washington to sign the bill. In 1791 the Bank of the United States was established for a 20-year period.

DIFFERENTIATED INSTRUCTION

Visual/Spatial Have students create a political cartoon that either supports or opposes the Bank of the United States. Encourage students to look at styles of political cartoons from the era and to use the types of tools that a satirist of the era may have used. Have students display their cartoons around the class. **L2**

☞ Refer to *Inclusion for the High School Social Studies Classroom Strategies and Activities* in the TCR.

The Whiskey Rebellion Hamilton believed the federal government also had to establish its right to impose direct taxes on the people. In his Second Report on Public Credit, issued in December 1790, Hamilton proposed an excise tax on American whiskey. An excise tax is a tax paid by the manufacturer of a product and passed on to those who buy the product. The sales tax many Americans pay today is an example of an excise tax.

In 1791 Congress approved Hamilton's proposal and enacted a high excise tax (about 25 percent) on whiskey. The tax hit Western farmers hard. Whiskey was used as a medium of exchange in the West, where bank notes and coins were not available in large quantities.

Complaints against the whiskey tax began in 1791, but it was not until the summer of 1794 that rebellion erupted. Farmers in western Pennsylvania began terrorizing tax collectors, robbing the mail, and destroying the whiskey-making stills of those who paid the tax. Determined to uphold federal authority to impose taxes, President Washington sent nearly 13,000 troops to crush the **Whiskey Rebellion.** The huge army caused the rebels to disperse without a fight.

✓ **Reading Check** **Explaining** Why did Alexander Hamilton propose an excise tax on American whiskey?

The Rise of Political Parties

During Washington's first term in office, disagreement over Hamilton's financial program had split Congress into factions. These factions became the nation's first political parties. Hamilton's supporters called themselves Federalists. Their opponents, led by Madison and Jefferson, took the name Democratic-Republicans. They were commonly referred to as Republicans. (The party became known as the Democratic Party later in the 1800s.)

Hamilton favored a strong national government led by the "rich, well born, and able." He believed that democracy was dangerous to liberty. Hamilton also believed that manufacturing and trade were the basis of national wealth and power. He favored policies that supported these areas of the economy. The Federalist Party included many artisans, merchants, manufacturers, and bankers. The party also attracted urban workers and Eastern farmers who benefited from trade.

Thomas Jefferson emerged as the leader of the Democratic-Republicans. Jefferson believed that the strength of the United States was its independent farmers. As long as most people owned their own land, they would fight to preserve the Republic.

Competing National Visions

Hamilton and the Federalists	Jefferson and the Democratic-Republicans
Strong national government	Strong state government
Ruling power given to wealthy, educated	Ruling power given to *all* landowners
Government should promote manufacturing	Government should promote agriculture
Loose interpretation of the Constitution	Strict interpretation of the Constitution
Protective tariffs protect domestic industries	Protective tariffs burden farmers

Chart Skills

1. **Interpreting Charts** Which party did not support tariffs, and why?
2. **Making Generalizations** Which party usually attracted bankers and manufacturers?

In general, Democratic-Republicans supported agriculture over commerce and trade. They feared that too much emphasis on commerce would lead to a society divided between the rich who owned everything and the poor who worked for wages. Over time, the Democratic-Republicans came to stand for the rights of states against the federal government. The party had a strong base in the rural South and West.

✓ **Reading Check** **Identifying** What were the nation's first two political parties, and what issues did each favor?

Washington's Foreign Policy

Shortly after Washington was inaugurated in 1789, the French Revolution began in Europe. At first, most Americans sympathized with the revolutionaries, who seemed to be fighting for the same rights Americans had won a few years earlier. By spring 1793, however, a group of French radicals had seized power. They stripped aristocrats of their property and executed thousands of people, including the French king, Louis XVI, and the queen, Marie Antoinette. The violence and chaos turned many Federalists against the French. Many Republicans, however, continued to support the Revolution, viewing it as a fight for liberty.

HISTORY Online

Student Web Activity Visit the *American Republic Since 1877* Web site at tarvol2.glencoe.com and click on *Student Web Activities— Chapter 4* for an activity on early political parties.

CHAPTER 4
Section 1, 152–159

✓ **Reading Check**

Answer: to establish the right to impose taxes directly on the people

Chart *Skills*

Answers:
1. Democratic-Republicans, because tariffs hurt farmers
2. Federalists

Chart Skills Practice
Ask: What example indicates the Federalists' support for a loose interpretation of the Constitution? *(the Bank of the United States, which was not specifically described in the Constitution)*

✓ **Reading Check**

Answer: Federalists favored a strong central government led by the rich and an economy based on manufacturing and trade. Democratic-Republicans favored many people owning land, an economy based on agriculture, and strong state governments.

HISTORY Online

Objectives and answers to the student activity can be found in the **Web Activity Lesson Plan** at tarvol2.glencoe.com.

INTERDISCIPLINARY CONNECTIONS ACTIVITY

Economics Have students use the Treasury Department's Web site to research the national debt for the years 1800, 1900, and 2000. Have students explain why it is not appropriate to compare these numbers directly. Encourage students to use an inflation calculator to calculate the debt figures in comparable dollars. Provide students with the Internet addresses shown below. **L2**

The Public Debt Online—http://www.publicdebt.treas.gov/opd/opd.htm
CJR Dollar Conversion Calculator—http://www.cjr.org/resources/inflater.asp

Writing a Report Have students use library and Internet resources to research a current issue related to most-favored-nation clauses (often called permanent normal trade relations). Then have them write a three- to five-page report on the topic. **L3**

📁 Use the rubric for writing a book review, research report, or position paper on pages 79–80 in the *Performance Assessment Activities and Rubrics.*

🎌 **Analyzing** *Political Cartoons*

Answer: They believed the treaty was pro-British.
Ask: With so much anger about the treaty, why did Washington implement it? *(to prevent a war with Great Britain and to protect the American economy)*

✓ **Reading Check**

Answer: to avoid being drawn into a European conflict

↗ CURRICULUM CONNECTION

Science Engineer Pierre Charles L'Enfant created a plan for the new national capital that featured wide boulevards connecting the branches of government, the national monuments, parks, and entry gates. He envisioned the Capitol building as a central point in a square grid of streets occupying the land between the Potomac and Anacostia rivers.

🎌 **Analyzing** *Political Cartoons*

A Fiery Protest Antifederalists burned at the stake a figure representing John Jay after Jay's Treaty with England was signed in 1794. *Why were people angry about the treaty?*

The turmoil within France soon led to conflict with other European kingdoms. When France declared war against Great Britain in 1793, the United States found itself in a difficult position. The Treaty of 1778 with France required the United States to help defend France's colonies in the Caribbean. Fulfilling this agreement might mean war with Great Britain. In an effort to avoid the conflict, President Washington issued a proclamation on April 22, 1793, declaring the United States to be "friendly and impartial" toward both warring powers.

Jay's Treaty Remaining neutral proved difficult. Britain used its navy to block the delivery of goods to French ports, seizing hundreds of American ships. At the same time, the British were reportedly inciting Native American attacks in the West, where British soldiers still occupied some forts they had promised to evacuate after the American Revolution. These activities pushed the United States to the brink of war in the spring of 1794.

156 CHAPTER 4 Federalists and Republicans

Desperate for a diplomatic solution, Washington sent John Jay to Britain. The British were busy fighting France and did not want to fight the United States as well. They agreed to sign what came to be called **Jay's Treaty.**

The British drove a hard bargain, however, knowing that the Americans depended on trade with Britain. They refused to stop seizing American ships or to compensate American merchants for lost cargoes. Instead, they agreed to create an international commission to hear the merchants' claims. They also insisted on establishing another commission to consider the claims of British subjects seeking repayment of pre-Revolutionary debts.

Although he gave ground on many issues, Jay was able to persuade the British to give the United States most-favored nation status. This meant that Americans would not be discriminated against when they traded with Britain but would receive the same treatment as other favored nations. Britain also agreed to allow limited American trade with its Caribbean colonies and to evacuate its forts in American territory.

When the public learned the terms of Jay's Treaty, the Democratic-Republicans immediately accused the Federalists of being pro-British. Across much of the country, public meetings were held condemning the treaty. George Washington deliberated long and hard but finally agreed to implement it. His decision prevented war with Great Britain and protected the fragile American economy.

Pinckney's Treaty Jay's Treaty also helped the United States win concessions from Spain, which still controlled Florida and territory west of the Mississippi River. In 1795 Spain joined France in its struggle against Britain. The signing of Jay's Treaty raised fears in Spain that the British and Americans might now join forces to seize Spain's North American holdings. Spain quickly offered to negotiate all outstanding issues with the United States.

Also in 1795 the Spanish signed the Treaty of San Lorenzo—better known as **Pinckney's Treaty,** after the American negotiator, Thomas Pinckney. The treaty granted the United States the right to navigate the Mississippi and to deposit goods at the port of New Orleans. Spain also agreed to accept the 31st parallel as the northern boundary of western Florida.

✓ **Reading Check** **Explaining** Why did President Washington choose neutrality in the war between Britain and France?

CRITICAL THINKING ACTIVITY

Understanding Cause and Effect Write the following on the board: Causes of French-British Rivalry. Have students suggest causes. *(desire to be the strongest world power, to colonize the largest area, to find new markets for goods, to rule the seas)* Then ask students: Where will the French-British rivalry affect the United States? Why? *(on land because both countries claim land on the American continent, on the seas because the United States sails the seas, in the trading of goods because both countries are trading partners)* **L2**

A New Administration

George Washington served two terms in office. By the end of his second term, however, he had grown exasperated by party politics and the attacks on his character in Democratic-Republican newspapers. Although many people urged him to run again, Washington decided to retire.

Before leaving office, the president wrote a long letter to the American people. Published on September 19, 1796, and widely reprinted, **Washington's Farewell Address** urged Americans to support the federal government and avoid sectionalism—dividing the country into North against South, or East against West. Washington also warned against the dangers of political parties, comparing party fervor to a fire that could easily burn out of control. Washington further advised Americans against excessively strong attachments to foreign countries: "'Tis our true policy to steer clear of permanent alliances with any portion of the foreign world."

With Washington stepping down, the United States held its first openly contested presidential election in 1796. The Federalists nominated John Adams, and the Republicans chose Thomas Jefferson. Anger over Jay's Treaty made the election close, but when the votes were counted, John Adams had won.

Adams and the Quasi-War One of Adams's first challenges was dealing with French aggression at sea. France, still at war with Britain, had been enraged by Jay's Treaty. The French had begun stopping American ships and seizing their goods if they were going to Britain. These actions led many Federalists to call for war against France. Although critical of the French, Adams, like Washington, was reluctant to involve the United States in a major war. Instead he sent Charles Pinckney, Elbridge Gerry, and John Marshall to negotiate with France in 1797.

After weeks of waiting, the Americans were finally approached by three French officials, referred to in later documents as X, Y, and Z. They asked for a bribe of $250,000 to initiate talks, along with an American loan of $12 million. Pinckney's indignant reply—"No, no, not a sixpence"—inspired pro-war Federalists to coin a stirring slogan: "Millions for defense, but not one cent for tribute."

The **XYZ Affair** heightened tensions with France. In June 1798, Congress voted to suspend all trade with France and to allow the navy to capture armed French ships. The two nations were soon fighting an undeclared war at sea, which came to be known as the **Quasi-War.**

In the fall of 1798, France proposed new negotiations. To the Federalists' dismay, Adams agreed to the talks. In September 1800, the two countries signed the Convention of 1800, ending the Quasi-War. The United States gave up all claims against France for damages to American shipping. France released the United States from the Treaty of 1778.

Domestic Troubles At home, divisions between the two political parties had been deepening. Many Federalists suspected pro-French Republicans of stirring up the people so much that they would attempt to overthrow the government. They also resented the harsh criticisms printed in Republican newspapers. Taking advantage of their congressional majorities, the Federalists decided to strike back at the opposing party.

In the spring and summer of 1798, the Federalists pushed four laws through Congress that became known as the **Alien and Sedition Acts.** The first three laws were aimed at aliens, people living in the country who were not citizens. The Federalists knew that

Picturing History

Compromise and the Capital City Southern states that had already paid their war debts accepted Hamilton's financial program on the condition that the new national capital be located along the Potomac River. Why did Southerners think having a Southern capital would benefit them?

Discussing a Topic Ask students if they know of any other armed confrontations that could be labeled quasi-wars. Ask students how such conflicts compared to the Quasi-War with France. **L2**

Picturing History

Answer: It would offset the strength of the Northern states in Congress. **Ask:** Before the decision to locate the capital in the area along the Potomac, where do you think the nation's capital would have been located? Why? (*Philadelphia because it was the site of the Constitutional Convention; New York because it was one of the nation's largest cities; Boston because colonists made such a strong statement of independence*)

The Tradition of Tribute The Romans made the countries they conquered pay tribute. The payment was seen as a sign of submission or the price of peace and protection. Tributes were also paid in feudal times. By the time of the XYZ Affair, the word tribute was synonymous with bribe.

EXTENDING THE CONTENT

The French Revolution After the American Revolution, the French fought for major changes in their own nation. In many ways the French society of the late 1700s was feudal. By law, people belonged to one of three classes, or estates. A person's social status, political rights, and economic privileges were determined by the estate to which he or she belonged. Many people in all of the estates were dissatisfied with their positions because of unequal privileges. This and the heavy burden of taxation placed on the poor were major causes of the French Revolution.

Geography *Skills*

Answers:

1. Pennsylvania, Maryland, North Carolina

2. Northern states, because of their support for trade and manufacturing

Geography Skills Practice

Ask: Which candidate did the western states favor? Why? *(Jefferson; he supported agriculture and states' rights.)*

3 ASSESS

Assign Section 1 Assessment as homework or as an in-class activity.

⊕ Have students use the **Interactive Tutor Self-Assessment CD-ROM.**

L1/ELL

Reading Essentials and Study Guide 4–1

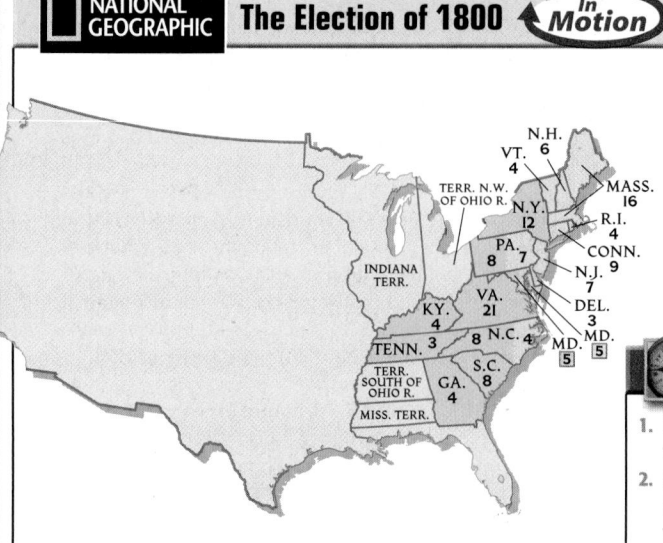

NATIONAL GEOGRAPHIC | **The Election of 1800** ◀ **In Motion**

Presidential Election, 1800			
Candidate	Popular Vote	Electoral Vote	Political Party
Jefferson	Unknown	73	Democratic Republican
Adams	Unknown	65	Federalist
Burr	Unknown	73	Democratic Republican
Pinckney	Unknown	64	Federalist
Jay	Unknown	1	Federalist

Geography *Skills*

1. **Interpreting Maps** Which states split their electoral votes between the two parties?
2. **Applying Geography Skills** Where did the Federalists have strong support? What policies did they favor that would account for their strength there?

*According to the Constitution, each elector in the Electoral College voted for two people in a presidential election. The person receiving the most votes became president, and the person receiving the second-highest number of votes became vice president. Under this system a tie was possible, as happened in the case of the tie between Thomas Jefferson and Aaron Burr in 1800. The House of Representatives then elected Jefferson after 35 rounds of voting in which there was no clear winner. To prevent such confusion in the future, the Twelfth Amendment was added to the Constitution in 1804. The amendment stipulates that electoral votes for president and vice president are counted and listed separately.

many recent immigrants had come from France and Ireland. These immigrants were often anti-British and tended to vote for the Republican Party once they gained citizenship. The first law required immigrants to wait 14 years before becoming citizens, thus weakening Republican support. The next two laws gave the president the power to deport without trial any alien deemed dangerous to the United States.

The fourth law made it a federal crime to utter or print anything "false, scandalous, and malicious" against the federal government or any federal official. In short, the act deprived citizens of their right to criticize public officials. The government indicted 15 people under this act, including leading Republicans.

In 1798 and 1799, the Republican-controlled legislatures of Kentucky and Virginia passed resolutions, secretly written by Jefferson and Madison, criticizing the Alien and Sedition Acts. Both resolutions argued that the Constitution was an agreement among the states. The states therefore had the power to judge whether a federal law was unconstitutional.

This idea that states have authority over the Constitution is called state sovereignty. It is different from the idea of states' rights. Americans today often

believe the federal government is above the state governments in power, but the Constitution originally intended to divide power between the states and the federal government. Defenders of states' rights wanted to prevent the federal government from exercising powers that should belong to the states. Both the Virginia and the Kentucky Resolutions were trying to protect states' rights, but in doing so, they developed the new idea of state sovereignty.

The Virginia Resolutions introduced the theory of interposition. They argued that if the federal government did something unconstitutional, the states could interpose between the federal government and the people to stop the action. The Kentucky Resolutions advanced a similar theory called nullification. According to this theory, if the federal government passed an unconstitutional law, the states had the right to nullify the law, or declare it invalid.

Although the **Kentucky and Virginia Resolutions** had little immediate effect, states used these ideas later to defend their interests. During the War of 1812, for example, New England states refused to enforce federal laws restricting trade. In

158 CHAPTER 4 Federalists and Republicans

Reading Strategy ◀ READING THE TEXT

Checking Comprehension After students have read through the section, ask them to write on a piece of paper what they remember about John Adams's presidency. Then, have students reread the section and review the statements they have written. Students should correct statements that are wrong and add more statements to fill in information that is missing. **L1**

📂 Refer to *Inclusion for the High School Social Studies Classroom Strategies and Activities* in the TCR.

the years before the Civil War, Southern states cited the resolutions to protect their trade and to preserve slavery.

✓ **Reading Check** **Analyzing** What was the purpose of the Alien and Sedition Acts?

The Election of 1800

Although John Adams hoped to win re-election in 1800, he faced a difficult battle. The Alien and Sedition Acts had angered many people, as had a new tax the Federalists had introduced on houses, land, and enslaved Africans. The Republican nominees for president and vice president, Thomas Jefferson and Aaron Burr, campaigned against the new taxes and the national bank. They accused the Federalists of favoring monarchy and discouraging political participation.

The election was closely contested and had an unexpected outcome, one that revealed a flaw in the system for selecting the president. The Constitution does not let citizens vote directly for the chief executive. Instead each state chooses a number of electors equal to its number of senators and representatives in Congress. This group, known as the Electoral College, then votes for the president.

The Constitution specified that each elector would vote for two candidates. The candidate receiving the most votes would become president; the runner-up would become vice president. Ties would be decided by the House of Representatives.

To avoid a tie between Jefferson and Burr, the Republicans had intended for all their electors to vote for Jefferson, and for all but one to vote for Burr. Somehow the plan went awry. When the votes were counted, Adams had 65, and Jefferson and Burr each had 73. Now the Federalist-controlled House of Representatives had to choose the president from the top two vote getters, who were both Republicans.

Some Federalists in the House hoped to use the deadlock to keep their party in power. Some despised Jefferson and wanted to select Burr. Other Federalists, including Burr's archenemy Alexander Hamilton, gave their support to Jefferson. This led to a tie in the House of Representatives. Finally, in February 1801, Jefferson informed Federalist James Bayard that if elected, he would not undo Hamilton's financial system. Bayard then cast a blank ballot, ensuring that Jefferson would have more votes than Burr. Jefferson became the new president.

The election of 1800 was an important turning point in American history. The Republicans had won not only the presidency but a majority of seats in Congress. The Federalists, who controlled the army as well as the government, could have refused to step down. Instead, they upheld the Constitution. The election of 1800 established that power in the United States could be peacefully transferred despite disagreements between political parties. The election also led to the Twelfth Amendment in 1804, which provided for separate ballots for the president and vice president.

✓ **Reading Check** **Summarizing** What changes did the election of 1800 bring?

HISTORY Online **Study Central™** To review this section, go to tarvol2.glencoe.com and click on **Study Central™**.

SECTION 1 ASSESSMENT

Checking for Understanding
1. **Define:** cabinet, bond, speculator, enumerated powers, implied powers, excise tax, most-favored nation, alien, interposition, nullification.
2. **Identify:** Whiskey Rebellion, XYZ Affair.
3. **Explain** how the Alien and Sedition Acts interfered with the lives of people living in the United States.

Reviewing Themes
4. **Global Connections** How did Great Britain and France test American neutrality during the presidencies of Washington and Adams?

Critical Thinking
5. **Synthesizing** Why did Hamilton think the United States should take responsibility for the debts of both the Confederation and the states?
6. **Organizing** Use a graphic organizer similar to the one below to list the first political parties, their leaders and supporters, and their positions on issues.

Political Party	Leaders	Supporters	Policy Positions

Analyzing Visuals
7. **Comparing Charts and Maps** Study the chart on page 155 and the map on page 158. How did the election results reflect the Democratic-Republican position on protective tariffs?

Writing About History
8. **Expository Writing** Write an editorial that responds to George Washington's Farewell Address. Defend or dispute Washington's opinion that political parties and permanent foreign alliances are dangerous.

CHAPTER 4 Federalists and Republicans **159**

SECTION 1 ASSESSMENT ANSWERS

1. Terms are in blue.
2. Whiskey Rebellion (p. 155), XYZ Affair (p. 157)
3. restricted residents' rights and rights of citizens to criticize the government
4. Both interfered with shipping.

5. He wanted to create confidence in government.
6. Answers should reflect text; in brief, Eastern commercial groups supported Federalists; farmers, especially in West, supported Democratic-Republicans.

7. The Democratic-Republican candidates received support from agricultural areas in the South and West.
8. Editorials should focus on party issues and permanent foreign alliances.

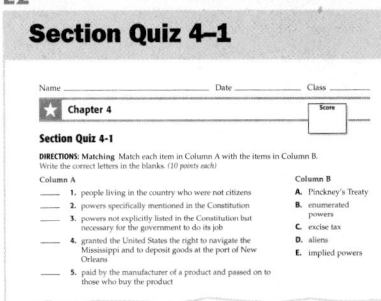

L2

Section Quiz 4–1

Name _____ Date _____ Class _____

★ Chapter 4   Score ☐

Section Quiz 4-1

DIRECTIONS: Matching Match each item in Column A with the items in Column B. Write the correct letters in the blanks. *(10 points each)*

Column A
____ 1. people living in the country who were not citizens
____ 2. powers specifically mentioned in the Constitution
____ 3. powers not explicitly listed in the Constitution but necessary for the government to do its job
____ 4. granted the United States the right to navigate the Mississippi and to deposit goods at the port of New Orleans
____ 5. paid by the manufacturer of a product and passed on to those who buy the product

Column B
A. Pinckney's Treaty
B. enumerated powers
C. excise tax
D. aliens
E. implied powers

✓ **Reading Check**

Answer: to strengthen the Federalists' hold on Congress

Reteach
Have students write and answer a question for each of the major headings in this section. Invite students to ask volunteers to answer them.

Enrich
Have students use library and Internet resources to research the origins of current political parties. Ask students to write a paragraph about each of the major parties.

✓ **Reading Check**

Answer: Republicans won both the presidency and control of Congress.

HISTORY Online

Study Central™ provides summaries, interactive games, and online graphic organizers to help students review section content.

4 CLOSE

Have students create a time line similar to the one on page 152, adding other important events that occurred during the time period.

159

TEACH

Reading a Flowchart Explain to students that flowcharts show connections among events. One event may be directly connected to two or three other events.

Have students prepare a flowchart that shows the steps they take to prepare for a test in their history class. Have students compare their flowcharts and revise them based on the feedback they receive.

Additional Practice
L1

Reinforcing Skills Activity 4

Name _____ Date _____ Class _____

★ Reinforcing Skills Activity 4

Reading a Flowchart
☐ LEARNING THE SKILL
Flowcharts can help you see the sequence of a series of events so you can better understand how the events are related. To read a flowchart, first look at the title or caption to find out the purpose of the chart. Then read the sentences or labels within each section of the chart. Look for numbers or arrows to show you the sequence or direction of movement between events.

☐ PRACTICING THE SKILL
DIRECTIONS: Study the flowchart below listing the events of the election of 1800. Then answer the questions that follow on a separate sheet of paper.

The Election of 1800

GLENCOE
TECHNOLOGY

CD-ROM
Glencoe Skillbuilder Interactive Workbook CD-ROM, Level 2

This interactive CD-ROM reinforces student mastery of essential social studies skills.

Social Studies
SKILLBUILDER

Reading a Flowchart

Why Learn This Skill?

Sometimes, determining a sequence of events can be confusing, particularly when many events are occurring at the same time. Reading a flowchart can help you understand how events are related and how one event leads to others.

Learning the Skill

Flowcharts show the steps in a process or a sequence of events. A flowchart could be used to show the movement of goods through a factory, of people through a training program, or of a bill through Congress. The following steps explain how to read a flowchart:

- Read the title or caption of the flowchart to find out what you are studying.
- Read all of the labels or sentences on the flowchart.
- Look for numbers indicating sequence or arrows showing the direction of movement.
- Evaluate the information in the flowchart.

Practicing the Skill

The flowchart on this page shows a sequence of events that led to the expansion of territory within the United States. Analyze the information in the flowchart and then answer the questions.

❶ What does the flowchart show?

❷ How do you know in what sequence the events took place?

❸ What inspired Napoleon to acquire the Louisiana Territory from Spain?

❹ How did the United States react to France's acquisition of the Louisiana Territory?

❺ What additional information from the chapter could you add to the flowchart to show a further sequence of events?

Circumstances Leading to the Louisiana Purchase

French leader Napoleon plans to rebuild France's empire in North America.

Napoleon convinces Spain to give the Louisiana Territory back to France.

President Jefferson sends ambassador Robert Livingston to France to try to block the deal.

Napoleon later wants to conquer Europe, but he needs funds to carry out his plans.

President Jefferson agrees to purchase Louisiana Territory.

Skills Assessment

Complete the Practicing Skills questions on page 175 and the Chapter 4 Skill Reinforcement Activity to assess your mastery of this skill.

Applying the Skill

Making a Flowchart Gather information about the steps necessary to apply to college. Then make up a flowchart outlining the steps. Present your flowchart to the class.

Glencoe's **Skillbuilder Interactive Workbook CD-ROM, Level 2,** provides instruction and practice in key social studies skills.

ANSWERS TO PRACTICING THE SKILL

❶ the circumstances leading to the Louisiana Purchase

❷ by the order of the boxes and the arrows indicating a top-to-bottom flow

❸ his plan to rebuild the French empire in North America

❹ They tried to block the deal.

❺ Possible answer: The Senate overwhelmingly ratified the Louisiana Purchase.

Applying the Skill
Students' flowcharts will vary. Flowcharts should include logical steps the college application process requires.

SECTION 2 The Republicans Take Power

Guide to Reading

Main Idea
President Jefferson limited the scope of the federal government and made the Louisiana Purchase. President Madison led the country into the War of 1812.

Key Terms and Names
judicial review, Louisiana Purchase, contraband, impressment, embargo, War Hawks

Reading Strategy
Sequencing As you read about the presidencies of Thomas Jefferson and James Madison, complete a time line similar to the one below to record major events of their administrations.

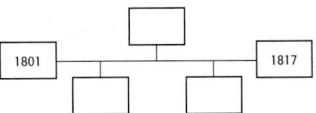

1801 ___ ___ 1817

Reading Objectives
• **Summarize** the changes Thomas Jefferson brought to the federal government.
• **Describe** the causes and the outcome of the War of 1812.

Section Theme
Government and Democracy The Supreme Court asserted the power to decide whether laws passed by Congress were constitutional.

Preview of Events

♦1800   ♦1805   ♦1810   ♦1815

1803
Supreme Court decides *Marbury* v. *Madison;* Louisiana Purchase

1807
British attack the *Chesapeake;* Embargo Act passed

1808
Madison elected president

1812
United States declares war on Britain

1814
British troops raid Washington, D.C.

★ An American Story ★

Thomas Jefferson

March 4, 1801, was Inauguration Day in Washington, D.C. The still unfinished capital of the United States was only a tiny village. Stumps and mud holes filled Pennsylvania Avenue, and a swampy wilderness separated Capitol Hill from the president's mansion. A Washington resident described the modest inauguration ceremony:

66The sun shone bright on that morning. . . . Mr. Jefferson . . . walk[ed] from his lodgings, which were not far distant. . . . Soon afterwards he entered . . . and bowing to the Senate, who arose to receive him, he approached a table on which the Bible lay and took the oath which was administered to him by the Chief Justice. . . . At dinner . . . A gentleman from Baltimore, . . . asked permission to wish him joy. 'I would advise you,' answered Mr. Jefferson smiling, 'to follow my example on nuptial occasions when I always tell the bridegroom I will wait till the end of the year before offering my congratulations.' And this was the only and solitary instance of any notice taken of the event of the morning.99

—quoted in *The Life of Thomas Jefferson*

Thomas Jefferson Takes Office

Thomas Jefferson privately referred to his election as the "Revolution of 1800." Believing that Washington and Adams had acted too much like royalty, the new president opted for less pomp and ceremony. Jefferson was the first president to begin his

CHAPTER 4   Federalists and Republicans   **161**

1 FOCUS

Section Overview
This section explores the administrations of Thomas Jefferson and James Madison.

BELLRINGER
Skillbuilder Activity

Project transparency and have students answer the question.

Daily Focus Skills Transparency 4–2

Reading Preview

Answers to Graphic: Students' time lines should include significant events in addition to those listed in the time line on this page.

Preteaching Vocabulary
Have students create cards with the Key Terms and Names on one side and definitions or explanations on the other side to prepare for assessments.

SECTION RESOURCES

📂 **Reproducible Masters**
• Reproducible Lesson Plan 4–2
• Daily Lecture and Discussion Notes 4–2
• Guided Reading Activity 4–2
• Section Quiz 4–2
• Reading Essentials and Study Guide 4–2
• Interpreting Political Cartoons
• Supreme Court Case Studies

🖹 **Transparencies**
• Daily Focus Skills Transparency 4–2

Multimedia
🔘 Interactive Tutor Self-Assessment CD-ROM
🔘 ExamView® Pro Testmaker CD-ROM
🔘 Presentation Plus! CD-ROM
🔘 TeacherWorks™ CD-ROM
🔘 Audio Program

2 TEACH

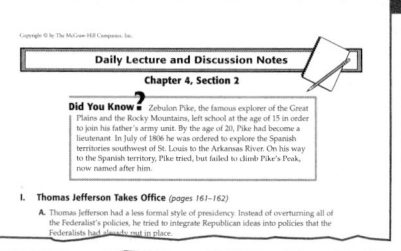
Preparing an Oral Presentation

Have students use library and Internet resources to learn more about one of the people or events mentioned in this section. Ask students to prepare a one-minute presentation about the person or event. **L1**

 Use the rubric for preparing an oral presentation, monologue, song, or skit on pages 67–68 in the *Performance Assessment Activities and Rubrics.*

Picturing History

Answer: *Marbury v. Madison*

Ask: What was John Marshall's lasting influence? *(He built the Supreme Court into a powerful, influential, and independent branch of the federal government.)*

✓ Reading Check

Answer: It established the Court's right of judicial review, the power to decide whether laws passed by Congress are constitutional.

Picturing History

John Marshall During his Supreme Court tenure, this staunch Federalist was concerned with establishing a strong federal government. *What case established the principle of judicial review?*

term at the new capital, Washington, D.C., and he used this opportunity to break with his predecessors' style. He rode on horseback rather than in carriages, and he substituted intimate dinners for formal receptions. In addition to setting a new style, Jefferson also reversed some of his predecessors' policies, but he did not overturn the entire Federalist program.

Restraining Federal Power A strong believer in small government, Jefferson hoped to limit the scope of federal power. Many Federalists expected him to dismantle the Bank of the United States. However, Jefferson's secretary of the treasury, **Albert Gallatin,** supported Hamilton's system and convinced the president to keep the national bank. Instead of maintaining the public debt and paying interest on it, though, Jefferson began paying it off. He cut government spending, did away with all excise taxes, including the hated whiskey tax, and trimmed the armed forces.

Conflict With the Courts Jefferson also hoped to weaken the Federalists' control of the judiciary. Just before Congress had changed hands, the Federalist majority had passed the **Judiciary Act of 1801.** This

act created 16 new federal judgeships, which Adams filled with Federalists. Adams supposedly stayed up until midnight on his last day in office, signing their appointments.

One of the first acts of the new Republican Congress was to repeal the Judiciary Act of 1801, abolishing the offices of the "midnight judges." The Republicans then tried to remove other Federalists from the bench by impeachment. Republican leaders believed that the impeachment power was one of the Constitution's checks and balances. Congress could therefore remove judges for arbitrary and unfair decisions, not just for criminal behavior. Only two judges were brought to trial, however, and only one was ousted. The attempt to remove the judges established the tradition that judges could only be removed for criminal behavior, not simply because Congress disagreed with their decisions.

Jefferson tried a different tactic with William Marbury. In his last days as president, Adams had appointed Marbury to be justice of the peace in Washington, D.C. Jefferson told his new secretary of state, James Madison, to withhold the documents that would confirm the appointment.

Marbury asked the Supreme Court for a writ, or court order, directing Madison to deliver the documents. The Court might have been expected to comply. After all, the Judiciary Act of 1789 empowered the Supreme Court to issue such writs.

In 1803 in *Marbury* v. *Madison,* Chief Justice **John Marshall** and his fellow justices unanimously agreed that Marbury should be given his documents, but that the Supreme Court could not issue the court order because it had no jurisdiction. Marshall pointed out that the Constitution was very specific about the kind of cases that could be taken directly to the Supreme Court rather than a lower court. Thus the section of the Judiciary Act of 1789 that authorized the Supreme Court to issue writs was unconstitutional and invalid. 📖 *(See page 963 for information on* Marbury v. Madison.)

Although the ruling did not help Marbury, it was a landmark decision for the Supreme Court. The Court had asserted its right of judicial review, the power to decide whether laws passed by Congress are constitutional and to strike down those that are not. Marshall remained as Chief Justice for more than 30 years, building the Supreme Court into a powerful, influential, and independent branch of the federal government.

✓ Reading Check Evaluating Why was *Marbury* v. *Madison* significant?

📖 Reading Strategy ◄ READING THE TEXT

Understanding Vocabulary As students read passages or literature selections in the social studies, they should be aware of the differences between denotation and connotation. *Denotation* is a word's dictionary definition. *Connotation* is the emotional value associated with a word. For example, *house* and *home* are synonyms, but *home* has a warm, personal meaning that is not stated in its dictionary definition. **L1**

 Refer to *Inclusion for the High School Social Studies Classroom Strategies and Activities* in the TCR.

The United States Expands West

Jefferson strongly supported the country's westward expansion, which had begun well before his presidency. During Washington's terms, Americans had flocked to the fertile region between the Appalachian Mountains and the Mississippi River. In 1792 Kentucky had enough people to become a new state, and Tennessee gained statehood in 1796. Meanwhile, settlers from Pennsylvania and Virginia were moving into the Northwest Territory, but they were coming into conflict with Native Americans there.

President Washington sent General Anthony Wayne to put down Native American resistance by force. In August 1794, at the Battle of Fallen Timbers in Ohio, Wayne's troops won a decisive victory. In August 1795, 12 Native American nations signed the **Treaty of Greenville.** In exchange for a yearly payment of $10,000 from the federal government, they gave up land near present-day Chicago and Detroit, as well as a large area in southern Ohio and Indiana. The flow of Americans into the region rapidly increased. By 1803 Ohio had enough settlers to become a state.

The Louisiana Purchase While Americans were pushing west, the French were hoping to rebuild their empire in North America. French leader Napoleon Bonaparte convinced Spain to give Louisiana back to France in 1800. Jefferson was uneasy about France controlling the lower Mississippi. He ordered the American ambassador to Paris, Robert Livingston, to try to gain concessions for the United States.

Livingston accomplished little at first. By 1803, however, Napoleon had begun making plans to conquer Europe. To gain funds and to pre-empt an alliance between the United States and Great Britain, Napoleon offered to sell all of the Louisiana Territory, as well as New Orleans, to the United States. Livingston immediately agreed. On April 30, 1803, the United States bought Louisiana from France for $11.25 million. It also agreed to take on French debts owed to Americans, worth about $3.75 million, making the total cost about $15 million.

The Senate overwhelmingly ratified the **Louisiana Purchase.** For less than three cents an acre, the United States had more than doubled its size and gained control of the entire Mississippi River.

GEOGRAPHY

Lewis and Clark and Zebulon Pike Even before Louisiana became a part of the United States, Jefferson convinced Congress to fund an expedition to explore the territory. Led by Meriwether Lewis and William Clark, the expedition headed west up the Missouri River in May 1804. Sacagawea, a Shoshone woman, acted as a guide during much of the voyage. Other Native Americans led the group along a path through the Rocky Mountains, and the explorers eventually traced the Columbia River to the Pacific Ocean. The **Lewis and Clark expedition** not only provided a wealth of information about Louisiana, it also gave the United States a claim to the Oregon Territory.

Zebulon Pike also explored the Louisiana Territory. In 1805 he mapped much of the upper Mississippi River. In 1806 he headed west to Colorado, where he encountered the mountain now known as Pikes Peak. Pike later mapped part of the Rio Grande and traveled across northern Mexico and southern Texas. His account of this trip gave Americans detailed information about the Great Plains and the Rocky Mountains.

The Essex Junto The Louisiana Purchase alarmed many New England Federalists. They knew that as new states appeared in the South and West, New England would lose political influence. In Massachusetts, a small group of Federalists known as the **Essex Junto** drafted a plan to take New England out of the Union.

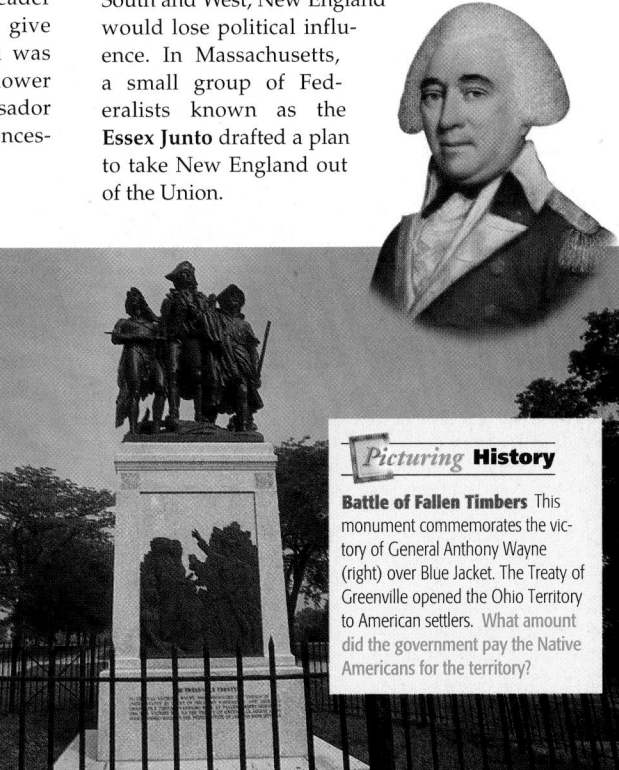

Picturing **History**

Battle of Fallen Timbers This monument commemorates the victory of General Anthony Wayne (right) over Blue Jacket. The Treaty of Greenville opened the Ohio Territory to American settlers. **What amount did the government pay the Native Americans for the territory?**

IN HISTORY

✓ **Reading Check**

Answer: The purchase would more than double the size of the United States, as well as provide control of the Mississippi River. This would greatly aid expansion.

Background: When William Henry Harrison was serving as governor of Indiana, he told Tecumseh that only the president had the authority to return the disputed lands to the Native Americans. Tecumseh replied: "Well, as the great chief is to decide the matter, I hope the Great Spirit will put sense enough into his head to induce him to give up this land. It is true, he is so far off he will not be injured by the war; he may sit still in his town and drink his wine, while you and I will have to fight it out." Tecumseh's prediction came true.

Ask: What was Tecumseh's fear about the future of all Native Americans? *(that they would lose their hunting grounds and be pushed farther to the west)*

In 1806 President Thomas Jefferson urged Congress to pass a law prohibiting the importation of enslaved people. The next year, Congress passed a law making the slave trade illegal as of January 1, 1808. Nevertheless, smuggling of enslaved peoples continued.

Vice President Aaron Burr, sympathetic to their goal, agreed to run for governor of New York in 1804. During the campaign, Alexander Hamilton called Burr "a dangerous man, and one who ought not be trusted with the reins of government." When Hamilton's remarks were published, Burr challenged him to a duel. Hamilton agreed, and on July 11, 1804, Burr shot and killed Hamilton. The nation had lost a brilliant leader and one of its founders.

✓ **Reading Check** **Explaining** Why did Thomas Jefferson want to purchase the Louisiana Territory?

Rising International Tensions

Foreign affairs preoccupied President Jefferson during his second term in office. France had resumed its war against Britain in mid-1803, and the United States had proclaimed its neutrality. In 1806 and 1807, however, both France and Britain adopted policies forbidding neutral countries from trading with the enemy. Any vessels traveling to Europe became subject to search and seizure by one side or the other.

Soon British warships were regularly stopping American merchant ships and searching them for contraband—smuggled goods—and for British sailors who had fled their vessels. If the British found deserters, they practiced impressment, a legalized form of kidnapping, to force the sailors back into service. They also used impressment to take American sailors.

Calls for War In June 1807, tensions between the United States and Britain reached the boiling point when the British warship *Leopard* stopped an American warship, the *Chesapeake*. When the *Chesapeake's* captain refused to submit to a search, the *Leopard* opened fire, killing three Americans. The British then boarded the *Chesapeake* and seized four sailors.

Profiles IN HISTORY

Tecumseh
c.1768–1813

Tecumseh was a Shawnee chief born near present-day Springfield, Ohio. The Shawnee had taken part in many wars in the Northwest Territory. After the Treaty of Greenville in 1795, Tecumseh and many other Shawnee moved to the Indiana territory to escape white settlers.

Tecumseh urged all Native Americans to unite. They were all one people, he said, and should cooperate in a confederacy to control their destiny. He was furious when the Delaware and Potawatomi agreed to cede about 3 million acres (1.2 million ha) to the United States. The land belonged to all Native Americans, Tecumseh argued. How could one group cede it?

In the end, Tecumseh saw no choice but to fight the whites: "The hunting grounds are fast disappearing and they are driving the red man farther and farther to the west." Ominously, he warned, "Surely [this] will be the fate of all tribes if the power of the whites is not forever crushed. . . ."

During the War of 1812, Tecumseh allied himself with the British. A superb commander, he met his end at the Battle of the Thames River, fought near Chatham, Ontario, in October 1813. There, 400 British troops commanded by General Henry Proctor and about 1,000 Native Americans led by Tecumseh fought some 3,000 American troops led by General William Henry Harrison. During the battle, the British broke ranks and fled, leaving Tecumseh's men to face the American forces alone. After Tecumseh fell, his confederacy collapsed, leaving the United States in firm control of the Northwest Territory.

The attack enraged the public. Anti-British mobs rioted in several cities, and protesters marched through the streets. President Jefferson, like Washington and Adams before him, did not want to be drawn into a European conflict. Instead, he decided to use economic sanctions against both Britain and France.

Jefferson asked Congress to pass the **Embargo Act of 1807,** halting all trade between the United States and Europe. The embargo, a government ban on trade with other countries, wound up hurting the United States more than Britain or France. In the Northeast, once-lucrative shipping businesses came to a standstill, while farmers saw the demand for their crops fall. Realizing that the embargo was costing the Republican Party support, Congress repealed it in March 1809.

Shortly before its repeal, Jefferson left office, having decided not to seek a third term but to retire to Monticello, his estate in Virginia. Jefferson had succeeded in limiting the role of the federal government, but he also left his successor with a foreign policy crisis.

New Economic Pressures The new Republican president, James Madison, had easily won the election of 1808.

INTERDISCIPLINARY CONNECTIONS ACTIVITY

Economics Have students use the Internet, library, and other resources to study the major economic issues facing the United States from 1800 to 1815, such as the Embargo Act of 1807. Have students make a chart of each issue detailing what caused it and how the United States dealt with it. **L2**

Like Jefferson, Madison preferred to avoid war if at all possible. To force the British to stop seizing American ships, he asked Congress to pass the **Non-Intercourse Act** in 1809. This act prohibited commerce with France and Britain but promised to resume trade with whichever country first dropped its own trade restrictions. When the act had no effect, Congress replaced it with Macon's Bill Number Two. This new law stated that if either France or Britain removed its trade restrictions, the United States would stop importing goods from the other nation. France eventually took some conciliatory steps, and Congress passed a nonimportation act against Britain in early 1811.

By early 1812, the refusal of the United States to buy British goods had begun to hurt British merchants and manufacturers. They began to pressure their government to repeal its restrictions on trade, but by the time Britain agreed, the United States had declared war.

The War Hawks Most of the members of Congress who wanted to declare war came from the South and West. Nicknamed the War Hawks, they were led by Henry Clay of Kentucky, John C. Calhoun of South Carolina, and Felix Grundy of Tennessee.

Americans living in the South and West were angry at Britain for several reasons. Southern planters and western farmers earned much of their income from exports of tobacco, rice, wheat, and cotton, so Britain's trade restrictions hurt them badly. Eastern merchants paid low prices for the farmers' crops and charged them high shipping fees to cover the potential loss of their ships bound for Europe.

Westerners also blamed Britain for their problems with Native Americans. In the early 1800s, settlers had begun moving past the line established by the Treaty of Greenville and onto Native American land. As clashes with Native Americans mounted, many settlers suspected that the British in Canada were arming the Native Americans.

A key incident occurred in November 1811, near the Tippecanoe River in the Indiana territory. The governor there, William Henry Harrison, decided to strike at Tenskwatawa (also known as "the Prophet"), the brother of Shawnee leader **Tecumseh**. Both men had been urging Native Americans to unify in order to hold on to their lands. The bloody **Battle of Tippecanoe** left about one-fourth of Harrison's troops dead or wounded, but its impact on the Native Americans was far greater. The clash shattered Native American confidence in the Prophet's leadership. Many, including Tecumseh, fled to Canada. This convinced some Americans that the British had indeed been aiding the Native Americans, as did the

The Star-Spangled Banner, 1779–1818 The Stars and Stripes flag gained two more stars and two more stripes in 1795, after Kentucky and Vermont joined the Union. This flag flew over Fort McHenry during the War of 1812 and inspired Francis Scott Key to write "The Star-Spangled Banner."

Congress realized that the flag would become too large if a stripe were added for every new state. It decided to keep the stripes at 13—for the 13 original colonies—and to add a star for each new state.

British-made rifles the Shawnee forces had left behind after the battle. Many western farmers argued that a war against Britain would enable the United States to seize Canada and end Native American attacks.

In early June 1812, President Madison gave in to the pressure and asked Congress to declare war. The vote split along regional lines. Most of the South and West voted for war, while the Northeast, fearing it would hurt trade, did not.

 Reading Check **Examining** How did people in the South and the West feel about declaring war against Great Britain? Why did each group feel the way it did?

The War of 1812

At the start of the War of 1812, conquering Canada was the primary objective of the United States. Most American leaders predicted that Canada would fall easily. Military commanders planned to invade from three directions—from Detroit, from Niagara Falls, and up the Hudson River valley toward Montreal. The British foiled all three attacks.

Perry's Victory on Lake Erie The following year, the United States had more success after Commodore **Oliver Perry** secretly arranged for the construction of a fleet on Lake Erie in Ohio. There, on September 10, 1813, Perry's ships attacked the British fleet. After a grueling four-hour battle, the British surrendered. As Perry famously reported, "We have met the enemy and they are ours."

Perry's victory gave the Americans control of Lake Erie. British ships had used the lake to shuttle troops back and forth quickly to meet American attacks.

CHAPTER 4 Federalists and Republicans **165**

Congress approved the first official flag of the United States on June 14, 1777. It included 13 alternating red and white stripes and a blue field with 13 white stars. In 1818 Congress decided that there would always be 13 stripes, one for each of the original 13 colonies. Stars would be added on July 4 in the year following a state's admission to the Union. The exact shades of red, white, and blue were standardized in 1934.

Reading Check

Answer: South: supported war because Britain's trade restrictions harmed their businesses; West: supported war because they blamed Britain for problems with Native Americans

CURRICULUM CONNECTION

Language Arts The plight of sailors thrown into unemployment by the embargo prompted a 13-year-old Massachusetts boy to write a poem in 1808. The writer, William Cullen Bryant, went on to become one of America's leading poets and newspaper editors. He was editor of the *New York Evening Post* from 1829 until his death in 1878.

CRITICAL THINKING ACTIVITY

Formulating an Opinion Have students reread the section "Calls for War" on page 164. Ask students to identify ways in which they think Jefferson violated his principles of individual freedom and limited federal power. Then ask them if they think that presidents should violate their principles for the good of the whole country. Have them explain the reasons for their opinion. **L1**

Geography *Skills*

Answers:

1. Ft. Michilimackinac
2. It crippled the ability of the British to quickly move troops to meet American attacks.

Geography Skills Practice

Ask: How did Andrew Jackson defend his troops? *(He built a barricade of cotton bales that absorbed the British bullets.)*

3 ASSESS

Assign Section 2 Assessment as homework or as an in-class activity.

⊙ Have students use the **Interactive Tutor Self-Assessment CD-ROM.**

L1/ELL

Reading Essentials and Study Guide 4–2

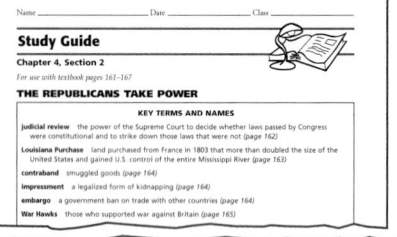

L2

Section Quiz 4–2

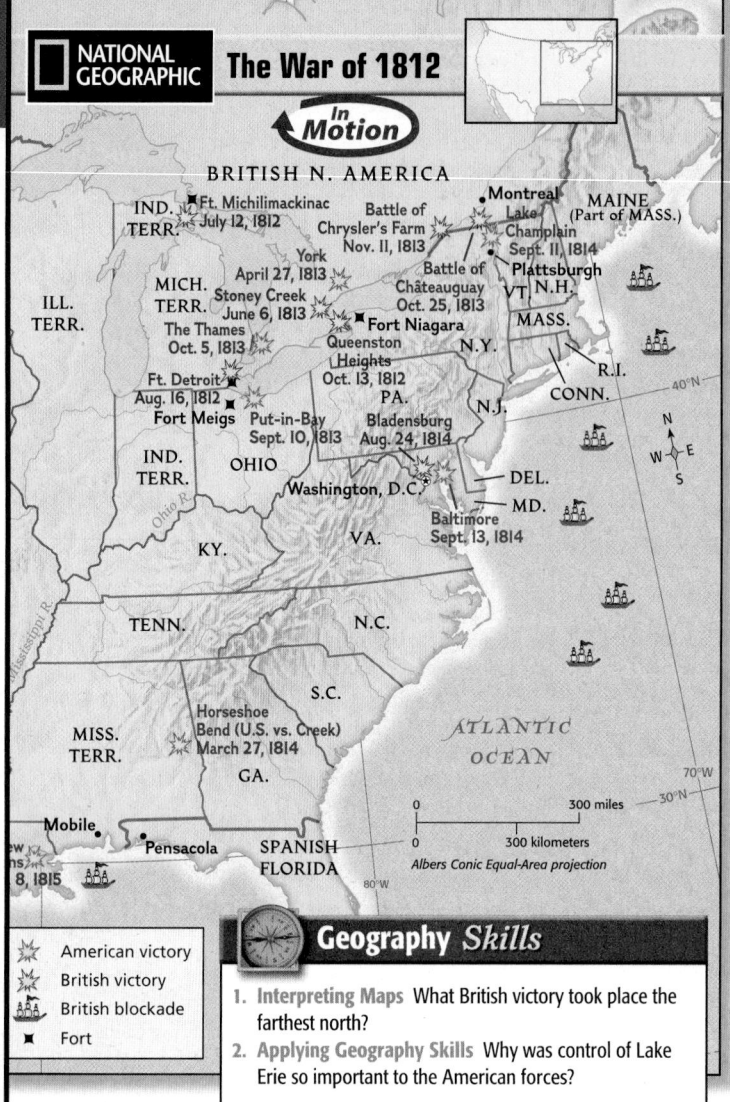

NATIONAL GEOGRAPHIC — The War of 1812

In Motion

BRITISH N. AMERICA

Map labels:
- Ft. Michilimackinac July 12, 1812
- Battle of Chrysler's Farm Nov. 11, 1813
- Montreal
- Lake Champlain Sept. 11, 1814
- MAINE (Part of MASS.)
- York April 27, 1813
- Plattsburgh
- N.H.
- Battle of Châteauguay Oct. 25, 1813
- VT
- Stoney Creek June 6, 1813
- Fort Niagara
- The Thames Oct. 5, 1813
- Queenston Heights Oct. 13, 1812
- N.Y.
- MASS.
- R.I.
- Ft. Detroit Aug. 16, 1812
- Fort Meigs
- Put-in-Bay Sept. 10, 1813
- Bladensburg Aug. 24, 1814
- CONN.
- PA.
- N.J.
- IND. TERR.
- OHIO
- Washington, D.C.
- DEL.
- MD.
- Baltimore Sept. 13, 1814
- VA.
- KY.
- TENN.
- N.C.
- S.C.
- Horseshoe Bend (U.S. vs. Creek) March 27, 1814
- MISS. TERR.
- GA.
- ATLANTIC OCEAN
- Mobile
- Pensacola
- SPANISH FLORIDA
- New Orleans Jan. 8, 1815
- ILL. TERR.
- MICH. TERR.
- IND. TERR.
- Ohio R.
- Mississippi R.

300 miles / 300 kilometers
Albers Conic Equal-Area projection

Legend:
- ✶ American victory
- ✶ British victory
- ⚓ British blockade
- ■ Fort

Geography *Skills*

1. **Interpreting Maps** What British victory took place the farthest north?
2. **Applying Geography Skills** Why was control of Lake Erie so important to the American forces?

Now their ability to respond to American attacks was more limited. Shortly afterward, William Henry Harrison, now a general, marched from Detroit into Canada. At the battle of the Thames River, Harrison defeated a combined force of British troops and Native Americans led by Tecumseh. Tecumseh died during the fighting, and the Native American confederacy soon collapsed.

Harrison expected to meet up with American troops coming from Niagara Falls. After learning that they had been defeated at the Battle of Stony Creek, however, Harrison retreated to Detroit. By the end of 1813, the United States still had not conquered any territory in Canada.

166 CHAPTER 4 Federalists and Republicans

The Battle of Lake Champlain In the early years of the War of 1812, the British were also fighting France. That changed in 1814 when Napoleon's empire fell apart. The British were then able to send many more troops to the United States.

In September 1814, about 15,000 well-trained and well-equipped British soldiers advanced southward from Montreal, intending to take New York. They were stopped when the American naval force on Lake Champlain, led by Commodore Thomas Macdonough, defeated the British fleet on September 11. When the British realized that the Americans could use their control of the lake to surround them, they retreated to Montreal.

Raids on Washington, D.C., and Baltimore With attention focused on Canada, a British fleet sailed into Chesapeake Bay in August 1814 and marched troops into Washington, D.C. Government officials hastily fled without a fight. The British set fire to both the White House and the Capitol and proceeded to Baltimore.

Unlike Washington, Baltimore was prepared. Some 13,000 militia troops and 1,000 American soldiers stood ready to defend the city. Throughout the night of September 13, the British bombarded Fort McHenry in Baltimore Harbor. Early the next morning, they abandoned their attack. **Francis Scott Key**, a young lawyer held aboard a British ship during the shelling, was elated to see the American flag still flying at dawn. On the back of a letter, he scribbled a poem that would later become the national anthem. The final lines of the first verse evoke the powerful symbolism of the flag:

> ❝O! say, does that Star-Spangled Banner yet wave,
> O'er the land of the free and the home of the brave?❞

Events in New England and New Orleans Opposition to the War of 1812 centered in New England. In December 1814, Federalists in Massachusetts organized delegates from Rhode Island, Connecticut, New Hampshire, and Vermont to

---

EXTENDING THE CONTENT

Military History When British troops took over Washington, D.C., in 1814, British admiral Sir George Cockburn ordered them to burn the Capitol, the White House, and the Navy Arsenal. Destruction to the city was not total, because a violent rainstorm struck the same night, and the accompanying winds destroyed houses, killed 30 British soldiers, and dismantled cannons. An accidental gunpowder explosion and a false rumor that American troops were mustering to retake Washington so demoralized the British that they left the city, never to return.

meet with them in Hartford, Connecticut. Some delegates urged New England to secede, or withdraw, from the United States. More moderate delegates refused to support such extreme action. Instead, the **Hartford Convention** ended by calling for constitutional amendments to increase the region's political power.

Less than a month after the Hartford Convention began, an American victory in the South put a stop to Federalist complaints. In January 1815, a British fleet landed about 7,500 men near New Orleans. American General Andrew Jackson quickly improvised a defense by building a barricade out of cotton bales from the nearby fields. The thick bales absorbed the British bullets, while the British advancing in the open provided easy targets for the American troops. After a brief battle, the British withdrew. It was a decisive victory for the United States.

The **Battle of New Orleans** made Jackson a hero. It also helped to destroy the Federalist Party. The smashing American victory led to a surge of patriotism, making the Federalists' actions at the Hartford Convention appear divisive. The Federalists never recovered politically. The battle, however, had little value militarily. It occurred two weeks after the war had officially ended and the peace treaty had been signed.

The Treaty of Ghent Peace talks began even before the major battles of 1814 in the European city of Ghent. Both sides agreed to sign the **Treaty of Ghent**

History *Through Art*

Inspiring Battle This Battle of New Orleans scene by John Landis shows General Andrew Jackson's cotton-bale defense of the Southern city. *Did the battle have an impact on the war's end? Why or why not?*

on December 24, 1814. This treaty restored prewar boundaries but did not mention neutral rights or impressment, and no territory changed hands. It did, however, create commissions to settle fishing rights and boundary disputes. Still, the War of 1812 increased the nation's prestige overseas and generated a new spirit of patriotism and national unity.

Four years later in the Convention of 1818, the United States and Great Britain set the U.S.-Canadian border from what is now Minnesota to the Rocky Mountains at 49° north latitude. The countries also agreed to claim jointly for the next ten years a region farther west known as the Oregon Country.

✓ **Reading Check** **Summarizing** What were the effects of the Battle of New Orleans?

HISTORY Online **Study Central™** To review this section, go to tarvol2.glencoe.com and click on **Study Central™**.

SECTION 2 ASSESSMENT

Checking for Understanding

1. **Define:** judicial review, contraband, impressment, embargo, War Hawk.
2. **Identify:** Louisiana Purchase.
3. **Summarize** why the Essex Junto and some Hartford Convention members wanted New England to secede from the United States.

Reviewing Themes

4. **Government and Democracy** How did *Marbury* v. *Madison* strengthen the Supreme Court?

Critical Thinking

5. **Comparing and Contrasting** In what ways was Jefferson similar to and different from Washington and Adams in terms of presidential style and policies?
6. **Categorizing** Use a graphic organizer to list the causes and effects of the War of 1812.

War of 1812		
Causes	Key Events	Effects

Analyzing Visuals

7. **Analyzing Art** Study John Landis's depiction of the Battle of New Orleans on this page. What has the artist done to portray General Andrew Jackson (far right, on horseback) as a heroic figure?

Writing About History

8. **Descriptive Writing** Imagine you are a member of the Lewis and Clark or Zebulon Pike expedition exploring unknown territory in the Far West. Write a journal entry describing a day's activities and sights.

SECTION 2 ASSESSMENT ANSWERS

1. Terms are in blue.
2. Louisiana Purchase *(p. 163)*
3. They were afraid that New England would lose political power as new states joined the union.
4. It asserted the Supreme Court's right to judicial review.
5. Similarities: foreign policy based on neutrality; Differences: Jefferson

was much more informal, and he wanted to limit the role of the federal government
6. Causes: blockades and impressments; effects: halted trade between United States and Europe, halted shipping businesses in the Northeast, and cut demand for crops from South and West

7. Jackson is in the thick of battle; horse is reared; he is in command.
8. Journal entries should focus on what a member of the expedition might have experienced using all senses.

History *Through Art*

Background: Militia units from surrounding states joined local troops in defending Louisiana. These included mounted militia and dragoons, which were mounted troops who rode into battle, dismounted, and fought on foot.
Answer: It had no real impact on the war's end, since the war officially ended two weeks earlier, when the peace treaty had been signed.
Ask: How did the battle affect Andrew Jackson? *(It made him a hero.)*

Reteach

Have students create a list of the changes Thomas Jefferson made to the federal government.

Enrich

Have students use library and Internet resources to learn more about Thomas Jefferson's life after his presidency and write a short report on their findings.

✓ **Reading Check**

Answer: It led to a surge in patriotism and effectively destroyed the Federalist party.

HISTORY Online

Study Central™ provides summaries, interactive games, and online graphic organizers to help students review section content.

4 CLOSE

Have students outline the effects of the War of 1812.

167

Geography&History

1 FOCUS

Tell students that the expedition traveled more than 7,600 miles to the Pacific. During the trip William Clark constructed 60 maps depicting the expedition's route. Have students identify the various landforms shown on the map, including rivers, mountains, and passes.

2 TEACH

Analyzing Information Have students study the map and read the feature. Have students create questions for a trivia game based on the information they have read. Have students pose their questions and see which student can answer them most quickly. If you choose, you can keep score and provide a small prize to the winners. **L1**

Mental Mapping Tell students to create a mental map of the route they take to school. Have students draw the map on a piece of paper. Encourage them to add appropriate details and include a legend. **L2**

FYI

Travelers' Rest is located southwest of present-day Lolo, Montana. The Lewis and Clark expedition camped here in 1805 and 1806. Native Americans also camped here. Although the name of the camp sounds inviting, the cold weather made the camp quite unpleasant.

168

The Journey West

● ● ● Route west

‑ ‑ ‑ ‑ Continental Divide

△ Camp

Scale of map varies in this perspective

BITTERROOT RANGE

Ajax Peak
10,030 ft. (3057 m)

Lost Trail Pass
7,014 ft. (2138 m)

Lolo Pass
5,233 ft. (1595 m)

Bitterroot River

△ **TRAVELER'S REST**
September 9, 1805

BEAVERHEAD MOUNTAINS

Lemhi Pass
7,373 ft. (2247 m)

Anaconda Range

SAPPHIRE MOUNTAINS

Mt. Evans
10,640 ft. (3243 m)

Baldy Mt.
10,568 ft. (3221 m)

Flint Creek Range

Clark Fork River

Red M
9,409 ft. (28

△ **CAMP FORTUNATE**
August 17, 1805

Beaverhead River

Crow Peak
9,413 ft. (2869 m)

GATES OF THE ROCKY MOUNTA

Jefferson River

ROUTE OF THE CORPS OF DISCOVERY

Missouri River

Madison River

△ **THREE FORKS**
July 27, 1805

Mt. Edith
9,504 ft. (2897 m)

BIG BELT MOUNTAINS

Smith

Area enlarged

British Territory

Claimed by Britain, Spain, and Russia

LOUISIANA PURCHASE 1803

St. Louis

UNITED STATES and Territories

Pacific Ocean

Spanish Territory

Atlantic Ocean

Gulf of Mexico

This locator map shows Lewis and Clark's route from St. Louis to the Pacific Ocean. The expedition collected valuable information about the people, plants, animals, and geography of the West. Americans soon followed in the footsteps of the intrepid explorers to open up the American West.

168 CHAPTER 4 Federalists and Republicans

EXTENDING THE CONTENT

Science and Nature Since many of the plants and animals that Lewis and Clark encountered were unknown to them, they collected and preserved many specimens including prairie dog, jackrabbit, black-tailed deer, pronghorn, and mountain sheep. Huge grizzly bears were common threats to the expedition. They also found some huge bones that may have been those of a dinosaur. As an avid collector of mastodon bones (the word dinosaur was not coined until 1840), Thomas Jefferson sent William Clark in search of more bones to add to his collection in 1807.

Westward to the Pacific

An accomplished geographer and cartographer, William Clark compiled this detailed map of the expedition's route around the Great Falls of the Missouri River.

Area of Clark's map in log book shown above

Sun River

GREAT FALLS
June 13, 1805

Camp above the falls

Camp below the falls

On May 26, 1805, from a bluff above the Missouri River, Meriwether Lewis "beheld the Rocky Mountains for the first time."

I n May 1804, the Corps of Discovery—Meriwether Lewis, William Clark, and about 40 others—set sail up the Missouri River from their camp outside of St. Louis. Their mission was to find the so-called Northwest Passage—a water route across the continent to the Pacific Ocean. However, after crossing the Great Plains, they discovered the enormous obstacle between them and the Pacific: the Rocky Mountains. Tackling those "terrible mountains," wrote Lewis, proved "the most perilous and difficult part of our voyage" (see map at left).

One of their first challenges was to get beyond the Great Falls of the Missouri. It took them nearly a month to move their boats and supplies almost 18 miles (29 km) around the falls to a more navigable part of the river. Clear of the falls, they pressed on, up through a deep canyon known as the Gates of the Rocky Mountains —"the most remarkable cliffs that we have yet seen," recalled Lewis. From here, the Missouri River ran fast, and its current was strong. In late July 1805, the expedition arrived at Three Forks. After trekking up each fork of the river, Lewis and Clark opted for the western branch, which they named for President Thomas Jefferson. From here, progress slowed. The men often had to wade through the increasingly shallow water, drag-

ging their boats behind them. Soon they would have to abandon the boats altogether; but first they needed horses to carry their supplies over the mountains.

Lewis and three men went on ahead. On August 12 they crossed the Continental Divide at Lemhi Pass, becoming the first explorers from the United States to do so. As Lewis and his party descended the steep mountains, they encountered a band of Shoshone. Lewis convinced Cameahwait, their leader, to go back to meet the others. To everyone's astonishment, the Shoshone recognized their Native American guide, Sacagawea, as a member of their band who had been kidnapped long ago. Sacagawea suddenly realized Chief Cameahwait was her brother, and she joyfully embraced him.

With Sacagawea's help, Lewis convinced the Shoshone to sell them horses and provide a guide. The Corps crossed into the Bitterroot Range around Lost Trail Pass. After a pause at Traveler's Rest, the expedition headed over the massive peaks. They climbed the snow-covered slopes and struggled around the fallen trees, watching in horror as their horses slipped and rolled down. Game was so scarce that the famished explorers were forced to kill and eat three of their colts. Despite the hardships, the weary party trudged on until they arrived at a village of the Nez Perce, who provided food and water. The explorers finally reached a tributary of the Columbia River, built dugout boats, abandoned their horses, and floated west all the way to the Pacific Ocean.

LEARNING FROM GEOGRAPHY

1. Why were Lewis and Clark unable to complete their mission?

2. Imagine that you are a member of the expedition. Write a letter home detailing some of the sights you have seen.

169

ANSWERS TO LEARNING FROM GEOGRAPHY

1. There was no navigable water route to the Pacific Ocean. They encountered rapids, shallows, and the Rocky Mountains.
2. Students' letters will vary. Encourage students to be as descriptive and specific as possible.

Remind them that one of the reasons the journey of Lewis and Clark is so well-known is that they kept detailed records.

NATIONAL GEOGRAPHIC

Geography&History

Creating a Drawing Tell students that accurate descriptions and drawings made Lewis and Clark's observations valuable. Have students look out a window in the classroom or go outside and choose an example of flora (plants) or fauna (animals). Have students draw and describe it so exactly that someone who had never seen it would be able to recognize it. **L2**

L2

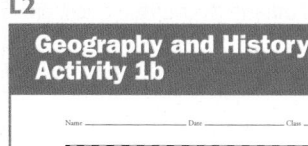

Geography and History Activity 1b

Name _____ Date _____ Class _____

⊕ GEOGRAPHY AND HISTORY ACTIVITY 1-B 🧭

The Missouri: A Powerful River

RIVER HIGHWAYS
When traveling across the country today, Americans use four-lane highways or airplanes. During the early explorations of our country, however, the "transportation systems" used most often were rivers. The rivers that carried explorers such as Meriwether Lewis, William Clark, Zebulon Pike, and Stephen Long to the West played an important role in their experiences and the development of the young United States. (See Map 1.)

river. If they arrived at this section of the river much earlier, the entire party could have been buried by the falling cliffs. Dangerous situations continued along most of the Missouri to the headwaters, or source, of the river. The Missouri's source is where the Gallatin, Madison, and Jefferson Rivers come together near present-day Three Forks, Montana. (See Map 1 inset.)

A RIVER IN MOTION
A river on a wide floodplain like the Missouri does not flow in a straight line

UNIT 1

3 ASSESS

Have students answer the Learning from Geography questions.

4 CLOSE

Ask students to list the challenges that faced the Lewis and Clark expedition.

NGS ONLINE

Access National Geographic's Web site for current events, atlas updates, activities, links, interactive features, and archives at www.nationalgeographic.com.

169

1 FOCUS

Section Overview

This section focuses on the swell of patriotism and national pride that followed the War of 1812.

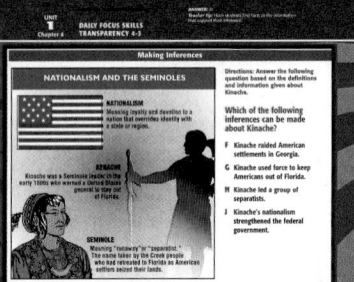
Reading Preview

Answers to Graphic: creation of new national bank, imposition of protective tariff, Supreme Court decisions established dominance of the nation over states, invasion of Florida, proclamation of the Monroe Doctrine

Preteaching Vocabulary
Have students write a sentence that uses at least two of the Key Terms and Names.

SECTION 3 The Growth of American Nationalism

Guide to Reading

Main Idea
Americans developed powerful feelings of patriotism and national unity after the War of 1812.

Key Terms and Names
revenue tariff, protective tariff, *McCulloch v. Maryland*, Seminole, Monroe Doctrine

Reading Strategy
Organizing As you read about the nation after the War of 1812, complete a graphic organizer by listing actions that strengthened the federal government at home and abroad.

Actions

Reading Objectives
• **Analyze** how John Marshall strengthened the Supreme Court.
• **Evaluate** how nationalism affected American foreign policy after the War of 1812.

Section Theme
Continuity and Change Increased national pride marked the period immediately following the War of 1812.

Preview of Events

♦1815	♦1820	♦1825

1816
Second Bank of the United States established; Monroe elected president

1819
Spain cedes Florida to United States; *McCulloch* v. *Maryland*

1823
Monroe Doctrine announced

1824
Gibbons v. *Ogden*

★ An American Story ★

James Monroe

On a March day in 1817, a dignified group of government officials gathered in Washington, D.C., to witness the inauguration of the fifth president of the United States. The attentive audience was full of hope and optimism as James Monroe delivered his Inaugural Address.

66 Never did a government commence under auspices so favorable, nor ever was success so complete. If we look to the history of other nations, ancient or modern, we find no example of a growth so rapid, so gigantic, of a people so prosperous and happy. In contemplating what we have still to perform, the heart of every citizen must expand with joy when he reflects how near our Government has approached to perfection. . . . If we persevere in the career in which we have advanced so far and in the path already traced, we can not fail, under the favor of a gracious Providence, to attain the high destiny which seems to await us. 99

—from James Monroe's Inaugural Address, March 1817

Political Unity

President Monroe's words emphasized the sense of nationalism that swept the United States after the War of 1812. More and more Americans began to consider themselves to be part of a whole. Their loyalty to the United States overrode their identity with state or region. Riding this wave of nationalism, the new president made a goodwill tour of the

---

SECTION RESOURCES

📁 Reproducible Masters
• Reproducible Lesson Plan 4–3
• Daily Lecture and Discussion Notes 4–3
• Guided Reading Activity 4–3
• Section Quiz 4–3
• Reading Essentials and Study Guide 4–3
• Supreme Court Case Studies

📄 Transparencies
• Daily Focus Skills Transparency 4–3

Multimedia
🖱 Interactive Tutor Self-Assessment CD-ROM
🖱 ExamView® Pro Testmaker CD-ROM
🖱 Presentation Plus! CD-ROM
🖱 TeacherWorks™ CD-ROM
🎧 Audio Program

country, finding enthusiastic crowds at every stop. The *Columbian Centinal,* a Boston newspaper, declared that an **Era of Good Feelings** had dawned.

Harmony in national politics reached a new high, mostly because only one party, the Republicans, had any power. At the same time, the war had taught Americans that a stronger federal government was advantageous. In the postwar years, Republican leaders shifted their focus from world affairs to national growth.

✓ **Reading Check** **Explaining** Why is the Monroe presidency known as the Era of Good Feelings?

Economic Nationalism

As Monroe's presidency began, Congress prepared an ambitious economic program. It included creating a new national bank, protecting American manufacturers from foreign competition, and building new roads and canals.

The Second Bank of the United States Republicans had blocked the rechartering of the First Bank of the United States in 1811 but offered nothing in its place. The results were disastrous. State-chartered banks and other private banks greatly expanded their lending with bank notes that were used as money. Without the regulatory presence of the national bank, prices rose rapidly during the War of 1812.

In 1816 Representative John C. Calhoun of South Carolina introduced a bill proposing the Second Bank of the United States. The bill passed and was signed by outgoing President Madison. It empowered the bank to control state banks and to issue notes that would serve as a national currency.

ECONOMICS

The Protective Tariff Protecting manufacturers from foreign competition was another Republican goal. Because the Embargo of 1807 and the War of 1812 had kept Americans from buying British goods, American industries had increased their output to meet demand. Once the war was over, British goods flowed into the United States at low prices, severely threatening American companies.

Congress responded with the Tariff of 1816. Unlike earlier revenue tariffs, intended to provide federal income, this was a protective tariff, aimed at protecting American manufacturers by taxing imports.

Internal Improvements The Republicans also wanted to improve the nation's transportation system. The difficulties of moving troops and supplies during the war highlighted the need for better roads and canals. In 1816 Calhoun sponsored a bill to fund such improvements. President Madison vetoed it, however, arguing that the Constitution did not empower Congress to improve transportation. Nevertheless, road and canal construction soon began in earnest with support from private businesses and state and local governments.

✓ **Reading Check** **Identifying** What were three examples of economic nationalism after the War of 1812?

Judicial Nationalism

The judicial philosophy of the Chief Justice of the United States, John Marshall, provided another boost to postwar nationalism. He interpreted the Constitution broadly to support federal power. Between 1816 and 1824, several important cases established the power of the nation over the states.

McCulloch v. Maryland The 1819 case of *McCulloch* v. *Maryland* involved Maryland's attempt to tax the Baltimore branch of the Second Bank of the

Profiles IN HISTORY

John C. Calhoun
1782–1850

John C. Calhoun of South Carolina was an influential member of Congress and, at least for a time, a close friend of Henry Clay. Like Clay, Calhoun was a War Hawk—one who urged war with Great Britain in 1812—and an ardent nationalist in his early career. After the War of 1812, Calhoun helped introduce congressional bills for a new Bank of the United States, a permanent road system to bind the nation together, and a tariff to protect the nation's industries.

In the 1830s Calhoun abandoned his nationalist stance in favor of states' rights and sectional interests. Fearing that the North intended to dominate the South, Calhoun spent the rest of his career trying to prevent the federal government from weakening states' rights and from interfering with the Southern way of life.

CHAPTER 4 Federalists and Republicans **171**

2 TEACH

Daily Lecture and Discussion Notes 4–3

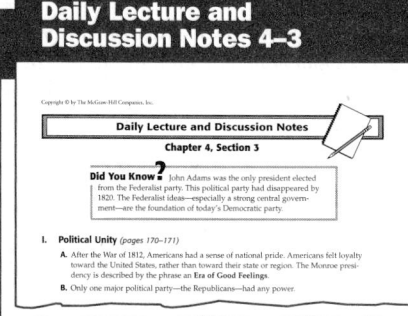

Copyright © by The McGraw-Hill Companies, Inc.

Daily Lecture and Discussion Notes
Chapter 4, Section 3

Did You Know? John Adams was the only president elected from the Federalist party. This political party had disappeared by 1820. The Federalist ideas—especially a strong central government—are the foundation of today's Democratic party.

I. **Political Unity** *(pages 170–171)*
   A. After the War of 1812, Americans had a sense of national pride. Americans felt loyalty toward the United States, rather than toward their state or region. The Monroe presidency is described by the phrase an Era of Good Feelings.
   B. Only one major political party—the Republicans—had any power.

Analyzing Information Have students use library, Internet, and other resources to study the tariffs of 1807, 1812, and 1816. Have them write a short paper analyzing the effects of these tariffs. **L2**

✓ **Reading Check**

Answer: because of a strong sense of national pride and enthusiasm

✓ **Reading Check**

Answer: a national bank, protective tariffs, internal improvements

Profiles IN HISTORY

John C. Calhoun served in both Houses of Congress, as secretary of state, and as vice president.

L1/ELL

Guided Reading Activity 4–3

Name _____ Date _____ Class _____

★ **Guided Reading Activity 4-3**

DIRECTIONS: Filling in the Blanks In the space provided, write the word or words that best complete the sentence. Refer to your textbook to fill in the blanks.
1. When James Monroe took office in 1817, a Boston newspaper used the phrase _____ to describe his presidency.
2. The War of 1812 had taught a new generation of Republican leaders that a stronger _____ was advantageous.
3. Without the regulatory presence of the _____, prices rose rapidly during the War of 1812.
4. In 1816 outgoing President Madison signed a bill to establish the Second Bank of the United States, which would control _____ and issue notes that would serve as a _____.
5. The Tariff of 1816 was a _____ designed to protect American manufac- _____.

| **Reading Strategy** | **READING THE TEXT** |

Taking Notes Students can use notes to group, outline, and organize information. As they read this section, have students list the main ideas about the growth of nationalism in the United States. Under each main idea, they should list at least two events that demonstrate how people's identity with the nation overrode their identity with a state or region. **L1**

📂 Refer to *Inclusion for the High School Social Studies Classroom Strategies and Activities* in the TCR.

Chart *Skills*

Answers:
1. *Marbury* v. *Madison*
2. possible answer: No, *McCulloch* v. *Maryland* emphasized the idea of implied powers.

✓ Reading Check

Answer: It interpreted the Constitution broadly to support federal power.

History *and the* Humanities

🏴 American Music: Hits Through History: "College Hornpipe," "Belle Catherine"

🏴 American Music: Cultural Traditions: "The Rose Tree," "Hull's Victory," "Hunters of Kentucky"

📁 Use *Supreme Court Case Study 2, McCulloch* v. *Maryland.*

📁 Use *Supreme Court Case Study 3, Dartmouth College* v. *Woodward.*

📁 Use *Supreme Court Case Study 4, Gibbons* v. *Ogden.*

3 ASSESS

Assign Section 3 Assessment as homework or as an in-class activity.

🖳 Have students use the **Interactive Tutor Self-Assessment CD-ROM.**

Major Supreme Court Decisions, 1801–1824

Case	Decision
Marbury v. Madison (1803)	Declared congressional act unconstitutional; Court asserts power of judicial review
Fletcher v. Peck (1810)	Protected contracts from legislative interference; Court could overturn state laws that opposed specific provisions of Constitution
Martin v. Hunter's Lessee (1816)	Court can accept appeals of state court decisions and review state decisions that involve federal statutes or treaties; asserted the Supreme Court's sovereignty over state courts
McCulloch v. Maryland (1819)	Upheld constitutionality of the Bank of the United States; doctrine of "implied powers" provided Congress more flexibility to enact legislation
Cohens v. Virginia (1821)	Reasserted federal judicial authority over state courts; argued that when states ratified Constitution, they gave up some sovereignty to federal courts
Gibbons v. Ogden (1824)	Revoked an existing state monopoly; Court gave Congress the right to regulate interstate commerce

Source: *The Oxford Companion to the Supreme Court of the United States*

Chart *Skills*

1. **Interpreting Charts** In which case did Chief Justice Marshall assert the Court's right of judicial review?
2. **Analyzing** Was Marshall a strict interpreter of the Constitution? Use a case to support your answer.

United States. Before addressing Maryland's right to tax the national bank, the Supreme Court first ruled on the federal government's right to create a national bank in the first place. In the Court's opinion, written by John Marshall, the bank was constitutional, even though the Constitution did not specifically give Congress the power to create one. Marshall observed that the Constitution gave the federal government the power to collect taxes, to borrow money, to regulate commerce, and to raise armies and navies. He noted that the national bank helped the federal government exercise these powers. He concluded that the "necessary and proper" clause allowed the federal government to use its powers in any way not specifically prohibited by the Constitution. 📖 *(See page 963 for more information on* McCulloch v. Maryland.*)*

Opponents argued that the necessary and proper clause meant the government could only take action that was absolutely necessary, but Marshall specifically rejected that idea. Instead, he held that "necessary and proper" meant the government could use any method that was convenient for carrying out its powers as long as the Constitution did not expressly forbid it.

Marshall then went on to argue that the federal government was "supreme in its own sphere of action." This meant that a state government could not interfere with an agency of the federal government exercising its specific constitutional powers within a state's borders. Taxing the national bank was a form of interference and was therefore ruled unconstitutional.

Gibbons v. Ogden The 1824 case of *Gibbons v. Ogden* dealt with interstate commerce. A company with a state-granted monopoly over steamboat traffic in New York waters also wanted exclusive control of steamboats crossing the Hudson River to New Jersey. The Supreme Court declared the original monopoly unconstitutional. In the Court's opinion, written by Marshall, a state could regulate commerce within its own borders, but navigation of a waterway between two states was interstate commerce, and the Constitution specifically granted the federal government control over interstate commerce.

In broadening the definition of interstate commerce beyond the exchange of goods between states, Marshall ensured that federal law would take precedence over state law in interstate transportation. Defenders of states' rights attacked many of Marshall's decisions, as his views helped make the "necessary and proper" clause and the interstate commerce clause vehicles for expanding federal power. 📖 *(See page 963 for more information on* Gibbons v. Ogden.*)*

✓ Reading Check **Explaining** How did the Supreme Court strengthen the power of the federal government over the states?

Nationalist Diplomacy

Postwar nationalism influenced foreign as well as domestic affairs. Feeling proud and confident, the United States under President Monroe expanded its borders and asserted itself on the world stage.

DIFFERENTIATED INSTRUCTION

Gifted and Talented Have students work in pairs to recreate the arguments of one of the cases in this section. Have the pairs work together to decide which side of the issue each of them will present. Have them research the case and present a summary of the arguments to the class. Encourage the pairs to pretend that they are arguing their case before the Supreme Court. Allow the class, acting as the court, to ask questions of each person. **L3**

📁 Refer to *Inclusion for the High School Social Studies Classroom Strategies and Activities* in the TCR.

Jackson Invades Florida During the early 1800s, Spanish-held Florida was a source of frustration for Southerners. Many runaway slaves hid there, and the **Seminoles,** a Native American group, often clashed with American settlers across the border in Georgia. Spain was unable to control the border, and many Americans demanded the United States step in. As tensions heightened, a Seminole leader named Kinache warned Americans to stay out of Florida:

❝You charge me with killing your people, stealing your cattle and burning your houses; it is I that have cause to complain of the Americans. . . . I shall use force to stop any armed Americans from passing my towns or my lands.❞

–quoted in *The Seminoles of Florida*

The warning fell on deaf ears. Former representative Calhoun, now secretary of war, authorized action against the Seminoles. In 1818 Andrew Jackson led U.S. troops into Florida and quickly seized Spanish settlements at Pensacola and St. Marks.

The Spanish government demanded that American officials punish Jackson, but Secretary of State John Quincy Adams blamed Spain for failing to keep order in Florida. Adams then put pressure on Spain in ongoing border questions. Occupied with problems throughout its Latin American empire, Spain gave in and ceded all of Florida to the United States in the **Adams-Onís Treaty** of 1819.

The Monroe Doctrine Spain had good reason to worry about Latin America. Many of Spain's colonies there were declaring their independence.

Meanwhile, some European monarchies expressed their interest in helping Spain suppress these Latin American revolutions.

Neither Great Britain nor the United States wanted Spain to regain control of its colonies. Both were trading with Latin America. In August 1823, Britain suggested that the United States join it in issuing a statement supporting Latin American independence.

John Quincy Adams urged President Monroe to issue his own statement on behalf of United States interests. The Monroe administration also had concerns at this time about Russia's growing interest in the American northwest. In 1821 Russia had announced that its empire extended south from Alaska to the Oregon territory.

Under these circumstances, Monroe decided to issue a statement in December 1823. In the **Monroe Doctrine,** the president declared that the American continents should no longer be viewed as open to colonization. He specifically advised Europe to respect the sovereignty of new Latin American nations. 📖 *(See page 952 for more information on the Monroe Doctrine.)*

The Monroe Doctrine was a bold act for a young nation. The United States might not have been able to back up its new stand if it had been challenged. The doctrine upheld Washington's policy of avoiding European entanglements and also guided American foreign policy for years.

✓ **Reading Check** **Examining** How did the Adams-Onís Treaty and the Monroe Doctrine demonstrate a strong approach to foreign policy?

 HISTORY Online **Study Central**™ To review this section, go to tarvol2.glencoe.com and click on **Study Central**™.

SECTION 3 ASSESSMENT

Checking for Understanding
1. **Define:** revenue tariff, protective tariff.
2. **Identify:** *McCulloch* v. *Maryland,* Seminole, Monroe Doctrine.
3. **Explain** how the Supreme Court rulings in *McCulloch* v. *Maryland* and *Gibbons* v. *Ogden* strengthened the federal government.

Reviewing Themes
4. **Continuity and Change** Did the Monroe Doctrine represent a continuation or change in President Washington's foreign policy? Explain.

Critical Thinking
5. **Analyzing** How did nationalism affect the foreign affairs of the United States?
6. **Organizing** Use a graphic organizer to list examples of nationalism in the United States after the War of 1812.

Examples of Nationalism		
Economic	Judicial	Diplomatic

Analyzing Visuals
7. **Posing Questions** Study the chart of Supreme Court decisions on page 172. Use the information to construct a 10-question quiz to give to your classmates to assess their understanding of the Marshall Court.

Writing About History
8. **Expository Writing** Imagine you are a newspaper editor in Georgia or Spanish-held Florida. Write an editorial in which you criticize or defend Andrew Jackson's actions in seizing Spanish settlements in Florida.

CHAPTER 4 Federalists and Republicans **173**

SECTION 3 ASSESSMENT ANSWERS

1. Terms are in blue.
2. *McCulloch* v. *Maryland (p. 171),* Seminole *(p. 173),* Monroe Doctrine *(p. 173)*
3. *McCulloch* v. *Maryland:* doctrine of "implied powers" gave Congress more flexibility to enact legislation; *Gibbons* v. *Ogden:* gave Congress right to regulate interstate trade

4. continuation, because it upheld policy of avoiding European entanglements
5. Nationalism led to the invasion of Florida and the declaration of the Monroe Doctrine.
6. economic nationalism: protective tariffs; judicial nationalism: the court strengthened the power of

the federal government at the expense of the states; diplomatic nationalism: Monroe Doctrine
7. Have students exchange quizzes and answer the questions.
8. Editorials should clearly support one side of the issue or the other.

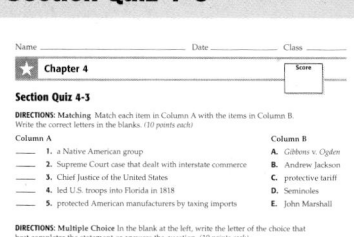

L1/ELL

Reading Essentials and Study Guide 4–3

Name _____ Date _____ Class _____

Study Guide

Chapter 4, Section 3
For use with textbook pages 170–173

THE GROWTH OF AMERICAN NATIONALISM

KEY TERMS AND NAMES

revenue tariff tax on goods that provides income for the federal government (page 171)

protective tariff tax on goods to help domestic manufacturers by taxing imports to drive up their prices (page 171)

McCulloch v. Maryland Supreme Court case that upheld the national bank and the power of Congress to be flexible in making laws (page 171)

Seminole a Native American group in Florida (page 173)

Monroe Doctrine President Monroe's declaration that the American continents were no longer open to colonization (page 173)

L2

Section Quiz 4–3

Name _____ Date _____ Class _____

⭐ **Chapter 4** Score _____

Section Quiz 4-3

DIRECTIONS: Matching Match each item in Column A with the items in Column B. Write the correct letters in the blanks. *(10 points each)*

Column A	Column B
___ 1. a Native American group	A. *Gibbons v. Ogden*
___ 2. Supreme Court case that dealt with interstate commerce	B. Andrew Jackson
___ 3. Chief Justice of the United States	C. protective tariff
___ 4. led U.S. troops into Florida in 1818	D. Seminoles
___ 5. protected American manufacturers by taxing imports	E. John Marshall

DIRECTIONS: Multiple Choice In the blank at the left, write the letter of the choice that best completes the statement or answers the question. *(10 points each)*

___ 6. Spain ceded all of Florida to the United States in the

Reteach
Ask students to list the ways that John Marshall strengthened the Supreme Court.

Enrich
Have students create a display on how Americans have shown patriotism throughout history.

✓ **Reading Check**

Answer: Both demonstrated that the United States could speak strongly for the Western Hemisphere.

 HISTORY Online

Study Central™ provides summaries, interactive games, and online graphic organizers to help students review section content.

4 CLOSE

At the top of the board, write Cause: Nationalism. Ask volunteers to write on the board specific effects that nationalism had during the time period.

GLENCOE TECHNOLOGY

MindJogger Videoquiz
Use the **MindJogger Videoquiz** to review Chapter 4 content.

⊙ Available in DVD

Reviewing Key Terms
Students' answers will vary. The pages where the words appear in the text are shown in parentheses.

1. **cabinet** (p. 153)
2. **bond** (p. 153)
3. **speculator** (p. 154)
4. **enumerated powers** (p. 154)
5. **implied powers** (p. 154)
6. **excise tax** (p. 155)
7. **most-favored nation** (p. 156)
8. **alien** (p. 157)
9. **interposition** (p. 158)
10. **nullification** (p. 158)
11. **judicial review** (p. 162)
12. **contraband** (p. 164)
13. **impressment** (p. 164)
14. **embargo** (p. 164)
15. **War Hawk** (p. 165)
16. **revenue tariff** (p. 171)
17. **protective tariff** (p. 171)

Reviewing Key Facts
18. XYZ Affair (p. 157), Monroe Doctrine (p. 173)
19. First eight amendments offered safeguards for the rights of individuals against actions by the federal government.
20. He believed that Congress lacked the authority to create the bank.
21. Tensions rose due to the increase in the number of western settlers and the continuing westward expansion.
22. British impressments of American sailors, British seizure of American cargo, and British role in Native American attacks on western settlers
23. Answers should include three of the

Reviewing Key Terms
On a sheet of paper, use each of these terms in a sentence.

1. cabinet
2. bond
3. speculator
4. enumerated powers
5. implied powers
6. excise tax
7. most-favored nation
8. alien
9. interposition
10. nullification
11. judicial review
12. contraband
13. impressment
14. embargo
15. War Hawk
16. revenue tariff
17. protective tariff

Reviewing Key Facts
18. **Identify:** XYZ Affair, Monroe Doctrine.
19. What was the main focus of the first eight amendments in the Bill of Rights?
20. Why did James Madison oppose the establishment of a national bank?
21. Why did tensions between Western settlers and Native Americans increase during Washington's presidency?
22. What events led to the War of 1812?
23. What were three actions that strengthened the federal government after the War of 1812?

Critical Thinking
24. **Analyzing Themes: Government and Democracy** What was the most important task for Congress after the U.S. Constitution was ratified? Explain your answer.
25. **Categorizing** Use a graphic organizer like the one below to list the differences between the first political parties in the United States.

Federalists	Republicans

26. **Interpreting Primary Sources** In *McCulloch* v. *Maryland,* the Supreme Court was asked whether Congress had the power to set up the Bank of the United States. The following excerpt is from Chief Justice John Marshall's ruling. Read the excerpt and answer the questions that follow.

❝The government of the United States . . . though limited in its powers, is supreme; and its laws, when made in pursuance of the constitution, form the supreme law of the land. . . . Among the enumerated powers, we do not find establishing a bank or creating a corporation. But there is no phrase in the instrument which . . . requires that everything granted shall be expressly and minutely described. . . . Among the enumerated powers

Chapter Summary

George Washington
- Established legitimacy of the new government
- Created executive departments
- Favored neutrality
- Used troops to stop Native American resistance in the West

Thomas Jefferson
- Republican leader; worked to limit power of national government
- Favored land ownership for all people
- Supported farmers over commerce and trade
- Negotiated purchase of the Louisiana Territory

John Adams
- Federalist leader in favor of strong national government
- Supported commerce and trade
- Favored neutrality; negotiated treaties with Britain and France to avoid war
- Angered farmers and landowners with taxes; angered political opponents with Alien and Sedition Acts

James Madison
- Republican who favored neutrality
- Asked Congress to declare war on Britain to protect trade interest in the East and farmers and settlers in the West
- Under his administration, the War of 1812 generated feelings of nationalism, and the Treaty of Ghent established fishing rights and boundaries with Canada

following: creation of new national bank, imposition of protective tariffs, Supreme Court decisions establishing dominance of the nation over states, invasion of Florida, or the proclamation of the Monroe Doctrine.

Critical Thinking
24. Any of the following are acceptable as long as they are supported: creation of cabinet, the Judiciary Act of 1789, the Bill of Rights, creation of a national bank.

25. Federalists favored a strong federal government and an economy based on manufacturing and trade. Republicans favored states' rights and supported agriculture.

26. **a.** It had both enumerated powers and implied powers and its powers were supreme. **b.** It confirmed the power of the government to act for the nation in areas such as raising funds, declaring wars, and regulating commerce.

HISTORY Online

Self-Check Quiz

Visit the *American Republic Since 1877* Web site at tarvol2.glencoe.com and click on *Self-Check Quizzes—Chapter 4* to assess your knowledge of chapter content.

of government . . . we find the great powers to lay and collect taxes; to borrow money; to regulate commerce; to declare war and conduct a war; and to raise and support armies and navies. . . . A government entrusted with such ample powers . . . must also be entrusted with ample means for their execution. . . . All means which are appropriate, which are plainly adapted to that end, which are not prohibited, but consist with the letter and spirit of the constitution, are constitutional. . . . **99**

—from *McCulloch* v. *Maryland*

a. What was Marshall's opinion about the power of the government of the United States?

b. Why do you think the ruling in *McCulloch* v. *Maryland* made American nationalism stronger?

Practicing Skills

27. Reading a Flowchart Reread the passage about Rising International Tensions on pages 164–165 from Section 2. Then complete the following flowchart of events leading to the War of 1812.
a. British warship attacks the *Chesapeake*.
b. _____
c. Madison asks Congress to pass the Non-Intercourse Act.
d. _____
e. France takes conciliatory steps.
f. _____
g. Congress declares war.

Writing Activity

28. Expository Writing Imagine that you are a newspaper editor in 1817. You have been asked to write an article on the high and low points of the first four presidential administrations. Use evidence to support your reflections.

Chapter Activity

29. American History Primary Source Document Library CD-ROM Under *A New Nation*, read George Washington's Farewell Address and Thomas Jefferson's First Inaugural Address. Debate modern political party performance with your classmates, using the opinions of Washington and Jefferson demonstrated in these primary sources.

NATIONAL GEOGRAPHIC | **Treaty of Greenville, 1795**

Lake Huron
Lake Michigan
Lake Erie
N.Y.
Ft. Miami
Ft. Defiance
PA.
NORTHWEST TERR.
Ft. Recovery
Ft. Washington
Greenville Treaty Line, 1795
VA.
Ohio R.
KY.

☐ Land ceded by Native Americans in Treaty of Greenville, 1795
■ Fort

0 ___ 100 miles
0 ___ 100 kilometers
Albers Conic Equal-Area projection

Geography and History

30. The map above shows land acquired in the Treaty of Greenville. Study the map and answer the questions below.
a. Interpreting Maps In the Treaty of Greenville, Native Americans ceded most of which present-day state?
b. Applying Geography Skills Why was the land the Native Americans gave up valuable to white settlers?

Standardized Test Practice

Directions: Choose the best answer to the following question.

Which of the following actions reflect President Jefferson's goal of limiting the power of the federal government?

F He increased the size of the army.

G He proposed renewing the Alien and Sedition Acts.

H He dissolved the Republican Party to eliminate political conflict.

J He cut the federal budget.

Test-Taking Tip: Think about the word *limit.* It means to reduce or restrict. Therefore, you can eliminate answer F—it gave the government more power.

HISTORY Online

Have students visit the Web site at tarvol2.glencoe.com to review Chapter 4 and take the Self-Check Quiz.

Standardized Test Practice

Answer: J
Test-Taking Tip: In addition to ruling out answers that they know are wrong, have students look for the main ideas in the question. For example, this question asks about Jefferson's goal of limiting the power of the federal government, which eliminates F and G because they increase federal authority.

Bonus Question ?

Ask: Who was the first president to live in the nation's new capital, Washington, D.C.? *(John Adams)*

Practicing Skills

27. b. Jefferson asks Congress to pass the Embargo Act of 1807; **d.** Macon's Bill Number Two passed by Congress; **f.** Congress passes a nonimportation act against Britain.

28. Articles should be written in a news report style. Have students review expository newspaper articles before writing their own articles.

29. Conduct the debate using formal debating rules and techniques.

Geography and History

30. a. Ohio; **b.** gave them a vast amount of farmland and greater access to the Ohio River

175

Timesaving Tools

TeacherWorks™ All-In-One Planner and Resource Center

- **Interactive Teacher Edition** Access your Teacher Wraparound Edition and your classroom resources with a few easy clicks.
- **Interactive Lesson Planner** Planning has never been easier! Organize your week, month, semester, or year with all the lesson helps you need to make teaching creative, timely, and relevant.

Use Glencoe's **Presentation Plus!** multimedia teacher tool to easily present dynamic lessons that visually excite your students. Using Microsoft PowerPoint® you can customize the presentations to create your own personalized lessons.

TEACHING TRANSPARENCIES

Graphic Organizer 5 L2

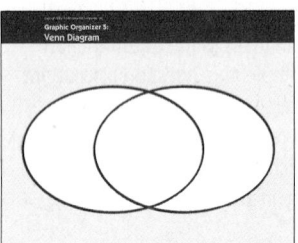

Why It Matters Chapter Transparency 5 L2

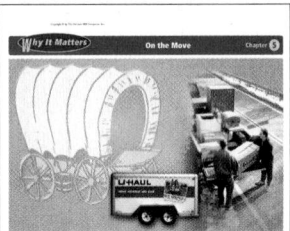

APPLICATION AND ENRICHMENT

Linking Past and Present Activity 5 L2

Enrichment Activity 5 L3

Primary Source Reading 5 L2

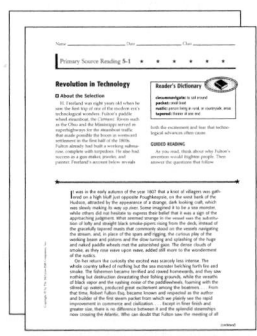

REVIEW AND REINFORCEMENT

Reteaching Activity 5 L1

Vocabulary Activity 5 L1

Time Line Activity 5 L2

Critical Thinking Skills Activity 5 L2

Meeting NCSS Standards

The following standards are covered in Chapter 5:

Section 1	VIII	Science, Technology, and Society: A, B, C
Section 2	VI	Power, Authority, and Governance: A, B, C, E, F, I
Section 3	V	Individuals, Groups & Institutions: A, B, D, E, F, G
Section 4	II	Time, Continuity, and Change: B, C, D

Local Standards

Chapter 5 Resources

ASSESSMENT AND EVALUATION

Chapter 5 Test
Form A L2

Chapter 5 Test
Form B L2

Standardized Test Practice
Workbook Activity 5 L2

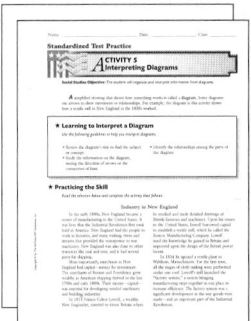

Performance Assessment
Activities and Rubrics 5 L1/ELL

ExamView® Pro
Testmaker CD-ROM

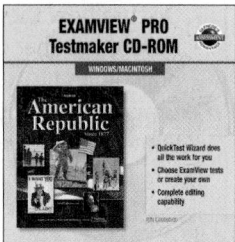

MULTIMEDIA

- Vocabulary PuzzleMaker CD-ROM
- Interactive Tutor Self-Assessment CD-ROM
- ExamView® Pro Testmaker CD-ROM
- Audio Program
- American History Primary Source Documents Library CD-ROM
- MindJogger Videoquiz
- Presentation Plus! CD-ROM
- TeacherWorks™ CD-ROM
- Interactive Student Edition CD-ROM
- Glencoe Skillbuilder Interactive Workbook CD-ROM, Level 2
- The *American Republic Since 1877* Video Program
- American Music: Hits Through History
- American Music: Cultural Traditions

SPANISH RESOURCES

The following Spanish language materials are available:

- Spanish Reading Essentials and Study Guide
- Spanish Guided Reading Activities
- Spanish Reteaching Activities
- Spanish Quizzes and Tests
- Spanish Vocabulary Activities
- Spanish Summaries
- The Declaration of Independence and United States Constitution Spanish Translation

The following videotape programs are available from Glencoe as supplements to Chapter 5:

- **Andrew Jackson: A Man for the People** (ISBN 1-56-501647-5)
- **The Alamo** (ISBN 1-56-501784-6)

To order, call Glencoe at 1-800-334-7344. To find classroom resources to accompany many of these videos, check the following home pages:
A&E Television: www.aande.com
The History Channel: www.historychannel.com

Use our Web site for additional resources. All essential content is covered in the Student Edition.

You and your students can visit tarvol2.glencoe.com, the Web site companion to the *American Republic Since 1877.* This innovative integration of electronic and print media offers your students a wealth of opportunities. The student text directs students to the Web site for the following options:

- **Chapter Overviews**
- **Self-Check Quizzes**
- **Student Web Activities**
- **Textbook Updates**

Answers to the student Web activities are provided for you in the **Web Activity Lesson Plans.** Additional Web resources and Interactive Tutor Puzzles are also available.

Chapter 5 Resources

SECTION RESOURCES

Daily Objectives	Reproducible Resources	Multimedia Resources
SECTION 1 **A Growing Nation** 1. Discuss how the Industrial Revolution changed methods of production and fostered urbanization. 2. Explain why cotton dominated the Southern economy.	Reproducible Lesson Plan 5–1 Daily Lecture and Discussion Notes 5–1 Guided Reading Activity 5–1* Section Quiz 5–1* Reading Essentials and Study Guide 5–1* Performance Assessment Activities and Rubrics	Daily Focus Skills Transparency 5–1 Interactive Tutor Self-Assessment CD-ROM ExamView® Pro Testmaker CD-ROM* Presentation Plus! CD-ROM TeacherWorks™ CD-ROM Skillbuilder Interactive Workbook, Level 2 Audio Program ABCNews Interactive™ Historic America Electronic Field Trips
SECTION 2 **The Age of Jackson** 1. Discuss the origin and terms of the Missouri Compromise. 2. Describe how President Jackson dealt with the nullification crisis, Native Americans, and the national bank.	Reproducible Lesson Plan 5–2 Daily Lecture and Discussion Notes 5–2 Guided Reading Activity 5–2* Section Quiz 5–2* Reading Essentials and Study Guide 5–2* Performance Assessment Activities and Rubrics Interpreting Political Cartoons	Daily Focus Skills Transparency 5–2 Interactive Tutor Self-Assessment CD-ROM ExamView® Pro Testmaker CD-ROM* Presentation Plus! CD-ROM TeacherWorks™ CD-ROM Audio Program
SECTION 3 **The Reform Spirit** 1. Explain the goals of the temperance movement, prison reform, educational reform, and the women's movement. 2. Discuss the growth of the abolition movement and reaction to it.	Reproducible Lesson Plan 5–3 Daily Lecture and Discussion Notes 5–3 Guided Reading Activity 5–3* Section Quiz 5–3* Reading Essentials and Study Guide 5–3* Performance Assessment Activities and Rubrics American History in Graphic Novel	Daily Focus Skills Transparency 5–3 American Art & Architecture Interactive Tutor Self-Assessment CD-ROM ExamView® Pro Testmaker CD-ROM* Presentation Plus! CD-ROM TeacherWorks™ CD-ROM Audio Program American Music: Hits Through History American Music: Cultural Traditions
SECTION 4 **Manifest Destiny** 1. Describe the pioneers of the 1840s, explain why and how they journeyed west, and discuss where they settled. 2. Discuss the founding of the Republic of Texas and the major events and outcome of the war with Mexico.	Reproducible Lesson Plan 5–4 Daily Lecture and Discussion Notes 5–4 Guided Reading Activity 5–4* Section Quiz 5–4* Reading Essentials and Study Guide 5–4* Performance Assessment Activities and Rubrics	Daily Focus Skills Transparency 5–4 American Art & Architecture Interactive Tutor Self-Assessment CD-ROM ExamView® Pro Testmaker CD-ROM* Presentation Plus! CD-ROM TeacherWorks™ CD-ROM Vocabulary PuzzleMaker CD-ROM Audio Program American Music: Hits Through History ABCNews Interactive™ Historic America Electronic Field Trips

0:00 OUT OF TIME?
Assign the Chapter 5 **Reading Essentials and Study Guide.**

*Also Available in Spanish

Printed Materials	Transparency	CD-ROM	DVD
Poster	Music Program	Audio Program	Videocassette

NATIONAL GEOGRAPHIC **Teacher's Corner**

INDEX TO NATIONAL GEOGRAPHIC MAGAZINE

The following articles relate to this chapter.
- "America's First Highway," March 1998
- "The Cherokee," May 1995
- "Daniel Boone: First Hero of the Frontier," December 1985
- "Erie Canal: Living Link to Our Past," November 1990

NATIONAL GEOGRAPHIC SOCIETY PRODUCTS

To order the following, call National Geographic at 1-800-368-2728:
- *Historical Atlas of the United States* (Atlas)
- *Washington, D.C.* (Video)

NGS ONLINE

Access National Geographic's Web site for current events, atlas updates, activities, links, interactive features, and archives.
www.nationalgeographic.com

MEETING SPECIAL NEEDS

In addition to the Differentiated Instruction strategies found in each section, the following resources are also suitable for your special needs students:

- *ExamView® Pro Testmaker CD-ROM* allows teachers to tailor tests by reducing answer choices.
- The *Audio Program* includes the entire narrative of the student edition so that less-proficient readers can listen to the words as they read them.
- The *Reading Essentials and Study Guide* provides the same content as the student edition but is written two grade levels below the textbook.
- *Guided Reading Activities* give less-proficient readers point-by-point instructions to increase comprehension as they read each textbook section.

KEY TO ABILITY LEVELS

Teaching strategies have been coded.

L1 BASIC activities for all students
L2 AVERAGE activities for average to above-average students
L3 CHALLENGING activities for above-average students
ELL ENGLISH LANGUAGE LEARNER activities

From the Classroom of...

John C. Horton
Covington Catholic High School
Covington, KY

Immigration: The Numbers
Speak Volumes

This activity helps students understand why 3.5 million Germans and Irish left their countries and immigrated to the U.S. between 1815 and 1860. We analyze the reasons they immigrated and where they settled once they arrived.

After I organize the class into two groups and label them the German Study Group and the Irish Study Group, I give them a day to research what political, economic, religious, or social conditions caused these mass emigrations from these two countries. I ask each group to boil their research down into three basic causes.

I then give them two days to create two types of visuals. The first is a bar graph that shows immigration numbers every 10 years from 1820 to 1860 for Germans and Irish. The second is a map that shows general settlement patterns (rural/urban).

We end the unit by having each group give a ten-minute presentation and using a question-and-answer format to open up discussion.

ADDITIONAL RESOURCES FROM GLENCOE

- American Music: Cultural Traditions
- American Art & Architecture
- Outline Map Resource Book
- U.S. Desk Map
- Building Geography Skills for Life
- Inclusion for the High School Social Studies Classroom Strategies and Activities
- Teaching Strategies for the American History Classroom (Including Block Scheduling Pacing Guides)
- Dinah Zike's High School American History Reading and Study Skills Foldables

 Block Schedule

Activities that are suited to use within the block scheduling framework are identified by:

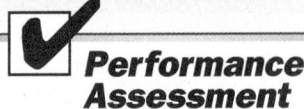

Why It Matters Activity

Ask students to identify significant events that occurred between 1816 and 1848 that caused the growth of sectional division. Students should evaluate their answers after they have completed the chapter.

GLENCOE
TECHNOLOGY

The *American Republic Since 1877* Video Program
To learn more about America from 1816 to 1848, have students view the Chapter 5 video, "Manifest Destiny," from the *American Republic Since 1877* Video Program.

MindJogger Videoquiz
Use the **MindJogger Videoquiz** to preview Chapter 5 content.

  Both programs available in DVD

CHAPTER
5 The Young Republic *1816–1848*

Why It Matters

After the War of 1812, new roads and canals helped connect the nation. Industry prospered in the North, while an agricultural economy dependent on slavery grew strong in the South. Although political, social, and religious reforms were key themes of the period, these reforms could not silence the growing sectionalism that increasingly gripped the nation. The addition of new territories only heightened sectional tensions.

The Impact Today

Many developments of this period shape our lives today.
- *Many Americans have a strong sense of national loyalty.*
- *Federal authority over interstate commerce helped create a truly national economy.*
- *Americans believe ordinary citizens should be able to qualify for all political offices.*

 The **American Republic Since 1877** *Video The Chapter 5 video, "Manifest Destiny," tells the story of the war between Texas and Mexico from the Mexican point of view.*

United States PRESIDENTS

1806
- Congress agrees to provide funds to construct National Road

Madison 1809–1817

1820
- Missouri Compromise proposed by Henry Clay

Monroe 1817–1825

1825
- Erie Canal opens

1831
- Nat Turner slave rebellion

J.Q. Adams 1825–1829

1832
- Democrats hold their first presidential nominating convention

Jackson 1829–1837

1810   *1820*   *1830*

World

1815
- Napoleon Bonaparte defeated at the Battle of Waterloo

1817
- Exploration of Australia's interior begins

1821
- Mexican independence proclaimed

1829
- Slavery abolished in Mexico

1832
- Male voting rights expanded in England

176

⟩ **Reading Strategy** **PURPOSE FOR READING**

Concept Maps Like web diagrams, concept maps are a way for students to visualize the components of a concept or key term. To begin, students should write and circle "Industrial Revolution" in the center of a piece of paper. Then to the left, right, and below, write and circle each of the following three sub-categories: "What is it? How did the Industrial Revolution aid in developing today's technology? How did the Industrial Revolution transform the economy and society of the United States?" Link each of the three sub-categories to the Industrial Revolution bubble by a line. Have students complete the concept map as they read the chapter by filling in brief answers in small bubbles around each sub-category. Link each answer to the corresponding sub-category bubble by a line. **L1** **ELL**

Election Day in Philadelphia by John L. Krimmel, 1815

HISTORY Online

Introduce students to chapter content and key terms by having them access the **Chapter 5 Overview** at tarvol2.glencoe.com.

More About the Art

John Krimmel (1789-1821) is considered one of America's first genre painters. His work expresses democratic and moralizing themes within the political and social changes affecting Philadelphia and the nation. Krimmel, born in Germany, immigrated to the United States in 1810. Much of his work, including *Election Day in Philadelphia,* contains hints of sarcasm.

TIME LINE ACTIVITY

Have students choose one of the events on the world time line and write a paragraph about how the event affected the United States. Instruct students to use library or Internet resources to learn more about the event they select.

1836
• Battle of the Alamo fought

1838
• Cherokee are driven from Georgia and embark on Trail of Tears

1845
• Congress votes to annex Republic of Texas

1846
• United States begins war with Mexico

1848
• Treaty of Guadalupe Hidalgo ends war with Mexico

Van Buren 1837–1841

W. Harrison 1841

Tyler 1841–1845

Polk 1845–1849

Taylor 1849–1850

Fillmore 1850–1853

1840

1850

HISTORY Online

Chapter Overview
Visit the *American Republic Since 1877* Web site at tarvol2.glencoe.com and click on **Chapter Overviews— Chapter 5** to preview chapter information.

1836
• First botany textbook published

1842
• China opened by force to foreign trade

1843
• Charles Dickens's *A Christmas Carol* published

1845
• Irish potato famine begins

1848
• Karl Marx and Frederich Engels's *The Communist Manifesto* published

177

FOLDABLES™ Study Organizer

Dinah Zike's Foldables are three-dimensional, interactive graphic organizers that help students practice basic writing skills, review key vocabulary terms, and identify main ideas. Have students complete the foldable activity in the *Dinah Zike's Reading and Study Skills Foldables* booklet.

GRAPHIC ORGANIZER ACTIVITY

Organizing Information Have students take notes on Chapter 5 by completing a table similar to the one shown. Students' notes should be concise and address the concepts or themes found in the chapter.

Religious Revival	Charles G. Finney
Prison Reform	Dorothea Dix
Education Reform	Horace Mann, Calvin Wiley
Women's Education	Emma Willard, Mary Lyon
Women's Rights	Lucretia Mott, Elizabeth Cady Stanton
Abolitionism	William Lloyd Garrison, Frederick Douglass

1 FOCUS

Section Overview

This section discusses industrialization in the North and the continuing importance of agriculture and slavery in the South.

BELLRINGER
Skillbuilder Activity

Project transparency and have students answer the question.

Daily Focus Skills Transparency 5–1

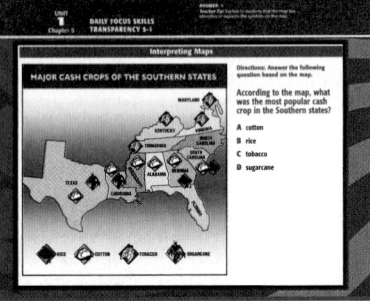

Reading Preview

Answers to Graphic: Milestones may include: 1811, National Road begun; 1817, Erie Canal begun; 1789, Slater builds spinning mill in Rhode Island; 1814, Lowell opens textile mill; 1820, canning process introduced

Preteaching Vocabulary
Have students use three entries from Key Terms and Names in a sentence. See how well they understand the concepts and individuals chosen.

SECTION 1 A Growing Nation

Guide to Reading

Main Idea
In the early 1800s, canals, railroads, and new industries transformed the North, while slavery expanded in the South.

Key Terms and Names
Robert Fulton, Peter Cooper, Industrial Revolution, Francis C. Lowell, Eli Whitney, interchangeable parts, nativism, Know-Nothing, labor union, strike, cotton gin, yeoman farmer, driver

Reading Strategy
Categorizing As you read about changes that occurred in the United States in the early 1800s, complete a graphic organizer similar to the one below by filling in milestones in transportation and industrialization.

Transportation	Industrialization

Reading Objectives
- **Discuss** how the Industrial Revolution changed methods of production and fostered urbanization.
- **Explain** why cotton dominated the Southern economy.

Section Theme
Science and Technology New technology increased trade and agricultural production and improved communications within the United States.

Preview of Events

♦1790		♦1810		♦1830
1793 Eli Whitney invents the cotton gin	**1808** Congress bans foreign slave trade		**1822** Denmark Vesey executed	**1825** Erie Canal opens	**1831** Nat Turner rebellion

Constructing the Erie Canal

★ **An American Story** ★

On July 4, 1817, New York state officials gathered in Rome, New York. They had come to launch the greatest engineering challenge in American history up to that time: the building of a canal connecting the Hudson River to Lake Erie. The longest canal in the nation at that time ran about 28 miles (45 km). The new canal, known as the Erie Canal, would be a colossal 363 miles (584.1 km) long and 40 feet (12.2 m) wide. At the ceremony, New York Commissioner Samuel Young explained the importance of the project:

❝We have assembled to commence the excavation of the Erie Canal. This work when accomplished will connect our western inland seas with the Atlantic Ocean. . . . By this great highway, unborn millions will easily transport their surplus productions to the shores of the Atlantic, procure their supplies, and hold a useful and profitable intercourse with all the maritime nations of the earth.❞

—quoted in *Erie Water West*

A Revolution in Transportation

Over the next few years, thousands of workers dug their way through dirt, rock and swamp. They built 83 locks and 18 aqueducts. When completed in October 1825, the Erie Canal cut the travel time from New York to Buffalo from 20 days to 6 days. The canal helped settle the Midwest and greatly increased the flow of goods. Using roads, four horses could pull a ton of goods 12 miles per day. Using the canal, two horses could pull a 100-ton barge 24 miles per day. The Erie Canal's success marked the beginning of a transportation revolution that swept through the Northern states in the early 1800s.

178 CHAPTER 5   The Young Republic

SECTION RESOURCES

📂 Reproducible Masters
- Reproducible Lesson Plan 5–1
- Daily Lecture and Discussion Notes 5–1
- Guided Reading Activity 5–1
- Section Quiz 5–1
- Reading Essentials and Study Guide 5–1

Transparencies
- Daily Focus Skills Transparency 5–1

Multimedia
- Interactive Tutor Self-Assessment CD-ROM
- ExamView® Pro Testmaker CD-ROM
- Presentation Plus! CD-ROM
- TeacherWorks™ CD-ROM
- Audio Program
- ABCNews Interactive™ Historic America Electronic Field Trips

Roads and Turnpikes In 1806 the nation took the first steps toward a transportation revolution when Congress funded the building of a major east-west highway, the **National Road.** In 1811 laborers started cutting the roadbed westward from Cumberland, Maryland. Paved with crushed stones, the National Road stretched to Vandalia, Illinois, by 1838. Pioneers in Conestoga wagons headed west on this road, while farmers from the interior drove their livestock and produce the opposite way, toward Eastern markets.

The National Road turned out to be the only great U.S.-funded transportation project of its time. Although some members of Congress pushed the federal government to make more internal improvements, American leaders disagreed on whether the Constitution permitted this.

Instead, states, localities, and private businesses took the initiative. Private companies laid down hundreds of miles of toll roads, often called **turnpikes** because of the spiked poles that forced travelers to stop at intervals and pay a toll. Turnpikes were profitable mainly in the East, where traffic was heavy.

TECHNOLOGY

Steamboats Rivers offered a faster, more efficient, and cheaper way to move goods than did early roads, which were often little more than wide paths. A single barge could hold many wagonloads of grain or coal. Loaded boats and barges, however, could usually travel only downstream, as trips against the current with heavy cargoes were impractical.

The steamboat changed all that. The first successful such vessel, the *Clermont,* was developed by **Robert Fulton** and promoted by Robert R. Livingston. At its debut in 1807, the *Clermont* stunned the nation by cruising 150 miles up the Hudson River from New York City to Albany in just 32 hours. Steamboats made river travel speedier and more reliable. By 1850 over 700 steamboats, also called riverboats, traveled the Mississippi, the Great Lakes, and other waterways.

The "Iron Horse" Another mode of transportation, railroads, also appeared in the early 1800s. A wealthy, self-educated industrialist named **Peter Cooper** built the *Tom Thumb,* a tiny but powerful locomotive based on engines originally developed in Great Britain. In 1830 the *Tom Thumb* pulled the nation's first load of train passengers along 13 miles of track in Maryland, chugging along at the then incredible speed of 10 miles per hour.

Some people complained about the noise and dirt of the new machines. In the 1800s people often regarded cities as noisy, crowded, and unhealthy. Sick people often traveled to the country to rest and recover their health. Some people feared that railroads would bring urban problems to the countryside. People realized, however, that trains traveled much faster than stagecoaches or wagons, and unlike steamboats, they could go nearly anywhere track was laid. Perhaps more than any other kind of transportation, trains helped settle the West and expand trade among the nation's different regions.

✓ **Reading Check** **Evaluating** What were two advantages of trains over other kinds of transportation in the 1800s?

Industrialization Sweeps the North

Along with dramatic changes in transportation, a revolution occurred in business and industry. The **Industrial Revolution,** which began in Britain in the middle 1700s, consisted of several basic developments. Manufacturing shifted from hand tools to large, complex machines. Individual artisans gave way to organized workforces. Factories, some large enough for hundreds of machines and workers, replaced home-based workshops. Manufacturers sold their wares nationwide or abroad instead of just locally.

By the early 1800s, these innovations had reached the United States. They transformed not only the economy but society as well.

Iron Horse Peter Cooper's *Tom Thumb* races a horse.

2 TEACH

Daily Lecture and Discussion Notes 5–1

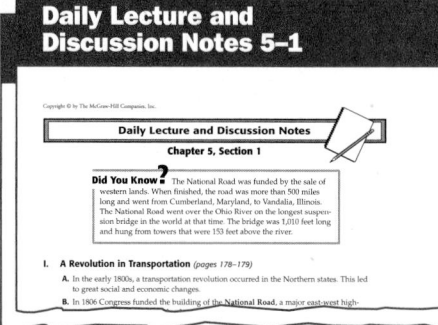

Copyright © by The McGraw-Hill Companies, Inc.

Daily Lecture and Discussion Notes
Chapter 5, Section 1

Did You Know? The National Road was funded by the sale of western lands. When finished, the road was more than 500 miles long and went from Cumberland, Maryland, to Vandalia, Illinois. The National Road went over the Ohio River on the longest suspension bridge in the world at that time. The bridge was 1,010 feet long and hung from towers that were 153 feet above the river.

I. A Revolution in Transportation *(pages 178–179)*

A. In the early 1800s, a transportation revolution occurred in the Northern states. This led to great social and economic changes.

B. In 1806 Congress funded the building of the **National Road,** a major east-west high-

Creating a Thematic Map
Provide students with an outline map of the United States without state borders. Instruct students to draw in the Ohio and Mississippi Rivers and their major tributaries. Tell students that they are planning a steamboat trip in 1850 from Wheeling, West Virginia, to New Orleans, Louisiana. Have students draw in the state borders that surround their route of travel and locate and label the major cities along the route. **L1** ELL

📁 Use the rubric for creating a map, display, or chart on pages 65–66 in the *Performance Assessment Activities and Rubrics.*

✓ **Reading Check**

Answer: Trains traveled much faster than stagecoaches or wagons and could go anywhere track could be laid.

COOPERATIVE LEARNING ACTIVITY

Writing a Script Organize students into small groups. Have the groups research the lives of children who worked in the textile mills. Based on their research, have the groups write a script of an event that might have occurred in the life of such a child. Examples include an encounter between a foreman and a worker who has fallen asleep, a dialogue with another worker as they are on their way home from a day's work, or a monologue of the child's thoughts as he or she trudges to work on a hot summer's day. Encourage groups to perform the script for the class.

Use the rubric for a cooperative group management plan on pages 71–72 in the *Performance Assessment Activities and Rubrics.*

L1/ELL

L1/ELL
Guided Reading Activity 5-1

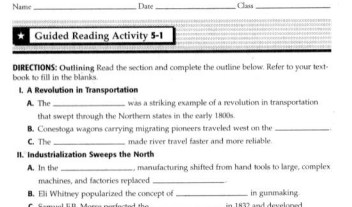

Name _____ Date _____ Class _____

★ Guided Reading Activity 5-1

DIRECTIONS: Outlining Read the section and complete the outline below. Refer to your text-book to fill in the blanks.
I. A Revolution in Transportation
  A. The _____ was a striking example of a revolution in transportation that swept through the Northern states in the early 1800s.
  B. Conestoga wagons carrying migrating pioneers traveled west on the _____.
  C. The _____ made river travel faster and more reliable.
II. Industrialization Sweeps the North
  A. In the _____, manufacturing shifted from hand tools to large, complex machines, and factories replaced _____.
  B. Eli Whitney popularized the concept of _____ in gunmaking.
  C. Samuel F.B. Morse perfected the _____ in 1832 and developed

Geography *Skills*

Answers:
1. Georgia
2. The North had more industry and more money to invest in canal building.

Geography Skills Practice
Ask: What modes of transportation could you have used to travel from New York to Baltimore in 1840? *(by rail, road, or sea)*

FYI

Listing Cause and Effect Write the words Industrial Revolution on the board. Ask students to list the causes and effects of the Industrial Revolution. For example, a cause was division of labor and its effect was the rise of labor unions. Then ask students to discuss whether they think these effects would have happened without industrialization.
L2

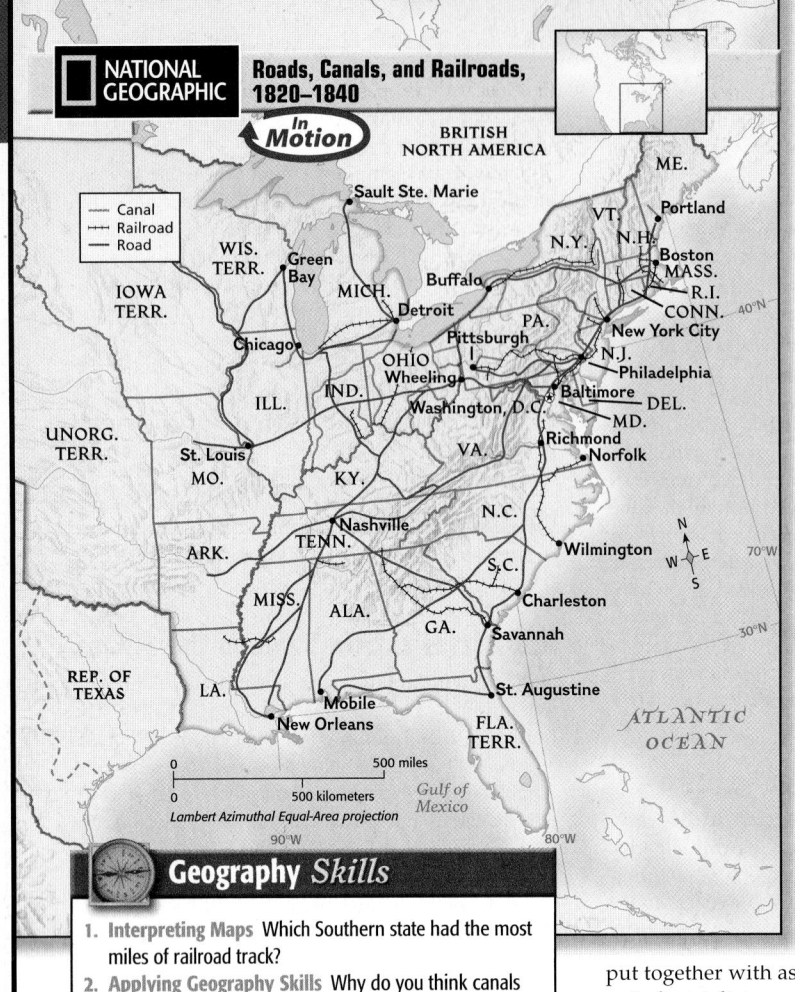

NATIONAL GEOGRAPHIC
Roads, Canals, and Railroads, 1820–1840
In Motion

- Canal
- Railroad
- Road

Geography *Skills*

1. **Interpreting Maps** Which Southern state had the most miles of railroad track?
2. **Applying Geography Skills** Why do you think canals were more common in the North than in other areas?

A New System of Production The United States industrialized quickly for several reasons. Perhaps the key factor was the American system of free enterprise based on private property rights. People could acquire and use capital without strict governmental controls while competition between companies encouraged them to try new technologies. The era's low taxes also meant that entrepreneurs had more money to invest.

Beginning in the 1830s, many states encouraged industrialization by passing general incorporation laws. These laws let companies become corporations and raise money by issuing stock without having to get a charter from the state legislature. They also limited liability. If people bought stock in a company and it went bankrupt, they were not responsible for the company's debts. The new laws thereby encouraged people to invest money, spurring economic growth.

Industrialization began in the Northeast, where many swift-flowing streams provided factories with water-power. The region was also home to many entrepreneurs who were willing to invest in British technology.

Although Britain had passed strict laws to block the export of its technology, an English textile worker named **Samuel Slater** took the risk. He moved to Rhode Island in 1789 and built a British water frame for spinning cotton into thread. In 1814 Francis Lowell opened mills in Massachusetts that not only spun cotton into thread but also produced cloth. His company even built a town that housed hundreds of workers, mostly women. By 1840 textile mills had sprung up throughout the Northeast.

In the early 1800s, a New Englander named Eli Whitney popularized the use of inter-changeable parts, or standard components, in gun-making. Machines turned out identical pieces that workers quickly put together with assembly-line techniques.

Industrialists used these techniques to produce lumber, shoes, leather, wagons, and other products. The sewing machine allowed inexpensive clothes to be mass produced. In the 1820s, William Underwood and Thomas Kensett began sealing foods in airtight tin containers. Canning allowed many foods to be stored and transported without fear of spoilage.

Advances in Communications In 1832 a major improvement in communications took place when **Samuel F.B. Morse** perfected the telegraph and developed Morse code. In 1844 he sent his first long-distance telegraph message, tapping out in code the words "What hath God wrought?" over a wire from Washington, D.C., to Baltimore.

Journalists began using the telegraph to speedily relay news. In 1848 a group of newspapers in New York created the Associated Press to collect and share news over the wires. By 1860 more than 50,000 miles of telegraph wire connected most parts of the country.

DIFFERENTIATED INSTRUCTION

At-Risk Students Ask students to select one of the common means of transportation that was used in the early 1800s. Have students create a model of their choice. Encourage students to be able to explain the materials used to construct the model and how it worked. Have students share their models with the class. **L1** **ELL**

📂 Refer to *Inclusion for the High School Social Studies Classroom Strategies and Activities* in the TCR.

Urban Growth and Immigration The industrialization of the United States drew thousands of people from farms and villages to towns in search of higher-paying factory jobs. Many city populations doubled or tripled. In 1820 only New York boasted more than 100,000 residents. By 1860 eight other cities had reached that size.

Immigrants hoping for a better life in the United States also contributed to urban growth. Between 1815 and 1860, over 5 million foreigners journeyed to America. While thousands of newcomers, particularly Germans, became farmers in the rural West, many others settled in cities, providing a steady source of cheap labor. A large number of Irish—over 44,000—arrived in 1845, after a devastating potato blight caused widespread famine in their homeland.

While immigrants often found a new sense of freedom and opportunity in America, some encountered prejudice. The presence of people from different cultures, with different languages and different religions, produced feelings of nativism, a preference for native-born people and a desire to limit immigration. Several societies sprang up to keep foreign-born persons and Catholics—the main religion of the Irish and many Germans—from holding public office. In 1854 delegates from some of these groups formed the American Party. This party came to be called the **Know-Nothings** because its members, when questioned about their activities, were supposed to answer, "I know nothing."

Women in the Workforce The growing cities also provided expanded work opportunities for women. Those from the poorer classes typically found jobs in factories or took positions as domestic laborers. Many middle-class women gravitated to publishing, an industry that was growing quickly to meet the rising demand for reading materials. America had always claimed a high literacy rate, and by 1840 over 75 percent of the total population and over 90 percent of the white population could read. Leading editors and writers included Sarah Buell Hale and Lydia Howard Huntley Sigourney.

Workers Begin to Organize Factory workers numbered roughly 1.3 million by 1860. They included many women and children, who would accept lower wages than men. Not even men were well paid, however, and factory workers typically toiled for 12 or more drudgery-filled hours a day.

Hoping to gain higher wages or shorter workdays, some workers began to organize in labor unions—groups of workers who press for better working conditions and member benefits. During the late 1820s and early 1830s, about 300,000 men and women belonged to these organizations. Most of the organizations were local and focused on a single trade, such as printing or shoemaking.

Early labor unions had little power. Most employers refused to bargain with them, and the courts often saw them as unlawful conspiracies that limited free enterprise. Unions did make some gains, however. In 1840 President Martin Van Buren showed his gratitude for labor's political support by reducing the workday for federal employees to 10 hours. In 1842 in the case of *Commonwealth v. Hunt,* the Massachusetts Supreme Court ruled that union strikes, or work stoppages, were legal. Still, decades would pass before organized labor achieved real influence.

✓ **Reading Check** **Describing** How did industrialization affect cities?

Lowell Girl This young girl worked in the new textile factories of the Northeast.

Creating a Graph Have students create a graph using the following U.S. Census Bureau data about the six largest cities in 1860. **L2**

City	Pop. in 1860	Pop. in 1820
New York, NY	813,669	123,706
Philadelphia, PA	565,529	63,802
Brooklyn, NY	266,661	7,175
Baltimore, MD	212,418	62,738
Boston, MA	177,840	43,298
New Orleans, LA	168,675	27,176

Use the rubric for creating a map, display, or chart on pages 65–66 in the *Performance Assessment Activities and Rubrics.*

✓ **Reading Check**

Answer: Industrialization caused an increase in urban populations.

ABCNEWS INTERACTIVE™

 VIDEOCASSETTE
Historic America Electronic Field Trips

View **Tape 2, Chapter 4:** "Lowell Factories."

Writing a Profile Have students write a profile of one of the following "Lowell Girls": Harriet Farley, Harriet Hanson Robinson, or Sarah Bagley. **L2**

INTERDISCIPLINARY CONNECTIONS ACTIVITY

Science Organize students into small groups. Have the groups use library and Internet resources to research how a lock in a canal works, then build a working model of a lock. Encourage students to create drawings and select appropriate materials for the model. A brief written explanation of how the model works should accompany the model. **L3**

Creating an Annotated Map
Provide students with a map of the Southern states. Have students list the crops grown in each state. As a class, identify various regions based on the crops grown and explain the reasons that certain crops grow better in certain states. **L1**

📁 Use the rubric for creating a map, display, or chart on pages 65–66 in the *Performance Assessment Activities and Rubrics.*

TECHNOLOGY & History

Background: Eli Whitney showed mechanical skill when he built a violin at the early age of 12. He never made much money from his cotton gin. It was so easy to build that few planters bothered to buy one.
Answer: It created a boom in cotton production in the South.

you don't say...

Origin of Lint The term *lint* refers to the cotton fibers. Ginning is the process that removes the lint from the seed.

The Continuing Importance of Agriculture

Despite the trend toward urban and industrial growth, agriculture remained the country's leading economic activity. Until the late 1800s, farming employed more people and produced more wealth than any other kind of work.

In the first half of the 1800s, the North had more than a million farms devoted mostly to growing corn, wheat, and other grains and to raising livestock. Farming was even more important in the South, which had few cities and less industry.

The South thrived on the production of several major cash crops. In the upper Southern states—Maryland, Virginia, Kentucky, and Tennessee—farmers grew tobacco. Rice paddies dominated the coastal regions of South Carolina and Georgia. In Louisiana and parts of eastern Texas, fields of sugarcane stretched for miles. No crop, however, played a greater role in the South's fortunes during this period than cotton, which was grown in a wide belt stretching from inland South Carolina west into Texas.

The Land of Cotton During a visit to the South in 1793, Eli Whitney, an inventive young New Englander, noticed how laborious it was to remove cotton seeds from the fluffy bolls by hand. In a mere 10 days, Whitney built a simple cotton gin—"gin" being short for engine—that quickly and efficiently did the task. Whitney's invention coincided with the expansion of Europe's textile industry. Mills in England and France were clamoring for all the cotton they could get.

In 1792, the year before Whitney invented his cotton gin, the South produced about 6,000 bales of cotton. By 1801 annual production had soared to 100,000 bales. Cotton soon dominated the region. In 1860 production reached almost 4 million bales. That year, Southern cotton accounted for nearly two-thirds of the total export trade of the United States. Southerners began saying, rightly, "Cotton is King."

The boom in cotton production allowed some smaller-scale planters to rapidly ascend the social ladder. As they expanded their property, they joined the ranks of the wealthy plantation owners who wielded enormous political power. This group, however,

---

TECHNOLOGY & History

The Cotton Gin

While visiting Catherine Greene's Georgia plantation in 1793, Eli Whitney had an inspiration. He built a device that removed the seeds of the "green-seed" cotton variety that grew in abundance throughout the South. Whitney devised a "gin" (short for *engine*) that combed the seeds out of the cotton. This simple cotton gin was easy to mass produce, and it increased cotton's profitability for many Southern farmers. *How did the invention of the cotton gin affect the South's economy?*

1 Cotton bolls are dumped into the **hopper.**

2 A crank turns the **cylinder** with wire teeth. The teeth pull the cotton past a grate.

3 Slots in the **grate** allow the cotton, but not its seeds, to pass through.

4 A second cylinder with **brushes** pulls the cotton off the toothed cylinder and sends it out of the gin.

crank grate hopper
brushes
cylinder

📖 Reading Strategy READING THE TEXT

Writing Free Writes Use *free writes* to explore students' background knowledge and check their reading comprehension. Ask students to play one of the following roles: a plantation owner, a yeoman farmer, enslaved person, ship's captain, textile mill owner, or textile mill worker. Have students write a letter to Eli Whitney describing to the inventor the impact of the cotton gin on their lives. Have students exchange their letters and write a response, playing the role of Eli Whitney. **L1**

📁 Refer to **Inclusion for the High School Social Studies Classroom Strategies and Activities** in the TCR.

History *Through Art*

Plantation Life *The Wedding* by E.L. Henry depicts Southern gentry's lavish lifestyle. They purchased enslaved labor at auctions advertised in local newspapers (right). *What invention made cotton production so profitable?*

represented less than half of 1 percent of white Southern families in 1850. Ordinary farmers, often called yeoman farmers, and their families still made up the vast majority of the white population. Mark Twain gives his impressions of a small Southern farm in his novel *The Adventures of Huckleberry Finn:*

> 66 A rail fence around a two-acre yard . . . big double log house for the white folks—hewed logs, with the chinks stopped up with mud or mortar . . . outside of the fence a garden and a watermelon patch; then the cotton fields begin. . . . 99

While agriculture brought prosperity to Southern states, they lagged behind the North in industrialization. The region had scattered iron works, textile mills, and coal, iron, salt, and copper mines, but it accounted for only 16 percent of the nation's manufacturing total. For the most part, the South remained rural, with only three large cities: Baltimore, Charleston, and New Orleans. Agriculture's influence was so great that even many city dwellers in the South invested in or owned farms.

Reading Check **Synthesizing** What effect did the cotton gin have on the Southern economy?

Enslaved and Free African Americans

While the spread of cotton plantations boosted the Southern economy, it also made the demand for slave labor skyrocket. Congress had outlawed the foreign slave trade in 1808, but a high birthrate among enslaved women—encouraged by slaveholders—kept the population growing. Between 1820 and 1850, the number of slaves in the South rose from about 1.5 million to nearly 3.2 million, to account for almost 37 percent of the total Southern population.

In a Southern white population of just over 6.1 million, a total of 347,725 families—about 30 percent—were slaveholders. Of this number, around 37,000 were plantation owners with 20 or more slaves. Fewer than 8,000 of these planters held 50 or more people in slavery, and only 11 held 500 or more. Thus wealthy slaveholders who exploited large workforces were somewhat rare.

The overwhelming majority of enslaved African Americans toiled in the fields on small farms. Some, however, became house servants. Others worked in the South's few industrial plants or in skilled trades such as blacksmithing, carpentry, and barrel making.

CHAPTER 5 The Young Republic **183**

EXTENDING THE CONTENT

Music of the Times One of the most popular composers of this time was Stephen Foster, who was famous for his songs idealizing the South. Foster used African American melodies to create lively songs. He wrote mostly for the popular minstrel shows, which incorporated the songs, dance, and instruments of African Americans. In the cities, opera was growing in popularity. European musicians, mostly German immigrants, delighted audiences with band concerts. Other European performers, such as the singer Jenny Lind, the "Swedish nightingale," toured the country and drew huge crowds.

ABCNEWS INTERACTIVE™

VIDEOCASSETTE
Historic America Electronic Field Trips

View **Tape 1, Chapter 9:** "Frederick Douglass's Home."

3 ASSESS

Assign Section 1 Assessment as homework or as an in-class activity.

🔘 Have students use the **Interactive Tutor Self-Assessment CD-ROM.**

L1/ELL

Reading Essentials and Study Guide 5–1

Name	Date	Class

Study Guide

Chapter 5, Section 1
For use with textbook pages 178–185

A GROWING NATION

KEY TERMS AND NAMES

Robert Fulton American inventor who designed and built the *Clermont*, the steamboat that traveled upstream on the Hudson River in 1807 *(page 179)*

Peter Cooper wealthy industrialist who built the *Tom Thumb*, a tiny but powerful locomotive *(page 179)*

Industrial Revolution time of change in business and industry in which manufacturing shifted from hand tools to large, complex machines; goods were made in factories instead of workshops in homes *(page 179)*

Francis C. Lowell opened a series of textile mills in Massachusetts; introduced mass production of cotton cloth to the U.S. *(page 180)*

L2

Section Quiz 5–1

Name	Date	Class

★ **Chapter 5**   Score

Section Quiz 5–1

DIRECTIONS: Matching Match each item in Column A with the items in Column B. Write the correct letters in the blanks. *(10 points each)*

Column A
_____ 1. an enslaved minister who believed God had chosen him to bring his people out of bondage
_____ 2. standard components first used in gun making
_____ 3. a textile worker who built a successful spinning mill
_____ 4. engine that quickly and efficiently removed cotton seeds from the bolls
_____ 5. developed the first successful steamboat

Column B
A. Samuel Slater
B. cotton gin
C. Nat Turner
D. Robert Fulton
E. interchangeable parts

DIRECTIONS: Multiple Choice In the blank at the left, write the letter of the choice that best completes the statement or answers the question. *(10 points each)*

Field Workers Enslaved African Americans who worked in the fields were organized along two basic labor systems. In the 1700s and early 1800s, a **task system** prevailed. Workers were given a specific set of jobs to accomplish every day. They worked until these were complete, and then they were allowed to spend the remainder of the day on their own. They could earn money through their artisanship, cultivate personal gardens, or hunt for extra food.

In the 1800s, as cotton production became more common and slavery became more widespread, many slaveholders adopted the **gang system** of labor. Under this more rigid system, enslaved persons were organized into work gangs that labored from sunup to sundown—plowing, planting, cultivating, or picking, depending on the season. A **driver** directed the gang, ensuring that the workers kept laboring throughout the day. The drivers were often slaves themselves, chosen for their intelligence or leadership abilities.

Coping with Enslavement All enslaved persons, no matter how well treated, suffered indignities. State slave codes forbade enslaved men and women from owning property, leaving a slaveholder's premises without permission, or testifying in court against a white person. Laws even banned them from learning to read and write. Frederick Douglass, who rose from slavery to become a prominent opponent of the institution, recalled how life as an enslaved person affected him:

❝My natural elasticity was crushed; my intellect languished; the disposition to read departed; the cheerful spark that lingered about my eye died out; the dark night of slavery closed in upon me, and behold a man transformed to a brute.❞

—from *Narrative of the Life of Frederick Douglass*

Music helped many African Americans endure the horrors of slavery. Field workers often sang to pass the long workday and to communicate with one another. Some songs were more provocative than most plantation owners knew, using subtle language and secret meanings to lament the singers' bondage and express a continuing hope for freedom.

Songs also played a key role in one of the most important parts of African American culture: religion. By the early 1800s, large numbers of African Americans were Christians, though their Christianity sometimes incorporated religious traditions from Africa. During their worship services, enslaved persons often sang spirituals—religious songs—and prayed for freedom or a better life in the next world.

Many enslaved men and women found ways to actively resist the dreadful lifestyle forced on them. Some quietly staged work slowdowns. Others broke tools or set fire to houses and barns. Still others risked beatings or mutilations by running away.

Some enslaved persons turned to violence, killing their owners or plotting revolts. In 1822 **Denmark Vesey,** a free African American in Charleston, South Carolina, was accused of planning a large armed uprising. After someone betrayed the group, the authorities arrested and hung Vesey and dozens of his followers before they could act.

The deadliest rebellion occurred in Virginia on August 22, 1831. Leading the attack was **Nat Turner,** an enslaved minister who believed God had chosen him to bring his people out of bondage. Turner and a small band of accomplices went from house to house, killing more than 50 white men, women, and children and recruiting followers until they numbered about 60. State and local troops put down the uprising, but it took them until October 30 to find Turner. They quickly tried and hung him along with 15 of his supporters.

Free African Americans Not all African Americans of the time lived in bondage. By 1850

"the dark night of slavery closed in upon me"

—*Frederick Douglass*

CRITICAL THINKING ACTIVITY

Comparing Have students research the task system and the gang system of organizing slave labor. Have students create a chart that compares and contrasts the systems from either the point of view of the landowner or of the enslaved person. **L2**

over 225,000 free African Americans resided in the South, mostly in the towns and cities of Maryland and Virginia. A few had descended from Africans brought to the United States as indentured servants in the 1700s before the slave system became universal. Some had earned their freedom fighting in the American Revolution, and still others were the half-white children of slaveholders, who had granted them freedom. There were also some former enslaved persons who had managed to purchase their freedom or whose owners had freed them.

Free African Americans occupied an ambiguous position in Southern society. In cities like Charleston and New Orleans, some were successful enough to become slaveholders themselves. Cecee McCarty, for example, a wealthy dry goods retailer in New Orleans, had a sales force of 32 slaves.

Another 197,700 free African Americans lived in the North, where slavery had been outlawed, but they were not embraced there either. Racial prejudice, lamented one, was "ever at my elbow." Still, free African Americans could organize their own churches and voluntary associations, plus earn money from the jobs they held. James Forten of Philadelphia was one success story.

Forten worked aboard ships as a teenager and later became a maker of sails. By the age of 32, he

owned a thriving sail factory employing 40 African American and white workers. Forten devoted much of his wealth to the cause of abolishing slavery.

✓ **Reading Check** **Describing** What was life like for enslaved African Americans in the South?

Profiles IN HISTORY

Nat Turner *1800–1831*

The man who led perhaps the nation's best-known slave revolt believed from an early age—through his mother's encouragement—that he was divinely inspired. "I was intended for some great purpose," he once declared.

Although many considered Nat Turner a religious fanatic—he claimed to take his directions from mysterious voices and the movements of heavenly bodies—others knew him to have a sharp mind. "He certainly never had the advantages of education," said the man later appointed to be his lawyer, "but he can read and write . . . and for natural intelligence and quickness of apprehension is surpassed by few men I have ever seen."

As he awaited execution, Turner reportedly showed little remorse for his deeds, certain that he had acted in the name of God to free his people. "I am here loaded with chains and willing to suffer the fate that awaits me," he said.

Turner's lack of remorse chilled those around him, including his lawyer, who described the calm, deliberate composure with which Turner spoke of what he had done. "I looked on him," the lawyer wrote, "and my blood curdled in my veins."

Turner's revolt sent a wave of terror through the South and heightened fears of future uprisings. As a result, many states adopted even harsher restrictions on both enslaved and free African Americans.

Profiles IN HISTORY

Ask: How did Turner's revolt affect the lives of enslaved people in the short term? *(Many states adopted even harsher restrictions on enslaved people.)*

✓ **Reading Check**

Answer: Enslaved people could not own property, leave the premises without permission, possess firearms, testify against a white person, or learn to read or write.

Reteach

Ask students to explain why cotton dominated the Southern economy.

Enrich

Invite students to choose a topic from this section and write a report using Internet and library resources.

Study Central™ provides summaries, interactive games, and online graphic organizers to help students review section content.

HISTORY Online **Study Central**™ To review this section, go to tarvol2.glencoe.com and click on **Study Central**™.

SECTION 1 ASSESSMENT

Checking for Understanding

1. **Define:** interchangeable parts, nativism, labor union, strike, cotton gin, yeoman farmer.
2. **Identify:** Robert Fulton, Peter Cooper, Industrial Revolution, Francis C. Lowell, Eli Whitney, Know-Nothing, driver.

Reviewing Themes

3. **Science and Technology** How did interchangeable parts revolutionize the manufacturing process?

Critical Thinking

4. **Synthesizing** Why did Southerners say "Cotton is King"?
5. **Organizing** Use a graphic organizer similar to the one below to list the effects of some of the technological advances of the early 1800s.

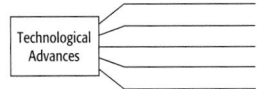

Analyzing Visuals

6. **Analyzing Art** Study the painting of a Southern wedding on page 183. How has the artist embellished the scene to suggest the lifestyle of the Southern planter class?

Writing About History

7. **Expository Writing** Imagine you have just taken a ride on one of the early American railroads. Write a letter to the editor of a newspaper detailing the journey.

CHAPTER 5 The Young Republic **185**

4 CLOSE

Call on volunteers to offer opinions about the development or invention that made the greatest contribution to the Industrial Revolution in the United States.

SECTION 1 ASSESSMENT ANSWERS

1. Terms are in blue.
2. Robert Fulton *(p. 179)*, Peter Cooper *(p. 179)*, Industrial Revolution *(p. 179)*, Francis C. Lowell *(p. 180)*, Eli Whitney *(p. 180)*, Know-Nothing *(p. 181)*, driver *(p. 184)*
3. Production became increasingly based on the more efficient assem-

bly line.
4. Cotton dominated the region and accounted for nearly two-thirds of United States exports.
5. Possible answers include steam boat: made river transportation reliable and extended range of transportation; railroad: helped settle the West and expanded trade

among the nation's different regions
6. wealthy home, richly dressed planters and happy slaves, Eden-like yard
7. Letters should describe an imagined trip by rail.

TEACH

Reading a Line Graph Remind students to look carefully at the graph to determine what information is being presented. Titles, labels, and legends are important parts of any graph.

Have students create a double-line graph using the data for the average height of children.

Age	Girls	Boys
6 years	46.00 in.	46.75 in.
7 years	48.00 in.	49.00 in.
8 years	50.75 in.	51.00 in.
9 years	53.25 in.	53.25 in.
10 years	55.50 in.	55.25 in.
11 years	58.50 in.	57.25 in.
12 years	60.50 in.	59.00 in.
13 years	61.25 in.	61.00 in.

Additional Practice
L1

Reinforcing Skills Activity 5

GLENCOE
TECHNOLOGY

CD-ROM
Glencoe Skillbuilder Interactive Workbook CD-ROM, Level 2

This interactive CD-ROM reinforces student mastery of essential social studies skills.

186

Social Studies
SKILLBUILDER

Reading a Line Graph

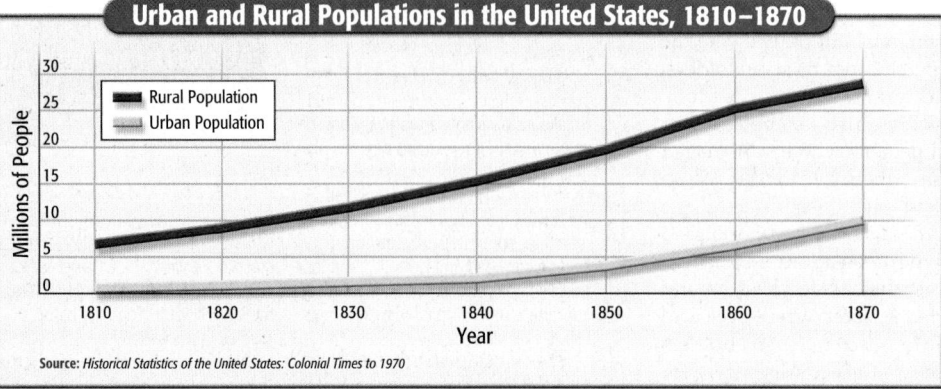

Urban and Rural Populations in the United States, 1810–1870

Source: *Historical Statistics of the United States: Colonial Times to 1970*

Why Learn This Skill?

Line graphs are a way of showing numbers visually, making them easier to read and understand. Learning to read line graphs will help you compare changes over time or differences between places, groups of people, or related events.

Learning the Skill

Line graphs are often used to show changes in number or quantity over time. They show information in two dimensions. The horizontal axis (or x-axis) is the line along the bottom of the graph. If the graph shows information over time, this axis usually shows the time period. The vertical axis (or y-axis) is the line that runs up the side of the graph. This axis usually displays the quantity, or amount, of whatever is being measured in the graph.

A double-line graph shows more than one line, recording two related quantities. For instance, you and a friend might both record your running speeds for footraces over a period of time on one graph, using a line of a different color for each of you. Before trying to understand any graph, be sure to read the labels on both axes and the key for each line.

Practicing the Skill

Study the line graph and answer the following questions.
1. What kind of information does the graph compare?
2. What are the time intervals on the horizontal axis?
3. What quantity is measured on the vertical axis?
4. What trend does the graph seem to show?
5. What two phenomena from the chapter explain the changes in the population?

Skills Assessment

Complete the Practicing Skills questions on page 213 and the Chapter 5 Skill Reinforcement Activity to assess your mastery of this skill.

Applying the Skill

Reading a Line Graph Create a line graph comparing the urban and rural population figures from 1910 to 1970. Compare your graph with the one on this page and write a summary of the differences you notice between the two.

Glencoe's **Skillbuilder Interactive Workbook CD-ROM, Level 2,** provides instruction and practice in key social studies skills.

186

ANSWERS TO PRACTICING THE SKILL

1. urban and rural populations
2. ten-year intervals
3. number of people
4. Increase in population is higher in rural areas.
5. immigration and industrialization

Applying the Skill
Summaries should reflect several key points about the population between 1910 and 1970: (1) little change in rural population, (2) continual increase in urban population, and (3) urban population exceeds rural population after 1920.

SECTION 2 The Age of Jackson

Guide to Reading

Main Idea
Sectionalism increased after the War of 1812. Jackson's election in 1828 ushered in a new era of American politics.

Key Terms and Names
Missouri Compromise, "favorite son," "corrupt bargain," mudslinging, spoils system, caucus, secede, Indian Removal Act, Trail of Tears, Nicholas Biddle, Whig, Specie Circular

Reading Strategy
Categorizing As you read about growing sectionalism, complete a graphic organizer similar to the one below by filling in the conflicts triggered by the divisive issues of the 1820s listed, along with their outcomes.

Issue	Conflict	Outcome
Westward expansion of slavery		
The tariff		

Reading Objectives
- **Discuss** the origin and terms of the Missouri Compromise.
- **Describe** how President Jackson dealt with the nullification crisis, Native Americans, and the national bank.

Section Theme
Government and Democracy Democracy expanded to serve a wider segment of the population during the Jackson era.

Preview of Events

◆1815	◆1825	◆1835	◆1845

1820
Missouri Compromise proposed

1825
John Quincy Adams named president by the House of Representatives

1828
Andrew Jackson elected president

1830
Webster-Hayne debate held in Senate

1838
U.S. Army drives Cherokee out of Georgia

★ **An American Story** ★

As May approached in 1820, Thomas Jefferson should have been enjoying his retirement from public life. Instead, a bitter political controversy had him feeling deeply troubled. After more than a year of debate, Congress finally had crafted a plan to allow the Missouri Territory to enter the Union as a slave state while Maine came in as a free state. This arrangement preserved the delicate balance in the number of free and slave states. The arrangement, known as the Missouri Compromise, highlighted the growing dispute over slavery's expansion into the Western territories—a dispute that Jefferson feared could tear the nation apart:

❝This momentous question, like a firebell in the night, awakened and filled me with terror. I considered it at once as the knell [funeral bell] of the Union. It is hushed, indeed, for the moment. But this is a reprieve only, not a final sentence.❞

—quoted in *The Annals of America*

Thomas Jefferson

The Resurgence of Sectionalism

As the matter of statehood for Missouri stirred up passionate disagreements, the Monroe administration's Era of Good Feelings began to dissolve. Increasingly, sectional disputes came to divide Americans.

The Missouri Compromise In 1819 the Union consisted of 11 free and 11 slave states. While Northerners already dominated the House of Representatives, admitting any new state, either slave or free, would upset the balance of political power in the Senate.

CHAPTER 5 The Young Republic **187**

---

1 FOCUS

Section Overview
This section focuses on the country's increasing sectionalism after the War of 1812.

BELLRINGER
Skillbuilder Activity

Project transparency and have students answer the question.

Daily Focus Skills Transparency 5–2

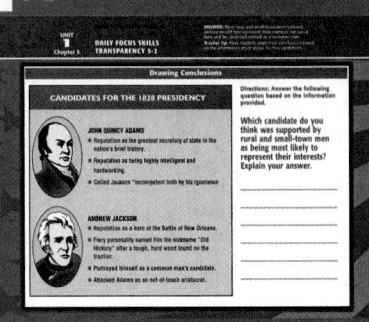

Reading Preview

Answers to Graphic: Westward expansion of slavery–Conflict: Would new states be slave or free states? Outcome: Missouri admitted as slave state; Maine admitted as free state; slavery was prohibited in areas north of Missouri. The tariff–Conflict: South Carolina wanted to nullify national tariffs. Outcome: Nation lowered tariffs; South Carolina repealed nullification and did not secede.

Preteaching Vocabulary
Have students identify a person that can be tied to each of the Key Terms.

SECTION RESOURCES

📂 Reproducible Masters
- Reproducible Lesson Plan 5–2
- Daily Lecture and Discussion Notes 5–2
- Guided Reading Activity 5–2
- Section Quiz 5–2
- Reading Essentials and Study Guide 5–2
- Performance Assessment Activities and Rubrics
- Interpreting Political Cartoons

🖨 Transparencies
- Daily Focus Skills Transparency 5–2

Multimedia
- 💿 Interactive Tutor Self-Assessment CD-ROM
- 💿 ExamView® Pro Testmaker CD-ROM
- 💿 Presentation Plus! CD-ROM
- 💿 TeacherWorks™ CD-ROM
- 🔊 Audio Program

2 TEACH

Daily Lecture and Discussion Notes 5–2

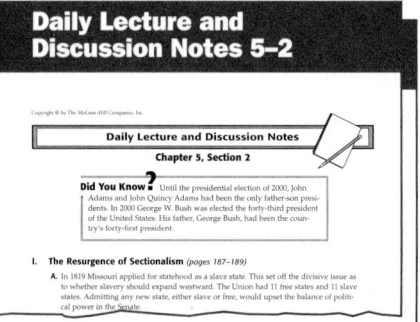

Creating a Table Have students create a table illustrating the four main candidates for president in 1824. Instruct students to include the candidates' names, party affiliations, home states, and positions on issues. **L1** ELL

 Use the rubric for creating a map, display, or chart on pages 65–66 in the *Performance Assessment Activities and Rubrics*.

Geography *Skills*

Answers:
1. Missouri and Maine
2. They believed the land was unsuitable for farming.

Geography Skills Practice
Ask: At what latitude is the Missouri Compromise line?
(36°30'N)

 Use *Interpreting Political Cartoons*, Cartoon 7.

188

Many Northerners opposed extending slavery into the western territories because they believed that human bondage was morally wrong. The South feared that if slavery could not expand, new free states would eventually give the North enough votes in the Senate to outlaw slaveholding.

Missouri's territorial government requested admission into the Union as a slave state in 1819. Acting for slavery's opponents, Congressman James Tallmadge, Jr., of New York proposed a resolution that prohibited slaveholders from bringing new slaves into Missouri. He also called for all enslaved children in Missouri to be freed at age 25. The House accepted the proposal, but the Senate rejected it.

A solution emerged later that year when Maine, then a part of Massachusetts, sought statehood. The Senate decided to combine its request with Missouri's and voted to admit Maine as a free state and Missouri as a slave state. The Senate added an amendment to prohibit slavery in the rest of the Louisiana Territory north of Missouri's southern boundary. Southerners agreed, viewing this Northern region as unsuitable for farming anyway.

Henry Clay carefully steered the amended bill through the House of Representatives, which passed it by a close vote in March 1820. In July, however, the **Missouri Compromise** became threatened by a proposed clause in the Missouri constitution that would infringe on the rights of free African Americans. Clay again engineered a solution, and Missouri became the twenty-fourth state in 1821.

The Missouri Compromise temporarily settled the dispute over the westward expansion of slavery. Like Jefferson, however, many leaders feared more trouble ahead. "I take it for granted," wrote John Quincy Adams, President Monroe's secretary of state, "that the present question is a mere preamble—a title page to a great tragic volume."

A Disputed Election Politics reflected the regional divisions of the day. Although the Republicans remained the only official political party, sectionalism

188 CHAPTER 5 The Young Republic

NATIONAL GEOGRAPHIC **The Missouri Compromise, 1820**

- ⊠ States admitted under conditions of the Missouri Compromise
- ☐ States and territories closed to slavery
- ▒ States and territories open to slavery

Geography *Skills*

1. **Interpreting Maps** The Missouri Compromise allowed which two states to enter the Union?
2. **Applying Geography Skills** Why did the South readily agree to making slavery illegal in the unorganized Louisiana Territory?

---

was strong in the election campaign of 1824. Four Republicans ran for president that year. All were "favorite sons," men who enjoyed popularity and political support in their home state and region. Two candidates, Henry Clay of Kentucky and Andrew Jackson of Tennessee, were rivals from the West. John Quincy Adams hailed from Massachusetts and was New England's favorite son. William Crawford of Georgia had the support of the South.

On Election Day, Jackson led in the popular vote and in the Electoral College, but he did not win the necessary majority of electoral votes. In accordance with constitutional procedure, the decision went to the House of Representatives, whose members would select the president from the top three vote-getters. Clay, who had placed fourth, was eliminated.

As the Speaker of the House, Henry Clay enjoyed tremendous influence, and he threw his support to Adams. Clay hoped Adams would champion his American System, a plan to promote domestic production by means of protective tariffs, a strong national bank, and new roads and canals. On February 9, 1825, Adams won the House election easily, with 13 votes to Jackson's 7 and Crawford's 4.

Reading Strategy | READING THE TEXT

Monitoring Comprehension As students read the section, they may encounter text or information they do not understand, requiring them to adjust their reading strategies to clarify the ideas. Model how this is done by reading the section aloud. As you read, say things such as "What do I think this subtopic might be about based on the heading?" *(predicting);* "Where are these territories located in relation to the states?" *(visualizing);* "What have I heard about this topic and is it correct based on the information described here?" *(activating prior knowledge)* Modeling how you read helps students think about strategies they can use as they read independently. **L1**

A Return to Two Parties Upon taking office, the new president named Clay as his secretary of state. Jackson's supporters immediately accused the pair of striking a "corrupt bargain," whereby Clay had secured votes for Adams in return for a cabinet post. Adams and Clay denied any wrongdoing, and no evidence of a deal ever emerged. Still, Jackson's outraged supporters decided to break with the faction of the party allied with Adams. The Jacksonians called themselves **Democratic Republicans,** later shortened to Democrats. Adams and his followers became known as **National Republicans.**

☑ **Reading Check** **Summarizing** How did John Quincy Adams win the election of 1824?

A New Era in Politics

John Quincy Adams, son of the second president, was highly intelligent and hardworking. He proposed ambitious internal improvements and funding for a national university, astronomical observatories, and scientific research. Congress, however, rejected most of Adams's ideas as too extravagant. When he ran for re-election in 1828, Adams could cite few accomplishments as president. Furthermore, his chilly manner cost him popular support at a time when more and more Americans were voting.

States Expand Voting Rights Throughout the first decades of the 1800s, hundreds of thousands of white males gained the right to vote. This was largely because many states lowered or eliminated property ownership as a voting qualification. They did so partly to reflect the ideals of the Declaration of Independence and the social equality of frontier life. In addition, as cities and towns grew, the percentage of working people who did not own property increased. These people paid taxes and had an interest in the political affairs of their communities, and so they wanted a say in electing those who represented them.

The expansion of voting rights was very much in evidence by 1828. That year, more than 1.13 million citizens voted for president, compared with about 355,000 in 1824.

Jackson Becomes "the People's President" The campaign of 1828 pitted John Quincy Adams against Andrew Jackson, who believed that the presidency had been unjustly denied him four years earlier. The candidates quickly resorted to mudslinging, attacking each other's personalities and morals. Adams

called his opponent "incompetent both by his ignorance and by the fury of his passions." Jackson portrayed himself as the candidate of the common man and criticized Adams as an out-of-touch, untrustworthy aristocrat.

When the results came in, Jackson had 56 percent of the popular vote and 178 of the 261 electoral votes, a clear victory. Much of his support came from the West and South, where rural and small-town residents, many voting for the first time, saw Jackson as the candidate most likely to represent their interests.

Orphaned at the age of 14, Andrew Jackson had received little formal education and had been a fighter all his life. When he entered the White House at age 61, he was newly widowed and plagued by various ailments. Jackson had an inner toughness, however. He was nicknamed "Old Hickory" after a hardwood found on the frontier, and he performed the duties of his office with a firm and steady hand.

As president, Jackson actively tried to make the government more inclusive. At his inauguration, he took the unprecedented step of inviting the masses to his White House reception. In an effort to

John Quincy Adams

CHAPTER 5 The Young Republic **189**

L1/ELL

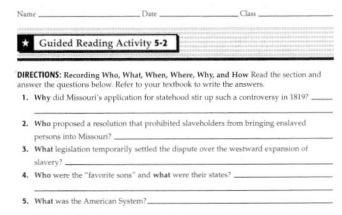

Guided Reading Activity 5-2

Name _____ Date _____ Class _____

★ Guided Reading Activity 5-2

DIRECTIONS: Recording Who, What, When, Where, Why, and How Read the section and answer the questions below. Refer to your textbook to write the answers.

1. Why did Missouri's application for statehood stir up such a controversy in 1819? _____
2. Who proposed a resolution that prohibited slaveholders from bringing enslaved persons into Missouri? _____
3. What legislation temporarily settled the dispute over the westward expansion of slavery? _____
4. Who were the "favorite sons" and what were their states? _____
5. What was the American System? _____
6. What was the "corrupt bargain"? _____

 ☑ **Reading Check**

Answer: Even though Jackson won the popular vote, no candidate won a majority in the Electoral College. When the election went to the House of Representatives, John Quincy Adams won the election.

CURRICULUM CONNECTION

Government Use a table similar to the one shown below to help students understand the election results of 1824. Note that the number of votes in the House represents the number of state delegations that voted for the candidate.

Candidate	Pop. Vote	Elect. Coll.	House of Rep.
Adams	108,740	84	13 states
Jackson	153,544	99	7 states
Crawford	46,618	41	4 states
Clay	47,136	37	*

*Only the three candidates who received the most votes in the Electoral College were included.

DIFFERENTIATED INSTRUCTION

Verbal/Linguistic Have students select one of the following political figures: Henry Clay, John Quincy Adams, Andrew Jackson, or William Crawford. Have students create and present an oral biography of the political figure. Encourage students to use quotes that express their figure's political views. **L2**

☞ Refer to *Inclusion for the High School Social Studies Classroom Strategies and Activities* in the TCR.

History *Through Art*

Background: Andrew Jackson's determined character made him a man not to be crossed. He once killed a man in a duel, a way to settle disputes in his day. When he considered something a matter of honor, there was no compromising.
Answer: He was not well educated.
Ask: What Washington building is pictured? *(the White House)*

FYI

In 1809 Andrew Jackson and his wife, Rachel Donelson Jackson, adopted one of Rachel's nephews and named him Andrew Jackson, Jr. In addition to their son, the Jacksons reared several other nephews, including Andrew Jackson Donelson.

Donelson and his wife Emily accompanied the Jacksons to Washington. The plan was for Donelson to serve as his uncle's secretary while Emily kept her aunt company.

After Rachel's death in December 1828, Jackson asked Emily to serve as his hostess. By all accounts, she did an excellent job of helping the president while also taking care of her growing family. When Emily became ill with tuberculosis, Jackson's daughter-in-law, Sarah Yorke Jackson, stepped in as his official hostess.

strengthen democracy, he vigorously utilized the spoils system, the practice of appointing people to government jobs based on party loyalty and support. In his view, he was getting rid of a permanent office-holding class and opening up the government to more ordinary citizens.

Jackson's supporters also moved to make the political system—specifically, the way in which presidential candidates were chosen—more democratic. At that time, political parties used the caucus system to select presidential candidates. The members of the party who served in Congress would hold a closed meeting, or caucus, to choose the party's nominee. Jackson's supporters believed that such a method restricted access to office to mainly the elite and well connected. The Jacksonians replaced the caucus with the national nominating convention, where delegates from the states gathered to decide on the party's presidential nominee.

✔ **Reading Check** **Examining** Why was there a large increase in the number of voters in the United States in 1828?

The Nullification Crisis

Jackson had not been in office long before he had to focus on a national crisis. It centered on South Carolina but highlighted the growing rift between the nation's northern and southern regions.

During the early 1800s, South Carolina's economy had been growing increasingly weak. Many residents blamed their troubles on the nation's tariffs. With little state industry, South Carolina purchased many of its tools, cooking utensils, and other manufactured goods from England. Tariffs made them extremely expensive, however. When Congress levied a new tariff in 1828—which critics called the Tariff of Abominations—many South Carolinians threatened to secede, or withdraw, from the union.

The growing turmoil particularly troubled Vice President **John C. Calhoun,** who was from South Carolina. To pave the way for his home state to legally resist the tariff, Calhoun had put forth the idea of nullification in 1828. He anonymously published *The South Carolina Exposition and Protest,* which argued that because the states had created the federal union, they had the right to declare a federal law null, or not valid.

The issue of nullification intensified in January 1830, when Robert Hayne of South Carolina and Daniel Webster of Massachusetts met for a Senate debate. Hayne, asserting that the Union was no more than a voluntary association of states, advocated "liberty first and Union afterward." Webster, perhaps the greatest orator of his day, countered that neither liberty nor the Union could survive without binding federal laws. He ended his speech with a stirring call: "Liberty *and* Union, now and for ever, one and inseparable!"

History *Through Art*

Jackson's Inaugural Hundreds of ordinary citizens celebrated Andrew Jackson's election at the White House. Jackson's portrait (left) by painter Asher Durand shows the president's determined character. **How was Jackson different from previous presidents?**

INTERDISCIPLINARY CONNECTIONS ACTIVITY

Economics In preparation for the discussion on the Panic of 1837, ask the economics teacher to prepare a presentation to explain the conditions that can cause a bank panic such as the one in 1837. Include in the discussion the problems caused by individual banks printing their own money. Also discuss the results of bank panics such as banks collapsing, loans becoming hard to obtain, and so on. Based on the discussion, have students create cause-and-effect charts to explain the economic impact of bank panics. **L2**

NATIONAL GEOGRAPHIC — Native American Removal, 1832–1841

In Motion

In 1832 Sauk and Fox warriors led by Chief Black Hawk fought to reclaim territory east of the Mississippi River, but were defeated.

The Cherokee took their refusal to move to the Supreme Court–and won. Federal troops forced them to leave in 1838.

Chief Osceola led the Seminole in rebellion.

- ☐ Ceded by Native Americans
- ☐ Ceded to Native Americans
- ← Multi-Group Removal Route
- — Trail of Tears
- ✕ Fort
- — 1840 border

0   200 miles
0   200 kilometers
Albers Conic Equal-Area projection

Geography *Skills*

1. **Interpreting Maps** Name two Native American groups in the northern half of the United States that were forced to move.
2. **Applying Geography Skills** Where did the Trail of Tears end?

Several months later, during a political dinner, President Jackson made his position clear. Looking directly at Calhoun, he offered this toast: "Our federal Union—It must be preserved."

The war of words erupted into an explosive situation in 1832 when Congress passed yet another tariff law. South Carolinians stepped up their call for secession, while a special session of the state legislature voted to nullify the law. Jackson considered nullification an act of treason and sent a warship to Charleston. As tensions rose, Senator Henry Clay managed to defuse the crisis. At Clay's insistence, Congress passed a bill that would lower tariffs gradually until 1842. South Carolina then repealed its nullification of the tariff law.

✓ **Reading Check** **Summarizing** What caused the nullification crisis?

Other Domestic Matters

Of the other issues of the day, slavery remained a divisive question. However, President Jackson, a slaveholder himself, largely ignored the rising voices of antislavery activists. He focused instead on two other matters—Native Americans and the national bank.

Policies Toward Native Americans Although Jackson wanted to ensure the survival of Native American peoples, he accelerated an effort that had been going on for years—moving them out of the way of white settlers. In 1830 Jackson signed the **Indian Removal Act,** which helped the states relocate Native Americans to largely uninhabited regions west of the Mississippi River.

The Cherokee in Georgia fought back by appealing to the Supreme Court, hoping that their territorial rights would be legally recognized. In *Cherokee Nation v. Georgia* (1831), Chief Justice Marshall supported the Cherokees' right to control their land. In *Worcester v. Georgia* (1832), the Court again ordered state officials to honor the Native Americans' property rights. Jackson refused to carry out this decision. "Marshall

CHAPTER 5   The Young Republic   **191**

CRITICAL THINKING ACTIVITY

Formulating Questions Point out to students that they might be able to comprehend written material more fully if they use it to create questions. As an example, ask students to form a question related to the first subheading in this section. Set a time limit—perhaps one minute—for students to find the answer in the text. Suggest that they use this method as they read the entire text.
L1 ELL

Analyzing *Political Cartoons*

Answer: the Constitution

Ask: What is Andrew Jackson holding in his left hand? *(a veto)*

✓ **Reading Check**

Answer: the name given to the forced relocation route of the Cherokee from Georgia to Oklahoma

3 ASSESS

Assign Section 2 Assessment as homework or as an in-class activity.

◉ Have students use the **Interactive Tutor Self-Assessment CD-ROM.**

L1/ELL

Reading Essentials and Study Guide 5–2

Name _____ Date _____ Class _____

Study Guide

Chapter 5, Section 2
For use with textbook pages 187–193

THE AGE OF JACKSON

KEY TERMS AND NAMES

Missouri Compromise agreement for admitting to the Union Maine as a free state and Missouri as a slave state *(page 188)*

"favorite son" man who enjoyed popularity and political support in his own state and region *(page 188)*

"corrupt bargain" accusation that Henry Clay won votes for John Quincy Adams in the House of Representatives in the presidential election of 1824 in exchange for a cabinet post *(page 189)*

mudslinging political campaign in which candidates criticize each other's personalities and principles *(page 189)*

spoils system the practice of appointing people to government jobs on the basis of party

L2

Section Quiz 5–2

Name _____ Date _____ Class _____

★ **Chapter 5** ___ Score ___

Section Quiz 5-2

DIRECTIONS: Matching Match each item in Column A with the items in Column B. Write the correct letters in the blanks. *(10 points each)*

Column A

___ 1. President Jackson issued this order that all payments for public lands be made in silver or gold

___ 2. men who enjoyed popularity and political support in their home state and region

___ 3. temporarily settled the dispute over the westward expansion of slavery

___ 4. candidates attacking each other's personalities and morals

___ 5. practice of appointing people to government jobs based on party loyalty and support

Column B

A. mudslinging
B. Specie Circular
C. favorite sons
D. Missouri Compromise
E. spoils system

---

has made his opinion," the president reportedly said, "now let him enforce it." 📖 *(See page 965 for more information on* Worcester v. Georgia.*)*

In 1838 Jackson's successor, Martin Van Buren sent in the army to forcibly move the Cherokee. Roughly 2,000 Cherokee died in camps while waiting for the westward march to begin. On the journey, known to the Cherokee as the **Trail of Tears,** about 2,000 others died of starvation, disease, and exposure.

Missionary-minded religious groups and a few members of Congress, like Henry Clay, declared that Jackson's policies toward Native Americans stained the nation's honor. Most citizens, however, supported them. By 1838 the majority of Native Americans still living east of the Mississippi had been forced onto government reservations. The Seminole of Florida were among the few holdouts. Even after the death of their leader, Chief **Osceola,** the Seminole in the Everglades resisted resettlement until the 1840s.

ECONOMICS

Jackson Battles the National Bank One of the most contentious developments of Jackson's presidency was his campaign against the national bank. Along with most Westerners and working people, the president distrusted the Second Bank of the United States. The Bank had done a good job of stabilizing the economy, but Jackson resented the power that its wealthy stockholders exercised. He disliked the Bank's aristocratic president, **Nicholas Biddle.** Jackson also believed the bank to be unconstitutional, despite the Supreme Court's ruling in *McCulloch v. Maryland.* He further believed in the equality of the different branches of the federal government and did not believe that, as president, he had to accept the Court's ruling.

The Bank's charter was scheduled to run out in 1836. In 1832, however, while Jackson was running for re-election, his foes in Congress passed a bill to extend the charter for another 20 years. Jackson vetoed the bill, and many Americans supported him.

When Jackson easily won a second term, he saw his victory as a mandate to destroy the Bank at once. He withdrew the government's deposits from the Bank, prompting Biddle to call in outstanding loans and stop new lending. By putting an end to the Bank of the United States, Jackson had won a considerable political victory. Later, however, critics would charge that the end of the Bank helped cause the financial woes that plagued the country in the years ahead.

✓ **Reading Check** **Interpreting** What was the Trail of Tears?

A New Party Emerges

By the mid-1830s, Jackson's critics had formed a new political party, the **Whigs.** Led by former National Republicans like Henry Clay, John Quincy Adams, and Daniel Webster, the Whigs wanted to expand the federal government, encourage industrial and commercial development, and create a centralized economy. Such policies differed from those of the Democrats, who favored a limited federal government.

The Whigs ran three candidates for president in the election of 1836. Jackson's continuing popularity, however, helped assure victory for his handpicked successor, Democrat Martin Van Buren.

Van Buren's Troubled Presidency Shortly after Van Buren took office, a crippling economic crisis hit the nation. The roots of the crisis stretched back

Analyzing *Political Cartoons*

Kingly Rule? Jackson's strong-willed leadership attracted many critics. Here a cartoonist portrays Jackson as an absolute monarch. What does Jackson appear to be trampling underfoot?

EXTENDING THE CONTENT

Sequoya and the Cherokee Language Prior to the 1800s, the Cherokee had no written language. The monumental task of creating a written Cherokee language took Native American scholar Sequoya about 12 years. Through the painstaking process of breaking down every Cherokee word into syllables, Sequoya found that all the sounds in the language could be represented by 86 symbols. He decided to borrow symbols from the Greek and Roman alphabets because existing printing presses could reproduce them. He introduced the writing system in 1821, and within four years the majority of Cherokee adults had mastered it.

to the end of Jackson's term, a period in which investment in roads, canals, and railroads boomed and prompted a wave of land speculation and bank lending. This heavy spending pushed up inflation, which Jackson feared eventually would render the nation's paper currency worthless. Just before leaving office, therefore, Jackson issued the **Specie Circular,** which ordered that all payments for public lands must be made in the form of silver or gold.

Jackson's directive set off the **Panic of 1837.** With easy paper credit no longer available, land sales plummeted and economic growth slowed. As a result, many banks and businesses failed and thousands of farmers lost their land through foreclosures. Van Buren, a firm believer in his party's philosophy of limited federal government, did little to ease the crisis.

"Tippecanoe and Tyler Too" With Van Buren clearly vulnerable, the Whigs looked forward to winning the White House in 1840. They nominated General William Henry Harrison, a hero of the battle against Native Americans at Tippecanoe in 1811. John Tyler, a Southerner and former Democrat who had left his party in protest over the nullification issue, joined the ticket as the vice presidential candidate. Campaigning with the slogan "Tippecanoe and Tyler too," the Whigs won a decisive victory.

On March 4, 1841, Harrison delivered his inauguration speech, speaking for nearly two hours in the bitter cold with no coat or hat. He came down with pneumonia and died one month after taking office. Vice President John Tyler then took over.

Major American Political Parties Since 1789

- Federalist
- Democratic-Republican
- National Republican
- Democratic
- Whig
- Republican

1789 1796 1804 1812 1820 1828 1836 1844 1852 1860 1868 1876 1884 1892 1900 1908 1916 1924 1932 1940 1948 1956 1964 1972 1980 1988 1996 2002

Source: *Governing by Consent*

Graph Skills

1. **Interpreting Graphs** What party shown had the shortest life span?
2. **Comparing** How long have Republicans and Democrats been major political rivals?

Tyler's ascendancy to the presidency dismayed Whig leaders. Tyler sided with the Democrats on numerous key issues, refusing to support a higher tariff or a new national bank. The new president did win praise, however, for the 1842 Webster-Ashburton Treaty, which established a firm boundary between the United States and Canada.

✓ **Reading Check** **Explaining** What caused the Panic of 1837?

HISTORY Online **Study Central™** To review this section, go to tarvol2.glencoe.com and click on **Study Central™**.

SECTION 2 ASSESSMENT

Checking for Understanding

1. **Define:** "favorite son," "corrupt bargain," mudslinging, spoils system, caucus, secede.
2. **Identify:** Missouri Compromise, Indian Removal Act, Trail of Tears, Nicholas Biddle, Whig, Specie Circular.

Reviewing Themes

3. **Government and Democracy** How did President Jackson try to make government more inclusive and democratic?

Critical Thinking

4. **Interpreting** How did President Jackson contribute to the Panic of 1837?
5. **Categorizing** Use a graphic organizer similar to the one below to identify key facts about the political parties active in the 1830s.

Party	Leaders	Policies
Democrats		
Whigs		

Analyzing Visuals

6. **Analyzing Photographs** Examine the daguerrotype of John Quincy Adams on page 189. What characteristics of Adams does this image highlight?

Writing About History

7. **Persuasive Writing** Imagine you are a Native American living in the United States during Andrew Jackson's presidency. Write a letter to President Jackson giving your opinion of the Indian Removal Act.

SECTION 2 ASSESSMENT ANSWERS

1. Terms are in blue.
2. Missouri Compromise *(p. 188),* Indian Removal Act, *(p. 191),* Trail of Tears *(p. 192),* Nicholas Biddle *(p. 192),* Whig *(p. 192),* Specie Circular *(p. 193)*
3. He used the spoils system and replaced the caucus system with a national nominating convention.
4. He issued the Specie Circular.
5. Democrats—Leaders: Jackson, Van Buren; Policies: limiting federal government; Whigs—Leaders: Clay, Adams; Policies: expanding federal government, industrial development, centralizing the economy
6. possible answer: his chilly, stern manner
7. Letters should express emotions that would have been felt by those being forced to relocate.

Graph Skills

Answers:
1. National Republican
2. since the mid-1850s

Geography Skills Practice
Ask: In what year did the Whig party begin? *(1836)*

✓ **Reading Check**

Answer: Jackson's order that all payments for public lands be made in silver or gold

Reteach

Have students write a one-sentence description of each of these administrations: Jackson, Van Buren, Harrison, and Tyler.

Enrich

Have interested students prepare an oral presentation focusing on one of the crises that occurred during Jackson's presidency.

HISTORY Online

Study Central™ provides summaries, interactive games, and online graphic organizers to help students review section content.

4 CLOSE

Ask students to explain how the land in the Louisiana Purchase played an important role in American life from the 1820s to the 1840s.

SECTION 3 The Reform Spirit

1 FOCUS

Section Overview

This section describes the social and cultural changes that occurred during the early and mid-1800s, including the Second Great Awakening.

BELLRINGER
Skillbuilder Activity

Project transparency and have students answer the question.

Daily Focus Skills Transparency 5–3

Reading Preview

Answers to Graphic:
1789: Baptists recommend abolition
1816: American Colonization Society forms
1831: the *Liberator* founded
1832: William Lloyd Garrison founds the New England Antislavery Society
1833: William Lloyd Garrison founds the American Antislavery Society
1845: autobiography of Frederick Douglass published

Preteaching Vocabulary
Have students use two Key Terms and Names in a sentence.

Guide to Reading

Main Idea
Strong faith and individualism led to an era of reform.

Key Terms and Names
Second Great Awakening, benevolent society, transcendentalism, utopia, temperance, Elizabeth Cady Stanton, abolition, emancipation, Frederick Douglass

Reading Strategy
Sequencing As you read about the abolitionist movement, complete a time line similar to the one below to record key events.

```
        1816   1832
1789                    1845
        1831   1833
```

Reading Objectives
• **Explain** the goals of the temperance movement, prison reform, educational reform, and the women's movement.
• **Discuss** the growth of the abolition movement and reaction to it.

Section Theme
Groups and Institutions Abolitionist reformers challenged the morality of slavery in the United States.

Preview of Events

♦1830	♦1840	♦1850	♦1860
1833 American Antislavery Society founded	**1840** Liberty Party runs first presidential candidate	**1848** Seneca Falls Convention	**1851** Maine passes first state prohibition law	**1855** Walt Whitman's *Leaves of Grass* published

★ An American Story ★

Dorothea Dix

By 1841 Dorothea Dix had been a schoolteacher in Massachusetts for many years. That year, a clergymember asked her to lead a Sunday school class at a local prison. What Dix saw there appalled her. Mentally ill persons lay neglected in dirty, unheated rooms. Putting aside her teaching career, she began a crusade to improve prison conditions for the mentally ill and to provide them with the treatment they needed.

In 1843 Dix composed a letter to the Massachusetts legislature calling for such reforms. She pointed to the example of one local woman as evidence that more humane treatment might help many of the mentally ill. "Some may say these things cannot be remedied," she wrote. "I *know* they can. . . . A young woman, a pauper . . . was for years a raging maniac. A cage, chains, and the whip were the agents for controlling her, united with harsh tones and profane language." Dix explained that a local couple took the woman in and treated her with care and respect. "They are careful of her diet. They keep her very clean. She calls them 'father' and 'mother.' Go there now, and you will find her 'clothed,' and though not perfectly in her 'right mind,' so far restored as to be a safe and comfortable inmate."

—adapted from *Old South Leaflets*

A Religious Revival

Largely through the efforts of Dorothea Dix, more than a dozen states enacted sweeping prison reforms and created special institutions for the mentally ill. As influential as she was, Dix was just one of many citizens who worked to reform various aspects of American society in the mid-1800s.

194 CHAPTER 5 The Young Republic

SECTION RESOURCES

📁 Reproducible Masters
• Reproducible Lesson Plan 5–3
• Daily Lecture and Discussion Notes 5–3
• Guided Reading Activity 5–3
• Section Quiz 5–3
• Reading Essentials and Study Guide 5–3

📑 Transparencies
• Daily Focus Skills Transparency 5–3

Multimedia
• Interactive Tutor Self-Assessment CD-ROM
• ExamView® Pro Testmaker CD-ROM
• Presentation Plus! CD-ROM
• TeacherWorks™ CD-ROM
• Audio Program
• American Music: Cultural Traditions
• American Music: Hits Through History

The reform movement stemmed in large part from a revival of religion that began at the turn of the century. Many church leaders sensed that the growth of scientific knowledge and rationalism were challenging the doctrine of faith. In the early 1800s, religious leaders organized to revive Americans' commitment to religion. The resulting movement came to be called the **Second Great Awakening.** Various Protestant denominations—most often the Methodists, Baptists, and Presbyterians—held camp meetings where thousands of followers sang, prayed, and participated in emotional outpourings of faith. One of the most successful ministers was **Charles G. Finney.** He pioneered many methods of revivalism still used by evangelists today.

New Religious Groups Emerge As membership in many Protestant churches swelled, other religious groups also flourished. Among them were Unitarianism, Universalism, and the Church of Jesus Christ of Latter-day Saints, whose followers are commonly known as Mormons.

Joseph Smith began preaching the Mormon faith in New York in the 1820s. After enduring much harassment in New York, Ohio, Missouri, and elsewhere, Mormons across the Midwest moved to Illinois. There the group prospered, and their settlement of Nauvoo grew to about 15,000 in 1844. Persecution continued, however, and following the murder of Joseph Smith the Mormons headed west, finally putting down permanent roots in the Utah Territory.

The Reform Spirit Revivalists preached the power of individuals to improve themselves and the world. **Lyman Beecher,** one of the nation's most prominent Presbyterian ministers, insisted that the nation's citizenry, more than its government, was responsible for building a better society.

Associations known as benevolent societies sprang up in cities and towns across the country. At first, they focused on spreading the word of God and attempting to convert nonbelievers. Soon, however, they sought to combat a number of social problems. One of the most striking features of the reform effort was the overwhelming presence of women. Young women in particular had joined the revivalist movement in much larger numbers than men. One reason was that many unmarried women with uncertain futures discovered in religion a foundation on which to build their lives. As more women turned to the church, many of them also joined religious-based reform groups.

 Reading Check **Examining** What sparked the reform movement of the mid-1800s?

A Literary Renaissance

The spirit of reform and the revival of religious feeling in the early 1800s coincided with a flowering of American literature. American essayists, poets, and novelists who were previously overshadowed by European writers now became widely admired.

The Transcendentalists One notable group of philosophers and writers in New England were the transcendentalists. Transcendentalism was based on the idea that people can transcend, or overcome, the mind's limits. The transcendentalists emphasized feeling over reason and sought communion with the natural world. The most influential transcendentalist was **Ralph Waldo Emerson,** who published his best-known essay, *Nature,* in 1836. Other leaders of the movement included **Margaret Fuller** and **Henry David Thoreau,** the author of *Walden.*

Distinctively American Voices Many of the nation's writers set out to create uniquely American works that celebrated the people, history, and natural beauty of the United States. James Fenimore Cooper romanticized Native Americans and frontier life in his Leatherstocking Tales, the most famous being *The Last of the Mohicans* (1826). Nathaniel Hawthorne, who produced more than 100 tales and novels, explored the Puritan heritage of New Englanders in books like *The Scarlet Letter* (1850). Herman Melville, another New Englander, wrote the whaling adventure *Moby Dick* (1851), a masterpiece of American fiction. Edgar Allan Poe achieved fame as a poet and writer of macabre short stories and detective tales. Henry Wadsworth Longfellow drew upon American

History *Through Art*

Religious Zeal J. Maze Burban's *Religious Camp Meeting* shows a charismatic preacher reaching many in the audience. From studying the image, can you suggest other reasons people might want to attend?

2 TEACH

Daily Lecture and Discussion Notes 5–3

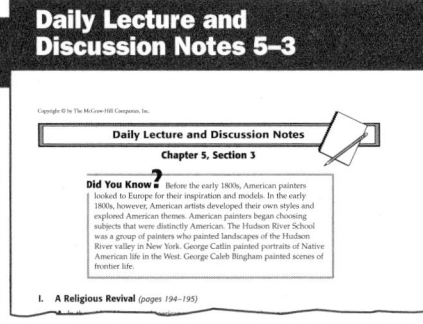

Copyright © by The McGraw-Hill Companies, Inc.

Daily Lecture and Discussion Notes

Chapter 5, Section 3

Did You Know? Before the early 1800s, American painters looked to Europe for their inspiration and models. In the early 1800s, however, American artists developed their own styles and explored American themes. American painters began choosing subjects that were distinctly American. The Hudson River School was a group of painters who painted landscapes of the Hudson River valley in New York. George Catlin painted portraits of Native American life in the West. George Caleb Bingham painted scenes of frontier life.

I. **A Religious Revival** (pages 194–195)

Creating a Poster Have students work in pairs to create a poster advocating reform in one of the areas mentioned in this section. Encourage students to use library and Internet resources to learn more about the reform issue. **L1** **ELL**

Use the rubric for creating a map, display, or chart on pages 65–66 in the *Performance Assessment Activities and Rubrics.*

 Reading Check

Answer: revival of religion

 History *Through Art*

Answer: It was a social gathering where people could enjoy meeting and being part of a crowd.
Ask: What is seen in the background that helps you understand the name of these meetings? *(tents)*

Reading Strategy **READING THE TEXT**

Classifying and Categorizing Information Students can use note cards to group and organize information. Have students form small groups. Give each group 10 note cards. Ask each group to write 10 questions that can be answered with the name of a person or reform movement discussed in the section. Direct the groups to arrange their questions into the following categories: literature, social reform, education reform, women's movement, or abolition movement. Collect the questions and have groups challenge each other to answer their questions. **L1**

Refer to *Inclusion for the High School Social Studies Classroom Strategies and Activities* in the TCR.

L1/ELL

Guided Reading Activity 5–3

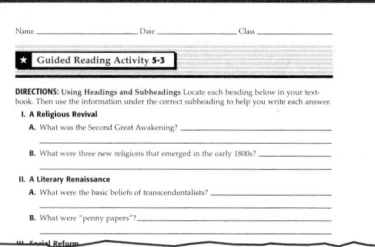

✔ **Reading Check**

Answer: Ralph Waldo Emerson, Margaret Fuller, Henry David Thoreau

🖌 **History** *Through Art*

Background: Nathaniel Currier's brother Charles introduced him to Jim Ives. Nathaniel Currier and Ives became close friends and eventually formed their well-known partnership, Currier & Ives.
Answer: A woman and child are seen weeping as the house burns.
Ask: Why did reformers consider alcohol so much of a problem?
(They argued that no other social vice caused as many problems.)

On the Wagon The phrase "on the wagon," referring to a recovering alcoholic, originated during the temperance movement. To publicize their cause, reformers pulled a water wagon through the streets and urged people to climb on. Over time "going on the wagon" came to mean accepting the temperance cause and staying sober.

---

history to create poems like "Paul Revere's Ride" (1863) and the "Song of Hiawatha" (1855) about a legendary Iroquois chief.

Perhaps the most provocative American writer of the day was **Walt Whitman,** who pioneered a new kind of poetry with *Leaves of Grass* (1855). Rejecting traditional rhyme and meter for free verse, Whitman exalted nature, the common people, democracy, and the human body and spirit.

The Penny Press A less literary but greatly influential phenomenon at this time was the rise of the mass newspaper. Before the early 1800s, most newspapers catered to well-educated readers and were too costly for the average worker. As more Americans learned to read and gained the right to vote, however, publishers began creating inexpensive "penny papers" that satisfied the popular craving for local news, crime reports, and gossip.

General-interest magazines that catered to particular groups also emerged around this time. Louis A. Godey founded *Godey's Lady's Book* in 1830, the first American magazine for women. In 1857 the poet James Russell Lowell launched the *Atlantic Monthly* for the well-educated. *Harper's Weekly* appealed to literate readers with its lavish illustrations and articles on everything from books to national news.

✔ **Reading Check** **Identifying** Who were some of the leading transcendentalists during America's literary renaissance?

🖌 **History** *Through Art*

Drunkard's Progress In 1846 Nathaniel Currier made this lithograph engraving (right). It clearly lays out the path to degradation that begins in Step 1, a glass of alcohol with a friend. Some innkeepers advertised their temperance principles with a sign such as the one above. From looking at the lithograph, how can you tell that women were often temperance supporters?

Social Reform

The optimism and the emphasis on the individual that infused much of American literature and religion in the mid-1800s also gave rise to dozens of new communities. The people who formed these communities believed that the way to a better life was to separate themselves from the corrupting influence of the larger society and form their own utopia, or ideal society. They typically practiced cooperative living and rejected the idea of private property. Some utopian settlements, like **Brook Farm** near Boston, were based on social or political ideologies. Others were religious in origin, like the communities founded by Shakers. The **Shakers** got their name from a ritual shaking dance that members performed. They reached their peak in the mid-1800s with some 6,000 members.

In general, however, only a few Americans chose to live in utopian communities. Many more, inspired by a strong faith in human goodness, attempted not to escape society but to reform it.

The Temperance Movement A number of reformers argued that no social vice caused more crime, poverty, or family damage than the excessive use of alcohol. In small towns throughout the West, people drank to ease the loneliness of rural life. In eastern cities, many workers made drinking in the pubs and saloons their main leisure activity.

Although advocates of temperance, or moderation in the consumption of alcohol, had been active since the late 1700s, the new reformers energized the campaign. Temperance groups formed across the country, preaching the evils of alcohol and urging

THE DRUNKARDS PROGRESS.
FROM THE FIRST GLASS TO THE GRAVE.

DIFFERENTIATED INSTRUCTION

Reading Support Have students select a reform movement mentioned in the section. Then have them create a pamphlet similar to those distributed in the early to mid-1800s encouraging people to join the cause. Tell students that they may need to research the movement in order to create the pamphlet. **L2**

📁 Refer to *Inclusion for the High School Social Studies Classroom Strategies and Activities* in the TCR.

heavy drinkers to give up liquor. In 1833 a number of groups formed a national organization, the **American Temperance Union,** to strengthen the movement.

While persuading people not to drink, temperance societies pushed to halt the sale of liquor. In 1851 Maine passed the first state prohibition law, an example a dozen other states followed by 1855. Other states passed "local option" laws, which allowed towns and villages to prohibit liquor sales within their boundaries.

Prison Reform One of society's most glaring ills, reformers insisted, was its prison system. Inmates of all kinds, ranging from violent offenders to debtors to the mentally ill, often were indiscriminately crowded together in jails and prisons, which in some cases were literally holes in the ground. One jail in Connecticut, for example, was an abandoned mineshaft.

Around 1816 many states began replacing these facilities with new penitentiaries where prisoners were to be rehabilitated rather than merely locked up. Officials developed forms of rigid discipline to rid inmates of the laziness that had led them astray. Solitary confinement was meant to give prisoners the chance to meditate on their wrongdoing.

✓**Reading Check** **Identifying** What were two aspects of American society targeted by reformers?

Educational Reform

Although the idea of state-supported schools dated back as far as the Massachusetts General School Act of 1647, there were few public schools in America in the Jacksonian Era. In the early 1800s, reformers began to push states to fund public schools for several reasons. For one thing, new technology created a demand for better-educated workers. It also seemed necessary to educate the increasing number of immigrants coming to the United States. The surging voting rolls in the 1820s and 1830s offered another compelling reason for

Prudence Crandall
1803–1890

In 1831 Prudence Crandall was running a successful school for girls in Canterbury, Connecticut, when Sarah Harris, the daughter of a prominent African American farmer, sought admission. When Crandall agreed to let her in, local parents objected, and many withdrew their children from the school.

Crandall then reorganized her school as a teacher-training institution for African American women. The citizens of Canterbury erupted in protest. To combat Crandall's effort, the state legislature passed the "Black Law," which forbade Connecticut schools from admitting out-of-state African American students and severely limited the type of schools that in-state African Americans could attend.

Crandall ignored the law and was arrested in August 1833. In a highly publicized case, prosecutors convicted her, but her conviction was overturned on appeal. In the wake of the trial, residents terrorized Crandall's school, dirtying its well, refusing it supplies, and creating other hardships. In 1834 Crandall closed her school.

Upon her death nearly 60 years later, a friend recalled her willingness to fight for what she believed in. "She had deep convictions of right. . . . Neither death, life, angels, principalities, things present, things to come, heights, depths, nor any other creature could keep her from following her convictions."

broader public education. After all, democracy demanded an informed and educated electorate.

Horace Mann Fights for Public Schooling One of the leaders of the education movement was Horace Mann. After helping to create the Massachusetts Board of Education in 1837, he served as its secretary for 12 years. During that time, he doubled teachers' salaries, opened 50 new high schools, and established schools for teacher training called **normal schools.**

By the 1850s, tax-supported elementary schools had gained widespread support in the Northeastern states and had begun to spread to the rest of the country. Rural areas responded more slowly, because children there were needed to help with planting and harvesting.

Horace Mann

In the South, a reformer named Calvin Wiley played a similar role in North Carolina to that of Horace Mann in Massachusetts. In 1839 North Carolina began providing support to local communities that established taxpayer-funded schools. Wiley traveled throughout the state building support for public education. By

✓**Reading Check**

Answer: temperance and prison reform

Profiles IN HISTORY

Background: The South outlawed public education for African American children. In 1828 there were only 2 schools in New York for 15,000 African Americans and only 3 schools in Philadelphia for 20,000 African American students.

Ask: What other event in history seems remarkably similar to the incident described in the profile of Prudence Crandall? *(desegregation during the 1950s and 1960s)*

Comparing and Contrasting Discuss the similarities and differences between educational reform in the 1800s and in the twenty-first century. Create a table on the board listing the similarities and differences. **L2**

Horace Mann carried his ideas on education from Massachusetts to Ohio, where he became the first president of Antioch College. There he fought for equal educational opportunities for women.

INTERDISCIPLINARY CONNECTIONS ACTIVITY

Sociology Invite a professor or women's rights activist to speak to your class about issues that face women in today's society in the United States and in other countries. The presentation should include social and economic issues. Ask the speaker to address topics that are appropriate for the young adult audience. Have them work with the students to compare and contrast today's reform movements to those in the early- and mid-1800s. **L2**

✓ Reading Check

Answer: to educate workers for skills involving new technologies, to educate increasing numbers of immigrants, and to educate voters

Determining Point of View

Read aloud the following response made by a Cincinnati, Ohio, milk deliverer when asked why Americans spent so much time reading newspapers.

"How should freemen spend their time, but looking after their government and watching that them fellers as we gives offices to, doos their duty and gives themselves no airs?"

Tell students to paraphrase the milk deliverer's explanation and discuss the links between education and democracy it suggests. **L2**

ABCNEWS INTERACTIVE™

📼 VIDEOCASSETTE
Historic America Electronic Field Trips

View **Tape 2, Chapter 6:** "Seneca Falls."

What *Life* Was Like...

Old-Fashioned School Days

Public schools in the early to mid-1800s were rough-and-ready affairs. Students came in all ages and sizes, teachers often had little training, and books and supplies were hard to obtain.

School ink jar

One-Room Schoolhouse
The painting *New England School* by Charles Frederick Bosworth tells the tale of teachers' challenges in early public schools. With a mixed-aged class, the teacher had to teach a few students at a time, leaving the others to their own education—or entertainment.

School lunch pail

1860 about two-thirds of North Carolina's white children attended school part of the year. The South as a whole responded less quickly, and only about one-third of Southern white children were enrolled in public schools by 1860. African American children were excluded entirely.

Women's Education When officials talked about educating voters, they had men in mind, since women were still not allowed to cast a ballot in the 1800s. Nonetheless, a number of women took advantage of the reform movement to create more educational opportunities for girls and women.

Emma Willard, who founded a girls' boarding school in Vermont in 1814, was an early women's educational pioneer. Her school went beyond the usual subjects for young women, such as cooking and etiquette, to include academic subjects like history, math, and literature. In 1837 another educator, Mary Lyon, opened the first higher education institution for women, Mount Holyoke Female Seminary, in Massachusetts. Eighty students arrived the first year; the second year, more than 200 applied for enrollment.

✓ Reading Check
Explaining Why was a better public education system needed in the early 1800s?

198   CHAPTER 5   The Young Republic

The Women's Movement

In the early 1800s, the industrial revolution began to change the economic roles of men and women. In the 1700s, most economic activity took place in or near the home because most people lived on farms. Although husbands and wives had distinct chores, running the farm and raising the family was the focus of their efforts. The rise of factories and other work centers in the 1800s began to separate the home from the workplace. Men now left home to go to work, while women tended the house and children.

Most people believed the home was the proper place for women, partly because the outside world was seen as dangerous and partly because of the era's ideas about the family. For many parents, raising children was treated as a solemn responsibility because it prepared young people for a proper Christian life. Women, in particular, were viewed as more moral and charitable than men, and better able to serve as models of piety and virtue for their families.

Magazine articles and novels reinforced the value of women's role at home. In 1841 **Catherine Beecher,** daughter of the minister Lyman Beecher, wrote *A Treatise on Domestic Economy.* The popular volume argued that women could find fulfillment at home and gave instruction on childcare, cooking, and health matters. At that time, most women did not feel that their role in life was too limited. Instead, the

---

CRITICAL THINKING ACTIVITY

Synthesizing Organize students into debate teams and explain the format that you will be using for the debate. The setting for the debate is the 1830s. Tell students they will debate the following resolution:

Resolved: Public education should be funded by taxes on all citizens of the United States. **L2**

First Readers
Generations of students used McGuffey's Readers, first produced in the 1830s by William McGuffey. His readers—the first Eclectic Reader is pictured here—ranged from simple to advanced and aimed to give students a happy, positive feeling. A college president at the end of his life, McGuffey began teaching in frontier Ohio schools when he was only 13.

School desk

era's ideas implied that wives were partners with their husbands, and, in some ways, morally superior.

The idea that women had an important role in building a virtuous home was soon expanded to society. As women became involved in reform movements, some argued for the right to promote their ideas.

In 1848 activists **Lucretia Mott** and **Elizabeth Cady Stanton** organized the Seneca Falls Convention in New York. This gathering of women reformers marked the beginning of an organized woman's movement. The convention issued the **Declaration of Sentiments and Resolutions,** better known as the Seneca Falls Declaration. It began with words expanding the Declaration of Independence: "We hold these truths to be self-evident: that all men and women are created equal. . . ." (See page 952 for more information on the Seneca Falls Declaration.)

Although Stanton shocked the women present when she proposed that they focus on gaining suffrage, or the right to vote, the convention narrowly passed her proposal. Throughout the 1850s, women organized conventions to promote greater rights for themselves. These conventions drew attention to their cause, paving the way for a stronger movement to emerge after the Civil War.

✓ **Reading Check** **Examining** How did society's view of women change in the early 1800s?

The Abolitionist Movement

Of all the reform movements that began in the early 1800s, the movement calling for abolition, or the immediate end to slavery, was the most divisive. By pitting North against South, it polarized the nation and helped bring about the Civil War.

Early Opposition to Slavery Opposition to slavery in the United States had actually begun as early as the Revolutionary War era. Quakers and Baptists in the North and South agreed not to enslave people, viewing the practice as a sin that corrupted both slaveholder and slave. In Virginia in 1789, the Baptists recommended "every legal measure to [wipe out] this horrid evil from the land."

One notable antislavery effort in the early 1800s was the formation of the **American Colonization Society** (ACS) in December 1816. This group, supported by such prominent figures as President James Monroe and Chief Justice John Marshall, encouraged African Americans to resettle in Africa. The privately funded ACS chartered ships and helped relocate between 12,000 and 20,000 African Americans along the west coast of Africa in what became the nation of **Liberia.** Still, there were over 1.5 million enslaved persons in the United States in 1820. Many of them, already two or three generations removed from Africa, strongly objected to the idea of resettlement.

TURNING POINT

The New Abolitionists The antislavery movement gained new momentum in the 1830s, thanks largely to **William Lloyd Garrison.** In his twenties, Garrison had worked for an antislavery newspaper in Baltimore. In 1831, at the age of 25, he cofounded his own paper in Boston with fellow abolitionist Isaac Knapp. In the *Liberator*, Garrison wrote caustic attacks on slavery and called for the immediate emancipation, or freeing, of enslaved persons. He had no patience with those who were put off by his militant stand:

> ❝I am aware that many object to the severity of my language; but is there not cause for severity? I will be as harsh as truth and as uncompromising as justice. On this subject I do not wish to think, or speak, or write with moderation. No! No! . . . urge me not to use moderation . . . I am in earnest, I will not equivocate, I will not excuse; I will not retreat a single inch—AND I WILL BE HEARD.❞
>
> —from the *Liberator*

✓ **Reading Check**

Answer: The idea that women had an important role in building a virtuous home was expanded to include society as a whole.

Drawing Conclusions Point out to students that the Constitution allowed slavery, it was against the law to help enslaved African Americans escape, and the law required runaway enslaved persons to be returned to their masters. Many abolitionists broke the law. Give students five minutes to write their thoughts about the following: "Are there some situations in which breaking the law is an acceptable protest?" Then have students participate in a class discussion about whether abolitionists should have broken the law to help enslaved persons escape. Extend the discussion to include other situations in which it might be acceptable to break the law as a form of protest.

History *and the* Humanities

🎵 American Music: Hits Through History: "Welcome Gospel Kindred," "Nabucca's Quick Step"

🎵 American Music: Cultural Traditions: "Kneebone Bend," "Come Life, Shaker Life," "The Handcart Song"

🎨 American Art & Architecture: Shaker Retiring Room

EXTENDING THE CONTENT

Etiquette In the early 1800s, a strict code of behavior governed relationships between unmarried men and women. Public displays of affection of any sort were prohibited. Modesty required that words referring to body parts were never spoken in mixed company. In 1839 English novelist Frederick Marryat toured the United States and was surprised by Americans' obsession with modesty. He visited a girls' school and found a grand piano in the parlor. The piano stood on its four "limbs" and, much to his surprise, each piano leg had been covered with a frilly trouser.

Geography Skills

Answers:
1. South Carolina and Louisiana
2. Virginia was less dependent on slave labor.

Geography Skills Practice

Ask: In which states did the percentage of African Americans as a percentage of the total population increase from 1820 to 1860? *(North Carolina, South Carolina, Alabama, Mississippi, Tennessee, and Arkansas)*

Sojourner Truth Her legal name was Isabella van Wagener, but she chose to use the name Sojourner Truth.

3 ASSESS

Assign Section 3 Assessment as homework or as an in-class activity.

☺ Have students use the **Interactive Tutor Self-Assessment CD-ROM.**

L1/ELL

Reading Essentials and Study Guide 5–3

NATIONAL GEOGRAPHIC **African American Populations, 1820 and 1860**

African American Percentage of Total Population
10.0 1820   **10.0** 1860
* 1830 data (Florida)
** Includes present-day West Virginia (Virginia)
*** No data for 1820 (Texas)

William Lloyd Garrison

Geography Skills

1. **Interpreting Maps** What two states had the highest percentage of African American population in 1820?
2. **Applying Geography Skills** Why do you think support for colonization might have been stronger in Virginia than in South Carolina?

Garrison soon attracted enough followers to found the **New England Antislavery Society** in 1832 and the **American Antislavery Society** in 1833. Both organizations thrived. By 1838 more than 1,350 chapters had formed, with over 250,000 members.

Orator Wendell Phillips, poet John Greenleaf Whittier, and many other dedicated people became active in the cause. Theodore Weld was one of the most effective leaders, recruiting and training many abolitionists for the American Antislavery Society. Arthur and Lewis Tappan, two devout and wealthy brothers from New York City, were also influential. Despite the risk of taunts and beatings, abolitionists worked tirelessly to end what they saw as a hideous wrong.

Many women also gave their efforts to the abolitionist cause. Prudence Crandall worked as a teacher and abolitionist in Connecticut. Lucretia Mott, a strong advocate of women's rights, also spoke out in favor of abolition. Some Southern women also joined the crusade. Among the earliest were Sarah and Angelina Grimké, South Carolina sisters who moved north to work openly against slavery.

200 CHAPTER 5 The Young Republic

African American Abolitionists Not surprisingly, free African Americans took a prominent role in the abolitionist movement. The most famous was **Frederick Douglass,** who had escaped from slavery in Maryland. A brilliant thinker and an electrifying speaker, Douglass drew many African Americans to the antislavery moment. He published his own antislavery newspaper, the *North Star,* and wrote an autobiography that quickly sold 4,500 copies after its publication in 1845.

Another important African American abolitionist was **Sojourner Truth.** She gained freedom in 1827 when New York freed all remaining enslaved persons in the state. In the 1840s her eloquent and deeply religious antislavery speeches attracted huge crowds.

Northern Views In the North, citizens responded to the abolitionist movement with everything from support to indifference to opposition. While many Northerners disapproved of slavery, some objected to abolitionism even more. They regarded the movement as a dangerous threat to the existing social system. Some whites, including many prominent businesspeople, warned that it would produce a destructive war between the North and the South. Others feared it might bring a great influx of freed African Americans to the North, overwhelming the

---

INTERDISCIPLINARY CONNECTIONS ACTIVITY

Music Tell students that one way enslaved people learned how to use the Underground Railroad was through a folk song entitled "Following the Drinking Gourd." The drinking gourd represents the Big Dipper. An explanation of the song can be found at http://quest.arc.nasa.gov/ltc/special/mlk/gourd2.html. Ask students to research the lyrics and write one or two paragraphs explaining what the "drinking gourd" was and how directions the song provided helped African Americans who were trying to escape slavery by way of the Underground Railroad. **L2**

labor and housing markets. Many Northerners also had no desire to see the South's economy crumble. If that happened, they might lose the huge sums Southern planters owed to Northern banks as well as the Southern cotton that fed Northern textile mills.

Given such attitudes, violence against abolitionists was hardly surprising. William Lloyd Garrison was nearly killed by an angry mob in 1834. Another abolitionist publisher, the Reverend Elijah P. Lovejoy, did indeed die in a mob attack in 1837. Yet Northerners also resented Southern slave-catchers who kidnapped African American runaways in the North and hauled them back to the South. In response, several Northern states passed laws restricting slave recapture.

Reaction in the South To most Southerners, slavery was a "peculiar institution," one that was distinctive and vital to the Southern way of life. While the North was building cities and factories, the South remained mostly agricultural, becoming increasingly tied to cotton and the enslaved people who planted and picked it. Southerners responded to the growing attacks against slavery by vehemently defending the institution. South Carolina's governor called it a "national benefit," while Thomas Dew, a leading academic of the South, claimed that most slaves had no desire for freedom, as they enjoyed a close and beneficial relationship with their slaveholders.

In 1831, when the Nat Turner rebellion left more than 50 white Virginians dead, Southerners were outraged. They cracked down on slaves throughout the region and railed against the North. Further, they demanded the suppression of abolitionist material as a condition for remaining in the Union. Southern

Frederick Douglass (center left) attending an abolitionist rally in Cazenovia, New York, in August 1850

postal workers refused to deliver abolitionist newspapers. In 1836, under Southern pressure, the House of Representatives passed a "gag rule" providing that all abolitionist petitions be shelved without debate.

Such measures did not deter the foes of slavery. Although the abolitionist movement was still relatively small, it continued to cause an uproar, and the North-South split continued to widen.

✓ **Reading Check** **Summarizing** How did Northerners and Southerners view abolitionism?

SECTION 3 ASSESSMENT

HISTORY Online **Study Central™** To review this section, go to tarvol2.glencoe.com and click on **Study Central™**.

Checking for Understanding

1. **Define:** benevolent society, transcendentalism, utopia, temperance, abolition, emancipation.
2. **Identify:** Second Great Awakening, Elizabeth Cady Stanton, Frederick Douglass.

Reviewing Themes

3. **Groups and Institutions** Which groups of Americans opposed slavery and which supported it? What efforts did they take to achieve their goals?

Critical Thinking

4. **Understanding Cause and Effect** How did the Second Great Awakening affect the reform spirit of the mid-1800s?
5. **Categorizing** Use a graphic organizer similar to the one below to identify some of the leading figures of the era discussed in this section.

Key Figures	Key Contributions
Abolitionists	
Other Social Reformers	
Literary Figures	
Religious Leaders	

Analyzing Visuals

6. **Analyzing Art** Look closely at the painting of a New England School on page 198. How is the room heated? What kinds of supplies did the students have?

Writing About History

7. **Persuasive Writing** Imagine that you are active in one of the reform movements of the early 1800s. Write an editorial to persuade others to support your cause.

SECTION 3 ASSESSMENT ANSWERS

1. Terms are in blue.
2. Second Great Awakening *(p. 195)*, Elizabeth Cady Stanton *(p. 199)*, Frederick Douglass *(p. 200)*
3. Students' responses should match information in the text.
4. Revivalists preached the power of individuals to improve themselves and the world and many sought social reform.
5. Key figures and contributions should match the text.
6. A fireplace provides heat; there are no individual desks, but each student has a book.
7. Editorials should include a call for action.

L2

✓ **Reading Check**

Answer: People in the North had varying views about abolitionism. There was some support, some opposition, and some indifference. Abolition was widely opposed in the South.

FYI

Sarah and Angelina Grimké's father was a slaveholder. The sisters moved to Philadelphia, became Quakers, and were among the first women to speak out for both abolition and women's rights.

Reteach

Have students use the headings in this section to create an outline of the reform movements.

Enrich

Invite students to take on the role of an abolitionist and prepare a speech, poster, or pamphlet supporting the movement.

 HISTORY Online

Study Central™ provides summaries, interactive games, and online graphic organizers to help students review section content.

4 CLOSE

Ask students to explain the connection between religious and social reform.

1 FOCUS

Section Overview
This section describes the nation's westward expansion.

BELLRINGER
Skillbuilder Activity

Project transparency and have students answer the question.

Daily Focus Skills Transparency 5–4

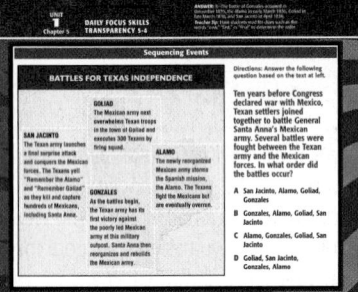

Reading Preview

Answers to Graphic: settlement of Texas: war between Texas and Mexico; Texas's fight for independence: gains independence; War with Mexico: United States gains 500,000 square miles and sets Rio Grande as border of Texas; Oregon's division: compromise with Britain to establish border at 49th parallel

Preteaching Vocabulary
Have students select one of the Key Terms and Names to learn about so that they can teach the class the meaning.

SECTION 4 Manifest Destiny

Guide to Reading

Main Idea
In the 1840s, the nation expanded as settlers moved west.

Key Terms and Names
Manifest Destiny, squatter, Pre-emption Act, *Tejano, empresario,* Antonio López de Santa Anna, Sam Houston, annexation, Bear Flag Republic, Treaty of Guadalupe Hidalgo

Reading Strategy
Organizing As you read about the settling of the West, complete a graphic organizer similar to the one below to describe the outcomes of disputes that arose as the United States expanded.

Dispute	Outcome

Reading Objectives
• **Describe** the pioneers of the 1840s, explain why and how they journeyed west, and discuss where they settled.
• **Discuss** the founding of the Republic of Texas and the major events and outcome of the war with Mexico.

Section Theme
Continuity and Change American settlers in Mexican lands continued to speak English and practice American customs.

Preview of Events

1836	1841	1845	1849

1836 — Texas declares independence from Mexico

1841 — Pre-emption Act passed

1845 — Texas becomes a state

1846 — Congress declares war on Mexico

1846 — Oregon boundary dispute settled

1848 — Treaty of Guadalupe Hidalgo signed

★ An American Story ★

Stephen F. Austin

In July 1821, Stephen F. Austin set off from Louisiana for the Texas territory in the northeastern corner of Mexico. The Spanish government had promised to give his father, Moses, a huge tract of Texas land if the elder Austin settled 300 families there from the United States. Moses, however, died before he could fulfill his end of the deal. On his deathbed, his dying wish was that Stephen take his place in Texas.

Stephen Austin was favorably impressed with the region. As he surveyed the land grant between the Brazos and Colorado Rivers, he noted its natural abundance:

❝The Prairie comes bluff to the river . . . and affords a most beautiful situation for a Town or settlement. . . . The country . . . is as good in every respect as man could wish for, Land all first rate, plenty of timber, fine water, beautifully rolling.❞

—quoted in *Stephen F. Austin: Empresario of Texas*

The Western Pioneers

Austin was not alone in seeing possibilities in Texas. Thousands of people would depart the United States to start a new life in this area by 1836. Around the same time, many more Americans began pushing into the Midwest and beyond, journeying all the way to California and the Oregon Territory. Between the late 1830s and early 1860s, more than 250,000 Americans braved great obstacles to venture west along overland trails. The opportunity to farm fertile soil, enter the fur trade, or trade with foreign nations across the Pacific lured farmers, adventurers, and merchants alike. Whatever their reasons, most emigrants, like the majority of Americans, believed in Manifest Destiny. Manifest Destiny was the

---

SECTION RESOURCES

📁 **Reproducible Masters**
• Reproducible Lesson Plan 5–4
• Daily Lecture and Discussion Notes 5–4
• Guided Reading Activity 5–4
• Section Quiz 5–4
• Reading Essentials and Study Guide 5–4

📖 **Transparencies**
• Daily Focus Skills Transparency 5–4

Multimedia
🖥 Interactive Tutor Self-Assessment CD-ROM
🖥 ExamView® Pro Testmaker CD-ROM
🖥 Presentation Plus! CD-ROM
🖥 TeacherWorks™ CD-ROM
🎧 Audio Program
🎵 American Music: Hits Through History
📺 ABCNews Interactive™ Historic America Electronic Field Trips

idea that the nation was meant to spread to the Pacific. 📖 *(See page 931 for more information on Manifest Destiny.)*

Farmers in the Midwest In 1800 only about 400,000 Americans were living west of the Appalachian Mountains. By 1850 over 4 million settlers had advanced across the Appalachian Mountains and into Ohio, Indiana, Illinois, Michigan, and Wisconsin.

Some of the first pioneers were called squatters, because they settled on lands they did not own. In 1841, however, Congress passed the **Pre-emption Act.** This law allowed squatters to buy up to 160 acres before the land went up for public sale.

The Push to the Pacific Latecomers to the Midwest set their sights on California and Oregon, although other nations had already claimed parts of these lands. The United States and Great Britain had agreed in 1818 to occupy the Oregon land jointly. The British dominated the region until about 1840, when the enthusiastic reports of American missionaries began to attract large numbers of would-be farmers to the region.

California was a frontier province of Mexico. Because few Mexicans wanted to make their homes in California, the local government welcomed foreign settlers. By 1845 more than 700 Americans lived in and around the Sacramento Valley. Though the central government in Mexico City relied on these American settlers, it was suspicious about their national loyalties.

GEOGRAPHY

The Trails West Between the frontier jumping-off points and the Pacific lay a vast expanse of difficult terrain. By the 1840s, several east-to-west routes had been carved out by early adventurers such as Kit

NATIONAL GEOGRAPHIC

Overland Trails West, 1840–1860

--- Continental Divide
)(Pass
■ Fort
— 1860 border

A wagon train headed west

Geography *Skills*

1. **Interpreting Maps** Name two Missouri cities that served as starting points for western emigrants.
2. **Applying Geography Skills** Why did emigrants bypass the open territory of the Great Plains for a grueling journey to the Far West?

---

2 TEACH

Daily Lecture and Discussion Notes 5–4

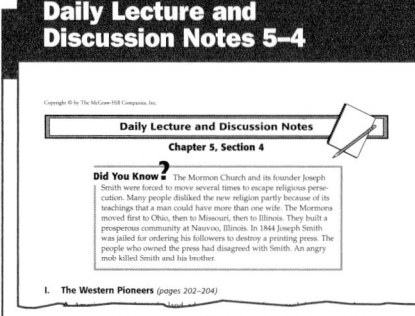

Copyright © by The McGraw-Hill Companies, Inc.

Daily Lecture and Discussion Notes
Chapter 5, Section 4

Did You Know ? The Mormon Church and its founder Joseph Smith were forced to move several times to escape religious persecution. Many people disliked the new religion partly because of its teachings that a man could have more than one wife. The Mormons moved first to Ohio, then to Missouri, then to Illinois. They built a prosperous community at Nauvoo, Illinois. In 1844 Joseph Smith was jailed for ordering his followers to destroy a printing press. The people who owned the press had disagreed with Smith. An angry mob killed Smith and his brother.

I. **The Western Pioneers** *(pages 202–204)*

Creating a Map Provide students with an outline map of the United States with all of the current state boundaries. Have students use the map to locate and label one of the trails shown on the map on page 203. Instruct students to name the current states and major geographic landmarks along the trail. **L1** ELL

📁 Use the rubric for creating a map, display, or chart on pages 65–66 in the *Performance Assessment Activities and Rubrics.*

Geography *Skills*

Answers:
1. Possible answers: St. Louis, St. Joseph, and Independence
2. They assumed the land was not good for farming and they feared the Plains Indians.

Geography Skills Practice
Ask: What mail route ran from Fort Smith, Arkansas, to El Paso, Texas? *(Butterfield Overland Mail)*

COOPERATIVE LEARNING ACTIVITY

Creating a Thematic Map Organize students into small groups. Have each group select one of the trails west. For the trail chosen, have students research the plant or animal life that early settlers were likely to encounter on their trip. Have students use their research to prepare a thematic map that shows where the plant or animal species were likely to be found. The group should include a picture and brief description of each plant or animal. Encourage students to include at least 12 types of plant or animal life.

Use the rubric for a cooperative group management plan on pages 71–72 in the *Performance Assessment Activities and Rubrics.*

Guided Reading Activity 5–4

Name _____ Date _____ Class _____

★ **Guided Reading Activity 5-4**

DIRECTIONS: Recalling Facts Read the section and answer the questions below. Refer to your textbook to write the answers.

1. Why did Americans head west? _____
2. What was Manifest Destiny? _____
3. Who were squatters? _____
4. How long did the typical trip west take? _____
5. What were the elements of the Treaty of Fort Laramie? _____
6. Why did Mexico decide to invite Americans and other foreigners to settle in the Texas region? _____

✓ **Reading Check**

Answer: Initially the Plains Indians were helpful, but they came to resent the disruption to their way of life. When white settlers violated the Treaty of Fort Laramie, the Native Americans became hostile.

Picturing History

Background: This poster was basically a "help wanted" ad for soldiers for hire.

Answer: It was more beneficial for the Texas war effort if the settlers stayed longer.

Ask: Who might have placed such an ad? *(an empresario)*

you don't say...

Texas The name *Texas* comes from a Native American word meaning "friend" or "ally." Spanish settlers used the word to refer to the Native Americans who were occupying the area when they arrived.

Carson and African American Jim Beckwourth. The most popular route was the **Oregon Trail**. Other trails included the California Trail and the Santa Fe Trail. The typical trip west took five to six months, with the wagon trains progressing about 15 miles (24 km) a day.

Crossing the Great Plains Most Americans assumed that the treeless Great Plains contained poor land for farming. Reports of hostile Plains Indians further discouraged settlement in this "Great American Desert." Early pioneers heading west through the region, however, often found that the Native Americans there were helpful and would provide food, water, fresh horses, and valuable information.

As the overland traffic increased, the Plains Indians came to resent the threat it posed to their way of life. They relied on the buffalo for food, shelter, warm clothing, and tools. Now they feared that the increasing flow of settlers across their hunting grounds would cause the buffalo herds to die off or migrate elsewhere.

Hoping to ensure peace, the federal government negotiated the **Treaty of Fort Laramie** in 1851. Eight Plains Indian groups agreed to specific geographic boundaries, while the United States promised that the defined territories would belong to the Native Americans forever. White settlers still streamed across the plains, however, provoking Native American hostility.

✓ **Reading Check** **Evaluating** What kind of relationship did the Plains Indians and white settlers have?

Americans Settle in Texas

When Stephen Austin arrived in Texas in 1821, most Spanish-speaking inhabitants, called *Tejanos,* lived in the southern part of the region. To the north lay the territory of the Apache, Comanche, and other Native American groups.

The sparse settlement in Texas posed a problem for the newly independent Mexican government. It worried that the United States might try to take over the region if Mexico left it underpopulated for long. Unable to persuade its own citizens to move closer to the Native American groups, Mexico continued the Spanish policy of inviting foreigners into Texas. Between 1823 and 1825, Mexico passed three colonization laws that offered cheap land to nearly anyone willing to come. The last law granted new immigrants a 10-year exemption from paying taxes but required that they become Mexican citizens, live under Mexican law, and convert to Roman Catholicism.

Americans began flooding into Texas with the encouragement of *empresarios*—agents who contracted with the Mexican government to bring in a certain number of residents in exchange for large grants of Texas land. The *empresarios* advertised for settlers, assigned a plot to each family, and governed the colonies they established. Stephen Austin was the first and most successful *empresario*. By the mid-1830s, Austin had persuaded some 1,500 American families to immigrate.

The Americans who relocated to Texas initially accepted Mexican citizenship. Few, however, adopted Mexican customs, learned Spanish, or developed a loyalty to Mexico. The Spanish Catholic Church was alien to them, and most had little contact with native Mexicans, who lived farther south.

Many Mexicans, in turn, distrusted the new settlers because of their American lifestyle and dismissal of Mexican ways. The Mexicans' unease increased in 1826, when *empresario* Haden Edwards's brother Benjamin rebelled against Mexican authority and proclaimed that American settlements in Texas were now an independent nation, **Fredonia.** Edwards gained few followers, however, and Stephen Austin led an American force that helped Mexico crush the revolt.

TEXAS!!

Emigrants who are desirous of assisting Texas at this important crisis of her affairs may have a free passage and equipments, by applying at the

NEW-YORK and PHILADELPHIA HOTEL,

On the Old Levee, near the Blue Stores.

Now is the time to ensure a fortune in Land: To all who remain in Texas during the War will be allowed 1280 Acres.
To all who remain Six Months, 640 Acres.
To all who remain Three Months, 320 Acres.
And as Colonists, 4600 Acres for a family and 1470 Acres for a Single Man.

New Orleans, April 23d, 1836.

Picturing History

Land in Texas This April 1836 poster from New Orleans sought volunteers during the Texas war for independence. The offer of land also drew settlers to Texas before the war. Why do you think the sponsors offered more land to settlers who stayed longer?

204 CHAPTER 5 The Young Republic

DIFFERENTIATED INSTRUCTION

Reading Support To help students gain a better understanding of what life was like on the westward trails, have them locate and read excerpts from diaries written by people who traveled West between 1820 and 1860. The names of some known diarists are shown below. **L1**

James Akin, Jr.	James Madison Coon	Amelia Stewart Knight	Catherine Sager Pringle
William H. Ashley	Nancy Miller Coon	William Porter	Narcissa Whitman

☛ Refer to *Inclusion for the High School Social Studies Classroom Strategies and Activities* in the TCR.

Profiles IN HISTORY

Lorenzo de Zavala
1788–1836

Lorenzo de Zavala demonstrated his fierce support of democratic principles both in his native Mexico and as a citizen of the Republic of Texas.

Born in the Yucatán peninsula, Zavala was jailed in his youth for advocating Mexican independence from Spain. Soon after Mexico gained independence in 1821, Zavala was elected to the new national congress. Battles for political power in early Mexico were intense. Zavala was forced into exile but granted a huge tract of land in southeastern Texas.

Politics in Texas proved no less intense than in Mexico. Most Mexicans in Texas were loyal to Mexico, but Zavala's disapproval of Santa Anna's policies led him to support Texan independence. As a speaker of both Spanish and English, he helped draft the new republic's constitution and design its flag. He also served as vice president of the Republic-in-Arms until ill health forced him to resign.

Sam Houston
1793–1863

Standing over six feet tall, Sam Houston seemed larger than life. A military hero in the Creek wars, he had a brief political career in Tennessee before heading to Texas in 1832. He soon revived his military career and led the army of the Republic of Texas to victory over Mexico at the Battle of San Jacinto. Texans elected him president of the Republic and later, when Texas joined the Union, Houston served as a U.S. senator.

Despite being a slaveholder himself, Houston voted with the antislavery faction because he believed a compromise was necessary to save the Union. When the Civil War broke out, Houston refused to take an oath of loyalty to the new Southern government, and he was removed from office. In his farewell address, he declared, "Oh my fellow countrymen, the fearful conflict will fill our land with untold suffering, misfortune, and disaster." He died in July 1863 at the height of the Civil War.

Suspicious of Americans' intentions in Texas, Mexico closed its borders to further American immigration in 1830. This action infuriated American settlers. Without immigration, their settlements could not grow and relatives back home could not join them. Worst of all, the Mexican government was telling them what they could and could not do.

✓ **Reading Check** **Examining** What did Mexico offer people willing to settle in northern Texas, and what did it require of these settlers?

Texas Fights for Independence

With tensions simmering, settlers met at two conventions in San Felipe in 1832 and 1833. The first convention asked Mexico to reopen Texas to American immigrants and to loosen the taxes on imports. The second convention was more aggressive. It recommended separating Texas from Coahuila, the Mexican state it was then part of, and designated Stephen Austin to travel to Mexico City to negotiate with the Mexican government. In the fall of 1833, when the negotiations stalled, an angry Austin wrote back to San Antonio to suggest that Texas should start peacefully organizing its own state government.

After sending his letter, Austin managed to win several concessions from President **Antonio López de Santa Anna.** Meanwhile, Mexican officials had intercepted Austin's letter. They arrested him for treason on January 3, 1834, and jailed him without trial in Mexico City.

After Austin was granted amnesty in July 1835, he concluded that negotiation with Santa Anna was impossible. In April 1834, Santa Anna had abruptly made himself a dictator, disavowing the country's democratic constitution and declaring that his word was law. In September 1835, Austin urged Texans to organize an army, which they quickly did.

The settler army first faced a Mexican force in October 1835. At the military post of Gonzales, about 75 miles east of San Antonio, Mexican soldiers ordered the Texans to surrender their arms. In response, the rebels pointed a cannon at the Mexican troops and held up a sign that read, "Come and Take It." Having no orders to attack, the Mexicans retreated to San Antonio. The Texans, who numbered only about 300, followed them and drove the much larger Mexican force out of San Antonio in mid-December 1835.

HISTORY Online

Student Web Activity Visit the *American Republic Since 1877* Web site at tarvol2.glencoe.com and click on **Student Web Activities— Chapter 5** for an activity on Manifest Destiny.

CHAPTER 5 The Young Republic **205**

✓ **Reading Check**

Answer: It offered cheap land and a ten-year tax exemption. In return, the settlers were required to become Mexican citizens, live under Mexican law, and convert to Roman Catholicism.

Profiles IN HISTORY

What did Santa Anna do in 1834 that might have influenced Zavala to support independence for Texas? What led to Sam Houston's removal from office? *(Santa Anna denounced Mexico's Constitution and made himself a dictator. Sam Houston refused to take an oath of loyalty to the new Southern government at the beginning of the Civil War.)*

HISTORY Online

Objectives and answers to the student activity can be found in the **Web Activity Lesson Plan** at tarvol2.glencoe.com.

History and the Humanities

🏳️ American Music: Hits Through History: "De Boatman's Dance"
✍️ American Art & Architecture: *The Great Blue Heron*

INTERDISCIPLINARY CONNECTIONS ACTIVITY

Government Explain to students that Texas draws on a rich history that includes having been a part of Mexico. Have students research the various flags that have flown over Texas throughout its history. Have students prepare displays showing each flag and explaining when and why each was used. L2

Geography *Skills*

Answers:

1. March 6, 1836

2. It united Texans behind their new country.

Geography Skills Practice

Ask: What river did Texas claim as its boundary with Mexico? (*Rio Grande*)

ABCNEWS INTERACTIVE™

VIDEOCASSETTE
Historic America Electronic Field Trips

View **Tape 1, Chapter 10:** "The Alamo."

Name Origins The building that is now called "the Alamo" was originally the chapel of a Franciscan mission. How it came to be called "the Alamo" is not clear. *Alamo* is the Spanish word for cottonwood. Some historians believe there were cottonwood trees in the area, thus the name. Other historians believe the name came from a city in Mexico—Alamo de Parras, Coahuila. This was the hometown of a cavalry unit housed at the old mission in the early 1800s. The Alamo now is a symbol of the war Texas fought to gain its freedom.

The Alamo Despite this early success, the Texans faced tremendous difficulties. They had to scramble to organize a government, and few of the men had any military training. In the meantime, Santa Anna was personally leading a Mexican force of about 6,000 to put down the rebellion. When Santa Anna's troops arrived at San Antonio in February 1836, they found about 150 rebels and 24 noncombatants holed up in a former Spanish mission called the Alamo. The Texan commander, Lieutenant Colonel **William B. Travis,** quickly sent a plea for help to fellow Texans and U.S. citizens:

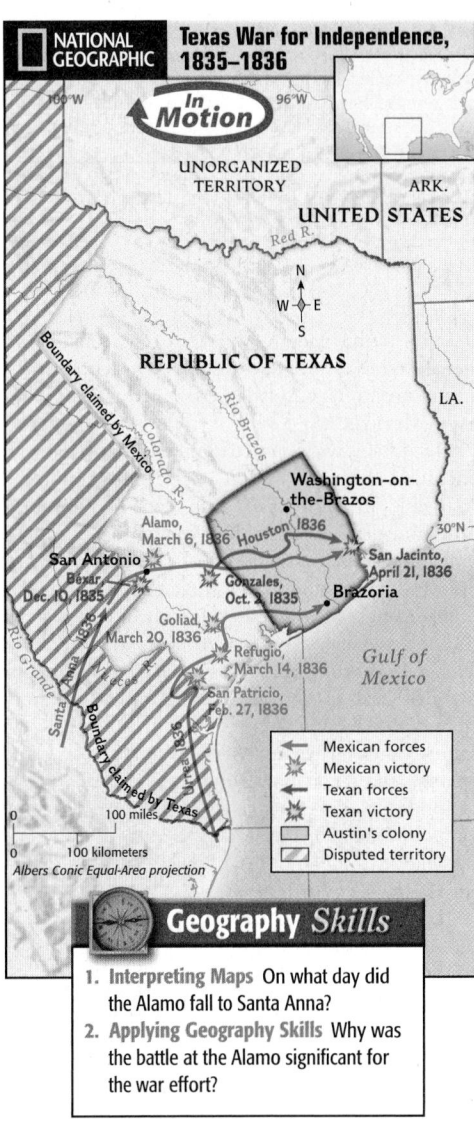

Geography *Skills*

1. **Interpreting Maps** On what day did the Alamo fall to Santa Anna?
2. **Applying Geography Skills** Why was the battle at the Alamo significant for the war effort?

206   CHAPTER 5   The Young Republic

> ❝I call on you, in the name of liberty, of patriotism, and everything dear to American character, to come to our aid with all dispatch. . . . Victory or death!❞
>
> —from *History of Texas*

The call for reinforcements went almost unanswered. Only 32 settlers from Gonzales arrived to join the fight. Still, the small band of Texans held off Santa Anna's army for 13 days. During the standoff, on March 2, the new Texas government met at **Washington-on-the-Brazos** and formally declared independence from Mexico.

On March 6, 1836, Santa Anna's army stormed the mission. The Texans fought off the attackers for several hours, killing or wounding over 600 before the Alamo was finally overrun. Only women, children, and some servants survived; the dead included famed frontiersmen **Davy Crockett** and **Jim Bowie.**

Two weeks later, the Mexican army overwhelmed troops led by **James W. Fannin** at Goliad, a town southeast of San Antonio. The Texans surrendered, hoping for clemency. Santa Anna, however, insisted on the usual punishment for captured foreigners—execution. At dawn on March 27, Fannin and more than 300 others died at the hands of a firing squad.

The losses at the Alamo and Goliad devastated Texans but also united them behind their new country. They regarded the Battle of the Alamo as a heroic struggle for freedom, and the Goliad massacre as evidence of Santa Anna's cruelty.

TURNING POINT

The Battle of San Jacinto Back in Washington-on-the-Brazos, the commander in chief of the Texas forces, **Sam Houston,** desperately needed time to recruit fresh volunteers and to train the soldiers who remained. He retreated east and waited for Santa Anna to make a mistake. His chance came on the afternoon of April 21, when the Texans caught Santa Anna's soldiers napping in their camp by the San Jacinto River. The Texans' surprise attack threw the Mexicans into a panic. They were used to acting only on orders, and with no time for officers to direct them, they suffered a quick defeat.

The Battle of San Jacinto lasted less than 20 minutes, but the bloodshed continued for hours. Yelling "Remember the Alamo" and "Remember Goliad," Houston's men killed hundreds of the enemy and took over 700 prisoners. Among those captured was Santa Anna. Knowing that the Mexican leader feared for his life, Houston compelled Santa Anna to withdraw his army from Texas and sign a treaty recognizing the

Reading Strategy   READING THE TEXT

Sequencing Information Understanding the order in which events took place will help students synthesize important information. Have students write the title "Texas Independence" on a sheet of paper. Then, have them draw a horizontal line and write "1820" on the left end and "1836" on the right end. Working independently, have students enter the major events in the struggle for independence in Texas on this time line. Ask students to use the information in their time line to write a chronological summary of the Texas Revolution. **L1** ELL

☞ Refer to *Inclusion for the High School Social Studies Classroom Strategies and Activities* in the TCR.

✓ **Reading Check**

Answer: Sam Houston was elected president and the vote was overwhelmingly in favor of annexation by the United States.

History *Through Art*

Battle of San Jacinto H.A. McArdle's painting (above) and this monument (right) commemorate the pivotal battle of the war between Texas and Mexico. **Why were Santa Anna and his troops surprised by Houston's attack?**

republic's independence. The Mexican government never accepted the treaty, but it was unwilling and unable to launch another military campaign. Texas had become a new nation.

The Republic of Texas In September 1836, the citizens of Texas elected Sam Houston president and voted 3,277 to 91 in favor of annexation—absorption—by the United States. Although proud of their republic, the settlers still regarded themselves as Americans.

Given that Americans had enthusiastically supported the war, most Texans assumed the United States would want to annex the republic. However, Texas wished to enter the Union as a slave state, which antislavery leaders opposed. In addition, Mexico continued to claim ownership of Texas. To avoid conflict, President Andrew Jackson made no move toward annexation. The Lone Star Republic, as Texas was nicknamed, would exist for almost a decade before joining the United States.

✓ **Reading Check** **Identifying** What was the outcome of the first election in Texas?

Texas and Oregon Enter the Union

John Tyler, who became president in 1841, hoped to bring Texas into the Union. In early 1844, he proposed a treaty to annex Texas. He blundered, however, by including in the supporting documents a letter written by Secretary of State John C. Calhoun that contained a defense of slavery. Outraged Northerners argued that the letter proved annexation was a plot to expand slavery. By a vote of 35 to 16, the Senate refused to annex Texas.

The Election of 1844 As the presidential race began in 1844, Texas statehood became a key issue. The Democrats nominated James K. Polk of Tennessee, who promised to annex not only Texas but also the contested Oregon Territory in the Northwest. In addition, he vowed to buy California from Mexico. The platform appealed to both Northerners and Southerners because it furthered Manifest Destiny while promising to maintain the delicate balance between free and slave states.

The Whig nominee, Henry Clay, originally opposed annexing Texas. He later announced his support of annexation if it could be done without causing war with Mexico. Many Whigs opposed to slavery felt so betrayed that they gave their support to James G. Birney of the pro-abolition Liberty Party. With the Whig vote split, Polk won the election.

Dividing Oregon High on President Polk's agenda was resolution of the Oregon question. "Oregon fever" was drawing more and more Americans to the Northwest. Despite Britain's long-standing claims, Polk maintained that the United States had a right to the entire Oregon country all the way to its northern border, on the line of 54° 40′ north latitude. During the election of 1844, Polk's supporters chanted "Fifty-four Forty or Fight." The British believed the boundary should be the Columbia River, which flowed near the 46th parallel.

In June 1846, the two countries agreed to a compromise, dividing the territory along the 49th parallel. The British took what is now the Canadian province of British Columbia, and the Americans received the land that later became the states of Washington, Oregon, and Idaho.

CHAPTER 5 The Young Republic **207**

EXTENDING THE CONTENT

Vice President of the Republic of Texas One of the Texans who thought it was time to break with Mexico was Lorenzo de Zavala. He had helped to found the Mexican Republic and had served as its ambassador to France. When Santa Anna became a dictator, Zavala resigned and settled in Texas. In 1836 Zavala was chosen vice president of the Republic of Texas.

Geography *Skills*

Answers:

1. Sloat

2. land that is now California, Nevada, Utah, most of Arizona and New Mexico, and parts of Colorado and Wyoming

Geography Skills Practice

Ask: In what body of water was the naval blockade? *(the Gulf of Mexico)*

✓ Reading Check

Answer: Oregon—a compromise with the British; Texas—Congress passed a resolution to annex it

3 ASSESS

Assign Section 4 Assessment as homework or as an in-class activity.

🌐 Have students use the **Interactive Tutor Self-Assessment CD-ROM.**

L1/ELL

Reading Essentials and Study Guide 5–4

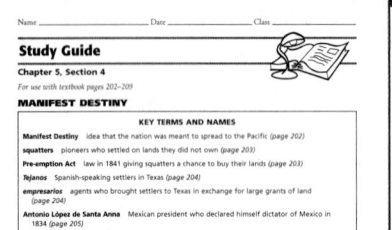

Study Guide

Chapter 5, Section 4

For use with textbook pages 202–209

MANIFEST DESTINY

KEY TERMS AND NAMES

Manifest Destiny idea that the nation was meant to spread to the Pacific *(page 202)*

squatters pioneers who settled on lands they did not own *(page 203)*

Pre-emption Act law in 1841 giving squatters a chance to buy their lands *(page 203)*

Tejanos Spanish-speaking settlers in Texas *(page 204)*

empresarios agents who brought settlers to Texas in exchange for large grants of land *(page 204)*

Antonio López de Santa Anna Mexican president who declared himself dictator of Mexico in 1834 *(page 205)*

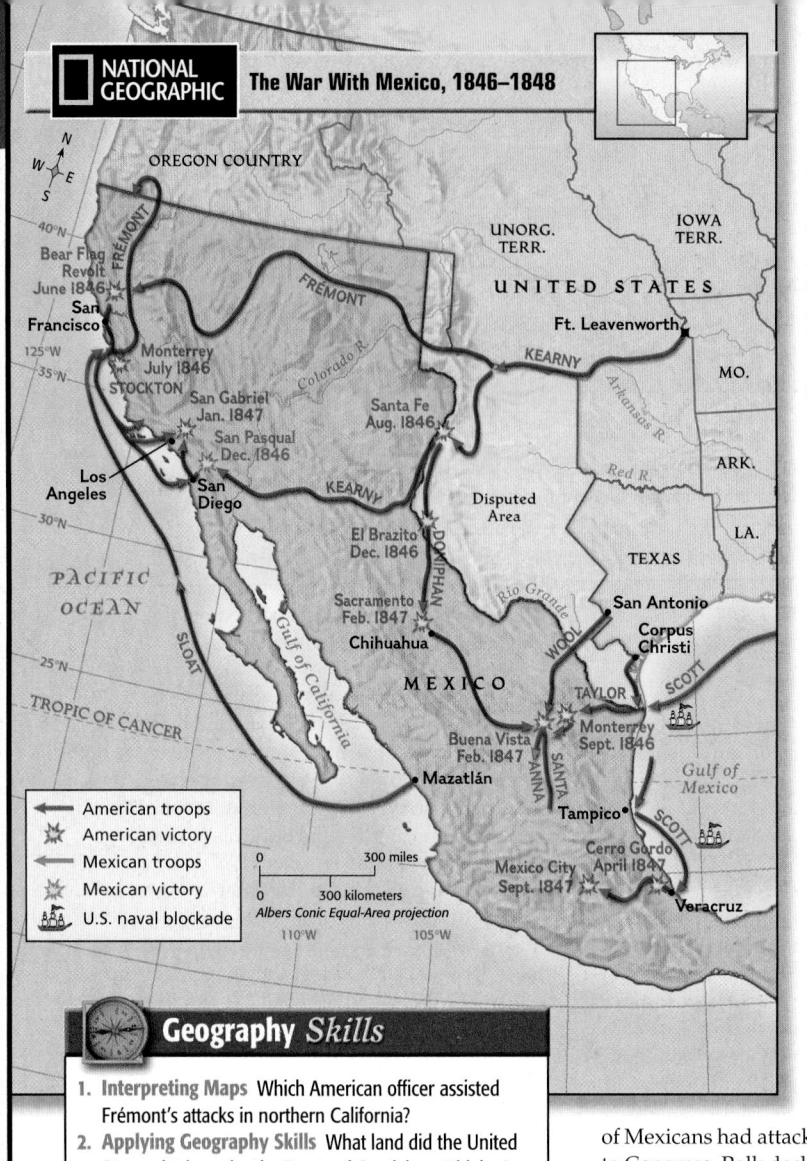

NATIONAL GEOGRAPHIC The War With Mexico, 1846–1848

- ← American troops
- ✶ American victory
- ← Mexican troops
- ✶ Mexican victory
- ⚓ U.S. naval blockade

0 300 miles
0 300 kilometers
Albers Conic Equal-Area projection

Geography *Skills*

1. **Interpreting Maps** Which American officer assisted Frémont's attacks in northern California?

2. **Applying Geography Skills** What land did the United States obtain under the Treaty of Guadalupe Hidalgo?

Annexing Texas The acquisition of Texas had been assured even before Polk took office. In February 1845, at the urging of outgoing president Tyler, Congress passed a joint resolution to annex Texas. The resolution succeeded because it needed only a simple majority of both houses rather than the two-thirds majority in the Senate necessary to ratify a standard treaty. In December 1845, Texas became a state.

✓ Reading Check **Explaining** How did the United States gain Oregon and Texas?

War With Mexico

Texas's entry into the Union outraged the Mexican government, which promptly broke diplomatic relations with the United States. Matters worsened when the two countries disputed Texas's southwestern border. Mexico insisted it was the Nueces River. The United States argued, as Texans had all along, that it was the Rio Grande—a claim that covered far more territory.

Polk's designs on California added to the conflict. In November 1845, he sent **John Slidell** to Mexico City to try to purchase the area and resolve other differences. Mexico's new president, **José Joaquín Herrera,** refused even to meet with Slidell.

Herrera's snub ended any realistic chance of a diplomatic solution. In January 1846, Polk ordered General **Zachary Taylor** to lead troops across the Nueces River into territory claimed by both the United States and Mexico. Polk wanted Mexican troops to fire the first shot. If he could say Mexico was the aggressor, he could more easily win support for a war. Finally, on May 9, news reached him that a force of Mexicans had attacked Taylor's men. In an address to Congress, Polk declared that the United States was at war "by the act of Mexico herself."

Many Whigs opposed the war as yet another plot to extend slavery. Nonetheless, most Washington politicians recognized that however questionable Polk's actions, the United States now had no choice but to fight. On May 13, 1846, the Senate voted 40 to 2 and the House 174 to 14 in favor of the war.

The Battle Plan Polk and his advisers developed a three-pronged strategy. Taylor's troops would cross the Rio Grande near the Gulf of Mexico. A separate force would capture Santa Fe, an important trading center in what is now New Mexico, and then march west to take control of California with the help of the

---

CRITICAL THINKING ACTIVITY

Predicting Consequences Present the following situation to students: What if James K. Polk had not won the presidential election of 1844? Would the war with Mexico have taken place? Why or why not? How would this have affected the United States's acquisition of western lands? Encourage students to write their answers to these questions in paragraph form. Call on volunteers to read and discuss their paragraphs. **L2**

American navy. Finally, U.S. troops would advance to Mexico City and force Mexico to surrender.

To implement the ambitious plan, Congress authorized the president to call for 50,000 volunteers. Men from every part of the country rushed to enlist.

The Fighting Begins In early May, several days before Polk signed the declaration of war, Taylor's troops twice defeated Mexican forces at Palo Alto and at Resaca de la Palma. Taylor then moved south, overcoming more enemy forces at Matamoros. By late September he had marched inland and captured Monterrey.

In the meantime, Colonel Stephen W. Kearny led troops from Fort Leavenworth, near Missouri's western boundary, toward Santa Fe. The long march through the dry countryside was brutal, but when Kearny's men reached the city in August, the Mexican force there had already fled. With Santa Fe secured, a small U.S. force headed on to California.

Before Kearny's troops arrived—and even before war with Mexico was officially declared—settlers in northern California, led by American general **John C. Frémont,** had begun an uprising. The official Mexican presence in the territory had never been strong, and the settlers had little trouble overcoming it. On June 14, 1846, they declared California independent and renamed the region the **Bear Flag Republic.** Within a month, American navy forces arrived to occupy the ports of San Francisco and San Diego and claim the republic for the United States.

Although Mexico had lost vast amounts of territory, its leaders refused to surrender. Polk decided to press on with the third phase of his battle plan and put General **Winfield Scott** in charge of seizing Mexico City. Scott's forces and his soldiers traveled by ship to the Gulf Coast town of Veracruz, landing in March 1847. From there they headed west toward the capital, battling the enemy along the way. In September, they finally captured Mexico City.

The Peace Treaty Defeated, Mexico's leaders signed the **Treaty of Guadalupe Hidalgo** on February 2, 1848. Mexico gave the United States more than 500,000 square miles (1,295,000 sq. km) of territory—what are now the states of California, Nevada, and Utah, as well as most of Arizona and New Mexico and parts of Colorado and Wyoming. Mexico also accepted the Rio Grande as the southern border of Texas. In return, the United States paid Mexico $15 million and took over $3.25 million in debts the Mexican government owed to American citizens.

With Oregon and the former Mexican territories now under the U.S. flag, the dream of Manifest Destiny was realized, but this expansion had cost more than 12,000 American lives. Furthermore, the question of whether the new lands should allow slavery would soon lead the country into another bloody conflict.

✓ **Reading Check** **Summarizing** What was President Polk's three-pronged strategy in the War with Mexico?

HISTORY Online **Study Central™** To review this section, go to tarvol2.glencoe.com and click on **Study Central™**.

SECTION 4 ASSESSMENT

Checking for Understanding

1. **Define:** Manifest Destiny, squatter, *Tejano, empresario,* annexation.

2. **Identify:** Pre-emption Act, Antonio López de Santa Anna, Sam Houston, Bear Flag Republic, Treaty of Guadalupe Hidalgo.

Reviewing Themes

3. **Continuity and Change** Many Americans who settled in Texas were Southerners. How did the issue of slavery later affect efforts to annex Texas?

Critical Thinking

4. **Evaluating** Was the United States justified in fighting the war with Mexico? Explain.

5. **Categorizing** Use a graphic organizer similar to the one below to list key events in Texas's history and explain why they occurred.

Event	Period or Date	Cause(s)

Analyzing Visuals

6. **Analyzing Posters** Examine the poster on page 204 advertising land to Texas settlers. How were permanent settlers and soldiers for hire rewarded differently?

7. **Examining Art** Study the painting of the Battle of San Jacinto on page 207. Why do you think the artist depicted a clearing blue sky in the top right corner of the painting?

Writing About History

8. **Descriptive Writing** Imagine that you are part of a wagon train headed west. Write a letter to a friend in the East describing your daily life.

CHAPTER 5   The Young Republic   **209**

SECTION 4 ASSESSMENT ANSWERS

1. Terms are in blue.
2. Pre-emption Act (p. 203), Antonio López de Santa Anna (p. 205), Sam Houston (p. 206), Bear Flag Republic (p. 209), Treaty of Guadalupe Hidalgo (p. 209)
3. Opposition to admitting Texas as a slave state held up Texas annexation for a decade.

4. Answers should demonstrate analytical thinking.
5. Answers should reflect text. In brief, 1823–1825: Mexico encourages settlement; 1830: Mexico halts immigration; 1835: Texas begins war for independence; 1836: Texas declares independence.

6. Permanent settlers were given more land.
7. Possible answer: to show a new day is dawning in Texas history.
8. Letters should describe the difficulty of the journey as well as new experiences.

L2

Section Quiz 5–4

Name _____ Date _____ Class _____

★ **Chapter 5**   Score ____

Section Quiz 5-4

DIRECTIONS: Matching Match each item in Column A with the items in Column B. Write the correct letters in the blanks. *(10 points each)*

Column A
___ 1. absorption
___ 2. famed frontiersman who died at the Alamo
___ 3. agents who contracted with the Mexican government to bring in a certain number of residents in exchange for large grants of Texas land
___ 4. settled on land they did not own
___ 5. the idea that the nation was meant to spread all the way to the Pacific

Column B
A. squatters
B. empresarios
C. Jim Bowie
D. Manifest Destiny
E. annexation

DIRECTIONS: Multiple Choice In the blank at the left, write the letter of the choice that

✓ **Reading Check**

Answer: Taylor's troops would cross the Rio Grande near the Gulf of Mexico; another force would capture Santa Fe and then march west to take control of California with the help of the American navy. U.S. troops would advance to Mexico City and force Mexico to surrender.

Reteach

Ask students to chronicle the American settlement of Texas.

Enrich

Have students write a short essay on what life would be like in the southwestern United States if the land had remained a part of Mexico. Have students use the point of view of someone living in the territory.

HISTORY Online

Study Central™ provides summaries, interactive games, and online graphic organizers to help students review section content.

4 CLOSE

Have students explain who the key figures were in Texas's fight for independence.

209

TEACH

Eulogy

Ask students the following questions after they have read the recollections of Chief Joseph.

- **What did Old Joseph tell his son his responsibility was?** *(to guide his people and to never sell or give away his land)*

- **Why do you think Old Joseph told his son to stop his ears when asked to sign a treaty?** *(Answers may vary. He suggests that the terms of the treaty might sound good and reasonable, but that his son should not even listen to the white man nor sell his father's grave.)*

Baseball

Have students compare these rules to the modern rules. **Ask: Which rules are still part of the game of baseball?** *(bases 90 feet apart in diamond shape; only nine players per side; at first base, a fielder can simply tag the bag to make an out)* **Which rules no longer apply? What rules have replaced them?** *(pitches will be thrown underhand replaced with pitches thrown overhand; ball caught on first bounce is an out replaced with catching the ball before it hits the ground; nine balls is a walk replaced with four balls is a walk)* **Why do you think rules of games change over time?** *(possible answers: to speed play, to reduce injuries, to make the game more challenging)*

Visit the TIME Web site at www.time.com for up-to-date news, weekly magazine articles, editorials, online polls, and an archive of past magazine and Web articles.

Eulogy

CHIEF JOSEPH *(above), a leader of the Nez Perce of the Wallowa Valley in eastern Oregon, remembers his father, Old Joseph. The Nez Perce were forced to leave the Wallowa Valley less than a decade after Old Joseph's death.*

MY FATHER SENT FOR ME. I SAW HE WAS DYING. I TOOK HIS HAND IN MINE. He said, "My son, my body is returning to my mother earth, and my spirit is going very soon to see the Great Spirit Chief. When I am gone, think of your country. You are the chief of these people. They look to you to guide them. Always remember that your father never sold his country. You must stop your ears whenever you are asked to sign a treaty selling your home. A few years more, and white men will be all around you. They have their eyes on this land. My son, never forget my dying words. This country holds your father's body. Never sell the bones of your father and your mother."

I pressed my father's hand and told him I would protect his grave with my life. My father smiled and passed to the spirit land.

I buried him in that beautiful valley of winding rivers. I love that land more than all the rest of the world. A man who would not love his father's grave is worse than a wild animal.

Baseball for Beginners

Thinking of taking up the new game of baseball? Watch out! The rules keep changing!

1845
- Canvas bases will be set 90 feet apart in a diamond shape.
- Only nine men will play on each side.
- Pitches are to be thrown underhanded.
- A ball caught on the first bounce is an out.

1846
- At first base, a fielder can tag the bag before the runner reaches it and so make an out.

1847
- Players may no longer throw the ball at a runner to put him out.

These changes may be coming:
- A poor pitch is a ball; nine balls gives the runner first base, a walk.
- A ball caught on the first bounce is no longer an out.

The New York baseball team

COOPERATIVE LEARNING ACTIVITY

Creating a Magazine Spread Organize the class into four groups. Assign each group one of the following decades: 1810–1819, 1820–1829, 1830–1839, or 1840–1849, and ask them to create their own two-page magazine spread for the decade. Encourage students to consider the Time Notebook design but to be creative as they select information that is of particular interest. Students should look at current magazines and books for design ideas. This activity can be completed using desktop publishing software or the more traditional cut-and-paste method.

Use the rubric for a cooperative group management plan on pages 71–72 in the *Performance Assessment Activities and Rubrics.*

WESTERN WORD PLAY

Word Watch

Can you talk Western? Match the word to its meaning.

1. maverick
2. Hangtown fry
3. grubstake
4. bonanza
5. palo alto
6. pard or rawwheel

a. gold rush favorite, made of eggs, bacon, and oysters

b. inexperienced '49er, Eastern type not used to wearing boots

c. a lucky discovery of gold; a source of sudden wealth

d. a style of hat worn by gold rush miners

e. a lone dissenter who takes an independent stand, from the name of a Texas cattleman who left his herd unbranded

f. food provided by an investor to a gold prospector in exchange for a share of whatever gold he finds

answers: 1.e; 2.a; 3.f; 4.c; 5.d; 6.b

Milestones

SETTLED, 1847. THE VALLEY OF THE GREAT SALT LAKE, by Brigham Young, leader of the Mormons, and a party of 143, to escape hostility toward their group in Illinois. Young plans to return to Council Bluffs, Iowa, and lead the rest of the members of his faith to a permanent home in Utah.

MOVED, 1845. HENRY DAVID THOREAU, writer, to Walden Pond, Concord, Massachusetts. Thoreau intends to build his own house on the shore of the pond and earn his living by the labor of his hands only. "Many of the so-called comforts of life," writes Thoreau, "are not only not indispensable, but positive hindrances to the elevation of mankind."

AILING, 1847. EDGAR ALLAN POE, in Baltimore, following the death of his wife, Virginia. Other than a poem on death, Poe has written little this year, devoting his dwindling energies to plagiarism suits against other authors.

Frederick Douglass

LIBRARY OF CONGRESS/CORBIS

EMIGRATED, 1845. FREDERICK DOUGLASS, former slave, author, and abolitionist leader, to England to escape the danger of re-enslavement in reaction to his autobiography, *Narrative of the Life of Frederick Douglass.* On his 1845 trip across the Atlantic, Douglass was not permitted cabin accommodations. After a lecture during the crossing, some passengers threatened to throw him overboard.

DISCOVERED, 1846. THE PLANET NEPTUNE, by German astronomer Johann Galle.

NUMBERS

18,000 Miles from New York to California by sea route around Cape Horn

90,000 People arriving in California in 1849, half by sea, half by overland route

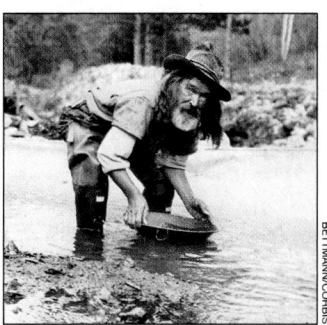

BETTMANN/CORBIS

Panning for gold

$20 Average earned per day by California gold miners in 1849

$18 Average expenses per day for California gold miners in 1849

$390 Value of miners' average daily earnings in 2001 dollars

50 Number of years after the signing of the Declaration of Independence that Thomas Jefferson and John Adams die—within hours of each other.

17,069,453 U.S. population in 1840

55,000 Number of emigrants moving west along the Oregon Trail in 1850

Portfolio Writing Project

Have students research one of the following people: Chief Joseph, Brigham Young, Henry David Thoreau, Edgar Allan Poe, Frederick Douglass, or Johann Galle. Ask students to write a one-page essay about the person's contribution to history.

Creating a Thematic Map Have students research the population of the states that were part of the United States at the end of 1850. Also have them find the population of these states using the 2000 census figures. Tell students to use an outline map of the United States to shade the states that were part of the Union in 1850 and label them with the name of the state, its population in 1850, and its population in 2000.

CLOSE

Have students work in small groups to create lists of words that we associate with certain regions of the country.

EXTENDING THE CONTENT

The Pathfinder John C. Frémont was a member of the United States Corps of Topographical Engineers, an agency that surveyed and mapped the country's unorganized territories. In 1842 on his first major expedition to the West, Frémont surveyed a section of the Oregon Trail along the Platte River to the South Pass through the Rocky Mountains. During 1843 and 1844, Frémont went north along the Rocky Mountains to the South Pass, west to the Columbia River, and then south along the Cascade and Sierra Nevada mountains in California. Frémont's return journey took him across the Great Basin to the Great Salt Lake and then over the Rocky Mountains. These explorations in the West earned Frémont the nickname "The Pathfinder."

GLENCOE TECHNOLOGY

MindJogger Videoquiz
Use the **MindJogger Videoquiz** to review Chapter 5 content.

 Available in DVD

Reviewing Key Terms
Students' answers will vary. The pages where the words appear in the text are shown in parentheses.

1. interchangeable parts (p. 180); **2. nativism** (p. 181); **3. labor union** (p. 181); **4. strike** (p. 181); **5. cotton gin** (p. 182); **6. yeoman farmer** (p. 183); **7. "favorite son"** (p. 188); **8. "corrupt bargain"** (p. 189); **9. mudslinging** (p. 189); **10. spoils system** (p. 190); **11. caucus** (p. 190); **12. secede** (p. 190); **13. benevolent society** (p. 195); **14. transcendentalism** (p. 195); **15. utopia** (p. 196); **16. temperance** (p. 196); **17. abolition** (p. 199); **18. emancipation** (p. 199); **19. Manifest Destiny** (p. 202); **20. squatter** (p. 203); **21. Tejano** (p. 204); **22. empresario** (p. 204); **23. annexation** (p. 207)

Reviewing Key Facts
24. Industrial Revolution (p. 179), Indian Removal Act, (p. 191), Second Great Awakening (p. 195), Bear Flag Republic (p. 209)

25. The invention of the cotton gin allowed the production of cotton to soar.

26. the expansion of slavery into new states

27. spoils system gave more people the opportunity to participate in government, caucus system replaced by national nominating convention, which gave more people the opportunity to participate in political party activities

28. Most Americans supported it. Missionary-minded religious groups and a few members of Congress opposed it because it stained the nation's honor.

Reviewing Key Terms
On a sheet of paper, use each of these terms in a sentence.

1. interchangeable parts
2. nativism
3. labor union
4. strike
5. cotton gin
6. yeoman farmer
7. "favorite son"
8. "corrupt bargain"
9. mudslinging
10. spoils system
11. caucus
12. secede
13. benevolent society
14. transcendentalism
15. utopia
16. temperance
17. abolition
18. emancipation
19. Manifest Destiny
20. squatter
21. *Tejano*
22. *empresario*
23. annexation

Chapter Summary

Nationalism in Society
- Steamboats and railroads link the nation's regions
- Factory system increases production of goods
- Telegraph establishes fast, long-distance communication

Sectionalism Emerges
- South's agricultural economy relies on labor of enslaved persons
- Northern leaders view slavery as morally wrong
- Missouri Compromise pits Northern leaders against Southern leaders
- Congress votes almost strictly along sectional lines

The Second Great Awakening Inspires Reform
- Commitment to religion swells church congregations
- New religions established
- Availability of education expands
- Abolitionist movement grows steadily

Manifest Destiny
- Large numbers of Americans move to Oregon in 1840
- Great Britain and United States divide territory without conflict
- Growing numbers of American settlers in Texas, California, and southwestern United States leads to war with Mexico
- By end of war in 1848, United States stretches from Atlantic to Pacific Ocean

Reviewing Key Facts
24. Identify: Industrial Revolution, Indian Removal Act, Second Great Awakening, Bear Flag Republic.

25. What helped cotton become king in the South?

26. What issue did the Missouri Compromise temporarily settle?

27. In what two ways did President Andrew Jackson expand democracy?

28. Who supported the Indian Removal Act, and who opposed it? What were their reasons for opposing it?

29. What were the main beliefs of transcendentalists?

30. How did Horace Mann improve public education in Massachusetts?

31. What were the results of the Seneca Falls Convention?

32. What was the goal of the American Colonization Society, an early antislavery group?

33. How did African Americans like Frederick Douglass and Sojourner Truth combat slavery?

34. Why did settlers in Texas declare war against Mexico?

35. What did the United States gain from the Treaty of Guadalupe Hidalgo?

Critical Thinking
36. Analyzing Themes: Groups and Institutions How did music and religion help African Americans cope with slavery?

37. Forming an Opinion Eli Whitney invented the cotton gin in 1793. Do you think the cotton gin had a positive or a negative effect on the nation? Explain your answer.

38. Interpreting Primary Sources In April of 1847, Charles Sumner of Massachusetts presented his views on the causes of the Mexican War in his "Report on the War with Mexico" to the Commonwealth of Massachusetts. Read the excerpt and answer the questions that follow.

❝It can no longer be doubted that this is a war of conquest. . . . In a letter to Commodore Sloat, . . . the Secretary [of War] says, 'You will take such measures as will render that vast region [California] a desirable place of residence for emigrants from our soil.' In a letter to

29. Transcendentalism urged people to transcend, or overcome, the limits of their minds and emphasized feeling over reason.

30. He helped create the Massachusetts Board of Education, doubled teachers' salaries, opened new school districts, and established teacher training schools.

31. beginning of an organized women's movement and Declaration of Sentiments and Resolutions

32. advocated the relocation of African Americans to a colony in Africa

33. by writing and speaking against it and telling of their experiences with it

34. Texans felt that negotiations to peacefully organize its own state government were hopeless. Thus, independence was the only option.

HISTORY Online

Self-Check Quiz

Visit the *American Republic Since 1877* Web site at tarvol2.glencoe.com and click on *Self-Check Quizzes—Chapter 5* to assess your knowledge of chapter content.

Colonel Kearny, . . . he says: 'Should you conquer and take possession of New Mexico and Upper California, you will establish civil governments therein. You may assure the people of these provinces that it is the wish and design of the United States to provide for them a free government with the least possible delay. . . . ""

—quoted in *Readings in American History*

a. According to Charles Sumner, why did the United States become involved in the war with Mexico?

b. What evidence does Sumner provide to show that this was the U.S. government's intention?

39. Organizing Use a graphic organizer similar to the one below to list the effects of the Industrial Revolution.

Effects of the Industrial Revolution

Practicing Skills

40. Multimedia Plan Develop a plan for a multimedia presentation on the social and cultural changes in the United States discussed in Section 3. Consider the following points to help guide you.

a. What specific examples would you use to show the different social and cultural changes taking place in the country?

b. What form of media would you use for each example?

Chapter Activity

41. Research Project Conduct research to learn more about one of the reformers discussed in the chapter. Then role-play the person by introducing yourself to the class and describing your background and your reform goals.

Writing Activity

42. Informative Writing On the American History Primary Source Document Library CD-ROM, read "Women's Rights" by Sojourner Truth. Imagine you are a newspaper reporter, and write an article reviewing Truth's speech. Explain her arguments for women's rights and describe how members of the convention reacted to her words.

NATIONAL GEOGRAPHIC — The United States in 1824

Geography and History

43. The map above shows the United States in 1824. Study the map and answer the questions below.

a. Interpreting Maps What international boundary was in dispute in 1824?

b. Applying Geography Skills What geographic features determined the eastern boundary of the Louisiana Purchase?

Standardized Test Practice

Directions: Choose the best answer to the following question.

On which of the following reform movements did William Lloyd Garrison have a major impact?

A The temperance movement

B The abolitionist movement

C The education reform movement

D The prison reform movement

Test-Taking Tip: Try to remember the names of the publication and the two organizations that Garrison established. Recalling these names will help you select the correct answer.

CHAPTER 5 The Young Republic **213**

HISTORY Online

Have students visit the Web site at tarvol2.glencoe.com to review Chapter 5 and take the Self-Check Quiz.

temperance movement or abolitionist movement; **b.** possible answers—photographs, speeches, other written documents, historical artifacts

Chapter Activity

41. You may have students present the role plays without stating the person's name and have the class determine the person's identity.

Writing Activity

42. Students' articles will vary. Students should review news articles for the correct style.

Geography and History

43. a. the northern boundary of Maine; **b.** the Mississippi River

---

Standardized Test Practice

Answer: B

Test-Taking Tip: Remind students that Garrison cofounded the *Liberator,* and ask them which answer choice fits in with the theme implied in the publication's name.

Bonus Question ?

Ask: More than 44,000 Irish came to the United States in 1845. Why did so many leave Ireland during that time? *(A devastating blight wiped out the potato crop. Faced with starvation, thousands chose to immigrate to the United States.)*

213

---

35. over 500,000 square miles of territory and resolution of the location of the southern border of Texas

Critical Thinking

36. music—to pass time and to communicate with one another; religion—prayed for freedom and hoped for a better life in the next world

37. Students' answers will vary. Positive—it increased production and enriched the region; negative—increased reliance on slave labor

38. a. to gain land; **b.** letters to Sloat and Kearney from the Secretary of War

39. shift from hand tools to large, complex machines; skilled artisans replaced with workers organized by specific tasks; factories replaced home-based workshops

Practicing Skills

40. a. possible answers—changes in education, women's rights, treatment of prisoners and mentally ill,

SUGGESTED PACING CHART

Unit 2 (1 Day)	Chapter 6 (4 Days)	Chapter 7 (6 Days)	Unit 2 (2 Days)
Day 1 Introduction	**Day 1** Chapter 6 Intro, Section 1 **Day 2** Section 2 **Day 3** Section 3 **Day 4** Chapter 6 Assessment	**Day 1** Chapter 7 Intro, Section 1 **Day 2** Section 2 **Day 3** Section 3 **Day 4** Section 4 **Day 5** Section 5 **Day 6** Chapter 7 Assessment	**Day 1** Wrap-Up/Project **Day 2** Unit 2 Assessment

GLENCOE'S ASSESSMENT ADVANTAGE

Use the following tools to easily assess student learning in a variety of ways:

- Performance Assessment Activities and Rubrics
- Chapter and Unit Tests
- Section Quizzes
- Standardized Test Practice Workbook

- tarvol2.glencoe.com
- Interactive Tutor Self-Assessment CD-ROM
- MindJogger Videoquiz
- ExamView® Pro Testmaker CD-ROM
- SAT I/II Test Practice

TEACHING TRANSPARENCIES

Unit 2 Map Overlay Transparencies
L2

Cause-and-Effect Transparency 2
L2

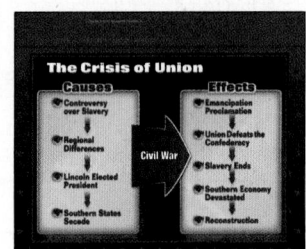

READING SUPPORT FROM JAMESTOWN EDUCATION

- **Timed Readings Plus in Social Studies** help students increase their reading rate and fluency while maintaining comprehension. The 400-word passages are similar to those found on state and national assessments.

- **Reading in the Content Area: Social Studies** concentrates on six essential reading skills that help students better comprehend what they read. The book includes 75 high-interest nonfiction passages written at increasing levels of difficulty.

- **Reading Fluency** helps students read smoothly, accurately, and expressively.

- **Jamestown's Reading Improvement,** by renowned reading expert Edward Fry, focuses on helping build your students' comprehension, vocabulary, and skimming and scanning skills.

- **Critical Reading Series** provides high-interest books, each written at three reading levels.

For more information about these products, see the Jamestown Education materials in the Classroom Solutions in the front of this Teacher Wraparound Edition. To order these products, call Glencoe at 1-800-334-7344.

ASSESSMENT

Unit 2 Pretests L2

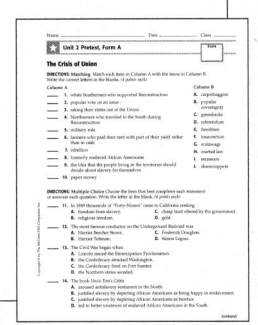

Unit 2 Posttests L2

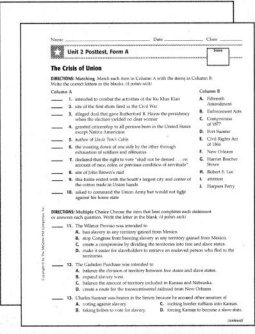

APPLICATION AND ENRICHMENT

American Biography 2 L2

History Simulation and Problem Solving 2 L1

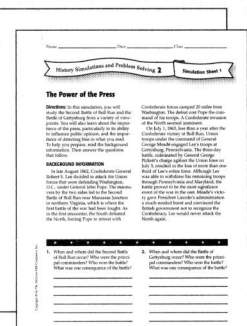

GEOGRAPHY

Geography and History Activity 2 L2

INTERDISCIPLINARY ACTIVITIES

American Literature Reading 2 L2

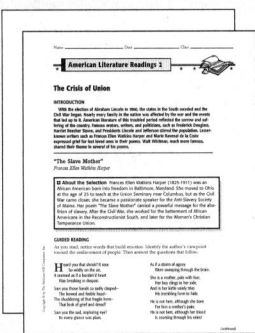

Economics and History Activity 2 L2

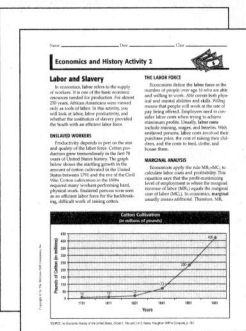

Team-Teaching Interdisciplinary Strategies and Activities 2 L2

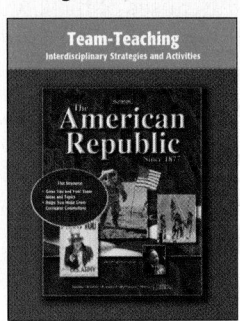

Reading List Generator CD-ROM

GLENCOE BOOKLINK

The Glencoe BookLink CD-ROM is a database that allows you to search more than 15,000 titles to create a customized reading list for your students.

- Reading lists can be organized by students' reading level, author, genre, theme, or area of interest.

- The database provides Degrees of Reading Power™ (DRP) and Lexile™ readability scores for all selections.

- A brief summary of each selection is included.

Leveled reading suggestions for this unit:

For students at a Grade 8 reading level:
- *Harriet Tubman: Antislavery Activist,* by M.W. Taylor.

For students at a Grade 9 reading level:
- *Portraits of War,* by George Sullivan.

For students at a Grade 10 reading level:
- *Been in the Storm So Long: The Aftermath of Slavery,* by Leon F. Litwack.

Extending the Content

Readings for the Teacher
- *America Goes to War.* Fine Communications, 1997.

Multimedia Resources
- *Living American History Series. U.S. History II: 1840–1876.* Private Learning Systems. VHS. (2 Apple diskettes, guide)

⏱ **0:00 Out of Time?**

If time does not permit teaching each chapter in this unit, you may want to use the **Reading Essentials and Study Guide** summaries.

Unit Overview

Unit 2 explores the crisis faced by the United States between 1848 and 1877. **Chapter 6** covers the years leading up to the Civil War, from 1848 to 1860. **Chapter 7** focuses on the Civil War and Reconstruction, from 1861 to 1877.

Unit Objectives

After studying this unit, students will be able to:
1. Identify the causes of the Civil War.
2. Detail the major battles and strategies used by the North and South during the Civil War.
3. Describe the process of Reconstruction after the Civil War.

Why It Matters Activity

Discuss the issues of racism and civil rights in American society today. Make generalizations about how the problems of America's past contribute to the issues faced by citizens today.

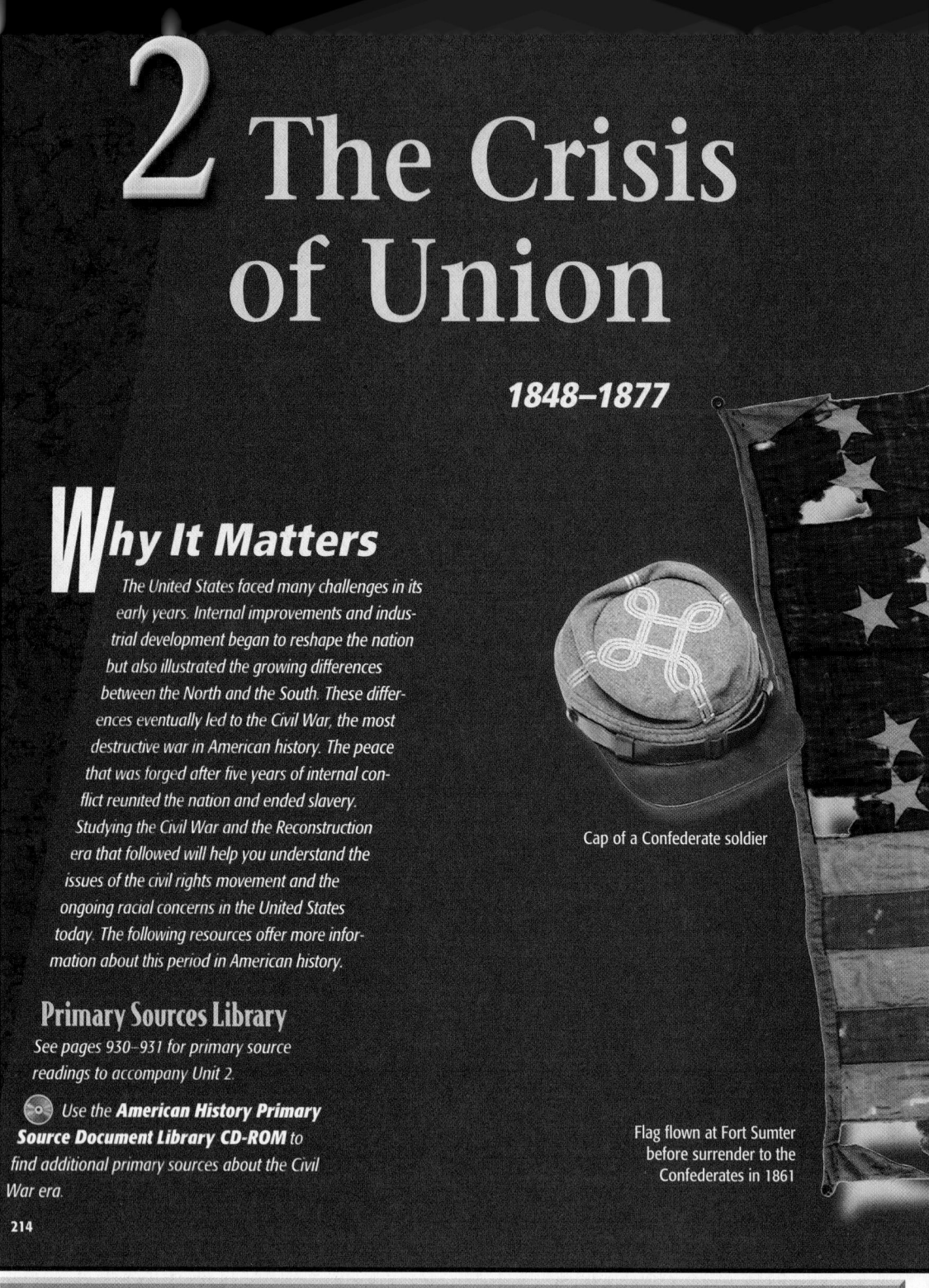

2 The Crisis of Union

1848–1877

Why It Matters

The United States faced many challenges in its early years. Internal improvements and industrial development began to reshape the nation but also illustrated the growing differences between the North and the South. These differences eventually led to the Civil War, the most destructive war in American history. The peace that was forged after five years of internal conflict reunited the nation and ended slavery. Studying the Civil War and the Reconstruction era that followed will help you understand the issues of the civil rights movement and the ongoing racial concerns in the United States today. The following resources offer more information about this period in American history.

Cap of a Confederate soldier

Primary Sources Library

See pages 930–931 for primary source readings to accompany Unit 2.

💿 Use the **American History Primary Source Document Library CD-ROM** to find additional primary sources about the Civil War era.

Flag flown at Fort Sumter before surrender to the Confederates in 1861

214

TEAM TEACHING ACTIVITY

Language Arts Have the language arts teacher discuss the personal accounts of the Civil War contained in letters between soldiers and their families. As a class discuss the role that bias plays in first-hand accounts of events. Have the teacher point out examples of bias and personal opinions in a letter. Then have students work in groups to review other letters from the Civil War and identify bias. 📦

"We shall nobly save, or meanly lose, the last best hope of earth."

—Abraham Lincoln, 1862

More About the Photo

Point out to students that over 600,000 Americans died during the Civil War, the most of any conflict involving the United States. Although the country remained united as a political entity, deep feelings of mistrust remained for a long time following the war. Ask students how unified they think the country is today and what the American flag symbolizes to them. *(Students' answers will vary. Encourage them to think about the flag as a symbol of unity.)*

Glencoe Literature Library

The following novel from the *High School American History Literature Library* may be used to enrich the study of this unit:

• *Red Badge of Courage* by Stephen Crane

SERVICE-LEARNING PROJECT

Organize students into small groups. Have each group select a civil rights issue that exists in your community today. Have students evaluate community response to the issue and then write an editorial supporting community efforts or suggesting constructive ways to resolve a civil rights problem. After reviewing the editorial, encourage groups to send their editorials to the local newspaper.

Refer to **Building Bridges: Connecting Classroom and Community through Service-Learning in Social Studies** from the National Council for the Social Studies for information about service-learning.

Chapter 6 Resources

Timesaving Tools

TeacherWorks™ All-In-One Planner and Resource Center

- **Interactive Teacher Edition** Access your Teacher Wraparound Edition and your classroom resources with a few easy clicks.
- **Interactive Lesson Planner** Planning has never been easier! Organize your week, month, semester, or year with all the lesson helps you need to make teaching creative, timely, and relevant.

Use Glencoe's **Presentation Plus!** multimedia teacher tool to easily present dynamic lessons that visually excite your students. Using Microsoft PowerPoint® you can customize the presentations to create your own personalized lessons.

TEACHING TRANSPARENCIES

Graphic Organizer 6 L2

Why It Matters Chapter Transparency 6 L2

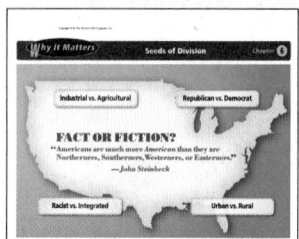

APPLICATION AND ENRICHMENT

Linking Past and Present Activity 6 L2

Enrichment Activity 6 L3

Primary Source Reading 6 L2

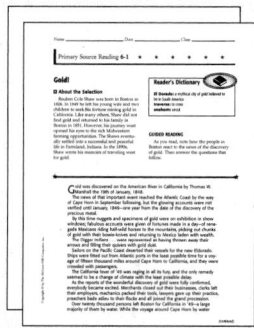

REVIEW AND REINFORCEMENT

Reteaching Activity 6 L1

Vocabulary Activity 6 L1

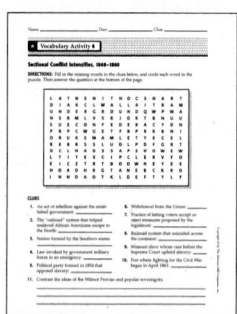

Time Line Activity 6 L2

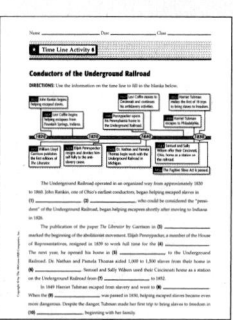

Critical Thinking Skills Activity 6 L2

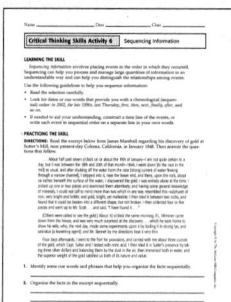

Meeting NCSS Standards

The following standards are covered in Chapter 6:

Section 1	III	People, Places, and Environments: G, H, I
Section 2	V	Individuals, Groups, and Institutions: B, C, F
Section 3	X	Civic Ideals and Practices: B, C, E, J

Local Standards

_____

_____

_____

_____

_____

_____

Chapter 6 Resources

ASSESSMENT AND EVALUATION

**Chapter 6 Test
Form A** L2

**Chapter 6 Test
Form B** L2

**Standardized Test Practice
Workbook Activity 6** L2

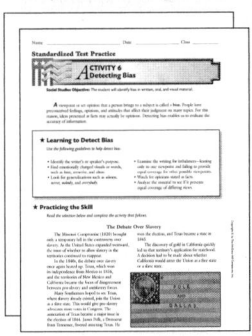

**Performance Assessment
Activities and Rubrics 6**
L1/ELL

**ExamView® Pro
Testmaker CD-ROM**

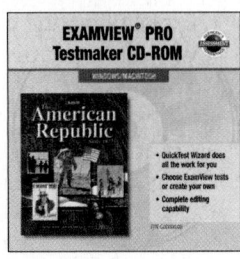

MULTIMEDIA

- Vocabulary PuzzleMaker CD-ROM
- Interactive Tutor Self-Assessment CD-ROM
- ExamView® Pro Testmaker CD-ROM
- Audio Program
- American History Primary Source Documents Library CD-ROM
- MindJogger Videoquiz
- Presentation Plus! CD-ROM
- TeacherWorks™ CD-ROM
- Interactive Student Edition CD-ROM
- Glencoe Skillbuilder Interactive Workbook CD-ROM, Level 2
- The *American Republic Since 1877* Video Program
- American Music: Hits Through History
- American Music: Cultural Traditions

SPANISH RESOURCES

The following Spanish language materials are available:

- Spanish Reading Essentials and Study Guide
- Spanish Guided Reading Activities
- Spanish Reteaching Activities
- Spanish Quizzes and Tests
- Spanish Vocabulary Activities
- Spanish Summaries
- The Declaration of Independence and United States Constitution Spanish Translation

The following videotape programs are available from Glencoe as supplements to Chapter 6:

- **Frederick Douglass** (ISBN 0-76-700120-6)
- **Underground Railroad** (ISBN 0-76-701679-3)

To order, call Glencoe at 1-800-334-7344. To find classroom resources to accompany many of these videos, check the following home pages:
A&E Television: www.aande.com
The History Channel: www.historychannel.com

Use our Web site for additional resources. All essential content is covered in the Student Edition.

You and your students can visit tarvol2.glencoe.com, the Web site companion to the *American Republic Since 1877*. This innovative integration of electronic and print media offers your students a wealth of opportunities. The student text directs students to the Web site for the following options:

- **Chapter Overviews**
- **Student Web Activities**
- **Self-Check Quizzes**
- **Textbook Updates**

Answers to the student Web activities are provided for you in the **Web Activity Lesson Plans.** Additional Web resources and Interactive Tutor Puzzles are also available.

Chapter 6 Resources

Daily Objectives	Reproducible Resources	Multimedia Resources
SECTION 1 **Slavery and Western Expansion** 1. Explain how the government dealt with slavery in the territories acquired after the war with Mexico. 2. Evaluate how both the Fugitive Slave Act and the transcontinental railroad heightened sectional tension.	Reproducible Lesson Plan 6–1 Daily Lecture and Discussion Notes 6–1 Guided Reading Activity 6–1* Section Quiz 6–1* Reading Essentials and Study Guide 6–1* Performance Assessment Activities and Rubrics	Daily Focus Skills Transparency 6–1 Interactive Tutor Self-Assessment CD-ROM ExamView® Pro Testmaker CD-ROM* Presentation Plus! CD-ROM TeacherWorks™ CD-ROM Skillbuilder Interactive Workbook, Level 2 Audio Program ABCNews Interactive™ Historic America Electronic Field Trips
SECTION 2 **The Crisis Deepens** 1. Describe the origins of the Republican Party and the fate of the Whigs and the Know-Nothings. 2. Explain the significance of the Dred Scott decision, the Lincoln-Douglas debates of 1858, and John Brown's raid on Harpers Ferry.	Reproducible Lesson Plan 6–2 Daily Lecture and Discussion Notes 6–2 Guided Reading Activity 6–2* Section Quiz 6–2* Reading Essentials and Study Guide 6–2* Performance Assessment Activities and Rubrics Interpreting Political Cartoons Supreme Court Case Studies	Daily Focus Skills Transparency 6–2 American Art & Architecture Interactive Tutor Self-Assessment CD-ROM ExamView® Pro Testmaker CD-ROM* Presentation Plus! CD-ROM TeacherWorks™ CD-ROM Audio Program American Music: Hits Through History American Music: Cultural Traditions
SECTION 3 **The Union Dissolves** 1. Discuss the presidential election of 1860. 2. Explain how and why the Civil War began.	Reproducible Lesson Plan 6–3 Daily Lecture and Discussion Notes 6–3 Guided Reading Activity 6–3* Section Quiz 6–3* Reading Essentials and Study Guide 6–3* Performance Assessment Activities and Rubrics American History in Graphic Novel	Daily Focus Skills Transparency 6–3 Interactive Tutor Self-Assessment CD-ROM ExamView® Pro Testmaker CD-ROM* Presentation Plus! CD-ROM TeacherWorks™ CD-ROM Vocabulary PuzzleMaker CD-ROM Audio Program

0:00 OUT OF TIME?
Assign the Chapter 6 **Reading Essentials and Study Guide.**

*Also Available in Spanish

 Printed Materials   Transparency   CD-ROM   DVD

Poster   Music Program   Audio Program   Videocassette

NATIONAL GEOGRAPHIC Teacher's Corner

INDEX TO NATIONAL GEOGRAPHIC MAGAZINE

The following articles relate to this chapter.

- "America's Poet: Walt Whitman," December 1994
- "C.S.S. *Alabama*," December 1994
- "Philadelphia's African Americans," August 1990
- "The Underground Railroad," July 1984

NATIONAL GEOGRAPHIC SOCIETY PRODUCTS

To order the following, call National Geographic at 1-800-368-2728:

- *Historical Atlas of the United States* (Atlas)
- *Immigration: The Triumph of Hope* (Video)
- *Steal Away: The Harriet Tubman Story* (Video)

NGS ONLINE

Access National Geographic's Web site for current events, atlas updates, activities, links, interactive features, and archives.

www.nationalgeographic.com

MEETING SPECIAL NEEDS

In addition to the Differentiated Instruction strategies found in each section, the following resources are also suitable for your special needs students:

- *ExamView® Pro Testmaker CD-ROM* allows teachers to tailor tests by reducing answer choices.

- The *Audio Program* includes the entire narrative of the student edition so that less-proficient readers can listen to the words as they read them.

- The *Reading Essentials and Study Guide* provides the same content as the student edition but is written two grade levels below the textbook.

KEY TO ABILITY LEVELS

Teaching strategies have been coded.

L1 BASIC activities for all students
L2 AVERAGE activities for average to above-average students
L3 CHALLENGING activities for above-average students
ELL ENGLISH LANGUAGE LEARNER activities

From the Classroom of...

Tim Palone
Elsik Ninth Grade Center
Alief, TX

Growing Sectionalism

For the period from 1848 to 1860, students will analyze speeches, editorials, and political cartoons found on the Internet, in local library archives, and in textbooks. Their analyses should address content and rhetorical style. Students will then present the speech, editorial, or cartoon to the class in a dramatic fashion, followed by their analysis.

In the next step the document will be placed on a time line, with students noting whether the rhetoric intensified over time.

Discuss the following questions with the class:

1. Did issues for Northerners and Southerners change over time, and if so, how?

2. Was conciliatory language ever used, and did the tone and style used change over time?

3. At what point do you feel the sides were too far apart for compromise?

ADDITIONAL RESOURCES FROM GLENCOE

- American Music: Cultural Traditions
- American Art & Architecture
- Outline Map Resource Book
- U.S. Desk Map
- Building Geography Skills for Life
- Inclusion for the High School Social Studies Classroom Strategies and Activities
- Teaching Strategies for the American History Classroom (Including Block Scheduling Pacing Guides)
- Dinah Zike's High School American History Reading and Study Skills Foldables

Block Schedule

Activities that are suited to use within the block scheduling framework are identified by:

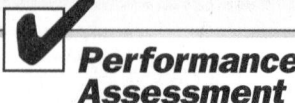

☑ Performance Assessment

Refer to Activity 6 in the Performance Assessment Activities and Rubrics booklet. 📖

Why It Matters Activity

Have students look at the time line on pages 216 and 217 and choose the event that they think is most significant. Students should evaluate their choices after they have completed the chapter.

GLENCOE TECHNOLOGY

The *American Republic Since 1877* Video Program

To learn more about the sectional conflicts that resulted in the Civil War, have students view the Chapter 6 video, "Tales from the Underground Railroad," from the *American Republic Since 1877* Video Program.

MindJogger Videoquiz

Use the **MindJogger Videoquiz** to preview Chapter 6 content.

⊙ Both programs available in DVD

6 Sectional Conflict Intensifies *1848–1860*

Why It Matters

When the nation gained new territory, the slavery controversy intensified. Would new states be slave or free? Who would decide? States that allowed slavery were determined to prevent free states from gaining a majority in the Senate. Political compromise broke down by 1860, and when Lincoln was elected president, many Southern states decided to secede.

The Impact Today

The political and social debates of this period continue to have influence on the United States.
* *Older sectional loyalties still define some regions of the country.*
* *The modern Republican Party grew in part from opposition to slavery.*

⊙ **The American Republic Since 1877 Video** *The Chapter 6 video, "Tales From the Underground Railroad," features a dramatization of enslaved African Americans using the Underground Railroad to reach freedom.*

1849
* California Gold Rush begins

1850
* Compromise of 1850 adopted in an attempt to ease sectional tensions

1854
* Republican Party founded

United States PRESIDENTS

Taylor 1849–1850 | Fillmore 1850–1853 | Pierce 1853–1857

1846   1850   1854

World

1847
* Working hours limited in Britain

1848
* Serfdom abolished in Austrian Empire

1853
* Crimean War pitting Russia against Great Britain and the Ottoman Empire begins

216

▌ Reading Strategy ◀ PURPOSE FOR READING

Problem-Solution Notes Have students use this strategy to examine a specific issue. Begin by saying, "The total population of the United States increased by 8 million during the 1850s. With railroads solving the transportation problems in the Midwest, its population grew rapidly, and people started moving westward. What problems or issues resulted from westward movement?" Then, have students create a two-column table. In left-hand column, they should list the following four questions: "What is the problem or issue? What are the effects of the problem? What are the causes of the problem? What are the solutions to the problem?" Have students record the answers to their questions in the right-hand column. **L1**

View of Harpers Ferry by Ferdinand Richardt, 1858, depicts the peaceful town a year before a raid on the federal arsenal there triggered a crisis for the Union.

1856
• "Bleeding Kansas" conflict between pro-slavery and antislavery forces begins

1858
• Lincoln-Douglas debates take place during the Illinois Senate campaign

1859
• John Brown attempts to arm and free enslaved African Americans by raiding the federal arsenal at Harpers Ferry, Virginia

1860
• South Carolina secedes from the Union

1861
• Fort Sumter bombarded by Confederate forces; the Civil War begins

Buchanan 1857–1861

Lincoln 1861–1865

1858   *1862*

1857
• Indians rebel against British rule

1859
• Darwin's *Origin of Species* published

HISTORY Online

Chapter Overview
Visit the *American Republic Since 1877* Web site at tarvol2.glencoe.com and click on **Chapter Overviews— Chapter 6** to preview chapter information.

217

HISTORY Online

Introduce students to chapter content and key terms by having them access the **Chapter 6 Overview** at tarvol2.glencoe.com

More About the Art

Harpers Ferry is located at the confluence of the Potomac and Shenandoah Rivers. In addition, it is where the Baltimore & Ohio Railroad crosses the northern Shenandoah Valley. During the war, the town changed hands eight times.

TIME LINE

ACTIVITY

Have students use the time line to determine the relative chronology of events by identifying who was president of the United States when each event occurred. Quiz the students by asking events out of order. Gold Rush begins *(Taylor)*, Compromise of 1850 *(Fillmore)*, Republican Party founded *(Pierce)*, "Bleeding Kansas" *(Pierce)*, Lincoln-Douglas debates *(Buchanan)*, Harpers Ferry *(Buchanan)*, South Carolina secedes *(Buchanan)*, Fort Sumter attacked *(Lincoln)*

FOLDABLES
Study Organizer

Dinah Zike's Foldables are three-dimensional, interactive graphic organizers that help students practice basic writing skills, review key vocabulary terms, and identify main ideas. Have students complete the foldable activity in the *Dinah Zike's Reading and Study Skills Foldables* booklet.

GRAPHIC ORGANIZER ACTIVITY

Organizing Information Have students create a graphic organizer similar to the one shown below to explain the events that occurred during each of the presidencies that increased sectional tensions. *(A–D: transcontinental railroad, Kansas-Nebraska Act, territorial civil war in Kansas, caning of Charles Sumner; E–F: Dred Scott decision, Kansas's Lecompton constitution)*

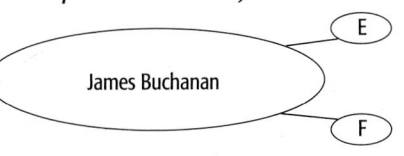

Franklin Pierce

James Buchanan

217

1 FOCUS

Section Overview

This section focuses on the growing sectional tensions between the North and South as westward expansion continued.

BELLRINGER
Skillbuilder Activity

 Project transparency and have students answer the question.

Daily Focus Skills Transparency 6–1

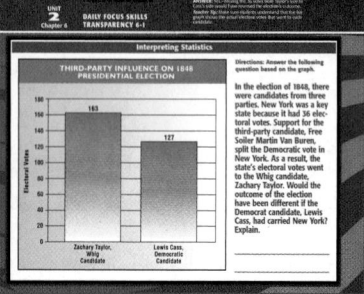

Reading Preview

Answers to Graphic: Clay: tried to find a compromise; Calhoun: defender of Southern rights; Douglass: abolitionist and powerful orator; Tubman: conductor on the Underground Railroad; Stowe: author of *Uncle Tom's Cabin*; Douglas: crafted the Kansas-Nebraska Act

Preteaching Vocabulary
Have students make a table with columns labeled North and South, then place Key Terms and Names in the appropriate columns.

SECTION 1 Slavery and Western Expansion

Guide to Reading

Main Idea
Continuing disagreements over the westward expansion of slavery increased sectional tensions between the North and the South.

Key Terms and Names
Wilmot Proviso, popular sovereignty, secession, Underground Railroad, Harriet Tubman, transcontinental railroad

Reading Strategy
Categorizing As you read about the deepening North–South tensions, complete a graphic organizer identifying key people of the era.

Key Figures	Significance
Henry Clay	
John Calhoun	
Frederick Douglass	
Harriet Tubman	
Harriet Beecher Stowe	
Stephen Douglas	

Reading Objectives
• **Explain** how the government dealt with slavery in the territories acquired after the war with Mexico.
• **Evaluate** how both the Fugitive Slave Act and the transcontinental railroad heightened sectional tensions.

Section Theme
Geography and History The acquisition of new lands heightened sectional tensions over slavery.

Preview of Events

♦1846	♦1850	♦1854	♦1858

1846
Wilmot Proviso proposed

1850
Compromise of 1850 adopted

1852
Uncle Tom's Cabin published

1854
Kansas-Nebraska Act adopted

1856
Charles Sumner attacked in Senate

★ *An American Story* ★

Early one cold morning in January 1847, Mrs. Crosswait woke to the sound of pistol shots. Without a word she rushed to her sleeping children, while her husband ran downstairs to bolt the door. The Crosswaits knew instantly the danger they were facing. Kidnappers had come to snatch them from their Michigan home and drag them back to Kentucky—and slavery.

The family had fled north after learning, to their horror, that the man who held them in slavery planned to sell them away from each other. They ended up in Marshall, Michigan. Home to a strong community of Quakers, Marshall welcomed them warmly.

Now, clutching her children, Mrs. Crosswait peeked fearfully from an upper window as three strangers fired bullet after bullet into their front door and demanded that the family surrender. She heard her husband pushing furniture against the door.

Then over the din came the voice of a neighbor, urging people to aid the family. Soon, friends came running. Shouting threats at the intruders, the townspeople intimidated them into leaving, thereby saving the family.

—adapted from *Black Pioneers: An Untold Story*

Notice of escaped enslaved person's capture

The Impact of the War With Mexico

The Crosswaits' struggle with kidnappers was not unique. Although many people escaped from slavery and headed north into free territory, even there they were not safe. Southerners believed that Article 4, Section 2, of the Constitution gave them the right to

218 CHAPTER 6 Sectional Conflict Intensifies

SECTION RESOURCES

📂 Reproducible Masters
• Reproducible Lesson Plan 6–1
• Daily Lecture and Discussion Notes 6–1
• Guided Reading Activity 6–1
• Section Quiz 6–1
• Reading Essentials and Study Guide 6–1

📄 Transparencies
• Daily Focus Skills Transparency 6–1

Multimedia
🔘 Interactive Tutor Self-Assessment CD-ROM
🔘 ExamView® Pro Testmaker CD-ROM
🔘 Presentation Plus! CD-ROM
🔘 TeacherWorks™ CD-ROM
🔘 Audio Program
📺 ABCNews Interactive™ Historic America Electronic Field Trips

retrieve an enslaved person who fled across state lines. Some Northerners, however, held strong beliefs to the contrary and helped runaways.

The war with Mexico only heightened these opposing viewpoints. The war opened vast new lands to American settlers, again raising the divisive issue of whether slavery should be allowed to spread westward.

GOVERNMENT

The Wilmot Proviso In August 1846, Representative David Wilmot, a Democrat from Pennsylvania, proposed an addition to a war appropriations bill. His amendment, known as the **Wilmot Proviso,** proposed that in any territory the United States gained from Mexico, "neither slavery nor involuntary servitude shall ever exist."

Despite fierce Southern opposition, a coalition of Northern Democrats and Whigs passed the Wilmot Proviso in the House of Representatives. The Senate, however, refused to vote on it. Senator John C. Calhoun of South Carolina argued that all the states owned U.S. territories in common, that Americans settling there had the right to bring along their property, including enslaved laborers, and that Congress had no power to ban slavery in the territories. Calhoun warned that civil war would surely erupt if the North failed to heed Southern concerns.

Popular Sovereignty For the next few years, Wilmot's proposal continued to be raised in Congress, deepening divisions between the North and South. Many moderate politicians began searching for a solution that would spare Congress from having to wrestle with the issue of slavery in the territories.

Senator **Lewis Cass** of Michigan proposed one solution. Cass suggested that the citizens of each new territory should be allowed to decide for themselves if they wanted to permit slavery or not. This idea came to be called popular sovereignty.

Popular sovereignty appealed strongly to many members of Congress because it removed the slavery issue from national politics. It also appeared democratic, since the settlers themselves would make the decision. Abolitionists, however, argued that it still denied African Americans their right not to be enslaved.

The Free-Soil Party As the 1848 election approached, both major parties sidestepped the slavery issue. The Whig candidate, General Zachary Taylor, avoided it and stressed his leadership experience in the war with Mexico. The Democrats' nominee, Lewis

Cass, downplayed his support for popular sovereignty to gain support in the South. Instead he emphasized his promise to veto the Wilmot Proviso, should Congress ever pass it.

Northern opponents of slavery had little enthusiasm for either Taylor or Cass. Many antislavery Whigs and Democrats decided to join with members of the abolitionist Liberty Party to form the **Free-Soil Party,** which opposed the spread of slavery onto the "free soil" of the western territories.

Although some Free-Soilers condemned slavery as immoral, most members of the new party simply wanted to preserve the territories in the West for white farmers. Allowing slavery to expand, they warned, would make it difficult for free men to find work. Adopting the slogan "Free soil, free speech, free labor, and free men," they chose former president Martin Van Buren as their candidate.

On Election Day, support for the Free-Soilers pulled votes away from the Democrats. When the ballots were counted, the Whig candidate, Zachary Taylor, had won a narrow victory.

✓ **Reading Check** **Evaluating** How did the war with Mexico affect the slavery issue?

Poster calling for antislavery meeting

CHAPTER 6 Sectional Conflict Intensifies **219**

2 TEACH

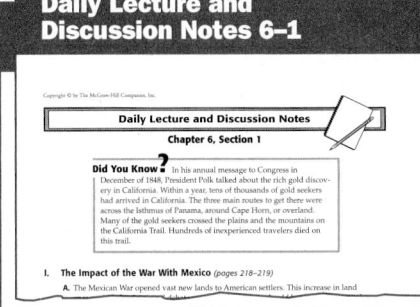

Daily Lecture and Discussion Notes 6–1

Copyright © by The McGraw-Hill Companies, Inc.

Daily Lecture and Discussion Notes

Chapter 6, Section 1

Did You Know? In his annual message to Congress in December of 1848, President Polk talked about the rich gold discovery in California. Within a year, tens of thousands of gold seekers had arrived in California. The three main routes to get there were across the Isthmus of Panama, around Cape Horn, or overland. Many of the gold seekers crossed the plains and the mountains on the California Trail. Hundreds of inexperienced travelers died on this trail.

I. The Impact of the War With Mexico (pages 218–219)

A. The Mexican War opened vast new lands to American settlers. This increase in land

Writing an Editorial Have students write an editorial explaining why slaveholding would be the major issue of the 1848 presidential election in spite of the major parties' efforts to ignore it. **L1**

✓ **Reading Check**

Answer: The war opened vast new territory for settlers and this raised the divisive issue of whether slavery should be allowed in the western territories.

you don't say...

Predicting Civil War John C. Calhoun died on March 31, 1850. Earlier that year, he predicted the dissolution of the Union "within twelve years or three presidential terms."

COOPERATIVE LEARNING ACTIVITY

Making an Oral Presentation Organize the class into eight groups. Read the following quote made by Sidney George Fisher, a Philadelphia lawyer, in 1844: "Every day the difference between the North and the South is becoming more prominent and apparent. The difference exists in everything which forms the life of the people—in institutions, laws, opinions, manners, feelings, education, pursuits, climate and soil." Assign each group one thing which "forms the life of the people" to prepare a brief oral presentation about the growing differences between the North and South.

Use the rubric for a cooperative group management plan on pages 71–72 in the **Performance Assessment Activities and Rubrics.**

Guided Reading Activity 6–1

Name _____ Date _____ Class _____

★ Guided Reading Activity 6-1

DIRECTIONS: Using Headings and Subheadings Locate each heading below in your textbook. Then use the information under the correct subheading to help you write each answer.
I. The Impact of the War With Mexico
  A. What did Southerners believe that Article 4, Section 2, of the Constitution gave them the right to do? _____
  B. What was popular sovereignty? _____
  C. What was the main platform of the Free-Soil Party? _____
II. Congress Struggles for a Compromise
  A. What led to California's application for statehood? _____
  B. Who was nicknamed "The Great Compromiser" and why? _____

Chart *Skills*

Answers:
1. the South
2. Answers may vary. The South probably achieved slightly more because its basic way of life did not have to change.

Chart Skills Practice
Ask: What did the Compromise of 1850 not prohibit in the District of Columbia? *(It did not prohibit owning enslaved people.)*

Locating Primary Sources

Have students use library and Internet resources to locate reproductions of primary sources illustrating antislavery activities. Have students prepare a short oral report about one of their findings. **L2**

 VIDEOCASSETTE
Historic America Electronic Field Trips

View **Tape 1, Chapter 11:** "Sutter's Mill."

Congress Struggles for a Compromise

Within a year of President Taylor's inauguration, the issue of slavery took center stage. The discovery of gold in California had quickly led to that territory's application for statehood. A decision had to be made about whether California would enter the Union as a free state or a slave state.

Forty-Niners Rush for Gold In January 1848, carpenter James Marshall was building a sawmill in Sacramento for a man named John Sutter. When Marshall found traces of gold in a stream near the sawmill, the two men tried to keep the secret to themselves. Word leaked out by spring, however, and San Franciscans abandoned their homes and businesses to pile into wagons and head to the mountains in search of gold. During the summer, news of the find swept all the way to the East Coast and beyond, and the California Gold Rush was on.

By the end of 1849, over 80,000 **"Forty-Niners"** had arrived in California hoping to make their fortunes. Mining towns sprang up overnight, and the frenzy for gold led to chaos and violence. Needing a strong government to maintain order, Californians decided to seek statehood. With the encouragement of President Taylor, California applied to enter the Union as a free state in December 1849.

The Debate Begins At the time, there were 15 free states and 15 slave states. If California tipped the balance, the slaveholding states would become a minority in the Senate. Southerners dreaded losing power in national politics, fearful it would lead to limits on slavery. A few Southern politicians began to talk of secession—taking their states out of the Union.

In early 1850, one of the most senior and influential leaders in the Senate, Henry Clay of Kentucky, tried to find a compromise that would enable California to join the Union and resolve other sectional disputes. Clay, nicknamed "The Great Compromiser" because of his role in promoting the Missouri Compromise in 1820 and solving the nullification crisis in 1833, proposed eight resolutions.

The first pair would allow California to come in as a free state but would organize the rest of the Mexican cession without any restrictions on slavery. The second pair would settle a boundary dispute between New Mexico and Texas in favor of New Mexico, but it would compensate Texas by having the federal government take on its debts.

Clay's third pair of resolutions would outlaw the slave trade in the District of Columbia but not slavery itself. The final two resolutions were concessions to the South. Congress would be prohibited from interfering with the domestic slave trade and would pass a stronger law to help Southerners recover enslaved African Americans who had fled north. These measures were intended to assure the South that the North would not try to abolish slavery after California joined the Union.

Clay's proposal triggered a massive debate in Congress. Senator Calhoun, the great defender of the South's rights, was unyielding. Although he was now dying from tuberculosis and too weak to address the Senate himself, he composed a reply to Clay and then sat, hollow-eyed and shrouded in blankets, as another senator read his words. Calhoun asserted that Northern agitation against slavery threatened to destroy the South, and that Clay's compromise would not save the Union. The South needed an acceptance of its rights, the return of fugitive slaves, and a guarantee of balance between the sections. Otherwise, secession was the only honorable solution.

The Compromise of 1850

Legislative Item	Victory for?
• California admitted to the Union as free state	Clear victory for the North
• Popular sovereignty to determine slavery issue in Utah and New Mexico territories	Moderate victory for both sides
• Texas border dispute with New Mexico resolved • Texas receives $10 million	Moderate Southern victories
• Slave trade, but not slavery itself, abolished in the District of Columbia	Moderate Northern victory
• Strong federal enforcement of new Fugitive Slave Act	Clear victory for the South

Chart *Skills*

1. **Interpreting Charts** Did the new Fugitive Slave Act appeal to the North or the South?
2. **Generalizing** Which side, North or South, achieved more of its goals in the Compromise of 1850?

DIFFERENTIATED INSTRUCTION

At-Risk Students Sometimes inattention is caused by the difficulty of the material. Have students preview Section 1 to assess components that they might find difficult. Discuss the factors that might affect their ability to maintain attention. For example, ask the following questions: On which subsection is it easier for you to maintain attention, "Congress Struggles for a Compromise" or "The Fugitive Slave Act"? Why? **L1**

☞ Refer to **Inclusion for the High School Social Studies Classroom Strategies and Activities** in the TCR.

Three days later, Senator **Daniel Webster** of Massachusetts pleaded for the Senate to put national unity above sectional loyalties. He voiced his support for Clay's plan, which he believed to be the only hope of keeping the Union intact:

> ❝I wish to speak to-day, not as a Massachusetts man, nor as a Northern man, but as an American. . . . I speak today for the preservation of the Union. . . . Peaceable secession is an utter impossibility. . . . I see as plainly as I see the sun in heaven what that disruption itself must produce; I see that it must produce war, and such a war as I will not describe.❞
>
> —from the *Congressional Globe,* 31st Congress

The Compromise of 1850 In the end, Congress did not pass Clay's bill, in part because President Taylor opposed it. Taylor, however, died unexpectedly in July 1850. Vice President Millard Fillmore succeeded him and quickly threw his support behind the compromise.

By the end of summer, Calhoun had also died, Webster had retired, and Clay was exhausted, leaving leadership of the Senate to younger men. Thirty-seven-year-old Stephen A. Douglas of Illinois deftly divided much of the large compromise initiative into several smaller bills. This allowed his colleagues from different sections to abstain or vote against whatever parts they disliked while supporting the rest. By September, Congress had passed all parts of the **Compromise of 1850** and President Fillmore had signed them into law, fulfilling Clay's original vision.

✔ **Reading Check** **Summarizing** Why did the Gold Rush create a new crisis over slavery?

The Fugitive Slave Act

To Northerners, one of the most objectionable components of the Compromise of 1850 was the **Fugitive Slave Act.** Under this law, a slaveholder or slavecatcher had only to point out alleged runaways to have them taken into custody. The accused would then be brought before a federal commissioner. With no right to testify on their own behalf, even those who had earned their freedom years earlier had no way to prove their case. An affidavit asserting that the captive had escaped from a slaveholder, or testimony by white witnesses, was all a court needed to order the person sent South. Furthermore, federal commissioners had a financial incentive to rule in favor of slaveholders; such judgments earned them a $10 fee, but judgments in favor of the accused paid only $5.

Heroic Figure Harriet Tubman escaped from slavery when she was around 29 years old. She helped many others do the same, guiding them along the freedom route, the Underground Railroad.

The Fugitive Slave Act also required federal marshals to assist slavecatchers. Marshals could even deputize citizens on the spot to help them capture an alleged fugitive. Anyone who refused to cooperate could be jailed.

Newspaper accounts of the unjust seizure of African Americans fueled Northern indignation. However, it was the requirement that ordinary citizens help capture runaways that drove many Northerners into active defiance. The abolitionist Frederick Douglass, himself an escapee from slavery, would work crowds into a furor over this part of the law. In emotional speeches, he would ask his audience if they would give a helpless runaway over to the "pursuing bloodhounds." "No!" the crowd would roar.

Northerners justified their defiance of the Fugitive Slave Act on moral grounds. In his 1849 essay "Civil Disobedience," Henry David Thoreau wrote that if the law "requires you to be the agent of injustice to another, then I say, break the law." In helping runaways, Northerners risked heavy fines and prison terms. Sometimes they even resorted to violence themselves. In a pamphlet, Douglass proposed "The True Remedy for the Fugitive Slave Law—A good revolver, a steady hand, and a determination to shoot down any man attempting to kidnap."

The Underground Railroad A key to many African Americans' escape from the South was the Underground Railroad. This informal but well-organized network of abolitionists began to expand in the early 1830s and helped thousands of enslaved persons flee north. "Conductors" transported runaways in secret, gave them shelter and food along the way, and saw them to freedom in the Northern states or Canada with some money for a fresh start. Conductors used secret signals to communicate about how to proceed safely—a hand lifted palm outwards, for example, or a certain kind of tug at the ear. The most famous conductor was **Harriet Tubman,**

CHAPTER 6 Sectional Conflict Intensifies **221**

Writing an Essay Have students write an essay describing the conditions in cities and towns in which escapees from slavery lived. Tell students to write from the point of view of either a federal marshal or a citizen who had just been deputized against his will or from the point of view of an escapee who simply wanted to lead a normal life. **L3**

CURRICULUM CONNECTION

Geography Stephen Douglas believed that the expansion of slavery would be decided by "the laws of climate, and of production, and of physical geography." In other words, slavery would expand into only those areas that were suitable for large-scale production of cotton.

INTERDISCIPLINARY CONNECTIONS ACTIVITY

Political Science Have students discuss the reasons the North and South disagreed on the Kansas-Nebraska Act. List the reasons on the board under the headings North and South. Tell students that much of the reasoning was the result of nationalism versus states' rights. Conclude by emphasizing the differences between the politics of the North and the South. **L2**

Geography *Skills*

Answers:
1. to the Canadian border
2. 11

Geography Skills Practice

Ask: What means of transportation was likely used to free enslaved people from Charleston, South Carolina? *(boats or ships)*

 Reading Check

Answer: It created active hostility toward slavery among Northerners.

CURRICULUM CONNECTION

World History *Uncle Tom's Cabin* had a tremendous impact on British politicians. Lord Palmerston, who served as prime minister in the late 1850s, read the book three times.

FYI

Slaveholders offered $40,000 for Harriet Tubman's capture. After the Civil War began, she worked as a cook, nurse, and even as a spy for the Union forces.

NATIONAL GEOGRAPHIC **Slavery and the Underground Railroad 1830–1860**

In Motion

The Underground Railroad existed as early as 1786, but its spread throughout most of the North occurred after 1830.

Ashtabula, OHIO–site of Hubbard House, one of the end points on the route north

Battle Creek, MICH.–burial site of abolitionist Sojourner Truth

Thousands of African Americans escaped slavery through the Underground Railroad between 1830 and 1860.

- More than 50% of people enslaved
- 10–50%
- Less than 10%
- No enslaved or data
- ← Underground RR routes
- — 1860 border

Doll of runaway child

Geography *Skills*

1. **Interpreting Maps** How far north did many underground routes reach?
2. **Applying Geography Skills** How many states had areas where more than 50 percent of the people were enslaved?

herself a runaway. Again and again, she risked journeys into the slave states to bring out men, women, and children.

Levi Coffin, a Quaker, sheltered a reported 2,000 escaped African Americans in his home in Indiana, where three Underground Railroad routes from the South converged. Coffin later moved to Cincinnati, Ohio, where he assisted another 1,300 slaves who had come from Kentucky to freedom.

Uncle Tom's Cabin Another Cincinnati resident at one time was the author **Harriet Beecher Stowe.** Her exposure to runaway slaves and the tragic reports she heard later about victims of the Fugitive Slave Law inspired her to "write something that would make this whole nation feel what an accursed thing slavery is."

In 1851, from her home in Brunswick, Maine, Stowe began writing *Uncle Tom's Cabin.* After first running as a newspaper serial, the story came out the next year in book form and sold an astounding 300,000 copies. Stowe's depiction of the enslaved hero, Tom, and the villainous overseer, Simon Legree, aroused passionate antislavery sentiment in the North.

Southerners were outraged at Stowe's novel, and some accused Stowe of writing distortions and falsehoods. Despite Southern outrage, the book eventually sold millions of copies. It had such a dramatic impact on public opinion that many historians consider it a cause of the Civil War.

 Reading Check **Analyzing** In what sense did the Fugitive Slave Act hurt the Southern cause?

222 CHAPTER 6 Sectional Conflict Intensifies

Reading Strategy   READING THE TEXT

Identifying Cause and Effect The cause-and-effect structure is used to explore the reasons for something happening and to examine the results of previous events. Copy the following headings on the board: CAUSES → EVENT → EFFECTS. Under Event, write Kansas-Nebraska Act, 1854. As students read through the section, have them complete the chain by adding the causes and effects related to passage of the Kansas-Nebraska Act. *(Causes: desire to organize new territories; desire to resolve the issue of expanding slaveholding; Effects: Northern anger over spread of slavery to "free" land; outbreak of violence in Kansas)* **L1**

New Territorial Troubles

In 1852 Franklin Pierce was elected president. As a pro-slavery Democrat from New Hampshire, he hoped he could help bridge the divide between North and South. Unfortunately, sectional tensions only worsened during his administration.

A Transcontinental Railroad

By the early 1850s, many Americans no longer perceived the Great Plains region as the "Great American Desert." Eager to survey and settle the fertile lands west of Missouri and Iowa, many farmers and land speculators called for the federal government to organize them as a territory.

At the same time, the opening of the Oregon country and the admission of California to the Union had convinced many business leaders, members of Congress, and farmers of the need for a transcontinental railroad—one that would cross the whole country. In the 1850s, getting to the West Coast required weeks of grueling overland travel or a long sea voyage around the tip of South America. A transcontinental railroad would reduce the journey to four relatively easy days and promote further growth in the territories along the route.

The transcontinental railroad had broad appeal, but the choice of its eastern starting point became a new cause of tension in the sectional conflict. Two central routes, a northern route, and a southern route were initially proposed.

Many Southerners favored the southern route, from New Orleans to San Diego, but the geography of the Southwest would require the railroad to pass through northern Mexico. Secretary of War Jefferson Davis, a strong supporter of the South's interests, found a solution. He urged President Pierce to send James Gadsden, a South Carolina politician and railroad promoter, to buy land from Mexico. In 1853 Mexico accepted $10 million for the **Gadsden Purchase**—a 30,000-square-mile strip of land that today is part of southern Arizona and New Mexico.

Meanwhile, Democratic Senator Stephen A. Douglas of Illinois had his own ideas for a transcontinental railroad. Douglas was from Illinois, and he wanted the eastern starting point to be in Chicago. He knew, however, that any route from the north would run through the unsettled lands west of Missouri and Iowa.

In 1853 Douglas prepared a bill to organize the region into a new territory to be called Nebraska. Although the House of Representatives passed the bill quickly, key Southern committee leaders prevented it from coming to a vote in the Senate. These senators made it clear that before Nebraska could be organized, Congress would have to repeal part of the Missouri Compromise and allow slavery in the new territory.

The Kansas-Nebraska Act

Stephen Douglas knew that any attempt to overturn the Missouri Compromise would create an uproar. Nevertheless, he wanted to open the northern Great Plains to settlement. At first, Douglas tried to dodge the issue and gain Southern support for his bill by saying that any states organized in the new Nebraska territory would be allowed to exercise popular sovereignty, deciding themselves whether to allow slavery.

This did not satisfy Southern leaders in the Senate. Therefore, in his next version of the bill, Douglas proposed to repeal the antislavery provision of the Missouri Compromise. He also proposed dividing the region into two territories. Nebraska would be the northernmost, adjacent to the free state of Iowa, and Kansas would be to the south, west of the slave state of Missouri. It appeared that Kansas would become a slave state while Nebraska would be a free state.

Northern Democrats and Whigs were outraged by Douglas's bill. At first, so was President Pierce. However, when Douglas and Jefferson Davis warned the president that failure to go along might cause the South to secede, Pierce gave in and backed the bill.

Picturing **History**

Bleeding Kansas These antislavery settlers in Topeka, Kansas, were among those on both sides who resorted to violence. What act triggered violence in Kansas?

CHAPTER 6 Sectional Conflict Intensifies **223**

Picturing **History**

Answer: Kansas-Nebraska Act
Ask: Why did antislavery settlers meet in Topeka? *(to draft a constitution prohibiting slavery)*

Drawing a Thematic Map Have students use library and Internet resources to learn more about the area acquired in the Gadsden Purchase. Instruct students to create/draw a thematic map showing the Mexican border before and after the Gadsden Purchase. **L2**

Use the rubric for creating a map, display, or chart on pages 65–66 in the *Performance Assessment Activities and Rubrics.*

3 ASSESS

Assign Section 1 Assessment as homework or as an in-class activity.

Have students use the **Interactive Tutor Self-Assessment CD-ROM.**

L1/ELL

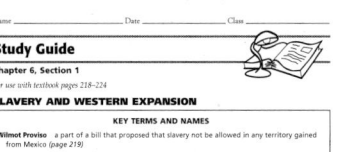

Reading Essentials and Study Guide 6–1

Name _____ Date _____ Class _____

Study Guide

Chapter 6, Section 1

For use with textbook pages 218–224

SLAVERY AND WESTERN EXPANSION

KEY TERMS AND NAMES

Wilmot Proviso a part of a bill that proposed that slavery not be allowed in any territory gained from Mexico *(page 219)*

popular sovereignty the idea that people living in a territory had the right to decide by voting whether to allow slavery in the territory *(page 219)*

secession the process of leaving the Union that Southern states threatened *(page 220)*

Underground Railroad an organized system for helping enslaved persons escape *(page 221)*

Harriet Tubman a conductor of the Underground Railroad *(page 221)*

transcontinental railroad railroad that connected the West Coast to the rest of the country *(page 223)*

EXTENDING THE CONTENT

Northerners Use Southern Argument States' rights had long been accepted as part of the Southern political culture. In the 1850s, Northerners used the idea to support opposition to the Fugitive Slave Act. For example, in 1854 the Wisconsin Supreme Court freed a man who had been jailed by a federal judge for violating the Fugitive Slave Act. The Wisconsin court said the act was unconstitutional. Five years later, the U.S. Supreme Court reversed the decision, saying that states had no right to interfere in federal cases.

L2

Section Quiz 6–1

✓ **Reading Check**

Answer: to allow two states in the Nebraska region—one free and one slave

Reteach

Ask students to explain how the government dealt with slavery in the territories acquired after the war with Mexico.

Enrich

Have students create a fact or fiction game surrounding the events discussed in the section. Have other students play the game and give feedback about what they have learned.

HISTORY
Online

Study Central™ provides summaries, interactive games, and online graphic organizers to help students review section content.

4 CLOSE

Have students list the reasons that the acquisition of new territory heightened the sectional tension over slavery.

The president's support did nothing to calm Northern fury. Free-Soilers and antislavery Democrats charged that repealing the Missouri Compromise would break a solemn promise to limit the spread of slavery. Editorials, speeches, and sermons condemned the bill, and all of the state legislatures in the North except Illinois refused to endorse it. Finally, however, in May 1854, Congress passed the **Kansas-Nebraska Act.**

Bleeding Kansas Kansas became the first battleground between those favoring the extension of slavery and those opposing it. Hordes of Northerners hurried into the territory, intent on creating an antislavery majority. Before the March elections of 1855, however, thousands of armed Missourians—called "border ruffians" in the press—swarmed across the border to vote illegally in Kansas, helping to elect a pro-slavery legislature. Furious antislavery settlers countered by holding a convention in Topeka and drafting their own constitution that prohibited slavery. By March 1856, Kansas had two governments, one opposed to slavery and the other supporting it.

In the spring of 1856, border ruffians, worked up by the arrival of more Northern settlers, attacked the town of Lawrence, a stronghold of antislavery settlers. The attackers wrecked newspaper presses, plundered shops and homes, and then burned a hotel and the home of the elected free-state governor.

"Bleeding Kansas," as newspapers dubbed the territory, became the scene of a territorial civil war between pro-slavery and antislavery settlers. By the end of 1856, 200 people had died in the fighting and $2 million worth of property had been destroyed.

The Caning of Charles Sumner The growing violence over slavery soon came to the very center of government. In May 1856, Senator **Charles Sumner** of Massachusetts, a fiery abolitionist, delivered a speech accusing pro-slavery senators of forcing Kansas into the ranks of slave states. He singled out Senator Andrew P. Butler of South Carolina for an unusually personal attack.

Butler's cousin, Representative Preston Brooks, later approached Sumner at his desk in the Senate chamber. Shouting that Sumner had defamed his home state and his cousin, Brooks raised a gold-handled cane and savagely beat the senator, leaving him severely injured and bleeding on the floor.

Many Southerners considered Brooks to be a hero. Some Southerners even sent him canes to replace the broken original one. Northerners, shocked by the attack and by the flood of support for Brooks, strengthened their determination to resist the "barbarism of slavery." One New York clergyman confided in his journal that "no way is left for the North, but to strike back, or be slaves."

✓ **Reading Check** **Explaining** Why did Stephen Douglas propose repealing part of the Missouri Compromise?

HISTORY Online | **Study Central™** To review this section, go to tarvol2.glencoe.com and click on **Study Central™**.

SECTION 1 ASSESSMENT

Checking for Understanding

1. **Define:** popular sovereignty, secession, Underground Railroad, transcontinental railroad.

2. **Identify:** Wilmot Proviso, Harriet Tubman.

Reviewing Facts

3. **Explain** why violence broke out in "Bleeding Kansas."

Reviewing Themes

4. **Geography and History** How did the war with Mexico, the Gold Rush, and the goal of a transcontinental railroad affect the slavery issue?

Critical Thinking

5. **Evaluating** Antislavery activists defied the Fugitive Slave Act on the grounds that it was immoral. Do you think it is better to use civil disobedience or to work through the political or legal system in response to unjust laws?

6. **Organizing** Use a graphic organizer similar to the one below to list the main effects of the Fugitive Slave Act.

Fugitive Slave Act → Effects

Analyzing Visuals

7. **Examining Photographs** Study the poster on page 219 advertising an antislavery meeting. What was one main reason that the poster designers opposed slavery?

8. **Analyzing Maps** Study the map on page 222 of slavery and the Underground Railroad. What two main cities are shown to be destinations from Southern port cities?

Writing About History

9. **Expository Writing** Write a research report about the Underground Railroad, the California Gold Rush, or the Great Compromiser, Henry Clay.

224   CHAPTER 6   Sectional Conflict Intensifies

SECTION 1 ASSESSMENT ANSWERS

1. Terms are in blue.
2. Wilmot Proviso *(p. 219)*, Harriet Tubman *(p. 221)*
3. Hot-tempered proslavery and antislavery settlers rushed in hoping to decide the future of slavery in Kansas.
4. Each affected whether territories would become free or slave states.

5. Answers will vary. Students should support their points of view with specific examples.
6. greatly angered many Northerners who defied the law; led to publication of *Uncle Tom's Cabin*
7. They believed that the expansion of slavery would take work away from free laborers.

8. Portland, Maine, and Boston, Massachusetts
9. Reports should be well organized with a clear outline, introduction, body, and conclusion.

Critical Thinking SKILLBUILDER

Predicting Consequences

Why Learn This Skill?

Did you ever wish you could see into the future? Although predicting future events is very difficult, you can develop skills that will help you identify the logical consequences of decisions or actions.

Learning the Skill

Follow these steps to help you accurately predict consequences:

• Review what you already know about a situation by listing facts, events, and people's responses. The list will help you recall events and how they affected people.

• Analyze patterns. Try to determine what the patterns show.

• Use your knowledge and observations of similar situations. In other words, ask yourself, "What were the consequences of a similar decision or action that occurred in the past?"

• Analyze each of the potential consequences by asking, "How likely is it that this will occur?"

• Make a prediction.

Practicing the Skill

Candidates for public office often make campaign promises based on how they think voters will respond. Use the information in the chart on this page to help you predict what type of candidate would be elected president in 1848. Then answer the questions that follow.

❶ What event initially forced candidates to address the issue of slavery in new territories?

❷ Review the facts and events listed on the chart. Do you notice any patterns? What do the facts tell you about the 1840s?

❸ What kind of president do you think Northerners would want? Southerners?

Events of the 1840s	Results and Reactions
Victory in war with Mexico creates new territory in Southwest.	→ Americans torn over whether area should be free or slave territory.
Wilmot Proviso proposes ban on slavery in any area taken from Mexico.	→ Southerners are outraged.
Members of Congress try to avoid issue of slavery in territories.	→ Northerners and Southerners continue to angrily debate the issue.
Popular sovereignty lets settlers decide whether territories should be free or not.	→ Abolitionists argue against popular sovereignty; many Northerners support it.
Whig Party nomination of Zachary Taylor angers some party members.	→ Many Northern Whigs split and join with others to create the Free-Soil Party.

Skills Assessment

Complete the Practicing Skills questions on page 241 and the Chapter 6 Skill Reinforcement Activity to assess your mastery of this skill.

Applying the Skill

Predicting Consequences Read several newspaper articles about an event affecting your community today. Make an educated prediction about what will happen, and explain your reasoning. Write a letter to the editor, summarizing your prediction. You may want to check back at a later time to see if your prediction came true.

 Glencoe's **Skillbuilder Interactive Workbook CD-ROM, Level 2,** provides instruction and practice in key social studies skills.

225

1 FOCUS

Section Overview

This section explains the breakdown of the major political parties and the growth in hostility between the North and South resulting from the issue of slavery.

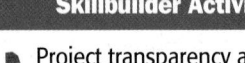

BELLRINGER
Skillbuilder Activity

Project transparency and have students answer the question.

Daily Focus Skills Transparency 6–2

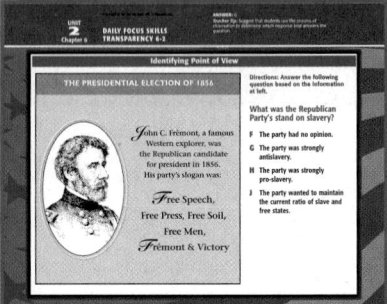

Reading Preview

Answers to Graphic:
The Crisis Deepens
I. Political Developments
   A. The Birth of the Republican Party
   B. The Election of 1856
II. Sectional Divisions Grow
Students should complete the outline by including all heads in the section.

Preteaching Vocabulary
Have students locate a date or write a phrase to help clarify the significance of the terms and names.

Guide to Reading

Main Idea
The slavery controversy accelerated the breakdown of the major political parties and the growth of hostility between North and South.

Key Terms and Names
Republican Party, Dred Scott, referendum, insurrection, Harpers Ferry

Reading Strategy
Taking Notes As you read about the widening split between the North and the South, use the major headings of the section to complete the outline started below.

The Crisis Deepens
I. Political Developments
   A.
   B.
II.
   A.
   B.

Reading Objectives
- **Describe** the origins of the Republican Party and the fate of the Whigs and the Know-Nothings.
- **Explain** the significance of the *Dred Scott* decision, the Lincoln-Douglas debates of 1858, and John Brown's raid on Harpers Ferry.

Section Theme
Groups and Institutions Americans forged new political alliances in the 1850s.

Preview of Events

◆1854	◆1856	◆1858	◆1860
1854 Republican Party founded	**1857** Lecompton constitution drafted in Kansas / **1857** Supreme Court announces *Dred Scott* decision	**1858** Lincoln-Douglas debates	**1859** John Brown and followers raid Harpers Ferry

Abraham Lincoln

★ An American Story ★

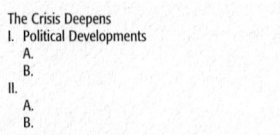

By the 1850s, feelings were running high among Northerners and Southerners over whether slavery should be allowed in new territories. These strong feelings also tore old political parties apart and created new ones. Soon after Abraham Lincoln, a congressman from Illinois, was defeated in his race for senator, he wrote to a Springfield friend:

❝I think I am a Whig; but others say there are not Whigs, and that I am an abolitionist. . . . I now do no more than oppose the extension of slavery. I am not a Know-Nothing. . . . How could I be? How can any one who abhors the oppression of negroes, be in favor of degrading classes of white people? . . . As a nation, we began by declaring 'all men are created equal.' We now practically read it 'all men are created equal except negroes.' When the Know-Nothings get control, it will read 'all men are created equal, except negroes, and foreigners, and catholics.' When it comes to this I should prefer emigrating to some country where they make no pretence of loving liberty—to Russia for instance. . . .❞

—quoted in *Abraham Lincoln*

Political Developments

When the Kansas-Nebraska Act made the delicate balance previously maintained by the Missouri Compromise obsolete, it enraged many opponents of slavery because it reopened the territories to slavery. While a few people struck back with violence, others worked for change through the political system.

SECTION RESOURCES

📁 **Reproducible Masters**
- Reproducible Lesson Plan 6–2
- Daily Lecture and Discussion Notes 6–2
- Guided Reading Activity 6–2
- Section Quiz 6–2
- Reading Essentials and Study Guide 6–2

📖 **Transparencies**
- Daily Focus Skills Transparency 6–2

- American Art & Architecture

Multimedia
- 💿 Interactive Tutor Self-Assessment CD-ROM
- 💿 ExamView® Pro Testmaker CD-ROM
- 💿 Presentation Plus! CD-ROM
- 💿 TeacherWorks™ CD-ROM
- 🎵 Audio Program
- 🎵 American Music: Hits Through History

The Birth of the Republican Party The Kansas-Nebraska Act shattered the Whig Party. Every Northern Whig in Congress had voted against the bill, while most Southern Whigs had supported it. "We Whigs of the North," wrote one member from Connecticut, "are unalterably determined never to have even the slightest political correspondence or connexion" with the Southern Whigs.

Many Northern Whigs left their party and joined forces with Free-Soilers and a few antislavery Democrats during the congressional elections of 1854. These antislavery coalitions officially organized as the **Republican Party** in July 1854. They chose that name to link themselves to Jefferson's original Democratic-Republican Party. Just as Jefferson had wanted to prevent the United States from becoming a monarchy, the new Republicans wanted to stop Southern planters from becoming an aristocracy that controlled the government.

Republicans did not agree on whether slavery should be abolished in the Southern states, but they did agree that it had to be kept out of the territories. A large majority of Northern voters seemed to agree, enabling the Republicans to make great strides in the elections of 1854.

At the same time, public anger against the Northern Democrats enabled the American Party—better known as the Know-Nothings—to make gains as well, particularly in the Northeast. The American Party was an anti-Catholic and nativist party. It hoped to prolong the naturalization process, weakening immigrant influence. In the 1840s and early 1850s, a large number of immigrants, many of them Irish and German Catholics, had begun to arrive. Prejudice and fears that immigrants would take away jobs enabled the Know-Nothings to win many seats in Congress and the state legislatures in 1854.

The party quickly began to founder, however. Soon after the 1854 elections, Know-Nothings from the Upper South split with Know-Nothings from the North over their support for the Kansas-Nebraska Act. Furthermore, most Americans considered slavery a far more important issue than immigration. Eventually, the Republican Party absorbed the Northern Know-Nothings, strengthening Republican power in the North.

The Election of 1856 To gain the widest possible support in the 1856 presidential campaign, the Republicans nominated John C. Frémont, a famous

Political Parties of the Era

Party	Characteristics	Major Leaders
Whig (1834–1854)	Party strongly divided into sectional factions; united only in opposition to Democratic Party	Daniel Webster, Henry Clay
Democrat (1828–present)	Largely controlled federal government from 1828 to 1860 but increasingly dominated by Southern Democrats after 1840	John C. Calhoun
Liberty (1839–c. 1844)	Promoted abolition of slavery; after Liberty Party's failure, members supported Free-Soil and Republican Parties	James Birney
Free-Soil (1848–1854)	Composed of Liberty Party members, antislavery Whigs, and antislavery New York Democrats	Martin Van Buren, Charles Francis Adams
Republican (c. 1854–present)	Composed of Northern Whigs and Free-Soilers; opposed further expansion of slavery	Abraham Lincoln
American Party (Know-Nothings) (1849–c. 1860)	Anti-immigrant and anti-Catholic	Millard Fillmore (former Whig)

Source: *Encarta Encyclopedia*

Chart *Skills*

1. **Interpreting Charts** Which party had the shortest life span?
2. **Drawing Conclusions** Which party listed did not have an obvious connection to the slavery issue?

CHAPTER 6 Sectional Conflict Intensifies **227**

---

2 TEACH

Daily Lecture and Discussion Notes 6–2

Copyright © The McGraw-Hill Companies, Inc.

Daily Lecture and Discussion Notes
Chapter 6, Section 2

Did You Know ? Abraham Lincoln volunteered for service in the Illinois militia during the Black Hawk War. Lincoln served with men from the New Salem, Illinois, area. The men elected Lincoln captain because of his friendliness, honesty, skill at storytelling, and his sportsmanship in contests. After the war, Lincoln ran for the state legislature, but he lost. Then he and a partner, William F. Berry, bought a New Salem store on credit. The store failed shortly thereafter, and left both men in debt. When Berry died two years later, all the debt fell on Lincoln. He eventually paid off the debt, helping him earn the nickname, "Honest Abe."

I. **Political Developments** *(pages 226–228)*

Reading Strategy

Synthesizing Information Have students reread Lincoln's statement on page 226. Discuss as a class the reasons that Lincoln could not support the Know-Nothings. **L1**

Chart *Skills*

Answer:
1. Liberty Party
2. Know-Nothings

Chart Skills Practice
Ask: Why do you think the Whigs did not last as a political party? *(They split over the Kansas–Nebraska Act, which caused such dissension among them that the party collapsed.)*

History *and the* Humanities

- American Music: Hits Through History: "Joshua Fit the Battle of Jericho," "John Brown's Dream"
- American Music: Cultural Traditions: "Hard Times Come Again No More," "Get Off the Track!"
- American Art & Architecture: *John Brown Going to His Hanging*

Reading Strategy | READING THE TEXT

Using Word Parts Have students use prefixes to unlock the meanings of unknown words. A *prefix* is a word part that comes before a base word or a root and changes the meaning of the word. For example, *dis-* means "the opposite of" and is found in words such as disobey, displease, or disown. *In-* means "not". Have students provide examples of words that use this prefix *(inactive, incorrect, inability, incomplete).* **L1** ELL

📖 Refer to **Inclusion for the High School Social Studies Classroom Strategies and Activities** in the TCR.

L1/ELL

Guided Reading Activity 6–2

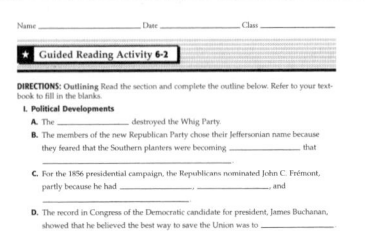

Name _____ Date _____ Class _____

★ Guided Reading Activity 6-2

DIRECTIONS: Outlining Read the section and complete the outline below. Refer to your text-book to fill in the blanks.
I. Political Developments
  A. The _____ destroyed the Whig Party.
  B. The members of the new Republican Party chose their Jeffersonian name because they feared that the Southern planters were becoming _____ that
  C. For the 1856 presidential campaign, the Republicans nominated John C. Frémont, partly because he had _____ and _____
  D. The record in Congress of the Democratic candidate for president, James Buchanan, showed that he believed the best way to save the Union was to _____
II. Sectional Divisions

✔ Reading Check

Answer: the division in the Whig party over the Kansas-Nebraska Act

🖼 Picturing **History**

Answer: They appear to be respectable people whose clothing indicates non-slave and middle-class status.

Ask: What was Dred Scott's basic argument before the Court? *(He lived in a free territory and should therefore be given his freedom.)*

Making Predictions Ask students to predict which justices were likely to side with Dred Scott and which were not. (Curtis and McLean dissented.) L2

Justice	Home State at the Time of Appointment to the Court
John Archibald Campbell	Alabama
John Catron	Tennessee
Benjamin R. Curtis	Massachusetts
Peter Vivian Daniel	Virginia
Robert Cooper Grier	Pennsylvania
John McLean	Ohio
Samuel Nelson	New York
Roger Brooke Taney	Maryland
James Moore Wayne	Georgia

🖼 Picturing **History**

Front Page News Chief Justice Roger B. Taney (right) delivered the Supreme Court's ruling in the *Dred Scott* case. The decision made Scott a topic for the nation's press. What impression of Scott's family do you get from the engravings shown here?

Western explorer nicknamed "The Pathfinder." Frémont had helped California become a free state and had spoken in favor of Kansas becoming a free state as well. Frémont had little political experience, but he also had few enemies and no embarrassing record to defend.

The Democrats nominated James Buchanan, a Pennsylvanian who could deliver the many electoral votes of his home state, then the second-largest in the Union. Despite his Northern roots, Buchanan also appealed to Southern Democrats because he had been serving as ambassador to

Britain during the debate over the Kansas-Nebraska Act and had not taken a public stand on the issue. Yet Buchanan's previous record in Congress showed that he believed the best way to save the Union was to make concessions to the South.

The American Party tried to reunite its Northern and Southern members at its convention, but most of the Northern delegates walked out when the party refused to call for the repeal of the Kansas-Nebraska Act. The remaining Know-Nothings then chose former president Millard Fillmore to represent them.

The campaign was really two separate contests, Buchanan against Frémont in the North, and Buchanan against Fillmore in the South. Buchanan had solid support in the South and only needed his home state of Pennsylvania and one other in the North to win the presidency. Democrats campaigned on the idea that only he could save the Union. When the votes were counted, Buchanan had won easily.

✔ Reading Check **Summarizing** What events led to the founding of the Republican Party?

Sectional Divisions Grow

Buchanan took office determined to adopt policies that would calm the growing sectional strife in the country. Yet a series of events during the opening months of his presidency helped to drive Northerners and Southerners even further apart.

The *Dred Scott* Decision Just two days after Buchanan's inauguration, the Supreme Court ruled in a landmark case involving slavery, *Dred Scott* v. *Sandford*. **Dred Scott** was a Missouri slave who had been taken north to work in free territory for several years. After he returned with his slaveholder to Missouri, Scott sued to end his slavery, arguing that living in free territory had made him a free man.

On March 6, 1857, the Supreme Court ruled against Scott. Chief Justice Roger B. Taney first stated that African Americans could not be U.S. citizens and that Scott thus had no right to sue in the federal courts. Taney then held that Scott's residence in free territory did not alter his enslaved status. Furthermore, Taney said, Congress's ban on slavery in the western territories, enacted as part of the Missouri Compromise, was unconstitutional and void. He reasoned that the Fifth Amendment protected slaveholders from being deprived of their property.

DIFFERENTIATED INSTRUCTION

Reading Support Have interested students write a script for a "You Are There" radio program on the reaction to the *Dred Scott* decision. Suggest that the scripts include an introduction that provides background information and interviews with lawyers, Dred Scott, John F. A. Sandford, other eyewitnesses at the court, and various experts on the Supreme Court. Encourage students to "broadcast" their scripts for the rest of the class. **L2**

📁 Refer to *Inclusion for the High School Social Studies Classroom Strategies and Activities* in the TCR.

While Democrats cheered the *Dred Scott* decision, Republicans called it a "willful perversion" of the Constitution, containing "gross historical falsehoods." They also claimed that the decision about slavery in the territories was not binding. If Dred Scott could not legally bring suit, they argued, then the Supreme Court should have dismissed the case without considering the constitutionality of the Missouri Compromise. 📖 *(For more on* Dred Scott v. Sandford, *see page 962.)*

Kansas's Lecompton Constitution After the *Dred Scott* decision, the conflict in "Bleeding Kansas" intensified. President Buchanan, hoping to end the troubles, urged the territory to apply for statehood. The pro-slavery legislature scheduled an election for delegates to a constitutional convention, but antislavery Kansans boycotted it. The resulting constitution, drafted in 1857 in the town of Lecompton, legalized slavery in the territory.

An antislavery majority then voted down the **Lecompton constitution** in a territory-wide referendum, or popular vote on an issue. Under pressure from Southern members of Congress, Buchanan ignored the vote and asked Congress to admit Kansas as a slave state. Stephen Douglas strongly disagreed, but the Senate endorsed statehood. Republicans and Northern Democrats in the House blocked the measure, arguing that it ignored the people's will.

Finally, in 1858, President Buchanan and Southern leaders in Congress agreed to allow another referendum in Kansas. If settlers did not approve the Lecompton constitution this time, they would have to defer statehood until their population reached 90,000—a significant delay. Nonetheless, the voters in Kansas overwhelmingly rejected the Lecompton constitution. They did not want slavery in their state. Not until 1861 did Kansas become a state—a free one.

✓ **Reading Check** **Explaining** Why did Dred Scott sue the slaveholder who held him?

Lincoln and Douglas

In 1858 Illinois Republicans chose a relative unknown named Abraham Lincoln to run for the Senate against the Democratic incumbent, Stephen A. Douglas. Lincoln launched his campaign in June with a memorable speech about the rift in the country:

> ❝A house divided against itself cannot stand. I believe this Government cannot endure, permanently

Fact	Fiction	Folklore

"Born in a Log Cabin" The image of a "common man" president was appealing to campaign managers in the 1800s. As voting rights spread beyond landowners, the candidate with humble roots was a potent political image. Although many nineteenth-century candidates sought to appeal to the masses, only five presidents were actually born in a log home: Andrew Jackson, James K. Polk, James Buchanan, Abraham Lincoln, and James Garfield. Of these five, Jackson, Lincoln, and Garfield experienced serious poverty in childhood. William Henry Harrison campaigned with images of a log cabin childhood, but he was actually born into an elite Virginia family that was acquainted with George Washington.

half *slave* and half *free.* I do not expect the Union to be *dissolved*—I do not expect the house to *fall*—but I do expect it will cease to be divided. It will become *all* one thing or *all* the other.❞

—quoted in *The Civil War, An Illustrated History*

The nationally prominent Douglas, a short, stocky man nicknamed "The Little Giant," regularly drew large crowds on the campaign trail. Seeking to overcome Douglas's fame, Lincoln proposed a series of debates, which would expose him to larger audiences than he could attract on his own. Douglas agreed to seven debates across the state.

Lincoln had entered politics after modest beginnings as a storekeeper, rail-splitter, and frontier lawyer. He proved himself a gifted debater, mixing logic with witty remarks, quotations from scripture, and appealing, homespun stories.

Although he was not an abolitionist, Lincoln believed slavery to be morally wrong, and he opposed its spread into western territories. Douglas, by contrast, supported popular sovereignty. He would accept any decision, for or against slavery, if the settlers voted for it. During a debate in Freeport, Lincoln asked Douglas if the people of a territory could legally exclude slavery before achieving statehood. If Douglas said yes, he would appear to be championing popular sovereignty and opposing the *Dred Scott* ruling, which would cost him Southern

Fact	Fiction	Folklore

Many candidates for political office try to make connections with ordinary people.
Ask: Can you think of things the current president does to make connections with ordinary people? *(Answers will vary. Some students might identify activities such as visiting a factory or a school, attending religious services, or other local activities.)*

✓ **Reading Check**

Answer: His slaveholder had taken him to live in a free territory before returning to Missouri. Scott argued that since he had spent time in a free territory, he was free.

The sons of Peter Blow, Dred Scott's original slaveholder, helped pay Scott's legal bills. Following the Supreme Court's decision, these childhood friends bought Scott and his wife Harriet and freed them. Scott died within the year.

Explaining a Quote Ask students to explain the words of Abraham Lincoln that are quoted on pages 229 and 230. Ask students to explain how Lincoln's words foreshadowed the direction the country would take by the end of his presidency. L2

📁 Use *Interpreting Political Cartoons,* Cartoon 8.

📁 Use *Supreme Court Case Study 5, Dred Scott* v. *Sandford.*

INTERDISCIPLINARY CONNECTIONS ACTIVITY

Language Arts Encourage students to act as reporters attending the Lincoln-Douglas debates. Ask them to write a news story on the debates, detailing the major issues raised and the exchanges between Lincoln and Douglas. Recommend that students review recent news articles to help them understand the style used in good news reporting. L2

✓ Reading Check

Answer: Douglas supported popular sovereignty. Although Lincoln was not an abolitionist, he believed slavery to be morally wrong and opposed its spread into western territories.

History *Through Art*

Answer: He used the debates to put forth the principles of the Republican Party and to establish his reputation as a clear, insightful thinker who could argue with force and eloquence.
Ask: From the picture, what similarities and differences do you see between this debate and modern televised presidential debates? *(possible answers—similarities: both candidates well dressed, both have a glass of water available, patriotic trappings surround them; differences: today only the candidates are on the podium, no supporting signs would be displayed)*

FYI

Even though Lincoln and Douglas debated publicly, their fate was in the hands of the Illinois state legislature. Douglas was reelected to the U.S. Senate by a vote of 54 to 46. In 1913 the Seventeenth Amendment established direct election of senators.

3 ASSESS

Assign Section 2 Assessment as homework or as an in-class activity.

◉ Have students use the **Interactive Tutor Self-Assessment CD-ROM.**

support. If he said no, it would seem as if he had abandoned popular sovereignty, the principle on which he had built his national following.

Douglas tried to avoid the dilemma, formulating an answer that became known as the **Freeport Doctrine.** He replied that he accepted the *Dred Scott* decision, but he argued that people could still keep out slavery by refusing to pass the laws needed to regulate and enforce it. "Slavery cannot exist . . . anywhere," said Douglas, "unless it is supported by local police regulations." Douglas's response pleased Illinois voters but angered Southerners.

Lincoln also attacked Douglas for claiming that he "cared not" whether Kansans voted for or against slavery. Denouncing the idea that slavery was as acceptable as freedom, Lincoln asked:

> ❝Has any thing ever threatened the existence of this Union save and except this very institution of slavery? What is it that we hold most dear amongst us? Our own liberty and prosperity. What has ever threatened our liberty and prosperity save and except this institution of slavery? If this is true, how do you propose to improve the condition of things by enlarging slavery—by spreading it out and making it bigger? You may have a wen [sore] or cancer upon your person and not be able to cut it out lest you bleed to death; but surely it is no way to cure it, to engraft it and spread it over your whole body. That is no proper way of treating what you regard a wrong.❞
> —quoted in *The Civil War: Opposing Viewpoints*

Douglas won the election, retaining his Senate seat, but Lincoln did not come away empty-handed. He had seized the opportunity in the debates to make clear the principles of the Republican Party. He had also established a national reputation for himself as a clear, insightful thinker who could argue with force and eloquence.

✓ Reading Check **Comparing** How did Stephen Douglas and Abraham Lincoln differ in their positions on slavery?

History *Through Art*

Charleston Confrontation Lincoln and Douglas matched wits seven times during the 1858 senatorial campaign. This painting by Robert Root shows them in Charleston, Illinois. One Republican and one Democratic newspaper published every word. How did the debates help Lincoln?

CRITICAL THINKING ACTIVITY

Analyzing Information Have students work in pairs to analyze the effects of the growth of slavery. Tell them that in 1790, there were 694,000 enslaved people in the United States. By 1860 there were 3,950,000 enslaved people in the South. Ask each pair to list reasons why political compromise over the slavery questions may have been easier right after the American Revolution than during the 1850s. *(possible reasons—Slavery had spread throughout the South by the 1850s, the economy of the South depended on slavery, and a better political climate for compromise may have existed after the Revolution.)* Discuss student responses as a class. **L2**

John Brown's Raid

About a year after the Lincoln-Douglas debates, national attention shifted to **John Brown,** a fervent abolitionist who opposed slavery not with words but with a gun. Brown had inflamed the violence in the Kansas conflict. After pro-slavery forces sacked the town of Lawrence, Brown took revenge by abducting and murdering five pro-slavery settlers living near Pottawatomie Creek.

In 1859 Brown developed a plan to incite an insurrection, or rebellion, against slaveholders. He would first conduct a raid into the Appalachian foothills, then move southward in hopes of attracting enslaved African Americans as he went. In his efforts, Brown had encouragement and financial aid from several Eastern abolitionists.

To obtain weapons, Brown planned to seize the federal arsenal at **Harpers Ferry,** Virginia (now West Virginia). On the night of October 16, 1859, Brown and about 18 followers attacked the arsenal. To the terrified night watchman, he announced, "I came here from Kansas, and this is a slave state; I want to free all the [African Americans] in this state; I have possession now of the United States armory, and if the citizens interfere with me I must only burn the town and have blood."

Soon, however, Brown was facing a contingent of U.S. Marines rushed to Harpers Ferry from Washington, D.C., and commanded by Colonel Robert E. Lee. After 10 of his men were killed, Brown surrendered—less than 36 hours after his attack had begun. A Virginia court tried and convicted him and sentenced him to death. In his last words to the court, Brown, repenting nothing, declared:

> ❝I believe that to have interfered as I have done, as I have always freely admitted I have done in behalf of [God's] despised poor, I did no wrong, but right. Now if it is deemed necessary that I should forfeit my life for the furtherance of the ends of justice and mingle my blood . . . with the blood of millions in this slave country whose rights are disregarded by wicked, cruel and unjust enactments, I say, let it be done!❞
>
> —quoted in *John Brown, 1800–1859*

On December 2, the day of his execution, Brown handed one of his jailers a prophetic note: "I, John Brown, am now quite *certain* that the crimes of this *guilty land* will never be purged *away* but with Blood. I had . . . *vainly* flattered myself that without *very much* bloodshed it might be done."

Many Northerners viewed Brown as a martyr in a noble cause. The execution, Henry David Thoreau predicted, would strengthen abolitionist feeling in the North. "He is not old Brown any longer," Thoreau declared, "he is an angel of light."

For most Southerners, however, Brown's raid offered all the proof they needed that Northerners were actively plotting the murder of slaveholders. "Defend yourselves!" cried Georgia senator Robert Toombs. "The enemy is at your door!"

✓ **Reading Check** **Evaluating** In what ways might a Northerner and a Southerner view John Brown's action?

HISTORY Online **Study Central™** To review this section, go to tarvol2.glencoe.com and click on **Study Central™.**

SECTION 2 ASSESSMENT

Checking for Understanding

1. **Define:** referendum, insurrection.
2. **Identify:** Republican Party, Dred Scott, Harpers Ferry.

Reviewing Facts

3. **Summarize** the ideas of the Freeport Doctrine.

Reviewing Themes

4. **Groups and Institutions** What were the main goals of the Republican and American Parties?

Critical Thinking

5. **Synthesizing** How did the ruling in *Dred Scott* v. *Sandford* increase sectional division?
6. **Categorizing** Use a graphic organizer similar to the one below to group key events of the period according to whether they were executive, legislative, judicial, or nongovernmental.

Executive	
Legislative	
Judicial	
Nongovernmental	

Analyzing Visuals

7. **Analyzing Photographs** Study the photograph on page 228 of the newspaper clipping depicting the Dred Scott family. What do you notice about the way the family is dressed? How would you describe their social class?

Writing About History

8. **Expository Writing** Imagine you have just read a newspaper report on the Supreme Court's ruling in the *Dred Scott* case or on John Brown's raid on Harpers Ferry. Write a letter to the editor explaining your reaction.

CHAPTER 6 Sectional Conflict Intensifies **231**

SECTION 2 ASSESSMENT ANSWERS

1. Terms are in blue.
2. Republican Party *(p. 227),* Dred Scott, *(p. 228),* Harpers Ferry *(p. 231)*.
3. Slavery could be restricted if local citizens did not pass and enforce necessary laws.
4. Republican Party: limit southern planters, prevent spread of slavery;

American Party: limit immigration
5. Northerners saw it as spreading slavery. Southerners saw it as protecting their livelihood.
6. Executive: Buchanan elected in 1856; legislative: Kansas's Lecompton constitution authorized slavery in territory; judicial: *Dred Scott* decision; nongovernmental:

John Brown's raid on Harpers Ferry's federal arsenal
7. plain but well-dressed; middle class
8. Editorials should express well-thought-out arguments.

L1/ELL

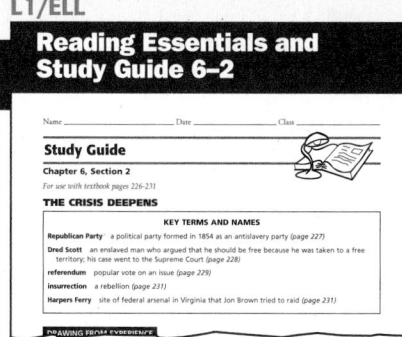

Reading Essentials and Study Guide 6–2

L2

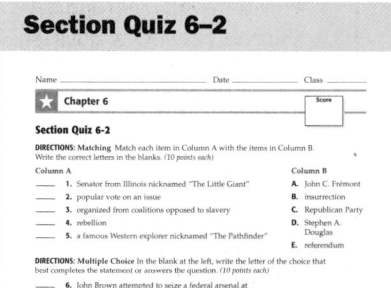

Section Quiz 6–2

✓ **Reading Check**

Answer: Northerners: a martyr for the cause of abolition; Southerners: fear of attacks from Northerners

Reteach

Have students chronicle the Lincoln-Douglas Senate campaign of 1858.

Enrich

Have students use library and Internet resources to create a profile of one of the people mentioned in this section.

HISTORY Online

Study Central™ provides summaries, interactive games, and online graphic organizers to help students review section content.

4 CLOSE

Ask students to write one sentence about the events that increased tensions before the war.

231

1 FOCUS

Section Overview

This section focuses on the events leading up to the attack on Fort Sumter and the secession of the Lower South.

BELLRINGER
Skillbuilder Activity

Project transparency and have students answer the question.

Daily Focus Skills Transparency 6–3

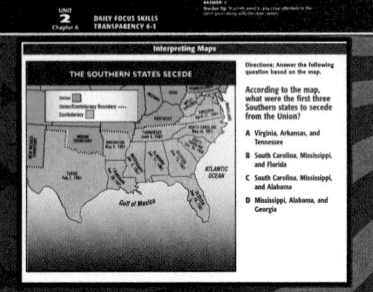

Reading Preview

Answers to Graphic: John Brown's raid on Harpers Ferry: Southerners angered; Lincoln's election: secession of lower southern states; convention in Montgomery, Alabama, on February 8, 1861: Confederacy formed; Fort Sumter falls: Civil War begins

Preteaching Vocabulary
Have students select and learn about one of the Key Terms and Names so they can teach the class the meaning.

Guide to Reading

Main Idea
The election of Abraham Lincoln as president and the secession of Southern states pushed the nation into civil war.

Key Terms and Names
Crittenden's Compromise, Confederacy, Jefferson Davis, Fort Sumter, martial law

Reading Strategy
Organizing As you read this section, complete a graphic organizer similar to the one below to list the chain of events that led to civil war.

Triggering Events	Effects

Reading Objectives
• **Discuss** the presidential election of 1860.
• **Explain** how and why the Civil War began.

Section Theme
Civic Rights and Responsibilities In the troubled days after Lincoln's election, many Southerners who placed loyalty to their states above loyalty to the Union spearheaded secession.

Preview of Events

◆ January 1861 ◆ March 1861 ◆ May 1861

December 1860
South Carolina secedes from the Union

February 1861
Confederate States of America formed

April 12
Fort Sumter bombarded

April 17
Virginia secedes

★ *An American Story* ★

Mary Chesnut

"I do not pretend to sleep," wrote Mary Chesnut of the night of April 12, 1861. "How can I?"

Hours earlier, her husband, former South Carolina senator James Chesnut, had gone by rowboat to Fort Sumter in Charleston Harbor. He was delivering an ultimatum to U.S. Army Major Robert Anderson to surrender the fort by four o'clock in the morning or be fired upon by the South Carolina militia.

Through the long night Mary Chesnut lay awake, until she heard chimes from a local church ring four times. The hour of surrender had arrived, and, she confessed, "I beg[a]n to hope." But her hopes of a peaceful outcome faded when, a half hour later, she heard the cannons begin to boom. "I sprang out of bed. And on my knees . . . I prayed as I never prayed before."

In a nightgown and shawl, Chesnut ran to the roof, where others had gathered to watch the bombardment of Fort Sumter. The sectional conflict that had brewed in debate and broken out in periodic violence had become a war. On her rooftop, Mary Chesnut shivered and felt the first terrifying evidence of the horrors to come. "The regular roar of the cannon— there it was. And who could tell what each volley accomplished of death and destruction."

—adapted from *Mary Chesnut's Civil War*

The Election of 1860

John Brown's raid on Harpers Ferry was a turning point for the South. The possibility of an African American uprising had long haunted many Southerners. Now they were terrified and enraged by the idea that Northerners would deliberately try to arm enslaved people and encourage them to rebel.

SECTION RESOURCES

Reproducible Masters
• Reproducible Lesson Plan 6–3
• Daily Lecture and Discussion Notes 6–3
• Guided Reading Activity 6–3
• Section Quiz 6–3
• Reading Essentials and Study Guide 6–3
• Performance Assessment Activities and Rubrics

Transparencies
• Daily Focus Skills Transparency 6–3

Multimedia
🔵 Interactive Tutor Self-Assessment CD-ROM
🔵 ExamView® Pro Testmaker CD-ROM
🔵 Presentation Plus! CD-ROM
🔵 TeacherWorks™ CD-ROM
🔵 Audio Program

Although Republican leaders quickly denounced Brown's raid, many Southern newspapers and politicians blamed Republicans for the attack. To many Southerners, the key point was that both the Republicans and John Brown opposed slavery. With the elections of 1860 looming, Senator Robert Toombs of Georgia warned that the South would "never permit this Federal government to pass into the traitorous hands of the Black Republican party."

The Democrats Split In April 1860, with the South still in an uproar, Democrats from across the United States began arriving in Charleston, South Carolina, to choose their nominee for president. Southern Democrats wanted their party to uphold the *Dred Scott* decision and defend slaveholders' rights in the territories. Northern Democrats, led by Stephen Douglas, preferred to continue supporting popular sovereignty. When Northerners also rebuffed the idea of a federal slave code in the territories, 50 Southern delegates stormed out of the convention. The walkout meant that neither Douglas nor anyone else could muster the two-thirds majority needed to become the party's nominee. After 57 ballots, the tired and angry delegates decided to adjourn.

In June 1860, the Democrats reconvened in Baltimore. Again, after more wrangling, Southern delegates walked out. The Democrats who remained then chose Stephen Douglas to run for president. The Southerners who had bolted organized their own convention in Richmond and nominated **John C. Breckinridge** of Kentucky, the sitting vice president.

Meanwhile, many former Whigs and others were alarmed at the prospect of Southern secession. They created a new party, the Constitutional Union Party, and chose former Tennessee senator **John Bell** as their presidential candidate. The party took no position on the issues dividing North and South. Their purpose, they said, was to uphold both the Constitution and the Union.

TURNING POINT

Lincoln Is Elected The Republicans, realizing they stood no chance in the South, needed a candidate who could sweep most of the North. They turned to Abraham Lincoln, who had gained a national reputation during his earlier debates with Douglas.

During the campaign, the Republicans tried to persuade voters that they were more than just an antislavery party. Although they remained true to

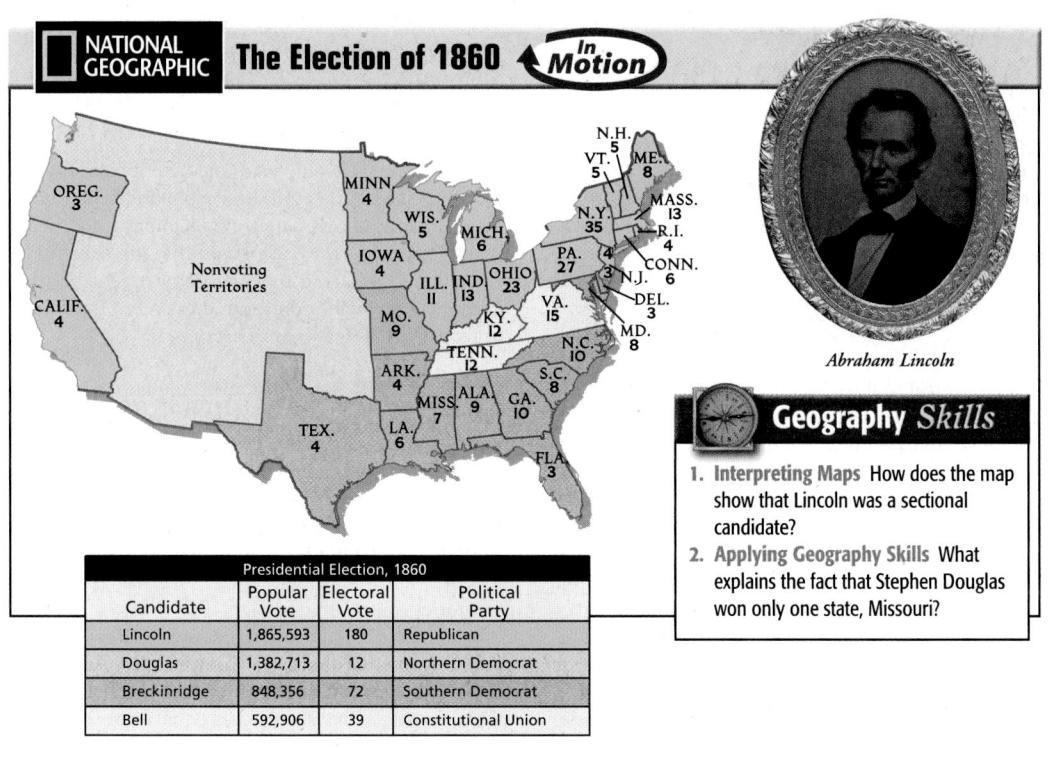

The Election of 1860 — In Motion

Abraham Lincoln

 Geography *Skills*

1. **Interpreting Maps** How does the map show that Lincoln was a sectional candidate?
2. **Applying Geography Skills** What explains the fact that Stephen Douglas won only one state, Missouri?

Presidential Election, 1860			
Candidate	Popular Vote	Electoral Vote	Political Party
Lincoln	1,865,593	180	Republican
Douglas	1,382,713	12	Northern Democrat
Breckinridge	848,356	72	Southern Democrat
Bell	592,906	39	Constitutional Union

CHAPTER 6 Sectional Conflict Intensifies 233

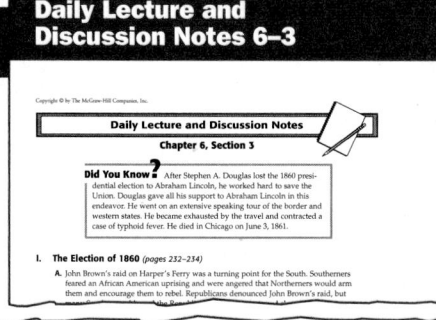

2 TEACH

Daily Lecture and Discussion Notes 6–3

Creating a Circle Chart Have students use the data shown in The Election of 1860 graphic to create a pair of circle charts illustrating the results of the presidential election of 1860. **L1**

Use the rubric for creating a map, display, or chart on pages 65–66 in the *Performance Assessment Activities and Rubrics.*

Geography *Skills*

Answers:
1. He won no states south of the Ohio River.
2. He lost the North to Lincoln and he was not proslavery enough for the South.

Geography Skills Practice
Ask: What do the election results tell you about the Northern and Southern populations in 1860? *(The North had a much larger population than the South.)*

Reading Strategy **READING THE TEXT**

Using Context Clues Students can often determine the meaning of a word they do not know by using context—the words and sentences that surround an unfamiliar word. Synonyms often appear in context when two things are compared. Antonyms appear in context most often when two things are contrasted. Definitions often are surrounded by commas, dashes, or parentheses. The use of examples reveals the meaning of an unfamiliar word. As students read the section and encounter words they do not know, remind them to use these clues to identify the word's meaning. **L1**

Refer to *Inclusion for the High School Social Studies Classroom Strategies and Activities* in the TCR.

L1/ELL
Guided Reading Activity 6–3

Name _____ Date _____ Class _____

★ Guided Reading Activity 6-3

DIRECTIONS: Recalling Facts Read the section and answer the questions below. Refer to your textbook to write the answers.

1. What aspect of John Brown's raid on Harpers Ferry terrified and enraged Southerners? _____

2. What were the elements of the disagreement between the Southern Democrats and the Northern Democrats? _____

3. What was the purpose of the new Constitutional Union Party? _____

4. Why did the Republicans choose Abraham Lincoln as their candidate for president in 1860? _____

🏛 **Analyzing** *Political Cartoons*

Answer: He once worked as a rail-splitter.

Ask: How does the cartoonist make Lincoln appear stronger than the others? *(He placed Lincoln in the foreground and showed him standing tall.)*

✓ **Reading Check**

Answer: the election of Lincoln, a Republican president

States seceded in this order: South Carolina, December 20, 1860; Mississippi, January 9, 1861; Florida, January 10, 1861; Alabama, January 11, 1861; Georgia, January 19, 1861; Louisiana, January 26, 1861; Texas, February 1, 1861; Virginia, April 17, 1861; Arkansas, May 6, 1861; and North Carolina, May 20, 1861. The Tennessee legislature adopted a "Declaration of Independence" on May 7, 1861, effectively breaking with the Union. Convention delegates did not formally accept secession until passing a referendum on June 8, 1861.

THE NATIONAL GAME. THREE "OUTS" AND ONE "RUN".
ABRAHAM WINNING THE BALL.

🏛 **Analyzing** *Political Cartoons*

Baseball and Politics In this cartoon, baseball terms are used to explain Lincoln's 1860 victory. John Bell is sad the opponents struck out. Stephen Douglas claims Lincoln had the advantage of his "rail," and John Breckinridge admits they were "skunk'd." Why is Lincoln pictured with a rail?

---

their free-soil principles, they reaffirmed the right of the Southern states to preserve slavery within their borders. They also supported higher tariffs to protect manufacturers and workers, a new homestead law for settlers in the West, and federal funds for a transcontinental railroad.

The Republican proposals greatly angered many Southerners. As expected, Lincoln won no Southern states; in fact, his name did not even appear on the ballot in some states. The Lower South went for Breckinridge, while Douglas divided the votes of the border states with Bell. The Republicans won in only their second national campaign. Lincoln won with the electoral votes of all of the free states except New Jersey, whose votes he split with Douglas.

Secession Many Southerners viewed Lincoln's election as a threat to their society and culture, even their lives. For many, there was now no choice but to secede.

The dissolution of the Union began with South Carolina, where secessionist sentiment had been burning the hottest for many years. Shortly after Lincoln's election, the state legislature called for a convention. On December 20, 1860, amid marching bands, fireworks, and militia drills, the convention unanimously voted to repeal the state's ratification of the Constitution and dissolve its ties to the Union.

By February 1, 1861, six more states in the Lower South—Mississippi, Florida, Alabama, Georgia, Louisiana, and Texas—had also voted to secede. Although some people in these states did not want to leave the Union, many Southerners viewed secession as similar to the American Revolution—a necessary course of action to uphold people's rights.

✓ **Reading Check** **Identifying** What event triggered the secession of the Lower South?

Compromise Fails

Although Lincoln was elected president in November 1860, he would not be inaugurated until the following March. The Union's initial response to secession was the responsibility of President Buchanan. Declaring that the government had no authority to forcibly preserve the Union, Buchanan urged Congress to be conciliatory.

Peace Efforts In December, Senator John J. Crittenden of Kentucky proposed a series of amendments to the Constitution. **Crittenden's Compromise,** as the newspapers called it, would guarantee slavery where it already existed. It would also reinstate the Missouri Compromise line and extend it all the way to the California border. Slavery would be prohibited in all territories north of the line and protected in all territories south of the line.

At Lincoln's request, congressional Republicans voted against Crittenden's Compromise. Accepting slavery in any of the territories, Lincoln argued, "acknowledges that slavery has equal rights with liberty, and surrenders all we have contended for."

234 CHAPTER 6 Sectional Conflict Intensifies

DIFFERENTIATED INSTRUCTION

Gifted and Talented Ask students to use library and Internet resources to research information about the stated political platforms and principles of the 1854–1876 Republican Party and the Republican Party today. Based on their research, have students write a three- to five-page report comparing the party then and now. **L3**

➤ Refer to *Inclusion for the High School Social Studies Classroom Strategies and Activities* in the TCR.

Finally, in a last-ditch effort to reverse secession, delegates from 21 states held a peace conference in Washington, D.C., in February 1861. No representatives showed up from the secessionist states, however, and the conference achieved little.

Founding the Confederacy On the same day the peace conference opened, delegates from the seceding states met at a convention in Montgomery, Alabama. There, on February 8, they declared themselves to be a new nation—the Confederate States of America, also known as the Confederacy. They drafted a frame of government based largely on the U.S. Constitution but with some important changes. The Confederate Constitution acknowledged the independence of each state, guaranteed slavery in Confederate territory, banned protective tariffs, and limited the president to a single six-year term.

The convention delegates chose former Mississippi senator **Jefferson Davis** to be president. In his inaugural address, Davis declared, "The time for compromise has now passed. The South is determined to . . . make all who oppose her smell Southern powder and feel Southern steel." He then called on the remaining Southern states to join the Confederacy.

Jefferson Davis

✓**Reading Check** **Summarizing** What measures were taken to try and reverse the South's secession?

The Civil War Begins

In the months between his election and the time he took office, Lincoln had watched anxiously as the nation fell apart. In his inaugural speech on March 4, 1861, Lincoln addressed the seceding states directly. He repeated his commitment not to interfere with slavery where it already existed, but insisted that "the Union of these States is perpetual." He did not threaten to attack the seceded states, but he did announce his intention to "hold, occupy, and possess" federal property in those states. Lincoln also made an eloquent plea for reconciliation:

❝In *your* hands, my dissatisfied fellow-countrymen, and not in *mine* is the momentous issue of civil war. The government will not assail *you.* You can have no conflict, without yourselves being the aggressors. . . . We must not be enemies. Though passion may have strained, it must not break our bonds of affection.❞

—from Lincoln's Inaugural Address, March 4, 1861

Fort Sumter Falls In April Lincoln announced that he intended to send needed supplies to **Fort Sumter** in Charleston Harbor, one of the few federal military bases that Southerners had not already seized. The Confederacy now faced a dilemma. To tolerate U.S. troops in the South's most vital Atlantic harbor seemed unacceptable for a sovereign nation. However, firing on the supply ship would undoubtedly provoke war with the United States.

President Jefferson Davis decided to demand the surrender of Fort Sumter before the supply ship arrived, but U.S. Army Major Robert Anderson stood fast. Confederate forces then bombarded Fort Sumter for 33 hours on April 12 and 13, until Anderson and his exhausted men gave up. No one had been killed, but the Civil War had begun.

GEOGRAPHY

Hanging On to the Border States After the fall of Fort Sumter, President Lincoln called for 75,000 volunteers to serve in the military for 90 days. Lincoln's action created a crisis in the Upper South. Many people in those states did not want to secede, but they were not willing to take up arms against fellow Southerners. Between April 17 and June 8, 1861, four more states chose to leave the Union—Virginia, Arkansas, North Carolina, and Tennessee. The Confederate Congress then established Richmond, Virginia, as the capital.

With the Upper South gone, Lincoln could not afford to lose the slaveholding border states as well. Delaware seemed safe, but Lincoln worried about Kentucky, Missouri, and particularly Maryland. Virginia's secession had placed a Confederate state

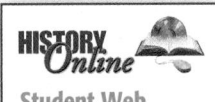

Student Web Activity Visit the *American Republic Since 1877* Web site at tarvol2.glencoe.com and click on *Student Web Activities— Chapter 6* for an activity on sectional conflicts.

✓**Reading Check**

Answer: Crittenden's Compromise proposed, peace conference held in Washington, D.C., in February 1861

Creating a Thematic Map Have students create a map that John J. Crittenden could have used as a visual aid when he presented his compromise to Congress. **L2**

📁 Use the rubric for creating a map, display, or chart on pages 65–66 in the *Performance Assessment Activities and Rubrics.*

Objectives and answers to the student activity can be found in the **Web Activity Lesson Plan** at tarvol2.glencoe.com.

3 ASSESS

Assign Section 3 Assessment as homework or as an in-class activity

💿 Have students use the **Interactive Tutor Self-Assessment CD-ROM.**

L1/ELL

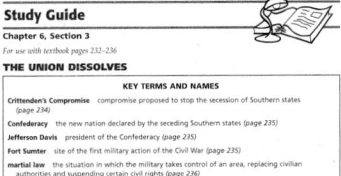

Reading Essentials and Study Guide 6–3

Name_____ Date_____ Class_____

Study Guide

Chapter 6, Section 3
For use with textbook pages 232–236

THE UNION DISSOLVES

KEY TERMS AND NAMES

Crittenden's Compromise compromise proposed to stop the secession of Southern states (page 234)

Confederacy the new nation declared by the seceding Southern states (page 235)

Jefferson Davis president of the Confederacy (page 235)

Fort Sumter site of the first military action of the Civil War (page 235)

martial law the situation in which the military takes control of an area, replacing civilian authorities and suspending certain civil rights (page 236)

INTERDISCIPLINARY CONNECTIONS ACTIVITY

Geography Provide students with an outline map of the United States with the current state boundaries. Have students create a thematic map by labeling and shading in one color all the states that were part of the Union on June 8, 1861, and labeling and shading in another color all the states that had seceded. Then have students shade the remaining area and label it "Territories." **L1**

L2

Section Quiz 6–3

Name	Date	Class

★ **Chapter 6** | **Score** |

Section Quiz 6-3

DIRECTIONS: Matching Match each item in Column A with the items in Column B
Write the correct letters in the blanks. *(10 points each)*

Column A | **Column B**
___ 1. military rule | A. South Carolina
___ 2. chosen to be president of the Confederate States of America | B. martial law
___ 3. first state to secede from the Union | C. Harpers Ferry
___ 4. site of John Brown's raid that was a turning point for the South | D. Virginia
___ 5. state where the Confederate capital was established | E. Jefferson Davis

DIRECTIONS: Multiple Choice In the blank at the left, write the letter of the choice that best completes the statement or answers the question. *(10 points each)*

✓ Reading Check

Answer: If Maryland seceded, Washington, D.C. would be completely surrounded by Confederate territory.

Graphic Organizer → Skills

Answer: Answers will vary, but should be supported.

Graphic Organizer Skills Practice

Ask: What type of legislation resulted from the Civil War? *(civil rights laws and legislation abolishing slavery)*

Reteach

Ask students to describe the various attempts to find a compromise between the demands of the North and the South.

Enrich

Have students create a chart listing the states in one of three categories: Free States, Slave States that Seceded, Slave States that did not Secede.

HISTORY Online

Study Central™ provides summaries, interactive games, and online graphic organizers to help students review section content.

4 CLOSE

Ask students to briefly explain why the Civil War began.

236

---

across the Potomac River from the nation's capital. If Maryland joined the South, Washington, D.C., would be surrounded by Confederate territory.

To prevent Maryland's secession, Lincoln imposed martial law—military rule—in Baltimore, where angry mobs had already attacked federal troops. Under martial law, anyone supporting secession could be arrested and held without trial. Although many people objected to this suspension of their rights, Maryland stayed in the Union.

In the border states of Kentucky and Missouri, fighting erupted. Kentucky initially declared neutrality in the conflict, but when Confederate troops occupied part of Kentucky, the state declared war on the Confederacy, and Lincoln sent troops to help. In Missouri, despite strong public support for the Confederacy, the state convention voted to stay in the Union. A struggle then erupted between convention leaders who organized a pro-Union government and secessionists led by the governor.

In the end, Missouri stayed in the Union with the support of federal forces. There and elsewhere, the war shattered old loyalties and made enemies of former friends. For the next several years, the bloody war between the states divided Americans and resulted in hundreds of thousands of casualties.

✓ Reading Check **Explaining** Why was Maryland important to the Union?

Causes and Effects of the Civil War

Causes

- Disagreement over the legality, morality, and politics of slavery
- Kansas-Nebraska Act sparked violence in Kansas.
- *Dred Scott* ruling voided any limitations on expansion of slavery.
- John Brown's raid on Harpers Ferry polarized North and South.
- Southern states seceded from the Union.
- Confederates attacked Fort Sumter in South Carolina.

Effects

- Slavery was outlawed in the United States.
- Southern states rebuilt their economy.
- African Americans gained citizenship and voting rights.
- The first U.S. civil rights laws were passed.

Graphic Organizer → Skills

Mounting sectional tensions erupted into open warfare in 1861.

Analyzing What do you think was the most important cause of the Civil War? Why?

HISTORY Online
Study Central™ To review this section, go to tarvol2.glencoe.com and click on **Study Central™**.

SECTION 3 ASSESSMENT

Checking for Understanding
1. **Define:** Confederacy, martial law.
2. **Identify:** Crittenden's Compromise, Jefferson Davis, Fort Sumter.

Reviewing Facts
3. **State** who the president of the Confederacy was.

Reviewing Themes
4. **Civic Rights and Responsibilities** Secessionists believed they had the right to break from the Union, just as the American colonists felt they had the right to declare independence from Britain. How were the two situations similar? How were they different?

Critical Thinking
5. **Evaluating** Although Confederates fired the first shots of the Civil War, Jefferson Davis argued that the North was to blame for having provoked the Fort Sumter attack. In your opinion, which side began the war? Explain.
6. **Categorizing** Use a graphic organizer similar to the one below to list the candidates in the 1860 election and their political positions.

Party	Candidate	Position
Northern Democrats		
Southern Democrats		
Constitutional Unionists		
Republicans		

Analyzing Visuals
7. **Examining Maps** Study the map on page 233 showing the results of the presidential election in 1860. Which candidate won the border states between the North and the Deep South?
8. **Analyzing Political Cartoons** Study the cartoon on page 234 about the presidential election of 1860. What does the use of a baseball comparison imply about politics?

Writing About History
9. **Persuasive Writing** Imagine you are an adviser to President Lincoln, and you have just heard about the firing on Fort Sumter. Write a brief report for the president, advising him on what steps to take next.

236 CHAPTER 6 Sectional Conflict Intensifies

SECTION 3 ASSESSMENT ANSWERS

1. Terms are in blue.
2. Crittenden's Compromise *(p. 234)*, Jefferson Davis *(p. 235)*, Fort Sumter *(p. 235)*
3. Jefferson Davis
4. Similarity: both believed their rights had been violated; difference: South had active role in U.S. government while American colonists did not
5. Students should state specific reasons for their point of view.
6. Candidates' positions should match the text.
7. John Bell
8. There is a clear winner and loser in an election and in baseball. Both are contests and there are strategies involved in each endeavor.
9. Students' reports will vary. Reports should include recommendations for action.

Frederick Douglass was born into slavery in Maryland in 1818. During the course of his incredible life, he escaped from slavery and eventually became renowned for eloquent lectures and writings for the causes of abolition and liberty. One of his most famous works is his autobiography about growing up under the shadow of slavery. In the following excerpt, Douglass is around eight years old, and Mrs. Auld, the wife of his slaveholder, has begun to teach him to read. Mr. Auld discovers what his wife has been doing, and his reaction causes young Frederick to decide to learn to read on his own, no matter what.

Read to Discover

Why did some slaveholders not want the enslaved to learn to read?

Reader's Dictionary

sentiments: feelings

revelation: discovery

conscious: aware

diligently: with great effort

from Narrative of the Life of Frederick Douglass

by Frederick Douglass

"Now," said [Mr. Auld], "if you teach that [boy] how to read, there would be no keeping him. It would forever unfit him to be a slave. He would at once become unmanageable, and of no value to his master. As to himself, it could do him no good, but a great deal of harm. It would make him discontented and unhappy." These words sank deep into my heart, stirred up sentiments within that lay slumbering, and called into existence an entirely new train of thought. It was a new and special revelation, explaining dark and mysterious things, with which my youthful understanding had struggled, but struggled in vain. . . . From that moment, I understood the pathway from slavery to freedom. It was just what I wanted, and I got it at a time when I least expected it. Whilst I was saddened by the thought of losing the aid of my kind mistress, I was gladdened by the invaluable instruction which, by the merest accident, I had gained from my master. Though conscious of the difficulty of learning without a teacher, I set out with high hope, and a fixed purpose, at whatever cost of trouble, to learn to read. . . . That which to [Mr. Auld] was a great evil, to be carefully shunned, was to me a

great good, to be diligently sought; and the argument which he so warmly urged, against my learning to read, only served to inspire me with a desire and determination to learn. In learning to read, I owe almost as much to the bitter opposition of my master, as to the kindly aid of my mistress. I acknowledge the benefit of both.

Analyzing Literature

1. **Recall** Why did Mr. Auld oppose the idea of Douglass learning to read?
2. **Interpret** What do you think Douglass means when he speaks of "a revelation, explaining dark and mysterious things"?
3. **Evaluate and Connect** How would you feel if someone had forbidden you to learn to read?

Interdisciplinary Activity

Art Design a poster promoting literacy. Include reasons why everyone should learn to read and write and get an education.

Block Schedule

Team Teaching This selection from *Narrative of the Life of Frederick Douglass* can be presented in conjunction with English or Language Arts.

Read to Discover

Answer: If enslaved people could read, they would think for themselves and question their status.

Reinforcing Vocabulary

Ask students to use each of the terms in a sentence that is not related to the reading.

Historical Connection

Narrative of the Life of Frederick Douglass was the first of two volumes of Frederick Douglass's autobiography. Douglass felt the need to tell his life story because white abolitionists could never convey a complete picture of slavery.

Portfolio Writing Activity

Ask students to write a short essay on Douglass's attitude toward education.

Refer to tarvol2.glencoe.com for additional Glencoe Literature titles, lesson plans, and study guides related to this unit.

Answers to Analyzing Literature

1. It would make him forever unfit to be a slave.
2. possible answer: why education had been denied to him
3. possible answer: frustrated that others could do something important that you could not

Interdisciplinary Activity
Posters should support reading and education in highly visual and creative ways.

1 FOCUS

This feature discusses the reasons for the creation of the Declaration of Independence.

Why It Matters

Ask students to discuss why they think the Declaration of Independence was created, and how they think it encouraged the Southern cause.

2 TEACH

Creating a List On the board write Basic Rights of Individuals that the Government Should Respect. Have the class brainstorm ideas they believe belong on the list of individual rights. Use this list as a starting point for a discussion about the Southern and Northern points of view about government and individual rights. **L1**

Predicting Consequences Have students form small groups to discuss the quote by Jefferson Davis that appears on page 238. Ask the groups to also discuss the likely consequences of dissolving government today. Have the groups share their ideas with the entire class. Then ask: Did Jefferson Davis really intend to abolish the government? Why or why not? *(Students should recognize that he intended to abolish one form and replace it with another; he was not advocating anarchy.)* **L2**

The Declaration of Independence

Why It Matters As late as 1860, Jefferson Davis was delivering speeches calling for peace and discouraging Southern secessionists. In 1861, however, delegates from seceding states met in Montgomery and elected Davis president of the Confederacy. Despite his fears about the South's ability to win the war, Davis spoke eloquently in his inaugural address about the justice of the Southern cause. Like many Southerners, Davis believed they were following the principle on which the nation was founded: that people should not have to live under a government that infringes on their basic rights.

The North's point of view was quite different: Southerners were destroying the nation by placing their authority above that of the federal government. The origins of this feud trace back to the Declaration of Independence. In crafting this document, the Founders advocated an entirely new relationship between a government and its citizens. They prompted a continuing debate over how to balance individual and states' rights with the power of a central authority.

Steps to . . . the Declaration of Independence

Over many centuries, there was little development in political theory that addressed the relationship between the individual and the government. The changes that came about after the period known as the Enlightenment culminated in the 1700s with the American Declaration of Independence.

Government by and for the People With very few exceptions, the world knew only monarchies and absolute rulers at the time the Declaration of Independence was written.

Drawing from new political theories, the Declaration put forth a different idea: governments derive "their just powers from the consent of the governed." In other words, governments exist to serve the people.

The main function of a government, the document declared, was to protect the "unalienable rights" of its citizens—the most important of which were the rights to "Life, Liberty and the pursuit of Happiness." When a government failed to live up to this obligation, the people had the right to "throw off such Government, and to provide new Guards for their future security."

In shaping this political philosophy, the Founders looked to the works of many people, including such classical thinkers as Aristotle, who had identified

> *"Our present condition . . . illustrates the American idea that governments rest upon the consent of the governed, and that it is the right of the people to alter or abolish governments whenever they become destructive to the ends for which they were established."*
>
> —*Jefferson Davis, 1861*

238

EXTENDING THE CONTENT

Secession Most people associate secession with the Civil War, but threats of secession abounded during and after the Revolutionary War. While the fighting raged, Ethan Allen schemed to make Vermont a province of Canada, although he may have been trying to force Congress to recognize Vermont as a separate state, rather than a territory of New York. At the same time, James Wilkinson, a Revolutionary officer working secretly for Spain, tried to annex Kentucky to Spain.

Signing of the Declaration of Independence in Philadelphia

three forms of government—democracy, oligarchy, and monarchy. The Founders believed the best government would combine all three forms of government and balance them against each other. The Constitution partly reflects these ideas. The president received powers similar to a monarch; the Senate was intended to protect the elite; and the House of Representatives, elected by the people, was the most democratic. The Founders also looked to the ideas of eighteenth-century Enlightenment thinkers. The greatest influence on American thinking, however, was probably the English philosopher John Locke. Locke's writings promoted the idea that power in society rested ultimately with its citizens.

A List of Grievances In declaring their independence from Britain, colonial leaders argued that the British government had failed to live up to its obligations to the colonists. In a section that has become known as the list of grievances, the Declaration of Independence spells out precisely how the British king had suppressed the rights of the colonists and failed to look out for their interests.

These 27 charges against the king were patterned after several documents, including the English Bill of Rights (1689), which criticized various actions of the king. Ideas for the Declaration's list of grievances also came from several papers of the Stamp Act Congress and the First and Second Continental Congress.

A Debate Over the Constitution The underlying belief of the Declaration of Independence was that government derives its power from the people. This core idea led to a great debate in 1787 over whether to ratify the U.S. Constitution. Those who supported the Constitution, known as Federalists, favored a strong central government in order to create a more organized and unified nation. Antifederalists, those who opposed the Constitution, feared that the creation of a strong central government eventually would lead to

the same kind of tyranny that the colonists had endured under Britain.

In particular, the Antifederalists criticized the fact that the proposed Constitution did not contain a bill of rights to protect the personal liberties of the people. The absence of such protections, argued one Antifederalist leader, "put Civil Liberty and happiness of the people at the Mercy of Rulers who may possess the great unguarded powers given."

Promoting Limited Government In the end, the Federalists agreed to add a bill of rights to the Constitution. The Bill of Rights is the name given to the first ten amendments to the Constitution. These amendments guarantee Americans protection of their basic civil rights, some of which they had demanded in the Declaration of Independence. These included the right to oppose or petition the government for change, the right to a trial by jury, and the right to refuse the quartering of soldiers.

In various other ways, the U.S. Constitution sought to limit the power of government and promote the rights of the people. It created three distinct branches of government: the executive, the legislative, and the judicial. The colonists distrusted concentrated political power, and so the separation of power among the branches was meant to prevent any such concentration.

To reinforce the Founders' goal of limited government, the Constitution also implemented a system of checks and balances among the branches so that no one branch could become too powerful. It also granted members of Congress only a certain number of years in office before they had to run again for election. These limits were meant to prevent any one person or groups of persons from gaining too much political power over the nation.

Checking for Understanding

1. According to the Declaration of Independence, what is the main duty of a government?
2. How did Aristotle's ideas influence the Founders' approach to the Constitution?

Critical Thinking

1. How is the U.S. Constitution a compromise between the Federalists and Antifederalists?
2. Do you agree or disagree that the secession of the Southern states marked a second American Revolution? Explain.

---

3 ASSESS

Assign the feature assessment questions as homework or as an in-class activity.

4 CLOSE

Tell students that the lines in the Declaration of Independence that read, ". . . whenever any Form of Government becomes destructive to these ends, it is the Right of the People to alter or to abolish it. . ." was considered an act of treason by the British government. Americans, of course, considered it justified. Conduct a class discussion about the situations in which students think the alteration or abolishment of a government is justified. Then ask if the South had justifiable reasons. Discuss students' points of view on this subject.

Checking for Understanding

1. to protect the rights of citizens
2. Aristotle identified three forms of government: monarchy, oligarchy, and democracy. The Founders created the presidency, Senate, and House of Representatives to combine these three forms into one government.

Critical Thinking

1. By including the Bill of Rights, the Constitution balances the rights of government and the rights of the people.
2. Answers will vary. Students should support their point of view using reasoning related to the Declaration of Independence.

MindJogger Videoquiz
Use the **MindJogger Videoquiz** to review Chapter 6 content.

 Available in DVD

Reviewing Key Terms
Students' answers will vary. The pages where the words appear in the text are shown in parentheses.

1. **popular sovereignty** (p. 219)
2. **secession** (p. 220)
3. **Underground Railroad** (p. 221)
4. **transcontinental railroad** (p. 223)
5. **referendum** (p. 229)
6. **insurrection** (p. 231)
7. **Confederacy** (p. 235)
8. **martial law** (p. 236)

Reviewing Key Facts

9. Harriet Tubman (p. 221), John Brown (p. 231), Fort Sumter (p. 235)
10. California admitted to the Union as a free state; Texas border dispute resolved with New Mexico; slave trade, but not slavery, abolished in the District of Columbia; federal enforcement of the new Fugitive Slave Act, Congress not allowed to interfere with interstate slave trade
11. When California entered the Union as a free state, the slaveholding states became the minority in the Senate; Southerners feared losing power.
12. They considered it immoral.
13. Republicans denounced John Brown's raid and reaffirmed the rights of Southern states to preserve slavery within their borders.
14. Northerners viewed John Brown as a martyr. Southerners feared that Northerners would actively try to murder slaveholders. This polarized the two sides.
15. Douglas and Breckinridge split the Democratic vote.

Reviewing Key Terms
On a sheet of paper, use each of these terms in a sentence.

1. popular sovereignty
2. secession
3. Underground Railroad
4. transcontinental railroad
5. referendum
6. insurrection
7. Confederacy
8. martial law

Chapter Summary

Key Events of the 1850s:

- California entered Union as a free state, giving free states a Senate majority
- Fugitive Slave Act passed to help Southerners recover enslaved people who escaped to North; act caused outrage in North
- *Uncle Tom's Cabin* published, angered many Southerners
- Kansas-Nebraska Act passed

Kansas-Nebraska Act heightened tensions:

- Angered Northerners by repealing Missouri Compromise
- Popular sovereignty regarding slavery issue led to violence in "Bleeding Kansas"
- Republican Party formed by former Whigs and members of Free-Soil Party
- *Dred Scott* decision by Southern-dominated Supreme Court angered Northerners
- Debates in Senate over Kansas led to caning of Charles Sumner
- Events in Kansas angered John Brown, who then raided Harpers Ferry

Election of 1860:

- Democratic Party split between North and South
- Republicans nominated eventual winner Abraham Lincoln
- Southern states established Confederacy in February 1861
- Fort Sumter fired upon in April 1861, starting the Civil War

240   CHAPTER 6   Sectional Conflict Intensifies

Reviewing Key Facts

9. **Identify:** Harriet Tubman, John Brown, Fort Sumter.
10. What were the main elements of the Compromise of 1850?
11. Why did Southern politicians begin talking about secession?
12. Why did Northerners resist the Fugitive Slave Act?
13. How did the Republican Party appeal to voters in the presidential election of 1860?
14. Why is John Brown's Harpers Ferry raid considered a turning point on the road to war?
15. Why was Lincoln able to win the 1860 election?
16. What efforts were made to prevent the outbreak of war?
17. What border states did Lincoln want to keep in the Union?

Critical Thinking

18. **Analyzing Themes: Civic Rights and Responsibilities** How did the Fugitive Slave Act and the *Dred Scott* decision affect formerly enslaved African Americans living in the North?
19. **Evaluating** Why did many members of Congress support popular sovereignty?
20. **Organizing** Use a graphic organizer similar to the one below to list the main events that pushed the nation into civil war.

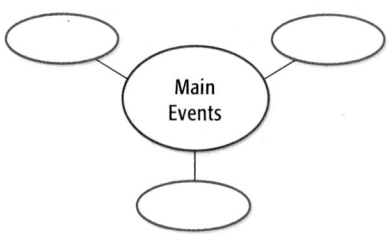

21. **Interpreting Primary Sources** Many people have written essays on the causes of the Civil War. Edward A. Pollard of Virginia was the editor of the *Daily Richmond Examiner* during the Civil War. He wrote a book, *The Lost Cause,* about the Civil War from a Southern point of view. Read the excerpt and answer the questions that follow.

❝In the ante-revolutionary period, the differences between the populations of the Northern and Southern colonies had already been strongly developed. The early colonists did not bear with them from the mother-country to the shores of the New World any greater degree of congeniality than existed among them at

16. Crittenden Compromise and a peace conference
17. Kentucky, Maryland, and Missouri

Critical Thinking

18. Many were captured and sent back to slavery. Many defied the act and helped slaves escape to freedom. All were probably angered by them.

19. They believed in people's rights to self-determination, and they wanted to preserve the Union.
20. Kansas-Nebraska Act, *Dred Scott* decision, John Brown's raid on Harpers Ferry
21. **a.** when the first colonists immigrated; **b.** They came from different social classes and different religious and political backgrounds.

Self-Check Quiz

Visit the *American Republic Since 1877* Web site at tarvol2.glencoe.com and click on *Self-Check Quizzes—Chapter 6* to assess your knowledge of chapter content.

home. They had come not only from different stocks of population, but from different feuds in religion and politics. There could be no congeniality between . . . New England, and the . . . South. . . .99

—from *The Lost Cause*

a. According to Pollard, when did the differences between the North and South begin?

b. According to Pollard, what caused the differences between Northerners and Southerners?

Practicing Skills

22. **Predicting Consequences** Review the skill on predicting consequences on page 225. Then read the following statements and predict three consequences for each. Rank the three consequences in order of most likely to occur to least likely to occur.

   a. A person elected to a political office does not support the issues he or she claimed to represent while campaigning for election.

   b. Engineers develop an effective, efficient automobile powered by solar energy.

Writing Activity

23. **Portfolio Writing: Mock Peace Convention** Hold a mock peace convention to try and reverse the secession of the Southern states. As a class, create a convention in which students are delegates from Union or secessionist states. Students should write a position paper for their assigned state proposing an idea that could help the states compromise. Write a summary of the proceedings and place it in your portfolio.

Chapter Activity

24. **Technology Activity: Developing a Multimedia Presentation** Use the Internet and other sources to find a map showing the routes of the Underground Railroad, photos of conductors and fugitive slaves, and primary source documents from conductors and fugitive slaves, such as diaries or journals. Create a multimedia report about the Underground Railroad. Present your report to the class.

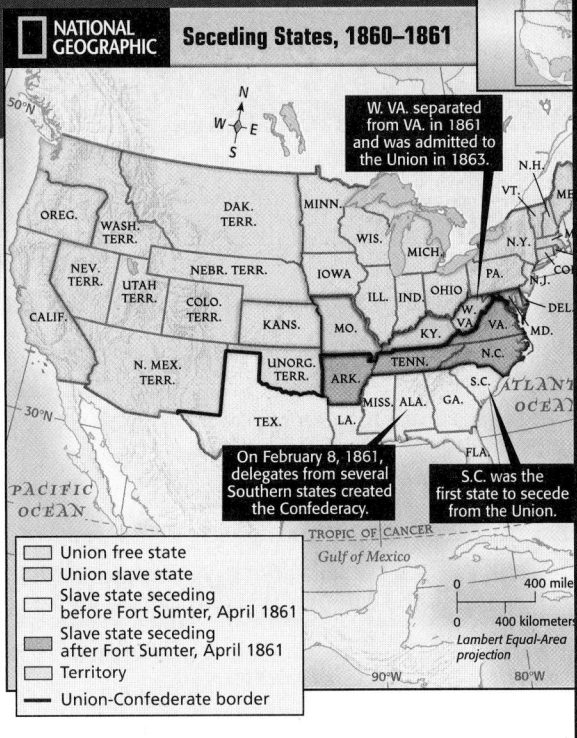

NATIONAL GEOGRAPHIC **Seceding States, 1860–1861**

W. VA. separated from VA. in 1861 and was admitted to the Union in 1863.

On February 8, 1861, delegates from several Southern states created the Confederacy.

S.C. was the first state to secede from the Union.

- Union free state
- Union slave state
- Slave state seceding before Fort Sumter, April 1861
- Slave state seceding after Fort Sumter, April 1861
- Territory
- Union-Confederate border

Lambert Equal-Area projection

Geography and History

25. The map above shows seceding states from 1860 to 1861. Study the map and answer the questions below.

   a. **Interpreting Maps** Which slave states remained in the Union after the Fort Sumter attack?

   b. **Applying Geography Skills** Which states did not secede until after the Fort Sumter attack?

Standardized Test Practice

Many Northerners saw John Brown as a martyr to the cause of the abolition of slavery. Southerners were afraid of John Brown because they felt he might

A increase the chances of electing a Republican president.

B destroy the Underground Railroad.

C convince Native Americans to fight against the South in the Civil War.

D encourage a slave revolt.

Test-Taking Tip: Look for clues in the question to help you find the answer. For example, if John Brown believed in the *abolition of slavery,* it is unlikely that he would have destroyed the Underground Railroad (answer B).

CHAPTER 6 Sectional Conflict Intensifies **241**

Have students visit the Web site at tarvol2.glencoe.com to review Chapter 6 and take the Self-Check Quiz.

Geography and History

25. **a.** Missouri, Kentucky, West Virginia, Maryland, Delaware; **b.** Virginia, North Carolina, Tennessee, Arkansas

Standardized Test Practice

Answer: D

Test-Taking Tip: Explain to students that paying attention to the precise wording of a question often gives them enough information to answer the question, or at least enough to make an intelligent guess.

Bonus Question ?

Ask: Who were Simon Legree and Tom in *Uncle Tom's Cabin*? (*Tom is the enslaved hero of the tale; Simon Legree is the evil slaveholder.*)

Practicing Skills

22. **a.** possible answers: 1. loses support of electorate, 2. people don't really object to changed point of view, 3. people support changed point of view; **b.** 1. market for cars explodes, 2. the price of gasoline goes down, 3. pollution declines

Writing Activity

23. Students' position papers should reflect their assigned position and should include attempts to find a compromise position.

Chapter Activity

24. Students' reports should include a variety of media, have a clear focus, and be well researched.

Chapter 7 Resources

Timesaving Tools

TeacherWorks™ All-In-One Planner and Resource Center

- **Interactive Teacher Edition** Access your Teacher Wraparound Edition and your classroom resources with a few easy clicks.
- **Interactive Lesson Planner** Planning has never been easier! Organize your week, month, semester, or year with all the lesson helps you need to make teaching creative, timely, and relevant.

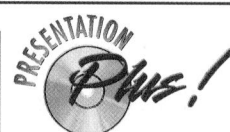

Use Glencoe's **Presentation Plus!** multimedia teacher tool to easily present dynamic lessons that visually excite your students. Using Microsoft PowerPoint® you can customize the presentations to create your own personalized lessons.

TEACHING TRANSPARENCIES

Graphic Organizer 7 L2

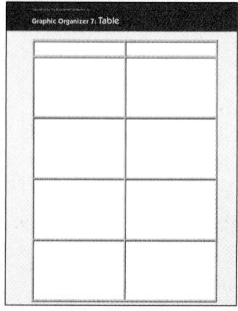

Why It Matters Chapter Transparency 7 L2

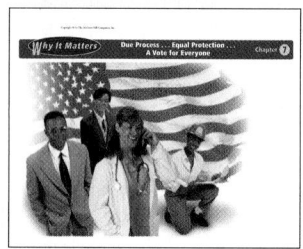

APPLICATION AND ENRICHMENT

Linking Past and Present Activity 7 L2

Enrichment Activity 7 L3

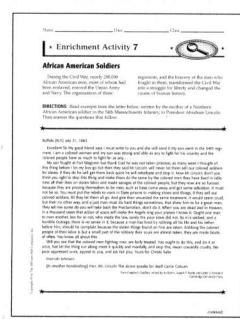

Primary Source Reading 7 L2

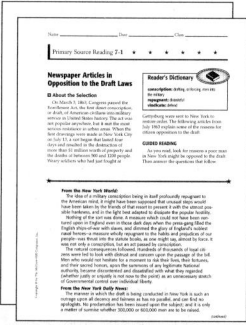

REVIEW AND REINFORCEMENT

Reteaching Activity 7 L1

Vocabulary Activity 7 L1

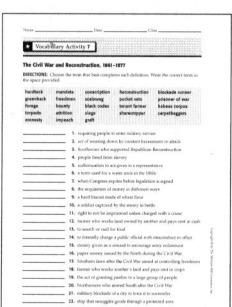

Time Line Activity 7 L2

Critical Thinking Skills Activity 7 L2

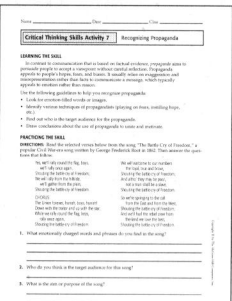

Meeting NCSS Standards

Local Standards

The following standards are covered in Chapter 7:

Section 1	V	Individuals, Groups, and Institutions: B, C, D
Section 2	III	People, Places, and Environments: B, E, I
Section 3	III	People, Places, and Environments: B, E, I
Section 4	V	Individuals, Groups, and Institutions: A, B, C, F, G
Section 5	VII	Production, Distribution, and Consumption: A, D

Chapter 7 Resources

Chapter 7 Test Form A L2

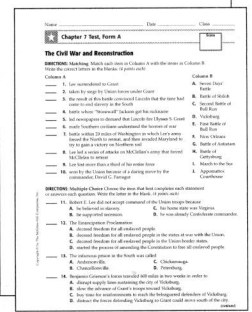

Chapter 7 Test Form B L2

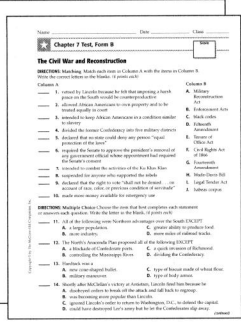

Standardized Test Practice Workbook Activity 7 L2

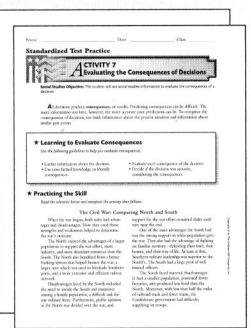

Performance Assessment Activities and Rubrics 7 L1/ELL

ExamView® Pro Testmaker CD-ROM

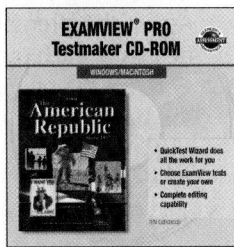

MULTIMEDIA

- Vocabulary PuzzleMaker CD-ROM
- Interactive Tutor Self-Assessment CD-ROM
- ExamView® Pro Testmaker CD-ROM
- Audio Program
- American History Primary Source Documents Library CD-ROM
- MindJogger Videoquiz
- Presentation Plus! CD-ROM
- TeacherWorks™ CD-ROM
- Interactive Student Edition CD-ROM
- Glencoe Skillbuilder Interactive Workbook CD-ROM, Level 2
- The *American Republic Since 1877* Video Program
- American Music: Hits Through History
- American Music: Cultural Traditions

SPANISH RESOURCES

The following Spanish language materials are available:

- Spanish Reading Essentials and Study Guide
- Spanish Guided Reading Activities
- Spanish Reteaching Activities
- Spanish Quizzes and Tests
- Spanish Vocabulary Activities
- Spanish Summaries
- The Declaration of Independence and United States Constitution Spanish Translation

The following videotape programs are available from Glencoe as supplements to Chapter 7:

- **American Civil War** (ISBN 0-7670-0-102-8)
- **Images of the Civil War** (ISBN 1-56501-171-6)

To order, call Glencoe at 1-800-334-7344. To find classroom resources to accompany many of these videos, check the following home pages:
A&E Television: www.aande.com
The History Channel: www.historychannel.com

Use our Web site for additional resources. All essential content is covered in the Student Edition.

You and your students can visit tarvol2.glencoe.com, the Web site companion to the **American Republic Since 1877**. This innovative integration of electronic and print media offers your students a wealth of opportunities. The student text directs students to the Web site for the following options:

- **Chapter Overviews**
- **Student Web Activities**
- **Self-Check Quizzes**
- **Textbook Updates**

Answers to the student Web activities are provided for you in the **Web Activity Lesson Plans.** Additional Web resources and Interactive Tutor Puzzles are also available.

Chapter 7 Resources

SECTION RESOURCES

Daily Objectives	Reproducible Resources	Multimedia Resources
SECTION 1 **The Opposing Sides** 1. Assess the strengths and weaknesses of each region's economy. 2. Contrast the political situations of the Union and the Confederacy.	Reproducible Lesson Plan 7–1 Daily Lecture and Discussion Notes 7–1 Guided Reading Activity 7–1* Section Quiz 7–1* Reading Essentials and Study Guide 7–1* Performance Assessment Activities and Rubrics	Daily Focus Skills Transparency 7–1 American Art & Architecture Interactive Tutor Self-Assessment CD-ROM ExamView® Pro Testmaker CD-ROM* Presentation Plus! CD-ROM TeacherWorks™ CD-ROM
SECTION 2 **The Early Stages** 1. Describe the progress of the war in the West and the East. 2. Evaluate the soldiers' wartime experiences.	Reproducible Lesson Plan 7–2 Daily Lecture and Discussion Notes 7–2 Guided Reading Activity 7–2* Section Quiz 7–2* Reading Essentials and Study Guide 7–2* Performance Assessment Activities and Rubrics	Daily Focus Skills Transparency 7–2 American Art & Architecture Interactive Tutor Self-Assessment CD-ROM ExamView® Pro Testmaker CD-ROM* Presentation Plus! CD-ROM Skillbuilder Interactive Workbook, Level 2
SECTION 3 **The Turning Point** 1. Evaluate the importance of events at Vicksburg and Gettysburg. 2. Discuss Lee's surrender and the events of the war's aftermath.	Reproducible Lesson Plan 7–3 Daily Lecture and Discussion Notes 7–3 Guided Reading Activity 7–3* Section Quiz 7–3* Reading Essentials and Study Guide 7–3* Performance Assessment Activities and Rubrics	Daily Focus Skills Transparency 7–3 Interactive Tutor Self-Assessment CD-ROM ExamView® Pro Testmaker CD-ROM* Presentation Plus! CD-ROM TeacherWorks™ CD-ROM Audio Program ABCNews Interactive™: Historic America Electronic Field Trips
SECTION 4 **Reconstruction Begins** 1. Discuss life in the South immediately after the war. 2. Describe the major features of congressional Reconstruction and its political impact.	Reproducible Lesson Plan 7–4 Daily Lecture and Discussion Notes 7–4 Guided Reading Activity 7–4* Section Quiz 7–4* Reading Essentials and Study Guide 7–4* Performance Assessment Activities and Rubrics Supreme Court Case Studies	Daily Focus Skills Transparency 7–4 Interactive Tutor Self-Assessment CD-ROM ExamView® Pro Testmaker CD-ROM* Presentation Plus! CD-ROM TeacherWorks™ CD-ROM Audio Program
SECTION 5 **Reconstruction and Republican Rule** 1. Discuss Republican rule in the South during Reconstruction. 2. Explain how Reconstruction ended, and contrast the New South and the Old South.	Reproducible Lesson Plan 7–5 Daily Lecture and Discussion Notes 7–5 Guided Reading Activity 7–5* Section Quiz 7–5* Reading Essentials and Study Guide 7–5* Performance Assessment Activities and Rubrics Interpreting Political Cartoons	Daily Focus Skills Transparency 7–5 Interactive Tutor Self-Assessment CD-ROM ExamView® Pro Testmaker CD-ROM* Presentation Plus! CD-ROM TeacherWorks™ CD-ROM Audio Program American Music: Cultural Traditions

0:00 OUT OF TIME?
Assign the Chapter 7 **Reading Essentials and Study Guide.**

*Also Available in Spanish

 Printed Materials   Transparency   CD-ROM   DVD

 Poster   Music Program   Audio Program   Videocassette

NATIONAL GEOGRAPHIC Teacher's Corner

INDEX TO NATIONAL GEOGRAPHIC MAGAZINE

The following articles relate to this chapter.

- "Colonial Florida Fort Recalls a Shining Moment in Black History," February 1997
- "The Cruelest Commerce: African Slave Trade," September 1992
- "C.S.S. *Alabama*," December 1994

NATIONAL GEOGRAPHIC SOCIETY PRODUCTS

To order the following, call National Geographic at 1-800-368-2728:

- *Historical Atlas of the United States*
- *Millennium in Maps Series: Battlefields of the Civil War*

NGS ONLINE

Access National Geographic's Web site for current events, atlas updates, activities, links, interactive features, and archives.

www.nationalgeographic.com

MEETING SPECIAL NEEDS

In addition to the Differentiated Instruction strategies found in each section, the following resources are also suitable for your special needs students:

- *ExamView® Pro Testmaker CD-ROM* allows teachers to tailor tests by reducing answer choices.
- The *Audio Program* includes the entire narrative of the student edition so that less-proficient readers can listen to the words as they read them.
- The *Reading Essentials and Study Guide* provides the same content as the student edition but is written two grade levels below the textbook.

KEY TO ABILITY LEVELS

Teaching strategies have been coded.

L1 BASIC activities for all students
L2 AVERAGE activities for average to above-average students
L3 CHALLENGING activities for above-average students
ELL ENGLISH LANGUAGE LEARNER activities

From the Classroom of...

Al Cate
Central High School
Memphis, TN

Sharecropping and the Cycle of Debt in the South

To help students understand the issue of sharecropping and debt peonage in the South, tell them this story about Big Daddy and Jim Brown.

"Jim Brown and his wife bring their eight children to Cateville to sharecrop 40 acres of Big Daddy's land. Big Daddy loans Jim one mule, tools, and seed. Jim will receive one-third of the profits from the crop, and credit at Big Daddy's store. The deal sounds good so Jim puts his X on the contract.

Because Jim Brown cannot avoid the inflated store prices and never knows what his profit from the crop will be, he goes deeper and deeper into debt. After the harvest, Brown goes to receive his money. Big Daddy merely hands Brown a bill for $100 and asks, "How do you want to settle accounts?"

Discuss Brown's options with students. Ask them to find the flaws in the contract between the two men.

ADDITIONAL RESOURCES FROM GLENCOE

- American Music: Cultural Traditions
- American Art & Architecture
- Outline Map Resource Book
- U.S. Desk Map
- Building Geography Skills for Life
- Inclusion for the High School Social Studies Classroom Strategies and Activities
- Teaching Strategies for the American History Classroom (Including Block Scheduling Pacing Guides)
- Dinah Zike's High School American History Reading and Study Skills Foldables

 Block Schedule

Activities that are suited to use within the block scheduling framework are identified by:

7 The Civil War and Reconstruction
1861–1877

Why It Matters Activity

Have selected students read the Fourteenth and Fifteenth Amendments aloud. Ask students what impact they think each amendment has had on Americans. Students should evaluate their answers after they have completed the chapter.

GLENCOE TECHNOLOGY

The *American Republic Since 1877* Video Program
To learn more about the Civil War, have students view the Chapter 7 video, "Lincoln and the Civil War," from the *American Republic Since 1877* Video Program.

MindJogger Videoquiz
Use the **MindJogger Videoquiz** to preview Chapter 7 content.

⊙ Both programs available in DVD

Why It Matters

The Civil War was a milestone in American history. The four-year-long struggle determined the nation's future. With the North's victory, slavery was abolished. The war itself introduced modern military innovations such as the use of railroads to move troops, the telegraph to speed communications, and reliance on conscription in a "total war" effort. After the war, the nation struggled to bring the South back into the Union during a contentious period known as Reconstruction.

The Impact Today

The Civil War and Reconstruction permanently changed the nation.
• The Thirteenth Amendment abolished slavery, while the Fourteenth and Fifteenth Amendments provided constitutional protections for all American citizens.
• The power of the federal government was strengthened.
• The Radical Republicans' rule so antagonized the South that the region remained solidly Democratic for nearly a century.

⊙ **The *American Republic Since 1877* Video**
The Chapter 7 video, "Lincoln and the Civil War," chronicles the president's efforts to solve the problems between the North and the South.

1861
• First Battle of Bull Run

1863
• Lincoln issues Emancipation Proclamation
• Battle of Gettysburg

1865
• Lee surrenders to Grant at Appomattox Courthouse
• John Wilkes Booth assassinates Lincoln

1868
• House impeaches President Johnson

United States PRESIDENTS

Lincoln 1861–1865 · *1861*

A. Johnson 1865–1869 · *1865*

Grant 1869–1877 · *1869*

World

1861
• Czar Alexander II emancipates Russian serfs

1863
• French troops occupy Mexico City

1865
• Gregor Mendel's Law of Heredity stated

1868
• Meiji Restoration begins Japanese modernization

1869
• First ships pass through Suez Canal

242

📖 **Reading Strategy** ▸ **PURPOSE FOR READING**

RAFT This is a writing tool that allows students to look at a topic from a different perspective. Make the following announcement: "Wanted: Soldiers to fight for the Union! Skilled soldiers needed for the 9th regiment of Boston. Volunteers, sign up today." Based on the announcement, have students take on the **R**ole of an army recruiter addressing a specific **A**udience—the men in their community. Using the **F**ormat of a longer newspaper article, have students write 5 reasons on the **T**opic of why the men should enlist in the Union Army. **L1**

📁 Refer to *Inclusion for the High School Social Studies Classroom Strategies and Activities* in the TCR.

Charge by Don Troiani, 1990, depicts the advance of the Eighth Pennsylvania Cavalry during the Battle of Chancellorsville.

1870
• Fifteenth Amendment ratified

1873
• Panic of 1873 paralyzes nation

1875
• "Whiskey Ring" scandal breaks

1877
• Compromise of 1877 ends Reconstruction efforts

*Hayes
1877–1881*

1873

1877

1871
• Unification of Germany completed; German Empire proclaimed

1873
• Sigmund Freud enters Vienna University

1874
• First Impressionist art exhibit launches Modern Art movement

1876
• Belgian king Leopold II begins establishing trading posts in Africa; European nations begin dividing control of Africa

HISTORY Online

Chapter Overview
Visit the *American Republic Since 1877* Web site at tarvol2.glencoe.com and click on **Chapter Overviews—Chapter 7** to preview chapter information.

243

GRAPHIC ORGANIZER ACTIVITY

Organizing Information Have students use a graphic organizer similar to the one shown below to illustrate the sequence and results of the Civil War battles mentioned in this chapter. Students' organizers should be more extensive than what is shown here.

Date	Battle Name	Outcome
1861	Fort Sumter	War begins
	First Battle of Bull Run	Confederate victory
1862	Battle of Antietam	Union victory

HISTORY Online

Introduce students to chapter content and key terms by having them access the **Chapter 7 Overview** at tarvol2.glencoe.com

More About the Art

Don Troiani is an artist and historian who was born in 1949 in New York City. He is well known for his realistic portrayals of Civil War and Revolutionary War scenes based on extensive research. To help him achieve his goal of presenting historical accuracy through art, Troiani maintains an extensive collection of military artifacts dating from 1754 to 1865. **Ask: How do you think the artist's research is reflected in the painting *Charge* shown on page 243?** *(Students' answers will vary. Answers might focus on the detail shown in the soldiers' uniforms, weapons, and equipment.)* **What kinds of resources do you think the author might have used in his research?** *(historical documents, letters, newspapers, and artifacts from the time period)*

TIME LINE ACTIVITY

Have students create a time line for events in the United States from 1861 through 1877 using the chapter time line and the section time lines. Instruct students to include months for all events.

FOLDABLES
Study Organizer

Dinah Zike's Foldables are three-dimensional, interactive graphic organizers that help students practice basic writing skills, review key vocabulary terms, and identify main ideas. Have students complete the foldable activity in the *Dinah Zike's Reading and Study Skills Foldables* booklet.

243

1 FOCUS

Section Overview

This section focuses on the advantages and disadvantages that each side had at the beginning of the Civil War.

BELLRINGER
Skillbuilder Activity

 Project transparency and have students answer the question.

Daily Focus Skills Transparency 7–1

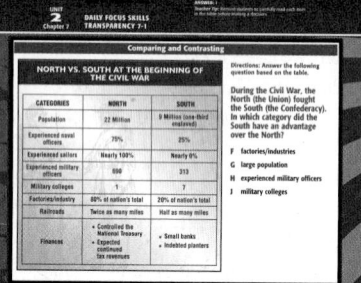

Reading Preview

Answers to Graphic:
I. Choosing Sides
II. The Opposing Economies
    A. Industry and Agriculture
Students should complete the outline by including all heads in the section.

Preteaching Vocabulary
Assign one of the Key Terms and Names to each student. Have each student prepare a 30-second oral presentation related to his or her term or name.

SECTION 1 The Opposing Sides

Guide to Reading

Main Idea
The North and the South each had distinct advantages and disadvantages at the beginning of the Civil War.

Key Terms and Names
Robert E. Lee, Legal Tender Act, greenback, War Democrat, Copperhead, conscription, habeas corpus, *Trent* Affair, attrition, Anaconda Plan

Reading Strategy
Taking Notes As you read about the North and South's advantages and disadvantages at the start of the Civil War, use the major headings of the section to create an outline similar to the one below.

    I. Choosing Sides

    II.
        A.
        B.

Reading Objectives
• **Assess** the strengths and weaknesses of each region's economy.
• **Contrast** the political situations of the Union and the Confederacy.

Section Theme
Groups and Institutions The Confederacy's weak central government had difficulty coordinating the war effort.

Preview of Events

◆April 1861	◆October 1861	◆April 1862

April 1861	**November 1861**	**February 1862**	**April 1862**
Robert E. Lee resigns from the U.S. Army	*Trent* Affair begins	Congress passes Legal Tender Act	Confederate Congress passes conscription law

---

★ An American Story ★

Theodore Upson

While husking corn on his family's Indiana farm in April 1861, 16-year-old Theodore Upson heard a neighbor tell his father Jonathan that "the Rebels have fired upon and taken Fort Sumter."

"Father said little," Upson remembered. However, when the family sat down for dinner later, the boy saw that his father "looked ten years older."

Upson later recalled, "We sat down to the table. Grandma wanted to know what was the trouble. Father told her and she began to cry. 'Oh, my poor children in the South. Now they will suffer!'"

Upson's father offered to let their Southern relatives come and stay with them at the farm, where he thought they would be safer. "No, they will not do that," the grandmother replied. "There is their home. There they will stay. Oh, to think that I should have lived to see the day when Brother should rise against Brother."

—**adapted from *With Sherman to the Sea***

Choosing Sides

On the same day that he learned his home state of Virginia had voted to secede from the Union, **Robert E. Lee**—one of the best senior officers in the United States Army—received an offer from General Winfield Scott to command Union troops. Although Lee had spoken against secession and considered slavery "a moral and political evil," he wrote, "I cannot raise my hand against my birthplace, my home, my children." Instead, he resigned from the army and offered his services to the Confederacy.

244 CHAPTER 7   The Civil War and Reconstruction

SECTION RESOURCES

📂 **Reproducible Masters**
• Reproducible Lesson Plan 7–1
• Daily Lecture and Discussion Notes 7–1
• Guided Reading Activity 7–1
• Section Quiz 7–1
• Reading Essentials and Study Guide 7–1

📖 **Transparencies**
• Daily Focus Skills Transparency 7–1

• American Art & Architecture

Multimedia
🖫 Interactive Tutor Self-Assessment CD-ROM
🖫 ExamView® Pro Testmaker CD-ROM
🖫 Presentation Plus! CD-ROM
🖫 TeacherWorks™ CD-ROM
🎧 Audio Program

Lee was only one of hundreds of military officers who resigned to join the Confederacy. These officers enabled the South to organize an effective fighting force quickly. So too did the strong military tradition in the South. In 1860 seven of the nation's eight military colleges were in the South. These colleges provided the South with a large number of trained officers to lead its armies.

Just as the South had a strong military tradition, the North had a strong naval tradition. More than three-quarters of the United States Navy's officers came from the North. At the same time, the crews of American merchant ships were almost entirely from the North. They provided a large pool of trained sailors for the Union navy as it expanded.

Reading Check **Explaining** Why was the South able to quickly organize an army?

The Opposing Economies

Although the South had many experienced officers to lead its troops in battle, the North had several economic advantages. In 1860 the population of the North was about 22 million, while the South had about 9 million people. The North's larger population gave it a great advantage in raising an army and in supporting the war effort.

ECONOMICS
Industry and Agriculture The North's industries also gave the region an important economic advantage

over the South. In 1860 almost 90 percent of the nation's factories were located in the Northern states. Thus, the North could provide its troops with ammunition and other supplies more easily.

In addition, the South had only half as many miles of railroad track as the North and had only one line—from Memphis to Chattanooga—connecting the western states of the Confederacy to the east. This made it much easier for Northern troops to disrupt the Southern rail system and prevent the movement of supplies and troops.

Financing the War Both the North and the South had to act quickly to raise money for the war. The North enjoyed several financial advantages. In addition to controlling the national treasury, the Union could expect continued revenue from tariffs. Many Northern banks also held large reserves of cash, which they loaned the government by purchasing bonds.

In order to make more money available for emergency use, Congress passed the **Legal Tender Act** in February 1862. This act created a national currency and allowed the government to issue paper money. The paper money came to be known as greenbacks, because of its color. Although the use of paper money helped to cause inflation—a decline in the value of money—it also enabled the government to pay its bills and keep the war effort going.

In contrast to the Union, the Confederacy's financial situation was not good, and it became worse over

Resources of the Union and of the Confederacy

Union | Confederacy

Category	Union	Confederacy
Population	71%	29%
Manufactured goods	92%	8%
Exports	56%	44%
Merchant ships	90%	10%
Miles of railroad track	72%	28%
Grain production	69%	31%
Number of farms	67%	33%
Iron production	94%	6%
Banking capital	82%	18%

Source: *Historical Statistics of the United States*

Chart *Skills*
1. **Interpreting Graphs** In which category is the difference between the Union and the Confederacy the greatest?
2. **Making Inferences** What additional factors are not considered when comparing population percentages between the Union and the Confederacy?

2 *TEACH*

Daily Lecture and Discussion Notes 7–1

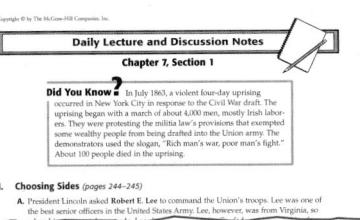

Copyright © by The McGraw-Hill Companies, Inc.

Daily Lecture and Discussion Notes
Chapter 7, Section 1

Did You Know? In July 1863, a violent four-day uprising occurred in New York City in response to the Civil War draft. The uprising began with a march of about 4,000 men, mostly Irish laborers. They were protesting the militia law's provisions that exempted some wealthy people from being drafted into the Union army. The demonstrators used the slogan, "Rich man's war, poor man's fight." About 100 people died in the uprising.

I. Choosing Sides *(pages 244–245)*

A. President Lincoln asked **Robert E. Lee** to command the Union's troops. Lee was one of the best senior officers in the United States Army. Lee, however, was from Virginia, so

Reading Strategy

Drawing Conclusions Have students read the paragraph on page 244 that describes Robert E. Lee's position. As a class, make a list of the things Lee may have weighed as he made his decision. Have students draw conclusions about what factors weighed most heavily in his decision to turn down Lincoln's offer and volunteer his service to the Confederacy. **L1** **ELL**

Reading Check

Answer: The South had more military officers. Seven of the eight military colleges in the nation were in the South.

Graphic Organizer → *Skills*

Answers:
1. iron production
2. possible answers: willingness of the people to fight, strength of leadership, demographic make-up of the population

Graphic Organizer Skills Practice
Ask: In what category are the two sides nearly equal? *(exports)*

Guided Reading Activity 7–1

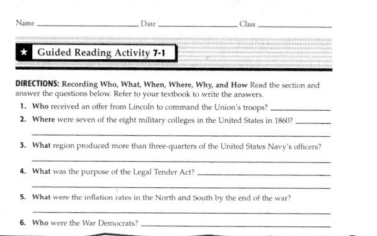

Name _____ Date _____ Class _____

★ Guided Reading Activity 7-1

DIRECTIONS: Recording Who, What, When, Where, Why, and How Read the section and answer the questions below. Refer to your textbook to write the answers.

1. Who received an offer from Lincoln to command the Union's troops? _____
2. Where were seven of the eight military colleges in the United States in 1860? _____
3. What region produced more than three-quarters of the United States Navy's officers? _____
4. What was the purpose of the Legal Tender Act? _____
5. What were the inflation rates in the North and South by the end of the war? _____
6. Who were the War Democrats? _____

 Reading Check

Answer: advantage in raising an army and supporting the war effort

CURRICULUM CONNECTION

Civics Life in the northwestern counties of Virginia was very different from life in the lowland areas. Small farms, not plantations worked by enslaved persons, dominated the landscape. The northwestern Virginians did not see why they should leave the Union to protect the rights of slaveholders. In August 1861 the northwestern counties broke away to apply for statehood as West Virginia.

 Linking Past & Present

While the federal income tax is the greatest source of federal government funding, state governments have the right to impose additional income taxes on citizens. Some states, such as Alaska, Florida, Nevada, South Dakota, Texas, Washington, and Wyoming, do not impose a personal income tax.

---

time. Most Southern planters were in debt and unable to buy bonds. At the same time, Southern banks were small and had few cash reserves. As a result, they could not buy many bonds either.

The best hope for the South to raise money was by taxing trade. Shortly after the war began, however, the Union Navy blockaded Southern ports, which reduced trade and revenues. The Confederacy then resorted to direct taxation of its people, but many Southerners refused to pay.

The Confederacy also printed paper money to pay its bills. This caused rapid inflation in the South, and Confederate paper money eventually became almost worthless. By the end of the war, the South had experienced 9,000 percent inflation, compared to only 80 percent in the North.

 Reading Check **Examining** How was having a larger population than the South an advantage for the North?

 Linking Past & Present

The Income Tax

Past: Funding the War
On July 1, 1862, a new tax law gave the United States a comprehensive federal income tax. A temporary way of funding the war debt, the tax was repealed in 1872. Another income tax passed in 1894 was challenged in court, and the Supreme Court ruled that a direct tax on incomes was unconstitutional. The Sixteenth Amendment (1913) again made the income tax legal.

$5 greenback

Present: The IRS Today
Today the income tax is the biggest source of federal government funding. The Internal Revenue Service (IRS) administers the tax, receiving and processing about 200 million returns every year.

246 CHAPTER 7 The Civil War and Reconstruction

The Political Situation

As both sides worked to address their various economic dilemmas, they also had to contend with a variety of political problems, including opposition to the war in the North and quarrels over war policies in the South.

Party Politics and Dissent in the North As the Civil War began, President Lincoln had to grapple with divisions within his own party. Many members of the Republican Party were abolitionists. Lincoln's goal, however, was to preserve the Union, even if it meant allowing slavery to continue.

The Republican president also had to contend with the Democrats, who were divided themselves. One faction, called **War Democrats,** strongly supported a war to restore the Union but opposed ending slavery. Another faction of Northern Democrats were known as the Peace Democrats. This group opposed the war and called for the reunion of the states by negotiation rather than force. Many Republicans viewed them as traitors and referred to them as **Copperheads,** after the poisonous snake.

One major disagreement between Republicans and Democrats concerned the enactment in 1862 of a militia law that allowed states to use conscription—or forcing people through a draft into military service—if this was necessary to fill their regiments. Many Democrats opposed the law, and riots erupted in several strongly Democratic districts in Indiana, Ohio, Pennsylvania, and Wisconsin.

Criticism also greeted President Lincoln's decision to suspend writs of habeas corpus. Habeas corpus refers to a person's right not to be imprisoned unless charged with a crime and given a trial. A writ of habeas corpus is a court order that requires the government to either charge an imprisoned person with a crime or let the person go free. When writs of habeas corpus are suspended, a person can be imprisoned indefinitely without trial. In this case, President Lincoln suspended the writ for anyone who openly supported the rebels or encouraged others to resist the militia draft. In taking such action, Lincoln justified limits on speech in wartime: "Must I shoot a simple-minded soldier boy who deserts," the president asked, "while I must not touch a hair of a wily agitator who induces him to desert?"

GOVERNMENT

Weak Southern Government Although the South had no organized opposition party, Confederate president Jefferson Davis still faced political problems. The

---

DIFFERENTIATED INSTRUCTION

At-Risk Students Students with reading problems sometimes have difficulty locating information necessary to answer questions. Point out that some answers are stated in the text, while other questions require the reader to put together information. Help students differentiate between these two question types by providing examples of them from "The Opposing Economies" section of the text. **L1**

📁 Refer to *Inclusion for the High School Social Studies Classroom Strategies and Activities* in the TCR.

Confederate constitution emphasized states' rights and limited the central government's power. This often interfered with Davis's ability to conduct the war with a united commitment from every Confederate state government.

Although many Southern leaders supported the war, some opposed Jefferson Davis when he supported conscription and established martial law early in 1862. They objected to the Confederacy forcing people to join the army. They also opposed the suspension of writs of habeas corpus, which the South had also introduced.

✓ Reading Check **Summarizing** How were the Northern Democrats divided over the Civil War?

The Diplomatic Challenge

The outbreak of the Civil War put the major governments of Europe in a difficult situation. The United States government did not want the Europeans interfering in the war. Confederate leaders wanted the Europeans, particularly the British, to recognize the South and provide it with military assistance.

Southern leaders knew that European textile factories depended on Southern cotton. To pressure the British and French, many Southern planters agreed to stop selling their cotton in these markets until the Europeans recognized the Confederacy.

In the autumn of 1861, as the European nations considered their course of action, two Confederate diplomats set out from Havana, Cuba, aboard the British vessel *Trent* to meet with European officials. When the *Trent* left Havana, the Union warship *San Jacinto* intercepted it and arrested the men.

After several tense weeks, the United States freed the men, and they continued on their journey to seek European allies. Although their arrest in the so-called *Trent* **Affair** had excited interest worldwide, their diplomatic mission failed. In the end, both Britain and France chose not to go to war against the United States.

✓ Reading Check **Explaining** Why was it important for the Confederate States to be recognized by the industrialized European nations?

The First Modern War

As they readied for battle, the North and South were about to embark on what was, in many respects, the first modern war. Most of the wars fought in Europe during the previous two centuries were fought by small, disciplined armies with limited goals. In contrast, the Civil War involved huge armies that consisted mostly of civilian volunteers and which required vast amounts of supplies and equipment.

Military Technology and Tactics The Civil War introduced new styles of fighting. Traditionally, troops would march toward the enemy in tight columns, firing in massed volleys. These were necessary tactics earlier in the century because soldiers used smoothbore muskets loaded with round metal balls. These muskets were very inaccurate except at close range.

By the 1850s, French and American inventors had developed an inexpensive conoidal—or cone-shaped—bullet that could be used in rifles. Rifles firing conoidal bullets were accurate at much greater distances. This meant that troops charging at enemy lines would be fired upon with more accuracy, producing much higher casualties.

At the same time, instead of standing in a line, troops defending positions in the Civil War began to use trenches and barricades to protect themselves. The combination of rifles and protective cover created situations where the attacking force often suffered very high casualties. High casualties meant that armies had to keep replacing their soldiers. Attrition—the wearing down of one side by the other through exhaustion of soldiers and resources—thus played a critical role as the war dragged on.

World History Connection

Gunpowder
The cannon and rifle fire that echoed throughout the valleys of Tennessee during Grant's campaign had become a familiar sound on the battlefields of the United States and the rest of the world by the mid-1800s. The key ingredient in these powerful weapons was gunpowder. Scholars believe that the Chinese invented this explosive mixture and were using it in fireworks and signals as early as the 900s. In 1304 the Arabs used the powder to develop the first gun. In the centuries that followed, numerous nations would develop and improve on the gun—which made all other weapons before it obsolete. *For what peaceful purposes can gunpowder be used?*

CHAPTER 7   The Civil War and Reconstruction   **247**

✓ Reading Check

Answer: War Democrats favored fighting to preserve the Union but opposed ending slavery. Peace Democrats wanted to avoid war and find a negotiated settlement that would reunite the states.

✓ Reading Check

Answer: for diplomatic gains and to get military assistance

World History Connection

Answer: fireworks
Ask: How were Civil War rifles more deadly than earlier weapons? *(The conoidal bullet made them more accurate at a longer range.)*

3 ASSESS

Assign Section 1 Assessment as homework or as an in-class activity.

🌐 Have students use the **Interactive Tutor Self-Assessment CD-ROM.**

INTERDISCIPLINARY CONNECTIONS ACTIVITY

Physics Invite a physics teacher or a physicist to demonstrate the science behind the effectiveness of the conoidal bullet. Ask the speaker to use and define scientific terminology, and to demonstrate the applicable laws of physics. **L2**

L1/ELL

Reading Essentials and Study Guide 7–1

Name _____ Date _____ Class _____

Study Guide

Chapter 7, Section 1
For use with textbook pages 244–248

CHOOSING SIDES

KEY TERMS AND NAMES

Robert E. Lee senior officer in the United States Army, who joined the Confederacy as a military leader (page 244)

Legal Tender Act created a national currency and allowed the government to issue paper money (page 245)

greenback green-colored paper money that was created as a national currency in 1862 (page 245)

War Democrats Democrats who supported a war to restore the Union but opposed ending slavery (page 246)

Copperheads a group of Northern Democrats, known as Peace Democrats, who opposed the

L2

Section Quiz 7–1

Name _____ Date _____ Class _____

⭐ Chapter 7   Score ☐

Section Quiz 7-1

DIRECTIONS: Matching Match each item in Column A with the items in Column B. Write the correct letters in the blanks. *(10 points each)*

Column A
___ 1. caused worldwide interest when a ship carrying two Confederate diplomats was intercepted by a Union warship
___ 2. opposed the war and called for reuniting the states through negotiation rather than force
___ 3. the wearing down of one side by the other through exhaustion of soldiers and resources
___ 4. a name the Republicans called the Peace Democrats
___ 5. paper money

Column B
A. Peace Democrats
B. greenbacks
C. *Trent* Affair
D. attrition
E. Copperheads

✓ **Reading Check**

Answer: His strategy was to attack, but to retreat when necessary to avoid heavy losses, hoping to wear down the North over time.

Reteach

Ask students to assess the strengths and weaknesses of each region's economy.

Enrich

Invite students to prepare a two-minute oral presentation on one of the persons mentioned in this section.

HISTORY Online

Study Central™ provides summaries, interactive games, and online graphic organizers to help students review section content.

4 CLOSE

Have students contrast the political situations of the Union and the Confederacy.

The Anaconda Plan

- Blockade Southern ports on the Atlantic
- Isolate the Confederacy from European aid and trade
- Cut off flow of supplies, equipment, money, food and cotton
- Exhaust Southern resources, forcing surrender
- Control the Mississippi with Union gunboats
- Divide the eastern part of the Confederacy from the western part
- Capture New Orleans, Vicksburg, and Memphis
- Cut off shipping to and from interior

The South's Strategy Early in the war, Jefferson Davis imagined a struggle similar to the American war for independence against Britain. Like George Washington, Southern generals would pick their battles carefully, attacking and retreating when necessary to avoid heavy losses. By waging a defensive war of attrition, Davis believed the South could force the Union to spend its resources until it became tired of the war and agreed to negotiate.

Much like Lincoln in the North, however, President Davis felt pressure to strike for a quick victory. Many strategists of this era were influenced by Napoleon's battle strategy in his European wars: Victory should come with one climactic battle. Many Southerners

also believed that their military traditions made them superior fighters, and they scorned defensive warfare. In the war, Southern troops went on the offensive in eight battles, suffering 20,000 more casualties than the Union by charging enemy lines. These were heavy losses the South could not afford.

The Union's Anaconda Plan Early in the war, the general in chief of the United States, Winfield Scott, proposed a strategy for defeating the South. Scott suggested that the Union blockade Confederate ports and send gunboats down the Mississippi River to divide the Confederacy in two. The South, thus separated, would gradually run out of resources and surrender. The plan would take time, Scott admitted, but it would defeat the South with the least amount of bloodshed.

Many Northerners rejected the plan as too slow and indirect for certain victory, favoring instead a strong, quick invasion of the South. Northern newspapers scorned this strategy, which they called the **Anaconda Plan,** after the snake that slowly strangles its prey to death. Lincoln eventually agreed to implement Scott's suggestions and imposed a blockade of Southern ports. Ultimately, however, he and other Union leaders realized that only a long war that focused on destroying the South's armies had any chance of success.

✓ **Reading Check** **Describing** What war strategy did Jefferson Davis develop for the South?

HISTORY Online **Study Central™** To review this section, go to tarvol2.glencoe.com and click on **Study Central™**.

SECTION 1 ASSESSMENT

Checking for Understanding

1. **Define:** greenback, conscription, habeas corpus, attrition.
2. **Identify:** Robert E. Lee, Legal Tender Act, War Democrat, Copperhead, *Trent* Affair, Anaconda Plan.
3. **Explain** why Robert E. Lee refused Lincoln's offer to command Union troops.

Reviewing Themes

4. **Groups and Institutions** How did a belief in states' rights hamper the South during the war?

Critical Thinking

5. **Comparing** Why did the North have an economic advantage over the South?
6. **Analyzing** Why did the South resort to using paper money during the war?
7. **Organizing** Using a graphic organizer similar to the one below, list the military innovations of the Civil War era.

Military Innovations

Analyzing Visuals

8. **Analyzing Charts** Examine the chart on the Anaconda Plan on this page. How would a naval blockade accomplish several goals of the Anaconda Plan at once?

Writing About History

9. **Descriptive Writing** Imagine that you are living in one of the border states at the beginning of the Civil War. Write a letter to a relative explaining why you plan to join either the Union or Confederate army.

248 CHAPTER 7 The Civil War and Reconstruction

SECTION 1 ASSESSMENT ANSWERS

1. Terms are in blue.
2. Robert E. Lee *(p. 244)*, Legal Tender Act *(p. 245)*, War Democrat *(p. 246)*, Copperhead *(p. 246)*, *Trent* Affair *(p. 247)*, Anaconda Plan *(p. 248)*
3. He could not fight against his birthplace.
4. The South lacked the strong central

government needed to coordinate the war effort.
5. The Union had a larger population, much more industry, controlled the treasury, collected tariffs, and had large cash reserves in the banks.
6. They had no other resources.
7. rifles, conoidal bullets, trenches,

barricades
8. It would isolate the South and prevent supplies from reaching the Confederacy, thereby exhausting or disrupting Southern resources.
9. Students' letters should offer plausible scenarios.

Guide to Reading

Main Idea
Union forces suffered defeat in Virginia, advanced down the Mississippi, and stopped the South's invasion of Maryland.

Key Terms and Names
"Stonewall" Jackson, bounty, blockade runner, David G. Farragut, Ulysses S. Grant, Emancipation Proclamation, hardtack, prisoner of war

Reading Strategy
Categorizing As you read about the early battles of the Civil War, complete a chart similar to the one below by filling in the results of each battle listed.

Battle	Results
First Battle of Bull Run	
Battle of Shiloh	
Seven Days' Battle	
Second Battle of Bull Run	

Reading Objectives
• **Describe** the progress of the war in the West and the East.
• **Evaluate** the soldiers' wartime experiences.

Section Theme
Geography and History The Union hoped to seize the Mississippi River valley and cut the Confederacy in two.

Preview of Events

♦1861	♦1862	♦1863

1861
Confederates defeat Union forces at First Battle of Bull Run (Manassas)

April 1862
20,000 casualties at Battle of Shiloh

September 1862
23,000 casualties at Battle of Antietam

1863
The Emancipation Proclamation takes effect

1 FOCUS

Section Overview
This section focuses on Union forces suffering defeat in Virginia, advancing down the Mississippi, and stopping the South's invasion of Maryland.

BELLRINGER
Skillbuilder Activity

Project transparency and have students answer the question.

Daily Focus Skills Transparency 7–2

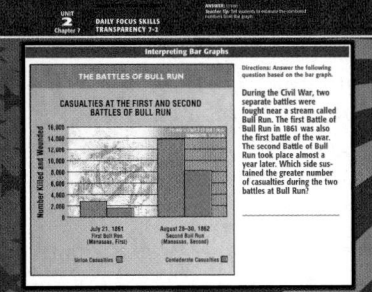

Reading Preview

Answers to Graphic:
First Battle of Bull Run: Confederate victory; Battle of Shiloh: Union victory, both sides suffer high casualties; Seven Days' Battle: no decisive victory, Union forced to retreat; Second Battle of Bull Run: Confederate victory, invasion of Maryland

Preteaching Vocabulary
For each of the Key Terms and Names, have students write a phrase or short sentence that will help them remember its significance.

★ An American Story ★

On July 21, 1861—a hot, sultry Sunday perfect for family outings—hundreds of people from Washington, D.C., picnicked along Bull Run near the northern Virginia town of Manassas Junction. They had gathered to watch the first battle between the Union and Confederate forces.

"The spectators were all excited," one reporter wrote, "and a lady with an opera glass who was near me was quite beside herself when an unusually heavy discharge roused the current of her blood: "That is splendid! Oh, my! Is not that first-rate?"

The spectators who came to Bull Run expected a short, exciting fight and a quick surrender by the rebel troops. Unexpectedly, the Confederates routed the Union army. A reporter with the Boston *Journal,* Charles Coffin, described the chaos:

❝Men fall. . . . They are bleeding, torn, and mangled. . . . The trees are splintered, crushed, and broken, as if smitten by thunderbolts. . . . There is smoke, dust, wild talking, shouting; hissings, howlings, explosions. It is a new, strange, unanticipated experience to the soldiers of both armies, far different from what they thought it would be.❞

—**quoted in** *Voices of the Civil War*

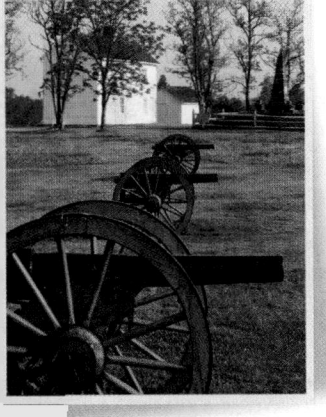

Civil War cannon near Bull Run in Manassas National Battlefield Park

Mobilizing the Troops

During the first few months of the war, President Lincoln felt tremendous pressure to strike hard against the South. He approved an assault on Confederate troops gathered only 25 miles (40 km) south of Washington, D.C. The **First Battle of Bull Run,** as it came to be called, started well for the Union as it forced Confederate troops to retreat.

CHAPTER 7 The Civil War and Reconstruction **249**

SECTION RESOURCES

🗁 Reproducible Masters
• Reproducible Lesson Plan 7–2
• Daily Lecture and Discussion Notes 7–2
• Guided Reading Activity 7–2
• Section Quiz 7–2
• Reading Essentials and Study Guide 7–2

📖 Transparencies
• Daily Focus Skills Transparency 7–2

• American Art & Architecture

Multimedia
🕮 Interactive Tutor Self-Assessment CD-ROM
🕮 ExamView® Pro Testmaker CD-ROM
🕮 Presentation Plus! CD-ROM
🕮 TeacherWorks™ CD-ROM
🕮 Audio Program

2 TEACH

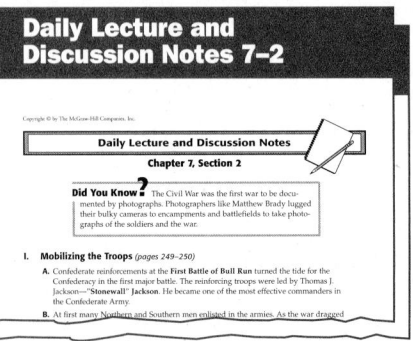

Creating a Thematic Map

Provide students with an outline map of the United States that includes state borders. As they read the section, have students use the map on page 252 to label their outline maps with the states in which battles were fought. Have them use different symbols to indicate Union and Confederate victories. **L1** **ELL**

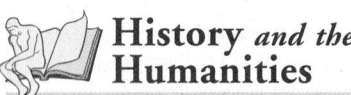 Use the rubric for creating a map, display, or chart on pages 65–66 in the *Performance Assessment Activities and Rubrics.*

Reading Check

Answer: It became clear that the North would need a large, well-trained army to defeat the South.

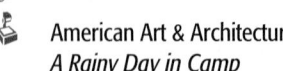

History *and the* Humanities

American Art & Architecture: *A Rainy Day in Camp*

The Confederate cause was saved when reinforcements from Virginia under Thomas J. Jackson arrived. The commander of the retreating troops yelled: "There is Jackson standing like a stone wall! Rally behind the Virginians!" Jackson became known as **"Stonewall" Jackson,** and he went on to become one of the Confederate army's most effective commanders. With the help of Jackson's reinforcements, the Union assault at Bull Run failed.

The Union defeat at the First Battle of Bull Run made it clear that the North would need a large, well-trained army to defeat the South. President Lincoln had originally called for 75,000 men to serve for three months. The day after Bull Run, he signed another bill for the enlistment of 500,000 men for three years.

The North initially tried to encourage voluntary enlistment by offering a bounty—a sum of money given as a bonus—to individuals who promised three years of military service. Eventually, however, both the Union and the Confederacy instituted the draft.

✓ **Reading Check**) **Summarizing** What was the significance of the First Battle of Bull Run?

The Naval War

While the Union and Confederacy mobilized their armies, President Lincoln proclaimed a blockade of all Confederate ports in an effort to cut Confederate trade with the world. Although the blockade became increasingly effective as the war dragged on, Union vessels were thinly spread and found it difficult to stop the blockade runners—small, fast vessels the South used to smuggle goods past the blockade, usually at night. By using blockade runners, the South could ship at least some of its cotton to Europe in exchange for shoes, rifles, and other supplies.

GEOGRAPHY

Farragut Captures New Orleans As part of its effort to close Southern ports, the Union navy developed a plan to seize New Orleans and gain control of the lower Mississippi River. In February 1862, **David G. Farragut** took command of a combined Union force consisting of 42 warships and 15,000 soldiers led by General Benjamin Butler.

In early April, Farragut's fleet began bombarding Confederate forts defending the lower Mississippi River, 75 miles south of New Orleans. When the attack failed to destroy the forts, Farragut made a daring move. In the early hours of April 24, 1862, his ships headed upriver past the forts in single file, exposing themselves to attack. The forts opened fire with more than 80 guns, while Confederate gunboats rammed the Union fleet. Remarkably, all but four of Farragut's ships survived the battle and continued upriver.

Ironclads Clash at Sea, March 9, 1862

Southerners hoped to break the Union blockade with a secret weapon—an iron-plated ship built by covering the hull of the wooden ship *Merrimack,* a captured Union warship, with iron. The armored vessel, renamed the *Virginia,* could easily withstand Union cannon fire.

On March 8, 1862, the *Virginia* sank two Union ships guarding the James River at Hampton Roads, Virginia. On the worst day of the war for the Union navy, 240 sailors died. The next day, the Union's own ironclad ship, the newly completed *Monitor,* challenged the *Virginia.* The two ships fought for hours, but neither could deliver a decisive blow. Although the vessels never fought again, the *Monitor's* presence kept the *Virginia* from breaking the Northern blockade.

Young boys known as "powder monkeys" often carried the explosive charges on Union naval vessels.

COOPERATIVE LEARNING ACTIVITY

Writing a Letter Organize students into pairs. Tell the pairs that they can select one of the battles listed in the section and that one person will be a Union soldier and the other a Confederate soldier. Explain that they are to write letters to their families immediately after the battle has ended. The letters should describe what they saw, felt, and heard during the battle. Have the pairs read each other's letters and discuss how the outcome of the battle affected their attitudes as they composed their letters.

Use the rubric for a cooperative group management plan on pages 71–72 in the *Performance Assessment Activities and Rubrics.*

On April 25, 1862, Farragut arrived at New Orleans. Six days later, General Butler's troops took control of the city. The South's largest city, and a center of the cotton trade, was now in Union hands.

✓ **Reading Check** **Explaining** How did the Confederates try to break the Union blockade?

The War in the West

In February 1862, as Farragut prepared for his attack on New Orleans, Union general **Ulysses S. Grant** began a campaign to seize control of two rivers: the Cumberland River, which flowed west past Nashville through Tennessee, and the Tennessee River, which flowed through northern Alabama and western Tennessee. Control of these rivers would cut Tennessee in two and provide the Union with a river route deep into Confederate territory.

Backed by armored gunboats, Grant first seized Fort Henry, the Confederacy's main fort on the Tennessee River. He then marched his troops east and surrounded Fort Donelson on the Cumberland River, forcing its surrender. With the fall of Fort Donelson and Fort Henry, all of Kentucky and most of western Tennessee came under Union control.

Grant next headed up the Tennessee River to attack Corinth, Mississippi. Seizing Corinth would cut the Confederacy's only rail line connecting Mississippi and western Tennessee to the east.

Early on April 6, 1862, Confederate forces launched a surprise attack on Grant's troops, which were camped about 20 miles (32 km) north of Corinth near a small church named Shiloh. The Union won the Battle of Shiloh the following day, but both sides paid an enormous cost. Twenty thousand troops had been killed or wounded, more than in any other battle up to that point. When newspapers demanded Grant be fired because of the high casualties, Lincoln refused, saying, "I can't spare this man; he fights."

✓ **Reading Check** **Evaluating** What was the significance of the Battle of Shiloh?

The War in the East

At the same time Union and Confederate troops were struggling for control of the Mississippi River and other regions in the West, another major campaign was being waged in the East to capture Richmond, Virginia, the Confederate capital. After General Irwin McDowell's failure at the First Battle

Fact | Fiction | Folklore

Same Battles, Different Names Many Civil War battles have two names. The Union usually named battles after the nearest body of water, while the Confederacy usually named them after the nearest settlement. Therefore, the battle known as the Battle of Bull Run (a creek) in the North was known as the Battle of Manassas (a town) in the South. Likewise, the Battle of Antietam was remembered in the South as the Battle of Sharpsburg.

of Bull Run, Lincoln relieved him of command and chose General George B. McClellan to lead the Union army in the East.

McClellan's Peninsula Campaign After several months of preparation, McClellan began transporting his troops by ship to the mouth of the James River, southeast of Yorktown, Virginia. From there he intended to march on Richmond, only 70 miles (113 km) away.

As McClellan advanced toward Richmond, he allowed his forces to become divided by the Chickahominy River. Seizing this opportunity, the Confederate commander, General Joseph E. Johnston, attacked McClellan's army, inflicting heavy casualties. After Johnston was wounded in the battle, General Robert E. Lee was placed in command.

In late June 1862, Lee began a series of attacks on McClellan's army that became known collectively as the Seven Days' Battle. Although Lee was unable to decisively defeat the Union army, he did force McClellan to retreat. Together the two sides had suffered over 30,000 casualties. Despite McClellan's protests, Lincoln ordered him to withdraw from the peninsula and bring his troops back to Washington.

TURNING POINT

The Battle of Antietam As McClellan's troops withdrew, Lee decided to attack the Union forces defending Washington. The maneuvers by the two sides led to another battle at Bull Run, near Manassas Junction, the site of the first major battle of the war. The South again forced the North to retreat, leaving the Confederate forces only 20 miles (32 km) from Washington, D.C. Soon after, Lee's forces invaded Maryland.

Lee decided to invade Maryland for several reasons. Both he and Jefferson Davis believed that only an invasion would convince the North to accept the

CHAPTER 7 The Civil War and Reconstruction **251**

Guided Reading Activity 7–2

Name _____ Date _____ Class _____

★ **Guided Reading Activity 7-2**

DIRECTIONS: Filling in the Blanks In the space provided, write the word or words that best complete the sentence. Refer to your textbook to fill in the blanks.

1. During the First Battle of Bull Run, the Confederate army's luck changed for the better when _____ and his forces arrived from _____.
2. The Union defeat at the First Battle of Bull Run made it clear that the North would need a _____ to defeat the South.
3. President Lincoln proclaimed a blockade of all _____, but it was hard to prevent _____ from getting through.
4. In spite of a powerful attack by the Confederates, all but four of the ships commanded by _____ survived to arrive at New Orleans on April 25, 1862.
5. Union General Ulysses S. Grant began a campaign to seize control of the _____ and _____ Rivers.

✓ **Reading Check**

Answer: by using small, fast vessels known as blockade runners to slip past the Union ships at night

✓ **Reading Check**

Answer: Despite winning, the Union suffered heavy casualties and there were demands that Grant be fired.

Fact | Fiction | Folklore

As part of the American Battlefield Protection Program, the National Park Service maintains a Web page with links to information on over 300 Civil War battles. Information about alternative names for battles is included. The address for the site is http://www2.cr.nps.gov/abpp/battles/bystate.htm.

FYI

Although David Glasgow Farragut was born in Tennessee, raised in Louisiana, and lived in Virginia, he was a Union hero. In 1866 he was awarded the rank of admiral—a first for the United States Navy. Farragut was touted as a possible presidential candidate in 1868, but he expressed no interest in politics. He died in 1870.

DIFFERENTIATED INSTRUCTION

Visual/Spatial Have students create a multimedia presentation that shows Farragut's capture of New Orleans beginning with the bombardment of the Confederate forts and ending with Butler's capture of the city. Suggest that students combine drawings with captions and recorded descriptions to create an effective and informative presentation. **L2**

👉 Refer to *Inclusion for the High School Social Studies Classroom Strategies and Activities* in the TCR.

Geography *Skills*

Answers:

1. Students should name any four of the following: Hampton Roads, Roanoke Island, Cape Hatteras, Fort Sumter, Port Royal, Fort Pulaski, St. Augustine.

2. They hoped to cut off the South's ability to ship cotton to and receive goods from Europe.

Geography Skills Practice

Ask: What battles were fought in Texas? *(Galveston, Sabine Pass, and Sabine Cross Roads)*

CURRICULUM CONNECTION

World History The military strategy courses taught at West Point—where most of the senior officers in both armies received their training—were based on the work of Henri de Jomini. A soldier and a historian, Jomini had served on Napoleon Bonaparte's general staff. By studying Napoleon's campaigns, Jomini developed a number of rules on fighting a war: offense is better than defense, bring the greatest possible force against the weakest point of the enemy's line, and constantly harass the enemy's lines of communication. Jomini's ideas influenced the way both Union and Confederate generals fought in the early stages of the war.

NATIONAL GEOGRAPHIC — **Civil War in the West and East, 1861–1863** — *In Motion*

Map legend:
- Confederate states
- Union states
- Confederate victory
- Union victory
- Union blockade
- Union routes
- Confederate routes
- **1863** Date West Virginia admitted to Union

IOWA • ILL. • IND. • OHIO • PA. • N.J. • MD. • DEL. • W. VA. (1863) • KY. • VA. • N.C. • S.C. • GA. • ALA. • MISS. • LA. • ARK. • MO. • UNORG. TERR. • TEXAS • FLA.

Battles/locations:
- Gettysburg July 1–3, 1863
- Antietam Sept. 17, 1862
- Bull Run July 21, 1861 & Aug. 29–30, 1862
- Chancellorsville May 1–4, 1863
- Seven Days July 1, 1862
- Washington, D.C.
- Fredericksburg Dec. 13, 1862
- Richmond
- Hampton Roads Mar. 9, 1862
- Roanoke Island Feb. 8, 1862
- Cape Hatteras Aug. 28–29, 1861
- Ft. Sumter Apr. 12–14, 1861
- Port Royal Nov. 7, 1861
- Ft. Pulaski Apr. 10–11, 1862
- St. Augustine Mar. 8, 1862
- Perryville Oct. 8, 1862
- Ft. Donelson Feb. 16, 1862
- Wilson's Creek Aug. 10, 1861
- Pea Ridge Mar. 7–8, 1862
- Shiloh Apr. 6–7, 1862
- Memphis
- Stone's River Dec. 31, 1862–Jan. 2, 1863
- Chattanooga Nov. 23–25, 1863
- Chickamauga Sept. 19–20, 1863
- Iuka Sept. 19, 1862
- Vicksburg July 4, 1863
- Jackson
- Montgomery
- Mobile
- New Orleans May 1, 1862
- Port Hudson July 9, 1863
- Sabine Cross Roads Apr. 8, 1864
- Sabine Pass Sept. 8, 1863
- Galveston Jan. 1, 1863
- Houston
- San Antonio
- Austin
- Dallas
- Laredo

Mississippi R. • Ohio R. • Gulf of Mexico • ATLANTIC OCEAN • 30°N • 25°N • 95°W • 90°W

0 300 miles / 0 300 kilometers
Albers Conic Equal-Area projection

Geography *Skills*

1. **Interpreting Maps** Name four battles that occurred along the eastern seaboard.
2. **Applying Geography Skills** What purpose did the North have in fighting so many battles along the coasts?

South's independence. They also thought that a victory on Northern soil might help the South win recognition from the British and help the Peace Democrats gain control of Congress in the upcoming midterm elections. By heading north, Lee also could feed his troops from Northern farms and draw Union troops out of Virginia during harvest season.

When he learned that McClellan had been sent after him, Lee ordered his troops to congregate near Sharpsburg, Maryland. Meanwhile, McClellan's troops took position along Antietam (an·TEE·tuhm) Creek, east of Lee's forces. On September 17, 1862, McClellan ordered his troops to attack. The **Battle of Antietam,** the bloodiest one-day battle in American history, ended with over 6,000 men killed

and around another 16,000 wounded. Although McClellan did not break Lee's lines, he inflicted so many casualties that Lee decided to retreat to Virginia.

The Battle of Antietam was a crucial victory for the Union. The British government had been ready to intervene in the war as a mediator if Lee's invasion had succeeded. Britain also had begun making plans to recognize the Confederacy in the event the North rejected mediation. Lee's defeat at Antietam changed everything. The British again decided to

252 CHAPTER 7 The Civil War and Reconstruction

INTERDISCIPLINARY CONNECTIONS ACTIVITY

Geography Have the geography teacher help students learn about the role that geography played in Civil War battles. Have students work in groups to build a model of the Battle of Antietam. The model should focus on the landforms in the area and should show the progress of the battle. As a starting point for researching information about the battle, visit the National Park Service's Web site about the battle at http://www.nps.gov/anti/home.htm. **L2**

wait and see how the war progressed. With this decision, the South lost its best chance at gaining international recognition and support. The South's defeat at Antietam had an even more important political impact in the United States. It convinced Lincoln that the time had come to end slavery in the South.

✓ **Reading Check** **Explaining** What was the significance of the Battle of Antietam?

The Emancipation Proclamation

Although most Democrats opposed any move to end slavery, Republicans were divided on the issue. Many Republicans were strong abolitionists. Others, like Lincoln, did not want to endanger the loyalty of the slaveholding border states that had chosen to remain in the Union. The war's primary purpose, in their opinion, was to preserve the Union.

With Northern casualties rising to staggering levels, however, more Northerners began to agree that slavery had to end, in part to punish the South and in part to make the soldiers' sacrifices worthwhile. George Julian, a Republican from Indiana, summed up the argument for freeing the slaves in a speech delivered early in 1862:

❝When I say that this rebellion has its source and life in slavery, I only repeat a simple truism. . . . The mere suppression of the rebellion will be an empty mockery of our sufferings and sacrifices, if slavery shall be spared to canker the heart of the nation anew, and repeat its diabolical misdeeds.❞

—quoted in *Battle Cry of Freedom*

On September 22, 1862, encouraged by the Union victory at Antietam, Lincoln publicly announced that he would issue the **Emancipation Proclamation**—a decree freeing all enslaved persons in states still in rebellion after January 1, 1863. Because the Proclamation freed enslaved African Americans only in states at war with the Union, it did not address slavery in the border states. Short of a constitutional amendment, however, Lincoln could not end slavery in the border states, nor did he want to endanger their loyalty. 📖 *(See page 953 for more on the Emancipation Proclamation.)*

The Proclamation, by its very existence, transformed the conflict over preserving the Union into a war of liberation. "We were no longer merely the soldiers of a political controversy," recalled Union officer Regis de Trobiand. "We were now the missionaries of a great work of redemption, the armed liberators of millions."

✓ **Reading Check** **Examining** Why did Lincoln issue the Emancipation Proclamation?

Life During the Civil War

The Emancipation Proclamation would bring great change to the lives of many African Americans. However, they were not the only group affected by the war. From the battlefront to the home front, the great conflict touched the lives of millions of Americans and turned life for many into a daily struggle.

The Wartime Economies As the war intensified, the economies of the North and South went in different directions. By the end of 1862, the South's economy had begun to suffer greatly. Although many farms had converted from cotton to food crops, the collapse of the South's transportation system and the presence of Union troops in several important agricultural regions led to severe food shortages in the winter of 1862. At the same time, rapid inflation drove up the prices of the food that was available.

The food shortages hurt Southern morale, and people began to question the sacrifices they were being asked to make—or to demand of others. In several communities, food shortages led to riots. Hearing of such hardships, many Confederate soldiers deserted to return home to help their families.

In contrast, the North actually experienced an economic boom because of the war. With its large, well-established banking industry, the North raised money for the war more easily than the South. Its growing industries also supplied Union troops with clothes, munitions, and other necessities.

Innovations in agriculture helped minimize the loss of labor as men left to fight. Greater use of mechanical reapers and mowers made farming possible with fewer workers, many of whom were women. Women also filled labor shortages in various

HISTORY Online

Student Web Activity Visit the *American Republic Since 1877* Web site at tarvol2.glencoe.com and click on *Student Web Activities— Chapter 7* for an activity on the Civil War.

✓ **Reading Check**

Answer: The South lost an opportunity to gain international support and recognition, and Lincoln decided that slavery had to end.

✓ **Reading Check**

Answer: to make the sacrifice of the soldiers worthwhile and to punish the South

HISTORY Online

Objectives and answers to the student activity can be found in the **Web Activity Lesson Plan** at tarvol2.glencoe.com.

Interpreting a Quotation Write the following quotation on the board: "The arm of the slave is the best defense against the arm of the slaveholder. Who would be free themselves must strike the blow." Frederick Douglass, March 5, 1863. **Ask:** What historical circumstances prompted Douglass to say this? Discuss student answers. (*As the Civil War dragged on, Douglass felt that African Americans could deliver the decisive blow if they were allowed to fight.*) **L2**

Reading Strategy **READING THE TEXT**

Analyzing Information Tell students that the governor of Massachusetts referred to the Emancipation Proclamation as "a poor *document*, but a mighty *act*." Explain that his statement reflected the fact that the importance of the Emancipation Proclamation was not in the number of enslaved persons who were immediately freed, but in the fact that slavery was made the central issue of the war. Have the class make a list of the issues that divided the United States before the proclamation. Then discuss how making slavery the main issue of the war helped the Union cause. **L2**

📂 Refer to *Inclusion for the High School Social Studies Classroom Strategies and Activities* in the TCR.

✓ **Reading Check**

Answer: hurt morale as people began to question the sacrifices they were being asked to make, and prompted desertions as soldiers returned home to help their families survive

Picturing **History**

Answer: 54th Massachusetts
Ask: Why did the Emancipation Proclamation bring so many African Americans into the Union army?
(They were now allowed to join, and they had a sense of purpose in fighting to end slavery for all African Americans.)

✓ **Reading Check**

Answer: exposure to illness, unsanitary water supplies, and extreme medical practices

3 ASSESS

Assign Section 2 Assessment as homework or as an in-class activity.

🔘 Have students use the **Interactive Tutor Self-Assessment CD-ROM.**

L1/ELL

Reading Essentials and Study Guide 7–2

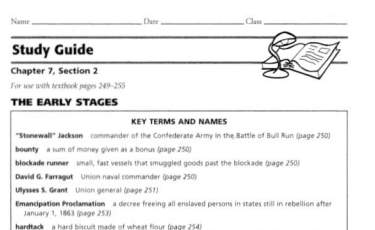

Name _____ Date _____ Class _____

Study Guide

Chapter 7, Section 2
For use with textbook pages 249–255

THE EARLY STAGES

KEY TERMS AND NAMES
"Stonewall" Jackson commander of the Confederate Army in the Battle of Bull Run *(page 250)*
bounty a sum of money given as a bonus *(page 250)*
blockade runner small, fast vessels that smuggled goods past the blockade *(page 250)*
David G. Farragut Union naval commander *(page 250)*
Ulysses S. Grant Union general *(page 251)*
Emancipation Proclamation a decree freeing all enslaved persons in states still in rebellion after January 1, 1863 *(page 253)*
hardtack a hard biscuit made of wheat flour *(page 254)*

industries, particularly in clothing and shoemaking factories where women were already prominent members of the labor force.

✓ **Reading Check** **Explaining** What were the effects of food shortages on the South?

Military Life

Union and Confederate soldiers endured a hard life with few comforts. Many Southern soldiers slept without blankets and walked barefoot, while soldiers on both sides learned to gulp down tasteless food. For the Union soldier, meals often consisted of hardtack (a hard biscuit made of wheat flour), potatoes, and beans, flavored at times with dried salt pork and washed down with coffee. Confederate soldiers had little coffee, and their hardtack was usually made of cornmeal.

Both Union and Confederate soldiers also faced the constant threat of disease. In the mid-1800s, the medical profession had little understanding of infectious germs. Doctors used the same unsterilized instruments on patient after patient, and infection spread quickly in the field hospitals as a result.

In many cases, regiments lost about half their men to illness before ever going into battle. Crowded together in army camps, many soldiers, especially those from rural areas, were exposed to illnesses they had never had before, such as measles and mumps. Smallpox, when it erupted, could be deadly, as could dysentery, typhoid, and pneumonia, which were typically caused by unsanitary water supplies.

Picturing **History**

African American Soldiers Battery A of the 2nd U.S. Colored Light Artillery was one of many groups of African Americans who fought for their freedom. What was the Union's first official African American regiment?

254 CHAPTER 7 The Civil War and Reconstruction

Battlefield physicians also used extreme measures in treating the wounded. Faced with appalling injuries, doctors routinely amputated arms and legs to prevent gangrene and other infections from spreading from the wounded limb to the rest of the body.

As brutal as life was for soldiers on the front, it was equally as miserable for prisoners of war—soldiers captured by the enemy in battle. As the war dragged on, both the North and the South found themselves with a growing numbers of prisoners of war. Taking care of them proved difficult, especially in the South. While conditions were bad in Northern prisons, the South was not able to adequately feed their prisoners because of food shortages.

The most infamous prison in the South, Andersonville in southwest Georgia, was an open camp with no shade or shelter for its huge population. Exposure, overcrowding, lack of food, and disease sometimes killed more than 100 men per day during the sweltering summer of 1864. In all, 13,000 of the 45,000 prisoners sent to Andersonville died in the camp. After the war, Henry Wirz, the commander at Andersonville, became the only person executed for war crimes during the Civil War.

✓ **Reading Check** **Summarizing** What medical problems did Union and Confederate soldiers face?

African Americans and Women

While the war brought hardship to many Americans, it also offered new opportunities for African Americans and women. The Emancipation Proclamation officially permitted African Americans to enlist in the Union army and navy. Almost immediately, thousands of African Americans rushed to join the military.

The first African American regiment officially organized in the North was the 54th Massachusetts, which became one of the most famous regiments in the war. The regiment fought valiantly at Fort Wagner near Charleston Harbor in July 1863, losing nearly half of its soldiers in the battle.

Although women helped in the war effort at home by managing family farms and businesses, perhaps their most important contribution to the Civil War was in serving as nurses to the wounded. One of the most prominent war nurses was **Clara Barton,** who left her job in a Washington patent office to aid soldiers on the battlefield. With her face sometimes bluish from gunpowder, Barton fed the sick, bandaged the wounded, and even removed bullets with her own small knife. An army surgeon, impressed

EXTENDING THE CONTENT

Effectiveness of the Union Blockade Historians disagree over whether or not the Union blockade of the Confederacy was a success. While it has been documented that between 1861 and 1865 approximately five out of six blockade runners made it through the blockade, their impact on the war's outcome remains questionable. By the end of the war, the Confederacy was suffering from a lack of supplies, weakening its ability to continue fighting. The supply shortage was due, in part, to the fact that the blockade runners that did slip through were designed to be fast and maneuverable, and therefore they were limited in the amount of supplies they could carry. Furthermore, when pursued, blockade runners often dumped part or all of their cargo to increase speed.

Picturing History

Battlefield Medicine The greatest impact women had on the battlefield was through serving as nurses. In what non-military ways did women contribute to the war effort?

with Barton's kindness and courage, called her "the true heroine of the age, the angel of the battlefield."

Although Southern women were encouraged to stay at home and support the troops by making bandages and other supplies, many voluntarily founded small hospitals or braved the horrors of the battlefield. Kate Cumming of Mobile, Alabama, served as a nurse following the Battle of Shiloh. In her diary she vividly described the spectacle of war in a makeshift hospital:

66Nothing that I had ever heard or read had given me the faintest idea of the horrors witnessed here. . . . The men are lying all over the house. . . . The foul air from this mass of human beings at first made me giddy and sick, but I soon got over it. . . .99

—quoted in *Battle Cry of Freedom*

The Civil War was a turning point for the American nursing profession. The courage shown by women helped break down the belief that women were emotionally weaker than men. In the meantime, the war dragged on, and by 1863 the stage was set for a series of pivotal battles.

Reading Check **Analyzing** Why do you think so many African Americans were willing to volunteer to fight in the Civil War?

HISTORY Online **Study Central™** To review this section, go to tarvol2.glencoe.com and click on **Study Central™**.

SECTION 2 ASSESSMENT

Checking for Understanding

1. **Define:** bounty, blockade runner, hardtack, prisoner of war.
2. **Identify:** "Stonewall" Jackson, David G. Farragut, Ulysses S. Grant, Emancipation Proclamation.
3. **State** two factors that contributed to food shortages in the South during the Civil War.

Reviewing Themes

4. **Geography and History** Why was seizing control of the Mississippi River an important strategy of the Union navy?

Critical Thinking

5. **Analyzing** In what ways do you think the Civil War changed people's opinion about women's capabilities?
6. **Organizing** Complete a graphic organizer similar to the one below to explain President Lincoln's reasons for issuing the Emancipation Proclamation and the effects the Proclamation had on the war.

Reasons for → Emancipation Proclamation → Effect on War

Analyzing Visuals

7. **Examining Art** Study the painting of the battle between the *Monitor* and the *Virginia* on page 250. What made these vessels superior to other warships used by the Union and the Confederacy?

Writing About History

8. **Persuasive Writing** Imagine that you are asked to advise President Lincoln about issuing the Emancipation Proclamation. Write a short paper in which you explain the reasons for the advice you give him.

SECTION 2 ASSESSMENT ANSWERS

1. Terms are in blue.
2. "Stonewall" Jackson *(p. 250)*, David G. Farragut *(p. 250)*, Ulysses S. Grant *(p. 251)*, Emancipation Proclamation *(p. 253)*
3. collapse of the South's transportation system and Union troops in several important agricultural regions
4. because New Orleans was the South's largest city and the center of the cotton trade
5. They saw that women were capable of great bravery and heroism.
6. Reasons for: to justify the sacrifice, to punish the South; effects on war: transformed the war into a war of liberation
7. Durable metal hulls made them resistant to regular cannon fire and less likely to burn.
8. Papers should offer specific advice, including rationale.

L2

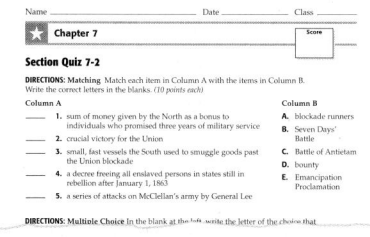

Section Quiz 7-2

Name _____ Date _____ Class _____

⭐ Chapter 7   Score ____

Section Quiz 7-2

DIRECTIONS: Matching Match each item in Column A with the items in Column B. Write the correct letters in the blanks. *(10 points each)*

Column A
_____ 1. sum of money given by the North as a bonus to individuals who promised three years of military service
_____ 2. crucial victory for the Union
_____ 3. small, fast vessels the South used to smuggle goods past the Union blockade
_____ 4. a decree freeing all enslaved persons in states still in rebellion after January 1, 1863
_____ 5. a series of attacks on McClellan's army by General Lee

Column B
A. blockade runners
B. Seven Days' Battle
C. Battle of Antietam
D. bounty
E. Emancipation Proclamation

DIRECTIONS: Multiple Choice In the blank at the left, write the letter of the choice that

✓**Reading Check**

Answer: They had a moral cause to fight for the freedom of enslaved African Americans.

Picturing History

Answer: They managed farms and businesses, made bandages and other supplies, and served as nurses tending to the sick and wounded.
Ask: What functions did battlefield nurses perform? *(They fed the sick, bandaged the wounded, gave comfort, and occasionally operated.)*

Reteach
Have students make a list comparing and contrasting the eastern and western campaigns.

Enrich
Invite students to write a short paper about military life.

HISTORY Online

Study Central™ provides summaries, interactive games, and online graphic organizers to help students review section content.

4 CLOSE

Ask students to contrast the effects of the war on the regional economies.

255

TEACH

Evaluating a Web Site Point out that virtually anyone can create and post a Web page. There are hosting sites that allow individuals to post Web pages at no charge. This means that Web sites are of varying degrees of quality.

Ask students to search for authoritative Web sites about one of the people mentioned in the chapter. Have them print the home page of the site and write a brief explanation of how they rate the site using the criteria listed on page 256.

Additional Practice

L1

Reinforcing Skills Activity 7

Name _____ Date _____ Class _____

★ Reinforcing Skills Activity **7**

Evaluating a Web Site

☐ **LEARNING THE SKILL**
The Internet is a wonderful research tool, but all the information you find there is not necessarily accurate or reliable. To evaluate a Web site, consider how well the facts presented are documented and the sources used for background information. Ask yourself whether the links are up-to-date and look for the credentials of the site author. Also consider the site design and the ease of accessing information.

☐ **PRACTICING THE SKILL**
DIRECTIONS: Visit the following two Web sites. Search both sites for information related to Presidents Lincoln and Johnson. Then answer the questions below in the space provided.
http://www.whitehouse.gov/history/presidents/
http://gi.grolier.com/presidents/preshome.html

GLENCOE TECHNOLOGY

CD-ROM
Glencoe Skillbuilder Interactive Workbook CD-ROM, Level 2

This interactive CD-ROM reinforces student mastery of essential social studies skills.

Evaluating a Web Site

Why Learn This Skill?

The Internet has become a valuable research tool. It is convenient to use, and the information contained on the Internet is plentiful. However, some Web site information is not necessarily accurate or reliable. When using the Internet as a research tool, you will need to distinguish between quality information and inaccurate or incomplete information.

Learning the Skill

There are a number of issues to consider when evaluating a Web site. Most important is to check the accuracy of the source and content. The author and publisher or sponsor of the site should be clearly indicated, and the user must also determine the usefulness of the site. The information on the site should be current, and the design and organization of the site should be appealing and easy to navigate.

To evaluate a Web site, ask yourself the following questions:

- Are the facts on the site documented?
- Is more than one source used for background information within the site?
- Are the links within the site appropriate and up-to-date?
- Is the author clearly identified?
- Does the site contain links to other useful resources?
- Is the information easy to access? Is it properly labeled?
- Is the design appealing?

Practicing the Skill

Visit the following Web site and answer the questions that follow.
http://sunsite.utk.edu/civil-war/

❶ Who is the author or sponsor of the Web site?

❷ What links does the site contain? Are they appropriate to the topic?

❸ What sources were used for the information contained on the site?

❹ Is the design of the site appealing? Why or why not?

❺ How is the home page organized?

Skills Assessment

Complete the Practicing Skills questions on page 281 and the Chapter 7 Skill Reinforcement Activity to assess your mastery of this skill.

Applying the Skill

Comparing Web Sites Locate two other Web sites about the Civil War. Evaluate them for accuracy and usefulness, and then compare them to the site featured above. Be certain to go through the various links that the site includes so that you can do a thorough evaluation of the site. Share your findings with the class.

 Glencoe's **Skillbuilder Interactive Workbook, CD-ROM Level 2,** provides instruction and practice in key social studies skills.

ANSWERS TO PRACTICING THE SKILL

❶ George H. Hoemann

❷ links to the Civil War Resources page and to various other sites that are appropriate

❸ various historical, biographical, miscellaneous sources

❹ Answers may vary. The site is easy to navigate and has appealing visuals and sound.

❺ by category

Applying the Skill
Students' evaluations will vary, but should use the criteria listed in the skillbuilder activity.

Guide to Reading

Main Idea
With the help of key victories at Vicksburg and Gettysburg, the North defeated the South after four long years of fighting.

Key Terms and Names
foraging, siege, Pickett's Charge, Gettysburg Address, William Tecumseh Sherman, torpedo, mandate, Thirteenth Amendment, Appomattox Courthouse

Reading Strategy
Categorizing As you read about battles that led to a turning point in the war, complete a chart by listing the results of the battles shown.

Battle	Results
Vicksburg	
Chancellorsville	
Gettysburg	
Chickamauga Creek	
Missionary Ridge	

Reading Objectives
- **Evaluate** the importance of events at Vicksburg and Gettysburg.
- **Discuss** Lee's surrender and the events of the war's aftermath.

Section Theme
Geography and History The Union victories at Vicksburg and Gettysburg turned the tide of the war firmly in favor of the North.

Preview of Events

♦July 1863		♦August 1864		♦April 1865

July 1–3, 1863
Battle of Gettysburg

July 4, 1863
Vicksburg falls

November 19, 1863
Lincoln delivers Gettysburg Address

April 9, 1865
Lee surrenders at Appomattox Courthouse

April 14, 1865
Lincoln assassinated

---

1 FOCUS

Section Overview
This section describes the events at Vicksburg and Gettysburg and explains how these events turned the tide of the war in favor of the Union.

BELLRINGER
Skillbuilder Activity

Project transparency and have students answer the question.

Daily Focus Skills Transparency 7–3

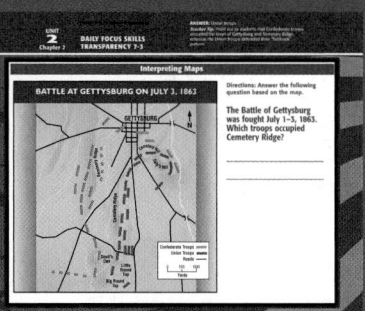

★ An American Story ★

At Gettysburg, Pennsylvania, in early July of 1863, Samuel Wilkeson sat to write his account of the battle that had raged for three days near the town. As he composed his dispatch, the body of Lieutenant Bayard Wilkeson, his son, lay dead beside him.

Wilkeson recorded the events that destroyed the peace of the Gettysburg countryside. He recalled "the singing of a bird, which had a nest in a peach tree within the tiny yard of the whitewashed cottage" that served as the Union army headquarters:

66In the midst of its warbling a shell screamed over the house, instantly followed by another and another and in a moment the air was full of the most complete artillery prelude to an infantry battle that was ever exhibited. Every size and form of shell known to British and to American gunnery shrieked, moaned, whirled, whistled, and wrathfully fluttered over our ground.99

—quoted in *Eyewitness to History*

Farmhouse used by General George Meade for his headquarters at Gettysburg

Vicksburg Falls

Gettysburg was only one of a series of horrific encounters in 1863. The first battle took place farther west, where a vital part of the Union strategy involved gaining control of the Mississippi River. In April 1862, Commander David Farragut had captured New Orleans and secured Union control of the Mississippi River delta. Later that year, Ulysses S. Grant seized control of the river as far south as Memphis after his victory at Shiloh. If the Union could capture Vicksburg, Mississippi, the last major Confederate stronghold on the river, the North could cut the South in two.

CHAPTER 7   The Civil War and Reconstruction   **257**

Reading Preview

Answers to Graphic: Vicksburg: Union victory cut South in two; Chancellorsville: Confederate victory; Gettysburg: Union victory and turning point of war; Chickamauga Creek: Confederate victory; Missionary Ridge: Union victory, fall of Chattanooga

Preteaching Vocabulary
Have students create a note card for each of the Key Terms and Names with the word at the top and a definition below it.

SECTION RESOURCES

Reproducible Masters
- Reproducible Lesson Plan 7–3
- Daily Lecture and Discussion Notes 7–3
- Guided Reading Activity 7–3
- Section Quiz 7–3
- Reading Essentials and Study Guide 7–3

Transparencies
- Daily Focus Skills Transparency 7–3

Multimedia
- Interactive Tutor Self-Assessment CD-ROM
- ExamView® Pro Testmaker CD-ROM
- Presentation Plus! CD-ROM
- TeacherWorks™ CD-ROM
- Audio Program
- ABCNews Interactive™ Historic America Electronic Field Trips

2 TEACH

Daily Lecture and Discussion Notes 7–3

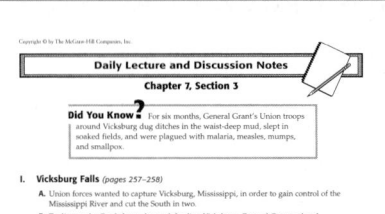

Copyright © by The McGraw-Hill Companies, Inc.

Daily Lecture and Discussion Notes
Chapter 7, Section 3

Did You Know? For six months, General Grant's Union troops around Vicksburg dug ditches in the waist-deep mud, slept in soaked fields, and were plagued with malaria, measles, mumps, and smallpox.

I. **Vicksburg Falls** (pages 257–258)
   A. Union forces wanted to capture Vicksburg, Mississippi, in order to gain control of the Mississippi River and cut the South in two.
   B. To distract the Confederate forces defending Vicksburg, General Grant ordered Benjamin Grierson to take a troop on a cavalry raid through Mississippi. This enabled Grant to land his troops south of Vicksburg.

Holding a Discussion Hold a class discussion on the characteristics of military leaders. Write the characteristics that students list on the board. **L1**

Answer: about a month and a half

Answer: to cut the South in two

History and the Humanities

- American Music: Hits Through History: "Johnny Comes Marching Home," "The Battle Hymn of the Republic"
- American Music: Cultural Traditions: "Bonnie Blue Flag," "Glory! Glory! Hallelujah! (John Brown's Body)"

Vicksburg Besieged Union troops used this house as a headquarters during the siege of Vicksburg. Nearby are Union trenches and the opening to a tunnel being dug under Confederate lines. *For how long was the city of Vicksburg under siege by Grant's Union forces?*

Grierson's Raid The city of Vicksburg was located on the east bank of the Mississippi River. At first Grant tried to approach the city from the north, but the land was too swampy, and the rivers in the area were covered with vegetation and blocked by trees. To get at Vicksburg, Grant decided to move his troops across the Mississippi to the west bank and then march south. Once past the city, Grant intended to cross back to the east bank of the river and attack the city from the south.

To distract the Confederates while he carried out this difficult maneuver, Grant ordered Benjamin Grierson to take 1,700 troops on a cavalry raid through Mississippi. Grierson's forces traveled 600 miles (965 km) in about two weeks, tearing up railroads, burning depots, and fighting skirmishes. His raid distracted the Confederate forces defending Vicksburg and enabled Grant to move his troops south of the city.

The Siege of Vicksburg After returning to the east bank of the Mississippi, Grant embarked on a daring march east, ordering his troops to live off the country. Foraging—or searching and raiding for food—as they marched, Grant's troops headed east into Mississippi and captured the town of Jackson before turning back west toward Vicksburg. Grant's troops marched an astonishing 180 miles (290 km) in 17 days, fought 5 battles, and inflicted 7,200 casualties on the Confederates. The march ended by driving the Confederate forces back into their defenses at Vicksburg.

On May 19, 1863, Grant launched an all-out assault on Vicksburg, but the city's defenders repulsed the attack and inflicted high casualties. On

May 22, Grant tried again, but Vicksburg's defenses were still too strong. He decided that the only way to take the city was to put it under siege—cutting off its food and supplies and bombarding the city until its defenders gave up. On July 4, 1863, with his troops literally on the verge of starvation, the Confederate commander at Vicksburg surrendered. The Union victory had cut the Confederacy in two.

Reading Check **Explaining** Why did President Lincoln want the Union army to capture Vicksburg?

Gettysburg

Shortly after McClellan's victory at Antietam in September 1862, Lincoln had become frustrated again with the general. McClellan could have destroyed Lee's army at Antietam, but he let the Confederates slip away. On November 7, 1862, Lincoln fired McClellan.

The president gave command of the army to General Ambrose Burnside and then to General Joseph Hooker, both of whom had little success against Lee's troops, who were entrenched in the hills south of Fredericksburg, Virginia. At the Battle of Fredericksburg and again at the Battle of Chancellorsville, Lee's outnumbered army defeated the Union troops.

Despite the fact that both sides suffered heavy casualties during the fighting, Lee's victory emboldened the Confederate general. Once again, he decided to invade the North.

TURNING POINT

The Battle of Gettysburg In June 1863, Lee marched into Pennsylvania, where his troops seized livestock, food, and clothing. Hooker's failure to stop Lee convinced Lincoln that the general lacked the decisiveness necessary to win the war. Lincoln removed Hooker from command and appointed General George Meade as his replacement. Meade immediately headed north to intercept Lee.

At the end of June, as Lee's army foraged in the Pennsylvania countryside, some of his troops headed into the town of **Gettysburg,** hoping to seize a supply of shoes. When they arrived near the town, they discovered two brigades of Union cavalry. On July 1, 1863, the Confederates pushed the Union troops out of the town and into the hills to the south. At the same time, the main forces of both armies hurried to the scene of the fighting.

On July 2, Lee attacked, but the Union troops held their ground. The following day, Lee ordered nearly 15,000 men under the command of General

---

Reading Strategy **READING THE TEXT**

Sequencing Events Understanding the order in which events took place will help students synthesize and understand important information. Have students create a wall calendar for 1863. Suggest that they locate a perpetual calendar to correctly match dates with days of the week. Instruct students to add the events mentioned in this section to the calendar as they read. **L1 ELL**

Refer to *Inclusion for the High School Social Studies Classroom Strategies and Activities* in the TCR.

George E. Pickett and General A.P. Hill to make a massive assault. The attack became known as **Pickett's Charge.** As the mile-wide line of Confederate troops marched across open farmland toward Union forces at Cemetery Ridge, Union cannons and guns opened fire, inflicting 7,000 casualties in less than half an hour of fighting.

Aftermath of the Battle

Pickett's Charge failed to break the Union lines. Fewer than 5,000 men made it up the ridge, and Union troops quickly overwhelmed those who did. "It is all my fault," said Lee. "It is I who have lost this fight." Despite the defeat, Lee quickly rallied his troops, withdrew from Gettysburg on a rainy July 4, and retreated back to Virginia. At Gettysburg, the Union suffered 23,000 casualties, but the South's toll was an estimated 28,000 casualties, more than one-third of Lee's entire force.

The disaster at Gettysburg proved to be the turning point of the war in the East. The Union's victory strengthened the Republicans politically and ensured once again that the British would not recognize the Confederacy. For the remainder of the war, Lee's forces remained on the defensive, slowly giving ground to the advancing Union army.

The Gettysburg Address

In November 1863, Lincoln came to Gettysburg to dedicate a part of the battlefield as a cemetery. His speech, the **Gettysburg Address,** became one of the best-known orations in American history. In it, Lincoln reminded his listeners that the nation was "conceived in liberty, and dedicated to the proposition that all men are created equal":

> ❝It is . . . for us to be here dedicated to the great task remaining before us—that from these honored dead we take increased devotion to that cause for which they gave the last full measure of devotion; that we here highly resolve that these dead shall not have died in vain; that this, nation, under God, shall have a new birth of freedom; and that the government of the people, by the people, and for the people, shall not perish from the earth.❞
>
> —from the Gettysburg Address

📖 *(See page 954 for the complete text of the Gettysburg Address.)*

✓ **Reading Check** **Summarizing** What was the result of Pickett's Charge?

TECHNOLOGY & History

The Telegraph

Invented by Samuel Morse in 1837, the telegraph was indispensable during the Civil War. It was used to send battle orders and to verify the locations of troops. With no telegraph in the White House, President Lincoln often visited the War Department's telegraph room to receive current information. Telegraph operators sent messages by pressing a key in a pattern of short and long clicks, following Morse's alphabetic code. *In what other areas of life was the telegraph useful?*

1. The telegraph operator pressed a switch, called the **key,** breaking an electric current .

2. The electric current activated a **sounder,** an electromagnet consisting of coiled wire wrapped around an iron core. The changing electric current created a clicking sound.

3. Skilled operators were able to send up to 60 **messages** each hour, keying a message with one hand while translating incoming messages with the other hand.

4. Telegraph wires allowed the clicking codes to be transmitted geographically.

sounder

key

L1/ELL

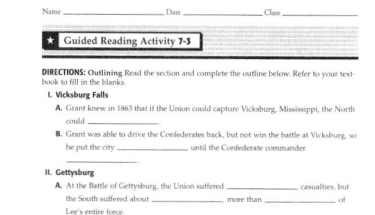

Guided Reading Activity 7-3

Name _____ Date _____ Class _____

★ **Guided Reading Activity 7-3**

DIRECTIONS: Outlining Read the section and complete the outline below. Refer to your textbook to fill in the blanks.

I. Vicksburg Falls
  A. Grant knew in 1863 that if the Union could capture Vicksburg, Mississippi, the North could _____
  B. Grant was able to drive the Confederates back, but not win the battle at Vicksburg, so he put the city _____ until the Confederate commander

II. Gettysburg
  A. At the Battle of Gettysburg, the Union suffered _____ casualties, but the South suffered about _____ more than _____ of Lee's entire force.
  B. _____

✓ **Reading Check**

Answer: It failed to break Union lines and resulted in heavy Confederate casualties.

TECHNOLOGY & History

Background: The men who operated the telegraph were known as the signal corps. When telegraph lines could not be run, the signal corps also transmitted messages using flags during the day and torches at night. The signal corps had to memorize all the signals and codes and were not permitted to carry anything that would be useful to the enemy in case they were captured.

Answer: to transmit news, to transact business, and to communicate with distant family members

---

ABCNEWS INTERACTIVE™

 VIDEOCASSETTE
Historic America Electronic Field Trips

View **Tape 1, Chapter 8:** "Gettysburg."

DIFFERENTIATED INSTRUCTION

Gifted and Talented Have students develop a list of 10 questions to ask General Ulysses S. Grant about the victory at Vicksburg. Then have them research the types of answers that Grant might have given to their questions. Have students work in pairs to select the best of both their questions and responses and then conduct an interview for the class between a reporter and General Grant. **L3**

👉 Refer to *Inclusion for the High School Social Studies Classroom Strategies and Activities* in the TCR.

Geography *Skills*

Answers:

1. Virginia

2. June 1864 to April 1865; it cut off the rail line supplying Lee's forces and thus allowed Union forces to entrap the retreating Lee at Appomattox Courthouse

Geography Skills Practice

Ask: Which wars have been the costliest to the United States in terms of human deaths? (*Civil War and World War II*)

FYI

In August 1861, the Confederacy signed treaties with a number of the Native American peoples living in the Indian Territory. In return for Confederate protection against the United States, the Native Americans promised to be "loyal allies." Indeed, groups of the Cherokee, Creek, Seminole, and Osage fought for the Confederacy in a number of battles in the West. General Stand Watie, a Cherokee leader, was one of the last Confederate commanders to surrender.

Creating a Circle Chart Have students use the number of American war deaths in the circle chart on page 260 to calculate the percentage of total American war deaths that each war represents. Have them recreate the circle chart showing percentages rather than actual numbers. Then have students create a series of questions that can be answered using the percentages. **L2**

 Final Campaigns of the Civil War, 1864–1865

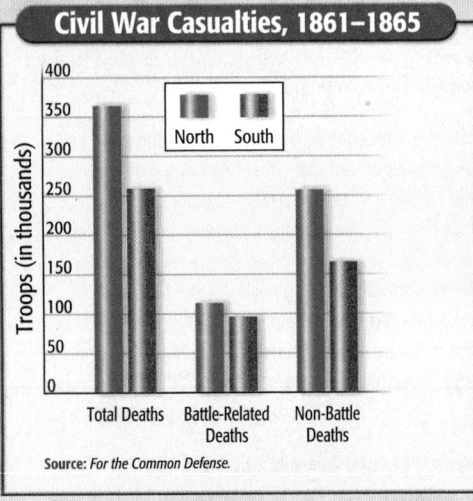

Civil War Casualties, 1861–1865

Source: *For the Common Defense.*

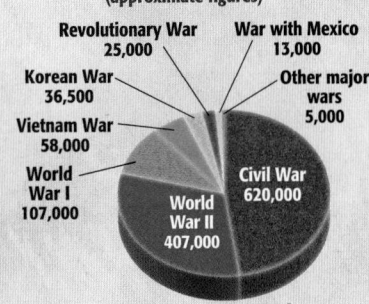

American War Deaths
(approximate figures)

- Revolutionary War 25,000
- War with Mexico 13,000
- Korean War 36,500
- Other major wars 5,000
- Vietnam War 58,000
- World War I 107,000
- World War II 407,000
- Civil War 620,000

Source: United States Civil War Center; *For the Common Defense*

Geography *Skills*

1. **Interpreting Maps** In what state did Lee surrender?
2. **Applying Geography Skills** How long did the siege of Petersburg last, and what significance did it have for the war?

Grant Secures Tennessee

After the Union's major victories at Vicksburg and Gettysburg, fierce fighting erupted in Tennessee near Chattanooga. Chattanooga was a vital railroad junction. Both the North and the South knew that if the Union forces captured Chattanooga, they would control a major railroad running south to Atlanta. The way would be open for a Union advance into Georgia.

Chattanooga had been in the hands of Confederate forces led by General Braxton Bragg. In early September 1863, however, Union general William Rosecrans pushed Bragg's troops out of the town. Bragg did not retreat far. When Rosecrans advanced into Georgia, Bragg launched an assault

against him at Chickamauga Creek on September 19, 1863. Rosecrans quickly ordered his troops to fall back to Chattanooga, where they found themselves surrounded by Bragg's forces.

In an effort to save the Union forces in Chattanooga, Lincoln decided to send some of Meade's forces to help Rosecrans. General Grant also hurried to Chattanooga and quickly took charge of the Union forces gathered there.

In late November, Grant ordered an attack on Confederate positions on Lookout Mountain. Charging uphill through swirling fog, the Union troops quickly forced the Southern troops to fall back. Confederates retreating from Lookout Mountain hurried to join the Southern forces at Missionary Ridge

INTERDISCIPLINARY CONNECTIONS ACTIVITY

Language Arts Tell students that Stephen Crane's novel, *The Red Badge of Courage*, presents a realistic view of the war. Have the language arts teacher select a few passages from the book that demonstrate how Crane paints a picture of the war. Then tell students that Crane did not actually fight in the Civil War. He based his book on war stories told by veterans and on the photographs taken by Mathew Brady, a famous Civil War photographer. Discuss the difference between participating in an event and having the event described by others. **L2**

east of Chattanooga. Although outnumbered, they secured a rugged position on high ground.

Grant did not intend to storm Missionary Ridge. He believed an all-out assault would be suicidal. Instead he ordered General **William Tecumseh Sherman** to attack Confederate positions on the north end of the ridge. When Sherman failed to break through, Grant ordered 23,000 men under General George Thomas to launch a limited attack against the Confederates in front of Missionary Ridge as a diversion.

To Grant's astonishment, Thomas's troops overran the Confederate trenches and charged up the steep slope of Missionary Ridge. The rapid charge scattered the surprised Confederate soldiers who retreated in panic, leaving Missionary Ridge—and Chattanooga—to the Union army.

By the spring of 1864, Grant had accomplished two crucial objectives for the Union. His capture of Vicksburg had given the Union control of the Mississippi River, while his victory at Chattanooga had secured eastern Tennessee and cleared the way for an invasion of Georgia.

Lincoln rewarded Grant by appointing him general in chief of the Union forces and promoting him to lieutenant general, a rank no one had held since George Washington. The president had finally found a general he trusted to win the war.

✓ **Reading Check** **Examining** Why was capturing Chattanooga important for the Union?

Grant Versus Lee

By the spring of 1864, Union leaders knew that the only way to end the long and bloody war was to defeat Lee's army. Accordingly, General Grant put his most trusted subordinate, William Sherman, in charge of Union operations in the West. Grant then headed to Washington, D.C., to take command of the Union troops facing Lee.

From Wilderness to Cold Harbor "Whatever happens, there will be no turning back," Grant promised Lincoln. He was determined to march southward, attacking Lee's forces until the South surrendered.

The first battle of Grant's campaign erupted in the Wilderness, a densely forested area near Fredericksburg, Virginia. Despite suffering heavy casualties in the two-day battle, Grant did not pause. He headed southeast toward Spotsylvania Courthouse. First in terrible heat and then in pouring rain, the two armies battled near

Spotsylvania for over a week, often in bloody hand-to-hand combat that left many traumatized.

Unable to break Lee's lines at Spotsylvania, Grant headed toward Cold Harbor, a strategic crossroads northeast of Richmond. Convinced that his relentless attacks had weakened and demoralized Lee's troops, Grant decided to launch an all-out assault at Cold Harbor. The attack failed miserably, costing the Union 7,000 casualties, compared to only 1,500 for the South.

The Siege of Petersburg Stopped by Lee at Cold Harbor, Grant tried another plan. He ordered General Philip Sheridan to stage a cavalry raid north and west of Richmond. While Sheridan's troops distracted Lee, Grant headed south past Richmond to cross the James River. His goal was to capture the nearby town of **Petersburg** and thus cut off the rail line supplying Richmond and Lee's forces.

When Union troops reached the outskirts of Petersburg, they paused. The city was defended by 20-foot thick barricades, 15-foot deep ditches, and carefully positioned cannons. The strength of the city's defenses intimidated the Union troops, who were already exhausted and demoralized. Realizing a full-scale frontal assault would be suicidal, Grant ordered his troops to lay siege to the city.

✓ **Reading Check** **Summarizing** Why did General Grant want to capture Petersburg?

Union Victories in the South

South of Virginia, General William Sherman marched his army from Chattanooga toward Atlanta, Georgia. Meanwhile, the Union navy sealed up the last major Confederate port on the Gulf of Mexico east of the Mississippi—Mobile, Alabama.

Farragut Attacks Mobile On August 5, 1864, David Farragut took 18 ships past the three Confederate forts defending Mobile Bay. As the fleet headed into the bay, a mine, which was called a torpedo in the 1860s, blew up a Union ship. The explosion brought the fleet to a halt directly in front of a fort's guns. "Damn the torpedoes! Full speed ahead!" cried Farragut, whose flagship led the way. After getting past the Confederate forts, Farragut's ships destroyed a Confederate fleet defending Mobile Bay. Although Farragut did not capture Mobile, he did seal off the bay.

Sherman Takes Georgia In late August 1864, General Sherman's army tried to encircle Atlanta. To avoid being trapped in the city, Confederate General

✓ **Reading Check**

Answer: They would control the major rail line running to Atlanta.

✓ **Reading Check**

Answer: to cut off the rail line that was supplying resources to Lee's troops

 CURRICULUM CONNECTION

Music The two songs that many people identify with the Civil War, "Dixie" and "The Battle Hymn of the Republic," were ironically both borrowed from the other side. Dan Emmett, the son of an Ohio abolitionist, wrote "Dixie" as a Northern minstrel tune. Julia Ward Howe wrote the words to "The Battle Hymn of the Republic" to the melody of a Southern camp meeting hymn.

FYI

Some historians believe baseball originated from a 1600s English game called rounders, which was played by the American colonists. Others have argued that Abner Doubleday of Cooperstown, New York, created specific rules for the game and called it base ball (two words). Baseball spread during the Civil War largely because Union soldiers played it for recreation between battles. Confederate prisoners and other troops watched the game and learned it. Before long, people around the country were playing baseball.

CRITICAL THINKING ACTIVITY

Synthesizing Information Use a map showing the western battles to review and discuss with students Grant's campaigns in the West. Then call on volunteers to explain how these campaigns fit in with the Union's strategy for the war. *(to gain control of the Mississippi River and to split the Confederacy in two)* L2

Profiles IN HISTORY

Background: On April 7, 1865, Grant wrote Lee the following: ". . . I regard it as my duty to shift from myself the responsibility of any further effusion of blood, by asking of you the surrender of that portion of the Confederate Southern army known as the Army of Northern Virginia." Lee replied: "I reciprocate your desire to avoid useless effusion of blood, and therefore, before considering your proposition, ask the terms you will offer on condition of its surrender."

Ask: What were the differences in these two men's military careers before the Civil War? *(Grant was undistinguished both at the military academy and as an army officer. Lee was an outstanding student at the military academy and a brilliant and courageous officer during the war with Mexico.)*

✓ **Reading Check**

Answer: to make Southern civilians understand the horrors of war and to pressure them into giving up the struggle

3 ASSESS

Assign Section 3 Assessment as homework or as an in-class activity.

💿 Have students use the **Interactive Tutor Self-Assessment CD-ROM.**

John B. Hood evacuated the city. Taking the city easily, Sherman's troops set fires to destroy railroads, warehouses, mills, and factories. The fires spread quickly, destroying more than one-third of the city.

On November 15, 1864, Sherman led his troops east across Georgia in what became known as the **March to the Sea.** The purpose of the march was to make Southern civilians understand the horrors of war and to pressure them into giving up the struggle. Sherman's troops cut a path of destruction through Georgia that was at times 60 miles (97 km) wide. They ransacked houses, burned crops, and killed livestock. By December 21, 1864, they had reached the coast and seized Georgia's first settlement, the city of Savannah.

After reaching the Atlantic coast, Sherman turned north and headed into South Carolina, the state that many people believed had started the Civil War. "The whole army," Sherman wrote, "is burning with an insatiable desire to wreak vengeance upon South Carolina." As one of Sherman's soldiers declared about South Carolina, "Here is where treason began and . . . here is where it shall end."

Sherman's troops burned and pillaged nearly everything in front of them. At least 12 towns were set on fire, including Columbia, the state capital,

which Sherman seized in February 1865. The march greatly demoralized Southerners. As one South Carolinian wrote, "All is gloom, despondency and inactivity. Our army is demoralized and the people panic stricken . . . to fight longer seems madness."

✓ **Reading Check** **Examining** Why did General Sherman march his army to the sea?

The South Surrenders

As Sherman and Grant began their campaigns in the spring of 1864, Lincoln worried greatly about his chances for re-election. Sensing the public's growing anger over the costly war, Lincoln even confided to an army officer, "I am going to be beaten." He did not know that the war was rapidly approaching its conclusion—and the South was headed toward collapse.

The Election of 1864 The capture of Atlanta came just in time to revitalize Northern support for the war and for Lincoln himself. On Election Day, voters elected the president to another term. Lincoln interpreted his re-election as an approval of his war policies and as a **mandate,** or clear sign from the voters, to end slavery permanently by amending the

---

Profiles IN HISTORY

Ulysses S. Grant
1822–1885

Before his victories in Kentucky and Tennessee, Ulysses S. Grant had been a mediocre West Point cadet, a failed businessperson, and an undistinguished army officer. More than any other Union commander, however, Grant changed the strategy—and the outcome—of the Civil War. Grant's restless urge for offensive fighting and his insistence on "unconditional surrender" at Fort Donelson convinced Lincoln to place the general in command of all the Union troops in 1864. Lincoln's confidence was not misplaced. Despite mounting casualties and accusations that he was a "butcher," Grant pushed relentlessly until he finally accepted Lee's surrender at Appomattox, Virginia.

The Union's enthusiasm for its victorious general made Grant a two-term president after the war, although scandals in his administration marred his reputation. The Civil War had been the high point of Grant's life, the challenge that brought out his best qualities. More than any monument or memorial—including Grant's Tomb, in New York City—Lincoln's defense of his embattled general during the war sums up Grant's character and achievement: "I can't spare this man; he fights."

Robert E. Lee
1807–1870

The son of a distinguished—though not wealthy—Virginia family, Robert E. Lee was raised in the socially exclusive world of the aristocratic South. From the beginning, he seemed marked by fate for brilliant success. At West Point he excelled in both his studies and his social life, impressing teachers and fellow cadets with his talent and good nature. As an army officer in the war with Mexico, he performed with brilliance and courage.

Offered command of the Union troops at the beginning of the Civil War, Lee refused, unable to oppose his fellow Virginians. He later commanded the army of Northern Virginia.

A hero to Southerners during the war, Lee felt a responsibility to set an example of Southern honor in defeat. His swearing of renewed allegiance to the United States after the war inspired thousands of former Confederate soldiers to follow his example. As president of Washington College in Virginia (later renamed Washington and Lee), Lee encouraged his students to put the war behind them and to behave as responsible citizens.

Lee died at age 63. In his last moments, he seemed to give orders to his troops, and then at last called out, "Strike the tent!"

262 CHAPTER 7 The Civil War and Reconstruction

EXTENDING THE CONTENT

Photography Mathew Brady captured the Civil War forever on film. He was one of America's first photojournalists—photographers who record the news in photographs. He traveled with the Union army, carrying his equipment in an old delivery wagon. Brady transported not only the camera, but also all the supplies needed to develop and process the photographs. By war's end, he and his many assistants had recorded in more than 10,000 photographs the battles, the camps, and the lives and deaths of Union soldiers.

Constitution. To get the amendment through Congress, Republicans appealed to Democrats who were against slavery to help them. On January 31, 1865, the **Thirteenth Amendment** to the Constitution, banning slavery in the United States, was narrowly passed by the House of Representatives and was sent to the states for ratification.

Surrender Meanwhile, back in the trenches near Petersburg, Lee knew that time was running out. On April 1, 1865, Union troops led by Philip Sheridan cut the last rail line into Petersburg at the Battle of Five Forks. The following night, Lee's troops withdrew from their positions near the city and raced west.

Lee's desperate attempt to escape Grant's forces failed when Sheridan's cavalry got ahead of Lee's troops and blocked the road at **Appomattox Courthouse.** When his troops failed to break through, Lee sadly observed, "There is nothing left for me to do but go and see General Grant, and I would rather die a thousand deaths." With his ragged and battered troops surrounded and outnumbered, Lee surrendered to Grant on April 9, 1865.

Grant's generous terms of surrender guaranteed that the United States would not prosecute Confederate soldiers for treason. When Grant agreed to let Confederates take their horses home "to put in a crop to carry themselves and their families through the next winter," Lee thanked him, adding that the kindness would "do much toward conciliating our people." As Lee left he shook hands with Ely Parker, a Senecan who served as Grant's secretary. "I am glad to see a real American here," Lee told the Native American. Parker replied, "We are all Americans."

Lincoln's Assassination With the war over, Lincoln delivered a speech describing his plan to restore the Southern states to the Union. In the speech, he mentioned including African Americans in Southern state governments. One listener, actor John Wilkes Booth, sneered to a friend, "That is the last speech he will ever make."

Although his advisers had repeatedly warned him not to appear unescorted in public, Lincoln went to Ford's Theater with his wife to see a play on the evening of April 14, 1865. Just after 10 P.M., Booth slipped quietly behind the president and shot him in the back of the head. Lincoln died the next morning.

The president's death shocked the nation. Once viewed as an unsophisticated man unsuited for the presidency, Lincoln had become the Union's greatest champion. Tens of thousands of men, women, and children lined railroad tracks across the nation as Lincoln's body was transported back to Springfield, Illinois.

Aftermath of the Civil War The North's victory in the Civil War saved the Union and strengthened the power of the federal government over the states. It transformed American society by ending slavery, but it also left the South socially and economically devastated, and many questions unresolved.

No one knew how to bring the Southern states back into the Union or what the status of African Americans would be in Southern society. Americans from the North and the South tried to answer these questions in the years following the Civil War—an era known as Reconstruction.

✓ **Reading Check** **Explaining** Why did President Lincoln doubt he could win the 1864 election?

HISTORY Online **Study Central**™ To review this section, go to tarvol2.glencoe.com and click on **Study Central**™.

SECTION 3 ASSESSMENT

Checking for Understanding
1. **Define:** foraging, siege, torpedo, mandate.
2. **Identify:** Pickett's Charge, Gettysburg Address, William Tecumseh Sherman, Thirteenth Amendment, Appomattox Courthouse.
3. **Describe** how General Grant conducted the Confederate surrender.

Reviewing Themes
4. **Geography and History** Why was capturing Vicksburg important for the Union?

Critical Thinking
5. **Analyzing** How might the outcome of the war have been different if the Confederates had won at Gettysburg? Why?
6. **Organizing** Complete a graphic organizer by listing the purpose for the Union march on Atlanta and the effect of the city's capture on both sides.

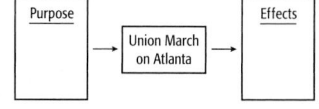
Purpose → Union March on Atlanta → Effects

Analyzing Visuals
7. **Examining Graphs** Examine the graphs of war deaths on page 260. What would account for the thousands of non-battle deaths listed in one of the graphs?

Writing About History
8. **Descriptive Writing** Take on the role of a Confederate or Union soldier at the Battle of Gettysburg. Write a journal entry describing the battle and your feelings about its result.

CHAPTER 7   The Civil War and Reconstruction   **263**

SECTION 3 ASSESSMENT ANSWERS

1. Terms are in blue.
2. Pickett's Charge (p. 259), Gettysburg Address (p. 259), William Tecumseh Sherman (p. 261), Thirteenth Amendment (p. 263), Appomattox Courthouse (p. 263)
3. Grant's generous terms allowed soldiers to go home without fear of prosecution for treason, and with their horses to help plow the fields.
4. It cut the South in two.
5. A Confederate win at Gettysburg might have convinced Britain to recognize the Confederacy and help the South defeat the Union.
6. Purpose: make citizens of Atlanta feel the hardship of war and destroy Atlanta's military value. Effect: more than one-third of the city was destroyed by fire.
7. diseases and unsanitary living conditions
8. Entries should be detailed and thoughtful.

✓ **Reading Check**

Answer: The war had been costly and long, angering many voters.

L1/ELL

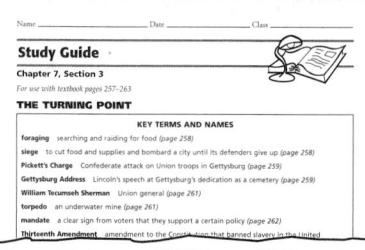

Reading Essentials and Study Guide 7-3

L2

Section Quiz 7-3

Reteach
Have students explain how battles in Tennessee helped turn the war in favor of the Union.

Enrich
Have interested students research and report on one aspect of American popular culture during the Civil War.

HISTORY Online

Study Central™ provides summaries, interactive games, and online graphic organizers to help students review section content.

4 CLOSE

Have students describe the events at Vicksburg and Gettysburg.

NATIONAL GEOGRAPHIC # Geography&History

1 FOCUS

Tell students that Gettysburg lies about 50 miles northwest of Baltimore, Maryland. On February 11, 1895, Congress made Gettysburg a National Military Park as a memorial to the armies that fought the bloodiest battle of the Civil War.

2 TEACH

Analyzing Information Have students read Lee's quote about the defeat. Ask students why they think Lee took responsibility for the defeat. Then ask students to explain how taking responsibility was a mark of leadership. Finally, have students relate examples from their own lives that demonstrate people taking responsibility for their actions. **L1**

Comparing and Contrasting Tell students that the Union and Confederate armies were very similar. Have students use library and Internet resources to identify ways in which the armies were similar and the ways they were different. To get them started, tell students that both armies used similar weapons. You may recommend that students visit http://www.nps.gov/gett/index.htm as a starting point for their research. **L2**

Benner's Hill

Wolf Hill

Hanover Road

Johnson

Rock Creek

Baltimore

Culp's Hill

Power's Hill

Early

12th Corps
SLOCUM
8,700

Army of the Potomac
General George G. Meade

Town of
GETTYSBURG

Cemetery
Hill

11th Corps
HOWARD
5,800

3rd C
BIR
6,4

2nd Corps
EWELL
15,000

Cemetery Ridge

2nd Corps
GIBBON
6,800

Taneytown Road

1st Corps
NEWTON
6,000

Pickett's Charge

Rodes

12,500
3 pm

Plum Run

Seminary Ridge

Pettigrew

Garnett

nderson

Kemper

3rd Corps
HILL
15,200

Armistead

Lang

Wilcox

Emmitsburg Road

Trimble

Peach
Orchard

Pickett

Army of Northern Virginia
General Robert E. Lee

McLaws

1st Corps
LONGSTREE
15,500

PENNSYLVANIA

Harrisburg

Carlisle

Chambersburg

Gettysburg

York

Frederick

Baltimore

Winchester

MARYLAND

Front
Royal

Washington, D.C.

VIRGINIA

Chancellorsville

Fredericksburg

INVADING THE NORTH

After their victory at Chancellorsville in May 1863, the Confederates invaded the North (red arrow). Using the Blue Ridge Mountains to screen their movements, the Confederates advanced down the Shenandoah Valley, crossed the Potomac River, and pushed into Pennsylvania. The Federal army (blue arrow) placed itself between the Rebels and Washington. On July 1, the two armies met at the crossroads town of Gettysburg, Pennsylvania.

A nurse poses with wounded soldiers outside one of the 400 tents set up as a temporary hospital at Gettysburg. During the battle, the Union army suffered 23,000 casualties, the Confederates 28,000.

EXTENDING THE CONTENT

The Hero of Little Round Top The extreme left flank of the Union lines at Gettysburg—a hill called Little Round Top—was commanded by Colonel Joshua Lawrence Chamberlain, a college professor who had taken a leave from teaching to fight in the war. Chamberlain knew that if the Confederates took Little Round Top, they would have a view of the whole Union line. Although greatly outnumbered, Chamberlain's forces withstood numerous attacks. Finally, Chamberlain led his troops in a bayonet charge that drove the Confederates from the field. Chamberlain received the Medal of Honor for his bravery at Gettysburg.

CANNON BOMBARDMENT
Pickett's Charge was preceded by a massive artillery bombardment. However, much of the Confederate artillery overshot the Federal positions on Cemetery Ridge, landing well to the rear of the frontline troops.

11th AC Hospital

Artillery Reserves

th Corps
SYKES
9,500

6th Corps
SEDGWICK
13,600

Little Round Top

Big Round Top

heat eld

Devil's Den

Hood

Hood

Gettysburg Forces

⚔	Union troops
🐎	Confederate troops
3rd Corps	Corp
HILL	Commander
15,200	Number of troops (as of noon, July 3rd)

Scale of map varies in this perspective (distance from Gettysburg to Big Round Top 3 miles)

Gettysburg: The Final Day

The Confederate invasion of Union territory in the summer of 1863 had been a bold stroke. By moving north, the Confederate commander of the Army of Northern Virginia, General Robert E. Lee, had relieved pressure on battle-ravaged Virginia. He had threatened the Federal capital of Washington, D.C., and gained access to the rich farms and other resources of Pennsylvania. Indeed, it was the prospect of finding shoes and other army supplies that lured the Confederates to Gettysburg.

By the morning of July 3, however, Lee was lamenting the lost opportunities. When his troops arrived in Gettysburg on July 1, they had driven the Federals out of the town. Quickly grasping the advantages of defending the high ground, Major General George Meade had ordered his Federal Army of the Potomac to take up positions in the hills south of town. The Federal line stretched from Culp's Hill and Cemetery Hill south along Cemetery Ridge to another hill called Little Round Top. The Confederates had taken up a position along a roughly parallel ridge to the west known as Seminary Ridge. Between the two positions stretched pastureland and fields of wheat. On July 2, Lee's troops had attacked Federal positions on Culp's Hill, Cemetery Hill and Little Round Top, but were pushed back. Now, on the morning of July 3, Lee was determined to punch a hole in the Federal line. Among the officers preparing to attack was Major General George Pickett, who would give his name to the day's infantry charge.

At about 3:00 p.m., more than 12,000 Confederates set out from Seminary Ridge. Three-quarters of a mile away, the Federals waited atop Cemetery Ridge. Federal artillery ripped holes in the Confederate line as it advanced. When the Rebels were 200 yards from the crest of Cemetery Ridge, the Federals unleashed volley after volley. Still the Confederates pressed on. Hundreds made it all the way up the slope of the ridge, but as they did, Federal reinforcements rushed in. Firing at point-blank range, stabbing with bayonets, bludgeoning with the butt ends of rifles, the Federals drove the Confederates back down the slope. Pickett's Charge had been repulsed. Lee retreated to Virginia and the tide of war turned in favor of the North.

LEARNING FROM GEOGRAPHY

1. How did the Confederate army use the mountains of Virginia in its invasion of the North?

2. Why was the Federal army in such a strong position at Gettysburg?

"It's all my fault. It is I who have lost this fight," Lee told the survivors as they struggled back after Pickett's Charge.

Creating a Relief Map Have students work in groups to create a relief map depicting one day at Gettysburg. Each student should be assigned the role of researcher, designer, or artist. Researchers find information about the day's battles, designers create plans for the maps that the artists can use to create the maps. **L3**

3 ASSESS

Have students answer the Learning from Geography questions.

4 CLOSE

Ask students to name the landforms on the map and to explain how the armies used the landforms.

NGS ONLINE

Access National Geographic's Web site for current events, atlas updates, activities, links, interactive features, and archives at www.nationalgeographic.com.

L2

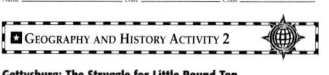

Geography and History
Activity 2

Name _____ Date _____ Class _____

◆ GEOGRAPHY AND HISTORY ACTIVITY 2

Gettysburg: The Struggle for Little Round Top

THE PHYSICAL GEOGRAPHY OF GETTYSBURG
In 1863 Gettysburg, Pennsylvania, was a small town surrounded by orchards, fields, woodlands, valleys, and hills. The geography and topography of the area—the patterns and placement of the hills, ridges, boulders, woods, and open areas—influenced how the Battle of Gettysburg was fought and its eventual outcome.
The Union forces, led by Major General George Meade, were positioned just south of Gettysburg in an upside-down fishhook

Map 1–Sites on the Gettysburg Battlefield

ANSWERS TO LEARNING FROM GEOGRAPHY

1. They used the mountains to screen their movements as they marched north.

2. It occupied the high ground, such as Cemetery Ridge, Culp's Hill, Cemetery Hill, and Little Round Top.

265

1 FOCUS

Section Overview

This section focuses on the plans to rebuild and reunite the nation following the Civil War.

BELLRINGER
Skillbuilder Activity

Project transparency and have students answer the question.

Daily Focus Skills Transparency 7–4

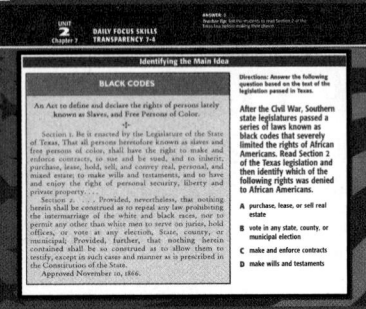

Reading Preview

Answers to Graphic: A key position of Lincoln's plan was that 10 percent of a former Confederate state's voters took a loyalty oath to the United States; for the Radical Republicans' plan, a key feature aimed at guaranteeing African Americans the right to vote.

Preteaching Vocabulary

Have each student write a brief explanation of one term from Key Terms and Names.

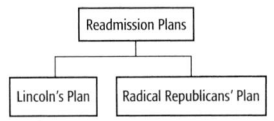

Guide to Reading

Main Idea
In the months after the Civil War, the nation began the effort to rebuild and reunite.

Key Terms and Names
Reconstruction, amnesty, pocket veto, freedmen, Freedmen's Bureau, black codes, Fourteenth Amendment, Military Reconstruction Act, impeach, Fifteenth Amendment

Reading Strategy
Organizing As you read about Reconstruction, complete a graphic organizer similar to the one below to compare the plans of President Lincoln and the Radical Republicans for readmitting Southern states to the Union.

Readmission Plans
Lincoln's Plan
Radical Republicans' Plan

Reading Objectives
- **Discuss** life in the South immediately after the war.
- **Describe** the major features of congressional Reconstruction and its political impact.

Section Theme
Groups and Institutions Northerners disagreed on which policies would best rebuild the South and safeguard the rights of African Americans.

Preview of Events

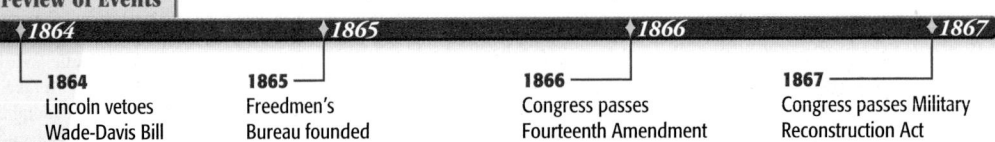

| ◆1864 | ◆1865 | ◆1866 | ◆1867 |

1864
Lincoln vetoes Wade-Davis Bill

1865
Freedmen's Bureau founded

1866
Congress passes Fourteenth Amendment

1867
Congress passes Military Reconstruction Act

Artist depiction of an emancipated African American

FREE!

★ An American Story ★

Houston Holloway was ready for freedom. By 1865 the 20-year-old enslaved man had toiled under three different slaveholders. President Lincoln's Emancipation Proclamation, delivered in 1863, had freed him—but only in theory. The proclamation freed enslaved persons in the Confederacy, but because the Union could not enforce its laws in Confederate territory, many African American men and women in the South remained enslaved. Holloway knew that his only hope of freedom was a Northern victory in the Civil War.

The time of that victory finally arrived. On the spring day in 1865 when Union troops overran his community in Georgia on their way to defeating the Confederacy, Holloway rejoiced upon reaching true freedom:

❝I felt like a bird out of a cage. Amen. Amen. Amen. I could hardly ask to feel better than I did that day. . . . The week passed off in a blaze of glory.❞

—quoted in *A Short History of Reconstruction*

Reconstruction Battle Begins

At the end of the Civil War, the South was a defeated region with a devastated economy. While some Southerners were bitter over the Union military victory, for many the more important struggle after the conflict was rebuilding their land and their lives. Meanwhile, the president and Congress grappled with the difficult task of Reconstruction, or rebuilding the nation after the war. Among other things, they had to decide under what terms and conditions the former Confederate states would be permitted to rejoin the Union.

266 CHAPTER 7   The Civil War and Reconstruction

SECTION RESOURCES

📖 Reproducible Masters
- Reproducible Lesson Plan 7–4
- Daily Lecture and Discussion Notes 7–4
- Guided Reading Activity 7–4
- Section Quiz 7–4
- Reading Essentials and Study Guide 7–4
- Supreme Court Case Studies

🖥 Transparencies
- Daily Focus Skills Transparency 7–4

Multimedia
- 💿 Interactive Tutor Self-Assessment CD-ROM
- 💿 ExamView® Pro Testmaker CD-ROM
- 💿 Presentation Plus! CD-ROM
- 💿 TeacherWorks™ CD-ROM
- 🎵 Audio Program

Lincoln's Plan In December 1863, President Lincoln set forth his plan for reuniting the country in the Proclamation of Amnesty and Reconstruction. Lincoln wanted a moderate policy that would reconcile the South with the Union instead of punishing it for treason. He offered a general amnesty, or pardon, to all Southerners who took an oath of loyalty to the United States and accepted the Union's proclamations concerning slavery. When 10 percent of a state's voters in the 1860 presidential election had taken this oath, they could organize a new state government. Certain people were excluded from taking the oath, however, and would not be pardoned. These included all Confederate government officials and officers in the Confederate army, as well as all judges, members of Congress, and military officers who had left their posts to help the Confederacy.

The Radical Republicans Resistance to Lincoln's plan surfaced at once among a group of Republicans in Congress known as **Radical Republicans.** Led by Representative **Thaddeus Stevens** of Pennsylvania and Senator Charles Sumner of Massachusetts, the radicals did not want to reconcile with the South. They wanted, in Stevens's words, to "revolutionize Southern institutions, habits, and manners."

The Radical Republicans had three main goals. First, they wanted to prevent the leaders of the Confederacy from returning to power after the war. Second, they wanted the Republican Party to become a powerful institution in the South. Finally, and perhaps most importantly, they wanted the federal government to help African Americans achieve political equality by guaranteeing their right to vote in the South.

Congressional Republicans knew that the abolition of slavery would give the South more seats in the House of Representatives. Before the Civil War, enslaved people had only counted in Congress as three-fifths of a free person. Now that African Americans were free, the South was entitled to more seats in Congress. This would endanger Republican control of Congress, unless Republicans could find a way to protect African American voting rights in the South.

Although the radicals knew that giving African Americans in the South the right to vote would help the Republican Party win elections, most were not acting cynically. Many of them had been abolitionists before the Civil War and had pushed Lincoln into making emancipation a goal of the war. They believed in equality for all Americans, regardless of their race. Senator Henry Wilson of Massachusetts summarized their position by saying:

66[Congress] must see to it that the man made free by the Constitution is a freeman indeed; that he can go where he pleases, work when and for whom he pleases . . . go into schools and educate himself and his children; that the rights and guarantees of the common law are his, and that he walks the earth proud and erect in the conscious dignity of a free man.99

The Wade-Davis Bill Caught between Lincoln and the Radical Republicans were many moderate Republicans. The moderates thought Lincoln was being too lenient, but they also thought the radicals were going too far in their support for African American equality and voting rights.

By the summer of 1864, the moderates and radicals had come up with a plan for Reconstruction that they could both support as an alternative to Lincoln's plan. The compromise between the moderates and the radicals was the **Wade-Davis Bill** of 1864. This bill required the majority of the adult white men in a former Confederate state to take an oath of allegiance to the Union. The state could then hold a constitutional convention to create a new state government. Furthermore, the people chosen to attend the constitutional convention had to take an "ironclad" oath asserting that they had never fought against the Union or supported the Confederacy in any way. Each state's convention would then have to abolish slavery, reject all debts the state had acquired as part of the Confederacy,

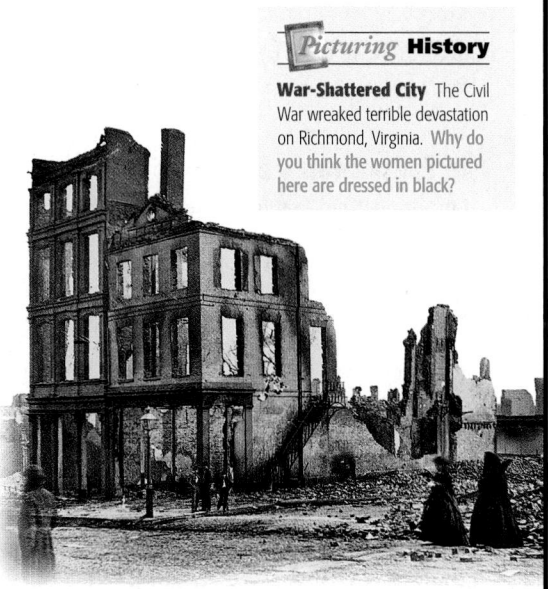

Picturing **History**

War-Shattered City The Civil War wreaked terrible devastation on Richmond, Virginia. Why do you think the women pictured here are dressed in black?

2 TEACH

Daily Lecture and Discussion Notes 7-4

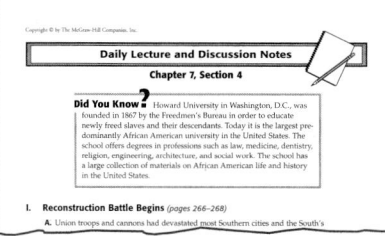

Copyright © by The McGraw-Hill Companies, Inc.

Daily Lecture and Discussion Notes

Chapter 7, Section 4

Did You Know ? Howard University in Washington, D.C., was founded in 1867 by the Freedmen's Bureau in order to educate newly freed slaves and their descendants. Today it is the largest predominantly African American university in the United States. The school offers degrees in professions such as law, medicine, dentistry, religion, engineering, architecture, and social work. The school has a large collection of materials on African American life and history in the United States.

I. **Reconstruction Battle Begins** (pages 266–268)

A. Union troops and cannons had devastated most Southern cities and the South's

 Reading Strategy

Making a List Have students read the quote on page 267. Then have students make a list of the things a free person can do according to Henry Wilson. Then have students add to the list other freedoms that they think freed African Americans may have valued. **Ask:** If you had been enslaved, which of the freedoms on our list would you value most? Why? **L1**

Picturing **History**

Answer: They are in mourning, perhaps for relatives who died in the war. **Ask:** What do you think these citizens of Richmond may have been feeling? *(possible answers—defeated, angry, determined, hopeless)*

FYI

In addition to the devastation of Southern cities, the war brought even greater disruption to the countryside. Southern cotton production, the mainstay of the Southern economy, did not reach its 1860 levels again until 1879.

Reading Strategy **READING THE TEXT**

Using Word Maps A word map can be any kind of graphic that is designed to show relationships between words or concepts. A commonly used word map or concept web map shows a central bubble containing a key word or idea. Bubbles that surround the center bubble may be used to show semantic relationships or to explain structure relationships. Choose a word or concept in the section and create a word map on the board. Have students complete the surrounding bubbles to clarify the relationship. **L1**

Refer to *Inclusion for the High School Social Studies Classroom Strategies and Activities* in the TCR.

L1/ELL
Guided Reading Activity 7–4

Name _____ Date _____ Class _____

★ Guided Reading Activity 7-4

DIRECTIONS: Recalling Facts Read the section and answer the questions below. Refer to your textbook to write the answers.

1. What was the condition of the South in 1865? _____
2. What was the purpose of Reconstruction? _____
3. What were the three goals of the Radical Republicans? _____
4. What was the belief of the moderate Republicans, caught between Lincoln and the Radicals? _____
5. Under what proposed bill would each state hold a constitutional convention to create a new state government? _____
6. How did Lincoln block this bill? _____

Why It Matters

The Fourteenth Amendment was proposed on June 13, 1866. The ratification process finally was completed in July 1868. Even after the ratification process was completed, states continued to ratify the amendment. On March 18, 1976, Kentucky finally ratified the amendment 109 years after initially rejecting it.

Ask: What are the three main provisions of the Fourteenth Amendment? *(1. Grants citizenship to all persons born or naturalized in the United States. 2. Forbids states from depriving any person of life, liberty, or property without due process of law. 3. Provides equal protection of the law.)*

Reading Check

Answer: He believed harsher terms would be counterproductive to the United States.

📁 Use *Supreme Court Case Study 6, Ex Parte Milligan.*

Why It Matters

The Fourteenth Amendment

Key provisions of the Fourteenth Amendment (1868) made all persons born in the United States citizens of both the nation and the state where they resided. States were prohibited from abridging the rights of citizenship or depriving persons of due process and equal protection of the law. The Supreme Court has often cited the Fourteenth Amendment when reviewing whether state or federal laws and actions violate the Constitution. The Court continues to do so today.

1954
In *Brown* v. *Board of Education,* the Court found that segregated education denied minority schoolchildren like Linda Brown (far left), the equal protection of the laws provided by the Fourteenth Amendment. This decision partially reversed *Plessy* v. *Ferguson.*

Testing the 14th Amendment
◆ *1896* ◆ *1954*

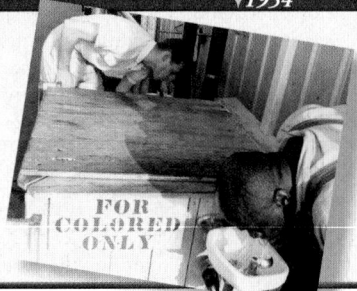

1896
In *Plessy* v. *Ferguson,* the Supreme Court decided that Jim Crow laws—state-mandated segregation of public facilities such as railroad cars—did not violate the Fourteenth Amendment. The Court ruled that separate facilities could be equal and allowed segregation to continue.

and deprive all former Confederate government officials and military officers of the right to vote or hold office.

Although Congress passed the Wade-Davis Bill, Lincoln blocked it with a pocket veto, that is, he let the session of Congress expire without signing the legislation. Although Lincoln sympathized with some of the radical goals, he felt that imposing a harsh peace on the South would be counterproductive.

> ✓ **Reading Check** **Summarizing** Why did Lincoln favor a generous Reconstruction policy toward the South?

The Freedmen's Bureau

Lincoln realized that harsh Reconstruction terms would only alienate many whites in the South. Also, the South was already in chaos. The devastation of the war and the collapse of the economy left hundreds of thousands of people unemployed, homeless, and hungry. At the same time, the victorious Union armies had to try to accommodate the large numbers of African Americans who flocked to Union lines as the war progressed. As Sherman marched through Georgia and South Carolina, thousands of freed African Americans—now known as freedmen—began following his troops seeking food and shelter.

As the different programs for assisting Southern refugees—both white and African American—got underway, support began to build in Congress for the creation of a federal agency to help with the refugee crisis. In March 1865, Congress established the Bureau of Refugees, Freedmen, and Abandoned Lands, better known as the **Freedmen's Bureau.** The Bureau was given the task of feeding and clothing war refugees in the South using surplus army supplies. Beginning in September 1865, the Bureau issued nearly 30,000 rations a day for the next year.

The Bureau also helped formerly enslaved people find work on plantations. It negotiated labor contracts with planters, specifying pay and hours of work. Although many people in the North applauded the Bureau's efforts, they argued those who were formerly enslaved should be given land—commonly referred to as "forty acres and a mule"—to support themselves now that they were free. To others, however, taking land from plantation owners and giving it to freedmen seemed to violate the nation's cherished commitment to individual property rights. As a result, Congress refused to confirm the right of African Americans to own the lands that had been seized from plantation owners and given to them.

Although the Freedmen's Bureau could not provide African Americans with land, it made an important contribution in education. The Bureau worked closely with Northern charities to educate formerly

DIFFERENTIATED INSTRUCTION

Reading Support Immediately after students read this section, lead a discussion about the Reconstruction plans of President Lincoln and the Radical Republicans. Tell students that you will be using some important terms from the text. Have students write each term they hear that also appeared in the text. Suggested terms include: Reconstruction, amnesty, Radical Republicans, Wade-Davis Bill, and pocket veto. **L1**

📁 Refer to *Inclusion for the High School Social Studies Classroom Strategies and Activities* in the TCR.

1963
In *Gideon* v. *Wainwright*, the Supreme Court ruled that the state of Florida had violated the due process clause when it refused to appoint a lawyer to represent Clarence Gideon (right). The ruling extended the Bill of Rights to state courts.

♦ 1963   ♦ 2000

2000
In the presidential race between George W. Bush and Al Gore (at right), the Supreme Court case of *Bush* v. *Gore* was based on the Fourteenth Amendment. Justices argued that a lack of uniform standards for hand recounts of ballots in Florida violated the equal protection of all the state's voters. The decision allowed Bush to claim a controversial victory.

enslaved African Americans. It provided housing for schools, paid teachers, and helped train African American teachers.

Many freed African Americans served in the U.S. Cavalry in units formed after 1866. Most were stationed in the southwestern United States, where they became known as buffalo soldiers.

✓ **Reading Check** **Explaining** Why was the Freedmen's Bureau established?

Johnson Takes Office

Shortly after Congress established the Freedmen's Bureau, Lincoln was assassinated. Although his successor, Vice President Andrew Johnson, was a Democrat from Tennessee, he had remained loyal to the Union. Like Lincoln, he believed in a moderate policy to bring the South back into the Union.

Johnson's Plan In the summer of 1865, with Congress in recess, Johnson began to implement what he called his restoration program, which closely resembled Lincoln's plan. In late May 1865, he issued a new Proclamation of Amnesty to supplement the one Lincoln had issued earlier. Johnson offered to pardon all former citizens of the Confederacy who took an oath of loyalty to the Union and to return their property. He excluded from the pardon the same peo-

ple Lincoln had excluded, such as former Confederate officers and officials. Those who were excluded could apply to the president individually for a pardon. Like Lincoln, Johnson also required Southern states to ratify the Thirteenth Amendment abolishing slavery.

The former Confederate states, for the most part, met Johnson's conditions. They then organized new governments and elected people to Congress. By the time Congress gathered for its next session in December 1865, Johnson's plan was well underway. Many members of Congress were astonished and angered when they realized that Southern voters had elected dozens of Confederate leaders to Congress. Moderate Republicans joined with the Radical Republicans and voted to reject the new Southern members of Congress.

The Black Codes Another development in the South also angered congressional Republicans. The new Southern state legislatures had passed laws known as black codes limiting the rights of African Americans in the South.

These codes varied from state to state, but all of them seemed intended to keep African Americans in a condition similar to slavery. African Americans were generally required to enter into annual labor contracts. Those who did not could be arrested for vagrancy and forced into involuntary servitude. Several codes established specific hours of labor and also required them to get licenses to work in non-agricultural jobs.

✓ **Reading Check** **Summarizing** Who did President Johnson blame for the Civil War?

Congressional Reconstruction

With the election of former Confederates to office and the introduction of the black codes, more and more moderate Republicans joined the radicals. Finally, in late 1865, House and Senate leaders created a Joint Committee on Reconstruction to develop their own program for rebuilding the Union.

The Fourteenth Amendment In March 1866, congressional Reconstruction began with the passage of an act intended to override the black codes. The **Civil Rights Act** of 1866 granted citizenship to all persons born in the United States except for Native Americans. The act guaranteed the rights of African Americans to own property, and it stated that they were to be treated equally in court. It also gave the federal government the power to sue people who violated those rights.

CHAPTER 7 The Civil War and Reconstruction **269**

✓ **Reading Check**

Answer: to help with the refugee problem created by the war

✓ **Reading Check**

Answer: the wealthy planter aristocracy

FYI

In 1867, under the direction of Secretary of State William H. Seward, the United States purchased Alaska from Russia for $7,200,000. Until rich veins of gold were discovered before the turn of the century, the purchase of Alaska was ridiculed. Some critics labeled the territory "Seward's Folly" or "Seward's Icebox."

Reading Strategy

Identifying Absolute Chronology Write the title "Reconstruction During Andrew Johnson's Presidency" on the board. Below the title, draw a time line and write "1865" at one end and "1868" at the other. Call on volunteers to come to the board and enter the major events in the process of Reconstruction during these years. Ask students to use information on the time line to write a chronological summary of Reconstruction up to the presidential election of 1868. **L2**

Andrew Johnson was a tailor by trade, and he made his own clothes up until the time he was elected to Congress and went to Washington, D.C.

Geography *Skills*

Answers:

1. Tennessee

2. about 5 years

Geography Skills Practice

Ask: Who was the military district commander for Texas and Louisiana? *(General Philip Sheridan)*

In October 1865, Robert E. Lee signed the oath of loyalty to the Union and sought a pardon from the United States government. Officials in Washington, D.C., however, misplaced the oath. Without it, Lee could neither get a pardon nor have his citizenship rights restored. More than 100 years later, the oath was discovered wrapped in a bundle of government documents in the National Archives. Shortly after, Congress issued a resolution restoring Lee's citizenship. President Gerald R. Ford signed it into law in August 1975.

3 ASSESS

Assign Section 4 Assessment as homework or as an in-class activity.

⏺ Have students use the **Interactive Tutor Self-Assessment CD-ROM.**

L1/ELL

Reading Essentials and Study Guide 7–4

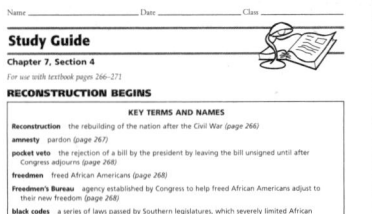

Name _____ Date _____ Class _____

Study Guide

Chapter 7, Section 4

For use with textbook pages 266–271

RECONSTRUCTION BEGINS

KEY TERMS AND NAMES

Reconstruction the rebuilding of the nation after the Civil War *(page 266)*

amnesty pardon *(page 267)*

pocket veto the rejection of a bill by the president by leaving the bill unsigned until after Congress adjourns *(page 268)*

freedmen freed African Americans *(page 268)*

Freedmen's Bureau agency established by Congress to help freed African Americans adjust to their new freedom *(page 268)*

black codes a series of laws passed by Southern legislatures, which severely limited African Americans' rights in the South *(page 269)*

Johnson vetoed the Civil Rights Act, arguing that it was unconstitutional and would "[cause] discord among the races." The veto convinced the remaining moderate Republicans to join with the radicals to override Johnson's veto, and the act became law.

Fearing that the Civil Rights Act might later be overturned in court, however, the radicals introduced the **Fourteenth Amendment** to the Constitution. This amendment granted citizenship to all persons born or naturalized in the United States and declared that no state could deprive any person of life, liberty, or property "without due process of law." It also declared that no state could deny any person "equal protection of the laws." In June 1866, Congress passed the amendment and sent it to the states for ratification. It was ratified in 1868.

Military Reconstruction Begins President Johnson attacked the Fourteenth Amendment and made it the major issue of the 1866 congressional elections. He hoped Northerners would vote out the Radical Republicans and elect a new majority in Congress that would support his plan for Reconstruction.

Events on Election Day dashed Johnson's hopes. When the votes were counted, the Republicans achieved an overwhelming victory, winning approximately a three-to-one majority in Congress. They now had the strength of numbers to override any presidential veto and could claim that they had a mandate, or command, from the American people to enact their own Reconstruction program in place of President Johnson's plan.

In March 1867, Congress passed the **Military Reconstruction Act,** which essentially nullified Johnson's programs. The act divided the former Confederacy, except for Tennessee—which had ratified the Fourteenth Amendment in 1866—into five military districts. A Union general was placed in charge of each district with orders to maintain peace and "protect the rights of persons and property."

In the meantime, each former Confederate state had to hold another constitutional convention to design a constitution acceptable to Congress. The new state constitutions had to give the right to vote to all adult male citizens, regardless of their race. After a state had ratified its new constitution, it also had to ratify the Fourteenth Amendment before it would be allowed to elect people to Congress.

Johnson's Impeachment

The Republicans knew that they had the votes to override any presidential veto of their policies, but they also knew that President Johnson could still interfere with their plans by refusing to enforce the laws they passed. Although they distrusted Johnson, Congressional Republicans knew that Secretary of War Edwin M. Stanton supported their program. They also trusted

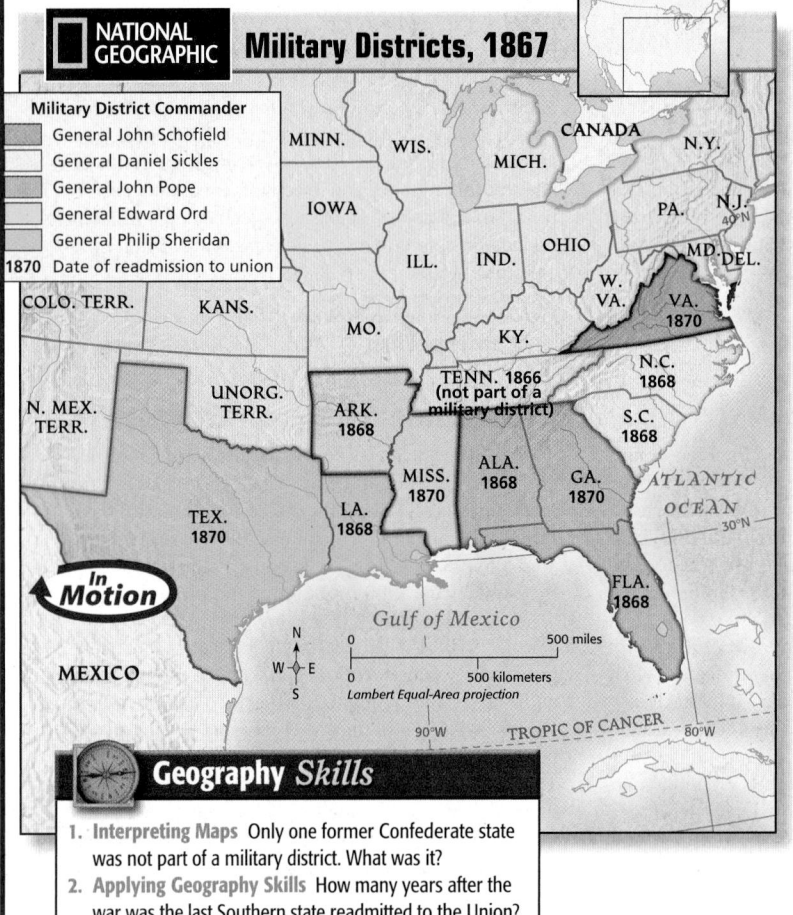

NATIONAL GEOGRAPHIC **Military Districts, 1867**

Military District Commander
- General John Schofield
- General Daniel Sickles
- General John Pope
- General Edward Ord
- General Philip Sheridan

1870 Date of readmission to union

CANADA

MINN. WIS. MICH. N.Y.

IOWA PA. N.J. 40°N

ILL. IND. OHIO MD. DEL.

COLO. TERR. KANS. W. VA. VA. 1870

MO. KY.

N. MEX. TERR. UNORG. TERR. ARK. 1868 TENN. 1866 (not part of a military district) N.C. 1868

MISS. 1870 ALA. 1868 GA. 1870 S.C. 1868

TEX. 1870 LA. 1868 ATLANTIC OCEAN 30°N

FLA. 1868

In Motion

Gulf of Mexico 0 500 miles

MEXICO N W E S 0 500 kilometers
Lambert Equal-Area projection

TROPIC OF CANCER

90°W 80°W

Geography *Skills*

1. **Interpreting Maps** Only one former Confederate state was not part of a military district. What was it?

2. **Applying Geography Skills** How many years after the war was the last Southern state readmitted to the Union?

CRITICAL THINKING ACTIVITY

Making a Decision Organize students into several small groups and have groups consider the following: **If you had been a member of the House of Representatives in 1868, would you have voted for or against the impeachment of President Andrew Johnson?** Explain the reasons for your choice. Call on group representatives to present their decisions and reasons to the rest of the class. **L2**

General Grant, the head of the army, to support the policies of Congress.

To prevent Johnson from bypassing Grant and Stanton, Congress passed two new laws: the Command of the Army Act and the Tenure of Office Act. The Command of the Army Act required all orders from the president to go through the headquarters of the general of the army—Grant's headquarters. The Tenure of Office Act required the Senate to approve the president's removal of any government official whose appointment had required the Senate's consent.

Andrew Johnson

Determined to challenge the Tenure of Office Act, Johnson fired Stanton on February 21, 1868. Three days later, the House of Representatives voted to impeach Johnson, meaning that they charged him with "high crimes and misdemeanors" in office. The main charge against Johnson was that he had broken the law by refusing to uphold the Tenure of Office Act.

As provided in the Constitution, the Senate then put the president on trial. If two-thirds of the senators found the president guilty of the charges, he would be removed from office. In May 1868 the Senate voted 35 to 19 that Johnson was guilty of high crimes and misdemeanors. This was just one vote short of what was needed for conviction.

The Election of 1868 Although Johnson remained in office, he finished his term quietly and did not run for election in 1868. That year, the Republicans

nominated Grant. During the campaign, Union troops in the South enabled African Americans to vote in large numbers. As a result, Grant won six Southern states and most of the Northern states. The Republicans also retained large majorities in both houses of Congress.

With their majority securely established and a sympathetic president in office, congressional Republicans moved rapidly to expand their Reconstruction program. Recognizing the importance of African American suffrage, the Republican-led Congress passed the **Fifteenth Amendment** to the Constitution. This amendment declared that the right to vote "shall not be denied . . . on account of race, color, or previous condition of servitude." In March 1870, the Fifteenth Amendment was ratified by the states and became part of the Constitution.

Radical Reconstruction had a dramatic impact on the South, particularly in the short term. It dramatically changed Southern politics by bringing hundreds of thousands of African Americans into the political process for the first time. It also began to change Southern society. As it did so, it angered many white Southerners, who began to fight back against the federal government's policies.

Reading Check **Identifying** What two laws did the Radical Republicans pass to reduce presidential power?

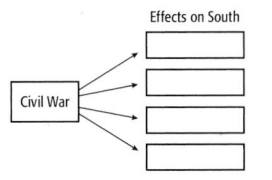

HISTORY Online | **Study Central™** To review this section, go to tarvol2.glencoe.com and click on **Study Central™**.

SECTION 4 ASSESSMENT

Checking for Understanding

1. **Define:** Reconstruction, amnesty, pocket veto, freedmen, black codes, impeach.
2. **Identify:** Freedmen's Bureau, Fourteenth Amendment, Military Reconstruction Act, Fifteenth Amendment.

Reviewing Themes

3. **Groups and Institutions** What were the Radical Republicans' three major goals?

Critical Thinking

4. **Evaluating** Do you think Presidents Lincoln and Johnson were wise in not seeking harsh treatment of the Southern states? Why or why not?
5. **Categorizing** Use a graphic organizer to describe the effects of the Civil War.

Effects on South

Civil War → ☐ ☐ ☐ ☐

Analyzing Visuals

6. **Interpreting Maps** Study the map of military districts on page 270. Then list the Confederate states that were readmitted to the Union in 1868, the earliest year for any such state to gain readmission.

Writing About History

7. **Persuasive Writing** Imagine that you are a citizen living during President Andrew Johnson's administration. Write a letter urging members of Congress to vote either for or against Johnson's impeachment. Include reasons for your position.

CHAPTER 7   The Civil War and Reconstruction   **271**

SECTION 4 ASSESSMENT ANSWERS

1. Terms are in blue.
2. Freedmen's Bureau (*p. 268*), Fourteenth Amendment (*p. 270*), Military Reconstruction Act (*p. 270*), Fifteenth Amendment (*p. 271*)
3. prevent leaders of the Confederacy from returning to power, make the

Republican Party more powerful in the South, guarantee African Americans' right to vote
4. Many students will agree that offering generous terms would help heal the wounds of war.
5. Effects included: ruined economy, destroyed cities, and improve-

ments for African Americans
6. North Carolina, South Carolina, Florida, Alabama, Louisiana, Arkansas
7. Students' letters will vary.

L2

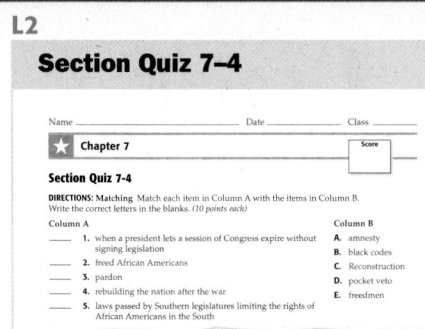

Section Quiz 7–4

Name _____ Date _____ Class _____

★ **Chapter 7**   Score ☐

Section Quiz 7-4

DIRECTIONS: Matching Match each item in Column A with the items in Column B. Write the correct letters in the blanks. (10 points each)

Column A
___ 1. when a president lets a session of Congress expire without signing legislation
___ 2. freed African Americans
___ 3. pardon
___ 4. rebuilding the nation after the war
___ 5. laws passed by Southern legislatures limiting the rights of African Americans in the South

Column B
A. amnesty
B. black codes
C. Reconstruction
D. pocket veto
E. freedmen

Reading Check

Answer: Command of the Army Act and Tenure of Office Act

Reteach

Have a class discussion about life in the South immediately after the war.

Enrich

Invite interested students to investigate who would have been president if Andrew Johnson had been removed from office. Encourage students to use library and Internet resources for their research.

HISTORY Online

Study Central™ provides summaries, interactive games, and online graphic organizers to help students review section content.

4 CLOSE

Have students describe the major features of Congressional Reconstruction.

1 FOCUS

Section Overview

This section deals with life in the South during Reconstruction.

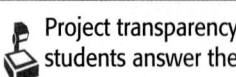

BELLRINGER
Skillbuilder Activity

Project transparency and have students answer the question.

Daily Focus Skills Transparency 7–5

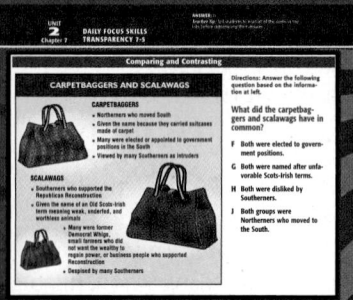

Reading Preview

Answers to Graphic:
Reconstruction and Republican Rule
I. Republican Rule in the South
   A. Carpetbaggers and Scalawags
   B. African Americans Enter Politics
   C. Republican Reforms in the South
Students should complete the outline by including all heads in the section.

Preteaching Vocabulary
Have volunteer students write a definition for a Key Term on the board. Then have others offer changes to clarify the definition.

SECTION 5

Reconstruction and Republican Rule

Guide to Reading

Main Idea
Under Republican rule, the South began to rebuild. African Americans gained new opportunities, and some Southerners organized to resist the Republicans.

Key Terms and Names
carpetbagger, scalawag, graft, Panic of 1873, Compromise of 1877, tenant farmer, sharecropper

Reading Strategy
Taking Notes As you read about Southern society and the end of Reconstruction, use the major headings of the section to create an outline similar to the one below.

Reconstruction and Republican Rule
I. Republican Rule in the South
   A.
   B.
   C.

Reading Objectives
• **Discuss** Republican rule in the South during Reconstruction.
• **Explain** how Reconstruction ended, and contrast the New South and the Old South.

Section Theme
Economic Factors After Reconstruction, the South tried to create a new economy, but many problems remained.

Preview of Events

♦1866	♦1870	♦1874	♦1878
1866 Ku Klux Klan formed	**1870** First Enforcement Act passed	**1873** Panic of 1873 paralyzes nation	**1877** Compromise of 1877 reached

Early KKK robe and hood

★ An American Story ★

On a moonlit December night in the late 1860s, Essic Harris, a formerly enslaved man, woke suddenly after hearing loud noises outside his small home in Chatham County, North Carolina. He peered out his bedroom window and a wave of terror rushed over him. Thirty men in white robes and hoods stood around the house. Many held shotguns. They were members of the Ku Klux Klan, an organization that used violence and intimidation to force African Americans and white Republicans out of Southern politics. They had come to harass Harris, who was active in local politics.

As Klan members began firing shotgun blasts at his home, Harris pushed his family into a corner and grabbed his own shotgun. He rushed to the front door and fired back, then shouted to one of his children, "Boy, bring my five-shooter!" Harris had no such gun, but his bluff worked. The Klan members cursed Harris and rode off, but they would return. They continued harassing Harris until he abandoned his home and moved to another county.

—**adapted from *The Fiery Cross***

Republican Rule in the South

By the fall of 1870, all of the former Confederate states had rejoined the Union under the congressional Reconstruction plan. Reunification, however, did little to restore harmony between the North and the South. Because of past disloyalty, some Southern whites were barred from voting or holding office in the new Southern governments, and many others

272   CHAPTER 7   The Civil War and Reconstruction

SECTION RESOURCES

📂 Reproducible Masters
• Reproducible Lesson Plan 7–5
• Daily Lecture and Discussion Notes 7–5
• Guided Reading Activity 7–5
• Section Quiz 7–5
• Reading Essentials and Study Guide 7–5

📖 Transparencies
• Daily Focus Skills Transparency 7–5

Multimedia
🔘 Interactive Tutor Self-Assessment CD-ROM
🔘 ExamView® Pro Testmaker CD-ROM
🔘 Presentation Plus! CD-ROM
🔘 TeacherWorks™ CD-ROM
🔘 Vocabulary Puzzlemaker CD-ROM
🎵 Audio Program
🎵 American Music: Cultural Traditions

simply refused to do so. As a result, a coalition of Northerners, Southern-born whites, and African Americans created Republican governments in the Southern states. While the governments instituted various reforms, most white Southerners scorned them.

Carpetbaggers and Scalawags During Reconstruction, a large number of Northerners traveled to the South. Many were eventually elected or appointed to positions in the South's new state governments. Southerners, particularly supporters of the Democratic Party, referred to these newcomers as carpetbaggers because some arrived with their belongings in suitcases made of carpet fabric. Many local residents viewed the Northerners as intruders seeking to exploit the South's postwar turmoil for their own gain.

While many Southerners despised carpetbaggers, they also disliked white Southerners who worked with the Republicans and supported Reconstruction. They called these people scalawags—an old Scotch-Irish term for weak, underfed, worthless animals.

The scalawags were a diverse group of people. Some were former Whigs who had grudgingly joined the Democratic Party before the war. Many were owners of small farms who did not want the wealthy planters to regain power. Still others were business people who favored Republican plans for developing the South's economy.

African Americans Enter Politics Thousands of formerly enslaved people also took part in governing the South. Having gained the right to vote, African Americans quickly began organizing politically. Within a few remarkable years, African Americans went from enslaved workers to legislators and administrators on nearly all levels of government. Hundreds of formerly enslaved people served as delegates to the conventions that created the new state constitutions. They also won election to numerous local offices, from mayor to police chief to school commissioner. During Reconstruction, dozens of African Americans also served in Southern state legislatures, while 14 were elected to the House of Representatives and 2 others served in the Senate.

While African Americans participated in the South's Reconstruction governments, they by no means

controlled them. The Republican Party took power in the South because it had the support of a large number of white Southerners. These were usually poor white farmers, who resented the planters and Democratic Party that had dominated the South before the Civil War.

Republican Reforms in the South The newly elected Republican governments in the South quickly instituted a number of reforms. In addition to repealing the black codes, they established state hospitals and institutions for orphans. They rebuilt roads, railways, and bridges damaged during the Civil War and provided funds for the construction of new railroads and industries in the South.

The Republican reforms did not come without cost. Many state governments were forced to borrow money and to impose high property taxes to pay for the repairs and new programs. Many property owners, unable to pay these new taxes, lost their land.

Although Republican leaders in the South demonstrated a devotion to public service, some of the more self-seeking members caused Southern Democrats to accuse the "carpetbag governments" of corruption. One Republican governor admitted accepting more than $40,000 in bribes. Graft, or gaining money illegally through politics, was common in the South, just as it was in the North at the time.

✓ **Reading Check** **Summarizing** What three groups of people helped to create Republican governments in the South during Reconstruction?

Profiles IN HISTORY

Hiram Revels *1822–1901*

For a man reluctant to enter politics, Hiram Revels went a long way—becoming the first African American in the United States Senate. Revels was born to free parents in Fayetteville, North Carolina. In 1845 he became a minister in the African Methodist Church. Soon after, Revels settled in Baltimore, where he worked as a church pastor and as the principal of an African American school.

After the Civil War, Revels settled in Natchez, Mississippi, where he continued his religious work. At first, Revels expressed reluctance to wade too

deeply into politics, but he overcame this concern and won the respect of both whites and African Americans. In 1870 Revels was elected to the Senate. As the first African American senator, he served in a subdued manner, speaking much less than other African American members of Congress. Upon his retirement from the Senate, Revels served twice as president of Alcorn University, an African American college in Mississippi.

CHAPTER 7   The Civil War and Reconstruction   **273**

2 TEACH

Daily Lecture and Discussion Notes 7–5

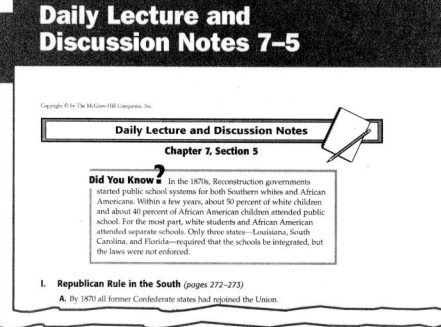

Copyright © by The McGraw-Hill Companies, Inc.

Daily Lecture and Discussion Notes
Chapter 7, Section 5

Did You Know? In the 1870s, Reconstruction governments started public school systems for both Southern whites and African Americans. Within a few years, about 50 percent of white children and about 40 percent of African American children attended public school. For the most part, white students and African American attended separate schools. Only three states—Louisiana, South Carolina, and Florida—required that the schools be integrated, but the laws were not enforced.

I. **Republican Rule in the South** (pages 272–273)
   A. By 1870 all former Confederate states had rejoined the Union.

Profiles IN HISTORY

Hiram Revels served in the United States Senate for just over one year—February 23, 1870 to March 3, 1871. In 1875, Mississippi again elected an African American to the Senate, but not until 1966 was another African American elected to serve in the U.S. Senate.

Writing a Profile Have students research and then write a short profile of one of the following African Americans who served in the U.S. House of Representatives between 1870 and 1901: Richard H. Cain, Henry P. Cheatham, Jeremiah Haralson, John A. Hyman, John M. Langston, Jefferson F. Long, John R. Lynch, Alonzo J. Ransier. **L1**

✓ **Reading Check**

Answer: African Americans, carpetbaggers, and poor white farmers

COOPERATIVE LEARNING ACTIVITY

Creating an Exhibit Organize the class into small groups which will develop an exhibit to illustrate Reconstruction. Groups may focus on an important person; an important event such as the impeachment of President Johnson; the culture of the period, such as hair and clothing styles, songs, and available reading material; or an important idea, such as what people expected of a Reconstruction policy. Exhibits should include illustrations, short written descriptions, and primary sources. 🖎

Use the rubric for a cooperative group management plan on pages 71–72 in the *Performance Assessment Activities and Rubrics.*

L1/ELL

Guided Reading Activity 7–5

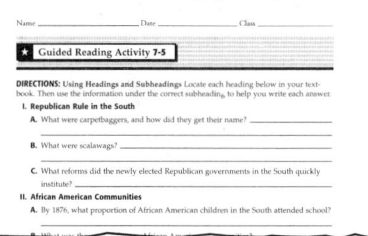

Name _____ Date _____ Class _____

★ Guided Reading Activity 7-5

DIRECTIONS: Using Headings and Subheadings Locate each heading below in your text-book. Then use the information under the correct subheading to help you write each answer.

I. Republican Rule in the South

A. What were carpetbaggers, and how did they get their name? _____

B. What were scalawags? _____

C. What reforms did the newly elected Republican governments in the South quickly institute? _____

II. African American Communities

A. By 1876, what proportion of African American children in the South attended school?

✓ Reading Check

Answer: The number of schools, African American students, and African American teachers gradually increased.

Picturing History

Background: Oliver Otis Howard, a Union officer and graduate of West Point, was named head of the Freedmen's Bureau by Andrew Johnson. Howard University in Washington, D.C., was named for him.
Answer: African Americans were eager to learn and parents were eager for their children to get an education.
Ask: Do you think the school shown in this picture was similar to schools for white children? *(Answers will vary. Remind students that one-room schoolhouses with all ages together were then common.)*

✓ Reading Check

Answer: to combat violence in the South, and outlaw the activities of the Ku Klux Klan

History *and the* Humanities

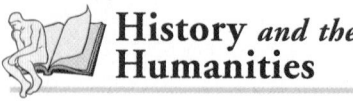

American Music: Cultural Traditions: "Roll, Jordan, Roll"

African American Communities

In addition to their efforts on the political stage, African Americans worked to improve their lives in other ways during Reconstruction. Upon gaining their freedom, many African Americans desired an education, something they had been denied under slavery. In the first years of Reconstruction, the Freedmen's Bureau, with the help of Northern charities, had established schools for African Americans across the South.

Gradually, the number of both African American students and teachers increased, and by 1876 about 40 percent of all African American children (roughly 600,000 students) attended school in the region.

With the same determination they showed in pursuing an education, formerly enslaved people across the South worked to establish their own churches. Religion had long played a central role in the lives of many African Americans, and with the shackles of slavery now gone, the building of churches quickly began. Churches served as the center of many African American communities, as they housed schools and hosted social events and political gatherings.

✓ Reading Check **Examining** How did education for African Americans change during Reconstruction?

Picturing History

Schools for African Americans O.O. Howard, head of the Freedmen's Bureau, is pictured here (far right) with the students of a Freedmen's school. *Why do you think these schools were so successful?*

274 CHAPTER 7 The Civil War and Reconstruction

Southern Resistance

At the same time these changes were taking place in the South, African Americans often faced intense resentment from many Southern whites. Many Southerners also despised the Republican governments, which they believed vindictive Northerners had forced upon them.

Unable to strike openly at the Republicans running their states, some Southern opponents of Reconstruction organized secret societies to undermine Republican rule. The largest of these groups was the **Ku Klux Klan.** Started in 1866 by former Confederate soldiers in Pulaski, Tennessee, the Klan spread rapidly throughout the South. Hooded, white-robed Klan members rode in bands at night terrorizing African Americans, white Republicans, carpetbaggers, teachers in African American schools, and others who supported the Republican governments. Republicans and African Americans responded to the attacks by organizing their own militias to fight back.

As the violence on both sides increased, President Grant and Congress took action. In 1870 and 1871, Congress passed three Enforcement Acts, one of which outlawed the activities of the Klan. Throughout the South, local authorities and federal agents, acting under the Enforcement Acts, arrested more than 3,000 Klan members. Southern juries convicted only about 600, however, and fewer still served any time in prison.

✓ Reading Check **Describing** Why did Congress pass the Enforcement Acts?

The Troubled Grant Administration

Despite his decisive actions against the Ku Klux Klan, Ulysses S. Grant was not a forceful president. He believed that the president's role was to carry out the laws and leave the development of policy to Congress. Eventually, Grant's lack of political experience and drive helped to divide the Republican Party and undermine public support for Reconstruction.

Throughout Grant's first term, a growing number of Republicans expressed concerns that men who were in office to make money and

DIFFERENTIATED INSTRUCTION

English Learners Students who are English learners sometimes have difficulty separating important information from supporting details. Help them to listen effectively by cueing them when you come to an important point. Alert students to some key guiding phrases such as "the definition of," "the main point," or "the most important feature." Have them write down the information you give following one of these key phrases. **L1/ELL**

📂 Refer to *Inclusion for the High School Social Studies Classroom Strategies and Activities* in the TCR.

sell influence were beginning to dominate the Republican Party. These critics also argued that the economic policies most Republicans supported, such as high tariffs, favored the rich over the poor. Eventually these critics, known as Liberal Republicans, broke with the Republican Party in 1872 and nominated their own candidate, the influential newspaper publisher Horace Greeley. Despite this split, Grant easily won re-election.

During Grant's second term, a series of scandals damaged his administration's reputation. In one scandal, Grant's secretary of war, **William Belknap,** was found to have accepted bribes from merchants operating at army posts in the West. He was impeached but resigned before the Senate could try him. Then, in 1875, the **"Whiskey Ring"** scandal broke. A group of government officials and distillers in St. Louis cheated the government out of millions of dollars by filing false tax reports. It was reported that Orville E. Babcock, Grant's private secretary, was in this group, although the charges were never proven.

In addition to these political scandals, Grant and the nation endured a staggering and long-lasting economic crisis that began during Grant's second term. The turmoil started in 1873, when a series of bad railroad investments forced the powerful banking firm of Jay Cooke and Company to declare bankruptcy. A wave of fear known as the **Panic of 1873** quickly spread though the nation's financial community. The panic prompted scores of smaller banks to close and caused the stock market to plummet. It soon set off a full-fledged depression that lasted until almost the end of the decade.

The scandals in the Grant administration and the nation's deepening economic depression hurt the Republicans politically. In the 1874 midterm elections, the Democrats won back control of the House of Representatives and made gains in the Senate.

✓Reading Check **Explaining** Why did the Liberal Republicans oppose President Grant?

 NATIONAL GEOGRAPHIC **The Election of 1876**

Legend:
- ▢ Disputed
- ▢ Territories

Presidential Election, 1876			
Candidate	Electoral Vote	Popular Vote	Political Party
Hayes	185	4,036,572	Republican
Tilden	184	4,284,020	Democrat

 Geography *Skills*

1. **Interpreting Maps** In which states were election results disputed?
2. **Applying Geography Skills** In what regions of the country did Hayes win support?

Reconstruction Ends

The rising power of the Democrats in Congress made enforcing Reconstruction more difficult. At the same time, Northerners were becoming more concerned with the government scandals and their own economic problems than with the situation in the South.

In the 1870s, Democrats began to regain power in the South. They did so in part through intimidation and fraud, and in part by defining the elections as a struggle between whites and African Americans. They also won back support by promising to cut the high taxes the Republicans had imposed and by accusing Republicans of corruption. Southern Democrats viewed their efforts to regain power as a crusade to help save the South from Republican rule. By 1876 the Democrats had taken control of all but three Southern state legislatures.

That year, the nation's presidential election pitted Republican Rutherford B. Hayes, a former governor of Ohio, against Democrat Samuel Tilden, a wealthy corporate lawyer and former governor of New York. On Election Day, twenty electoral votes were disputed. Nineteen of the votes were in the three Southern states controlled by Republicans.

CHAPTER 7 The Civil War and Reconstruction **275**

INTERDISCIPLINARY CONNECTIONS ACTIVITY

Economics Ask the economics teacher to describe the labor force and to explain how jobs are classified into agricultural, manufacturing, or service. Have students estimate what the trends in each category have been from colonial times to the present. Then have students use resources such as the *Statistical Abstract of the United States* to research the trends over time in the number of people employed in the agriculture, manufacturing, and service industries. Have them create line charts using the data to see if their estimations about the trends were accurate. **L3**

Different Viewpoints

Different Viewpoints

Answers:

1. Answers may vary. Students should note that Lowe's characterization seems more arbitrary and emotion-based than Morton's. That tends to make Morton's view seem more accurate.

2. Answers will vary. Possible questions include—Morton: As a Northerner, how do you know what will help the South? Lowe: Are you saying that Democrats never have the wrong motives for running for elected office?

✓ Reading Check

Answer: who would be president

3 ASSESS

Assign Section 5 Assessment as homework or as an in-class activity.

🔘 Have students use the **Interactive Tutor Self-Assessment CD-ROM.**

L1/ELL

Reading Essentials and Study Guide 7–5

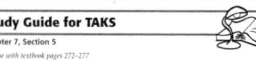

Name _____ Date _____ Class _____

Study Guide for TAKS

Chapter 7, Section 5

For use with textbook pages 272–277

RECONSTRUCTION AND REPUBLICAN RULE

KEY TERMS AND NAMES

carpetbagger name given to Northern whites who moved South after the war and supported Republicans *(page 273)*

scalawag name given by former Confederates to Southern whites who supported Republican Reconstruction of the South *(page 273)*

graft gaining money illegally through politics *(page 273)*

Panic of 1873 an economic crisis *(page 275)*

Compromise of 1877 the method used to reach an outcome in the 1876 presidential election *(page 276)*

tenant farmers farmers who paid rent for the land they farmed *(page 277)*

sharecroppers farmers who paid a share of their crops to cover their rent and the equipment

Carpetbaggers: Corrupt or Well-Intentioned?

According to Southerners, many carpetbaggers were corrupt Northerners who came south to get rich or to get elected. Films like *Gone with the Wind* influenced many generations to accept this view. The opposing interpretation argues that Northerners were not necessarily corrupt but often simply wanted to make new lives or aid African Americans.

In 1871 Oliver Morton, a Radical Republican senator from Indiana, defended Northerners who relocated to the South, claiming they were beneficial to that region:

"When the war ended many men who had been in the Union army remained in the South, intending to make it their home. . . . Others emigrated from the North, taking with them large capital, believing that the South presented fine prospects for business. . . . It so happened, and was, in fact, necessary, that many of these men should be elected to office. This was their right and the natural result of the circumstances by which they were surrounded. . . . Emigration is a part of the genius of the American people. . . . it is an odious and anti-American doctrine that a man has no right to be elected to an office in a State because he was not born in it. . . . What the South needs is emigrants with carpet bags well filled with capital to revive industry. . . ."

—quoted in *Reconstruction: Opposing Viewpoints*

In an 1871 question-and-answer session before Congress, William Manning Lowe, a former Confederate colonel and Alabama lawyer, criticized his state's U.S. senators, Willard Warner and George Spencer. Both were originally from Northern states:

"[A] carpet-bagger is generally understood to be a man who comes here for office sake, of an ignorant or bad character, and who seeks to array the Negroes against the whites . . . in order to get office through them. . . . (The term) does not apply to all northern men who come here. . . . We regard any republican or any man as a man of bad character, whether he is native or foreign born, who seeks to obtain office from the Negroes by exciting their passions and prejudices against the whites. We think that a very great evil—very great. We are intimately associated with the Negro race; we have a large number in the country, and we think it essential that we shall live in peace together. . . . No, sir; the term is never applied to a democrat under any circumstances. . . ."

—quoted in *Reconstruction: Opposing Viewpoints*

Learning From History

1. **Evaluating** Which of these two viewpoints most accurately describes carpetbaggers? Why?
2. **Analyzing** Choose one of the viewpoints above. Write three questions you would like to ask your chosen speaker.

As a result, congressional leaders worked out an agreement known as the **Compromise of 1877.**

Historians are not sure if a deal really took place or what its exact terms were. The compromise reportedly included the following conditions: Southern Democrats agreed to give the election to Hayes, and in return, the Republicans promised that a Southerner would become postmaster general. This was an important position because of the many federal jobs it controlled. The Republicans reportedly also promised funds for internal improvements in the South. Most importantly, they agreed to withdraw the remaining federal troops from the South. In April 1877, after assuming the presidency, Hayes did pull federal troops out of the South. Without soldiers to support

them, the last remaining Republican governments in the South quickly collapsed. Reconstruction had come to an end.

✓ Reading Check
Explaining What major issue was settled by the Compromise of 1877?

A "New South" Arises

During his inaugural speech in March 1877, President Hayes expressed his desire to move the country beyond the quarrelsome years of Reconstruction in part by putting an end to the nation's regional distinctions. He hoped to narrow the divisions of sectionalism that had long plagued the nation:

Reading Strategy — READING THE TEXT

Analyzing Concepts Analyzing concepts will help students understand the main ideas of a passage or section they are reading. As students read this section, remind them that one goal of the Radical Republicans was equal citizenship for African Americans. Then, ask students to consider the following question: Why do you think Radical Republicans had difficulty putting equal citizenship into effect during Reconstruction? Discuss student responses. Conclude by asking students to write a paragraph discussing whether equal citizenship is a reality today. **L2**

☛ Refer to **Inclusion for the High School Social Studies Classroom Strategies and Activities** in the TCR.

66Let me assure my countrymen of the Southern States that it is my earnest desire to regard and promote their truest interests—the interests of the white and colored people both equally—and to put forth my best efforts in behalf of a civil policy which will forever wipe out . . . the distinction between North and South, to the end that we may have not merely a united North or a united South, but a united country.99

—quoted in *Rutherford B. Hayes*

Eventually the South did develop closer ties with the North. Southern leaders realized the South could never return to the pre–Civil War agricultural economy dominated by the planter elite. Instead, these Southerners called for the creation of a "New South." They were convinced that the region had to develop a strong industrial economy. An alliance between Southerners and Northern financiers brought great economic changes to some parts of the South. Northern capital helped to build thousands of miles of railroads and dozens of new industries.

The South, however, changed very little. Despite its industrial growth, the region remained largely agricultural. As late as 1900, its number of manufacturing establishments equaled only 4 percent of its number of farms. For many African Americans in particular, the end of Reconstruction meant a return to the "old South" and an end to their hopes of being granted their own land. Instead many returned to the plantations owned by whites, where they, along with many poor white farmers, either worked for wages or became tenant farmers paying rent for the land they farmed. After the Civil War, the South's weak economy did not have enough cash available and the cost of borrowing money was high. Many farmers could

Picturing **History**

A New South? While the developing downtown area of Houston, Texas, in the 1890s was similar to other Southern urban areas, most of the South remained agricultural in the decades following the Civil War. *What did the leaders of the "New South" movement support?*

not afford to buy their own land. As a result, most tenant farmers became sharecroppers. Sharecroppers did not pay their rent in cash. Instead they paid a share of their crops, often as much as two-thirds, to cover their rent as well as the cost of the seed, fertilizer, tools and animals they needed.

Although sharecropping allowed African American farmers to control their work schedules and working conditions for the first time in their lives, they rarely had enough crops left over to sell to enable them to buy their own land. The Civil War ended slavery, but Reconstruction's failure left many African Americans, as well as many whites, trapped in economic circumstances beyond their control.

✓ **Reading Check** **Summarizing** What alliance brought economic change in the South?

HISTORY **Study Central**™ To review this section, go to **tarvol2.glencoe.com** and click on **Study Central**™.

SECTION 5 ASSESSMENT

Check for Understanding

1. **Define:** carpetbagger, scalawag, graft, tenant farmer, sharecropper.
2. **Identify:** Panic of 1873, Compromise of 1877.
3. **Describe** how some white Southerners reacted to the Republican Party gaining power in the South.

Reviewing Themes

4. **Economic Factors** What factors contributed to improving the economy of the South after Reconstruction?

Critical Thinking

5. **Analyzing** Why did Southerners resent both carpetbaggers and scalawags?
6. **Organizing** Use a graphic organizer similar to the one below to identify the problems that President Grant's administration faced.

Problems Faced by Grant's Administration

Analyzing Visuals

7. **Examining Photographs** Study the photograph of O.O. Howard and a Freedmen's school on page 274. How would you describe the children depicted in this photograph?

Writing About History

8. **Expository Writing** Write a short essay explaining what you consider to be the three most important events of the Reconstruction period. Explain why you chose these events.

CHAPTER 7   The Civil War and Reconstruction   **277**

SECTION 5 ASSESSMENT ANSWERS

1. Terms are in blue.
2. Panic of 1873 (*p. 275*), Compromise of 1877 (*p. 276*)
3. They scorned them.
4. investment by Northern financiers; rebuilt roads, railways, and bridges; provided funds for construction of new railroads and industries

5. Carpetbaggers and scalawags both wanted to change the South while many Southerners wanted things to remain as they were.
6. perception that wealthy Americans were influential; Belknap and Whiskey Ring scandals; Panic of 1873

7. serious and nicely dressed for portrait
8. Essays should include three events and an explanation for each.

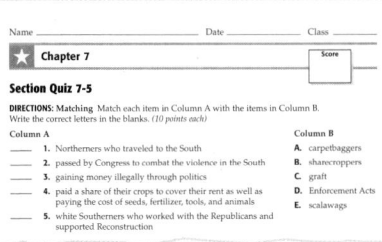
✓**Reading Check**

Answer: the alliance between Southerners and Northern financiers

Picturing **History**

Answer: more industry for the South
Ask: How successful was the South in developing industry after the Civil War? *(Despite industrial growth, the South remained largely agricultural.)*

Reteach

Ask students to list the effects of Republican rule in the South during Reconstruction.

Enrich

Have students use historical statistical abstracts to find data on African American enrollment in schools from 1860 to 1900.

Study Central™ provides summaries, interactive games, and online graphic organizers to help students review section content.

4 CLOSE

Ask students to identify the major differences between the Old South and the New South.

TIME NOTEBOOK

TEACH

Eyewitness

Tell students that some historians view Edmund Ross as courageous, while others view him as politically expedient. Organize the class into small groups and assign the groups to research Edmund Ross and his decision not to convict Andrew Johnson. Assign half the groups to write an editorial expressing the opinion that Ross was a courageous man and martyr. Assign the other half to write an editorial expressing the opinion that Ross was a scoundrel, using his vote for political favors. "Publish" the editorials and distribute them to the class. As a class, discuss how our understanding of events is influenced by the opinions of contemporary writers and historians.

Presidential Superlatives

Have students select one of the U.S. presidents and create a list of interesting facts and firsts about him or his presidency. Compile the various lists, placing them in sequential order, and create a display about our presidents for the school.

Visit the TIME Web site at www.time.com for up-to-date news, weekly magazine articles, editorials, online polls, and an archive of past magazine and Web articles.

Eyewitness

PHOTOWORLD/FPG

WILLIAM H. CROOKE *served as a bodyguard for President Andrew Johnson and witnessed the decisive vote by Edmund Ross during the impeachment trial in the Senate on Saturday, May 16, 1868. Here, Crooke recalls the scene:*

The tension grew. There was a weary number of names before that of Ross was reached. When the clerk called it, and Ross [senator from Kansas] stood forth, the crowd held its breath.

'Not guilty,' called the senator from Kansas. It was like the babbling [sic] over of a caldron. The Radical Senators, who had been laboring with Ross only a short time before, turned to him in rage; all over the house people began to stir. The rest of the roll-call was listened to with lessened interest. . . . When it was over, and the result—35 to 19—was announced, there was a wild outburst, chiefly groans of anger and disappointment, for the friends of the president were in the minority.

It was all over in a moment, and Mr. Johnson was ordering some whiskey from the cellar. [President Johnson was not convicted.]

VERBATIM

❝If the South is ever to be made a safe Republic, let her lands be cultivated by the toil of the owners, or the free labor of intelligent citizens.❞
 THADDEUS STEVENS,
 arguing for land redistribution in the South during Reconstruction

❝In the South, the [Civil] war is what A.D. is elsewhere; they date from it.❞
 MARK TWAIN,
 from Life on the Mississippi

❝For we colored people did not know how to be free and the white people did not know how to have a free colored person about them.❞
 HOUSTON HARTSFIELD HOLLOWAY,
 freedman, on the problem of Reconstruction

❝As in the war, freedom was the keynote of victory, so now is universal suffrage the keynote of Reconstruction.❞
 ELIZABETH CADY STANTON,
 arguing for universal suffrage, 1867

❝We thought we was goin' to be richer than the white folks, 'cause we was stronger and knowed how to work, and the whites didn't and they didn't have us to work for them anymore. But it didn't turn out that way. We soon found out that freedom could make folks proud but it didn't make 'em rich.❞
 FELIX HAYWOOD,
 former slave

PRESIDENTIAL SUPERLATIVES

BETTMANN/CORBIS

Andrew Johnson

While he was neither "first in war, first in peace" nor "first in the hearts of his countrymen," President Andrew Johnson left his mark on history:

- First to have never attended school
- First to be impeached
- First to be elected to the Senate both before and after being president
- First to host a queen at the White House

- First tailor/president who made his own clothes
- Last not to attend successor's inauguration
- Most vetoes overridden
- Father of the Homestead Act

COOPERATIVE LEARNING ACTIVITY

Creating a Magazine Spread Organize the class into groups of four or five. Have each group select one of the following time periods: 1860–1865, 1866–1870, or 1871–1877. Have each group create its own two-page magazine spread for the period selected. Encourage students to use elements similar to those in the Time Notebook but to be creative as they select information. Students should look at current magazines and books for ideas about page design. This activity can be completed using desktop publishing software or the more traditional cut-and-paste method.

Use the rubric for a cooperative group management plan on pages 71–72 in the *Performance Assessment Activities and Rubrics.*

(Re)inventing America

Patents awarded to African American inventors during the Reconstruction period:

ALEXANDER ASHBOURNE biscuit cutter

LANDROW BELL locomotive smokestack

LEWIS HOWARD LATIMER water closets (toilets) for railway cars, electric lamp with cotton filament, dough kneader

THOMAS ELKINS refrigerator with cooling coils

THOMAS J. MARTIN fire extinguisher

ELIJAH McCOY automatic oil cup and 57 other devices and machine parts, including an ironing board and lawn sprinkler

Refrigerators keep foods cool.

BETTMANN/CORBIS

NUMBERS

$7,200,000
Purchase price paid by U.S. to Russia for Alaska in 1867

2¢ Price paid per acre for Alaska

$30 Boarding and tuition, per quarter, at Saint Frances Academy, boarding school for African American girls in Baltimore, Maryland. Students come from states as distant as Florida and Missouri for an education "productive of the happiest effects among individuals and in society."

$5 Extra charge for instruction in embroidery

$25 Extra charge for instruction in making wax fruit

$3 Tuition, per quarter, for local "day scholars"

5,407 Number of pupils in Mississippi Freedmen's schools in 1866

50 Number of schools established for freed African Americans in Mississippi in 1866

20% Percentage of state income of Mississippi spent on artificial arms and legs for war veterans in 1866

Milestones

REEXAMINED. THE ROMANTIC STORY OF POCAHONTAS, based on the written account of Captain John Smith. The *London Spectator*, reporting on the work of Mr. E. Neils, debunks Smith's tale of the young Pocahontas flinging herself between him and her father's club. The young girl was captured and held prisoner on board a British ship and then forcibly married to Mr. John Rolfe. Comments *Appleton's Journal* in 1870: "All that is heroic, picturesque, or romantic in history seems to be rapidly disappearing under the microscopic scrutiny of modern critics."

FOUNDED, 1877. NICODEMUS, KANSAS, by six African American and two white Kansans. On the high, arid plains of Graham County, the founders hope to establish a community of homesteading former slaves.

TOPPED, 1875. THE ONE MILLION MARK FOR POPULATION, by New York City. New York is the ninth city in the history of the world to achieve a population level of more than one million. The first was Rome in 133 B.C.

Pocahontas

MPI/HULTON GETTY PICTURE LIBRARY/LIAISON

EXTINGUISHED, 1871. THE PESHTIGO FOREST FIRE in Wisconsin. The conflagration caused 2,682 deaths. The Peshtigo tragedy has been overshadowed by the Great Chicago Fire of the same year, which killed 300.

PUBLISHED, 1865. *DRUM TAPS*, by Walt Whitman. Based on his experiences as a hospital volunteer, Whitman's new poems chronicle the horrors of the Civil War.

THROWN, 1867. FIRST CURVEBALL, by William A. "Candy" Cummings of the Brooklyn Excelsiors. In a game against Harvard, pitcher Cummings put a spin on the ball to make it swerve downward. Most spectators thought the ball's curved path was an illusion.

Freedmen's classroom

LIBRARY OF CONGRESS

EXTENDING THE CONTENT

Elizabeth Cady Stanton One of the founders of the National Woman Suffrage Association, Elizabeth Cady Stanton worked throughout her life to secure rights for women. She learned early in life that women did not have the same opportunities as men. She was the only girl who took the mathematics and language courses offered in her school. She was barred from attending college and practicing law simply because she was a woman. The National Woman Suffrage Association, formed in 1869, sought to gain voting rights for women. Stanton also worked to gain economic and political equality for women.

CHAPTER 7 ASSESSMENT and ACTIVITIES

Reviewing Key Terms
Students' answers will vary. The pages where the words appear in the text are shown in parentheses.

1. **greenback** *(p. 245)*
2. **conscription** *(p. 246)*
3. **habeas corpus** *(p. 246)*
4. **attrition** *(p. 247)*
5. **bounty** *(p. 250)*
6. **blockade runner** *(p. 250)*
7. **hardtack** *(p. 254)*
8. **prisoner of war** *(p. 254)*
9. **forage** *(p. 258)*
10. **siege** *(p. 258)*
11. **torpedo** *(p. 261)*
12. **mandate** *(p. 262)*
13. **Reconstruction** *(p. 266)*
14. **amnesty** *(p. 267)*
15. **pocket veto** *(p. 268)*
16. **freedmen** *(p. 268)*
17. **black codes** *(p. 269)*
18. **impeach** *(p. 271)*
19. **carpetbagger** *(p. 273)*
20. **scalawag** *(p. 273)*
21. **graft** *(p. 273)*
22. **tenant farmer** *(p. 277)*
23. **sharecropper** *(p. 277)*

Reviewing Key Facts
24. Robert E. Lee *(p. 244),* Copperhead *(p. 246), Trent* Affair *(p. 247),* Anaconda Plan *(p. 248),* Ulysses S. Grant *(p. 251),* Military Reconstruction Act *(p. 270)*
25. transformed the war from a conflict over preservation of the Union into a war of liberation

Reviewing Key Terms
On a sheet of paper, use each of these terms in a sentence.

1. greenback
2. conscription
3. habeas corpus
4. attrition
5. bounty
6. blockade runner
7. hardtack
8. prisoner of war
9. forage
10. siege
11. torpedo
12. mandate
13. Reconstruction
14. amnesty
15. pocket veto
16. freedmen
17. black codes
18. impeach
19. carpetbagger
20. scalawag
21. graft
22. tenant farmer
23. sharecropper

Reviewing Key Facts
24. **Identify:** Robert E. Lee, Copperhead, *Trent* Affair, Anaconda Plan, Ulysses S. Grant, Military Reconstruction Act.
25. What effects did the Emancipation Proclamation have on the war?
26. How did the Civil War affect the South's economy?
27. How did the Thirteenth, Fourteenth, and Fifteenth Amendments advance civil rights?

28. What did President Johnson do that convinced Congress that he was not carrying out the laws Congress had passed for Reconstruction?
29. What were said to be the provisions of the Compromise of 1877?

Critical Thinking
30. **Analyzing Themes: Civic Rights and Responsibilities** President Lincoln suspended writs of habeas corpus to prevent interference with the draft. Do you think suspending civil liberties is justified in some situations? Why or why not?
31. **Interpreting Primary Sources** At the beginning of the Civil War, Robert E. Lee wrote to his sister, Mrs. Anne Marshall, of his decision to resign from the U.S. Army. Read the excerpt and answer the questions that follow.

> 66With all my devotion to the Union and the feeling of loyalty and duty of an American citizen, I have not been able to make up my mind to raise my hand against my relatives, my children, my home. I have, therefore, resigned my commission in the Army, and, save in defense of my native state . . . I hope I may never be called on to draw my sword. I know you will blame me; but you must think as kindly of me as you can. . . .99
>
> —from *Personal Reminiscences, Anecdotes, and Letters of General Robert E. Lee*

Chapter Summary

Civil War

1861
• First Battle of Bull Run (Manassas)

1863
• Emancipation Proclamation issued
• North wins decisive victories at Gettysburg and Vicksburg

1862
• Monitor and Virginia battle to a draw
• South introduces conscription for military service; David Farragut captures New Orleans
• Battle of Antietam

1865
• Thirteenth Amendment passed
• South surrenders
• John Wilkes Booth assassinates Lincoln

Reconstruction

1866
• Fourteenth Amendment passed

1868
• Andrew Johnson impeached
• Ulysses S. Grant wins presidency

1870
• Fifteenth Amendment passed

1867
• Military Reconstruction Act passed

1873
• Economic panic strikes U.S

1877
• Compromise of 1877 ends Reconstruction

1861 ♦*1869* ♦*1877*

26. devastated the Southern economy–agriculture disrupted, rails destroyed
27. Thirteenth abolished slavery; Fourteenth granted citizenship rights to all persons born or naturalized in the United States and required states to grant due process to all citizens; Fifteenth granted voting rights to citizens of all races.
28. He challenged congressional authority and the Tenure of Office Act by firing Secretary of War Edwin Stanton.

29. granted Hayes the presidency, promised that a Southerner would be postmaster general, promised funds for improvements in the South, and agreed to withdrawal of all remaining troops in the South

Critical Thinking
30. Answers will vary. Students who support suspending civil rights should be very specific about the conditions under which they could be suspended. Students who

Self-Check Quiz
Visit the *American Republic Since 1877* Web site at tarvol2.glencoe.com and click on **Self-Check Quizzes— Chapter 7** to assess your knowledge of chapter content.

a. What were Robert E. Lee's feelings about the war?

b. Why did Lee feel it necessary to resign from the Union army and become a Confederate army commander?

32. **Organizing** Complete a graphic organizer similar to the one below by listing the effects of the Civil War on the nation.

Results of Civil War

Practicing Skills

33. **Evaluating a Web Site** Go through the steps described on page 256 for evaluating a Web site. Then search the Internet for Web sites that deal with prisoners of war during the Civil War. Write a report describing the best and worst site you find, listing reasons for your evaluations.

Economics and History

34. The graph on this page shows agricultural production in the South from 1860 to 1900. Study the graph and answer the questions below.
    a. **Interpreting Graphs** Which crops surpassed pre–Civil War levels of production by 1890?
    b. **Synthesizing** What factors do you think might have contributed to the increase in agricultural production levels in the South in the late 1800s?

Writing Activity

35. **Portfolio Writing** Choose one of the events of the Civil War or Reconstruction discussed in the chapter. Imagine that the radio had been invented at that time. Write a radio news segment in which you provide information about the event and your view of it. Include the script for the radio segment in your portfolio.

Chapter Activity

36. **Research Projects** Use library sources to find examples of political cartoons from the Civil War or Reconstruction era. Create a display of these cartoons and write a summary of how they illustrate the major issues of the time period.

Agricultural Production in the South, 1860–1900

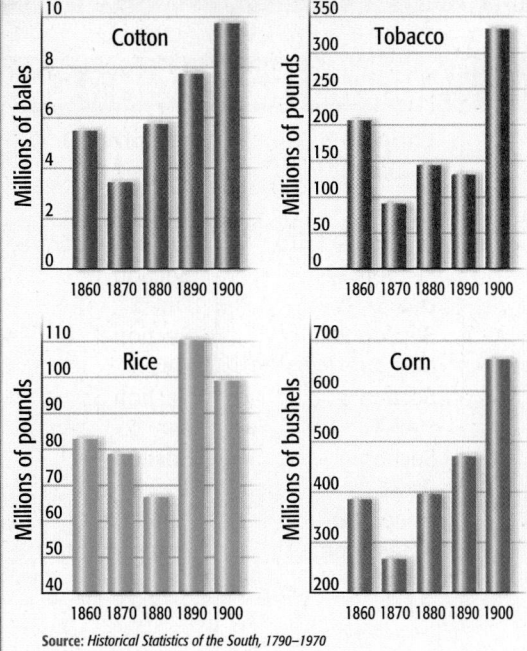

Source: *Historical Statistics of the South, 1790–1970*

Standardized Test Practice

Directions: Choose the phrase that best completes the statement below.

One advantage that Southern states held during the Civil War was that

A they received military and financial support from the British and the French.

B many battles occurred on lands with which Southerners were more familiar.

C the largest weapons factories were located in the South.

D most people agreed with the position of the Southern states.

Test-Taking Tip: When you are not sure of an answer, it can be helpful to use the process of elimination. For example, you probably remember that the North had a greater population than the South. Therefore, answer D is probably incorrect.

Have students visit the Web site at tarvol2.glencoe.com to review Chapter 7 and take the Self-Check Quiz.

Economics and History

34. **a.** cotton, rice, and corn, **b.** possible answers: increased demand, better railroad systems to reach more distant markets

Writing Activity

35. Scripts will vary but should present the facts in a style typical of radio news broadcasts.

Chapter Activity

36. Political cartoons selected will vary. The displays should be well-organized and the summaries should indicate a clear understanding of the events and the meaning of the cartoons.

Standardized Test Practice

Answer: B
Test-Taking Tip: Tell students that if they are unsure of the answer, they should create a list of things they do know about the Southern states to help them locate the best answer or to at least eliminate answers that they know are incorrect.

Bonus Question ?

Ask: What similarities existed between slavery and share-cropping? *(Both systems trapped African Americans in poverty.)*

---

do not support suspending civil rights should provide adequate reasoning for their point of view.

31. **a.** He hoped he would not have to fight. **b.** He could not fight against his own relatives and place of birth.

32. possible answers: ended slavery; strengthened the federal government; left South economically devastated; gave African Americans new political, economic, and social opportunities; allowed the Republicans to control Reconstruction; promoted nursing as a profession for women

Practicing Skills

33. Evaluations should include an assessment of the authoritativeness of the sites.

Unit 3 (1 Day)	Chapter 8 (4 Days)	Chapter 9 (5 Days)	Chapter 10 (5 Days)	Chapter 11 (4 Days)	Unit 3 (2 Days)
Day 1 Introduction	**Day 1** Chapter 8 Intro, Section 1 **Day 2** Section 2 **Day 3** Section 3 **Day 4** Chapter 8 Assessment	**Day 1** Chapter 9 Intro, Section 1 **Day 2** Section 2 **Day 3** Section 3 **Day 4** Section 4 **Day 5** Chapter 9 Assessment	**Day 1** Chapter 10 Intro, Section 1 **Day 2** Section 2 **Day 3** Section 3 **Day 4** Section 4 **Day 5** Chapter 10 Assessment	**Day 1** Chapter 11 Intro, Section 1 **Day 2** Section 2 **Day 3** Section 3 **Day 4** Chapter 11 Assessment	**Day 1** Wrap-Up/Project **Day 2** Unit 3 Assessment

GLENCOE'S ASSESSMENT ADVANTAGE

Use the following tools to easily assess student learning in a variety of ways:

- Performance Assessment Activities and Rubrics
- Chapter and Unit Tests
- Section Quizzes
- Standardized Test Practice Workbook

- tarvol2.glencoe.com
- Interactive Tutor Self-Assessment CD-ROM
- MindJogger Videoquiz
- ExamView® Pro Testmaker CD-ROM
- SAT I/II Test Practice

TEACHING TRANSPARENCIES

Unit 3 Map Overlay Transparencies L2

Cause-and-Effect Transparency 3 L2

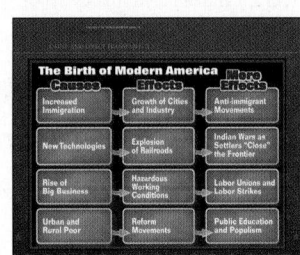

READING SUPPORT FROM JAMESTOWN EDUCATION

- ***Timed Readings Plus in Social Studies*** help students increase their reading rate and fluency while maintaining comprehension. The 400-word passages are similar to those found on state and national assessments.

- ***Reading in the Content Area: Social Studies*** concentrates on six essential reading skills that help students better comprehend what they read. The book includes 75 high-interest nonfiction passages written at increasing levels of difficulty.

- ***Reading Fluency*** helps students read smoothly, accurately, and expressively.

- ***Jamestown's Reading Improvement,*** by renowned reading expert Edward Fry, focuses on helping build your students' comprehension, vocabulary, and skimming and scanning skills.

- ***Critical Reading Series*** provides high-interest books, each written at three reading levels.

For more information about these products, see the Jamestown Education materials in the Classroom Solutions in the front of this Teacher Wraparound Edition. To order these products, call Glencoe at 1-800-334-7344.

ASSESSMENT

APPLICATION AND ENRICHMENT

American Biography 3 L2

History Simulation and Problem Solving 3 L1

GEOGRAPHY

Geography and History Activity 3 L2

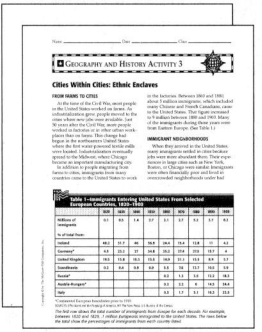

INTERDISCIPLINARY ACTIVITIES

American Literature Reading 3 L2

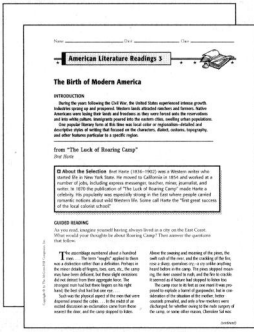

Economics and History Activity 3 L2

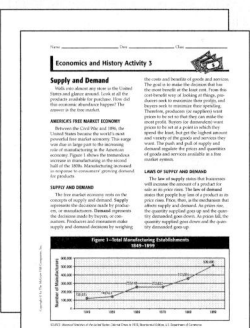

Team-Teaching Interdisciplinary Strategies and Activities 3 L2

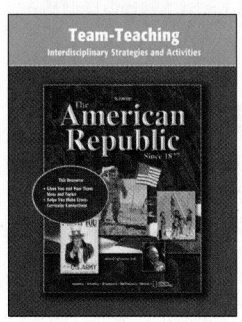

Reading List Generator CD-ROM

GLENCOE BOOKLINK

The Glencoe BookLink CD-ROM is a database that allows you to search more than 15,000 titles to create a customized reading list for your students.

- Reading lists can be organized by students' reading level, author, genre, theme, or area of interest.

- The database provides Degrees of Reading Power™ (DRP) and Lexile™ readability scores for all selections.

- A brief summary of each selection is included.

Leveled reading suggestions for this unit:

For students at a Grade 8 reading level:
- *Full Steam Ahead,* by Rhoda Blumberg.

For students at a Grade 9 reading level:
- *A Strange and Distant Shore: Indians of the Great Plains in Exile,* by Brent Ashabranner.

For students at a Grade 10 reading level:
- *Twenty Years at Hull House,* by Jane Addams.

Extending the Content

Readings for the Teacher
- *The Muckrakers,* edited by Arthur Weinberg and Lila Shaffer Weinberg. University of Illinois Press, 2001.

Multimedia Resources
- *Nez Perce: Portrait of a People.* National Park Service. VHS. (23 minutes)

0:00 **Out of Time?**

If time does not permit teaching each chapter in this unit, you may want to use the **Reading Essentials and Study Guide** summaries.

Unit Overview

Unit 3 explores the transformation of the United States from a rural nation into an industrial, urban nation during the period from 1865 to 1900. **Chapter 8** covers the settling of the West from 1865 to 1900. **Chapter 9** focuses on the industrialization of America from 1865 to 1901. **Chapter 10** explores urban America from 1865 to 1896. **Chapter 11** examines the political and reform movements that responded to industrialization from 1877 to 1896.

Unit Objectives

After studying this unit, students will be able to:
1. Describe the settlement of the West.
2. Explain the changes to American society that resulted from industrialization.
3. Analyze the role immigration played in industrialization.
4. Describe the political response to the economic problems of the period.

Why It Matters Activity

Have students consider the changes that have occurred in their lifetimes as a result of technological changes. Then have them make generalizations about the effects of technological change on peoples' lives.

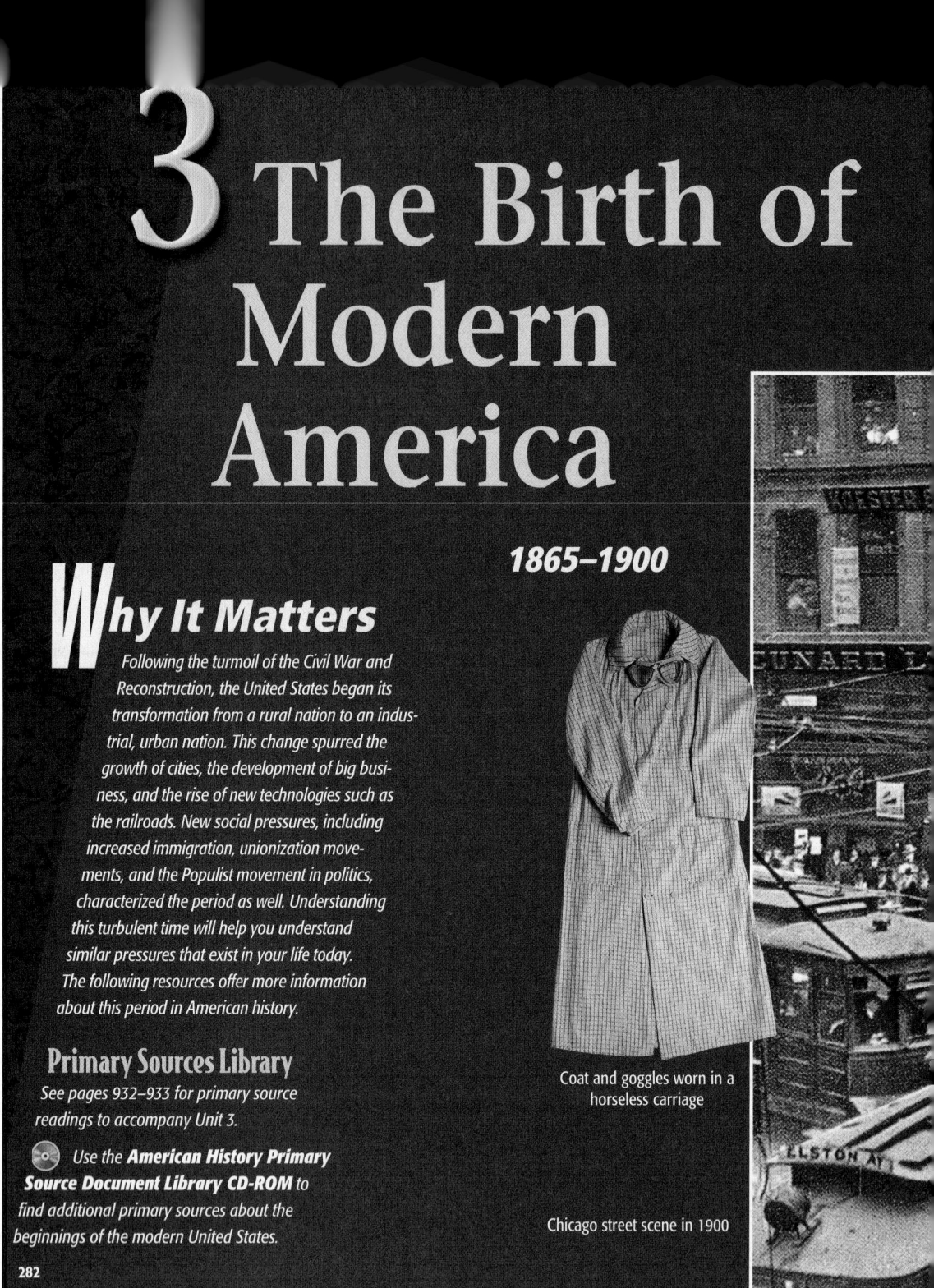

3 The Birth of Modern America

1865–1900

Why It Matters

Following the turmoil of the Civil War and Reconstruction, the United States began its transformation from a rural nation to an industrial, urban nation. This change spurred the growth of cities, the development of big business, and the rise of new technologies such as the railroads. New social pressures, including increased immigration, unionization movements, and the Populist movement in politics, characterized the period as well. Understanding this turbulent time will help you understand similar pressures that exist in your life today. The following resources offer more information about this period in American history.

Primary Sources Library

See pages 932–933 for primary source readings to accompany Unit 3.

Use the **American History Primary Source Document Library CD-ROM** to find additional primary sources about the beginnings of the modern United States.

282

Coat and goggles worn in a horseless carriage

Chicago street scene in 1900

TEAM TEACHING ACTIVITY

Economics Have the economics teacher compare and contrast small, entrepreneurial businesses with big businesses, and family farms with large agricultural enterprises. After the presentation, have a class discussion using the following questions: How are workers treated differently in different types of enterprises? How is family life affected by the various enterprises? How does the type of enterprise in which your family is involved affect where and how you live? What effect do economic changes such as recessions have on these types of enterprises?

"The city is the nerve center of our civilization. It is also the storm center."

—Josiah Strong, 1885

A BUSY DAY ON DEARBORN AND RANDOLPH STREETS CHICAGO

GLENCOE TECHNOLOGY

CD-ROM
American History
Primary Source
Document Library
CD-ROM

Use the **American History Primary Source Document Library CD-ROM** to access primary source documents related to this period in history.

More About the Photo

Point out to students that the late 1800s and early 1900s saw significant changes in modes of transportation. Have students identify the various forms of transportation in the picture and speculate on the function and usefulness of each form. Tell students that congested streets are still a feature of most large urban areas and that pedestrians are still a major feature of large urban centers.

Glencoe Literature Library

The following novels from the *High School American History Literature Library* may be used to enrich the study of this unit:

• *The Adventures of Huckleberry Finn* by Mark Twain
• *My Ántonia* by Willa Cather
• *The Yearling* by Marjorie Rawlings

SERVICE-LEARNING PROJECT

Have a person from your local historical society describe the types of records they keep. Organize students into small groups. Have the groups select a significant event or period from your local history. Then have the groups work together to prepare a display about the event or period. Encourage students to contact people who remember the event and to gather and properly display historical primary source materials. If possible, have the displays set up in a public place such as a library for the community to enjoy.

Refer to **Building Bridges: Connecting Classroom and Community through Service-Learning in Social Studies** from the National Council for the Social Studies for information about service-learning.

Chapter 8 Resources

Timesaving Tools

TeacherWorks™ All-In-One Planner and Resource Center

● **Interactive Teacher Edition** Access your Teacher Wraparound Edition and your classroom resources with a few easy clicks.

● **Interactive Lesson Planner** Planning has never been easier! Organize your week, month, semester, or year with all the lesson helps you need to make teaching creative, timely, and relevant.

Use Glencoe's **Presentation Plus!** multimedia teacher tool to easily present dynamic lessons that visually excite your students. Using Microsoft PowerPoint® you can customize the presentations to create your own personalized lessons.

TEACHING TRANSPARENCIES

Graphic Organizer 8 L2

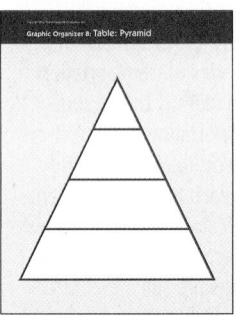

Why It Matters Chapter Transparency 8 L2

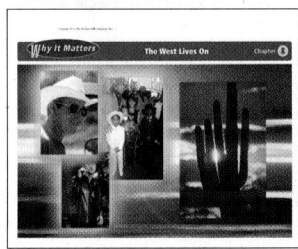

APPLICATION AND ENRICHMENT

Linking Past and Present Activity 8 L2

Enrichment Activity 8 L3

Primary Source Reading 8 L2

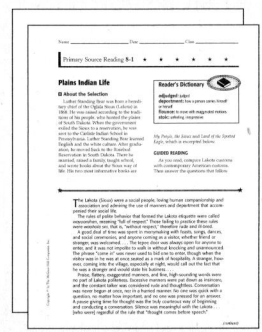

REVIEW AND REINFORCEMENT

Reteaching Activity 8 L1

Vocabulary Activity 8 L1

Time Line Activity 8 L2

Critical Thinking Skills Activity 8 L2

Meeting NCSS Standards

Local Standards

The following standards are covered in Chapter 8:

Section 1	VII	Production, Distribution, and Consumption: B, F, I
Section 2	III	People, Places, and Environments: A, B
Section 3	IV	Individual Development and Identity: E, G

Chapter 8 Resources

**Chapter 8 Test
Form A L2**

**Chapter 8 Test
Form B L2**

**Standardized Test Practice
Workbook Activity 8 L2**

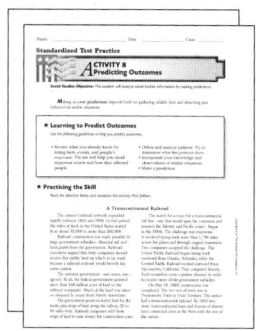

**Performance Assessment
Activities and Rubrics 8
L1/ELL**

**ExamView® Pro
Testmaker CD-ROM**

MULTIMEDIA

- Vocabulary PuzzleMaker CD-ROM
- Interactive Tutor Self-Assessment CD-ROM
- ExamView® Pro Testmaker CD-ROM
- Audio Program
- American History Primary Source Documents Library CD-ROM
- MindJogger Videoquiz
- Presentation Plus! CD-ROM
- TeacherWorks™ CD-ROM
- Interactive Student Edition CD-ROM
- Glencoe Skillbuilder Interactive Workbook CD-ROM, Level 2
- The *American Republic Since 1877* Video Program
- American Music: Hits Through History
- American Music: Cultural Traditions

SPANISH RESOURCES

The following Spanish language materials are available:

- Spanish Reading Essentials and Study Guide
- Spanish Guided Reading Activities
- Spanish Reteaching Activities
- Spanish Quizzes and Tests
- Spanish Vocabulary Activities
- Spanish Summaries
- The Declaration of Independence and United States Constitution Spanish Translation

---

THE HISTORY CHANNEL®

The following videotape programs are available from Glencoe as supplements to Chapter 8:

- **Buffalo Bill: Showman of the West** (ISBN 1-56-501940-7)
- **Crazy Horse** (ISBN 1-56-501597-5)
- **Geronimo** (ISBN 1-56-501939-3)
- **Sitting Bull: Chief of the Lakota Nation** (ISBN 1-56-501684-X)

To order, call Glencoe at 1-800-334-7344. To find classroom resources to accompany many of these videos, check the following home pages:
A&E Television: www.aande.com
The History Channel: www.historychannel.com

Use our Web site for additional resources. All essential content is covered in the Student Edition.

You and your students can visit tarvol2.glencoe.com, the Web site companion to the *American Republic Since 1877.* This innovative integration of electronic and print media offers your students a wealth of opportunities. The student text directs students to the Web site for the following options:

- **Chapter Overviews**
- **Self-Check Quizzes**
- **Student Web Activities**
- **Textbook Updates**

Answers to the student Web activities are provided for you in the **Web Activity Lesson Plans.** Additional Web resources and Interactive Tutor Puzzles are also available.

Chapter 8 Resources

SECTION RESOURCES

Daily Objectives	Reproducible Resources	Multimedia Resources
SECTION 1 **Miners and Ranchers** 1. Trace the growth of the mining industry in the West. 2. Describe the ways that new technology changed open-range ranching.	Reproducible Lesson Plan 8–1 Daily Lecture and Discussion Notes 8–1 Guided Reading Activity 8–1* Section Quiz 8–1* Reading Essentials and Study Guide 8–1* Performance Assessment Activities and Rubrics Supreme Court Case Studies	Daily Focus Skills Transparency 8–1 American Art & Architecture Interactive Tutor Self-Assessment CD-ROM ExamView® Pro Testmaker CD-ROM* Presentation Plus! CD-ROM TeacherWorks™ CD-ROM Audio Program American Music: Hits Through History
SECTION 2 **Farming the Plains** 1. Explain why and how people began settling the Plains. 2. Trace the growth of commercial farming on the Plains.	Reproducible Lesson Plan 8–2 Daily Lecture and Discussion Notes 8–2 Guided Reading Activity 8–2* Section Quiz 8–2* Reading Essentials and Study Guide 8–2* Performance Assessment Activities and Rubrics American History in Graphic Novel	Daily Focus Skills Transparency 8–2 Interactive Tutor Self-Assessment CD-ROM ExamView® Pro Testmaker CD-ROM* Presentation Plus! CD-ROM Skillbuilder Interactive Workbook, Level 2 TeacherWorks™ CD-ROM Audio Program American Music: Cultural Traditions
SECTION 3 **Native Americans** 1. Discuss conflicts that arose between the Plains Indians and American settlers. 2. Summarize problems caused by attempts to assimilate Native Americans.	Reproducible Lesson Plan 8–3 Daily Lecture and Discussion Notes 8–3 Guided Reading Activity 8–3* Section Quiz 8–3* Reading Essentials and Study Guide 8–3* Performance Assessment Activities and Rubrics Interpreting Political Cartoons American History in Graphic Novel	Daily Focus Skills Transparency 8–3 American Art & Architecture Interactive Tutor Self-Assessment CD-ROM ExamView® Pro Testmaker CD-ROM* Presentation Plus! CD-ROM TeacherWorks™ CD-ROM Vocabulary PuzzleMaker CD-ROM Audio Program ABCNews Interactive™ Historic America Electronic Field Trips American Music: Hits Through History

0:00 OUT OF TIME?
Assign the Chapter 8 **Reading Essentials and Study Guide.**

*Also Available in Spanish

 Printed Materials   Transparency   CD-ROM   DVD

 Poster   Music Program   Audio Program   Videocassette

NATIONAL GEOGRAPHIC — Teacher's Corner

INDEX TO NATIONAL GEOGRAPHIC MAGAZINE

The following articles relate to this chapter.

- "Along the Santa Fe Trail," March 1991
- "Buffalo: Back Home on the Range," November 1994
- "Geronimo," October 1992
- "John Wesley Powell," April 1994
- "Ogallala Aquifer," March 1993
- "Wide Open Wyoming," January 1993

NATIONAL GEOGRAPHIC SOCIETY PRODUCTS

To order the following, call National Geographic at 1-800-368-2728:

- *Heritage of the Black West* (Video)
- *Immigration: The Triumph of Hope* (Video)
- *The West That Was* (Video)

NGS ONLINE

Access National Geographic's Web site for current events, atlas updates, activities, links, interactive features, and archives.

www.nationalgeographic.com

MEETING SPECIAL NEEDS

In addition to the Differentiated Instruction strategies found in each section, the following resources are also suitable for your special needs students:

- *ExamView® Pro Testmaker CD-ROM* allows teachers to tailor tests by reducing answer choices.
- The *Audio Program* includes the entire narrative of the student edition so that less proficient readers can listen to the words as they read them.
- The *Reading Essentials and Study Guide* provides the same content as the student edition but is written two grade levels below the textbook.

KEY TO ABILITY LEVELS

Teaching strategies have been coded.

- **L1** BASIC activities for all students
- **L2** AVERAGE activities for average to above-average students
- **L3** CHALLENGING activities for above-average students
- **ELL** ENGLISH LANGUAGE LEARNER activities

From the Classroom of...

Teresa Squires Osborne
Reynolds High School
Troutdale, OR

Immigration Panel

Create a panel of students, from your class and/or from the school, made up of first and second generation immigrants to the U.S. After panel members have shown their country of origin on a map, have the student panel address the following information:

1. What is the story of your family's arrival here? Where and when did you or your parents arrive in the U.S.?
2. Why did your family choose to leave your native country?
3. What is different or similar about life in the U.S. compared to your family's native country?
4. How would your life be different if you or your parents had remained?

Have students compare the answers of the panel with the experiences of earlier immigrant groups.

ADDITIONAL RESOURCES FROM GLENCOE

- American Music: Cultural Traditions
- American Art & Architecture
- Outline Map Resource Book
- U.S. Desk Map
- Building Geography Skills for Life
- Inclusion for the High School Social Studies Classroom Strategies and Activities
- Teaching Strategies for the American History Classroom (Including Block Scheduling Pacing Guides)
- Dinah Zike's High School American History Reading and Study Skills Foldables

Block Schedule

Activities that are suited to use within the block scheduling framework are identified by:

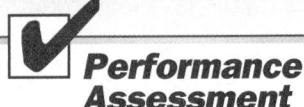

✓ **Performance Assessment**

Refer to Activity 8 in the Performance Assessment Activities and Rubrics booklet.

Why It Matters Activity

Ask students how the settlement of the West affects their lives today. Students should evaluate their answers after they have completed the chapter.

GLENCOE
TECHNOLOGY

The *American Republic Since 1877* **Video Program**
To learn more about early days of Western settlement in the United States, have students view the Chapter 8 video, "Life in the West," from the *American Republic Since 1877* **Video Program.**

MindJogger Videoquiz
Use the **MindJogger Videoquiz** to preview Chapter 8 content.

 Both programs available in DVD

CHAPTER

 8 Settling the West
1865–1900

Why It Matters

After the Civil War, a dynamic period in American history opened—the settlement of the West. The lives of Western miners, farmers, and ranchers were often filled with great hardships, but the wave of American settlers continued. Railroads hastened this migration. During this period, many Native Americans lost their homelands and their way of life.

The Impact Today

Developments of this period are still evident today.
* *Native American reservations still exist in the United States.*
* *The myth of the Western hero is prominent in popular culture.*

 The **American Republic Since 1877** *Video The Chapter 8 video, "Life in the West," chronicles the early days of western settlement in the United States.*

1859
* Comstock Lode of gold and silver discovered in Nevada

1864
* Sand Creek Massacre

1867
* Chisholm Trail cattle drive begins

1881
* President Garfield assassinated

1876
* Battle of the Little Bighorn

United States PRESIDENTS

| Lincoln 1861–1865 | A. Johnson 1865–1869 | Grant 1869–1877 | Hayes 1877–1881 | Garfield 1881 | Arthur 1881–188 |

1860   *1870*   *1880*

World

1867
* Diamonds discovered in South Africa

1871
* Otto von Bismarck unifies the many German states into modern Germany

1877
* First Wimbledon tennis tournament held

1868
* Cro-Magnon skeleton discovered in France

1881
* Japanese emperor Mutsuhito promises to establish national legislature

284

📖 **Reading Strategy   PURPOSE FOR READING**

Think/Write–Pair–Share This strategy engages students in the subject matter through discussion. Have students **T**hink silently about what they know concerning the settlement of the West and the hardships the settlers faced. Ask them to **W**rite down three to five of these hardships. Have students **P**air with a partner and **S**hare their ideas. Conclude with a class discussion. **L1**

📁 Refer to *Inclusion for the High School Social Studies Classroom Strategies and Activities* in the TCR.

Mother and child in a Wyoming wheat field

1885
• First skyscraper built in Chicago

1887
• Dawes Act eliminates communal ownership of Native American reservations

1896
• *Plessy* v. *Ferguson* creates "separate but equal" doctrine

Cleveland
1885–1889

B. Harrison
1889–1893

Cleveland
1893–1897

McKinley
1897–1901

1890

1900

1888
• Brazil ends slavery

1894
• China begins war against Japan

1896
• Modern Olympics begin in Athens, Greece

HISTORY
Online

Chapter Overview
Visit the *American Republic Since 1877* Web site at tarvol2.glencoe.com and click on *Chapter Overviews— Chapter 8* to preview chapter information.

285

More About the Photo

Joseph E. Stimson was the official photographer for the Union Pacific Railroad in Cheyenne, Wyoming, from 1889 to 1903. He often photographed Native Americans in Wyoming during his travels for the railroad. The mother and child who appear on page 285 stood in a field of Red Cross and Turkey Red Wheat at a U.S. experimental station at Newcastle, Wyoming.

TIME LINE
ACTIVITY

Have students write a short biographical profile of one of the presidents shown on the time line on pages 284 and 285. Instruct students to include information about how the president they select influenced the settlement of the West.

FOLDABLES™
Study Organizer

Dinah Zike's Foldables are three-dimensional, interactive graphic organizers that help students practice basic writing skills, review key vocabulary terms, and identify main ideas. Have students complete the foldable activity in the *Dinah Zike's Reading and Study Skills Foldables* booklet.

GRAPHIC ORGANIZER ACTIVITY

Organizing Information Have students create an integrated time line using the chapter and section time lines. Instruct students to use absolute chronology in placing significant events on the time line.

1 FOCUS

Section Overview

This section focuses on the westward migration of people searching for economic opportunities as miners and ranchers.

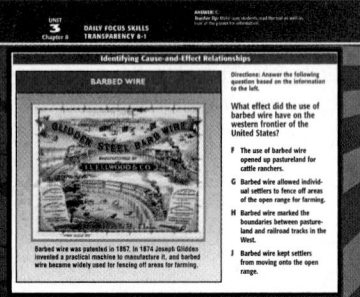
Reading Preview

Answers to Graphic: silver in Nevada (Comstock Lode); lead and silver in Leadville, Colorado; gold in Colorado; gold in Dakota Territory; copper in Montana

Preteaching Vocabulary
Have students look up the meanings of the Key Terms and use the words in a sentence.

Guide to Reading

Main Idea
Miners and ranchers settled large areas of the West.

Key Terms and Names
placer mining, quartz mining, Henry Comstock, vigilance committee, open range, long drive, Chisholm Trail, maverick, barbed wire

Reading Strategy
Organizing As you read about the development of the mining industry, complete a graphic organizer listing the locations of mining booms and the discoveries made there.

Mining Booms & Discoveries

Reading Objectives
• **Trace** the growth of the mining industry in the West.
• **Describe** the ways that new technology changed open-range ranching.

Section Theme
Economic Factors People migrated to the West in search of economic opportunity.

Preview of Events

| ♦1858 | ♦1868 | ♦1878 | ♦1888 |

1858	**1859**	**1867**	**1875**	**1886–1887**
Gold discovered in Colorado	Comstock Lode discovered in Nevada	Cattle drives begin on Chisholm Trail	Gold rush begins in Dakota Territory	Blizzards devastate western ranches

★ An American Story ★

Miner working the Comstock Lode

Jacob Waldorf arrived in Virginia City, Nevada, in 1873 to seek his fortune in the fabled silver mines of the Comstock Lode. Like many others, he found work at one of the big mining companies. Seven days a week he toiled in a dangerous mine shaft, earning enough to support his family and buy a little stock in local mining companies. As his son John recalled:

66The favorite game with our father was stocks. . . . Mother used to say to me, 'Some day we're going back east,' but for years none of the stocks in which Dad invested showed any disposition to furnish us with the price of transportation.99

In 1877 the stock Waldorf owned skyrocketed in value. "Dad's holdings rose . . . to $10,000 and mother began to talk of buying a farm," John wrote. "The stock kept going upward. Dad was worth $15,000 for at least a minute." He waited for the stock to go even higher before selling, but instead it plummeted: "The bottom fell out of Ophi [a mining stock], and Mother's dream farm fell with it, for Dad was broke."

Jacob Waldorf overcame this financial setback. Earning the respect of his fellow workers, he headed the miners' union in 1880 and later served as a state legislator.

—adapted from *A Kid on the Comstock*

Growth of the Mining Industry

The story of western mining is bigger than the individual stories of fortune seekers like Waldorf. The West's rich deposits of gold, silver, and copper served the needs of growing industries in the East. They also brought the first wave of settlers that populated the mountain states of the West.

SECTION RESOURCES

📁 **Reproducible Masters**
• Reproducible Lesson Plan 8–1
• Daily Lecture and Discussion Notes 8–1
• Guided Reading Activity 8–1
• Section Quiz 8–1
• Reading Essentials and Study Guide 8–1

🖨 **Transparencies**
• Daily Focus Skills Transparency 8–1

• American Art & Architecture

Multimedia
🖥 Interactive Tutor Self-Assessment CD-ROM
🖥 ExamView® Pro Testmaker CD-ROM
🖥 Presentation Plus! CD-ROM
🖥 TeacherWorks™ CD-ROM
🔊 Audio Program
🎵 American Music: Hits Through History

News of a mineral strike in an area would start a stampede of prospectors desperately hoping to strike it rich. Early prospectors would extract the shallow deposits of ore largely by hand in a process called *placer mining*, using simple equipment like picks, shovels, and pans. After these surface deposits dwindled, corporations would move in to begin *quartz mining*, which dug deep beneath the surface. As those deposits dried up, commercial mining either disappeared or continued on a restricted basis.

ECONOMICS

The Big Strike in Nevada The story of the Comstock Lode is similar to other stories of gold, silver, and copper strikes throughout the West. In 1859 a prospector named **Henry Comstock** staked a claim in Six-Mile Canyon, Nevada. The sticky, blue-gray mud found there turned out to be nearly pure silver ore. News of the Comstock strike brought hordes of miners to Virginia City, Nevada. Almost overnight the town went from a frontier outpost to a boomtown of about 30,000, boasting an opera house, shops with furniture and fashions from Europe, several newspapers, and a six-story hotel with the West's first elevator, called a "rising room." When the silver veins were exhausted several years later, the mines closed. Without the mines, the town's economy collapsed,

and most of the townspeople moved on in search of new opportunities. This cycle of boom and bust—from boomtown to ghost town—was repeated throughout the mountainous West.

During the booms, crime posed a serious problem. Prospectors fought over claims, and thieves haunted the streets and trails. Law enforcers were scarce, and self-appointed volunteers sometimes formed **vigilance committees** to track down and punish wrongdoers. In some cases, they punished the innocent or let the guilty go free, but most people in these communities respected the law and tried to deal firmly but fairly with those accused of crimes.

Mining towns such as Virginia City at first were inhabited mostly by men, but soon they attracted more women. Some women owned property and were influential community leaders. Others worked as cooks or in laundries. Still other women worked at "hurdy-gurdy" houses (named after the mechanical musical instrument), where they danced with men for the price of a drink.

Other Bonanzas Mining also spurred the development of Colorado, the Dakota Territory, and Montana. The discovery of gold near Pikes Peak in 1858 set miners on a frantic rush. Coining the phrase "Pikes Peak

TECHNOLOGY & History

Mining Sluice

Western prospectors used sluices to search riverbeds more quickly than they could with the backbreaking panning method. A sluice diverted the current of a river into earthen or wooden trenches. The water was directed to a box with metal "riffle" bars that disturbed the current, causing heavier minerals to settle to the bottom of the box. A screen at the end of the riffle box prevented the minerals from flowing out. *Why was the sluice more efficient than panning for precious minerals?*

1 Sluices were sometimes simple trenches dug into the ground. Others were made of wood.

2 The **riffle box** agitated the water flow with metal bars, or sometimes cobble stones or small holes.

3 The box, sometimes called a "**tom**," had a **screen** to prevent the separated minerals from escaping with the water and sediment.

screen

sluice

riffle box

COOPERATIVE LEARNING ACTIVITY

Constructing a Plan Organize students into several small groups and ask groups to construct a plan for a late-1800s Western town. Suggest that groups consider the following points in preparing their plans: the buildings they will include and their location; the building materials, energy sources, and landscaping they want to use; and the public facilities they will include. Have groups draw pictorial maps of their towns and accompany them with short reports explaining the choices they made in planning.

Use the rubric for a cooperative group management plan on pages 71–72 in the *Performance Assessment Activities and Rubrics.*

---

2 TEACH

Daily Lecture and Discussion Notes 8–1

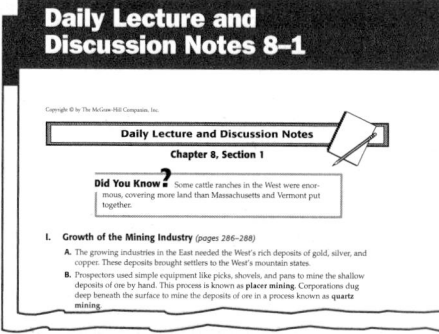

Copyright © by The McGraw-Hill Companies, Inc.

Daily Lecture and Discussion Notes

Chapter 8, Section 1

Did You Know? Some cattle ranches in the West were enormous, covering more land than Massachusetts and Vermont put together.

I. Growth of the Mining Industry *(pages 286–288)*

  A. The growing industries in the East needed the West's rich deposits of gold, silver, and copper. These deposits brought settlers to the West's mountain states.

  B. Prospectors used simple equipment like picks, shovels, and pans to mine the shallow deposits of ore by hand. This process is known as **placer mining**. Corporations dug deep beneath the surface to mine the deposits of ore in a process known as **quartz mining**.

Creating a Thematic Map Have students create a thematic map showing the locations mentioned under the heading "Growth of the Mining Industry." **L1**

Use the rubric for creating a map, display, or chart on pages 65–66 in the *Performance Assessment Activities and Rubrics.*

TECHNOLOGY & History

Background: Sometimes a V-shaped cut would be made in a hill, and a system of sluice boxes would be installed to separate the material washed down the hillside. Gold and silver were separated from the worthless rock. Mounds of worthless rock still exist in some places today, lasting evidence of the miners' work.

Answer: searches for minerals went more quickly and efficiently using sluices

Guided Reading Activity 8–1

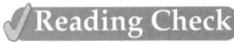

Name _____ Date _____ Class _____

★ Guided Reading Activity 8-1

DIRECTIONS: Filling in the Blanks In the space provided, write the word or words that best complete the sentence. Refer to your textbook to fill in the blanks.

1. _____ was a hand process that used simple equipment like picks, shovels, and pans.

2. _____ dug deep beneath the surface.

3. _____ staked a claim in Six-Mile Canyon that turned out to be nearly pure silver ore.

4. Almost overnight Virginia City, Nevada, went from a _____ to a _____ of about 30,000.

5. In mining, the cycle of _____ was repeated throughout the mountainous West.

6. During the booms, law enforcers were scarce, and self-appointed volunteers sometimes

✓ Reading Check

Answer: The Dakota Territory was divided into the states of North Dakota, South Dakota, and Montana.

Creating a Thematic Graph

Write the following data on the board.

Population of Denver, Colorado

1870	4,759
1880	35,629
1890	106,713
1900	133,859

Ask students to create a thematic graph showing the trend of Denver's population from 1870 to 1900. **L2**

📁 Use the rubric for creating a map, display, or chart on pages 65–66 in the *Performance Assessment Activities and Rubrics.*

Linking Past & Present

The residents of Virginia City, Nevada, which was first known as Virginny Town, got some of their news from the *Territorial Enterprise*. The newspaper employed a young reporter from Hannibal, Missouri, named Sam Clemens. Most of the readers knew him by his pen name, Mark Twain.

---

or Bust," many panned for gold without success and headed home, complaining of a "Pikes Peak hoax."

In truth, there was plenty of gold and silver in the Colorado mountains, but much of it was hidden beneath the surface and hard to extract. One of the richest strikes occurred in the late 1870s in Leadville, so called for deep deposits of lead that contained large amounts of silver. By the summer of 1879, as many as 1,000 newcomers per week were pouring into Leadville, creating one of the most legendary boomtowns dotting the mining frontier.

Overall, operations at Leadville and other mining towns in Colorado yielded more than $1 billion worth of silver and gold (many billions in today's money). This bonanza spurred the building of railroads through the Rocky Mountains and transformed Denver, the supply point for the mining areas, into the second largest city in the West after San Francisco.

The discovery of gold in the Black Hills of the Dakota Territory and copper in Montana led to rapid development of the northern Great Plains. Miners flooded into the region in the 1870s. After railroads were built in the 1880s, many farmers and ranchers moved to the territory. In 1889, Congress divided the Dakota Territory and admitted North Dakota and South Dakota, as well as Montana, as new states.

✓ Reading Check
Explain How did the creation of new states change the political boundaries of the Great Plains?

Linking Past & Present

Virginia City

Past: Comstock Boomtown
The wealth of its silver mines turned Virginia City, Nevada, from a leaky-tent mining town into a metropolis with five newspapers and a stock exchange. Express companies carried out silver and brought in supplies for the city's 30,000 people.

Present: Tourist Center
Unlike many mining towns that became ghost towns, Virginia City still exists. The community depends on the tourist industry. Visitors can see the old school building, the opera house, and a mining museum. Virginia City is just a short drive from Carson City and Lake Tahoe.

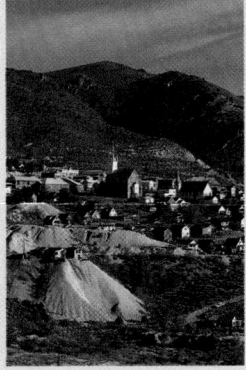

288 CHAPTER 8 Settling the West

Ranching and Cattle Drives

While many Americans headed to the Rocky Mountains to mine gold and silver after the Civil War, others began building vast cattle ranches on the Great Plains. In the early 1800s, Americans did not think cattle ranches on the Great Plains were practical. Water was scarce, and cattle from the East could not survive on the tough prairie grasses. Farther south, however, in Texas, there existed a breed of cattle adapted to living on the Great Plains.

The Texas longhorn was a breed descended from Spanish cattle that had been brought to Mexico two centuries earlier. Ranchers in Mexico and Texas had allowed their cattle to run wild, and slowly a new breed—the longhorn—had emerged. Lean and rangy, the longhorn could easily survive in the harsh climate of the Plains, and by 1865, as many as 5 million of them roamed the grasslands of Texas.

Mexicans had introduced cattle ranching in New Mexico, California, and Texas before these areas became part of the United States. The industry grew in part because of the open range—a vast area of grassland owned by the government. The open range covered much of the Great Plains and provided land where ranchers could graze their herds free of charge and unrestricted by the boundaries of private farms.

Mexican cowhands developed the tools and techniques for rounding up and driving cattle. These Hispanic herders taught American cowhands their trade and enriched the English vocabulary with words of Spanish origin, including "lariat," "lasso," and "stampede."

DIFFERENTIATED INSTRUCTION

Kinesthetic Have interested students build a model to demonstrate either the process of panning for gold and silver or using a sluice to find the minerals. Have students demonstrate the process to the class using their models. Tell students to be prepared to answer questions about their models. **L2**

📁 Refer to *Inclusion for the High School Social Studies Classroom Strategies and Activities* in the TCR.

NATIONAL GEOGRAPHIC **Mining Country and Cattle Trails, 1848–1890**

In Motion

Helena, Montana in 1865

■ Gold	—— Cattle trails
■ Silver	···· Railroads
—— 1890 border	

Cowhands on a cattle drive

Geography Skills

1. **Interpreting Maps** What cities were destination points for the Chisholm Trail?
2. **Applying Geography Skills** Why do you think the destination cities at the end of the cattle trails are all located along railroad lines?

Before the Civil War, ranchers had little incentive to round up the longhorns. Beef prices were low, and moving the cattle to eastern markets was not practical. Two developments changed this situation: the Civil War and the construction of the railroads. During the Civil War, eastern cattle were slaughtered in huge numbers to feed the armies of the Union and the Confederacy. After the war, beef prices soared, making it worthwhile to round up the longhorns if a way could be found to move them east.

By the 1860s, railroads had reached the Great Plains. Lines ended at Abilene and Dodge City in Kansas and at Sedalia in Missouri. Ranchers and livestock dealers realized that if the longhorns were rounded up and driven north several hundred miles to the railroad, they could be sold for a huge profit and shipped east to market.

In 1866 ranchers rounded up cattle and drove about 260,000 of them to Sedalia, Missouri. Although only a fraction of the herds survived this first long drive, the drive overall was a tremendous success, proving that cattle could be driven north to the rail lines and sold for 10 times the price they could get in Texas.

Other trails soon opened. The route to Abilene, Kansas, became the major route north. Between 1867 and 1871, cowboys drove nearly 1.5 million head of cattle up the **Chisholm Trail** to Abilene—a town that, when filled with cowboys at the end of a drive, rivaled the mining towns in terms of rowdiness. As the railroads expanded in the West, other trails reached from Texas to more towns in Kansas, Nebraska, Montana, and Wyoming.

The Long Drive A long drive was a spectacular sight. It began with the spring roundup when ranchers met with their cowboys to collect cattle from the

CHAPTER 8 Settling the West **289**

CURRICULUM CONNECTION

Language Arts Hamlin Garland vividly recorded the hard life of the Plains farmers. In books such as *Main-Travelled Roads* (1891) and *A Son of the Middle Border* (1917), Garland told "a tale of toil that's never done." Although his stories included many moments of joy, such as harvest time, and of great beauty, such as the arrival of spring, Garland refused to paint life on the Plains as always perfect. "I will not lie," he wrote. "A proper portion of the sweat, flies, heat, dirt, and drudgery shall go in."

History *and the* Humanities

🎵 American Music: Hits Through History: "I'm an Old Cowhand"
🏛 American Art & Architecture: *The Stampede*

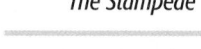 Use *Supreme Court Case Study 7, Slaughterhouse* Cases.

INTERDISCIPLINARY CONNECTIONS ACTIVITY

Economics Have the economics teacher explain the basic principles of supply and demand in a free market economy. Have students formulate generalizations on the impact of supply and demand on the boom and bust in the Texas cattle industry. *(Example: Because of a large supply of cattle and a huge demand for meat, profits in the cattle industry increased. Profits decreased when the supply of meat was greater than demand for it.)* Discuss students' generalizations and use the generalizations to construct a basic supply-and-demand graph. **L2**

3 ASSESS

Assign Section 1 Assessment as homework or as an in-class activity.

🌐 Have students use the **Interactive Tutor Self-Assessment CD-ROM.**

L1/ELL

Reading Essentials and Study Guide 8–1

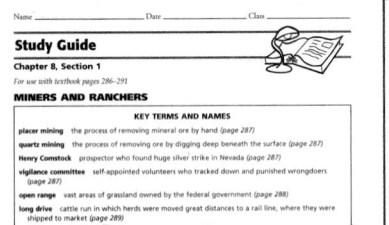

L2

Section Quiz 8–1

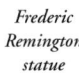

Frederic Remington statue

Breaking Camp This painting by Charles M. Russell captures the excitement of a long cattle drive. Ranchers hired cowboys to move thousands of cattle north to railroad towns, where the cattle were then shipped east for butchering and sale in the cities. How did the Civil War encourage the start of long cattle drives?

open range. Stock from many different owners made up these herds. Only their brands showing which rancher owned the cattle distinguished them from one another. Stray calves with no identifying symbols were called **mavericks.** These were divided and branded. The combined herds moving onto the trail could number anywhere from 2,000 to 5,000 cattle.

Cowboys for major ranchers went north with the herds. Most of the cowboys in the early years of the cattle drives were former Confederate army soldiers escaping the harsh life in the South during Reconstruction. A few were Hispanic, and many were African Americans such as Nat Love. Born an enslaved man in Tennessee in 1854, Love was freed at the end of the Civil War. He went west in 1869 and applied for work with a cattle-driving outfit that included several other African American cowhands:

> 66After breakfast I asked the camp boss for a job as a cow boy. He asked me if I could ride a wild horse. I said 'yes sir.' He said if you can I will give you a job. So he spoke to one of the colored cow boys called Bronko Jim, and told him to go out and rope old Good Eye, saddle him and put me on his back. Bronko Jim gave me a few pointers and told me to look out for the horse was especially bad. . . . This

proved the worst horse to ride I had ever mounted in my life, but I stayed with him and the cow boys were the most surprised outfit you ever saw, as they had taken me for a tenderfoot, pure and simple. After the horse got tired and I dismounted the boss said he would give me a job and pay me $30.00 per month and more later on.99

—quoted in *Life and Adventures of Nat Love*

Life for Love and the other cowboys on the trail demanded discipline, endurance, and courage, but those who survived the many dangers collected wages to spend in the towns at the end of the trail. Life in these towns was exciting, but many cowboys told exaggerated tales of daring that often supplied material for what were called "dime novels." These adventure books sold for a dime and helped spread the myths of the "Wild West" in eastern towns and cities.

Ranching Becomes Big Business Cowboys drove millions of cattle north from Texas to Kansas and points beyond. Some of the cattle went straight to slaughterhouses, but many were sold to ranchers who were building up herds and grazing them in Wyoming, Montana, and other territories. When sheep herders moved their flocks onto the range and when farmers settled there, blocking the trails,

290 CHAPTER 8 Settling the West

"range wars" broke out among competing groups. Eventually, and after considerable loss of life, the range was largely fenced off with a new invention—**barbed wire**—which enabled hundreds of square miles to be fenced off cheaply and easily.

At first, ranchers saw barbed wire as more of a threat than an opportunity. They did not want to abandon open grazing and complained when farmers put up barriers that prevented the ranchers' livestock from roaming. Soon, however, ranchers used barbed wire to shut out those competing with them for land and to keep their animals closer to sources of food and water. For cowhands, however, barbed wire ended the excitement of long cattle drives.

The fencing in of the range was not the only reason the long drives ended. Investors from the East and from Britain poured money into the booming cattle business, causing an oversupply of animals on the market. Prices dropped dramatically in the mid-1880s and many ranchers went bankrupt. Then, in the winter of 1886 to 1887, blizzards covered the ground with snow so deep that the cattle could not dig down to the grass. Temperatures fell to more than 40 degrees below zero.

The cattle industry survived this terrible blow, but it was changed forever. The day of the open range had ended. From that point on, herds were raised on fenced-in ranches. New European breeds replaced longhorns, and the cowboy became a ranch hand.

✓ **Reading Check** **Analyzing** How did heavy investment in the cattle industry affect the industry as a whole?

World Geography Connection

The Cowboys of Argentina

While cowboys are often considered a unique part of the American heritage, they also belong to the history of another nation, Argentina. Like the cowboys of the American West, this group of hardy and daring individuals made their living during the 1800s trying to tame the "pampas"—Argentina's frontier grasslands. Known as "gauchos," they rounded up wild cattle and horses on the pampas and sold their hides. Like their counterparts to the north, gauchos wore distinctive clothing—wide-brim hats, ponchos, and loose trousers tucked into low boots—and became highly romanticized and revered figures. They also went the same way as the American cowboy, eventually becoming ranch hands as big business took greater control of the cattle and herding industry. *What were the similarities between the American cowboys and the gauchos?*

lariat

spurs

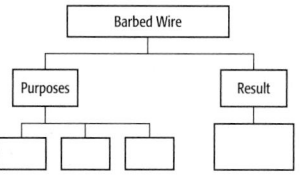

HISTORY Online **Study Central**™ To review this section, go to <u>tarvol2.glencoe.com</u> and click on **Study Central**™.

SECTION 1 ASSESSMENT

Checking for Understanding
1. **Define:** placer mining, quartz mining, open range, long drive, maverick.
2. **Identify:** Henry Comstock, vigilance committee, Chisholm Trail, barbed wire.
3. **List** the factors that contributed to the rise of the cattle industry.
4. **Explain** how cattle ranching shifted from open range to an organized business operation.

Reviewing Themes
5. **Economic Factors** What two developments in the late 1800s led to the decline of the cattle business?

Critical Thinking
6. **Evaluating** How did the mining industry contribute to the development of the West?
7. **Organizing** Use a graphic organizer similar to the one below to list the ways barbed wire was used and the result of using barbed wire on the Great Plains.

```
          Barbed Wire
         /          \
    Purposes        Result
   /   |   \          |
 [ ] [ ] [ ]         [ ]
```

Analyzing Visuals
8. **Examining Maps** Study the map detailing the western mining country and cattle trails on page 289. Then create your own thematic map detailing either the cattle country or the mining country.

Writing About History
9. **Descriptive Writing** Write a summary for a story line for a Hollywood movie. Your script should realistically portray the lives of either a miner or rancher in the West in the mid- to late 1800s. Be sure to include descriptions of people living in a western settlement.

SECTION 1 ASSESSMENT ANSWERS

1. Terms are in blue.
2. Henry Comstock (p. 287), vigilance committee (p. 287), Chisholm Trail (p. 289), barbed wire (p. 291)
3. Factors include emergence of the longhorn breed, higher beef prices, and railroad transportation.
4. Barbed wire eliminated long drives, and the cowboy became a ranch hand.
5. An oversupply of cattle drove down prices, and the winter of 1886 to 1887 killed a large number of cattle.
6. People moved west, towns sprung up, and railroads expanded.
7. Purposes: keep out competitors, keep animals closer to food and water supplies, keep livestock from roaming freely; result: ended the long cattle drives
8. Maps should include rail lines, towns, and trails.
9. Students' summaries will vary.

FYI

When ranchers and farmers settled the Southwest, they displaced many of the Mexican Americans who had lived there for generations. Land Acts passed by Congress required these earlier settlers to provide detailed legal proof. However, most titles were either not specific, were recorded in Mexico, or became lost.

World Geography Connection

Answer: They were hardy individuals who wore distinctive clothing and lived on the frontier.
Ask: Where did gauchos work? *(in the pampas of Argentina)*

Reteach
Have students trace the growth of the mining industry.

Enrich
Have students research the conflict among cattle ranchers, sheepherders, and farmers and write a few paragraphs on how this conflict might have been resolved without violence.

✓ **Reading Check**

Answer: It caused an oversupply of cattle, which drove prices down. Many ranchers went bankrupt.

HISTORY Online

Study Central™ provides summaries, interactive games, and online graphic organizers to help students review section content.

4 CLOSE

Have students describe the ways new technology changed open-range ranching.

291

1 FOCUS

Section Overview

This section focuses on the people who settled the Great Plains.

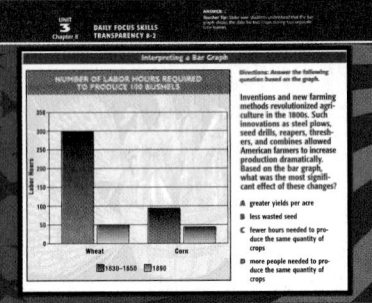
Reading Preview

Answers to Graphic: Homestead Act, Morrill Act, and promoting railroad construction

Preteaching Vocabulary
Have students skim the section to preview each of the Key Terms and Names.

Guide to Reading

Main Idea
After 1865, settlers staked out homesteads and began farming the Great Plains.

Key Terms and Names
Great Plains, Stephen Long, Homestead Act, homestead, dry farming, sodbuster, Wheat Belt, bonanza farm

Reading Strategy
Organizing As you read about the settlement of the Great Plains, complete a graphic organizer similar to the one below listing the ways the government encouraged settlement.

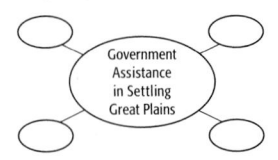
Government Assistance in Settling Great Plains

Reading Objectives
• **Explain** why and how people began settling the Plains.
• **Trace** the growth of commercial farming on the Plains.

Section Theme
Science and Technology The need for new farming techniques in the West led to several technological innovations.

Preview of Events

♦1860	♦1870	♦1880	♦1890
1862 Homestead Act	**1873** Timber Culture Act	**late 1870s** Bonanza farming begins on Great Plains	**late 1880s** Western farmlands hit by drought

★ An American Story ★

Well hand pump

On September 15, 1884, the O'Kieffe family left their home in Nebraska and headed west across the state in a covered wagon to start a challenging new life on the open plains. The O'Kieffes faced a new environment that lacked many things that people in the East took for granted, including easy access to water and wood for building a house. Without trees to use as timber, they built their house from chunks of sod, densely packed soil held together by grass roots. To obtain water, the family had to drill a well 134 feet deep and operate the pump by hand. They let nothing go to waste. In summer, they ate the weeds from their garden as well as the vegetables, obeying the rule, "If you can't beat 'em, eat 'em."

There were other settlers in the area, and they would gather to socialize and help each other. When disaster struck, however, each family had to be prepared to face the trouble alone. In January 1888, a three-day blizzard struck without warning. As Charley, the youngest son, reflected: "By the end of the three-day blizzard we were in fine shape to take care of our stock. Many others did not fare so well; but that's life. After all, we said to each other, this was a new country and folks had to learn how to look after themselves."

—adapted from *Western Story: Recollections of Charley O'Kieffe*

Geography of the Plains

The O'Kieffes were early settlers in a region known today as the **Great Plains.** This region extends westward to the Rocky Mountains from around the 100th meridian—an imaginary line running north and south from the central Dakotas through western Texas. Rainfall on the Plains averages less than 20 inches per year, and trees grow naturally only

---

SECTION RESOURCES

📖 Reproducible Masters
• Reproducible Lesson Plan 8–2
• Daily Lecture and Discussion Notes 8–2
• Guided Reading Activity 8–2
• Section Quiz 8–2
• Reading Essentials and Study Guide 8–2
• Performance Assessment Activities and Rubrics

📽 Transparencies
• Daily Focus Skills Transparency 8–2

Multimedia
🖲 Interactive Tutor Self-Assessment CD-ROM
🖲 ExamView® Pro Testmaker CD-ROM
🖲 TeacherWorks™ CD-ROM
🎧 Audio Program
🎵 American Music: Cultural Traditions

along rivers and streams. For centuries this open country had been home to vast herds of buffalo that grazed on the prairie grasses. Nomadic Native American groups had hunted the buffalo for food and used buffalo hides for clothing and shelter.

Major **Stephen Long,** who explored the region with an army expedition in 1819, called it the "Great American Desert" and concluded that it was "almost wholly unfit for cultivation." He predicted that the scarcity of wood and water would prove to be "an insuperable obstacle in . . . settling the country."

✓ **Reading Check** **Examining** What geographic factors created challenges to the settlement of the Great Plains in the late 1800s?

The Beginnings of Settlement

During the late 1800s several factors undermined the belief that the Plains was a "Great American Desert." One important factor was the construction of the railroads, which provided easy access to the Great Plains. Railroad companies sold land along the rail lines at low prices and provided credit to prospective settlers. Railroads opened offices throughout the United States and in major cities in Europe where land was scarce. Posters and pamphlets proclaimed that booking passage to the Plains was a ticket to prosperity.

The catchy slogan "Rain follows the plow," coined by a Nebraskan to sell the idea that cultivating the Plains would increase rainfall, encouraged settlers.

As if to prove the saying correct, the weather cooperated. For more than a decade beginning in the 1870s, rainfall on the Plains was well above average. The lush green of the endless prairies contradicted the popular belief that the region was a desert.

In 1862, the government also supported settlement in the Great Plains region by passing the **Homestead Act.** For a $10 registration fee, an individual could file for a homestead—a tract of public land available for settlement. A homesteader could claim up to 160 acres of public land and could receive title to that land after living there for five years. Later government acts increased the size of the tracts available. The Homestead Act provided a legal method for settlers to acquire clear title to property in the West. With their property rights secured, settlers were more willing to move to the Plains.

When settlers arrived on the Plains, they often found life very difficult. The lack of trees and water forced them to build their first homes from sod cut from the ground and to drill wells up to 300 feet deep. Summer temperatures often soared over 100° Fahrenheit. Prairie fires were a constant danger. Sometimes swarms of grasshoppers swept over farms and destroyed the crops. In winter there were terrible blizzards and extreme cold. Despite these challenges, most homesteaders persisted and learned how to live in the harsh environment.

✓ **Reading Check** **Analyzing** What is the relationship between private property rights and the settlement of the Great Plains?

Picturing **History**

Farming the Great Plains Technology made farming the vast open plains of America feasible. Here horse-drawn binders are being used to gather hay in the late 1800s. What other factors encouraged settlement on the Great Plains?

CHAPTER 8
Section 2, 292–295

2 TEACH

Daily Lecture and Discussion Notes 8–2

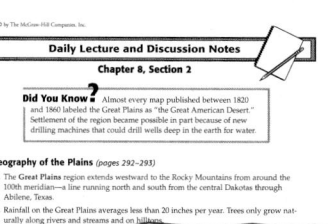

Copyright © by The McGraw-Hill Companies, Inc.

Daily Lecture and Discussion Notes
Chapter 8, Section 2

Did You Know ? Almost every map published between 1820 and 1860 labeled the Great Plains as "the Great American Desert." Settlement of the region became possible in part because of new drilling machines that could drill wells deep in the earth for water.

I. **Geography of the Plains** (pages 292–293)

A. The Great Plains region extends westward to the Rocky Mountains from around the 100th meridian—a line running north and south from the central Dakotas through Abilene, Texas.

B. Rainfall on the Great Plains averages less than 20 inches per year. Trees only grow naturally along rivers and streams and on hilltops.

Reading Strategy

Summarizing Information
Have students list the problems and solutions in settling the land and in accessing transportation. L1

✓ **Reading Check**

Answer: low rainfall and few trees

Picturing **History**

Answer: Railroads sold the land along tracks cheaply; the government sold tracts at reduced prices.
Ask: **How did many farmers get their land?** *(They could claim 160 acres by filing for a homestead and living on the land for five years.)*

✓ **Reading Check**

Answer: The Homestead Act secured individual private property rights to settlers, which made people more willing to move there.

History *and the* **Humanities**

🏳 American Music: Cultural Traditions: "Little Old Sod Shanty"

Reading Strategy **READING THE TEXT**

Using Possible Sentences Possible Sentences is a strategy that allows students to speculate about word meanings. Choose ten vocabulary words and write them on the board. Write sentences using the words either correctly or incorrectly. Then ask students to comment on whether the sentences are "possible." As students encounter the key vocabulary during the reading, have them note each term's usage in the selection's context. After reading, students should reread the sentences and revise them as necessary. L1

📂 Refer to *Inclusion for the High School Social Studies Classroom Strategies and Activities* in the TCR.

Why It Matters

Justin Smith Morrill, a U.S. Representative from Vermont, introduced the Land-Grant College Act of 1862, also known as the Morrill Act. The Morrill Act of 1890 required states to use funds from the first Morrill Act to educate both African American and white students. The result was the establishment of 16 African American land-grant colleges across the South.

3 ASSESS

Assign Section 2 Assessment as homework or as an in-class activity.

🖭 Have students use the **Interactive Tutor Self-Assessment CD-ROM.**

Why It Matters

Land-Grant Colleges

To promote agriculture and manufacturing, the 1862 Morrill Act gave states large tracts of federal lands, with the requirement that part of the land be used to set up and maintain colleges. The colleges were required to offer programs in agriculture and engineering as well as traditional academic subjects. Military training programs were also required at these "land-grant colleges." Most state agricultural and engineering schools were established under the Morrill Act. Today every state, as well as Puerto Rico, has at least one land-grant college.

◄ **4-H Programs**
Extension services associated with land-grant colleges coordinate the 4-H programs that help train future farmers. 4-H offers many programs for young people ages 5 to 19.

ROTC ►
The Reserve Officer Training Corps (ROTC) programs set up at land-grant colleges have been instrumental in providing training for the U.S. military. The program continues to provide scholarships for young Americans around the nation.

The Wheat Belt

For those who had the financial resources, farming could be very profitable on the Plains. Many inventions and new farming methods revolutionized agriculture.

One approach, called dry farming, was to plant seeds deep in the ground where there was enough moisture for them to grow. By the 1860s, farmers on the Plains were employing newly designed steel plows, seed drills, reapers, and threshing machines. The new machines made dry farming possible. Unfortunately, prairie soil often blew away, especially in a dry season. Many sodbusters, as those who plowed the soil on the Plains were called, eventually lost their homesteads through the combined effects of drought, wind erosion, and overuse of the land.

Large landholders faced similar problems, but they were able to make quick profits with the help of mechanical reapers, which speeded the harvest. Mechanical binders tied the stalks into bundles for collection. Threshing machines knocked kernels loose from the stalks. These innovations were well suited for harvesting wheat, which had the advantage of withstanding drought better than corn and some other crops. Wheat became as important to the Great Plains as cotton was to the South.

During the 1880s, many wheat farmers from Minnesota and other Midwestern states moved to the Great Plains to take advantage of the inexpensive land and the new farming technology. This productive new **Wheat Belt** began at the eastern edge of the Great Plains and encompassed much of the Dakotas and the western parts of Nebraska and Kansas.

Commercial Farming The new machines allowed a single family to bring in a substantial harvest on a wheat farm covering several hundred acres. Some wheat farms covered up to 50,000 acres. These were called bonanza farms because they often yielded big profits. Like mine owners, bonanza farmers formed companies, made large investments in property and equipment, and hired laborers as needed.

ECONOMICS

Farmers Fall on Hard Times The bountiful harvests in the Wheat Belt helped the United States become the world's leading exporter of wheat by the 1880s. American wheat growers faced rising competition, however, from other wheat-producing nations. In the 1890s, a glut of wheat on the world market caused prices to drop.

Some farmers tried to make it through lean periods by mortgaging their land—that is, they took bank loans based on the value of their property. If they failed to meet their mortgage payments, they forfeited the land to the bank and had to abandon

294 CHAPTER 8 Settling the West

DIFFERENTIATED INSTRUCTION

Reading Support Have students select two of the following states: Texas, Wisconsin, California, Minnesota, Oregon, Kansas, Nevada, or Nebraska. For their selected states, have students use historical data from the Census Bureau to chart their population growth from 1870 to 1890. Have the students use the charts to help them write a paragraph analyzing the Census Bureau's claim that the frontier was closing. **L2**

👝 Refer to *Inclusion for the High School Social Studies Classroom Strategies and Activities* in the TCR.

their farms or work them as tenants for the new owner. By 1900 tenants cultivated about one-third of the farms in the corn and wheat areas.

Beginning in the late 1880s, farmers also faced a prolonged drought that destroyed crops and farms. Kansas newspaper editor William Allen White described a farm family returning from the West:

> 66These movers . . . had seen it stop raining for months at a time. They had heard the fury of the winter wind as it came whining across the short burned grass. . . . They have tossed through hot nights, wild with worry, and have arisen only to find their worst nightmares grazing in reality on the brown stubble in front of their sun-warped doors.99

In hard times, some homesteaders gave up and headed home, but others soon took their place.

✓ **Reading Check** **Identifying** What technological innovations helped farmers cultivate the Plains?

Closing the Frontier

On April 22, 1889, the government opened one of the last large territories for settlement, land that later became the state of Oklahoma. Within hours, over 10,000 people raced to stake claims in the event known as the Oklahoma Land Rush.

The next year, the Census Bureau reported that settlement throughout the West had been so rapid "that there can hardly be said to be a frontier line." In reality, much land was still unoccupied, and new

settlement continued at a brisk pace into the 1900s. The news that the frontier was closing, however, concerned those who saw it as the end of an era. They believed that unoccupied land at the frontier had provided a "safety-valve of social discontent," the idea that Americans could always make a fresh start.

Most settlers did indeed make a fresh start, adjusting to the often hostile environment of the Plains. Water from their deep wells enabled them to plant trees and gardens. Railroads brought lumber and brick to replace sod as a building material and coal as fuel.

The O'Kieffes were typical of small-scale, self-sustaining homesteaders. They never got rich, but they got by. Those who struggled as the O'Kieffes did to support themselves emerged with a more realistic view of the West. It was not a land of limitless opportunity. As Charley O'Kieffe learned, the real story of the West was not about heroes who rode off into the sunset. It was about ordinary people who settled down and built homes and communities through great effort—"sterling and steady men and women whose lives were spent doing the work as it needed to be done."

✓ **Reading Check** **Examining** Why did some people feel that the closing of the frontier was the end of an era?

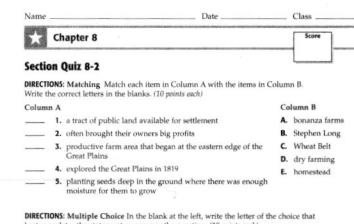

Student Web Activity Visit the *American Republic Since 1877* Web site at tarvol2.glencoe.com and click on *Student Web Activities— Chapter 8* for an activity on settling the West.

HISTORY Online Study Central™ To review this section, go to tarvol2.glencoe.com and click on **Study Central™**.

SECTION 2 ASSESSMENT

Checking for Understanding
1. **Define:** homestead, dry farming, sodbuster, bonanza farm.
2. **Identify:** Great Plains, Stephen Long, Homestead Act, Wheat Belt.
3. **Explain** why the Great Plains was not suitable for homesteading.

Reviewing Themes
4. **Science and Technology** How did the need for new farming techniques on the Great Plains result in technological innovations in agriculture?

Critical Thinking
5. **Analyzing** What factors contributed to the making of the Wheat Belt in the Great Plains and then to troubled times for wheat farmers in the 1890s?
6. **Categorizing** Use a graphic organizer similar to the one below to list the effects of technology on farming in the Great Plains.

Invention	Advantage for Farmers

Analyzing Visuals
7. **Examining Photographs** Study the photograph on page 293 of farmers using binding machines in western Wisconsin. Based on the terrain and the type of work they needed to do, what other types of technology would have helped farmers on the Plains?

Writing About History
8. **Persuasive Writing** Write an advertisement persuading people from the East and from Europe to establish homesteads in the Great Plains.

CHAPTER 8 Settling the West **295**

SECTION 2 ASSESSMENT ANSWERS

1. Terms are in blue.
2. Great Plains (p. 292), Stephen Long (p. 293), Homestead Act (p. 293), Wheat Belt (p. 294)
3. geography and climate
4. Mechanical reapers, binders, and threshing machines were all created to help farmers har-

vest large tracts of farmland quickly.
5. The Homestead Act, new farming techniques and equipment; good harvests, world competition caused a glut that caused prices to drop.
6. mechanical reapers: speeded harvesting; mechanical binders: tied

stalks; threshing machines: knocked kernels loose
7. possible answer: windmills to supply power and irrigation
8. Advertisements will vary but should reflect information presented in the section.

Section Quiz 8–2

Name _____ Date _____ Class _____

★ **Chapter 8** Score ___

Section 8-2

DIRECTIONS: Matching Match each item in Column A with the items in Column B. Write the correct letters in the blanks. (10 points each)

Column A
___ 1. a tract of public land available for settlement
___ 2. often brought their owners big profits
___ 3. productive farm area that began at the eastern edge of the Great Plains
___ 4. explored the Great Plains in 1819
___ 5. planting seeds deep in the ground where there was enough moisture for them to grow

Column B
A. bonanza farms
B. Stephen Long
C. Wheat Belt
D. dry farming
E. homestead

DIRECTIONS: Multiple Choice In the blank at the left, write the letter of the choice that best completes the statement or answers the question. (10 points each)

HISTORY Online

Objectives and answers to the student activity can be found in the **Web Activity Lesson Plan** at tarvol2.glencoe.com.

✓ **Reading Check**

Answer: mechanical reapers, mechanical binders, threshing machines, and seed drills

Reteach
Have students explain why people settled the Plains.

Enrich
Have students research the founding of at least 10 land-grant colleges.

✓ **Reading Check**

Answer: They felt it ended the chance to make a fresh start.

Study Central™ provides summaries, interactive games, and online graphic organizers to help students review section content.

---

4 CLOSE

Have students study commercial farming in the Plains.

295

TEACH

Interpreting Statistics Point out that two sets of data are not necessarily related. For example, if the local movie theater reports an increase in attendance and the local bookstore reports a dip in sales, it does not necessarily mean that people are going to the movies instead of buying books.

Assign students to find statistics related to your school and your community. Have students create a graphic or tabular display of the information. As a class, identify possible correlations and determine whether they are positive or negative.

Additional Practice
L1

Reinforcing Skills Activity 8

Name _____ Date _____ Class _____

★ Reinforcing Skills Activity 8

Interpreting Statistics

☐ **LEARNING THE SKILL**

Statistics can help you support an opinion or make a point. Statistics are data collected and organized to help identify effects and make predictions. To interpret statistics, first read the title and any labels to get an overall idea of the information being shown. Analyze the numbers shown by looking for decreases, increases, similarities, and differences. Look for sets of numbers or data that seem to be related or that have some correlation. Draw conclusions from the information based on the relationships and trends you find.

☐ **PRACTICING THE SKILL**

DIRECTIONS: Study the statistical information, then answer the questions below on a separate sheet of paper.

GLENCOE
TECHNOLOGY

CD-ROM
Glencoe Skillbuilder Interactive Workbook CD-ROM, Level 2

This interactive CD-ROM reinforces student mastery of essential social studies skills.

Social Studies
SKILLBUILDER

Interpreting Statistics

The Railroad and Native American Population

Year	1860	1870	1880	1890	1900
Approximate miles of railroad track in U.S.:	30,000	53,000	116,000	208,000	259,000
Approximate Native American population:	351,000	323,000	318,000	265,000	248,000

Why Learn This Skill?

Often presented in graphs and tables, statistics are collections of data that are used to support a claim or an opinion. The ability to interpret statistics allows us to understand probable effects and to make predictions.

Learning the Skill

Use the following steps to help you interpret statistical information.

• **Scan** the graph or table, reading the title and labels to get an idea of what is being shown.

• **Examine** the statistics shown, looking for increases and decreases, similarities and differences.

• **Look** for a *correlation* in the statistics. Two sets of data may be related or unrelated. If they are related, we say that there is a correlation between them. In a positive correlation, as one number rises, so does the other number. In a negative correlation, as one number rises, the other number falls. For example, there is a positive correlation between academic achievement and wages, and there is a negative correlation between smoking and life expectancy. Sometimes, statistics may try to show a correlation when none exists. For example, a report that "people who go fishing are less likely to get cancer" may be statistically true but lack any real correlation.

• **Determine** the conclusions you can draw from the statistics.

Practicing the Skill

Study the table above, and then answer the following questions.

❶ What claim does this set of statistics seem to support?

❷ Is there a correlation between miles of railroad tracks and the Native American population? Is the correlation positive or negative? Explain.

Skills Assessment

Complete the Practicing Skills questions on page 305 and the Chapter 8 Skill Reinforcement Activity to assess your mastery of this skill.

Delivering a presentation

Applying the Skill

Interpreting Statistics Create a survey with two questions for which you believe the answers will show a correlation. For example, you might ask, "How many hours of television do you watch per day?" and "How many hours of sleep do you usually get at night?" Organize your statistics in a chart or graph. Then, look for a correlation in your data and evaluate your results. Write a paragraph summarizing your evaluation.

Glencoe's **Skillbuilder Interactive Workbook CD-ROM, Level 2,** provides instruction and practice in key social studies skills.

ANSWERS TO PRACTICING THE SKILL

❶ As the number of miles of railroad track increased, the Native American population declined.

❷ Students may see a negative correlation, but other data would be needed to support the conclusion that an increase in railroad track caused a reduction in Native American population.

Applying the Skill

Students' graphs and paragraphs will vary. Paragraphs should be supported by the data collected.

SECTION 3 Native Americans

Guide to Reading

Main Idea
The settlement of the West dramatically changed the way of life of the Plains Indians.

Key Terms and Names
nomad, annuity, Little Crow, Indian Peace Commission, George A. Custer, Ghost Dance, assimilate, allotment, Dawes Act

Reading Strategy
Sequencing As you read about the crisis facing Native Americans during the late 1800s, complete a time line to record the battles between Native Americans and the U.S. government and the results of each.

Reading Objectives
• **Discuss** conflicts that arose between the Plains Indians and American settlers.
• **Summarize** problems caused by attempts to assimilate Native Americans.

Section Theme
Individual Action Some Native American groups fought the federal government in an attempt to keep their ancestral homelands.

Preview of Events

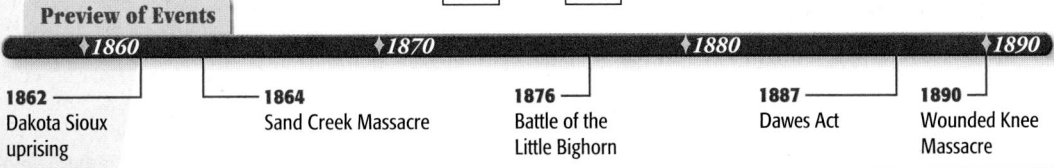

| ♦1860 | ♦1870 | ♦1880 | ♦1890 |

1862 — Dakota Sioux uprising

1864 — Sand Creek Massacre

1876 — Battle of the Little Bighorn

1887 — Dawes Act

1890 — Wounded Knee Massacre

Ten Bears

★ An American Story ★

In October 1867, a Comanche chief named Ten Bears arrived with other Native American leaders and their followers at Medicine Lodge Creek in present-day Kansas to meet with federal treaty-makers and army officers. The federal officials wanted them to sign a treaty agreeing to move to confined areas called reservations and to submit to American authority. In return, the government offered them food, housing, instruction in farming, and other assistance. After listening to the treaty-makers, Ten Bears spoke against moving to a reservation:

❝That which you say we must now live on is too small. The Texans have taken away the places where the grass grew the thickest. . . . The white man has the country which we loved, and we only wish to wander on the prairie until we die.❞

In the end, Ten Bears and the other chiefs had little choice but to sign the treaty. The army's main representative at the council, General William Tecumseh Sherman, told them bluntly that they would have to accept the deal: "You can no more stop this than you can stop the sun or moon; you must submit and do the best you can."

—adapted from *Tribes of the Southern Plains*

Culture of the Plains Indians

For centuries the Great Plains was home to many Native American nations. Some lived in communities as farmers and hunters, but most were nomads who roamed vast distances, following their main source of food—the buffalo.

Despite their differences, the groups of Plains Indians were similar in many ways. They lived in extended family networks and had a close relationship with nature. Plains

---

1 FOCUS

Section Overview
This section focuses on how Western settlement affected the Plains Indians.

BELLRINGER
Skillbuilder Activity

Project transparency and have students answer the question.

Daily Focus Skills Transparency 8–3

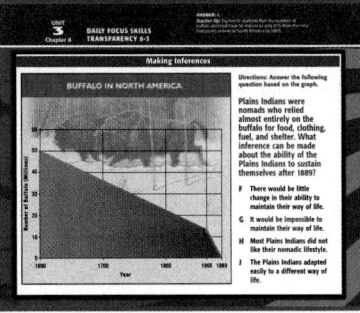

Reading Preview

Answers to Graphic:
1862–Dakota Sioux Uprising: deaths of settlers and Native Americans; 1864–Sand Creek Massacre: formation of the Indian Peace Commission; 1866–Fetterman's Massacre: U.S. Army defeat; 1876–Battle of Little Bighorn: Native American victory; 1890–Wounded Knee: about 200 Lakota died

Preteaching Vocabulary
Have students identify a person who can be tied to each of the Key Terms.

SECTION RESOURCES

📁 Reproducible Masters
• Reproducible Lesson Plan 8–3
• Daily Lecture and Discussion Notes 8–3
• Guided Reading Activity 8–3
• Section Quiz 8–3
• Reading Essentials and Study Guide 8–3
• Interpreting Political Cartoons

📀 Transparencies
• Daily Focus Skills Transparency 8–3
Multimedia
• Interactive Tutor Self-Assessment CD-ROM
• ExamView® Pro Testmaker CD-ROM
• TeacherWorks™ CD-ROM
• Audio Program
• ABCNews Interactive™ Historic America Electronic Field Trips

2 TEACH

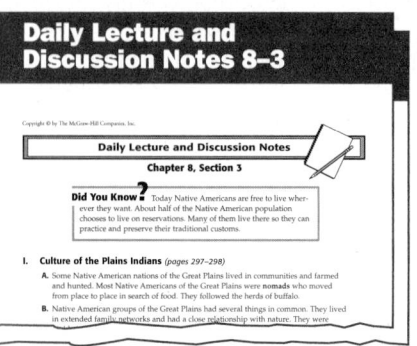
Reading Check

Answer: They lived in extended family networks. They practiced a religion centered on the natural world. Tasks were assigned by gender.

Creating a Display Have students use library and Internet resources to create a display showcasing the history and traditions of the Plains Indians, especially those that signed the Medicine Lodge Peace Treaty in 1867—Apache, Arapaho, Cheyenne, Comanche, or Kiowa. **L1**

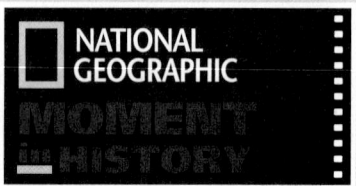

Ask: Why did the Crow people cooperate with American settlers and soldiers? *(ancient enmity with Sioux and to secure good relations with the United States)*

Indian nations, sometimes numbering several thousand people, were divided into bands consisting of up to 500 people. A governing council headed each band, but most members participated in making decisions. Gender determined the assignment of tasks. Women generally performed domestic tasks: rearing children, cooking, and preparing hides. Men performed tasks such as hunting, trading, and supervising the military life of the band. Most Plains Indians practiced a religion based on a belief in the spiritual power of the natural world.

✓ **Reading Check** **Comparing** In what ways were different groups of Plains Indians similar?

Cultures Under Pressure

As ranchers, miners, and farmers moved onto the Plains, they deprived Native Americans of their hunting grounds, broke treaties guaranteeing certain lands to the Plains Indians, and often forced them to relocate to new territory. Native Americans resisted by attacking wagon trains, stagecoaches, and ranches. Occasionally an entire group would go to war against nearby settlers and troops. The first major clash on the Plains began in 1862, when the Sioux people in Minnesota launched a major uprising.

The Dakota Sioux Uprising The Dakota Sioux had agreed to live on a small reservation in Minnesota. In exchange for moving to the reservation, the United States government issued annuities, or payments to reservation dwellers, at least once per year. The annuities, however, amounted to only between 5 and 30 cents an acre, and much of that money ended up in the hands of American traders. These traders often made up stories about debts owed to them by the Dakota, and they took the annuities as payments.

Congress made things worse for the Dakota in 1862 by delaying annuities. By August the payments were a month late, and some of the Dakota were starving. Chief **Little Crow** asked traders to provide his people food on credit. "If they are hungry," trader Andrew Myrick replied, "let them eat grass or their

NATIONAL GEOGRAPHIC
MOMENT IN HISTORY

THE END OF A WAY OF LIFE

Medicine Crow, a war chief of the Crow people, solemnly poses for a photographer during a conference in Washington, D.C., in 1880. The Crow and the Sioux were ancestral enemies, and so Medicine Crow and his warriors agreed to act as scouts against the Sioux for the soldiers and settlers of the Great Plains. The Crows' valiant service, however, could not preserve their independence. By 1890 all of the Plains Indians, including the Crow, had been confined to reservations.

298 CHAPTER 8 Settling the West

Reading Strategy **READING THE TEXT**

Predicting Consequences Provide students with a map showing the location of the various Native American nations during the mid-1800s. Have students compare that map with the one on page 289 that shows the railroad lines. Then ask them to decide what conflicts could have been predicted before the railroads were built. As they read the section, have students review the maps and their predictions. **L1** ELL

📁 Refer to *Inclusion for the High School Social Studies Classroom Strategies and Activities* in the TCR.

wn dung." Two weeks later, the Dakota rose up in rms, and Myrick was found shot to death with grass tuffed in his mouth.

Little Crow reluctantly agreed to lead this uprising. He wanted to wage war against soldiers, not civilians, but he was unable to keep angry Dakota from slaughtering settlers in the area. Hundreds died before troops arrived from St. Paul and put down the uprising.

A military tribunal sentenced 307 Dakota to death for taking part in the hostilities, but President Lincoln reviewed the evidence and reduced the number executed to 38. Many others who fled the reservation when the troops arrived became exiles in a region that bore their name—the Dakota Territory.

Lakota Sioux Defend Their Territory Following the Dakota uprising, the army sent patrols far out onto the northern Great Plains to prevent further trouble among the Sioux there. This action did more to stir up hostilities than to prevent them, for it brought troops into contact with another branch of the Sioux—the nomadic Lakota—who had offered refuge to Native Americans from Minnesota. The Lakota fought hard to keep control of their hunting grounds, which extended from the Black Hills westward to the Bighorn Mountains. They had battled rival groups for this country and did not intend to let settlers have it. Leading them were chiefs Red Cloud, Crazy Horse, and Sitting Bull.

The army suffered a stunning defeat at the hands of Red Cloud's forces in Wyoming in December 1866. Army troops were operating a fort on the Bozeman Trail, used by prospectors to reach gold mines in Montana. Crazy Horse, a religious leader as well as a war chief, lured the troops into a deadly trap. He tricked the fort's commander into sending Captain William Fetterman and about 80 soldiers out to pursue what they thought was a small raiding party. Hundreds of warriors were waiting in ambush and wiped out the entire detachment.

Sand Creek **Fetterman's Massacre,** as this battle came to be called, was just one example of the growing hostilities between settlers and Native Americans. Another incident, the **Sand Creek Massacre,** took place along Sand Creek in eastern Colorado.

In the 1860s, tensions began to rise between the Cheyenne and Arapaho peoples and the miners who had flocked to Colorado in search of gold and silver. As the number of settlers increased, bands of Native Americans began raiding wagon trains and stealing cattle and horses from ranches. By the summer of 1864, travelers heading to Denver or the mining camps were no longer safe. Trade had come to a

standstill, dozens of ranches had been burned, and an estimated 200 settlers had been killed. The territorial governor, John Evans, ordered the Native Americans to surrender at Fort Lyon, where he said they would be given food and protection. Those who failed to report would be subject to attack.

Although several hundred Native Americans surrendered at the fort, many others did not. In November 1864, Chief Black Kettle brought several hundred Cheyenne to the fort, not to surrender but to negotiate a peace deal. The fort's commander did not have the authority to negotiate, and he told Black Kettle to make camp at Sand Creek while he waited for orders. Shortly afterward, Colonel John Chivington of the Colorado Volunteers was ordered to attack the Cheyenne at Sand Creek.

When Chivington stopped at Fort Lyon, he was told that the Native Americans at Sand Creek were waiting to negotiate. Chivington replied that since the Cheyenne had been attacking settlers, including women and children, there could be no peace.

What actually happened at Sand Creek is unclear. Some witnesses stated afterward that Black Kettle had been flying both an American flag and a white flag of truce, which Chivington ignored. Others reported the American troops fired on the unsuspecting Native Americans, then brutally murdered hundreds of women and children. Still others described a savage battle in which both sides fought ferociously for two days. Fourteen soldiers died, but the number of Native Americans reported killed varied from 69 to 600, with some witnesses stating that very few

Fact | Fiction | Folklore

Buffalo Bill's Wild West Show Many Americans who never set foot on the Great Plains enjoyed a make-believe excursion there through a Wild West show. Various promoters staged these popular extravaganzas, but the most famous was Buffalo Bill's Wild West Show.

Members of the cast performed a mock buffalo hunt with real buffalo, and they reenacted Custer's defeat at the Little Bighorn. Among the stars of the show was Annie Oakley, a sharpshooter from Ohio who appeared in Western outfit and dazzled both the audience and her fellow performers.

BUFFALO BILL'S WILD WEST
CONGRESS, ROUGH RIDERS OF THE WORLD.

MISS ANNIE OAKLEY,
THE PEERLESS LADY WING-SHOT.

Fact | Fiction | Folklore

Annie Get Your Gun, a musical interpretation of Annie Oakley's exploits, opened on Broadway in 1946 with Ethel Merman starring as Oakley. Irving Berlin wrote the music and lyrics based on the book written by Herbert and Dorothy Fields. The musical had a long run on Broadway, was made into a movie, and is a favorite for school and community productions. Perhaps the most recognizable songs from the show are "Anything You Can Do (I can do better)" and "There's No Business Like Show Business."

L1/ELL

Guided Reading Activity 8–3

Name _____ Date _____ Class _____

★ **Guided Reading Activity 8-3**

DIRECTIONS: Recalling Facts Read the section and answer the questions below. Refer to your textbook to write the answers.

1. How did most Native Americans of the Great Plains live? _____

2. Among most Native American groups, how were tasks assigned? _____

3. What took a serious toll on Native Americans? _____

4. What agreement did the Dakota Sioux make with the United States government? _____

5. What happened to the money the Dakota Sioux received from the government? _____

Telling a Story Ask students to develop a story describing one of the events mentioned under the heading "Cultures Under Pressure." Instruct students to develop their stories from the point of view of one of the participants. Encourage students to use library and Internet resources to learn more about the event. Invite students to tell their stories in class. **L2**

📁 Use the rubric for a diary, short story, memorandum, or letter on pages 69–70 in the *Performance Assessment Activities and Rubrics.*

DIFFERENTIATED INSTRUCTION

Reading Support Have students select an event in this section and write a journal entry as if they had participated in the event. Tell students to write from the perspective of an American soldier, a Native American warrior, a settler in the region, or as a child observing the event and its results. Encourage students to describe their feelings, as well as the actions they took. **L2**

📁 Refer to *Inclusion for the High School Social Studies Classroom Strategies and Activities* in the TCR.

History *and the* Humanities

🎵 American Music: Hits Through History: "Kiowa Hymn II"

🏛 American Art & Architecture: *The Buffalo Chase, Mouth of the Yellowstone; Merced River, Yosemite Valley; Chief Joseph*

Reading Check

Answer: creation of two large reservations on the Plains: one in the Black Hills for the Sioux and the other in the Indian Territory (Oklahoma) for southern Plains Indians

Geography *Skills*

Answers:

1. at Bear Paw Mountain in Montana

2. The steady increase in white settlers and their focus on mining, cattle ranching, and buffalo hunting contributed to significant changes in the Native American way of life.

Geography Skills Practice

Ask: In what states and territories were the Native American battles fought? *(Arizona Territory, Colorado, Montana, and South Dakota)*

women or children died. General Nelson Miles later called Chivington's attack "the foulest and most unjustifiable crime in the annals of America," but a Senate committee investigating the incident decided that Chivington should not be charged. The truth of what really happened remains unknown.

GOVERNMENT

A Doomed Plan for Peace Fetterman's Massacre and the Sand Creek Massacre, along with several other incidents, convinced Congress that something had to be done to end the growing conflict with Native Americans on the Great Plains. In 1867 Congress formed an **Indian Peace Commission,** which proposed creating two large reservations on the Plains, one for the Sioux and another for southern Plains Indians. Agents from the federal government's Bureau of Indian Affairs would run the reservations. The army would be given authority to deal with any groups that refused to report or remain there.

This plan was doomed to failure. Pressuring Native American leaders into signing treaties, as negotiators had done at Medicine Lodge Creek in 1867, did not ensure that chiefs or their followers would abide by the terms. Those who did move to reservations faced much the same conditions that drove the Dakota Sioux to violence—poverty, despair, and the corrupt practices of American traders.

Reading Check ✓ **Explaining** What proposal did the Indian Peace Commission present to the Plains Indians?

NATIONAL GEOGRAPHIC
Native American Battles and Reservations, late 1800s

In Motion

CANADA

PACIFIC OCEAN

CASCADE RANGE

WASH.

Bear Paw Mountain 1877

MONT.

Little Bighorn 1876

N. DAK.

MINN.

OREG.

IDAHO

Rosebud 1876

S. DAK.

Black Hills

WIS.

MICH.

NEV.

WYO.

Wounded Knee 1890

IOWA

ILL.

IND.

FORT LARAMIE TREATIES
1851: Native Americans agree to the construction of roads and forts on their lands.
1868: The Sioux agree to move to a reservation in the Black Hills.

Ft. Laramie

NEBR.

1867 TREATY OF MEDICINE LODGE
Southern Plains Indians agree to move to Indian Territory.

UTAH TERR.

Sand Creek 1864

COLO.

KANS.

MO.

KY.

CALIF.

Ft. Lyon

Medicine Lodge

ARIZ. TERR.

Ft. Defiance

Canyon de Chelly 1864

NO MAN'S LAND

CHEROKEE OUTLET

OSAGE

CHEROKEE

CHEYENNE AND ARAPAHO

CREEK

SEMINOLE

ARK.

TENN.

120°W

BOSQUE REDONDO (1863–1868)

GREER COUNTY (CLAIMED BY TEXAS)

CHICKASAW

CHOCTAW

MISS.

ALA.

Ft. Sumner

N. MEX. TERR.

UNASSIGNED LANDS

COMANCHE, KIOWA, AND APACHE

LA.

0   400 miles
0   400 kilometers
Lambert Equal-Area projection

TEX.

Apache leader Geronimo surrenders at Skeleton Canyon in 1886.

Legend:
- ✖ Fort
- ✳ Battle
- △ Treaty Site
- ─── 1890 border
- ▨ Reservation in 1890
- ⬅ Route of the Navajo's Long Walk, 1864
- ⬅ Route of Chief Joseph and the Nez Perce, 1877

Geography *Skills*

1. **Interpreting Maps** Where did Chief Joseph finally give up his flight from the U.S. Army?
2. **Applying Geography Skills** What physical and geographic factors contributed to Native Americans being located to reservations?

INTERDISCIPLINARY CONNECTIONS ACTIVITY

Performing Arts Have students select one of the Native American nations mentioned in the section. Tell them to use library and Internet resources to research the dances and music associated with the rituals performed by the nation. Have students create a display that shows how the dance was performed and explains what the elements mean. Encourage students to include examples of the instruments used by the Native Americans to accompany the dance. **L3**

The Last Native American Wars

By the 1870s, many Native Americans on the southern Plains had left the reservations in disgust. They preferred hunting buffalo on the open Plains, so they joined others who had also shunned the reservations. Buffalo, however, were rapidly disappearing. Beginning with the Gold Rush, migrants crossing the Plains had killed off thousands of the animals.

Following the Civil War, professional buffalo hunters invaded the area, seeking buffalo hides for markets in the East. Other hunters killed merely for sport, leaving carcasses to rot. Then railroad companies hired sharpshooters to kill large numbers of buffalo that were obstructing rail traffic. The army, determined to force Native Americans onto reservations, encouraged buffalo killing. By 1889 very few of the animals remained.

Battle of the Little Bighorn In 1876 fortune hunters overran the Lakota Sioux reservation in South Dakota to mine gold in the Black Hills. The Lakota saw no reason why they should abide by a treaty that American settlers were violating, and many left the reservation that spring to hunt near the Bighorn Mountains in southeastern Montana.

The government responded by sending an expedition commanded by General Alfred H. Terry. Lieutenant Colonel **George A. Custer,** commander of the Seventh Cavalry, was with the expedition. An impulsive officer, Custer underestimated the fighting capabilities of the Lakota and Cheyenne.

On June 25, 1876, Custer launched a three-pronged attack in broad daylight on one of the largest groups of Native American warriors ever assembled on the Great Plains. It consisted of about 2,500 Lakota and Cheyenne warriors camped along the Little Bighorn River.

The Native American warriors first repulsed a cavalry charge from the south. Then they turned on Custer and a detachment of 210 soldiers and killed them all. One Lakota warrior recalled the scene afterward: "The soldiers were piled one on top of another, dead, with here and there, an Indian among the soldiers. Horses lay on top of men, and men on top of horses."

Newspapers portrayed Custer as the victim of a massacre. The army stepped up its campaign against the Native Americans. Sitting Bull fled with followers to Canada, but the other Lakota were forced to return to the reservation and give up the Black Hills.

Farther west, members of the Nez Perce, led by Chief Joseph, refused to be moved to a smaller reservation in Idaho in 1877. When the army came to relocate them, they fled their homes and embarked on a flight of more than 1,300 miles. Finally, in October 1877, Chief Joseph surrendered, and his followers were exiled to Oklahoma. His speech summarized the hopelessness of the Native American cause:

> 66 Our chiefs are killed. . . . The little children are freezing to death. My people . . . have no blankets, no food. . . . Hear me, my chiefs; I am tired; my heart is sick and sad. From where the sun now stands I will fight no more forever. 99

—quoted in *Bury My Heart at Wounded Knee*

Tragedy at Wounded Knee Native American resistance to federal authority finally came to a tragic end on the Lakota Sioux reservation in 1890. Defying

Profiles IN HISTORY

Sitting Bull
1831–1890

In June 1876, a showdown loomed between Custer's troops and the Lakota Sioux who had left their reservation. Lakota chief Sitting Bull sought help for his people from the supreme power they called *Wakan Tanka,* or the "Great Mystery," by performing the Sun Dance.

Before dancing, an assistant made many small cuts in the chief's arms and shoulders. Then Sitting Bull raised his bleeding arms to heaven and danced around a sacred pole with his eyes on the sun. He continued to dance through the night and into the next day, when he entered a death-like trance. When he revived, he told of a vision in which he saw white soldiers upside down. The Lakota were encouraged by Sitting Bull's dream and the sacrifice he had made for them. Many felt that his Sun Dance helped bring them victory over Custer.

Sitting Bull remained devoted to the traditional religious practices of his people even after he and his followers reluctantly returned to the reservation under pressure from the army. Federal authorities regarded ceremonies like the Sun Dance—practiced in one form or another by many Plains Indians—as heathen and subversive. In 1883 the federal government outlawed the Sun Dance and many other Native American religious rites.

Profiles IN HISTORY

For a time in the mid-1880s, Sitting Bull traveled with Buffalo Bill's Wild West Show.

Ask: Why do you think federal authorities outlawed the Sun Dance and other religious rites? *(Students might answer that federal authorities felt it would be better for everyone if Native Americans abandoned their culture and assimilated into American society as defined by white Christians.)*

ABCNEWS INTERACTIVE™

 VIDEOCASSETTE
Historic America Electronic Field Trips

View **Tape 2, Chapter 3:** "Little Bighorn."

3 ASSESS

Assign Section 3 Assessment as homework or as an in-class activity.

⊕ Have students use the **Interactive Tutor Self-Assessment CD-ROM.**

L1/ELL

Reading Essentials and Study Guide 8–3

Name _____ Date _____ Class _____

Study Guide

Chapter 8, Section 3

For use with textbook pages 297–302

NATIVE AMERICANS

KEY TERMS AND NAMES
nomads people who roam great distances *(page 297)*
annuity payment to reservation dwellers *(page 298)*
Little Crow a Chief of the Dakota *(page 298)*
Indian Peace Commission a commission formed by Congress in 1867, which created two reservations on the Great Plains *(page 300)*
George A. Custer United States military leader in the Battle of the Little Bighorn *(page 301)*
Ghost Dance a ritual performed by the Lakota Sioux *(page 302)*
assimilate to be absorbed into *(page 302)*

CRITICAL THINKING ACTIVITY

Synthesizing Read the following statement made by Chief Joseph in an appeal to President Rutherford B. Hayes. "Let me be a free man—free to travel, free to stop, free to work, free to trade where I choose, free to choose my own teachers, free to follow the religion of my father, free to think and talk and act for myself—and I will obey every law or submit to the penalty." Ask students: In what ways does Chief Joseph's statement not address the concerns of either the Native Americans or the settlers? *(It does not mention control of the land or settlers' concerns about Native American attacks.)* Why do you think Joseph wrote his appeal in this way? *(to create sympathy for Native Americans who were being denied freedom)* **L2**

L2

Section Quiz 8–3

Name	Date	Class
★ **Chapter 8**		Score
Section Quiz 8-3		

DIRECTIONS: Matching Match each item in Column A with the items in Column B. Write the correct letters in the blanks. *(10 points each)*

Column A		Column B
____	1. leader of the Nez Perce people	**A.** Chief Joseph
____	2. site of a murderous battle between U.S. soldiers and Lakota men, women, and children	**B.** assimilate
____	3. to be absorbed	**C.** annuities
____	4. main source of food for many Native Americans	**D.** Wounded Knee Creek
____	5. payments to reservation dwellers	**E.** buffalo

DIRECTIONS: Multiple Choice In the blank at the left, write the letter of the choice that best completes the statement or answers the question. *(10 points each)*

✓ Reading Check

Answer: The U.S. Army's defeat caused it to step up its campaign which eventually forced some Lakota to the reservation.

Reteach

Have students discuss the conflicts that arose between Plains Indians and white settlers.

Enrich

Have students research life on reservations today. They should review the effects of past legislation, such as the Indian Reorganization Act of 1934 and the termination policy of the 1950s. Suggest that students include information on both problems and successes.

✓ Reading Check

Answer: Her book sparked discussions of better treatment for Native Americans.

Study Central™ provides summaries, interactive games, and online graphic organizers to help students review section content.

4 CLOSE

Have students summarize problems caused by attempts to assimilate Native Americans.

302

---

the orders of the government agent, the Lakota continued to perform the **Ghost Dance,** a ritual that celebrated a hoped-for day of reckoning when settlers would disappear, the buffalo would return, and Native Americans would reunite with their deceased ancestors. The government agent blamed the latest defiance on Sitting Bull, who had returned to the reservation from Canada, and he sent police to arrest the chief. Sitting Bull's supporters resisted the police, and the chief himself died in an exchange of gunfire.

The participants of the Ghost Dance then fled the reservation, and U.S. troops went after them. On December 29, 1890, as troops tried to disarm the Native Americans at Wounded Knee Creek, gunfire broke out. A deadly battle ensued, costing the lives of 25 U.S. soldiers and approximately 200 Lakota men, women, and children.

✓ Reading Check **Summarizing** What was the outcome of the battle at the Little Bighorn River?

Assimilation

Some Americans had long opposed the treatment of Native Americans. Author Helen Hunt Jackson described the years of broken promises and assaults on Native Americans in her book, *A Century of Dishonor,* published in 1881. Jackson's descriptions of events such as the massacre at Sand Creek sparked discussions—even in Congress—of better treatment for Native Americans. Some people believed that the situation would improve only if Native Americans could assimilate, or be absorbed,

into American society as landowners and citizens. That meant breaking up reservations into individual allotments, where families could become self-supporting.

This policy became law in 1887 when Congress passed the **Dawes Act.** This act allotted to each head of household 160 acres of reservation land for farming; single adults received 80 acres, and 40 acres were allotted for children. The land that remained after all members had received allotments would be sold to American settlers, with the proceeds going into a trust for Native Americans.

This plan failed to achieve its goals. Some Native Americans succeeded as farmers or ranchers, but many had little training or enthusiasm for either pursuit. Like homesteaders, they often found their allotments too small to be profitable, and so they sold them. Some Native American groups had grown attached to their reservations and hated to see them transformed into homesteads for settlers as well as Native Americans.

In the end, the assimilation policy proved a dismal failure. No legislation could provide a satisfactory solution to the Native American issue, because there was no entirely satisfactory solution to be had. The Plains Indians were doomed because they were dependent on buffalo for food, clothing, fuel, and shelter. When the herds were wiped out, Native Americans on the Plains had no way to sustain their way of life, and few were willing or able to adopt American settlers' lifestyles in place of their traditional cultures.

✓ Reading Check **Cause and Effect** What effect did Helen Hunt Jackson's book *A Century of Dishonor* have?

HISTORY Online **Study Central™** To review this section, go to tarvol2.glencoe.com and click on **Study Central™**.

SECTION 3 ASSESSMENT

Checking for Understanding

1. **Define:** nomad, annuity, assimilate, allotment.
2. **Identify:** Little Crow, Indian Peace Commission, George A. Custer, Ghost Dance, Dawes Act.
3. **Analyze** how Native Americans responded to land lost due to white settlement of the Great Plains.

Reviewing Themes

4. **Individual Action** How did Chief Joseph resist the government's attempts to move the Nez Perce to reservations?

Critical Thinking

5. **Analyzing** Why do you think the government's policy of assimilation of Native Americans was a failure?
6. **Organizing** Use a graphic organizer similar to the one below to list the reasons that the government's plans to move the Plains Indians onto reservations failed to bring peace.

Reasons for Failure

Analyzing Visuals

7. **Analyzing Maps** Examine the map of battle sites and reservations on page 300. Then, from the point of view of a historian, explain the actions taken against Native Americans within the historical context of the time.

Writing About History

8. **Descriptive Writing** Assume the role of a Plains Indian affected by the assimilation policy of the Dawes Act. Write a journal entry describing how you feel about the policy and how it has affected your life.

302 CHAPTER 8 Settling the West

SECTION 3 ASSESSMENT ANSWERS

1. Terms are in blue.
2. Little Crow *(p. 298)*, Indian Peace Commission *(p. 300)*, George A. Custer *(p. 301)*, Ghost Dance *(p. 302)*, Dawes Act *(p. 302)*
3. attacked wagon trains and ranches, and killed settlers and soldiers
4. Chief Joseph and the Nez Perce

fled 1,300 miles before surrendering.
5. After the buffalo herds were wiped out, Native Americans were unwilling or unable to live like American settlers.
6. Native Americans preferred life on the Plains; leaders were pressured

into signing treaties; reservations were plagued by poverty, despair, and outside corruption.
7. Answers may vary. Accept different viewpoints as long as the reasoning is sound and based on facts.
8. Students' journal entries will vary. Entries should be written from the perspective of a Native American.

American LITERATURE

Gertrude Simmons Bonnin (Zitkala Sa) was a talented and educated Native American woman who spent her life fighting against prejudice toward Native American culture and women. Through her contributions in the fields of literature, music, and politics, Bonnin aimed at creating understanding between the dominant white and Native American cultures. As a woman of mixed white and Native American ancestry, she embodied the need for the two cultures to live cooperatively. In the following excerpt from her essay, *An Indian Teacher Among Indians,* she describes a reunion with her mother after being away from home teaching for several years.

Read to Discover

What evidence do you see of the "generation gap"—the differences between parents and children—in the passage?

Reader's Dictionary

position: job

steadfastly: faithfully

avenge: get even for

from An Indian Teacher Among Indians

by Gertrude Simmons Bonnin

"Mother, why is not your house cemented? Do you have no interest in a more comfortable shelter? . . ."

"You forget, my child, that I am now old, and I do not work with beads any more. Your brother Dawee, too, has lost his position, and we are left without means to buy even a morsel of food," she replied.

Dawee was a government clerk in our reservation when I last heard from him. I was surprised upon hearing what my mother said concerning his lack of employment. Seeing the puzzled expression on my face, she continued: "Dawee! Oh, has he not told you that the Great Father at Washington sent a white son to take your brother's pen from him? Since then Dawee has not been able to make use of the education the Eastern school has given him."

I found no words with which to answer satisfactorily. I found no reason with which to cool my inflamed feelings. . . .

Turning to my mother, I urged her to tell me more about Dawee's trouble, but she only said: "Well, my daughter, this village has been these many winters a refuge for white robbers. The Indian cannot complain to the Great Father in Washington without suffering outrage for it here. . . .

A Native American reservation

"My child, there is only one source of justice, and I have been praying steadfastly to the Great Spirit to avenge our wrongs," she said, seeing I did not move my lips.

My shattered energy was unable to hold longer any faith, and I cried out desperately: "Mother, don't pray again! The Great Spirit does not care if we live or die!"

Analyzing Literature

1. **Recall and Interpret** Why did Bonnin's brother lose his job?
2. **Evaluate and Connect** How does Bonnin's mother react to the injustice of the "Great Father in Washington"? How does Bonnin herself react?

Interdisciplinary Activity

Drama In small groups, assume the roles of Bonnin, her mother, and her brother, and extend the passage by imagining what might happen when Dawee returns.

 Block Schedule

Team Teaching This selection from *An Indian Teacher Among Indians* can be presented in conjunction with English or Language Arts.

Read to Discover

Answer: Zitkala Sa criticizes her mother for not keeping up her house and for praying to the Great Spirit.

Reading Strategy

Reinforcing Vocabulary

Have students look up the meaning of any other unfamiliar words, such as *morsel, inflamed,* or *refuge.*

Historical Connection

Bonnin devoted her life to working for Native Americans. In 1926 she founded the National Council of American Indians.

Portfolio Writing Activity

Have students write a short narrative about a conflict between generations of the same family.

Refer to tarvol2.glencoe.com for additional Glencoe Literature titles, lesson plans, and study guides related to this unit.

Answers to Analyzing Literature

1. Even though Dawee was educated in an Eastern school, he lost his job and was replaced by a white man.

2. Bonnin's mother prays for the Great Spirit to avenge wrongs. Bonnin tells her mother to stop praying because the Great Spirit does not care about them.

Interdisciplinary Activity
Students' answers will vary. Encourage students to present their role plays to the class.

CHAPTER 8

ASSESSMENT and ACTIVITIES

Reviewing Key Terms
The pages where the words appear in the text are shown in parentheses.

1. **placer mining** (p. 287)
2. **quartz mining** (p. 287)
3. **open range** (p. 288)
4. **long drive** (p. 289)
5. **maverick** (p. 290)
6. **homestead** (p. 293)
7. **dry farming** (p. 294)
8. **sodbuster** (p. 294)
9. **bonanza farm** (p. 294)
10. **nomad** (p. 297)
11. **annuity** (p. 298)
12. **assimilate** (p. 302)
13. **allotment** (p. 302)

Reviewing Key Facts
14. Henry Comstock (p. 287), Great Plains (p. 292), Stephen Long (p. 293), Little Crow (p. 298), Indian Peace Commission (p. 300), George A. Custer (p. 301), Dawes Act (p. 302)
15. the discovery of copper, gold, or silver; when the lode played out, mines closed and the towns' economies collapsed
16. barbed wire
17. Railroad companies sold land along rail lines at low prices, provided credit to prospective settlers, and advertised the benefits of booking passage to the Plains.
18. Wheat could be cultivated using dry farming.
19. White settlers' moving west, railroad construction, buffalo slaughtered, and wars

Reviewing Key Terms
On a sheet of paper, use each of these terms in a sentence.

1. placer mining
2. quartz mining
3. open range
4. long drive
5. maverick
6. homestead
7. dry farming
8. sodbuster
9. bonanza farm
10. nomad
11. annuity
12. assimilate
13. allotment

Reviewing Key Facts
14. **Identify:** Henry Comstock, Great Plains, Stephen Long, Little Crow, Indian Peace Commission, George A. Custer, Dawes Act.
15. What led to the start of boomtowns, and what caused their decline?
16. What new invention finally brought an end to the open range on the Great Plains?
17. How did the railroads boost the settlement of the West?
18. Why was wheat a suitable crop to grow on the Great Plains?
19. What events brought the way of life of the Plains Indians to an end?

Critical Thinking
20. **Analyzing Themes: Economic Factors** Do you think that people moved to and settled in the West primarily for economic reasons? Why or why not?

21. **Drawing Conclusions** Why do you think that so many people were willing to give up their homes and move to mining towns and homesteads in the West?
22. **Forming an Opinion** How do you think a peaceful settlement might have been reached between the Native Americans and the U.S. government?
23. **Interpreting Primary Sources** In the late 1860s, the U.S. government adopted a policy of forcing Native Americans onto small reservations in the Black Hills of Dakota and barren regions of Oklahoma. The government forced many Native American chiefs to sign treaties and to promise to move onto the reservations. Many Native Americans, however, refused to move and fought to maintain their traditional way of life. In the excerpt that follows, Satanta, a chief of the Kiowa, responds to the government's policy. Read the excerpt and answer the questions that follow:

❝I have heard that you intend to settle us on a reservation near the mountains. I don't want to settle. I love to roam over the prairies. There I feel free and happy, but when we settle down we grow pale and die. I have laid aside my lance, bow, and shield, and yet I feel safe in your presence. I have told you the truth. I have no little lies hid about me, but I don't know how it is with the commissioners. Are they as clear as I am? A long time ago this land belonged to our fathers; but when I go up to the river I see camps of soldiers on its banks. These soldiers cut down my timber; they kill my buffalo;

Chapter Summary

Mining and Ranching
- Discovery of gold, silver, and copper attracted settlers to Colorado, the Dakota Territory, Nevada, and Montana
- Growth of cattle and sheep ranching attracted settlers to Texas, Montana, Wyoming, and other western areas

Farming
- Cheap land of Homestead Act encouraged settlement
- Farming technology and climate moderation made the Great Plains into the Wheat Belt

Native Americans
- Federal government forced Plains Indians off their lands with promise of receiving new land
- White settlers moved into lands promised to Native Americans
- Slaughter of buffalo removed a major part of Native American way of life

Role of Railroads

Provided easy way to ship sheep and cattle to Eastern markets	Brought scarce timber and coal to the Great Plains; advertised for settlers	Helped displace Native Americans by moving settlers west, taking lands, and promoting buffalo slaughter

Critical Thinking
20. Many did move for the hope of riches; others for adventure, freedom, or a fresh start.
21. Many settlers thought that they could prosper in the West.
22. Students' answers will vary. Discuss ideas as a class.
23. **a.** He enjoyed his nomadic life. **b.** He thinks the white man does not respect the land. He says white men kill buffalo recklessly.

24. prospects of getting rich from mining, opportunity to purchase land at a reasonable price, chance to escape the South following the Civil War

Practicing Skills
25. **a.** negative; **b.** It will continue to decline.

Self-Check Quiz
Visit the *American Republic Since 1877* Web site at tarvol2.glencoe.com and click on **Self-Check Quizzes—Chapter 8** to assess your knowledge of chapter content.

and when I see that, my heart feels like bursting; I feel sorry. . . . Has the white man become a child that he should recklessly kill and not eat? When the red men slay game, they do so that they may live and not starve. 🙶

—quoted in *Bury My Heart at Wounded Knee*

a. What reasons does Satanta give for not wanting to settle on a reservation?

b. How does Satanta view the white settlers' approach to the land and the resources on it?

24. Organizing Use a graphic organizer to list the factors that promoted the settlement of the West.

Reasons for Settling the West

Practicing Skills

25. Interpreting Statistics Examine the chart on Native American populations displayed on this page. Then use the steps you learned about interpreting statistics to answer the following questions.

a. According to this data, is there a positive or a negative correlation between Native American population and the passage of time?

b. Based on this correlation, what conclusions can you draw about Native American population after 1900?

Writing Activity

26. Portfolio Writing Watch an older movie about the West. Look critically at the movie's depiction of cowhands and Native Americans. Write a movie review in which you assess how accurately the movie portrays the West. Place the review in your portfolio.

Chapter Activity

27. Technology: Using the Internet Search the Internet for sites about old mining towns (ghost towns) in the West. Many of these towns are tourist attractions today. Find out the location and history of a few of these towns, as well as the points of interest. Incorporate the information in a brochure for tourists interested in taking a "ghost town" vacation.

Native American Population

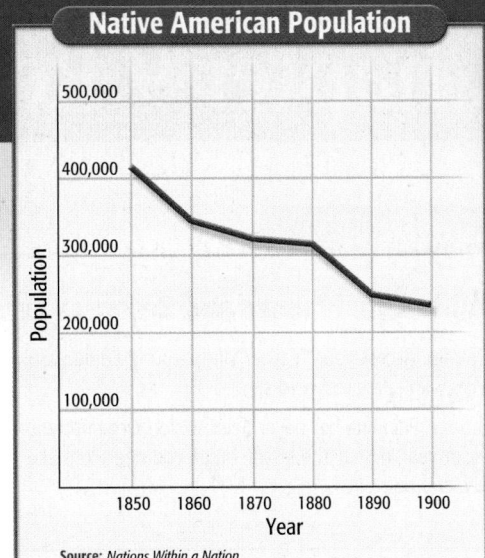

Source: *Nations Within a Nation.*

Geography and History

28. The graph above shows Native American population from 1850 to 1900. Study the graph and answer the questions below.

a. Interpreting Graphs What does the graph indicate about Native American populations between 1850 and 1900?

b. Understanding Cause and Effect What factor caused the Native American populations to decline sharply between 1880 and 1890?

Standardized Test Practice

Directions: Choose the best answer to the following question.

Which of the following factors provided an incentive for people to try to farm the Great Plains?

A Long cattle drives

B Barbed wire

C The Homestead Act

D Placer mining

Test-Taking Tip: When you are not sure of an answer, it can be helpful to use the process of elimination. Eliminate the answers that you know are incorrect. For instance, long cattle drives had to do with ranching, not farming. Therefore, you can eliminate answer A.

Have students visit the Web site at tarvol2.glencoe.com to review Chapter 8 and take the Self-Check Quiz.

Standardized Test Practice

Answer: C
Test-Taking Tip: Encourage students to read the question carefully and eliminate answers they know are incorrect. It may be helpful to have them list the subject to which each answer choice relates (answers A and B to ranching, answer C to farming, and answer D to mining).

Bonus Question ?

Ask: How did dry farming damage the ecology of the prairie? *(Dry farming contributed to soil erosion and massive dust storms.)*

CHAPTER 8 Settling the West **305**

Writing Activity
26. Reviews should note differences between historical facts and movie portrayals of events.

Chapter Activity
27. Encourage students to create an informative brochure that will interest tourists in the ghost towns.

Geography and History
28. a. They declined steadily. **b.** Students should note that Native Americans suffered high casualty rates in conflicts with white settlers.

Timesaving Tools

TeacherWorks™ All-In-One Planner and Resource Center

- **Interactive Teacher Edition** Access your Teacher Wraparound Edition and your classroom resources with a few easy clicks.
- **Interactive Lesson Planner** Planning has never been easier! Organize your week, month, semester, or year with all the lesson helps you need to make teaching creative, timely, and relevant.

Use Glencoe's **Presentation Plus!** multimedia teacher tool to easily present dynamic lessons that visually excite your students. Using Microsoft PowerPoint® you can customize the presentations to create your own personalized lessons.

TEACHING TRANSPARENCIES

Graphic Organizer 9 L2

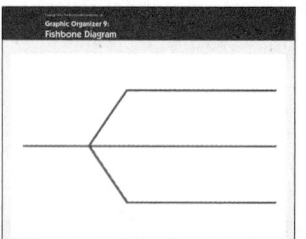

Why It Matters Chapter Transparency 9 L2

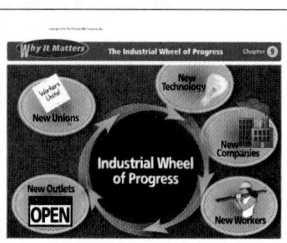

APPLICATION AND ENRICHMENT

Linking Past and Present Activity 9 L2

Enrichment Activity 9 L3

Primary Source Reading 9 L2

REVIEW AND REINFORCEMENT

Reteaching Activity 9 L1

Vocabulary Activity 9 L1

Time Line Activity 9 L2

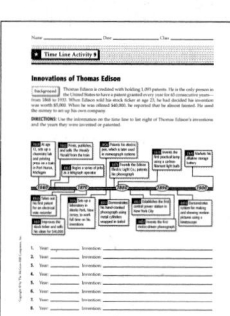

Critical Thinking Skills Activity 9 L2

Meeting NCSS Standards

The following standards are covered in Chapter 9:

Section 1	VII	Production, Distribution, and Consumption: A, B
Section 2	IV	Individual Development and Identity: G
Section 3	VII	Production, Distribution, and Consumption: A, B, D, E
Section 4	IV	Individual Development and Identity: A, C

Local Standards

_____

_____

_____

_____

_____

_____

Chapter 9 Resources

ASSESSMENT AND EVALUATION

**GLENCOE'S
ASSESSMENT
ADVANTAGE**

**Chapter 9 Test
Form A** L2

**Chapter 9 Test
Form B** L2

**Standardized Test Practice
Workbook Activity 9** L2

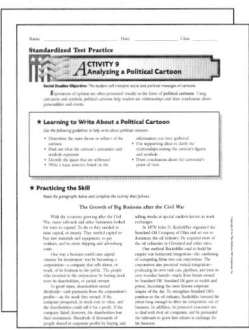

**Performance Assessment
Activities and Rubrics 9**
L1/ELL

**ExamView® Pro
Testmaker CD-ROM**

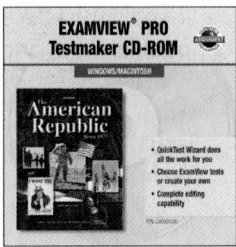

MULTIMEDIA

- **Vocabulary PuzzleMaker CD-ROM**
- **Interactive Tutor Self-Assessment CD-ROM**
- **ExamView® Pro Testmaker CD-ROM**
- **Audio Program**
- **American History Primary Source Documents Library CD-ROM**
- **MindJogger Videoquiz**
- **Presentation Plus! CD-ROM**
- **TeacherWorks™ CD-ROM**
- **Interactive Student Edition CD-ROM**
- **Glencoe Skillbuilder Interactive Workbook CD-ROM, Level 2**
- **The *American Republic Since 1877* Video Program**
- **American Music: Hits Through History**
- **American Music: Cultural Traditions**

SPANISH RESOURCES

The following Spanish language materials are available:

- Spanish Reading Essentials and Study Guide
- Spanish Guided Reading Activities
- Spanish Reteaching Activities
- Spanish Quizzes and Tests
- Spanish Vocabulary Activities
- Spanish Summaries
- The Declaration of Independence and United States Constitution Spanish Translation

---

THE HISTORY CHANNEL.

The following videotape programs are available
from Glencoe as supplements to Chapter 9:

- **Legacy of King Coal, Empires of American Industry** (ISBN 0-76-700621-6)
- **Dow and Jones: Wizards of Wall Street** (ISBN 0-76-700203-2)

To order, call Glencoe at 1-800-334-7344. To find classroom resources to
accompany many of these videos, check the following home pages:
A&E Television: www.aande.com
The History Channel: www.historychannel.com

Use our Web site for additional resources. All essential content is covered in the Student Edition.

You and your students can visit tarvol2.glencoe.com, the Web site
companion to the ***American Republic Since 1877.*** This innovative
integration of electronic and print media offers your students a wealth
of opportunities. The student text directs students to the Web site for
the following options:

- **Chapter Overviews**
- **Self-Check Quizzes**
- **Student Web Activities**
- **Textbook Updates**

Answers to the student Web activities are provided for you in the **Web
Activity Lesson Plans.** Additional Web resources and Interactive Tutor
Puzzles are also available.

Chapter 9 Resources

Daily Objectives	Reproducible Resources	Multimedia Resources
SECTION 1 **The Rise of Industry** 1. Identify the effects of expanding population on industry. 2. Explain the effects of technological innovations such as the telephone and telegraph on American development.	Reproducible Lesson Plan 9–1 Daily Lecture and Discussion Notes 9–1 Guided Reading Activity 9–1* Section Quiz 9–1* Reading Essentials and Study Guide 9–1* Performance Assessment Activities and Rubrics	Daily Focus Skills Transparency 9–1 Interactive Tutor Self-Assessment CD-ROM ExamView® Pro Testmaker CD-ROM* Presentation Plus! CD-ROM TeacherWorks™ CD-ROM Audio Program Skillbuilder Interactive Workbook, Level 2 ABCNews Interactive™ Historic America Electronic Field Trips
SECTION 2 **The Railroads** 1. Discuss ways in which the railroads spurred industrial growth. 2. Analyze how the railroads were financed and how they grew.	Reproducible Lesson Plan 9–2 Daily Lecture and Discussion Notes 9–2 Guided Reading Activity 9–2* Section Quiz 9–2* Reading Essentials and Study Guide 9–2* Performance Assessment Activities and Rubrics	Daily Focus Skills Transparency 9–2 Interactive Tutor Self-Assessment CD-ROM ExamView® Pro Testmaker CD-ROM* Presentation Plus! CD-ROM TeacherWorks™ CD-ROM Audio Program
SECTION 3 **Big Business** 1. Analyze how large corporations came to dominate American business. 2. Evaluate how Andrew Carnegie's innovations transformed the steel industry.	Reproducible Lesson Plan 9–3 Daily Lecture and Discussion Notes 9–3 Guided Reading Activity 9–3* Section Quiz 9–3* Reading Essentials and Study Guide 9–3* Performance Assessment Activities and Rubrics Interpreting Political Cartoons	Daily Focus Skills Transparency 9–3 American Art & Architecture Interactive Tutor Self-Assessment CD-ROM ExamView® Pro Testmaker CD-ROM* Presentation Plus! CD-ROM TeacherWorks™ CD-ROM Audio Program
SECTION 4 **Unions** 1. Describe industrial working conditions in the United States in the late 1800s. 2. List the barriers to labor union growth.	Reproducible Lesson Plan 9–4 Daily Lecture and Discussion Notes 9–4 Guided Reading Activity 9–4* Section Quiz 9–4* Reading Essentials and Study Guide 9–4* Performance Assessment Activities and Rubrics	Daily Focus Skills Transparency 9–4 Interactive Tutor Self-Assessment CD-ROM ExamView® Pro Testmaker CD-ROM* Presentation Plus! CD-ROM TeacherWorks™ CD-ROM Vocabulary PuzzleMaker CD-ROM Audio Program

0:00 OUT OF TIME?
Assign the Chapter 9 **Reading Essentials and Study Guide.**

*Also Available in Spanish

 Printed Materials Transparency CD-ROM DVD

 Poster Music Program Audio Program Videocassette

NATIONAL GEOGRAPHIC | Teacher's Corner

INDEX TO NATIONAL GEOGRAPHIC MAGAZINE

The following articles relate to this chapter.

- "Geronimo," October 1992
- "New Life for Ellis Island," September 1990
- "Pittsburgh—Stronger than Steel," December 1991

NATIONAL GEOGRAPHIC SOCIETY PRODUCTS

To order the following, call National Geographic at 1-800-368-2728:

- *Full Steam Ahead: The Race to Build a Transcontinental Railroad*
- *Historical Atlas of the United States* (Atlas)
- *Immigration: The Triumph of Hope*

NGS ONLINE

Access National Geographic's Web site for current events, atlas updates, activities, links, interactive features, and archives.

www.nationalgeographic.com

From the Classroom of...

Tom Beaman
Reynolds High School
Troutdale, OR

Strategic Inventions

The rise of the United States to an industrial power started after the Civil War. The period between 1865 and 1901 saw rapid industrialization.

Give students a list of 10 to 15 items invented during this time period that contributed to the growth of industry in the United States. Consider items such as the light bulb, the elevator brake, the ice machine, the telephone, the electric streetcar, and the gasoline-powered car.

Students should research the background of one item's invention. They should then comment on how it contributed to the growth of industry.

MEETING SPECIAL NEEDS

In addition to the Differentiated Instruction strategies found in each section, the following resources are also suitable for your special needs students:

- *ExamView® Pro Testmaker CD-ROM* allows teachers to tailor tests by reducing answer choices.
- The *Audio Program* includes the entire narrative of the student edition so that less proficient readers can listen to the words as they read them.
- The *Reading Essentials and Study Guide* provides the same content as the student edition but is written two grade levels below the textbook.

ADDITIONAL RESOURCES FROM GLENCOE

- American Music: Cultural Traditions
- American Art & Architecture
- Outline Map Resource Book
- U.S. Desk Map
- Building Geography Skills for Life
- Inclusion for the High School Social Studies Classroom Strategies and Activities
- Teaching Strategies for the American History Classroom (Including Block Scheduling Pacing Guides)
- Dinah Zike's High School American History Reading and Study Skills Foldables

KEY TO ABILITY LEVELS

Teaching strategies have been coded.

- **L1** BASIC activities for all students
- **L2** AVERAGE activities for average to above-average students
- **L3** CHALLENGING activities for above-average students
- **ELL** ENGLISH LANGUAGE LEARNER activities

Block Schedule

Activities that are suited to use within the block scheduling framework are identified by:

Performance Assessment

Refer to Activity 9 in the Performance Assessment Activities and Rubrics booklet.

Why It Matters Activity

Ask students to explain how the industrialization of the United States in the late 1800s affects their shopping habits in the 2000s. Students should evaluate their answers after they have completed the chapter.

GLENCOE
TECHNOLOGY

The *American Republic Since 1877* Video Program

To learn more about the industrial expansion of the United States, have students view the Chapter 9 video, "Building America," from the *American Republic Since 1877* Video Program.

MindJogger Videoquiz

Use the **MindJogger Videoquiz** to preview Chapter 9 content.

Both programs available in DVD

9 Industrialization
1865–1901

Why It Matters

The rise of the United States as an industrial power began after the Civil War. Many factors promoted industry, including cheap labor, new inventions and technology, and plentiful raw materials. Railroads rapidly expanded. Government policies encouraged growth, and large corporations became an important part of the economy. As industry expanded, workers tried to form unions to fight for better wages and working conditions.

The Impact Today

Trends which began in this era can still be seen today.
* *Corporations continue to play an important role.*
* *Technology continues to change American life.*
* *Unions remain powerful in many industries.*

The American Republic Since 1877 Video
The Chapter 9 video, "Building America," examines industrial expansion in the United States in the late 1800s.

1869
• Transcontinental railroad completed

1876
• Alexander Graham Bell invents telephone

1882
• Standard Oil forms trust

1879
• Edison perfects lightbulb

United States PRESIDENTS

A. Johnson 1865–1869 | Grant 1869–1877 | Hayes 1877–1881 | Garfield 1881 | Arthur 1881–1885 | Cleveland 1885–1889

1865   *1875*   *1885*

World

1867
• British colonies unite to form Dominion of Canada

1876
• Korea forced to trade with Japan

1869
• Chemist Dmitri Mendeleyev creates periodic table of elements

1881
• Russian czar Alexander II assassinated

306

Reading Strategy   PURPOSE FOR READING

Free Writes and Picture Notes These strategies explore students' background knowledge and engage students using visual representations. Ask students to imagine that they will be choosing outstanding modern inventions, such as machines, processes, materials, medicinal drugs, and new treatments, to exhibit at a technical fair being held in their community. Have students draw visual representations of the inventions that might be included in such an exhibit. Tell them these drawings do not have to be perfect, merely rough drafts. Have students break into groups of three or four to share and explain their sketches to one another. **L1**

This painting by twentieth-century artist Aaron Bohrod captures the dynamism of an industrializing nation. Bohrod titled his work *The Big Blow: the Bessemer Process.*

1886
• Haymarket Square riot

1892
• Homestead strike occurs

1894
• Pullman strike begins

1901
• J.P. Morgan forms U.S. Steel

1903
• Women's Trade Union League founded

B. Harrison 1889–1893

Cleveland 1893–1897

McKinley 1897–1901

T. Roosevelt 1901–1909

1895

1905

1892
• Rudolf Diesel patents diesel engine

1896
• Athens hosts first modern Olympic games

1900
• Boxer Rebellion begins in China

HISTORY Online

Chapter Overview
Visit the *American Republic Since 1877* Web site at tarvol2.glencoe.com and click on **Chapter Overviews—Chapter 9** to preview chapter information.

307

HISTORY Online

Introduce students to chapter content and key terms by having them access the **Chapter 9 Overview** at tarvol2.glencoe.com.

More About the Art

Aaron Bohrod (1907–1992) was well known during his lifetime as a painter, sculptor, printmaker, ceramist, and illustrator. Many of his paintings exhibit social realism and attention to detail.

TIME LINE ACTIVITY

Have students write a paragraph about how the events listed on the time line have affected their lives within the last year. Invite students to share their experiences with the class.

FOLDABLES™ Study Organizer

Dinah Zike's Foldables are three-dimensional, interactive graphic organizers that help students practice basic writing skills, review key vocabulary terms, and identify main ideas. Have students complete the foldable activity in the *Dinah Zike's Reading and Study Skills Foldables* booklet.

GRAPHIC ORGANIZER ACTIVITY

Organizing Information Have students use a graphic organizer similar to the one shown below to link these areas of industrialization to key names in this chapter.

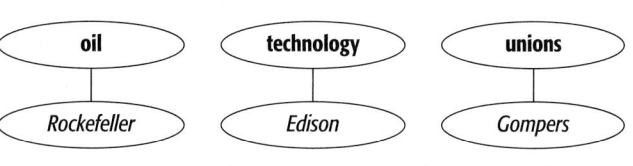

Industrialization

railroads	steel	oil	technology	unions
Vanderbilt	*Carnegie*	*Rockefeller*	*Edison*	*Gompers*

307

1 FOCUS

Section Overview

This section focuses on how American industry grew and brought changes to society.

BELLRINGER
Skillbuilder Activity

Project transparency and have students answer the question.

Daily Focus Skills Transparency 9–1

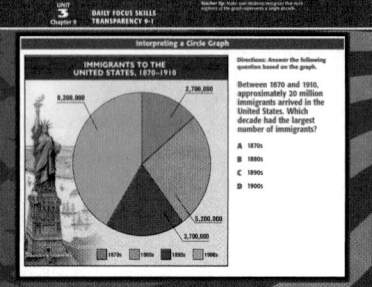

Reading Preview

Answers to Graphic: abundance of raw materials, oil production, population increase, free enterprise system, large free trade area, new inventions

Preteaching Vocabulary
Have students scan the section and write a sentence using each of the Key Terms and Names in context.

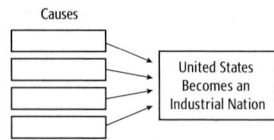

SECTION 1 The Rise of Industry

Guide to Reading

Main Idea
American industry grew rapidly after the Civil War, bringing revolutionary changes to American society.

Key Terms and Names
gross national product, Edwin Drake, laissez-faire, entrepreneur, Morrill Tariff, Alexander Graham Bell, Thomas Alva Edison

Reading Strategy
Organizing As you read about the changes brought about by industrialization, complete a graphic organizer similar to the one below listing the causes of industrialization.

Causes → United States Becomes an Industrial Nation

Reading Objectives
- **Identify** the effects of expanding population on industry.
- **Explain** the effects of technological innovations such as the telephone and telegraph on American development.

Section Theme
Economic Factors The free enterprise system nurtured the growth of American industry.

Preview of Events

| ♦1860 | ♦1870 | ♦1880 | ♦1890 |

1859
Edwin Drake drills first oil well

1865
Thaddeus Lowe invents ice machine

1876
Alexander Graham Bell invents telephone

1879
Thomas Edison perfects lightbulb

c. 1893
Northrop automatic loom introduced

★ An American Story ★

Thomas Edison

On October 21, 1879, Thomas Alva Edison and his team of workers were too excited to sleep. For weeks they had worked to create an electric incandescent lamp, or lightbulb, that would burn for more than a few minutes. For much of the 1800s, inventors had struggled to develop a form of lighting that would be cheaper, safer, and brighter than traditional methods such as candles, whale oil, kerosene, and gas. If Edison and his team could do it, they would change the world. Finally, after weeks of dedicated effort, they turned night into day. Edison later recalled:

❝We sat and looked and the lamp continued to burn and the longer it burned the more fascinated we were. None of us could go to bed and there was no sleep for over 40 hours; we sat and just watched it with anxiety growing into elation. It lasted about 45 hours and then I said, 'If it will burn 40 hours now I know I can make it burn a hundred.'❞

—quoted in *Eyewitness to America*

The United States Industrializes

Although the Industrial Revolution began in the United States in the early 1800s, the nation was still largely a farming country when the Civil War erupted. Out of a population of more than 30 million, only 1.3 million Americans worked in industry in 1860. After the Civil War, industry rapidly expanded, and millions of Americans left their farms to work in mines and factories.

By the early 1900s, Americans had transformed the United States into the world's leading industrial nation. By 1914 the nation's gross national product (GNP)—the total

308 CHAPTER 9 Industrialization

SECTION RESOURCES

📁 **Reproducible Masters**
- Reproducible Lesson Plan 9–1
- Daily Lecture and Discussion Notes 9–1
- Guided Reading Activity 9–1
- Section Quiz 9–1
- Reading Essentials and Study Guide 9–1

📖 **Transparencies**
- Daily Focus Skills Transparency 9–1

Multimedia
- 💿 Interactive Tutor Self-Assessment CD-ROM
- 💿 ExamView® Pro Testmaker CD-ROM
- 💿 Presentation Plus! CD-ROM
- 💿 TeacherWorks™ CD-ROM
- 🎧 Audio Program
- 📺 ABCNews Interactive™ Historic America Electronic Field Trips

value of all goods and services produced by a country—was eight times greater than it had been when the Civil War ended.

Natural Resources An abundance of raw materials was one reason for the nation's industrial success. The United States contained vast natural resources upon which industry in the 1800s depended, including water, timber, coal, iron, and copper. The presence of these resources meant that American companies could obtain them cheaply and did not have to import them from other countries. Many of the nation's resources were located in the mountains of the American West. The settlement of this region after the Civil War helped to accelerate industrialization, as did the construction of the transcontinental railroad. Railroads brought settlers and miners to the region, and carried the resources back to factories in the East.

At the same time, a new resource, petroleum, began to be exploited. Even before the invention of the automobile, petroleum was in high demand because it could be turned into kerosene. Kerosene was used in lanterns and stoves. The American oil industry was built on the demand for kerosene. It began in western Pennsylvania, where residents had long noticed oil bubbling to the surface of area springs and streams. In 1859 **Edwin Drake** drilled the first oil well near Titusville, Pennsylvania. By 1900 oil fields from Pennsylvania to Texas had been opened. As oil production rose, it fueled economic expansion.

A Large Workforce The human resources available to American industry were as important as natural resources in enabling the nation to industrialize rapidly. Between 1860 and 1910, the population of the United States almost tripled. This population provided industry with a large workforce and also created greater demand for the consumer goods that factories produced.

Population growth stemmed from two causes—large families and a flood of immigrants. American industry began to grow at a time when social and economic conditions in China and eastern Europe convinced many people to leave their nations and move to the United States in search of a better life. Between 1870 and 1910, roughly 20 million immigrants arrived in the United States. These multitudes added to the growing industrial workforce, helping factories increase their production and furthering demand for industrial products.

✓ **Reading Check** **Explaining** How did oil production affect the American economy?

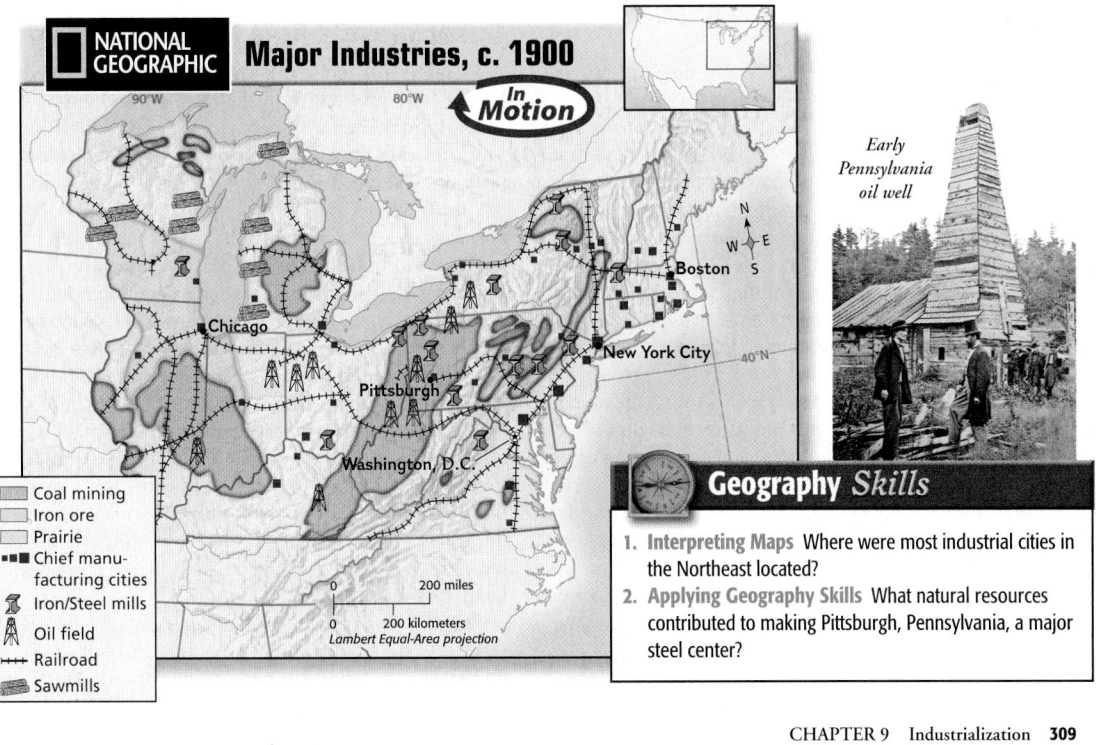

NATIONAL GEOGRAPHIC

Major Industries, c. 1900

In Motion

- Coal mining
- Iron ore
- Prairie
- ■■■ Chief manufacturing cities
- Iron/Steel mills
- Oil field
- Railroad
- Sawmills

Boston
Chicago
New York City
Pittsburgh
Washington, D.C.

0   200 miles
0   200 kilometers
Lambert Equal-Area projection

Early Pennsylvania oil well

Geography *Skills*

1. **Interpreting Maps** Where were most industrial cities in the Northeast located?
2. **Applying Geography Skills** What natural resources contributed to making Pittsburgh, Pennsylvania, a major steel center?

CHAPTER 9 Industrialization **309**

2 TEACH

Daily Lecture and Discussion Notes 9–1

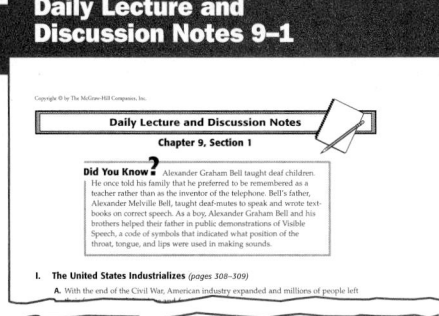

Copyright © by The McGraw-Hill Companies, Inc.

Daily Lecture and Discussion Notes
Chapter 9, Section 1

Did You Know? Alexander Graham Bell taught deaf children. He once told his family that he preferred to be remembered as a teacher rather than as the inventor of the telephone. Bell's father, Alexander Melville Bell, taught deaf-mutes to speak and wrote textbooks on correct speech. As a boy, Alexander Graham Bell and his brothers helped their father in public demonstrations of Visible Speech, a code of symbols that indicated what position of the throat, tongue, and lips were used in making sounds.

I. The United States Industrializes *(pages 308–309)*

A. With the end of the Civil War, American industry expanded and millions of people left

Geography *Skills*

Answers:
1. on rail lines
2. iron ore and coal

Geography Skills Practice
Ask: Which states had sawmills?
(Michigan and Wisconsin)

✓ **Reading Check**

Answer: fueled economic expansion

Writing a Magazine Article
Have students write a magazine article about one of the new inventions mentioned in this section. Instruct students to write the article as it might have appeared at the time the invention was introduced. **L1**

 Use the rubric for creating a magazine, newspaper, Web site article, or help wanted ad on pages 75–76 in the *Performance Assessment Activities and Rubrics.*

Reading Strategy ◄ **READING THE TEXT**

Taking Notes Students can use notes to group, outline, and organize information. As students read this section, have them create an outline, using heads and subheads, of the main ideas about the rise of industry in America. Then have students write a few sentences summarizing the main ideas they listed in their outline. **L1**

📁 Refer to *Inclusion for the High School Social Studies Classroom Strategies and Activities* in the TCR.

L1/ELL
Guided Reading Activity 9–1

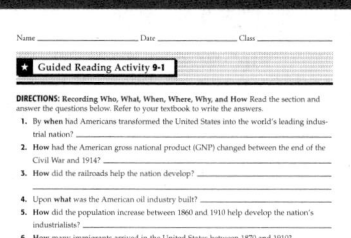

✓ Reading Check

Answer: Laissez-faire relies on supply and demand rather than the government to regulate prices and wages.

Creating a Time Line Have students research one of the inventions featured on the time line that appears on pages 310 and 311. Instruct students to create a time line for significant events related to the chosen invention. For example, a time line for the telephone might include the dates for the invention of the telephone keypad, the cordless telephone, and the cell phone. Encourage students to use library and Internet resources for this project. **L2**

📂 Use the rubric for creating a map, display, or chart on pages 65–66 in the *Performance Assessment Activities and Rubrics.*

American Inventions

1876 Alexander Graham Bell, telephone

1865 Thaddeus Lowe, ice machine

1850

1852 Elisha Otis, elevator brake

1864 George Pullman, rail sleeping car

1865

1874 Stephen Dudley Field, electric streetcar

Free Enterprise

Another important factor that enabled the United States to industrialize rapidly was the free enterprise system. In the late 1800s, many Americans embraced the idea of laissez-faire (leh·say·FAR), literally "let do," a French phrase meaning "let people do as they choose." Supporters of laissez-faire believe the government should not interfere in the economy other than to protect private property rights and maintain peace. These supporters argue that if the government regulates the economy, it increases costs and eventually hurts society more than it helps.

Laissez-faire relies on supply and demand rather than the government to regulate prices and wages. Supporters claim that a free market with competing companies leads to greater efficiency and creates more wealth for everyone. Laissez-faire advocates also support low taxes to ensure that private individuals, not the government, will make most of the decisions about how the nation's wealth is spent. They also believe that the government's debt should be kept limited since money the government borrows from banks is not available to be loaned to individuals for their own uses.

In the United States, the profit motive attracted people of high ability and ambition into business. American entrépreneurs—people who risk their capital in organizing and running a business—appreciated the challenges and rewards of building a business and making profits for themselves.

In the late 1800s, the prospect of making money in manufacturing and transportation attracted many entrepreneurs. The savings that New Englanders accumulated through trade, fishing, whaling, textile mills, and shoe manufacturing helped build hundreds of factories and thousands of miles of railroad track. An equally important source of private capital was Europe, especially Great Britain. Foreign investors saw more opportunity for profit and growth in the United States than at home, and their money also helped to fund the nation's industrial buildup.

✓ Reading Check **Explaining** What does it mean when a government has a laissez-faire economic policy?

Government's Role in Industrialism

In many respects, the United States practiced laissez-faire economics in the late 1800s. State and federal governments kept taxes and spending low and did not impose costly regulations on industry. Nor did they try to control wages and prices. In other ways, the government went beyond laissez-faire and adopted policies intended to help industry, although these policies frequently produced results other than what had been intended.

Since the early 1800s, the struggle between the northeastern states and the southern states had shaped the economic debate in the United States. Northern leaders wanted high tariffs to protect American industry from foreign competition. They also sought federal subsidies for companies building roads, canals, and railroads to the west. Southern leaders opposed subsidizing internal improvements, and they favored low tariffs to promote trade and to keep the cost of imported manufactured goods low.

The Civil War ended this debate. When the South seceded, the Republicans were left in control of Congress. They quickly passed the **Morrill Tariff,**

310 CHAPTER 9 Industrialization

DIFFERENTIATED INSTRUCTION

Reading Support Have each student list the electrical equipment he or she uses during a typical week. Then ask students to identify two adults, one between 40 and 50 years old, and a second between 60 and 70 years old. Have the adults check off the electrical appliances they used as teenagers. Have students discuss what the lists reflect about the recent explosion of inventions. **L1**

📂 Refer to *Inclusion for the High School Social Studies Classroom Strategies and Activities* in the TCR.

1877
Thomas Edison, phonograph

1887
Granville T. Woods, electromechanical brake

1893
Charles and J. Frank Duryea, gasoline-powered car

↟*1880*

↟*1895*

1879
Thomas Edison, incandescent lightbulb

1879
James Ritty, cash register

1883
Jan E. Matzeliger, shoemaking machine

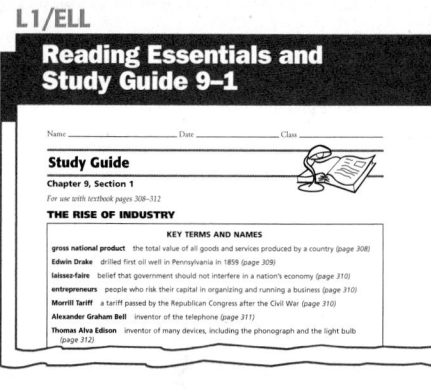

3 ASSESS

Assign Section 1 Assessment as homework or as an in-class activity.

◉ Have students use the **Interactive Tutor Self-Assessment CD-ROM.**

L1/ELL

Reading Essentials and Study Guide 9–1

Name _____ Date _____ Class _____

Study Guide
Chapter 9, Section 1
For use with textbook pages 308–312
THE RISE OF INDUSTRY

KEY TERMS AND NAMES

gross national product the total value of all goods and services produced by a country *(page 308)*
Edwin Drake drilled first oil well in Pennsylvania in 1859 *(page 309)*
laissez-faire belief that government should not interfere in a nation's economy *(page 310)*
entrepreneurs people who risk their capital in organizing and running a business *(page 310)*
Morrill Tariff a tariff passed by the Republican Congress after the Civil War *(page 310)*
Alexander Graham Bell inventor of the telephone *(page 311)*
Thomas Alva Edison inventor of many devices, including the phonograph and the light bulb *(page 312)*

L2

Section Quiz 9–1

Name _____ Date _____ Class _____

★ **Chapter 9**   Score ___

Section Quiz 9-1

DIRECTIONS: Matching Match each item in Column A with the items in Column B. Write the correct letters in the blanks. *(10 points each)*

Column A
___ 1. people who risk their capital in organizing and running a business
___ 2. the total value of all goods and services produced by a country
___ 3. act that reversed years of declining tariffs
___ 4. "let do," a French phrase meaning "let people do as they choose"
___ 5. resource that could be turned into kerosene

Column B
A. Morrill Tariff
B. laissez-faire
C. gross national product
D. petroleum
E. entrepreneurs

DIRECTIONS: Multiple Choice In the blank at the left, write the letter of the choice that

✓ **Reading Check**

Answer: Students' answers will vary. Students might mention that while higher tariffs hurt consumers, they spurred industrialization.

---

reversing years of declining tariffs. By the end of the Civil War, tariffs had risen sharply. Congress also gave vast tracts of western land and millions of dollars in loans to western railroads. The government also sold public lands with mineral resources for much less than their market value. Historians still dispute whether these policies helped to industrialize the country.

Supporters of laissez-faire generally favor free trade and oppose subsidies, believing that tariffs and subsidies drive up prices and protect inefficient companies. They point out that one reason the United States industrialized so rapidly in the 1800s was because it was one of the largest free trade areas in the world. Unlike Europe, which was divided into dozens of states, each with tariffs, the entire United States was open to trade. The Constitution bans states from imposing tariffs, and there were few federal regulations to impede the movement of goods across the country. Similarly, the United States practiced free trade in labor, placing very few restrictions on immigration.

High tariffs, however, contradicted laissez-faire ideas and hurt many Americans. When the United States raised tariffs against foreign goods, other countries raised their tariffs against American goods. This hurt American companies trying to sell goods overseas, and in particular, it hurt farmers who sold their products to Europe. Ironically, the problems farmers faced may have helped speed up industrialization, as many rural Americans decided to leave their farms and take jobs in the new factories.

Despite the problems tariffs created for trade, many business leaders and members of Congress believed they were necessary. Much of Western Europe had already industrialized, and few believed that the new American industries could compete with the large established European factories unless tariffs were put in place to protect them. By the early 1900s, many American industries were large and highly competitive. Business leaders increasingly began to push for free trade because they believed they could compete internationally and win.

✓ **Reading Check** **Analyzing** Do you think government policies at this time helped or hindered industrialization? Why?

New Inventions

A flood of important inventions helped increase the nation's productive capacity and improved the network of transportation and communications that was vital to the nation's industrial growth. New inventions led to the founding of new corporations, which produced new wealth and new jobs.

TECHNOLOGY

Bell and the Telephone One of the most dramatic inventions in the late 1800s came in the field of communications. In 1874 a young Scottish-American inventor named **Alexander Graham Bell** suggested the idea of a telephone to his assistant, Thomas Watson. Watson recalled, "He had an idea by which he believed it would be possible to talk by telegraph." Bell intended to make an electrical current of varying intensity transmit sound.

Bell worked until 1876 before he succeeded in transmitting his voice. Picking up the crude telephone, he called to the next room, "Come here, Watson, I want you." Watson heard and came. The telephone

CHAPTER 9 Industrialization **311**

INTERDISCIPLINARY CONNECTIONS ACTIVITY

Science Invite a science teacher or a representative of a telephone company to demonstrate the science behind the invention of the telephone and discuss the science involved in cellular communications. Encourage students to ask questions. After the presentation, discuss how the standard telephone and cellular telephone have changed the way people communicate with one another. List the advantages and disadvantages of telephone communications. **L2**

ABCNEWS INTERACTIVE™

VIDEOCASSETTE
Historic America Electronic Field Trips

View **Tape 2, Chapter 5**: "Thomas Edison's Lab."

Reteach
Have students identify the effects of expanding population on industry.

Enrich
Have interested students write a report on the various uses of petroleum, including kerosene, diesel fuel, and gasoline.

Reading Check

Answer: revolutionized business by opening up entirely new markets for inventions and goods to sell

HISTORY Online

Study Central™ provides summaries, interactive games, and online graphic organizers to help students review section content.

4 CLOSE

Have students explain the effects of technological innovations such as the telephone and telegraph on American industrial development.

---

revolutionized both business and personal communication. In 1877 Bell and others organized the Bell Telephone Company, which eventually became the American Telephone and Telegraph Company (AT&T).

Edison and Electricity Perhaps the most famous inventor of the late 1800s was **Thomas Alva Edison.** A great innovator, Edison worked tirelessly to invent new products and to improve devices created by others. His laboratory at Menlo Park, New Jersey, staffed by skilled assistants, became the forerunner of the modern research laboratory. Edison stood as a symbol for the emerging age of technology.

Edison first achieved international fame in 1877 with the invention of the phonograph. Two years later, Edison perfected the lightbulb and the electric generator. His laboratory then went on to invent or improve several other major devices, including the battery, the dictaphone, the mimeograph (an early copying machine), and the motion picture.

In 1882 the Edison Electric Illuminating Company launched a new industry and began the transformation of American society when it began to supply electric power to customers in New York City. In 1889 several of Edison's companies merged to form the Edison General Electric Company, which today is known as GE.

Technology's Impact As knowledge about technology grew, almost everyone in the United States felt its effects. Shortly after the Civil War, Thaddeus Lowe invented the ice machine, the basis of the refrigerator.

In the early 1870s, Gustavus Swift hired an engineer to develop a refrigerated railroad car. In 1877 Swift shipped the first refrigerated load of fresh meat. The widespread use of refrigeration allowed food to be kept fresh longer and reduced the risk of disease from food poisoning.

The textile industry had long depended on machines to turn fibers into cloth. By the mid-1800s, the introduction of the Northrop automatic loom allowed cloth to be made at an even faster rate. Bobbins, which previously had been changed by hand, were now changed automatically without stopping the loom.

Great changes also took place in the clothing industry. Standard sizes, developed from measurements taken of Union soldiers during the Civil War, were used in the manufacture of ready-made clothes. Power-driven sewing machines and cloth cutters rapidly moved the clothing business from small tailor shops to large factories.

Similar changes took place in shoemaking. New processes and inventions made increased production possible in the shoe industry. Large factories could mass-produce shoes more cheaply and efficiently than local cobblers and could pass these savings on to their customers in the form of lower prices. By 1900 local cobblers had nearly disappeared. Prices of many other products also dropped as the United States industrialized.

✓ **Reading Check** **Explaining** How did the use of electric power affect the economic development of the United States?

HISTORY Online **Study Central™** To review this section, go to **tarvol2.glencoe.com** and click on **Study Central™**.

SECTION 1 ASSESSMENT

Checking for Understanding
1. **Define:** gross national product, laissez-faire, entrepreneur.
2. **Identify:** Edwin Drake, Morrill Tariff, Alexander Graham Bell, Thomas Alva Edison.
3. **Explain** how an abundance of natural resources contributed to economic growth in the United States in the late 1800s.

Reviewing Themes
4. **Economic Factors** How did the principles of the free enterprise system, laissez-faire, and profit motive encourage the rise of industry?

Critical Thinking
5. **Synthesizing** What role did the federal government play in increasing industrialization in the United States after the Civil War?
6. **Organizing** Use a graphic organizer similar to the one below to indicate how the inventions listed affected the nature of American work and business.

Invention	Effects
telephone	
lightbulb	
automatic loom	

Analyzing Visuals
7. **Applying Time Lines** Copy the time line on pages 310 and 311 onto a separate sheet of paper. Add other inventions you have learned about to the time line in proper chronological order. Be sure to include the date for each invention.

Writing About History
8. **Descriptive Writing** Imagine you are a young person living in this country in the late 1800s. Choose one of the inventions discussed in the section, and write a journal entry describing its impact on your life. Use standard grammar, spelling, sentence structure, and punctuation.

312 CHAPTER 9 Industrialization

SECTION 1 ASSESSMENT ANSWERS

1. Terms are in blue.
2. Edwin Drake *(p. 309)*, Morrill Tariff *(p. 310)*, Alexander Graham Bell *(p. 311)*, Thomas Alva Edison *(p. 312)*
3. Americans did not have to import resources from other countries, saving resources for internal growth.

4. They put development in the hands of entrepreneurs, not the government.
5. Congress subsidized railroads; sold lands below market value
6. telephone: better communications; lightbulb: cheap lighting; automatic loom: made cloth faster

7. possible answers: 1859, first oil well dug; 1882, Edison Electric Illuminating Company supplies electric power to New York City; 1877, first refrigerated railroad car; 1893, Northrup automatic loom
8. Students' journal entries will vary.

The Wright Brothers Triumph at Kitty Hawk

Why Learn the Skill?

Just as you are about to leave home to catch your school bus, you hear a radio report. Firefighters are battling a blaze near the bus garage. Your bus is late. Although no one told you, you know that the fire disrupted the bus schedule. You have made an *inference*. From the limited facts available, you formed a conclusion. By combining facts and general knowledge, you inferred that the fire trucks delayed your bus.

Learning the Skill

Learning how to make inferences will help you draw conclusions about particular situations. To make accurate inferences, follow these steps:

- Read or listen carefully for stated facts and ideas.
- Review what you already know about the same topic or situation.
- Use logic and common sense to form a conclusion about the topic.
- If possible, find information that proves or disproves your inference.

Practicing the Skill

Read the following passage about early airplanes, and then answer the questions that follow.

On December 8, 1903, Samuel Langley was ready for his second attempt at flying a manned, self-propelled aircraft. This had never been done before.

Langley used a $50,000 U.S. government grant to build a plane based on unmanned aircraft designs, adding a very powerful engine. The plane broke apart on takeoff and crashed into the Potomac River.

In contrast, Wilbur and Orville Wright used a little more than $1,000 of their personal savings to build their aircraft. The brothers carefully studied the problems with previous planes and designed one with better wings, a more efficient propeller, and a strong but light engine. On December 17, 1903, these intrepid Americans made the first manned, powered flight in history on the sand dunes of Kitty Hawk, North Carolina.

First flight at Kitty Hawk, December 17, 1903

❶ What are the facts regarding Langley's attempt?

❷ What are the facts regarding the Wright brothers' attempt?

❸ What inferences might you draw based on the success of the Wright brothers and failure of Langley?

Skills Assessment

Complete the Practicing Skills questions on page 333 and the Chapter 9 Skill Reinforcement Activity to assess your mastery of this skill.

Applying the Skill

Making Inferences Reread the American Story about Thomas Edison on page 308, then answer these questions.

1. What device did inventors struggle to develop for much of the 1800s?

2. Why did Edison want to develop this new device?

3. Based on these facts, what inference can you make about Thomas Edison's methods? What inference can you make about how his invention would affect the economy?

 Glencoe's **Skillbuilder Interactive Workbook CD-ROM, Level 2,** provides instruction and practice in key social studies skills.

313

TEACH

Making Inferences Point out to students that we make inferences daily. Their accuracy is based on previous knowledge and experiences, fact-gathering, and using logic.

Read students an encyclopedia entry on Thomas Alva Edison. Have students list the facts in the article. Then ask them to make inferences about Edison's life and the company he founded.

Additional Practice

L1

Reinforcing Skills Activity 9

Name _____ Date _____ Class _____

★ Reinforcing Skills Activity 9

Making Inferences

◻ LEARNING THE SKILL

When you make inferences, you "read between the lines," or draw conclusions that are not stated directly. To help draw inferences, first read carefully for stated facts and ideas. Summarize the information and list the important facts. Then apply related information that you may already know to make inferences. Use your knowledge and insight to develop some conclusions about the facts.

◻ PRACTICING THE SKILL

DIRECTIONS: The excerpt below is taken from a personal memo written by Andrew Carnegie in 1868. Read the excerpt, and then answer the questions below in the space provided.

Man must have an idol—The amassing of wealth is one of the worst species of idolatry. No idol more debasing than the worship of money. Whatever I engage in I must push inordinately there-

GLENCOE
TECHNOLOGY

 CD-ROM
Glencoe Skillbuilder Interactive Workbook CD-ROM, Level 2

This interactive CD-ROM reinforces student mastery of essential social studies skills.

ANSWERS TO PRACTICING THE SKILL

❶ He used a large government grant and a powerful engine. The plane broke apart and crashed.

❷ The Wrights used their own money, studied previous designs, built a lightweight engine and better wings, and successfully flew.

❸ Possible inferences are that government grants cannot substitute for entrepreneurial initiative and the willingness to learn from mistakes.

Applying the Skill

1. the electric incandescent lamp or light bulb

2. Light bulbs would be cheaper, safer, and brighter than existing methods.

3. Answers will vary but may include that light bulbs would lead to an electrical industry and make candles and oil lamps obsolete.

The Railroads

1 FOCUS

Section Overview

This section focuses on how the growth of railroads affected the growth of industries.

Reading Preview

Answers to Graphic: development of time zones, sped long-distance transportation, longer and heavier trains used, rate per mile declined, united America's regions, promoted a national market

Preteaching Vocabulary
Have students write short sentences to describe each of the Key Names.

Main Idea
After the Civil War, the rapid construction of railroads accelerated the nation's industrialization and linked the country together.

Key Terms and Names
Pacific Railway Act, Grenville Dodge, Leland Stanford, Cornelius Vanderbilt, time zone, land grant, Jay Gould, Crédit Mobilier, James J. Hill

Reading Strategy
Organizing As you read about the development of a nationwide rail network, complete a graphic organizer similar to the one below listing the effects of this rail network on the nation.

Nationwide Rail Network → Effects

Reading Objectives
- **Discuss** ways in which the railroads spurred industrial growth.
- **Analyze** how the railroads were financed and how they grew.

Section Theme
Individual Action The railroads provided new ways for some Americans to amass wealth.

Preview of Events

◆1870   ◆1875   ◆1880   ◆1885

1869
First transcontinental railroad completed

1872
Crédit Mobilier scandal takes place

1873
First direct rail service between New York and Chicago begins

1883
Time zones instituted

★ An American Story ★

Grenville Dodge

At Promontory Summit, Utah, on May 10, 1869, hundreds of spectators gathered to watch a historic event. Dignitaries from the East and the West met to hammer gold and silver spikes into the final rails that would join two great railroad lines—the Union Pacific and Central Pacific—and span the entire country.

Telegraph offices around the country stood ready to receive news that the last spike had been driven. When the news arrived, bells pealed across the nation, and even the Liberty Bell was rung. In Chicago a seven-mile procession paraded through the streets, and the pealings of church bells resonated throughout the nation's small towns. General Grenville Dodge, who had overseen part of the construction, observed:

❝The trains pulled up facing each other, each crowded with workmen who sought advantageous positions to witness the ceremonies. . . . The officers and invited guests formed on each side of the track. . . . Prayer was offered; a number of spikes were driven in the two adjoining rails . . . and thus the two roads were welded into one great trunk line from the Atlantic to the Pacific.❞

—quoted in *Mine Eyes Have Seen*

Linking the Nation

In 1865 the United States had about 35,000 miles of railroad track, almost all of it east of the Mississippi River. After the Civil War, railroad construction expanded dramatically, linking the distant regions of the nation in a transportation network. By 1900 the United States, now a booming industrial power, boasted over 200,000 miles of track.

SECTION RESOURCES

📁 **Reproducible Masters**
- Reproducible Lesson Plan 9–2
- Daily Lecture and Discussion Notes 9–2
- Guided Reading Activity 9–2
- Section Quiz 9–2
- Reading Essentials and Study Guide 9–2
- Performance Assessment Activities and Rubrics

🎞 **Transparencies**
- Daily Focus Skills Transparency 9–2

Multimedia
- 💿 Interactive Tutor Self-Assessment CD-ROM
- 💿 ExamView® Pro Testmaker CD-ROM
- 💿 Presentation Plus! CD-ROM
- 💿 TeacherWorks™ CD-ROM
- 🎧 Audio Program

The railroad boom began in 1862 when President Abraham Lincoln signed the **Pacific Railway Act.** This act provided for the construction of a transcontinental railroad by two corporations, the Union Pacific and the Central Pacific railroad companies. To encourage rapid construction, the government offered each company land along its right-of-way. Feverish competition between the two companies developed, as each sought to obtain as much public land and money as possible.

The Union Pacific and Grenville Dodge Under the direction of engineer **Grenville Dodge,** a former Union general, the Union Pacific began pushing westward from Omaha, Nebraska, in 1865.

The laborers faced blizzards in the mountains, scorching heat in the desert, and sometimes angry Native Americans. Labor, money, and engineering problems plagued the supervisors of the project. As Dodge observed:

> ❝At one time we were using at least ten thousand animals, and most of the time from eight to ten thousand laborers. . . . To supply one mile of track with material and supplies required about forty cars. . . . Everything—rails, ties, bridging, fastenings, all

railway supplies, fuel for locomotives and trains, and supplies for men and animals on the entire work— had to be transported from the Missouri River.❞

—quoted in *The Growth of the American Republic*

The railroad workers included Civil War veterans, new immigrants from Ireland recruited especially for the task, frustrated miners and farmers, cooks, adventurers, and ex-convicts. At the height of the project, the Union Pacific employed about 10,000 workers. While most of the laborers camped along the line, about one-fourth of them slept three-deep in bunk beds on rolling boarding cars. Camp life was rough, dirty, and dangerous, with lots of gambling, hard drinking, and fighting.

The Big Four and the Central Pacific The Central Pacific Railroad began as the dream of engineer Theodore Dehone Judah, who convinced the California legislature to organize a state railroad convention to support his idea. He sold stock in his fledgling Central Pacific Railroad Company to four Sacramento merchants: grocer Leland Stanford, shop owner Charley Crocker, and hardware store owners Mark Hopkins and Collis P. Huntington.

These so-called "Big Four" eventually made huge fortunes from their investment. **Leland Stanford**

Picturing **History**

Engineering Victory The Union Pacific and Central Pacific were joined near Ogden, Utah. The last spike driven was made of gold. It was quickly removed and kept as a symbol. What did the event mean for the nation's commerce?

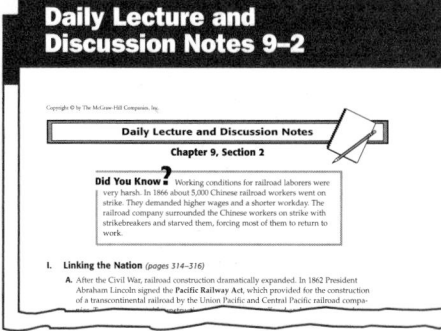
2 TEACH

Daily Lecture and Discussion Notes 9–2

Picturing **History**

Answer: The country now had the means to ship raw materials and finished goods coast to coast.
Ask: Who do you think the men who are shaking hands are? *(representatives of the Union Pacific and the Central Pacific railroads)*

Creating a Thematic Map Tell students that before railroads stretched across the country, communities determined their own times. Have students discuss why railroads needed to standardize times. Then have students create a time zone map of the continental United States and Canada that could be posted in a train depot. **L1**

📁 Use the rubric for creating a map, display, or chart on pages 65–66 in the *Performance Assessment Activities and Rubrics.*

Reading Strategy | READING THE TEXT

Making Inferences When students make inferences, they use their reason and their experience to make educated guesses about what an author implies or suggests. To help students learn how to make inferences, show them how to look for clues in the text. Encourage students to notice descriptions, events, or relationships that might signal information a writer is suggesting. Ask students to think about what they already know, either from prior text clues or from their own experiences. **L1**

📁 Refer to *Inclusion for the High School Social Studies Classroom Strategies and Activities* in the TCR.

Guided Reading Activity 9–2

Reading Check

Answer: a shortage of laborers in California

World History Connection

Background: A passenger train traveling the Trans-Siberian route takes seven days to complete the journey from Moscow to Vladivostok.

Answer: Towns would prosper during and after the construction.

Ask: How different do you think the conditions were for workers on the Trans-Siberian line compared to the transcontinental railroad in the United States? *(Students' answers will vary. They might mention that weather conditions might have been worse in Siberia.)*

HISTORY Online

Objectives and answers to the student activity can be found in the **Web Activity Lesson Plan** at tarvol2.glencoe.com.

became governor of California and later served as a United States senator after founding Stanford University in 1885.

Because of a shortage of labor in California, the Central Pacific Railroad hired about 10,000 workers from China. All the equipment—rails, cars, locomotives, and machinery—was shipped from the East, either around Cape Horn at the tip of South America or over the Isthmus of Panama in Central America.

Reading Check **Examining** Why were many workers on the Central Pacific Railroad recruited from China?

Railroads Spur Growth

The transcontinental railroad was the first of many lines that began to crisscross the nation after the Civil War. This expansion spurred American industrial growth. By linking the nation, railroads helped increase the size of markets for many products. Huge consumers themselves, the railroads also stimulated the economy by spending extraordinary amounts of money on steel, coal, timber, and other necessities.

Linking Other Lines In the early 1800s, most railroads had been built to promote specific cities or to serve local needs. By 1865 hundreds of small

World History Connection

The Trans-Siberian Railroad

Nearly 50 years after Americans completed their transcontinental railroad, the Russians hammered the final spike into their own cross-country rail line. Begun in 1891 and completed in 1916, the Trans-Siberian Railroad was the longest in the world, running nearly 5,800 miles (9,330 km) from Moscow in the west to Vladivostok on the Sea of Japan in the east. Like the American railroads, the Trans-Siberian line opened up the way for trade and settlement throughout Russia's frontier—an arctic, windswept land known as Siberia.
How might the construction of a railroad affect towns along the line?

unconnected lines existed. The challenge for eastern capitalists was to create a single rail transportation system from this maze of small companies.

Railroad consolidation proceeded rapidly from 1865 to 1900. Large rail lines took over about 400 small railroads, and by 1890 the Pennsylvania Railroad was a consolidation of 73 smaller companies. Eventually seven giant systems with terminals in major cities and scores of branches reaching into the countryside controlled most rail traffic.

One of the most famous and successful railroad consolidators was **Cornelius Vanderbilt**, a former boat captain who had built the largest steamboat fleet in America. By 1869 Vanderbilt had purchased and merged three short New York railroads to form the New York Central, running from New York City to Buffalo. Within four years he had extended his control over lines all the way to Chicago, which enabled him to offer the first direct rail service between New York City and Chicago. In 1871 Vanderbilt began construction of New York's Grand Central terminal.

The Benefits of a National System Before the 1880s each community set its clocks by the sun's position in the sky at high noon. At noon in Chicago, for example, it was 12:50 P.M. in Washington, D.C., 12:09 P.M. in Louisville, Kentucky, and 11:41 A.M. in St. Paul, Minnesota. Local time interfered with train scheduling and at times even threatened passenger safety. When two trains traveled on the same track, collisions could result from scheduling errors caused by variations in time.

To make rail service safer and more reliable, in 1883 the American Railway Association divided the country into four time zones in regions where the same time was kept. The federal government ratified this change in 1918.

Large integrated railroad systems benefited the nation. They were able to shift cars from one section of the country to another according to seasonal needs and in order to speed long-distance transportation. At the same time, new locomotive technology and the introduction of air brakes enabled railroads to put longer and heavier trains on their lines. The new rail systems, along with more powerful locomotives,

HISTORY Online

Student Web Activity Visit the *American Republic Since 1877* Web site at tarvol2.glencoe.com and click on **Student Web Activities—Chapter 9** for an activity on industrialization.

DIFFERENTIATED INSTRUCTION

Gifted and Talented Encourage students to use library and Internet resources to find drawings and diagrams of Edwin Drake's oil well. Then have students make a model of the well. Allow students to choose the construction material they wish to use. For students who need additional guidance, suggest making the model using 1-inch by 1-inch pinewood trim and 1.5-inch flat pine molding on a plywood base. Models should have labels explaining the parts and how they worked. **L3**

Refer to *Inclusion for the High School Social Studies Classroom Strategies and Activities* in the TCR.

NATIONAL GEOGRAPHIC Railroads, 1870 and 1890
In Motion

Pacific Time Zone
Mountain Time Zone
Central Time Zone
Eastern Time Zone
+++ Railroads built by 1870
+++ Railroads built by 1890
*Time zones and borders shown as of 1890

Miles of Track, 1870–1890

Total Miles of Railroad Operating (in thousands)

Source: *Historical Statistics of the United States: Colonial Times to 1970.*

Geography *Skills*

1. **Interpreting Maps** What part of the United States saw the greatest expansion in rail lines by 1890?
2. **Applying Geography Skills** In which time zone did the Central Pacific originate?

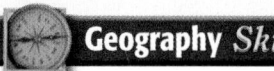

Geography *Skills*

Answers:
1. Great Plains
2. Pacific

Geography Skills Practice
Ask: What was the only California city that you could reach by train in 1870? *(San Francisco)*

✔ **Reading Check**

Answer: to make rail service safer and more reliable

✔ **Reading Check**

Answer: land grants

3 ASSESS

Assign Section 2 Assessment as homework or as an in-class activity.

🔵 Have students use the **Interactive Tutor Self-Assessment CD-ROM.**

L1/ELL

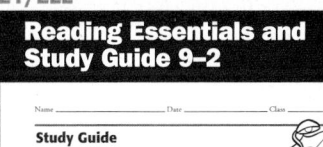

Reading Essentials and Study Guide 9–2

---

made railroad operation so efficient that the average rate per mile for a ton of freight dropped from two cents in 1860 to three-fourths of a cent in 1900.

The nationwide rail network also helped unite Americans in different regions. Looking back at a quarter century of railroad travel, the *Omaha Daily Republican* observed in 1883 that railroads had "made the people of the country homogeneous, breaking through the peculiarities and provincialisms which marked separate and unmingling sections." This was, perhaps, an overstatement, but it recognized a significant contribution that railroads made to the nation.

✔ **Reading Check** **Explaining** Why did the American Railway Association divide the country into four time zones?

The Land Grant System

Building and operating railroad lines, especially across the vast unsettled regions of the West, often required more money than most private investors could raise on their own. To encourage railroad construction, the federal government gave land grants to many railroad companies. Railroads would then

sell the land to settlers, real estate companies, and other businesses to raise the money they needed to build the railroad.

In the 1850s, the federal government granted individual states over 28 million acres of public lands to give to the railroads. After the Pacific Railway Acts of 1862 and 1864, the government gave the land directly to the railroad companies.

During the 1850s and 1860s, the federal land grant system awarded railroad companies over 120 million acres of land, an area larger than New England, New York, and Pennsylvania combined. Several railroad companies, including the Union Pacific and the Central Pacific, earned enough money from the government's generous land grants to cover much of the cost of building their lines.

✔ **Reading Check** **Summarizing** How did the government help finance railroads?

Robber Barons

The great wealth many railroad entrepreneurs acquired in the late 1800s led to accusations that they had built their fortunes by swindling investors and

CHAPTER 9 Industrialization **317**

INTERDISCIPLINARY CONNECTIONS ACTIVITY

Daily Life Tell students that the transcontinental railroad that was completed in 1869 was built with a great deal of immigrant labor, especially immigrants newly arrived from Ireland and China. Have interested students consider the daily experiences that Irish and Chinese railroad laborers faced while constructing the transcontinental railroad and then have them write a letter to family members back home detailing these daily experiences. Tell students that the letters should reflect the challenges faced by someone newly arrived in the United States at that time, but also demonstrate any opportunities being in the United States would provide. **L2**

Time Tales Opponents of standard time called local time "God's time" because it was based on the laws of nature—the sun's position in the sky. Not until 1918 was Congress able to pass a law that standardized time zones.

Reteach

Have students analyze how the railroads were financed.

Enrich

Have students research and write a report on one of the railroad tycoons.

Answer: shipped goods both ways, operated without aid, and was a financial success

HISTORY Online

Study Central™ provides summaries, interactive games, and online graphic organizers to help students review section content.

4 CLOSE

Have students discuss ways in which the railroads spurred industrial growth.

taxpayers, bribing government officials, and cheating on their contracts and debts. The person with probably the worst reputation for this kind of activity was **Jay Gould,** who often practiced "insider trading." He used information he received as a railroad owner to manipulate stock prices to his benefit.

Bribery occurred frequently in this era, partly because the state and federal governments were so deeply entangled in funding the railroads. Railroad investors quickly discovered that they could make more money by acquiring government land grants than by operating the railroad. As a result, many investors bribed members of Congress and the state legislatures to vote for more grants.

The Crédit Mobilier Scandal The corruption in the railroad industry became public in 1872 when the Crédit Mobilier scandal erupted. **Crédit Mobilier** was a construction company set up by several stockholders of the Union Pacific, including Oakes Ames, a member of Congress. Acting for both the Union Pacific and Crédit Mobilier, the investors signed contracts with themselves. Crédit Mobilier greatly overcharged Union Pacific for the work it did, and since the same investors controlled both companies, the railroad agreed to pay the inflated bills.

By the time the Union Pacific railroad was completed, the investors had made several million dollars, but the railroad itself had used up its federal grants and was almost bankrupt. To convince Congress to give the railroad more grants, Ames gave other members of Congress shares in the Union Pacific at a price well below their market value.

During the election campaign of 1872, a disgruntled associate of Ames sent a letter to the *New York Sun* listing the members of Congress who had accepted shares. The scandal led to an investigation that implicated several members of Congress, including Speaker of the House James G. Blaine and James Garfield, who later became president. It also revealed that Vice President Schuyler Colfax had accepted stock from the railroad.

The Great Northern The Crédit Mobilier scandal provided sensational newspaper headlines. It created the impression that all railroad entrepreneurs were robber barons—people who loot an industry and give nothing back—but the term was not always deserved.

One railroad entrepreneur who was clearly not a robber baron was **James J. Hill.** Hill built and operated the Great Northern Railroad from St. Paul, Minnesota, to Everett, Washington, without any federal land grants or subsidies. He built the Great Northern across good land, carefully planning his route to pass by towns in the region. To increase business, he offered low fares to settlers who homesteaded along his route. He then identified American products that were in demand in China, including cotton, textiles, and flour, and arranged to haul those goods to Washington for shipment to Asia. This enabled the railroad to earn money by hauling goods both east and west, instead of simply sending lumber and farm products east and coming back empty, as many other railroads did. Operating without government subsidies or land grants, the Great Northern became the most successful transcontinental railroad and the only one that was not eventually forced into bankruptcy.

✓ **Reading Check** **Describing** How was the Great Northern different from other railroads of the time?

HISTORY Online **Study Central™** To review this section, go to **tarvol2.glencoe.com** and click on **Study Central™**.

SECTION 2 ASSESSMENT

Checking for Understanding
1. **Define:** time zone, land grant.
2. **Identify:** Pacific Railway Act, Grenville Dodge, Leland Stanford, Cornelius Vanderbilt, Jay Gould, Crédit Mobilier, James J. Hill.
3. **Explain** the provisions of the Pacific Railway Act.

Reviewing Themes
4. **Individual Action** How did Grenville Dodge contribute to the economic growth of the United States in the late 1800s?

Critical Thinking
5. **Synthesizing** How did railroad expansion in the United States lead to industrial growth?
6. **Organizing** Use a graphic organizer similar to the one below to list the different ways that railroads were financed.

Ways Railroads Were Financed

Analyzing Visuals
7. **Examining Maps and Graphs** Study the map and the graph on page 317. Then make up a quiz of at least five questions based on the information presented.

Writing About History
8. **Persuasive Writing** Take on the role of an employee of a major railroad corporation. Your job assignment is to write an advertisement to recruit workers for your corporation. After writing the advertisement, present it to your class.

318   CHAPTER 9   Industrialization

SECTION 2 ASSESSMENT ANSWERS

1. Terms are in blue.
2. Pacific Railway Act (p. 315), Grenville Dodge (p. 315), Leland Stanford (p. 315), Cornelius Vanderbilt (p. 316), Jay Gould (p. 318), Crédit Mobilier (p. 318), James J. Hill (p. 318)
3. provided for the construction of the transcontinental railroad
4. supervised the Union Pacific's westward expansion
5. increased size of markets, spent great amounts of money on resources
6. land grants, private investment, gifts of public lands to railroads, money generated from running the railroads
7. Students' quizzes will vary. Students should include answers for their quiz questions.
8. Students' advertisements will vary. Advertisements should include a list of benefits.

Guide to Reading

Main Idea
After the Civil War, big business assumed a more prominent role in American life.

Key Terms and Names
corporation, stockholder, stock, economies of scale, fixed costs, operating costs, pool, Andrew Carnegie, Bessemer process, vertical integration, horizontal integration, monopoly, trust, holding company

Reading Strategy
Organizing As you read about the rise of corporations in the United States, complete a graphic organizer similar to the one below to describe the steps large business owners took to weaken or eliminate competition.

Slashed prices temporarily → □ → □ → □

Reading Objectives
• **Analyze** how large corporations came to dominate American business.
• **Evaluate** how Andrew Carnegie's innovations transformed the steel industry.

Section Theme
Economic Factors Large national corporations formed in the United States in the mid-1800s and contributed to greater production.

Preview of Events

♦1865	♦1875	♦1885	♦1895

1862 John D. Rockefeller buys first oil refinery

1875 Andrew Carnegie opens steel mill in Pittsburgh

1879 Woolworth's chain store opens

1882 Dow Jones & Company founded

1901 J.P. Morgan forms U.S. Steel

★ *An American Story* ★

In the 1860s, the oil industry in the United States was highly competitive. One highly efficient company was Standard Oil, owned by John D. Rockefeller and his associates. Because his company shipped so much oil, Rockefeller was able to negotiate rebates, or refunds, from railroads that wanted his business. This gave his company an advantage, and he began to pressure other oil companies to sell out to him.

Oil producer Franklin Tarbell pledged never to surrender. Tarbell's daughter Ida later recalled her father's indignation over Rockefeller's maneuvers:

66 It was as if somebody had tried to crowd me off the road. . . . There were rules, you couldn't use the road unless you obeyed those rules. . . . The railroads—so said my father—ran through the valley by the consent of the people; they had given them a right of way. The road on which I trotted was a right of way. One man had the same right as another, but the railroads had given to one something they would not give to another. . . . The strong wrested from the railroads the privilege of preying upon the weak. 99

—quoted in *All in the Day's Work*

Cartoon of John D. Rockefeller

The Rise of Big Business

Before the Civil War, the personal wealth of a few people operating in partnership financed most businesses, including many early factories. Most manufacturing enterprises were very small. By 1900 everything had changed. Big businesses dominated the economy, operating vast complexes of factories, warehouses, offices, and distribution facilities.

CHAPTER 9 Industrialization **319**

---

1 FOCUS

Section Overview
This section focuses on how big business became important in American life.

BELLRINGER
Skillbuilder Activity

Project transparency and have students answer the question.

Daily Focus Skills Transparency 9–3

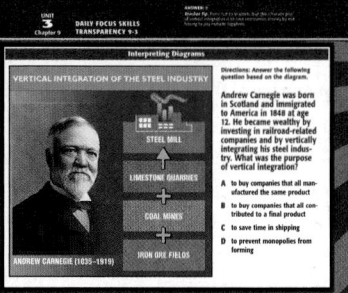

Reading Preview

Answers to Graphic: pools, vertical and horizontal integration, holding companies, trusts

Preteaching Vocabulary
Have students use a standard dictionary to look up the Key Terms in this section to gain a better understanding of them.

SECTION RESOURCES

📂 **Reproducible Masters**
• Reproducible Lesson Plan 9–3
• Daily Lecture and Discussion Notes 9–3
• Guided Reading Activity 9–3
• Section Quiz 9–3
• Reading Essentials and Study Guide 9–3

📖 **Transparencies**
• Daily Focus Skills Transparency 9–3

• American Art & Architecture

Multimedia
🞂 Interactive Tutor Self-Assessment CD-ROM
🞂 ExamView® Pro Testmaker CD-ROM
🞂 Presentation Plus! CD-ROM
🞂 TeacherWorks™ CD-ROM
🞂 Audio Program

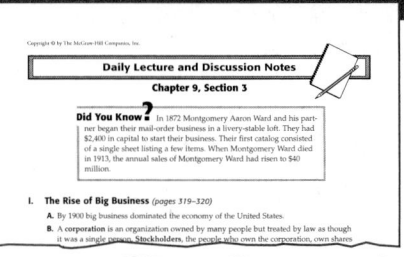

2 TEACH

**Daily Lecture and
Discussion Notes 9–3**

Copyright © by The McGraw-Hill Companies, Inc.

Daily Lecture and Discussion Notes

Chapter 9, Section 3

Did You Know? In 1872 Montgomery Aaron Ward and his partner began their mail-order business in a livery-stable loft. They had $2,400 in capital to start their business. Their first catalog consisted of a single sheet listing a few items. When Montgomery Ward died in 1913, the annual sales of Montgomery Ward had risen to $40 million.

I. The Rise of Big Business *(pages 319–320)*

A. By 1900 big business dominated the economy of the United States.

B. A **corporation** is an organization owned by many people but treated by law as though it was a single person. **Stockholders**, the people who own the corporation, own shares

 Reading Check

Answer: general incorporation laws and economies of scale

Creating a Profile Encourage students to use library and Internet resources to learn about a local philanthropist—past or present. Instruct students to prepare a short fact sheet for the person they select. **L1**

FYI

In 1898, although Carnegie Steel's output had risen threefold over the previous few years, the number of workers needed to produce the steel had decreased by 400. The use of electricity to drive automatic machinery was largely responsible for the decline in the workforce.

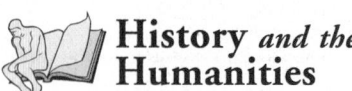
History *and the* Humanities

 American Art & Architecture: Smoking Room of the John D. Rockefeller House

---

ECONOMICS

The Role of Corporations Big business would not have been possible without the corporation. A corporation is an organization owned by many people but treated by law as though it were a single person. A corporation can own property, pay taxes, make contracts, and sue and be sued. The people who own the corporation are called **stockholders** because they own shares of ownership called **stock.** Issuing stock allows a corporation to raise large amounts of money for big projects while spreading out the financial risk.

Before the 1830s, there were few corporations in the United States because entrepreneurs had to convince a state legislature to issue them a charter. Beginning in the 1830s, however, states began passing general incorporation laws, allowing companies to become corporations and issue stock without charters from the legislature.

Economies of Scale With the money they raised from the sale of stock, corporations could invest in new technologies, hire a large workforce, and purchase many machines, greatly increasing their efficiency. This enabled them to achieve what is called economies of scale, in which corporations make goods more cheaply because they produce so much so quickly using large manufacturing facilities.

All businesses have two kinds of costs, fixed costs and operating (or variable) costs. Fixed costs are costs a company has to pay, whether or not it is operating. For example, a company would have to pay its loans, mortgages, and taxes, regardless of whether it was operating. Operating costs are costs that occur when running a company, such as paying wages and shipping charges and buying raw materials and other supplies.

The small manufacturing companies that had been typical before the Civil War usually had very low fixed costs but very high operating costs. If sales dropped, it was cheaper to shut down and wait for better economic conditions. By comparison, big companies had very high fixed costs because it took so much money to build and maintain a factory. Compared to their fixed costs, big businesses had low operating costs. Wages and transportation costs were such a small part of a corporation's costs that it made sense to keep operating, even in a recession.

In these circumstances, big corporations had several advantages. They could produce goods more cheaply and efficiently. They could continue to operate in poor economic times by cutting prices to increase sales, rather than shutting down. Many were

320 CHAPTER 9 Industrialization

---

also able to negotiate rebates from the railroads, thus lowering their operating costs even further.

Small businesses with high operating costs found it difficult to compete against large corporations, and many were forced out of business. At the time, many people criticized corporations for cutting prices and negotiating rebates. They believed the corporations were behaving unethically by using their wealth to drive small companies out of business. In many cases, the changing nature of business organization and the new importance of fixed costs that caused competition to become so severe forced many small companies out of business.

✓ **Reading Check** **Describing** What factors led to the rise of big business in the United States?

The Consolidation of Industry

Many corporate leaders did not like the intense competition that had been forced on them. Although falling prices benefited consumers, they cut into profits. To stop prices from falling, many companies organized pools, or agreements to maintain prices at a certain level.

American courts and legislatures were suspicious of pools because they interfered with competition and property rights. As a result, companies that formed pools had no legal protection and could not enforce their agreements in court. Pools generally did not last long. They broke apart whenever one member cut prices to steal the market share from another, which then allowed competition to resume. By the 1870s, competition had reduced many industries to a few large and highly efficient corporations.

Andrew Carnegie and Steel The remarkable life of **Andrew Carnegie** illustrates many of the different factors that led to industrialism and the rise of big business in the United States. He was born in Scotland, the son of a poor hand weaver who emigrated to the United States in 1848. At a young age, Carnegie worked as a bobbin boy in a textile factory earning $1.20 per week. At 14 he became a messenger in a telegraph office, then served as private secretary to Thomas Scott, a superintendent and later president of the Pennsylvania Railroad. Carnegie's energy impressed Scott, and when Scott was promoted, Carnegie succeeded him as superintendent.

As a railroad supervisor, Carnegie knew that he could make a lot of money by investing in companies that served the railroad industry. He bought shares in iron mills and factories that made sleeping cars and

---

Reading Strategy | READING THE TEXT

Analyzing Information Have students create a chart with the following headings: *corporation, economies of scale, pool, vertical integration, horizontal integration, trust,* and *holding company.* Students should fill in the space under each heading with information as they read this section. For each of these items, they should define what they are, identify their exact features, and determine how they impacted business in the United States. **L1**

Refer to *Inclusion for the High School Social Studies Classroom Strategies and Activities* in the TCR.

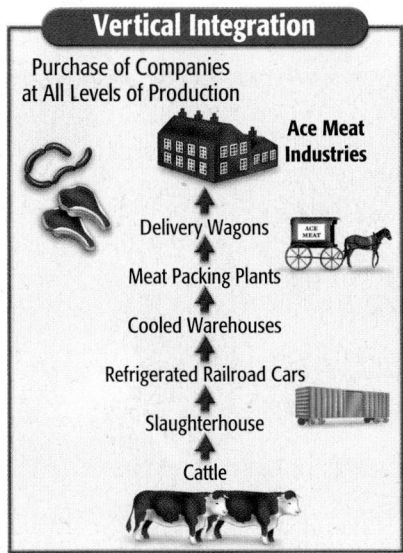

Vertical Integration

Purchase of Companies at All Levels of Production

Ace Meat Industries

Delivery Wagons

Meat Packing Plants

Cooled Warehouses

Refrigerated Railroad Cars

Slaughterhouse

Cattle

Horizontal Integration

Purchase of Competing Companies in Same Industry

U.S. Oil Company

Independent Oil Refineries

> ## Chart *Skills*
>
> Horizontal and vertical integration were the two most common business combinations in the late 1800s.
> **Evaluating** Which combination do you think would yield the most efficient business? Why?

Guided Reading Activity 9–3

Name _____ Date _____ Class _____

★ Guided Reading Activity 9-3

DIRECTIONS: Using Headings and Subheadings Locate each heading below in your textbook. Then use the information under the correct subheading to help you write each answer.

I. The Rise of Big Business

A. Why did the number of American corporations increase beginning in the 1830s? _____

B. How did corporations achieve economies of scale? _____

C. Rather than unethical behavior on the part of corporations, what was likely the cause of small companies going out of business? _____

II. The Consolidation of Industry

A. How did corporations keep prices from falling? _____

> ## Chart *Skills*
>
> **Answer:** Answers may vary. Both could be highly efficient if well managed. Some students may favor vertical integration since they may argue that horizontal integration reduces competition and may lead to less efficient giant business.
>
> **Chart Skills Practice**
> **Ask:** What potential problems exist if one large business buys all its competitors? *(The resulting monopoly can charge high prices; it has less reason to be highly efficient.)*

locomotives. He also invested in a company that built railroad bridges. In his early 30s, he was earning $50,000 per year, and he decided to quit his job with the railroad to concentrate on his own business affairs.

As part of his business activities, Carnegie frequently traveled to Europe to sell railroad bonds. On one trip, he met the English inventor, Sir Henry Bessemer, who had invented a new process for making high quality steel efficiently and cheaply. After meeting Bessemer, Carnegie decided to concentrate his investments in the steel industry. He opened a steel company in Pittsburgh in 1875 and quickly adapted his steel mills to use the **Bessemer process.** Carnegie often boasted about how cheaply he could produce steel:

> ❝Two pounds of iron stone mined upon Lake Superior and transported nine hundred miles to Pittsburgh; one pound and one-half of coal mined and manufactured into coke, and transported to Pittsburgh; one-half pound of lime, mined and transported to Pittsburgh; a small amount of manganese ore mined in Virginia and brought to Pittsburgh—and these four pounds of materials manufactured into one pound of steel, for which the consumer pays one cent.❞
>
> —quoted in *The Growth of the American Republic*

Vertical and Horizontal Integration To increase manufacturing efficiency even further, Carnegie took the next step in building a big business. He did this by beginning the vertical integration of the steel industry. A vertically integrated company owns all of the different businesses on which it depends for its operation. Instead of paying companies for coal, lime, and iron, Carnegie's company bought coal mines, limestone quarries, and iron ore fields. Vertical integration saved companies money while enabling big companies to become even bigger.

Successful business leaders like Carnegie also pushed for horizontal integration, or combining many firms engaged in the same type of business into one large corporation. Horizontal integration took place frequently as companies competed. When a company began to lose market share, it would often sell out to competitors to create a larger organization. By 1880, for example, a series of buyouts had enabled Rockefeller's Standard Oil to gain control of approximately 90 percent of the oil refining industry in the United States. When a single company achieves control of an entire market, it becomes a monopoly. Many Americans feared monopolies because they believed that a company with a monopoly could charge whatever it wanted for its products. Others, however, supported monopolies. They believed that monopolies had to keep prices low because raising prices would encourage competitors to reappear and offer the products for a lower price. In some industries companies had a virtual monopoly in the United States but were competing on a global scale. Standard Oil, for example, came very close to having a monopoly in the United States, but competition with other

Discussing a Topic Have students compare the game of Monopoly with the monopolies built by Rockefeller and other magnates. **L1**

Today the Organization of Petroleum Exporting Countries (OPEC) tries to maintain stability in the oil industry to ensure profits. This is called a *cartel*. Since 1970 OPEC has controlled approximately one-third to one-half of the world's oil supply. In 2001 member nations included Algeria, Indonesia, Iran, Iraq, Kuwait, Libya, Nigeria, Qatar, Saudi Arabia, the United Arab Emirates, and Venezuela.

CHAPTER 9   Industrialization   **321**

DIFFERENTIATED INSTRUCTION

Gifted and Talented Have interested students research how by-products of oil such as kerosene, paint, or paraffin are produced. Ask students to show the process by creating a poster or flowchart that includes drawings and explanatory labels. Display the posters and flowcharts and have students answer questions about the process. **L3**

☛ Refer to *Inclusion for the High School Social Studies Classroom Strategies and Activities* in the TCR.

3 ASSESS

Assign Section 3 Assessment as homework or as an in-class activity.

🌐 Have students use the **Interactive Tutor Self-Assessment CD-ROM.**

L1/ELL

Reading Essentials and Study Guide 9–3

Name _____ Date _____ Class ____

Study Guide

Chapter 9, Section 3
For use with textbook pages 319–323

BIG BUSINESS

KEY TERMS AND NAMES
corporation an organization owned by many people but treated by law as though it were a single person (page 320)
stockholders people who own a corporation through shares of ownership (page 320)
stock shares of ownership (page 320)
economies of scale ability of large manufacturing facilities to produce more goods more cheaply (page 320)
fixed costs costs a company has to pay whether it is operating or not (page 320)
operating costs costs that occur when running a company (page 320)
pool agreement among companies to maintain prices at a certain level (page 320)

L2

Section Quiz 9–3

Name _____ Date _____ Class ____

⭐ Chapter 9   Score ____

Section Quiz 9-3

DIRECTIONS: Matching Match each item in Column A with the items in Column B.
Write the correct letters in the blanks. *(10 points each)*

Column A	Column B
___ **1.** process for making high-quality steel efficiently and cheaply	**A.** Woolworth's
___ **2.** agreements to maintain prices at a certain level	**B.** pools
___ **3.** when a company owns all the different businesses on which it depends for its operation	**C.** Bessemer process
___ **4.** became one of the most successful retail chains in American history	**D.** monopoly
___ **5.** a single company achieves control of an entire market	**E.** vertical integration

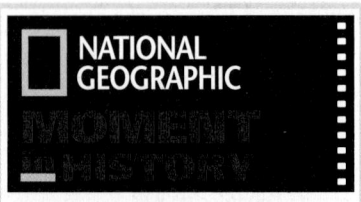

NATIONAL GEOGRAPHIC
MOMENT IN HISTORY

Before the advent of the electric vacuum cleaner, the ritual of spring-cleaning involved moving furniture aside and taking carpets and rugs outdoors to beat the dust out of them.

✓**Reading Check**

Answer: pools, vertical and horizontal integration, monopolies, trusts, and holding companies

NATIONAL GEOGRAPHIC
ARGENT HISTORY

LABOR SAVERS
American inventiveness and the nation's growing industrial might combined to provide turn-of-the-century consumers with an ever-increasing array of products. Here, a homemaker wields an early electric vacuum cleaner. Mass-produced household devices had a tremendous impact on the lifestyles and buying habits of millions of middle-class Americans. In cities, huge shopping emporiums replaced the cozy dry goods stores of the 1800s. Even rural customers could buy an almost endless variety of merchandise from mail-order catalogues such as Sears, Roebuck and Montgomery Ward.

oil companies throughout the world forced the Standard Oil Company to keep its prices low.

Trusts By the late 1800s, many Americans had grown suspicious of large corporations and feared the power of monopolies. To preserve competition and prevent horizontal integration, many states made it illegal for one company to own stock in another without specific permission from the state legislature. In 1882 Standard Oil formed the first trust, a new way of merging businesses that did not violate the laws against owning other companies. A trust is a legal concept that allows one person to manage another person's property. The person who manages another person's property is called a trustee.

Instead of buying a company outright, which was often illegal, Standard Oil had stockholders give their stocks to a group of Standard Oil trustees. In exchange, the stockholders received shares in the trust, which entitled them to receive a portion of the trust's profits. Since the trustees did not own the stock but were merely managing it for someone else,

they were not violating the law. This arrangement enabled the trustees to control a group of companies as if they were one large merged company.

Holding Companies Beginning in 1889 the state of New Jersey further accelerated the rise of big business with a new general incorporation law. This law allowed corporations chartered in New Jersey to own stock in other businesses without any need for special legislative action. Many companies immediately used the New Jersey law to create a new organization called a holding company. A holding company does not produce anything itself. Instead, it owns the stock of companies that do produce goods. The holding company controls all of the companies it owns, effectively merging them into one large enterprise. By 1904 the United States had 318 holding companies. Together these giant corporations controlled over 5,300 factories and were worth more than $7 billion.

✓**Reading Check** **Explaining** What techniques did corporations use to consolidate their industries?

322   CHAPTER 9   Industrialization

INTERDISCIPLINARY CONNECTIONS ACTIVITY

Economics Invite a representative from the Small Business Administration to speak to the class about the impact of small businesses on the community. Ask the speaker to address the basics of how one goes about setting up a small business. As a class, discuss the various ways that businesses can be financed. **L2**

Selling the Product

The vast array of products that American industries churned out led retailers to look for new ways to market and sell goods. N.W. Ayer and Son of Philadelphia, for example, developed bold new formats for advertising. Large display ads with illustrations replaced the small-type line ads that had been standard in newspapers. By 1900 retailers were spending over $90 million a year on advertising in newspapers and magazines sold across the nation. Advertising attracted readers to the newest retail business, the department store.

In 1877 advertisements billed John Wanamaker's new Philadelphia department store, the Grand Depot, as the "largest space in the world devoted to retail selling on a single floor." When Wanamaker's opened, only a handful of department stores existed in the United States; soon hundreds sprang up. Department stores changed the idea of shopping by bringing a huge array of different products together in a large, elegant building. They created an atmosphere that made shopping seem glamorous and exciting.

Chain stores, a group of similar stores owned by the same company, first appeared in the mid-1800s. In contrast to department stores, which offered many services, chain stores focused on thrift, offering low prices instead of elaborate service and decor. Woolworth's, a chain store that opened in 1879, became one of the most successful retail chains in American history.

To reach the millions of people who lived in rural areas in the late 1800s—far from chain stores or department stores—retailers began issuing

mail-order catalogs. Two of the largest mail-order retailers were Montgomery Ward and Sears, Roebuck. Their huge catalogs, widely distributed through the mail, used attractive illustrations and friendly descriptions to advertise thousands of items for sale.

Fact | Fiction | Folklore

The New York Stock Exchange In 1792 business-people met in New York City to establish a stock exchange—a marketplace for buying and selling stock in companies. At first, the new stock exchange was located under a buttonwood tree on Wall Street.

The organization took its present name, the New York Stock Exchange, in 1863. Huge amounts of the capital required for the nation's industrialization after the Civil War passed through the New York Stock Exchange.

As stock trading grew, investors across the nation needed financial news. In 1882 Henry Charles Dow and Edward D. Jones founded Dow Jones & Company. This new company sent bulletins on the day's business to Wall Street's financial houses. The day's last delivery contained a news sheet, which became the *Wall Street Journal* in July 1889.

Reading Check **Identifying** What innovations did retailers introduce in the late 1800s to sell goods to consumers?

HISTORY Online **Study Central™** To review this section, go to tarvol2.glencoe.com and click on **Study Central™**.

SECTION 3 ASSESSMENT

Checking for Understanding
1. **Define:** corporation, economies of scale, fixed costs, operating costs, pool, vertical integration, horizontal integration, monopoly, trust, holding company.
2. **Identify:** stockholder, stock, Andrew Carnegie, Bessemer process.
3. **List** the new methods of advertising and selling that helped push consumer goods in the late 1800s.

Reviewing Themes
4. **Economic Factors** What factors allowed corporations to develop in the United States in the late 1800s?

Critical Thinking
5. **Forming an Opinion** Do you think an individual today can rise from "rags to riches" like Andrew Carnegie did? Why or why not?
6. **Organizing** Use a graphic organizer like the one below to list ways business leaders in the late 1800s tried to eliminate competition.

Attempts to Eliminate Competition

Analyzing Visuals
7. **Analyzing Photographs** Study the photograph on page 322 of a woman using an early electric vacuum cleaner. How would you compare this to today's vacuum cleaners? How do you think new mass-produced appliances such as this one affected the lives of women in this era?

Writing About History
8. **Expository Writing** Write a newspaper editorial in which you explain why entrepreneurs such as John D. Rockefeller and Andrew Carnegie were a positive or a negative force on the U.S. economy in the late 1800s.

CHAPTER 9 Industrialization **323**

SECTION 3 ASSESSMENT ANSWERS

1. Terms are in blue.
2. stockholder *(p. 320)*, stock *(p. 320)*, Andrew Carnegie *(p. 320)*, Bessemer process *(p. 321)*
3. large display ads in newspapers, department stores, chain stores, mail-order catalogs
4. general incorporation laws
5. Students' answers will vary.
6. pools, trusts, monopolies, vertical and horizontal integration
7. today's are lighter; gave women more leisure time
8. Editorials should use clear arguments.

1 FOCUS

In 1870 the Standard Oil Company of Ohio was one of 26 oil refineries in Cleveland. At the time of the company's creation in January of that year, Standard Oil controlled 10 percent of the nation's petroleum refining. Over the next 10 years, John D. Rockefeller gained control of over 90 percent of the oil refining in the U.S. through mergers, elimination of competition, and the use of rebates to lower shipping costs. In 1899 George Rice complained to the U.S. Industrial Commission.

2 TEACH

Discussing an Issue Ask students to look at the current economic environment and discuss the pros and cons of the chief advantages listed by John D. Rockefeller as they relate to another industry, such as the airlines, computers, cell phones, or health care. L2

you don't say...

Board of Trustees Even though it is now illegal to operate a business as a trust, many corporations continue to refer to the group who directs the business as the "board of trustees."

You're *the* Historian

John D. Rockefeller

Investigating Standard Oil

By the 1880s, the Standard Oil Company, under the direction of John D. Rockefeller and his associates, had gained control of more than 90 percent of the oil refining business in the United States. Did Standard Oil use unfair tactics? The United States Industrial Commission investigated, calling Rockefeller himself to testify. Rockefeller said his success was due to the efficiency of his company. George Rice, an independent refiner from Marietta, Ohio, told the Industrial Commission that Standard Oil's advantage was criminal collusion with the railroads. Was he right? You're the historian.

Read the following excerpts from the Industrial Commission hearings of 1899. Then complete the questions and activities on the next page.

Standard Oil stock

From John D. Rockefeller's testimony

Question: To what advantages, or favors, or methods of management do you ascribe chiefly the success of the Standard Oil Company?

Answer [Rockefeller]: I ascribe the success of the Standard to its consistent policy to make the volume of its business large through the merits and cheapness of its products. It has spared no expense in finding, securing, and utilizing the best and cheapest methods of manufacture. It has sought for the best superintendents and workmen and paid the best wages. It has not hesitated to sacrifice old machinery and old plants for new and better ones. It has placed its manufactories at the points where they could supply markets at the least expense. It has not only sought markets for its principal products, but for all possible by-products, sparing no expense in introducing them to the public.

It has not hesitated to invest millions of dollars in methods of cheapening the gathering and distribution of oils by pipe lines, special cars, tank steamers, and tank wagons. . . .

Question: What are, in your judgment, the chief advantages from industrial combinations—(a) financially to stockholders; (b) to the public?

Answer: All the advantages which can be derived from a cooperation of person and aggregation of capital. . . . It is too late to argue about advantages of industrial combinations. They are a necessity. And if Americans are to have the privilege of extending their business in all the States of the Union, and into foreign countries as well, they are a necessity on a large scale, and require the agency of more than one corporation. Their chief advantages are:

1. Command of necessary capital.
2. Extension of limits of business.
3. Increase the number of persons interested in the business.
4. Economy in the business.
5. Improvements and economies which are derived from knowledge of many interested persons of wide experience.
6. Power to give the public improved products at less prices and still make a profit from stockholders.
7. Permanent work and good wages for laborers.

Cartoon criticizing Standard Oil

EXTENDING THE CONTENT

Point of View Historians disagree about some of the issues surrounding the business practices employed by John D. Rockefeller and the Standard Oil Trust. For example, while it was common practice for the railroads to offer rebates to big shippers in a variety of industries, some historical accounts indicate that in addition to rebates, Rockefeller got inside information from the railroads about the business activities of his competitors. Discrepancies can also be found in historical accounts of the business practices of George Rice. Some accounts characterize Rice as a reputable businessman, while others paint him as a charlatan and con man.

Oil derricks

SOHIO GASOLINE

ETHYL
(TRADE MARK)
REG U.S. PATENT OFF.
BRAND OF
ANTI-KNOCK
COMPOUND
ETHYL GASOLINE
CORPORATION
NEW YORK, U.S.A.

From George Rice's testimony

I am a citizen of the United States. . . . Producer of petroleum for more than 30 years, and a refiner of same for 20 years, but my refinery has been shut down during the past 3 years, owing to the powerful and all-prevailing machinations of the Standard Oil Trust, in criminal collusion and conspiracy with the railroads to destroy my business of 20 years of patient industry, toil, and money in building up, wholly by and through unlawful freight discriminations. I have been driven from pillar to post, from one railway line to another, for 20 years, in the absolutely vain endeavor to get equal and just freight rates with the Standard Oil Trust, so as to be able to run my refinery at anything approaching a profit, but which I have been utterly

unable to do. I have had to consequently shut down, with my business absolutely ruined and my refinery idle. This has been a very sad, bitter, and ruinous experience for me to endure, but I have endeavored to the best of my circumstances and ability to combat it the utmost I could for many a long waiting year, expecting relief through the honest and proper execution of our laws, which have as yet, however, never come. . . .

Outside of rebates or freight discriminations I had no show with the Standard Oil trust, because of their unlawfully acquired monopoly, by which they could temporarily cut only my customers' prices, and below cost, leaving the balance of the town, nine-tenths, uncut. This they can easily do without any appreciable harm to

their general trade, and thus effectually wipe out all competition, as fully set forth. Standard Oil prices generally were so high that I could sell my goods 2 to 3 cents a gallon below their prices and make a nice profit, but these savage attacks and cuts upon my customers' goods, and their consequent loss, plainly showed them their power for evil, and the uselessness to contend against such odds, and they would buy no more of my oil. . . .

Understanding the Issue

1. What potential advantages could companies like Standard Oil offer consumers?
2. What did George Rice believe to be the reason Standard Oil was so successful?
3. How would you assess the credibility of the two accounts?

Activities

1. **Investigate** Today many industries, unions, and special interest groups lobby Congress for favorable legislation. What are the most powerful groups? How do they operate?
2. **Check the News** Are there any companies that recently have been investigated for unfair or monopolistic practices? Collect headlines and news articles and create a bulletin board display.

PORTFOLIO ACTIVITY

1 FOCUS

Section Overview

This section focuses on the formation of labor unions during the late 1800s.

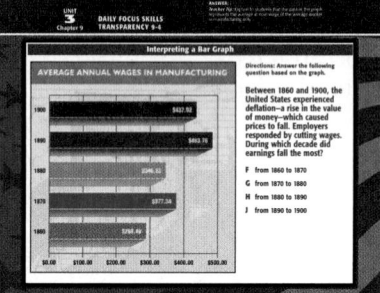
Reading Preview

Answers to Graphic: 1877: Great Railroad Strike involves 80,000 workers in 11 states, government troops break up strike, millions of dollars in damage and more than 100 people killed; 1886: Haymarket Riot kills 11 people and greatly weakens the Knights of Labor; 1894: Pullman Strike against railroads nearly paralyzes economy, federal troops force an end to strike, and the ARU collapses

Preteaching Vocabulary

Have students skim this section to glean the meaning or significance of each of the Key Terms and Names.

SECTION 4 Unions

Guide to Reading

Main Idea
In an attempt to improve their working conditions, industrial workers came together to form unions in the late 1800s.

Key Terms and Names
deflation, trade union, industrial union, blacklist, lockout, Marxism, Knights of Labor, arbitration, closed shop

Reading Strategy
Sequencing As you read about the increase of American labor unions in the late 1800s, complete a time line similar to the one below by filling in the incidents of labor unrest discussed and the results of each incident.

1877

Reading Objectives
• **Describe** industrial working conditions in the United States in the late 1800s.
• **List** the barriers to labor union growth.

Section Theme
Individual Action People like Samuel Gompers and Mother Jones strove to balance the power of corporations with the needs of workers.

Preview of Events

♦1875	♦1885	♦1895	♦1905
1877 Great Railroad Strike	**1886** American Federation of Labor founded	**1886** Riot in Chicago's Haymarket Square	**1894** Pullman Strike	**1903** Women's Trade Union League founded

★ An American Story ★

Avondale Mine disaster

On September 6, 1869, hundreds of miners' wives and children heard the repeated shrill blasts of the Avondale Mine's whistle, which signaled an accident. The families ran to the mine's entry and beheld a terrifying sight: hot smoke billowing from the mine shaft.

The owners of the Avondale Coal Mine in Luzerne County, Pennsylvania, had not built a second entrance. Without an escape route, the 179 miners trapped below soon died. Songs to commemorate the disaster later gave voice to the silenced victims:

> ❝And as their souls ascended
> To God who gave them breath
> They plead against the company
> Whose greed had caused their death❞

Following the deaths at Avondale, John Siney, an Irish immigrant and union leader, urged his fellow miners to unionize:

> ❝Men, if you must die with your boots on, die for your families, your homes, your country, but do not longer consent to die like rats in a trap. . . .❞

> —quoted in *Labor's Untold Story*

Working in the United States

Life for workers in industrial America was difficult. As machines replaced skilled labor, work became monotonous. Workers had to perform highly specific, repetitive tasks and could take little pride in their work. In addition, working conditions were

SECTION RESOURCES

📁 Reproducible Masters
• Reproducible Lesson Plan 9–4
• Daily Lecture and Discussion Notes 9–4
• Guided Reading Activity 9–4
• Section Quiz 9–4
• Reading Essentials and Study Guide 9–4
• Performance Assessment Activities and Rubrics

📖 Transparencies
• Daily Focus Skills Transparency 9–4

Multimedia
◎ Interactive Tutor Self-Assessment CD-ROM
◎ ExamView® Pro Testmaker CD-ROM
◎ Presentation Plus! CD-ROM
◎ TeacherWorks™ CD-ROM
◎ Audio Program

often unhealthy and dangerous. Workers breathed in lint, dust, and toxic fumes. Heavy machines lacking safety devices caused a high number of injuries.

Despite the difficult working conditions, industrialism brought about a dramatic rise in the standard of living. While only a few entrepreneurs became rich, real wages earned by the average worker rose by about 50 percent between 1860 and 1890.

Despite the rise in the standard of living, the uneven division of income between the wealthy and the working class caused resentment among workers. In 1900 the average industrial worker made 22¢ per hour and worked 59 hours per week.

At the same time, an economic phenomenon of the late 1800s made relations between workers and employers even more difficult. Between 1865 and 1897, the United States experienced deflation, or a rise in the value of money. Throughout the late 1800s, deflation caused prices to fall, which increased the buying power of workers' wages. Although companies cut wages regularly in the late 1800s, prices fell even faster, so that wages were actually still going up in buying power. Workers, however, believed that companies wanted to pay them less money for the same work. Eventually, many workers decided that the only way to improve their working conditions was to organize unions. With a union, they could bargain collectively to negotiate higher wages and better working conditions.

✔ Reading Check

Describing What aspects of industrial life caused frustration for workers in the late 1800s?

Early Unions

There were two basic types of industrial workers in the United States in the 1800s—craft workers and common laborers. Craft workers had special skills and training. They included machinists, iron molders, stonecutters, glassblowers, shoemakers, printers, carpenters, and many others. Craft workers generally received higher wages and

had more control over how they organized their time on the shop floor. Common laborers had few skills and received lower wages.

In the 1830s, as industrialism began to spread, craft workers began to form trade unions—unions limited to people with specific skills. By the early 1870s, there were over 30 national trade unions in the United States. Among the largest and most successful were the Iron Molders' International Union, the International Typographical Union, and the Knights of St. Crispin—the shoemakers' union.

Industry Opposes Unions Employers were often forced to recognize and negotiate with trade unions because they represented workers whose skills they needed. However, employers generally regarded unions as illegitimate conspiracies that interfered with their property rights. Owners of large corporations particularly opposed industrial unions, which united all craft workers and common laborers in a particular industry.

Companies used several techniques to prevent unions from forming. They required workers to take oaths or sign contracts promising not to join a union,

Picturing **History**

Unsafe Working Conditions Workers in the late 1800s often faced unsafe working conditions. Many began to join labor unions in an attempt to improve these conditions. *What unsafe conditions does this photograph of a steel mill show?*

CHAPTER 9 Industrialization **327**

2 TEACH

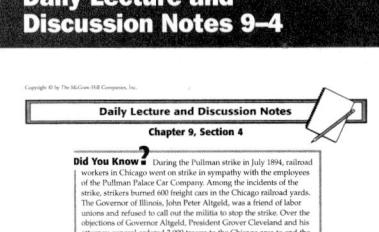

Daily Lecture and Discussion Notes 9–4

Copyright © by The McGraw-Hill Companies, Inc.

Daily Lecture and Discussion Notes
Chapter 9, Section 4

Did You Know❓ During the Pullman strike in July 1894, railroad workers in Chicago went on strike in sympathy with the employees of the Pullman Palace Car Company. Among the incidents of the strike, strikers burned 600 freight cars in the Chicago railroad yards. The Governor of Illinois, John Peter Altgeld, was a friend of labor unions and refused to call out the militia to stop the strike. Over the objections of Governor Altgeld, President Grover Cleveland and his attorney general ordered 2,000 troops to the Chicago area to end the Pullman strike.

I. Working in the United States (pages 326–327)

📖 Reading Strategy

Analyzing Information Read the following quote by George Pullman: "Last year [1892], I made only 4.5 percent profit and this year it will be less than 4 percent. I am entitled to make more money than that. My workers will have to take a pay cut." **Ask:** Was Pullman justified in asking his workers to take a cut in pay and, if so, why? Discuss why present-day companies ask employees to take pay cuts. **L1**

Picturing **History**

Answer: Workers are dangerously close to molten steel.
Ask: What problems resulted from unsafe working conditions? *(injuries, deaths, and illnesses)*

✔ Reading Check

Answer: working conditions, low pay, highly specific and repetitive tasks

📖 **Reading Strategy**   **READING THE TEXT**

Activating Prior Knowledge Before students begin to absorb any new knowledge, prepare them by bringing to mind what they already know. Use the key concepts and boldfaced terms in the text to frame general questions that encourage students to think about the topic and to share ideas. Then provide specific information that will enhance their understanding of the subject. **L1**

📂 Refer to *Inclusion for the High School Social Studies Classroom Strategies and Activities* in the TCR.

327

Name _____ Date _____ Class _____

★ Guided Reading Activity 9-4

DIRECTIONS: Filling in the Blanks In the space provided, write the word or words that best complete the sentence. Refer to your textbook to fill in the blanks.

1. Despite the difficult working conditions of industrial America, industrialism brought about a dramatic rise in _____

2. In 1900 the average industrial worker made approximately _____ an hour and worked an average of _____ a week.

3. _____ generally received higher wages and had more control over how they organized their time on the shop floor.

4. In the 1800s, craft workers began to form _____—unions limited to people with specific skills.

5. Owners of large corporations opposed _____—unions that united all craft workers and common laborers in a particular industry.

Profiles IN HISTORY

Mary Harris Jones published her life story, *The Autobiography of Mother Jones*, in 1925 when she was 95 years old.

Ask: What was Mother Jones's main message? *(The only way workers could help themselves was to work together with other workers.)*

✓ Reading Check

Answer: They associated unions with immigrants, revolution, and anarchy.

📖 Reading Strategy

Organizing Information Have students create a graphic organizer similar to the one shown below to categorize the obstacles facing immigrants coming to the United States in the late 1800s. Students should include as many rows as they need. **L1**

Working Conditions	Family Life	City Life	Social Life

---

and they hired detectives to go undercover and identify union organizers. Workers who tried to organize a union or strike were fired and placed on a **blacklist**—a list of "troublemakers." Once blacklisted, a laborer could get a job only by changing residence, trade, or even his or her name.

If workers formed a union, companies often used a lockout to break it. They locked workers out of the property and refused to pay them. If the union called a strike, employers would hire replacement workers, or **strikebreakers,** also known as scabs.

Political and Social Opposition
Workers who wanted to organize a union faced several major problems. There were no laws giving workers the right to organize or requiring owners to negotiate with them. Courts frequently ruled that strikes were "conspiracies in restraint of trade," for which labor leaders might be fined or jailed.

Unions also suffered from the perception that they threatened American institutions. In the late 1800s, the ideas of Karl Marx, called Marxism, had become very influential in Europe. Marx argued that the basic force shaping capitalist society was the class struggle between workers and owners. He believed that workers would eventually revolt, seize control of the factories, and overthrow the government.

Marxists claimed that after the revolution, the government would seize all private property and create a socialist society where wealth was evenly divided. Eventually, Marx thought, the state would wither away, leaving a Communist society where classes did not exist. Marxism strongly shaped the thinking of European unions.

While many labor supporters agreed with Marx, a few supported anarchism. Anarchists believe that society does not need any government. At the time, some believed that with only a few acts of violence, they could ignite a revolution to topple the government. In the late 1800s, anarchists assassinated government officials and set off bombs all across Europe, hoping to trigger a revolution.

As Marxist and anarchist ideas spread in Europe, tens of thousands of European immigrants began arriving in the United States. Nativism—anti-immigrant feelings—was already strong in the United States. As people began to associate immigrant workers with revolution and anarchism, they became increasingly suspicious of unions. These fears, as well as the government's duty to maintain law and order, often led officials to use the courts, the police, and even the army to crush strikes and break up unions.

✓ Reading Check Identifying
Why were some Americans suspicious of Unions?

The Struggle to Organize

Although workers attempted on many occasions to create large industrial unions, they rarely succeeded. In many cases the confrontations with owners and the government led to violence and bloodshed. In 1868 William Sylvis, president of the Iron Molders Union and leader of the National Labor Union, wrote to Karl Marx to encourage Marx's work and express his own hopes:

> ❝Our cause is a common one. . . . Go ahead in the good work that you have undertaken, until the most glorious success crowns your efforts . . . monied

Profiles IN HISTORY

Mother Jones *1830–1930*

Mary Harris "Mother" Jones emigrated to the United States from Ireland in 1835 at the age of five. Jones became the nation's most prominent woman union leader after a tragic personal loss. In 1867 her husband George, a union organizer, and their four children died from yellow fever.

Widowed and childless, Jones moved to Chicago and opened a dressmaker's shop. From her shop window, Jones could see the effects of the economic downturn of the 1870s: "poor shivering wretches, jobless and hungry." At night she attended rallies for the Knights of Labor.

By 1890 Jones had become an organizer for the United Mine Workers. In 1897 she traveled to West Virginia. The intrepid labor organizer trudged from camp to camp along railroad tracks or rode atop farm wagons. She slept in a tent.

A journalist who followed Jones on her trip reported that Jones began her speeches slowly, encouraging her listeners to "look on yourselves, and upon each other. Let us consider this together for I am one of you, and I know what it is to suffer." Then Mother Jones would make an impassioned plea for the miners to join the union. "You pity yourselves, but you do not pity your brothers, or you would stand together to help one another."

DIFFERENTIATED INSTRUCTION

Reading Support Have students play the role of a reporter assigned to cover the railroad strike of 1877. Tell them to write investigative articles that tell when, what, where, why, and how things occurred. Ask students to do independent research to find facts such as dates. Have volunteers read their articles to the class. **L2**

📂 Refer to *Inclusion for the High School Social Studies Classroom Strategies and Activities* in the TCR.

NATIONAL GEOGRAPHIC **Strikes and Labor Unrest, 1870–1890**

Coeur d'Alene, 1892, 1899

Baltimore Rail Strike, 1877

Haymarket Riot, 1886

Pullman, 1894

Leadville, 1896

Cripple Creek, 1903–04

Homestead, 1892

Texas and Pacific R.R., 1886

Birmingham-Bessemer 1894

400 miles
400 kilometers
Lambert Equal-Area projection

🚂 Railroad strike
✕ Miners' strike
⚒ Other strike or riot
▨ Counties with strike activity, 1881–1894
☐ No strikes reported
— 1890 border

Geography *Skills*

1. **Interpreting Maps** In what part of the nation did most of the strikes occur?
2. **Applying Geography Skills** Why did most of the labor conflicts take place where they did?

Geography *Skills*

Answers:
1. Northeast, Midwest, West
2. They were sites of major industrial development.

Geography Skills Practice
Ask: In which states did mining strikes occur? (*Alabama, Colorado, Idaho*)

Designing a Board Game Have students design a game based on life in the late 1800s. Invite interested students to play some of the games and explain the connections to the 1800s. **L3**

🖾 Use the rubric for creating a cooperative group management plan on pages 71–72 in the *Performance Assessment Activities and Rubrics*.

FYI

A century after the railroad strike of 1877, another group of transportation workers, air traffic controllers, went on strike demanding higher wages and fewer working hours. In August 1981, over 11,000 striking air traffic controllers were fired.

you don't say...

Hard Work Strict rules were enforced in the workplace in the late 1800s. Many bosses forbade singing, drinking, joking, smoking, or conversation on the job. They also denied immigrant workers time to celebrate their national holidays and holy days, and they did not accommodate workers who did not want to work on the Sabbath.

power is fast eating up the substance of the people. We have made war upon it, and we mean to win it. If we can we will win through the ballot box; if not, we will resort to sterner means. A little bloodletting is sometimes necessary in desperate causes.❞

—quoted in *Industrialism and the American Worker*

The Great Railroad Strike of 1877 In 1873 a severe recession known as the Panic of 1873 struck the American economy and forced many companies to cut wages. In July 1877, as the recession continued, several railroads announced another round of wage cuts. This triggered the first nationwide labor protest. The day after the cuts took effect, railroad workers in Martinsburg, West Virginia, walked off the job and blocked the tracks.

As word spread, railroad workers across the country walked off the job. The strike eventually involved 80,000 railroad workers in 11 states and affected two-thirds of the nation's railways. Angry strikers smashed equipment, tore up tracks, and blocked rail service in New York, Baltimore, Pittsburgh, St. Louis,

and Chicago. The governors of several states called out their militias to stop the violence. In many places, gun battles erupted between the militia and striking workers.

Determined to stop the violence, President Hayes ordered the army to open the railroad between Philadelphia and Pittsburgh. He then sent troops to Chicago, where the strike had paralyzed the entire city. The troops restored order, but by the time the strike ended, more than 100 people lay dead, and millions of dollars of property had been destroyed.

The Knights of Labor The failure of the Great Railroad Strike convinced many labor organizers that workers across the nation needed to be better organized. By the late 1870s, enough workers had joined a new organization, the **Knights of Labor,** to make it the first nationwide industrial union.

The Knights called for an eight-hour workday and a government bureau of labor statistics. They also supported equal pay for women, the abolition of child labor, and the creation of worker-owned factories. The Knights' leaders initially opposed the use of strikes, preferring to use boycotts to pressure

CHAPTER 9   Industrialization   **329**

INTERDISCIPLINARY CONNECTIONS ACTIVITY

Economics Have students use magazines to create a collage of today's American workforce. Instruct students to insert text callouts to highlight how today's workforce is similar to and different from the workforce the late 1800s. **L1**

Writing a Report Have students write a report about one of the labor issues mentioned in this section. Encourage students to use library and Internet resources for their research. **L1**

3 ASSESS

Assign Section 4 Assessment as homework or as an in-class activity.

💿 Have students use the **Interactive Tutor Self-Assessment CD-ROM.**

L1/ELL

Reading Essentials and Study Guide 9–4

Name _____ Date _____ Class _____

Study Guide

Chapter 9, Section 4
For use with textbook pages 326–331

UNIONS

KEY TERMS AND NAMES

deflation a rise in the value of money *(page 327)*

trade unions unions that were limited to people with specific skills *(page 327)*

industrial union unions that represented all craft workers and common laborers in a particular industry *(page 327)*

blacklist a list of people who tried to organize a union or strike and were considered trouble-makers by employers *(page 328)*

lockout a method used by employers to prevent unions from forming *(page 328)*

Marxism the ideas of Karl Marx *(page 328)*

L2

Section Quiz 9–4

Name _____ Date _____ Class _____

⭐ **Chapter 9** _____ Score ____

Section Quiz 9-4

DIRECTIONS: Matching Match each item in Column A with the items in Column B. Write the correct letters in the blanks. *(10 points each)*

Column A		Column B
___ 1.	process whereby an impartial third party helps workers and management reach an agreement	A. Knights of Labor
___ 2.	a rise in the value of money	B. Women's Trade Union League
___ 3.	first national association dedicated to promoting women's labor issues	C. arbitration
___ 4.	unions limited to people with specific skills	D. deflation
___ 5.	first nationwide industrial union	E. trade unions

DIRECTIONS: Multiple Choice In the blank at the left, write the letter of the choice that best completes the statement or answers the question. *(10 points each)*

---

employers. They also supported arbitration, a process in which an impartial third party helps workers and management reach an agreement.

In the early 1880s, the Knights began to use strikes, and they achieved great success initially. After striking Knights convinced one of Jay Gould's railroads to reverse wage cuts in 1885, membership in the union leapt from 100,000 to 700,000 in less than a year. The following year, 1886, marked the peak of their success. In the spring of that year, an event known as the **Haymarket Riot** undermined the Knights' reputation, and the union rapidly declined.

The Haymarket Riot In the early 1880s, the movement for an eight-hour workday began to build support. In 1886 organizers called for a nationwide strike on May 1 to show support for the idea. On that date, strikes took place in many cities, including Chicago.

On May 3, a clash between strikers and police in Chicago left one striker dead. The next evening, an anarchist group organized a meeting in Chicago's Haymarket Square to protest the killing. Around 3,000 people gathered to hear the speeches. When police entered the square, someone threw a bomb. The police opened fire, and workers shot back. Seven police officers and four workers were killed.

Police arrested eight people for the bombing. Seven of those arrested were German immigrants and advocates of anarchism. The incident horrified people across the country.

No one knew who threw the bomb. Although the evidence was weak, all eight men were convicted, and four were later executed. Unfortunately for the Knights of Labor, one of the men arrested was a member of the union. The incident badly hurt the Knights' reputation, and they began to lose members rapidly.

The Pullman Strike Although the Haymarket Riot set back the drive to create industrial unions, other labor organizers continued their efforts. In 1893 railroad workers created the American Railway Union (ARU) under the leadership of Eugene V. Debs. One of the companies the ARU unionized was the Pullman Palace Car Company.

The Pullman Company was based in Illinois. It had built a town named Pullman near its factory and required its workers to live in the town and to buy goods from company stores. In 1893 a depression

struck the United States, causing the Pullman Company to slash wages. The wage cuts made it difficult for workers to pay their rent or the high prices at the company stores. In May 1894, after Pullman fired three workers who complained, a strike began. In support, the ARU stopped handling Pullman cars all across the United States.

The boycott of Pullman cars tied up railroads and threatened to paralyze the economy. Determined to break the union, railroad managers arranged for U.S. mail cars to be attached to the Pullman cars. If the strikers refused to handle the Pullman cars, they would be interfering with the U.S. mail, a violation of federal law. President Grover Cleveland then sent in troops, claiming it was his responsibility to keep the mail running. When a federal court issued an injunction ordering the union to halt the boycott, the strike at Pullman and the ARU both collapsed.

✓ **Reading Check** **Analyzing** Why did industrial unions frequently fail in the late 1800s?

The American Federation of Labor

Although large-scale industrial unions generally failed in the late 1800s, trade unions continued to prosper. In 1886 delegates from over 20 of the nation's trade unions organized the **American Federation of Labor** (AFL). The AFL's first leader was **Samuel Gompers.** His approach to labor relations—which he called "plain and simple" unionism—helped unions to become accepted in American society.

Gompers believed that unions should stay out of politics. He rejected socialist and communist ideas. Rather, he believed that the AFL should fight for small gains—such as higher wages and better working conditions—within the American system. He was willing to use the strike but preferred to negotiate.

Samuel Gompers

Under Gompers's leadership, the AFL had three main goals. First, it tried to convince companies to recognize unions and to agree to collective bargaining. Second, it pushed for closed shops, meaning that companies could only hire union members. Third, it promoted an eight-hour workday.

The AFL grew slowly, but by 1900 it was the biggest union in the country, with over 500,000 members. Still, at that time, the AFL represented less than 15 percent of all non-farm workers. All unions, including railroad

---

CRITICAL THINKING ACTIVITY

Synthesizing Ask students to describe stereotypes associated with unions. Have students then explain how these stereotypes were formed. Then ask students to explain the impact of these stereotypes on the efforts of organized labor. Finally, ask students to evaluate if these stereotypes about unions are still held by people today. **L1**

unions, represented only 18 percent. As the 1900s began, the vast majority of workers remained unorganized, and unions were relatively weak.

✓ **Reading Check** **Analyzing** What AFL policies contributed to its growth as a union?

Working Women

Throughout the 1800s, most wage-earning workers in the United States were men. After the Civil War, the number of women wage earners began to increase. By 1900 women made up more than 18 percent of the labor force.

The type of jobs women did outside the home in the late 1800s and early 1900s reflected society's ideas about what constituted "women's work." Roughly one-third of women worked as domestic servants. Another third worked as teachers, nurses, sales clerks, and secretaries. The remaining third were industrial workers, but they were employed in light industrial jobs that people believed appropriate to their gender. Many worked in the garment industry and food processing plants.

Regardless of their employment, women were paid less than men even when they performed the same jobs. It was assumed that a woman had a man helping to support her, either her father or her husband, and that a man needed higher wages to support a family. For this reason, most unions, including the AFL, excluded women.

In 1903 two woman labor organizers, Mary Kenney O'Sullivan and Leonora O'Reilly, decided to establish a separate union for women. With the help

Picturing **History**

Detail Work These women worked in the National Elgin Watch Company's gilding room, where they gilded metal watches with thin layers of gold. What do you notice about their working conditions?

of Jane Addams and Lillian Wald—the founders of the settlement house movement—they established the **Women's Trade Union League** (WTUL), the first national association dedicated to promoting women's labor issues. The WTUL pushed for an eight-hour day, the creation of a minimum wage, an end to evening work for women, and the abolition of child labor. The WTUL also collected funds to support women on strike.

✓ **Reading Check** **Comparing** How were female industrial workers treated differently than male workers in the late 1800s?

HISTORY Online **Study Central™** To review this section, go to tarvol2.glencoe.com and click on **Study Central™**.

SECTION 4 ASSESSMENT

Checking for Understanding
1. **Define:** deflation, trade union, industrial union, lockout, Marxism, arbitration, closed shop.
2. **Identify:** blacklist, Knights of Labor.
3. **List** the groups of workers represented by the Knights of Labor and the American Federation of Labor.

Reviewing Themes
4. **Individual Action** What political contribution did Mary Harris "Mother" Jones make to American society?

Critical Thinking
5. **Analyzing** Why did early labor unions fail?
6. **Organizing** Use a graphic organizer similar to the one below to list the factors that led to an increase in unions in the late 1800s.

Factors Contributing to Unionization

Analyzing Visuals
7. **Analyzing Photographs** Examine the photograph at the top of this page of workers in a watch factory. Most of the people in the picture are women. What do you think the jobs were of the men in the photograph?

Writing About History
8. **Persuasive Writing** Imagine that you are an American worker living in one of the nation's large cities. Write a letter to a friend explaining why you support or oppose the work of labor unions.

Reading Check
Answer: emphasis on collective bargaining, closed shops, eight-hour workday

Picturing **History**
Answer: women workers working close together, uncomfortable chairs, dressed more formally than workers today
Ask: Why do you think this constituted women's work? (*It was light industrial work that did not involve heavy machinery.*)

Reteach
Have students list the barriers to labor union growth.

Enrich
Encourage students to write a profile of one of the leading labor unions today, such as the AFL-CIO or the Teamsters.

Reading Check
Answer: excluded from unions, paid less than male counterparts, employed in jobs deemed appropriate for women

HISTORY Online
Study Central™ provides summaries, interactive games, and online graphic organizers to help students review section content.

4 CLOSE
Have students describe industrial working conditions in the United States in the late 1800s.

SECTION 4 ASSESSMENT ANSWERS

1. Terms are in blue.
2. blacklist (*p. 328*), Knights of Labor (*p. 329*)
3. industrial workers, trade workers
4. She became a key organizer for the United Mine Workers union.
5. confrontations led to violence, courts ruled against them, frequent strikes, fought for many things all at the same time, blacklisting
6. concern about working conditions, concern about pay, concern about job security, economic challenges such as deflation
7. managers or supervisors
8. Students' letters will vary. Letters should express a point of view.

Reviewing Key Terms
Students' answers will vary. The pages where the words appear in the text are shown in parentheses.

1. **gross national product** (p. 308)
2. **laissez-faire** (p. 310)
3. **entrepreneur** (p. 310)
4. **time zone** (p. 316)
5. **land grant** (p. 317)
6. **corporation** (p. 320)
7. **economies of scale** (p. 320)
8. **fixed costs** (p. 320)
9. **operating costs** (p. 320)
10. **pool** (p. 320)
11. **vertical integration** (p. 321)
12. **horizontal integration** (p. 321)
13. **monopoly** (p. 321)
14. **trust** (p. 322)
15. **holding company** (p. 322)
16. **deflation** (p. 327)
17. **trade union** (p. 327)
18. **industrial union** (p. 327)
19. **lockout** (p. 328)
20. **Marxism** (p. 328)
21. **arbitration** (p. 330)
22. **closed shop** (p. 330)

Reviewing Key Facts
23. Morrill Tariff (p. 310), Andrew Carnegie (p. 320)
24. iron ore, water, copper, coal, timber; large families, and floods of immigrants
25. helped increase the nation's productive capacity, improved transportation and communication

Reviewing Key Terms
On a sheet of paper, use each of these terms in a sentence.

1. gross national product
2. laissez-faire
3. entrepreneur
4. time zone
5. land grant
6. corporation
7. economies of scale
8. fixed costs
9. operating costs
10. pool
11. vertical integration
12. horizontal integration
13. monopoly
14. trust
15. holding company
16. deflation
17. trade union
18. industrial union
19. lockout
20. Marxism
21. arbitration
22. closed shop

Chapter Summary

Factors Behind Industrialization
- Abundant natural resources
- Cheap immigrant labor force
- High tariffs that reduced foreign goods
- National communication and transportation networks

Growth of Business
- Little or no government intervention
- Development of pools, trusts, holding companies, and monopolies
- Small businesses could not compete with economies–of–scale of large businesses
- Practices of some big businesses sometimes limited competition

Changing Workplace
- Rural migration and immigration created large, concentrated workforce
- In large–scale industries, low wages, long hours, and dangerous working conditions were common
- First large unions formed but had little bargaining power against large companies

Reviewing Key Facts
23. **Identify:** Morrill Tariff, Andrew Carnegie.
24. The United States had an advantage in industrializing due to its resources and large workforce. What resources did the nation have? Why was its workforce large?
25. How did inventions contribute to economic growth in the United States in the late 1800s?
26. How did the federal government encourage railroad companies to construct railroads?
27. What new methods of selling products were developed in the late 1800s?
28. Why did workers try to organize labor unions in the United States in the late 1800s?
29. What were the two basic types of workers in American industry at this time?

Critical Thinking
30. **Analyzing Themes: Individual Action** List the names and actions of five people who contributed to American economic growth in the late 1800s.
31. **Organizing** Use a graphic organizer similar to the one below to list the factors that led to making the United States an industrial nation.

32. **Interpreting Primary Sources** Americans like Ida Tarbell criticized large corporations such as the Standard Oil Company. In the following excerpt from *History of the Standard Oil Company,* she warns of the results of Rockefeller's business practices on the nation's morality. Read the excerpt and answer the questions that follow:

❝Very often people who admit the facts, who are willing to see that Mr. Rockefeller has employed force and fraud to secure his ends, justify him by declaring, 'It's business.' That is, 'It's business' has come to be a legitimate excuse for hard dealing, sly tricks, special privileges. It is a common enough thing to hear men arguing that the ordinary laws of morality do not apply in business.

26. by offering land grants
27. large display advertisements in newspapers, department stores, chain stores, mail-order catalogs
28. to change poor working conditions, low pay, and job security
29. craft workers and common laborers

Critical Thinking
30. Students' answers will vary. Names may include inventors and industrialists.
31. large labor force, inventions, abundant natural resources, free enterprise system
32. **a.** force and fraud; **b.** the "it's just business" attitude that excused immoral actions

HISTORY Online

Self-Check Quiz
Visit the *American Republic Since 1877* Web site at tarvol2.glencoe.com and click on **Self-Check Quizzes—Chapter 9** to assess your knowledge of chapter content.

As for the ethical side, there is no cure but in an increasing scorn of unfair play. . . . When the businessman who fights to secure special privileges, to crowd his competitor off the track by other than fair competitive methods, receives the same summary disdainful ostracism by his fellows that the doctor or lawyer who is 'unprofessional,' the athlete who abuses the rules, receives, we shall have gone a long way toward making commerce a fit pursuit for our young men.99

—quoted in *Readings in American History*

a. According to Tarbell, what practices had Rockefeller used to establish the Standard Oil Company?

b. In what way did Tarbell believe the attitudes of the American people contributed to Rockefeller's business practices?

33. **Analyzing** Analyze the impact of technological innovations and industrialization on the American labor movement.

Practicing Skills

34. **Making Inferences** Reread the passage titled "Working in the United States" from Section 4, page 326. Then answer the following questions.

a. What facts are stated about working conditions in the United States during this time period?

b. Based on your answer to the previous question, what can you infer about the attitude of employers toward their workers during this time?

Writing Activity

35. **Portfolio Writing: Persuasive Writing** Think of a product that you think is essential to life today. Write an advertisement for this product that would persuade people to purchase it.

Chapter Activity

36. **American History Primary Source Document Library CD-ROM** Read "Driving the Golden Spike" by Alexander Toponce, under *Reshaping the Nation*. For further background, reread your textbook's coverage of the same subject on page 315. Then prepare a presentation for your classmates. In it, describe what Toponce had to say about the workers during the celebration and what Grenville Dodge

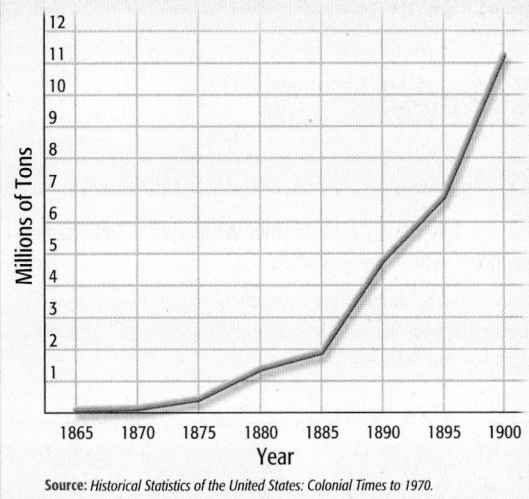

Steel Production, 1865–1900

Millions of Tons (y-axis: 1–12) / Year (x-axis: 1865, 1870, 1875, 1880, 1885, 1890, 1895, 1900)

Source: *Historical Statistics of the United States: Colonial Times to 1970.*

had to say about their experience during the project. What attitudes do you think each man had toward the workers?

Economics and History

37. The graph above shows steel production from 1865 to 1900. Study the graph and answer the questions below.

a. **Interpreting Graphs** Between what years did steel production have the greatest increase?

b. **Making Inferences** How did increased steel production contribute to American industrialism?

HISTORY Online

Have students visit the Web site at tarvol2.glencoe.com to review Chapter 9 and take the Self-Check Quiz.

Writing Activity
35. Advertisements should be clearly persuasive yet factually accurate.

Chapter Activity
36. Presentations should contrast the two men's views about the railroad workers.

Economics and History
37. **a.** 1895 and 1900; **b.** allowed railroads to be built, improving transportation and benefitting industry

Standardized Test Practice

Answer: G
Test-Taking Tip: Tell students not to be misled by answer choices that are only partially correct. In order to make the right choice, students must make sure *both* parts of the answer they choose are accurate.

Bonus Question ?

Ask: What are some of the reasons the United States had become the world's leading industrial nation by the early 1900s? *(possible answers include: abundant natural resources, large workforce, free enterprise system)*

33. Inventions such as electric power and the automatic loom led to large manufacturing companies and industrialization but created a host of challenges for workers, such as harsh working conditions. This led workers to unite and join labor unions.

Practicing Skills

34. **a.** Working conditions were often unhealthy and dangerous. Workers breathed lint, dust, and toxic fumes. The lack of safety devices in heavy machinery caused a high number of injuries. **b.** Students' answers will vary. They might suggest that employers were not concerned with the welfare of their workers.

Chapter 10 Resources

Timesaving Tools

TeacherWorks™ All-In-One Planner and Resource Center

- **Interactive Teacher Edition** Access your Teacher Wraparound Edition and your classroom resources with a few easy clicks.
- **Interactive Lesson Planner** Planning has never been easier! Organize your week, month, semester, or year with all the lesson helps you need to make teaching creative, timely, and relevant.

Use Glencoe's **Presentation Plus!** multimedia teacher tool to easily present dynamic lessons that visually excite your students. Using Microsoft PowerPoint® you can customize the presentations to create your own personalized lessons.

TEACHING TRANSPARENCIES

Graphic Organizer 10 L2

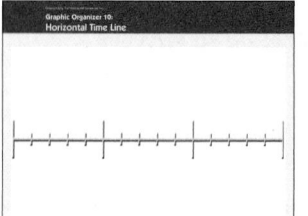

Why It Matters Chapter Transparency 10 L2

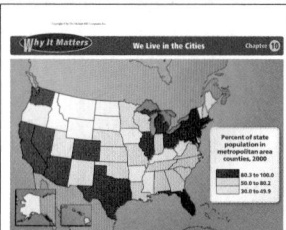

APPLICATION AND ENRICHMENT

Linking Past and Present Activity 10 L2

Enrichment Activity 10 L3

Primary Source Reading 10 L2

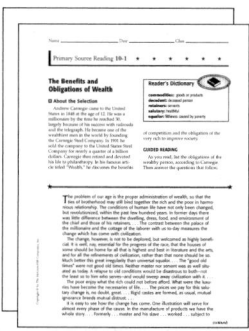

REVIEW AND REINFORCEMENT

Reteaching Activity 10 L1

Vocabulary Activity 10 L1

Time Line Activity 10 L2

Critical Thinking Skills Activity 10 L2

Meeting NCSS Standards

The following standards are covered in Chapter 10:

Section 1 III People, Places, and Environments: B, C, H, I
Section 2 VI Power, Authority, and Governance: B, C, H
Section 3 I Culture: A, C
Section 4 IV Individual Development and Identity: A, B, C, D

Local Standards

_____

_____

_____

_____

_____

Chapter 10 Resources

ASSESSMENT AND EVALUATION

Chapter 10 Test Form A L2

Chapter 10 Test Form B L2

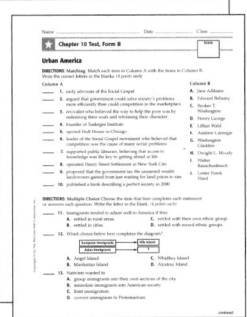

Standardized Test Practice Workbook Activity 10 L2

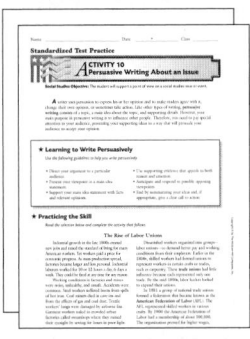

Performance Assessment Activities and Rubrics 10 L1/ELL

ExamView® Pro Testmaker CD-ROM

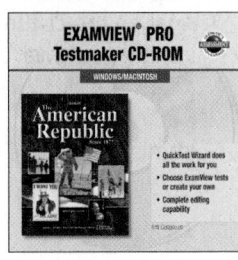

MULTIMEDIA

- Vocabulary PuzzleMaker CD-ROM
- Interactive Tutor Self-Assessment CD-ROM
- ExamView® Pro Testmaker CD-ROM
- Audio Program
- American History Primary Source Documents Library CD-ROM
- MindJogger Videoquiz
- Presentation Plus! CD-ROM
- TeacherWorks™ CD-ROM
- Interactive Student Edition CD-ROM
- Glencoe Skillbuilder Interactive Workbook CD-ROM, Level 2
- The *American Republic Since 1877* Video Program
- American Music: Hits Through History
- American Music: Cultural Traditions

SPANISH RESOURCES

The following Spanish language materials are available:

- Spanish Reading Essentials and Study Guide
- Spanish Guided Reading Activities
- Spanish Reteaching Activities
- Spanish Quizzes and Tests
- Spanish Vocabulary Activities
- Spanish Summaries
- The Declaration of Independence and United States Constitution Spanish Translation

---

THE HISTORY CHANNEL®

The following videotape programs are available from Glencoe as supplements to Chapter 10:

- **Ellis Island** (3 pack) (ISBN 0-76-700005-6)
- **Textiles: Birth of an American Industry** (ISBN 0-76-700624-0)

To order, call Glencoe at 1-800-334-7344. To find classroom resources to accompany many of these videos, check the following home pages:
A&E Television: www.aande.com
The History Channel: www.historychannel.com

Use our Web site for additional resources. All essential content is covered in the Student Edition.

You and your students can visit tarvol2.glencoe.com, the Web site companion to the *American Republic Since 1877*. This innovative integration of electronic and print media offers your students a wealth of opportunities. The student text directs students to the Web site for the following options:

- **Chapter Overviews**
- **Self-Check Quizzes**
- **Student Web Activities**
- **Textbook Updates**

Answers to the student Web activities are provided for you in the **Web Activity Lesson Plans**. Additional Web resources and Interactive Tutor Puzzles are also available.

Chapter 10 Resources

Daily Objectives	Reproducible Resources	Multimedia Resources
SECTION 1 **Immigration** 1. Analyze the circumstances surrounding the great wave of immigration after the Civil War. 2. Evaluate how nativism affected immigration policies.	Reproducible Lesson Plan 10–1 Daily Lecture and Discussion Notes 10–1 Guided Reading Activity 10–1* Section Quiz 10–1* Reading Essentials and Study Guide 10–1* Performance Assessment Activities and Rubrics Interpreting Political Cartoons	Daily Focus Skills Transparency 10–1 Interactive Tutor Self-Assessment CD-ROM ExamView® Pro Testmaker CD-ROM* Presentation Plus! CD-ROM TeacherWorks™ CD-ROM Audio Program American Music: Cultural Traditions ABCNews Interactive™ Historic America Electronic Field Trips
SECTION 2 **Urbanization** 1. Explain the technological developments that made the growth of cities possible. 2. Evaluate the role that political machines played in urban politics in the late 1800s.	Reproducible Lesson Plan 10–2 Daily Lecture and Discussion Notes 10–2 Guided Reading Activity 10–2* Section Quiz 10–2* Reading Essentials and Study Guide 10–2* Performance Assessment Activities and Rubrics Interpreting Political Cartoons	Daily Focus Skills Transparency 10–2 American Art & Architecture Interactive Tutor Self-Assessment CD-ROM ExamView® Pro Testmaker CD-ROM* Presentation Plus! CD-ROM TeacherWorks™ CD-ROM Audio Program
SECTION 3 **The Gilded Age** 1. Evaluate the doctrine of Social Darwinism and the impact it had on American industry. 2. Explain how industrialization promoted leisure time and encouraged new forms of entertainment.	Reproducible Lesson Plan 10–3 Daily Lecture and Discussion Notes 10–3 Guided Reading Activity 10–3* Section Quiz 10–3* Reading Essentials and Study Guide 10–3* Performance Assessment Activities and Rubrics	Daily Focus Skills Transparency 10–3 American Art & Architecture Interactive Tutor Self-Assessment CD-ROM ExamView® Pro Testmaker CD-ROM* Presentation Plus! CD-ROM TeacherWorks™ CD-ROM Audio Program American Music: Hits Through History American Music: Cultural Traditions
SECTION 4 **The Rebirth of Reform** 1. Explain the methods that social critics advocated to improve society. 2. Evaluate efforts to help the urban poor.	Reproducible Lesson Plan 10–4 Daily Lecture and Discussion Notes 10–4 Guided Reading Activity 10–4* Section Quiz 10–4* Reading Essentials and Study Guide 10–4* Performance Assessment Activities and Rubrics	Daily Focus Skills Transparency 10–4 Interactive Tutor Self-Assessment CD-ROM ExamView® Pro Testmaker CD-ROM* Presentation Plus! CD-ROM TeacherWorks™ CD-ROM Skillbuilder Interactive Workbook, Level 2 Vocabulary PuzzleMaker CD-ROM Audio Program

0:00 OUT OF TIME?
Assign the Chapter 10 **Reading Essentials and Study Guide.**

*Also Available in Spanish

 Printed Materials   Transparency   CD-ROM   DVD

Poster   Music Program   Audio Program   Videocassette

Chapter 10 Resources

NATIONAL GEOGRAPHIC — Teacher's Corner

INDEX TO NATIONAL GEOGRAPHIC MAGAZINE

The following articles relate to this chapter.
- "Boston's North Enders," October 2000
- "Chicago: Welcome to the Neighborhood," May 1991
- "New Life for Ellis Island," September 1990
- "New York's Chinatown," August 1998

NATIONAL GEOGRAPHIC SOCIETY PRODUCTS

To order the following, call National Geographic at 1-800-368-2728:
- *Historical Atlas of the United States*
- "Immigration: The Triumph of Hope" (Video)

NGS ONLINE

Access National Geographic's Web site for current events, atlas updates, activities, links, interactive features, and archives.
www.nationalgeographic.com

MEETING SPECIAL NEEDS

In addition to the Differentiated Instruction strategies found in each section, the following resources are also suitable for your special needs students:

- *ExamView® Pro Testmaker CD-ROM* allows teachers to tailor tests by reducing answer choices.
- The *Audio Program* includes the entire narrative of the student edition so that less-proficient readers can listen to the words as they read them.
- The *Reading Essentials and Study Guide* provides the same content as the student edition but is written two grade levels below the textbook.
- *Guided Reading Activities* give less-proficient readers point-by-point instructions to increase comprehension as they read each textbook section.

KEY TO ABILITY LEVELS

Teaching strategies have been coded.

L1 BASIC activities for all students
L2 AVERAGE activities for average to above-average students
L3 CHALLENGING activities for above-average students
ELL ENGLISH LANGUAGE LEARNER activities

From the Classroom of...

Heather Pang
Castilleja School
Palo Alto, CA

Urban America

Select 10 to 15 images from Jacob Riis's *How the Other Half Lives* (available online at http://www.cis.yale.edu/amstud/inforev/riis/title.html and in most libraries). Images of children are particularly effective for this exercise. Show these pictures to the students (slides, scanned images, or photocopies).

Organize the students into small groups and assign each group one of the following roles: city police, local school board, charitable organization, philanthropic guild, schoolchildren, garment district workers, and a merchants' association. Each group should use the pictures as evidence to prepare a report titled "Poverty in the City: What Is to Be Done?" Remind the students that each of these groups will have different reactions to the Riis images depending on their own backgrounds. Each report should list the most significant problems shown in the images and provide suggestions for solutions.

It might be helpful to start the lesson with a short introduction to Riis and the tradition of muckraking journalism.

ADDITIONAL RESOURCES FROM GLENCOE

- American Music: Cultural Traditions
- American Art & Architecture
- Outline Map Resource Book
- U.S. Desk Map
- Building Geography Skills for Life
- Inclusion for the High School Social Studies Classroom Strategies and Activities
- Teaching Strategies for the American History Classroom (Including Block Scheduling Pacing Guides)
- Dinah Zike's High School American History Reading and Study Skills Foldables

 Block Schedule

Activities that are suited to use within the block scheduling framework are identified by:

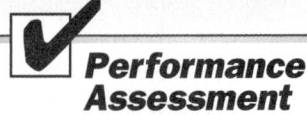
Performance Assessment

Refer to Activity 10 in the Performance Assessment Activities and Rubrics booklet. 📀

Why It Matters Activity

Ask students if they think people from rural America and immigrants from other countries migrate to American cities now for the same reasons they did in the late 1800s. Students should evaluate their answers after they have completed the chapter.

GLENCOE
TECHNOLOGY

The *American Republic Since 1877* Video Program

To learn more about the problems the nation faced during this period of urbanization, have students view the Chapter 10 video, "Huddled Masses in the City," from the *American Republic Since 1877* Video Program.

MindJogger Videoquiz

Use the **MindJogger Videoquiz** to preview Chapter 10 content.

 Both programs available in DVD

CHAPTER
10 Urban America
1865–1896

Why It Matters

European and Asian immigrants arrived in the United States in great numbers during the late 1800s. Providing cheap labor, they made rapid industrial growth possible. They also helped populate the growing cities. The immigrants' presence affected both urban politics and labor unions. Reactions to immigrants and to an urban society were reflected in new political organizations and in literature and philosophy.

The Impact Today

Industrialization and urbanization permanently influenced American life.
* *The United States continues to be a magnet for immigrants seeking a better way of life.*
* *The cities of the United States continue to draw new residents in search of opportunity.*

The *American Republic Since 1877* **Video** The Chapter 10 video, "Huddled Masses in the City," depicts one of the problems the nation faced during its urbanization period.

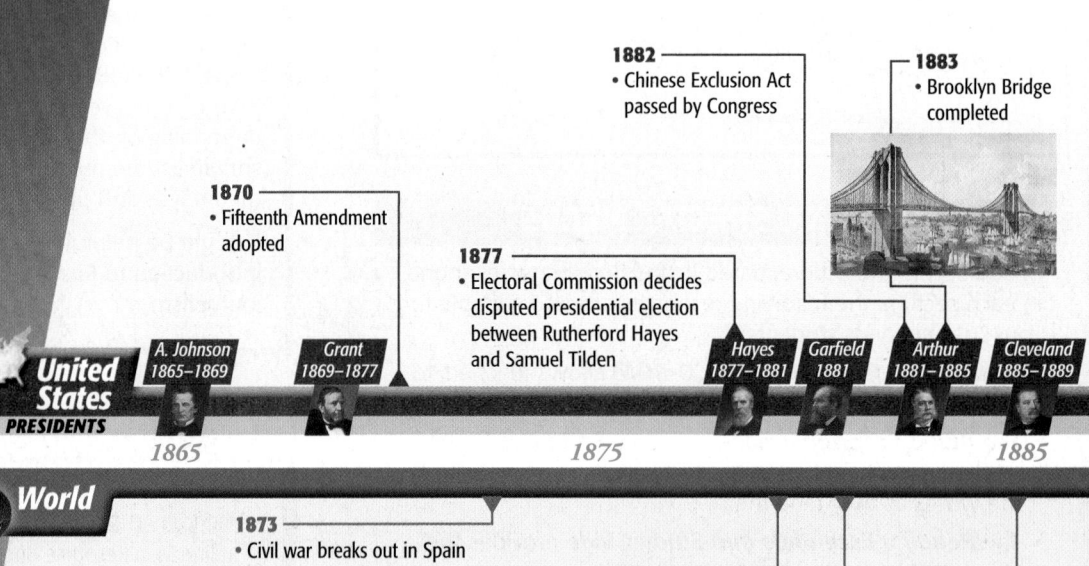

1882
• Chinese Exclusion Act passed by Congress

1883
• Brooklyn Bridge completed

1870
• Fifteenth Amendment adopted

1877
• Electoral Commission decides disputed presidential election between Rutherford Hayes and Samuel Tilden

United States PRESIDENTS

| A. Johnson 1865–1869 | Grant 1869–1877 | | Hayes 1877–1881 | Garfield 1881 | Arthur 1881–1885 | Cleveland 1885–1889 |

1865   *1875*   *1885*

World

1873
• Civil war breaks out in Spain

1878
• Independent Serbia recognized

1879
• Chile engages in war with Bolivia and Peru

1885
• Indian National Congre organizes for independ from Great Britain

334

Reading Strategy **PURPOSE FOR READING**

Dialogue Journal These pre-reading activities bring out students' background knowledge and allow them to exchange thoughts with a partner through writing. Tell students that before 1890, most immigrants to the United States came from northern and western Europe. Between 1890 and 1914, the majority immigrated from Italy, Russia, Poland, Austria-Hungary, Greece, Romania, and Turkey. Have students find these places on the world map on pages RA16–RA17. Ask students to write in their journals why they think this shift in immigration took place. Have students exchange journals, read one another's entries, and respond in writing. **L1**

Immigrants arriving at Ellis Island

1888
- First electric trolley line opened in Richmond, Virginia

1891
- James Naismith invents basketball

1896
- National Association of Colored Women founded

1899
- Scott Joplin's "Maple Leaf Rag" published

MAPLE LEAF RAG

Scott Joplin

B. Harrison
1889–1893

Cleveland
1893–1897

McKinley
1897–1901

T. Roosevelt
1901–1909

1895

1905

1886
- Gold discovered in Transvaal region of South Africa

1901
- Victorian era ends with death of Britain's Queen Victoria

HISTORY Online

Chapter Overview
Visit the *American Republic Since 1877* Web site at tarvol2.glencoe.com and click on *Chapter Overviews— Chapter 10* to preview chapter information.

335

HISTORY Online

Introduce students to chapter content and key terms by having them access the **Chapter 10 Overview** at tarvol2.glencoe.com.

More About the Photo

Between 1892 and 1954, approximately 12 million people who entered the United States through the port of New York were legally and medically inspected at Ellis Island, a small island in New York Harbor.

TIME LINE ACTIVITY

Have students work in pairs to duplicate the United States portion of the time line that appears on pages 334 and 335. Instruct students to use absolute chronology to add the events shown on the section time lines. Suggest that students color-code the events by section to help identify the themes.

FOLDABLES
Study Organizer

Dinah Zike's Foldables are three-dimensional, interactive graphic organizers that help students practice basic writing skills, review key vocabulary terms, and identify main ideas. Have students complete the foldable activity in the *Dinah Zike's Reading and Study Skills Foldables* booklet.

GRAPHIC ORGANIZER ACTIVITY

Organizing Information Have students use an outline map of the United States to label the cities where the various immigrant groups settled. Have students use a color code or small symbols to identify the different groups. Then ask students to use the maps to draw conclusions about immigration and its impact on urban America.

1 FOCUS

Section Overview

This section focuses on immigrants coming to the United States after the Civil War.

BELLRINGER
Skillbuilder Activity

 Project transparency and have students answer the question.

Daily Focus Skills Transparency 10–1

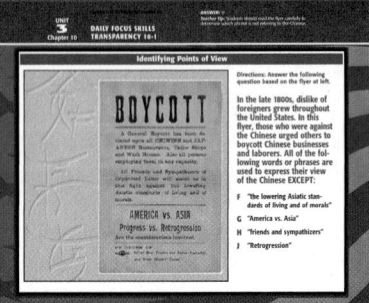

Reading Preview

Answers to Graphic: Push Factors: avoid forced military service, avoid religious persecution; Pull Factors: jobs, chance to move up the social ladder

Preteaching Vocabulary
Have students skim this section to find time references for each of the Key Terms and Names.

SECTION 1 Immigration

Guide to Reading

Main Idea
After the Civil War, millions of immigrants from Europe and Asia settled in the United States.

Key Terms and Names
steerage, Ellis Island, Jacob Riis, Angel Island, nativism, Chinese Exclusion Act

Reading Strategy
Categorizing Complete a graphic organizer similar to the one below by filling in the reasons people left their homelands to immigrate to the United States.

Reasons for Immigrating	
Push Factors	Pull Factors

Reading Objectives
• **Analyze** the circumstances surrounding the great wave of immigration after the Civil War.
• **Evaluate** how nativism affected immigration policies.

Section Theme
Geography and History Immigrants from all over the world enriched the cultural life of the United States.

Preview of Events

♦1880   ♦1890   ♦1900   ♦1910

1882
Chinese Exclusion Act passed

1886
Haymarket Riot in Chicago

1887
American Protective Association founded

1892
Ellis Island immigration center opens

1910
United States opens Angel Island facility for Asian immigrants

---

★ An American Story ★

Samuel Goldwyn

Samuel Goldwyn was born in Warsaw, Poland, in 1879. His family lived in a tiny two-room apartment. As Jews they feared the pogroms—anti-Jewish riots—that often erupted in the city. At age 16, Goldwyn set out for America, first walking 500 miles to the port of Hamburg, Germany. When he arrived in the United States, Goldwyn worked first as a floor sweeper and then as a cutter in a glove factory, putting in 13-hour days. At night, he went to school. Within two years he was a foreman, and soon after he became a successful glove salesman.

In 1913 Goldwyn visited a nickelodeon, an early movie theater. As he watched the film, he became convinced that this new industry would grow into something big. He used his savings to set up a film company, and in 1914 he released his first movie. The film was an instant success. During his career, Goldwyn helped found three film companies: Paramount Studios, Metro-Goldwyn-Mayer (MGM), and United Artists. All three still make movies today. Looking back on his rise from poverty to wealth, Goldwyn commented:

❝When I was a kid . . . the only place I wanted to go was America. I had heard them talking about America, about how free people were in America. . . . Even then America, actually only the name of a faraway country, was a vision of paradise.❞

—adapted from *Goldwyn: A Biography*

Europeans Flood Into the United States

By 1900, more than half of all immigrants in the United States were eastern and southern Europeans, including Italians, Greeks, Poles, Slavs, Slovaks, Russians, and Armenians. Like Samuel Goldwyn, many of the 14 million immigrants who came to the United States between 1860 and 1900 were eastern European Jews.

336 CHAPTER 10   Urban America

SECTION RESOURCES

📖 Reproducible Masters
• Reproducible Lesson Plan 10–1
• Daily Lecture and Discussion Notes 10–1
• Guided Reading Activity 10–1
• Section Quiz 10–1
• Reading Essentials and Study Guide 10–1
• Interpreting Political Cartoons

🖥 Transparencies
• Daily Focus Skills Transparency 10–1

Multimedia
🔘 Interactive Tutor Self-Assessment CD-ROM
🔘 ExamView® Pro Testmaker CD-ROM
🔘 Presentation Plus! CD-ROM
🔘 TeacherWorks™ CD-ROM
🎧 Audio Program
🎵 American Music: Cultural Traditions

NATIONAL GEOGRAPHIC

"Old" and "New" Immigrants, 1870–1900

"Old" Immigrants
Northern & Western Europe

"New" Immigrants
Southern & Eastern Europe

7,876,122

10,961,744
Total

3,085,622

Canadian
Immigrants
820,669

28,409

243,860 Asian Immigrants

215,451

Latin American
Immigrants
91,792

ALASKA
U.S.

CANADA

ASIA

JAPAN

CHINA

Ellis Island

Angel Island
UNITED STATES

MEXICO

EUROPE

ATLANTIC
OCEAN

AFRICA

SOUTH
AMERICA

PACIFIC
OCEAN

AUSTRALIA

ARCTIC CIRCLE

TROPIC OF CANCER

EQUATOR

TROPIC OF CAPRICORN

0   1500 miles
0   1500 kilometers
Mercator projection

N W E S

Immigration, 1870–1900

Immigrants (thousands)

500
400
300
200
100

1870   1880   1890   1900
Year

From northern and
western Europe
From southern and
eastern Europe
From the Americas
From Asia

Push Factors
- Farm poverty & worker uncertainty
- Wars & compulsory military service
- Political tyranny
- Religious oppression

Pull Factors
- Plenty of land & plenty of work
- Higher standard of living
- Democratic political system
- Opportunity for social advancement

Geography Skills

1. **Analyzing Maps** From which region did the majority of U.S. immigrants come?
2. **Applying Geography Skills** In what year did immigration from northern and western Europe peak?

Europeans abandoned their homelands and headed to the United States for many reasons. Many poor rural farmers came simply because the United States had plenty of jobs available and few immigration restrictions. Yet Europe in the late 1800s offered plenty of jobs in its booming industrial cities, so economic factors were not the only reason people migrated. Many moved to avoid forced military service, which in some nations could last for many years. Others, especially Jews living in Poland and Russia, fled to avoid religious persecution.

By the late 1800s, most European states had made moving to the United States easy. Immigrants were allowed to take their savings with them, and most countries had repealed old laws that had forced peasants to stay in their villages and had banned skilled workers from leaving the country. At the same time, moving to the United States offered a chance to break away from Europe's class

system and move to a democratic nation where they had a chance to move up the social ladder.

The Atlantic Voyage Getting to the United States was often very difficult. Most immigrants booked passage in steerage, the most basic and cheapest accommodations on a steamship. Edward Steiner, an Iowa clergyman who posed as an immigrant in order to write a book on immigration, described the miserable quarters:

> Narrow, steep and slippery stairways lead to it. Crowds everywhere, ill smelling bunks, uninviting washrooms—this is steerage. The odors of scattered orange peelings, tobacco, garlic and disinfectants meeting but not blending. No lounge or chairs for

CHAPTER 10 Urban America **337**

2 TEACH

Daily Lecture and Discussion Notes 10–1

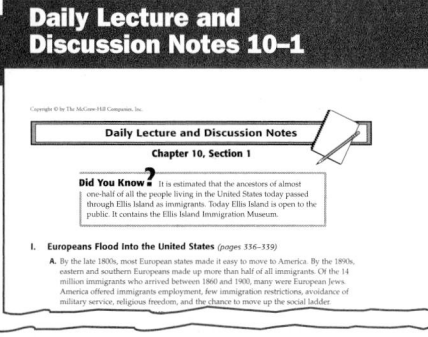

Copyright © by The McGraw-Hill Companies, Inc.

Daily Lecture and Discussion Notes
Chapter 10, Section 1

Did You Know? It is estimated that the ancestors of almost one-half of all the people living in the United States today passed through Ellis Island as immigrants. Today Ellis Island is open to the public. It contains the Ellis Island Immigration Museum.

I. Europeans Flood Into the United States (pages 336–339)
A. By the late 1800s, most European states made it easy to move to America. By the 1890s, eastern and southern Europeans made up more than half of all immigrants. Of the 14 million immigrants who arrived between 1860 and 1900, many were European Jews. America offered immigrants employment, few immigration restrictions, avoidance of military service, religious freedom, and the chance to move up the social ladder.

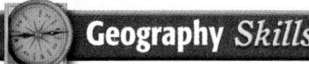

Geography Skills

Answers:
1. Europe
2. around 1882

Geography Skills Practice
Ask: Where did most Asian immigrants arrive in the United States? (Angel Island, California)

Creating a Collage Have students create a collage on the origins of immigrants to the United States after 1880. Encourage students to clip photos from newsmagazines to make the collage. **L1** ELL

L1/ELL

Guided Reading Activity 10–1

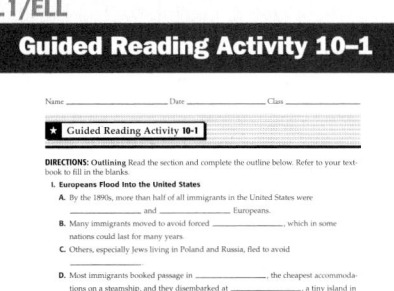

Name _____ Date _____ Class _____

★ **Guided Reading Activity 10–1**

DIRECTIONS: Outlining Read the section and complete the outline below. Refer to your textbook to fill in the blanks.

I. Europeans Flood Into the United States
A. By the 1890s, more than half of all immigrants were _____ and _____ Europeans.
B. Many immigrants moved to avoid forced _____, which in some nations could last for many years.
C. Others, especially Jews living in Poland and Russia, fled to avoid _____.
D. Most immigrants booked passage in _____, the cheapest accommodations on a steamship, and they disembarked at _____, a tiny island in New York Harbor.

Reading Strategy READING THE TEXT

Analyzing Information Organize students into groups of three or four to trace the arrival of an immigrant family in the United States. Each group should choose a different nationality and point of entry. Have students discuss the reasons why immigrants left their native countries, what mode of transportation they took, where they arrived in America, and how they settled into life in their new country. Students should also point out the problems the immigrants faced as they settled into their new lives. **L1**

Refer to *Inclusion for the High School Social Studies Classroom Strategies and Activities* in the TCR.

Different Viewpoints

Two Views of Immigration

The history of immigration to the United States has been both celebrated and criticized. Many millions of immigrants arrived in the United States in the late 1800s. The newcomers sought opportunity, enriched American culture, and caused concerns. Here, two political cartoons address the immigration issue.

Anti-Immigration

"Columbia's Unwelcome Guests" shows another view of immigration. In this 1885 cartoon, the figure of Columbia bars entry to anarchists, Socialists, and Communists who enter from the sewers of Europe's darker society. Some of the inscriptions on the column pedestal beside Columbia read "Anarchy is not liberty," and "When a Man's Rights End, His Neighbor's Begin."

Pro-Immigration

Uncle Sam plays the role of Noah in this cartoon. As immigrants file two by two into the safety of the ark, they leave behind the dangers of Europe that are darkening the sky. A sign lists some reasons people came to the United States to begin a new life.

Learning From History

1. According to the cartoon, why were people concerned about immigrants coming to the United States?
2. Which cartoon best expresses your own views on immigration today? Why?

comfort, and a continual babble of tongues—this is steerage. The food, which is miserable, is dealt out of huge kettles into the dinner pails provided by the steamship company. When it is distributed, the stronger push and crowd. . . ."

—quoted in *World of Our Fathers*

At the end of a 14-day journey, the passengers usually disembarked at **Ellis Island,** a tiny island in New York Harbor. There, a huge three-story building served as the processing center for many of the immigrants arriving on the East Coast after 1892.

Ellis Island Most immigrants passed through Ellis Island in about a day. They would not soon forget their hectic introduction to the United States. A medical examiner who worked there later described how "hour after hour, ship load after ship load . . . the stream of human beings with its kaleidoscopic variations

was . . . hurried through Ellis Island by the equivalent of 'step lively' in every language of the earth."

In Ellis Island's enormous hall, crowds of immigrants filed past the doctor for an initial inspection. "Whenever a case aroused suspicion," an inspector wrote, "the alien was set aside in a cage apart from the rest . . . and his coat lapel or shirt marked with colored chalk" to indicate the reason for the isolation. About one out of five newcomers was marked with an "H" for heart problems, "K" for hernias, "Sc" for scalp problems, or "X" for mental disability. Newcomers who failed the inspection might be separated from their families and returned to Europe.

GEOGRAPHY

Ethnic Cities Many of those who passed the Ellis Island inspections settled in the nation's cities. By the 1890s, immigrants made up significant percentages of

338　CHAPTER 10　Urban America

Creating Circle Charts Provide the census data below and have students create four circle charts to show the proportion of the U.S. population made up of persons born in the United States and persons born in foreign countries. **L2**

	U.S. Born	Foreign Born
1870	32,676,000	5,480,000
1880	42,869,000	6,499,000
1890	52,919,000	9,198,000
1900	64,344,000	10,263,000

ABCNEWS INTERACTIVE™

VIDEOCASSETTE
Historic America Electronic Field Trips

View **Tape 2, Chapter 7:** "Ellis Island."

History *and the* Humanities

American Music: Cultural Traditions: "No Irish Need Apply," "Polka Wiesniaczka"

DIFFERENTIATED INSTRUCTION

Verbal/Linguistic Oral histories are a good way to preserve the immigrant experience. Have students interview a person who immigrated to the United States. Their questions might include: reasons for immigrating to the United States; a description of the journey; feelings upon entering the United States; and problems faced such as finding employment or overcoming the language barrier. **L2**

📂 Refer to ***Inclusion for the High School Social Studies Classroom Strategies and Activities*** in the TCR.

some of the country's largest cities, including New York, Chicago, Milwaukee, and Detroit. **Jacob Riis,** a Danish-born journalist, observed in 1890 that a map of New York City, "colored to designate nationalities, would show more stripes than on the skin of a zebra."

In the cities, immigrants lived in neighborhoods that were often separated into ethnic groups, such as "Little Italy" or the Jewish "Lower East Side" in New York City. There they spoke their native languages and re-created the churches, synagogues, clubs, and newspapers of their homelands.

How well immigrants adjusted depended partly on how quickly they learned English and adapted to American culture. Immigrants also tended to adjust well if they had marketable skills or money, or if they settled among members of their own ethnic group.

As many as one in three immigrants returned to Europe shortly after coming to the United States. Some had never planned to stay and had come simply to make a little money before returning home.

✓ **Reading Check** **Explaining** How did immigration affect demographic patterns in the United States?

Asian Immigration to America

Many Chinese immigrants began crossing the Pacific to arrive in the United States in the mid-1800s. By that time, China's population had reached about 430 million, and the country was suffering from severe unemployment, poverty, and famine.

The 1848 discovery of gold in California began to lure Chinese immigrants to the United States. Then, in 1850, the Taiping Rebellion erupted in their homeland. This insurrection against the Chinese government took some 20 million lives and caused such suffering that thousands of Chinese left for the United States. In the early 1860s, as the Central Pacific Railroad began construction of its portion of the transcontinental railroad, the demand for railroad workers further increased Chinese immigration.

Chinese immigrants mainly settled in western cities, where they often worked as laborers or servants or in skilled trades. Others worked as merchants. Because native-born Americans kept them out of many businesses, some Chinese immigrants opened their own. To save enough to buy his own laundry, one immigrant, Lee Chew, had to work for two years as a servant:

❝I did not know how to do anything, and I did not understand what the lady said to me, but she showed me how to cook, wash, iron, sweep, dust, make beds, wash dishes, clean windows, paint and brass, polish the knives and forks, etc., by doing the things herself and then overseeing my efforts to imitate her.❞
—quoted in *A Sunday Between Wars*

Another group of Asians, the Japanese, also immigrated to the United States. Until 1900, however, their numbers remained small. Between 1900 and 1908, large numbers of Japanese migrated to the United States as Japan began building both an industrial economy and an empire. Both developments disrupted the economy of Japan and caused hardships for its people, thus stimulating emigration.

Until 1910 Asian immigrants arriving in San Francisco first stopped at a two-story shed at the wharf. As many as 500 people at a time were often squeezed into this structure, which Chinese immigrants from Canton called *muk uk,* or "wooden house."

In January 1910, California opened a barracks on **Angel Island** to accommodate the Asian immigrants. Most of the immigrants were young males in their teens or twenties, who nervously awaited the results of their immigration hearings in dormitories packed with double or triple tiers of bunks. This unpleasant delay could last for months. On the walls of the detention barracks, the immigrants wrote anonymous poems in pencil or ink. Some even carved their verse into the wood.

✓ **Reading Check** **Making Generalizations** Why did Chinese immigrants come to the United States?

Angel Island Over 200,000 immigrants from Japan and China arrived on the West Coast during the late 1800s.

HISTORY Online

Student Web Activity Visit the *American Republic Since 1877* Web site at tarvol2.glencoe.com and click on **Student Web Activities— Chapter 10** for an activity on immigration.

✓ **Reading Check**

Answer: larger population and a more urban population

HISTORY Online

Objectives and answers to the student activity can be found in the **Web Activity Lesson Plan** at tarvol2.glencoe.com.

✓ **Reading Check**

Answer: high unemployment, poverty, and famine in China; Taiping Rebellion; availability of railroad jobs in the United States

📁 Use *Interpreting Political Cartoons,* Cartoon 14.

3 ASSESS

Assign Section 1 Assessment as homework or as an in-class activity.

💡 Have students use the **Interactive Tutor Self-Assessment CD-ROM.**

L1/ELL

Reading Essentials and Study Guide 10–1

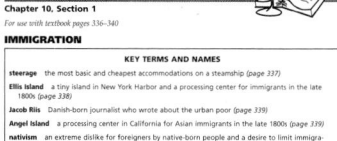

Name _____ Date _____ Class _____

Study Guide

Chapter 10, Section 1
For use with textbook pages 336–340

IMMIGRATION

KEY TERMS AND NAMES

steerage the most basic and cheapest accommodations on a steamship *(page 337)*
Ellis Island a tiny island in New York Harbor and a processing center for immigrants in the late 1800s *(page 338)*
Jacob Riis Danish-born journalist who wrote about the urban poor *(page 339)*
Angel Island a processing center in California for Asian immigrants in the late 1800s *(page 339)*
nativism an extreme dislike for foreigners by native-born people and a desire to limit immigration *(page 340)*
Chinese Exclusion Act a law that barred Chinese immigration for 10 years and prevented the Chinese already in the country from becoming citizens *(page 340)*

INTERDISCIPLINARY CONNECTIONS ACTIVITY

Sociology Write the word *Assimilation* in a circle on the board. Have students add spokes out from the circle and label each spoke with a way in which immigrants in the late 1800s and early 1900s were asked to assimilate into American culture. Repeat the process by writing *Assimilation Today* in another circle on the board. Have students add descriptive spokes to the wheel. As a class, discuss how the expectation of immigrants to assimilate has changed and how it is still the same. **L2**

L2

Section Quiz 10–1

Name _____ Date _____ Class _____

★ Chapter 10   Score ☐

Section Quiz 10–1

DIRECTIONS: Matching Match each item in Column A with the items in Column B.
Write the correct letters in the blanks. (10 points each)

Column A
_____ 1. the most basic and cheapest accommodations on a steamship
_____ 2. an anti-immigrant organization
_____ 3. insurrection against the Chinese government that caused an increase of Chinese immigrants
_____ 4. location of a barracks in California to accommodate Asian immigrants
_____ 5. an extreme dislike for foreigners by native-born people and a desire to limit immigration

Column B
A. Angel Island
B. steerage
C. American Protective Association
D. nativism
E. Taiping Rebellion

Reteach

Have students analyze the circumstances surrounding the great wave of European immigration after the Civil War.

Enrich

Invite interested students to create a display that showcases a cultural tradition that immigrants brought to the United States. For example, families from the Netherlands continued the children's tradition of setting out wooden shoes in hopes that St. Nicholas would bring treats on December 6. Encourage students to share information about their own family traditions that are based on cultural heritage.

✓ Reading Check

Answer: to limit Chinese immigration; it was a reaction to the violence in California and a reflection of the era's prejudices

HISTORY
Online

Study Central™ provides summaries, interactive games, and online graphic organizers to help students review section content.

4 CLOSE

Have students evaluate how nativism affected immigration policies.

340

The Resurgence of Nativism

Eventually the wave of immigration led to increased feelings of nativism on the part of many Americans. Nativism is a preference for native-born people and a desire to limit immigration. It had surfaced earlier in the 1800s during another large wave of immigration. In the 1840s and 1850s, it had focused primarily on Irish immigrants. Now anti-immigrant feelings focused on Asians, Jews, and eastern Europeans.

Nativists opposed immigration for many reasons. Some feared that the influx of Catholics from Ireland and southern and eastern Europe would swamp the mostly Protestant United States, giving the Catholic Church too much power in the American government. Many labor unions also opposed immigration, arguing that immigrants would work for low wages or accept work as strikebreakers, thus undermining American-born workers.

Nativists Organize   In the Northeast and Midwest, increased feelings of nativism led to the founding of two major anti-immigrant organizations. One, called the **American Protective Association,** was founded in 1887. The organization's founder, Henry Bowers, despised Catholicism and committed his group to stopping Catholic immigration. Membership of the organization peaked at about one million but declined rapidly after the economic recession of 1893 ended.

In the West, where sentiment against the Chinese was very strong, widespread racial violence erupted. Denis Kearney, himself an Irish immigrant, organized the **Workingman's Party of California** in the 1870s to fight Chinese immigration. The party won seats in California's legislature and made opposition to Chinese immigration a national issue.

Congress Passes New Immigration Laws   Even though several presidents vetoed other laws that would have stemmed the steady flow of new immigrants, concern over unchecked immigration stimulated the passage of a new federal law. Enacted in 1882, the law banned convicts, paupers, and the mentally disabled from immigrating to the United States. The new law also placed a 50¢ head tax on each newcomer.

That same year, Congress passed the **Chinese Exclusion Act**. The law barred Chinese immigration for 10 years and prevented the Chinese already in the country from becoming citizens. The Chinese in the United States did not accept the new law quietly. They protested that white Americans did not oppose immigration by Italians, Irish, or Germans. Some Chinese organized letter-writing campaigns, petitioned the president, and even filed suit in federal court.

These efforts, however, proved fruitless. Congress renewed the Chinese Exclusion Act in 1892 and then made it permanent in 1902. In 1890 the number of Chinese living in the United States totaled 105,000. By 1900 that total had dropped to just above 74,000. In the 40 years after the passage of the act, the Chinese population in the United States continued to decrease. The act was not repealed until 1943.

✓ Reading Check   **Explaining** Why did the federal government pass the Chinese Exclusion Act?

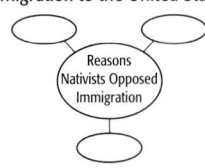

HISTORY *Online*   **Study Central**™ To review this section, go to **tarvol2.glencoe.com** and click on **Study Central**™.

SECTION 1 ASSESSMENT

Checking for Understanding
1. **Define:** steerage, nativism.
2. **Identify:** Ellis Island, Jacob Riis, Angel Island, Chinese Exclusion Act.
3. **Describe** where most immigrants to the United States settled in the late 1800s.
4. **Explain** why nativist organizations sought to limit immigration.

Reviewing Themes
5. **Geography and History** What routes did European and Asian immigrants take to get to the United States?

Critical Thinking
6. **Analyzing** Why did some Americans blame immigrants for the nation's problems?
7. **Organizing** Complete a graphic organizer by listing reasons nativists opposed immigration to the United States.

    (Reasons Nativists Opposed Immigration)

Analyzing Visuals
8. **Analyzing Political Cartoons** Compare the cartoons on page 338. What conclusions can you draw about American views on immigration in the late 1880s? Why do you think various people viewed immigration differently?

Writing About History
9. **Descriptive Writing** Imagine that you are an immigrant who arrived in the country in the 1800s. Write a letter to a relative in your home country describing your feelings during processing at either Ellis Island or Angel Island.

340   CHAPTER 10   Urban America

SECTION 1 ASSESSMENT ANSWERS

1. Terms are in blue.
2. Ellis Island *(p. 338)*, Jacob Riis *(p. 339)*, Angel Island *(p. 339)*, Chinese Exclusion Act *(p. 340)*
3. neighborhoods of large cities
4. disliked their religion; perceived to take jobs from Americans
5. Europeans generally entered through Ellis Island, New York, Asians through Angel Island, San Francisco.
6. They were blamed for economic recession and stigmatized for their religion and political beliefs.
7. influx of Catholics would give Catholic Church too much power, immigrants would weaken unions, would take jobs from Americans
8. Some Americans embraced immigrants and others were threatened by new arrivals.
9. Letters might express joy, fear, or frustration.

Guide to Reading

Main Idea
During the three decades following the Civil War, the United States transformed rapidly from a rural nation to a more urban one.

Key Terms and Names
skyscraper, Louis Sullivan, tenement, political machine, party boss, George Plunkitt, graft, William M. "Boss" Tweed

Reading Strategy
Organizing As you read about urbanization in the United States in the late 1800s, complete a graphic organizer similar to the one below by filling in the problems the nation's urban areas faced.

Urban Problems

Reading Objectives
• **Explain** the technological developments that made the growth of cities possible.
• **Evaluate** the role that political machines played in urban politics in the late 1800s.

Section Theme
Government and Democracy Political bosses grew powerful in urban areas by helping immigrants find work and necessities.

Preview of Events

♦1875	♦1880	♦1885	♦1890

1874
"Boss" Tweed sentenced to prison

1883
Brooklyn Bridge completed

1885
First steel girder construction used in building in Chicago

1888
Nation's first electric trolley line opens in Richmond, Virginia

1890
Jacob Riis publishes *How the Other Half Lives*

★ An American Story ★

Frank Lloyd Wright

With just $3.10 in his pocket, a young man from Wisconsin named Frank Lloyd Wright wandered the streets of Chicago in the late spring of 1887. Sixteen years earlier, almost four square miles of the city had burned in the Chicago Fire of 1871. Now the rebuilt city's towering new buildings beckoned the young visitor who, within a few decades, would become one of the most famous architects in the world.

In Chicago, Wright saw electric lights and cable cars for the first time. What surprised him most about the big city, however, were the signs that seemed to be everywhere:

66There were glaring signs on the glass shop-fronts against the lights inside, . . . HURRAH signs. STOP signs. COME ON IN signs. HELLO signs set out before the blazing windows on the sidewalks . . . food shops, barber shops, eating houses, saloons, restaurants, groceries, laundries—and [they all] became chaos in a wilderness of Italian, German, Irish, [Polish], Greek, English, Swedish, French, Chinese and Spanish names. . . .99

—quoted in *Eyewitness to America*

Americans Migrate to the Cities

During the three decades after the Civil War, the urban population of the United States—those living in towns with a population of 2,500 or more—grew from around 10 million in 1870 to over 30 million in 1900. New York City alone, which had over 800,000 inhabitants in 1860, grew to almost 3.5 million by 1900. Frank Lloyd Wright observed Chicago during an even faster growth period. The Midwestern city swelled from 109,000 residents in 1860 to more than 1.6 million by 1900. The United States had only 131 cities in 1840; by 1900 that number had risen to over 1,700.

CHAPTER 10 Urban America **341**

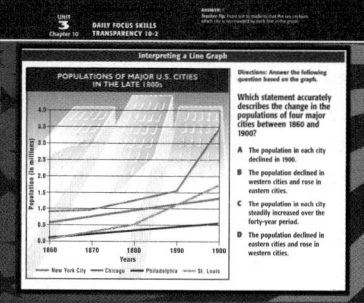
---

2 TEACH

Daily Lecture and Discussion Notes 10–2

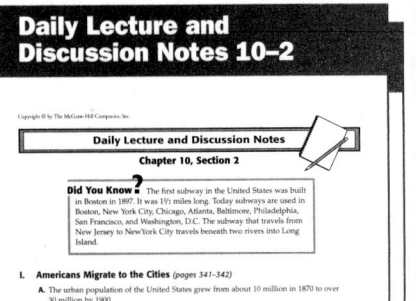

Daily Lecture and Discussion Notes
Chapter 10, Section 2

Did You Know? The first subway in the United States was built in Boston in 1897. It was 1½ miles long. Today subways are used in Boston, New York City, Chicago, Atlanta, Baltimore, Philadelphia, San Francisco, and Washington, D.C. The subway that travels from New Jersey to New York City travels beneath two rivers into Long Island.

I. Americans Migrate to the Cities (pages 341–342)

  A. The urban population of the United States grew from about 10 million in 1870 to over 30 million by 1900.

  B. Immigrants remained in the cities, where they worked long hours for little pay. Still,

✓ **Reading Check**

Answer: Cities offered more and better-paying jobs.

Creating a Postcard Have students imagine that they are immigrants living in New York City in the late 1800s. Instruct them to create a postcard that shows a scene of the city. **L1** ELL

📁 Use the rubric for creating a political cartoon, pamphlet, or handbill on pages 77–78 in the *Performance Assessment Activities and Rubrics.*

FYI

During the construction of the Brooklyn Bridge, John Roebling, who designed the bridge, was killed on the job. His son continued directing the work until being injured. The work was then taken over by John's wife, who completed the project with her son's direction.

History *and the* Humanities

✏️ American Art & Architecture: *Let Us Prey,* Guaranty Building, *Cliff Dwellers*

Most of the immigrants who poured into the United States in the late 1800s lacked the money to buy farms and the education to obtain higher-paying jobs. They therefore remained in the nation's growing cities, where they toiled long hours for little pay in the rapidly expanding factories of the United States. Despite the harshness of their new lives, most immigrants found that the move had still improved their standard of living.

The United States offered immigrants a chance at social mobility, or moving upward in society. Although only a few immigrants rose from poverty to great wealth, many seized the opportunities the American system offered and rose from the working class to the middle class. In much of Europe, on the other hand, people born into a particular social class were expected to stay there. Although some immigrants faced prejudice, most Americans accepted the idea that people in the lower classes could rise in society. The lack of a rigid class system in the United States gave immigrants a degree of freedom they had never known before.

Many rural Americans also began moving to the cities at this time. Farmers moved to the cities because urban areas offered more and better-paying jobs than did rural areas. Cities had much to offer, too—bright lights, running water, and modern plumbing, plus many things to do and see, including museums, libraries, and theaters.

✓ **Reading Check** **Explaining** Why did rural Americans move to the cities in the late 1800s?

The New Urban Environment

As millions of people flooded into the nation's cities, engineers and architects developed new approaches to housing and transporting such a large number of people.

Skyscrapers As city populations grew, demand raised the price of land, giving owners greater incentive to grow upward rather than outward. Soon, tall steel frame buildings called skyscrapers began to appear on American skylines. Chicago's ten-story Home Insurance Building, built in 1885, was the first skyscraper, but other buildings quickly dwarfed it. New York City boasted more skyscrapers than any other city in the world. With limited land, New Yorkers had to build up, not out.

No one contributed more to the design of skyscrapers than Chicago's **Louis Sullivan,** whose students included Frank Lloyd Wright. Sullivan's lofty structures featured simple lines and spacious windows using new durable plate glass.

The Technology of Urbanization

Before the mid-1800s, few buildings exceeded four or five stories. To make wooden and stone structures taller required enormously thick walls in the lower levels.

By the late 1800s, steel companies were making girders capable of bearing a building's weight. Walls no longer had to support the building—a steel frame skeleton was all that was needed. Meanwhile, Elisha Otis invented the safety elevator in 1852, and by the late 1880s, the first electric elevators had been installed, making tall buildings practical.

Steel also changed the way bridges were built. New technology enabled engineers to suspend bridges from steel towers using cables also made of steel. Using this technique, John A. Roebling, a German American engineer, designed New York's Brooklyn Bridge—the largest suspension bridge in the world at the time it was completed in 1883.

Brooklyn Bridge under construction

New York City's Flatiron Building

Reading Strategy   READING THE TEXT

Understanding Vocabulary Have students become familiar with different types of words. Point out to students that *Homophones* are words that sound the same but have different meanings and usually different spellings. For example, *base* is a foundation whereas *bass* is a deep tone. *Homographs* are words that are spelled the same but have different meanings and different origins. Some homographs have different pronunciations. For example, a *bow* may accompany an arrow but it also may be a part of a ship. **L1**

📁 Refer to *Inclusion for the High School Social Studies Classroom Strategies and Activities* in the TCR.

Mass Transit Various kinds of mass transit developed in the late 1800s to move huge numbers of people around cities quickly. At first, almost all cities relied on the horsecar—a railroad car pulled by horses. In 1890 horsecars moved about 70 percent of urban traffic in the United States.

More than 20 cities, beginning with San Francisco in 1873, installed cable cars, which were pulled along tracks by underground cables. Then, in 1887, engineer **Frank J. Sprague** developed the electric trolley car. The following year, Richmond, Virginia, opened the country's first electric trolley line.

In the largest cities, congestion became so bad that engineers began looking for ways to move mass transit off the streets. Chicago responded by building an elevated railroad, while Boston, followed by New York, built America's first subway systems.

✓ **Reading Check** **Summarizing**
What new technologies helped people in the late 1800s get to and from work?

Separation by Class

In the growing cities, wealthy people and the working class lived in different parts of town. So too did the middle class. The boundaries between neighborhoods can still be seen in many cities today.

High Society During the last half of the 1800s, the wealthiest families established fashionable districts in the hearts of cities. Americans with enough money could choose to construct a feudal castle, an English manor house, a French château, a Tuscan villa, or a Persian pavilion. In Chicago, merchant and real estate developer Potter Palmer chose a castle. In New York, Cornelius Vanderbilt's grandson commissioned a $3 million French château equipped with a two-story dining room, a gymnasium, and a marble bathroom.

Middle-Class Gentility American industrialization not only made the wealth of people like Potter Palmer possible; it also helped create a growing middle class. The nation's rising middle class included doctors, lawyers, engineers, managers, social workers, architects, and teachers. It was typical for many people in the emerging middle class to move away from the central city. Some took advantage of the new commuter rail lines to move to "streetcar suburbs."

Profiles IN HISTORY

Michael Pupin
1858–1935

Many immigrants came to America seeking freedom. One example was inventor Michael Pupin. As a young boy in Hungary, Pupin became fascinated with electricity after reading about Ben Franklin's experiments. He tried to study in Prague, but anti-Jewish prejudice made it impossible. He decided that only in America would he be free to study what he wanted.

At age 16, Pupin headed to New York. Once there he took odd jobs, including chopping wood and mowing hay, to pay for his education. Five years later, he won a scholarship to Columbia University. In 1889 Pupin became a professor of electrical engineering at Columbia University, and he went on to invent several important devices. He improved the x-ray machine, making it much more useful for doctors. He invented one device that improved long-distance telephone transmissions and another device that helped tune radio transmissions. In addition, his autobiography, *From Immigrant to Inventor,* won the Pulitzer Prize in 1924.

During this period, middle-class salaries were about twice that of the average factory worker. In 1905 a college professor earned a middle-class salary of $1,100.

The Working Class The majority of American city dwellers at the turn of the century would have considered an eight-room house an absolute luxury. In New York, three out of four residents squeezed into tenements, dark and crowded multi-family apartments. To supplement the average industrial worker's annual income of $490, many families sent their young children to work in factories or rented precious space to a boarder. Zalmen Yoffeh, a journalist, lived in a New York tenement as a child. He recalled:

❝With . . . one dollar a day [our mother] fed and clothed an ever-growing family. She took in boarders. Sometimes this helped; at other times it added to the burden of living. Boarders were often out of work and penniless; how could one turn a hungry man out? She made all our clothes. She walked blocks to reach a place where meat was a penny cheaper, where bread was a half cent less. She collected boxes and old wood to burn in the stove. . . .❞

—quoted in *How We Lived*

✓ **Reading Check** **Explaining** What social class grew as a result of industrialization in the late 1800s?

CHAPTER 10 Urban America **343**

L1/ELL
Guided Reading Activity 10-2

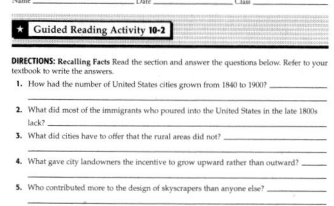

✓ **Reading Check**
Answer: cable cars, trolleys, elevated railroads, and subway systems

Profiles IN HISTORY

Background: Pupin received 34 patents for his inventions and was awarded 5 medals and 18 honorary degrees. Serbian King Alexander also awarded him the Order of the White Eagle
Ask: How was Pupin's experience similar to other immigrants coming to the U.S.? *(He came seeking freedom, worked odd jobs to pay for his education, and moved to a large city.)*

✓ **Reading Check**
Answer: middle class

CURRICULUM CONNECTION

Economics In the 1870s people thought that typing was physically too strenuous and intellectually too complicated for women. As a result, most secretaries were men. The Young Women's Christian Association (YWCA) conducted a survey and found that stenography was a lucrative career. In order to help working-class girls who came to urban areas for jobs, the YWCA offered shorthand and typing classes for women.

DIFFERENTIATED INSTRUCTION

At-Risk Students Some students feel most comfortable when they are permitted to tape lectures and discussions. This helps bypass the writing problem but creates another problem—time needed to review the lecture. This process can be more efficient if students are cued by the teacher as to when to turn on the recorder. As you discuss the problems of urban population increases, use a prearranged cueing system to help students. **L1**

📁 Refer to *Inclusion for the High School Social Studies Classroom Strategies and Activities* in the TCR.

Many tenement buildings began as tenant houses. These were often large residences of wealthy people who had moved away from the city. Real-estate agents subdivided the large rooms into smaller ones for immigrants. Agents, eager to make money, sometimes subdivided the rooms without considering lighting or ventilation.

✓ Reading Check

Answer: Sewage, street waste, smoke, soot, and ash contributed to health problems and epidemics of contagious diseases.

📂 Use *Interpreting Political Cartoons,* Cartoons 12 and 13.

3 ASSESS

Assign Section 2 Assessment as homework or as an in-class activity.

💿 Have students use the **Interactive Tutor Self-Assessment CD-ROM.**

L1/ELL

Reading Essentials and Study Guide 10–2

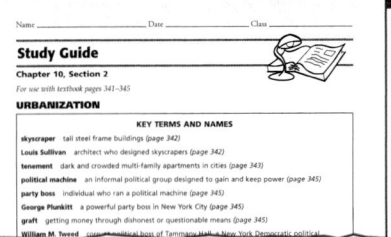

Name _____ Date _____ Class _____

Study Guide

Chapter 10, Section 2

For use with textbook pages 341–345

URBANIZATION

KEY TERMS AND NAMES

skyscraper tall steel frame buildings *(page 342)*

Louis Sullivan architect who designed skyscrapers *(page 342)*

tenement dark and crowded multi-family apartments in cities *(page 343)*

political machine an informal political group designed to gain and keep power *(page 345)*

party boss individual who ran a political machine *(page 345)*

George Plunkitt a powerful party boss in New York City *(page 345)*

graft getting money through dishonest or questionable means *(page 345)*

William M. Tweed corrupt political boss of Tammany Hall, a New York Democratic political...

NATIONAL GEOGRAPHIC

MOMENT IN HISTORY

TEEMING TENEMENTS

The swelling tide of immigration to U.S. cities in the late 1800s led to deplorable living conditions and almost unbearable congestion. By 1890, more than two-thirds of New York's 1.5 million residents lived in overcrowded apartment buildings called tenements. On the Lower East Side, one of the most densely populated areas in the world, people frequented vibrant outdoor markets such as this one on Hester Street for goods from eggs to rugs to pots and pans. Gossip, haggling, and cries of street peddlers—mostly in Yiddish in this Jewish neighborhood—echoed down the street from dawn to dusk.

Urban Problems

City living posed threats such as crime, violence, fire, disease, and pollution, especially for the working poor like Yoffeh and his family. The rapid growth of cities only made these problems worse. Minor criminals, such as pickpockets, swindlers, and thieves, thrived in crowded urban living conditions. Major crimes multiplied as well. From 1880 to 1900, the murder rate jumped sharply from 25 per million people to more than 100 per million people. In comparison, the murder rate in 1999 was 57 per million people.

Native-born Americans often blamed immigrants for the increase in crime and violence. In reality, the crime rate for immigrants was not significantly higher than that for other Americans.

Alcohol did contribute to violent crime, both inside and outside the home. Danish immigrant Jacob Riis, who documented slum life in his 1890 book *How the Other Half Lives,* accused saloons of "breeding poverty," corrupting politics, bringing suffering to the wives and children of drunkards, and fostering "the corruption of the child" by selling beer to minors.

Disease and pollution posed even bigger threats. Improper sewage disposal contaminated city drinking water and triggered epidemics of typhoid fever and cholera. Though flush toilets and sewer systems existed in the 1870s, pollution remained a severe problem as horse waste was left in the streets, smoke belched from chimneys, and soot and ash accumulated from coal and wood fires.

✓ Reading Check **Drawing Conclusions** Why were diseases and pollution big problems in American cities in the late 1800s?

Urban Politics

A new kind of political system developed to meet these urban problems. This system provided essential city services in return for political power.

INTERDISCIPLINARY CONNECTIONS ACTIVITY

Literature Have students obtain a copy of *How the Other Half Lives* by Jacob A. Riis. Have students investigate the legislation Riis advocated to improve slum conditions and research how he went about securing this legislation. Ask students to present their findings as if they were asking Congress to pass a law to protect urban dwellers. **L3**

The Political Machine and the Party Boss The political machine, an informal political group designed to gain and keep power, came about partly because cities had grown much faster than their governments. New city dwellers needed jobs, housing, food, heat, and police protection. In exchange for votes, political machines and the party bosses who ran them eagerly provided these necessities.

George Plunkitt, an Irish immigrant who rose to be one of New York City's most powerful party bosses, explained how the system worked when a fire burned a neighborhood:

❝I just get [housing] for them, buy clothes for them if their clothes were burned up, and fix them up till they get things runnin' again. It's philanthropy, but it's politics too—mighty good politics. Who can tell how many votes one of these fires bring me? The poor are the most grateful people in the world, and, let me tell you, they have more friends in their neighborhoods than the rich have in theirs.❞

—quoted in *In Search of America*

As Plunkitt observed, the payoff for party bosses came on Election Day. Urban immigrant groups, which wielded tremendous voting strength, voted in overwhelming numbers for the political machines.

Graft and Fraud The party bosses who ran the political machines also controlled the city's finances. Many machine politicians grew rich as the result of fraud or graft—getting money through dishonest or questionable means. Plunkitt defended what he called "honest graft." For example, a politician might find out in advance where a new park was to be built and buy the land near the site. The politician would then sell the land to the city for a profit. As Plunkitt stated, "I see my opportunity and I take it."

Outright fraud occurred when party bosses accepted bribes from contractors, who were supposed to compete fairly to win contracts to build streets, sewers, and buildings. Corrupt bosses also sold permits to their friends to operate public utilities, such as railroads, waterworks, and power systems.

Tammany Hall Tammany Hall, the New York Democratic political machine for which George Plunkitt performed his labors, was the most famous such organization. **William M. "Boss" Tweed** was its corrupt leader during the 1860s and 1870s. Tweed's corruption led him to prison in 1874.

Other cities' machines controlled all the city services, including the police department. For example, St. Louis's boss never feared arrest when he called out to his supporters at the police-supervised voting booth, "Are there any more repeaters out here that want to vote again?" Based in Kansas City, Missouri, the Pendergast brothers, James and Thomas, ran state and city politics from the 1890s until the 1930s.

Opponents of political machines, such as political cartoonist Thomas Nast, blasted bosses for their corruption. Defenders, though, argued that machines provided necessary services and helped to assimilate the masses of new city dwellers.

✓ **Reading Check** **Evaluating** Why did political machines help city dwellers in the late 1800s?

L2

Section Quiz 10–2

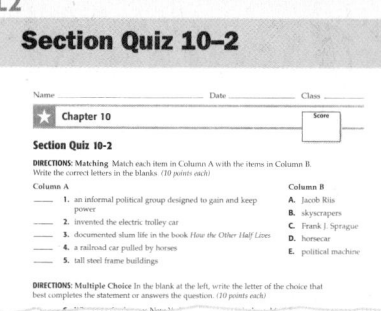

Section Quiz 10-2
DIRECTIONS: Matching Match each item in Column A with the items in Column B. Write the correct letters in the blanks. *(10 points each)*

Column A
___ 1. an informal political group designed to gain and keep power
___ 2. invented the electric trolley car
___ 3. documented slum life in the book *How the Other Half Lives*
___ 4. a railroad car pulled by horses
___ 5. tall steel frame buildings

Column B
A. Jacob Riis
B. skyscrapers
C. Frank J. Sprague
D. horsecar
E. political machine

DIRECTIONS: Multiple Choice In the blank at the left, write the letter of the choice that best completes the statement or answers the question. *(10 points each)*

Reteach
Have students list the technological developments that made the growth of cities possible.

Enrich
Have students create a three-column table illustrating social problems, solutions, and alternatives. Instruct students to use the first column to list the social problems described in this section. In the second column, students should describe the solutions used. Students should explain their alternative solutions in the third column.

✓ **Reading Check**

Answer: to gain immigrant votes and thus maintain political power

Study Central™ provides summaries, interactive games, and online graphic organizers to help students review section content.

Study Central™ To review this section, go to **tarvol2.glencoe.com** and click on **Study Central™.**

SECTION 2 ASSESSMENT

Checking for Understanding
1. **Define:** skyscraper, tenement, political machine, party boss, graft.
2. **Identify:** Louis Sullivan, George Plunkitt, William M. "Boss" Tweed.
3. **Explain** what two technologies made the building of skyscrapers possible in the late 1800s.

Reviewing Themes
4. **Government and Democracy** How did political machines respond to the needs of the people?

Critical Thinking
5. **Comparing** Compare the conditions under which the wealthy class, the middle class, and the working class lived in the United States in the late 1800s.
6. **Organizing** Complete a graphic organizer similar to the one below by listing the effects of many Americans moving from rural to urban areas in the late 1800s.

Migration	→	Effects

Analyzing Visuals
7. **Examining Photographs** Study the photographs on page 342 of the Brooklyn Bridge and the Flatiron Building. Why was it advantageous to construct taller buildings rather than purchase more land?

Writing About History
8. **Persuasive Writing** Take on the role of an urban planner living in one of the nation's major cities in the late 1800s. Write a letter to members of the city government listing specific reasons for the importance of setting aside city land for a park and recreational area.

CHAPTER 10   Urban America   **345**

SECTION 2 ASSESSMENT ANSWERS

1. Terms are in blue.
2. Louis Sullivan *(p. 342)*, George Plunkitt *(p. 345)*, William M. ("Boss") Tweed *(p. 345)*
3. steel frames and durable plate glass
4. provided jobs, housing, food, heat, police protection
5. wealthy lived in grand homes in fashionable areas, middle class in comfortable homes in streetcar suburbs, and working class in tenements
6. new demographic patterns included more urban population and more disease; also growth of political machines
7. land was limited and expensive; allowed more people to work in the cities
8. Students' letters will vary. Letters should include specific reasons for parks and recreational areas.

4 CLOSE

Have students evaluate the role that political machines played in urban politics in the late 1800s.

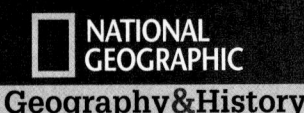

1 FOCUS

Tell students that Jane Addams's efforts in Hull House were modeled on Toynbee Hall, a settlement house in England. She provided various experiences for immigrants, including visits to art galleries, classes in English, and the use of a gymnasium.

2 TEACH

Making Generalizations As a class, discuss urban living as presented in the chapter and from the students' own experiences with urban areas. Have students make generalizations about living in urban areas. Write these generalizations on the board. Allow students to refine or change their generalizations as the discussion progresses. **L1**

Analyzing Information
Organize the class into small groups and assign each group one of the immigrant groups listed on the Hull House Neighborhood inset map. Have each group research what industries or jobs were held by their assigned immigrant group. Have each group list its findings on the board. As a class, discuss how immigrant groups contributed to Chicago life. **L2**

The Hull House Neighborhood

Bohemian	French Canadian	Irish	Russian
Chinese	French	Italian	Scandinavian
English speaking	German	Polish	Swiss
	Non-residential		

Chicago's apartment buildings, or tenements, were squeezed onto lots that measured 25 by 125 feet (7.6 by 38.1 m). These lots typically held three families and their boarders. Unlike New York City's tenements, most were only two or three stories tall.

346 CHAPTER 10 Urban America

EXTENDING THE CONTENT

Urban Problems Urban problems are not new. Many cities in ancient times were large and crowded. Some historians place Rome's population at more than 1 million by the start of the first century A.D. Within 100 years overcrowding resulted in many of Rome's citizens living in apartment houses. Some apartments were 5 or 6 stories high and sheltered about 200 people each. Many of the city's residential structures were poorly constructed, and living conditions paralleled those in the impoverished sections of 1800s New York or Chicago.

Immigrants Arrive In Chicago

A major port and a conduit for the nation's east-west rail travel, Chicago was a booming industrial center for the lumber, grain, meatpacking, and mail-order businesses at the end of the 1800s. Since the early 1870s, more ships had been docking in Chicago than in New York, Baltimore, Philadelphia, Charleston, and San Francisco combined. The city's expansion was phenomenal. In 50 years, it grew from a modest frontier town to the second-largest city in the country.

Immigrants swarmed into Chicago seeking jobs. Poles found work slaughtering livestock; Irish laying railroads; Russian and Polish Jews making clothes; Swedes constructing buildings and Italians forging steel. Women established boardinghouses, took in sewing to do at home, and worked in factories. In most factories, the hours were long and the working conditions difficult: noisy, hot, grimy, and overcrowded. By the beginning of the 1900s, three-fourths of the people in this teeming metropolis were European immigrants and their American-born children.

Ethnic neighborhoods dotted the city, as did blocks of tenements thrown up to house the flood of newcomers. The inset map at left—an enlargement of the highlighted rectangle on the lithograph—shows the Hull House neighborhood in Chicago's West Side in 1893. Hull House was established by social reformer Jane Addams to "investigate and improve the conditions in the industrial districts of Chicago." The neighborhood was one of the city's poorest. Its tenement buildings were disease-ridden and dangerous, crowding about 270 residents into each acre. Jane Addams wrote: "The streets are inexpressibly dirty, the number of schools inadequate, sanitary legislation unenforced, the street lighting bad, the paving miserable and altogether lacking in the alleys."

The neighborhood was also one of the most ethnically diverse. As the inset shows, the bewildered new immigrants tended to settle in enclaves that had already been established by others from their homeland. They banded together as they learned about the ways of the new land. Many immigrants found comfort in social life centered on the church or synagogue. Younger immigrants were more eager to abandon their old customs. Many of them quickly adopted American clothes and manners, learned to speak English, and tried to make American friends.

A visiting nurse puts drops in an infant's eyes. Crowded conditions threatened the health of many of the immigrants in Chicago's tenements.

LEARNING FROM GEOGRAPHY

1. How did the location of Chicago influence its development?

2. Pose and answer five questions about the geographic distribution and patterns shown on this model.

CHAPTER 10 Urban America **347**

ANSWERS TO LEARNING FROM GEOGRAPHY

1. Since it developed on the waterfront, Chicago developed both as a port city and a rail city. Ships would transport goods to the city and the goods would be shipped across the country from the rail lines.

2. Students' questions and answers will vary. You may have students trade questions and then have the pairs discuss the answers.

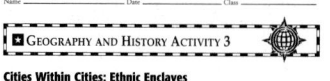

SECTION 3 The Gilded Age

1 FOCUS

Section Overview

This section focuses on how American society's thinking and behavior changed in the late 1800s.

BELLRINGER
Skillbuilder Activity

Project transparency and have students answer the question.

Daily Focus Skills Transparency 10–3

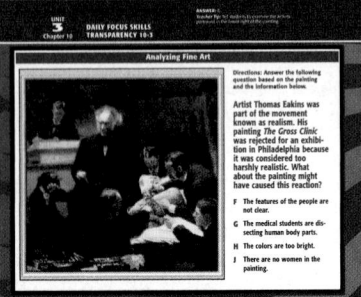

Reading Preview

Answers to Graphic: Social Darwinism: the theory that human society evolves through competition and natural selection–survival of the fittest; Laissez-faire: an economic doctrine that opposed government programs that interfered with business; Gospel of Wealth: the philosophy that wealthy people should give to public charity; Realism: movement in art and literature to portray people realistically

Preteaching Vocabulary
Have students write three questions that can be answered using the Key Terms and Names.

Guide to Reading

Main Idea
Industrialism and urbanization changed American society's ideas and culture in the late 1800s.

Key Terms and Names
Gilded Age, Social Darwinism, Gospel of Wealth, philanthropy, realism, vaudeville, ragtime, Scott Joplin

Reading Strategy
Categorizing Complete a graphic organizer similar to the one below by filling in the main idea of each of the theories and movements listed.

Theory or Movement	Main Idea
Social Darwinism	
Laissez-Faire	
Gospel of Wealth	
Realism	

Reading Objectives
- **Evaluate** the doctrine of Social Darwinism and the impact it had on American industry.
- **Explain** how industrialization promoted leisure time and encouraged new forms of entertainment.

Section Theme
Culture and Traditions The Gilded Age was an era of great cultural change in the United States.

Preview of Events

♦1870 ♦1880 ♦1890 ♦1900

1869
The Cincinnati Red Stockings become the first salaried baseball team

1884
Mark Twain publishes *Huckleberry Finn*

1891
James Naismith invents basketball

1899
Scott Joplin publishes "The Maple Leaf Rag"

William Graham Sumner

★ An American Story ★

In 1872, at the age of 32, William Graham Sumner became a professor of political and social science at Yale College. Sumner's classes were very popular. One of his students, William Lyon Phelps, illustrated Sumner's tough, no-nonsense approach with this example of a class discussion:

Student: "Professor, don't you believe in any government aid to industries?"
Sumner: "No! It's root, hog, or die."
Student: "Yes, but hasn't the hog got a right to root?"
Sumner: "There are no rights. The world owes nobody a living."
Student: "You believe then, Professor, in only one system, the contract-competitive system?"
Sumner: "That's the only sound economic system. All others are fallacies."
Student: "Well, suppose some professor of political economy came along and took your job away from you. Wouldn't you be sore?"
Sumner: "Any other professor is welcome to try. If he gets my job, it is my fault. My business is to teach the subject so well that no one can take the job away from me."

—adapted from *Social Darwinism in American Thought*

A Changing Culture

In 1873 Mark Twain and Charles Warner wrote a novel together entitled *The Gilded Age*. Historians later adopted the term and applied it to the era in American history that begins about 1870 and ends around 1900.

348 CHAPTER 10 Urban America

SECTION RESOURCES

📖 Reproducible Masters
- Reproducible Lesson Plan 10–3
- Daily Lecture and Discussion Notes 10–3
- Guided Reading Activity 10–3
- Section Quiz 10–3
- Reading Essentials and Study Guide 10–3

🖥 Transparencies
- Daily Focus Skills Transparency 10–3

- American Art & Architecture

Multimedia
- Interactive Tutor Self-Assessment CD-ROM
- ExamView® Pro Testmaker CD-ROM
- Presentation Plus! CD-ROM
- TeacherWorks™ CD-ROM
- Audio Program
- American Music: Hits Through History
- American Music: Cultural Traditions

This era was in many ways a time of marvels. Amazing new inventions led to rapid industrial growth. Cities expanded to sizes never seen before. Masses of workers thronged the streets. Skyscrapers reached to the sky, and electric lights banished the darkness. Newly wealthy entrepreneurs built spectacular mansions.

By calling this era the **Gilded Age,** Twain and Warner were sounding an alarm. Something is gilded if it is covered with gold on the outside but made of cheaper material inside. A gilded age might appear to sparkle, but Twain, Warner, and other writers tried to point out that beneath the surface lay corruption, poverty, crime, and great disparities in wealth between the rich and the poor.

Whether the era was golden or merely gilded, it was certainly a time of great cultural activity. Industrialism and urbanization altered the way Americans looked at themselves and their society, and these changes gave rise to new values, new art, and new forms of entertainment.

The Idea of Individualism One of the strongest beliefs of the era—and one that remains strong today—was the idea of **individualism.** Many Americans firmly believed that no matter how humble their origins, they could rise in society and go as far as their talents and commitment would take them. In 1885 the wealthy cotton manufacturer Edward Atkinson gave a speech to a group of workers at a textile factory in Rhode Island. He told them they had no reason to complain:

> 66There is always plenty of room on the front seats in every profession, every trade, every art, every industry. . . . There are men in this audience who will fill some of those seats, but they won't be boosted into them from behind.99
>
> —quoted in *America's History*

Horatio Alger No one expressed the idea of individualism better than Horatio Alger. A minister from Massachusetts, Alger eventually left the clergy and moved to New York. There he wrote more than 100 "rags-to-riches" novels, in which a poor person goes to the big city and becomes successful. Many young people loved reading these tales. Inspired by Alger's novels they concluded that no matter how many obstacles they faced, success was possible.

✓ **Reading Check** **Describing** What was the main idea behind individualism?

Social Darwinism

Another powerful idea of the era was Social Darwinism, which strongly reinforced the idea of individualism. English philosopher **Herbert Spencer** first proposed this idea. Historian John Fiske, political scientist William Graham Sumner, and the magazine *Popular Science Monthly* all popularized it in the United States.

Herbert Spencer Philosopher Herbert Spencer applied **Charles Darwin's** theory of evolution and natural selection to human society. In his 1859 book, *On the Origin of Species by Means of Natural Selection,* Darwin argued that plant and animal life had evolved over the years by a process he called natural selection. In this process, those species that cannot adapt to the environment in which they live gradually die out, while those that do adapt thrive and live on.

Spencer took this biological theory, intended to explain developments over millions of years, and argued that human society also evolved through competition and natural selection. He argued that society progressed and became better because only the fittest people survived.

Herbert Spencer

Spencer and others who shared his views became known as Social Darwinists, and their ideas were known as **Social Darwinism.** "Survival of the fittest" became the catchphrase of their philosophy. By 1902 over 350,000 copies of Spencer's books had been sold in the United States.

 Horatio Alger novel

2 TEACH

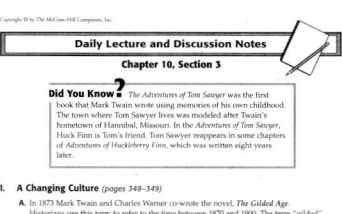

Daily Lecture and Discussion Notes 10–3

Copyright © The McGraw-Hill Companies, Inc.

Daily Lecture and Discussion Notes
Chapter 10, Section 3

Did You Know? *The Adventures of Tom Sawyer* was the first book that Mark Twain wrote using memories of his own childhood. The town where Tom Sawyer lives was modeled after Twain's hometown of Hannibal, Missouri. In the *Adventures of Tom Sawyer,* Huck Finn is Tom's friend. Tom Sawyer reappears in some chapters of *Adventures of Huckleberry Finn,* which was written eight years later.

I. **A Changing Culture** (pages 348–349)

A. In 1873 Mark Twain and Charles Warner co-wrote the novel, *The Gilded Age.* Historians use this term to refer to the time between 1870 and 1900. The term "gilded"

✓ **Reading Check**

Answer: that regardless of background, a person could rise in society and go as far as his or her talents and commitment would take them

📖 **Reading Strategy**

Creating a Profile Have students chose one of the persons mentioned in this section and write a short biographical profile emphasizing the person's connection to the Gilded Age. **L1**

📇 Use the rubric for creating a book review, research report, or handbill on pages 77–78 in the *Performance Assessment Activities and Rubrics.*

History *and the* Humanities

🎵 American Music: Hits Through History: "Maple Leaf Rag"

🎵 American Music: Cultural Traditions: "Maple Leaf Rag," "St. Louis Tickle"

🏛 American Art & Architecture: *In the Garden,* Favrile Glass Vase

📖 **Reading Strategy** **READING THE TEXT**

Evaluation Information Tell students that they are going to create a national magazine that would appeal to the general public in the late 1800s. In this magazine they will discuss the changes in society in the late 1800s, the influence of Social Darwinism, realism in art and literature, and the emergence of popular culture. Organize students into four groups and assign one of the topics to each of the groups. As students read the section, have them write short articles for the magazine based on the information they have gathered in the section. Within each group, students should divide subtopics and help one another if they don't understand a concept or idea. **L1**

History *Through Art*

Background: Thomas Eakins was a painter, sculptor, photographer, and art teacher. Many of his portrait subjects did not appreciate his realistic approach, and his insistence on the use of nude models for teaching also presented problems. Both his realistic style and his teaching techniques achieved great acceptance after his death. Eakins's work is now exhibited in some of America's most prestigious museums, including the Art Institute of Chicago, the Metropolitan Museum of Art, and the National Gallery of Art.

Answer: the everyday subject matter

Ask: What artistic movement did realism follow? *(romanticism)*

✓ Reading Check

Answer: that human society evolves through competition and natural selection—survival of the fittest

---

Social Darwinism also paralleled the economic doctrine of laissez-faire that opposed any government programs that interfered with business. Not surprisingly, industrial leaders like John D. Rockefeller heartily embraced the theory. Rockefeller maintained that survival of the fittest, as demonstrated by the growth of huge businesses like his own Standard Oil, was "merely the working out of the law of nature and the law of God."

Darwinism and the Church Rockefeller may have appreciated Spencer's interpretation of evolution, but Charles Darwin's conclusions about the origin of new species frightened and outraged many devout Christians as well as some leading scientists. They rejected the theory of evolution because they believed it contradicted the Bible's account of creation. Some American scholars and ministers, however, concluded that evolution may have been God's way of creating the world. Henry Ward Beecher of Plymouth Church in Brooklyn called himself a "cordial Christian evolutionist." Beecher accepted Spencer's ideas of Social Darwinism and championed the success of American business.

History *Through Art*

Baseball Players Practicing Thomas Eakins painted this work in 1875. A member of the Realist school of art, Eakins tried to depict everyday events in detail. **What elements of this painting reflect the Realist movement?**

Carnegie's Gospel of Wealth A wealthy and prominent business leader of the time, Andrew Carnegie believed wholeheartedly in Social Darwinism and laissez-faire. Speaking of the law of unregulated competition, he wrote:

> ❝It ensures the survival of the fittest in every department. We accept and welcome, therefore, as conditions to which we must accommodate ourselves, great inequality of environment, the concentration of business, . . . in the hands of a few, and the laws of competition . . . as being not only beneficial, but essential for the future progress of the race.❞
>
> —quoted in *Voices from America's Past*

Believing that those who profited from society owed it something in return, Carnegie attempted to extend and soften the harsh philosophy of Social Darwinism with the **Gospel of Wealth.** This philosophy held that wealthy Americans bore the responsibility of engaging in philanthropy—using their great fortunes to further social progress. Carnegie himself, for example, donated millions of dollars as the "trustee and agent for his poorer brethren." Other industrialists also contributed to social causes. 📖 *(See page 933 for more information on the Gospel of Wealth.)*

✓ Reading Check

Summarizing What was the main idea of Social Darwinism?

Realism

Just as Darwin had looked at the natural world scientifically, a new movement in art and literature known as realism attempted to portray people realistically instead of idealizing them as romantic artists had done.

Realism in Art Realist painters rejected the idealistic depictions of the world of the earlier 1800s. One such painter, **Thomas Eakins** of Philadelphia, Pennsylvania, considered no day-to-day

---

DIFFERENTIATED INSTRUCTION

Reading Support Ask students to choose a sport that was played during the time period covered in this section. Pair students and ask them to teach one another how to play their chosen sports. Instructions should be limited to verbal cues only. As a class, discuss the problems in teaching an activity without visual aids or written directions. **L2**

👉 Refer to *Inclusion for the High School Social Studies Classroom Strategies and Activities* in the TCR.

subject beneath his interest and careful observation. On his canvases, with their realistic detail and precise lighting, young men swam, surgeons operated, and scientists experimented. Eakins even dared to paint President Hayes working in shirtsleeves instead of in more traditional formal dress.

Realism in Literature Writers also attempted to capture the world as they saw it. In several novels, **William Dean Howells** presented realistic descriptions of American life. For example, his 1885 novel *The Rise of Silas Lapham* described the attempts of a self-made businessperson to enter Boston society. Also an influential literary critic, Howells was the first to claim Mark Twain to be an American genius and hailed him as "incomparable, the Lincoln of our literature."

Twain, a Missouri native whose real name was Samuel Clemens, wrote his masterpiece, *Adventures of Huckleberry Finn,* in 1884. In this novel, the title character and his friend Jim, an escaped slave, float down the Mississippi River on a raft. Through their innocent eyes, readers gain a piercing view of American society in the pre–Civil War era. Twain wrote in local dialect with a lively sense of humor. Nevertheless, Howells realized that Twain was more than a humorist. He had written a true American novel, in which the setting, subject matter, characters, and style were unmistakably American.

Howells also recognized talent in the work of a very different writer, **Henry James,** who lived most of his adult life in England. In novels such as *Portrait of a Lady* (1881), James realistically characterized the inner lives of the upper class. Isabel Archer, the lady of the title, reflects one of the prime values of her class—the concern to maintain social position by marrying well. Ultimately Isabel's wealth interferes with her ability to pursue her own happiness.

Edith Wharton, who also concerned herself with the upper class she knew, modeled her realistic writing after those of James. She won a Pulitzer Prize for her novel *The Age of Innocence,* a stark portrait of upper-class New York society in the 1870s.

✓ Reading Check **Explaining** What was the significance of Mark Twain's *Adventures of Huckleberry Finn*?

Popular Culture

Popular culture changed considerably in the late 1800s. Industrialization improved the standard of living for many people, enabling them to spend money on entertainment and recreation. Increasingly, urban Americans, unlike rural people, divided their lives

| Fact | Fiction | Folklore |

The Seventh-Inning Stretch This baseball tradition, where fans often stand up to stretch in the middle of the seventh inning, does not have a completely reliable history. One claim is that in 1869, all the Cincinnati Red Stockings players stood during the seventh inning to seek relief from the hard wooden benches on which they were sitting. Another popular story asserts that in 1910, President William Howard Taft stood to stretch himself; thinking that the president was leaving, fans at the Washington Senators game also stood out of respect.

Moses Fleetwood Walker, early African American baseball player

into separate units—that of work and that of home. Furthermore, people began looking for things to do outside the home and began "going out" to public entertainment.

The Saloon As Frank Lloyd Wright had noted when he arrived in Chicago, the city's saloons far outnumbered its groceries and meat markets. Functioning like community centers, saloons played a major role in the life of male workers in the 1800s. They also served as political centers. Saloonkeepers often served as key figures in political machines.

Saloons offered free toilets, water for horses, and free newspapers for customers. They even offered the first "free lunch": salty food that made patrons thirsty and eager to drink more. Saloons developed loyal customers. The first workers from the night shift would stream in at 5:00 A.M., and the last would stay until late at night.

Amusement Parks and Sports While saloons catered mostly to men, working-class families or single adults who sought excitement and escape could go to amusement parks such as New York's **Coney Island.** Amusements there such as water slides and railroad rides cost only a nickel or dime.

Watching professionals box or play baseball also first became popular during the late 1800s. A game much like baseball, known as rounders and derived from the game of cricket, had enjoyed limited popularity in Great Britain in the early 1800s. Versions of the modern game of baseball began to appear in

| Fact | Fiction | Folklore |

Although organized baseball was played as early as the 1850s, the game really took off after the Civil War. Returning veterans helped to form teams, and by 1866 there were 202 teams in 17 states.

FYI

Football became a popular spectator sport during the Gilded Age, with college games proving to be the biggest draw. Rutgers and Princeton played in the first collegiate contest in 1869. Throughout the late 1800s, three Eastern universities—Harvard, Yale, and Princeton—dominated the sport.

✓ Reading Check

Answer: It was one of the first truly American novels.

3 ASSESS

Assign Section 3 Assessment as homework or as an in-class activity.

💿 Have students use the **Interactive Tutor Self-Assessment CD-ROM.**

L1/ELL

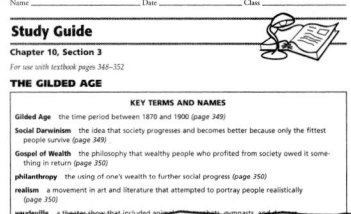

Reading Essentials and Study Guide 10–3

Name _____ Date _____ Class _____

Study Guide
Chapter 10, Section 3
For use with textbook pages 348–352
THE GILDED AGE

KEY TERMS AND NAMES
Gilded Age the time period between 1870 and 1900 *(page 349)*
Social Darwinism the idea that society progresses and becomes better because only the fittest people survive *(page 349)*
Gospel of Wealth the philosophy that wealthy people who profited from society owed it something in return *(page 350)*
philanthropy the using of one's wealth to further social progress *(page 350)*
realism a movement in art and literature that attempted to portray people realistically *(page 350)*
vaudeville a theater show that included songs...

INTERDISCIPLINARY CONNECTIONS ACTIVITY

Performing Arts Invite a performing arts teacher or artist to work with your students to produce a vaudeville-style show. Ask the guest to help students understand the kinds of acts performed in vaudeville, and offer suggestions about resources students can use to learn more about vaudeville. Arrange for students to perform for an audience. **L2**

L2

Section Quiz 10–3

Picturing History

Answer: syncopated rhythms that grew out of the music of vaudeville and honky-tonk pianists and banjo players

Ask: What do you think is the role of the man wearing a business suit in the middle of the picture? *(may have been a promoter or manager)*

Reteach
Have students explain how industrialization promoted leisure time and new forms of entertainment.

Enrich
Invite interested students to learn more about popular culture in the late 1800s. Suggest that they work in pairs to create a trivia game that can be played in class.

Reading Check
Answer: functioned as community centers and political centers for men

Study Central™ provides summaries, interactive games, and online graphic organizers to help students review section content.

4 CLOSE
Have students evaluate the doctrine of Social Darwinism and its impact on industry.

352

---

the United States in the early 1800s. As the game grew in popularity, it became a source of profit. The first salaried team, the Cincinnati Red Stockings, was formed in 1869. Other cities soon fielded professional teams, and in 1903 the first modern World Series was played between the Boston Red Sox and the Pittsburgh Pirates.

The second most popular game, football, appealed first to the upper classes, in part because it began in private colleges and universities that the middle and working classes could not afford. By the late 1800s, the game had spread to public universities.

As work became less physically strenuous, many people looked for leisure activities that involved physical exercise. Lawn tennis, golf, and croquet became popular. James Naismith, a Canadian working as an athletic director for a college in Springfield, Massachusetts, invented the game of basketball in 1891.

Vaudeville and Ragtime The many people living in the cities provided large and eager markets for other types of entertainment. Adapted from French theater, vaudeville took on an American flavor in the early 1880s with its hodgepodge of animal acts, acrobats, gymnasts, and dancers. The fast-moving acts, like the tempo of big-city life, went on in continuous shows all day and night.

Picturing History
Ragtime Band This group of African American musicians traveled around the country playing ragtime music at motion picture shows. What are some of the roots of ragtime music?

Like vaudeville, ragtime music echoed the hectic pace of city life. Its syncopated rhythms grew out of the music of riverside honky-tonk, saloon pianists, and banjo players, using the patterns of African American music. **Scott Joplin,** one of the most important African American ragtime composers, became known as the "King of Ragtime." He published his signature piece, "The Maple Leaf Rag," in 1899.

✓ **Reading Check** Describing What importance did the saloon have in nineteenth-century life?

Study Central™ To review this section, go to tarvol2.glencoe.com and click on **Study Central™**.

SECTION 3 ASSESSMENT

Checking for Understanding
1. **Define:** philanthropy, realism, vaudeville, ragtime.
2. **Identify:** Gilded Age, Social Darwinism, Gospel of Wealth, Scott Joplin.
3. **Describe** how changes in art and literature reflected the issues and characteristics of the late nineteenth century.

Reviewing Themes
4. **Culture and Traditions** What were the defining characteristics of the Gilded Age?

Critical Thinking
5. **Synthesizing** Do you think the idea of the Gospel of Wealth is still alive today? Why or why not?
6. **Organizing** Complete a graphic organizer similar to the one below by filling in new forms of entertainment that Americans turned to in the late 1800s.

New Entertainment

Analyzing Visuals
7. **Examining Photographs** Analyze the photograph at the top of this page. How does the clothing the musicians are wearing compare with the clothing worn by musicians today?

Writing About History
8. **Descriptive Writing** Imagine that you are a newspaper editor in the late 1800s. Write an editorial in which you support or oppose the philosophy of Social Darwinism. Include reasons to support your position.

352 CHAPTER 10 Urban America

SECTION 3 ASSESSMENT ANSWERS

1. Terms are in blue.
2. Gilded Age *(p. 349)*, Social Darwinism *(p. 349)*, Gospel of Wealth *(p. 350)*, Scott Joplin *(p. 352)*
3. Art and literature became more realistic as artists and writers depicted the world as they believed it to be, not as they thought it should be.
4. individualism, urbanization, new values, art, and forms of entertainment
5. Explanations will likely focus on current philanthropy of wealthy individuals.
6. saloons, sports, amusement parks, vaudeville
7. Students might mention that some groups of musicians dress alike and others do not, some wear suits and others do not, some wear clothing similar to what their audiences wear and others wear costumes.
8. Students' editorials will vary.

Guide to Reading

Main Idea
The pressing problems of the urban poor in the late 1800s and early 1900s eventually stimulated attempts to reform industrial society.

Key Terms and Names
Henry George, Lester Frank Ward, Edward Bellamy, naturalism, Jane Addams, settlement house, Americanization

Reading Strategy
Taking Notes As you read about reform movements in the United States in the late 1800s, complete an outline like the one below by listing the people whose ideas influenced the movements.

The Rebirth of Reform
I. Social Criticism
  A.
  B.
  C.
II. Naturalism in Literature

Reading Objectives
• **Explain** the methods that social critics advocated to improve society.
• **Evaluate** efforts to help the urban poor.

Section Theme
Individual Action Many middle- and upper-class individuals worked to soften social and economic inequality.

Preview of Events

◆1880	◆1885	◆1890	◆1895

1879
Henry George's *Progress and Poverty* published

1881
Booker T. Washington founds Tuskegee Institute

1889
Jane Addams founds Hull House

1893
Stephen Crane's *Maggie: A Girl of the Streets* published

1896
National Association of Colored Women founded

Lillian Wald

★ **An American Story** ★

On a drizzly March morning in 1893, a nursing student named Lillian Wald was teaching a public health class to residents of New York's poor Lower East Side. Suddenly a girl broke in, disrupting the lesson. The child's mother desperately needed a nurse. The interruption changed Wald's life. She followed the girl to a squalid tenement, where she found a family of seven sharing their two rooms with boarders. The sick woman lay on a dirty bed. Wald later wrote:

❝That morning's experience was a baptism of fire. Deserted were the laboratory and the academic work of the college. I never returned to them. . . . To my inexperience it seemed certain that conditions such as these were allowed because people did not *know,* and for me there was a challenge to know and to tell. . . . If people knew things,—and "things" meant everything implied in the condition of this family,—such horrors would cease to exist. . . .❞

—quoted in *The House on Henry Street*

In 1895 Wald and her friend Mary Brewster established the Henry Street Settlement. The young nurses offered medical care, education, labor organization, and social and cultural programs to the neighborhood residents.

Social Criticism

The tremendous changes brought about by industrialism and urbanization triggered a debate among Americans as to how best to address society's problems. While many Americans embraced the ideas of individualism and Social Darwinism, others disagreed,

CHAPTER 10   Urban America   **353**

---

1 FOCUS

Section Overview
This section focuses on the efforts to help the urban poor.

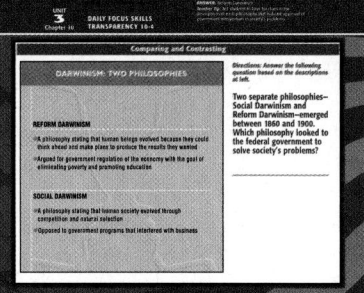

BELLRINGER
Skillbuilder Activity

Project transparency and have students answer the question.

Daily Focus Skills Transparency 10–4

Reading Preview

Answers to Graphic:
The Rebirth of Reform
  I. Social Criticism
    A. Henry George on Progress and Poverty
    B. Reform Darwinism
    C. Looking Backward
  II. Naturalism in Literature
Students should complete the outline by including all heads in the section.

Preteaching Vocabulary
Have students write a one-sentence definition for each of the Key Terms.

SECTION RESOURCES

📁 **Reproducible Masters**
• Reproducible Lesson Plan 10–4
• Daily Lecture and Discussion Notes 10–4
• Guided Reading Activity 10–4
• Section Quiz 10–4
• Reading Essentials and Study Guide 10–4
• Performance Assessment Activities and Rubrics

🖥 **Transparencies**
• Daily Focus Skills Transparency 10–4

Multimedia
🖲 Interactive Tutor Self-Assessment CD-ROM
🖲 ExamView® Pro Testmaker CD-ROM
🖲 Presentation Plus! CD-ROM
🖲 TeacherWorks™ CD-ROM
🎧 Audio Program

2 TEACH

Daily Lecture and Discussion Notes 10–4

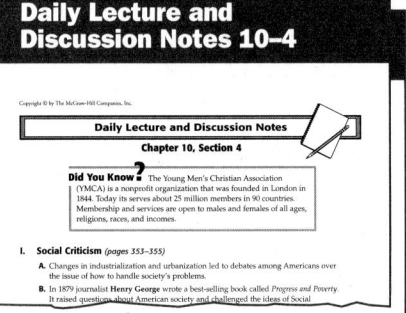

Copyright © by The McGraw-Hill Companies, Inc.

Daily Lecture and Discussion Notes
Chapter 10, Section 4

Did You Know? The Young Men's Christian Association (YMCA) is a nonprofit organization that was founded in London in 1844. Today its serves about 25 million members in 90 countries. Membership and services are open to males and females of all ages, religions, races, and incomes.

I. **Social Criticism** (pages 353–355)
   A. Changes in industrialization and urbanization led to debates among Americans over the issue of how to handle society's problems.
   B. In 1879 journalist **Henry George** wrote a best-selling book called *Progress and Poverty.* It raised questions about American society and challenged the ideas of Social

Posing and Answering Questions

Assign half the class to pose questions about Henry George's theory and the other half to pose questions about Lester Frank Ward's theory. The half of the class that is not posing questions should answer the questions based on information in the textbook or on conclusions that they have drawn. **L1**

Graph *Skills*

Answers:

1. almost 200 out of every 100,000 people

2. that conditions improved from the start to the end of the 1900s

Graph Skills Practice

Ask: Why do you think a larger percentage of students graduate from high school today than in 1900?

(possible answer: fewer have to go to work fulltime while in their teens, education is more important for the types of jobs available today)

---

arguing that society's problems could be fixed only if Americans and their government began to take a more active role in regulating the economy and helping those in need.

Henry George on Progress and Poverty In 1879 journalist **Henry George** published *Progress and Poverty.* His book quickly became a national best-seller. "The present century has been marked by a prodigious increase in wealth-producing power," George observed, which should have made poverty "a thing of the past." Instead, he argued:

> 66It becomes no easier for the masses of our people to make a living. On the contrary it becomes harder. . . . The gulf between the employed and the employer is growing wider; social contrasts are becoming sharper; as liveried carriages appear, so do barefoot children.99
>
> —from *Progress and Poverty*

Most economists now argue that George's analysis was flawed. Industrialism did make some Americans very wealthy, but it also improved the standard of living for most other Americans as well. At the time,

however, in the midst of the poverty, crime, and harsh working conditions, many Americans did not believe things were improving.

George offered a simple solution. Land, he argued, was the basis of wealth, and people could grow wealthy just by waiting for land prices to rise. George proposed a "single tax" on this unearned wealth to replace all other taxes. He believed it would help make society more equal and also provide the government with enough money to help the poor.

Economists have since rejected George's economic theory. His real importance to American history is that he raised questions about American society and led the way in challenging the ideas of Social Darwinism and laissez-faire economics. Many future reform leaders first became interested in reform because of George's book.

Reform Darwinism Four years after Henry George challenged the ideas of Social Darwinism, **Lester Frank Ward** published *Dynamic Sociology.* Ward took the ideas of Darwinism and used them to reach a very different conclusion than Spencer had. He argued that human beings were different from other animals in nature because they

---

Social Conditions: Past and Present

Death Rates for Specific Causes (per 100,000 people)

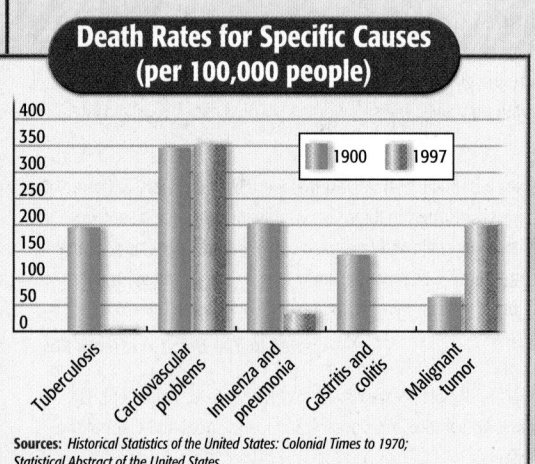

Legend: 1900, 1997

Y-axis: 0, 50, 100, 150, 200, 250, 300, 350, 400

X-axis: Tuberculosis, Cardiovascular problems, Influenza and pneumonia, Gastritis and colitis, Malignant tumor

Sources: *Historical Statistics of the United States: Colonial Times to 1970; Statistical Abstract of the United States.*

High School Graduation Rates

1900 — 6.4% Graduated, 93.6% Did Not Graduate

1997 — 69% Graduated, 31% Did Not Graduate

Sources: *Historical Statistics of the United States, Colonial Times to 1970; Statistical Abstract of the United States.*

Life Expectancy

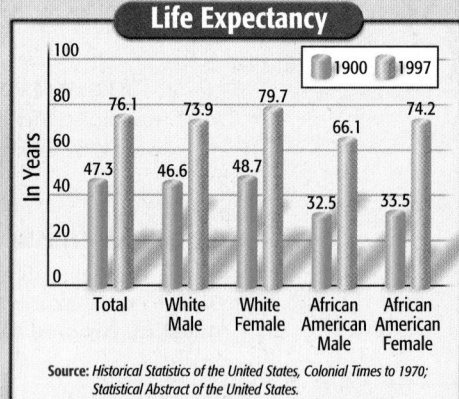

Legend: 1900, 1997

Y-axis (In Years): 0, 20, 40, 60, 80, 100

- Total: 47.3, 76.1
- White Male: 46.6, 73.9
- White Female: 48.7, 79.7
- African American Male: 32.5, 66.1
- African American Female: 33.5, 74.2

Source: *Historical Statistics of the United States, Colonial Times to 1970; Statistical Abstract of the United States.*

Graph *Skills*

1. **Analyzing Graphs** How many people per 100,000 died of tuberculosis in the year 1900?
2. **Understanding Cause and Effect** Collectively, what do these graphs tell you about social conditions as the twentieth century progressed?

Reading Strategy   READING THE TEXT

Taking Notes Students can use notes to group, outline, and organize information. As students read this section, have them list the main ideas about the rebirth of reform in the United States in the late 1800s. Under each main idea, they should list at least two items that demonstrate how reformers reacted to the changes industrialization brought to the United States. **L1**

Refer to *Inclusion for the High School Social Studies Classroom Strategies and Activities* in the TCR.

had the ability to think ahead and make plans to produce the future outcomes they desired.

Ward's ideas came to be known as Reform Darwinism. People, he insisted, had succeeded in the world not because of their ability to compete but because of their ability to cooperate. Ward believed that competition was wasteful and time consuming. Government, he argued, could regulate the economy, cure poverty, and promote education more efficiently than could competition in the marketplace. While some disagreed with Ward's conclusions, others did think that government should do more to solve society's problems. Among these were the people who became reformers in the late 1800s.

Looking Backward By the late 1880s, some critics of Social Darwinism and laissez-faire economics had moved to the opposite extreme. In 1888 **Edward Bellamy** published *Looking Backward, 2000–1887,* a novel about a young Bostonian who falls asleep in 1887 and awakens in the year 2000 to find that the United States has become a perfect society with no crime, poverty, or politics. In this fictional society, the government owns all industry and shares the wealth equally with all Americans. Bellamy's ideas were essentially a form of socialism. His book quickly became a bestseller, and although few people were willing to go as far as Bellamy suggested, his ideas, like those of George and Ward, helped to shape the thinking of American reformers in the late 1800s.

✓ Reading Check **Describing** What were Lester Frank Ward's views on government?

Naturalism in Literature

Criticism of industrial society also appeared in literature in a new style of writing known as naturalism. Social Darwinists and realists argued that people could control their lives and make choices to improve their situation. Naturalists challenged this idea by suggesting that some people failed in life simply because they were caught up in circumstances they could not control. In other words, leaving society and the economy unregulated did not always lead to the best result. Sometimes people's lives were destroyed through no fault of their own.

Among the most prominent naturalist writers were Stephen Crane, Frank Norris, Jack London, and Theodore Dreiser. Stephen Crane's novel, *Maggie, A Girl of the Streets* (1893), told the story of a girl's descent into prostitution and death. Frank Norris's work, *McTeague* (1899), described how a dentist and

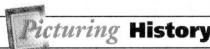
Picturing **History**

Urban Poverty The impoverished lifestyle of many Americans like this mother and child in Chicago was a growing concern among social reformers. What organizations were created to help the urban poor?

his wife are driven mad by greed and violence. Jack London's tales of the Alaskan wilderness demonstrated the power of the natural environment over civilization. Theodore Dreiser's stories, such as *Sister Carrie* (1900), painted a world where people sinned without punishment and where the pursuit of wealth and power often destroyed their character.

✓ Reading Check **Describing** How did the beliefs of naturalist writers differ from those of Social Darwinists?

Helping the Urban Poor

While naturalist writers expressed pessimism about the individual's life in an industrialized world, some critics of industrial society were working for reform. Their reform efforts gave rise to the Social Gospel movement, the Salvation Army and the YMCA, women's clubs, settlement houses, and temperance movements.

The Social Gospel From about 1870 until 1920, reformers in the Social Gospel movement worked to better conditions in cities according to the biblical ideals of charity and justice. An early advocate of the Social Gospel, **Washington Gladden,** a minister from Columbus, Ohio, tried to apply what he called "Christian law" to social problems. During a coal strike in 1884, for example, Gladden preached about

CHAPTER 10 Urban America **355**

L1/ELL

Guided Reading Activity 10–4

Name _____ Date _____ Class _____

★ Guided Reading Activity 10-4

DIRECTIONS: Identifying Supporting Details Read each main idea. Use your textbook to supply the details that support or explain each main idea.

☐ **Main Idea:** The tremendous changes industrialism and urbanization brought about triggered a debate among Americans as to how best to address society's problems.
  1. Detail: Industrialism made some Americans very wealthy, and it improved the _____ for most other Americans as well.
  2. Detail: Henry George argued that _____ was the basis of wealth.
  3. Detail: Ward insisted that people had succeeded in the world because of their ability to

☐ **Main Idea:** Criticism of industrial society appeared in literature, in a new style of writing known as naturalism.
  4. Detail: Naturalists suggested that some people failed in life simply because they were

Reading Strategy

Creating a Profile Have students choose one of the persons mentioned in this section and write a short biographical profile emphasizing the person's connection to the reform movement. **L1**

Use the rubric for writing a book review, research report, or handbill on pages 77–78 in the *Performance Assessment Activities and Rubrics.*

✓ Reading Check

Answer: He believed that government could regulate the economy, cure poverty, and promote education better than could an unregulated economy.

Picturing **History**

Answer: Salvation Army and YMCA
Ask: What evidence of poverty can you see in this photograph? *(worn and dirty clothes, used utensils, grime)*

✓ Reading Check

Answer: Social Darwinists believed people could make choices to improve their situation; naturalists believed some people failed because they were caught up in circumstances they could not control.

Researching a Topic Have students contact a social service agency in your community that provides services for the poor. Instruct students to learn about the agency's programs and its clients. Ask students to write a short report comparing their findings to the social service organizations that aided the urban poor in the late 1800s. **L2**

Use the rubric for writing a book review, research report, or handbill on pages 79–80 in the *Performance Assessment Activities and Rubrics.*

the "right and necessity of labor organizations," despite the fact that his congregation included top officers of the coal company.

Walter Rauschenbusch, a Baptist minister who spent nine years serving in a church in one of New York City's poorest neighborhoods, later led the Social Gospel movement. As he put it, "The Church must either condemn the world and seek to change it, or tolerate the world and conform to it." Unlike Social Darwinists, Rauschenbusch believed that competition was the cause of many social problems, causing good people to behave badly.

The efforts of leaders like Gladden and Rauschenbusch inspired many organized churches to expand their missions. These churches began to take on community functions designed to improve society. Some of their projects included building gyms and providing social programs and day care. Others focused exclusively on helping the poor.

The Salvation Army and the YMCA The combination of religious faith and interest in reform nourished the growth of the Christian Mission, a social welfare organization first organized in England by a minister named William Booth. Adopting a military-style organization, the group became known as the Salvation Army in 1878. It offered practical aid and religious counseling to the urban poor.

Like the Salvation Army, the Young Men's Christian Association (YMCA) also began in England. The YMCA tried to help industrial workers and the urban poor by organizing Bible studies, prayer meetings, citizenship training, and group activities. In the United States, YMCAs, or "Ys," quickly spread from Boston throughout the country. YMCA facilities included libraries, gymnasiums, swimming pools, auditoriums, and low-cost hotel rooms available on a temporary basis to those in need.

Revivalism and Dwight L. Moody One prominent organizer of the American YMCA was **Dwight L. Moody,** who was president of the Chicago YMCA in the late 1860s. A gifted preacher and organizer, Moody founded his own church in Chicago, today known as Moody Memorial Church. By 1867 Moody had begun to organize revival meetings in other

What If...

English Spelling Reform Had Been Accepted?

In 1906 the Simplified Spelling Board suggested a list of 300 words that it thought needed to be simplified. For example, it recommended spelling "axe" without the silent "e." The association also asked for more radical changes, such as replacing the "-ed" at the end of past-tense verbs with a "t." Thus, "kissed" and "missed" would be "kisst" and "misst." "Thoroughly" would be simplified to "thoroly."

Although the reforms were not accepted, they received support from such famous people as Mark Twain and President Theodore Roosevelt. After Roosevelt suggested that the Government Printing Office adopt the new spellings, Mark Twain tried to convince the Associated Press news agency to follow along:

❝If [you] will adopt and use our simplified forms . . . [W]e shall be rid of . . . pneumonia and . . . pterodactyl, and all those other insane words which no man . . . can try to spell. . . . What is the real function . . . of language? Isn't it merely to convey ideas and emotions . . . ? [I]f we can do it with words of fonetic brevity and compactness, why keep the present cumbersome forms?❞

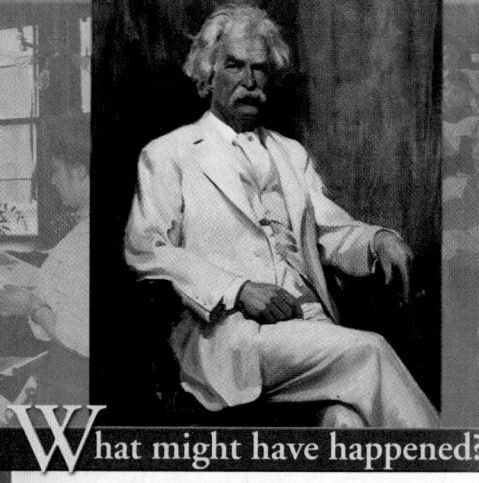

What might have happened?

1. Why do you think these spelling reforms were never accepted?

2. Would English be easier for immigrants to learn and understand if the reforms had been accepted? Why or why not?

INTERDISCIPLINARY CONNECTIONS ACTIVITY

Language Arts Have the language arts teacher present a discussion of realism and naturalism. Ask the teacher to focus on the essential characteristics of each form of literature. Then direct students to write a paragraph demonstrating each style of writing. Have volunteers share their paragraphs with the class without stating the style, and have the class identify the style. **L2**

Profiles IN HISTORY

Booker T. Washington
1856–1915

Born enslaved on a plantation in Virginia, Booker T. Washington spent his childhood working in the coal mines of West Virginia. At age 16 he heard about the Hampton Institute in Virginia, where African Americans could learn farming or a trade. With little money in his pockets, Washington left home and walked nearly 500 miles to the school, where he was able to work as a janitor to pay for his education.

After Washington completed his degree, Hampton hired him as an instructor in 1879. Two years later, Hampton's founder, Samuel Armstrong, asked Washington to organize an agricultural and industrial school for African Americans in Tuskegee, Alabama. The Tuskegee Institute's beginnings were modest. As Washington recalled, it began with 40 students and a "dilapidated shanty." By 1915 the school had over 100 buildings, about 2,000 students, and an endowment of nearly $2 million. Washington himself became a nationally known spokesperson for the African American community.

George Washington Carver
1864–1943

At about 10 years of age, George Washington Carver left his home in Missouri and began traveling on his own. He worked as a servant, hotel clerk, laundry worker, and farmhand in order to get a formal education. In 1894 he graduated from the Iowa State College of Agriculture and Mechanical Arts. Two years later, he became the director of agricultural research at the Tuskegee Institute, where he began experimenting with various crops.

To help Southern sharecroppers overcome their problems of depleted soil, poverty, and poor nutrition, Carver urged them to plant peanuts and soybeans. These plants restored the soil's nitrogen while providing extra protein in the farmers' diets. To make peanut farming profitable, Carver developed over 300 industrial uses for peanuts, including flour, inks, dyes, wood stains, soap, and cosmetics. By 1940 his research had made the peanut the South's second most lucrative crop after cotton.

American cities. In 1870 Moody met Ira Sankey, a hymn writer and singer. Together they introduced the gospel hymn into worship services in the United States and Great Britain. Moody's preaching and Sankey's hymns drew thousands of people to revival meetings in the 1870s and 1880s.

Moody strongly supported charities that helped the poor, but he rejected both the Social Gospel and Social Darwinism. He believed the way to help the poor was not by providing them with services but by redeeming their souls and reforming their character.

The Settlement House Movement In a way, the settlement house movement was an offshoot of the Social Gospel movement. It attracted idealistic reformers who believed it was their Christian duty to improve living conditions for the poor. During the late 1800s, reformers such as **Jane Addams** established settlement houses in poor neighborhoods. In these establishments, middle-class residents lived and helped poor residents, mostly immigrants.

Addams, who opened the famous Hull House in Chicago in 1889, inspired many more such settlements across the country, including the Henry Street Settlement run by Lillian Wald in New York City. The women who ran settlement houses provided everything from medical care, recreation programs, and

English classes to hot lunches for factory workers. Their efforts helped shape the social work profession, in which women came to play a major role.

Reading Check **Summarizing** What were the beliefs of Dwight L. Moody?

Public Education

As the United States became increasingly industrialized and urbanized, it needed more workers who were trained and educated. The demand for skilled workers led to a much greater focus on building schools and colleges in the late 1800s.

The Spread of Schools The number of public schools increased quickly after the Civil War. In 1870 around 6,500,000 children attended school. By 1900 that number had risen to over 17,300,000.

Public schools were often crucial to the success of immigrant children. It was there the children usually became knowledgeable about American culture, a process known as Americanization. To assimilate immigrants into American culture, schools taught immigrant children English, American history, and the responsibilities of citizenship. They also tried to instill discipline and a strong work ethic, values considered important to the nation's progress.

Profiles IN HISTORY

Background: The Tuskegee Institute in Alabama is now known as Tuskegee University.

Ask: Based on the information presented in the profiles on page 357, how were the early lives of Booker T. Washington and George Washington Carver similar? *(They both traveled far from home and worked to put themselves through college.)*

Reading Check

Answer: believed that the way to help the poor was to redeem their souls and reform their character

3 ASSESS

Assign Section 4 Assessment as homework or as an in-class activity.

🌐 Have students use the **Interactive Tutor Self-Assessment CD-ROM.**

L1/ELL

Reading Essentials and Study Guide 10–4

Name _____ Date _____ Class _____

Study Guide

Chapter 10, Section 4
For use with textbook pages 353–358

THE REBIRTH OF REFORM

KEY TERMS AND NAMES
Henry George a journalist who criticized the effects of industrialization *(page 354)*
Lester Frank Ward a writer who challenged the ideas of Social Darwinism *(page 354)*
Edward Bellamy a writer whose ideas were a form of socialism *(page 355)*
naturalism a new style of writing that suggested that some people failed in life because of circumstances beyond their control *(page 355)*
Jane Addams reformer who established settlement houses *(page 357)*
settlement house residences in poor neighborhoods in which middle-class people lived and helped poor people *(page 357)*

CRITICAL THINKING ACTIVITY

Comparing Present the following information to students: In the late 1800s, grade school was synonymous with learning by simple memorization. Virtually everything was drilled into students' minds through endless repetition. All subjects—arithmetic, reading, spelling, and handwriting—were taught in this manner. Ask students to compare the way in which students were taught in the late 1800s with how they themselves learned to read, spell, write, and do math. **L2**

L2

Section Quiz 10–4

Name	Date	Class

★ Chapter 10

Score

Section Quiz 10–4

DIRECTIONS: Matching Match each item in Column A with the items in Column B. Write the correct letters in the blanks. *(10 points each)*

Column A

___ 1. the idea that people succeed in the world not because of their ability to compete, but because of their ability to cooperate
___ 2. Baptist minister and leader in the Social Gospel movement
___ 3. prominent naturalist writer
___ 4. established in poor neighborhoods where middle-class residents lived and helped the poor residents
___ 5. the idea that some people failed in life simply because they were caught up in circumstances they could not control

Column B

A. naturalism
B. Reform Darwinism
C. settlement houses
D. Stephen Crane
E. Walter Rauschenbusch

FYI

Ungraded schools were common in rural areas. Children from 3 to 18 were often taught in the same classroom.

Reteach

Have students critique the efforts to help the urban poor.

Enrich

Have students play the role of a parent living in a rural area or an African American parent during the late 1800s. Have them write a letter to their congressional representative suggesting changes to improve the education system for their children.

✓ Reading Check

Answer: by teaching English and American values

HISTORY Online

Study Central™ provides summaries, interactive games, and online graphic organizers to help students review section content.

4 CLOSE

Have students pose and answer questions about the methods that social critics advocated to improve society.

Carnegie Library, Shelbyville, Indiana

Americanization could also pose a problem for immigrant children, however, because sometimes parents worried that it would make the children forget their own cultural traditions.

Not everyone had access to school. In the rush to fund education, cities were way ahead of rural areas. Many African Americans, also, did not have equal educational opportunities. To combat this discrimination, some African Americans started their own schools. The leader of this movement was Booker T. Washington, who founded the Tuskegee Institute in Alabama in 1881.

Education for the Workplace City schools helped immigrants assimilate, and they also helped future workers prepare for the jobs they hoped would lift their families out of poverty. The grammar school system in city schools divided students into eight grades and drilled them in timely attendance, neatness, and efficiency—necessary habits for success in the workplace. At the same time, vocational and technical education in the high schools provided students with skills required in specific trades.

Expanding Higher Education Colleges also multiplied in the late 1800s, helped by the Morrill Land Grant Act. This Civil War–era law gave federal land grants to states for the purpose of establishing agricultural and mechanical colleges. By 1900 land-grant colleges were established across the Midwest. The number of students enrolled expanded rapidly in this period. In 1870 around 50,000 students attended college, but by 1890 the number had more than tripled to 157,000.

Traditionally, women's educational opportunities lagged behind men's. Around this time, however, things began to change. The opening of private women's colleges such as Vassar, Wellesley, and Smith, along with new women's colleges on the campuses of Harvard and Columbia Universities, served to increase the number of women attending college.

Public Libraries Like public schools, free libraries also made education available to city dwellers. One of the strongest supporters of the public library movement was industrialist Andrew Carnegie, who believed access to knowledge was the key to getting ahead in life. Carnegie donated millions of dollars toward the construction of libraries all across the United States. These libraries, as well as the various educational and social reform movements that arose in the late 1800s, helped people cope with the harsher aspects of a newly industrialized society.

✓ Reading Check **Explaining** How did the United States try to Americanize immigrants?

HISTORY Online | **Study Central™** To review this section, go to tarvol2.glencoe.com and click on **Study Central™**.

SECTION 4 ASSESSMENT

Checking for Understanding

1. **Define:** naturalism, settlement house, Americanization.
2. **Identify:** Henry George, Lester Frank Ward, Edward Bellamy, Jane Addams.
3. **Describe** the way naturalist writers portrayed the fictional characters in their novels.

Reviewing Themes

4. **Individual Action** How did the efforts of Jane Addams and Mary Brewster help poor people in urban areas in the late 1800s?

Critical Thinking

5. **Analyzing** What role do you think the government should play in the economy? Give reasons to support your opinion.
6. **Categorizing** Complete a chart like the one below by listing names and goals of reform movements that arose in the late 1800s to help the urban poor.

Reform Movement	Goals

Analyzing Visuals

7. **Analyzing Graphs** Examine the graphs on page 354, and then develop a quiz with questions based on specific information found in the graphs. Include at least one broad question about a pattern you see. Give the quiz to some of your classmates.

Writing About History

8. **Descriptive Writing** Take on the role of an immigrant in the late 1800s. Write a diary entry in which you describe your feelings about your children becoming Americanized while attending the local public school.

358 CHAPTER 10 Urban America

SECTION 4 ASSESSMENT ANSWERS

1. Terms are in blue.
2. Henry George *(p. 354)*, Lester Frank Ward *(p. 354)*, Edward Bellamy *(p. 355)*, Jane Addams *(p. 357)*
3. as people who failed in life because they were caught up in circumstances beyond their control
4. provided medical care, recreation, English classes, and meals
5. Students' answers will vary but should be supported with facts.
6. Social Gospel movement tried to better conditions in cities according to biblical ideals of charity and justice, revivalism aimed to help the poor by redeeming their souls, and the settlement house movement focused on improving living conditions of the poor.
7. Students' quizzes will vary.
8. Students' diary entries should reflect both positive and negative feelings about Americanization.

SKILLBUILDER

Hypothesizing

Why Learn This Skill?

When you are reading new material, you may often encounter ideas and events that you do not immediately understand. One way to overcome this difficulty is to make educated guesses about what happened.

Learning the Skill

When you read things that you do not understand, you probably make guesses about what the material means. You may or may not have been able to prove these guesses, but you have taken a step toward deciphering the information. This step is called **hypothesizing.** When you hypothesize, you form one or more hypotheses, which are guesses that offer possible answers to a problem or provide possible explanations for an observation. When hypothesizing, follow these steps.

• Read the material carefully.

• Ask yourself what the material is actually saying. To do this, try to put the material in your own words.

• Determine what you might logically assume from your guesses. Then form one or more hypotheses.

• Test each hypothesis to determine whether or not it is correct. You can usually do this by asking yourself questions that relate to your hypothesis and then researching the answers.

• Based on your research, determine which hypothesis, if any, provides an explanation for the information that you originally read.

Hypotheses are only preliminary explanations. They must be accepted, rejected, or modified as the problem is investigated. Each hypothesis must be tested against the information gathered. Hypotheses that are supported by evidence can be accepted as explanations of the problem.

Practicing the Skill

Using the steps just discussed and what you have read in the chapter, test the following hypotheses and determine if they can be supported.

❶ Most immigrants who came to the United States came in search of work.

❷ Improved transportation led people to move to urban areas from rural areas.

❸ The general laissez-faire approach taken by the government toward growing cities was beneficial to businesses and citizens.

Students collaborating

Skills Assessment

Complete the Practicing Skills questions on page 361 and the Chapter 10 Skill Reinforcement Activity to assess your mastery of this skill.

Applying the Skill

Hypothesizing Reread the passage titled "The Resurgence of Nativism" in Section 1. Using the facts that you are given in these paragraphs, form at least two hypotheses that may explain what is being described. Test each hypothesis, then select the best one. Which hypothesis did you choose? Why?

 Glencoe's **Skillbuilder Interactive Workbook CD-ROM, Level 2,** provides instruction and practice in key social studies skills.

TEACH

Hypothesizing Remind students that it is important to test a hypothesis.

Instruct students to look at a newspaper photograph and read the caption without reading the accompanying article. Ask students to develop hypotheses based on the photo and caption. Record the hypotheses on the board. Ask students to read the newspaper article and test the hypotheses.

Additional Practice

L1

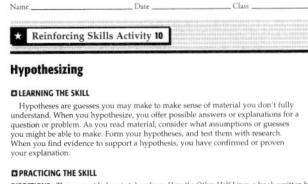

Reinforcing Skills Activity 10

Name _____ Date _____ Class _____

★ Reinforcing Skills Activity **10**

Hypothesizing

☐ **LEARNING THE SKILL**

Hypotheses are guesses you may make to make sense of material you don't fully understand. When you hypothesize, you offer possible answers or explanations for a question or problem. As you read material, consider what assumptions or guesses you might be able to make. Form your hypotheses, and test them with research. When you find evidence to support a hypothesis, you have confirmed or proven your explanation.

☐ **PRACTICING THE SKILL**

DIRECTIONS: The excerpt below is taken from *How the Other Half Lives,* a book written by Jacob Riis in 1890. Read the section in your text titled **Urban Problems** on page 344, and then read the excerpt below. Use both the text and the excerpt to answer the questions that follow on a separate sheet of paper.

GLENCOE
TECHNOLOGY

 CD-ROM
Glencoe Skillbuilder Interactive Workbook CD-ROM, Level 2

This interactive CD-ROM reinforces student mastery of essential social studies skills.

ANSWERS TO PRACTICING THE SKILL

❶ Students might say the hypothesis cannot be supported because there are no solid statistics in the text. They might suggest that the hypothesis could be revised to indicate that some immigrants came in search of work.

❷ Students might note that transportation is not a reason listed in the text.

❸ Students might say that the laissez-faire approach was not beneficial to all citizens.

Applying the Skill

Students' answers will vary. Students should follow the five steps outlined on page 359 as they complete this assignment.

CHAPTER 10 ASSESSMENT and ACTIVITIES

CHAPTER 10

GLENCOE
TECHNOLOGY

MindJogger Videoquiz
Use the **MindJogger Videoquiz** to review Chapter 10 content.

○ Available in DVD

Reviewing Key Terms
Students' answers will vary. The pages where the words appear in the text are shown in parentheses.

1. **steerage** *(p. 337)*
2. **nativism** *(p. 340)*
3. **skyscraper** *(p. 342)*
4. **tenement** *(p. 343)*
5. **political machine** *(p. 345)*
6. **party boss** *(p. 345)*
7. **graft** *(p. 345)*
8. **philanthropy** *(p. 350)*
9. **realism** *(p. 350)*
10. **vaudeville** *(p. 352)*
11. **ragtime** *(p. 352)*
12. **naturalism** *(p. 355)*
13. **settlement house** *(p. 357)*
14. **Americanization** *(p. 357)*

Reviewing Key Facts
15. Ellis Island *(p. 338),* Angel Island *(p. 339),* Louis Sullivan *(p. 342),* George Plunkitt *(p. 345),* William M. ("Boss") Tweed *(p. 345),* Gilded Age *(p. 349),* Herbert Spencer *(p. 349),* Lester Frank Ward *(p. 354),* Jane Addams *(p. 357)*

16. organized letter-writing campaigns, petitioned the president, filed suit in federal court

17. set up American Protective Association, set up Working Man's Party of California, worked to get Chinese Exclusion Act passed

18. congestion, crime, violence, fire, disease, pollution

Reviewing Key Terms
On a sheet of paper, use each of these terms in a sentence.

1. steerage
2. nativism
3. skyscraper
4. tenement
5. political machine
6. party boss
7. graft
8. philanthropy
9. realism
10. vaudeville
11. ragtime
12. naturalism
13. settlement house
14. Americanization

Reviewing Key Facts

15. **Identify:** Ellis Island, Angel Island, Louis Sullivan, George Plunkitt, William M. ("Boss") Tweed, Gilded Age, Herbert Spencer, Lester Frank Ward, Jane Addams.

16. How did the Chinese in the United States react to the Chinese Exclusion Act of 1882?

17. What attempts did nativist groups make to decrease immigration to the United States in the late 1800s?

18. What problems did cities in the United States face in the late 1800s?

19. What did realist authors such as Mark Twain and Henry James write about?

20. What movements in the late 1800s addressed urban problems?

Critical Thinking

21. **Analyzing Themes: Geography and History** What factors led so many people to immigrate to the United States in the late 1800s?

22. **Analyzing** What methods did political machines use to build support in the late 1800s?

23. **Evaluating** Recall the problems facing city dwellers in the late 1800s. What do you think is the biggest problem facing people living in large cities today? How do you think the problem should be solved?

24. **Interpreting Primary Sources** Reaction in the United States to "old" immigration was generally more favorable than reaction to "new" immigration. Some people, however, still favored all immigration. The following excerpt from an 1882 editorial in the *Commercial and Financial Chronicle* addresses the effects of immigration on the nation.

❝In the very act of coming and traveling to reach his destination, he [the immigrant] adds . . . to the immediate prosperity and success of certain lines of business. . . . Not only do the ocean steamers . . . get very large returns in carrying passengers of this description, but in forwarding them to the places chosen by the immigrants as their future homes the railroad companies also derive great benefit and their passenger traffic is greatly swelled. . . .

Chapter Summary

Immigration and Internal Migration

↓

Rapid Growth of Cities

↓

Urban Problems of Poverty, Crime, and Disease

Nativism leads to immigration restrictions and violence against immigrants.

Political machines develop to offer services to city dwellers in exchange for votes.

19. the world as they saw it
20. Social Gospel, revivalism, and settlement house movement

Critical Thinking
21. military conscription in their homeland, religious persecution, better job opportunities in the United States

22. They provided housing, jobs, food, heat, and police protection to new immigrants unfamiliar with the United States and its culture.

23. Students' answers will vary. They should compare and contrast urban problems then and now.

24. **a.** positive; **b.** editorial viewed it positively and focused on economic benefits; nativists opposed immigration and worried about cultural and economic threats

Self-Check Quiz

Visit the *American Republic Since 1877* Web site at tarvol2.glencoe.com and click on **Self-Check Quizzes—Chapter 10** to assess your knowledge of chapter content.

... These immigrants not only produce largely, ... but, having wants which they cannot supply themselves, create a demand for outside supplies.... Thus it is that the Eastern manufacturer finds the call upon him for his wares and goods growing more urgent all the time, thus the consumption of coal keeps on expanding notwithstanding the check to new railroad enterprises, and thus there is a more active and larger interchange of all commodities.... 99

a. According to the editorial, what kind of effect did immigration have on the nation's economy?

b. How is the editorial's view of the effects of immigration different from that of the nativists?

25. **Organizing** Complete a graphic organizer similar to the one below by listing the new technologies that contributed to urban growth in the late 1800s.

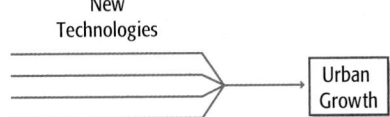

New Technologies → Urban Growth

Practicing Skills

26. **Hypothesizing** Reread the passage titled "The Spread of Schools" from Section 4. Using the information in this passage, form a hypothesis that describes the availability of education to people during this time. Write your hypothesis down and research the topic. Then state whether or not your hypothesis was correct.

Writing Activity

27. **Descriptive Writing** Find out about an individual in the 1800s who experienced a "rags-to-riches" success story. You might use one of the business leaders or other individuals discussed in the chapter. Write a brief sketch of the person, describing how he or she became a success.

Chapter Activity

28. **American History Primary Source Document Library CD-ROM** Read the article "The Need for Public Parks" by Frederick Law Olmsted, under *Reshaping the Nation*. Then work with a partner and create a design for a park that you think would meet the recreational needs of people in your community.

Immigration's Contribution to Population Growth, 1860–1900

People (in millions) — Year

Legend: Total population increase; Immigration

1861–1865, 1866–1870, 1871–1875, 1876–1880, 1881–1885, 1886–1890, 1891–1895, 1896–1900

Source: *Historical Statistics of the United States: Colonial Times to 1970.*

Geography and History

29. The graph above shows how much immigration contributed to population growth in the United States between 1860 and 1900. Study the graph and answer the questions below.

a. **Interpreting Graphs** By about how much did the population of the United States increase between 1861 and 1900?

b. **Understanding Cause and Effect** What is the relationship between immigration and population increase?

Standardized Test Practice

Directions: Choose the best answer to the following question.

Which of the following concepts is associated with both Social Darwinism and the Gospel of Wealth?

A Philanthropy

B Natural selection

C Governmental regulation

D Laissez-faire

Test-Taking Tip: Read the question carefully. Although more than one answer may apply to *either* Social Darwinism or the Gospel of Wealth, only one answer applies to *both*.

Have students visit the Web site at tarvol2.glencoe.com to review Chapter 10 and take the Self-Check Quiz.

Chapter Activity

28. The park designs should consider the needs of various ages and interests.

Geography and History

29. a. by about 2.5 million;
    b. Immigration played a significant role, especially in the period from 1881 to 1885.

Standardized Test Practice

Answer: D

Test-Taking Tip: Tell students that if they are not sure of the answer, they should use the process of elimination. Students should ask themselves if Social Darwinism and the Gospel of Wealth are both associated with the concept of philanthropy. The answer is no, so they can eliminate A. Ask the same question for each possible answer to eliminate B and C. The answer is D.

Bonus Question ?

Ask: What was the only ethnic group to be officially excluded by federal law from immigrating to the United States between 1870 and 1900? *(the Chinese)*

---

25. skyscrapers, cable cars, elevated railroads, subway systems

Practicing Skills

26. Students' answers will vary. Their hypothesis should be logical; however, it does not have to be correct. Students' research should support or refute their hypothesis.

Writing Activity

27. Students' sketches should include basic biographical facts and some insight into what enabled the person to go from rags to riches.

Chapter 11 Resources

Timesaving Tools

TeacherWorks™ All-In-One Planner and Resource Center

- **Interactive Teacher Edition** Access your Teacher Wraparound Edition and your classroom resources with a few easy clicks.
- **Interactive Lesson Planner** Planning has never been easier! Organize your week, month, semester, or year with all the lesson helps you need to make teaching creative, timely, and relevant.

Use Glencoe's **Presentation Plus!** multimedia teacher tool to easily present dynamic lessons that visually excite your students. Using Microsoft PowerPoint® you can customize the presentations to create your own personalized lessons.

TEACHING TRANSPARENCIES

Graphic Organizer 11 L2

Why It Matters Chapter Transparency 11 L2

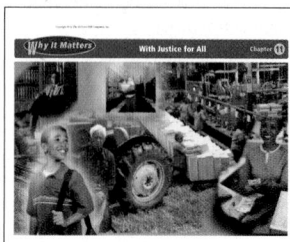

APPLICATION AND ENRICHMENT

Linking Past and Present Activity 11 L2

Enrichment Activity 11 L3

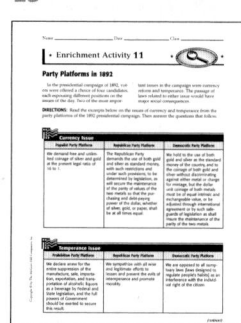

Primary Source Reading 11 L2

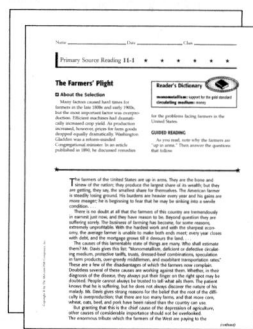

REVIEW AND REINFORCEMENT

Reteaching Activity 11 L1

Vocabulary Activity 11 L1

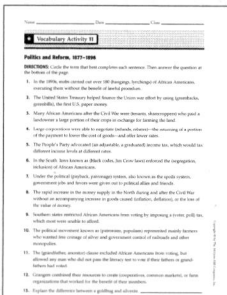

Time Line Activity 11 L2

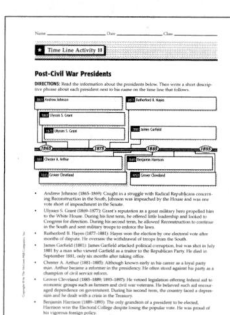

Critical Thinking Skills Activity 11 L2

Meeting NCSS Standards

Local Standards

The following standards are covered in Chapter 11:

Section 1 — II Time, Continuity, and Change: A, B, D
Section 2 — VII Production, Distribution, and Consumption: B, G, I
Section 3 — IV Individual Development and Identity: A, C, E, F

Chapter 11 Resources

ASSESSMENT AND EVALUATION

Chapter 11 Test Form A L2

Chapter 11 Test Form B L2

Standardized Test Practice Workbook Activity 11 L2

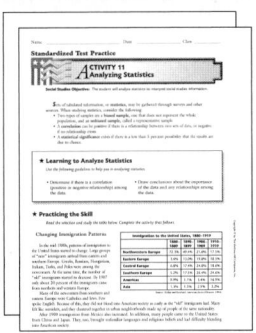

Performance Assessment Activities and Rubrics 11 L1/ELL

ExamView® Pro Testmaker CD-ROM

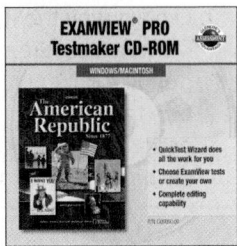

MULTIMEDIA

- Vocabulary PuzzleMaker CD-ROM
- Interactive Tutor Self-Assessment CD-ROM
- ExamView® Pro Testmaker CD-ROM
- Audio Program
- American History Primary Source Documents Library CD-ROM
- MindJogger Videoquiz
- Presentation Plus! CD-ROM
- TeacherWorks™ CD-ROM
- Interactive Student Edition CD-ROM
- Glencoe Skillbuilder Interactive Workbook CD-ROM, Level 2
- The *American Republic Since 1877* Video Program
- American Music: Hits Through History
- American Music: Cultural Traditions

SPANISH RESOURCES

The following Spanish language materials are available:

- Spanish Reading Essentials and Study Guide
- Spanish Guided Reading Activities
- Spanish Reteaching Activities
- Spanish Quizzes and Tests
- Spanish Vocabulary Activities
- Spanish Summaries
- The Declaration of Independence and United States Constitution Spanish Translation

---

The following videotape programs are available from Glencoe as supplements to Chapter 11:

- **Ku Klux Klan: A Secret History** (ISBN 0-76-700878-2)
- **J. Pierpont Morgan: Emperor of Wall Street** (ISBN 1-56-501957-1)

To order, call Glencoe at 1-800-334-7344. To find classroom resources to accompany many of these videos, check the following home pages:
A&E Television: www.aande.com
The History Channel: www.historychannel.com

Use our Web site for additional resources. All essential content is covered in the Student Edition.

You and your students can visit tarvol2.glencoe.com, the Web site companion to the *American Republic Since 1877.* This innovative integration of electronic and print media offers your students a wealth of opportunities. The student text directs students to the Web site for the following options:

- **Chapter Overviews**
- **Student Web Activities**
- **Self-Check Quizzes**
- **Textbook Updates**

Answers to the student Web activities are provided for you in the **Web Activity Lesson Plans.** Additional Web resources and Interactive Tutor Puzzles are also available.

Chapter 11 Resources

SECTION RESOURCES

Daily Objectives	Reproducible Resources	Multimedia Resources
SECTION 1 **Stalemate in Washington** 1. Explain why the Republicans and Democrats were so evenly matched during this period. 2. Cite the economic problems of the period and the basic viewpoints of each political party.	Reproducible Lesson Plan 11–1 Daily Lecture and Discussion Notes 11–1 Guided Reading Activity 11–1* Section Quiz 11–1* Reading Essentials and Study Guide 11–1* Performance Assessment Activities and Rubrics	Daily Focus Skills Transparency 11–1 Interactive Tutor Self-Assessment CD-ROM ExamView® Pro Testmaker CD-ROM* Presentation Plus! CD-ROM TeacherWorks™ CD-ROM Audio Program
SECTION 2 **Populism** 1. Explain why farmers wanted a greenback currency and why the adoption of the gold standard led to the Farmers' Alliance. 2. Describe who joined the Populist Party and what the party's goals were.	Reproducible Lesson Plan 11–2 Daily Lecture and Discussion Notes 11–2 Guided Reading Activity 11–2* Section Quiz 11–2* Reading Essentials and Study Guide 11–2* Performance Assessment Activities and Rubrics	Daily Focus Skills Transparency 11–2 Interactive Tutor Self-Assessment CD-ROM ExamView® Pro Testmaker CD-ROM* Presentation Plus! CD-ROM TeacherWorks™ CD-ROM Audio Program American Music: Cultural Traditions
SECTION 3 **The Rise of Segregation** 1. Discuss how African Americans in the South were disfranchised and how segregation was legalized. 2. Describe three major African American leaders' responses to discrimination.	Reproducible Lesson Plan 11–3 Daily Lecture and Discussion Notes 11–3 Guided Reading Activity 11–3* Section Quiz 11–3* Reading Essentials and Study Guide 11–3* Performance Assessment Activities and Rubrics Supreme Court Case Studies	Daily Focus Skills Transparency 11–3 Interactive Tutor Self-Assessment CD-ROM ExamView® Pro Testmaker CD-ROM* Presentation Plus! CD-ROM Skillbuilder Interactive Workbook, Level 2 TeacherWorks™ CD-ROM Vocabulary PuzzleMaker CD-ROM Audio Program

0:00 OUT OF TIME?
Assign the Chapter 11 **Reading Essentials and Study Guide.**

*Also Available in Spanish

 Printed Materials Transparency CD-ROM 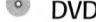 DVD

Poster   Music Program   Audio Program

NATIONAL GEOGRAPHIC **Teacher's Corner**

INDEX TO NATIONAL GEOGRAPHIC MAGAZINE

The following articles relate to this chapter.
- "Central Park: Oasis in the City," May 1993
- "Chicago: Welcome to the Neighborhood," May 1991
- "Miami," January 1992
- "New Life for Ellis Island," September 1990
- "New York's Chinatown," August 1998

NATIONAL GEOGRAPHIC SOCIETY PRODUCTS

To order the following, call National Geographic at 1-800-368-2728:
- *Historical Atlas of the United States*
- *Immigration: The Triumph of Hope* (Video)

NGS ONLINE

Access National Geographic's Web site for current events, atlas updates, activities, links, interactive features, and archives.
www.nationalgeographic.com

MEETING SPECIAL NEEDS

In addition to the Differentiated Instruction strategies found in each section, the following resources are also suitable for your special needs students:

- *ExamView® Pro Testmaker CD-ROM* allows teachers to tailor tests by reducing answer choices.
- The *Audio Program* includes the entire narrative of the student edition so that less-proficient readers can listen to the words as they read them.
- The *Reading Essentials and Study Guide* provides the same content as the student edition but is written two grade levels below the textbook.

KEY TO ABILITY LEVELS

Teaching strategies have been coded.

L1 BASIC activities for all students
L2 AVERAGE activities for average to above-average students
L3 CHALLENGING activities for above-average students
ELL ENGLISH LANGUAGE LEARNER activities

From the Classroom of...

Lindsay Linoff
Mesa School District
Mesa, AZ

Political Allegory in *Wizard of Oz*

Have the students read the original version of the *Wizard of Oz*. Point out that the story can be read on several levels. For example, the yellow brick road might represent the gold standard and Dorothy's silver shoes might represent the silver standard. (For students unfamiliar with the gold and silver standards, tell them that to fully appreciate the underlying political allegory, they need to research the time period in which Baum was writing and attempt to understand what the allegory refers to.)

Ask them to find at least five items in the book that might be allegorical and research the items' symbolism in society at that time. Help them connect the history of the time to Baum's story in the *Wizard of Oz*.

Have them write a report discussing the story and the underlying political allegory they discover.

ADDITIONAL RESOURCES FROM GLENCOE

- American Music: Cultural Traditions
- American Art & Architecture
- Outline Map Resource Book
- U.S. Desk Map
- Building Geography Skills for Life
- Inclusion for the High School Social Studies Classroom Strategies and Activities
- Teaching Strategies for the American History Classroom (Including Block Scheduling Pacing Guides)
- Dinah Zike's High School American History Reading and Study Skills Foldables

 Block Schedule

Activities that are suited to use within the block scheduling framework are identified by:

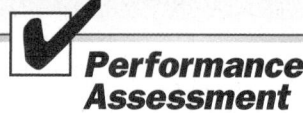

✓ Performance Assessment

Refer to Activity 11 in the Performance Assessment Activities and Rubrics booklet.

Why It Matters Activity

Have students discuss examples of segregation that may still remain in your community. Ask students what impact segregation has on people and on society as a whole. Students should evaluate their answers after they have completed the chapter.

GLENCOE
TECHNOLOGY

The *American Republic Since 1877* Video Program

To learn more about this period in American history, have students view the Chapter 11 video, "The 1893 Chicago World's Fair," from the *American Republic Since 1877* Video Program.

MindJogger Videoquiz

Use the **MindJogger Videoquiz** to preview Chapter 11 content.

 Both programs available in DVD

CHAPTER

11 Politics and Reform *1877–1896*

Why It Matters

During this period, political parties often focused on party competition rather than on important issues. Rural Americans were suffering economically, and they began to organize to obtain relief. Many states passed laws segregating African Americans and limiting their voting rights.

The Impact Today

Events of this period remain significant today.
* *To ensure fair hiring, a federal civil service system was created.*
* *Segregation created problems that Americans are still working to overcome.*

The American Republic Since 1877 Video
The Chapter 11 video, "The 1893 Chicago World's Fair," captures the feeling of this influential age.

1881
• President Garfield assassinated

1877
• Farmers' Alliance founded in Texas

1883
• Civil Service Act adopted

United States PRESIDENTS

Hayes 1877–1881

Garfield 1881

Arthur 1881–1885

Cleveland 1885–1889

1876   *1881*   *1886*

World

1878
• Russians defeat Turks in war over control of Balkans

1880
• France annexes Tahiti

1884
• First subway in London

362

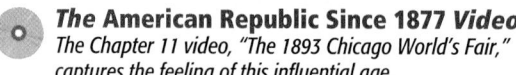 **Reading Strategy** **PURPOSE FOR READING**

Anticipation Guide Use anticipation guides to test background knowledge and focus students' reading in a chapter. Have students brainstorm: *What problems did Southern farmers face after the Civil War?* Write their ideas on the board or an overhead. After a sufficient list is established, have students select five problems they think are the most important. In complete sentences, have students write the ideas on a piece of paper, explaining why they think these were significant problems. As they read the chapter, have them revisit the sentences and correct any misconceptions. **L1**

Refer to *Inclusion for the High School Social Studies Classroom Strategies and Activities* in the TCR.

Electioneering in a Country Town by E.L. Henry

1887
- Florida initiates Jim Crow laws
- Interstate Commerce Act adopted

1890
- Sherman Antitrust Act passed

1895
- Booker T. Washington gives Atlanta Compromise speech

1896
- Democrats support free silver

B. Harrison
1889–1893

Cleveland
1893–1897

1891

1896

1893
- France acquires a protectorate over Laos

1894
- Sino-Japanese War breaks out

363

HISTORY Online

Chapter Overview
Visit the *American Republic Since 1877* Web site at tarvol2.glencoe.com and click on *Chapter Overviews—Chapter 11* to preview chapter information.

HISTORY Online

Introduce students to chapter content and key terms by having them access the **Chapter 11 Overview** at tarvol2.glencoe.com.

More About the Art

E.L. Henry (1841–1919) was a prolific artist who specialized in genre painting–paintings which depict everyday scenes, often in a sentimentalized or nostalgic style. He was also known for Civil War sketches in pencil and pastel crayon. Often, he sketched appealing behind-the-lines scenes of soldiers, horses, and wagons.
Ask: From the subject portrayed, what is the artist suggesting about local elections? *(that they are important, many are participating)*

TIME LINE ACTIVITY

Have students select one event on the time line that they would like to learn more about. Have them learn one new fact about the event to share with the class. Use the additional information to create an annotated class time line for the chapter.

FOLDABLES™ Study Organizer

Dinah Zike's Foldables are three-dimensional, interactive graphic organizers that help students practice basic writing skills, review key vocabulary terms, and identify main ideas. Have students complete the foldable activity in the *Dinah Zike's Reading and Study Skills Foldables* booklet.

GRAPHIC ORGANIZER ACTIVITY

Organizing Information Have students use a graphic organizer similar to the one shown below to identify the legislation that was passed during this period. Students' graphics will contain more lines than shown here.

Legislation	Intent
Pendleton Act	*filled federal jobs according to Civil Service Commission's rule*
McKinley Tariff	*lowered some tariffs, raised others*
Sherman Antitrust Act	*attempted to limit the power of trusts*

1 FOCUS

Section Overview
This section focuses on political struggles between the evenly matched Democrats and Republicans.

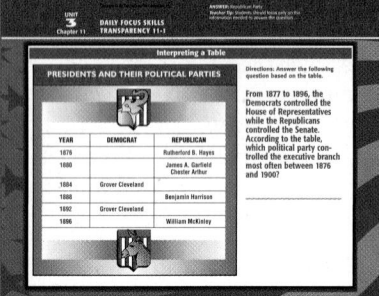
Reading Preview

Answers to Graphic: Stalwarts supported Reconstruction; Halfbreeds supported Pendleton Act

Preteaching Vocabulary
Have students look up the meaning of each of the Key Terms in the Glossary.

Guide to Reading

Main Idea
From 1877 to 1896, the Republicans and Democrats were so evenly matched that only a few reforms were possible at the national level.

Key Terms and Names
patronage, Stalwarts, Pendleton Act, rebate, Interstate Commerce Commission

Reading Strategy
Organizing As you read about the electoral politics of the 1880s, complete a graphic organizer similar to the one below by filling in the ideals of each Republican Party faction listed.

Stalwarts	Halfbreeds

Reading Objectives
- **Explain** why the Republicans and Democrats were so evenly matched during this period.
- **Cite** the economic problems of the period and the basic viewpoints of each political party.

Section Theme
Continuity and Change Political parties relied on support from different groups and regions of the country.

Preview of Events

♦1881	♦1884	♦1887	♦1890

1881
Garfield assassinated; succeeded by Chester A. Arthur

1883
Civil Service Act adopted

1887
Interstate Commerce Act adopted

1890
Sherman Antitrust Act adopted

Pitcher depicting James Garfield

★ An American Story ★

After the election of President James A. Garfield in 1880, many of his supporters tried to claim the "spoils of office"—the government jobs that follow an election victory. One of these job-seekers was Charles Guiteau. In the spring of 1881, Guiteau made daily trips to the White House or State Department, repeatedly asking for a job. Finally, the night of May 18, he had a crazed inspiration: "[I]f the president was out of the way," he thought, "everything would go better." Unlike Garfield, Guiteau reasoned, Vice President Chester Arthur was comfortable with the old spoils system. Arthur would give him the position he deserved. On July 2, 1881, Guiteau shot President Garfield in a train station near Capitol Hill. In a note left behind, Guiteau stated:

❝The President's tragic death was a sad necessity, but it will unite the Republican party and save the Republic. . . . I had no ill-will toward the President. His death was a political necessity. I am a lawyer, theologian, and politician. I am a Stalwart of the Stalwarts. . . .❞

—quoted in *Garfield*

A Campaign to Clean Up Politics

For many, the assassination of President Garfield highlighted the need to work seriously on reforming politics. Traditionally, under the spoils system, or patronage, government jobs went to supporters of the winning party in an election. Many Americans believed the spoils system prevented government from addressing the nation's issues and corrupted

---

SECTION RESOURCES

📁 Reproducible Masters
- Reproducible Lesson Plan 11–1
- Daily Lecture and Discussion Notes 11–1
- Guided Reading Activity 11–1
- Section Quiz 11–1
- Reading Essentials and Study Guide 11–1
- Performance Assessment Activities and Rubrics

📊 Transparencies
- Daily Focus Skills Transparency 11–1

Multimedia
- 💿 Interactive Tutor Self-Assessment CD-ROM
- 💿 ExamView® Pro Testmaker CD-ROM
- 💿 Presentation Plus! CD-ROM
- 💿 TeacherWorks™ CD-ROM
- 🎧 Audio Program

those who worked for the government. By the late 1870s, a movement to reform the civil service had begun to build support.

Stalwarts and Halfbreeds When Rutherford B. Hayes entered the White House in 1877, he attacked the practice of patronage by appointing reformers to his cabinet and replacing officials who owed their jobs to party bosses. His actions infuriated New York senator Roscoe Conkling, who, like other local bosses of Republican political machines, was called a "Stalwart" in the newspapers.

The Stalwarts were already angry with Hayes for abandoning Reconstruction, because this abandonment allowed Democrats to regain full control of the South. Conkling labeled the Republican reformers "Halfbreeds." He accused them of backing reform simply to create openings for their own supporters. "They are wolves in sheep's clothing," he charged. "Their real object is office and plunder."

As the presidential election of 1880 approached, Hayes honored his pledge not to seek a second term. The Republicans nominated a mixed ticket—a Halfbreed, James Garfield, for president, and a Stalwart, Chester A. Arthur, for vice president. Despite the party's feud, its ticket managed to win the election. A few months into his presidency, however, Garfield was assassinated.

The Pendleton Act Garfield's assassination further excited public opinion against the spoils system. In 1883 Congress responded by passing the **Pendleton Act.** This law allowed the president to decide which federal jobs would be filled according to rules laid down by a bipartisan Civil Service Commission. Candidates competed for these jobs through examinations, and appointments could be made only from the list of those who took the exams. Once appointed, a civil service official could not be removed for political reasons.

Although President Arthur was a Stalwart, he supported the Pendleton Act. He placed 14,000 jobs (about one-tenth of the total) under the control of the civil service. The federal government had finally begun to shift away from the spoils system.

✔ **Reading Check** **Explaining** Why did Garfield's assassination highlight the need for political reform?

Two Parties, Neck and Neck

Although many people thought corruption prevented the government from addressing the nation's problems, a major reason few new policies were introduced in the 1870s and 1880s was the political system itself. The Republicans held a voting edge in New England and the upper Midwest. As the party that had preserved the Union and established pensions for Civil War veterans, the Republicans had the support of former Union soldiers and Americans who were strongly patriotic. In addition, Republicans had the support of big business and strong support among farmers on the Great Plains. The Republicans were also seen as the party of reform because they supported abolition, temperance, and other reforms. Most Republicans were Protestants who viewed their party as the defender of traditional American morals and values.

While Republicans were sometimes seen as the "party of morality," Democrats portrayed themselves as the "party of personal liberty." The Democrats dominated the South, where white voters remained anti-Republican following the Civil War and Reconstruction. The Democrats also enjoyed strong support in big cities, where large numbers of Catholics and immigrants lived.

From 1877 to 1896, these voting patterns gave the Democrats an edge in the House of Representatives, where voters in each congressional district elected

Picturing **History**

National Tragedy A newspaper artist captured the attack on President Garfield. Why was Charles Guiteau obsessed with the idea of killing the president?

FRANK LESLIE'S
ILLUSTRATED
NEWSPAPER
NEW YORK, JULY 16, 1881.

WASHINGTON, D. C.—THE ATTACK ON THE PRESIDENT'S LIFE—MRS. SMITH SUPPORTING THE PRESIDENT WHILE AWAITING THE ARRIVAL OF THE AMBULANCE.

CHAPTER 11 Politics and Reform **365**

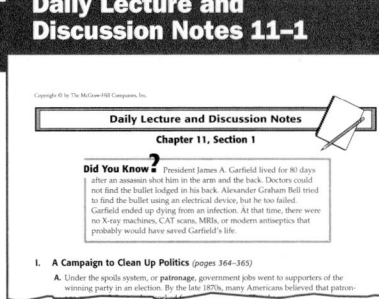

2 TEACH

Daily Lecture and Discussion Notes 11–1

Copyright © by The McGraw-Hill Companies, Inc.

Daily Lecture and Discussion Notes
Chapter 11, Section 1

Did You Know? President James A. Garfield lived for 80 days after an assassin shot him in the arm and the back. Doctors could not find the bullet lodged in his back. Alexander Graham Bell tried to find the bullet using an electrical device, but he too failed. Garfield ended up dying from an infection. At that time, there were no X-ray machines, CAT scans, MRIs, or modern antiseptics that probably would have saved Garfield's life.

I. **A Campaign to Clean Up Politics** (pages 364–365)
   A. Under the spoils system, or patronage, government jobs went to supporters of the winning party in an election. By the late 1870s, many Americans believed that patron-

Drawing a Time Line Ask students to draw a time line that shows U.S. presidents from 1877 to 1896, including names, party affiliations, and why they left office. **L1**

✔ **Reading Check**

Answer: The old spoils system had led to Garfield's assassination.

Picturing **History**

Answer: When Guiteau did not get the government job he wanted, he decided to kill Garfield, hoping Arthur would give him a job.
Ask: Do you think this illustration accurately represents the assassination scene? *(Students' answers will vary.)*

Reading Strategy · READING THE TEXT

Understanding Vocabulary Remind students about the difference between *synonyms,* which are words that have similar meanings, and *antonyms,* which are words that have opposite meanings. Tell students that they can easily remember this difference if they imagine that the "s" in synonyms stands for "same." As students read the text and encounter words that they are unfamiliar with, have them use a thesaurus to identify an appropriate synonym and antonym based on the words' context. **L1** ELL

☛ Refer to *Inclusion for the High School Social Studies Classroom Strategies and Activities* in the TCR.

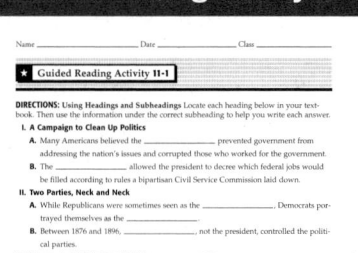

L1/ELL
Guided Reading Activity 11–1

Geography Skills

Answers:

1. West, Great Plains, Midwest, New England

2. New York, Pennsylvania, and Ohio; because they had the most electoral votes

Geography Skills Practice

Ask: Was the popular vote or the Electoral College vote closer? *(the popular vote)*

 Reading Check

Answer: Republicans won four of the six presidential elections.

Creating Circle Graphs Have students use the data below to make four circle graphs for the 1876 and 1888 elections. (One pair will show the electoral, and one the popular vote.) **L2**

1876 Candidate	Popular Vote	Electoral Vote
Hayes, Rep.	4,036,572	185
Tilden, Dem.	4,284,020	184

1888 Candidate	Popular Vote	Electoral Vote
Cleveland, Dem.	5,537,857	168
Harrison, Rep.	5,477,129	233

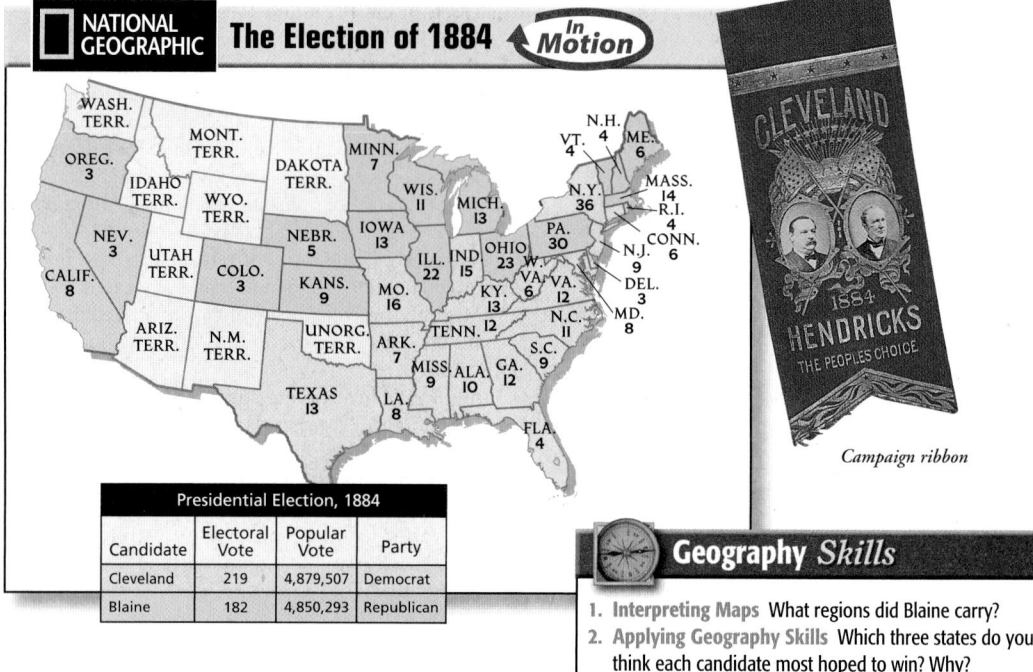

NATIONAL GEOGRAPHIC — The Election of 1884 — *In Motion*

Presidential Election, 1884			
Candidate	Electoral Vote	Popular Vote	Party
Cleveland	219	4,879,507	Democrat
Blaine	182	4,850,293	Republican

Campaign ribbon

Geography Skills

1. **Interpreting Maps** What regions did Blaine carry?
2. **Applying Geography Skills** Which three states do you think each candidate most hoped to win? Why?

members directly. The Republicans had the upper hand in the Senate, because state legislatures chose senators and Republicans generally controlled a majority of state governments.

Both parties were well organized to turn out the vote in elections, and narrow margins decided most presidential elections between 1876 and 1896. The elections of 1880 and 1888 came down to the swing states of New York, Ohio, and Pennsylvania, with their big blocks of electoral votes. Twice during this period, in 1876 and 1888, a candidate lost the popular vote but won the election. This happened because even if candidates win several states by slim popular vote margins, they still receive all the electoral votes in those states. These narrow victories then give the candidate an Electoral College majority, regardless of the overall popular vote count.

Although the Republicans won four of the six presidential elections between 1876 and 1896, the president often had to contend with a House controlled by Democrats and a Senate dominated by Republicans who did not always agree with him on the issues. Furthermore, this was an era when local political bosses, not the president, controlled the party. The nearly even division of power produced political deadlock at the federal level.

Reading Check **Summarizing** What were the results of most presidential elections between 1876 and 1896?

Democrats Reclaim the White House

As the election of 1884 approached, Democrats saw their best chance to win the White House since before the Civil War. Republicans remained divided over reform, and Democrats went after the votes of pro-reform Republicans by nominating Governor Grover Cleveland of New York. Cleveland was an opponent of **Tammany Hall,** the corrupt Democratic political machine in New York City.

Cleveland's Republican opponent was James G. Blaine, a former speaker of the House of Representatives and chairman of the Maine committee of the Republican Party since 1859. Blaine was wildly popular among party workers. When his name was placed in nomination at the Republican convention in Chicago, delegates launched into a riotous celebration. The cheers "deepened into a roar fully as deafening as the voice of Niagara," a witness reported. "The air quivered, the gas lights trembled and the walls fairly shook."

The campaign was sensational and frenzied. Because so many voters believed corruption was the main problem in American government, they focused their attention on the personal morals of the

366 CHAPTER 11 Politics and Reform

DIFFERENTIATED INSTRUCTION

At-Risk Students Spatial learners find it helpful to organize information with drawings and graphic organizers. Have students create a graphic organizer for each of the presidents mentioned in this section. The organizer should include their dates in office, their party affiliation, and one or two facts about their presidency. Encourage students to add other graphic organizers for other presidents and create a fact book for future reference. **L1**

📖 Refer to *Inclusion for the High School Social Studies Classroom Strategies and Activities* in the TCR.

candidates. The wild show of support for Blaine offended *New York Evening Post* editor Edwin L. Godkin, who called it a "disgrace to decency" and compared the celebration to a "mass meeting of maniacs." Godkin disliked Blaine, who had been accused during the Crédit Mobilier scandal of profiting financially from a political favor he did for the Union Pacific Railroad while serving as Speaker of the House in the 1870s.

Some Republican reformers were so unhappy with Blaine that they abandoned their party and supported Cleveland. These renegade reformers became known as **"Mugwumps,"** from an Algonquian word meaning "great chiefs." They thought of themselves as moral leaders who were more concerned with helping the nation than with helping a particular political party. Mugwumps believed that Blaine was too entrenched in the old system of politics to support their reform issues. Most Mugwumps came from New York and Massachusetts.

Cleveland, a bachelor, also faced moral criticism during the campaign when a newspaper revealed that he had fathered a child 10 years earlier. Aides asked Cleveland how they should respond to reporters seeking to know more about this story, and he replied, "Tell the truth." By admitting to the charge, Cleveland preserved his reputation for honesty and retained the support of many Mugwumps.

Blaine hoped that he could make up for the loss of the Mugwumps by persuading Roman Catholics to defect from the Democratic Party. His mother was an Irish Catholic, and there were half a million Irish Americans in New York state alone at the time. During the campaign, however, Blaine met with a Protestant minister who denounced the Democratic Party for its ties to Catholicism. Because Blaine was slow to denounce the remark, he lost most of the Irish American vote. To make matters worse for Blaine, many pro-temperance Republicans in upstate New York backed the candidate of the Prohibition Party, which was dedicated to banning the sale of alcohol. Cleveland won New York by a margin of about 1,000 votes out of more than 1,000,000 cast, and his victory there decided the election.

✓ **Reading Check** **Describing** From what sources did Grover Cleveland gain support in the 1884 presidential election?

A President Besieged by Problems

Grover Cleveland was an easy-going man who enjoyed the personal side of politics. Like his predecessors, he was shocked by the crowds that flocked to the White House seeking jobs. "This dreadful . . .

office-seeking hangs over me and surrounds me," he complained, "and makes me feel like resigning."

As the first elected Democratic president since 1856, he faced a horde of supporters who expected him to reward them with jobs. Mugwumps, on the other hand, expected him to multiply the number of positions covered under the merit system. Cleveland chose a middle course and wound up angering both sides. Economic issues, however, soon overshadowed the debate about political reform.

ECONOMICS

The Interstate Commerce Commission With greater industrialization and the growth of the labor movement, unrest among workers was mounting across the country. Many strikes occurred in this period, and police and paid guards sometimes attacked workers with clubs. This period of violence culminated in 1886 when a bomb exploded at a labor demonstration in Haymarket Square in Chicago.

The power of large corporations also concerned Americans. In particular, small businesses and farmers had become angry at the railroads. While large corporations such as Standard Oil were able to negotiate rebates—or partial refunds—and lower rates because of the volume of goods they shipped, others were forced to pay much higher rates. Although the high fixed costs and low operating costs of railroads caused much of this problem, many Americans believed railroads were gouging customers.

Neither Democrats nor Republicans moved quickly at the federal level to address these problems.

Analyzing *Political Cartoons*

Difficult Passage In Greek mythology, Scylla and Charybdis were sea monsters who threatened the hero Odysseus from opposite sides of a narrow strait. Why do you think the artist chose this image for Grover Cleveland in 1886?

CHAPTER 11 Politics and Reform **367**

Analyzing *Political Cartoons*

Answer: He was under pressure from both personal and political issues.
Ask: What did the Mugwumps expect? *(to add to the number of jobs under the merit system)*

Drawing a Political Cartoon
Have students choose one of the problems that President Grover Cleveland faced and create a political cartoon about it. **L3**

 Use the rubric for a political cartoon, pamphlet, or handbill on pages 77–78 in the *Performance Assessment Activities and Rubrics.*

FYI

Thomas Nast was responsible for creating the symbols of both the Democratic and Republican parties. To this day, the donkey symbolizes Democrats, and the elephant symbolizes Republicans.

✓ **Reading Check**

Answer: Mugwumps and Irish Americans

INTERDISCIPLINARY CONNECTIONS ACTIVITY

Government Have students make a poster using newspaper and magazine ads that advertise political issues or candidates. Ask students to write a caption for each illustration that explains the message that the ad presents. Have students share their work with a partner, critiquing each other's work and making needed improvements. Display the finished products in the classroom. **L2**

3 ASSESS

Assign Section 1 Assessment as homework or as an in-class activity.

🔵 Have students use the **Interactive Tutor Self-Assessment CD-ROM.**

L1/ELL

L2

Picturing History

Answer: government corruption and character of the candidates

Ask: What were the moral issues facing each of the candidates?

(Blaine had been implicated in the Crédit Mobilier scandal, and Cleveland, who was not married, had fathered a child.)

Reading Check

Answer: It had to rely on the courts to enforce its rulings.

Picturing History

Changing of the Guard Grover Cleveland delivers his inaugural speech in March 1885. His predecessor, Chester Arthur, is seen at left. What were the major issues of this election?

Both parties believed that government should not interfere with corporations' property rights, which courts had held to be the same as those of individuals. Many states had new laws regulating railroad freight rates. In 1886, however, the Supreme Court ruled in the case of *Wabash* v. *Illinois* that Illinois could not restrict the rates that the Wabash Railroad charged for traffic between states because only the federal government could regulate interstate commerce. 📖 *(See page 965 for a summary of* Wabash v. Illinois.*)*

Public pressure forced Congress to respond to the *Wabash* ruling. In 1887 Cleveland signed the Interstate Commerce Act creating the **Interstate Commerce Commission** (ICC). This act was the first federal law designed to regulate interstate commerce. The legislation limited railroad rates to what was "reasonable and just," forbade rebates to high-volume users, and made it illegal to charge higher rates for shorter hauls. The commission was not very effective in regulating the industry, however, because it had to rely on the courts to enforce its rulings.

Debating Tariffs Another important economic issue concerned tariffs. Although tariffs had been lowered slightly in the 1870s, they were still much higher than in the years before the Civil War. Many Democrats thought that Congress should cut tariffs

because these taxes had the effect of raising the prices of manufactured goods. While protecting weak domestic manufacturing after the Civil War may have made sense, many questioned the necessity of maintaining high tariffs in the 1880s, when large American companies were fully capable of competing internationally. High tariffs also forced other nations to respond in kind, making it difficult for farmers to export their surpluses.

In December 1887, President Cleveland proposed lowering tariffs. The House, with a Democratic majority, passed moderate tariff reductions, but the Republican-controlled Senate rejected the bill. With Congress deadlocked, tariff reduction became a major issue in the election of 1888.

☑ **Reading Check** **Examining** Why was the Interstate Commerce Commission unable to carry out its goals effectively?

Republicans Regain Power

The Republicans and their presidential candidate, Benjamin Harrison, received large contributions for the 1888 campaign from industrialists who benefited from tariff protection. Cleveland and the Democrats campaigned against unnecessarily high tariff rates. In one of the closest races in American history,

368 CHAPTER 11 Politics and Reform

CRITICAL THINKING ACTIVITY

Drawing Conclusions Have interested students research the nation's budget surpluses and deficits since 1860. Based on the information, create a line graph showing the changing trends. At each point where the trend shows a change of direction, identify the events that might have brought about these changes. Have students write a paragraph stating how political leaders have contributed to surpluses and deficits and whether their decisions helped or hurt the country. **L3**

Harrison lost the popular vote but won the electoral vote with narrow victories in New York and Indiana.

The McKinley Tariff The election of 1888 gave the Republicans control of both houses of Congress as well as the White House. Using this power, the party passed legislation to address points of national concern. One major piece of legislation was McKinley's tariff bill. Representative William McKinley of Ohio pushed through a tariff bill that cut tobacco taxes and tariff rates on raw sugar but greatly increased rates on other goods, such as textiles, to discourage people from buying those imports.

The **McKinley Tariff** lowered federal revenue and transformed the nation's budget surplus into a budget deficit. In 1890, furthermore, Congress passed a new pension law increasing payments to veterans and the number of veterans eligible to receive them. While securing more votes for the Republicans, the new pension plan greatly worsened the federal deficit.

Harrison paper lantern

The Sherman Antitrust Act The Republican-controlled Congress also responded to popular pressure to do something about the power of trusts, large combinations of companies that dominated certain markets. Senator John Sherman of Ohio introduced the **Sherman Antitrust Act** of 1890, which declared illegal any "combination in the form of trust . . . or conspiracy, in restraint of trade or commerce among the several States." The courts were responsible for enforcement, however, and judges saw nothing in this vaguely worded legislation that required them to make big companies change the way they did business. In 1895, for example, the Supreme Court agreed that the American Sugar Refining Company was a trust, enjoying a nearly complete monopoly of sugar manufacturing. Nevertheless, the Court ruled that the company's actions did not violate the Sherman Antitrust Act because manufacturing was not interstate commerce. In the years following passage of the act, businesses formed trusts and combinations at a great rate. In 1899 alone there were over 1,200 recorded mergers in manufacturing and mining firms. Like the ICC, the Sherman Antitrust Act was more important for establishing a precedent than for its immediate impact.

As the midterm congressional election of 1890 approached, some Americans concluded that the two-party system was incapable of solving the nation's problems. That conviction was strongest among farmers, who felt exploited by banks and railroads and neglected by the government. They doubted that either the Democrats or the Republicans would respond to their concerns.

☑ **Reading Check** **Summarizing** What were the results of the McKinley Tariff?

HISTORY Online | **Study Central™** To review this section, go to tarvol2.glencoe.com and click on **Study Central™**.

SECTION 1 ASSESSMENT

Checking for Understanding
1. **Define:** patronage, rebate.
2. **Identify:** Stalwart, Halfbreed, Interstate Commerce Commission.
3. **Explain** how the Pendleton Act created civil service reform.
4. **Describe** the events leading to the establishment of the Interstate Commerce Commission.

Reviewing Themes
5. **Continuity and Change** What groups and regions were strongholds for Republicans and Democrats in the 1880s? Where is their support today?

Critical Thinking
6. **Interpreting** Why was the Sherman Antitrust Act ineffective?
7. **Organizing** Use a graphic organizer similar to the one below to list the era's economic problems and the Harrison administration's solutions.

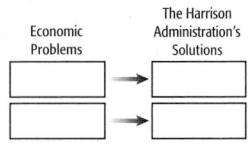

Analyzing Visuals
8. **Examining Photographs** Study the photograph on page 368. What similarities do you see between Cleveland's inauguration ceremony and the ones we have today? Do you see any differences between the ceremonies then and now?

Writing About History
9. **Persuasive Writing** Imagine that you are seeking a federal job in the early 1880s. Write a letter to your congressional representatives urging them to support or oppose the Pendleton Act.

CHAPTER 11 Politics and Reform **369**

The Interstate Commerce Commission no longer exists. It was terminated in 1995.

Reteach
Have students explain why the Republicans and Democrats were so evenly matched during this period.

Enrich
Have students research and report on how the Sherman Antitrust Act was used in the case to try to break up Microsoft.

✓ **Reading Check**

Answer: lowered federal revenue and transformed the nation's budget surplus into a budget deficit

Study Central™ provides summaries, interactive games, and online graphic organizers to help students review section content.

4 CLOSE

Have students cite the economic problems of the period and the basic viewpoints of each political party.

SECTION 1 ASSESSMENT ANSWERS

1. Terms are in blue.
2. Stalwart (p. 365), Halfbreed (p. 365), Interstate Commerce Commission (p. 368)
3. certain federal jobs filled according to newly created Civil Service Commission rules
4. worker and consumer unrest, fear of powerful corporations and industry, anger at railroads
5. Republicans: big business, Great Plains farmers, Protestants; Midwest, South, rural areas; Democrats: Catholics and immigrants, urban areas
6. The enforcing courts judged the legislation language too vague to rule against big companies.
7. Problems: price gouging, high tariffs, trusts; Solutions: ICC, McKinley Tariff, Sherman Antitrust Act
8. similar setup; differences: clothing; more women today
9. Students' letters will vary.

TIME NOTEBOOK

TEACH

Urban Poverty

Ask students the following questions after they have read the excerpt of the exposé by Jacob Riis.

- **What problems does Riis cite in this excerpt?** (*overcrowding, filth, poor water system, and all-night parties*)

- **How does Riis view the landlords of the building?** (*They are profiting at the expense of the tenants.*)

- **What problems may children encounter in such crowded conditions?** (*possible answers: sickness, lack of attention, a poor night's sleep, poor nutrition*)

Livin' in the City

Have students review the family budget, identifying items that would not be included today or are not necessary today. Then tell students to assume that they are married and have two children. Both spouses work, and their combined annual salary is $48,000. Have students work in pairs to prepare a balanced budget that includes some savings. After reviewing their budgets with another pair of students, they may make any necessary adjustments. As a class, discuss why living on a budget is wise.

Visit the **TIME** Web site at www.time.com for up-to-date news, weekly magazine articles, editorials, online polls, and an archive of past magazine and Web articles.

Eyewitness

In his exposé of urban poverty, How the Other Half Lives *(1890),* **JACOB RIIS** *documented the living conditions in New York City tenements:*

"The statement once made a sensation that between seventy and eighty children had been found in one tenement. It no longer excites even passing attention, when the sanitary police report counting 101 adults and 91 children in a Crosby Street house, one of twins, built together. The children in the others, if I am not mistaken, numbered 89, a total of 180 for two tenements! Or when midnight inspection in Mulberry Street unearths a hundred and fifty "lodgers" sleeping on filthy floors in two buildings. In spite of brown-stone fittings, plate-glass and mosaic vestibule floors, the water does not rise in summer to the second story, while the beer flows unchecked to the all-night picnics on the roof. The saloon with the side-door and the landlord divide the prosperity of the place between them, and the tenant, in sullen submission, foots the bill."

VERBATIM

❝Tell 'em quick, and tell 'em often.❞

WILLIAM WRIGLEY,
soap salesman and promoter of chewing gum, on his marketing philosophy

❝A pushing, energetic, ingenious person, always awake and trying to get ahead of his neighbors.❞

HENRY ADAMS,
historian, describing the average New Yorker or Chicagoan

❝We cannot all live in cities, yet nearly all seem determined to do so.❞

HORACE GREELEY,
newspaper editor

INDICATORS:
Livin' in the City

Moving off the farm for a factory job? Sharpen your pencil. You'll need to budget carefully to buy all you will need.

Here are the numbers for a Georgia family of four in 1890. The husband is a textile worker, and the wife works at home. There is one child, age 4, and a boarder. They share a two-room, wood-heated, oil-lighted apartment.

INCOME: (annual)

husband's income	$312.00
boarder's rent	10.00
TOTAL INCOME	**$322.00**

EXPENSES: (annual)

medical	$65.00
furniture	46.90
clothing	46.00
rent	21.00
flour/meal	25.00
hog products	17.00
other meat	13.00
vegetables	13.00
lard	6.50
potatoes	6.40
butter	5.00
sugar	4.00
charitable donations	6.10
vacation	3.25
alcohol	3.25
tobacco	3.00
molasses	2.00
other food	27.80
miscellaneous	68.20
TOTAL EXPENSES	**$382.40**

COOPERATIVE LEARNING ACTIVITY

Creating a Magazine Spread Organize the class into four groups. Have each group identify a current social problem and write an exposé-style essay for a magazine. Groups should research the problem and use facts in the essay. Then have groups create a magazine spread for the article. Students should look at magazines for ideas about page design and photo placement. This activity can be completed using desktop publishing software or the cut-and-paste method.

Use the rubric for a cooperative group management plan on pages 71–72 in the **Performance Assessment Activities and Rubrics.**

Milestones

ON THE RUN, 1881. THE JESSE JAMES GANG, after robbing a Chicago, Rock Island, and Pacific train near Winston, Missouri, and killing the conductor and a passenger.

OVERTURNED, 1878. By the Supreme Court, a Louisiana court decision that awarded damages to an African American woman who had been refused admission to a steamship stateroom reserved for whites.

PLAGUED BY GRASSHOPPERS, 1874. THE AMERICAN GREAT PLAINS. Insect swarms a mile wide blot out the midday sun. Two inches deep on the ground, they leave "nothing but the mortgage," as one farmer put it.

CELEBRATED IN EUROPE, 1887. ANNIE OAKLEY, star of Buffalo Bill's Wild West Show. Oakley shot a cigarette from the lips of Crown Prince Wilhelm of Germany. Years later, when the U.S. goes to war against Kaiser Wilhelm, Oakley will quip: "I wish I'd missed that day!"

Jesse James

Susan B. Anthony

REMOVED, 1884. IDA B. WELLS, journalist and former slave, from a ladies coach on a train. Wells refused to move to the smoking car where African Americans were to be seated.

ESTABLISHED, 1883. STANDARD TIME. To accommodate the railroad system, noon will no longer be the moment in a given locality when the sun stands highest in the sky but, instead will be standard across four time zones. Set your watches!

ARRESTED, 1872. SUSAN B. ANTHONY, for casting a ballot in Rochester, New York. Anthony argued that the Fourteenth and Fifteenth Amendments applied to women.

NUMBERS

1 in 12 Americans living in cities of 100,000 or more in 1865

A crowded New York City street

1 in 5 Americans living in cities in 1896

522 Inhabitants in a one-acre area in the Bowery, New York City

$2 Daily wage for a farm laborer, New York, 1869

$4 Daily wage for a plumber, New York City, 1869

50¢ Price of a pair of boy's knee pants, a parasol, button boots, or a necktie (1870s)

$8 Price of a "Fine All-Wool Suit," 1875

$3 Box seat for four at Gilmore's Concert Garden in New York City

4¢ Price for one pound of fancy white rice, 1896

25¢ Admission to "Barnum's American Museum" (featuring the smallest pair of human beings ever seen!), 1896

Portfolio Writing Project

Have students research one of the people or events listed in the Milestones. Have students write a descriptive essay about the person or event.

Using a Database Tell students to research interesting numbers from life today. They may include information on urban population, minimum wage, average wage rates or salaries for various jobs, prices of common goods and services, and prices of admission to various forms of entertainment. Have students organize the information into a database. Then have students create five questions that can be answered from the database. Have them trade databases and questions with another student and answer each other's questions.

CLOSE

As a class, discuss whether the quotes in the Verbatim section on page 370 are still valid today.

EXTENDING THE CONTENT

Urban Pollution In New York City in 1866, a report on sanitary conditions in the city listed the following problems: (1) filthy streets; (2) neglected garbage and domestic refuse; (3) obstructed and faulty sewers and drains; (4) neglected privies and stables; (5) cattle pens and large stables in the more populous districts; (6) neglected and filthy markets; (7) slaughterhouses and hide and fat depots in close proximity to populous streets; (8) droves of cattle and swine in crowded streets; (9) swill-milk stables; (10) bone boiling, fat melting . . . within the city limits; (11) . . . offensive exhalations . . . in gas manufacture; (12) . . . dumping grounds and manure yards in vicinity of populous streets; (13) . . . management of refuse and junk materials; (14) overcrowding of . . . public conveyances; (15) neglect of dead animals in the streets and gutters of the city.

1 FOCUS

Section Overview

This section focuses on the development of the Populist Party.

BELLRINGER
Skillbuilder Activity

Project transparency and have students answer the question.

Daily Focus Skills Transparency 11–2

Reading Preview

Answers to Graphic:
I. Unrest in Rural America
   A. The Money Supply
   B. Deflation Hurts Farmers
   C. The Grange Takes Action

Students should complete the outline by including all heads in the section.

Preteaching Vocabulary

Have students create a simple symbol, icon, or sketch for each of the Key Terms and Names. Ask students to label each drawing.

Populism

Guide to Reading

Main Idea

In the 1890s an independent political movement called populism emerged to challenge the two major parties.

Key Terms and Names

populism, greenback, inflation, deflation, Grange, cooperative, People's Party, graduated income tax, goldbug, silverite, William Jennings Bryan

Reading Strategy

Taking Notes As you read about the emergence of populism in the 1890s, use the major headings of the section to create an outline similar to the one below.

```
Populism
I.  Unrest in Rural America
    A.
    B.
II.
    A.
    B.
```

Reading Objectives

• **Explain** why farmers wanted a greenback currency and why the adoption of the gold standard led to the Farmers' Alliance.

• **Describe** who joined the Populist Party and what the party's goals were.

Section Theme

Economic Factors Currency and credit problems led to the rise of the Populist movement.

Preview of Events

♦1865	♦1875	♦1885	♦1895

1867 Grange founded to aid farmers

1873 Congress adopts a gold standard for currency

1877 Farmers' Alliance founded in Texas

1890 People's Party formed in Kansas

1892 National People's Party formed

★ An American Story ★

Populist farmers gather in Dickinson County, Kansas

On July 4, 1890, Leonidas L. Polk took a political gamble. He stepped up to make a speech to a crowd of 6,000 in a small town in Kansas. Polk was a Southerner, a lifelong Democrat, and a former Confederate soldier. He was not in friendly territory.

Polk had come to Kansas because he was now involved in a different kind of battle, one that cut across the lines dividing Northerners from Southerners and Democrats from Republicans. He was calling on farmers from both parties and both regions to unite for their common good. Polk urged the crowd to reject the two-party system and join the emerging movement that became known as populism:

❝I tell you this afternoon that from New York to the Golden Gate, the farmers have risen up and have inaugurated a movement such as the world has never seen. It is a revolution of thought. . . . The farmer of North Carolina, Georgia, Texas, South Carolina is your brother. . . . Some people have stirred up sectional feelings and have kept us apart for twenty-five years. . . . They know that if we get together and shake hands . . . their doom is sealed. . . . Congress could give us a bill in forty-eight hours that would relieve us, but Wall Street says nay. . . . I believe that both of the parties are afraid of Wall Street.❞

–quoted in *Democratic Promise: The Populist Movement in America*

Unrest in Rural America

Populism was the movement to increase farmers' political power and to work for legislation in their interest. The economic crisis that drove farmers to embrace this movement had its origins in the years immediately following the Civil War. A major

372 CHAPTER 11 Politics and Reform

SECTION RESOURCES

📖 Reproducible Masters
• Reproducible Lesson Plan 11–2
• Daily Lecture and Discussion Notes 11–2
• Guided Reading Activity 11–2
• Section Quiz 11–2
• Reading Essentials and Study Guide 11–2

📑 Transparencies
• Daily Focus Skills Transparency 11–2

Multimedia
🖸 Interactive Tutor Self-Assessment CD-ROM
🖸 ExamView® Pro Testmaker CD-ROM
🖸 Presentation Plus! CD-ROM
🖸 TeacherWorks™ CD-ROM
🔊 Audio Program
🎵 American Music: Cultural Traditions

problem was that farm prices had dropped due to new technology. Farmers were producing more crops, and greater supply tended to lower prices. At the same time, high tariffs increased the cost of manufactured goods farmers needed and made it harder for farmers to sell their goods overseas. Farmers also felt they were victimized by large and faraway entities: the banks from which they obtained loans and the railroads that set their shipping rates. The world that farmers now dealt with was more and more one of big business, and they felt they were losing power and influence.

The Money Supply One specific problem that greatly concerned farmers was the nation's money supply. To help finance the Union war effort, the United States Treasury had greatly expanded the money supply by issuing millions of dollars in greenbacks—paper currency that could not be exchanged for gold or silver coins. This rapid increase in the money supply without an accompanying increase in goods for sale caused inflation, or a decline in the value of money. As the paper money lost value, the prices of goods soared.

After the Civil War ended, the United States had three types of currency in circulation—greenbacks, gold and silver coins, and national bank notes backed by government bonds. To get inflation under control,

the federal government stopped printing greenbacks and began paying off its bonds. In 1873 Congress also decided to stop making silver into coins.

These decisions meant that the United States did not have a large enough money supply to meet the needs of the country's growing economy. In 1865, for example, there was about $30 in circulation for each American, but by 1895 it had sunk to about $23. As the economy expanded, deflation—or an increase in the value of money and a decrease in the general level of prices—began. As money increased in value, prices began to fall.

Deflation Hurts Farmers Deflation hit farmers especially hard. Most farmers had to borrow money for seed and other supplies to plant their crops. Because money was in short supply, interest rates began to rise, which increased the amount farmers owed. For those who wanted to expand their farms, rising interest rates also made mortgages more expensive. The falling prices of the period of deflation meant the farmers sold their crops for less. Nevertheless, they still had to make the same mortgage payments to the banks.

Realizing that their problems were due to a shortage of currency, many farmers concluded that Eastern bankers had pressured Congress into reducing the money supply. Some farmers called for the

Picturing **History**

Populist Territory This farm family in Nebraska represents the kind of people who typically supported populism. Why did farmers dislike Eastern bankers?

Brainstorming Organize students into groups of four or five. Give each group the topic of the Grange, the Farmers' Alliance, or the Populist Party. Using one piece of paper per group, have each student write a statement about the history of their topic during the late 1800s. Have them pass the paper around several times until they have written down all they know about their topic. Then have students review the statements and add any information that is missing. Have each group share their statements with the class. **L1**

📁 Refer to *Inclusion for the High School Social Studies Classroom Strategies and Activities* in the TCR.

2 *TEACH*

Daily Lecture and Discussion Notes 11–2

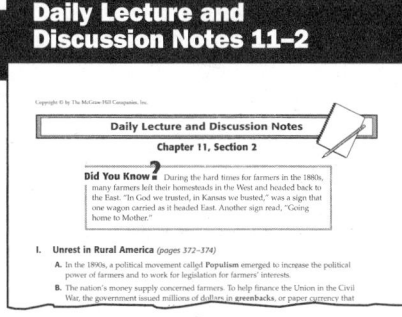

Copyright © by The McGraw-Hill Companies, Inc.

Daily Lecture and Discussion Notes
Chapter 11, Section 2

Did You Know? During the hard times for farmers in the 1880s, many farmers left their homesteads in the West and headed back to the East. "In God we trusted, in Kansas we busted," was a sign that one wagon carried as it headed East. Another sign read, "Going home to Mother."

I. Unrest in Rural America (pages 372–374)

  A. In the 1890s, a political movement called **Populism** emerged to increase the political power of farmers and to work for legislation for farmers' interests.

  B. The nation's money supply concerned farmers. To help finance the Union in the Civil War, the government issued millions of dollars in **greenbacks**, or paper currency that

Picturing **History**

Answer: Farmers thought that their problems were due to a shortage of currency and that Eastern bankers had pressured Congress into reducing the money supply.

Ask: What do you think it would be like to spend a winter in this type of dwelling? (*It would be cold and damp.*)

Drawing a Diagram Have students draw an inflation and deflation diagram. The diagram should show how the supply of money and goods and services changes under each condition, and how farmers were affected by deflation. You may want to consult the economics teacher to help review these concepts with students. **L1** ELL

373

L1/ELL

Guided Reading Activity 11-2

FYI

Farmers in 37 states belong to the Grange today. The organization still pursues its original goals of providing educational and social support to farmers and their families.

you don't say...

Rural Lingo Grange comes from the Middle Latin word *granica,* which is from the Latin *granum,* or "grain." At one time the grange was the farm of a monastery, where grain was stored.

CURRICULUM CONNECTION

Economics To quiet demands for a larger money supply, the government passed the Bland-Allison Act of 1878. The act authorized the U.S. Treasury to purchase silver and issue silver certificates for the first time. Silver certificates could be exchanged for silver dollars. The Treasury continued to exchange silver certificates for silver dollars until 1964. Silver certificates remain a legal form of currency in the United States.

---

printing of more greenbacks to expand the money supply. Others, particularly those living in the West where new silver mines had been found, wanted the government to begin minting silver coins. They referred to the decision to stop minting silver as **"The Crime of '73."** Increasingly, farmers realized that if they were going to convince the government to meet their demands, they needed to organize.

The Grange Takes Action In 1866 the United States Department of Agriculture sent Oliver H. Kelley to tour the rural South and report on the condition of the region's farmers. Realizing how isolated the farmers were from each other, the following year, Kelley founded the nation's first national farm organization, the Patrons of Husbandry, better known as the **Grange.**

At first Grangers got together largely for social and educational purposes. Then, in 1873, the nation plunged into a severe recession, and farm income fell sharply. Farmers looking for help joined the Grange in large numbers. By 1874 the Grange had between 800,000 and 1.5 million members.

Grangers responded to the crisis in three ways. Some pressured state legislatures to regulate railroad and warehouse rates, which they believed were too high. Others joined the Independent National Party. This new political party, nicknamed the Greenback Party, wanted the government to print more greenbacks to increase the money supply. Grangers also pooled their resources and tried to create cooperatives—marketing organizations that worked for the benefit of their members.

One of the reasons farmers could not charge higher prices for their crops was that there were so many farmers in competition. If a farmer raised prices, a buyer could always go elsewhere and pay

Farmers' Alliance This small band of farmers met in a cabin in Lampasas County, Texas, to form the Farmers' Alliance.

less. Cooperatives pooled farmers' crops and held them off the market in order to force up prices. Because a cooperative controlled a large quantity of farm products, it could also negotiate better shipping rates with the railroads.

The Grange Fails None of the strategies the Grangers employed improved farmers' economic condition. Several western states passed "Granger laws" setting maximum rates and prohibiting railroads from charging more for short hauls than for long ones. The railroads fought back by cutting services and refusing to lay new track until the laws were repealed. The 1886 Supreme Court ruling in *Wabash v. Illinois* then greatly limited the states' ability to regulate railroads by ruling that states could not regulate commerce that crossed state lines. 📖 *(See pages 368 and 965 for more information on* Wabash v. Illinois.*)*

Meanwhile the Greenback Party failed to gain much public support. Many Americans were very suspicious of paper money. They did not believe it would hold its value, and they considered the Greenback Party's proposal to print more paper money dangerous for the economy. The Grange's cooperatives also failed, partly because they were too small to have any effect on prices, and partly because Eastern businesses and railroads considered them to be similar to unions—illegitimate conspiracies in restraint of trade—and refused to do business with them. By the late 1870s, membership in the Grange had begun to fall, as farmers moved to other organizations that they hoped would better address their problems.

The Farmers' Alliance

Even as the Grange began to fall apart, a new organization, known as the **Farmers' Alliance,** began to form. The Farmers' Alliance began in Lampasas County, Texas, in 1877. By 1885 it had built a substantial following throughout the state. The following year, Charles W. Macune became the leader of the Alliance. Macune called for the organization to begin recruiting farmers outside of Texas.

The Alliance Grows During the late 1880s, Alliance members traveled across the South and West speaking to farmers and organizing local chapters. By 1890 the Alliance had between 1.5 and 3 million members. Its support was very strong in the South and on the Great Plains, particularly in Kansas, Nebraska, and North and South Dakota.

When Macune became the leader of the Alliance, he also announced a plan to organize very large cooperatives that the Alliance called exchanges.

DIFFERENTIATED INSTRUCTION

Verbal/Linguistic Farm families of the late 1800s bought many things through mail-order catalogs. Have pairs of students find reproductions of Sears or Montgomery Ward catalogs of the late 1800s and choose two sections for study. Have them list the types of goods sold in the sections, comparing them with current catalogs on types of items and price. Then ask students to compare the needs of families of the late 1800s with the needs of families today. **L2**

📁 Refer to *Inclusion for the High School Social Studies Classroom Strategies and Activities* in the TCR.

Picturing **History**

Hard Labor Southern farmers spent long hours working in their fields. Harvesting cotton (left) and husking corn (right) were family activities that were done by hand with no expensive mechanical equipment. What do you notice about the ages of the group husking corn?

Macune hoped these exchanges would be big enough to force farm prices up and to make loans to farmers at low interest rates. The exchanges had some success. The Texas Exchange successfully marketed cotton at prices slightly higher than those paid to individual farmers, while the Illinois Exchange negotiated slightly better railroad rates for wheat farmers.

The People's Party Despite their temporary success, the large cooperatives failed for several reasons. Many overextended themselves by loaning too much money at low interest rates that was never repaid. In many cases, wholesalers, manufacturers, railroads, and bankers discriminated against them, making it difficult for them to stay in business. The exchanges also failed because they still were too small to dramatically affect world prices for farm products.

By 1890 the failure of the Alliance to fix farmers' problems had started a power struggle within the organization. Some Alliance leaders, particularly in the Western states, wanted to form a new party and push for political reforms. Members of the Kansas Alliance formed the **People's Party,** also known as the Populists, and nominated candidates to run for Congress and the state legislature. Alliances in Nebraska, South Dakota, and Minnesota quickly followed Kansas's example.

The Subtreasury Plan Most Southern leaders of the Alliance, including Charles Macune, opposed the idea of a third party. They did not want to undermine the Democrats' control of the South. Instead, Macune suggested that the Alliance produce a list of demands and promise to vote for candidates who supported those demands. He hoped this strategy would force the Democrats to adopt the Alliance program.

As part of this strategy, Macune introduced the subtreasury plan, which called for the government to set up warehouses called subtreasuries. Farmers would store the crops in the warehouses, and the government would provide low-interest loans to the farmers. Macune believed that the plan would allow farmers to hold their crops off the market in large enough quantities to force prices up. He hoped that the Democrats would adopt the subtreasury plan and thereby win farmers' votes.

✓**Reading Check** **Explaining** How did the Farmers' Alliance try to help farmers?

The Rise of Populism

In 1890 members of the Farmers' Alliance met in Ocala, Florida, and issued what came to be known as the Ocala Demands. These demands were intended

CHAPTER 11 Politics and Reform **375**

INTERDISCIPLINARY CONNECTIONS ACTIVITY

Music Read or distribute the following folk song of the Populist movement. Then have students discuss how the song expresses the feelings of farmers in the late 1800s. **L2**

Starving to Death on My Government Claim

My name is Tom Hight,/An old bach'lor I am;/You'll find me out west/in the county of fame,/You'll find me out west/on an elegant plain,/Starving to death/on my government claim. Hurrah for Green County!/the land of the free;/The land of the bedbug,/grasshopper, and flea;/I'll sing of its praises,/I'll tell of its fame,/While starving to death/on my government claim.

Background: Mary Ellen Lease supported the popular election of senators, setting up postal savings banks, government control of the railroads, and federal supervision of corporations. She also spoke for woman suffrage and temperance.

Ask: What do you think critics of Mary Ellen Lease thought she should be doing rather than speaking for the People's Party? *(Some students might say that critics wanted her to behave like most other women.)*

Creating a Time Line Have students learn more about the nation's changing money supply. Have students create a time line from 1789 to the present that records significant events relating to the money supply, including the use of greenbacks and silver certificates, the use of the gold standard, and so on. **L3**

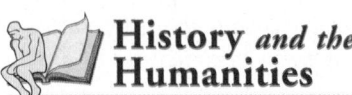

History *and the* Humanities

🎵 American Music: Cultural Traditions: "The Farmer Is the Man That Feeds Them All"

to guide farmers in choosing whom to vote for in 1890. The demands called for the adoption of the subtreasury plan, the free coinage of silver, an end to protective tariffs and national banks, tighter regulation of the railroads, and direct election of senators by voters instead of by state legislatures.

To prevent farmers from voting for Populists, the Republicans in Congress, led by Senator John Sherman, pushed through the **Sherman Silver Purchase Act of 1890.** This act authorized the United States Treasury to purchase 4.5 million ounces of silver per month. It put more money into circulation and may have reduced the deflation slightly, but it did little to help the farmers.

The midterm elections of 1890 seemed to suggest that both the Southern and Western strategies had worked for the farmers. In the South, four governors, all Democrats, were elected after promising to support the Alliance program. Several Southern legislatures now had pro-Alliance majorities, and over 40 Democrats who supported the Alliance program were elected to Congress. Meanwhile, the new People's Party did equally well in the West. Populists took control of the Kansas and Nebraska legislatures. Populists also held the balance of power in Minnesota and South Dakota. Eight Populists were elected to the U.S. House of Representatives and two to the Senate.

The South Turns to Populism At first Southern members were excited over their success in electing so many pro-Alliance Democrats to Congress and Southern state legislatures, but over the next two years, their excitement turned into frustration.

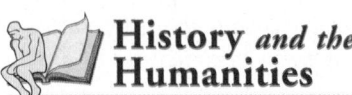

Mary Ellen Lease
1853–1933

Mary Ellen Lease, a former schoolteacher and daughter of an Irish political refugee, earned a law degree while raising four children on the Kansas frontier. She was one of the most passionate speakers for the People's Party in Kansas during the 1890 election campaign. Political opponents nicknamed her "Mary Yellin" and criticized the tall and forceful Lease for acting in an "unfeminine" manner by speaking in public.

Lease's blunt style, however, appealed to Kansas farmers. "Wall Street owns the country," she declared. "It is no longer a government of the people, for the people, by the people, but a government of Wall Street, for Wall Street, and by Wall Street." Lease urged farmers to spend less time raising crops and more time campaigning against the banks and railroads.

376 CHAPTER 11 Politics and Reform

Despite their promises, few Democrats followed through by supporting the Alliance program, either at the state or the federal level.

In May 1891, Western populists met with some labor and reform groups in Cincinnati. The meeting endorsed the creation of a new national People's Party to run candidates for president. Only a few Southerners attended the convention. By the following year, however, it had become obvious to many Southern members of the Alliance that the Democrats were not going to keep their promises to the Alliance. By early 1892 many Southern farmers had reached the point where they were willing to break with the Democratic Party and join the People's Party.

A Populist for President In July 1892, the People's Party held its first national convention in Omaha, Nebraska. There, members officially organized their party and nominated **James B. Weaver** to run for president. Weaver was a former Union Army General who had run for president before as the candidate of the Greenback Party. The Omaha convention also endorsed a platform, or program, that spelled out the party's positions in strong terms. First of all, the Omaha platform denounced the government's refusal to coin silver as a "vast conspiracy against mankind." To increase the money supply, it called for a return to unlimited coinage of silver at a ratio that gave 16 ounces of silver the same value as 1 ounce of gold. Other platform planks called for federal ownership of railroads and a graduated income tax, one that taxed higher earnings more heavily.

Above all, the Populists wanted to strengthen the hand of government so that it could defend the public against what they saw as greedy and irresponsible private interests. "We believe that the powers of government—in other words, of the people—should be expanded," the platform stated, "as rapidly and as far as the good sense of an intelligent people and the teachings of experience shall justify."

Although the Populists also adopted proposals designed to appeal to organized labor, workers found it hard to identify with the rural Populists. The Populists did have close ties to the Knights of Labor, but that organization was in decline, while the fast-growing American Federation of Labor steered clear of an alliance with them. The Omaha

CRITICAL THINKING ACTIVITY

Detecting Bias On the chalkboard, write the following partial quotation from a Nebraska newspaper.

"There are three great crops raised in Nebraska. One is a crop of corn, one a crop of freight rates, and one a crop of interest. One is produced by farmers, who sweat and toil on the land. The other two are produced by . . . "

Ask students to study the incomplete quotation and suggest how it might be concluded. *(possible answers: railroads and bankers)* Ask if the author of the quotation displays a bias, and if so, what is the bias. *(Yes, the author is biased in favor of farmers.)* **L2**

MOMENT in HISTORY

HARD LIFE ON THE PLAINS

English-born immigrant farmer David Hilton and his family proudly pose beside their pump organ on their home-stead in Nebraska. The organ, their prized possession, had been rescued from the Hiltons' sod-built dugout after the roof collapsed. Farm families on the sparsely-settled, treeless plains had to cope with isolation as well as a variety of natural haz-ards, including dust storms, tornadoes, erratic rainfall, and the occasional plague of destructive insects that could strip entire fields of crops in a matter of hours.

NATIONAL GEOGRAPHIC
MOMENT in HISTORY

The pump organ works by pushing your foot down on the two foot ped-als, which fills the bellows with air. The ten stops each give a different sound, such as the sound of a violin or bass. This Victorian-style organ was in many households across the United States in the late 1800s.

CURRICULUM CONNECTION

Government The Populist Party had an impact on politics and gov-ernment far beyond its showing in national elections. Minor parties have often served as vehicles for reform by taking clear-cut stands on controversial issues and proposing bold and original solutions. Among the Populist proposals that were adopted and are still in place today are the federal income tax (Sixteenth Amendment, 1913), direct election of U.S. senators (Seventeenth Amendment, 1913), the secret ballot (late 1890s), and primary elections (Wisconsin, 1903).

platform took positions popular with labor, includ-ing calling for an eight-hour workday, restricting immigration, and denouncing strikebreaking, but most urban workers still preferred to remain within the Democratic Party.

Democrats retained support in Northern cities by nominating the popular New Yorker, Grover Cleveland, who was seeking to return to the White House after his close defeat in 1888. The South also remained solidly Democratic, despite determined efforts by Populists. When the votes were counted, Cleveland had won a resounding victory in the Electoral College, with 277 votes to 145 for Harrison. The Populist candidate, James Weaver, had done remarkably well, winning four states and splitting two others for a total of 22 electoral votes.

The Panic of 1893 Not long after Cleveland's inau-guration in 1893, the nation plunged into the worst economic crisis it had ever experienced. The panic began in March when the Philadelphia and Reading Railroads declared bankruptcy. Many railroads had expanded too rapidly in the period before the panic and now found it hard to repay their loans. The stock market on Wall Street crashed, and banks closed their doors. By 1894 the economy was deep in a depression. About 690,000 workers went on strike that year, and more than 4.6 million more were unemployed, approximately 18 percent of the workforce.

Goldbugs and Silverites The Panic of 1893 also cre-ated a crisis for the United States Treasury. Many American and European investors owned U.S. govern-ment bonds, but as the economy worsened, they began cashing in their bonds for gold. This caused gold to drain out of the U.S. Treasury and left the federal gov-ernment's gold reserves at a dangerously low level.

Although President Cleveland could not stop the flow of gold to redeem bonds, he could protect the government's reserves in another way. Gold was also being lost every time people exchanged silver for gold under the Sherman Silver Purchase Act. Unlike many Democrats, Cleveland believed the United States should use gold as the basis for its cur-rency, not silver or paper money. In June 1893, he summoned Congress into a special session and pushed through the repeal of the Sherman Silver Purchase Act.

CHAPTER 11 Politics and Reform **377**

Bimetallists People who supported using both gold and silver as currency were known as bimetallists.

EXTENDING THE CONTENT

Thieves on the Campaign Trail During William Jennings Bryan's presidential campaign, he was faithfully followed by a band of pickpockets. To make the point that silver was as widely accepted as gold, Bryan would first ask people who carried gold to raise their hands. He would then ask those who carried silver to do the same. The thieves, unbeknownst to Bryan, worked the packed crowd, relieving both groups of their money.

FYI

After William Jennings Bryan delivered his speech at the Democratic convention in 1896, people were crying and rejoicing for an hour.

Picturing History

Background: William Jennings Bryan campaigned for the presidency in 1896, 1900, and 1908. He was unsuccessful all three times.
Answer: McKinley won
Ask: Which candidate's style is the closest to the way modern candidates campaign? *(Bryan's, because of the great distances he traveled seeking to win votes)*

✓ Reading Check

Answer: The Populist candidate, James Weaver, lost the election, but he did win 22 electoral votes.

3 ASSESS

Assign Section 2 Assessment as homework or as an in-class activity.

🔘 Have students use the **Interactive Tutor Self-Assessment CD-ROM.**
L1/ELL

Reading Essentials and Study Guide 11–2

Name _____ Date _____ Class _____

Study Guide
Chapter 11, Section 2
For use with textbook pages 372–379
POPULISM

KEY TERMS AND NAMES
populism the movement to increase farmers' political power and to work for legislation in their interest *(page 372)*
greenback paper currency that could not be exchanged for gold or silver coins *(page 373)*
inflation a decline in the value of money *(page 373)*
deflation an increase in the value of money and a decrease in the level of prices *(page 373)*
Grange the first national farmers' organization *(page 374)*
cooperatives marketing organizations that worked for the benefit of their members *(page 374)*
People's Party party formed by members of the Farmers' Alliance *(page 375)*

Picturing History

Campaigns in Contrast In 1896 Democrat William Jennings Bryan (left) ran an energetic campaign for president, traveling far and wide. Republican William McKinley (right) campaigned from the front porch of his Canton, Ohio, home. How did their campaign styles work out?

Cleveland's actions split the Democratic Party into two factions, nicknamed "goldbugs" and "silverites." The goldbugs believed the American currency should be based only on gold, while silverites believed coining silver in unlimited quantities would solve the nation's economic crisis.

✓ Reading Check

Summarizing What was the main outcome of the Populist campaign in the elections of 1892?

The Election of 1896

As the election of 1896 approached, leaders of the People's Party decided to make the silver issue the focus of their campaign. They also decided to hold their convention after the Republican and Democratic conventions. They believed the Republicans would endorse a gold standard, which they did. They also expected the Democrats to nominate Cleveland again and hoped that when the People's Party strongly endorsed silver, pro-silver Democrats would abandon their party and vote for the Populists in large numbers.

Unfortunately for the Populists, their political strategy failed. The Democrats did not waffle on the silver issue. Instead, they nominated **William Jennings Bryan,** a strong supporter of silver. When the Populists gathered in St. Louis for their own convention, they faced a difficult choice: endorse Bryan and risk undermining their identity as a separate party, or nominate their own candidate and risk splitting the silver vote. They eventually decided to support Bryan.

378 CHAPTER 11 Politics and Reform

Bryan's Campaign William Jennings Bryan, a former member of Congress from Nebraska, was only 36 years old when the Democrats and Populists nominated him for president. Bryan had served in Congress for two terms as a representative from Nebraska. He was a powerful speaker, and he won the nomination by delivering an electrifying address in defense of silver, one of the most famous in American political history. He began by telling delegates that he had come to speak "in defense of a cause as holy as the cause of liberty—the cause of humanity." With a few well-chosen words, Bryan transformed the campaign for silver into a crusade:

> ❝Having behind us the producing masses of this nation and the world, supported by the commercial interests, the laboring interests and the toilers everywhere, we will answer their demand for a gold standard by saying to them: You shall not press down upon the brow of labor this crown of thorns; you shall not crucify mankind upon a cross of gold.❞
>
> —quoted in *America in the Gilded Age*

Bryan waged an unusually energetic campaign for the presidency, traveling thousands of miles and making 600 speeches in 14 weeks. Some found his relentless campaigning undignified, however, and his crusade in favor of silver alienated others. Catholic immigrants and other city-dwellers cared little for the silver issue. They did not like Bryan's speaking style either. It reminded them of rural Protestant preachers, who were sometimes anti-Catholic.

Republicans knew that Bryan would be hard to beat in the South and the West. To regain the White House, they would have to sweep the Northeast and

---

COOPERATIVE LEARNING ACTIVITY

Creating Campaign Posters Assign students to work in small groups to make campaign posters for Cleveland, Harrison, and Weaver or for Bryan and McKinley. Tell students that the posters must reflect the beliefs of the candidates and their parties. Have each group choose a member to present the poster to the class. ELL

Use the rubric for a cooperative group management plan on pages 71–72 in the *Performance Assessment Activities and Rubrics.*

the Midwest. They thought that **William McKinley** of Ohio, a former governor and member of Congress, was the candidate who could do it.

The Front Porch Campaign In sharp contrast to the hectic travels of Bryan, McKinley stayed at his home in Canton, Ohio. He conducted what the newspapers called his "Front-Porch Campaign" by meeting with various delegations that came to visit him. Meanwhile, across the Midwest and Northeast, the Republican Party launched an intensive campaign on McKinley's behalf.

The Republicans campaigned against the Democrats by blaming Cleveland's administration for the depression and promising workers that McKinley would provide a "full dinner pail." This meant a lot more to most urban workers than the issue of silver money. At the same time, most business leaders supported the Republicans, convinced that unlimited silver coinage would ruin the country. They donated huge sums of money to the Republican campaign. Many employers warned their workers that if Bryan won, businesses would fail, unemployment would rise, and wages would be cut.

McKinley's reputation for moderation on labor issues and tolerance toward different ethnic groups helped improve the Republican Party's image with urban workers and immigrants. When the votes were counted, McKinley had won a decisive victory. He captured 51 percent of the popular vote and had a winning margin of 95 electoral votes—hefty numbers in an era of tight elections. As expected, Bryan won the South and most of the West, but few of the states he carried had large populations or delivered many electoral votes. By embracing populism and its rural base, Bryan and the Democrats lost the Northern industrial areas where votes were concentrated.

Populism Declines Opposition to the gold-based currency dwindled during McKinley's time in office. The depression was over, and prospectors found gold in Canada in 1896 and in Alaska in 1898. That wealth, combined with new gold strikes in South Africa and other parts of the world, increased the money supply without turning to silver. This meant that credit was easier to obtain and farmers were less distressed. In 1900 the United States officially adopted a gold-based currency when Congress passed the Gold Standard Act.

When the silver crusade died out, the Populists lost their momentum. Their efforts to ease the economic hardships of farmers and to regulate big business had not worked. Some of the reforms they favored, however, came about in the next century, including the graduated income tax and some governmental regulation of the economy.

✓ **Reading Check** **Evaluating** What were the results of the 1896 presidential election?

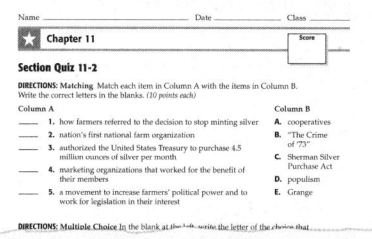

Student Web Activity Visit the *American Republic Since 1877* Web site at tarvol2.glencoe.com and click on *Student Web Activities— Chapter 11* for an activity on political changes in the late 1800s.

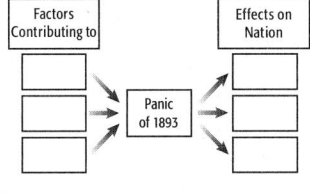

HISTORY Online **Study Central™** To review this section, go to tarvol2.glencoe.com and click on **Study Central™**.

SECTION 2 ASSESSMENT

Checking for Understanding
1. **Define:** populism, greenback, inflation, deflation, cooperative, graduated income tax, goldbug, silverite.
2. **Identify:** Grange, People's Party, William Jennings Bryan.
3. **List** the issues that the Democrats endorsed in the 1896 presidential election.

Reviewing Themes
4. **Economic Factors** What economic problems caused farmers to support populism?

Critical Thinking
5. **Analyzing** How did the Farmers' Alliance contribute to the rise of a new political party?
6. **Organizing** Use a graphic organizer similar to the one below to list the factors that contributed to the Panic of 1893 and its effects on the nation.

Factors Contributing to → Panic of 1893 → Effects on Nation

Analyzing Visuals
7. **Analyzing Photographs** Examine the photograph of David Hilton and his family on page 377, showing them with an organ they rescued from a collapsed sod house. Why do you think it was so important for them to rescue the organ?

Writing About History
8. **Persuasive Writing** Imagine you support the Populist Party and that you have been asked to write copy to be used in a campaign poster for your party's candidates. Include a slogan that provides reasons for people to support the Populists.

CHAPTER 11 Politics and Reform **379**

SECTION 2 ASSESSMENT ANSWERS

1. Terms are in blue.
2. Grange *(p. 374)*, People's Party *(p. 375)*, William Jennings Bryan *(p. 378)*
3. supported farmers and silver as a monetary base
4. deflation, falling farm prices, high tariffs, high rail shipping rates
5. Some Alliance members wanted to form a new party to get their programs passed.
6. Contributing factors: widespread railroad bankruptcies, stock market crash, bank closures; effects: unemployment rose, strikes, repeal of Sherman Silver Purchase Act
7. They may recognize that the organ was one of the few sources of entertainment for the family.
8. Slogans should have a clear connection to the issues or the candidates.

L2

Section Quiz 11-2

Name _____ Date _____ Class _____

⭐ Chapter 11   Score [ ]

Section Quiz 11-2

DIRECTIONS: Matching Match each item in Column A with the items in Column B. Write the correct letters in the blanks. *(10 points each)*

Column A	Column B
___ 1. how farmers referred to the decision to stop minting silver	**A.** cooperatives
___ 2. nation's first national farm organization	**B.** "The Crime of '73"
___ 3. authorized the United States Treasury to purchase 4.5 million ounces of silver per month	**C.** Sherman Silver Purchase Act
___ 4. marketing organizations that worked for the benefit of their members	**D.** populism
___ 5. a movement to increase farmers' political power and to work for legislation in their interest	**E.** Grange

DIRECTIONS: Multiple Choice In the blank at the left, write the letter of the choice that

Objectives and answers to the student activity can be found in the **Web Activity Lesson Plan** at tarvol2.glencoe.com.

Reteach
Have students explain why the adoption of the gold standard led to the Farmers' Alliance.

Enrich
Have students create a pair of circle graphs showing the results of the presidential election of 1896. One graph should reflect the popular vote, the other the Electoral College vote.

✓ **Reading Check**

Answer: McKinley victory, end of populism

Study Central™ provides summaries, interactive games, and online graphic organizers to help students review section content.

4 CLOSE

Have students describe who joined the Populist Party and what the party's goals were.

SECTION 3 The Rise of Segregation

Section Overview

This section focuses on how segregation grew in the late 1800s.

BELLRINGER
Skillbuilder Activity

Project transparency and have students answer the question.

Daily Focus Skills Transparency 11–3

Reading Preview

Answers to Graphic: poll taxes, literacy tests, Jim Crow laws, doctrine of "separate but equal," Supreme Court decision that overturned the Civil Rights Act of 1875

Preteaching Vocabulary
Have students write a paragraph using at least four of the Key Terms and Names.

Guide to Reading

Main Idea
In the late 1800s, Southern states passed laws that denied African Americans the right to vote and imposed segregation on them.

Key Terms and Names
sharecropper, poll tax, grandfather clause, segregation, Jim Crow laws, lynching, Ida B. Wells, W.E.B. Du Bois

Reading Strategy
Organizing As you read about the South in the 1890s, complete a web diagram like the one below by listing ways that states disfranchised African Americans and legalized discrimination.

Factors Contributing to Discrimination

Reading Objectives
• **Discuss** how African Americans in the South were disfranchised and how segregation was legalized.
• **Describe** three major African American leaders' responses to discrimination.

Section Theme
Individual Action African Americans stood up to fight against discrimination in the United States.

Preview of Events

♦1885   ♦1890   ♦1895   ♦1900

1886
Colored Farmers' National Alliance formed

1887
Florida passes Jim Crow laws

1890
Mississippi introduces voting restrictions

1895
Booker T. Washington proposes Atlanta Compromise

Tom Watson

★ *An American Story* ★

In the fall of 1892, H.S. Doyle, a young African American preacher, defied Georgia's power structure—dominated by whites and Democrats—by giving more than 60 speeches on behalf of a white Populist, Tom Watson, who was running for Congress.

Doyle took that risk because Watson was doing something almost unbelievable for a Southern politician. He was urging poor whites and blacks to unite against the wealthy white elite. "You are kept apart that you may be separately fleeced of your earnings," Watson told a racially mixed audience at one gathering. "The accident of color can make no difference in the interests of farmers."

Shortly before the election, Doyle himself received a death threat. Watson offered the preacher refuge in his home and alerted supporters in the area. An estimated 2,000 Populists gathered there with guns in hand. The crowd then marched to the local courthouse, where Watson vowed to protect Doyle and other African American Populists. "We are determined in this free country that the humblest white or black man that wants to talk our doctrine shall do it," he declared, "and the man doesn't live who shall touch a hair of his head, without fighting every man in the People's Party."

—adapted from *Tom Watson: Agrarian Rebel*

Resistance and Repression

For H.S. Doyle and other African Americans, the violence of the election of 1892 was not something they could shrug off. They could see that some Southern leaders were beginning to devise ways to keep them from voting. In the end, even Watson would betray his African

SECTION RESOURCES

📁 **Reproducible Masters**
• Reproducible Lesson Plan 11–3
• Daily Lecture and Discussion Notes 11–3
• Guided Reading Activity 11–3
• Section Quiz 11–3
• Reading Essentials and Study Guide 11–3
• Performance Assessment Activities and Rubrics
• Supreme Court Case Studies

📄 **Transparencies**
• Daily Focus Skills Transparency 11–3

Multimedia
🔘 Interactive Tutor Self-Assessment CD-ROM
🔘 ExamView® Pro Testmaker CD-ROM
🔘 Presentation Plus! CD-ROM
🔘 TeacherWorks™ CD-ROM
🔘 Audio Program

American supporters. He became a political boss in Georgia, cast aside his former ideals, and used crude racist rhetoric to appeal to white voters.

After Reconstruction, many African Americans in the rural South lived in conditions that were little better than slavery. They were technically free, but few escaped from grinding poverty. Most were sharecroppers, landless farmers who had to hand over to the landlord a large portion of their crops to cover the cost of rent, seed, tools, and other supplies. They were always in debt. Many eventually left farming and sought jobs in Southern towns or headed west to claim homesteads.

Exodus to Kansas In 1879, 70-year-old Benjamin "Pap" Singleton, himself formerly enslaved, took action to escape the conditions of the rural South. He organized a mass migration of thousands of African Americans from the rural South to Kansas. The newspapers called it "an Exodus," like the Hebrews' escape from Egyptian bondage. The migrants themselves came to be known as **"Exodusters."** One of them later explained why they went: "The whole South—every State in the South—had got into the hands of the very men that held us as slaves." A journalist named Henry King described the scene when the first group reached Kansas:

> 66 One morning in April, 1879, a Missouri steamboat arrived at Wyandotte, Kansas, and discharged a load of negro men, women and children, with . . . barrels, boxes, and bundles of household effects. . . . [T]heir garments were incredibly patched and tattered . . . and there was not probably a dollar in money in the pockets of the entire party. The wind was eager, and they stood upon the wharf shivering. . . . They looked like persons coming out of a dream. And, indeed, such they were . . . for this was the advance guard of the Exodus. 99
>
> —quoted in *Eyewitness: The Negro in History*

Forming a Separate Alliance While some African Americans fled the South, others joined with poor white farmers who had created the Farmers' Alliance.

Alliance leaders urged African Americans to form a similar organization. In 1886 African American farmers gathered in Texas at the home of a white minister named R.M. Humphrey and formed the Colored Farmers' National Alliance. By 1890 the organization had an estimated 1.2 million members.

The **Colored Farmers' National Alliance** worked to help its members economically by setting up cooperatives. When the Populist Party formed in 1891, many African American farmers joined the new organization. They hoped that the new People's Party would unite poor whites and poor blacks to challenge the Democratic Party's power in the South.

Crushing the Populist Revolt Populism posed a new challenge to the Democratic Party in the South. If enough poor whites left the party and joined with African American Populists, the coalition might become unbeatable.

To win back the poor white vote, Democratic leaders began appealing to racism, warning whites that support for Populists or joint Republican-Populist parties would return the South to "Black Republican" rule similar to Reconstruction. In addition, although many African Americans in the South were still able to vote as of 1890, election officials began using various methods to make it harder and harder for them to do so. As one Democratic leader in the South told a reporter, "Some of our people, some editors especially, deny that [African Americans] are hindered from voting; but what is the good of lying? They are interfered with, and we are obliged to do it, and we may as well tell the truth."

✓ **Reading Check** **Examining** Who were the Exodusters, and why did they migrate to Kansas in 1879?

Picturing **History**

A Kansas Home Many African Americans left the rural South to find a new life. They usually began with very little. Why were they called Exodusters?

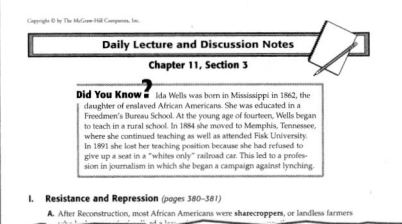
✓ **Reading Check**

Answer: African Americans who migrated from the rural South to Kansas in 1879; to escape discrimination

Picturing **History**

Answer: from the term *Exodus*, referring to the Hebrews' escape from Egypt
Ask: Why did the Exodusters have so little when they arrived in Kansas? *(because they were poor sharecroppers who were in debt)*

Drawing a Sketch Have students draw a sketch to accompany the Henry King quotation that appears on page 381. Then have students give an appropriate title to their drawing. Ask volunteers to display their drawings for the class. L1 ELL

📁 Use *Supreme Court Case Study 9*, *Plessy* v. *Ferguson*.

Reading Strategy   READING THE TEXT

Writing Free Writes Invite students to think about the ways in which African American rights were denied during Reconstruction. Remind them about the poll tax, literacy tests, grandfather clause, and Jim Crow laws. Have students write a diary entry as if they were an African American dealing with these issues. L1

📁 Refer to *Inclusion for the High School Social Studies Classroom Strategies and Activities* in the TCR.

381

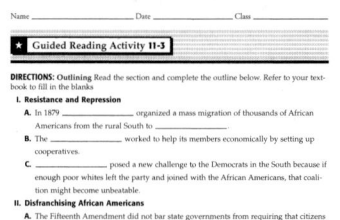

Profiles IN HISTORY

Background: Mary Church Terrell was one of the first African American women to earn a college degree. She continued her studies in Europe and became fluent in French, German, and Italian. She opposed segregation and supported woman suffrage. She was one of the founders of the National Association for the Advancement of Colored People (NAACP).
Ask: Would Mary Church Terrell's life have been different if she had chosen to stay in Europe? Why?
(Yes. She would have faced fewer racial barriers.)

✓ **Reading Check**

Answer: poll taxes and literacy tests

Creating a Display Have students create a display of photographs and drawings that help illustrate the Fourteenth and Fifteenth Amendments. **L1**

📁 Use the rubric for creating a map, display, or chart on pages 65–66 in the *Performance Assessment Activities and Rubrics.*

Disfranchising African Americans

The Fifteenth Amendment prohibited states from denying citizens the right to vote on the basis of "race, color, or previous condition of servitude." However, it did not bar the governments from requiring that citizens be literate or own property in order to vote. Using this loophole, Southern states began imposing restrictions that barred nearly all African Americans from voting, even though the restrictions seemed on the surface to apply to both races.

Mississippi took this step first in 1890 by requiring that all citizens registering to vote pay a poll tax of $2, a sum beyond the means of most poor African Americans. Mississippi also instituted a literacy test, requiring that prospective voters be able to read or understand the state constitution. More than half of all African Americans who came of age in the South after the Civil War were illiterate, and the literacy rate for those who had grown up under slavery was less than 20 percent. Even those who knew how to read often failed the literacy test because local officials deliberately picked complicated passages that few could understand.

Other Southern states later adopted similar restrictions, and the results were devastating. In Louisiana the number of African Americans registered to vote fell from about 130,000 in 1890 to around 5,300 in 1900. In Alabama the number fell from about 181,000 to around 3,700.

Election officials were far less strict in applying the poll tax and literacy requirements to whites, but the number of white voters also fell significantly. Local Democratic Party leaders were not sorry to see poor whites barred from voting, because they had helped fuel the Populist revolt. Some states gave whites a special break, however, by including a so-called grandfather clause in the restrictions. The grandfather clause in Louisiana allowed any man to vote if he had an ancestor on the voting rolls in 1867. The clause made almost all formerly enslaved Louisiana citizens ineligible to vote.

✓ **Reading Check** **Identifying** How did Southern states restrict African American voting in the 1890s?

Profiles IN HISTORY

Mary Church Terrell
1863–1954

Few African American women who grew up in the late 1800s had as many advantages in life as Mary Church Terrell. Her father, the son of a wealthy white man and an enslaved woman, had invested shrewdly in real estate in the South after the Civil War and became one of the nation's first African American millionaires. He spared no expense for his daughter's education. After she graduated from Oberlin College in 1884, he sent her to Europe to travel and study.

She could easily have remained in Europe where there were fewer racial barriers to overcome than in the United States, but Terrell chose to return home, she said, "to promote the welfare of my race." She taught at an African American high school in Washington, D.C., and in 1896 became the first president of the National Association of Colored Women. The organization offered day care and other services to the many African American women who worked to support their families while raising children.

Terrell continued to promote the welfare of African Americans until the last years of her life. In 1950, at the age of 86, she demanded service at a segregated restaurant in Washington, D.C. When the owner refused, she filed a lawsuit and won a ruling in the Supreme Court that desegregated restaurants in the nation's capital.

Legalizing Segregation

Discrimination in the late 1800s was not confined to the South. African Americans in the North had often been barred from many public places used by whites. In the South, segregation, or separation of the races, was different because laws enforced and perpetuated the discrimination. The statutes enforcing segregation were known as Jim Crow laws. The term probably came from the name of a character popularized by a slavery-era blackface minstrel—a white musical stage performer who darkened his face with makeup and crudely imitated supposed African American behavior.

In 1883 the Supreme Court set the stage for legalized segregation by overturning the Civil Rights Act of 1875. That law had prohibited keeping people out of public places on the basis of race, and it also prohibited racial discrimination in selecting jurors. White authorities

Segregation sign from the turn of the century

challenged the law in both the North and the South. The 1883 Supreme Court decision, however, said that the Fourteenth Amendment only provided that "no state" could deny citizens equal protection under the law. Thus, only state actions were subject to challenge. Private organizations and businesses, such as hotels, theaters, and railroads, were free to practice segregation.

Encouraged by the Supreme Court's ruling and by the decline of congressional support for civil rights, Southern states passed a series of laws that enforced segregation in virtually all public places. Southern whites and African Americans could no longer ride together in the same railroad cars, eat in the same dining halls, or even drink from the same water fountains. Restrooms, hotels, and swimming pools were all segregated.

In 1892 an African American named Homer Plessy challenged a Louisiana law that forced him to ride in a separate railroad car from whites. He was arrested for riding in a "whites-only" car and brought to trial before criminal court judge John H. Ferguson. Ferguson rejected Plessy's argument that the law was unconstitutional. In 1896 the Supreme Court, in *Plessy* v. *Ferguson*, upheld the Louisiana law and expressed a new legal doctrine endorsing "separate but equal" facilities for African Americans. 📖 *(See page 964 for more information on* Plessy v. Ferguson.*)*

The ruling established the legal basis for discrimination in the South for more than 50 years to come. While public facilities for African Americans in the South were always separate, they were far from equal. In many cases, they were inferior.

Racial Violence Even worse than the Jim Crow laws was the brutality leveled against African Americans. In the late 1800s, mob violence increased in the United States, particularly in the South. Between 1890 and 1899, there was an average of 187 lynchings—executions without proper court proceedings—carried out by mobs each year. Over 80 percent of the lynchings occurred in the South, and nearly 70 percent of the victims were African Americans.

✓ **Reading Check** **Summarizing** How did the Supreme Court help to legalize segregation?

The African American Response

In 1892 **Ida B. Wells,** a fiery young African American woman from Tennessee, launched a fearless crusade against lynching. Wells pointed out that

Picturing History

Crusading Journalist Ida B. Wells, seen here with her son, campaigned fiercely against lynching in the 1890s. *What two factors did Wells believe to be behind lynchings?*

greed, not just racial prejudice, was often behind these brutal acts. Writing in the *Memphis Free Speech* newspaper, she reported that three African American grocers lynched in Memphis had been guilty of nothing more than competing successfully against white grocers.

A mob destroyed the press that printed the *Memphis Free Speech* and drove Wells out of town, but she settled in Chicago and continued her campaign. In 1895 she published a book denouncing mob violence against African Americans and demanding "a fair trial by law for those accused of crime, and punishment by law after honest conviction." Although Congress rejected an anti-lynching bill, the number of lynchings decreased significantly in the 1900s due in great part to the efforts of activists such as Wells.

A Call for Compromise Some African American leaders like Wells chose the path of protest, but others recommended different solutions to discrimination. One such person was the influential educator **Booker T. Washington.** He proposed that African Americans concentrate on achieving economic goals rather than legal or political ones. In 1895

CHAPTER 11 Politics and Reform **383**

CHAPTER 11
Section 3, 380–384

✓ **Reading Check**

Answer: It upheld segregation and expressed a new legal doctrine endorsing "separate but equal" facilities for African Americans.

📷 *Picturing* **History**

Background: Ida B. Wells was raised in Mississippi. She worked to put herself through college and taught school in Tennessee. In addition to being an author, Wells used her talents as a speaker to campaign against lynching. She was one of the founders of the NAACP.

Answer: greed and racial prejudice

Ask: What did Wells cite to support her opinion about the causes of the lynchings? *(the 3 African American grocers in Memphis who had successfully competed against white grocers)*

3 ASSESS

Assign Section 3 Assessment as homework or as an in-class activity.

💿 Have students use the **Interactive Tutor Self-Assessment CD-ROM.**

L1/ELL

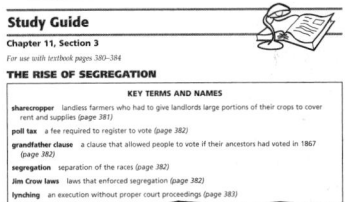

Reading Essentials and Study Guide 11–3

Name _____ Date _____ Class _____

Study Guide

Chapter 11, Section 3
For use with textbook pages 380–384

THE RISE OF SEGREGATION

KEY TERMS AND NAMES

sharecropper landless farmers who had to give landlords large portions of their crops to cover rent and supplies (page 381)

poll tax a fee required to register to vote (page 382)

grandfather clause a clause that allowed people to vote if their ancestors had voted in 1867 (page 382)

segregation separation of the races (page 382)

Jim Crow laws laws that enforced segregation (page 382)

lynching an execution without proper court proceedings (page 383)

INTERDISCIPLINARY CONNECTIONS ACTIVITY

Civics Tell students that disfranchisement was the technical term for the process that removed nearly all African Americans from the voting rolls of Southern states. Organize students into small groups and assign each group one of the Southern states. Have them use library and Internet resources to identify the specific methods that various states used to restrict voting. Have each group prepare a chart that lists the state, the various provisions of its voting law, and the year that the law or state constitutional amendment was passed. Have the groups present their charts to the class. **L2**

383

L2

Section Quiz 11–3

Background: W.E.B. Du Bois was educated at Harvard, where he earned three degrees—bachelor's, master's, and doctorate. He was one of the founders of the NAACP.

Answer: voting rights

Ask: Who gave the address known as the Atlanta Compromise?

(Booker T. Washington)

Reteach

Have students discuss how segregation was legalized.

Enrich

Invite interested students to learn more about Jim Crow laws and present a list of 10 examples to the other class members.

Answer: She wrote newspaper articles and a book denouncing lynching.

Study Central™ provides summaries, interactive games, and online graphic organizers to help students review section content.

4 CLOSE

Have students describe three major African American leaders' responses to discrimination.

384

"color discrimination is barbarism"

—*W.E.B. Du Bois*

he summed up his views in a speech before a mostly white audience at the Cotton States and International Exposition in Atlanta. Known as the **Atlanta Compromise,** the address came amid increasing acts of discrimination against African Americans. Washington urged his fellow African Americans to postpone the fight for civil rights and instead concentrate on preparing themselves educationally and vocationally for full equality:

❝The wisest among my race understand that the agitation of questions of social equality is the extremest folly, and that the enjoyment of all the privileges that will come to us must be the result of severe and constant struggle rather than of artificial forcing. . . . It is important and right that all privileges of the law be ours, but it is vastly more important that we be prepared for the exercise of these privileges. The opportunity to earn a dollar in a factory just now is worth infinitely more than the opportunity to spend a dollar in an opera-house.❞

–adapted from *Up From Slavery*

Voice of the Future The Atlanta Compromise speech provoked a strong challenge from **W.E.B. Du Bois,** the leader of a new generation of African American activists born after the Civil War. Du Bois pointed out in his 1903 book *The Souls of Black Folk* that white Southerners continued to strip African Americans of their civil rights. This was true in spite of the progress African Americans were making in education and vocational training. They could regain that lost ground and achieve full equality, Du Bois argued, only by demanding their rights. Du Bois was particularly concerned with protecting and exercising voting rights. "Negroes must insist continually, in season and out of season," he wrote, "that voting is necessary to proper manhood, that color discrimination is barbarism." In the years that followed, many African Americans worked to win the vote and end discrimination. The struggle, however, would prove to be a long one.

✓ **Reading Check** **Describing** How did Ida B. Wells attempt to stop the lynching of African Americans?

SECTION 3 ASSESSMENT

HISTORY Online **Study Central**™ To review this section, go to tarvol2.glencoe.com and click on **Study Central**™.

Reviewing Themes

1. **Define:** sharecropper, poll tax, grandfather clause, segregation, Jim Crow laws, lynching.
2. **Identify:** Ida B. Wells, W.E.B. Du Bois.
3. **Explain** what happened to Ida B. Wells after she began campaigning against lynching.

Reviewing Themes

4. **Individual Action** Why did Homer Plessy challenge a Louisiana law in 1892, and what was the significance of his action?

Critical Thinking

5. **Examining** After Reconstruction, why did many African Americans in the South live in conditions that were little better than slavery?
6. **Organizing** Use a graphic organizer similar to the one below to list the responses of some prominent African Americans to racial discrimination.

African American	Response to Discrimination
Ida B. Wells	
Booker T. Washington	
W.E.B. Du Bois	

Analyzing Visuals

7. **Analyzing Photographs** Examine the photograph of an "Exoduster" family on page 381. Pose questions about the photograph to your classmates in a quiz and then have them answer the questions.

Writing About History

8. **Expository Writing** Imagine that you are living in the 1890s. Write a letter to the editor of the local newspaper explaining your view of the Supreme Court ruling in *Plessy* v. *Ferguson.*

384 CHAPTER 11 Politics and Reform

SECTION 3 ASSESSMENT ANSWERS

1. Terms are in blue.
2. Ida B. Wells (p. 383), W.E.B. Du Bois (p. 384)
3. She was driven out of town and moved to Chicago to continue her campaign.
4. He argued that the law that forced him to ride in a separate railroad car from whites was unconstitutional; his challenge led to the "separate but equal" doctrine.
5. They owned no property and worked as sharecroppers.
6. Wells wrote against lynching. Washington urged African Americans to prepare themselves educationally and vocationally for equality. Du Bois campaigned for voting rights.
7. Students' questions will vary.
8. Students' letters will vary but their position should be based on information presented in the text.

Critical Thinking
SKILLBUILDER

Interpreting Points of View

Why Learn This Skill?

Suppose you want to see a new movie, but your friends' opinions range from "terrific" to "boring." People often have different opinions about the same people, events, or issues because they look at them from different points of view.

Learning the Skill

A point of view results from one's own beliefs and values. Many factors affect an individual's point of view, including age, gender, racial or ethnic background, economic class, and religion. To judge the accuracy or the objectivity of an argument, you must first identify the speaker's point of view.

To interpret point of view in written material, gather background information on the author that might reveal his or her point of view. Identify aspects of the topic that the author chooses to emphasize or exclude. Look for emotionally charged words such as *charming, vicious, heartwarming,* and *drastic.* Also notice metaphors and analogies that imply an opinion, such as, "If this budget can work, then pigs can fly."

Practicing the Skill

Read the following excerpts from William Jennings Bryan's "Cross of Gold" speech. Then answer the questions.

The humblest citizen in all the land, when clad in the armor of a righteous cause, is stronger than all the hosts of error. I come to speak to you in defense of a cause as holy as the cause of liberty—the cause of humanity. . . .

When you come before us and tell us that we are about to disturb your business interest, we reply that you have disturbed our business interests by your course. . . . We say not one word against those who live upon the Atlantic coast, but the hardy pioneers who have braved all the dangers of the wilderness, who have made the desert to blossom as the rose . . . it is for these that we speak. . . .

If they ask us why it is that we say more on the money question than we say upon the tariff question, I reply

that, if protection has slain its thousands, the gold standard has slain its tens of thousands. . . .

Having behind us the producing masses of this nation and the world, supported by the commercial interest, the laboring interests, and the toilers everywhere, we will answer their demand for a gold standard by saying to them: You shall not press down upon the brow of labor this crown of thorns, you shall not crucify mankind upon a cross of gold.

Cartoon portraying William Jennings Bryan

1. What subject is Bryan addressing? What group is he speaking for?
2. What is Bryan's point of view?
3. What emotionally charged words and phrases does Bryan use in his speech? How does this language help reveal his point of view?

Skills Assessment

Complete the Practicing Skills questions on page 387 and the Chapter 11 Skills Reinforcement Activity to assess your mastery of this skill.

Applying the Skill

Interpreting Points of View In a newspaper or magazine, find an editorial or letter to the editor that expresses a point of view on an issue. Write a paragraph analyzing the author's point of view. Compare it to your own and explain why you agree or disagree with the author.

 Glencoe's **Skillbuilder Interactive Workbook CD-ROM, Level 2,** provides instruction and practice in key social studies skills.

385

ANSWERS TO PRACTICING THE SKILL

1. money question, farmers
2. against the gold standard
3. "Hardy pioneers" expresses his view of the people for whom he speaks; references to biblical language attempt to connect his cause to righteous action.

Applying the Skill
Students' answers will vary. Paragraphs should include both an analysis of the author's point of view and a comparison to the students' own point of view.

CHAPTER 11 ASSESSMENT and ACTIVITIES

CHAPTER
11
ASSESSMENT and ACTIVITIES

GLENCOE TECHNOLOGY

MindJogger Videoquiz
Use the **MindJogger Videoquiz** to review Chapter 11 content.

Available in DVD

Reviewing Key Terms
Students' answers will vary. The pages where the words appear in the text are shown in parentheses.

1. **patronage** (p. 364)
2. **rebate** (p. 367)
3. **populism** (p. 372)
4. **greenback** (p. 373)
5. **inflation** (p. 373)
6. **deflation** (p. 373)
7. **cooperative** (p. 374)
8. **graduated income tax** (p. 376)
9. **goldbug** (p. 378)
10. **silverite** (p. 378)
11. **sharecropper** (p. 381)
12. **poll tax** (p. 382)
13. **grandfather clause** (p. 382)
14. **segregation** (p. 382)
15. **Jim Crow laws** (p. 382)
16. **lynching** (p. 383)

Reviewing Key Facts
17. Interstate Commerce Commission (p. 368), Sherman Antitrust Act (p. 369), Grange (p. 374), People's Party (p. 375), William Jennings Bryan (p. 378), Ida B. Wells (p. 383), W.E.B. Du Bois (p. 384)

18. There was a nearly even division of power between the Democrats and Republicans.

19. Problems included labor strikes, price gouging by railroads, and high tariffs.

Reviewing Key Terms
On a sheet of paper, use each of these terms in a sentence.

1. patronage
2. rebate
3. populism
4. greenback
5. inflation
6. deflation
7. cooperative
8. graduated income tax
9. goldbug
10. silverite
11. sharecropper
12. poll tax
13. grandfather clause
14. segregation
15. Jim Crow laws
16. lynching

Reviewing Key Facts

17. **Identify:** Interstate Commerce Commission, Sherman Antitrust Act, Grange, People's Party, William Jennings Bryan, Ida B. Wells, W.E.B. Du Bois

18. What contributed to political deadlock at the federal level between 1876 and 1896?

19. What economic problems did the United States face during the administration of President Cleveland?

20. How did the Grange attempt to solve farmers' problems in the late 1800s?

21. What was the significance of the Supreme Court's ruling in *Plessy* v. *Ferguson?*

Critical Thinking

22. **Analyzing Themes: Economic Factors** Why was the type of currency used in the United States an important issue to farmers in the late 1800s?

23. **Comparing** How did Booker T. Washington's answer to racial discrimination compare to that of W.E.B. Du Bois?

24. **Organizing** Use a graphic organizer similar to the one below to list the major reforms sought by the Populists in the 1892 presidential election.

Populist Reforms

25. **Interpreting Primary Sources** Reform movements in farming led to the organization of the Populist Party in 1891. In the following excerpt from an 1890 article, Washington Gladden, a Congregational minister, discusses the problems facing farmers in the United States.

❝The farmers of the United States are up in arms. . . . They produce the largest share of its wealth; but they are getting, they say, the smallest share for themselves. With the hardest work and with the sharpest economy, the average farmer is unable to make both ends meet;

Chapter Summary

Republican Party
- Popular in North and Midwest; appealed to rural and small town voters
- Party split over civil service reform
- Favored higher tariffs and the gold standard

Populist Party
- Sought government control over business to protect farmers
- Supported national control of railroads, increased money supply, and direct election of U.S. senators
- Support declined when gold crisis was resolved
- Lost presidential elections but inspired reforms that were later adopted

Democratic Party
- Strongly supported by Southerners, immigrants, and urban workers
- Supported civil service reform
- Supported cutting tariffs and regulating interstate commerce
- Party split over silver coinage

Political Inequality for African Americans
- Supreme Court overturned the Civil Rights Act of 1875
- Unfair voting laws disfranchised Southern African Americans
- *Plessy* v. *Ferguson* defended "separate but equal" public facilities

20. It pooled resources to create cooperatives, pressured legislatures to regulate railroad and warehouse rates, and encouraged the government to print more money.

21. Plessy's challenge of a state law forcing him to ride in a separate railroad car led to the Supreme Court decision establishing the "separate but equal" doctrine and continuing social segregation.

Critical Thinking

22. Without greenbacks and silver coins, the money supply could not meet the needs of the growing economy. The value of money increased, and crop prices began to fall.

23. Washington wanted to postpone the fight for voting rights and focus on educational and job training, while Du Bois pushed for voting rights.

HISTORY Online

Self-Check Quiz

Visit the *American Republic Since 1877* Web site at tarvol2.glencoe.com and click on *Self-Check Quizzes—Chapter 11* to assess your knowledge of chapter content.

every year closes with debt, . . . the average annual reward of the farm proprietor [of Connecticut] is $181.31, while the average annual wages of the ordinary hired man is $386.36.

. . . [T]he root of the difficulty is overproduction; that there are too many farms . . . [but] other causes . . . should not be overlooked. The enormous tribute which the farmers of the West are paying to the moneylenders of the East is one source of their poverty. . . .

[Farmers] believe that the miseries under which they are suffering are largely due to political causes and can be cured by legislation. . . . The prime object of the Farmers' Alliance is to better the condition of the farmers of America, mentally, morally, and financially; . . .

—quoted in *Forum*

a. According to Gladden, why were farmers up in arms?

b. What was the main purpose of the new Farmers' Alliance?

Practicing Skills

26. **Interpreting Points of View** Study the American Story on page 372 that gives an excerpt of Polk's speech on July 4, 1890. Then answer these questions.

a. How do historians analyze points of view?

b. What emotionally charged words and phrases does Polk use? How do they reveal his point of view?

Writing Activities

27. **Persuasive Writing** Imagine that you are living in 1881 and have just heard about President Garfield's assassination by a disappointed office-seeker. Write to your representatives in Congress, urging them either to pass civil service reform or to keep the current "spoils system" for appointments to federal offices. Explain why you believe your recommendation is rational.

28. **Chronology Quiz** Absolute chronology refers to specific dates, while relative chronology looks at when something occurred with reference to when other things occurred. Memorize the unit titles and time periods in your book, then close your book. Practice relative chronology by writing the unit titles in correct order. Then apply absolute chronology by writing the unit dates.

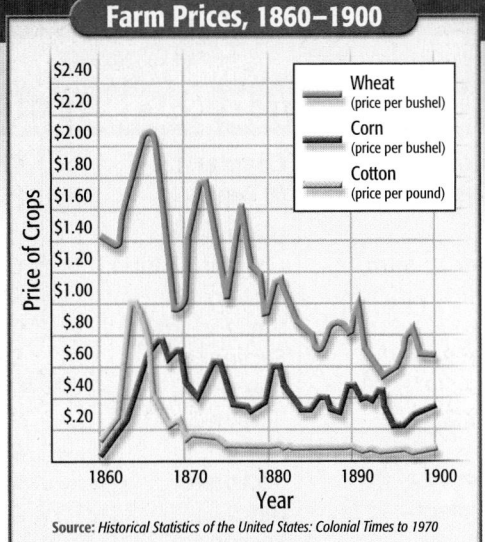

Farm Prices, 1860–1900

Wheat (price per bushel)
Corn (price per bushel)
Cotton (price per pound)

Price of Crops / Year

Source: *Historical Statistics of the United States: Colonial Times to 1970*

Economics and History

29. The graph above shows farm prices in the United States between 1860 and 1900. Study the graph and answer the questions below.

a. **Analyzing Graphs** What happened to prices of crops between 1865 and 1895?

b. **Understanding Cause and Effect** What factors might have contributed to this situation?

Standardized Test Practice

Directions: Choose the best answer to the following question.

The Sherman Antitrust Act of 1890 declared illegal "any combination . . . in restraint of trade or commerce." What *combination* was it originally intended to prevent?

A labor unions

B business mergers

C transcontinental railroads

D Farmers' Alliances

Test-Taking Tip: Make sure your answer reflects the original goal of the Antitrust Act. Only one answer reflects the reason Congress passed the law.

CHAPTER 11
Assessment and Activities

HISTORY Online

Have students visit the Web site at tarvol2.glencoe.com to review Chapter 11 and take the Self-Check Quiz.

Writing Activities

27. Letters should clearly state a point of view and reasons for the point of view.

28. Encourage students to review the chronologies for accuracy and to get an overview of U.S. history.

Economics and History

29. **a.** The trend for wheat and corn is downward. The price of cotton remained relatively constant during the period after an initial fluctuation. **b.** abundant crops, flat demand, high tariffs, or increased competition

Standardized Test Practice

Answer: B

Test-Taking Tip: Tell students to consider what they know about each of the choices. Which could realistically restrain trade? Labor unions and the Farmers' Alliance were combinations of workers and did not have the power to restrain trade.

Bonus Question ?

Ask: What were some of the difficulties that settlers encountered as they settled the Great Plains? *(possible answers include: isolation, tornadoes, destructive insects, harsh weather, and dust storms)*

---

24. return to silver coinage, federal ownership of railroads, eight-hour work day, restricting immigration

25. **a.** because they produced so much food and got so little profit in return; **b.** better the condition of farmers mentally, morally, and financially

Practicing Skills

26. **a.** analyze emotionally charged words in the context of surrounding historical events; **b.** possible answers: revolution (to support farmers' fighting strength), brother (to unite all farmers), Wall Street (refers to Wall Street as a power unrestrained, even by Congress)

Unit 4 (1 Day)	Chapter 12 (4 Days)	Chapter 13 (6 Days)	Chapter 14 (5 Days)	Unit 4 (2 Days)
Day 1 Introduction	**Day 1** Chapter 12 Intro, Section 1 **Day 2** Section 2 **Day 3** Section 3 **Day 4** Chapter 12 Assessment	**Day 1** Chapter 13 Intro, Section 1 **Day 2** Section 2 **Day 3** Section 3 **Day 4** Section 4 **Day 5** Section 5 **Day 6** Chapter 13 Assessment	**Day 1** Chapter 14 Intro, Section 1 **Day 2** Section 2 **Day 3** Section 3 **Day 4** Section 4 **Day 5** Chapter 14 Assessment	**Day 1** Wrap-Up/Project **Day 2** Unit 4 Assessment

GLENCOE'S **ASSESSMENT** ADVANTAGE

Use the following tools to easily assess student learning in a variety of ways:

- Performance Assessment Activities and Rubrics
- Chapter and Unit Tests
- Section Quizzes
- Standardized Test Practice Workbook

- tarvol2.glencoe.com
- Interactive Tutor Self-Assessment CD-ROM
- MindJogger Videoquiz
- ExamView® Pro Testmaker CD-ROM
- SAT I/II Test Practice

TEACHING TRANSPARENCIES

Unit 4 Map Overlay Transparencies L2

Cause-and-Effect Transparency 4 L2

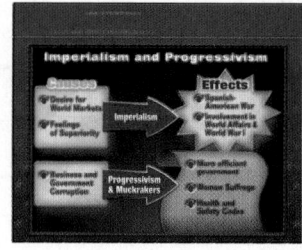

READING SUPPORT FROM
JAMESTOWN ⚓ EDUCATION

- ***Timed Readings Plus in Social Studies*** help students increase their reading rate and fluency while maintaining comprehension. The 400-word passages are similar to those found on state and national assessments.

- ***Reading in the Content Area: Social Studies*** concentrates on six essential reading skills that help students better comprehend what they read. The book includes 75 high-interest nonfiction passages written at increasing levels of difficulty.

- ***Reading Fluency*** helps students read smoothly, accurately, and expressively.

- ***Jamestown's Reading Improvement,*** by renowned reading expert Edward Fry, focuses on helping build your students' comprehension, vocabulary, and skimming and scanning skills.

- ***Critical Reading Series*** provides high-interest books, each written at three reading levels.

For more information about these products, see the Jamestown Education materials in the Classroom Solutions in the front of this Teacher Wraparound Edition. To order these products, call Glencoe at 1-800-334-7344.

Unit 4 Resources

ASSESSMENT

Unit 4 Pretests L2

Unit 4 Posttests L2

APPLICATION AND ENRICHMENT

American Biography 4 L2

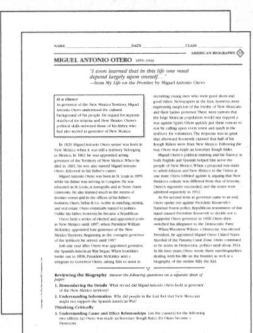

History Simulation and Problem Solving 4 L1

GEOGRAPHY

Geography and History Activity 4 L2

INTERDISCIPLINARY ACTIVITIES

American Literature Reading 4 L2

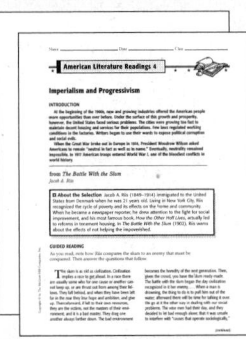

Economics and History Activity 4 L2

Team-Teaching Interdisciplinary Strategies and Activities 4 L2

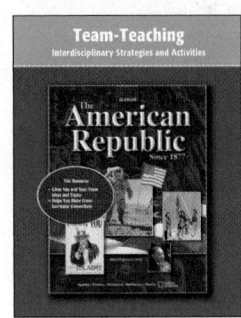

Reading List Generator CD-ROM

GLENCOE BOOKLINK

The Glencoe BookLink CD-ROM is a database that allows you to search more than 15,000 titles to create a customized reading list for your students.

- Reading lists can be organized by students' reading level, author, genre, theme, or area of interest.

- The database provides Degrees of Reading Power™ (DRP) and Lexile™ readability scores for all selections.

- A brief summary of each selection is included.

Leveled reading suggestions for this unit:

For students at a Grade 8 reading level:
- *Panama Canal: Gateway to the World,* by Judith St. George.

For students at a Grade 9 reading level:
- *Not for Ourselves Alone,* by Geoffrey Ward and Ken Burns.

For students at a Grade 10 reading level:
- *All Quiet on the Western Front,* by Erich Maria Remarque.

Extending the Content

Readings for the Teacher
- *An Illustrated History of the First World War,* by John Keegan, Knopf, 2001.

Multimedia Resources
- *Mirror of America.* National Archives. VHS. (36 minutes)

0:00 Out of Time?

If time does not permit teaching each chapter in this unit, you may want to use the **Reading Essentials and Study Guide** summaries.

Unit Overview

Unit 4 describes how the United States became a world power in the 1900s. **Chapter 12** explores imperialism and the Spanish-American War. **Chapter 13** focuses on the Progressive movement from 1890 to 1919. **Chapter 14** discusses World War I and its impact on America.

Unit Objectives

After studying this unit, students will be able to:

1. Analyze how a desire for more trade and markets led to political change.
2. Evaluate the legacy of the Progressive movement.
3. Analyze how the United States raised an army and won support for World War I.

Why It Matters Activity

Tell students that the federal government began regulating food and drugs when the Pure Food and Drug Act was passed in 1906. Ask students what impact they think this act has on the food they eat.

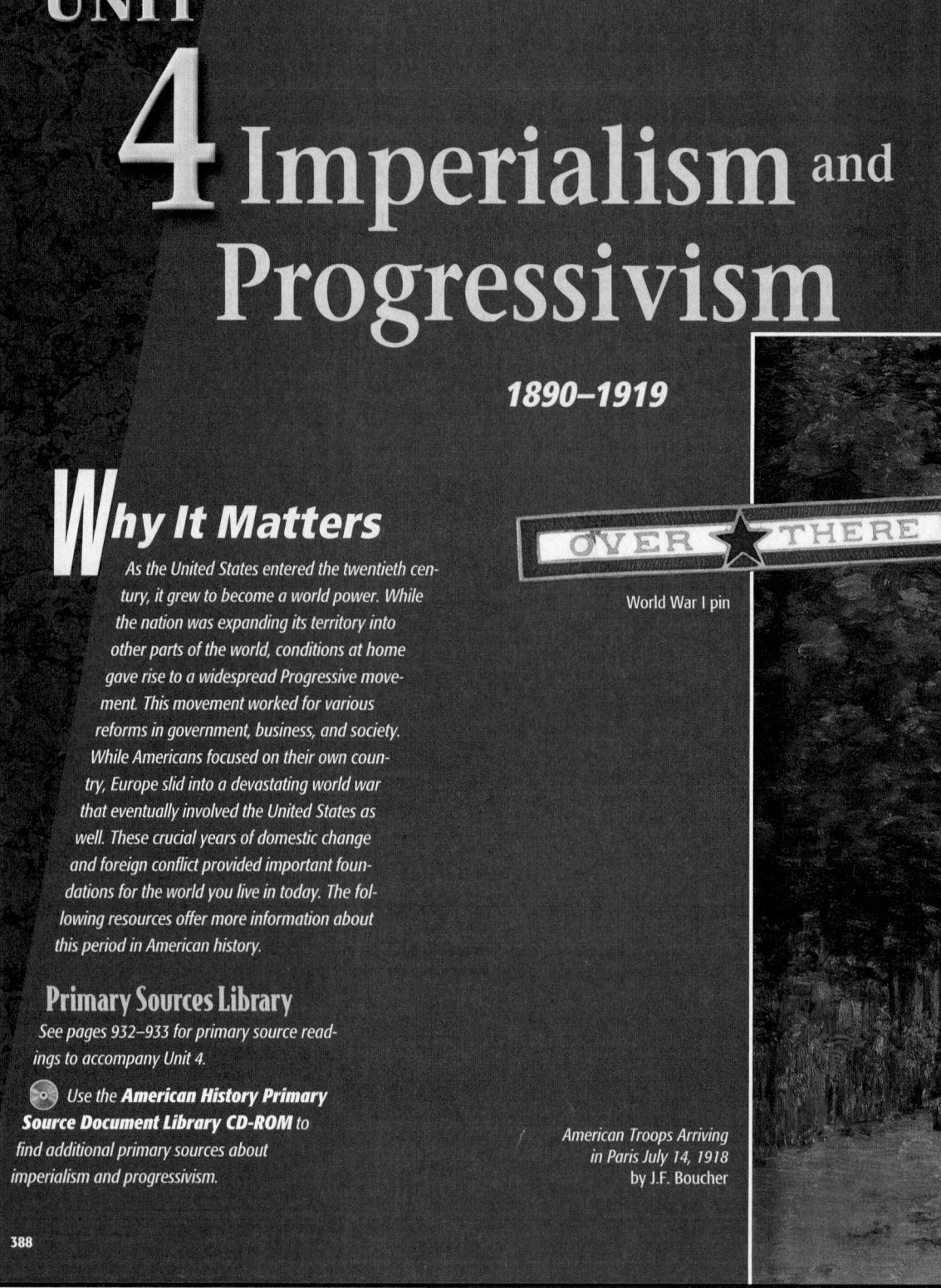

UNIT
4 Imperialism and Progressivism

1890–1919

Why It Matters

As the United States entered the twentieth century, it grew to become a world power. While the nation was expanding its territory into other parts of the world, conditions at home gave rise to a widespread Progressive movement. This movement worked for various reforms in government, business, and society. While Americans focused on their own country, Europe slid into a devastating world war that eventually involved the United States as well. These crucial years of domestic change and foreign conflict provided important foundations for the world you live in today. The following resources offer more information about this period in American history.

Primary Sources Library

See pages 932–933 for primary source readings to accompany Unit 4.

Use the **American History Primary Source Document Library CD-ROM** to find additional primary sources about imperialism and progressivism.

World War I pin

American Troops Arriving in Paris July 14, 1918 by J.F. Boucher

388

TEAM TEACHING ACTIVITY

Sociology Read to students the following lines written by poet Sarah Cleghorn in the early 1900s: The golf links lie so near the mill/That almost every day/The laboring children can look out/And see the men at play. Ask students what they think this quote tells them about the economic and social conditions in the United States in 1900. (Have the sociology or economics teacher come and explain the evolution of child labor laws and their impact on the business world.)

"It is hard to fail, but it is worse never to have tried to succeed."

— *Theodore Roosevelt, 1899*

GLENCOE
TECHNOLOGY

CD-ROM
American History
Primary Source
Document Library
CD-ROM
Use the **American History Primary Source Document Library CD-ROM** to access primary source documents related to this period in history.

More About the Art

Although the war itself was devastating to Europe, fanfare often accompanied American troops marching into large cities such as Paris. The United States's involvement in the war was brief compared to that of European powers, but the European people often viewed Americans as heroes who had saved Allied countries from complete destruction. Ask students to describe the tone and mood of the painting.

Glencoe Literature Library

The following novel from the *High School American History Literature Library* may be used to enrich the study of this unit:
- *To Kill a Mockingbird* by Harper Lee

SERVICE-LEARNING PROJECT

Work with an elementary school to set up a mentoring or tutoring program between your students and elementary school students. Have volunteers sign up to participate in the program. Tell students that their goal is to work with the elementary school student on any subject with which he or she is struggling. Arrange for all meetings to occur in a public place such as at the school or in a library. Help students develop creative ways to help mentor or tutor the younger students.

Refer to ***Building Bridges: Connecting Classroom and Community through Service-Learning in Social Studies*** from the National Council for the Social Studies for information about service-learning.

Chapter 12 Resources

Timesaving Tools

TeacherWorks™ All-In-One Planner and Resource Center

- **Interactive Teacher Edition** Access your Teacher Wraparound Edition and your classroom resources with a few easy clicks.
- **Interactive Lesson Planner** Planning has never been easier! Organize your week, month, semester, or year with all the lesson helps you need to make teaching creative, timely, and relevant.

Use Glencoe's **Presentation Plus!** multimedia teacher tool to easily present dynamic lessons that visually excite your students. Using Microsoft PowerPoint® you can customize the presentations to create your own personalized lessons.

TEACHING TRANSPARENCIES

Graphic Organizer 12 L2

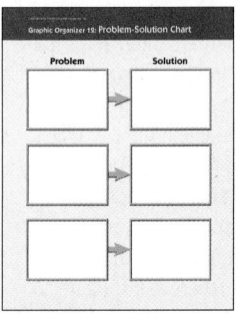

Why It Matters Chapter Transparency 12 L2

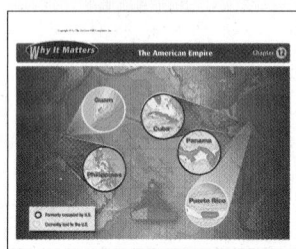

APPLICATION AND ENRICHMENT

Linking Past and Present Activity 12 L2

Enrichment Activity 12 L3

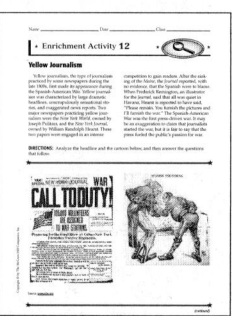

Primary Source Reading 12 L2

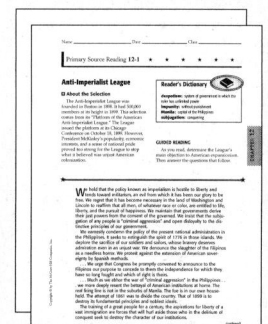

REVIEW AND REINFORCEMENT

Reteaching Activity 12 L1

Vocabulary Activity 12 L1

Time Line Activity 12 L2

Critical Thinking Skills Activity 12 L2

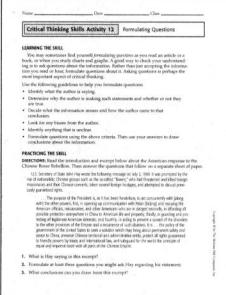

Meeting NCSS Standards

The following standards are covered in Chapter 12:

Section 1   IX   Global Connections: B, C, D

Section 2   VI   Power, Authority, and Governance: B, F, G, I

Section 3   II   Time, Continuity, and Change: B, C, D

Local Standards

Chapter 12 Resources

ASSESSMENT AND EVALUATION

Chapter 12 Test Form A L2

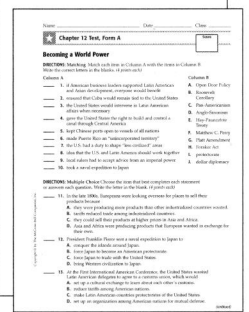

Chapter 12 Test Form B L2

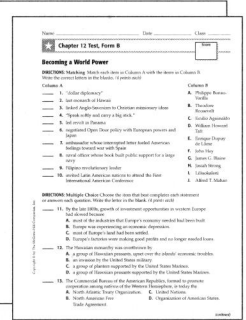

Standardized Test Practice Workbook Activity 12 L2

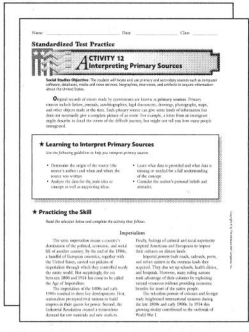

Performance Assessment Activities and Rubrics 12 L1/ELL

ExamView® Pro Testmaker CD-ROM

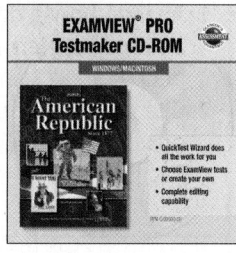

MULTIMEDIA

- Vocabulary PuzzleMaker CD-ROM
- Interactive Tutor Self-Assessment CD-ROM
- ExamView® Pro Testmaker CD-ROM
- Audio Program
- American History Primary Source Documents Library CD-ROM
- MindJogger Videoquiz
- Presentation Plus! CD-ROM
- TeacherWorks™ CD-ROM
- Interactive Student Edition CD-ROM
- Glencoe Skillbuilder Interactive Workbook CD-ROM, Level 2
- The *American Republic Since 1877* Video Program
- American Music: Hits Through History
- American Music: Cultural Traditions

SPANISH RESOURCES

The following Spanish language materials are available:

- Spanish Reading Essentials and Study Guide
- Spanish Guided Reading Activities
- Spanish Reteaching Activities
- Spanish Quizzes and Tests
- Spanish Vocabulary Activities
- Spanish Summaries
- The Declaration of Independence and United States Constitution Spanish Translation

The following videotape programs are available from Glencoe as supplements to Chapter 12:

- **Theodore Roosevelt: Roughrider to Rushmore** (ISBN 1-56-501806-0)
- **The Panama Canal** (ISBN 1-56-501243-7)

To order, call Glencoe at 1-800-334-7344. To find classroom resources to accompany many of these videos, check the following home pages:
A&E Television: www.aande.com
The History Channel: www.historychannel.com

Use our Web site for additional resources. All essential content is covered in the Student Edition.

You and your students can visit tarvol2.glencoe.com, the Web site companion to the *American Republic Since 1877*. This innovative integration of electronic and print media offers your students a wealth of opportunities. The student text directs students to the Web site for the following options:

- **Chapter Overviews**
- **Self-Check Quizzes**
- **Student Web Activities**
- **Textbook Updates**

Answers to the student Web activities are provided for you in the **Web Activity Lesson Plans.** Additional Web resources and Interactive Tutor Puzzles are also available.

Chapter 12 Resources

SECTION RESOURCES

Daily Objectives	Reproducible Resources	Multimedia Resources
SECTION 1 **The Imperialist Vision** 1. Analyze how a desire for more trade and markets led to political change between 1877 and 1898. 2. Cite the motivations for and methods of American expansion in the Pacific.	Reproducible Lesson Plan 12–1 Daily Lecture and Discussion Notes 12–1 Guided Reading Activity 12–1* Section Quiz 12–1* Reading Essentials and Study Guide 12–1* Performance Assessment Activities and Rubrics Interpreting Political Cartoons	Daily Focus Skills Transparency 12–1 Interactive Tutor Self-Assessment CD-ROM ExamView® Pro Testmaker CD-ROM* Presentation Plus! CD-ROM TeacherWorks™ CD-ROM Skillbuilder Interactive Workbook, Level 2 Audio Program American Music: Hits Through History
SECTION 2 **The Spanish-American War** 1. Describe the circumstances that led to war between the United States and Spain in 1898. 2. Explain how the war made the United States a world power.	Reproducible Lesson Plan 12–2 Daily Lecture and Discussion Notes 12–2 Guided Reading Activity 12–2* Section Quiz 12–2* Reading Essentials and Study Guide 12–2* Performance Assessment Activities and Rubrics	Daily Focus Skills Transparency 12–2 Interactive Tutor Self-Assessment CD-ROM ExamView® Pro Testmaker CD-ROM* Presentation Plus! CD-ROM TeacherWorks™ CD-ROM Audio Program American Music: Cultural Traditions
SECTION 3 **New American Diplomacy** 1. Critique Theodore Roosevelt's foreign policy as president. 2. Explain the Open Door policy and its effects on relations between the United States and Asia.	Reproducible Lesson Plan 12–3 Daily Lecture and Discussion Notes 12–3 Guided Reading Activity 12–3* Section Quiz 12–3* Reading Essentials and Study Guide 12–3* Performance Assessment Activities and Rubrics Interpreting Political Cartoons	Daily Focus Skills Transparency 12–3 Interactive Tutor Self-Assessment CD-ROM ExamView® Pro Testmaker CD-ROM* Presentation Plus! CD-ROM TeacherWorks™ CD-ROM Vocabulary PuzzleMaker CD-ROM Audio Program

0:00 OUT OF TIME?
Assign the Chapter 12 **Reading Essentials and Study Guide.**

*Also Available in Spanish

 Printed Materials Transparency ◉ CD-ROM ◉ DVD

▢ Poster Music Program Audio Program

Chapter 12 Resources

NATIONAL GEOGRAPHIC — Teacher's Corner

INDEX TO NATIONAL GEOGRAPHIC MAGAZINE

The following articles relate to this chapter.
- "Alone Across the Arctic Crown," April 1993
- "Kodiak, Alaska's Island Refuge," November 1993
- "Remember the *Maine*," February 1998
- "Wrangell-St. Elias: Alaska's Sky-High Wilderness," May 1994

NATIONAL GEOGRAPHIC SOCIETY PRODUCTS

To order the following, call National Geographic at 1-800-368-2728:
- *Hawaii: Strangers in Paradise* (Video)
- *Historical Atlas of the United States* (Atlas)

NGS ONLINE

Access National Geographic's Web site for current events, atlas updates, activities, links, interactive features, and archives.

www.nationalgeographic.com

MEETING SPECIAL NEEDS

In addition to the Differentiated Instruction strategies found in each section, the following resources are also suitable for your special needs students:

- *ExamView® Pro Testmaker CD-ROM* allows teachers to tailor tests by reducing answer choices.

- The *Audio Program* includes the entire narrative of the student edition so that less-proficient readers can listen to the words as they read them.

- The *Reading Essentials and Study Guide* provides the same content as the student edition but is written two grade levels below the textbook.

KEY TO ABILITY LEVELS

Teaching strategies have been coded.

- **L1** BASIC activities for all students
- **L2** AVERAGE activities for average to above-average students
- **L3** CHALLENGING activities for above-average students
- **ELL** ENGLISH LANGUAGE LEARNER activities

From the Classroom of...

Richard L. Manser, Ph.D.
Upper Merion High School
King of Prussia, PA

The Change in the Paradigm

The 1890s brought a change in the diplomatic paradigm from isolation to imperialism. Using the theses of Robert Beisner in *From the Old Diplomacy to the New, 1865–1900* (1974), students will research the end of the frontier including the Turner Thesis and the 1890 census; the 1893 Depression including causes, consequences, and Cleveland's policies; agrarian unrest including the Ocala Demands and Populist Party Platform; dominant personalities including Mahan, Roosevelt, Strong, and Beveridge; and the prevailing ideologies of democracy, capitalism, white man's burden, and Social Darwinism.

Write the events on the board and invite the class to make cause-and-effect relationships between the events, characters, and attitudes. The result should be a detailed explanation of the change in paradigm that resulted in the Spanish-American War, the Open Door, and the American response to the insurrection in the Philippines.

ADDITIONAL RESOURCES FROM GLENCOE

- American Music: Cultural Traditions
- American Art & Architecture
- Outline Map Resource Book
- U.S. Desk Map
- Building Geography Skills for Life
- Inclusion for the High School Social Studies Classroom Strategies and Activities
- Teaching Strategies for the American History Classroom (Including Block Scheduling Pacing Guides)
- Dinah Zike's High School American History Reading and Study Skills Foldables

Block Schedule

Activities that are suited to use within the block scheduling framework are identified by:

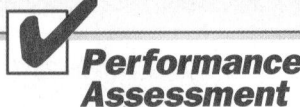

✓ Performance Assessment

Refer to Activity 12 in the Performance Assessment Activities and Rubrics booklet.

Why It Matters Activity

Assign half the class to learn an interesting fact about the Panama Canal and the other half to learn an interesting fact about Puerto Rico. After students have studied the chapter, have them evaluate whether the fact they discovered relates to events that occurred in the early 1900s. If there is a connection, have them identify the connection for the class.

GLENCOE
TECHNOLOGY

The *American Republic Since 1877* Video Program

To learn more about how the United States became a world power, have students view the Chapter 12 video, "Teddy Roosevelt and Yellow Journalism," from the *American Republic Since 1877* Video Program.

MindJogger Videoquiz

Use the **MindJogger Videoquiz** to preview Chapter 12 content.

Both programs available in DVD

CHAPTER
12 Becoming a World Power
1872–1912

Why It Matters

During this era, economic and military competition from world powers convinced the United States it must be a world power. The United States became an empire when it acquired the Philippines and territory in the Caribbean. American influence in Central and South America grew as the United States took a more active role in Latin American affairs.

The Impact Today

Events of this time continue to influence American politics.
- *The United States continues to use its navy to protect its overseas interests.*
- *The Panama Canal serves as a major route for international commerce.*
- *Puerto Rico remains tied to the United States as a commonwealth.*

○ *The* **American Republic Since 1877** *Video*
The Chapter 12 video, "Teddy Roosevelt and Yellow Journalism," chronicles the events leading to the United States becoming a world power.

1872
- Victoria Claflin Woodhull becomes first female candidate for U.S. president

1881
- President Garfield assassinated by Charles Guiteau

1889
- First Pan-American conference

United States PRESIDENTS

| Grant 1869–1877 | Hayes 1877–1881 | Garfield 1881 | Arthur 1881–1885 | Cleveland 1885–1889 |

1870   *1880*   *1890*

World

1874
- Britain annexes Fiji Islands

1876
- Nicholas Otto builds first practical gasoline engine

1880
- John Milne develops the seismograph

1889
- Gustave Eiffel completes tower for Paris World Exhibit

390

📖 Reading Strategy PURPOSE FOR READING

Carousel Brainstorming Divide the class into groups of three to four students. Give each group a sheet of paper and different colored markers (one color per student). Give half of the groups the topic: *What do you think it means to be a world power?* Give the other groups the topic: *What responsibilities does a world power have to the world community?* Instruct one student in each group to write down with a marker an idea or thought about the topic. Then, have the next student in the group add another item, using a different colored marker. Continue this process until each student in the group has listed at least two to three items. Display the sheets in the classroom. After completing the chapter, have students add new information they learned. **L1**

Artist's rendition of Theodore Roosevelt's charge up San Juan Hill

1893
• Americans overthrow Queen Liliuokalani of Hawaii

1898
• U.S. declares war on Spain

1899
• Hay sends Open Door notes

1901
• President McKinley assassinated

1904
• Panama Canal construction begins
• Roosevelt Corollary to Monroe Doctrine issued

SEAL OF THE CANAL ZONE ISTHMUS OF PANAMA

| B. Harrison 1889–1893 | Cleveland 1893–1897 | McKinley 1897–1901 | T. Roosevelt 1901–1909 | | Taft 1909–1913 |

1900   *1910*

1895
• Louis and Auguste Lumière introduce motion pictures

1899
• Boer War begins between Great Britain and South African Republic

1900
• Boxer Rebellion begins in China

1904
• Russo-Japanese War begins

391

HISTORY Online

Introduce students to chapter content and key terms by having them access the **Chapter 12 Overview** at tarvol2.glencoe.com.

More About the Art

On July 1, 1898, Theodore Roosevelt and his volunteer cavalry, the Rough Riders, joined in the capture of the San Juan Hill complex. They helped secure a U.S. victory in the Battle of Santiago, the decisive battle of the brief Spanish-American War. Two days after the battle, the Spanish fleet fled the harbor at Santiago, effectively surrendering control of Cuba to the United States.

HISTORY Online

Chapter Overview
Visit the *American Republic Since 1877* Web site at tarvol2.glencoe.com and click on **Chapter Overviews— Chapter 12** to preview chapter information.

TIME LINE
ACTIVITY

Have students select one of the people mentioned on the time line and prepare a brief profile of his or her life, including major accomplishments.

FOLDABLES™
Study Organizer

Dinah Zike's Foldables are three-dimensional, interactive graphic organizers that help students practice basic writing skills, review key vocabulary terms, and identify main ideas. Have students complete the foldable activity in the *Dinah Zike's Reading and Study Skills Foldables* booklet.

GRAPHIC ORGANIZER ACTIVITY

Organizing Information Have students use a graphic organizer similar to the one below to present the arguments for and against United States foreign expansion.

Arguments For
• *increases trade*
• *helps civilize people*
• *spreads American ideals*

→ **Foreign Expansion** ←

Arguments Against
• *too costly*
• *drives down American wages*
• *violates America's principles*

1 FOCUS

Section Overview

This section focuses on the United States becoming an imperialist power.

BELLRINGER
Skillbuilder Activity

Project transparency and have students answer the question.

Daily Focus Skills Transparency 12–1

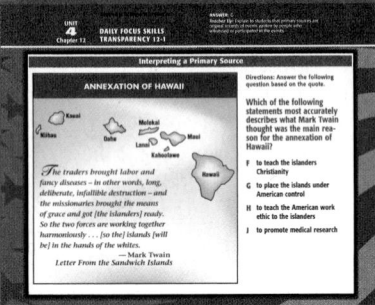

Reading Preview

Answers to Graphic:
I. Building Support for Imperialism
   A. A Desire for New Markets
   B. A Feeling of Superiority
II. Expansion in the Pacific
   A. Perry Opens Japan
   B. Annexing Hawaii
III. Trade and Diplomacy in Latin America
IV. Building a Modern Navy

Preteaching Vocabulary
Have students look up the proper pronunciations of the Key Terms and Names.

Guide to Reading

Main Idea
In the late 1800s, many Americans wanted the United States to expand its military and economic power overseas.

Key Terms and Names
imperialism, protectorate, Anglo-Saxonism, Matthew C. Perry, Queen Liliuokalani, Pan-Americanism, Alfred T. Mahan, Henry Cabot Lodge

Reading Strategy
Organizing As you read about the development of the United States as a world power, use the major headings of the section to create an outline similar to the one below.

The Imperialist Vision
I. Building Support for Imperialism
   A.
   B.
II.
   A.
   B.

Reading Objectives:
• **Analyze** how a desire for more trade and markets led to political change between 1877 and 1898.
• **Cite** the motivations for and methods of American expansion in the Pacific.

Section Theme
Global Connections America's growing trade with the world and rivalry with European nations led to a naval buildup and a search for territory overseas.

Preview of Events

1850 ———————— 1875 ———————— 1900

1853 Commodore Perry arrives in Japan

1888 Samoan Crisis erupts

1890 Alfred T. Mahan's *Influence of Sea Power Upon History, 1660–1783* published

1893 American settlers overthrow Queen Liliuokalani of Hawaii

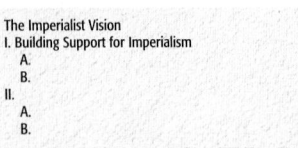

✴ An American Story ✴

John L. Stevens

On January 16, 1893, 162 United States Marines marched off the warship *Boston* and onto the shores of Oahu, one of the Hawaiian Islands. John L. Stevens, the American minister to Hawaii, had ordered the troops ashore. He claimed Hawaii's ruler, Queen Liliuokalani, had created widespread turmoil and endangered American lives and property. Stevens had other motives as well. He wanted to make Hawaii, with its profitable sugarcane plantations, part of the United States.

Stevens ordered the American troops to take up positions near Queen Liliuokalani's palace. Although the marines took no action against the Hawaiian government, their presence intimidated the queen's supporters. Within hours, the American settlers in Hawaii abolished the monarchy and set up a provisional—or temporary—government. On February 1, 1893, at the request of the provisional government, Stevens announced that Hawaii was now under American protection, and he hoisted the American flag over Hawaii's government buildings. Several weeks later, Stevens made his support for annexing Hawaii perfectly clear: "The Hawaiian pear is now fully ripe," he wrote, "and this is the golden hour for the United States to pluck it."

—adapted from *A History of the American People*

Building Support for Imperialism

John Stevens was not alone in his views. Many Americans cheered the events in Hawaii and favored expanding American power elsewhere in the world as well. The American public's enthusiasm, however, was a relatively new phenomenon. In the years

---

SECTION RESOURCES

📁 Reproducible Masters
• Reproducible Lesson Plan 12–1
• Daily Lecture and Discussion Notes 12–1
• Guided Reading Activity 12–1
• Section Quiz 12–1
• Reading Essentials and Study Guide 12–1
• Interpreting Political Cartoons

🖳 Transparencies
• Daily Focus Skills Transparency 12–1

Multimedia
🔘 Interactive Tutor Self-Assessment CD-ROM
🔘 ExamView® Pro Testmaker CD-ROM
🔘 Presentation Plus! CD-ROM
🔘 TeacherWorks™ CD-ROM
🔘 Audio Program

immediately following the Civil War, most Americans showed little interest in expanding their nation's territory and international influence. Instead, they focused on reconstructing the South, building up the nation's industries, and settling the West.

Beginning in the 1880s, however, American opinion began to shift. More people wanted to make the United States a world power. Economic and military competition from other nations, as well as a growing feeling of cultural superiority, led to this shift in opinion.

ECONOMICS

A Desire for New Markets While the United States focused inward, several European nations were expanding their power overseas. This expansion became known as the New Imperialism. Imperialism is the economic and political domination of a strong nation over other weaker nations.

The Europeans embarked upon a policy of expansion and imperialism for many reasons. By the late 1800s, most industrialized countries had placed high tariffs against each other. These tariffs were intended to protect a nation's industries from foreign competition. The tariffs reduced trade between industrial countries, forcing companies to look overseas for places to sell their products.

At the same time, the growth of investment opportunities in western Europe had slowed. Most of the factories, railroads, and mines that Europe's economy needed had been built. Increasingly, Europeans began looking overseas for places to invest their capital. They began investing in industries in other countries, particularly in Africa and Asia.

To protect their investments, the European nations began exerting control over those territories where they invested their capital and sold their products. Some areas became colonies. Many others became protectorates. In a protectorate, the imperial power allowed the local rulers to stay in control and protected them against rebellions and invasion. In exchange for this protection, the local rulers usually had to accept advice from the Europeans on how to govern their countries.

The expansion of European power overseas did not go unnoticed in the United States. As the United States industrialized, many Americans took interest in the new imperialism. Until the late 1800s, the United States had always been able to expand by settling more territory in North America. Now, with settlers finally filling up the western frontier, many Americans concluded that the nation had to develop new overseas markets to keep its economy strong. "We are raising more than we can consume," declared Indiana senator Albert J. Beveridge. "We are

making more than we can use. Therefore, we must find new markets for our produce, new occupation for our capital, new work for our labor."

A Feeling of Superiority In addition to economic concerns, certain other key ideas convinced many Americans to encourage their nation's expansion overseas. Many supporters of Social Darwinism argued that nations competed with each other politically, economically, and militarily, and that only the strongest would ultimately survive. They used this idea to justify expanding the power of the United States overseas.

Many Americans, such as the well-known writer and historian John Fiske, took this idea even further. Fiske argued that English-speaking nations had superior character, ideas, and systems of government, and were destined to dominate the planet:

> ❝The work which the English race began when it colonized North America is destined to go on until every land . . . that is not already the seat of an old civilization shall become English in its language, in its religion, in political habits and traditions, and to a predominant extent in the blood of its people.❞
>
> —quoted in *Expansionists of 1898*

This idea, known as **Anglo-Saxonism,** was popular in Britain and the United States. Many Americans saw it as part of the idea of Manifest Destiny. They believed it had been the nation's destiny to expand west to the Pacific Ocean. Now they believed it was

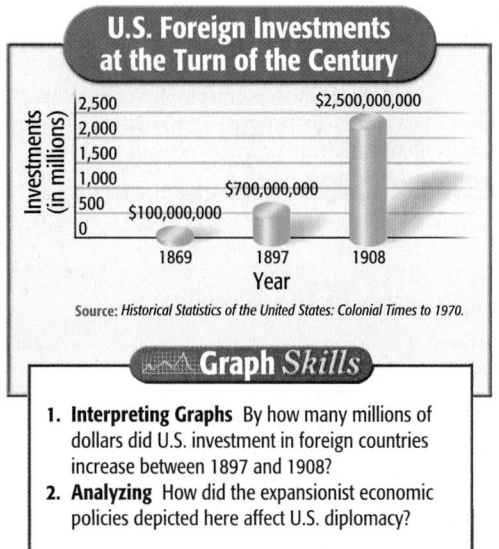

U.S. Foreign Investments at the Turn of the Century

Investments (in millions)

- 1869: $100,000,000
- 1897: $700,000,000
- 1908: $2,500,000,000

Year

Source: *Historical Statistics of the United States: Colonial Times to 1970.*

Graph *Skills*

1. **Interpreting Graphs** By how many millions of dollars did U.S. investment in foreign countries increase between 1897 and 1908?
2. **Analyzing** How did the expansionist economic policies depicted here affect U.S. diplomacy?

CHAPTER 12 Becoming a World Power **393**

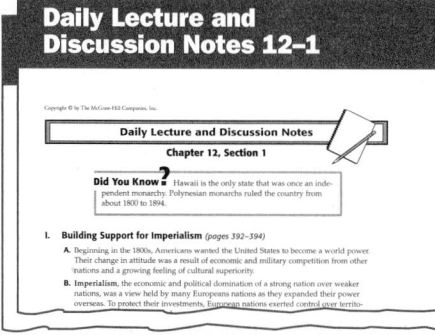

2 TEACH

Daily Lecture and Discussion Notes 12–1

Copyright © by The McGraw-Hill Companies, Inc.

Daily Lecture and Discussion Notes

Chapter 12, Section 1

Did You Know? Hawaii is the only state that was once an independent monarchy. Polynesian monarchs ruled the country from about 1800 to 1894.

I. Building Support for Imperialism (pages 392–394)

A. Beginning in the 1800s, Americans wanted the United States to become a world power. Their change in attitude was a result of economic and military competition from other nations and a growing feeling of cultural superiority.

B. Imperialism, the economic and political domination of a strong nation over weaker nations, was a view held by many Europeans nations as they expanded their power overseas. To protect their investments, European nations exerted control over territo-

Supporting Statements with Facts Write the following statements on the chalkboard:

1. United States emerges from isolationism.
2. United States seeks to open new markets.
3. United States changes its naval policy.
4. United States becomes a world power.

Ask students to find at least two facts in the text to support these statements. **L1** ELL

Graph *Skills*

Answers:
1. by $1,800 million
2. caused the U.S. to have greater trade and diplomatic contacts with Asia and Latin America

Graph Skills Practice

Ask: Why do you think such a dramatic increase in foreign investments made the United States feel superior? *(showed growing power of the United States around the world, opened new markets)*

Reading Strategy   READING THE TEXT

Using Word Parts Help students learn how suffixes can help them unlock the meaning of words. A suffix is a word part that comes after a base word or a root. It may change the meaning of the word or the way the word is used in the sentence. Provide students with these examples: *–less* means "without" (careless, powerless); *–ish* means "like" (childish, foolish); *–ful* means "full of" (playful, thoughtful). Have students find words with suffixes in the section and identify the root word's meaning. **L1**

Refer to *Inclusion for the High School Social Studies Classroom Strategies and Activities* in the TCR.

Picturing History

American Imperialism To open Japan to American trade, Commodore Matthew Perry led the U.S. Navy into what is now Tokyo Bay on July 8, 1853. This lithograph shows Perry's forces arriving in Yokohama in March 1854. How did Perry's action affect Japan?

Matthew C. Perry

the destiny of the United States to expand overseas and spread its civilization to other people.

Another influential advocate of Anglo-Saxonism was **Josiah Strong,** a popular American minister in the late 1800s. Strong linked Anglo-Saxonism to Christian missionary ideas. His ideas influenced many Americans. "The Anglo-Saxon," Strong declared, "[is] divinely commissioned to be, in a peculiar sense, his brother's keeper." By linking missionary work to Anglo-Saxonism, Strong convinced many Americans to support imperialism and an expansion of American power overseas.

✓ **Reading Check** **Summarizing** How did Americans' opinions on overseas expansion begin to change in the 1800s?

Expansion in the Pacific

From the earliest days of the Republic, Americans had expanded their nation by moving west. When Americans began looking overseas for new markets in the 1800s, therefore, they naturally tended to look westward. Even before imperialist ideas became popular, Americans had begun expanding across the Pacific Ocean toward East Asia. By the early 1800s, dozens of ships were making the long trip to China every year.

Perry Opens Japan Many American business leaders believed that the United States would benefit from trade with Japan as well as with China. Japan's rulers, however, believed that excessive contact with the West would destroy their culture and only allowed the Chinese and Dutch to trade with their nation.

In 1852, after receiving several petitions from Congress, President Franklin Pierce decided to force Japan to trade with the United States. He ordered Commodore **Matthew C. Perry** to take a naval expedition to Japan to negotiate a trade treaty.

On July 8, 1853, four American warships under Perry's command entered Yedo Bay (today known as Tokyo Bay). The Japanese had never seen steamships before and were impressed by the display of American technology and firepower. Perry's arrival in Japan forced the Japanese to make changes internally. Realizing that they could not compete against modern Western technology and weapons, the Japanese signed a treaty opening the ports of Simoda and Hakodadi to American trade on March 31, 1854.

DIFFERENTIATED INSTRUCTION

At-Risk Students To focus students' attention during classroom discussion, interrupt the discussion occasionally with the announcement of a "pop listening quiz." Award "listening points" to students who can answer quiz questions correctly. For example, when the class is discussing the annexation of Hawaii, pop the question, "Who pushed for the annexation of Hawaii—President Grover Cleveland, American sugar growers, or the Hawaiian people themselves?" **L1** ELL

📂 Refer to *Inclusion for the High School Social Studies Classroom Strategies and Activities* in the TCR.

The American decision to force Japan to open trade played an important role in Japanese history. Many Japanese leaders concluded that the time had come to remake their society. In 1868, after a long internal power struggle, Japanese leaders began to Westernize their country. They adopted Western technology and launched their own industrial revolution. By the 1890s, the Japanese had built a powerful modern navy, and they set out to build their own empire in Asia.

Annexing Hawaii As trade with China and Japan grew in the 1800s, many Americans became interested in Hawaii. Ships traveling between China and the United States regularly stopped in Hawaii to allow their crews to rest and to take on supplies. In 1820 a group of missionaries from New England settled in Hawaii. At about the same time, American whaling ships operating in the North Pacific began using Hawaii as a base.

The American settlers in Hawaii quickly discovered that the climate and soil of the islands were suitable for growing sugarcane. By the mid-1800s, many sugarcane plantations had been established in the islands. In 1872 a severe recession struck Hawaii's economy. Worried that the economic crisis might force the Hawaiians to turn to the British or French for help, the United States Senate ratified a trade treaty in 1875 that exempted Hawaiian sugar from tariffs. Several years later, when the treaty came up for renewal, the Senate insisted that the Hawaiians grant the United States exclusive rights to a naval base at Pearl Harbor.

The trade treaty led to a boom in the Hawaiian sugar industry and wealth for the planters. In 1887 prominent planters pressured the Hawaiian king into accepting a new constitution that limited the king's authority and increased the planters' power. These developments angered the Hawaiian people, who feared they were losing control of the country.

Tensions between the planters and the Hawaiians mounted. Congress passed the McKinley Tariff in 1890. Although the tariff eliminated all duties on sugar, it also gave subsidies to sugar producers in the United States. Hawaiian sugar was now more expensive than American sugar, despite the lack of tariffs. As sales of Hawaiian sugar declined, the islands' economy went into a tailspin.

In 1891 **Queen Liliuokalani** ascended the Hawaiian throne. Liliuokalani disliked the influence that American settlers had gained in Hawaii. In January 1893, she unsuccessfully attempted to impose a new constitution that would have reasserted her authority as ruler of the Hawaiian people.

Faced with the economic crisis and the queen's actions, the planters backed an attempt to overthrow the monarchy. Supported by the marines from the *Boston,* a group of planters forced the queen to give up power and set up a provisional government. They then requested that the United States annex Hawaii. President Cleveland strongly opposed imperialism. He withdrew the annexation treaty from the Senate and tried to restore Liliuokalani to power. Hawaii's new leaders refused to restore Liliuokalani, and they decided to wait until a new president took office who favored annexation. Five years later, the United States annexed Hawaii. 📖 *(See page 955 for more text on Hawaiian annexation.)*

✔**Reading Check** **Explaining** How did the desire to expand into new markets help push the United States to become a world power?

Trade and Diplomacy in Latin America

The Pacific was not the only region where the United States sought to increase its influence in the 1800s. It also focused on Latin America. Although the United States bought raw materials from this region, Latin Americans bought most of their manufactured goods from Europe. American business leaders and government officials wanted to increase the sale of American products to the region. They also wanted the Europeans to understand that the United States was the dominant power in the region.

James G. Blaine, who served as secretary of state in two administrations in the 1880s, led early efforts

Hawaiian Queen Liliuokalani

✔**Reading Check**

Answer: It led them to annex Hawaii and to open trade with Japan.

Creating a Thematic Map
Provide students with a map of the Pacific Ocean that includes both the West Coast of the United States and South America and the eastern coast of Asia. Have students research and map the routes taken by James Cook when he became the first European to visit the Hawaiian Islands, the trade routes used to export sugarcane, and strategic locations that allowed Hawaii to play a military role during the Spanish-American War. **L2**

📁 Use the rubric for creating a map, display, or chart on pages 65–66 in the *Performance Assessment Activities and Rubrics.*

you don't say...

Annex The word *annex* comes from Latin and literally means "to bind to."

FYI

In 1826, many years before the Pan-American conference was held in Washington, D.C., Simón Bolívar convened the Congress of Panama with the idea of creating an association of states in the Western Hemisphere. The OAS charter was signed in 1948. At the same conference, participants also signed the American Declaration of the Rights and Duties of Man, which was the first international statement expressing human rights principles.

TECHNOLOGY & History

Background: The U.S.S. *Texas* was the first commissioned battleship in the United States fleet. It was commissioned on August 15, 1895. The battleship carried two 12-inch and six 6-inch guns and was equipped with four 14-inch torpedo tubes. The ship was protected by 12-inch-thick steel armor. For its era, it was one of the most powerful ships in the world.

Answer: Captain Alfred Mahan whose *The Influence of Sea Power Upon History, 1660–1783,* persuaded many in government that a modern navy was necessary to protect America's expanding global trade

✓ Reading Check

Answer: He wanted to create a customs union between Latin America and the United States, and he wanted to create a system for American nations to work out their disputes peacefully.

3 ASSESS

Assign Section 1 Assessment as homework or as an in-class activity.

🌐 Have students use the **Interactive Tutor Self-Assessment CD-ROM.**

L1/ELL

Reading Essentials and Study Guide 12–1

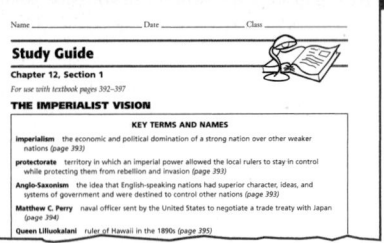

Name _____ Date _____ Class _____

Study Guide

Chapter 12, Section 1

For use with textbook pages 392–397

THE IMPERIALIST VISION

KEY TERMS AND NAMES
imperialism the economic and political domination of a strong nation over one weaker nations *(page 393)*
protectorate territory in which an imperial power allowed the local rulers to stay in control while protecting them from rebellion and invasion *(page 393)*
Anglo-Saxonism the idea that English-speaking nations had superior character, ideas, and systems of government and were destined to control other nations *(page 393)*
Matthew C. Perry naval officer sent by the United States to negotiate a trade treaty with Japan *(page 394)*
Queen Liliuokalani ruler of Hawaii in the 1890s *(page 395)*

TECHNOLOGY & History

Modern Battleships

In the 1880s, the United States Navy modernized its fleet of warships. Moving away from wooden ships powered solely by the wind, the new navy constructed steel-hulled ships with steam-powered engines as well as sails. Probably the most famous ship of this era was the USS *Maine,* one of the U.S. Navy's first armored battleships (depicted at right). It was one of the first U.S. naval vessels with electrical lighting. It had a top speed of 17 knots and a crew of 392 officers and enlisted men. *Which U.S. naval officer argued for the necessity of a modern navy?*

1 The *Maine* was designed for **sail power** as well as steam, but the sails were never fitted on the ship.

2 It had a maximum **armor** thickness of 12 inches.

3 Eight **steam boilers** powered two engines.

sail power

cowls

torpedo tubes

galley

steam boilers

magazine

armor

4 Cowls provided fresh air below decks.

5 Food was prepared in the galley.

6 Munitions were stored in the magazine.

to expand American influence in Latin America. Blaine proposed that the United States invite the Latin American nations to a conference in Washington, D.C. The conference would discuss ways in which the American nations could work together to support peace and to increase trade. The idea that the United States and Latin America should work together came to be called **Pan-Americanism.**

Blaine's idea became reality in 1889 when the Pan-American conference was held in Washington, D.C. Seventeen Latin American nations attended. Blaine had two goals for the conference. He wanted to create a customs union between Latin America and the United States, and he also wanted to create a system for American nations to work out their disputes peacefully.

A customs union would require all of the American nations to reduce their tariffs against each other and to treat each other equally in trade. Blaine hoped that a customs union would turn the Latin Americans away from European products and toward American products. He also hoped that a common system for settling disputes would keep the Europeans from meddling in American affairs.

Although the warm reception they received in the United States impressed the Latin American delegates

to the conference, they rejected both of Blaine's ideas. They did agree, however, to create the Commercial Bureau of the American Republics, an organization that worked to promote cooperation among the nations of the Western Hemisphere. This organization was later known as the Pan-American Union and is today called the **Organization of American States** (OAS).

✓ Reading Check Summarizing How did Secretary of State Blaine attempt to increase American influence in Latin America?

Building a Modern Navy

As imperialism and Anglo-Saxonism gained support in the late 1800s, the United States became increasingly assertive in foreign affairs. Three international crises illustrated this new approach. In 1888 the country was willing to go to war to prevent Germany from taking control of the Samoa Islands in the South Pacific. Three years later, when a mob in Chile attacked American sailors in the port of Valparaíso, the United States threatened to go to war unless Chile paid reparations for the lives lost. Then, in 1895, the United States backed

---

CRITICAL THINKING ACTIVITY

Analyzing Pose the following question to students: What problems arise when we view our own culture as so superior to others that we refuse to accept new ideas from other cultures? Ask students to write their analysis in the form of a letter to the editor. If possible, have students use a personal experience of a current event as a starting point for their letter. Have students share their letters with the class. **L2**

Venezuela against Great Britain in a border dispute with the colony of British Guiana. After Britain rejected an American ultimatum to settle the dispute, many newspapers and members of Congress called for war. All three crises were eventually solved peacefully.

As both the American people and their government became more willing to risk war in defense of American interests overseas, support for building a large modern navy began to grow. Supporters argued that if the United States did not build up its navy and acquire bases overseas, it would be shut out of foreign markets by the Europeans.

Captain **Alfred T. Mahan,** an officer in the U.S. Navy who taught at the Naval War College, best expressed this argument. In 1890 Mahan published his lectures in a book called *The Influence of Sea Power Upon History, 1660–1783.* In this book Mahan pointed out that many prosperous peoples in the past, such as the British and Dutch, had built large fleets of merchant ships in order to trade with the world. He then suggested that a nation also needed a large navy to protect its merchant ships and to defend its right to trade with other countries.

After arguing that the United States needed a large navy, Mahan observed that building a modern navy meant that the United States had to acquire territory for naval bases overseas. In the 1890s, navy warships burned coal to power their engines. To operate a navy far from home, a country needed bases and coaling stations in distant regions. This would allow the ships to be resupplied en route to their destination.

Mahan's book became a best-seller, and it helped to build public support for a big navy. In Congress two powerful senators, **Henry Cabot Lodge** and Albert J. Beveridge, pushed for the construction of a new navy. In the executive branch, Benjamin Tracy, secretary of the navy under President Harrison, and John D. Long, secretary of the navy under President McKinley, strongly supported Mahan's ideas—as did future president Theodore Roosevelt, who served as an assistant secretary of the navy in the late 1890s.

By the 1890s, several different ideas had come together in the United States. Business leaders wanted new markets overseas. Anglo-Saxonism had convinced many Americans that they had a destiny to dominate the world. Growing European imperialism threatened America's security. Combined with Mahan's influence, these ideas convinced Congress to authorize the construction of a modern American navy.

By the late 1890s, the United States was well on its way to becoming one of the top naval powers in the world. Although it was not yet an imperial power, it had the power to become one if the opportunity arose. That opportunity was not long in coming. In the spring of 1898, war erupted between Spain and the United States.

✓ **Reading Check** **Explaining** Why did Alfred T. Mahan and Henry Cabot Lodge call for the building of a strong U.S. navy?

 HISTORY Online **Study Central™** To review this section, go to **tarvol2.glencoe.com** and click on **Study Central™.**

SECTION 1 ASSESSMENT

Checking for Understanding

1. **Define:** imperialism, protectorate.
2. **Identify:** Anglo-Saxonism, Matthew C. Perry, Queen Liliuokalani, Pan-Americanism, Alfred T. Mahan, Henry Cabot Lodge.
3. **Explain** why Secretary of State James G. Blaine convened the Pan-American conference in 1889.

Reviewing Themes

4. **Global Connections** What events in the world convinced Americans to support a large navy?

Critical Thinking

5. **Forming an Opinion** Do you think the United States should have supported the planters in their attempt to overthrow Queen Liliuokalani of Hawaii? Why or why not?
6. **Organizing** Use a graphic organizer to list the factors that led to an imperialist policy in the United States in the 1800s.

Factors Leading to U.S. Imperialist Policy

Analyzing Visuals

7. **Analyzing Art** Study the painting on page 394. How is the U.S. Navy portrayed in relation to the Japanese residents of Yokohama? Do you think the artist shows any bias in this representation? Why or why not?

Writing About History

8. **Persuasive Writing** Imagine that you are living in the United States in the 1890s. Write a letter to the president persuading him to support or oppose an imperialist policy for the United States. Be sure to use standard grammar, spelling, sentence structure, and punctuation.

CHAPTER 12 Becoming a World Power **397**

SECTION 1 ASSESSMENT ANSWERS

1. Terms are in blue.
2. Anglo-Saxonism (p. 393), Mathew C. Perry (p. 394), Queen Liliuokalani (p. 395), Pan-Americanism (p. 396), Alfred T. Mahan (p. 397), Henry Cabot Lodge (p. 397)
3. He convened the conference to support peace and increase trade among the Americas.
4. Germany tried to control Samoa Islands; Chilean mob attacked American soldiers; U.S. backed Venezuela in border dispute
5. Students' answers will vary. Students should be able to defend their points of view.
6. feeling of superiority, interest in expanding trade, need for strategic military bases, European competition
7. probable bias; U.S. troops more numerous and surround Japanese representatives
8. Letters should express a clear point of view.

L2

Section Quiz 12–1

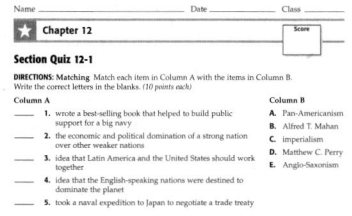

Name _____ Date _____ Class _____

★ Chapter 12 Score ☐

Section Quiz 12-1

DIRECTIONS: Matching Match each item in Column A with the items in Column B. Write the correct letters in the blanks. *(10 points each)*

Column A

___ 1. wrote a best-selling book that helped to build public support for a big navy

___ 2. the economic and political domination of a strong nation over other weaker nations

___ 3. idea that Latin America and the United States should work together

___ 4. idea that the English-speaking nations were destined to dominate the planet

___ 5. took a naval expedition to Japan to negotiate a trade treaty

Column B

A. Pan-Americanism
B. Alfred T. Mahan
C. imperialism
D. Matthew C. Perry
E. Anglo-Saxonism

Reteach

Have students analyze how a desire for more trade and markets led to political change between 1877 and 1898.

Enrich

Have students imagine that they were living in Tokyo at the time that Matthew C. Perry steamed into Yedo Bay. Have students write a letter to a friend in another part of Japan relaying the events that transpired.

✓ **Reading Check**

Answer: to protect merchant ships and defend the nation's right to trade with other countries

 HISTORY Online

Study Central™ provides summaries, interactive games, and online graphic organizers to help students review section content.

4 CLOSE

Have students cite the motivations for and the methods of American expansion in the Pacific.

TEACH

Using an Electronic Spreadsheet Spreadsheets use a standard row and column format to organize information. Cells, the intersection of a row and column, may contain text, numbers, or formulas.

Give students this assignment: Assume that you are in charge of a fund-raising activity for a community event. Create a spreadsheet that you could use to track money received, expenses, and money donated.

Additional Practice

L1

Reinforcing Skills Activity 12

Name _____ Date _____ Class _____

★ Reinforcing Skills Activity 12

Using an Electronic Spreadsheet

☐ LEARNING THE SKILL

A spreadsheet is an electronic worksheet that can manage numbers quickly and easily. All spreadsheets follow a basic design of rows and columns. Each column is assigned a letter, and each row is assigned a number. Each point where a column and row intersect is called a cell. The cell's position on the spreadsheet is labeled according to its corresponding column and row, so A1 is column A, row 1. Spreadsheets use formulas to calculate numbers. To create a formula, highlight the cell you want the results in. Type an equal sign (=) and then build the formula, step by step.

☐ PRACTICING THE SKILL

DIRECTIONS: Use the following data to create your own spreadsheet.

1. In cell A1, type the words population State. In cell B1, type A1. In cell A1, type the name of the

GLENCOE
TECHNOLOGY

CD-ROM
Glencoe Skillbuilder Interactive Workbook CD-ROM, Level 2

This interactive CD-ROM reinforces student mastery of essential social studies skills.

Using an Electronic Spreadsheet

Why Learn This Skill?

Electronic spreadsheets can help people manage numbers quickly and easily. Historians use spreadsheets to easily manipulate statistical data. You can use a spreadsheet any time a problem involves numbers that can be arranged in rows and columns.

Learning the Skill

A spreadsheet is an electronic worksheet that follows a basic design of rows and columns. Each *column* (vertical) is assigned a letter or number. Each *row* (horizontal) is assigned a number. Each point where a column and row intersect is called a *cell*. The cell's position on the spreadsheet is labeled according to its column and row. Therefore, Column A, Row 1 is referred to as cell A1; Column B, Row 2 is B2, and so on.

Spreadsheets use standard formulas to calculate numbers. You create a simple mathematical equation that uses these standard formulas, and the computer does the calculations for you.

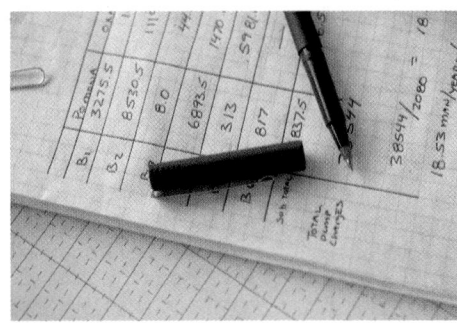

You can also create spreadsheets manually.

A1	B1	C1	D1	E1
A2	B2	C2	D2	E2
A3	B3	C3	D3	E3
A4	B4	C4	D4	E4
A5	B5	C5	D5	E5

Practicing the Skill

Use these steps to create a spreadsheet that will provide the population densities (population per square mile) of the states in the United States in 1900.

❶ In cell A1 type *State;* in cell B1 type *Population;* in cell C1 type *Land area (square miles);* in cell D1 type *Population per square mile.*

❷ In cells A2–A46, type each state's name. In cell A47, type the words *Total for the United States.*

❸ In cells B2–B46, enter the population of each of the states listed in cells A2–A46.

❹ In cells C2–C46, enter the land area (square miles) of each state shown in cells A2–A46.

❺ In cell D2, create a formula to calculate the population per square mile. The formula tells what cells (B2 ÷ C2) to divide. Copy this formula into cells D3–D46.

❻ Use the process in step 5 to create and copy a formula to calculate the nation's total population (B2 + B3 + B4 . . .) for cell B47.

❼ Use the process in step 5 to create and copy a formula to calculate the nation's population per square mile (B47 ÷ C47) for cell D47.

Skills Assessment

Complete the Practicing Skills questions on page 415 and the Chapter 12 Skill Reinforcement Activity to assess your mastery of this skill.

Applying the Skill

Using an Electronic Spreadsheet Use a spreadsheet to enter your test scores and homework grades. Following the grading period, create an equation that allows the spreadsheet to calculate your average grade.

 Glencoe's **Skillbuilder Interactive Workbook CD-ROM, Level 2,** provides instruction and practice in key social studies skills.

ANSWERS TO PRACTICING THE SKILL

Students will create a spreadsheet that gives the population density of each state. Have students use an almanac, a statistical abstract, or other reference source to obtain each state's land area and population in 1900. Remind students that Oklahoma, New Mexico, Arizona, Alaska, and Hawaii were not states in 1900.

Applying the Skill

Students' spreadsheets will vary. Rows and columns should be clearly labeled and the formula to calculate the average grade should be accurate.

SECTION 2 The Spanish-American War

Guide to Reading

Main Idea
The United States defeated Spain in a war, acquired new overseas territories, and became an imperial power.

Key Terms and Names
José Martí, William Randolph Hearst, Joseph Pulitzer, yellow journalism, jingoism, Theodore Roosevelt, Platt Amendment

Reading Strategy
Organizing As you read about the Spanish-American War, complete a graphic organizer like the one below by listing the circumstances that contributed to war with Spain.

Factors Contributing to Declaration of War

Reading Objectives:
• **Describe** the circumstances that led to war between the United States and Spain in 1898.
• **Explain** how the war made the United States a world power.

Section Theme
Government and Democracy The United States fought Spain to help Cubans gain their independence.

Preview of Events

| ♦January 1898 | ♦May 1898 | ♦September 1898 | ♦December 1898 |

February 1898
U.S.S. *Maine* explodes

April 1898
U.S. declares war on Spain

May 1898
Dewey destroys Spanish fleet in the Philippines

December 1898
Treaty of Paris ends Spanish-American War

★ An American Story ★

Clara Barton

Clara Barton, the founder and first president of the American National Red Cross, was working late in her villa overlooking the harbor in Havana, Cuba, on the evening of February 15, 1898. As she and an assistant reviewed some paperwork, an enormous blast lit up the sky. She later recalled:

❝The deafening roar was such a burst of thunder as perhaps one never heard before. And off to the right, out over the bay, the air filled with a blaze of light, and this in turn filled with black specks like huge specters flying in all directions.❞

Barton quickly learned what had happened. The U.S.S. *Maine,* anchored in the Havana harbor, had exploded. Barton rushed to a nearby hospital, where she took a firsthand look at the blast's devastation. The sailors' wounds, she wrote, "were all over them—heads and faces terribly cut, internal wounds, arms, legs, feet and hands burned to the live flesh."

—adapted from *The Spanish War*

The Coming of War

Of the 354 officers and sailors aboard the *Maine* that winter night, 266 died. No one is sure why the *Maine* exploded. The size of the explosion indicates that the ship's ammunition supplies blew up. Some experts think that a fire accidentally ignited the ammunition. Others argue that a mine detonated near the ship set off the ammunition.

CHAPTER 12 Becoming a World Power **399**

2 TEACH

History *Through Art*

Answer: because they regarded the Spanish as tyrants

Ask: What was Cuba's main export product? *(sugarcane)*

Reading Strategy

Making a List After students have read the part of this section titled "The Coming of War" ask students what events led up to the Spanish-American War. Write their answers on the board in the order that students respond. As a class, put the list in chronological order. **L1**

you don't say...

Strong Ego William Randolph Hearst sent artist Frederic Remington to Cuba to cover events after the explosion of the *Maine*. When the expected conflict between the United States and Spain did not immediately materialize, the artist asked if he should return home. Hearst cabled back, "You furnish the pictures, I'll furnish the war."

History *Through Art*

Cuban Rebellion During the Cuban Revolution in 1895, Spanish general Valeriano Weyler forced much of the Cuban population into guarded camps near military installations. Why were Americans supporting Cuba's fight against Spain?

When the explosion happened, many Americans blamed it on Spain. Cuba was a Spanish colony at the time, but it was in the midst of a revolution. The Cuban people were fighting for independence from Spain. Many Americans regarded the Spanish as tyrants and supported the Cubans in their struggle. These Americans quickly jumped to the conclusion that Spain had blown up the *Maine*. Within a matter of weeks, Spain and the United States were at war. Although the fighting only lasted a few months, the outcome dramatically altered the position of the United States on the world stage.

The Cuban Rebellion Begins Cuba was one of Spain's oldest colonies in the Americas. Its sugarcane plantations generated considerable wealth for Spain and produced nearly one-third of the world's sugar in the mid-1800s. Until Spain abolished slavery in 1886, about one-third of the Cuban population was enslaved and forced to work for wealthy landowners on the plantations.

In 1868 Cuban rebels declared independence and launched a guerrilla war against Spanish authorities. Lacking internal support, the rebellion collapsed in 1878. Many Cuban rebels then fled to the United States, where they began planning a new revolution.

One of the exiled leaders was **José Martí,** a writer and poet who was passionately committed to the cause of Cuban independence. While living in New York City in the 1880s, Martí brought together different Cuban exile groups living in the United States. The groups raised funds from sympathetic Americans, purchased weapons, and trained their troops in preparation for an invasion of Cuba.

By the early 1890s, the United States and Cuba had become closely linked economically. Cuba exported much of its sugar to the United States, and Americans had invested approximately $50 million in Cuba's mines, railroads, and sugar plantations. These economic ties created a crisis in 1894, when the United States imposed new tariffs—including a tariff on sugar—in an effort to protect its troubled economy from foreign competition. The new tariff wrecked the sale of Cuban sugar in the United States and devastated the island's economy.

With Cuba in an economic crisis, Martí's followers launched a new rebellion in February 1895. Although Martí died in battle shortly after returning to Cuba, the revolutionaries seized control of eastern Cuba, declared independence, and formally established the Republic of Cuba in September 1895.

Americans Support the Cubans When the uprising in Cuba began, President Grover Cleveland declared the United States neutral. Outside the White House, however, much of the public openly supported the rebels. Some citizens compared the Cubans' struggle to the American Revolution. A few sympathetic Americans even began smuggling guns from Florida to the Cuban rebels.

What led most Americans to support the rebels were the dramatic stories of Spanish atrocities reported in two of the nation's major newspapers, the *New York Journal* and the *New York World*. The *Journal*, owned by **William Randolph Hearst,** and the *World*, owned by **Joseph Pulitzer,** competed with each other to increase their circulation. The *Journal* reported outrageous stories of the Spanish feeding Cuban prisoners to sharks and dogs. Not to be outdone, the *World* described Cuba as a place with "blood on the roadsides, blood in the fields, blood on the doorsteps, blood, blood, blood!" This kind of sensationalist reporting, in which writers often exaggerated or even made up stories to attract readers, became known as yellow journalism.

Although the press invented sensational stories to sell more papers, there is no doubt that the Cuban people indeed suffered horribly. The Spanish dispatched nearly 200,000 troops to the island to put down

Reading Strategy   READING THE TEXT

Summarizing Information After students have read through the section, ask them to summarize the causes of the Spanish-American War. They should do this by writing a newspaper article from the following points of view: a Rough Rider, a yellow journalist, a wife of a crew member of the *Maine*, or a Cuban who was forced to live in a reconcentration camp. Have students pair up and critique one another's articles. **L1**

Refer to *Inclusion for the High School Social Studies Classroom Strategies and Activities* in the TCR.

the rebellion and appointed General Valeriano Weyler to serve as governor. Weyler's harsh policies quickly earned him the nickname *El Carnicero* ("The Butcher").

The Cuban rebels carried out a guerrilla war. They staged hit-and-run raids, burned plantations and sugar mills, tore up railroad tracks, and attacked supply depots. The rebels knew that many American businesses had invested in Cuba's railroads and plantations. They hoped that the destruction of American property would lead to American intervention in the war.

To prevent Cuban villagers from helping the rebels, Weyler herded hundreds of thousands of rural men, women, and children into "reconcentration camps," where tens of thousands died of starvation and disease. News reports of this brutal treatment of civilians enraged Americans and led to renewed calls for American intervention in the war.

Calling Out for War In 1897 Republican William McKinley became president of the United States. The new president did not want to intervene in the war, believing it would cost too many lives and hurt the economy. In September 1897, he asked the Spanish if the United States could help negotiate an end to the conflict. He made it clear that if the war did not end soon, the United States might have to intervene.

Pressed by McKinley, the Spanish government removed Weyler from power. Spain then offered the Cubans autonomy—the right to their own government—but only if Cuba remained part of the Spanish empire. The Cuban rebels refused to negotiate. They wanted full independence.

Spain's concessions to the rebels enraged many Spanish loyalists in Cuba. In January 1898, the loyalists rioted in Havana. Worried that American citizens in Cuba might be attacked, McKinley made the fateful decision to send the battleship *Maine* to Havana in case the Americans had to be evacuated.

In February 1898, the *New York Journal* printed a private letter written by **Enrique Dupuy de Lôme,** the Spanish ambassador to the United States. A Cuban agent had intercepted the letter and delivered it to the paper. It described McKinley as "weak and a bidder for the admiration of the crowd." The nation erupted in fury over the insult.

Ambassador de Lôme resigned, but before the furor could die down, the *Maine* exploded in the Havana harbor. The press promptly blamed Spain. Rapidly responding to the hysterical anger of the American public, Congress unanimously authorized the president to spend $50 million for war preparations. Shortly afterward, on March 28, 1898, a naval

court of inquiry concluded that a mine had destroyed the *Maine.* Throughout America, people began using the slogan "Remember the *Maine!*" as a rallying cry for war. By early April, President McKinley was under tremendous pressure to go to war. American mobs were demonstrating in the streets against Spain—and against McKinley for refusing to go to war.

Within the Republican Party, jingoism, or an attitude of aggressive nationalism, was very strong, especially among younger members of the party. These members were furious at McKinley for not declaring war. Assistant Secretary of the Navy **Theodore Roosevelt,** for one, raged that McKinley had "no more backbone than a chocolate éclair." Many Democrats were also demanding war, and Republicans feared that if McKinley did not go to war, the Democrats would win the presidency in 1900. Finally, on April 11, 1898, McKinley asked Congress to authorize the use of force to end the conflict in Cuba.

On April 19, Congress declared Cuba independent, demanded that Spain withdraw from the island, and authorized the president to use armed force if necessary. In response, on April 24, Spain declared war on the United States. For the first time in 50 years, the United States was at war with another nation.

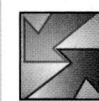 **Reading Check** **Examining** What conditions led to the Cuban rebellion in 1895?

A War on Two Fronts

The Spanish in Cuba were not prepared for war. Tropical diseases and months of hard fighting had weakened their soldiers. Their warships were old and their crews poorly trained. The United States had more battleships, and both sides knew that the war ultimately would be decided at sea. If the United States could defeat Spain's fleet, the Spanish would not be able to get supplies to its troops in Cuba. Eventually, they would have to surrender.

The United States Takes the Philippines The United States Navy was ready for war with Spain. The navy's North Atlantic Squadron blockaded Cuba, and the American fleet based in British Hong Kong was ordered to attack the Spanish fleet in the Philippines. The Philippines was a Spanish colony, and American naval planners were determined to prevent the fleet there from sailing east to attack the United States.

CHAPTER 12 Becoming a World Power **401**

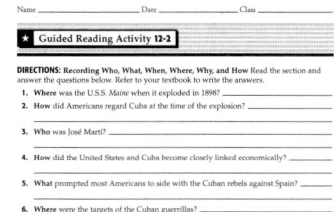
L1/ELL

Guided Reading Activity 12-2

Name _____ Date _____ Class _____

★ **Guided Reading Activity 12-2**

DIRECTIONS: Recording Who, What, When, Where, Why, and How Read the section and answer the questions below. Refer to your textbook to write the answers.
1. Where was the U.S.S. *Maine* when it exploded in 1898? _____
2. How did Americans regard Cuba at the time of the explosion? _____
3. Who was José Martí? _____
4. How did the United States and Cuba become closely linked economically? _____
5. What prompted most Americans to side with the Cuban rebels against Spain? _____
6. Where were the targets of the Cuban guerrillas? _____

 Reading Check

Answer: Spanish oppression, Spanish economic exploitation

CURRICULUM CONNECTION

Language Arts "Yellow" journalism takes its name from the "Yellow Kid" comic strip, which featured a scrappy little bald kid in a flashy yellow nightshirt. Drawn by R.F. Outcault, the comic strip first ran in 1895 in Joseph Pulitzer's *New York World.* The bright yellow ink attracted readers. Thereafter, yellow journalism came to refer to flashy, unsubstantiated news accounts.

FYI

When President McKinley asked Congress for a declaration of war, the House of Representatives voted 311 to 6 in support of the declaration. The Senate was more evenly divided, voting 42 to 35. To appease some reluctant members of Congress, the Teller Amendment was added to the declaration. The amendment called for the United States to help Cuba become an independent country once the war had ended.

DIFFERENTIATED INSTRUCTION

Reading Support Summarizing requires students to choose key ideas or events and state them concisely. Ask students to pick one of the key events in the section and draw it. *(Most students will choose the battleship explosion.)* Then have students write a sentence that explains one event that preceded the event they drew and one event that came after it. Label the sequence 1, 2, and 3. Explain that students have used drawings and descriptions to summarize a section of text. **L1**

👉 Refer to **Inclusion for the High School Social Studies Classroom Strategies and Activities** in the TCR.

Geography Skills

Answers:
1. in the Caribbean and in the Philippines
2. about 320 miles (515 kilometers)

Geography Skills Practice
Ask: Who was the leader of the Spanish fleet in the Caribbean?
(Cervera)

Creating an Absolute Chronology Have students find the dates of events in 1898 that were part of the Spanish-American War. Draw a line across the board and label it 1898. Divide the line into 12 segments to represent the months of the year. Have students enter the events in the appropriate places. Note: one source of events related to the Spanish-American War can be found at http://lcweb.loc.gov/rr/hispanic/1898/chronology.html. L2

The Tenth Cavalry was one of four African American units to serve in Cuba. Although their courage was highly praised, they were not considered equals. The U.S. Army did not abolish segregated units until 1948.

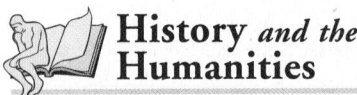

History and the Humanities

American Music: Cultural Traditions: "Battleship of Maine"

NATIONAL GEOGRAPHIC
Spanish-American War in the Philippines and the Caribbean, 1898

In Motion

Geography Skills

1. **Interpreting Maps** The main battles of the Spanish-American War occurred in which parts of the world?
2. **Applying Geography Skills** How far is the Havana harbor from the port of Tampa, Florida?

U.S. Deaths in the Spanish-American War

385 in battle

2,061 of food poisoning and disease

Source: *The Nystrom Atlas of United States History.*

A short time after midnight, on May 1, 1898, Commodore **George Dewey** led his squadron into Manila Bay in the Philippines. As dawn broke, Dewey's fleet opened fire and rapidly destroyed or captured the severely outgunned Spanish warships.

Dewey's quick victory took McKinley and his advisers by surprise. The army was not yet ready to send troops to help Dewey capture the Philippines. Hastily, the army assembled 20,000 troops to sail from San Francisco to the Philippines. On the way to the Philippines, the American troops also seized the island of Guam, another Spanish possession in the Pacific.

While waiting for the American troops to arrive, Dewey contacted **Emilio Aguinaldo,** a Filipino revolutionary leader who had staged an unsuccessful uprising against the Spanish in 1896. Aguinaldo quickly launched a new guerrilla war.

At first, Aguinaldo believed the Americans were his allies, but when American troops arrived in the islands he became suspicious. The Americans quickly seized the Philippine capital of Manila from the Spanish but refused to allow Aguinaldo's forces into the city. They also refused to recognize his rebel government. Hostility between the Filipinos and the Americans began to grow as both sides waited for the war with Spain to end.

American Forces Battle in Cuba Unlike the mobilization of the navy, which had been very efficient, the mobilization of the American army was very poorly conducted. Although volunteers flooded into army training camps, the army lacked the resources to train and equip them. In many camps, conditions were so unsanitary that epidemics broke out, and hundreds of Americans died. By the end of the war, far more Americans had died in training camps than in actual battle.

Finally, on June 14, 1898, a force of about 17,000 troops landed on the southern coast of Cuba, east of the city of Santiago. A Spanish fleet occupied Santiago Harbor, where it was well protected by powerful shore-based guns. American military planners wanted to capture those guns in order to

402 CHAPTER 12 Becoming a World Power

INTERDISCIPLINARY CONNECTIONS ACTIVITY

Language Arts Read the following quote from Walt Whitman, published in 1882:
"Long ere the second centennial arrives, there will be some forty to fifty great States, among them Canada and Cuba. . . . The Pacific will be ours, and the Atlantic mainly ours. There will be daily electric communication with every part of the globe. . . . The individuality of one nation must then, as always, lead the world. Can there be any doubt who the leader ought to be?" Discuss with students how Whitman expresses the expansionist views held by many Americans. L2

drive the Spanish fleet out of the harbor and into battle with the American fleet waiting nearby.

Among the American troops advancing toward Santiago was a volunteer cavalry unit from the American West. They were a flamboyant mix of cowboys, miners, and law officers known as the **"Rough Riders."** The commander of the Rough Riders was Colonel **Leonard Wood.** Second in command was Theodore Roosevelt, who had resigned from his post as assistant secretary of the navy to join the fight.

On July 1, American troops attacked the village of El Caney northeast of Santiago. Another force attacked the San Juan Heights, a series of hills overlooking the main road to Santiago. While one group of soldiers attacked San Juan Hill, the Rough Riders—who were on foot, not horseback—attacked Kettle Hill. After seizing Kettle Hill, Roosevelt and his men assisted in the capture of San Juan Hill.

The Rough Riders did not make their attack alone. Accompanying them up Kettle Hill were the all-black 9th and 10th Cavalry Regiments. Many African Americans had responded to the call for volunteers, and roughly one-fourth of the American troops fighting in Cuba were African American.

Four African American soldiers received the Medal of Honor for their bravery during the war.

The Spanish commander in Santiago panicked after the American victories at El Caney and the San Juan Heights. He immediately ordered the Spanish fleet in the harbor to flee. As the Spanish ships raced out of the harbor on July 3, the American warships guarding the entrance attacked them. In the ensuing battle, the American squadron sank or beached every Spanish vessel.

Spanish resistance in Cuba ended with the surrender of Santiago two weeks later. Soon after, American troops occupied the nearby Spanish colony of Puerto Rico. On August 12, 1898, Spain and the United States agreed to a cease-fire.

✓ **Reading Check** **Describing** How prepared was the U.S. Army to fight a war against Spain?

An American Empire is Born

As American and Spanish leaders met to discuss the terms for a peace treaty, Americans debated what to do about their newly acquired lands. Cuba would

NATIONAL GEOGRAPHIC
MOMENT IN HISTORY

FEISTY LEADER FOR A NEW CENTURY

Theodore Roosevelt (center) embodied the spirit of the United States at the turn of the century: full of vitality, brimming with confidence, and convinced that no job was impossible, no challenge insurmountable. Whether hunting big game in Africa, roping cattle from horseback on a Dakota ranch, or leading his "Rough Riders" cavalry (right) up San Juan Hill during the Spanish-American War, Roosevelt never did anything cautiously or quietly. As president, Roosevelt guided the country into its new, unaccustomed role as a world power.

CRITICAL THINKING ACTIVITY

Synthesizing Ask students to list reasons why a nation might be justified in declaring war on another nation. Have students incorporate their reasons into a paragraph that applies them to the United States's declaration of war on Spain in 1898. Invite volunteers to share their paragraphs with the class and discuss whether these reasons are justifiable. **L2**

Analyzing Information Have students reexamine the painting on page 391 after they have read "American Forces Battle in Cuba." **Ask:** What is the discrepancy between the painting and the facts? *(The Rough Riders were on foot, not on horseback.)* How do you think movies today affect the way that we view historical events? *(Encourage students to consider how* Saving Private Ryan *and* Pearl Harbor *mix facts with fiction.)* **L1**

✓ **Reading Check**

Answer: well prepared, with a plan to attack around Santiago to scare the Spanish fleet out of the harbor and into battle with the American Navy

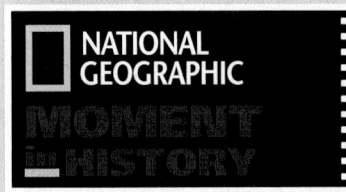
NATIONAL GEOGRAPHIC
MOMENT IN HISTORY

One of Theodore Roosevelt's greatest disappointments was President Woodrow Wilson's refusal to allow him to fight in World War I. Roosevelt was in his late 50s when the United States entered the war.

you don't say...

Literature Rudyard Kipling wrote "The White Man's Burden" in 1899 to persuade the Americans to make the Philippines a colony.

Reading Strategy

Interpreting Quotations Have students read the quote from McKinley on page 404. Then read the following quote from Andrew Carnegie: "You seem to have finished your work of civilizing the Filipinos; it is thought about 8,000 of them have been completely civilized and sent to heaven. I hope you like it." Ask students to interpret each quotation. **L2**

3 ASSESS

Assign Section 2 Assessment as homework or as an in-class activity.

⊙ Have students use the **Interactive Tutor Self-Assessment CD-ROM.**

L1/ELL

Reading Essentials and Study Guide 12–2

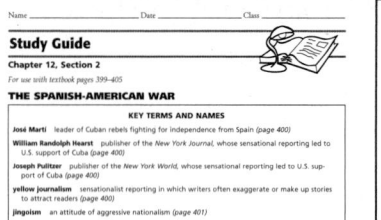

be given its freedom as promised, and Spain had agreed that the United States would annex Guam and Puerto Rico. The big question was what to do with the Philippines. The United States faced a difficult choice—remain true to its republican ideals or become an imperial power.

The Debate Over Annexation Many supporters of annexing the Philippines emphasized the economic and military benefits of taking the islands. They would provide the United States with a naval base in Asia, a stopover on the way to China, and a large market for American goods.

Other supporters believed America had a duty to teach "less civilized" peoples how to live properly. "Surely this Spanish war has not been a grab for empire," commented a New England minister, "but a heroic effort [to] free the oppressed, and to teach the millions of ignorant, debased human beings thus freed how to live."

Not all Americans supported annexation. Anti-imperialists included industrialist Andrew Carnegie, social worker Jane Addams, writer Samuel Clemens (Mark Twain), and the leader of the American Federation of Labor, Samuel Gompers. Carnegie argued that the cost of an empire far outweighed the economic benefits it provided. Gompers worried that competition from cheap Filipino labor would drive down American wages. Addams, Clemens, and others believed imperialism violated American principles.

President McKinley had to decide what to do with the Philippines. Ultimately, he decided to annex the islands. He later explained his reasoning to a group of ministers:

> ❝And one night late it came to me this way . . . (1) that we could not give them back to Spain—that would be cowardly and dishonorable; (2) that we could not turn them over to France or Germany . . . that would be bad for business and discreditable; (3) that we could not leave them to themselves—they were unfit for self-government . . . and (4) that there was nothing left for us to do but to take them all, and to educate the Filipinos, and uplift and civilize and Christianize them.❞
>
> —quoted in *A Diplomatic History of the American People*

On December 10, 1898, the United States and Spain signed the Treaty of Paris. Under the treaty, Cuba became an independent country, and the United States acquired Puerto Rico and Guam and agreed to pay Spain $20 million for the Philippines. After an intense

404 CHAPTER 12 Becoming a World Power

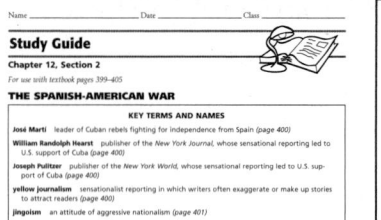
Picturing History

Building an Empire Two Filipino women nervously converse with American troops in the Philippines. Filipino civilians suffered many hardships while Filipino guerrillas fought American troops. Thousands perished from sickness, starvation, and other indirect effects of war. What American policy contributed to civilian hardships in the Philippines?

debate, the Senate ratified the treaty in February 1899. The United States had become an imperial power.

Rebellion in the Philippines The United States quickly learned that controlling its new empire would not be easy. Emilio Aguinaldo called the American decision to annex his homeland a "violent and aggressive seizure." He then ordered his troops to attack the American soldiers in the Philippines.

To fight the Filipino guerrillas, General Arthur MacArthur (the father of the future American general Douglas MacArthur) adopted many of the same policies that America had condemned Spain for using in Cuba. MacArthur set up reconcentration camps to separate guerrillas from civilians. The results were also similar to what had happened in Cuba. Thousands of Filipinos died from disease and starvation.

While MacArthur fought the guerrillas, the first U.S. civilian governor of the islands, William Howard Taft, tried to win over the Filipino people by reforming education, transportation, and health care. New railroads, bridges, and telegraph lines strengthened the economy. A public school system was set up, and new health care policies virtually eliminated severe diseases such as cholera and smallpox. These reforms slowly reduced Filipino hostility.

Emilio Aguinaldo

EXTENDING THE CONTENT

Puerto Rican Independence Eugenio María de Hostos y Bonilla championed the cause of independence for Puerto Rico. He lived and worked in New York City from 1898 to 1900 pursuing avenues to allow the people of Puerto Rico, through popular vote, to determine the future status of the island. He was a member of a delegation that delivered this demand to President McKinley. He was also a prolific writer who supported the causes of abolition and women's rights.

In March 1901, American troops captured Aguinaldo. The following month, Aguinaldo accepted American control of the islands and called on the guerrillas to surrender. By summer 1902, the United States had declared the war over. Eventually the United States allowed the Filipinos a greater role in governing their own country. By the mid-1930s, they were permitted to elect their own congress and president. Finally, in 1946, the United States granted independence to the Philippines.

GOVERNMENT

Governing Puerto Rico Another pressing question facing the United States government was how to govern Puerto Rico. In 1900 Congress passed the **Foraker Act,** making Puerto Rico an unincorporated territory. This meant that Puerto Ricans were not U.S. citizens and had no constitutional rights. The act also stated that Congress could pass whatever laws it wanted for the island.

Congress gradually allowed the inhabitants of Puerto Rico a certain degree of self-government. In 1917 the United States made Puerto Ricans citizens of the United States. In 1947 the island was given the right to elect its own governor. At this time a debate began over whether to grant Puerto Rico statehood, allow it to become an independent country, or continue it as a commonwealth of the United States. This debate over Puerto Rico's status continues today.

Cuba and the Platt Amendment After the war, the United States established a military government in Cuba. Although the United States had promised to grant Cuba its independence, President McKinley took steps to ensure that Cuba would remain tied to the United States. He allowed the Cubans to prepare a new constitution for their country, but he attached conditions. A special amendment that Senator Orville Platt attached to the 1901 army appropriations bill described those conditions.

The **Platt Amendment** specified the following: (1) Cuba could not make any treaty with another nation that would weaken its independence or allow another foreign power to gain territory in Cuba; (2) Cuba had to allow the United States to buy or lease naval stations in Cuba; (3) Cuba's debts had to be kept low to prevent foreign countries from landing troops to enforce payment; and (4) the United States would have the right to intervene to protect Cuban independence and keep order.

Although the Cubans rejected the Platt Amendment at first, they quickly realized that unless they accepted it, the United States would maintain its military government of the island. Reluctantly, they added the amendment to their constitution. The Platt Amendment governed relations between the United States and Cuba until its repeal in 1934. It effectively made Cuba an American protectorate.

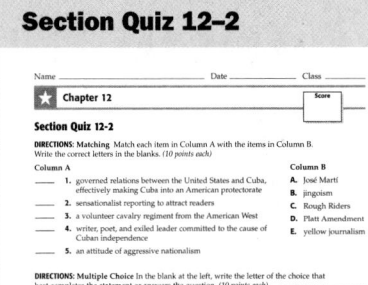

Student Web Activity Visit the *American Republic Since 1877* Web site at tarvol2.glencoe.com and click on **Student Web Activities— Chapter 12** for an activity on American imperialism.

Reading Check **Explaining** What were the arguments for and against establishing an American empire?

 Study Central™ To review this section, go to tarvol2.glencoe.com and click on **Study Central™.**

SECTION 2 ASSESSMENT

Checking for Understanding
1. **Define:** yellow journalism, jingoism.
2. **Identify:** José Martí, William Randolph Hearst, Joseph Pulitzer, Theodore Roosevelt, Platt Amendment.
3. **Explain** why many Americans blamed Spain for the explosion of the U.S.S. *Maine.*

Reviewing Themes
4. **Government and Democracy** Why did many Filipinos feel betrayed by the U.S. government after the Spanish-American War?

Critical Thinking
5. **Interpreting** Do you think President McKinley could have taken a different course of action with Spain over Cuba? If so, what kind? If not, why not?
6. **Categorizing** Complete a graphic organizer by summarizing the effects of the United States annexing lands obtained after the Spanish-American War.

Lands Annexed	Effects

Analyzing Visuals
7. **Analyzing Art** Examine the painting on page 391. Considering what you have learned about the Rough Riders and this battle, what is inaccurate about the painting? What kind of artistic bias is evident in this painting?

Writing About History
8. **Descriptive Writing** Imagine that you are a Filipino living during the time of the U.S. annexation of the Philippine Islands. Write a journal entry in which you describe your feelings about U.S. control of the islands.

CHAPTER 12 Becoming a World Power **405**

SECTION 2 ASSESSMENT ANSWERS

1. Terms are in blue.
2. José Martí (p. 400), William Randolph Hearst (p. 400), Joseph Pulitzer (p. 400), Theodore Roosevelt (p. 401), Platt Amendment (p. 405)
3. Cuba was fighting Spain for its independence, and many

Americans saw the Spanish as tyrants.
4. The Filipinos did not want their homeland annexed.
5. Students' answers will vary.
6. Puerto Rico: U.S. control of its government, Puerto Ricans: are U.S. citizens from 1917; Philippines: provide a naval base to guard U.S.

trade; some improvements in Filipino schools, roads, and healthcare
7. They are on horseback in the painting; they were actually on foot. It glorifies the Rough Riders.
8. Journal entries will vary. Entries should be written from the point of view of a Filipino.

L2

Section Quiz 12–2

Name _____ Date _____ Class _____

★ Chapter 12   Score

Section Quiz 12–2

DIRECTIONS: Matching Match each item in Column A with the items in Column B. Write the correct letters in the blanks. *(10 points each)*

Column A
____ 1. governed relations between the United States and Cuba, effectively making Cuba into an American protectorate
____ 2. sensationalist reporting to attract readers
____ 3. a volunteer cavalry regiment from the American West
____ 4. writer, poet, and exiled leader committed to the cause of Cuban independence
____ 5. an attitude of aggressive nationalism

Column B
A. José Martí
B. jingoism
C. Rough Riders
D. Platt Amendment
E. yellow journalism

DIRECTIONS: Multiple Choice In the blank at the left, write the letter of the choice that best completes the statement or answers the question. *(10 points each)*

Reteach
Have students explain the significance of 1898.

Enrich
Have students write reports explaining a commonwealth government.

HISTORY Online

Objectives and answers to the student activity can be found in the **Web Activity Lesson Plan** at tarvol2.glencoe.com.

Reading Check

Answer: For: a naval base in Asia and a market for American goods; to teach the less fortunate. Against: cost, cheap labor might drive down American wages, competition, and violated American principles

HISTORY Online

Study Central™ provides summaries, interactive games, and online graphic organizers to help students review section content.

4 CLOSE

Have students explain how the war made the United States a world power.

405

Remind students that improved technology can sometimes provide information about a historical event. Point out that even if we know the truth today, history was shaped by what people believed at the time.

2 TEACH

Researching a Topic Have students find a history book that was published before 1976, when Rickover's team of experts issued their conclusion. Instruct students to compare the content to what appears in this feature. Have students write a paragraph based on their findings. Instruct students to prepare a bibliographic citation for the book they use. **L2**

you don't say...

Military Hardware The word *ordnance* refers to weapons, ammunition, and military vehicles, along with the tools and equipment for maintenance.

Who Sank the *Maine*?

During Cuba's revolt against Spain, the American battleship *Maine* dropped anchor in the Havana harbor to protect American interests in Cuba. On the night of February 15, 1898, the ship exploded and 266 Americans lost their lives. The United States sent a court of inquiry to Havana on February 21. Despite the lack of evidence concerning the source of the explosion, American newspapers and many public officials claimed that Spain was responsible. Pressured on all sides, President McKinley sent Spain an ultimatum that led to war. Who—or what—really sank the *Maine*?

Read the following excerpts from testimony and evidence. Then answer the questions and complete the activities that follow.

Captain Charles Sigsbee

Newspaper headline

NEW YORK JOURNAL

DESTRUCTION OF THE WAR SHIP MAINE WAS THE WORK OF AN ENEMY

From the commander and an early interview

Telegraph from the commander of the *Maine* to the secretary of the navy, February 15:

"*Maine* blown up in Havana harbor at nine forty to-night and destroyed. Many wounded and doubtless more killed or drowned. . . . Public opinion should be suspended until further report. . . . Many Spanish officers, including representatives of General Blanco, now with us to express sympathy."

—Captain Charles D. Sigsbee

The court of inquiry was interested in discovering whether the explosion had come from inside or outside the ship. If it came from inside, was it sabotage or an accident? If it came from outside, who or what caused it? Before the court met, the *Washington Evening Star* published a February 18 interview with the U.S. Navy's leading ordnance expert:

"We know of no instances where the explosion of a torpedo or mine under the ship's bottom has exploded the magazine [powder and explosives] within. It has simply torn a great hole in the side or bottom, through which water entered, and in consequence of which the ship sunk. Magazine explosions, on the contrary, produce effects exactly similar to the effects of the explosion on the *Maine*. When it

comes to seeking the cause of the explosion of the *Maine's* magazine, we should naturally look not for the improbable or unusual causes. . . . The most common of these is through fires in the bunkers."

—Philip R. Alger

U.S.S. Maine

EXTENDING THE CONTENT

Artifacts from the *Maine* When the U.S.S. *Maine* was raised from Havana Harbor in 1911, some members of Congress wanted a piece. Frank B. Willis, a Representative from Ohio, claimed Captain Sigsbee's enameled-steel bathtub. After his hometown of Urbana turned down the gift of the bathtub, the people of Findlay, Ohio, claimed it. When the bathtub arrived in Findlay in 1913, disappointed citizens saw that the artifact was not quite the treasure they had hoped for. After being underwater for 14 years, the tub was rusted and ugly. Displayed in various places in Findlay over the years, it now resides in the Hancock Historical Museum.

Engraving of the explosion

From the inquiry and later reports

As the court of inquiry concluded its investigation, it considered reports of the divers who examined the *Maine* and evidence that suggested there had been two explosions. On March 11, 1898, Lieutenant Commander Adolph Marix, judge advocate of the court of inquiry, questioned Commander George A. Converse, who was brought in as a technical expert.

Marix: Looking at the plan of the *Maine*'s forward 10-inch and 6-inch magazines, would it be possible for them to have exploded, torn out the ship's side on both sides, and leave that part of the ship forward of frame 18 so water borne as to raise the after portion of that part of the ship, drag it aft, and bring the vertical keel into the condition you see in the sketch?

Converse: It is difficult for me to realize that that effect could have been produced by an explosion of the kind supposed.

Marix: Do you think, then, necessarily, there must have been an underwater mine to produce these explosions?

Converse: Indications are that an underwater explosion produced the conditions there.

In 1911 the U.S. Navy raised the *Maine* from Havana's harbor. The navy's board of inspection reexamined the ship, and its findings were similar to those of 1898. Then, in 1976, Admiral H.G. Rickover and other naval historians gathered a team of experts to examine the official court records of 1898 and 1911. This team's conclusions were very different.

1911 board conclusion:

The board finds that the injuries to the bottom of the *Maine* above described were caused by the explosion of a charge of a low form of explosive exterior to the ship between frames 28 and 31.

H.G. Rickover team conclusion:

The general character of the overall wrecked structure of the *Maine*, with hull sides and whole deck structures peeled back, leaves no doubt that a large internal explosion occurred. . . .

The mines available in 1898 are believed to have been incapable of igniting the *Maine* magazine if they exploded on the harbor bottom or against the ship side. . . . It is most unlikely that the *Maine* explosion was indeed initiated by a mine. . . .

The available evidence is consistent with an internal explosion alone. . . . The most likely source was heat from a fire in the coal bunker adjacent to the 6-inch reserve magazine.

Mast of the Maine *at Arlington National Cemetery*

Understanding the Issue

1. Why did the original investigation's conclusion that there was an underwater explosion lead to war with Spain?
2. If there had been an underwater explosion, was it logical to conclude that a Spanish person planted the mine? Why or why not? Is this an example of a biased opinion?
3. Why did the 1976 review conclude that the explosion came from inside the *Maine*?

Activities

1. **Rewriting History** Suppose that the initial court of inquiry had concluded that an internal explosion sank the *Maine.* Write a paragraph describing an alternate course history could have taken in the following year.
2. **Oral Report** Read a biography of one of these key players in the decision of the United States to go to war: Hearst, Roosevelt, or McKinley. Write a short oral presentation on this person's perspective and influence on the war.

3

Have
Under
questio.

Answers
Issue

1. People a
a torpedo
water expl
assumed tha
responsible fc
pedo and thus

2. Anyone who ha
harbor could hav
mine. Because of t.
relationship with S₁
Cuba, the Spanish w
viewed as enemies. T.
example of bias.

3. They were able to look a
wrecked structure with tl
hull sides and deck peelea
back. They also determined
that it could not have come
from outside because the
mines available in 1898 could
not have caused the kind of
damage that was inflicted on
the *Maine.*

Activities

1. Students' answers will vary.

2. Have volunteers share their oral reports with the class.

4 CLOSE

Ask students to locate information about the terrorist attack on the U.S.S. *Cole.* Have students comment on the ways that modern technology allows us to know the precise cause of tragedies in a shorter period of time.

PORTFOLIO ACTIVITY

Creating a Brochure Give students this assignment: Create a three-panel brochure explaining the history of the sinking of the *Maine.* Use the information presented in Section 2 and in this feature, along with other information gathered from library and Internet resources. Use display type and graphics to make the brochure interesting and attractive.

OCUS

Overview

on focuses on how
dency of Theodore
t helped increase
's power.

BELLRINGER
Skillbuilder Activity

Project transparency and have
students answer the question.

ly Focus Skills Transparency
–3

Reading Preview

Answers to Graphic: save time, save
money, help the United States remain
a world power

Preteaching Vocabulary
Have students choose one of the
proper names from the list of Key
Terms and Names. Ask students to
find the name and write a brief
description. Ask for volunteers to
share their explanations.

SECTION 3 New American Diplomacy

Guide to Reading

Main Idea
Under President Theodore Roosevelt, the
United States increased its power on the
world stage.

Key Terms and Names
sphere of influence, Open Door policy,
Boxer Rebellion, "Great White Fleet,"
Hay-Pauncefote Treaty, Roosevelt
Corollary, dollar diplomacy

Reading Strategy
Organizing As you read about the
increasing presence of the United States
in the world, complete a graphic organizer like the one below by listing the
reasons President Roosevelt gave for
wanting a canal in Central America.

Reasons to
Build Canal

Reading Objectives:
• **Critique** Theodore Roosevelt's foreign
policy as president.
• **Explain** the Open Door policy and its
effects on relations between the United
States and Asia.

Section Theme
Continuity and Change The commercial
interests of the United States spurred its
involvement in distant parts of the world,
such as China and Latin America.

Preview of Events

♦1898	♦1900	♦1902	♦1904

1899
Secretary of State Hay
sends first Open Door note

1900
Boxer Rebellion
erupts in China

1901
McKinley assassinated; Theodore
Roosevelt becomes president

1904
Construction of Panama
Canal begins

★ **An American Story** ★

Dr. William Gorgas

Upon arriving in Panama in 1904, Dr. William Crawford Gorgas, a U.S. Army
doctor and chief sanitary officer to the Panama Canal project, quickly realized that death
awaited American workers. The United States was about to begin constructing the Panama
Canal to connect the Atlantic and Pacific Oceans. The task would be daunting because the
dense jungles of Panama were home to swarms of mosquitoes that spread the deadly disease
of yellow fever.

Gorgas set out to lessen the threat of disease by keeping mosquitoes from breeding. He
and his crew drained swamps, gullies, and other sources of stagnant water, a main breeding
ground for mosquitoes. On those areas of water they could not drain, they spread kerosene
and oil, which killed the mosquito eggs before they hatched. They also fumigated nearly
every home in the region and destroyed many buckets, pots, and other outdoor containers
that local residents let fill up with rainwater. In two years Gorgas and his crew had wiped out
yellow fever in the area.

—adapted from *The Strength to Move a Mountain*

Theodore Roosevelt's Rise to Power

The construction of the Panama Canal might never have taken place had Theodore
Roosevelt not become president. "Teddy," as the press called him, gained the presidency
largely by accident. Roosevelt's exploits during the Spanish-American War had made

408 CHAPTER 12 Becoming a World Power

SECTION RESOURCES

📁 Reproducible Masters
• Reproducible Lesson Plan 12–3
• Daily Lecture and Discussion Notes 12–3
• Guided Reading Activity 12–3
• Section Quiz 12–3
• Reading Essentials and Study Guide 12–3
• Interpreting Political Cartoons

🔖 Transparencies
• Daily Focus Skills Transparency 12–3

Multimedia
🟦 Interactive Tutor Self-Assessment CD-ROM
🟦 ExamView® Pro Testmaker CD-ROM
🟦 Presentation Plus! CD-ROM
🟦 TeacherWorks™ CD-ROM
🎧 Audio Program

him famous and enabled him to win the election for governor of New York in November 1898. In 1900 President McKinley asked Roosevelt to run as his vice president. Less than a year later, a tragic turn of events thrust Roosevelt into the White House.

The Election of 1900 The election of 1900 once again pitted President McKinley against William Jennings Bryan. Bryan, an anti-imperialist, attacked the Republicans for their support of imperialism in Asia. McKinley focused on the country's increased prosperity. Employing the slogan "Four Years More of the Full Dinner Pail," the Republicans promised good times ahead if McKinley was reelected. He did indeed win the election by a wide margin, and Theodore Roosevelt became vice president.

On September 6, 1901, as President McKinley greeted the public during an appearance in Buffalo, New York, a gunman stepped from the crowd. The man was Leon Czolgosz, an avowed anarchist, who opposed all forms of government. Czolgosz fired two shots and hit the president. A few days later, McKinley died from his wounds.

Theodore Roosevelt, just 42 years old at the time, became the youngest person ever to become president. Roosevelt had been chosen as McKinley's running mate because Republican leaders knew his powerful charisma and heroic war record would be a great asset. They also hoped the relatively powerless position of vice president would quiet his reform-minded spirit. Now they cringed at the thought of a headstrong Roosevelt in the White House. Republican senator Mark Hanna exclaimed, "Now look, that . . . cowboy is president of the United States!"

Roosevelt Becomes President Roosevelt brought to the presidency an energy and enthusiasm rarely seen before in the office. Such vigor stemmed in part from his childhood. Born into a wealthy New York family, Roosevelt was a sickly child who endured a host of ailments, including poor eyesight and asthma.

Roosevelt pushed himself to overcome his frailties. He mastered marksmanship and horseback riding and could row up to 20 miles a day. He took up boxing and wrestling in college and continued with both throughout his life, practicing the belief that competition and conflict keep one healthy.

Roosevelt became a strong proponent of increasing American power on the world stage. Just as he refused to sit around idly in life, the

president warned Americans not to "sit huddled" and become "an assemblage of well-to-do hucksters who care nothing for what happens beyond." Roosevelt also accepted some of the ideas of Anglo-Saxonism. He believed that the United States had a duty to shape the "less civilized" corners of the earth. The new president intended to make the country a world power.

✓ **Reading Check** **Summarizing** What was President Roosevelt's opinion on the role of the United States as a world power?

American Diplomacy in Asia

In 1899 the United States was a major power in Asia, with naval bases all across the Pacific. Operating from those bases, the United States Navy—now the third largest in the world—was capable of exerting American power anywhere in East Asia.

The nation's primary interest in Asia, however, was not conquest but commerce. Between 1895 and 1900, American exports to China increased by four times. Although China bought only about two percent of all the goods exported by the United States, the vast Chinese markets excited American business leaders, especially those in the textile, oil, and steel industries.

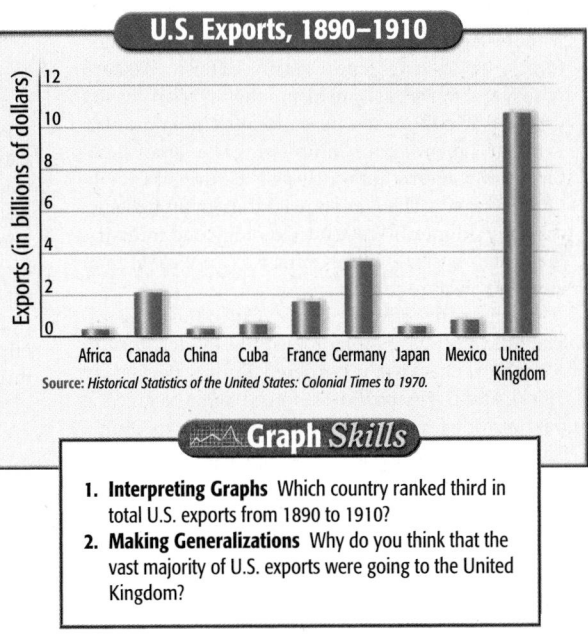

U.S. Exports, 1890–1910

Source: *Historical Statistics of the United States: Colonial Times to 1970.*

Graph *Skills*

1. **Interpreting Graphs** Which country ranked third in total U.S. exports from 1890 to 1910?
2. **Making Generalizations** Why do you think that the vast majority of U.S. exports were going to the United Kingdom?

CHAPTER 12   Becoming a World Power   **409**

2 TEACH

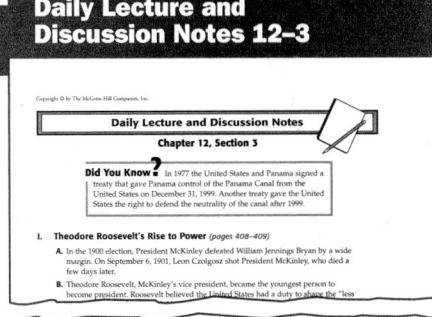

Daily Lecture and Discussion Notes 12–3

Copyright © by The McGraw-Hill Companies, Inc.

Daily Lecture and Discussion Notes
Chapter 12, Section 3

Did You Know? In 1977 the United States and Panama signed a treaty that gave Panama control of the Panama Canal from the United States on December 31, 1999. Another treaty gave the United States the right to defend the neutrality of the canal after 1999.

I. **Theodore Roosevelt's Rise to Power** *(pages 408–409)*

A. In the 1900 election, President McKinley defeated William Jennings Bryan by a wide margin. On September 6, 1901, Leon Czolgosz shot President McKinley, who died a few days later.

B. Theodore Roosevelt, McKinley's vice president, became the youngest person to become president. Roosevelt believed the United States had a duty to shape the "less

✓ **Reading Check**

Answer: that it should shape "less civilized" nations

Analyzing a Quote Read this statement by Theodore Roosevelt: "I wish to preach, not the doctrine of ignoble ease, but the doctrine of the strenuous life, the life of toil and effort, of labor and strife…." **Ask students:** How might Roosevelt conduct foreign affairs? *(He might try to expand the American empire, not content with American gains.)* **L1**

Graph *Skills*

Answers:
1. Canada
2. They had long been America's main trading partner.

Graph Skills Practice
Ask: Trade with China increased between 1895 and 1900, but how did it rank in 1910? *(at the bottom, with Africa and Japan)*

Reading Strategy   READING THE TEXT

Using Word Maps Graphic organizers, such as word maps, help students understand the structure of a chapter or section. Ask students to create a word map showing a central bubble with the name *Teddy Roosevelt.* Have students draw surrounding bubbles, linking each to the center bubble with a line. Ask students to fill in these bubbles with the main heads of the section. As they read through the section, have them write the main points of each sub-category in additional linking bubbles. **L1**

📁 Refer to *Inclusion for the High School Social Studies Classroom Strategies and Activities* in the TCR.

L1/ELL

Guided Reading Activity 12–3

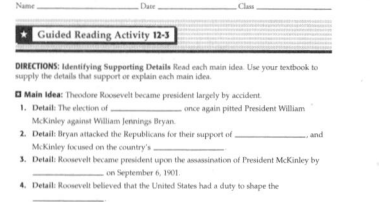

Name _____ Date _____ Class _____

★ Guided Reading Activity 12-3

DIRECTIONS: Identifying Supporting Details Read each main idea. Use your textbook to supply the details that support or explain each main idea.

☐ **Main Idea:** Theodore Roosevelt became president largely by accident.

1. **Detail:** The election of _____ once again pitted President William McKinley against William Jennings Bryan.
2. **Detail:** Bryan attacked the Republicans for their support of _____ and McKinley focused on the country's _____
3. **Detail:** Roosevelt became president upon the assassination of President McKinley by _____ on September 6, 1901.
4. **Detail:** Roosevelt believed that the United States had a duty to shape the

☐ **Main Idea:** The nation's interest in Asia was reawakened but somewhere

Why It Matters

In recent years, the volume of cargo passing through the Panama Canal has increased significantly with the growth of world trade.

FYI

The Boxers, also known as the Righteous and Harmonious Fists, were members of a secret society opposed to foreign influence in China. As the Boxers laid siege to the foreign legations in Beijing, diplomats, foreign civilians, and Chinese Christians were trapped behind barricades for nearly 60 days before an international rescue team ended the uprising.

you don't say...

Anti-Imperialist William Jennings Bryan was nominated for president three times. He lost in 1896, 1900, and 1908. In part his anti-imperialist stand helped defeat him. He did go on to become secretary of state under President Woodrow Wilson. In that post Bryan continued to oppose U.S. expansionist policies.

📁 Use *Interpreting Political Cartoons,* Cartoon 18.

Why It Matters

The Panama Canal

One of the most impressive feats of engineering in the world, the Panama Canal was built under a 1903 U.S. treaty with Panama. It took 10 years to build, required more than 40,000 laborers, and cost almost $390 million. The canal stretches 50 miles (80 km) across the mountainous regions of Panama. In 1977 a new treaty took effect that gave Panama control of the canal as of December 31, 1999.

A Cartoonist's View ➤
Many people criticized Roosevelt's role in building the Panama Canal. They believed that he was trying to dominate Latin America. The canal was also costly in terms of human life. Accidents and disease claimed the lives of 5,609 people, including about 4,500 Caribbean laborers.

THE MAN WHO CAN MAKE THE DIRT FLY.

▲ Trade
Nearly 13,000 oceangoing vessels pass through the canal annually. Roughly 60 percent of the cargo is coming from or going to U.S. ports. The canal's relative share of world cargo has declined somewhat, but its absolute volume has grown with the continued expansion of global trade.

The Open Door Policy In 1894 war erupted between China and Japan over Korea, which at that time was part of the Chinese empire. European and American leaders expected China, with its massive armed forces, to defeat Japan easily. These Western observers were astonished when Japan easily defeated China. In the peace treaty, China granted Korea independence. China also gave Japan territory in Manchuria that included the important city of Port Arthur. The war showed that Japan had successfully adopted Western technology and industry. It also demonstrated that China was far weaker than anyone had thought.

Japan's rising power greatly worried the Russians. They did not want Japan to acquire the territory in Manchuria, because it bordered Russia. Backed by France and Germany, Russia forced Japan to give the part of Manchuria it had acquired back to China. Then, in 1898, Russia demanded that China lease the territory to Russia instead.

Leasing a territory meant that it would still belong to China, even though a foreign government would maintain overall control. Germany and France demanded leaseholds in China, and Britain insisted on several as well. Each "leasehold" became

the center of a country's sphere of influence, an area where a foreign nation controlled economic development such as railroad construction and mining.

These events in northern China greatly worried the United States. President McKinley and Secretary of State John Hay both supported what they called an Open Door policy, in which all countries should be allowed to trade with China. In 1899 Hay sent notes to countries with leaseholds in China asking them not to discriminate against other nations that wanted to do business with the Chinese inside each leasehold. The Europeans and Japanese received the Open Door proposals coolly. Each power claimed to accept them in principle but refused to act on them unless all of the others agreed to do so as well. Hay refused to consider this a rebuff. Once he had received assurances from all of the great powers, he declared that the United States expected the other powers to abide by the plan.

The Boxer Rebellion While foreign countries debated who should control China, secret Chinese societies were organizing to get rid of foreign control. Westerners referred to one such group as the Boxers. In 1900 the group rose up to wipe out "foreign

410 CHAPTER 12 Becoming a World Power

DIFFERENTIATED INSTRUCTION

Visual/Spatial Provide students with a world map. Have them trace the water route from San Francisco to New York City around Cape Horn, using the map's scale to calculate the approximate distance. *(about 13,000 miles)* Next, have students trace the route by ship from San Francisco to New York City via the Panama Canal and calculate that distance. *(about 5,200 miles)* Have students write a sentence explaining how the Panama Canal improved United States trade and business. **L2**

📁 Refer to *Inclusion for the High School Social Studies Classroom Strategies and Activities* in the TCR.

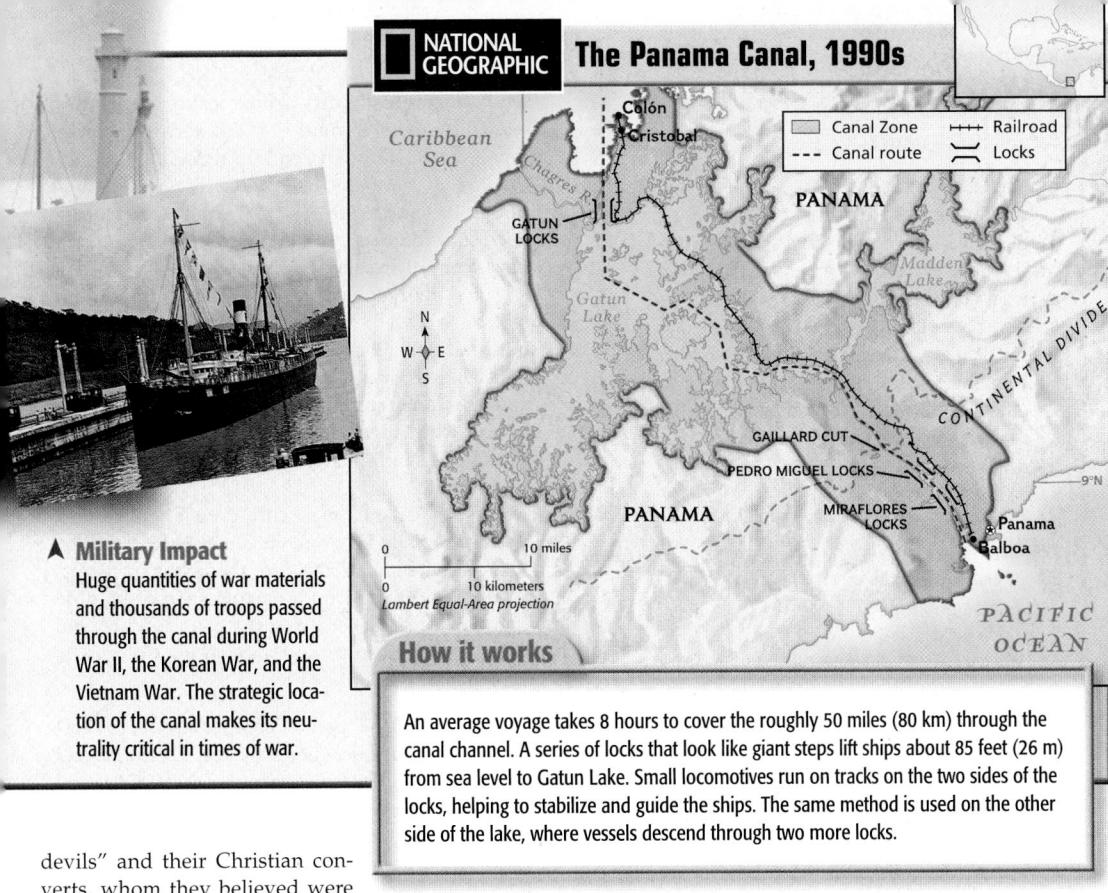

NATIONAL GEOGRAPHIC **The Panama Canal, 1990s**

Caribbean Sea

Colón
Cristobal

GATUN LOCKS

Chagres R.

Gatun Lake

Madden Lake

PANAMA

CONTINENTAL DIVIDE

GAILLARD CUT
PEDRO MIGUEL LOCKS
MIRAFLORES LOCKS

PANAMA

Panama
Balboa

9°N

PACIFIC OCEAN

Canal Zone   Railroad
Canal route   Locks

N
W   E
S

0   10 miles
0   10 kilometers
Lambert Equal-Area projection

▲ **Military Impact**
Huge quantities of war materials and thousands of troops passed through the canal during World War II, the Korean War, and the Vietnam War. The strategic location of the canal makes its neutrality critical in times of war.

How it works

An average voyage takes 8 hours to cover the roughly 50 miles (80 km) through the canal channel. A series of locks that look like giant steps lift ships about 85 feet (26 m) from sea level to Gatun Lake. Small locomotives run on tracks on the two sides of the locks, helping to stabilize and guide the ships. The same method is used on the other side of the lake, where vessels descend through two more locks.

CURRICULUM CONNECTION

Science Constructing the Panama Canal involved three main engineering projects. First, the workers had to excavate the Gaillard Cut, which was 300 feet (91 meters) wide across the isthmus. Next, they had to build a dam across the Chagres River to create an artificial lake. Finally, they had to construct the canal's locks. The hardest job was digging the Gaillard Cut, because the hill through which the cut runs consists of soft volcanic material. When workers dug a hole, more rock and earth would slide into the space or push up from below.

FYI

John Hay studied law in an office next to Abraham Lincoln. He was Lincoln's assistant private secretary when Lincoln was president.

you don't say...

Regulating the Canal Water flows in and out of the locks by gravity, so no pumps are needed. Locks are used to handle changes in elevation along the course of the canal and in tide level near the seacoast. *Cut* is an engineering term for an artificially created passageway or channel.

---

devils" and their Christian converts, whom they believed were corrupting Chinese society. In what became known as the **Boxer Rebellion,** group members besieged foreign embassies in Beijing, killing more than 200 foreigners and taking others prisoner. In August 1900, an international force that included U.S. troops stepped in and quashed the rebellion.

During the crisis, Secretary of State Hay and British leaders worked to persuade European nations not to use the Boxer Rebellion as an excuse to partition China. In a second set of Open Door notes, Hay convinced the participating powers to back away from a full-scale retaliation against China. He urged them instead to accept compensation from China for any damage that the rebellion caused. After some discussion, China was never broken up into colonies. As a result, the United States retained access to China's lucrative trade in tea, spices, and silk and maintained an increasingly larger market for its own goods.

Balancing Power in East Asia As president, Theodore Roosevelt supported the Open Door policy in China and worked to prevent any single nation from monopolizing trade there. This concern prompted Roosevelt to step in to help negotiate peace

in a war between Japan and Russia in 1905. At a peace conference in Portsmouth, New Hampshire, Roosevelt convinced the Russians to recognize Japan's territorial gains and persuaded the Japanese to stop fighting and to seek no further territory. For his efforts in ending the war, Roosevelt won the Nobel Peace Prize in 1906.

In the years after the peace treaty, relations between the United States and Japan steadily grew worse. As the two nations vied for greater influence in Asia, they held each other in check through a series of agreements. They agreed to respect each other's territorial possessions, to uphold the Open Door policy, and to support China's independence.

In 1907 President Roosevelt sent 16 battleships of the new United States Navy, known as the **"Great White Fleet,"** on a voyage around the world to showcase the nation's military might. The tour made a stop in Japan to demonstrate that the United States could and would uphold its interests in Asia. This visit did not help ease the growing tensions between the two countries throughout the early 1900s.

✓ **Reading Check** **Explaining** What was the purpose of the Open Door policy?

CHAPTER 12   Becoming a World Power   **411**

✓**Reading Check**

Answer: to ensure that all nations had access to China's market

---

INTERDISCIPLINARY CONNECTIONS ACTIVITY

Economics Ask students to use library and Internet resources to identify the products that were traded between the countries involved with China. Based on their research, have students create a chart showing the trading relationships among the various nations. Also, ask them to write a position paper supporting or opposing the Open Door policy. **L3**

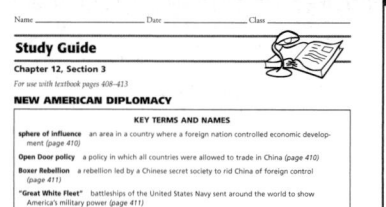

Answer: It reduced shipping time between Europe and Asia.

Ask: How do you think the Suez Canal affected Africa? *(It enriched Egypt, which controlled the canal, but it hurt ports along the western and southern coasts of Africa.)*

FYI

Many U.S. legislators opposed Roosevelt's corollary, claiming that his actions were unconstitutional because it was the Senate's right to make such decisions. Most Americans approved of the corollary, however, so the Senate agreed in 1907 to a treaty that maintained United States control of Dominican customs.

3 ASSESS

Assign Section 3 Assessment as homework or as an in-class activity.

⊕ Have students use the **Interactive Tutor Self-Assessment CD-ROM.**

L1/ELL

Reading Essentials and Study Guide 12–3

Name _____ Date _____ Class _____

Study Guide

Chapter 12, Section 3
For use with textbook pages 408–413

NEW AMERICAN DIPLOMACY

KEY TERMS AND NAMES

sphere of influence an area in a country where a foreign nation controlled economic development *(page 410)*
Open Door policy a policy in which all countries were allowed to trade in China *(page 410)*
Boxer Rebellion a rebellion led by a Chinese secret society to rid China of foreign control *(page 411)*
"Great White Fleet" battleships of the United States Navy sent around the world to show America's military power *(page 411)*
Hay-Pauncefote Treaty the treaty that gave the United States the exclusive right to build and control a canal through Central America *(page 412)*

World History
Connection

The Suez Canal

Forty-five years before the Panama Canal was completed, another canal opened that dramatically changed world trade patterns. In 1869 a French company, led by Ferdinand de Lesseps, completed work on the Suez Canal after more than 10 years of construction.

The Suez Canal is located in Egypt. It connects the Mediterranean Sea to the Red Sea, creating a shortcut for ships traveling from Europe to the Indian Ocean. Before the canal's opening, ships had to travel around Africa to reach India and countries in East Asia. The canal greatly reduced travel times between Europe and Asia and rapidly became one of the world's major shipping lanes. *How did the canal change world trade patterns?*

Route After Suez Canal

Route Before Suez Canal

A Growing Presence in the Caribbean

Theodore Roosevelt believed in a strong global military presence. He insisted that displaying American power to the world would make nations think twice about fighting, thus promoting global peace. He often expressed this belief with a West African saying, "Speak softly and carry a big stick." Roosevelt's "big stick" policy was perhaps most evident in the Caribbean.

GEOGRAPHY

The Panama Canal One of Roosevelt's most dramatic actions in the Caribbean was the acquisition of the Panama Canal Zone in 1903. Roosevelt and others viewed the construction of a canal through Central America as vital to American power in the world. A canal would save time and money for both commercial and military shipping.

As early as 1850, the United States and Great Britain had signed a treaty in which each nation had agreed not to build a canal without the other's participation. Because of its strong interest in a canal, however, the United States negotiated a new treaty. In 1901, the United States and Great Britain signed the

---

Hay-Pauncefote Treaty, which gave the United States the exclusive right to build and control any proposed canal through Central America.

A French company had begun digging a canal through Panama in 1881. By 1889, however, it abandoned its efforts because of bankruptcy and terrible losses from disease among the workers. The company was reorganized in 1894, but its operations practically ceased and its only hope was to sell its rights to digging the canal.

The United States had long considered two possible canal sites, one through Nicaragua and one through Panama. The French company eased this choice by offering to sell its rights and property in Panama to the United States.

In 1903 Panama was still part of Colombia. Secretary of State Hay offered Colombia $10 million and a yearly rent of $250,000 for the right to construct the canal and to control a narrow strip of land on either side of it. Considering the price too low and afraid of losing control of Panama, the Colombian government refused the offer.

Revolt in Panama Some Panamanians feared losing the commercial benefits of the canal. Panama had opposed Colombian rule since the mid-1800s, and the canal issue added to the tensions. In addition, the French company was still concerned that the United States would build the canal in Nicaragua instead. The French company's agent, Philippe Bunau-Varilla, and Panamanian officials decided that the only way to ensure the canal would be built was to declare independence and make their own deal with the United States. Bunau-Varilla arranged for a small army to stage an uprising in Panama.

On November 3, 1903, Bunau-Varilla's forces revolted. Meanwhile, President Roosevelt sent ships to Panama to prevent Colombian interference. Within a few days, the United States recognized Panama's independence. Less than two weeks later, the two nations signed a treaty allowing the canal to be built.

Protesters in the United States and throughout Latin America condemned Roosevelt's actions as unjustifiable aggression. The president countered that he had advanced "the needs of collective civilization" by building a canal that shortened the distance between the Atlantic and the Pacific by about 8,000 nautical miles (14,816 km).

The Roosevelt Corollary The growing American involvement in foreign affairs caused Roosevelt to expand his "big stick" diplomacy. In an address to Congress in 1904, the president defined what came

---

CRITICAL THINKING ACTIVITY

Analyzing Work with students to create a list of personal qualities and conditions that are essential for world leaders if they are to be successful mediators between antagonistic nations. Have students read about prominent world leaders, noting the tactics and negotiation strategies they have employed in order to resolve conflicts. Then have students develop a list of conflict resolution strategies to use in daily situations. **L2**

to be known as the **Roosevelt Corollary** to the Monroe Doctrine. To prevent European nations from sending troops to the Caribbean or Central America, he announced that the United States would intervene in Latin American affairs when necessary to maintain stability in the Western Hemisphere:

❝Chronic wrongdoing . . . may, in America, as elsewhere, ultimately require intervention by some civilized nation, and in the Western Hemisphere the adherence of the United States to the Monroe Doctrine may force the United States, however reluctantly . . . to the exercise of an international police power.❞

—quoted in *The Growth of the United States*

The United States first applied the Roosevelt Corollary in the Dominican Republic, which had fallen behind on its debt payments to European nations. In 1905, worried that the Europeans were getting ready to send troops, Roosevelt sent American marines to the Dominican Republic to collect customs tariffs to make the debt payments.

Latin American nations resented the growing American influence in the region. Roosevelt's successor, William Howard Taft, continued Roosevelt's policies, however, with an emphasis on helping Latin American industry. He believed that if American business leaders supported Latin American development, everyone would benefit. The United States would increase its trade, American businesses would increase their profits, and countries in Latin America would rise out of poverty and social disorder, and European nations would have no reason to intervene in the region. Taft's policy came to be called **dollar diplomacy.**

Analyzing *Political Cartoons*

American Imperialism This cartoon displays Roosevelt's belief that the United States should "speak softly and carry a big stick" in foreign affairs. In what part of the world did Roosevelt's quote originate?

Although Taft described his brand of diplomacy as "substituting dollars for bullets," in Nicaragua he used both. In 1911 American bankers began making loans to Nicaragua to support its shaky government. The following year, civil unrest forced the Nicaraguan president to appeal for greater assistance. American marines entered the country, replaced the collector of customs with an American agent, and formed a committee of two Americans and one Nicaraguan to control the customs commissions. American troops stayed to support both the government and customs until 1925.

Reading Check **Describing** What did the Roosevelt Corollary state?

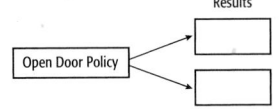
Study Central™ To review this section, go to **tarvol2.glencoe.com** and click on **Study Central™.**

SECTION 3 ASSESSMENT

Checking for Understanding

1. **Define:** sphere of influence, Open Door policy, dollar diplomacy.
2. **Identify:** Boxer Rebellion, "Great White Fleet," Hay-Pauncefote Treaty, Roosevelt Corollary.

Reviewing Themes

3. **Continuity and Change** Why do you think Latin American nations resented American influence in the region?

Critical Thinking

4. **Analyzing** How did the Open Door policy and dollar diplomacy affect U.S. relations with other countries?
5. **Organizing** Use a graphic organizer to summarize the results of the Open Door policy in China.

Open Door Policy → Results

Analyzing Visuals

6. **Analyzing Graphs** Examine the graph on page 409. Why do you think such a small number of U.S. exports went to China and Japan?

Writing About History

7. **Persuasive Writing** Imagine you are Theodore Roosevelt, and write a speech justifying the actions that led to the building of the Panama Canal. Be specific in your reasons.

SECTION 3 ASSESSMENT ANSWERS

1. Terms are in blue.
2. Boxer Rebellion (*p. 411*), "Great White Fleet" (*p. 411*), Hay Pauncefote Treaty (*p. 412*), Roosevelt Corollary (*p. 413*)
3. Students' answers will vary. Possible answers: They wanted the right to self-determination. They knew that America would act in its

own interests, not the interests of Latin American countries.
4. The Open Door policy kept China open to U.S. trade; dollar diplomacy generally created Latin American resentment.
5. all countries could trade with China; prevented warfare between competing nations

6. Possible answers: American products were in little demand; Chinese and Japanese could not afford them.
7. Students' speeches will vary. Speeches should include benefits to the United States and other countries.

Analyzing *Political Cartoons*

Answer: West Africa

Ask: How did a "big stick" promote peace? *(It would discourage nations from fighting.)*

Reteach

Have students critique Theodore Roosevelt's rise to the presidency.

Enrich

Have interested students create a game that illustrates the struggle among world powers for control of China's market in the early 1900s.

Reading Check

Answer: The United States would intervene in Latin America to prevent European intervention and to maintain stability in the Western Hemisphere.

Study Central™ provides summaries, interactive games, and online graphic organizers to help students review section content.

4 CLOSE

Have students explain the Open Door policy and its effects on relations between the United States and Asia.

413

CHAPTER 12 ASSESSMENT and ACTIVITIES

CHAPTER 12 ASSESSMENT and ACTIVITIES

GLENCOE TECHNOLOGY

MindJogger Videoquiz
Use the **MindJogger Videoquiz** to review Chapter 12 content.

⊙ Available in DVD

Reviewing Key Terms
Students' answers will vary. The pages where the words appear in the text are shown in parentheses.

1. **imperialism** *(p. 393)*
2. **protectorate** *(p. 393)*
3. **yellow journalism** *(p. 400)*
4. **jingoism** *(p. 401)*
5. **sphere of influence** *(p. 410)*
6. **Open Door policy** *(p. 410)*
7. **dollar diplomacy** *(p. 413)*

Reviewing Key Facts

8. Mathew C. Perry *(p. 394)*, Queen Liliuokalani *(p. 395)*, Alfred T. Mahan *(p. 397)*, Henry Cabot Lodge *(p. 397)*, José Martí *(p. 400)*, Theodore Roosevelt *(p. 401)*, "Great White Fleet" *(p. 411)*, Roosevelt Corollary *(p. 413)*

9. It wanted to compete economically and militarily with other countries, and there was a growing feeling of superiority.

10. Newspapers that practiced yellow journalism made up outrageous stories about the Spanish treatment of the Cuban people. They inflamed American citizens' negative sentiments toward the Spanish.

11. Cuba became an independent country, the United States acquired Puerto Rico and Guam, and the United States agreed to pay Spain $20 million for the Philippines.

12. He wanted to prevent any single nation from monopolizing trade in the Far East.

Reviewing Key Terms
On a sheet of paper, use each of these terms in a sentence.

1. imperialism
2. protectorate
3. yellow journalism
4. jingoism
5. sphere of influence
6. Open Door policy
7. dollar diplomacy

Reviewing Key Facts

8. **Identify:** Matthew C. Perry, Queen Liliuokalani, Alfred T. Mahan, Henry Cabot Lodge, José Martí, Theodore Roosevelt, "Great White Fleet," Roosevelt Corollary.

9. Why did the United States seek to become a world power in the 1890s?

10. How did yellow journalism contribute to American support of the Cuban revolution?

11. What were the provisions of the Treaty of Paris of 1898?

12. Why did President Theodore Roosevelt help negotiate peace between Japan and Russia?

13. What was dollar diplomacy?

Critical Thinking

14. **Analyzing Themes: Government and Democracy** Why did American sugarcane planters in Hawaii revolt against Queen Liliuokalani?

15. **Explaining** What was the significance of the year 1898 as a turning point for the United States?

16. **Evaluating** Do you think the Panama Canal was worth the cost in terms of money spent and lives lost? Analyze the effects of physical and human geographic factors on the building of the canal to determine your answer.

17. **Interpreting Primary Sources** After the Spanish-American War, Carl Schurz, the leader of the liberal wing of the Republican Party, opposed American expansion abroad. In the following excerpt, Schurz attacks the arguments for taking over the Philippine Islands.

❝Taking a general view of the Philippines as a commercial market for us, I need not again argue against the barbarous notion that in order to have a profitable trade with a country we must own it. . . . It is equally needless to show to any well-informed person that the profits of the trade with the islands themselves can never amount to the cost of making and maintaining the conquest of the Philippines.

But there is another point of real importance. Many imperialists admit that our trade with the Philippines themselves will not nearly be worth its cost; but they say that we must have the Philippines as a foothold, a sort of power station, for the expansion of our trade on the Asiatic continent, especially in China. Admitting this, for argument's sake, I ask what kind of a foothold we should really need. Coaling stations and docks for our fleet, and facilities for the establishment of commercial houses and depots. That is all. And now I ask further, whether we could not easily have had these things if we had, instead of making war upon the Filipinos, favored the independence of the islands. Everybody knows that we could. We might have those things now for the mere asking if we stopped the war and came to a friendly understanding with the Filipinos tomorrow. . . .❞

—quoted in *The Policy of Imperialism*

Chapter Summary

U.S. Actions

In the Pacific	In Latin America
• Expanded Chinese and Japanese markets • Annexed the Midway Islands as refueling depots for expanded navy • Built coaling stations on Samoan Islands • American business leaders led successful campaign for Hawaiian annexation • Victory over Spain gave U.S. control over Guam and the Philippines	• At Pan-American Conference, invited Latin American countries to trade with U.S. • Supported Cuba's rebellion against Spain, leading to Spanish-American War; victory over Spain gave U.S. control over Cuba, Puerto Rico • Built the Panama Canal • Issued the Roosevelt Corollary stating that the U.S. would intervene in Latin America to maintain stability

13. It was the policy that placed less emphasis on military force and more on investing American dollars in Latin America.

Critical Thinking
14. She attempted to impose a new constitution and to decrease the power of American planters.

15. The United States declared war on Spain. After the war the U.S. gained territory outside the continental United States and established itself as a world power. The United States also annexed Hawaii in 1898.

16. Students' answers will vary.

17. **a.** The cost of conquest and maintaining control is more than the potential profit. **b.** We could have favored and supported their independence and kept open communication.

Self-Check Quiz

Visit the *American Republic Since 1877* Web site at
tarvol2.glencoe.com and click on *Self-Check Quizzes—
Chapter 12* to assess your knowledge of chapter content.

a. How does Schurz counter the argument that annexation of the Philippines was necessary to make the nation a commercial market for the United States?

b. What action other than annexation does Schurz suggest the United States could have taken to obtain the coaling stations, docks, and depots it needed for trade with Asia?

18. **Organizing** Using a graphic organizer similar to the one below, list ways that American imperialism affected Hawaii, Cuba, and the Philippines.

Practicing Skills

19. **Using an Electronic Spreadsheet** Enter in a spreadsheet the land area of the territories that came under U.S. control as a result of the Spanish-American War (Puerto Rico, Guam, and the Philippines). Enter the current land area of the United States in the spreadsheet. Create an equation to calculate the percentage of land that each territory represents compared to the United States land area.

Writing Activity

20. **Portfolio Writing** Imagine that you are Dr. William Gorgas. You have just arrived in Havana, where you have been assigned to address the problems of workers suffering from yellow fever. Write a letter home describing some of the conditions, problems, and needs facing you as you search for a cure. Place the letter in your portfolio.

Chapter Activity

21. **Evaluating the Validity of a Source** Use the library or the internet to find writings by people in support of and against the Spanish-American War. Evaluate the authors' points based on the language and logic they use. Then evaluate the authors' backgrounds and experience to determine if they are reliable or objective sources.

Geography and History

22. The map on this page shows the expansion of the United States in 1900. Study the map and answer the following questions.

U.S. Possessions in the Pacific, 1899

U.S. possessions with date acquired

a. **Interpreting Maps** Approximately how far west is the island of Guam from the west coast of the United States?

b. **Applying Geography Skills** Why did the United States acquire so much island territory in the Pacific?

Standardized Test Practice

Directions: Choose the best answer to the following question.

Which of the following statements about the Platt Amendment is true?

A It guaranteed that Cuba would be independent by 1915.

B It prevented the United States from intervening in Cuban foreign affairs.

C It essentially made Cuba a U.S. protectorate.

D It opened up territory in Cuba to a variety of foreign powers.

Test-Taking Tip: Eliminate answers you know are incorrect. The Platt Amendment laid out conditions desired by the United States, and so you can eliminate answers that would not be beneficial to the United States.

HISTORY Online

Have students visit the Web site at tarvol2.glencoe.com to review Chapter 12 and take the Self-Check Quiz.

Chapter Activity

21. Students' evaluations should show that they can detect bias and point of view in the writings.

Geography and History

22. **a.** approximately 6,500 miles (10,500 kilometers); **b.** for military and trade purposes

Standardized Test Practice

Answer: C
Test-Taking Tip: Remind students that if they are unsure which answer is correct, they should focus on what is known about the topic. Students might remember that the Cubans did not readily accept the Platt Amendment and that they were reluctant to add it to their constitution. Now have students look at the answers and eliminate the ones that Cuba would not have objected to, such as A and B.

Bonus Question ?

Ask: What was the cause of the Boxer Rebellion in China? *(The fear of foreign control of China caused several secret societies to band together and attack foreign embassies.)*

---

18. Hawaii: eventually became a state. Cuba: U.S. set up a military government and forced them to add the Platt Amendment to their constitution effectively making them a protectorate until 1934. Philippines: U.S. controlled the Filipino government until, by the mid-1930s, Filipinos were granted some self-government. They were granted independence in 1946.

Practicing Skills

19. Spreadsheets should contain accurate data and all columns and rows should be appropriately labeled.

Writing Activity

20. The letters should describe the facts and should provide a sense of the magnitude of the problems he encountered.

Timesaving Tools

TeacherWorks™ All-In-One Planner and Resource Center

● **Interactive Teacher Edition** Access your Teacher Wraparound Edition and your classroom resources with a few easy clicks.

● **Interactive Lesson Planner** Planning has never been easier! Organize your week, month, semester, or year with all the lesson helps you need to make teaching creative, timely, and relevant.

Use Glencoe's **Presentation Plus!** multimedia teacher tool to easily present dynamic lessons that visually excite your students. Using Microsoft PowerPoint® you can customize the presentations to create your own personalized lessons.

TEACHING TRANSPARENCIES

Graphic Organizer 13 L2

Why It Matters Chapter Transparency 13 L2

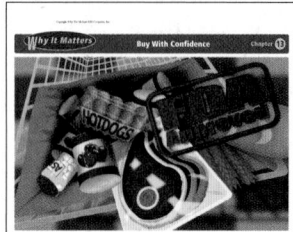

APPLICATION AND ENRICHMENT

Linking Past and Present Activity 13 L2

Enrichment Activity 13 L3

Primary Source Reading 13 L2

REVIEW AND REINFORCEMENT

Reteaching Activity 13 L1

Vocabulary Activity 13 L1

Time Line Activity 13 L2

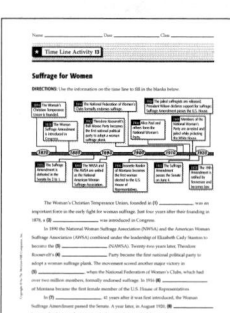

Critical Thinking Skills Activity 13 L2

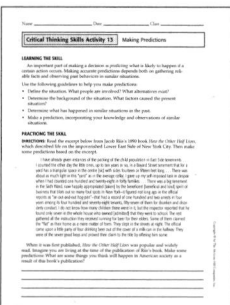

Meeting NCSS Standards

The following standards are covered in Chapter 13:

Section 1 VI Power, Authority, and Governance: A, B, I

Section 2 IV Individual Development and Identity: E, F

Section 3 II Time, Continuity, and Change: B, C, F

Section 4 VI Power, Authority, and Governance: A, F, I

Local Standards

Chapter 13 Resources

ASSESSMENT AND EVALUATION

Chapter 13 Test Form A L2

Chapter 13 Test Form B L2

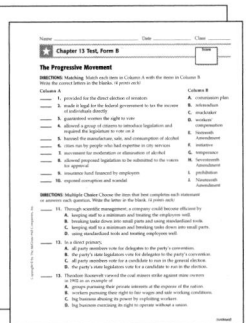

Standardized Test Practice Workbook Activity 13 L2

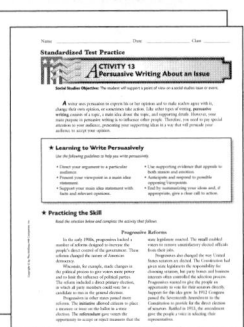

Performance Assessment Activities and Rubrics 13 L1/ELL

ExamView® Pro Testmaker CD-ROM

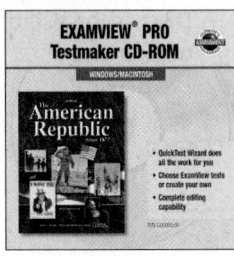

MULTIMEDIA

- Vocabulary PuzzleMaker CD-ROM
- Interactive Tutor Self-Assessment CD-ROM
- ExamView® Pro Testmaker CD-ROM
- Audio Program
- American History Primary Source Documents Library CD-ROM
- MindJogger Videoquiz
- Presentation Plus! CD-ROM
- TeacherWorks™ CD-ROM
- Interactive Student Edition CD-ROM
- Glencoe Skillbuilder Interactive Workbook CD-ROM, Level 2
- The *American Republic Since 1877* Video Program
- American Music: Hits Through History
- American Music: Cultural Traditions

SPANISH RESOURCES

The following Spanish language materials are available:

- Spanish Reading Essentials and Study Guide
- Spanish Guided Reading Activities
- Spanish Reteaching Activities
- Spanish Quizzes and Tests
- Spanish Vocabulary Activities
- Spanish Summaries
- The Declaration of Independence and United States Constitution Spanish Translation

The following videotape programs are available from Glencoe as supplements to Chapter 13:

- **Molly Brown: An American Legend** (ISBN 0-76-700767-0)
- **Susan B. Anthony: Rebel for the Cause** (ISBN 1-56-501646-7)

To order, call Glencoe at 1-800-334-7344. To find classroom resources to accompany many of these videos, check the following home pages:
A&E Television: www.aande.com
The History Channel: www.historychannel.com

Use our Web site for additional resources. All essential content is covered in the Student Edition.

You and your students can visit tarvol2.glencoe.com, the Web site companion to the *American Republic Since 1877*. This innovative integration of electronic and print media offers your students a wealth of opportunities. The student text directs students to the Web site for the following options:

- **Chapter Overviews**
- **Student Web Activities**
- **Self-Check Quizzes**
- **Textbook Updates**

Answers to the student Web activities are provided for you in the **Web Activity Lesson Plans**. Additional Web resources and Interactive Tutor Puzzles are also available.

Chapter 13 Resources

SECTION RESOURCES

Daily Objectives	Reproducible Resources	Multimedia Resources
SECTION 1 **The Roots of Progressivism** 1. Discuss the rise of the Progressive movement. 2. Evaluate the impact of initiative, referendum, and recall, and of the Seventeenth Amendment.	Reproducible Lesson Plan 13–1 Daily Lecture and Discussion Notes 13–1 Guided Reading Activity 13–1* Section Quiz 13–1* Reading Essentials and Study Guide 13–1* Performance Assessment Activities and Rubrics Interpreting Political Cartoons	Daily Focus Skills Transparency 13–1 Interactive Tutor Self-Assessment CD-ROM ExamView® Pro Testmaker CD-ROM* Presentation Plus! CD-ROM TeacherWorks™ CD-ROM Skillbuilder Interactive Workbook, Level 2 Audio Program
SECTION 2 **Roosevelt in Office** 1. Describe various efforts to regulate concentrated corporate power. 2. Discuss Theodore Roosevelt's interest in environmental conservation.	Reproducible Lesson Plan 13–2 Daily Lecture and Discussion Notes 13–2 Guided Reading Activity 13–2* Section Quiz 13–2* Reading Essentials and Study Guide 13–2* Performance Assessment Activities and Rubrics Supreme Court Case Studies	Daily Focus Skills Transparency 13–2 Interactive Tutor Self-Assessment CD-ROM ExamView® Pro Testmaker CD-ROM* Presentation Plus! CD-ROM TeacherWorks™ CD-ROM Audio Program
SECTION 3 **The Taft Administration** 1. Explain how Theodore Roosevelt helped Taft get elected. 2. Discuss why progressives were disappointed with Taft as president.	Reproducible Lesson Plan 13–3 Daily Lecture and Discussion Notes 13–3 Guided Reading Activity 13–3* Section Quiz 13–3* Reading Essentials and Study Guide 13–3* Performance Assessment Activities and Rubrics	Daily Focus Skills Transparency 13–3 Interactive Tutor Self-Assessment CD-ROM ExamView® Pro Testmaker CD-ROM* Presentation Plus! CD-ROM TeacherWorks™ CD-ROM Audio Program
SECTION 4 **The Wilson Years** 1. Describe Wilson's economic and social reforms. 2. Evaluate the legacy of the Progressive movement.	Reproducible Lesson Plan 13–4 Daily Lecture and Discussion Notes 13–4 Guided Reading Activity 13–4* Section Quiz 13–4* Reading Essentials and Study Guide 13–4* Performance Assessment Activities and Rubrics	Daily Focus Skills Transparency 13–4 Interactive Tutor Self-Assessment CD-ROM ExamView® Pro Testmaker CD-ROM* Presentation Plus! CD-ROM TeacherWorks™ CD-ROM Vocabulary PuzzleMaker CD-ROM Audio Program

0:00 OUT OF TIME?
Assign the Chapter 13 **Reading Essentials and Study Guide.**

*Also Available in Spanish

 Printed Materials   Transparency   CD-ROM   DVD

 Poster   Music Program   Audio Program

Chapter 13 Resources

NATIONAL GEOGRAPHIC   Teacher's Corner

INDEX TO NATIONAL GEOGRAPHIC MAGAZINE

The following articles relate to this chapter.

- "Central Park: Oasis in the City," May 1993
- "Chicago: Welcome to the Neighborhood," May 1991
- "Miami," January 1992
- "New Life for Ellis Island," September 1990
- "New York's Chinatown," August 1998

NATIONAL GEOGRAPHIC SOCIETY PRODUCTS

To order the following, call National Geographic at 1-800-368-2728:

- *Historical Atlas of the United States* (Atlas)
- *Immigration: The Triumph of Hope* (Video)

NGS ONLINE

Access National Geographic's Web site for current events, atlas updates, activities, links, interactive features, and archives.

www.nationalgeographic.com

MEETING SPECIAL NEEDS

In addition to the Differentiated Instruction strategies found in each section, the following resources are also suitable for your special needs students:

- *ExamView® Pro Testmaker CD-ROM* allows teachers to tailor tests by reducing answer choices.

- The *Audio Program* includes the entire narrative of the student edition so that less-proficient readers can listen to the words as they read them.

- The *Reading Essentials and Study Guide* provides the same content as the student edition but is written two grade levels below the textbook.

KEY TO ABILITY LEVELS

Teaching strategies have been coded.

- **L1** BASIC activities for all students
- **L2** AVERAGE activities for average to above-average students
- **L3** CHALLENGING activities for above-average students
- **ELL** ENGLISH LANGUAGE LEARNER activities

From the Classroom of...

Deborah Welch
Glade Valley High School
Glade Valley, NC

The Muckrakers

Organize the class into groups. Each will create a newspaper and divide the workload between editor and reporters. Each newspaper will then investigate a problem that reporters of the Progressive Era researched and prepare articles for inclusion in their paper. Possible topics include: workers' strikes and the courts, trust-busting, settlement houses, woman suffrage, presidential campaigns, temperance reform, and World War I and the issue of U.S. participation before 1917.

Encourage students to secure a "scoop." For example, one might create an interview with a resident of a settlement house. Another student might secure an interview with Roosevelt, Taft, or Wilson during the 1912 presidential campaign. Other interview subjects might include W.E.B. Du Bois in 1909 when the National Association for the Advancement of Colored People was formed.

Working with their editors, each group will put together their newspaper for the class to read. If time allows, the class might then debate the views presented in each newspaper.

ADDITIONAL RESOURCES FROM GLENCOE

- American Music: Cultural Traditions
- American Art & Architecture
- Outline Map Resource Book
- U.S. Desk Map
- Building Geography Skills for Life
- Inclusion for the High School Social Studies Classroom Strategies and Activities
- Teaching Strategies for the American History Classroom (Including Block Scheduling Pacing Guides)
- Dinah Zike's High School American History Reading and Study Skills Foldables

 Block Schedule

Activities that are suited to use within the block scheduling framework are identified by:

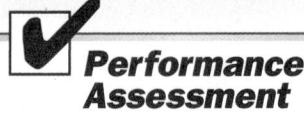

Performance Assessment

Refer to Activity 13 in the Performance Assessment Activities and Rubrics booklet.

Why It Matters Activity

Have students hypothesize how direct primaries and the direct election of senators changed politics in America. Students should evaluate their answers after they have completed the chapter.

GLENCOE
TECHNOLOGY

The *American Republic Since 1877* Video Program
To learn more about the meatpacking industry, have students view the Chapter 13 video, "The Stockyard Jungle," from the *American Republic Since 1877* Video Program.

MindJogger Videoquiz
Use the **MindJogger Videoquiz** to preview Chapter 13 content.

  Both programs available in DVD

CHAPTER
13 The Progressive Movement *1890–1919*

Why It Matters

Industrialization changed American society. Cities were crowded with new immigrants, working conditions were often bad, and the old political system was breaking down. These conditions gave rise to the Progressive movement. Progressives campaigned for both political and social reforms for more than two decades and enjoyed significant successes at the local, state, and national levels.

The Impact Today

Many Progressive-era changes are still alive in the United States today.
- *Political parties hold direct primaries to nominate candidates for office.*
- *The Seventeenth Amendment calls for the direct election of senators.*
- *Federal regulation of food and drugs began in this period.*

 The American Republic Since 1877 Video
The Chapter 13 video, "The Stockyard Jungle," portrays the horrors of the meatpacking industry first investigated by Upton Sinclair.

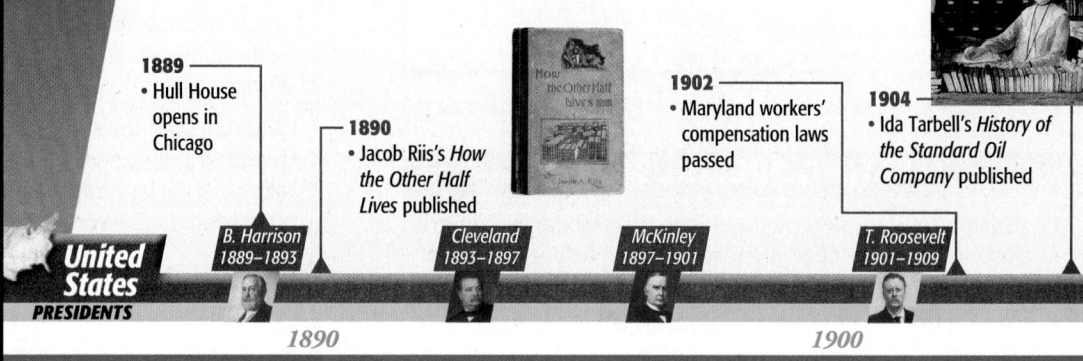

1889
• Hull House opens in Chicago

1890
• Jacob Riis's *How the Other Half Lives* published

1902
• Maryland workers' compensation laws passed

1904
• Ida Tarbell's *History of the Standard Oil Company* published

United States PRESIDENTS

| B. Harrison 1889–1893 | Cleveland 1893–1897 | McKinley 1897–1901 | T. Roosevelt 1901–1909 |

1890   *1900*

World

1884
• Toynbee Hall, first settlement house, established in London

1900
• Freud's *Interpretation of Dreams* published

1902
• Anglo-Japanese alliance formed

1903
• Russian Bolshevik Party established by Lenin

416

Reading Strategy   **PURPOSE FOR READING**

RAFT This strategy—**R**ole, **A**udience, **F**ormat, **T**opic—is a writing tool that directs students to look at a topic from a different perspective. Begin with a brief class discussion, asking students if anyone has ever served as a volunteer in an election campaign, including student council elections. Briefly have those students describe their experiences. If there are no students with such experiences, have the class discuss what campaigns might be like. Then ask all students to write in their journals about election campaigns. They should take on the **R**ole of a campaign manager addressing as their **A**udience the official running for office. Students should choose the **F**ormat of a list, in which they itemize the items needed for their **T**opic—a successful campaign. **L1**

Women marching for the vote in New York City, 1912

1905
• Industrial Workers of the World founded

1906
• Pure Food and Drug Act passed

1910
• Mann-Elkins Act passed

1913
• Seventeenth Amendment ratified

1920
• Nineteenth Amendment ratified, guaranteeing women's voting rights

VOTE YES Nov. 2

VOTE FOR WOMAN SUFFRAGE NOVEMBER 2nd

WOMAN SUFFRAGE VOTE YES OCTOBER 19

Taft 1909–1913

Wilson 1913–1921

1910

1920

1910
• Mexican Revolution

1914
• World War I begins in Europe

1905
• Einstein's theory of relativity formulated

417

HISTORY Online
Chapter Overview
Visit the *American Republic Since 1877* Web site at tarvol2.glencoe.com and click on *Chapter Overviews—Chapter 13* to preview chapter information.

HISTORY Online
Introduce students to chapter content and key terms by having them access the **Chapter 13 Overview** at tarvol2.glencoe.com.

More About the Photo

Demonstrations for woman suffrage were generally peaceful. However, some turned violent, and arrests were made. During World War I, militant suffragists demanded that President Wilson reverse his opposition to their cause. Some demonstrated by carrying banners comparing the president to Kaiser Wilhelm II of Germany. In the patriotic wartime climate, these banners inflamed hostility toward the protesters.

TIME LINE ACTIVITY

Have students select a world event that is shown on the time line and learn more about it. From their research, have them write a brief description of the impact the event had on American history.

FOLDABLES™
Study Organizer

Dinah Zike's Foldables are three-dimensional, interactive graphic organizers that help students practice basic writing skills, review key vocabulary terms, and identify main ideas. Have students complete the foldable activity in the *Dinah Zike's Reading and Study Skills Foldables* booklet.

GRAPHIC ORGANIZER ACTIVITY

Organizing Information Have students use a graphic organizer similar to the one shown at right to describe the details that support the main idea that progressives wanted to make government more responsive to the people. Students' details may include direct election of senators, direct primaries, legislation to protect the banking system, food supply, and so on.

More responsive government

1 FOCUS

Section Overview

This section focuses on the rise of the Progressive movement.

BELLRINGER
Skillbuilder Activity

 Project transparency and have students answer the question.

Daily Focus Skills Transparency 13–1

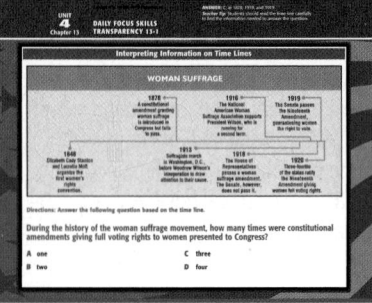

Reading Preview

Answers to Graphic: that people could improve society if they had strong faith in science, government should play an active role in solving society's problems, government needed to be more efficient, senators should be directly elected, women should vote

Preteaching Vocabulary
Have students create a database of the Key Terms and Names. Instruct students to add the definition and other helpful information as they find the terms and names while reading this section.

SECTION 1 The Roots of Progressivism

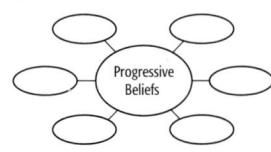

Guide to Reading

Main Idea
Progressivism was a diverse response to the problems posed by industrialism and modern life.

Key Terms and Names
progressivism, muckraker, Jacob Riis, commission plan, Robert La Follette, direct primary, initiative, referendum, recall, suffrage, Alice Paul, temperance, prohibition, socialism

Reading Strategy
Organizing As you read about the beginnings of progressivism, complete a graphic organizer similar to the one below by filling in the beliefs of progressives.

Progressive Beliefs

Reading Objectives
• **Discuss** the rise of the Progressive movement.
• **Evaluate** the impact of initiative, referendum, and recall, and of the Seventeenth Amendment.

Section Theme
Government and Democracy
Progressive reformers focused on political reforms to try to keep the nation true to its democratic ideals.

Preview of Events

◆1890	◆1900	◆1910	◆1920
1890 Jacob Riis's *How the Other Half Lives* published	**1901** Galveston, Texas, adopts commission system	**1913** Seventeenth Amendment provides for direct election of senators	**1920** Nineteenth Amendment gives women the vote

★ An American Story ★

A police officer arresting two suffragists in Washington, D.C.

In 1917 suffragist Rose Winslow and several other women, including Alice Paul, founder of the National Woman's Party, were arrested for obstructing traffic and blocking sidewalks. The women had been picketing the White House to draw attention to the fact that women did not yet have the right to vote in federal elections. After being sentenced to seven months in jail, Paul, Winslow, and other women prisoners went on a hunger strike. Prison authorities forced the prisoners to eat. Winslow smuggled details of their plight out to the public:

❝We have been in solitary for five weeks. . . . I have felt quite feeble the last few days—faint, so that I could hardly get my hair brushed, my arms ached so. But today I am well again. . . . [Alice Paul] dreaded forcible feeding frightfully, and I hate to think how she must be feeling. . . . I am really all right. If this continues very long I perhaps won't be. All the officers here know we are making this hunger strike [so] that women fighting for liberty may be considered political prisoners. . . . [W]e don't want women ever to have to do this over again.❞

—**quoted in *Jailed for Freedom***

The Rise of Progressivism

The struggle for the right of women to vote was only one of a series of reform efforts that transformed American society in the early 1900s. Historians refer to this era in American history—from about 1890 to 1920—as the Progressive Era.

418 CHAPTER 13 The Progressive Movement

SECTION RESOURCES

📖 Reproducible Masters
• Reproducible Lesson Plan 13–1
• Daily Lecture and Discussion Notes 13–1
• Guided Reading Activity 13–1
• Section Quiz 13–1
• Reading Essentials and Study Guide 13–1
• Interpreting Political Cartoons

📠 Transparencies
• Daily Focus Skills Transparency 13–1

Multimedia
🖥 Interactive Tutor Self-Assessment CD-ROM
🖥 ExamView® Pro Testmaker CD-ROM
🖥 Presentation Plus! CD-ROM
🖥 TeacherWorks™ CD-ROM
🔊 Audio Program

Who Were the Progressives?

Progressivism was not a tightly organized political movement with a specific set of reforms. Instead, it was a collection of different ideas and activities. Progressives had many different views about how to fix the problems they believed existed in American society.

Progressives generally believed that industrialism and urbanization had created many social problems. Most agreed that the government should take a more active role in solving society's problems. Progressives belonged to both major political parties and usually were urban, educated middle-class Americans. Many leaders of the Progressive movement worked as journalists, social workers, educators, politicians, and members of the clergy.

Beginnings of Progressivism

Progressivism was partly a reaction against laissez-faire economics and its emphasis on an unregulated market. After seeing the poverty of the working class and the filth and crime of urban society, these reformers began to doubt the free market's ability to address those problems. At the same time, they doubted that government in its present form could fix those problems. They concluded that government had to be fixed first before it could be used to fix other problems.

One reason progressives believed people could improve society was because they had a strong faith in science and technology. The application of scientific knowledge had produced the lightbulb, the telephone, the automobile, and the airplane. It had built skyscrapers and railroads. Science and technology had benefited people; thus progressives believed using scientific principles could also produce solutions for society.

The Muckrakers

Among the first people to articulate Progressive ideas was a group of crusading journalists who investigated social conditions and political corruption. These writers became known as muckrakers after a speech by President Theodore Roosevelt:

> ❝Now, it is very necessary that we should not flinch from seeing what is vile and debasing. There is filth on the floor and it must be scraped up with the muck-rake; and there are times and places where this service is the most needed of all the services that can be performed. . . .❞
>
> —Washington, D.C., April 14, 1906

By the early 1900s, American publishers were competing to see who could expose the most corruption and scandal. A group of aggressive 10¢ and 15¢ magazines grew in popularity at this time, including *McClure's, Collier's,* and *Munsey's.*

Muckrakers uncovered corruption in many areas. Some concentrated on exposing what they considered to be the unfair practices of large American corporations. In *McClure's,* for example, **Ida Tarbell** published a series of articles critical of the Standard Oil Company. In *Everybody's Magazine,* Charles Edward Russell attacked the beef industry.

Other muckrakers targeted government. David Graham Philips described how money influenced the Senate, while **Lincoln Steffens,** another *McClure's* reporter, reported on vote stealing and other corrupt practices of urban political machines. These were later collected into a book, *The Shame of the Cities.*

Still other muckrakers concentrated on social problems. In his influential book *How the Other Half Lives,* published in 1890, **Jacob Riis** described the poverty, disease, and crime that afflicted many immigrant neighborhoods in New York City. The

Picturing History

Muckrakers *McClure's* published Ida Tarbell's exposé on Standard Oil. What issues particularly concerned the muckrakers?

2 TEACH

Daily Lecture and Discussion Notes 13–1

Copyright © by The McGraw-Hill Companies, Inc.

Daily Lecture and Discussion Notes
Chapter 13, Section 1

Did You Know? Photographer Lewis Hine used his photographs to record social conditions and make them known to Americans. He made a large photographic study of immigrants and their lives in tenements and sweatshops in New York City. He also photographed children working under deplorable working conditions in factories, mills, and mines. His photographs of and comments by the children shocked the nation and greatly helped the reform movement to end child labor.

I. The Rise of Progressivism *(pages 418–420)*

  A. The era in American history from about 1890 to 1920 is known as the Progressive Era.

Listing Goals Ask students to find examples of the problems in American society that prompted Progressive objectives. Invite students to present the problems they found; have another student explain how each led to a Progressive goal. **L1**

HISTORY Online

Objectives and answers to the student activity can be found in the **Web Activity Lesson Plan** at tarvol2.glencoe.com.

Picturing History

Answer: social conditions, political corruption, and unfair practices in industry
Ask: What company did Ida Tarbell criticize? *(Standard Oil)*

📁 Use *Interpreting Political Cartoons,* Cartoon 19.

📖 Reading Strategy ▶ READING THE TEXT

Classifying and Categorizing Information Organize the class into groups of five students and supply each group with a flip chart or large sheets of paper. Ask each group to make a series of charts about the reforms discussed in the chapter. Within each group, one student can record information; the others can specialize in looking for information about the following: (1) areas of reform; (2) names of reformers; (3) suggested reforms; (4) success of the suggestions. When the charts are completed, take a class vote on the reform or reformer that students consider the most important. 📚 **L1**

📁 Refer to *Inclusion for the High School Social Studies Classroom Strategies and Activities* in the TCR.

Guided Reading Activity 13–1

Name _____ Date _____ Class _____

★ Guided Reading Activity **13-1**

DIRECTIONS: Using Headings and Subheadings Locate each heading below in your text-book. Then use the information under the correct subheading to help you write each answer.

I. The Rise of Progressivism

  A. What, generally, did progressives believe? _____

  B. Who were among the first to articulate Progressive ideas? _____

  C. What were some of the areas targeted by muckrakers? _____

II. Making Government Efficient

  A. What were the arguments of efficiency progressives? _____

✓ **Reading Check**

Answer: They investigated social conditions, and published their findings.

A City and a Storm In addition to Galveston, two Midwestern cities saw notable reforms during this time. In Toledo, Ohio, Mayor Samuel "Golden Rule" Jones established municipal ownership of public utilities and tackled police corruption. In Detroit, Michigan, Mayor Hazen Pingree set up new schools, parks, and work programs. **Ask: What form of local government do we have?** (Students' answers will vary depending on where they live.) **L2**

✓ **Reading Check**

Answer: because government could not carry out reforms unless it was reformed first

---

muckrakers' articles led to a general public debate on social and economic problems and put pressure on politicians to introduce reforms.

✓ **Reading Check** **Describing** How did the muckrakers help spark the Progressive movement?

Making Government Efficient

There were many different types of progressivism. Different causes led to different approaches, and progressives even took opposing positions on how to solve some problems.

One group of progressives focused on making government more efficient. They believed that many problems in society could be solved if government worked properly. Efficiency progressives took their ideas from business. These progressives believed business had become more efficient by applying the principles of scientific management.

The ideas of scientific management had been developed in the late 1800s and were popularized by Frederick W. Taylor in his book *The Principles of Scientific Management,* published in 1911. Taylor described how a company could become more efficient by managing time, breaking tasks down into small parts, and using standardized tools.

Efficiency progressives argued that managing a modern city required experts, not politicians. They did not want more democracy in government, for they believed that the democratic process led to compromise and corruption. In most American cities, the mayor or city council chose the heads of city departments. Traditionally, these jobs went to political supporters and friends, who often knew little about city services.

Efficiency progressives wanted either a commission plan or a council-manager system. Under the commission plan, a city's government would be divided into several departments, which would each be placed under the control of an expert commissioner. These progressives argued that a board of commissioners or a city manager with expertise in city services should hire the specialists to run city departments. Galveston, Texas, adopted the commission system in 1901. Other cities soon followed.

✓ **Reading Check** **Explaining** Why did progressives want to reorganize city government?

A City and a Storm

On September 8, 1900, a massive hurricane devastated the city of Galveston, Texas. About 6,000 people died. When the political machine that controlled the city government proved incapable of responding to the disaster, local business leaders convinced the state to let them take control. In April 1901, Galveston introduced the commission system of government. Under this system, Galveston chose five commissioners to replace the mayor and city council.

Four commissioners were local business leaders. When the city quickly recovered, reformers in other cities were impressed. Galveston's experience seemed to prove the benefits of running a city like a business by dividing its government into departments and placing each under an expert commissioner. Many other cities soon followed, adopting either the commission plan or the council-manager system.

DIFFERENTIATED INSTRUCTION

At-Risk Students This activity helps to address the particular needs of visual learners. Pair students to write slogans against child labor that could have been used in the early 1900s. Slogans should be brief and clear, with emotional appeal. Then ask students to bring in contemporary magazines or books with pictures showing politicians, religious leaders, celebrities, or protesters advocating some type of political, economic, or social reform. **L1**

📁 Refer to *Inclusion for the High School Social Studies Classroom Strategies and Activities* in the TCR.

Democracy and Progressivism

Not all progressives agreed with the efficiency progressives. Many believed that society needed more democracy, not less. They wanted to make elected officials more responsive to voters.

"Laboratory of Democracy" Political reform first came to the state level when Wisconsin voters elected Republican **Robert La Follette** to be governor. La Follette used his office to attack the way political parties ran their conventions. Because party bosses controlled the selection of convention delegates, they also controlled which candidates were chosen to run for office. La Follette pressured the state legislature to require each party to hold a direct primary, in which all party members could vote for a candidate to run in the general election.

La Follette's great reform success gave Wisconsin a reputation as the "laboratory of democracy." La

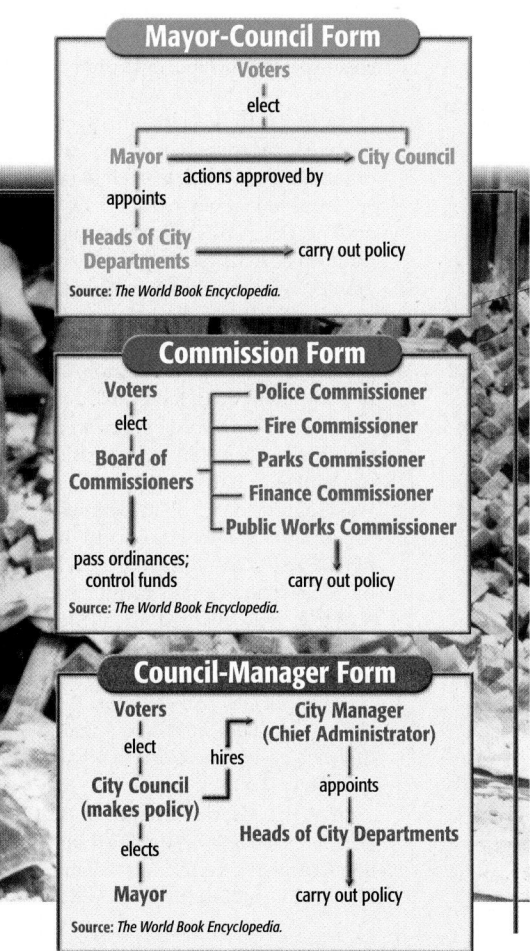

Mayor-Council Form

Voters
↓ elect

Mayor → City Council
actions approved by

↓ appoints

Heads of City Departments → carry out policy

Source: *The World Book Encyclopedia.*

Commission Form

Voters
↓ elect

Board of Commissioners

- Police Commissioner
- Fire Commissioner
- Parks Commissioner
- Finance Commissioner
- Public Works Commissioner

pass ordinances; control funds   carry out policy

Source: *The World Book Encyclopedia.*

Council-Manager Form

Voters
↓ elect

City Manager (Chief Administrator)
hires

City Council (makes policy) → appoints

Heads of City Departments

↓ elects

Mayor   carry out policy

Source: *The World Book Encyclopedia.*

Follette claimed, "Democracy is based upon knowledge. . . . The only way to beat the boss . . . is to keep the people thoroughly informed."

Inspired by La Follette, progressives in other states pushed for similar electoral changes. To force state legislators to respond to voters, three new reforms were introduced in many states. The initiative allowed a group of citizens to introduce legislation and required the legislature to vote on it. The referendum allowed proposed legislation to be submitted to the voters for approval. The recall allowed voters to demand a special election to remove an elected official from office before his or her term had expired.

GOVERNMENT

Direct Election of Senators Another reform the progressives favored affected the federal government—the direct election of senators. As originally written, the United States Constitution directed each state legislature to elect two senators from that state. Political machines or large trusts often influenced the election of senators, who then repaid their supporters with federal contracts and jobs. By the early 1900s, muckraker Charles Edward Russell charged that the Senate had become "only a chamber of butlers for industrialists and financiers."

To counter Senate corruption, progressives called for the direct election of senators by all state voters. In 1912 Congress passed a direct-election amendment. Although the direct election of senators was intended to end corruption, it also removed one of the state legislatures' checks on federal power. In 1913 the amendment was ratified, becoming the Seventeenth Amendment to the Constitution.

✓ **Reading Check** **Evaluating** What was the impact of the Seventeenth Amendment? What problem was it intended to solve?

The Suffrage Movement

In July 1848, Elizabeth Cady Stanton and Lucretia Mott organized the first women's rights convention in Seneca Falls, New York. Stanton proposed to the delegates that their first priority should be getting women the right to vote. The movement for women's voting rights became known as the suffrage movement. Suffrage is the right to vote.

Woman suffrage was an important issue for progressives. Although the suffrage movement began well before progressivism emerged, many progressives joined the movement in the late 1800s and early 1900s.

CHAPTER 13   The Progressive Movement   **421**

✓ **Reading Check**

Answer: Allowing the public to elect senators made the Senate more democratic. It was intended to end corruption but removed one of the state government's checks on federal power.

FYI

Point out that reforms often start at the local level and spread. In 1875 Nebraska established preferential primaries so voters could indicate their choices for senator. By 1912 more than one-half of the states had such primaries.

CURRICULUM CONNECTION

World History At the same time that American women were struggling for the right to vote, women in China were finally being freed from the disabling custom of foot-binding. Foot-binding had been practiced in China since the Song dynasty (A.D. 960–1279). It involved tightly wrapping strips of linen around young girls' feet to discourage growth. The practice extended to all social classes and left women throughout China virtually crippled in later life. The Chinese government officially banned the practice in 1912.

INTERDISCIPLINARY CONNECTIONS ACTIVITY

Government Invite someone from the local government to address your class about the form of government used in your community. If you live in an area where there are several kinds of governments in adjacent communities, invite representatives of each. Ask your guest(s) to prepare a short talk about the way the government operates and the kinds of services that it provides. Instruct students to prepare for the class by jotting down some questions for the speaker(s). **L2**

Background: Susan B. Anthony was the first woman depicted on a U.S. coin. Unfortunately, the Susan B. Anthony dollar was not well received by the general public. The coin is no longer minted.

Ask: How do you think employers have rationalized paying women less than their male counterparts?

(Students' answers will vary.)

Creating a Thematic Map Have students draw a map of the United States and indicate the states that allowed women to vote in 1912. **L1**

📂 Use the rubric for creating a map, display, or chart on pages 65–66 in the *Performance Assessment Activities and Rubrics.*

FYI

Mary Church Terrell, born in 1863, was the most prominent African American in the suffrage movement, but she also led a lifelong campaign against racial injustice. Terrell encouraged picketing and sit-ins years before the civil rights movement adopted those strategies. She also was a cofounder of the NAACP. Fittingly, Terrell lived long enough to see the Supreme Court's landmark ruling in *Brown* v. *Board of Education.*

Early Problems The suffrage movement got off to a slow start. Women suffragists were accused of being unfeminine and immoral. Several were physically attacked. The movement also remained weak because many of its supporters were abolitionists as well. In the years before the Civil War, they preferred to concentrate on abolishing slavery.

After the Civil War, the Republicans in Congress introduced the Fourteenth and Fifteenth Amendments to the Constitution to protect the voting rights of African Americans. Several leaders of the woman suffrage movement had wanted these amendments worded to give women the right to vote as well. They were bitterly disappointed when Republicans refused.

The debate over the Fourteenth and Fifteenth Amendments split the suffrage movement into two groups: the National Woman Suffrage Association, led by Elizabeth Cady Stanton and Susan B. Anthony, and the American Woman Suffrage Association, led by Lucy Stone and Julia Ward Howe. The first group wanted to focus on passing a constitutional amendment allowing woman suffrage. The second group believed that the best strategy was to convince state governments to give women the right to vote before trying to amend the Constitution.

This split reduced the movement's effectiveness. In 1878 a constitutional amendment granting woman suffrage was introduced in Congress, but it failed to pass. Few state governments granted women the right to vote either. By 1900 only Wyoming, Idaho, Utah, and Colorado had granted women full voting rights.

The Movement Builds Support In 1890 the two groups united to form the **National American Woman Suffrage Association** (NAWSA). The movement still did not make significant gains, however, until about 1910. Part of the problem was convincing women to become politically active. As the Progressive movement began, however, many middle-class women concluded that they needed the vote to promote social reforms they favored. Many working-class women also wanted the vote to ensure passage of labor laws protecting women.

As the suffrage movement grew, members began lobbying lawmakers, organizing marches, and delivering speeches on street corners. By the end of 1912, Washington, Oregon, California, Arizona, and Kansas had granted women full voting rights. On March 3, 1913, the day before President Wilson's inauguration, suffragists marched in Washington, D.C., to draw attention to their cause.

Alice Paul, a Quaker social worker who headed NAWSA's congressional committee, had organized the Washington march. Paul wanted to use protests to force President Wilson to take action on suffrage. Her activities alarmed other members of NAWSA who wanted to negotiate with Wilson. Paul left NAWSA and formed the National Woman's Party. Her supporters picketed the White House, blocked sidewalks, chained themselves to lampposts, and went on hunger strikes if arrested.

In 1915 **Carrie Chapman Catt** became NAWSA's leader. Catt developed what she called her "Winning Plan" to mobilize the suffrage

Profiles IN HISTORY

Susan B. Anthony
1820–1906

Susan B. Anthony was born in Adams, Massachusetts, to Quaker parents. Quakers were generally more supportive of women's rights than some other groups, and so Anthony was able to receive a good education. She finished her schooling at the age of 17. Anthony then worked as a teacher in New York, but she was fired after protesting that her pay was one-fifth the amount of her male colleagues. She found another job, however, as a principal at New York's Canajoharie Academy. Between 1848 and 1863, Anthony was involved in both the temperance and abolitionist movements.

Her involvement in the drive for women's equality began in 1851 after she met Elizabeth Cady Stanton. Between 1854 and 1860, the duo attempted to change discriminatory laws in New York. In 1869 Anthony and Stanton organized the National Woman Suffrage Association and began promoting an amendment to grant woman suffrage. Anthony and 12 other women illegally cast votes in the presidential election of 1872. They were arrested and convicted, but the judge feared that the jury would rule in Anthony's favor. He dismissed the jury and fined Anthony instead. She refused to pay the $100 fine, but the judge decided to let her go, afraid that appealing the case might generate sympathy for the suffrage movement.

In 1883 Anthony traveled to Europe, and she helped form the International Council of Women in 1888. This organization represented the rights of women in 48 countries. She died in Rochester, New York, in 1906. Though Anthony did not live to see her dream of woman suffrage become reality, the United States government honored her by placing her portrait on a new dollar coin in 1979.

422 CHAPTER 13 The Progressive Movement

CRITICAL THINKING ACTIVITY

Evaluating Have students research some social services available in their community. Instruct students to select a particular social issue and learn more about what services are available. Suggest that they focus on the following questions: What is the issue? What agencies or organizations provide services related to this issue? What kinds of services are provided? What impact are these services having on the community? Have students write a report answering these questions. **L2**

Woman Suffrage, 1869–1920

□ Full woman suffrage before 1920, with date granted
□ Partial woman suffrage before 1920
■ No woman suffrage until ratification of the Nineteenth Amendment
— 1920 border

Geography *Skills*

1. **Interpreting Maps** Which region led the way in granting woman suffrage?
2. **Applying Geography Skills** Based on the map, what region would you suggest had the least amount of campaigning for woman suffrage?

movement nation-wide in one final push to gain voting rights. She also threw NAWSA's support behind Wilson in the 1916 election. Although Wilson did not endorse a woman suffrage amendment, he supported the Democratic Party's call for states to give women the vote.

The Nineteenth Amendment As more states granted women the right to vote, Congress began to favor a constitutional amendment. In 1918 the House of Representatives passed a woman suffrage amendment. Wilson then addressed the Senate, asking it to vote for the amendment. Despite his efforts, the amendment failed to pass by two votes.

During the midterm elections of 1918, Catt used NAWSA's resources to defeat two anti-suffrage senators. The following year, in June 1919, the Senate finally passed the Nineteenth Amendment by just more than the two-thirds vote needed. On August 26, 1920, after three-fourths of the states had voted to ratify it, the Nineteenth Amendment guaranteeing women the right to vote went into effect.

✓ **Reading Check** **Evaluating** How successful were women in lobbying to achieve passage of the Nineteenth Amendment?

Social Welfare Progressivism

While many progressives focused on reforming the political system, others focused on social problems, such as crime, illiteracy, alcohol abuse, child labor, and the health and safety of Americans. These social welfare progressives created charities to help the poor and disadvantaged. They also pushed for new laws they hoped would fix social problems.

The Campaign Against Child Labor Probably the most emotional Progressive issue was the campaign against child labor. Children had always worked on family farms, but the factory work that many children performed was monotonous, and the conditions were often unhealthy. In 1900 over 1.7 million children under the age of 16 worked outside the home. Reformers established a National Child Labor Committee in 1904 to work to abolish child labor.

Muckraker John Spargo's 1906 book *The Bitter Cry of the Children* presented detailed evidence on child labor conditions. He told of coal mines where thousands of "breaker boys" were hired at age 9 or 10 to pick slag out of coal and were paid 60¢ for a 10-hour

CHAPTER 13 The Progressive Movement **423**

✓ **Reading Check**

Answer: Women were effective in lobbying, first at the state level. Their defeat of local candidates was especially persuasive in convincing Congress to pass the Nineteenth Amendment.

Geography *Skills*

Answers:
1. the West
2. the South

Geography Skills Practice
Ask: In which states did women have full voting rights in 1900? *(Wyoming, Idaho, Utah, and Colorado)*

Creating a Poster Have students create a poster or a sign that suffragists could have carried during one of their protests or marches. **L1**

📁 Use the rubric for creating a map, display, or chart on pages 65–66 in the *Performance Assessment Activities and Rubrics.*

FYI

Tennessee became the thirty-sixth state to ratify the Nineteenth Amendment in August 1920. With ratification of the necessary three-fourths of the states, Secretary of State Bainbridge Colby certified the ratification on August 26, 1920.

EXTENDING THE CONTENT

Western Women In addition to being allowed to own and run their own ranches and farms, Western women were the first to win the right to vote. The first seven states to grant woman suffrage were in the West, beginning with the territory of Wyoming in 1869. **L2**

The term *sweatshop* comes from the "sweating system" of subcontracting. A garment manufacturer, for instance, gave material to a go-between, who then subcontracted the work to tailors and seamstresses who worked at home or in small shops. Workers were paid by the piece, not by the hour. They therefore "sweated" because they had to work very fast.

FYI

The issue of labor relations was the central theme of one of the most popular books of the 1890s, Edward Bellamy's *Looking Backward, 2000–1887.* In this utopian novel, people worked in a national industrial army until they retired at age 45.

3 ASSESS

Assign Section 1 Assessment as homework or as an in-class activity.

⚫ Have students use the **Interactive Tutor Self-Assessment CD-ROM.**

L1/ELL

Reading Essentials and Study Guide 13–1

NATIONAL GEOGRAPHIC
MOMENT in HISTORY

YOUTHFUL PROTEST
Two young immigrants march in a New York City demonstration against child labor practices in 1907. Both young women wear banners proclaiming the same message—one in English, the other in Yiddish. Such protests helped publicize the exploitation of children in dingy, dangerous "sweatshops" in American cities. At the dawn of the twentieth century, more than a million children—some as young as eight—labored long hours in factories. The weight of popular opinion finally forced state governments to pass laws protecting young workers.

day. He described how the work bent their backs permanently and often crippled their hands. Reports like these convinced states to pass laws that set a minimum age for employment and established other limits on child labor, such as maximum hours children could work. At the same time, many states began passing compulsory education laws, requiring young children to be in school instead of at work.

By the early 1900s, the number of child laborers had begun to decline. For many families, the new wealth generated by industry enabled them to survive without having their children work. For others, the child labor and compulsory education laws meant that wives had to work instead.

Health and Safety Codes Many adult workers also labored in difficult conditions. Factories, coal mines, and railroads were particularly dangerous. For example, in 1911 a terrible fire swept through Triangle Shirtwaist Company in New York City. Nearly 150 women workers died, trapped by doors locked from the outside. Outrage at the deaths caused New York

City to pass strict building codes dealing with fire hazards and unsafe machinery and working conditions.

During the early 1900s, thousands of people died or were injured on the job, but they and their families received little compensation. Progressives joined union leaders to pressure states for workers' compensation laws. These laws established insurance funds financed by employers. Workers injured in industrial accidents received payments from the funds.

Some progressives also favored zoning laws as a method of protecting the public. These laws divided a town or city into zones for commercial, residential, or other development, thereby regulating how land and buildings could be used. Building codes set minimum standards for light, air, room size, and sanitation, and required buildings to have fire escapes. Health codes required restaurants and other facilities to maintain clean environments for their patrons.

The Prohibition Movement Many progressives believed alcohol was responsible for many problems in American life. Settlement house workers hated the

424   CHAPTER 13   The Progressive Movement

DIFFERENTIATED INSTRUCTION

Gifted and Talented American women who sought reform during this era needed to be persuasive. Have students demonstrate that reforming spirit by portraying one of the following women: Jane Addams or Lillian Wald arguing for better opportunities for the poor; Carrie Chapman Catt or Alice Paul arguing for woman suffrage; or Frances Willard or Carry Nation arguing for temperance. Ask students to speak or write what the reformer might have told a crowd. **L3**

📁 Refer to *Inclusion for the High School Social Studies Classroom Strategies and Activities* in the TCR.

effects of drinking on families. Scarce wages were spent on alcohol, and drinking sometimes led to physical abuse and sickness. Many Christians also opposed alcohol.

Some employers believed drinking hurt workers' efficiency, while political reformers viewed the saloon as the informal headquarters of the machine politics they opposed. The temperance movement, which advocated the moderation or elimination of alcohol, emerged from these concerns.

For the most part, women led the temperance movement. In 1874 a group of women formed the **Women's Christian Temperance Union** (WCTU). By 1911 the WCTU had nearly 250,000 members. In 1893 another organization—the Anti-Saloon League—was formed. At first the temperance movement worked to reduce alcohol consumption. Later it pressed for prohibition—laws banning the manufacture, sale, and consumption of alcohol.

> ✔ **Reading Check** **Examining** What actions did progressives take to deal with the issue of child labor?

Progressives Versus Big Business

A fourth group of progressives focused their efforts on regulating big business. Many progressives believed that wealth was concentrated in the hands of too few people. In particular, many became concerned about trusts and holding companies—giant corporations that dominated many industries.

Progressives disagreed, however, over how to regulate big business. Some believed government should break up big companies to restore competition. This idea led to the Sherman Antitrust Act in 1890. Others argued that big business was the most efficient way to organize the economy. They pushed instead for the creation of government agencies to regulate big companies and prevent them from abusing their power. The Interstate Commerce Commission (ICC), created in 1887, was an early example of this kind of Progressive thinking.

Some progressives went even further and advocated socialism—the idea that the government should own and operate industry for the community as a whole. They wanted the government to buy up large companies, especially industries that affected everyone, such as railroads and utilities.

At its peak, socialism had some national support. **Eugene Debs,** the former American Railway Union leader, won nearly a million votes as the American Socialist Party candidate for president in 1912. Most progressives and most Americans, however, believed in the superiority of the American system of free enterprise.

Efforts to regulate business were focused at the national level. Congress passed a number of proposals to regulate the economy under presidents Theodore Roosevelt, William Taft, and Woodrow Wilson.

> ✔ **Reading Check** **Evaluating** What was the impact of Eugene Debs and the Socialist Party on the 1912 election?

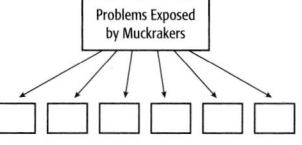

HISTORY Online **Study Central™** To review this section, go to tarvol2.glencoe.com and click on **Study Central™.**

SECTION 1 ASSESSMENT

Checking for Understanding

1. **Define:** progressivism, muckraker, commission plan, direct primary, initiative, referendum, recall, suffrage, temperance, prohibition, socialism.

2. **Identify:** Jacob Riis, Robert La Follette, Alice Paul.

3. **State** what was provided for by the Nineteenth Amendment to the Constitution.

Reviewing Themes

4. **Government and Democracy** How did initiative, referendum, and recall change democracy in the United States?

Critical Thinking

5. **Evaluating** What impact did Susan B. Anthony have on Progressive era reforms?

6. **Organizing** Use a graphic organizer similar to the one below to list the kinds of problems that muckrakers exposed.

Problems Exposed by Muckrakers

Analyzing Visuals

7. **Examining Charts** Study the charts on page 421. Under which system do voters seem to have the most control over department heads? Why do you think so?

Writing About History

8. **Persuasive Writing** Some women in the early 1900s suggested that the Constitution needed an equal rights amendment. Imagine you are living then. Write a letter to the editor of your local paper supporting or opposing such an amendment.

CHAPTER 13 The Progressive Movement **425**

SECTION 1 ASSESSMENT ANSWERS

1. Terms are in blue.
2. Jacob Riis (p. 419), Robert LaFollette (p. 421), Alice Paul (p. 422)
3. The Nineteenth Amendment granted women the right to vote.
4. They gave voters more power to introduce legislation, to approve

legislation, and to remove elected officials.
5. helped form early woman suffrage organizations
6. unfair business practices, corrupt political practices, social problems
7. mayor-council form or the commission form–voters elect the per-

son to whom the department heads report
8. Students' letters will vary. Letters should clearly express a point of view.

> ✔ **Reading Check**

Answer: established the NCLC, wrote books to expose problems, and helped pass laws

Reteach

Have students discuss the rise of the Progressive movement.

Enrich

Invite interested students to write a short biographical profile of one of the persons mentioned in this section.

> ✔ **Reading Check**

Answer: election showed socialism unlikely to succeed in the United States

Study Central™ provides summaries, interactive games, and online graphic organizers to help students review section content.

4 CLOSE

Have students evaluate the impact of initiative, referendum, and recall and the Seventeenth Amendment.

TEACH

Taking Notes Effective note taking is useful for much more than taking notes in class. Once students develop a system of note taking, for example, they can use it to take notes at meetings or to note upcoming events for social organizations. Point out that students' primary goal is to provide a way to recall important information as they need it.

Have students review the first section of Chapter 13, taking notes that they can use as they prepare for chapter or unit tests.

Additional Practice

L1

Reinforcing Skills Activity 13

Name _____ Date _____ Class _____

▶ Reinforcing Skills Activity **13**

Taking Notes

☐ **LEARNING THE SKILL**

Effective note taking involves breaking up much of the information you read or hear into meaningful parts so that you can understand and remember. As you listen or read, take note of key points that are emphasized. In written material, look for topic sentences and words in bold or italic type. Clues like these will help you identify important concepts. Your notes should be neatly written and should summarize in your own words the main ideas and supporting details of your subject.

☐ **PRACTICING THE SKILL**

DIRECTIONS: Read the material on pages 439 to 442 of your textbook. Fill in the missing information in the outline below to prepare notes.

Main Idea: Wilson's Character and Background

GLENCOE
TECHNOLOGY

CD-ROM
Glencoe Skillbuilder Interactive Workbook CD-ROM, Level 2

This interactive CD-ROM reinforces student mastery of essential social studies skills.

Taking Notes

Why Learn This Skill?

Taking notes is a way of recording the important parts of something you have read. Taking notes also helps you recall information. The guidelines below explain how to get the most out of your notes.

Learning the Skill

One of the best ways to remember something is to write it down. Taking notes involves writing down information in a brief and orderly form. This helps you remember information and makes it easier to study.

There are several styles of taking notes, but all clarify and put information in a logical order. Keep these guidelines in mind when you are taking notes:

- Identify the subject and write it at the top of the page. In your book, for example, look for chapter or section headings.

- Be selective in what information you include in your notes. For example, anything your teacher writes on the chalkboard or shows you from a transparency should be included. If your teacher emphasizes a point or spends a considerable amount of time on a given topic, this is also a clue to its importance. Similarly, if your textbook covers a single topic over several pages, take notes by seeking the topic sentences of paragraphs on the topic. Be certain to write down all words that are in bold or italicized type. Your goal is to listen or read carefully, paying attention to the main ideas or key points. Do not write down every word your teacher says. Your notes should consist of the main ideas and supporting details on the subject.

- Paraphrase the information. Put it in your own words rather than trying to take it down word for word. In order to save time, you might want to develop a personal form of shorthand. For example, eliminating vowels from words saves

Student success relies on good note-taking.

time: "develop" becomes "dvlp." Use symbols, arrows, or sketches: "&" in place of "and." Use your shorthand whenever you take notes.

- Make sure your notes are neat so you will be able to understand them when you study them later.

Practicing the Skill

After you have carefully read Section 4 of this chapter, follow the general guidelines to taking notes listed above and create notes for the subsection "The Limits of Progressivism."

Skills Assessment

Complete the Practicing Skills questions on page 445 and the Chapter 13 Skill Reinforcement Activity to assess your mastery of this skill.

Applying the Skill

Taking Notes Have a classmate quiz you on the section on which you took notes. How did you do? Did your notes work well? What can be improved about them? What would you change?

 GO TO Glencoe's **Skillbuilder Interactive Workbook CD-ROM, Level 2,** provides instruction and practice in key social studies skills.

ANSWERS TO PRACTICING THE SKILL

Students' notes should be organized by the heads and subheads of the section. For each head or subhead, the major event or topic and its significance should be referenced. Encourage students to adopt a consistent format.

Applying the Skill
Students' answers will vary. Students should identify weaknesses and offer suggestions for change.

Guide to Reading

Main Idea
With Theodore Roosevelt's succession to the presidency in September 1901, progressivism entered national politics.

Key Terms and Names
Square Deal, Northern Securities, United Mine Workers, arbitration, Hepburn Act, Upton Sinclair

Reading Strategy
Taking Notes As you read about the administration of President Theodore Roosevelt, use the major headings of the section to create an outline similar to the one below.

Roosevelt in Office
I. Roosevelt Revives the Presidency
   A.
   B.
   C.
   D.
II.

Reading Objectives
• **Describe** various efforts to regulate concentrated corporate power.
• **Discuss** Theodore Roosevelt's interest in environmental conservation.

Section Theme
Individual Action Progressive goals were carried to the national level when Theodore Roosevelt became president.

Preview of Events

♦1900	♦1902	♦1904	♦1906

1901
Theodore Roosevelt becomes president after William McKinley's death

1902
United Mine Workers go on strike

1903
Roosevelt sets up Bureau of Corporations

1906
Upton Sinclair's *The Jungle* published

1906
Meat Inspection Act passed

★ An American Story ★

Theodore Roosevelt

William McKinley's assassination brought Teddy Roosevelt to the presidency. Despite the tragic circumstances, he took to the office with great joy. A man who loved the outdoors and physical activity, Roosevelt impressed many people as a new kind of president. One visitor wrote that after spending time with Roosevelt, "you go home and wring the personality out of your clothes."

The famous muckraker, Lincoln Steffens, already knew Roosevelt as a fellow reformer. Steffens went to Washington to see his friend, and this is what he saw:

66His offices were crowded with people, mostly reformers, all day long. . . . He strode triumphant around among us, talking and shaking hands, dictating and signing letters, and laughing. Washington, the whole country, was in mourning, and no doubt the President felt he should hold himself down; he didn't; he tried to but his joy showed in every word and movement. . . . With his feet, his fists, his face and his free words, he laughed at his luck. . . . And he laughed with glee at the power and place that had come to him.99

—quoted in *Theodore Roosevelt, A Life*

Roosevelt Revives the Presidency

Theodore Roosevelt, better known as "Teddy," took office at age 42—the youngest person ever to serve as president. Roosevelt was intensely competitive, strong-willed, and extremely energetic. In international affairs, Roosevelt was a Social Darwinist. He believed the United States was in competition with the other nations of the world and that only the fittest would survive. Domestically, however, Roosevelt was a committed

CHAPTER 13 The Progressive Movement **427**

---

1 FOCUS

Section Overview
This section focuses on how Roosevelt brought Progressive thought to the national level.

BELLRINGER
Skillbuilder Activity

 Project transparency and have students answer the question.

Daily Focus Skills Transparency 13–2

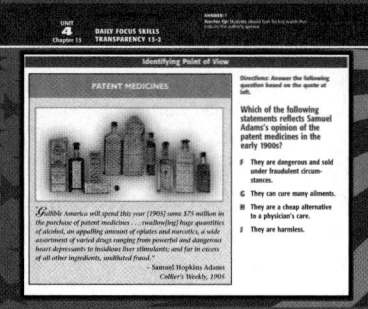

Reading Preview

Answers to Graphic:
I. Roosevelt Revives the Presidency
   A. Roosevelt Takes on the Trusts
   B. The Coal Strike of 1902
   C. The Bureau of Corporations
   D. Congress Follows
II. Social Welfare Action
III. Conservation
   A. Land Development in the West
   B. Gifford Pinchot
   C. Roosevelt's Legacy

Preteaching Vocabulary
Assign one of the Key Terms and Names to each student. Have the students prepare 30-second oral presentations on their terms and names.

SECTION RESOURCES

 Reproducible Masters
• Reproducible Lesson Plan 13–2
• Daily Lecture and Discussion Notes 13–2
• Guided Reading Activity 13–2
• Section Quiz 13–2
• Reading Essentials and Study Guide 13–2
• Supreme Court Case Studies

Transparencies
• Daily Focus Skills Transparency 13–2

Multimedia
• Interactive Tutor Self-Assessment CD-ROM
• ExamView® Pro Testmaker CD-ROM
• Presentation Plus! CD-ROM
• TeacherWorks™ CD-ROM
• Audio Program

Daily Lecture and Discussion Notes 13–2

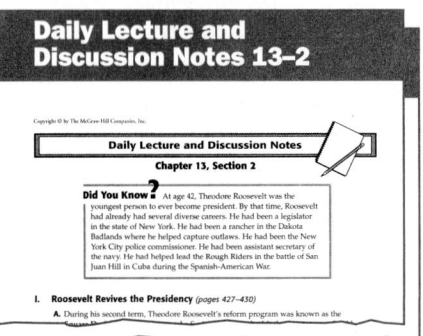

Copyright © by The McGraw-Hill Companies, Inc.

Daily Lecture and Discussion Notes
Chapter 13, Section 2

Did You Know? At age 42, Theodore Roosevelt was the youngest person to ever become president. By that time, Roosevelt had already had several diverse careers. He had been a legislator in the state of New York. He had been a rancher in the Dakota Badlands where he helped capture outlaws. He had been the New York City police commissioner. He had been assistant secretary of the navy. He had helped lead the Rough Riders in the battle of San Juan Hill in Cuba during the Spanish-American War.

I. **Roosevelt Revives the Presidency** (pages 427–430)

   A. During his second term, Theodore Roosevelt's reform program was known as the

---

Analyzing *Political Cartoons*

Answer: Wall Street was the major financial center of the nation.
Ask: How did the artist make his point of view known? *(by choosing a familiar story and by the relative size of the components of the drawing)*

Drawing a Political Cartoon
Have students draw a political cartoon focusing on Roosevelt. Suggest that students use characters from contemporary culture or traditional stories such as fairy tales. **L1**

 Use the rubric for creating a political cartoon, pamphlet, or handbill on pages 77–78 in the *Performance Assessment Activities and Rubrics.*

FYI

On December 3, 1901, Roosevelt made his first annual address to Congress. His speech focused on the need for the federal government to restrain large corporations and trusts. During his presidency, he initiated 44 lawsuits against trusts.

---

progressive, who firmly believed that government should actively balance the needs of competing groups in American society.

"I shall see to it," Roosevelt declared in 1904, "that every man has a square deal, no less and no more." During his second term, his reform programs became known as the Square Deal. To Roosevelt, it was not inconsistent to believe in Social Darwinism and Progressivism at the same time. He believed the United States needed to adopt progressive reforms in order to maintain an efficient society that could compete successfully against other nations.

Roosevelt Takes on the Trusts Although he admired competition, Roosevelt was also concerned with efficiency. He believed that trusts and other large business organizations were very efficient and part of the reason for America's prosperity. Yet Roosevelt remained concerned that in the pursuit of

Analyzing *Political Cartoons*

Corporate Giants This 1904 cartoon portrays Roosevelt as "Jack the Giant-Killer," but he actually restrained very few trusts. Why do you think the scene is set on Wall Street?

John D. Rockefeller

J.P. Morgan

James J. Hill

T. Roosevelt

their private interests, some trusts were hurting the public interest. He wanted to find a way to supervise big business without destroying its economic efficiency. When the *New York Sun* declared that Roosevelt was "bringing wealth to its knees," the president disagreed. "We draw the line against misconduct," he declared, "not against wealth."

During Roosevelt's first year in office, a fight for control of the Burlington Railroad erupted on the New York Stock Exchange. On one side was E.H. Harriman of the Union Pacific Railroad. On the other side were James J. Hill and J.P. Morgan of the Great Northern and Northern Pacific Railroads. The stock battle almost triggered a financial panic that could have plunged the nation into a recession. The three men ultimately compromised by creating a giant new holding company called **Northern Securities.**

The formation of the Northern Securities Company alarmed many Americans, including Roosevelt. The stock battle that led to its creation seemed a classic example of private interests acting in a way that threatened the nation as a whole. Roosevelt decided that the company was in violation of the Sherman Antitrust Act. In early 1902, he ordered his attorney general to file a lawsuit against Northern Securities.

In 1904 in *Northern Securities* v. *the United States,* the Supreme Court ruled five to four that Northern Securities had violated the Sherman Antitrust Act. The dissenting justices argued that the Sherman Antitrust Act did not ban companies from buying or selling stock to each other. They observed that Northern Securities had not hurt commerce. It had not tried to keep other companies from competing, and it had not tried to raise railroad rates. In fact, rates had fallen on railroads owned by Northern Securities. Although the court was sharply divided, Roosevelt declared the decision a great victory. Newspapers hailed Roosevelt as a "trustbuster," and his popularity soared. *(See page 964 for more information on* Northern Securities *v.* the United States*.)*

The Coal Strike of 1902 As president, Roosevelt regarded himself as the nation's head manager. He believed it was his job to keep society operating efficiently by preventing conflict between the nation's different groups and their interests. In the fall of 1902, he put these beliefs into practice.

The previous spring, the **United Mine Workers** (UMW) union had called a strike of the miners who dug anthracite, or hard coal. Nearly 150,000 workers

---

walked out of eastern Pennsylvania's anthracite mines demanding a pay increase, a reduction in work hours, and recognition for their union.

As the months passed and the strike continued, coal prices began to rise. To Roosevelt it was another example of groups pursuing their private interests at the expense of the nation. If the strike dragged on too long, the country would face a coal shortage that could shut down factories and leave many people's homes cold with winter fast approaching.

Roosevelt urged the union and the owners to accept arbitration—a settlement imposed by an outside party. The union agreed. The mine owners, determined to destroy the UMW, did not. One owner, George Baer, declared, "The rights and interests of the laboring man will be protected and cared for not by the labor agitators, but by the Christian men to whom God in His infinite wisdom has given the control of the property interests of the country."

The mine owners' stubbornness infuriated Roosevelt, as it did much of the public. Roosevelt threatened to order the army to run the mines. Fearful of this, the mine owners finally accepted arbitration. By intervening in the dispute, Roosevelt had taken the first step toward establishing the federal government as an honest broker between powerful groups in society.

The Bureau of Corporations Despite his lawsuit against Northern Securities and his role in the coal strike, Roosevelt was not opposed to big business. He believed most trusts benefited the economy and that breaking them up would do more harm than good. Instead, Roosevelt proposed the creation of a new federal agency to investigate corporations and publicize the results. He believed the most effective way to keep big business from abusing its power was through knowledge and publicity of the facts.

In 1903 Roosevelt convinced Congress to create the Department of Commerce and Labor. Within this department would be a division called the **Bureau of Corporations,** with the authority to investigate corporations and issue reports on their activities.

The following year, the Bureau of Corporations began investigating U.S. Steel, a gigantic holding company that had been created in 1901. Worried about a possible antitrust lawsuit, the company's leaders met privately with Roosevelt and offered a deal. They would open their account books and records to the Bureau of Corporations. In exchange, if the Bureau found anything wrong, the company would be advised privately and allowed to correct the problem without having to go to court.

Picturing **History**

Miner's Lot In the early 1900s, miners worked under dangerous conditions for little pay. How did Roosevelt respond when they went on strike?

Roosevelt accepted this "gentlemen's agreement," as he called it. Shortly afterward he made similar deals with other companies. These arrangements gave Roosevelt the ability to regulate big business without having to sacrifice economic efficiency by breaking up the trusts.

Congress Follows In addition to creating the Department of Commerce and Labor, Congress passed the Expedition Act, which gave federal antitrust suits precedence on the dockets of circuit courts. Then, in 1906, Roosevelt pushed the **Hepburn Act** through Congress. This act was intended to strengthen the Interstate Commerce Commission (ICC). An early effort to regulate the railroad industry, the ICC had been ineffective because it lacked sufficient authority.

The Hepburn Act tried to strengthen the ICC by giving it the power to set railroad rates. The agency originally was intended to regulate rates to ensure that companies did not compete unfairly. At first, railroad companies were suspicious of the ICC and tied up its decisions by challenging them in court. Eventually, the railroads realized that they could work with the ICC to set rates and regulations that limited competition and prevented new competitors from entering the industry. Over time the ICC

CHAPTER 13 The Progressive Movement **429**

CHAPTER 13
Section 2, 427–431

L1/ELL

Guided Reading Activity 13–2

Name _____ Date _____ Class _____

★ **Guided Reading Activity 13-2**

DIRECTIONS: Filling in the Blanks In the space provided, write the word or words that best complete the sentence. Refer to your textbook to fill in the blanks.

1. President Theodore Roosevelt was a Social Darwinist. He believed that the United States was in competition with other nations and that _____.
2. Roosevelt also wanted to find some way to supervise big business without destroying its _____.
3. Roosevelt believed it was his job to keep society operating efficiently by preventing _____ between the nation's different _____.
4. By intervening in the Coal Strike of 1902, Roosevelt made the first step toward establishing the _____ as an honest "broker" between powerful groups in society.
5. The _____, a division of the new Department of Commerce and Labor, had the authority to investigate _____ and issue _____.

Picturing **History**

Answer: He worked to get the labor union and mine owners to accept arbitration as a way to settle the strike. **Ask:** Why did mine owners finally accept arbitration as a way to settle the strike? *(Roosevelt threatened to bring in the military to run the mines.)*

Creating a Table Have students create a table to show the advantages and disadvantages of a gentlemen's agreement. **L2**

📁 Use *Supreme Court Case Study 10, Northern Securities Company v. United States.*

3 ASSESS

Assign Section 2 Assessment as homework or as an in-class activity.

🌐 Have students use the **Interactive Tutor Self-Assessment CD-ROM.**

DIFFERENTIATED INSTRUCTION

At-Risk Students Many students with reading comprehension or attention problems have difficulty covering material in a timely fashion. To help them, set a goal and a time limit. Give students a one-minute time goal to search for the major players in the 1902 coal strike. Repeat the process. **L1**

📁 Refer to *Inclusion for the High School Social Studies Classroom Strategies and Activities* in the TCR.

429

✔ **Reading Check**

Answer: regulated railroad rates so that companies did not compete unfairly; not very—lacked authority

Fact	Fiction	Folklore

Michtom's wife hand stitched the first bears. After they sold quickly, Michtom sent a bear to the president and asked for permission to name the bears "Teddy." After getting a positive response, Michtom made arrangements for mass production.

✔ **Reading Check**

Answer: Meat Inspection Act and Pure Food and Drug Act

L1/ELL

Reading Essentials and Study Guide 13–2

Name _____ Date _____ Class _____

Study Guide

Chapter 13, Section 2
For use with textbook pages 427–431

ROOSEVELT IN OFFICE

KEY TERMS AND NAMES

Square Deal the reform programs of President Roosevelt (page 428)
Northern Securities a giant holding company broken up by Theodore Roosevelt (page 428)
United Mine Workers a union for mine workers (page 428)
arbitration a settlement imposed by an outside party (page 429)
Hepburn Act a law intended to strengthen the Interstate Commerce Commission (page 429)
Upton Sinclair author of The Jungle, which described horrible conditions in the meatpacking industry (page 430)

L2

Section Quiz 13–2

Name _____ Date _____ Class _____

★ Chapter 13   Score ____

Section Quiz 13-2

DIRECTIONS: Matching Match each item in Column A with the items in Column B. Write the correct letters in the blanks. (10 points each)

Column A

___ 1. wrote The Jungle, a book with appalling descriptions of conditions in the meatpacking industry
___ 2. had the authority to investigate corporations and issue reports on their activities
___ 3. appointed to head the United States Forest Service
___ 4. a settlement imposed by an outside party
___ 5. Roosevelt's reform programs

Column B

A. Gifford Pinchot
B. Square Deal
C. Upton Sinclair
D. arbitration
E. Bureau of Corporations

DIRECTIONS: Multiple Choice In the blank at the left, write the letter of the choice that best completes the statement or answers the question. (10 points each)

430

---

became a supporter of the railroads' interests, and by 1920 it had begun setting rates at levels intended to ensure the industry's profits.

✔ **Reading Check** **Comparing** What was the purpose of the Interstate Commerce Commission, and how successful was it?

Social Welfare Action

When Roosevelt took office, he was not greatly concerned about consumer issues, but by 1905 consumer protection had become a national issue. That year, a journalist named Samuel Hopkins Adams published a series of articles in *Collier's* magazine describing the patent medicine business.

Many companies were patenting and marketing potions they claimed would cure a variety of ills. Many patent medicines were little more than alcohol, colored water, and sugar. Others contained caffeine, opium, cocaine, and other dangerous compounds. Consumers had no way to know what they were taking, nor did they receive any assurance that the medicines worked as claimed.

Many Americans were equally concerned about the food they ate. Dr. W.H. Wiley, chief chemist at the United States Department of Agriculture, had issued reports documenting the dangerous preservatives being used in what he called "embalmed meat." Then, in 1906, **Upton Sinclair** published *The Jungle.* Based on Sinclair's close observations of the

Fact	Fiction	Folklore

The Teddy Bear The soft and cuddly teddy bear was named after the gruff and rugged Theodore ("Teddy") Roosevelt. The idea for the toy stemmed from a hunting trip Roosevelt took to Mississippi in 1902. On the trip, the president refused to kill a defenseless bear cub. Cartoonist Clifford Berryman drew a whimsical reenactment of the scene for the *Washington Post,* which in turn inspired Morris Michtom, a toy shop owner in Brooklyn, to create the "teddy bear." The toy became a runaway success in the United States and abroad.

430 CHAPTER 13   The Progressive Movement

---

slaughterhouses of Chicago, the powerful book featured appalling descriptions of conditions in the meatpacking industry:

❝There would come all the way back from Europe old sausage that had been rejected, and that was moldy and white—it would be dosed with borax and glycerine, and dumped into the hoppers, and made over again for home consumption. . . . There would be meat stored in great piles in rooms; and the water from leaky roofs would drip over it, and thousands of rats would race about upon it.❞

—from *The Jungle*

Sinclair's book was a best-seller. It made consumers ill—and angry. Roosevelt and Congress responded with the **Meat Inspection Act.** It required federal inspection of meat sold through interstate commerce and required the Agriculture Department to set standards of cleanliness in meatpacking plants. The **Pure Food and Drug Act,** passed on the same day in 1906, prohibited the manufacture, sale, or shipment of impure or falsely labeled food and drugs.

✔ **Reading Check** **Summarizing** What two pieces of legislation were enacted due to the facts revealed in Upton Sinclair's *The Jungle*?

Conservation

Roosevelt put his stamp on the presidency most clearly in the area of environmental conservation. Realizing that the nation's bountiful natural resources were being used up at an alarming rate, Roosevelt urged Americans to conserve these resources.

An enthusiastic outdoorsman, Roosevelt valued the country's minerals, animals, and rugged terrain. He cautioned against unregulated exploitation of public lands and believed in conservation to manage the nation's resources. As president, Roosevelt eagerly assumed the role of manager. He argued that the government must distinguish "between the man who skins the land and the man who develops the country. I am going to work with, and only with, the man who develops the country."

GEOGRAPHY

Land Development in the West Roosevelt quickly applied his philosophy in the dry Western states, where farmers and city dwellers competed for scarce water. In 1902 Roosevelt supported passage of the **Newlands Reclamation Act,** authorizing the use of

---

INTERDISCIPLINARY CONNECTIONS ACTIVITY

Health Have students collect warning labels and labeling information from products and advertisements. Have students write a warning label for a product that they use or consume regularly. Have students display their labels with the appropriate product or a picture of it. **Ask:** Do you think that people read warning labels? Why is it important to have warning labels? **L2**

federal funds from public land sales to pay for irrigation and land development projects. Thus it was the federal government that began the large-scale transformation of the West's landscape and economy.

Gifford Pinchot Roosevelt also backed efforts to save the nation's forests through careful management of the timber resources of the West. He appointed his close friend Gifford Pinchot to head the United States Forest Service. "The natural resources," Pinchot said, "must be developed and preserved for the benefit of the many and not merely for the profit of a few."

As progressives, Roosevelt and Pinchot both believed that trained experts in forestry and resource management should apply the same scientific standards to the landscape that others were applying to the management of cities and industry. They rejected the laissez-faire argument that the best way to preserve public land was to sell it to lumber companies, who would then carefully conserve it because it was the source of their profits. With the president's support, Pinchot's department drew up regulations controlling lumbering on federal lands.

Roosevelt took other steps as well to conserve the nation's resources. He added over 100 million acres to the protected national forests, quadrupling their area, and established 5 new national parks and 51 federal wildlife reservations.

Roosevelt's Legacy President Roosevelt changed the role of the federal government and the nature of the presidency. Increasingly, Americans began to look to the federal government to solve the nation's economic and social problems. Under Roosevelt, the

Picturing **History**

Crowd Pleaser Teddy Roosevelt's energetic speaking style captivated audiences across the nation. *What impact did he have on the office of the presidency?*

executive branch of government had dramatically increased its power. The ICC could set rates, the Agriculture Department could inspect food, the Bureau of Corporations could monitor business, and the attorney general could rapidly bring antitrust lawsuits under the Expedition Act.

✓ **Reading Check** **Examining** How did Roosevelt's policies help the conservation of natural resources?

HISTORY Online **Study Central™** To review this section, go to tarvol2.glencoe.com and click on **Study Central™**.

SECTION 2 ASSESSMENT

Checking for Understanding
1. **Define:** Square Deal, arbitration.
2. **Identify:** Northern Securities, United Mine Workers, Hepburn Act, Upton Sinclair.
3. **Explain** what was provided for in the Hepburn Act.

Reviewing Themes
4. **Individual Action** How did Upton Sinclair contribute to involving the federal government in protecting consumers?

Critical Thinking
5. **Drawing Conclusions** What impact did Roosevelt's use of the Sherman Antitrust Act have on business?
6. **Organizing** Use a graphic organizer similar to the one below to list the results of the Coal Strike of 1902.

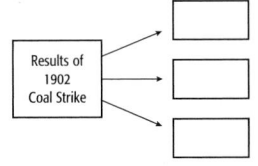
Results of 1902 Coal Strike

Analyzing Visuals
7. **Analyzing Political Cartoons** Look at the cartoon on page 428. Why are the giants depicted as they are? What do they represent? Roosevelt is called Jack the Giant-Killer. What fairy tale is being referred to?

Writing About History
8. **Descriptive Writing** Imagine that you are living in the early 1900s and that you have just read Upton Sinclair's *The Jungle*. Write a letter to a friend explaining what the novel is about and how it characterizes the Progressive era.

CHAPTER 13 The Progressive Movement **431**

SECTION 2 ASSESSMENT ANSWERS

1. Terms are in blue.
2. Northern Securities *(p. 428)*, United Mine Workers *(p. 428)*, Hepburn Act *(p. 429)*, Upton Sinclair *(p. 430)*
3. The Hepburn Act attempted to strengthen the ICC by giving it the power to set railroad rates.
4. His book *The Jungle* raised

awareness of conditions in the meatpacking industry.
5. It broke up Northern Securities and put big business on notice that Roosevelt would use the powers of the act if necessary.
6. coal prices rose, use of arbitration, established precedent for future strikes

7. They are very powerful men who forcefully dominate politics and the economy. *Jack and the Beanstalk*
8. Students' letters will vary. Letters should include as much detail as possible based on information presented in this section.

Reteach
Have students describe the various efforts to weaken concentrated corporate power.

Enrich
Invite interested students to read one of the books mentioned in this section and write a book report.

HISTORY Online

Study Central™ provides summaries, interactive games, and online graphic organizers to help students review section content.

4 CLOSE

Have students list the ways in which Theodore Roosevelt showed his interest in environmental conservation.

1 FOCUS

Read students the following quote from Theodore Roosevelt: "There can be nothing in the world more beautiful than the Yosemite, the groves of the giant sequoias and redwoods, the Canyon of the Colorado, the Canyon of the Yellowstone, the Three Tetons; and our people should see to it that they are preserved for their children and their children's children forever, with their majestic beauty all unmarred."

2 TEACH

Synthesizing Information Have students look at the photograph and caption that shows Theodore Roosevelt and John Muir. Then direct students to look at the map and name the various points Roosevelt and Muir would have likely seen from their vista. *(At a minimum, they could have seen Half Dome, Sentinel Rock, Yosemite Valley, and Cloud's Rest.)* **L1**

Creating a Display Organize students into nine groups and assign each group one of the national parks shown on the map on page 432. Have the groups create a display about the park and its natural beauty. **L2**

CATHEDRAL RANGE

Cloud
9,926 ft.

Yosemite
Point

Eagle
Peak

Upper
Yosemite Falls
1,430 ft. (436 m)

El Capitan
7,569 ft. (2,307 m)

Royal Arches

Yosemite Falls
total drop
2,425 ft. (739 m)

Cathe
Spire

Yosemite Valley
4,000 ft. (1,219 m)

Cathedral Rocks

Bridalveil Fall
620 ft. (189 m)

Merced River

Early National Parks

• Mount Rainier, 1899

• Crater Lake, 1902

• Sullys Hill, 1904

• Yellowstone, 1872

• Wind Cave, 1903

• Yosemite, 1890
• General Grant (Kings Canyon), 1890
• Sequoia, 1890

• Mesa Verde, 1906

Atlantic
Ocean

Pacific
Ocean

Gulf of Mexico

OUR GROWING HERITAGE

This map of the United States shows 9 of the national parks that existed by the end of President Theodore Roosevelt's administration. Roosevelt established 5 national parks, 4 of which still exist today. He also established 51 wildlife preserves and 150 national forests.

EXTENDING THE CONTENT

Conservationist Theodore Roosevelt first visited the Badlands in 1883. As an avid hunter, he came to hunt bison but soon learned that the animals were virtually extinct as a result of hide hunters and disease. As he spent more time in the West, Roosevelt became alarmed at the environmental damage being done to the land and the wildlife. He translated his concerns into action when he became president, creating national parks, bird and game reserves, and national forests.

The Story of Yosemite

The breathtaking beauty of the Yosemite Valley has always astounded visitors to California's High Sierra. In 1851 volunteer soldiers came upon the valley. One officer felt a "peculiar exalted sensation" as he marveled at his surroundings.

The officer's reaction was a natural one. Carved by glaciers and rivers, the seven-mile-long valley into which he and his men rode lies at an elevation of 4,000 feet (1219 m). Above them rose the near-vertical cliffs and great granite monoliths of El Capitan, Half Dome, and Cathedral Rocks. Down onto the valley floor poured the waters of Bridalveil Fall. A dozen other waterfalls spilled over sheer cliffs elsewhere in the valley, some of them— like Yosemite Falls at 2,425 feet (739 m)—among the highest on Earth. Within five years, horseback parties were coming to gaze at Bridalveil Fall and the face of El Capitan. The tourists had found Yosemite.

To guarantee that the public could continue to enjoy the beauty, in 1864 President Abraham Lincoln granted the valley to California as a wilderness preserve. In so doing, Lincoln laid the foundation for the national park system. (The first official national park, Yellowstone, was not created until eight years later.) By the late 1880s Yosemite was attracting about 5,000 visitors a year. John Muir and other conservationists were anxious to preserve the area. Muir had spent years tramping through the woods and up and down the

President Theodore Roosevelt and John Muir stand atop Glacier Point.

mountains and glaciers of the park. His compelling descriptions swayed many influential people. In 1890 Congress expanded the protected area and made Yosemite an official national park.

In many ways Yosemite established a pattern for our national park system. It started programs to teach visitors about native plants and wildlife and was the first park to build a museum to help visitors understand and enjoy the region.

In 1903 President Theodore Roosevelt visited the park with Muir. The natural beauty of the valley captivated the environmentalist president and stimulated his desire to protect vast areas of the country. "We are not building this country of ours for a day," declared Roosevelt. "It is to last through the ages." During his presidency Roosevelt enlarged Yosemite, established the U.S. Forest Service, and put millions of acres of land under federal protection. In 1916 the National Park Service was established, and today it manages more than 380 areas, including 57 national parks.

Glacier Point
7,214 ft. (2,199 m)

Nevada Falls
594 ft. (181 m)

Sentinel Rock

Sightseers admire Yosemite Falls as they ride along Glacier Point Trail in 1901. Today some 3.5 million tourists visit the park each year.

LEARNING FROM GEOGRAPHY

1. How was the Yosemite Valley formed?

2. How did the establishment of the national park system help to conserve natural resources?

433

FYI

After Roosevelt left office, he continued his adventures with nature. In 1913 he participated in an expedition to the Amazon River sponsored by the American Museum of Natural History. He and his companions traveled more than 1,000 miles on the previously uncharted Rio da Duvida.

3 ASSESS

Have students answer the Learning from Geography questions.

4 CLOSE

Have students who have visited Yosemite or another national park describe how they benefited from the experience.

NGS ONLINE

Access National Geographic's Web site for current events, atlas updates, activities, links, interactive features, and archives at www.nationalgeographic.com.

ANSWERS TO LEARNING FROM GEOGRAPHY

1. Yosemite Valley was created by glaciers and rivers.

2. It protected the land by establishing ways in which the land could be used, and it established programs to teach people about the rich plant and animal life.

1 FOCUS

Section Overview

This section focuses on how Progressives were disappointed with the Taft administration.

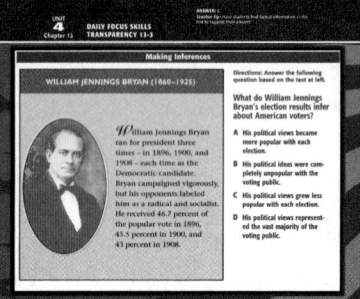
Reading Preview

Answers to Graphic: progressives' campaign to unseat Cannon as Speaker of the House, Payne-Aldrich Tariff, Ballinger-Pinchot controversy

Preteaching Vocabulary
Have students create note cards with the Key Terms and Names on the front of the cards. Instruct students to use the reverse side to make notes about the term or name.

SECTION 3 The Taft Administration

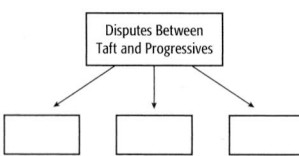
Guide to Reading

Main Idea
President Taft continued with Roosevelt's Progressive policies, but he did not live up to the expectations of many progressives.

Key Terms and Names
Joseph G. Cannon, Payne-Aldrich Tariff, Richard Ballinger, syndicate, insubordination

Reading Strategy
Organizing As you read about progressivism in this section, complete a graphic organizer similar to the one below listing Taft's conflicts with the progressives.

> Disputes Between
> Taft and Progressives

Reading Objectives
- **Explain** how Theodore Roosevelt helped Taft get elected.
- **Discuss** why progressives were disappointed with Taft as president.

Section Theme
Continuity and Change Political differences with Roosevelt caused President Taft to lose Progressive support, even though he supported many Progressive policies.

Preview of Events

♦1908	♦1910	♦1912

1908
Taft elected president

1909
Ballinger-Pinchot controversy

1910
Mann-Elkins Act passed

1911
Antitrust lawsuit filed against U.S. Steel

1912
Roosevelt challenges Taft for Republican nomination

★ An American Story ★

William Howard Taft

One evening in January 1908, President Theodore Roosevelt sat chatting with Secretary of War William Howard Taft and his wife, Nellie, in the second-floor White House library. The mood was relaxed. Seated comfortably in his easy chair, Roosevelt was talking about a subject he had often discussed with his guests: the future role of Taft. Roosevelt toyed with a couple of options. "At one time it looks like the presidency," he mused, considering a future role for his trusted lieutenant, "then again it looks like the chief justiceship."

The Tafts knew that Roosevelt had the power to bring about either of these options. "Make it the presidency," interrupted Nellie Taft, always ambitious about her husband's career. Taft himself was less convinced that he would make a good chief executive. "Make it the chief justiceship," he uttered.

In the end, Taft bowed to the wishes of his wife and his boss. Following George Washington's example and honoring his own promise of 1904, Roosevelt decided not to seek reelection in 1908. Instead, he endorsed an experienced administrator and moderate progressive to run for president on the Republican ticket: William Howard Taft.

—adapted from *The American Heritage Pictorial History of the Presidents of the United States*

Taft Becomes President

Roosevelt loved "Smiling Bill" Taft like a brother and believed him to be the ideal person to continue his policies. He was, Roosevelt said, a leader who possessed "a scorn of all that is base and mean, a hearty sympathy with the oppressed [and a] kindly generosity of nature which makes him feel that all of his countrymen are in very truth his friends and

434 CHAPTER 13 The Progressive Movement

SECTION RESOURCES

📁 **Reproducible Masters**
- Reproducible Lesson Plan 13–3
- Daily Lecture and Discussion Notes 13–3
- Guided Reading Activity 13–3
- Section Quiz 13–3
- Reading Essentials and Study Guide 13–3
- Performance Assessment Activities and Rubrics

📊 **Transparencies**
- Daily Focus Skills Transparency 13–3

Multimedia
- 💿 Interactive Tutor Self-Assessment CD-ROM
- 💿 ExamView® Pro Testmaker CD-ROM
- 💿 Presentation Plus! CD-ROM
- 💿 TeacherWorks™ CD-ROM
- 🎧 Audio Program

brothers." Taft had been Roosevelt's most trusted lieutenant. He had served as a judge, as governor of the Philippines, and as Roosevelt's secretary of war. In fact, Taft seemed acceptable to almost everyone. Thanks to Roosevelt's efforts, he easily received his party's nomination. His victory in the general election in November 1908 was a foregone conclusion. The Democratic candidate, twice-defeated William Jennings Bryan, lost once more.

Taft's Approach to Government

"My dear Theodore," Taft wrote to his old friend a couple of weeks after assuming office. "When I am addressed as 'Mr. President,' I turn to see whether you are at my elbow." The comment was telling.

In that same letter, Taft admitted some of his early fears about his presidency:

> ❝I have no doubt that when you return you will find me very much under suspicion. . . . I have not the prestige which you had. . . . I am not attempting quite as much as you did . . . and so I fear that a large part of the public will feel as if I had fallen away from your ideals; but you know me better and will understand that I am still working away on the same old plan.❞
>
> —quoted in *The American Heritage Pictorial History of the Presidents of the United States*

Roosevelt and Taft were very different people. Roosevelt was a dynamic person who loved the spotlight and the rough-and-tumble world of politics. He had grand ideas and schemes but left the details of administering them to others. Taft was the opposite in many ways. He was a skillful administrator and judge. He disliked political maneuvering and preferred to avoid conflict with others. Unlike Roosevelt, who acted quickly and decisively on issues, Taft responded slowly, approaching problems from a legalistic point of view. "I don't like politics," he wrote, "I don't like the limelight." Although committed to many progressive ideas, Taft's personality and approach to politics quickly brought him into conflict with progressives.

Picturing **History**

Presidential Ritual In 1910 President Taft threw out the first baseball of the season at Lincoln Park in Washington, D.C., as his wife Nellie looked on. Why do you think presidents often continue this practice today?

CHAPTER 13
Section 3, 434–437

2 TEACH

Daily Lecture and Discussion Notes 13–3

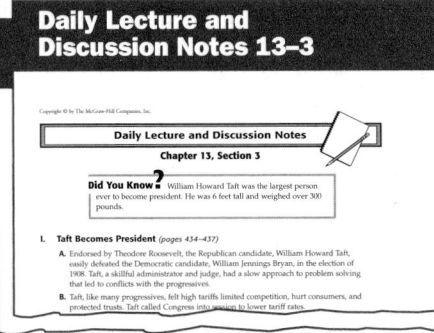

Copyright © by The McGraw-Hill Companies, Inc.

Daily Lecture and Discussion Notes
Chapter 13, Section 3

Did You Know? William Howard Taft was the largest person ever to become president. He was 6 feet tall and weighed over 300 pounds.

I. **Taft Becomes President** *(pages 434–437)*

   A. Endorsed by Theodore Roosevelt, the Republican candidate, William Howard Taft, easily defeated the Democratic candidate, William Jennings Bryan, in the election of 1908. Taft, a skillful administrator and judge, had a slow approach to problem solving that led to conflicts with the progressives.

   B. Taft, like many progressives, felt high tariffs limited competition, hurt consumers, and protected trusts. Taft called Congress into session to lower tariff rates.

Creating Circle Graphs Provide the data below and ask students to make a pair of circle graphs showing the results of the presidential election of 1908. **L1**

Candidate	Popular Vote	Electoral Vote
Taft, Rep.	7,675,320	321
Bryan, Dem.	6,412,294	162

📁 Use the rubric for creating a map, display, or chart on pages 65–66 in the *Performance Assessment Activities and Rubrics*.

Picturing **History**

Answer: Students might say it shows that the president is interested in the same things that other Americans enjoy.

Ask: What is different about the place from which Taft threw out the first pitch compared to presidents today? *(Taft was in the stands. Most dignitaries today are invited to throw out the pitch from the pitcher's mound.)*

Reading Strategy | READING THE TEXT

Using Possible Sentences This strategy allows students to speculate about word meanings. Choose ten vocabulary words and write them on the board. Write sentences using the words either correctly or incorrectly. Then ask students to comment on whether the sentences are "possible." As students encounter the key vocabulary during the reading, they should note the use of each term in the selection's context. After reading, students should re-read the sentences and revise them as necessary. **L1**

📁 Refer to *Inclusion for the High School Social Studies Classroom Strategies and Activities* in the TCR.

L1/ELL
Guided Reading Activity 13–3

Guided Reading Activity 13-3

DIRECTIONS: Outlining Read the section and complete the outline below. Refer to your textbook to fill in the blanks.

I. Taft Becomes President
   A. Thanks to the efforts of _____ William Howard Taft won the presidency in the election of 1908.
   B. Taft believed _____ limited competition, hurt consumers, and protected the trusts.
   C. Roosevelt had warned Taft to stay away from _____ because it would divide the _____.
   D. When Taft eventually accepted the _____, which cut tariffs hardly at all and actually raised them on some goods, his standing among _____ deteriorated.

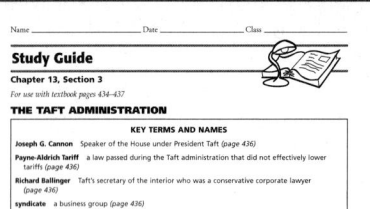

Picturing **History**

Answer: Pinchot was fired for insubordination, and a congressional commission cleared Ballinger.

Ask: How does this incident highlight Pinchot's Progressive views?
(showed he was ready to fight the president himself if he thought Progressive principles were being violated)

3 ASSESS

Assign Section 3 Assessment as homework or as an in-class activity.

⊙ Have students use the **Interactive Tutor Self-Assessment CD-ROM.**

L1/ELL

Reading Essentials and Study Guide 13–3

Name _____ Date _____ Class _____

Study Guide
Chapter 13, Section 3
For use with textbook pages 434–437
THE TAFT ADMINISTRATION

KEY TERMS AND NAMES
Joseph G. Cannon Speaker of the House under President Taft *(page 436)*
Payne-Aldrich Tariff a law passed during the Taft administration that did not effectively lower tariffs *(page 436)*
Richard Ballinger Taft's secretary of the interior who was a conservative corporate lawyer *(page 436)*
syndicate a business group *(page 436)*
insubordination disobedience *(page 437)*

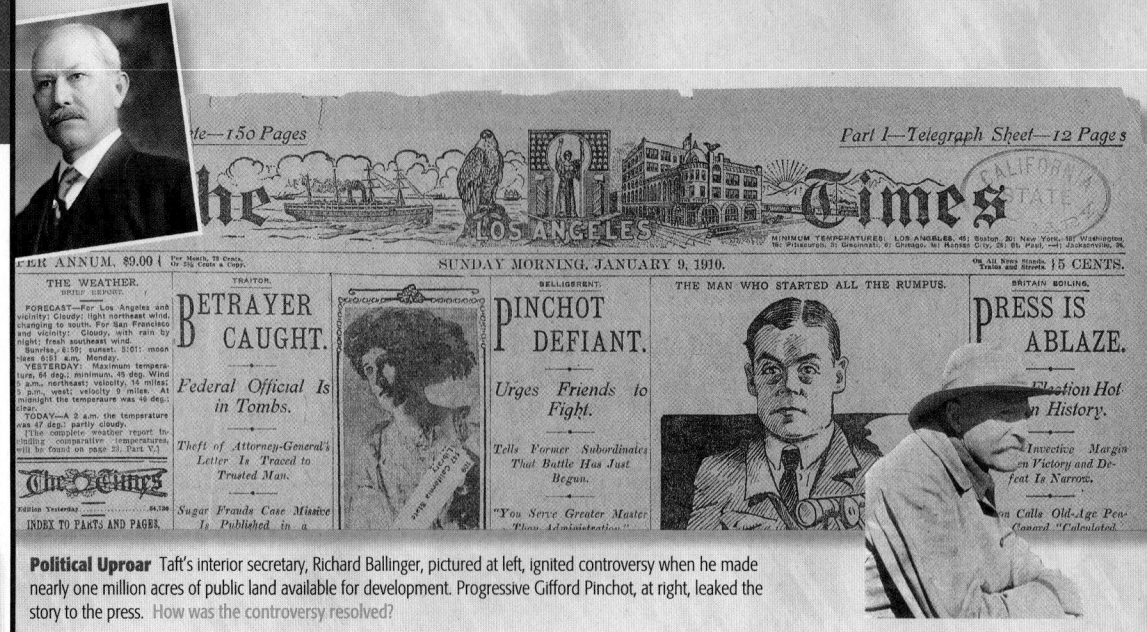

Political Uproar Taft's interior secretary, Richard Ballinger, pictured at left, ignited controversy when he made nearly one million acres of public land available for development. Progressive Gifford Pinchot, at right, leaked the story to the press. How was the controversy resolved?

The Payne-Aldrich Tariff Act Like many progressives, Taft believed high tariffs limited competition, hurt consumers, and protected trusts. Roosevelt had warned him to stay away from tariff reform because it would divide the Republican Party. Taft, however, went ahead and called Congress into special session to lower tariff rates.

To pass a new tariff, Taft needed the help of Speaker of the House **Joseph G. Cannon.** As Speaker, Cannon appointed all committees and decided which bills they handled. By exercising almost total control over debate, Cannon could push some bills through without discussion and see that others never came to a vote. Progressives, however, wanted to unseat Cannon because he often blocked their legislation.

Taft disagreed with the effort to unseat Cannon. He pressured progressive Republicans into stopping their campaign against Cannon. In exchange, Cannon quickly pushed the tariff bill through the House of Representatives. Taft's compromise angered many progressives. The following year, they defied the president by joining with House Democrats and removing Cannon from power.

Taft further alienated progressives when the tariff bill went to the Senate. The powerful head of the Senate Finance Committee, Republican Nelson Aldrich from Rhode Island, wanted to protect high tariffs, as did many other conservative senators. The result was the **Payne-Aldrich Tariff,** which cut tariffs hardly at all and actually raised them on some goods.

After discussions with Aldrich and other senators, however, Taft decided to accept the new tariff.

Progressives felt betrayed and outraged by Taft's decision: "I knew the fire had gone out of [the Progressive movement]," recalled chief forester Gifford Pinchot after Roosevelt left office. "Washington was a dead town. Its leader was gone, and in his place [was] a man whose fundamental desire was to keep out of trouble."

The Ballinger-Pinchot Controversy With Taft's standing among Republican progressives deteriorating, a sensational controversy broke out late in 1909 that helped destroy Taft's popularity with reformers for good. Many progressives had been unhappy when Taft replaced Roosevelt's secretary of the interior, James R. Garfield, an aggressive conservationist, with **Richard A. Ballinger,** a more conservative corporate lawyer. Suspicion of Ballinger grew when he tried to make nearly a million acres of public forests and mineral reserves available for private development.

In the midst of this mounting concern, Gifford Pinchot charged the new secretary with having once plotted to turn over valuable public lands in Alaska to a private syndicate, or business group, for personal profit. Pinchot took the charges to the president. Taft's attorney general investigated the charges and decided they were groundless.

Still not satisfied, Pinchot leaked the story to the press and asked Congress to investigate. Taft fired

436 CHAPTER 13 The Progressive Movement

DIFFERENTIATED INSTRUCTION

Reading Support This activity will be particularly helpful for students needing extra work on the basic points. Ask students to bring in pictures, newspaper or magazine stories, or objects that portray or represent the United States president in action. Discuss the many roles of the president, such as proposing legislation, representing the United States overseas, and commanding the military. L1 ELL

☞ Refer to *Inclusion for the High School Social Studies Classroom Strategies and Activities* in the TCR.

Pinchot for insubordination, or disobedience. The congressional committee appointed to study the controversy cleared Ballinger.

By signing the Payne-Aldrich Tariff Act, supporting Ballinger against Pinchot, and backing Cannon, Taft gave the impression that he had "sold the Square Deal down the river." Popular indignation was so great that the congressional elections of 1910 resulted in a sweeping Democratic victory, with Democrats taking the majority in the House and Democrats and Progressive Republicans grabbing control of the Senate from the conservatives.

☑ **Reading Check** **Summarizing** What problems did President Taft have with progressives on tariff issues?

Taft's Progressive Reforms

Despite his political problems, Taft also had several successes. Although Roosevelt was nicknamed the "trustbuster," Taft was a strong supporter of competition and actually brought twice as many antitrust cases in four years as his predecessor had in seven.

In other areas, too, Taft was at least as strong a progressive as Roosevelt. Taft established the **Children's Bureau,** a federal agency similar to Roosevelt's Bureau of Corporations. The Children's Bureau investigated and publicized problems with child labor. Taft also supported the **Mann-Elkins Act** of 1910, which increased the regulatory powers of the ICC.

The Ballinger-Pinchot controversy aside, Taft was also a dedicated conservationist. His contributions in this area actually equaled or surpassed those of Roosevelt. He set up the Bureau of Mines to monitor the activities of mining companies, expanded the national forests, and protected waterpower sites from private development.

After Taft took office in 1909, Roosevelt left for a big-game hunt in Africa followed by a tour of Europe. He did not return to the United States until June 1910. Although disturbed by stories of Taft's "betrayal" of progressivism, Roosevelt at first refused to criticize the president.

In October 1911, Taft announced an antitrust lawsuit against U.S. Steel, claiming that the company's decision to buy the Tennessee Coal and Iron Company in 1907 had violated the Sherman Antitrust Act. The lawsuit was the final straw for Roosevelt. As president, he had approved U.S. Steel's plan to buy the company.

Roosevelt believed Taft's focus on breaking up trusts was destroying the carefully crafted system of cooperation and regulation that Roosevelt had established with big business through the Bureau of Corporations. In November 1911, Roosevelt publicly criticized Taft's decision. Roosevelt argued that the best way to deal with the trusts was to allow them to exist while at the same time increasing government's ability to regulate them.

Having broken with Taft, it was only a matter of time before progressives convinced Roosevelt to reenter politics. In late February 1912, Roosevelt announced that he would enter the presidential campaign of 1912 and attempt to replace Taft as the Republican nominee for president.

☑ **Reading Check** **Evaluating** How did President Taft's accomplishments regarding conservation and trustbusting compare to President Roosevelt's?

HISTORY Online **Study Central**™ To review this section, go to tarvol2.glencoe.com and click on **Study Central**™.

SECTION 3 ASSESSMENT

Checking for Understanding
1. **Define:** syndicate, insubordination.
2. **Identify:** Joseph G. Cannon, Payne-Aldrich Tariff, Richard Ballinger.
3. **Describe** how Taft helped conservation efforts, alleviated child labor problems, and strengthened the ICC.

Reviewing Themes
4. **Continuity and Change** How did replacing Roosevelt's secretary of the interior cause a dispute between Taft and the progressives?

Critical Thinking
5. **Comparing** What was the difference between Roosevelt and Taft regarding the relationship between the president and Congress?
6. **Organizing** Use a graphic organizer like the one below to list Taft's Progressive reforms.

Taft's Progressive Reforms

Analyzing Visuals
7. **Examining Photographs** Study the photograph on page 435. Note the formal attire of the president and his wife. How would you compare the clothes the people in the photograph are wearing with today's style of dress for leisure activities?

Writing About History
8. **Descriptive Writing** Write a magazine article in which you defend or criticize President Taft's administration in terms of its support of progressivism.

CHAPTER 13 The Progressive Movement **437**

SECTION 3 ASSESSMENT ANSWERS

1. Terms are in blue.
2. Joseph G. Cannon (p. 436), Payne-Aldrich Tariff (p. 436), Richard Ballinger (p. 436)
3. expanded national forests, protected water sites, set up a commission to investigate child labor and supported the Mann-Elkins Act
4. Garfield, an aggressive conservationist, was replaced by Ballinger, a conservative corporate lawyer.
5. Roosevelt came up with great ideas and left administration up to others while Taft preferred administration.
6. Children's Bureau, Mann-Elkins Act, Bureau of Mines
7. The people in the photograph are more formally dressed than we dress today.
8. Students' articles should back up their defense or criticism with fact.

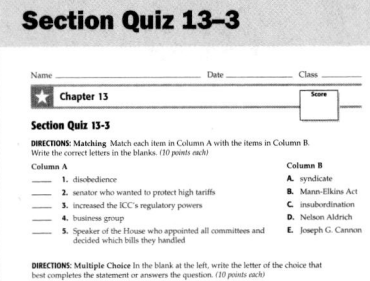

Section Quiz 13–3

☑ **Reading Check**

Answer: Taft alienated them when he did not veto the Payne-Aldrich Tariff, which hardly cut tariffs and actually raised a few.

Reteach
Have students explain how Theodore Roosevelt helped Taft get elected.

Enrich
Invite interested students to research the conservation efforts of the Taft administration. Encourage students to use library and Internet resources for their research.

☑ **Reading Check**

Answer: Taft equaled or surpassed Roosevelt's actions.

Study Central™ provides summaries, interactive games, and online graphic organizers to help students review section content.

4 CLOSE

Have students discuss why progressives were disappointed with Taft as president.

1 FOCUS

Section Overview

This section focuses on the many economic and social reforms of Wilson's Progressive agenda.

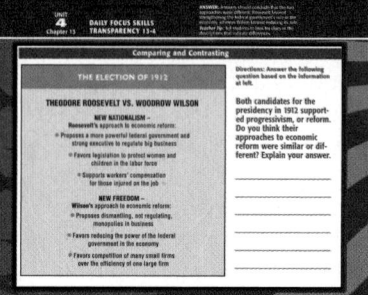
Reading Preview

Answers to Graphic: Economic: Federal Reserve Act, Antitrust Act, Underwood Tariff, Federal Trade Commission; Social: Keating-Owen Child Labor Act, Adamson Act

Preteaching Vocabulary
Have students identify a person who can be tied to each of the Key Terms. Have them identify an event that can be tied to each of the Key Names.

Guide to Reading

Main Idea
Woodrow Wilson pursued a Progressive agenda after his 1912 election victory.

Key Terms and Names
Progressive Party, New Nationalism, New Freedom, income tax, Federal Reserve Act, Federal Trade Commission, unfair trade practices, National Association for the Advancement of Colored People

Reading Strategy
Categorizing As you read about progressivism during the Wilson administration, complete a chart similar to the one below by listing Wilson's Progressive economic and social reforms.

Economic Reforms	Social Reforms

Reading Objectives
• **Describe** Wilson's economic and social reforms.
• **Evaluate** the legacy of the Progressive movement.

Section Theme
Government and Democracy Woodrow Wilson's reforms greatly increased the federal government's role in regulating the nation's economy.

Preview of Events

◆1912	◆1914	◆1916

1912
Woodrow Wilson elected president

1913
Federal Reserve Act passed

1914
Federal Trade Commission Act passed

1916
Keating-Owen Child Labor Act passed

★ An American Story ★

A Woodrow Wilson election poster

On September 15, 1910, in the Taylor Opera House in Trenton, New Jersey, a young progressive named Joseph Patrick Tumulty watched as a lean man with iron-gray hair made his way toward the stage. The man was Thomas Woodrow Wilson, the Democratic Party's nominee for governor.

Wilson was the choice of the party bosses. As Tumulty recalled, progressives were "feeling sullen, beaten, and hopelessly impotent." To Tumulty's astonishment, Wilson announced: "I shall enter upon the duties of the office of governor, if elected, with absolutely no pledge of any kind to prevent me from serving the people of the state with singleness of purpose."

Tumulty knew that Wilson was declaring his independence from the New Jersey political machine. It brought the progressives at the convention roaring to their feet. From one came the cry, "Thank God, at last, a leader has come!"

Two years later, Woodrow Wilson was the Democrats' nominee for the presidency, an office they had won only twice since the Civil War. This time they were confident of victory, for Wilson, a committed progressive, faced a Republican Party wracked by division.

—adapted from *Wilson: The Road to the White House*

The Election of 1912

The 1912 presidential campaign featured a current president, a former president, and an academic who had entered politics only two years earlier. The election's outcome determined the path of the Progressive movement and helped shape the nation's path in the 1900s.

SECTION RESOURCES

📂 Reproducible Masters
• Reproducible Lesson Plan 13–4
• Daily Lecture and Discussion Notes 13–4
• Guided Reading Activity 13–4
• Section Quiz 13–4
• Reading Essentials and Study Guide 13–4
• Performance Assessment Activities and Rubrics

📙 Transparencies
• Daily Focus Skills Transparency 13–4

Multimedia
🕤 Interactive Tutor Self-Assessment CD-ROM
🕤 ExamView® Pro Testmaker CD-ROM
🕤 Presentation Plus! CD-ROM
🕤 TeacherWorks™ CD-ROM
🎧 Audio Program

The Republican Party Splits Believing that President Taft had failed to live up to Progressive ideals, Theodore Roosevelt informed seven state governors that he was willing to accept the Republican nomination. "My hat is in the ring!" he declared. "The fight is on."

The struggle for control of the Republican Party reached its climax at the national convention in Chicago in June. Conservatives rallied behind Taft. Most of the progressives lined up for Roosevelt. When it became clear that Taft's delegates controlled the nomination, Roosevelt decided to leave the party and campaign as an independent. "We stand at Armageddon," he told his supporters, "and we battle for the Lord."

Declaring himself "fit as a bull moose," Roosevelt became the presidential candidate for the newly formed **Progressive Party,** nicknamed the Bull Moose Party. Because Taft had alienated so many groups, the election of 1912 became a contest between two progressives: the Bull Moose Roosevelt and the Democrat Wilson.

Wilson's Character and Background Woodrow Wilson entered politics as a firm progressive. As governor of New Jersey, he pushed one Progressive reform after another through the statehouse. He revamped election laws, established utility regulatory boards, and allowed cities to change to the commissioner form of government. In less than two years, New Jersey became a model of Progressive reform.

"New Freedom" Versus "New Nationalism" The election of 1912 was a contest between two men who supported progressivism, although they had different approaches to reform. Roosevelt accepted the economic power of the trusts as a fact of life and proposed a more powerful federal government and a strong executive to regulate them. Roosevelt also outlined a complete program of reforms. He favored legislation to protect women and children in the labor force and supported workers' compensation for those injured on the job. He also wanted a federal trade commission to regulate industry in a manner similar to the ICC's authority over railroads. Roosevelt called his program the **New Nationalism.**

Wilson countered with what he called the **New Freedom.** He criticized Roosevelt's program as one that supported "regulated monopoly." Monopolies, he believed, were evils to be destroyed, not regulated. Wilson argued that Roosevelt's approach gave the federal government too much power in the economy

and did nothing to restore competition. Freedom, in Wilson's opinion, was more important than efficiency. "The history of liberty," Wilson declared, "is the history of the limitation of governmental power. . . . If America is not to have free enterprise, then she can have freedom of no sort whatever."

Wilson Is Elected As expected, Roosevelt and Taft split the Republican voters, enabling Wilson to win the Electoral College and the election with 435 votes, even though he received less than 42 percent of the popular vote—less than Roosevelt and Taft combined. For the first time since Grover Cleveland's election in 1892, a Democrat became president of the United States.

✓ **Reading Check** **Summarizing** Who were the three major candidates in the presidential election of 1912?

Regulating the Economy

The new chief executive lost no time in embarking on his program of reform. He immediately took charge of the government. "The president is at liberty, both in law and conscience, to be as big a man as he can,"

Picturing **History**

The New Freedom Woodrow Wilson initially believed that government should break up trusts. Why did Wilson favor economic competition?

CHAPTER 13 The Progressive Movement **439**

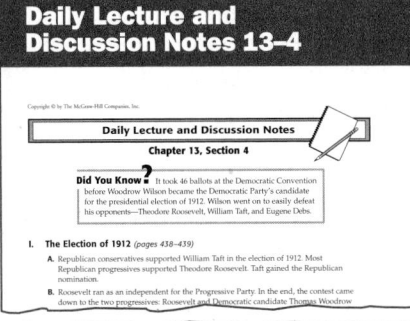

Reading Strategy

Using Social Studies Terminology To make certain that students understand the business and economics terminology in this section, have them write a paragraph in which they correctly use the following terms: *antitrust, competition, tariff,* and *monopoly.* Ask for volunteers to share their paragraphs with the class. Allow students time to ask questions to further clarify the meanings of these terms. **L1**

✓**Reading Check**

Answer: Theodore Roosevelt, William Howard Taft, and Woodrow Wilson

Picturing **History**

Answer: He believed economic freedom was more important than efficiency.
Ask: Of what state was Wilson governor? *(New Jersey)*

Reading Strategy **READING THE TEXT**

Previewing Students can quickly gain an understanding of what the text will be about by looking over features such as headings and subheadings, charted information, illustrations, captions, and graphics. Have students preview the section by looking at these elements before they begin reading so they know what they will be reading about. **L1**

Refer to ***Inclusion for the High School Social Studies Classroom Strategies and Activities*** in the TCR.

L1/ELL
Guided Reading Activity 13-4

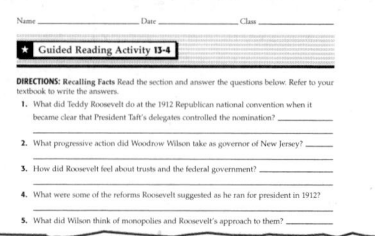

Creating a Table Have students create a table showing the major legislation mentioned in this section. Instruct students to include the date and name of the act and a brief description of its intended effect. **L2**

 Use the rubric for creating a map, display, or chart on pages 65–66 in the *Performance Assessment Activities and Rubrics.*

Geography *Skills*

Answers:
1. Texas
2. Students' answers will vary but may include population density and size of a region's economy.

Geography Skills Practice
Ask: What is the role of the Board of Governors? *(setting the branch banks' interest rates, thereby adjusting the amount of money in circulation nationally)*

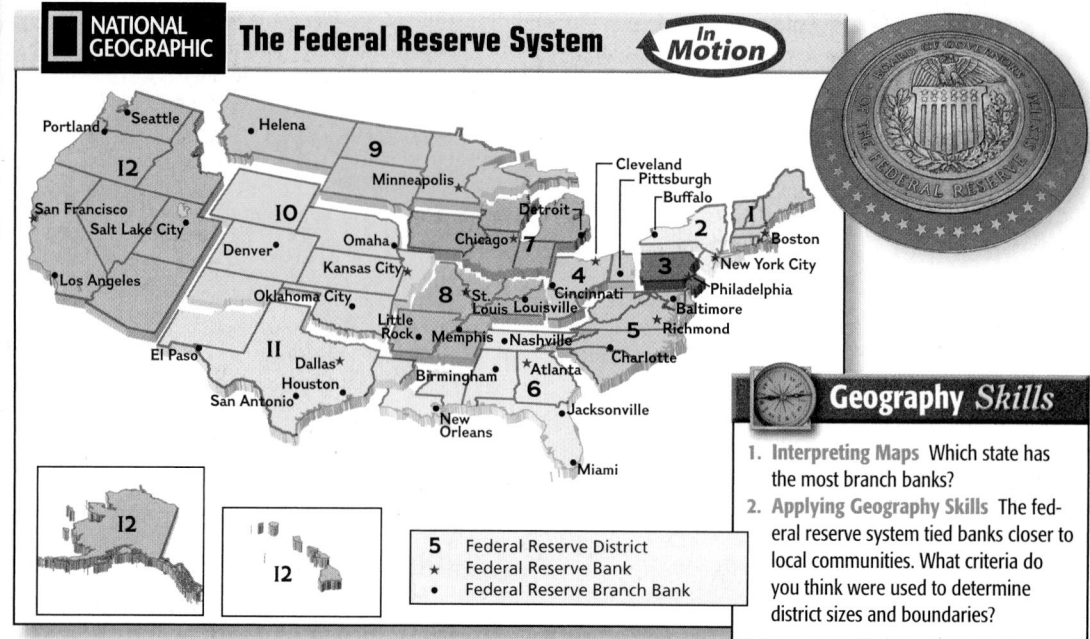

NATIONAL GEOGRAPHIC The Federal Reserve System *In Motion*

5	Federal Reserve District
★	Federal Reserve Bank
•	Federal Reserve Branch Bank

Geography *Skills*
1. **Interpreting Maps** Which state has the most branch banks?
2. **Applying Geography Skills** The federal reserve system tied banks closer to local communities. What criteria do you think were used to determine district sizes and boundaries?

Wilson had once written. "His capacity will set the limit." During his eight years as president, Wilson demonstrated his power as he crafted reforms affecting tariffs, the banking system, trusts, and workers' rights.

Reforming Tariffs Five weeks after taking office, Wilson appeared before Congress, the first president to do so since John Adams. He had come to present his bill to reduce tariffs.

He personally lobbied members of Congress to support the tariff reduction bill. Not even Roosevelt had taken such an active role in promoting special legislation. In Wilson's message to Congress, he declared that high tariffs had "built up a set of privileges and exemptions from competition behind which it was easy . . . to organize monopoly until . . . nothing is obliged to stand the tests of efficiency and economy."

Wilson believed that the pressure of foreign competition would lead American manufacturers to improve their products and lower their prices. Lower tariff rates, he claimed, would help businesses by putting them under the "constant necessity to be efficient, economical, and enterprising."

In 1913 the Democrat-controlled Congress passed the **Underwood Tariff** and Wilson signed it into law. This piece of legislation reduced the average tariff on imported goods to about 30 percent of the value of the goods, or about half the tariff rate of the 1890s.

An important section of the Underwood Tariff Act was the provision for levying an income tax, or a direct tax on the earnings of individuals and corporations. The Constitution originally prohibited direct taxes unless they were apportioned among the states on the basis of population. In other words, the states would be paying the income tax, not individuals, and states with more people would pay more tax. Passage of the Sixteenth Amendment in 1913, however, made it legal for the federal government to tax the income of individuals directly.

ECONOMY

Reforming the Banks The United States had not had a central bank since the 1830s. During the economic depressions that hit the country periodically after that time, hundreds of small banks collapsed, wiping out the life savings of many of their customers. The most recent of these crises had been in 1907.

To restore public confidence in the banking system, Wilson supported the establishment of a Federal Reserve system. Banks would have to keep a portion of their deposits in a regional reserve bank, which would provide a financial cushion against unanticipated losses.

At the center of the Federal Reserve system would be a Board of Governors, appointed by the president. The Board could set the interest rates the reserve

DIFFERENTIATED INSTRUCTION

English Learners Bring a game of Monopoly to class. Display the board and outline the basic rules of the game if necessary. Then have volunteers, working individually or with partners, present a lesson based upon the game. For example, they might purchase houses or buy up all of the railroads to explain what trusts were, how they operated in this era, and how the president tried to prevent them. **L1** ELL

 Refer to *Inclusion for the High School Social Studies Classroom Strategies and Activities* in the TCR.

banks charged other banks, thereby indirectly controlling the interest rates of the entire nation and the amount of money in circulation. This gave the Board the ability to fight inflation by raising interest rates and to stimulate the economy during a recession by lowering interest rates. Congress approved the new system at the end of 1913. The **Federal Reserve Act** became one of the most significant pieces of legislation in American history.

Antitrust Action During his campaign, Wilson had promised to restore competition to the economy by breaking up big business monopolies. Roosevelt argued that Wilson's ideas were unrealistic because big business was more efficient and unlikely to be replaced by smaller, more competitive firms. Once in office, Wilson's opinion shifted, and he came to agree with Roosevelt—but progressives in Congress continued to demand action against big business.

In the summer of 1914, at Wilson's request, Congress created the **Federal Trade Commission** (FTC) to monitor American business. The FTC had the power to investigate companies and issue "cease and desist" orders against companies engaging in unfair trade practices, or those which hurt competition. The FTC could be taken to court if a business disagreed with its rulings.

Wilson did not want the FTC to break up big business. Instead, it was to work with business to limit activities that unfairly limited competition. He deliberately appointed conservative business leaders to serve as the FTC's first commissioners.

Wilson's approach did not satisfy progressives in Congress, who responded by passing the **Clayton Antitrust Act.** The act banned tying agreements, which required retailers who bought from one company to stop selling a competitor's products. It also banned price discrimination. Businesses could not charge different customers different prices. Manufacturers could no longer give discounts to chain stores and other retailers who bought a large volume of goods.

Before the act passed, labor unions lobbied Congress to exempt unions from the antitrust laws. The Clayton Antitrust Act specifically declared that unions were not unlawful combinations in restraint of trade. When the bill became law, Samuel Gompers, head of the American Federation of Labor, called the Clayton Antitrust Act the worker's "Magna Carta," because it gave unions the right to exist.

✔ **Reading Check** **Evaluating** What was the impact of the passage of the Sixteenth Amendment?

Federal Aid and Social Welfare

By the fall of 1914, Wilson believed that his New Freedom program was essentially complete. As a result, he began to retreat from activism.

The congressional elections of 1914, however, shattered the president's complacency. Democrats suffered major losses in the House of Representatives, and voters who had supported the Bull Moose Party in 1912 began returning to the Republicans. Realizing that he would not be able to rely on a divided opposition when he ran for re-election in 1916, Wilson began to support further reforms.

In 1916, for example, Wilson signed the first federal law regulating child labor. The Keating-Owen Child Labor Act prohibited the employment of children under the age of 14 in factories producing goods for interstate commerce. The Supreme Court

The NAACP

Past
Violent race riots broke out in 1908 in Springfield, Illinois, as immigrants and African Americans vied with other residents for scarce jobs. In one riot, a mob killed several African Americans and destroyed much property. Responding to the growing racial violence in the nation, an integrated group of citizens met in New York City to discuss remedies. Out of that meeting, the National Association for the Advancement of Colored People (NAACP) was born.

THE CRISIS

Present
Today the NAACP works for such causes as school desegregation, fair housing and employment, voter registration, and equal health care and income opportunity. It plays a role in establishing legal precedents to improve the quality of life for African Americans across the nation.

The NAACP has chapters in all 50 states and the District of Columbia. It also has chapters in some foreign countries.

✔ **Reading Check**

Answer: The Sixteenth Amendment made it legal for the federal government to directly tax the income of individuals.

3 ASSESS

Assign Section 4 Assessment as homework or as an in-class activity.

⊙ Have students use the **Interactive Tutor Self-Assessment CD-ROM.**

L1/ELL

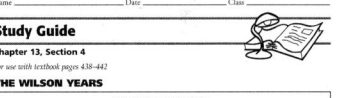

Reading Essentials and Study Guide 13–4

Name _____ Date _____ Class _____

Study Guide
Chapter 13, Section 4
For use with textbook pages 438–442
THE WILSON YEARS

KEY TERMS AND NAMES

Progressive Party newly formed political party, nicknamed the Bull Moose Party *(page 439)*
New Nationalism suggested reform programs of Theodore Roosevelt in the 1912 election *(page 439)*
New Freedom suggested reform programs of Woodrow Wilson in the 1912 election *(page 439)*
Income tax direct tax on the earnings of individuals and corporations *(page 440)*
Federal Reserve Act law that set up a central banking system in 1913 *(page 441)*
Federal Trade Commission agency created by Congress to monitor American business *(page 441)*
unfair trade practices business practices that unfairly limited competition *(page 441)*

INTERDISCIPLINARY CONNECTIONS ACTIVITY

Literature In 1903 W.E.B. Du Bois published one of his most famous works, *The Soul of Black Folk,* a collection of 15 essays. In one essay, Du Bois spelled out his differences with and praise for Booker T. Washington. "Manly self-respect," Du Bois claimed, was "worth more than land and houses." Have students select one of the essays from *The Soul of Black Folk* and prepare a one-minute presentation about it. Presentations should include a summary of the essay and the reader's reaction. **L2**

L2

Section Quiz 13–4

✓ Reading Check

Answer: created an eight-hour workday for railroad workers

Reteach
Have students list Wilson's economic and social reforms.

Enrich
Invite interested students to
research the early history of the
NAACP and report their findings to the class. Encourage students to use library and Internet
resources for their research.

✓ Reading Check

Answer: expanded democracy and
raised expectations of the federal
government's role in the economy
and society

HISTORY Online

Study Central™ provides summaries,
interactive games, and online graphic
organizers to help students review
section content.

4 CLOSE

Have students evaluate the
legacy of the Progressive
movement.

442

---

declared the law unconstitutional on the grounds
that child labor was not interstate commerce and
therefore only states could regulate it. Wilson's effort,
however, helped his reputation with progressive voters. Wilson also supported the Adamson Act, which
established the eight-hour workday for railroad
workers, and the Federal Farm Loan Act, which created 12 Federal Land Banks to provide farmers with
long-term loans at low interest rates.

✓ Reading Check Examining How did the Adamson
Act improve labor conditions in the United States?

The Legacy of Progressivism

During his presidency, Wilson had built upon
Roosevelt's foundation. He expanded the role of the
federal government and of the president.

A New Kind of Government Progressivism made
important changes in the political life of the United
States. Before this era, most Americans did not expect
the government to pass laws protecting workers or
regulating big business. In fact, many courts had previously ruled that it was unconstitutional for the government to do so.

By the end of the Progressive era, however, both
legal and public opinion had shifted. Increasingly,
Americans expected the government, particularly the
federal government, to play a more active role in regulating the economy and solving social problems.

The Limits of Progressivism The most conspicuous limit to progressivism was its failure to address
African American reform issues. African Americans
themselves, however, were absorbing the reform
spirit, which fueled their longstanding desire for
advancement.

In 1905 W.E.B. Du Bois and 28 other African
American leaders met at Niagara Falls to demand full
political rights and responsibilities for African
Americans. They met on the Canadian side of the falls
because no hotel on the American side would accept
them. There they launched what became known as the
Niagara Movement. This meeting was one of many
steps leading to the founding of the **National
Association for the Advancement of Colored People**
(NAACP) in 1909. Du Bois and other NAACP founders
believed that the vote was essential to bring about an
end to lynching and racial discrimination. "The power
of the ballot we need in sheer self-defense," Du Bois
said, "else what shall save us from a second slavery?"

Despite the failure of most progressives to focus on
racial issues, Progressive reform helped change
American society in many ways. Although they
excluded many groups from their efforts, the progressives expanded democracy and improved the quality
of life for millions of men, women, and children. As the
country entered World War I, however, Americans
soon turned from reforming their own society to a crusade to "make the world safe for democracy."

✓ Reading Check Evaluating How did progressivism
change American beliefs about the federal government?

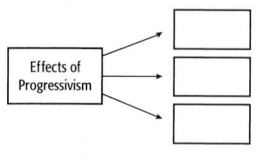

HISTORY Online **Study Central**™ To review this section, go to
tarvol2.glencoe.com and click on **Study Central**™.

SECTION 4 ASSESSMENT

Checking for Understanding
1. **Define:** income tax, unfair trade
practices.
2. **Identify:** Progressive Party, New
Nationalism, New Freedom, Federal
Reserve Act, Federal Trade Commission,
National Association for the
Advancement of Colored People.
3. **Explain** why President Wilson proposed
the establishment of the Federal
Reserve System.

Reviewing Themes
4. **Government and Democracy** What
new federal agencies increased the
government's power to regulate the
economy?

Critical Thinking
5. **Forming an Opinion** Which of
Wilson's reforms do you consider most
important? Why?
6. **Organizing** Use a graphic organizer
similar to the one below to list the effects
progressivism had on American society.

Effects of
Progressivism → [ ]
→ [ ]
→ [ ]

Analyzing Visuals
7. **Analyzing Photographs** Study the
photograph on page 443. What details
do you see in the image that might
have contributed to tainted meat?
When do you think the stamp above
the photo began to be used?

Writing About History
8. **Expository Writing** Imagine that you
are a newspaper editor during President
Wilson's administration. Write an article
on the shortcomings of the Progressive
movement in terms of its attitudes about
race. Provide ideas about how the
movement might have addressed
discrimination and segregation.

SECTION 4 ASSESSMENT ANSWERS

1. Terms are in blue.
2. Progressive Party *(p. 439)*, New
Nationalism *(p. 439)*, New
Freedom *(p. 439)*, Federal Reserve
Act *(p. 441)*, Federal Trade
Commission *(p. 441)*, National
Association for the Advancement
of Colored People *(p. 442)*
3. to restore public confidence in the
banking system
4. the Federal Reserve System and
the Federal Trade Commission
5. Students' answers will vary but
should include a reasonable
argument.
6. expanded democracy, improved
quality of life, expanded government role
7. condition of floors, wheelbarrow
carrying meat; after 1906
8. Students' editorials will vary.
Students should point out specific
shortcomings and suggest ways
that the progressives could have
addressed these social problems.

American LITERATURE

Born in Maryland in 1878, **Upton Sinclair** spent his life writing about and trying to change what he saw as wrong in the United States. One of his most famous novels, *The Jungle*, deals with working conditions and the rights of immigrants. The novel tells the story of Jurgis Rudkus, a Lithuanian immigrant who comes to the United States with his family in the early 1900s, dreaming of wealth and freedom. What he finds is "Packingtown," the bustling, filthy stockyards of Chicago. In the following excerpt, Sinclair describes the system Jurgis comes to know after gaining his first job in a meatpacking plant.

Read to Discover
What qualities did Sinclair believe a person must have to succeed in Packingtown?

Reader's Dictionary
pitted: set against each other

caldron: a large kettle or pot for boiling

knave: a tricky, deceitful person

from The Jungle
by Upton Sinclair

After Jurgis had been there awhile he would know that the plants were simply honeycombed with rottenness . . . —the bosses grafted off the men, and they grafted off each other; and some day the superintendent would find out about the boss, and then he would graft off the boss. . . . Here was Durham's, for instance, owned by a man who was trying to make as much money out of it as he could, and did not care in the least how he did it; and underneath him . . . were managers and superintendents and foremen, each one driving the man next below him and trying to squeeze out of him as much work as possible. And all the men of the same rank were pitted against each other. . . . So from top to bottom the place was simply a seething caldron of jealousies and hatreds; there was no loyalty or decency anywhere about it, there was no place in it where a man counted for anything against a dollar. . . .

Jurgis would find these things out for himself, if he stayed there long enough; it was the men [like him] who had to do all the dirty jobs. . . . Jurgis had come there, and thought he was going to make himself useful, and rise and become a skilled man; but he would soon find out his error—for nobody rose in Packingtown by doing good work. [I]f you met a man who was rising in Packingtown, you met a knave. . . . [T]he man who minded his own business and did his work— why, they would (wear) him out, and then . . . throw him into the gutter.

Analyzing Literature
1. According to the passage, what is the plant owner's main goal?
2. What does Sinclair mean when he says, ". . . there was no place in it where a man counted for anything against a dollar. . . ."?

Interdisciplinary Activity
Government When it was published, *The Jungle* was so shocking that it launched a government investigation of the meatpacking industry. The investigation eventually led to the establishment of laws regulating the industry. Using the Internet, research these laws and read about how they are enforced today. Write a short report on your findings.

CHAPTER 13 The Progressive Movement **443**

American LITERATURE

Block Schedule
Team Teaching This selection from *The Jungle* can be presented with English or Language Arts.

Read to Discover
Answer: greed, jealousy, and hatred

Reading Strategy

Reader's Dictionary
Have students look up words that might have a different meaning in this context, for example, *honeycombed* and *seething*.

Historical Connection
Upton Sinclair set out to expose the poor working conditions of immigrants but readers focused on how the meatpacking conditions affected *them*.

Portfolio Writing Activity
Have students write a short narrative about working conditions in a place a family member has worked.

Refer to tarvol2.glencoe.com for additional Glencoe Literature titles, lesson plans, and study guides related to this unit.

Answers to Analyzing Literature

1. His main goal is to make money.
2. He means that making money was more important than human life.

Interdisciplinary Activity
Students' reports will vary. Remind students to include bibliographic information about the sources they use.

CHAPTER
13 ASSESSMENT and ACTIVITIES

GLENCOE
TECHNOLOGY

MindJogger Videoquiz
Use the **MindJogger Videoquiz** to review Chapter 13 content.

 Available in DVD

Reviewing Key Terms

Students' answers will vary. The pages where the words appear in the text are shown in parentheses.

1. **progressivism** *(p. 419)*
2. **muckraker** *(p. 419)*
3. **commission plan** *(p. 420)*
4. **direct primary** *(p. 421)*
5. **initiative** *(p. 421)*
6. **referendum** *(p. 421)*
7. **recall** *(p. 421)*
8. **suffrage** *(p. 421)*
9. **temperance** *(p. 425)*
10. **prohibition** *(p. 425)*
11. **socialism** *(p. 425)*
12. **Square Deal** *(p. 428)*
13. **arbitration** *(p. 429)*
14. **syndicate** *(p. 436)*
15. **insubordination** *(p. 437)*
16. **income tax** *(p. 440)*
17. **unfair trade practices** *(p. 441)*

Reviewing Key Facts

18. Robert La Follette *(p. 421)*, Alice Paul *(p. 422)*, Hepburn Act *(p. 429)*, Upton Sinclair *(p. 430)*, Payne-Aldrich Tariff *(p. 436)*, Federal Reserve Act *(p. 441)*, Federal Trade Commission *(p. 441)*

19. belief that people could improve society, that government should play an active role in reform

20. He threatened to send in the army to work the mines. His threat finally got the mine owners to agree to arbitration.

21. He set up the Federal Reserve System to control the circulation of money in the United States.

Reviewing Key Terms

On a sheet of paper, use each of these terms in a sentence.

1. progressivism
2. muckraker
3. commission plan
4. direct primary
5. initiative
6. referendum
7. recall
8. suffrage
9. temperance
10. prohibition
11. socialism
12. Square Deal
13. arbitration
14. syndicate
15. insubordination
16. income tax
17. unfair trade practices

Reviewing Key Facts

18. **Identify:** Robert La Follette, Alice Paul, Hepburn Act, Upton Sinclair, Payne-Aldrich Tariff, Federal Reserve Act, Federal Trade Commission.
19. What were the characteristics of the Progressive era?
20. How did President Roosevelt influence the outcome of the 1902 coal strike?
21. How did President Wilson attempt to reform the banking industry?

Critical Thinking

22. **Analyzing Themes: Government and Democracy** How did Wisconsin governor La Follette help to expand democracy in the United States?
23. **Analyzing** How did Progressive reforms strengthen the cause of woman suffrage?
24. **Evaluating** What was the impact of reform leaders such as W.E.B. Du Bois and Robert La Follette on American society?
25. **Organizing** Use a graphic organizer similar to the one below to list the economic, political, and social welfare reforms brought about during the Progressive era.

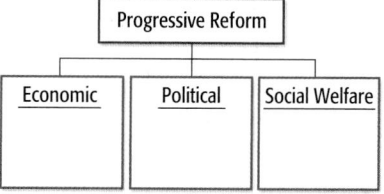

26. **Interpreting Primary Sources** Ida Husted Harper was a social reformer, a newspaper reporter, and a strong supporter of suffrage for women. In the following excerpt, she examines the attitudes of the time toward the kinds of work women should do.

Chapter Summary

Basic Beliefs of Progressives
• People could improve society by relying on science and knowledge.
• Industrialism and urbanization caused problems.
• Government should fix problems.
• To achieve reform, government itself had to be reformed.

Government Reforms
• Commission and city-manager forms of government were adopted.
• Direct primary system let citizens choose office candidates.
• Initiative, referendum, and recall were adopted.
• Seventeenth Amendment gave voters right to elect senators directly.
• Nineteenth Amendment gave women the right to vote.

Business Regulation
• Interstate Commerce Commission was strengthened.
• Consumer protection laws were passed.
• Federal Trade Commission was set up to regulate business.
• Federal Reserve System was set up to control money supply.

Social Reforms
• Zoning laws and building codes improved urban housing.
• Child labor laws were passed.
• Workers' compensation laws were passed.
• Temperance movement worked to ban alcohol.

444 CHAPTER 13 The Progressive Movement

Critical Thinking

22. pressured the state legislature to require each party to hold a direct primary, weakening the party caucus system

23. many middle class women concluded that they needed the vote to promote the social reforms they favored and to ensure the passage of labor laws to protect women

24. Du Bois helped establish the NAACP and La Follette helped create a more democratic government.

25. Economic: Federal Reserve Act, Sherman Antitrust Act, Underwood Tariff, Hepburn Act, Mann-Elkins Act, Newlands Reclamation Act; Political: city government structure, Nineteenth Amendment, direct primaries, direct election of senators, initiative, referendum, and recall; Social Welfare: Keating-Owen Child Labor Act, Adamson Act, Meat Inspection Act, Pure Food and Drug Act

HISTORY Online

Self-Check Quiz

Visit the *American Republic Since 1877* Web site at tarvol2.glencoe.com and click on *Self-Check Quizzes—Chapter 13* to assess your knowledge of chapter content.

“The moment we accept the theory that women must enter wage-earning occupations only when compelled to do so by poverty, that moment we degrade labor and lower the status of all women who are engaged in it. This theory prevailed throughout past ages, and it placed a stigma upon working women which is only beginning to be removed by the present generation. . . .

There is not, there never has been, an effort 'to create a sentiment that home is no place for a girl.' A good home is the one place above all others for a girl, as it is for a boy. It is her rest, her haven, her protection, but this does not necessarily imply that she must not engage in any work outside its limits. . . .

It is wholly impracticable to draw a dividing line between the employments which are suitable and those which are unsuitable for women. They have just as much right as men to decide this question for themselves. . . .

It is not intended to argue that every woman should leave the home and go into business, but only that those who wish to do so shall have the opportunity, and that men shall no longer monopolize the gainful occupations.”

—quoted in *The Independent,* 1901

a. What views does Ida Harper have on the kinds of work women should do?

b. What kinds of work-related issues do women face today?

Practicing Skills

27. **Taking Notes** Reread the subsection titled "The Coal Strike of 1902" on pages 428 and 429. Then use the steps you learned about taking notes on page 426 to take notes on the subsection.

Chapter Activities

28. **Technology** Search the Internet for an article written by a muckraker mentioned in the chapter. Using a word processor, prepare a two-page summary of the article and indicate how its contents may have sparked the demand for reform.

29. **Research Project** Worker safety was an important issue for progressives. Research three worker safety laws in your state, and describe how they benefit workers. Present your findings in a written report.

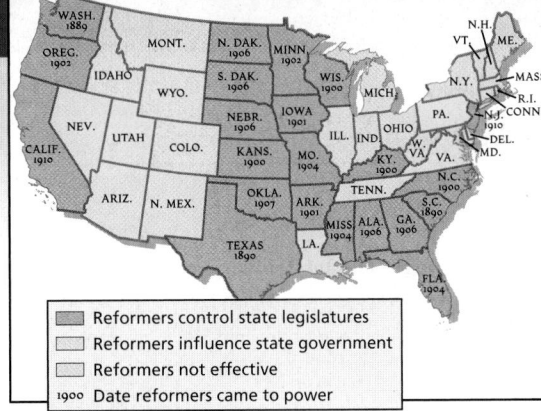

NATIONAL GEOGRAPHIC The Progressive Movement and State Governments 1889–1912

- Reformers control state legislatures
- Reformers influence state government
- Reformers not effective
- 1900 Date reformers came to power

Writing Activity

30. **Informative Writing** Imagine you are a reporter in 1906, assigned to interview Upton Sinclair. Reread pages 430 and 443, then prepare a list of questions to ask him during the interview.

Geography and History

31. The map above shows the relationship between the Progressive movement and state governments. Study the map and answer the questions below.

   a. Interpreting Maps Which three states came under the control of reformers before Wisconsin did?

   b. Applying Geography Skills What generalization can you make about progressives in state governments?

Standardized Test Practice

Directions: Choose the best answer to the following question.

In 1920 women won an important victory when the Nineteenth Amendment was ratified. What did this amendment accomplish?

A It required colleges to accept women.

B It guaranteed child care for workers' children.

C It granted women the right to vote.

D It guaranteed equal wages for equal work.

Test-Taking Tip: Some answers can be eliminated by using your own knowledge. For example, you probably know that child care is still an issue for parents today, so it cannot be guaranteed in the Nineteenth Amendment. Therefore, you can eliminate answer B.

HISTORY Online

Have students visit the Web site at tarvol2.glencoe.com to review Chapter 13 and take the Self-Check Quiz.

Writing Activity

30. Students' lists will vary but should show a keen understanding of the material presented on pages 430 and 443.

Geography and History

31. **a.** Texas, Washington, and South Carolina **b.** Reformers were most active in the South, Great Plains, and Far West.

Standardized Test Practice

Answer: C

Test-Taking Tip: Tell students to use the information in the stem of the question to help organize their thoughts. Most women were not worried about attending college in the 1920s, so they can eliminate A. Child care and equal wages are still issues facing women today, so they can also eliminate B and D.

Bonus Question ?

Ask: What does the term *suffrage* mean? *(the right to vote)*

---

26. **a.** She believed women could work at the same jobs as men. **b.** Possible answers: lower wages, sexual harassment, discrimination, difficulty finding child care

Practicing Skills

27. Have students trade their notes with a classmate and suggest improvements in their classmates' note-taking skills.

Chapter Activities

28. The summaries will vary but students should include an analysis of how the piece may have sparked the demand for reform.

29. The written reports should highlight the benefits of worker safety laws in your state.

Chapter 14 Resources

Timesaving Tools

TeacherWorks™ All-In-One Planner and Resource Center

- **Interactive Teacher Edition** Access your Teacher Wraparound Edition and your classroom resources with a few easy clicks.
- **Interactive Lesson Planner** Planning has never been easier! Organize your week, month, semester, or year with all the lesson helps you need to make teaching creative, timely, and relevant.

Use Glencoe's **Presentation Plus!** multimedia teacher tool to easily present dynamic lessons that visually excite your students. Using Microsoft PowerPoint® you can customize the presentations to create your own personalized lessons.

TEACHING TRANSPARENCIES

Graphic Organizer 14 L2

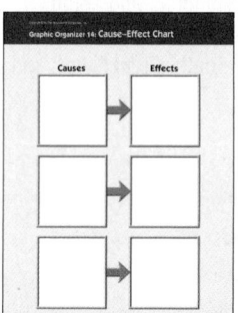

Why It Matters Chapter Transparency 14 L2

APPLICATION AND ENRICHMENT

Linking Past and Present Activity 14 L2

Enrichment Activity 14 L3

Primary Source Reading 14 L2

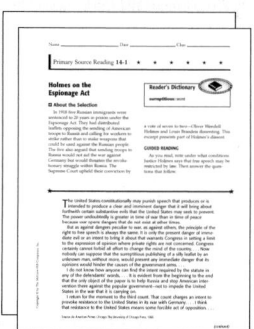

REVIEW AND REINFORCEMENT

Reteaching Activity 14 L1

Vocabulary Activity 14 L1

Time Line Activity 14 L2

Critical Thinking Skills Activity 14 L2

Meeting NCSS Standards

Local Standards

The following standards are covered in Chapter 14:

Section 1	II	Time, Continuity, and Change: B, C, F
Section 2	VI	Power, Authority, and Governance: B, C, D, I
Section 3	IV	Individual Development and Identity: A, D, E
Section 4	II	Time, Continuity, and Change: A, B, E

Chapter 14 Resources

ASSESSMENT AND EVALUATION

Chapter 14 Test Form A L2

Chapter 14 Test Form B L2

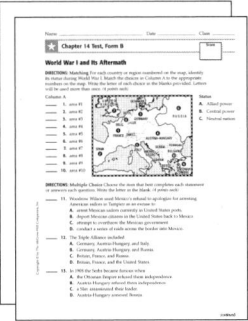

Standardized Test Practice Workbook Activity 14 L2

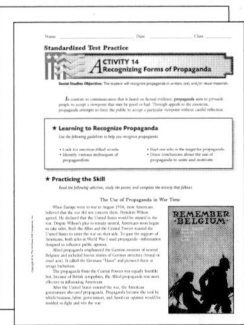

Performance Assessment Activities and Rubrics 14 L1/ELL

ExamView® Pro Testmaker CD-ROM

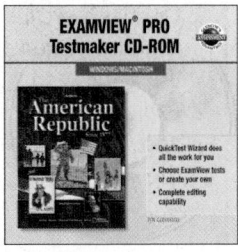

MULTIMEDIA

- Vocabulary PuzzleMaker CD-ROM
- Interactive Tutor Self-Assessment CD-ROM
- ExamView® Pro Testmaker CD-ROM
- Audio Program
- American History Primary Source Documents Library CD-ROM
- MindJogger Videoquiz
- Presentation Plus! CD-ROM
- TeacherWorks™ CD-ROM
- Interactive Student Edition CD-ROM
- Glencoe Skillbuilder Interactive Workbook CD-ROM, Level 2
- The *American Republic Since 1877* Video Program
- American Music: Hits Through History
- American Music: Cultural Traditions

SPANISH RESOURCES

The following Spanish language materials are available:

- Spanish Reading Essentials and Study Guide
- Spanish Guided Reading Activities
- Spanish Reteaching Activities
- Spanish Quizzes and Tests
- Spanish Vocabulary Activities
- Spanish Summaries
- The Declaration of Independence and United States Constitution Spanish Translation

THE HISTORY CHANNEL.

The following videotape programs are available from Glencoe as supplements to Chapter 14:

- **Woodrow Wilson: Reluctant Warrior** (ISBN 0-76-700101-X)
- **Pancho Villa: Outlaw Hero** (ISBN 0-76-700315-2)

To order, call Glencoe at 1-800-334-7344. To find classroom resources to accompany many of these videos, check the following home pages:
A&E Television: www.aande.com
The History Channel: www.historychannel.com

HISTORY Online

Use our Web site for additional resources. All essential content is covered in the Student Edition.

You and your students can visit tarvol2.glencoe.com, the Web site companion to the *American Republic Since 1877.* This innovative integration of electronic and print media offers your students a wealth of opportunities. The student text directs students to the Web site for the following options:

- **Chapter Overviews**
- **Self-Check Quizzes**
- **Student Web Activities**
- **Textbook Updates**

Answers to the student Web activities are provided for you in the **Web Activity Lesson Plans**. Additional Web resources and Interactive Tutor Puzzles are also available.

Chapter 14 Resources

SECTION RESOURCES

Daily Objectives	Reproducible Resources	Multimedia Resources
SECTION 1 **The United States Enters World War I** 1. Discuss the causes and results of American intervention in Mexico and the Caribbean. 2. Explain the causes of World War I and why the United States entered the war.	📁 Reproducible Lesson Plan 14–1 📁 Daily Lecture and Discussion Notes 14–1 📁 Guided Reading Activity 14–1* 📁 Section Quiz 14–1* 📁 Reading Essentials and Study Guide 14–1* 📁 Performance Assessment Activities and Rubrics 📁 American History in Graphic Novel	🖎 Daily Focus Skills Transparency 14–1 🖎 American Art & Architecture 💿 Interactive Tutor Self-Assessment CD-ROM 💿 ExamView® Pro Testmaker CD-ROM* 💿 Presentation Plus! CD-ROM 💿 TeacherWorks™ CD-ROM 🎧 Audio Program 🎵 American Music: Hits Through History 🎵 American Music: Cultural Traditions
SECTION 2 **The Home Front** 1. Analyze how the United States raised an army and won support for World War I. 2. Explain how the economy was controlled to support the war.	📁 Reproducible Lesson Plan 14–2 📁 Daily Lecture and Discussion Notes 14–2 📁 Guided Reading Activity 14–2* 📁 Section Quiz 14–2* 📁 Reading Essentials and Study Guide 14–2* 📁 Performance Assessment Activities and Rubrics 📁 Supreme Court Case Studies	🖎 Daily Focus Skills Transparency 14–2 💿 Interactive Tutor Self-Assessment CD-ROM 💿 ExamView® Pro Testmaker CD-ROM* 💿 Presentation Plus! CD-ROM 💿 TeacherWorks™ CD-ROM 🎧 Audio Program
SECTION 3 **A Bloody Conflict** 1. Discuss the fighting techniques used in World War I. 2. Characterize the American response to the Treaty of Versailles.	📁 Reproducible Lesson Plan 14–3 📁 Daily Lecture and Discussion Notes 14–3 📁 Guided Reading Activity 14–3* 📁 Section Quiz 14–3* 📁 Reading Essentials and Study Guide 14–3* 📁 Performance Assessment Activities and Rubrics	🖎 Daily Focus Skills Transparency 14–3 💿 Interactive Tutor Self-Assessment CD-ROM 💿 ExamView® Pro Testmaker CD-ROM* 💿 Presentation Plus! CD-ROM 💿 Skillbuilder Interactive Workbook, Level 2 💿 TeacherWorks™ CD-ROM 🎧 Audio Program
SECTION 4 **The War's Impact** 1. Describe the effects of the postwar recession on the United States. 2. Discuss the causes of and reaction to the Red Scare.	📁 Reproducible Lesson Plan 14–4 📁 Daily Lecture and Discussion Notes 14–4 📁 Guided Reading Activity 14–4* 📁 Section Quiz 14–4* 📁 Reading Essentials and Study Guide 14–4* 📁 Performance Assessment Activities and Rubrics 📁 Interpreting Political Cartoons	🖎 Daily Focus Skills Transparency 14–4 🖎 American Art & Architecture 💿 Interactive Tutor Self-Assessment CD-ROM 💿 ExamView® Pro Testmaker CD-ROM* 💿 Presentation Plus! CD-ROM 💿 TeacherWorks™ CD-ROM 💿 Vocabulary PuzzleMaker CD-ROM 🎧 Audio Program

`0:00` OUT OF TIME?
Assign the Chapter 14 **Reading Essentials and Study Guide.** 📁

*Also Available in Spanish

 Printed Materials   Transparency   💿 CD-ROM   DVD

 Poster   Music Program   Audio Program

NATIONAL GEOGRAPHIC Teacher's Corner

INDEX TO NATIONAL GEOGRAPHIC MAGAZINE

The following articles relate to this chapter.

- "The Bolshevik Revolution," October 1992
- "Riddle of the *Lusitania*," April 1994
- "St. Petersburg, Capital of the Tsars," December 1993
- "The Wings of War," March 1994

NATIONAL GEOGRAPHIC SOCIETY PRODUCTS

To order the following, call National Geographic at 1-800-368-2728:

- *Historical Atlas of the United States*
- *1917: Revolution in Russia* (Video)
- *1914–1918: World War I* (Video)

NGS ONLINE

Access National Geographic's Web site for current events, atlas updates, activities, links, interactive features, and archives.

www.nationalgeographic.com

MEETING SPECIAL NEEDS

In addition to the Differentiated Instruction strategies found in each section, the following resources are also suitable for your special needs students:

- *ExamView® Pro Testmaker CD-ROM* allows teachers to tailor tests by reducing answer choices.
- The *Audio Program* includes the entire narrative of the student edition so that less-proficient readers can listen to the words as they read them.
- The *Reading Essentials and Study Guide* provides the same content as the student edition but is written two grade levels below the textbook.

KEY TO ABILITY LEVELS

Teaching strategies have been coded.

L1 BASIC activities for all students
L2 AVERAGE activities for average to above-average students
L3 CHALLENGING activities for above-average students
ELL ENGLISH LANGUAGE LEARNER activities

From the Classroom of…

Lee Weber
Price Laboratory School
Cedar Falls, IA

U.S. Entrance into World War I

Place the following "Causes of American Entrance into World War I" on an overhead transparency:

- Loss of innocent lives
- Loss of trade
- Historical/cultural ties to British/French
- Defense of democracy against dictatorship
- Freedom of the seas
- The Zimmermann Note

Ask students to individually rank the causes from most important to least important. Then randomly group students and have them try to reach consensus. The interrelated nature of the six causes makes the task extremely difficult. If time permits, repeat the process and make a hypothetical change in the historical facts. For instance, suggest that Germany had a large surface navy and Britain developed unrestricted submarine warfare. How would U.S. policy have changed? Or, what if Germany were our major trading partner, not England and its allies?

ADDITIONAL RESOURCES FROM GLENCOE

- American Music: Cultural Traditions
- American Art & Architecture
- Outline Map Resource Book
- U.S. Desk Map
- Building Geography Skills for Life
- Inclusion for the High School Social Studies Classroom Strategies and Activities
- Teaching Strategies for the American History Classroom (Including Block Scheduling Pacing Guides)
- Dinah Zike's High School American History Reading and Study Skills Foldables

Block Schedule

Activities that are suited to use within the block scheduling framework are identified by: 🔳

Why It Matters Activity

Ask students how they think the United States's involvement in World War I affects their lives today. Students should evaluate their answers after they have completed the chapter.

GLENCOE TECHNOLOGY

The *American Republic Since 1877* Video Program

To learn more about how royal marriages and political alliances contributed to the war in Europe, have students view the Chapter 14 video, "Cousins: Royalty and World War I," from the ***American Republic Since 1877* Video Program.**

MindJogger Videoquiz

Use the **MindJogger Videoquiz** to preview Chapter 14 content.

 Both programs available in DVD

CHAPTER 14 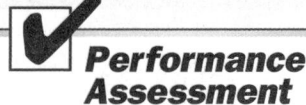 World War I and Its Aftermath

1914–1920

Why It Matters

The United States reluctantly entered World War I after German submarines violated American neutrality. After the war ended, President Wilson supported the Treaty of Versailles, believing its terms would prevent another war. The U.S. Senate, however, rejected the treaty. It did not want the country to be tied to European obligations. Instead, Americans turned their attention to the difficult adjustment to peacetime.

The Impact Today

The experience of World War I had a long-term effect on American history.
• The United States continues to be involved in European affairs.
• The horrors of the conflict helped reshape how people view warfare.

 The *American Republic Since 1877* Video The Chapter 14 video, "Cousins: Royalty and World War I," explains how royal marriages and complex political alliances contributed to the outbreak of war in Europe.

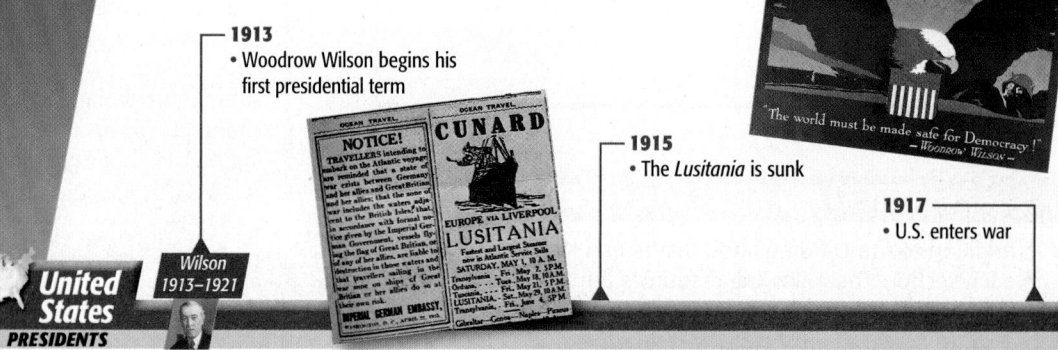

1913
• Woodrow Wilson begins his first presidential term

Wilson 1913–1921

United States PRESIDENTS

1915
• The *Lusitania* is sunk

1917
• U.S. enters war

1913   *1915*   *1917*

World

1914
• Archduke Franz Ferdinand assassinated; war begins in Europe

1915
• Italy joins Allies in war
• Japan gains rights in Chinese territory

1916
• British suppress Easter Rebellion in Ireland
• Battle of the Somme begins in July

1917
• Bolshevik Revolution begins in October
• Balfour Declaration favors setting up a Jewish homeland in Palestine

446

Reading Strategy ▶ PURPOSE FOR READING

Seed Discussion Students can lead their own discussion groups effectively by using this strategy. Organize the class into groups of five or six students. After the sinking of the *Lusitania,* President Wilson made this statement: "There is such a thing as a nation being so right that it does not need to convince others by force that it is right." Read the statement aloud and write it on the board. Ask the class: *What is Wilson's main point?* Instruct students to carry on a discussion within their group. Student #1 starts the seed discussion with his or her thoughts and ideas and becomes the recorder for the group. Student #2 adds an idea, or seed, and expands the discussion. Students should continue until all members have contributed. Conclude by posting the groups' reports in the classroom. **L1**

American soldiers in the 23rd Infantry fire on German positions in the Argonne Forest.

1918
- Congress passes Sedition Act
- Battle of Argonne Forest begins in September
- Armistice ends fighting on November 11

1919
- Race riots and strikes take place in Northern cities
- Red Scare and Palmer raids target Communists in the U.S.

Harding 1921–1923

1919

1921

1918
- Treaty of Brest-Litovsk ends Russian-German war

1919
- Treaty of Versailles conference begins

1920
- British government creates the Northern Ireland province

1921
- Irish Free State established by signed treaty

I WANT YOU *for the* **U.S. ARMY** ENLIST NOW

HISTORY
Online

Chapter Overview
Visit the *American Republic Since 1877* Web site at tarvol2.glencoe.com and click on *Chapter Overviews—Chapter 14* to preview chapter information.

447

HISTORY
Online
Introduce students to chapter content and key terms by having them access the **Chapter 14 Overview** at tarvol2.glencoe.com.

More About the Photo

Alvin C. York was one of the men on the battlefield at Argonne Forest. He is credited with almost single-handedly capturing 132 Germans. York kept a diary of the events, and his recollections of October 7, 1918, include the following description: "It was raining a little bit all day, drizzly and very damp. Lots of big shells bursting all around us. We were not up close enough for the machine guns to reach us, but airplanes were buzzing overhead most all the time, just like a lot of hornets. Lots of men were killed by the artillery fire. And lots more wounded." Ask students how the conditions of war produce heroes like York. *(Responses may typically refer to feelings for comrades.)*

TIME LINE

ACTIVITY

Have students use the chapter and section time lines to create a single time line that incorporates all of the significant dates related to World War I.

FOLDABLES™
Study Organizer

Dinah Zike's Foldables are three-dimensional, interactive graphic organizers that help students practice basic writing skills, review key vocabulary terms, and identify main ideas. Have students complete the foldable activity in the *Dinah Zike's Reading and Study Skills Foldables* booklet.

GRAPHIC ORGANIZER ACTIVITY

Organizing Information Have students create two maps of Europe, one showing Europe in 1914 and the other showing Europe after World War I. Encourage students to review these maps as they prepare for chapter assessments and to keep these maps for use with their study of World War II.

1 FOCUS

Section Overview

This section focuses on the events that led up to World War I and how the United States became involved.

BELLRINGER
Skillbuilder Activity

Project transparency and have students answer the question.

Daily Focus Skills Transparency 14–1

Reading Preview

Answers to Graphic: Balkan crisis, alliance system, naval race, assassination of Franz Ferdinand

Preteaching Vocabulary
For each of the Key Terms and Names, have students write a phrase or short sentence that will help them remember the significance of the term or name.

The United States Enters World War I

Guide to Reading

Main Idea
Although the United States tried to remain neutral, events soon pushed the nation into World War I.

Key Terms and Names
Pancho Villa, guerrilla, nationalism, self-determination, Franz Ferdinand, Allies, Central Powers, propaganda, contraband, U-boat, Sussex Pledge, Zimmermann telegram

Reading Strategy
Organizing As you read about the start of World War I, complete a graphic organizer similar to the one below by identifying the factors that contributed to the conflict.

Factors Contributing to World War I

Reading Objectives
• **Discuss** the causes and results of American intervention in Mexico and the Caribbean.
• **Explain** the causes of World War I and why the United States entered the war.

Section Theme
Continuity and Change Ties with the British influenced American leaders to enter World War I on the side of the Allies.

Preview of Events

| ♦1914 | ♦1915 | ♦1916 | ♦1917 |

April 1914
U.S. Marines occupy Veracruz, Mexico

June 1914
Assassination of Archduke Franz Ferdinand

July 1914
World War I begins

May 1915
Sinking of the *Lusitania*

April 1917
United States enters the war

Raising the flag at Veracruz

★ An American Story ★

Edith O'Shaughnessy could not sleep on the rainy night of April 20, 1914. Living at the American embassy in Mexico City, the wife of diplomat Nelson O'Shaughnessy was well aware of the growing crisis between Mexico and the United States. Earlier that day, President Wilson had asked Congress to authorize the use of force against Mexico. In her diary, O'Shaughnessy described the tensions in the Mexican capital:

66 I can't sleep. National and personal potentialities [possibilities] are surging through my brain. Three stalwart railroad men came to the Embassy this evening. They brought reports of a plan for the massacre of Americans in the street to-night, but, strange and wonderful thing, a heavy rain is falling. . . . Rain is as potent as shell-fire in clearing the streets, and I don't think there will be any trouble. 99

The next day, O'Shaughnessy reported that the conflict had begun: "We are in Mexico, in full intervention! . . . Marines are due to-day in Vera Cruz. . . ."

—adapted from *A Diplomat's Wife in Mexico*

Woodrow Wilson's Diplomacy

As president, Wilson resolved to "strike a new note in international affairs" and to see that "sheer honesty and even unselfishness . . . should prevail over nationalistic self-seeking in American foreign policy." Wilson strongly opposed imperialism. He also

---

SECTION RESOURCES

📁 Reproducible Masters
• Reproducible Lesson Plan 14–1
• Daily Lecture and Discussion Notes 14–1
• Guided Reading Activity 14–1
• Section Quiz 14–1
• Reading Essentials and Study Guide 14–1

Transparencies
• Daily Focus Skills Transparency 14–1

Multimedia
🔆 Interactive Tutor Self-Assessment CD-ROM
🔆 ExamView® Pro Testmaker CD-ROM
🔆 Presentation Plus! CD-ROM
🔆 TeacherWorks™ CD-ROM
🔊 Audio Program
🎵 American Music: Hits Through History
🎵 American Music: Cultural Traditions

believed that democracy was essential to a nation's stability and prosperity, and that the United States should promote democracy in order to ensure a peaceful world free of revolution and war. During Wilson's presidency, however, other forces at work at home and abroad frustrated his hope to lead the world by moral example. In fact, Wilson's first international crisis was awaiting him when he took office in March 1913.

The Mexican Revolution From 1884 to 1911, a dictator, Porfirio Díaz, ruled Mexico. Díaz encouraged foreign investment in Mexico to help develop the nation's industry. A few wealthy landowners dominated Mexican society. The majority of the people were poor and landless, and they were increasingly frustrated by their circumstances. In 1911 a revolution erupted, forcing Díaz to flee the country.

Francisco Madero, a reformer who appeared to support democracy, constitutional government, and land reform, replaced Díaz. Madero, however, proved to be an unskilled administrator. Frustrated with Mexico's continued decline, army officers plotted against Madero. Shortly before Wilson took office, General **Victoriano Huerta** seized power in Mexico, and Madero was murdered—presumably on Huerta's orders.

Huerta's brutality repulsed Wilson, who refused to recognize the new government. Wilson was convinced that without the support of the United States, Huerta soon would be overthrown. Wilson therefore tried to prevent weapons from reaching Huerta, and he permitted Americans to arm other political factions within Mexico.

Wilson Sends Troops Into Mexico In April 1914, American sailors visiting the city of Tampico were arrested after entering a restricted area. Though they were quickly released, their American commander demanded an apology. The Mexicans refused. Wilson used the refusal as an opportunity to overthrow Huerta. He sent marines to seize the Mexican port of Veracruz.

Although the president expected the Mexican people to welcome his action, anti-American riots broke out in Mexico. Wilson then accepted international mediation to settle the dispute. Venustiano Carranza, whose forces had acquired arms from the United States, became Mexico's president.

Mexican forces opposed to Carranza were not appeased, and they conducted raids into the United States hoping to force Wilson to intervene. **Pancho Villa** (VEE·yah) led a group of guerrillas—an

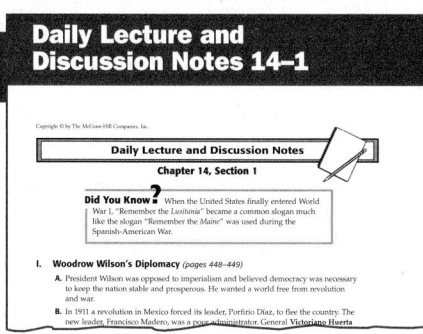

Picturing **History**

Moral Imperialism President Wilson sent General John Pershing (below) to stop Pancho Villa's (right) raids into the United States. Why was Villa conducting these raids?

armed band that uses surprise attacks and sabotage rather than open warfare—that burned the town of Columbus, New Mexico, and killed a number of Americans. Wilson responded by sending more than 6,000 U.S. troops under General **John J. Pershing** across the border to find and capture Villa. The expedition dragged on as Pershing failed to capture the guerrillas. Wilson's growing concern over the war raging in Europe finally caused him to recall Pershing's troops in 1917.

Wilson's Mexican policy damaged U.S. foreign relations. The British ridiculed the president's attempt to "shoot the Mexicans into self-government." Latin Americans regarded his "moral imperialism" as no improvement on Theodore Roosevelt's "big stick" diplomacy. In fact, Wilson followed Roosevelt's example in the Caribbean. During his first term, Wilson sent marines into Nicaragua, Haiti, and the Dominican Republic to preserve order and to set up governments that he hoped would be more stable and democratic than the current regimes.

✓ **Reading Check** **Examining** Why did President Wilson intervene in Mexico?

The Outbreak of World War I

Despite more than 40 years of general peace, tensions among European nations were building in 1914. Throughout the late 1800s and early 1900s, a number

CHAPTER 14   World War I and Its Aftermath   **449**

2 TEACH

Daily Lecture and Discussion Notes 14–1

Copyright © by The McGraw-Hill Companies, Inc.

Daily Lecture and Discussion Notes

Chapter 14, Section 1

Did You Know? When the United States finally entered World War I, "Remember the *Lusitania*" became a common slogan much like the slogan "Remember the *Maine*" was used during the Spanish-American War.

I.   Woodrow Wilson's Diplomacy *(pages 448–449)*

A. President Wilson was opposed to imperialism and believed democracy was necessary to keep the nation stable and prosperous. He wanted a world free from revolution and war.

B. In 1911 a revolution in Mexico forced its leader, Porfirio Díaz, to flee the country. The new leader, Francisco Madero, was a poor administrator. General **Victoriano Huerta**

Creating a Map Give students an outline map of Central America and have them identify and label all of the places mentioned in this section. **L1**

📁 Use the rubric for creating a map, display, or chart on pages 65–66 in the *Performance Assessment Activities and Rubrics.*

Picturing **History**

Answer: Mexicans were unhappy with the new Mexican president, who was receiving assistance from the United States. Villa was trying to force the United States to intervene.

Ask: How successful was Pershing's expedition to capture Pancho Villa? *(not a success; Pershing recalled)*

✓ **Reading Check**

Answer: first, to help support the overthrow of Huerta, later to suppress Villa

COOPERATIVE LEARNING ACTIVITY

Creating a News Magazine Have students create a special issue of a magazine that reports United States foreign policies from Wilson's inauguration on March 4, 1913, to his war message to Congress on April 2, 1917. Students might include news articles, news analysis, news features, editorials, and political cartoons. Advise students to determine specific tasks for each individual. Suggest that they choose an editor in chief to help organize the selection of topics so that the end product contains varied and accurate coverage of the foreign policy of the period. 📦

Use the rubric for a cooperative group management plan on pages 71–72 in the *Performance Assessment Activities and Rubrics.*

Guided Reading Activity 14–1

Name _____ Date _____ Class _____

★ **Guided Reading Activity 14-1**

DIRECTIONS: Recording Who, What, When, Where, Why, and How Read the section and answer the questions below. Refer to your textbook to write the answers.

1. Who seized power in Mexico shortly before Woodrow Wilson took office as president in 1913?
2. How did Wilson respond to a refusal of the Mexicans to apologize for arresting American sailors in April 1914?
3. How did Wilson respond to attacks on American soil by Mexican guerrilla Pancho Villa?
4. What was the result of this action?
5. How was the new surge of nationalism evident in Europe in the late 1800s?

Writing Newspaper Headlines
Have students choose three major events leading to World War I and write a newspaper headline for each event. Tell students to review newspaper headlines that focus on the United States's War on Terrorism in Afghanistan, Iraq, and elsewhere to see how editors use a few words for maximum impact. Point out that most newspapers use action verbs in headlines. For example, most editors would choose "U.S. Enters War" rather than "A Nation at War." **L2**

FYI

On Christmas Day 1914, the fighting stopped, and British and German soldiers met in no-man's-land to chat, play soccer, and pose for photographs. Officers quickly ended these goodwill meetings, and the soldiers returned to war.

---

of factors created problems among the powers of Europe and set the stage for a monumental war.

The Alliance System The roots of World War I date back to the 1860s. In 1864, while Americans fought the Civil War, the German kingdom of Prussia launched the first of a series of wars to unite the various German states into one nation. By 1871 Prussia had united Germany and proclaimed the birth of the German Empire. The new German nation rapidly industrialized and quickly became one of the most powerful nations in the world.

The creation of Germany transformed European politics. In 1870, as part of their plan to unify Germany, the Prussians had attacked and defeated France. They then forced the French to give up territory along the German border. From that point forward, France and Germany were enemies. To protect itself, Germany signed alliances with Italy and with Austria-Hungary, a huge empire that controlled much of southeastern Europe. This became known as the **Triple Alliance.**

The new alliance alarmed Russian leaders, who feared that Germany intended to expand eastward into Russia. Russia and Austria-Hungary were also competing for influence in southeastern Europe. Many of the people of southeastern Europe were Slavs—the same ethnic group as the Russians—and the Russians wanted to support them against Austria-Hungary. As a result, Russia and France had a common interest in opposing Germany and Austria-Hungary. In 1894 they signed the Franco-Russian Alliance.

The Naval Race While the other major powers of Europe divided into competing alliances, Great Britain remained neutral. Then, in 1898, the Germans began to build a navy challenging Great Britain's historical dominance at sea. By the early 1900s, an arms race had begun between Great Britain and Germany, as both sides raced to build warships. The naval race greatly increased tensions between Germany and Britain and convinced the British to establish closer relations with France and Russia. The British refused to sign a formal alliance, so their new relationship with the French and Russians became known as an "entente cordiale"—a friendly understanding. Britain, France, and Russia became known as the **Triple Entente.**

The Balkan Crisis By the late 1800s, nationalism, or a feeling of intense pride of one's homeland, had become a powerful idea in Europe. Nationalists place

Fateful Couple Archduke Franz Ferdinand and wife Sophia visit Sarajevo the day of the assassination.

primary emphasis on promoting their homeland's culture and interests above those of other countries. Nationalism was one of the reasons for the tensions among the European powers. Each nation viewed the others as competitors, and many people were willing to go to war to expand their nation at the expense of others.

One of the basic ideas of nationalism is the right to self-determination—the idea that people who belong to a nation should have their own country and government. In the 1800s, nationalism led to a crisis in southeastern Europe in the region known as the **Balkans.** Historically, the Ottoman Empire and the Austro-Hungarian Empire had ruled the Balkans. Both of these empires were made up of many different nations. As nationalism became a powerful force in the 1800s, the different national groups within these empires began to press for independence.

Among the groups pushing for independence were the Serbs, Bosnians, Croats, and Slovenes. These people all spoke similar languages and had come to see themselves as one people. They called themselves South Slavs, or Yugoslavs. The first of these people to obtain independence were the Serbs, who formed a nation called Serbia between the Ottoman and Austro-Hungarian empires. Serbs believed their nation's mission was to unite the South Slavs.

Russia supported the Serbs, while Austria-Hungary did what it could to limit Serbia's growth. In 1908 Austria-Hungary annexed Bosnia, which at the time belonged to the Ottoman Empire. The Serbs were furious. They wanted Bosnia to be part of their nation. The annexation demonstrated to the Serbs that Austria-Hungary had no intention of letting the Slavic people in its empire become independent.

A Continent Goes to War In late June 1914, the heir to the Austro-Hungarian throne, the Archduke **Franz Ferdinand,** visited the Bosnian capital

---

DIFFERENTIATED INSTRUCTION

Visual/Spatial Have students use a map in the text or an outline map that you provide to locate the members of the Triple Alliance and Triple Entente. Ask students to measure the distances between the capitals of the countries within the two groups. Then discuss the relative size and proximity of these groupings. **Ask:** Why might it be beneficial for allied nations to be located near each other? Does the distance matter if your allies are large and strong? **L1**

☞ Refer to *Inclusion for the High School Social Studies Classroom Strategies and Activities* in the TCR.

of Sarajevo. As he and his wife rode through the city, a Bosnian revolutionary named Gavrilo Princip rushed their open car and shot the couple to death. The assassin was a member of a Serbian nationalist group nicknamed the "Black Hand." The assassination took place with the knowledge of Serbian officials who hoped to start a war that would bring down the Austro-Hungarian Empire.

The Austro-Hungarian government blamed Serbia for the attack and decided the time had come to crush Serbia in order to prevent Slavic nationalism from undermining its empire. Knowing an

NATIONAL GEOGRAPHIC — European Alliances, 1914

In Motion

0   500 miles
0   500 kilometers
Lambert Azimuthal Equal-Area projection

NORWAY
St. Petersburg (Petrograd)
SWEDEN
Moscow
DENMARK
North Sea
Baltic Sea
UNITED KINGDOM
RUSSIA
London
NETH.
Berlin
BELG. GERMANY
LUX.
Paris
ATLANTIC OCEAN
FRANCE
SWITZ.
Vienna
Budapest
AUSTRIA-HUNGARY

June 28, 1914 Archduke Franz Ferdinand assassinated by Serb nationalist.

PORTUGAL
SPAIN
Corsica Fr.
ITALY
Sardinia It.
Rome
ALBANIA
Sarajevo
SERBIA
ROMANIA
Black Sea
MONTENEGRO
BULGARIA

Bulgaria joined the Central Powers in 1915. Romania joined the Allies in 1916.

Constantinople
GREECE
OTTOMAN EMPIRE

Italy refused to honor Central Powers alliance and joined Allied Powers on May 23, 1915.

Sicily It.

Greece did not enter the war until 1917.

SPANISH MOROCCO
MOROCCO Fr.
TUNISIA Fr.
ALGERIA Fr.
LIBYA It.
Crete Gr.
Cyprus U.K.
Mediterranean Sea
EGYPT U.K.

Legend:
- Allied Powers
- Central Powers
- Neutral nations
- → Initial troop movements of Central Powers

Geography Skills

1. **Interpreting Maps** Which nations comprised the Central Powers in 1914?
2. **Applying Geography Skills** What was the name of the southeastern European region that sparked the beginning of the war?

June 28
Assassination of Archduke Franz Ferdinand

July 28
Austria-Hungary declares war on Serbia

August 3
Germany declares war on France, begins invasion of Belgium

August 6
Austria-Hungary declares war on Russia

◆July 1914   ◆August 1914

July 30
Russia begins mobilizing troops in defense of Serbia

August 1
Germany declares war on Russia

August 4
Britain declares war on Germany

August 12
France and Great Britain declare war on Austria-Hungary

CHAPTER 14 World War I and Its Aftermath **451**

Geography Skills

Answers:
1. Germany, Austria-Hungary, Bulgaria, Ottoman Empire, Italy joined the Allies in 1915
2. Balkans

Geography Skills Practice
Ask: Into what country did the Central Powers send troops? *(France)*

Interpreting a Map Have students create a map of Europe at the beginning of World War I. Have students label the countries and indicate the order in which the countries involved in the conflict declared war. **L1**

📁 Use the rubric for creating a map, display, or chart on pages 65–66 in the *Performance Assessment Activities and Rubrics.*

FYI

The last Ottoman sultan with any political and military power was Abdul Hamid. He was responsible for the massacres of Armenian men, women, and children living in Anatolia from 1894 to 1896. Although there was widespread condemnation in the West, the Ottomans did gain one friend among European nations—Germany. Hamid was overthrown in 1908 by the Committee of Union and Progress (CUP). Two important members of CUP, Enver Bey and Talaat Bey, forged the alliance with Germany that would carry over into World War I.

INTERDISCIPLINARY CONNECTIONS ACTIVITY

Civics Have students research the reaction to the start of World War I of people who lived in your community at the beginning of the war. Suggest that students use library, museum, historical society, and government resources to locate information. Encourage students to investigate resources available from veterans organizations in the community. **L2**

Background: Although she represented all that suffragists were striving for, Rankin's vote against entering World War I alienated her from many suffragists. After she voted against the war, several suffragist groups in New York canceled her speaking engagements.

Ask: How did Jeannette Rankin demonstrate her commitment to pacifism? *(voting against entry into World War I, voting against entry into World War II, protesting against the Vietnam War)*

Answer: assassination of Archduke Franz Ferdinand and his wife

FYI

Until the outbreak of World War I, Europe had not had a major war for almost 100 years, since the end of the Napoleonic Wars in 1815.

History and the Humanities

🎵 American Music: Hits Through History: "Over There"

🎵 American Music: Cultural Traditions: "War Song Hits"

🖋 American Art & Architecture: "I Want You for the U.S. Army"

---

attack on Serbia might trigger a war with Russia, the Austrians asked their German allies for support. Germany promised to support Austria-Hungary if war erupted.

Austria-Hungary then issued an ultimatum to the Serbian government. The Serbs counted on Russia to back them up, and the Russians, in turn, counted on France. French leaders were worried that they might someday be caught alone in a war with Germany, so they were determined to keep Russia as an ally. They promised to support Russia if war began.

On July 28, Austria declared war on Serbia. Russia immediately mobilized its army, including troops stationed on the German border. On August 1, Germany declared war on Russia. Two days later, it declared war on France. World War I had begun.

Germany's Plan Fails Germany had long been prepared for war against France and Russia. It immediately launched a massive invasion of France, hoping to knock the French out of the war. It would then be able to send its troops east to deal with the Russians.

Profiles IN HISTORY

Jeannette Rankin
1880–1973

As he addressed the "Gentlemen of the Congress" on April 2, 1917, President Woodrow Wilson actually misspoke. Sitting in the chamber listening to the president's request for a declaration of war against Germany was Representative Jeannette Rankin—the first woman ever elected to Congress.

Rankin was born in Missoula, Montana, in 1880. She became a social worker and participated in the woman suffrage movement. In 1916 she was elected to the U.S. House of Representatives from Montana—one of the few states at that time that allowed women to vote. As a representative, Rankin sponsored legislation to grant federal voting rights for women and to provide health services for them.

Apart from her title as the first woman in Congress, Rankin is remembered most for her strong pacifism. She was one of 56 legislators who voted against the nation's entry into World War I. "I want to stand by my country," she said, "but I cannot vote for war."

In 1940 Rankin ran again for Congress as a representative from Montana. She ran on an isolationist policy and won. In 1941 she was the only member of Congress to vote against declaring war on Japan and entering World War II.

After leaving Congress in 1943, Rankin continued working for peace. In 1968, at 87 years of age, she led thousands of women in the March on Washington to oppose the Vietnam War.

452 CHAPTER 14 World War I and Its Aftermath

The German plan had one major problem. It required the German forces to advance through neutral Belgium in order to encircle the French troops. The British had guaranteed Belgium's neutrality. When German troops crossed the Belgian frontier, Britain declared war on Germany.

Those fighting for the Triple Entente were called the **Allies.** France, Russia, and Great Britain formed the backbone of the Allies along with Italy, which joined them in 1915 after the other Allies promised to cede Austro-Hungarian territory to Italy after the war. What remained of the Triple Alliance—Germany and Austria-Hungary—joined with the Ottoman Empire and Bulgaria to form the **Central Powers.**

The German plan seemed to work at first. German troops swept through Belgium and headed into France, driving back the French and British forces. Then, to the great surprise of the Germans, Russian troops invaded Germany. The Germans had not expected Russia to mobilize so quickly. They were forced to pull some of their troops away from the attack on France and send them east to stop the Russians. This weakened the German forces just enough to give the Allies a chance to stop them. The Germans drove to within 30 miles (48 km) of Paris, but stubborn resistance by British and French troops at the Battle of the Marne finally stopped the German advance. Because the swift German attack had failed to defeat the French, both sides became locked in a bloody stalemate along hundreds of miles of trenches that would barely change position for the next three years.

The Central Powers had greater success on the Eastern Front. German and Austrian forces stopped the Russian attack and then went on the offensive. They swept across hundreds of miles of territory and took hundreds of thousands of prisoners. Russia suffered 2 million killed, wounded, or captured in 1915 alone, but it kept fighting.

✓ **Reading Check** **Explaining** What incident triggered the beginning of World War I?

American Neutrality

When the fighting began, President Wilson declared the United States to be neutral in an attempt to keep the

---

CRITICAL THINKING ACTIVITY

Explaining Causes Write the following terms on the chalkboard: *imperialism, nationalism, militarism, balance of power.* Have students define each term. Using the text and additional research, ask them to explain how each contributed to war in Europe. Ask if students think any one nation or group of nations was primarily responsible for World War I. Have each student give evidence to support his or her opinion. **L2**

country from being drawn into a foreign war. "We must be impartial in thought as well as in action," Wilson stated. For many Americans, however, that proved difficult to do.

Americans Take Sides Despite the president's plea, many Americans showed support for one side or the other. This was especially true for recent immigrants from Europe. Many of the 8 million German Americans, for example, supported their homeland. The nation's 4.5 million Irish Americans, whose homeland endured centuries of British rule, also sympathized with the Central Powers.

In general, though, American public opinion favored the Allied cause. Many Americans valued the heritage, language, and political ideals they shared with Britain. Others treasured America's historic links with France, a great friend to America during the Revolutionary War.

Pro-British Sentiment One select group of Americans was decidedly pro-British: President Wilson's cabinet. Only Secretary of State William Jennings Bryan favored neutrality. The other cabinet members, as well as Bryan's chief adviser, Robert Lansing, and Walter Hines Page, the American ambassador to London, argued forcefully on behalf of Britain. American military leaders also backed the British. They believed that an Allied victory was the only way to preserve the international balance of power.

British officials worked diligently to win American support. One method they used was propaganda, or information designed to influence opinion. Both the Allies and the Central Powers used propaganda, but German propaganda was mostly anti-Russian and did not appeal to most Americans. British propaganda, on the other hand, was extremely skillful. Furthermore, Britain cut the transatlantic telegraph cable from Europe to the United States, limiting news about the war mainly to British reports. Stories arrived depicting numerous German war atrocities, including the charge that Germans used corpses from the battlefield to make fertilizer and soap. Although many such reports were questionable, enough Americans believed them to help sway American support in favor of the Allies.

ECONOMICS

Business Links American business interests also leaned toward the Allies. Companies in the United States, particularly on the East Coast, had strong ties with businesses in the Allied countries. As business leader Thomas W. Lamont stated, "Our firm had

never for one moment been neutral: we did not know how to be. From the very start we did everything that we could to contribute to the cause of the Allies."

Many American banks began to invest heavily in an Allied victory. American loans to the cash-hungry Allies skyrocketed. By 1917 such loans would total over $2 billion. Other American banks, particularly in the Midwest, where pro-German feelings were strongest, also lent some $27 million to Germany. Even more might have been lent, but most foreign loans required the approval of William McAdoo, the secretary of the Treasury. McAdoo was strongly pro-British and did what he could to limit loans to Germany. As a result, the country's prosperity was intertwined with the military fortunes of Britain, France, and Russia. If the Allies won, the money would be paid back; if not, the money might be lost forever.

✓ **Reading Check** **Evaluating** How was American prosperity intertwined with the military fortunes of the Allies?

Moving Toward War

Although most Americans supported the Allies and hoped for their victory, they did not want to join the conflict. However, a series of events gradually eroded American neutrality and drew the nation into the war firmly on the side of the Allies.

The British Blockade Shortly after the war began, the British deployed their navy to blockade Germany and keep it from obtaining supplies. The British planted mines in the North Sea and forced neutral ships into port for inspections in case they were trying to transport valuable materials to Germany or its neutral neighbors. British officials also expanded their definition of contraband, or prohibited materials, to prevent neutral countries from shipping food to Germany.

The Germans knew that the Allies depended on food, equipment, and other supplies from both the United States and their overseas empires. If Germany could strangle that trade, it could starve the British and French into surrendering. To get around Britain's blockade, the Germans deployed submarines known as U-boats—from the German

Student Web Activity Visit the *American Republic Since 1877* Web site at tarvol2.glencoe.com and click on *Student Web Activities— Chapter 14* for an activity on World War I.

✓ **Reading Check**

Answer: Many American banks invested in an Allied victory and made loans to the Allies.

HISTORY Online

Objectives and answers to the student activity can be found in the **Web Activity Lesson Plan** at tarvol2.glencoe.com.

Discussing a Topic Have students discuss the differences between news reporting, propaganda, and advertising. Ask students to identify the purpose of each and explain the value of each. **L2**

CURRICULUM CONNECTION

Government Concerning the Mexican Revolution, President Wilson cautioned "watchful waiting." Interventionists termed his policy "deadly drifting." One critic joked about Wilson's diplomacy by making up an ironic dance step he called the Wilson Tango. It consisted of one step forward, two steps back, one to the side, and then a hesitation.

EXTENDING THE CONTENT

Distress Signals From the early days of wireless telegraphy, a distress call has had absolute priority over all other communications. In 1904 the Marconi Company directed its ships to use the letters *CQD*, popularly defined as "Come Quick—Distress" or "Come Quick—Danger." These abbreviations were adopted by the British Post Office telegraph service. Because the letters CQ were also used for general calls, confusion often developed. The distress signal, therefore, was replaced in 1912 by *SOS*, popularly defined as "Sink or Swim" or "Save Our Ship." The distress call used in radio telephony, "Mayday," is a corruption of the French phrase *M'aidez*, "Help me."

Picturing History

Answer: Germans believed that any British passenger liners might contain supplies for the Allies.
Ask: Do you think military supplies might have been on passenger liners? *(Answers will vary.)*

3 ASSESS

Assign Section 1 Assessment as homework or as an in-class activity.

Have students use the **Interactive Tutor Self-Assessment CD-ROM.**

L1/ELL

Reading Essentials and Study Guide 14–1

L2

Section Quiz 14–1

FYI

The first German U-boat was built in 1906. During World War I, Germany was able to put several types of U-boats into service.

454

---

word *Unterseeboot* (meaning "underwater boat"). In February 1915, the Germans announced that they would attempt to sink without warning any ship they found in the waters around Britain.

Germany's announcement triggered outrage in the United States and elsewhere. Attacking civilian vessels without warning violated an international treaty stipulating that military vessels must reveal their intentions to merchant ships and make provisions for the safety of the targeted ship's crew and passengers before sinking it. The Germans claimed that many merchant ships were actually warships in disguise and that their U-boats would be placed at great risk if they revealed themselves before firing.

The issue reached a crisis on May 7, 1915. Despite warnings from Germany, the British passenger liner *Lusitania* entered the war zone. A submerged German submarine fired on the ship, killing nearly 1,200 passengers—including 128 Americans. Many Americans were outraged and regarded the attack as an act of terrorism, not war.

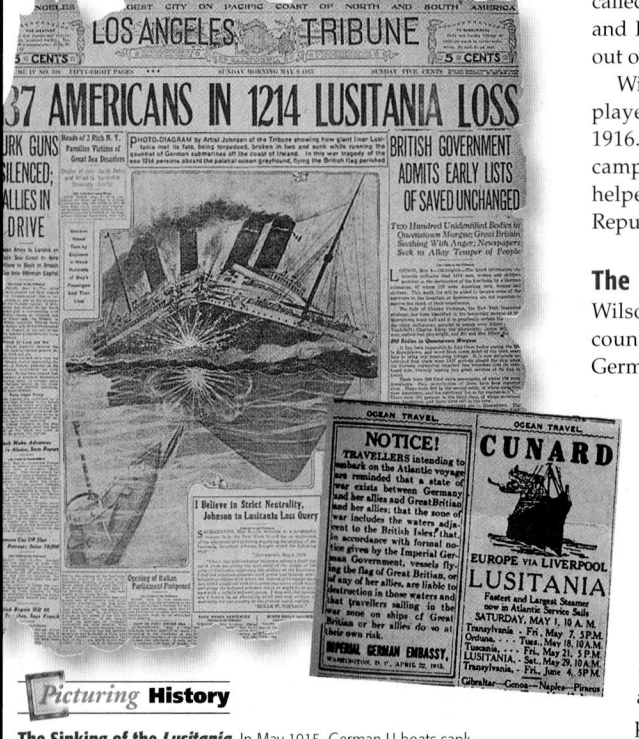

Picturing History

The Sinking of the *Lusitania* In May 1915, German U-boats sank the British passenger liner *Lusitania*. Among those who drowned were 128 Americans. Here the *Los Angeles Tribune* reports the attack, and a newspaper advertisement warns ship passengers to travel the Atlantic at their own risk. Why were the Germans sinking passenger liners?

454 CHAPTER 14 World War I and Its Aftermath

Others argued that the passengers traveling on ships of foreign nations did so at their own risk.

Wilson steered a middle course on the issue of the U-boats. He refused to take extreme measures against Germany, saying that the United States was "too proud to fight." Nevertheless, he sent several diplomatic notes to Germany insisting that its government safeguard the lives of noncombatants in the war zones.

Late in March 1916, Wilson's policy was tested when a U-boat torpedoed the French passenger ship *Sussex*, injuring several Americans on board. Although Wilson's closest advisers favored breaking off diplomatic relations with Germany immediately, the president, busy with the crisis in Mexico, chose to issue one last warning. He demanded that the German government abandon its methods of submarine warfare or risk war with the United States.

Germany did not want to strengthen the Allies by drawing the United States into the war. It promised with certain conditions to sink no more merchant ships without warning. The **Sussex Pledge,** as it was called, met the foreign-policy goals of both Germany and President Wilson by keeping the United States out of the war a little longer.

Wilson's efforts to keep American soldiers at home played an important part in his re-election bid in 1916. Campaigning as the "peace" candidate, his campaign slogan, "He kept us out of the war," helped lead Wilson to a narrow victory over the Republican nominee, Charles Evans Hughes.

The United States Declares War Following Wilson's re-election, events quickly brought the country to the brink of war. In January 1917, a German official named Arthur Zimmermann cabled the German ambassador in Mexico, instructing him to make an offer to the Mexican government. Zimmermann proposed that Mexico ally itself with Germany in the event of war between Germany and the United States. In return, Mexico would regain its "lost territory in Texas, New Mexico, and Arizona" after the war. Germany hoped Mexico would tie down the American forces and prevent them from being sent to Europe. British intelligence intercepted the **Zimmermann telegram.** Shortly afterward, it was leaked to American newspapers. Furious, many Americans now concluded war with Germany was necessary.

Then, on February 1, 1917, Germany resumed unrestricted submarine warfare. German military leaders believed that they could starve Britain into

---

Reading Strategy   READING THE TEXT

Reviewing Information Discuss with students what caused the outbreak of World War I. Make sure students include information they have gathered while reading the section. Aside from the assassination of Archduke Franz Ferdinand, the economic interests and military alliances of the European countries made war probable. Because of entangled treaties and continued colonial aspirations, Europe was poised for a war that could have been set off by any number of events. Ask students to explain how the Russian Revolution affected the war. *(Because of the revolution, Russia withdrew from the war. This meant Germany was free to concentrate its forces on the Western front.)* **L1**

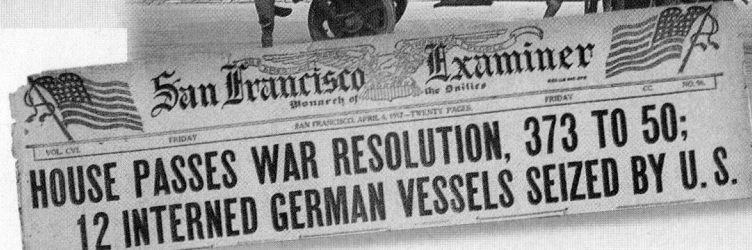

"The world must be made safe for democracy."

—Woodrow Wilson, April 1917

***Picturing* History**

Americans Go to War Congress voted heavily in favor of entering the European war. Here, excited Americans wave from an Army recruitment truck. What events pushed the United States to finally declare war?

***Picturing* History**

Answer: British blockade, sinking of the *Lusitania* and other passenger liners, Germany's attempt to ally with Mexico

Ask: By looking at this picture, what might you assume about public opinion related to the U.S. government's decision to enter the war? *(that people supported the decision)*

San Francisco Examiner

HOUSE PASSES WAR RESOLUTION, 373 TO 50; 12 INTERNED GERMAN VESSELS SEIZED BY U.S.

submission in four to six months if their U-boats could return to a more aggressive approach of sinking all ships on sight. Although they recognized that their actions might draw the United States into the war, the Germans did not believe that the Americans could raise an army and transport it to Europe in time to prevent the Allies from collapsing.

Between February 3 and March 21, German U-boats sank six American merchant ships without warning. Finally roused to action, President Wilson appeared before a special session of Congress on April 2, 1917, to ask for a declaration of war against Germany.

66It is a fearful thing to lead this great peaceful people into war. . . . But the right is more precious than peace, and we shall fight for the things which we have always carried nearest to our hearts—for democracy, for the right of those who submit to authority to have a voice in their own governments, for the rights and liberties of small nations. . . .99

—quoted in the *Congressional Record,* 1917

After a spirited debate, the Senate passed the resolution on April 4 by a vote of 82 to 6. The House concurred 373 to 50 on April 6, and Wilson signed the resolution. America was now at war.

✔ **Reading Check** **Summarizing** How did Germany's use of unrestricted submarine warfare lead to American entry into World War I?

Reteach

Have students explain the causes and results of American intervention in Mexico and the Caribbean.

Enrich

Invite interested students to develop a multimedia presentation to help explain the history of the Balkans. Encourage students to use library and Internet resources for this assignment.

✔ **Reading Check**

Answer: The Germans sank civilian passenger liners and U.S. merchant ships, which outraged the Americans, who then sided with the British.

HISTORY *Online*

Study Central™ provides summaries, interactive games, and online graphic organizers to help students review section content.

SECTION 1 ASSESSMENT

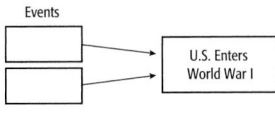
HISTORY *Online* **Study Central**™ To review this section, go to **tarvol2.glencoe.com** and click on **Study Central**™.

Checking for Understanding

1. **Define:** guerrilla, nationalism, self-determination, propaganda, contraband, U-boat.
2. **Identify:** Pancho Villa, Franz Ferdinand, Allies, Central Powers, Sussex Pledge, Zimmermann telegram.
3. **Name** the two alliances that Europe was divided into at the start of World War I.

Reviewing Themes

4. **Continuity and Change** Why did most of President Wilson's cabinet members support the British?

Critical Thinking

5. **Synthesizing** How did European nationalism contribute to the outbreak of World War I?
6. **Organizing** Use a graphic organizer similar to the one below to identify the events that led the United States to enter World War I.

Events

→ U.S. Enters World War I

Analyzing Visuals

7. **Analyzing Time Lines** Examine the time line on page 451. How does the order in which countries declared war reflect the European alliance system?

Writing About History

8. **Expository Writing** Imagine that you are a Mexican citizen living in Mexico between 1914 and 1917. Write a script for a radio newscast in which you express your feelings about American actions in Mexico. Include reasons for your feelings.

CHAPTER 14 World War I and Its Aftermath **455**

SECTION 1 ASSESSMENT ANSWERS

1. Terms are in blue.
2. Pancho Villa *(p. 449),* Franz Ferdinand *(p. 450),* Allies *(p. 452),* Central Powers *(p. 452),* Sussex Pledge *(p. 454),* Zimmermann telegram *(p. 454)*
3. Triple Alliance and Triple Entente
4. They believed that Allied victory was the only way to preserve the

international balance of power, and they cited the close historical ties with Britain and France.

5. Each major ethnic group in European empires wanted its own country.
6. unrestricted submarine warfare; Germany's attempt to ally with Mexico

7. When one country declared war, its allies declared war.
8. Students' scripts will vary. Encourage students to act out their scripts as if they were actually on the radio.

4 CLOSE

Have students discuss the causes of World War I and why the United States entered the war.

1 FOCUS

Section Overview

This section focuses on the efforts undertaken at home to mobilize the nation for war.

BELLRINGER
Skillbuilder Activity

Project transparency and have students answer the question.

Daily Focus Skills Transparency 14–2

Reading Preview

Answers to Graphic:
I. Building Up the Military
   A. Selective Service
   B. African Americans in the War
   C. Women in the Military
II. Organizing Industry

Students should complete the outline by including all heads in the section.

Preteaching Vocabulary
Have students create a simple symbol, icon, or sketch for each of the Key Terms and Names.

SECTION 2 The Home Front

Guide to Reading

Main Idea
To successfully fight the war, the United States had to mobilize the entire nation.

Key Terms and Names
conscription, War Industries Board, Bernard Baruch, victory garden, Liberty Bond, Victory Bond, Committee on Public Information, espionage

Reading Strategy
Taking Notes As you read about how the United States mobilized for war, use the major headings of the section to create an outline similar to the one below.

```
The Home Front
I. Building Up the Military
   A.
   B.
   C.
II.
   A.
   B.
```

Reading Objectives
• **Analyze** how the United States raised an army and won support for World War I.
• **Explain** how the economy was controlled to support the war.

Section Theme
Government and Democracy To fight the war, the federal government created new agencies to mobilize the economy, draft soldiers, and build public support.

Preview of Events

1917	1918	1919
1917 Selective Service Act and Espionage Act passed	**May 1918** Sedition Act passed	**September 1918** Eugene Debs imprisoned / **1919** *Schenck* v. *United States*

★ An American Story ★

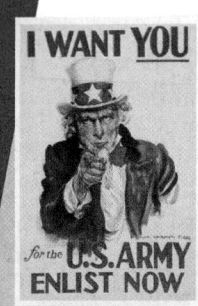

World War I recruiting poster

After Congress declared war on Germany in April 1917, young men from across the nation swamped recruiting offices eager to volunteer for the war. Historian William Langer, who served in World War I, recalled the enthusiasm of the young recruits:

66 What strikes me most, I think, is the eagerness of the men to get to France and above all to reach the front. One would think that, after almost four years of war, after the most detailed and realistic accounts of the murderous fighting . . . to say nothing of the day-to-day agony of trench warfare, it would have been all but impossible to get anyone to serve without duress. But it was not so. We and many thousands of others volunteered. Perhaps we were offended by the arrogance of the German U-boat campaign, and convinced Kaiserism must be smashed, once and for all. Possibly we already felt that, in the American interest, Western democracy must not be allowed to go under. But . . . most of us, young, were simply fascinated by the prospect of adventure and heroism. . . . Here was our one great chance for excitement and risk. We could not afford to pass it up. 99

—quoted in *Doughboy War*

Building Up the Military

When the United States declared war against Germany in April 1917, progressives controlled the federal government. They did not abandon their ideas simply because a war had begun. Instead, they applied progressive ideas to fighting the war.

Selective Service When the United States entered the war in 1917, the army and National Guard together had slightly more than 370,000 troops. Although many men volunteered after war was declared, many felt more soldiers needed to be drafted.

SECTION RESOURCES

📁 Reproducible Masters
• Reproducible Lesson Plan 14–2
• Daily Lecture and Discussion Notes 14–2
• Guided Reading Activity 14–2
• Section Quiz 14–2
• Reading Essentials and Study Guide 14–2
• Performance Assessment Activities and Rubrics
• Supreme Court Case Studies

🖥 Transparencies
• Daily Focus Skills Transparency 14–2

Multimedia
🔘 Interactive Tutor Self-Assessment CD-ROM
🔘 ExamView® Pro Testmaker CD-ROM
🔘 Presentation Plus! CD-ROM
🔘 TeacherWorks™ CD-ROM
🔘 Audio Program

Many progressives believed that conscription—forced military service—was a violation of democratic and republican principles. Realizing a draft was necessary, however, Congress, with Wilson's support, created a new system called **selective service.** Instead of having the military run the draft, the Selective Service Act of 1917 required all men between 21 and 30 to register for the draft. A lottery randomly determined the order they were called before a local draft board in charge of selecting or exempting people from military service.

The thousands of local boards were the heart of the system. The members of the draft boards were civilians from local communities. Progressives believed local people, understanding community needs, would know which men to draft. Eventually about 2.8 million Americans were drafted.

Volunteers for War Not all American soldiers were drafted. Approximately 2 million men volunteered for military service. Some had heard stories of German atrocities and wanted to fight back. Others believed democracy was at stake. Many believed they had a duty to respond to their nation's call. They had grown up listening to stories of the Civil War and the Spanish-American War. They saw this war as a great adventure and wanted to fight for their country's cause. To soldiers such as Justin Klingenberger, "War consisted of following the flag over a shell-torn field, with fixed bayonet . . . pushing the Hun back from trench to trench. . . ." Although the horrors of the war soon became clear to the American troops, their morale remained high, helping to ensure an Allied victory.

African Americans in the War Of the nearly 400,000 African Americans who were drafted, about 42,000 served overseas as combat troops. African American soldiers encountered discrimination and prejudice in the army. They served in racially segregated units almost always under white officers.

Despite these challenges, many African American soldiers fought with distinction in the war. For example, the African American 92nd and 93rd Infantry Divisions fought in bitter battles along the Western Front. Many of them won praise from both the French commander, Marshal Henri Pétain, and the United States commander, General John Pershing. The entire 369th Infantry Regiment won the highly prized French decoration, the Croix de Guerre ("war cross"), for gallantry in combat.

Women in the Military World War I was the first war in which women officially served in the armed forces, although only in noncombat positions. Women nurses had served in both the army and navy since the early 1900s, but as auxiliaries. Before World War I, nurses were not assigned ranks, and the women were not technically enlisted in the army or navy.

As the military prepared for war in 1917, it faced a severe shortage of clerical workers because so many men were assigned to active duty. Early in 1917, the navy authorized the enlistment of women to meet its clerical needs. By the end of the war, over 11,000 women had served in the navy. Although most performed clerical duties, others served as radio operators, electricians, pharmacists, and photographers.

The army still did not enlist women. Instead, it hired them as temporary clerical workers. The only women to actually serve in the army were in the **Army Nursing Corps.** Army nurses were the only women in the military sent overseas during the war. Over 20,000 nurses served in the army during the war, including more than 10,000 overseas.

✓ **Reading Check** **Describing** How did Congress ensure that the military had enough troops to fight the war?

Organizing Industry

The progressive emphasis on careful planning and scientific management shaped the federal government's approach to mobilizing the American war

Picturing **History**

Women and War Although not allowed in combat, many women served in auxiliary positions, such as nursing. Here, Birmingham, Alabama, women collect money during a Red Cross parade in 1918. In what other capacities did women serve during the war?

CHAPTER 14 World War I and Its Aftermath **457**

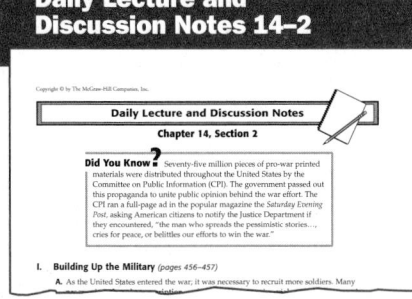
2 TEACH

Daily Lecture and Discussion Notes 14–2

Reading Strategy

Interpreting Quotations Have students note whether the following quotes support neutrality or war. **L1**

" . . . loans by American bankers to any foreign nation at war are inconsistent with the true spirit of neutrality."—William Jennings Bryan, 1914

"Our whole duty . . . is summed up in this motto: America first."—Woodrow Wilson, 1915

✓ Reading Check

Answer: The Selective Service Act of 1917 required all men ages 21 to 30 to register for the draft.

Picturing **History**

Answer: secretaries, radio operators, electricians, and pharmacists, among others

Ask: Why did the Navy finally enlist women? *(to meet its clerical needs)*

Reading Strategy   READING THE TEXT

Previewing Students can quickly gain an understanding of what the text will be about by looking over features such as headings and subheadings, charted information, illustrations, captions, and graphics. Have students preview the section by looking at these elements before they begin reading. **L1**

 Refer to *Inclusion for the High School Social Studies Classroom Strategies and Activities* in the TCR.

L1/ELL
Guided Reading Activity 14-2

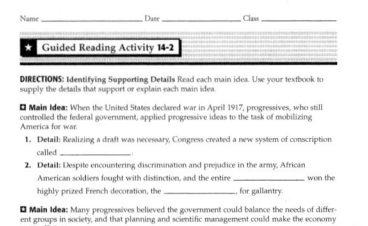

Name _____ Date _____ Class _____

⭐ Guided Reading Activity 14-2

DIRECTIONS: Identifying Supporting Details Read each main idea. Use your textbook to supply the details that support or explain each main idea.

☐ **Main Idea:** When the United States declared war in April 1917, progressives, who still controlled the federal government, applied progressive ideas to the task of mobilizing America for war.

1. **Detail:** Realizing a draft was necessary, Congress created a new system of conscription called _____.

2. **Detail:** Despite encountering discrimination and prejudice in the army, African American soldiers fought with distinction, and the entire _____ won the highly prized French decoration, the _____, for gallantry.

☐ **Main Idea:** Many progressives believed the government could balance the needs of different groups in society, and that planning and scientific management could make the economy more efficient.

✓ **Reading Check**

Answer: War Industries Board, Food Administration, Fuel Administration

Picturing **History**

Answer: The general theme is supporting the war effort. The posters were effective in reminding people of their patriotic duty.
Ask: What was the main message of each of these posters? *(Students' answers will vary. Some ideas might include encouraging men to enlist in the armed forces, coming together at work for the war effort, patriotic messages about democracy, and encouraging victory gardens.)*

Creating a Poster Have students create a poster that might have been used by the Committee on Public Information to boost support of the war effort. Encourage students to use the posters shown on this page as models. **L2**

📁 Use *Supreme Court Case Study 12, Schenck* v. *United States.*

economy. To efficiently manage the relationship between the federal government and private companies, Congress created special boards. These boards emphasized cooperation between big business and government. Business executives, professional managers, and government representatives staffed the boards. Their goal was to ensure the most efficient use of national resources to further the war effort.

The War Industries Board One of the first agencies established was the **War Industries Board** (WIB). Created in July 1917, the WIB's job was to coordinate the production of war materials. At first, President Wilson was reluctant to give the WIB much authority over the economy, but by March 1918, he decided industrial production needed better coordination. The WIB was reorganized and **Bernard Baruch** was appointed to run it. Under this Wall Street stockbroker's supervision, the WIB told manufacturers what to produce. It controlled the flow of raw materials, ordered the construction of new factories, and occasionally, with the president's approval, set prices.

Food and Fuel Perhaps the most successful government agency was the Food Administration, run by Herbert Hoover. This agency was responsible for increasing food production while reducing civilian consumption. Instead of using rationing, Hoover encouraged Americans to save food on their own. Using the slogan "Food Will Win the War—Don't Waste It," the Food Administration encouraged families to "Hooverize" by "serving just enough" and by having Wheatless Mondays, Meatless Tuesdays, and Porkless Thursdays. Hoover also encouraged citizens to plant victory gardens to raise their own vegetables, leaving more for the troops.

While Hoover managed food production, the Fuel Administration, run by Harry Garfield, tried to manage the nation's use of coal and oil. To conserve energy, Garfield introduced **daylight savings time** and shortened workweeks for factories that did not make war materials.

Paying for the War By the end of World War I, the United States was spending about $44 million a day—leading to a total expenditure of about $32 billion for the entire conflict. To fund the war effort, Congress raised income tax rates. Congress also placed new taxes on corporate profits and an extra tax on the profits of arms factories.

Taxes, however, could not pay for the war. To raise money, the government borrowed over $20 billion from the American people by selling **Liberty Bonds** and **Victory Bonds.** By buying the bonds, Americans were loaning the government money. The government agreed to repay the money with interest in a specified number of years. Posters, rallies, and "Liberty Loan sermons" encouraged people to buy the bonds as an act of patriotism.

✓ **Reading Check** **Summarizing** What federal agencies helped control American industries during the war?

Picturing **History**

Propaganda Posters George Creel's Committee on Public Information encouraged Americans to do all they could to support the war effort. What is the general theme of these posters? Do you think the posters were effective?

DIFFERENTIATED INSTRUCTION

Gifted and Talented Have students imagine that they are teens living in the United States when Wilson declared that the country would enter the war. Have students write a series of diary entries that describes their reactions to and feelings about entering the war and the preparations that were made on the home front as the nation geared up to fight. **L3**

📁 Refer to *Inclusion for the High School Social Studies Classroom Strategies and Activities* in the TCR.

Mobilizing the Workforce

While the WIB and other agencies tried to build cooperation between the government and business, officials knew that they also needed workers to cooperate if mobilization was to succeed. To prevent strikes from disrupting the war effort, the government established the **National War Labor Board** (NWLB) in March 1918. Chaired by William Howard Taft and Frank Walsh, a prominent labor attorney, the NWLB attempted to mediate labor disputes that might otherwise lead to strikes.

The NWLB frequently pressured industry to grant important concessions to workers, including wage increases, an eight-hour workday, and the right of unions to organize and bargain collectively. In exchange, labor leaders agreed not to disrupt war production with strikes or other disturbances. As a result, membership in unions increased by just over one million between 1917 and 1919.

Women Support Industry The war increased work opportunities for women, who filled industrial jobs vacated by men serving in the military. These included positions in the shipping, manufacturing, and railroad industries. These new jobs for women, however, were not permanent. After the war, when the servicemen returned home, most women returned to their previous jobs or stopped working.

The Great Migration Begins With the flow of immigrants from Europe cut off and large numbers of white workers being drafted, the war also opened new doors for African Americans. Wartime job openings and high wages drew thousands of African Americans to factories producing war materials. Encouraged by recruiting agents promising high wages and plentiful work, between 300,000 and 500,000 African Americans left the South to settle in Northern cities. This massive population movement became known as the "Great Migration." It greatly altered the racial makeup of such cities as Chicago, New York, Cleveland, and Detroit.

Mexican Americans Head North African Americans were not the only group to migrate north during the war. Continued political turmoil in Mexico and the wartime labor shortage in the United States convinced many Mexicans to head north. Between 1917 and 1920, over 100,000 Mexicans migrated into Texas, Arizona, California, and New Mexico, providing labor for the farms and ranches of the Southwest.

Meanwhile, tens of thousands of Mexican Americans headed north to Chicago, St. Louis,

Federal Mobilization Agencies

Agency	Purpose
War Industries Board	Organized industry to increase efficiency, maximizing production
Railroad Administration	Assumed temporary control of rail lines to modernize equipment and increase operating efficiency
Food Administration	Supervised agricultural production, promoted food conservation and rationing
Fuel Administration	Increased production of coal and oil; maintained conservation of fuel with such innovations as daylight savings time
National War Labor Board	Maintained cooperation between industry management and labor unions; acted as mediator to prevent and quickly settle disputes
Committee on Public Information	Provided propaganda to rally citizen support for all aspects of the war effort

Chart *Skills*

1. **Interpreting Charts** Which agency worked with manufacturers and labor unions?
2. **Analyzing** How did the Fuel Administration's daylight savings time plan achieve its goal?

Omaha, and other cities to take wartime factory jobs. Many Mexican Americans faced hostility and discrimination when they arrived in American cities. Like other immigrants before them, they tended to settle in their own separate neighborhoods, called **barrios,** where they could support each other.

✓ **Reading Check** **Evaluating** How permanent were women's advances in the wartime workplace?

Ensuring Public Support

Progressives in the government did not think coordinating business and labor was enough to ensure the success of the war effort. They also believed that the government should take steps to shape public opinion and build support for the war.

Chart *Skills*

Answer:
1. National War Labor Board
2. Because daylight savings time moved sunset one hour later, people used less fuel.

Chart Skills Practice
Ask: Which of the federal mobilization agencies do you think had the greatest impact on ordinary citizens? *(Many students will note that the Committee on Public Information had the broadest impact.)*

Finding an Artifact Encourage students to use library and Internet resources to find a photograph, piece of art, graph, or book about the Great Migration. Have students bring the artifacts or copies of them to class. Display them around the classroom. Then hold a class discussion on the Great Migration's impact. **L2**

✓ **Reading Check**

Answer: The gains were mostly temporary.

Some of the posters printed by the United States government contained highly charged language and images. One showed two German soldiers robbing a house after shooting the owner; the soldiers were labeled "Hindenburglers." Another, entitled "Halt the Hun," showed an American soldier preventing a German soldier from bayoneting a defenseless woman and her baby.

INTERDISCIPLINARY CONNECTIONS ACTIVITY

Music Tell students that George M. Cohan wrote his most famous song, "Over There," on the day war was declared. He sat down at the piano and wrote what he said was just a bugle call. Have students research other songs of World War I and study their lyrics. Then ask: How do the lyrics reflect the attitudes of the time? Are they idealistic, humorous, optimistic, patriotic, or sentimental? **L2**

Different Viewpoints

Answers:

1. inciting revolution
2. freedom of the press and freedom of speech

Ask: Why does Justice Holmes dissent from the majority opinion? *(He believed that the writers had constitutional protection in writing and publishing their leaflets.)*

FYI

The mass media of the World War I era consisted only of newsprint. Neither film nor radio had developed as a medium for spreading ideas. Considering these limitations, World War I propaganda was extremely effective.

3 ASSESS

Assign Section 2 Assessment as homework or as an in-class activity.

◉ Have students use the **Interactive Tutor Self-Assessment CD-ROM.**

L1/ELL

Reading Essentials and Study Guide 14–2

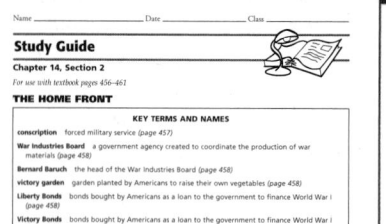

Name _____ Date _____ Class _____

Study Guide

Chapter 14, Section 2

For use with textbook pages 456–461

THE HOME FRONT

KEY TERMS AND NAMES

conscription forced military service *(page 457)*

War Industries Board a government agency created to coordinate the production of war materials *(page 458)*

Bernard Baruch the head of the War Industries Board *(page 458)*

victory garden garden planted by Americans to raise their own vegetables *(page 458)*

Liberty Bonds bonds bought by Americans as a loan to the government to finance World War I *(page 458)*

Victory Bonds bonds bought by Americans as a loan to the government to finance World War I *(page 458)*

Different Viewpoints

Abrams v. United States, 1919

The Espionage Act of 1917 made it a crime to "willfully utter, print, write, or publish any disloyal, profane, scurrilous or abusive language about the government." Although the act limited First Amendment freedoms, many Americans believed winning World War I was more important. 📖 *(See page 962 for more information on* Abrams v. the United States.)*

Justice John H. Clarke delivered the majority opinion:

It is argued, somewhat faintly, that the acts charged against the defendants were not unlawful because within the protection of that freedom . . . of speech and of the press . . . and that the entire Espionage Act is unconstitutional. . . .

. . . the plain purpose of their propaganda was to excite, at the supreme crisis of the war, disaffection, sedition, riots, and, as they hoped, revolution, in this country for the purpose of embarrassing, and, if possible, defeating the military plans of the Government in Europe. . . . [T]he language of these circulars was obviously intended to provoke and to encourage resistance to the United States in the war, as the third count runs, and the defendants, in terms, plainly urged and advocated a resort to a general strike of workers in ammunition factories for the purpose of curtailing the production of ordnance and munitions necessary and essential to the prosecution of the war. . . . Thus, it is clear not only that some evidence, but that much persuasive evidence, was before the jury tending to prove that the defendants were guilty as charged. . . .

Justice Oliver Wendell Holmes, Jr., dissenting:

It is only the present danger of immediate evil or an intent to bring it about that warrants Congress in setting a limit to the expression of opinion where private rights are not concerned. Congress certainly cannot forbid all effort to change the mind of the country. Now nobody can suppose that the surreptitious publishing of a silly leaflet by an unknown man, without more, would present any immediate danger that its opinions would hinder the success of the government arms or have any appreciable tendency to do so.

In this case, sentences of twenty years' imprisonment have been imposed for the publishing of two leaflets that I believe the defendants had as much right to publish as the Government has to publish the Constitution of the United States now vainly invoked by them. . . . I regret that I cannot put into more impressive words my belief that, in their conviction upon this indictment, the defendants were deprived of their rights under the Constitution of the United States.

Amendment I

—Congress shall make no law respecting an establishment of religion, or prohibiting the free exercise thereof; or abridging the freedom of speech, or of the press; or the right of the people peaceably to assemble, and to petition the Government for a redress of grievances.

Learning From History

1. What were the charges against the defendants?
2. On what key point did Holmes and Clarke disagree?

Selling the War A new government agency, the **Committee on Public Information,** had the task of "selling" the war to the American people. The head of the CPI was journalist George Creel, who recruited advertising executives, commercial artists, authors, songwriters, entertainers, public speakers, and motion picture companies to help sway public opinion in favor of the war.

The CPI distributed pamphlets and arranged for thousands of short patriotic talks, called "four-minute speeches," to be delivered at movie theaters and public halls and gathering places. The Four-Minute Men urged audiences to support the war in various ways, from buying war bonds to reporting draft dodgers to the proper authorities.

Civil Liberties Curtailed In addition to using propaganda and persuasion, the government also passed legislation to fight antiwar activities or enemies at home. Espionage, or spying to acquire secret government information, was addressed in the Espionage Act of 1917, which established penalties and prison terms for anyone who gave aid to the enemy. This act also penalized disloyalty, giving false reports, or otherwise interfering with the war effort. The Post Office even hired college professors to translate foreign periodicals to find out if they contained antiwar messages.

The Sedition Act of 1918 expanded the meaning of the Espionage Act to make illegal any public expression of opposition to the war. In practice, it allowed officials to prosecute anyone who criticized

---

CRITICAL THINKING ACTIVITY

Evaluating Ask students to identify actions the government took to organize for World War I (regulating industry, encouraging greater production, propaganda, keeping an eye on dissenters). Write the responses on the board. After students identify the actions, have them list the effects of those actions. Then ask students to identify the similarities and the differences between the government's preparation and explanation for entering World War I as compared to the government's decision to begin the War on Terrorism in Afghanistan and Iraq. **L2**

the president or the government. Combined, these laws generated over 1,500 prosecutions and 1,000 convictions.

A Climate of Suspicion The fear of spies and emphasis on patriotism quickly led to the mistreatment and persecution of German Americans. To avoid German-sounding names, advertisers began to call sauerkraut "Liberty cabbage" and hamburger "Salisbury steak." Many schools dropped German language classes from their curricula, and orchestras stopped performing the music of Beethoven, Schubert, Wagner, and other German composers. Anti-German feelings sometimes led to violence. Some citizens beat neighbors who were German-born. In Collinsville, Illinois, a mob lynched a German-born man whom they suspected of disloyalty.

German Americans were not the only ones under suspicion. Mobs attacked labor activists, socialists, and pacifists. Newspapers ads urged Americans to monitor the activities of their fellow citizens. Americans even formed private organizations, such as the American Protective League and the Boy Spies of America, to spy on neighbors and coworkers. Secretary of War Newton Baker expressed concern about the growing intolerance:

George Creel

66 There is a growing frenzy of suspicion and hostility toward disloyalty. I am afraid we are going to have a good many instances of people roughly treated on very slight evidence of disloyalty. Already a number of men and some women have been tarred and feathered, and a portion of the press is urging with great vehemence more strenuous efforts at detection and punishment. 99

—quoted in *Echoes of Distant Thunder*

The Supreme Court Limits Free Speech Despite protests against the government's tactics, however, the courts generally upheld the principle behind them. Although the First Amendment specifically states that "Congress shall make no law . . . abridging the freedom of speech, or of the press," the Supreme Court decided otherwise, departing from a strict literal interpretation of the Constitution.

In the landmark case of *Schenck* v. *the United States* (1919), the Supreme Court ruled that an individual's freedom of speech could be curbed when the words uttered constitute a "clear and present danger." The Court used as an example someone yelling "Fire!" in a crowded theater as a situation in which freedom of speech would be superseded by the theater-goers' right to safety. The Court's majority opinion stated, "When a nation is at war, many things that might be said in times of peace are such a hindrance to its effort that their utterance will not be endured so long as [soldiers] fight. . . ." 📖 *(See page 965 for more information on* Schenck v. the United States.*)*

✔ **Reading Check** **Explaining** Why did Congress pass the Espionage Act in 1917?

HISTORY Online **Study Central**™ To review this section, go to tarvol2.glencoe.com and click on **Study Central**™.

SECTION 2 ASSESSMENT

Checking for Understanding
1. **Define:** conscription, victory garden, espionage.
2. **Identify:** War Industries Board, Bernard Baruch, Liberty Bond, Victory Bond, Committee on Public Information.
3. **Describe** the contributions of African Americans during the war.

Reviewing Themes
4. **Government and Democracy** How did government efforts to ensure support for the war conflict with democratic ideals?

Critical Thinking
5. **Analyzing** How did World War I cause the federal government to change its relationship with the business world?
6. **Organizing** Use a graphic organizer similar to the one below to identify the effects of the war on the American workforce.

Effects of War on U.S. Workforce

Analyzing Visuals
7. **Analyzing Posters** Examine the posters on page 458. How do these images encourage support for the war? How effective do you think they would be today?

Writing About History
8. **Persuasive Writing** Imagine that you are working for the Committee on Public Information. Write text for an advertisement or lyrics to a song in which you attempt to sway public opinion in favor of the war.

SECTION 2 ASSESSMENT ANSWERS

1. Terms are in blue.
2. War Industries Board *(p. 458),* Bernard Baruch *(p. 458),* Liberty Bond *(p. 458),* Victory Bond *(p. 458),* Committee on Public Information *(p. 460)*
3. About 400,000 African Americans were drafted to serve in the war; many received high praise for their

courage from French generals.
4. limited free speech and freedom of the press
5. Special boards were created that encouraged cooperation between business and government.
6. Effects should include increased job opportunities for women and African Americans.

7. Supporting the war is portrayed as good; other answers will vary.
8. Answers will vary. Invite students to display or perform their work.

L2

Section Quiz 14–2

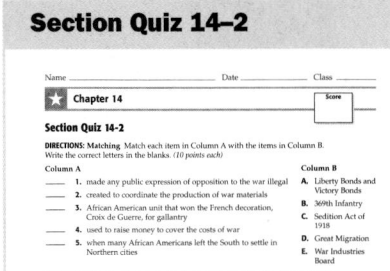

Reteach
Have students analyze how the United States raised an army and won support for World War I.

Enrich
Have students write newspaper editorials questioning the moral implications of using advertising to "sell" a war to a nation. Invite volunteers to read their editorials to the class. Then ask students what might have happened in 1917 to anyone who wrote such an editorial.

✔ **Reading Check**

Answer: to control public opinion and stop antiwar supporters

Study Central™ provides summaries, interactive games, and online graphic organizers to help students review section content.

4 CLOSE

Have students explain how the economy was controlled to support the war.

TEACH

World War I Firsts

Organize students into four groups. Assign each group one of the following: aerial combat, gas attacks and gas masks, donkey's ears, or Big Bertha. Have the groups research to learn more about their assigned item. Then have students research modern warfare to find either the state of the art in their assigned category (fighter planes and gas masks) or to find corollaries in modern warfare (for example, a corollary to donkey's ears may be night vision goggles or satellite tracking information). Have the groups prepare a display to present the information they have found.

Color My World

Have interested students research nonmilitary inventions that occurred between 1914 and 1918. Have students write a report on their findings. As a class, create a time line of the various inventions.

Visit the **TIME** Web site at www.time.com for up-to-date news, weekly magazine articles, editorials, online polls, and an archive of past magazine and Web articles.

BROWN BROTHERS

American soldiers set sail for Europe.

World War Firsts

Human ingenuity goes to work in the service of war:

AERIAL COMBAT, 1914. War takes to the air. Two Allied aircraft chase two German planes across Britain.

GAS ATTACKS, 1915. The German High Command admits to using chlorine gas bombs and shells on the field of combat. Deadly mustard gas is used in 1917.

GAS MASKS. Issued to Allied soldiers in 1915.

DONKEY'S EARS. A new trench periscope enables soldiers to observe the battleground from the relative safety of a trench without risking sniper fire.

BIG BERTHA. Enormous howitzer gun bombards Paris. "Big Bertha," named after the wife of its manufacturer, is thought to be located nearly 63 miles behind German lines. Moving at night on railroad tracks, the gun is difficult for the Allies to locate.

BROWN BROTHERS

Color My World

Some bright spots in a dark decade:

- Color newspaper supplements (1914)
- 3-D films (1915)
- Nail polish (1916)
- Three-color traffic lights (1918)
- Color photography introduced by Eastman Kodak (1914)

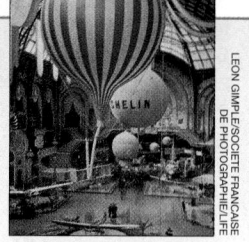

LEON GIMPEL/SOCIETE FRANCAISE DE PHOTOGRAPHIE/LIFE

One of the first color photographs

VERBATIM

❝My message was one of death for young men. How odd to applaud that.❞

WOODROW WILSON,
on returning to the White House after asking Congress for a declaration of war, 1917

❝Food is Ammunition—Don't Waste It❞

POSTER FROM U.S. FOOD ADMINISTRATION,
administered by Herbert Hoover

❝I have had a hard time getting over this war. My old world died.❞

RAY STANNARD BAKER,
journalist

❝Let us, while this war lasts, forget our special grievances and close our ranks shoulder to shoulder with our own white fellow citizens and the allied nations that are fighting for democracy.❞

W.E.B. DU BOIS,
African American scholar and leader, 1918

❝America has at one bound become a world power in a sense she never was before.❞

BRITISH PRIME MINISTER DAVID LLOYD GEORGE,
on the U.S. entry into World War I, 1917

❝In the camps I saw barrels mounted on sticks on which zealous captains were endeavoring to teach their men how to ride a horse.❞

THEODORE ROOSEVELT,
on touring U.S. military training facilities, 1917

❝The war was over, and it seemed as if everything in the world were possible, and everything was new, and that peace was going to be all we dreamed about.❞

FLORENCE HARRIMAN,
Red Cross volunteer, in Paris on Armistice Day, 1918

COOPERATIVE LEARNING ACTIVITY

Creating a Magazine Spread Organize the class into groups of four or five. Have students create a magazine spread about America's war on terrorism. Although students may use ideas from recent news magazines, encourage the groups to look for their own unique angle for the spread. Students should look at current magazines and books for ideas about page design. This activity can be completed using desktop publishing software or the more traditional cut-and-paste method.

Use the rubric for a cooperative group management plan on pages 71–72 in the *Performance Assessment Activities and Rubrics.*

How to Make a Doughboy

Take one American infantryman.

1. Arm with 107 pieces of fighting equipment, including:
   - rifle
   - rifle cartridges
   - cartridge belt
   - steel helmet
   - clubs
   - knives
   - gas mask
   - wire cutters
   - trench tool
   - bayonet and scabbard
   - grenades

2. Add 50 articles of clothing, including 3 wool blankets and a bedsack.

3. Equip with eating utensils and 11 cooking implements.

4. Train well.

TOTAL COST: $156.30

(not including training and transportation to Europe)

BROWN BROTHERS

Milestones

REPATRIATED, APRIL 10, 1917.
VLADIMIR ILYICH LENIN, to Russia, after an 11-year absence. The leader of the leftist Bolshevik party hopes to reorganize his revolutionary group.

Vladimir Lenin

CULVER PICTURES

SHOT DOWN AND KILLED, APRIL 22, 1918. "THE RED BARON," Manfred von Richthofen, Germany's ace pilot. Von Richthofen destroyed more than 80 Allied aircraft. On hearing of the Red Baron's death, English fighter pilot Edward Mannock said, "I hope he roasted all the way down."

Jeannette Rankin

BROWN BROTHERS

ELECTED, NOVEMBER 7, 1916.
JEANNETTE RANKIN of Montana, to the U.S. Congress. The first woman congressional representative explained her victory by saying that women "got the vote in Montana because the spirit of pioneer days was still alive."

EXECUTED, OCTOBER 15, 1917.
MATA HARI, in France, for espionage. The famous Dutch dancer was sentenced to death for spying for the Germans.

NUMBERS 1915

$1,040 Average annual income for workers in finance, insurance, and real estate

$687 Average income for industrial workers (higher for union workers, lower for nonunion workers)

$510 Average income for retail trade workers

$355 Average income for farm laborers

$342 Average income for domestic servants

$328 Average income for public school teachers

$11.95 Cost of a bicycle

BROWN BROTHERS

$1.15 Cost of a baseball

$1 Average cost of a hotel room

39¢ Cost of one dozen eggs

5¢ Cost of a glass of cola

7¢ Cost of a large roll of toilet paper

Portfolio Writing Project

Tell students that two popular reasons given when a volunteer was asked why he enlisted were "because people admire soldiers" and "to see the world." Based on these reasons, have students write a recruiting speech to be delivered at a local high school to recruit enlistees.

Writing a Profile Have students research information about the Doughboys, such as why they were given their name, what they did between battles, and life in the trenches. Based on their research, have students write a profile of the average World War I soldier.

CLOSE

Have students select one of the famous people mentioned in the Milestones. Ask each student to learn one new thing about the person selected. Have volunteers share their findings with the class.

EXTENDING THE CONTENT

Stars and Stripes *Stars and Stripes,* the armed forces newspaper staffed entirely by soldiers, was first published in 1918. In addition to being a source of information and morale for soldiers, it provided many young journalists and cartoonists with their first jobs. Two well-known cartoonists whose work appeared in *Stars and Stripes* were Milt Caniff ("Terry and the Pirates") and Bill Mauldin, who would win the Pulitzer Prize in 1945 for his "Willie" and "GI Joe" cartoons.

1 FOCUS

Section Overview

This section focuses on the military aspects of World War I.

Reading Preview

Answers to Graphic: airplanes, poison gas, machine guns, trenches, tanks

Preteaching Vocabulary
Have students identify the Key Terms and Names that refer to specific individuals and write a one-sentence description of each person.

Guide to Reading

Main Idea
After four years of fighting, the war in Europe ended in November 1918.

Key Terms and Names
"no man's land," convoy, Vladimir Lenin, Treaty of Brest-Litovsk, armistice, Fourteen Points, League of Nations, Treaty of Versailles, reparations

Reading Strategy
Organizing As you read about the battles of World War I, complete a graphic organizer similar to the one below by listing the kinds of warfare and technology used in the fighting.

(Warfare and Technology Used in World War I)

Reading Objectives
- **Discuss** the fighting techniques used in World War I.
- **Characterize** the American response to the Treaty of Versailles.

Section Theme
Individual Action American troops played a major role in helping end the war, while President Wilson played a major role in the peace negotiations.

Preview of Events

♦1915   ♦1917   ♦1919

July 1916
Battle of the Somme begins

November 1917
Communists seize power in Russia

March 1918
Treaty of Brest-Litovsk ends war between Russia and Germany

September 1918
Beginning of Battle of the Argonne Forest

November 1918
Armistice ends war

★ An American Story ★

John J. Pershing

General John J. Pershing, commander of the American forces in World War I, could not help but feel a sense of pride and excitement as he watched the Second Battalion of the First Division's 16th Infantry march through the streets of Paris on July 4, 1917:

❝. . . The battalion was joined by a great crowd, many women forcing their way into the ranks and swinging along arm in arm with the men. With wreaths about their necks and bouquets in their hats and rifles, the column looked like a moving flower garden. With only a semblance of military formation, the animated throng pushed its way through avenues of people to the martial strains of the French band and the still more thrilling music of cheering voices.❞

—quoted in *The Yanks Are Coming*

While his men marched through Paris, Pershing raced to Picpus Cemetery, the burial place of the Marquis de Lafayette, a French noble who had fought in the American Revolution. One of Pershing's officers, Colonel Charles E. Stanton, raised his hand in salute and acknowledged the continuing American-French relationship by proclaiming, "Lafayette, we are here!"

Combat in World War I

By the spring of 1917, World War I had devastated Europe and claimed millions of lives. Terrible destruction resulted from a combination of old-fashioned strategies and new technologies. Despite the carnage Europeans had experienced, many Americans believed their troops would make a difference and quickly bring the war to an end.

464 CHAPTER 14 World War I and Its Aftermath

SECTION RESOURCES

📁 Reproducible Masters
- Reproducible Lesson Plan 14–3
- Daily Lecture and Discussion Notes 14–3
- Guided Reading Activity 14–3
- Section Quiz 14–3
- Reading Essentials and Study Guide 14–3
- Performance Assessment Activities and Rubrics

🖳 Transparencies
- Daily Focus Skills Transparency 14–3

Multimedia
- Interactive Tutor Self-Assessment CD-ROM
- ExamView® Pro Testmaker CD-ROM
- Presentation Plus! CD-ROM
- TeacherWorks™ CD-ROM
- Audio Program

Trench Warfare The early offensives of 1914 quickly demonstrated that the nature of warfare had changed. Troops that dug themselves in and relied upon modern rifles and a new weapon—the rapid-fire machine gun—could easily hold off the attacking forces. On the Western Front, troops dug a network of trenches that stretched from the English Channel to the Swiss border. The space between the opposing trenches was known as **"no man's land,"** a rough, barren landscape pockmarked with craters from artillery fire.

To break through enemy lines, both sides began with massive artillery barrages. Then bayonet-wielding soldiers would scramble out of their trenches, race across no man's land, and hurl grenades into the enemy's trenches. The results were often disastrous. The artillery barrages rarely destroyed the enemy defenses, and troops crossing no man's land were easily stopped by enemy machine guns and rifle fire. These kind of assaults caused staggeringly high casualties. In major battles, both sides often lost several hundred thousand men.

These battles produced horrific scenes of death and destruction, as one American soldier noted in his diary:

❝Many dead Germans along the road. One heap on a manure pile . . . Devastation everywhere. Our barrage has rooted up the entire territory like a ploughed field. Dead horses galore, many of them have a hind quarter cut off—the Huns [Germans] need food. Dead men here and there.❞

—quoted in *The American Spirit*

New Technology As it became clear that charging enemy trenches could bring only limited success at great cost, both sides began to develop new technologies to help them break through enemy lines. In April 1915, the Germans first used poison gas in the Second Battle of Ypres. The fumes caused vomiting, blindness, and suffocation. Soon afterward the Allies also began using poison gas, and gas masks became a necessary part of a soldier's equipment.

In 1916 the British introduced the tank into battle. The first tanks were very slow and cumbersome, mechanically unreliable, and fairly easy to destroy. They could roll over barbed wire and trenches, but there were usually not enough of them to make a

An American Hero

Although the brutal trench warfare of World War I led to many acts of astonishing bravery, the heroism of one American, Corporal Alvin York, captured the nation's imagination. Born in 1887, York grew up poor in the mountains of Tennessee, where he learned to shoot by hunting wild game.

On October 8, 1918, during the Battle of the Argonne Forest, York's patrol lost its way and ended up behind enemy lines. When a German machine gun emplacement on a fortified hill fired on the patrol and killed nine men, York took command and charged the machine gun. Although the details of the battle are unclear, when it ended, York had killed between 9 and 25 Germans, captured the machine guns, and taken 132 prisoners. For his actions, he received the Medal of Honor and the French Croix de Guerre. After returning home, he used his fame to raise money for the Alvin York Institute—a school for underprivileged Tennessee children.

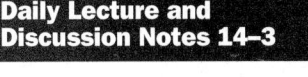

2 TEACH

Daily Lecture and Discussion Notes 14–3

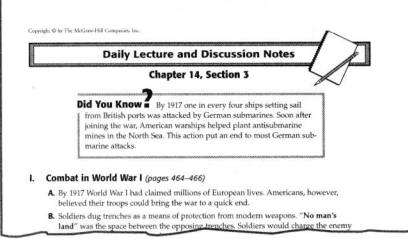

Copyright © by The McGraw-Hill Companies, Inc.

Daily Lecture and Discussion Notes

Chapter 14, Section 3

Did You Know? By 1917 one in every four ships setting sail from British ports was attacked by German submarines. Soon after joining the war, American warships helped plant antisubmarine mines in the North Sea. This action put an end to most German submarine attacks.

I. Combat in World War I *(pages 464–466)*

A. By 1917 World War I had claimed millions of European lives. Americans, however, believed their troops could bring the war to a quick end.

B. Soldiers dug trenches as a means of protection from modern weapons. "No man's land" was the space between the opposing trenches. Soldiers would charge the enemy

Writing a Letter Have students take on the role of a young soldier leaving for war. Instruct students to write a letter to a family member or close friend. The letter should explain why the person is going to war, what he or she fears, and what the friend or relative can do to help. **L1**

📁 Use the rubric for creating a diary, short story, memorandum, or letter on pages 69–70 in the *Performance Assessment Activities and Rubrics.*

Stalemate A stalemate occurs in the game of chess when one player cannot make any move without putting his or her king in a position to be captured, and thus lose the game. It is an apt term for the deadlock along the Western Front.

Reading Strategy   READING THE TEXT

Activating Prior Knowledge Before students begin to absorb any new knowledge, prepare them by bringing to mind what they already know. Use the key concepts and boldfaced terms in the text to frame general questions that encourage students to think about the topic and to share ideas. Then provide specific information that will enhance their understanding of the subject. **L1**

📁 Refer to *Inclusion for the High School Social Studies Classroom Strategies and Activities* in the TCR.

L1/ELL

Guided Reading Activity 14–3

Name _____ Date _____ Class _____

★ **Guided Reading Activity 14-3**

DIRECTIONS: Using Headings and Subheadings Locate each heading below in your textbook. Then use the information under the correct subheading to help you write each answer.

I. Combat in World War I

A. How did soldiers from both sides attempt to break through enemy lines? _____

B. What were the results of such actions? _____

C. Why did both sides begin to develop new technology? _____

D. When and where did the Germans first use poison gas? _____

E. What two military vehicles were introduced during World War I? _____

II. The Americans and Victory

✓ **Reading Check**

Answer: machine guns, tanks, airplanes, poison gas

Creating a Drawing Have interested students create drawings of the types of aircraft used by both the Allies and the Central Powers during World War I. Have students label and display their drawings. **L2**

FYI

Three pilots who flew bombers in World War I were among the best-known fighters of the war. American Eddie Rickenbacker shot down 22 planes during the war. Flying aces from other countries also became famous. Manfred von Richthofen of Germany, known as the "Red Baron," was credited with 80 victories, and Rene Fonck of France with 75.

Ace The term *ace* originally referred to a pilot who shot down five enemy planes. It later came to mean anyone who was exceptionally good at something.

NATIONAL GEOGRAPHIC **Battles of World War I, 1914–1918**
In Motion

- ❻ Lusitania sunk May 7, 1915
- ❸ Battles of Ypres Oct.–Nov. 1914
- ❹ Apr.–May 1915
- ❶ Tannenberg Aug. 1914
- ❽ Battle of the Somme July–Nov. 1916
- ❼ Battle of Verdun Feb.–Dec. 1916
- ❷ First Battle of the Marne Sept. 1914
- ❾ Caporetto Oct.–Dec. 1917
- ❺ Gallipoli Apr. 1915–Jan. 1916

Allied Powers
Central Powers
Neutral nations
German unrestricted submarine warfare zone
Allied offensives
Central Powers' offensives
Farthest advance of Central Powers
Line of trench warfare, 1915–1917
Allied victory
Central Powers' victory
Indecisive battle

Lambert Azimuthal Equal-Area projection

---

difference. While tanks did help troops, they did not revolutionize warfare in World War I.

World War I also saw the first use of airplanes in combat. At first, planes were used mainly to observe enemy activities. Soon, the Allies and Central Powers used them to drop small bombs. As technology advanced, they also attached machine guns to aircraft to engage in deadly air battles known as dogfights.

✓ **Reading Check** **Describing** What new technologies were introduced in World War I?

The Americans and Victory

Wave upon wave of American troops marched into this bloody stalemate—nearly 2 million before the war's end. These **"doughboys,"** a nickname for American soldiers, were largely inexperienced, but they were fresh, so their presence immediately boosted the morale of Allied forces.

Winning the War at Sea No American troopships were sunk on their way to Europe—an accomplishment due largely to the efforts of American Admiral William S. Sims. For most of the war, the British preferred to fight German submarines by sending warships to find them. Meanwhile, merchant ships would race across the Atlantic individually. The British approach had not worked well, and submarines had inflicted heavy losses on British shipping.

Sims proposed that merchant ships and troop transports be gathered into groups, called convoys, and escorted across the Atlantic by warships. If submarines wanted to attack a convoy, they would have to get past the warships protecting it. The convoy system greatly reduced shipping losses and ensured that American troops arrived safely in Europe. They arrived during a pivotal time in late 1917.

Russia Leaves the War In March 1917, riots broke out in Russia over the government's handling of the war and over the scarcity of food and fuel. On March

---

DIFFERENTIATED INSTRUCTION

English Learners To help improve reading comprehension for students with reading difficulties, help them create a list of key terms for this section. Start with the terms in the Guide to Reading. Add other names and unfamiliar words and phrases. Have students work in pairs to quiz each other on the meaning and importance of each name and term on the list. **L1 ELL**

📁 Refer to *Inclusion for the High School Social Studies Classroom Strategies and Activities* in the TCR.

Western Front, 1914–1918

Geography Skills

1. **Interpreting Maps** Where did the majority of World War I battles occur?
2. **Interpreting Charts** Which nation suffered the largest number of military deaths during World War I?

15, Czar Nicholas II, the leader of the Russian Empire, abdicated his throne. Political leadership in Russia passed into the hands of a provisional, or temporary, government, consisting largely of moderate representatives who supported Russia's continued participation in World War I. The government, however, was unable to adequately deal with the major problems, such as food shortages, that were afflicting the nation.

The **Bolsheviks,** a group of Communists, soon competed for power in Russia. In November 1917, **Vladimir Lenin,** the leader of the Bolshevik Party, overthrew the Russian government and established a Communist government.

Germany's military fortunes improved with the Bolshevik takeover of Russia. Lenin's first act after seizing power was to pull Russia out of the war and concentrate on establishing a Communist state. He accomplished this by agreeing to the **Treaty of Brest-Litovsk** with Germany on March 3, 1918. Under this treaty, Russia lost substantial territory, giving up Ukraine, its Polish and Baltic territories, and Finland. However, the treaty also removed the German army from the remaining Russian lands. With the Eastern Front settled, Germany was now free to concentrate its forces in the west.

The German Offensive Falters On March 21, 1918, the Germans launched a massive attack along the Western Front, beginning with gas attacks and a bombardment by over 6,000 artillery pieces. German forces, reinforced with troops transferred from the Russian front, pushed deeply into Allied lines. By early June, they were less than 40 miles (64 km) from Paris.

American troops played an important role in containing the German offensive. In late May, as the German offensive continued, the Americans launched their first major attack, quickly capturing the village of Cantigny. On June 1, American and French troops blocked the German drive on Paris at the town of Château-Thierry. On July 15, the Germans launched

CHAPTER 14   World War I and Its Aftermath   **467**

✓ **Reading Check**

Answer: to pull Russia out of the war and establish a Communist state

Picturing **History**

Answer: the Battle of the Argonne Forest
Ask: How many artillery pieces were used in the battle? *(roughly 4,000)*

3 ASSESS

Assign Section 3 Assessment as homework or as an in-class activity.

ⓘ Have students use the **Interactive Tutor Self-Assessment CD-ROM.**

L1/ELL

Reading Essentials and Study Guide 14–3

Name _____ Date _____ Class _____

Study Guide
Chapter 14, Section 3
For use with textbook pages 464–469
A BLOODY CONFLICT

KEY TERMS AND NAMES
"no man's land" the space between opposing trenches (page 465)
convoys groups of merchant ships and troop transports (page 466)
Vladimir Lenin leader of the Bolshevik Party (page 467)
Treaty of Brest-Litovsk treaty between Germany and Russia that ended Russia's involvement in World War I (page 467)
armistice a cease-fire (page 468)
Fourteen Points President Wilson's plan for peace after World War I (page 468)
League of Nations an association of nations organized to help keep peace and prevent future

L2

Section Quiz 14–3

Name _____ Date _____ Class _____

★ **Chapter 14**   Score ____

Section Quiz 14-3
DIRECTIONS: Matching Match each item in Column A with the items in Column B. Write the correct letters in the blanks. *(10 points each)*

Column A	Column B
___ 1. supreme commander of the Allied forces	A. General John J. Pershing
___ 2. a group of Communists	B. Marshall Ferdinand Foch
___ 3. commander of the American troops	C. "no man's land"
___ 4. payments for war damages	D. Bolsheviks
___ 5. the space between opposing trenches	E. reparations

DIRECTIONS: Multiple Choice In the blank at the left, write the letter of the choice that best completes the statement or answers the question. *(10 points each)*

---

one last massive attack in a determined attempt to take Paris, but American and French troops held their ground.

The Battle of the Argonne Forest With the German drive stalled, French Marshal Ferdinand Foch, supreme commander of the Allied forces, ordered massive counterattacks all along the front. In mid-September, American troops drove back German forces at the battle of Saint-Mihiel. The attack was a prelude to a massive American offensive in the region between the Meuse River and the Argonne Forest. General Pershing assembled over 600,000 American troops, some 40,000 tons of supplies, and roughly 4,000 artillery pieces for the most massive attack in American history.

The attack began on September 26, 1918. Slowly, one German position after another fell to the advancing American troops. The Germans inflicted heavy casualties on the American forces, but by early November, the Americans had shattered the German defenses and opened a hole in the German lines.

The War Ends While fighting raged along the Western Front, a revolution engulfed Austria-Hungary, and the Ottoman Turks surrendered. Faced with the surrender of their allies and a naval mutiny at Kiel in early November, the people of Berlin rose in rebellion on November 9 and forced the German emperor to step down. At the 11th hour on the 11th day of the 11th month, 1918, the fighting stopped. Germany had finally signed an armistice, or cease-fire, that ended the war.

✓ **Reading Check** **Explaining** What was Vladimir Lenin's first goal after controlling Russia in 1917?

Picturing **History**

American Artillery This photo shows some of the materials used to fight World War I. Artillery shells are piled at the feet of these American soldiers. What American battle demanded the largest amount of supplies and artillery pieces?

A Flawed Peace

In January 1919, a peace conference began in Paris to try to resolve the complicated issues arising from World War I. The principal figures in the negotiations were the "Big Four," the leaders of the victorious Allied nations: President Wilson of the United States, British prime minister David Lloyd George, French premier Georges Clemenceau, and Italian prime minister Vittorio Orlando. Germany was not invited to participate.

Wilson had presented his plan, known as the **Fourteen Points,** to Congress in January 1918. The Fourteen Points were based on "the principle of justice to all peoples and nationalities." In the first five points, the president proposed to eliminate the general causes of the war through free trade, disarmament, freedom of the seas, impartial adjustment of colonial claims, and open diplomacy instead of secret agreements. The next eight points addressed the right of self-determination. They also required the Central Powers to evacuate all of the countries invaded during the war, including France, Belgium, and Russia. The fourteenth point, perhaps the most important one to Wilson, called for the creation of a "general association of nations" known as the **League of Nations.** The League's member nations would help preserve peace and prevent future wars by pledging to respect and protect each other's territory and political independence. 📖 *(See page 956 for the text of the Fourteen Points.)*

The Treaty of Versailles As the peace talks progressed in the Palace of Versailles (vehr·SY), it became clear that Wilson's ideas did not coincide with the interests of the other Allied governments. They criticized his plan as too lenient toward Germany.

Despite Wilson's hopes, the terms of peace were harsh. The **Treaty of Versailles,** signed by Germany on June 28, 1919, had weakened or discarded many of Wilson's proposals. Under the treaty, Germany was stripped of its armed forces and was made to pay reparations, or war damages, in the amount of $33 billion to the Allies. This sum was far beyond Germany's financial means. Perhaps most humiliating, the treaty required Germany to acknowledge guilt for the outbreak of World War I and the devastation caused by the war.

The war itself resulted in the dissolution of four empires: the Russian Empire, the Ottoman Empire, which lost territory in the war and fell to revolution in 1922, the German Empire after the abdication of the emperor and loss of territory in the treaty, and

---

CRITICAL THINKING ACTIVITY

Supporting Key Ideas Write the following statement on the board: "The peace treaty in Europe did not establish a lasting peace." Have students work in pairs to locate evidence to support this statement. *(Evidence includes Germany's severe punishment and disputed national boundaries.)*
L2

Austria-Hungary, which was split into separate countries. Furthermore, nine new countries were established in Europe, including Yugoslavia, Poland, and Czechoslovakia.

While Wilson expressed disappointment in the treaty, he found consolation in its call for the creation of his cherished League of Nations. He returned home to win approval for the treaty.

The U.S. Senate Rejects the Treaty The Treaty of Versailles, especially the League of Nations, faced immediate opposition from numerous U.S. lawmakers. A key group of senators, nicknamed "the Irreconcilables" in the press, assailed the League as the kind of "entangling alliance" that Washington, Jefferson, and Monroe had warned against. These critics feared that the League might supersede the power of Congress to declare war and thus force the United States to fight in numerous foreign conflicts.

A larger group of senators, known as the "Reservationists," was led by the powerful chairman of the Foreign Relations committee, Henry Cabot Lodge. This group supported the League but would ratify the treaty only with amendments that would preserve the nation's freedom to act independently. Wilson feared such changes would defeat the basic purpose of the League and insisted that the Senate ratify the treaty without changes.

Convinced that he could defeat his opposition by winning public support, Wilson took his case directly to the American people. Starting in Ohio in September 1919, he traveled 8,000 miles and made over 30 major speeches in three weeks. The physical strain of his tour, however, proved too great. Wilson collapsed in Colorado on September 25 and returned to the White

World Geography Connection

Global War

Although World War I was fought mainly in Europe, it touched the lives of peoples throughout the world, including those in Africa and India. By the time the war broke out, much of Africa and India was under the control of European nations. While the British controlled much of India, no less than seven European powers had divided up Africa among themselves. As a result of living under the rule of Europeans, Africans and Indians took part in the great war. About one million Indians fought for the British in Europe, while nearly as many Africans served in the French army. The fighting also spread to Africa, as the Allies fought to seize control of Germany's African colonies. *Why is it accurate to characterize World War I as a global conflict?*

House. There, he suffered a stroke and was bedridden for months, isolated from even his closest advisers but determined not to compromise with the Senate.

The Senate voted in November 1919 and again in March 1920, but it refused to ratify the treaty. After Wilson left office in 1921, the United States negotiated separate peace treaties with each of the Central Powers. The League of Nations, the foundation of President Wilson's plan for lasting world peace, took shape without the United States.

Reading Check **Examining** What major issues did Wilson's Fourteen Points address?

SECTION 3 ASSESSMENT

HISTORY Online **Study Central™** To review this section, go to **tarvol2.glencoe.com** and click on **Study Central™**.

Checking for Understanding

1. **Define:** convoy, armistice, reparations.
2. **Identify:** "no man's land," Vladimir Lenin, Treaty of Brest-Litovsk, Fourteen Points, League of Nations, Treaty of Versailles.
3. **List** the four nations that dominated the Paris peace conference in 1919.

Reviewing Themes

4. **Individual Action** Why did President Wilson propose his Fourteen Points?

Critical Thinking

5. **Analyzing** What impact did John J. Pershing and the Battle of the Argonne Forest have on World War I?
6. **Organizing** Use a graphic organizer to list the results of World War I.

Results of World War I

Analyzing Visuals

7. **Analyzing Maps and Charts** Examine the map and chart on page 467. Prepare a quiz with questions based on information from both. Give the quiz to some of your classmates.

Writing About History

8. **Descriptive Writing** Imagine that you are an American soldier fighting in Europe during World War I. Write a letter home describing your situation, and explain why you are there.

SECTION 3 ASSESSMENT ANSWERS

1. Terms are in blue.
2. "no man's land" *(p. 465)*, Vladimir Lenin *(p. 467)*, Treaty of Brest-Litovsk *(p. 467)*, Fourteen Points *(p. 468)*, League of Nations *(p. 468)*, Treaty of Versailles *(p. 468)*
3. Italy, Britain, France, United States

4. He wanted to provide justice for all peoples and nationalities.
5. It shattered German defenses and opened a hole in the German line.
6. League of Nations, dissolution of four empires, nine new European countries, Germany pays reparations

7. Instruct students to provide answers for all questions posed.
8. Letters should focus on the soldier's reaction to his situation.

World Geography Connection

Answer: Although it was fought mainly in Europe, World War I was a global conflict because it involved people from many different parts of the world. Also, some of the fighting eventually spread to the African continent.

✓ Reading Check

Answer: free trade, disarmament, freedom of the seas, impartial adjustment of colonial claims, open diplomacy, self-determination, creation of the League of Nations

Reteach

Have students discuss fighting strategies of World War I.

Enrich

Invite interested students to research what happened to the League of Nations after the Treaty of Versailles.

HISTORY Online

Study Central™ provides summaries, interactive games, and online graphic organizers to help students review section content.

4 CLOSE

Have students characterize the American response to the Treaty of Versailles.

469

TEACH

Analyzing Information Point out that reading and understanding can be enhanced by students' ability to analyze information and place it in context with other knowledge they already possess.

To help students learn the process, ask them to analyze the information in a short newspaper or magazine article on a topic of personal interest. Suggest that they choose a topic that is not related to their schoolwork. Instruct them to follow the steps outlined on page 470.

Additional Practice

L1

Reinforcing Skills Activity 14

Name _____ Date _____ Class _____

★ Reinforcing Skills Activity **14**

Analyzing Information

▢ **LEARNING THE SKILL**

Before you can make a decision or form an opinion about a subject, you must analyze information about it. As you read about a subject, first identify the topic. Next, identify the main points made by the author and summarize the information in your own words. Use this information plus your previous knowledge about the topic to form your own statement on the topic.

▢ **PRACTICING THE SKILL**

DIRECTIONS: Read the excerpt below from A. Mitchell Palmer's "The Case Against the Reds." Then answer the questions that follow on a separate sheet of paper.

It has always been plain to me that when American citizens unite upon any national issue they are generally right...

The whole mass of evidence, accumulated from all parts of the country, was scrupulously...

GLENCOE
TECHNOLOGY

CD-ROM
Glencoe Skillbuilder
Interactive Workbook
CD-ROM, Level 2

This interactive CD-ROM reinforces student mastery of essential social studies skills.

Analyzing Information

Why Learn This Skill?

The ability to analyze information is important in deciding your position on a subject. For example, you need to analyze a political decision to determine if you should support it. You would also analyze a candidate's position statements to determine if you should vote for him or her.

Learning the Skill

To analyze information, use the following steps:

• Identify the topic that is being discussed.

• Examine how the information is organized. What are the main points?

• Summarize the information in your own words, and then make a statement of your own based on your understanding of the topic and on what you already know.

Practicing the Skill

Read the following information taken from Henry Cabot Lodge's *On the League of Nations* speech. Use the steps listed above to analyze the information and answer the questions that follow.

I am as anxious as any human being can be to have the United States render every possible service to the civilization and the peace of mankind. But I am certain that we can do it best by not putting ourselves in leading strings, or subjecting our policies and our sovereignty to other nations. The independence of the United States is not only more precious to ourselves, but to the world, than any single possession.

I will go as far as anyone in world service that the first step to world service is the maintenance of the United States. You may call me selfish if you will, conservative or reactionary, or use any other harsh adjective you see fit to apply. But an American I was born, an

American I've remained all my life. I can never be anything else but an American, and I must think of the United States first. And when I think of the United States first in an argument like this, I am thinking of what is best for the world. For if the United States fails, the best hope of mankind fails with it. I have never had but one allegiance; I cannot divide it now. I have loved but one flag and I cannot share that devotion and give affection to the mongrel banner invented for a league. Internationalism, illustrated by the Bolshevik and by the men to whom all countries are alike, provided they can make money out of them, is to me repulsive. National I must remain and in that way I, like all Americans, can render the amplest service to the world.

The United States is the world's best hope, but if you fetter her in the interest through quarrels of other nations, if you tangle her in the intrigues of Europe, you will destroy her powerful good, and endanger her very existence.

❶ What topic is being discussed?

❷ What are the main points of this excerpt from Senator Lodge's speech?

❸ Summarize the information in this excerpt, and then provide your analysis based on this information and what you know from the rest of the chapter.

Skills Assessment

Complete the Practicing Skills questions on page 477 and the Chapter 14 Skill Reinforcement Activity to assess your mastery of this skill.

Applying the Skill

Analyzing Information Find a short, informative piece of news, such as a political candidate's position paper, an editorial in a newspaper, or an explanation of a new law that will be enacted soon. Analyze the information and make a statement of your own.

 Glencoe's **Skillbuilder Interactive Workbook CD-ROM, Level 2,** provides instruction and practice in key social studies skills.

ANSWERS TO PRACTICING THE SKILL

❶ League of Nations

❷ Independence of the United States is precious to us and to the world; he cannot share his devotion to the United States with the League of Nations; getting involved in the intrigues of Europe will endanger the existence of the United States.

❸ Students' answers will vary but should demonstrate an understanding of the material in the chapter.

Applying the Skill
Students should show that they used the three-step process to analyze the information.

Guide to Reading

Main Idea
As American society moved from war to peace, turmoil in the economy and fear of communism caused a series of domestic upheavals.

Key Terms and Names
cost of living, general strike, Red Scare, A. Mitchell Palmer, J. Edgar Hoover, deport

Reading Strategy
Organizing As you read about the war's aftermath, complete a graphic organizer similar to the one below to list the effects of the end of World War I on the American economy.

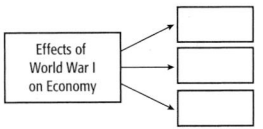

Reading Objectives:
• **Describe** the effects of the postwar recession on the United States.
• **Discuss** the causes of and reaction to the Red Scare.

Section Theme
Continuity and Change The postwar period proved a difficult readjustment period for the United States, in part because of economic turmoil and the fear of communism.

Preview of Events

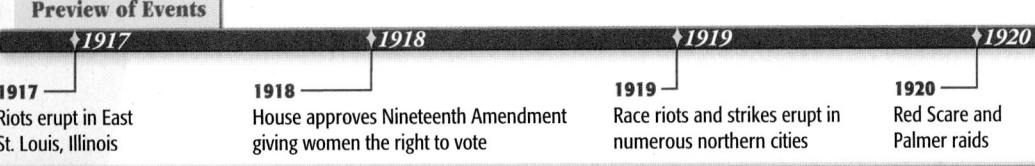

1917	1918	1919	1920
1917 Riots erupt in East St. Louis, Illinois	**1918** House approves Nineteenth Amendment giving women the right to vote	**1919** Race riots and strikes erupt in numerous northern cities	**1920** Red Scare and Palmer raids

★ An American Story ★

"Mother" Jones

On August 20, 1919, Mary Harris Jones, also known as "Mother" Jones, was thrown in jail in Homestead, Pennsylvania. The 89-year-old had just finished delivering a fiery, impassioned speech in an attempt to gain support for steel unions. Referring to the owners of the big steel companies, she said:

66 Our Kaisers sit up and smoke seventy-five cent cigars and have lackeys with knee pants bring them champagne while you starve, while you grow old at forty, stoking their furnaces. You pull in your belts while they banquet. They have stomachs two miles long and two miles wide and you fill them. . . . If Gary [chair of U.S. Steel] wants to work twelve hours a day, let him go in the blooming mill and work. What we want is a little leisure, time for music, playgrounds, a decent home, books, and the things that make life worthwhile. 99

—quoted in *Labor in Crisis*

An Economy in Turmoil

The end of World War I brought great upheaval to American society. When the war ended, government agencies removed their controls from the American economy. This released pent-up demand in the economy. People raced to buy goods that had been rationed, while businesses rapidly raised prices they had been forced to keep low during the war. The result was rapid inflation. In 1919 prices rose at an average of more than 15 percent. Inflation greatly increased the cost of living—the cost of food, clothing, shelter, and other essentials that people need to survive.

CHAPTER 14 World War I and Its Aftermath **471**

---

1 FOCUS

Section Overview
This section focuses on the impact World War I had on America when the war was over.

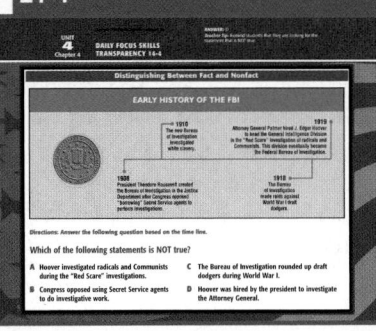
Reading Preview

Answers to Graphic: rapid inflation, mass demand for goods, strikes

Preteaching Vocabulary
Have students scan the section and write a sentence using each of the Key Terms and Names in context.

---

2 TEACH

Daily Lecture and Discussion Notes 14-4

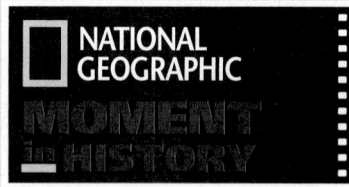

NATIONAL GEOGRAPHIC
MOMENT in HISTORY

Historians believe that the bands that accompanied African American regiments introduced jazz and ragtime to Europeans.

Reading Strategy

Creating an Outline Have students use the headings in this section to create a sentence outline as a guide to reading the section. **L1** **ELL**

FYI

As fresh memories of the war, economic problems, labor unrest, and racial tension combined to create a sense of disillusionment, scandal marred a symbol of American life. In 1919 eight members of the Chicago White Sox were accused of taking mob money to lose the World Series to the Cincinnati Reds. The players, dubbed the Black Sox, were acquitted in court but were banned from professional baseball for life.

Inflation Leads to Strikes Many companies had been forced to raise wages during the war, but inflation now threatened to wipe out all the gains workers had made. While workers wanted higher wages to keep up with inflation, companies wanted to hold down wages because inflation was also driving up their operating costs.

During the war, the number of workers in unions had increased dramatically. By the time the war ended, workers were better organized and much more capable of organizing strikes than they had been before. Many business leaders, on the other hand, were determined to break the power of the unions and roll back the gains labor had made. These circumstances led to an enormous wave of strikes in 1919. By the end of the year, more than 3,600 strikes involving more than 4 million workers had taken place.

The Seattle General Strike The first major strike took place in Seattle, when some 35,000 shipyard workers walked off the job demanding higher wages and shorter hours. Soon other unions in Seattle joined the shipyard workers and organized a general strike. A general strike is a strike that involves all workers living in a certain location, not just workers in a particular industry. The Seattle general strike involved more than 60,000 people and paralyzed the city for five days. Although the strikers returned to work without making any gains, their actions worried many Americans because the general strike was a common tactic used in Europe by Communists and other radical groups.

The Boston Police Strike Perhaps the most famous strike of 1919 took place in Boston, when roughly 75 percent of the police force walked off the job. Riots and looting soon erupted in the city, forcing the governor of Massachusetts, **Calvin Coolidge,** to send in the National Guard. When the strikers tried to return to work, the police commissioner refused to accept them. He fired the strikers and hired a new police force instead.

Despite protests, Coolidge agreed the men should be fired. He declared, "There is no right to strike

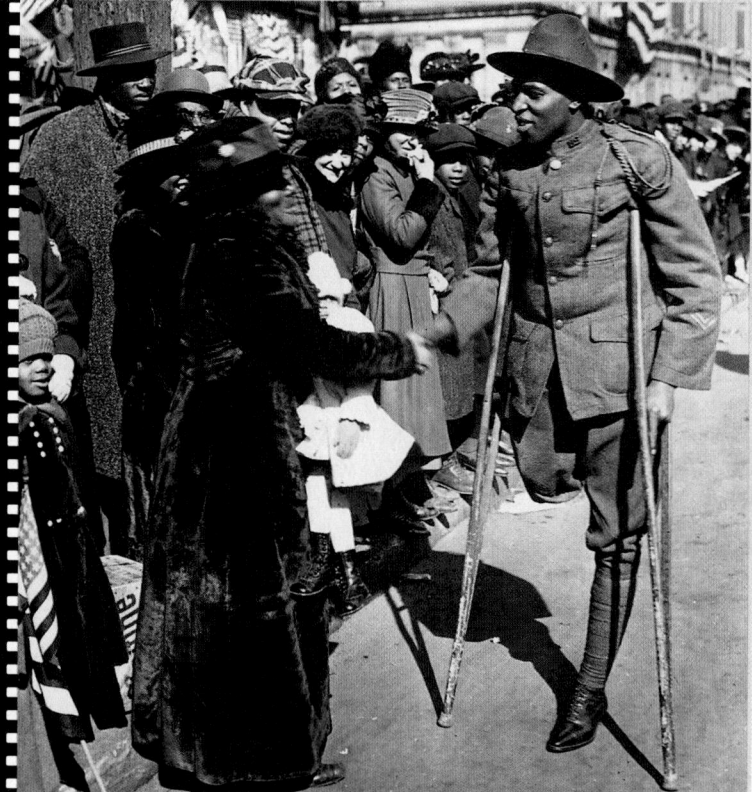

NATIONAL GEOGRAPHIC
MOMENT in HISTORY

HERO'S HOMECOMING
A wounded soldier of the 369th Regiment, the Harlem "Hell-Fighters," accepts congratulations during a victory parade through New York City in 1919. Facing discrimination within their own army, African American soldiers at the front received a warm reception from their French allies. "I have never before experienced what it meant really to be free, to taste real liberty," one soldier wrote home, "in a phrase, 'to be a man.'" Two African American infantry divisions suffered some 6,000 casualties, but at war's end, they still came home to a segregated American society.

472   CHAPTER 14   World War I and Its Aftermath

Reading Strategy   READING THE TEXT

Monitoring Comprehension As students read the section, they may encounter text or information that they do not understand. Point out to students they need to adjust their reading strategies to increase their comprehension. Model how this is done by reading the section aloud. As you read, say things such as "What do I think this subtopic might be about based on the heading?" *(predicting);* "What would worker strikes and raids on radical organizations have looked like?" *(visualizing);* "What have I heard about this topic and is it correct based on the information described here?" *(activating prior knowledge)* Modeling how you read helps students think about strategies they can use as they read independently. **L1**

Effects of World War I on the United States

Developments in the War

- War-torn economies of Europe
- Russian Revolution
- Industrial demand of wartime
- Sacrifices of wartime; disappointment with Versailles Peace Treaty

Effects on U.S.

- Boom in U.S. economy; emergence of U.S. as world industrial leader
- "Red Scare" in postwar U.S.; suspicion of immigrants
- Internal migration in U.S., especially African American migration to Northern cities
- Failure to join League of Nations

Graphic Organizer → Skills

World War I had profound effects on the United States.

Interpreting Why did the destruction of European economies cause an industrial boom in the United States?

Graphic Organizer → Skills

Answer: American industry was undamaged by the war and was needed to help rebuild Europe.

Graphic Organizer Skills Practice

Ask: What development during the war most contributed to the Red Scare? *(Russian Revolution)*

✓ **Reading Check**

Answer: Business attempted to break the wartime gains of unions and roll back wages.

✓ **Reading Check**

Answer: Returning soldiers and African Americans competed for jobs.

Organizing Information Have students use a graphic with columns labeled Who, Where, When, How Many, and Results to compare the three major strikes mentioned in this section. **L2**

📁 Use *Interpreting Political Cartoons*, Cartoon 20.

---

against the public safety by anybody, anywhere, anytime." Coolidge's response brought him to national attention and earned him widespread public support. It also convinced the Republicans to make Coolidge their vice presidential candidate in the 1920 election.

The Steel Strike Shortly after the police strike ended, one of the largest strikes in American history began when an estimated 350,000 steelworkers went on strike for higher pay, shorter hours, and recognition of their union. **Elbert H. Gary,** the head of U.S. Steel, refused even to talk to union leaders. Instead, the company set out to break the union by using anti-immigrant feelings to divide the workers.

Many steelworkers were immigrants. The company blamed the strike on foreign radicals and called for loyal Americans to return to work. Meanwhile, the company hired African Americans and Mexicans as replacement workers and managed to keep its steel mills operating despite the strike. Clashes between company guards and strikers were frequent, and in Gary, Indiana, a riot left 18 strikers dead. In early January of 1920, the strike collapsed. The failure of the strike set back the union cause in the steel industry. Steelworkers remained unorganized until 1937.

✓ **Reading Check** **Explaining** What caused the wave of strikes in 1919?

Racial Unrest

Adding to the nation's economic turmoil was the return of hundreds of thousands of American soldiers from Europe who needed to find employment.

Many African Americans who had moved north during the war were also competing for jobs and housing. Frustration and racism combined to produce violence. In the summer of 1919, over 20 race riots broke out across the nation.

The worst violence occurred in Chicago. On a hot July day, African Americans went to a whites-only beach. Both sides began throwing stones at each other. Whites also threw stones at an African American teenager swimming near the beach to prevent him from coming ashore, and he drowned. A full-scale riot then erupted in the city. Angry African Americans attacked white neighborhoods while whites attacked African American neighborhoods. The riot lasted for several days. In the end, 38 people died—15 white and 23 black—and over 500 were injured.

✓ **Reading Check** **Analyzing** Why did the end of the war lead to race riots?

The Red Scare

The wave of strikes in 1919 helped to fuel fears that Communists were conspiring to start a revolution in the United States. Americans had been stunned when Lenin and the Bolsheviks seized power and withdrew Russia from the war. Americans had become very anti-German as the war progressed, and when the Communists withdrew Russia from the war, they seemed to be helping Germany. American anger at Germany quickly expanded into anger at Communists as well. Americans began to associate communism with being unpatriotic and disloyal.

DIFFERENTIATED INSTRUCTION

Reading Support This activity helps to address the particular needs of visual learners. As students read this section, lead them through the photographs, charts, and other graphics as a way of informally telling the story of the section. Have students use the time lines to summarize events and to discuss absolute and relative chronology of events. Encourage students to add important dates to create a master time line in the classroom. **L1** ELL

📁 Refer to *Inclusion for the High School Social Studies Classroom Strategies and Activities* in the TCR.

History *and the* Humanities

American Art & Architecture: *Allies Day*

FYI

During the Red Scare, many Americans believed that people who promoted radical causes should be treated without regard for their rights. Others, such as journalist William Allen White, argued that the arrests and deportation of alleged Communists gave radical causes more publicity than they deserved.

3 ASSESS

Assign Section 4 Assessment as homework or as an in-class activity.

🖲 Have students use the **Interactive Tutor Self-Assessment CD-ROM.**

L1/ELL

Reading Essentials and Study Guide 14–4

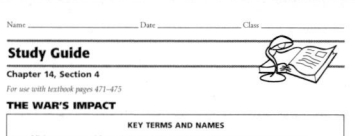

Name _____ Date _____ Class _____

Study Guide

Chapter 14, Section 4
For use with textbook pages 471–475

THE WAR'S IMPACT

KEY TERMS AND NAMES

cost of living the cost of food, clothing, shelter, and other essentials that people need to survive (page 471)

general strike a strike that involves all workers in a certain location, not just workers in a particular industry (page 472)

Red Scare a panic in the United States caused by the fear that Communists would seize power in the United States (page 474)

A. Mitchell Palmer Attorney General of the United States in 1919 (page 474)

J. Edgar Hoover head of the General Intelligence Division, which became the FBI (page 474)

deported to be expelled from a country (page 474)

Terror in the Streets After the House of Morgan—a bank in New York City—was damaged by a bomb in 1920, Attorney General A. Mitchell Palmer instituted raids on antigovernment activists and many immigrants, often violating their civil liberties in the process. Whom did Palmer appoint to coordinate these investigations?

Americans had long been suspicious of Communist ideas. Throughout the late 1800s, many Americans had accused immigrants of importing radical socialist and Communist ideas into the United States and blamed them for labor unrest and violence. Now Communists had seized control of an entire nation, and fears surged that they would try to incite revolutions elsewhere. These fears seemed to be confirmed in 1919, when the Soviet Union formed the **Communist International**—an organization for coordinating the activities of Communist parties in other countries.

The Red Scare Begins

As strikes erupted across the United States in 1919, the fear that Communists, or "reds," as they were called, might seize power led to a nationwide panic known as the **Red Scare.** Seattle's mayor, Ole Hanson, spoke for others when he condemned the leaders of the Seattle general strike as revolutionaries who wanted to "take possession of our American government and try to duplicate the anarchy of Russia."

In April the postal service intercepted more than 30 parcels addressed to leading businesspeople and politicians that were triggered to explode when opened. In June eight bombs in eight cities exploded within minutes of one another, suggesting a nationwide conspiracy. One of them damaged the home of United States Attorney General **A. Mitchell Palmer** in Washington, D.C. Most people believed the bombings were the work of Communists or other revolutionaries trying to destroy the American way of life.

The Palmer Raids

Declaring that a "blaze of revolution" was "burning up the foundations of society," Palmer took action. He established a special division within the Justice Department, the General Intelligence Division, headed by **J. Edgar Hoover.** This division eventually became the Federal Bureau of Investigation (FBI). From late 1919 to the spring of 1920, Palmer organized a series of raids on the headquarters of various radical organizations. Although evidence pointed to no single group as the bombers, Palmer's agents focused on foreign residents and immigrants. The authorities detained thousands of suspects and deported, or expelled from the country, approximately 500 of them.

474 CHAPTER 14 World War I and Its Aftermath

INTERDISCIPLINARY CONNECTIONS ACTIVITY

Music Have students work in small groups to write a song describing the turmoil of the early 1900s. Ask each group to choose an existing melody, or write their own, and then write lyrics that relate to one of these topics: fear of radicalism, racial unrest, or labor unrest. Encourage students to use the names of people, places, and events mentioned in this section. Invite students to perform their songs for the class. **L2**

Palmer's agents often disregarded the civil liberties of the suspects. Officers entered homes and offices without search warrants. People were mistreated and jailed for indefinite periods of time and were not allowed to talk to their attorneys.

For a while, Palmer was regarded as a national hero. His raids, however, failed to turn up any hard evidence of revolutionary conspiracy. When his dire prediction that violence would rock the nation on May Day 1920—a popular European celebration of workers—proved wrong, Palmer lost much of his credibility and soon faded from prominence.

The Red Scare greatly influenced people's attitudes during the 1920s. Americans often linked radicalism with immigrants, and that attitude led to a call for Congress to limit immigration.

✓ **Reading Check** **Examining** After World War I, why were Americans suspicious of some union leaders?

An End to Progressivism

Economic problems, labor unrest, and racial tensions, as well as the fresh memories of World War I, all combined to create a general sense of disillusionment in the United States. By 1920 Americans wanted an end to the upheaval. During the 1920 campaign, Ohio Governor James M. Cox and his running mate, Assistant Secretary of the Navy Franklin D. Roosevelt, ran on a platform of keeping alive Woodrow Wilson's progressive ideals. The Republican candidate, Warren G. Harding, called for a return to "normalcy." He urged that what the United States needed was a return to the simpler days before the Progressive Era reforms:

A. Mitchell Palmer and J. Edgar Hoover

❝[Our] present need is not heroics, but healing; not nostrums, but normalcy; not revolution, but restoration; not agitation, but adjustment; not surgery, but serenity; not the dramatic, but the dispassionate; . . . not submergence in internationality, but sustainment in triumphant nationality.❞

—quoted in *Portrait of a Nation*

Harding's sentiments struck a chord with voters, and he won the election by a landslide margin of over 7 million votes. Americans were weary of more crusades to reform society and the world. They hoped to put the country's racial and labor unrest and economic troubles behind them and build a more prosperous and stable society.

✓ **Reading Check** **Explaining** How was Harding able to win the presidential election of 1920?

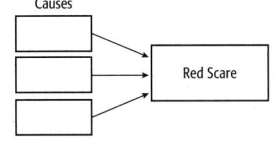 **Study Central™** To review this section, go to tarvol2.glencoe.com and click on **Study Central™**.

SECTION 4 ASSESSMENT

Checking for Understanding
1. **Define:** cost of living, general strike, deport.
2. **Identify:** Red Scare, A. Mitchell Palmer, J. Edgar Hoover.
3. **Describe** the conditions that African Americans faced after the end of World War I.

Reviewing Themes
4. **Continuity and Change** Why did Republican Warren G. Harding win the election of 1920?

Critical Thinking
5. **Analyzing** How did the Palmer raids deprive some citizens of their civil rights?
6. **Organizing** Use a graphic organizer similar to the one below to list the causes of the Red Scare in the United States.

Causes → Red Scare

Analyzing Visuals
7. **Analyzing Photographs** Study the photograph on page 472. How might parades such as this one mobilize African Americans to work for an end to discrimination?

Writing About History
8. **Descriptive Writing** Imagine that you are a European immigrant working in a factory in the United States in 1919. Write a letter to a relative in Europe explaining economic conditions in America and why workers are striking.

CHAPTER 14　World War I and Its Aftermath　**475**

SECTION 4 ASSESSMENT ANSWERS

1. Terms are in blue.
2. Red Scare (p. 474), A. Mitchell Palmer (p. 474), J. Edgar Hoover (p. 474)
3. They faced racism and intense competition for housing and jobs.
4. He campaigned on a return to "normalcy," which many wanted.
5. They abused civil liberties by

searching without a warrant, jailing suspects indefinitely, and limiting lawyer-client communication.
6. strikes, bombings and Palmer Raids, fear of Communists seizing power
7. African Americans would note that they had fought for their country and deserved to be treated equally.

8. Students' letters will vary. Letters should describe inflation, the cost of living, and business opposition to unions.

Section Quiz 14–4

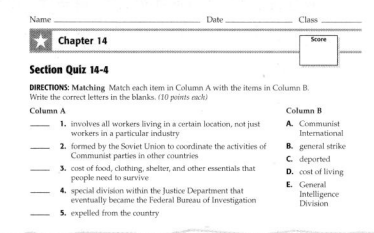

✓ **Reading Check**

Answer: They blamed union leaders for causing social unrest through strikes.

Reteach
Have students describe the effects of the postwar recession on the United States.

Enrich
Invite interested students to research one of the persons mentioned in this chapter and prepare a short biographical profile. Encourage students to use library and Internet resources for their research.

✓ **Reading Check**

Answer: by campaigning for a return to a simpler time before racial and labor unrest and economic troubles

Study Central™ provides summaries, interactive games, and online graphic organizers to help students review section content.

4 CLOSE

Have students create a graphic organizer showing the causes of and the reactions to the Red Scare.

475

CHAPTER 14 ASSESSMENT and ACTIVITIES

CHAPTER 14 ASSESSMENT and ACTIVITIES

GLENCOE TECHNOLOGY

MindJogger Videoquiz
Use the **MindJogger Videoquiz** to review Chapter 14 content.

○ Available in DVD

Reviewing Key Terms
Students' answers will vary. The pages where the words appear in the text are shown in parentheses.

1. **guerrilla** (p. 449)
2. **nationalism** (p. 450)
3. **self-determination** (p. 450)
4. **propaganda** (p. 453)
5. **contraband** (p. 453)
6. **U-boat** (p. 453)
7. **conscription** (p. 457)
8. **victory garden** (p. 458)
9. **espionage** (p. 460)
10. **convoy** (p. 466)
11. **armistice** (p. 468)
12. **reparations** (p. 468)
13. **cost of living** (p. 471)
14. **general strike** (p. 472)
15. **deport** (p. 474)

Reviewing Key Facts
16. Pancho Villa (p. 449), Franz Ferdinand (p. 450), Zimmermann telegram (p. 454), Bernard Baruch (p. 458), Committee on Public Information (p. 460), "no man's land" (p. 465), Vladimir Lenin (p. 467), Fourteen Points (p. 468), League of Nations (p. 468), A. Mitchell Palmer (p. 474), J. Edgar Hoover (p. 474)

17. the alliance system, the naval buildup, nationalism in the Balkans, and the assassination of Archduke Franz Ferdinand

18. Women filled noncombat positions such as nurses, clerical help, and other jobs vacated by men who had become soldiers.

Reviewing Key Terms
On a sheet of paper, use each of these terms in a sentence.

1. guerrilla
2. nationalism
3. self-determination
4. propaganda
5. contraband
6. U-boat
7. conscription
8. victory garden
9. espionage
10. convoy
11. armistice
12. reparations
13. cost of living
14. general strike
15. deport

Reviewing Key Facts
16. **Identify:** Pancho Villa, Franz Ferdinand, Zimmermann telegram, Bernard Baruch, Committee on Public Information, "no man's land," Vladimir Lenin, Fourteen Points, League of Nations, A. Mitchell Palmer, J. Edgar Hoover.

17. What factors contributed to the start of World War I in Europe?

18. What role did American women play in the war effort during World War I?

19. What did the American government do to solve the problem of supplying its troops?

20. What were the provisions of the Treaty of Versailles?

21. What were the Palmer raids?

Critical Thinking
22. **Analyzing Themes: Government and Democracy** Do you think government action to suppress opposition to World War I was justified? Why or why not?

23. **Interpreting Primary Sources** On September 12, 1918, Socialist leader Eugene V. Debs was convicted of violating the Espionage Act. Debs later spoke to the court at his sentencing. Read his speech and answer the questions that follow.

❝I look upon the Espionage laws as a despotic enactment in flagrant conflict with democratic principles and with the spirit of free institutions. . . . I am opposed to the social system in which we live. . . . I believe in fundamental change, but if possible by peaceful and orderly means. . . .

I am thinking this morning of the men in the mills and factories, . . . of the women who for a paltry wage

Chapter Summary

Mobilizing for War

→ **Armed Forces**
- Congress passed Selective Service Act which required young men ages 21–30 to register for the draft
- Employed women in non-combat roles

→ **Domestic Front**
- War Industries Board controlled war materials and production
- Committee on Public Information created war propaganda
- Government worked with employers and labor to ensure production
- Congress passed Espionage and Sedition Acts to limit opposition to the war
- Congress increased taxes and sold Liberty Bonds to pay for war

→ **Postwar Problems**
- Cost of living greatly increased
- Economic problems led to racial violence and widespread strikes
- Fear of communism led to Red Scare and Palmer raids

19. A draft was initiated to alleviate the shortage of troops; convoys ensured they–and supplies–could get to Europe safely.

20. Germany was stripped of its armed forces, forced to accept guilt for the war, and made to pay reparations to the Allies.

21. raids of various radical organizations to round up suspects to deport or imprison

Critical Thinking
22. A possible positive answer is that it protected American people from Communist propaganda. A possible negative answer is that it violated civil rights and liberties.

23. **a.** Problems: low wages, child labor, love of money; change should be peaceful and orderly **b.** He calls it despotic and states that it violates the principles of democracy. Students' responses should consider the need to balance liberty and safety.

HISTORY Online

Self-Check Quiz

Visit the *American Republic Since 1877* Web site at tarvol2.glencoe.com and click on *Self-Check Quizzes—Chapter 14* to assess your knowledge of chapter content.

---

are compelled to work out their barren lives; of the little children who in this system are robbed of their childhood and . . . forced into industrial dungeons. . . . In this high noon of our twentieth century Christian civilization, money is still so much more important than the flesh and blood of childhood. In very truth, gold is god. . . . "

—quoted in *Echoes of Distant Thunder*

a. According to Debs, what were some problems in American society at this time? How did he believe change should be brought about?

b. How did Debs seem to feel about the Espionage Act? Do you agree with him? Why or why not?

24. Organizing Use a table like the one below to list the significant events of each year from 1914 to 1918.

Year	Event	Significance
1914		
1915		
1916		
1917		
1918		

Practicing Skills

25. Analyzing Information Read the subsections titled "The Treaty of Versailles" and "The U.S. Senate Rejects the Treaty" on pages 468 and 469. Using the information on these pages, write an analysis of the effects of the treaty in the form that it was finally accepted.

Geography and History

26. The map on this page shows the geographical changes in Europe after World War I. Study the map and answer the questions below.

a. Interpreting Maps After World War I, what new countries were formed using territory that had belonged to Austria-Hungary?

b. Applying Geography Skills What countries acquired territory from the former Russian Empire?

Writing Activity

27. Persuasive Writing Take on the role of a newspaper editor in 1919. Write an editorial favoring or opposing ratification of the Treaty of Versailles.

NATIONAL GEOGRAPHIC **Europe After World War I, 1920**

Map features:
- Former Austria-Hungary boundary
- Former German boundary
- Former Russian boundary
- National boundary
- ⊛ Capital city

500 miles / 500 kilometers
Lambert Azimuthal Equal-Area projection

Chapter Activity

28. Research Project Both the British and the American governments used propaganda to garner support for the war. Use the library and other resources to find examples of these propaganda techniques. Compile your research in an illustrated and captioned poster, and display it in the classroom.

Standardized Test Practice

Directions: Choose the best answer to the following question.

Which of the following was one of the primary causes of World War I?

F A complex set of alliances among European nations

G The exile of Mexican General Victoriano Huerta

H The dissatisfaction of Russian peasants

J The breakup of the Austro-Hungarian Empire

Test-Taking Tip: Eliminate answers you know are incorrect. For example, the breakup of Austria-Hungary took place after World War I, so you can eliminate that answer. Similarly, the exile of Huerta occurred in Mexico, which had little effect on European nations. You also can eliminate that answer.

CHAPTER 14   World War I and Its Aftermath   **477**

HISTORY Online

Have students visit the Web site at tarvol2.glencoe.com to review Chapter 14 and take the Self-Check Quiz.

Chapter Activity

28. Posters should reflect the types of propaganda used during World War I.

Standardized Test Practice

Answer: F
Test-Taking Tip: After students have eliminated one or two of the answers, they can concentrate on what they know about the remaining possibilities. For example, students might know that one of the results of World War I was the breakup of several empires. This makes J less likely to be the correct answer. F is the correct answer.

Bonus Question ?

Ask: What was the name of the Austrian archduke whose assassination started World War I? (*Franz Ferdinand*)

---

24. 1914: beginning of World War I; 1915: *Lusitania* sunk, Americans side with British; 1916: fighting in trenches worsens; 1917: United States commits resources and soldiers to help Allies; 1918: Americans break through German lines leading to Germany's defeat

Practicing Skills

25. Students should use the skills they learned in the Skillbuilder Activity to analyze the treaty.

Geography and History

26. a. Czechoslovakia, Austria, Hungary, Romania, and parts of Yugoslavia, Italy, and Poland; **b.** Poland, Lithuania, Latvia, Estonia, Finland, and part of Romania

Writing Activity

27. Editorials will vary. Students should clearly express an opinion about ratification of the treaty.

SUGGESTED PACING CHART

Unit 5 (1 Day)	Chapter 15 (4 Days)	Chapter 16 (4 Days)	Chapter 17 (4 Days)	Chapter 18 (5 Days)	Unit 5 (2 Days)
Day 1 Introduction	**Day 1** Chapter 15 Intro, Section 1 **Day 2** Section 2 **Day 3** Section 3 **Day 4** Chapter 15 Assessment	**Day 1** Chapter 16 Intro, Section 1 **Day 2** Section 2 **Day 3** Section 3 **Day 4** Chapter 16 Assessment	**Day 1** Chapter 17 Intro, Section 1 **Day 2** Section 2 **Day 3** Section 3 **Day 4** Chapter 17 Assessment	**Day 1** Chapter 18 Intro, Section 1 **Day 2** Section 2 **Day 3** Section 3 **Day 4** Section 4 **Day 5** Chapter 18 Assessment	**Day 1** Wrap-Up/Project **Day 2** Unit 5 Assessment

GLENCOE'S ASSESSMENT ADVANTAGE

Use the following tools to easily assess student learning in a variety of ways:

- Performance Assessment Activities and Rubrics
- Chapter and Unit Tests
- Section Quizzes
- Standardized Test Practice Workbook

- tarvol2.glencoe.com
- Interactive Tutor Self-Assessment CD-ROM
- MindJogger Videoquiz
- ExamView® Pro Testmaker CD-ROM
- SAT I/II Test Practice

TEACHING TRANSPARENCIES

Unit 5 Map Overlay Transparencies
L2

Cause-and-Effect Transparency 5
L2

READING SUPPORT FROM JAMESTOWN EDUCATION

- ***Timed Readings Plus in Social Studies*** help students increase their reading rate and fluency while maintaining comprehension. The 400-word passages are similar to those found on state and national assessments.

- ***Reading in the Content Area: Social Studies*** concentrates on six essential reading skills that help students better comprehend what they read. The book includes 75 high-interest nonfiction passages written at increasing levels of difficulty.

- ***Reading Fluency*** helps students read smoothly, accurately, and expressively.

- ***Jamestown's Reading Improvement,*** by renowned reading expert Edward Fry, focuses on helping build your students' comprehension, vocabulary, and skimming and scanning skills.

- ***Critical Reading Series*** provides high-interest books, each written at three reading levels.

For more information about these products, see the Jamestown Education materials in the Classroom Solutions in the front of this Teacher Wraparound Edition. To order these products, call Glencoe at 1-800-334-7344.

ASSESSMENT

Unit 5 Pretests L2

Unit 5 Posttests L2

APPLICATION AND ENRICHMENT

American Biography 5 L2

History Simulation and Problem Solving 5 L1

GEOGRAPHY

Geography and History Activity 5 L2

INTERDISCIPLINARY ACTIVITIES

American Literature Reading 5 L2

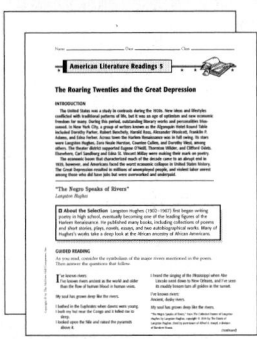

Economics and History Activity 5 L2

Team-Teaching Interdisciplinary Strategies and Activities 5

Reading List Generator CD-ROM

GLENCOE BOOKLINK

The Glencoe BookLink CD-ROM is a database that allows you to search more than 15,000 titles to create a customized reading list for your students.

- Reading lists can be organized by students' reading level, author, genre, theme, or area of interest.

- The database provides Degrees of Reading Power™ (DRP) and Lexile™ readability scores for all selections.

- A brief summary of each selection is included.

Leveled reading suggestions for this unit:

For students at a Grade 8 reading level:
- *A Woman Unafraid,* by Penny Colman.

For students at a Grade 9 reading level:
- *The Great Depression and the New Deal,* by Anne E. Schraff.

For students at a Grade 10 reading level:
- *Pride and Promise: The Harlem Renaissance,* by Kathryn Cryan-Hicks.

Extending the Content

Readings for the Teacher
- *Hoover, Conservation, and Consumerism: Engineering the Good Life,* by Kendrick A. Clements. University Press of Kansas, 2000.

Multimedia Resources
- *Brother, Can You Spare a Dime?* History in Action. Films for the Humanities. VHS. (20 minutes)

478B

0:00 Out of Time?

If time does not permit teaching each chapter in this unit, you may want to use the **Reading Essentials and Study Guide** summaries.

Unit Overview

Unit 5 describes the Boom and Bust cycles the United States experienced from 1920 to 1941. **Chapter 15** explores the jazz age and the African American cultural renaissance. **Chapter 16** focuses on the good times of the 1920s. **Chapter 17** discusses the beginning years of the Great Depression. **Chapter 18** focuses on Roosevelt and the New Deal.

Unit Objectives

After studying this unit, students will be able to:
1. Describe the clash of values in the 1920s and the changing status of women.
2. Analyze how the growing importance of the automobile and other new industries improved the U.S. standard of living.
3. Identify the causes of the Great Depression.
4. Explain the worsening situation in the U.S. banking system in the early 1930s.

Why It Matters Activity

Tell students that the economic problems that triggered the Great Depression brought a new awareness of economic cycles. Have students bring in an article to share with the class about the current state of the economy. Ask students how important they think economic news is to their daily lives.

5 Boom and Bust 1920–1941

Why It Matters

After World War I, the United States enjoyed a time of prosperity and confidence. The decade of the 1920s saw rising stock prices and increased consumer spending. It also witnessed cultural innovations such as jazz music and motion pictures. At the end of the 1920s, however, several economic problems combined to trigger the Great Depression that began in 1929. Understanding the events of these decades will help you understand American society today. The following resources offer more information about this period in American history.

Primary Sources Library

See page 934–935 for primary source readings to accompany Unit 5.

*Use the **American History Primary Source Document Library CD-ROM** to find additional primary sources about the Roaring Twenties and the Great Depression.*

Hatbox depicting a New York street scene

Sixth Avenue Elevated at Third St. by John Sloan, 1928

478

TEAM TEACHING ACTIVITY

Art Have the art teacher explain the Art Deco style and show classic examples of the style. Then have students research your local community for examples of Art Deco architecture, art, and design. If possible, have students take photos of the examples to present to the class. Have students explain why the samples they have shown illustrate this art style.

"*I have no fears for the future of our country. It is bright with hope.*"

—*Herbert Hoover, 1929*

GLENCOE TECHNOLOGY

CD-ROM
American History
Primary Source
Document Library
CD-ROM

Use the **American History Primary Source Document Library CD-ROM** to access primary source documents related to this period in history.

More About the Art

Flappers such as these are iconic depictions of the 1920s. Despite the carefree attitude many had during that decadent decade, the Great Depression soon followed, bringing with it hardship. Have students discuss why they think the 1920s was a decade of great cultural change.

Glencoe Literature Library

The following novel from the *High School American History Literature Library* may be used to enrich the study of this unit:
• *Picture Bride* by Yoshiko Uchida

SERVICE-LEARNING PROJECT

Tell students that no matter what the country's economic circumstances there are always people who do not have adequate food, clothing, or shelter. Have students learn about the needs of a local food or clothing pantry. After learning about their needs, have students plan a food or clothing drive for the benefit of the pantry.

Refer to *Building Bridges: Connecting Classroom and Community through Service-Learning in Social Studies* from the National Council for the Social Studies for information about service-learning.

Timesaving Tools

TeacherWorks™ All-In-One Planner and Resource Center

- **Interactive Teacher Edition** Access your Teacher Wraparound Edition and your classroom resources with a few easy clicks.
- **Interactive Lesson Planner** Planning has never been easier! Organize your week, month, semester, or year with all the lesson helps you need to make teaching creative, timely, and relevant.

Use Glencoe's **Presentation Plus!** multimedia teacher tool to easily present dynamic lessons that visually excite your students. Using Microsoft PowerPoint® you can customize the presentations to create your own personalized lessons.

TEACHING TRANSPARENCIES

Graphic Organizer 15 L2

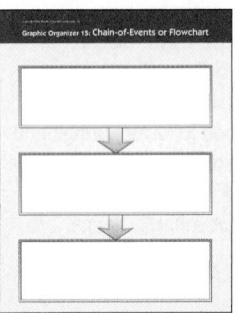

Why It Matters Chapter Transparency 15 L2

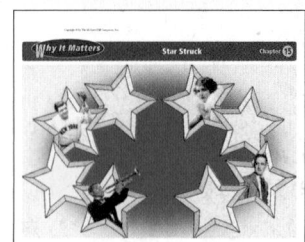

APPLICATION AND ENRICHMENT

Linking Past and Present Activity 15 L2

Enrichment Activity 15 L3

Primary Source Reading 15 L2

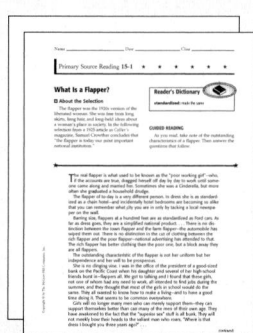

REVIEW AND REINFORCEMENT

Reteaching Activity 15 L1

Vocabulary Activity 15 L1

Time Line Activity 15 L2

Critical Thinking Skills Activity 15 L2

Meeting NCSS Standards

The following standards are covered in Chapter 15:

Section 1 II Time, Continuity, and Change: B, C, E, F
Section 2 I Culture: A, C
Section 3 V Individuals, Groups, and Institutions: B, C, E, F

Local Standards

Chapter 15 Resources

ASSESSMENT AND EVALUATION

Chapter 15 Test Form A L2

Chapter 15 Test Form B L2

Standardized Test Practice Workbook Activity 15 L2

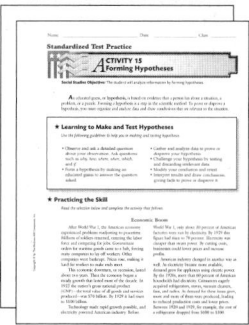

Performance Assessment Activities and Rubrics 15 L1/ELL

ExamView® Pro Testmaker CD-ROM

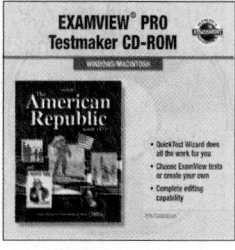

MULTIMEDIA

- Vocabulary PuzzleMaker CD-ROM
- Interactive Tutor Self-Assessment CD-ROM
- ExamView® Pro Testmaker CD-ROM
- Audio Program
- American History Primary Source Documents Library CD-ROM
- MindJogger Videoquiz
- Presentation Plus! CD-ROM
- TeacherWorks™ CD-ROM
- Interactive Student Edition CD-ROM
- Glencoe Skillbuilder Interactive Workbook CD-ROM, Level 2
- The *American Republic Since 1877* Video Program
- American Music: Hits Through History
- American Music: Cultural Traditions

SPANISH RESOURCES

The following Spanish language materials are available:

- Spanish Reading Essentials and Study Guide
- Spanish Guided Reading Activities
- Spanish Reteaching Activities
- Spanish Quizzes and Tests
- Spanish Vocabulary Activities
- Spanish Summaries
- The Declaration of Independence and United States Constitution Spanish Translation

The following videotape programs are available from Glencoe as supplements to Chapter 15:

- **Babe Ruth: His Life** (ISBN 1-56-501422-7)
- **The Monkey Trial: In Search of History** (ISBN 0-76-700609-7)
- **The Prohibition Era** (3 pack) (ISBN 0-76-700179-6)

To order, call Glencoe at 1-800-334-7344. To find classroom resources to accompany many of these videos, check the following home pages:
A&E Television: www.aande.com
The History Channel: www.historychannel.com

Use our Web site for additional resources. All essential content is covered in the Student Edition.

You and your students can visit tarvol2.glencoe.com, the Web site companion to the **American Republic Since 1877**. This innovative integration of electronic and print media offers your students a wealth of opportunities. The student text directs students to the Web site for the following options:

- **Chapter Overviews**
- **Self-Check Quizzes**
- **Student Web Activities**
- **Textbook Updates**

Answers to the student Web activities are provided for you in the **Web Activity Lesson Plans.** Additional Web resources and Interactive Tutor Puzzles are also available.

Chapter 15 Resources

SECTION RESOURCES

Daily Objectives	Reproducible Resources	Multimedia Resources
SECTION 1 **A Clash of Values** 1. Explain the rise in racism and nativism in the 1920s. 2. Describe the clash of values in the 1920s and the changing status of women.	Reproducible Lesson Plan 15–1 Daily Lecture and Discussion Notes 15–1 Guided Reading Activity 15–1* Section Quiz 15–1* Reading Essentials and Study Guide 15–1* Interpreting Political Cartoons Supreme Court Case Studies Performance Assessment Activities and Rubrics	Daily Focus Skills Transparency 15–1 Interactive Tutor Self-Assessment CD-ROM ExamView® Pro Testmaker CD-ROM* Presentation Plus! CD-ROM TeacherWorks™ CD-ROM Skillbuilder Interactive Workbook, Level 2 Audio Program
SECTION 2 **Cultural Innovations** 1. Describe the explosion of art and literature and the disillusionment of 1920s artists. 2. Summarize the effects of sports, movies, radio, and music on popular culture.	Reproducible Lesson Plan 15–2 Daily Lecture and Discussion Notes 15–2 Guided Reading Activity 15–2* Section Quiz 15–2* Reading Essentials and Study Guide 15–2* Performance Assessment Activities and Rubrics	Daily Focus Skills Transparency 15–2 American Art & Architecture Interactive Tutor Self-Assessment CD-ROM ExamView® Pro Testmaker CD-ROM* Presentation Plus! CD-ROM TeacherWorks™ CD-ROM Audio Program American Music: Hits Through History American Music: Cultural Traditions
SECTION 3 **African American Culture** 1. Describe the Harlem Renaissance and the rediscovery of African American cultural roots. 2. Explain the increase in African American political activism.	Reproducible Lesson Plan 15–3 Daily Lecture and Discussion Notes 15–3 Guided Reading Activity 15–3* Section Quiz 15–3* Reading Essentials and Study Guide 15–3* Performance Assessment Activities and Rubrics	Daily Focus Skills Transparency 15–3 Interactive Tutor Self-Assessment CD-ROM ExamView® Pro Testmaker CD-ROM* Presentation Plus! CD-ROM TeacherWorks™ CD-ROM Vocabulary PuzzleMaker CD-ROM Audio Program American Music: Hits Through History American Music: Cultural Traditions

0:00 OUT OF TIME?
Assign the Chapter 15 **Reading Essentials and Study Guide.**

*Also Available in Spanish

 Printed Materials   Transparency   CD-ROM   DVD

 Poster   Music Program   Audio Program

Chapter 15 Resources

NATIONAL GEOGRAPHIC   Teacher's Corner

INDEX TO
NATIONAL GEOGRAPHIC MAGAZINE

The following articles relate to this chapter.
- "Growing up in East Harlem," May 1990
- "Offbeat New Orleans," January 1995
- "Traveling the Blues Highway," April 1999

NATIONAL GEOGRAPHIC SOCIETY PRODUCTS

To order the following, call National Geographic at 1-800-368-2728:
- *Eyewitness to the 20th Century* (Book)
- *Historical Atlas of the United States* (Atlas)

NGS ONLINE

Access National Geographic's Web site for current events, atlas updates, activities, links, interactive features, and archives.
www.nationalgeographic.com

MEETING SPECIAL NEEDS

In addition to the Differentiated Instruction strategies found in each section, the following resources are also suitable for your special needs students:

- *ExamView® Pro Testmaker CD-ROM* allows teachers to tailor tests by reducing answer choices.

- The *Audio Program* includes the entire narrative of the student edition so that less-proficient readers can listen to the words as they read them.

- The *Reading Essentials and Study Guide* provides the same content as the student edition but is written two grade levels below the textbook.

- *Guided Reading Activities* give less-proficient readers point-by-point instructions to increase comprehension as they read each textbook section.

- *Enrichment Activities* includes a stimulating collection of readings and activities for gifted and talented students.

KEY TO ABILITY LEVELS

Teaching strategies have been coded.

L1 BASIC activities for all students
L2 AVERAGE activities for average to above-average students
L3 CHALLENGING activities for above-average students
ELL ENGLISH LANGUAGE LEARNER activities

From the Classroom of...

Jennifer G. Lange
Forest Hills High School
Forest Hills, NY

The Culture of Slang

Provide the students with a list of slang expressions from the Jazz Age. Do not give them the explanations of the slang. Ask students to try to decide what the words mean (some of the expressions we still use today). Ask students to explain how the new vocabulary reflected the culture of the Jazz Age. Ask students to describe the role that slang plays in their lives today. Some slang terms that developed in the period include:

- cat's meow (or cat's pajamas)—something fantastic
- crush—an infatuation with someone
- gatecrasher—someone who "crashes" a party
- blind date—dating someone you have never met
- big cheese—the boss
- bump off—murder or kill
- goofy—silly
- gams—a woman's legs
- heebie jeebies—jitters
- high hat—snub
- flapper—the "new woman" of the 1920s
- gyp—cheat
- darb—something truly wonderful
- gin mill—a speakeasy

ADDITIONAL RESOURCES FROM GLENCOE

- American Music: Cultural Traditions
- American Art & Architecture
- Outline Map Resource Book
- U.S. Desk Map
- Building Geography Skills for Life
- Inclusion for the High School Social Studies Classroom Strategies and Activities
- Teaching Strategies for the American History Classroom (Including Block Scheduling Pacing Guides)
- Dinah Zike's High School American History Reading and Study Skills Foldables

Block Schedule

Activities that are suited to use within the block scheduling framework are identified by:

✓ **Performance Assessment**

Refer to Activity 15 in the Performance Assessment Activities and Rubrics booklet.

Why It Matters Activity

Read the title of Section 1 and the main idea statement from the Guide to Reading. Ask students to jot down ideas about why this time in history matters today. Repeat for Sections 2 and 3. Ask students to evaluate and revise their responses after they have completed the chapter. Invite students to share their ideas with the class.

GLENCOE TECHNOLOGY

The *American Republic Since 1877* Video Program
To learn more about Harlem's art and music, have students view the Chapter 15 video, "The Harlem Renaissance," from the *American Republic Since 1877* Video Program.

MindJogger Videoquiz
Use the **MindJogger Videoquiz** to preview Chapter 15 content.

 Both programs available in DVD

CHAPTER

15 The Jazz Age
1921–1929

Why It Matters

The 1920s was an era of rapid change and clashing values. Many Americans believed society was losing its traditional values, and they took action to preserve these values. Other Americans embraced new values associated with a freer lifestyle and the pursuit of individual goals. Writers and artists pursued distinctively American themes, and the Harlem Renaissance gave African Americans new pride.

The Impact Today

The 1920s left permanent legacies to American culture.
- *National celebrities in sports and film emerged.*
- *Jazz music became part of American culture.*
- *F. Scott Fitzgerald and Ernest Hemingway wrote classics of American literature.*

The American Republic Since 1877 *Video* *The Chapter 15 video, "The Harlem Renaissance," focuses on Harlem's lively arts and music scene and the movement's contributions to American culture.*

1915
- New Ku Klux Klan founded

1921
- Emergency Quota Act passed, limiting immigration

1922
- Antilynching bill passes in House

1920
- Marcus Garvey leads march through Harlem

United States PRESIDENTS

Wilson 1913–1921

Harding 1921–1923

1915   *1920*

World

1917
- British government's Balfour Declaration supports national home for Jewish people in Palestine

1921
- Ireland becomes an independent country

1922
- Mussolini and Fascists take power in Italy

480

Reading Strategy ▶ **PURPOSE FOR READING**

Listen/Write/Free Response Students listen, question, speculate, and find meaning by free writing in this prereading activity. Bring to class a recording by a famous jazz musician from the early era of Jazz. Instruct students to listen for the distinctive rhythms of the music, and if there are lyrics, ask students to listen for the theme. After students have listened to the piece, have them write in their journals about how the piece made them feel and how they would describe the mood and theme of the piece. Emphasize that there are no wrong answers. Conclude this activity by telling students they will learn more about jazz in this chapter. **L1**

This photograph of jazz musicians captures the boisterous spirit of the 1920s.

1925
• Scopes trial begins
• F. Scott Fitzgerald's *The Great Gatsby* published

1924
• National Origins Act passed

Coolidge
1923–1929

1926
• Langston Hughes's *The Weary Blues* published

1927
• First feature film with sound debuts
• Lindbergh completes first solo transatlantic flight

Hoover
1929–1933

1925   *1930*

1924
• Britain recognizes the USSR

1923
• Turkish Republic founded

1926
• Pavlov's *Conditioned Reflexes* published

1928
• Chiang Kai-shek elected president of China

481

HISTORY *Online*

Introduce students to chapter content and key terms by having them access the **Chapter 15 Overview** at tarvol2.glencoe.com.

More About the Photo

Clothing styles were beginning to change before World War I. The pace of change accelerated after the war. For women, scooped necklines, knee-length hems, and sleeveless dresses departed radically from the frumpy styles of the Victorian era. Clothing styles reflected the carefree, happy-go-lucky feeling of the time.

TIME LINE ACTIVITY

Have students re-create the United States portion of the chapter time line on a separate piece of paper. Instruct students to link the Key Terms and Names from this chapter to an appropriate event on the time line. Remind students that the terms and names appear in the Guide to Reading at the beginning of each section.

HISTORY *Online*

Chapter Overview
Visit the *American Republic Since 1877* Web site at tarvol2.glencoe.com and click on **Chapter Overviews—Chapter 15** to preview chapter information.

FOLDABLES™
Study Organizer

Dinah Zike's Foldables are three-dimensional, interactive graphic organizers that help students practice basic writing skills, review key vocabulary terms, and identify main ideas. Have students complete the foldable activity in the *Dinah Zike's Reading and Study Skills Foldables* booklet.

GRAPHIC ORGANIZER ACTIVITY

Organizing Information Have students create a graphic organizer similar to the one shown below to explain the forms of entertainment that were popular in the 1920s and to give an example of a person or form of each. (Answers may vary from those shown here.)

Popular Forms of Entertainment

Movies	*Sports*	*Dancing*	*Jazz*
Charlie Chaplin	*Babe Ruth*	*Charleston*	*Louis Armstrong*

1 FOCUS

Section Overview

This section focuses on the rise of racism and nativism during the 1920s.

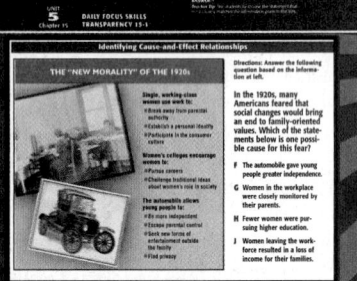
Reading Preview

Answers to Graphic: Causes: job competition, European immigrant influx, eugenics, economic recession; **Effects:** return of KKK, Sacco-Vanzetti case, governmental control of immigration.

Preteaching Vocabulary
Have students look up the meaning of each of the Key Terms in the Glossary and write the definition on a sheet of paper to use while they are studying the section.

SECTION 1 A Clash of Values

Guide to Reading

Main Idea
During the 1920s, clashes between traditional and modern values shook the United States.

Key Terms and Names
anarchist, eugenics, Ku Klux Klan, Emergency Quota Act, flapper, Fundamentalism, evolution, creationism, police powers, speakeasy

Reading Strategy
Organizing As you read about Americans' reactions to immigrants in the 1920s, complete a graphic organizer similar to the one below by filling in the causes and effects of anti-immigrant prejudices.

Causes → Anti-Immigrant Prejudices → Effects

Reading Objectives
- **Explain** the rise in racism and nativism in the 1920s.
- **Describe** the clash of values in the 1920s and the changing status of women.

Section Theme
Continuity and Change The rapid changes of the early 1900s challenged Americans who wanted to preserve traditional values.

Preview of Events

♦1919 ———— ♦1924 ———— ♦1929 ———— ♦1934

1919 Eighteenth Amendment ratified

1921 Emergency Quota Act passed

1924 National Origins Act passed

1927 Sacco and Vanzetti executed

1933 Prohibition repealed

★ An American Story ★

In 1911 Alfred Levitt left a small town in Russia to immigrate to New York City. Like many immigrants before and since, he had big ambitions, despite his poor English and lack of education. He wanted to forget his Russian heritage and become a successful American:

❝My conscious drive when I got here was to escape the rigors of poverty, to become somebody of importance. This I don't mean economically, but someone who can justify his presence on the planet. I wonder: Who am I? What am I here for? At seventeen years, the first question for me, though, was: What was I going to do? What will I become? . . . I made up my mind, as young as I was, that I'm going to amount to something in the world, and I'm not going to continue being one of those who starve.❞

—quoted in *Centenarians: The Story of the Twentieth Century by the Americans Who Lived It*

Alfred Levitt (standing)

Levitt did indeed "amount to something." A successful artist, he lived the rest of his life in New York City. Twenty of his paintings are part of the permanent collection of the city's Metropolitan Museum of Art.

Nativism Resurges

As the 1920s opened, an economic recession, an influx of immigrants, and racial and cultural tensions combined to create an atmosphere of disillusionment and intolerance. The fear and prejudice many felt toward Germans and Communists expanded to include all immigrants. This triggered a general rise in racism and in nativism, the desire to protect the interests of old-stock Americans against those of immigrants.

482 CHAPTER 15 The Jazz Age

SECTION RESOURCES

Reproducible Masters
- Reproducible Lesson Plan 15–1
- Daily Lecture and Discussion Notes 15–1
- Guided Reading Activity 15–1
- Section Quiz 15–1
- Reading Essentials and Study Guide 15–1
- Interpreting Political Cartoons
- Supreme Court Case Studies

Transparencies
- Daily Focus Skills Transparency 15–1

Multimedia
- Interactive Tutor Self-Assessment CD-ROM
- ExamView® Pro Testmaker CD-ROM
- Presentation Plus! CD-ROM
- TeacherWorks™ CD-ROM
- Audio Program

During World War I, immigration to the United States had dropped sharply. By 1921, however, it had returned to prewar levels, with the majority of immigrants at this time coming from southern and eastern Europe. Many Americans saw immigrants as a threat to stability and order. The arrival of millions of immigrants also seemed to pose a threat to the four million recently demobilized military men and women searching for work in an economy with soaring unemployment and rising prices.

As the new immigrants, many of whom were unskilled workers, sought to enter the workforce and establish a foothold in American life, many of them encountered ethnic and religious prejudices. The experience of two Italian immigrants, Nicola Sacco and Bartolomeo Vanzetti, exemplified the prejudices and fears of the period.

The Sacco-Vanzetti Case Shortly after 3:00 P.M. on April 15, 1920, two men shot and killed two employees of the Slater & Morrill Shoe Company in South Braintree, Massachusetts, and robbed the company of its $15,000 payroll. Police subsequently arrested Nicola Sacco, a shoemaker, and Bartolomeo Vanzetti, a fish peddler.

The **Sacco and Vanzetti case** created a furor, as newspapers around the country revealed that the two immigrants were anarchists, or people who oppose all forms of government. They also discovered that Sacco owned a gun similar to the murder weapon and that the bullets used in the murders matched those in Sacco's gun. Although no one at the time knew if Sacco and Vanzetti were guilty, many people leaped to that conclusion because the two men were Italian immigrants and anarchists. Others viewed the case as an example of prejudice against people based on their ethnic origin and political beliefs.

On July 14, 1921, a jury found Sacco and Vanzetti guilty, and the judge sentenced them to death. Many Americans, caught up in the antiforeign fever of the time, applauded the verdict and the penalty. Over the next six years, lawyers filed numerous appeals for a new trial, but all were denied. In April 1927, a special Massachusetts commission studied the case and upheld the verdict. Four months later, on August 23, 1927, Sacco and Vanzetti were executed, proclaiming their innocence all the while. 📖 *(See You're the Historian on pages 490–491 for more information on Sacco and Vanzetti.)*

Pseudo-Scientific Racism Nativist and racist feelings in the 1920s were reinforced by the beliefs of the eugenics movement. Eugenics is a pseudo-science (or false science) that deals with improving hereditary traits. Developed in Europe in the early 1900s, eugenics emphasized that human inequalities were inherited and warned against breeding the "unfit" or "inferior." Eugenics fueled the nativists' argument for the superiority of the "original" American stock—white Protestants of northern European descent. Political, intellectual, and cultural figures like Woodrow Wilson and Henry Cabot Lodge embraced eugenics. By doing so, they lent authority to racist theories, which reinvigorated the nativist argument for strict immigration control.

Return of the Ku Klux Klan At the forefront of the movement to restrict immigration was the **Ku Klux Klan,** or KKK. The old KKK had flourished in the South after the Civil War and used threats and violence to intimidate newly freed African Americans. The new Klan had other targets as well—Catholics, Jews, immigrants, and other groups believed to represent "un-American" values.

William J. Simmons founded the new Ku Klux Klan in Atlanta, Georgia, in 1915. A former circuit-riding Methodist preacher, Simmons pledged to preserve America's white, Protestant civilization. In the 1920s, Klan publicity claimed that the organization was fighting for "Americanism."

The Klan attracted few members until 1920, when Simmons hired public relations entrepreneurs Edward Young Clarke and Elizabeth Tyler, paying

Analyzing *Political Cartoons*

New Immigrants This cartoon portrays the feelings of many Americans who were opposed to immigration. What comment does the cartoon make about immigrants?

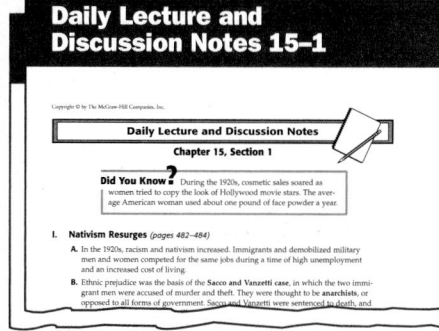
Discussing a Topic Ask students to offer examples of how adults show bias toward teenagers. Invite students to share how they feel when they encounter bias. Have students consider reasons for the bias and discuss ways to initiate a dialogue to lessen the bias. **L1**

Analyzing *Political Cartoons*

Answer: It implies that other countries were sending their unwanted citizens to the United States.

Ask: Why did some people have such a strong opposition to the new wave of immigrants? *(competition for scarce jobs, fear that immigrants were anarchists and revolutionaries)*

Reading Strategy READING THE TEXT

Identifying Cause and Effect The cause-and-effect structure is used to explore the reasons for something happening and to examine the results of previous events. Copy the following headings on the board: CAUSES → EVENT → EFFECTS. Under Event, write "Nativism." As students read through the section, have them complete the chain by adding the causes and effects related to the rise of nativism during the 1920s. *(Causes: influx of immigrants; rise in racism; economic recession; Effects: eugenics movement; return of the Ku Klux Klan; Emergency Quota and National Origins Acts)* **L1**

📂 Refer to *Inclusion for the High School Social Studies Classroom Strategies and Activities* in the TCR.

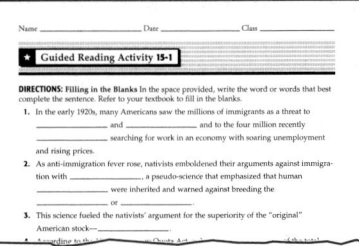

✓ Reading Check

Answer: fear of Communists, nativism, economic competition, eugenics

Interpreting Statistics Have students use library and Internet resources to locate historical immigration statistics for 1890, 1900, 1910, 1920, and 1930. Tell them to select two countries to compare, one from Western Europe and one from Eastern Europe. Have students use the data to construct an immigration chart that shows the effects of the immigration laws of 1921 and 1924. Ask students to write a brief explanation of the significance of their findings. **L2**

✓ Reading Check

Answer: Students might suggest that Hispanics made the United States more ethnically and linguistically diverse.

them a commission of $8 of every $10 initiation fee for a new Klan recruit. Clarke and Tyler divided the nation into regions and paid more than 1,000 "sales-people" to promote the Klan. As a result of their strategy, membership in the Ku Klux Klan exploded, reaching nearly 4 million by 1924 as it spread beyond the South and into Northern cities.

The Klan began to decline in the late 1920s, how-ever, largely as a result of scandals and power struggles involving its leaders. Membership shrank, and politicians whom the Klan supported were voted out of office. The sharp reduction in immigrants due to new immigration laws further disabled the Klan, depriving it of a major issue. The Klan never again had a major impact on politics.

✓ **Reading Check** **Explaining** Why did many Americans oppose immigration after World War I?

Controlling Immigration

After World War I, American immigration poli-cies changed in response to the postwar recession and nativist pleas to "Keep America American." Even big business, which previously favored unre-stricted immigration as a source of cheap labor, now feared the new immigrants as radicals.

In 1921 President Harding signed the **Emergency Quota Act,** which established a temporary quota sys-tem, limiting immigration. According to this act, only three percent of the total number of people in any ethnic group already living in the United States, as indicated in the 1910 census, could be admitted in a single year. This theoretically restricted the number of immigrants from all countries, but in practice it discriminated heavily against people from southern and eastern Europe. Ethnic identity and national ori-gin thus determined admission to the United States.

Henry Curran, the commissioner of Ellis Island from 1922 to 1926, commented on the heartbreak caused by the Emergency Quota Act:

> ❝The hardest quota cases were those that sepa-rated families. When part of the family had been born in a country with a quota still open, while the other part had been born in a country whose quota was exhausted, the law let in the first part and deported the other part. Mothers were torn from children, hus-bands from wives. The law came down like a sword between them.❞
>
> —quoted in *Ellis Island: Echoes from a Nation's Past*

GOVERNMENT

The National Origins Act of 1924 In 1924 the National Origins Act made immigrant restriction a permanent policy. The law also tightened the quota system, setting quotas at two percent of each national group residing in the country in 1890. By moving back the year to 1890, an even larger pro-portion of the quotas were allotted to immigrants from northwestern Europe.

A second part of the act, which took effect in 1929, replaced the 1924 quotas with a limit of 150,000 immigrants admitted per year. In addition, the percentage allotted to each nationality would now be based on the 1920 census. This resulted in northwestern European countries accounting for 87 percent of the total immigration quota.

Hispanic Immigration to the United States The immigration acts of 1921 and 1924 reduced the available labor pool in the United States. While workers and unions rejoiced at the reduction in competition for jobs, employers desperately needed laborers for agriculture, mining, and rail-road work. Mexican immigrants helped to fill this need.

The first wave of Mexican immigration to the United States followed the passage of the Newlands Reclamation Act of 1902, which pro-vided funds for irrigation projects in the arid Southwest. Factory farms soon dominated the land-scape, and they needed large numbers of agricul-tural laborers. By 1914 more than 70,000 Mexican immigrants had poured into the United States, many of them fleeing the terror and aftermath of the Mexican Revolution of 1910.

A larger wave of immigration brought more than 600,000 Mexicans to the United States between 1914 and the end of the 1920s. The National Origins Act of 1924 exempted natives of the Western Hemisphere from the quota system. As the demand for cheap farm labor in California and the Southwest steadily increased, Mexican immigrants crossed the border in record numbers.

✓ **Reading Check** **Explaining** How did Hispanic immigrants shape the national identity of the United States?

The New Morality

Many groups that wanted to restrict immigration also wanted to preserve what they considered to be traditional values. They feared that a "new morality" was taking over the nation. Challenging traditional

---

DIFFERENTIATED INSTRUCTION

English Learners To help address the needs of students who have difficulty reading, have stu-dents create an outline using the subheadings in this section. Once they have done that, encour-age them to listen to the Audio Program and highlight or circle the topics in their outline as they are discussed. **L1/ELL**

📂 Refer to *Inclusion for the High School Social Studies Classroom Strategies and Activities* in the TCR.

ways of seeing and thinking, the new morality glorified youth and personal freedom and influenced various aspects of American society.

The New Morality Ideals of the loving family and personal satisfaction—views popularized in magazines and other media—influenced popular views on relationships. As the loving and emotional aspects of marriage grew in importance, the ideas of romance, pleasure, and friendship became linked to successful marriages. Advice books in the 1920s dispensed such hints as, "Have lots of pleasure that both husband and wife enjoy . . . and above all, be good friends."

Women in the workforce also began to define the new morality. Many single, working-class women held jobs simply because they needed the wages for themselves or for their families. For some young, single women, work was a way to break away from parental authority and establish a personal identity. Work also provided the wages that allowed women to participate in the consumer culture.

Women who attended college in the 1920s often found support for their emerging sense of independence. Women's colleges, in particular, encouraged their students to pursue careers and to challenge traditional ideas about the nature of women and their role in society.

The automobile also played a role in encouraging the new morality. The nation's youth loved cars because cars made them more independent and allowed them to escape the careful watch of their parents. Instead of socializing at home with the family, many youths could now use cars to seek new forms of entertainment with their friends and to find privacy.

Women in the 1920s Fashion took on a modern look during the 1920s, as women "bobbed," or shortened, their hair and wore flesh-colored silk stockings. It also emphasized the youthful appearance of

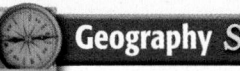

European Immigration Totals, 1890–1920

Number of People Immigrating to the United States by region, 1890–1920

488,099	2,135,312
672,223	3,060,151
1,130,656	3,695,828
1,195,628	3,859,297
— 1914 border	

500 miles
500 kilometers
Lambert Azimuthal Equal-Area projection

In Motion

Geography *Skills*

1. **Interpreting Maps** Between 1890 and 1920, what European regions sent more than three million immigrants to the United States?
2. **Applying Geography Skills** Why were so many people willing to leave their homelands to come to the United States?

glamorous stage and screen stars. In this new culture, the carefree, chic "flapper" played a prominent role.

Though hardly typical of American women at the time, the **flapper**—a young, dramatic, stylish, and unconventional woman—personified women's changing behavior in the 1920s. The flapper smoked cigarettes, drank prohibited liquor, and dressed in attire considered too revealing by previous generations.

While flappers pursued social freedoms, other women sought financial independence by entering the workforce, many of them as salesclerks, secretaries, or telephone operators. A few made contributions in science, medicine, law, or literature. In science, Florence Sabin's medical research led to a

CHAPTER 15 The Jazz Age **485**

Geography *Skills*

Answers:
1. Italy, Austro-Hungarian Empire and Serbia, and Russian Empire
2. They hoped to find greater opportunities.

Geography Skills Practice
Ask: From what countries did the fewest number of people emigrate? *(France, the Netherlands, Belgium, Luxembourg, and Switzerland)*

Making a Table Have students make a table showing areas where women's roles changed in the 1920s. Ask them to include visuals and examples for each area on the chart. **L1**

Use the rubric for creating a map, display, or chart on pages 65–66 in the *Performance Assessment Activities and Rubrics.*

FYI

The first Miss America was crowned in 1921. It seems fitting that sixteen-year-old Margaret Gorman was from the nation's capital–Washington, D.C.

Use *Interpreting Political Cartoons,* Cartoon 21.

Use *Supreme Court Case Study 15, Olmsted* v. *United States.*

Use *Supreme Court Case Study 16, Near* v. *Minnesota.*

INTERDISCIPLINARY CONNECTIONS ACTIVITY

Economics Have interested students research the number of women in the workforce in 1900, 1910, 1920, and 1930. Also, have them find the average annual wage that women earned in each of these years. Have students use the statistics to create a line graph showing the economic gains that women made during the early 1900s. **L2**

What *Life* Was Like...

Ask: How does modern clothing compare to clothing of the 1920s? *(possible answers: less formal, more synthetic fabrics; in both eras, boldly colored hats were popular and clothing expressed a person's identity with a group)*

✓ **Reading Check**

Answer: Some pursued social freedoms, entered the workforce, and contributed to medicine, literature, and science. Many others focused on enhancing traditional marriage relationships.

Creating a Cause-and-Effect Graphic Have students use a graphic organizer similar to the one shown below to illustrate some of the causes and effects of Prohibition. Invite students to share their graphics with the class. Create a composite graphic from the various student responses. **L2**

Prohibition

FYI

Charismatic preacher Aimee Semple McPherson gained added notoriety for a five-week disappearance she claimed was a kidnapping and for the many lawsuits filed against her in the following years, often for libel or slander.

What *Life* Was Like...

Flappers

Perhaps no other symbol of the 1920s captured the spirit of the time like the flapper. Psychologist G. Stanley Hall wrote his observation of a typical flapper:

❝She wore a knitted hat, with hardly any brim, of a flame or bonfire hue; a henna scarf; two strings of Betty beads, of different colors, twisted together; an open short coat, with ample pockets; a skirt with vertical stripes. . . . Her stockings were woolen and of brilliant hue. But most noticeable of all were her high overshoes, or galoshes. One seemed to be turned down at the top and entirely unbuckled, while the other was fastened below and flapped about her trim ankle in a way that compelled attention.❞

—quoted in *We, the American Women*

Modern Clothing
Women's clothing changed significantly in the 1920s. Hemlines were much shorter and showed more of the body. Stylish new hats also emphasized bold colors and a freer design.

New Forms of Expression
Rebelling against older, more formal dancing styles, these Charleston dancers perform steps that one observer described as "knock-kneed and pigeon-toed."

dramatic drop in death rates from tuberculosis. In literature, Edith Wharton received the Pulitzer Prize for her novel *The Age of Innocence.* Public health nurse Margaret Sanger, believing that the standard of living could be improved if families limited the number of children they had, founded the American Birth Control League in 1921. This organization became Planned Parenthood in the 1940s. In 1928 **Margaret Mead,** one of the first woman anthropologists, published the highly regarded study, *Coming of Age in Samoa,* which described life in a Pacific island culture.

✓ **Reading Check** **Identifying** What political, social, and economic contributions did women make to American society in the 1920s?

The Fundamentalist Movement

While many Americans embraced the new morality, millions more feared that the country was losing its traditional values. To these Americans, the modern consumer culture, relaxed ethics, and growing urbanism symbolized the nation's moral decline. Many of these people, especially those in small rural

towns, responded by joining a religious movement known as **Fundamentalism**—a name derived from a series of pamphlets titled *The Fundamentals,* published by oil millionaire Lyman Stewart.

Fundamentalist Beliefs Fundamentalists believed that the Bible was literally true and without error. They defended the Protestant faith against ideas that implied that human beings derived their moral behavior from society and nature, not God. In particular, Fundamentalists rejected Charles Darwin's theory of evolution, which said that human beings had developed from lower forms of life over the course of millions of years. Instead, they believed in creationism—the belief that God created the world as described in the Bible.

Two popular evangelical preachers, **Billy Sunday** and **Aimee Semple McPherson,** stirred Fundamentalists' passions by preaching traditional religious and moral values in very nontraditional ways. A former professional baseball player, Sunday drew huge crowds with his rapid-fire sermons and on-stage showmanship. McPherson conducted her revivals and faith healings in Los Angeles in a

CRITICAL THINKING ACTIVITY

Making Generalizations Initiate a discussion by asking the following questions: What sorts of attempts have been made to limit alcohol consumption in recent years? *(raising the minimum legal age for alcohol purchase, restrictions on hard liquor advertisements on television, warning labels on alcohol products, high alcohol taxes, education programs, MADD, SADD)* Ask whether students think these attempts have been successful and whether other initiatives should be considered. **L2**

Charleston
The Charleston, named after the city of Charleston, South Carolina, was the dance craze of the 1920s. Women who did the Charleston were called flappers, perhaps because of the way they flapped their arms while doing the dance.

flamboyant theatrical style, using stage sets and costumes that expressed the themes of her highly emotional sermons.

The Scopes Trial Evolutionists and creationists eventually clashed in a historic trial. In 1925 Tennessee passed the Butler Act, which outlawed any teaching that denied "the story of the Divine Creation of man as taught in the Bible," and taught instead that "man descended from a lower order of animals." The American Civil Liberties Union (ACLU) advertised for a teacher who would be willing to be arrested for teaching evolution. John T. Scopes, a high school biology teacher in Dayton, Tennessee, volunteered to be the test case. He taught evolution and was subsequently arrested and put on trial.

The trial took place in the summer of 1925. William Jennings Bryan, a three-time Democratic presidential candidate, was the prosecutor and represented the creationists. Clarence Darrow, one of the country's most celebrated trial lawyers, defended Scopes. After eight days of trial, Scopes was found guilty and fined $100, although the conviction was later overturned on a technicality. Parts of the trial had been broadcast over

the radio, and Darrow's blistering cross-examination of Bryan did little for the Fundamentalist cause. Increasingly, Fundamentalists found themselves isolated from mainstream Protestantism, and their commitment to political activism declined.

> ✓ **Reading Check** **Explaining** What were the major beliefs of Fundamentalists?

Prohibition

The movement to ban alcohol had been building throughout the late 1800s. By the early 1900s, many progressives and traditionalists supported prohibition. Many people believed the prohibition of alcohol would help reduce unemployment, domestic violence, and poverty. Their support helped pass the Eighteenth Amendment, which took effect in January 1920.

To try to enforce the amendment, Congress passed the National Prohibition Act, also known as the **Volstead Act.** Enforcing Prohibition became the responsibility of the U.S. Treasury Department. Treasury agents had enforced federal tax laws for many years, but police powers—a government's power to control people and property in the interest of public safety, health, welfare, and morals—had generally been reserved for the state governments. The Eighteenth Amendment granted federal and state governments the power to enforce Prohibition, marking a dramatic increase in federal police powers.

The Treasury Department's new Prohibition Unit struggled to enforce Prohibition. During the 1920s, treasury agents made more than 540,000 arrests, but Americans persisted in blatantly ignoring the law. People flocked to secret bars called speakeasies, where they could purchase alcohol. In New York City alone, an estimated 32,000 such bars sold liquor illegally. Liquor also was readily available in rural

New Words The youth culture of the twenties produced a number of new words and phrases that became a part of their own language. In the mid-1920s, partygoers urged fellow dancers to "Get hot! Get hot!" Young Americans also invented such terms as *beauts, cat's pajamas,* and *cat's whiskers* to describe attractive young women. The terms *lounge lizards, jelly beans,* and *jazzbos* described attractive young men, while the phrase *hard-boiled eggs* described tough guys.

> ✓ **Reading Check**

Answer: They believed in the authority of the Bible and creationism.

Fact Fiction Folklore

Prohibition also expanded American vocabulary. *Bootlegger, speakeasy,* and *hip flask* became part of common speech. It also gave new meaning to the words *wet* and *dry.*

FYI

Tennessee's law against teaching evolution remained on the books until 1967.

3 ASSESS

Assign Section 1 Assessment as homework or as an in-class activity.

🖱 Have students use the **Interactive Tutor Self-Assessment CD-ROM.**

L1/ELL

Reading Essentials and Study Guide 15–1

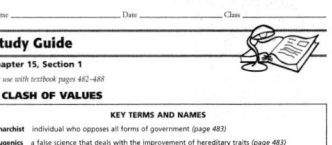

Name _____ Date _____ Class _____

Study Guide
Chapter 15, Section 1
For use with textbook pages 482–488
A CLASH OF VALUES

KEY TERMS AND NAMES
anarchist individual who opposes all forms of government *(page 483)*
eugenics a false science that deals with the improvement of hereditary traits *(page 483)*
Ku Klux Klan a society set up to restore white Protestant America by terrorizing African Americans and other minorities *(page 483)*
Emergency Quota Act law that established a temporary quota system and limited immigration *(page 484)*
flapper a young, dramatic, stylish, and unconventional woman *(page 485)*
Fundamentalism religious movement that focused on the authority of the Bible *(page 486)*

EXTENDING THE CONTENT

Agents of Prohibition Isador Einstein, known as Izzy, and his partner, Moe Smith, worked as a team to trap lawbreakers during Prohibition. Masters of disguise, they were a flamboyant pair who used any number of methods to enforce the law. Izzy was particularly adept at going through diverse neighborhoods because he spoke five languages. He once nabbed an unsuspecting speakeasy owner by disguising himself as a pickle salesman. Together Izzy and Moe made some 4,000 arrests and hauled in around $15 million worth of alcohol. Have students research Einstein and Smith to learn more about their actions during Prohibition.

L2

Section Quiz 15–1

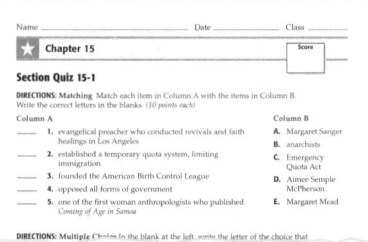

Picturing History

Answer: not very successful
Ask: How did the American public respond to Prohibition? Give some examples. *(many blatantly ignored the law; speakeasies, organized crime supplied alcohol, bootlegging, smuggling)*

Reteach

Have students explain the reasons for the rise in racism and nativism in the 1920s, especially toward immigrants.

Enrich

Invite interested students to create a collage showcasing the changing role of women in the 1920s.

✓ Reading Check

Answer: Many people believed Prohibition would help reduce unemployment, domestic violence, and poverty.

Study Central™ provides summaries, interactive games, and online graphic organizers to help students review section content.

4 CLOSE

Have students explain the resurgence, impact, and decline of the Ku Klux Klan.

488

Picturing History

Prohibition in Action Federal revenue agents carried out the laws of Prohibition by destroying barrels of alcohol. **How successful were their enforcement efforts?**

America, where bootlegging—the illegal production and distribution of liquor—was common.

Organized crime specialized in supplying and often running these speakeasies, which popped up all over the country. The huge profits that could be made supplying liquor encouraged some people to become smugglers, bringing liquor into the United States from Canada and the Caribbean. Smuggling and the consumption of liquor by millions helped create an illegal billion-dollar industry for gangsters. More than 70 federal agents were killed while enforcing Prohibition in the 1920s.

Crime became big business, and some gangsters had enough money to corrupt local politicians. Al Capone, one of the most successful and violent gangsters of the era, had many police officers, judges, and other officials on his payroll. Capone dominated organized crime in Chicago, where he ran bootlegging and other criminal rackets. Finally, Eliot Ness, the leader of a special Treasury Department task force, brought Capone to justice.

The battle to repeal Prohibition began almost as soon as the Eighteenth Amendment was ratified. Supporters of repeal associated Prohibition with "priggish fanaticism." The ratification of the Twenty-first Amendment in 1933 repealed the Eighteenth Amendment and ended federally-mandated Prohibition. It was a defeat for the supporters of traditional values and those who favored the use of federal police powers to achieve moral reform.

✓ Reading Check **Analyzing** Analyze the reasons for the adoption of the Eighteenth Amendment.

SECTION 1 ASSESSMENT

HISTORY Online | **Study Central**™ To review this section, go to **tarvol2.glencoe.com** and click on **Study Central**™.

Checking for Understanding

1. **Define:** anarchist, eugenics, flapper, evolution, creationism, police powers, speakeasy.
2. **Identify:** Ku Klux Klan, Emergency Quota Act, Fundamentalism.
3. **Explain** why the Eighteenth Amendment was repealed.

Reviewing Themes

4. **Continuity and Change** How did the passage of the Eighteenth Amendment and the Volstead Act change the federal government's role?

Critical Thinking

5. **Synthesizing** Why were immigrants from Mexico not included in the quota system set by the immigration acts?
6. **Categorizing** Use a graphic organizer similar to the one below to list the provisions of the immigration acts passed in the 1920s.

Act	Provisions

Analyzing Visuals

7. **Analyzing Photographs** Study the image on this page of the federal agent destroying barrels of alcohol. Why do you think the barrels were destroyed in public with a crowd watching?

Writing About History

8. **Persuasive Writing** Imagine it is the 1920s. Write a letter to your senator to persuade him or her to either continue to support Prohibition or to work for its repeal.

488 CHAPTER 15 The Jazz Age

SECTION 1 ASSESSMENT ANSWERS

1. Terms are in blue.
2. Ku Klux Klan *(p. 483)*, Emergency Quota Act *(p. 484)*, Fundamentalism *(p. 486)*
3. People recognized that Prohibition was not successful.
4. The federal government obtained police powers to enforce the law.
5. They provided cheap labor.

6. 1921 Emergency Quota Act limited the number of immigrants to 3 percent of the existing immigrant population based on the 1910 census; 1924 National Origins Act limited the number of immigrants to 2 percent of the existing immigrant population based on the 1890 census

7. to intimidate people, hoping to make them fearful and submissive in the face of federal authority
8. Letters should clearly express a point of view.

Synthesizing Information

Why Learn This Skill?

The authors of this book gathered information from many sources to present a story of how the United States came about and how the country's people lived. To combine the information into a logical story, the authors used a process called *synthesis*. Being able to synthesize information can be a useful skill for you as a student when you need to gather data from several sources for a report or a presentation.

Learning the Skill

The skill of synthesizing involves combining and analyzing information gathered from separate sources or at different times to make logical connections. Follow these steps to synthesize information:

• Select important and relevant information.

• Analyze the information and build connections.

• Reinforce or modify the connections as you acquire new information.

Suppose you need to write a research paper on the status of women in the 1920s. You would need to synthesize what you learn to inform others. You could begin by detailing the ideas and information you already have about the status of women in the 1920s. A graphic organizer such as the one on this page could help categorize the facts.

Then you could select an article about women in the 1920s, such as the following:

In 1923 the National Woman's Party first proposed an equal rights amendment to the Constitution. This amendment stated that "men and women shall have equal rights throughout the United States and every place subject to its jurisdiction." The National Woman's party pointed out that legislation discriminating against women existed in every state. . . .

Some progressive women reformers, however, opposed the goals of the National Woman's Party. These progressives favored protective legislation, which had brought shorter hours and better working conditions for many women. The efforts of the progressives helped defeat the equal rights amendment.

Women's Status in the 1920s	
Economic:	Many more women worked in factories and other jobs outside the home.
Social:	Women had much more social freedom, including greater choices in clothing styles and public behavior.
Educational:	Many women had a high school education, and more than ever were attending college.

Practicing the Skill

Use the graphic organizer and the passage on this page to answer the following questions.

❶ What information is presented in the table?

❷ What is the main idea of the passage? What information does the passage add to your knowledge of this topic?

❸ By synthesizing the two sources and using what you know from reading Section 1 of this chapter, what conclusions can you draw about the role of women in 1920s society?

Skills Assessment

Complete the Practicing Skills questions on page 507 and the Chapter 15 Skill Reinforcement Activity to assess your mastery of this skill.

Applying the Skill

Synthesizing Information Find two sources of information on the same topic and write a short report. In your report, answer these questions: What kinds of sources did you use—primary or secondary? What are the main ideas in these sources? How does each source add to your understanding of the topic? Do the sources support or contradict each other?

Glencoe's **Skillbuilder Interactive Workbook CD-ROM, Level 2,** provides instruction and practice in key social studies skills.

489

TEACH

Synthesizing Information Point out that synthesizing information is a skill that people use every day. To properly prepare for a test, a student would have to know what kind of information will be on the test, when the test will be, how much time the student needs to study, and when the student has available time to study.

Ask students to share some other examples of how they synthesize information in their daily lives.

Additional Practice
L1

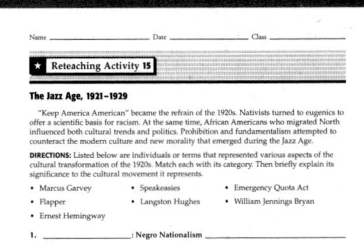

Reteaching Activity 15

Name _____ Date _____ Class _____

★ Reteaching Activity 15

The Jazz Age, 1921–1929

"Keep America American" became the refrain of the 1920s. Nativists turned to eugenics to offer a scientific basis for racism. At the same time, African Americans who migrated North influenced both cultural trends and politics. Prohibition and fundamentalism attempted to counteract the modern culture and new morality that emerged during the Jazz Age.

DIRECTIONS: Listed below are individuals or terms that represented various aspects of the cultural transformation of the 1920s. Match each with its category. Then briefly explain its significance to the cultural movement it represents.

• Marcus Garvey	• Speakeasies	• Emergency Quota Act
• Flapper	• Langston Hughes	• William Jennings Bryan
• Ernest Hemingway		

1. _____ : Negro Nationalism _____

GLENCOE
TECHNOLOGY

CD-ROM
Glencoe Skillbuilder Interactive Workbook CD-ROM, Level 2

This interactive CD-ROM reinforces student mastery of essential social studies skills.

ANSWERS TO PRACTICING THE SKILL

❶ status of women in the 1920s

❷ An amendment dedicated to women's rights was proposed in 1923, but it was defeated with the help of women who opposed it.

❸ Women pursued social freedom, entered the workforce, and made contributions in medicine, literature, and science.

Applying the Skill
Students' reports will vary. Students should correctly identify the sources they used as primary or secondary.

Remind students that the American criminal justice system is based on the presumption of innocence. The judge and the foreman of the jury that convicted Sacco and Vanzetti presumed that the defendants were guilty before the evidence was heard.

2 TEACH

Analyzing Information Tell students that many of the people who testified for the two defendants were Italians who spoke English poorly. Much of their testimony had to be taken in Italian and translated for the judge and jury. Ask students: **How do you think the witnesses' inability to speak English well affected their credibility?** (*Students should recognize that it should not have affected their credibility, but that bias toward immigrants might have unfairly influenced the jury.*) **Do you think people who do not speak English well face similar bias in the United States today?** (*Answers will vary. Students may note that they do not face the same degree of bias, but that bias still exists.*) **L2**

The Sacco-Vanzetti Case

Painting supporting the accused

On April 15, 1920, in South Braintree, Massachusetts, armed robbers murdered two factory employees during a payroll holdup. Police arrested two Italian immigrants and anarchists—Nicola Sacco and Bartolomeo Vanzetti—as suspects. After a court found the two men guilty, defense attorneys fought for six years for a new trial. The attorneys believed the trial had shown signs of prejudice, intimidation, and dishonesty. Did Sacco and Vanzetti receive a fair trial, or were they victims of the troubled atmosphere in the United States at the time? You're the historian.

Read the following excerpts from testimony and evidence. Then complete the questions and activities that follow.

From trial testimony

The defense produced several people who supported the defendants' alibis. When arrested, Nicola Sacco had been carrying a pistol. The prosecuting attorney questioned Captain Proctor, a Massachusetts State Police ballistics expert, about the gun.

Q. Captain Proctor, have you an opinion as to whether bullet three was fired from the Colt automatic which is in evidence [Sacco's pistol]?

A. I have.

Q. And what is your opinion?

A. My opinion is that it is consistent with being fired by that pistol.

Defense experts, however, testified that in their judgment, bullet three had not been fired from Sacco's gun. The defense called on Sacco to testify, which gave the prosecution an opportunity to ask Sacco about his political beliefs.

Q. Did you say yesterday you love a free country?

A. Yes, sir.

Q. Did you love this country in the month of May 1917? [At this time, Sacco had gone to Mexico to escape military service.]

A. If you can, Mr. Katzman, if you give me that, —I could explain.

Q. There are two words you can use, Mr. Sacco, yes or no.

A. Yes.

[later]

Q. What did you mean when you said yesterday you loved a free country?

A. . . .When I came to this country I saw there was not what I was thinking before. . . . I could see the best men, intelligent, education, they been arrested and sent to prison and died in prison . . . and Debs, one of the great men in his country, he is in prison . . . because he is a socialist. He wanted the laboring class to have better conditions . . . but they put him in prison. . . . They want the working class to be low all the times.

The jury returned a verdict of guilty. In the sentencing phase, Bartolomeo Vanzetti was asked to explain why he should not be sentenced to death.

I am suffering because I am a radical, and indeed I am a radical. I have suffered because I am an Italian, and indeed I am an Italian. I have suffered more for my family and for my beloved than for myself, but I am so convinced to be right that if you could execute me two times, and if I could be reborn two other times, I would live again to do what I have done already. . . . You know I am innocent. That is the same words I pronounced seven years ago. You condemn two innocent men.

EXTENDING THE CONTENT

Due Process The Sacco-Vanzetti case influenced the Supreme Court's actions in the 1950s and 1960s under the leadership of Chief Justice Earl Warren. In more than one case, the Court ruled that the due process clause of the Bill of Rights extended to the states. This, in effect, altered the legal system in many states. Massachusetts had already changed its laws in 1939 to allow a new trial not only if the verdict violated the law, but also if it went against the evidence presented at the trial.

Headline announcing the execution

The Boston Daily Globe

MADEIROS, SACCO, VANZETTI DIED IN CHAIR THIS MORNING
Electrocuted in That Order Soon After Midnight—All Reject Religious Consolation to the Last—Two Make Statements

Comments on the case

The Sacco-Vanzetti case aroused indignation among intellectuals from the 1920s on. They generally agreed that the two were found guilty because they were Italian radicals, not because there was clear evidence against them. However, two students of the case, Robert Hanson, a local historian, and Francis Russell, who wrote two books on the case, believe Sacco and Vanzetti received a fair trial. Russell cites James Graham, an attorney for Sacco:

We spent considerable time with him [Vanzetti] at the Plymouth County Jail as the case was drawing to a close. . . . Toward the end of the discussion Mr. Vahey said to Vanzetti, in substance, "I can advise you as to what the District Attorney may inquire about the effect of your failure to take the stand, but you are the one who has to make the decision as to whether you will testify or not."

Vanzetti replied,

I don't think I can improve on the alibi which has been established. I had better not take the stand.

Russell also reports that Carlo Tresca, an anarchist who had supported the two Italians, told friends that Sacco was guilty, Vanzetti innocent. Then Russell quotes a letter from labor writer Paul Jacobs:

. . . I had a close friend, Anthony Ramuglia. . . . One day he came to me and said he had a story he wanted me to write. . . . The story was that when he was a young man around the anarchist movement in Boston, he had been approached by one of Sacco's witnesses for his alibi in the restaurant at lunch. My friend Tony agreed, and evidently, was carefully coached in what he was to say, when suddenly he remembered that on the day in question

he had actually been in jail in St. Louis and so might obviously be found out as a perjurer. He told someone about this and was relieved of his responsibilities. . . . I asked Tony whether he thought Sacco and Vanzetti were really guilty, and he replied in much the same way as you quote Tresca. "Sacco could have done it but Vanzetti was never capable of such a thing."

Workers showing support for Sacco (right) and Vanzetti (left)

Understanding the Issue

1. Why did the defense attorneys believe that the defendants were not given a fair trial?
2. Why do you think the prosecution questioned Sacco on his political beliefs?
3. After studying the historical context of the case and the frame of reference of the jury, how might a modern historian argue that Sacco and Vanzetti did not receive a fair trial?

Activities

1. **Investigate** Check your local library or the Internet and prepare a report on the latest information on the case.
2. **Create a Simulation** Recreate the trial. Research the testimony and the people involved in the case. Assign roles to class members, including witnesses, jury members, a prosecutor, a defense attorney, and a judge.

CHAPTER 15   The Jazz Age   **491**

3 ASSESS

Have students answer the Understanding the Issues questions and complete the Activities.

Understanding the Issues

1. They argued that the defendants were found guilty because of their political views, not because of the evidence against them.
2. They wanted to establish that his radical views made him dangerous, regardless of whether he actually committed the crime.
3. A historian might argue that since the evidence was inconclusive, the verdict was unfounded.

Activities

1. Reports should consider the quality of the arguments presented.
2. Encourage students to prepare for their assigned roles. At the end of the trial, have the jury read its verdict, then discuss as a class the various opinions and thoughts about the event.

4 CLOSE

Ask students to explain how public opinion can affect the outcome of a trial.

PORTFOLIO ACTIVITY

Court Drawings Ask students to select one moment in the trial and create a drawing about it similar to the ones done by court artists today. Have students write a paragraph describing the scene they have drawn. **L2**

1 FOCUS

Section Overview

This section focuses on the cultural innovations of the 1920s including art, literature, mass media, music, and sports.

BELLRINGER
Skillbuilder Activity

Project transparency and have students answer the question.

Daily Focus Skills Transparency 15–2

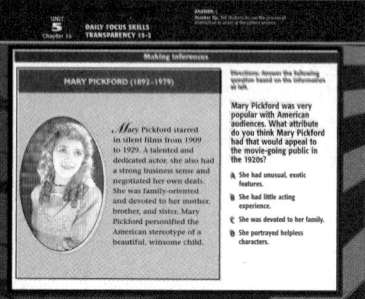

Reading Preview

Answers to Graphic: Art: diverse, individual expression influenced by European art movement; Literature: various styles and subject matter, themes of disillusionment and emptiness; Popular Culture: sports heroes, Hollywood allure, radio shows, jazz, and blues

Preteaching Vocabulary
Have students skim the section to preview each of the Key Terms and Names.

SECTION 2 Cultural Innovations

Guide to Reading

Main Idea
An era of exciting and innovative cultural trends, the 1920s witnessed changes in art and literature. This period also saw a dramatic increase in the country's interest in sports and other forms of popular culture.

Key Terms and Names
Bohemian, Carl Sandburg, Eugene O'Neill, Ernest Hemingway, F. Scott Fitzgerald, mass media

Reading Strategy
Organizing As you read about the 1920s, complete a graphic organizer like the one below by filling in the main characteristics of art, literature, and popular culture that reflect the era.

Cultural Movement	Main Characteristics
Art	
Literature	
Popular Culture	

Reading Objectives
• **Describe** the explosion of art and literature and the disillusionment of 1920s artists.
• **Summarize** the effects of sports, movies, radio, and music on popular culture.

Section Theme
Culture and Traditions American culture in the 1920s saw a rise in both the arts and popular entertainment.

Preview of Events

♦1922   ♦1924   ♦1926   ♦1928

1923
Coca-Cola creates the six-pack

1925
F. Scott Fitzgerald's *The Great Gatsby* published

1927
Babe Ruth hits 60 home runs

1927
First feature-length sound motion picture, *The Jazz Singer*

1927
Charles Lindbergh makes solo transatlantic flight

Charles Lindbergh and his Spirit of St. Louis

★ An American Story ★

On May 20, 1927, a lanky, sandy-haired young man named Charles Lindbergh took off from an airfield on Long Island, New York, in a small, single-engine plane called the *Spirit of St. Louis* and headed east across the Atlantic Ocean. The next evening—more than 33 hours after Lindbergh left New York—thousands of people waited anxiously at the small Le Bourget airfield outside Paris, France. Attention was riveted on the sky, and the spectators strained their eyes as they watched Lindbergh's small airplane softly slip out of the darkness. When the plane landed, the crowd ecstatically greeted the pilot, who had just completed a historic event—the first solo nonstop flight across the Atlantic Ocean.

In an era when people questioned ideals and heroes, Lindbergh's historic flight symbolized American progress in the modern age, and his solo triumph restored Americans' belief in the courageous, pioneering individual. American writer F. Scott Fitzgerald said of Lindbergh:

❝A young Minnesotan who seemed to have nothing to do with his generation did a heroic thing, and for the moment people set down their glasses in country clubs and speakeasies and thought of their old dreams.❞

—**quoted in *Echoes of the Jazz Age***

Art and Literature

The modern age symbolized by Lindbergh's historic transatlantic flight was reflected strongly in American art, literature, and popular culture. During the 1920s, American artists and writers challenged traditional ideas. These artists explored what

---

SECTION RESOURCES

📂 Reproducible Masters
• Reproducible Lesson Plan 15–2
• Daily Lecture and Discussion Notes 15–2
• Guided Reading Activity 15–2
• Section Quiz 15–2
• Reading Essentials and Study Guide 15–2

📃 Transparencies
• Daily Focus Skills Transparency 15–2

Multimedia
🖲 Interactive Tutor Self-Assessment CD-ROM
🖲 ExamView® Pro Testmaker CD-ROM
🖲 Presentation Plus! CD-ROM
🖲 TeacherWorks™ CD-ROM
🎧 Audio Program
🎵 American Music: Hits Through History
🎵 American Music: Cultural Traditions

it meant to be "modern," and they searched for meaning in the emerging challenges of the modern world.

Greenwich Village and the South Side

Many artists, writers, and intellectuals of the era flocked to Manhattan's Greenwich Village and Chicago's South Side. As writer Brooks Atkinson noted in a memoir,

> 66 The Village was no prude . . . no matter what you did you could hardly be conspicuous. On my street the middle-aged lady in knickers who aired her cat on a pink ribbon twice a day and the rosy-cheeked damsel in overalls who split kindling wood on the side walk . . . were hardly more conspicuous than the formal citizenry. To become conspicuous you would probably have to shoot someone in the street. 99
>
> —from *New York's Greenwich Village*

The artistic and unconventional, or Bohemian, lifestyle of these neighborhoods offered young artists and writers new lifestyles.

Modern American Art

European art movements greatly influenced the modernists of American art. Perhaps most striking was the diverse range of artistic styles, each attempting to express the individual, modern experience.

Taking his cue from the bold and colorful Impressionism of French artist Paul Cézanne, American painter John Marin drew on nature as well as the urban dynamics of New York for inspiration, explaining, "the whole city is alive; buildings, people, all are alive; and the more they move me the more I feel them to be alive." Painter Charles Scheeler applied the influences of photography and the geometric forms of Cubism to urban and rural American landscapes. **Edward Hopper** revived the visual accuracy of Realism in his haunting scenes. His paintings conveyed a modern sense of disenchantment and isolation.

Poets and Writers

Poets and writers of the 1920s varied greatly in their styles and subject matter. Chicago poet **Carl Sandburg** used common speech to glorify the Midwest and the expansive nature of American life. In Greenwich Village, Edna St.

Vincent Millay, in her poem "First Fig," expressed women's freedom and equality and praised a life intensely lived:

> 66 My candle burns at both ends;
> It will not last the night;
> But ah, my foes, and oh, my friends—
> It gives a lovely light. 99

Several poets of this time had an important impact on the literary culture. Gertrude Stein, for example, was supposed to have been able to make or break a writer's career with a few well-placed remarks. Poets such as Ezra Pound, Amy Lowell, and William Carlos Williams used clear, concise images to express moments in time.

Some poets concentrated on what they considered the negative effects of modernism. In his poem "The Hollow Men," for example, **T.S. Eliot** described a world filled with empty dreams and "hollow men," and he foresaw a world that would end "not with a bang but a whimper."

Among playwrights, one of the most innovative was **Eugene O'Neill.** His plays, filled with bold artistry and modern themes, portrayed realistic characters and situations, offering a vision of life that sometimes touched on the tragic.

Many novelists, affected by the experiences of World War I, wrote about disillusionment and reevaluated the myths of American heroes. They often created characters who were "heroic antiheroes"—flawed individuals who still had heroic qualities of mind and spirit. **Ernest Hemingway,** who served as an ambulance driver in Italy during World War I, was one such writer. His fiction presented a new literary style characterized by direct, simple, and concise prose, as when he wrote about war in such works as *For Whom the Bell Tolls* and *A Farewell to Arms.*

History *Through Art*

Lonely People Like many of his works, Edward Hopper's *Nighthawks* depicts isolated people. How do you think this painting reflects the experience of small-town people who moved to the cities?

2 TEACH

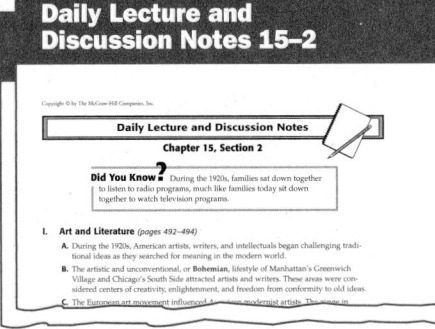

Daily Lecture and Discussion Notes 15–2

Copyright © by The McGraw-Hill Companies, Inc.

Daily Lecture and Discussion Notes

Chapter 15, Section 2

Did You Know? During the 1920s, families sat down together to listen to radio programs, much like families today sit down together to watch television programs.

I. Art and Literature *(pages 492–494)*

A. During the 1920s, American artists, writers, and intellectuals began challenging traditional ideas as they searched for meaning in the modern world.

B. The artistic and unconventional, or **Bohemian,** lifestyle of Manhattan's Greenwich Village and Chicago's South Side attracted artists and writers. These areas were considered centers of creativity, enlightenment, and freedom from conformity to old ideas.

C. The European art movement influenced American modernist artists. The range in

History *Through Art*

Answer: Many would have felt lonely and alienated.

Ask: What style did Edward Hopper use in this painting? *(realism)*

Reading Strategy

Creating a Thematic Table

Have students create a thematic table listing the names of the writers mentioned in this section, the medium or media used by the writer, and a brief description of the theme or characteristics of the author's works. **L1**

📁 Use the rubric for creating a map, display, or chart on pages 65–66 in the *Performance Assessment Activities and Rubrics.*

L1/ELL

Guided Reading Activity 15–2

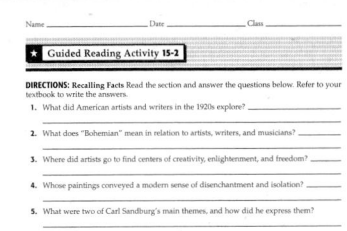

Name _____ Date _____ Class _____

★ Guided Reading Activity 15–2

DIRECTIONS: Recalling Facts Read the section and answer the questions below. Refer to your textbook to write the answers.

1. What did American artists and writers in the 1920s explore? _____

2. What does "Bohemian" mean in relation to artists, writers, and musicians? _____

3. Where did artists go to find centers of creativity, enlightenment, and freedom? _____

4. Whose paintings conveyed a modern sense of disenchantment and isolation? _____

5. What were two of Carl Sandburg's main themes, and how did he express them? _____

Reading Strategy — READING THE TEXT

Summarizing Information Summarizing information teaches students to reduce information and to rethink what they have read. Have students read the paragraphs under "Popular Culture" and then summarize what they have just read. Remind students that only the main ideas should be included in their summaries. When the summaries are complete, have students determine whether they have included all the main ideas by asking themselves: Can my summary be easily understood by someone who has not read the selection? **L1**

📁 Refer to *Inclusion for the High School Social Studies Classroom Strategies and Activities* in the TCR.

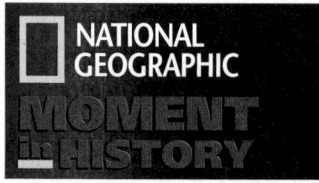

NATIONAL GEOGRAPHIC

MOMENT in HISTORY

The Kelly Air Mail Act of 1925 allowed private carriers to deliver air mail. The act supported the fledgling airline industry, which was still considered by many people to be a novelty, partly because of the barnstormers.

History *and the* Humanities

- 🎵 American Music: Hits Through History: "Can the Circle Be Unbroken"
- 🎵 American Music: Cultural Traditions: "Wildwood Flower"
- 🎨 American Art & Architecture: *Yellow Cactus Flower*

3 ASSESS

Assign Section 2 Assessment as homework or as an in-class activity.

💿 Have students use the **Interactive Tutor Self-Assessment CD-ROM.**

John Dos Passos, a critic of America's capitalist culture, experimented with the form of the novel in his innovative trilogy *U.S.A.,* which combined fiction, biography, news headlines, and prose poems. Sinclair Lewis wrote about the absurdities of traditional life in small-town America in his novels *Main Street* and *Babbitt.* **F. Scott Fitzgerald,** perhaps the most famous writer of the era, created colorful, glamorous characters who chased futile dreams in *The Great Gatsby,* a novel that poignantly exposed the emptiness and superficiality of much of modern society.

✓ **Reading Check** **Examining** Why did many artists, writers, and intellectuals flock to New York City's Greenwich Village and Chicago's South Side during the 1920s?

Popular Culture

The economic prosperity of the 1920s provided many Americans with more leisure time and more spending money, which they devoted to making their lives more enjoyable. Millions of Americans eagerly watched and participated in sports and enjoyed music, theater, and other forms of popular entertainment. They also fell in love with radio shows and motion pictures.

Baseball, Boxing, and Other Sports Thanks to radio and motion pictures, sports such as baseball and boxing reached new heights of popularity in the 1920s. Baseball star **Babe Ruth** became a national hero, famous for hitting hundreds of home runs. As one broadcaster later remarked, "He wasn't a baseball player. He was a worldwide celebrity, an international star, the likes of which baseball has never seen since."

Sports fans also idolized boxer Jack Dempsey. Dempsey held the title of world heavyweight champion from 1919 until 1926, when he lost it to Gene Tunney. When Dempsey attempted to win back the title in 1927, fans' enthusiasm for the rematch reached such a frenzy that one store sold $90,000 worth of radios—an incredible sum at that time—in the two weeks before the event.

NATIONAL GEOGRAPHIC

MOMENT in HISTORY

ENTERTAINMENT FOR A NEW ERA

In the 1920s, the United States developed an almost insatiable appetite for daredevils and death-defying stunts. Itinerant pilots, known as "barnstormers," crisscrossed the country offering airplane rides for a dollar and performing dangerous aerial maneuvers for delighted spectators. Some pilots banded together to form "flying circuses." Competition was fierce as these troupes dreamed up ever more complex and hair-raising stunts to thrill audiences. Here, the "Flying Black Hats" engage in an airborne tennis match.

DIFFERENTIATED INSTRUCTION

Gifted and Talented Have students read a poem or study a piece of art from the period covered in this section. Instruct students to use library and Internet resources to learn more about the style or characteristics of the works of the author or artist. Encourage students to make journal entries while they are doing their research. Have students share their experiences with the class. **L3**

📂 Refer to **Inclusion for the High School Social Studies Classroom Strategies and Activities** in the TCR.

Americans eagerly followed other sports and sports figures, too. Newspaper coverage helped generate enthusiasm for college football. One of the most famous players of the 1920s was Red Grange of the University of Illinois. Grange was known as the "Galloping Ghost" because of his speed and ability to evade members of opposing teams.

Millions of sports fans also were thrilled by the achievements of Bobby Jones, the best golfer of the decade, and tennis players Bill Tilden and Helen Wills, who dominated world tennis. In 1926 Jones became the first golfer to win the U.S. Open and the British Open in the same year. In 1927 swimmer Gertrude Ederle enchanted Americans when she shattered records by swimming the English Channel in a little over 14 hours.

The Rise of Hollywood Although sports became increasingly popular in the 1920s, nothing quite matched the allure of motion pictures. Technology had not yet made sound possible in films, so theaters hired piano players to provide music during the feature, while subtitles revealed the plot. Audiences thronged to see such stars as Mary Pickford, Charlie Chaplin, Tom Mix, Douglas Fairbanks, Gloria Swanson, Rudolph Valentino, and Clara Bow. In 1927 the first "talking" picture—*The Jazz Singer*—was produced, and the golden age of Hollywood began.

Popular Radio Shows and Music Radio also enjoyed a large following during the Jazz Age. In 1920, in one of the first commercial radio broadcasts in history, listeners of station KDKA in Pittsburgh learned the news of Warren G. Harding's landslide victory in the presidential election. Within two years, Americans could turn the dial to more than 400 different radio stations around the country.

Most stations in the 1920s played the popular music of the day, such as "Yes! We Have No Bananas" and "Lover Come Back Again." Broadcasts such as *The Eveready Hour* offered everything from classical music to comedy. In one of the most popular radio shows, *Amos 'n' Andy*, the trials and tribulations of two African American characters (portrayed by white actors) captured the nation's attention every evening.

The mass media—radio, movies, newspapers, and magazines aimed at a broad audience—did more than just entertain. Their easy availability to millions helped break down patterns of provincialism, or narrow focus on local interests. They fostered a sense of shared national experience that helped unify the nation and spread the new ideas and attitudes of the time.

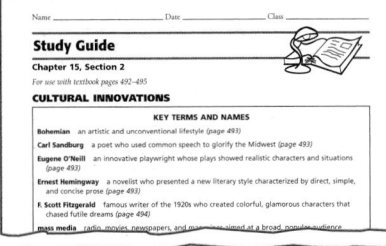

Babe Ruth

✓ **Reading Check** **Summarizing** How did the American economy of the 1920s affect popular culture?

Study Central™ To review this section, go to tarvol2.glencoe.com and click on **Study Central™.**

SECTION 2 ASSESSMENT

Checking for Understanding
1. **Define:** Bohemian, mass media.
2. **Identify:** Carl Sandburg, Eugene O'Neill, Ernest Hemingway, F. Scott Fitzgerald.
3. **Describe** the main themes of artists and writers during the 1920s.

Reviewing Themes
4. **Culture and Traditions** How did writers, artists, and popular culture of the 1920s affect traditional ideas in the United States?

Critical Thinking
5. **Synthesizing** How did World War I influence the literature written during the 1920s?
6. **Organizing** Use a graphic organizer similar to the one below to list the effects of mass media on American culture.

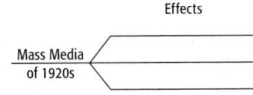

Effects

Mass Media of 1920s

Analyzing Visuals
7. **Interpreting Art** Study the Edward Hopper painting, *Nighthawks,* on page 493. How do different elements of this piece work to convey a sense of isolation?

Writing About History
8. **Descriptive Writing** Imagine that you have moved to New York's Greenwich Village in the 1920s. Write a letter to a friend describing the atmosphere in your neighborhood.

CHAPTER 15 The Jazz Age **495**

SECTION 2 ASSESSMENT ANSWERS

1. Terms are in blue.
2. Carl Sandburg *(p. 493)*, Eugene O'Neill *(p. 493)*, Ernest Hemingway *(p. 493)*, F. Scott Fitzgerald *(p. 494)*
3. disenchantment, isolation, disillusionment, and emptiness
4. They broke down patterns of narrow focus on local interest.
5. It led many writers to portray disillusionment and to reevaluate the myths of American heroes.
6. broke down patterns of provincialism, unified Americans through shared national experience, spread new ideas and attitudes
7. One man eats by himself, there are only three customers in the diner, there is only one person working at the diner, and there are no people on the sidewalk or in the street.
8. Letters should include words and phrases popular at the time.

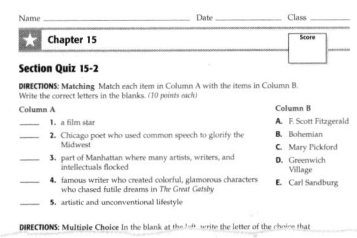
Reteach
Have students describe the disillusionment of 1920s artists.

Enrich
Invite interested students to locate and view a silent movie and prepare a brief report on how silent movies differ from movies made today.

✓ **Reading Check**

Answer: Economic prosperity allowed Americans more leisure time and more spending money to pursue different kinds of popular culture.

Study Central™ provides summaries, interactive games, and online graphic organizers to help students review section content.

4 CLOSE
Have students summarize the effects of sports, movies, radio, and music on popular culture.

495

1 FOCUS

Ask students to consider what life would be like in the United States today if the goverment had the power to force everyone to practice the same religion. Tell students that freedom of religion is a fundamental guarantee of the Constitution.

2 TEACH

Identifying the Main Idea

Write on the board the words of the First Amendment that protect freedom of religion. Tell students that some citizens believe that some of the court rulings have gone to the extreme of advocating freedom from religion, meaning that one's religious beliefs should not be expressed in any public forum. As a class discuss the difference between freedom of religion and freedom from religion. **L1**

Predicting Consequences

Have groups of students research President George W. Bush's faith-based initiatives and discuss potential court challenges to the initiative. After the groups have completed their research, ask them to write a two-page position paper expressing their support or opposition for such initiatives. **L2**

Religious Freedom in the United States

Why It Matters During the summer of 1925, a young teacher, John Scopes, was put on trial for teaching evolution in defiance of Tennessee law. The Scopes trial involved more than a debate between science and religion. It also involved the constitutional principle of the separation of church and state. This principle is based on the First Amendment, which states that the federal government cannot establish an official religion or interfere with a person's right to practice a religion. In 1926 an appeals court upheld Tennessee's law. In 1968, however, the United States Supreme Court ruled that laws banning the teaching of evolution were unconstitutional because they indirectly helped to establish an official religion. From early colonial times, Americans have struggled to preserve their right to worship as they choose and to define the proper relationship between the church and the government.

Steps to . . . Religious Freedom

The American tradition of religious freedom began in the 1600s. England's government persecuted people who did not worship in the manner required by the Church of England. Among the persecuted were Puritans, Catholics, and Quakers, many of whom moved to America in search of religious freedom.

Colonial Beginnings In 1620 the Pilgrims established the Plymouth colony so that they could practice their faith freely. Ten years later, thousands of Puritans, led by John Winthrop, established the colony of Massachusetts. In 1634 Lord Baltimore established Maryland as a refuge for Catholics fleeing persecution, and in 1681 William Penn, a Quaker, founded Pennsylvania, promising religious tolerance to all who settled there.

Church and State At first the Massachusetts Puritans did not practice separation of church and state. Instead they enacted policies that promoted the Puritan faith. For example, taxes supported the Puritan churches; laws required citizens to attend church; and only church members were allowed to vote. People who expressed ideas contrary to Puritan beliefs could be banished.

In the 1630s, Massachusetts banished many people for their religious beliefs, including Roger Williams and Anne Hutchinson. Williams, Hutchinson, and others joined together to create the colony of Rhode

"The Civil rights of none shall be abridged on account of religious belief or worship, nor shall any national religion be established. . . ."

—*James Madison*

496

EXTENDING THE CONTENT

Passing the Amendment After the Bill of Rights was debated and passed in each house of Congress, a committee met to agree to the final wording. The House version of the First Amendment read: "Congress shall make no law establishing religion, or to prevent the free exercise thereof, or to infringe the rights of conscience." The Senate version read: "Congress shall make no law establishing articles of faith or a mode of worship, or prohibiting the free exercise of religion." The final wording was accepted by the House on September 24, 1789, and by the Senate on September 25, 1789.

Virginia colonists attending Old Bruton Church

Island, where church and state were kept separate and the government did not try to coerce religious belief. Meanwhile, in 1639, settlers in Connecticut adopted the Fundamental Orders of Connecticut. These Orders allowed non-church members to vote.

The Great Awakening
During the early 1700s, a period of religious revivalism known as the Great Awakening strengthened the idea of religious freedom. Ministers began preaching the importance of each individual's commitment to faith. The Great Awakening divided many congregations and led to the rise of the Baptists and Presbyterians. It also led to greater religious tolerance. By the time of the American Revolution, the idea of freedom of religion was widely accepted in the American colonies.

The Virginia Statute for Religious Freedom
In 1786, shortly after the American Revolution, Virginia passed the Statute for Religious Freedom. Its author, Thomas Jefferson, believed religious toleration to be one of the most important aspects of a free society. The Virginia statute stated that "all men shall be free to profess… their opinion in matters of religions, and that the same shall in no wise…affect their civil capacities."

A Constitutional Guarantee
American leaders guaranteed religious freedom in the new U.S. Constitution. The First Amendment states that "Congress shall make no law respecting an establishment of religion, or prohibiting the free exercise thereof." This sentence consists of two parts. The establishment clause forbids the federal government from creating an official religion or supporting religious activities. The free exercise clause forbids the government from suppressing freedom of religious worship.

Continuing Issues
Like many other ideas in the Constitution, the idea of religious freedom has been reinterpreted over time. In the 1879 case *Reynolds* v. *United States,* the U.S. Supreme Court ruled that freedom of religion is not absolute. Religious practices that violate the law or undermine the public interest, the Court declared, were not protected by the First Amendment.

One of the most controversial issues has been the role of religion in the public schools. In 1962, in *Engel* v. *Vitale,* the Court ruled that states could not require official prayers to be recited in schools. In 1963, in *Abingdon School District* v. *Schempp,* the Court also ruled out daily Bible readings in schools. In 1990, however, the Court ruled that student groups could study the Bible and pray together because they were private individuals, not school officials. With religion an integral part of many Americans' lives, the nation continues to grapple with the problem of balancing freedom of religion with the need to avoid federal support of a particular church.

Checking for Understanding
1. How did the Great Awakening promote greater religious tolerance?
2. What did the Supreme Court rule in *Reynolds* v. *United States?*

Critical Thinking
1. How has the establishment clause of the First Amendment been applied to public schools?
2. Why do you think freedom of religion is such an important and controversial right?

Looking Back...

Creating a Political Cartoon
Encourage students to create a political cartoon that expresses one of the current positions on freedom of religion in the United States. **L2**

3 ASSESS

Have students trace the historical developments in the colonial period that helped establish the principle of religious freedom.

FYI

Many of the founders were Deists in religion. Deists believe in one god. They are inspired by the design found in the universe. They do not support the idea of divine revelation, nor do they have a holy book.

4 CLOSE

Review with students the fundamental reasons that religious freedom was so important to the founders of the country.

Checking for Understanding
1. The Great Awakening fostered the founding of many new churches. These many new churches increased religious toleration.
2. According to *Reynolds* v. *United States,* religious practices that violated the law or undermined the public interest were not protected by the First Amendment.

Critical Thinking
1. Two Supreme Court decisions, *Engel* v. *Vitale* and *Abingdon School District* v. *Schempp* ruled that school-sponsored prayers are unconstitutional. The issue continues to be debated.
2. Answers will vary. Encourage students to use specific examples in their responses.

1 FOCUS

Section Overview

This section focuses on African American culture during the 1920s, including the Harlem Renaissance and political activism.

BELLRINGER
Skillbuilder Activity

 Project transparency and have students answer the question.

Daily Focus Skills Transparency 15–3

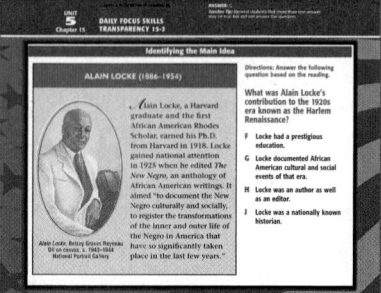

Reading Preview

Answers to Graphic: Causes: Great Migration and racial pride; **Effects:** important African American writers, jazz, blues, theater; also sparked political change

Preteaching Vocabulary
Have students write a paragraph using at least four of the Key Terms and Names.

SECTION 3 African American Culture

Guide to Reading

Main Idea
During World War I, the prospect of employment and greater freedoms spurred the "Great Migration" of African Americans from the rural South to industrial cities in the North.

Key Terms and Names
Great Migration, Harlem Renaissance, Claude McKay, Langston Hughes, jazz, Cotton Club, blues, Marcus Garvey

Reading Strategy
Organizing As you read about the African American experience in the 1920s, complete a graphic organizer similar to the one below by filling in the causes and effects of the Harlem Renaissance.

Causes   Effects

Harlem Renaissance

Reading Objectives
• **Describe** the Harlem Renaissance and the rediscovery of African American cultural roots.
• **Explain** the increase in African American political activism.

Section Theme
Groups and Institutions African Americans played stronger political and cultural roles in the 1920s than they had in previous decades.

Preview of Events

♦1922	♦1924	♦1926	♦1928
1922 Antilynching bill passes in the House but not in the Senate	**1924** The Negro League holds its first world series	**1926** Langston Hughes's *The Weary Blues* published	**1928** Claude McKay's *Home to Harlem* published

---

★ An American Story ★

Louis Armstrong

On August 8, 1922, a young cornet player named Louis Armstrong took the train from New Orleans to Chicago. His hero, the bandleader Joe "King" Oliver, had sent a telegram to Armstrong offering him a job. Here, Armstrong recalls his trip:

❝When I got to the station in Chicago, I couldn't see Joe Oliver anywhere . . . I'd never seen a city that big. All those tall buildings, I thought they were universities. I said, no, this is the wrong city. I was just fixing to take the next train back home . . . when a red cap [train porter] Joe had left word with came up to me. He took me to the Lincoln Gardens and when I got to the door there and heard Joe and his band wailing so good, I said to myself, 'No, I ain't supposed to be in this band. They're too good.'❞

The next night, near the end of the show, Oliver let Armstrong perform a solo. Armstrong later recalled his feelings: "I had hit the big time. I was up North with the greats. I was playing with my idol, the King, Joe Oliver. My boyhood dream had come true at last."

—quoted in *The African American Family Album*

The Harlem Renaissance

Louis Armstrong's first impressions of Chicago and his desire to fulfill a dream were probably similar to the first impressions and desires of hundreds of thousands of other African Americans who joined in what was called the **Great Migration** from the rural

---

SECTION RESOURCES

📖 Reproducible Masters
• Reproducible Lesson Plan 15–3
• Daily Lecture and Discussion Notes 15–3
• Guided Reading Activity 15–3
• Section Quiz 15–3
• Reading Essentials and Study Guide 15–3

📑 Transparencies
• Daily Focus Skills Transparency 15–3

Multimedia
🖥 Interactive Tutor Self-Assessment CD-ROM
🖥 ExamView® Pro Testmaker CD-ROM
🖥 Presentation Plus! CD-ROM
🖥 TeacherWorks™ CD-ROM
🎧 Audio Program
🎵 American Music: Hits Through History
🎵 American Music: Cultural Traditions

South to industrial cities in the North. By moving north, African Americans sought to escape the segregated society of the South, to find economic opportunities, and to build better lives. After World War I, black populations swelled in large northern cities. The cities were full of nightclubs and music, particularly in the New York City neighborhood of Harlem—the heart and soul of the African American renaissance. It was there that African Americans created an environment that stimulated artistic development, racial pride, a sense of community, and political organization. The result was a flowering of African American arts that became known as the **Harlem Renaissance.**

The Writers Considered the first important writer of the Harlem Renaissance, **Claude McKay** emigrated from Jamaica to New York. There, he translated the shock of American racism into *Harlem Shadows*, a collection of poetry published in 1922. In such poems as "The Lynching" and "If We Must Die," McKay's eloquent verse expressed a proud defiance and bitter contempt of racism—two striking characteristics of Harlem Renaissance writing.

One of the most prolific, original, and versatile writers of the Harlem Renaissance was **Langston Hughes.** Born in Joplin, Missouri, Hughes became a leading voice of the African American experience in the United States. 📖 *(See American Literature on page 503 for more information on Langston Hughes.)*

Harlem Renaissance authors continue to influence writers today. **Zora Neale Hurston** published her first novels, *Jonah's Gourd Vine* and *Their Eyes Were Watching God*, in the 1930s. These works influenced such contemporary authors as Ralph Ellison and Toni Morrison. Hurston's personal and spirited portrayals of rural African American culture, often set in Florida where she grew up, were also the first major stories featuring African American females as central characters. Other notable writers of the Harlem Renaissance include Countee Cullen, Alain Locke, Dorothy West, and Nella Larsen.

Jazz, Blues, and the Theater Shortly after **Louis Armstrong** arrived in Chicago from New Orleans, he introduced an improvisational, early form of jazz, a style of music influenced by Dixieland music and ragtime, with its ragged rhythms and syncopated melodies.

In 1925, three years after joining Joe "King" Oliver's band, Armstrong awed fellow musicians with a series of recordings made with his group, the "Hot Five." In these recordings, especially in the song "Cornet Chop Suey," Armstrong broke away from the New Orleans tradition of ensemble or group playing by performing highly imaginative solos. He became the first great cornet and trumpet soloist in jazz music.

Ragtime also influenced the composer, pianist, and bandleader **Duke Ellington,** who listened as a teenager to ragtime piano players in Washington, D.C. In 1923 Ellington formed a small band, moved to New York, and began playing in speakeasies and clubs. He soon created his own sound, a blend of improvisation and orchestration using different combinations of instruments. The Ellington style appeared in such hits as "Mood Indigo" and "Sophisticated Lady."

Like many other African American entertainers, Ellington got his start at the **Cotton Club,** one of the most famous Harlem nightspots. Years later, reflecting on the music of this era, Ellington said, "Everything, and I repeat, *everything* had to swing. And that was just it, those cats really had it; they had that soul. And you know you can't just play some of this music without soul. Soul is very important."

Picturing **History**

Renaissance Writers Claude McKay wrote about his Jamaican homeland, while Zora Neale Hurston celebrated the courage of African Americans in the rural South. *How did these writers contribute to African Americans' cultural identity?*

HISTORY *Online*

Objectives and answers to the student activity can be found in the **Web Activity Lesson Plan** at tarvol2.glencoe.com.

2 **TEACH**

Daily Lecture and Discussion Notes 15–3

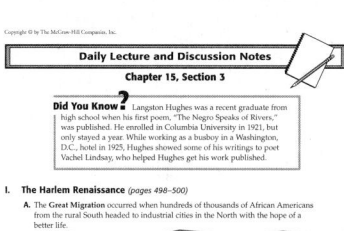

Reading Strategy

Reading Poetry Have students select a poem by an African American poet of the Harlem Renaissance and prepare to read it aloud for the class. Suggest that students work in pairs as they practice reading the poetry with the proper rhythm and intonation. **L1**

Picturing **History**

Answer: by writing proudly about their own experience
Ask: What two striking characteristics of Harlem Renaissance writing are evident in some of McKay's poetry? *(proud defiance and bitter contempt of racism)*

Reading Strategy **READING THE TEXT**

Activating Prior Knowledge Before students begin to absorb any new knowledge, prepare them by bringing to mind what they already know. Ask students what they know about the Harlem Renaissance. Use specific information found in this section to help foster discussion that will enhance their understanding of the subject. **L1**

☞ Refer to *Inclusion for the High School Social Studies Classroom Strategies and Activities* in the TCR.

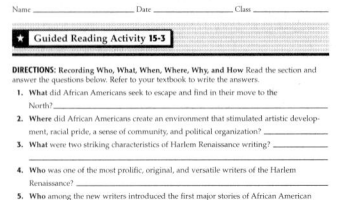

Name _____ Date _____ Class _____

★ Guided Reading Activity **15-3**

DIRECTIONS: Recording Who, What, When, Where, Why, and How Read the section and answer the questions below. Refer to your textbook to write the answers.

1. What did African Americans seek to escape and find in their move to the North?

2. Where did African Americans create an environment that stimulated artistic development, racial pride, a sense of community, and political organization?

3. What were two striking characteristics of Harlem Renaissance writing?

4. Who was one of the most prolific, original, and versatile writers of the Harlem Renaissance?

5. Who among the new writers introduced the first major stories of African American female characters?

Picturing **History**

Answer: After World War I, many African Americans moved to large cities. There they found many night-clubs that welcomed them as performers. The African American community in these cities stimulated artistic development, racial pride, a sense of community, and political organization.
Ask: Although they made economic gains, what persistent problems still existed for African Americans? *(segregation and racial prejudice)*

Reading Check

Answer: They developed the rhythms and sound of jazz and the blues; their literature reflected the African American as a part of American life.

History *and the* Humanities

🎵 American Music: Hits Through History: "Ain't Misbehavin'," "These Foolish Things"

🎵 American Music: Cultural Traditions: "Muskrat Ramble," "Downhearted Blues"

Bessie Smith seemed to symbolize soul. Her emotional singing style and commanding voice earned her the title "the Empress of the Blues." Smith sang of unfulfilled love, poverty, and oppression—the classic themes of the blues, a soulful style of music that evolved from African American spirituals. Born in Tennessee, Smith started performing in tent shows, saloons, and small theaters in the South. Discovered by Ma Rainey, one of the first great blues singers, Smith later performed with many of the greatest jazz bands of the era, including those of Louis Armstrong, Fletcher Henderson, and Benny Goodman. Her first recorded song, "Down Hearted Blues," became a major hit in 1923.

While jazz and blues filled the air during the Harlem Renaissance, the theater arts were also flourishing. *Shuffle Along,* the first musical written, produced, and performed by African Americans, made its debut on Broadway in 1921. The show's success helped launch a number of careers, including those of Florence Mills and Paul Robeson.

Paul Robeson, a celebrated singer and actor, received wide acclaim in the title role of a 1924 New York production of *Emperor Jones,* a play by Eugene O'Neill. In 1928 Robeson gained fame for his work in the musical *Show Boat.* He also often appeared at the Apollo Theater, another famous entertainment club in Harlem. Robeson's fame ultimately spread to Europe, where he became well known as a singer and actor.

Perhaps the most daring performer of the era, Josephine Baker transformed a childhood knack for flamboyance into a career as a well-known singer and dancer. Baker performed on Broadway but went to Paris to dance in 1925. Baker took Paris by storm, launching an international career.

The Harlem Renaissance succeeded in bringing international fame to African American arts. It also sparked a political transformation in the United States.

✓ **Reading Check** **Analyzing** Analyze how African Americans helped shape the national identity through the use of music and literature.

Picturing **History**

Harlem Renaissance The growing fame of African American artists, who often performed (but could not be patrons) at Harlem's "Cotton Club," encouraged a flamboyant lifestyle. What conditions encouraged the growth of African American art?

DIFFERENTIATED INSTRUCTION

Auditory/Musical Have interested students create a presentation titled "Introduction to Jazz." Encourage students to create a multimedia presentation that provides a musical overview of the musical patterns and themes common in jazz. **L2**

👉 Refer to *Inclusion for the High School Social Studies Classroom Strategies and Activities* in the TCR.

African American Politics

The racial pride that sparked the artistic achievements of the Harlem Renaissance also fueled the political and economic aspirations of many African Americans. The postwar years saw the development of new attitudes among African Americans, who forged new roles in life and in politics. For many, the sight of the 1,300 African American men of the Fifteenth Regiment of New York's National Guard, returning from the war and marching through Manhattan and home to Harlem, symbolized these aspirations. W.E.B. Du Bois, editor of *The Crisis,* captured the new sense of dignity and defiance of African Americans:

> 66We return.
> We return from fighting.
> We return fighting.
> Make way for democracy! We saved it in France, and
> by the Great Jehovah, we will save it in the United
> States of America, or know the reason why.99
>
> —from *When Harlem Was in Vogue*

The Black Vote in the North The Great Migration had a significant impact on the political power of African Americans in the North. As their numbers grew in certain city neighborhoods, African Americans became a powerful voting bloc that could sometimes sway the outcome of elections.

At election time, most African American voters in the North cast their votes for Republicans, the party of Abraham Lincoln. In 1928 African American voters in Chicago achieved a significant political breakthrough. Voting as a bloc, they helped elect **Oscar DePriest,** the first African American representative in Congress from a Northern state. During his three terms in Congress, DePriest introduced laws to provide pensions to formerly enslaved African Americans over 75 years old, to declare Lincoln's birthday a public holiday, and to fine and imprison officials who allowed lynchings of prisoners.

The NAACP Battles Lynching On the legal front, the National Association for the Advancement of Colored People (NAACP) battled valiantly but often unsuccessfully against segregation and discrimination against African Americans. Its efforts focused primarily on lobbying public officials and working through the court system.

From its beginning in 1909, the NAACP lobbied and protested against the horrors of lynching. The NAACP's persistent efforts led to the passage of anti-lynching legislation in the House of

Jazz's Global Roots

Jazz may be an American creation, but its roots stretch across the Atlantic Ocean to Europe and Africa. The music Louis Armstrong and Duke Ellington helped to make famous originated from the spirituals and work songs of African slaves. These songs were a blend of African rhythms and European melodies and harmonies, which African slaves encountered after arriving in North America. This music evolved into ragtime during the late 1800s and early 1900s. By the 1920s, artists had combined aspects of ragtime with the uniquely African American sounds of the blues, and thus jazz was born. *Why do you think music often spreads easily across different cultures?*

Representatives in 1922. The Senate defeated the bill, but the NAACP continued to lobby against lynching throughout the 1920s and 1930s. Its ongoing efforts kept the issue in the news and probably helped to reduce the number of lynchings that took place.

One of the NAACP's greatest political triumphs occurred in 1930 with the defeat of Judge John J. Parker's nomination to the U.S. Supreme Court. The NAACP joined with labor unions to launch a highly organized national campaign against the North Carolina judge, who allegedly was racist and anti-labor. By a narrow margin, the Senate refused to confirm Parker's nomination. His defeat demonstrated that African American voters and lobby groups had finally begun to achieve enough influence to affect national politics and change decisions in Congress.

While some people were fighting for integration and improvement in the economic and political position of African Americans, other groups began to emphasize black nationalism and black pride. Eventually, some began to call for black separation from white society.

Black Nationalism and Marcus Garvey A dynamic black leader from Jamaica, **Marcus Garvey,** captured the imagination of millions of African Americans with his call for "Negro Nationalism," which glorified the black culture and traditions of the past.

Inspired by Booker T. Washington's call for self-reliance, Garvey founded the Universal Negro Improvement Association (UNIA), an organization aimed at promoting black pride and unity. The central message of Garvey's Harlem-based movement was that African Americans could gain economic and

CHAPTER 15   The Jazz Age   **501**

World History Connection

Answer: There is no language barrier; everyone can appreciate instrumental music.
Ask: What elements were blended together to create jazz? *(ragtime and blues)*

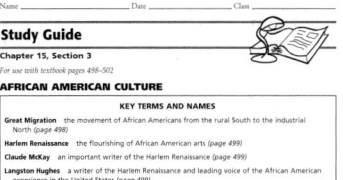

All That Jazz The origin of the term *jazz* is one notable dispute in American English. It may have come from the word *Chaz,* the nickname of an early ragtime drummer named Charles Washington, or from *chasse,* a kind of dance step. African and Creole sources are also possibilities.

3 ASSESS

Assign Section 3 Assessment as homework or as an in-class activity.

🔹 Have students use the **Interactive Tutor Self-Assessment CD-ROM.**

L1/ELL

Reading Essentials and Study Guide 15–3

Name _____ Date _____ Class _____

Study Guide

Chapter 15, Section 3

For use with textbook pages 498–502

AFRICAN AMERICAN CULTURE

KEY TERMS AND NAMES
Great Migration   the movement of African Americans from the rural South to the industrial North (page 498)
Harlem Renaissance   the flourishing of African American arts (page 499)
Claude McKay   an important writer of the Harlem Renaissance (page 499)
Langston Hughes   a writer of the Harlem Renaissance and leading voice of the African American experience in the United States (page 499)
jazz   a style of music influenced by Dixieland music and ragtime (page 499)
Cotton Club   a famous Harlem nightspot (page 499)

INTERDISCIPLINARY CONNECTIONS ACTIVITY

Music Have students listen to recordings of jazz and blues performances by popular musicians from the 1920s, such as Duke Ellington and Bessie Smith. Instruct students to use the library, Internet, and other resources to learn more about the performer they have selected. Have students prepare a profile of the life of their chosen performer. Encourage students to include a look at their music and their personal lives. **L2**

L2

Section Quiz 15–3

Chapter 15

Score

Section Quiz 15-3

DIRECTIONS: Matching Match each item in Column A with the items in Column B.
Write the correct letters in the blanks. *(10 points each)*

Column A
1. first African American representative in Congress from a Northern state
2. "the Empress of the Blues"
3. the first musical written, produced, and performed by African Americans
4. flowering of African American arts
5. author whose work continues to influence writers today

Column B
A. Zora Neale Hurston
B. Oscar DePriest
C. *Shuffle Along*
D. Bessie Smith
E. Harlem Renaissance

DIRECTIONS: Multiple Choice In the blank at the left, write the letter of the choice that best completes the statement or answers the question. *(10 points each)*

Picturing History

Answer: He was convicted of mail fraud and deported. His attempts to revive his movement worldwide failed.

Reading Check

Answer: African Americans saw themselves as defenders of democracy and thus entitled to all the rights of citizens.

Reteach
Have students describe the rediscovery of African American cultural roots.

Enrich
Invite students to read one of the novels mentioned in the section and write a book report.

HISTORY Online

Study Central™ provides summaries, interactive games, and online graphic organizers to help students review section content.

---

4 CLOSE

Have students explain the increase in African American political activism.

Picturing History

Black Nationalism Marcus Garvey's Universal Negro Improvement Association advocated African American self-reliance and separation from whites and white society. *What eventually happened to Garvey and his movement?*

political power by educating themselves. Garvey also advocated separation and independence from whites.

In 1920, at the height of his power, Garvey presided over an international conference in the UNIA Liberty Hall in Harlem. After the convention, about 50,000 people, led by Garvey, marched through the streets of Harlem in a show of support. Garvey told his followers they would never find justice or freedom in America, and he proposed to lead them to Africa.

Garvey's plan to create a settlement in the African country of Liberia alarmed France and Great Britain, which governed surrounding territories. In the United States, the emerging African American middle class and intellectuals distanced themselves from Garvey and his push for racial purity and separation. FBI officials saw UNIA as a dangerous catalyst for black uprisings in urban areas. Garvey also alienated key figures in the Harlem Renaissance by characterizing them as "weak-kneed and cringing . . . [flatterers of] the white man."

Garvey was convicted of mail fraud in 1923 and served time in prison. In 1927 President Coolidge commuted Garvey's sentence and used Garvey's immigrant status to have him deported to Jamaica. Garvey's subsequent attempts to revitalize his movement from abroad failed.

Despite Garvey's failure to keep his movement alive, he inspired millions of African Americans with a sense of pride in their heritage and hope for the future. That sense of pride and hope survived long after Garvey and his "back to Africa" movement was gone. This pride and hope reemerged strongly during the 1950s and played a vital role in the civil rights movement of the 1960s.

Reading Check **Summarizing** How did World War I change attitudes among African Americans toward themselves and their country?

HISTORY Online **Study Central**™ To review this section, go to **tarvol2.glencoe.com** and click on **Study Central**™.

SECTION 3 ASSESSMENT

Checking for Understanding
1. **Define:** jazz, blues.
2. **Identify:** Great Migration, Harlem Renaissance, Claude McKay, Langston Hughes, Cotton Club, Marcus Garvey.
3. **Explain** how Bessie Smith's music conveyed universal themes.
4. **Explain** the importance of the defeat of Judge John Parker's nomination to the U.S. Supreme Court.
5. **Describe** the goals of Marcus Garvey's Universal Negro Improvement Association.

Reviewing Themes
6. **Groups and Institutions** What actions did the NAACP take to expand political rights for African Americans?

Critical Thinking
7. **Synthesizing** How did the Great Migration affect the political power of African Americans in the North?
8. **Analyzing** How did Duke Ellington create a new musical style that grew out of the ragtime tradition?
9. **Organizing** Use a graphic organizer similar to the one below to describe the impact of the Harlem Renaissance on U.S. society.

Impact of Harlem Renaissance

Analyzing Visuals
10. **Examining Photographs** Study the pictures on page 500 of the Cotton Club and African Americans posing by their car. What are some elements of these pictures that show African Americans adopting parts of the 1920s social culture?

Writing About History
11. **Descriptive Writing** Imagine that you witnessed the African American men of the Fifteenth Regiment of New York's National Guard, who had come back from the war, march through Manhattan and home to Harlem. Write a paragraph describing your feelings upon seeing these men.

SECTION 3 ASSESSMENT ANSWERS

1. Terms are in blue.
2. Great Migration (p. 498), Harlem Renaissance (p. 499), Claude McKay (p. 499), Langston Hughes (p. 499), Cotton Club (p. 499), Marcus Garvey (p. 501)
3. She sang of love, poverty, and oppression.
4. showed political strength of African Americans
5. emphasized black pride and separate African American society
6. lobbied and worked through the courts
7. created a strong voting bloc
8. distinctive orchestration and improvisation
9. literature; new styles of music; theater; political influence
10. style of clothing
11. Students' paragraphs should focus on emotional responses.

American LITERATURE

Selected Poems by Langston Hughes

Langston Hughes was born in Joplin, Missouri, in 1902. After high school Hughes went on to Columbia University to study engineering, but he soon dropped out to pursue his first love—poetry. Hughes eventually became known as the "Poet Laureate of Harlem." The following poems are representative of Hughes's work. In "I, Too" he describes the disenfranchisement many African Americans felt in the United States in the 1920s, and their willingness to stand up and take pride in their heritage. In "The Negro Speaks of Rivers," Hughes reveals a profound love of his heritage.

Read to Discover
What is Hughes's perception of the place of African Americans in society at the time he wrote these poems?

Reader's Dictionary
Euphrates: River in the Middle East

Congo and **Nile:** Rivers in Africa

lulled: calmed; soothed

The Negro Speaks of Rivers

I've known rivers:
I've known rivers ancient as the
    world and older than the
flow of human blood in human veins.

My soul has grown deep like the
    rivers.

I bathed in the Euphrates when
    dawns were young.
I built my hut near the Congo and it
    lulled me to sleep.
I looked upon the Nile and raised
    the pyramids above it.
I heard the singing of the Mississippi
    when Abe Lincoln went down to
    New Orleans, and I've seen its
    muddy bosom turn all golden in
    the sunset.

I've known rivers:
Ancient, dusky rivers

My soul has grown deep like the
    rivers.

I, Too

I, too, sing America.

I am the darker brother.
They send me to eat in the kitchen
When company comes,
But I laugh,
And eat well,
And grow strong.

Tomorrow,
I'll be at the table
When company comes.
Nobody'll dare
Say to me,
"Eat in the kitchen,"
Then.

Besides,
They'll see how beautiful I am
And be ashamed—

I, too, am America.

Analyzing Literature

1. **Recall and Interpret** How do you think Hughes's use of punctuation and line breaks helps convey his point?
2. **Evaluate and Connect** Do you think these poems convey a positive message or a negative one? Why?

Interdisciplinary Activity
Response Writing The poem "I, Too" is a response to Walt Whitman's poem, "I Hear America Singing." Using the Internet or other resources, find and read Whitman's poem. In small groups, try to figure out how Hughes's poem ties in to Whitman's. Then write your own response poem to "I Hear America Singing."

CHAPTER 15 The Jazz Age **503**

American LITERATURE

American LITERATURE

Block Schedule

Team Teaching This selection of poems by Langston Hughes can be presented in conjunction with English or Language Arts.

Read to Discover
Answer: The poem indicates that African Americans are not currently accepted in American society but they will be in the future.

Reinforcing Vocabulary
Have students locate and label the rivers on a world map.

Historical Connection
Point out that "I, Too" demonstrates the racial pride that was characteristic of the Harlem Renaissance.

Portfolio Writing Activity
Have students read "The Weary Blues" and listen to a recording by blues singer Bessie Smith. Instruct students to write a short paper on the poem and blues music.

HISTORY Online
Refer to tarvol2.glencoe.com for additional Glencoe Literature titles, lesson plans, and study guides related to this unit.

Answers to Analyzing Literature

1. Answers will vary. The use of punctuation and line breaks forces the reader to pause and reflect on the line just read.

2. Possible response: a positive, hopeful message; the poet suggests that while things are not good now, there is hope for the future

Interdisciplinary Activity
Students' answers will vary. Encourage students to reflect on their own experiences in composing their response.

TEACH

Appreciation

Have students work in groups to select one Louis Armstrong recording and find photos to illustrate the mood and tone of the piece. Have the groups combine the music and the photos into a multimedia tribute to the jazz legend. Have the groups share their presentations with the class and, if possible, select several of the presentations to be made to a wider audience.

Verbatim

Have students select one of the quotes and find a list of specific examples that support or refute the statement. Have students use their lists to write a letter to the person named in the quote. The letter should either offer support of their point of view or refute their statement.

Visit the **TIME** Web site at www.time.com for up-to-date news, weekly magazine articles, editorials, online polls, and an archive of past magazine and Web articles.

Appreciation

LOUIS DANIEL ARMSTRONG *Writer Stanley Crouch remembers Louis Armstrong, a Jazz Age great.*

Pops. Sweet Papa Dip. Satchmo. He had perfect pitch and perfect rhythm. His improvised melodies and singing could be as lofty as a moon flight or as low-down as the blood drops of a street thug dying in the gutter. The extent of his influence across jazz and across American music continues to this day.

Not only do we hear Armstrong in trumpet players who represent the present renaissance in jazz, we can also detect his influence in certain rhythms that sweep from country-and-western music to rap.

Louis Daniel Armstrong was born in New Orleans on August 4, 1901. It was at a home for troubled kids that young Louis first put his lips to the mouthpiece of a cornet and later, a trumpet.

In 1922 Armstrong went to Chicago, where he joined King Oliver and his Creole Jazz Band. The band brought out the people and all the musicians, black and white, who wanted to know how it was truly done.

When he first played in New York City in 1924, his improvisations set the city on its head. The stiff rhythms of the time were slashed away by his combination of the percussive and the soaring. He soon returned to Chicago, perfected what he was doing, and made one record after another.

Louis Armstrong was so much, in fact, that every school of jazz since has had to address how he interpreted the basics of the idiom—swing, blues, ballads, and Afro-Hispanic rhythms. His freedom, his wit, and his discipline give his music a perpetual position in the wave of the future that is the station of all great art.

VERBATIM

❝The great creators of the government . . . thought of America as a light to the world, as created to lead the world in the assertion of the right of peoples and the rights of free nations.❞

WOODROW WILSON,
in defense of the League of Nations, 1920

❝We seek no part in directing the destinies of the Old World.❞
WARREN G. HARDING,
Inaugural Address, 1921

❝Here was a new generation, . . . dedicated more than the last to the fear of poverty and the worship of success; grown up to find . . . all wars fought, all faiths in man shaken.❞

F. Scott Fitzgerald

F. SCOTT FITZGERALD,
author, This Side of Paradise

❝There has been a change for the worse during the past year in feminine dress, dancing, manners and general moral standards. [One should] realize the serious ethical consequences of immodesty in girls' dress.❞
from the **PITTSBURGH OBSERVER**

❝[In New York] I saw 7,000,000 two-legged animals penned in an evil smelling cage, . . . streets as unkempt as a Russian steppe, . . . rubbish, waste paper, cigar butts. . . . One glance and you know no master hand directs.❞
article in Soviet newspaper **PRAVDA**
describing New York City in 1925

COOPERATIVE LEARNING ACTIVITY

Creating a Magazine Spread Organize the class into small groups. Tell the groups that they are to create a magazine spread that includes articles or items about each section of Chapter 15. Students should look at current magazines and books for ideas about page design. This activity can be completed using desktop publishing software or the more traditional cut-and-paste method.

Use the rubric for a cooperative group management plan on pages 71–72 in the **Performance Assessment Activities and Rubrics.**

BROWN BROTHERS

Hide the Hooch

Ingenious Americans are finding unusual places to store their liquor under Prohibition:

- canes
- hot water bottles
- shoe heels
- rolled newspaper
- folds of coats
- perfume bottles

Milestones

EMBARRASSED, 1920. TEXAS SENATOR MORRIS SHEPPARD, a leading proponent of the Eighteenth Amendment, when a large whiskey still is found on his farm.

ERASED, 1922. THE WORD "OBEY," from the Episcopal marriage ceremony, by a vote of American Episcopal bishops.

DIED, 1923. HOMER MOREHOUSE, 27, in the 87th hour of a record-setting 90-hour, 10-minute dance marathon.

EXONERATED, 1921. EIGHT CHICAGO WHITE SOX PLAYERS charged with taking bribes to throw the 1919 World Series. The players were found "not guilty" when grand jury testimony disappeared. Newly appointed commissioner of baseball Kenesaw Mountain Landis banned the "Black Sox" from baseball.

CULVER PICTURES

MAKING A COMEBACK. SANTA CLAUS, after falling into low favor in the last decade. Aiming at children, advertisers are marketing St. Nick heavily.

WHAT'S NEW
Invented This Decade
How did we live without . . .

- push-button elevators
- neon signs
- oven thermostats
- electric razors
- tissues
- spiral-bound notebooks
- motels
- dry ice
- zippers
- pop-up toasters
- flavored yogurt
- car radios
- adhesive tape
- food disposals
- water skiing
- automatic potato peeler
- self-winding wristwatch

Beautiful Goodrich ZIPPERS
BROWN BROTHERS

NUMBERS

60,000
Families with radios in 1922

9,000,000
Motor vehicles registered in U.S. in 1920

$2,467,946
Income tax paid by Henry Ford in 1924

500,000
People who wrote to Henry Ford in 1924 begging for money

33.5 Number of hours Charles Lindbergh spent in his nonstop flight from New York to Paris on May 20, 1927

1,800 Tons of ticker tape and shredded paper dropped on Charles Lindbergh in his parade in New York City

$16,000 Cost of cleaning up after the parade

7,000 Job offers received by Lindbergh

3.5 million
Number of letters received by Lindbergh

BROWN BROTHERS
Charles Lindbergh

Portfolio Writing Project

Have students research one of the inventions mentioned in the magazine spread. They should discover what preceded the invention, who invented it, and what improvements were made to the product. Students should also decide if the invention is still relevant today or has become obsolete. Based on their research, students should write a two-page report about their chosen invention.

Compare and Contrast

Have students create two political cartoons, one expressing the popular sentiment about Prohibition and one expressing the concerns over alcohol consumption today.

CLOSE

Have students select one of the numbers and find a correlating statistic for today. For example, a student could identify the number of motor vehicles registered in the United States in the current year.

EXTENDING THE CONTENT

Banned From the Game Commissioner Landis banned all White Sox players from professional baseball, saying that "regardless of the verdict of the juries, no player who throws a ball game, no player who undertakes or promises to throw a ball game, no player who sits in confidence with a bunch of crooked players and does not promptly tell his club about it, will ever play professional baseball." The ban remained in effect, and none of the players were ever allowed to participate in professional baseball again.

GLENCOE TECHNOLOGY

MindJogger Videoquiz
Use the **MindJogger Videoquiz** to review Chapter 15 content.

 Available in DVD

Reviewing Key Terms
Students' answers will vary. The pages where the words appear in the text are shown in parentheses.

1. **anarchist** (p. 483)
2. **eugenics** (p. 483)
3. **flapper** (p. 485)
4. **evolution** (p. 486)
5. **creationism** (p. 486)
6. **police powers** (p. 487)
7. **speakeasy** (p. 487)
8. **Bohemian** (p. 493)
9. **mass media** (p. 495)
10. **jazz** (p. 499)
11. **blues** (p. 500)

Reviewing Key Facts
12. Emergency Quota Act (p. 484), Fundamentalism (p. 486), Carl Sandburg (p. 493), Eugene O'Neill (p. 493), Ernest Hemingway (p. 493), F. Scott Fitzgerald (p. 494), Great Migration (p. 498), Harlem Renaissance (p. 499), Claude McKay (p. 499), Langston Hughes (p. 499), Marcus Garvey (p. 501)
13. influx of immigrants and a recession
14. Emergency Quota Act and National Origins Act
15. Southern and Eastern Europeans
16. allowed them to escape parents' control
17. It was a religious movement to reassert the Bible's authority in life.
18. The communities offered freedom from conformity and traditional ideas.
19. because of its large, concentrated African American population
20. Harlem Renaissance and African American experience in World War I

506

Reviewing Key Terms
On a sheet of paper, use each of these terms in a sentence.

1. anarchist
2. eugenics
3. flapper
4. evolution
5. creationism
6. police powers
7. speakeasy
8. Bohemian
9. mass media
10. jazz
11. blues

Chapter Summary

Cultural Changes
- The "new morality" emphasized youth and beauty
- Young people and women gained more independence
- The working class enjoyed more leisure time
- The mass media expanded

African American Renaissance

Harlem Renaissance
- Breakthrough period for African American arts
- Literature revealed racial pride and contempt of racism
- Jazz and blues popularized

Political Renaissance
- Great Migration created strong African American voting blocs in Northern cities
- First African American elected to Congress from a Northern state
- NAACP battled segregation and discrimination

Revitalized Traditional Values
- Fundamentalists preached traditional religious values
- Emphasis on family and moral values
- Traditionalists supported Prohibition

Nativism
- Nativists used eugenics as a pseudo-scientific basis for ethnic and religious prejudice
- The new Ku Klux Klan targeted African Americans, Jews, Catholics, immigrants, and other groups they considered to be "un-American"
- Congress established immigration quotas

506 CHAPTER 15 The Jazz Age

Reviewing Key Facts
12. **Identify:** Emergency Quota Act, Fundamentalism, Carl Sandburg, Eugene O'Neill, Ernest Hemingway, F. Scott Fitzgerald, Great Migration, Harlem Renaissance, Claude McKay, Langston Hughes, Marcus Garvey.
13. Why was there a rise in racism and nativism in the 1920s?
14. What actions did Congress and the president take during the first half of the 1920s to restrict immigration?
15. What national groups were affected most by the new restrictions on immigration?
16. What role did the automobile play in changing the way that young people in the United States lived and socialized?
17. What was the Fundamentalist movement?
18. Why did artists and writers move to Greenwich Village and Chicago's South Side in the 1920s?
19. Why was Harlem the center of the African American renaissance?
20. What were two reasons for the rise in African American political activism?

Critical Thinking
21. **Analyzing Themes: Groups and Institutions** In what ways did the new morality change American family life?
22. **Interpreting** Why was Charles Lindbergh a symbol of modern America?
23. **Determining Cause and Effect** Analyze the causes and effects of the changing role of women in the 1920s.
24. **Identifying** List three works of American art or literature that convey universal themes.
25. **Analyzing** Analyze the impact that Clarence Darrow and William Jennings Bryan had on American society as the lawyers in the Scopes trial.
26. **Categorizing** Use a graphic organizer similar to the one below to list the major organizations and movements of the 1920s and their goals or purposes.

Organizations/Movements	Goals/Purposes

27. **Interpreting Primary Sources** Arna Bontemps was a poet who started his writing career during the Harlem Renaissance. Read the poem and answer the questions that follow.

Critical Thinking
21. The new morality increased youth's independence and allowed women to develop a personal identity that was demonstrated in work and fashion.
22. His solo flights restored Americans' belief in the courageous, pioneering individual.
23. Causes: new morality, more education, and job experience; Effects: greater public freedom, women's contributions in new fields

24. Students' answers will vary but should include reasonable examples from the text.
25. They caused a debate over science and religion.
26. the new morality aimed to expand individual freedom; Fundamentalism aimed to restore the Bible's authority; Prohibition aimed to ban alcohol
27. **a.** He has worked hard all his life but has little to show for it. **b.** disillusionment

HISTORY Online

Self-Check Quiz

Visit the *American Republic Since 1877* Web site at tarvol2.glencoe.com and click on *Self-Check Quizzes– Chapter 15* to assess your knowledge of chapter content.

A Black Man Talks of Reaping

I have sown beside all waters in my day.
I planted deep, within my heart the fear
That wind or fowl would take the grain away.
I planted safe against this stark, lean year.

I scattered seed enough to plant the land
In rows from Canada to Mexico
But for my reaping only what the hand
Can hold at once is all that I can show.

Yet what I sowed and what the orchard yields
My brother's sons are gathering stalk and root,
Small wonder then my children glean in fields
They have not sown, and feed on bitter fruit.

a. What does Bontemps mean by "what the hand can hold at once is all that I can show" and "bitter fruit"?

b. What major theme of Harlem Renaissance writing is evident in this poem?

Practicing Skills

28. **Synthesizing Information** Read the subsections titled "Nativism Resurges" and "Pseudo-Scientific Racism" at the beginning of Section 1. What information is presented in the first subsection? The second? Synthesize the information in these two subsections and write a short statement that describes American attitudes toward immigrants during the 1920s.

Chapter Activities

29. **Research Project** Work with another student to research the art of Georgia O'Keeffe made in the 1920s. Examine how her efforts reflect the characteristics of the Jazz Age, such as experimentation and innovation. Present your findings to the class.

30. **American History Primary Source Document Library CD-ROM** Under *The Roaring Twenties,* read "The Movies" by Preston William Slossen. Work with a few of your classmates to write an article that compares and contrasts the motion picture industry in the 1920s with the motion picture industry today.

Writing Activity

31. **Persuasive Writing** Imagine that you are living during the early 1920s. Marcus Garvey is campaigning to lead African Americans to a new settlement to be founded in Liberia.

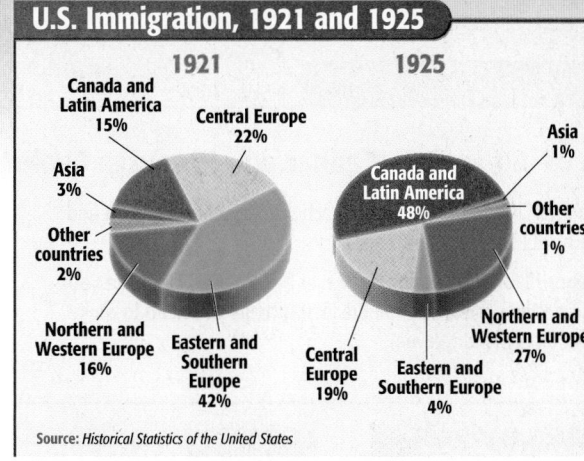

U.S. Immigration, 1921 and 1925

1921

Canada and Latin America 15%
Central Europe 22%
Asia 3%
Other countries 2%
Northern and Western Europe 16%
Eastern and Southern Europe 42%

1925

Asia 1%
Canada and Latin America 48%
Other countries 1%
Northern and Western Europe 27%
Central Europe 19%
Eastern and Southern Europe 4%

Source: *Historical Statistics of the United States*

Write a letter to a newspaper editor in which you take a position on the merits of Garvey's plan. In your letter, describe how you think this plan will affect the nation and your own community.

Geography and History

32. The circle graphs above show immigration numbers in the United States in 1921 and 1925. Study the graphs and answer the questions below.
  a. **Interpreting Graphs** What significant changes in immigration do the circle graphs show?
  b. **Applying Geography Skills** Why did these changes in immigration occur between 1921 and 1925?

Standardized Test Practice

Directions: Choose the best answer to the following question.

Which of the following events of the 1920s contributed to a renewed nativist movement?

A Economic recession

B Harlem Renaissance

C Scopes trial

D Prohibition

Test-Taking Tip: First you must be clear on the meaning of *nativism.* Then use the process of elimination to rule out the answers that do not seem related to the definition of nativism.

CHAPTER 15 The Jazz Age 507

CHAPTER 15 The Jazz Age **507**

HISTORY Online

Have students visit the Web site at tarvol2.glencoe.com to review Chapter 15 and take the Self-Check Quiz.

Writing Activity

31. Letters to the editor will vary but should express a clear point of view.

Geography and History

32. a. They show a dramatic increase in the percentage of immigrants from Latin America and a dramatic decrease in the percentage of immigrants from Eastern and Southern Europe. **b.** changes in immigration laws

---

Standardized Test Practice

Answer: A
Test-Taking Tip: If students know that nativism means favoring native-born people over immigrants, they can probably rule out answers B, C, and D, which are not related to this definition.

Bonus Question?

Ask: Billy Sunday and Aimee Semple McPherson are both regarded as examples of what religious movement of the 1920s? *(Fundamentalism)*

Practicing Skills

28. Students' statements will vary but should reflect the difficulties faced by immigrants during the 1920s.

Chapter Activities

29. Multimedia presentations featuring O'Keeffe and her works are ideal.

30. Students' comparisons will vary and should include specific examples.

Chapter 16 Resources

Timesaving Tools

TeacherWorks™ All-In-One Planner and Resource Center

- **Interactive Teacher Edition** Access your Teacher Wraparound Edition and your classroom resources with a few easy clicks.
- **Interactive Lesson Planner** Planning has never been easier! Organize your week, month, semester, or year with all the lesson helps you need to make teaching creative, timely, and relevant.

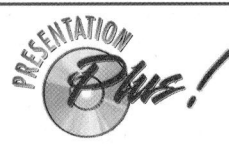

Use Glencoe's **Presentation Plus!** multimedia teacher tool to easily present dynamic lessons that visually excite your students. Using Microsoft PowerPoint® you can customize the presentations to create your own personalized lessons.

TEACHING TRANSPARENCIES

Graphic Organizer 1 L2

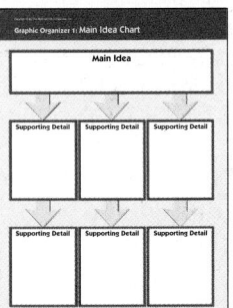

Why It Matters Chapter Transparency 16 L2

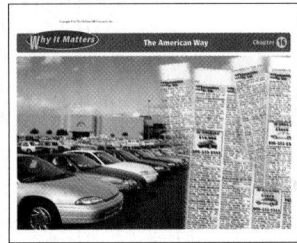

APPLICATION AND ENRICHMENT

Linking Past and Present Activity 16 L2

Enrichment Activity 16 L3

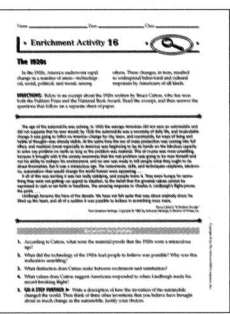

Primary Source Reading 16 L2

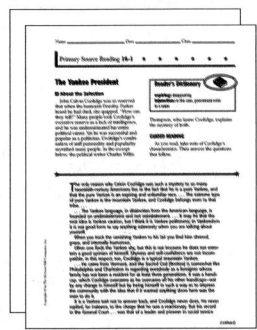

REVIEW AND REINFORCEMENT

Reteaching Activity 16 L1

Vocabulary Activity 16 L1

Time Line Activity 16 L2

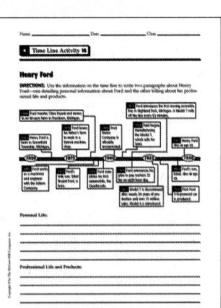

Critical Thinking Skills Activity 16 L2

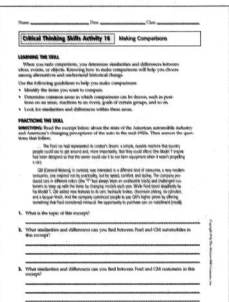

Meeting NCSS Standards

The following standards are covered in Chapter 16:

Section 1	VI	Power, Authority, and Governance: B, E
Section 2	VIII	Science, Technology, and Society: A, B, C
Section 3	VII	Production, Distribution, and Consumption: A, D, F

Local Standards

_____

_____

_____

_____

_____

Chapter 16 Resources

ASSESSMENT AND EVALUATION

**Chapter 16 Test
Form A L2**

**Chapter 16 Test
Form B L2**

**Standardized Test Practice
Workbook Activity 16 L2**

**Performance Assessment
Activities and Rubrics 16
L1/ELL**

**ExamView® Pro
Testmaker CD-ROM**

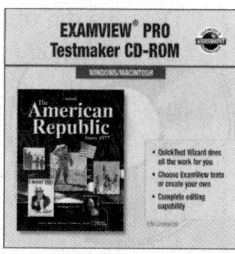

MULTIMEDIA

- Vocabulary PuzzleMaker CD-ROM
- Interactive Tutor Self-Assessment CD-ROM
- ExamView® Pro Testmaker CD-ROM
- Audio Program
- American History Primary Source Documents Library CD-ROM
- MindJogger Videoquiz
- Presentation Plus! CD-ROM
- TeacherWorks™ CD-ROM
- Interactive Student Edition CD-ROM
- Glencoe Skillbuilder Interactive Workbook CD-ROM, Level 2
- The *American Republic Since 1877* Video Program
- American Music: Hits Through History
- American Music: Cultural Traditions

SPANISH RESOURCES

The following Spanish language materials are available:

- Spanish Reading Essentials and Study Guide
- Spanish Guided Reading Activities
- Spanish Reteaching Activities
- Spanish Quizzes and Tests
- Spanish Vocabulary Activities
- Spanish Summaries
- The Declaration of Independence and United States Constitution Spanish Translation

---

The following videotape programs are available from Glencoe as supplements to Chapter 16:

- **Amelia Earhart** (ISBN 1-56-501960-1)
- **Henry Ford: Tin Lizzy Tycoon** (ISBN 1-56-501380-8)
- **Radio: Out of Thin Air** (ISBN 0-76-700464-7)

To order, call Glencoe at 1-800-334-7344. To find classroom resources to accompany many of these videos, check the following home pages:
A&E Television: www.aande.com
The History Channel: www.historychannel.com

Use our Web site for additional resources. All essential content is covered in the Student Edition.

You and your students can visit tarvol2.glencoe.com, the Web site companion to the *American Republic Since 1877*. This innovative integration of electronic and print media offers your students a wealth of opportunities. The student text directs students to the Web site for the following options:

- **Chapter Overviews**
- **Self-Check Quizzes**
- **Student Web Activities**
- **Textbook Updates**

Answers to the student Web activities are provided for you in the **Web Activity Lesson Plans.** Additional Web resources and Interactive Tutor Puzzles are also available.

Chapter 16 Resources

SECTION RESOURCES

Daily Objectives	Reproducible Resources	Multimedia Resources
SECTION 1 **Presidential Politics** 1. Describe the corruption that tainted the Harding administration. 2. Explain how Calvin Coolidge restored public confidence after assuming the presidency.	Reproducible Lesson Plan 16–1 Daily Lecture and Discussion Notes 16–1 Guided Reading Activity 16–1* Section Quiz 16–1* Reading Essentials and Study Guide 16–1* Performance Assessment Activities and Rubrics	Daily Focus Skills Transparency 16–1 Interactive Tutor Self-Assessment CD-ROM ExamView® Pro Testmaker CD-ROM* Presentation Plus! CD-ROM TeacherWorks™ CD-ROM Audio Program
SECTION 2 **A Growing Economy** 1. Analyze how the growing importance of the automobile and other new industries improved the U.S. standard of living. 2. Analyze the growing economic crisis in farming in the 1920s.	Reproducible Lesson Plan 16–2 Daily Lecture and Discussion Notes 16–2 Guided Reading Activity 16–2* Section Quiz 16–2* Reading Essentials and Study Guide 16–2* Performance Assessment Activities and Rubrics	Daily Focus Skills Transparency 16–2 Interactive Tutor Self-Assessment CD-ROM ExamView® Pro Testmaker CD-ROM* Presentation Plus! CD-ROM TeacherWorks™ CD-ROM Audio Program
SECTION 3 **The Policies of Prosperity** 1. Explain Andrew Mellon's economic strategies for maintaining prosperity. 2. Describe how the United States remained involved in world affairs without joining the League of Nations.	Reproducible Lesson Plan 16–3 Daily Lecture and Discussion Notes 16–3 Guided Reading Activity 16–3* Section Quiz 16–3* Reading Essentials and Study Guide 16–3* Performance Assessment Activities and Rubrics	Daily Focus Skills Transparency 16–3 American Art & Architecture Interactive Tutor Self-Assessment CD-ROM ExamView® Pro Testmaker CD-ROM* Presentation Plus! CD-ROM Skillbuilder Interactive Workbook, Level 2 TeacherWorks™ CD-ROM Vocabulary PuzzleMaker CD-ROM Audio Program American Music: Hits Through History

0:00 OUT OF TIME?
Assign the Chapter 16 **Reading Essentials and Study Guide.**

*Also Available in Spanish

 Printed Materials   Transparency   CD-ROM   DVD

 Poster   Music Program   Audio Program

NATIONAL GEOGRAPHIC

Teacher's Corner

INDEX TO NATIONAL GEOGRAPHIC MAGAZINE

The following articles relate to this chapter.

- "Growing up in East Harlem," May 1990
- "Offbeat New Orleans," January 1995
- "Traveling the Blues Highway," April 1999

NATIONAL GEOGRAPHIC SOCIETY PRODUCTS

To order the following, call National Geographic at 1-800-368-2728:

- *Eyewitness to the 20th Century* (Book)
- *Historical Atlas of the United States* (Atlas)

NGS ONLINE

Access National Geographic's Web site for current events, atlas updates, activities, links, interactive features, and archives.
www.nationalgeographic.com

MEETING SPECIAL NEEDS

In addition to the Differentiated Instruction strategies found in each section, the following resources are also suitable for your special needs students:

- *ExamView® Pro Testmaker CD-ROM* allows teachers to tailor tests by reducing answer choices.
- The *Audio Program* includes the entire narrative of the student edition so that less-proficient readers can listen to the words as they read them.
- The *Reading Essentials and Study Guide* provides the same content as the student edition but is written two grade levels below the textbook.
- *Guided Reading Activities* give less-proficient readers point-by-point instructions to increase comprehension as they read each textbook section.
- *Enrichment Activities* includes a stimulating collection of readings and activities for gifted and talented students.

KEY TO ABILITY LEVELS

Teaching strategies have been coded.

L1   BASIC activities for all students
L2   AVERAGE activities for average to above-average students
L3   CHALLENGING activities for above-average students
ELL ENGLISH LANGUAGE LEARNER activities

From the Classroom of...

F. Rick Johnston
Shroder Paideia Academy
Cincinnati, OH

"All the News That's Fit to Print"

Introduce the activity by asking students to predict the types of news stories that will be found in a daily newspaper. Responses may include: sports; business; classified; national, international, and local news; entertainment; and editorial. List these quickly on the board.

Ask: If a current newspaper provides a good way to get a sense of national issues and concerns, could newspapers from earlier times in U.S. history reflect the issues and concerns of that era? Why or why not?

Point out that this chapter focuses on the 1920s. Introduce the era of the postwar decade. Explain that the class will be using the format of modern newspapers to create a 1920s newspaper. As the class reads the chapter, have students select "stories" to "cover." Students should label their stories according to the type of "news" it is. For example, the Scopes trial would go on the national news page. The stories should represent the social, economic, and political developments in the chapter.

ADDITIONAL RESOURCES FROM GLENCOE

- American Music: Cultural Traditions
- American Art & Architecture
- Outline Map Resource Book
- U.S. Desk Map
- Building Geography Skills for Life
- Inclusion for the High School Social Studies Classroom Strategies and Activities
- Teaching Strategies for the American History Classroom (Including Block Scheduling Pacing Guides)
- Dinah Zike's High School American History Reading and Study Skills Foldables

Block Schedule

Activities that are suited to use within the block scheduling framework are identified by:

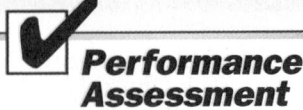

✔ Performance Assessment

Refer to Activity 16 in the Performance Assessment Activities and Rubrics booklet. 📁

Why It Matters Activity

Have students interview five adults whom they know and ask them when and how they got their first automobile. After students have conducted their interviews, ask them to report their findings. Then ask students how important they think automobiles are to the American way of life. Students should evaluate their answers after they have completed the chapter.

GLENCOE TECHNOLOGY

The *American Republic Since 1877* Video Program

To learn more about the importance of the radio in American life, have students view the Chapter 16 video, "Tuning in to Radio in the 1920s," from the *American Republic Since 1877* Video Program.

MindJogger Videoquiz

Use the **MindJogger Videoquiz** to preview Chapter 16 content.

 Both programs available in DVD

CHAPTER

16 Normalcy and Good Times

1921–1929

Why It Matters

Prosperity was the theme of the 1920s, and national policy favored business. Although farmers were going through an economic depression, most people remained optimistic about the economy. The middle class bought on credit the many new convenience products available. One of the most popular purchases of the day was the automobile, which had a major impact on how Americans lived.

The Impact Today

Important elements of American life were first seen at this time.
- *The automobile remains central to American transportation.*
- *Credit is a standard means for making purchases.*

🔘 *The* **American Republic Since 1877 Video** *The Chapter 16 video, "Tuning in to Radio in the 1920s," describes the growth of a mass media culture in the United States and the importance of the radio.*

1920
- Women vote in national election for the first time

1921
- Washington Conference convenes
- Farm Bloc organized in U.S. Congress

1923
- Teapot Dome scandal erupts
- Ford Motor Company gains 50 percent of the new car market
- President Harding dies

1924
- Dawes Plan negotiated with France, Britain, and Germany
- Calvin Coolidge elected president

United States PRESIDENTS

Harding 1921–1923

Coolidge 1923–1929

1921   *1923*   *1925*

World

1923
- Hitler's Munich coup fails

1924
- Leader of Soviet Union, Vladimir Lenin, dies

1925
- Soldier-leader Reza Khan pronounced shah of Iran

508

📖 **Reading Strategy** **PURPOSE FOR READING**

Mindstreaming Use this strategy to bring out students' background knowledge before beginning a new chapter. Have students pair up. Then have student A talk for one minute about the 1920s, telling everything he or she knows, while student B listens and encourages. Reverse roles for another minute. Finally, solicit the information discussed by the pairs. **L1**

📁 Refer to *Inclusion for the High School Social Studies Classroom Strategies and Activities* in the TCR.

HISTORY Online

Introduce students to chapter content and key terms by having them access the **Chapter 16 Overview** at tarvol2.glencoe.com.

More About the Art

Howard A. Thain was born in Dallas, Texas. He studied art in St. Louis, Chicago, and New York City. The Impressionist influence can be seen in this oil painting celebrating the opening of Florenz Ziegfeld's "No Foolin'." In the upper right hand corner of the painting, you can see part of the Globe Theater's marquee—"No Foolin'—Globe—Glorifying the American Girl."

Opening Night, Ziegfeld Follies by Howard A. Thain captures the excitement surrounding the opening of a new musical revue in New York City.

TIME LINE ACTIVITY

Have students select an event from the time lines on pages 508–509, 510, 514, and 521. Ask students to read the corresponding portion of the chapter to identify the cause(s) and effect(s) of the events.

1927
• 15 millionth Model T built

1926
• British General Strike paralyzes the British economy

1928
• Kellogg-Briand Pact proposes an end to war

1929
• U.S. radio sales exceed $800 million

Hoover 1929–1933

1929
• Lateran Treaties with Italy make the Vatican sovereign territory

1927

1929

HISTORY Online

Chapter Overview
Visit the *American Republic Since 1877* Web site at tarvol2.glencoe.com and click on *Chapter Overviews— Chapter 16* to preview chapter information.

FOLDABLES Study Organizer

Dinah Zike's Foldables are three-dimensional, interactive graphic organizers that help students practice basic writing skills, review key vocabulary terms, and identify main ideas. Have students complete the foldable activity in the *Dinah Zike's Reading and Study Skills Foldables* booklet.

509

GRAPHIC ORGANIZER ACTIVITY

Organizing Information Have students create a graphic organizer similar to the one below to classify members of Harding's administration as effective, ineffective, or involved in scandal.

Effective	Ineffective	Involved in Scandal
Charles Evans Hughes, Secretary of State	Charles Sawyer, White House Physician	Charles R. Forbes, head of Veterans Bureau
Herbert Hoover, Secretary of Commerce	Daniel Crissinger, Chairman of the Federal Reserve	Albert B. Fall, Secretary of the Interior

1 FOCUS

Section Overview

This section focuses on the Harding and Coolidge administrations.

BELLRINGER
Skillbuilder Activity

Project transparency and have students answer the question.

Daily Focus Skills Transparency 16–1

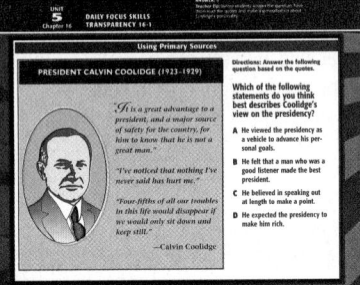

Reading Preview

Answers to Graphic:
Presidential Politics
I. The Harding Administration
   A. A Self-Doubter in the White House
   B. The Ohio Gang
   C. The Teapot Dome Scandal
II. The Coolidge Administration
   A. "Silent Cal" Takes Over
   B. The Election of 1924

Preteaching Vocabulary
Have students list the Key Terms and Names and add information to clarify their significance.

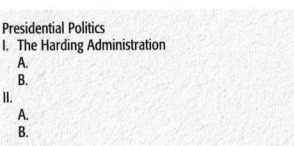

Guide to Reading

Main Idea
Warren Harding's administration suffered from several scandals. His successor, Calvin Coolidge, promised to support business.

Key Terms and Names
normalcy, Ohio Gang, Albert B. Fall, Teapot Dome scandal, immunity, Progressive Party, Robert M. La Follette

Reading Strategy
Taking Notes As you read about Presidents Harding and Coolidge, use the major headings of the section to create an outline similar to the one below.

Presidential Politics
I. The Harding Administration
   A.
   B.
II.
   A.
   B.

Reading Objectives
• **Describe** the corruption that tainted the Harding administration.
• **Explain** how Calvin Coolidge restored public confidence after assuming the presidency.

Section Theme
Government and Democracy The "Ohio Gang" of the Harding administration created scandals and political upheaval.

Preview of Events

| ♦1920 | ♦1922 | ♦1924 | ♦1926 |

1920
Women vote in national election for the first time; Warren G. Harding elected president

1923
Teapot Dome scandal; Harding dies; Calvin Coolidge becomes president

1924
Coolidge elected president in his own right

★ An American Story ★

Calvin Coolidge (right) being sworn in as president after his 1924 election

In August 1923, Vice President Calvin Coolidge was taking a short vacation at his family's homestead in Plymouth Notch, Vermont. The straitlaced Coolidge went to bed at 9:00 as usual on August 2, but at 2:30 A.M., his father woke him. "I noticed that his voice trembled," Coolidge said later. "I knew that something of the gravest nature had occurred." After learning that President Warren G. Harding was dead, Coolidge dressed hurriedly and went downstairs. Shortly afterward, in a small, sparsely furnished room lit by a flickering kerosene lamp, the elder Coolidge, a farmer and justice of the peace, got out the family Bible and administered the presidential oath of office to his son.

Later, while painting a portrait of the new president, artist Charles Hopkinson asked, "Mr. Coolidge, what was the first thought that came into your mind when you were told that Mr. Harding was dead and the presidency was yours?" Coolidge replied, "I thought I could swing it."

—adapted from *Flappers, Bootleggers, "Typhoid Mary" and the Bomb*

The Harding Administration

Coolidge assumed the presidency during a time when Americans yearned to go back to simpler and steadier times after the carnage of World War I. Coolidge's predecessor, Warren G. Harding, had tailored his presidency to this goal. The oldest of eight children, Harding was born in 1865 in Corsica, Ohio. As an adult, he was active in civic and fraternal organizations, and he also published the *Marion Daily Star.* In 1898 Harding was elected to the Ohio legislature. He fit in comfortably with the powerful Ohio Republican

510 CHAPTER 16 Normalcy and Good Times

SECTION RESOURCES

📁 Reproducible Masters
• Reproducible Lesson Plan 16–1
• Daily Lecture and Discussion Notes 16–1
• Guided Reading Activity 16–1
• Section Quiz 16–1
• Reading Essentials and Study Guide 16–1
• Performance Assessment Activities and Rubrics

💿 Transparencies
• Daily Focus Skills Transparency 16–1

Multimedia
🔵 Interactive Tutor Self-Assessment CD-ROM
🔵 ExamView® Pro Testmaker CD-ROM
🔵 Presentation Plus! CD-ROM
🔵 TeacherWorks™ CD-ROM
🔊 Audio Program

political machine and won election as lieutenant governor in 1903. He failed in his bid for governor in 1910 but was elected to the United States Senate four years later. After serving one term in the Senate, Harding ran for and won the presidency in 1920.

A Self-Doubter in the White House With his silver hair and impressive bearing, Harding looked like a president, but he thought he lacked the intellectual qualifications for the job. "I have such a sure understanding of my own inefficiency," he once said, "that I should really be ashamed to presume myself fitted to reach out for a place of such responsibility."

Despite such doubts, Harding's political philosophy fit in well with the times. He ran on the campaign slogan to return to normalcy, or a return to "normal" life after the war. Harding's charm and genial manner endeared him to the nation. The quiet gloom of President Wilson's last years was replaced by the open, easygoing atmosphere of the first days of the Harding administration. On the day of his election, he went out to play a round of golf—a confident, relaxed gesture.

GOVERNMENT

The Ohio Gang Harding made several distinguished appointments to the cabinet, including former Supreme Court justice Charles Evans Hughes as secretary of state, former Food Administrator Herbert Hoover as secretary of commerce, and business tycoon Andrew Mellon as secretary of the treasury.

Many of Harding's other appointments, however, were disastrous. He gave many cabinet posts and other high-level jobs to friends and political allies from Ohio. Harding named Charles "Doc" Sawyer from Marion, Ohio, as White House physician, a post that came with the rank of brigadier general. Harding made his boyhood friend Daniel Crissinger chairman of the Federal Reserve Board and selected Colonel Charles R. Forbes—another Ohio acquaintance—to head the Veterans Bureau.

Harding felt more comfortable among his old poker-playing friends, known as the **Ohio Gang,** than he did around such sober and serious people as Herbert Hoover. Alice Roosevelt Longworth, the daughter of Theodore Roosevelt, was a keen observer of Washington society. She wrote that it was common to find the Ohio Gang in the White House study, and here she describes a typical scene:

> ❝The air [would be] heavy with tobacco smoke, trays with bottles containing every imaginable brand of whiskey . . . cards and poker chips at hand—a general atmosphere of waistcoat unbuttoned, feet on desk, and spittoons alongside.❞
>
> —quoted in *The Perils of Prosperity, 1914–1932*

The Ohio Gang did more than drink, smoke, and play poker with the president. Some members used their positions to sell government jobs, pardons, and protection from prosecution. Forbes sold scarce medical supplies from veterans hospitals and kept the money for himself, costing the taxpayers over $200 million. When Harding learned what was going on, he complained privately that he had been betrayed. He said that he had no troubles with his enemies, but his friends were a different story: "They're the ones that keep me walking the floor nights!"

Inkwell depicting Warren Harding

Picturing History

Return to Normalcy Warren Harding did some of his campaigning from his front porch in Ohio. Why do you think Harding's slogan, "Return to Normalcy," was successful?

2 TEACH

Daily Lecture and Discussion Notes 16–1

Copyright © by The McGraw-Hill Companies, Inc.

Daily Lecture and Discussion Notes

Chapter 16, Section 1

Did You Know? Most historians rank President Warren G. Harding as one of the country's weakest presidents. They believe he failed as president because he was weak-willed and a poor judge of character.

I. **The Harding Administration** (pages 510–512)

A. In 1920, when Warren G. Harding ran for president, most Americans wanted to return to simpler times. His campaign slogan to return to **normalcy**, or a "normal" life after the war, made him very popular and he won the presidency.

B. Harding made a few distinguished appointments to the cabinet, but most appointments were given to friends. His old poker-playing friends became known as the "Ohio Gang." Some members used their government positions to sell jobs, pardons,

Drawing a Political Cartoon Have students draw a political cartoon to illustrate one of the scandals of the Harding Administration. Remind them that the cartoon should express a clear point of view. **L1**

📁 Use the rubric for creating a political cartoon, pamphlet, or handbill on pages 77–78 in the *Performance Assessment Activities and Rubrics.*

Picturing History

Answer: Many people wanted a less activist government after the war.

Ask: What characteristics made Harding look presidential? *(handsome, silver hair, impressive bearing)*

Reading Strategy   READING THE TEXT

Taking Notes Students can use notes to group, outline, and organize information. As students read this section, have them list the main ideas about Warren Harding's and Calvin Coolidge's presidencies in an outline format. At the end of the section, ask students to write a one-paragraph summary of the section using their outlines. **L1** ELL

📁 Refer to *Inclusion for the High School Social Studies Classroom Strategies and Activities* in the TCR.

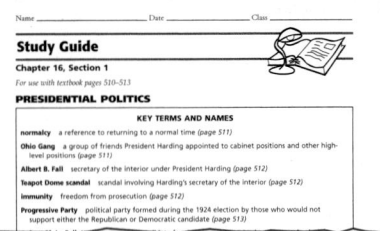

The news media popularized the elephant and donkey symbols in election coverage.

✓ **Reading Check**

Answer: Americans yearned for simpler times after World War I.

🏛 **Analyzing** *Political Cartoons*

Answer: Secretary of the Interior Albert Fall; because he was involved in the Teapot Dome scandal

3 ASSESS

Assign Section 1 Assessment as homework or as an in-class activity.

💿 Have students use the **Interactive Tutor Self-Assessment CD-ROM.**

L1/ELL

Reading Essentials and Study Guide 16-1

Name _____ Date _____ Class _____

Study Guide
Chapter 16, Section 1
For use with textbook pages 510–513

PRESIDENTIAL POLITICS

KEY TERMS AND NAMES

normalcy a reference to returning to a normal time *(page 511)*

Ohio Gang a group of friends President Harding appointed to cabinet positions and other high-level positions *(page 511)*

Albert B. Fall secretary of the interior under President Harding *(page 512)*

Teapot Dome scandal involving Harding's secretary of the interior *(page 512)*

immunity freedom from prosecution *(page 512)*

Progressive Party political party formed during the 1924 election by those who would not support either the Republican or Democratic candidate *(page 513)*

Cartoon Symbols Political cartoonists routinely use symbols to get their message across. Two of the most enduring have been the donkey, representing the Democrats, and the elephant, representing the Republicans (also known as the GOP, or the Grand Old Party). On November 7, 1874, cartoonist Thomas Nast became the first to use the symbols in a cartoon that appeared in *Harper's Weekly.*

In June 1923, amid the scandal in the Veterans Bureau and rumors of other unethical behavior, Harding and the First Lady left to tour the West. En route from Alaska to California, he became ill with what was probably a heart attack. He died in San Francisco on August 2, shortly before the news of the Forbes scandal broke.

The Teapot Dome Scandal Other scandals also came to light. Harding's secretary of the interior, **Albert B. Fall,** secretly allowed private interests to lease lands containing U.S. Navy oil reserves at Teapot Dome, Wyoming, and Elk Hills, California. In return, Fall received bribes from these private interests totaling more than $300,000. Eventually the Senate investigated what the newspapers named the **Teapot Dome scandal,** and Secretary Fall became the first cabinet officer in history to go to prison.

The last Harding administration scandal involved Attorney General Harry Daugherty, Harding's former campaign manager. It concerned a German-owned American company that the American government had seized during World War I as enemy property. To acquire the company and its valuable chemical patents, a German agent bribed a "go-between" politician, and a portion of the bribe ended up in an Ohio bank account that Daugherty controlled.

Under investigation by his own Justice Department, Daugherty refused to turn over requested files and bank records. He also refused to testify under oath, claiming immunity, or freedom from prosecution, on the grounds that he had had confidential dealings with the president. Daugherty's actions disgusted the new president, Calvin Coolidge, who demanded his resignation. The tattered reputation of Harding's presidency dissolved in scandal and corruption.

✓ **Reading Check** **Describing** Why was Harding's emphasis on "normalcy" an effective campaign strategy?

512 CHAPTER 16 Normalcy and Good Times

The Coolidge Administration

Just as Harding's promise of "normalcy" had appealed to war-weary voters in 1920, the virtue of his successor came as a welcome change from the turmoil of the Harding administration's corruption. Born on July 4, 1872, John Calvin Coolidge grew up on the Vermont farm that his family had worked for five generations. While governor of Massachusetts, Coolidge rose to national prominence for his handling of the Boston police strike in 1919. Shortly afterward, he was asked to run as Harding's vice president.

"Silent Cal" Takes Over Coolidge was very different from Harding. Harding had enjoyed the easy conversation and company of old friends. Coolidge, joked a critic, could be "silent in five languages." With his simple and frugal manner, he contrasted not only with Harding but also with the spirit of the time, the booming, materialistic era of the Roaring Twenties.

Coolidge quickly distanced himself from the Harding administration. He named Harlan Fiske Stone, dean of the Columbia Law School, to replace Daugherty as attorney general. He also asked the most capable cabinet members—Hughes, Mellon, and Hoover—to stay on.

🏛 **Analyzing** *Political Cartoons*

Teapot Dome Scandal In this cartoon, Democrats are enjoying the troubles the Teapot Dome scandal has caused for the GOP elephant. Who is shown being dragged along by the scandal? Why?

© N. Y. "Tribune."

DIFFERENTIATED INSTRUCTION

Reading Support Have students write campaign slogans for the 1920 presidential election campaign. Instruct students to write two slogans for each candidate that reflect their stands on issues in the 1920 campaign. Encourage students to use library and Internet resources to find examples of recent campaign slogans. Students should also compare the 1920 election issues and candidate policies to the issues and policies discussed in the recent presidential election. **L2**

👉 Refer to *Inclusion for the High School Social Studies Classroom Strategies and Activities* in the TCR.

Coolidge's philosophy of government was simple. He believed that prosperity rested on business leadership and that part of his job as president was to make sure that government interfered with business and industry as little as possible. He once said, "Four-fifths of all our troubles in this life would disappear if we would only sit down and keep still."

Calmly and cautiously, Coolidge worked to restore integrity to the presidency. In the year following Harding's death and the revelations of scandals, Coolidge's presidency avoided crises and continued the nation's expanding prosperity. Coolidge easily won the Republican Party's nomination for president in 1924.

The Election of 1924 Even though the scandals of the Harding administration presented the Democrats with a ready-made issue, they lost the chance for victory. Deeply divided between their urban Eastern constituency and their rural following in the South and West, the Democrats had difficulty agreeing on a nominee. They finally compromised on John W. Davis of West Virginia after 103 attempts to find someone acceptable to a majority of the delegates.

The Republicans effectively campaigned on the slogan "Keep Cool with Coolidge," and they urged Americans to retain the party that favored business. In his economic policies, Coolidge aligned himself—and the government—with prosperity and big business.

Not everyone was content to choose between the Republicans and Democrats. Defectors from both parties joined farm, labor, and religious activists to form the new Progressive Party, nominating Wisconsin senator **Robert M. La Follette** as their candidate. Although La Follette captured 16.6

 History

Cool Coolidge President Coolidge believed the nation would run more smoothly if the government was less involved. How did the public react to Coolidge's message on Election Day?

percent of the popular vote, or a total of almost 5 million, he and Davis combined could not keep the Republicans from winning the election. Coolidge won easily with more than half the popular vote and 382 electoral votes.

In a speech to the American Society of Newspaper Editors in 1925, Coolidge said, "The chief business of the American people is business. The man who builds a factory builds a temple. The man who works there worships there." The *Wall Street Journal* joyously exclaimed, "Never before, here or anywhere else, has a government been so completely fused with business." By avoiding war, reform, and scandal, Coolidge promised to give the United States the normalcy Harding had failed to deliver.

✓ **Reading Check** **Summarizing** How did Calvin Coolidge restore public confidence after becoming president?

 History

Answer: positively, by awarding him more than half of the popular vote and 382 electoral votes

Reteach
Have students list the Harding administration scandals.

Enrich
Ask interested students to investigate what happened to Albert Fall or Harry Daugherty.

✓ **Reading Check**
Answer: He distanced himself from the Harding administration.

Study Central™ provides summaries, interactive games, and online graphic organizers to help students review section content.

SECTION 1 ASSESSMENT

HISTORY Online **Study Central™** To review this section, go to tarvol2.glencoe.com and click on **Study Central™**.

Checking for Understanding
1. **Define:** normalcy, immunity.
2. **Identify:** Ohio Gang, Albert B. Fall, Teapot Dome scandal, Robert M. La Follette.
3. **Evaluate** the effects of the Teapot Dome scandal on citizens' views of the federal government.

Reviewing Themes
4. **Government and Democracy** How did the Ohio Gang tarnish the Harding Administration?

Critical Thinking
5. **Interpreting** How did the Democrats lose the chance for victory in the election of 1924?
6. **Categorizing** Use a graphic organizer similar to the one below to compare and contrast the politics and presidencies of Harding and Coolidge.

	Politics	Presidency
Harding		
Coolidge		

Analyzing Visuals
7. **Analyzing Photographs** Examine the photograph of Calvin Coolidge on this page. How did Coolidge's actions demonstrate effective leadership following the Harding administration?

Writing About History
8. **Expository Writing** Imagine you are a newspaper reporter during President Harding's term. Write an article breaking the news of the Teapot Dome scandal.

CHAPTER 16 Normalcy and Good Times **513**

---

4 CLOSE
Have students explain how Calvin Coolidge restored public confidence after assuming the presidency.

SECTION 1 ASSESSMENT ANSWERS

1. Terms are in blue.
2. Ohio Gang (p. 511), Albert B. Fall (p. 512), Teapot Dome scandal (p. 512), Robert M. La Follette (p. 513)
3. viewed government as corrupt
4. used their positions for personal advantage
5. could not agree on a nominee
6. Harding: open politics, scandal-ridden presidency; Coolidge: simple politics, business-oriented presidency
7. avoided scandal, supported business prosperity
8. Students' articles will vary. Articles' style should be similar to a news story with an attention-grabbing lead.

1 FOCUS

Section Overview

This section focuses on the economic growth of the 1920s.

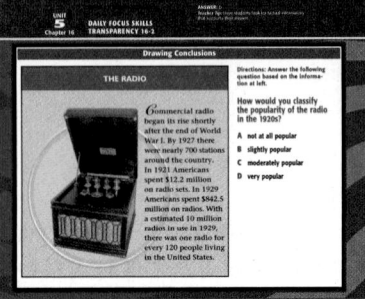
Reading Preview

Answers to Graphic: Industry: air travel, automobiles, consumer goods, radio; society: consumer-oriented, consumer credit, workers shifting from farming to industry, labor saving devices, growing mobility

Preteaching Vocabulary
Have students skim this section to find time references for each of the Key Terms and Names.

SECTION 2 A Growing Economy

Guide to Reading

Main Idea
The United States experienced stunning economic growth during the 1920s.

Key Terms and Names
mass production, assembly line, Model T, Charles Lindbergh, National Broadcasting Company, Columbia Broadcasting System, welfare capitalism, open shop

Reading Strategy
Organizing As you read about the booming era of the 1920s, complete a graphic organizer to analyze the causes of economic growth and prosperity in the 1920s.

Changes in 1920s

Industry   Society

Reading Objectives
• **Analyze** how the growing importance of the automobile and other new industries improved the U.S. standard of living.
• **Analyze** the growing economic crisis in farming in the 1920s.

Section Theme
Science and Technology New technology such as the automobile and radio helped reshape American lifestyles.

Preview of Events

◆1920   ◆1923   ◆1926   ◆1929

1920
First commercial radio broadcast

1922
Congress passes Fordney-McCumber Act

1923
Ford gains 50 percent of the new car market

1927
The 15 millionth Ford Model T rolls off the assembly line

1929
U.S. radio sales exceed $800 million

★ *An American Story* ★

Henry Ford

At around 2:00 A.M. on June 4, 1896, Henry Ford and his friend Jim Bishop readied Ford's "horseless carriage" for a test. The shop doors were too small for the contraption to pass through, so Ford immediately seized a sledgehammer and began knocking out an opening in the brick. Ford later recalled the scene that followed:

❝Mr. Bishop had his bicycle ready to ride ahead and warn drivers of horse-drawn vehicles—if indeed any were to be met with at such an hour. . . . I set the choke and spun the flywheel. As the motor roared and sputtered to life, I climbed aboard and started off. . . .❞

There were many such trips in the following days. Bishop would bicycle ahead, stopping at saloons and stores to warn people that they should come out and hold their horses. Many of the onlookers responded by calling out, "Crazy Henry!" As he climbed out of the car, Ford invariably responded, "Yes, crazy. Crazy like a fox."

—**adapted from** *The Fords: An American Epic*

The Rise of New Industries

Although neither Ford nor Bishop realized it at the time, "Crazy Henry's" horseless carriage would revolutionize American transportation and with it American society. By the 1920s, the automobile had become an accepted part of American life. In a 1925 survey conducted in Muncie, Indiana, 21 out of 26 families who owned cars did not have bathtubs with running water. Explaining why her family decided a car was more important than indoor plumbing, a farm wife said, "You can't ride to town in a bathtub."

514 CHAPTER 16 Normalcy and Good Times

The automobile was just one part of a rising standard of living that Americans experienced in the 1920s. Real per capita earnings, essentially unchanged during the previous 30 years, soared 22 percent. Meanwhile, as Americans' wages increased, their work hours decreased. In 1923 U.S. Steel cut its daily work shift from 12 hours to 8 hours. In 1926 Henry Ford cut the workweek for his employees from six days to five, and International Harvester, a maker of trucks, tractors, and other farm machinery, instituted an annual two-week paid vacation for employees.

At the same time, the rise of mass production, or large-scale product manufacturing usually done by machinery, created more supply and reduced consumer costs. This formula reshaped the American economy. Within this prosperous and productive atmosphere, innovation thrived and new industries emerged.

TECHNOLOGY

The Assembly Line Another major industrial development enormously increased manufacturing efficiency. First adopted by carmaker Henry Ford, the assembly line divided operations into simple tasks that unskilled workers could do and cut unnecessary

motion to a minimum. In 1913, Ford installed the first moving assembly line at his plant in Highland Park, Michigan. By the following year, workers were building automobiles every 93 minutes. Previously, the task had taken 12 hours. By 1925 a Ford car was rolling off the line every 10 seconds. "The way to make automobiles," Ford said, "is to make one automobile like another . . . to make them come through the factory all alike, just as one pin is like another pin when it comes from the pin factory."

Ford's assembly-line product was the **Model T**— affectionately called the "Tin Lizzie" or "Flivver." In 1908, the Model T's first year, it sold for $850. In 1914 mass production reduced the price to $490. Three years later, improved assembly-line methods and a high volume of sales brought the price down to $360. By 1924 Model Ts were selling for $295, and Ford sold millions of them. His business philosophy was simple: lower the cost per car and thereby increase the volume of sales. "Every time I reduce the charge for our car by one dollar," he boasted, "I get a thousand new buyers." In this way, Ford made the automobile available to millions of American consumers.

Ford also increased his workers' wages in 1914 to an unprecedented $5 a day and reduced the workday

2 TEACH

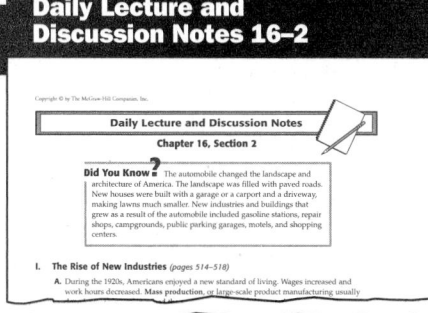

Daily Lecture and Discussion Notes 16–2

Demonstrating a Concept
Have students work in small groups to demonstrate the efficiency concept behind the assembly line. Suggest that students use children's building toys for their demonstrations. **L1**

TECHNOLOGY & History

Background: Committed to large-volume production of the Model T, Henry Ford innovated mass-production techniques at his plant in Highland Park, Michigan. The plant opened in 1910, but Ford did not introduce the moving assembly line until 1913. "The step forward in assembly line," Ford said, "came when we began taking the work to the men instead of the men to the work."
Answer: The price fell as the time to manufacture the vehicle decreased.
Ask: What kind of injuries are assembly line workers prone to? (repetitive stress injuries)

TECHNOLOGY & History

The Assembly Line

The idea of an assembly line had existed before Henry Ford, but he helped popularize its use in manufacturing. Ford combined sub-assembly lines into one continuously moving line, which was positioned at waist level to reduce back strain. Ford's Highland Park factory featured a multistoried assembly line that reduced the construction time of a single Model T from 12 hours, 8 minutes to 1 hour, 33 minutes. *How did Ford's assembly technique affect the price of his product?*

1 Tires were assembled and delivered downstairs using chutes.

2 Engines and gas tanks were assembled at other ends of the factory floor and delivered to the chassis sub-assembly.

3 Automobile were assembled and dropped onto the separately-assembled chassis with a pully.

In 1914 Ford Motor Company produced 308,162 automobiles—more than all other auto manufacturers combined.

Reading Strategy — READING THE TEXT

Analyzing Information Organize the class into groups of five students each. Assign the following roles to one member of each group: advertising executive, assembly line worker, housewife, farmer, and union leader. Pose this question: How has the automobile affected your life and other Americans like you? Students should play their assigned roles when answering the question. Encourage members of the group to share information and ask questions of each other until everyone in the group has a good understanding of the effect the automobile had on society. **L1**

Refer to *Inclusion for the High School Social Studies Classroom Strategies and Activities* in the TCR.

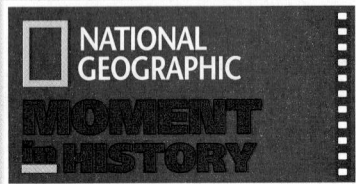
Making Comparisons Have students place images of a Model T and a popular contemporary family vehicle on a display board or large piece of paper. Ask them to compare the features of the vehicles. Suggest that students use callouts to highlight the differences and similarities. **L1**

NATIONAL GEOGRAPHIC
MOMENT in HISTORY

In 1920 there were about 8 million cars on the road but fewer than 36,000 miles of paved roads. Few roads had names, numbers, or signs to warn drivers of imminent danger. From 1920 to 1930, about 100,000 miles of road were paved—the government's second-greatest expense.

---

to eight-hour shifts. Ford took these dramatic steps to build up workers' loyalty and to undercut union organizers.

There were strings attached, however, to the wage increase. Ford created a "Sociological Department," which set requirements workers had to meet. For instance, the common practice of renting living space to nonfamily members was strictly forbidden. Investigators visited employees' homes to verify their eligibility and to see that they spent their wages in approved ways. Workers who transgressed could be disqualified from extra pay, suspended, or even fired.

The low prices made possible by Ford's mass-production methods not only created an immense market for his cars but also spawned imitators. By the mid-1920s, other car manufacturers, notably General Motors and Chrysler, competed successfully with Ford.

The auto industry spurred growth in other industries, such as rubber, plate glass, nickel, and lead. Automaking alone consumed 15 percent of the nation's steel, and the flood of cars stimulated a tremendous expansion of the petroleum industry.

The Social Impact of the Automobile Just as he had revolutionized manufacturing, Henry Ford was the force behind a social revolution related to the automobile. He almost single-handedly changed the auto from a toy of the wealthy to an affordable necessity for the middle class.

Cars revolutionized American life. Although many small businesses declined during the 1920s, the automobile created new small-business opportunities for such enterprises as garages and gas stations.

The automobile eased the isolation of rural life, putting towns within reach of many farmers and the countryside a mere ride away for city dwellers. Cars also enabled more people to live farther from work. An entirely new kind of consumer and worker, the auto commuter, appeared. Commuters lived in growing suburban communities and drove to work in the city.

The Consumer Goods Industry Many other new goods came on the market to take advantage of rising disposable income. Americans bought such innovations as electric razors, disposable facial tissues, frozen foods, and home hair dye.

NATIONAL GEOGRAPHIC
MOMENT in HISTORY

ON THE ROAD
The United States first felt the sweeping impact of the automobile during the 1920s. Mass production, pioneered by Henry Ford with his famous Model T, reduced costs and put practical, reliable cars within the reach of millions of middle-class Americans. Adventurous families—like the one shown here driving an upscale, open touring car through a giant Sequoia tree in Yosemite National Park—set out to explore the country. They used a network of roads that had been little more than rutted wagon trails two decades earlier.

516   CHAPTER 16   Normalcy and Good Times

DIFFERENTIATED INSTRUCTION

Reading Support Have students make journal entries about American dependence on the automobile over a period of several days. Remind students that their experience is not limited to driving or riding in a car, but includes where they go and what they do. Instruct students to write an essay based on their journal entries. **L2**

📂 Refer to *Inclusion for the High School Social Studies Classroom Strategies and Activities* in the TCR.

Profiles IN HISTORY

Bessie Coleman *c. 1892–1926*

Bessie Coleman was the first African American woman to receive a pilot's license and the first to become a stunt pilot. She performed in her first air show in September 1922 in Garden City, Long Island.

Coleman was born in Atlanta, Texas, to an African American mother and a Choctaw father. Too poor to attend college for more than one term, she moved to Chicago to become a pilot. No flight school she applied to, however, was willing to admit an African American. With the help of a Chicago publisher, Coleman then went to France to train. Back home, she championed the African American cause through her public statements and impressive flying feats.

Coleman's achievements inspired the founding of Chicago's Coffey School of Aeronautics. Its graduates helped train the U.S. military's first African American pilots, the Tuskegee Airmen, who served with distinction in World War II.

Amelia Earhart *1897–1937*

Amelia Earhart, perhaps the world's most celebrated woman pilot, saw her first airplane at the Iowa State Fair when she was 10 years old. She was unimpressed: "It was a thing of rusty wire and wood and not at all interesting. . . ." In her early 20s, however, she attended a California "aerial meet," a fateful decision.

Known for promoting women's flying, Earhart seemed destined for celebrity from early on. By 1932 she was flying solo across the Atlantic.

Earhart's most daring flight was her last. In 1937 she set out to fly around the world with her navigator. Two-thirds of the trip was covered when their plane disappeared. On the trip, she had written her husband, "Please know I am quite aware of the hazards. . . . I want to do it because I want to do it. Women must try to do things as men have tried."

Many of the new products were created for the home. As indoor plumbing became more common, Americans' concern for hygiene spawned the development of numerous household cleaning products. By appealing to people's health concerns, advertisers were able to convince homemakers to buy cleansers to protect their families from disease.

New appliances advertised as labor-savers changed the home. Electric irons, vacuum cleaners, washing machines, refrigerators, gas stoves, and improved glass cookware changed the way people cleaned their homes and prepared meals.

Another lucrative category of consumer products focused on Americans' concerns with fashion, youthful appearance, and success in personal and business endeavors. Mouthwash, deodorants, cosmetics, and perfumes became popular products in the 1920s.

The Airline Industry After the successful flight of the Wright brothers at Kitty Hawk in 1903, the aviation industry began to develop rapidly. Leading the way was American inventor Glenn Curtiss. Curtiss owned a motorcycle company in Hammondsport, New York. Fascinated by airplanes, he agreed in 1907 to become director of experiments at the Aerial Experiment Association, an organization founded by Alexander Graham Bell.

Within a year, Curtiss had invented ailerons—surfaces attached to wings that can be tilted to steer the plane. Ailerons made it possible to build rigid wings and much larger aircraft. They are still used on aircraft today. In 1912 Curtiss designed the first flying boat. In 1919 one of his flying boats became the first aircraft to cross the Atlantic.

Curtiss's company began building aircraft, and it made the first airplane sales in the United States. The company grew from a single factory to a huge industrial enterprise during World War I, as orders flooded in from allied governments for his biplanes and engines. Although Curtiss retired in 1920, his inventions made possible the airline industry that emerged in the 1920s.

After entrepreneurs such as Curtiss started building practical aircraft, the federal government began to support the airline industry. President Wilson's postmaster general had introduced the world's first regular airmail service in 1918 by hiring pilots to fly mail between Washington, D.C., and New York. In 1919 the Post Office expanded airmail service across the continent. The aviation industry received an economic boost in 1925 with the passage of the Kelly Act, which authorized postal officials to contract with private airplane operators to carry mail.

In 1926 the aviation industry received another boost with the passage of the Air Commerce Act, which provided federal aid for building airports. It was the extraordinary transatlantic solo flight of former airmail pilot **Charles Lindbergh** in 1927, however, that demonstrated the possibilities of aviation

INTERDISCIPLINARY CONNECTIONS ACTIVITY

Economics Have interested students research the economic impact of the airline industry in the United States during the 1900s. Have students create either a table or a chart showing the growth of the airline industry and its impact on the American economy. Tell students that they can focus on the revenues generated by the industry or on the number of people employed in the industry. **L2**

Reading Check

Answer: Technological innovations increased manufacturing efficiency and reduced the need to hire skilled workers.

Making a Collage Have students make a collage using copies of advertisements for consumer products from the 1920s paired with current advertisements for similar products. **L1**

FYI

Born in 1902, Charles Lindbergh grew up in Minnesota. After two years at the University of Wisconsin, he started flying as a stunt pilot. Lindbergh completed flight training to become an Army Air Service Reserve pilot. Later he flew mail between Chicago and St. Louis. An offer of $25,000 to become the first pilot to fly nonstop from New York to Paris inspired Lindbergh's famous flight.

Analyzing Economics Tell students that by the end of the 1920s, up to 90 percent of durable goods were purchased on credit. Ask students why they think people were more confident about going into debt and making purchases using credit, and what the benefits and consequences are of using credit to buy things.

Washing machine advertisement

and won popular support for commercial flight. By the end of 1928, 48 airlines were serving 355 American cities.

Advertisers praised the benefits of commercial flying for business executives, as in this 1928 ad for the Ford Motor Company's "Trimotor" plane: "When the occasion comes for your first time up, it will not be to 'joy-ride' in an antiquated and hazardous machine; but far more probably it will be to reach some distant meeting-place in advance of business competition!"

The Radio Industry In 1912 Edwin Armstrong, an American engineer, invented a special circuit that made long-range radio transmission of voice and music practical. The radio industry began a few years later. In November 1920, the Westinghouse Company broadcast the news of Harding's landslide election victory from station KDKA in Pittsburgh—one of the first public broadcasts in history. That success persuaded Westinghouse to open other stations.

In 1926 the **National Broadcasting Company**

(NBC) established a permanent network of stations to distribute daily programs. By 1927 almost 700 stations dotted the country, and the Federal Radio Commission had been established to regulate them. Sales of radio equipment skyrocketed from $12.2 million in 1921 to $842.5 million in 1929, by which time 10 million radio sets were in use in the United States.

In 1928 the **Columbia Broadcasting System** (CBS) assembled a coast-to-coast network of stations to rival NBC. The two networks sold advertising time and hired popular musicians, actors, and comedians from vaudeville, movies, and the nightclub circuit to appear on their shows. In 1928 Americans experienced complete coverage of the first presidential election campaign conducted over the airwaves, when the radio networks sold more than $1 million in advertising time to the Republican and Democratic Parties.

Reading Check **Analyzing** How did technological innovations such as the assembly line impact the nature of work?

The Consumer Society

Higher wages and shorter workdays resulted in a decade-long buying spree that kept the economy booming. Shifting from traditional attitudes of thrift and prudence, Americans in the 1920s enthusiastically accepted their new role as consumers.

ECONOMICS

Easy Consumer Credit One notable aspect of the economic boom was the growth of individual borrowing. The prosperity of the 1920s gave many Americans the confidence to go into debt to buy new consumer goods.

Credit had been available before the boom, but most Americans had considered debt to be shameful. Now, however, American attitudes toward debt started changing as people began believing in their ability to pay their debts over time. Many listened to the sales pitch, "Buy now and pay in easy installments," and racked up debts for the family car, radio, furniture, washing machine, and vacuum cleaner. Americans bought 75 percent of their radios and 60 percent of their automobiles on the installment plan. Some started buying on credit at a faster rate than their incomes increased.

Mass Advertising When inventor Otto Rohwedder developed a commercial bread slicer in 1928, he faced a problem common to new inventions: the bread slicer was a device that made a product—sliced bread—that no one knew they needed. To create consumers for

CRITICAL THINKING ACTIVITY

Analyzing Write the following sentence on the board: *The business technology of the 1920s created an era of prosperity.* Have students find three facts in the section to support the generalization. Write supporting facts on the board as students state them. Then have students make a generalization about the early radio industry and find three facts to support their generalization. **L1**

their new products, manufacturers turned to advertising, another booming industry in the 1920s.

Advertisers created appealing, persuasive messages that linked their clients' products with qualities associated with the modern era, such as progress, convenience, leisure, success, fashion, and style. In a 1924 magazine advertisement for deodorant, the headline read, "Flappers they may be—but they know the art of feminine appeal!" An advertisement for a prepared spaghetti product told the busy homemaker that heating is the same as cooking: "Just one thing to do and it's ready to serve." Advertisers also preyed on consumers' fears and anxieties, whether they be jarred nerves due to the hectic pace of modern life or insecurities about one's status or weight.

The Managerial Revolution
By the early 1920s, many industries had begun to create modern organizational structures. Companies were divided into divisions with different functions, such as sales, marketing, accounting, and operations. To run these divisions, businesses needed to hire managers. Managers freed executives and owners from the day-to-day business of running their companies and allowed them to develop long-range plans and goals.

The managerial revolution in companies created a new career—the professional manager—and companies began to hire large numbers of people with managerial training from business schools. The large numbers of managers helped to expand the size of the middle class, which in turn added to the nation's prosperity. Similarly, so many companies relied on new technology to drive their business that engineers were also in very high demand. They too joined the ranks of the rapidly growing middle class.

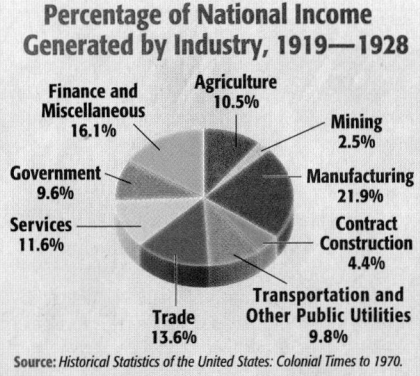

Percentage of National Income Generated by Industry, 1919—1928

- Finance and Miscellaneous 16.1%
- Agriculture 10.5%
- Mining 2.5%
- Government 9.6%
- Manufacturing 21.9%
- Services 11.6%
- Contract Construction 4.4%
- Trade 13.6%
- Transportation and Other Public Utilities 9.8%

Source: Historical Statistics of the United States: Colonial Times to 1970.

Welfare Capitalism Middle-class Americans were not the only members of the new consumer society. Industrial workers also prospered in the 1920s, partly due to rising wages and partly because many corporations introduced what came to be called welfare capitalism. Companies allowed workers to buy stock, participate in profit sharing, and receive benefits such as medical care and pensions.

Benefits programs also made unions seem unnecessary to many workers. During the 1920s, unions lost both influence and membership. Employers promoted the open shop—a workplace where employees were not required to join a union.

With benefits covering some of their basic needs, workers were able to spend more of their income. Many eagerly purchased consumer goods they previously could not afford.

✓ **Reading Check** **Analyzing Bias** How did advertisers try to convince Americans to buy their products?

The Farm Crisis Returns

American farmers did not share in the prosperity of the 1920s. As a group, they earned less than one-third of the average income for workers in the rest of the economy. Technological advances in fertilizers, pesticides, seed varieties, and farm machinery allowed them to produce more, but higher yields without a corresponding increase in demand meant that they received lower prices. Between 1920 and 1921, corn prices dropped almost 19 percent, and

Farm Wages

Monthly Wages (including room and board)

$55 $50 $45 $40 $35 $30

1920 1922 1924 1926 1928 1930

Year

Source: Historical Statistics of the United States: Colonial Times to 1970.

Graph Skills

1. **Interpreting Graphs** How far did farm wages fall between 1920 and 1930?
2. **Understanding Cause and Effect** What caused the decline in wages? Do you think farmers could have done anything to prevent this?

CHAPTER 16 Normalcy and Good Times **519**

✓ **Reading Check**

Answer: preyed on consumers' fears and anxieties; linked products to progress and success

Graph Skills

Answers:
1. about $13 per month
2. higher production rates, increased debt, and a drop in foreign sales

Graph Skills Practice
Ask: From 1920 to 1930, when were farm wages lowest and highest? (lowest in 1922, highest in 1920)

3 ASSESS

Assign Section 2 Assessment as homework or as an in-class activity.

⊙ Have students use the **Interactive Tutor Self-Assessment CD-ROM.**

L1/ELL

Reading Essentials and Study Guide 16–2

Name _____ Date _____ Class _____

Study Guide

Chapter 16, Section 2
For use with textbook pages 514–520

A GROWING ECONOMY

KEY TERMS AND NAMES

mass production large-scale product manufacturing usually done by machinery (page 515)

assembly line a manufacturing system that divided operations into simple tasks that unskilled workers could do (page 515)

Model T assembly-line automobile manufactured in Henry Ford's plants (page 515)

Charles Lindbergh former airmail pilot who made transatlantic solo flight (page 517)

National Broadcasting Company company that established a permanent network of radio stations to distribute daily programs (page 518)

Columbia Broadcasting System company that established a coast-to-coast network of radio stations (page 518)

EXTENDING THE CONTENT

Industry Growth and Decline While the automobile helped boost some industries and activities, it led to decline or even obsolescence in other areas. Railroads, for example, declined as personal cars and the burgeoning trucking industry brought more flexibility to both personal and commercial transport. Some thriving towns on railroad lines became virtual ghost towns as railway travel fell out of favor. City streets and downtown areas also suffered. New road designs and layouts catered to auto circulation and speed; the results were rarely pedestrian-friendly. The premium on parking turned many downtown buildings into lifeless parking lots and garages.

L2

Section Quiz 16–2

Picturing **History**

Answer: producing more; greater European competition after the war

Reteach

Have students analyze the growing importance of the automobile.

Enrich

Suggest that students work in groups to discuss the changes in people's attitudes toward big business that took place in the 1920s.

Reading Check

Answer: a decline in foreign markets and increased productivity

HISTORY Online

Study Central™ provides summaries, interactive games, and online graphic organizers to help students review section content.

4 CLOSE

Have students explain the growing economic crisis in farming.

Picturing **History**

Price of Progress With the help of improved technology in the 1920s, farm production went up—and farm prices and farmers' income went down. How do you explain this "quiet depression"?

wheat went from $1.83 a bushel to $1.03. The cost to farmers of the improved technology, meanwhile, continued to increase.

Changing Market Conditions Many factors contributed to this "quiet depression" in American agriculture. During the war, the government had urged farmers to produce more to meet the great need for food supplies in Europe. Many farmers borrowed heavily to buy new land (at inflated prices) and new machinery in order to raise more crops. Sales were strong, prices were high, and farmers prospered. After the war, however, European farm output rose, and the debt-ridden countries of Europe had little to spend on

American farm products. Congress had unintentionally made matters worse when it passed the Fordney-McCumber Act in 1922. This act raised tariffs dramatically in an effort to protect American industry from foreign competition. By dampening the American market for foreign goods, it provoked a reaction in foreign markets against American agricultural products. Farmers in the United States could no longer sell as much of their output overseas, and prices tumbled.

Helping Farmers Some members of Congress tried to help the farmers sell their surplus. Every year from 1924 to 1928, Senator Charles McNary of Oregon and Representative Gilbert Haugen of Iowa proposed the McNary-Haugen Bill, which called for the federal government to purchase surplus crops and sell them abroad while protecting the American market with a high tariff. McNary and Haugen argued that the plan would immediately raise the domestic price of crops, and it would aid farmers just as the Fordney-McCumber tariffs helped manufacturers.

Congress passed the bill twice, but President Coolidge vetoed it both times. He argued that with money flowing to farmers under this law, the farmers would be encouraged to produce even greater surplus volumes, which the government would be unable to sell in glutted overseas markets. American farmers remained mired in recession throughout the 1920s. Their problems would only grow worse when the Great Depression began in 1929.

Reading Check **Synthesizing** What factors led to the growing economic crisis in farming in the 1920s?

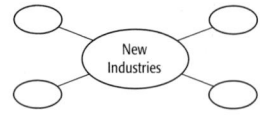 **Study Central™** To review this section, go to **tarvol2.glencoe.com** and click on **Study Central™**.

SECTION 2 ASSESSMENT

Checking for Understanding

1. **Define:** mass production, assembly line, welfare capitalism, open shop.
2. **Identify:** Model T, Charles Lindbergh, National Broadcasting Company, Columbia Broadcasting System.
3. **Summarize** the factors that led to the new consumer society in the United States during the 1920s.

Reviewing Themes

4. **Science and Technology** How did the automobile impact American society?

Critical Thinking

5. **Identifying Cause and Effect** How did the United States government help spur the growth of the airline industry?
6. **Organizing** Use a graphic organizer similar to the one below to list some of the new industries that grew in importance during the 1920s.

[Graphic organizer: central oval labeled "New Industries" with connecting ovals]

Analyzing Visuals

7. **Analyzing Advertisements** Examine the advertisement on page 518. How did the growing consumer culture impact the nation's economy?

Writing About History

8. **Expository Writing** Write an article for a contemporary newspaper analyzing the impact of Charles Lindbergh's transatlantic flight on the development of aviation in the United States and the world.

SECTION 2 ASSESSMENT ANSWERS

1. Terms are in blue.
2. Model T (p. 515), Charles Lindbergh (p. 517), National Broadcasting Company (p. 518), Columbia Broadcasting System (p. 518)
3. mass production, easy credit, mass advertisement, and economic prosperity
4. eased rural isolation, allowed workers to live farther away from work
5. governmental airmail service and funds for airports
6. airline, automobile, consumer goods, radio
7. raised standard of living, encouraged Americans to buy new goods
8. Students' articles will vary but should contain factual information.

SECTION 3 The Policies of Prosperity

Guide to Reading

Main Idea
Economic policies of the United States government encouraged the prosperity of the 1920s.

Key Terms and Names
supply-side economics, cooperative individualism, isolationism, Charles G. Dawes, Charles Evans Hughes, moratorium, Kellogg-Briand Pact

Reading Strategy
Organizing As you read about government policies in the 1920s, complete a graphic organizer similar to the one below by filling in ways the government attempted to stimulate economic growth and prosperity.

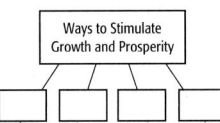

Ways to Stimulate
Growth and Prosperity

Reading Objectives
- **Explain** Andrew Mellon's economic strategies for maintaining prosperity.
- **Describe** how the United States remained involved in world affairs without joining the League of Nations.

Section Theme
Economic Factors After World War I, the United States had to pay down a large amount of war debt while maintaining economic growth.

Preview of Events

| ♦1920 | ♦1923 | ♦1926 | ♦1929 |

1921
Washington Conference begins discussing naval disarmament

1922
Fordney-McCumber Act passed

1924
Dawes Plan negotiated with France, Britain, and Germany

1928
Kellogg-Briand Pact signed by 15 nations

★ An American Story ★

Andrew W. Mellon

After Election Day 1920, President-elect Harding began searching for qualified Americans for his cabinet. One of the most important posts would be secretary of the treasury. The nation faced a large national debt, and many worried that the country would not easily pull out of its postwar recession.

Harding was considering Andrew W. Mellon, a successful banker and industrialist, but he worried about Mellon's ties to industry and his relative anonymity. Harding's campaign manager, Harry Daugherty, reassured the president with a ringing endorsement of Mellon:

❝A man who can quietly make the millions this modest-looking man has gathered in is little short of a magician. If there is one thing he knows it's money. He will make for you the greatest Secretary of the Treasury since Alexander Hamilton. . . .❞

—adapted from *Mellon's Millions*

Promoting Prosperity

Harry Daugherty's confidence in Andrew Mellon proved to be well founded. Mellon became the chief architect of economic policy in the United States in the 1920s, and he served as secretary of the treasury in three successive Republican administrations. His policies encouraged growth and led to a stock market boom.

CHAPTER 16 Normalcy and Good Times **521**

---

1 FOCUS

Section Overview
This section focuses on the economic policies of the federal government during the 1920s.

BELLRINGER
Skillbuilder Activity

Project transparency and have students answer the question.

Daily Focus Skills Transparency 16–3

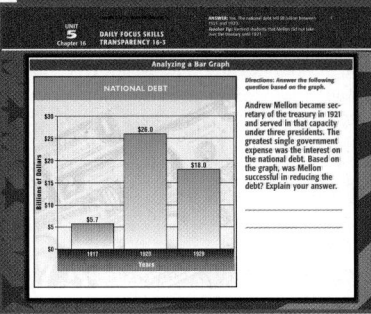

Reading Preview

Answers to Graphic: less government regulation of business, tax cuts, refinancing of the national debt, and reduced government spending

Preteaching Vocabulary
Have students create a database of the Key Terms and Names. Instruct students to add definitions and other helpful information as they read the section.

SECTION RESOURCES

Reproducible Masters
- Reproducible Lesson Plan 16–3
- Daily Lecture and Discussion Notes 16–3
- Guided Reading Activity 16–3
- Section Quiz 16–3
- Reading Essentials and Study Guide 16–3

Transparencies
- Daily Focus Skills Transparency 16–3

Multimedia
- Interactive Tutor Self-Assessment CD-ROM
- ExamView® Pro Testmaker CD-ROM
- Presentation Plus! CD-ROM
- TeacherWorks™ CD-ROM
- Audio Program
- American Music: Hits Through History

Picturing **History**

Answer: He cut government spending, refinanced the debt to a lower interest rate, and convinced the Federal Reserve to lower its interest rates.

Discussing a Topic Have students discuss isolationism. Ask students what types of global activities, if any, they think isolationists would support. **L1**

✓ **Reading Check**

Answer: tax cuts, lowering the interest rate on the national debt, lowering Federal Reserve interest rates

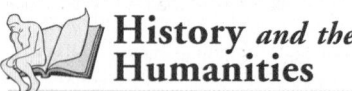

History *and the* Humanities

📖 American Music: Hits Through History: "Yes Sir! That's My Baby"

🎨 American Art & Architecture: Empire State Building

Picturing **History**

Harding's Cabinet Some members of Harding's cabinet (posing here with the president, seated center, in 1921) were effective administrators. How did Secretary of the Treasury Andrew Mellon lower the national debt between 1921 and 1929?

ECONOMICS

The Mellon Program Mellon firmly believed that the government should apply business principles to its operations. In 1921 he convinced Congress to create both the Bureau of the Budget to prepare a unified federal budget and the General Accounting Office to track government spending.

When Mellon took office, he had three major goals—to balance the budget, to reduce the government's debt, and to cut taxes. He was convinced that these policies would promote economic growth and ensure prosperity.

Mellon began by cutting government spending. The federal budget fell from $6.4 billion to less than $3 billion in seven years. One major expense was the interest on the national debt. World War I costs had raised the debt from $5.7 billion in 1917 to almost $26 billion by 1920. Mellon refinanced the debt to lower the interest on it and persuaded the Federal Reserve to lower its interest rates as well. These steps, combined with increased tax revenue from the nation's economic boom, reduced the debt by $7 billion between 1921 and 1929.

In addition to trimming government spending, Mellon focused on reducing tax rates. He believed that high taxes reduced the money available for private investment and prevented business expansion. Mellon further argued that high tax rates actually reduced the amount of tax money the government collected. If taxes were lower, businesses and consumers would spend and invest their extra money, causing the economy to grow. As the economy grew, Americans would earn more money, and the government would actually

---

collect more taxes at a lower rate than it would if it kept tax rates high. This idea is known today as supply-side economics.

At Mellon's urging, Congress dramatically reduced tax rates. When Mellon took office, most taxpayers paid 4 percent federal income tax, while wealthy Americans in the highest bracket paid 73 percent. By 1928 Congress had reduced the rate most Americans paid to .5 percent and cut the rate for the wealthiest Americans to 25 percent.

Hoover's Cooperative Individualism Mellon's program was only one part of the government's effort to promote economic growth. Secretary of Commerce Herbert Hoover also sought to promote economic stability in various industries. Hoover tried to balance government regulation with his own philosophy of cooperative individualism. This idea involved encouraging manufacturers and distributors to form their own trade associations, which would voluntarily share information with the federal government. Hoover believed this system would reduce costs and promote economic efficiency.

To assist American businesses, Hoover also created several other agencies. He expanded the Bureau of Foreign and Domestic Commerce to find new markets and business opportunities for American companies. He also established the Bureau of Aviation to regulate and support the airline industry and the Federal Radio Commission, which set rules regarding the use of radio frequencies and the power of radio transmitters.

✓ **Reading Check** **Evaluating** What government policies were intended to promote economic growth and improve business efficiency in the 1920s?

Trade and Arms Control

Before World War I the United States had owed billions of dollars more to foreign investors than foreigners owed to Americans. By the end of the war, the situation was reversed. Former wartime allies owed the United States more than $10 billion in war debts incurred for food and armaments. By the 1920s the United States was the dominant economic power in the world—its national income far greater than that of Britain, Germany, France, and Japan combined. This new power presented the United States with a unique diplomatic challenge.

Isolationism In his victory speech after the 1920 election, President Harding declared the issue of American involvement in the League of Nations

---

"deceased." The majority of Americans, tired of being entangled in the baffling, mutually hostile, and dangerous politics of Europe, favored isolationism. They simply wanted to be left alone to pursue prosperity.

The United States, however, was too powerful, too economically interconnected with other countries, and too widely involved in international affairs to retreat into isolationism. American delegations participated in many League conferences. It was United States policy to promote peace through agreements with individual countries rather than doing so through the collective efforts of the League.

The Dawes Plan The United States's former wartime allies had difficulty making the payments on their immense war debts. They claimed that high American tariffs had closed the American market to their products and hampered their economic recovery. If they could not sell their products in the United States, they could not acquire the money they needed to pay off their war debts. They also argued that the United States should be willing to bear more of the financial burden because it had suffered far fewer wartime casualties than its allies.

The United States government took the stance that American taxpayers should not be asked to assume the debts of others. American officials argued further that America's allies had gained new territory as a result of the victory over Germany, while the United States had gained nothing. These countries also were receiving reparations—huge cash payments Germany was required to make as punishment for starting the war and causing so much destruction. These payments, however, were completely crippling the German economy.

It was vital for the United States that European economies be healthy so that the Europeans could buy American exports and repay their war debts. Thus, in 1924, **Charles G. Dawes,** an American banker and diplomat, negotiated an agreement with France, Britain, and Germany by which American banks would make loans to the Germans that would enable them to meet their reparations payments. At the same time, Britain and France would accept less in reparations and pay more on their war debts.

Although well intended, the Dawes Plan did little to ease Europe's economic problems. Britain, France, and Germany went through the motions of paying what they owed while in fact going deeper into debt to American banks and corporations.

The Washington Conference Despite severe economic hardship, the major powers were involved in a costly postwar naval arms race. To help halt this arms race, the United States invited representatives from eight major countries—Great Britain, France, Italy, China, Japan, Belgium, the Netherlands, and

The Washington Conference, November 1921–February 1922

Treaty	Signers	Terms	Weaknesses
Four-Power Treaty	United States, Great Britain, France, Japan	• All agreed to respect the others' territory in the Pacific • Full and open negotiations in the event of disagreements	• Mutual defense of other co-signers not specified
Five-Power Treaty	United States, Great Britain, France, Japan, Italy	• All agreed to freeze naval production at 1921 levels and halt production of large warships for 10 years • U.S. and Great Britain would not build new naval bases in the western Pacific	• No restrictions on the construction of smaller battle craft such as submarines and naval destroyers • Did not place restrictions on the ground forces
Nine-Power Treaty	United States, Great Britain, France, Japan, Italy, Belgium, China, the Netherlands, Portugal	• All agreed to preserve equal commercial rights to China—a reassertion of the "Open Door Policy"	• No enforcement of the terms of the "Open Door Policy" specified

Chart Skills

1. **Interpreting Charts** Which countries signed the Five-Power Treaty?
2. **Analyzing** Why do you think the terms of the treaties focused on the Pacific region?

CHAPTER 16
Section 3, 521–524

L1/ELL

Guided Reading Activity 16–3

Name _____ Date _____ Class _____

★ Guided Reading Activity 16-3

DIRECTIONS: Using Heads and Subheadings Locate each heading below in your textbook. Then use the information under the correct subheading to help you write each answer.

I. Promoting Prosperity

A. Who was Andrew Mellon? _____

B. What did Andrew Mellon believe about high taxes? _____

C. What would happen if taxes were lower? _____

D. What would happen as the economy grew? _____

E. What was cooperative individualism? _____

Chart *Skills*

Answer:

1. United States, Great Britain, France, Japan, Italy

2. U.S. government concerns about Japanese power and the China market

Chart Skills Practice

Ask: Which countries signed all three treaties? *(United States, Great Britain, France, and Japan)*

3 ASSESS

Assign Section 3 Assessment as homework or as an in-class activity.

📀 Have students use the **Interactive Tutor Self-Assessment CD-ROM.**

L1/ELL

Reading Essentials and Study Guide 16–3

Name _____ Date _____ Class _____

Study Guide

Chapter 16, Section 3
For use with textbook pages 521–524

THE POLICIES OF PROSPERITY

KEY TERMS AND NAMES

supply-side economics the idea that the economy would grow by lowering taxes, which would increase spending and investing (page 522)

cooperative individualism an idea promoted by Herbert Hoover that encouraged manufacturers and distributors to form trade associations and voluntarily share information with the federal government (page 522)

isolationism philosophy that a nation should limit its involvement in international affairs (page 523)

Charles G. Dawes American banker and diplomat who negotiated a loan repayment plan with France, Britain, and Germany (page 523)

DIFFERENTIATED INSTRUCTION

Gifted and Talented Have a group develop an alternative to the Dawes Plan that would have achieved the following goals: maximizing repayments of debts to the United States, encouraging economic stability in Europe, and helping Europe rebuild from the war. Encourage groups to present their ideas in the form of an economic stabilization and development plan. **L3**

📁 Refer to *Inclusion for the High School Social Studies Classroom Strategies and Activities* in the TCR.

Section Quiz 16-3

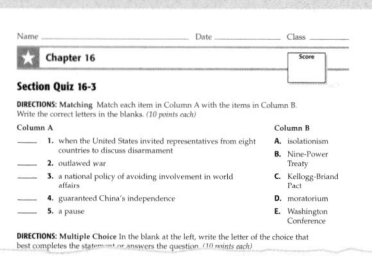

Fact | Fiction | Folklore

The identities of the three other soldiers buried in the Tomb of the Unknown Soldier are, in fact, unknown. In 1998, however, DNA analysis allowed the Vietnam War soldier buried there to be identified. He is U.S. Air Force First Lieutenant Michael Joseph Blassie.

Reteach

Have students explain Andrew Mellon's economic strategies for maintaining prosperity.

Enrich

Have students write a paragraph explaining why they think a written agreement to end war could or could not be an effective deterrent to war.

Reading Check

Answer: It caused Britain, France, and Germany to go further into debt.

HISTORY Online

Study Central™ provides summaries, interactive games, and online graphic organizers to help students review section content.

4 CLOSE

Have students explain how the United States remained involved in world affairs without being a League of Nations member.

Fact | Fiction | Folklore

The Tomb of the Unknown Soldier On March 4, 1921, Congress approved the burial of an unidentified World War I soldier in Arlington National Cemetery on a hill that overlooks Washington, D.C. This burial site, which was dedicated on November 11, 1921, is called the Tomb of the Unknown Soldier.

In 1958 two unknown soldiers from World War II and the Korean War were buried alongside the original unknown soldier. In 1984 a Vietnam War soldier was added.

On the side of the original tomb are inscribed the words: "Here rests in honored glory an American soldier known but to God." The Tomb is guarded year-round, day and night, regardless of weather.

Portugal—to Washington to discuss disarmament. The Washington Conference opened on November 12, 1921.

In his address to the delegates, Secretary of State **Charles Evans Hughes** proposed a 10-year moratorium—or pause—on the construction of major new warships. He also proposed a list of warships in each country's navy to be destroyed, beginning with some American battleships. The delegates cheered Hughes's speech and then entered into lengthy negotiations.

Their efforts produced three agreements. In the **Five-Power Naval Limitation Treaty,** Britain, France, Italy, Japan, and the United States essentially formalized Hughes's proposal. The **Four-Power Treaty** between the United States, Japan, France, and Britain recognized each country's island possessions in the Pacific. Finally, all the participating countries signed the **Nine-Power Treaty,** which guaranteed China's independence.

As a long-term effort to prevent war, the conference had some serious shortcomings. It did nothing to limit land forces. It also angered the Japanese because it required Japan to maintain a smaller navy than either the United States or Great Britain. It did, however, give Americans cause to look forward to a period of peace, recovery, and prosperity.

Abolishing War The apparent success of the Washington Conference boosted the belief that written agreements could end war altogether. Perhaps the highest expression of that idea occurred when U.S. Secretary of State Frank Kellogg and French Foreign Minister Aristide Briand proposed a treaty to outlaw war. On August 27, 1928, the United States and 14 other nations signed the **Kellogg-Briand Pact.** Eventually 62 nations ratified it.

Though it had no binding force, the pact was hailed as a victory for peace. It stated that all signing nations agreed to abandon war and to settle all disputes by peaceful means. The Kellogg-Briand Pact and the Dawes Plan were perhaps the most notable foreign policy achievements of the Coolidge administration.

Reading Check **Identifying** Why did the Dawes Plan fail to ease Europe's economic problems?

HISTORY Online
Study Central™ To review this section, go to tarvol2.glencoe.com and click on **Study Central**™.

SECTION 3 ASSESSMENT

Checking for Understanding

1. **Define:** supply-side economics, cooperative individualism, isolationism, moratorium.

2. **Identify:** Charles G. Dawes, Charles Evans Hughes, Kellogg-Briand Pact.

Reviewing Themes

3. **Economic Factors** Why did Andrew Mellon work to reduce federal tax rates?

Critical Thinking

4. **Evaluating** What efforts did the United States make to promote permanent peace and worldwide economic recovery? Were these efforts successful? Explain your answer.

5. **Categorizing** Use a graphic organizer like the one below to list the major terms of the treaties resulting from the Washington Conference.

Major Terms of Treaties

Analyzing Visuals

6. **Analyzing Photographs** Study the photograph on page 522 of President Harding's cabinet of advisers. What differences do you see between politics and the media then and now?

Writing About History

7. **Persuasive Writing** Imagine you are an American business owner or farmer in the 1920s. Write a letter to your representatives in Congress explaining why you think cutting tax rates is a good or bad idea.

SECTION 3 ASSESSMENT ANSWERS

1. Terms are in blue.
2. Charles G. Dawes (p. 523), Charles Evans Hughes (p. 524), Kellogg-Briand Pact (p. 524)
3. He believed that lowering tax rates would spur the economy by encouraging businesses and consumers to invest and spend.
4. Students' answers should reflect analysis of text information, including the Dawes Plan and the Washington Naval Conference.
5. Answers should match information in the text.
6. Students should note that media coverage in both cases is often staged. However, today there is almost instant access by the media to politicians.
7. Letters should be written from the point of view of a business owner or a farmer.

Distinguishing Fact From Opinion

Why Learn This Skill?

Imagine that you are watching two candidates for president debate the merits of the college loan program. One candidate says, "In my view, the college loan program must be reformed. Sixty percent of students do not repay their loans on time."

The other candidate responds, "College costs are skyrocketing, but only 30 percent of students default on their loans for more than one year. I believe we should spend more money on this worthy program."

How can you tell who or what to believe? First, you must learn to distinguish a fact from an opinion. Then you will be better prepared to evaluate the statements that other people make.

Learning the Skill

A **fact** is a statement that can be proven. In the example above, the statement "Sixty percent of students do not repay their loans on time" may be a fact. By reviewing statistics on the number of student loan recipients who repay their loans, we can determine whether the statement is true or false. To identify potential facts, look for words and phrases indicating specific people, places, events, dates, amounts, or times.

An **opinion,** on the other hand, expresses a personal belief, viewpoint, or emotion. Because opinions are subjective, we cannot prove or disprove them. In the example above, most statements by the candidates are opinions. To identify opinions, look for qualifying words and phrases such as *I think, I believe, probably, seems to me, may, might, could, ought, should, in my judgment,* and *in my view.* Also, look for expressions of approval or disapproval such as *good, bad, poor,* and *satisfactory.* Be aware of superlatives such as *greatest, worst, finest,* and *best,* and notice words with negative meanings and implications such as *squander, contemptible,* and *disgrace.* Also, identify generalizations such as *none, every, always,* and *never.*

Practicing the Skill

For each pair of statements below, determine which is a fact and which is an opinion. Give a reason for each of your choices.

❶ **a.** President Harding was born in Ohio in 1865.

　　b. Harding later became the most scandalous president in United States history.

❷ **a.** Harding's administration suffered numerous public scandals, including the Teapot Dome scandal.

　　b. Calvin Coolidge was probably disgusted with Harding's poor performance in the White House.

❸ **a.** Harding stated that the United States needed a return to normalcy, but he did not do anything to help the country.

　　b. Coolidge took over the White House after Harding's death and led the nation for the next several years.

❹ **a.** Henry Ford significantly lowered the price of the automobile with his mass production methods.

　　b. Ford's Model T was the most significant invention of the 20th century.

Skills Assessment

Complete the Practicing Skills questions on page 527 and the Chapter 16 Skill Reinforcement Activity to assess your mastery of this skill.

Applying the Skill

Distinguishing Fact From Opinion In a newspaper, find a news article and an editorial on the same topic or issue. Identify five facts and five opinions from these sources.

 Glencoe's **Skillbuilder Interactive Workbook CD-ROM, Level 2,** provides instruction and practice in key social studies skills.

ANSWERS TO PRACTICING THE SKILL

❶ **a.** fact, it can be proven; **b.** opinion, expresses a viewpoint, includes the word *most*

❷ **a.** fact, it can be proven; **b.** opinion, includes the word *probably*

❸ **a.** opinion, expresses a viewpoint; **b.** fact, it can be proven

❹ **a.** fact, it can be proven; **b.** opinion, expresses a point of view, includes the phrase *most significant*

Applying the Skill
Students' lists will vary. Students should be able to distinguish between fact and opinion.

CHAPTER
16 ASSESSMENT and ACTIVITIES

Reviewing Key Terms
Students' answers will vary. The pages where the words appear in the text are shown in parentheses.

1. **normalcy** *(p. 511)*
2. **immunity** *(p. 512)*
3. **mass production** *(p. 515)*
4. **assembly line** *(p. 515)*
5. **welfare capitalism** *(p. 519)*
6. **open shop** *(p. 519)*
7. **supply-side economics** *(p. 522)*
8. **cooperative individualism** *(p. 522)*
9. **isolationism** *(p. 523)*
10. **moratorium** *(p. 524)*

Reviewing Key Facts
11. Albert B. Fall *(p. 512)*, Teapot Dome scandal *(p. 512)*, Charles Lindbergh *(p. 517)*, Charles G. Dawes *(p. 523)*, Charles Evans Hughes *(p. 524)*, Kellogg-Briand Pact *(p. 524)*
12. Inefficiency and scandal plagued his presidency.
13. Coolidge distanced himself from the Harding administration and named the most capable individuals to his cabinet.
14. automobile-related industries such as garage and gas stations, the consumer goods, airlines, and radio industries
15. He increased workers' wages and reduced the workday, weakening the power of unions.
16. reduce taxes, reduce federal debt, balance the budget

Reviewing Key Terms
On a sheet of paper, use each of the following terms in a sentence.

1. normalcy
2. immunity
3. mass production
4. assembly line
5. welfare capitalism
6. open shop
7. supply-side economics
8. cooperative individualism
9. isolationism
10. moratorium

Reviewing Key Facts
11. **Identify:** Albert B. Fall, Teapot Dome scandal, Charles Lindbergh, Charles G. Dawes, Charles Evans Hughes, Kellogg-Briand Pact.
12. What was the presidency of Warren G. Harding like?
13. How did President Coolidge restore public confidence?
14. What were four new industries, besides the automobile industry, that grew in importance during the 1920s?
15. How did Henry Ford increase worker loyalty and impact the labor movement?
16. What were Andrew Mellon's strategies for maintaining postwar American prosperity?

Critical Thinking
17. **Analyzing Themes: Culture and Traditions** How did automobiles change the standard of living during the 1920s?

18. **Evaluating** How effective were President Coolidge's attempts to distance himself from the Harding administration? Explain your answer.
19. **Forming an Opinion** The former World War I allies felt that the United States should have borne more of the financial burden after the war. Do you agree or disagree? Explain your answer.
20. **Identifying Cause and Effect** Examine the graph on page 519. What caused the trend illustrated in this graph?
21. **Interpreting Primary Sources** In December 1928, President Coolidge delivered his annual State of the Union message to Congress. Read the excerpt and answer the questions that follow.

❝The great wealth created by our enterprise and industry, and saved by our economy, has had the widest distribution among our own people, and has gone out in a steady stream to serve the charity and the business of the world. The requirements of existence have passed beyond the standard of necessity into the region of luxury. . . . The country can regard the present with satisfaction and anticipate the future with optimism.

The main source of these unexplained blessings lies in the integrity and character of the American people. They have had great faith, which they have supplemented with mighty works. . . . Yet these remarkable powers would have been exerted almost in vain

Chapter Summary

Government's Role	Business Innovation	New Consumer Society
• Minimal interference with business • Cut government spending and debt • Eliminated or reduced taxes • High tariffs	• Mass production reduced prices • Technology such as autos, airplanes, and radios led to new industries • New consumer goods fueled manufacturing boom	• More disposable income • More leisure time • Easily available credit • Mass advertising

Prosperity

Critical Thinking
17. Automobiles allowed people to travel much greater distances more quickly and allowed workers to live outside cities. Rural Americans' sense of isolation also decreased. Successful mass production resulted in new and cheaper consumer goods.
18. Coolidge was quite successful in distancing himself from Harding. He did this by choosing effective cabinet members and associating himself with prosperity and big business.

19. Opinions will vary. Students should note that the United States was not an original combatant in the war but that the United States played a major role in the war, including contributing to the destruction in Europe.
20. mass production created a large supply, rising cost of farm machinery, decrease in demand due to tariffs

without the constant cooperation and careful administration of the Federal Government. . . .⁹⁹

—from President Coolidge's Annual Message
to Congress, December 4, 1928

a. According to Coolidge, how should Americans feel about
the present economy and the future economy?

b. Whom does Coolidge credit for U.S. prosperity?

22. **Organizing** Use a graphic organizer like the one below to
list the factors that helped create a new consumer society in
the United States during the 1920s.

New Consumer Society

Practicing Skills

23. **Distinguishing Fact From Opinion** Read the following
statements. Determine which are facts and which are opinions. Give a reason for each of your choices.

a. American farmers earned less than one-third the average
income for workers in the rest of the economy in the
1920s.

b. President Harding's choice to appoint Colonel Charles R.
Forbes to head the Veterans Bureau was his worst decision in office.

c. The Kelly Act authorized postal officials to contract with
private airplane operators to carry mail.

Chapter Activity

24. **American History Primary Source Document Library
CD-ROM** Under *The Roaring Twenties,* read "Ford and the
Model T" by Charles E. Sorenson. Work with a few of your
classmates to create a diorama of the first Model T assembly
line based on the information in the article.

Writing Activity

25. **Persuasive Writing** Use the Internet or other resources to
research advertisements and products from the 1920s. Then,
based on the style of these advertisements, create an ad for a
personal-care product that became popular in the 1920s,
such as mouthwash, deodorant, cosmetics, or perfume.

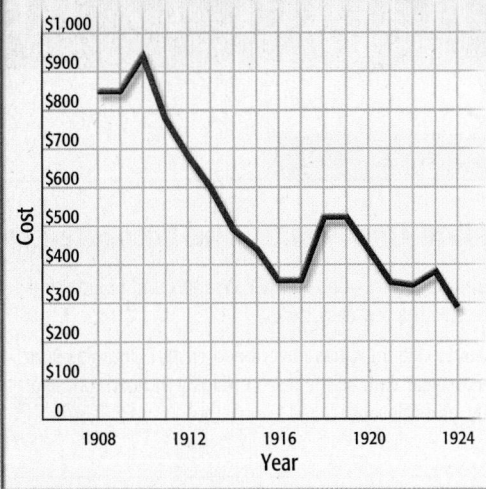

Cost of a Model T, 1908—1924

Economics and History

26. The graph above shows the cost of a new Model T automobile between 1908 and 1924. Study the graph and answer
the questions below.

a. **Interpreting Graphs** By how much did the cost of the
Model T drop from 1908 to 1920?

b. **Evaluating** How was Henry Ford able to lower the price
of the Model T?

Standardized Test Practice

**Directions: Choose the phrase that best
completes the following sentence.**

One of the effects of World War I on the American
economy was

A a sharp rise in unemployment.

B stronger government control over industry.

C a sharp decrease in taxes.

D the abolition of labor unions, which were seen as
unpatriotic.

Test-Taking Tip: This question is asking for a cause-and-
effect relationship. Look for an answer that can be *directly
related* to the needs of a wartime economy. During the war,
it was necessary to produce supplies and munitions for the
armed forces (which also needed more personnel), so
answer A must be incorrect. In fact, there were more jobs
and fewer workers to fill them, so unemployment is not a
logical choice.

Writing Activity

25. The ad should persuade consumers
to purchase the product.

Economics and History

26. **a.** about $400; **b.** decreased produc-
tion costs, increased productivity
level and sales volume

Standardized Test Practice

Answer: B
Test-Taking Tip: For this question
students need to think of things a
government would need to do to
support the war. The United States
had to raise revenue to pay for the
war, which led to a rise in taxes during
the war. Thus, answer C is incorrect.

Bonus Question ?

Ask: What was the Teapot Dome
scandal? *(During the Harding administration, government lands containing large reserves of oil in Teapot
Dome, Wyoming, were leased to
private interests.)*

---

21. a. Coolidge says they should be satisfied and
optimistic. **b.** He credits the American people.

22. shorter workday, higher wages, mass production techniques, easy consumer credit, mass advertising, managerial revolution

Practicing Skills

23. a. fact, it can be proven; **b.** opinion, expresses a point
of view, uses the word *worst*; **c.** fact, it can be proven

Chapter Activity

24. The diorama should demonstrate the efficiency of the
assembly line.

Timesaving Tools

TeacherWorks™ All-In-One Planner and Resource Center

- **Interactive Teacher Edition** Access your Teacher Wraparound Edition and your classroom resources with a few easy clicks.
- **Interactive Lesson Planner** Planning has never been easier! Organize your week, month, semester, or year with all the lesson helps you need to make teaching creative, timely, and relevant.

Use Glencoe's **Presentation Plus!** multimedia teacher tool to easily present dynamic lessons that visually excite your students. Using Microsoft PowerPoint® you can customize the presentations to create your own personalized lessons.

TEACHING TRANSPARENCIES

Graphic Organizer 2 L2

Why It Matters Chapter Transparency 17 L2

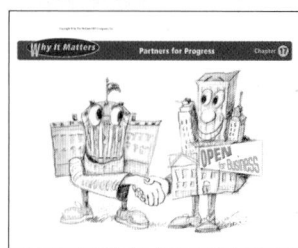

APPLICATION AND ENRICHMENT

Linking Past and Present Activity 17 L2

Enrichment Activity 17 L3

Primary Source Reading 17 L2

REVIEW AND REINFORCEMENT

Reteaching Activity 17 L1

Vocabulary Activity 17 L1

Time Line Activity 17 L2

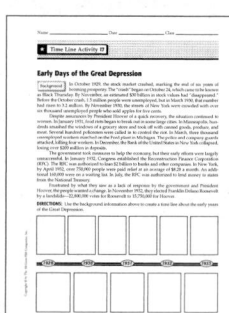

Critical Thinking Skills Activity 17 L2

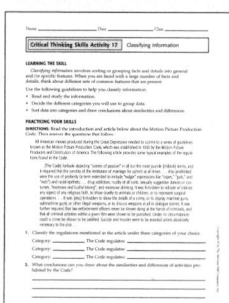

Meeting NCSS Standards

The following standards are covered in Chapter 17:

Section 1 VII Production, Distribution, and Consumption: A, B, D

Section 2 I Culture: A, C

Section 3 V Individuals, Groups, and Institutions: B, C, F, G

Local Standards

Chapter 17 Resources

ASSESSMENT AND EVALUATION

Glencoe's ASSESSMENT ADVANTAGE

Chapter 17 Test Form A L2

Chapter 17 Test Form B L2

Standardized Test Practice Workbook Activity 17 L2

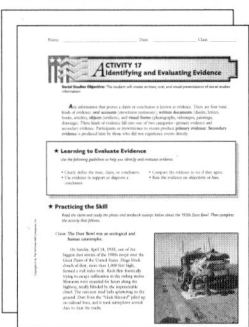

Performance Assessment Activities and Rubrics 17 L1/ELL

ExamView® Pro Testmaker CD-ROM

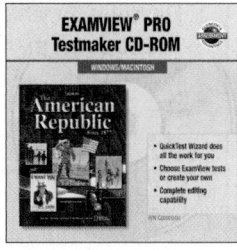

MULTIMEDIA

- Vocabulary PuzzleMaker CD-ROM
- Interactive Tutor Self-Assessment CD-ROM
- ExamView® Pro Testmaker CD-ROM
- Audio Program
- American History Primary Source Documents Library CD-ROM
- MindJogger Videoquiz
- Presentation Plus! CD-ROM
- TeacherWorks™ CD-ROM
- Interactive Student Edition CD-ROM
- Glencoe Skillbuilder Interactive Workbook CD-ROM, Level 2
- The *American Republic Since 1877* Video Program
- American Music: Hits Through History
- American Music: Cultural Traditions

SPANISH RESOURCES

The following Spanish language materials are available:

- Spanish Reading Essentials and Study Guide
- Spanish Guided Reading Activities
- Spanish Reteaching Activities
- Spanish Quizzes and Tests
- Spanish Vocabulary Activities
- Spanish Summaries
- The Declaration of Independence and United States Constitution Spanish Translation

---

THE HISTORY CHANNEL.

The following videotape programs are available from Glencoe as supplements to Chapter 17:

- **Dow and Jones: Wizards of Wall Street** (ISBN 0-76-700203-2)
- **The Stock Exchange** (ISBN 0-76-700562-7)

To order, call Glencoe at 1-800-334-7344. To find classroom resources to accompany many of these videos, check the following home pages:
A&E Television: www.aande.com
The History Channel: www.historychannel.com

HISTORY Online

Use our Web site for additional resources. All essential content is covered in the Student Edition.

You and your students can visit tarvol2.glencoe.com, the Web site companion to the *American Republic Since 1877.* This innovative integration of electronic and print media offers your students a wealth of opportunities. The student text directs students to the Web site for the following options:

- **Chapter Overviews**
- **Self-Check Quizzes**
- **Student Web Activities**
- **Textbook Updates**

Answers to the student Web activities are provided for you in the **Web Activity Lesson Plans.** Additional Web resources and Interactive Tutor Puzzles are also available.

Chapter 17 Resources

SECTION RESOURCES

Daily Objectives	Reproducible Resources	Multimedia Resources
SECTION 1 **Causes of the Depression** 1. Describe the characteristics of the 1920s stock market. 2. Identify the causes of the Great Depression.	Reproducible Lesson Plan 17–1 Daily Lecture and Discussion Notes 17–1 Guided Reading Activity 17–1* Section Quiz 17–1* Reading Essentials and Study Guide 17–1* Performance Assessment Activities and Rubrics	Daily Focus Skills Transparency 17–1 Interactive Tutor Self-Assessment CD-ROM ExamView® Pro Testmaker CD-ROM* Presentation Plus! CD-ROM TeacherWorks™ CD-ROM Audio Program
SECTION 2 **Life During the Depression** 1. Describe how the Great Depression affected American families. 2. Discuss how artists portrayed the effects of the Depression.	Reproducible Lesson Plan 17–2 Daily Lecture and Discussion Notes 17–2 Guided Reading Activity 17–2* Section Quiz 17–2* Reading Essentials and Study Guide 17–2* Performance Assessment Activities and Rubrics Interpreting Political Cartoons	Daily Focus Skills Transparency 17–2 American Art & Architecture Interactive Tutor Self-Assessment CD-ROM ExamView® Pro Testmaker CD-ROM* Presentation Plus! CD-ROM TeacherWorks™ CD-ROM Audio Program American Music: Hits Through History American Music: Cultural Traditions
SECTION 3 **Hoover Responds** 1. Evaluate President Hoover's attempts to revive the economy. 2. Analyze the limitations of Hoover's recovery plans.	Reproducible Lesson Plan 17–3 Daily Lecture and Discussion Notes 17–3 Guided Reading Activity 17–3* Section Quiz 17–3* Reading Essentials and Study Guide 17–3* Performance Assessment Activities and Rubrics	Daily Focus Skills Transparency 17–3 Interactive Tutor Self-Assessment CD-ROM ExamView® Pro Testmaker CD-ROM* Presentation Plus! CD-ROM Skillbuilder Interactive Workbook, Level 2 TeacherWorks™ CD-ROM Vocabulary PuzzleMaker CD-ROM Audio Program

0:00 OUT OF TIME?
Assign the Chapter 17 **Reading Essentials and Study Guide.**

*Also Available in Spanish

 Printed Materials   Transparency   CD-ROM   DVD

 Poster   Music Program   Audio Program

Chapter 17 Resources

NATIONAL GEOGRAPHIC Teacher's Corner

INDEX TO NATIONAL GEOGRAPHIC MAGAZINE

The following articles relate to this chapter.
• "The Okies—Beyond the Great Depression," September 1984

NATIONAL GEOGRAPHIC SOCIETY PRODUCTS

To order the following, call National Geographic at 1-800-368-2728:
• *1929–1941: The Great Depression* (Video)
• *Historical Atlas of the United States* (Atlas)
• *National Geographic World Atlas for Young Explorers—Classroom Library Edition* (Teacher's Guide, Transparencies, Resource Masters)

NGS ONLINE

Access National Geographic's Web site for current events, atlas updates, activities, links, interactive features, and archives.
www.nationalgeographic.com

MEETING SPECIAL NEEDS

In addition to the Differentiated Instruction strategies found in each section, the following resources are also suitable for your special needs students:

• *ExamView® Pro Testmaker CD-ROM* allows teachers to tailor tests by reducing answer choices.

• The *Audio Program* includes the entire narrative of the student edition so that less-proficient readers can listen to the words as they read them.

• The *Reading Essentials and Study Guide* provides the same content as the student edition but is written two grade levels below the textbook.

• *Guided Reading Activities* give less-proficient readers point-by-point instructions to increase comprehension as they read each textbook section.

• *Enrichment Activities* includes a stimulating collection of readings and activities for gifted and talented students.

KEY TO ABILITY LEVELS

Teaching strategies have been coded.

L1 BASIC activities for all students
L2 AVERAGE activities for average to above-average students
L3 CHALLENGING activities for above-average students
ELL ENGLISH LANGUAGE LEARNER activities

From the Classroom of...

Jon Lever
Green River High School
Green River, WY

Beginning of the Great Depression: 1929–1932

As a class, read from the text or other source about life in the early part of the Depression. Focus on the lifestyle changes that occurred as a result of the deepening Depression. This provides the background for the activity.

Once the students show an understanding of the changes in life during the Depression, have the students visit the American Memories Web site, located at memory.loc.gov and find three different pictures of the time period from three different regions. Once the students have found their pictures, they are to write a short story describing the background of that picture based on the life changes in America.

ADDITIONAL RESOURCES FROM GLENCOE

• American Music: Cultural Traditions
• American Art & Architecture
• Outline Map Resource Book
• U.S. Desk Map
• Building Geography Skills for Life
• Inclusion for the High School Social Studies Classroom Strategies and Activities
• Teaching Strategies for the American History Classroom (Including Block Scheduling Pacing Guides)
• Dinah Zike's High School American History Reading and Study Skills Foldables

Block Schedule

Activities that are suited to use within the block scheduling framework are identified by:

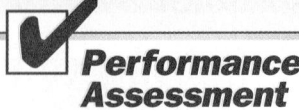

☑ **Performance Assessment**

Refer to Activity 17 in the Performance Assessment Activities and Rubrics booklet. 📘

Why It Matters Activity

Ask students to describe how they think businesses and government cooperate today. Then ask if they think this cooperation helps workers and consumers. Students should evaluate their answers after they have completed the chapter.

GLENCOE
TECHNOLOGY

The *American Republic Since 1877* Video Program

To learn more about life during the Great Depression, have students view the Chapter 17 video, "Brother, Can You Spare a Dime?" from the ***American Republic Since 1877* Video Program.**

MindJogger Videoquiz

Use the **MindJogger Videoquiz** to preview Chapter 17 content.

 Both programs available in DVD

CHAPTER
17 The Great Depression Begins
1929–1932

Why It Matters

Prosperity in the United States seemed limitless before the Great Depression struck. Overproduction and agricultural problems contributed to the economic catastrophe. President Hoover looked to voluntary business action and limited government relief as solutions, but these efforts failed. Meanwhile, millions of Americans lost their jobs and life savings. Artists and writers depicted this suffering, and many people turned to lighthearted films to escape their difficult lives.

The Impact Today

Events of this period remain important.
* *Hoover's model of business-government cooperation is still influential.*
* *John Steinbeck's novel* The Grapes of Wrath *and Grant Wood's painting* American Gothic *are permanent artistic legacies.*

 The *American Republic Since 1877 Video*
The Chapter 17 video, "Brother, Can You Spare a Dime?" chronicles Depression-era life in the United States.

October 29, 1929
* Stock market crashes on Black Tuesday

June 1930
* Hawley-Smoot Tariff passed

1930
* Grant Wood paints *American Gothic*

United States
PRESIDENTS

Hoover 1929–1933

1929   *1930*   *1931*

World

1929
* Remarque's *All Quiet on the Western Front* published

1930
* Ras Tafari becomes Emperor Haile Selassie of Ethiopia

1931
* Gandhi released from prison in India, ending second passive resistance campaign against British rule

528

📖 **Reading Strategy** ► **PURPOSE FOR READING**

Concept Map Like web diagrams, concept maps help students visualize the components of a concept or key term. To begin, students should write and circle "Economic Depression" in the center of a piece of paper. Then to the left, right, and below, have them write and circle each of the following three sub-categories: "What is it? What are its properties? What are some examples?" Students should link each of the three sub-categories to the center bubble by a line. Have students complete the concept map as they read the chapter by filling in brief answers in small bubbles around each sub-category, linking each answer to the corresponding sub-category bubble by a line. **L1**

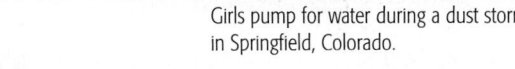

Girls pump for water during a dust storm in Springfield, Colorado.

HISTORY
Online

Introduce students to chapter content and key terms by having them access the **Chapter 17 Overview** at tarvol2.glencoe.com.

More About the Photo

Lawrence Svobida, an eyewitness to the Dust Bowl days, remembers, ". . . With the gales came the dust. Sometimes it was so thick that it completely hid the sun. Visibility ranged from nothing to fifty feet, the former when the eyes were filled with dirt which could not be avoided, even with goggles."

TIME LINE

ACTIVITY

Ask students to select one of the political or economic events on the United States portion of the time line and identify at least one cause and one effect of the event.

October 1931
• National Credit Corporation created

1932
• Drought sweeps Great Plains

July 1932
• Bonus Marchers forced out of Washington, D.C.

January 1932
• Reconstruction Finance Corporation created

F. Roosevelt 1933–1945

1932

1933

September 21, 1931
• Britain abandons gold standard

1932
• Salazar becomes premier of Portugal

February 1932
• Japan sets up puppet government in Manchukuo in northern China

HISTORY
Online
Chapter Overview
Visit the *American Republic Since 1877* Web site at tarvol2.glencoe.com and click on *Chapter Overviews— Chapter 17* to preview chapter information.

529

FOLDABLES™
Study Organizer

Dinah Zike's Foldables are three-dimensional, interactive graphic organizers that help students practice basic writing skills, review key vocabulary terms, and identify main ideas. Have students complete the foldable activity in the *Dinah Zike's Reading and Study Skills Foldables* booklet.

GRAPHIC ORGANIZER ACTIVITY

Organizing Information Have students use a graphic organizer similar to the one below to help them identify the chains of events that led to the Great Depression.

| Stock prices fall. | → | *Margin calls occur.* | → | *People take money from banks and default on loans.* | → | Banks fail. |

| Farm prices decline. | → | *Dust storms destroy topsoil.* | → | *Farm families head west to find work.* | → | Families live in makeshift camps. |

1 FOCUS

Section Overview

This section focuses on the stock market crash of 1929 and the causes of the Great Depression.

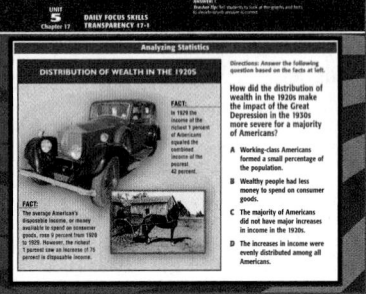
Reading Preview

Answers to Graphic: Hoover: Republican, Quaker, engineer, eight years as Secretary of Commerce, favored Prohibition; Smith: Democrat, Catholic, four-time governor of New York, opposed Prohibition

Preteaching Vocabulary
Have students write a paragraph using at least five of the Key Terms and Names.

SECTION 1 Causes of the Depression

Guide to Reading

Main Idea
Inflated stock prices, overproduction, high tariffs, and mistakes by the Federal Reserve led to the Great Depression.

Key Terms and Names
Alfred E. Smith, stock market, bull market, margin, margin call, speculation, Black Tuesday, installment, Hawley-Smoot Tariff

Reading Strategy
Categorizing As you read about the election of 1928, complete a graphic organizer similar to the one below comparing the backgrounds and issues of the presidential candidates.

1928 Presidential Campaign		
Candidate	Background	Issues

Reading Objectives
• **Describe** the characteristics of the 1920s stock market.
• **Identify** the causes of the Great Depression.

Section Theme
Economic Factors The Great Depression was caused by a combination of various economic problems and government policies.

Preview of Events

◆November 1928	◆September 1929	◆July 1930

November 1928
Herbert Hoover elected president

October 24, 1929
Stocks fall during Black Thursday

October 29, 1929
Black Tuesday stock market crash

June 1930
Congress passes Hawley-Smoot Tariff

★ An American Story ★

Bank run

In the years just after the 1929 stock market crash, Annetta Gibson taught English in a Rockford, Illinois, grade school. As a teacher, Gibson was lucky because she was at least able to keep her job, unlike many other American workers.

❝Everyone knew that the teachers' salaries were being held up. . . . The stores charged anything we wanted, and we'd pay them when we got paid, so it wasn't too bad.
The one thing that was bad was that we had worked hard at school to get the children to save. . . . The children would bring, oh, maybe just a few pennies that they would put in their banks. Some of them had nice little bank accounts when the Depression hit, and some of them never got their money back. It wasn't too good a lesson . . . because they thought they might as well spend their money as save it and then have it gone.❞

—quoted in *Centenarians: The Story of the Twentieth Century by the Americans Who Lived It*

The Election of 1928

The economic collapse that began in 1929 had seemed unimaginable only a year earlier. In the election of 1928, the presidential candidates vied with each other to paint a rosy picture of the future. Republican Herbert Hoover declared, "We are nearer to the final triumph over poverty than ever before in the history of any land."

530 CHAPTER 17 The Great Depression Begins

SECTION RESOURCES

📂 **Reproducible Masters**
• Reproducible Lesson Plan 17–1
• Daily Lecture and Discussion Notes 17–1
• Guided Reading Activity 17–1
• Section Quiz 17–1
• Reading Essentials and Study Guide 17–1
• Performance Assessment Activities and Rubrics

📽 **Transparencies**
• Daily Focus Skills Transparency 17–1

Multimedia
💿 Interactive Tutor Self-Assessment CD-ROM
💿 ExamView® Pro Testmaker CD-ROM
💿 Presentation Plus! CD-ROM
💿 TeacherWorks™ CD-ROM
🎧 Audio Program

The Candidates When Calvin Coolidge decided not to run for president in 1928, he cleared the way for Herbert Hoover to head the Republican ticket. A successful engineer and former head of the Food Administration during World War I, Hoover had also spent over seven years as secretary of commerce in the Harding and Coolidge administrations. The Democrats chose **Alfred E. Smith,** four-time governor of New York. Smith was an Irish American from New York's Lower East Side and the first Roman Catholic ever nominated to run for president.

Campaign Issues By 1928 Prohibition had become a major issue among voters. Because he favored the ban on liquor sales, Hoover was considered a "dry" in the popular language of the day. Smith, who disliked the ban, was a "wet."

The candidates' religious differences sparked a smear campaign against Smith. Many Protestants were willing to believe that the Catholic Church financed the Democratic Party and would rule the United States if Smith got into the White House. These slurs embarrassed Hoover, a Quaker, and he tried to quash them, but the charges seriously damaged Smith's candidacy.

Smith's biggest problem, however, was the prosperity of the 1920s, for which the Republicans took full credit. Republican candidates promised to continue the trend with such slogans as "two cars in every garage." Hoover received over 6 million more votes than Smith and won the Electoral College in a landslide, 444 to 87.

On March 4, 1929, an audience of 50,000 stood in the rain to hear Hoover's inaugural speech. Sound movie cameras covered the inauguration for the first time and radios broadcast the address worldwide. "I have no fears for the future of our country," Hoover said. "It is bright with hope."

 Reading Check **Examining** What campaign issues led to Herbert Hoover's election to the presidency?

The Long Bull Market

The wave of optimism that swept Hoover into the White House also drove stock prices to new highs. The stock market was established as a system for buying and selling shares of companies. Sometimes circumstances in the stock market lead to a long period of rising stock prices, which is known as a bull market. In the late 1920s a prolonged bull market convinced many Americans to invest heavily in stocks. By 1929 about 3 million Americans, or roughly 10 percent of households, owned stocks.

As the market continued to soar, many investors began buying stocks on margin, meaning they made only a small cash down payment—as low as 10 percent of the price. With $1,000 an investor could buy $10,000 worth of stock. The other $9,000 would come as a loan from a stockbroker, who earned both a commission on the sale and interest on the loan. The broker held the stock as collateral.

As long as stock prices kept rising, buying on margin was safe. For example, an investor who borrowed money to buy $10,000 worth of stocks had to wait only a short time for them to rise to $11,000 in value. The investor could then sell the stock, repay the loan, and make $1,000 in profit. The problem came if the stock price began to fall. To protect the loan, a broker could issue a margin call, demanding the investor repay the loan at once. As a result, many investors were very sensitive to any fall in stock prices. If prices fell, they had to sell quickly, or they might not be able to repay their loans.

Before the late 1920s, the prices investors paid for stocks had generally reflected the stocks' true value. If a company made a profit or had good future sales prospects, its stock price rose, while a drop in earnings or an aging product line could send the price down. In the late 1920s, however, hordes of new investors bid prices up without regard to a company's earnings and profits. Buyers, hoping to make a fortune overnight, engaged in speculation. Instead of investing in the future of the companies whose shares they bought,

Picturing **History**

Herbert Hoover The nation and its new president felt confident about the future in early 1929. Why were Americans so optimistic?

2 **TEACH**

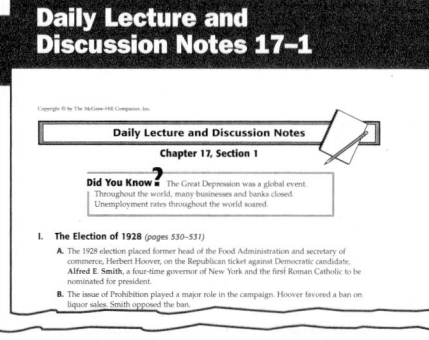

Daily Lecture and Discussion Notes 17–1

Copyright © by The McGraw-Hill Companies, Inc.

Daily Lecture and Discussion Notes
Chapter 17, Section 1

Did You Know? The Great Depression was a global event. Throughout the world, many businesses and banks closed. Unemployment rates throughout the world soared.

I. **The Election of 1928** (pages 530–531)

A. The 1928 election placed former head of the Food Administration and secretary of commerce, Herbert Hoover, on the Republican ticket against Democratic candidate, **Alfred E. Smith,** a four-time governor of New York and the first Roman Catholic to be nominated for president.

B. The issue of Prohibition played a major role in the campaign. Hoover favored a ban on liquor sales. Smith opposed the ban.

Reading Strategy

Making Comparisons Write on the board the three Ps that guided the outcome of the 1928 presidential election: prosperity, Prohibition, and Protestantism. Ask students to write on a piece of paper one example for each, showing how it worked for Hoover and against Smith. Have volunteers share their answers with the class. **L1**

Reading Check

Answer: Prohibition, religious values, economic prosperity

Picturing **History**

Background: Herbert Hoover was born in Iowa, grew up in Oregon, and graduated from Stanford University.
Answer: The economy and stock market were growing.
Ask: What campaign slogan did Hoover use to assure Americans of continuing prosperity? (*two cars in every garage*)

Reading Strategy **READING THE TEXT**

Monitoring Comprehension One of the most important reading strategies students can learn is that they must monitor his or her reading comprehension. As students read, they should be aware of when they have missed something. They can monitor comprehension by questioning themselves as they read. If they do not understand an important idea, they need to re-read, review, or read on to clarify what is unclear. **L1** **ELL**

Refer to *Inclusion for the High School Social Studies Classroom Strategies and Activities* in the TCR.

Guided Reading Activity 17–1

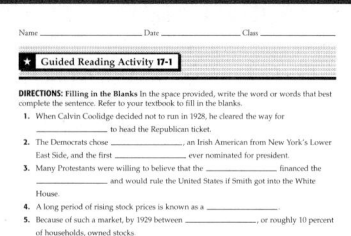

Name _____ Date _____ Class _____

★ Guided Reading Activity **17-1**

DIRECTIONS: Filling in the Blanks In the space provided, write the word or words that best complete the sentence. Refer to your textbook to fill in the blanks.

1. When Calvin Coolidge decided not to run in 1928, he cleared the way for _____ to head the Republican ticket.

2. The Democrats chose _____, an Irish American from New York's Lower East Side, and the first _____ ever nominated for president.

3. Many Protestants were willing to believe that the _____ financed the _____ and would rule the United States if Smith got into the White House.

4. A long period of rising stock prices is known as a _____.

5. Because of such a market, by 1929 _____ between _____, or roughly 10 percent of households, owned stocks.

📈 Graph *Skills*

Answers:

1. 1924

2. It resulted in falling demand for textiles, oil, steel, and rubber. Businesses in these industries laid off workers.

Graph Skills Practice

Ask: How did tariffs affect the Great Depression? *(High tariffs reduced foreign demand for American goods.)*

✓ Reading Check

Answer: bull market, a long period of rising stock prices

⟷ CURRICULUM CONNECTION

Economics The growing gap between the rich and poor in the 1920s reveals that many business leaders had forgotten Henry Ford's insight into the importance of paying workers enough so that they could buy the products they were making.

The Great Depression

Causes

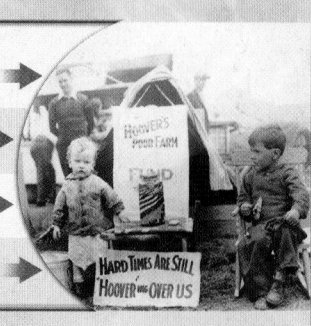

- Overproduction and low demand leads to employee layoffs
- Low wages reduce consumer buying power
- High tariffs restrict foreign demand for American goods
- Unemployment reduces buying power further

Cyclical Effect

Automobile sales declined. This loss of demand meant less demand for:

Textiles — Oil — Steel — Rubber

Which helped contribute further to...

Lower wages — Unemployment

Industry slowed, which caused:

Stock Prices, 1920–1932

Price per Share: $350, $300, $250, $200, $150, $100, $50, 0

— Annual high
— Annual low

1920 1922 1924 1926 1928 1930 1932
Dow-Jones Industrial Averages

Source: Standard and Poor's *Security Price Index Record.*

📈 Graph *Skills*

1. **Interpreting Graphs** Stock prices peaked in 1929. Before this peak, when did they begin to rise sharply?
2. **Making Generalizations** How did the decline in auto sales affect many other industries?

speculators took risks, betting that the market would continue to climb, thus enabling them to sell the stock and make money quickly.

✓ Reading Check **Summarizing** What was the stock market like in the 1920s?

The Great Crash

The bull market lasted only as long as investors continued putting new money into it. By the latter half of 1929, the market was running out of new customers. In September professional investors sensed danger and began to sell off their holdings. Prices slipped. Other investors sold shares to pay the interest on their brokerage loans. Prices fell further.

TURNING POINT

Crash! On Monday, October 21, Groucho Marx, the comic star of stage and screen, was awakened by a telephone call from his broker. "You'd better get

down here with some cash to cover your margin," the broker said. The stock market had plunged. The dazed comedian had to pay back the money he had borrowed to buy stocks, which were now selling for far less than he had paid.

Other brokers made similar margin calls. Frightened customers put their stocks up for sale at a frenzied pace, driving the market into a tailspin. When Marx arrived at the brokerage, he found ticker tape "knee-deep on the floor." He further recalled, "People were shouting orders to sell and others were frantically scribbling checks in vain efforts to save their original investments."

On October 24, a day that came to be called Black Thursday, the market plummeted further. Marx was wiped out. He had earned a small fortune from plays and films, and now it was gone in the blink of an eye. Like many other investors, he was deeply in debt. Arthur Marx recalled his father's final visit to the brokerage, as Groucho looked around and spotted his broker:

❝He was sitting in front of the now-stilled ticker-tape machine, with his head buried in his hands. Ticker tape was strewn around him on the floor, and

---

DIFFERENTIATED INSTRUCTION

At-Risk Students For students who have reading difficulties, you may wish to have them outline this rather complex section. Ask them to copy the main ideas and subheads in their notebooks, leaving plenty of space after each head for their notes about key events and concepts. Remind students to use the chapter and section time lines to preview the events that they will read about. **L1**

☞ Refer to *Inclusion for the High School Social Studies Classroom Strategies and Activities* in the TCR.

the place . . . looked as if it hadn't been swept out in a week. Groucho tapped [him] on the shoulder and said, 'Aren't you the fellow who said nothing could go wrong?' 'I guess I made a mistake,' the broker wearily replied. 'No, I'm the one who made a mistake,' snapped Groucho. 'I listened to you.'99

—quoted in *1929: The Year of the Great Crash*

The following week, on October 29, a day later dubbed **Black Tuesday,** prices took the steepest dive yet. That day stocks lost $10 to $15 billion in value.

By mid-November stock prices had dropped by over one-third. Some $30 billion was lost, a sum roughly equal to the total wages earned by Americans in 1929. The stock market crash was not the major cause of the Great Depression, but it undermined the economy's ability to hold out against its other weaknesses.

Banks in a Tailspin The market crash severely weakened the nation's banks in two ways. First, many banks had lent money to stock speculators. Second, many banks had invested depositors' money in the stock market, hoping for higher returns than they could get by using the money for conventional loans.

When stock values collapsed, the banks lost money on their investments, and the speculators defaulted on their loans. Having suffered serious losses, many banks cut back drastically on the loans they made. With less credit available, consumers and businesses were unable to borrow as much money as they had previously. This helped to put the economy into a recession.

For some banks, the losses they suffered in the crash were more than they could absorb, and they were forced to close. At that time, the government did not insure bank deposits; therefore, if a bank collapsed, customers lost their savings. The bank failures in 1929 and early 1930 triggered a crisis of confidence in the banking system.

News of bank failures worried many Americans. They began to make runs on the nation's banks, causing the banks to collapse. A bank run takes place when many depositors decide to withdraw their money at one time, usually for fear the bank is going to collapse.

Most banks make a profit by lending money received from depositors and collecting interest on the loans. The bank holds on to only a fraction of the depositors' money to cover everyday business, such as occasional withdrawals. Ordinarily that reserve is enough to meet the bank's needs, but if too many people withdraw their money, the bank will eventually collapse. During the first two years

of the Depression, more than 3,000 banks—over 10 percent of the nation's total—were forced to close.

 Reading Check **Evaluating** How did bank failures contribute to the Great Depression?

The Roots of the Great Depression

The stock market crash helped put the economy into a recession. Yet the crash would not have led to a long-lasting depression if other forces had not been at work. The roots of the Great Depression were deeply entangled in the economy of the 1920s.

The Uneven Distribution of Income Most economists agree that overproduction was a key cause of the Depression. More efficient machinery increased the production capacity of both factories and farms.

Most Americans did not earn enough to buy up the flood of goods they helped produce. While manufacturing output per person-hour rose 32 percent, the average worker's wage increased only 8 percent. In 1929 the top 5 percent of all American households earned 30 percent of the nation's income. By contrast, about two-thirds of families earned less than $2,500 a year, leaving them little expendable income.

History *Through Art*

Wall Street Panic This painting shows the confusion and chaos surrounding the financial industry in October 1929. How does the artist depict a sense of disorder?

 Reading Check

Answer: The bank failures triggered a crisis of confidence in the banking system. Many people made runs on the banks, causing them to collapse.

History *Through Art*

Answer: the urgent sense of movement; the paper littered on the floor; the shocked look of several figures
Ask: **What occurred on Black Tuesday?** *(Stocks lost $10 to $15 billion in value in their steepest drop.)*

FYI

By 1932 the nation's manufacturing output stood at 47 percent of its 1929 level.

3 ASSESS

Assign Section 1 Assessment as homework or as an in-class activity.

⊙ Have students use the **Interactive Tutor Self-Assessment CD-ROM.**

L1/ELL

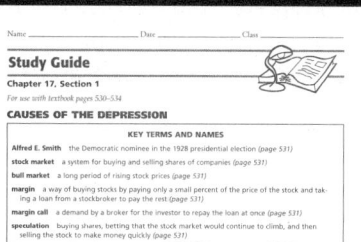

Reading Essentials and Study Guide 17–1

Name _____ Date _____ Class _____

Study Guide

Chapter 17, Section 1
For use with textbook pages 530–534

CAUSES OF THE DEPRESSION

KEY TERMS AND NAMES

Alfred E. Smith the Democratic nominee in the 1928 presidential election (page 531)
stock market a system for buying and selling shares of companies (page 531)
bull market a long period of rising stock prices (page 531)
margin a way of buying stocks by paying only a small percent of the price of the stock and taking a loan from a stockbroker to pay the rest (page 531)
margin call a demand by a broker for the investor to repay the loan at once (page 531)
speculation buying shares, betting that the stock market would continue to climb, and then selling the stock to make money quickly (page 531)

INTERDISCIPLINARY CONNECTIONS ACTIVITY

Economics Invite an economist or an economics teacher to speak to the class about the safeguards that are now in place to help prevent a depression as serious as the Great Depression. Ask the speaker to look at other drops in the stock market and how these safeguards have worked at these times. Ask the speaker to provide an activity or pretest that students can complete in advance of the presentation. **L2**

FYI

Some of the country's leading financiers had tried to avert the crash by pumping money into the market, but others wanted to profit from the panic. The president of Chase National Bank sold 42,506 shares of his own bank's stock, bought them back later in the year at a lower price, and made a profit of $4 million.

Reteach

Have students describe the characteristics of the 1920s stock market.

Enrich

Ask students to hypothesize how the crash might have affected the business of a toy company and the business of a dairy company.

✓ Reading Check

Answer: Tariffs damaged American sales abroad and discouraged imports.

HISTORY Online

Study Central™ provides summaries, interactive games, and online graphic organizers to help students review section content.

4 CLOSE

Have students list the causes of the Great Depression.

Newspaper headline the day after Black Tuesday

During the 1920s many Americans bought high-cost items, such as refrigerators and cars, on the installment plan, under which they would make a small down payment and pay the rest in monthly installments. Some buyers reached a point where paying off their debts forced them to reduce other purchases. This low consumption then led manufacturers to cut production and lay off employees.

The slowdown in retail manufacturing had repercussions throughout the economy. When radio sales slumped, for example, makers cut back on their orders for copper wire, wood cabinets, and glass radio tubes. Montana copper miners, Minnesota lumberjacks, and Ohio glassworkers, in turn, lost their jobs. Jobless workers had to cut back purchases, further reducing sales. This kind of chain reaction put more and more Americans out of work.

The Loss of Export Sales Many jobs might have been saved if American manufacturers had sold more goods abroad. As the bull market of the 1920s accelerated, U.S. banks made high-interest loans to stock speculators instead of lending money to foreign companies. Without these loans from U.S. banks, foreign companies purchased fewer products from American manufacturers.

Matters grew worse after June 1930, when Congress passed the **Hawley-Smoot Tariff** raising the average tariff rate to the highest level in American history. Rates went up on more than 900 manufactured items. The Hawley-Smoot Tariff aimed to protect American manufacturers from foreign competition, but it damaged American sales abroad. Because imports now cost much more, Americans bought fewer of them. Foreign countries responded by raising their own tariffs against American products, and this caused fewer American products to be sold overseas. In 1932 U.S. exports fell to about one-fifth of what they had been in 1929, which hurt both American companies and farmers.

Mistakes by the Federal Reserve Just as consumers were able to buy more goods on credit, access to easy money propelled the stock market. Instead of raising interest rates to curb excessive speculation, the Federal Reserve Board kept its rates very low throughout the 1920s.

The Board's failure to raise interest rates significantly helped cause the Depression in two ways. First, by keeping rates low, it encouraged member banks to make risky loans. Second, its low interest rates led business leaders to think the economy was still expanding. As a result, they borrowed more money to expand production, a serious mistake because it led to overproduction when sales were falling. When the Depression finally hit, companies had to lay off workers to cut costs. Then the Fed made another mistake. It raised interest rates, tightening credit. The economy continued to spiral downward.

✓ Reading Check
Examining How did the decline in worldwide trade contribute to the Depression?

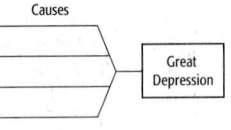 **HISTORY Online** | **Study Central™** To review this section, go to tarvol2.glencoe.com and click on **Study Central™**.

SECTION 1 ASSESSMENT

Checking for Understanding

1. **Define:** stock market, bull market, margin, margin call, speculation, installment.
2. **Identify:** Alfred E. Smith, Black Tuesday, Hawley-Smoot Tariff.
3. **Explain** the significance of the year 1929.

Reviewing Themes

4. **Economic Factors** How did the practices of buying on margin and speculation cause the stock market to rise?

Critical Thinking

5. **Determining Cause and Effect** Why did the stock market crash cause banks to fail?
6. **Organizing** Use a graphic organizer similar to the one below to list the causes of the Great Depression.

Causes → Great Depression

Analyzing Visuals

7. **Analyzing Graphs** Study the graphs on page 532. Note that decreased demand for automobiles ultimately led to layoffs. These layoffs further decreased the demand for automobiles. What do you think might have ended this cycle?

Writing About History

8. **Expository Writing** Write an article for a financial magazine explaining the rapid decline of the stock market in 1929 and the reasons for the Black Tuesday crash.

SECTION 1 ASSESSMENT ANSWERS

1. Terms are in blue.
2. Alfred E. Smith *(p. 531)*, Black Tuesday *(p. 533)*, Hawley-Smoot Tariff *(p. 534)*
3. The Great Depression began.
4. Speculation drove up market prices beyond the stock's value.
5. Banks had lent money to stock speculators and had invested depositors' money in stocks.
6. uneven distribution of wealth, decline in sales, mistakes by the Federal Reserve
7. Answers will vary. Students may suggest that businesses could have avoided layoffs or that the government could have intervened.
8. Students' articles will vary but should include appropriate vocabulary.

Guide to Reading

Main Idea
Many people were impoverished during the Great Depression, but some found ways to cope with the hard times.

Key Terms and Names
bailiff, shantytown, Hooverville, hobo, Dust Bowl, Walt Disney, soap opera, Grant Wood, John Steinbeck, William Faulkner

Reading Strategy
Taking Notes As you read about life in the United States during the Great Depression, use the major headings of the section to create an outline similar to the one below.

Life During the Depression
I. The Depression Worsens
   A.
   B.
   C.
II.

Reading Objectives
• **Describe** how the Great Depression affected American families.
• **Discuss** how artists portrayed the effects of the Depression.

Section Theme
Culture and Traditions Radio and motion pictures provided ways to escape the worries that plagued people during the Depression's early years.

Preview of Events

♦1930 ♦1935 ♦1940

1930
Grant Wood paints *American Gothic*

1932
Drought sweeps Great Plains

1934
Dust storms destroy 300 million acres

1937
Walt Disney releases *Snow White and the Seven Dwarfs*

1939
Popular musical *The Wizard of Oz* released

☆ An American Story ☆

A young girl with the unusual name of Dynamite Garland was living with her family in Cleveland, Ohio, in the 1930s when her father, a railroad worker, lost his job. Unable to afford rent, they gave up their home and moved into a two-car garage.

The hardest aspect of living in a garage was getting through the frigid winters. "We would sleep with rugs and blankets over the top of us," Garland later recalled. "In the morning we'd . . . get some snow and put it on the stove and melt it and wash 'round our faces." When Garland's father found a part-time job in a Chinese restaurant, the family "lived on those fried noodles."

On Sundays the family looked at houses for sale. "That was a recreation during the Depression," said Garland. "You'd go and see where you'd put this and where you could put that, and this is gonna be my room." In this way, the family tried to focus on better times. Movies and radio programs also provided a brief escape from their troubles, but the struggle to survive left little room for pleasure.

—adapted from *Hard Times*

An unemployed man advertising his skills

The Depression Worsens

In 1930, 1,352 banks suspended operations across the nation, more than twice the number of bank failures in 1929. The Depression grew steadily worse during Hoover's administration. By 1933 more than 9,000 banks had failed. In 1932 alone some 30,000 companies

1 FOCUS

Section Overview
This section focuses on life during the Great Depression, including the hardships and the diversions.

BELLRINGER
Skillbuilder Activity

Project transparency and have students answer the question.

Daily Focus Skills Transparency 17–2

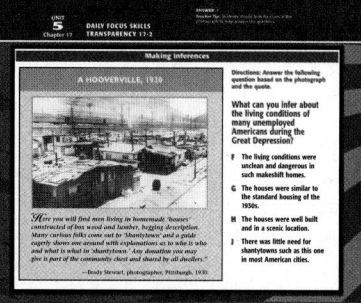

Reading Preview

Answers to Graphic:
I. The Depression Worsens
   A. Lining up at Soup Kitchens
   B. Living in Makeshift Villages
   C. The Dust Bowl
II. Escaping the Depression
   A. The Hollywood Fantasy Factory
   B. On the Air
III. The Depression in Art

Preteaching Vocabulary
Have students create a simple symbol, icon, or sketch for each of the Key Terms and Names.

SECTION RESOURCES

📁 Reproducible Masters
• Reproducible Lesson Plan 17–2
• Daily Lecture and Discussion Notes 17–2
• Guided Reading Activity 17–2
• Section Quiz 17–2
• Reading Essentials and Study Guide 17–2

🗒 Transparencies
• Daily Focus Skills Transparency 17–2

Multimedia
• 💿 Interactive Tutor Self-Assessment CD-ROM
• 💿 ExamView® Pro Testmaker CD-ROM
• 💿 Presentation Plus! CD-ROM
• 💿 TeacherWorks™ CD-ROM
• 🎧 Audio Program
• 🎵 American Music: Hits Through History
• 🎵 American Music: Cultural Traditions

2 TEACH

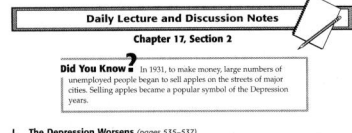

Copyright © by The McGraw-Hill Companies, Inc.

Daily Lecture and Discussion Notes
Chapter 17, Section 2

Did You Know? In 1931, to make money, large numbers of unemployed people began to sell apples on the streets of major cities. Selling apples became a popular symbol of the Depression years.

I. The Depression Worsens (pages 535–537)

A. By 1933 thousands of banks had closed and millions of American workers were unemployed. Unemployed workers often stood at **bread lines** to receive free food or at **soup kitchens** where private charities gave a free meal to the poor.

B. Americans unable to pay their mortgage or rent lost their homes. Those unable or unwilling to move had a court-ordered eviction notice delivered by a court officer or

Discussing a Topic Ask students to consider both negative and positive emotions and activities a major depression might cause in a nation. **L1**

During the 1930s, the Resettlement Administration trained recreational leaders by having them gather the folk music of many immigrant groups. Today the Library of Congress has the song sheets from this project.

History *and the* Humanities

🎵 American Music: Hits Through History: "Brother, Can You Spare a Dime?" "Flores Negras"

🎵 American Music: Cultural Traditions: "Talking Dust Bowl"

🏛 American Art & Architecture: "Migrant Mother"

MOMENT IN HISTORY

IMAGE OF AN ERA

Lasting a decade, the Great Depression deprived many Americans of jobs, land, and livelihoods. Plummeting crop prices and farms withering under drought and dust clouds forced many families to take to the road in search of work, often with little success. Dismayed by scenes of destitution and homelessness, photographer Dorothea Lange joined the Resettlement Administration in 1935. In 1936 in rural Nipomo, California, Lange photographed this "Migrant Mother," a 32-year-old woman with seven children. She had just sold her car tires to buy food.

went out of business. By 1933 more than 12 million workers were unemployed—about one-fourth of the workforce. Average family income dropped from $2,300 in 1929 to $1,600 a few years later.

Lining Up at Soup Kitchens

People without jobs often went hungry. Whenever possible they joined **bread lines** to receive a free handout of food or lined up outside **soup kitchens,** which private charities set up to give poor people a meal.

Peggy Terry, a young girl in Oklahoma City during the Depression, later told an interviewer how each day after school, her mother sent her to the soup kitchen:

> ❝If you happened to be one of the first ones in line, you didn't get anything but water that was on top. So we'd ask the guy that was ladling out soup into the buckets—everybody had to bring their own bucket to get the soup—he'd dip the greasy, watery stuff off the top. So we'd ask him to please dip down to get some meat and potatoes from the bottom of the kettle. But he wouldn't do it.❞
>
> —quoted in *Hard Times*

Living in Makeshift Villages

Families or individuals who could not pay their rent or mortgage lost their homes. Some of them, paralyzed by fear and humiliation over their sudden misfortune, simply would not or could not move. Their landlord would then ask the court for an eviction notice. Court officers called **bailiffs** then ejected the nonpaying tenants, piling their belongings in the street.

Throughout the country, newly homeless people put up shacks on unused or public lands, forming communities called **shantytowns.** Blaming the president for their plight, people referred to such places as **Hoovervilles.**

In search of work or a better life, many homeless and unemployed Americans began to wander around the country, walking, hitchhiking, or, most often, "riding the rails." These wanderers, called **hobos,** would sneak past railroad police to slip into open boxcars on freight trains for a ride to somewhere else. They camped in "hobo jungles," usually situated near rail yards. Hundreds of thousands of people, mostly boys and young men, wandered from place to place in this fashion.

536 CHAPTER 17 The Great Depression Begins

Reading Strategy READING THE TEXT

Reviewing Information Have students work in pairs and ask each other interview questions that a journalist might have asked someone during the Great Depression. The questions should concern the government's responses to the Depression and the interviewee's opinions about the response, either pro or con. Students should try to include as much of the information they have gathered while reading this section as possible. **L1**

📁 Refer to *Inclusion for the High School Social Studies Classroom Strategies and Activities* in the TCR.

GEOGRAPHY

The Dust Bowl Farmers soon faced a new disaster. Since the beginnings of homesteading on the Great Plains, farmers had gambled with nature. Their plows had uprooted the wild grasses that held the soil's moisture. The new settlers then blanketed the region with wheat fields.

When crop prices dropped in the 1920s, however, Midwestern farmers left many of their fields uncultivated. Then, beginning in 1932, a terrible drought struck the Great Plains. With neither grass nor wheat to hold the scant rainfall, the soil dried to dust. From the Dakotas to Texas, America's pastures and wheat fields became a vast "Dust Bowl."

Winds whipped the arid earth, blowing it aloft and blackening the sky for hundreds of miles. When the dust settled, it buried crops and livestock and piled up against farmhouses like snow. No matter how carefully farm families sealed their homes, dust covered everything in the house. As the drought persisted, the number of yearly dust storms grew, from 22 in 1934 to 72 in 1937.

Some Midwestern and Great Plains farmers managed to hold on to their land, but many had no chance. If their withered fields were mortgaged, they had to turn them over to the banks. Then, nearly penniless, many families packed their belongings into old cars or trucks and headed west, hoping for a better life in California. Since many migrants were from Oklahoma, they became known as "Okies." In California, they lived in makeshift roadside camps and remained homeless and impoverished.

✓ **Reading Check**

Explaining What chain of events turned the once-fertile Great Plains into the Dust Bowl?

Escaping the Depression

Despite the devastatingly hard times, Americans could escape—if only for an hour or two—through entertainment. Most people could scrape together the money to go to the movies, or they could sit with their families and listen to one of the many radio programs broadcast across the country.

Student Web Activity Visit the *American Republic Since 1877* Web site at tarvol2.glencoe.com and click on *Student Web Activities—Chapter 17* for an activity on the Great Depression.

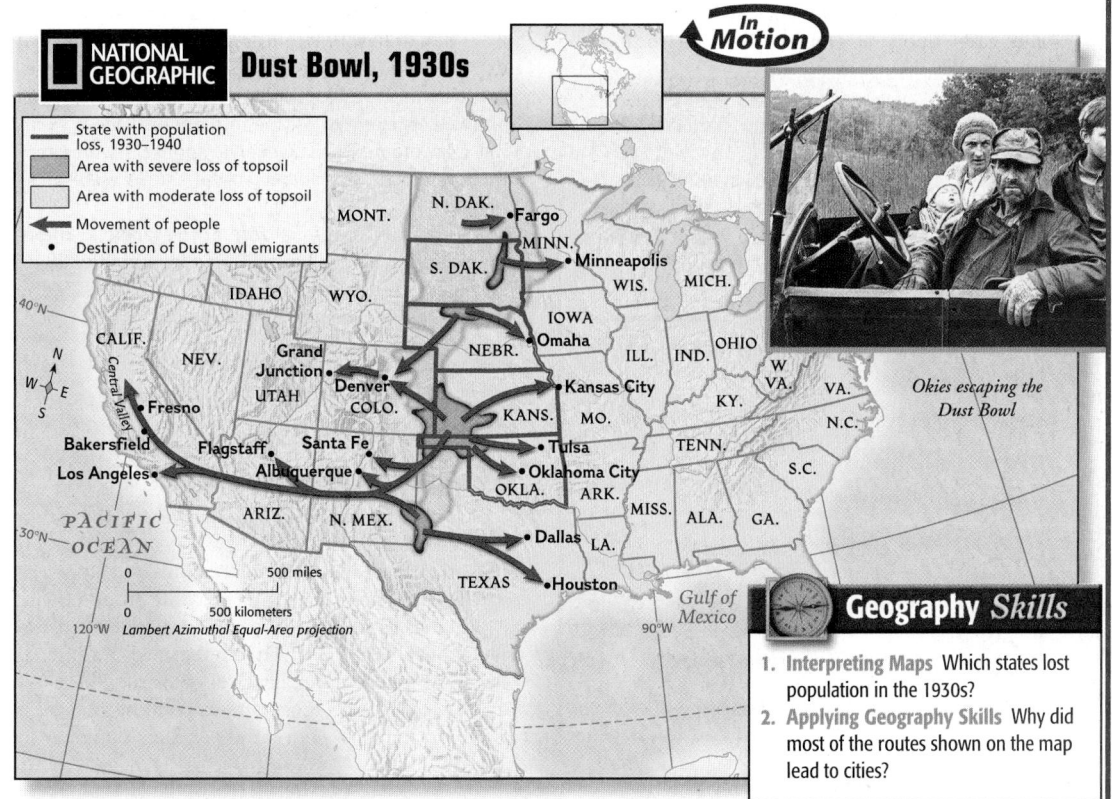

Dust Bowl, 1930s

Legend:
— State with population loss, 1930–1940
Area with severe loss of topsoil
Area with moderate loss of topsoil
← Movement of people
• Destination of Dust Bowl emigrants

Okies escaping the Dust Bowl

Geography Skills

1. **Interpreting Maps** Which states lost population in the 1930s?
2. **Applying Geography Skills** Why did most of the routes shown on the map lead to cities?

HISTORY Online

Objectives and answers to the student activity can be found in the **Web Activity Lesson Plan** at tarvol2.glencoe.com.

✓ **Reading Check**

Answer: uprooting the wild grasses, a drop in crop prices, and terrible drought

Geography Skills

Answers:
1. South Dakota, Nebraska, Kansas, Oklahoma
2. Cities had more job possibilities.

Geography Skills Practice
Ask: To what city did North Dakota farmers migrate? *(Fargo)*

📁 Use *Interpreting Political Cartoons,* Cartoon 23.

DIFFERENTIATED INSTRUCTION

At-Risk Students Encourage students to use library and Internet resources to learn more about hobo signs. Have students create a pictorial message using the hobo signs. Have students present their messages to the class and have other class members try to decipher them. Discuss how the secret signs used by hobos helped them survive. **L1**

📁 Refer to *Inclusion for the High School Social Studies Classroom Strategies and Activities* in the TCR.

Background: At the height of the Great Depression there may have been as many as 250,000 teenage hobos.

Ask: Why do you think teens took up the hobo lifestyle? *(running away, orphaned or abandoned, looking for work)*

✔ **Reading Check**

Answer: comedies, westerns, soap operas

3 ASSESS

Assign Section 2 Assessment as homework or as an in-class activity.

🌐 Have students use the **Interactive Tutor Self-Assessment CD-ROM.**

L1/ELL

Reading Essentials and Study Guide 17–2

L2

Section Quiz 17–2

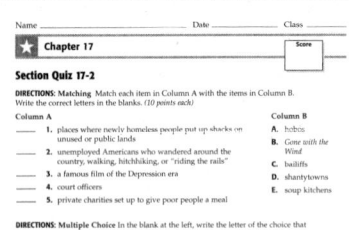

The Hollywood Fantasy Factory Ordinary citizens often went to the movies to see people who were rich, happy, and successful. The 60 to 90 million weekly viewers walked into a fantasy world of thrills and romance. Comical screenplays offered a welcome release from daily worries. Groucho Marx wisecracked while his brothers' antics provoked hilarity in such films as *Animal Crackers.*

Many European actors, writers, and directors, fleeing economic hardship and the threat of dictatorships, went to Hollywood in the 1920s and 1930s. Two European women emerged as superstars. Germany's **Marlene Dietrich** portrayed a range of roles with subtlety. Swedish actress **Greta Garbo** often played a doomed beauty, direct and unhesitating in her speech and actions.

Moviegoers also loved cartoons. **Walt Disney** produced the first feature-length animated film, *Snow White and the Seven Dwarfs,* in 1937. Its box office appeal may have spurred MGM two years later to produce *The Wizard of Oz,* a colorful musical that lifted viewers' spirits.

Even when films focused on serious subjects, they usually contained a note of optimism. In *Mr. Smith Goes to Washington,* James Stewart plays a naïve youth leader who becomes a senator. He dramatically exposes the corruption of some of his colleagues and calls upon his fellow senators to see the American political system as the peak of "what man's carved out for himself after centuries of fighting for something better than just jungle law."

Gone with the Wind, an elaborately costumed film nearly four hours long, topped the Depression-era epics. Its heroine, Scarlett O'Hara, played by British actress Vivien Leigh, struggles to maintain her life on a Georgia plantation during and after the Civil War. Romance enters as Clark Gable, playing the masterful Rhett Butler, woos Scarlett. Audiences found inspiration in Scarlett's unassailable will to survive.

On the Air While movie drama captured the imagination, radio offered entertainment on a more personal level. People listened to the radio every day, gathering around the big wooden box in the living room. It could have been the voice of the president or a newscaster that held their attention. More often it was the comedy of Jack Benny or George Burns and Gracie Allen, or the adventures of a hero like the Green Hornet.

One of the most popular heroes was the Lone Ranger, who fought injustice in the Old West with the help of his "faithful Indian companion," Tonto. The listener needed only to picture the hero with a black mask hiding his identity, as he fired a silver bullet to knock a gun from an outlaw's hand.

Daytime radio dramas carried their stories over from day to day. Programs such as *The Guiding Light* depicted middle-class families confronting illness, conflict, and other problems. These short dramas allowed listeners to escape into a world more exciting than their own. The shows' sponsors were often makers of laundry soaps, so the shows were nicknamed soap operas.

While the Depression tore at the fabric of many towns, radio created a new type of community. Even strangers found common ground in discussing the lives of radio characters.

✔ **Reading Check** **Evaluating** What movies and radio shows entertained Americans during the Depression?

The Depression in Art

Art and literature also flourished in the harsh and emotional 1930s. The homeless and unemployed became the subject of pictures and stories as artists and writers tried to portray life around them. **Thomas Hart Benton** and **Grant Wood** led the regionalist school, which emphasized traditional American values, especially those of the rural Midwest and South. Wood's most famous painting, *American Gothic,* portrays a stern farmer and his daughter in

---

Fact | Fiction | Folklore

Hobo Signs The hundreds of thousands of hobos who roamed the country developed intricate symbols that they wrote on trees, fences, or buildings to warn or inform other hobos. Many became a part of American folklore.

☺	(a closed eye) This community is indifferent toward hobos.
◉	(an open eye) The authorities here are alert; be careful.
🏠	This is a dangerous neighborhood.
〰️	Fresh water and a safe campsite.
🔲	This is dangerous drinking water.
⊗	This is a good place for a handout.
🐟	You may sleep in the hayloft here.

Source: *Hobo Signs.*

INTERDISCIPLINARY CONNECTIONS ACTIVITY

Mathematics Ask students to make a graph of the unemployment rates in the 1930s. Provide the data shown below. **L2**

Year	Rate	Year	Rate	Year	Rate
1930	9%	1934	22%	1938	19%
1931	16%	1935	21%	1939	17%
1932	24%	1936	17%		
1933	25%	1937	15%		

front of their humble farmhouse. The portrait pays tribute to no-nonsense Midwesterners while at the same time gently making fun of their severity.

Novelists such as **John Steinbeck** added flesh and blood to journalists' reports of poverty and misfortune. Their writing evoked both sympathy for their characters and indignation at social injustice. In *The Grapes of Wrath*, published in 1939, Steinbeck tells the story of an Oklahoma family fleeing the Dust Bowl to find a new life in California. Steinbeck had seen firsthand the plight of migrant farm families uprooted by the Dust Bowl. After visiting camps of these families he had a better understanding of their fears. He described "people in flight" along Route 66. Inside one old jalopy sat the members of a family, worrying:

> 66There goes a gasket. Got to go on. Find a nice place to camp. . . . The food's getting low, the money's getting low. When we can't buy no more gas—what then? Danny in the back seat wants a cup a water. Little fella's thirsty.99
>
> —from *The Grapes of Wrath*

Other novelists of this time influenced literary style itself. In *The Sound and the Fury*, for example, author **William Faulkner** shows what his characters are thinking and feeling before they speak. Using this stream of consciousness technique, he exposes hidden attitudes of Southern whites and African Americans in a fictional Mississippi county. Another

Profiles IN HISTORY

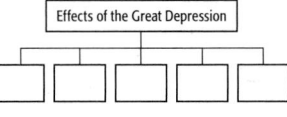

Dorothea Lange *1895–1965*

Before she had ever used a camera, Dorothea Lange knew she wanted to be a photographer. After finishing high school, she took a photography course in New York, then traveled around the world. Lange earned her keep by taking and selling photos. Her trip ended in San Francisco.

In San Francisco, Lange photographed homeless people and uncovered the desperation of her subjects. One day, while driving through California's Central Valley, Lange noticed a sign: "Pea-Pickers Camp." On impulse, she stopped. She approached a woman and her children gazing listlessly out of a tattered tent. Lange took five pictures while the mother "sat in that lean-to tent with her children huddled around her, and seemed to know that my pictures might help her, and so she helped me."

In the mid-1930s, Lange traveled through the Dust Bowl states, capturing the ravages of dust storms. When the images were reproduced in a best-selling book, *American Exodus*, the state of California created camps to shelter migrant workers.

Southern writer, Thomas Wolfe, used the facts of his own life to examine the theme of artistic creation in such powerful novels as *Look Homeward Angel*.

While the written word remained powerful, the printed image was growing in influence. Magazine photographers roamed the nation armed with the new 35-millimeter cameras, seeking new subjects. Photojournalist **Margaret Bourke-White's** striking pictures, displayed in *Fortune* magazine, showed the ravages of drought. In 1936 *Time* magazine publisher Henry Luce introduced *Life*, a weekly photojournalism magazine that enjoyed instant success.

✓**Reading Check** **Examining** How did artists, photographers, and writers, such as John Steinbeck, reflect the characteristics of the 1930s?

SECTION 2 ASSESSMENT

HISTORY Online **Study Central™** To review this section, go to **tarvol2.glencoe.com** and click on **Study Central™**.

Checking for Understanding

1. **Define:** bailiff, shantytown, Hooverville, hobo, Dust Bowl, soap opera.
2. **Identify:** Walt Disney, Grant Wood, John Steinbeck, William Faulkner.
3. **Explain** what caused the Dust Bowl conditions on the Great Plains.

Reviewing Themes

4. **Culture and Traditions** In what ways did people seek to forget about the Depression?

Critical Thinking

5. **Making Inferences** Why do you think *Life* magazine was so popular during the 1930s?
6. **Organizing** Use a graphic organizer to list the effects of the Great Depression.

Effects of the Great Depression

Analyzing Visuals

7. **Analyzing Photos** Study the photograph on page 536. Think of three adjectives that you would use to describe the people in the photograph. Using these adjectives, write a paragraph describing the family pictured.

Writing About History

8. **Descriptive Writing** Imagine that you are living during the Great Depression. Write a journal entry describing a day in your life.

CHAPTER 17 The Great Depression Begins **539**

SECTION 2 ASSESSMENT ANSWERS

1. Terms are in blue.
2. Walt Disney *(p. 538)*, Grant Wood *(p. 538)*, John Steinbeck *(p. 539)*, William Faulkner *(p. 539)*
3. uncultivated fields, depletion of grasslands protecting soil, and drought
4. Americans looked to radio and motion pictures as an escape.
5. Its photos provided a powerful commentary on American life.
6. bank failures, unemployment, hunger, homelessness, and hardship
7. Students' paragraphs will vary. Possible adjectives are desperate, defeated, and discouraged.
8. Students' journal entries will vary. Encourage students to take on the role of someone living during the Depression.

Profiles IN HISTORY

Background: Lange started her career as a portrait photographer, often taking pictures of wealthy individuals and families. Lange worked for several government agencies documenting American life.
Ask: How do you think Lange's photographs helped officials in California decide to create camps to shelter migrant workers? *(Her work brought the problem to officials' attention, and made it seem more real.)*

Reteach

Have students pose and answer questions about how the Great Depression affected American families.

Enrich

Invite interested students to learn more about an artist or author whose work depicts the Depression. Have students create an oral presentation about the subject they select.

✓**Reading Check**

Answer: by depicting the homeless and unemployed in their works

HISTORY Online

Study Central™ provides summaries, interactive games, and online graphic organizers to help students review section content.

4 CLOSE

Have students discuss how artists captured the effects of the Depression.

NATIONAL GEOGRAPHIC Geography&History

1 FOCUS

Tell students Hoover Dam is about 660 feet (201 meters) thick at its base. It has 17 generators. Hydroelectric power is both a renewable and inexpensive source of electricity.

2 TEACH

Analyzing Information Have students study the map and read the feature. Have students create questions for a trivia game based on the information they have read. Have students pose their questions and see which student can answer the question most quickly. If you choose, you can keep score and provide a small prize to the winners. **L1**

Creating a Database Have students work in small groups to gather facts about Hoover Dam and other large hydroelectric power producers. Have students create an electronic database using these facts. As a starting point for their research, you may recommend the following Web site: http://www.hooverdam.usbr.gov/ **L2**

L2

Geography and History Activity 5

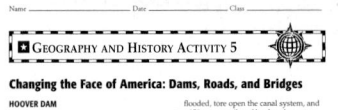

Name _____ Date _____ Class _____

⊕ GEOGRAPHY AND HISTORY ACTIVITY 5 🌐

Changing the Face of America: Dams, Roads, and Bridges

HOOVER DAM

Hoover Dam was one of many projects, large and small, built during the Great Depression that changed the landscape of the United States. Hoover Dam tamed one of this country's wildest rivers—the Colorado. The Colorado River challenged settlers, ranchers, and farmers in the water-starved West and Southwest. They saw the 1,400-mile-long river as a potential source of water and power. The Colorado, however, could not be relied on to cooperate with

flooded, tore open the canal system, and put 150 square miles of land under water. After several more floods, there was much public outcry for a dam. In 1920 the Boulder Canyon Project was formed. After four years of surveys and tests, the Black Canyon on the Arizona-Nevada border was chosen as the site to harness the Colorado River.

By the time construction of the Hoover Dam started in 1931, the country was in the grips of the Great Depression. Unemployment in the United States reached a high of almost 13 million in 1933. (See Figure 1.)

540

THE FLOW OF ELECTRICITY

Today Hoover Dam generates more than 4 billion kilowatt-hours of electricity per year—enough to keep machines humming and lights burning for over a million people. More than half of that electricity is sent to California; the remainder goes to Nevada and Arizona (see inset map).

540 CHAPTER 17 The Great Depression Begins

EXTENDING THE CONTENT

Protecting the Dam During World War II, Hoover Dam was considered a prime target because it supplied water and electricity to so many people. Pillbox gun emplacements were scattered in the hills surrounding the dam. These emplacements were manned 24 hours a day during the war. One of the emplacements on the Arizona side of the dam remains. The dam is still protected around the clock. Security measures vary, but no vehicle is allowed to stop on the dam, and no pedestrian traffic is allowed around or on the dam at night. At times of heightened alert, the authorities restrict the types of vehicles that can drive on the road over the dam.

Hoover Dam

American farmers and settlers in the low-lying valleys of southern California and southwestern Arizona have been tapping the waters of the Colorado River for more than a century. Thanks to irrigation canals, the parched desert valleys became year-round gardens that provided fruit and vegetables for the nation. At times, however, the unpredictable river would decrease to a trickle. Other times, it became a raging torrent, destroying all in its path. The federal government decided to dam the Colorado to control it. In 1931 construction began in Black Canyon, whose high rock walls made it an ideal site. Here, on the border between Arizona and Nevada, would rise one of the most ambitious engineering projects the world had ever seen: the Hoover Dam.

Named after President Herbert Hoover, the dam was built in the middle of a forbidding desert. Everything had to be imported, including labor. There was no shortage of candidates. The country was in the grips of the Great Depression; thousands of unemployed workers flocked to the remote canyon. To accommodate them, an entire town was built—Boulder City, Nevada.

The new arrivals faced brutal conditions. Men worked in three shifts around the clock. Summer temperatures climbed higher than 120 degrees in the canyon, and even those who worked at night had to endure temperatures of more than 85 degrees. Still, the project was completed in less than five years. Lake Mead, the 115-mile-long reservoir created by the dam, is large enough to hold two years' worth of the average flow of the Colorado River—enough to cover the entire state of New York with one foot of water. The benefits to the Southwest were immense. Hoover Dam created much-needed employment. It also provided a regular supply of water, irrigating over a million acres of rich agricultural land and producing hydroelectric power, which has allowed Southwestern cities to grow.

Suspended on ropes, "high scalers" armed with dynamite and jackhammers prepare the walls of Black Canyon to take the concrete of Hoover Dam. Such work was hazardous. Twenty-four workers fell to their deaths during construction of the dam.

Hoover Dam and Environs

- .... State boundary
- – – – Aqueduct
- —— Road
- ✶—✶ Power line
- ▬▬ Urban area

Scale varies in this perspective

McCullough Range

Henderson

River Mountains

to Las Vegas

Aqueduct

Las Vegas Bay

Swallow Bay

Hoover Dam, a major supplier of hydroelectric power, is more than 700 feet (213 m) tall and contains about 4,360,000 cubic yards of concrete—enough for a two-lane highway from Los Angeles to Boston.

LEARNING FROM GEOGRAPHY

1. Why did the federal government decide to dam the Colorado River?

2. Why did engineers choose the Black Canyon site?

541

Drawing Conclusions Tell students that Lake Mead has become a recreational lake that tourists visit throughout the year. Remind students that the dam was built to control the unpredictable flow of the Colorado River and to provide water and power to the Southwest. **Ask:** Why do you think the recreational uses for the lake were not part of the planning? (*The government goal was not to create a recreational site.*) What benefits do you think having the lake as a recreational destination have created for Arizona and Nevada? (*Students should note that it created a reason for people to live in the area after the dam was built; it also created jobs and revenues from tourism.*) **L2**

3 ASSESS

Have students answer the Learning from Geography questions.

4 CLOSE

Ask students to recount the dangers faced by workers who constructed the dam.

NGS ONLINE

Access National Geographic's Web site for current events, atlas updates, activities, links, interactive features, and archives at www.nationalgeographic.com.

ANSWERS TO LEARNING FROM GEOGRAPHY

1. The river was dammed to control its unpredictable flow.

2. The high rock walls made Black Canyon the preferred site for the dam.

1 FOCUS

Section Overview

This section focuses on Hoover's responses to the Depression.

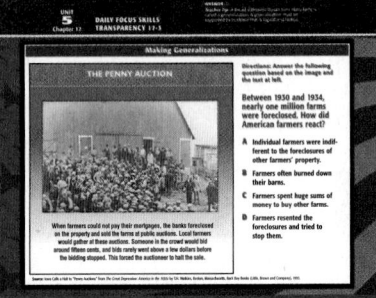
Reading Preview

Answers to Graphic: Industry was to keep factories open and stop slashing wages, but business leaders did not follow through; to increase public works, but this had little effect; to pump money into the economy, but this was too limited and could not reverse the accelerating collapse.

Preteaching Vocabulary
Have students make a list of the Key Terms and Names and write a helpful phrase next to each term or name.

SECTION 3 Hoover Responds

Guide to Reading

Main Idea
President Hoover's philosophy of government guided his response to the Depression.

Key Terms and Names
public works, Reconstruction Finance Corporation, relief, foreclose, Bonus Army

Reading Strategy
Categorizing As you read about Hoover's response to the Depression, complete a graphic organizer by listing his major initiatives and their results.

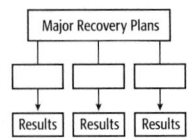

Major Recovery Plans

Results | Results | Results

Reading Objectives
- **Evaluate** President Hoover's attempts to revive the economy.
- **Analyze** the limitations of Hoover's recovery plans.

Section Theme
Groups and Institutions President Hoover began using new government agencies to improve the nation's slumping economy.

Preview of Events

♦1931   ♦1932   ♦1933

October 1931
National Credit Corporation created

January 1932
Congress approves Reconstruction Finance Corporation

July 1932
Congress passes Emergency Relief and Construction Act; soldiers rout the Bonus Marchers

---

★ An American Story ★

Joseph Heffernan

In December 1929, Mayor Joseph Heffernan of Youngstown, Ohio, listened impatiently to fellow public officials assembled in the Cleveland Chamber of Commerce hall. He had been called to one of a series of conferences on unemployment that President Hoover had arranged. At the conference, Heffernan grew restless as he listened to the other speakers. He felt that it would take too long to pass their confident proposals for ending unemployment, and by that time, it would be too late to prevent a depression. He asked the other conference members, "Why not tell people the truth?"

Youngstown business leaders criticized Heffernan for trying to tell his constituents how bad the economic outlook was. Heffernan later recalled that one of them said to him, "Don't emphasize hard times and everything will be all right."

The man who rebuked Mayor Heffernan expressed what many, including President Hoover himself, believed in late 1929: The country merely needed to regain its confidence. As the crisis worsened, Hoover took steps to help the economy recover, but only within the limits of his philosophy of government.

—adapted from *The Great Depression*

Promoting Recovery

On Friday, October 25, the day after Black Thursday, President Hoover issued a statement assuring the nation that industry was "on a sound and prosperous basis." In March 1930 he told the public that "the worst effects of the crash . . . will have passed during the next 60 days." Critics derided his optimism as conditions worsened. Hoover,

---

SECTION RESOURCES

📖 Reproducible Masters
- Reproducible Lesson Plan 17–3
- Daily Lecture and Discussion Notes 17–3
- Guided Reading Activity 17–3
- Section Quiz 17–3
- Reading Essentials and Study Guide 17–3
- Performance Assessment Activities and Rubrics

Transparencies
- Daily Focus Skills Transparency 17–3

Multimedia
- Interactive Tutor Self-Assessment CD-ROM
- ExamView® Pro Testmaker CD-ROM
- Presentation Plus! CD-ROM
- TeacherWorks™ CD-ROM
- Audio Program

however, hoped to downplay the public's fears. He wanted to avoid more bank runs and layoffs by urging consumers and business leaders to become more rational in their decision making.

Voluntary Efforts and Public Works Despite his soothing words, Hoover was seriously worried about the economy. He organized a series of conferences, bringing together the heads of banks, railroads, and other big businesses, as well as labor and government officials.

He won a pledge from industry to keep factories open and to stop slashing wages. By 1931, however, business leaders had abandoned those pledges. Hoover's next step was to increase public works—government-financed building projects. The resulting construction jobs could replace some of those lost in the private sector. He urged governors and mayors throughout the nation to increase public works spending.

Hoover's actions did spur construction increases, but the effort made up for only a small fraction of the jobs lost in the private sector. The only way the government could create enough new jobs would be to massively increase government spending, which Hoover refused to do.

The problem was that someone had to pay for public works projects. If the government raised taxes to pay for them, it would take money away from consumers and hurt businesses that were already struggling. If the government decided to keep taxes low and run a budget deficit instead—spending more money than it collected in taxes—it would have to borrow the money from banks. If the government did this, less

2 TEACH

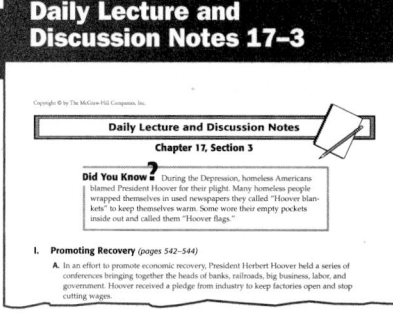

Daily Lecture and Discussion Notes 17–3

Copyright © by The McGraw-Hill Companies, Inc.

Daily Lecture and Discussion Notes
Chapter 17, Section 3

Did You Know? During the Depression, homeless Americans blamed President Hoover for their plight. Many homeless people wrapped themselves in used newspapers they called "Hoover blankets" to keep themselves warm. Some wore their empty pockets inside out and called them "Hoover flags."

I. **Promoting Recovery** (pages 542–544)
A. In an effort to promote economic recovery, President Herbert Hoover held a series of conferences bringing together the heads of banks, railroads, big business, labor, and government. Hoover received a pledge from industry to keep factories open and stop cutting wages.

Discussing a Concept Conduct a class discussion about the role of government in the economy by asking students what the government should do to help those who are unemployed and what responsibility the government has to keep the economy healthy. **L1**

Different Viewpoints

What Should the Government's Role in the Economy Be?

The government's role in the economy was an important issue in the 1932 presidential election, when the country was in the throes of the Depression. President Herbert Hoover explained in a 1928 speech why a limited government role was best, while President Franklin Roosevelt argued in his inaugural address in 1933 that an expanded government role was necessary.

from Hoover's Madison Square Garden Address, 1928

"During one hundred and fifty years we have built up a form of self-government and a social system which is peculiarly our own. . . . It is founded upon a particular conception of self-government in which decentralized local responsibility is the very base. . . .

During the war we necessarily turned to the government to solve every difficult economic problem. . . . However justified in time of war, if continued in peacetime it would destroy . . . our progress and freedom. . . . The acceptance of these ideas would have meant the destruction of self-government through centralization of government. It would have meant the undermining of the individual initiative and enterprise through which our people have grown to unparalleled greatness."

from Roosevelt's Inaugural Address, 1933

"Our greatest primary task is to put people to work. This is no unsolvable problem if we face it wisely and courageously. It can be accomplished in part by direct recruiting by the Government itself, treating the task as we would treat the emergency of a war, but at the same time, through this employment, accomplishing greatly needed projects to stimulate and reorganize the use of our natural resources.

. . . The task can be helped . . . by national planning for and supervision of all forms of transportation and of communications and other utilities which have a definitely public character. There are many ways in which it can be helped, but it can never be helped merely by talking about it. We must act and act quickly.

. . . We now realize as we have never realized before our interdependence on each other; . . . that if we are to go forward, we must move as a trained and loyal army willing to sacrifice for the good of a common discipline."

Learning From History

1. **Analyzing Arguments** What did Hoover fear would happen if government programs started during World War I were continued after the war?
2. **Making Inferences** Do you think Roosevelt would have agreed with Hoover's assessment of the government's role during World War I? Why or why not?

Different Viewpoints

Answers:

1. It would destroy freedom and initiative.

2. Yes, because during a national emergency—whether World War I or the Great Depression—Roosevelt believed the government should take more responsibility for the economy

Ask: Do you think that Hoover might have changed his mind by the time Roosevelt was inaugurated? (*Students' answers will vary.*)

Reading Strategy   READING THE TEXT

Identifying the Main Idea Students should identify main ideas as they read. Text features, such as headings, subheadings, boldfaced terms, and graphics, are good indicators of main or key ideas. As students read, have them make a list of ideas by creating an outline or drawing a graphic organizer. **L1** ELL

Refer to *Inclusion for the High School Social Studies Classroom Strategies and Activities* in the TCR.

L1/ELL

Guided Reading Activity 17–3

Name_____ Date_____ Class_____

★ **Guided Reading Activity 17-3**

DIRECTIONS: Recalling Facts Read the section and answer the questions below. Refer to your textbook to write the answers.

1. Of what did President Hoover assure the nation on Friday, October 25, 1929, the day after Black Thursday?

2. What did President Hoover win from industry, and what was the result?

3. What did President Hoover see as problems with government-paid public works jobs?

4. What was President Hoover's fear about deficit spending?

5. What was the purpose of the National Credit Corporation (NCC)?

✓ **Reading Check**

Answer: He believed it would delay an economic recovery.

CURRICULUM CONNECTION

Music The music of Woody Guthrie gave an uplifting voice to people who struggled through the Depression. Unlike swing or big-band songs, Guthrie's lyrics told of rough living and fighting back. The guitarist drew upon the traditional tunes of farmers and workers to write workers' anthems for decades to come.

✓ **Reading Check**

Answer: He felt that only state and city governments should give out relief.

FYI

Ironically the board game Monopoly was invented during the Depression. Charles Darrow was an unemployed Pennsylvania engineer when he designed the famous game in the early 1930s.

---

money would be available for businesses that wanted to expand and for consumers who wanted mortgages or other loans. Hoover feared that deficit spending would actually delay an economic recovery.

The Midterm Election As the congressional elections of 1930 approached, most Americans felt that worsening unemployment posed a grave threat to their well-being. Citizens blamed the party in power for the stumbling economy. The Republicans lost 49 seats and their majority in the House of Representatives; they held on to the Senate by a single vote.

✓ **Reading Check** **Examining** Why did Hoover oppose deficit spending?

Pumping Money Into the Economy

Hoover soon turned his attention to the problem of money. There was very little in the economy now that so many banks had collapsed. The government, he believed, had to make sure that banks could make loans to corporations so they could expand production and rehire workers.

White Angel Breadline In 1932 a wealthy woman nicknamed the "White Angel" set up a breadline in San Francisco. Dorothea Lange captured the hopelessness of the Depression in this famous photograph of the breadline.

GOVERNMENT

Trying to Rescue the Banks The president asked the Federal Reserve Board to put more currency into circulation, but the Board refused. In an attempt to ease the money shortage, Hoover set up the National Credit Corporation (NCC) in October 1931. The NCC created a pool of money to enable troubled banks to continue lending money in their communities. Hoover then persuaded a number of New York bankers to contribute to the NCC. Their contributions, however, did not meet the nation's needs.

By 1932 Hoover concluded that the only way to provide funding for borrowers was for the government to do the lending. He requested that Congress set up the **Reconstruction Finance Corporation** (RFC) to make loans to banks, railroads, and agricultural institutions. By early 1932, the RFC had lent about $238 million to approximately 160 banks, 60 railroads, and 18 building-and-loan organizations. The RFC was overly cautious, however. It failed to increase its loans in sufficient amounts to meet the need, and the economy continued its decline.

Direct Help for Citizens From the start, Hoover strongly opposed the federal government's participation in relief—money that went directly to impoverished families. He believed that only state and city governments should dole out relief. By the spring of 1932, however, they were running out of money.

In 1932 political support was building for a relief measure, and Congress passed the Emergency Relief and Construction Act. Although reluctant, Hoover signed the bill on July 21. The new act called for $1.5 billion for public works and $300 million in loans to the states for direct relief. By this time, however, the new program could not reverse the accelerating collapse.

✓ **Reading Check** **Summarizing** Why did Hoover oppose the federal government's participation in relief programs?

In an Angry Mood

In the months after the Wall Street crash, Americans had seemed resigned to bad economic news. By 1931, however, they were growing increasingly discontented, and open acts of revolt began to occur.

Hunger Marches In January 1931, around 500 men and women in Oklahoma City, shouting angrily about hunger and joblessness, broke into a grocery store and looted it. Crowds began showing

---

DIFFERENTIATED INSTRUCTION

Reading Support Tell students that library use surged during the 1930s; one Indiana town, for example, found that the circulation of books rose 145 percent between 1929 and 1933. Ask students to identify the relationship between the economic circumstances of the day and the increased reading of books. Ask them to suggest the types of books people would logically choose. **L2**

☞ Refer to *Inclusion for the High School Social Studies Classroom Strategies and Activities* in the TCR.

Picturing **History**

Poverty and Plenty Spattered with milk, dairy farmers are shown here destroying their product in a vain effort to drive up prices. For the hungry and unemployed, like the families at left, the farmers' actions were unthinkable. *Why did the farmers think their actions would drive up prices?*

Picturing **History**

Answer: By lowering supply, they hoped to raise prices.

Ask: Why is the image of a child carrying this sign especially powerful? *(It plays on emotions and highlights the innocent victims.)*

3 ASSESS

Assign Section 3 Assessment as homework or as an in-class activity.

🕐 Have students use the **Interactive Tutor Self-Assessment CD-ROM.**

L1/ELL

Reading Essentials and Study Guide 17–3

Name _____ Date _____ Class _____

Study Guide

Chapter 17, Section 3
For use with textbook pages 542–546

HOOVER RESPONDS

KEY TERMS AND NAMES
public works government-financed building projects *(page 543)*
Reconstruction Finance Corporation organization set up by Congress to make loans to businesses *(page 544)*
relief money that went directly to people in poverty *(page 544)*
foreclosed taken possession of by creditors *(page 545)*
Bonus Army a group of World War I veterans who marched on Washington to demand the payment of bonuses that Congress promised *(page 545)*

L2

Section Quiz 17–3

Name _____ Date _____ Class _____

★ Chapter 17   Score [ ]

Section Quiz 17-3

DIRECTIONS: Matching Match each item in Column A with the items in Column B. Write the correct letters in the blanks. *(10 points each)*

Column A		Column B
___ 1. money that went directly to impoverished families		A. National Credit Corporation
___ 2. World War I veterans who marched to Washington, D.C.		B. budget deficit
___ 3. created when the government spends more money than it collects in taxes		C. relief
___ 4. created a pool of money to rescue troubled banks		D. public works
___ 5. government-financed building projects		E. Bonus Army

DIRECTIONS: Multiple Choice In the blank at the left, write the letter of the choice that best completes the statement or answers the question. *(10 points each)*

up at rallies and "hunger marches" held by the American Communist Party, which was eager to take advantage of national problems to change the American form of government. On December 5, 1932, a freezing day in the nation's capital, around 1,200 hunger marchers assembled and chanted, "Feed the hungry, tax the rich." Police herded them into a blocked-off area, where they had to spend the night sleeping on the sidewalk or in trucks. The police denied them food, water, and medical treatment until some members of Congress insisted on the marchers' right to petition their government. They were then released and permitted to march to Capitol Hill.

Farmers Revolt In the summer of 1932, farmers also took matters into their own hands. Beginning in the boom days of World War I, many farmers had heavily mortgaged their land to pay for seed, feed, and equipment. After the war, prices sank so low that farmers could not even earn back their costs, let alone make a profit. Between 1930 and 1934 creditors foreclosed on nearly one million farms, taking possession of them and evicting the families.

Some farmers began destroying their crops in a desperate attempt to raise crop prices by reducing the supply. In Nebraska grain growers burned corn

to heat their homes in the winter. In Iowa food growers forcibly prevented the delivery of vegetables to distributors. Georgia dairy farmers blocked highways and stopped milk trucks, emptying the milk cans into ditches.

The Bonus Marchers In appreciation of the World War I service of American soldiers and sailors, Congress in 1924 had enacted a $1,000 bonus for each veteran, to be distributed in 1945. The economic crisis, however, made the wait more difficult. In 1931 Texas congressman Wright Patman introduced a bill in the House of Representatives that authorized early payment of the veterans' bonuses. The bill later passed the House and moved to the Senate for debate.

In May 1932 several hundred Portland, Oregon, veterans set off on a month-long march to Washington to lobby Congress to pass the legislation. As they moved east, other veterans joined them until they numbered about 1,000. Wearing ragged military uniforms, they trudged along the highways or rode the rails, singing old war songs and reminiscing about army days. The press termed the marchers the **"Bonus Army."**

Once in Washington, the marchers camped in Hoovervilles. As weeks went by, additional veterans joined them, until the Bonus Army swelled to

INTERDISCIPLINARY CONNECTIONS ACTIVITY

Sociology Point out to students that acting selflessly is a survival mechanism for groups as a whole. Often the most selfless people are those who have the least. Tell students that in *The Grapes of Wrath,* Ma Joad says, "If you're in trouble or hurt or need—go to poor people. They're the only ones that'll help." Ask students to analyze this statement and then write a paragraph that discusses why they feel that acting selflessly might be a group survival mechanism. Have students use examples to support their analysis. **L2**

Picturing History

Answer: They had a negative reaction toward Hoover.

Ask: What alternatives do you think the government had? (Students' answers will vary.)

FYI

In 1931 a Christmas tree was placed amid the rubble from some demolished buildings. Workers who still had jobs decorated the tree with tin cans and paper. A few years later at the same site, the official Rockefeller Center tree tradition was inaugurated.

Reteach

Have students evaluate President Hoover's attempts to invigorate the economy.

Enrich

Invite interested students to interview someone who lived during the Depression. Suggest that they pose questions to learn about housing, food, clothing, entertainment, and emotions during the era.

Reading Check

Answer: Reactions included hunger marches, farmers' revolts, and the Bonus Army march.

HISTORY Online

Study Central™ provides summaries, interactive games, and online graphic organizers to help students review section content.

4 CLOSE

Have students analyze the limitations of Hoover's recovery plans.

Picturing History

Clearing Out the Bonus Marchers Fierce battles resulted when President Hoover ordered the Washington, D.C., police to evict the Bonus Army from public buildings and land they had been occupying. How did the public feel when they saw or heard about this event?

15,000. President Hoover acknowledged the veterans' petition rights but refused to meet with them.

When the Senate voted the new bonus bill down, veterans waiting outside the Capitol began to grumble, until one of their leaders started them singing "America." Gradually their anger cooled, and many returned home. A significant number of the marchers, however, stayed on since they had no job prospects. Some moved from the camps to unoccupied buildings downtown.

In late July, Hoover ordered the buildings cleared. The police made the first try, but one of them panicked and fired into a crowd, killing two veterans. The Washington, D.C., government then called in the army. Army chief of staff Douglas MacArthur ignored Hoover's orders to clear the buildings but to leave the camps alone. He sent cavalry, infantry, and tanks to clear the veterans from the city.

A Federal Trade Commission member, A. Everette McIntyre, watched as the infantry "fixed their bayonets and also fixed their gas masks over their faces. At orders they brought their bayonets at thrust and moved in. The bayonets were used to jab people to make them move." Soon unarmed veterans were on the run with 700 soldiers at their heels. The soldiers tear-gassed stragglers and burned the shacks. Tear gas killed a baby boy.

The nationwide press coverage and newsreel images of veterans under assault by troops presented an ugly picture to the public. The routing of the veterans hounded the president throughout his 1932 re-election campaign.

Hoover failed to resolve the crisis of the Depression, but he did more to expand the economic role of the federal government than any previous president. The Reconstruction Finance Corporation marked the first time the federal government had established a federal agency to stimulate the economy during peacetime. It was the image of the routed Bonus Marchers and the lingering Depression, however, that shaped the public's perception of President Hoover.

✓ Reading Check **Evaluating** How did Americans react as the Depression continued?

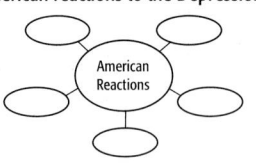
HISTORY Online | **Study Central**™ To review this section, go to **tarvol2.glencoe.com** and click on **Study Central**™.

SECTION 3 ASSESSMENT

Checking for Understanding

1. **Define:** public works, relief, foreclose.
2. **Identify:** Reconstruction Finance Corporation, Bonus Army.
3. **Summarize** three major initiatives taken by Hoover to improve the economy and the results of each.

Reviewing Themes

4. **Groups and Institutions** What did business leaders promise Hoover they would do to help the economy? Did they keep their promises?

Critical Thinking

5. **Interpreting** How did President Hoover's philosophy of government guide his response to the Depression?
6. **Organizing** Use a graphic organizer similar to the one below to list American reactions to the Depression.

American Reactions

Analyzing Visuals

7. **Picturing History** Study the photographs on page 545. The farmers shown would rather dump their milk than sell it. What did they hope to achieve by their actions?

Writing About History

8. **Persuasive Writing** Imagine that you are a veteran of World War I. Write a letter to members of Congress explaining your circumstances and asking them to give you your bonus early.

546 CHAPTER 17 The Great Depression Begins

SECTION 3 ASSESSMENT ANSWERS

1. Terms are in blue.
2. Reconstruction Finance Corporation (p. 544), Bonus Army (p. 545)
3. Conferences with industry leaders did not secure cooperation; funding from the National Credit Corporation and the Reconstruction Finance Corporation was insufficient.
4. They promised to keep factories open and stop slashing wages; no.
5. Belief in volunteerism and loans, rather than direct relief, restricted his actions.
6. bonus marchers, discontent, farmers' revolts, hunger strikes, squatting
7. They hoped to drive up prices by limiting supply.
8. Students' letters will vary. Letters should be written from the perspective of a World War I veteran.

Technology
SKILLBUILDER

Building a Database

Why Learn This Skill?

Do you have a collection of sports cards, CDs, or DVDs? Have you ever kept a list of the names, addresses, and phone numbers of friends and relatives? If you have collected information and kept it in a list or file, then you have created a database.

Learning the Skill

An electronic database is a collection of facts that are stored in a file on a computer. The information is organized in fields.

A database can be organized and reorganized in any way that is useful to you. By using a database management system (DBMS)—special software developed for record keeping—you can easily add, delete, change, or update information. You give commands to the computer that tell it what to do with the information, and it follows these commands. When you want to retrieve information, the computer searches through the file, finds the information, and displays it on the screen.

Practicing the Skill

The Great Depression is a well-known period in American history. Follow these steps to build a database containing the events that led to the Great Depression and its effects on the country.

❶ Determine what facts you want to include in your database.

❷ Follow instructions to set up fields in the DBMS that you are using. Then enter each item of data in its assigned field.

❸ Determine how you want to organize the facts in the database—chronologically by the date of the event, or alphabetically by the name of the event.

❹ Follow the instructions in your computer program to place the information in the order you selected.

Skills Assessment

Complete the Practicing Skills questions on page 549 and the Chapter 17 Skill Reinforcement Activity to assess your mastery of this skill.

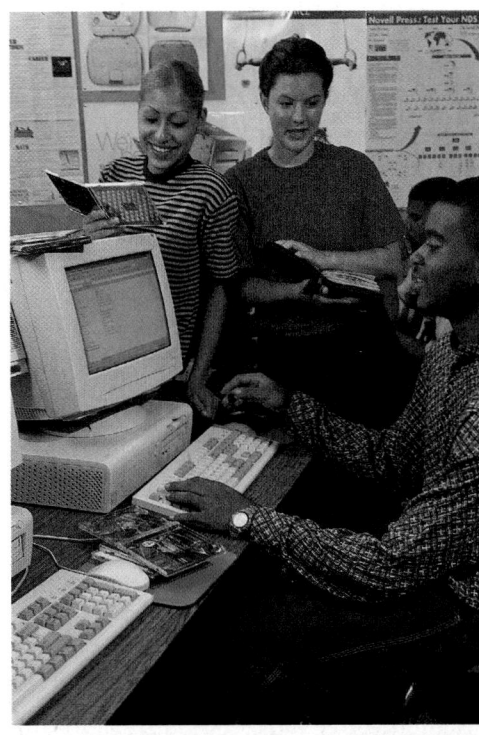

Applying the Skill

Building a Database Bring current newspapers or news magazines to class. Using the steps just described, build a database of current political events in the United States. Include a brief explanation of why the database is organized the way it is and how it might be used in class.

 Glencoe's **Skillbuilder Interactive Workbook CD-ROM, Level 2,** provides instruction and practice in key social studies skills.

547

Technology
SKILLBUILDER

TEACH

Building a Database Remind students that a database is a way to organize information. Explain that database management systems allow people to organize large amounts of information according to selected categories; they can then search for specific data or manipulate the categories to draw conclusions.

Additional Practice

L1

Reinforcing Skills Activity 17

Name _____ Date _____ Class _____

★ Reinforcing Skills Activity 17

Building a Database

▶ LEARNING THE SKILL

An electronic database is a collection of data—names, facts, and statistics—that are stored in a file on the computer. People use databases to organize large amounts of information. The database organizes information into categories call *fields*, such as Name, Event, or Date. A database management system (DBMS) will electronically store, sort, and display information from your database on screen.

▶ PRACTICING THE SKILL

DIRECTIONS: Use the information from Section 2 of your text to create a database containing Depression Era artists and entertainers. Use resources from your library or the Internet to add fields with additional information as your teacher directs.

1. Using the fields listed below as your categories, build your database by filling in as much information as you are able to locate.

GLENCOE
TECHNOLOGY

CD-ROM
Glencoe Skillbuilder Interactive Workbook CD-ROM, Level 2

This interactive CD-ROM reinforces student mastery of essential social studies skills.

ANSWERS TO PRACTICING THE SKILL

❶ Facts should surround the events of the Great Depression.

❷ Encourage students to identify fields that will fit with the facts they have gathered.

❸ and ❹ Explain to students that data can be sorted in various ways. Encourage students to experiment with different choices.

Applying the Skill
Students' databases and explanations will vary. The explanations should readily help a person understand the information contained in the database.

547

GLENCOE TECHNOLOGY

MindJogger Videoquiz
Use the **MindJogger Videoquiz** to review Chapter 17 content.

Available in DVD

Reviewing Key Terms
Students' answers will vary. The pages where the words appear in the text are shown in parentheses.

1. **stock market** (p. 531)
2. **bull market** (p. 531)
3. **margin** (p. 531)
4. **margin call** (p. 531)
5. **speculation** (p. 531)
6. **installment** (p. 534)
7. **bailiff** (p. 536)
8. **shantytown** (p. 536)
9. **Hooverville** (p. 536)
10. **hobo** (p. 536)
11. **Dust Bowl** (p. 537)
12. **soap opera** (p. 538)
13. **public works** (p. 543)
14. **relief** (p. 544)
15. **foreclose** (p. 545)

Reviewing Key Facts
16. Black Tuesday (p. 533), Hawley-Smoot Tariff (p. 534), Walt Disney (p. 538), Grant Wood (p. 538), John Steinbeck (p. 539), Reconstruction Finance Corporation (p. 544), Bonus Army (p. 545)

17. It was a bull market that crashed because stocks were overvalued and many people had purchased stocks on margin.

18. They focused on pictures and stories of the homeless and unemployed.

19. They migrated searching for work. Many ended up working as homeless migrant laborers.

Reviewing Key Terms
On a sheet of paper, use each of these terms in a sentence.

1. stock market
2. bull market
3. margin
4. margin call
5. speculation
6. installment
7. bailiff
8. shantytown
9. Hooverville
10. hobo
11. Dust Bowl
12. soap opera
13. public works
14. relief
15. foreclose

Reviewing Key Facts
16. **Identify:** Black Tuesday, Hawley-Smoot Tariff, Walt Disney, Grant Wood, John Steinbeck, Reconstruction Finance Corporation, Bonus Army.

17. What was the character of the stock market in the late 1920s, and what caused it to crash?

18. How did artists and writers capture the effects of the Great Depression?

19. Why did "Okies" migrate to California during the Great Depression, and what happened to them once they got there?

20. What three major initiatives did President Hoover take to try to help the economy of the United States?

21. What did World War I veterans do to try to get their service bonuses early?

Critical Thinking
22. **Analyzing Themes: Culture and Traditions** Many people in the United States were impoverished during the Depression, yet 60 to 90 million weekly viewers paid to see movies. Why do you think movies were so popular?

23. **Evaluating** Do you think President Hoover could have done more to end the Great Depression? Why or why not?

24. **Identifying** What approaches were used in literature and photography to highlight social problems during the Depression?

25. **Categorizing** Use a graphic organizer similar to the one below to list the causes and effects of the Great Depression.

Causes	Effects

26. **Interpreting Primary Sources** E.Y. Harburg lived during the Great Depression. After he lost his business, he became a poet and lyricist. He wrote the lyrics to one of the most famous songs of the time, "Brother, Can You Spare a Dime?" Read an excerpt of the lyrics to this song and answer the questions that follow.

“They used to tell me I was building a dream
With peace and glory ahead—
Why should I be standing on line
Just waiting for bread?

Chapter Summary

Stock Market Helps Trigger Depression
• Bull market encouraged widespread speculation.
• Many investors bought stocks on margin.
• Sharp drop in market prices left investors in debt.
• Bank closings left many in debt.

Underlying Causes of Great Depression
• Overproduction and low interest rates
• Uneven distribution of income, which led to low demand
• Depressed farm sector
• Weak international market with high tariffs

Downward Momentum of the Great Depression

Low Sales → Job Layoffs → Less Income → Fewer Purchases → Lower Sales → More Job Layoffs

548 CHAPTER 17 The Great Depression Begins

20. voluntary conferences with industry leaders, National Credit Corporation, Reconstruction Finance Corporation

21. They marched to Washington to petition Congress and then became squatters in unoccupied buildings.

Critical Thinking
22. Movies gave people an escape from their own lives.

23. Students' answers will vary. Possible explanations: Yes, the government should have gotten more involved in relief efforts. No, the problems were so great that there was nothing more the government could do.

24. Writing and visual styles evoked sympathy for the homeless and unemployed. Stream-of-consciousness writing illuminated peoples' thoughts and emotions.

CHAPTER 17
Assessment and Activities

Self-Check Quiz

Visit the *American Republic Since 1877* Web site at tarvol2.glencoe.com and click on *Self-Check Quizzes—Chapter 17* to assess your knowledge of chapter content.

"Once I built a railroad, made it run,
Made it run against time.
Once I built a railroad,
Now it's done—
Brother, can you spare a dime?

Once I built a tower to the sun.
Brick and rivet and lime,
Once I built a tower,
Now it's done—
Brother, can you spare a dime?"

a. How was the narrator's life different before the Great Depression than it was during it?

b. During the 1932 presidential campaign, the Republicans tried to discourage the radio networks from playing this song. Why do you think they did that?

Practicing Skills

27. **Building a Database** Use the business section of your local newspaper to prepare a database that lists the prices of three different stocks for one week. Use the following information in your database:

- Stock symbol
- Date
- Stock price at the end of each day (closing price)

Be sure to follow these steps to build your database:

a. Follow instructions in the DBMS that you are using. Then enter each item in its assigned field.

b. Determine how you want to organize the information in the database.

c. Place the information in the order you choose (by date, alphabetically by symbol, by price, etc.).

d. Check the accuracy of the information. Make necessary changes.

Writing Activity

28. **Creating a Dictionary** Create a dictionary of words and phrases that grew out of the Great Depression. If possible, include pictures or photographs that illustrate the entries.

Chapter Activity

29. **Creative Presentations** Analyze the statistical information you gathered in building the computer database in

Crop Prices, 1910–1935

Price of Crops
- $2.60
- $2.20
- $1.80
- $1.40
- $1.00
- $0.60
- $0.20

Wheat (price per bushel)
Corn (price per bushel)
Cotton (price per pound)

Year: 1910 1915 1920 1925 1930 1935

Source: *Historical Statistics of the United States: Colonial Times to 1970.*

question 27. Write a short report describing the progress of the stocks you followed. Create a chart and a graph as a visual aid to present your findings to the class.

Economics and History

30. The graph above shows changes in crop prices from 1910 to 1935. Study the graph and answer the questions below.

a. **Interpreting Graphs** What trend does this graph show about wheat and corn prices in the 1930s?

b. **Analyzing** Between which 10-year span did the greatest increase and decrease in farm prices occur?

Standardized Test Practice

Directions: Choose the phrase that best completes the following sentence.

A major reason for the collapse of the American economy after 1929 was

A high interest rates.

B decreased farm production.

C low tariffs at home and abroad.

D overproduction of consumer goods.

Test-Taking Tip: If you are not sure of the answer, use the process of elimination. For example, farmers were not prosperous in the 1920s because their huge crops forced down agricultural prices. Therefore, answer B is incorrect.

HISTORY Online

Have students visit the Web site at tarvol2.glencoe.com to review Chapter 17 and take the Self-Check Quiz.

Chapter Activity

29. Students' reports should accurately summarize the information in the database.

Economics and History

30. **a.** They declined sharply in the early 1930s, then rose steadily.
    b. For the most *volatile* ten-year period, students will choose 1915 to 1925 when graph lines rise and plummet dramatically; for the ten-year period in which there was the *greatest overall difference* in farm prices, students should add the price points of all three crops and figure the difference, yielding the answer *between 1910 and 1920.*

Standardized Test Practice

Answer: D

Test-Taking Tip: The Hawley-Smoot Tariff, passed in 1930, was the highest tariff ever. This means you can eliminate C. Because interest rates were low, business leaders continued to overproduce. This means you can eliminate answer A. The correct answer is D.

Bonus Question ?

Ask: What does the phrase "Dust Bowl" refer to? *(Starting in 1932, a prolonged drought caused great clouds of dust to blanket the region from Texas to the Dakotas.)*

---

25. Causes: overproduction, uneven distribution of wealth, decline in exports and sales, mistakes by the Federal Reserve, stock market crash; Effects: unemployment, poverty, migration, government programs to influence the economy

26. **a.** He was a productive worker, now is unemployed.
    b. Students might say that hearing the song suggested criticism of society and discouraged the unemployed.

Practicing Skills

27. Databases should reflect accurate information about the three stocks.

Writing Activity

28. Dictionaries will vary. Encourage students to check standard dictionary entries as they write their own dictionaries.

Timesaving Tools

TeacherWorks™ All-In-One Planner and Resource Center

- **Interactive Teacher Edition** Access your Teacher Wraparound Edition and your classroom resources with a few easy clicks.
- **Interactive Lesson Planner** Planning has never been easier! Organize your week, month, semester, or year with all the lesson helps you need to make teaching creative, timely, and relevant.

Use Glencoe's **Presentation Plus!** multimedia teacher tool to easily present dynamic lessons that visually excite your students. Using Microsoft PowerPoint® you can customize the presentations to create your own personalized lessons.

TEACHING TRANSPARENCIES

Graphic Organizer 3 L2

Why It Matters Chapter Transparency 18 L2

APPLICATION AND ENRICHMENT

Linking Past and Present Activity 18 L2

Enrichment Activity 18 L3

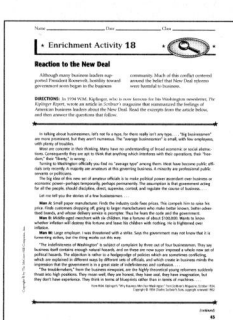

Primary Source Reading 18 L2

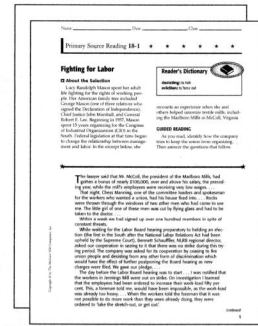

REVIEW AND REINFORCEMENT

Reteaching Activity 18 L1

Vocabulary Activity 18 L1

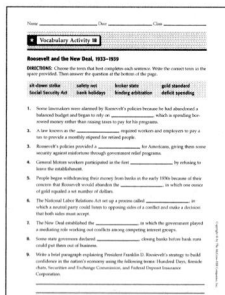

Time Line Activity 18 L2

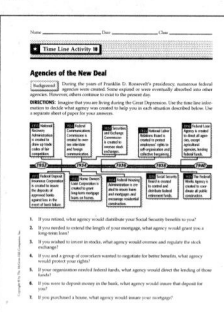

Critical Thinking Skills Activity 18 L2

Meeting NCSS Standards

Local Standards

The following standards are covered in Chapter 18:

Section 1	IV	Individual Development and Identity: D, F, H
Section 2	V	Individuals, Groups, and Institutions: B, C, F, G
Section 3	VI	Power, Authority, and Governance: A, B, C, H, I
Section 4	V	Individuals, Groups, and Institutions: A, B, E

Chapter 18 Resources

Chapter 18 Test Form A L2

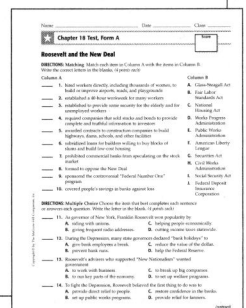

Chapter 18 Test Form B L2

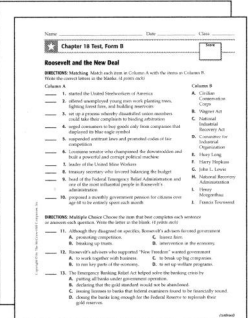

Standardized Test Practice Workbook Activity 18 L2

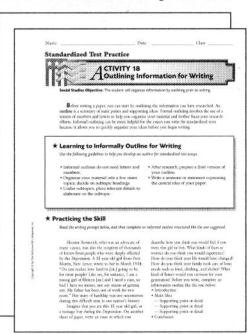

Performance Assessment Activities and Rubrics 18 L1/ELL

ExamView® Pro Testmaker CD-ROM

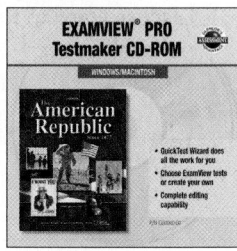

MULTIMEDIA

- Vocabulary PuzzleMaker CD-ROM
- Interactive Tutor Self-Assessment CD-ROM
- ExamView® Pro Testmaker CD-ROM
- Audio Program
- American History Primary Source Documents Library CD-ROM
- MindJogger Videoquiz
- Presentation Plus! CD-ROM
- TeacherWorks™ CD-ROM
- Interactive Student Edition CD-ROM
- Glencoe Skillbuilder Interactive Workbook CD-ROM, Level 2
- The *American Republic Since 1877* Video Program
- American Music: Hits Through History
- American Music: Cultural Traditions

SPANISH RESOURCES

The following Spanish language materials are available:

- Spanish Reading Essentials and Study Guide
- Spanish Guided Reading Activities
- Spanish Reteaching Activities
- Spanish Quizzes and Tests
- Spanish Vocabulary Activities
- Spanish Summaries
- The Declaration of Independence and United States Constitution Spanish Translation

---

THE HISTORY CHANNEL®

The following videotape programs are available from Glencoe as supplements to Chapter 18:

- **FDR: The Years of Crisis** (ISBN 1-56-501511-8)
- **Eleanor Roosevelt: A Restless Spirit** (ISBN 1-56-501405-7)
- **The Great Depression** (ISBN 0-76-700859-6)

To order, call Glencoe at 1-800-334-7344. To find classroom resources to accompany many of these videos, check the following home pages:
A&E Television: www.aande.com
The History Channel: www.historychannel.com

HISTORY Online

Use our Web site for additional resources. All essential content is covered in the Student Edition.

You and your students can visit tarvol2.glencoe.com, the Web site companion to the **American Republic Since 1877**. This innovative integration of electronic and print media offers your students a wealth of opportunities. The student text directs students to the Web site for the following options:

- **Chapter Overviews**
- **Self-Check Quizzes**
- **Student Web Activities**
- **Textbook Updates**

Answers to the student Web activities are provided for you in the **Web Activity Lesson Plans**. Additional Web resources and Interactive Tutor Puzzles are also available.

Chapter 18 Resources

Daily Objectives	Reproducible Resources	Multimedia Resources
SECTION 1 **Roosevelt Takes Office** 1. Discuss Franklin Roosevelt's early political career. 2. Explain the worsening situation in the U.S. banking system in the early 1930s.	Reproducible Lesson Plan 18–1 Daily Lecture and Discussion Notes 18–1 Guided Reading Activity 18–1* Section Quiz 18–1* Reading Essentials and Study Guide 18–1* Performance Assessment Activities and Rubrics	Daily Focus Skills Transparency 18–1 American Art & Architecture Interactive Tutor Self-Assessment CD-ROM ExamView® Pro Testmaker CD-ROM* Presentation Plus! CD-ROM TeacherWorks™ CD-ROM Audio Program American Music: Cultural Traditions
SECTION 2 **The First New Deal** 1. List three programs of the First New Deal that provided jobs for the unemployed. 2. Discuss why New Dealers believed that sometimes the government needs to regulate industry and labor.	Reproducible Lesson Plan 18–2 Daily Lecture and Discussion Notes 18–2 Guided Reading Activity 18–2* Section Quiz 18–2* Reading Essentials and Study Guide 18–2* Performance Assessment Activities and Rubrics Interpreting Political Cartoons American History in Graphic Novel	Daily Focus Skills Transparency 18–2 Interactive Tutor Self-Assessment CD-ROM ExamView® Pro Testmaker CD-ROM* Presentation Plus! CD-ROM Skillbuilder Interactive Workbook, Level 2 TeacherWorks™ CD-ROM Audio Program
SECTION 3 **The Second New Deal** 1. Describe the political challenges Roosevelt faced in the mid-1930s. 2. Explain why the Social Security Act is still regarded as an important piece of legislation.	Reproducible Lesson Plan 18–3 Daily Lecture and Discussion Notes 18–3 Guided Reading Activity 18–3* Section Quiz 18–3* Reading Essentials and Study Guide 18–3* Performance Assessment Activities and Rubrics Supreme Court Case Studies	Daily Focus Skills Transparency 18–3 Interactive Tutor Self-Assessment CD-ROM ExamView® Pro Testmaker CD-ROM* Presentation Plus! CD-ROM TeacherWorks™ CD-ROM Audio Program
SECTION 4 **The New Deal Coalition** 1. Explain the achievements and the defeats of Roosevelt's second term. 2. Analyze how the New Deal affected Americans' sense of security and their attitude toward the role of government.	Reproducible Lesson Plan 18–4 Daily Lecture and Discussion Notes 18–4 Guided Reading Activity 18–4* Section Quiz 18–4* Reading Essentials and Study Guide 18–4* Performance Assessment Activities and Rubrics	Daily Focus Skills Transparency 18–4 Interactive Tutor Self-Assessment CD-ROM ExamView® Pro Testmaker CD-ROM* Presentation Plus! CD-ROM TeacherWorks™ CD-ROM Vocabulary PuzzleMaker CD-ROM Audio Program

0:00 OUT OF TIME?
Assign the Chapter 18 **Reading Essentials and Study Guide.**

*Also Available in Spanish

 Printed Materials   Transparency CD-ROM DVD

Poster   Music Program   Audio Program

NATIONAL GEOGRAPHIC Teacher's Corner

INDEX TO NATIONAL GEOGRAPHIC MAGAZINE

The following articles relate to this chapter.
• "The Okies—Beyond the Great Depression," September 1984

NATIONAL GEOGRAPHIC SOCIETY PRODUCTS

To order the following, call National Geographic at 1-800-368-2728:
• *Eyewitness to the 20th Century* (Book)
• *1929–1941: The Great Depression* (Video)
• *Historical Atlas of the United States* (Atlas)
• *National Geographic World Atlas for Young Explorers—Classroom Library Edition* (Teacher's Guide, Transparencies, Resource Masters)

NGS ONLINE

Access National Geographic's Web site for current events, atlas updates, activities, links, interactive features, and archives.
www.nationalgeographic.com

MEETING SPECIAL NEEDS

In addition to the Differentiated Instruction strategies found in each section, the following resources are also suitable for your special needs students:

• *ExamView® Pro Testmaker CD-ROM* allows teachers to tailor tests by reducing answer choices.

• The *Audio Program* includes the entire narrative of the student edition so that less-proficient readers can listen to the words as they read them.

• The *Reading Essentials and Study Guide* provides the same content as the student edition but is written two grade levels below the textbook.

• *Guided Reading Activities* give less-proficient readers point-by-point instructions to increase comprehension as they read each textbook section.

• *Enrichment Activities* includes a stimulating collection of readings and activities for gifted and talented students.

KEY TO ABILITY LEVELS

Teaching strategies have been coded.

L1 BASIC activities for all students
L2 AVERAGE activities for average to above-average students
L3 CHALLENGING activities for above-average students
ELL ENGLISH LANGUAGE LEARNER activities

From the Classroom of...

Rick Harris
Cincinnati Public Schools
Cincinnati, OH

Understanding the TVA

The Tennessee Valley Authority (TVA) demonstrates the profound effects of the New Deal on the United States. After introducing the unit, I give the groups two research days, one day to prepare, and a day to present. I assign groups one of the following areas:

• **Map:** This group creates a map showing all areas shaped by the TVA, including the states affected, the dams and reservoirs created, reforested areas, and diverted roads and rail lines.

• **Time Line:** Students create a detailed time line that shows the major milestones of the TVA.

• **Budget:** This group creates graphs to show the TVA's original budget, its final budget, and its budget in modern dollars. Students should show how specific congressional appropriations provided TVA funding.

• **Long-term Impact:** Students present a photographic essay of the long-term impact of the TVA. Examples include before and after shots of areas where dams created reservoirs and recreational areas.

ADDITIONAL RESOURCES FROM GLENCOE

• American Music: Cultural Traditions
• American Art & Architecture
• Outline Map Resource Book
• U.S. Desk Map
• Building Geography Skills for Life
• Inclusion for the High School Social Studies Classroom Strategies and Activities
• Teaching Strategies for the American History Classroom (Including Block Scheduling Pacing Guides)
• Dinah Zike's High School American History Reading and Study Skills Foldables

Block Schedule

Activities that are suited to use within the block scheduling framework are identified by:

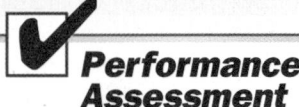

W*hy It Matters Activity*

Ask students how they think Social Security benefits people today. **Ask:** Is Social Security used in the ways in which it was originally intended? Students should evaluate their answers after they have completed the chapter.

GLENCOE
TECHNOLOGY

The *American Republic Since 1877* Video Program
To learn more about the personal and political challenges FDR faced as president, have students view the Chapter 18 video, "Franklin Roosevelt and the New Deal," from the *American Republic Since 1877* Video Program.

MindJogger Videoquiz
Use the **MindJogger Videoquiz** to preview Chapter 18 content.

💿 Both programs available in DVD

CHAPTER

18 Roosevelt and the New Deal
1933–1939

Why It Matters

Unlike Herbert Hoover, Franklin Delano Roosevelt was willing to employ deficit spending and greater federal regulation to revive the depressed economy. In response to his requests, Congress passed a host of new programs. Millions of people received relief to alleviate their suffering, but the New Deal did not really end the Depression. It did, however, permanently expand the federal government's role in providing basic security for citizens.

The Impact Today

Certain New Deal legislation still carries great importance in American social policy.
- *The Social Security Act still provides retirement benefits, aid to needy groups, and unemployment and disability insurance.*
- *The National Labor Relations Act still protects the right of workers to unionize.*
- *Safeguards were instituted to help prevent another devastating stock market crash.*
- *The Federal Deposit Insurance Corporation still protects bank deposits.*

💿 **The American Republic Since 1877 Video** The Chapter 18 video, "Franklin Roosevelt and the New Deal," describes the personal and political challenges Franklin Roosevelt faced as president.

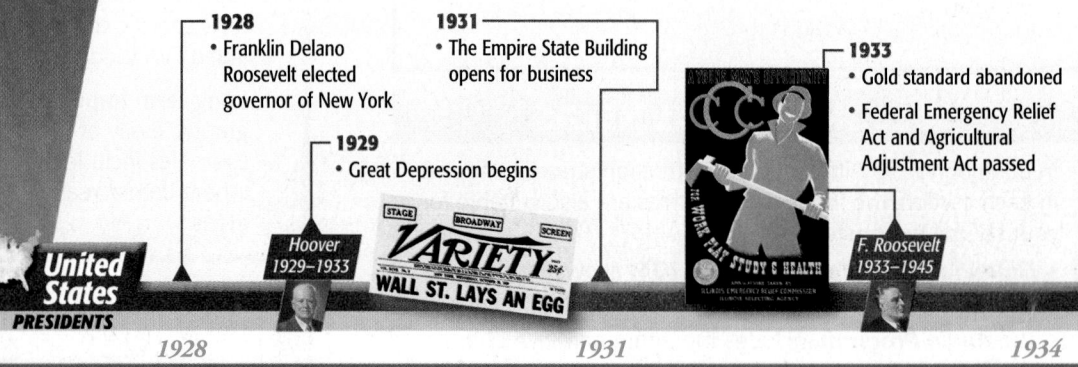

United States PRESIDENTS

1928
- Franklin Delano Roosevelt elected governor of New York

1929
- Great Depression begins

Hoover 1929–1933

1931
- The Empire State Building opens for business

1933
- Gold standard abandoned
- Federal Emergency Relief Act and Agricultural Adjustment Act passed

F. Roosevelt 1933–1945

1928   *1931*   *1934*

World

1928
- Alexander Fleming discovers penicillin

1930
- Germany's Nazi Party wins 107 seats in Reichstag

1931
- German unemployment reaches 5.6 million
- Surrealist artist Salvador Dali paints *Persistence of Memory*

1933
- Adolf Hitler appointed German chancellor
- Japan withdraws from League of Nations

550

📖 **Reading Strategy**   **PURPOSE FOR READING**

Pre- and Post-Reading Graphic Organizer Working in pairs, have students draw a line down the middle of a sheet of paper. Have students write "Programs/Actions Before Reading" on the top left side of the paper and "Programs/Actions After Reading" on the top right side. On the far left, ask students to write the following words, leaving ample space between them: "Government," "Business," and "Banking." Then have each pair brainstorm what programs or actions taken by the government, businesses, and banks might have eased the devastating effects of the Depression. Students should record their thoughts on the left side of the graphic organizer. After reading the chapter, have students reexamine their lists and enter the actions actually taken during the 1930s. **L1**

In this Ben Shahn mural detail, New Deal planners (at right) design the town of Jersey Homesteads as a home for impoverished immigrants.

1935
- Supreme Court strikes down NIRA
- Social Security Act passed

1937
- Court-packing bill defeated
- "Roosevelt recession" begins

1938
- Fair Labor Standards Act passed

1937

1940

1936
- Civil War erupts in Spain

1938
- Hitler annexes Austria

1939
- World War II begins

HISTORY Online

Chapter Overview
Visit the *American Republic Since 1877* Web site at tarvol2.glencoe.com and click on *Chapter Overviews— Chapter 18* to preview chapter information.

551

HISTORY Online

Introduce students to chapter content and key terms by having them access the **Chapter 18 Overview** at tarvol2.glencoe.com.

More About the Art

Born in Lithuania, Ben Shahn immigrated to the United States in 1906. During the Depression, he enlisted in one of Roosevelt's New Deal programs for the arts. The program provided funds for the production of public murals. The Resettlement Administration built the town of Jersey Homesteads depicted in this fresco to house Jewish garment workers from New York City.

TIME LINE
ACTIVITY

Have students select and research a world event from the time line. Then have them write a brief description of the impact the event had on American history.

FOLDABLES
Study Organizer

Dinah Zike's Foldables are three-dimensional, interactive graphic organizers that help students practice basic writing skills, review key vocabulary terms, and identify main ideas. Have students complete the foldable activity in the *Dinah Zike's Reading and Study Skills Foldables* booklet.

GRAPHIC ORGANIZER ACTIVITY

Organizing Information Have students create a time line of New Deal legislation. Ask them to include the years 1933 to 1938. Have students identify the significant legislation passed in each of these years and the purpose of the legislation.

1 FOCUS

Section Overview

This section focuses on Franklin Delano Roosevelt's early life and election as president.

Reading Preview

Answers to Graphic: love of the outdoors, polio, assistant secretary of the navy, governor of New York

Preteaching Vocabulary
Have students skim this section to glean the meaning or significance of each of the Key Terms and Names.

Guide to Reading

Main Idea
Franklin Delano Roosevelt's character and experiences prepared him for the presidency of a nation in crisis.

Key Terms and Names
New Deal, polio, gold standard, bank holiday

Reading Strategy
Organizing As you read about Franklin Roosevelt's background, complete a graphic organizer similar to the one below by listing the early influences and experiences that helped shape Roosevelt as a politician.

Influences and Experiences

Reading Objectives
- **Discuss** Franklin Roosevelt's early political career.
- **Explain** the worsening situation in the U.S. banking system in the early 1930s.

Section Theme
Individual Action Franklin Roosevelt's optimism, determination, and outgoing personality shaped his approach to politics.

Preview of Events

◆1905	◆1915	◆1925	◆1935
1905 Franklin Roosevelt and Eleanor Roosevelt marry	**1910** Roosevelt elected to New York State Senate	**1921** Roosevelt stricken with polio	**1928** Roosevelt elected governor of New York

⋆ **An American Story** ⋆

Franklin D. Roosevelt as a young man

When Louis Howe was a child in Saratoga Springs, New York, a bicycle accident left his face scarred. As an adult and a reporter for his father's newspaper, he cheerfully described himself as "one of the four ugliest men in the state of New York." Howe dressed sloppily, perhaps to demonstrate how little importance he attached to appearance. He worked hard, however, and was respected for his reporting.

In the winter of 1911, Howe traveled to Albany to interview a Democratic state senator, Franklin Delano Roosevelt—or FDR, as he was called. Howe found himself fascinated by the tall, intense young man with the gold-rimmed glasses who paced back and forth in front of him, earnestly answering his questions. He admired the dashing appearance Roosevelt made.

During the interview Roosevelt declared his intention to challenge the party bosses. The usually skeptical Howe found himself believing the young legislator.
"I made up my mind," Howe later recalled, "that nothing but an accident could keep him from becoming president."

—adapted from *The Crisis of the Old Order*

Roosevelt's Rise to Power

In mid-June 1932, with the country deep in the Depression, Republicans gathered in Chicago and nominated Herbert Hoover to run for a second term as president. The mood at the convention was somber. Delegates knew the Depression had turned many voters against Hoover.

552 CHAPTER 18 Roosevelt and the New Deal

SECTION RESOURCES

📁 Reproducible Masters
- Reproducible Lesson Plan 18–1
- Daily Lecture and Discussion Notes 18–1
- Guided Reading Activity 18–1
- Section Quiz 18–1
- Reading Essentials and Study Guide 18–1

📖 Transparencies
- Daily Focus Skills Transparency 18–1

- American Art & Architecture

Multimedia
- 💿 Interactive Tutor Self-Assessment CD-ROM
- 💿 ExamView® Pro Testmaker CD-ROM
- 💿 Presentation Plus! CD-ROM
- 💿 TeacherWorks™ CD-ROM
- 🎧 Audio Program
- 🎵 American Music: Cultural Traditions

Later that month, the Democrats also met in Chicago to choose their own candidate for president. It took four ballots and a great deal of negotiating, but the party eventually chose the popular governor of New York, Franklin Delano Roosevelt. When he won the nomination, Roosevelt broke with tradition by flying to Chicago to deliver the first acceptance speech ever made to a nominating convention. Roosevelt's speech set the tone for his campaign:

> 66 The appearance before a National Convention of its nominee for President . . . is unprecedented and unusual, but these are unprecedented and unusual times. . . . Let it also be symbolic that in so doing I broke traditions. Let it be from now on the task of our Party to break foolish traditions. . . . It is inevitable that the main issue of this campaign should revolve about . . . a depression so deep that it is without precedent. . . . Republican leaders not only have failed in material things, they have failed in national vision, because in disaster they have held out no hope. . . . I pledge you, I pledge myself, to a new deal for the American people. 99

—quoted in *The Public Papers and Addresses of Franklin D. Roosevelt*

The next day, a cartoonist used the words "new deal" to stand for Roosevelt's program. From that point forward, Roosevelt's policies for ending the Depression became known as the **New Deal.** Roosevelt's confidence that he could make things better contrasted sharply with Hoover's apparent failure to do anything effective. On Election Day, Roosevelt won the Electoral College in a landslide, 472 votes to 59, and he received nearly 23 million votes to slightly less than 16 million for Hoover in the general election.

Picturing **History**

The Young Roosevelts Franklin Roosevelt and Eleanor Roosevelt were married in 1905. They were distantly related through former president Theodore Roosevelt—her uncle and his cousin. What sort of childhood did Franklin Roosevelt have growing up in Hyde Park, New York?

Roosevelt's Background Franklin Roosevelt—a distant cousin of President Theodore Roosevelt—was born in 1882 to a wealthy New York family. Roosevelt grew up on his family's estate at Hyde Park on the Hudson River. There, Roosevelt learned to hunt, fish, ride horses, and sail, and he developed his lifelong commitment to conservation and a love of rural America. Roosevelt was educated at Harvard and Columbia Law School. While at Harvard, he became friends with Theodore Roosevelt's niece, Eleanor. Soon afterward, they were married.

Roosevelt was intensely competitive. He enjoyed winning and liked to be in control. He also liked being around people. His charming personality, deep rich voice, and wide smile expressed confidence and optimism. He could also be very persuasive. Overall, FDR's personality seemed made for a life in politics.

FDR's Early Political Career Shortly after leaving law school, Roosevelt plunged into politics. In 1910 he won a seat in the New York State Senate, where he earned a reputation as a progressive reformer willing to stand up to the party bosses. Roosevelt strongly supported Woodrow Wilson's presidential campaign in 1912. After winning the election, Wilson rewarded Roosevelt by appointing him assistant secretary of the navy, a position he held through World War I.

2 TEACH

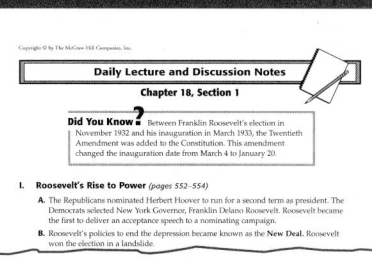

Copyright © by The McGraw-Hill Companies, Inc.

Daily Lecture and Discussion Notes

Chapter 18, Section 1

Did You Know? Between Franklin Roosevelt's election in November 1932 and his inauguration in March 1933, the Twentieth Amendment was added to the Constitution. This amendment changed the inauguration date from March 4 to January 20.

I. Roosevelt's Rise to Power *(pages 552–554)*

A. The Republicans nominated Herbert Hoover to run for a second term as president. The Democrats selected New York Governor, Franklin Delano Roosevelt. Roosevelt became the first to deliver an acceptance speech to a nominating campaign.

B. Roosevelt's policies to end the depression were known as the **New Deal.** Roosevelt won the election in a landslide.

Creating Circle Graphs Provide the data below and ask students to make a pair of circle graphs showing the results of the presidential election of 1932. **L2**

Candidate	Popular Vote	Electoral Vote
Roosevelt, Dem.	22,809,638	472
Hoover, Rep.	15,758,901	59
Thomas, Social.	881,951	0

Picturing **History**

Answer: life of privilege, wealth, education

Ask: How would you describe Franklin Roosevelt's personality? *(possible answers: competitive, confident, optimistic, persuasive)*

History *and the* Humanities

American Music: Cultural Traditions: "Franklin D. Roosevelt's Back Again"

American Art & Architecture: Fallingwater

Reading Strategy   **READING THE TEXT**

Writing Free Writes Remind students of the hardships faced by many Americans during the early years of the Depression. Then have students read the quote by Franklin Roosevelt on page 554. Based on what they have learned about the Depression, have students write a letter to a friend about the winter of 1932 as though they were an unemployed factory worker, a banker whose bank has just collapsed, or a farmer who has lost his land. **L1**

Refer to *Inclusion for the High School Social Studies Classroom Strategies and Activities* in the TCR.

Linking Past & Present

A twentieth-century vaccine was developed not only for polio but also for smallpox. By 1980 the disease had been eradicated except for small samples kept for research.

✓ Reading Check

Answer: privileged upbringing, love of the outdoors, polio, service in political office

3 ASSESS

Assign Section 1 Assessment as homework or as an in-class activity.

⦿ Have students use the **Interactive Tutor Self-Assessment CD-ROM.**

L1/ELL

Reading Essentials and Study Guide 18–1

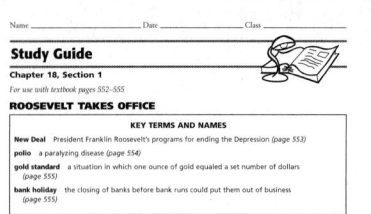

In 1920, hoping his name would win votes, the Democrats nominated Roosevelt as their candidate for vice president. After losing the election, Roosevelt temporarily withdrew from politics. The next year he came down with a fever and soon felt numbness in both legs. He had caught the dreaded and paralyzing disease known as **polio.** Although there was no cure, Roosevelt refused to give in. He began a vigorous exercise program to restore muscle control. Eventually, by wearing heavy steel braces on his legs, he was able to appear to walk by leaning on a cane and someone's arm and swinging his legs forward by moving his hips.

While recovering from polio, Roosevelt depended on his wife to keep his name prominent in the New York Democratic Party. Although shy, Eleanor Roosevelt became an effective public speaker. Her efforts during this time kept her husband's political career alive.

Linking Past & Present

Roosevelt Dime

Past: Search for a Cure
In 1921 Franklin Roosevelt contracted polio, a disease that paralyzed his legs. Few people knew of his physical limitations when he became president. His only freedom from braces came when he swam. After Roosevelt established a foundation for polio victims at Warm Springs, Georgia, entertainer Eddie Cantor suggested that everyone in the country send a dime for polio research to the president. This campaign, which became known as the March of Dimes, produced 150,000 letters a day. In 1945 Congress voted to honor Roosevelt by placing his image on the dime.

Present: A Threat Eliminated
In the early 1950s, Dr. Jonas Salk discovered the polio vaccine. Today polio is no longer the threat to health that it once was.

Governor of New York By the mid-1920s, Roosevelt was again active in the Democratic Party. He became a strong supporter of New York's governor, Alfred E. Smith. When the Democratic Party nominated Smith for president in 1928, Smith urged Roosevelt to run for governor of New York. Roosevelt campaigned hard to demonstrate that his illness had not slowed him down, and he narrowly won the election.

Roosevelt's policies as governor made him very popular. He cut taxes for farmers and worked to reduce the rates charged by public utilities. In 1931, as the Depression worsened, Roosevelt convinced the New York legislature to set up a new state agency to help unemployed New Yorkers. The agency distributed over $25 million in aid that provided relief to about 10 percent of New York's families.

Roosevelt's popularity in New York paved the way for his presidential nomination in 1932. Many Americans applauded his use of the government's power to help people in economic distress. Others believed that his struggle against polio had given him a better understanding of their hardships.

Perhaps most important, Americans saw in Roosevelt an energy and optimism that gave them hope despite the tough economic times. After Roosevelt became president, his serenity and confidence amazed many people. When one aide commented on his attitude, Roosevelt replied, "If you had spent two years in bed, trying to wiggle your big toe, after that anything else would seem easy."

✓ **Reading Check Interpreting** What events in Roosevelt's life shaped his ideas and character?

Roosevelt Is Inaugurated

Although Roosevelt won the presidency in November 1932, the country's unemployed and homeless had to endure one more winter as they waited for his inauguration on March 4, 1933. All through the winter, unemployment continued to rise. Theater director Harold Clurman later wrote about the fear:

> ❝Yes, we could smell the depression in the air, that historically cruel winter of 1932–33, which chilled so many of us like a world's end. . . . It was like a raw wind; the very houses we lived in seemed to be shrinking, hopeless of real comfort.❞
>
> —quoted in *Franklin Roosevelt and the New Deal*

DIFFERENTIATED INSTRUCTION

Reading Support Remind students of the hardships faced by many Americans during the early years of the Depression. Then have students read the quote by Franklin Roosevelt on page 554. Based on what they have learned about the Depression, have students compose a poem about the winter of 1932 as though they were either an unemployed factory worker, a banker whose bank has just collapsed, or a farmer who has lost his land. **L2**

📁 Refer to *Inclusion for the High School Social Studies Classroom Strategies and Activities* in the TCR.

> *" . . . the only thing we have to fear is fear itself . . . "*
>
> —*Franklin D. Roosevelt*

Picturing History

Inspiring Words President Roosevelt used his first Inaugural Address of March 1933 to rally the nation's spirits. What problems had made the nation anxious and fearful?

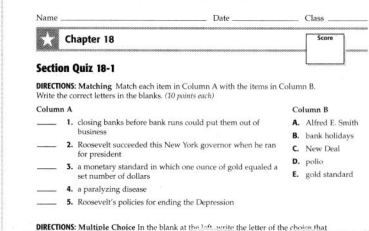
Meanwhile, bank runs greatly increased, further threatening the nation's banking system. Some of the bank runs occurred because people feared Roosevelt would abandon the gold standard and reduce the value of the dollar in order to fight the Depression. Under the gold standard, one ounce of gold equaled a set number of dollars. To reduce the value of the dollar, the United States would have to stop exchanging dollars for gold. Many Americans, and many foreign investors with deposits in American banks, decided to take their money out of the banks and convert it to gold before it lost its value.

Across the nation, people stood in long lines with paper bags and suitcases, waiting to withdraw their money from banks. By March 1933, over 4,000 banks

had collapsed, wiping out 9 million savings accounts. In 38 states, governors declared **bank holidays**— closing the remaining banks before bank runs could put them out of business.

By the day of Roosevelt's inauguration, most of the nation's banks were closed. One in four workers was unemployed. The economy seemed paralyzed. Roosevelt knew he had to restore the nation's confidence. "First of all," the president declared in his Inaugural Address, "let me assert my firm belief that the only thing we have to fear is fear itself. . . . This nation asks for action, and action now!"

 Reading Check **Summarizing** What was the nation's condition when Roosevelt took office?

Picturing History

Answer: high unemployment, massive bank failures, and the weak economy

Reteach
Have students discuss Franklin Roosevelt's early political career.

Enrich
Have students write a summary of Roosevelt's first inaugural address.

HISTORY Online **Study Central**™ To review this section, go to tarvol2.glencoe.com and click on **Study Central**™.

SECTION 1 ASSESSMENT

Checking for Understanding
1. **Define:** gold standard.
2. **Identify:** New Deal, polio, bank holiday.
3. **Describe** the ways in which early influences and experiences shaped Roosevelt as a politician.

Reviewing Themes
4. **Individual Action** Why did Roosevelt's election lead to an increase in bank runs?

Critical Thinking
5. **Explaining** How did FDR's experiences as governor of New York prepare him for the presidency?
6. **Organizing** Use a graphic organizer like the one below to list early influences on Roosevelt's political career.

Early Political Influences

Analyzing Visuals
7. **Analyzing Photographs** Study the photograph on this page. What did the president mean when he said "the only thing we have to fear is fear itself"?

Writing About History
8. **Persuasive Writing** Imagine you are living during the Depression. In your hometown, there has been a run on the bank. Write a letter to the president describing this event. In your letter, ask him to take steps to cure the bank crisis.

 Reading Check

Answer: 25% unemployment, many bank failures

HISTORY Online

Study Central™ provides summaries, interactive games, and online graphic organizers to help students review section content.

4 CLOSE

Have students discuss America's banking system in the early 1930s.

CHAPTER 18 Roosevelt and the New Deal **555**

SECTION 1 ASSESSMENT ANSWERS

1. Term is in blue.
2. New Deal *(p. 553)*, polio *(p. 554)*, bank holiday *(p. 555)*
3. Roosevelt was influenced by his experience with polio, his competitive nature, and his support for Wilson's presidency.
4. People feared that Roosevelt would

take the United States off the gold standard, and that their paper money would become worthless.
5. He used government's power to help New Yorkers in economic distress.
6. family, love of outdoors, political service

7. Fear would drive people to stop trying to get the economy out of its tailspin. If people could avoid fearing the future, they would be able to improve conditions.
8. Letters should express a point of view.

1 FOCUS

Section Overview

This section focuses on the first 100 days of Roosevelt's presidency.

BELLRINGER
Skillbuilder Activity

Project transparency and have students answer the question.

Daily Focus Skills Transparency 18–2

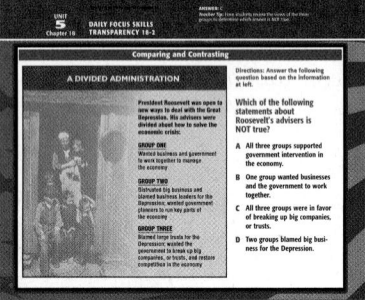

Reading Preview

Answers to Graphic: Problems addressed include: bank runs, unprotected bank deposits, stock fraud, and the plight of farmers.

Preteaching Vocabulary
Provide the following list and have students match one of the Key Terms and Names with each item on the list: new laws, radio, stocks, banks, farms, and forests.

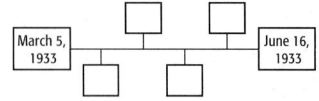

SECTION 2 The First New Deal

Guide to Reading

Main Idea
In the first 100 days of Roosevelt's presidency, his team initiated a series of laws that transformed the United States.

Key Terms and Names
Hundred Days, fireside chats, Securities and Exchange Commission, Federal Deposit Insurance Corporation, Agricultural Adjustment Administration, Civilian Conservation Corps

Reading Strategy
Sequencing As you read about President Roosevelt's first three months in office, complete a time line similar to the one below to record the major problems he addressed during this time.

March 5, 1933 — □ □ — June 16, 1933

Reading Objectives
• **List** three programs of the First New Deal that provided jobs for the unemployed.
• **Discuss** why New Dealers believed that sometimes the government needs to regulate industry and labor.

Section Theme
Groups and Institutions FDR's attempts to end the Depression resulted in many new government agencies.

Preview of Events

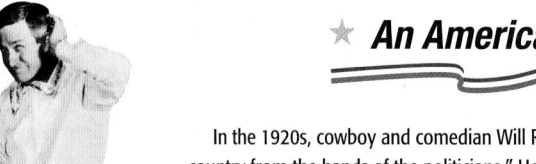

♦March 1933   ♦May 1933   ♦July 1933

March 4, 1933
FDR inaugurated

March 31, 1933
Civilian Conservation Corps created

May 12, 1933
Federal Emergency Relief Act; Agricultural Adjustment Act

June 16, 1933
National Industrial Recovery Act; Glass-Steagall Banking Act; Farm Credit Act

---

★ **An American Story** ★

Will Rogers

In the 1920s, cowboy and comedian Will Rogers said that his life's work was "to rescue the country from the hands of the politicians." He used his sharp wit to go after these public figures. A friend of presidents and politicians of both parties, Rogers nevertheless satirized them mercilessly in public appearances and on the radio.

With FDR, however, Rogers changed his tune: "President Roosevelt closed the banks before lunch and called Congress into session while he was having dessert. . . . The whole country is with him. . . . Even if he does what is wrong they are with him, just so he does something. . . . If he burned down the Capitol, we would cheer and say, 'Well, we at least got a fire started anyhow.'"

As Roosevelt's New Deal gained momentum, Rogers praised the resulting flurry of legislation: "Mr. Roosevelt just makes out a little list of things every morning that he wants [Congress] to do . . . and the whole country is better off."

—adapted from *Will Rogers: A Biography*

The Hundred Days Begins

Roosevelt and his advisers, sometimes called the Brain Trust, came into office bursting with ideas for recovery from the Depression. Roosevelt had no clear agenda. The previous spring, during his campaign for the presidential nomination, Roosevelt had revealed the approach he would take as president. "The country needs," Roosevelt explained, "bold, persistent experimentation. . . . Above all, try something."

The new president began to send bill after bill to Congress. Between March 9 and June 16, 1933—which came to be called the **Hundred Days**—Congress passed 15 major acts to

---

SECTION RESOURCES

📁 Reproducible Masters
• Reproducible Lesson Plan 18–2
• Daily Lecture and Discussion Notes 18–2
• Guided Reading Activity 18–2
• Section Quiz 18–2
• Reading Essentials and Study Guide 18–2
• Interpreting Political Cartoons

📠 Transparencies
• Daily Focus Skills Transparency 18–2

Multimedia
🔵 Interactive Tutor Self-Assessment CD-ROM
🔵 ExamView® Pro Testmaker CD-ROM
🔵 Presentation Plus! CD-ROM
🔵 TeacherWorks™ CD-ROM
🎵 Audio Program

meet the economic crisis, setting a pace for new legislation that has never been equaled. Together, these programs made up what would later be called the First New Deal.

Origins of the New Deal The New Deal was not based on a clear strategy shaped by a single philosophy. Roosevelt was not an intellectual, nor did he have a strong political ideology. He was a practical politician. FDR was willing to try a variety of approaches both to see whether they worked and whether they were helping or hurting him politically.

To generate new ideas and programs, Roosevelt sought advice from a wide range of advisers with experience in academia, business, agriculture, government, law, and social work. The president deliberately chose advisers who disagreed with each other. He wanted to hear many different points of view, and by setting his advisers against one another, Roosevelt ensured that he alone made the final decision on what policies to pursue.

A Divided Administration Roosevelt's advisers were divided roughly into three main groups. Despite their disagreements, most of the advisers had grown up in the Progressive Era, and their approaches reflected progressive ideas. They generally favored some form of government intervention in the economy—although they disagreed over what the government's role should be.

One group that was very influential during the early years of Roosevelt's administration supported the "New Nationalism" of Theodore Roosevelt. These advisers believed that business and government should work together to manage the economy. They had been very impressed by business-government cooperation on the War Industries Board during World War I. They believed that if government agencies worked with businesses to regulate wages, prices, and production, they could lift the economy out of the Depression.

A second group of advisers in the Roosevelt administration went even further. They distrusted big business and blamed business leaders for causing the Depression. These advisers wanted government planners to run key parts of the economy.

A third group in Roosevelt's administration supported the "New Freedom" of Woodrow Wilson. They too blamed large trusts for the Depression, but they believed the government had to restore competition to the economy. These advisers wanted Roosevelt to support "trust busting" by breaking up big companies and allowing competition to set wages, prices, and production levels. They also thought the government should impose regulations on the economy to keep competition fair.

✓ **Reading Check** **Summarizing** What ideas did Roosevelt's advisers support?

Fixing the Banks and the Stock Market

As the debate over policies and programs swirled around him, President Roosevelt took office with one thing clear in his mind. Very few of the proposed solutions would work as long as the nation's banks remained closed. The first thing he had to do was restore confidence in the banking system.

The Emergency Banking Relief Act On his very first night in office, Roosevelt told Secretary of the Treasury William H. Woodin he wanted an emergency banking bill ready for Congress in less than five days. The following afternoon, Roosevelt declared a national bank holiday, temporarily closing all banks, and called Congress into a special session scheduled to begin on March 9, 1933.

On the day Congress convened, the House of Representatives unanimously passed the Emergency Banking Relief Act after only 38 minutes of debate.

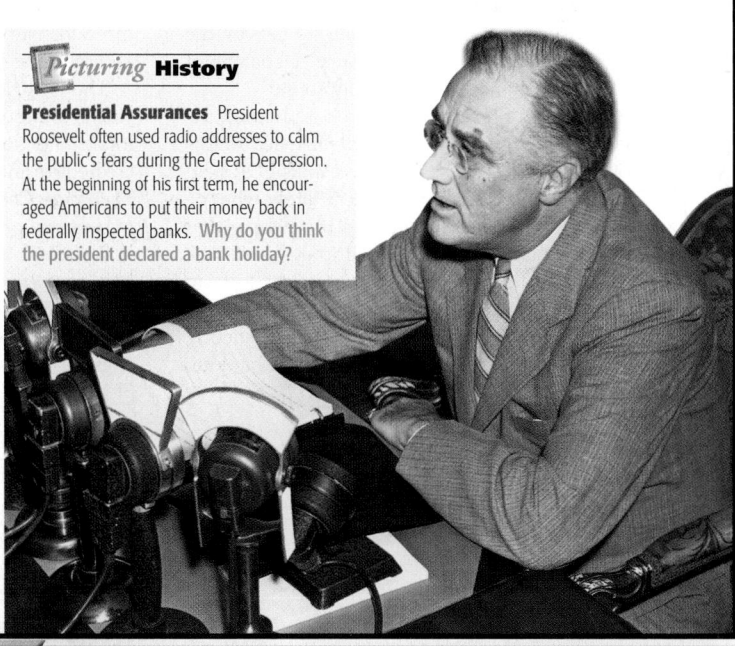

Picturing **History**

Presidential Assurances President Roosevelt often used radio addresses to calm the public's fears during the Great Depression. At the beginning of his first term, he encouraged Americans to put their money back in federally inspected banks. **Why do you think the president declared a bank holiday?**

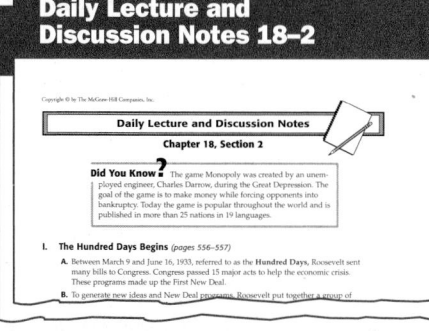
✓ **Reading Check**

Answer: One group wanted joint government-business cooperation; another wanted government control of business; another wanted more competition.

Discussing a Topic Ask students to comment on the following statement: "The New Deal was a continuation of the Progressive era." Have students who agree with the statement list specific ways in which the New Deal resembled the Progressive era. Have those who disagree point out the differences between the New Deal and Progressivism. **L1**

Picturing **History**

Answer: It would provide a brief interval during which depositors could not withdraw money. Roosevelt hoped to restore confidence in the banking system.

Ask: How many people listened to Roosevelt's fireside chat on March 12, 1933? *(60 million)*

Reading Strategy — READING THE TEXT

Predicting Before students learn about actual New Deal programs, organize them into groups of four or five. Ask each student to design his or her own "new deal" program. Each student in the group should tackle a different issue, such as creating jobs, providing emergency relief, bolstering business, or safeguarding bank deposits. As students read the section, have them review and compare the actual New Deal programs to the programs they developed. **L1**

📖 Refer to *Inclusion for the High School Social Studies Classroom Strategies and Activities* in the TCR.

L1/ELL

Guided Reading Activity 18-2

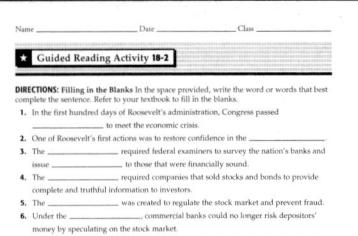

Name _____ Date _____ Class _____

★ **Guided Reading Activity 18-2**

DIRECTIONS: Filling in the Blanks In the space provided, write the word or words that best complete the sentence. Refer to your textbook to fill in the blanks.

1. In the first hundred days of Roosevelt's administration, Congress passed _____ to meet the economic crisis.

2. One of Roosevelt's first actions was to restore confidence in the _____.

3. The _____ required federal examiners to survey the nation's banks and issue _____ to those that were financially sound.

4. The _____ required companies that sold stocks and bonds to provide complete and truthful information to investors.

5. The _____ was created to regulate the stock market and prevent fraud.

6. Under the _____, commercial banks could no longer risk depositors' money by speculating on the stock market.

Why It Matters

Background: The TVA's original mission focused on making the Tennessee River navigable and controlling floods. In addition, reforestation and land reclamation were part of the mission. The agency was also charged with the responsibility of generating electrical power and assisting with industrial and agricultural development. Today the TVA's mission focuses on the sustained, integrated development of the region. Supplying reliable, economical power, supporting the river system, and stimulating economic growth are key to the mission.

Ask: Which seven states are directly affected by the TVA? *(Alabama, Georgia, Kentucky, Mississippi, North Carolina, Tennessee, and Virginia)*

you don't say...

FDIC Since 1933 the Federal Deposit Insurance Corporation (FDIC) has insured bank deposits. Originally the FDIC insured each bank account for up to $5,000. Today accounts are insured up to $100,000.

Why It Matters

The TVA

Perhaps no New Deal program produced as many visible benefits as the Tennessee Valley Authority (TVA). This dam-building project was a bold venture to control floods, conserve forestlands, and bring electricity to rural America. The TVA created a comprehensive plan for developing a vast seven-state region drained by the Tennessee and Cumberland Rivers and populated mainly by poor farmers working worn-out land. The TVA erected 20 dams, employing up to 40,000 workers at a time. The agency also reforested millions of acres, built fertilizer factories and power plants, and strung thousands of miles of wire to bring electricity to rural families for the first time.

◄ **Recreation**
Millions of people each year fish, swim, ski, white-water raft, or go boating on the reservoirs. Sometimes the reservoir system is referred to as the "Great Lakes of the South."

NATIONAL GEOGRAPHIC **The TVA, 1940** *In Motion*

Area supplied with power from the TVA
— Dam
■ Steam power plant

The Senate approved the bill that evening, and Roosevelt signed it into law shortly afterward. The new law required federal examiners to survey the nation's banks and issue Treasury Department licenses to those that were financially sound.

On March 12, President Roosevelt addressed the nation by radio. Sixty million people listened to this first of many "fireside chats," direct talks FDR held with the American people to let them know what he was trying to accomplish. He told the people that their money would now be secure if they put it back into the banks. "I assure you that it is safer to keep your money in a reopened bank than under the mattress." When banks opened the day after the speech, deposits far outweighed withdrawals. The banking crisis was over.

Regulating Banks and Brokers Although President Roosevelt had restored confidence in the banking system, many of his advisers who favored trust-busting and fair competition urged him to go further. They pushed for new regulations for both banks and the stock market. Roosevelt agreed with their ideas and threw his support behind the Securities Act of 1933 and the Glass-Steagall Banking Act.

The Securities Act required companies that sold stocks and bonds to provide complete and truthful information to investors. The following year Congress created an independent agency, the **Securities and Exchange Commission** (SEC), to regulate the stock market and prevent fraud.

The Glass-Steagall Act separated commercial banking from investment banking. Commercial banks handle everyday transactions. They take deposits, pay interest, cash checks, and loan money for mortgages and other business activities. Under the Glass-Steagall Act, these banks were no longer permitted to risk depositors' money by using it to speculate on the stock market.

To further protect depositors, the Glass-Steagall Act also created the **Federal Deposit Insurance Corporation** (FDIC) to provide government insurance

---

DIFFERENTIATED INSTRUCTION

Reading Support Have students work in pairs to create a diagram showing how the banking system worked before and after the Glass-Steagall Act and the creation of the Federal Deposit Insurance Corporation. Suggest that students use visuals, such as play money, to make their diagrams interesting. **L2**

📁 Refer to *Inclusion for the High School Social Studies Classroom Strategies and Activities* in the TCR.

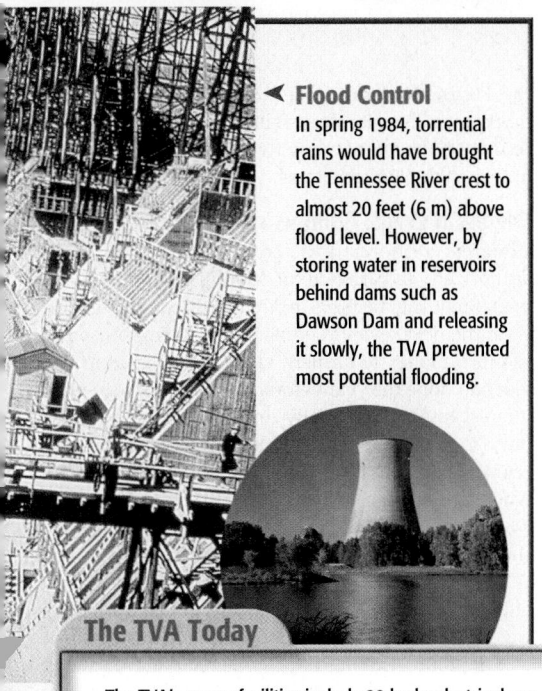

◄ Flood Control

In spring 1984, torrential rains would have brought the Tennessee River crest to almost 20 feet (6 m) above flood level. However, by storing water in reservoirs behind dams such as Dawson Dam and releasing it slowly, the TVA prevented most potential flooding.

The TVA Today

The TVA's power facilities include 29 hydroelectric dams, 11 fossil-fuel plants, 3 nuclear power plants, 4 combustion-turbine plants, a pumped-storage facility, and 17,000 miles of transmission lines. These facilities provide power to nearly 8 million people in the seven-state region.

for bank deposits up to a certain amount. By protecting depositors in this way, the FDIC greatly increased public confidence in the banking system.

✓ **Reading Check** **Explaining** How did the government restore confidence in the banking system?

Managing Farms and Industry

Many of Roosevelt's advisers believed that both farmers and businesses were suffering because prices were too low and production too high. Several advisers believed competition was inefficient and bad for the economy. They wanted business and government to work together and favored the creation of federal agencies to manage the economy.

The Agricultural Adjustment Administration
The nation's farmers had been hit hard by the Depression. One week after calling Congress into special session, Roosevelt announced plans for a new farm program. Working closely with the leaders of the nation's farm organizations, Secretary of Agriculture Henry Wallace raced to complete a new farm bill before planting season began.

The Agricultural Adjustment Act that Roosevelt asked Congress to pass was based on a simple idea—that prices for farm goods were low because farmers grew too much food. Under Roosevelt's program, the government would pay farmers *not* to raise certain livestock, such as hogs, and *not* to grow certain crops, such as cotton, corn, wheat, and tobacco. The farm program was administered by the **Agricultural Adjustment Administration** (AAA).

By the time the AAA was organized, however, farmers had already planted their crops for the year and begun raising the season's livestock. To prevent cotton—which was already at a very low price—from reaching the market, the AAA paid cotton farmers about $100 million to plow under about 25 percent of their crop. Similarly, hog producers slaughtered 6 million piglets instead of fattening them for market.

Over the next two years, farmers withdrew millions of acres from production and received more than $1 billion in support payments. The program accomplished its goal: The farm surplus fell greatly by 1936. Food prices then rose, as did total farm income, which quickly increased by more than 50 percent.

In a nation caught in a Depression, however, raising food prices drew harsh criticism. Furthermore, not all farmers benefited. Large commercial farmers, who concentrated on one crop, profited more than smaller farmers who raised several products. Worse, thousands of poor tenant farmers—many of them African Americans—became homeless and jobless when landlords chose their fields to be taken out of production.

A Blueprint for Industrial Recovery The government turned its attention from farming to manufacturing in June 1933, when Roosevelt and Congress enacted the **National Industrial Recovery Act** (NIRA). The NIRA suspended the antitrust laws and allowed business, labor, and government to cooperate in setting up voluntary rules for each industry.

These rules were known as codes of fair competition. Some codes set prices, established minimum wages, and limited factories to two shifts per day so production could be spread to as many firms as possible. Other codes shortened workers' hours with the goal of creating additional jobs. Another provision in the law guaranteed workers the right to form unions.

Under the leadership of Hugh Johnson, the **National Recovery Administration** (NRA) ran the entire program. Business owners who signed code agreements received signs displaying the NRA's symbol—a blue eagle—and the slogan, "We do our part." Since the NRA had limited power to enforce the

CHAPTER 18 Roosevelt and the New Deal **559**

✓**Reading Check**

Answer: Roosevelt ordered a bank holiday, signed the Emergency Banking Relief Act into law, and addressed the nation in a "fireside chat." He also supported the Glass-Steagall Act, which created the FDIC to provide government insurance for bank deposits.

Drawing Conclusions Ask students to discuss whether it is a citizen's duty to follow the suggestion of a president such as Roosevelt's to redeposit money in a bank. Ask students if a president has made a similar request during their lifetime. Then ask how citizens responded to the request. (If students cannot identify a similar request, direct the discussion towards likely reactions from citizens to such requests.) **L1**

FYI

Throughout his presidency Franklin Roosevelt averaged two press conferences a week. These were informal affairs, with as many as 200 reporters cramming into the Oval Office to hear Roosevelt's pronouncements. He answered questions off the cuff and seemed to know each reporter by name.

 Use *Interpreting Political Cartoons*, Cartoon 24.

INTERDISCIPLINARY CONNECTIONS ACTIVITY

Language Arts Have students write a persuasive speech that Franklin Roosevelt could have used during the Hundred Days to promote his solutions to the banking crisis or to defend his emergency relief measures. Students may want to study transcripts or recordings of some of Roosevelt's speeches to get a sense of his speaking style. Students should also identify characteristics of the audience and write a speech targeted to those characteristics. **L2**

codes, it used public opinion to pressure companies into going along. It urged consumers to buy goods only from companies that displayed the blue eagle.

The NRA did produce a revival of a few industries, but the gains proved short-lived. Small companies complained, justifiably, that large corporations wrote the codes to favor themselves. More efficient companies disliked price fixing, which limited competition and made it hard for them to increase their market share by cutting prices. Employers disliked codes that gave workers the right to form unions and bargain collectively over wages and hours. They also argued that paying high minimum wages forced them to charge higher prices to cover their costs.

The codes were also very difficult to administer, and business leaders often ignored them. It became obvious that the NRA was failing when industrial production actually fell after the organization was established. By the time the Supreme Court declared the NRA to be unconstitutional in 1935, it had already lost much of its political support.

✓ **Reading Check** **Examining** What were the provisions of the Agricultural Adjustment Act and the National Industrial Recovery Act?

Providing Debt Relief

While some of Roosevelt's advisers believed low prices had caused the Depression, others believed that debt was the main obstacle to economic recovery. With incomes falling, people had to use most of their money to pay their debts and had little left over to buy goods or pay for services. Many Americans, terrified of losing their homes and farms, deliberately cut back on their spending to make sure they could pay their mortgages. President Roosevelt responded to the crisis by introducing several policies intended to assist Americans with their debts.

The Home Owners' Loan Corporation To help homeowners pay their mortgages, Roosevelt asked Congress to establish the Home Owners' Loan Corporation (HOLC). The HOLC bought the mortgages of many homeowners who were behind in their payments. It then restructured them with longer terms of repayment and lower interest rates. Roughly 10 percent of the nation's homeowners received a HOLC loan.

The HOLC did not help everyone. It only made loans to homeowners who were still employed. When people lost their jobs and could no longer pay their mortgages, the HOLC foreclosed on their property, just as a bank would have done. By 1938

560 CHAPTER 18 Roosevelt and the New Deal

the HOLC had foreclosed on more than 100,000 mortgages. Despite these failures, the HOLC helped refinance one out of every five mortgages on private homes in the United States.

The Farm Credit Administration Three days after Congress authorized the creation of the HOLC, it authorized the Farm Credit Administration (FCA) to begin helping farmers refinance their mortgages. Over the next seven months, the FCA lent four times as much money to farmers as the entire banking system had done the year before. It was also able to push interest rates substantially lower. "I would be without a roof over my head if it hadn't been for the government loan," wrote one of the millions of farmers who were saved by FCA loans.

Although FCA loans helped many farmers in the short term, their long-term value can be questioned. FCA loans helped less efficient farmers keep their land, but giving loans to poor farmers meant that the money was not available to loan to more efficient businesses in the economy. Although FCA loans may have slowed the overall economic recovery, they did help many desperate and impoverished people hold onto their land.

✓ **Reading Check** **Identifying** What New Deal programs helped farmers and homeowners?

Spending and Relief Programs

While many of Roosevelt's advisers emphasized tinkering with prices and providing debt relief in order to cure the Depression, others maintained that the fundamental cause of the Depression was low consumption. People were simply not buying enough products to keep the economy going. The fastest way out of the Depression, these advisers asserted, was to get money directly into the hands of needy individuals.

Neither President Roosevelt nor his advisers wanted simply to give money to the unemployed. They argued that recipients were more likely to maintain work skills and self-respect if they earned their

Picturing **History**

The NRA Eagle As a symbol of the National Recovery Administration, this eagle informed consumers about industries that were meeting the standards of the National Industrial Recovery Act. How successful was the NRA?

CRITICAL THINKING ACTIVITY

Analyzing Media Have students listen to a recording of one of Roosevelt's fireside chats. Then have students view a live broadcast of a speech by the current president. Have students discuss how the two speeches compare. Ask students how the styles reflect the individuals in office and how the styles reflect the events occurring in the country at the time the speeches were given. (Recordings of some fireside chats are available at libraries and on the Internet.) **L2**

The First New Deal, 1933–1935

Agency	Established	Function
Civilian Conservation Corps (CCC)	March 1933	Employed single men, ages 18–25, for natural resource conservation
Tennessee Valley Authority (TVA)	May 1933	Built hydroelectric plants and dams aimed at improving seven Southern states and attracting industry to the South
Agricultural Adjustment Act (AAA)	May 1933	Reduced agricultural surplus and raised prices for struggling farmers
Federal Emergency Relief Administration (FERA)	May 1933	Granted federal money to state and local governments to be used to help the unemployed
National Recovery Administration (NRA)	June 1933	Controlled industrial production and prices with industry-created codes of fair competition
Federal Deposit Insurance Corporation (FDIC)	June 1933	Guaranteed bank deposits up to $2,500
Public Works Administration (PWA)	June 1933	Provided employment in construction of airports, parks, schools, and roads
Civil Works Administration (CWA)	November 1933 (cancelled 1934)	Provided employment in construction of airports, parks, schools, and roads
Securities and Exchange Commission (SEC)	June 1934	Regulated the stock market to avoid dishonest practices

Chart Skills

1. **Interpreting Charts** Which of the programs listed was cancelled the year after it was established?
2. **Examining** What steps did the AAA take to ensure its listed function?

money. As a result, Roosevelt urged Congress to establish a series of government agencies that would organize work programs for the unemployed.

The CCC The most highly praised New Deal work relief program was the **Civilian Conservation Corps** (CCC), which combined Roosevelt's love of nature and commitment to conservation with the need to help the unemployed. Beginning in March 1933, the CCC offered unemployed young men 18 to 25 years old the opportunity to work under the direction of the national forestry service planting trees, fighting forest fires, and building reservoirs.

The young men lived in camps near their work areas and earned $30 a month. By midsummer the CCC had created some 1,500 camps. The average CCC worker returned home after six months to a year of service better nourished than before and with greater self-respect. "I weighed about 160 pounds when I went there, and when I left, I was 190," said one. "It made a man of me, all right." By the time it closed down in 1942, the CCC had put 3 million young men to work outdoors.

Public Works and Emergency Relief A few weeks after authorizing the CCC, Congress established the Federal Emergency Relief Administration (FERA). FERA did not initially create projects for the unemployed. Instead, it channeled money—a half-billion dollars in all—to state and local agencies to fund

their relief projects. The leader of FERA was Harry Hopkins, whose nervous energy and sarcastic manner put off many people. Despite his personality, Hopkins became one of the most influential people in Roosevelt's administration.

Half an hour after meeting with Roosevelt to discuss his new job, Hopkins set up a desk in the hallway of his new office. In the next two hours, he spent $5 million on relief projects. When critics charged that some of the projects did not make sense in the long run, Hopkins replied, "People don't eat in the long run—they eat every day."

In June 1933, Congress authorized the creation of another federal relief agency—the **Public Works Administration** (PWA). Roosevelt knew that nearly one-third of the nation's unemployed were in the construction industry. To put them back to work, the PWA began a series of construction projects to build and improve highways, dams, sewer systems, water-works, schools, and other government facilities.

In most cases, the PWA did not hire workers directly, but instead awarded contracts to construction companies. By insisting that contractors hire African Americans, the agency broke down some of the long-standing racial barriers in the construction trades.

Chart Skills

Answer:
1. Civil Works Administration
2. AAA paid farmers not to raise certain livestock, not to raise certain crops, to plow under cotton, and to slaughter piglets.

Chart Skills Practice
Ask: How much money did the **FERA spend?** *(half a billion dollars)*

Making Predictions Ask students if they think young people today would be interested in joining a group similar to the Civilian Conservation Corps. Have students explain their reasoning. **L1**

3 ASSESS

Assign Section 2 Assessment as homework or as an in-class activity.

⊙ Have students use the **Interactive Tutor Self-Assessment CD-ROM.**

L1/ELL

Reading Essentials and Study Guide 18–2

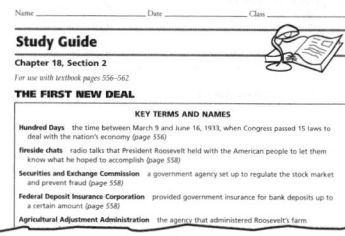

EXTENDING THE CONTENT

Recovery Projects Besides working on a national level, the Public Works Administration (PWA) revitalized local economies throughout the United States. For example, in 1934 the PWA granted New York Mills, a small town in Minnesota, money to build a village water system. All the town's unemployed men went back to work during this construction project. In addition, engineering contractors, plumbing and electrical companies, and materials suppliers gained new business from the project.

Section Quiz 18–2

Picturing **History**

Answer: 1942

Ask: Why do you think the CCC was closed down in 1942? *(The United States entered World War II.)*

Reteach
Have students describe three programs of the early New Deal that provided work relief to the unemployed.

Enrich
Have students prepare an oral report on a member of Roosevelt's administration.

Reading Check
Answer: Civilian Conservation Corps, Public Works Administration, Civil Works Administration

HISTORY Online
Study Central™ provides summaries, interactive games, and online graphic organizers to help students review section content.

4 CLOSE
Have students discuss why many members of Roosevelt's administration believed that the government should regulate industry and labor.

Picturing **History**

The Civilian Conservation Corps FDR satisfied both the nation's need for employment and his love of nature with the CCC. Workers planted forests, built reservoirs, and received a monthly salary. In what year did the CCC halt operations?

The CWA By the fall of 1933, neither FERA nor the PWA had reduced unemployment significantly. Hopkins realized that unless the federal government acted quickly, a huge number of unemployed would be in severe distress once winter began. After Hopkins explained the situation, President Roosevelt authorized him to set up the **Civil Works Administration** (CWA).

Unlike the PWA, the CWA hired workers directly and put them on the federal government's payroll. That winter the CWA employed 4 million people, 300,000 of them women. Under Hopkins's direction, the agency built or improved 1,000 airports,

500,000 miles of roads, 40,000 school buildings, and 3,500 playgrounds, parks, and playing fields.

The cost of the CWA was huge—the program spent nearly $1 billion in just five months. A former colleague remembered Hopkins as "the kind of guy that seldom wrote a letter. He'd just call and say, 'Send a million dollars to Arkansas, and five million to New York. People are in need.'"

Although the CWA helped many people get through the winter, President Roosevelt was alarmed at how quickly the agency was spending money. He did not want Americans to get used to the federal government providing them with jobs. Warning that the CWA would "become a habit with the country," Roosevelt insisted that it be shut down. "We must not take the position," the president explained, "that we are going to have a permanent depression in this country." By early April 1934, Hopkins had shut down the CWA and fired the 4 million workers the agency had hired.

By the end of his first year in office, President Roosevelt had convinced Congress to pass an astonishing array of programs and policies. The programs passed during the first New Deal did not restore prosperity, but they all reflected Roosevelt's zeal for action, his willingness to experiment, and his openness to new ideas. Perhaps the most important result of the first New Deal was a noticeable change in the spirit of the American people. Roosevelt's actions had inspired hope and optimism, and Americans' faith in their nation had been restored.

Reading Check **Identifying** What three New Deal programs provided work relief to the unemployed?

Study Central™ To review this section, go to **tarvol2.glencoe.com** and click on **Study Central™**.

SECTION 2 ASSESSMENT

Checking for Understanding
1. **Define:** fireside chats.
2. **Identify:** Hundred Days, Securities and Exchange Commission, Federal Deposit Insurance Corporation, Agricultural Adjustment Administration, Civilian Conservation Corps.
3. **Summarize** the different viewpoints of Roosevelt's advisers.

Reviewing Themes
4. **Groups and Institutions** How did the Glass-Steagall Act and the Federal Deposit Insurance Corporation help make the banking industry safer?

Critical Thinking
5. **Interpreting** Did the CCC, CWA, and PWA achieve their goals? Explain your answer.
6. **Organizing** Use a graphic organizer like the one below to list the major agencies of the First New Deal.

(Roosevelt's New Agencies)

Analyzing Visuals
7. **Analyzing Charts** Examine the chart on page 561. How did the various agencies listed change the historical role of the federal government?

Writing About History
8. **Expository Writing** Research the Agricultural Adjustment Act by rereading the text on page 559. Use library resources and the Internet to complete your research. Then write an article explaining the benefits and drawbacks of this piece of legislation.

SECTION 2 ASSESSMENT ANSWERS
1. Term is in blue.
2. Hundred Days (p. 556), Securities and Exchange Commission (p. 558), Federal Deposit Insurance Corporation (p. 558), Agricultural Adjustment Administration (p. 559), Civilian Conservation Corps (p. 561)
3. One group wanted government-business cooperation; another wanted greater government control; another wanted to increase competition.
4. The Glass-Steagall Act protected depositors' money from speculation and the FDIC insured bank deposits.
5. They temporarily employed workers, but did not reduce unemployment significantly.
6. Answers should match text information.
7. Answers should explain the various ways the government increased its role.
8. Articles should cover both sides of the issue.

Study and Writing SKILLBUILDER

Outlining

Why Learn This Skill?

To draw a scene, first you would sketch the rough shape, or outline, of the picture. Then you would fill in this rough shape with details. Outlining written material is a similar process. You begin with the rough shape of the material and gradually fill in the details.

Learning the Skill

When studying written material, outlining helps you identify main ideas and group together related facts. In writing, it helps you put information in a logical order.

There are two kinds of outlines—*formal* and *informal*. An informal outline is similar to taking notes. You write only words and phrases needed to remember ideas. Under the main ideas, jot down related but less important details. This kind of outline is useful for reviewing material before a test.

A formal outline has a standard format. In a formal outline, label main heads with Roman numerals, subheads with capital letters, and details with Arabic numerals. Each level must have at least two entries and should be indented from the previous level. All entries use the same grammatical form. For example, if one entry is a complete sentence, all other entries at that level must also be complete sentences.

When outlining written material, first read the material to identify the main ideas. In textbooks, section heads provide clues to main topics. Next, identify the subheads. List details that support or explain subheads underneath the appropriate subhead.

Practicing the Skill

Study the outline on this page on Roosevelt's New Deal. Then answer the following questions.

❶ Is this an example of a formal or an informal outline?

❷ What are the main headings?

❸ How do the subheads under "Managing Farm and Industry" relate to the main idea?

❹ Give two examples of grammatical inconsistency in this outline:

I. The Hundred Days Begins
  A. Origins of the New Deal
  B. A Divided Administration
    1. Some advisers wanted government and business cooperation.
    2. Others wanted government to run the economy or regulate competition.

II. Fixing the Banks and Stock Market
  A. The Emergency Banking Relief Act
    1. All banks closed temporarily.
    2. The banks reopened and were monitored by federal examiners.
  B. Regulating Banks and Brokers
    1. The Securities Act ensured complete and truthful investment information.
    2. The Glass-Steagall Act separated commercial banking from investment banking.

III. Managing Farms and Industry
  A. The Agricultural Adjustment Administration
    1. Addressed the oversupply of farm products
    2. Increased farm income
  B. A Blueprint for Industrial Recovery
    1. The National Recovery Administration established "fair competition" for industry.
    2. Set minimum wages for employees
    3. The codes were difficult to administer and gains were short-lived.

Skills Assessment

Complete the Practicing Skills questions on page 579 and the Chapter 18 Skill Reinforcement Activity to assess your mastery of this skill.

> #### Applying the Skill
>
> **Outlining** Write a formal or informal outline for Section 4 of this chapter.
>
> Glencoe's **Skillbuilder Interactive Workbook CD-ROM, Level 2,** provides instruction and practice in key social studies skills.

ANSWERS TO PRACTICING THE SKILL

❶ formal
❷ the entries beginning with Roman numerals
❸ They all deal with addressing problems during the Hundred Days.
❹ IIIA1 and IIIB2 are not complete sentences while other numbered points are.

Applying the Skill
Students' outlines will vary. Outlines should be consistent with the content of the text.

1 FOCUS

Section Overview

This section focuses on the new programs Roosevelt introduced to help unions, the elderly, and the unemployed.

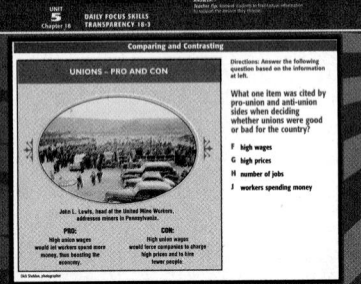
Reading Preview

Answers to Graphic: Graphic organizers should include information from the chart on page 567. In addition, they should include the Wagner Act, which guaranteed workers the right to organize without interference and the right to collective bargaining.

Preteaching Vocabulary
Have students group Key Terms with Key Names associated with the terms.

SECTION 3 The Second New Deal

Guide to Reading

Main Idea
In 1935 Roosevelt introduced new programs to help unions, the elderly, and the unemployed.

Key Terms and Names
deficit spending, American Liberty League, Works Progress Administration, National Labor Relations Board, binding arbitration, sit-down strike, Social Security Act

Reading Strategy
Organizing As you read about President Roosevelt's Second New Deal, complete a graphic organizer similar to the one below by filling in his main legislative successes during this period.

Legislation	Provisions

Reading Objectives
- **Describe** the political challenges Roosevelt faced in the mid-1930s.
- **Explain** why the Social Security Act is still regarded as an important piece of legislation.

Section Theme
Government and Democracy The Second New Deal was a political response to growing criticism from both the left and the right.

Preview of Events

◆April 1935   ◆June 1935   ◆August 1935   ◆October 1935

April 1935 — Works Progress Administration founded

May 1935 — Supreme Court strikes down NIRA

July 1935 — National Labor Relations Act becomes law

August 1935 — Social Security Act adopted

November 1935 — John L. Lewis forms Committee for Industrial Organization

---

★ *An American Story* ★

Harry Hopkins

Harry Hopkins, head of the Federal Emergency Relief Administration, worked long hours in his Washington office, a bare, dingy room with exposed water pipes. He preferred this space to the grandeur of the more conventional offices of high-ranking officials. Here he often defended the New Deal's work relief programs when reporters dropped by, and he lashed out at New Deal critics with headline-making phrases. "Some people just can't stand to see others make a decent living," he said, or, "Hunger is not debatable."

Sometimes Hopkins went on the road to talk about his job. Once, on a trip to his home state of Iowa, Hopkins was extolling New Deal policies to a sympathetic audience when a voice from the crowd shouted, "Who's going to pay for it?" Without a word Hopkins peeled off his jacket, loosened his tie, and rolled up his sleeves. Then his voice ripped through the utter stillness, "You are!"

—adapted from *The Politics of Upheaval*

Challenges to the New Deal

President Roosevelt appreciated Harry Hopkins's feistiness. He needed effective speakers who were willing to contend with his adversaries. Although Roosevelt had been tremendously popular during his first two years in office, opposition to his policies had begun to grow.

The New Deal had been in effect for two years, yet the economy had shown only a slight improvement. Although more than 2 million new jobs had been created, more than 10 million workers remained unemployed, and the nation's total income remained about half of what it had been in 1929. As one of Harry Hopkins's aides reported on a visit to

---

Houston, Texas, "Nobody seems to think any more that the thing [the New Deal] is going to work."

Criticism From Left and Right

Hostility toward Roosevelt came from both the right wing and the left wing of the political spectrum. People on the right generally believed the New Deal had imposed too many regulations on business. The right wing also included many Southern Democrats who believed the New Deal had expanded the federal government's power at the expense of states' rights.

The right wing had opposed the New Deal from the beginning, but by late 1934, the opposition began to increase. To pay for his programs, Roosevelt had begun deficit spending. He had abandoned a balanced budget and begun borrowing money to pay for his programs. Many business leaders became greatly alarmed at the government's growing deficit.

In August 1934, business leaders and anti–New Deal politicians from both parties joined together to create the **American Liberty League.** Its purpose was to organize opposition to the New Deal and "teach the necessity of respect for the rights of person and property."

While criticisms from the right threatened to split the Democratic Party and reduce business support for Roosevelt, another serious challenge to the New Deal came from the left. People on the left believed Roosevelt had not gone far enough. They wanted the government to intervene even more dramatically in the economy to shift wealth from the rich to middle-income and poor Americans.

Huey Long

Perhaps the most serious threat from the left came from Democratic senator Huey Long of Louisiana. Long captivated audiences with folksy humor and fiery oratory. As governor of Louisiana, Long had championed the downtrodden. He had improved schools, colleges, and hospitals, and had built roads and bridges. These benefits made Long very popular and enabled him to build a powerful and corrupt political machine.

Long's attacks on the rich gave him a national following, too. His supporters organized some 27,000 "Share Our Wealth" clubs across the country. Pollsters estimated that if he ran against Roosevelt as a third-party candidate in 1936, Long would win

Critics From the Left Huey Long and Father Charles Coughlin claimed the New Deal did not do enough to help the poor.

several million votes—enough, they believed, to ensure a Republican victory.

Father Coughlin

Huey Long's challenge to Roosevelt became even more credible when his supporters were combined with those of Father Charles Coughlin, a Catholic priest in Detroit. Coughlin had a popular radio show that attracted a weekly audience of about 30 to 45 million Americans.

Originally a New Deal supporter, Coughlin had become impatient with its moderate reforms. He called instead for heavy taxes on the wealthy and nationalization of the banking system. In the spring of 1935, Coughlin organized the National Union for Social Justice, which some Democrats feared was the first step to creating a new political party.

The Townsend Plan

A third left-wing challenge to Roosevelt came from Dr. Francis Townsend, a former public health official. Townsend proposed that the federal government pay citizens over age 60 a pension of $200 a month. Recipients would have to retire and spend their entire pension check each month. He believed the plan would increase spending and remove people from the labor force, freeing up jobs for the unemployed.

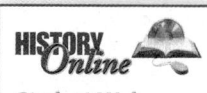
Student Web Activity Visit the *American Republic Since 1877* Web site at tarvol2.glencoe.com and click on **Student Web Activities— Chapter 18** for an activity on the New Deal.

2 TEACH

Daily Lecture and Discussion Notes 18–3

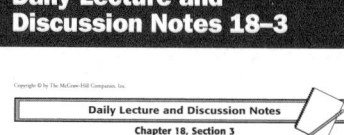

Copyright © by The McGraw-Hill Companies, Inc.

Daily Lecture and Discussion Notes

Chapter 18, Section 3

Did You Know? The National Youth Administration (NYA) was created in 1935 to provide job training for unemployed youth and part-time jobs for needy students. More than 2 million high school and college students worked in part-time clerical jobs at their schools.

I. **Challenges to the New Deal** *(pages 564–566)*

A. Support of Roosevelt and his New Deal began to fade in 1935. The effectiveness of the New Deal was questioned by right and left wing politicians.

B. Roosevelt used **deficit spending** to pay for his programs. He abandoned a balanced budget and borrowed money to pay for his programs.

Making Comparisons Ask students to think of radio personalities who express their political views. Have one student act as recorder, listing the names on the board, with other students offering a description of radio personalities' views. Then **ask:** How is their use of radio similar to Father Coughlin's? **L1**

Objectives and answers to the student activity can be found in the **Web Activity Lesson Plan** at tarvol2.glencoe.com.

The American Liberty League had two objectives: to teach respect for the rights of person and property, and to teach that it was the duty of government to encourage private enterprise and protect property.

COOPERATIVE LEARNING ACTIVITY

Playing a Role Organize the class into discussion groups. Each group member should play one of the following roles: Franklin Roosevelt, a farm laborer, a factory worker, an unemployed person, a business leader, or a retired person. Have the groups read Section 3 to find out what each person's criticism of Roosevelt would be and how Roosevelt would respond to that criticism. Then have each group role-play a meeting between the citizens and Roosevelt.

Use the rubric for a cooperative group management plan on pages 71–72 in the **Performance Assessment Activities and Rubrics.**

Guided Reading Activity 18–3

Name _____ Date _____ Class _____

★ **Guided Reading Activity 18-3**

DIRECTIONS: Using Headings and Subheadings Locate each heading below in your textbook. Then use the information under the correct subheading to help you write each answer.

I. Challenges to the New Deal

A. What did the right wing think of the New Deal? _____

B. What did the left wing think of the New Deal? _____

C. What did Father Coughlin call for to make life better for many Americans? _____

D. How did Dr. Francis Townsend propose to free up jobs for the unemployed? _____

II. Launching the Second New Deal

✓ **Reading Check**

Answer: Right: American Liberty League (business leaders and anti-New Deal politicians)—organize opposition and teach necessity of respect for rights of person and property; Left: Democrats (Huey Long)—share wealth with all; National Union for Social Justice (Fr. Charles Coughlin)—heavy taxes on rich and nationalization of banks; Townsend Plan (Dr. Francis Townsend)—universal pension

NATIONAL GEOGRAPHIC MOMENT in HISTORY

This is one of only two photographs that show Roosevelt seated in a wheelchair. In January 2001 a new portion of the Roosevelt Memorial in Washington, D.C., was unveiled. The statue shows Roosevelt seated in a wheelchair. After initial resistance, his family now supports the addition of the statue. His grandson David Roosevelt said, "I hope that when young people—a young person who goes to visit the FDR Memorial who perhaps is in a wheelchair herself or himself—when they first see the entrance and when they see FDR in a wheelchair, they will say, 'I can do that, too.'"

Townsend's proposal attracted millions of supporters, especially among the elderly, who mobilized as a political force for the first time in American history. Townsend's program was particularly popular in the West. When combined with Long's support in the Midwest and South and Coughlin's support among urban Catholics in the Northeast, there was a real possibility of a coalition that would draw enough votes away from Roosevelt to prevent his re-election in 1936.

✓ **Reading Check** **Examining** What groups of people challenged Roosevelt and the New Deal? What concerns did they have?

Launching the Second New Deal

Although he remained tremendously popular with the American people, Roosevelt realized that his political support could be undermined by the attacks from left and right. He was also disturbed by the failure of the New Deal to generate a rapid economic recovery. In 1935 he launched what came to be called the Second New Deal—another series of programs and reforms that he hoped would speed up the nation's recovery, provide economic security to every American, and ensure his re-election in 1936.

The WPA In January 1935, Roosevelt began by asking Congress for nearly $5 billion "for work relief and to increase employment by providing useful projects." Much of the money would be given to the **Works Progress Administration** (WPA), a new federal agency headed by Harry Hopkins. "The big boss is ready to go places in a big way," Hopkins told a colleague.

Over the next several years, the WPA spent $11 billion. Its 8.5 million workers constructed about 650,000 miles of highways, roads, and streets, 125,000 public buildings, and more than 8,000 parks. It built or improved more than 124,000 bridges and 853 airports.

The WPA's most controversial program was "Federal Number One," a section of the Professional Projects Division that offered work to artists, musicians, theater people, and writers. "They've got to eat just like other people," Hopkins commented to critics of the program. The artists created thousands of murals and sculptural works to beautify the walls and halls of public buildings. Musicians established 30

NATIONAL GEOGRAPHIC MOMENT in HISTORY

BRIEF RESPITE FOR FDR Enjoying a short break from the pressures of dealing with the country's economic woes, President Franklin D. Roosevelt holds his beloved dog Fala while chatting with the granddaughter of the family gardener at his Hyde Park, New York, estate. The president and his staff, with the help of the press, took great pains to conceal his polio-induced paralysis. He was never filmed or photographed being wheeled or carried from place to place. This rare snapshot is one of the few known to exist that shows Roosevelt seated in his wheelchair.

DIFFERENTIATED INSTRUCTION

At-Risk Students To help students with reading disabilities, have them list the headings of the section. Then have them scan the information under each heading to find out what sector of society leveled certain criticisms at Roosevelt and how Roosevelt reacted. Ask students to list this information under each heading on their list to make an outline for studying. **L1/ELL**

📁 Refer to *Inclusion for the High School Social Studies Classroom Strategies and Activities* in the TCR.

city symphony orchestras, as well as hundreds of smaller musical groups. The Federal Theater Project financed playwrights, actors, and directors. The program also funded historians who interviewed former slaves to document American history.

The Supreme Court's Role

When Roosevelt asked Congress to fund the WPA in January 1935, he had expected quick action on the bill. He quickly discovered that opposition to his programs was growing in Congress. The bill creating the WPA did not pass until April 1935. By late May, Congress was preparing to adjourn for the summer, leaving Roosevelt with very few accomplishments.

Suddenly, the political situation shifted. On May 27, 1935, the Supreme Court unanimously struck down the National Industrial Recovery Act in *Schechter* v. *United States.* The Schechter brothers, who had a poultry business in Brooklyn, New York, had been convicted in 1933 of violating the NIRA's Live Poultry Code. They had sold diseased chickens and violated the code's wage-and-hour provisions. 📖 *(See page 964 for more about* Schechter v. United States.*)*

In what became known as the "sick chicken case," the Court ruled that the Constitution did not allow Congress to delegate its powers to the executive branch. Thus it considered the NIRA codes unconstitutional. The decision worried Roosevelt. The ruling suggested that the Court could soon strike down the rest of the New Deal as well.

Shortly after the Schechter decision, Roosevelt sprang into action. With the Court threatening to strike down the New Deal and with growing challenges from the left and right, the president knew he needed a new series of programs to keep voters' support. He called congressional leaders to a White House conference. Pounding his desk, he thundered that Congress could not go home until it passed his new bills. That summer, Congress began what the press nicknamed the "second hundred days" and worked feverishly to pass Roosevelt's programs.

✓ **Reading Check** **Examining** How did the Supreme Court's ruling affect the New Deal?

The Second New Deal, 1935

Agency/Legislation	Function
Works Progress Administration (WPA)	Combated unemployment; created jobs throughout economy
Rural Electrification Administration (REA)	Brought electricity to isolated agricultural areas
Social Security Act	Created unemployment system, disability insurance, old-age pension, and child welfare benefits
Public Utility Holding Company Act	Eliminated unfair practices and abuses of utility companies
Banking Act	Strengthened the Federal Reserve
Resettlement Act	Assisted poor families and sharecroppers in beginning new farms or purchasing land

Chart *Skills*

1. **Interpreting Charts** What did the Resettlement Act try to accomplish?
2. **Understanding Cause and Effect** How did these acts create a safety net for American citizens?

The Rise of Industrial Unions

When the Supreme Court ruled against the NIRA, it also struck down the section of the law that established labor's right to organize. President Roosevelt and the Democrats in Congress knew that the working-class vote was very important in winning re-election in 1936. They also believed that unions could help end the Depression. They thought that high union wages would let workers spend more money, thereby boosting the economy. Opponents disagreed, arguing that high wages forced companies to charge higher prices and to hire fewer people. Despite these concerns, Congress pushed ahead with new labor legislation.

The National Labor Relations Act In July 1935, Congress passed the National Labor Relations Act, also called the Wagner Act after its author, Democratic senator Robert Wagner of New York. The act guaranteed workers the right to organize unions without interference from employers and to bargain collectively. The law set up the **National Labor Relations Board** (NLRB), which organized factory elections by secret ballot to determine whether workers wanted a union. The NLRB then certified the successful unions.

The new law also set up a process whereby dissatisfied union members could take their complaints to binding arbitration, in which a neutral party would listen to both sides and decide the issues. The NLRB was authorized to investigate the

CHAPTER 18   Roosevelt and the New Deal   **567**

Chart *Skills*

Answer:
1. The act assisted poor families and sharecroppers in beginning new farms or purchasing land.
2. They protected laborers, created insurance for the unemployed and the elderly, and strengthened the economy.

Chart Skills Practice
Ask: **What problem did the Rural Electrification Administration address?** *(the lack of electricity in isolated rural areas)*

FYI

Among the most exciting and innovative projects of the WPA was the Federal Theater. In 1936 a gifted young director named Orson Welles staged Shakespeare's *Macbeth,* setting it in the West Indies and using an all African American cast. Many Federal Theater productions used the "living newspaper" technique, often taking on the style and method of radio and documentary cinema to build morality plays about current events.

📁 Use *Supreme Court Case Study 19,* West Coast Hotel v. *Parrish.*

✓ Reading Check

Answer: By threatening to derail the New Deal, the ruling caused Roosevelt and Congress to pass much legislation very quickly.

INTERDISCIPLINARY CONNECTIONS ACTIVITY

Performing and Visual Arts Invite an actor, director, or drama teacher to speak to your class about the role government has played in the past and currently plays in funding and encouraging the performing arts. After hearing the presentation, have students write a position paper explaining their support for or opposition to government funding for the arts. Encourage students to use reasoned arguments to support their positions. **L3**

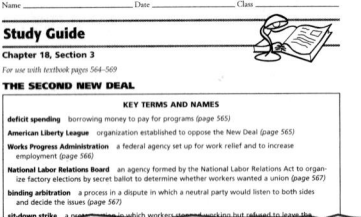

3 ASSESS

Assign Section 3 Assessment as homework or as an in-class activity.

🖲 Have students use the **Interactive Tutor Self-Assessment CD-ROM.**

L1/ELL

Reading Essentials and Study Guide 18–3

Name _____ Date _____ Class _____

Study Guide

Chapter 18, Section 3
For use with textbook pages 564–569

THE SECOND NEW DEAL

KEY TERMS AND NAMES

deficit spending borrowing money to pay for programs *(page 565)*

American Liberty League organization established to oppose the New Deal *(page 565)*

Works Progress Administration a federal agency set up for work relief and to increase employment *(page 566)*

National Labor Relations Board an agency formed by the National Labor Relations Act to organize factory elections by secret ballot to determine whether workers wanted a union *(page 567)*

binding arbitration a process in a dispute in which a neutral party would listen to both sides and decide the issues *(page 567)*

sit-down strike a protest in which workers stopped working but refused to leave the

---

actions of employers and had the power to issue "cease and desist" orders against unfair practices.

The CIO The Wagner Act stimulated a burst of labor activity. In the mid-1930s, the United Mine Workers union, led by John L. Lewis, began working with several other unions to organize workers in industries where unions did not yet exist. They formed the **Committee for Industrial Organization** (CIO) in 1935.

The CIO set out to organize industrial unions, or unions that included all workers in a particular industry, skilled and unskilled. The CIO began by focusing on the automobile and steel industries—two of the largest industries in America where workers were not yet organized into unions.

Sit-Down Strikes In late December 1936, officials at the General Motors auto-body plant in Cleveland, Ohio, demoted two union men. In an unplanned protest, a shift of 135 workers sat down and launched an unprecedented kind of strike. They stopped working but refused to leave the factory. A few days later, the workers at the company's plant in Flint, Michigan, launched their own sit-down strike,

as the press quickly dubbed it. Workers at other plants followed suit or carried out traditional strikes.

Bruce Bliven, editor of *The New Republic* magazine, was among the few journalists allowed into the plant. Regarding the condition of the strike, he reported:

> 66 The place was remarkably neat and tidy, at least as clean as it is under normal conditions. Beds were made up on the floor of each car, the seats being removed if necessary. . . . I could not see—and I looked for it carefully—the slightest damage done anywhere to the General Motors Corporation. The nearly completed car bodies, for example, were as clean as they would be in the salesroom, their glass and metal shining. 99
>
> —quoted in *The Great Depression*

Violence broke out in Flint when police launched a tear gas assault on one of the smaller plants. The strikers turned back the attack with whatever was at hand—door hinges, bottles, stones, and balls of ice. The police wounded more than a dozen strikers with gunfire, but the strike held. On February 11, 1937, the company gave in and recognized the CIO's United

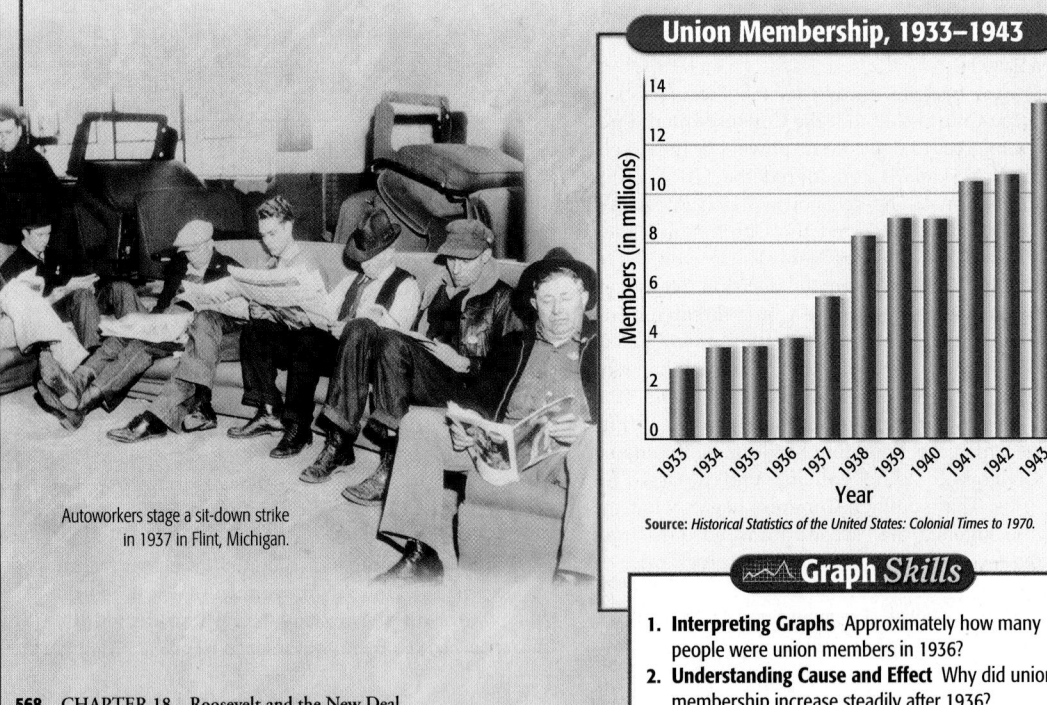

Trying to Improve Working Conditions

Autoworkers stage a sit-down strike in 1937 in Flint, Michigan.

Union Membership, 1933–1943

Source: Historical Statistics of the United States: Colonial Times to 1970.

Graph Skills

1. **Interpreting Graphs** Approximately how many people were union members in 1936?
2. **Understanding Cause and Effect** Why did union membership increase steadily after 1936?

568 CHAPTER 18 Roosevelt and the New Deal

Reading Strategy   READING THE TEXT

Analyzing Information Although President Roosevelt did not fully support the Wagner Act, he believed that the Supreme Court's invalidation of the National Industrial Recovery Act made it imperative to restore labor's rights. The National Labor Relations Board, which the Wagner Act established, supported the right of workers to organize unions. Organize students into two groups, with one developing arguments for unionization, and the other developing arguments against unionization. Ask each group to present its view. **L1**

📭 Refer to ***Inclusion for the High School Social Studies Classroom Strategies and Activities*** in the TCR.

Auto Workers (UAW) as its employees' sole bargaining agent. The UAW quickly became one of the most powerful unions in the United States.

The United States Steel Corporation, the nation's largest steel producer, decided it did not want to repeat the General Motors experience. The company recognized the CIO's United Steelworkers of America, which won a 40-hour workweek and a 10-percent pay raise. Smaller steel producers did not initially recognize unions, and strikes broke out around the country. By 1941, however, the steelworkers' union had contracts with the entire industry.

In the late 1930s, workers in other industries also sat down at their jobs to gain union recognition. In only six years, total union membership tripled from roughly 3 million in 1933 to about 9 million in 1939. In 1938 the CIO changed its name to the Congress of Industrial Organizations and became a federation of industrial unions.

✓ **Reading Check** **Examining** What provisions did the National Labor Relations Act establish?

The Social Security Act

After passing the Wagner Act, Congress began work on a bill that ranks as one of the most important pieces of legislation in American history. This was the Social Security Act, which became law in August 1935. Its major goal was to provide some security for the elderly and for unemployed workers.

With the support of Secretary of Labor Frances Perkins, Roosevelt and his team spent months preparing the bill. The framers viewed it primarily as an insurance bill. Workers earned the right to receive benefits because they paid premiums. The legislation also provided modest welfare payments to other needy people, including those with disabilities and poor families with young dependent children.

The core of Social Security was the monthly retirement benefit, which people could collect when they stopped working at age 65. Another important benefit, unemployment insurance, supplied a temporary income to unemployed workers looking for new jobs. Some critics did not like the fact that the money came from payroll taxes imposed on workers and employers, but to Roosevelt these taxes were crucial: "We put those payroll contributions there so as to give the contributors a legal, moral, and political right to collect their pensions and the unemployment benefits."

Since the people receiving benefits had already paid for them, he explained, "no politician can ever scrap my social security program." What Roosevelt did not anticipate was that in the future, Congress would borrow money from the Social Security fund to pay for other programs while failing to raise payroll deductions enough to pay for the benefits.

Social Security helped many people, but initially it left out many of the neediest members of society—farm and domestic workers. Some 65 percent of all African American workers in the 1930s fell into these two categories. Nevertheless, Social Security established the principle that the federal government should be responsible for those who, through no fault of their own, were unable to work.

✓ **Reading Check** **Explaining** How did the Social Security Act protect workers?

HISTORY Online **Study Central™** To review this section, go to tarvol2.glencoe.com and click on **Study Central™**.

SECTION 3 ASSESSMENT

Checking for Understanding
1. **Define:** deficit spending, binding arbitration, sit-down strike, Social Security Act.
2. **Identify:** American Liberty League, Works Progress Administration, National Labor Relations Board.
3. **Contrast** the ideas of Father Charles Coughlin, Senator Huey Long, and Dr. Francis Townsend.

Reviewing Themes
4. **Government and Democracy** How did the New Deal contribute to the growth of industrial unions?

Critical Thinking
5. **Analyzing** Why is the Social Security Act an important piece of legislation?
6. **Organizing** Use a graphic organizer similar to the one below to list the political challenges Roosevelt faced in his first term.

Political Challenges

Analyzing Visuals
7. **Analyzing Graphs** Examine the photo and graph on page 568. How did successful strikes such as the sit-down strike shown in the photograph lead to a rise in union membership?

Writing About History
8. **Descriptive Writing** Imagine you are either a General Motors worker or a member of management during the sit-down strike in Flint, Michigan. Write a letter to your local newspaper describing the strike and explaining your actions during it.

CHAPTER 18 Roosevelt and the New Deal **569**

SECTION 3 ASSESSMENT ANSWERS

1. Terms are in blue.
2. American Liberty League (p. 565), Works Progress Administration (p. 566), National Labor Relations Board (p. 567)
3. Coughlin: tax the rich and nationalize the banking system; Long: share the wealth; Townsend: pensions for the elderly

4. Legislation such as the Wagner Act encouraged workers to organize unions where none existed and set up a process to protect unions as they developed.
5. It forced the government to protect the unemployed.
6. American Liberty League, left-wing Democrats, urban Catholics

7. As workers saw that unions helped them, more workers supported and joined unions.
8. Letters should clearly express a point of view.

L2

✓ **Reading Check**

Answer: the right to organize unions without interference, and collective bargaining

Reteach
Have students describe the kinds of political challenges Roosevelt faced in the mid-1930s.

Enrich
Remind students that Roosevelt's goals when he took office were relief, recovery, and reform. Ask students to write an essay that evaluates his success in achieving these goals.

✓ **Reading Check**

Answer: It provided temporary income to unemployed workers looking for new jobs and provided a small pension for retired workers.

HISTORY *Online*

Study Central™ provides summaries, interactive games, and online graphic organizers to help students review section content.

4 CLOSE

Have students explain why the Social Security Act is still regarded as an important piece of legislation.

Looking Back...

The Role of the Federal Government

TEACH

Identifying the Main Idea

Draw a triangle on the board and label one branch of government as each point of the triangle. Have students come to the board and write next to each leg of the triangle the ways in which one branch of the government limits the power of the other branches. Then ask students to give recent examples of when one branch has limited another branch. Examples include recent presidential vetos and Congress not ratifying a treaty or rejecting a presidential appointment. **L1**

Analyzing Concepts
Have students research the Supreme Court's rulings in the 2000 presidential election. Ask them to find out if either side in the case cited the *Martin* v. *Hunter's Lessee* ruling. Then have students write a paragraph stating how the 2000 presidential election case revisited the issue between states' rights and federal authority. **L3**

Why It Matters The New Deal dramatically expanded the federal government's role. To address the Depression, federal programs were directed at everything from the economy to caring for the country's unemployed, aged, and sick. Many critics opposed this new federal activity, and the Supreme Court struck down several New Deal programs as unconstitutional. At the same time, the Court also issued decisions that dramatically increased the federal government's role. The debate over the power and role of the federal government echoed debates from earlier times in the nation's history.

Steps To . . . a Strong Federal Government

The growth of federal power began with the writing of the Constitution itself. When the American Revolution began, the individual state governments were very suspicious of centralized power. They did not want to create a strong national government that might endanger their liberties.

Federalism In drafting the new Constitution in 1787, the Founders adopted the idea of federalism. Federalism refers to a system under which power is shared between the national or federal government and the state governments. The Constitution divides government authority. It gives the national government specific powers but reserves all other powers to the states or to the people.

The Founders saw federalism as a way to forge a strong union while preserving the states as a check on federal power.

Necessary and Proper Clause The Constitution also gives the federal government implied powers. These are powers that the government has, even though they are not written down, because without them the government could not carry out the powers it has been expressly given.

The basis for implied powers is the Constitution's necessary and proper clause (art. 1, sec. 8). This clause gives Congress the power to make laws that are "necessary and proper" for it to execute its powers under the Constitution. The necessary and proper clause has been used many times to expand the federal government's power.

The debate over implied powers began in George Washington's administration in a dispute about the

> *"The government of the United States, then, though limited in its powers is supreme; and its laws, when made in pursuance of the Constitution, form the supreme law of the land . . . "*
>
> —*U.S. Supreme Court Chief Justice John Marshall, 1819*

EXTENDING THE CONTENT

Fighting Poverty Fighting poverty has been at the root of most of the efforts to move powers from either private organizations or state governments to the federal government. Before the Great Depression, most people in need looked to charities and churches for relief. The massive unemployment and poverty created by the Great Depression was beyond the means of existing charities. Government programs such as the New Deal under Roosevelt, the Great Society under Johnson, and Supplemental Security Income under Nixon greatly increased the role of the federal government in providing relief. More recent presidents have reduced the federal government's role in fighting poverty because of the fear that existing programs fostered dependency. President Clinton's welfare reforms are one example.

The Federal System

Powers of the National Government	Powers Shared by National and State Governments	Powers Reserved for State Governments
• Regulate interstate and foreign trade	• Collect taxes	• Regulate trade within the state
• Raise/support armed forces	• Borrow money	• Write business/corporate laws
• Declare war/make peace	• Make and enforce laws	• Establish and maintain public schools
• Coin and print money	• Establish and maintain courts	• Set up local governments
• Grant patents/copyrights	• Charter banks	• Pass marriage/divorce laws
• Establish federal courts	• Provide for public welfare	• Conduct elections
• Govern territories and admit new states		• Ratify constitutional amendments
• Set weights/measures		
• Establish a postal system		
• Regulate immigration		

ASSESS

Have students examine the chart on page 571, then choose one item from each column—a federal power, a shared power, and a power reserved to state governments. They should then write a paragraph suggesting why each power has probably been designated for the federal or state government, or why it is shared. (For example, only the federal government coins money because separate state monetary systems would inhibit interstate commerce.)

CLOSE

Review with students how power is structured in a republic and why the country's founders felt so strongly about limiting the power of the federal government.

creation of a national bank. Alexander Hamilton believed a bank was convenient and not prohibited in carrying out the government's treasury functions, while Thomas Jefferson believed the federal government could not create a bank since it was not absolutely necessary. Washington sided with Hamilton, and the bank was created.

The Supreme Court, under the leadership of Chief Justice John Marshall, strongly defended the idea that the necessary and proper clause gave the federal government wide-ranging powers. In 1819, in *McCulloch* v. *Maryland*, the Court ruled that the necessary and proper clause allowed the federal government to use any method that was convenient for carrying out its express powers, as long as it was not specifically forbidden in the Constitution.

The Commerce Clause Another clause in the Constitution that has been used to expand the federal government's power is the commerce clause. The Constitution gives the federal government the power to regulate commerce with foreign nations and between the states. Over time, the definition of the word *commerce* has played an important role in determining the powers of the federal government.

In 1824 the Supreme Court ruled in *Gibbons* v. *Ogden* that the commerce clause meant that anything crossing state lines could be regulated by the federal government. In the late 1800s and early 1900s, however, the Court ruled that federal laws regulating industry, agriculture, child labor, and

unions were unconstitutional because such activities took place within states, not across state lines. During the New Deal, however, the Supreme Court's opinion shifted. In 1937 it ruled in *NLRB* v. *Jones and Laughlin Steel* that the commerce clause allowed the federal government to regulate industry within states.

The Fourteenth Amendment Perhaps the most dramatic increase in federal power took place following the Civil War. The new Fourteenth Amendment banned states from depriving people of their life, liberty, or property "without due process of law" and prohibited states from denying people the "equal protection of the laws." Both the due process clause and the equal protection clause have been used repeatedly by the Supreme Court to extend the Bill of Rights to the states and to end segregation of African Americans. As a result, by the late twentieth century, the federal government had acquired powers far beyond those envisioned in 1787.

Checking for Understanding
1. What is the necessary and proper clause in the Constitution?
2. In what ways did the Supreme Court use the commerce clause?

Critical Thinking
1. Do you agree with Jefferson's or Hamilton's view of implied powers? Explain.
2. How did the Fourteenth Amendment increase federal power?

Checking for Understanding
1. Article 1, Section 8 creates implied powers: Congress may pass laws necessary and proper to carrying out the federal government's constitutional powers.
2. The Court has often used the clause to expand federal power by interpreting *commerce* broadly. In the late 1800s, it used the clause to limit federal regulatory power by interpreting it narrowly.

Critical Thinking
1. Some students will say the government should only be allowed to do what is absolutely necessary; others may say that anything that is convenient and not prohibited should be allowed.
2. Due process and equal protection clauses allowed the Supreme Court to expand federal power and to apply the Bill of Rights to the states.

1 FOCUS

Section Overview

This section focuses on Roosevelt's second term as president.

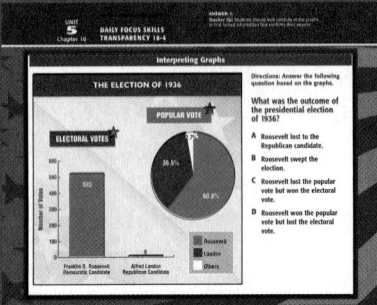
Reading Preview

Answers to Graphic:
I. Roosevelt's Second Term
   A. The Election of 1936
   B. The Court-Packing Plan
   C. The Roosevelt Recession
II. The Last New Deal Reforms
   A. The National Housing Act
   B. The Farm Security Administration
   C. The Fair Labor Standards Act
III. The Legacy of The New Deal
   A. The Broker State
   B. Government's New Role

Preteaching Vocabulary
Have students identify the Key Terms and Names that refer to specific individuals and write a one-sentence description of each person.

SECTION 4 The New Deal Coalition

Guide to Reading

Main Idea

Backed by a new coalition of voters, Roosevelt easily won a second term, but the opposition of conservatives weakened his ability to achieve additional reforms.

Key Terms and Names

Frances Perkins, court-packing, Henry Morgenthau, John Maynard Keynes, broker state, safety net

Reading Strategy

Taking Notes As you read about the New Deal coalition, use the major headings of the section to create an outline similar to the one below.

The New Deal Coalition
I. Roosevelt's Second Term
   A.
   B.
   C.
II.
   A.
   B.

Reading Objectives
• **Explain** the achievements and the defeats of Roosevelt's second term.
• **Analyze** how the New Deal affected Americans' sense of security and their attitude toward the role of government.

Section Theme

Groups and Institutions The Democratic Party's victory in 1936 resulted from a new alignment in politics that lasted for several decades.

Preview of Events

1936	1937	1937	1938
FDR reelected	Court-packing bill defeated; Farm Tenant Act; National Housing Act	Roosevelt Recession begins	Fair Labor Standards Act passed

Robert Vann

★ An American Story ★

One day in 1932, Emma Guffey Miller, the sister of Democratic senator Joseph Guffey, was having her nails done at a salon in Pittsburgh. Her manicurist mentioned that Robert Vann, publisher of the *Pittsburgh Courier,* a leading African American newspaper, wanted to see the senator. When Senator Guffey met Vann, Vann told him that the Democrats could win most of the 280,000 African American votes in Pennsylvania if they made the effort.

Since the Civil War, most African Americans had voted for the Republicans. Now times had changed. The Depression had hit the African American community very hard, and Republicans had done little to help. In talks to African American voters, Vann often said, "My friends, go home and turn Lincoln's picture to the wall. That debt has been paid in full."

Guffey was impressed. He persuaded party leaders to appoint Vann to lead "the first really effective Negro division a Democratic campaign committee ever had." By 1936 the majority of African American voters had switched their support to the Democratic Party.

—adapted from *The Politics of Upheaval*

Roosevelt's Second Term

The dramatic shift in party allegiance by African Americans was part of a historic political realignment triggered by FDR's New Deal. As the election of 1936 approached, millions of voters owed their jobs, mortgages, or salvaged bank accounts to the New Deal, and they knew it.

Profiles IN HISTORY

Mary McLeod Bethune
1875–1955

Mary McLeod Bethune was born into a poor South Carolina family, the 15th of 17 children. Although she worked from a young age picking cotton and washing clothes, Bethune was determined to get an education. She won a scholarship to a seminary in North Carolina and later graduated from the Moody Bible Institute in Chicago. Bethune then began teaching at the Haines Institute. In 1904 she founded a school in Florida for the children of African American railroad workers. "I rang doorbells," she later recalled. "I wrote articles . . . distributed leaflets, [and] invaded churches, clubs, lodges, [and] chambers of commerce." Gradually she raised enough money to found the Daytona Normal and Industrial School, later known as Bethune College.

Bethune's efforts gained her a national reputation. In the 1920s, she visited the White House to discuss African American affairs. She also became a good friend of Eleanor Roosevelt. In 1936 FDR appointed her director of the Negro Division of the National Youth Administration (NYA), which provided job training for young people. Bethune also founded the National Council of Negro Women to support civil rights. In later years, she advised Presidents Truman and Eisenhower.

Frances Perkins
1882–1965

From the moment she became FDR's secretary of labor at the age of 50, Frances Perkins confronted the challenge of being the first female cabinet member in the nation's history.

Perkins studied social work at Columbia University. Early in her career, she assisted Jane Addams at Hull House and worked with Florence Kelley of the Consumers' League. From her lobbying efforts there, Perkins learned how to deal with politicians.

Perkins first met Roosevelt when she worked for the New York Committee on Safety, lobbying state legislators to limit the workweek for women to 54 hours. When Roosevelt became governor in 1928, he appointed Perkins state industrial commissioner. After Roosevelt won the presidency in 1932, he asked Perkins to head the Department of Labor. Upon taking the job, Perkins found many areas that needed improvement: offices that were run down, disorganized files, and lax work schedules, conditions she quickly remedied.

Given her background, it was fitting that one of Perkins's major tasks was to head the team that designed the Social Security program. She also supervised implementation of the Fair Labor Standards Act and built up the Bureau of Labor Statistics.

The white South, which had been the core of the Democratic Party, now became just one part of a new coalition that included farmers, laborers, African Americans, new immigrants, ethnic minorities, women, progressives, and intellectuals. First Lady Eleanor Roosevelt helped bring about the change in the African American and women's vote. She had demonstrated strong sympathies toward these groups, with whom she spoke in her many tours of the country. She recounted her experiences to her husband and persuaded him to address at least some of their problems in his New Deal programs.

African Americans and women made some modest gains during the New Deal. For example, the president appointed a number of African Americans to positions in his administration; informally, they became known as the Black Cabinet. Roosevelt also tried to see that New Deal relief programs did not exclude African Americans.

A similar approach guided New Deal policies toward women. Roosevelt appointed the first woman to a cabinet post, Secretary of Labor **Frances Perkins,** and assigned many women to lower-level jobs in the federal bureaucracy. Even so, the general view was

that women did not need federal government action to ensure equal treatment, but rather to provide certain protections for them.

The Election of 1936 To oppose Roosevelt, the Republicans nominated Kansas Governor Alfred Landon. Although Landon favored some New Deal policies, he declared it was time "to unshackle initiative and free the spirit of American enterprise." As the election neared, Landon became more aggressive. The New Deal "violates the basic ideals of the American system," he declared. "If we are to preserve our American form of government, this administration must be defeated."

Despite Landon's attacks, Roosevelt and the New Deal remained overwhelmingly popular with the American people. The challenge from left-wing radicals also proved much weaker than expected—primarily because Huey Long had been assassinated in Louisiana in September of 1935. Long's supporters joined with those of Father Coughlin and Francis Townsend in the summer of 1936 to form a new political movement called the **Union Party,** but without a strong leader, the party had no chance.

CHAPTER 18   Roosevelt and the New Deal   **573**

---

2 TEACH

Daily Lecture and Discussion Notes 18–4

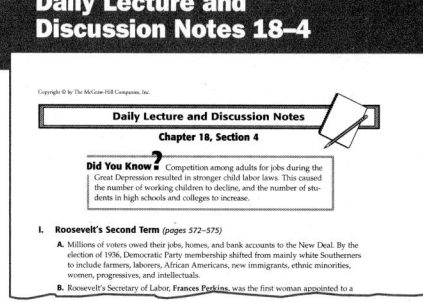

Daily Lecture and Discussion Notes
Chapter 18, Section 4

Did You Know? Competition among adults for jobs during the Great Depression resulted in stronger child labor laws. This caused the number of working children to decline, and the number of students in high schools and colleges to increase.

I.   Roosevelt's Second Term *(pages 572–575)*

A. Millions of voters owed their jobs, homes, and bank accounts to the New Deal. By the election of 1936, Democratic Party membership shifted from mainly white Southerners to include farmers, laborers, African Americans, new immigrants, ethnic minorities, women, progressives, and intellectuals.

B. Roosevelt's Secretary of Labor, **Frances Perkins,** was the first woman appointed to a

Profiles IN HISTORY

Background: Bethune started her school with $1.50 and five students. Today Bethune-Cookman College in Daytona Beach, Florida, has more than 2,500 students and an endowment worth more than $25 million. **Ask:** How did Bethune and Perkins help today's working women? *(Answers will vary.)*

Creating Circle Graphs Provide the data below and ask students to make a pair of circle graphs showing the results of the presidential election of 1936. **L1**

Candidate	Popular Vote	Electoral Vote
Roosevelt, Dem.	27,752,869	523
Landon, Rep.	16,674,665	8
Lemke, Union	882,479	0

Use the rubric for a map, display, or chart on pages 65–66 in the *Performance Assessment Activities and Rubrics.*

Reading Strategy ▶ READING THE TEXT

Using Word Parts Have students use prefixes to unlock the meanings of unknown words. A *prefix* is a word part that comes before a base word or a root and changes the meaning of the word. For example, *dis-* means "the opposite of" and is found in words such as disobey, displease, or disown. *In-* means "not." Have student provide examples of words that use this prefix *(inactive, incorrect, inability, incomplete).* **L1 ELL**

Refer to *Inclusion for the High School Social Studies Classroom Strategies and Activities* in the TCR.

L1/ELL

Guided Reading Activity 18–4

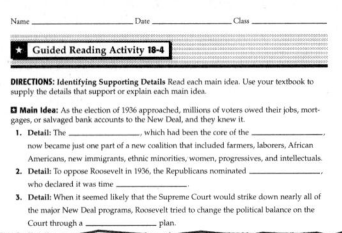

Name _____ Date _____ Class _____

★ **Guided Reading Activity 18-4**

DIRECTIONS: Identifying Supporting Details Read each main idea. Use your textbook to supply the details that support or explain each main idea.

■ **Main Idea:** As the election of 1936 approached, millions of voters owed their jobs, mortgages, or salvaged bank accounts to the New Deal, and they knew it.

1. **Detail:** The _____ which had been the core of the _____ now became just one part of a new coalition that included farmers, laborers, African Americans, new immigrants, ethnic minorities, women, progressives, and intellectuals.

2. **Detail:** To oppose Roosevelt in 1936, the Republicans nominated _____ who declared it was time _____.

3. **Detail:** When it seemed likely that the Supreme Court would strike down nearly all of the major New Deal programs, Roosevelt tried to change the political balance on the Court through a _____ plan.

Writing a Biographical Profile
Have students write a short biographical profile of one of the people mentioned in this section. Encourage them to select the person whose actions they most admire. **L2**

FYI

As part of the New Deal, the WPA produced posters publicizing a variety of programs and events. Over 2,000 of these graphically diverse posters are known to exist today. The Library of Congress has more than 900 of the them.

Picturing History

Answer: farmers, union members, African Americans, new immigrants, ethnic minorities, women, intellectuals, progressives

Ask: Why do you think so many different groups supported Roosevelt's bid for re-election? *(Many people were benefiting from the initiatives of his first term in office.)*

On Election Day, Roosevelt swept to victory in one of the largest landslides in American history. He won more than 60 percent of the popular vote and carried every state except Maine and Vermont.

The Court-Packing Plan Although popular opinion supported most of the president's programs, the Supreme Court saw things differently. In January 1936, the Court declared the Agricultural Adjustment Act to be unconstitutional. With cases pending on Social Security and the Wagner Act, it seemed likely the Court would strike down nearly all of the major New Deal programs.

Roosevelt was furious that a handful of jurists, "nine old men" as he called them, were blocking the wishes of a majority of the people. After winning re-election, he decided to try to change the political balance on the Supreme Court. Claiming that the Court was overburdened with work, Roosevelt sent Congress a bill to increase the number of justices: If any justice had served for 10 years and did not retire within six months after reaching the age of 70, the president could appoint an additional justice to the Court. Since four justices were in their 70s and two more were in their late 60s, the bill, if passed, would allow Roosevelt to quickly appoint as many as six new justices.

The **court-packing** plan, as the press called it, was Roosevelt's first serious political mistake as president. Although Congress had the power to change

Picturing History

Campaigning in 1936 During the 1936 election, FDR's Democratic Party brought together farmers, like this North Dakotan, and many other groups of Americans to form a new coalition of political supporters. This coalition helped give Roosevelt a strong re-election victory. What different groups made up this coalition?

---

the size of the Court, the scheme created the impression that the president was trying to interfere with the Constitution's separation of powers and undermine the Court's independence.

The issue split the Democratic Party. Many Southern Democrats feared Roosevelt's plan would put justices on the Court who would overturn segregation. At the same time, African American leaders worried that once Roosevelt set the precedent of changing the Court's makeup, a future president might pack the Court with justices opposed to civil rights. Many Americans believed the plan would give the president too much power.

Despite the uproar over the scheme, Roosevelt's actions appeared to force the Supreme Court to back down. In April 1937, the Court upheld the Wagner Act, and in May it declared the Social Security Act to be constitutional. Shortly afterward, one of the more conservative judges resigned, enabling Roosevelt to appoint a supporter of the New Deal to the Court.

In mid-July, the Senate quietly killed the court-packing bill without bringing it to a vote. Although Roosevelt had achieved his goal of changing the Court's view of the New Deal, the fight over the plan had hurt his reputation with the American people and encouraged conservative Democrats in Congress to work with Republicans to oppose further New Deal proposals.

ECONOMICS

The Roosevelt Recession In late 1937, Roosevelt's reputation suffered another blow when unemployment suddenly surged. Earlier in the year, the economy had seemed to be on the verge of full recovery. Industrial output was almost back to the level it had reached before the Depression began, and many people believed the worst was over.

Although unemployment remained high, Roosevelt decided it was time to balance the budget. Concerned about the dangers of too much debt, Roosevelt ordered the WPA and the PWA to be cut significantly. Unfortunately, Roosevelt cut spending just as the first Social Security payroll taxes removed $2 billion from the economy. Almost immediately the economy plummeted. By the end of 1937, about two million people had been thrown out of work.

The recession of 1937 led to a debate inside Roosevelt's administration over what to do. Treasury Secretary **Henry Morgenthau** favored balancing the budget and cutting spending. This would reassure business leaders and

---

DIFFERENTIATED INSTRUCTION

Kinesthetic Have interested students play the role of the Supreme Court justices at the time that Roosevelt sent his court plan to Congress. First have students conduct biographical research on the justices. Then have the students create a dramatic reenactment of the justices' first meeting after the plan was announced. Encourage students to rehearse their roles and present their reenactment to the class. **L2**

☛ Refer to *Inclusion for the High School Social Studies Classroom Strategies and Activities* in the TCR.

encourage them to invest in the economy. Harry Hopkins, head of the WPA, and **Harold Ickes,** head of the PWA, both disagreed with Morgenthau and pushed for more government spending. They pointed to a new theory called "Keynesianism" to support their arguments.

Keynesianism was based on the theories of an influential British economist named **John Maynard Keynes.** In 1936 Keynes published a book that discussed the causes of recessions. He argued that the government should spend heavily during a recession, even if it had to run a deficit, in order to jump-start the economy.

According to Keynesian economics, Roosevelt had done exactly the wrong thing when he cut back programs in 1937. At first Roosevelt was reluctant to begin deficit spending again. Many critics of his policies had argued that the recession proved the American people were becoming too dependent on government spending, and Roosevelt worried they might be right. Finally, in the spring of 1938, with no recovery in sight, he asked Congress for $3.75 billion for the PWA, the WPA, and other programs.

✓ Reading Check **Summarizing** What events weakened Roosevelt's reputation in 1937?

The Last New Deal Reforms

In his second inaugural speech, Roosevelt had pointed out that despite the nation's progress in climbing out of the Depression, many Americans still endured crippling poverty:

> ❝In this nation I see tens of millions of its citizens—a substantial part of its whole population—who at this very moment are denied the greater part of what the very lowest standards of today call the necessities of life. . . . I see one-third of a nation ill-housed, ill-clad, ill-nourished. . . . The test of our progress is not whether we add more to the abundance of those who have much; it is whether we provide enough for those who have too little.❞
>
> —quoted in *Public Papers and Addresses of Franklin D. Roosevelt*

Despite the president's idealistic goals, the fight over the court-packing scheme and the recession of 1937 had weakened Roosevelt politically. Although he pushed ahead with a new series of New Deal programs, his successes were far more limited than they had been in previous years.

"Come along. We're going to the Trans-Lux to hiss Roosevelt."

 Analyzing *Political Cartoons*

Traitor to His Class By 1936 many wealthy Americans believed that FDR had turned his back on his own upbringing, and they actively worked to prevent his re-election. How did the New Deal change the way many people view government?

The National Housing Act One of the president's goals for his second term was to provide better housing for the nation's poor. The Home Owners Loan Corporation had helped many middle-class citizens, but it had not provided housing for those who could not afford a mortgage. Eleanor Roosevelt, who had toured poverty-stricken regions of Appalachia and the Deep South, was among those urging the president to do something.

Senator Wagner, who shared the First Lady's concerns, prepared a new housing bill with Roosevelt's full support. The 1937 National Housing Act established the United States Housing Authority, which received $500 million to subsidize loans for builders willing to buy blocks of slums and build low-cost housing.

The Farm Security Administration Before the Supreme Court struck it down, the Agricultural Adjustment Administration had paid many farmers to take land out of production to force food prices to rise. The price-support program raised farm income, but it badly hurt tenant farmers. Landowners often

CHAPTER 18 Roosevelt and the New Deal **575**

 Analyzing *Political Cartoons*

Answer: Many people came to view government as the provider of a safety net for Americans.
Ask: Why do you think wealthy Americans believed that FDR had turned his back on his upbringing? *(They believed that his programs took money from wealthier groups and gave it to lower-income people.)*

Understanding Vocabulary Tell students that the "paradox of thrift" was Keynes's idea that in times of unemployment and economic crisis, saving money leads to more unemployment and economic crisis. Have students find the definition of the word "paradox" and suggest other situations that are paradoxes.

✓ Reading Check

Answer: Events included the fight over the New Deal plan in the Court, the court-packing plan, and the recession.

Making Predictions Have students list the reasons they think Roosevelt might be reelected and the reasons he might not be reelected. Instruct students to review their lists and predict the outcome of the 1940 presidential race. **L2**

CURRICULUM CONNECTION

Economics FDR favored a stronger role for federal government in improving the lives of all Americans. These improvements cost money. Under FDR the public debt increased more than it had in the nation's history, reaching $43 billion in 1940 compared with $16.2 billion in 1930.

INTERDISCIPLINARY CONNECTIONS ACTIVITY

Civics Organize the class into groups of three. Have each member of the groups prepare to debate the issue of adding additional members to the Supreme Court. All three members of the group should be prepared to debate either side of the issue. Invite groups to debate in front of the class. Assign the sides randomly and ask the third member of the group to be the moderator. **L2**

What *Life* Was Like...

Ask students to compare and contrast 1930s entertainment with today's entertainment. **L2**

Creating a Display Have students research one aspect of entertainment in the 1930s, such as dancing, movies, or board games. Have students create displays based on their research.

✓ Reading Check

Answer: farmers, the poor, workers, and children

3 ASSESS

Assign Section 4 Assessment as homework or as an in-class activity.

🅐 Have students use the **Interactive Tutor Self-Assessment CD-ROM.**

L1/ELL

Reading Essentials and Study Guide 18–4

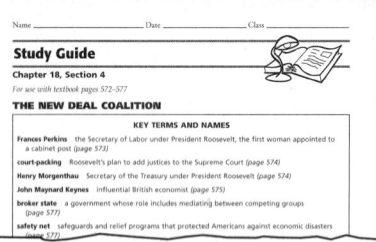

Name _____ Date _____ Class _____

Study Guide

Chapter 18, Section 4

For use with textbook pages 572–577

THE NEW DEAL COALITION

KEY TERMS AND NAMES

Frances Perkins the Secretary of Labor under President Roosevelt, the first woman appointed to a cabinet post (page 573)

court-packing Roosevelt's plan to add justices to the Supreme Court (page 574)

Henry Morgenthau Secretary of the Treasury under President Roosevelt (page 574)

John Maynard Keynes influential British economist (page 575)

broker state a government whose role includes mediating between competing groups (page 575)

safety net safeguards and relief programs that protected Americans against economic disasters (page 577)

What *Life* Was Like...

1930s Entertainment

During the Depression, people needed entertainment more than ever. Movies topped the list of ways to escape everyday hardship, but music and dance were popular as well. For really cheap entertainment, one could stay at home and play cards or board games.

Movie Escapism
Movies cost less than 25¢ in many places, so children could afford to go, too. These children display door prizes handed out during a matinee in California.

Dance Craze
Dance marathons got their start in the manic 1920s, but they gained wide popularity in the 1930s. Couples might dance hundreds of hours, until they were exhausted. The last couple standing could win substantial prize money.

expelled tenants from the land in order to take it out of production. About 150,000 white and 195,000 African American tenants left farming during the 1930s for this reason.

To stop this trend, the Farm Security Administration was created in 1937 to give loans to tenants so they could purchase farms. Over the next four years it extended loans of about $1 billion. Members of Congress, many of whom believed the program made agricultural problems worse by increasing farm production and driving down prices, kept its appropriations at a low level.

The Fair Labor Standards Act In 1938 New Dealers were still trying to reinstate important pro-labor regulations to make up for the Supreme Court's dismantling of the NIRA in 1935. The Fair Labor Standards Act of 1938 provided more protection for workers, abolished child labor, and established a 40-hour workweek for many workers to come into effect within three years.

Congress, however, was beginning to turn against the New Deal. The recession of 1937 enabled the Republicans to win many seats in Congress in the midterm elections of 1938. Together with conservative Southern Democrats, they began blocking further New Deal legislation.

Roosevelt, meanwhile, became increasingly preoccupied with the growing international threat posed by Germany and Japan. By 1939 the New Deal era had come to an end.

✓ Reading Check **Examining** What groups did Roosevelt's last New Deal programs try to help?

The Legacy of the New Deal

In terms of its main goal of ending the Depression, the New Deal was only a limited success. Unemployment remained high, and economic recovery was not complete until after World War II. Even so, the New Deal gave many Americans a stronger sense of security and stability.

The Broker State As a whole, the New Deal tended to operate so that it balanced competing economic interests. Business leaders, farmers, workers, consumers, homeowners, and others now looked to government to protect their interests.

The federal government's ability to take on this new role was enhanced by two important Supreme Court decisions. In 1937, in *NLRB* v. *Jones and Laughlin Steel,* the Court ruled that the federal government had the constitutional authority, under the

CRITICAL THINKING ACTIVITY

Comparing and Contrasting Tell students that in 1936 about 38 percent of the families in the United States had annual incomes of less than $1,000. The poverty line at that time was $1,330. Ask students to use sources such as the *Statistical Abstract of the United States* to find the most recent poverty figures. Have students compare the poverty situation today to that of the mid-1930s. Then ask them to discuss the following question: What changes made in the 1930s may help us deal with poverty today? **L2**

Music and Monopoly

The legendary Jimmie Lunceford Orchestra was one of many big band orchestras of the 1930s. Whether touring the country in one-night gigs or playing on the radio, they drew a huge following. Monopoly was a major 1930s fad. Players of this board game moved pieces around, buying and developing "property" in a race to amass a fortune in fake money.

interstate commerce clause, to regulate production within a state. In 1942, in *Wickard* v. *Filburn*, the Court used a similar argument to allow the federal government to regulate consumption in the states. These decisions increased federal power over the economy and allowed it to mediate between competing groups. 📖 *(See pages 964 and 965 for more information on these Supreme Court cases.)*

In taking on this mediating role, the New Deal established what some have called the broker state,

working out conflicts among different interests. This broker role has continued under the administrations of both parties ever since.

Government's New Role Probably the biggest change the New Deal brought about was the new public attitude toward government. Roosevelt's programs had succeeded in creating something of a safety net for average Americans—safeguards and relief programs that protected them against economic disaster. By the time the Roosevelt years were over, the American people felt that the government had a duty to maintain this safety net even though it required a larger, more expensive federal government than at any time in American history.

Critics continued to argue that the New Deal made the government too powerful. Another legacy of the New Deal, therefore, is a debate that has continued to the present over how much the government should intervene in the economy or support the disadvantaged.

Throughout the hard times of the Depression, most Americans maintained a surprising degree of confidence in the American system. Journalist Dorothy Thompson expressed this feeling in 1940:

66 We have behind us eight terrible years of a crisis. . . . Here we are, and our basic institutions are still intact, our people relatively prosperous and most important of all, our society relatively affectionate. . . . No country is so well off. 99

✔ **Reading Check** **Summarizing** What was the legacy of Roosevelt's New Deal?

SECTION 4 ASSESSMENT

HISTORY Online **Study Central™** To review this section, go to tarvol2.glencoe.com and click on **Study Central™**.

Checking for Understanding

1. **Define:** broker state, safety net.
2. **Identify:** Frances Perkins, court-packing, Henry Morgenthau, John Maynard Keynes.
3. **Explain** Roosevelt's court-packing plan and how it was received.

Reviewing Themes

4. **Groups and Institutions** What groups made up the New Deal coalition?

Critical Thinking

5. **Interpreting** How did the New Deal change attitudes toward government?
6. **Categorizing** Use a chart like the one below to list the achievements and defeats of Roosevelt's second term.

Achievements	Defeats

Analyzing Visuals

7. **Analyzing Photographs** Study the photograph on page 574. What does it suggest about Roosevelt's method of campaigning?

Writing About History

8. **Persuasive Writing** Write an essay evaluating the effectiveness of New Deal measures in ending the Depression.

CHAPTER 18 Roosevelt and the New Deal **577**

SECTION 4 ASSESSMENT ANSWERS

1. Terms are in blue.
2. Frances Perkins *(p. 573)*, court-packing *(p. 574)*, Henry Morgenthau *(p. 574)*, John Maynard Keynes *(p. 575)*
3. wanted to change the political balance of the Supreme Court; seen as interfering with separation of powers

4. African Americans, farmers, labor, minorities, new immigrants, women, intellectuals, and progressives
5. Americans felt government had a duty to maintain a safety net.
6. Achievements: Court upholds reforms, National Housing Act, Fair Labor Standards Act; Defeats:

Depression continued, WPA/PWA, court-packing plan
7. shows he went directly to the people
8. Essays should reflect that the New Deal was a mixed success.

L2

Section Quiz 18–4

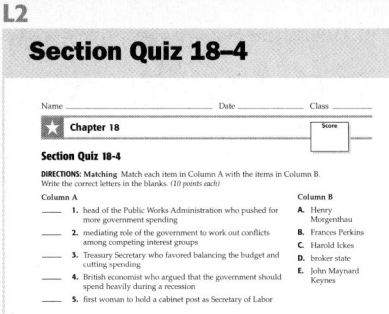

Reteach
Have students explain the achievements and the defeats of Roosevelt's second term.

Enrich
Have students select one segment of the American population, such as women, Native Americans, African Americans, or farmers. Have them research how their chosen group fared under the New Deal programs and write a one-page analysis of the group's gains or losses during the 1930s.

✔ **Reading Check**

Answer: The New Deal increased the government's role and fostered the attitude that the government was responsible for providing a safety net.

Study Central™ provides summaries, interactive games, and online graphic organizers to help students review section content.

4 CLOSE

Have students analyze how the New Deal affected Americans' sense of security and their attitude toward the role of government.

CHAPTER
18 ASSESSMENT and ACTIVITIES

GLENCOE
TECHNOLOGY

MindJogger Videoquiz
Use the **MindJogger Videoquiz** to review Chapter 18 content.

 Available in DVD

Reviewing Key Terms

Students' answers will vary. The pages where the words appear in the text are shown in parentheses.

1. **gold standard** *(p. 555)*
2. **fireside chats** *(p. 558)*
3. **deficit spending** *(p. 565)*
4. **binding arbitration** *(p. 567)*
5. **sit-down strike** *(p. 568)*
6. **Social Security Act** *(p. 569)*
7. **broker state** *(p. 577)*
8. **safety net** *(p. 577)*

Reviewing Key Facts

9. New Deal *(p. 553)*, bank holiday *(p. 555)*, Hundred Days *(p. 556)*, Securities and Exchange Commission *(p. 558)*, Federal Deposit Insurance Corporation *(p. 558)*, Agricultural Adjustment Administration *(p. 559)*, Works Progress Administration *(p. 566)*, National Labor Relations Board *(p. 567)*, Frances Perkins *(p. 573)*, court-packing *(p. 574)*, John Maynard Keynes *(p. 575)*

10. He was concerned about too much debt and its repercussions, especially on the business community.

11. The programs were designed to speed up economic recovery by providing income to American workers.

12. The Supreme Court overturned some of the New Deal legislation by declaring it unconstitutional.

13. The Wagner Act gave workers the right to organize without interference and forced companies to recognize unions as bargaining agents.

14. He was frustrated with the defeats he had suffered and wanted to change the makeup of the Supreme Court.

Reviewing Key Terms
On a sheet of paper, use each of these terms in a sentence.

1. gold standard
2. fireside chats
3. deficit spending
4. binding arbitration
5. sit-down strike
6. Social Security Act
7. broker state
8. safety net

Reviewing Key Facts

9. **Identify:** New Deal, bank holiday, Hundred Days, Securities and Exchange Commission, Federal Deposit Insurance Corporation, Agricultural Adjustment Administration, Works Progress Administration, National Labor Relations Board, Frances Perkins, court-packing, John Maynard Keynes.

10. Why was President Roosevelt reluctant to use deficit spending to help the American economy recover from the Great Depression?

11. Why did the federal government create work programs during the Depression?

12. How did the Supreme Court challenge the New Deal?

13. How did the Wagner Act contribute to the growth of unions?

14. Why did President Roosevelt devise the court-packing plan?

15. What impact did New Deal legislation have on the role of the federal government in state commerce?

Critical Thinking

16. **Analyzing Themes: Economic Factors** What caused the recession in 1937, and how did Keynesian economics explain this recession?

17. **Analyzing** Choose one of the New Deal programs. Describe its goals and evaluate its success.

18. **Forming an Opinion** Which method should be used to settle differences between unions and companies—binding arbitration or strikes? Explain your answer.

19. **Interpreting Primary Sources** In her autobiography, Eleanor Roosevelt wrote about discussions she had with people across the country. Read the excerpt and answer the questions that follow.

66This trip to the mining areas was my first contact with the work being done by the Quakers. I liked the idea of trying to put people to work to help themselves. The men were started on projects and taught to use their abilities to develop new skills. The women were encouraged to revive any household arts they might once have known but which they had neglected in the drab life of the mining village.

This was only the first of many trips into the mining districts but it was the one that started the homestead

Chapter Summary

Major New Deal Programs

Financial and Debt
- Emergency Banking Relief Act regulated banks.
- Federal Deposit Insurance Corporation insured bank deposits.
- Farm Credit Administration refinanced farm mortgages.
- Home Owners' Loan Corporation financed homeowners' mortgages.

Work and Relief
- Civilian Conservation Corps created forestry jobs for young men.
- Federal Emergency Relief Administration funded city and state relief programs.
- Public Works Administration created work programs to build public projects, such as roads, bridges, and schools.

Agriculture and Industry
- Agricultural Adjustment Administration paid farmers to limit surplus production.
- National Industrial Recovery Act limited industrial production and set prices.
- National Labor Relations Act gave workers the right to organize unions and bargain collectively.
- Tennessee Valley Authority financed rural electrification and helped develop the economy of a seven-state region.

Social "Safety Net"
- Social Security Act provided:
  – income for elderly, handicapped, and unemployed.
  – monthly retirement benefit for people over 65

578 CHAPTER 18 Roosevelt and the New Deal

15. *NLRB* v. *Jones and Laughlin Steel* gave the federal government power to regulate production in a state.

Critical Thinking
16. A reduction in government spending at the same time that the payroll tax went into effect was the main cause of the recession. Keynesian economics argued that government should increase spending during a recession.

17. Students' answers will vary. They should realistically evaluate the program's successes and failures.

18. Binding arbitration is a fair compromise because a neutral party listens to both sides and decides issues. Strikes might be used where employers are resisting negotiation.

HISTORY Online

Self-Check Quiz

Visit the *American Republic Since 1877* Web site at tarvol2.glencoe.com and click on *Self-Check Quizzes—Chapter 18* to assess your knowledge of chapter content.

idea [placing people in planned communities with homes, farms, and jobs]. . . . It was all experimental work, but it was designed to get people off relief, to put them to work building their own homes and to give them enough land to start growing food. **"**

a. Why did Eleanor Roosevelt like the Quaker project?

b. Based on this excerpt, do you think that Eleanor Roosevelt supported her husband's New Deal programs? Explain your answer.

20. Categorizing Use a graphic organizer like the one below to list groups of people helped by each program.

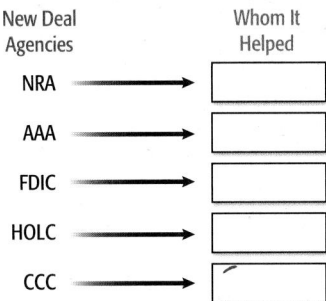

New Deal Agencies		Whom It Helped
NRA	→	
AAA	→	
FDIC	→	
HOLC	→	
CCC	→	

Practicing Skills

21. Outlining Study the subheads of Section 3, "The Second New Deal," and Section 4, "The New Deal Coalition," to review the sections. Then do the following exercises.

a. Make a formal outline of Section 3. Pay special attention to forming complete sentences.

b. Make an informal outline of Section 4.

Writing Activity

22. Expository Writing Under *Economic Crisis and the New Deal* on the American History Primary Source Document Library CD-ROM, read Roosevelt's First Inaugural Address. Work with another student to write a commentary on the address and then present it as a radio broadcast to the class. Your commentary should include opinions about Roosevelt's economic ideas.

Chapter Activity

23. Technology Activity: Researching the Internet Use the Internet to research two New Deal agencies: the FDIC and

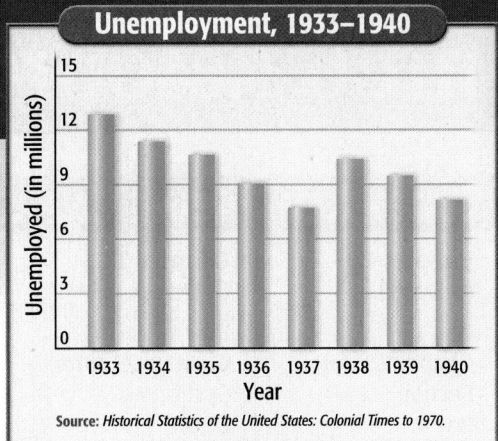

Unemployment, 1933–1940

Source: *Historical Statistics of the United States: Colonial Times to 1970.*

the SEC. Write a short report explaining how they continue to affect the lives of U.S. citizens and the U.S. economy today.

Economics and History

24. Examine the graph above showing unemployment figures, and then answer the questions below.

a. Interpreting Graphs What was the difference in unemployment between 1937 and 1938?

b. Analyzing Why did unemployment decline between 1933 and 1937? Why did it increase in 1938?

Standardized Test Practice

Directions: Choose the best answer to the following question.

Which of the following is true of the bills passed during the first Hundred Days of FDR's presidency?

F They were intended to provide long-term relief to American citizens.

G They were known as the Second New Deal.

H They were designed as temporary measures to restart the economy.

J They were the subject of divisive and protracted debate in Congress.

Test-Taking Tip: Remember, this question asks for the true statement. Read through each answer carefully to see if it is true of FDR's first Hundred Days. Since answer G refers to the *Second* New Deal, it could not refer to the *first* Hundred Days, so you can eliminate that answer.

HISTORY Online

Have students visit the Web site at tarvol2.glencoe.com to review Chapter 18 and take the Self-Check Quiz.

Chapter Activity

23. Reports will vary but should be based on solid sources and contain appropriate bibliographic references.

Economics and History

24. a. It increased from approximately 8 million to 10.5 million. **b.** It declined due to the New Deal programs and an improving economy. It increased in 1938 as a result of recession and reduced funding for some New Deal programs.

Standardized Test Practice

Answer: H

Test-Taking Tip: Have students look for information in the question stem that will help them find the correct answer. For example, 100 days is less than four months. It does not seem likely that much could have been accomplished if Congress was involved in divisive and protracted debate. Therefore, students can rule out answer J.

Bonus Question ?

Ask: What board game became a national fad during the 1930s? (Monopoly)

---

19. a. It emphasized individual initiative in improving the lives of miners. **b.** She did support his New Deal programs and often advised him on people's needs.

20. NRA: industrial workers; AAA: farmers; FDIC: bank depositors; HOLC: middle-class homeowners; CCC: single men ages 18–25

Practicing Skills

21. Students' outlines should follow rules for formal and informal outline techniques and be based on the content of the two sections.

Writing Activity

22. Allow time for students to present their radio broadcasts. Students could place the script or recording in their portfolios.

SUGGESTED PACING CHART

Unit 6 (1 Day)	Chapter 19 (5 Days)	Chapter 20 (6 Days)	Chapter 21 (5 Days)	Chapter 22 (5 Days)	Unit 6 (2 Days)
Day 1 Introduction	**Day 1** Chapter 19 Intro, Section 1	**Day 1** Chapter 20 Intro, Section 1	**Day 1** Chapter 21 Intro, Section 1	**Day 1** Chapter 22 Intro, Section 1	**Day 1** Wrap-Up/Project **Day 2** Unit 6 Assessment
	Day 2 Section 2	**Day 2** Section 2	**Day 2** Section 2	**Day 2** Section 2	
	Day 3 Section 3	**Day 3** Section 3	**Day 3** Section 3	**Day 3** Section 3	
	Day 4 Section 4	**Day 4** Section 4	**Day 4** Section 4	**Day 4** Section 4	
	Day 5 Chapter 19 Assessment	**Day 5** Section 5	**Day 5** Chapter 21 Assessment	**Day 5** Chapter 22 Assessment	
		Day 6 Chapter 20 Assessment			

GLENCOE'S ASSESSMENT ADVANTAGE

Use the following tools to easily assess student learning in a variety of ways:

- Performance Assessment Activities and Rubrics
- Chapter and Unit Tests
- Section Quizzes
- Standardized Test Practice Workbook

- tarvol2.glencoe.com
- Interactive Tutor Self-Assessment CD-ROM
- MindJogger Videoquiz
- ExamView® Pro Testmaker CD-ROM
- SAT I/II Test Practice

TEACHING TRANSPARENCIES

Unit 6 Map Overlay Transparencies
L2

Cause-and-Effect Transparency 6
L2

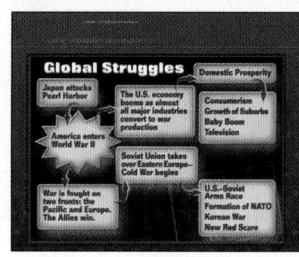

READING SUPPORT FROM JAMESTOWN EDUCATION

- ***Timed Readings Plus in Social Studies*** help students increase their reading rate and fluency while maintaining comprehension. The 400-word passages are similar to those found on state and national assessments.

- ***Reading in the Content Area: Social Studies*** concentrates on six essential reading skills that help students better comprehend what they read. The book includes 75 high-interest nonfiction passages written at increasing levels of difficulty.

- ***Reading Fluency*** helps students read smoothly, accurately, and expressively.

- ***Jamestown's Reading Improvement,*** by renowned reading expert Edward Fry, focuses on helping build your students' comprehension, vocabulary, and skimming and scanning skills.

- ***Critical Reading Series*** provides high-interest books, each written at three reading levels.

For more information about these products, see the Jamestown Education materials in the Classroom Solutions in the front of this Teacher Wraparound Edition. To order these products, call Glencoe at 1-800-334-7344.

APPLICATION AND ENRICHMENT

Unit 6 Pretests L2

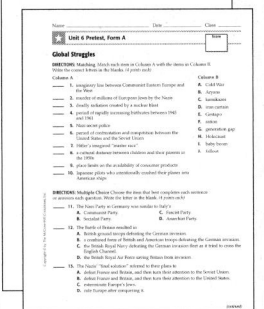

Unit 6 Posttests L2

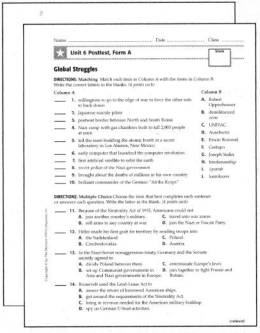

American Biography 6 L2

History Simulation and Problem Solving 6 L1

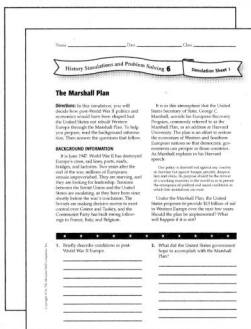

GEOGRAPHY

INTERDISCIPLINARY ACTIVITIES

Geography and History Activity 6 L2

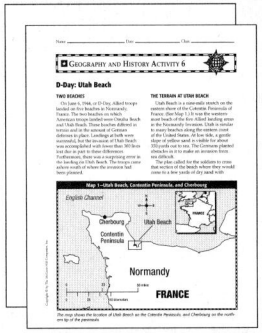

American Literature Reading 6 L2

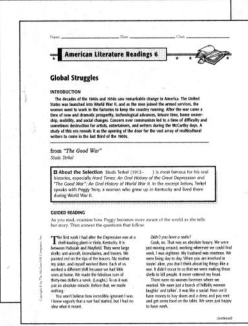

Economics and History Activity 6 L2

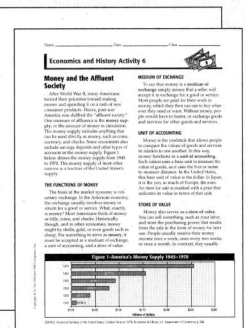

Team-Teaching Interdisciplinary Strategies and Activities 6 L2

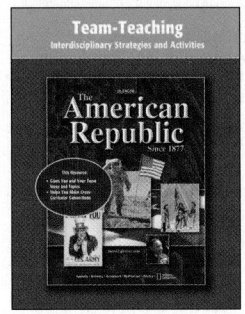

Reading List Generator CD-ROM

The Glencoe BookLink CD-ROM is a database that allows you to search more than 15,000 titles to create a customized reading list for your students.

- Reading lists can be organized by students' reading level, author, genre, theme, or area of interest.

- The database provides Degrees of Reading Power™ (DRP) and Lexile™ readability scores for all selections.

- A brief summary of each selection is included.

Leveled reading suggestions for this unit:

For students at a Grade 8 reading level:
- *Joseph McCarthy and the Cold War,* by Victoria Sherrow.

For students at a Grade 9 reading level:
- *Navajo Code Talkers,* by Nathan Aaseng.

For students at a Grade 10 reading level:
- *Tell Them We Remember: The Story of the Holocaust,* by Susan D. Bachrach.

Extending the Content

Readings for the Teacher
- *Life in a Japanese American Internment Camp,* by Diane Yancey. Lucent Books, 1998.

Multimedia Resources
- *December 7th.* National Archives. VHS. (34 minutes)

0:00 Out of Time?

If time does not permit teaching each chapter in this unit, you may want to use the **Reading Essentials and Study Guide** summaries.

Unit Overview

Unit 6 explores the global struggles faced by the United States between 1931 and 1960. **Chapter 19** covers the ten years leading up to World War II, 1931–1941. **Chapter 20** focuses on America and World War II, 1941–1945. **Chapter 21** details the beginning of the Cold War, 1945–1960. **Chapter 22** focuses on postwar America, 1945–1960.

Unit Objectives

After studying this unit, students will be able to:
1. Identify events leading up to World War II.
2. Detail the major battles and strategies of World War II.
3. Explain how the Cold War began.
4. Describe life in postwar America.

Why It Matters Activity

Discuss the reasons countries become involved in wars. Ask students to identify places where wars or armed conflicts are currently taking place. Ask students if they think another world war is possible.

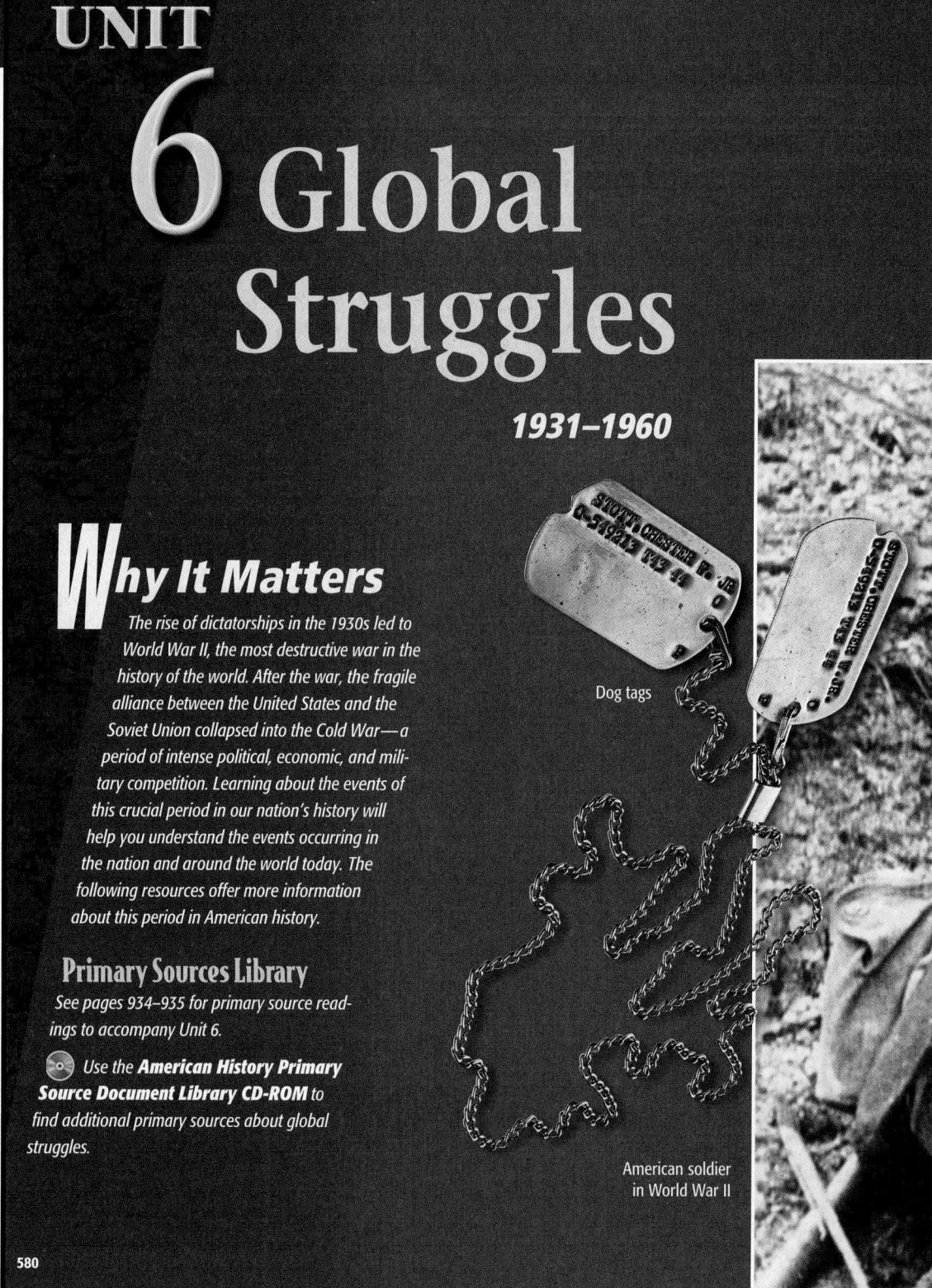

UNIT
6 Global Struggles
1931–1960

Why It Matters

The rise of dictatorships in the 1930s led to World War II, the most destructive war in the history of the world. After the war, the fragile alliance between the United States and the Soviet Union collapsed into the Cold War—a period of intense political, economic, and military competition. Learning about the events of this crucial period in our nation's history will help you understand the events occurring in the nation and around the world today. The following resources offer more information about this period in American history.

Primary Sources Library

See pages 934–935 for primary source readings to accompany Unit 6.

Use the **American History Primary Source Document Library CD-ROM** to find additional primary sources about global struggles.

Dog tags

American soldier in World War II

580

TEAM TEACHING ACTIVITY

Economics The booming postwar economy affected millions of Americans during 1945–1960 and the effects are still felt today. Cold War military spending, new home construction, and demand for consumer goods all played a role in the healthy economy. Work with the economics teacher to coordinate the study of the economic trends of postwar America.

"More than an end to war, we want an end to the beginning of all wars."

—*Franklin D. Roosevelt, 1945*

GLENCOE
TECHNOLOGY

CD-ROM
American History
Primary Source
Document Library
CD-ROM
Use the **American History Primary Source Document Library CD-ROM** to access primary source documents related to this period in history.

More About the Photo

Point out to students that over 400,000 Americans died in World War II. Most Americans personally knew someone who died or was injured during the war—a friend, relative, or neighbor. Have students describe what they see in the photograph and ask them what sacrifices were made by American soldiers. *(Students' answers will vary. They might mention the physical surroundings of the soldier shown in the photograph, time away from family, and the threat of injury or death.)*

Glencoe Literature Library

The following novels from the *High School American History Literature Library* may be used to enrich the study of this unit:
• *And the Earth Did Not Devour Him* by Tomás Rivera
• *A Separate Peace* by John Knowles

SERVICE-LEARNING PROJECT

Organize students into small groups. Have each group use music from the 1930s and 1940s to prepare an "Evening of Musical Entertainment." Arrange for each group to share its program at a local assisted living or nursing home facility. Encourage students to be creative in their presentation. Have each group member write a few paragraphs about his or her experience.

Refer to **Building Bridges: Connecting Classroom and Community through Service-Learning in Social Studies** from the National Council for the Social Studies for information about service-learning.

Timesaving Tools

TeacherWorks™ All-In-One Planner and Resource Center

- **Interactive Teacher Edition** Access your Teacher Wraparound Edition and your classroom resources with a few easy clicks.
- **Interactive Lesson Planner** Planning has never been easier! Organize your week, month, semester, or year with all the lesson helps you need to make teaching creative, timely, and relevant.

Use Glencoe's **Presentation Plus!** multimedia teacher tool to easily present dynamic lessons that visually excite your students. Using Microsoft PowerPoint® you can customize the presentations to create your own personalized lessons.

TEACHING TRANSPARENCIES

Graphic Organizer 4 L2

Why It Matters Chapter Transparency 19 L2

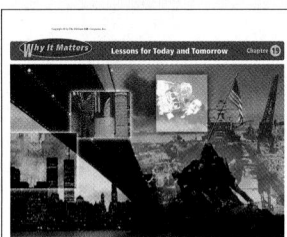

APPLICATION AND ENRICHMENT

Linking Past and Present Activity 19 L2

Enrichment Activity 19 L3

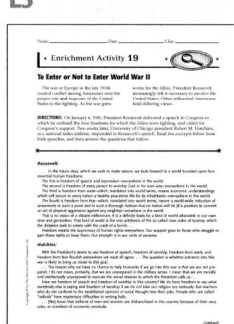

Primary Source Reading 19 L2

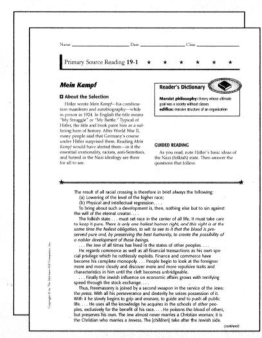

REVIEW AND REINFORCEMENT

Reteaching Activity 19 L1

Vocabulary Activity 19 L1

Time Line Activity 19 L2

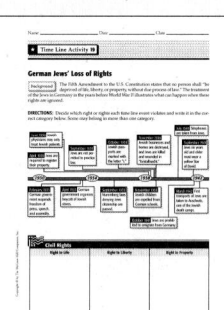

Critical Thinking Skills Activity 19 L2

Meeting NCSS Standards

The following standards are covered in Chapter 19:

Section 1 IX Global Connections: B, E, F
Section 2 II Time, Continuity, and Change: B, C
Section 3 X Civic Ideals and Practices: B, F, G, J
Section 4 IV Individual Development and Identity: A, C, F

Local Standards

Chapter 19 Resources

ASSESSMENT AND EVALUATION

Chapter 19 Test Form A L2

Chapter 19 Test Form B L2

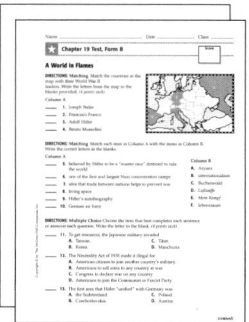

Standardized Test Practice Workbook Activity 19 L2

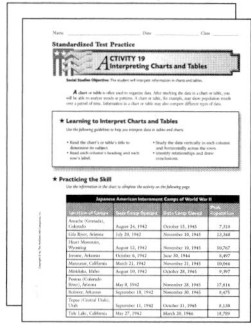

Performance Assessment Activities and Rubrics 19 L1/ELL

ExamView® Pro Testmaker CD-ROM

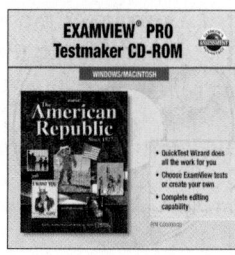

MULTIMEDIA

- Vocabulary PuzzleMaker CD-ROM
- Interactive Tutor Self-Assessment CD-ROM
- ExamView® Pro Testmaker CD-ROM
- Audio Program
- American History Primary Source Documents Library CD-ROM
- MindJogger Videoquiz
- Presentation Plus! CD-ROM
- TeacherWorks™ CD-ROM
- Interactive Student Edition CD-ROM
- Glencoe Skillbuilder Interactive Workbook CD-ROM, Level 2
- The *American Republic Since 1877* Video Program
- American Music: Hits Through History
- American Music: Cultural Traditions

SPANISH RESOURCES

The following Spanish language materials are available:

- Spanish Reading Essentials and Study Guide
- Spanish Guided Reading Activities
- Spanish Reteaching Activities
- Spanish Quizzes and Tests
- Spanish Vocabulary Activities
- Spanish Summaries
- The Declaration of Independence and United States Constitution Spanish Translation

The following videotape program is available from Glencoe as a supplement to Chapter 19:

- **The War in Europe** (ISBN 1-56-501993-8)

To order, call Glencoe at 1-800-334-7344. To find classroom resources to accompany this video, check the following home pages:
A&E Television: www.aande.com
The History Channel: www.historychannel.com

Use our Web site for additional resources. All essential content is covered in the Student Edition.

You and your students can visit tarvol2.glencoe.com, the Web site companion to the ***American Republic Since 1877***. This innovative integration of electronic and print media offers your students a wealth of opportunities. The student text directs students to the Web site for the following options:

- **Chapter Overviews**   **Student Web Activities**
- **Self-Check Quizzes**   **Textbook Updates**

Answers to the student Web activities are provided for you in the **Web Activity Lesson Plans.** Additional Web resources and Interactive Tutor Puzzles are also available.

Chapter 19 Resources

Daily Objectives	Reproducible Resources	Multimedia Resources
SECTION 1 **America and the World** 1. Describe how postwar conditions contributed to the rise of antidemocratic governments in Europe. 2. Explain why many Americans supported a policy of isolationism in the 1930s.	Reproducible Lesson Plan 19–1 Daily Lecture and Discussion Notes 19–1 Guided Reading Activity 19–1* Section Quiz 19–1* Reading Essentials and Study Guide 19–1* Performance Assessment Activities and Rubrics Supreme Court Case Studies	Daily Focus Skills Transparency 19–1 Interactive Tutor Self-Assessment CD-ROM ExamView® Pro Testmaker CD-ROM* Presentation Plus! CD-ROM TeacherWorks™ CD-ROM Audio Program
SECTION 2 **World War II Begins** 1. Explain why Hitler was able to take over Austria and Czechoslovakia. 2. Describe the early events of the war and why Britain was able to resist the Nazis.	Reproducible Lesson Plan 19–2 Daily Lecture and Discussion Notes 19–2 Guided Reading Activity 19–2* Section Quiz 19–2* Reading Essentials and Study Guide 19–2* Performance Assessment Activities and Rubrics	Daily Focus Skills Transparency 19–2 Interactive Tutor Self-Assessment CD-ROM ExamView® Pro Testmaker CD-ROM* Presentation Plus! CD-ROM TeacherWorks™ CD-ROM Audio Program
SECTION 3 **The Holocaust** 1. Describe Nazi prejudices against Jews and early persecution of German Jews. 2. Explain the methods Hitler used to try to exterminate Europe's Jewish population.	Reproducible Lesson Plan 19–3 Daily Lecture and Discussion Notes 19–3 Guided Reading Activity 19–3* Section Quiz 19–3* Reading Essentials and Study Guide 19–3* Performance Assessment Activities and Rubrics	Daily Focus Skills Transparency 19–3 Interactive Tutor Self-Assessment CD-ROM ExamView® Pro Testmaker CD-ROM* Presentation Plus! CD-ROM TeacherWorks™ CD-ROM Audio Program ABCNews Interactive™ Historic America Electronic Field Trips
SECTION 4 **America Enters the War** 1. Explain how Roosevelt helped Britain while maintaining official neutrality. 2. Trace the events that led to increasing tensions, and ultimately war, between the United States and Japan.	Reproducible Lesson Plan 19–4 Daily Lecture and Discussion Notes 19–4 Guided Reading Activity 19–4* Section Quiz 19–4* Reading Essentials and Study Guide 19–4* Performance Assessment Activities and Rubrics Interpreting Political Cartoons	Daily Focus Skills Transparency 19–4 Interactive Tutor Self-Assessment CD-ROM ExamView® Pro Testmaker CD-ROM* Presentation Plus! CD-ROM Skillbuilder Interactive Workbook, Level 2 TeacherWorks™ CD-ROM Vocabulary PuzzleMaker CD-ROM Audio Program ABCNews Interactive™ Historic America Electronic Field Trips

0:00 OUT OF TIME?
Assign the Chapter 19 **Reading Essentials and Study Guide.**

*Also Available in Spanish

 Printed Materials   Transparency   CD-ROM   DVD

 Poster   Music Program   Audio Program   Videocassette

Chapter 19 Resources

NATIONAL GEOGRAPHIC Teacher's Corner

INDEX TO NATIONAL GEOGRAPHIC MAGAZINE

The following articles relate to this chapter.

- "The Bismarck Found," November 1989
- "Blueprints for Victory," May 1995
- "Douglas MacArthur: An American Soldier," March 1992
- "Hiroshima," August 1995
- "Living with Radiation," April 1989
- "Pearl Harbor: A Return to the Day of Infamy," December 1991
- "Remembering the Blitz," July 1991

NATIONAL GEOGRAPHIC SOCIETY PRODUCTS

To order the following, call National Geographic at 1-800-368-2728:

- *Eyewitness to the 20th Century* (Book)
- *Historical Atlas of the United States*
- *Lost Fleet of Guadalcanal* (Video)

NGS ONLINE

Access National Geographic's Web site for current events, atlas updates, activities, links, interactive features, and archives.
www.nationalgeographic.com

From the Classroom of...

Wendy FitzHenry
Trinity Lutheran School
Bend, OR

Pre-World War II German Family Dilemma

Organize students into "families" with each student assigned a role such as mom, dad, and oldest son. Describe the following scenario to them:

It is 1938. You are a German family who has become close friends with the Jewish family next door. In the past few years, Jewish citizens have had to abide by nightly curfews and have often been the victims of violence. One night, the family asks you if they can hide in your basement.

Discuss their request as a family. Remember, if caught, all of you would be subjected to the same punishment as your Jewish neighbors.

Make a list of difficulties your family would face if you say yes. How would you keep their existence a secret? What about food and clothing? What if you are inspected by German soldiers?

You must make a final decision either yes or no. The dad has the final say. Justify your reason.

MEETING SPECIAL NEEDS

In addition to the Differentiated Instruction strategies found in each section, the following resources are also suitable for your special needs students:

- *ExamView® Pro Testmaker CD-ROM* allows teachers to tailor tests by reducing answer choices.

- The *Audio Program* includes the entire narrative of the student edition so that less-proficient readers can listen to the words as they read them.

KEY TO ABILITY LEVELS

Teaching strategies have been coded.

- **L1** BASIC activities for all students
- **L2** AVERAGE activities for average to above-average students
- **L3** CHALLENGING activities for above-average students
- **ELL** ENGLISH LANGUAGE LEARNER activities

ADDITIONAL RESOURCES FROM GLENCOE

- American Music: Cultural Traditions
- American Art & Architecture
- Outline Map Resource Book
- U.S. Desk Map
- Building Geography Skills for Life
- Inclusion for the High School Social Studies Classroom Strategies and Activities
- Teaching Strategies for the American History Classroom (Including Block Scheduling Pacing Guides)
- Dinah Zike's High School American History Reading and Study Skills Foldables

Block Schedule

Activities that are suited to use within the block scheduling framework are identified by:

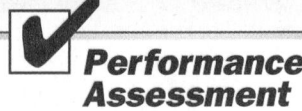
Performance Assessment

Refer to Activity 19 in the Performance Assessment Activities and Rubrics booklet.

Why It Matters Activity

Ask students if they would support or oppose U.S. involvement in a conflict between other countries if it might result in a world war. *(Students should give reasons for their positions.)* Point out that the issue of involvement was very important before the onset of World War II.

GLENCOE
TECHNOLOGY

The *American Republic Since 1877* Video Program
To learn more about this period in U.S. history, have students view the Chapter 19 video, "Holocaust Stories," from the *American Republic Since 1877* Video Program.

MindJogger Videoquiz
Use the **MindJogger Videoquiz** to preview Chapter 19 content.

Both programs available in DVD

CHAPTER
19 A World in Flames *1931–1941*

Why It Matters

After World War I, Europe was unstable. Fascists led by Benito Mussolini seized power in Italy, and Adolf Hitler and the Nazis took control of Germany. Meanwhile, Japan expanded its territory in Asia. As the Nazis gained power, they began a campaign of violence against Jews. When Germany attacked Poland, World War II began. The United States clung to neutrality until Japan attacked Pearl Harbor.

The Impact Today

European events of this time serve as lessons for American leaders.
*   *The danger of ethnic and religious prejudice is more readily recognized than it was before.*
*   *Many American leaders believe that international aggression cannot be ignored.*

 The American Republic Since 1877 Video *The Chapter 19 video, "Holocaust Stories," presents firsthand accounts from survivors of the Holocaust.*

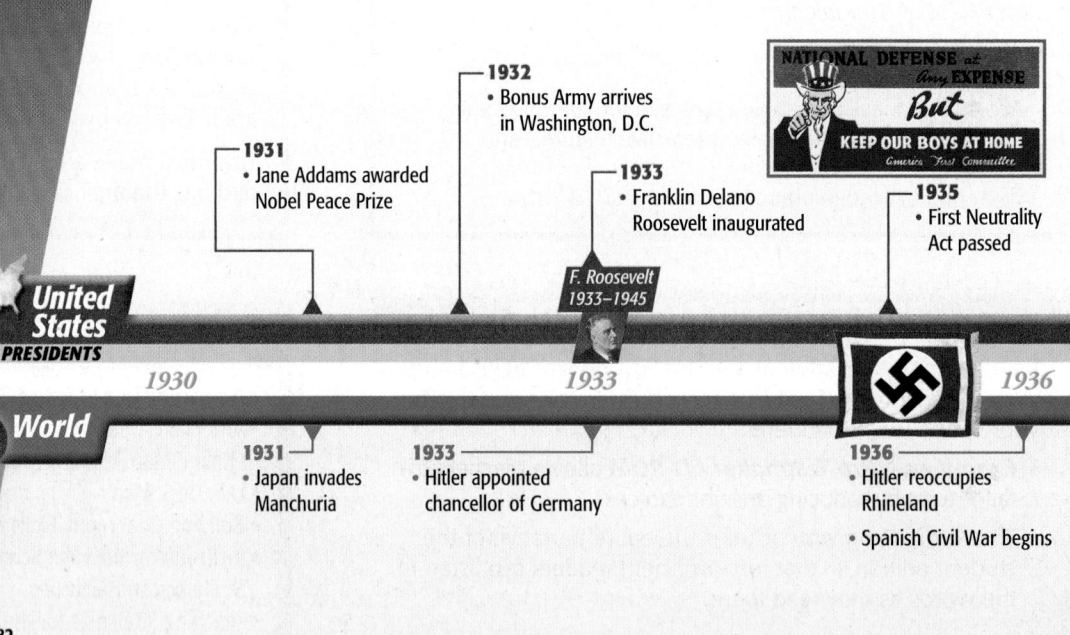

1931
• Jane Addams awarded Nobel Peace Prize

1932
• Bonus Army arrives in Washington, D.C.

1933
• Franklin Delano Roosevelt inaugurated

1935
• First Neutrality Act passed

NATIONAL DEFENSE at *any* EXPENSE
But
KEEP OUR BOYS AT HOME
America First Committee

United States PRESIDENTS

F. Roosevelt 1933–1945

1930   *1933*   *1936*

World

1931
• Japan invades Manchuria

1933
• Hitler appointed chancellor of Germany

1936
• Hitler reoccupies Rhineland
• Spanish Civil War begins

582

⊳⊳ **Reading Strategy** ⊳ **PURPOSE FOR READING**

Carousel Brainstorming This activity generates students' background knowledge. Write each of the following topics on the top of its own sheet of large paper: *President Roosevelt, Winston Churchill, Adolph Hitler, Benito Mussolini, Joseph Stalin, Nazi Party, Holocaust,* and *Pearl Harbor.* Post these sheets around the classroom. Organize the class into eight groups and assign each group one of the topics. Giving each group a different colored marker, have students write anything they think they know about the topic on the paper. After two minutes, have each group carousel to the next topic. This time, have the groups make corrections or additions to the existing lists. Continue until each group is back to their original topic. Conclude the activity with each group reviewing the added information. **L1**

German chancellor Adolf Hitler reviews a parade of Nazi troops.

1937
• Neutrality Act limits trade with all warring nations

1938
• Munich Conference appeases Hitler

1939
• SS *St. Louis* denied permission to dock in United States

1939
• World War II begins with Hitler's attack on Poland

1940
• Roosevelt makes "destroyers-for-bases" deal with Britain

1940
• France falls to the Nazis

1941
• Roosevelt and Churchill coauthor Atlantic Charter

December 7, 1941
• Japan attacks Pearl Harbor

1939

1942

HISTORY Online

Chapter Overview
Visit the *American Republic Since 1877* Web site at tarvol2.glencoe.com and click on *Chapter Overviews— Chapter 19* to preview chapter information.

583

GRAPHIC ORGANIZER ACTIVITY

Organizing Information Have students use a graphic organizer like the one shown at right to help them identify the steps that Roosevelt took to aid the Allied cause.

Step

Step

Step

Step

HISTORY Online

Introduce students to chapter content and key terms by having them access the **Chapter 19 Overview** at tarvol2.glencoe.com.

More About the Photo

Ask students what symbols they see in the photo that are traditionally associated with Hitler or the Third Reich. *(swastika and Hitler's salute)* The swastika, a symbol in the form of a Greek cross with the ends of the arms extended, was used in ancient times to symbolize prosperity and as a good luck symbol. The Nazi Party adopted it as a symbol of its goals of German expansionism and anti-Semitism.

TIME LINE
ACTIVITY

Have students select an event shown on the time line and research more about it. From their research have them write a brief description of the event and the impact it had on American history.

FOLDABLES™
Study Organizer

Dinah Zike's Foldables are three-dimensional, interactive graphic organizers that help students practice basic writing skills, review key vocabulary terms, and identify main ideas. Have students complete the foldable activity in the *Dinah Zike's Reading and Study Skills Foldables* booklet.

1 FOCUS

Section Overview

This section examines how anti-democratic governments came to power in Europe and Asia.

Reading Preview

Answers to Graphic:
America and the World
 I. The Rise of Dictators
    A. Mussolini and Fascism in Italy
    B. Stalin Takes Over the USSR
    C. Hitler and Nazism in Germany
    D. Militarists Gain Control of Japan
 II. America Turns to Neutrality

Preteaching Vocabulary
Have students write a paragraph using at least three of the Key Terms and Names.

SECTION 1 America and the World

Guide to Reading

Main Idea
In the years following World War I, aggressive and expansionist governments took power in both Europe and Asia.

Key Terms and Names
Benito Mussolini, fascism, Vladimir Lenin, Joseph Stalin, Adolf Hitler, Manchuria, Neutrality Act of 1935, internationalism

Reading Strategy
Taking Notes As you read about the events in Europe and Asia after World War I, use the major headings of the section to create an outline similar to the one below.

America and the World
I. The Rise of Dictators
    A.
    B.
    C.
    D.
II.

Reading Objectives
• **Describe** how postwar conditions contributed to the rise of antidemocratic governments in Europe.
• **Explain** why many Americans supported a policy of isolationism in the 1930s.

Section Theme
Global Connections German and Japanese actions in the 1930s led President Roosevelt to work to prevent aggression.

Preview of Events

♦1922	♦1927	♦1932	♦1937
1922 Fascist Party takes power in Italy; USSR established	**1931** Japan takes control of Manchuria	**1933** Hitler takes power in Germany	**1935** Congress passes first Neutrality Act · **1937** Japan attacks China

★ An American Story ★

Dorothy Thompson

In August 1934, American journalist Dorothy Thompson received an urgent call from the porter at her Berlin hotel. A member of Germany's secret state police wanted to talk to her. Thompson had been reporting on Adolf Hitler's rise to power, and she had written various anti-Nazi articles for the American press. In one she described the beautiful singing she had heard at a Hitler youth camp, where thousands of boys ages 10 to 16 marched and sang. The boys' lovely voices echoing across the hills stirred Thompson, but the words on an enormous banner hanging across one hillside chilled her:

❝It was so prominent that every child could see it many times a day. It was white, and there was a swastika painted on it, and besides that only seven words, seven immense black words: YOU WERE BORN TO DIE FOR GERMANY.❞

When Thompson met with the police, they ordered her to leave Germany immediately. "I, fortunately, am an American," Thompson observed, "so I was merely sent to Paris. Worse things can happen to one."

—quoted in *The Women Who Wrote the War*

The Rise of Dictators

Less than 20 years before the dictatorial German government expelled Dorothy Thompson, the future of democracy in Europe seemed bright. When World War I ended in 1918, President Woodrow Wilson had announced, "Everything for which America fought has been accomplished." Wilson had hoped that the United States could "aid in

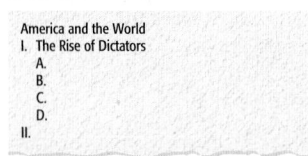

the establishment of just democracy throughout the world." Instead, the treaty that ended the war, along with the economic depression that followed, contributed to the rise of antidemocratic governments in both Europe and Asia.

Mussolini and Fascism in Italy One of Europe's first major dictatorships arose in Italy. There, a former schoolmaster and journalist named **Benito Mussolini** returned from World War I convinced that his country needed a strong leader.

In 1919 Mussolini founded Italy's Fascist Party. Fascism was a kind of aggressive nationalism. Fascists believed that the nation was more important than the individual. They argued that individualism made countries weak and that a strong government led by a dictator was needed to impose order on society. Fascists believed a nation became great by expanding its territory and building up its military.

Fascism was also strongly anticommunist. After the Communist revolution in Russia, many Europeans feared that Communists, allied with labor unions, were trying to bring down their governments. Mussolini exploited these fears by portraying fascism as a bulwark against the Communists. Fascism began to stand for the protection of private property and of the middle class. Mussolini also offered the working class full employment and social security. He stressed national prestige, pledging to return Italy to the glories of the Roman Empire.

Backed by the Fascist militia known as the Blackshirts, Mussolini threatened to march on Rome in 1922, claiming he was coming to defend Italy against a Communist revolution. Liberal members of the Italian parliament insisted that the king declare martial law. When he refused, the cabinet resigned. Conservative advisers then persuaded the king to appoint Mussolini as the premier.

Once in office, Mussolini worked quickly to destroy democracy and set up a dictatorship. Weary of strikes and riots, many Italians welcomed Mussolini's leadership. With the support of industrialists, landowners, and the Roman Catholic Church, Mussolini—who took the title of *Il Duce*, or "The Leader"—embarked on an ambitious program of bringing order to Italy.

Stalin Takes Over the USSR The Communists were a much larger force in Russia than in Italy. After the Russian Revolution began in 1917, the Bolshevik Party, led by **Vladimir Lenin**, established Communist governments throughout the Russian empire. In 1922 they renamed these territories the Union of Soviet Socialist Republics (USSR). They then proceeded to establish control over these territories. To

do this, the Communists instituted one-party rule, suppressed individual liberties, and punished opponents. After Lenin died in 1924, a power struggle began. By 1926, **Joseph Stalin** had become the new Soviet dictator. In 1927 Stalin began a massive effort to industrialize his country. Tolerating no opposition, the effort brought about the deaths of 8 to 10 million peasants who resisted the Communist policies.

Hitler and Nazism in Germany Adolf Hitler was a fervent anticommunist and an admirer of Mussolini. Hitler had fought for Germany in World War I. Germany's surrender and the subsequent Versailles Treaty left him and many other Germans with a smoldering hatred for the victorious Allies and for the German government that had accepted the peace terms.

The political and economic chaos in postwar Germany led to the rise of new political parties. One of these was the National Socialist German Workers' Party, or the **Nazi Party.** The party did not represent the working class, as its name suggested, but was nationalistic and anticommunist. Adolf Hitler was one of the party's first recruits.

In November 1923, the Nazis tried to seize power by marching on city hall in Munich, Germany. Hitler intended to seize power locally

Picturing **History**

Supreme Soviets Joseph Stalin (right) took over control of the Soviet Union after Lenin's death in 1924. He was determined to modernize and industrialize his nation. *How many people died while opposing Stalin's leadership?*

2 TEACH

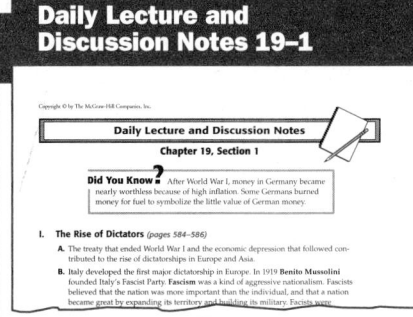

Daily Lecture and Discussion Notes 19–1

Comparing Have students compare the goals of Mussolini and Hitler. Ask students: What objectives did the two leaders have in common? *(desire for a totalitarian state, building up the military, and territorial expansion)* L1

you don't say...

Political Symbols The word *fascist* comes from the Latin word *fasces,* or the rods and axes that Roman officials carried in ancient times to represent their authority.

Picturing **History**

Answer: 8 to 10 million people
Ask: How did the Bolsheviks establish control over the territories of the former Russian Empire? *(They established Communist governments, instituted one-party rule, suppressed individual liberties, and punished opponents.)*

Use *Supreme Court Case Study 15, DeJonge v. Oregon.*

Reading Strategy — READING THE TEXT

Summarizing Information Organize the students into three groups. Assign each group one of the following: Tojo, Hitler, or Mussolini. Have each group discuss the growth of dictatorships in either Japan, Germany, or Italy, listing the reasons for aggressive policies in the early to mid-1930s. Then have one person from each group summarize their list and present it to the entire class. L1

Refer to *Inclusion for the High School Social Studies Classroom Strategies and Activities* in the TCR.

L1/ELL

Guided Reading Activity 19–1

Name _____ Date _____ Class _____

★ **Guided Reading Activity 19-1**

DIRECTIONS: Using Headings and Subheadings Locate each heading below in your text-book. Then use the information under the correct subheading to help you write each answer.

I. The Rise of Dictators

A. Where was the first major European dictatorship? _____

B. Who was the new dictator, and what did he believe was needed? _____

C. What were the elements of fascism? _____

D. Why did many Italians welcome Mussolini's leadership? _____

E. Who supported Mussolini in his rise to power? _____

F. How did the Communists establish control in the new Union of Soviet Socialist Republics (USSR)?

Writing an Editorial Tell students to choose an international-ist or isolationist point of view. Have students write a newspaper editorial expressing their point of view while trying to convince readers to join with them. Have students present their editorials to the class. **L2**

FYI

A section of Amy Tan's popular novel *The Joy Luck Club* was set during the troubles between China and Japan during the 1930s.

Picturing History

Answer: Both were extreme national-ists who wanted to expand their terri-tories and build up their military.

✓ Reading Check

Answer: Political inequities caused by the Versailles Treaty ending World War I fueled nationalism. Widespread economic depression and social unrest created desperation among the people for new, stronger leader-ship. Dictators were able to capitalize on these feelings to seize control of governments.

and then march on Berlin, the German capital, but the plan failed and Hitler was arrested.

While in prison, Hitler wrote his autobiography, titled *Mein Kampf* ("My Struggle"). In the book, Hitler called for the unification of all Germans under one government. He claimed that Germans, particularly blond, blue-eyed Germans, belonged to a "master race" called Aryans. He argued that Germans needed more lebensraum, or living space, and called for Germany to expand east into Poland and Russia. According to Hitler, the Slavic people of Eastern Europe belonged to an inferior race, which Germans should enslave. Hitler's prejudice was strongest, however, toward Jews. He believed that Jews were responsible for many of the world's problems, espe-cially for Germany's defeat in World War I.

After his release from prison, Hitler changed his tactics. Instead of trying to seize power violently, he focused on getting Nazis elected to the Reichstag, the lower house of the German parliament. When the Great Depression struck Germany, many desperate Germans began to vote for radical parties, including the Nazis and Communists. By 1932 the Nazis were the largest party in the Reichstag.

Many traditional German leaders supported Hitler's nationalism. They believed that if they helped Hitler become leader of Germany legally, they could control him. In 1933 the German president appointed Hitler as chancellor, or prime minister.

After taking office, Hitler called for new elections. He then ordered the police to crack down on the Socialist and Communist Parties. Storm Troopers, as

Picturing History

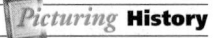

Meeting of Minds Mussolini and Hitler are shown here meeting in October 1940. *What beliefs did they share?*

the Nazi paramilitary units were called, began intimi-dating voters. After the election, the Reichstag, domi-nated by the Nazis and other right-wing parties, voted to give Hitler dictatorial powers. In 1934 Hitler became president, which gave him control of the army. He then gave himself the new title of führer, or "leader." The following year, he began to rebuild Germany's military, in violation of the Treaty of Versailles.

Militarists Gain Control of Japan In Japan, as in Germany, difficult economic times helped under-mine the political system. Japanese industries had to import nearly all of the resources they needed to produce goods. During the 1920s, Japan did not earn enough money from its exports to pay for its imports, which limited economic growth and increased unemployment. When the Depression struck, other countries raised their tariffs. This made the situation even worse.

Many Japanese military officers blamed the coun-try's problems on corrupt politicians. Most officers believed that Japan was destined to dominate East Asia. Many also believed that democracy was "un-Japanese" and bad for the country.

Japanese military leaders and the civilians who supported them argued that the only way for Japan to get needed resources was to seize territory. They targeted the resource-rich province of **Manchuria** in northern China as the perfect place to conquer.

A group of Japanese officers decided to act without the government's permission. In September 1931, the Japanese army invaded Manchuria. After the inva-sion began, the Japanese government tried to end the war, but when the Japanese prime minister began negotiations, officers assassinated him. From that point forward, the military was effectively in control. Although Japan still had a civilian gov-ernment, it now supported the nationalist policy of expanding the empire, and it appointed several mili-tary officers to serve as prime minister.

✓ Reading Check

Examining How did postwar conditions contribute to the rise of dictatorships in Europe?

DIFFERENTIATED INSTRUCTION

Reading Support Have students create a thematic map of Europe that shows the territorial changes included in the Treaty of Versailles. Include new countries created, land gained by Italy, France, Belgium, and Denmark, and demilitarized areas. Have students use their maps to explain why Germany felt slighted by the treaty and how that affected later events. **L2**

☛ Refer to *Inclusion for the High School Social Studies Classroom Strategies and Activities* in the TCR.

America Turns to Neutrality

The rise of dictatorships and militarism after World War I discouraged many Americans. The sacrifices they had made during the war seemed pointless. Once again, Americans began to support isolationism, or the belief that the United States should avoid international commitments that might drag the nation into another war.

The Nye Committee Isolationist ideas became even stronger in the early 1930s for two reasons. When the Depression began, many European nations found it difficult to repay money they had borrowed during World War I. In June 1934, all of the debtor nations except Finland announced they would no longer repay their war debts.

At about the same time, dozens of books and articles appeared arguing that arms manufacturers had tricked the United States into entering World War I. In 1934 Senator Gerald P. Nye of North Dakota held hearings to investigate the country's involvement in World War I. The **Nye Committee** documented the huge profits that arms factories had made during the war. The report created the impression that these businesses influenced the United States to go to war. The European refusal to repay their loans and the Nye Committee's findings turned even more Americans toward isolationism.

Legislating Neutrality Worried that growing German and Italian aggression might lead to war, Congress passed the **Neutrality Act of 1935.** Based on the belief that arms sales had helped bring the United States into World War I, the act made it illegal for Americans to sell arms to any country at war.

In 1936 a rebellion erupted in Spain after a coalition of Republicans, Socialists, and Communists was elected. General **Francisco Franco** led the rebellion. Franco was backed by the Falangists, or Spanish Fascists, army officers, landowners, and Catholic Church leaders.

The revolt quickly became a civil war and attracted worldwide attention. The Soviet Union provided arms and advisers to the government forces, while Germany and Italy sent tanks, airplanes, and soldiers to help Franco. To keep the United States neutral, Congress passed another neutrality act, banning the sale of arms to either side in a civil war.

Shortly after the **Spanish Civil War** began in 1936, Hitler and Mussolini signed an agreement pledging to cooperate on several international issues. Mussolini referred to this new relationship with Germany as the Rome-Berlin Axis. The following

Anti-Fascist Propaganda Spanish general Francisco Franco led the Fascist rebellion that received support from Hitler and Mussolini. This poster translates to "The claw of the Italian invader intends to make slaves of us." How did the United States respond to these events?

month, Japan aligned itself with Germany and Italy when it signed the **Anti-Comintern Pact** with Germany. The pact required the two countries to exchange information about Communist groups. Together Germany, Italy, and Japan became known as the **Axis Powers,** although they did not formally become allies until September 1940.

With the situation in Europe getting worse, Congress passed the Neutrality Act of 1937. This act continued the ban on selling arms to nations at war, but it also required warring countries to buy nonmilitary supplies from the United States on a "cash-and-carry" basis. If a country at war wanted goods from the United States, it had to send its own ships to pick up the goods, and it had to pay cash. Loans were not allowed. Isolationists knew that attacks on neutral American ships carrying supplies to Europe had helped bring the country into World War I. They were determined to prevent it from happening again.

CHAPTER 19   A World in Flames   **587**

3 ASSESS

Assign Section 1 Assessment as homework or as an in-class activity.

◆ Have students use the **Interactive Tutor Self-Assessment CD-ROM.**

L1/ELL

Reading Essentials and Study Guide 19–1

Name _____ Date _____ Class _____

Study Guide
Chapter 19, Section 1
For use with textbook pages 584–588
AMERICA AND THE WORLD

KEY TERMS AND NAMES

Benito Mussolini Fascist dictator of Italy (page 585)
fascism a kind of aggressive nationalism (page 585)
Vladimir Lenin leader of the Bolshevik Party in Russia (page 585)
Joseph Stalin dictator of the Soviet Union (page 585)
Adolf Hitler Nazi leader of Germany (page 585)
Manchuria province in northern China (page 586)
Neutrality Act of 1935 law that made it illegal for Americans to sell arms to any country at war (page 587)

L2

Section Quiz 19–1

Name _____ Date _____ Class _____

★ Chapter 19 | Score _____

Section Quiz 19-1

DIRECTIONS: Matching Match each item in Column A with the items in Column B. Write the correct letters in the blanks. (10 points each)

Column A
___ 1. Germany, Italy, and Japan
___ 2. idea that a country should focus on its own problems and avoid international commitments
___ 3. Adolph Hitler's autobiography written while he was in prison
___ 4. a kind of aggressive nationalism
___ 5. resource-rich province of China invaded by the Japanese army

Column B
A. isolationism
B. Axis Powers
C. fascism
D. *Mein Kampf*
E. Manchuria

DIRECTIONS: Multiple Choice In the blank at the left, write the letter of the choice that

---

INTERDISCIPLINARY CONNECTIONS ACTIVITY

Life Skills Have students choose a leader from this period and create a résumé that includes pertinent details of the leader's education, career experience, political offices held, and major events in which the person participated. Also have them include any skills, activities, and memberships that might present a fuller picture of the person. Possible subjects include Adolf Hitler, Benito Mussolini, Joseph Stalin, Hideki Tojo, Winston Churchill, and Franklin Roosevelt. **L2**

Picturing History

Answer: He argued that arms sales could be made since war had not been officially declared.

Ask: What did internationalists believe about the economy? (*They believed trade between nations created prosperity, helped prevent war.*)

FYI

During their invasion of China, the Japanese used extreme violence in the capital of Nanking. This incident, which became known as the "Rape of Nanking," helped prompt President Roosevelt to sell weapons to China.

Reteach

Ask students to summarize how postwar conditions affected the rise of dictatorships in Europe.

Enrich

Have students view the video *For Whom the Bell Tolls.* Have them write a few paragraphs related to the film on the themes of isolationism and neutrality. Discuss these themes and how they relate to the period between World War I and World War II.

✓ Reading Check

Answer: They felt remaining apart from European conflicts would avoid another war.

Study Central™ provides summaries, interactive games, and online graphic organizers to help students review section content.

4 CLOSE

Have students draw a political cartoon that expresses the feelings of internationalists or isolationists.

588

GOVERNMENT

Roosevelt and Internationalism When he took office in 1933, President Roosevelt declared that "our international relations, though vastly important, are in point of time and necessity secondary to the establishment of a sound national economy." Roosevelt knew that ending the Depression was his first priority, but he was not an isolationist. He supported internationalism, the idea that trade between nations creates prosperity and helps to prevent war. Internationalists also believed the United States should try to preserve peace in the world.

Roosevelt supported internationalism but knew that the public wanted neutrality. He warned that the neutrality acts "might drag us into war instead of keeping us out," but he did not veto the bills. Isolationism was too strong to resist.

In July 1937, Japanese forces in Manchuria launched a full-scale attack on China. Roosevelt decided to help the Chinese. Since neither China nor Japan had actually declared war, Roosevelt claimed the Neutrality Act of 1937 did not apply, and he authorized the sale of weapons to China. He warned that the nation should not stand by and let an "epidemic of lawlessness" infect the world:

❝When an epidemic of physical disease starts to spread, the community . . . joins in a quarantine of the patients in order to protect the health of the community against the spread of the disease. . . . War is a contagion, whether it be declared or undeclared. . . . There is no escape through mere isolation or neutrality. . . .❞

—quoted in *Freedom from Fear*

Picturing History

Imperial Expansion In 1931 Japan occupied the northeast Chinese province of Manchuria. In 1937 the Japanese invaded all of China, prompting FDR to authorize the sale of arms to the Chinese Army. How did Roosevelt justify his actions in light of the Neutrality Act?

Despite Roosevelt's words, Americans were still not willing to risk another war to stop aggression overseas. "It is a terrible thing," the president said, "to look over your shoulder when you are trying to lead—and find no one there."

✓ Reading Check **Evaluating** Why did many Americans support isolationism?

HISTORY *Online* **Study Central**™ To review this section, go to **tarvol2.glencoe.com** and click on **Study Central**™.

SECTION 1 ASSESSMENT

Checking for Understanding
1. **Define:** fascism, internationalism.
2. **Identify:** Benito Mussolini, Vladimir Lenin, Joseph Stalin, Adolf Hitler, Manchuria, Neutrality Act of 1935.
3. **Explain** why isolationism was strong in the United States in the early 1930s.

Reviewing Themes
4. **Global Connections** What events caused President Roosevelt to become more of an internationalist?

Critical Thinking
5. **Interpreting** Why did antidemocratic governments rise to power in postwar Europe and Asia?
6. **Categorizing** Use a graphic organizer similar to the one below to compare the antidemocratic governments that arose in Europe and Asia.

Country	Dictator	Ideology

Analyzing Visuals
7. **Analyzing Art** Study the Spanish Civil War era propaganda poster reproduced on page 587. Without being told the phrase, how would you be able to discover the poster's meaning?

Writing About History
8. **Persuasive Writing** Write a newspaper editorial urging fellow citizens to embrace either isolationism or internationalism after World War I. Be certain to include reasons your readers should back a specific position.

588 CHAPTER 19 A World in Flames

SECTION 1 ASSESSMENT ANSWERS

1. Terms are in blue.
2. Benito Mussolini (*p. 585*), Vladimir Lenin (*p. 585*), Joseph Stalin (*p. 585*), Adolf Hitler (*p. 585*), Manchuria (*p. 586*), Neutrality Act of 1935 (*p. 587*)
3. unpaid European war debts; belief that arms manufacturers influenced U.S. to enter World War I

4. Japanese invasion of China
5. unhappiness with Treaty of Versailles terms; worldwide economic depression
6. Italy: Mussolini, Fascism; USSR: Stalin, Communism; Germany: Hitler, Nazism; Japan: Japanese military, militarism

7. a cruel claw-like hand is trying to grasp the country; colors of Italian flag superimposed on hand
8. Answers will vary but should include text material.

World War II Begins

Guide to Reading

Main Idea
World War II officially began with the Nazi invasion of Poland and the French and British declaration of war on Germany in September 1939.

Key Terms and Names
Anschluss, appeasement, blitzkrieg, Maginot Line, Winston Churchill, Battle of Britain

Reading Strategy
Sequencing As you read about the events leading up to the beginning of World War II, record them by completing a time line similar to the one below.

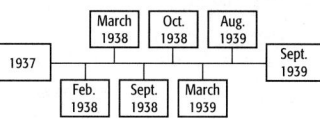

Reading Objectives
• **Explain** why Hitler was able to take over Austria and Czechoslovakia.
• **Describe** the early events of the war and why Britain was able to resist the Nazis.

Section Theme
Continuity and Change The desire of the French and British to avoid another war helped encourage Hitler's aggression in Europe.

Preview of Events

♦1938	♦1939	♦1940	♦1941

March 1938
Hitler announces German-Austrian unification

August 1939
Hitler and Stalin sign Nazi-Soviet pact

September 1939
World War II begins

June 1940
France surrenders to Germany

August 1940
Battle of Britain begins

---

1 FOCUS

Section Overview
This section focuses on the beginning of World War II in Europe.

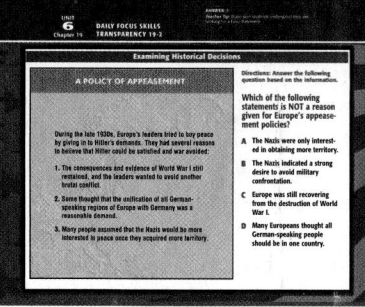
Reading Preview

Answers to Graphic: Hitler calls for German unity; Hitler threatens to invade Austria; the *Anschluss*; Germany claims Sudetenland; Germany demands return of Danzig; Germany annexes Czechoslovakia; Nazi-Soviet Nonaggression Pact; Germany invades Poland

Preteaching Vocabulary
Assign one of the Key Terms and Names to each student. Have each student prepare a 30-second oral presentation related to the selected term or name.

Sumner Welles

★ An American Story ★

In February 1940, President Franklin Roosevelt sent Undersecretary of State Sumner Welles to Europe to report on the political situation. A few months earlier, Germany had invaded Poland, and Roosevelt hoped to negotiate peace before wider hostilities erupted.

In Italy Welles found Mussolini intent on war and judged that "there was not the slightest chance of any successful negotiation." In Paris Welles glumly noted the "sullen apathy" in people's faces and concluded that France had little will to resist a German onslaught. After speaking to Hitler, Welles concluded that a negotiated peace settlement was impossible: "It was only too tragically plain that all decisions had already been made." In London, Welles did not feel the sense of doom he had in Paris. The British, he reported, would "fight to the very last ditch." Welles later reflected on his mission:

❝Only one thing could have deflected Hitler from his purpose: the sure knowledge that the power of the United States would be directed against him if he attempted to carry out his intention of conquering the world by force. . . . At that time no representative of this government could have been authorized to intimate any such thing. . . . My mission, therefore, was a forlorn hope.❞

—quoted in *Roosevelt and Churchill*

"Peace in Our Time"

Whether or not the United States could have forced Hitler to negotiate is uncertain. By 1940 the German army had been rebuilt, and Hitler was bent on conquest. What is known is that in the years before Welles visited Europe, when the Nazi regime was

---

SECTION RESOURCES

📁 Reproducible Masters
• Reproducible Lesson Plan 19–2
• Daily Lecture and Discussion Notes 19–2
• Guided Reading Activity 19–2
• Section Quiz 19–2
• Reading Essentials and Study Guide 19–2
• Performance Assessment Activities and Rubrics

📽 Transparencies
• Daily Focus Skills Transparency 19–2

Multimedia
🔘 Interactive Tutor Self-Assessment CD-ROM
🔘 ExamView® Pro Testmaker CD-ROM
🔘 Presentation Plus! CD-ROM
🔘 TeacherWorks™ CD-ROM
🎧 Audio Program

2 TEACH

Daily Lecture and Discussion Notes 19–2

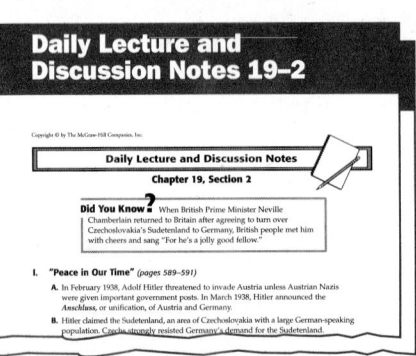

Copyright © by The McGraw-Hill Companies, Inc.

Daily Lecture and Discussion Notes

Chapter 19, Section 2

? Did You Know? When British Prime Minister Neville Chamberlain returned to Britain after agreeing to turn over Czechoslovakia's Sudetenland to Germany, British people met him with cheers and sang "For he's a jolly good fellow."

I.   **"Peace in Our Time"** *(pages 589–591)*
   A. In February 1938, Adolf Hitler threatened to invade Austria unless Austrian Nazis were given important government posts. In March 1938, Hitler announced the *Anschluss*, or unification, of Austria and Germany.
   B. Hitler claimed the Sudetenland, an area of Czechoslovakia with a large German-speaking population. Czechs strongly resisted Germany's demand for the Sudetenland.

Reading Strategy

Organizing Information Have the students make a list of the regions or countries that Germany annexed or invaded between 1935 and 1941. *(Rhineland, Austria, Sudetenland, Czechoslovakia, Polish Corridor, Poland, Norway, Denmark, the Netherlands, Belgium, Luxembourg, France)* Ask students what some of the motivations were for expanding the territory. *(Answers will vary but should include the unification of German-speaking peoples, lebensraum, and access to more natural resources.)* **L1**

FYI

The Baltic city of Gdansk (Danzig in German) has alternated through its history between being a politically free city, or part of Poland or German-speaking Prussia. It was a part of Prussia until the Treaty of Versailles, when it became a free city again. Identification with Germany has been strong however. In the 1930s, Nazi officials were voted into the majority of the city assembly. Gunter Grass writes of this era in his book *The Tin Drum.*

Appeasement in Action At Munich in September 1938, Mussolini (second from left), Britain's Neville Chamberlain (left), and Hitler (second from right) were among those deciding Czechoslovakia's fate.

much weaker, European leaders did not try to stop Hitler. Instead, they vainly tried to buy peace by giving in to his demands.

Europe's leaders had several reasons for believing—or wanting to believe—that Hitler could be satisfied and war avoided. First, the shadow of World War I loomed large, making many leaders fearful of another bloody conflict. Second, some thought Hitler's demand that all German-speaking regions of Europe be united with Germany was reasonable. Third, many people assumed that the Nazis would be more interested in peace once they gained more territory.

The Austrian *Anschluss* Hitler's first demands concerned Austria and Czechoslovakia. In late 1937 Hitler stepped up his call for the unification of all German-speaking people, including those in Austria and Czechoslovakia. Seizing Austria and Czechoslovakia would also gain food supplies, defensible frontiers, and soldiers for Germany. Hitler believed that Germany could only expand its territory by "resort[ing] to force with its attendant risks."

In February 1938 Hitler threatened to invade German-speaking Austria, his native land, unless Austrian Nazis were given important government posts. Austria's chancellor quickly gave in to this demand. Several weeks later, the chancellor tried to put the matter of unification with Germany to a democratic vote. Fearing the outcome, Hitler sent troops into Austria in March and announced the *Anschluss,* or unification, of Austria and Germany.

The Munich Crisis and Appeasement Shortly after Germany annexed Austria, Hitler announced German claims to the Sudetenland, an area of Czechoslovakia with a large German-speaking

590 CHAPTER 19 A World in Flames

population. Since Austrians shared a common culture and language with Germany, many people had accepted the *Anschluss.* In Czechoslovakia, on the other hand, people spoke several different languages. In addition, while Austria had an authoritarian government, Czechoslovakia was a democracy. Furthermore, Austria had no allies to help it defend itself, but Czechoslovakia was allied with France and the Soviet Union.

The Czechs strongly resisted Germany's demands for the Sudetenland. France threatened to fight if Germany attacked, and the Soviet Union also promised assistance. British prime minister **Neville Chamberlain** publicly promised to support France, Britain's ally.

To prevent another war, representatives of Britain, France, Italy, and Germany agreed to meet in Munich to decide Czechoslovakia's fate. At the Munich Conference on September 29, 1938, Britain and France agreed to Hitler's demands, a policy that came to be known as appeasement. Appeasement is the policy of giving concessions in exchange for peace. Supporters of appeasement mistakenly believed that Hitler had a few limited demands. They felt that if they gave Hitler what he wanted, he would be satisfied and war would be avoided. Czechoslovakia was informed that it must give up the Sudetenland or fight Germany on its own.

Chamberlain had gambled that sacrificing part of Czechoslovakia would satisfy Hitler. He also knew that Britain's military was not ready for war, so he was buying time. When Chamberlain returned home he promised "a peace with honor . . . peace in our time," but he also began to speed up British rearmament.

The following March, in brazen violation of the Munich agreement, Germany sent troops into Czechoslovakia and broke up the country. Slovakia became independent in name, but it was actually a satellite state under German control. The Czech lands became a German protectorate.

Danzig and the Polish Corridor After the Munich conference, Hitler turned his sights on Poland. In October 1938 he demanded the return of Danzig, a Baltic Sea port with strong German roots, to German control. Although Danzig was more than 90 percent German, it had been separated from Germany at the end of World War I to give Poland access to the sea. Hitler also requested a highway and railroad across the Polish Corridor, which separated western Germany from the German state of East Prussia.

Hitler's demands on Poland convinced the British and French that appeasement had failed. On March 31,

Reading Strategy   READING THE TEXT

Sequencing Information As students read through the section, ask them to create a time line that includes the following information: the Austrian *Anschluss,* the Munich Conference, the Nazi-Soviet Nonaggression Pact, the invasion of Poland, the invasion of France, and the evacuation of Dunkirk. Have students include an explanation of how each event contributed to the official beginning of World War II. **L1**

☛ Refer to *Inclusion for the High School Social Studies Classroom Strategies and Activities* in the TCR.

1939, the British announced that if Poland went to war to defend its territory, Britain and France would come to its aid. This encouraged the Polish government to refuse Hitler's demands.

In May 1939, Hitler ordered the German army to prepare to invade Poland. He also ordered his foreign minister to begin negotiations with the USSR. If Germany was going to fight Britain and France, Hitler did not want to have to fight the Soviets too.

The Nazi-Soviet Nonaggression Pact When German officials proposed a nonaggression treaty to the Soviets, Stalin agreed. He believed the best way to protect the USSR was to turn the capitalist nations against each other. If the treaty worked, Germany would go to war against Britain and France, and the USSR would be safe.

On August 23, 1939, Germany and the USSR signed the nonaggression pact. The Nazi-Soviet pact shocked the world. Communism and Nazism were supposed to be totally opposed to each other. Leaders in Britain and France understood, however,

that Hitler had made the deal to free himself for war against their countries and Poland. What they did not know was that the treaty also contained a secret deal between Germany and the Soviet Union to divide Poland between them.

✓ **Reading Check** **Explaining** What were three reasons European leaders agreed to a policy of appeasement?

The War Begins

On September 1, 1939, Germany invaded Poland from the west, and soon after the Soviets invaded from the east. On September 3, Britain and France declared war on Germany, marking the start of World War II.

Blitzkrieg in Poland Poland bravely resisted Germany's onslaught, but to no avail. The Germans used a new type of warfare called blitzkrieg, or lightning war. Blitzkrieg used large numbers of massed tanks to break through and rapidly encircle enemy

NATIONAL GEOGRAPHIC

Axis Expansion, 1935–1941 In Motion

Axis nations
Axis satellite states
Axis conquests
Allied control
Neutral countries
→ Axis advance
— International boundary, Jan. 1938
⌇⌇ Maginot Line

0   500 miles
0   500 kilometers
Lambert Azimuthal Equal-Area projection

Geography Skills

1. **Interpreting Maps** Satellite states were independent in name, but they were under German control. What was the French satellite state called?
2. **Applying Geography Skills** Why was Czechoslovakia physically in danger once the *Anschluss* took place?

L1/ELL

Guided Reading Activity 19–2

Name _____ Date _____ Class _____

★ Guided Reading Activity 19-2

DIRECTIONS: Filling in the Blanks In the space provided, write the word or words that best complete the sentence. Refer to your textbook to fill in the blanks.

1. Hitler sent troops into Austria in March 1938, and announced the _____ or _____ of Austria and Germany.
2. _____ is the policy of giving concessions in exchange for peace.
3. At the _____, Czechoslovakia's leaders were informed that they must give up the _____ or fight Germany on their own.
4. Hitler's demands on Poland convinced the _____ and _____ that appeasement had failed.
5. When German officials proposed a _____ to the Soviets, Stalin agreed.
6. The Germans used a new type of warfare called _____, or lightning war.

✓ **Reading Check**

Answer: wished to avoid war; the goal of unifying German-speaking regions seemed reasonable; thought the Nazis would be more interested in peace once they acquired more territory

Expressing an Opinion Ask students to reread this section and assess whether appeasement was justified. **L2**

Geography Skills

Answers:
1. Vichy
2. It was nearly surrounded by Germany and German-controlled Austria.

Geography Skills Practice
Ask: Why was Hitler interested in negotiating the nonaggression pact with the USSR before invading Poland? *(Germany did not want to fight a war on its eastern and western fronts simultaneously.)*

DIFFERENTIATED INSTRUCTION

Verbal/Linguistic Have students imagine that they are newspaper editors in London at the time of the Munich crisis. Have students write an editorial supporting or opposing Neville Chamberlain's actions, especially his agreement to the policy of appeasement. Have students review newspaper editorials for proper style. **L2**

📁 Refer to *Inclusion for the High School Social Studies Classroom Strategies and Activities* in the TCR.

Creating a Thematic Map Have students research and map the Maginot Line and the Siegfried Line. During World War II the Siegfried Line was a defensive line in western Germany along the border between Germany and France. Ask the students to discover when the plan was put forward and by whom, what was proposed, why more of the planned fortifications were not built, and why, ultimately, the line did not achieve its purpose.

 Use the rubric for creating a map, display, or chart on pages 65–66 in the *Performance Assessment Activities and Rubrics.*

FYI

At the time of the invasion, the Polish military consisted of outdated infantry and horse cavalry. They were ineffectual against the 1,500 planes, including *Stuka* dive bombers, and the panzers, or German tanks. Also, they were not prepared for their invaders, whom Hitler had instructed to "close their hearts to pity."

Fact | Fiction | Folklore

Despite the success of the evacuation of Dunkirk, Churchill warned Parliament, "Wars are not won by evacuations."

positions. Supporting the tanks were waves of aircraft that bombed enemy positions and dropped paratroopers to cut their supply lines. Blitzkrieg depended on radios to coordinate the tanks and aircraft. The Polish army was unable to cope with the German attack. On September 27, the Polish capital of Warsaw fell to the Germans. By October 5, 1939, the Polish army had been defeated.

GEOGRAPHY

The Fall of France In contrast to the war in Poland, western Europe remained eerily quiet. The Germans referred to this situation as the *sitzkrieg*, or sitting war. The British called it the "Bore War," while American newspapers nicknamed it the "Phony War." The British had sent troops to France, but both countries remained on the defensive, waiting for the Germans to attack.

After World War I, the French had built a line of concrete bunkers and fortifications called the **Maginot Line** along the German border. Rather than risk their troops by attacking, the French preferred to wait behind the Maginot Line for the Germans to approach. Unfortunately, this decision allowed Germany to concentrate on Poland first before turning west to face the British and French.

After taking Poland, Hitler and his generals decided to attack Norway and Denmark before invading France. Germany's industry depended on iron ore from Sweden that had to be shipped down Norway's coast part of the year. If the British sent

Fact | Fiction | Folklore

The Battle of Dunkirk Hitler's invasion of Poland fueled the fears of Americans who preferred not to become involved in Europe's conflict. In contrast, the evacuation from Dunkirk less than a year later generated very different reactions. For example, soon after the evacuation, the *New York Times* wrote:

❝So long as the English tongue survives, the word Dunkirk will be spoken with reverence. For in that harbor, in such a hell as never blazed on earth before, at the end of a lost battle, the rages and blemishes that have hidden the soul of democracy fell away. There, beaten but unconquered, in shining splendor, she faced the enemy.❞

Indeed, the Battle of Dunkirk would soon help to lift the United States out of its isolationism.

592 CHAPTER 19 A World in Flames

troops to Norway, they could block the iron shipments. On April 9, 1940, the attack began, and within a month, Germany controlled both countries.

With his northern flank secure, Hitler turned his attention to France. Hitler planned to go around the Maginot Line, which protected France's border with Germany but not France's border with Belgium and Luxembourg. To get around the Maginot Line, the Germans would have to invade the Netherlands, Belgium, and Luxembourg first—which is exactly what they did. On May 10, Hitler launched a new blitzkrieg in the west. While German troops parachuted into the Netherlands, an army of tanks rolled into Belgium and Luxembourg.

The British and French had expected the German attack. As soon as it began, British and French forces raced north into Belgium. This was a mistake. Instead of sending their tanks through the open countryside of central Belgium, the Germans sent their main force through the Ardennes Mountains of Luxembourg and eastern Belgium. The French did not think that large numbers of tanks could move through the mountains, and they had left only a few troops to defend that part of the border. The Germans easily smashed through the French lines, then raced west across northern France to the English Channel. The British and French armies were still in Belgium and could not move back into France quickly enough. They were now trapped in Belgium.

The Miracle at Dunkirk After trapping the Allied forces in Belgium, the Germans began to drive them toward the English Channel. The only hope for Britain and France was to evacuate their surviving troops by sea, but the Germans had captured all but one port, **Dunkirk,** a small town in northern France near the Belgian border.

As German forces closed in on Dunkirk, Hitler suddenly ordered them to stop. No one is sure why he gave this order. Historians know that Hitler was nervous about risking his tank forces, and he wanted to wait until more infantry arrived. Hermann Goering, the head of the German air force, was also assuring Hitler that aircraft alone could destroy the trapped soldiers. There is also some evidence that Hitler thought that the British would be more willing to accept peace if the Germans did not humiliate them by destroying their forces at Dunkirk.

Whatever Hitler's reasons, his order provided a three-day delay. This gave the British time to strengthen their lines and begin the evacuation. Some 850 ships of all sizes, from navy warships to small sailboats operated by civilian volunteers, headed to

INTERDISCIPLINARY CONNECTIONS ACTIVITY

Literature Locate a copy of Paul Gallico's short story *The Snow Goose.* The story describes how a disabled man in England was able to help with the evacuation of Dunkirk. Read the story to the students. Ask them to prepare a written response describing how the story made them feel and why they think that so many citizens wanted to find a way to contribute to the war effort. L3

NATIONAL GEOGRAPHIC

MOMENT IN HISTORY

NEVER GIVE IN

Few photographs capture the British resolve to keep a stiff upper lip better than this one. Night after night between September 1940 and May 1941, German warplanes rained bombs on London, Coventry, and other British cities. The attacks were intended to destroy British morale and war production, but Royal Air Force pilots shot down bombers faster than Germany could replace them. Plucky British civilians, like this milkman making his rounds through a debris-strewn London street, remained determined to carry on as usual each morning.

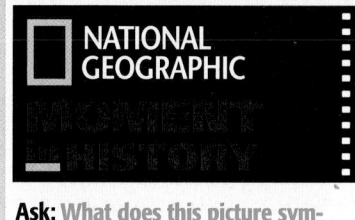

NATIONAL GEOGRAPHIC

Ask: What does this picture symbolize? *(British determination to live their usual lives despite the war)*

3 ASSESS

Assign Section 2 Assessment as homework or as an in-class activity.

◗ Have students use the **Interactive Tutor Self-Assessment CD-ROM.**

L1/ELL

Reading Essentials and Study Guide 19–2

Study Guide
Chapter 19, Section 2
For use with textbook pages 589–594
WORLD WAR II BEGINS

KEY TERMS AND NAMES
Anschluss the unification of Austria and Germany (page 590)
appeasement giving concessions in exchange for peace (page 590)
blitzkrieg lightning war (page 591)
Maginot Line a line of bunkers and fortifications built by the French along the German border (page 592)
Winston Churchill prime minister of Great Britain (page 593)
Battle of Britain an all-out German air attack against the British Royal Air Force (page 594)

L2

Section Quiz 19–2

★ **Chapter 19**   Score

Section Quiz 19-2

DIRECTIONS: Matching Match each item in Column A with the items in Column B. Write the correct letters in the blanks. *(10 points each)*

Column A
____ 1. lightning war
____ 2. unification
____ 3. a line of concrete bunkers and fortifications built by the French along the German border
____ 4. the policy of giving concessions in exchange for peace
____ 5. a Polish port with strong German roots

Column B
A. blitzkrieg
B. Danzig
C. Maginot Line
D. appeasement
E. *Anschluss*

DIRECTIONS: Multiple Choice In the blank at the left, write the letter of the choice that best completes the statement or answers the question. *(10 points each)*

Dunkirk from England. The British had hoped to rescue about 45,000 troops. Instead, when the evacuation ended on June 4, an estimated 338,000 British and French troops had been saved. This stunning success led British newspapers to refer to the evacuation as the "Miracle at Dunkirk."

The evacuation had its price, however. Almost all of the British army's equipment remained at Dunkirk—90,000 rifles, 7,000 tons of ammunition, and 120,000 vehicles. If Hitler invaded Britain, it would be almost impossible to stop him from conquering the country.

Three weeks later, on June 22, 1940, Hitler accepted the French surrender in the same railway car in which the Germans had surrendered at the end of World War I. Germany now occupied much of northern France and its Atlantic coastline. To govern the rest of the country, Germany installed a puppet government at the town of Vichy and made Marshal Philippe Pétain the new government's figurehead leader. Pétain predicted that Britain "will have her neck wrung like a chicken."

☑ **Reading Check** **Summarizing** Why was Germany able to overtake Poland?

Britain Remains Defiant

Neither Pétain nor Adolf Hitler anticipated the bravery of the British people or the spirit of their leader, **Winston Churchill,** who had replaced Neville Chamberlain as prime minister. Hitler fully expected the British to negotiate peace after France surrendered. For Winston Churchill, however, peace was not an option. The war was a fight to defend civilization. On June 4, 1940, Churchill delivered a defiant speech in Parliament, intended not only to rally the British people but to alert the isolationist United States to Britain's plight:

❝Even though large tracts of Europe have fallen . . . we shall not flag or fail. . . . We shall defend our island, whatever the cost may be, we shall fight on the beaches, we shall fight on the landing grounds, we shall fight in the fields and in the streets, we shall fight in the hills; we shall never surrender.❞

—quoted in *Freedom from Fear*

When Hitler realized that Britain would not surrender, he ordered his commanders to prepare to invade. Only the choppy waters of the narrow

CHAPTER 19 A World in Flames **593**

CRITICAL THINKING ACTIVITY

Analyzing Consequences Have students reexamine the photo on page 593. Ask students to explain what the German goal was in bombing civilian targets. *(to demoralize resistance)* Then ask students to explain why they think British resolve was actually strengthened as a result of the bombings. Ask students to suggest other factors that might influence a population's response to aerial attacks on civilians. **L2**

☑ **Reading Check**

Answer: Germans used a new type of warfare, the *blitzkrieg,* that used large numbers of tanks, infantry, and air power in a coordinated attack.

FYI

During the bombing of Great Britain from August 1940 to May 1941, large areas of London and the entire city of Coventry were reduced to rubble.

Reteach

Have students explain why Hitler was able to take over Austria and Czechoslovakia.

Enrich

Invite interested students to create a model depicting the evacuation of Dunkirk. Encourage students to use library and Internet resources for this project.

✔ **Reading Check**

Answer: Germany had few transport ships to send troops across the English Channel; the British had developed radar.

Study Central™ provides summaries, interactive games, and online graphic organizers to help students review section content.

4 CLOSE

Summarize with the class the content of the section by creating a time line of the major events.

594

Picturing **History**

Never Surrender Hitler ordered Nazi aircraft to bomb British cities, intending to weaken the people's will. Though shaken, the British, like the dome of St. Paul's Cathedral (right), stood firm. What technology allowed the outnumbered Royal Air Force to resist the German *Luftwaffe*?

English Channel separated Britain from Germany's powerful army, but getting across the Channel posed a major challenge. Germany had few transport ships, and the British air force would sink them if they tried to land troops in England. To invade, therefore, Germany first had to defeat the British air force.

In June 1940, the German air force, called the *Luftwaffe*, began to attack British shipping in the English Channel. Then, in mid-August, the *Luftwaffe* launched an all-out air battle to destroy the British Royal Air Force. This air battle, which lasted into the fall of 1940, became known as the **Battle of Britain.**

On August 23, German bombers accidentally bombed London, the British capital. This attack on civilians enraged the British, who responded by bombing Berlin the following night. For the first time in the war, bombs fell on the German capital. Infuriated, Hitler ordered the *Luftwaffe* to stop its attacks on British military targets and to concentrate on bombing London.

Hitler's goal now was to terrorize the British people into surrendering. The British people endured, however, hiding out in the city's subway tunnels whenever German bombers appeared.

Although the Royal Air Force was greatly outnumbered, the British had one major advantage. They had developed a new technology called radar. Using radar stations placed along their coast, the British were able to detect incoming German aircraft and direct British fighters to intercept them.

Day after day, the British fighters inflicted more losses on the Germans than they suffered. The skill of a few hundred pilots saved Britain from invasion. Praising the pilots, Churchill told Parliament, "Never in the field of human conflict was so much owed by so many to so few." On October 12, 1940, Hitler cancelled the invasion of Britain.

✔ **Reading Check** **Evaluating** Why was Britain able to resist Hitler and the Nazis?

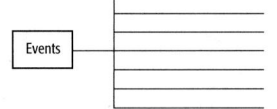
Study Central™ To review this section, go to **tarvol2.glencoe.com** and click on **Study Central™.**

SECTION 2 ASSESSMENT

Checking for Understanding

1. **Define:** appeasement, blitzkrieg.
2. **Identify:** *Anschluss,* Maginot Line, Winston Churchill, Battle of Britain.
3. **Explain** why Hitler was able to take over Austria and Czechoslovakia.

Reviewing Themes

4. **Continuity and Change** How did the policy of appeasement affect France and Great Britain?

Critical Thinking

5. **Evaluating** Why were the British able to prevent the Germans from invading their country?
6. **Organizing** Use a graphic organizer similar to the one below to list the early events of the war in Poland and western Europe.

   Events ─┬──────────
          ├──────────
          ├──────────
          └──────────

Analyzing Visuals

7. **Analyzing Photographs** Study the photographs on pages 593 and 594. How do they reflect the British resolve to "never surrender"?

Writing About History

8. **Expository Writing** Using library or Internet resources, find more information on the German annexation of Czechoslovakia. Use the information to write a report detailing the events leading up to and including the annexation. Share your report with the class.

594 CHAPTER 19 A World in Flames

SECTION 2 ASSESSMENT ANSWERS

1. Terms are in blue.
2. *Anschluss* (p. 590), Maginot Line (p. 592), Winston Churchill (p. 593), Battle of Britain (p. 594)
3. Britain and France gave in to Hitler's demands.
4. France was not prepared for German attack; Britain left to fight alone

5. Britain was an island, with a strong air force, navy, and radar stations.
6. Germany and Soviets invade Poland; Britain and France enter the war; Germany invades Norway, Denmark, Belgium, the Netherlands, Luxembourg, and France

7. shows British desire to continue with their daily routines and activities in spite of devastation
8. Reports should include details about the political and social structure of Czechoslovakia before the annexation.

SECTION 3 The Holocaust

Guide to Reading

Main Idea
The Nazis believed Jews to be subhuman. They steadily increased their persecution of Jews and eventually set up death camps and tried to kill all the Jews in Europe.

Key Terms and Names
Holocaust, Shoah, Nuremberg Laws, Wannsee Conference, concentration camp, extermination camp

Reading Strategy
Organizing As you read about the Holocaust, complete a graphic organizer similar to the one below by listing examples of Nazi persecution of German Jews.

Examples of Persecution

Reading Objectives
• **Describe** Nazi prejudices against Jews and early persecution of German Jews.
• **Explain** the methods Hitler used to try to exterminate Europe's Jewish population.

Section Theme
Civic Rights and Responsibilities The Nazis systematically deprived Jews of their rights, while other nations refused to accept many Jewish refugees.

Preview of Events

◆1933   ◆1936   ◆1939   ◆1942

Autumn 1935
Nuremberg Laws deprive German Jews of citizenship

November 1938
Anti-Jewish violence erupts during *Kristallnacht*

June 1939
SS *St. Louis* denied permission to dock in the United States

January 1942
Nazis' Wannsee Conference determines "final solution" for Jews

---

★ An American Story ★

Mira Ryczke

Mira Ryczke was born in 1923 to a middle-class Jewish family in Danzig, Poland, a port on the Baltic Sea. After World War II broke out in September 1939, the Nazis expelled Danzig's Jews to Warsaw, where they were forced to live in deplorable conditions in a special area known as the Warsaw ghetto. In 1943 the Nazis emptied the Warsaw ghetto. The Ryczkes had to ride for three days in a suffocating cattle car headed for Auschwitz, the infamous Nazi death camp, and its neighboring camp of Birkenau.

After arriving at the camps, the terrified newcomers learned that a selection was to take place. When 20-year-old Mira asked what the selection was for, an old-time prisoner pointed to chimneys on top of a building and replied, "Selected for the gas chambers to go up in smoke." Mira later wrote:

❝[W]e were told by the old-timers to try to look strong, healthy, and to walk in an upright position when our turn came. . . . Because the women I was with were young, only a few were taken out. Their numbers, tattooed on their left arms, were written down by the SS, and after a few days during roll call, their tattoo numbers were called out and these women were marched to the gas chamber.❞

—quoted in *Echoes from the Holocaust*

Nazi Persecution of the Jews

Mira Ryczke and her family were only a few of the millions of Jews who suffered terrible persecution before and during World War II. During the Holocaust, the catastrophe that ravaged Europe's Jews, the Nazis killed nearly 6 million Jews. The Nazis also killed

CHAPTER 19   A World in Flames   **595**

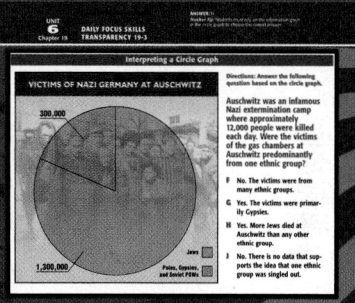

2 TEACH

Daily Lecture and Discussion Notes 19-3

Profiles IN HISTORY

Background: Because they were persecuted in Germany, a number of brilliant Jewish German scientists immigrated to the United States in the 1930s.

Ask: When and why did Einstein leave Germany? *(in 1933 when Hitler became chancellor; Hitler's policies were anti-Semitic)*

Discussing a Topic Ask students to discuss how a dictator acquires and maintains power, for example, by promising security and threatening violence. **L1**

ABCNEWS INTERACTIVE™

VIDEOCASSETTE
Historic America Electronic Field Trips

View **Tape 2, Chapter 9:** "The Holocaust Museum."

Profiles IN HISTORY

Albert Einstein
1879–1955

Among the Jews who left Nazi Germany in the early 1930s was Albert Einstein, whose brilliant scientific theories revolutionized physics. Einstein gained international fame in 1919 when the Royal Society of London announced that calculations had supported his general theory of relativity. Einstein's fame increased after he won the Nobel Prize for Physics in 1921. Lecture invitations poured in from around the world.

Einstein never actively practiced Judaism, but he did proudly identify himself as a Jew. As anti-Semitism took hold in Germany, Einstein's worldwide fame contrasted with the insults he faced in Berlin for practicing "Bolshevism [Communism] in physics." His public support for Zionism, the right of Jews to settle in Palestine (later Israel), aroused further anger among Nazis.

Soon after Hitler became Germany's chancellor in 1933, Einstein renounced his citizenship and left Germany for Belgium. Fears for his life prompted friends to take him secretly by private yacht to England. He later settled in Princeton, New Jersey.

A pacifist who had opposed World War I, Einstein ironically saw his scientific ideas applied to the creation of a powerful and destructive weapon, the atomic bomb. After the United States detonated the first atomic bomb in combat over Hiroshima, Japan, in 1945, Einstein devoted his final years to promoting pacifism. The scientist's greatest legacy, however, would be the revolutionary scientific discoveries he had made in the early 1900s. As Einstein himself had observed, "Politics are for the moment. An equation is for eternity."

---

millions of people from other groups they considered inferior. The Hebrew term for the Holocaust is **Shoah,** meaning "catastrophe," but it is often used specifically to refer to the Nazi campaign to exterminate the Jews during World War II.

Nazi Ideology Once the Nazis took power in Germany, they acted swiftly to implement the political racial policies Hitler had outlined in *Mein Kampf.* Although the Nazis persecuted anyone who dared oppose them, as well as the disabled, Gypsies, homosexuals, and Slavic peoples, they reserved their strongest hatred for the Jews. This loathing went far beyond the European anti-Semitism common at the time. Over the centuries, people who were prejudiced against Jews had put down Jewish religious practices and discriminated against Jews in many ways. For example, Jews were sometimes segregated in ghettos or prohibited from owning land. For the Nazis, however, all Jewish

people were evil no matter what their religion, occupation, or education.

The Nuremberg Laws After the Nazis took power, they quickly moved to deprive German Jews of many rights that all citizens had long taken for granted. In September 1935 the **Nuremberg Laws** took citizenship away from Jewish Germans and banned marriage between Jews and other Germans. Two months later, another decree defined a Jew as a person with at least one Jewish grandparent and prohibited Jews from holding public office or voting. Other laws forbade Jews from employing female German servants under age 35 and compelled Jews with German-sounding names to adopt "Jewish" names. Soon the passports of Jews were marked with a red "J" to clearly identify them as Jewish.

By the summer of 1936, at least half of Germany's Jews were jobless, having lost the right to work as civil servants, journalists, farmers, teachers, and actors. In 1938 the Nazis also banned Jews from practicing law and medicine and from operating businesses. With no source of income, life became very difficult.

Despite worsening conditions, many Jews chose to remain in Germany during the early years of Nazi rule. Well integrated into German society before this time, they were reluctant to leave and give up the lives they had built there. Many also thought that conditions would surely improve after a time. In fact, they soon became worse.

Kristallnacht On November 7, 1938, a young Jewish refugee named Herschel Grynszpan shot and killed a German diplomat in Paris. Grynszpan's father and 10,000 other Jews had been deported from Germany to Poland, and the distraught young man was seeking revenge for this act and for the persecution of the Jews in general.

In retaliation for the killing, an infuriated Hitler ordered his minister of propaganda, Joseph Goebbels, to stage attacks against the Jews that would appear to be a spontaneous popular reaction to news of the murder. On the night of November 9, this plan played out in a spree of destruction.

596 CHAPTER 19 A World in Flames

COOPERATIVE LEARNING ACTIVITY

Analyzing Concepts Organize students into small groups and have them research one of the following topics: *Kristallnacht,* the Warsaw ghetto, German use of slave labor, artwork stolen from occupied countries by Germany. Have each group present their findings to the class as a panel. Each member of the group should present one aspect of the topic. When the panel is finished, they should field questions from other members of the class.

Use the rubric for a cooperative group management plan on pages 71–72 in the *Performance Assessment Activities and Rubrics.*

In Vienna a Jewish child named Frederick Morton watched in terror that night as 10 young Nazi Storm Troopers broke into his family's apartment:

> ❝They yanked out every drawer in every one of our chests and cupboards, and tossed each in the air. They let the cutlery jangle across the floor, the clothes scatter, and stepped over the mess to fling the next drawer.... 'We might be back,' the leader said. On the way out he threw our mother-of-pearl ashtray over his shoulder, like confetti. We did not speak or move or breathe until we heard their boots against the pavement.❞
>
> —quoted in *Facing History and Ourselves*

The anti-Jewish violence that erupted throughout Germany and Austria that night came to be called *Kristallnacht*, or "night of broken glass," because broken glass littered the streets afterward. When daylight came, more than 90 Jews lay dead, hundreds were badly injured, and thousands more were terrorized. The Nazis had forbidden police to interfere while roving bands of thugs destroyed 7,500 Jewish businesses and wrecked over 180 synagogues.

The lawlessness of *Kristallnacht* did not end with the dawn. Following that night of violence, the **Gestapo,** the government's secret police, arrested at least 20,000 wealthy Jews, releasing them only if they agreed to emigrate and surrender all their possessions. The state also confiscated insurance payments owed to Jewish owners of ruined businesses.

The week after *Kristallnacht*, Nazi interior minister Hermann Goering added insult to injury by fining the Jewish community to pay for the damage. "German Jewry," he proclaimed "shall, as punishment for their abominable crimes . . . have to make a contribution for one billion marks. . . . I would like to say that I would not like to be a Jew in Germany."

Jewish Refugees Try to Flee
Kristallnacht and its aftermath marked a significant escalation in the Nazi policy of persecution against the Jews. Many Jews, including Frederick Morton's family, decided that it was time to leave and fled to the United States. Between 1933, when Hitler took power, and the start of World War II in 1939, some 350,000 Jews escaped Nazi-controlled Germany. These emigrants included prominent scientists such as Albert Einstein and businesspeople like Otto Frank, who resettled his family in Amsterdam in 1933. Otto's daughter **Anne Frank** would later keep a diary of her family's life in hiding after the Nazis overran the Netherlands.

By 1938 the American consulate in Stuttgart, Germany, had a backlog of over 100,000 visa applications from Jews trying to leave Germany and come to the United States. Following the Nazi *Anschluss,* 3,000 Austrian Jews each day applied for American visas. Many never received visas to the United States

The Final Solution

Before the war, a Jewish family in Germany poses for a photograph during a family outing. Few members of this family would survive the war.

On *Kristallnacht,* roaming bands of thugs destroyed Jewish property and menaced Jewish families throughout Germany.

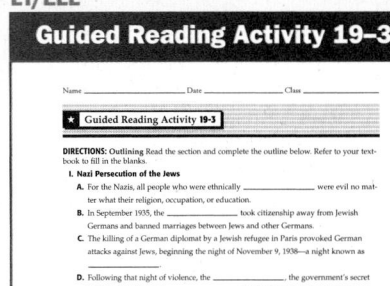

Guided Reading Activity 19–3

Name _____ Date _____ Class _____

★ Guided Reading Activity **19-3**

DIRECTIONS: Outlining Read the section and complete the outline below. Refer to your text-book to fill in the blanks.

I. Nazi Persecution of the Jews

  A. For the Nazis, all people who were ethnically _____ were evil no matter what their religion, occupation, or education.

  B. In September 1935, the _____ took citizenship away from Jewish Germans and banned marriages between Jews and other Germans.

  C. The killing of a German diplomat by a Jewish refugee in Paris provoked German attacks against Jews, beginning the night of November 9, 1938—a night known as _____.

  D. Following that night of violence, the _____, the government's secret police, arrested around _____ wealthy Jews, releasing them only if

Creating a Thematic Chart
Have students use the information presented in this section, including the maps, to create a chart to illustrate the following: the number of Jews who fled Germany from 1933 to 1939, the number of immigrants allowed to enter the U.S. each year, the number of Jews killed at Auschwitz, and the number of Jews killed in Europe. Encourage students to create visuals that reflect the statistics for the map. **L2**

📂 Use the rubric for creating a map, display, or chart on pages 65–66 in the *Performance Assessment Activities and Rubrics.*

Complete Destruction *Holocaust* means a sacrifice consumed by fire, especially a complete or thorough sacrifice or destruction.

DIFFERENTIATED INSTRUCTION

Logical/Mathematical Have students examine the effects of propaganda by selecting a major war in American history and examining the positive and negative roles of propaganda. To report their findings, have students create a chart that shows benefits and drawbacks of propaganda, listing examples of each classification. **L2**

📂 Refer to *Inclusion for the High School Social Studies Classroom Strategies and Activities* in the TCR.

Creating a Chart Have students work in pairs to prepare a chart that compares the United States Bill of Rights and the rights that Nazis denied the Jews. Use the charts as a basis for a class discussion about the effects of Nazi rule on the Jews. **L2**

📁 Use the rubric for creating a map, display, or chart on pages 65–66 in the *Performance Assessment Activities and Rubrics.*

CURRICULUM CONNECTION

World History In addition to the Jews, millions of others were exterminated by the Nazis. To learn more about how the Poles were treated by the Nazis, read *Forgotten Holocaust: The Poles Under German Occupation, 1934–1944,* by R. C. Lukas (Lexington, Kentucky, 1986).

✓ Reading Check

Answer: Jews remained because of restrictions on immigration to other countries, because they thought conditions would improve, because Germany was their home, or because they either had no money or their savings would be lost if they emigrated.

or to the other countries where they applied. As a result, millions of Jews remained trapped in Nazi-dominated Europe.

Several factors limited Jewish immigration to the United States. First, Nazi orders prohibited Jews from taking more than about four dollars out of Germany. Second, many countries refused to accept Jewish immigrants. In the United States, laws restricted granting a visa to anyone "likely to become a public charge." American customs officials tended to assume that this applied to Jews since Germany had forced them to leave any wealth behind. High unemployment rates in the 1930s also made immigration politically unpopular. Few Americans wanted to raise immigration quotas, even to accommodate European refugees. The existing immigration policy allowed only a total of 150,000 immigrants annually, with a fixed quota from each country. The law permitted no exceptions for refugees or victims of persecution.

At an international conference on refugees in 1938, several European countries, the United States, and Latin America stated their regret that they could not take in more of Germany's Jews without raising their immigration quotas. Meanwhile, Nazi propaganda chief Joseph Goebbels announced that "if there is any country that believes it has not enough Jews, I shall gladly turn over to it all our Jews." Hitler also declared himself "ready to put all these criminals at the disposal of these countries . . . even on luxury ships."

As war loomed in 1939, many ships departed from Germany crammed with Jews desperate to escape. Some of their visas, however, had been forged or sold illegally, and Mexico, Paraguay, Argentina, and Costa Rica all denied access to Jews with such documents. So too did the United States.

On May 27, 1939, the **SS St. Louis** entered the harbor in Havana, Cuba, with 930 Jewish refugees on board. Most of these passengers hoped to go to the United States eventually, but they had certificates improperly issued by Cuba's director of immigration giving them permission to land in Cuba. When the ships arrived in Havana, the Cuban government, partly in response to anti-Semitic sentiment stirred up by Nazi propaganda, revoked the certificates and refused to let the refugees come ashore. For several days, the ship's captain steered his ship in circles off the coast of Florida, awaiting official permission to dock at a United States port. Denied such permission, the ship turned back toward Europe on June 6. The forlorn passengers finally disembarked in France, Holland, Belgium, and Great Britain. Within two years, the first three of these countries fell under Nazi domination. Many of the refugees brought to these countries aboard the SS *St. Louis* perished in the Nazis' "final solution."

✓ **Reading Check** **Analyzing** Why did many Jews remain in Germany even though they were persecuted?

After the war broke out, the Nazis methodically deprived Jews of their rights, confining many to overcrowded ghettos. After weeks of fierce resistance, Jews in the Warsaw ghetto were rounded up for deportation to concentration camps in May 1943.

INTERDISCIPLINARY CONNECTIONS ACTIVITY

Current Events Journalist C.L. Sulzberger reported that after General Eisenhower first visited a concentration camp, "He cabled Washington and London to send journalists and members of Congress and Parliament to Germany as soon as possible." Eisenhower wanted no one to doubt the extent of the atrocities that had been committed. His fears have been partly justified, for today some individuals insist that the Holocaust did not take place. Have students research who has tried to deny the Holocaust and how their denials have been received. Urge students to describe the kinds of evidence that are available to determine what actually happened in the camps. **L3**

The Final Solution

On January 20, 1942, 15 Nazi leaders met at the **Wannsee Conference,** held in a Berlin suburb, to determine the "final solution of the Jewish question." Previous "solutions" had included rounding up Jews, Gypsies, and Slavs from conquered areas, shooting them, and piling them into mass graves. Another method required forcing Jews and other "undesirables" into trucks and then piping in exhaust fumes to kill them. These methods, however, had proven too slow and inefficient for the Nazis.

At Wannsee, the Nazis made plans to round up Jews from the vast areas of Nazi-controlled Europe and take them to detention centers known as concentration camps. There, healthy individuals would work as slave laborers until they dropped dead of exhaustion, disease, or malnutrition. Most others, including the elderly, the infirm, and young children, would be sent to extermination camps, attached to many of the concentration camps, to be executed in massive gas chambers.

Concentration Camps

The Nazis had established their first concentration camps in 1933 to jail political opponents. After the war began, the Nazis built concentration camps throughout Europe.

Buchenwald, one of the first and largest concentration camps, was built near the town of Weimar in Germany in 1937. During its operation, over 200,000 prisoners worked 12-hour shifts as slave laborers in nearby factories. Though Buchenwald had no gas chambers, hundreds of prisoners died there every month as a result of exhaustion and the horrible living conditions.

Leon Bass, a young American soldier, described viewing a barracks in Buchenwald at the end of the war. Built to hold 50 people, the room had housed more than 150, with bunks built almost to the ceiling. Bass recalled:

> ❝I looked at a bottom bunk and there I saw one man. He was too weak to get up; he could just barely turn his head. He was skin and bones. He looked like a skeleton; and his eyes were deep set. He didn't utter a sound; he just looked at me with those eyes, and they still haunt me today.❞
>
> —quoted in *Facing History and Ourselves*

Extermination Camps

After the Wannsee Conference, the Nazis built extermination facilities in a number of the concentration camps, mostly in Poland, to kill Jews more efficiently. At these camps, including the infamous Treblinka and Auschwitz, Jews were the Nazis' main victims. **Auschwitz** alone housed about 100,000 people in 300 prison barracks. Its gas chambers, built to kill 2,000 people at a time, sometimes gassed 12,000 people in a day. Of the

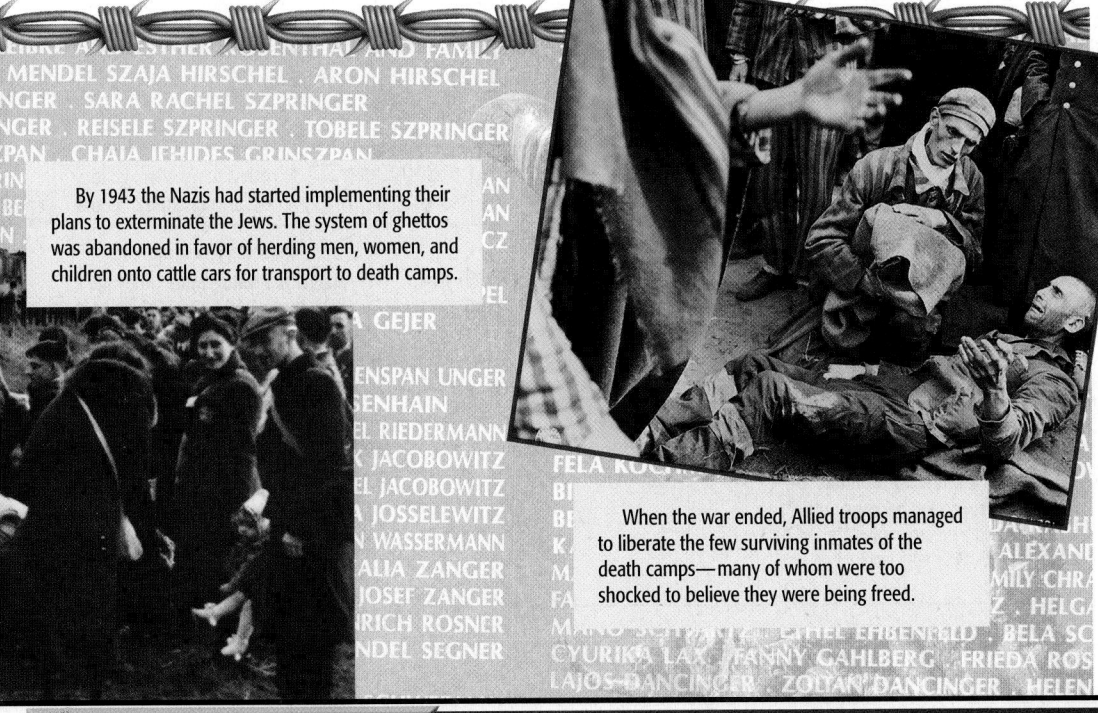

By 1943 the Nazis had started implementing their plans to exterminate the Jews. The system of ghettos was abandoned in favor of herding men, women, and children onto cattle cars for transport to death camps.

When the war ended, Allied troops managed to liberate the few surviving inmates of the death camps—many of whom were too shocked to believe they were being freed.

Interpreting a Map Have students locate the major concentration and extermination camps and calculate the distance of each from the nearest large city. Then ask students to discuss how residents of the cities must have reacted, what they must have known, and why they did not act to rescue the people in the camps. **L2**

3 ASSESS

Assign Section 3 Assessment as homework or as an in-class activity.

🕮 Have students use the **Interactive Tutor Self-Assessment CD-ROM.**

L1/ELL

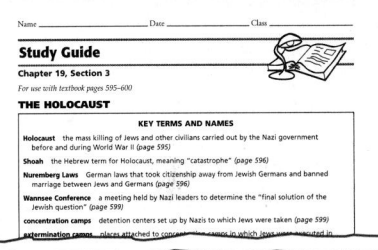

Reading Essentials and Study Guide 19–3

Name _____ Date _____ Class _____

Study Guide

Chapter 19, Section 3
For use with textbook pages 595–600

THE HOLOCAUST

KEY TERMS AND NAMES

Holocaust the mass killing of Jews and other civilians carried out by the Nazi government before and during World War II *(page 595)*

Shoah the Hebrew term for Holocaust, meaning "catastrophe" *(page 596)*

Nuremberg Laws German laws that took citizenship away from Jewish Germans and banned marriage between Jews and Germans *(page 596)*

Wannsee Conference a meeting held by Nazi leaders to determine the "final solution of the Jewish question" *(page 599)*

concentration camps detention centers set up by Nazis to which Jews were taken *(page 599)*

extermination camps places attached to concentration camps in which Jews were executed in

L2

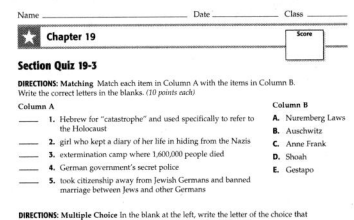

Section Quiz 19–3

Name _____ Date _____ Class _____

⭐ **Chapter 19** · · · · · · · · · · · · Score

Section Quiz 19–3

DIRECTIONS: Matching Match each item in Column A with the items in Column B. Write the correct letters in the blanks. *(10 points each)*

Column A	Column B
___ 1. Hebrew for "catastrophe" and used specifically to refer to the Holocaust	A. Nuremberg Laws
___ 2. girl who kept a diary of her life in hiding from the Nazis	B. Auschwitz
___ 3. extermination camp where 1,600,000 people died	C. Anne Frank
___ 4. German government's secret police	D. Shoah
___ 5. took citizenship away from Jewish Germans and banned marriage between Jews and other Germans	E. Gestapo

DIRECTIONS: Multiple Choice In the blank at the left, write the letter of the choice that best completes the statement or answers the question. *(10 points each)*

Reading Strategy   READING THE TEXT

Analyzing Information Tell students that wars have always involved the killing of innocent civilians. After reading the section, ask students to explain what made the killing of the Jewish people by the Nazis in World War II different. Students should use specific examples from the section to support their views. Based on the class discussion, have students write a descriptive essay that compares and contrasts the collateral killing of civilians during a war with the intentional killing of people in concentration and execution camps. **L1**

☞ Refer to *Inclusion for the High School Social Studies Classroom Strategies and Activities* in the TCR.

Geography *Skills*

Answers:

1. Poland (3 million)

2. Fascists were not as anti-Semitic as the Nazis.

Geography Skills Practice

Ask: Which of the Soviet Socialist Republics had the smallest percentage of their Jewish population killed under the Nazis? *(Russian S.S.R.)*

Reteach

Have students describe Nazi prejudice against Jews and early persecution of German Jews.

Enrich

Invite interested students to read, or reread, an excerpt from Anne Frank's diary. Ask students to share their feelings about what they read.

Reading Check

Answer: Some died of exhaustion, disease, or malnutrition in concentration camps. Others were executed in gas chambers at extermination camps.

HISTORY *Online*

Study Central™ provides summaries, interactive games, and online graphic organizers to help students review section content.

4 CLOSE

Have students summarize the gradually intensifying steps of Hitler's campaign against the Jews.

NATIONAL GEOGRAPHIC **Jewish Losses, 1939–1945** *In Motion*

DENMARK 500

Baltic Sea

BALTIC STATES 228,000

RUSSIAN S.S.R. 107,000

North Sea

NETHERLANDS 105,000

BYELORUSSIAN S.S.R. 245,000

BELGIUM 40,000

GERMANY AND AUSTRIA 210,000

POLAND 3,000,000

UKRAINIAN S.S.R. 900,000

CZECHOSLOVAKIA 155,000

FRANCE 90,000

HUNGARY 450,000

ROMANIA 300,000

ITALY 8,000

YUGOSLAVIA 26,000

Black Sea

BULGARIA 14,000

Percentage of Jewish Population Annihilated
- 83–90
- 65–77
- 50–60
- 11–26

FRANCE 90,000 **Number of Jews killed under Nazi racial policies**

GREECE 54,000

0 200 miles

0 200 kilometers

Lambert Azimuthal Equal-Area projection

Geography *Skills*

1. **Interpreting Maps** What country had the highest number of Jews in its population killed?

2. **Applying Geography Skills** A relatively low percentage of Italy's Jewish population died in the Holocaust. From this information, how would you compare Fascists and Nazis in terms of their Jewish policies?

estimated 1,600,000 people who died at Auschwitz, about 1,300,000 were Jews. The other 300,000 were Poles, Soviet prisoners-of-war, and Gypsies.

Upon arrival at Auschwitz, healthy prisoners such as Mira Ryczke were selected for slave labor. Elderly or disabled people, the sick, and mothers and children went immediately to the gas chambers, after which their bodies were burned in giant crematoriums. In her memoirs, Ryczke described "columns of people marching slowly toward the gas chambers" and "the horrible stench in the air—the smell of burning human flesh. I have never forgotten that smell."

In only a few years, Jewish culture, which had existed in Europe for over 1,000 years, had been virtually obliterated by the Nazis in the lands they conquered. Despite exhaustive debate, there is still great controversy about why and how an event so horrifying as the Holocaust could have occurred. No consensus has been reached, but most historians point to a number of factors: the German people's sense of injury after World War I; severe economic problems; Hitler's control over the German nation; the lack of a strong tradition of representative government in Germany; German fear of Hitler's secret police; and a long history of anti-Jewish prejudice and discrimination in Europe.

Reading Check **Summarizing** What methods did Hitler use to try to exterminate Europe's Jewish population?

HISTORY Online **Study Central™** To review this section, go to tarvol2.glencoe.com and click on **Study Central™**.

SECTION 3 ASSESSMENT

Checking for Understanding

1. **Define:** Holocaust, concentration camp, extermination camp.

2. **Identify:** Shoah, Nuremberg Laws, Wannsee Conference.

3. **List** the groups of people who were persecuted by the Nazis.

Reviewing Themes

4. **Civic Rights and Responsibilities** Do you think the German people or other nations could have prevented the Holocaust? Why or why not?

Critical Thinking

5. **Analyzing** What are some factors that attempt to explain the Holocaust?

6. **Organizing** Use a graphic organizer similar to the one below to list the methods used to try to exterminate Europe's Jewish population.

Extermination Methods

Analyzing Visuals

7. **Analyzing Photographs** Study the photographs of the Final Solution on pages 597–599. How do the photographs show the systematic destruction of Jewish life?

Writing About History

8. **Descriptive Writing** Take on the role of a person living in Germany during *Kristallnacht*. Write a diary entry describing the events of that night. Include a description of events during the days following *Kristallnacht* as well.

SECTION 3 ASSESSMENT ANSWERS

1. Terms are in blue.
2. Shoah *(p. 596),* Nuremberg Laws *(p. 596),* Wannsee Conference *(p. 599)*
3. Jews, disabled, Gypsies, homosexuals, Slavic peoples
4. Students' answers will vary but

should be based on reasoned argument.

5. Hitler's dictatorship, European anti-Semitism, propaganda, fear
6. gas chambers, malnutrition, untreated disease, worked to death
7. shows stages of Hitler's campaign,

from civil discrimination and violence to deportation to camps

8. Students' diary entries should focus on events surrounding *Kristallnacht,* as told from a Jewish perspective.

Guide to Reading

Main Idea
After World War II began, the United States attempted to continue its prewar policy of neutrality.

Key Terms and Names
America First Committee, Lend-Lease Act, hemispheric defense zone, Atlantic Charter, strategic materials

Reading Strategy
Organizing As you read about the efforts of the United States to stay neutral in the war, complete a graphic organizer similar to the one below by naming two events that shifted American opinion toward helping the Allies.

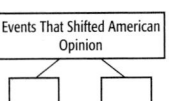
Events That Shifted American Opinion

Reading Objectives
• **Explain** how Roosevelt helped Britain while maintaining official neutrality.
• **Trace** the events that led to increasing tensions, and ultimately war, between the United States and Japan.

Section Theme
Individual Action Even while the United States was officially neutral, President Roosevelt found ways to help the British fight Germany.

Preview of Events

◆September 1940	◆March 1941	◆August 1941	◆December 1941

September 1940
FDR makes destroyers-for-bases deal with Britain

March 1941
Congress passes Lend-Lease Act

August 1941
Roosevelt and Churchill sign Atlantic Charter

October 1941
Germans sink *Reuben James*

December 7, 1941
Japan attacks Pearl Harbor

★ An American Story ★

Daniel Inouye after joining the U.S. Army's 442nd Infantry

December 7, 1941, dawned like any other Sunday in Hawaii, where teenager Daniel Inouye lived with his family. Like other Americans who lived through the experience, Inouye would never forget what he was doing the moment American isolationism ended:

❝As soon as I finished brushing my teeth and pulled on my trousers, I automatically clicked on the little radio that stood on the shelf above my bed. I remember that I was buttoning my shirt and looking out the window . . . when the hum of the warming set gave way to a frenzied voice. 'This is no test,' the voice cried out. 'Pearl Harbor is being bombed by the Japanese!'❞

The Inouye family ran outside and gazed toward the naval base at Pearl Harbor:

❝And then we saw the planes. They came zooming up out of that sea of gray smoke, flying north toward where we stood and climbing into the bluest part of the sky, and they came in twos and threes, in neat formations, and if it hadn't been for that red ball on their wings, the rising sun of the Japanese Empire, you could easily believe that they were Americans, flying over in precise military salute.❞

—quoted in *Eyewitness to America*

FDR Supports England

The Japanese attack surprised many Americans. Most people had believed that Germany posed the greatest danger. What Americans did not realize was that the causes of the Japanese attack could be traced back more than two years to President Roosevelt's policies for helping Britain against Germany.

CHAPTER 19   A World in Flames   **601**

1 FOCUS

Section Overview
This section focuses on the events that led to the United States entering World War II.

BELLRINGER
Skillbuilder Activity

Project transparency and have students answer the question.

Daily Focus Skills Transparency 19–4

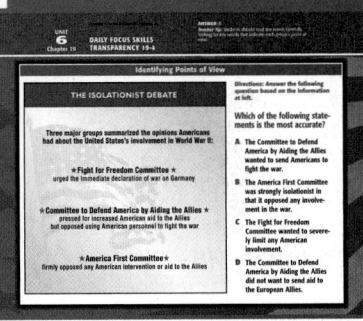

Reading Preview

Answers to Graphic: Britain's struggle with Germany, Japan's attack on Pearl Harbor

Preteaching Vocabulary
Have students write a sentence explaining the significance of each of the Key Names.

SECTION RESOURCES

📁 Reproducible Masters
• Reproducible Lesson Plan 19–4
• Daily Lecture and Discussion Notes 19–4
• Guided Reading Activity 19–4
• Section Quiz 19–4
• Reading Essentials and Study Guide 19–4

📀 Transparencies
• Daily Focus Skills Transparency 19–4

Multimedia
⊙ Interactive Tutor Self-Assessment CD-ROM
⊙ ExamView® Pro Testmaker CD-ROM
⊙ Presentation Plus! CD-ROM
⊙ TeacherWorks™ CD-ROM
⊙ Audio Program
📺 ABCNews Interactive™ Historic America Electronic Field Trips

2 TEACH

Analyzing *Political Cartoons*

Answer: instituted a cash-and-carry policy for arms sales to France and Britain; Roosevelt's destroyers-for-bases deal

Reading Check

Answer: They were adjusted to allow the United States to sell arms to warring countries as long as they paid cash and carried the goods away on their own ships.

Expressing Points of View

Organize the class into three groups representing the views in the isolationist debate. Assign one group to be the Fight for Freedom Committee, one to be the Committee to Defend America by Aiding the Allies, and one to be the America First Committee. Have each group develop a one-paragraph position statement and present it to the class. Discuss the reasons for the varying opinions as a class. **L1**

Analyzing *Political Cartoons*

Peace Above All Many Americans were willing to help European democracies but did not want to sell them arms. In what ways did the United States assist these nations?

The Neutrality Act of 1939 President Roosevelt officially proclaimed the United States neutral two days after Britain and France declared war on Germany. Despite this declaration, he was determined to do all he could to help the two countries in their struggle against Hitler. Soon after the war began, Roosevelt called Congress into a special session to revise the neutrality laws. He asked Congress to eliminate the ban on arms sales to nations at war. Public opinion strongly supported the president. Congress passed the new law, but isolationists demanded a price for the revision. Under the Neutrality Act of 1939, warring nations could buy weapons from the United States only if they paid cash and carried the arms on their own ships.

Destroyers-for-Bases Deal In the spring of 1940, the United States faced its first test in remaining neutral. In May British Prime Minister Winston Churchill began asking Roosevelt to transfer old American destroyers to Britain. Britain had lost nearly half its destroyers and needed more to protect its cargo ships from German submarines and to block any German attempt to invade Britain.

Determined to give Churchill the destroyers, Roosevelt used a loophole in the provision of the Neutrality Act that required cash for purchases. In exchange for the right to build American bases on British-controlled Newfoundland, Bermuda, and islands in the Caribbean, Roosevelt sent 50 old American destroyers to Britain. Since the deal did not involve an actual sale, the Neutrality Act did not apply. On September 3, 1940, he announced his action to an astonished press.

✓ **Reading Check** **Examining** How were the Neutrality Acts revised?

The Isolationist Debate

Widespread public acceptance of the destroyers-for-bases deal demonstrated a marked change in American public opinion. The shift began after the German invasion of France and the rescue of Allied forces at Dunkirk. By July 1940 most Americans favored offering limited aid to the Allies.

The Range of Opinion American opinion was hardly unanimous. In fact, beginning in the spring of 1940, a spirited debate took place between people who wanted greater American involvement in World War II and those who felt that the United States should remain neutral.

At one extreme was the Fight for Freedom Committee, a group which urged the repeal of all neutrality laws and wanted stronger action against Germany. Closer to the center, the Committee to Defend America by Aiding the Allies, headed by journalist William Allen White, pressed for increased American aid to the Allies but opposed armed intervention.

Roosevelt's destroyers-for-bases deal led to the founding of the **America First Committee,** a staunchly isolationist group that firmly opposed any American intervention or aid to the Allies. The group had many famous members, including aviator Charles Lindbergh, former governor Philip LaFollette, and Senator Gerald Nye.

The Election of 1940 The heated debate over neutrality took place in the midst of the 1940 presidential election campaign. For months Americans had wondered whether President Roosevelt would follow long-standing tradition by retiring at the end of his second term. With the United States in a precarious position, a change of leaders might not be in the country's best interest. Roosevelt decided to run for an unprecedented third term.

Reading Strategy ◁ READING THE TEXT

Using Context Clues Provide students with these tips to use context to determine meaning: look before, at, and after the unfamiliar word for a context clue; connect what you already know with what the author has written; predict a possible meaning; apply the meaning in the sentence; decide if the meaning makes sense; if the meaning does not make sense, try again. **L1** ELL

🡒 Refer to *Inclusion for the High School Social Studies Classroom Strategies and Activities* in the TCR.

During the campaign, FDR steered a careful course between neutrality and intervention. The Republican nominee, Wendell Willkie, did the same, promising that he too would stay out of the war but assist the Allies. The voters re-elected Roosevelt by a wide margin, preferring to stick with a president they knew during this crisis period.

✓ Reading Check **Analyzing** Why did Roosevelt win an unprecedented third term in office?

Edging Toward War

With the election safely over, Roosevelt expanded the nation's role in the war. Britain was fighting for democracy, he said, and the United States had to help. Speaking to Congress, he listed the "Four Freedoms" for which both the United States and Great Britain stood: freedom of speech, freedom of worship, freedom from want, and freedom from fear. 📖 *(See page 957 for an excerpt from this speech.)*

The Lend-Lease Act By December 1940, Great Britain had run out of funds to wage its war against Germany. President Roosevelt came up with a way to remove the cash requirement of the Neutrality Act. With the **Lend-Lease Act,** the United States would be able to lend or lease arms to any country considered "vital to the defense of the United States." This act meant that the United States could send weapons to Britain if Britain promised to return or pay rent for them after the war.

The president warned that if Britain fell, an "unholy alliance" of Germany, Japan, and Italy would keep trying to conquer the world, and then "all of us in all the Americas would be living at the point of a gun." The president argued that the United States should become the "great arsenal of democracy" to keep the British fighting and make it unnecessary for Americans to go to war.

The America First Committee disagreed, but Congress passed the Lend-Lease Act by a wide margin. By the time the program ended, the United States had contributed more than $40 billion in weapons, vehicles, and other supplies to the Allied war effort.

While shipments of supplies to Britain began at once, lend-lease aid eventually went to the Soviet Union as well. After calling off the invasion of Britain, Hitler returned to his original goal of carving out lebensraum for Germany in eastern Europe. In June 1941, in violation of the Nazi-Soviet pact, Hitler launched a massive invasion of the Soviet Union. Although Churchill detested communism and considered Stalin a harsh dictator, he vowed that any person or state "who fights against Nazism will have our aid." Roosevelt, too, supported this policy.

The Hemispheric Defense Zone Congressional approval of the Lend-Lease Act did not solve the problem of how to get American arms and supplies to Britain. German submarines patrolling the Atlantic Ocean were sinking hundreds of thousands of tons of shipping each month, and the British navy simply did not have enough ships in the Atlantic to stop them.

Roosevelt could not simply order the U.S. Navy to protect British cargo ships, since the United States was still technically neutral. Instead, he developed the idea of a hemispheric defense zone. Roosevelt declared that the entire western half of the Atlantic was part of the Western Hemisphere and therefore neutral. He then ordered the U.S. Navy to patrol the western Atlantic and reveal the location of German submarines to the British.

The Atlantic Charter In August 1941 Roosevelt and Churchill met face-to-face on board American and British warships anchored near Newfoundland. During these meetings, the two men agreed on the text of the **Atlantic Charter.** It committed the two

Picturing **History**

Neutrality Debate The America First Committee strongly opposed the increasingly weak neutrality of the United States. Here an American soldier confronts an isolationist marching outside the White House. How did the Lend-Lease Act further weaken the nation's official neutrality?

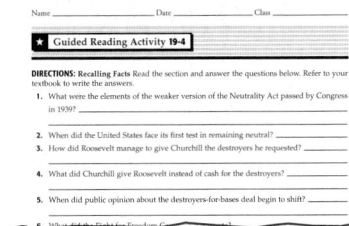
L1/ELL
Guided Reading Activity 19–4

✓ **Reading Check**

Answer: Americans wanted to stay with a president that they knew during this period of unrest.

Organizing Information Have students create a graphic to illustrate the ways America edged toward war economically and militarily. L1

FYI

Isolationist sentiment in the United States arose in part from the fact that the nation was an ocean away from the conflict in Europe and Asia.

Picturing **History**

Answer: It involved the United States in the war by lending or leasing arms to any country fighting Hitler.
Ask: What messages were protesters trying to convey? *(support for the country but not for the war)*

📁 Use *Interpreting Political Cartoons,* Cartoon 25.

DIFFERENTIATED INSTRUCTION

English Learners Help students organize events by having them make four columns on a sheet of paper and labeling them Allied Powers, Axis Powers, Axis-controlled Countries, and Neutral Countries. Students should then use the text, including maps, to identify and list the countries under the appropriate headings. L1 ELL

📁 Refer to *Inclusion for the High School Social Studies Classroom Strategies and Activities* in the TCR.

ABCNEWS INTERACTIVE™

📼 VIDEOCASSETTE
Historic America Electronic Field Trips

View **Tape 2, Chapter 8:** "The *U.S.S. Arizona* Memorial."

✓ Reading Check

Answer: by getting arms to the Allies

📖 Reading Strategy

Organizing Information Have students outline the ways Roosevelt discouraged Japan from attacking the British Empire. **L2**

CURRICULUM CONNECTION

Geography To gain direct access to natural resources, Japanese military leaders aimed to build an empire in the Pacific. The U.S. Pacific Fleet was headquartered at Oahu island in Hawaii–approximately 70 warships, including 8 battleships and 24 auxiliary vessels, were stationed at Pearl Harbor on the island. Thus, Japanese military leaders saw the fleet as an obstacle that had to be destroyed if they were to achieve their goals.

---

leaders to a postwar world of democracy, non-aggression, free trade, economic advancement, and freedom of the seas. Churchill later said that FDR pledged to "force an 'incident' . . . which would justify him in opening hostilities" with Germany.

An incident quickly presented itself. In early September a German U-boat fired on the American destroyer *Greer*, which had been radioing the U-boat's position to the British. Roosevelt promptly responded by ordering American ships to follow a "shoot-on-sight" policy toward German submarines.

The Germans escalated hostilities the following month, targeting two American destroyers. One of them, the **Reuben James,** broke in two after being torpedoed. It sank into the frigid waters of the North Atlantic, where 115 sailors died. As the end of 1941 grew near, Germany and the United States continued a tense standoff in the North Atlantic.

✓ Reading Check Evaluating How did the Lend-Lease Act help the Allied war effort?

Japan Attacks the United States

Despite the growing tensions in the Atlantic, the Japanese attack on Pearl Harbor was what finally brought the United States into World War II. Ironically, Japan's decision to attack the United States was a direct result of Roosevelt's efforts to help Britain in its war against Germany.

America Embargoes Japan Between August 1939 and December 1941, Roosevelt's primary goal was to help Britain and its allies defeat Germany. He knew that one of the problems Britain faced was the need to keep much of its navy in Asia to protect British territories there from Japanese attack. As German submarines began sinking British shipping, the British began moving warships from Southeast Asia to the Atlantic, leaving their empire vulnerable. In response, Roosevelt introduced policies to discourage the Japanese from attacking the British Empire.

NATIONAL GEOGRAPHIC **Pearl Harbor, Hawaii, December 7, 1941** In Motion

---

INTERDISCIPLINARY CONNECTIONS ACTIVITY

Communication Many Americans who were alive on December 7, 1941, remember the attack on Pearl Harbor. Have students interview three residents of the community who remember the day of the attack. Encourage students to work in pairs to prepare sample interview questions, such as what people were doing when they heard about the attack, how they reacted, and how the attack affected them. Have students write a newspaper article based on their interviews. If possible, students should include an appropriate photograph with their article. **L2**

Roosevelt began by putting economic pressure on Japan. Japan depended on the United States for many key materials, including scrap iron, steel, and especially oil. Approximately 80 percent of Japan's oil came from the United States. In July 1940, Congress passed the Export Control Act, giving Roosevelt the power to restrict the sale of strategic materials (materials important for fighting a war) to other nations. Roosevelt immediately blocked the sale of airplane fuel and scrap iron to Japan. Furious, the Japanese signed an alliance with Germany and Italy, formally becoming a member of the Axis.

In 1941 Roosevelt began sending lend-lease aid to China. Japan had invaded China in 1937, and by 1941, it controlled much of the Chinese coast. Roosevelt hoped that lend-lease aid would enable the Chinese to tie down the Japanese and prevent them from attacking elsewhere. The strategy failed. By July 1941, the Japanese had sent troops into southern Indochina, posing a direct threat to the British Empire. Japanese aircraft were now in position to

strike British shipping in the Strait of Malacca and bomb Hong Kong and Singapore.

Roosevelt responded very quickly to the Japanese threat. He froze all Japanese assets in the United States, reduced the amount of oil being shipped to Japan, and sent General Douglas MacArthur to the Philippines to build up American defenses there.

Roosevelt made it clear that he would lift the oil embargo only if Japan withdrew from Indochina and made peace with China. With the war against China now in jeopardy because of a lack of oil and other resources, the Japanese military began making plans to attack the resource-rich British and Dutch colonies in Southeast Asia. They also decided to seize the Philippines and to attack the American fleet at Pearl Harbor. They could not risk leaving the United States with a navy in the Pacific to oppose their plans. While the Japanese prepared for war, negotiations with the United States continued, but neither side would back down. On November 26, 1941, six Japanese aircraft carriers, two battleships, and several other warships set sail for Hawaii.

Japan Attacks Pearl Harbor
The Japanese government appeared to be continuing negotiations with the United States in good faith. American intelligence, however, had decoded Japanese communications that made it clear that Japan was preparing to go to war against the United States.

On November 27, American commanders at the Pearl Harbor naval base received a war warning from Washington, but Hawaii was not mentioned as a possible target. It was a great distance from Japan to Hawaii, and Washington officials doubted Japan would try to launch such a long-range attack.

The failure to collect sufficient information and the failure of the branches of the U.S. military to share the information available left Pearl Harbor an open target. The result was devastating. Japan's surprise attack on December 7, 1941, sank or damaged 21 ships of the U.S. Pacific Fleet, including 8 battleships, 3 cruisers, 4 destroyers, and

Student Web Activity Visit the *American Republic Since 1877* Web site at tarvol2.glencoe.com and click on *Student Web Activities— Chapter 19* for an activity on Pearl Harbor.

❶ 6:45 A.M.: The destroyer *Ward* sinks a Japanese midget submarine near the entrance to Pearl Harbor.

❷ 7:02 to 7:39 A.M.: Army radar at Opana tracks a cloud of aircraft approaching from the north. An officer at Fort Shafter concludes it is a flight of B-17s due in from California.

❸ 7:49 A.M.: The first wave of 183 Japanese planes is ordered to attack. The force includes 40 torpedo bombers and 49 high-altitude bombers—each armed with a single projectile—bound for Battleship Row. Other bombers and Zero fighters attack airfields.

❹ 8:55 A.M.: The second wave of 167 planes renews the attack on airfields and ships. Oil tanks and most ship-repair facilities are ignored, an omission the Japanese later regret.

Americans responded heroically to Japan's attack on Pearl Harbor: 16 men received the Medal of Honor, the nation's highest award; 5 were awarded the Distinguished Service Cross; and 69 received the Silver Star. The Navy Cross was awarded to another 51, including Dorie Miller, World War II's first recognized African American hero, who bravely operated an antiaircraft gun on his ship during the Japanese attack.

"above and beyond the call of duty"

DORIE MILLER

CHAPTER 19 A World in Flames **605**

HISTORY Online

Objectives and answers to the student activity can be found in the **Web Activity Lesson Plan** at tarvol2.glencoe.com.

Interpreting a Map To help students understand how geography affected the war, have them calculate the distance between each of these locations and Washington, D.C.: Hawaii, Tokyo, and San Francisco. Ask students what they notice about the distances. **L1**

3 ASSESS

Assign Section 4 Assessment as homework or as an in-class activity.

🌐 Have students use the **Interactive Tutor Self-Assessment CD-ROM.**

L1/ELL

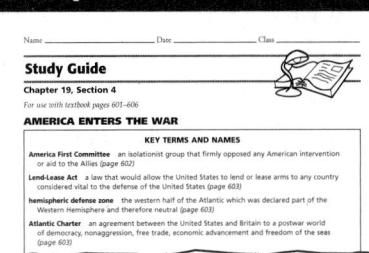

Reading Essentials and Study Guide 19–4

Name _____ Date _____ Class _____

Study Guide

Chapter 19, Section 4
For use with textbook pages 601–606

AMERICA ENTERS THE WAR

KEY TERMS AND NAMES

America First Committee an isolationist group that firmly opposed any American intervention or aid to the Allies (page 602)

Lend-Lease Act a law that would allow the United States to lend or lease arms to any country considered vital to the defense of the United States (page 603)

hemispheric defense zone the western half of the Atlantic which was declared part of the Western Hemisphere and therefore neutral (page 603)

Atlantic Charter an agreement between the United States and Britain to a postwar world of democracy, nonaggression, free trade, economic advancement and freedom of the seas (page 603)

CRITICAL THINKING ACTIVITY

Comparing Remind students of the embargo cutting off exports of scrap metal to Japan ordered by Roosevelt in 1940. The embargo was later extended to other products with military uses. Discuss the embargoes imposed against Iraq in 1990 and Haiti in 1993. Ask students to write their opinions on whether embargoes are successful in preventing war or accomplishing the goals established by the nations who impose them. **L3**

Section Quiz 19–4

Name _____ Date _____ Class _____

★ Chapter 19   Score ☐

Section Quiz 19-4

DIRECTIONS: Matching Match each item in Column A with the items in Column B.
Write the correct letters in the blanks. (10 points each)

Column A
____ 1. materials important for fighting a war
____ 2. revised to allow warring countries to buy arms from the United States on a cash-and-carry basis
____ 3. American destroyer torpedoed and sunk by a German submarine
____ 4. stated the United States could lend or lease arms to any country considered "vital to the defense of the United States"
____ 5. the entire western half of the Atlantic Ocean that Roosevelt declared as neutral territory

Column B
A. Lend-Lease Act
B. hemispheric defense zone
C. Neutrality Act of 1939
D. strategic materials
E. Reuben James

World Geography Connection

Answer: Since much of East-West trade went through the strait, its control would allow the Japanese to keep other powers out of the region.

Reteach
Have students explain how Roosevelt helped Britain under a neutrality policy.

Enrich
Invite students to write a report on the accuracy of a World War II film.

✔ Reading Check

Answer: attack on Pearl Harbor

HISTORY Online

Study Central™ provides summaries, interactive games, and online graphic organizers to help students review section content.

4 CLOSE

Have students create a relative chronology explaining the events that eventually led to war between the United States and Japan.

World Geography Connection

Geography and War

Throughout history, geography has played a key role in wars. In 1941, for example, Japan attacked Malaya and Indonesia to gain access to oil and rubber. It also wanted control of the Strait of Malacca, an important waterway linking the Indian Ocean with the South China Sea. Geography can also influence a war's outcome, as it did in the Vietnam War. There, miles of dense jungle allowed guerrillas to wage war first against French troops and then against American forces. *Why do you think the Strait of Malacca was so important?*

6 other vessels. The attack also destroyed 188 airplanes and killed 2,403 Americans. Another 1,178 were injured.

On the night of the attack, a gray-faced Roosevelt met with his cabinet to tell them the country now faced the most serious crisis since the outbreak of the Civil War. The next day, the president asked Congress to declare war:

❝Yesterday, December 7, 1941—a date which will live in infamy—the United States of America was suddenly and deliberately attacked by the naval and air forces of Japan. . . . I believe I interpret the will of the Congress and of the people when I assert that we will not only defend ourselves to the uttermost, but we will make very certain that this form of treachery shall never endanger us again. . . . No matter how long it may take us . . . the American people in their righteous might will win through to absolute victory.❞

—quoted in *Franklin D. Roosevelt: A Rendezvous with Destiny*

Following the president's speech, the Senate voted 82 to 0 and the House 388 to 1 to declare war on Japan.

Germany Declares War Although Japan was now at war with the United States, Hitler did not have to declare war on the Americans. The terms of the alliance with Japan specified that Germany only had to come to Japan's aid if Japan was attacked, not if Japan attacked another country. Hitler, however, had grown frustrated with the American navy's attacks on German submarines, and he believed the time had come to declare war.

Hitler greatly underestimated the strength of the United States, and he expected the Japanese to easily defeat the Americans in the Pacific. He hoped that by helping Japan now, he could count on Japanese support against the Soviet Union once the Americans had been beaten. On December 11, Germany and Italy both declared war on the United States.

✔ Reading Check
Examining What finally caused the United States to become involved in World War II?

HISTORY Online **Study Central™** To review this section, go to **tarvol2.glencoe.com** and click on **Study Central™**.

SECTION 4 ASSESSMENT

Checking for Understanding
1. **Define:** hemispheric defense zone, strategic materials.
2. **Identify:** America First Committee, Lend-Lease Act, Atlantic Charter.

Reviewing Themes
3. **Individual Action** After Roosevelt made the destroyers-for-bases deal with Britain, some Americans called him a dictator. Do you think Roosevelt was right or wrong in his actions? Explain your answer.

Critical Thinking
4. **Interpreting** Why was the United States unprepared for Japan's attack on Pearl Harbor?
5. **Organizing** Use a graphic organizer to list how Roosevelt helped Britain while maintaining official neutrality.

Help to Britain
☐ ☐ ☐

Analyzing Visuals
6. **Analyzing Maps** Study the map on pages 604–605. Based on the geography of Oahu, why was the location of Pearl Harbor perfect for a naval base?

Writing About History
7. **Persuasive Writing** Take on the role of an American in 1940. Write a letter to the editor of your newspaper explaining why you think the United States should either remain neutral or become involved in World War II.

SECTION 4 ASSESSMENT ANSWERS

1. Terms are in blue.
2. America First Committee (p. 602), Lend-Lease Act (p. 603), Atlantic Charter (p. 603)
3. Some may say it was important to stop Germany; others that Roosevelt violated the Neutrality Act.
4. The United States was still negotiating with Japan and had failed to collect sufficient information. The U.S. military had not shared information among the various branches.
5. destroyers for bases, Lend-Lease Act, hemispheric defense zone
6. It was sheltered and provided easy access to the ocean.
7. Students' letters will vary but should express a clear and reasoned opinion.

Making Generalizations

Why Learn This Skill?

Have you heard statements such as "Only tall people play basketball well," or "Dogs make better pets than cats"? Do you accept these statements at face value, or do you stop and consider whether or not they are valid?

Learning the Skill

The statements listed above are called *generalizations*, which are broad statements about a topic. To be valid, a generalization must be based on accurate information.

Let's examine the generalization, "Only tall people play basketball well." We can find many examples of tall basketball players, but there are also many shorter players who excel at this sport.

In this case, we began with a generalization and looked for facts to support or disprove it. In other cases, you will start with a group of facts about a topic and then make a generalization from these facts. To make a valid generalization, first collect information relevant to the topic. This information must consist of accurate facts, not opinions.

Suppose that you want to make a generalization about the relative danger of airplane travel compared to automobile travel. First, you would collect accident statistics involving airplanes and cars. Your next step would be to classify the information into categories. Then you would look for relationships between these categories. For example, you might put the airplane and automobile statistics in separate categories. You might also categorize the number of accidents and the number of fatalities. Finally, you should make a generalization that is consistent with most of the facts you gathered.

Practicing the Skill

Reread the passage about the Austrian *Anschluss* on page 590, and then answer these questions.

❶ What facts about the *Anschluss* are presented?

❷ Organize these facts into categories.

❸ How does the vote held in Austria relate to the other facts?

❹ What generalization can you make about Austria regarding the *Anschluss?*

Skills Assessment

Complete the Practicing Skills questions on page 609 and the Chapter 19 Skill Reinforcement Activity to assess your mastery of this skill.

Applying the Skill

Making Generalizations Review the information in the chapter about appeasement as it related to the countries of Czechoslovakia, France, and Britain. Write a generalization about Czechoslovakia's role in the appeasement policy. Support your generalization with at least five facts.

Glencoe's **Skillbuilder Interactive Workbook CD-ROM, Level 2,** provides instruction and practice in key social studies skills.

TEACH

Making Generalizations

Explain that generalizations are broad statements that should be based on observable or accurate information.

Organize the class into small groups. Have each group develop three generalizations based on information they have learned about American history. Have the groups share their generalizations as the other groups state the type of information that would support or refute the generalization.

Additional Practice

L1

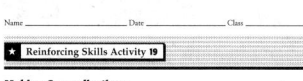

Reinforcing Skills Activity 19

Name _____ Date _____ Class _____

★ Reinforcing Skills Activity 19

Making Generalizations

☐ **LEARNING THE SKILL**
To generalize means to draw inferences from or make general conclusions about a set of statements or information. The quality of the information you use determines the accuracy of the generalizations you make. Information that consists of facts, not opinions, is essential to drawing accurate generalizations. As you gather facts, begin to group the information into categories, and look for relationships among the categories. Based on those relationships, you can begin to make new generalizations or test existing ones.

☐ **PRACTICING THE SKILL**
DIRECTIONS: Is the generalization below accurate? Read or review Section 1 of your textbook to find support for the generalization. Complete the table below to help you organize your information and find relationships.

GLENCOE
TECHNOLOGY

 CD-ROM
Glencoe Skillbuilder Interactive Workbook CD-ROM, Level 2

This interactive CD-ROM reinforces student mastery of essential social studies skills.

ANSWERS TO PRACTICING THE SKILL

❶ Hitler demanded *Anschluss* on the basis of common language. He wanted to expand German territory and resources. He used threats and force to achieve it.

❷ Possible categories: Hitler's actions, Austria's response

❸ The vote was held after Hitler's troops were already in Austria.

❹ Possible answers: Austrians could not have prevented the *Anschluss*; Austrians shared language and culture with Germans.

Applying the Skill
Students' answers should support the generalization.

CHAPTER 19 ASSESSMENT and ACTIVITIES

CHAPTER 19
ASSESSMENT and ACTIVITIES

GLENCOE TECHNOLOGY

MindJogger Videoquiz
Use the **MindJogger Videoquiz** to review Chapter 19 content.

Available in DVD

Reviewing Key Terms
Students' answers will vary. The pages where the words appear in the text are shown in parentheses.

1. **fascism** (p. 585)
2. **internationalism** (p. 588)
3. **appeasement** (p. 590)
4. **blitzkrieg** (p. 591)
5. **Holocaust** (p. 595)
6. **concentration camp** (p. 599)
7. **extermination camp** (p. 599)
8. **hemispheric defense zone** (p. 603)
9. **strategic materials** (p. 605)

Reviewing Key Facts
10. Benito Mussolini (p. 585), Vladimir Lenin (p. 585), Adolf Hitler (p. 585)
11. Germany, Italy, Japan
12. Austrians spoke German and had an authoritarian government. Czechoslovakians spoke several languages and had a democratic government and allies.
13. Nazis took away their civil liberties, seized their property, imprisoned them, and killed them.
14. Roosevelt made a destroyers-for-bases deal, got Congress to pass the Lend-Lease Act, and developed the hemispheric defense zone strategy.

Critical Thinking
15. Answers will vary. A possible reason for a positive answer is that the attack on Pearl Harbor was the result of the United States's efforts to help Britain in the war against Germany. A possible reason for a negative answer is that Hitler seemed bent on world domination so that

Reviewing Key Terms
On a sheet of paper, use each of these terms in a sentence.

1. fascism
2. internationalism
3. appeasement
4. blitzkrieg
5. Holocaust
6. concentration camp
7. extermination camp
8. hemispheric defense zone
9. strategic materials

Reviewing Key Facts
10. **Identify:** Benito Mussolini, Vladimir Lenin, Adolf Hitler.
11. Where did antidemocratic governments arise in Europe and Asia after World War I?
12. Why was Austria easier for Hitler to annex than Czechoslovakia?
13. What were four ways that Nazis persecuted Jews?
14. In what three ways did Roosevelt help Britain while maintaining an American policy of neutrality?

Critical Thinking
15. **Analyzing Themes: Global Connections** If Roosevelt's internationalist policy had been fully pursued, do you think it could have prevented World War II?
16. **Evaluating** Why were the British able to stop the German invasion of their country?
17. **Determining Cause and Effect** How did the rise of dictatorships and the attack on Pearl Harbor cause the United States to become involved in World War II?
18. **Organizing** Use a graphic organizer similar to the one below to list countries that Hitler and the Nazis seized between 1936 and 1940.

Countries Seized by Hitler and the Nazis

Chapter Summary

Axis

Italy

- Mussolini's Fascist Party believed in supreme power of the state
- Cooperated with Germany from 1936 onward

Germany
- Hitler's Nazi Party believed in all-powerful state, territorial expansion, and ethnic purity
- Invaded Poland in 1939, France in 1940, and the USSR in 1941

Japan
- Military leaders pushed for territorial expansion
- Attacked Manchuria in 1931
- Invaded China in 1937
- Attacked Pearl Harbor in 1941

Allies

United States
- Passed Neutrality Acts in 1935, 1937, and 1939
- Gave lend-lease aid to Britain, China, and the USSR
- Declared war on Japan in 1941

Great Britain

- Tried to appease Hitler by allowing territorial growth
- Declared war on Germany in 1939
- Resisted German attack in 1940
- Received U.S. aid through lend-lease program and cash-and-carry provision

France
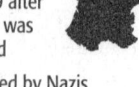
- Along with Great Britain, tried to appease Hitler
- Declared war on Germany in 1939 after Poland was invaded
- Occupied by Nazis in 1940

USSR
- Communists, led by harsh dictator Joseph Stalin, created industrial power
- Signed non-aggression pact with Germany in 1939
- Received U.S. aid; eventually fought with Allies to defeat Germany

U.S. interests would eventually have needed protection.

16. the British use of radar; skill of British air force
17. The United States sided with democratically-based governments, particularly after Nazi Germany attacked France and Britain; Pearl Harbor was an outright attack on the United States.
18. Austria, Czechoslovakia, Poland, Denmark, Belgium, France, Luxembourg, the Netherlands, Norway

19. **a.** Lindbergh believed that many Americans were against entering the war and that in a democratic nation, their wishes should be listened to. **b.** Students' answers will vary. It might not have changed his mind; he believed we needed to protect ourselves.

HISTORY Online

Self-Check Quiz

Visit the *American Republic Since 1877* Web site at tarvol2.glencoe.com and click on *Self-Check Quizzes—Chapter 19* to assess your knowledge of chapter content.

19. **Interpreting Primary Sources** The America First Committee was one group organized to prevent American involvement in the war. On April 24, 1941, a leading spokesperson for this committee, aviator Charles Lindbergh, delivered a speech in New York. Read the excerpt from his speech and answer the questions that follow.

   ❝War is not inevitable for this country. Such a claim is defeatism in the true sense. No one can make us fight abroad unless we ourselves are willing to do so. No one will attempt to fight us here if we arm ourselves as a great nation should be armed. Over a hundred million people in this nation are opposed to entering the war. If the principles of democracy mean anything at all, that is reason enough for us to stay out. If we are forced into war against the wishes of an overwhelming majority of our people, we will have proved democracy such a failure at home that there will be little use fighting for it abroad.❞

   a. Why did Lindbergh favor isolationism?

   b. How do you think Lindbergh might have felt about isolationism after the attack on Pearl Harbor?

Practicing Skills

20. **Making Generalizations** Read the passage below and answer the questions that follow.

   ❝Hitler and the Nazis believed the Germanic people to be superior to all others. He often referred to Germans as the Aryan race, a completely fictitious racial ethnic type. The groups the Nazis held in low regard included homosexuals, the disabled, Gypsies, and Slavic peoples. The Nazis reserved their most virulent hatred for the Jews, however. . . . For the Nazis, all people who were ethnically Jewish were completely evil no matter what their religion, occupation, or education.❞

   a. What facts are presented about the attitude of Hitler and the Nazis toward Germans and Jews?

   b. What generalization can be made from these facts?

Geography and History

21. The map on this page shows Nazi concentration and extermination camps. Study it and answer these questions.

   a. **Interpreting Maps** In which two countries were most of the concentration and extermination camps located?

Nazi Concentration and Extermination Camps, 1933–1945

- ⊛ Capital city
- ■ Nazi concentration camp/ death camp

200 miles
200 kilometers
Lambert Azimuthal Equal-Area projection

   b. **Applying Geography Skills** What can you conclude about the extent of the Nazis' "final solution"?

Chapter Activity

22. **Research Project** Research and write a short biography of Winston Churchill. Then describe his career, involvement in World War II, and beliefs to the class.

Writing Activity

23. **Descriptive Writing** Using the Internet and the library, find firsthand accounts of Holocaust survivors. Create a report on these survivors, and present the report to your classmates.

HISTORY Online

Have students visit the Web site at tarvol2.glencoe.com to review Chapter 19 and take the Self-Check Quiz.

Standardized Test Practice

Answer: D

Test-Taking Tip: Instruct students to ask themselves what they know about the timing of the event. This will help them rule out A since the Depression was largely over by this time. Then have them ask themselves who the Axis powers were. Once they realize that Germany, Italy, and Japan were not democratic countries, they can rule out B. Finally, ask if supplying aid to one side is likely to allow the country to remain neutral. By ruling out C, they are left with the answer D.

Bonus Question ?

Ask: What is the name of the German-born Nobel prize-winning physicist whose scientific theories revolutionized modern physics? *(Albert Einstein)*

Practicing Skills

20. **a.** Hitler believed in faulty concepts of race, that Germans were a superior race, and that Jews were an evil race. **b.** Hitler and the Nazis were racists.

Geography and History

21. **a.** Germany and Poland; **b.** The Nazis applied the "Final Solution" in Germany and in all the countries he conquered.

Chapter Activity

22. Students' biographies of Churchill will vary. The biographies should focus on his career, his involvement in the war, and his beliefs.

Writing Activity

23. Reports will vary depending on the research. All should include accounts of survivors' experiences and will to live.

Timesaving Tools

TeacherWorks™ All-In-One Planner and Resource Center

● **Interactive Teacher Edition** Access your Teacher Wraparound Edition and your classroom resources with a few easy clicks.

● **Interactive Lesson Planner** Planning has never been easier! Organize your week, month, semester, or year with all the lesson helps you need to make teaching creative, timely, and relevant.

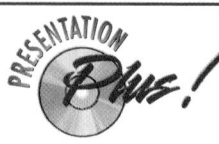

Use Glencoe's **Presentation Plus!** multimedia teacher tool to easily present dynamic lessons that visually excite your students. Using Microsoft PowerPoint® you can customize the presentations to create your own personalized lessons.

TEACHING TRANSPARENCIES

Graphic Organizer 5 L2

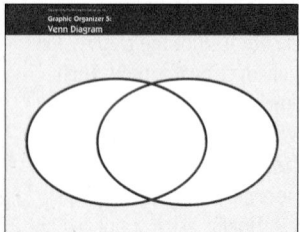

Why It Matters Chapter Transparency 20 L2

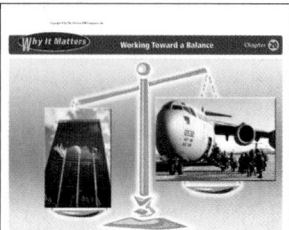

APPLICATION AND ENRICHMENT

Linking Past and Present Activity 20 L2

Enrichment Activity 20 L3

Primary Source Reading 20 L2

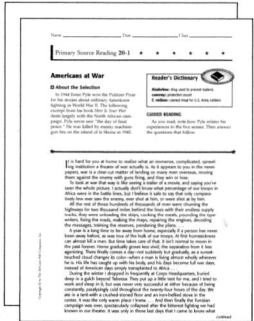

REVIEW AND REINFORCEMENT

Reteaching Activity 20 L1

Vocabulary Activity 20 L1

Time Line Activity 20 L2

Critical Thinking Skills Activity 20 L2

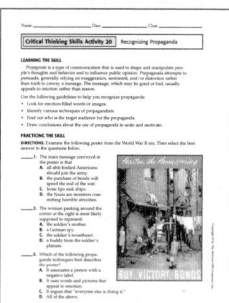

Meeting NCSS Standards

The following standards are covered in Chapter 20:

Section 1	V	Individuals, Groups, and Institutions: B, D, E
Section 2	I	Culture: A, B, D
Section 3	II	Time, Continuity, and Change: B, C, F
Section 4	III	People, Places, and Environments: A, F, H
Section 5	VII	Production, Distribution, and Consumption: A, F

Local Standards

_____

_____

_____

_____

_____

Chapter 20 Resources

ASSESSMENT AND EVALUATION

Chapter 20 Test Form A L2

Chapter 20 Test Form B L2

Standardized Test Practice Workbook Activity 20 L2

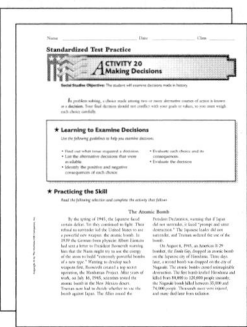

Performance Assessment Activities and Rubrics 20 L1/ELL

ExamView® Pro Testmaker CD-ROM

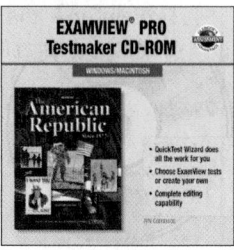

MULTIMEDIA

- Vocabulary PuzzleMaker CD-ROM
- Interactive Tutor Self-Assessment CD-ROM
- ExamView® Pro Testmaker CD-ROM
- Audio Program
- American History Primary Source Documents Library CD-ROM
- MindJogger Videoquiz
- Presentation Plus! CD-ROM
- TeacherWorks™ CD-ROM
- Interactive Student Edition CD-ROM
- Glencoe Skillbuilder Interactive Workbook CD-ROM, Level 2
- The *American Republic Since 1877* Video Program
- American Music: Hits Through History
- American Music: Cultural Traditions

SPANISH RESOURCES

The following Spanish language materials are available:

- Spanish Reading Essentials and Study Guide
- Spanish Guided Reading Activities
- Spanish Reteaching Activities
- Spanish Quizzes and Tests
- Spanish Vocabulary Activities
- Spanish Summaries
- The Declaration of Independence and United States Constitution Spanish Translation

The following videotape programs are available from Glencoe as a supplement to Chapter 20:

- **FDR: The War Years** (1-56-501458-8)
- **The Best Kept Secret: D Day** (0-76-700680-1)
- **Propaganda Wars: Japan and the U.S.** (1-56-501320-4)
- **The War in the Pacific** (1-56-501994-6)

To order, call Glencoe at 1-800-334-7344. To find classroom resources to accompany many of these videos, check the following home pages:
A&E Television: www.aande.com
The History Channel: www.historychannel.com

HISTORY Online

Use our Web site for additional resources. All essential content is covered in the Student Edition.

You and your students can visit tarvol2.glencoe.com, the Web site companion to the *American Republic Since 1877*. This innovative integration of electronic and print media offers your students a wealth of opportunities. The student text directs students to the Web site for the following options:

- **Chapter Overviews**
- **Self-Check Quizzes**
- **Student Web Activities**
- **Textbook Updates**

Answers to the student Web activities are provided for you in the **Web Activity Lesson Plans.** Additional Web resources and Interactive Tutor Puzzles are also available.

Chapter 20 Resources

Daily Objectives	Reproducible Resources	Multimedia Resources
SECTION 1 **Mobilizing for War** 1. Explain how the United States mobilized its economy. 2. Describe the issues involved in raising an American army.	Reproducible Lesson Plan 20–1 Daily Lecture and Discussion Notes 20–1 Guided Reading Activity 20–1* Section Quiz 20–1* Reading Essentials and Study Guide 20–1* Performance Assessment Activities and Rubrics	Daily Focus Skills Transparency 20–1 Interactive Tutor Self-Assessment CD-ROM ExamView® Pro Testmaker CD-ROM* Presentation Plus! CD-ROM TeacherWorks™ CD-ROM Audio Program
SECTION 2 **The Early Battles** 1. Analyze how the Allies were able to fight a war on two fronts and turn the war against the Axis in the Pacific, Russia, and North Atlantic. 2. Explain why Stalingrad is considered a major turning point of World War II.	Reproducible Lesson Plan 20–2 Daily Lecture and Discussion Notes 20–2 Guided Reading Activity 20–2* Section Quiz 20–2* Reading Essentials and Study Guide 20–2* Performance Assessment Activities and Rubrics	Daily Focus Skills Transparency 20–2 Interactive Tutor Self-Assessment CD-ROM ExamView® Pro Testmaker CD-ROM* Presentation Plus! CD-ROM Skillbuilder Interactive Workbook, Level 2 TeacherWorks™ CD-ROM Audio Program
SECTION 3 **Life on the Home Front** 1. Describe how the wartime economy created opportunities for women and minorities. 2. Discuss how Americans coped with shortages and rapidly rising prices.	Reproducible Lesson Plan 20–3 Daily Lecture and Discussion Notes 20–3 Guided Reading Activity 20–3* Section Quiz 20–3* Reading Essentials and Study Guide 20–3* Supreme Court Case Studies	Daily Focus Skills Transparency 20–3 American Art & Architecture Interactive Tutor Self-Assessment CD-ROM ExamView® Pro Testmaker CD-ROM* Presentation Plus! CD-ROM American Music: Cultural Traditions
SECTION 4 **Pushing the Axis Back** 1. Describe the goals of the two major offensives the Allies launched in Europe in 1943. 2. Explain the American strategy for pushing the Japanese back in the Pacific.	Reproducible Lesson Plan 20–4 Daily Lecture and Discussion Notes 20–4 Guided Reading Activity 20–4* Section Quiz 20–4* Reading Essentials and Study Guide 20–4* Performance Assessment Activities and Rubrics	Daily Focus Skills Transparency 20–4 Interactive Tutor Self-Assessment CD-ROM ExamView® Pro Testmaker CD-ROM* Presentation Plus! CD-ROM TeacherWorks™ CD-ROM Audio Program
SECTION 5 **The War Ends** 1. Explain the tactics the Allies used to invade Germany and to defeat Japan. 2. Outline the reasons the Allies created the United Nations and held war crimes trials.	Reproducible Lesson Plan 20–5 Daily Lecture and Discussion Notes 20–5 Guided Reading Activity 20–5* Section Quiz 20–5* Reading Essentials and Study Guide 20–5* Performance Assessment Activities and Rubrics	Daily Focus Skills Transparency 20–5 Interactive Tutor Self-Assessment CD-ROM ExamView® Pro Testmaker CD-ROM* Presentation Plus! CD-ROM TeacherWorks™ CD-ROM Vocabulary PuzzleMaker CD-ROM Audio Program American Music: Cultural Traditions

0:00 OUT OF TIME?
Assign the Chapter 20 **Reading Essentials and Study Guide.**

*Also Available in Spanish

 Printed Materials   Transparency   CD-ROM   DVD

 Poster   Music Program   Audio Program

NATIONAL GEOGRAPHIC Teacher's Corner

INDEX TO NATIONAL GEOGRAPHIC MAGAZINE

The following articles relate to this chapter.

- "The *Bismarck* Found," November 1989
- "Blueprints for Victory," May 1995
- "Douglas MacArthur: An American Soldier," March 1992
- "Hiroshima," August 1995
- "Living with Radiation," April 1989
- "Pearl Harbor: A Return to the Day of Infamy," December 1991
- "Remembering the Blitz," July 1991

NATIONAL GEOGRAPHIC SOCIETY PRODUCTS

To order the following, call National Geographic at 1-800-368-2728:

- *Eyewitness to the 20th Century* (Book)
- *Historical Atlas of the United States*
- *Lost Fleet of Guadalcanal* (Video)
- *PicturePack: World War II Era* (Transparencies)
- *PictureShow: World War II Era* (CD-ROM)

NGS ONLINE

Access National Geographic's Web site for current events, atlas updates, activities, links, interactive features, and archives.

www.nationalgeographic.com

MEETING SPECIAL NEEDS

In addition to the Differentiated Instruction strategies found in each section, the following resources are also suitable for your special needs students:

- *ExamView® Pro Testmaker CD-ROM* allows teachers to tailor tests by reducing answer choices.
- The *Audio Program* includes the entire narrative of the student edition so that less-proficient readers can listen to the words as they read them.

KEY TO ABILITY LEVELS

Teaching strategies have been coded.

L1 BASIC activities for all students
L2 AVERAGE activities for average to above-average students
L3 CHALLENGING activities for above-average students
ELL ENGLISH LANGUAGE LEARNER activities

From the Classroom of...

Ellen Closs
Okemos Public Schools
Okemos, MI

Reporters and the Times

Ask students to try to adopt the point of view of someone living in the 1940s. Organize the class into groups of 3 people each (reporter, soldier, and someone on the home front). Instruct the reporter to interview both the soldier and the person on the home front about how America's role in the war has changed their lives. How have they themselves changed as people? Has the war changed their view of the American government or the world? If possible, give them primary resources, such as letters and autobiographies from the time to help them prepare their questions.

Have them present their interviews to the class, acting as people who are living during World War II.

ADDITIONAL RESOURCES FROM GLENCOE

- American Music: Cultural Traditions
- American Art & Architecture
- Outline Map Resource Book
- U.S. Desk Map
- Building Geography Skills for Life
- Inclusion for the High School Social Studies Classroom Strategies and Activities
- Teaching Strategies for the American History Classroom (Including Block Scheduling Pacing Guides)
- Dinah Zike's High School American History Reading and Study Skills Foldables

Block Schedule

Activities that are suited to use within the block scheduling framework are identified by:

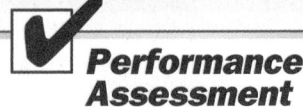

Why It Matters Activity

Have students explain how they think World War II continues to have an impact on the lives of Americans. Students should evaluate their answers after they have completed the chapter.

GLENCOE
TECHNOLOGY

The *American Republic Since 1877* Video Program
To learn more about America's role in World War II, have students view the Chapter 20 video, "Japanese American Internment Camps," from the ***American Republic Since 1877* Video Program.**

MindJogger Videoquiz
Use the **MindJogger Videoquiz** to preview Chapter 20 content.

 Both programs available in DVD

CHAPTER
20 America and World War II
1941–1945

Why It Matters

The United States entered World War II unwillingly and largely unprepared. The American people, however, quickly banded together to transform the American economy into the most productive and efficient war-making machine in the world. American forces turned the tide in Europe and the Pacific, and they played a crucial role in the defeat of Germany, Italy, and Japan.

The Impact Today

Many changes that began in World War II are still shaping our lives today.
- *The United Nations was founded.*
- *Nuclear weapons were invented.*
- *The United States became the most powerful nation in the world.*

 The *American Republic Since 1877* Video *The Chapter 20 video, "Japanese American Internment Camps," chronicles the treatment of Japanese Americans during World War II.*

1943
- Detroit race riots
- Zoot suit riots in Los Angeles

1941
- President Roosevelt forbids racial discrimination in defense industries
- United States enters World War II

1942
- Women's Army Auxiliary Corps established
- Japanese American relocation ordered

United States PRESIDENTS
F. Roosevelt 1933–1945

1941 *1942* *1943*

World

1941
- Japan attacks Pearl Harbor and the Philippines

1942
- Japan takes Philippines; MacArthur vows: "I shall return."
- Americans turn the tide in the Pacific at the Battle of Midway

1943
- Battle of Tarawa
- Germans defeated at Stalingrad
- Allied forces land in Italy

610

Reading Strategy   PURPOSE FOR READING

Venn Diagram Using these diagrams helps students compare and/or contrast two or more items. Tell students there were two major opponents of the United States in World War II—Germany and Japan. Have students draw two overlapping circles on their papers. Label one "Germany," one "Japan," and the overlapping area "Both." As students study the chapter, have them compare and contrast Germany and Japan by writing information for each in the appropriate circle. Students should list information that applies to both countries in the overlapping area. **L1** ELL

📁 Refer to ***Inclusion for the High School Social Studies Classroom Strategies and Activities*** in the TCR.

Allied soldiers landing at Omaha Beach in Normandy on D-Day—June 6, 1944

More About the Photo

Landing craft were used to transport troops and equipment on D-Day. Have students imagine that they are one of these soldiers. Ask them what they were experiencing as their landing craft's ramp was lowered. *(Students may describe the physical conditions such as the cold, salty water or the emotions that the soldiers likely experienced such as determination or fear.)*

TIME LINE
ACTIVITY

Have students use a globe or world map to identify the approximate location where the world events on the time line occurred.

FOLDABLES™
Study Organizer

Dinah Zike's Foldables are three-dimensional, interactive graphic organizers that help students practice basic writing skills, review key vocabulary terms, and identify main ideas. Have students complete the foldable activity in the *Dinah Zike's Reading and Study Skills Foldables* booklet.

1944
• Supreme Court rules in *Korematsu v. the United States* that Japanese American relocation is constitutional

1945
• Franklin Roosevelt dies in office; Harry S Truman becomes president

Truman 1945–1953

1944

1945

1944
• Eisenhower leads D-Day invasion
• Battle of Leyte Gulf

1945
• United States drops atomic bomb on Japan
• World War II ends

HISTORY
Online

Chapter Overview
Visit the *American Republic Since 1877* Web site at tarvol2.glencoe.com and click on *Chapter Overviews— Chapter 20* to preview chapter information.

611

GRAPHIC ORGANIZER ACTIVITY

Organizing Information Have students take notes on Chapter 20 by completing a table similar to the one shown below. Students' notes should be concise, addressing the concepts or themes found in the chapter.

Allied Power	Axis Power
Britain	Germany
Russia	Italy
United States	Japan

1 FOCUS

Section Overview

This section describes the preparations the U.S. made in anticipation of entering the war.

BELLRINGER
Skillbuilder Activity

Project transparency and have students answer the question.

Daily Focus Skills Transparency 20–1

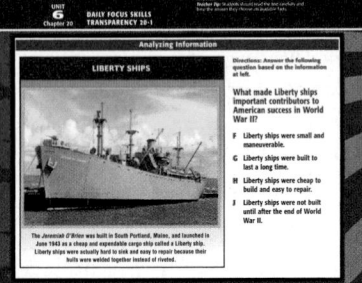

Reading Preview

Answers to Graphic: A restructured Reconstruction Finance Corporation, War Production Board, Office of War Mobilization, draft board (under Selective Service and Training Act)

Preteaching Vocabulary
Have students write two questions that can be answered using the Key Terms.

Guide to Reading

Main Idea
The United States quickly mobilized its economy and armed forces to fight World War II.

Key Terms and Names
cost-plus, Reconstruction Finance Corporation, Liberty ship, War Production Board, Selective Service and Training Act, disfranchise

Reading Strategy
Organizing As you read about American mobilization for World War II, complete a graphic organizer like the one below by filling in the agencies the U.S. government created to mobilize the nation's economy for war.

Government Agencies Created to Mobilize the Economy

Reading Objectives
- **Explain** how the United States mobilized its economy.
- **Describe** the issues involved in raising an American army.

Section Theme
Individual Action The success of the United States in mobilizing for war was due largely to the cooperation of individual American citizens.

Preview of Events

♦1940	♦1941	♦1942	♦1943

1940
Fall of France; Selective Service Act

December 7, 1941
Japan attacks Pearl Harbor

1942
Women's Army Auxiliary Corps (WAAC) established

1943
Office of War Mobilization (OWM) established

★ An American Story ★

Franklin D. Roosevelt

Shortly after 1:30 P.M. on December 7, 1941, Secretary of the Navy Frank Knox phoned President Roosevelt at the White House. "Mr. President," Knox said, "it looks like the Japanese have attacked Pearl Harbor." A few minutes later, Admiral Harold Stark, chief of naval operations, phoned and confirmed the attack.

As Eleanor Roosevelt passed by the president's study, she knew immediately something very bad had happened:

"All the secretaries were there, two telephones were in use, the senior military aides were on their way with messages." Eleanor also noticed that President Roosevelt remained calm: "His reaction to any event was always to be calm. If it was something that was bad, he just became almost like an iceberg, and there was never the slightest emotion that was allowed to show."

Turning to his wife, President Roosevelt expressed anger at the Japanese: "I never wanted to have to fight this war on two fronts. We haven't got the Navy to fight in both the Atlantic and Pacific. . . . We will have to build up the Navy and the Air Force and that will mean we will have to take a good many defeats before we can have a victory."

—adapted from *No Ordinary Time*

Converting the Economy

Although the difficulties of fighting a global war troubled the president, British Prime Minister Winston Churchill was not worried. Churchill knew that victory in modern war depended on a nation's industrial power. He compared the American economy

---

SECTION RESOURCES

📁 **Reproducible Masters**
- Reproducible Lesson Plan 20–1
- Daily Lecture and Discussion Notes 20–1
- Guided Reading Activity 20–1
- Section Quiz 20–1
- Reading Essentials and Study Guide 20–1
- Performance Assessment Activities and Rubrics

🖐 **Transparencies**
- Daily Focus Skills Transparency 20–1

Multimedia
- 💿 Interactive Tutor Self-Assessment CD-ROM
- 💿 ExamView® Pro Testmaker CD-ROM
- 💿 Presentation Plus! CD-ROM
- 💿 TeacherWorks™ CD-ROM
- 🔊 Audio Program

to a gigantic boiler: "Once the fire is lighted under it there is no limit to the power it can generate."

Churchill was right. The industrial output of the United States during the war astounded the rest of the world. American workers were twice as productive as German workers and five times more productive than Japanese workers. American war production turned the tide in favor of the Allies. In less than four years, the United States achieved what no other nation had ever done—it fought and won a two-front war against two powerful military empires, forcing each to surrender unconditionally.

The United States was able to expand its war production so rapidly after the attack on Pearl Harbor in part because the government had begun to mobilize the economy before the country entered the war. When the German blitzkrieg swept into France in May 1940, President Roosevelt declared a national emergency and announced a plan to build 50,000 warplanes a year. Shocked by the success of the German attack, many Americans were willing to build up the country's defenses.

Roosevelt and his advisers believed that the best way to rapidly mobilize the economy was to give industry an incentive to move quickly. As Henry Stimson, the new secretary of war, wrote in his diary: "If you are going to try and go to war, or to prepare for war, in a capitalist country, you have got to let business make money out of the process or business won't work."

Normally when the government needed military equipment, it would ask companies to bid for the contract, but that system was too slow in wartime. Instead of asking for bids, the government signed cost-plus contracts. The government agreed to pay a company whatever it cost to make a product plus a guaranteed percentage of the costs as profit. Under the cost-plus system, the more a company produced and the faster it did the work, the more money it would make. The system was not cheap, but it did get war materials produced quickly and in quantity.

Although cost-plus convinced many companies to convert to war production, others could not afford to reequip their factories to make military goods. To convince more companies to convert, Congress gave new authority to the **Reconstruction Finance Corporation** (RFC). The RFC, a government agency set up during the Depression, was now permitted to make loans to companies to help them cover the cost of converting to war production.

✓ Reading Check **Analyzing** What government policies helped American industry to produce large quantities of war materials?

American Industry Gets the Job Done

By the fall of 1941, much had already been done to prepare the economy for war, but it was still only partially mobilized. Although many companies were producing military equipment, most still preferred to make consumer goods. The Depression was ending and sales were rising. The Japanese attack on Pearl Harbor, however, changed everything. By the summer of 1942, almost all major industries and some 200,000 companies had converted to war production. Together they made the nation's wartime "miracle" possible.

ECONOMICS

Tanks Replace Cars The automobile industry was uniquely suited to the mass production of military equipment. Automobile factories began to produce trucks, jeeps, and tanks. This was critical in modern warfare because the country that could move troops and supplies most quickly usually

 History *Through Art*

WW II Posters War posters were designed to help encourage and inform the American public. How would you have felt to see a poster such as this one?

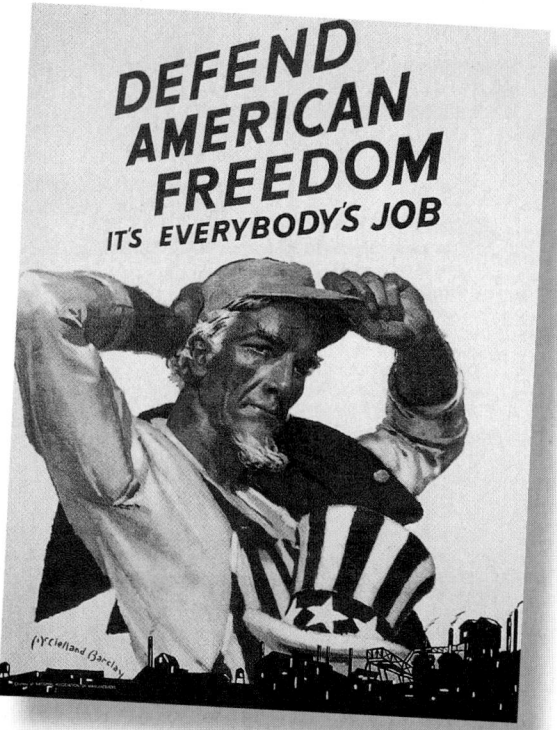

CHAPTER 20 America and World War II **613**

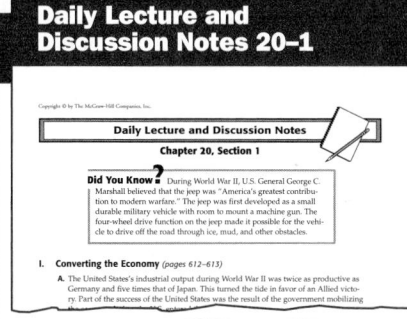

2 TEACH

Daily Lecture and Discussion Notes 20–1

Copyright © by The McGraw-Hill Companies, Inc.

Daily Lecture and Discussion Notes

Chapter 20, Section 1

Did You Know? During World War II, U.S. General George C. Marshall believed that the jeep was "America's greatest contribution to modern warfare." The jeep was first developed as a small durable military vehicle with room to mount a machine gun. The four-wheel drive function on the jeep made it possible for the vehicle to drive off the road through ice, mud, and other obstacles.

I. Converting the Economy (pages 612–613)

A. The United States's industrial output during World War II was twice as productive as Germany and five times that of Japan. This turned the tide in favor of an Allied victory. Part of the success of the United States was the result of the government mobilizing

Designing a Bulletin Board
Have students create a bulletin board on one of the topics in this section. Students should focus on either industry or government as the nation prepared for war. **L1** ELL

📁 Use the rubric for creating a map, display, or chart on pages 65–66 in the *Performance Assessment Activities and Rubrics.*

✓ Reading Check

Answer: The cost-plus program encouraged companies to produce many products quickly and in quantity. The RFC made loans to help companies convert to war production.

 History *Through Art*

Answer: Students may say it would have encouraged them to consider the threats to American freedom.

Reading Strategy   READING THE TEXT

Using Word Parts Have students use prefixes to unlock the meanings of unknown words. A *prefix* is a word part that comes before a base word or a root and changes the meaning of the word. For example, *dis-* means "the opposite of" and is found in words such as disobey, displease, or disown. *In-* means "not". Have students provide examples of words that use this prefix *(inactive, incorrect, inability, incomplete).* **L1** ELL

📁 Refer to *Inclusion for the High School Social Studies Classroom Strategies and Activities* in the TCR.

L1/ELL

Guided Reading Activity 20–1

Name _____ Date _____ Class _____

★ Guided Reading Activity **20-1**

DIRECTIONS: Recording Who, What, When, Where, Why, and How Read the section and answer the questions below. Refer to your textbook to write the answers.
1. Why was Winston Churchill not worried about America's ability to fight a global war?
2. Why did the industrial output of the United States during the war astound the rest of the world?
3. How did cost-plus contracts work?
4. What was the Reconstruction Finance Corporation (RFC)?
5. What industry was uniquely suited to the mass production of military equipment?

Analyzing Information Have students look carefully at the photograph and graphs on pages 614–615. Using what they see in the photo and graphs, along with the content of this section, have students write a paragraph describing what they think was happening when the photograph was taken. **L2**

⎍⎍⎍ Graph *Skills*

Answers:
1. As the production of cars decreases, the production of tanks increases. When tank production is at its highest, auto production is at its lowest. When the production of tanks decreases the production of autos increases.
2. The graphs show that producing tanks to help win the war took precedence over producing automobiles.

Graph Skills Practice
Ask: Why does the production of tanks jump so sharply between 1941 and 1942? *(U.S. entered the war at the end of 1941.)*

won the battle. As General George C. Marshall, chief of staff for the United States Army, observed:

❝The greatest advantage the United States enjoyed on the ground in the fighting was . . . the jeep and the two-and-a-half ton truck. These are the instruments that moved and supplied United States troops in battle, while the German army . . . depended on animal transport. . . . The United States, profiting from the mass production achievements of its automotive industry . . . had mobility that completely outclassed the enemy.❞

—quoted in *Miracle of World War II*

Automobile factories did not just produce vehicles. They also built artillery, rifles, mines, helmets, pontoon bridges, cooking pots, and dozens of other pieces of military equipment. Henry Ford launched one of the most ambitious projects when he created an assembly line for the enormous B-24 bomber known as "the Liberator" at Willow Run Airport near Detroit. By the end of the war, the factory had built over 8,600 aircraft. Overall, the automobile industry produced nearly one-third of the military equipment manufactured during the war.

Building the Liberty Ships Henry Kaiser's shipyards more than matched Ford's achievement in aircraft production. Kaiser's shipyards built many ships, but they were best known for their production of Liberty ships. The Liberty ship was the basic cargo ship used during the war. Most Liberty ships were welded instead of riveted. Welded ships were cheap, easy to build, and very hard to sink compared to riveted ships.

When a riveted ship was hit, the rivets often came loose, causing the ship to fall apart and sink. A welded ship's hull was fused into one solid piece of steel. A torpedo might blow a hole in it, but the hull would not come apart. A damaged Liberty ship could often get back to port, make repairs, and return to service.

The War Production Board As American companies converted to war production, many business leaders became frustrated with the mobilization process. Government agencies argued constantly about supplies and contracts and whose orders had the highest priority.

After Pearl Harbor, President Roosevelt tried to improve the system by creating the **War Production Board** (WPB). He gave the WPB the authority to set

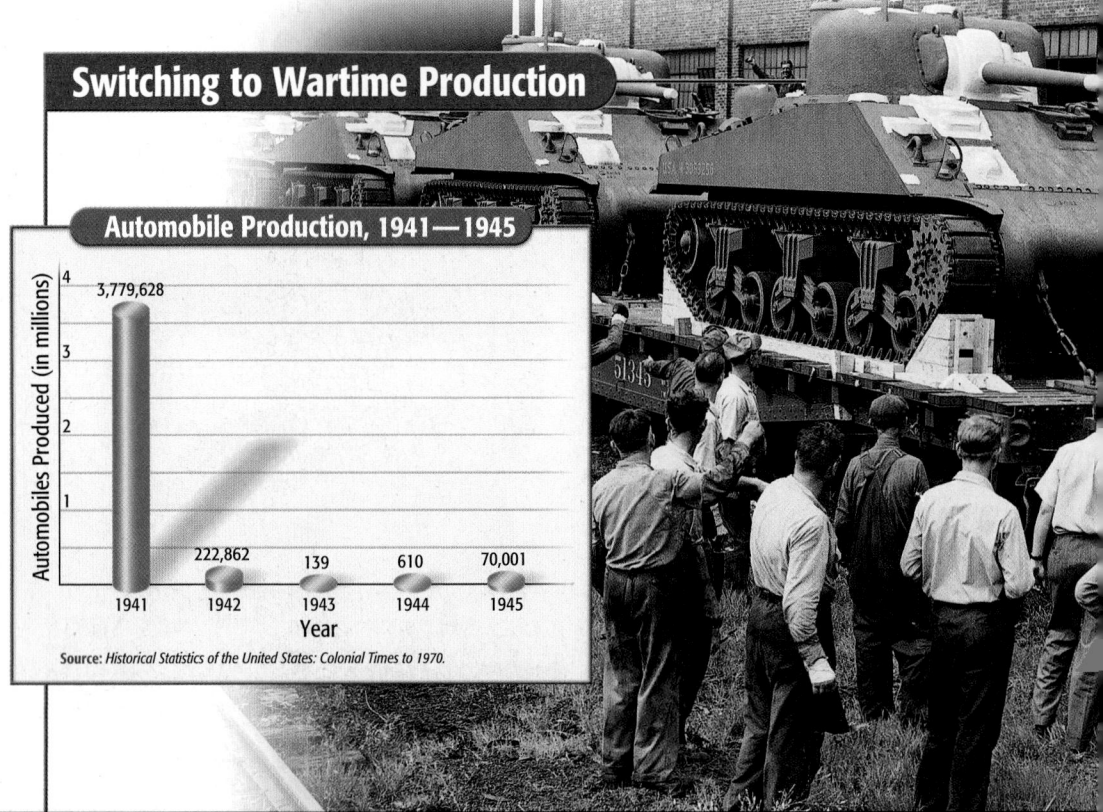

Switching to Wartime Production

Automobile Production, 1941—1945

Automobiles Produced (in millions)

- 1941: 3,779,628
- 1942: 222,862
- 1943: 139
- 1944: 610
- 1945: 70,001

Year

Source: Historical Statistics of the United States: Colonial Times to 1970.

DIFFERENTIATED INSTRUCTION

At-Risk Students Students with language-based learning disabilities often know a variety of strategies for studying text, but they sometimes forget to employ these strategies appropriately. Ask students to preview Section 1 to determine the topics presented. List the topics on the board and ask students to think of strategies and skills they have employed throughout the text that might help in learning the information in this section. **L1** ELL

🖿 Refer to *Inclusion for the High School Social Studies Classroom Strategies and Activities* in the TCR.

priorities and production goals and to control the distribution of raw materials and supplies. Almost immediately, the WPB clashed with the military. Military agencies continued to sign contracts without consulting with the WPB. Finally, in 1943, Roosevelt established the **Office of War Mobilization** (OWM) to settle arguments between the different agencies.

✓ **Reading Check** **Explaining** What military need led to the production of Liberty ships?

Building an Army

Converting factories to war production was only part of the mobilization process. If the United States was actually going to fight and win the war, the country also needed to build up its armed forces.

Creating an Army Within days of Germany's attack on Poland, President Roosevelt expanded the army to 227,000 soldiers. After France surrendered to Germany in June 1940, two members of Congress

introduced the **Selective Service and Training Act,** a plan for the first peacetime draft in American history. Before the spring of 1940, college students, labor unions, isolationists, and most members of Congress had opposed a peacetime draft. Opinions changed after Germany defeated France. In September Congress approved the draft by a wide margin.

You're in the Army Now At first the flood of draftees overwhelmed the army's training facilities. Many recruits had to live in tents and use temporary facilities. The army also endured equipment shortages. Troops carried sticks representing guns, threw stones simulating grenades, and practiced maneuvers with trucks carrying signs that read "TANK."

New draftees were initially sent to a reception center, where they were given physical exams and injections against smallpox and typhoid. The draftees were then issued uniforms, boots, and whatever equipment was available. The clothing bore the label "G.I.," meaning "Government Issue," which is why American soldiers were called "GIs."

After taking aptitude tests, recruits were sent to basic training for eight weeks. They learned how to handle weapons, load backpacks, read maps, pitch tents, and dig trenches. Trainees drilled and exercised constantly and learned how to work as a team.

After the war, many veterans complained that basic training had been useless. Soldiers were rushed through too quickly, and the physical training left them too tired to learn the skills they needed. A sergeant in Italy told a reporter for *Yank* magazine that during a recent battle, a new soldier had held up his rifle and yelled, "How do I load this thing?"

Despite its problems, basic training helped to break down barriers between soldiers. Recruits came from all over the country, and training together made them into a unit. Training created a "special sense of kinship," one soldier noted. "The reason you storm the beaches is not patriotism or bravery. It's that sense of not wanting to fail your buddies."

A Segregated Army Although basic training promoted unity, most recruits did not encounter Americans from every part of society. At the start of the war, the U.S. military was completely segregated. White recruits did not train alongside African Americans. African Americans had separate barracks, latrines, mess halls, and recreational facilities.

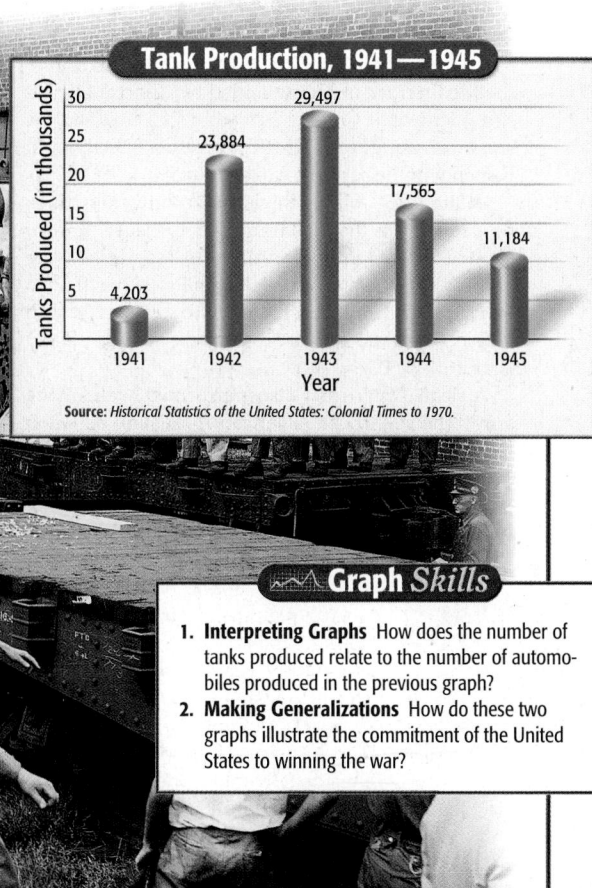

Tank Production, 1941—1945

Tanks Produced (in thousands)

- 1941: 4,203
- 1942: 23,884
- 1943: 29,497
- 1944: 17,565
- 1945: 11,184

Source: *Historical Statistics of the United States: Colonial Times to 1970.*

Graph *Skills*

1. **Interpreting Graphs** How does the number of tanks produced relate to the number of automobiles produced in the previous graph?
2. **Making Generalizations** How do these two graphs illustrate the commitment of the United States to winning the war?

CHAPTER 20 America and World War II **615**

Creating a Chart Have students use the data in the chart that appears on page 615 to create a circle graph showing what proportion of all tanks made between 1941–1945 were made in each of the years. Tell them to use different color slices for each year and to prepare a legend to correlate the colors with the years. **L3**

Writing a Report Have students research the effects of new training bases in one of the Southwestern states. Point out to students that these locations were chosen because of the reliable weather conditions.

World War II Terms A term commonly used by GIs during World War II was *O-dark-30.* The expression means *early in the morning* and refers to military time of 30 minutes past midnight.

From 1948 until 1973, during both peacetime and periods of conflict, men were drafted to fill vacancies in the armed forces which could not be filled through voluntary means. The draft ended in 1973 and the U.S. converted to an all-volunteer military.

INTERDISCIPLINARY CONNECTIONS ACTIVITY

Government Ask students to discuss current U.S. policy regarding readiness for a draft. Ask the following questions: Do you think that current policy would allow the government to mobilize effectively? How do you feel about requiring persons of specific ages, gender, and citizenship status to register? Do you think that women should be required to register? Why or why not? The Selective Service System Web site at www.sss.gov provides information about current policy and answers to frequently asked questions. **L2**

3 ASSESS

Assign Section 1 Assessment as homework or as an in-class activity.

🖰 Have students use the **Interactive Tutor Self-Assessment CD-ROM.**

L1/ELL

Reading Essentials and Study Guide 20–1

L2

Section Quiz 20–1

Picturing History

Background: By the war's end, the Tuskegee Airmen had shot down 111 enemy aircraft, destroyed 150 enemy aircraft on the ground, and, in a rare feat, used machine gun fire from the air to sink a German destroyer.

Answer: European

Ask: Why did the military begin to recruit African Americans?

(President Roosevelt ordered them to recruit African Americans.)

Once trained, African Americans were organized into their own military units, but white officers were generally in command of them. Most military leaders also wanted to keep African American soldiers out of combat and assigned them to construction and supply units.

Pushing for "Double V" Some African Americans did not want to support the war. As one student at a black college noted: "The Army Jim Crows us. . . . Employers and labor unions shut us out. Lynchings continue. We are disenfranchised . . . and spat upon. What more could Hitler do to us than that?" By **disfranchised,** the student meant that African Americans were often denied their right to vote. Despite the bitterness, most African Americans agreed with African American writer Saunders Redding that they should support their country:

❝There are many things about this war I do not like . . . yet I believe in the war. . . . We know that whatever the mad logic of [Hitler's] New Order there is no hope for us under it. The ethnic theories of the Hitler 'master folk' admit of no chance of freedom. . . . This is a war to keep [people] free. The struggle to broaden and lengthen the road of freedom—our own private and important war to enlarge freedom here in America—will come later. . . . I believe in this war because I believe in America. I believe in what America professes to stand for. . . . ❞

—quoted in *America at War*

Picturing History

Tuskegee Airmen The Tuskegee Airmen distinguished themselves in combat, yet they were not allowed to serve in integrated units. In what theater of the war did the Tuskegee Airmen serve?

Benjamin O. Davis, Sr.

Many African American leaders combined patriotism with protest. In 1941 the National Urban League asked its members to encourage African Americans to join the war effort. It also asked them to make plans for building a better society in the United States after the war. The *Pittsburgh Courier*, a leading African American newspaper, launched the **"Double V" campaign.** The campaign urged African Americans to support the war in order to achieve a double victory—a victory over Hitler's racism abroad and America's racism at home.

Under pressure from African American leaders, President Roosevelt ordered the army air force, navy, and marines to recruit African Americans, and he told the army to put African Americans into combat. He also promoted **Colonel Benjamin O. Davis, Sr.,** the highest-ranking African American officer, to the rank of brigadier general.

African Americans in Combat In early 1941, the army air force created its first African American unit, the 99th Pursuit Squadron. The pilots trained in Tuskegee, Alabama, and became known as the **Tuskegee Airmen.** In April 1943, after General Davis urged the military to put African Americans into combat as soon as possible, the squadron was sent to the Mediterranean. Commanded by General Davis's son, Lieutenant Colonel Benjamin O. Davis, Jr., the squadron fought in North Africa and Sicily, and helped win the battle of Anzio in Italy.

In late 1943, Colonel Davis took command of three new squadrons that had trained at Tuskegee. Known as the 332nd Fighter Group, these squadrons were ordered to protect American bombers as they flew to their targets. The 332nd Fighter Group flew 200 such missions and did not lose a single bomber to enemy aircraft.

African Americans also performed well in the army. The all-African American 761st Tank Battalion was commended for its service during the Battle of the Bulge. Fighting in northwest Europe, African Americans in the 614th Tank Destroyer Battalion won 8 Silver Stars for distinguished service, 28 Bronze Stars, and 79 Purple Hearts.

Although the military did not end all segregation during the war, it did integrate military bases in 1943 and steadily expanded the role of African Americans within the armed forces. These successes paved the way for President Truman's decision to fully integrate the military in 1948.

CRITICAL THINKING ACTIVITY

Analyzing Events World War II resulted in the devastation of lives and property. Ask students the following questions: Could World War II have been avoided? Why or why not? *(Answers will vary. Some students might say that it could have been avoided if the Allies had not used the policy of appeasement with Hitler in the late 1930s. They might also indicate that it could have been avoided if the League of Nations had been given greater power after World War I. Other students might say that a war could not have been avoided, because force was the only way to stop the military aggression of Germany and Japan.)* **L2**

Women Join the Armed Forces As in World War I, women joined the armed forces. The army enlisted women for the first time, although they were barred from combat. Instead, as the army's recruiting slogan suggested, women were needed to "release a man for combat." Many jobs in the army were administrative and clerical. By assigning women to these jobs, more men would be available for combat.

Congress first allowed women in the military in May 1942, when it established the **Women's Army Auxiliary Corps** (WAAC) and appointed **Oveta Culp Hobby**, an official with the War Department, to serve as its first director. Although pleased about the establishment of the WAAC, many women were unhappy that it was an auxiliary corps and not part of the regular army. A little over a year later, the army replaced the WAAC with the **Women's Army Corps** (WAC). Director Hobby was assigned the rank of colonel. "You have a debt and a date," Hobby explained to those training to be the nation's first women officers. "A debt to democracy, a date with destiny." The Coast Guard, the navy, and the marines quickly followed the army and set up their own women's units. In addition to serving in these new organizations, another 68,000 women served as nurses in the army and navy.

Americans Go to War The Americans who went to war in 1941 were not well trained. Most of the troops had no previous military experience. Most of the officers had never led men in combat. The armed forces mirrored many of the tensions and prejudices of American society. Despite these challenges, the United States armed forces performed well in battle.

Picturing **History**

Women Pilots General Barney M. Giles inspects the guard of honor of the Women Airforce Service Pilots (WASPS) at Avenger Field in Sweetwater, Texas. Many pilots wore Filfinella patches (right) for good luck. Why do you think the army refused to allow women to fly in combat?

Of all the major powers involved in the war, the United States suffered the fewest casualties in combat.

American troops never adopted the spit-and-polish style of the Europeans. When they arrived at the front, Americans' uniforms were usually a mess, and they rarely marched in step. When one Czechoslovakian was asked what he thought of the sloppy, unprofessional American soldiers, he commented, "They walk like free men."

✓ **Reading Check** **Summarizing** How did the status of women and African Americans in the armed forces change during the war?

 Study Central™ To review this section, go to **tarvol2.glencoe.com** and click on **Study Central™.**

SECTION 1 ASSESSMENT

Checking for Understanding
1. **Define:** cost-plus, Liberty ship, disfranchise.
2. **Identify:** Reconstruction Finance Corporation, War Production Board, Selective Service and Training Act.
3. **Describe** the role of the OWM in the war production effort.

Reviewing Themes
4. **Individual Action** Why do you think African Americans were willing to fight in the war even though they suffered discrimination in American society?

Critical Thinking
5. **Evaluating** How effectively did American industry rally behind the war effort? Give examples to support your opinion.
6. **Categorizing** Use a graphic organizer like the one below to list the challenges facing the United States as it mobilized for war.

Challenges to Mobilization

Analyzing Visuals
7. **Analyzing Graphs** Study the graphs of automobile and tank production on pages 614 and 615. Why did automobile production decrease while tank production increased?

Writing About History
8. **Descriptive Writing** Take on the role of a draftee who has just completed the first week of basic training. Write a letter to your parents telling them about basic training and what you hope to accomplish once the training is over.

CHAPTER 20 America and World War II **617**

SECTION 1 ASSESSMENT ANSWERS

1. Terms are in blue.
2. Reconstruction Finance Corporation (p. 613), War Production Board (p. 614), Selective Service and Training Act (p. 615)
3. The OWM resolved conflicts among mobilization agencies.
4. They opposed Hitler's ethnic theories, believed America should wage this war, and demonstrated their support for democracy and equality at home and overseas.
5. By 1942, almost all major industries were producing trucks, jeeps, and tanks.
6. converting to wartime economy, building an army, training troops
7. Auto manufacturers were producing tanks rather than cars.
8. Answers should be in the form of a letter.

Picturing **History**

Answer: Before the war women's education and career choices were limited. It is likely that army officials thought that women were not mentally or physically capable of combat. **Ask:** Which service was the first to allow women's units? *(the army)*

Reteach
Have students create a two-column chart. In one column, have them list the industries affected by the war mobilization effort. In the other column, have students list how the industries were affected.

Enrich
Have students research one of the persons or organizations mentioned in this section using library and Internet resources to write a one-page paper about the topic.

✓ **Reading Check**
Answer: African Americans had several units that gave distinguished service. Women were allowed to serve in non-combat units.

Study Central™ provides summaries, interactive games, and online graphic organizers to help students review section content.

4 CLOSE

Ask students to speculate on how their lives might be different if the U.S. had not begun to prepare for war when it did.

617

1 FOCUS

Section Overview

This section describes the early battles of World War II.

BELLRINGER
Skillbuilder Activity

Project transparency and have students answer the question.

Daily Focus Skills Transparency 20–2

Reading Preview

Answers to Graphic: April 1942, Doolittle Raid, Allies; May 1942, Philippines, Axis; May 1942, Coral Sea, Allies; June 1942, Midway, Allies; November 1942, Stalingrad, Allies; May 1943, North Africa, Allies

Preteaching Vocabulary
Have students write a paragraph containing at least four of the Key Terms and Names introduced in this section.

The Early Battles

Guide to Reading

Main Idea
By late 1942, the Allies had stopped the German and Japanese advance.

Key Terms and Names
Chester Nimitz, Douglas MacArthur, James Doolittle, periphery, George Patton, convoy system

Reading Strategy
Sequencing As you read about the military campaigns of 1942, complete a time line similar to the one below to record the major battles discussed and the victor in each.

```
           ┌──────┐
    ┌──────┤      │
1942 │     └──────┘     │ 1943
    │      ┌──────┐     │
    └──────┤      ├─────┘
           └──────┘
```

Reading Objectives
• **Analyze** how the Allies were able to fight a war on two fronts and turn the war against the Axis in the Pacific, Russia, and the North Atlantic.
• **Explain** why Stalingrad is considered a major turning point of the war.

Section Theme
Individual Action Many American soldiers made heroic sacrifices in order to turn the tide against the Axis Powers.

Preview of Events

♦1942	♦1943	♦1944

May 1942
Fall of the Philippines; Battle of the Coral Sea

June 1942
Battle of Midway

February 1943
Germans defeated at Stalingrad

May 1943
Germans driven out of North Africa

★ An American Story ★

James S. Thach

On June 4, 1942, Lieutenant Commander James Thach climbed into his F4F Wildcat fighter plane. Thach knew that the Japanese Zero fighter planes were better than his Wildcat. To improve his chances against them, he had developed a new tactic he called the "Thach weave." At the Battle of Midway, he had his first chance to try it:

❝So we boarded our planes. All of us were highly excited and admittedly nervous. . . . A very short time after, Zero fighters came down on us—I figured there were twenty. . . . The air was just like a beehive, and I wasn't sure that anything would work. And then my weave began to work! I got a good shot at two Zeros and burned them . . . then Ram, my wingman, radioed: 'There's a Zero on my tail.' . . . I was really angry then. I was mad because my poor little wingman had never been in combat before [and] this Zero was about to chew him to pieces. I probably should have ducked under the Zero, but I lost my temper and decided to keep my fire going into him so he'd pull out. He did, and I just missed him by a few feet. I saw flames coming out of his airplane. This was like playing chicken on the highway with two automobiles headed for each other, except we were shooting at each other as well.❞

—quoted in *The Pacific War Remembered*

Holding the Line Against Japan

While officers like James Thach developed new tactics to fight the Japanese, the commander of the United States Navy in the Pacific, Admiral **Chester Nimitz,** began planning operations against the Japanese navy. Although the Japanese had badly damaged the American fleet at Pearl Harbor, they had missed the American aircraft carriers,

---

SECTION RESOURCES

📁 Reproducible Masters
• Reproducible Lesson Plan 20–2
• Daily Lecture and Discussion Notes 20–2
• Guided Reading Activity 20–2
• Section Quiz 20–2
• Reading Essentials and Study Guide 20–2
• Performance Assessment Activities and Rubrics

📊 Transparencies
• Daily Focus Skills Transparency 20–2

Multimedia
🔘 Interactive Tutor Self-Assessment CD-ROM
🔘 ExamView® Pro Testmaker CD-ROM
🔘 Presentation Plus! CD-ROM
🔘 TeacherWorks™ CD-ROM
🔊 Audio Program

which were at sea on a mission. The United States had several carriers in the Pacific, and Nimitz was determined to use them. In the days just after Pearl Harbor, however, he could do little to stop Japan's advance into Southeast Asia.

The Fall of the Philippines A few hours after they bombed Pearl Harbor, the Japanese attacked American airfields in the Philippines. Two days later, Japanese troops landed in the islands. The American and Filipino forces defending the Philippines were badly outnumbered. Their commander, General **Douglas MacArthur,** decided to retreat to the Bataan Peninsula. Using the peninsula's rugged terrain, MacArthur's troops held out for more than three months. Gradually, the lack of supplies along with diseases such as malaria, scurvy, and dysentery took their toll. Realizing MacArthur's capture would demoralize the American people, President Roosevelt ordered the general to evacuate to Australia. In Australia MacArthur made a promise: "I came through, and I shall return."

On April 9, 1942, the weary defenders of Bataan finally surrendered. Nearly 78,000 prisoners of war were forced to march—sick, exhausted, and starving—65 miles (105 km) to a Japanese prison camp. Thousands died on this march, which came to be known as the **Bataan Death March.** Here one captured American, Leon Beck, recalls the nightmare:

66 They'd halt us in front of these big artesian wells . . . so we could see the water and they wouldn't let us have any. Anyone who would make a break for water would be shot or bayoneted. Then they were left there. Finally, it got so bad further along the road that you never got away from the stench of death. There were bodies laying all along the road in various degrees of decomposition—swollen, burst open, maggots crawling by the thousands. . . . 99

—quoted in *Death March: The Survivors of Bataan*

Although the troops in the Bataan Peninsula surrendered, a small force held out on the island of **Corregidor** in Manila Bay. Finally, in May 1942, Corregidor surrendered. The Philippines had fallen.

The Doolittle Raid Even before the fall of the Philippines, President Roosevelt was searching for a way to raise the morale of the American people. He wanted to bomb Tokyo, but American planes could reach Tokyo only if an aircraft carrier brought them close enough. Unfortunately, Japanese ships in the North Pacific prevented carriers from getting close enough to Japan to launch their short-range bombers.

In early 1942, a military planner suggested replacing the carrier's usual short-range bombers with long-range B-25 bombers that could attack from farther away. Although B-25s could take off from a carrier, they could not land on its short deck. After attacking Japan, they would have to land in China.

President Roosevelt put Lieutenant Colonel **James Doolittle** in command of the mission. At the end of March, a crane loaded sixteen B-25s onto the aircraft carrier *Hornet.* The next day the *Hornet* headed west across the Pacific. On April 18, American bombs fell on Japan for the first time.

Striking Back: The Doolittle Raid, April 18, 1942

The plan for the Doolittle raid was to launch B-25 bombers from aircraft carriers between 450 and 650 miles from Japan. The planes would bomb selected targets, and fly another 1,200 miles to airfields in China.

All went well until the Japanese discovered the carriers more than 150 miles from the proposed launch site. Instead of canceling the mission, the bombers took off early. The planes reached Japan and dropped their bombs, but they did not have enough fuel to reach the friendly airfields in China. The crews were forced to bail out or crash-land, and only 71 of the 80 crew members survived. Nevertheless, the raid provided an instant boost to sagging American morale.

Planes arrive in China
Carriers launch B-25s
Tokyo is bombed

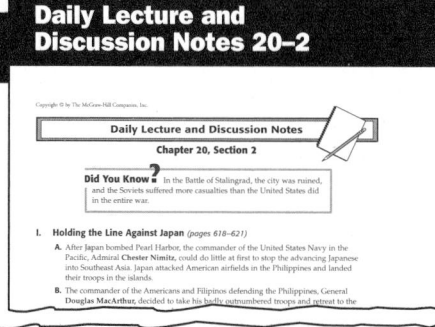

2 TEACH

Daily Lecture and Discussion Notes 20–2

Copyright © by The McGraw-Hill Companies, Inc.

Daily Lecture and Discussion Notes
Chapter 20, Section 2

Did You Know ? In the Battle of Stalingrad, the city was ruined, and the Soviets suffered more casualties than the United States did in the entire war.

I. **Holding the Line Against Japan** (pages 618–621)

A. After Japan bombed Pearl Harbor, the commander of the United States Navy in the Pacific, Admiral **Chester Nimitz,** could do little at first to stop the advancing Japanese into Southeast Asia. Japan attacked American airfields in the Philippines and landed its troops in the islands.

B. The commander of the Americans and Filipinos defending the Philippines, General **Douglas MacArthur,** decided to take his badly outnumbered troops and retreat to the

Writing a Press Release
Organize the class into two groups. Have one group represent Roosevelt. Have the other group represent the Japanese leaders. As you review each of the major battles in the Pacific front discussed in this section, have each group write a press release intended for publication to their people the day after the battle. **L1**

More About the Photo

In addition to the B-25 bombers used for the Doolittle raid, the U.S. also used B-24 and B-29 bombers and P-38 and P-40 fighter planes during the course of World War II. Ask students why they think American leaders decided not to cancel the mission. *(Because the Japanese had bombed American soil and captured U.S. forces, American leaders felt that bombing Japan would raise American morale.)*

Geography *Skills*

Background: Before World War II, few of the indigenous peoples of the islands of the South Pacific had encountered people from other parts of the world.

Answers:

1. June 4, 1942, 4:30 A.M.

2. Aircraft carriers reduced the distance planes had to fly and the amount of fuel they consumed.

Geography Skills Practice

Ask: What general direction did the *Enterprise* and *Hornet* take? *(southwest)*

Writing a Report Ask students to prepare a one-page report on the career of a World War II military leader. The report should address how the leader contributed to the war effort and what the leader did earlier or later in his career. **L2**

📁 Use the rubric for creating a book review, research report, or position paper on pages 79–80 in the *Performance Assessment Activities and Rubrics.*

L1/ELL

Guided Reading Activity 20–2

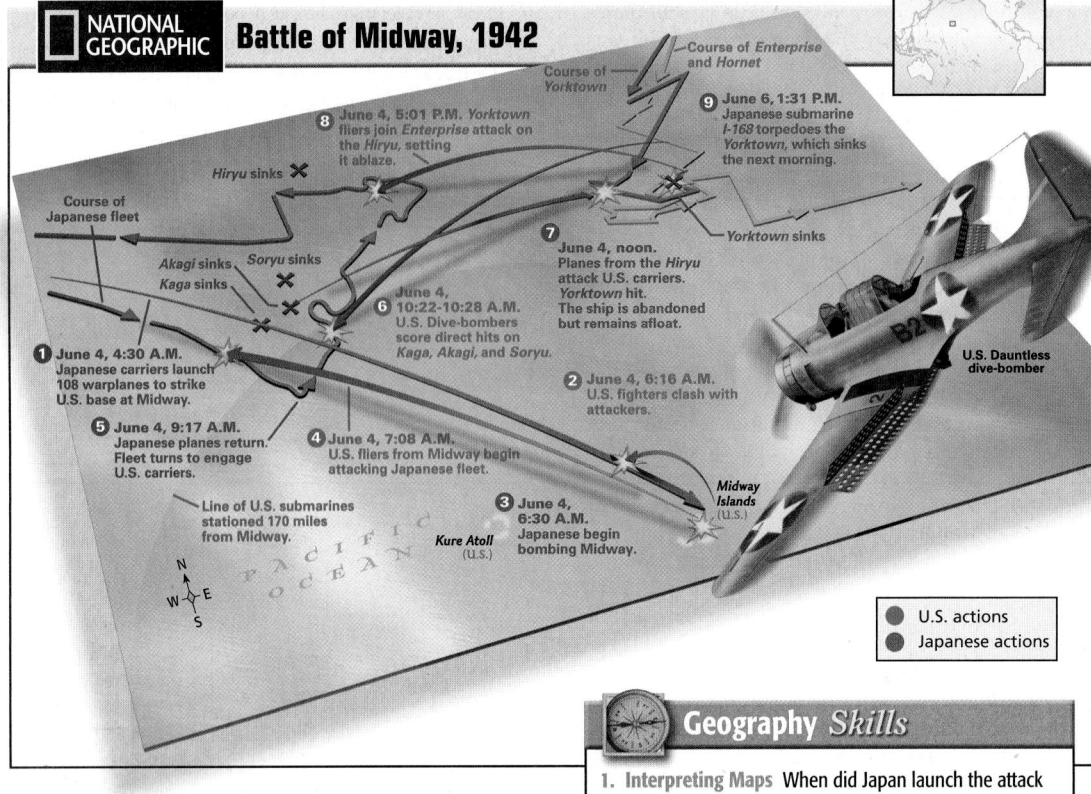

NATIONAL GEOGRAPHIC **Battle of Midway, 1942**

Course of Enterprise and Hornet

Course of Yorktown

8 June 4, 5:01 P.M. *Yorktown* fliers join *Enterprise* attack on the *Hiryu*, setting it ablaze.

9 June 6, 1:31 P.M. Japanese submarine *I-168* torpedoes the *Yorktown*, which sinks the next morning.

Hiryu sinks ✕

Course of Japanese fleet

Akagi sinks *Soryu sinks*

Kaga sinks

Yorktown sinks

7 June 4, noon. Planes from the *Hiryu* attack U.S. carriers. *Yorktown* hit. The ship is abandoned but remains afloat.

6 June 4, 10:22-10:28 A.M. U.S. Dive-bombers score direct hits on *Kaga*, *Akagi*, and *Soryu*.

1 June 4, 4:30 A.M. Japanese carriers launch 108 warplanes to strike U.S. base at Midway.

2 June 4, 6:16 A.M. U.S. fighters clash with attackers.

5 June 4, 9:17 A.M. Japanese planes return. Fleet turns to engage U.S. carriers.

4 June 4, 7:08 A.M. U.S. fliers from Midway begin attacking Japanese fleet.

3 June 4, 6:30 A.M. Japanese begin bombing Midway.

Midway Islands (U.S.)

Line of U.S. submarines stationed 170 miles from Midway.

Kure Atoll (U.S.)

PACIFIC OCEAN

N W E S

U.S. Dauntless dive-bomber

● U.S. actions
● Japanese actions

Geography *Skills*

1. **Interpreting Maps** When did Japan launch the attack on Midway?
2. **Applying Geography Skills** Why were aircraft carriers so vital to the war in the Pacific?

A Change in Japanese Strategy While Americans were overjoyed that the air force had finally struck back, Japanese leaders were aghast. Doolittle's bombs could have killed the emperor. The Doolittle raid convinced Japanese leaders to change their strategy.

Before the raid, the Japanese Navy had been arguing about what to do next. The officers in charge of the navy's planning wanted to cut American supply lines to Australia by capturing the south coast of New Guinea. The commander of the fleet, Admiral Yamamoto, wanted to attack Midway Island—the last American base in the North Pacific west of Hawaii. Yamamoto believed that attacking Midway would lure the American fleet into battle and enable his fleet to destroy it.

After Doolittle's raid, the planners dropped their opposition to Yamamoto's plan. The American fleet had to be destroyed in order to protect Tokyo from bombing. The attack on New Guinea would still go ahead, but only three aircraft carriers were assigned to the mission. All of the other carriers were ordered to prepare for an assault on Midway.

620 CHAPTER 20 America and World War II

The Battle of the Coral Sea The Japanese believed that they could proceed with two different attacks. They thought the United States was unaware of Japan's activity and would not be able to respond in time. Japan did not know that an American team of code breakers, based in Hawaii, had already broken the Japanese Navy's secret code for conducting operations.

In March 1942, decoded Japanese messages alerted the United States to the Japanese attack on New Guinea. In response, Admiral Nimitz sent two carriers, the *Yorktown* and the *Lexington*, to intercept the Japanese in the Coral Sea. There, in early May, carriers from both sides launched all-out airstrikes against each other. Although the Japanese sank the *Lexington* and badly damaged the *Yorktown*, the American attacks forced the Japanese to call off their landing on the south coast of New Guinea. The American supply lines to Australia stayed open.

DIFFERENTIATED INSTRUCTION

English Learners Have students select one portion of Section 2 to teach to another student. Ask students to read the passage and then to teach it to a partner. Have the student doing the teaching ask questions about what has been taught. Direct the teaching student to review any concepts that the learner did not understand. **L1** ELL

📁 Refer to *Inclusion for the High School Social Studies Classroom Strategies and Activities* in the TCR.

JAPANESE FORCES To destroy the U.S. Pacific Fleet, crippled by the 1941 attack on Pearl Harbor, Japan plots an occupation of two Aleutian islands and an invasion of Midway. Strategists believe that the twin actions will lure U.S. carriers to their doom. Two Japanese carriers and 58 other ships sail for the Aleutians. For Midway, Japan commits 4 large carriers, 2 light carriers, 280 planes, 7 battleships, 14 cruisers, 15 submarines, 42 destroyers, and more than 30 supporting ships. These include transports carrying 5,000 troops to take Midway.

U.S. FORCES No battleships guard U.S. carriers sent to Midway to engage the enemy fleet. Into combat go 3 carriers, including battle-damaged Yorktown. Protecting them are 8 cruisers and 16 destroyers. The U.S. has a total of 360 aircraft, including 234 carrier-based fighters and small bombers. Based on Midway are 28 fighters, 46 small bombers, 31 PBY Catalina scout planes, 4 Marauder medium bombers, and 17 Flying Fortresses. Most pilots on Midway have never flown in combat.

TURNING POINT

The Battle of Midway Back at Pearl Harbor, the code-breaking team that had alerted Nimitz to the attack on New Guinea now learned of the plan to attack Midway. With so many ships at sea, Admiral Yamamoto transmitted the plans for the Midway attack by radio, using the same code the Americans had already cracked.

Admiral Nimitz had been waiting for the opportunity to ambush the Japanese fleet. He immediately ordered carriers to take up positions near Midway. Unaware they were heading into an ambush, the Japanese launched their aircraft against Midway on June 4, 1942. The island was ready. The Japanese planes ran into a blizzard of antiaircraft fire, and 38 of them were shot down.

As the Japanese prepared a second wave to attack Midway, aircraft from the American carriers *Hornet, Yorktown,* and *Enterprise* launched a counterattack. The American planes caught the Japanese carriers with fuel, bombs, and aircraft exposed on their flight decks. Within minutes three Japanese carriers were reduced to burning wrecks. A fourth was sunk a few hours later. By nightfall it was apparent that the Americans had

dealt the Japanese navy a deadly blow. Admiral Yamamoto ordered his remaining ships to retreat.

The Battle of Midway was a turning point in the war. The Japanese Navy lost four of its largest carriers—the heart of its fleet. Just six months after Pearl Harbor, the United States had stopped the Japanese advance in the Pacific. As Admiral Ernest King, the commander in chief of the U.S. Navy, later observed, Midway "put an end to the long period of Japanese offensive action." The victory was not without cost, however. The battle killed 362 Americans and 3,057 Japanese. Afterward, one naval officer wrote to his wife: "Let no one tell you or let you believe that this war is anything other than a grim, terrible business."

Reading Check **Explaining** Why was the Battle of Midway considered a turning point?

Turning Back the German Army

In 1942 Allied forces began to win victories in Europe as well. Almost from the moment the United States entered the war, Joseph Stalin, the leader of the Soviet Union, urged President Roosevelt to open a second front in Europe. Stalin appreciated the Lend-Lease supplies that the United States had sent, but the Soviet people were still doing most of the fighting. If British and American troops opened a second front by attacking Germany from the west, it would take pressure off the Soviet Union.

Roosevelt wanted to get American troops into battle in Europe, but Prime Minister Churchill urged caution. He did not believe the United States and Great Britain were ready to launch a full-scale invasion of Europe. Instead Churchill wanted to attack the periphery, or edges, of the German empire. Roosevelt agreed, and in July 1942 he ordered the invasion of Morocco and Algeria—two French territories indirectly under German control.

The Struggle for North Africa Roosevelt decided to invade Morocco and Algeria for two reasons. First, the invasion would give the army some experience without requiring a lot of troops. More importantly, once American troops were in North Africa, they would be able to help British troops fighting the Germans in Egypt.

 Student Web Activity Visit the *American Republic Since 1877* Web site at tarvol2.glencoe.com and click on *Student Web Activities–Chapter 20* for an activity on America and World War II.

Creating a Thematic Map Have students create a map of the Pacific region with labels for major landforms and bodies of water. Students should also label the countries to show whether they were an Allied nation, a neutral nation, or part of the Japanese Empire. **L2**

Use the rubric for creating a map, display, or chart on pages 65–66 in the *Performance Assessment Activities and Rubrics.*

Reading Check

Answer: The Japanese lost four large carriers and their initiative.

FYI

The Japanese flag shown on page 621 is the regimental flag for the Japanese cavalry and infantry. The national flag of Japan since 1870 has consisted of a white background with a red circle in the middle. The red circle is said to symbolize the rising sun.

Objectives and answers to the student activity can be found in the **Web Activity Lesson Plan** at tarvol2.glencoe.com.

INTERDISCIPLINARY CONNECTIONS ACTIVITY

Visual Arts Have students work in groups to research and report on the military vessels and planes used in World War II. Ask students to organize their research to show the development of the vessels during the course of the war. Have students illustrate their work with photos, drawings, and models. Create a display area to showcase students' work. **L2**

Profiles IN HISTORY

Use a Venn diagram to compare and contrast the lives and military careers of Nimitz and Yamamoto.

3 ASSESS

Assign Section 2 Assessment as homework or as an in-class activity.

⊙ Have students use the **Interactive Tutor Self-Assessment CD-ROM.**

L1/ELL

Reading Essentials and Study Guide 20–2

Name _____ Date _____ Class _____

Study Guide

Chapter 20, Section 2
For use with textbook pages 618–623

THE EARLY BATTLES

KEY TERMS AND NAMES

Chester Nimitz the commander of the United States Navy in the Pacific *(page 618)*

Douglas MacArthur the commander of the American and Filipino forces in the Philippines *(page 619)*

James Doolittle lieutenant colonel and head of the mission to bomb Tokyo *(page 619)*

periphery the edges *(page 621)*

George Patton commander of the American forces in Morocco during the American invasion of North Africa *(page 622)*

convoy system a system in which cargo ships traveled in groups and were escorted by navy warships *(page 623)*

L2

Section Quiz 20–2

Name _____ Date _____ Class _____

★ **Chapter 20** — Score _____

Section Quiz 20-2

DIRECTIONS: Matching Match each item in Column A with the items in Column B. Write the correct letters in the blanks. *(10 points each)*

Column A
___ 1. cargo ships traveled in groups and were escorted by navy warships
___ 2. turning point in the war that put the Germans on the offensive
___ 3. edges
___ 4. turning point in the war that stopped the Japanese advance in the Pacific
___ 5. when 78,000 prisoners of war were forced to march 65 miles to a Japanese prison camp

Column B
A. Battle of Midway
B. Battle of Stalingrad
C. Bataan Death March
D. convoy system
E. periphery

Profiles IN HISTORY

Fleet Admiral Chester W. Nimitz 1885–1966

Taking command of the Pacific Fleet after the bombing of Pearl Harbor, Admiral Chester Nimitz did not view the Japanese attack as a complete disaster. The United States still had its aircraft carriers, and base facilities were in good repair. Even though the battle fleet was at the bottom of the harbor, most of the ships could be retrieved and repaired. If the Japanese had attacked the fleet at sea, nothing would have been salvageable.

Nimitz believed that the only way to win the war was to keep constant pressure on the Japanese. He ordered attacks in early 1942 and firmly backed the Doolittle raid. Nimitz planned the American campaigns that turned the tide of war at Midway and Guadalcanal. Nimitz kept the pressure on the Japanese throughout the war, and he signed the Japanese surrender document as the official representative of the United States government in 1945. In less than four years, he had taken a badly damaged fleet and made it victorious throughout the Pacific.

Admiral Isoroku Yamamoto 1884–1943

The son of a schoolmaster, Isoroku Yamamoto spent his entire adult life in the military. In the 1930s he was one of the few Japanese leaders who opposed war with the United States. Yamamoto did so not because he was a pacifist, but because he feared Japan would lose.

When he realized that Japan's leaders were intent on war, Yamamoto became convinced that Japan's only hope lay in launching a surprise attack that would destroy the American Pacific Fleet. Although some officers opposed his plan, Yamamoto won out, and he planned and implemented the attack on Pearl Harbor. During the first years of the war, he enjoyed tremendous prestige because of Japanese victories he helped engineer.

In April 1943 the admiral took an inspection flight of several islands. Having already broken the Japanese codes, the Americans knew of the flight. On April 18, American fighters shot down Yamamoto's plane in the South Pacific, and the admiral was killed in the attack.

Egypt was very important to Britain because of the Suez Canal. Most of Britain's empire, including India, Hong Kong, Singapore, Malaya, and Australia, used the canal to send supplies to Britain. The German forces in the area, known as the "Afrika Korps," were commanded by General Erwin Rommel—a brilliant leader whose success earned him the nickname "Desert Fox."

The British forced Rommel to retreat at the battle of El Alamein, but his forces remained a serious threat. On November 8, 1942, the American invasion of North Africa began under the command of General Dwight D. Eisenhower. The American forces in Morocco, led by General **George Patton,** quickly captured the city of Casablanca, while those in Algeria seized the cities of Oran and Algiers. The Americans then headed east into Tunisia, while British forces headed west into Libya. The plan was to trap Rommel between the two Allied forces.

When the American troops advanced into the mountains of western Tunisia, they had to fight the German army for the first time. They did not do well. At the **Battle of Kasserine Pass,** the Americans were outmaneuvered and outfought. They suffered roughly 7,000 casualties and lost nearly 200 tanks. Eisenhower fired the general who led the attack and put Patton in

command. Together, the American and British forces finally pushed the Germans back. On May 13, 1943, the last German forces in North Africa surrendered.

The Battle of the Atlantic As American and British troops fought the German army in North Africa, the war against German submarines in the Atlantic Ocean continued to intensify. After Germany declared war on the United States, German submarines entered American coastal waters. They found American cargo ships to be easy targets, especially at night when the glow from the cities in the night sky silhouetted the vessels. To protect the ships, cities on the East Coast dimmed their lights every evening. People also put up special "blackout curtains" and drove with their headlights off.

By August 1942, German submarines had sunk about 360 American ships along the American coast. So many oil tankers were sunk that gasoline and fuel oil had to be rationed. To keep oil flowing, the government built the first long-distance oil pipeline, stretching some 1,250 miles (2,010 km) from the Texas oil fields to Pennsylvania.

The loss of so many ships convinced the U.S. Navy to set up a convoy system. Under this system, cargo ships traveled in groups and were escorted by navy warships. The convoy system improved the

622 CHAPTER 20 America and World War II

Reading Strategy — READING THE TEXT

Comparing and Contrasting After reading the section, ask students to review the information by comparing and contrasting the early battles that the Allies fought against the Japanese and the Germans. In small groups, have students prepare charts showing the similarities and differences that they discover. Have the groups post their charts in the class. Give the groups time to review the charts. Then hold a class discussion on what they discovered. **L1**

▸ Refer to *Inclusion for the High School Social Studies Classroom Strategies and Activities* in the TCR.

situation dramatically. It made it much harder for a submarine to torpedo a cargo ship and escape without being attacked.

The spring of 1942 marked the high point of the German submarine campaign. In May and June alone, over 1.2 million tons of shipping were sunk. Yet in those same two months, American and British shipyards built over 1.1 million tons of new shipping. From July 1942 onward, American shipyards produced more ships than German submarines managed to sink. At the same time, American airplanes and warships began to use new technology, including radar, sonar, and depth charges, to locate and attack submarines. As the new technology began to take its toll on German submarines, the Battle of the Atlantic slowly turned in favor of the Allies.

TURNING POINT

Stalingrad In the spring of 1942, before the Battle of the Atlantic turned against Germany, Adolf Hitler was very confident he would win the war. Rommel's troops were pushing the British back in Egypt. German submarines were sinking American ships rapidly, and the German army was ready to launch a new offensive to knock the Soviets out of the war.

Hitler was convinced that the only way to defeat the Soviet Union was to destroy its economy. In May 1942, he ordered his army to capture strategic oil fields, industries, and farmlands in southern Russia and Ukraine. The key to the attack was the city of Stalingrad. The city controlled the Volga River and was a major railroad junction. If the German army captured Stalingrad, the Soviets would be cut off from the resources they needed to stay in the war.

When German troops entered Stalingrad in mid-September, Stalin ordered his troops to hold the city

Picturing **History**

Halting the German Advance Soviet troops assault German positions in Stalingrad in November 1942. *Why did the Soviet army need to hold on to the city of Stalingrad?*

at all cost. Retreat was forbidden. The Germans were forced to fight from house to house, losing thousands of soldiers in the process.

On November 23, Soviet reinforcements arrived and surrounded Stalingrad, trapping almost 250,000 German troops. When the battle ended in February 1943, 91,000 Germans had surrendered, although only 5,000 of them survived the Soviet prison camps and returned home after the war. The Battle of Stalingrad was a major turning point in the war. Just as the Battle of Midway put the Japanese on the defensive for the rest of the war, the Battle of Stalingrad put the Germans on the defensive as well.

✓ **Reading Check** **Evaluating** What did the Allies do to win the Battle of the Atlantic?

HISTORY Online **Study Central™** To review this section, go to tarvol2.glencoe.com and click on **Study Central™.**

SECTION 2 ASSESSMENT

Checking for Understanding

1. **Define:** periphery, convoy system.
2. **Identify:** Chester Nimitz, Douglas MacArthur, James Doolittle, George Patton.
3. **Explain** the American strategy in North Africa.

Reviewing Themes

4. **Individual Action** How did the Doolittle raid help boost American morale?

Critical Thinking

5. **Analyzing** How did code breakers help stop Japanese advances?
6. **Evaluating** How were the Americans able to win the Battle of the Atlantic?
7. **Organizing** Use a graphic organizer like the one below to list the reasons the Battle of Midway was a major turning point in the war.

> Battle of Midway

Analyzing Visuals

8. **Examining Maps** Study the map of Midway on page 620. Why do you think the Japanese forces attacked when they did?

Writing About History

9. **Descriptive Writing** Take on the role of an American soldier fighting in the Pacific in World War II. Write a letter to your family explaining what conditions are like for you and what you hope to accomplish during the war.

CHAPTER 20 America and World War II **623**

Picturing **History**

Answer: to keep their supply lines open

Ask: What was the result of the battle for Stalingrad? *(The battle put the Germans on the defensive and was a turning point of the war.)*

Reteach
List the significant events that were discussed in this section on the board. Have students identify which Axis power was involved in each event.

Enrich
Have students create a table showing every geographical location named in this section, along with an explanation of the location's significance as it related to World War II. Have students locate and mark each location on a world map.

✓ **Reading Check**

Answer: In addition to using the convoy system to protect cargo ships, the Allies used new technology to locate and attack German submarines.

HISTORY Online

Study Central™ provides summaries, interactive games, and online graphic organizers to help students review section content.

4 CLOSE

Ask students to speculate on what happened to the 91,000 German troops who surrendered at Stalingrad.

SECTION 2 ASSESSMENT ANSWERS

1. Terms are in blue.
2. Chester Nimitz *(p. 618),* Douglas MacArthur *(p. 619),* James Doolittle *(p. 619),* George Patton *(p. 622)*
3. The North African campaign gave the army some experience and helped the British in Egypt.
4. Americans felt they had avenged

Pearl Harbor by attacking Japanese soil.

5. They alerted the U.S. to the imminent attacks on New Guinea and Midway.
6. the convoy system protected cargo ships; radar, sonar, and depth charges located and damaged German submarines

7. Japanese navy lost four carriers; stopped the Japanese advance in the Pacific; ended Japanese offensive
8. Answers may note that early morning attacks held an element of surprise.
9. Letters should focus on soldiers' emotions and activities.

TEACH

Reading a Thematic Map This skill emphasizes the importance of maps to understanding many historical events. By learning to read military maps using the legends, map scale, and other visuals, students gain an appreciation for the influence of geography on history.

Have students trace the troop movements of the Japanese and U.S. forces. Ask students to identify the main battles that occurred on the Bataan Peninsula.

Additional Practice

L1

Reinforcing Skills Activity 20

GLENCOE TECHNOLOGY

CD-ROM
Glencoe Skillbuilder Interactive Workbook CD-ROM, Level 2

This interactive CD-ROM reinforces student mastery of essential social studies skills.

Social Studies SKILLBUILDER

Reading a Thematic Map

Why Learn This Skill?

In your study of American history, you will often encounter thematic maps. Knowing how to read a thematic map will help you get more out of it.

Learning the Skill

Military maps use colors, symbols, and arrows to show major battles, troop movements, and defensive positions during a particular battle or over a period of time. When reading a military map, follow these steps:

- **Read the map title.** This will indicate the location and time period covered on the map.
- **Read the map key.** This tells what the symbols on the map represent. For example, battle sites may be indicated by crossed swords or burst shells.
- **Study the map itself.** This will reveal the actual event or sequence of events that took place. Notice the geography of the area, and try to determine how it could affect military strategy.
- **Use the map to draw conclusions.**

Practicing the Skill

The map on this page shows troop movements in the Philippines from December 1941 to May 1942. Analyze the information on the map, then answer the following questions.

❶ What part of the world does the map show?

❷ When did MacArthur leave for Australia? What information on the map shows you this?

❸ Where did the Japanese imprison the survivors of the Bataan Death March?

❹ What geographic features did the Japanese encounter on the Bataan Peninsula?

Skills Assessment

Complete the Practicing Skills questions on page 651 and the Chapter 20 Skill Reinforcement Activity to assess your mastery of this skill.

NATIONAL GEOGRAPHIC
Bataan and Corregidor, December 1941–May 1942

Map key:
- ← U.S. retreat to Bataan
- ← Japanese forces
- ← MacArthur to Australia
- ◄--- "Death March" of U.S. prisoners
- ▲▲▲▲ U.S. defensive line at date shown
- ✳ Japanese victory
- ⊛ USAFFE HQ
- ▨ Occupied by Japanese

Lambert Equal-Area projection

0 ——— 15 miles
0 ——— 15 kilometers

Applying the Skill

Reading a Thematic Map Study the map of the Battle of Midway on pages 620–621. Use the information on the map to answer the following questions.

1. When was the battle fought?

2. What American aircraft carriers took part in the battle?

3. What was the fate of the *Hiryu*?

 Glencoe's **Skillbuilder Interactive Workbook CD-ROM, Level 2,** provides instruction and practice in key social studies skills.

ANSWERS TO PRACTICING THE SKILL

❶ Bataan and Corregidor, in Southeast Asia

❷ March 12, the date beside the troop movement arrow

❸ Camp O'Donnell

❹ mountainous terrain

Applying the Skill

1. June 4–6, 1942

2. *Enterprise, Hornet,* and *Yorktown*

3. It sank.

Guide to Reading

Main Idea
World War II placed tremendous demands on Americans at home and led to new challenges for all Americans.

Key Terms and Names
Rosie the Riveter, A. Philip Randolph, Sunbelt, zoot suit, rationing, victory garden, E bond

Reading Strategy
Categorizing As you read about the challenges facing Americans on the home front, complete a graphic organizer listing opportunities for women and African Americans before and after the war. Also evaluate what progress still needed to be made after the war.

Opportunities			
	Before War	After War	Still Needed
Women			
African Americans			

Reading Objectives
- **Describe** how the wartime economy created opportunities for women and minorities.
- **Discuss** how Americans coped with shortages and rapidly rising prices.

Section Theme
Civic Rights and Responsibilities To win the war, American citizens at home made countless changes in work patterns and lifestyles.

Preview of Events

♦1941	♦1942	♦1943	♦1944

June 1941
Executive Order 8802 forbids race discrimination in industries with government contracts

August 1941
Roosevelt creates the Office of Price Administration

February 1942
Japanese American relocation ordered

June 1943
Race riots in Detroit; zoot suit riots in Los Angeles

1 FOCUS

Section Overview
This section describes life in the United States during World War II.

BELLRINGER
Skillbuilder Activity

Project transparency and have students answer the question.

Daily Focus Skills Transparency 20–3

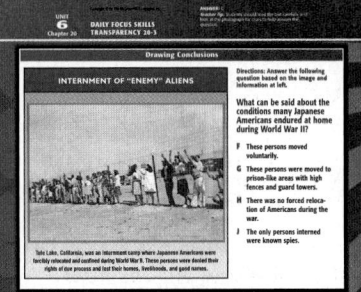

Reading Preview

Answers to Graphic: Women– Before war, few worked outside the home and job opportunities were limited to low-paying jobs. After war women were more accepted in the workforce. African Americans–Before war, African Americans had limited employment opportunities. After war, they were protected by the Fair Employment Practices Commission. Students' ideas about what is still needed for both groups will vary.

Preteaching Vocabulary
Have students create two posters that feature the Key Terms and Names.

★ An American Story ★

Laura Briggs was a young woman living on a farm in Idaho when World War II began. As with many other Americans, the war completely changed her outlook on life:

66When I was growing up, it was very much depression times. . . . As farm prices [during the war] began to get better and better, farm times became good times. . . . We and most other farmers went from a tarpaper shack to a new frame house with indoor plumbing. Now we had an electric stove instead of a wood-burning one, and running water at the sink. . . . The war made many changes in our town. I think the most important is that aspirations changed. People suddenly had the idea, 'Hey I can reach that. I can have that. I can do that. I could even send my kid to college if I wanted to.'99

—quoted in *Wartime America: The World War II Home Front*

"Rosie the Riveter" symbolized new roles for women

Women and Minorities Gain Ground

As American troops fought their first battles against the Germans and Japanese, the war began to dramatically change American society at home. In contrast to the devastation the war brought to large parts of Europe and Asia, World War II had a positive effect on American society. The war finally put an end to the Great Depression. Mobilizing the economy created almost 19 million new jobs and nearly doubled the average family's income.

When the war began, American defense factories wanted to hire white men. With so many men in the military, there simply were not enough white men to fill all of the jobs. Under pressure to produce, employers began to recruit women and minorities.

CHAPTER 20 America and World War II **625**

SECTION RESOURCES

Reproducible Masters
- Reproducible Lesson Plan 20–3
- Daily Lecture and Discussion Notes 20–3
- Guided Reading Activity 20–3
- Section Quiz 20–3
- Reading Essentials and Study Guide 20–3

Transparencies
- Daily Focus Skills Transparency 20–3

- American Art & Architecture

Multimedia
- Interactive Tutor Self-Assessment CD-ROM
- ExamView® Pro Testmaker CD-ROM
- Presentation Plus! CD-ROM
- TeacherWorks™ CD-ROM
- Audio Program
- American Music: Cultural Traditions

2 TEACH

Daily Lecture and Discussion Notes 20–3

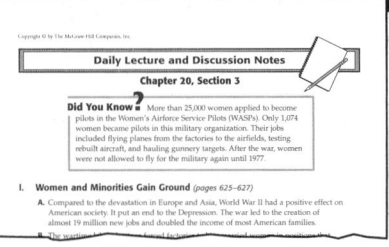

Copyright © by The McGraw-Hill Companies, Inc.

Daily Lecture and Discussion Notes
Chapter 20, Section 3

Did You Know? More than 25,000 women applied to become pilots in the Women's Airforce Service Pilots (WASPs). Only 1,074 women became pilots in this military organization. Their jobs included flying planes from the factories to the airfields, testing rebuilt aircraft, and hauling gunnery targets. After the war, women were not allowed to fly for the military again until 1977.

I. Women and Minorities Gain Ground (pages 625–627)

A. Compared to the devastation in Europe and Asia, World War II had a positive effect on American society. It put an end to the Depression. The war led to the creation of almost 19 million new jobs and doubled the income of most American families.

Writing a Letter Have students take on the role of a young woman who just took a job working in a defense factory during the war and is writing to her grandmother about her first few days on the job. **L1**

📁 Use the rubric for creating a diary, short story, memorandum, or letter on pages 69–70 in the *Performance Assessment Activities and Rubrics.*

Profiles IN HISTORY

One of the advantages of using Navajo code talkers was that a three-line English message could be encoded, transmitted, and decoded in about 20 seconds. Code machines in use at the time took at least 30 minutes to perform the same task.

Ask: What is the significance of the Navajo language being a "hidden language"? *(Because the language has no written alphabet and was known only to a few people, it was a very secure code.)*

Women in the Defense Plants During the Depression, many people believed married women should not work outside the home, especially if it meant taking jobs away from men trying to support their families. Most women who did work were young, single, and employed in traditional female jobs. The wartime labor shortage, however, forced factories to recruit married women to do industrial jobs that traditionally had been reserved for men.

Although the government hired nearly 4 million women for mostly clerical jobs, it was the women in the factories who captured the public's imagination. The great symbol of the campaign to hire women was **"Rosie the Riveter,"** a character from a popular song by the Four Vagabonds. The lyrics told of Rosie, who worked in a factory while her boyfriend served in the marines. Images of Rosie appeared on posters, in newspapers, and in magazines. Eventually 2.5 million women went to work in shipyards, aircraft factories, and other manufacturing plants. For many older middle-class women like Inez Sauer, working in a factory changed their perspective:

Profiles IN HISTORY

The Navajo Code Talkers
1942–1945

When American marines stormed an enemy beach, they used radios to communicate. Using radios, however, meant that the Japanese could intercept and translate the messages. In the midst of the battle, however, there was no time to use a code machine. Acting upon the suggestion of Philip Johnston, an engineer who had lived on a Navajo reservation as a child, the marines recruited Navajos to serve as "code talkers."

The Navajo language was a "hidden language"—it had no written alphabet and was known only to the Navajo and a few missionaries and anthropologists. The Navajo recruits developed a code using words from their own language to represent military terms. For example, the Navajo word *jay-sho,* or "buzzard," was code for bomber; *lotso,* or "whale," meant battleship; and *na-ma-si,* or "potatoes," stood for grenades.

Code talkers proved invaluable in combat. They could relay a message in

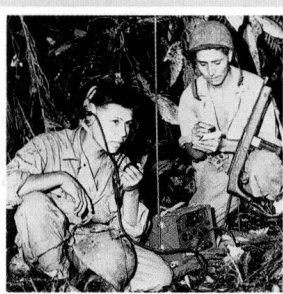

minutes that would have taken a code machine operator hours to encipher and transmit. At the battle of Iwo Jima, code talkers transmitted more than 800 messages during the first 48 hours as the marines struggled to get ashore under intense bombardment.

Over 400 Navajo served in the marine corps as code talkers. Sworn to secrecy, their mission was not revealed until many years after the war. In 2001 Congress awarded the code talkers the Congressional Gold Medal to recognize their unique contribution to the war effort.

626 CHAPTER 20 America and World War II

❝I learned that just because you're a woman and have never worked is no reason you can't learn. The job really broadened me. . . . I had always been in a shell; I'd always been protected. But at Boeing I found a freedom and an independence I had never known. After the war I could never go back to playing bridge again, being a clubwoman. . . . when I knew there were things you could use your mind for. The war changed my life completely.❞

—quoted in *Eyewitness to World War II*

Although most women left the factories after the war, their success permanently changed American attitudes about women in the workplace.

African Americans Demand War Work Although factories were hiring women, they resisted hiring African Americans. Frustrated by the situation, **A. Philip Randolph,** the head of the Brotherhood of Sleeping Car Porters—a major union for African American railroad workers—decided to take action.

He informed President Roosevelt that he was organizing "from ten to fifty thousand [African Americans] to march on Washington in the interest of securing jobs . . . in national defense and . . . integration into the military and naval forces."

In response, Roosevelt issued Executive Order 8802, on June 25, 1941. The order declared, "there shall be no discrimination in the employment of workers in defense industries or government because of race, creed, color or national origin." To enforce the order, the president created the Fair Employment Practices Commission—the first civil rights agency established by the federal government since the Reconstruction era.

Mexicans Become Farmworkers The wartime economy needed workers in many different areas. To help farmers in the Southwest overcome the labor shortage, the government introduced the **Bracero Program** in 1942. *Bracero* is Spanish for worker. The federal government arranged for Mexican farmworkers to help in the harvest. Over 200,000 Mexicans came to the United States to help harvest

---

Reading Strategy ▸ READING THE TEXT

Varying Reading Rate Students will learn that some text selections are more difficult to read than others, and they must make adjustments to their reading rate. Remind students to slow down when they encounter difficult concepts, connections to previous ideas, new vocabulary, or text that contains a great deal of information. **L1** ELL

📁 Refer to *Inclusion for the High School Social Studies Classroom Strategies and Activities* in the TCR.

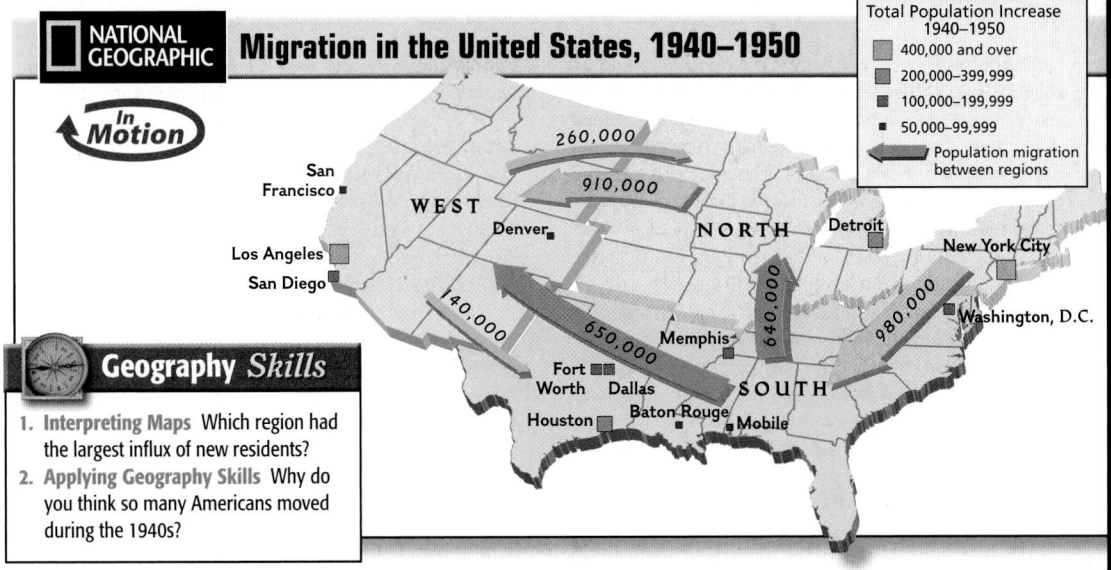

Migration in the United States, 1940–1950

Total Population Increase 1940–1950
- 400,000 and over
- 200,000–399,999
- 100,000–199,999
- 50,000–99,999
- → Population migration between regions

WEST — 260,000 — 910,000
San Francisco
Los Angeles
San Diego
Denver
140,000
650,000
NORTH
Detroit
New York City
Washington, D.C.
640,000
980,000
Memphis
Fort Worth
Dallas
Houston
Baton Rouge
Mobile
SOUTH

Geography *Skills*

1. **Interpreting Maps** Which region had the largest influx of new residents?
2. **Applying Geography Skills** Why do you think so many Americans moved during the 1940s?

Geography *Skills*

Background: Remind students that during World War II the United States consisted of only 48 states. Alaska and Hawaii had not yet become states.

Answers:

1. the West, with 1,560,000 (650,000 from the South and 910,000 from the North)
2. job opportunities

Geography Skills Practice
Give students a list of the 48 states and ask them to use the map to classify the states by region.

---

fruit and vegetables in the Southwest. Many also helped to build and maintain railroads. The Bracero Program continued until 1964. Migrant farmworkers became an important part of the Southwest's agricultural system.

✓ **Reading Check** **Describing** How did mobilizing the economy help end the Depression?

A Nation on the Move

The wartime economy created millions of new jobs, but the Americans who wanted these jobs did not always live nearby. To get to the jobs, 15 million Americans moved during the war. Although the assembly plants of the Midwest and the shipyards of the Northeast attracted many workers, most Americans headed west and south in search of jobs.

Taken together, the growth of southern California and the expansion of cities in the Deep South created a new industrial region—the Sunbelt. For the first time since the Industrial Revolution began in the United States, the South and West led the way in manufacturing and urbanization.

The Housing Crisis Perhaps the most difficult task facing cities with war industries was deciding where to put the thousands of new workers. Many people had to live in tents and tiny trailers. To help solve the housing crisis, the federal government allocated over $1.2 billion to build public housing, schools, and community centers during the war.

Although prefabricated government housing had tiny rooms, thin walls, poor heating, and almost no privacy, it was better than no housing at all. Nearly two million people lived in government-built housing during the war.

Racism Explodes Into Violence African Americans began to leave the South in great numbers during World War I, but this **"Great Migration,"** as historians refer to it, slowed during the Depression. When jobs in war factories opened up for African Americans during World War II, the Great Migration resumed. When African Americans arrived in the crowded cities of the North and West, however, they were often met with suspicion and intolerance. Sometimes these attitudes led to violence.

The worst racial violence of the war erupted in Detroit on Sunday, June 20, 1943. The weather that day was sweltering. To cool off, nearly 100,000 people crowded into Belle Isle, a park on the Detroit River. Fights erupted between gangs of white and African American teenage girls. These fights triggered others, and a full-scale riot erupted across the city. By the time the violence ended, 25 African Americans and 9 whites had been killed. Despite the appalling violence in Detroit, African American leaders remained committed to their Double V campaign.

The Zoot Suit Riots Wartime prejudice erupted elsewhere as well. In southern California, racial tensions became entangled with juvenile delinquency. Across the nation, crimes committed by young people rose dramatically. In Los Angeles, racism against Mexican Americans and the fear of juvenile crime became linked because of the "zoot suit."

CHAPTER 20 America and World War II **627**

✓ **Reading Check**

Answer: Mobilizing the economy for war production created nearly 19 million new jobs and nearly doubled the average family's income.

L1/ELL

Guided Reading Activity 20–3

History *and the* Humanities

♪ American Music: Cultural Traditions: "Take Me Back to Tulsa," "Boogie Woogie Bugle Boy"

🏛 American Art & Architecture: *The Red Stairway*

DIFFERENTIATED INSTRUCTION

At-Risk Students Have students work in small groups to create a short play about daily life in the United States during the war. Encourage students to use props and costumes that represent the period. Have the groups present their plays to the rest of the class. As a class, discuss what students have learned about the daily lives of people in the United States during World War II. **L1** ELL

📁 Refer to *Inclusion for the High School Social Studies Classroom Strategies and Activities* in the TCR.

Expressing an Opinion Provide the following information: In March 1942, United States General John DeWitt, acting under War Department orders, began the evacuation of all persons of Japanese descent from the western half of Washington, Oregon, and California, and from southern Arizona. Most of the evacuees were American citizens. DeWitt explained the evacuation by saying, "It makes no difference whether a Japanese is theoretically a citizen. He is still Japanese . . ." Organize the class into groups and have each group draft a response to DeWitt's statement. **L2**

📁 Use *Supreme Court Case Study 23,* Endo v. *United States.*

📁 Use *Supreme Court Case Study 24,* Korematsu v. *United States.*

NATIONAL GEOGRAPHIC

List the names and locations of the following camps on the board and have students use a map to point out the general locations of the camps: Amache, Colorado; Gila River, Arizona; Heart Mountain, Wyoming; Jerome, Arkansas; Manzanar, California; Minidoka, Idaho; Poston, Arizona; Rohwer, Arkansas; Topaz, Utah; and Tule Lake, California. Ask students to look at the picture and describe the emotions that these young boys are probably feeling.

A **zoot suit** had very baggy, pleated pants and an overstuffed, knee-length jacket with wide lapels. Accessories included a wide-brimmed hat and a long key chain. Zoot-suit wearers usually wore their hair long, gathered into a ducktail. The zoot suit angered many Americans. In order to save fabric for the war, most men wore a **"victory suit"**—a suit with no vest, no cuffs, a short jacket, and narrow lapels. By comparison, the zoot suit seemed unpatriotic.

In California, Mexican American teenagers adopted the zoot suit. In June 1943, after hearing rumors that zoot suiters had attacked several sailors, 2,500 soldiers and sailors stormed into Mexican American neighborhoods in Los Angeles. They attacked Mexican American teenagers, cut their hair, and tore off their zoot suits. The police did not intervene, and the violence continued for several days. The city of Los Angeles responded by banning the zoot suit.

Racial hostility against Mexican Americans did not deter them from joining the war effort. Approximately 500,000 Hispanic Americans served in the armed forces during the war. Most—about 400,000—were Mexican American. Another 65,000 were from Puerto Rico. They fought in Europe, North Africa, and the Pacific, and by the end of the war, 17 Mexican Americans had received the Medal of Honor.

Japanese American Relocation When Japan attacked Pearl Harbor, many West Coast Americans turned their anger against Japanese Americans. Mobs attacked Japanese American businesses and homes. Banks would not cash their checks, and grocers refused to sell them food.

Newspapers printed rumors about Japanese spies in the Japanese American community. Members of Congress, mayors, and many business and labor leaders demanded that all people of Japanese ancestry be removed from the West Coast. They did not believe that Japanese Americans would remain loyal to the United States in the face of war with Japan.

On February 19, 1942, President Roosevelt gave in to pressure and signed an order allowing the War Department to declare any part of the United States to be a military zone and to remove anybody they wanted from that zone. Secretary of War Henry Stimson declared most of the West Coast a military zone and ordered all people of Japanese ancestry to evacuate to 10 internment camps.

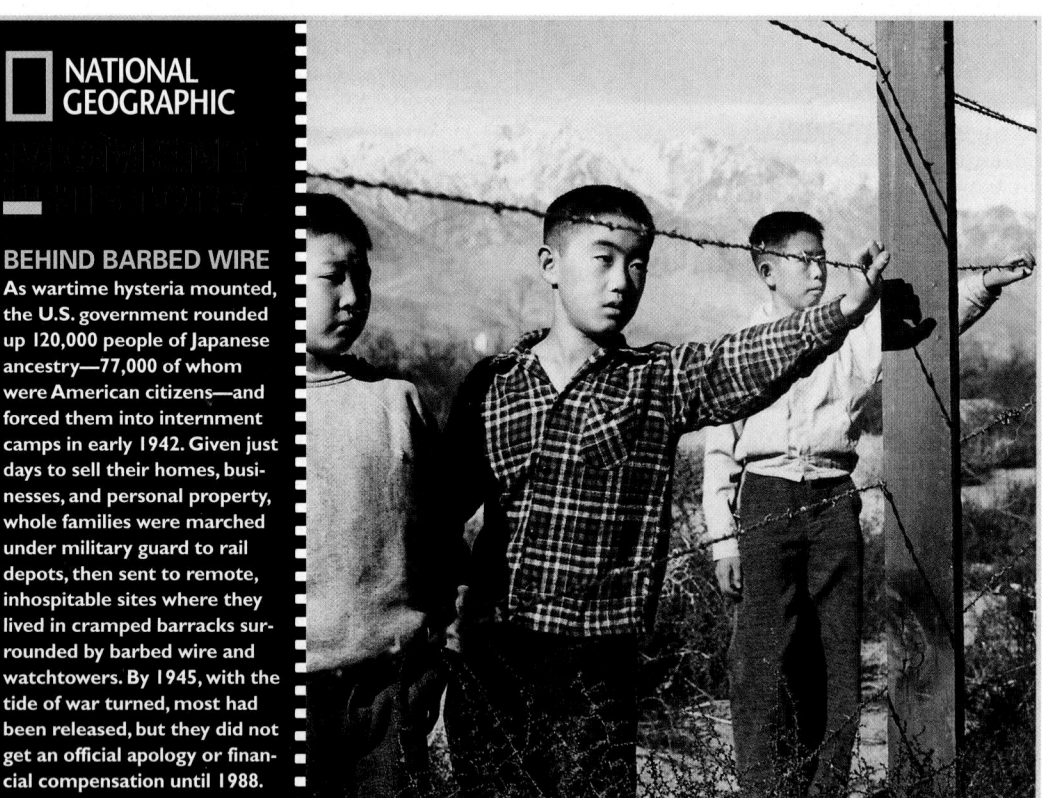

NATIONAL GEOGRAPHIC

BEHIND BARBED WIRE

As wartime hysteria mounted, the U.S. government rounded up 120,000 people of Japanese ancestry—77,000 of whom were American citizens—and forced them into internment camps in early 1942. Given just days to sell their homes, businesses, and personal property, whole families were marched under military guard to rail depots, then sent to remote, inhospitable sites where they lived in cramped barracks surrounded by barbed wire and watchtowers. By 1945, with the tide of war turned, most had been released, but they did not get an official apology or financial compensation until 1988.

INTERDISCIPLINARY CONNECTIONS ACTIVITY

Economics Have students work in small groups to explore the effects of inflation on consumer prices. Ask the groups to research the way in which inflation is measured, especially the makeup of the Consumer Price Index (CPI). Ask the groups to prepare tabletop displays showing the effects of inflation from 1900 to 1999. Encourage groups to link the periods of high or low inflation to political and social events. **L3**

Not all Japanese Americans accepted the relocation without protest. Fred Korematsu argued that his rights had been violated and took his case to the Supreme Court. In December 1944, in *Korematsu v. the United States*, the Supreme Court ruled that the relocation was constitutional because it was based not on race, but on "military urgency." Shortly afterward, the Court did rule in *Ex Parte Endo* that loyal American citizens could not be held against their will. In early 1945, therefore, the government began to release the Japanese Americans from the camps. 📖 *(See page 963 for more information on* Korematsu v. the United States.*)*

Despite the fears and rumors, no Japanese American was ever tried for espionage or sabotage. Japanese Americans served as translators for the army during the war in the Pacific. The all-Japanese 100th Battalion, later integrated into the **442nd Regimental Combat Team,** was the most highly decorated unit in World War II.

After the war, the **Japanese American Citizens League** (JACL) tried to help Japanese Americans who had lost property during the relocation. In 1988 President Reagan apologized to Japanese Americans on behalf of the U.S. government and signed legislation granting $20,000 to each surviving Japanese American who had been interned.

✓ **Reading Check** **Comparing** Why did racism lead to violence in Detroit and Los Angeles in 1943?

Daily Life in Wartime America

Housing problems and racial tensions were serious difficulties during the war, but mobilization strained society in many other ways as well. Prices rose, materials were in short supply, and the question of how to pay for it all loomed ominously over the entire war effort.

ECONOMICS

Wage and Price Controls As the economy mobilized, the president worried about inflation. Both wages and prices began to rise quickly during the war because of the high demand for workers and raw materials. To stabilize both wages and prices, Roosevelt created the **Office of Price Administration** (OPA) and the Office of Economic Stabilization (OES). The OES regulated wages and the price of farm products. The OPA regulated all other prices. Despite some problems with labor unions, the OPA and OES were able to keep inflation under control.

Picturing **History**

Rationing Products War rationing affected everyone. Women painted seams on their legs to make it appear they were wearing stockings, because silk was needed to make parachutes instead of stockings. Why was rationing so vital to the war effort?

While the OPA and OES worked to control inflation, the War Labor Board (WLB) tried to prevent strikes that might endanger the war effort. In support, most American unions issued a "no strike pledge," and instead of striking, asked the WLB to serve as a mediator in wage disputes. By the end of the war, the WLB had helped to settle over 17,000 disputes involving more than 12 million workers.

Blue Points, Red Points The demand for raw materials and supplies created shortages. The OPA began rationing, or limiting the availability of, many products to make sure enough were available for military use. Meat and sugar were rationed to provide enough for the army. To save gasoline and rubber, gasoline was rationed, driving was restricted, and the speed limit was set at 35 miles per hour.

Every month each household would pick up a book of ration coupons. Blue coupons, called blue points, controlled processed foods. Red coupons, or red points, controlled meats, fats, and oils. Other coupons controlled items such as coffee and sugar. When people bought food, they also had to give enough coupon points to cover their purchases.

CHAPTER 20 America and World War II **629**

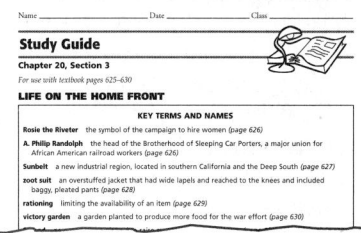

Reading Essentials and Study Guide 20–3

Name _____ Date _____ Class _____

Study Guide

Chapter 20, Section 3
For use with textbook pages 625–630

LIFE ON THE HOME FRONT

KEY TERMS AND NAMES

Rosie the Riveter the symbol of the campaign to hire women *(page 626)*
A. Philip Randolph the head of the Brotherhood of Sleeping Car Porters, a major union for African American railroad workers *(page 626)*
Sunbelt a new industrial region, located in southern California and the Deep South *(page 627)*
zoot suit an overstuffed jacket that had wide lapels and reached to the knees and included baggy, pleated pants *(page 628)*
rationing limiting the availability of an item *(page 629)*
victory garden a garden planted to produce more food for the war effort *(page 630)*

CRITICAL THINKING ACTIVITY

Evaluating Decisions In 1942 the U.S. government removed more than 100,000 people of Japanese birth and ancestry from their homes on the Pacific Coast to relocation centers. There was also a desire to relocate Americans of German and Italian descent from the West Coast, but only 10,000 were moved. Ask students the following question: Do you think the government ever has the right to relocate or keep a group in detention? Why or why not? *(Answers will vary. Students who oppose the relocation policy might suggest that it was a violation of civil rights; those who agree with the policy might indicate that sometimes the country's security takes precedence over the issue of a group's rights.)* L2

L2

Section Quiz 20–3

Name _____ Date _____ Class _____

★ Chapter 20   Score ☐

Section Quiz 20-3

DIRECTIONS: Matching Match each item in Column A with the items in Column B.
Write the correct letters in the blanks. (10 points each)

Column A	Column B
___ 1. first civil rights agency established by the federal government since the Reconstruction era	A. Japanese American Citizens League
___ 2. gardens planted to produce more food for the war effort	B. victory gardens
___ 3. tried to help Japanese Americans who had lost property during the relocation	C. "Rosie the Riveter"
___ 4. created to stabilize both wages and prices	D. Office of Price Administration
___ 5. symbol of the campaign to hire women during the wartime labor shortage	E. Fair Employment Practices Commission

Analyzing *Political Cartoons*

Answer: to be conscious of the dangers their city lights pose to American sailors

Reteach

Have students create a poster encouraging efforts such as rationing, victory gardens, or war bonds.

Enrich

Have students prepare a two-minute oral presentation on one of the neutral countries shown on the map on page 642 explaining the reasons for neutrality.

Reading Check

Answer: Rationing limited access to common products, but allowed people to purchase necessities.

HISTORY
Online

Study Central™ provides summaries, interactive games, and online graphic organizers to help students review section content.

4 CLOSE

As a class, discuss the effects of prejudice in society by focusing on groups discriminated against in the 1940s and today.

630

Illumination for the Shooting Gallery

Analyzing *Political Cartoons*

Turning Off the Lights Early in the war, lights from eastern cities silhouetted ships along the east coast, making them easy targets for German submarines. Americans were asked to turn out lights or put up dark curtains. What point is the cartoon making to Americans?

Victory Gardens and Scrap Drives Americans also planted gardens to produce more food for the war effort. Any area of land might become a garden—backyards, schoolyards, city parks, and empty lots. The government encouraged victory gardens by praising them in film reels, pamphlets, and official statements.

Certain raw materials were so vital to the war effort that the government organized scrap drives. Americans collected spare rubber, tin, aluminum, and steel. They donated pots, tires, tin cans, car bumpers, broken radiators, and rusting bicycles. Oils and fats were so important to the production of explosives that the WPB set up fat-collecting stations. Americans would exchange bacon grease and meat drippings for extra ration coupons. The scrap drives were very successful and one more reason for the success of American industry during the war.

Paying for the War The United States had to pay for all of the equipment and supplies it needed. The federal government spent more than $300 billion during World War II—more money than it had spent from Washington's administration to the end of Franklin Roosevelt's second term.

To raise money, the government raised taxes. Because most Americans opposed large tax increases, Congress refused to raise taxes as high as Roosevelt requested. As a result, the extra taxes collected covered only 45 percent of the cost of the war.

To raise the rest of the money, the government issued war bonds. When Americans bought bonds, they were loaning money to the government. In exchange for the money, the government promised that the bonds could be cashed in at some future date for the purchase price plus interest. The most common bonds were **E bonds,** which sold for $18.75 and could be redeemed for $25.00 after 10 years. Individual Americans bought nearly $50 billion worth of war bonds. Banks, insurance companies, and other financial institutions bought the rest—over $100 billion worth of bonds.

"V" for Victory Despite the hardships, the overwhelming majority of Americans believed the war had to be fought. Although the war brought many changes to the United States, most Americans remained united behind one goal—winning the war.

Reading Check **Evaluating** How did rationing affect daily life in the United States? How did it affect the economy?

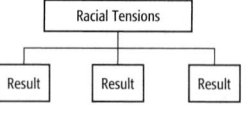

Study Central™ To review this section, go to tarvol2.glencoe.com and click on **Study Central**™.

SECTION 3 ASSESSMENT

Checking for Understanding

1. **Define:** Sunbelt, rationing, victory garden.
2. **Identify:** Rosie the Riveter, A. Philip Randolph, zoot suit, E bond.
3. **Explain** how the federal government expanded during the war.

Reviewing Themes

4. **Civic Rights and Responsibilities** What changes did American citizens and industry have to make to adapt to the war?

Critical Thinking

5. **Evaluating** If you had been a government official during the war, how would you have proposed paying for the war?
6. **Categorizing** Use a graphic organizer like the one below to list the results of increased racial tensions during the war.

Racial Tensions
→ Result | Result | Result

Analyzing Visuals

7. **Examining Maps** Study the map on page 627. Which cities had populations over 400,000?
8. **Analyzing Photographs** Study the photograph on page 628. Why were Japanese Americans interned?

Writing About History

9. **Persuasive Writing** Write a newspaper editorial urging fellow citizens to conserve resources so that these resources can be diverted to the war effort.

SECTION 3 ASSESSMENT ANSWERS

1. Terms are in blue.
2. Rosie the Riveter *(p. 626)*, A. Philip Randolph *(p. 626)*, zoot suit *(p. 628)*, E bond *(p. 630)*
3. New government agencies controlled the economy, raised taxes, and issued war bonds.
4. Industry and workers accepted wage and price controls and agreed to settle wage disputes by using WLB mediators. Citizens accepted rationing, planted victory gardens, recycled, and purchased war bonds.
5. Students' answers should include a rationale for their plan.
6. racial violence in Detroit, juvenile delinquency, Japanese internment
7. Los Angeles, Houston, New York
8. Many believed that they would not remain loyal to the United States.
9. Students' editorials should follow the style of a newspaper editorial.

SECTION 4 Pushing the Axis Back

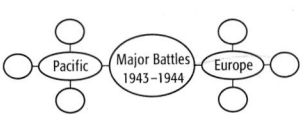

Guide to Reading

Main Idea
The Allies slowly pushed back the German and Japanese forces in 1943 and 1944.

Key Terms and Names
Casablanca Conference, Operation Overlord, D-Day, Omar Bradley, amphtrac, Guadalcanal, kamikaze

Reading Strategy
Organizing As you read about the major battles of 1943 and 1944, complete a graphic organizer similar to the one below by filling in the names of the battles fought. Indicate whether each battle was an Allied or an Axis victory.

Pacific — Major Battles 1943–1944 — Europe

Reading Objectives
• **Describe** the goals of the two major offensives the Allies launched in Europe in 1943.
• **Explain** the American strategy for pushing the Japanese back in the Pacific.

Section Theme
Geography and History The United States fought the war by landing troops in Italy and France and island-hopping across the Pacific toward Japan.

Preview of Events

♦1943		♦1944		♦1945
January 1943 Casablanca Conference	**July 1943** The Allies invade Italy	**November 1943** Roosevelt, Churchill, and Stalin meet at Tehran	**June 6, 1944** D-Day invasion begins	**October 20, 1944** MacArthur returns to the Philippines

---

1 FOCUS

Section Overview
This section describes the Allied strategies and the battles of the later years of World War II.

BELLRINGER
Skillbuilder Activity

 Project transparency and have students answer the question.

Daily Focus Skills Transparency 20–4

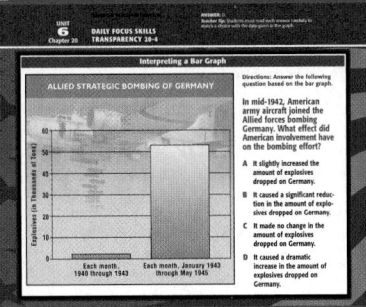

Reading Preview

Answers to Graphic: Pacific–Tarawa Atoll, Gilbert Islands, 1943, Allies; Guam, August 1944, Allies; Europe–Sicily, July–August 1943, Allies; D-Day, June 1944, Allies

Preteaching Vocabulary
Have students write three questions that can be answered using the Key Terms and Names. Remind them to use all the terms and names.

★ An American Story ★

Men board a landing craft on D-Day

On the morning of June 6, 1944, Lieutenant John Bentz Carroll of the 16th Infantry Regiment scrambled down a net ladder from his troop ship to a small landing craft tossing in the waves 30 feet (9 m) below. The invasion of France had begun. Carroll's platoon would be among the first Americans to land in Normandy. Their objective was a beach, code-named "Omaha":

❝Two hundred yards out, we took a direct hit. . . . [A machine gun] was shooting a rat-tat-tat on the front of the boat. Somehow or other, the ramp door opened up . . . and the men in front were being struck by machine gun fire. Everyone started to jump off into the water. They were being hit as they jumped, the machine gun fire was so heavy. . . . The tide was moving us so rapidly. . . . We would grab out on some of those underwater obstructions and mines built on telephone poles and girders, and hang on. We'd take cover, then make a dash through the surf to the next one, fifty feet beyond. The men would line up behind those poles. They'd say, 'You go—you go—you go,' and then it got so bad everyone just had to go anyway, because the waves were hitting with such intensity on these things.❞

—quoted in *D-Day: Piercing the Atlantic Wall*

Striking Back at the Third Reich

As Lieutenant Carroll's experience shows, storming a beach under enemy control can be a terrifying ordeal. There is no cover on a beach, no place to hide, and no way to turn back. Launching an invasion from the sea is very risky. Unfortunately, the Allies had no choice. If they were going to win the war, they had to land their troops in Europe and on islands in the Pacific.

CHAPTER 20   America and World War II   **631**

SECTION RESOURCES

Reproducible Masters
• Reproducible Lesson Plan 20–4
• Daily Lecture and Discussion Notes 20–4
• Guided Reading Activity 20–4
• Section Quiz 20–4
• Reading Essentials and Study Guide 20–4
• Performance Assessment Activities and Rubrics

Transparencies
• Daily Focus Skills Transparency 20–4

Multimedia
🖸 Interactive Tutor Self-Assessment CD-ROM
🖸 ExamView® Pro Testmaker CD-ROM
🖸 Presentation Plus! CD-ROM
🖸 TeacherWorks™ CD-ROM
🖸 Audio Program

2 TEACH

Daily Lecture and Discussion Notes 20-4

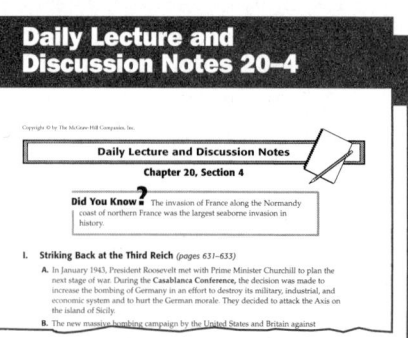

Copyright © by The McGraw-Hill Companies, Inc.

Daily Lecture and Discussion Notes
Chapter 20, Section 4

Did You Know? The invasion of France along the Normandy coast of northern France was the largest seaborne invasion in history.

I. Striking Back at the Third Reich (pages 631–633)

A. In January 1943, President Roosevelt met with Prime Minister Churchill to plan the next stage of war. During the **Casablanca Conference**, the decision was made to increase the bombing of Germany in an effort to destroy its military, industrial, and economic system and to hurt the German morale. They decided to attack the Axis on the island of Sicily.

B. The new massive bombing campaign by the United States and Britain against

Creating a Database Have students create a database of the battles presented in this section. The database should include such information as site, dates, results, and casualties. Encourage students to conduct independent research to fill in any missing fields in the database. Have students use the database to pose and answer questions about the battles fought in Europe.

Picturing History

Background: Being in the infantry meant working as a team. Each soldier had a specific role, and the team counted on each member to perform that role efficiently.

Answer: The Allies thought that the Italians would quit the war if their territory was invaded.

Ask: Who led the Allied forces on the ground during the invasion of Sicily? *(General Patton for the United States and General Montgomery for the British)*

The first large Allied invasion of the war—the attack on North Africa in November 1942—had shown that the Allies could mount a large-scale invasion from the sea. The success of the landings convinced Roosevelt that it was again time to meet with Churchill to plan the next stage of the war. In January 1943, the president headed to Casablanca, Morocco, to meet the prime minister.

At the **Casablanca Conference,** Roosevelt and Churchill agreed to step up the bombing of Germany. The goal of this new campaign was "the progressive destruction of the German military, industrial, and economic system, and the undermining of the morale of the German people." The Allies also agreed to attack the Axis on the island of Sicily. Churchill called Italy the "soft underbelly" of Europe and was convinced that the Italians would quit the war if the Allies invaded their homeland.

Strategic Bombing The Allies had been bombing Germany even before the Casablanca Conference. Britain's Royal Air Force had dropped an average of 2,300 tons (2,093 t) of explosives on Germany every month for over three years. The United States Eighth Army Air Force had joined the campaign in the summer of 1942, and they had dropped an additional 1,500 tons (1,365 t) of bombs by the end of the year.

These numbers were tiny, however, compared to the massive new campaign. Between January 1943 and May 1945, the Royal Air Force and the United States Eighth Army Air Force dropped approximately 53,000 tons (48,230 t) of explosives on Germany every month.

Picturing History

Softening the Gustav Line Infantrymen fire an 81-millimeter mortar to soften the German Gustav Line near the Rapido River. Why do you think the Allies decided to attack first in Italy rather than in France?

The bombing campaign did not destroy Germany's economy or undermine German morale, but it did cause a severe oil shortage and wrecked the railroad system. It also destroyed so many aircraft factories that Germany's air force could not replace its combat losses. By the time the Allies landed in France, they had total control of the air, ensuring that their troops would not be bombed.

Striking at the Soft Underbelly As the bombing campaign against Germany intensified, the plan for the invasion of Sicily moved ahead as well. General Dwight D. Eisenhower was placed in overall command of the invasion. General Patton and the British General Bernard Montgomery were put in charge of the actual forces on the ground. The invasion began before dawn on July 10, 1943. Despite bad weather, the Allied troops made it ashore with few casualties. A new vehicle, the **DUKW**—an amphibious truck—proved very effective in bringing supplies and artillery to the soldiers on the beach.

Eight days after the troops came ashore, American tanks led by General Patton smashed through enemy lines and captured the western half of the island. After capturing western Sicily, Patton's troops headed east, staging a series of daring end-runs around the German positions, while the British, under Montgomery, attacked from the south. By August 18, the Germans had evacuated the island.

The attack on Sicily created a crisis within the Italian government. The king of Italy, Victor Emmanuel, and a group of Italian generals decided that it was time to get rid of Mussolini. On July 25, 1943, the king invited the dictator to his palace. "My dear Duce," the king began, "it's no longer any good. Italy has gone to bits. The soldiers don't want to fight anymore. At this moment, you are the most hated man in Italy." The king then placed Mussolini under arrest, and the new Italian government began secretly negotiating with the Allies for Italy's surrender.

On September 8, 1943, the Italian government publicly announced Italy's surrender. The following day, American troops landed at Salerno. Although stunned by the surrender, Hitler was not about to lose Italy to the Allies. German troops went into action at once. They seized control of northern Italy, including Rome, attacked the Americans at Salerno, and put Mussolini back in power. To stop the Allied advance, the German army took up positions near the heavily

COOPERATIVE LEARNING ACTIVITY

Researching Organize the class into groups of four or five. Have each group report on one of the battles described in this section. Reports should include more in-depth coverage than what is provided in the textbook. Each group should assign a special responsibility to each member in the group such as research, writing, or graphic presentation. Have each group present their report to the rest of the class.

Use the rubric for a cooperative group management plan on pages 71–72 in the *Performance Assessment Activities and Rubrics.*

L1/ELL

Guided Reading Activity 20–4

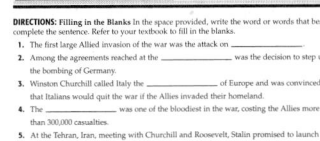

Name _____ Date _____ Class _____

★ Guided Reading Activity 20-4

DIRECTIONS: Filling in the Blanks In the space provided, write the word or words that best complete the sentence. Refer to your textbook to fill in the blanks.

1. The first large Allied invasion of the war was the attack on _____.
2. Among the agreements reached at the _____ was the decision to step up the bombing of Germany.
3. Winston Churchill called Italy the _____ of Europe and was convinced that Italians would quit the war if the Allies invaded their homeland.
4. The _____ was one of the bloodiest in the war, costing the Allies more than 300,000 casualties.
5. At the Tehran, Iran, meeting with Churchill and Roosevelt, Stalin promised to launch a _____ against the Germans when the Allies invaded France in 1944.
6. Stalin also promised that once Germany was beaten, the Soviet Union would help

fortified town of Cassino. The terrain near Cassino was steep, barren, and rocky. Instead of attacking such difficult terrain, the Allies chose to land at Anzio, behind German lines. They hoped the maneuver would force the Germans to retreat. Instead of retreating, however, the Germans surrounded the Allied troops near Anzio.

It took the Allies five months to break through the German lines at **Cassino** and **Anzio.** Finally, in late May 1944, the Germans were forced to retreat. Less than two weeks later, the Allies captured Rome. Fighting in Italy continued, however, until May 2, 1945. The Italian campaign was one of the bloodiest in the war. It cost the Allies more than 300,000 casualties.

Roosevelt Meets Stalin at Tehran
Roosevelt wanted to meet with Stalin before the Allies launched the invasion of France. In late 1943 Stalin agreed, and he proposed that Roosevelt and Churchill meet him in Tehran, Iran.

The leaders reached several agreements. Stalin promised to launch a full-scale offensive against the Germans when the Allies invaded France in 1944. Roosevelt and Stalin then agreed to break up Germany after the war so that it would never again threaten world peace. Stalin also promised that once Germany was beaten, the Soviet Union would help the United States defeat Japan. He also accepted Roosevelt's proposal to create an international organization to help keep the peace after the war.

✓ **Reading Check** **Explaining** What two major decisions did the Allies make at Casablanca?

The Big Three Stalin, Roosevelt, and Churchill meet at Tehran.

Landing in France

After the conference in Tehran, Roosevelt headed to Cairo, Egypt, where he and Churchill continued planning the invasion of France. One major decision still had to be made. The president had to choose the commander for **Operation Overlord**—the code name for the planned invasion. Roosevelt wanted to appoint General George C. Marshall, Chief of Staff for the United States Army, but he depended on Marshall for military advice and did not want to send him to Europe. Instead, the president selected General Eisenhower to command the invasion.

Planning Operation Overlord Knowing that the Allies would eventually invade France, Hitler had fortified the coast. Although these defenses were formidable, the Allies did have one advantage—the element of surprise. The Germans did not know when or where the Allies would land. They believed that the Allies would land in Pas-de-Calais—the area of France closest to Britain. To convince the Germans they were right, the Allies placed inflated rubber tanks, empty tents, and dummy landing craft along the coast across from Calais. To German spy planes, the decoys looked real, and they succeeded in fooling the Germans. The real target was not Pas-de-Calais, but Normandy.

By the spring of 1944, everything was ready. Over 1.5 million American soldiers, 12,000 airplanes, and more than 5 million tons (4.6 million t) of equipment had been sent to England. Only one

CHAPTER 20 America and World War II **633**

More About the Photo

Background: Tehran is the capital of Iran. Tehran was an ideal location for the meeting because it was not a combat area and not a home to any of the big three Allied powers.

Discussing a Topic As a class, discuss how each of the following influenced Operation Overlord: the weather, the decoys placed along the coast opposite Calais, and the choice of five beaches for landing the troops. L1 ELL

FYI

The Women's Airforce Service Pilots tested new and rebuilt fighter planes and flew military aircraft from factories to bases in the United States and Europe. Despite their outstanding service, they did not receive recognition or veterans benefits until 1977.

✓ **Reading Check**

Answer: to step up the bombing of Germany and attack the Axis at Sicily

DIFFERENTIATED INSTRUCTION

At-Risk Students Ask interested students to sketch the typical battle gear of Allied soldiers. Students should include the standard weapons used by the infantry. Have students write a paragraph to accompany each sketch that describes the item and how it was used. L1 ELL

☞ Refer to *Inclusion for the High School Social Studies Classroom Strategies and Activities* in the TCR.

Creating a Table Have students create a table to illustrate these four important conferences: Arcadia, Casablanca, Tehran, and Yalta. The table should include the dates, the city and country where the conference was held, which world leaders attended, and the outcomes. Have students use their tables to pose and answer questions about the purposes and results of the various conferences. **L2**

What If...

A good way to help students understand the importance of historical events is to have them think about what might have happened if things had turned out differently. Have students read the passage and answer the questions on their own. Organize students into small groups and have them discuss their answers.

Answers:
1. Students' answers will vary. Likely answers will focus on how fog and rain would have hindered visibility for landing craft crews, troops approaching the beach, and pilots.
2. Students' answers will vary. Likely answers will focus on the potential casualties and a prolonging of the war if the Germans had known about the attack.

thing was left to do—pick the date and give the command to go. The invasion had to begin at night to hide the ships crossing the English Channel. The ships had to arrive at low tide so that they could see the beach obstacles. The low tide had to come at dawn so that gunners bombarding the coast could see their targets. Before the main landing on the beaches, paratroopers would be dropped behind enemy lines. They required a moonlit night in order to see where to land. Perhaps most important of all, the weather had to be good. A storm would ground the airplanes, and high waves would swamp the landing craft.

Given all these conditions, there were only a few days each month when the invasion could begin. The first opportunity would last from June 5 to 7, 1944. Eisenhower's planning staff referred to the day any operation began by the letter D. The date for the invasion, therefore, came to be known as **D-Day.** Heavy cloud cover, strong winds, and high waves made it impossible to land on June 5. A day later the weather briefly improved. The Channel was still rough, but the landing ships and aircraft could operate. It was a difficult decision. Eisenhower's advisers were split on what to do. After looking at weather forecasts one last time, shortly after midnight on June 6, 1944, Eisenhower gave the final order: "OK, we'll go."

The Longest Day Nearly 7,000 ships carrying more than 100,000 soldiers set sail for the coast of Normandy on June 6, 1944. At the same time, 23,000 paratroopers were dropped inland, east and west of the beaches. Allied fighter-bombers raced up and down the coast, hitting bridges, bunkers, and radar sites. As dawn broke, the warships in the Allied fleet let loose with a tremendous barrage of fire. Thousands of shells rained down on the beaches, code-named "Utah," "Omaha," "Gold," "Sword," and "Juno."

The American landing at Utah Beach went very well. The German defenses were weak, and in less than three hours American troops had captured the beach and moved inland, suffering less than 200 casualties in the process. On the eastern flank, the British and Canadian landings also went well. By the end of the day, British and Canadian forces were several miles inland.

Omaha Beach, however, was a different story. Under intense German fire, the American assault almost disintegrated. As General **Omar Bradley,** the commander of the American forces landing at Omaha

What If...

Operation Overlord Had Failed?

In what some historians believe was the most important weather prediction in military history, Group Captain James Stagg, chief meteorologist for the Royal Air Force, predicted gradual clearing for Normandy, France, on June 6, 1944. The prediction was critical for General Dwight D. Eisenhower, Supreme Commander of the Allied Expeditionary Forces. He had already delayed Operation Overlord once. The invasion forces of Operation Overlord were assembled and ready to go at a moment's notice. Everything depended upon a break in the bad weather so that the assault would take the Germans by surprise. Eisenhower trusted the weather prediction and believed in the battle plan. The day before the invasion, however, he wrote the following note on a small piece of paper—a message he would deliver in the event the invasion failed. He mistakenly jotted "July 5" on the bottom and stuck the note in his wallet.

❝Our landings in the Cherbourg-Havre area have failed to gain a satisfactory foothold and I have withdrawn the troops. My decision to attack at this time and place was based upon the best information available. The troops, the air and the Navy did all that Bravery and devotion to duty could do. If any blame or fault attaches to the attempt it is mine alone.❞

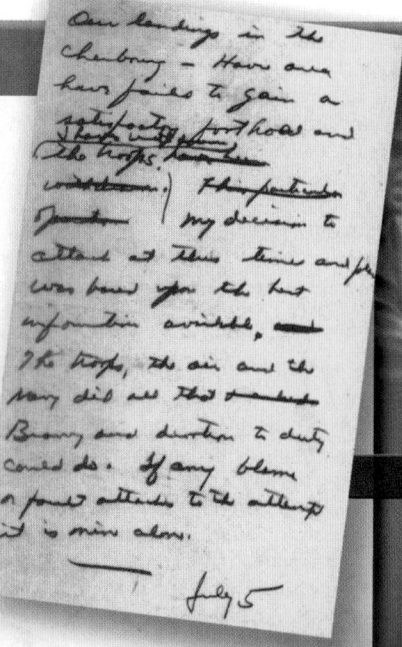

INTERDISCIPLINARY CONNECTIONS ACTIVITY

Performing Arts Have students work in teams to research popular songs and films from this period to determine if the war had an impact on these arts. Have students prepare a short written report along with in-class presentations of their findings. Encourage them to integrate performances into their presentations. Costumes, singing, lip-synching to recorded music, dancing, and skits are all appropriate. **L1** **ELL**

and Utah, grimly watched the carnage, he began making plans to evacuate Omaha. Slowly, however, the American troops began to knock out the German defenses. More landing craft arrived, ramming their way through the obstacles to get to the beach. Nearly 2,500 Americans were either killed or wounded on Omaha, but by early afternoon Bradley received this message: "Troops formerly pinned down on beaches . . . [are] advancing up heights behind beaches." By the end of the day, nearly 35,000 American troops had landed at Omaha, and another 23,000 had landed at Utah. Over 75,000 British and Canadian troops were on shore as well. The invasion had succeeded.

✓ **Reading Check** **Summarizing** What conditions had to be met before Eisenhower could order D-Day to begin?

Driving the Japanese Back

While the buildup for the invasion of France was taking place in Britain, American military leaders were also developing a strategy to defeat Japan. The American plan called for a two-pronged attack. The Pacific Fleet, commanded by Admiral Nimitz, would

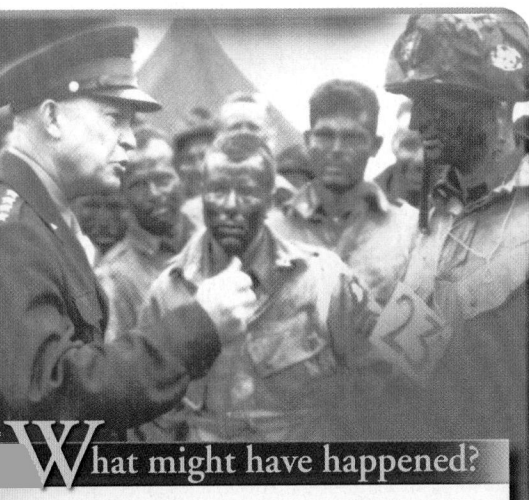

What might have happened?

1. What might have happened if the weather had not changed and the troops had landed amidst fog and rain?

2. What if the invasion had been delayed and the element of surprise lost?

advance through the central Pacific by hopping from one island to the next, closer and closer to Japan. Meanwhile, General MacArthur's troops would advance through the Solomon Islands, capture the north coast of New Guinea, and then launch an invasion to retake the Philippines.

GEOGRAPHY

Island-Hopping in the Pacific By the fall of 1943, the navy was ready to launch its island-hopping campaign, but the geography of the central Pacific posed a problem. Many of the islands were coral reef atolls. The water over the coral reef was not always deep enough to allow landing craft to get to the shore. If the landing craft ran aground on the reef, the troops would have to wade to the beach. As some 5,000 United States Marines learned at Tarawa Atoll, wading ashore could cause very high casualties.

Tarawa, part of the Gilbert Islands, was the Navy's first objective in the Pacific. When the landing craft hit the reef, at least 20 ships ran aground. The marines had to plunge into shoulder-high water and wade several hundred yards to the beach. Raked by Japanese fire, only one marine in three made it ashore. Once the marines reached the beach the battle was still far from over. As reporter Robert Sherrod wrote, the marines faced savage hand-to-hand fighting:

66 A Marine jumped over the seawall and began throwing blocks of fused TNT into a coconut-log pillbox. . . . Two more Marines scaled the seawall, one of them carrying a twin-cylindered tank strapped to their shoulders, the other holding the nozzle of the flame thrower. As another charge of TNT boomed inside the pillbox, causing smoke and dust to billow out, a khaki-clad figure ran out the side entrance. The flame thrower, waiting for him, caught him in its withering stream of intense fire. As soon as it touched him, the [Japanese soldier] flared up like a piece of celluloid. He was dead instantly . . . charred almost to nothingness. 99

—from *Tarawa: The Story of a Battle*

Over 1,000 marines died on Tarawa. Photos of bodies lying crumpled next to burning landing craft shocked Americans back home. Many people began to wonder how many lives it would cost to defeat Japan.

Although many troops died wading ashore, one vehicle had been able to cross the reef and deliver its troops onto the beaches. The vehicle was the LVT—a boat with tank tracks. Nicknamed the "Alligator," the

CHAPTER 20 America and World War II **635**

✓ **Reading Check**

Answer: The invasion had to begin at night, the ships had to arrive at low tide, and the weather had to be relatively good.

you don't say...

Banzai On the final night of the battle of Tarawa, the Japanese made a last desperate charge against the American lines. This type of suicidal charge became known as a *banzai* attack, because the Japanese would yell, "Tenno heika banzai!" (Long Live the Emperor!)

Creating a Drawing Have interested students use the quote on page 635 as the basis for a pencil or chalk drawing that might have accompanied a news story filed by Robert Sherrod. Have students include the quote at the bottom of the drawing so that people viewing the drawing will have a frame of reference. **L3**

 CURRICULUM CONNECTION

Science American soldiers carried a first aid pouch attached to their waist belt. The pouch contained a package of sulfa powder and a bandage to dress wounds. The use of the sulfa drug Sulfanilamide significantly reduced the mortality rate during World War II, because the sulfa powder immediately went to work to fight bacterial infections. Sulfa drugs are still in use today.

Reading Strategy **READING THE TEXT**

Synthesizing Information After students have read the section, have them explain the significance of the promises that Stalin made at the Tehran Conference. *(By agreeing to launch a full-scale offensive against the Germans when the Allies invaded France, Stalin guaranteed that Germany would be defending itself on two fronts. Stalin's promise to declare war on Japan as soon as Germany was beaten meant that the Japanese would be fighting on two fronts.)* **L1**

☞ Refer to *Inclusion for the High School Social Studies Classroom Strategies and Activities* in the TCR.

Geography Skills

Answers:

1. Leyte Gulf: Oct. 23–26, 1944

2. to acquire bases to move supplies and troops closer and closer to Japan

Geography Skills Practice

Ask: What are the approximate distances between Hawaii and the Gilbert Islands *(appx. 2,500 miles [4,000 km])*, Hawaii and Guam *(appx. 4,300 miles [7,000 km])*, and Hawaii and Midway *(appx. 1,600 miles [2,600 km])*?

3 ASSESS

Assign Section 4 Assessment as homework or as an in-class activity.

🖱 Have students use the **Interactive Tutor Self-Assessment CD-ROM.**

L1/ELL

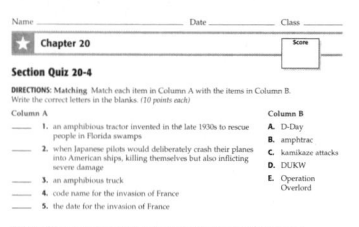

L2

Section Quiz 20–4

NATIONAL GEOGRAPHIC Island-Hopping in the Pacific, 1942–1945

Geography Skills

1. **Interpreting Maps** Where did the first major battle between the American and Japanese forces in the South Pacific take place?

2. **Applying Geography Skills** Why do you think Americans adopted the policy of island-hopping?

amphibious tractor, or *amphtrac,* had been invented in the late 1930s to rescue people in Florida swamps. It had never been used in combat, and not until 1941 did the navy decide to buy 200 of them. Had more been available at Tarawa, the number of American casualties probably would have been much lower.

The assault on the next major objective—Kwajalein Atoll in the Marshall Islands—went much more smoothly. This time all of the troops went ashore in amphtracs. Although the Japanese resisted fiercely, the marines captured Kwajalein and nearby Eniwetok with far fewer casualties.

After the Marshall Islands, the navy targeted the Mariana Islands. American military planners wanted to use the Marianas as a base for a new heavy bomber, the B-29 Superfortress. The B-29 could fly farther than any other plane in the world. From airfields in the

Marianas, B-29s could bomb Japan. Admiral Nimitz decided to invade three of the Mariana Islands: Saipan, Tinian, and Guam. Despite strong Japanese resistance, American troops captured all three by August 1944. A few months later, B-29 bombers began bombing Japan.

MacArthur Returns to the Philippines As the forces under Admiral Nimitz hopped across the central Pacific, General MacArthur's troops began their own campaign in the southwest Pacific. The campaign began with the invasion of **Guadalcanal** in August 1942. It continued until early 1944, when MacArthur's troops finally captured enough islands to surround Rabaul, the main Japanese base in the region. In response the Japanese withdrew their ships and aircraft from the base, although they left 100,000 troops behind to hold the island.

Worried that the navy's advance across the central Pacific was leaving him behind, MacArthur ordered his forces to leap nearly 600 miles (966 km) past Rabaul to capture the Japanese base at Hollandia on

EXTENDING THE CONTENT

Clare Boothe Luce Although women did not participate in combat during World War II, some were assigned to cover the fighting as journalists, broadcasters, or photographers. Before she became well known as a member of Congress (1942–1946) and as an ambassador, Clare Boothe Luce (1903–1987) was a playwright and worked for *Life* magazine during World War II. She endured battle experiences ranging from bombing raids in Europe and the Pacific to arrest in Trinidad by British customs officials who were upset by her accurate article about poor military preparedness in Libya. As a result of her article, Luce's longtime friend Winston Churchill changed Great Britain's Middle Eastern military policy.

the north coast of New Guinea. Shortly after securing New Guinea, MacArthur's troops seized the island of Morotai—the last stop before the Philippines.

To take back the Philippines, the United States assembled an enormous invasion force. In October 1944, more than 700 ships carrying over 160,000 troops sailed for Leyte Gulf in the Philippines. On October 20, the troops began to land on Leyte, an island on the eastern side of the Philippines. A few hours after the invasion began, MacArthur headed to the beach. Upon reaching the shore, he strode to a radio and spoke into the microphone: "People of the Philippines, I have returned. By the grace of Almighty God, our forces stand again on Philippine soil."

To stop the American invasion, the Japanese sent four aircraft carriers toward the Philippines from the north and secretly dispatched another fleet to the west. Believing the Japanese carriers were leading the main attack, most of the American carriers protecting the invasion left Leyte Gulf and headed north to stop them. Seizing their chance, the Japanese warships to the west raced through the Philippine Islands into Leyte Gulf and ambushed the remaining American ships.

The Battle of Leyte Gulf was the largest naval battle in history. It was also the first time that the Japanese used *kamikaze* attacks. *Kamikaze* means "divine wind" in Japanese. It refers to the great storm that destroyed the Mongol fleet during its invasion of Japan in the thirteenth century. Kamikaze pilots would deliberately crash their planes into American ships, killing themselves but also inflicting severe damage. Luckily for the Americans, just as their situation was becoming

A Triumphant Return In October 1944, Douglas MacArthur fulfilled his promise and returned to the Philippines.

desperate, the Japanese commander, believing more American ships were on the way, ordered a retreat.

Although the Japanese fleet had retreated, the campaign to recapture the Philippines from the Japanese was long and grueling. Over 80,000 Japanese were killed; less than 1,000 surrendered. MacArthur's troops did not capture Manila until March 1945. The battle left the city in ruins and over 100,000 Filipino civilians dead. The remaining Japanese retreated into the rugged terrain north of Manila, and they were still fighting when word came in August 1945 that Japan had surrendered.

Reading Check **Describing** What strategy did the United States Navy use to advance across the Pacific?

More About the Photo

Writing about his return to the Philippines, MacArthur said, "It took me only 30 or 40 strides to reach dry land, but that was one of the most meaningful walks I ever took."

Reteach
Write the years 1941–1945 on the board. Have students list important events that occurred during these years and explain how they affected U.S. foreign and domestic policy.

Enrich
In addition to the 6 major powers, over 50 other nations were at war during World War II. Some countries entered the war as early as 1939, while others did not make a commitment until 1945. Have students work in pairs to research the roles five other countries played in World War II.

Reading Check

Answer: They moved from island to island, advancing slowly toward Japan.

Study Central™ provides summaries, interactive games, and online graphic organizers to help students review section content.

SECTION 4 ASSESSMENT

HISTORY Online **Study Central™** To review this section, go to tarvol2.glencoe.com and click on **Study Central™**.

Checking for Understanding
1. **Define:** amphtrac, kamikaze.
2. **Identify:** Casablanca Conference, Operation Overlord, D-Day, Omar Bradley, Guadalcanal.
3. **Explain** why D-Day's success was so vital to an Allied victory.

Reviewing Themes
4. **Geography and History** How did the geography of the Pacific affect American strategy?

Critical Thinking
5. **Analyzing** What made the invasion of Normandy so important?
6. **Organizing** Use a graphic organizer to explain the significance of each leader listed below.

Leader	Significance
Dwight Eisenhower	
George Patton	
George Marshall	
Omar Bradley	
Douglas MacArthur	

Analyzing Visuals
7. **Examining Photographs** Study the photograph on this page. What effect do you think MacArthur's return had on Philippine morale?

Writing About History
8. **Expository Writing** Using library or Internet resources, find more information on one of the battles discussed in this section. Use the information to write a report detailing the importance of the battle. Share your report with the class.

SECTION 4 ASSESSMENT ANSWERS

1. Terms are in blue.
2. Casablanca Conference *(p. 632)*, Operation Overlord *(p. 633)*, D-Day *(p. 634)*, Omar Bradley *(p. 634)*, Guadalcanal *(p. 636)*
3. It would force the Germans to fight on two fronts.
4. Coral reefs around some of the atolls made landing craft hard to

maneuver. They began using amphtracs to land the soldiers.
5. The Germans now had to fight a two-front war, which stretched their resources even further. The Soviet Union had promised help in defeating the Japanese once the Germans were defeated.

6. Answers should match chapter content.
7. Answers may vary. They welcomed him because they had been treated harshly by the Japanese.
8. Reports should include details that do not appear in the student text.

4 CLOSE

Ask students to discuss why they think it was so important for the Allies to recapture the Philippines.

1 FOCUS

Have students consider the obstacles faced by an invading army. **Ask:** What kinds of landing sites were the Allies looking for when they were planning to invade Europe in 1944? (*a sheltered coastline somewhere between Denmark and Portugal with flat, firm beaches and within range of fighter planes based in England*)

2 TEACH

Writing a Narrative Have students choose one of the groups that landed at Omaha Beach and describe their journey after reaching the beach. Include information about the distance and direction traveled, the geography traversed, and German defenses encountered. **L1**

Practicing Map Skills Have students calculate the approximate distances Canadian, British, and U.S. troops traveled from England to France on D-Day. Have students use a table to report the starting point, distance traveled, landing site, and nationality of troops for each of the five beaches along the coast of Normandy. **L2**

SLOW GOING

Allied planners had hoped that American forces landing at Omaha early on June 6, 1944, would advance 5 to 10 miles after 24 hours of fighting. Stiff German resistance, however, stopped the invaders cold on the beach. Progress inland was excruciatingly slow and painful. The Americans reached their first-day objective (dotted blue line on map) only after more than two days of bloody fighting. Despite terrible losses, American forces successfully carried out one of the most crucial missions of the war.

638 CHAPTER 20 America and World War II

EXTENDING THE CONTENT

Military Inventions For centuries French farmers had erected high banks of earth around every small field to fence in livestock and protect crops from coastal winds. These natural barriers, known as hedgerows, grew thick with the roots of shrubs and trees. Although Allied tanks could ride up over these hedgerows, they exposed their undersides to antitank fire. The enemy was able to attack the tanks at their most vulnerable point. A creative sergeant solved the problem by adding tusks to the fronts of the tanks. The tusks would get caught in the underbrush and hold the tank in place as the engine propelled it forward through the mound of dirt.

A Day for Heroes

The selection of a site for the largest amphibious landing in history was one of the biggest decisions of World War II. Allied planners needed a sheltered location with flat, firm beaches and within range of friendly fighter planes based in England.

There had to be enough roads and paths to move jeeps and trucks off the beaches and to accommodate the hundreds of thousands of American, Canadian, and British troops set to stream ashore following the invasion. An airfield and a seaport that the Allies could use were also needed. Most important was a reasonable expectation of achieving the element of surprise.

Five beaches on the northern coast of Normandy, France, met all the criteria and were chosen as invasion sites. On D-Day the attack on four beaches—Utah in the west and Gold, Juno, and Sword in the east (inset, opposite page)—went according to plan. But at Omaha Beach (map), between Utah and Gold, the bravery and determination of the U.S. 1st Infantry Division was tested in one of the fiercest battles of the war.

Surrounded at both ends by cliffs that rose wall-like from the sea, Omaha was only four miles long. It was the only sand beach in the area, however, and thus the only place for a landing. Unless the Allies were to leave a 20-mile gap between Utah and Gold, they would have to come ashore at Omaha Beach.

Troops crowd into a landing craft to head across the English Channel to Omaha Beach.

To repel the Allies at the water's edge, the Germans built a fortress atop the cliffs at Pointe du Hoc overlooking Omaha from the west. They dug trenches and guns into the 150-foot bluffs lining the beach and along five ravines leading off it (see map).

Wading into the surf, the Americans advanced toward Omaha Beach. Many men were cut down as the doors of their landing craft opened. The survivors had to cross more than 300 yards across a tidal flat strewn with man-made obstacles. Winds and a current pushed landing craft into clumps as the men moved ashore. As a result, soldiers ran onto the beach in groups and became easy targets. Of the more than 9,000 Allied casualties on D-Day, Omaha accounted for about one-third.

Although many died, the Americans took control of the beach and fought their way inland. As General Omar Bradley later wrote, **"Every man who set foot on Omaha Beach that day was a hero."**

D-Day Forces

A-L	U.S. Company — 200 men
116th	U.S. Battalion — 900 men
Rn.	U.S. Rangers
916th	German infantry — forces associated with German battalion
	German resistance point
	German coastal defense
	U.S. stronghold
	Landing craft
	Landing craft — sunk
	Battleship
	Cruiser
	Transport
	Hedgerows
o	Town

Scale varies in this perspective

Wounded infantrymen from the American 1st Division wait to be evacuated after landing on Omaha Beach.

LEARNING FROM GEOGRAPHY

1. Why did the Allies choose Normandy as the site of the invasion?

2. Why was the landing at Omaha Beach so much more difficult than U.S. leaders expected?

639

3 ASSESS

Have students answer the Learning from Geography questions.

4 CLOSE

Ask students to describe what might have happened had the casualties at Omaha Beach been even greater than they were. Ask students how they think their lives would be different if the invasion of France had been unsuccessful.

NGS ONLINE

Access National Geographic's Web site for current events, atlas updates, activities, links, interactive features, and archives at www.nationalgeographic.com.

ANSWERS TO LEARNING FROM GEOGRAPHY

1. The Allies chose Normandy because it was a sheltered location with flat, firm beaches and was within range of friendly fighter planes based in England. There were roads or paths to lead jeeps, trucks, and troops off the beaches. There was an airfield and a seaport that could be used by the Allies. There was a reasonable expectation of achieving the element of surprise.

2. Winds and steady currents pushed landing craft into clumps as the men moved to shore. As groups of soldiers ran onto the beach they became easy targets for the Germans who had built strong defenses atop the cliffs overlooking Omaha Beach.

1 FOCUS

Section Overview

This section describes the end of World War II, including the dropping of the atomic bomb.

BELLRINGER
Skillbuilder Activity

 Project transparency and have students answer the question.

Daily Focus Skills Transparency 20–5

Reading Preview

Answers to Graphic:

The War Ends
I. The Third Reich Collapses
  A. The Battle of the Bulge
  B. V-E Day: War Ends in Europe
II. Japan Is Defeated
  A. Uncommon Valor on Iwo Jima

Students should complete the outline by including all heads in the section.

Preteaching Vocabulary

Organize the class into eight groups. Assign each group one of the Key Terms and Names. Have each group prepare a brief presentation for its assigned term.

SECTION 5   The War Ends

Guide to Reading

The Main Idea

The ferocious military campaigns of 1945 finally convinced the Axis powers to surrender and the Allies to set up organizations to prevent another global war.

Key Terms and Names

hedgerow, Battle of the Bulge, V-E Day, Harry S Truman, Curtis LeMay, napalm, Manhattan Project, V-J Day, United Nations, charter

Reading Strategy

Taking Notes As you read about the end of World War II and the organizations set up to maintain global peace, use the major headings of the section to create an outline similar to the one below.

The War Ends
I. The Third Reich Collapses
  A.
  B.
II.
  A.
  B.

Reading Objectives

• **Explain** the tactics the Allies used to invade Germany and to defeat Japan.
• **Outline** the reasons the Allies created the United Nations and held war crimes trials.

Section Theme

Groups and Institutions Allied leaders forged plans for an international organization to prevent future wars.

Preview of Events

♦1944   ♦1945   ♦1946

December 16, 1944
Battle of the Bulge begins

February 19, 1945
American troops invade Iwo Jima

April 12, 1945
Franklin Roosevelt dies; Harry Truman becomes president

May 7, 1945
Germany surrenders

August 15, 1945
V-J Day, Japan surrenders

⋆ An American Story ⋆

Jewish prisoners at a German concentration camp

In 1945 Captain Luther Fletcher entered the German concentration camp at Buchenwald with a group of Germans who were being forced to see what their country had done. In his diary Fletcher described what they witnessed:

❝They saw blackened skeletons and skulls in the ovens of the crematorium. In the yard outside, they saw a heap of white human ashes and bones. . . . [The] dead were stripped of their clothing and lay naked, many stacked like cordwood waiting to be burned at the crematory. At one time 5,000 had been stacked on the vacant lot next to the crematory. . . . At headquarters of the SS troops who ran the place were lamp shades made from human skin. . . . Often, the guide said, the SS wished to make an example of someone in killing him. . . . They used what I call hay hooks, catching him under the chin and the other in the back of the neck. He hung in this manner until he died.❞

—**quoted in** *World War II: From the Battle Front to the Home Front*

The Third Reich Collapses

Well before the war ended, President Roosevelt and other Allied leaders were aware that the Nazis were committing atrocities. In 1943 the Allies officially declared that they would punish the Nazis for their crimes after the war. Meanwhile, Roosevelt was convinced that the best way to put an end to the concentration camps was to destroy the Nazi regime. To do that, he believed the Allies had to dedicate their resources to breaking out of Normandy, liberating France, and conquering Germany.

640   CHAPTER 20   America and World War II

SECTION RESOURCES

📁 Reproducible Masters

• Reproducible Lesson Plan 20–5
• Daily Lecture and Discussion Notes 20–5
• Guided Reading Activity 20–5
• Section Quiz 20–5
• Reading Essentials and Study Guide 20–5

🖥 Transparencies

• Daily Focus Skills Transparency 20–5

Multimedia

• Interactive Tutor Self-Assessment CD-ROM
• ExamView® Pro Testmaker CD-ROM
• Presentation Plus! CD-ROM
• TeacherWorks™ CD-ROM
• Audio Program
• American Music: Hits Through History
• American Music: Cultural Traditions

Although D-Day had been a success, it was only the beginning. Surrounding many fields in Normandy were hedgerows—dirt walls, several feet thick, covered in shrubbery. The hedgerows had been built to fence in cattle and crops, but they also enabled the Germans to fiercely defend their positions. The battle of the hedgerows ended on July 25, 1944, when 2,500 American bombers blew a hole in the German lines, enabling American tanks to race through the gap.

As the Allies broke out of Normandy, the French Resistance—French civilians who had secretly organized to resist the German occupation of their country—staged a rebellion in Paris. When the Allied forces liberated Paris on August 25, they found the streets filled with French citizens celebrating their victory. Three weeks later, American troops were within 20 miles (32 km) of the German border.

The Battle of the Bulge

As the Allies closed in on Germany, Hitler decided to stage one last desperate offensive. His goal was to cut off Allied supplies coming through the port of Antwerp, Belgium. The attack began just before dawn on December 16, 1944. Six inches (15 cm) of snow covered the ground, and the weather was bitterly cold. Moving rapidly, the Germans caught the American defenders by surprise. As the German troops raced west, their lines bulged outward, and the attack became known as the **Battle of the Bulge.**

Part of the German plan called for the capture of the town of Bastogne, where several important roads converged. If the Allies held Bastogne, it would greatly delay the German advance. American reinforcements raced to the town, arriving just ahead of the Germans. The Germans then surrounded the town and demanded that the Americans surrender. The American commander sent back a one-word reply: "Nuts!"

Shortly after the Germans surrounded the Americans, Eisenhower ordered General Patton to rescue them. Three days later, faster than anyone expected in the midst of a snowstorm, Patton's troops slammed into the German lines. As the weather cleared, Allied aircraft began hitting German fuel depots. On Christmas Eve, out of fuel and weakened by heavy losses, the German troops driving toward Antwerp were forced to halt. Two days later, Patton's troops broke through to Bastogne.

Although fighting continued for three weeks, the United States had won the Battle of the Bulge. On January 8, the Germans began to withdraw. They had suffered more than 100,000 casualties and lost many tanks and aircraft. They now had very little left to prevent the Allies from entering Germany.

V-E Day: The War Ends in Europe While American and British forces fought to liberate France, the Soviet Union began a massive attack on German troops in Russia. By the time the Battle of the Bulge ended, the Soviets had driven Hitler's forces out of Russia and back across Poland. By February 1945, Soviet troops had reached the Oder River. They were only 35 miles (56 km) from Berlin.

As the Soviets crossed Germany's eastern border, American forces attacked Germany's western border. By the first week of March, 1945, American troops had fought their way to the Rhine River, Germany's last major line of defense in the west. Then on March 7, American soldiers captured the heights above the town of Remagen. Gazing down at the town, platoon leader Emmet J. Burrows was amazed at what he saw. The Ludendorf Bridge across the Rhine was still intact. The Germans had not blown it up. The American troops raced across the bridge, driving

Picturing **History**

Soldiers and Friends The Americans and the Soviets join forces in a long-awaited meeting. The alliance is symbolized here by Lieutenants William D. Robertson of the U.S. First Army and Alexander Sylvashko of the First Ukrainian Army, in a meeting near Torgau on the Elbe River. What was the Allied strategy during the closing days of the war?

2 TEACH

Daily Lecture and Discussion Notes 20–5

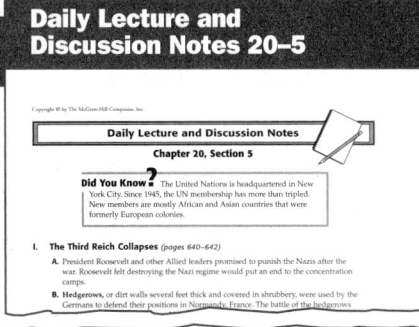

Copyright © by The McGraw-Hill Companies, Inc.

Daily Lecture and Discussion Notes

Chapter 20, Section 5

Did You Know? The United Nations is headquartered in New York City. Since 1945, the UN membership has more than tripled. New members are mostly African and Asian countries that were formerly European colonies.

I. **The Third Reich Collapses** *(pages 640–642)*

  A. President Roosevelt and other Allied leaders promised to punish the Nazis after the war. Roosevelt felt destroying the Nazi regime would put an end to the concentration camps.

  B. **Hedgerows,** or dirt walls several feet thick and covered in shrubbery, were used by the Germans to defend their positions in Normandy, France. The battle of the hedgerows

Analyzing Information As a class discuss the troop movements of the Allies and the Axis during the Battle of the Bulge. Ask students to identify good and poor strategic moves related to the battle. Then ask students how the strategy used by each side affected the outcome of the battle. **L1**

Picturing **History**

Background: The American lieutenant stands on the left, and the Ukrainian soldier is on the right. They can be identified by their uniforms. The high, stiff-necked collar signifies a soldier in the Russian army.

Answer: The U.S. and British troops worked to liberate France, while the Soviet troops began a massive attack on German troops in Russia.

Ask: What does V-E stand for? *(victory in Europe)*

Reading Strategy | **READING THE TEXT**

Team Review Group students into home teams of four and assign each member of the team a number from 1 to 4. Divide the section up into four parts and number the parts. Have everyone with the number 1 meet to study and discuss part 1 of the section. Do the same for each of the other parts. Reunite the home teams and have each member of the team share his or her knowledge about this section. **L1**

Refer to *Inclusion for the High School Social Studies Classroom Strategies and Activities* in the TCR.

L1/ELL

Guided Reading Activity 20–5

Name _____ Date _____ Class _____

★ **Guided Reading Activity 20-5**

DIRECTIONS: Outlining Read the section and complete the outline below. Refer to your textbook to fill in the blanks.

I. The Third Reich Collapses

  A. While American and British forces fought to liberate _____, the _____ began a massive attack on German troops in the _____.

  B. By the end of February 1945, American troops had fought their way to the _____ Germany's last major line of defense in the west.

  C. On May 7, 1945, Germany surrendered _____, and the next day was proclaimed _____ for _____.

II. Japan Is Defeated

  A. So that the B-29 Superfortress bombers would have enough fuel for efficient bombing of Japan, the _____ captured the bombers _____ within the island _____

Interpreting a Quotation

When Vice President Truman heard that Roosevelt had died, he said that he felt "like the moon, the stars, and all the planets have fallen on me." Ask students to offer their interpretation of his words. **L1**

Making an Oral Presentation

As a class, discuss the ideas of valor (courage) and identify some examples of people who have acted with valor. Organize students into pairs. Ask the pairs to identify a person who has displayed valor and have them work together to prepare an oral presentation describing the courage that person has shown. Ask each pair to present their example of courage to the class. **L2**

📁 Use the rubric for an oral presentation, monologue, song, or skit on pages 67–68 in the *Performance Assessment Activities and Rubrics.*

☑ **Reading Check**

Answer: The Germans lost over 100,000 troops and most of their tanks and aircraft.

NATIONAL GEOGRAPHIC

World War II in Europe and Africa, 1939–1945

- Major Axis powers
- Greatest extent of Axis control
- Allied or Allied-controlled
- Neutral powers
- ← Allied advance
- ← Supply line
- — International boundary, Jan. 1938

Supply lines from U.S.

D-Day June 6, 1944

German central armies destroyed May-July, 1944

Nov. 8, 1942

Aug. 15, 1944

July 10, 1943

Oct. 23, 1942

Supply line to Soviet Union from the Middle East

0   500 miles
0   500 kilometers
Lambert Azimuthal Equal-Area projection

---

back the German defenders. By the end of the day, American tanks were across the Rhine. Hearing the news, General Bradley yelled, "Hot dog . . . this will bust them wide open."

As German defenses crumbled, American troops raced east, closing to within 70 miles (113 km) of Berlin. On April 16, Soviet troops finally smashed through the German defenses on the Oder River. Five days later, they reached the outskirts of Berlin.

Deep in his Berlin bunker, Adolf Hitler knew the end was near. On April 30, 1945, he put a pistol in his mouth and pulled the trigger. His secretary, Martin Bormann, carried Hitler's body outside, doused it in gasoline, and set it on fire. Before killing himself, Hitler chose Grand Admiral Karl Doenitz to be his successor. Doenitz tried to surrender to the

Americans and British while continuing to fight the Soviets, but Eisenhower insisted on unconditional surrender. On May 7, 1945, Germany surrendered unconditionally. The next day—May 8, 1945—was proclaimed **V-E Day,** for "Victory in Europe."

✓ **Reading Check**   **Explaining** Why was the Battle of the Bulge such a disastrous defeat for Germany?

Japan Is Defeated

Unfortunately, President Roosevelt did not live to see the defeat of Germany. On April 12, 1945, while vacationing in Warm Springs, Georgia, he suffered a stroke and died. His vice president, **Harry S Truman,** became president during this difficult time.

DIFFERENTIATED INSTRUCTION

Reading Support There are several feature films on World War II. Students might get a flavor of the period from any of the following films: *The Bridge on the River Kwai* (1957), *A Bridge Too Far* (1977), *Guns of Navarone* (1961), *Saving Private Ryan* (1998), *Summer of My German Soldier* (1978), and *They Were Expendable* (1945). Have students prepare a two- to three-minute critique of the movie they watched. **L1**

📁 Refer to *Inclusion for the High School Social Studies Classroom Strategies and Activities* in the TCR.

Rise and Fall of Axis Powers

1939

Axis Expansion The Axis powers included Germany, Italy, Austria, and the Sudetenland.

1942

Axis Control At their height, the Axis controlled almost all of Europe and North Africa.

1945

Axis Collapse The Allies invaded Germany from the east and the west.

Military and Civilian Deaths in World War II		
Country	Military Deaths	Civilian Deaths
USSR	11,000,000	6,700,000
Germany	3,250,000	2,350,000
Japan	1,740,000	393,000
China	1,400,000	8,000,000
Poland	110,000	5,300,000
United States	405,000	2,000
Great Britain	306,000	61,000
Italy	227,000	60,000
France	122,000	470,000

Source: *World War II: A Statistical Survey.* (Figures are approximate.)

WW I

Military 86%

Civilian 14%

WW II

Military 46%

Civilian 54%

War Casualties World War II took more lives than any other war in history. More civilians than soldiers died in the war.

Geography *Skills*

1. **Interpreting Maps** Which European countries remained neutral during the war?
2. **Applying Geography Skills** How did the Soviet Union receive supplies during the war?

The next day, Truman told reporters: "Boys, if you ever pray, pray for me now. . . . When they told me yesterday what had happened, I felt like the moon, the stars, and all the planets had fallen on me." Despite feeling overwhelmed, Truman began at once to make decisions about the war. Although Germany surrendered a few weeks later, the war with Japan continued to intensify, and Truman was forced to make some of the most difficult decisions of the war during his first six months in office.

Uncommon Valor on Iwo Jima On November 24, 1944, bombs fell on Tokyo for the first time since the 1942 Doolittle raid. Above the city flew 80 B-29

Superfortress bombers that had traveled over 1,500 miles (2,414 km) from new American bases in the Mariana Islands.

At first the B-29s did little damage because they kept missing their targets. Japan was simply too far away: By the time the B-29s reached Japan, they did not have enough fuel left to fix their navigational errors or to adjust for high winds. The solution was to capture an island closer to Japan, where the B-29s could refuel. After studying the problem, American military planners decided to invade **Iwo Jima.**

Iwo Jima was perfectly located, roughly halfway between the Marianas and Japan, but its geography

CHAPTER 20 America and World War II **643**

Geography *Skills*

Background: Stalin had originally cooperated with Hitler. Churchill and Roosevelt delayed an attack in Europe, forcing the Soviets to face the Germans alone. This increased the Soviets' losses and weakened them as a postwar power.

Answers:
1. Ireland, Portugal, Spain, Sweden, Switzerland, and Turkey
2. They received supplies across the Atlantic, around the Scandinavian Peninsula, and across the Arctic Circle, through Iran and across the Caspian Sea.

Geography Skills Practice
Ask: Which countries had the highest number of military and civilian deaths during World War II? *(military: USSR; civilian: China)*

CURRICULUM CONNECTION

Music After announcing the death of President Franklin D. Roosevelt from a cerebral hemorrhage, the NBC Radio Network played Samuel Barber's *Adagio for Strings.* Since that time, this sad, serene piece of music has been linked to occasions of public mourning. It has been used as a lament in hundreds of funerals and memorials all over the world.

INTERDISCIPLINARY CONNECTIONS ACTIVITY

Mathematics Have students add the total number of military and civilian deaths displayed on the charts on page 643. Then have students determine the percentages of military and civilian deaths for each country. Next have students create a third column for the table adding the number of civilian and military deaths for each country. Have them total the new column and again find the percentages. Have students refer to their percentages as you ask several questions about them. For example, what percentage of total civilian deaths did Poland experience? *(21.3%)* L2

Expressing an Opinion Tell students that the firebombing of Japan has long been controversial because so many civilians were killed. Have students discuss their ideas about the lengths a military campaign should take to ensure that the fewest number of civilians are killed. Encourage students to express their opinions and explain their reasoning. **L2**

Picturing **History**

Background: The monument based on this famous photo pays tribute to the nearly 7,000 Americans who gave their lives in the battle of Iwo Jima. The monument was sculpted by Felix W. de Weldon over a nine-year period. The sculptor made plaster casts of the faces of the three members of the flag raisers who survived World War II. The other three figures were created from photos. The monument stands near Arlington National Cemetery in the nation's capital.
Answer: They boosted American morale because they saw the American forces gaining ground and winning victories.
Ask: What do you think Nimitz meant by his quote? *(He meant that doing the heroic was commonplace among the soldiers who landed on Iwo Jima.)*

FYI

In addition to the Los Alamos facility in New Mexico, two other facilities were constructed for the Manhattan Project. A facility in Oak Ridge, Tennessee, was built to separate uranium 235 from uranium 238, the more common form. Nuclear reactors used to produce plutonium were built in Hanford, Washington.

---

was formidable. At its southern tip was Mount Suribachi, a dormant volcano. The terrain was rugged, with rocky cliffs, jagged ravines, and dozens of caves. Volcanic ash covered the ground. Even worse, the Japanese had built a vast network of caves and concrete bunkers connected by miles of tunnels.

On February 19, 1945, 60,000 U.S. Marines landed on Iwo Jima. As the troops leapt from the amphtracs, they sank up to their ankles in the soft ash. Meanwhile, Japanese artillery began to pound the invaders. Robert Sherrod, who had been on Tarawa, was shocked: "[The marines] died with the greatest possible violence. Nowhere in the Pacific have I seen such badly mangled bodies. Many were cut squarely in half. Legs and arms lay 50 feet (15 m) away from any body."

Inch by inch, the marines crawled inland, using flamethrowers and explosives to attack the Japanese bunkers. More than 6,800 marines were killed before the island was captured. Admiral Nimitz later wrote that on Iwo Jima, "uncommon valor was a common virtue."

Firebombing Devastates Japan While American engineers prepared airfields on Iwo Jima, General **Curtis LeMay,** commander of the B-29s based in the Marianas, decided to change strategy. To help the B-29s hit their targets, he ordered them to drop bombs filled with napalm—a kind of a jellied gasoline. The bombs were designed not only to explode but also to start fires. Even if the B-29s missed their targets, the fires they started would spread to the intended targets.

The use of firebombs was very controversial because the fires would also kill civilians; however, LeMay could think of no other way to destroy Japan's war production quickly. Loaded with firebombs, B-29s attacked Tokyo on March 9, 1945. As strong winds fanned the flames, the firestorm grew so intense that it sucked the oxygen out of the air, asphyxiating thousands. As one survivor later recalled:

> ❝The fires were incredible . . . with flames leaping hundreds of feet into the air. . . . Many people were gasping for breath. With every passing moment the air became more foul . . . the noise was a continuing crashing roar. . . . Fire-winds filled with burning particles rushed up and down the streets. I watched people . . . running for their lives. . . . The flames raced after them like living things, striking them down. . . . Wherever I turned my eyes, I saw people . . . seeking air to breathe.❞
>
> —quoted in *New History of World War II*

"uncommon valor was a common virtue"
—*Admiral Chester W. Nimitz*

Picturing **History**

Planting the Flag Photographer Joe Rosenthal won the Pulitzer Prize for this photo of five marines and a navy medical corpsman raising the flag on Iwo Jima. How do you think photographs such as this one affected American morale? Why?

CRITICAL THINKING ACTIVITY

Synthesizing After students read the "Different Viewpoints" that appears on pages 646–647, ask them to formulate a series of questions that they would like to ask Gar Alperovitz in order to get a better understanding of his position. *(Students' answers will vary; examples of appropriate questions include: How close were the Soviets to invading Japan? What was the likelihood of a successful invasion? How many lives would have been lost in an invasion? What changes in the terms of surrender would you suggest to make surrender more acceptable to Japan?)* **L2**

The Tokyo firebombing killed over 80,000 people and destroyed more than 250,000 buildings. By the end of June 1945, Japan's six most important industrial cities had been firebombed, destroying almost half of their total urban area. By the end of the war, the B-29s had firebombed 67 Japanese cities.

The Invasion of Okinawa Despite the massive damage the firebombing caused, there were few signs in the spring of 1945 that Japan was ready to quit. Many American officials believed the Japanese would not surrender until Japan had been invaded. To prepare for the invasion, the United States needed a base near Japan to stockpile supplies and build up troops. Iwo Jima was small and still too far away. After much discussion, military planners chose Okinawa—only 350 miles (563 km) from Japan.

American troops landed on Okinawa on April 1, 1945. Instead of defending the beaches, the Japanese troops took up positions in the island's rugged mountains. To dig the Japanese out of their caves and bunkers, the Americans had to fight their way up steep slopes against constant machine gun and artillery fire. More than 12,000 American soldiers, sailors, and marines died during the fighting, but by June 22, 1945, Okinawa had finally been captured.

The Terms for Surrender Shortly after the United States captured Okinawa, the Japanese emperor urged his government to find a way to end the war. The biggest problem was the American demand for unconditional surrender. Many Japanese leaders were willing to surrender but on one condition—the emperor had to stay in power.

American officials knew that the fate of the emperor was the most important issue for the Japanese. Most Americans, however, blamed the emperor for the war and wanted him removed from power. President Truman was reluctant to go against public opinion. Furthermore, he knew the United States was almost ready to test a new weapon that might force Japan to surrender without any conditions. The new weapon was the atomic bomb.

The Manhattan Project In 1939 Leo Szilard, one of the world's top physicists, learned that German scientists had split the uranium atom. Szilard had been the first scientist to suggest that splitting the atom might release enormous energy. Worried that the Nazis were working on an atomic bomb, Szilard convinced the world's best-known physicist, Albert

Picturing **History**

Ship Attacks Kamikaze attacks intensified in 1945, hitting the USS *Bunker Hill* and many other American ships. Why do you think these Japanese kamikaze pilots were willing to fly suicide missions?

Einstein, to sign a letter Szilard had drafted and send it to President Roosevelt. In the letter Einstein warned that by using uranium, "extremely powerful bombs of a new type may . . . be constructed."

Roosevelt responded by setting up a scientific committee to study the issue. The committee remained skeptical until 1941, when they met with British scientists who were already working on an atomic bomb. The British research so impressed the Americans that they convinced Roosevelt to begin a program to build an atomic bomb.

The American program to build an atomic bomb was code-named the **Manhattan Project** and was headed by General Leslie R. Groves. The project's first breakthrough came in 1942, when Szilard and Enrico Fermi, another physicist, built the world's first nuclear reactor at the University of Chicago. Groves organized a team of engineers and scientists to build an atomic bomb at a secret laboratory in Los Alamos, New Mexico. J. Robert Oppenheimer led the team. On July 16, 1945, they detonated the world's first atomic bomb near Alamogordo, New Mexico.

The Decision to Drop the Bomb Even before the bomb was tested, American officials began to debate how to use it. Admiral William Leahy, chairman of the Joint Chiefs of Staff, opposed using the bomb because

Picturing **History**

Background: The inset photo captures a kamikaze attack. During the invasion of Okinawa, kamikazes scored hundreds of hits on United States naval vessels.
Answer: They were willing to die for the emperor, and the empire would see them as heroes.
Ask: What were the terms that Japan wanted to surrender? (*They wanted the emperor to stay in power.*)

you don't say...

Different Results The effects of a nuclear explosion depend on the size of the bomb, weather conditions, terrain, and the point of the explosion in relationship to the earth's surface. Two different types of bombs were dropped on Hiroshima and Nagasaki. The one dropped on Hiroshima was smaller. However, more people were killed in Hiroshima due to the city's flat terrain.

History *and the* Humanities

- American Music: Hits Through History: "Comin' In on a Wing and a Prayer," "Blue Moon of Kentucky," "Take the A Train," "Hard Day Blues"
- American Music: Cultural Traditions: "Jersey Bounce," "It's Mighty Dark to Travel"

EXTENDING THE CONTENT

Japanese Surrender On September 2, 1945, as U.S. bombers flew above, the Japanese formally surrendered to the Allies in a ceremony aboard the battleship U.S.S. *Missouri* in Tokyo Bay. General Douglas MacArthur signed for the Allies, and Mamoru Shigemitsu signed for the Japanese.

Analyzing a Course of Action

Ask: If a decision or action solves an immediate problem, how heavily should future effects of the action be weighed? Have students give examples from their own experience to demonstrate their thinking. **L2**

3 ASSESS

Assign Section 5 Assessment as homework or as an in-class activity.

🌐 Have students use the **Interactive Tutor Self-Assessment CD-ROM.**

L1/ELL

Reading Essentials and Study Guide 20–5

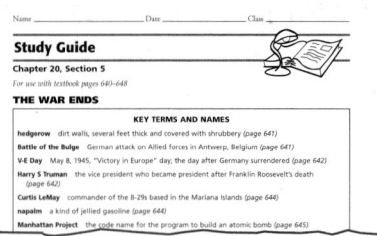

L2

Section Quiz 20–5

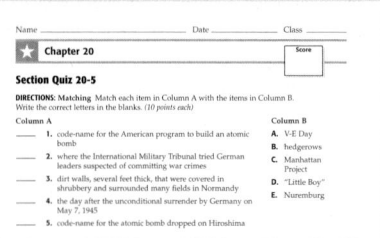

it killed civilians indiscriminately. He believed that an economic blockade and conventional bombing would convince Japan to surrender. Secretary of War Henry Stimson wanted to warn the Japanese about the bomb while at the same time telling them that they could keep the emperor if they surrendered. Secretary of State James Byrnes, however, wanted to drop the bomb without any warning to shock Japan into surrendering.

President Truman later wrote that he "regarded the bomb as a military weapon and never had any doubts that it should be used." His advisers had warned him to expect massive casualties if the United States invaded Japan. Truman believed it was his duty as president to use every weapon available to save American lives.

The Allies threatened Japan with "prompt and utter destruction" if the nation did not surrender unconditionally, but the Japanese did not reply. Truman then ordered the military to drop the bomb. On August 6, 1945, a B-29 bomber named the *Enola Gay* dropped an atomic bomb, code-named "Little Boy," on Hiroshima, an important industrial city. The bomb was dropped at 8:15 A.M. Forty-three seconds later, it exploded. Heat, radiation, and an enormous shock wave slammed into Hiroshima.

The bomb destroyed 76,000 buildings—about 63 percent of the city. Somewhere between 80,000 and 120,000 people died instantly, and thousands more died later from burns and radiation sickness. Everywhere, as witness Nozaki Kiyoshi recalled, were "horrific scenes":

> ❝The center of the city was still burning bright red, like live charcoal. Roof tiles were popping. We passed numerous war dead who had been carbonized. . . . We found five or six half-burned roofless streetcars. Inside were piles of corpses smoldering under white smoke. . . . A young mother lay face down, her baby tucked under her breast. They looked more like pink wax dolls than human beings.❞

> —quoted in *Senso: The Japanese Remember the Pacific War*

Different Viewpoints

Dropping the Atomic Bomb: Was It the Right Decision?

More than half a century later, people continue to debate what some historians have called the most important event of the twentieth century—President Truman's order to drop the atomic bomb on Japan. Did his momentous decision shorten the war and save lives on both sides, or was it prompted by Truman's fear that the Soviet Union, poised to invade, would gain control of Japan after the war?

A historian opposes Truman's decision:

Historian Gar Alperovitz maintains that Truman possessed alternatives to the atomic bomb but chose to use the weapon in order to force Japan's surrender before the Soviet Union could mount an invasion and subsequently occupy Japanese territory.

"Quite simply, it is not true that the atomic bomb was used because it was the only way to save the 'hundreds of thousands' or 'millions' of lives as was subsequently claimed. The readily available options were to modify the surrender terms and/or await the shock of the Russian attack.

Perhaps it is here, most poignantly, that we confront our own reluctance to ask the difficult questions—for even if one were to accept the most inflated estimates of lives saved by the atomic bomb, the fact remains that it was an act of violent destruction aimed at large concentrations of noncombatants."

—quoted in *The Decision to Use the Atomic Bomb, and the Architecture of an American Myth*

Hiroshima in the aftermath of the atomic bomb

COOPERATIVE LEARNING ACTIVITY

Creating Graphs Organize students into groups of three or four. Have each group research the number of military deaths that occurred during World War II. Ask each group to prepare two circle graphs, one showing the Allied losses and one showing the Axis losses. Each piece of the circles should represent the losses suffered by each of the major countries on the two sides. Encourage groups to label the graphs clearly. 📦

Use the rubric for a cooperative group management plan on pages 71–72 in the **Performance Assessment Activities and Rubrics.**

The bombing stunned Japan. Three days later, on August 9, the Soviet Union declared war on Japan. Later that day, the United States dropped another atomic bomb, code-named "Fat Man," on the city of Nagasaki, killing between 35,000 and 74,000 people.

Faced with such massive destruction and the shock of the Soviets joining the war, the Japanese emperor ordered his government to surrender. On August 15, 1945—**V-J Day**—Japan surrendered. On the other side of the world, Americans celebrated. For American soldiers the news was especially good. As one veteran recalled: "We would not be obliged to run up the beaches near Tokyo assault firing while being mortared and shelled. . . . We were going to live. We were going to grow up to adulthood after all." The long war was finally over. The United States and its allies, after a tremendous effort, had freed Europe from Nazi tyranny and put an end to Japanese aggression in Asia.

✓**Reading Check** **Analyzing** What issues did Truman consider before using the atomic bomb?

A historian defends Truman's decision:

Historian Herbert Feis argues that Truman's desire to avoid an invasion of Japan, thus saving thousands of lives on both sides, motivated his decision to drop the bomb.

"Our right, legal and historical, to use the bomb may thus well be defended; but those who made the decision to use it were not much concerned over these considerations, taking them for granted. Their thoughts about its employment were governed by one reason which was deemed imperative: that by using the bomb, the agony of war might be ended more quickly.

The primary and sustaining aim from the start of the great exertion to make the bomb was military, and the impelling reason for the decision to use it was military—to end the war victoriously as soon as possible."

—quoted in *Japan Subdued: The Atomic Bomb and the End of the War in the Pacific*

Learning From History
1. Which of the above interpretations do you think is the most valid? Why?
2. Using the Internet or other resources, find an account of the bombing from the point of a Japanese citizen. How does it differ from the accounts above, and why?

Family Sacrifices Millions of American homes proudly displayed banners such as these during the war. The blue star on the flag indicated that a family member was serving in the military. A gold star proclaimed that an individual had been killed. Many homes displayed banners with several stars, indicating the family had sent many members off to war.

Building a New World

Well before the war ended, President Roosevelt had begun to think about what the world would be like after the war. The president had wanted to ensure that war would never again engulf the world.

Creating the United Nations President Roosevelt believed that a new international political organization could prevent another world war. In 1944, at the Dumbarton Oaks Estate in Washington, D.C., delegates from 39 countries met to discuss the new organization, which was to be called the **United Nations** (UN).

The delegates at the conference agreed that the UN would have a General Assembly, where every member nation in the world would have one vote. The UN would also have a Security Council with 11 members. Five countries would be permanent members of the Security Council: Britain, France, China, the Soviet Union, and the United States—the five big powers that had led the fight against the Axis. These five permanent members would each have veto power.

On April 25, 1945, representatives from 50 countries came to San Francisco to officially organize the United Nations and design its charter, or constitution. The General Assembly was given the power to vote on resolutions, to choose the non-permanent members of the Security Council, and to vote on the UN budget. The Security Council was responsible for international peace and security. It could investigate any international problem and propose settlements to countries that had disputes with each other. It could also take action to preserve the peace, including asking its members to use military force to uphold a UN resolution.

CHAPTER 20   America and World War II   **647**

✓**Reading Check**

Answer: the potentially massive casualties involved in a ground invasion of Japan and his duty to save American lives

Fact Fiction Folklore

It is not uncommon for Americans to display symbols to signify their support for family and friends who serve in the military. Point out that during the Persian Gulf War in 1991, many Americans tied yellow ribbons on trees and poles to show their support for the American troops.

Different Viewpoints

Organize the students into small groups to research Truman's decision to use the atomic bomb. Ask them to debate the following: Truman's decision to drop the atomic bomb was or was not morally and ethically justified.
Answers:
1. Answers will vary but should focus on the use of evidence and potential bias.
2. Answers will vary but should include details from the selected narrative.

INTERDISCIPLINARY CONNECTIONS ACTIVITY

Government Organize the class into small groups. Assign each group one of the following topics related to the United Nations: how it is funded, what it has accomplished, what types of humanitarian aid it provides, what influence it has today, and how the leader is chosen. Have each group prepare an oral presentation of their findings. Encourage groups to use charts, pictures, tables, and other visual aids during their presentations. **L2**

Picturing **History**

Background: The identity of the nurse and sailor remained a mystery until recently. The nurse has been identified as Edith Shain, while the sailor's identity remains uncertain.

Answer: It captured the joy of the war's end.

Reteach

Have students select a significant date mentioned in this section to write a newspaper headline for the day.

Enrich

Read students the following quotation by President Truman announcing the use of the atomic bomb: "[The Japanese] may expect a rain from the air, the like of which has never been seen on this earth." Ask them to discuss the ways in which the atomic bomb altered international politics.

Reading Check

Answer: a General Assembly of all member nations and an 11-member Security Council with 5 permanent members, each of whom has veto power over UN actions

HISTORY Online

Study Central™ provides summaries, interactive games, and online graphic organizers to help students review section content.

Picturing **History**

V-J Day Photographer Alfred Eisenstaedt captured this image of a nurse and a sailor in Times Square during the victory celebration on V-J Day. Why did this photograph become so famous?

Putting the Enemy on Trial Although the Allies had declared their intention to punish German and Japanese leaders for their war crimes, they did not work out the details until the summer of 1945. In early August, the United States, Britain, France, and the Soviet Union created the **International Military** Tribunal (IMT). At the **Nuremberg trials** in Nuremberg, Germany, the IMT tried German leaders suspected of committing war crimes.

Twenty-two leaders of Nazi Germany were prosecuted at Nuremberg. Three were acquitted and another seven were given prison sentences. The remaining 12 were sentenced to death by hanging. Trials of lower-ranking government officials and military officers continued until April 1949. Those trials led to the execution of 24 more German leaders. Another 107 were given prison sentences.

Similar trials were held in Tokyo for the leaders of wartime Japan. The IMT for the Far East charged 25 Japanese leaders with a variety of war crimes. Significantly, the Allies did not indict the Japanese emperor. They feared that any attempt to put him on trial would lead to an uprising by the Japanese people. Eighteen Japanese defendants were sentenced to prison. The rest were sentenced to death by hanging.

The war crimes trials punished many of the people responsible for World War II and the Holocaust, but they were also part of the American plan for building a better world. As Robert Jackson, chief counsel for the United States at Nuremberg, observed in his opening statement to the court: "The wrongs we seek to condemn and punish have been so calculated, so malignant and so devastating, that civilization cannot tolerate their being ignored because it cannot survive their being repeated."

Reading Check **Describing** How is the United Nations organized?

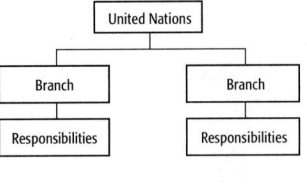
HISTORY Online

Study Central™ To review this section, go to **tarvol2.glencoe.com** and click on **Study Central**™.

SECTION 5 ASSESSMENT

Checking for Understanding
1. **Define:** hedgerow, napalm, charter.
2. **Identify:** Battle of the Bulge, V-E Day, Harry S Truman, Curtis LeMay, Manhattan Project, V-J Day, United Nations.
3. **List** the major campaigns on the European and Pacific fronts in 1945.
4. **Explain** how the United States developed the atomic bomb.
5. **Describe** the war crimes trials.

Reviewing Themes
6. **Continuity and Change** Why do you think the goal of world peace has yet to be achieved?

Critical Thinking
7. **Analyzing** If you had been an adviser to President Truman, what advice would you have given him about dropping the atomic bomb? Give reasons why you would have given this advice.
8. **Categorizing** Using a graphic organizer like the one below, fill in the structure of the United Nations.

United Nations → Branch → Responsibilities; Branch → Responsibilities

Analyzing Visuals
9. **Examining Photographs** Study the photograph on page 646 of Hiroshima after the atomic bomb was dropped. What effect do you think this photograph may have had on the American public? Why?

Writing About History
10. **Descriptive Writing** Imagine you are a war correspondent who has seen the D-Day beaches and Nazi concentration camps. Write an editorial explaining why the American sacrifices were necessary and whether or not Americans have a civic duty to fight for their country.

SECTION 5 ASSESSMENT ANSWERS

4 CLOSE

Ask students if the Allies would have indicted Adolf Hitler and if an indictment of Hitler would have influenced the decision about indicting Emperor Hirohito.

1. Terms are in blue.
2. Battle of the Bulge (p. 641), V-E Day (p. 642), Harry S Truman (p. 642), Curtis LeMay (p. 644), Manhattan Project (p. 645), V-J Day (p. 647), United Nations (p. 647)
3. Battle of the Bulge, Iwo Jima, Okinawa
4. secretly in New Mexico
5. 3 Nazis acquitted, 7 imprisoned, 12 executed; 18 Japanese imprisoned, 7 executed
6. Answers will vary.
7. Answers will vary but should be defensible.
8. General Assembly: voting body; Security Council: international security
9. Answers will vary. Many would have been shocked by the devastation.
10. Student editorials will vary but may mention the need to preserve freedom, to protect civilians, to defend rights, and to stop atrocities.

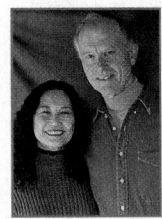

American LITERATURE

from Farewell to Manzanar
by Jeanne Wakatsuki Houston *and* James D. Houston

The following excerpt describes Jeanne Wakatsuki's first impressions as she and her family arrived at the internment camp.

We drove past a barbed-wire fence, through a gate, and into an open space where trunks and sacks and packages had been dumped from the baggage trucks that drove out ahead of us. I could see a few tents set up, the first rows of black barracks, and beyond them . . . rows of barracks that seemed to spread for miles across the plain. People were sitting on cartons or milling around . . . waiting to see which friends or relatives might be on this bus. . . .

We had pulled up just in time for dinner. The mess halls weren't completed yet. . . . They issued us army mess kits, the round metal kind that fold over, and plopped in scoops of canned Vienna sausage, canned string beans, steamed rice that had been cooked too long, and on top of the rice a serving of canned apricots. The caucasian servers were thinking that the fruit poured over rice would make a dessert. Among the Japanese, of course, rice is never eaten with sweet foods, only with salty or savory foods. . . .

After dinner we were taken to Block 16, a cluster of fifteen barracks. . . . The shacks were built of one thickness of pine planking covered with tarpaper. . . . We were assigned two of these for the twelve

people in our family group; and our official family "number" was enlarged by three digits—16 plus the number of this barracks. We were issued steel army cots, two brown army blankets, each, and some mattress covers, which my brothers stuffed with straw.

Jeanne Wakatsuki Houston was born in Inglewood, California. In 1942, when she was seven years old, her family was uprooted from their home and sent to live at the Manzanar internment camp in California. The detainees had committed no crimes. They were detained simply because of their heritage.

Farewell to Manzanar is the story of the Wakatsuki family's attempt to survive the indignities of forced detention and living behind barbed wire in the United States.

Read to Discover
How does Jeanne Wakatsuki Houston describe the internment camp that is to be her new home? What does her description remind you of?

Reader's Dictionary
barracks: plain and barren lodgings usually used to house soldiers
milling: wandering
savory: seasoned with spices

Analyzing Literature
1. **Recall and Interpret** How did the food served at the camp show a lack of understanding of Japanese culture?
2. **Evaluate and Connect** Why do you think the families in the camps were assigned numbers?

Interdisciplinary Activity
Art and Architecture Draw plans for a community memorial for remembering Japanese Americans who were treated unfairly during World War II.

Block Schedule

Team Teaching This selection from *Farewell to Manzanar* can be presented in a team teaching context, in conjunction with English or Language Arts.

Read to Discover
Answer: The barracks are crudely built and unfinished. Students may see a parallel between these camps and the Nazi camps built in Europe.

Reinforcing Vocabulary
Ask students to use each of the terms in a sentence that is not related to the reading.

Historical Connection
In 1983 the Commission of Wartime Relocation and Internment of Civilians reported in *Personal Justice Denied* that there was no military necessity for internment.

Portfolio Writing Activity
Ask students to interview an older family member, neighbor, or friend. Ask them to describe how the most important historical event of his or her lifetime affected them. Write the results of the interview in a question-and-answer format.

HISTORY *Online*

Refer to tarvol2.glencoe.com for additional Glencoe Literature titles, lesson plans, and study guides related to this unit.

Answers to Analyzing Literature

1. Students' answers will vary depending on their understanding of Japanese culture. Answers should mention that rice is never eaten with sweet foods.
2. Students' answers will vary. Camp officials likely chose to use numbers because they found Japanese names difficult to spell and pronounce.

Interdisciplinary Activity
The plans for the memorial should show details including the size and shape of the memorial. The plans should emphasize how community members might interact with the memorial.

CHAPTER
20 ASSESSMENT and ACTIVITIES

Reviewing Key Terms
Students' answers will vary. The pages where the words appear in the text appear below.

1. cost-plus (p. 613); **2. Liberty ship** (p. 614); **3. disfranchise** (p. 616); **4. periphery** (p. 621); **5. convoy system** (p. 622); **6. Sunbelt** (p. 627); **7. rationing** (p. 629); **8. victory garden** (p. 630); **9. amphtrac** (p. 636); **10. kamikaze** (p. 637); **11. hedgerow** (p. 641); **12. napalm** (p. 644); **13. charter** (p. 647);

Reviewing Key Facts
14. Selective Service and Training Act (p. 615), Chester Nimitz (p. 618), Douglas MacArthur (p. 619), George Patton (p. 622), E bond (p. 630), Casablanca Conference (p. 632), D-Day (p. 634), Manhattan Project (p. 645), United Nations (p. 647)

15. It was a campaign to enlist support in the African American community for the war effort. Double V stood for double victory–victory over Hitler's racism and victory over racism in the United States.

16. 15 million Americans moved during the war, usually for work opportunities; some moved to the Northeast, but most moved to the Sunbelt.

17. Women and African Americans were able to get jobs not normally available to them. The gains were short lived.

18. It boosted America's morale by striking on Japanese soil.

19. They used rationing, encouraged victory gardens, and controlled wages and prices.

Reviewing Key Terms
On a sheet of paper, use each of these terms in a sentence.

1. cost-plus
2. Liberty ship
3. disfranchise
4. periphery
5. convoy system
6. Sunbelt
7. rationing
8. victory garden
9. amphtrac
10. kamikaze
11. hedgerow
12. napalm
13. charter

Reviewing Key Facts
14. Identify: Selective Service and Training Act, Chester Nimitz, Douglas MacArthur, George Patton, E bond, Casablanca Conference, D-Day, Manhattan Project, United Nations.

15. What was the "Double V" campaign?

16. How did the war change patterns of population movement and settlement in the United States?

17. How did the war effort change employment opportunities for women and African Americans?

18. Why was the Doolittle raid so important to Americans?

19. How did the American government ensure that there were enough necessities to supply the war effort?

20. Why did the United States adopt a policy of island-hopping in the Pacific?

21. Explain the significance of the following dates in American history: 1941–1945.

22. Why were the victories on Iwo Jima and Okinawa so vital to the Allies?

23. What did the Allies do to punish Axis leaders after the war?

Critical Thinking
24. Interpreting Primary Sources Many historians believe that the civil rights movement of the 1950s and 1960s had its roots in the Double V campaign and the March on Washington. Alexander Allen, a member of the Urban League during the war, believed that World War II was a turning point for African Americans. Read the excerpt and answer the questions that follow.

❝Up to that point the doors to industrial and economic opportunity were largely closed. Under the pressure of war, the pressures of government policy, the pressures of world opinion, the pressures of blacks themselves and their allies, all this began to change. . . . The war forced the federal government to take a stronger position with reference to discrimination, and things began to change as a result. There was a tremendous attitudinal change that grew out of the war. There had been a new experience for blacks, and many weren't willing to go back to the way it was before. ❞

—quoted in *Wartime America*

a. How did the war change the status of African Americans in American society?

b. Why do you think the war forced the government to take a stronger position on discrimination in the workplace?

25. Analyzing Themes: Global Connections How did World War II underscore the importance of an international organization such as the United Nations?

Chapter Summary

	1941	1942	1943	1944	1945
The Pacific	Japan attacks Pearl Harbor on December 7.	The United States defeats Japan in the Battles of the Coral Sea and Midway.	The United States launches its island-hopping campaign.	The United States retakes the Philippines.	The United States drops atomic bombs; Japan surrenders on August 15.
Europe and North Africa		The Allies turn the tide in the Battle of the Atlantic.	The Allies invade Italy; Germans surrender at Stalingrad.	The Allies invade Normandy on June 6.	Germany surrenders unconditionally on May 7.
The Home Front	President Roosevelt forbids race discrimination in defense industries.	WAAC is established; Japanese American relocation is ordered.	OWM is established; Detroit and Zoot Suit Riots occur.	The case of *Korematsu* v. *United States* is decided.	The UN charter is signed.

---

20. It was a way to efficiently move materials and troops closer to Japan.

21. The United States committed its manpower and economic resources to fight in World War II.

22. It gave Americans landing areas within striking distance of Japan.

23. The Nuremberg trials and trials of the Japanese leaders convicted many of the Axis leaders of war crimes, imprisoned some and executed others, but spared the emperor of Japan.

Critical Thinking
24. a. It allowed many to work in industry and benefit from such work for the first time. Most were not willing to return to the way things had been. **b.** Possible answers: the war effort demanded a large domestic workforce; wished to avoid work stoppages

HISTORY Online

Self-Check Quiz

Visit the *American Republic Since 1877* Web site at tarvol2.glencoe.com and click on *Self-Check Quizzes—Chapter 20* to assess your knowledge of chapter content.

26. **Analyzing Effects** Do you think the opportunities that opened up for women during World War II would have developed if the United States had stayed out of the war? Explain your answer.

27. **Synthesizing** Why do you think the United States was able to successfully fight a war on multiple fronts?

28. **Categorizing** Use a concept web similar to the one below to list the major campaigns in the Pacific and in Europe.

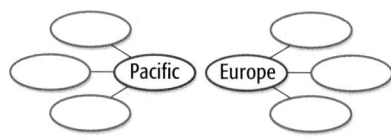

Practicing Skills

29. **Reading a Thematic Map** Study the map of migration patterns on page 627. Then use the steps you learned about reading thematic maps on page 624 to answer the following questions.
    a. **Interpreting Maps** Which regions had a net loss of residents to other regions during this period?
    b. **Synthesizing Information** How were the locations of the four fastest growing cities similar?

Chapter Activities

30. **Research Project** Use library or Internet resources to find information on the United Nations today. Use what you find to design an illustrated brochure highlighting the organization's work.

31. **Analyzing Geographic Patterns and Distributions** Look at the chart on Military and Civilian Deaths in World War II found on page 643. Create a thematic map indicating each country and the deaths that occurred there. Then write a quiz based on the chart about the distribution of casualties around the world and the patterns this suggests.

Writing Activity

32. **Persuasive Writing** Assume the role of an immigrant who fled Fascist Europe in 1933 and who has become a U.S. citizen. You have just read about the proposed United Nations, and you want to write your senator to urge that the United States join the organization or boycott it. Choose which position you support, and write a letter trying to convince the senator to support your position.

NATIONAL GEOGRAPHIC

Battle of the Bulge, December 1944–January 1945

U.S. forces
British forces
German forces
Front line at date shown.

Albers Conic Equal-Area projection

American units at Bastogne were encircled on Dec. 19, and relieved on Dec. 26.

Geography and History

33. The map above shows troop movements at the Battle of the Bulge. Study the map and answer the questions below.
    a. **Interpreting Maps** At what location did the Germans surround American forces on December 25?
    b. **Applying Geography Skills** What geographic features did the Germans encounter as they attacked? What information on the map shows you this?

Standardized Test Practice

Directions: Choose the best answer to the following question.

Why did Britain and France finally declare war in 1939?

A Because Germany annexed part of Czechoslovakia

B Because Germany invaded Poland

C Because Italy invaded France

D Because of the non-aggression pact between Russia and Germany

Test-Taking Tip: Use the process of elimination to rule out answers you know are wrong. For example, it is unlikely that a non-aggression pact between Russia and Germany would cause Britain and France to declare war.

HISTORY Online

Have students visit the Web site at tarvol2.glencoe.com to review Chapter 20 and take the Self-Check Quiz.

31. Maps should reflect data in charts and quizzes should be based on the maps.

Writing Activity

32. Letters should express a clear and reasoned opinion using standard grammar, spelling, sentence structure, and punctuation.

Geography and History

33. **a.** Bastogne; **b.** rivers and mountainous terrain; the dark shading in the south, as opposed to flatter northern areas

Standardized Test Practice

Answer: B

Test-Taking Tip: Ask students to use the process of elimination to rule out answers they know are wrong. For example, it is unlikely that a non-aggression pact between Russia and Germany would cause Britain and France to declare war.

Bonus Question ?

Ask: Why was the Battle of Midway so crucial to the war in the Pacific? *(Losing four carriers gutted the heart of the Japanese fleet and stopped Japan's ability to advance in the Pacific.)*

25. It pointed out the need to investigate and propose settlements to international disputes before war erupted.

26. Answers may vary. Students should use knowledge of women's past experiences as part of their answer.

27. Answers will vary. Students should note that most industrial production was geared to supporting both fronts and that the United States had personnel available to wage both fronts of the war.

28. Pacific: Battle of Coral Sea, Battle of Midway, Guadalcanal, Iwo Jima, Okinawa; Europe: North African campaign, Battle of the Atlantic, Stalingrad, D-Day, Battle of the Bulge

Practicing Skills

29. **a.** Northeast and South; **b.** They were all located on large bodies of water.

Chapter Activities

30. Brochures should reflect current information about the United Nations.

65

Chapter 21 Resources

TEACHING TRANSPARENCIES

Graphic Organizer 6 L2

Why It Matters Chapter Transparency 21 L2

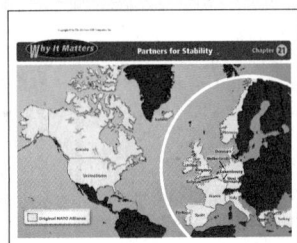

APPLICATION AND ENRICHMENT

Linking Past and Present Activity 21 L2

Enrichment Activity 21 L3

Primary Source Reading 21 L2

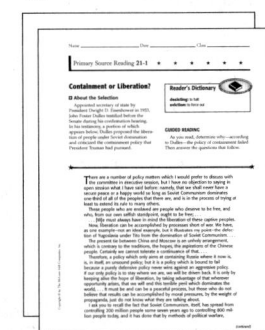

REVIEW AND REINFORCEMENT

Reteaching Activity 21 L1

Vocabulary Activity 21 L1

Time Line Activity 21 L2

Critical Thinking Skills Activity 21 L2

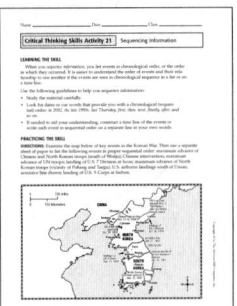

Meeting NCSS Standards

The following standards are covered in Chapter 21:

Section 1   IX   Global Connections: B, D, E, G
Section 2   IX   Global Connections: B, C, D, E, G
Section 3   X   Civic Ideals and Practices: C, F
Section 4   VIII   Science, Technology, and Society: B, C

Local Standards

Chapter 21 Resources

ASSESSMENT AND EVALUATION

Chapter 21 Test Form A L2

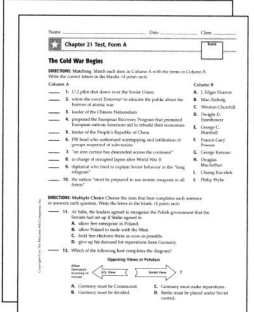

Chapter 21 Test Form B L2

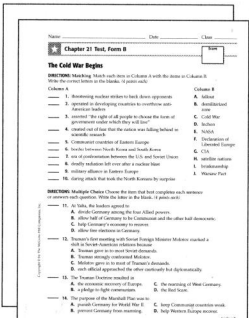

Standardized Test Practice Workbook Activity 21 L2

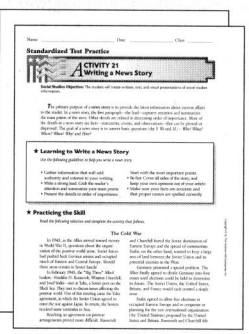

Performance Assessment Activities and Rubrics 21 L1/ELL

ExamView® Pro Testmaker CD-ROM

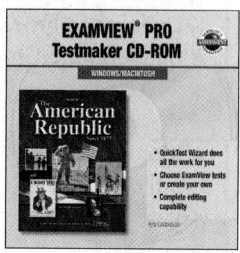

MULTIMEDIA

- Vocabulary PuzzleMaker CD-ROM
- Interactive Tutor Self-Assessment CD-ROM
- ExamView® Pro Testmaker CD-ROM
- Audio Program
- American History Primary Source Documents Library CD-ROM
- MindJogger Videoquiz
- Presentation Plus! CD-ROM
- TeacherWorks™ CD-ROM
- Interactive Student Edition CD-ROM
- Glencoe Skillbuilder Interactive Workbook CD-ROM, Level 2
- The *American Republic Since 1877* Video Program
- American Music: Hits Through History
- American Music: Cultural Traditions

SPANISH RESOURCES

The following Spanish language materials are available:

- Spanish Reading Essentials and Study Guide
- Spanish Guided Reading Activities
- Spanish Reteaching Activities
- Spanish Quizzes and Tests
- Spanish Vocabulary Activities
- Spanish Summaries
- The Declaration of Independence and United States Constitution Spanish Translation

The following videotape programs are available from Glencoe as supplements to Chapter 21:

- **Dwight D. Eisenhower: Commander-in-Chief** (1-56-501807-9)
- **Senator Joseph McCarthy: An American Inquisitor** (1-56-501610-6)
- **The Rosenbergs** (0-76-700193-1)
- **Harry S Truman: A New View** (1-56-501449-9)

To order, call Glencoe at 1-800-334-7344. To find classroom resources to accompany many of these videos, check the following home pages:
A&E Television: www.aande.com
The History Channel: www.historychannel.com

Use our Web site for additional resources. All essential content is covered in the Student Edition.

You and your students can visit tarvol2.glencoe.com, the Web site companion to the *American Republic Since 1877*. This innovative integration of electronic and print media offers your students a wealth of opportunities. The student text directs students to the Web site for the following options:

- **Chapter Overviews**
- **Student Web Activities**
- **Self-Check Quizzes**
- **Textbook Updates**

Answers to the student Web activities are provided for you in the **Web Activity Lesson Plans.** Additional Web resources and Interactive Tutor Puzzles are also available.

Chapter 21 Resources

SECTION RESOURCES

Daily Objectives	Reproducible Resources	Multimedia Resources
SECTION 1 **Origins of the Cold War** 1. Explain the growing tensions between the United States and the Soviet Union at the end of World War II. 2. Identify the goals of Stalin's foreign policy immediately after the war.	Reproducible Lesson Plan 21–1 Daily Lecture and Discussion Notes 21–1 Guided Reading Activity 21–1* Section Quiz 21–1* Reading Essentials and Study Guide 21–1* Performance Assessment Activities and Rubrics	Daily Focus Skills Transparency 21–1 Interactive Tutor Self-Assessment CD-ROM ExamView® Pro Testmaker CD-ROM* Presentation Plus! CD-ROM TeacherWorks™ CD-ROM Audio Program American Music: Cultural Traditions
SECTION 2 **The Early Cold War Years** 1. Describe the American view of the Soviet Union and the policy of containment. 2. Explain the causes of the Korean War.	Reproducible Lesson Plan 21–2 Daily Lecture and Discussion Notes 21–2 Guided Reading Activity 21–2* Section Quiz 21–2* Reading Essentials and Study Guide 21–2* Performance Assessment Activities and Rubrics Supreme Court Case Studies	Daily Focus Skills Transparency 21–2 Interactive Tutor Self-Assessment CD-ROM ExamView® Pro Testmaker CD-ROM* Presentation Plus! CD-ROM TeacherWorks™ CD-ROM Audio Program
SECTION 3 **The Cold War and American Society** 1. Describe the new Red Scare. 2. Discuss how American society reflected fears of the nuclear age.	Reproducible Lesson Plan 21–3 Daily Lecture and Discussion Notes 21–3 Guided Reading Activity 21–3* Section Quiz 21–3* Reading Essentials and Study Guide 21–3* Performance Assessment Activities and Rubrics American History in Graphic Novel	Daily Focus Skills Transparency 21–3 Interactive Tutor Self-Assessment CD-ROM ExamView® Pro Testmaker CD-ROM* Presentation Plus! CD-ROM TeacherWorks™ CD-ROM Audio Program
SECTION 4 **Eisenhower's Policies** 1. Evaluate Eisenhower's military policy known as the "New Look." 2. Debate the effectiveness of Eisenhower's foreign policy.	Reproducible Lesson Plan 21–4 Daily Lecture and Discussion Notes 21–4 Guided Reading Activity 21–4* Section Quiz 21–4* Reading Essentials and Study Guide 21–4* Performance Assessment Activities and Rubrics	Daily Focus Skills Transparency 21–4 Interactive Tutor Self-Assessment CD-ROM ExamView® Pro Testmaker CD-ROM* Presentation Plus! CD-ROM Skillbuilder Interactive Workbook, Level 2 TeacherWorks™ CD-ROM Vocabulary PuzzleMaker CD-ROM Audio Program

0:00 OUT OF TIME?
Assign the Chapter 21 **Reading Essentials and Study Guide.**

Also Available in Spanish

 Printed Materials   Transparency   CD-ROM   DVD

 Poster   Music Program   Audio Program

NATIONAL GEOGRAPHIC Teacher's Corner

INDEX TO NATIONAL GEOGRAPHIC MAGAZINE

The following articles relate to this chapter.

- "Bikini's Nuclear Graveyard," June 1992
- "Douglas MacArthur: An American Soldier," March 1992

NATIONAL GEOGRAPHIC SOCIETY PRODUCTS

To order the following, call National Geographic at 1-800-368-2728:

- *Historical Atlas of the United States* (Atlas)
- *National Geographic World Atlas For Young Explorers—Classroom Library Edition* (Teacher's Guide, Transparencies, Resource Masters)
- *1945–1989: The Cold War*
- "The Rise and Fall of the Soviet Union" (Video)

NGS ONLINE

Access National Geographic's Web site for current events, atlas updates, activities, links, interactive features, and archives.

www.nationalgeographic.com

MEETING SPECIAL NEEDS

In addition to the Differentiated Instruction strategies found in each section, the following resources are also suitable for your special needs students:

- *ExamView® Pro Testmaker CD-ROM* allows teachers to tailor tests by reducing answer choices.
- The *Audio Program* includes the entire narrative of the student edition so that less-proficient readers can listen to the words as they read them.
- The *Reading Essentials and Study Guide* provides the same content as the student edition but is written two grade levels below the textbook.

KEY TO ABILITY LEVELS

Teaching strategies have been coded.

- L1 BASIC activities for all students
- L2 AVERAGE activities for average to above-average students
- L3 CHALLENGING activities for above-average students
- ELL ENGLISH LANGUAGE LEARNER activities

From the Classroom of...

Tricia Hock
Heritage Academy
Fort Walton Beach, FL

Cold War Interviews

Students work in groups, pairs, or individually to conduct interviews with persons who were alive during the Cold War. Interviews can be with people of different ages, but similar questions can be asked, such as:

- What year were you born? How old were you when you realized the U.S. was in a "Cold War"?
- If you were in school during the Cold War years, did your school conduct air raid drills? How were they conducted?
- Were you afraid the United States would be the target of bombs or missiles? Who did you think would fire them?
- Did anyone you know have a bomb shelter? Did you ever see one? If so, what was it like?
- Did TV, books, or the media heighten the fear of nuclear attack? How?
- When did you realize that the Cold War was over, or coming to an end?

Students should report their findings to the class.

ADDITIONAL RESOURCES FROM GLENCOE

- American Music: Cultural Traditions
- American Art & Architecture
- Outline Map Resource Book
- U.S. Desk Map
- Building Geography Skills for Life
- Inclusion for the High School Social Studies Classroom Strategies and Activities
- Teaching Strategies for the American History Classroom (Including Block Scheduling Pacing Guides)
- Dinah Zike's High School American History Reading and Study Skills Foldables

 Block Schedule

Activities that are suited to use within the block scheduling framework are identified by:

Why It Matters Activity

Ask students how they think the Cold War and the fear of communism might have affected life in the 1950s. Students should evaluate their answers after they have completed the chapter.

GLENCOE
TECHNOLOGY

The *American Republic Since 1877* Video Program
To learn more about the crisis of the Berlin airlift, have students view the Chapter 21 video, "Symbols of the Cold War," from the ***American Republic Since 1877* Video Program.**

MindJogger Videoquiz
Use the **MindJogger Videoquiz** to preview Chapter 21 content.

💿 Both programs available in DVD

CHAPTER
21 The Cold War Begins *1945–1960*

Why It Matters

After World War II, an intense rivalry developed between the United States and the Soviet Union—two superpowers with very different political and economic systems. This rivalry, known as the Cold War, led to a massive buildup of military weapons on both sides. The determination of American leaders to contain communism also led to the Korean War, in which over 36,500 Americans died.

The Impact Today

The effects of Cold War events are still evident today.
* *The NATO alliance works to guarantee the security of many democratic countries.*
* *The math and science training important to the space race remains an educational priority.*

💿 ***The American Republic Since 1877* Video** *The Chapter 21 video, "Symbols of the Cold War," examines the era by focusing on the crisis of the Berlin airlift.*

1947
* Truman Doctrine declared

1945
* Yalta conference
* Franklin Roosevelt dies

1948
* Berlin airlift begins

1949
* NATO established

1950
* McCarthy charges that Communists staff the U.S. State Department
* Korean War begins

United States PRESIDENTS

Truman 1945–1953

1945

1950

World

1945
* Italian women gain right to vote

1946
* Orwell's *Animal Farm* published

1948
* State of Israel created

1949
* People's Republic of China established

1952
* Britain produces an atomic bomb

652

Reading Strategy ◀ PURPOSE FOR READING

Concept Map Like web diagrams, concept maps help students visualize the components of a concept or key term. To begin, students should write and circle "Communism" in the center of a piece of paper. Then to the left, right, and below, have them write and circle each of the following three sub-categories: "What is it? What are its properties? What are some examples?" Students should link each of the three sub-categories to the center bubble by a line. Have students complete the concept map as they read the chapter by filling in brief answers in small bubbles around each sub-category, linking each answer to the corresponding sub-category bubble by a line. Tell students they will explore post World War II, communism, and the Cold War in this chapter. **L1**

During Nixon's 1959 visit to Moscow, the vice president exchanged angry words with Soviet leader Nikita Khrushchev during the "kitchen" debate at an exhibit at the U.S. Trade and Cultural Fair.

1953
• Rosenbergs executed for treason
• Armistice reached in Korean War

1959
• Khrushchev and Eisenhower hold summit

1960
• U-2 incident

Eisenhower 1953–1961

1955

1960

1953
• Stalin dies

1956
• Suez Canal crisis
• Hungarians rise up against their Communist government

1957
• Soviet Union launches *Sputnik*

HISTORY *Online*

Chapter Overview
Visit the *American Republic Since 1877* Web site at tarvol2.glencoe.com and click on **Chapter Overviews–Chapter 21** to preview chapter information.

653

GRAPHIC ORGANIZER ACTIVITY

Organizing Information Have students compare the Soviet and American views of world affairs that led to the Cold War by completing the following graphic organizers. Students' answers will vary but should show the vastly different approaches taken by the two powers.

Soviet Views → **World Affairs** ← American Views

HISTORY *Online*

Introduce students to chapter content and key terms by having them access the **Chapter 21 Overview** at tarvol2.glencoe.com.

More About the Photo

The day after this meeting, *The New York Times* published a transcript of the exchange between Nixon and Khrushchev. After asking Nixon how long America had existed, Khrushchev is reported to have said, "One hundred and fifty years? Well then we will say America has been in existence for 150 years and this is the level she has reached. We have existed not quite 42 years and in another seven years we will be on the same level as America. . . . Plainly speaking, if you want capitalism you can live that way. That is your own affair and doesn't concern us. We can still feel sorry for you, but since you don't understand us—live as you do understand."

TIME LINE
ACTIVITY

Have students create a time line for events in the United States spanning 1945 through 1960 using the chapter time line and the section time lines. Instruct students to include months for all events.

FOLDABLES™
Study Organizer

Dinah Zike's Foldables are three-dimensional, interactive graphic organizers that help students practice basic writing skills, review key vocabulary terms, and identify main ideas. Have students complete the foldable activity in the *Dinah Zike's Reading and Study Skills Foldables* booklet.

653

SECTION 1 Origins of the Cold War

1 FOCUS

Section Overview

This section focuses on the growing tensions between the United States and the Soviet Union at the end of World War II.

BELLRINGER
Skillbuilder Activity

Project transparency and have students answer the question.

Daily Focus Skills Transparency 21–1

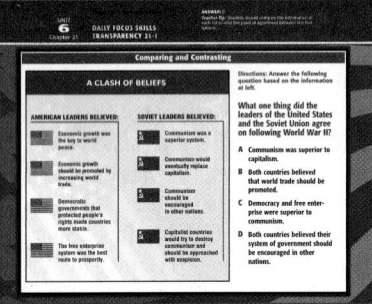

Reading Preview

Answers to Graphic: Yalta: Poland's government recognized, Poland to have free elections, Declaration of Liberated Europe, Germany divided into four zones, terms of German reparations set; Potsdam: New border established between Germany and Poland, Germany's reparations to the Soviet Union restructured

Preteaching Vocabulary
Have students write a paragraph using all the Key Terms and Names.

Guide to Reading

Main Idea
The detonation of the atomic bomb and the end of World War II led to disagreements among the "Big Three" wartime Allies and a shift in American attitudes toward the Soviet Union.

Key Terms and Names
Cold War, Potsdam, satellite nation, iron curtain

Reading Strategy
Categorizing As you read about the origins of the Cold War, complete a graphic organizer similar to the one below by filling in the names of the conferences held among the "Big Three" Allies and the outcomes of each.

Conferences	Outcomes

Reading Objectives
- **Explain** the growing tensions between the United States and the Soviet Union at the end of World War II.
- **Identify** the goals of Stalin's foreign policy immediately after the war.

Section Theme
Global Connections As World War II was ending, the United States and the Soviet Union began to negotiate to influence the shape of the postwar world.

Preview of Events

◆February 1945   ◆July 1945   ◆December 1945   ◆May 1946

February 1945
Yalta conference held in the USSR

April 1945
President Roosevelt dies

July 1945
Potsdam conference convenes in Germany

March 1946
Churchill delivers "iron curtain" speech

Harry S Truman

★ An American Story ★

On April 23, 1945, President Harry S Truman welcomed Soviet Foreign Minister Vyacheslav Molotov into the Oval Office of the White House. Truman had been president for less than two weeks, but he was determined to get tough with Molotov.

Truman told the Soviet diplomat how disgusted he was with Moscow's refusal to permit free elections in Poland, expressing his "deep disappointment" that the Soviet Union was not carrying out its agreements. Bluntly, he warned Molotov that Soviet defiance would seriously shake the confidence of the United States and Great Britain in their wartime ally.

Molotov began to explain the Soviet position, but Truman interrupted again and again, repeating his demand that Stalin "carry out that agreement in accordance with his word." Astonished, Molotov blurted out, "I have never been talked to like that in my life!"

"Carry out your agreements," the president snapped back, "and you won't get talked to like that!"

—adapted from *The Cold War: A History*

A Clash of Interests

Even before World War II ended, the wartime alliance between the United States and the Soviet Union had begun to show signs of strain. President Roosevelt had hoped that a victory over the Axis and the creation of the United Nations would lead to a more peaceful world. Instead, the United States and the Soviet Union became increasingly hostile toward each other after the war. This led to an era of confrontation and competition between the United States and the Soviet Union that lasted from about 1946 to 1990. This era became known as the Cold War.

654 CHAPTER 21 The Cold War Begins

SECTION RESOURCES

📂 Reproducible Masters
- Reproducible Lesson Plan 21–1
- Daily Lecture and Discussion Notes 21–1
- Guided Reading Activity 21–1
- Section Quiz 21–1
- Reading Essentials and Study Guide 21–1

✒ Transparencies
- Daily Focus Skills Transparency 21–1

Multimedia
- 💿 Interactive Tutor Self-Assessment CD-ROM
- 💿 ExamView® Pro Testmaker CD-ROM
- 💿 Presentation Plus! CD-ROM
- 💿 TeacherWorks™ CD-ROM
- 🎧 Audio Program
- 🎵 American Music: Cultural Traditions

Soviet Security Concerns

Tensions between the United States and the Soviet Union began to increase because the two sides had different goals. As the war ended, Soviet leaders became concerned about security. Germany had invaded Russia twice in less than 30 years. The Soviets wanted to keep Germany weak and make sure that the countries between Germany and the Soviet Union were under Soviet control.

Although security concerns influenced their thinking, Soviet leaders were also Communists. They believed that communism was a superior economic system that would eventually replace capitalism and that the Soviet Union should encourage communism in other nations. Soviet leaders also accepted Lenin's theory that capitalist countries eventually would try to destroy communism. This made Soviet leaders suspicious of capitalist nations.

American Economic Concerns

While Soviet leaders focused on securing their borders, American leaders focused on economic problems. Many American officials believed that the Depression had caused World War II. Without it, Hitler would never have come to power, and Japan would not have wanted to expand its empire.

American advisers also thought the Depression had been overly severe because countries cut back on trade. They believed that when nations seal themselves off economically, it forces them to go to war to get the resources they need. By 1945 President Roosevelt and his advisers were convinced that economic growth was the key to world peace. They wanted to promote economic growth by increasing world trade.

Similar reasoning convinced American leaders to promote democracy and free enterprise. They believed that democratic government with protections for people's rights made countries more stable and peaceful. They also thought that the free enterprise system, with private property rights and limited government intervention in the economy, was the best route to prosperity.

✓ Reading Check

Describing Why did U.S. leaders promote both international trade and free enterprise?

The Yalta Conference

In February 1945, Roosevelt, Churchill, and Stalin met at the Soviet resort of **Yalta** to plan the postwar world. There, Stalin reaffirmed the Soviet pledge to enter the war against Japan after Germany was defeated. Several agreements reached at Yalta, however, later played an important role in causing the Cold War.

Poland The first issue discussed at Yalta was what to do about Poland. Shortly after the Germans invaded Poland, the Polish government leaders had fled to Britain. In 1944, however, Soviet troops drove back the Germans and entered Poland. As they liberated Poland from German control, the Soviets encouraged Polish Communists to set up a new government. This meant there were now two governments claiming the right to govern Poland, one Communist and one non-Communist.

President Roosevelt and Prime Minister Churchill both argued that the Poles should be free to choose their own government. "This is what we went to war against Germany for," Churchill explained, "that Poland should be free and sovereign."

Stalin quickly responded to Churchill's comments. According to Stalin, the Polish government had to be friendly to the Soviet Union. It was a matter of "life and death." Eventually, the three leaders compromised. Roosevelt and Churchill agreed to recognize the Polish government set up by the Soviets. Stalin agreed that the government would include members

Germany in Ruins World War II devastated many German cities. Here a woman sits among the ruins of Cologne, a northern city on the Rhine River.

2 TEACH

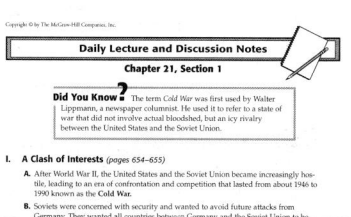

Daily Lecture and Discussion Notes 21–1

Daily Lecture and Discussion Notes

Chapter 21, Section 1

Did You Know? The term *Cold War* was first used by Walter Lippmann, a newspaper columnist. He used it to refer to a state of war that did not involve actual bloodshed, but an icy rivalry between the United States and the Soviet Union.

I. **A Clash of Interests** (pages 654–655)

A. After World War II, the United States and the Soviet Union became increasingly hostile, leading to an era of confrontation and competition that lasted from about 1946 to 1990 known as the **Cold War**.

B. Soviets were concerned with security and wanted to avoid future attacks from Germany. They wanted all countries between Germany and the Soviet Union to be

✓ Reading Check

Answer: in hopes that trade and free enterprise would increase prosperity and peace

 Reading Strategy

Organizing Information Have students make a two-column list showing the postwar concerns of the Soviet Union and the United States. Use them to guide a class discussion on mounting tensions. **L1** ELL

FYI

The only two superpowers left after World War II were the United States and the Soviet Union; they had as much productive capacity between them as the rest of the world combined.

 History *and the* Humanities

🏴 American Music: Cultural Traditions: "Old Man Atom"

 Reading Strategy | **READING THE TEXT**

Using Word Parts Help students learn how suffixes can help them unlock the meaning of words. A suffix is a word part that comes after a base word or a root. It may change the meaning of the word or the way the word is used in the sentence. Provide students with these examples: *–less* means "without" (careless, powerless); *–ish* means "like" (childish, foolish); *–ful* means "full of" (playful, thoughtful). Have students find words with suffixes in the section and identify the root word's meaning. **L1** ELL

📩 Refer to *Inclusion for the High School Social Studies Classroom Strategies and Activities* in the TCR.

Guided Reading Activity 21-1

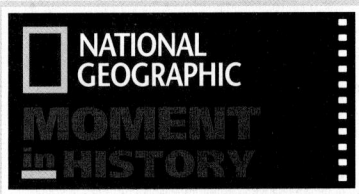

Name _____ Date _____ Class _____

★ Guided Reading Activity 21-1

DIRECTIONS: Recalling Facts Read the section and answer the questions below. Refer to your textbook to write the answers.

1. Why did the Soviet Union want to keep Germany weak? _____

2. What was Lenin's theory about capitalism? _____

3. What did American advisers believe happens when nations seal themselves off economically? _____

4. What did President Roosevelt and his advisers believe was the best way to create prosperity? _____

5. What were the _____ decisions among Roosevelt, Churchill, and Stalin as to ...

NATIONAL GEOGRAPHIC
MOMENT in HISTORY

As a neutral country, Switzerland accepted refugees from the war, although it did close its borders during part of the war. Those who were able to support themselves were allowed to live and work freely in Switzerland. Those who could not support themselves lived in work camps run by the Swiss police.

Creating a Thematic Map Have students create a thematic map that shows the countries affected by Yalta. Instruct students to indicate where the Soviets did not abide by the Yalta agreement. **L2**

 Use the rubric for creating a map, display, or chart on pages 65–66 in the *Performance Assessment Activities and Rubrics.*

FYI

Over 750 years old, Berlin has been a major European cultural center since the 1700s. Following the reunification of Germany in 1990, Berlin was reestablished as the capital in 1991.

---

of the prewar Polish government and that free elections would be held as soon as possible.

Declaration of Liberated Europe After reaching a compromise on Poland, Roosevelt, Churchill, and Stalin agreed to issue the **Declaration of Liberated Europe.** The declaration asserted "the right of all people to choose the form of government under which they will live."

The Allies promised that the people of Europe would be allowed "to create democratic institutions of their own choice." They also promised to create temporary governments that represented "all democratic elements" and pledged "the earliest possible establishment through free elections of governments responsive to the will of the people."

Dividing Germany After agreeing to a set of principles for liberating Europe, the conference focused on Germany. Roosevelt, Churchill, and Stalin agreed to divide Germany into four zones. Great Britain, the United States, the Soviet Union, and France would each control one zone. The same four countries would also divide the city of Berlin, even though it was in the Soviet zone.

Although pleased with the decision to divide Germany, Stalin also wanted to weaken the country economically. He demanded that Germany pay heavy reparations for the war damage it caused. Roosevelt agreed, but he insisted reparations be based on Germany's ability to pay. He also suggested, and Stalin agreed, that Germany pay reparations with trade goods and products instead of cash. The Allies would also be allowed to remove industrial machinery, railroad cars, and other equipment from Germany as reparations.

This decision did not resolve the issue. Over the next few years, arguments about reparations and economic policy in Germany increased tensions between the United States and the Soviet Union. These arguments became one of the major causes of the Cold War.

Tensions Begin to Rise The Yalta decisions shaped the expectations of the United States. Two weeks after Yalta, the Soviets pressured the King of Romania into

NATIONAL GEOGRAPHIC
MOMENT in HISTORY

AID FOR WAR'S YOUNGEST VICTIMS

The gift of a new pair of shoes from the American Red Cross lights up the face of a young Austrian refugee. Millions of people across Europe were uprooted by almost six years of fighting that seldom distinguished between combatants and civilians. Millions more fled as victorious Soviet troops advanced through Eastern Europe into Germany at the end of World War II. The fate of the refugees became enmeshed in the growing power struggle between the United States and the Soviet Union, which turned the former allies into Cold War enemies.

DIFFERENTIATED INSTRUCTION

At-Risk Students Winston Churchill's metaphor of an iron curtain to describe Soviet control in Eastern Europe is very evocative. Have students work individually or with partners to come up with words and images they associate with the words *iron* (for example, strength, its use in the making of weapons) and *curtain* (for example, its ability to cut off contact with others or to hide what lies behind it). Allow students to draw as well as list the images that come to mind. **L1**

 Refer to *Inclusion for the High School Social Studies Classroom Strategies and Activities* in the TCR.

appointing a Communist government. The United States accused the Soviets of violating the Declaration of Liberated Europe.

Soon afterward, the Soviets refused to allow more than three non-Communist Poles to serve in the 18-member Polish government. There was also no indication that they intended to hold free elections in Poland as promised. On April 1, President Roosevelt informed the Soviets that their actions in Poland were not acceptable. Eleven days later, with Soviet-American relations deteriorating, President Roosevelt died, and Vice President Harry Truman took office.

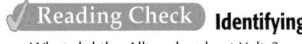

Reading Check Identifying
What did the Allies decide at Yalta?

Picturing **History**

Potsdam Trio Issues about Germany dominated the Potsdam meeting, which was attended by (from left to right) Britain's Clement Attlee, President Truman, and Soviet leader Joseph Stalin. *What agreement did they reach regarding reparations?*

Truman Takes Control

Although inexperienced in diplomacy, Truman already had his own views about how to deal with the Soviets. Truman was strongly anticommunist and suspicious of Stalin. He believed World War II had begun because Britain had tried to appease Hitler. He was determined not to make the same mistake with Stalin. "We must stand up to the Russians," he told Secretary of State Edward Stettinius, the day after taking office.

Ten days later, Truman did exactly that during his meeting with Soviet Foreign Minister Molotov. Truman immediately brought up the issue of Poland and demanded that Stalin hold free elections as he promised at Yalta. Molotov took the unexpectedly strong message back to Stalin. The meeting marked an important shift in Soviet-American relations and set the stage for further confrontations.

The Potsdam Conference In July 1945, with the war against Japan still raging, Truman finally met Stalin at **Potsdam,** near Berlin. Both men had come to Potsdam primarily to work out a deal on Germany.

Truman was now convinced that German industry was critical. Unless Germany's economy was allowed to revive, the rest of Europe would never recover, and the German people might turn to communism out of desperation.

Stalin and his advisers were equally convinced that they needed reparations from Germany. The war had devastated their economy. Soviet troops had begun stripping their zone in Germany of its machinery and industrial equipment for use back home, but Stalin wanted Germany to pay much more.

At the conference, Truman took a firm stand against heavy reparations. He insisted that Germany's industry had to be allowed to recover. Truman suggested that the Soviets take reparations from their zone, while the Allies allowed industry to revive in the other zones. Stalin opposed this idea since the Soviet zone was mostly agricultural. It could not provide all of the reparations the Soviets wanted.

To get the Soviets to accept the deal, Truman offered Stalin a small amount of German industrial equipment from the other zones but required the Soviets to pay for part of it with food shipments from their zone. He also offered to accept the new German-Polish border the Soviets had established.

Stalin did not like Truman's proposal. At Potsdam, Truman learned that the atomic bomb had been successfully tested, and he told Stalin about the test. Stalin suspected Truman was trying to bully him into a deal and that the Americans were trying to limit reparations to keep the Soviets weak.

Despite his suspicions, Stalin had to accept the deal. American and British troops controlled

CHAPTER 21 The Cold War Begins **657**

✓ **Reading Check**

Answer: They decided Poland's government and border, Europeans' right to choose their own government, and the division of Germany into four zones.

Picturing **History**

Answer: Soviets would take reparations from their zone, while Great Britain, the United States, and France would allow industry to revive.

3 ASSESS

Assign Section 1 Assessment as homework or as an in-class activity.

💿 Have students use the **Interactive Tutor Self-Assessment CD-ROM.**

L1/ELL

Reading Essentials and Study Guide 21–1

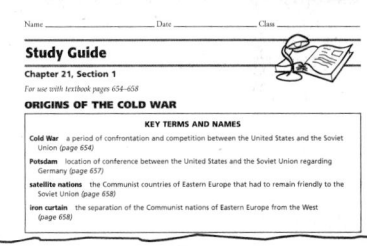

Name _____ Date _____ Class _____

Study Guide

Chapter 21, Section 1
For use with textbook pages 654–658

ORIGINS OF THE COLD WAR

KEY TERMS AND NAMES

Cold War a period of confrontation and competition between the United States and the Soviet Union (page 654)

Potsdam location of conference between the United States and the Soviet Union regarding Germany (page 657)

satellite nations the Communist countries of Eastern Europe that had to remain friendly to the Soviet Union (page 658)

iron curtain the separation of the Communist nations of Eastern Europe from the West (page 658)

L2

Section Quiz 21–1

Name _____ Date _____ Class _____

★ **Chapter 21** [Score]

Section Quiz 21-1

DIRECTIONS: Matching Match each item in Column A with the items in Column B. Write the correct letters in the blanks. *(10 points each)*

Column A

_____ 1. located near Berlin, where Truman and Stalin met to work out a deal on Germany

_____ 2. the Communist countries of Eastern Europe

_____ 3. issued by Roosevelt, Churchill, and Stalin and declared "the right of all people to choose the form of government under which they will live"

_____ 4. a Soviet resort on the Black Sea where Roosevelt, Churchill, and Stalin met to plan the postwar world

_____ 5. an era of confrontation and competition between the United States and the Soviet Union that lasted from about 1946 to 1990

Column B

A. Declaration of Liberated Europe
B. satellite nations
C. Cold War
D. Potsdam
E. Yalta

INTERDISCIPLINARY CONNECTIONS ACTIVITY

Geography Tell students that several nations in eastern Europe have a long history of being overrun by more powerful nations. Organize students into small groups. Give the groups a blank outline map of eastern Europe today and several overhead transparencies. Have the groups research and show how the boundaries of these countries have changed by creating a series of overlays for the map. Suggest that students show the boundaries at the turn of each century or on other significant dates from 1500 to the present. **L2**

Geography Skills

Answers:

1. Germany
2. They were occupied by Soviet troops and forced to seat Communist governments.

Geography Skills Practice

Ask: With which Communist countries did Austria share a border? *(Yugoslavia, Hungary, and Czechoslovakia)*

Reading Check

Answer: It increased tension because Stalin suspected that Truman wanted to limit reparations to keep the Soviet Union weak.

Reteach

Have students explain the growing tensions between the United States and the Soviet Union at the end of World War II.

Enrich

Ask students to read and analyze Winston Churchill's "iron curtain" speech.

Study Central™ provides summaries, interactive games, and online graphic organizers to help students review section content.

4 CLOSE

Have students identify the goals of Stalin's foreign policy immediately after the war.

658

NATIONAL GEOGRAPHIC **Divided Europe, 1948**

Communist nations
Non-Communist nations

Geography Skills

1. **Interpreting Maps** What nation was divided into Communist and non-Communist zones?
2. **Applying Geography Skills** Why did so many Eastern European nations have Communist governments?

Germany's industrial heartland, and there was no way for the Soviets to get any reparations except by cooperating. Nevertheless, the Potsdam conference marked yet another increase in tensions between the Soviets and the Americans, further paving the way for the Cold War.

The Iron Curtain Descends Although Truman had won the argument over reparations, he had less success on other issues at Potsdam. The Soviets refused to make any stronger commitments to uphold the

---

Declaration of Liberated Europe. The presence of the Soviet army in Eastern Europe ensured that eventually, pro-Soviet Communist governments would be established in Poland, Romania, Bulgaria, Hungary, and Czechoslovakia. "This war is not as in the past," Stalin commented. "Whoever occupies a territory also imposes his own social system. . . . It cannot be otherwise."

The Communist countries of Eastern Europe came to be called **satellite nations.** Although not under direct Soviet control, they had to remain Communist and friendly to the Soviet Union. They also had to follow policies that the Soviets approved.

As he watched the Communist takeover in Eastern Europe, Winston Churchill coined a phrase to describe what had happened. On March 5, 1946, in a speech delivered in Fulton, Missouri, Churchill said:

> ❝From Stettin in the Baltic to Trieste in the Adriatic, an iron curtain has descended across the continent. Behind that line lie all the capitals of the ancient states of central and Eastern Europe. . . . All are subject, in one form or another, not only to Soviet influence, but to a very high and increasing measure of control from Moscow.❞
>
> —quoted in *The United States and the Origins of the Cold War, 1941–1947*

With the iron curtain separating the Communist nations of Eastern Europe from the West, the World War II era had come to an end. The Cold War was about to begin.

Reading Check **Explaining** How did the Potsdam conference hurt Soviet-American relations?

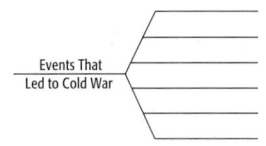

HISTORY Online **Study Central™** To review this section, go to tarvol2.glencoe.com and click on **Study Central™**.

SECTION 1 ASSESSMENT

Checking for Understanding

1. **Define:** Cold War, iron curtain.
2. **Identify:** Potsdam, satellite nation.
3. **Reviewing Facts** Why did tensions grow between the United States and the Soviet Union after World War II?

Reviewing Themes

4. **Global Connections** At Yalta, what agreement did the "Big Three" come to about Germany's future after World War II?

Critical Thinking

5. **Synthesizing** Do you think Roosevelt could have prevented the Cold War? Why or why not?
6. **Organizing** Use a graphic organizer similar to the one below to list events that led to the Cold War.

Events That
Led to Cold War

Analyzing Visuals

7. **Analyzing Maps** Study the map on this page. Why did the Soviet Union want the countries on its western border to have strong Communist governments?

Writing About History

8. **Expository Writing** Imagine you are an adviser to President Truman. Write a report explaining your interpretation of Churchill's iron curtain speech.

SECTION 1 ASSESSMENT ANSWERS

1. Terms are in blue.
2. Potsdam *(p. 657),* satellite nation *(p. 658)*
3. had different goals for Germany and Eastern Europe
4. Germany was divided into four zones controlled by Great Britain, France, the Soviet Union, and the United States.

5. Students who think the Cold War could have been prevented might mention that Soviet needs might have been accommodated. Students who think the Cold War was inevitable may say that the Soviets had already broken several promises.
6. disagreement over Germany,

Soviets' refusal to honor Declaration of Liberated Europe, Soviet actions in Poland, Potsdam Conference
7. to protect itself from invasion by Germany
8. Students' reports will vary. Reports should include specific references to Churchill's speech.

SECTION 2 The Early Cold War Years

Guide to Reading

Main Idea
As the Cold War began, the United States struggled to oppose Communist aggression in Europe and Asia through political, economic, and military measures.

Key Terms and Names
George Kennan, containment, Marshall Plan, NATO, limited war

Reading Strategy
Sequencing As you read about the Cold War, complete a time line similar to the one below by recording the major events involving the Korean War.

Reading Objectives
• **Describe** the American view of the Soviet Union and the policy of containment.
• **Explain** the causes of the Korean War.

Section Theme
Global Connections Beliefs about Soviet goals and actions had a lasting effect on American policies abroad and on the agencies used to carry them out.

Preview of Events

♦1947 ♦1948 ♦1949 ♦1950

March 1947 — Truman Doctrine declared

June 1948 — Berlin airlift begins

April 1949 — NATO forms

October 1949 — People's Republic of China established

June 1950 — Korean War begins

★ An American Story ★

Lieutenant Gail Halvorsen

Air Force lieutenant Gail Halvorsen was one of the pilots who airlifted supplies into Berlin in 1948. On one of his days off, he was shooting a home movie outside Berlin's Tempelhof Airport and soon drew a crowd of curious boys and girls. As a wartime pilot, Halvorsen had met children in other cities. They would playfully confront American soldiers, asking, "Any gum, chum?" While digging into his pockets for gum, Halvorsen had an idea. He said that if the children would wait at the end of the runway the next day, he would drop candy from his airplane.

The next day, eager children gathered at the airport. As Halvorsen's plane flew overhead, three small white parachutes floated down with a payload of candy. Halvorsen's "chocolate bombs" became a routine, earning him the nickname *Schokoladenflieger* ("chocolate-flyer"). Other pilots joined in, and by the end of the airlift, American pilots had dropped 250,000 candy parachutes for the children of Berlin.

—adapted from *Berlin in the Balance*

Containing Communism

The early Cold War shaped the politics and economics of many parts of the world, especially Europe. The airlift of supplies to Berlin, like Halvorsen's own candy airlift, reassured Europeans that the United States would help them rebuild their lives, even in the shadow of growing Soviet hostility.

CHAPTER 21   The Cold War Begins   **659**

---

1 FOCUS

Section Overview
This section focuses on the political, economic, and military measures the United States used to oppose communism.

BELLRINGER
Skillbuilder Activity

Project transparency and have students answer the question.

Daily Focus Skills Transparency 21–2

Reading Preview

Answers to Graphic: Answers might include: 1945: Soviet-U.S. division of Korea at the end of World War II; June 1950: North Korean troops invade South Korea; November 1950: China intervenes; April 1951: MacArthur fired

Preteaching Vocabulary
Have students select one of the Key Terms and Names to write a one-paragraph description explaining its significance.

SECTION RESOURCES

📁 Reproducible Masters
• Reproducible Lesson Plan 21–2
• Daily Lecture and Discussion Notes 21–2
• Guided Reading Activity 21–2
• Section Quiz 21–2
• Reading Essentials and Study Guide 21–2
• Supreme Court Case Studies

📊 Transparencies
• Daily Focus Skills Transparency 21–2

Multimedia
• Interactive Tutor Self-Assessment CD-ROM
• ExamView® Pro Testmaker CD-ROM
• Presentation Plus! CD-ROM
• TeacherWorks™ CD-ROM
• Audio Program

659

2 TEACH

Daily Lecture and Discussion Notes 21–2

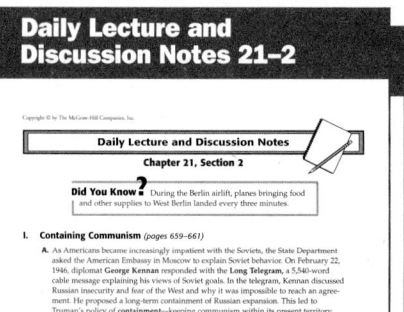

Daily Lecture and Discussion Notes
Chapter 21, Section 2

Did You Know? During the Berlin airlift, planes bringing food and other supplies to West Berlin landed every three minutes.

I. Containing Communism (pages 659–661)

A. As Americans became increasingly impatient with the Soviets, the State Department asked the American Embassy in Moscow to explain Soviet behavior. On February 22, 1946, diplomat **George Kennan** responded with the **Long Telegram**, a 5,540-word cable message explaining his views of Soviet goals. In the telegram, Kennan discussed Russian insecurity and fear of the West and why it was impossible to reach an agreement. He proposed a long-term containment of Russian expansion. This led to Truman's policy of **containment**—keeping communism within its present territory through...

Graphic Organizer → Skills

Answer: Most students will likely focus on Soviet control of Eastern Europe or the exploding of the atomic bombs. Students should present reasons for their choices.

Graphic Organizer Skills Practice
Ask: Which of the effects was likely a direct result of the superpowers' atomic bombs? *(American and Soviet arms race)*

Analyzing Points of View

Have half the students develop a list of reasons that the Truman administration should support the policy of containment. Have the other half develop a list of reasons that the administration should oppose the policy. Have each group present their lists, then have the class vote to select the position that makes the most sense to them. **L2**

Causes and Effects of the Cold War

Causes
- Soviet Union controls Eastern Europe after World War II.
- Chinese Communists win control of mainland China.
- United States and Soviet Union explode atomic bombs.

Effects
- Marshall Plan provides aid to Western Europe.
- Western nations form NATO; Communist nations respond with Warsaw Pact.
- Korean War erupts.
- American and Soviet arms race begins.
- Red Scare leads to hunt for Communists in the United States.

Graphic Organizer → Skills

The Cold War between the United States and the Soviet Union dominated postwar politics.

Evaluating What do you think was the most important cause of the Cold War? Why?

Despite the growing tensions between the Soviet Union and the United States, many American officials continued to believe cooperation with the Soviets was possible. In late 1945, the foreign ministers of the former wartime Allies met first in London, then in Moscow, to discuss the future of Europe and Asia.

Although Ernest Bevin, the British foreign minister, and James Byrnes, the American secretary of state, pushed the Soviets to hold free elections in Eastern Europe, the Soviets refused to budge. "Our relations with the Russians," Bevin gloomily concluded, "are drifting into the same condition as that in which we had found ourselves with Hitler."

The Long Telegram Increasingly exasperated by the Soviets' refusal to cooperate, officials at the State Department asked the American Embassy in Moscow to explain Soviet behavior. On February 22, 1946, diplomat **George Kennan** responded with what came to be known as the **Long Telegram,** a 5,540-word cable message explaining his views of Soviet goals.

According to Kennan, the Soviets' view of the world came from a traditional "Russian sense of insecurity" and fear of the West, intensified by the Communist ideas of Lenin and Stalin. Because Communists believed that they were in a long-term historical struggle against capitalism, Kennan argued, it was impossible to reach any permanent settlement with them.

Kennan therefore proposed what became the basic American policy throughout the Cold War: "a long-term, patient but firm and vigilant containment of

Russian expansive tendencies." Kennan explained that, in his opinion, the Soviet system had several major economic and political weaknesses. If the United States could keep the Soviets from expanding their power, it was only a matter of time until the Soviet system would fall apart. Communism could be beaten without going to war. The Long Telegram circulated widely in Truman's administration. It gave rise to the policy of containment—keeping communism within its present territory through the use of diplomatic, economic, and military actions.

Crisis in Iran While Truman's administration discussed Kennan's ideas, a series of crises erupted in the spring and summer of 1946. These crises seemed to prove that Kennan was right about the Soviets. The first crisis began in Iran in March 1946.

During World War II, the United States had put troops in southern Iran while Soviet troops occupied northern Iran to secure a supply line from the Persian Gulf. After the war, instead of withdrawing as promised, the Soviet troops remained in northern Iran. Stalin then began demanding access to Iran's oil supplies. To increase the pressure, Soviet troops helped local Communists in northern Iran establish a separate government.

To American officials, these actions signaled a Soviet push into the Middle East. Secretary of State James Byrnes sent Moscow a strong message demanding that they withdraw. At the same time, the battleship USS *Missouri* sailed into the eastern Mediterranean. The pressure seemed to work. Soviet forces withdrew, having been promised a joint Soviet-Iranian oil company. The Iranian parliament later rejected the plan.

660 CHAPTER 21 The Cold War Begins

Reading Strategy — READING THE TEXT

Discussing the War Use a panel-discussion format to help students focus on the issues of the Korean War. Call on volunteers to portray President Truman, Douglas MacArthur, a representative from the United Nations, a Chinese diplomat, a South Korean civilian, and a North Korean civilian. Then invite other students to ask the panel questions about why there is a war in Korea, why the United States forces are fighting there, and how the fighting can be ended. Work with students to compile a list of memorable statements from the discussion for review purposes. **L1**

📁 Refer to *Inclusion for the High School Social Studies Classroom Strategies and Activities* in the TCR.

The Truman Doctrine Frustrated in Iran, Stalin turned to Turkey. There the straits of the Dardanelles were a vital route from Soviet Black Sea ports to the Mediterranean. For centuries Russia had wanted to control this strategic route. In August 1946, Stalin demanded joint control of the Dardanelles with Turkey. Presidential adviser **Dean Acheson** saw this move as the first step in a Soviet plan to control the Mideast, and he advised Truman to make a show of force. The president declared, "We might as well find out whether the Russians are bent on world conquest." He then ordered the new aircraft carrier *Franklin D. Roosevelt* to join the *Missouri* in protecting Turkey and the eastern Mediterranean.

While the United States supported Turkey, Britain tried to help Greece. In August 1946, Greek Communists launched a guerrilla war against the Greek government. For about six months, British troops helped the Greeks fight the guerrillas. The effort strained Britain's economy, which was still weak from World War II. In February 1947, Britain informed the United States that it could no longer afford to help Greece.

On March 12, 1947, Truman went before Congress to ask for $400 million to fight Communist aggression in Greece and Turkey. His speech outlined a policy which became known as the **Truman Doctrine.** Its goal was to aid "free peoples who are resisting attempted subjugation by armed minorities or by outside pressures." Its immediate effects were to stabilize the Greek government and ease Soviet demands in Turkey. In the long run, it pledged the United States to fight communism worldwide. *(See page 958 for more on the Truman Doctrine.)*

ECONOMICS

The Marshall Plan Meanwhile, postwar Western Europe faced grave problems. Economies were in ruin, people were near starvation, and political chaos was at hand. The terrible winter of 1946 made things worse.

In June 1947, Secretary of State George C. Marshall proposed the European Recovery Program, or **Marshall Plan,** which would give European nations American aid to rebuild their economies. Truman saw the Marshall Plan and the Truman Doctrine as "two halves of the same walnut," both essential

George Marshall

for containment. Marshall offered help to all nations planning a recovery program:

> ❝Our policy is not directed against any country or doctrine, but against hunger, poverty, desperation and chaos. Its purpose should be the revival of a working economy in the world so as to permit the emergence of political and social conditions in which free institutions can exist. . . .❞
>
> —quoted in *Marshall: A Hero for Our Times*

The Soviet Union and its satellite nations in Eastern Europe rejected the offer. Instead, the Soviets developed their own economic program. This action further separated Europe into competing regions. The Marshall Plan pumped billions of dollars worth of supplies, machinery, and food into Western Europe. Western Europe's recovery weakened the appeal of communism and opened new markets for trade.

✔ **Reading Check** **Summarizing** What were the goals of the Truman Doctrine and the Marshall Plan?

The Berlin Crisis

The Marshall Plan was only one part of the American strategy for rebuilding Europe. President Truman and his advisers believed that Western Europe's prosperity depended on Germany's recovery. The Soviets, however, still wanted Germany to pay reparations to the Soviet Union. Eventually, the dispute over Germany brought the United States and the Soviet Union to the brink of war.

West Germany Is Founded By early 1948, U.S. officials had concluded that the Soviets were deliberately trying to undermine Germany's economy. In response, the United States, Great Britain, and France announced that they were merging their zones in Germany and allowing the Germans to have their own government. They also agreed to merge their zones in Berlin and to make West Berlin part of the new German republic.

The new nation was officially called the Federal Republic of Germany, but it became known as West Germany. West Germany's economy was completely separate from the Soviet zone, which eventually became known as East Germany. West Germany was not allowed to have a military, but in most respects, it was independent.

L1/ELL

Guided Reading Activity 21–2

✔ **Reading Check**

Answer: fight Soviet aggression in Greece and Turkey, stabilize Europe's economy to defeat communism

Creating a Chart Have students create a chart showing examples of Truman's containment policies in Iran, Turkey, Greece, Germany, and China. **L2**

📁 Use the rubric for creating a map, display, or chart on pages 65–66 in the *Performance Assessment Activities and Rubrics.*

you don't say...

Marshall Opposition Senator Robert A. Taft opposed the Marshall Plan, calling it a "global give-away program." He was concerned that the plan would bankrupt the United States.

📁 Use *Supreme Court Case Study 27, Dennis v. United States.*

DIFFERENTIATED INSTRUCTION

English Learners It is often difficult for students with poor vocabularies to understand the emotional impact of words and how these words shape our feelings about events. Have students examine the quote on page 661 and make a list of words they believe have an emotional impact. Then ask what emotions these words held for people in the United States and for people who lived in postwar Europe. **L1** ELL

📁 Refer to *Inclusion for the High School Social Studies Classroom Strategies and Activities* in the TCR.

Answer: 11 months
Ask: What did the Berlin airlift symbolize? *(American determination to support the divided city)*

Reading Check

Answer: Soviet blockade of West Berlin

Creating a Map On an outline map of Europe, have students show the division between East and West by shading the European countries that made up the NATO alliance in 1949 in one color and those that made up the Warsaw Pact in 1955 in another color. **L1**

Use the rubric for creating a map, display, or chart on pages 65–66 in the *Performance Assessment Activities and Rubrics.*

FYI

During the Berlin airlift, a plane flew into the city every three minutes. Without the supplies those planes carried, West Berliners would have had to back down.

Picturing **History**

Bucking the Blockade The Berlin airlift became a symbol of American determination to resist the Soviet Union's effort to control Berlin. **For how many months did American pilots supply Berlin with food and supplies?**

The Berlin Airlift The decision to create West Germany convinced the Soviets that they would never get the reparations they wanted. In late June 1948, Soviet troops cut all road and rail traffic to West Berlin. The blockade provoked a crisis. President Truman sent long-range bombers with atomic weapons to bases in Britain. General Lucius Clay, the American commander in Germany, warned that if Berlin fell, West Germany would be next. "If we mean to hold Europe against communism, then we must not budge," he said.

The challenge was to keep West Berlin alive without provoking war with the Soviets. In June 1948, Truman ordered the **Berlin airlift** to begin. For 11 months, cargo planes supplied Berliners with food, medicine, and coal. The airlift continued through the spring of 1949, bringing in over 2 million tons of supplies. Stalin finally lifted the blockade on May 12. The Berlin airlift became a symbol of American determination to stand by the divided city.

NATO The Berlin blockade convinced many Americans that the Soviets were bent on conquest. Both the public and Congress began to support a military alliance with Western Europe. By April 1949, an agreement had been reached to create the North Atlantic Treaty Organization (NATO)—a mutual defense alliance.

NATO initially included 12 countries: the United States, Canada, Britain, France, Italy, Belgium, Denmark, Portugal, the Netherlands, Norway, Luxembourg , and Iceland. NATO members agreed to come to the aid of any member who was attacked. For the first time in its history, the United States had committed itself to maintaining peace in Europe. Six years later, the United States and its allies decided to allow West Germany to rearm and join NATO. This decision alarmed Soviet leaders. They responded by organizing a military alliance in Eastern Europe, which became known as the **Warsaw Pact.**

Reading Check **Evaluating** What triggered the beginning of the Berlin airlift?

The Cold War Spreads to East Asia

The Cold War eventually spread beyond Europe. Conflicts also emerged in Asia, where events in China and Korea brought about a new attitude toward Japan.

Civil War and Revolution in China In China, Communist forces led by **Mao Zedong** had been struggling against the Nationalist government led by Chiang Kai-shek since the late 1920s. During World War II, the two sides suspended their war to resist Japanese occupation. With the end of World War II, however, civil war broke out again. Although Mao made great gains, neither side could win, and neither would accept a compromise.

To prevent a Communist revolution in Asia, the United States sent the Nationalist government $2 billion in aid beginning in the mid-1940s, but it squandered this advantage with poor military planning and corruption. By 1949 the Communists had captured the Chinese capital of Beijing and moved southward, while support for the Nationalists declined.

In August 1949, the State Department discontinued aid to the Chinese Nationalists. The defeated Nationalists then fled the Chinese mainland for the small island of Taiwan (Formosa). The victorious Communists established the People's Republic of China in October 1949.

After the Fall China's fall to communism shocked Americans. To make matters worse, in September 1949 the Soviet Union announced that it had successfully

---

INTERDISCIPLINARY CONNECTIONS ACTIVITY

Government Berlin remained a focal point throughout the Cold War. In 1961 the government of East Germany built the Berlin Wall to prevent its people from moving to West Germany. The dismantling of the Berlin Wall in 1989 foreshadowed the end of the Communist domination of Eastern Europe. Encourage students to use library and Internet resources to learn more about the reunification of Germany and the reestablishment of Berlin as Germany's capital.

tested its first atomic weapon. Then, early in 1950, the People's Republic of China and the Soviet Union signed a treaty of friendship and alliance. Many Western leaders feared that China and the Soviet Union would support Communist revolutions in other nations.

The United States kept formal diplomatic relations with only the Nationalists in Taiwan. It used its veto power in the UN Security Council to keep representatives of the new Communist China out of the UN, allowing the Nationalists to retain their seat.

The Chinese revolution brought about a significant change in American policy toward Japan. At the end of World War II, General Douglas MacArthur had taken charge of occupied Japan. His mission was to introduce democracy and keep Japan from

threatening war again. Once the United States lost China as its chief ally in Asia, it adopted policies to encourage the rapid recovery of Japan's industrial economy. Just as the United States viewed West Germany as the key to defending all of Europe against communism, it saw Japan as the key to defending Asia.

✓ **Reading Check** **Analyzing** How did the revolution in China affect American foreign policy with Japan?

The Korean War

At the end of World War II, American and Soviet forces entered Korea to disarm the Japanese troops stationed there. The Allies divided Korea at the 38th

NATIONAL GEOGRAPHIC **Korean War, 1950–1953** *In Motion*

June 25, 1950–November 24, 1950
- ▢ UN-held territory, Sept. 15, 1950
- ← North Korean advance
- ← UN counteroffensive
- — UN front line, Nov. 24, 1950

SOVIET UNION
CHINA
Yalu River
40°N
NORTH KOREA
Pyongyang
❸ Taken by UN, Oct. 19, 1950
38th Parallel
❷ Liberated by UN, Sept. 28, 1950
Seoul
Inchon
❶ MacArthur lands, Sept. 15, 1950
SOUTH KOREA
Sea of Japan
Yellow Sea
•Pusan
0 100 miles
0 100 kilometers
Lambert Conformal Conic projection
JAPAN

SOVIET UNION
N W E S
CHINA
❹ Chinese counteroffensive, Nov. 26, 1950
Yalu River
40°N
NORTH KOREA
Pyongyang
Sea of Japan
38th Parallel
Panmunjom•
Seoul
Inchon
❺ Armistice line, July 27, 1953
SOUTH KOREA
•Taegu
•Pusan
Yellow Sea
0 100 miles
0 100 kilometers
Lambert Conformal Conic projection
130°E
JAPAN

November 24, 1950–July 27, 1953
- — UN front line, Nov. 24, 1950
- ← Chinese counteroffensive, Nov. 25, 1950
- — Farthest Chinese advance, Jan. 24, 1951
- ← UN advance, Jan. 25, 1951

Geography *Skills*

1. **Interpreting Maps** Along what latitude was Korea divided into two nations after World War II?
2. **Applying Geography Skills** In debates over expanding the Korean War, why do you think Truman opposed MacArthur's request to bomb bridges on the Yalu River?

CHAPTER 21 The Cold War Begins **663**

✓ **Reading Check**

Answer: The United States adopted policies to encourage the rapid recovery of Japan's industrial economy.

Geography *Skills*

Answers:
1. 38°N
2. Truman did not want to risk bringing the Chinese into the war, or to use the atomic bomb.

Geography Skills Practice
Ask: What was the importance of the Yalu River in the Korean War? *(It was the boundary between China and North Korea.)*

you don't say...

Chinese Changes In October 2000 the Library of Congress and other U.S. libraries joined the international community and began using the Pinyin standard to convert Chinese characters. Pinyin has been widely used since 1979. In the older Wade-Giles system, it was Mao Tse-tung. In the Pinyin system, it is Mao Zedong.

FYI

Douglas MacArthur and his father are the only father and son to have both received the Medal of Honor for people who perform extraordinary acts of heroism.

CRITICAL THINKING ACTIVITY

Making Judgments The Truman administration's policy toward China was met with criticism. Have students answer the following questions: Could the United States have saved China from Communist domination? If so, how? If not, why not? *(Students' answers will vary. Some might suggest that the United States should have given the Nationalists more military and economic aid. Other students might suggest that the conflict in China was a civil war and thus beyond the control of the U.S. government.)* **L2**

Different Viewpoints

Learning from History
Answers:
1. MacArthur believed Truman's policy would lead to war later. Truman did not want to widen the conflict, or lose allies.
2. The president is commander in chief.

Creating a Time Line Have students create a time line for the Korean War. Suggest that they use the time lines in this chapter as a reference. Encourage them to illustrate the time line with drawings or photographs. **L2**

3 ASSESS

Assign Section 2 Assessment as homework or as an in-class activity.

⊙ Have students use the **Interactive Tutor Self-Assessment CD-ROM.**

L1/ELL

Reading Essentials and Study Guide 21–2

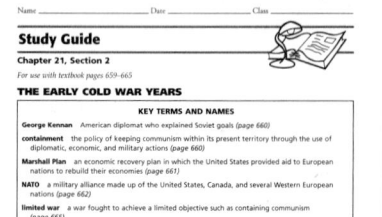

Name _____ Date _____ Class _____

Study Guide

Chapter 21, Section 2

For use with textbook pages 659–665

THE EARLY COLD WAR YEARS

KEY TERMS AND NAMES

George Kennan American diplomat who explained Soviet goals (page 660)

containment the policy of keeping communism within its present territory through the use of diplomatic, economic, and military actions (page 660)

Marshall Plan an economic recovery plan in which the United States provided aid to European nations to rebuild their economies (page 661)

NATO a military alliance made up of the United States, Canada, and several Western European nations (page 662)

limited war a war fought to achieve a limited objective such as containing communism (page 665)

Different Viewpoints

Should the War in Korea Be Expanded?

A controversy between President Harry S Truman and General Douglas MacArthur began shortly after the outbreak of the Korean War. It reached a climax when the president relieved MacArthur of his command. Truman believed in a limited war in Korea, while MacArthur wanted total victory.

President Harry S Truman defends limited war:

The Kremlin [Soviet Union] is trying, and has been trying for a long time, to drive a wedge between us and the other nations. It wants to see us isolated. It wants to see us distrusted. It wants to see us feared and hated by our allies. Our allies agree with us in the course we are following. They do not believe that we should take the initiative to widen the conflict in the Far East. If the United States were to widen the conflict, we might well have to go it alone.

If we go it alone in Asia, we may destroy the unity of the free nations against aggression. Our European allies are nearer to Russia than we are. They are in far greater danger. . . . Going it alone brought the world to the disaster of World War II. . . .

I do not propose to strip this country of its allies in the face of Soviet danger. The path of collective security is our only sure defense against the dangers that threaten us.

General Douglas MacArthur addresses Congress, April 19, 1951:

History teaches with unmistakable emphasis that appeasement but begets new and bloodier war. . . . Like blackmail, it lays the basis for new and successively greater demands, until, as in blackmail, violence becomes the only other alternative. Why, my soldiers asked of me, surrender military advantage to an enemy in the field? I could not answer.

It was my constant effort to preserve them and end this savage conflict honorably and with the least loss of time and minimum sacrifice of life.

I am closing 52 years of military service. . . . But I still remember the refrain of one of the most popular barrack ballads of that day which proclaimed most proudly that—

"Old soldiers never die, they just fade away." And like the old soldier of that ballad, I now close my military career and just fade away—an old soldier who tried to do his duty as God gave him the light to see that duty. Good-by.

Learning From History

1. **Identifying Central Issues** How did MacArthur view Truman's decision to fight a limited war in Korea? How did Truman see it?
2. **Making Inferences** On the basis of what authority did Truman fire MacArthur?

---

parallel of latitude. Soviet troops controlled the north, while American troops controlled the south.

As the Cold War began, talks to reunify Korea broke down. A Communist Korean government was organized in the north, while an American-backed government controlled the south. Both governments claimed authority over all of Korea, and border clashes were common. The Soviet Union provided extensive military aid to the North Koreans, who quickly built up a large, well-equipped army. On June 25, 1950, North Korean troops invaded into the south, rapidly driving back the poorly equipped South Korean forces.

The UN Intervenes Truman saw the Communist invasion of South Korea as a test of the containment policy and ordered United States naval and airpower

into action. He then called on the United Nations to act. Truman succeeded because the Soviet delegate was boycotting the Security Council over its China policy and was not present to veto the American proposal. With the pledge of UN troops, Truman ordered General MacArthur to send American troops from Japan to the Korean peninsula.

The American and South Korean troops were driven back into a small pocket of territory near the port of Pusan. Inside the "Pusan perimeter," as it came to be called, the troops stubbornly resisted the North Korean onslaught, buying time for MacArthur to organize reinforcements.

EXTENDING THE CONTENT

Chinese Civil War The civil war between the Chinese Nationalists and the Chinese Communists might have been avoided had the Nationalists kept their promises to the people. By denying peasants the land they were promised, by forcing friendly Communists out of the government, and by ignoring corruption, the Nationalists practically guaranteed their unpopularity and the struggle for power with the Communists.

On September 15, MacArthur ordered a daring invasion behind enemy lines at the port of Inchon. The Inchon landing took the North Koreans by surprise. Within weeks they were in full retreat back across the 38th parallel. Truman then gave the order to pursue the North Koreans beyond the 38th parallel. MacArthur pushed the North Koreans north to the Yalu River, the border with China.

China Enters the War

The Communist Chinese government saw the advancing UN troops as a threat and warned the forces to halt their advance. When those warnings were ignored, China launched a massive attack across the Yalu River in November. Hundreds of thousands of Chinese troops flooded across the border, driving the UN forces back across the 38th parallel.

As his troops fell back, an angry MacArthur demanded approval to expand the war against China. He asked for a blockade of Chinese ports, the use of Chiang Kai-shek's Nationalist forces, and the bombing of Chinese cities with atomic weapons.

Truman Fires MacArthur

President Truman refused MacArthur's demands because he did not want to expand the war into China or to use the atomic bomb. MacArthur persisted. He publicly criticized the president, saying, "There is no substitute for victory."

Determined to maintain control of policy and show that the president commanded the military, an exasperated Truman fired MacArthur for insubordination in April 1951. MacArthur, who remained popular despite being fired, returned home to parades and a hero's welcome. Despite criticism, Truman remained committed to limited war—a war fought to achieve a limited objective, such as containing communism.

Changes in Policy

Truman chose General Matthew Ridgway to replace MacArthur. By mid-1951, the UN forces had pushed the Chinese and North Korean forces back across the 38th parallel. The war then settled down into a series of relatively small battles over hills and other local objectives. In November 1951, peace negotiations began, but an armistice would not be signed until July 1953. More than 33,600 American soldiers died in action in the Korean War, and more than 2,800 died from accidents or from disease.

The Korean War marked an important turning point in the Cold War. Until 1950 the United States had preferred to use political pressure and economic aid to contain communism. After the Korean War began, the United States embarked on a major military buildup.

The Korean War also helped expand the Cold War to Asia. Before 1950 the United States had focused on Europe as the most important area in which to contain communism. After the Korean War began, the United States became more militarily involved in Asia. Defense agreements were signed with Japan, South Korea, Taiwan, the Philippines, and Australia. American aid also began to flow to the French forces fighting Communist guerrillas in Vietnam.

✓ **Reading Check** **Analyzing** How did President Truman view the Communist invasion of South Korea?

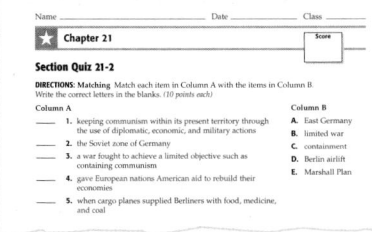

Student Web Activity Visit the *American Republic Since 1877* Web site at tarvol2.glencoe.com and click on *Student Web Activities— Chapter 21* for an activity on the Cold War.

HISTORY Online **Study Central™** To review this section, go to tarvol2.glencoe.com and click on **Study Central™**.

SECTION 2 ASSESSMENT

Checking for Understanding

1. **Define:** containment, limited war.
2. **Identify:** George Kennan, Marshall Plan, NATO.
3. **Review Facts** How did the Truman Doctrine and the Marshall Plan address the spread of communism?

Reviewing Themes

4. **Global Connections** What long-term Cold War strategy did the United States follow?

Critical Thinking

5. **Evaluating** How did the Long Telegram influence American policy?
6. **Categorizing** Use a graphic organizer similar to the one below to list early conflicts between the USSR and the U.S.

Conflicts Between the USSR and the U.S.

Analyzing Visuals

7. **Analyzing Maps** Study the maps of the Korean War on page 663. When did the United Nations control the most territory in Korea? When did both sides finally agree upon an armistice line?

Writing About History

8. **Persuasive Writing** Write a letter to the editor of a newspaper explaining whether you agree or disagree with President Truman's firing of General MacArthur.

CHAPTER 21 The Cold War Begins **665**

SECTION 2 ASSESSMENT ANSWERS

1. Terms are in blue.
2. George Kennan *(p. 660)*, Marshall Plan *(p. 661)*, NATO *(p. 662)*
3. They would help any country fight against communism and they would help rebuild economies to strengthen the resistance to communism.
4. the policy of containing communism through international aid, diplomacy, and a strong military
5. It recommended patient but firm and vigilant containment of Russian expansion.
6. crisis in Iran, Berlin crisis, Korean War
7. November 1950; July 27, 1953
8. Students' letters will vary. Letters should express a point of view based on facts.

Section Quiz 21–2

Name _____ Date _____ Class _____

★ Chapter 21 Score ☐

Section Quiz 21-2

DIRECTIONS: Matching Match each item in Column A with the items in Column B. Write the correct letters in the blanks. *(10 points each)*

Column A
____ 1. keeping communism within its present territory through the use of diplomatic, economic, and military actions
____ 2. the Soviet zone of Germany
____ 3. a war fought to achieve a limited objective such as containing communism
____ 4. gave European nations American aid to rebuild their economies
____ 5. when cargo planes supplied Berliners with food, medicine, and coal

Column B
A. East Germany
B. limited war
C. containment
D. Berlin airlift
E. Marshall Plan

Objectives and answers to the student activity can be found in the **Web Activity Lesson Plan** at tarvol2.glencoe.com.

✓ **Reading Check**

Answer: Truman viewed it as a test of the United States containment policy.

Reteach

Have students describe the American view of the Soviet Union and containment.

Enrich

Invite interested students to write an editorial expressing an opinion about when, if ever, it is appropriate for a military leader to override a president's decision.

Study Central™ provides summaries, interactive games, and online graphic organizers to help students review section content.

4 CLOSE

Have students create a cause-and-effect organizer for the Korean War.

1 FOCUS

After students have read the Looking Back. . . feature, review the reasons stated in the Why It Matters paragraph. Then have students reread Patrick Henry's words at the bottom of page 666. Discuss what his words mean in today's context.

2 TEACH

Demonstrating the Main Idea

At the beginning of class, have students take out a sheet of paper for a pop quiz. Give them five very difficult questions over material that they have not yet studied. Tell students that the quiz grades will count the same as a test. Amid students' protestations, ask students how your actions represent tyranny. Review with students the meanings of the following words: tyranny, oppression, and despotism. **L1**

Analyzing Concepts
Have students list recent examples of tyranny in the world. Ask students what role the United States has played in defending those who lost their natural rights as a result of tyranny. Also, ask them to evaluate the effectiveness of current American policies about granting people basic human rights. **L2**

The American Revolution

Why It Matters The Cold War between the United States and the Soviet Union stemmed from a number of factors, from mutual fear and mistrust to a desire by both superpowers to spread their influence around the world. On another level, however, the effort to contain communism reflected a basic tradition of Americans first seen in the American Revolution: standing up to tyranny and fighting for freedom.

The United States was founded on the principles of individual liberty and democratic rule. Since then, Americans have felt a special duty to promote these ideals and challenge any attempt to undermine them abroad as well as at home. In confronting the Soviet Union, Americans believed they were carrying on a long tradition of battling oppression and despotism.

 ## Steps to . . . the American Revolution

A central idea behind the American Revolution was that the colonists had a right to rebel because the British were suppressing their basic rights. Americans have remained committed to this political principle. By contrast, many of these rights—for example, the right to free speech or to own property—were not recognized in the Soviet Union.

Samuel Adams Few colonists were as unyielding in their opposition to British rule as Samuel Adams. Adams was one the most outspoken of the patriots and the founder of the prominent resistance group, the Sons of Liberty. He admired the ideas of English philosopher John Locke, agreeing with Locke that every citizen enjoyed the natural rights of life, liberty, and property.

A government, Adams declared, "has no right to absolute, arbitrary power over the lives of and fortunes of the people. . . ."

Thomas Jefferson Perhaps no colonist did more to advance freedom than Thomas Jefferson, one of the main authors of the Declaration of Independence. When the debate over whether to fight Great Britain began, Jefferson was one of many who argued that personal liberty and self-determination were worth fighting for.

"We have counted the cost of this contest and find nothing so dreadful as voluntary slavery," Jefferson stated in a 1775 declaration cowritten with

"If we wish to be free; if we mean to preserve inviolate those inestimable privileges for which we have been so long contending; if we mean not basely to abandon the noble struggle in which we have been so long engaged, . . . we must fight!"

—*Patrick Henry, 1775*

EXTENDING THE CONTENT

Stalin's Response The impact of the Soviets' lack of a free press—one of the keystones of the American constitutional system— is demonstrated by some of Stalin's statements. For example, after Winston Churchill's "iron curtain" speech, Stalin came up with his own characterization of geopolitical changes. Stalin claimed that the West was racist. He compared the West to "Hitler and his friends," and said Churchill was arguing that "only nations speaking the English language are fully valuable nations. . . ." Under the Soviet system, no journalist or scholar could challenge the accuracy of Stalin's statement.

American vs. Soviet Government Systems

U.S. Constitutional System	Soviet System
Bill of Rights to protect individual rights with access to independent judiciary	Soviet constitution states protections, but they are not enforced; no independent judiciary
Free elections	Government-controlled elections
Representative government at federal, state, and local levels	Central Committee of Communist Party in control of central, state, and local government
Police under civilian control	Police under party control; active secret police unit to control dissent
Free press	State-controlled press
Military under control of elected civilian government bodies	Military under control of central leadership of Communist Party
Extensive private property ownership	State ownership of major industries; very limited private ownership

John Dickinson. "Honor, justice, and humanity forbid us tamely to surrender that freedom which we received from our gallant ancestors, and which our [descendants] have a right to receive from us."

George Washington During the Revolution, George Washington's duties were mostly military, but he believed strongly in civilian government. He showed his political beliefs at the end of the Revolutionary War, when he learned that a group of military officers who had not been paid were considering seizing control of the government. He criticized the plotters and expressed his disgust with the idea of military rule. Such an action, Washington declared, "has something so shocking in it that humanity revolts at the idea. . . ." Washington's position reflected his commitment to a government by the people.

Benjamin Franklin Benjamin Franklin, the American philosopher, diplomat, and inventor, also supported independence. For a long time, Franklin was friendly to Great Britain, but he eventually came to see British rule as oppressive. In a satirical 1773 piece entitled *Rules by Which a Great Empire May Be Reduced to a Small One,* Benjamin Franklin explained that Britain was following all the necessary steps to create a colonial rebellion:

"If you are told of discontents in your colonies, never believe that they are general, or that you have

given occasion for them; therefore, do not think of applying any remedy, or of changing any offensive measure. . . ."

Free Speech and Free Press Free speech and freedom of the press were important freedoms for which the colonists fought. Before the American Revolution, colonists could be charged with sedition for criticizing the government. After the Revolution, many state constitutions guaranteed the right to free speech and a free press.

The Virginia Declaration of Rights of 1776 stated that "the freedom of the press is one of the greatest bulwarks of liberty and can never be restrained but by despotic governments." These ideas led to the lines in the First Amendment of the Constitution guaranteeing free speech and freedom of the press. These freedoms are rarely found in Communist societies or in military dictatorships. Protecting these freedoms was one more reason the United States opposed the spread of communism.

Check for Understanding

1. What doctrine of John Locke did Samuel Adams promote?
2. What principle did George Washington believe was important in the relationship between government and the military?

Critical Thinking

1. Why do you think that dictatorships and other tyrannical forms of governments oppose freedom of the press?
2. In what ways were the revolutionary leaders mentioned here similar to American leaders during the Cold War?

---

3 ASSESS

Reteach

Review the seven elements in the chart on page 667 listing specific rights under the American Constitution. Have students consider working examples of these rights in their own community. Call on students in a class discussion to elicit their examples.

Enrich

Have students choose one of the four American leaders treated in the Looking Back. . . feature—Samuel Adams, Thomas Jefferson, George Washington, Benjamin Franklin. Students should conduct further research in the library or on the Internet to deepen their understanding of the ideas excerpted here, and then write a short report on this research.

4 CLOSE

Ask students to consider when, if ever, freedom of the press should be limited and how. Have students give specific examples.

Checking for Understanding

1. Samuel Adams promoted Locke's concept of natural human rights.
2. Washington believed that the civil government should be supreme and that the military should not interfere in politics.

Critical Thinking

1. Without a free press, citizens have very limited means to express their discontent or protests.
2. Answers will vary. Students should mention their commitment to a freely elected government and their commitment to natural human rights.

1 FOCUS

Section Overview

This section focuses on the impact of the Cold War on American society.

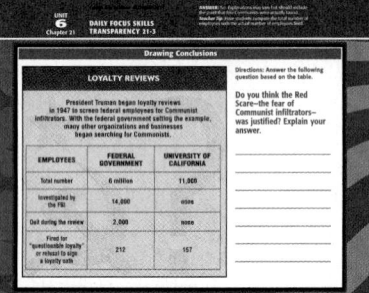
Reading Preview

Answers to Graphic:
The Cold War and American Society
I. The New Red Scare
   A. The Loyalty Review Program
   B. HUAC
   C. Alger Hiss
   D. The Rosenbergs
   E. Project Venona
   F. The Red Scare Spreads
Students should complete the outline by including all heads in the section.

Preteaching Vocabulary
Have students create a study card for each Key Term and Name with the term on one side and a definition or description on the other side.

Guide to Reading

Main Idea
The Cold War heightened Americans' fears of Communist infiltration and atomic attack.

Key Terms and Names
subversion, loyalty review program, Alger Hiss, perjury, McCarran Act, McCarthyism, censure, fallout, fallout shelter

Reading Strategy
Taking Notes As you read about American reaction to the Cold War, use the major headings of the section to create an outline similar to the one below.

The Cold War and American Society
I. A New Red Scare
   A. The Loyalty Review Program
   B.
   C.
   D.

Reading Objectives
• **Describe** the new Red Scare.
• **Discuss** how American society reflected fears of the nuclear age.

Section Theme
Civic Rights and Responsibilities In the early part of the Cold War, the fear of communism led to a hunt for spies and to intolerance and suspicion of people with radical ideas in the United States.

Preview of Events

♦1947	♦1950	♦1953
March 1947 Loyalty Review Board established	**February 1950** McCarthy claims to have a list of Communists in the State Department	**September 1950** McCarran Act passed **June 1953** Rosenbergs executed

★ *An American Story* ★

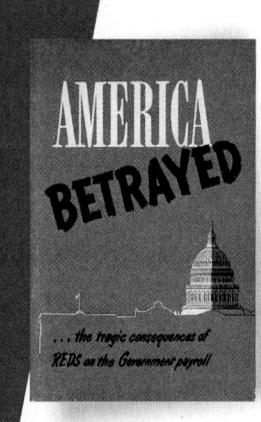

Book produced during the Red Scare of the 1950s

In the 1940s, Ruth Goldberg belonged to the Parent-Teacher Association in Queens, New York. In 1947 she agreed to run for PTA president, but the campaign turned nasty. Because Goldberg had associated with people with left-wing interests, a rumor spread through the neighborhood that she was a Communist. Suddenly Goldberg's quiet life became terrifying. Callers threatened her, and the local priest denounced her in his sermons. One afternoon, Goldberg's eight-year-old son came home in tears. A playmate had told him, "You know, your mother's a Red. She should be put up against a wall and shot."

Looking back much later, Goldberg saw the PTA campaign as part of a bigger and more complex pattern of distrust and hatred. "It was a small thing, but it was an indication of what had happened with the Cold War, with this Red specter—that somebody like me could be a danger to a community."

—adapted from *Red Scare*

A New Red Scare

During the 1950s, thousands of ordinary people—from teachers to autoworkers to high government officials—shared Ruth Goldberg's disturbing experience. Rumors and accusations of Communists in the United States and of Communist infiltration of the government tapped into fears that the Communists were trying to take over the world.

SECTION RESOURCES

📁 Reproducible Masters
• Reproducible Lesson Plan 21-3
• Daily Lecture and Discussion Notes 21-3
• Guided Reading Activity 21-3
• Section Quiz 21-3
• Reading Essentials and Study Guide 21-3
• Interpreting Political Cartoons

📇 Transparencies
• Daily Focus Skills Transparency 21-3

Multimedia
🔘 Interactive Tutor Self-Assessment CD-ROM
🔘 ExamView® Pro Testmaker CD-ROM
🔘 Presentation Plus! CD-ROM
🔘 TeacherWorks™ CD-ROM
🔘 Audio Program

The Red Scare began in September 1945, when a clerk named Igor Gouzenko walked out of the Soviet Embassy in Ottawa, Canada, and defected. Gouzenko carried documents revealing a massive effort by the Soviet Union to infiltrate organizations and government agencies in Canada and the United States with the specific goal of obtaining information about the atomic bomb.

The Gouzenko case stunned Americans. It implied that spies had infiltrated the American government. Soon, however, the search for spies escalated into a general fear of Communist subversion. Subversion is the effort to secretly weaken a society and overthrow its government. As the Cold War intensified in 1946 and early 1947, Americans began to fear that Communists were secretly working to subvert the American government.

GOVERNMENT

The Loyalty Review Program In early 1947, just nine days after his powerful speech announcing the Truman Doctrine, the president established a **loyalty review program** to screen all federal employees. Rather than calm public suspicion, Truman's action seemed to confirm fears that Communists had infiltrated the government and helped increase the fear of communism sweeping the nation.

Between 1947 and 1951, over 6 million federal employees were screened for their loyalty—a term difficult to define. A person might become a suspect for reading certain books, belonging to various groups, traveling overseas, or even seeing certain foreign films. About 14,000 employees were subject to intensive scrutiny from the Federal Bureau of Investigation (FBI). Some 2,000 employees quit their jobs during the check, many under pressure. Another 212 were fired for "questionable loyalty," though no actual evidence against them was uncovered.

HUAC Although the FBI helped screen federal employees, FBI Director **J. Edgar Hoover** was not satisfied. In 1947 Hoover went before the House Un-American Activities Committee (HUAC). Formed in 1938 to investigate both Communist and Fascist activities in the United States, HUAC was a relatively minor committee until Hoover catapulted it to prominence.

Hoover urged HUAC to hold public hearings on Communist subversion. The committee, Hoover said, could reveal "the diabolical machinations of sinister figures

engaged in un-American activities." Once Communists were identified, he explained, the public would isolate them and end their influence. Hoover's aim was to expose not just Communists but also "Communist sympathizers" and "fellow travelers." Under Hoover's leadership, the FBI sent agents to infiltrate groups suspected of subversion and wiretapped thousands of telephones.

Alger Hiss In 1948 **Whittaker Chambers,** a *Time* magazine editor and former Communist Party member, testified to HUAC that several government officials were also former Communists or spies.

The most prominent government official named by Chambers was **Alger Hiss,** a lawyer and diplomat who had served in Roosevelt's administration, attended the Yalta conference, and taken part in organizing the United Nations. After Hiss sued him for libel, Chambers testified before a grand jury that in 1937 and 1938 Hiss gave him secret documents from the State Department. Hiss denied being either a spy or a member of the Communist Party, and he also denied ever having known Chambers.

The committee was ready to drop the investigation until Representative Richard Nixon of California convinced his colleagues to continue the hearings to determine whether Hiss or Chambers had lied. As the committee continued to question Hiss, he admitted that he had indeed met Chambers in the 1930s. When Chambers continued to claim that Hiss was a Communist, Hiss sued him, claiming that his accusations were unfounded and malicious.

To defend himself, Chambers produced copies of secret documents along with microfilm that he had hidden in a hollow pumpkin on his farm. These "pumpkin papers," Chambers claimed, proved that

Picturing **History**

Convicted of Conspiracy Ethel and Julius Rosenberg were convicted of transmitting atomic secrets to Soviet Russia. What sentence did they receive?

2 TEACH

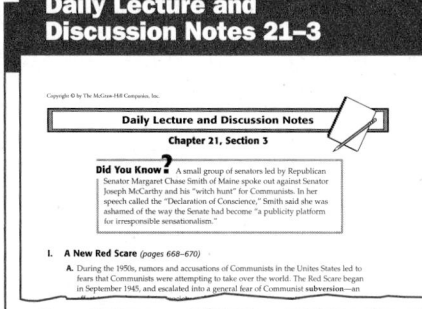

Daily Lecture and Discussion Notes 21–3

Copyright © by The McGraw-Hill Companies, Inc.

Daily Lecture and Discussion Notes

Chapter 21, Section 3

Did You Know? A small group of senators led by Republican Senator Margaret Chase Smith of Maine spoke out against Senator Joseph McCarthy and his "witch hunt" for Communists. In her speech called the "Declaration of Conscience," Smith said she was ashamed of the way the Senate had become "a publicity platform for irresponsible sensationalism."

I.   A New Red Scare *(pages 668–670)*

   A. During the 1950s, rumors and accusations of Communists in the Unites States led to fears that Communists were attempting to take over the world. The Red Scare began in September 1945, and escalated into a general fear of Communist **subversion**—an

Organizing Information Have students create a chart of the major players in the new Red Scare. Instruct students to include the names of the persons involved, a description of their involvement, and an explanation of the outcome of their involvement. **L1** ELL

📁 Use the rubric for creating a map, display, or chart on pages 65–66 in the *Performance Assessment Activities and Rubrics.*

Picturing **History**

Answer: condemned to death for espionage
Ask: Do you think the Soviet Union could have produced an atomic bomb without help? Why or why not? *(Most students will likely note that it probably would have taken the Soviet Union longer without help.)*

Reading Strategy **READING THE TEXT**

Writing Free Writes To better understand the Cold War fears, have students take the role of a person during that time and write a journal entry. They should take one of the following roles: a history teacher finding out that the FBI is investigating her; a blacklisted actor having just returned from an audition; an office worker who has discussed the Hiss or Rosenberg case with coworkers; or someone whose family is discussing building a fallout shelter. **L1**

📁 Refer to *Inclusion for the High School Social Studies Classroom Strategies and Activities* in the TCR.

L1/ELL
Guided Reading Activity 21–3

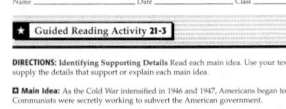

Name _____ Date _____ Class _____

★ **Guided Reading Activity 21-3**

DIRECTIONS: Identifying Supporting Details Read each main idea. Use your textbook to supply the details that support or explain each main idea.

☐ **Main Idea:** As the Cold War intensified in 1946 and 1947, Americans began to fear that Communists were secretly working to subvert the American government.

1. **Detail:** _____ is the effort to secretly weaken a society and overthrow its government.

2. **Detail:** FBI Director _____ urged the _____ formed in 1938 to investigate Communist and fascist activities in the United States, to hold public hearings on Communist subversion.

3. **Detail:** In 1948 _____ admitted he had been a Communist courier between 1934 and 1937, and he claimed that several government officials had been Communists or _____ at that time.

✓ Reading Check

Answer: to check for Communists who might have infiltrated the government of the United States

---

Writing an Article Have students write an article for a history journal about the impact of accusations of disloyalty. For example, anyone accused of disloyalty had a very difficult time finding a job. Encourage students to use library and Internet resources. **L2**

📁 Use the rubric for creating a magazine/newspaper/Web site article or help-wanted ad on pages 75–76 in the *Performance Assessment Activities and Rubrics.*

FYI

Many people, including Albert Einstein and Pope Pius XII, urged clemency for the Rosenbergs. Files released after the fall of the Soviet Union seem to indicate that the Rosenbergs were guilty. However, information based on a 1996 interview with David Greenglass, Ethel Rosenberg's brother, puts Ethel's guilt in doubt.

---

he was telling the truth. A jury agreed and convicted Hiss of perjury, or lying under oath.

The Rosenbergs Another sensational spy case centered around accusations that American Communists had sold the secrets of the atomic bomb. Many people did not believe that the Soviet Union could have produced an atomic bomb in 1949 without help. This belief intensified the hunt for spies.

In 1950 the hunt led to Klaus Fuchs, a British scientist who admitted sending information to the Soviet Union. His testimony led the FBI to arrest **Julius and Ethel Rosenberg,** a New York couple who were members of the Communist Party. The government charged them with heading a Soviet spy ring.

The Rosenbergs denied the charges but were condemned to death for espionage. Many people believed that they were not leaders or spies, but victims caught up in the wave of anti-Communist frenzy. Appeals, public expressions of support, and pleas for clemency failed, however, and the couple was executed in June 1953.

Project Venona The American public hotly debated the guilt or innocence of individuals like the Rosenbergs who were accused as spies. There was, however, solid evidence of Soviet espionage, although very few Americans knew it at the time. In 1946 American cryptographers working for a project code-named "Venona" cracked the Soviet spy code of the time, enabling them to read approximately 3,000 messages between Moscow and the United States collected during the Cold War. The messages confirmed extensive Soviet spying and sent federal investigators on a massive hunt. To keep the Soviets from learning how thoroughly the United States had penetrated their codes, authorities chose not to make the intercepted messages public. Not until 1995 did the government reveal **Project Venona's** existence. The Venona documents provided strong evidence that the Rosenbergs were guilty.

The Red Scare Spreads Following the federal government's example, many state and local governments, universities, businesses, unions, and churches began their own efforts to find Communists. The University of California required its 11,000 faculty members to take loyalty oaths and fired 157 who refused to do so. Many Catholic groups became strongly anticommunist and urged their members to identify Communists within the church.

The Taft-Hartley Act required union leaders to take oaths that they were not Communists, but many union leaders did not object. Instead they launched their own efforts to purge Communists from their organizations. The president of the CIO called Communist sympathizers "skulking cowards" and "apostles of hate." The CIO eventually expelled 11 unions that refused to remove Communist leaders from their organization.

✓ **Reading Check** **Explaining** What was the purpose of the loyalty review boards and HUAC?

Hollywood on Trial

One of HUAC's first hearings focused on the film industry as a powerful cultural force that Communists might use and manipulate. Its interviews routinely began, "Are you now, or have you ever been, a member of the Communist Party?" As fear of Communists in Hollywood spread, producers then drew up a blacklist and agreed not to hire anyone in the film industry who was believed to be a Communist or who refused to cooperate with the committee. The blacklist created an atmosphere of distrust and fear. People could be blacklisted for making chance remarks, criticizing HUAC, or knowing a suspected Communist.

Ronald Reagan, head of the Screen Actors Guild at the time, testified that there were Communists in Hollywood.

Ten screenwriters, known as the "Hollywood Ten" (shown here with their lawyers), used their Fifth Amendment right to protect themselves from self-incrimination and refused to testify before HUAC.

DIFFERENTIATED INSTRUCTION

Reading Support To help demonstrate the impact of McCarthyism, invite two volunteers to portray a HUAC member and someone called to testify before the committee. Have the HUAC member question the witness for several minutes about Communist influence in his or her workplace and among his or her friends and family. Afterward, ask participants and listeners to share their reactions. **L2**

📁 Refer to *Inclusion for the High School Social Studies Classroom Strategies and Activities* in the TCR.

"A Conspiracy So Immense"

In 1949 the Red Scare intensified even further. That year, the Soviet Union successfully tested an atomic bomb, and China fell to communism. To many Americans these events seemed to prove that the United States was losing the Cold War. Deeply concerned, they wanted an explanation as to why their government was failing. As a result, many continued to believe that Communists had infiltrated the government and remained undetected.

In February 1950, soon after Alger Hiss's perjury conviction, a little-known Wisconsin senator gave a political speech to a Republican women's group in West Virginia. Halfway through his speech, Senator **Joseph R. McCarthy** made a surprising statement:

> 66While I cannot take the time to name all the men in the State Department who have been named as members of the Communist Party and members of a spy ring, I have here in my hand a list of 205 that were known to the Secretary of State as being members of the Communist Party and who nevertheless are still working and shaping the policy of the State Department.99
>
> —quoted in *The Fifties*

By the next day, the Associated Press had picked up the statement and sent it to papers all over the country. When McCarthy arrived at the Denver airport, reporters crowded around him and asked to see his list of Communists in the state department. McCarthy replied that he would be happy to show them the list, but unfortunately, it was packed in his bag on the plane. In fact, the list never appeared. McCarthy, however, continued to make charges and draw attention.

McCarthy's Charges Born in 1908 near Appleton, Wisconsin, Joseph R. McCarthy studied law and served in World War II before his first run for the Senate. McCarthy's 1946 political campaign sounded the keynote of his career. Without making any specific charges or offering any proof, McCarthy accused his opponent, Robert M. La Follette, Jr., of being "communistically inclined." Fear of communism, plus McCarthy's intense speeches, won him the election.

After becoming a senator, McCarthy continued to proclaim that Communists were a danger both at home and abroad. To some of his audiences, he distributed a booklet called "The Party of Betrayal," which accused Democratic Party leaders of corruption and of protecting Communists. Secretary of State Dean Acheson was a frequent target. According to McCarthy, Acheson was incompetent and a tool of Stalin. He wildly accused George C. Marshall, the former army chief of staff and secretary of state, of disloyalty as a member of "a conspiracy so immense as to dwarf any previous such ventures in the history of man."

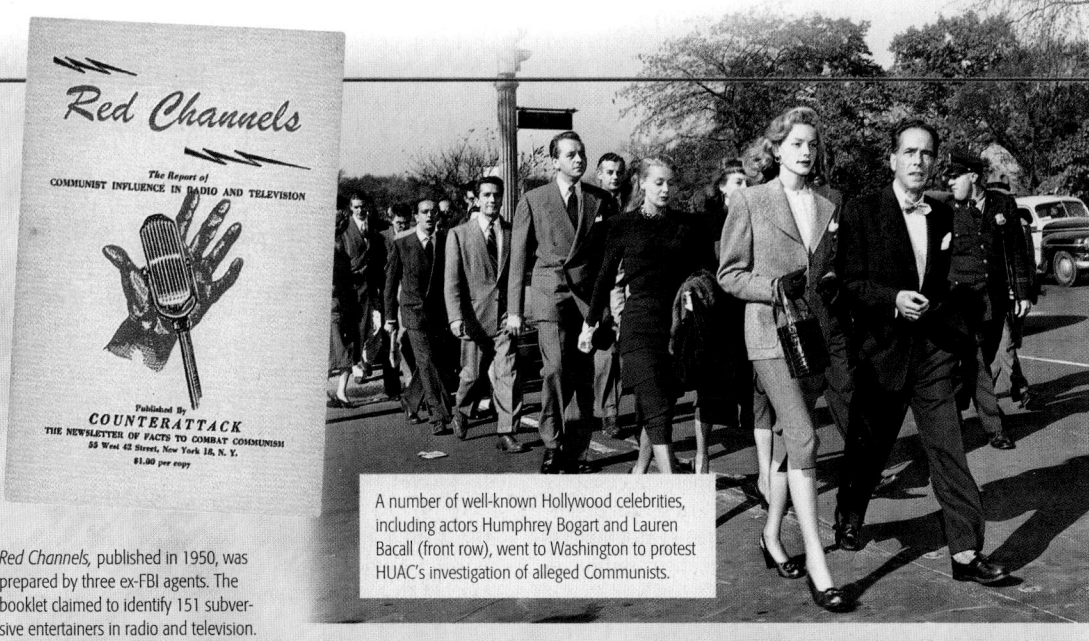

Red Channels, published in 1950, was prepared by three ex-FBI agents. The booklet claimed to identify 151 subversive entertainers in radio and television.

A number of well-known Hollywood celebrities, including actors Humphrey Bogart and Lauren Bacall (front row), went to Washington to protest HUAC's investigation of alleged Communists.

CHAPTER 21 The Cold War Begins **671**

Drawing a Political Cartoon
Have students draw a political cartoon on the effect Senator Joseph McCarthy had on the American people. The cartoon should express a clear opinion about McCarthy's tactics. **L2**

 Use the rubric for creating a political cartoon, pamphlet, or handbill on pages 77–78 in the *Performance Assessment Activities and Rubrics.*

 CURRICULUM CONNECTION

Literature In his 1953 play, *The Crucible,* playwright Arthur Miller wrote about the witch trials in Salem, Massachusetts, in the 1600s. Despite the setting, Miller made it clear that the play was referring to the McCarthy era.

FYI

Of the film industry people investigated by HUAC, ten went to prison. This group, often referred to as "The Hollywood Ten," consisted of Alvah Bessie, Herbert J. Biberman, Lester Cole, Edward Dmytryk, Ring Lardner, Jr., John Howard Lawson, Albert Maltz, Samuel Ornitz, Adrian Scott, and Dalton Trumbo.

INTERDISCIPLINARY CONNECTIONS ACTIVITY

Psychology Have students use library and Internet resources to learn how mass hysteria contributed to the hunt for Communists in the United States in the 1950s. Ask students to write a report that answers the following questions: What fears did people have that made them so worried about Communist infiltration? How did media and government actions fuel these fears? **L2**

Answer: Television drew national attention to the hearings. When people saw McCarthy's bullying tactics, the support for his accusations waned. **Ask:** Who finally stood up to McCarthy? *(an army lawyer named Joseph Welch)*

Creating Relative Chronology

Have students chronicle the major events of the McCarthy era by creating a chart listing significant events in the order they occurred. Encourage students to use library and Internet resources to learn more about the events of the McCarthy era. **L2**

📁 Use the rubric for creating a map, display, or chart on pages 65–66 in the *Performance Assessment Activities and Rubrics.*

FYI

Many Americans were afraid to challenge McCarthy. Even Dwight D. Eisenhower, running for president in 1952, did not speak out against him, though Eisenhower disliked McCarthy's tactics. Once he was elected president, he worked with congressional leaders to undermine McCarthy's authority.

📁 Use *Interpreting Political Cartoons,* Cartoon 26.

Picturing History

McCarthy Goes Too Far Army lawyer Joseph Welch listens to Senator McCarthy during the televised Army-McCarthy hearings. How did televising the hearings affect McCarthyism?

McCarthy was not alone in making such charges. In the prevailing mood of anxiety about communism, many Americans were ready to believe them.

The McCarran Internal Security Act

In 1950, with the Korean War underway and McCarthy and others arousing fears of Communist spies, Congress passed the Internal Security Act, usually called the **McCarran Act.** Declaring that "world Communism has as its sole purpose the establishment of a totalitarian dictatorship in America," Senator Pat McCarran of Nevada offered a way to fight "treachery, infiltration, sabotage, and terrorism." The act made it illegal to "combine, conspire, or agree with any other person to perform any act which would substantially contribute to . . . the establishment of a totalitarian government." The law required all Communist Party and "Communist-front" organizations to register with the United States attorney general and publish their records. The act also created other restrictions for Communists. For example, they could not get passports to travel abroad.

The McCarran Act did not stop there. In case of a national emergency, it allowed the arrest and detention of Communists and Communist sympathizers. Unwilling to punish people for their opinions, Truman vetoed the bill, but Congress easily passed it

over his veto in 1950. Later Supreme Court cases, however, ensured that the McCarran Act would never be very effective.

McCarthy's Tactics

After the 1952 election gave the Republicans control of Congress, McCarthy became chairman of the Senate subcommittee on investigations. Using the power of his committee to force government officials to testify about alleged Communist influences, McCarthy turned the investigation into a witch hunt—a search for disloyalty based on flimsy evidence and irrational fears. His tactic of damaging reputations with vague and unfounded charges became known as **McCarthyism.**

McCarthy's theatrics and sensational accusations drew the attention of the press, which put him in the headlines and quoted him widely. When he questioned witnesses, McCarthy would badger them and then refuse to accept their answers. His tactics left a cloud of suspicion that McCarthy and others interpreted as guilt. Furthermore, people were afraid to challenge him for fear of becoming targets themselves.

McCarthy's Downfall

In 1954 McCarthy began to look for Soviet spies in the United States Army. Alerted to his intentions, the army conducted its

CRITICAL THINKING ACTIVITY

Assessing Outcomes The McCarthy era officially ended with McCarthy's death in 1957. In the end few spies were purged from the United States government. Yet for many people, the impact of McCarthy was felt for a lifetime. During the 1950s, many workers in a variety of industries lost their jobs because they were accused of having Communist sympathies. Although some of those accused probably were Communists, many others were not. **Ask:** Why do you think that fellow workers might have been afraid to stand up for their friends? *(for fear of being attacked themselves)* **L2**

own internal investigation and found no spies or any suspicion of espionage. Furious at the denial, McCarthy took his investigation onto television. He questioned and challenged officers in a harsh voice, harassing them about trivial details and accusing them of misconduct.

During weeks of televised **Army-McCarthy hearings** in the spring of 1954, millions of Americans watched McCarthy bully witnesses. His popular support started to fade. Finally, to strike back at the army lawyer, Joseph Welch, McCarthy brought up the past of a young lawyer in Welch's firm who had been a member of a Communist-front organization during his law school years. Welch, who was fully aware of the young man's past, now exploded at McCarthy for possibly ruining the young man's career: "Until this moment, I think I never really gauged your cruelty or your recklessness. . . . You have done enough. Have you no sense of decency, sir, at long last? Have you left no sense of decency?"

Spectators cheered. Welch had said aloud what many Americans had been thinking. One senator on the committee, Stuart Symington of Missouri, was also repelled: "The American people have had a look at you for six weeks. You are not fooling anyone." McCarthy had lost the power to arouse fear. Newspaper headlines repeated, "Have you no sense of decency?"

Later that year, the Senate passed a vote of censure, or formal disapproval, against McCarthy—one of the most serious criticisms it can level against a member. His influence gone, McCarthy faded from public view. Although he remained in the Senate, he had little influence. He died in 1957, a broken and embittered man.

✓ **Reading Check** **Evaluating** What were the effects of McCarthyism?

Life During the Early Cold War

The Red Scare and the spread of nuclear weapons had a profound impact on life in the 1950s. Fear of communism and of nuclear war dominated life for ordinary Americans as well as for government leaders throughout the era.

Facing the Bomb Already upset by the first Soviet atomic test in 1949, Americans were shocked when the USSR again successfully tested the much more powerful hydrogen bomb, or H-bomb, in 1953. This was less than a year after the United States had tested its own H-bomb.

Americans prepared for a surprise Soviet attack. Schools set aside special areas as bomb shelters. In bomb drills, students learned to duck under their

Picturing **History**

Signs of the Times During the Cold War, the media often gave survival tips for the nuclear holocaust many saw just around the corner. At right, a California resident works on his fallout shelter. How did such fears affect American politics?

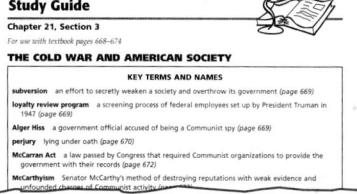

EXTENDING THE CONTENT

Nuclear Powers In 1945 the United States exploded the first atomic bomb in New Mexico. The Soviet Union tested its first atomic bomb in 1949. China, France, Great Britain, India, and Pakistan have also exploded nuclear weapons. In addition to the countries that have tested nuclear weapons, there are several countries believed to possess nuclear capabilities. **L2**

L2

Section Quiz 21-3

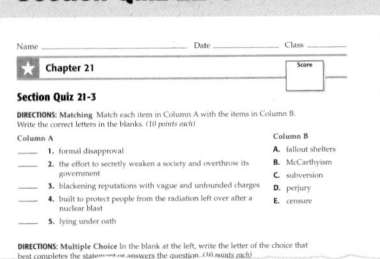

Fact | Fiction | Folklore

The Cold War inspired the marketing of Nuclear Attack Survival Kit Water, which was bottled water claiming to be "impervious to nuclear fallout."

✓ Reading Check

Answer: Americans prepared for a surprise Soviet attack, worried about a nuclear war, and watched films and read books about Communist infiltration of the United States.

Reteach

Have students describe the new Red Scare.

Enrich

Have interested students make a poster using headlines and sayings from the McCarthy era.

HISTORY Online

Study Central™ provides summaries, interactive games, and online graphic organizers to help students review section content.

4 CLOSE

Have students discuss how American society reflected fears of the nuclear age.

674

Fact | Fiction | Folklore

Cold War Words The development of nuclear weapons and artificial satellites created not only new anxieties but also new words and expressions.

"*Sputnik,*" the name of the Soviet satellite, started its own language trend, as words gained a *-nik* ending for a foreign-sounding effect. One new word, *beatnik,* described a young person influenced by the style of Beat writers such as Jack Kerouac and Allen Ginsberg. Another word, *peacenik,* was used to describe a peace activist.

The atomic bomb test on Bikini Atoll gave the Nuclear Age two new words: *fallout,* the term for the harmful radiation left over after an atomic blast, and *bikini,* a skimpy swimsuit that French designers promised would produce an "explosion" on the beach.

desks, turn away from the windows, and cover their heads with their hands. These "duck-and-cover" actions were supposed to protect them from a nuclear bomb blast.

"Duck-and-cover" might have made people feel safe, but it would not have protected them from deadly nuclear radiation. According to experts, for every person killed outright by a nuclear blast, four more would die later from fallout, the radiation left over after a blast. To protect themselves, some families built backyard fallout shelters and stocked them with canned food.

Popular Culture in the Cold War Worries about nuclear war and Communist infiltration filled people's imaginations. Cold War nightmares soon appeared in films and popular fiction.

Matt Cvetic was an FBI undercover informant who secretly infiltrated the Communist Party in Pittsburgh. His story captivated magazine readers in the *Saturday Evening Post* in 1950 and came to the screen the next year as *I Was a Communist for the FBI.* Another suspense film, *Walk East on Beacon* (1951), features the FBI's activities in an espionage case. In 1953 television took up the theme with a series about an undercover FBI counterspy who was also a Communist Party official. Each week, *I Led Three Lives* kept television viewers on edge.

In 1954 author Philip Wylie published *Tomorrow!* This novel describes the horrific effects of nuclear war on an unprepared American city. As an adviser on civil defense, Wylie had failed to convince the federal government to play a strong role in building bomb shelters. Frustrated, he wrote this novel to educate the public about the horrors of atomic war.

At the same time these fears were haunting Americans, the country was enjoying postwar prosperity and optimism. That spirit, combined with McCarthyism, witch hunts, fears of Communist infiltration, and the threat of atomic attack, made the early 1950s a time of contrasts. As the 1952 election approached, Americans were looking for someone or something that would make them feel secure.

✓ Reading Check **Describing** How did the Cold War affect life in the 1950s?

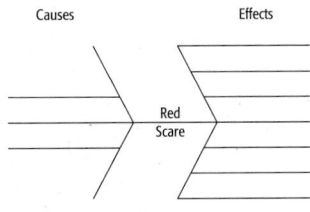

HISTORY Online **Study Central™** To review this section, go to tarvol2.glencoe.com and click on **Study Central™**.

SECTION 3 ASSESSMENT

Checking for Understanding

1. **Define:** subversion, perjury, censure, fallout, fallout shelter.
2. **Identify:** loyalty review program, Alger Hiss, McCarran Act, McCarthyism.
3. **Explain** the goals of Project Venona.
4. **Review Facts** What did the McCarran Act propose to do?

Reviewing Themes

5. **Civic Rights and Responsibilities** How did McCarthyism and the Red Scare change American society and government?

Critical Thinking

6. **Interpreting** Why did McCarthy initially receive a lot of support for his efforts to expose Communists?
7. **Organizing** Use a graphic organizer to list the causes and effects of the new Red Scare.

Causes   Effects

Red Scare

Analyzing Visuals

8. **Analyzing Photographs** Study the photograph on page 672 of the Army-McCarthy hearings. From their postures, how would you describe the attitude of army lawyer Joseph Welch toward Senator Joseph McCarthy? Do you think Welch respects McCarthy's presentation?

Writing About History

9. **Persuasive Writing** Imagine you are a newspaper editor during the McCarthy hearings. Write an editorial supporting or condemning Senator McCarthy. Defend your position.

674 CHAPTER 21 The Cold War Begins

SECTION 3 ASSESSMENT ANSWERS

1. Terms are in blue.
2. loyalty review program *(p. 669),* Alger Hiss *(p. 669),* McCarran Act *(p. 672),* McCarthyism *(p. 672)*
3. to crack the Soviet spy code, and confirm Soviet spying
4. to make it illegal to associate with or be a Communist

5. While people were enjoying postwar prosperity and optimism, they feared communism and an atomic attack.
6. People feared communism.
7. Causes: Gouzenko case, Alger Hiss trial, Rosenbergs, Russia's successful test of an atomic bomb; Effects: Loyalty Review Program, HUAC,

McCarran Act, McCarthyism, fallout shelters, etc.
8. Students might suggest disgust or annoyance.
9. Students' editorials will vary. Editorials should address the tactics McCarthy used and express a clear point of view.

Guide to Reading

Main Idea
As president, Eisenhower developed plans to reduce world tensions while containing and competing with communism.

Key Terms and Names
massive retaliation, *Sputnik,* brinkmanship, covert, Central Intelligence Agency, developing nation, military-industrial complex

Reading Strategy
Organizing As you read about Eisenhower's presidency, complete a graphic organizer similar to the one below by filling in aspects of Eisenhower's "New Look".

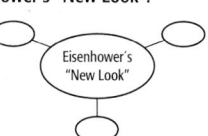
Eisenhower's "New Look"

Reading Objectives
• **Evaluate** Eisenhower's military policy known as the "New Look."
• **Debate** the effectiveness of Eisenhower's foreign policy.

Section Theme
Science and Technology Nuclear technology enabled Eisenhower to change American military policy, while new missile technology marked the beginning of the space age.

Preview of Events

◆1952	◆1955	◆1958	◆1961

July 1953
Armistice in Korean War

October 1956
Hungarian revolution

October 1956
Suez Canal crisis

October 4, 1957
Soviet Union launches *Sputnik*

May 1960
U-2 incident

⭐ An American Story ⭐

On May 1, 1960, CIA pilot Francis Gary Powers sat in the cockpit of his U-2 spy plane, flying at more than 60,000 feet over Afghanistan. His mission was to fly over suspected Soviet missile bases and photograph them.

As Powers passed over the forbidden border into the Soviet Union, he felt a familiar thrill. "There was no abrupt change in topography," he remembered, "yet the moment you crossed the border, you sensed the difference. . . . Knowing there were people who would shoot you down if they could created a strange tension. . . . I wondered how the Russians felt, knowing I was up here, unable to do anything about it. . . . I could imagine their frustration and rage."

Suddenly, Powers heard a dull thump. A surface-to-air missile exploded nearby in a flash of orange. The plane's wings snapped off, leaving the spinning aircraft plummeting down towards the earth. Powers screamed, "I've had it now!"

The downing of Powers's plane set off one of the major confrontations of the Cold War during the presidency of Dwight D. Eisenhower.

–adapted from *May-Day: The U-2 Affair*

Francis Gary Powers

Eisenhower's "New Look"

By the end of 1952, many Americans were ready for a change in leadership. The Cold War had much to do with that attitude. Many Americans believed that Truman's foreign policy was not working. The Soviet Union had acquired the atomic bomb and consolidated its hold on Eastern Europe. China had fallen to communism, and American troops had been sent across the Pacific to fight in the Korean War.

CHAPTER 21 The Cold War Begins **675**

1 FOCUS

Section Overview
This section focuses on Eisenhower's plans to reduce world tensions and contain and compete with communism.

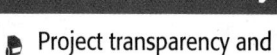

BELLRINGER
Skillbuilder Activity

Project transparency and have students answer the question.

Daily Focus Skills Transparency 21–4

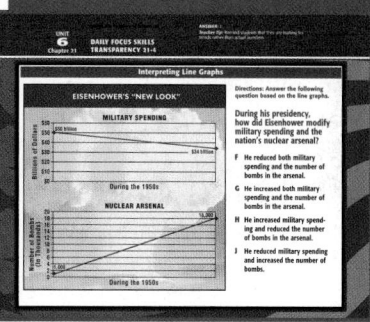

Reading Preview

Answers to Graphic: brinkmanship, covert action, massive retaliation

Preteaching Vocabulary
Have students select two of the Key Terms and Names and use them in a sentence.

SECTION RESOURCES

📖 Reproducible Masters
• Reproducible Lesson Plan 21–4
• Daily Lecture and Discussion Notes 21–4
• Guided Reading Activity 21–4
• Section Quiz 21–4
• Reading Essentials and Study Guide 21–4
• Performance Assessment Activities and Rubrics

📄 Transparencies
• Daily Focus Skills Transparency 21–4

Multimedia
🔘 Interactive Tutor Self-Assessment CD-ROM
🔘 ExamView® Pro Testmaker CD-ROM
🔘 Presentation Plus! CD-ROM
🔘 TeacherWorks™ CD-ROM
🔊 Audio Program

2 TEACH

Daily Lecture and Discussion Notes 21–4

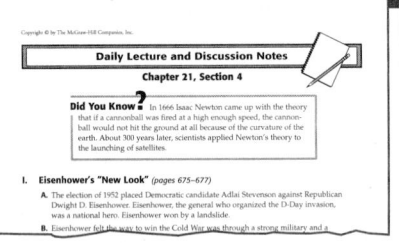

Daily Lecture and Discussion Notes
Chapter 21, Section 4

Did You Know? In 1666 Isaac Newton came up with the theory that if a cannonball was fired at a high enough speed, the cannonball would not hit the ground at all because of the curvature of the earth. About 300 years later, scientists applied Newton's theory to the launching of satellites.

I. **Eisenhower's "New Look"** *(pages 675–677)*

  A. The election of 1952 placed Democratic candidate Adlai Stevenson against Republican Dwight D. Eisenhower. Eisenhower, the general who organized the D-Day invasion, was a national hero. Eisenhower won by a landslide.

  B. Eisenhower felt the way to win the Cold War was through a strong military and a

Creating an Outline Have students create an outline illustrating Eisenhower's approach to nuclear war, massive retaliation, a smaller army, and a strong economy. **L1** **ELL**

TECHNOLOGY & History

Background: The Soviets also had a highly secret program to create a hydrogen bomb. A famous Orthodox monastery housed the design team, which successfully tested the Soviet hydrogen bomb on August 12, 1953.

Answer: The primary device sets off a smaller atomic explosion, creating x-ray radiation pressure. The secondary device creates the fusion process when pressure from the first device builds inside the bomb casing.

Ask: Why did Eisenhower favor nuclear weapons? *(He believed the cost to fight a conventional war was too great; having nuclear weapons would create sufficient threat to deter war and be more cost efficient.)*

Tired of the criticism and uncertain he could win, Truman decided not to run again. The Democrats nominated Adlai Stevenson, governor of Illinois. The Republicans chose Dwight D. Eisenhower, the general who had organized the D-Day invasion.

Despite Stevenson's charming personality and skilled speech making, he had no chance against a national hero who had helped win World War II. Americans were looking for someone they could trust to lead the nation in its Cold War struggle against communism. Eisenhower won in a landslide.

"More Bang for the Buck" The Cold War shaped Eisenhower's thinking from the moment he took office. Eisenhower was convinced that the key to victory in the Cold War was not simply military might but also a strong economy. The United States had to show the world that free enterprise could produce a better and more prosperous society than communism. At the same time, economic prosperity would prevent Communists from gaining support in the United States and protect society from subversion.

As a professional soldier, Eisenhower knew the costs associated with large-scale conventional war. Preparing for that kind of warfare, he believed, would cost far too much money. "We cannot defend the nation in a way which will exhaust our economy," Eisenhower declared. A "New Look" in defense policy was needed. Instead of maintaining a large and expensive army, the nation "must be prepared to use atomic weapons in all forms." Nuclear weapons, he said, gave "more bang for the buck."

Massive Retaliation The Korean War had convinced Eisenhower that the United States could not contain communism by fighting a series of small wars. Such wars were unpopular and too expensive. Instead, they had to be prevented from happening in the first place. The best way to do that seemed to be to threaten to use nuclear weapons if a Communist state tried to seize territory by force. This policy came to be called massive retaliation.

The new policy enabled Eisenhower to cut military spending from $50 billion to $34 billion. He did this by cutting back the army, which required a lot of money to maintain. At the same time, he increased America's nuclear arsenal from about 1,000 bombs in 1953 to about 18,000 bombs in 1961.

The *Sputnik* Crisis The New Look's emphasis on nuclear weapons required new technology to deliver them. In 1955 the air force unveiled the huge B-52

TECHNOLOGY & History

The Hydrogen Bomb

The atomic bomb dropped on Hiroshima in 1945 had an explosive force of 20,000 tons of TNT. As devastating as that bomb was, the hydrogen bomb was exponentially more powerful. Designed by Edward Teller and Stanislaw Ulam, the hydrogen test bomb, nicknamed "Mike," was first detonated on November 1, 1952. Its explosive force was equal to 10 million tons of TNT. *How did the two explosive devices combine to create an explosion?*

1 The **plutonium core** provides the radiation from plutonium essential for a fusion reaction.

uranium shield

Plutonium 239

High explosive charges

2 The **primary device** sets off a smaller atomic explosion that creates x-ray radiation pressure.

3 In the **secondary device**, the fusion process begins when pressure builds inside the bomb casing from the release of radiation.

Reading Strategy | READING THE TEXT

Creating Posters After students have read the section, organize the class into groups of three or four. Have each group plan and prepare a poster explaining Eisenhower's approach to one of the following events: the Korean War, the *Sputnik* crisis, the Taiwan crisis, the Suez crisis, or the covert battle against communism. Have the groups display their posters and then discuss the ways in which Eisenhower changed military priorities. **L1**

📁 Refer to *Inclusion for the High School Social Studies Classroom Strategies and Activities* in the TCR.

bomber, which was designed to fly across continents and drop nuclear bombs anywhere in the world. Because bombers could be shot down, Eisenhower also began development of intercontinental ballistic missiles (ICBMs) that could deliver bombs anywhere in the world. He also began a program to build submarines capable of launching nuclear missiles.

As the United States began to develop long-range nuclear missiles, Americans were stunned to discover the Soviet Union had already developed their own. On October 4, 1957, the Soviets launched *Sputnik,* the first artificial satellite to orbit the earth. This technological triumph alarmed Americans, who took it as a sign that the United States was falling behind the Soviet Union in missile technology.

Eisenhower insisted he was not worried just because the Soviets "put one small ball into the air." Members of Congress, on the other hand, feared the nation was falling behind in scientific research. The following year, Congress created the **National Aeronautics and Space Administration** (NASA) to coordinate research in rocket science and space exploration. It also passed the **National Defense Education Act** (NDEA), which provided funds for education and training in science, math, and foreign languages.

✓ **Reading Check** **Summarizing** How did Eisenhower alter the nature of defense spending?

Brinkmanship In Action

President Eisenhower's apparent willingness to threaten nuclear war to maintain the peace worried some people. Secretary of State **John Foster Dulles,** however, the dominant figure in the nation's foreign policy in the 1950s, strongly defended the policy:

> ❝You have to take chances for peace, just as you must take chances in war. Some say that we were brought to the verge of war. Of course we were brought to the verge of war. The ability to get to the verge without getting into the war is the necessary art. . . . If you try to run away from it, if you are scared to go to the brink, you are lost. We've had to look it square in the face. . . . We walked to the brink and we looked it in the face. We took strong action.❞
>
> —quoted in *Rise to Globalism*

Critics called this brinkmanship—the willingness to go to the brink of war to force the other side to back down—and argued that it was too dangerous.

"So Russia Launched a Satellite, but Has It Made Cars With Fins Yet?"

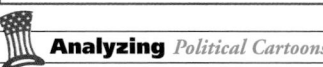

Analyzing *Political Cartoons*

Cold War Worries The speaker here is comparing American prosperity with the Soviets' launching of *Sputnik.* **What is the cartoonist's intent?**

Several times, however, President Eisenhower felt compelled to threaten nuclear war during a crisis.

The Korean War Ends During his campaign for the presidency, Eisenhower had said, "I shall go to Korea," promising to end the costly and increasingly unpopular war. On December 4, 1952, just weeks after his election, he kept his promise. Bundled against the freezing Korean winter, the president-elect talked with frontline commanders and their troops.

Eisenhower became convinced that the ongoing battle was costing too many lives and bringing too few victories. "Small attacks on small hills," the former general declared, "[will] not end this war." The president then quietly let the Chinese know that the United States might continue the Korean War "under circumstances of our own choosing"—a hint at nuclear attack.

The threat to go to the brink of nuclear war seemed to work. In July 1953, negotiators signed an armistice. The battle line between the two sides, which was very near the prewar boundary, became the border between North Korea and South Korea. A "demilitarized zone" (DMZ) separated them. There was no victory, but the war had at least stopped the spread of communism in Korea—the goal of containment. American troops are still based in Korea, helping South Korea defend its border.

L1/ELL

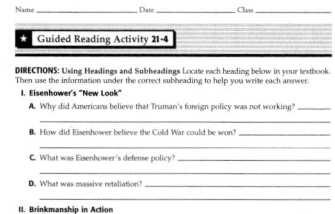

Guided Reading Activity 21–4

Name _____ Date _____ Class _____

★ Guided Reading Activity 21-4

DIRECTIONS: Using Headings and Subheadings Locate each heading below in your textbook. Then use the information under the correct subheading to help you write each answer.

I. Eisenhower's "New Look"

   A. Why did Americans believe that Truman's foreign policy was not working? _____

   B. How did Eisenhower believe the Cold War could be won? _____

   C. What was Eisenhower's defense policy? _____

   D. What was massive retaliation? _____

II. Brinkmanship in Action

✓ **Reading Check**

Answer: He cut military spending from $50 billion to $34 billion while increasing America's nuclear arsenal.

Analyzing *Political Cartoons*

Answer: The cartoonist is conveying anxiety in an ironic manner—the United States has built fancy consumer goods, but it is behind in space technology.

Ask: Do you think the cartoonist would have supported Eisenhower's defense plans? *(The cartoonist likely would have supported his plans.)*

DIFFERENTIATED INSTRUCTION

Gifted and Talented Have students write and present a verse that either supports or opposes the concept of brinkmanship. Encourage students to examine different styles of poetry before writing their verse. Have volunteers present their verses to the class and have the class identify whether they express support or opposition for brinkmanship. **L3**

📁 Refer to *Inclusion for the High School Social Studies Classroom Strategies and Activities* in the TCR.

677

Creating a Chart Have students create a chart to list the five countries most directly involved in the Suez Crisis and each country's role in the crisis. **L2**

 Use the rubric for creating a map, display, or chart on pages 65–66 in the *Performance Assessment Activities and Rubrics.*

FYI

The Suez Canal, which connects the Mediterranean and Red Seas, opened in 1869. It cut approximately 4,000 miles off voyages between Britain and India.

CURRICULUM CONNECTION

World History Many historians recognize Gamal Abdel Nasser's move to seize control of the Suez Canal as the beginning of a process that would eventually dissolve the British Empire.

 Geography *Skills*

Answers:
1. eight; nine if one views the Soviet Union as European, which some scholars do at least to the Ural Mountains

Geography Skills Practice
Ask: Which major nation on the Adriatic Sea was Communist but not a member of the Warsaw Pact?
(Yugoslavia)

The Taiwan Crisis Shortly after the war ended, a new crisis erupted in Asia. Although the Chinese Communists had taken power in mainland China, the Chinese Nationalists still controlled Taiwan and several small islands along China's coast.

In the fall of 1954, China threatened to seize two of the islands from the Nationalists. Eisenhower saw Taiwan as part of the "anticommunist barrier" in Asia. When China began shelling the islands and announced that Taiwan would soon be liberated, Eisenhower asked Congress to authorize the use of force to defend Taiwan.

Eisenhower then warned the Chinese that any attempt to invade Taiwan would be resisted by American naval forces stationed nearby. He and Dulles hinted that they would use nuclear weapons to stop an invasion. Soon afterward, China backed down.

The Suez Crisis The year after Eisenhower went to the brink of war with China, a serious crisis erupted in the Middle East. Eisenhower's goal in the Middle East was to prevent Arab nations from aligning with the Soviet Union. To build support among Arabs, Dulles offered to help Egypt finance the construction of a dam on the Nile River. The Egyptians eagerly accepted the American offer.

The deal ran into trouble in Congress, however, because Egypt had bought weapons from Communist Czechoslovakia. Dulles was forced to withdraw the offer. A week later, Egyptian troops seized control of the Suez Canal from the Anglo-French company that had controlled it. The Egyptians intended to use the canal's profits to pay for the dam.

The British and French responded quickly to the Suez Crisis. In October 1956, British and French troops invaded Egypt. Eisenhower was furious with Britain and France. He declared they had made a "complete mess and botch of things." The situation became even more tense when the Soviet Union threatened rocket attacks on Britain and France and offered to send troops to help Egypt. Eisenhower immediately put American nuclear forces on alert, noting, "If those

NATIONAL GEOGRAPHIC **NATO and the Warsaw Pact, 1955** *In Motion*

Legend:
- "Iron Curtain"
- Communist nations not in Warsaw Pact
- Warsaw Pact countries
- Non-Communist nations not in NATO
- NATO countries
- ⊛ Capital

500 miles / 500 kilometers
Lambert Azimuthal Equal-Area projection

Geography *Skills*

By the mid-1950s, two powerful military alliances, NATO and the Warsaw Pact, were facing each other in Europe. **Applying Geography Skills** How many European nations had Communist governments in 1955?

INTERDISCIPLINARY CONNECTIONS ACTIVITY

Communication Have students work as a team to prepare a thirty-minute special news report about the 1956 Suez Canal crisis. Organize students into groups of at least five students. Instruct each group to organize itself into a team, including a segment producer, researchers, and writers. After the segments are produced, ask for volunteers to present the special report. Remind students that a news report will include graphics. **L2**

fellows start something, we may have to hit them—and if necessary, with everything in the bucket."

Under strong American pressure, the British and French called off their invasion. The Soviet Union had won a major diplomatic victory, however, by supporting Egypt. Soon afterward, other Arab nations began accepting Soviet aid as well.

✓ **Reading Check** **Identifying** What was brinkmanship?

Fighting Communism Covertly

President Eisenhower relied on brinkmanship on several occasions, but he knew it could not work in all situations. It could prevent war, but it could not, for example, prevent Communists from staging revolutions within countries. To prevent Communist uprisings in other countries, Eisenhower decided to use covert, or hidden, operations conducted by the **Central Intelligence Agency** (CIA).

Containment in Developing Nations Many of the CIA's operations took place in developing nations—nations with primarily agricultural economies. Many of these countries blamed European imperialism and American capitalism for their problems. Their leaders looked to the Soviet Union as a model of how to industrialize their countries. They often threatened to nationalize, or put under government control, foreign businesses operating in their countries.

American officials feared that these leaders might align their nations with the Soviet Union or even stage a Communist revolution. One way to stop developing nations from moving into the Communist camp was to provide them with financial aid, as Eisenhower had tried to do in Egypt. In some cases, however, where the threat of communism seemed stronger, the CIA staged covert operations to overthrow anti-American leaders and replace them with pro-American leaders.

Iran and Guatemala Two examples of covert operations that achieved American objectives took place in Iran and Guatemala. By 1953 Iranian prime minister Mohammed Mossadegh had already nationalized the Anglo-Iranian Oil Company. He seemed ready to make an oil deal with the Soviet Union. In 1953 Mossadegh moved against the pro-American Shah of Iran, who was temporarily forced into exile. Dulles quickly sent agents to organize street riots and arrange a coup that ousted Mossadegh, and the Shah returned to power.

Picturing **History**

Distinguished Brothers John Foster Dulles (right) became secretary of state under Eisenhower; his brother Allen Dulles (center) was director of the CIA in the 1950s. With what policy is John Foster Dulles associated?

The following year, the CIA acted to protect American-owned property in Guatemala. In 1951 Jacobo Arbenz Guzmán won election as president of Guatemala with Communist support. His land reform program took over large estates, including those of the American-owned United Fruit Company. In May 1954, Communist Czechoslovakia delivered arms to Guatemala. The CIA responded by arming the Guatemalan opposition and training them at secret camps in Nicaragua and Honduras. Shortly after these CIA-trained forces invaded Guatemala, Arbenz Guzmán left office.

Uprising in Hungary Covert operations did not always work as Eisenhower hoped. In 1953 Stalin died, and a power struggle began in the Soviet Union. By 1956 **Nikita Khrushchev** had emerged as the leader of the Soviet Union. That year, Khrushchev delivered a secret speech to Soviet leaders. He attacked Stalin's policies and insisted there were

CHAPTER 21   The Cold War Begins   **679**

✓ **Reading Check**

Answer: Brinkmanship is the willingness to go to the brink of war to force the other side to back down.

Picturing **History**

Answer: brinkmanship
Ask: Who coined the term brinkmanship? *(critics of Eisenhower's willingness to threaten nuclear war to get the other side to back down)*

FYI

Many people in Iran resented the Shah's close ties with the West. Their anger at the Shah's attachment to Western ideas and customs helped fuel the 1979 revolt against him. Mohammed Reza Shah Pahlavi died in exile in 1980.

3 ASSESS

Assign Section 4 Assessment as homework or as an in-class activity.

🔵 Have students use the **Interactive Tutor Self-Assessment CD-ROM.**

L1/ELL

Reading Essentials and Study Guide 21–4

Name _____ Date _____ Class _____

Study Guide
Chapter 21, Section 4
For use with textbook pages 675–680
EISENHOWER'S POLICIES

KEY TERMS AND NAMES

massive retaliation the policy of threatening Communist states with nuclear war if the state tried to take territory by force (page 676)

Sputnik developed by the Soviet Union, the first artificial satellite to orbit the earth (page 677)

brinkmanship the willingness to go to the brink of war to force the other side to back down (page 677)

covert hidden (page 679)

Central Intelligence Agency an agency that conducted covert operations (page 679)

developing nation nation with a primarily agricultural economy (page 679)

CRITICAL THINKING ACTIVITY

Evaluating Action The overthrow of the leftist Guatemalan government was made possible by the activities of the Central Intelligence Agency. Ask students the following questions: **Is secret aggression, such as that by the CIA, justifiable? Why or why not? What events in your lifetime have helped shape your opinion? L2**

L2

Section Quiz 21-4

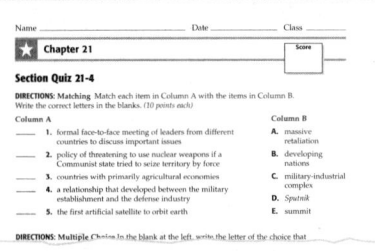

✓ Reading Check

Answer: He used covert actions to secretly help countries fight communism and overthrow anti-American leaders.

✓ Reading Check

Answer: He thought that a military-industrial complex could threaten democracy.

Reteach

Have students rate the changes Eisenhower brought to the White House as positive or negative.

Enrich

Have interested students research the social, cultural, and historical factors that affected the Hungarians' reaction to Communist control. Encourage students to use library and Internet resources.

Study Central™ provides summaries, interactive games, and online graphic organizers to help students review section content.

4 CLOSE

Have students debate the effectiveness of Eisenhower's foreign policy.

---

many ways to build a Communist society. Although the speech was secret, the CIA obtained a copy. With Eisenhower's permission, the CIA arranged for it to be broadcast to Eastern Europe.

Many Eastern Europeans had long been frustrated with Communist rule. Hearing Khrushchev's speech further discredited communism. In June 1956, riots erupted in Eastern Europe. By late October, a full-scale uprising had begun in Hungary. Although Khrushchev was willing to tolerate greater freedom in Eastern Europe, he had never meant to imply that the Soviets would tolerate an end to communism in Eastern Europe. Soon after the uprising began, Soviet tanks rolled into Budapest, the capital of Hungary, and crushed the rebellion.

✓ **Reading Check** **Explaining** Why did Eisenhower use covert operations?

Continuing Tensions

The uprising in Hungary forced Khrushchev to reassert Soviet power and the superiority of communism. Previously, he had supported "peaceful coexistence" with capitalism. Now he accused the "capitalist countries" of starting a "feverish arms race." In 1957, after the launch of Sputnik, Khrushchev boasted, "We will bury capitalism. . . . Your grandchildren will live under communism."

In late 1958 Khrushchev demanded that the United States, Great Britain, and France withdraw their troops from West Berlin. Secretary of State Dulles rejected Khrushchev's demands. If the Soviets threatened Berlin, Dulles announced, NATO would respond, "if need be by military force." Brinkmanship worked again, and Khrushchev backed down.

To try to improve relations, Eisenhower invited Khrushchev to visit the United States in late 1959. The visit went well, and the two leaders agreed to hold a summit in Paris in 1960. A **summit** is a formal face-to-face meeting of leaders from different countries to discuss important issues.

Shortly before the summit was to begin, the Soviet Union shot down the American U-2 spy plane piloted by **Francis Gary Powers.** At first, Eisenhower claimed that the aircraft was a weather plane that had strayed off course. Then Khrushchev dramatically produced the pilot. Eisenhower refused to apologize, saying the flights had protected American security. In response, Khrushchev broke up the summit.

In this climate of heightened tension, President Eisenhower prepared to leave office. In January 1961, he delivered a farewell address to the nation. In the address, he pointed out that a new relationship had developed between the military establishment and the defense industry. He warned Americans to be on guard against the immense influence of this military-industrial complex in a democracy. Although he had avoided war and kept communism contained, Eisenhower admitted to some frustration: "I confess I lay down my official responsibility in this field with a definite sense of disappointment. . . . I wish I could say that a lasting peace is in sight."

✓ **Reading Check** **Evaluating** Why did Eisenhower warn Americans about the military-industrial complex?

Study Central™ To review this section, go to tarvol2.glencoe.com and click on **Study Central™.**

SECTION 4 ASSESSMENT

Checking for Understanding

1. **Define:** massive retaliation, brinkmanship, covert, developing nation, military-industrial complex.
2. **Identify:** *Sputnik,* Central Intelligence Agency.
3. **Reviewing Facts** What was the significance of the Soviet Union's launching of *Sputnik* in 1957?

Reviewing Themes

4. **Science and Technology** How did technology shape Eisenhower's military policy?

Critical Thinking

5. **Interpreting** Do you think Eisenhower's foreign policy was successful? Why or why not?
6. **Organizing** Use a graphic organizer similar to the one below to list Eisenhower's strategies for containing Communism.

```
        Strategies for
        Containing
        Communism
   ┌────┬────┬────┬────┐
   │    │    │    │    │
   └────┴────┴────┴────┘
```

Analyzing Visuals

7. **Analyzing Maps** Study the map on page 678. How many nations belonged to NATO? How many nations belonged to the Warsaw Pact? Which nations did not belong to either NATO or the Warsaw Pact?

Writing About History

8. **Persuasive Writing** Imagine you are a member of Eisenhower's cabinet. Defend or attack brinkmanship as a foreign policy tactic. Be sure to provide specific reasons for your point of view.

SECTION 4 ASSESSMENT ANSWERS

1. Terms are in blue.
2. *Sputnik* (p. 677), Central Intelligence Agency (p. 679)
3. It stunned Americans and led to the creation of NASA and the passage of the NDEA.
4. It allowed him to pursue the policy of brinkmanship since the nuclear arsenal was a real threat. It also allowed covert operations in Iran and Guatemala.
5. Students' answers will vary. Students should cite specific events to support their conclusion.
6. strong economy, nuclear weapons for massive retaliation, brinkmanship, covert operations
7. 12 NATO on map (Iceland also a member, but not shown on map); 8 Warsaw Pact; 7 did not belong to NATO or the Warsaw Pact
8. Students' answers should express a point of view supporting or opposing brinkmanship.

Critical Thinking

SKILLBUILDER

Making Decisions

Why Learn This Skill?

Suppose you have been given the choice of taking an art class or a music class during your free period during school. How will you decide which class to take?

Learning the Skill

When you make a decision, you are making a choice between alternatives. In order to make that choice, you must be informed and aware. There are five key steps you should follow that will help you through the process of making decisions.

- Identify the problem. What are you being asked to choose between?
- Gather information to identify and consider various alternatives that are possible.
- Determine the consequences for each alternative. Identify both positive and negative consequences.
- Evaluate the consequences. Consider both the positive and negative consequences for each alternative.
- Determine which alternative seems to have more positive than negative consequences. Then make your decision.

Practicing the Skill

Decisions throughout history have affected the outcome of events and defined history as we know it today. Identify the alternatives and describe their consequences for each of the following events that occurred after World War II. Each of these events took place as a result of a decision made by a person or a group of people.

❶ Britain and the United States recognize the Soviet-backed government that takes control in Poland.

❷ The United States orchestrates the Berlin airlift to assist residents of West Berlin after Stalin cuts off surface transportation bringing supplies from the West.

President Truman and Dean Acheson

❸ The Marshall Plan for rebuilding war-torn Western Europe is approved.

❹ President Truman relieves General Douglas MacArthur of his command because of insubordination.

Skills Assessment

Complete the Practicing Skills questions on page 683 and the Chapter 21 Skill Reinforcement Activity to assess your mastery of this skill.

Applying the Skill

Making Decisions Use a newspaper or magazine to find a current issue that directly affects your life. Identify the issue, and then review the facts and what you already know about the issue. Identify various alternatives and determine the consequences for each. Use this information to evaluate both positive and negative consequences. Make a sound decision about which alternative would be best for you, and write a paragraph defending your decision.

 Glencoe's **Skillbuilder Interactive Workbook CD-ROM, Level 2,** provides instruction and practice in key social studies skills.

681

Critical Thinking

SKILLBUILDER

TEACH

Making Decisions Have students select one of the leaders discussed in this chapter. Then have students identify a specific decision of that leader and possible alternatives the leader may have had. Have students write two or three paragraphs explaining whether a different decision was defensible.

Additional Practice
L1

Reinforcing Skills Activity 21

Name _____ Date _____ Class _____

★ Reinforcing Skills Activity 21

Making Decisions

◻ **LEARNING THE SKILL**
To make a good decision, you need to analyze the information available and weigh the possible consequences. Decision making involves: (1) identifying the problem; (2) gathering information and considering alternatives; (3) identifying possible positive and negative consequences; (4) evaluating the consequences; and (5) selecting the most favorable alternative.

◻ **PRACTICING THE SKILL**
DIRECTIONS: Read the excerpt below from Truman's speech to Congress, delivered March 12, 1947, which came to be known as the Truman Doctrine. Based on this excerpt and Section 2 of your text, answer the following questions on a separate sheet of paper.

The peoples of a number of countries of the world have recently had totalitarian regimes forced upon them against their will. The Government ...

GLENCOE
TECHNOLOGY

 CD-ROM
Glencoe Skillbuilder Interactive Workbook CD-ROM, Level 2

This interactive CD-ROM reinforces student mastery of essential social studies skills.

ANSWERS TO PRACTICING THE SKILL

❶ Nonrecognition leads to tension and possible war.
❷ No airlift makes Berlin residents suffer and the United States look weak.
❸ No Marshall Plan hurts Europe's economy and its political stability.

❹ Leaving MacArthur in command might lead to war with China and greater American involvement in Asia.

Applying the Skill
Students' reasoning should be clearly evident.

681

CHAPTER 21 ASSESSMENT and ACTIVITIES

CHAPTER
21
ASSESSMENT and ACTIVITIES

GLENCOE TECHNOLOGY

MindJogger Videoquiz
Use the **MindJogger Videoquiz** to review Chapter 21 content.

○ Available in DVD

Reviewing Key Terms
Students' answers will vary. The pages where the words appear in the text are shown in parentheses.

1. **Cold War** *(p. 654)*
2. **iron curtain** *(p. 658)*
3. **containment** *(p. 660)*
4. **limited war** *(p. 665)*
5. **subversion** *(p. 669)*
6. **perjury** *(p. 670)*
7. **censure** *(p. 673)*
8. **fallout** *(p. 674)*
9. **fallout shelter** *(p. 674)*
10. **massive retaliation** *(p. 676)*
11. **brinkmanship** *(p. 677)*
12. **covert** *(p. 679)*
13. **developing nation** *(p. 679)*
14. **military-industrial complex** *(p. 680)*

Reviewing Key Facts
15. Potsdam *(p. 657)*, Marshall Plan *(p. 661)*, NATO *(p. 662)*, McCarthyism *(p. 672)*

16. Stalin's push for German reparations and for a Communist government in Poland conflicted with United States desire for democracy in Poland and economic recovery for Germany.

17. NATO was formed to maintain peace and freedom for European nations and the Warsaw Pact was formed to achieve Soviet foreign policy goals.

18. The long-term strategy was to fight the spread of communism worldwide.

Reviewing Key Terms
On a sheet of paper, use each of these terms in a sentence.

1. Cold War
2. iron curtain
3. containment
4. limited war
5. subversion
6. perjury
7. censure
8. fallout
9. fallout shelter
10. massive retaliation
11. brinkmanship
12. covert
13. developing nation
14. military-industrial complex

Reviewing Key Facts
15. **Identify:** Potsdam, Marshall Plan, NATO, McCarthyism.
16. How did Stalin's postwar foreign policy goals add to the growing tensions between the United States and the USSR?
17. Why were NATO and the Warsaw Pact formed?
18. What was the long-term strategy of the United States during the Cold War?
19. What were the effects of the new Red Scare on federal employees?
20. What was President Eisenhower's "new look" for the military?

Critical Thinking
21. **Analyzing Themes: Global Connections** How did the Truman Doctrine and the Marshall Plan cause the United States to change its foreign policy goal of isolationism?

22. **Evaluating** How did the Korean War affect American domestic and international policy?

23. **Organizing** Use a graphic organizer similar to the one below to list the causes of the Cold War.

24. **Interpreting Primary Sources** Margaret Chase Smith, a Republican from Maine, was elected to the Senate in 1948. As a newcomer and the only woman in the Senate, she had very little power. Smith was upset by Joseph McCarthy's accusations, but she hoped her senior colleagues would reprimand him. When they failed to do so, Smith made her "Declaration of Conscience" speech. Read the excerpt and answer the questions that follow.

Chapter Summary

The Cold War

	Soviet Union		Western Allies
General Goals	• To create a protective sphere of Communist countries along European border • To promote the spread of communism		• To contain the spread of communism by supporting capitalist democratic governments
In Europe	• Occupied Eastern European nations and saw that Communist governments were established		• Expected free elections to occur in Soviet-controlled Eastern Europe
In the Middle East	• Sought access to oil in Iran • Aided Communists in Greece and pressured Turkey for access to the Mediterranean		• Forced Soviet withdrawal from Iran • Pledged aid to halt Soviet threats to Turkey and Greece
In Asia	• Communists seize power in China in 1949 • China and Soviet Union signed treaty of friendship and alliance • Communist North Korea invaded South Korea to start Korean War • Chinese troops fought for North Korea		• Aided China's Nationalist government • Dedicated money and troops to establish democratic stronghold in Japan • United Nations troops sent to fight for South Korea in Korean War
At Home	• Promoted development of high-technology weapons and surveillance		• Focused on the development of advanced technology weapons

19. Federal employees faced stricter screening and termination if they were suspected of being disloyal.

20. Eisenhower favored the use of atomic weapons, instead of maintaining a large and expensive army.

Critical Thinking
21. They highlighted the possibility of Communist influence in Turkey, Greece, and Europe, resulting in the containment policy and increased foreign aid.

22. domestic: reinforced the idea of containment and greater military readiness; international: brought the Cold War to Asia, and led to United States defense agreements with Asian countries

Self-Check Quiz

Visit the *American Republic Since 1877* Web site at tarvol2.glencoe.com and click on *Self-Check Quizzes—Chapter 21* to assess your knowledge of chapter content.

66As a United States Senator, I am not proud of the way in which the Senate has been made a publicity platform for irresponsible sensationalism. I am not proud of the reckless abandon in which unproved charges have been hurled from this side of the aisle. I am not proud of the obviously staged, undignified countercharges that have been attempted in retaliation from the other side of the aisle. . . . I am not proud of the way we smear outsiders from the Floor of the Senate and hide behind the cloak of congressional immunity. . . .

As an American, I am shocked at the way Republicans and Democrats alike are playing directly into the Communist design of 'confuse, divide, and conquer'. . . . I want to see our nation recapture the strength and unity it once had when we fought the enemy instead of ourselves.99

a. With whom is Smith angry, and why?

b. According to Smith, who is really dividing the nation?

Practicing Skills

25. **Making Decisions** Study the text on the Truman Doctrine on page 661. Then use the steps you learned about making decisions on page 681 to identify the alternatives the president had in making a decision to ask for aid to fight Soviet aggression in Turkey and Greece. Create a graphic organizer to list the alternatives you have identified.

Chapter Activity

26. **Technology Activity: Developing a Multimedia Presentation** Use the Internet and other resources to find out more about American popular culture during the Cold War. Then create a multimedia report about popular culture at this time, and present your report to the class. Your report could discuss films, books, and magazine articles.

Writing Activity

27. **Persuasive Writing** Imagine that you have witnessed the crowds giving General MacArthur a hero's welcome. Write an opinion piece for a magazine justifying his reception or criticizing it because of his disagreement with Truman.

NATIONAL GEOGRAPHIC **The Occupation of Berlin After World War II, 1945**

Map legend:
- Airports
- American sector
- British sector
- French sector
- Soviet sector

0   5 miles
0   5 kilometers
Albers Conic Equal-Area projection

Geography and History

28. The map above shows the occupation of Berlin after World War II. Study the map and answer the questions below.

   a. Interpreting Maps How was West Berlin's location a disadvantage? How did Stalin use this disadvantage against the Western Allies?

   b. Applying Geography Skills What transportation advantage did West Berlin have over East Berlin? How did the United States use this advantage when West Berlin was stranded?

CHAPTER 21   The Cold War Begins   **683**

Have students visit the Web site at tarvol2.glencoe.com to review Chapter 21 and take the Self-Check Quiz.

Chapter Activity

26. Multimedia reports will vary but should reflect elements of popular culture from the 1950s.

Writing Activity

27. Students' opinion pieces will vary but should clearly express a reasoned opinion supporting or opposing MacArthur's reception.

Geography and History

28. **a.** It was completely surrounded by East Germany; blockaded it; **b.** It had three airports that were used to shuttle food and supplies to the Berliners.

Standardized Test Practice

Answer: D
Test-Taking Tip: Tell students to try using the process of elimination to help rule out answers that cannot possibly be correct. For example, if a student knows that communism often takes hold in poor countries, he or she can eliminate B.

Bonus Question ?

Ask: How long did the era called the Cold War last? *(from 1946 to 1991)*

23. Soviet-U.S. conflict over Soviet control of Eastern Europe and Soviet reparations demands from Germany; U.S. fear of Communist influence or control in the Middle East and Asia

24. **a.** with the Senate because of its behavior in pursuing suspected Communists; **b.** believed the Republicans and Democrats were dividing the nation

Practicing Skills

25. Problem: USSR demanded control of Dardanelles and Greek Communists began guerrilla warfare; alternatives: allow USSR and Communists to control and expand or stand up to the USSR in Turkey and support the Greek government; consequences: further expansion of communism, fewer overseas entanglements, and less spending overseas, or increased overseas involvement, more security for United States, and halt spread of communism

Timesaving Tools

TeacherWorks™ All-In-One Planner and Resource Center

- **Interactive Teacher Edition** Access your Teacher Wraparound Edition and your classroom resources with a few easy clicks.
- **Interactive Lesson Planner** Planning has never been easier! Organize your week, month, semester, or year with all the lesson helps you need to make teaching creative, timely, and relevant.

Use Glencoe's **Presentation Plus!** multimedia teacher tool to easily present dynamic lessons that visually excite your students. Using Microsoft PowerPoint® you can customize the presentations to create your own personalized lessons.

TEACHING TRANSPARENCIES

Graphic Organizer 7 L2

Why It Matters Chapter Transparency 22 L2

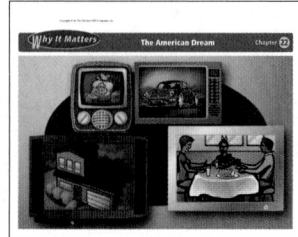

APPLICATION AND ENRICHMENT

Linking Past and Present Activity 22 L2

Enrichment Activity 22 L3

Primary Source Reading 22 L2

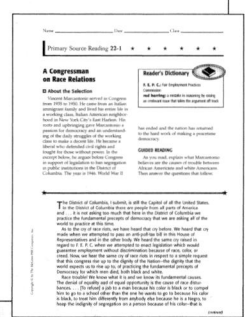

REVIEW AND REINFORCEMENT

Reteaching Activity 22 L1

Vocabulary Activity 22 L1

Time Line Activity 22 L2

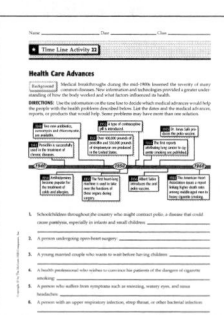

Critical Thinking Skills Activity 22 L2

Meeting NCSS Standards

The following standards are covered in Chapter 22:

Section 1 VII Production, Distribution, and Consumption: A, B, D, F

Section 2 II Time, Continuity, and Change: C, E

Section 3 I Culture: A, C

Section 4 II Time, Continuity, and Change: B, E

Local Standards

Chapter 22 Resources

ASSESSMENT AND EVALUATION

GLENCOE'S **ASSESSMENT** ADVANTAGE

Chapter 22 Test Form A L2

Chapter 22 Test Form B L2

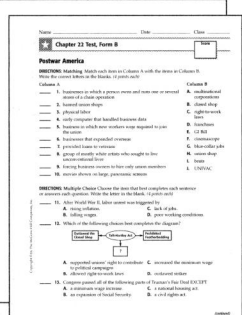

Standardized Test Practice Workbook Activity 22 L2

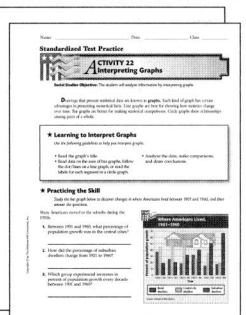

Performance Assessment Activities and Rubrics 22 L1/ELL

ExamView® Pro Testmaker CD-ROM

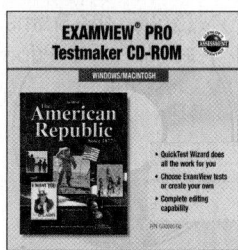

MULTIMEDIA

- Vocabulary PuzzleMaker CD-ROM
- Interactive Tutor Self-Assessment CD-ROM
- ExamView® Pro Testmaker CD-ROM
- Audio Program
- American History Primary Source Documents Library CD-ROM
- MindJogger Videoquiz
- Presentation Plus! CD-ROM
- TeacherWorks™ CD-ROM
- Interactive Student Edition CD-ROM
- Glencoe Skillbuilder Interactive Workbook CD-ROM, Level 2
- The *American Republic Since 1877* Video Program
- American Music: Hits Through History
- American Music: Cultural Traditions

SPANISH RESOURCES

The following Spanish language materials are available:

- Spanish Reading Essentials and Study Guide
- Spanish Guided Reading Activities
- Spanish Reteaching Activities
- Spanish Quizzes and Tests
- Spanish Vocabulary Activities
- Spanish Summaries
- The Declaration of Independence and United States Constitution Spanish Translation

---

A&E HOME VIDEO. **B**iography® THE HISTORY CHANNEL.

The following videotape programs are available from Glencoe as supplements to Chapter 22:

- **Harry S Truman: A New View** (ISBN 1-56-501449-9)
- **Dwight D. Eisenhower: Commander-in-Chief** (ISBN 1-56-501807-9)
- **The Television: Window to the World** (ISBN 0-76-700137-0)

To order, call Glencoe at 1-800-334-7344. To find classroom resources to accompany many of these videos, check the following home pages:
A&E Television: www.aande.com
The History Channel: www.historychannel.com

HISTORY *Online*

Use our Web site for additional resources. All essential content is covered in the Student Edition.

You and your students can visit tarvol2.glencoe.com, the Web site companion to the *American Republic Since 1877.* This innovative integration of electronic and print media offers your students a wealth of opportunities. The student text directs students to the Web site for the following options:

- **Chapter Overviews**
- **Self-Check Quizzes**
- **Student Web Activities**
- **Textbook Updates**

Answers to the student Web activities are provided for you in the **Web Activity Lesson Plans.** Additional Web resources and Interactive Tutor Puzzles are also available.

Chapter 22 Resources

SECTION RESOURCES

Daily Objectives	Reproducible Resources	Multimedia Resources
SECTION 1 **Truman and Eisenhower** 1. Explain the Truman administration's efforts on the domestic front. 2. Describe President Eisenhower's domestic agenda.	Reproducible Lesson Plan 22–1 Daily Lecture and Discussion Notes 22–1 Guided Reading Activity 22–1* Section Quiz 22–1* Reading Essentials and Study Guide 22–1* Performance Assessment Activities and Rubrics	Daily Focus Skills Transparency 22–1 Interactive Tutor Self-Assessment CD-ROM ExamView® Pro Testmaker CD-ROM* Presentation Plus! CD-ROM TeacherWorks™ CD-ROM Audio Program
SECTION 2 **The Affluent Society** 1. Explain the reasons for and the effects of the nation's economic boom. 2. Describe changes to the American family that took place during the 1950s.	Reproducible Lesson Plan 22–2 Daily Lecture and Discussion Notes 22–2 Guided Reading Activity 22–2* Section Quiz 22–2* Reading Essentials and Study Guide 22–2* Performance Assessment Activities and Rubrics	Daily Focus Skills Transparency 22–2 Interactive Tutor Self-Assessment CD-ROM ExamView® Pro Testmaker CD-ROM* Presentation Plus! CD-ROM TeacherWorks™ CD-ROM Audio Program
SECTION 3 **Popular Culture of the 1950s** 1. Explain the characteristics of the new youth culture. 2. Discuss the contributions of African Americans to 1950s culture.	Reproducible Lesson Plan 22–3 Daily Lecture and Discussion Notes 22–3 Guided Reading Activity 22–3* Section Quiz 22–3* Reading Essentials and Study Guide 22–3* Performance Assessment Activities and Rubrics	Daily Focus Skills Transparency 22–3 American Art & Architecture Interactive Tutor Self-Assessment CD-ROM ExamView® Pro Testmaker CD-ROM* Presentation Plus! CD-ROM TeacherWorks™ CD-ROM Audio Program American Music: Hits Through History American Music: Cultural Traditions
SECTION 4 **The Other Side of American Life** 1. Identify those groups that found themselves left out of the American economic boom following World War II. 2. Explain the factors that contributed to the poverty among various groups.	Reproducible Lesson Plan 22–4 Daily Lecture and Discussion Notes 22–4 Guided Reading Activity 22–4* Section Quiz 22–4* Reading Essentials and Study Guide 22–4* Performance Assessment Activities and Rubrics	Daily Focus Skills Transparency 22–4 Interactive Tutor Self-Assessment CD-ROM ExamView® Pro Testmaker CD-ROM* Presentation Plus! CD-ROM Skillbuilder Interactive Workbook, Level 2 TeacherWorks™ CD-ROM Vocabulary PuzzleMaker CD-ROM Audio Program

0:00 OUT OF TIME?
Assign the Chapter 22 **Reading Essentials and Study Guide.**

*Also Available in Spanish

 Printed Materials   Transparency   CD-ROM   DVD

 Poster   Music Program   Audio Program

NATIONAL GEOGRAPHIC Teacher's Corner

INDEX TO NATIONAL GEOGRAPHIC MAGAZINE

The following articles relate to this chapter.

- "Alone Across the Arctic Crown," April 1993
- "Kodiak, Alaska's Island Refuge," November 1993
- "Wrangell-St. Elias: Alaska's Sky-High Wilderness," May 1994

NATIONAL GEOGRAPHIC SOCIETY PRODUCTS

To order the following, call National Geographic at 1-800-368-2728:

- *1945–1989: The Cold War* (Video)
- *Eyewitness to the 20th Century* (Book)
- *Historical Atlas of the United States*
- *National Geographic World Atlas for Young Explorers— Classroom Library Edition* (Guide, Transparencies, Resource Masters)

NGS ONLINE

Access National Geographic's Web site for current events, atlas updates, activities, links, interactive features, and archives.

www.nationalgeographic.com

From the Classroom of...

Dr. Jerry A. Micelle
Calcasieu Career Center
Lake Charles, LA

American History Journal

Ask students to find and analyze five pictures that span the time period from 1945 to 1960. Consider the following questions and others that come to mind.

- Where is the photograph taken?
- What is occurring? What are the expressions on the subjects' faces, and why might that be important?
- What types of objects are being held or used?
- What might that tell you?
- What does the photograph tell you about the level of science and technology during the era?
- What does the photograph tell you about clothing styles and fashion?

Next, have students find quotations they can relate to each picture. Finally, have them write reports on their five pictures.

MEETING SPECIAL NEEDS

In addition to the Differentiated Instruction strategies found in each section, the following resources are also suitable for your special needs students:

- *ExamView® Pro Testmaker CD-ROM* allows teachers to tailor tests by reducing answer choices.
- The *Audio Program* includes the entire narrative of the student edition so that less-proficient readers can listen to the words as they read them.

ADDITIONAL RESOURCES FROM GLENCOE

- American Music: Cultural Traditions
- American Art & Architecture
- Outline Map Resource Book
- U.S. Desk Map
- Building Geography Skills for Life
- Inclusion for the High School Social Studies Classroom Strategies and Activities
- Teaching Strategies for the American History Classroom (Including Block Scheduling Pacing Guides)
- Dinah Zike's High School American History Reading and Study Skills Foldables

KEY TO ABILITY LEVELS

Teaching strategies have been coded.

- L1 BASIC activities for all students
- L2 AVERAGE activities for average to above-average students
- L3 CHALLENGING activities for above-average students
- ELL ENGLISH LANGUAGE LEARNER activities

 Block Schedule

Activities that are suited to use within the block scheduling framework are identified by:

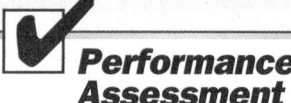

Why It Matters Activity

Ask students to conduct brief interviews with five adults. Tell them to ask each one the following questions about his or her childhood: favorite television programs, number of televisions at home, and times television was watched. Based on their brief interviews, have students draw conclusions about the influence of television in America. Students should evaluate their answers after they have completed the chapter.

GLENCOE TECHNOLOGY

The *American Republic Since 1877* Video Program

To learn more about the cultural impact of the automobile, have students view the Chapter 22 video, "America Takes to the Roads," from the *American Republic Since 1877* Video Program.

MindJogger Videoquiz

Use the **MindJogger Videoquiz** to preview Chapter 22 content.

 Both programs available in DVD

CHAPTER 22
Postwar America
1945–1960

Why It Matters

After World War II, the country enjoyed a period of economic prosperity. Many more Americans could now aspire to a middle-class lifestyle, with a house in the suburbs and more leisure time. Television became a favorite form of entertainment. This general prosperity, however, did not extend to many Hispanics, African Americans, Native Americans, or people in Appalachia.

The Impact Today

The effects of this era can still be seen.
• The middle class represents a large segment of the American population.
• Television is a popular form of entertainment for many Americans.

 The American Republic Since 1877 Video The Chapter 22 video, "America Takes to the Roads," describes the cultural impact of the automobile and its importance to the growing baby boom generation.

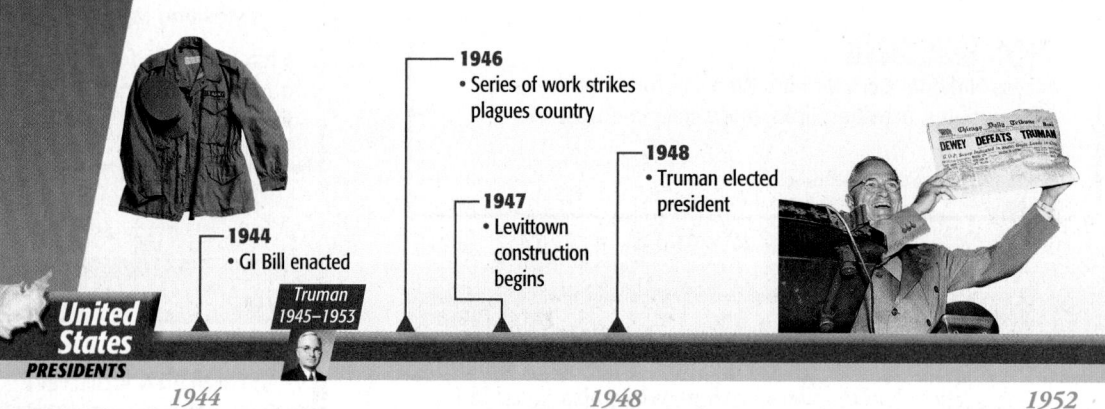

1946
• Series of work strikes plagues country

1948
• Truman elected president

1947
• Levittown construction begins

1944
• GI Bill enacted

Truman 1945–1953

United States PRESIDENTS

1944   *1948*   *1952*

World

1946
• Juan Perón elected president of Argentina

1948
• South Africa introduces apartheid

1952
• Scientists led by Edward Teller develop hydrogen bomb

684

HISTORY Online

Introduce students to chapter content and key terms by having them access the **Chapter 22 Overview** at tarvol2.glencoe.com.

More About the Photo

Tell students that the life of middle-class citizens in the United States was very different from that of the poor. Middle-class families in the suburbs could afford automobiles. Family vacations often revolved around driving to national parks or amusement centers across the country. Many poor, on the other hand, had to rely on public transportation. This often meant that poor workers had limited access to jobs. Ask students to explain how they think automobiles affected the growth of suburbs.

TIME LINE ACTIVITY

Have students select one of the people listed on the time line to research. Have students make a bulleted list of the person's achievements and honors received.

FOLDABLES
Study Organizer

Dinah Zike's Foldables are three-dimensional, interactive graphic organizers that help students practice basic writing skills, review key vocabulary terms, and identify main ideas. Have students complete the foldable activity in the *Dinah Zike's Reading and Study Skills Foldables* booklet.

These confident newlyweds capture the prosperous attitude of postwar America.

1953
• Lucille Ball gives birth in real life and on her television show

1955
• Salk polio vaccine becomes widely available

1956
• Elvis Presley appears on *The Ed Sullivan Show*
• Federal Highway Act passed

1957
• Estimated 40 million television sets in use in United States

1958
• Galbraith's *The Affluent Society* published

Eisenhower 1953–1961

1956 *1960*

1954
• Gamal Abdel Nasser takes power in Egypt

1956
• Suez Canal crisis erupts

1957
• USSR launches *Sputnik I* and *Sputnik II* satellites

HISTORY Online

Chapter Overview
Visit the *American Republic Since 1877* Web site at tarvol2.glencoe.com and click on **Chapter Overviews—Chapter 22** to preview chapter information.

685

GRAPHIC ORGANIZER ACTIVITY

Organizing Information Have students create web diagrams similar to the ones below to show the experiences of the middle class and the poor during the 1950s. Have students list at least four characteristics for each group.

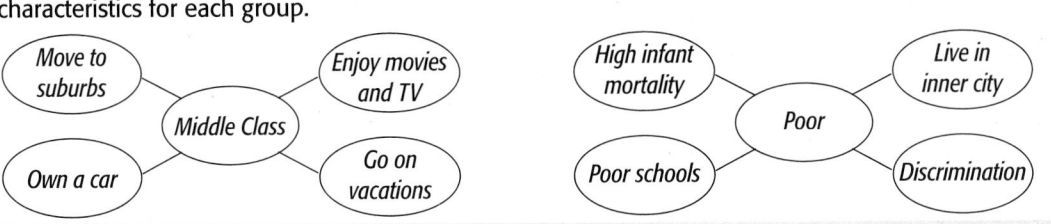

Move to suburbs — Enjoy movies and TV — **Middle Class** — Own a car — Go on vacations

High infant mortality — Live in inner city — **Poor** — Poor schools — Discrimination

685

1 FOCUS

Section Overview

This section focuses on the post-war administrations of Truman and Eisenhower.

BELLRINGER
Skillbuilder Activity

Project transparency and have students answer the question.

Daily Focus Skills Transparency 22–1

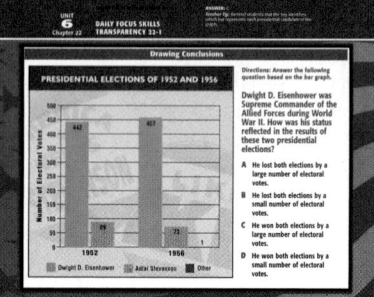

Reading Preview

Answers to Graphic: increased consumer spending, higher prices, rising inflation, labor unrest

Preteaching Vocabulary
Have students make a two-column list with the headings Truman and Eisenhower and write the Key Terms and Names in the appropriate columns.

SECTION 1 Truman and Eisenhower

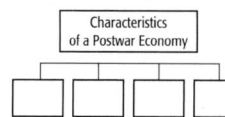
Guide to Reading

Main Idea
After World War II, the Truman and Eisenhower administrations set out to help the nation adjust to peacetime.

Key Terms and Names
GI Bill, closed shop, right-to-work law, union shop, featherbedding, "Do-Nothing Congress," Fair Deal, dynamic conservatism, Federal Highway Act

Reading Strategy
Categorizing As you read about the Truman and Eisenhower administrations, complete a graphic organizer similar to the one below by listing the characteristics of the postwar economy of the United States.

Characteristics of a Postwar Economy

Reading Objectives
• **Explain** the Truman administration's efforts on the domestic front.
• **Describe** President Eisenhower's domestic agenda.

Section Theme
Economic Factors Following World War II, the federal government supported programs that helped the economy make the transition to peacetime production.

Preview of Events

♦1944   ♦1947   ♦1950   ♦1953

1944
Congress passes GI Bill

1946
Strikes take place across the country

1948
Harry S Truman wins presidential election

1952
Dwight D. Eisenhower wins presidential election

Army fatigues and college diploma

★ An American Story ★

As World War II ended, Robert Eubanks was worried as he prepared for his discharge from the army. He had joined the army because, as an African American, it was hard for him to find a job that paid well. Then he heard about something known as the GI Bill, a government program that paid veterans' tuition for college and provided a living allowance.

Eubanks took advantage of the program and enrolled at the Illinois Institute of Technology. He earned three degrees on the GI Bill and eventually became a professor at the University of Illinois.

Years later Eubanks recalled how his life was changed by the bill. "It's very hard to explain how things were during the 1940s," he said. "The restrictions on blacks then were rough. The GI Bill gave me my start on being a professional instead of a stock clerk."

—adapted from *When Dreams Came True*

Return to a Peacetime Economy

After the war many Americans feared the return to a peacetime economy. They worried that after military production halted and millions of former soldiers glutted the labor market, unemployment and recession might sweep the country.

Despite such worries, the economy continued to grow after the war as increased consumer spending helped ward off a recession. After 17 years of economic depression and wartime shortages, Americans rushed out to buy the luxury goods they had long desired.

686   CHAPTER 22   Postwar America

SECTION RESOURCES

📖 **Reproducible Masters**
• Reproducible Lesson Plan 22–1
• Daily Lecture and Discussion Notes 22–1
• Guided Reading Activity 22–1
• Section Quiz 22–1
• Reading Essentials and Study Guide 22–1
• Performance Assessment Activities and Rubrics

🎞 **Transparencies**
• Daily Focus Skills Transparency 22–1

Multimedia
💿 Interactive Tutor Self-Assessment CD-ROM
💿 ExamView® Pro Testmaker CD-ROM
💿 Presentation Plus! CD-ROM
💿 TeacherWorks™ CD-ROM
🎧 Audio Program

The Servicemen's Readjustment Act, popularly called the **GI Bill,** further boosted the economy. The act provided generous loans to veterans to help them establish businesses, buy homes, and attend college.

Inflation and Strikes The postwar economy was not without its problems. A greater demand for goods led to higher prices, and this rising inflation soon triggered labor unrest. As the cost of living rose, workers across the country went on strike for better pay. Work stoppages soon affected the automobile, electrical, steel, and mining industries.

Afraid that the nation's energy supply would be drastically reduced because of the striking miners, President Truman forced the miners to return to work after one strike that had lasted over a month. Truman ordered government seizure of the mines while pressuring mine owners to grant the union most of its demands. The president also halted a strike that shut down the nation's railroads by threatening to draft the striking workers into the army.

Republican Victory Labor unrest and high prices prompted many Americans to call for a change. The Republicans seized upon these sentiments during the 1946 congressional elections, winning control of both houses of Congress for the first time since 1930.

Disgusted with the rash of strikes that was crippling the nation, the new conservative Congress quickly set out to curb the power of organized labor. Legislators proposed a measure known as the **Taft-Hartley Act,** which outlawed the closed shop, or the practice of forcing business owners to hire only union members. Under the law, states could pass right-to-work laws, which outlawed union shops (shops in which new workers were required to join the union). The measure also prohibited featherbedding, the practice of limiting work output in order to create more jobs. Furthermore, the bill forbade unions from using their money to support political campaigns. When the bill reached Truman, however, he vetoed it, arguing:

> 66 . . . [It would] reverse the basic direction of our national labor policy, inject the government into private economic affairs on an unprecedented scale, and conflict with important principles of our democratic society. Its provisions would cause more strikes, not fewer. 99
>
> —quoted in *The Growth of the American Republic*

The president's concerns did little to sway Congress, which passed the Taft-Hartley Act in 1947 over Truman's veto. Its supporters claimed the law held irresponsible unions in check just as the Wagner Act of 1935 had restrained anti-union activities and employers. Labor leaders called the act a "slave labor" law and insisted that it erased many of the gains that unions had made since 1933.

Reading Check

Explaining Why did Truman veto the Taft-Hartley Act?

Truman's Domestic Program

The Democratic Party's loss of members in the 1946 elections did not dampen President Truman's spirits or his plans. Shortly after taking office, Truman had proposed a series of domestic measures that sought to continue the work done as part of Franklin Roosevelt's New Deal. During his tenure in office, Truman worked to push this agenda through Congress.

Truman's Legislative Agenda Truman's proposals included the expansion of Social Security benefits; the raising of the legal minimum wage from 40¢ to 75¢ an hour; a program to ensure full employment through aggressive use of federal spending and investment; public housing and slum clearance; long-range environmental and public works planning; and a system of national health insurance.

Truman also boldly asked Congress in February 1948 to pass a broad civil rights bill that would

The GI Bill African American soldiers review the benefits of the GI Bill, which included loans to attend college and to buy homes.

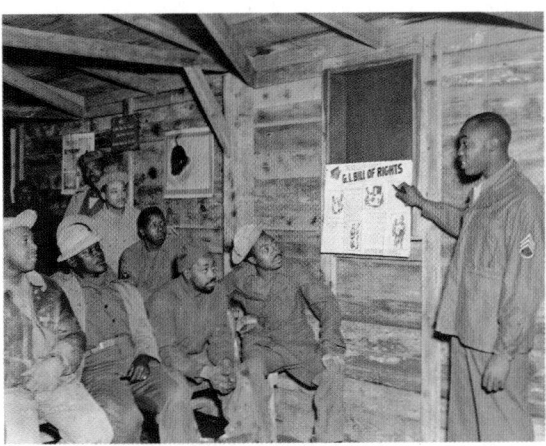

2 TEACH

Daily Lecture and Discussion Notes 22–1

Objectives and answers to the student activity can be found in the **Web Activity Lesson Plan** at tarvol2.glencoe.com.

Reading Check

Answer: He felt it injected the government into private economic affairs on an unprecedented scale and would cause more strikes without contributing to economic stability and progress.

Discussing a Concept Explain that President Truman favored an increase in the minimum wage, and Congress supported him. In 1949 the minimum wage went from 40 cents to 75 cents per hour; in 1955 the hourly rate reached $1. Have students discuss the positive and negative results of raising the minimum wage. **L1** ELL

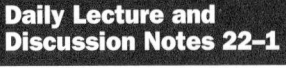

Student Web Activity Visit the *American Republic Since 1877* Web site at tarvol2.glencoe.com and click on *Student Web Activities— Chapter 22* for an activity on postwar America.

Reading Strategy — READING THE TEXT

Using Graphic Organizers Venn diagrams are ways for students to compare and/or contrast two or more items. Have students draw two overlapping circles on their papers. Label one circle "Truman," one circle "Eisenhower," and the overlapping area "Both." Ask students to list the main domestic policy approaches of each president in the appropriate area. Students should list the policies that both presidents adopted in the overlapping area. **L1**

☛ Refer to *Inclusion for the High School Social Studies Classroom Strategies and Activities* in the TCR.

Guided Reading Activity 22–1

Name _____ Date _____ Class _____

★ **Guided Reading Activity 22-1**

DIRECTIONS: Filling in the Blanks In the space provided, write the word or words that best complete the sentence. Refer to your textbook to fill in the blanks.

1. After the war, many Americans worried that after _____ halted and millions of former soldiers glutted the labor market, _____ and _____ might sweep the country.

2. To end a miners' strike, President Truman ordered _____ of the mines while pressuring the mine owners to grant the union _____.

3. The Taft-Hartley Act outlawed the _____, or the practice of forcing business owners to hire only _____.

4. In February 1948, Truman asked Congress to pass a broad civil rights bill that would protect African Americans' _____, abolish _____, and make _____ a federal crime.

5. He also issued _____ barring dis...

Picturing History

Answer: supported a civil rights bill, issued an executive order banning discrimination in federal employment, and ended segregation in the armed forces

Ask: What three groups provided a great deal of support for Truman in 1948? *(laborers, African Americans, and farmers)*

Making a Comparison Have students research the cost of a modest suburban home built in their community during the 1950s and the cost of the same home today. Instruct students to include an exterior sketch or photograph, a floor plan, and a description of special features such as a patio or garage. Encourage students to use library and Internet resources to locate real estate records. Use the reports as a starting point for a discussion about the affordability of housing in the 1950s and today. **L2**

In addition to providing low interest loans to help veterans buy homes and farms, the GI Bill provided unemployment benefits for veterans who could not find jobs.

---

protect African Americans' right to vote, abolish poll taxes, and make lynching a federal crime. He also issued an executive order barring discrimination in federal employment, and he ended segregation in the armed forces.

Most of Truman's legislative efforts, however, met with little success, as a coalition of Republicans and conservative Southern Democrats defeated many of his proposals. While these defeats angered Truman, the president soon had to worry about other matters.

The Election of 1948 As the presidential election of 1948 approached, most observers gave Truman little chance of winning. Some Americans still believed that he lacked the stature for the job, and they viewed his administration as weak and inept.

Divisions within the Democratic Party also seemed to spell disaster for Truman. At the Democratic Convention that summer, two factions abandoned the party altogether. Reacting angrily to Truman's support of civil rights, a group of Southern Democrats formed the States' Rights, or Dixiecrat, Party and nominated South Carolina governor **Strom Thurmond** for president. At the same time, the party's more liberal members were frustrated by Truman's ineffective domestic policies and critical of his anti-Soviet foreign policy. They formed a new Progressive Party, with Henry A. Wallace as their presidential candidate. In addition, the president's Republican opponent was New York governor Thomas Dewey, a dignified and popular candidate who seemed unbeatable. After polling 50 political writers, *Newsweek* magazine declared three weeks before the election, "The landslide for Dewey will sweep the country."

Picturing History

African Americans Rally for Truman During the 1948 election, President Truman spoke at many rallies similar to this one in New York City. What legislative proposals by President Truman built African American political support?

Perhaps the only one who gave Truman a chance to win was Truman himself. "I know every one of those 50 fellows," he declared about the writers polled in *Newsweek*. "There isn't one of them has enough sense to pound sand in a rat hole." Ignoring the polls, the feisty president poured his efforts into an energetic campaign. He traveled more than 20,000 miles by train and made more than 350 speeches. Along the way, Truman attacked the majority Republican Congress as "do-nothing, good-for-nothing" for refusing to enact his legislative agenda.

Truman's attacks on the **"Do-Nothing Congress"** did not mention that both he and Congress had been very busy dealing with foreign policy matters. Congress had passed the Truman Doctrine's aid program to Greece and Turkey, as well as the Marshall Plan. It had also created the Department of Defense and the CIA and established the Joint Chiefs of Staff as a permanent organization. The 80th Congress, therefore, did not "do nothing" as Truman charged, but its accomplishments were in areas that did not affect most Americans directly. As a result, Truman's charges began to stick, and to the surprise of almost everyone, his efforts paid off.

With a great deal of support from laborers, African Americans, and farmers, Truman won a narrow but stunning victory over Dewey. Perhaps just as remarkable as the president's victory was the resurgence of the Democratic Party. When the dust had cleared after Election Day, Democrats had regained control of both houses of Congress.

GOVERNMENT

The Fair Deal Truman's State of the Union message to the new Congress repeated the domestic agenda he had put forth previously. "Every segment of our population and every individual," he declared, "has a right to expect from . . . government a fair deal." Whether intentional or not, the president had coined a name—the **Fair Deal**—to set his program apart from the New Deal.

The 81st Congress did not completely embrace Truman's Fair Deal. Legislators did raise the legal minimum wage to 75¢ an hour. They also approved an important expansion of the Social Security system, increasing benefits by 77 percent and extending them to 10 million additional people. Congress also passed the National Housing Act of 1949, which provided for the construction of more than 800,000 units of low-income housing, accompanied by long-term rent subsidies.

Congress refused, however, to pass national health insurance or to provide subsidies for farmers or

---

DIFFERENTIATED INSTRUCTION

Kinesthetic Meeting and talking with people, punctuated by shaking hands, is an important part of election campaigns. Invite four students to represent one of the candidates in the 1948 presidential election campaign—Truman, Dewey, Thurmond, or Wallace. Have the remaining students meet and greet the "candidates." Encourage the candidates to shake hands with their constituents and talk about their qualifications and their proposed programs. **L2**

📁 Refer to *Inclusion for the High School Social Studies Classroom Strategies and Activities* in the TCR.

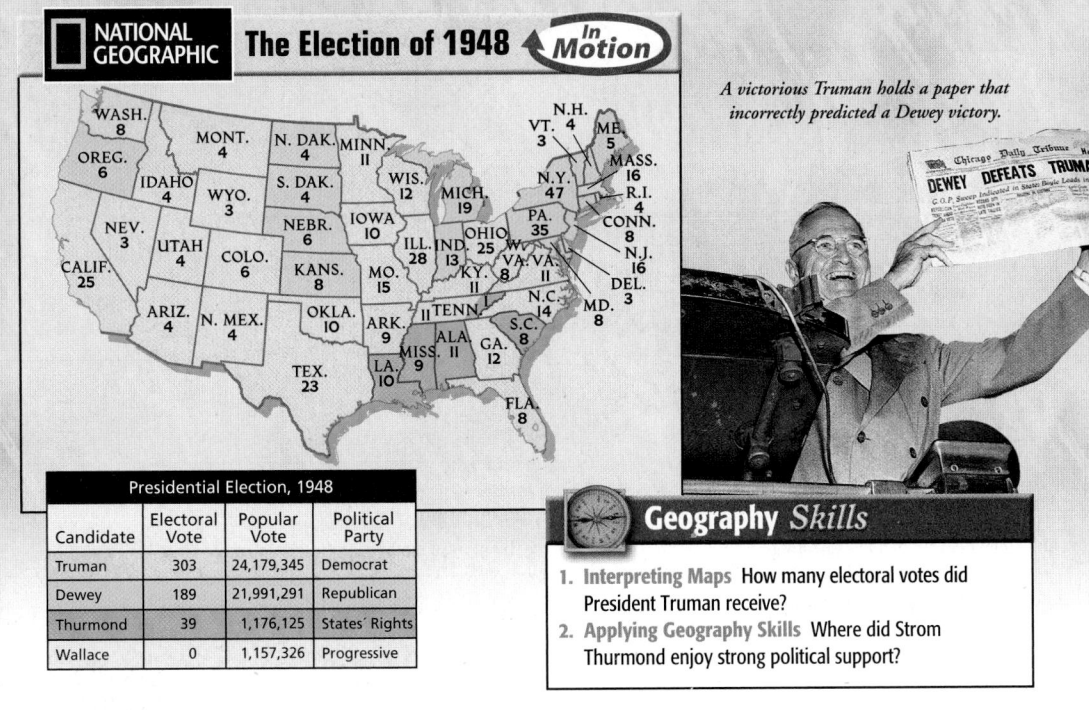

NATIONAL GEOGRAPHIC — The Election of 1948 — In Motion

Presidential Election, 1948			
Candidate	Electoral Vote	Popular Vote	Political Party
Truman	303	24,179,345	Democrat
Dewey	189	21,991,291	Republican
Thurmond	39	1,176,125	States' Rights
Wallace	0	1,157,326	Progressive

A victorious Truman holds a paper that incorrectly predicted a Dewey victory.

Geography *Skills*

1. **Interpreting Maps** How many electoral votes did President Truman receive?
2. **Applying Geography Skills** Where did Strom Thurmond enjoy strong political support?

Geography *Skills*

Answers:
1. 303
2. Alabama, Louisiana, Mississippi, South Carolina, and eastern Tennessee

Geography Skills Practice
Ask: In which Western state did the voters turn out for Dewey?
(Oregon)

Reading Check

Answer: The victory of Truman and the Democrats paved the way for the Fair Deal legislation, some of which was approved by Congress.

Creating Circle Graphs Have students use the data on the map on this page to make a pair of circle graphs showing the results of the presidential election of 1948. One graph should show the results of the popular vote and the other should show the results of the electoral vote. **L1**

📁 Use the rubric for creating a map, display, or chart on pages 65–66 in the *Performance Assessment Activities and Rubrics.*

---

federal aid for schools. In addition, legislators opposed Truman's efforts to enact civil rights legislation.

Reading Check **Describing** What was the impact of the election of 1948?

The Eisenhower Years

In 1950 the United States went to war in Korea. The war consumed the nation's attention and resources and basically ended Truman's Fair Deal. By 1952, with the war a bloody stalemate and his approval rating dropping quickly, Truman declined to run again for the presidency. With no Democratic incumbent to face, Republicans pinned their hopes of regaining the White House on a popular World War II hero.

The Election of 1952 Dwight Eisenhower decided to run as the Republican nominee for president in 1952. His running mate was a young California senator, Richard Nixon. The Democrats nominated Illinois governor Adlai Stevenson, a witty and eloquent speaker who had the support of leading liberals and organized labor.

The Republicans adopted the slogan: "It's time for a change!" The warm and friendly Eisenhower, known as "Ike," promised to end the war in Korea. "I like Ike" became the Republican rallying cry.

Eisenhower's campaign soon came under fire as reports surfaced that Richard Nixon had received gifts from California business leaders totaling $18,000 while he was a senator. For a while, it looked as if Nixon might be dropped from the ticket. In a nationwide speech broadcast on radio and television, Nixon insisted the funds had been used for legitimate political purposes. He did admit that his family had kept one gift, a cocker spaniel puppy named "Checkers." He declared, "The kids love the dog, [and] regardless about what they say about it, we're going to keep it." This so-called "Checkers speech" won praise from much of the public and kept Nixon on the ticket.

Eisenhower won the election by a landslide, carrying the Electoral College 442 votes to 89. The Republicans also gained an eight-seat majority in the House, while the Senate became evenly divided between Democrats and Republicans.

Ike as President President Eisenhower had two favorite phrases. "Middle of the road" described his political beliefs, which fell midway between conservative and liberal. He also referred to the notion of "dynamic conservatism," which meant balancing economic conservatism with some activism.

INTERDISCIPLINARY CONNECTIONS ACTIVITY

Government Have students illustrate how Truman's Fair Deal fared in Congress. **L2**

Fair Deal Legislation	Fair Deal Programs Not Enacted
increase in minimum wage	*national health insurance*
expansion of the Social Security system	*farm subsidies*
National Housing Act	*federal aid to schools*
	civil rights legislation

Why It Matters

Background: The numbering system for interstate highways is a good example of effective planning. One- and two-digit numbers designate all major routes. The north-south routes use odd numbers while the east-west routes use even numbers. East-west routes begin with the lowest numbers along the southern border of the United States and north-south routes begin with the lowest numbers along the West Coast.

Ask: Assuming that you drive 10 hours a day for 4.5 days, what is your average speed in traveling the 2,800 miles across country? *(10 hrs. × 4.5 days = 45 hours of driving time; 2,800 ÷ 45 = 62.2 miles per hour)* Have students compare their result to the average speed of Eisenhower's convoy.

3 ASSESS

Assign Section 1 Assessment as homework or as an in-class activity.

🖲 Have students use the **Interactive Tutor Self-Assessment CD-ROM.**

L1/ELL

Reading Essentials and Study Guide 22–1

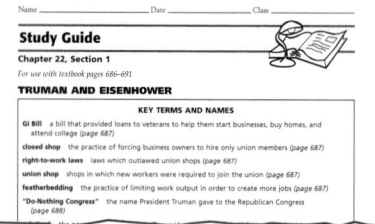

Name _____ Date _____ Class _____

Study Guide

Chapter 22, Section 1

For use with textbook pages 686–691

TRUMAN AND EISENHOWER

KEY TERMS AND NAMES

GI Bill   a bill that provided loans to veterans to help them start businesses, buy homes, and attend college *(page 687)*

closed shop   the practice of forcing business owners to hire only union members *(page 687)*

right-to-work laws   laws which outlawed union shops *(page 687)*

union shop   shops in which new workers were required to join the union *(page 687)*

featherbedding   the practice of limiting work output in order to create more jobs *(page 687)*

"Do-Nothing Congress"   the name President Truman gave to the Republican Congress *(page 688)*

Why It Matters

Interstate Highways

As Cold War tensions rose, American officials realized that the ability to move troops and military equipment across the country quickly and efficiently could very well determine whether the nation could survive attack. Since the haphazard system of two-lane highways that crisscrossed America could not handle such a task, the Eisenhower administration proposed a 41,000-mile network of multi-lane interstate highways. The interstate system changed American life in several significant ways.

The Interstate System, 2000
NATIONAL GEOGRAPHIC

CANADA

EAST
INTERSTATE
ARIZONA
10

HAWAII

MEXICO

Gulf of Mexico

ATLANTIC OCEAN

TROPIC OF CANCER

110°W   100°W   90°W   80°W

0   200 miles
0   200 kilometers

0   500 k
Albers Conic Eq
projection

Interst
highwa
Interst
highwa

More Efficient Distribution of Goods ➤
The interstates made the distribution of goods faster and more efficient. In the 1990s, trucks moved more than 6 billion tons of goods each year, nearly half of all commercial transports in the United States. Most of these trucks used interstates.

Eisenhower wasted little time in showing his conservative side. The new president's cabinet appointments included several business leaders. Under their guidance, Eisenhower ended government price and rent controls, which many conservatives had viewed as unnecessary federal control over the business community. The Eisenhower administration viewed business growth as vital to the nation. The president's secretary of defense, formerly the president of General Motors, declared to the Senate that "what is good for our country is good for General Motors, and vice versa."

Eisenhower's conservatism showed itself in other ways as well. In an attempt to curb the federal budget, the president vetoed a school construction bill and agreed to slash government aid to public housing. Along with these cuts, he supported some modest tax reductions.

Eisenhower also targeted the federal government's continuing aid to businesses, or what he termed "creeping socialism." Shortly after taking office, the president abolished the Reconstruction Finance Corporation (RFC), which since 1932 had lent money to banks, railroads, and other large institutions in financial trouble. Another Depression-era agency, the Tennessee Valley Authority (TVA), also came under Eisenhower's economic scrutiny. During his presidency, appro-

priations for the TVA fell from $185 million to $12 million.

In some areas, President Eisenhower took an activist role. For example, he advocated the passage of two large government projects. During the 1950s, as the number of Americans who owned cars increased, so too did the need for greater and more efficient travel routes. In 1956 Congress responded to this growing need by passing the **Federal Highway Act,** the largest public works program in American history. The act appropriated $25 billion for a 10-year effort to construct more than 40,000 miles (64,400 km) of interstate highways. Congress also authorized construction of the Great Lakes-St. Lawrence Seaway to connect the Great Lakes with the Atlantic Ocean through a series of locks on the St. Lawrence River. Three previous presidents had been unable to reach agreements with Canada to build this waterway to aid international shipping. Through Eisenhower's efforts, the two nations finally agreed on a plan to complete the project.

Extending the New Deal Although President Eisenhower cut federal spending and worked to limit the federal government's role in the nation's economy, he also agreed to extend the Social Security system to an additional 10 million people. He also extended unemployment compensation to an additional 4 million citizens and agreed to increase

690 CHAPTER 22   Postwar America

CRITICAL THINKING ACTIVITY

Determining a Point of View The Taft-Hartley Act created controversy for the Truman administration. Have students determine their position on the following statement: The president should have the right to halt economically damaging strikes for a "cooling off" period. Students should provide reasons for their positions. *(Students' answers will vary, but their positions need to be substantiated with specific reasons.)* **L2**

◀ **Suburbanization and Urban Sprawl**
The interstate system contributed to the growth of suburban communities and the eventual geographic spread of center-less cities. Using the interstates, suburbanites could commute to their jobs miles away.

A New Road Culture ➤
The interstates created an automobile society. In 1997, $687 billion were spent on private automobiles compared to $22.8 billion for public transit. Additionally, chains of fast food restaurants and motels replaced independent operators across the country.

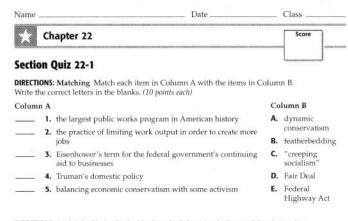

Speed of Travel

The interstate highways drastically decreased the time it took to travel across the continent. In 1919 a young Dwight D. Eisenhower joined 294 other members of the army to travel the 2,800 miles from Washington, D.C., to San Francisco. They made the trip in 62 days, averaging 5 miles per hour. During World War II, General Eisenhower was impressed with the modern design of Germany's freeway system, the Autobahn. "The old convoy," he said, "had started me thinking about good, two-lane highways, but Germany had made me see the wisdom of broader ribbons across the land." Wide lanes and controlled entrance and exit points allowed cars to travel at much higher speeds. Using the interstate highways, Eisenhower's trip would now take 4½ days.

Travel Times: Washington, D.C., to San Francisco

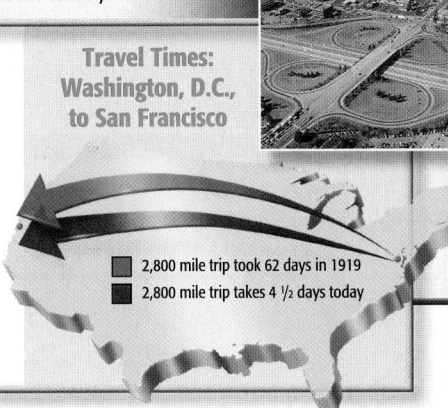

■ 2,800 mile trip took 62 days in 1919
■ 2,800 mile trip takes 4 ½ days today

the minimum hourly wage from 75¢ to $1 and to continue to provide some government aid to farmers.

By the time Eisenhower ran for a second term in 1956—a race he won easily—the nation had successfully completed the transition from a wartime to a peacetime economy. The battles between liberals and conservatives over whether to continue New Deal policies would continue. In the meantime, however, most Americans focused their energy on enjoying what had become a decade of tremendous prosperity.

✓ **Reading Check** **Evaluating** What conservative and activist measures did Eisenhower take during his administration?

 Study Central™ To review this section, go to tarvol2.glencoe.com and click on **Study Central™**.

SECTION 1 ASSESSMENT

Checking for Understanding
1. **Define:** closed shop, right-to-work law, union shop, featherbedding, dynamic conservatism.
2. **Identify:** GI Bill, "Do-Nothing Congress," Fair Deal, Federal Highway Act.

Reviewing Themes
3. **Economic Factors** How did President Eisenhower aid international shipping during his administration?

Critical Thinking
4. **Interpreting** In what ways did the Taft-Hartley Act hurt labor unions?
5. **Categorizing** Use a graphic organizer to compare the agendas of the Truman and Eisenhower administrations.

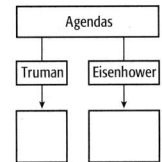

Agendas

Truman | Eisenhower

Analyzing Visuals
6. **Analyzing Maps** Study the map on page 689. Which parts of the country did Dewey win? Why do you think he did so well in these areas?

Writing About History
7. **Persuasive Writing** Take on the role of a member of Congress during the Truman administration. Write a speech in which you try to persuade the 81st Congress to either pass or defeat Truman's Fair Deal measures.

CHAPTER 22 Postwar America **691**

SECTION 1 ASSESSMENT ANSWERS

1. Terms are in blue.
2. GI Bill *(p. 687)*, "Do-Nothing Congress" *(p. 688)*, Fair Deal *(p. 688)*, Federal Highway Act *(p. 690)*
3. He authorized the Great Lakes-St. Lawrence Seaway, which connected the Great Lakes with the Atlantic Ocean.
4. It outlawed closed shops, allowed states to outlaw union shops, and prohibited featherbedding.
5. Truman: increase government involvement in business, expand federal spending; Eisenhower: limit government involvement in business, curb federal spending
6. Northeast, Great Plains; governor of New York, strong in traditional Republican areas
7. Students' speeches will vary. Speeches should focus on several components of the Fair Deal.

✓ **Reading Check**

Answer: reduced government control over business, cut spending on public housing; passed the Federal Highway Act, extended the Social Security System, and increased the minimum wage

Reteach
Have students explain Truman's domestic policy.

Enrich
Invite interested students to write and deliver the opening paragraph of a speech that a presidential candidate could have used in 1948, 1952, or 1956.

HISTORY Online

Study Central™ provides summaries, interactive games, and online graphic organizers to help students review section content.

4 CLOSE

Have students describe President Eisenhower's domestic agenda.

1 FOCUS

Section Overview

This section focuses on the postwar economic boom.

BELLRINGER
Skillbuilder Activity

 Project transparency and have students answer the question.

Daily Focus Skills Transparency 22–2

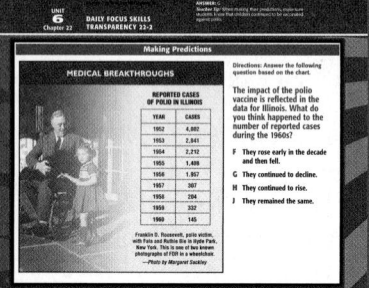

Reading Preview

Answers to Graphic: 1946, earliest computer; 1947, transistor developed; 1955, injection polio vaccine developed; 1958, satellite launched

Preteaching Vocabulary
Have students write a word or phrase next to each name and term to help clarify its meaning.

SECTION 2 The Affluent Society

Guide to Reading

Main Idea
The postwar economic boom brought great changes to society, including the ways many Americans worked and lived.

Key Terms and Names
John Kenneth Galbraith, white-collar, blue-collar, multinational corporation, franchise, David Riesman, Levittown, baby boom, Jonas Salk

Reading Strategy
Sequencing As you read about American society in the 1950s, complete a time line similar to the one below by recording the scientific and technological breakthroughs of the time.

1946 — 1958

Reading Objectives
- **Explain** the reasons for and the effects of the nation's economic boom.
- **Describe** changes to the American family that took place during the 1950s.

Section Theme
Continuity and Change Americans became avid consumers in the atmosphere of postwar abundance.

Preview of Events

♦1946	♦1950	♦1954	♦1958
1947 Construction of Levittown begins	**1950** David Riesman's *The Lonely Crowd* published	**1955** Salk polio vaccine becomes widely available	**1958** John Kenneth Galbraith's *The Affluent Society* published

---

★ An American Story ★

Kemmons Wilson on magazine cover

In the summer of 1951, Kemmons Wilson traveled with his family from Memphis, Tennessee, to Washington, D.C. He noticed that some of the motels they stayed in were terrible. Each added a $2 charge per child to the standard room price, and many were located far from restaurants, forcing travelers back into their cars to search for meals.

Frustrated, Wilson decided to build a motel chain that would provide interstate travelers with comfortable lodgings. They would be located near good family restaurants and allow kids to stay free. Together with a group of investors, Wilson began building the Holiday Inn motel chain. Families loved his motels, and soon Holiday Inns were sprouting up all over the country.

Wilson said he never doubted the success of his endeavor. "I like to think that I'm so . . . normal that anything I like, everybody else is going to like too," he said. "The idea that my instincts are out of line just doesn't occur to me." His prosperity mirrored a growing affluence in the nation. This time of prosperity made the shortages of the Great Depression and World War II a distant memory.

—adapted from *The Fifties*

American Abundance

Wilson's motel chain proved successful largely because the 1950s was a decade of incredible prosperity. In 1958 economist **John Kenneth Galbraith** published *The Affluent Society*, in which he claimed that the nation's postwar prosperity was a new phenomenon. In the past, Galbraith said, all societies had an "economy of scarcity,"

 SECTION RESOURCES

📁 **Reproducible Masters**
- Reproducible Lesson Plan 22–2
- Daily Lecture and Discussion Notes 22–2
- Guided Reading Activity 22–2
- Section Quiz 22–2
- Reading Essentials and Study Guide 22–2
- Performance Assessment Activities and Rubrics

🖥 **Transparencies**
- Daily Focus Skills Transparency 22–2

Multimedia
- 💿 Interactive Tutor Self-Assessment CD-ROM
- 💿 ExamView® Pro Testmaker CD-ROM
- 💿 Presentation Plus! CD-ROM
- 💿 TeacherWorks™ CD-ROM
- 🔊 Audio Program

meaning that a lack of resources and overpopulation had limited economic productivity. Now, the United States and a few other industrialized nations had created what Galbraith called an "economy of abundance." New business techniques and improved technology enabled these nations to produce an abundance of goods and services for their people—all of which allowed many of them to enjoy a standard of living never before thought possible.

The Spread of Wealth Some critics accused Galbraith of overstating the situation, but the facts and figures seemed to support his theory. Between 1940 and 1960, the average income of American families roughly tripled. Americans in all income brackets—poor, middle-class, and wealthy—experienced this rapid rise in income. The dramatic rise in home ownership also showed that the income of average families had risen significantly. Between 1940 and 1960, the number of Americans owning their own homes rose from about 43 to about 62 percent.

Accompanying the country's economic growth were dramatic changes in work environments. Mechanization in farms and factories meant that fewer farmers and laborers were needed to provide the public with food and goods. As a result, more Americans began working in what are called white-collar jobs, such as those in sales and management. In 1956, for the first time, white-collar workers outnumbered blue-collar workers, or people who perform physical labor in industry.

Multinationals and Franchises Many white-collar employees worked for large corporations. As these businesses competed with each other, some expanded overseas. These multinational corporations located themselves closer to important raw materials and benefited from a cheaper labor pool, which made them more competitive.

The 1950s also witnessed the rise of franchises, in which a person owns and runs one or several stores of a chain operation. Because many business leaders believed that consumers valued dependability and familiarity, the owners of chain operations often demanded that their franchises present a uniform look and style.

The Organization Man Like franchise owners, many corporate leaders also expected their employees to conform to company standards. In general, corporations did not desire free-thinking individuals or people who might speak out or criticize the company.

Some social observers recognized this phenomenon and disapproved of it. In his 1950 book, *The Lonely Crowd,* sociologist **David Riesman** argued that this conformity was changing people. Formerly, he claimed, people were "inner-directed," judging themselves on the basis of their own values and the esteem of their families. Now, however, people were becoming "other-directed," concerning themselves with winning the approval of the corporation or community.

In his 1956 book *The Organization Man,* writer **William H. Whyte, Jr.,** assailed the similarity many business organizations cultivated in order to keep any individual from dominating. "In group doctrine," Whyte wrote, "the strong personality is viewed with overwhelming suspicion," and the person with ideas is considered "a threat."

The New Consumerism The conformity of the 1950s included people's desires to own the same new products as their neighbors. With more disposable income, Americans bought more luxury items, such as refrigerators, washing machines, vacuum cleaners, and air conditioners. Americans also bought a variety of labor-saving machines. As *House and Garden* magazine boasted in a 1954 article, coffeemakers, blenders, and lawn trimmers "[replaced] the talents of caretaker, gardener, cook, [and] maid."

"He never wastes a minute, J.P.—that's his lunch."

Analyzing *Political Cartoons*

The Organization Man In the 1950s, more and more people worked in white-collar corporate jobs. Some social critics worried that this development emphasized conformity. In what other ways did society encourage people to conform?

---

2 TEACH

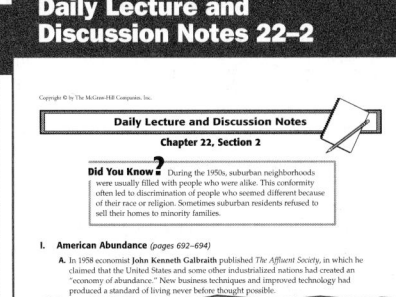

Daily Lecture and Discussion Notes 22–2

Copyright © by The McGraw-Hill Companies, Inc.

Daily Lecture and Discussion Notes

Chapter 22, Section 2

Did You Know? During the 1950s, suburban neighborhoods were usually filled with people who were alike. This conformity often led to discrimination of people who seemed different because of their race or religion. Sometimes suburban residents refused to sell their homes to minority families.

I. American Abundance (pages 692–694)

A. In 1958 economist John Kenneth Galbraith published *The Affluent Society,* in which he claimed that the United States and some other industrialized nations had created an "economy of abundance." New business techniques and improved technology had produced a standard of living never before thought possible.

Discussing a Concept Have students discuss how lifestyles have changed since World War II. Ask them to consider the number of entertainment items their family owns, from televisions to computers, CD players, and sports equipment. Ask them to suggest the kind of leisure-related possessions families probably owned in the 1920s and 1930s. **L2**

Evaluating Trends The 1950s was a time of conformity in the workplace. Ask students if they think encouraging conformity and adherence to company standards is a good idea or not. How do they think it would affect worker productivity? **L2**

Analyzing *Political Cartoons*

Answer: social pressure to purchase similar consumer goods and homes, pressure to "keep up with the Joneses"

Ask: What distinguishes a white-collar job from a blue-collar job? *(White-collar workers are employed in sales and management positions, while blue-collar workers perform physical labor in industry.)*

Reading Strategy | **READING THE TEXT**

Summarizing Information Summarizing information teaches students to reduce information and to rethink what they have read. Have students read the paragraphs under "American Abundance" and then summarize what they have just read. Remind students that only the main ideas should be included in their summaries. When the summaries are complete, have students determine whether they have included all the main ideas by asking themselves: Can my summary be easily understood by someone who has not read the selection? **L1**

👉 Refer to *Inclusion for the High School Social Studies Classroom Strategies and Activities* in the TCR.

L1/ELL

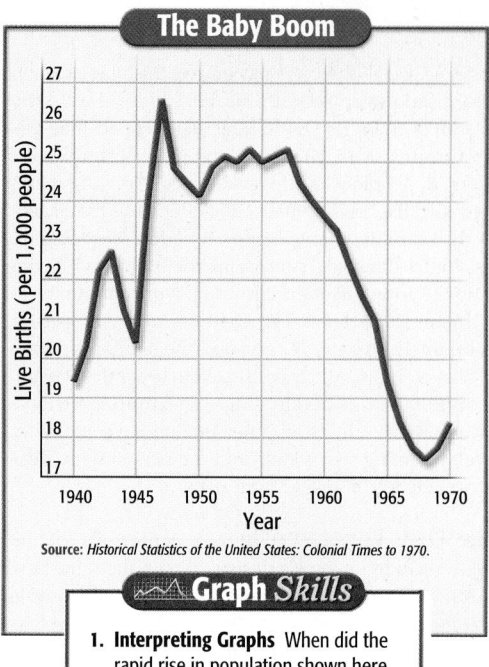

The Baby Boom

Source: *Historical Statistics of the United States: Colonial Times to 1970.*

Graph *Skills*

1. **Interpreting Graphs** When did the rapid rise in population shown here reach its peak?
2. **Analyzing Cause and Effect** What factors contributed to this rapid rise in births?

Graph *Skills*

Answers:

1. about 1947

2. Couples had delayed marriage until after the war and could now afford a family, and popular culture celebrated pregnancy, parenthood, and large families.

Graph Skills Practice

Ask: What do you suppose caused the birth rate to rise again in the late 1960s? *(The first baby boomers were having children of their own.)*

Reading Check

Answer: causes: new business techniques and improved technology; effects: answers may include consumerism and growth of suburbs

CURRICULUM CONNECTION

Geography Three Levittowns were built, the first on Long Island, the second in Bucks County, Pennsylvania, and the third in Willingboro, New Jersey. These planned communities allowed people to live in smaller communities but commute to larger cities.

Accompanying the nation's spending spree was the growth of more sophisticated advertising. Advertising became the fastest-growing industry in the United States, as manufacturers employed new marketing techniques to sell their products. These techniques were carefully planned to whet the consumer's appetite. The purpose of these advertisers was to influence choices among brands of goods that were essentially the same. According to the elaborate advertising campaigns of the time, a freezer became a promise of plenty, a second car became a symbol of status, and a mouthwash became the key to immediate success.

The Growth of Suburbia Advertisers targeted their ads to consumers who had money to spend. Many of these consumers lived in the nation's growing suburbs that grew up around cities.

Levittown, New York, was one of the earliest of the new suburbs. The driving force behind this planned residential community was Bill Levitt, who mass-produced hundreds of simple and similar-looking homes in a potato field 10 miles east of New York City. Between 1947 and 1951, thousands of families rushed to buy the inexpensive homes, and

soon other communities similar to Levittown sprang up throughout the United States.

Suburbs became increasingly popular throughout the 1950s, accounting for about 85 percent of new home construction. The number of suburban dwellers doubled, while the population of cities themselves rose only 10 percent. Reasons for the rapid growth of suburbia varied. Some people wanted to escape the crime and congestion of city neighborhoods. Others viewed life in the suburbs as a move up to a better life for themselves and their children. In contrast to city life, suburbia offered a more picturesque environment. As developers in earlier periods had done, the developers of the 1950s attracted home buyers with promises of fresh air, green lawns, and trees.

Affordability became a key factor in attracting home buyers to the suburbs. Because the GI Bill offered low-interest loans, new housing was more affordable during the postwar period than at any other time in American history. Equally attractive was the government's offer of income tax deductions for home mortgage interest payments and property taxes. For millions of Americans, the suburbs came to symbolize the American dream. They owned their homes, sent their children to good schools, lived in safe communities, and enjoyed economic security.

Nevertheless, some social commentators, such as architect Lewis Mumford and writer John Keats, viewed such plain and identical-looking communities as another sign of conformity. "You too can find a box of your own," wrote Keats, "inhabited by people whose age, income, number of children, problems, habits, conversations, dress, possessions, perhaps even blood types are almost precisely like yours."

Reading Check
Interpreting What were two causes and effects of the economic boom of the 1950s?

The 1950s Family

In addition to all the other transformations taking place in the nation during the 1950s, the American family also was changing. Across the country, many families grew larger, and more married women entered the workforce.

The Baby Boom The American birthrate exploded after World War II. From 1945 to 1961, a period known as the baby boom, more than 65 million children were born in the United States. At the height of the baby boom, a child was born every seven seconds.

Several factors contributed to the baby boom. First, young couples who had delayed marriage during

---

DIFFERENTIATED INSTRUCTION

At-Risk Students To address the needs of visual learners, have students work with a map of a large metropolitan area. Have them identify the suburbs and the city center. Also, have students label or identify the major shopping malls around the city. Discuss how suburbs changed the landscape and the lifestyles of people in the 1950s. **L1**

Refer to *Inclusion for the High School Social Studies Classroom Strategies and Activities* in the TCR.

World War II and the Korean War could now marry, buy homes, and begin their families. In addition, the government encouraged the growth of families by offering generous GI benefits for home purchases. Finally, on television and in magazines, popular culture celebrated pregnancy, parenthood, and large families.

Women in the Fifties Many women focused on their traditional role of homemaker during the 1950s. Even though 8 million American women had gone to work during the war, the new postwar emphasis on having babies and establishing families now discouraged women from seeking employment. Many Americans assumed that a good mother should stay home to take care of her children.

"Let's face it, girls," declared one female writer in *Better Homes and Gardens* in April 1955, "that wonderful guy in your house—and in mine—is building your house, your happiness and the opportunities that will come to your children." The magazine advised stay-at-home wives to "set their sights on a happy home, a host of friends and a bright future through success in HIS job."

Despite the popular emphasis on homemaking, however, the number of women who held jobs outside the home actually increased during the 1950s. Most women who went to work did so in order to help their families maintain their comfortable lifestyles. By 1960 nearly one-third of all married women were part of the paid workforce.

✔ **Reading Check** **Evaluating** What were three factors that contributed to the baby boom?

Technological Breakthroughs

As the United States underwent many social changes during the postwar era, the nation also witnessed several important scientific advances. In medicine, space exploration, and electronics, American scientists broke new ground during the 1950s.

Advances in Electronics The electronics industry made rapid advances after World War II. In 1947 three American physicists—John Bardeen, Walter H. Brattain, and William Shockley—developed the transistor, a tiny device that generated electric signals and made it possible to miniaturize radios and calculators.

The age of computers also dawned in the postwar era. In 1946 scientists working under a U.S. Army contract developed one of the nation's earliest computers—known as ENIAC (Electronic Numerical Integrator and Computer)—to make military calculations. Several years later, a newer model called UNIVAC (Universal Automatic Computer) would handle business data and launch the computer revolution. The computer, along with changes and improvements in communication and transportation systems, allowed many Americans to work more quickly and efficiently. As a result, families in the 1950s had more free time, and new forms of leisure activity became popular.

Medical Miracles The medical breakthroughs of the 1950s included the development of powerful antibiotics to fight infection; the introduction of new drugs to combat arthritis, diabetes, cancer, and heart

The Incredible Shrinking Computer

Past: The First Computer
ENIAC (Electronic Numerical Integrator and Computer) was the first large-scale digital computer. Operating from 1946 to 1955, its primary function was to provide data for the military. It weighed more than 30 tons and took up 1,800 square feet—more than some houses!

Present: Modern Marvels
Modern computers are very small and very fast. Many personal computers now fit easily in a briefcase or backpack. They are also more efficient. While the ENIAC could perform approximately 5,000 calculations per second, the typical home computer performs about 70 million calculations per second—14,000 times faster!

Suburban Dream Developers attracted homebuyers to the suburbs with the promise of fresh air, green lawns, and trees. The names of many suburbs and subdivisions echoed that promise by including words such as park, forest, woods, grove, or hills.

✔ **Reading Check**

Answer: delayed marriages, affordable housing, and popular culture

Even if you do not have your own personal computer or laptop, you use computer technology everyday. Computers designed to handle specific functions control many appliances. For example, a small computer program that determines the setting and timing used to pop a perfect batch of popcorn is behind the "popcorn" setting on a microwave oven.

Creating a Chart Provide the data below and ask students to chart the U.S. home ownership rate from 1900 to 2000. Ask students to offer explanations for noticeable trends. **L2**

Year	Rate	Year	Rate
2000	67.40%	1940	43.60%
1990	64.20%	1930	47.80%
1980	64.40%	1920	45.60%
1970	62.90%	1910	45.90%
1960	61.90%	1900	46.70%
1950	55.00%		

INTERDISCIPLINARY CONNECTIONS ACTIVITY

Science Have students research one of the technological or medical advances discussed in this section. Have them identify the inventor or researcher who discovered and developed the advance, the way in which it changed American society, and whether it is still in use today. If the advance has become obsolete, have students identify its replacement. Students should present their findings in an illustrated report. **L2**

FYI

Parents of baby boomers seized the opportunity to give their children what they themselves never had. Memories of rationing and limited supplies during the Great Depression and World War II often fueled their enthusiasm for activities such as music lessons and Little League.

3 ASSESS

Assign Section 2 Assessment as homework or as an in-class activity.

🌐 Have students use the **Interactive Tutor Self-Assessment CD-ROM.**

L1/ELL

Reading Essentials and Study Guide 22–2

Picturing History

Polio Epidemic In the 1940s and 1950s, Americans were very concerned about the wave of polio cases that struck so many young children. Here, devices known as iron lungs help polio patients breathe. *How did people try to safeguard against the spread of the disease?*

disease; and groundbreaking advances in surgical techniques. Polio, however, continued to baffle the medical profession.

Periodic polio epidemics had been occurring in the United States since 1916. The disease had even struck the young Franklin Roosevelt and forced him to use a wheelchair. In the 1940s and 1950s, however, polio struck the nation in epidemic proportions. Officially known as infantile paralysis because it generally targeted the young, the disease brought a wave of terror to the country. No one knew where or when polio would strike, but an epidemic broke out in some area of the country each summer, crippling and killing its victims. People watched helplessly while neighbors fell sick. Many died, and those who did not were often confined to iron lungs—large metal tanks with pumps that helped patients breathe. If they eventually recovered, they were often paralyzed for the rest of their lives.

Because no one knew what caused the disease, parents searched for ways to safeguard their families each summer. Some sent their children to the country to avoid excessive contact with others. Public swimming pools and beaches were closed. Parks and playgrounds across the country stood deserted. Nevertheless, the disease continued to strike. In 1952 a record 58,000 new cases were reported.

Finally, a research scientist named **Jonas Salk** developed an injectable vaccine that prevented polio. Salk first tested the vaccine on himself, his wife, and his three sons. It was then tested on 2 million schoolchildren. In 1955 the vaccine was declared safe and effective and became available to the general public. The results were spectacular. New cases of polio fell to 5,700 in 1958 and then to 3,277 in 1960. American scientist Albert Sabin then developed an oral vaccine for polio. Because it was safer and more convenient than Salk's injection vaccine, the Sabin vaccine became the most common form of treatment against the disease. In the years to come, the threat of polio would almost completely disappear.

Conquering Space After the Soviet Union launched *Sputnik,* the world's first space satellite, in October 1957, the United States hastened to catch up with its

CRITICAL THINKING ACTIVITY

Determining Cause and Effect During the 1950s, American economic production was quite high. To ensure that people bought enough to match the output, business and government often followed certain policies or practices: (1) built-in obsolescence meant that consumers needed to replace a product often—a new car every year, for example; (2) advertising to create new demand; (3) the shipping of excess food and technology to less-advantaged nations; and (4) public programs, such as interstate highways, that required massive consumption. Ask students to discuss what would happen if an oversupply of goods vanished. How would these policies change in an economy of scarcity? **L1**

Cold War rival. Less than four months later, on January 31, 1958, the United States launched its own satellite from Cape Canaveral, Florida. Reporter Milton Bracker described the jubilant scene:

66As the firing command neared, a deadly silence fell on those who were watching. In the glare of the searchlights, a stream of liquid oxygen could be seen venting like a lavender cloud from the side of the seventy-foot rocket. . . . At fourteen and one-half seconds after time zero, after the priming fuel had ignited almost invisibly, the main stage engine came to life with an immeasurable thrust of flame in all directions. . . . With thousands of eyes following it, the rocket dug into the night and accelerated as its sound loudened. Spectators on near-by beaches pointed and craned their necks and cried, 'There it is!' and began to cheer.99

—quoted in *Voices from America's Past*

Meanwhile, engineers were building smoother and faster commercial planes. Poet Carl Sandburg wrote about taking the first American jet flight from New York to Los Angeles. The trip took only five and a half hours. "You search for words to describe the speed of this flight," wrote an amazed Sandburg.

Profiles IN HISTORY

Dr. Jonas Salk
1914–1995

The man who developed the vaccine for one of the nation's most feared diseases almost did not go into medicine. Jonas Salk enrolled in college as a pre-law student but soon changed his mind. "My mother didn't think I would make a very good lawyer," Salk said, "probably because I could never win an argument with her." Salk switched his major to premed and went on to become a research scientist.

Salk initially directed the search for a cure to the dreaded ailment of polio at the University of Pittsburgh's Virus Research Laboratory. Every so often, Salk would make rounds in the overcrowded polio wards of nearby Municipal Hospital, where nurses described their feelings of pity and helpless rage as paralyzed children cried for water. As one nurse said, "I can remember how the staff used to kid Dr. Salk—kidding in earnest—telling him to hurry up and do something."

Salk became famous for his breakthrough vaccine. The shy doctor, however, did not desire fame. About his becoming a celebrity, Salk observed that it was "a transitory thing and you wait till it blows over. Eventually people will start thinking, 'That poor guy,' and leave me alone. Then I'll be able to get back to my laboratory."

"You are whisked . . . from an ocean on one side of the continent to an ocean on the opposite side in less time than it takes the sun to trace a 90-degree arc across the sky."

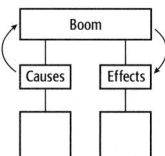 **Reading Check** **Examining** What medical and technological advances met specific needs in the late 1940s and 1950s?

HISTORY Online **Study Central™** To review this section, go to tarvol2.glencoe.com and click on **Study Central™**.

SECTION 2 ASSESSMENT

Checking for Understanding

1. **Define:** white-collar, blue-collar, multinational corporation, franchise, baby boom.
2. **Identify:** John Kenneth Galbraith, David Riesman, Levittown, Jonas Salk.
3. **Describe** how and why the suburbs became popular places to live.

Reviewing Themes

4. **Continuity and Change** How was the affluent society of the United States in the 1950s different from previous decades?

Critical Thinking

5. **Interpreting** What caused the advertising industry boom in the 1950s?
6. **Organizing** Use a graphic organizer similar to the one below to list the causes and effects of the economic boom of the 1950s.

```
        Boom
       /    \
  Causes    Effects
    □          □
```

Analyzing Visuals

7. **Analyzing Photographs** Study the photograph on page 696 of children suffering from polio. What do you think it was like to live in such an environment? Do Americans today face similar medical fears?

Writing About History

8. **Descriptive Writing** Write an article for a magazine such as *Better Homes and Gardens* describing changes the American family underwent during the 1950s.

CHAPTER 22 Postwar America **697**

SECTION 2 ASSESSMENT ANSWERS

1. Terms are in blue.
2. John Kenneth Galbraith (p. 692), David Riesman (p. 693), Levittown (p. 694), Jonas Salk (p. 696)
3. some wanted to escape urban problems; more people were able to afford homes and automobiles
4. The lives of many Americans improved significantly.
5. Advertisers competed for Americans' disposable income.
6. Causes: new business techniques, improved technology; effects: answers may include consumerism and suburban growth
7. Descriptions will vary. It must have been depressing and frustrating both for the patients and the people treating them.
8. Articles should use realistic examples and offer explanations for the changes.

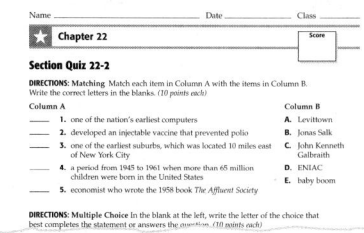
Profiles IN HISTORY

Salk received his medical degree from New York University in 1939.

✓**Reading Check**

Answer: antibiotics; drugs for arthritis, diabetes, cancer, and heart disease; new surgical techniques; polio vaccine

Reteach

Have students explain the effects the nation's economic boom had on American society.

Enrich

Invite students to research scientific advances not mentioned in the section and report back to the class.

Study Central™ provides summaries, interactive games, and online graphic organizers to help students review section content.

4 CLOSE

Have students describe changes in the American family that took place during the 1950s.

1 FOCUS

Section Overview

This section focuses on the popular culture that grew out of postwar prosperity.

BELLRINGER
Skillbuilder Activity

Project transparency and have students answer the question.

Daily Focus Skills Transparency 22–3

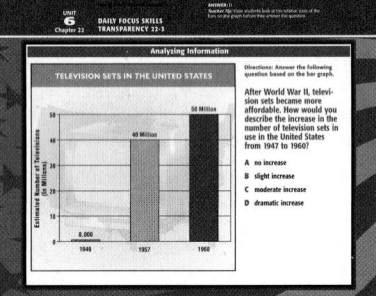

Reading Preview

Answers to Graphic: Television: action shows, game shows, situation comedies, variety shows; radio: recorded music, news, weather, talk shows; cinema: cinemascope, 3-D movies; music: rock 'n' roll; literature: the beat movement

Preteaching Vocabulary
Have students create a database for the Key Terms and Names in this section.

SECTION 3 Popular Culture of the 1950s

Guide to Reading

Main Idea
During the carefree and prosperous 1950s, Americans turned to television, new forms of music, cinema, and literature to entertain themselves.

Key Terms and Names
Ed Sullivan, Alan Freed, Elvis Presley, generation gap, Jack Kerouac, Little Richard

Reading Strategy
Categorizing As you read about the popular culture of the 1950s, complete a graphic organizer similar to the one below comparing new forms of mass media during the 1950s.

New Forms of Mass Media	Description

Reading Objectives
• **Explain** the characteristics of the new youth culture.
• **Discuss** the contributions of African Americans to 1950s culture.

Section Theme
Culture and Traditions The 1950s added such elements as rock 'n' roll music and sitcom television to modern culture.

Preview of Events

♦1955	♦1956	♦1957	♦1958
1955 The quiz show *The $64,000 Question* debuts	**1956** Elvis Presley appears on the *Ed Sullivan Show*; Allen Ginsberg's "Howl" published	**1957** 40 million television sets in use in the United States	**1958** TV quiz show scandals begin to surface

Lucille Ball and Desi Arnaz

★ An American Story ★

In 1953 Lucille Ball and her real-life husband, Desi Arnaz, were starring in one of the most popular shows on American television, *I Love Lucy.* In January, Ball had a baby—both in real life and on her show. Her pregnancy and the birth of her baby became a national event that captivated her audience. A pre-filmed segment of the show showed Lucy and her husband going to the hospital to have the baby, and the show was broadcast only a few hours after the real birth. More than two-thirds of the nation's television sets tuned in, an audience of around 44 million viewers. Far fewer people watched the next day when television broadcast a presidential inauguration.

I Love Lucy was so popular that some people actually set up their work schedules around the show. Marshall Field's, which had previously held sales on the same night the show was on, eventually switched its sales to a different night. A sign on its shop window explained, "We love Lucy too, so we're closing on Monday nights." A relatively new medium, television had swept the nation by the mid-1950s.

—adapted from *Watching TV: Four Decades of American Television*

The New Mass Media

Although regular television broadcasts had begun in the early 1940s, there were few stations, and sets were expensive. By the end of the 1950s, however, the small, black-and-white-screened sets sat in living rooms across the country. Television's popularity

698 CHAPTER 22 Postwar America

SECTION RESOURCES

📖 Reproducible Masters
• Reproducible Lesson Plan 22–3
• Daily Lecture and Discussion Notes 22–3
• Guided Reading Activity 22–3
• Section Quiz 22–3
• Reading Essentials and Study Guide 22–3

✍ Transparencies
• Daily Focus Skills Transparency 22–3

Multimedia
🖥 Interactive Tutor Self-Assessment CD-ROM
🖥 ExamView® Pro Testmaker CD-ROM
🖥 Presentation Plus! CD-ROM
🖥 TeacherWorks™ CD-ROM
🎧 Audio Program
🎵 American Music: Hits Through History
🎵 American Music: Cultural Traditions

forced the other forms of mass media—namely motion pictures and radio—to innovate in order to keep their audiences.

The Rise of Television Popularity

During World War II, televisions became more affordable for consumers. In 1946 it is estimated there were between 7,000 and 8,000 sets in the entire United States. By 1957 there were 40 million television sets in use. Over 80 percent of households had televisions.

By the late 1950s, television news had become an important vehicle for information. Television advertising spawned a growing market for many new products. Advertising, after all, provided television with the money that allowed it to flourish. As one critic concluded, "Programs on television are simply a device to keep the advertisements and commercials from bumping loudly together." Televised athletic events gradually made professional and college sports one of the most prominent sources of entertainment.

Comedy, Action, and Games

Early television programs fell into several main categories including comedy, action and adventure, and variety-style entertainment. Laughter proved popular in other formats besides the half-hour situation comedy. Many of the early television comedy shows, such as those starring Bob Hope and Jack Benny, were adapted from popular old radio shows. Benny enjoyed considerable television success with his routines of bad violin playing and stingy behavior.

Television watchers in the 1950s also relished action shows. Westerns such as *Hopalong Cassidy, The Lone Ranger,* and *Gunsmoke* grew quickly in popularity. Viewers also enjoyed police programs such as *Dragnet,* a hugely successful show featuring Joe Friday and his partner hunting down a new criminal each week.

Variety shows such as **Ed Sullivan's** *Toast of the Town* provided a mix of comedy, opera, popular song, dance, acrobatics, and juggling. Quiz shows attracted large audiences, too, after the 1955 debut of *The $64,000 Question.* In this show and its many imitators, two contestants tried to answer questions from separate glass-encased booths. The questions, stored between shows in a bank vault, arrived at the studio at airtime in the hands of a stern-faced bank executive flanked by two armed guards. The contestants competed head-to-head, with the winner returning the following week to face a new challenger.

TV Nation

Television programming depicted a narrow view of American culture in the 1950s. Most television shows during these years centered around a common image of American life—an image that was predominantly white, middle-class, and suburban, epitomized by the popular situation comedy *The Adventures of Ozzie and Harriet.* Such shows also reinforced traditional gender roles, showing fathers working and mothers staying home to raise children and take care of the house.

Westerns were also popular at the time, especially *The Lone Ranger,* in which a mysterious masked man helped people in distress. *The Howdy Doody Show,* which featured Buffalo Bob and his freckle-faced marionette, was the first network kids' show to run five days a week, the first television show ever broadcast in color, and the first show ever to air more than 1,000 continuous episodes.

Ozzie and Harriet

Tonto and the Lone Ranger

Howdy Doody

COOPERATIVE LEARNING ACTIVITY

Depicting a Culture Organize the students into small groups and encourage them to create a mural that illustrates the broad theme "America in the 1950s." The mural should depict the expansion and prosperity of the American middle-class during this era. Have students divide the work so that everyone participates in choosing what to depict. Some students can work on the layout; some can research for artistic accuracy; and some can provide sketches and lettering. Display the murals outside your classroom for others in the school to enjoy.

Use the rubric for a cooperative group management plan on pages 71–72 in the ***Performance Assessment Activities and Rubrics.***

2 TEACH

Daily Lecture and Discussion Notes 22–3

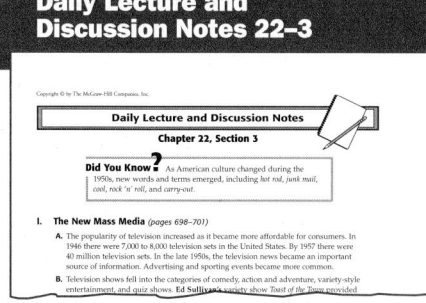

Copyright © by The McGraw-Hill Companies, Inc.

Daily Lecture and Discussion Notes

Chapter 22, Section 3

Did You Know? As American culture changed during the 1950s, new words and terms emerged, including *hot rod, junk mail, cool, rock 'n' roll,* and *carry-out.*

I. **The New Mass Media** (pages 698–701)

A. The popularity of television increased as it became more affordable for consumers. In 1946 there were 7,000 to 8,000 television sets in the United States. By 1957 there were 40 million television sets. In the late 1950s, the television news became an important source of information. Advertising and sporting events became more common.

B. Television shows fell into the categories of comedy, action and adventure, variety-style entertainment, and quiz shows. **Ed Sullivan's** variety show *Toast of the Town* provided

Discussing a Topic Have students develop a list of the various types of television shows such as situation comedies, dramas, reality shows, and game shows. Tell students to pick their three favorite types. Tally the student responses and indicate the top five vote-getters. Then ask students why they think different types of shows have been popular in different periods of television history. **L1**

TV Nation Ask: What segments of society do you think were usually not depicted on television? (*African Americans, Hispanics, poor, farmers*)

FYI

Invented in the 1930s, television became popular in the late 1940s. By 1960 nearly 90 percent of American families owned at least one set—mostly black and white. Although the Columbia Broadcasting System presented the first commercial color telecast in 1953, color television remained too expensive during the 1950s for widespread use.

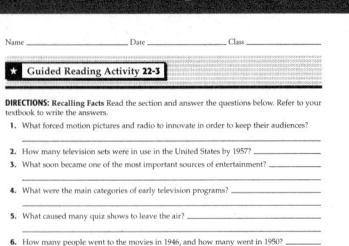

Fact	Fiction	Folklore

The Swanson Company created its first frozen meals in 1952 and started using the name "Swanson TV Dinner" in 1954. Swanson sold 10 million TV dinners the first year they were distributed nationally. By the time the TV dinner celebrated its 45th birthday, Americans were buying 3 million a week. The famous compartmentalized aluminum tray was retired in 1986 and replaced with microwave-safe packaging.

Creating a Culture Dictionary

Have students select a movie video that depicts the 1950s, such as *Back to the Future*, *American Graffiti*, or *Grease* or watch a rerun of a television program that depicts or was popular during the 1950s such as *I Love Lucy*, *Laverne and Shirley*, or *The Many Loves of Dobie Gillis*. Tell them to make a list of the styles, slang expressions, attitudes, and behaviors that are different from those of today. Discuss the lists and then compile them into a 1950s culture dictionary. **L2**

Fact	Fiction	Folklore

Quick and Easy Eats Along with the television came . . . TV dinners! Capitalizing on the television boom of the 1950s, these frozen individual meals offered an entrée, a side dish or two, and a dessert, all on an aluminum tray divided into compartments.

Not everyone actually ate TV dinners in front of the television, but the meals were popular because they offered convenience. Noted one food industry executive of the time, "When Mary Smith rushes home from work late in the afternoon, she wants to buy food that not only will look pretty on the table but is something she can get ready in the half hour before her husband comes home for dinner."

In 1956 the quiz show *Twenty-One* caused an uproar across the nation after **Charles Van Doren,** a young assistant professor with a modest income, won $129,000 during his weeks on the program. The viewing public soon learned, however, that Van Doren and many of the other contestants had received the answers to the questions in advance. Before a congressional committee in 1959, Van Doren admitted his role in the scandal and apologized to his many fans, saying, "I was involved, deeply involved, in a deception." In the wake of the *Twenty-One* fraud, many quiz shows went off the air.

Hollywood Adapts to the Times As the popularity of television grew, movies lost viewers. "Hollywood's like Egypt," lamented producer David Selznick in 1951. "Full of crumbling pyramids." While the film business may not have been collapsing, it certainly did suffer after the war. Attendance dropped from 82 million in 1946 to 36 million by 1950. By 1960, when some 50 million Americans owned a television, one-fifth of the nation's movie theaters had closed.

Throughout the decade, Hollywood struggled mightily to recapture its audience. "Don't be a 'Living Room Captive,'" one industry ad pleaded. "Step out and see a great movie!" When contests, door prizes, and an advertising campaign announcing that "Movies Are Better Than Ever" failed to lure people out of their homes, Hollywood began to try to make films more exciting. Between 1952 and 1954, audiences of 3-D films received special

glasses that gave the impression that a monster or a knife was lunging directly at them from off the screen. Viewers, however, soon tired of both the glasses and the often ridiculous plots of 3-D movies.

Cinemascope, movies shown on large, panoramic screens, finally gave Hollywood a reliable lure. Wide-screen spectacles like *The Robe, The Ten Commandments,* and *Around the World in 80 Days* cost a great deal of money to produce. These blockbusters, however, made up for their cost by attracting huge audiences and netting large profits. The movie industry also made progress by taking the "if you can't beat 'em, join 'em" approach. Hollywood eventually began to film programs especially for television and also sold old movies, which could be rebroadcast cheaply, to the networks.

Like television, the films of the fifties for the most part adhered to the conformity of the times. Roles for single women who did not want families were few and far between. For example, each of Marilyn Monroe's film roles featured the blond movie star as married, soon to be married, or unhappy that she was not married.

Movies with African Americans routinely portrayed them in stereotypical roles, such as maids, servants, or sidekicks for white heroes. Even when African Americans took leading roles, they were often one-dimensional characters who rarely showed human emotions or characteristics. African American actor Sidney Poitier resented having to play such parts:

> ❝The black characters usually come out on the screen as saints, as the other-cheek-turners, as people who are not really people: who are so nice and good. . . . As a matter of fact, I'm just dying to play villains.❞
>
> —quoted in *The Fifties: The Way We Really Were*

Radio Draws Them In Television also lured away radio listeners and forced the radio industry, like Hollywood, to develop new ways to win back audiences. After television took over many of radio's concepts of comedies, dramas, and soap operas, for example, many radio stations began to specialize in presenting recorded music, news, talk shows, weather, public-service programming, and shows for specific audiences.

As a result of this targeted programming, radio stations survived and even flourished. Their numbers more than doubled between 1948, when 1,680

DIFFERENTIATED INSTRUCTION

Reading Support The 1950s often are looked back upon as a time of strong families and friendships. Ask students to think about TV shows that present such an image of the decade. Then review some of the topics covered in the text—the baby boom, the growth of the suburbs, increased consumerism, the rise of TV, and the emergence of rock 'n' roll. Ask students to write some thoughts about possible effects of each topic on people's relationships. **L2**

📁 Refer to *Inclusion for the High School Social Studies Classroom Strategies and Activities* in the TCR.

stations were broadcasting to the nation, and 1957, when more than 3,600 stations filled the airwaves.

 Reading Check **Identifying** How did the television industry affect the U.S. economy?

The New Youth Culture

While Americans of all ages embraced the new mass media, some of the nation's youth rebelled against such a message. During the 1950s, a number of young Americans turned their backs on the conformist ideals adult society promoted. Although these youths were a small minority, their actions brought them widespread attention. In general, these young people longed for greater excitement and freedom, and they found an outlet for such feelings of restlessness in new and controversial styles of music and literature.

Rock 'n' Roll In the early 1950s, rock 'n' roll emerged as the distinctive music of the new generation. In 1951 at a record store in downtown Cleveland,

Ohio, radio disc jockey **Alan Freed** noticed white teenagers buying African American rhythm and blues records and dancing to the music in the store. A week later, Freed won permission from his station manager to play the music on the air. Just as the disc jockey had suspected, the listeners went crazy for it. Soon, white artists began making music that stemmed from these African American rhythms and sounds, and a new form of music, **rock 'n' roll,** had been born.

With a loud and heavy beat that made it ideal for dancing along with lyrics about romance, cars, and other themes that spoke to young people, rock 'n' roll grew wildly popular among the nation's teens. Before long boys and girls around the country were rushing out to buy the latest hits from such artists as Buddy Holly, Chuck Berry, and Bill Haley and the Comets. In 1956 teenagers found their first rock 'n' roll hero in **Elvis Presley.** Presley, who had been born in rural Mississippi and grown up poor in Memphis, Tennessee, eventually claimed the title of "King of Rock 'n' Roll."

While in high school, Presley had learned to play guitar and sing by imitating the rhythm and blues

 Reading Check

Answer: Television spawned a growing market for many new products through advertising and damaged the movie industry until it adapted.

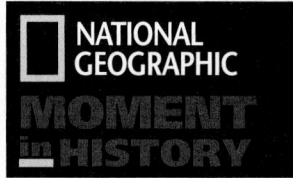

Dancing became extremely popular among teenagers in the 1950s. Teenagers continued to dance the jitterbug that their parents had originated, in addition to their own creations such as line dances, the twist, the bop, the Watusi, the stroll, the slide, the pony, and the monkey.

FYI

Elvis Presley's leather jacket and ducktail haircut became standard dress for young men in the 1950s.

 History *and the* Humanities

- American Music: Hits Through History: "Chances Are," "Little Joe Cook and The Thrillers," "Jet Song," "I'll Fly Away," "I Walk the Line"
- American Music: Cultural Traditions: "Rocket 88," "Rock Around the Clock"
- American Art & Architecture: *Finny Fish,* Rock and Roll Hall of Fame Museum

THE KING OF ROCK
Elvis Presley, shown here signing autographs after a performance in Houston, took American youth in the 1950s by storm. Parents, on the other hand, were less than thrilled with his music—a blend of African American-inspired rhythm and blues and early rock 'n' roll—and his hip-swiveling gyrations on stage. For Presley's first appearance on The Ed Sullivan Show, the host insisted that cameras show him only from the waist up. Elvis added to his fame by starring in a string of films that audiences loved but critics panned.

CHAPTER 22 Postwar America **701**

INTERDISCIPLINARY CONNECTIONS ACTIVITY

Music One way to trace the beginnings of the generation gap is to review the top-selling records during the 1950s. In 1952, for example, such hits as "Blue Tango" and "I Saw Mommy Kissing Santa Claus" dominated the pop charts. By 1956 Doris Day's "Whatever Will Be, Will Be (Que Sera Sera)" competed with Elvis Presley's "Hound Dog." By 1959 rock 'n' roll was pushing for ever-greater dominance on the charts. Ask students to discuss how the music reflected a changing American society. Consider playing music from the 1950s during the discussion. **L2**

✓ Reading Check

Answer: It provided an outlet for feelings of restlessness, separated children and parents, and created a bond among the young.

3 ASSESS

Assign Section 3 Assessment as homework or as an in-class activity.

🌑 Have students use the **Interactive Tutor Self-Assessment CD-ROM.**

L1/ELL

Reading Essentials and Study Guide 22–3

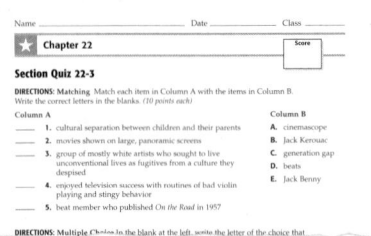

L2

Section Quiz 22–3

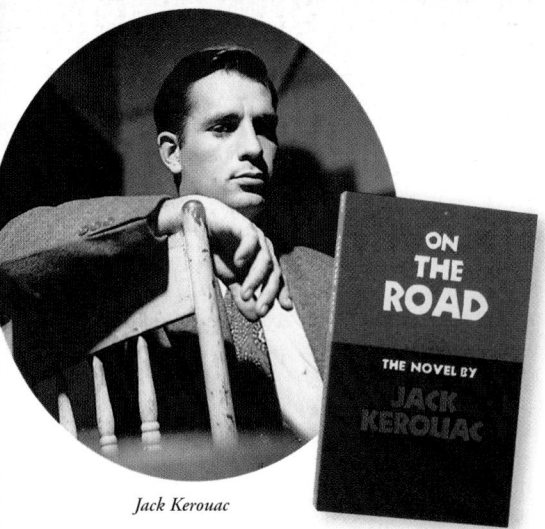

Jack Kerouac

music he heard on the radio. By 1956 Elvis had a record deal with RCA Victor, a movie contract, and public appearances on several television shows. At first the popular television variety show host Ed Sullivan refused to invite Presley on, insisting that the rock 'n' roll music was not fit for a family-oriented show. When a competing show featuring Presley upset his own high ratings, however, Sullivan relented. He ended up paying Presley $50,000 per performance for three appearances, more than triple the amount he had paid any other performer.

The dark-haired and handsome Presley owed his wild popularity as much to his moves as to his music. During his performances he would gyrate his hips and dance in other suggestive ways that shocked many in the audience. Presley himself admitted the importance of this part of his act:

❝I'm not kidding myself. My voice alone is just an ordinary voice. What people come to see is how I use it. If I stand still while I'm singing, I'm dead, man. I might as well go back to driving a truck.❞

—quoted in *God's Country: America in the Fifties*

Not surprisingly, parents—many of whom listened to Frank Sinatra and other more mellow and main-stream artists—condemned rock 'n' roll as loud, mindless, and dangerous. The city council of San Antonio, Texas, actually banned rock 'n' roll from the jukeboxes at public swimming pools. The music, the council declared, "attracted undesirable elements given to practicing their gyrations in abbreviated bathing suits." A minister in Boston complained that "rock and roll inflames and excites youth."

The rock 'n' roll hits that teens bought in record numbers united them in a world their parents did not share. Thus in the 1950s rock 'n' roll helped to create what became known as the generation gap, or the cultural separation between children and their parents.

The Beat Movement If rock 'n' roll helped to create a generation gap, a group of mostly white artists who called themselves the **beats** highlighted a values gap in the 1950s United States. The term *beat* may have come from the feeling among group members of being "beaten down" by American culture, or from jazz musicians who would say, "I'm beat right down to my socks."

The beats sought to live unconventional lives as fugitives from a culture they despised. Beat poets, writers, and artists harshly criticized what they considered the sterility and conformity of American life, the meaninglessness of American politics, and the emptiness of popular culture.

In 1956, 29-year-old beat poet **Allen Ginsberg** published a long poem called "Howl," which blasted modern American life. Another beat member, **Jack Kerouac,** published *On the Road* in 1957. Although Kerouac's book about his freewheeling adventures with a car thief and con artist shocked some readers, the book went on to become a classic in modern American literature.

✓ Reading Check **Summarizing** How did rock 'n' roll help create the generation gap?

African American Entertainers

While artists such as Jack Kerouac rejected American culture, African American entertainers struggled to find acceptance in a country that often treated them as second-class citizens. With a few notable exceptions, television tended to shut out African Americans. In 1956, NBC gave a popular African American singer named Nat King Cole his own 15-minute musical variety show. In 1958, after 64 episodes, NBC canceled the show after failing to secure a national sponsor for a show hosted by an African American.

African American rock 'n' roll singers had more luck gaining acceptance. The talented African American singers and groups who recorded hit songs in the fifties included **Chuck Berry, Ray Charles, Little Richard,** and the **Drifters.** The latter years of the 1950s also saw the rise of several African American women's groups, including the

---

Reading Strategy ⟩ **READING THE TEXT**

Identifying Assumptions Increased spending and the use of consumer credit are trends of the 1950s that imply two assumptions—that Americans believed they deserved the latest and best products and that the economy would continue to prosper. Ask students to review Section 3 and identify other assumptions they can link with specific trends and developments. **L2**

👉 Refer to *Inclusion for the High School Social Studies Classroom Strategies and Activities* in the TCR.

Little Richard

Fats Domino

Picturing **History**

African American Entertainers Rhythm and blues music provided the roots of the 1950s rock 'n' roll sound. Did African American rock 'n' roll artists experience the same acceptance as artists like Elvis Presley? Why or why not?

Picturing **History**

Answer: No, television tended to shut them out, and they often were treated as second-class citizens.
Ask: Why was Nat King Cole's television show canceled before it aired? *(The network was unable to find a sponsor willing to back an African American performer.)*

Crystals, the **Chiffons,** the **Shirelles,** and the **Ronettes.** With their catchy, popular sound, these groups became the musical ancestors of the famous late 1960s groups **Martha and the Vandellas** and the **Supremes.**

Over time, the music of the early rock 'n' roll artists had a profound influence on music throughout the world. Little Richard and Chuck Berry, for example, provided inspiration for the Beatles, whose music swept Britain and the world in the 1960s. Elvis's music transformed generations of rock 'n' roll bands that were to follow him and other pioneers of rock.

Despite the innovations in music and the economic boom of the 1950s, not all Americans were part of the affluent society. For much of the country's minorities and rural poor, the American dream remained well out of reach.

Reading Check **Evaluating** What impact did American rock 'n' roll artists have on the rest of the world?

✓ **Reading Check**

Answer: They influenced music throughout the world and inspired such bands as the Beatles.

Reteach
Have students present a skit, complete with costumes and props, to highlight the characteristics of the new youth culture.

Enrich
Encourage interested students to interview someone who was a teenager or young adult during the 1950s and write a magazine-style article about what life was like.

SECTION 3 ASSESSMENT

HISTORY Online Study Central™ To review this section, go to tarvol2.glencoe.com and click on **Study Central™**.

Checking for Understanding
1. **Define:** generation gap.
2. **Identify:** Ed Sullivan, Alan Freed, Elvis Presley, Jack Kerouac, Little Richard.
3. **Explain** what happened to motion pictures and radio when television became popular.

Reviewing Themes
4. **Culture and Traditions** What roles did African Americans play in television and rock 'n' roll?

Critical Thinking
5. **Comparing** How did the themes of television shows of the 1950s differ from the themes of the literature of the beat movement?
6. **Organizing** Use a graphic organizer similar to the one below to list the styles of music and literature that made up the new youth culture of the 1950s.

[Graphic organizer: New Youth Culture]

Analyzing Visuals
7. **Analyzing Photographs** Study the photographs on pages 698 and 699. Many people have criticized these television programs for presenting a one-sided view of American life. Do you agree with this criticism? Why or why not?

Writing About History
8. **Expository Writing** Imagine you are a beat writer in the 1950s. Explain to your readers how the themes you write about are universal themes that could apply to everyone.

CHAPTER 22 Postwar America **703**

HISTORY Online

Study Central™ provides summaries, interactive games, and online graphic organizers to help students review section content.

4 CLOSE
Have students pose a series of questions that can be used to stimulate discussion about the contributions of African Americans to 1950s culture.

SECTION 3 ASSESSMENT ANSWERS

1. Terms are in blue.
2. Ed Sullivan *(p. 699),* Alan Freed *(p. 701),* Elvis Presley *(p. 701),* Jack Kerouac *(p. 702),* Little Richard *(p. 702)*
3. Motion picture attendance and radio listenership dropped for a while.
4. They had limited opportunities on television but more success in the music industry.
5. Television shows depicted middle-class values endorsing American society; beat literature depicted it as meaningless and sterile.
6. rock 'n' roll and beat literature

7. Students' answers will vary. Most will likely agree that the view was somewhat one-sided.
8. Students' papers will vary. Papers should describe beat themes as being applicable to more than just American culture.

TEACH

Reading Strategy

Verbatim

Have students review the quotes in the Verbatim section and discuss each item as it relates to the people and themes found in the textbook. Have students research a current political, economic, or social issue. Have them find quotations about the issue and create a brief statement explaining the quotes, identifying the people quoted, and describing how the quotes relate to the issue. Ask students to share their lists in a class discussion.

American Scene

Have students look at the graph on page 705 and explain the differences between 1950 and 1960. **Ask:** Why is there an increase in each category? *(As the number of children grew, so did the number participating in sports and recreation.)*

Be Prepared

Have students review the information about bomb shelters. **Ask:** Have you experienced or heard about any similar kind of preparedness effort? *(Answers will vary, but many students will have had personal experience with preparations for Y2K or for natural disasters such as tornadoes.)*

Translation, Please

Have students interview friends and relatives who were teenagers in the 1950s to learn about more teenage lingo. Make a list of all the words and definitions that students bring in.

Numbers 1957

Have students research the current numbers for each item on the list and create a table to show the dollar amounts in 1957 and today.

TIME NOTEBOOK

BETTMANN/CORBIS

Profile

JAMES DEAN *had a brief but spectacular career as a film star. His role in* Rebel Without a Cause *made him an icon for American youth in the mid-50s. In 1955 Dean was killed in a car crash. He was 24.*

"I guess I have as good an insight into this rising generation as any other young man my age. Therefore, when I do play a youth, I try to imitate life. *Rebel Without a Cause* deals with the problems of modern youth. . . . If you want the kids to come and see the picture, you've got to try to reach them on their own grounds. If a picture is psychologically motivated, if there is truth in the relationships in it, then I think that picture will do good."

—from an interview for Rebel Without a Cause

VERBATIM

❝It will make a wonderful place for the children to play in, and it will be a good storehouse, too.❞
MRS. RUTH CALHOUN,
mother of three, on her backyard fallout shelter, 1951

❝Riddle: What's college? That's where girls who are above cooking and sewing go to meet a man they can spend their lives cooking and sewing for.❞
ad for Gimbel's department store campus clothes, 1952

❝Radioactive poisoning of the atmosphere and hence annihilation of any life on Earth has been brought within the range of technical possibilities.❞
ALBERT EINSTEIN,
physicist, 1950

❝If the television craze continues with the present level of programs, we are destined to have a nation of morons.❞
DANIEL MARSH,
President of Boston University, 1950

❝Every time the Russians throw an American in jail, the House Un-American Activities Committee throws an American in jail to get even.❞
MORT SAHL,
comedian, 1950s

WINNERS & LOSERS

POODLE CUTS
Short, curly hairstyle gains wide popularity and acceptance

TV GUIDE
New weekly magazine achieves circulation of 6.5 million by 1959

PALMER PAINT COMPANY OF DETROIT
Sells 12 million paint-by-number kits ranging from simple landscapes and portraits to Leonardo da Vinci's *The Last Supper*

THE DUCKTAIL
Banned in several Massachusetts schools in 1957

COLLIER'S
The respected magazine loses circulation, publishes its final edition on January 4, 1957

LEONARDO DA VINCI'S *THE LAST SUPPER*
Now everyone can paint their own copy to hang in their homes

ARCHIVE PHOTOS

Poodle Cut

SUPER STOCK

The Ducktail

COOPERATIVE LEARNING ACTIVITY

Creating a Magazine Spread Organize the class into small groups and ask them to create their own two-page magazine spread for one year between 1950 and 1960. Encourage students to use elements similar to those that appear in the text but to be creative as they select information. Students should look at current magazines and books for ideas about page design. This activity can be completed using desktop publishing software or the more traditional cut-and-paste method.

Use the rubric for a cooperative group management plan on pages 71–72 in the *Performance Assessment Activities and Rubrics.*

1950s WORD PLAY
Translation, Please!
Match the word to its meaning.

Teen-Age Lingo

1. cool
2. hang loose
3. hairy
4. yo-yo

a. a dull person, an outsider
b. worthy of approval
c. formidable
d. don't worry

answers: 1. b; 2. d; 3. c; 4. a

Bauer/Corbis

Bomb Shelter

Be Prepared

"Know the Bomb's True Dangers. Know the Steps You Can Take to Escape Them!—You Can Survive."
Government pamphlet, 1950

DIGGING YOUR OWN BOMB SHELTER? Better go shopping. Below is a list of items included with the $3,000 Mark I Kidde Kokoon, designed to accommodate a family of five for a three- to five-day underground stay.

- air blower
- radiation detector
- protective apparel suit
- face respirator
- radiation charts (4)
- hand shovel combination (for digging out after the blast)
- gasoline driven generator
- gasoline (10 gallons)

- chemical toilet
- toilet chemicals (2 gallons)
- bunks (5)
- mattresses and blankets (5)
- air pump (for blowing up mattresses)
- incandescent bulbs (2) 40 watts
- fuses (2) 5 amperes
- clock—non-electric

- first aid kit
- waterless hand cleaner
- sterno stove
- canned water (10 gallons)
- canned food (meat, powdered milk, cereal, sugar, etc.)
- paper products

NUMBERS 1957

3¢ Cost of first-class postage stamp

19¢ Cost of loaf of bread

25¢ Cost of issue of *Sports Illustrated*

35¢ Cost of movie ticket

50¢ Cost of gallon of milk (delivered)

$2.05 Average hourly wage

$2,845 Cost of new car

POPPERFOTO/ARCHIVE PHOTO

$5,234 Median income for a family of four

$19,500 Median price to buy a home

American Scene, 1950–1960
(MILLIONS)

	1950	1960
Children 5–14	24.3	35.5
Girl Scouts & Brownies	1.8	4.0
Bicycle Production	2.0	3.8
National Forest Campers	1.5	6.6
Outboard Motors in Use	2.8	5.8

CHAPTER 22 Postwar America **705**

EXTENDING THE CONTENT

Music Popular music in the 1950s included doo-wop. Groups named for birds such as Flamingos and Cardinals, cars such as Cadillacs and El Dorados, or household items such as Coasters or Cufflinks appeared on stage dressed in perfectly matched suits. One member of the group sang falsetto, while the others chimed in with complicated harmonies and syncopated rhythms. Nonsense syllables such as "oooh, oo-wee-oooh" were repeated by the bass singer. Fans loved the romantic, moving sounds and the rhythms. Doo-wop remained at the top of pop music charts until it was displaced by Beatles hits in the early 1960s.

1 FOCUS

Section Overview

This section focuses on the difficulties faced by those who were not included in the postwar economic boom.

BELLRINGER
Skillbuilder Activity

Project transparency and have students answer the question.

Daily Focus Skills Transparency 22–4

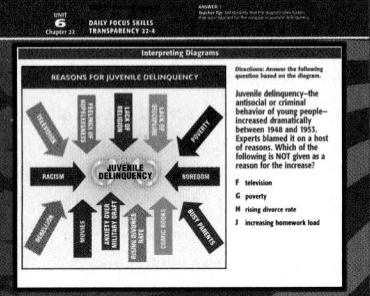

Reading Preview

Answers to Graphic:
The Other Side of American Life
I. Poverty Amidst Prosperity
  A. The Decline of the Inner City
  B. African Americans
  C. Hispanics
  D. Native Americans
  E. Appalachia
II. Juvenile Delinquency

Preteaching Vocabulary
Have students write a short paragraph using at least three of the Key Names or Terms.

SECTION 4   The Other Side of American Life

Main Idea
Not everyone in the United States prospered during the nation's postwar boom, as millions of minorities and rural whites struggled daily with poverty.

Key Terms and Names
poverty line, Michael Harrington, urban renewal, Bracero program, termination policy, juvenile delinquency

Reading Strategy
Taking Notes As you read about social problems in the United States in the 1950s, use the major headings of the section to create an outline similar to the one below.

The Other Side of American Life
I. Poverty Amidst Prosperity
  A.
  B.
  C.
  D.
  E.
II.

Reading Objectives
• **Identify** those groups that found themselves left out of the American economic boom following World War II.
• **Explain** the factors that contributed to the poverty among various groups.

Section Theme
Continuity and Change For some groups, poverty continued during the apparent abundance of the 1950s.

Preview of Events

◆1953   ◆1956   ◆1959   ◆1962

1953
Federal government institutes termination policy directed at Native Americans

1955
Rudolf Flesch's *Why Johnny Can't Read* published

1959
A Raisin in the Sun opens on Broadway

1962
Michael Harrington's *The Other America* published

★ An American Story ★

Lorraine Hansberry

In 1959 Lorraine Hansberry's play, *A Raisin in the Sun,* opened on Broadway. The play told the story of a working-class African American family struggling against poverty and racism. The title referred to a Langston Hughes poem that wonders what happens to an unrealized dream: "Does it dry up like a raisin in the sun?" Hansberry's play won the New York Drama Critics Circle Award for the best play of the year. Reflecting later upon the play's theme, she wrote:

❝Vulgarity, blind conformity, and mass lethargy need not triumph in the land of Lincoln and Frederick Douglass. . . . There is simply no reason why dreams should dry up like raisins or prunes or anything else in the United States. . . . I believe that we can impose beauty on our future.❞

—adapted from *To Be Young, Gifted, and Black*

Poverty Amidst Prosperity

The booming 1950s saw a tremendous expansion of the middle class. In 1950, about 1 in 3 Americans were poor. By 1959, only 1 in 5 were poor. Despite these dramatic gains, about 30 million people still lived below the poverty line, a figure set by the government to reflect the minimum income required to support a family. Such poverty

---

SECTION RESOURCES

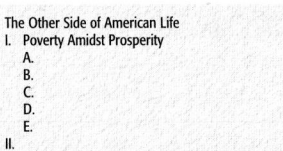

📂 **Reproducible Masters**
• Reproducible Lesson Plan 22–4
• Daily Lecture and Discussion Notes 22–4
• Guided Reading Activity 22–4
• Section Quiz 22–4
• Reading Essentials and Study Guide 22–4
• Performance Assessment Activities and Rubrics

🖥 **Transparencies**
• Daily Focus Skills Transparency 22–4

Multimedia
🖱 Interactive Tutor Self-Assessment CD-ROM
🖱 ExamView® Pro Testmaker CD-ROM
🖱 Presentation Plus! CD-ROM
🖱 TeacherWorks™ CD-ROM
🔊 Audio Program

remained invisible to most Americans, who assumed that the country's general prosperity had provided everyone with a comfortable existence. The writer **Michael Harrington,** however, made no such assumptions. During the 1950s, Harrington set out to chronicle poverty in the United States. In his book, *The Other America,* published in 1962, he alerted those in the mainstream to what he saw in the run-down and hidden communities of the country:

> ❝Tens of millions of Americans are, at this very moment, maimed in body and spirit, existing at levels beneath those necessary for human decency. If these people are not starving, they are hungry, and some-times fat with hunger, for that is what cheap foods do. They are without adequate housing and educa-tion and medical care.❞
>
> —from *The Other America*

The poor included single mothers and the elderly; minority immigrants such as Puerto Ricans and Mexicans; rural Americans, black and white; and inner city residents, who remained stuck in crowded slums as wealthier citizens fled to the suburbs. Poverty also gripped many Americans in the nation's Appalachian region, which stretches from Pennsylvania to Georgia, as well as Native Americans, many of whom endured grinding poverty whether they stayed on reservations or migrated to cities.

ECONOMICS

The Decline of the Inner City The poverty in the 1950s was most apparent in the nation's urban centers. As white families moved to the suburbs, many inner cities became home to poorer, less educated minority groups. The centers of many cities deteriorated, because as the middle class moved out, their tax money went with them. This deprived inner cities of the tax dollars necessary to provide adequate public transportation, housing, and other services.

When government tried to help inner city residents, it often made matters worse. During the 1950s, for example, urban renewal programs tried to eliminate poverty by tearing down slums and erecting new high-rise buildings for poor residents. The crowded, anonymous conditions of these high-rise projects, however, often created an atmosphere of violence. The government also unwittingly encouraged the residents of public housing to remain poor by evicting them as soon as they began to earn any money.

In the end, urban renewal programs actually destroyed more housing space than they created. Too often in the name of urban improvement, the wrecking ball destroyed poor people's homes to make way for roadways, parks, universities, tree-lined boulevards, or shopping centers.

African Americans Many of the citizens left behind in the cities as families fled to the suburbs were African American. The large number of African American inner city residents resulted largely from the migration of more than 3 million African Americans from the South to the North between 1940 and 1960.

Many African Americans had migrated in the hopes of finding greater economic opportunity and escaping violence and racial intimidation. For many of these migrants, however, life proved to be little better in Northern cities. Fewer and fewer jobs were available as numerous factories and mills left the cities for suburbs and smaller towns in order to cut their costs. Long-standing patterns of racial discrimination in schools, housing, hiring, and salaries in the North kept inner-city African Americans poor. The last hired and the first fired for good jobs, they often remained stuck in the worst-paying occupations. In 1958 African American salaries, on average, equaled only 51 percent of what whites earned.

Picturing **History**

Inner-City Poverty This young African American girl in Chicago's inner city struggles to fill a bowl with water that has frozen due to lack of heat. Why did the numbers of poor in the country's inner cities grow in the 1950s?

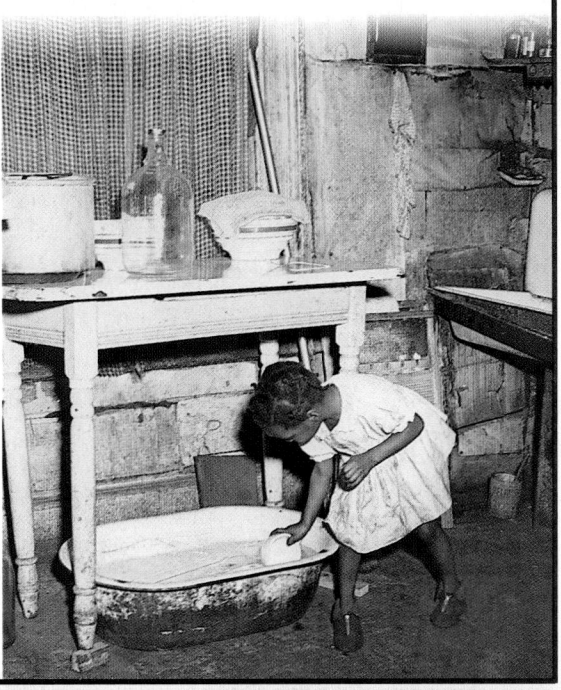

2 TEACH

Daily Lecture and Discussion Notes 22–4

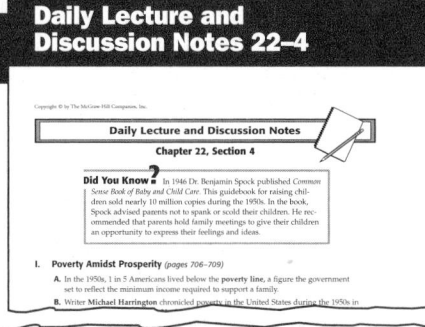

Copyright © by The McGraw-Hill Companies, Inc.

Daily Lecture and Discussion Notes

Chapter 22, Section 4

Did You Know In 1946 Dr. Benjamin Spock published *Common Sense Book of Baby and Child Care.* This guidebook for raising children sold nearly 10 million copies during the 1950s. In the book, Spock advised parents not to spank or scold their children. He recommended that parents hold family meetings to give their children an opportunity to express their feelings and ideas.

I. **Poverty Amidst Prosperity** *(pages 706–709)*
   A. In the 1950s, 1 in 5 Americans lived below the **poverty line,** a figure the government set to reflect the minimum income required to support a family.
   B. Writer **Michael Harrington** chronicled poverty in the United States during the 1950s in

Brainstorming Explain that between 1941 and 1945, one out of every five Americans moved from one area of the country to another. During that time, more than 700,000 African Americans left the South for the North and the West. Ask students to consider what kinds of problems such migration presented for individuals and communities. **L1**

Picturing **History**

Answer: Poor immigrants as well as African Americans from the South moved to the cities.

Ask: How did government programs make things worse for the urban poor? *(Urban renewal replaced slums with high-rise buildings that were plagued by violence. The government unwittingly contributed to poverty by evicting the poor from government housing when they earned too much money.)*

Reading Strategy ▸ **READING THE TEXT**

Using Possible Sentences This strategy allows students to speculate about word meanings. Choose ten vocabulary words and write them on the board. Write sentences using the words either correctly or incorrectly. Then ask students to comment on whether the sentences are "possible." As students encounter the words in the section, they should note the use of each term in the selection's context. After reading, students should reread the sentences and revise them as necessary. **L1** **ELL**

📂 Refer to *Inclusion for the High School Social Studies Classroom Strategies and Activities* in the TCR.

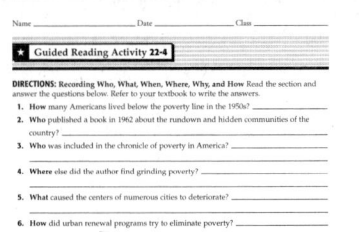

L1/ELL

Guided Reading Activity 22–4

Name _____ Date _____ Class _____

★ Guided Reading Activity 22-4

DIRECTIONS: Recording Who, What, When, Where, Why, and How Read the section and answer the questions below. Refer to your textbook to write the answers.

1. How many Americans lived below the poverty line in the 1950s? ____
2. Who published a book in 1962 about the rundown and hidden communities of the country? ____
3. Who was included in the chronicle of poverty in America? ____
4. Where else did the author find grinding poverty? ____
5. What caused the centers of numerous cities to deteriorate? ____
6. How did urban renewal programs try to eliminate poverty? ____

Picturing **History**

Answer: The government intended to raise their standard of living by integrating them into American society.
Ask: What was the termination policy? (It removed all official recognition of Native American groups as legal entities, making Native Americans subject to the same laws as white citizens.)

Predicting Consequences

Remind students that the life of the poor in the 1950s was very different from the life that middle-class Americans were enjoying. Have students discuss the differences that existed among the classes in the United States. Then ask students to predict the problems that were likely to result from these differences. **L2**

FYI

Lorraine Hansberry achieved another first on April 7, 1959, when she became the first African American, and only the fifth woman, to win the prestigious New York Drama Critics Circle Award for her first play, *A Raisin in the Sun*.

Poverty and racial discrimination also deprived many African Americans of other benefits, such as decent medical care. Responding to a correspondent who had seen *A Raisin in the Sun*, Lorraine Hansberry wrote, "The ghettos are killing us; not only our dreams . . . but our very bodies. It is not an abstraction to us that the average [African American] has a life expectancy of five to ten years less than the average white." Several African American groups, such as the NAACP and the Congress of Racial Equality (CORE), pressed for greater economic opportunity for African Americans. In general, however, these organizations met with little success.

Hispanics African Americans were not the only minority group that struggled with poverty. Much of the nation's Hispanic population faced the same problems. During the 1950s and early 1960s, the **Bracero program** brought nearly 5 million Mexicans to the United States to work on farms and ranches in the Southwest. The Braceros were temporary contract workers, and many later returned home. Some came with their families, however, and about 350,000 settled permanently in the United States.

These laborers, who worked on large farms throughout the country, lived a life of extreme poverty and hardship. They toiled long hours for little pay in conditions that were often unbearable. As Michael Harrington noted, "[The nation's migrant

Picturing **History**

Vocational Training Native American Franklin Beaver learns to become a stone mason at this vocational school sponsored by the U.S. Indian Bureau. Why was the government trying to bring Native Americans into mainstream society?

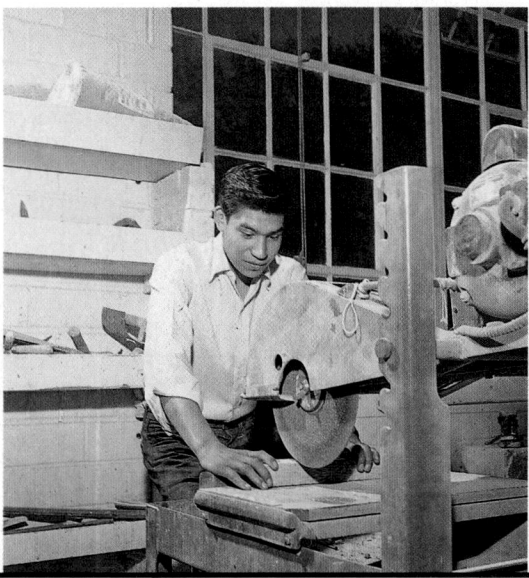

laborers] work ten-eleven-twelve hour days in temperatures over one hundred degrees. Sometimes there is no drinking water. . . . Women and children work on ladders and with hazardous machinery. Babies are brought to the field and are placed in 'cradles' of wood boxes."

Away from the fields, many Mexican families lived in small, crudely built shacks, while some did not even have a roof over their heads. "They sleep where they can, some in the open," Harrington noted about one group of migrant workers. "They eat when they can (and sometimes what they can)." The nation would pay little attention to the plight of Mexican farm laborers until the 1960s, when the workers began to organize for greater rights.

Native Americans Native Americans also faced challenges throughout the postwar era of prosperity. By the middle of the 1900s, Native Americans—who made up less than one percent of the population—were the poorest group in the nation. Average annual family income for Native American families, for example, was $1,000 less than that for African Americans.

After World War II, during which many Native American soldiers had served with distinction, the U.S. government launched a program to bring Native Americans into mainstream society—whether they wanted to assimilate or not. Under the plan, which became known as the termination policy, the federal government withdrew all official recognition of the Native American groups as legal entities and made them subject to the same laws as white citizens. At the same time, the government encouraged Native Americans to blend in to larger society by helping them move off the reservations to cities such as Minneapolis, Minnesota.

Although the idea of integrating Native Americans into mainstream society began with good intentions, some of its supporters had more selfish goals. Speculators and developers sometimes gained rich farmland at the expense of destitute Native American groups.

Most Native Americans found termination a disastrous policy that only deepened their poverty. In the mid-1950s, for example, the Welfare Council of Minneapolis described Native American living conditions in that city as miserable. "One Indian family of five or six, living in two rooms, will take in relatives and friends who come from the reservations seeking jobs until perhaps fifteen people will be crowded into the space," the council reported. During the 1950s, Native Americans in Minneapolis could expect to live only 37 years, compared to 46

DIFFERENTIATED INSTRUCTION

Gifted and Talented Tell students that music has long been a way for people to express their emotions, whether they are joyful or sad. Challenge interested students to take the impressions that they have gained while reading the chapter to compose and perform a song expressing the plight of one of the ethnic groups mentioned in this section. **L3**

📂 Refer to *Inclusion for the High School Social Studies Classroom Strategies and Activities* in the TCR.

Picturing **History**

Poverty in Appalachia This mining family lived in the kind of extreme poverty that was often overlooked in the 1950s. Eight people lived in this three-room house lined with newspaper. *Why was infant mortality so high in Appalachia?*

years for all Minnesota Native Americans and 68 years for other Minneapolis residents. Benjamin Reifel, a Sioux, described the widespread despair that the termination policy produced:

> ❝The Indians believed that when the dark clouds of war passed from the skies overhead, their rising tide of expectations, though temporarily stalled, would again reappear. Instead they were threatened by termination. . . . Soaring expectations began to plunge. Termination took on the connotation of extermination for many.❞
>
> —quoted in *The Earth Shall Weep*

Appalachia The nation's minorities were not the only people dealing with poverty. The picturesque streams and mountains of Appalachia hid the ruined mines, scarred hills, and abandoned farms of impoverished families who had dwelled in these hills for generations.

During the 1950s, 1.5 million people abandoned Appalachia to seek a better life in the nation's cities. They left behind elderly and other less mobile residents. "Whole counties," wrote one reporter who visited the region, "are precariously held together by a flour-and-dried-milk paste of surplus foods. . . . The men who are no longer needed in the mines and the farmers who cannot compete . . . have themselves become surplus commodities in the mountains."

A host of statistics spoke to Appalachia's misery. Studies revealed high rates of nutritional deficiency and infant mortality. Appalachia had fewer doctors per thousand people than the rest of the country, and the doctors it did have were older than their counterparts in other areas. In addition, schooling in the region was considered even worse than in inner city slums.

✓ **Reading Check** **Identifying** Which groups of people were left out of the country's economic boom of the 1950s?

Juvenile Delinquency

During the 1950s, many middle-class white Americans found it easy to ignore the poverty and racism that afflicted many of the nation's minorities, since they themselves were removed from it. Some social problems, however, became impossible to ignore.

One problem at this time was a rise in, or at least a rise in the reporting of, juvenile delinquency—antisocial or criminal behavior of young people. Between 1948 and 1953, the United States saw a 45 percent rise in juvenile crime rates. A popular 1954 book titled *1,000,000 Delinquents* correctly calculated that in the following year, about 1 million young people would get into some kind of criminal trouble. Car thefts topped the list of juvenile crimes, but people were

CHAPTER 22 Postwar America **709**

Picturing **History**
Answer: nutritional deficiencies, few doctors, and poor living conditions
Ask: Why do you think newspapers cover the walls in this house? *(to provide some insulation, to keep out cold drafts and insects)*

✓ **Reading Check**
Answer: African Americans, Hispanics, Native Americans, people in Appalachia

FYI

James Baldwin created a vivid description of African American life in the postwar years in his novel *Go Tell It on the Mountain.* The novel describes a day in the lives of members of a church in Harlem, and, through flashbacks, their ancestors. Baldwin was recognized as a leading African American novelist noted for his powerful treatment of bigotry and oppression in American society.

3 ASSESS

Assign Section 4 Assessment as homework or as an in-class activity.

🖥 Have students use the **Interactive Tutor Self-Assessment CD-ROM.**

L1/ELL

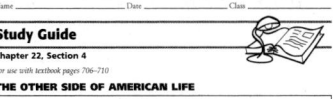

Reading Essentials and Study Guide 22–4

Name _____ Date _____ Class _____

Study Guide
Chapter 22, Section 4
For use with textbook pages 706–710

THE OTHER SIDE OF AMERICAN LIFE

KEY TERMS AND NAMES

poverty line a figure the government set to reflect the minimum income required to support a family *(page 706)*

Michael Harrington author who wrote *The Other America,* which reported on poverty in the United States *(page 707)*

urban renewal type of program that tried to eliminate poverty by tearing down slums and building high-rise buildings for poor residents *(page 707)*

Bracero program a program that brought millions of Mexicans to the United States to help fill the nation's farm labor needs *(page 708)*

termination policy government plan that withdrew all official recognition of the Native

---

INTERDISCIPLINARY CONNECTIONS ACTIVITY

Performing Arts Organize students into small groups and have them discuss what life was like in the 1950s for one of the groups mentioned in this section. Have students produce a skit depicting one aspect of life for the group they selected. Encourage students to use appropriate music to set the tone for their skits. Make arrangements for students to perform for their classmates. **L2**

Section Quiz 22–4

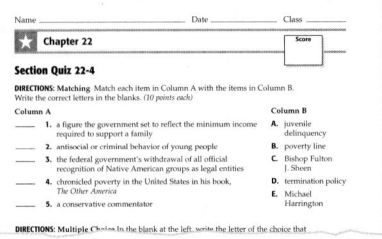

✓ Reading Check

Answer: The educational system could not keep up with population growth and there was a lack of scientific and technical education.

Discussing a Topic Have students discuss the causes of juvenile delinquency. Ask if they think the same conditions exist today. Explore the similarities and differences that they note. L2

Reteach
Identify those groups that found themselves left out of the American economic boom following World War II.

Enrich
Invite interested students to research the life of migrant workers today and compare today's situation to the situation in the 1950s.

Study Central™ provides summaries, interactive games, and online graphic organizers to help students review section content.

4 CLOSE

Explain the factors that contributed to the poverty among various groups.

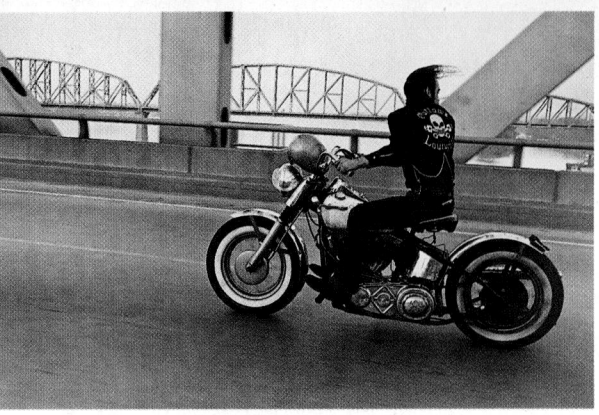

Rebelling Against Conformity This biker, one of the Louisville "Outlaws," fits the stereotype of the 1950s juvenile delinquent.

also alarmed at the behavior of young people who belonged to street gangs and committed muggings, rape, and even murder.

Americans could not agree on what had triggered the rise in delinquency. Experts blamed it on a host of reasons, including poverty, lack of religion, television, movies, comic books, racism, busy parents, a rising divorce rate, and anxiety over the military draft. Some cultural critics claimed that young people were rebelling against the hypocrisy and conformity of their parents. Conservative commentators pinned the blame on a lack of discipline. Doting parents, complained Bishop Fulton J. Sheen, had raised bored children who sought new thrills, such as "alcohol, marijuana, even murder." Liberal observers preferred to pinpoint social causes, blaming teen violence on poverty and feelings of hopelessness among underprivileged youths. Delinquency in the 1950s, however, cut across class

and racial lines—the majority of car thieves, for example, had grown up in middle-class homes.

Most teens, of course, steered clear of gangs, drugs, and crime. Nonetheless, the public tended to stereotype young people as juvenile delinquents, especially those teens who favored unconventional clothing, long hair, or street slang.

Many parents were also growing concerned over the nation's educational system. As baby boomers began entering the school system, they ignited a spurt in school construction. During the 1950s, school enrollments increased by 13 million. School districts struggled to erect new buildings and hire new teachers. Nevertheless, shortages sprang up in both buildings and the people to staff them.

Americans' education worries only intensified in 1957 after the Soviet Union launched the world's first space satellites, *Sputnik I* and *Sputnik II*. Many Americans felt they had fallen behind their Cold War enemy and blamed what they felt was a lack of technical education in the nation's schools. *Life* magazine proclaimed a "Crisis in Education," and offered a grim warning: "What has long been an ignored national problem, *Sputnik* has made a recognized crisis." In the wake of the *Sputnik* launches, efforts began to improve math and science education in the schools. Profound fears about the country's young people, it seemed, dominated the end of a decade that had brought great progress for many Americans.

✓ Reading Check
Evaluating How did many Americans feel about the education system of the 1950s?

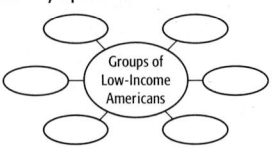

Study Central™ To review this section, go to tarvol2.glencoe.com and click on **Study Central™**.

SECTION 4 ASSESSMENT

Checking for Understanding
1. **Define:** poverty line, urban renewal, termination policy, juvenile delinquency.
2. **Identify:** Michael Harrington, Bracero program.
3. **Evaluate** how the federal government's termination policy affected Native Americans.

Reviewing Themes
4. **Continuity and Change** Why did urban renewal fail the poor of the inner cities?

Critical Thinking
5. **Interpreting** What were some possible reasons for a dramatic rise in juvenile delinquency in the 1950s?
6. **Organizing** Use a graphic organizer similar to the one below to list the groups of Americans who were left out of the country's postwar economic boom.

Groups of Low-Income Americans

Analyzing Visuals
7. **Analyzing Photographs** Study the photograph on this page. What in the photograph might attract young people to this type of life? Why would others oppose such a life?

Writing About History
8. **Expository Writing** Using library or Internet resources, find information about juvenile delinquency in the United States today to write a report. Compare today's problems with those of the 1950s. Share your report with the class.

SECTION 4 ASSESSMENT ANSWERS

1. Terms are in blue.
2. Michael Harrington (p. 707), Bracero program (p. 708)
3. The policy deepened their poverty.
4. The high-rise buildings were too crowded, destroyed more housing than they created, and created an atmosphere of violence.
5. Reasons offered included poverty, lack of supervision, media influences, racism, lack of discipline or of religion.
6. single mothers, elderly, minority immigrants, rural Americans, inner city residents, people in Appalachia
7. Shows a lone cyclist crossing a bridge, unconventional clothes, chance to rebel; many would oppose it because it suggests a rejection of many traditional values
8. Students' reports will vary.

Study and Writing
SKILLBUILDER

Writing a Journal

Why Learn This Skill?

Journal writing is personal writing with a casual style. The style in which you write is not as important as what you write about—your experiences, interests, and feelings. Journal writing can help you generate new ideas, and it can also give you a clearer picture of your thoughts and help you put them in order.

Learning the Skill

A journal is a written account that records what you have learned or experienced. In a journal you can express your feelings about a subject, summarize key topics, describe difficulties or successes in solving particular problems, and draw maps or other visuals. To help you get started writing in your journal, follow these steps.

- Jot down notes or questions about a specific topic or event as you read your textbook. Then look for details and answers about it as you continue reading.

- Describe your feelings as you read a selection or look at a photograph. Are you angry, happy, frustrated, or sad? Explain why you are reacting in this way.

- Ask yourself if drawing a map or flowchart would help you understand an event better. If so, draw in your journal.

Practicing the Skill

The following excerpt is a journal entry describing the launching of the nation's first satellite in 1958. Read the excerpt, and then use the following questions to help you write entries in your own journal.

"As the firing command neared, a deadly silence fell on those who were watching. . . . At fourteen and one-half seconds after time zero, after the priming fuel had ignited almost invisibly, the main stage engine came to life with an immeasurable thrust of flame in all directions. . . . With

thousands of eyes following it, the rocket dug into the night and accelerated as its sound loudened. Spectators on nearby beaches pointed and craned their necks and cried, 'There it is!' and began to cheer."

❶ What is particularly interesting about this description?

❷ What are your feelings as you read the excerpt?

❸ Note the descriptive phrases and details that make the event come to life. Try to use similar techniques when writing in your journal.

❹ Draw a map or other visual to help you understand the situation described here.

Cover from a World War II journal

Skills Assessment

Complete the Practicing Skills questions on page 713 and the Chapter 22 Skill Reinforcement Activity to assess your mastery of this skill.

Applying the Skill

Writing a Journal Imagine that you have had the chance to take part in a great adventure—for instance, serving in the armed forces during a war overseas or participating in a spaceflight. Make notes for a journal entry describing what you have done and seen.

 Glencoe's **Skillbuilder Interactive Workbook CD-ROM, Level 2,** provides instruction and practice in key social studies skills.

711

Study and Writing
SKILLBUILDER

TEACH

Journal Writing Tell students that journal writing can help with generating ideas, with placing events or reactions in context, and with being able to put their thoughts in order.

Encourage students to keep a journal about their lives and experiences for a week. Ask volunteers to share one thing that they learned about themselves or their experiences in the process.

Additional Practice

L1

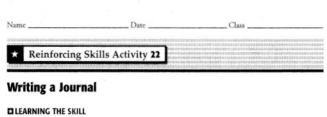

Reinforcing Skills Activity 22

Name _____ Date _____ Class _____

★ Reinforcing Skills Activity 22

Writing a Journal

□ **LEARNING THE SKILL**
Journals contain personal accounts, feelings, and reflections on experiences. Writing in a journal can help you express your thoughts, gain understanding, and think creatively. A journal might include maps or other visuals, as well as personal writing. To write a journal entry in response to your reading, begin by writing questions or thoughts about the subject matter, and then look for answers or related material as you read. Describe your reactions and feelings as you read. Consider drawing visuals such as a flowchart to help you understand the material better.

□ **PRACTICING THE SKILL**
DIRECTIONS: Read the excerpt below from Robert Friedman's "The Baby Boom Turns 50." On a separate sheet of paper, use the questions that follow to help you write journal entries in response to the reading.

GLENCOE
TECHNOLOGY

 CD-ROM
Glencoe Skillbuilder Interactive Workbook CD-ROM, Level 2

This interactive CD-ROM reinforces student mastery of essential social studies skills.

ANSWERS TO PRACTICING THE SKILL

Possible answers:
❶ the precision and moment-by-moment quality of the description
❷ suspense, excitement
❸ Answers will vary.

❹ Visual representations will vary. Have students share them with the class.

Applying the Skill
Journal entries will vary. Encourage students to use the techniques learned in this Skillbuilder activity.

Reviewing Key Terms

Students' answers will vary. The pages where the words appear in the text are shown in parentheses.

1. **closed shop** (p. 687)
2. **right-to-work law** (p. 687)
3. **union shop** (p. 687)
4. **featherbedding** (p. 687)
5. **dynamic conservatism** (p. 689)
6. **white-collar** (p. 693)
7. **blue-collar** (p. 693)
8. **multinational corporation** (p. 693)
9. **franchise** (p. 693)
10. **baby boom** (p. 694)
11. **generation gap** (p. 702)
12. **poverty line** (p. 706)
13. **urban renewal** (p. 707)
14. **termination policy** (p. 708)
15. **juvenile delinquency** (p. 709)

Reviewing Key Facts

16. GI Bill (p. 687), Fair Deal (p. 688), John Kenneth Galbraith (p. 692), David Riesman (p. 693), Ed Sullivan (p. 699), Alan Freed (p. 701), Elvis Presley (p. 701), Jack Kerouac (p. 702), Michael Harrington (p. 707)

17. The three characteristics of the post-war economy were abundant goods, low unemployment, and a housing boom.

18. The economic boom was the result of consumerism and the GI Bill.

19. They wanted to escape urban crime and make a better life for their families. They had automobiles to transport them to and from work.

Reviewing Key Terms

On a sheet of paper, use each of these terms in a sentence.

1. closed shop
2. right-to-work law
3. union shop
4. featherbedding
5. dynamic conservatism
6. white-collar
7. blue-collar
8. multinational corporation
9. franchise
10. baby boom
11. generation gap
12. poverty line
13. urban renewal
14. termination policy
15. juvenile delinquency

Reviewing Key Facts

16. **Identify:** GI Bill, Fair Deal, John Kenneth Galbraith, David Riesman, Ed Sullivan, Alan Freed, Elvis Presley, Jack Kerouac, Michael Harrington.

17. What were three characteristics of the economy of the United States after World War II?

18. What were two reasons for the economic boom of the 1950s?

19. What caused many Americans to move to the suburbs in the 1950s?

20. How did the scientific discovery of the transistor affect communications?

21. Which groups of Americans found themselves left out of the postwar economic boom?

Critical Thinking

22. **Analyzing Themes: Continuity and Change** How has mass media changed since the 1950s?

23. **Evaluating** What factors led to a rise in juvenile delinquency in the United States during the 1950s?

24. **Comparing and Contrasting** Harry S Truman was a Democrat, and Dwight D. Eisenhower was a Republican. How were the domestic agendas of these two presidents different? How were they similar?

25. **Interpreting Primary Sources** George Gallup, one of the nation's first pollsters, spoke at the University of Iowa in 1953 about the importance of mass media in the United States. Read the excerpt and answer the questions that follow.

❝One of the real threats to America's future place in the world is a citizenry which duly elects to be entertained and not informed. From the time the typical citizen arises and looks at his morning newspaper until he turns off his radio or television set before going to bed,

Chapter Summary

	Signs of Prosperity	Signs of Inequality
Economy	• The GI Bill provided loans to millions of war veterans. • Consumer spending increased rapidly. • More Americans owned homes than ever before.	• Workers went on strike for higher wages. • Truman's civil rights bill did not pass. • Eisenhower cut back New Deal programs.
Population Patterns	• The U.S. population grew dramatically. • The number of working women increased.	• Financially able people moved from crowded cities to new suburbs. • Many poor people remained in cities that now faced major economic and social problems.
Science, Technology, and Medicine	• Medical breakthroughs included the polio vaccine, antibiotics, and treatments for heart disease, arthritis, cancer, and diabetes. • Improvements in communication, transportation, and electronics allowed Americans to work more efficiently.	• Many poor people in inner cities and rural areas had limited access to health care.
Popular Culture	• Popular culture included new forms of music, radio, cinema, and literature. • Television replaced radio as the nation's newest form of mass media.	• African Americans and other minorities were, for the most part, not depicted on television. • Many television programs promoted stereotypical gender roles.

20. The transistor made the miniaturization of radios and calculators possible and resulted in improvements in communication and transportation.

21. Single mothers, the elderly, minority immigrants, rural Americans, inner-city residents, African Americans, Hispanics, Native Americans, and people in Appalachia were left out of the postwar economic boom.

Critical Thinking

22. Mass media has become more pervasive. Hundreds of radio and television stations, as well as the Internet, are available 24 hours a day, 7 days a week.

23. Different reasons were suggested, including poverty, lack of supervision, media influences, racism, lack of discipline or of religion.

HISTORY Online

Self-Check Quiz
Visit the *American Republic Since 1877* Web site at tarvol2.glencoe.com and click on **Self-Check Quizzes–Chapter 22** to assess your knowledge of chapter content.

he has unwittingly cast his vote a hundred times for entertainment or for education. Without his knowing it, he has helped to determine the very character of our three most important media of communication—the press, radio, and television. . . . 99

—quoted in *Vital Speeches of the Day*

a. According to Gallup, what is a threat to the future of the United States in the world?

b. How do American citizens determine what is read, seen, and heard in the mass media?

26. **Organizing** Use a graphic organizer similar to the one below to list the changes to the American family during the 1950s.

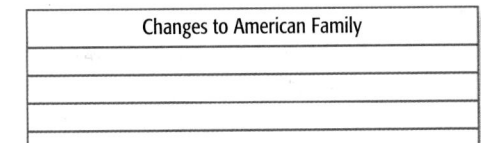

Changes to American Family

Practicing Skills

27. **Writing a Journal** Imagine that you are Dr. Jonas Salk, and you realize that you have just discovered the world's first successful polio vaccine. Write a journal entry that describes how you feel about this accomplishment and what impact it will have on the world.

Writing Activity

28. **Writing a Book Report** Read one of the books about American society in the 1950s, such as *Why Johnny Can't Read* or *The Other America*. Write a book report explaining the main concepts of the book and whether or not the issues are similar to or different from the main issues in American society today.

Chapter Activities

29. **American History Primary Source Document Library CD-ROM** Read the speech "On Television" by Newton Minow, under *The Postwar World*. Working with a few of your classmates, evaluate whether television has improved since Minow's critical assessment. Has television content changed since the 1950s? If so, how? Present your findings and comparisons to your class.

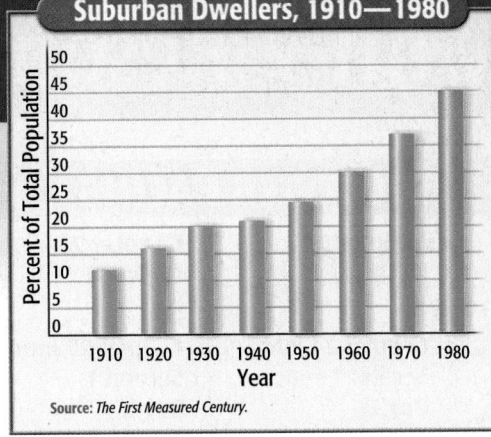

Suburban Dwellers, 1910—1980

Source: *The First Measured Century.*

30. **Research Project** Work with a small group to research advertisements from the 1950s. Write a report comparing and contrasting advertisements from that decade with advertisements today. Present one or more of the advertisements along with your comparisons to your class.

Geography and History

31. The graph above shows the number of suburban dwellers in the United States as a percentage of the total population. Study the data displayed in the graph and answer the questions below.

a. **Interpreting Graphs** What trend in the percentage of suburban dwellers does this graph show?

b. **Understanding Cause and Effect** How might the trend of suburban dwellers shown on this graph have affected life in suburbs and cities?

Standardized Test Practice

Directions: Choose the phrase that best completes the following statement.

Which of the following did the Eisenhower administration work to achieve?

F Fixing wage and price controls

G Defeating the Federal Highway Act

H Repealing right-to-work laws

J Extending the Social Security system

Test-Taking Tip: Pay careful attention to the wording of the question. Note that three of the four answer choices were not part of Eisenhower's programs.

HISTORY Online

Have students visit the Web site at tarvol2.glencoe.com to review Chapter 22 and take the Self-Check Quiz.

Writing Activity
28. Students' reports will vary. Be sure students include some comparison to problems in society today.

Chapter Activities
29. Students' findings should point out differences and similarities in content. Their assessments of television should reflect a critical look at available programs.

30. Students' comparisons will vary. Encourage students to share their findings with the class.

Geography and History
31. **a.** rising; **b.** caused urban life to decline and suburban life to become the ideal

---

Standardized Test Practice

Answer: J
Test-Taking Tip: Encourage students to consider the goals of dynamic conservatism. **Ask:** Which answer is most consistent with those goals?

Bonus Question ?

Ask: What does the term Baby Boom refer to? *(a sixteen-year period from 1945 to 1961 when 65 million children were born in the United States)*

---

24. Differences: Truman's policies included aggressive federal spending, the creation of public housing, and a system of national health insurance. Eisenhower's policies included curbing federal spending, ending government price and rent controls, and cutting aid to public housing and business. Similarities: Both presidents expanded Social Security and raised the minimum wage.

25. **a.** He feared a citizenry that chose to be entertained and not informed. **b.** They do it by the choices they make in forms of entertainment.

26. the move to suburbs, travel by automobile, growing gap between generations

Practicing Skills
27. Journal entries should reflect what the students know about Salk, such as the fact that he preferred research to celebrity.

Unit 7 (1 Day)	Chapter 23 (4 Days)	Chapter 24 (4 Days)	Chapter 25 (5 Days)	Chapter 26 (5 Days)	Unit 7 (2 Days)
Day 1 Introduction	**Day 1** Chapter 23 Intro, Section 1	**Day 1** Chapter 24 Intro, Section 1	**Day 1** Chapter 25 Intro, Section 1	**Day 1** Chapter 26 Intro, Section 1	**Day 1** Wrap-Up/Project **Day 2** Unit 7 Assessment
	Day 2 Section 2	**Day 2** Section 2	**Day 2** Section 2	**Day 2** Section 2	
	Day 3 Section 3	**Day 3** Section 3	**Day 3** Section 3	**Day 3** Section 3	
	Day 4 Chapter 23 Assessment	**Day 4** Chapter 24 Assessment	**Day 4** Section 4	**Day 4** Section 4	
			Day 5 Chapter 25 Assessment	**Day 5** Chapter 26 Assessment	

GLENCOE'S ASSESSMENT ADVANTAGE

Use the following tools to easily assess student learning in a variety of ways:

- Performance Assessment Activities and Rubrics
- Chapter and Unit Tests
- Section Quizzes
- Standardized Test Practice Workbook

- tarvol2.glencoe.com
- Interactive Tutor Self-Assessment CD-ROM
- MindJogger Videoquiz
- ExamView® Pro Testmaker CD-ROM
- SAT I/II Test Practice

READING SUPPORT FROM JAMESTOWN EDUCATION

TEACHING TRANSPARENCIES

Unit 7 Map Overlay Transparencies
L2

Cause-and-Effect Transparency 7
L2

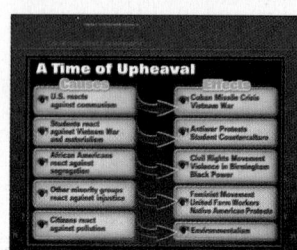

- **Timed Readings Plus in Social Studies** help students increase their reading rate and fluency while maintaining comprehension. The 400-word passages are similar to those found on state and national assessments.

- **Reading in the Content Area: Social Studies** concentrates on six essential reading skills that help students better comprehend what they read. The book includes 75 high-interest nonfiction passages written at increasing levels of difficulty.

- **Reading Fluency** helps students read smoothly, accurately, and expressively.

- **Jamestown's Reading Improvement,** by renowned reading expert Edward Fry, focuses on helping build your students' comprehension, vocabulary, and skimming and scanning skills.

- **Critical Reading Series** provides high-interest books, each written at three reading levels.

For more information about these products, see the Jamestown Education materials in the Classroom Solutions in the front of this Teacher Wraparound Edition. To order these products, call Glencoe at 1-800-334-7344.

ASSESSMENT

GLENCOE'S
ASSESSMENT
ADVANTAGE

Unit 7 Pretests L2

Unit 7 Posttests L2

APPLICATION AND ENRICHMENT

American Biography 7 L2

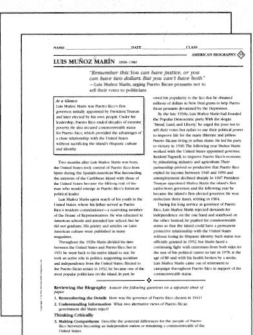

History Simulation and Problem Solving 7 L1

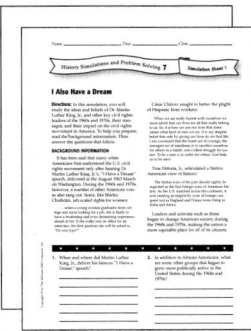

GEOGRAPHY

Geography and History Activity 7 L2

INTERDISCIPLINARY ACTIVITIES

American Literature Reading 7 L2

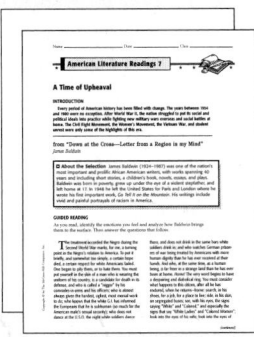

Economics and History Activity 7 L2

Team-Teaching Interdisciplinary Strategies and Activities 7 L2

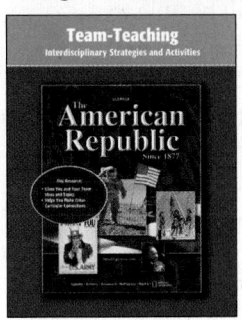

Reading List Generator CD-ROM

GLENCOE BOOKLINK

The Glencoe BookLink CD-ROM is a database that allows you to search more than 15,000 titles to create a customized reading list for your students.

- ■ Reading lists can be organized by students' reading level, author, genre, theme, or area of interest.

- ■ The database provides Degrees of Reading Power™ (DRP) and Lexile™ readability scores for all selections.

- ■ A brief summary of each selection is included.

Leveled reading suggestions for this unit:

For students at a Grade 8 reading level:
- ■ *Our Poisoned Sky,* by Edward F. Dolan.

For students at a Grade 9 reading level:
- ■ *Mississippi Challenge,* by Mildred Pitts Walter.

For students at a Grade 10 reading level:
- ■ *A Thousand Days: John F. Kennedy in the White House,* by Arthur M. Schlesinger, Jr.

Extending the Content

Readings for the Teacher
- ■ *Divided Minds: Intellectuals and the Civil Rights Movement,* by Carol Polsgrove. W.W. Norton & Company, 2001.

Multimedia Resources
- ■ *America and the World Since World War II, 1961–1975.* Volume III ABC News. VHS. (52 minutes)

0:00 **Out of Time?**

If time does not permit teaching each chapter in this unit, you may want to use the **Reading Essentials and Study Guide** summaries.

Unit Overview

Unit 7 describes the upheavals that occurred from 1954 to 1980. **Chapter 23** explores the New Frontier and the Great Society. **Chapter 24** focuses on the civil rights movement. **Chapter 25** explores the Vietnam War. **Chapter 26** discusses the politics of protest.

Unit Objectives

After studying this unit, students will be able to:

1. Summarize Kennedy's economic policies.
2. Discuss the changing role of the federal government in civil rights enforcement.
3. Describe how President Johnson deepened American involvement in Vietnam.
4. Describe the workplace concerns that fueled the growth of the women's movement.

Why It Matters Activity

Have students interview someone who was growing up or an adult in the late 1960s and the 1970s. Interviews should center around finding out how this era influenced the United States today. Students should prepare a transcript of the interview. Ask for volunteers to share insightful portions of their transcripts as you discuss the importance of this era to life in America today.

7 A Time of Upheaval *1954–1980*

Why It Matters

From a presidential assassination to massive governmental programs, from the Vietnam War to the civil rights movement, the post–World War II decades immensely affected the lives of Americans. The nation struggled to put its social and political ideals into practice while fighting military wars overseas and social wars at home. Understanding how these events unfolded provides a window to the world you live in today. The following resources offer more information about this period in American history.

Primary Sources Library

See pages 936–937 for primary source readings to accompany Unit 7.

Use the American History Primary Source Document Library CD-ROM to find additional primary sources about this eventful era.

MARCH ON WASHINGTON FOR JOBS AND FREEDOM AUGUST 28, 1963

We Shall Overcome

Poster from the March on Washington

Dr. Martin Luther King

SOUP without MEAT

Mural on building in Davenport, Iowa

714

TEAM TEACHING ACTIVITY

Music Have the music teacher share classic examples of the protest music that was popular in the 1960s and 1970s. Have students examine the lyrics and pose questions to the teacher about what particular phrases mean. Have students compile a database of the new words they learn, along with their meanings. Encourage students to add to this database as they study this unit.

"What we won when all of our people united . . . must not now be lost in suspicion, distrust, selfishness, and politics. . . ."

—Lyndon Johnson, 1968

We Must learn to live together as brothers or perish together as fools.

True Peace is not merely the absence of tension, it is the Presence of Justice.

A sound Mind has no specific color in which to be heard from carries out an emphati message of every hum race. Sherwin Q. Robinson

NELSON MANDELA

GLENCOE
TECHNOLOGY

CD-ROM
American History
Primary Source
Document Library
CD-ROM

Use the **American History Primary Source Document Library CD-ROM** to access primary source documents related to this period in history.

More About the Photo

The social movements of the late 1960s and the 1970s encouraged many artists to paint murals on buildings, usually in inner-city neighborhoods and near freeways. African Americans and Hispanics created many of the murals that can be seen in cities across the nation. With several thousand murals on city walls, Los Angeles may be the "mural capital" of the United States.

Glencoe Literature Library

The following novel from the *High School American History Literature Library* may be used to enrich the study of this unit:
• *And the Earth Did Not Devour Him* by Tomás Rivera

SERVICE-LEARNING PROJECT

Tell students that many Vietnam War veterans felt abandoned by American society. Unlike veterans of other wars, many Vietnam veterans did not return to a heroes' welcome. They often took protests about the war to mean that their country did not value their sacrifices or that they had done something wrong by serving. Have the class prepare a display honoring the Vietnam veterans living in the local community. Arrange to have the display exhibited in a public location for the community to enjoy.

Refer to **Building Bridges: Connecting Classroom and Community through Service-Learning in Social Studies** from the National Council for the Social Studies for information about service-learning.

Chapter 23 Resources

Timesaving Tools

TeacherWorks™ All-In-One Planner and Resource Center

- **Interactive Teacher Edition** Access your Teacher Wraparound Edition and your classroom resources with a few easy clicks.
- **Interactive Lesson Planner** Planning has never been easier! Organize your week, month, semester, or year with all the lesson helps you need to make teaching creative, timely, and relevant.

Use Glencoe's **Presentation Plus!** multimedia teacher tool to easily present dynamic lessons that visually excite your students. Using Microsoft PowerPoint® you can customize the presentations to create your own personalized lessons.

TEACHING TRANSPARENCIES

Graphic Organizer 8 L2

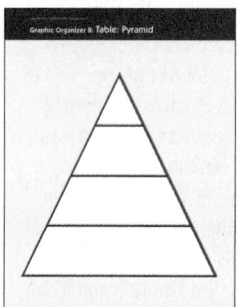

Why It Matters Chapter Transparency 23 L2

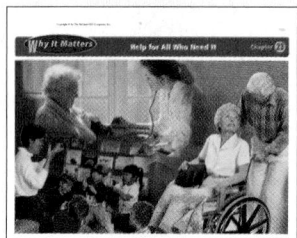

APPLICATION AND ENRICHMENT

Linking Past and Present Activity 23 L2

Enrichment Activity 23 L3

Primary Source Reading 23 L2

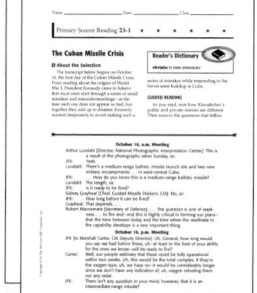

REVIEW AND REINFORCEMENT

Reteaching Activity 23 L1

Vocabulary Activity 23 L1

Time Line Activity 23 L2

Critical Thinking Skills Activity 23 L2

Meeting NCSS Standards

The following standards are covered in Chapter 23:

Section 1	X	Civic Ideals and Practices: A, C, F
Section 2	VIII	Science, Technology, and Society: A, B, C
Section 3	VI	Power, Authority, and Governance: A, B, C, H, I

Local Standards

Chapter 23 Resources

ASSESSMENT AND EVALUATION

Chapter 23 Test Form A L2

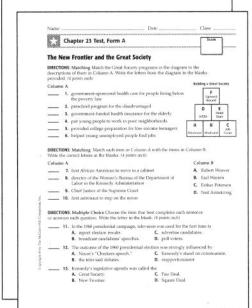

Chapter 23 Test Form B L2

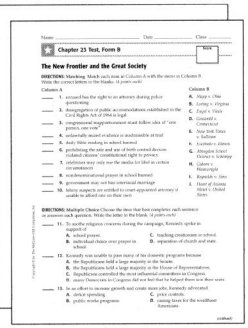

Standardized Test Practice Workbook Activity 23 L2

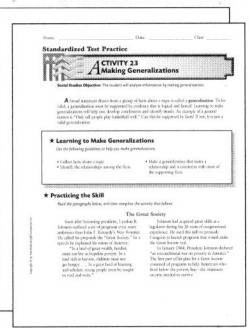

Performance Assessment Activities and Rubrics 23 L1/ELL

ExamView® Pro Testmaker CD-ROM

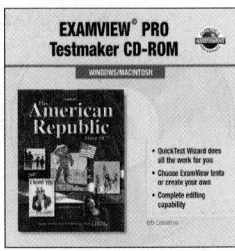

MULTIMEDIA

- **Vocabulary PuzzleMaker CD-ROM**
- **Interactive Tutor Self-Assessment CD-ROM**
- **ExamView® Pro Testmaker CD-ROM**
- **Audio Program**
- **American History Primary Source Documents Library CD-ROM**
- **MindJogger Videoquiz**
- **Presentation Plus! CD-ROM**
- **TeacherWorks™ CD-ROM**
- **Interactive Student Edition CD-ROM**
- **Glencoe Skillbuilder Interactive Workbook CD-ROM, Level 2**
- **The *American Republic Since 1877* Video Program**
- **American Music: Hits Through History**
- **American Music: Cultural Traditions**

The following videotape programs are available from Glencoe as supplements to Chapter 23:

- **John F. Kennedy: A Personal Story** (ISBN 0-76-700010-2)
- **Lyndon Johnson: Triumph and Tragedy** (ISBN 0-76-700109-5)
- **Bay of Pigs Cuban Missile Crisis** (ISBN 0-76-701199-6)
- **Malcolm X: A Search for Identity** (ISBN 1-56-501674-2)

To order, call Glencoe at 1-800-334-7344. To find classroom resources to accompany many of these videos, check the following home pages:
A&E Television: www.aande.com
The History Channel: www.historychannel.com

SPANISH RESOURCES

The following Spanish resources are available:

- **Spanish Reading Essentials and Study Guide**
- **Spanish Guided Reading Activities**
- **Spanish Reteaching Activities**
- **Spanish Quizzes and Tests**
- **Spanish Vocabulary Activities**
- **Spanish Summaries**
- **The Declaration of Independence and United States Constitution Spanish Translation**

Use our Web site for additional resources. All essential content is covered in the Student Edition.

You and your students can visit tarvol2.glencoe.com, the Web site companion to the *American Republic Since 1877.* This innovative integration of electronic and print media offers your students a wealth of opportunities. The student text directs students to the Web site for the following options:

- **Chapter Overviews**
- **Self-Check Quizzes**
- **Student Web Activities**
- **Textbook Updates**

Answers to the student Web activities are provided for you in the **Web Activity Lesson Plans.** Additional Web resources and Interactive Tutor Puzzles are also available.

Chapter 23 Resources

SECTION RESOURCES

Daily Objectives	Reproducible Resources	Multimedia Resources
SECTION 1 **The New Frontier** 1. Summarize Kennedy's economic policies. 2. Explain why Congress often did not support Kennedy's proposals.	Reproducible Lesson Plan 23–1 Daily Lecture and Discussion Notes 23–1 Guided Reading Activity 23–1* Section Quiz 23–1* Reading Essentials and Study Guide 23–1* Performance Assessment Activities and Rubrics Supreme Court Case Studies	Daily Focus Skills Transparency 23–1 Interactive Tutor Self-Assessment CD-ROM ExamView® Pro Testmaker CD-ROM* Presentation Plus! CD-ROM TeacherWorks™ CD-ROM Audio Program
SECTION 2 **JFK and the Cold War** 1. Describe Kennedy's plan for the armed forces. 2. Explain how the Cold War influenced foreign aid and the space program.	Reproducible Lesson Plan 23–2 Daily Lecture and Discussion Notes 23–2 Guided Reading Activity 23–2* Section Quiz 23–2* Reading Essentials and Study Guide 23–2* Performance Assessment Activities and Rubrics Interpreting Political Cartoons	Daily Focus Skills Transparency 23–2 Interactive Tutor Self-Assessment CD-ROM ExamView® Pro Testmaker CD-ROM* Presentation Plus! CD-ROM TeacherWorks™ CD-ROM Audio Program
SECTION 3 **The Great Society** 1. Explain what inspired Johnson's Great Society programs. 2. Identify several specific health and employment programs of the Johnson administration.	Reproducible Lesson Plan 23–3 Daily Lecture and Discussion Notes 23–3 Guided Reading Activity 23–3* Section Quiz 23–3* Reading Essentials and Study Guide 23–3* Performance Assessment Activities and Rubrics	Daily Focus Skills Transparency 23–3 Interactive Tutor Self-Assessment CD-ROM ExamView® Pro Testmaker CD-ROM* Presentation Plus! CD-ROM Skillbuilder Interactive Workbook, Level 2 TeacherWorks™ CD-ROM Vocabulary PuzzleMaker CD-ROM Audio Program

0:00 OUT OF TIME?
Assign the Chapter 23 **Reading Essentials and Study Guide.**

*Also Available in Spanish

 Printed Materials   Transparency   CD-ROM   DVD

Poster   Music Program   Audio Program

NATIONAL GEOGRAPHIC Teacher's Corner

INDEX TO NATIONAL GEOGRAPHIC MAGAZINE

The following articles relate to this chapter.

- "I Dream a World: America's Black Women," August 1989
- "National Trail to Recall Civil Rights Marches," March 1994
- "Philadelphia's African Americans," August 1990
- "Selma to Montgomery: The Road to Equality," February 2000

NATIONAL GEOGRAPHIC SOCIETY PRODUCTS

To order the following, call National Geographic at 1-800-368-2728:

- *Historical Atlas of the United States* (Atlas)
- *NGS PictureShow: Civil Rights* (CD-ROM, Transparencies)

NGS ONLINE

Access National Geographic's Web site for current events, atlas updates, activities, links, interactive features, and archives.

www.nationalgeographic.com

MEETING SPECIAL NEEDS

In addition to the Differentiated Instruction strategies found in each section, the following resources are also suitable for your special needs students:

- *ExamView® Pro Testmaker CD-ROM* allows teachers to tailor tests by reducing answer choices.
- The *Audio Program* includes the entire narrative of the student edition so that less-proficient readers can listen to the words as they read them.
- The *Reading Essentials and Study Guide* provides the same content as the student edition but is written two grade levels below the textbook.

KEY TO ABILITY LEVELS

Teaching strategies have been coded.

L1 BASIC activities for all students
L2 AVERAGE activities for average to above-average students
L3 CHALLENGING activities for above-average students
ELL ENGLISH LANGUAGE LEARNER activities

From the Classroom of...

Joe Naumann
Ferguson-Florissant
School District
St. Louis, MO

U.S. Foreign Policy: Cold War Map and Time Line

Select 10 to 15 events that the U.S. reacted to or was involved in during the Cold War. Students receive the list of events and a blank map of the world or a part of the world if the events relate to only one region. If student map skills are weak, draw arrows to the places on the map and have the students write the place-names next to the appropriate arrow. If you do not supply the dates of the events, students could research that information.

Tell the students to arrange the list of events on a time line, allowing students to see the geographical dimensions of the events as well as the sequence of events.

Consider expanding the project with a written assignment where students explain the connections among events or why the United States got involved in some places while choosing not to get involved in others at that time.

ADDITIONAL RESOURCES FROM GLENCOE

- American Music: Cultural Traditions
- American Art & Architecture
- Outline Map Resource Book
- U.S. Desk Map
- Building Geography Skills for Life
- Inclusion for the High School Social Studies Classroom Strategies and Activities
- Teaching Strategies for the American History Classroom (Including Block Scheduling Pacing Guides)
- Dinah Zike's High School American History Reading and Study Skills Foldables

Block Schedule

Activities that are suited to use within the block scheduling framework are identified by:

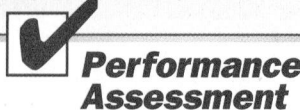

✔ *Performance Assessment*

Refer to Activity 23 in the Performance Assessment Activities and Rubrics booklet.

Why It Matters Activity

Contact your local Social Security Administration office to obtain brochures describing the Medicaid and Medicare programs and benefits. Have students review these brochures and provide a brief overview of these programs. Ask students why they think these programs were instituted. Students should evaluate their answers after they have completed the chapter.

GLENCOE TECHNOLOGY

The *American Republic Since 1877* Video Program

To learn more about the American space program, have students view the Chapter 23 video, "A New Frontier: The Space Race," from the *American Republic Since 1877* Video Program.

MindJogger Videoquiz

Use the **MindJogger Videoquiz** to preview Chapter 23 content.

Both programs available in DVD

CHAPTER 23
The New Frontier and the Great Society
1961–1968

Why It Matters

President John F. Kennedy urged Americans to work for progress and to stand firm against the Soviets. Cold War tensions and the threat of nuclear war peaked during the Cuban missile crisis. Kennedy's assassination changed the nation's mood, but President Lyndon Johnson embraced ambitious goals, including working toward the passage of major civil rights legislation and eradicating poverty.

The Impact Today

Initiatives introduced in this era remain a part of American society.
- Medicaid and Medicare legislation provides major health benefits for elderly and low-income people.
- The Head Start program provides early educational opportunities for disadvantaged children.

The American Republic Since 1877 Video The Chapter 23 video, "A New Frontier: The Space Race," explores the dramatic history of the American space program.

November 1963
- Kennedy assassinated; Lyndon Johnson becomes president

April 1961
- Bay of Pigs invasion

December 1961
- Presidential Commission on the Status of Women created

June 1963
- Kennedy visits Berlin Wall

October 1962
- Cuban missile crisis

Kennedy 1961–1963

L. Johnson 1963–1969

United States PRESIDENTS

1960   *1962*   *1964*

World

1959
- Cuban revolution brings Castro to power

April 1961
- Eichmann goes on trial for crimes against Jews

August 1961
- Construction of Berlin Wall begins

1964
- South Africa's Nelson Mandela sentenced to life in prison

716

Reading Strategy ▶ PURPOSE FOR READING

Read and Say Something This strategy helps students with reading comprehension—especially for difficult reading material. Bring copies of President John F. Kennedy's Inaugural Address to class and give each student a copy. Have students read one paragraph, then turn to a partner and say something about the reading. Tell students they should say anything they want related to the selection, such as their reactions to ideas, descriptions, images, or anything they find confusing. Solicit information from the entire class about what each pair discussed. Inform students that they will be studying the Kennedy era and the Johnson years in this chapter. **L1**

President John F. Kennedy at his inaugural ball in 1961

July 1965
• Congress establishes Medicare and Medicaid programs

October 1966
• Fair Packaging and Labeling Act passed

March 1968
• Lyndon Johnson announces that he will not run for re-election

1966　　　　　　　　　　　　　*1968*

1966
• Indira Gandhi becomes prime minister of India

1968
• Student riots paralyze France

HISTORY Online

Chapter Overview
Visit the *American Republic Since 1877* Web site at tarvol2.glencoe.com and click on *Chapter Overviews—Chapter 23* to preview chapter information.

717

GRAPHIC ORGANIZER ACTIVITY

Organizing Information Have students identify the important legislation and government programs passed during the Kennedy and Johnson administrations by completing a graphic organizer similar to the one below.

Legislation and Government Programs	
Kennedy	**Johnson**
increase in minimum wage	*Economic Opportunity Act*
Area Redevelopment Act	*VISTA*
Housing Act	*Medicare and Medicaid*

1 FOCUS

Section Overview

This section focuses on the domestic aspects of the Kennedy administration.

BELLRINGER
Skillbuilder Activity

Project transparency and have students answer the question.

Daily Focus Skills Transparency 23–1

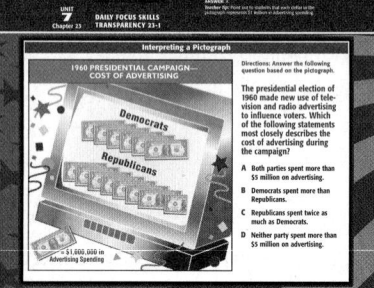

Reading Preview

Answers to Graphic: Successes: more funds in defense and space exploration, some advance in women's rights, economic improvement; **Setbacks:** health insurance for the elderly, a Department of Urban Affairs, federal aid to education, aid for migrant workers

Preteaching Vocabulary
Have students define the Key Terms in their own words.

Guide to Reading

Main Idea
John F. Kennedy encountered both success and setbacks on the domestic front.

Key Terms and Names
missile gap, New Frontier, Earl Warren, reapportionment, due process

Reading Strategy
Categorizing As you read about the presidency of John F. Kennedy, complete a graphic organizer similar to the one below by filling in the domestic successes and setbacks of Kennedy's administration.

Successes	Setbacks

Reading Objectives
• **Summarize** Kennedy's economic policies.
• **Explain** why Congress often did not support Kennedy's proposals.

Section Theme
Civic Rights and Responsibilities The Supreme Court made decisions that protected individual rights, including the "one man, one vote" decision.

Preview of Events

◆1960	◆1961	◆1962	◆1963
1960 John Kennedy defeats Richard Nixon for the presidency	**1961** Kennedy creates Presidential Commission on the Status of Women	**1962** Supreme Court issues *Baker* v. *Carr* ruling	**1963** Kennedy signs Equal Pay Act for women

★ **An American Story** ★

John F. Kennedy and Richard Nixon in the 1960 debate

On September 26, 1960, at 9:30 P.M. eastern standard time, streets all across the United States grew strangely still. An estimated 75 million people sat indoors, focused on their television sets, where they saw two men standing behind lecterns. One was John F. Kennedy, and the other was Richard M. Nixon.

For the first time, thanks to the wonders of television, two presidential candidates were coming right into the nation's living rooms to debate. Americans were enthralled: "You hear each man directly," observed one. "There's nothing between you and what he says," added another. "You can see which man gets rattled easily."

The man who seemed to get rattled easily was Nixon. Kennedy, the Democratic nominee, looked healthy, strong, and confident. Nixon, the Republicans' choice, came across as tired and frazzled. "He appeared ill," one viewer commented. In fact, Nixon had been ill recently. Kennedy had a glowing tan, while Nixon's face was pale and drawn, shadowed by the stubble of a beard. As one observer noted, "Nixon's eyes darted around, perspiration was clearly noticeable on his chin, and with the tight shots . . . these things were more obvious."

—adapted from *The Great Debate*

The Election of 1960

The television debates of the 1960 presidential election had enormous impact. Following the first debate, the media focused more strongly on the appearance of the candidates. Suddenly the whole country seemed to have become experts on makeup and tele-

---

SECTION RESOURCES

📁 Reproducible Masters
• Reproducible Lesson Plan 23–1
• Daily Lecture and Discussion Notes 23–1
• Guided Reading Activity 23–1
• Section Quiz 23–1
• Reading Essentials and Study Guide 23–1
• Performance Assessment Activities and Rubrics
• Supreme Court Case Studies

📋 Transparencies
• Daily Focus Skills Transparency 23–1

Multimedia
🔘 Interactive Tutor Self-Assessment CD-ROM
🔘 ExamView® Pro Testmaker CD-ROM
🔘 Presentation Plus! CD-ROM
🔘 TeacherWorks™ CD-ROM
🔘 Audio Program

vision lighting. One Republican leader even wondered if the Democrats had supplied Nixon's makeup.

With that debate, the era of television politics had begun. Though television had been used in campaigns as early as 1948, it was not until the 1960 election that a large majority of voters used the medium as a voting tool. The nation itself seemed on the brink of a new age. Having lived through a decade of unprecedented prosperity and the onset of the Cold War and the atomic age, Americans looked to the future with excitement and anxiety.

Both candidates shared the desire to lead the nation through the challenges of a new decade, but they differed in many ways. Kennedy, a Catholic, came from a wealthy and influential Massachusetts family. Nixon, a Quaker, was a Californian from a financially struggling family. Kennedy seemed outgoing and relaxed, while Nixon struck many as formal and even stiff in manner.

A New Kind of Campaign Compared to earlier campaigns, the 1960 presidential race made new use of television, with both major parties spending substantial amounts of money on television ads. The Democrats spent over $6 million in television and radio spots, while the Republicans spent more than $7.5 million.

Not everyone was happy with this new emphasis on image. Television news commentator Eric Sevareid complained that the candidates had become "packaged products," and he stated that "the Processed Politician has finally arrived."

The Main Issues The campaign centered on the economy and the Cold War. Although the candidates presented different styles, they differed little on these two issues. Both promised to boost the economy, and both portrayed themselves as "Cold Warriors" determined to stop the forces of communism.

Kennedy argued that the nation faced serious threats from the Soviets. In Cuba, Fidel Castro was allying himself with the Soviet Union. At home, many people lived in fear of a Soviet nuclear attack. Kennedy voiced his concern about a suspected "missile gap," in which the United States lagged behind the Soviets in weaponry. (Decades later, Americans learned that, in fact, the only area where the Soviet Union was briefly ahead was in rocketry). The nation, Kennedy argued, had grown complacent and aimless. "It is time to get this country moving again."

Nixon countered that the United States was on the right track under the current administration. "I'm tired of hearing our opponents downgrade the United States," the vice president said. Nixon also warned that the Democrats' fiscal policies would boost inflation, and that only he had the necessary foreign policy experience to guide the nation.

Kennedy came under scrutiny about his religion. The United States had never had a Catholic president, and many Protestants had concerns about Kennedy. Kennedy decided to confront this issue openly in a speech. "I believe in an America where the separation of the church and state is absolute," he said, "where no Catholic prelate would tell the president, should he be a Catholic, how to act."

The four televised debates strongly influenced the outcome of the election, one of the closest in American history. Kennedy won the popular vote by 119,000 out of 68 million votes cast and the Electoral College by 303 votes to 219. In several states only a few thousand votes could have swung the Electoral College numbers the other way.

✓ **Reading Check** **Identifying** What were two main issues of the 1960 presidential election?

The Kennedy Mystique

Despite his narrow victory, John F. Kennedy, commonly referred to as JFK, captured the imagination of the American public as few presidents before him had. During the campaign, many had been taken with Kennedy's youth and optimism. The new president strongly reinforced this impression when he gave his Inaugural Address.

Inauguration Day, January 20, 1961, was crisp and cold in Washington, D.C. At the site of the ceremony, a crowd gathered, wrapped in coats and blankets. As Kennedy rose to take the oath of office, he wore neither a coat nor a hat. During his speech, the new president declared, "The torch has been passed to a new generation," and he called on his fellow citizens to take a more active role in making the United States a better place. "My fellow Americans," he exclaimed, "ask not what your country can do for you—ask what you can do for your country."

Kennedy, his wife Jacqueline, their children Caroline and John, and their large extended family seemed to have been created for media coverage. Reporters followed the family everywhere.

Kennedy tie clasp (left) and Nixon pendant from 1960 presidential campaign

2 TEACH

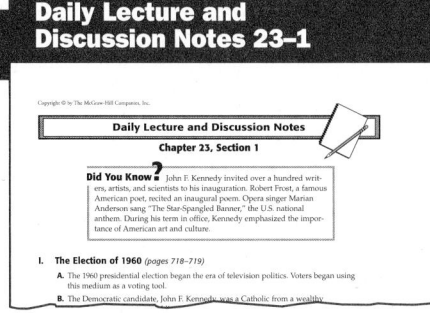

Daily Lecture and Discussion Notes 23–1

Copyright © by The McGraw-Hill Companies, Inc.

Daily Lecture and Discussion Notes

Chapter 23, Section 1

Did You Know? John F. Kennedy invited over a hundred writers, artists, and scientists to his inauguration. Robert Frost, a famous American poet, recited an inaugural poem. Opera singer Marian Anderson sang "The Star-Spangled Banner," the U.S. national anthem. During his term in office, Kennedy emphasized the importance of American art and culture.

I. **The Election of 1960** (pages 718–719)
  A. The 1960 presidential election began the era of television politics. Voters began using this medium as a voting tool.
  B. The Democratic candidate, John F. Kennedy, was a Catholic from a wealthy

Identifying a Strategy Organize the class into two groups. Have one group represent Nixon's staff and the other represent Kennedy's staff. After students have read page 719, have each group identify the campaign strategies that each should use to overcome their weaknesses, to explain their goals for the country, and to encourage undecided voters to vote for them. Have each group present their strategies. As a class, discuss why the election results were so close. **L1**

✓ **Reading Check**

Answer: The issues were the economy and the Cold War.

FYI

The 1960 vote was so close that Nixon considered demanding a recount, but then decided against it. He explained that if there were a recount, "the organization of the new administration and the orderly transfer of responsibility from the old to the new might be delayed for months. The situation within the entire federal government would be chaotic."

COOPERATIVE LEARNING ACTIVITY

Researching the Candidates Organize the class into six groups. Assign each group one of the following topics: Kennedy's childhood and family background, Kennedy's college years and military service, Kennedy's political background, Nixon's childhood and family background, Nixon's college years and military service, or Nixon's political background. Have the groups research their topic. Then have the Kennedy groups and the Nixon groups work together to prepare a display providing a portrait of the two men. 📦

Use the rubric for a cooperative group management plan on pages 71–72 in the *Performance Assessment Activities and Rubrics.*

Guided Reading Activity 23–1

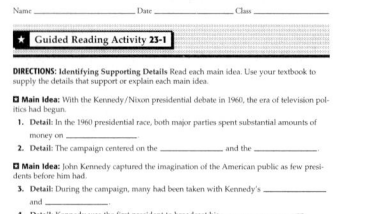

Name _____ Date _____ Class _____

★ **Guided Reading Activity 23-1**

DIRECTIONS: Identifying Supporting Details Read each main idea. Use your textbook to supply the details that support or explain each main idea.

❏ **Main Idea:** With the Kennedy/Nixon presidential debate in 1960, the era of television politics had begun.

1. **Detail:** In the 1960 presidential race, both major parties spent substantial amounts of money on _____

2. **Detail:** The campaign centered on the _____ and the _____

❏ **Main Idea:** John Kennedy captured the imagination of the American public as few presidents before him had.

3. **Detail:** During the campaign, many had been taken with Kennedy's _____ and _____

4. **Detail:** Kennedy was the first president to broadcast his _____ on _____

Picturing **History**

Background: In 2001 the Metropolitan Museum of Art and the John F. Kennedy Library organized an exhibit of clothing worn by Jacqueline Kennedy while she was First Lady.
Answer: Students' answers will vary. Students might suggest that the young family provided good stories for the media, and the family encouraged the attention.
Ask: What technology helped make scrutiny of the Kennedys possible? *(television)*

✓ Reading Check

Answer: Kennedy inspired the nation with his optimism, his youth, and his ability to handle the media.

FYI

John Kennedy, his wife, and their two small children were the youngest family to live in the White House since Theodore Roosevelt's days.

Picturing **History**

The Kennedy White House Jacqueline Kennedy (center right) brought youthful elegance and style to the White House. Why do you think the media scrutinized the First Family so much?

Kennedy himself was a master of the media, particularly television. He was the first to broadcast his press conferences live on television.

The Kennedy charisma inspired many of his staff members. His press secretary, Pierre Salinger, put this feeling into words:

> 66None of us will ever have a better job as long as we live. . . . The big *plus*—the fringe benefit that made it all worthwhile—was JFK himself. . . . Our faith in him and in what he was trying to do was absolute, and he could impart to our work together a sense of challenge and adventure—a feeling that he was moving, and the world with him, toward a better time.99
>
> —quoted in *With Kennedy*

✓ **Reading Check** **Summarizing** In what ways did John F. Kennedy inspire the nation?

Success and Setback on the Domestic Front

Not everyone in the nation fell for the Kennedy mystique. His high culture, elite Northeast upbringing, and Catholicism irritated some Americans. Congress also was less than taken with the new president. Upon entering office, President Kennedy set out to implement a legislative agenda, which became known as the **New Frontier.** He hoped to increase aid to education, provide health insurance to the elderly, create a Department of Urban Affairs, and help migrant workers. He

would soon find that transforming lofty ideals into real legislation was no easy task on Capitol Hill.

Kennedy Struggles With Congress Although the Democratic Party enjoyed large majorities in both houses of Congress, Kennedy was unable to push through many of his domestic programs. Kennedy had trailed Nixon in many Democratic districts and had not helped many Democrats get elected. Those who did win, therefore, did not feel they owed him anything. As one Democrat in Congress told *U.S. News & World Report,* "A good many [congressional representatives] were elected in 1960 in spite of his presence on the ticket rather than because his name was there." As a result, legislators found it easy to follow their own interests rather than those of the president.

In addition, Republicans as well as conservative Southern Democrats—who were responsible for holding the Democratic majority in Congress—viewed the New Frontier as too big and too costly. Senator Everett Dirksen, Republican minority leader from Illinois, claimed that Kennedy's efforts to increase the power and reach of the federal government would push the nation down an ominous path.

In the end, Congress defeated a number of JFK's proposals, including health insurance for the elderly, a Department of Urban Affairs, and federal aid to education. The president often resisted calls to push harder for his agenda. He decided not to fight every battle on Capitol Hill and preferred to reserve his bargaining power for issues that were both truly important and winnable.

ECONOMICS

Strengthening the Economy Kennedy did achieve some victories in Congress, particularly in his efforts to improve the nation's economy. The American economy, which had soared through much of the 1950s, had slowed by the end of the decade. From 1960 to 1961, the growth rate of the gross national product was only 2 percent, while the unemployment rate hovered near 7 percent of the workforce, the second-highest figure since World War II.

In an effort to increase growth and create more jobs, Kennedy advocated the New Deal strategy of deficit spending, first implemented during Franklin Roosevelt's presidency. The new president convinced Congress to invest more funds in defense and in space exploration. Such spending did indeed create more jobs and stimulate economic growth. Reluctant to rely too heavily on deficit spending, which tends to cause inflation, Kennedy also sought to boost the economy by increasing business production and efficiency. In

720 CHAPTER 23 The New Frontier and the Great Society

DIFFERENTIATED INSTRUCTION

Reading Support Arrange to videotape students as you conduct mock debates on topics of interest to students. As a class watch the videotapes and have students select which debaters look comfortable and which look uncomfortable. Have students note particular mannerisms or actions that make people look comfortable in front of the camera. **L1**

📁 Refer to *Inclusion for the High School Social Studies Classroom Strategies and Activities* in the TCR.

addition, his administration asked businesses to hold down prices and labor leaders to hold down pay increases.

Prodded by Secretary of Labor Arthur Goldberg, labor unions in the steel industry agreed to reduce their demands for higher wages. In 1962, however, several steel companies raised prices sharply.

The president threatened to have the Department of Defense buy cheaper steel from foreign companies and instructed the Justice Department to investigate whether the steel industry was guilty of price-fixing. In response to Kennedy's tactics, the steel companies backed down and cut their prices. To achieve this victory, however, the president had strained his relations with the nation's business community.

In an effort to get the economy moving, Kennedy also adopted supply-side ideas and pushed for a cut in tax rates. When opponents argued that a tax cut would only help the wealthy, Kennedy asserted that lower taxes meant businesses would have more money to expand, which would create new jobs and benefit everybody. "A rising tide lifts all boats," Kennedy explained, as a way to illustrate how tax cuts would stimulate the economy and help all Americans.

Congress refused to pass the tax cut because many members feared it would cause inflation. However, they did support Kennedy's request to raise the minimum wage and his proposal for an Area Redevelopment Act and a Housing Act. These two programs provided funds to poor areas. They helped to clear slums, create jobs, and build low-income housing.

Women's Rights Kennedy also helped women make strides during the 1960s. Although Kennedy never appointed a woman to his cabinet, a number of women worked in prominent positions in his administration, including **Esther Peterson,** assistant secretary of labor and director of the Women's Bureau of the Department of Labor.

Kennedy advanced women's rights in other ways as well. In 1961 he created the **Presidential Commission on the Status of Women.** The commission called for federal action against gender discrimination and affirmed the right of women to equally paid employment. Kennedy responded by issuing an executive order ending gender discrimination in the federal civil service, and in 1963 he signed the Equal Pay Act for women. The commission also sparked the creation of similar groups on the state level and inspired many women to work together to further their interests.

✓ Reading Check **Evaluating** Why did Kennedy have difficulty getting his New Frontier legislation passed?

Warren Court Reforms

During the Kennedy years, the Supreme Court also took an active role in social issues. In 1953 President Eisenhower had nominated **Earl Warren,** the popular Republican governor of California, to become Chief Justice of the United States. More so than previous courts, the Warren Court took an activist stance, helping to shape national policy by taking a forceful stand on a number of key issues of the day.

GOVERNMENT

"One Man, One Vote" One of the Warren Court's more notable decisions had a powerful impact on who would hold political power in the United States. This decision concerned reapportionment, or the way in which states draw up political districts based on changes in population. By 1960 many more Americans resided in cities and suburbs than in rural areas. Yet many states had failed to restructure their electoral districts to reflect that change.

In Tennessee, for example, a rural county with only 2,340 voters had 1 representative in the state assembly, while an urban county with 133 times more voters had only 7. The vote of a city dweller counted for less than the vote of a rural resident. Some Tennessee voters took the matter to court.

The *Baker* v. *Carr* case reached the Supreme Court after a federal court ruled that the issue should be

---

| Fact | Fiction | Folklore |

Camelot In December 1960, *Camelot,* a musical starring Richard Burton and Julie Andrews, opened on Broadway in New York City. The Kennedys attended the show, which told the legend of the heroism of King Arthur and the Knights of the Round Table, and so enjoyed it that they listened to the music often. The president's favorite song included the lines: "Don't let it be forgot, that once there was a spot, for one brief shining moment that was known as Camelot."

In later years, the Kennedy presidency became known as "Camelot," largely because of Mrs. Kennedy. Shortly after the president's death in 1963, she told a journalist that all she could think about was the president's favorite line. She went on to say: "There'll be great presidents again, . . . but there'll never be another Camelot again." Journalist Theodore H. White later wrote that "all she could repeat was, 'Tell people there will never be that Camelot again.'"

Making a Collage Have students make a collage using images of important events in the Kennedy administration. Invite students to post their collages and explain any unique elements that they included. **L1**

CURRICULUM CONNECTION

Civics Tell students that Eleanor Roosevelt had remained a popular and active political figure after her husband's death. During the 1960 presidential campaign, she appeared in a television commercial urging people to vote for Kennedy because he was the man to improve human rights. Her appearance indicated to traditional Democrats and women that Kennedy was the man for the job.

| Fact | Fiction | Folklore |

In the legendary Camelot, leaders sat at a round table. With no head of the table, it was implied that rule was by all, not just by one.

 Use *Supreme Court Case Study 33, Baker* v. *Carr.*

✓ Reading Check

Answer: The legislation was perceived as too expensive and too broad in scope.

INTERDISCIPLINARY CONNECTIONS ACTIVITY

Language Arts Tell students that John F. Kennedy won a Pulitzer Prize in biography for his book, *Profiles in Courage.* Encourage students to find the book in the library, read one of the profiles, and write a report on the person profiled. Have volunteers share their reports with the class. Then as a class, discuss the virtue of courage and how the people Kennedy selected represented it. **L2**

Civil Rights	
Brown v. *Board of Education* (1954)	Segregation in public schools unconstitutional
Baker v. *Carr* (1962)	Established that federal courts can hear lawsuits seeking to force state authorities to redraw electoral districts
Reynolds v. *Sims* (1964)	State legislative districts should be equal in population
Heart of Atlanta Motel v. *United States* (1964)	Desegregation of public accommodations established in the Civil Rights Act of 1964 is legal
Loving v. *Virginia* (1967)	States may not ban interracial marriage
Due Process	
Mapp v. *Ohio* (1961)	Unlawfully seized evidence is inadmissible at trial
Gideon v. *Wainwright* (1963)	Suspects are entitled to court-appointed attorney if unable to afford one on their own
Escobedo v. *Illinois* (1964)	Accused has the right to an attorney during police questioning
Miranda v. *Arizona* (1966)	Police must inform suspects of their rights during the arrest process
Freedom of Religion and Freedom of Speech	
Engel v. *Vitale* (1962)	State-mandated prayer in school banned
Abington School District v. *Schempp* (1963)	State-mandated Bible readings in school banned
New York Times v. *Sullivan* (1964)	Celebrities may sue the media for libel only in certain circumstances

Chart *Skills*

Answers:
1. Students should discuss school integration and reapportionment.
2. It affected civil rights, due process, and freedom of religion and speech.

Chart Skills Practice
Ask: Which cases are related to the separation of church and state?
(Engel *v.* Vitale *and* Abington School District *v.* Schempp)

📁 Use *Supreme Court Case Study 32, Mapp* v. *Ohio; 34, Engel* v. *Vitale; 35, Abington School District* v. *Schempp; 36, Gideon* v. *Wainwright; 37, Escobedo* v. *Illinois; 38, Reynolds* v. *Sims; 41, Miranda* v. *Arizona.*

Chart *Skills*

1. **Interpreting Charts** Analyze the effects *Brown* v. *Board of Education* and *Reynolds* v. *Sims* had on the nation.
2. **Summarizing** What three major areas of policy did the Warren Court's decisions affect?

3 ASSESS

Assign Section 1 Assessment as homework or as an in-class activity.

🌐 Have students use the **Interactive Tutor Self-Assessment CD-ROM.**

L1/ELL

Reading Essentials and Study Guide 23–1

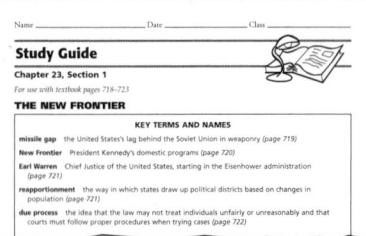

Name _____ Date _____ Class _____

Study Guide

Chapter 23, Section 1
For use with textbook pages 718–723

THE NEW FRONTIER

KEY TERMS AND NAMES

missile gap the United States's lag behind the Soviet Union in weaponry *(page 719)*
New Frontier President Kennedy's domestic programs *(page 720)*
Earl Warren Chief Justice of the United States, starting in the Eisenhower administration *(page 721)*
reapportionment the way in which states draw up political districts based on changes in population *(page 721)*
due process the idea that the law may not treat individuals unfairly or unreasonably and that courts must follow proper procedures when trying cases *(page 722)*

solved by legislation. The Fourteenth Amendment specifically gives Congress authority to enforce voting rights. In 1962 the Supreme Court ruled that the federal courts did have jurisdiction and sent the matter back to the lower courts. 📖 *(See page 962 for more information on* Baker v. Carr.*)*

Two years later, in June 1964, the Supreme Court ruled in *Reynolds* v. *Sims* that the current apportionment system in most states was indeed unconstitutional. In a decision that helped to promote the principle of "one man, one vote," the Warren Court required state legislatures to reapportion electoral districts so that all citizens' votes would have equal weight. The Court's decision was a momentous one, for it shifted political power throughout the country from rural and often conservative areas to urban areas, where more liberal voters resided. The Court's decision also boosted the political power of African Americans and Hispanics, who typically lived in cities. 📖 *(See page 964 for more information on* Reynolds v. Sims.*)*

Extending Due Process In a series of historic rulings in the 1960s, the U.S. Supreme Court began to use the Fourteenth Amendment to apply the Bill of Rights to the states. Originally, the Bill of Rights

applied only to the federal government. Many states had their own bill of rights, but some federal rights did not exist at the state level. The Fourteenth Amendment specifically stated that "no state shall . . . deprive any person of life, liberty, or property without due process of law." Due process means that the law may not treat individuals unfairly, arbitrarily, or unreasonably, and that courts must follow proper procedures and rules when trying cases. Due process ensures that all people are treated the same by the court system. In the 1960s, the Supreme Court ruled in several cases that upholding due process meant applying the federal bill of rights to the states.

In 1961 the Supreme Court ruled in *Mapp* v. *Ohio* that state courts could not consider evidence obtained in violation of the federal Constitution. In *Gideon* v. *Wainwright* (1963), the Court ruled that a defendant in a state court had the right to a lawyer, regardless of his or her ability to pay. The following year, in *Escobedo* v. *Illinois*, the justices ruled that a

722   CHAPTER 23   The New Frontier and the Great Society

📖 Reading Strategy   READING THE TEXT

Understanding Vocabulary Ask students the meaning of the word *frontier*. As a class, discuss both the denotation of the word (what the word means) and the connotation (what the word suggests beyond the literal meaning). Then ask students why they think Kennedy named his program the New Frontier. **L1**

📁 Refer to *Inclusion for the High School Social Studies Classroom Strategies and Activities* in the TCR.

suspect must be allowed access to a lawyer and must be informed of his or her right to remain silent before being questioned by the police. *Miranda* v. *Arizona* (1966) went even further, requiring that authorities immediately give suspects a fourfold warning. The warning consisted of informing suspects that they have the right to remain silent, that anything they say can and will be used against them in court, that they have a right to a lawyer while being questioned, and that if they cannot afford a lawyer, the court will appoint one for them. Today these warnings are known as the Miranda rights. *(See pages 963–964 for more information on* Mapp v. Ohio, Gideon v. Wainwright, Escobedo v. Illinois, *and* Miranda v. Arizona.)

Many citizens and police departments and even some of the Supreme Court justices accused the Warren Court of favoring criminals. Others cheered the decisions, seeing them as promoting the rights of all citizens, even the less privileged.

Prayer and Privacy The Supreme Court also handed down decisions affecting the relationship between church and state. The Court applied the First Amendment to the states in *Engel* v. *Vitale* (1962). In this ruling, the Court decided that states could not compose official prayers and require those prayers to be recited in state public schools. The following year, in *Abington School District* v. *Schempp*, it ruled against state-mandated Bible readings in public schools. Weighing in on another controversial issue, the Court ruled in *Griswold* v. *Connecticut* (1965) that prohibiting the sale and use of birth control devices violated citizens' constitutional right to privacy. *(See pages 962–963 for more information on these Supreme Court cases.)*

Activist Court The Warren Court poses for its official portrait in 1962, with Chief Justice Earl Warren front and center.

As with most rulings of the Warren Court, these decisions delighted some and deeply disturbed others. What most people did agree upon, however, was the Court's pivotal role in shaping national policy. The Warren Court, wrote *New York Times* columnist Anthony Lewis, "has brought about more social change than most Congresses and most Presidents."

From the political arena to the legal system to people's everyday lives, the Warren Court indeed left its imprint on the nation. Meanwhile, away from the domestic arena, President Kennedy worked to make his mark on the country's foreign affairs during a time of rising Cold War tensions.

✓ **Reading Check** **Examining** What was the significance of the Warren Court's "One Man, One Vote" ruling?

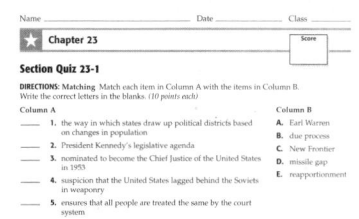

More About the Photo

In 1962 the members of the Warren Court included two members appointed by Franklin Delano Roosevelt, one appointed by Harry S Truman, four appointed by Eisenhower, and two appointed by John F. Kennedy.

Reteach
Have students summarize Kennedy's economic policies.

Enrich
Invite interested students to learn more about the life and career of one of the justices who served on the Warren Court. Encourage students to use library and Internet resources.

✓ **Reading Check**

Answer: All citizens' votes would have equal weight regardless of where they lived.

Study Central™ provides summaries, interactive games, and online graphic organizers to help students review section content.

SECTION 1 ASSESSMENT

HISTORY Online **Study Central™** To review this section, go to tarvol2.glencoe.com and click on **Study Central™.**

Checking for Understanding
1. **Define:** missile gap, reapportionment, due process.
2. **Identify:** New Frontier, Earl Warren.
3. **Summarize** the progress made for women's rights during Kennedy's administration.

Reviewing Themes
4. **Civic Rights and Responsibilities** Name three decisions of the Warren Court that protected civil rights.

Critical Thinking
5. **Interpreting** In what way was the 1960 presidential election a turning point in campaign history?
6. **Organizing** Use a graphic organizer similar to the one below to list the economic policies of the Kennedy administration.

Economic Policies	

Analyzing Visuals
7. **Analyzing Charts** Study the chart of Warren Court decisions on page 722. How did the Court expand the rights of the accused? Were these sound decisions? Why or why not?

Writing About History
8. **Expository Writing** In his Inaugural Address, President Kennedy asked his fellow Americans to "Ask what you can do for your country." Respond to this statement in an essay.

SECTION 1 ASSESSMENT ANSWERS

1. Terms are in blue.
2. New Frontier *(p. 720),* Earl Warren *(p. 721)*
3. Presidential Commission on the Status of Women, ending gender discrimination in federal civil service, and the Equal Pay Act
4. Answers should include any of the civil rights decisions listed on page 722.
5. Television played a more influential role.
6. a cut in tax rates, an increase in funds for defense and space exploration, an increase in the minimum wage, housing and redevelopment
7. Students should summarize the chart's due process decisions and weigh individual rights against police concerns.
8. Students' essays will vary but should focus on the meaning of Kennedy's statement.

4 CLOSE
Have students explain why Congress often did not support Kennedy's proposals.

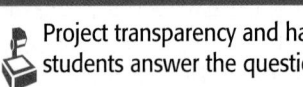

1 FOCUS

Section Overview

This section focuses on the Cold War during the Kennedy administration.

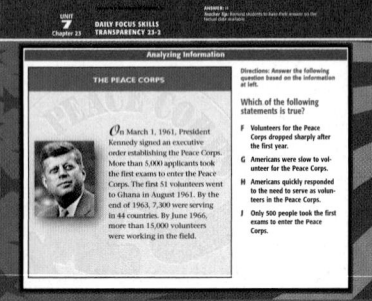

BELLRINGER
Skillbuilder Activity

Project transparency and have students answer the question.

Daily Focus Skills Transparency 23–2

Reading Preview

Answers to Graphic: January 1959, Castro's overthrow of Batista; April 17, 1961, Bay of Pigs; June 1961, Kennedy and Khrushchev meet in Vienna; October 1962, Cuban missile crisis; October 1962, Soviets agree to remove missiles from Cuba

Preteaching Vocabulary
Have students select one of the Key Terms and Names and write several questions about the term or name. Then have students work in pairs to answer the questions.

Guide to Reading

Main Idea
As president, John F. Kennedy had to confront the challenges and fears of the Cold War.

Key Terms and Names
flexible response, Peace Corps, space race, Berlin Wall, Warren Commission

Reading Strategy
Sequencing As you read about the crises of the Cold War, complete a time line similar to the one below to record the major events of the Cold War in the late 1950s and early 1960s.

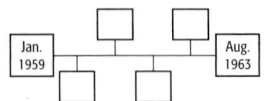

Reading Objectives
- **Describe** Kennedy's plan for the armed forces.
- **Explain** how the Cold War influenced foreign aid and the space program.

Section Theme
Science and Technology During the Cold War, the nation devoted much of its scientific and technological resources to competing with the Soviet Union, especially in getting to the moon.

Preview of Events

| ♦1961 | ♦1962 | ♦1963 | ♦1964 |

April 1961
Bay of Pigs invasion

May 1961
Kennedy informs Congress of moon expedition goal

October 1962
Cuban missile crisis

September 1963
Senate ratifies Limited Test Ban Treaty

November 22, 1963
Kennedy assassinated

★ An American Story ★

Emergency water supplied by Department of Defense

Like millions of other Americans in late October 1962, Tami Gold was having trouble concentrating on anything. For several tension-filled days that fall, the world seemed headed for nuclear destruction. U.S. officials had discovered that the Soviet Union had placed missiles in Cuba—a mere 90 miles (145 km) from the shores of the United States. When the Soviets refused to remove the weapons, a bitter weeklong standoff ensued in which the two superpowers hurled threats and warnings at each other and moved to the brink of nuclear war. Gold, then a seventh-grade student in Long Island, New York, recalled the events of one particular day:

❝I remember I was in the bathroom of the school . . . when they had said over the loud speaker . . . that everyone had to return to their homerooms immediately and get instruction from their homeroom teacher. And it was probably one of the scariest moments of my life, it was like the sensation that our country could go to war and I didn't understand at all what it was about, but the fact that the country could go to war at any moment was really really present. . . . It was chilling, it was scary, it was really nauseating. . . .❞

—quoted in *Collective Memories of the Cuban Missile Crisis*

Kennedy Confronts Global Challenges

The Cuban missile crisis, as the standoff came to be called, may have been the most dramatic foreign policy episode Kennedy faced. It was not the only one, however. As Kennedy entered the White House, the nation's dangerous rivalry with the Soviet Union continued to intensify.

724 CHAPTER 23 The New Frontier and the Great Society

SECTION RESOURCES

Reproducible Masters
- Reproducible Lesson Plan 23–2
- Daily Lecture and Discussion Notes 23–2
- Guided Reading Activity 23–2
- Section Quiz 23–2
- Reading Essentials and Study Guide 23–2
- Interpreting Political Cartoons

Transparencies
- Daily Focus Skills Transparency 23–2

Multimedia
- Interactive Tutor Self-Assessment CD-ROM
- ExamView® Pro Testmaker CD-ROM
- Presentation Plus! CD-ROM
- TeacherWorks™ CD-ROM
- Audio Program

Kennedy appeared ready to stand up to the Soviets. Upon taking the oath of office, the new president devoted much of his Inaugural Address to the role of the United States in a divided world:

> ❝Let the word go forth from this time and place . . . that the torch has been passed to a new generation of Americans—born in this century, tempered by war, disciplined by a hard and bitter peace, proud of our ancient heritage—and unwilling to witness or permit the slow undoing of those human rights to which this nation has always been committed. . . . Let every nation know, whether it wishes us well or ill, that we shall pay any price, bear any burden, meet any hardship, support any friend, oppose any foe, to assure the survival and the success of liberty.❞
>
> —quoted in *Let the Word Go Forth*

A More Flexible Response Kennedy took office at a time of growing global instability. Nationalism was exploding throughout the developing world, and the Soviet Union actively supported "wars of national liberation." *Newsweek* magazine wrote that the "greatest single problem that faces John Kennedy is how to meet the aggressive power of the Communist bloc."

Kennedy felt that Eisenhower had relied too heavily on nuclear weapons, which could only be used in extreme situations. To allow for a "flexible response" if nations needed help against Communist movements, the president pushed for a buildup of conventional troops and weapons.

In adopting this plan, Kennedy supported the Special Forces, a small army unit created in the 1950s to wage guerrilla warfare in limited conflicts. Kennedy expanded it and allowed the soldiers to wear their distinctive "Green Beret" headgear.

Aid to Other Countries One area of the world where Kennedy wanted to renew diplomatic focus was Latin America. Conditions in much of Latin American society were not good: Governments were often in the hands of the wealthy few and many of their citizens lived in extreme poverty. In some Latin American countries, these conditions spurred the growth of left-wing movements aimed at overthrowing their governments. When the United States was involved in Latin America, it was usually to help existing governments stay in power in order to prevent Communist movements from flourishing. Poor Latin Americans resented this intrusion, just as they resented American corporations that had business operations in their countries, a presence that was seen as a kind of imperialism.

To improve relations between the United States and Latin America, President Kennedy proposed an **Alliance for Progress,** a series of cooperative aid projects with Latin American governments. The alliance was designed to create a "free and prosperous Latin America" that would be less likely to support Communist-inspired revolutions.

Over a 10-year period, the United States pledged $20 billion to help Latin American countries establish better schools, housing, health care, and fairer land distribution. The results were mixed. In some countries—notably Chile, Colombia, Venezuela, and the Central American republics—the alliance did promote real reform. In others, governing rulers used the money to keep themselves in power.

The Peace Corps Another program aimed at helping less developed nations fight poverty was the **Peace Corps,** an organization that sent young Americans to perform humanitarian services in these countries.

After rigorous training, volunteers spent two years in countries that had requested assistance. They laid out sewage systems in Bolivia and trained medical technicians in Chad. Others taught English or helped to build roads. By late 1963 thousands of Peace Corps volunteers were serving in over 30 countries. Today, the Peace Corps is still active and remains one of Kennedy's most enduring legacies.

TECHNOLOGY

The Cold War Moves Into Space In 1961 Yuri Gagarin, a Soviet astronaut, became the first person to orbit the earth. Again, as in 1957 when they launched *Sputnik,* the first satellite, the Soviets had beaten the United States in the space race. President Kennedy worried about the impact of the flight on the Cold War. Soviet successes in space might convince the world that communism was better than capitalism. "Is there any place we can catch them?" Kennedy asked Vice President Johnson.

After consulting experts, Johnson gave Kennedy an idea. Less than six weeks after the Soviet flight, the president appeared before Congress. "Whatever mankind must undertake, free men must fully share," Kennedy announced. "I believe that this nation should commit itself to achieving the goal, before this decade

HISTORY Online

Student Web Activity Visit the *American Republic Since 1877* Web site at tarvol2.glencoe.com and click on *Student Web Activities— Chapter 23* for an activity on the New Frontier.

CHAPTER 23 The New Frontier and the Great Society **725**

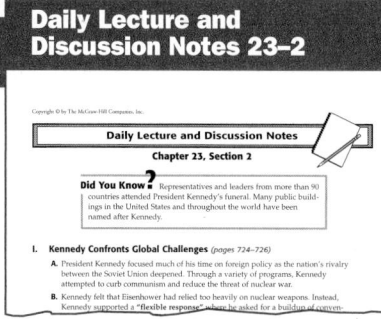

Daily Lecture and Discussion Notes 23–2

Copyright © by The McGraw-Hill Companies, Inc.

Daily Lecture and Discussion Notes
Chapter 23, Section 2

Did You Know? Representatives and leaders from more than 90 countries attended President Kennedy's funeral. Many public buildings in the United States and throughout the world have been named after Kennedy.

I. Kennedy Confronts Global Challenges *(pages 724–726)*

 A. President Kennedy focused much of his time on foreign policy as the nation's rivalry between the Soviet Union deepened. Through a variety of programs, Kennedy attempted to curb communism and reduce the threat of nuclear war.

 B. Kennedy felt that Eisenhower had relied too heavily on nuclear weapons. Instead, Kennedy supported a "**flexible response**" where he asked for a buildup of conven-

Discussing a Topic Have students discuss how President Kennedy's plans for space exploration reflected the Cold War. **L1** ELL

FYI

Since the Peace Corps was established in 1961, over 160,000 volunteers have served in 135 countries. Volunteer sectors include education, environment, health, business, and agriculture. In 2001 there were 7,300 Peace Corps volunteers serving in 72 countries.

HISTORY Online

Objectives and answers to the student activity can be found in the **Web Activity Lesson Plan** at tarvol2.glencoe.com.

Evaluating Information As access to print materials and electronic resources increases, students need to be able to evaluate what they read. Evaluating requires making a judgment or forming an opinion. To help students learn how to evaluate information, pose the following questions and remind them to use these when they read: Is the author qualified to write on this subject? Is the point of view biased? Is there another point of view not expressed here? Are opinions backed with facts, statistics, and examples? **L1**

📁 Refer to *Inclusion for the High School Social Studies Classroom Strategies and Activities* in the TCR.

L1/ELL
Guided Reading Activity 23-2

Name _____ Date _____ Class _____

★ **Guided Reading Activity 23-2**

DIRECTIONS: Using Headings and Subheadings Locate each heading below in your textbook. Then use the information under the correct subheading to help you write each answer.

I. Kennedy Confronts Global Challenges

A. What may have been the most dramatic foreign episode President Kennedy faced? _____

B. How did Kennedy attempt to reduce the threat of nuclear war and stem communism? _____

C. What was Kennedy's "flexible response"? _____

D. Where did Kennedy want to renew diplomatic focus? _____

E. What was the Peace Corps? _____

Why It Matters

Background: When the Soviets launched *Sputnik I* on October 4, 1957, American scientists were concerned about the military implications. The launching of *Sputnik II* a month later caused even more concern. Much larger than its predecessor and carrying a passenger—a dog named Laika—*Sputnik II* was propelled into space by an incredibly powerful rocket, which might, it seemed, be modified to carry missiles against the United States.

✓ Reading Check

Answer: the spread of communism, the Cuban missile crisis, Latin American relations, and reducing the threat of nuclear war

FYI

The names of the early manned space programs, Mercury, Gemini, and Apollo, were based on mythology. In Roman mythology, for example, Mercury was the messenger of the gods. In Greek mythology, Apollo carried the sun across the sky in his chariot each day.

Why It Matters

The Space Program

In 1962 President Kennedy responded to those who questioned the nation's effort to reach the moon: "But why, some say, the moon? Why choose this as our goal? And they may well ask, why climb the highest mountain? Why, 35 years ago, fly the Atlantic? . . . We choose to go to the moon. We choose to go to the moon in this decade and do the other things, not because they are easy, but because they are hard, because that goal will serve to organize and measure the best of our energies and skills, because that challenge is one that we are willing to accept, one we are unwilling to postpone, and one which we intend to win. . . ."

The Saturn V moon rocket is the most powerful rocket ever built.

Buzz Aldrin on the moon, July 1969

New Products ➤

By the time Neil Armstrong and Buzz Aldrin walked on the moon, NASA had spent over $33 billion. Since then, the space program has greatly benefited Americans. Space research has led to many new products, technologies, and manufacturing processes.

is out, of landing a man on the moon."

Kennedy's speech set in motion a massive effort by NASA and American industry to produce the necessary technology. In early 1962 John Glenn became the first American to orbit the earth. By 1965 American spacecraft had begun carrying two men at a time into orbit. Three years later the United States launched three men into orbit in a capsule called *Apollo. Apollo* was launched using the Saturn V, the largest and most powerful rocket ever built. Standing 363 feet (111 m) tall, the Saturn V was capable of giving both *Apollo* and the lunar module—which astronauts would use to land on the moon—enough velocity to escape Earth's gravitational pull and reach the moon.

On July 16, 1969, a Saturn V lifted off a launch pad in Florida carrying three American astronauts: Neil Armstrong, Edwin "Buzz" Aldrin, and Michael Collins. On July 20, Armstrong and Aldrin boarded their lunar module, named *Eagle,* and headed down to the moon. After a few tense minutes, Armstrong radioed the NASA flight center in Texas: "Houston . . . the *Eagle* has landed."

Armstrong opened the hatch and climbed down to the surface, becoming the first human being to walk on the moon. As he set foot on the lunar soil,

Armstrong announced: "That's one small step for man, one giant leap for mankind." American technology and determination had reached out across 238,000 miles to put men on the moon. America had won the space race and decisively demonstrated its technological superiority over the Soviet Union.

✓ Reading Check **Examining** What global challenges did Kennedy face during his presidency?

Crises of the Cold War

President Kennedy's efforts to combat Communist influence in other countries led to some of the most intense crises of the Cold War. At times these crises left Americans and people in many other nations wondering whether the world would survive.

The Bay of Pigs The first crisis occurred in Cuba, only 90 miles (145 km) from American shores. There, Fidel Castro had overthrown the corrupt Cuban dictator Fulgencio Batista in 1959. Almost immediately, Castro established ties with the Soviet Union, instituted drastic land reforms, and seized foreign-owned businesses, many of them American. Cuba's alliance

726 CHAPTER 23 The New Frontier and the Great Society

DIFFERENTIATED INSTRUCTION

Visual/Spatial Many Americans found inspiration in Kennedy's idealism, grieved at his death, and recaptured some hope for their country in President Johnson's determination. Ask students to create a poster that they feel captures the essence of President Kennedy's "New Frontier" or of his handling of international issues. **L1**

▸ Refer to *Inclusion for the High School Social Studies Classroom Strategies and Activities* in the TCR.

▼ **Assistance for People With Disabilities**
The NASA tele-operator and robot technology was used to develop a voice-controlled wheelchair and manipulator. Using a minicomputer, the wheelchair responds to 35 single-word voice commands, helping physically challenged people perform tasks like picking up packages, opening doors, and turning on appliances.

Increased Safety ➤
Remote-controlled robots reduce human injury levels because they can perform hazardous tasks men and women used to carry out. Robots can also perform operations no human being ever could, such as volcano research on the Puna Ridge of Kilauea, Hawaii.

Communication Advances

A communications satellite now in development will provide better telephone, television, and data service between western Europe, the Americas, and Africa. Another communications satellite has improved ship-to-shore communications, which used to be interrupted frequently by bad weather.

Writing a Speech Have students write speeches that President Kennedy might have given during the Cuban missile crisis. Ask volunteers to present their speeches to the class. **L3**

📁 Use the rubric for an oral presentation, monologue, song, or skit on pages 67–68 in the *Performance Assessment Activities and Rubrics.*

Proud Words Almost two years after the Berlin Wall was built, President Kennedy paid tribute to the spirit of Berliners when he spoke to a crowd gathered near the wall. He said, "All free men, wherever they may live, are citizens of Berlin. And, therefore, as a free man, I take pride in the words 'Ich bin ein Berliner' (I am a Berliner)."

Although the city of Berlin had been divided into East Berlin and West Berlin since the end of World War II, in August 1961 an actual wall of concrete, barbed wire, and stone was erected.

📁 Use *Interpreting Political Cartoons,* Cartoon 27.

---

with the Soviets worried many Americans. The Communists were now too close for comfort, and Soviet Premier Nikita Khrushchev had indicated he would strengthen Cuba's military.

Fearing that the Soviets would use Cuba as a base to spread revolution throughout the Western Hemisphere, President Eisenhower authorized the Central Intelligence Agency (CIA) to secretly train and arm Cuban exiles, known as La Brigada, to invade the island. The invasion was intended to ignite a popular uprising against Castro.

When Kennedy became president, his advisers approved the plan. In office fewer than three months and trusting his experts, Kennedy agreed to the operation with some changes. On April 17, 1961, 1,400 armed Cuban exiles landed at the **Bay of Pigs** on the south coast of Cuba. The invasion was a disaster. La Brigada's boats ran aground on coral reefs, Kennedy cancelled their air support to keep United States involvement a secret, and the expected popular uprising never happened. Within two days, Castro's forces killed or captured almost all the members of La Brigada. The outcome alarmed Kennedy. The action exposed an American plot to overthrow a neighbor's government and made the United States look weak and disorganized.

The Berlin Wall Goes Up Still reeling from the Bay of Pigs fiasco, Kennedy faced another foreign policy challenge in June 1961 when he met with Khrushchev in Vienna, Austria. Khrushchev wanted to stop the flood of Germans pouring out of Communist East Germany into West Berlin. He demanded that the Western powers recognize East Germany and that the United States, Great Britain, and France withdraw from Berlin, a city lying completely within East Germany. Kennedy refused and reaffirmed the West's commitment to West Berlin.

Khrushchev retaliated by building a wall through Berlin, sealing off the Soviet sector. Guards posted along the wall shot at anyone trying to escape from the East. For nearly 30 years afterward, the **Berlin Wall** stood as a visible symbol of the Cold War division between East and West.

The Cuban Missile Crisis By far the most terrifying crisis of the Kennedy era occurred the next year. Once again, the crisis dealt with Cuba. Over the summer of

---

INTERDISCIPLINARY CONNECTIONS ACTIVITY

Language Arts Tell students that through the Peace Corps, American volunteers offer help to developing nations around the world. Ask students to imagine that they want to join the Peace Corps today. Have them research the process and write a short report about what they learn. Encourage students to use library and Internet resources for their research. Remind students that they are to gather information. They should not actually submit an application to the Peace Corps. The Internet address for the Peace Corps is www.peacecorps.gov. **L2**

Reading Check

Answer: It was resolved through negotiations. The Soviet Union agreed to remove the missiles and Kennedy publicly agreed not to invade Cuba. Privately, Kennedy agreed to remove missiles from Turkey.

Picturing **History**

Answer: He announced the existence of the missiles, ordered a naval blockade, demanded the dismantling of the sites, warned that the U.S. was ready to respond with force to any attack, and negotiated a settlement with the Soviet Union.

3 ASSESS

Assign Section 2 Assessment as homework or as an in-class activity.

🌐 Have students use the **Interactive Tutor Self-Assessment CD-ROM.**

L1/ELL

Reading Essentials and Study Guide 23-2

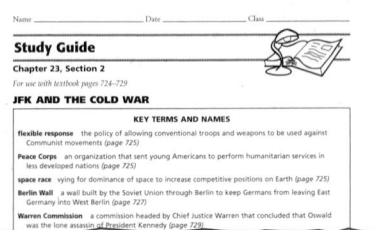

Name _____ Date _____ Class _____

Study Guide

Chapter 23, Section 2
For use with textbook pages 724–729

JFK AND THE COLD WAR

KEY TERMS AND NAMES

flexible response the policy of allowing conventional troops and weapons to be used against Communist movements (page 725)

Peace Corps an organization that sent young Americans to perform humanitarian services in less developed nations (page 725)

space race vying for dominance of space to increase competitive positions on Earth (page 725)

Berlin Wall a wall built by the Soviet Union through Berlin to keep Germans from leaving East Germany into West Berlin (page 727)

Warren Commission a commission headed by Chief Justice Warren that concluded that Oswald was the lone assassin of President Kennedy (page 729)

1962, American intelligence agencies learned that Soviet technicians and equipment had arrived in Cuba. On October 22, President Kennedy announced on television that American spy planes had taken aerial photographs showing that the Soviet Union had placed long-range missiles in Cuba. Enemy missiles stationed so close to the United States posed a dangerous threat.

Kennedy ordered a naval blockade to stop the Soviets from delivering more missiles, and he demanded that they dismantle existing missile sites. As Soviet ships headed toward the blockade, Americans braced themselves for war.

After a flurry of secret negotiations, the Soviet Union offered a deal. It would remove the missiles if the United States promised not to invade Cuba and to remove its missiles from Turkey near the Soviet border.

Neither Kennedy nor Khrushchev wanted nuclear war. "Only lunatics . . . who themselves want to perish and before they die destroy the world, could do this," wrote the Soviet leader. On October 28, the leaders reached an agreement. Kennedy publicly agreed not to invade Cuba and privately agreed to remove the Turkish missiles; the Soviets agreed to remove their missiles from Cuba. The world could breathe again.

The Impact of the Cuban Missile Crisis The Cuban missile crisis brought the world closer to nuclear war than at any time since World War II. Both the United States and the Soviet Union had been forced to consider the consequences of such a war. In the following months, each country seemed ready to work to lessen world tensions. In August 1963, the United States and the Soviet Union concluded years of negotiation by agreeing to a treaty to ban the testing of nuclear weapons in the atmosphere—the first step toward mutual arms reduction since the beginning of the Cold War.

In the long run, however, the missile crisis had ominous consequences. The humiliating retreat the United States forced upon the Soviet leadership contributed to Nikita Khrushchev's fall from power in October 1964. Perhaps more important, the crisis gave the Soviets evidence of their military inferiority and helped produce a dramatic Soviet arms buildup over the next two decades. This buildup contributed to a comparable military increase in the United States in the early 1980s.

Reading Check **Summarizing** How was the Cuban missile crisis resolved?

The Death of a President

Soon after the Senate ratified the test ban treaty, John F. Kennedy's presidency came to a shocking and

Picturing **History**

Cold War Peak Fears of communism peaked during the Cuban missile crisis. Routine reconnaissance flights over Cuba revealed the construction of missile sites, fueling facilities, and launch pads. **What steps did Kennedy take to deal with the crisis?**

CRITICAL THINKING ACTIVITY

Comparing Most people in the United States alive at the time of President Kennedy's assassination remember what they were doing when they heard the news. Ask students to compare the impact of the assassination on the lives of Americans to the impact of the events of September 11, 2001. In small groups have students compare the two tragedies in terms of their impact on the lives of Americans. **L2**

tragic end. On November 22, 1963, Kennedy and his wife traveled to Texas with Vice President Lyndon Johnson for a series of political appearances. As the presidential motorcade rode slowly through the crowded streets of Dallas, gunfire rang out. Someone had shot the president twice—once in the throat and once in the head. Horrified government officials sped Kennedy to a nearby hospital, where he was pronounced dead moments later.

Lee Harvey Oswald, the man accused of killing Kennedy, appeared to be a confused and embittered Marxist who had spent time in the Soviet Union. He himself was shot to death while in police custody two days after the assassination. The bizarre situation led some to speculate that the second gunman, local nightclub owner Jack Ruby, killed Oswald to protect others involved in the crime. In 1964 a national commission headed by Chief Justice Warren concluded that Oswald was the lone assassin. The report of the **Warren Commission** left some questions unanswered, and theories about a conspiracy to kill the president have persisted, though none has gained wide acceptance.

In the wake of the assassination, the United States and the world went into mourning. Americans across the land sobbed in public. Thousands traveled to Washington, D.C., and waited in a line that stretched for several miles outside the Capitol in order to walk silently past the president's flag-draped casket. Millions of others spent hours in front of their televisions, simply watching people file past the casket.

John F. Kennedy served as president for little more than 1,000 days. Yet his powerful personality and active approach to the presidency made a profound impression on most Americans. Aided by the tidal

A Final Salute John F. Kennedy, Jr. (right) bravely salutes his father's coffin during the state funeral. *How did people around the world react to JFK's assassination?*

wave of emotion that followed the president's death, his successor, Lyndon Johnson, set out to implement the programs Kennedy had left behind.

 Evaluating How did Kennedy's presidency end?

HISTORY Online **Study Central™** To review this section, go to tarvol2.glencoe.com and click on **Study Central™**.

SECTION 2 ASSESSMENT

Checking for Understanding
1. **Define:** flexible response, space race.
2. **Identify:** Peace Corps, Berlin Wall, Warren Commission.
3. **Explain** the goals of the Alliance for Progress.

Reviewing Themes
4. **Science and Technology** What was Kennedy's goal for the United States in the space race?

Critical Thinking
5. **Interpreting** What was the role of foreign aid in the relations between the United States and Latin America?
6. **Organizing** Use a graphic organizer similar to the one below to list the programs that Kennedy used to reduce the threat of nuclear war and to try to stem communism.

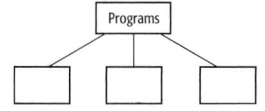

Analyzing Visuals
7. **Analyzing Photographs** Study the photographs on pages 726–727. Explain how space exploration has led to other innovations that have affected our daily lives and standard of living.

Writing About History
8. **Descriptive Writing** Take on the role of an American citizen during the Cuban missile crisis. Write a journal entry describing the mood of the country during that time.

SECTION 2 ASSESSMENT ANSWERS

1. Terms are in blue.
2. Peace Corps (p. 725), Berlin Wall (p. 727), Warren Commission (p. 729)
3. The goals were to create cooperative aid projects that helped establish better schools, improve housing, distribute land more equitably, and improve health care.
4. to beat the Soviets to the moon
5. to help governments stay in power and prevent Communist revolutions
6. conventional weaponry program, aid to foreign governments, the Peace Corps
7. Space discoveries have provided new solutions to problems faced by the disabled as well as scientists.
8. Journal entries will vary but should focus on emotions.

L2
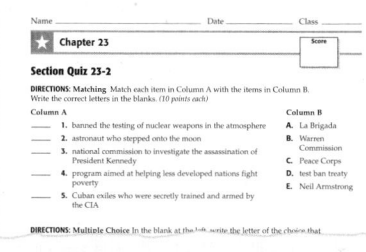

Section Quiz 23–2

Picturing **History**

Answer: People brought flowers to American embassies or wept.

Ask: When was President Kennedy assassinated? *(November 22, 1963)*

Reteach
Have students describe Kennedy's plan for the armed forces.

Enrich
Invite interested students to work in pairs to videotape interviews with people about what they remember about the day of President Kennedy's assassination and the days leading up to and including the funeral.

Reading Check

Answer: He was assassinated.

Study Central™ provides summaries, interactive games, and online graphic organizers to help students review section content.

4 CLOSE

Have students explain how the Cold War influenced foreign aid and the space program.

TEACH

Eyewitness

Tell students that President Johnson delivered his speech six months after Kennedy's assassination. His words set a clear agenda for the nation. Ask students to identify the particular phrases that they found inspiring. Then ask why they think this speech was important both for the president and for the American public. Have interested students use library and Internet resources to read Johnson's entire speech.

Reading Strategy

Verbatim

Have students review the quotes in the Verbatim section and discuss each item as it related to the people and themes found in their textbook. Have students research a current political, economic, or social issue. Have them create a list of quotations about the issue along with a brief statement explaining the quote, identifying the person quoted, and how the quote relates to the issue. Ask students to share their lists in a class discussion.

What Is a Pip, Anyway?

Have students work in pairs to create a matching game that lists popular groups today in one column and the lead singer(s) in the other column. Have students see how other students, their parents or guardians, or their younger siblings do on the quiz.

Visit the **TIME** Web site at www.time.com for up-to-date news, weekly magazine articles, editorials, online polls, and an archive of past magazine and Web articles.

BETTMANN/CORBIS

Eyewitness

On May 22, 1964, **PRESIDENT LYNDON JOHNSON** *delivered a speech in Ann Arbor, Michigan, outlining his domestic agenda that would become known as "The Great Society." Speechwriter and policy adviser Richard Goodwin watched the speech on videotape the next morning back in Washington. He recalls his reaction:*

Then, with the cheers, at first muted as if the audience were surprised at their own response, then mounting toward unrestrained, accepting delight, Johnson concluded: "There are those timid souls who say . . . we are condemned to a soulless wealth. I do not agree. We have the power to shape civilization. . . . But we need your will, your labor, your hearts. . . . So let us from this moment begin our work, so that in the future men will look back and say: It was then, after a long and weary way, that man turned the exploits of his genius to the full enrichment of his life."

Watching the film in the White House basement, almost involuntarily I added my applause to the tumultuous acclaim coming from the sound track. . . . I clapped for the President, and for our country.

WHAT IS A PIP, ANYWAY?

Match these rock 'n' roll headliners with their supporting acts.

1. Paul Revere and   a. the Union Gap
2. Martha and   b. the Supremes
3. Gary Puckett and   c. the Miracles
4. Gladys Knight and   d. the Vandellas
5. Smokey Robinson and   e. the Raiders
6. Diana Ross and   f. the Pips

answers: 1. e; 2. d; 3. a; 4. f; 5. c; 6. b

VERBATIM

"Is there any place we can catch them? What can we do? Are we working 24 hours a day? Can we go around the moon before them?"

PRESIDENT JOHN F. KENNEDY,
to Lyndon B. Johnson, after hearing that Soviet cosmonaut Yuri Gagarin had orbited the earth, 1961

"It was quite a day. I don't know what you can say about a day when you see four beautiful sunsets. . . . This is a little unusual, I think."
COLONEL JOHN GLENN,
in orbit, 1962

"There are tens of millions of Americans who are beyond the welfare state. Taken as a whole there is a culture of poverty . . . bad health, poor housing, low levels of aspiration and high levels of mental distress. Twenty percent of a nation, some 32,000,000."
MICHAEL HARRINGTON,
The Culture of Poverty, 1962

"I have a dream."
MARTIN LUTHER KING,
1963

"I don't see an American dream; . . . I see an American nightmare . . . Three hundred and ten years we worked in this country without a dime in return."
MALCOLM X,
1964

"The Great Society rests on abundance and liberty for all. It demands an end to poverty and racial injustice."
LYNDON B. JOHNSON,
1964

"In 1962, the starving residents of an isolated Indian village received 1 plow and 1,700 pounds of seeds. They ate the seeds."
PEACE CORPS AD,
1965

COOPERATIVE LEARNING ACTIVITY

Creating a Magazine Spread Organize the class into small groups. Assign each group one of the years in the 1960s and ask them to create their own two-page magazine spread for the year. Encourage students to use elements similar to those that appear in the Time Notebook, but to be creative as they select information that is of particular interest. Students should look at current magazines and books for ideas about page design. This activity can be completed using desktop publishing software or the more traditional cut-and-paste method.

Use the rubric for a cooperative group management plan on pages 71–72 in the *Performance Assessment Activities and Rubrics.*

Space Race

Want to capture some of the glamour and excitement of space exploration? Create a new nickname for your city. You won't be the first.

CITY	NICKNAME
Danbury, CT	Space Age City
Muscle Shoals, AL	Space Age City
Houston, TX	Space City, USA
Galveston, TX	Space Port, USA
Cape Kennedy, FL	Spaceport, USA
Blacksburg, VA	Space Age Community
Huntsville, AL	~~Rocket City, USA~~
	~~Space City, USA~~
	~~Space Capital of the Nation~~
	Space Capital of the World

John Glenn, first American to orbit Earth

RALPH MORSE/TIMEPIX

Milestones

PERFORMED IN ENGLISH, 1962. THE CATHOLIC MASS, following Pope John XXIII's Second Vatican Council. "Vatican II" allows the Latin mass to be translated into local languages around the world.

ENROLLED, 1962. JAMES MEREDITH, at the University of Mississippi, following a Supreme Court ruling that ordered his admission to the previously segregated school. Rioting and a showdown with state officials who wished to bar his enrollment preceded Meredith's entrance to classes.

BROKEN, 1965. 25-DAY FAST BY CÉSAR CHÁVEZ, labor organizer. His protest convinced others to join his nonviolent strike against the grape growers; shoppers boycotted table grapes in sympathy.

STRIPPED, 1967. MUHAMMAD ALI, of his heavyweight champion title, after refusing induction into the army following a rejection of his application for conscientious objector status. The boxer was arrested, given a five-year sentence, and fined $10,000.

PICKETED, 1968. The Miss America Pageant in Atlantic City, by protesters who believe the contest's emphasis on women's physical beauty is degrading and minimizes the importance of women's intellect.

AP

REMOVED, 1968. TOY GUNS, from the Sears, Roebuck Christmas catalog after the assassinations of Martin Luther King, Jr., and Robert Kennedy.

NUMBERS

7% of African American adults registered to vote in Mississippi in 1964 before passage of the Voting Rights Act of 1965

67% of African American adults in Mississippi registered to vote in 1969

70% of white adults registered to vote in 1964, nationwide

90% of white adults registered to vote nationwide in 1969

57 Number of days senators filibustered to hold up passage of the Civil Rights Bill in 1964

14½ Hours duration of all-night speech delivered by Senator Robert Byrd before a cloture vote stopped the filibuster

72% of elementary and high school teachers approve of corporal punishment as a disciplinary measure in 1961

HULTON-DEUTSCH COLLECTION/CORBIS

$80-90 Weekly pay for a clerk/typist in New York in 1965

$200 Rent for a two-bedroom apartment at Broadway and 72nd Street on New York City's Upper West Side in 1965

Portfolio Writing Project

Have students research one of the following people: John Glenn, Pope John XXIII, James Meredith, César Chávez, Muhammad Ali, Martin Luther King, Jr., or Robert Kennedy. Ask students to write a one-page essay about the person's contributions to history.

Creating a Nickname Have students research whether their city or county has a nickname, and what local history might have led to it. Then have students work in small groups to find a new nickname based on contemporary events, products, or reputation. Encourage students to be creative, but to select something that positively characterizes the area. List the groups' ideas on ballots. Have students vote for their top three choices. Tally the responses and identify the new nickname for the area. Have students give their suggested nickname to a local political leader.

CLOSE

Have students find out the number of registered voters who voted in the last presidential election. Students may focus on either national results or those from their own state or community.

EXTENDING THE CONTENT

Popular Culture In 1963 the top 10 television programs were: 1. *The Beverly Hillbillies,* 2. *Bonanza,* 3. *The Dick Van Dyke Show,* 4. *Petticoat Junction,* 5. *The Andy Griffith Show,* 6. *The Lucy Show,* 7. *Candid Camera,* 8. *The Ed Sullivan Show,* 9. *The Danny Thomas Show,* and 10. *My Favorite Martian.* The Limbo Rock, introduced by Chubby Checker, was the popular dance craze. The Beach Boys, with their melodic songs about hot rods and surfing, had five hit songs in 1963. *Cleopatra,* a film starring Elizabeth Taylor and Richard Burton, opened and was the most expensive film ever made to that date.

1 FOCUS

Section Overview
This section focuses on the Johnson administration.

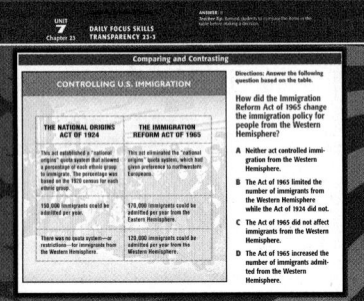

Reading Preview

Answers to Graphic: Programs include Higher Education Act, HUD, Job Corps, Medicaid, Medicare, Project Head Start. (See chart, page 736 for summary.)

Preteaching Vocabulary
Have students create a database of the Key Terms and Names that includes a definition and other important facts.

Guide to Reading

Main Idea
Lyndon Johnson succeeded John F. Kennedy as president and greatly expanded Kennedy's agenda with far-reaching programs in many areas.

Key Terms and Names
consensus, war on poverty, VISTA, Great Society, Medicare, Medicaid, Head Start, Robert Weaver

Reading Strategy
Organizing As you read about Lyndon Johnson's presidency, complete a graphic organizer similar to the one below to list the social and economic programs started during his administration.

Johnson's Programs

Reading Objectives
- **Explain** what inspired Johnson's Great Society programs.
- **Identify** several specific health and employment programs of the Johnson administration.

Section Theme
Government and Democracy In a time of prosperity, President Johnson won support for extending government aid to the poor and elderly.

Preview of Events

♦November 1963	♦June 1964	♦January 1965	♦August 1965

November 1963
Johnson becomes president upon Kennedy's death

August 1964
Congress enacts Economic Opportunity Act

November 1964
Johnson wins election as president

July 1965
Congress passes Medical Care Act, establishing Medicare and Medicaid

---

★ An American Story ★

Urban poverty in Chicago

In 1961, 61-year-old John Rath lived in a sparsely furnished room in Chicago. In the room sat a stove, a sink, a package of cereal, and a tiny icebox. The plaster on the wall was crumbling, the ceiling was cracked, and the window shades were smudged. Telling his story to an interviewer, Rath said:

❝I come home to an empty room. I don't even have a dog. No, this is not the kind of life I would choose. If a man had a little piece of land or something, a farm, or well . . . anyway, you've got to have something. You sit down in a place like this, you grit your teeth, you follow me? So many of them are doing that, they sit down, they don't know what to do, they go out. I see 'em in the middle of the night, they take a walk. Don't know what to do. Have no home environment, don't have a dog, don't have nothing . . . just a big zero.❞

—quoted in *Division Street: America*

Johnson Takes the Reins

John Rath's life was not the image that many Americans had of their country in the mid-1960s. The United States that President Lyndon Johnson inherited from John F. Kennedy appeared to be a booming, bustling place. From new shopping malls to new roads with new cars to fill them, everything in the country seemed to shout prosperity.

Away from the nation's affluent suburbs, however, was another country, one inhabited by the poor, the ill-fed, the ill-housed, and the ill-educated. Writer Michael Harrington examined the nation's impoverished areas in his 1962 book, *The Other America.* Harrington claimed that while the truly poor numbered almost 50 million, they remained largely

732 CHAPTER 23 The New Frontier and the Great Society

---

hidden in city slums, in rural areas, in the Deep South, and on Native American reservations.

Harrington's book moved many Americans and inspired both President Kennedy and his successor, Lyndon Johnson, to make the elimination of poverty a major policy goal. The nation was prosperous, and many leaders had come to believe that the economy could be managed so that prosperity would be permanent. They believed the federal government could afford to fund a new antipoverty program.

Lyndon Johnson decided to continue with Kennedy's plan soon after taking office. Immediately after President Kennedy was pronounced dead, officials whisked Johnson to the airport. At 2:38 P.M. on November 22, 1963, he stood in the cabin of Air Force One, the president's plane, with Jacqueline Kennedy on one side of him and his wife, Lady Bird, on the other. Johnson raised his right hand, placed his left hand on a Bible, and took the oath of office.

Johnson knew that he had to assure a stunned public that he could hold the nation together, that he was a leader. He later recalled the urgency with which he had to act:

66A nation stunned, shaken to its very heart, had to be reassured that the government was not in a state of paralysis . . . that the business of the United States would proceed. I knew that not only the nation but the whole world would be anxiously following every move I made—watching, judging, weighing, balancing. . . . It was imperative that I grasp the reins of power and do so without delay. Any hesitation or wavering, any false step, any sign of self-doubt, could have been disastrous.99

—quoted in *Lyndon Johnson and the American Dream*

Days after the assassination, Johnson appeared before Congress and urged the nation to move on. "The ideas and ideals which [Kennedy] so nobly represented must and will be translated into effective action," he stated. "John Kennedy's death commands what his life conveyed—that America must move forward."

Johnson's Leadership Style
Lyndon Baines Johnson was born and raised in the "hill country" of central Texas, near the banks of the Pedernales River. He remained a Texan in his heart and in his life.

Johnson's style posed a striking contrast with Kennedy's. He was a man of impressive stature who spoke directly, convincingly, and even roughly at times. His style was more that of a persuasive and personable politician than of the elegant society man. Finding it difficult to gain acceptance from the Eastern establishment in the nation's capital, he often reveled in his rough image.

Johnson had honed his style in long years of public service. By the time he became president at age 55, he already had 26 years of congressional experience behind him. He had been a congressional staffer, a member of the U.S. House of Representatives, a U.S. senator, Senate majority leader, and vice president.

As he moved up the political ladder, Johnson developed a reputation as a man who got things done. He did favors, twisted arms, bargained, flattered, and threatened. The tactics he used to persuade others became known throughout Washington as the "Johnson treatment." Several writers described this often overpowering and intimidating style:

66The Treatment could last ten minutes or four hours. . . . Its tone could be supplication, accusation, cajolery, exuberance, scorn, tears, complaint, the hint of threat. It was all these together. . . . Interjections from the target were rare. Johnson anticipated them

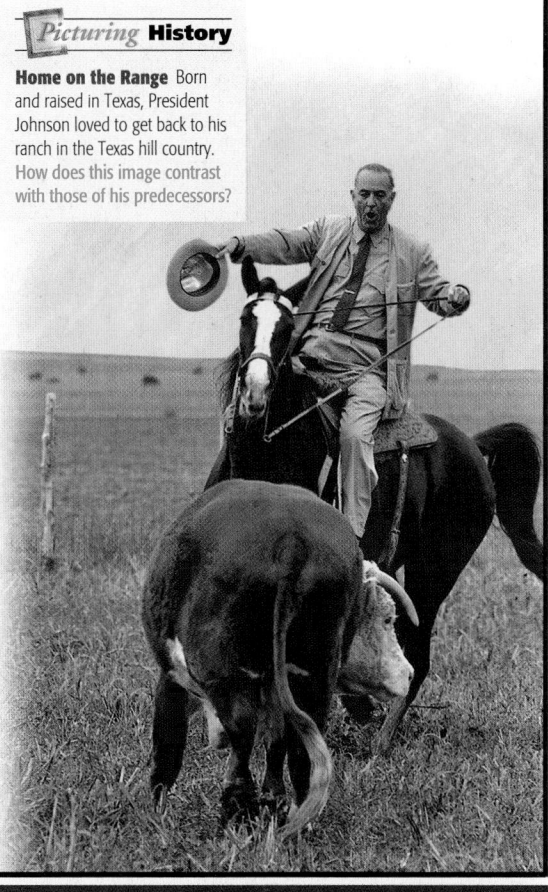

Picturing History

Home on the Range Born and raised in Texas, President Johnson loved to get back to his ranch in the Texas hill country. How does this image contrast with those of his predecessors?

2 TEACH

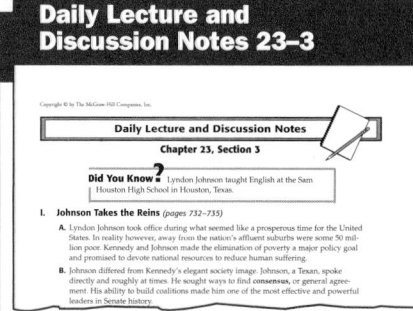

Daily Lecture and Discussion Notes 23–3

Daily Lecture and Discussion Notes
Chapter 23, Section 3

Did You Know? Lyndon Johnson taught English at the Sam Houston High School in Houston, Texas.

I. **Johnson Takes the Reins** (pages 732–735)

A. Lyndon Johnson took office during what seemed like a prosperous time for the United States. In reality however, away from the nation's affluent suburbs were some 50 million poor. Kennedy and Johnson made the elimination of poverty a major policy goal and promised to devote national resources to reduce human suffering.

B. Johnson differed from Kennedy's elegant society image. Johnson, a Texan, spoke directly and roughly at times. He sought ways to find consensus, or general agreement. His ability to build coalitions made him one of the most effective and powerful leaders in Senate history.

Creating a Poster Have students create a poster that illustrates one of the Great Society initiatives. Encourage students to use a before-and-after technique in which the poster shows both the need for the initiative and the proposed result of the program. **L1** ELL

you don't say...

What's in a Name? Lyndon Baines Johnson was the second man named Johnson to assume the mantle of the presidency after an assassination. Andrew Johnson became president after President Lincoln was killed.

Picturing History

Answer: Students should recognize that Johnson's image was considered rough compared to Kennedy's.
Ask: Where was Johnson born? (*Texas*)

Reading Strategy | READING THE TEXT

Using Word Parts A *root* is the part of the word that contains its basic meaning. Unlike a base word, a root is not a word by itself. Many roots come from Greek or Latin. For example, *bio* means "life" (biology, biography); *tele* means "distant" (television, telescope); *dent* means "tooth" (dentist, trident). Have students find root words in their study of the section and find their meanings using a dictionary. **L1** ELL

Refer to **Inclusion for the High School Social Studies Classroom Strategies and Activities** in the TCR.

L1/ELL

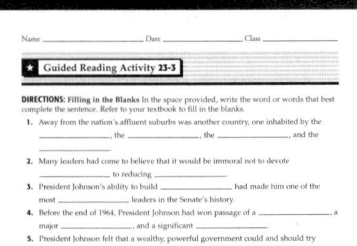
Writing a Letter Have students play the role of a member of one of the groups that had not experienced economic prosperity after World War II. From the point of view of the person they are playing, have students write a letter to President Johnson explaining what life is like and asking him to help. **L2**

📁 Use the rubric for a diary, short story, memorandum, or letter on pages 69–70 in the *Performance Assessment Activities and Rubrics.*

📷 *Picturing* History

Background: The images in this picture present a sharp contrast to the prosperity many Americans had experienced in the years after World War II.

Answer: He had known hard times and felt a wealthy nation should try to improve living standards for all.

Ask: What was the name of Johnson's antipoverty program? *(the war on poverty)*

---

before they could be spoken. He moved in close, his face a scant millimeter from his target, his eyes widening and narrowing, his eyebrows rising and falling. From his pocket poured clippings, memos, statistics. Mimicry, humor, and the genius of analogy made The Treatment an almost hypnotic experience and rendered the target stunned and helpless. 99

—from *Lyndon Johnson: The Exercise of Power*

With every technique he could think of, Johnson sought to find consensus, or general agreement. His ability to build coalitions had made him one of the most effective and powerful leaders in the Senate's history.

A War on Poverty As president, Johnson used his considerable talents to push through a number of Kennedy's initiatives. Before the end of 1964, he won passage of a tax cut, a major civil rights bill, and a significant anti-poverty program.

Why was this powerful man so concerned about poor people? Johnson liked to exaggerate the poor conditions of his childhood for dramatic effect, but he had in fact known hard times. He had also seen extreme poverty firsthand in a brief career as a teacher in a low-income area. Johnson understood suffering, and he believed deeply in social action. He felt that a wealthy, powerful government could and should try to improve the lives of its citizens. Kennedy himself had said of Johnson, "He really cares about this nation." Finally, there was Johnson's ambition. He wanted to achieve great things so that history would record him as a great president. Attacking poverty was a good place to begin.

Plans for an anti-poverty program were already in place when Johnson took office, and he knew that he would be able to command strong support for any program that could be linked to Kennedy. In his State of the Union address to Congress in 1964, barely seven weeks after taking office, President Johnson told his audience: "Unfortunately, many Americans live on the outskirts of hope, some because of their poverty and some because of their color and all too many because of both." Johnson concluded his speech by announcing that his administration was declaring an "unconditional war on poverty in America."

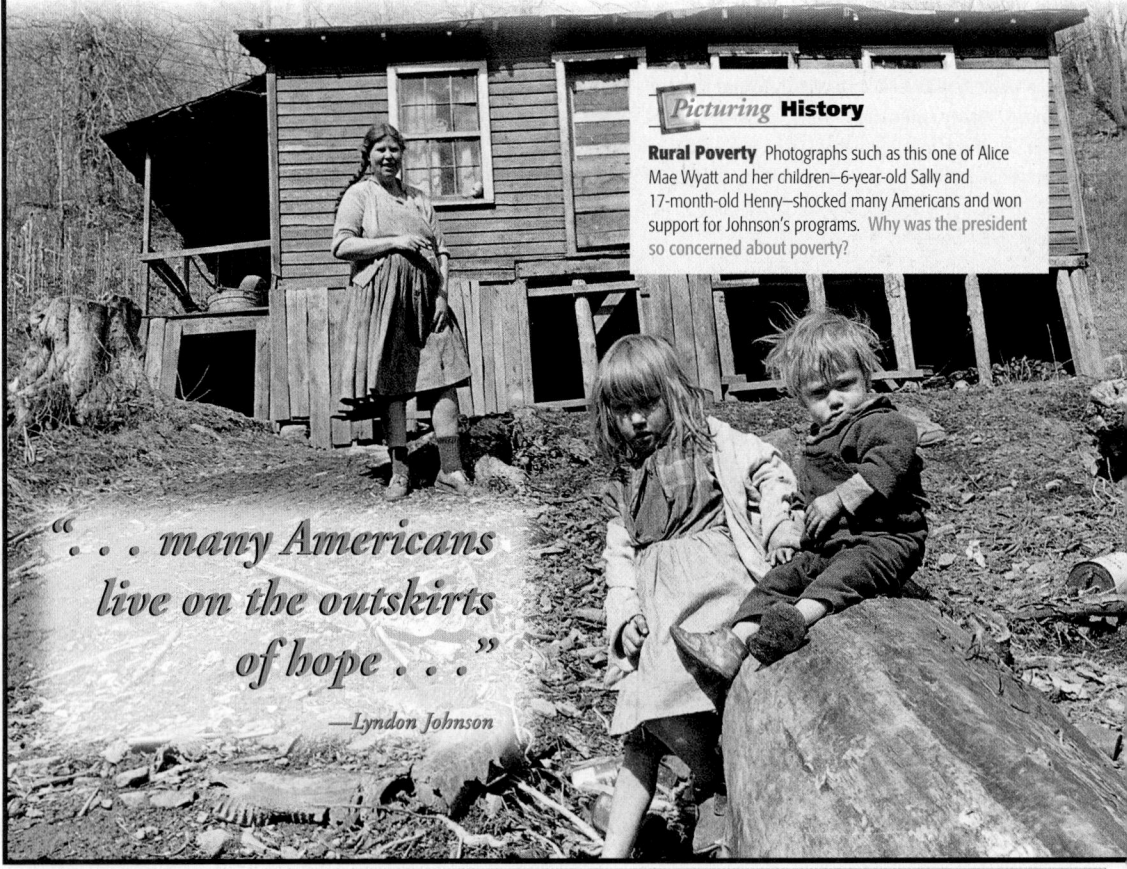

📷 *Picturing* History

Rural Poverty Photographs such as this one of Alice Mae Wyatt and her children—6-year-old Sally and 17-month-old Henry—shocked many Americans and won support for Johnson's programs. Why was the president so concerned about poverty?

" . . . *many Americans live on the outskirts of hope . . .*"

—*Lyndon Johnson*

DIFFERENTIATED INSTRUCTION

Visual/Spatial Have interested students examine the photograph on page 734 and then research other scenes of poverty from the 1960s. Based on their research, have students draw or paint a scene depicting the reality of poverty. Encourage students to focus on the expressions of the people living in poverty. **L2**

📁 Refer to *Inclusion for the High School Social Studies Classroom Strategies and Activities* in the TCR.

By the summer of 1964, Johnson had convinced Congress to pass the Economic Opportunity Act. The act established a wide range of programs aimed at creating jobs and fighting poverty. It also created a new government agency, the Office of Economic Opportunity (OEO) to coordinate the new programs. Many of the new programs were directed at young Americans living in the inner city. The Neighborhood Youth Corps provided work-study programs to help underprivileged young men and women earn a high school diploma or college degree. The Job Corps tried to help young unemployed people find jobs. One of the more dramatic programs introduced was **VISTA** (Volunteers in Service to America), which was essentially a domestic Peace Corps. VISTA put young people with skills and community-minded ideals to work in poor neighborhoods and rural areas to help people overcome poverty.

The Election of 1964 As early as April 1964, *Fortune* magazine declared, "Lyndon Johnson has achieved a breadth of public approval few observers would have believed possible when he took office." Johnson had little time to enjoy such praise, for he was soon to run for the office he had first gained through a tragic event.

Johnson's Republican opponent in the 1964 presidential election was **Barry Goldwater** of Arizona, a senator known for his outspoken conservatism. He set the tone for his campaign when he accepted his party's nomination, declaring, "Extremism in the defense of liberty is no vice! And let me remind you also that moderation in the pursuit of justice is no virtue!"

Few Americans were ready to embrace Goldwater's message, which was too aggressive for a nation nervous about nuclear war. On Election Day, Johnson won in a landslide, winning all but five southern states and Arizona. "For the first time in my life," he said later, "I truly felt loved by the American people."

✓ Reading Check **Examining** What inspired the war on poverty?

The Great Society

After his election, Johnson began working with Congress to create the "Great Society" he had promised during his campaign. In this same period, major goals of the civil rights movement were achieved with the passage of the Civil Rights Act of 1964, which barred discrimination of many kinds, and the Voting Rights Act of 1965, which ensured African Americans' right to vote.

Picturing **History**

Conservative Stance Senator Barry Goldwater's conservative ideas were not very popular in 1964, and they posed little challenge to President Johnson. How many states did Goldwater win?

The **Great Society** was Johnson's vision of the more perfect and equitable society the United States could and should become. According to Bill Moyers, who served as Johnson's press secretary, Johnson admired Franklin Roosevelt and wanted to fulfill FDR's mission. To do that would require a program that would be on the same large scale as the New Deal.

Johnson's goals were consistent with the times for several reasons. The civil rights movement had brought the grievances of African Americans to the forefront, reminding many that greater equality of opportunity had yet to be realized. Economics also supported Johnson's goal. The economy was strong, and many believed it would remain so indefinitely. There was no reason, therefore, that poverty could not be significantly reduced—especially when some had so much and others had so little.

Johnson first elaborated on the goals of the Great Society during a speech at the University of Michigan. It was clear that the president did not intend only to expand relief to the poor or to confine government efforts to material things. The president wanted, he said, to build a better society for all, a society "where leisure is a welcome chance to build and reflect, . . . where the city of man serves not only the needs of the body and the demands of commerce but the desire for beauty and the hunger for community. . . ."

Picturing **History**

Answer: Goldwater carried six states— five Southern states and his home state of Arizona.
Ask: How did people react to Goldwater's aggressive message? *(They were nervous about nuclear war and did not respond positively to Goldwater's aggressiveness.)*

Creating Circle Graphs Provide the data below and ask students to make a pair of circle graphs showing the results of the presidential election of 1964. **L2**

Candidate	Popular Vote	Electoral Vote
Goldwater, Rep.	27,178,188	52
Johnson, Dem.	43,129,566	486

Use the rubric for creating a map, display, or chart on pages 65–66 in the *Performance Assessment Activities and Rubrics.*

✓ Reading Check

Answer: the existence of pockets of extreme poverty in a generally prosperous society

When Head Start began, it was a summer program, but by 1970 most programs were year round. In 1999 Head Start enrollment was over 800,000 and cost an average of $5,400 per child.

INTERDISCIPLINARY CONNECTIONS ACTIVITY

Economics Ask the economics teacher to discuss with your class transfer payments by which the government transfers money from taxpaying citizens to needy people. Have the teacher provide statistics on transfer payments and discuss why Americans accept transfer payments as a way to deal with the problems of poverty. As a class, discuss the reasons that Americans approve of this role of the federal government. **L3**

Explaining Symbolism
President Johnson signed the Elementary and Secondary Education Act at his one-room schoolhouse, the Voting Rights Act in the room where Abraham Lincoln signed the Emancipation Proclamation, and the Immigration Act in the shadow of the Statue of Liberty. Ask students to explain the symbolism of each of these locations. **L2**

Chart *Skills*

Answers:
1. The Office of Economic Opportunity oversaw many inner-city programs.
2. Students' answers will vary but they should be able to explain how their chosen programs changed society.

Chart Skills Practice
Ask: How did health and welfare programs promote education?
(Child nutrition made students better able to learn from the educational programs offered.)

This ambitious vision encompassed a multitude of programs. In the three years between 1965 and 1968, more than 60 programs were passed. Among the most significant programs were **Medicare** and **Medicaid.** Health care reform had been a major issue since the days of Harry Truman. By the 1960s, public support for better health care benefits had solidified. Medicare had especially strong support since it was directed at the entire elderly population—in 1965, around half of those over the age of 65 had no health insurance.

Johnson convinced Congress to set up Medicare as a health insurance program funded through the Social Security system. Medicare's twin program, Medicaid, financed health care for welfare recipients, those who were living below the poverty line. Like the New Deal's Social Security program, both programs created what have been called "entitlements," that is, they entitle certain categories of Americans to benefits. Today, the cost of these programs has become a permanent part of the U.S. budget.

Great Society programs also strongly supported education. For Johnson, who had taught school when he was a young man, education was a personal passion. Vice President Hubert Humphrey once said that Johnson "was a nut on education. . . . [He] believed in it, just like some people believe in miracle cures."

The Elementary and Secondary Education Act of 1965 granted millions of dollars to public and private schools for textbooks, library materials, and special education programs. Efforts to improve education also extended to preschoolers, where Project **Head Start,** administered by the Office of Economic Opportunity, was directed at disadvantaged children who had "never looked at a picture book or scribbled with a crayon." Another program, Upward Bound, was designed to provide college preparation for low-income teenagers.

Improvements in health and education were only the beginning of the Great Society programs. Because of the deterioration of inner cities, Johnson told Congress that "America's cities are in crisis." Conditions in the cities—poor schools, crime, slum housing, poverty, and pollution—blighted the lives of those who lived there. Johnson urged Congress to act on several pieces of legislation addressing this issue.

Major Great Society Programs

Health and Welfare	Education	The "War on Poverty"	Consumer and Environmental Protection
Medicare (1965) established a comprehensive health insurance program for all elderly people; financed through the Social Security system.	**The Elementary and Secondary Education Act** (1965) targeted aid to students and funded related activities such as adult education and education counseling.	**The Office of Economic Opportunity** (1964) oversaw many programs to improve life in inner cities, including Job Corps, an education and job training program for at-risk youth.	**The Water Quality Act and Clean Air Acts** (1965) supported development of standards and goals for water and air quality.
Medicaid (1965) funded by federal and state governments, provided health and medical assistance to low-income families.	**Higher Education Act** (1965) supported college tuition scholarships, student loans, and work-study programs for low- and middle-income students.	**Housing and Urban Development Act** (1965) established new housing subsidy programs and made federal loans and public housing grants easier to obtain.	**The Highway Safety Act** (1966) supported highway safety by improving federal, state, and local coordination and by creating training standards for emergency medical technicians.
Child Nutrition Act (1966) established a school breakfast program and expanded the school lunch program and milk program to improve poor children's nutrition.	**Project Head Start** (1965) funded a preschool program for the disadvantaged.	**Demonstration Cities and Metropolitan Development Act** (1966) helped revitalize urban areas through a variety of social and economic programs.	**The Fair Packaging and Labeling Act** (1966) required all consumer products to have true and informative labels.

Chart *Skills*

1. **Interpreting Charts** What was the purpose of the Office of Economic Opportunity?
2. **Evaluating** Which Great Society program do you think had the most impact on American society? Why?

CRITICAL THINKING ACTIVITY

Evaluating Policies Tell students that Franklin Roosevelt appointed 27-year-old Lyndon Baines Johnson to serve as the national youth administrator for the state of Texas. Under Johnson's leadership, thousands of young people returned to high school, and thousands found work on government or private projects. Ask students how Johnson's early experience under Franklin Roosevelt's New Deal influenced his Great Society legislation in the 1960s. **L2**

YOUTH'S HELPING HAND

In 1965 VISTA (Volunteers in Service to America) was created as part of President Johnson's war on poverty. Roused by the social consciousness of the early 1960s, thousands of students and young people focused their energy into working with local agencies in low-income communities around the nation. One of VISTA's basic themes was to help local communities mobilize their own resources. Since 1993 VISTA has been a part of the AmeriCorps network of service programs.

Ask: How do you think programs such as VISTA brought out the positive, giving side of Americans? *(It allowed them to help people who were less fortunate.)*

✓ **Reading Check**

Answer: They included health, housing, job, and education programs.

3 ASSESS

Assign Section 3 Assessment as homework or as an in-class activity.

🖳 Have students use the **Interactive Tutor Self-Assessment CD-ROM.**

L1/ELL

Reading Essentials and Study Guide 23–3

Name _____ Date _____ Class _____

Study Guide

Chapter 23, Section 3

For use with textbook pages 732–738

THE GREAT SOCIETY

KEY TERMS AND NAMES
consensus general agreement *(page 734)*
war on poverty a program announced by President Johnson to fight poverty in the United States *(page 734)*
VISTA a Great Society program in which young people were put to work in poor school districts *(page 735)*
Great Society the domestic programs and goals of President Johnson's administration *(page 735)*
Medicare a government health insurance program for the elderly *(page 736)*
Medicaid a government health care program ...

One created a new cabinet agency, the Department of Housing and Urban Development, in 1965. Its first secretary, **Robert Weaver,** was the first African American to serve in a cabinet. A broad-based program informally called "Model Cities" authorized federal subsidies to many cities nationwide. The funds, matched by local and state contributions, supported an array of programs, including transportation, health care, housing, and policing. Since many depressed urban areas lacked sufficient or affordable housing, legislation also authorized about $8 billion to build houses for low- and middle-income people.

One notable Great Society measure changed the composition of the American population: the Immigration Reform Act of 1965. For a brief time, this act maintained a strict limit on the number of immigrants admitted to the United States each year: 170,000 from the Eastern Hemisphere and 120,000 from the Western Hemisphere. It did, however, eliminate the national origins system established in the 1920s, which had given preference to northern European immigrants. The new measure opened wider the door of the United States to newcomers from all parts of Europe, as well as from Asia and Africa.

✓ **Reading Check** **Summarizing** What were the Great Society programs?

Legacy of the Great Society

The Great Society programs touched nearly every aspect of American life and improved thousands if not millions of lives. In the years since President Johnson left office, however, debate has continued over whether or not the Great Society was truly a success.

In many ways, the impact of the Great Society was limited. In his rush to get as much done as he could, Johnson did not calculate exactly how his programs might work. As a result, some of them did not work as well as people had hoped. Furthermore, the programs grew so quickly they were often unmanageable and difficult to evaluate.

Cities, states, and groups eligible for aid began to expect immediate and life-changing benefits. These

CHAPTER 23 The New Frontier and the Great Society **737**

EXTENDING THE CONTENT

Social Security Administration The Social Security Administration has many service facilities around the country, employing thousands. In Johnson's Great Society, it participated in community projects to identify, train, and motivate unemployed and underemployed people. It worked with college placement officers, especially in African American colleges, to communicate information about government careers. It also worked with local community groups such as the Opportunities Industrialization Center, Metropolitan Employment Councils, and Equal Opportunity Commissions to reach the chronically unemployed.

Section Quiz 23–3

Profiles
IN HISTORY

Ask: For what causes did Esther Peterson fight? (*women's rights, trade unions, and consumer rights*)

Reteach
Have students explain what inspired the Great Society programs.

Enrich
Have students research LBJ's plan for Model Cities and write a report on the plans and how they were later modified.

 Reading Check

Answer: It improved millions of lives and reshaped government.

HISTORY Online

Study Central™ provides summaries, interactive games, and online graphic organizers to help students review section content.

4 CLOSE
Have students identify several specific health and employment programs of the Johnson era.

738

Profiles IN HISTORY

Esther Peterson
1906–1997

In the 1930s, Boston employers asked women who sewed aprons for them to switch from square pockets to a more difficult heart-shaped pocket, but they did not offer any increase in pay. Esther Peterson, a local teacher and outspoken advocate for women's rights, led the workers in a strike for more money. The women won their pay raise. For 60 years, Esther Peterson continued to use her tact and will to fight for women's rights, trade unions, and consumers.

Born in Provo, Utah, as Esther Eggertsen, Peterson became a teacher in the 1930s. She taught milliners, telephone operators, and garment workers at the innovative Bryn Mawr Summer School for Women Workers in Industry. In 1961 President Kennedy selected her to serve as Assistant Secretary of Labor and Director of the Women's Bureau.

Peterson then encouraged Kennedy to create a Presidential Commission on the Status of Women to focus attention on working women.

Under President Johnson, Peterson served as Special Assistant for Consumer Affairs, where she worked on consumer concerns. Lynda Johnson Robb, daughter of President Johnson, described Peterson this way: "She had a velvet hammer and talked people into doing what was right, even if we didn't know it at the time." Peterson continued to use her "velvet hammer" for the public good throughout her long life. At the time of her death at the age of 91, she was actively promoting senior citizens' health issues.

---

expectations often left many feeling frustrated and angry. Other Americans opposed the massive growth of federal programs and criticized the Great Society for intruding too much into their lives.

A lack of funds also hurt the effectiveness of Great Society programs. The programs themselves were expensive enough. When Johnson attempted to fund both his grand domestic agenda and the increasingly costly war in Vietnam, the Great Society eventually suffered. Some Great Society initiatives have survived

to the present, however. These include Medicare and Medicaid, two cabinet agencies—the Department of Transportation and the Department of Housing and Urban Development (HUD)—and Project Head Start. Overall, the programs provided some important benefits to poorer communities and gave political and administrative experience to minority groups.

An important legacy of the Great Society was the questions it produced, questions Americans continue to consider. How can the federal government help its disadvantaged citizens? How much government help can a society have without weakening the private sector? How much help can its people receive without losing motivation to fight against hardships on their own?

Lyndon Johnson came into office determined to change the United States in a way few other presidents had attempted. If he fell short, it was perhaps that the goals he set were so high. In evaluating the administration's efforts, the *New York Times* wrote, "The walls of the ghettos are not going to topple overnight, nor is it possible to wipe out the heritage of generations of social, economic, and educational deprivation by the stroke of a Presidential pen."

✓ Reading Check **Evaluating** What was the impact of the Great Society?

HISTORY Online
Study Central™ To review this section, go to **tarvol2.glencoe.com** and click on **Study Central**™.

SECTION 3 ASSESSMENT

Checking for Understanding
1. **Define:** consensus, war on poverty.
2. **Identify:** VISTA, Great Society, Medicare, Medicaid, Head Start, Robert Weaver.
3. **Describe** how the Great Society programs were inspired.

Reviewing Themes
4. **Government and Democracy** How did Johnson's war on poverty strive to ensure greater fairness in American society?

Critical Thinking
5. **Interpreting** What were three legacies of the Great Society?
6. **Organizing** Use a graphic organizer similar to the one below to list five Great Society initiatives that have survived to the present.

Great Society Initiatives

Analyzing Visuals
7. **Photographs** Study the photograph on page 734. Why do you think pictures such as this one would help build support for the war on poverty?

Writing About History
8. **Descriptive Writing** Take on the role of a biographer. Write a chapter in a biography of Lyndon Johnson in which you compare and contrast his leadership style to that of John Kennedy.

SECTION 3 ASSESSMENT ANSWERS

1. Terms are in blue.
2. VISTA (*p. 735*), Great Society (*p. 735*), Medicare (*p. 736*), Medicaid (*p. 736*), Head Start (*p. 736*), Robert Weaver (*p. 737*)
3. Johnson wanted to fulfill FDR's mission for a nation of equal opportunity.
4. by offering the less fortunate education, training, and access to jobs
5. Answers should reflect text, for example, Medicare and Medicaid, political experience for minorities, Head Start.
6. Medicare, Medicaid, Department of Transportation, Department of Housing and Urban Development, Project Head Start
7. Answers will vary. Students should describe the emotions evoked by such photographs.
8. Chapters should include specific information about the leadership styles of the two men.

Problem Solving

Why Learn This Skill?

Imagine you have just done poorly on a chemistry exam. You wonder why you cannot do better since you always go to class, take notes, and study for exams. In order to improve your grades, you need to identify the specific problem and then take actions to solve it.

Learning the Skill

There are six key steps you should follow that will help you through the problem-solving process.

- Identify the problem. In the case listed above, you know that you are not doing well on chemistry exams.

- Gather information. You know that you always go to class and take notes. You study by yourself for about two hours each day for two or three days before the exam. You also know that you sometimes forget details or get confused about things as you are taking the exam.

- List and consider possible solutions. For example, instead of studying by yourself, you might try studying with a friend or a group. You might also study for shorter timespans to avoid overloading yourself with information.

- Consider the advantages and disadvantages of each solution.

- Now that you have listed and considered the possible options, you need to choose the best solution to your problem. Choose what you think is the right solution, and carry it out.

- Evaluate the effectiveness of the solution. This will help you determine if you have solved the problem. If you earn better scores on the next few chemistry tests, you will know that you have solved your problem.

Practicing the Skill

Reread the material in Section 1 on page 720 under the heading "Kennedy Struggles with Congress." Use that information and the steps listed on this page to answer the following questions.

❶ What problem did Kennedy encounter as he tried to pass domestic policy legislation through Congress?

❷ What options were available to the president in facing this opposition? What were the advantages and disadvantages?

❸ Explain the solution Kennedy implemented to solve his problem.

❹ Evaluate the effectiveness of Kennedy's solution. Was it successful? How do you determine this?

Skills Assessment

Complete the Practicing Skills questions on page 743 and the Chapter 23 Skill Reinforcement Activity to assess your mastery of this skill.

Applying the Skill

Problem Solving The conservation club at your school has no money to continue its recycling project. The school district allocated money to the club at the beginning of the year, but that money has been spent. As a member of the club, you have been asked to join a committee to save the conservation club and its projects. Write an essay describing the problem, the list of options and their advantages and disadvantages, a solution, and an evaluation of the chosen solution.

Glencoe's **Skillbuilder Interactive Workbook CD-ROM, Level 2,** provides instruction and practice in key social studies skills.

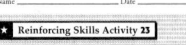

TEACH

Problem Solving Tell students that when they encounter problems the first step is identifying the problem.

As a class, students should select a problem that the community is facing. Have students work in pairs to use the problem-solving process to identify the best solution. Have the class reach a consensus on the best solution. Submit the class's suggestion to local political leaders or other decision makers who may be working on the problem.

Additional Practice

L1

Reinforcing Skills Activity 23

Name _____ Date _____ Class _____

★ Reinforcing Skills Activity 23

Problem Solving

☐ LEARNING THE SKILL

The first step in identifying a problem is clearly defining it. After you have identified a problem, begin to gather information about it. Then consider possible solutions to the problem, and weigh the advantages and disadvantages of each solution you have identified. Use your list of positives and negatives to pick the best solution. As you begin to put your solution into action, monitor the results. Has your solution been effective in solving your problem? If not, make adjustments to your solution as necessary.

☐ PRACTICING THE SKILL

DIRECTIONS: Read the excerpt below from page 725 of your text. Then answer the questions that follow on a separate sheet of paper.

GLENCOE
TECHNOLOGY

CD-ROM
Glencoe Skillbuilder
Interactive Workbook
CD-ROM, Level 2

This interactive CD-ROM reinforces student mastery of essential social studies skills.

ANSWERS TO PRACTICING THE SKILL

❶ congressional resistance

❷ He could push harder for all aspects of his agenda or reserve his bargaining power for only the issues that were truly important and winnable.

❸ He chose to reserve his bargaining power.

❹ Students' answers will vary. Students might mention that many of JFK's proposals were defeated, or that he lacked political leverage no matter what strategy he used.

Applying the Skill
Students' essays will vary. Encourage students to use the steps on this page as they plan their essays.

1 FOCUS

Remind students that the Anti-Federalists were the primary supporters of the Bill of Rights because they feared the power of a strong central government. Federalists, such as George Washington, Benjamin Franklin, and James Madison, did not believe that the Bill of Rights was necessary. They argued that the necessary protections were already in either the Constitution or in state constitutions.

2 TEACH

Analyzing a Concept List each of the basic rights on the board. Have students think of specific examples from the colonial period in which the British or other foreign entities denied these rights to colonists. Have students write their examples on the board to create a chart that they can use for later reference. Encourage students to use their text's Table of Contents and Index to help them find and review the examples. **L1**

Creating a Song Have interested students create a song or jingle that they can use to help them remember the basic guarantees of the Bill of Rights. Have students perform their songs or jingles for the class. **L2**

The Bill of Rights

Why It Matters In 1962 Clarence Earl Gideon was arrested for breaking into a Florida pool hall. When he asked for a lawyer, the judge refused. Defendants in Florida were not entitled to a court-appointed lawyer except in death penalty cases. Gideon then appealed to the Supreme Court, arguing that the Constitution's Sixth Amendment guaranteed the right to a lawyer. In 1963, in *Gideon* v. *Wainright,* the Supreme Court decided that the Sixth Amendment applied to both state and federal courts. The court ruled that having a lawyer in a criminal case is a fundamental right.

For over 200 years, the first ten amendments to the Constitution, known as the Bill of Rights, have protected the rights of Americans. Five of the amendments specify rights Americans have in federal court. In the 1960s, the Supreme Court extended many of these rights to the state and local levels.

Steps To . . . the Bill of Rights

During the Middle Ages, kings had great power, but to pass a new law they usually obtained the consent of a council of important nobles. This custom of ruling with "noble consent" was not written into law until 1215.

From Liberties to Rights In 1215 King John of England faced a rebellion of many of the English nobles. Under pressure, he signed the **Magna Carta.** In this document the king promised "to all freemen of our kingdom . . . all the underwritten liberties, to be had and held by them and their heirs, of us and our heirs forever." After 1215 the English king was expected to rule in accordance with the Magna Carta.

When the Enlightenment began in the 1600s, a new idea of rights emerged. Several writers argued that kings could not give rights to people. Instead, every person was born with rights that the government could not violate. **John Locke** was an advocate of this new idea. His book, *Two Treatises of Government,* became very influential in the American colonies.

The Magna Carta

In 1688 the English Parliament helped remove King James II from the throne in what was known as the Glorious Revolution. Before the new king and queen took the throne, Parliament demanded they accept the **English Bill of Rights.** The English Bill of Rights strongly influenced American ideas. When the American Revolution began, revolutionaries accused the British of violating many of these rights.

"We hold these truths to be self-evident, that all men are created equal, that they are endowed by their Creator with certain unalienable rights, that among these are Life, Liberty, and the pursuit of Happiness."

—Thomas Jefferson, The Declaration of Independence

740

EXTENDING THE CONTENT

Magna Carta Although the Magna Carta placed some legal restraints on the king, it extended rights only to nobles (who were the freemen) and did nothing for the common people. Throughout Europe's kingdoms, the rights of individuals were very limited. In France dukes who determined the rights of common people on the lands they controlled held most of the power. Even when a French legislature was created, the townspeople were given only one collective vote as the third estate.

Origins of the Bill of Rights

Basic Rights	Magna Carta (1215)	English Bill of Rights (1689)	Virginia Declaration of Rights (1776)	Virginia Statute for Religious Freedom (1786)	American Bill of Rights (1791)
No state religion				●	●
Freedom of worship		● limited	●	●	●
Freedom of speech		●	●		●
Right to petition		● limited			●
Right to bear arms					●
No quartering troops in private homes without permission				●	●
No searches and seizures without a specific search warrant	●		●		●
Government cannot take away life, liberty, or property unless it follows proper court procedures (due process)	●	●	●		●
Right to a speedy public trial by jury and to a lawyer	●	●	●	●	●
No excessive bail, fines, or cruel and unusual punishment	●	●			●

The American Revolution In the 1760s, in order to stop smuggling in the American colonies, the British began sending accused smugglers to vice admiralty courts. These courts had no juries. In the Declaration of Independence, Americans accused the British of "depriving us . . . of the benefits of trial by jury" as guaranteed in the Magna Carta and the English Bill of Rights. Americans later wrote the Fifth and Sixth Amendments of the Bill of Rights to prevent similar abuses by the American federal government.

Also to stop smuggling, the British issued "writs of assistance" authorizing officials to search private property as they saw fit. Americans later wrote the Fourth Amendment to prevent officials from conducting searches without specific search warrants.

Free Speech In England, free speech was limited by laws against sedition. Sedition is the encouraging of opposition to the government. The only exception applied to Parliament. The English Bill of Rights stated that "freedom of speech . . . in parliament, ought not to be . . . questioned."

The Founders of the United States knew that the American Revolution could not have happened had they been unable to make speeches or print their ideas in newspapers. When the Bill of Rights was submitted, a ban on any federal law restricting free speech or freedom of the press was prominent in the First Amendment.

Putting Rights Into the Constitution When the Constitution was drafted, it did not include a list of rights because supporters believed the new federal government's checks and balances would protect people's rights. When the Constitution was submitted to the states for ratification, however, opponents argued that without a list of rights, the Constitution would lead to a tyrannical federal government.

George Mason, who drafted Virginia's Declaration of Rights, was a leader of the opposition. To get the Constitution ratified, supporters promised a Bill of Rights. In September 1789, James Madison prepared 12 amendments to the Constitution. In wording these amendments, Madison relied heavily on Virginia's Declaration of Rights. Ten of the amendments were ratified. Together, they make up the Bill of Rights.

Checking for Understanding
1. How many rights are in the Bill of Rights?
2. Which amendments in the Bill of Rights protect rights the British violated in the 1760s?

Critical Thinking
1. Which right do you think is the most important? Why?
2. Do Americans have any other rights other than those listed in the Bill of Rights? What are they?

Looking Back...

Writing an Essay Explain to students that the Supreme Court has ruled that the right to freedom of speech is quite broad. Have interested students write an essay describing some of the forms of speech that the Supreme Court has ruled are protected under the First Amendment, and some that are not protected. **L3**

3 ASSESS

Have students answer the Checking for Understanding and Critical Thinking questions.

Ask interested students to research their state courts to learn about how court-appointed lawyers are selected, including the criteria for determining whether a defendant needs a court-appointed lawyer. Students should report their findings in an essay.

4 CLOSE

Ask students to consider when, or if, any of the rights listed in the Bill of Rights should be suspended, for example in times of war. Hold a class discussion on this topic.

Checking for Understanding
1. The Bill of Rights contains 10 basic rights.
2. In the 1760s, the British violated the right to proper court procedures (Fifth Amendment), the right to a speedy public trial (Sixth Amendment), and the right to be protected from searches and seizures without a warrant (Fourth Amendment).

Critical Thinking
1. Students should state specific reasons for their choices.
2. Students should recognize that Americans have other rights under the Constitution, the other amendments to the Constitution, and, to a certain extent, under individual state constitutions.

CHAPTER
23 ASSESSMENT and ACTIVITIES

Reviewing Key Terms
Students' answers will vary. The pages
where the words appear in the text are
shown in parentheses.

1. **missile gap** *(p. 719)*
2. **reapportionment** *(p. 721)*
3. **due process** *(p. 722)*
4. **flexible response** *(p. 725)*
5. **space race** *(p. 725)*
6. **consensus** *(p. 734)*
7. **war on poverty** *(p. 734)*

Reviewing Key Facts
8. New Frontier *(p. 720)*, Earl Warren *(p. 721)*, Peace Corps *(p. 725)*, Warren Commission *(p. 729)*, Great Society *(p. 735)*, Head Start *(p. 736)*
9. The campaign marked the first time that television played a major role, including the televised debate between Kennedy and Nixon.
10. They focused on the economy and the Cold War.
11. Kennedy won the popular vote by only 118,000, with 68 million votes cast. In the Electoral College, the margin was greater: 303 to 219.
12. He threatened to buy steel from foreign companies and investigated price fixing.
13. He used deficit spending, invested in space exploration and defense to create jobs, and asked businesses to hold down prices and labor leaders to hold down pay increase requests.
14. conventional weaponry program, foreign aid, the Peace Corps
15. Johnson's personal experiences and the nation's ability to finance programs

Reviewing Key Terms
On a sheet of paper, use each of these terms in a sentence.

1. missile gap
2. reapportionment
3. due process
4. flexible response
5. space race
6. consensus
7. war on poverty

Reviewing Key Facts
8. **Identify:** New Frontier, Earl Warren, Peace Corps, Warren Commission, Great Society, Head Start.
9. How was the 1960 presidential election a new kind of campaign?
10. What main issues did Nixon and Kennedy discuss in their televised debate?
11. How close was the outcome of the 1960 presidential election between Nixon and Kennedy?
12. What was Kennedy's response to the steel industry's decision to raise prices sharply?
13. What were three measures Kennedy took to strengthen the economy?
14. What were three programs set up by Kennedy to reduce the threat of nuclear war and to try to stem communism?
15. What inspired President Johnson's war on poverty?
16. What was the purpose of Medicare, passed during Johnson's administration?
17. Which Great Society initiatives are still in effect today?

Critical Thinking
18. **Analyzing Themes: Government and Democracy** Why were Medicare and Medicaid landmark pieces of legislation in American history?
19. **Evaluating** In the 1960 presidential debate, most radio listeners thought Nixon had won, while most television viewers thought Kennedy had. Why do you think this was so?
20. **Drawing Conclusions** How did Kennedy help prevent Communist movements from flourishing in Latin America?
21. **Analyzing** President Kennedy was unable to pass civil rights legislation. What were some of the factors that allowed President Johnson to push civil rights forward after Kennedy's assassination?
22. **Organizing** Use a graphic organizer similar to the one below to list the crises of the Cold War during the Kennedy administration.

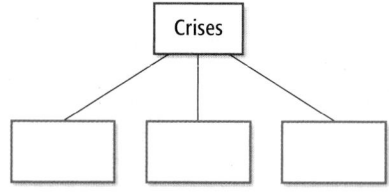

23. **Evaluating** How did the Warren Court decisions in *Baker* v. *Carr* and *Reynolds* v. *Sims* affect voting power in the nation?
24. **Interpreting Primary Sources** Although the standard of living for most Americans rose dramatically throughout the

---

Chapter Summary

The New Frontier and the Great Society

Domestic Programs	Foreign Policy	Supreme Court Cases
• Office of Economic Opportunity fights illiteracy, unemployment, and disease. • Civil Rights Act of 1964 prohibits race discrimination and social segregation. • Voting Rights Act protects the right to vote. • Medicare and Medicaid Acts provide federal medical aid to the elderly and poor. • Elementary and Secondary Education Act increases aid for public schools.	• "Flexible response" policy maintains opposition to communism. • U.S. pledges aid to struggling Latin American nations. • Peace Corps offers humanitarian aid in poor countries. • Nuclear Test Ban Treaty with the Soviet Union eases Cold War tensions.	• *Reynolds* v. *Sims* boosts voting power of urban dwellers, including many minorities. • Extension of due process gives more protection to people accused of crimes. • Court rules that states could not require prayer and Bible readings in public schools.

742 CHAPTER 23 The New Frontier and the Great Society

---

16. Medicare was designed as a health insurance program for the elderly.
17. Among programs or agencies still in effect are Medicare, Medicaid, Head Start, Department of Transportation, and Department of Housing and Urban Development.

Critical Thinking
18. They represented the first time that the U.S. government had funded health care on a large scale.

19. Kennedy's physical appearance and demeanor made a positive impact on the television audience. Their reaction to Nixon's appearance and demeanor was negative. Because they could only hear the candidates, radio listeners had a different reaction.
20. He provided aid to Latin America so that countries would be less likely to support communist-inspired revolutions.
21. the civil rights movement, Kennedy's death, Johnson's style of leadership

Self-Check Quiz

Visit the *American Republic Since 1877* Web site at tarvol2.glencoe.com and click on *Self-Check Quizzes— Chapter 23* to assess your knowledge of chapter content.

1960s, some Americans remained mired in poverty. Reread the excerpt on page 732 in which John Rath discusses his personal experiences with coping with poverty in his sparsely furnished room in Chicago. Then answer the following questions.

a. What does Rath think might help him to have some purpose in his life?

b. What does Rath mean when he says: "You sit down in a place like this, you grit your teeth. . . ."?

Practicing Skills

25. **Problem Solving** Reread the passage on pages 727–728 titled "The Cuban Missile Crisis." Use that information to answer the following questions.

a. What problem did Kennedy encounter in Cuba?

b. What options were available to the president in this situation? What were the advantages and disadvantages of each option?

c. Explain the solution Kennedy used to resolve the Cuban missile crisis.

d. Was Kennedy's solution successful? Why or why not?

Chapter Activity

26. **Technology Activity: Using the Internet** Search the Internet to check the status of Great Society programs today. Find out how these programs have changed since they were initiated. Make a chart showing the provisions of the programs in the 1960s compared to the provisions of the programs today.

Writing Activity

27. **Expository Writing** Assume the role of a historian. Evaluate the effectiveness of Kennedy's New Frontier and Johnson's Great Society programs. Write an article for a historical journal explaining the successes and setbacks of each president's policy agendas.

Geography and History

28. The map on this page shows the results of the presidential election of 1960. Study the map and answer the questions below.

a. **Interpreting Maps** Which regions of the country supported Kennedy? Which regions supported Nixon?

b. **Applying Geography Skills** What would have happened if Kennedy had lost New York to Nixon?

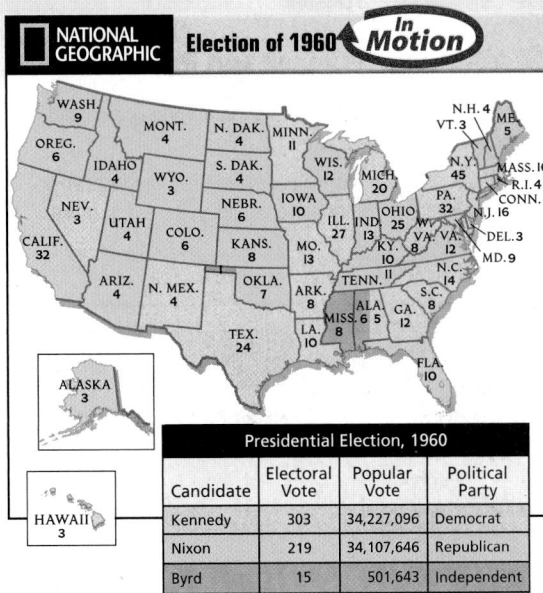

NATIONAL GEOGRAPHIC   **Election of 1960** *In Motion*

Presidential Election, 1960			
Candidate	Electoral Vote	Popular Vote	Political Party
Kennedy	303	34,227,096	Democrat
Nixon	219	34,107,646	Republican
Byrd	15	501,643	Independent

Standardized Test Practice

Directions: Choose the best answer to the following question.

Which of the following was an effect of a ruling by the Warren Court?

A State-mandated Bible readings allowed in schools

B Extended rights for people accused of crimes

C Unlawfully seized evidence is admissible at trial

D Increased state authority at the expense of federal authority

Test-Taking Tip: Use the process of elimination to answer this question. The Warren Court expanded individual civil liberties and the power of the judicial branch. Eliminate answers that go against these ideas.

Have students visit the Web site at tarvol2.glencoe.com to review Chapter 23 and take the Self-Check Quiz.

Chapter Activity

26. Students' charts will vary. You may want to have students work in pairs on this activity.

Writing Activity

27. Students' articles will vary but should use the perspective of history to evaluate the successes and failures of the programs.

Geography and History

28. **a.** Nixon: Midwest, West; Kennedy: Northeast, some Southern and Midwestern states; **b.** Nixon would have won the election by six electoral votes.

Standardized Test Practice

Answer: B

Test-Taking Tip: Even if students do not know all the rulings of the Warren Court, they can eliminate some of the answers by applying the knowledge they do have. For example, since answer C would obviously limit rather than expand civil liberties, they can eliminate that answer.

Bonus Question ?

Ask: Which president started the Peace Corps? *(Kennedy)*

---

22. Bay of Pigs, Berlin Wall, Cuban missile crisis

23. In *Baker* v. *Carr,* the court ruled that the federal government has the right to enforce voting rights in the states. In *Reynolds* v. *Sims,* the court ruled that many states' apportionment plans were unconstitutional.

24. **a.** owning his home; **b.** The statement shows helplessness, desperation, and frustration.

Practicing Skills

25 **a.** long-range missiles; **b.** acceptance of the missiles (unacceptable for national security); threats to use nuclear weapons (nuclear devastation); negotiation backed by threat of force (actual choice); **c.** negotiations; **d.** Solution was successful for the immediate problem but it led to arms buildup.

Timesaving Tools

TeacherWorks™ All-In-One Planner and Resource Center

- **Interactive Teacher Edition** Access your Teacher Wraparound Edition and your classroom resources with a few easy clicks.
- **Interactive Lesson Planner** Planning has never been easier! Organize your week, month, semester, or year with all the lesson helps you need to make teaching creative, timely, and relevant.

Use Glencoe's **Presentation Plus!** multimedia teacher tool to easily present dynamic lessons that visually excite your students. Using Microsoft PowerPoint® you can customize the presentations to create your own personalized lessons.

TEACHING TRANSPARENCIES

Graphic Organizer 9 L2

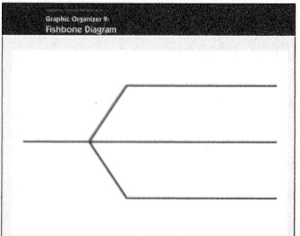

Why It Matters Chapter Transparency 24 L2

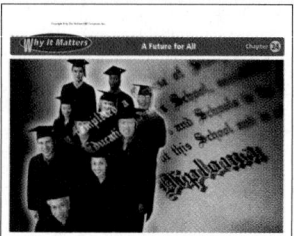

APPLICATION AND ENRICHMENT

Linking Past and Present Activity 24 L2

Enrichment Activity 24 L3

Primary Source Reading 24 L2

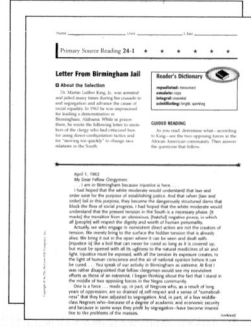

REVIEW AND REINFORCEMENT

Reteaching Activity 24 L1

Vocabulary Activity 24 L1

Time Line Activity 24 L2

Critical Thinking Skills Activity 24 L2

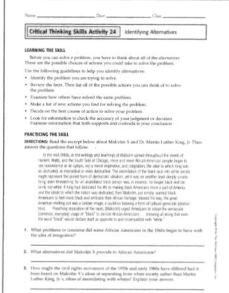

Meeting NCSS Standards

The following standards are covered in Chapter 24:

Section 1 VI Power, Authority, and Governance: A, C, D, F, H, I
Section 2 VIII Science, Technology, and Society: A, B, C
Section 3 X Civic Ideals and Practices: A, C, E, F, G, J

Local Standards

Chapter 24 Resources

ASSESSMENT AND EVALUATION

**Chapter 24 Test
Form A L2**

**Chapter 24 Test
Form B L2**

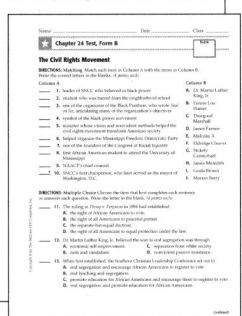

**Standardized Test Practice
Workbook Activity 24 L2**

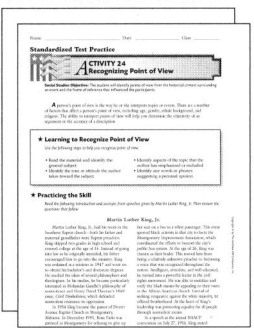

**Performance Assessment
Activities and Rubrics 24
L1/ELL**

**ExamView® Pro
Testmaker CD-ROM**

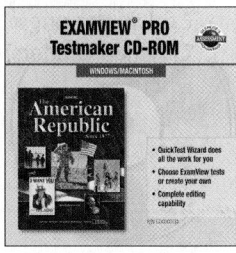

MULTIMEDIA

- Vocabulary PuzzleMaker CD-ROM
- Interactive Tutor Self-Assessment CD-ROM
- ExamView® Pro Testmaker CD-ROM
- Audio Program
- American History Primary Source Documents
  Library CD-ROM
- MindJogger Videoquiz
- Presentation Plus! CD-ROM
- TeacherWorks™ CD-ROM
- Interactive Student Edition CD-ROM
- Glencoe Skillbuilder Interactive Workbook
  CD-ROM, Level 2
- The *American Republic Since 1877* Video Program
- American Music: Hits Through History
- American Music: Cultural Traditions

SPANISH RESOURCES

The following Spanish resources are available:

- Spanish Reading Essentials and Study Guide
- Spanish Guided Reading Activities
- Spanish Reteaching Activities
- Spanish Quizzes and Tests
- Spanish Vocabulary Activities
- Spanish Summaries
- The Declaration of Independence and United States Constitution
  Spanish Translation

The following videotape programs are available
from Glencoe as supplements to Chapter 24:

- **Martin Luther King, Jr.: The Man and the Dream** (ISBN 0-76-701057-4)
- **Thurgood Marshall: Justice for All** (ISBN 0-76-700121-4)
- **Malcolm X: A Search for Identity** (ISBN 1-56-501674-2)

To order, call Glencoe at 1-800-334-7344. To find classroom resources to
accompany many of these videos, check the following home pages:
A&E Television: www.aande.com
The History Channel: www.historychannel.com

Use our Web site for additional resources. All essential content is covered in the Student Edition.

You and your students can visit tarvol2.glencoe.com, the Web site
companion to the *American Republic Since 1877.* This innovative
integration of electronic and print media offers your students a wealth
of opportunities. The student text directs students to the Web site for
the following options:

- **Chapter Overviews**
- **Self-Check Quizzes**
- **Student Web Activities**
- **Textbook Updates**

Answers to the student Web activities are provided for you in the **Web
Activity Lesson Plans.** Additional Web resources and Interactive Tutor
Puzzles are also available.

Chapter 24 Resources

Daily Objectives	Reproducible Resources	Multimedia Resources
SECTION 1 **The Movement Begins** 1. Explain the origin of the Southern Christian Leadership Conference. 2. Discuss the changing role of the federal government in civil rights enforcement.	Reproducible Lesson Plan 24–1 Daily Lecture and Discussion Notes 24–1 Guided Reading Activity 24–1* Section Quiz 24–1* Reading Essentials and Study Guide 24–1* Performance Assessment Activities and Rubrics Supreme Court Case Studies	Daily Focus Skills Transparency 24–1 Interactive Tutor Self-Assessment CD-ROM ExamView® Pro Testmaker CD-ROM* Presentation Plus! CD-ROM TeacherWorks™ CD-ROM Audio Program
SECTION 2 **Challenging Segregation** 1. Evaluate the Civil Rights Act of 1964. 2. Summarize the efforts to establish voting rights for African Americans.	Reproducible Lesson Plan 24–2 Daily Lecture and Discussion Notes 24–2 Guided Reading Activity 24–2* Section Quiz 24–2* Reading Essentials and Study Guide 24–2* Performance Assessment Activities and Rubrics	Daily Focus Skills Transparency 24–2 Interactive Tutor Self-Assessment CD-ROM ExamView® Pro Testmaker CD-ROM* Presentation Plus! CD-ROM TeacherWorks™ CD-ROM Audio Program American Music: Hits Through History American Music: Cultural Traditions
SECTION 3 **New Issues** 1. Describe the division between Dr. Martin Luther King, Jr., and the black power movement. 2. Discuss the direction and progress of the civil rights movement after 1968.	Reproducible Lesson Plan 24–3 Daily Lecture and Discussion Notes 24–3 Guided Reading Activity 24–3* Section Quiz 24–3* Reading Essentials and Study Guide 24–3* Performance Assessment Activities and Rubrics Supreme Court Case Studies	Daily Focus Skills Transparency 24–3 Interactive Tutor Self-Assessment CD-ROM ExamView® Pro Testmaker CD-ROM* Presentation Plus! CD-ROM Skillbuilder Interactive Workbook, Level 2 TeacherWorks™ CD-ROM Vocabulary PuzzleMaker CD-ROM Audio Program

0:00 OUT OF TIME?
Assign the Chapter 24 **Reading Essentials and Study Guide.**

*Also Available in Spanish

 Printed Materials   Transparency   CD-ROM   DVD

 Poster   Music Program   Audio Program

Chapter 24 Resources

NATIONAL GEOGRAPHIC   Teacher's Corner

INDEX TO NATIONAL GEOGRAPHIC MAGAZINE

The following articles relate to this chapter.

- "I Dream a World: America's Black Women," August 1989
- "National Trail to Recall Civil Rights Marches," March 1994
- "Philadelphia's African Americans," August 1990
- "Selma to Montgomery: The Road to Equality," February 2000

NATIONAL GEOGRAPHIC SOCIETY PRODUCTS

To order the following, call National Geographic at 1-800-368-2728:

- *Historical Atlas of the United States* (Atlas)
- *NGS PictureShow: Civil Rights* (CD-ROM, Transparencies)

NGS ONLINE

Access National Geographic's Web site for current events, atlas updates, activities, links, interactive features, and archives.

www.nationalgeographic.com

MEETING SPECIAL NEEDS

In addition to the Differentiated Instruction strategies found in each section, the following resources are also suitable for your special needs students:

- *ExamView® Pro Testmaker CD-ROM* allows teachers to tailor tests by reducing answer choices.
- The *Audio Program* includes the entire narrative of the student edition so that less-proficient readers can listen to the words as they read them.
- The *Reading Essentials and Study Guide* provides the same content as the student edition but is written two grade levels below the textbook.

KEY TO ABILITY LEVELS

Teaching strategies have been coded.

- **L1** BASIC activities for all students
- **L2** AVERAGE activities for average to above-average students
- **L3** CHALLENGING activities for above-average students
- **ELL** ENGLISH LANGUAGE LEARNER activities

From the Classroom of...

Jason Follett
Malcolm Price Laboratory School
Cedar Falls, IA

Birmingham's 16th Street Baptist Church Bombing Lesson Plan

This activity helps students understand how the civil rights movement in the United States affected students their own age.

First, read and discuss literature that focuses on the tensions in Birmingham in 1963. Present Associated Press file photos of the era and discuss the Robert Chambliss trial. Then watch, discuss, and take notes on Spike Lee's documentary *4 Little Girls.* To end this section, have students read the latest news surrounding this event.

Students should build a story map with the climax and resolution clearly identified. Using the story map, students create a hand-drawn or computer-drawn comic book of the bombing and a student guide to drawing a comic book. Examples of non-humor comic books can be obtained through the Federal Reserve System. The best way to evaluate these comic books is to use a rubric.

ADDITIONAL RESOURCES FROM GLENCOE

- American Music: Cultural Traditions
- American Art & Architecture
- Outline Map Resource Book
- U.S. Desk Map
- Building Geography Skills for Life
- Inclusion for the High School Social Studies Classroom Strategies and Activities
- Teaching Strategies for the American History Classroom (Including Block Scheduling Pacing Guides)
- Dinah Zike's High School American History Reading and Study Skills Foldables

Block Schedule

Activities that are suited to use within the block scheduling framework are identified by:

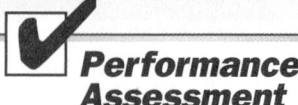

Performance Assessment

Refer to Activity 24 in the Performance Assessment Activities and Rubrics booklet.

W*hy It Matters Activity*

Ask students what kind of an impact they think the civil rights movement had on their communities. Students should evaluate their answers after they have completed the chapter.

GLENCOE
TECHNOLOGY

The *American Republic Since 1877* **Video Program**
To learn more about milestones of the movement to win rights for African Americans, have students view the Chapter 24 video, "The Civil Rights Movement," from the *American Republic Since 1877* **Video Program.**

MindJogger Videoquiz
Use the **MindJogger Videoquiz** to preview Chapter 24 content.

Both programs available in DVD

CHAPTER
24 The Civil Rights Movement *1954–1968*

Why It Matters

In the 1950s and 1960s, African Americans made major strides. They began by challenging segregation in the South. With the Montgomery bus boycott, Martin Luther King, Jr., achieved national and worldwide recognition. His peaceful resistance inspired many, especially students. After King's assassination, the civil rights movement shifted focus. Many people in the movement began to see economic opportunity as the key to equality.

The Impact Today

Changes brought about by the civil rights movement are still with us.
• *Civil rights legislation provides protection against discrimination for all citizens.*
• *Economic programs for inner-city residents by government and social service agencies continue.*

The *American Republic Since 1877* ***Video*** *The Chapter 24 video, "The Civil Rights Movement," chronicles the milestones of the movement to win rights for African Americans.*

1954
• *Brown v. Board of Education* ruling issued by Supreme Court

1955
• Rosa Parks refuses to give up bus seat; Montgomery bus boycott begins in Alabama

1957
• Eisenhower sends troops to a Little Rock, Arkansas, high school to ensure integration

1960
• Sit-in protests begin

United States
PRESIDENTS

Eisenhower 1953–1961

Kennedy 1961–1963

1953   *1957*   *1961*

World

1955
• West Germany admitted to NATO

1958
• Pasternak's *Dr. Zhivago* awarded Nobel Prize for Literature

1959
• Mary Leakey discovers 1.7 million-year-old hominid skull fragment in Tanzania

1960
• France successfully tests nuclear weapons

744

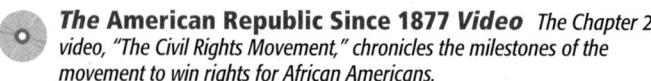

Reading Strategy   PURPOSE FOR READING

Free Writes This strategy helps engage students in the subject matter and explores students' background knowledge. Bring to class several books or magazines that show pictures of the civil rights movement. Ask students to examine the photos without reading captions or words. Tell them to look closely at the facial expressions and body language of the participants. Have students write in their journals what they can learn from the pictures about the civil rights movement. Emphasize that there are no wrong answers to the question. Conclude this activity by telling students they will be studying the civil rights movement in this chapter. **L1**

Americans march from Selma, Alabama, to Montgomery in support of the civil rights movement.

1963
• Over 200,000 civil rights supporters march on Washington, D.C.

1965
• Malcolm X assassinated
• Race riots erupt in Los Angeles neighborhood of Watts

1968
• Civil Rights Act of 1968 passed
• Martin Luther King, Jr., assassinated

Johnson 1963–1969

1965   *1969*

1963
• Organization of African Unity formed
• Kenya becomes an independent nation

1965
• China's Cultural Revolution begins

1967
• Arab-Israeli War brings many Palestinians under Israeli rule

745

More About the Photo

Tell students that in 1963, Selma, Alabama, was a small town of about 30,000 people. At the time only about 1 percent of the African Americans eligible to vote in Dallas County, where Selma is located, was registered. The system there strongly discouraged African Americans from registering to vote. Ask students how they think the civil rights movement showed both how far African Americans had come and how far they still had to go to obtain full rights as citizens of the United States.

TIME LINE ACTIVITY

Have students write a paragraph about how the events listed on the time line have affected their lives within the last year. Invite students to share their paragraphs with the class.

FOLDABLES™ Study Organizer

Dinah Zike's Foldables are three-dimensional, interactive graphic organizers that help students practice basic writing skills, review key vocabulary terms, and identify main ideas. Have students complete the foldable activity in the *Dinah Zike's Reading and Study Skills Foldables* booklet.

GRAPHIC ORGANIZER ACTIVITY

Organizing Information Have students complete a graphic organizer similar to the one below to help them focus on the results of various events in the civil rights movement. Student answers will vary but should include: the Montgomery bus boycott; challenging segregation at the voting booths and in public transportation, housing, and facilities; the sit-in movement; the formation of SNCC; the registration of African American voters; and the challenge to segregation in the Democratic party.

Civil Rights Confrontation	Reactions and Results

745

1 FOCUS

Section Overview

This section focuses on the beginning of the civil rights movement.

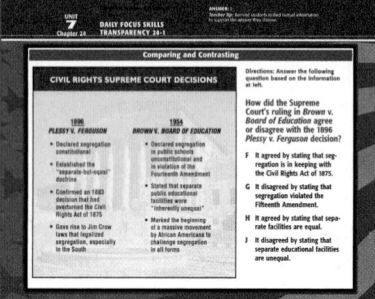
Reading Preview

Answers to Graphic: segregation, lack of voting rights, African American experiences in World War II

Preteaching Vocabulary
Have students create a database using the Key Terms and Names. Have them add facts as they learn more about each term, person, event, or group.

SECTION 1 The Movement Begins

Guide to Reading

Main Idea
After World War II, African Americans and other supporters of civil rights challenged segregation in the United States.

Key Terms and Names
separate-but-equal, de facto segregation, NAACP, sit-in, Thurgood Marshall, Linda Brown, Dr. Martin Luther King, Jr., Southern Christian Leadership Conference

Reading Strategy
Organizing As you read about the birth of the civil rights movement, complete a graphic organizer similar to the one below by filling in the causes of the civil rights movement.

➡️ Civil Rights Movement

Reading Objectives
- **Explain** the origin of the Southern Christian Leadership Conference.
- **Discuss** the changing role of the federal government in civil rights enforcement.

Section Theme
Government and Democracy In the 1950s, African Americans began a movement to win greater social equality.

Preview of Events

♦1954	♦1955	♦1956	♦1957
1954 Brown v. Board of Education of Topeka, Kansas, decision	**1955** Rosa Parks refuses to give up bus seat in Montgomery, Alabama	**1956** Group of 101 Southern members of Congress sign Southern Manifesto	**1957** Southern Christian Leadership Conference formed

Rosa Parks

★ An American Story ★

On December 1, 1955, Rosa Parks left her job as a seamstress in Montgomery, Alabama, and boarded a bus to go home. In 1955 buses in Montgomery reserved seats in the front for whites and seats in the rear for African Americans. Seats in the middle were open to African Americans, but only if there were few whites on the bus.

Rosa Parks took a seat just behind the white section. Soon all of the seats on the bus were filled. When the bus driver noticed a white man standing at the front of the bus, he told Parks and three other African Americans in her row to get up and let the white man sit down. Nobody moved. The driver cautioned, "You better make it light on yourselves and let me have those seats." The other three African Americans rose, but Rosa Parks did not. The driver then called the Montgomery police, who took Parks into custody.

News of the arrest soon reached E.D. Nixon, a former president of the local chapter of the National Association for the Advancement of Colored People (NAACP). Nixon wanted to challenge bus segregation in court, and he told Parks, "With your permission we can break down segregation on the bus with your case." Parks told Nixon, "If you think it will mean something to Montgomery and do some good, I'll be happy to go along with it."

—adapted from *Parting the Waters: America in the King Years*

The Origins of the Movement

When Rosa Parks agreed to challenge segregation in court, she did not know that her decision would launch the modern civil rights movement. Within days of her arrest, African Americans in Montgomery had organized a boycott of the bus system. Mass

---

SECTION RESOURCES

📁 **Reproducible Masters**
- Reproducible Lesson Plan 24–1
- Daily Lecture and Discussion Notes 24–1
- Guided Reading Activity 24–1
- Section Quiz 24–1
- Reading Essentials and Study Guide 24–1
- Supreme Court Case Studies

📄 **Transparencies**
- Daily Focus Skills Transparency 24–1

Multimedia
- 💿 Interactive Tutor Self-Assessment CD-ROM
- 💿 ExamView® Pro Testmaker CD-ROM
- 💿 Presentation Plus! CD-ROM
- 💿 TeacherWorks™ CD-ROM
- 🔊 Audio Program

protests began across the nation. After decades of segregation and inequality, many African Americans had decided the time had come to demand equal rights.

The struggle would not be easy. The Supreme Court had declared segregation to be constitutional in *Plessy* v. *Ferguson* in 1896. The ruling had established the "separate-but-equal" doctrine. Laws segregating African Americans were permitted as long as equal facilities were provided for them.

After the *Plessy* decision, laws segregating African Americans and whites spread quickly. These laws, nicknamed "Jim Crow" laws, segregated buses and trains, schools, restaurants, swimming pools, parks, and other public facilities. Jim Crow laws were common throughout the South, but segregation existed in other states as well. Often it was left up to each local community to decide whether to pass segregation laws. Areas without laws requiring segregation often had de facto segregation—segregation by custom and tradition. 📖 *(See page 964 for more information on* Plessy v. Ferguson.*)*

Court Challenges Begin The civil rights movement had been building for a long time. Since 1909, the **National Association for the Advancement of Colored People** (NAACP) had supported court cases intended to overturn segregation. Over the years, the NAACP achieved some victories. In 1935, for example, the Supreme Court ruled in *Norris* v. *Alabama* that Alabama's exclusion of African Americans from juries violated their right to equal protection under the law. In 1946 the Court ruled in *Morgan* v. *Virginia* that segregation on interstate buses was unconstitutional. In 1950 it ruled in *Sweatt* v. *Painter* that state law schools had to admit qualified African American applicants, even if parallel black law schools existed. 📖 *(See pages 964–965 for more information on these cases.)*

HISTORY Online

Student Web Activity Visit the *American Republic Since 1877* Web site at tarvol2.glencoe.com and click on *Student Web Activities—Chapter 24* for an activity on the civil rights movement.

HISTORY Online

Objectives and answers to the student activity can be found in the **Web Activity Lesson Plan** at tarvol2.glencoe.com.

2 TEACH

Daily Lecture and Discussion Notes 24–1

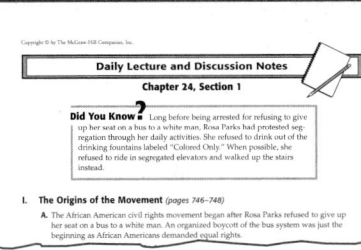

Discussing a Topic To help students identify with Linda Brown and James Meredith, give them a few minutes to write diary notes about how it might have felt to attend a school where he or she was unwanted. **L1** ELL

NATIONAL GEOGRAPHIC
MOMENT in HISTORY

AMERICAN SEGREGATION

In an Oklahoma City streetcar station in 1939, a man takes a drink from a water cooler labeled "COLORED." Racially segregated facilities—waiting rooms, railroad cars, lavatories, and drinking fountains—were prevalent all across the South. Under the so-called Jim Crow system, African Americans were legally entitled to "separate-but-equal" education, housing, and social services. In practice, however, only a small percentage of public funds earmarked for schools, streets, police, and other expenses found its way to African American neighborhoods.

CHAPTER 24 The Civil Rights Movement **747**

NATIONAL GEOGRAPHIC
MOMENT in HISTORY

Ask: How did the disparity between white and "colored" facilities indicate that America had not changed its views on race? *(It showed that African Americans were still being treated as second-class citizens.)*

Reading Strategy READING THE TEXT

Using Context Clues Students can often determine the meaning of a word they do not know by using context—the words and sentences that surround an unfamiliar word. Synonyms often appear in context when two things are compared. Antonyms may appear in context when two things are contrasted. Definitions often are surrounded by commas, dashes, or parentheses. Examples within the text can reveal the meaning of an unfamiliar word. As students read the section and encounter words they do not know, remind them to use these clues to identify the word's meaning. **L1** ELL

➥ Refer to *Inclusion for the High School Social Studies Classroom Strategies and Activities* in the TCR.

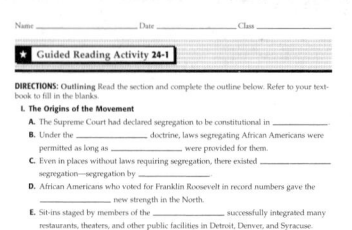

Name _____ Date _____ Class _____

★ **Guided Reading Activity 24-1**

DIRECTIONS: Outlining Read the section and complete the outline below. Refer to your text-book to fill in the blanks.
I. The Origins of the Movement
A. The Supreme Court had declared segregation to be constitutional in _____
B. Under the _____ doctrine, laws segregating African Americans were permitted as long as _____ were provided for them.
C. Even in places without laws requiring segregation, there existed _____ segregation—segregation by _____.
D. African Americans who voted for Franklin Roosevelt in record numbers gave the _____ new strength in the North.
E. Sit-ins staged by members of the _____ successfully integrated many restaurants, theaters, and other public facilities in Detroit, Denver, and Syracuse.
II. The Civil Rights Movement...

Analyzing a Decision Have interested students research the NAACP's strategy of ending school segregation. Ask students to report their findings to the class. As a class, analyze why the NAACP might have chosen to challenge school segregation rather than segregation in other areas of American life. **Ask:** What do you think would have happened if the NAACP had lost in the Supreme Court? **L2**

FYI

Rosa Parks and her husband both lost their jobs as a result of taking part in the bus boycott.

 Use *Supreme Court Case Study 29, Brown v. Board of Education of Topeka, Kansas.*

✓ Reading Check

Answer: The ruling said the segregation was constitutional as long as equal facilities were provided for African Americans.

New Political Power In addition to a string of court victories, African Americans enjoyed increased political power. Before World War I, most African Americans lived in the South, where they were largely excluded from voting. During the Great Migration, many moved to Northern cities, where they were allowed to vote. Increasingly, Northern politicians sought their votes and listened to their concerns.

During the 1930s, many African Americans benefited from FDR's New Deal programs. Thus they began supporting the Democratic Party, giving it new strength in the North. This wing of the party was now able to counter Southern Democrats, who often supported segregation.

The Push for Desegregation During World War II, African American leaders began to use their new political power to demand more rights. Their efforts helped end discrimination in factories that held government contracts and increased opportunities for African Americans in the military.

In Chicago in 1942, James Farmer and George Houser founded the **Congress of Racial Equality** (CORE). CORE began using **sit-ins**, a form of protest first used by union workers in the 1930s. In 1943 CORE attempted to desegregate restaurants that refused to serve African Americans. Using the sit-in strategy, members of CORE went to segregated restaurants. If they were denied service, they sat down and refused to leave. The sit-ins were intended to shame restaurant managers into integrating their restaurants. Using these protests, CORE successfully integrated many restaurants, theaters, and other public facilities in Chicago, Detroit, Denver, and Syracuse.

✓ Reading Check

Examining How had the ruling in *Plessy* v. *Ferguson* contributed to segregation?

Separate but Unequal Linda Brown's court case ended decades of official segregation in the South.

The Civil Rights Movement Begins

When World War II ended, many African American soldiers returned home optimistic that their country would appreciate their loyalty and sacrifice. In the 1950s, when change did not come as quickly as hoped, their determination to change prejudices in the United States led to protests and marches—and to the emergence of the civil rights movement.

Brown v. Board of Education After World War II, the NAACP continued to challenge segregation in the courts. From 1939 to 1961, the NAACP's chief counsel and director of its Legal Defense and Education Fund was the brilliant African American attorney **Thurgood Marshall.** After World War II, Marshall focused his efforts on ending segregation in public schools.

In 1954 the Supreme Court decided to combine several different cases and issue a general ruling on segregation in schools. One of the cases involved a young African American girl named **Linda Brown,** who was denied admission to her neighborhood school in Topeka, Kansas, because of her race. She was told to attend an all-black school across town. With the help of the NAACP, her parents then sued the Topeka school board.

On May 17, 1954, the Supreme Court ruled unanimously in the case of *Brown* v. *Board of Education of Topeka, Kansas,* that segregation in public schools was unconstitutional and violated the equal protection clause of the Fourteenth Amendment. Chief Justice Earl Warren summed up the Court's decision when he wrote: "In the field of public education, the doctrine of separate but equal has no place. Separate educational facilities are inherently unequal." 📖 *(See pages 959 and 962 for information on* Brown v. Board of Education.*)*

The Southern Manifesto The Brown decision marked a dramatic reversal of the ideas expressed in the *Plessy* v. *Ferguson* case. *Brown* v. *Board of Education* applied only to public schools, but the ruling threatened the entire system of segregation. Although it convinced many African Americans that the time had come to challenge other forms of segregation, it also angered many white Southerners, who became even more determined to defend segregation, regardless of what the Supreme Court ruled.

Although some school districts in border states integrated their schools in compliance with the Court's ruling, anger and opposition was a far more common reaction. In Washington, D.C., Senator Harry F. Byrd of Virginia called on Southerners to

---

DIFFERENTIATED INSTRUCTION

Gifted and Talented Have students work in pairs to write song lyrics to be sung at a civil rights march. Have them base the lyrics on the events mentioned in this section. Recommend that they research some of the traditional songs used during the era for examples and style. Encourage students to set the lyrics to music. Invite students to perform their songs for the class. **L3**

📁 Refer to *Inclusion for the High School Social Studies Classroom Strategies and Activities* in the TCR.

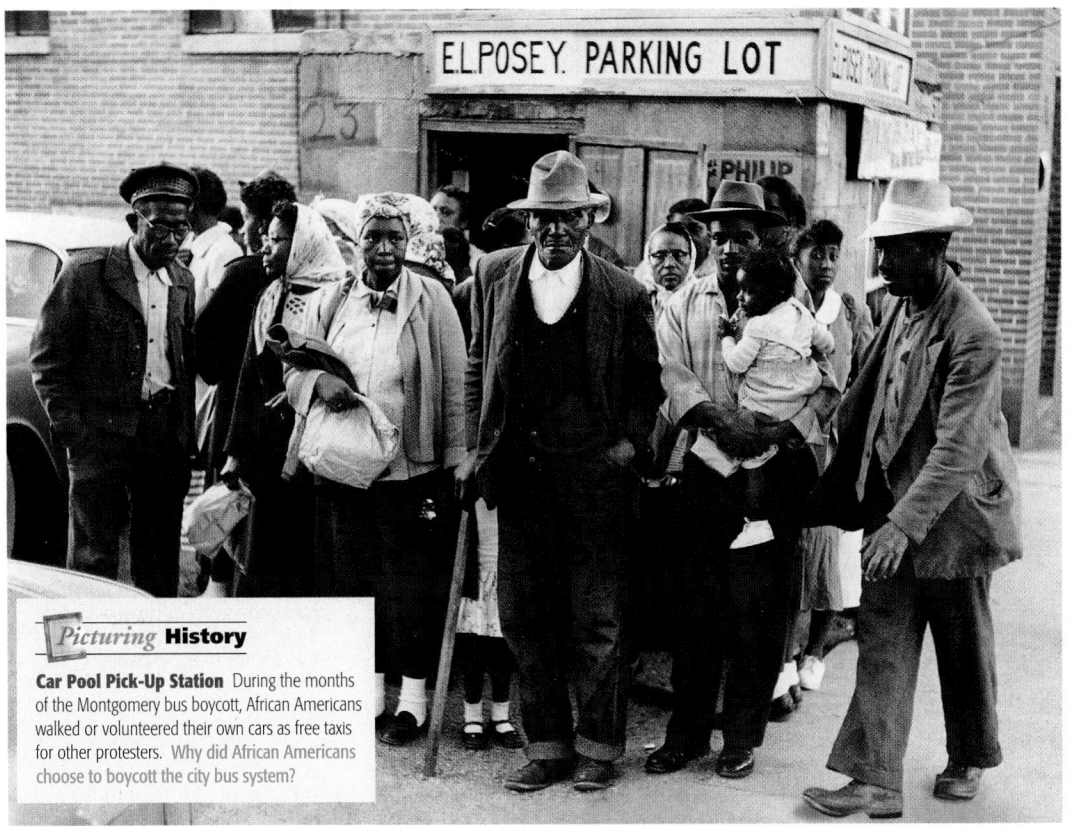

Car Pool Pick-Up Station During the months of the Montgomery bus boycott, African Americans walked or volunteered their own cars as free taxis for other protesters. Why did African Americans choose to boycott the city bus system?

adopt "massive resistance" against the ruling. Across the South, hundreds of thousands of white Americans joined citizens' councils to pressure their local governments and school boards into defying the Supreme Court. Many states adopted pupil assignment laws. These laws created an elaborate set of requirements other than race that schools could use to prevent African Americans from attending white schools.

The Supreme Court inadvertently encouraged white resistance when it followed up its decision in *Brown* v. *Board* a year later. The Court ordered school districts to proceed "with all deliberate speed" to end school segregation. The wording was vague enough that many districts were able to keep their schools segregated for many more years.

Massive resistance also appeared in the halls of Congress. In 1956 a group of 101 Southern members of Congress signed the **Southern Manifesto,** which denounced the Supreme Court's ruling as "a clear abuse of judicial power" and pledged to use "all lawful means" to reverse the decision. Although the Southern

Manifesto had no legal standing, the statement encouraged white Southerners to defy the Supreme Court.

The Montgomery Bus Boycott In the midst of the uproar over the *Brown* v. *Board of Education* case, Rosa Parks made her decision to challenge segregation of public transportation. Outraged by Parks's arrest, Jo Ann Robinson, head of a local organization called the Women's Political Council, called on African Americans to boycott Montgomery's buses on the day Rosa Parks appeared in court.

The boycott was a dramatic success. That afternoon, several African American leaders formed the Montgomery Improvement Association to run the boycott and to negotiate with city leaders for an end to segregation. They elected a 26-year-old pastor named **Martin Luther King, Jr.,** to lead them.

On the evening of December 5, 1955, a meeting was held at Dexter Avenue Baptist Church, where Dr. King was pastor. In the deep, resonant tones and powerful phrases that characterized his speaking style, King encouraged the people to continue their

CHAPTER 24 The Civil Rights Movement **749**

INTERDISCIPLINARY CONNECTIONS ACTIVITY

Communication Invite a journalist who covered events in your community during the civil rights movement to address your class about his or her experiences and perceptions of how minorities are portrayed in the media. Ask the speaker to suggest an activity that students can do to prepare for the presentation, such as reading an article or researching a topic. **L2**

Profiles IN HISTORY

Ask: What did Thurgood Marshall mean when he said, "The true miracle of the Constitution was not the birth of the Constitution, but its life"? *(Students' answers should recognize that he thought the Constitution was a living document which could be interpreted and amended to meet a changing society.)*

✓ **Reading Check**

Answer: Public school segregation was ruled unconstitutional because it violated the Fourteenth Amendment.

Creating a Display Have students base a display on African Americans who broke racial barriers. Ask each student to bring an image and a caption to contribute to the display. Encourage students to search a variety of fields, including entertainment, sports, sciences, and arts. **L2**

📁 Use the rubric for creating a map, display, or chart on pages 65–66 in the *Performance Assessment Activities and Rubrics.*

---

protest. "There comes a time, my friends," he said, "when people get tired of being thrown into the abyss of humiliation, where they experience the bleakness of nagging despair." He explained, however, that the protest had to be peaceful:

> 66Now let us say that we are not advocating violence. . . . The only weapon we have in our hands this evening is the weapon of protest. If we were incarcerated behind the iron curtains of a communistic nation—we couldn't do this. If we were trapped in the dungeon of a totalitarian regime—we couldn't do this. But the great glory of American democracy is the right to protest for right!99
>
> —quoted in *Parting the Waters: America in the King Years*

King had earned a Ph.D. in theology from Boston University. He believed that the only moral way to end segregation and racism was through nonviolent passive resistance. He told his followers, "We must use the weapon of love. We must realize that so many people are taught to hate us that they are not totally responsible for their hate." African Americans, he urged, must say to racists and segregationists: "We will soon wear you down by our capacity to suffer, and in winning our freedom we will so appeal to your heart and conscience that we will win you in the process."

King drew upon the philosophy and techniques of Indian leader Mohandas Gandhi, who had used nonviolent resistance effectively against British rule in India. Like Gandhi, King encouraged his followers to disobey unjust laws. Believing in people's ability to transform themselves, King was certain that public opinion would eventually force the government to end segregation.

Stirred by King's powerful words, African Americans in Montgomery continued their boycott for over a year. Instead of riding the bus, they organized car pools or walked to work. They refused to be intimidated, yet they avoided violence. Meanwhile Rosa Parks's legal challenge to bus segregation worked its way through the courts. Finally, in December 1956, the Supreme Court

---

Profiles IN HISTORY

Thurgood Marshall
1908–1993

Over his long lifetime, Thurgood Marshall made many contributions to the civil rights movement. Perhaps his most famous accomplishment was representing the NAACP in the *Brown* v. *Board of Education* case.

Marshall's speaking style was both simple and direct. During the *Brown* case, Justice Frankfurter asked Marshall for a definition of equal. "Equal means getting the same thing, at the same time and in the same place," Marshall answered.

Born into a middle-class Baltimore family in 1908, Marshall earned a law degree from Howard University Law School. The school's dean, Charles Hamilton Houston, enlisted Marshall to work for the NAACP. Together the two laid out the legal strategy for challenging discrimination in many arenas of American life.

Marshall became the first African American on the Supreme Court when President Lyndon Johnson appointed him in 1967. On the Court, he remained a voice for civil rights. In his view, the Constitution was not perfect because it had accepted slavery. Its ideas of liberty, justice, and equality had to be refined. "The true miracle of the Constitution," he once wrote, "was not the birth of the Constitution, but its life."

affirmed the decision of a special three-judge panel declaring Alabama's laws requiring segregation on buses to be unconstitutional.

✓ **Reading Check** **Describing** What was the ruling in *Brown v. Board of Education?*

African American Churches

Martin Luther King, Jr., was not the only prominent minister in the bus boycott. Many of the other leaders were African American ministers. The boycott could not have succeeded without the support of the African American churches in the city. As the civil rights movement gained momentum, African American churches continued to play a critical role. They served as forums for many of the protests and planning meetings, and they also mobilized many of the volunteers for specific civil rights campaigns.

After the Montgomery bus boycott demonstrated that nonviolent protest could be successful, African American ministers led by King established the **Southern Christian Leadership Conference** (SCLC) in 1957. The SCLC set out to eliminate segregation from American society and to encourage

---

CRITICAL THINKING ACTIVITY

Comparing Philosophies Martin Luther King, Jr., took many of his nonviolent ideas from those of Mohandas K. Gandhi, leader of India's nationalist movement against Britain. Ask students to research Gandhi's philosophy and his work. Have them compare each man's philosophy. **Ask:** How are they similar? How are they different? What impact did each leader have on his nation? How successful was each in reaching his goals? Have students present their findings orally for class discussion. **L2**

African Americans to register to vote. Dr. King served as the SCLC's first president. Under his leadership, the organization challenged segregation at the voting booths and in public transportation, housing, and public accommodations.

Reading Check **Summarizing** What role did African American churches play in the civil rights movement?

Eisenhower and Civil Rights

President Eisenhower sympathized with the goals of the civil rights movement, and he personally disagreed with segregation. Following the precedent set by President Truman, he ordered navy shipyards and veterans' hospitals to be desegregated.

At the same time, however, Eisenhower disagreed with those who wanted to roll back segregation through protests and court rulings. He believed that people had to allow segregation and racism to end gradually as values changed. With the nation in the midst of the Cold War, he worried that challenging white Southerners on segregation might divide the nation and lead to violence at a time when the country

had to pull together. Publicly, he refused to endorse the *Brown v. Board of Education* decision. Privately, he remarked, "I don't believe you can change the hearts of men with laws or decisions."

Despite his belief that the *Brown v. Board of Education* decision was wrong, Eisenhower felt he had to uphold the authority of the federal government, including its court system. As a result, he became the first president since Reconstruction to send federal troops into the South to protect the constitutional rights of African Americans.

Crisis in Little Rock In September 1957, the school board in Little Rock, Arkansas, won a court order to admit nine African American students to Central High, a school with 2,000 white students. Little Rock was a racially moderate Southern city, as was most of the state of Arkansas. A number of Arkansas communities, as well as the state university, had already begun to desegregate their schools.

The governor of Arkansas, Orval Faubus, was believed to be a moderate on racial issues, unlike many other Southern politicians. Faubus was determined to win re-election, however, and so he began to campaign

Picturing **History**

Crisis in Little Rock Fifteen-year-old Elizabeth Eckford (in sunglasses at right) braves an angry crowd of Central High School students in Arkansas. How did Governor Orval Faubus react to attempts to integrate the high school?

✓**Reading Check**

Answer: They supported boycotts, nonviolent demonstrations, and voter registration.

Picturing **History**

Answer: He ordered National Guard troops to prevent the African American students from entering the school.
Ask: How do you think Elizabeth Eckford felt on the day this picture was taken? *(Students' answers will vary. Students might indicate that she was frightened, lonely, sad, or angry.)*

3 ASSESS

Assign Section 1 Assessment as homework or as an in-class activity.

⏺ Have students use the **Interactive Tutor Self-Assessment CD-ROM.**

L1/ELL

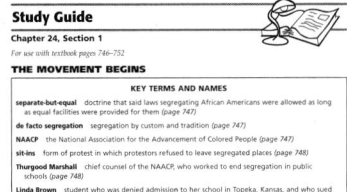

Reading Essentials and Study Guide 24–1

EXTENDING THE CONTENT

Sports In 1947 Jackie Robinson became the first African American to play major-league baseball. Other professional sports integrated at different times. African American prizefighters and jockeys had been successful even before 1904 when Charles W. Follis became the first African American professional football player. It was not until 1950 that the Boston Celtics of the National Basketball Association signed Charles "Chuck" Cooper to be the first African American player in the league.

L2

Section Quiz 24–1

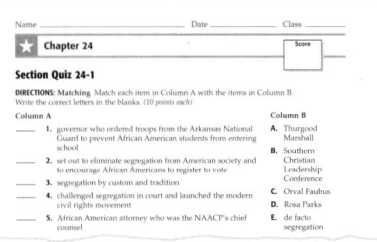

Reteach
Have students explain the origin of the Southern Christian Leadership Conference.

Enrich
Invite interested students to prepare a presentation about one of the persons mentioned in this section. Encourage students to use library and Internet resources.

✓ **Reading Check**

Answer: He intervened because the governor of Arkansas had used armed forces to oppose the authority of the federal government. After the governor withdrew the National Guard troops, Eisenhower used federal troops to stop the violence and enforce the law.

HISTORY Online

Study Central™ provides summaries, interactive games, and online graphic organizers to help students review section content.

4 CLOSE

Have students discuss the changing role of the federal government in civil rights enforcement.

---

as a defender of white supremacy. He ordered troops from the Arkansas National Guard to prevent the nine African American students from entering the school. The next day, as the National Guard troops surrounded the school, an angry white mob joined the troops to protest the integration plan and to intimidate the African American students trying to register.

Television coverage of this episode placed Little Rock at the center of national attention. Faubus had used the armed forces of a state to oppose the authority of the federal government—the first such challenge to the Constitution since the Civil War. Eisenhower knew that he could not allow Faubus to defy the federal government. After a conference between Eisenhower and Faubus proved fruitless, the district court ordered the governor to remove the troops. Instead of ending the crisis, however, Faubus simply left the school to the mob. After the African American students entered the school, angry whites beat at least two African American reporters and broke many of the school's windows. The mob came so close to capturing the terrified African American students that the police had to take them away to safety.

The mob violence finally pushed President Eisenhower's patience to the breaking point. Federal authority had to be upheld. He immediately ordered the U.S. Army to send troops to Little Rock. By nightfall 1,000 soldiers of the elite 101st Airborne Division had arrived. By 5:00 A.M. the troops had encircled the school, bayonets ready. A few hours later, the nine African American students arrived in an army station wagon, and they walked into the high school. The law had been upheld, but the troops were forced to remain in Little Rock for the rest of the school year.

New Civil Rights Legislation The same year that the Little Rock crisis began, Congress passed the first civil rights law since Reconstruction. The **Civil Rights Act of 1957** was intended to protect the right of African Americans to vote. Eisenhower believed firmly in the right to vote, and he viewed it as his responsibility to protect voting rights. He also knew that if he sent a civil rights bill to Congress, conservative Southern Democrats would try to block the legislation. In 1956 he did send the bill to Congress, hoping not only to split the Democratic Party but also to convince more African Americans to vote Republican.

Several Southern senators did try to stop the Civil Rights Act of 1957, but the Senate majority leader, Democrat Lyndon Johnson, put together a compromise that enabled the act to pass. Although its final form was much weaker than originally intended, the act still brought the power of the federal government into the civil rights debate. The act created a civil rights division within the Department of Justice and gave it the authority to seek court injunctions against anyone interfering with the right to vote. It also created the United States Commission on Civil Rights to investigate allegations of denial of voting rights. After the bill passed, the SCLC announced a campaign to register 2 million new African American voters.

✓ **Reading Check** **Explaining** Why did President Eisenhower intervene in the civil rights controversy?

HISTORY Online | **Study Central™** To review this section, go to tarvol2.glencoe.com and click on **Study Central™**.

SECTION 1 ASSESSMENT

Checking for Understanding
1. **Define:** separate-but-equal, de facto segregation, sit-in.
2. **Identify:** NAACP, Thurgood Marshall, Linda Brown, Martin Luther King, Jr., Southern Christian Leadership Conference.
3. **State** the outcome of the *Brown* v. *Board of Education* case.

Reviewing Themes
4. **Government and Democracy** Why did the role of the federal government in civil rights enforcement change?

Critical Thinking
5. **Interpreting** Do you think the civil rights movement would have been successful in gaining civil rights for African Americans without the help of the NAACP and the SCLC? Explain.
6. **Organizing** Use a graphic organizer similar to the one below to list the efforts made to end segregation.

Efforts to End Segregation

Analyzing Visuals
7. **Examining Photographs** Study the photograph of Central High School students on page 751. How would you describe Elizabeth Eckford's demeanor compared to those around her? What might this tell you about her character?

Writing About History
8. **Expository Writing** Take on the role of an African American soldier returning to the United States after fighting in World War II. Write a letter to the editor of your local newspaper describing your expectations of civil rights as an American citizen.

752 CHAPTER 24 The Civil Rights Movement

SECTION 1 ASSESSMENT ANSWERS

1. Terms are in blue.
2. NAACP *(p. 747)*, Thurgood Marshall *(p. 748)*, Linda Brown *(p. 748)*, Martin Luther King, Jr. *(p. 749)*, Southern Christian Leadership Conference *(p. 750)*
3. Segregation in public schools is unconstitutional.

4. because its authority and decisions were challenged by individual states
5. Students should recognize that the NAACP and the SCLC provided financial support, leadership, and organization to the civil rights movement.

6. founding of CORE, NAACP court challenges, bus boycott, voter registration movement
7. Students' answers will vary but should recognize her courage.
8. Letters should include specific expectations.

Guide to Reading

Main Idea
African American citizens and white supporters created organizations that directed protests, targeted specific inequalities, and attracted the attention of the mass media and the government.

Key Terms and Names
Jesse Jackson, Ella Baker, Freedom Riders, filibuster, cloture, Civil Rights Act of 1964, poll tax

Reading Strategy
Organizing As you read about challenges to segregation in the South, complete a cause/effect chart like the one below.

Cause	Effect
Sit-In Movement	
Freedom Riders	
	African American support of Kennedy
	African American voter registration

Reading Objectives
- **Evaluate** the Civil Rights Act of 1964.
- **Summarize** the efforts to establish voting rights for African Americans.

Section Theme
Science and Technology The civil rights movement gained momentum in the early 1960s due to national television coverage.

Preview of Events

◆1960	◆1962	◆1964	◆1966

May 1961
Freedom Riders attempt to desegregate interstate buses in the South

Spring 1963
Martin Luther King, Jr., jailed in Birmingham

August 28, 1963
March on Washington

July 1964
President Johnson signs Civil Rights Act of 1964

1965
Voting Rights Act passed

★ An American Story ★

In the fall of 1959, four young African Americans—Joseph McNeil, Ezell Blair, Jr., David Richmond, and Franklin McCain—enrolled at North Carolina Agricultural and Technical College in Greensboro. The four freshmen became close friends and spent evenings talking about the civil rights movement. In January 1960, McNeil told his friends that he thought the time had come to take action, and he suggested a sit-in at the whites-only lunch counter in the nearby Woolworth's department store.

"All of us were afraid," Richmond later recalled, "but we went and did it." On February 1, 1960, the four friends entered the Woolworth's. They purchased school supplies and then sat at the lunch counter and ordered coffee. When they were refused service, Blair said, "I beg your pardon, but you just served us at [the checkout] counter. Why can't we be served at the counter here?" The students stayed at the counter until it closed, then announced that they would sit at the counter every day until they were given the same service as white customers.

As they left the store, the four were excited. McNeil recalled, "I just felt I had powers within me, a superhuman strength that would come forward." McCain was also energized, saying, "I probably felt better that day than I've ever felt in my life."

—adapted from *Civilities and Civil Rights*

Four North Carolina college students after they participated in a lunch counter sit-in

The Sit-In Movement

News of the daring sit-in at the Woolworth's store spread quickly across Greensboro. The following day, 29 African American students arrived at Woolworth's determined to sit at the counter until served. By the end of the week, over 300 students were taking part.

CHAPTER 24   The Civil Rights Movement   **753**

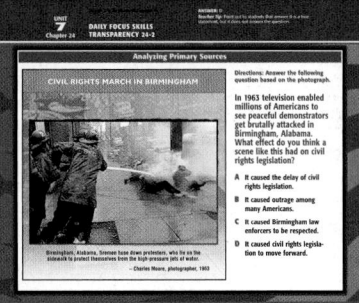

2 TEACH

**Daily Lecture and
Discussion Notes 24–2**

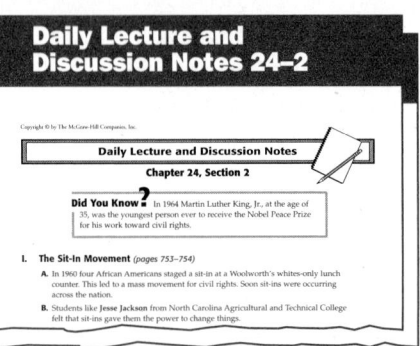

Copyright © by The McGraw-Hill Companies, Inc.

Daily Lecture and Discussion Notes

Chapter 24, Section 2

Did You Know? In 1964 Martin Luther King, Jr., at the age of 35, was the youngest person ever to receive the Nobel Peace Prize for his work toward civil rights.

I. The Sit-In Movement *(pages 753–754)*

　　A. In 1960 four African Americans staged a sit-in at a Woolworth's whites-only lunch counter. This led to a mass movement for civil rights. Soon sit-ins were occurring across the nation.

　　B. Students like **Jesse Jackson** from North Carolina Agricultural and Technical College felt that sit-ins gave them the power to change things.

Creating a Chart Have students create a chart similar to the one shown below to illustrate the activities of the persons mentioned in this section. **L1** ELL

Working for Civil Rights	
Name	Involvement

Working to Maintain Segregation	
Name	Involvement

✓**Reading Check**

Answer: It got the nation's attention and gave people a way to get involved in the civil rights movement.

Picturing **History**

Answer: They were nervous.
Ask: How did young people staging sit-ins generally behave? *(They were nonviolent.)*

✓**Reading Check**

Answer: She urged students to create SNCC.

Starting with just four students, a new mass movement for civil rights had begun. Within two months, sit-ins had spread to 54 cities in 9 states. Sit-ins were staged at segregated stores, restaurants, hotels, movie theaters, and swimming pools. By 1961 sit-ins had been held in more than 100 cities.

The sit-in movement brought large numbers of idealistic and energized college students into the civil rights struggle. Many African American students had become discouraged by the slow pace of desegregation. Students like **Jesse Jackson,** a student leader at North Carolina Agricultural and Technical College, wanted to see things change. The sit-in offered them a way to take matters into their own hands.

At first the leaders of the NAACP and the SCLC were nervous about the sit-in movement. They feared that students did not have the discipline to remain nonviolent if they were provoked enough. For the most part, the students proved them wrong. Those conducting sit-ins were heckled by bystanders, punched, kicked, beaten with clubs, and burned with cigarettes, hot coffee, and acid—but most did not fight back. They remained peaceful, and their heroic behavior grabbed the nation's attention.

✓**Reading Check** **Examining** What were the effects of the sit-in movement?

SNCC

As the sit-ins spread, student leaders in different states realized that they needed to coordinate their efforts. The person who brought them together was **Ella Baker,** the 55-year-old executive director of the SCLC. In April 1960, Baker invited student leaders to attend a convention at Shaw University in Raleigh, North Carolina. At the convention, Baker urged students to create their own organization instead of joining the NAACP or the SCLC. Students, she said, had "the right to direct their own affairs and even make their own mistakes."

The students agreed with Baker and established the **Student Nonviolent Coordinating Committee** (SNCC). Among SNCC's early leaders were **Marion Barry,** who later served as mayor of Washington, D.C., and John Lewis, who later became a member of Congress. African American college students from all across the South made up the majority of SNCC's members, although many whites also joined.

Between 1960 and 1965, SNCC played a key role in desegregating public facilities in dozens of Southern communities. SNCC also began sending volunteers into rural areas of the Deep South to register African Americans to vote. The idea for what came to be called the Voter Education Project began with Robert Moses, an SNCC volunteer from New York. Moses pointed out that the civil rights movement tended to focus on urban areas. He urged SNCC to fill in the gap by helping rural African Americans. Moses himself went to rural Mississippi, where African Americans who tried to register to vote frequently met with violence.

Despite the danger, many SNCC volunteers headed to Mississippi and other parts of the Deep South. Several had their lives threatened, and others were beaten. In 1964 local officials in Mississippi brutally murdered three SNCC workers as the workers attempted to register African American voters.

One SNCC organizer, a former sharecropper named **Fannie Lou Hamer,** had been evicted from her farm after registering to vote. She was then arrested in Mississippi for urging other African Americans to register, and she was severely beaten by the police while in jail. She then helped organize the Mississippi Freedom Democratic Party, and she challenged the legality of the segregated Democratic Party at the 1964 Democratic National Convention.

✓**Reading Check** **Explaining** What role did Ella Baker play in forming SNCC?

The Freedom Riders

Despite rulings outlawing segregation in interstate bus service, bus travel remained segregated in much of the South. In 1961 CORE leader James Farmer asked teams of African Americans and whites to travel into the South to draw attention to

Picturing **History**

Sit-Ins Fight Segregation African American students challenged Southern segregation laws by demanding equal service at lunch counters. How did the NAACP initially feel about the sit-in movement?

COOPERATIVE LEARNING ACTIVITY

Registering to Vote Organize the class into two groups to research the ease or difficulty of registering to vote in the 1960s versus today. One group can research the tactics used before 1965 to keep African Americans from registering to vote. Students should look for examples of actions taken in the North as well as the South. The other group can contact the local election board to find out how to register to vote in their community. Have students make a display showing the process, including options such as registering in person, by mail, or online.

Use the rubric for a cooperative group management plan on pages 71–72 in the **Performance Assessment Activities and Rubrics.**

the South's refusal to integrate bus terminals. The teams became known as the Freedom Riders.

In early May 1961, the first Freedom Riders boarded several southbound interstate buses. When the buses carrying them arrived in Anniston, Birmingham, and Montgomery, Alabama, angry white mobs attacked them. The mobs slit the bus tires and threw rocks at the windows. In Anniston, someone threw a firebomb into one bus, although fortunately no one was killed.

In Birmingham the riders emerged from a bus to face a gang of young men armed with baseball bats, chains, and lead pipes. They beat the riders viciously. One witness later reported, "You couldn't see their faces through the blood." The head of the police in Birmingham, Public Safety Commissioner Theophilus Eugene ("Bull") Connor, explained that there had been no police at the bus station because it was Mother's Day, and he had given many of his officers the day off. FBI evidence later showed that Connor had contacted the local Ku Klux Klan and told them he wanted the Freedom Riders beaten until "it looked like a bulldog got a hold of them."

The violence in Alabama made national news, shocking many Americans. The attack on the Freedom Riders came less than four months after President John F. Kennedy took office. The new president felt compelled to do something to get the violence under control.

 Reading Check **Summarizing** What was the goal of the Freedom Riders?

John F. Kennedy and Civil Rights

While campaigning for the presidency in 1960, John F. Kennedy promised to actively support the civil rights movement if elected. His brother, Robert F. Kennedy, had used his influence to get Dr. King released from jail after a demonstration in Georgia. African Americans responded by voting overwhelmingly for Kennedy. Their votes helped him narrowly win several key states, including Illinois, which Kennedy won by less than 9,000 votes. Once in office, however, Kennedy at first seemed as cautious as Eisenhower on civil rights, which disappointed many African Americans. Kennedy knew that he needed the support of many Southern senators to get

Riding Into Danger On May 14, 1961, Freedom Riders were driven from their bus outside of Anniston, Alabama, when angry townspeople set the bus on fire. Which civil rights protest organization coordinated the Freedom Riders?

other programs he wanted through Congress, and that any attempt to push through new civil rights legislation would anger them.

Kennedy did, however, name approximately 40 African Americans to high-level positions in the federal government. He also appointed Thurgood Marshall to a judgeship on the Second Circuit Appeals Court in New York—one level below the Supreme Court and the highest judicial position an African American had attained to that point. Kennedy also created the **Committee on Equal Employment Opportunity** (CEEO) to stop the federal bureaucracy from discriminating against African Americans when hiring and promoting people.

The Justice Department Takes Action Although President Kennedy was unwilling to challenge Southern Democrats in Congress, he allowed the Justice Department, run by his brother Robert, to actively support the civil rights movement. Robert Kennedy tried to help African Americans register to vote by having the civil rights division of the Justice Department file lawsuits throughout the South.

When violence erupted against the Freedom Riders, the Kennedys came to their aid as well, although not at first. At the time the Freedom Riders took action, President Kennedy was preparing for a meeting with Nikita Khrushchev, the leader of the Soviet Union. Kennedy did not want violence in the South to disrupt the meeting by giving the impression that his country was weak and divided.

After the Freedom Riders were attacked in Montgomery, the Kennedys publicly urged them to

L1/ELL

Guided Reading Activity 24–2

Name _____ Date _____ Class _____

★ Guided Reading Activity 24-2

DIRECTIONS: Recalling Facts Read the section and answer the questions below. Refer to your textbook to write the answers.

1. Who organized a convention at Shaw University and urged students to create the Student Nonviolent Coordinating Committee (SNCC)? _____
2. Who, as an SNCC volunteer from New York, urged the SNCC to help rural African Americans register to vote? _____
3. Who helped organize the Mississippi Freedom Democratic Party, and then challenged the legality of the segregated Democratic Party at the 1964 Democratic National Convention? _____
4. Why did President Kennedy seem cautious at first on civil rights? _____
5. What was the purpose of the Committee on Equal Employment Opportunity? _____

Picturing **History**

Answer: CORE (Congress of Racial Equality)
Ask: Who was responsible for the violence against the Freedom Riders in Birmingham, Alabama? *(Ku Klux Klan)*

 Reading Check

Answer: CORE wanted to draw attention to segregation in Southern bus terminals.

FYI

Presidential aide John Siegenthaler recounted the mob scene at the bus terminal: "The Freedom Riders emerging from the bus were being mauled. It looked like two hundred, three hundred people all over them. There were screams and shouts…." The one white man aboard the bus, Jim Zwerg, was viciously attacked—as if the mob was furious that he would side with African Americans.

History *and the* Humanities

🎵 American Music: Hits Through History: "Why? (Am I Treated So Bad)"

🎵 American Music: Cultural Traditions: "We Shall Not Be Moved"

DIFFERENTIATED INSTRUCTION

Reading Support Ask students to listen to an audio recording of the "I Have a Dream" speech delivered by Martin Luther King, Jr., at the 1963 March on Washington. Instruct students not to take notes. After listening to the speech have the students jot down their impressions. Play the recording again and allow students to take notes. Discuss the speech elements that make it powerful, such as word choice, delivery, and timing. **L2**

📩 Refer to *Inclusion for the High School Social Studies Classroom Strategies and Activities* in the TCR.

Creating a Brochure Have students create a brochure encouraging people to register to vote. Suggest that they contact the local board of elections and organizations that encourage voting, such as the League of Women Voters, to get examples of actual brochures. **L2**

📂 Use the rubric for creating a political cartoon, pamphlet, or handbill on pages 77–78 in the *Performance Assessment Activities and Rubrics.*

CURRICULUM CONNECTION

Government Like many leading political figures in Southern states, George Wallace opposed integration. Elected in 1962 as the governor of Alabama, his actions and words, such as his statement, "segregation now, segregation tomorrow, segregation forever," openly defied the federal government's efforts. So strong was Southern anger over the segregation issue that Wallace would garner much support in his 1968 and 1972 presidential bids. Wallace eventually apologized for his racist beliefs.

stop the rides and give everybody a "cooling off" period. James Farmer replied that African Americans "have been cooling off now for 350 years. If we cool off anymore, we'll be in a deep freeze." Instead he announced that the Freedom Riders planned to head into Mississippi on their next trip.

To stop the violence, President Kennedy made a deal with Senator James Eastland of Mississippi, a strong supporter of segregation. If Eastland would use his influence in Mississippi to prevent violence, Kennedy would not object if the Mississippi police arrested the Freedom Riders. Eastland kept the deal. No violence occurred when the buses arrived in Jackson, Mississippi, but the riders were arrested.

The cost of bailing the Freedom Riders out of jail used up most of CORE's funds, which meant that the rides would have to end unless more money could be found. When Thurgood Marshall learned of the situation, he offered James Farmer the use of the NAACP's Legal Defense Fund's huge bail bond account to keep the rides going.

When President Kennedy returned from his meeting with Khrushchev and found that the Freedom Riders were still active, he changed his position and ordered the Interstate Commerce Commission to tighten its regulations against segregated bus terminals. In the meantime, Robert Kennedy ordered the Justice Department to take legal action against Southern cities that were maintaining segregated bus terminals. The continuing pressure of CORE and the actions of the ICC and the Justice Department finally produced results. By late 1962, segregation in interstate travel had come to an end.

James Meredith As the Freedom Riders were trying to desegregate bus terminals, efforts continued to integrate Southern schools. On the very day John F. Kennedy was inaugurated, an African American air force veteran named **James Meredith** applied for a transfer to the University of Mississippi. Up to that point, the university had avoided complying with the Supreme Court ruling ending segregated education.

In September 1962, Meredith tried to register at the university's admissions office, only to find Ross Barnett, the governor of Mississippi, blocking his path. Although Meredith had a court order directing the university to register him, Governor Barnett stated emphatically, "Never! We will never surrender to the evil and illegal forces of tyranny."

Frustrated, President Kennedy dispatched 500 federal marshals to escort Meredith to the campus. Shortly after Meredith and the marshals arrived, an

angry white mob attacked the campus, and a full-scale riot erupted. The mob hurled rocks, bottles, bricks, and acid at the marshals. Some people fired shotguns at them. The marshals responded with tear gas, but they were under orders not to fire.

The fighting continued all night. By morning, 160 marshals had been wounded. Reluctantly Kennedy ordered the army to send several thousand troops to the campus. For the rest of the year, Meredith attended classes at the University of Mississippi under federal guard. He graduated the following August.

Violence in Birmingham The events in Mississippi frustrated Martin Luther King, Jr., and other civil rights leaders. Although they were pleased that Kennedy had intervened to protect Meredith's rights, they were disappointed that the president had not seized the moment to push for a new civil rights law. When the Cuban missile crisis began the following month, civil rights issues dropped out of the news, and for the next several months, foreign policy became the main priority at the White House.

Reflecting on the problem, Dr. King came to a difficult decision. It seemed to him that only when violence and disorder got out of hand would the federal government intervene. "We've got to have a crisis to bargain with," one of his advisers observed. King agreed. In the spring of 1963, he decided to launch demonstrations in Birmingham, Alabama, knowing they would probably provoke a violent response. He believed it was the only way to get President Kennedy to actively support civil rights.

The situation in Birmingham was volatile. Public Safety Commissioner Bull Connor, who had arranged for the attack on the Freedom Riders, was now running for mayor. Eight days after the protests began, King was arrested and held for a time in solitary confinement. While in prison, King began writing on scraps of paper that had been smuggled into his cell. The "Letter From a Birmingham Jail" that he produced is one of the most eloquent defenses of nonviolent protest ever written.

In his letter, King explained that although the protesters were breaking the law, they were following a higher moral law based on divine justice. To the charge that the protests created racial tensions, King argued that the protests "merely bring to the surface the hidden tension that is already alive." Injustice, he insisted, had to be exposed "to the light of human conscience and the air of national opinion before it can be cured." 📖 *(See page 936 for more on "Letter From a Birmingham Jail.")*

756 CHAPTER 24 The Civil Rights Movement

INTERDISCIPLINARY CONNECTIONS ACTIVITY

Civics Tell students that protests have always been a part of the American tradition and that many protests have involved demonstrations in Washington, D.C. Have students research and write a report about one of the marches or rallies in Washington that occurred between 1960 and 1980. Examples of appropriate subjects for research are the Poor People's Campaign, 1968; ERA, 1978; Earth Day, 1970; or antinuclear protests, 1980. **L2**

After King was released, the protests, which had been dwindling, began to grow again. Bull Connor responded with force, ordering the police to use clubs, police dogs, and high-pressure fire hoses on the demonstrators, including women and children. Millions of people across the nation watched the graphic violence on television. Outraged by the brutality and worried that the government was losing control, Kennedy ordered his aides to prepare a new civil rights bill.

 Reading Check **Evaluating** How did President Kennedy help the civil rights movement?

The Civil Rights Act of 1964

Determined to introduce a civil rights bill, Kennedy now waited for a dramatic opportunity to address the nation on the issue. Shortly after the violence in Birmingham had shocked the nation, Alabama's governor, George Wallace, gave the president his chance. Wallace was committed to segregation. At his inauguration, he had stated, "I draw a line in the dust . . . and I say, Segregation now! Segregation tomorrow! Segregation forever!" On June 11, 1963, Wallace personally stood in front of the University of Alabama's admissions office to block the enrollment of two African Americans. He stayed until federal marshals ordered him to stand aside.

President Kennedy seized the moment to announce his civil rights bill. That evening, he went on television to speak to the American people about a "moral issue . . . as old as the scriptures and as clear as the American Constitution":

❝The heart of the question is whether . . . we are going to treat our fellow Americans as we want to be treated. If an American, because his skin is dark, cannot eat lunch in a restaurant open to the public, if he cannot send his children to the best public school available, if he cannot vote for the public officials who will represent him . . . then who among us would be content to have the color of his skin changed and stand in his place?

One hundred years of delay have passed since President Lincoln freed the slaves, yet their heirs, their grandsons, are not fully free. . . . And this nation, for all its hopes and all its boasts, will not be fully free until all its citizens are free. . . . Now the time has come for this nation to fulfill its promise.❞

—from Kennedy's White House Address, June 11, 1963

TURNING POINT

The March on Washington Dr. King realized that Kennedy would have a very difficult time pushing his civil rights bill through Congress. Therefore, he searched for a way to lobby Congress and to build more public support. When A. Philip Randolph suggested a march on Washington, King agreed.

On August 28, 1963, more than 200,000 demonstrators of all races flocked to the nation's capital. The audience heard speeches and sang hymns and songs as they gathered peacefully near the Lincoln Memorial. Dr. King then delivered a powerful speech outlining his dream of freedom and equality for all Americans:

Picturing **History**

Forcing Change Birmingham police used high-pressure hoses to force civil rights protesters to stop their marches. Why did King's followers offer no resistance?

 Reading Check

Answer: He appointed some African Americans to federal positions in his administration, protected civil rights through federal involvement with the states, and prepared a civil rights bill.

Creating a Graph Provide the data below and ask students to create a graph illustrating the percentage of total voters and African American voters in national elections between 1964 and 1974. Ask students to explain any trends. **L2**

Percentage of Voting Age Population That Voted

Year	Total	African American
1974	44.7%	33.8%
1972	63.0%	52.1%
1970	54.6%	43.5%
1968	67.8%	57.6%
1966	55.4%	41.7%
1964	69.3%	58.5%

Use the rubric for creating a map, display, or chart on pages 65–66 in the *Performance Assessment Activities and Rubrics.*

Picturing **History**

Answer: They believed in the strategy of nonviolence.
Ask: What happened to Martin Luther King, Jr., following the March on Birmingham? *(He was arrested.)*

CRITICAL THINKING ACTIVITY

Analyzing Gains Although African Americans have gained many rights and opportunities as a result of the civil rights movement, much remains to be done. Ask students to identify areas where they think more could be done to ensure that all Americans have equal rights. Have students write their ideas in the form of a letter to their representative in Congress. Invite students to read their letters aloud to the class. **L2**

Answer: Civil Rights Act of 1964
Ask: How long did it take after the March on Washington for the Civil Rights Act of 1964 to be passed? *(a little over ten months)*

Analyzing Decisions Explain to students that President Kennedy decided to support the civil rights movement in the summer of 1963. The country had watched with revulsion as the drama in Birmingham played itself out. Tell them that the mood of the country was changing and that Kennedy was working to get out in front of a movement that was gaining momentum. Discuss with students their opinions about Kennedy's decision and its timing in light of the March on Washington and his political strength in Congress. **L2**

FYI

In 1989 the Southern Poverty Law Center dedicated the Civil Rights Memorial to those who died during the struggle for civil rights in the South. Located in Montgomery, Alabama–the scene of so many of the events in that cause–the memorial serves to inform and educate young people about the civil rights movement. Maya Lin, the creator of the Vietnam Veterans Memorial in Washington, D.C., designed the monument.

"I have a dream"
—*Martin Luther King, Jr.*

Picturing **History**

A Dream Deferred The 1963 March on Washington was the emotional high point of the civil rights movement. Its nonviolent atmosphere and Dr. King's eloquent speech made it one of the most momentous American events of the twentieth century. What significant legislation resulted from the March on Washington?

> ❝I have a dream that one day this nation will rise up and live out the true meaning of its creed . . . that all men are created equal. . . . I have a dream that one day . . . the sons of former slaves and the sons of former slave owners will be able to sit together at the table of brotherhood. . . . I have a dream that my four little children will one day live in a nation where they will not be judged by the color of their skin but by the content of their character. I have a dream . . . when all of God's children, black men and white men, Jews and Gentiles, Protestants and Catholics, will be able to join hands and sing . . . 'Free at last, Free at last, Thank God Almighty, we are free at last.'❞

> —quoted in *Freedom Bound: A History of America's Civil Rights Movement*

King's speech and the peacefulness and dignity of the March on Washington had built momentum for the civil rights bill. Opponents in Congress, however, continued to do what they could to slow the bill down, dragging out their committee investigations and using procedural rules to delay votes. 📖 *(See page 960 for an excerpt from Dr. King's "I Have a Dream" speech.)*

The Civil Rights Bill Becomes Law Although the civil rights bill was likely to pass the House of Representatives, where a majority of Republicans and Northern Democrats supported the measure, it faced a much more difficult time in the Senate. There, a small group of determined senators would try to block the bill indefinitely.

In the U.S. Senate, senators are allowed to speak for as long as they like when a bill is being debated. The Senate cannot vote on a bill until all senators have finished speaking. A **filibuster** occurs when a small group of senators take turns speaking and refuse to stop the debate and allow a bill to come to a vote. Today a filibuster can be stopped if at least 60 senators vote for **cloture,** a motion which cuts off debate and forces a vote. In the 1960s, however, 67

EXTENDING THE CONTENT

Commitment to Nonviolence Ralph Abernathy's church and home were bombed shortly after Martin Luther King, Jr., had organized the Atlanta conference in January 1957. In the face of this and many other acts of violence, King and his followers stuck to their commitment to nonviolence.

senators had to vote for cloture to stop a filibuster. This meant that a minority of senators opposed to civil rights could easily prevent the majority from enacting new civil rights laws.

Worried the bill would never pass, many African Americans became even more disheartened. Then President Kennedy was assassinated in Dallas, Texas, on November 22, 1963, and his vice president, Lyndon Johnson, became president. Johnson was from Texas and had been the leader of the Senate Democrats before becoming vice president. Although he had helped push the Civil Rights Acts of 1957 and 1960 through the Senate, he had done so by weakening their provisions and by compromising with other Southern senators.

To the surprise of the civil rights movement, Johnson committed himself wholeheartedly to getting Kennedy's program, including the civil rights bill, through Congress. Unlike Kennedy, Johnson was very familiar with how Congress operated, having served there for many years. He knew how to build public support, how to put pressure on members of Congress, and how to use the rules and procedures to get what he wanted.

In February 1964, President Johnson's leadership began to produce results. The civil rights bill passed the House of Representatives by a majority of 290 to 130. The debate then moved to the Senate. In June, after 87 days of filibuster, the Senate finally voted to end debate by a margin of 71 to 29—four votes over the two-thirds needed for cloture. On July 2, 1964, President Johnson signed the **Civil Rights Act of 1964** into law.

The Civil Rights Act of 1964 was the most comprehensive civil rights law Congress had ever enacted. It gave the federal government broad power to prevent racial discrimination in a number of areas. The law made segregation illegal in most places of public accommodation, and it gave citizens of all races and nationalities equal access to such facilities as restaurants, parks, libraries, and theaters. The law gave the attorney general more power to bring lawsuits to force school desegregation, and it required private employers to end discrimination in the workplace. It also established the **Equal Employment Opportunity Commission** (EEOC) as a permanent agency in the federal government. This commission monitors the ban on job discrimination by race, religion, gender, and national origin.

✓ **Reading Check** **Examining** How did Dr. King lobby Congress to expand the right to participate in the democratic process?

The Struggle for Voting Rights

Even after the Civil Rights Act of 1964 was passed, voting rights were far from secure. The act had focused on segregation and job discrimination, and it did little to address voting issues. The Twenty-fourth Amendment, ratified in 1964, helped somewhat by eliminating poll taxes, or fees paid in order to vote, in federal (but not state) elections. African Americans still faced hurdles, however, when they tried to vote. As the SCLC and SNCC stepped up their voter registration efforts in the South, their members were often attacked and beaten, and several were murdered.

Across the South, bombs exploded in African American businesses and churches. Between June and October 1964, arson and bombs destroyed 24 African American churches in Mississippi alone. Convinced that a new law was needed to protect African American voting rights, Dr. King decided to stage another dramatic protest.

The Selma March In January 1965, the SCLC and Dr. King selected Selma, Alabama, as the focal point for their campaign for voting rights. Although African Americans made up a majority of Selma's

Voting Rights In the early 1960s, African Americans focused on increasing their political power.

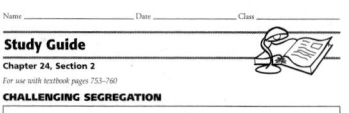

CHAPTER 24
Section 2, 753–760

Creating a Poster Have students create a poster highlighting one of the struggles of the civil rights movement. Have students decide on the message they want to convey and then select images and words that convey the message. **L2**

✓ **Reading Check**

Answer: with the March on Washington and his speech at the Lincoln Memorial

3 ASSESS

Assign Section 2 Assessment as homework or as an in-class activity.

🔹 Have students use the **Interactive Tutor Self-Assessment CD-ROM.**

L1/ELL

Reading Essentials and Study Guide 24–2

Name _____ Date _____ Class _____

Study Guide
Chapter 24, Section 2
For use with textbook pages 753–760
CHALLENGING SEGREGATION

KEY TERMS AND NAMES

Jesse Jackson student leader in the sit-in movement to end segregation (page 754)

Ella Baker executive director of the SCLC, who urged African American students to start their own organization (page 754)

Freedom Riders teams of African Americans and white Americans who traveled through the South to draw attention to the South's refusal to integrate bus terminals (page 755)

filibuster a tactic in which senators take turns speaking and refuse to stop the debate and allow a bill to come to a vote (page 758)

cloture a motion which cuts off debate and forces a vote (page 758)

Civil Rights Act of 1964 law that made segregation illegal in most public places (page 759)

▌▌**Reading Strategy** ▶ **READING THE TEXT**

Analyzing Information Organize students into small groups and discuss the major events of the civil rights movement during the Kennedy and Johnson administrations. Ask if they think the nonviolent aspect of the movement helped or hindered success. In their analyses, have each group compare the results of early actions of the movement to those taken as the movement progressed. Have each group present its analysis to the class. To conclude, have the class as a whole come to a consensus on the effectiveness of nonviolent resistance. **L1**

📩 Refer to *Inclusion for the High School Social Studies Classroom Strategies and Activities* in the TCR.

L2

Section Quiz 24–2

Name _____ Date _____ Class _____

★ Chapter 24   Score ☐

Section Quiz 24-2

DIRECTIONS: Matching Match each item in Column A with the items in Column B.
Write the correct letters in the blanks. (10 points each)

Column A   **Column B**

_____ 1. when a small group of senators take turns speaking and   **A.** Fannie Lou
         refuse to stop the debate and allow a bill to come to vote   Hamer
_____ 2. teams of African Americans and white Americans who   **B.** filibuster
         traveled into the South to draw attention to the South's
         refusal to integrate bus terminals   **C.** "march for
_____ 3. African American air force veteran who applied for   freedom"
         a transfer to the University of Mississippi
                                                                    D. James Meredith
_____ 4. former sharecropper and Student Nonviolent Coordinating
         Committee organizer   **E.** Freedom Riders
_____ 5. a march from Selma to Montgomery, Alabama, organized
         by Dr. King and SNCC

Reteach

Have students summarize the efforts to establish voting rights for African Americans.

Enrich

Invite interested students to locate photographs and artifacts from your community that illustrate "separate but equal." Encourage students to use museum, library, and Internet resources.

✓ **Reading Check**

Answer: It eliminated poll taxes in federal elections.

HISTORY Online

Study Central™ provides summaries, interactive games, and online graphic organizers to help students review section content.

4 CLOSE

Have students evaluate the Civil Rights Act of 1964.

760

---

population, they comprised only 3 percent of registered voters. To prevent African Americans from registering to vote, Sheriff Jim Clark had deputized and armed dozens of white citizens. His posse terrorized African Americans and frequently attacked demonstrators with clubs and electric cattle prods.

Just weeks after receiving the Nobel Peace Prize in Oslo, Norway, for his work in the civil rights movement, Dr. King stated, "We are not asking, we are demanding the ballot." King's demonstrations in Selma led to approximately 2,000 African Americans, including schoolchildren, being arrested by Sheriff Clark. Clark's men attacked and beat many of the demonstrators, and Selma quickly became a major story in the national news.

To keep pressure on the president and Congress to act, Dr. King joined with SNCC activists and organized a "march for freedom" from Selma to the state capitol in Montgomery, a distance of about 50 miles (80 km). On Sunday, March 7, 1965, the march began. The SCLC's Hosea Williams and SNCC's John Lewis led 500 protesters toward U.S. Highway 80, the route that marchers had planned to follow to Montgomery.

As the protesters approached the Edmund Pettus Bridge, which led out of Selma, Sheriff Clark ordered them to disperse. While the marchers kneeled in prayer, more than 200 state troopers and deputized citizens rushed the demonstrators. Many were beaten in full view of television cameras. This brutal attack, known later as "Bloody Sunday," left 70 African Americans hospitalized and many more injured.

The nation was stunned as it viewed the shocking footage of law enforcement officers beating peaceful demonstrators. Watching the events from the White House, President Johnson became furious. Eight days later, he appeared before a nationally televised joint session of the legislature to propose a new voting rights law.

The Voting Rights Act of 1965 On August 3, 1965, the House of Representatives passed the voting rights bill by a wide margin. The following day, the Senate also passed the bill. The **Voting Rights Act of 1965** authorized the attorney general to send federal examiners to register qualified voters, bypassing local officials who often refused to register African Americans. The law also suspended discriminatory devices such as literacy tests in counties where less than half of all adults had been allowed to vote.

The results were dramatic. By the end of the year, almost 250,000 African Americans had registered as new voters. The number of African American elected officials in the South also increased, from about 100 in 1965 to more than 5,000 in 1990.

The passage of the Voting Rights Act of 1965 marked a turning point in the civil rights movement. The movement had now achieved its two major legislative goals. Segregation had been outlawed, and new federal laws were in place to prevent discrimination and protect voting rights.

After 1965 the movement began to shift its focus. It began to pay more attention to the problem of achieving full social and economic equality for African Americans. As part of that effort, the movement turned its attention to the problems of African Americans trapped in poverty and living in ghettos in many of the nation's major cities.

✓ **Reading Check** **Summarizing** How did the Twenty-fourth Amendment affect African American voting rights?

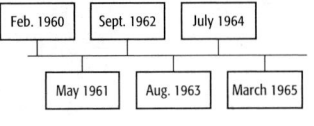

HISTORY Online **Study Central™** To review this section, go to **tarvol2.glencoe.com** and click on **Study Central™**.

SECTION 2 ASSESSMENT

Checking for Understanding

1. **Define:** Freedom Riders, filibuster, cloture, poll tax.
2. **Identify:** Jesse Jackson, Ella Baker, Civil Rights Act of 1964.
3. **Describe** the provisions of the Civil Rights Act of 1964 aimed at ending segregation and racial discrimination.

Reviewing Themes

4. **Science and Technology** How did television help the civil rights movement?

Critical Thinking

5. **Evaluating** How did protesting and lobbying lead to the passage of the Voting Rights Act of 1965?
6. **Sequencing** Use a time line like the one below to show relative chronology of events in the civil rights movement.

Feb. 1960	Sept. 1962	July 1964

May 1961	Aug. 1963	March 1965

Analyzing Visuals

7. **Examining Photographs** Study the photographs in this section. What elements of the photographs show the sacrifices African Americans made in the civil rights movement?

Writing About History

8. **Descriptive Writing** Take on the role of a journalist for the student newspaper of a college in 1960. Write an article for the newspaper describing the sit-in movement taking place across the country.

760 CHAPTER 24 The Civil Rights Movement

SECTION 2 ASSESSMENT ANSWERS

1. Terms are in blue.
2. Jesse Jackson *(p. 754)*, Ella Baker *(p. 754)*, Civil Rights Act of 1964 *(p. 759)*
3. The act gave the federal government broad powers to prevent racial discrimination in a number of areas.
4. Television brought national attention to the civil rights movement.
5. Police resistance to peaceful protests, seen on TV, raised sympathy for the civil rights cause.
6. 1960: sit-ins in Greensboro; 1961: Freedom Riders; 1962: James Meredith enters the University of Mississippi; 1963: March on Washington; 1964: Civil Rights Act; 1965: Selma march
7. Photographs show the humiliations African Americans endured.
8. Students' articles will vary but must be historically accurate.

SECTION 3 New Issues

Guide to Reading

Main Idea
In the mid-1960s, civil rights leaders began to understand that merely winning political rights for African Americans would not address the problem of African Americans' economic status.

Key Terms and Names
racism, Chicago Movement, Richard Daley, black power, Stokely Carmichael, Malcolm X, Black Panthers

Reading Strategy
Organizing As you read about the changing focus of the civil rights movement, complete a chart similar to the one below. Fill in five major violent events and their results.

Event	Result

Reading Objectives
• **Describe** the division between Dr. Martin Luther King, Jr., and the black power movement.
• **Discuss** the direction and progress of the civil rights movement after 1968.

Section Theme
Civic Rights and Responsibilities In the late 1960s, the civil rights movement tried to address the persistent economic inequality of African Americans.

Preview of Events
♦1965   ♦1966   ♦1967   ♦1968

1965
Watts riots break out in Los Angeles; Malcolm X assassinated

1966
Chicago Movement fails

1967
Kerner Commission studies problems of inner cities

1968
Dr. Martin Luther King, Jr., assassinated

★ An American Story ★

Thursday, July 12, 1965, was hot and humid in Chicago. That evening Dessie Mae Williams, a 23-year-old African American woman, stood on the corner near the firehouse at 4000 West Wilcox Street. A firetruck sped out of the firehouse, and the driver lost control. The truck smashed into a stop sign near Williams, and the sign struck and killed her.

African Americans had already picketed this firehouse because it was not integrated. Hearing of Williams's death, 200 neighborhood young people streamed into the street, surrounding the firehouse. For two nights, rioting and disorder reigned. Angry youths threw bricks and bottles at the firehouse and nearby windows. Shouting gangs pelted police with rocks and accosted whites and beat them. Approximately 75 people were injured.

African American detectives, clergy, and National Guard members eventually restored order. Mayor Richard Daley then summoned both white and black leaders to discuss the area's problems. An 18-year-old man who had been in the riot admitted that he had lost his head. "We're sorry about the bricks and bottles," he said, "but when you get pushed, you shove back. Man, you don't like to stand on a corner and be told to get off it when you got nowhere else to go."

—adapted from *Anyplace But Here*

Dr. Martin Luther King, Jr., marching with protesters in Chicago

Problems Facing Urban African Americans

Civil rights leaders had made great progress in the decade following the Montgomery bus boycott, but full equality still eluded many African Americans. Until 1965 the civil rights movement had focused on ending segregation and restoring the voting rights of

---

1 FOCUS

Section Overview
This section focuses on the attention paid by African American leaders to improving the economic status of African Americans.

BELLRINGER
Skillbuilder Activity

 Project transparency and have students answer the question.

Daily Focus Skills Transparency 24–3

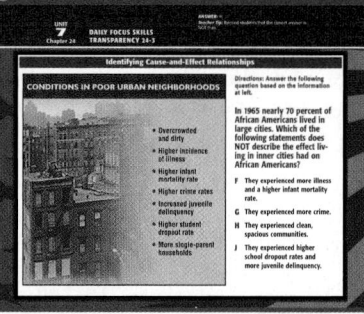

Reading Preview

Answers to Graphic: *Event:* Dessie Mae Williams is killed, *Result:* riots; *Event:* Watts Riot, *Result:* Kerner Commission report on urban riots; *Event:* Malcolm X breaks with the Nation of Islam, *Result:* Malcolm X assassinated; *Event:* King supports strike by African American sanitation workers in Memphis, *Result:* King assassinated

Preteaching Vocabulary
Have students scan the section to preview the Key Terms and Names.

SECTION RESOURCES

📖 Reproducible Masters
• Reproducible Lesson Plan 24–3
• Daily Lecture and Discussion Notes 24–3
• Guided Reading Activity 24–3
• Section Quiz 24–3
• Reading Essentials and Study Guide 24–3
• Supreme Court Case Studies

🖥 Transparencies
• Daily Focus Skills Transparency 24–3

Multimedia
🔵 Interactive Tutor Self-Assessment CD-ROM
🔵 ExamView® Pro Testmaker CD-ROM
🔵 Presentation Plus! CD-ROM
🔵 TeacherWorks™ CD-ROM
🔵 Audio Program

2 TEACH

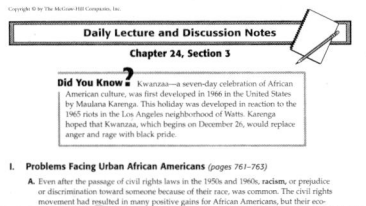

Summarizing Concepts Discuss with students the discontent among many African Americans. Then have them summarize in a list the tactics used by groups such as SNCC, CORE, and the Black Panthers. Discuss as a class the effect of these tactics on the attitudes of white Americans. **L1** ELL

Art Many African American artists used African motifs in their creations, which often expressed outrage with society or portrayed scenes from African American history. An example is *Wall of Love* by William Walker.

Analyzing *Political Cartoons*

Answer: Allegations of police brutality sparked the riots.

Ask: What symbol does the cartoon use to highlight the problems of riots, tension, and racial violence in cities? *(mines)*

African Americans in the South. These were goals that could be achieved through court decisions and by convincing Congress to pass new laws.

Despite the passage of several civil rights laws in the 1950s and 1960s, racism—prejudice or discrimination toward someone because of his or her race—was still common in American society. Changing the law could not change people's attitudes immediately, nor could it help those African Americans trapped in poverty in the nation's big cities.

In 1965 nearly 70 percent of African Americans lived in large cities. Many had moved from the South to the big cities of the North and West during the Great Migration of the 1920s and 1940s. There, they often found the same prejudice and discrimination that had plagued them in the South. Many whites refused to live with African Americans in the same neighborhood. When African Americans moved into a neighborhood, whites often moved out. Real estate agents and landlords in white neighborhoods refused to rent or sell to African Americans, who often found it difficult to arrange for mortgages at local banks.

Even if African Americans had been allowed to move into white neighborhoods, poverty trapped many of them in inner cities while whites moved to

Analyzing *Political Cartoons*

"Perilous Going" This political cartoon highlights the problems that American cities were experiencing in the mid-1960s. Why did riots break out in the Los Angeles neighborhood of Watts?

762   CHAPTER 24   The Civil Rights Movement

the suburbs. Many African Americans found themselves channeled into low-paying jobs. They served as custodians and maids, porters and dock workers, with little chance of advancement. Those who did better typically found employment as blue-collar workers in factories, but very few advanced beyond that. In 1965 only 15 percent of African Americans held professional, managerial, or clerical jobs, compared to 44 percent of whites. Almost half of all African American families lived in poverty, and the median income of an African American family was only 55 percent of that of the average white family. African American unemployment was typically twice that of whites.

Poor neighborhoods in the nation's major cities were overcrowded and dirty, leading to higher rates of illness and infant mortality. At the same time, the crime rate increased in the 1960s, particularly in low-income neighborhoods. Incidents of juvenile delinquency rose, as did the rate of young people dropping out of school. Complicating matters even more was a rise in the number of single-parent households. All poor neighborhoods suffered from these problems, but because more African Americans lived in poverty, their communities were disproportionately affected.

Many African Americans living in urban poverty knew the civil rights movement had made enormous gains, but when they looked at their own circumstances, nothing seemed to be changing. The movement had raised their hopes, but their everyday problems were economic and social, and therefore harder to address. As a result, their anger and frustration began to rise—until it finally erupted.

The Watts Riot Just five days after President Johnson signed the Voting Rights Act, a race riot broke out in Watts, an African American neighborhood in Los Angeles. Allegations of police brutality had served as the catalyst of this uprising, which lasted for six days and required over 14,000 members of the National Guard and 1,500 law officers to restore order. Rioters burned and looted entire neighborhoods and destroyed about $45 million in property. They killed 34 people, and about 900 suffered injuries.

More rioting was yet to come. Race riots broke out in dozens of American cities between 1965 and 1968. It seemed that they could explode at any place and at any time. The worst riot took place in Detroit in 1967. Burning, looting, and skirmishes with police and National Guard members resulted in 43 deaths and over 1,000 wounded. Eventually the U.S. Army sent in tanks and soldiers armed with machine guns to get control of the situation. Nearly 4,000 fires destroyed

Reading Strategy **READING THE TEXT**

Using Word Maps A word map is a graphic designed to show relationships between words or concepts. A commonly used word map or concept web map shows a central bubble containing a key word or idea. Surrounding bubbles connected to the center bubble by lines are used to show semantic relationships or to explain structure relationships. Choose a word or concept from the section, such as *Black Power,* and create a word map on the board. Have students complete the surrounding bubbles to clarify the relationship. **L1**

Refer to *Inclusion for the High School Social Studies Classroom Strategies and Activities* in the TCR.

1,300 buildings, and the damage in property loss was estimated at $250 million. The governor of Michigan, who viewed the smoldering city from a helicopter, remarked that Detroit looked like "a city that had been bombed."

GOVERNMENT

The Kerner Commission In 1967 President Johnson appointed the National Advisory Commission on Civil Disorders, headed by Governor Otto Kerner of Illinois, to study the causes of the urban riots and to make recommendations to prevent them from happening again in the future. The **Kerner Commission,** as it became known, conducted a detailed study of the problem. The commission blamed white society and white racism for the majority of the problems in the inner city. "Our nation is moving toward two societies, one black, one white—separate and unequal," it concluded.

The commission recommended the creation of 2 million new jobs in the inner city, the construction of 6 million new units of public housing, and a renewed federal commitment to fight de facto segregation. President Johnson's war on poverty, however, which addressed some of the same concerns for inner-city jobs and housing, was already underway. Saddled with massive spending for the Vietnam War, however, President Johnson never endorsed the recommendations of the commission.

✓ **Reading Check** **Explaining** What was the federal government's response to the race riots in Los Angeles and Detroit?

The Shift to Economic Rights

By the mid-1960s, a number of African American leaders were becoming increasingly critical of Martin Luther King's nonviolent strategy. They felt it had failed to improve the economic position of African Americans. What good was the right to dine at restaurants or stay at hotels if most African Americans could not afford these services anyway? Dr. King became sensitive to this criticism, and in 1965 he began to focus on economic issues.

In 1965 Albert Raby, president of a council of community organizations that worked to improve conditions for Chicago's poor, invited Dr. King to visit the city. Dr. King and his staff had never conducted a civil rights campaign in the North. By focusing on the problems that African Americans faced in Chicago, Dr. King believed he could call greater attention to poverty and other racial problems that lay beneath the urban race riots.

To call attention to the deplorable housing conditions that many African American families faced, Dr. King and his wife Coretta moved into a slum apartment in an African American neighborhood in Chicago. Dr. King and the SCLC hoped to work with local leaders to improve the economic status of African Americans in Chicago's poor neighborhoods.

The **Chicago Movement,** however, made little headway. When Dr. King led a march through the all-white suburb of Marquette Park to demonstrate the need for open housing, he was met by angry white mobs similar to those in Birmingham and Selma. Mayor **Richard Daley** ordered the Chicago police to protect the marchers, but he wanted to avoid any repeat of the violence. He met with Dr. King and proposed a new program to clean up the slums. Associations of realtors and bankers also agreed to promote open housing. In theory, mortgages and rental property would be available to everyone, regardless of race. In practice, very little changed.

✓ **Reading Check** **Describing** How did Dr. King and SCLC leaders hope to address economic concerns?

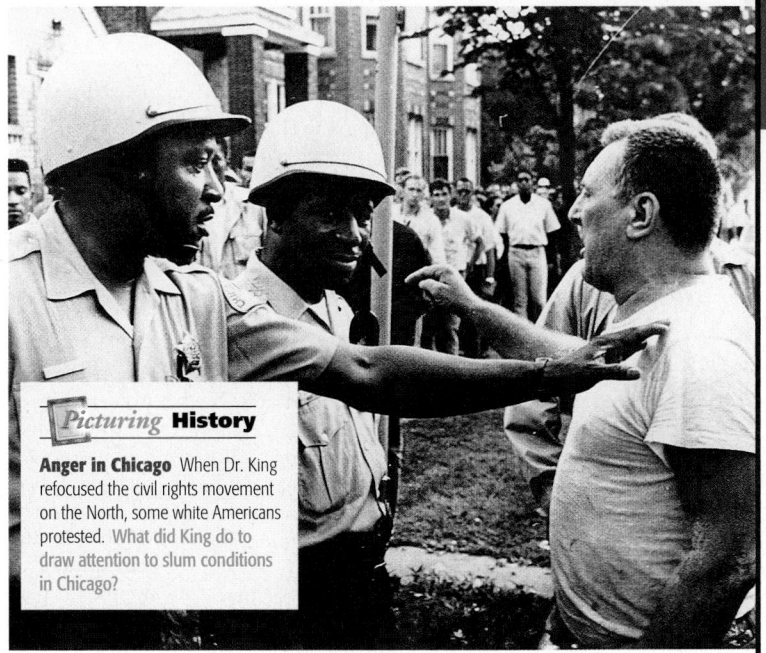

Picturing **History**

Anger in Chicago When Dr. King refocused the civil rights movement on the North, some white Americans protested. **What did King do to draw attention to slum conditions in Chicago?**

CHAPTER 24   The Civil Rights Movement   **763**

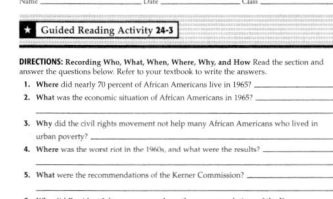

L1/ELL
Guided Reading Activity 24–3

Name _____ Date _____ Class _____

★ Guided Reading Activity **24-3**

DIRECTIONS: Recording Who, What, When, Where, Why, and How Read the section and answer the questions below. Refer to your textbook to write the answers.
1. Where did nearly 70 percent of African Americans live in 1965? _____
2. What was the economic situation of African Americans in 1965? _____
3. Why did the civil rights movement not help many African Americans who lived in urban poverty? _____
4. Where was the worst riot in the 1960s, and what were the results? _____
5. What were the recommendations of the Kerner Commission? _____
6. Why did President Johnson never endorse the recommendations of the Kerner Commission? _____

✓ **Reading Check**

Answer: United States Army troops were deployed, and the Kerner Commission recommended reforms to prevent further riots.

Picturing **History**

Answer: King and his wife moved into a slum apartment in Chicago.
Ask: Why did whites protest when the civil rights movement moved to the North? *(There was prejudice and racism in the North.)*

✓ **Reading Check**

Answer: by meeting with local leaders to discuss housing and economic reforms

Writing an Article Have students research the Watts riot using library and Internet resources. Then have them write a headline and a brief newspaper article describing the riot.

📁 Use the rubric for a magazine/newspaper/Web site article or help-wanted ad on pages 75–76 in the *Performance Assessment Activities and Rubrics.*

DIFFERENTIATED INSTRUCTION

Reading Support Form volunteers into two groups to conduct a debate. Ask one group to present arguments supporting African American nationalism, the other opposing it. Give students time to consider their arguments. Have each side present its views to the class. Make sure each side presents evidence to support its views. As the students discuss the pros and cons of African American nationalism, encourage the class to reach a consensus. **L2**

📁 Refer to *Inclusion for the High School Social Studies Classroom Strategies and Activities* in the TCR.

Conducting an Interview Have students draw up questions in order to conduct an interview with someone who lived through or participated in the civil rights movement. Help students prepare questions that will get the interviewee to tell how his or her life changed as a result of the civil rights movement. Have students conduct the interviews and then present their findings to the class. Discuss how the interviews add to the information in the text. **L3**

📁 Use the rubric for an interview on pages 83–84 in the *Performance Assessment Activities and Rubrics.*

📁 Use *Supreme Court Case Study 30, Yates v. United States.*

Picturing History

Background: Because they were treated as property, very few enslaved people had last names. If they did have a last name, it was often the name of their slaveholder. Members of the Nation of Islam adopted the "X" to eliminate the historical ties to their enslaved past.

Answer: The X was a symbol for the family name of his African ancestors.

Ask: What belief did Malcolm X share with Marcus Garvey? *(Both believed that African Americans should form their own self-governing communities; Malcolm X later abandoned separatism.)*

Black Power

Dr. King's failure in Chicago seemed to show that nonviolent protests could do little to change economic problems. After 1965 many African Americans, especially young people living in cities, began to turn away from King. Some leaders called for more aggressive forms of protest. Their new strategies ranged from armed self-defense to the suggestion that the government set aside a number of states where African Americans could live free from the presence of whites.

As African Americans became more assertive, they placed less emphasis on cooperation with sympathetic whites in the civil rights movement. Some African American organizations, including CORE and SNCC, voted to expel all whites from leadership positions within their organizations, believing that African Americans alone should determine the course and direction of their struggle.

Many young African Americans called for black power, a term that had many different meanings. A few interpreted black power to mean that physical self-defense and even violence were acceptable in defense of one's freedom—a clear rejection of Dr. King's philosophy. To most, including **Stokely Carmichael,** the leader of SNCC in 1966, the term meant that African Americans should control the social, political, and economic direction of their struggle:

❝This is the significance of black power as a slogan. For once, black people are going to use the words they want to use—not just the words whites want to hear. . . . The need for psychological equality is the reason why SNCC today believes that blacks must organize in the black community. Only black people

Picturing History

Malcolm X Makes His Point Once the most visible spokesperson for the Nation of Islam, Malcolm X originally disagreed with Dr. King's passive protest tactics. What did the "X" in his name symbolize?

can . . . create in the community an aroused and continuing black consciousness. . . . Black people must do things for themselves; they must get . . . money they will control and spend themselves; they must conduct tutorial programs themselves so that black children can identify with black people.❞

—from the *New York Review of Books,* September 1966

Black power also stressed pride in the African American cultural group. It emphasized racial distinctiveness rather than **cultural assimilation**—the process by which minority groups adapt to the dominant culture in a society. African Americans showed pride in their racial heritage by adopting new Afro hairstyles and African-style clothing. Many also took on African names. In universities, students demanded that African and African American Studies courses be adopted as part of the standard school curriculum. Dr. King and some other leaders criticized black power as a philosophy of hopelessness and despair. The idea was very popular, however, in the poor urban neighborhoods where many African Americans resided.

Malcolm X and the Nation of Islam By the early 1960s, a man named **Malcolm X** had become a symbol of the black power movement that was sweeping the nation. Born Malcolm Little in Omaha, Nebraska, he experienced a difficult childhood and adolescence. He drifted into a life of crime, and in 1946, he was convicted of burglary and sent to prison for six years.

Prison transformed Malcolm. He began to educate himself, and he played an active role in the prison debate society. Eventually he joined the **Nation of Islam,** commonly known as the Black Muslims, who were led by Elijah Muhammad. Despite their name, the Black Muslims do not hold the same beliefs as mainstream Muslims. The Nation of Islam preached black nationalism. Like Marcus Garvey in the 1920s, Black Muslims believed that African Americans should separate themselves from whites and form their own self-governing communities.

Shortly after joining the Nation of Islam, Malcolm Little changed his name to Malcolm X. The "X" stood as a symbol for the family name of his African ancestors who had been enslaved. Malcolm argued that his true family name had been stolen from him by slavery, and he did not intend to use the name white society had given him.

The Black Muslims viewed themselves as their own nation and attempted to make themselves as economically self-sufficient as possible. They ran their own businesses, organized their own schools, established

INTERDISCIPLINARY CONNECTIONS ACTIVITY

Citizenship Have students work in pairs to read about and find photo images of one of the radical African American groups such as the Black Panther Party or the Nation of Islam. Have the pairs create a photo essay of their chosen group. Tell students that the essay should involve photos and descriptive captions that give readers insight into the goals of the organization and motives for specific actions. **L2**

their own weekly newspaper *(Muhammad Speaks)*, and encouraged their members to respect each other and to strengthen their families. Although the Black Muslims did not advocate violence, they did advocate self-defense. Malcolm X was a powerful and charismatic speaker, and his criticisms of white society and the mainstream civil rights movement gained national attention for the Nation of Islam.

By 1964 Malcolm X had broken with the Black Muslims. Discouraged by scandals involving the Nation of Islam's leader, he went to the Muslim holy city of Makkah (also called Mecca) in Saudi Arabia. After seeing Muslims from many different races worshipping together, he concluded that an integrated society was possible. In a revealing letter describing his pilgrimage to Makkah, he stated that many whites that he met during the pilgrimage displayed a spirit of brotherhood that gave him a new, positive insight into race relations.

After Malcolm X broke with the Nation of Islam, he continued to criticize the organization and its leader, Elijah Muhammad. Because of this, three organization members shot and killed him in February 1965 while he was giving a speech in New York. Although Malcolm X left the Nation of Islam before his death, his speeches and ideas from those years with the Black Muslims are those for which he is most remembered. In Malcolm's view, African Americans may have been victims in the past, but they did not have to allow racism to victimize them in the present. His ideas have influenced African Americans to take pride in their own culture and to believe in their ability to make their way in the world.

The Black Panthers Malcolm X's ideas influenced a new generation of militant African American leaders who also preached black power, black nationalism, and economic self-sufficiency. In 1966 in Oakland, California, Huey Newton, Bobby Seale, and Eldridge Cleaver organized the Black Panther Party for Self-Defense, or the **Black Panthers,** as they were known. They considered themselves the heirs of Malcolm X, and they recruited most of their members from poor urban communities across the nation.

The Black Panthers believed that a revolution was necessary in the United States, and they urged African Americans to arm themselves and confront white society in order to force whites to grant them equal rights. Black Panther leaders adopted a "Ten-Point Program," which called for black empowerment, an end to racial oppression, and control of major institutions and services in the African American community, such as schools, law enforcement, housing, and medical

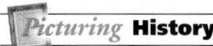
Picturing **History**

Black Power U.S. athletes Tommie Smith and John Carlos give the black power salute during the medal ceremony at the 1968 Olympic Games in Mexico City. How did black power supporters demonstrate their belief in the movement?

facilities. **Eldridge Cleaver,** who served as the minister of culture, articulated many of the organization's objectives in his 1967 best-selling book, *Soul on Ice.*

✓ **Reading Check** **Describing** What caused a division between Dr. Martin Luther King, Jr., and the black power movement?

The Assassination of Martin Luther King, Jr.

By the late 1960s, the civil rights movement had fragmented into dozens of competing organizations with philosophies for reaching equality. At the same time, the emergence of black power and the call by some African Americans for violent action angered many white civil rights supporters. This made further legislation to help blacks economically less likely.

In this atmosphere, Dr. King went to Memphis, Tennessee, to support a strike of African American sanitation workers in March 1968. At the time, the SCLC had been planning a national "Poor People's Campaign" to promote economic advancement for

CHAPTER 24 The Civil Rights Movement **765**

Picturing **History**

Answer: They gave this same black power salute by raising a clenched fist.

✓ **Reading Check**

Answer: King was nonviolent; the black power movement advocated aggressive self-defense, even violence.

Understanding Relative Chronology Have students create a fact sheet tracing the changing tactics of the civil rights movement. **L2**

3 ASSESS

Assign Section 3 Assessment as homework or as an in-class activity.

🖲 Have students use the **Interactive Tutor Self-Assessment CD-ROM.**

L1/ELL

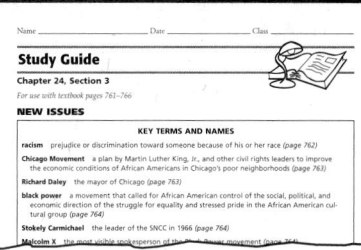

Reading Essentials and Study Guide 24–3

Name _____ Date _____ Class _____

Study Guide

Chapter 24, Section 3
For use with textbook pages 761–766

NEW ISSUES

KEY TERMS AND NAMES
racism prejudice or discrimination toward someone because of his or her race *(page 762)*
Chicago Movement a plan by Martin Luther King, Jr., and other civil rights leaders to improve the economic conditions of African Americans in Chicago's poor neighborhoods *(page 763)*
Richard Daley the mayor of Chicago *(page 763)*
black power a movement that called for African American control of the social, political, and economic direction of the struggle for equality and stressed pride in the African American cultural group *(page 764)*
Stokely Carmichael the leader of the SNCC in 1966 *(page 764)*
Malcolm X the most visible spokesperson of the Black Power movement *(page 764)*

CRITICAL THINKING ACTIVITY

Analyzing Concepts Ask students to consider the following questions and write their thoughts and responses on a sheet of paper. Is violence in self-defense, or in response to violence, justifiable? Is nonviolent civil disobedience an effective strategy for attaining full equality? After students have had a chance to write down their thoughts, conduct a class discussion about the differences between violent and nonviolent protests. Encourage students to share differing views as they explore these complex concepts. **L2**

L2

Section Quiz 24–3

Picturing **History**

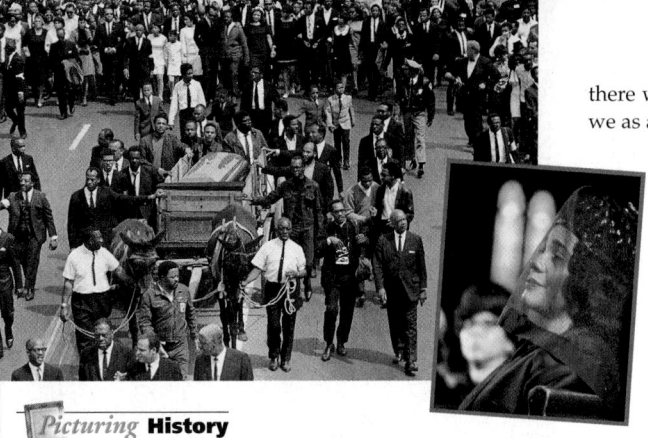

Picturing **History**

Atlanta Mourns Martin Luther King, Jr. The nation joined Coretta Scott King (right) in sorrow following the assassination of her husband in 1968. Why was King in Memphis at the time of his death?

Picturing **History**

Answer: to support a strike by African American sanitation workers

---

Reteach

Have students describe the division between Dr. Martin Luther King, Jr., and the black power movement.

Enrich

Have interested students write a paragraph explaining why the Kerner Commission was largely ignored.

✓ **Reading Check**

Answer: The Poor People's Campaign promoted economic advancement for all impoverished Americans.

HISTORY Online

Study Central™ provides summaries, interactive games, and online graphic organizers to help students review section content.

---

4 CLOSE

Have students discuss the direction and progress of the civil rights movement after 1968.

---

all impoverished Americans. The purpose of this campaign, the most ambitious one that Dr. King would ever lead, was to lobby the federal government to commit billions of dollars to end poverty and unemployment in the United States. People of all races and nationalities were to converge on the nation's capital, as they had in 1963 during the March on Washington, where they would camp out until both Congress and President Johnson agreed to pass the requested legislation to fund the proposal.

On the evening of April 4, 1968, as he stood on his hotel balcony in Memphis, Dr. King was assassinated by a sniper. Ironically, he had told a gathering at a local African American church just the previous night, "I've been to the mountaintop. . . . I've looked over and I've seen the Promised Land. I may not get there with you, but I want you to know tonight that we as a people will get to the Promised Land."

Dr. King's assassination touched off both national mourning and riots in more than 100 cities, including Washington, D.C. The Reverend **Ralph Abernathy,** who had served as a trusted assistant to Dr. King for many years, led the Poor People's Campaign in King's absence. The demonstration, however, did not achieve any of the major objectives that either King or the SCLC had hoped it would.

In the wake of Dr. King's death, Congress passed the Civil Rights Act of 1968. The act contained a fair housing provision outlawing discrimination in housing sales and rentals and gave the Justice Department authority to bring suits against such discrimination.

Dr. King's death marked the end of an era in American history. Although the civil rights movement continued, it lacked the unity of purpose and vision that Dr. King had given it. Under his leadership, and with the help of tens of thousands of dedicated African Americans, many of whom were students, the civil rights movement transformed American society. Although many problems remain to be resolved, the achievements of the civil rights movement in the 1950s and 1960s dramatically improved life for African Americans, creating new opportunities where none had existed before.

✓ **Reading Check** **Summarizing** What were the goals of the Poor People's Campaign?

HISTORY Online

Study Central™ To review this section, go to **tarvol2.glencoe.com** and click on **Study Central**™.

SECTION 3 ASSESSMENT

Checking for Understanding

1. **Define:** racism, black power.
2. **Identify:** Chicago Movement, Richard Daley, Stokely Carmichael, Malcolm X, Black Panthers.
3. **Explain** the goals of the Nation of Islam in the 1960s.
4. **Summarize** the findings of the Kerner Commission.

Reviewing Themes

5. **Civic Rights and Responsibilities** How was the Civil Rights Act of 1968 designed to help end discrimination?

Critical Thinking

6. **Identifying Cause and Effect** What were the effects of the assassination of Dr. Martin Luther King, Jr.?
7. **Categorizing** Using a graphic organizer like the one below, list the main views of the three leaders listed.

Leader	Views
Dr. Martin Luther King, Jr.	
Malcolm X	
Eldridge Cleaver	

Analyzing Visuals

8. **Analyzing Political Cartoons** The cartoon on page 762 suggests that the violence of the mid-1960s was as bad as the violence of the Vietnam War going on at the same time. What images does the cartoonist use to compare violence at home with the violence of the war?

Writing About History

9. **Expository Writing** Take on the role of a reporter in the late 1960s. Imagine you have interviewed a follower of Dr. King and a Black Panther member. Write out a transcript of each interview.

---

766 CHAPTER 24 The Civil Rights Movement

SECTION 3 ASSESSMENT ANSWERS

1. Terms are in blue.
2. Chicago Movement *(p. 763),* Richard Daley *(p. 763),* Stokely Carmichael *(p. 764),* Malcolm X *(p. 764),* Black Panthers *(p. 765)*
3. It wanted separate self-governing communities for African Americans.
4. It blamed racism for inner-city problems and urged job and housing programs.
5. by outlawing housing discrimination
6. It touched off both national mourning and riots; the Civil Rights Act of 1968 was passed.
7. King: nonviolent protest; Malcolm X: self-defense and separatism; Cleaver: revolution
8. the ocean ships, floating mines
9. Students' articles will vary but should be written as if a reporter were describing an interview.

SKILLBUILDER

Preparing a Bibliography

Why Learn This Skill?

When you write research reports, you should include a list of the sources used to find your information. This list, called a *bibliography*, allows you to credit the sources you cited and supports the report's accuracy.

Learning the Skill

A bibliography is a list of sources used in a research report. These sources include books; articles from newspapers, magazines, and journals; interviews; and other sources.

There are two main reasons to write a bibliography. First, those who read your report may want to learn more about the topic. Second, a bibliography supports the reliability of your report.

A bibliography follows an established format. The entry for each source contains all the information needed to find that source, including the author, title, page numbers, publisher information, and publication date. You should document this information as you carry out your research. If you neglect this step early in your research, you must locate your sources again in order to credit them in your report.

You should arrange bibliographic entries alphabetically by the author's last name. The following are acceptable formats, followed by sample entries. Note that all lines after the first line are indented.

Books:

Author's last name, first name. *Full Title.* Place of publication: publisher, copyright date.

Hay, Peter. *Ordinary Heroes: The Life and Death of Chana Szenes, Israel's National Heroine.* New York: Paragon House, 1986.

Articles:

Author's last name, first name. "Title of Article." *Name of Periodical* in which article appears, volume number (date of issue): page numbers.

Watson, Bruce. "The New Peace Corps in the New Kazakhstan." *Smithsonian*, Vol. 25 (August 1994): pp. 26–35.

Other Sources:

For other kinds of sources, adapt the format for book entries as needed.

Practicing the Skill

Review the sample bibliography below from a report on Martin Luther King, Jr. Then answer the questions that follow.

Patrick, Diane. *Martin Luther King, Jr.* New York: Franklin Watts, 1990.

Franklin, John H. "Jim Crow Goes to School: The Genesis of Legal Segregation in Southern Schools." *South Atlantic Quarterly*, 57 (1956): pp. 225–235.

Washington, James Melvin, ed. *A Testament of Hope: The Essential Writings of Martin Luther King, Jr.* San Francisco: Harper & Row.

King, Jr., Martin Luther. Time for Freedom has Come. New York Times Magazine (Sept. 10, 1961).

❶ Are the bibliography entries in the correct order? Why or why not?

❷ What is missing from the second book listing?

❸ What features are missing from the second article listing?

Skills Assessment

Complete the Practicing Skills questions on page 769 and the Chapter 24 Skill Reinforcement Activity to assess your mastery of this skill.

Applying the Skill

Preparing a Bibliography Put together a bibliography of at least five sources that you could use for a report on the civil rights movement. Include books, periodicals, and any other sources you wish.

Glencoe's **Skillbuilder Interactive Workbook CD-ROM, Level 2,** provides instruction and practice in key social studies skills.

TEACH

Preparing a Bibliography

Provide students with information about acceptable styles for a bibliography for this class. Point out that while there is more than one acceptable format, a teacher, department, or school often selects one style to be used by all students. This is also common at the college level and in the business world.

Additional Practice

L1

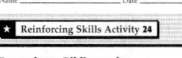

Reinforcing Skills Activity 24

Name _____ Date _____ Class _____

★ Reinforcing Skills Activity 24

Preparing a Bibliography

☐ LEARNING THE SKILL

A bibliography is a list of the resources used in writing a report. It establishes the reliability of your research and helps those who read your report to know where to find more information on your topic. Bibliographies follow an established format. Entries are listed in alphabetical order and include the author, title, publisher information, publication date, and page numbers. Sample entries are shown below.

Books:
Hay, Peter. *Ordinary Heroes: The Life and Death of Chana Szenes, Israel's National Heroine.* New York: Paragon House, 1986.

Articles:
Watson Bruce. "The New Peace Corps in the New Kazakhstan." *Smithsonian,* Vol. 25 (August 1994): pp. 26–35.

GLENCOE
TECHNOLOGY

CD-ROM
Glencoe Skillbuilder
Interactive Workbook
CD-ROM, Level 2

This interactive CD-ROM reinforces student mastery of essential social studies skills.

ANSWERS TO PRACTICING THE SKILL

❶ No, they should be in alphabetical order using the last name of each author.

❷ publication date

❸ quotes around the title of the article, and italics for the *New York Times Magazine*

Applying the Skill
Students' bibliographies will vary. Students should follow the guidelines on this page or other guidelines you provide.

CHAPTER 24 ASSESSMENT and ACTIVITIES

CHAPTER 24 ASSESSMENT and ACTIVITIES

GLENCOE
TECHNOLOGY

MindJogger Videoquiz
Use the **MindJogger Videoquiz** to review Chapter 24 content.

 Available in DVD

Reviewing Key Terms
Students' answers will vary. The pages where the words appear in the text are shown in parentheses.

1. **separate-but-equal** (p. 747)
2. **de facto segregation** (p. 747)
3. **sit-in** (p. 748)
4. **Freedom Riders** (p. 755)
5. **filibuster** (p. 758)
6. **cloture** (p. 758)
7. **poll tax** (p. 759)
8. **racism** (p. 762)
9. **black power** (p. 764)

Reviewing Key Facts
10. NAACP (p. 747), Thurgood Marshall (p. 748), Linda Brown (p. 748), Martin Luther King, Jr. (p. 749), Southern Christian Leadership Conference (p. 750), Jesse Jackson (p. 754), Chicago Movement (p. 763), Stokely Carmichael (p. 764), Malcolm X (p. 764)

11. Rosa Parks's arrest led to the bus boycott.

12. It was the first case in which the Court found segregation to be unconstitutional.

13. It worked for desegregation of public facilities and voter registration.

14. It sent in National Guard and U.S. Army troops, and appointed the Kerner Commission.

15. It moved from focusing on ending segregation to focusing on full social and economic equality. It also moved from nonviolent resistance to militancy.

Reviewing Key Terms
On a sheet of paper, use each of these terms in a sentence.

1. separate-but-equal
2. de facto segregation
3. sit-in
4. Freedom Riders
5. filibuster
6. cloture
7. poll tax
8. racism
9. black power

Reviewing Key Facts
10. **Identify:** NAACP, Thurgood Marshall, Linda Brown, Martin Luther King, Jr., Southern Christian Leadership Conference, Jesse Jackson, Chicago Movement, Stokely Carmichael, Malcolm X.

11. What event led to the bus boycott in Montgomery, Alabama?

12. Why was the decision in *Brown* v. *Board of Education* a significant step toward ending segregation?

13. What was the role of SNCC in the civil rights movement?

14. How did the government react to race riots in cities such as Los Angeles and Detroit?

15. What were two changes in the focus of the civil rights movement in the mid-1960s?

Critical Thinking
16. **Analyzing Themes: Civic Rights and Responsibilities** Do you agree with the viewpoint of Dr. Martin Luther King, Jr., or with that of the Black Panthers concerning the civil rights movement? Explain your answer.

17. **Evaluating** Why did the civil rights movement make fewer gains after 1968?

Chapter Summary

Major Events in Civil Rights Movement

1954
- *Brown* v. *Board of Education* attacks school segregation.
- Separate-but-equal doctrine in education is ruled unconstitutional.

1955
- Rosa Parks inspires Montgomery bus boycott.

1957
- SCLC is formed to fight segregation and encourage African Americans to vote.
- Eisenhower sends army troops to Little Rock, Arkansas.

1960
- Sit-ins begin and spread to over 100 cities.
- SNCC is formed and leads fight against segregated public facilities.

1961
- Freedom Rides begin.

1963
- Birmingham demonstrations and the March on Washington help build support for the civil rights movement.

1964
- Twenty-fourth Amendment abolishes poll tax.
- Civil Rights Act of 1964 outlaws discrimination based on race, gender, religion, or national origin, and gives equal access to public facilities.

1965
- Voting Rights Act ensures African Americans of the right to vote.
- Watts riot sparks several years of urban racial violence.
- Splinter groups within the civil rights movement advocate more aggressive means of gaining racial equality.

1968
- Dr. Martin Luther King, Jr. assassinated.
- Civil Rights Act of 1968 outlaws discrimination in the sale and rental of housing.

1954 — *1961* — *1968*

Critical Thinking
16. Students' answers will vary. Students should refer to the results and reactions in this chapter in discussing their opinions.

17. After Martin Luther King, Jr., was assassinated, the movement fragmented; also, economic gains were harder to win.

18. It was a nonviolent protest that offered immediate results and gained sympathy from many people in the nation.

19. Civil Rights Act of 1957: created the civil rights division of the Department of Justice to support the right to vote, created the United States Commission of Civil Rights; Twenty-Fourth Amendment: ended poll taxes; Voting Rights Act: authorized the attorney general to send federal examiners to register qualified voters;

HISTORY Online

Self-Check Quiz

Visit the *American Republic Since 1877* Web site at tarvol2.glencoe.com and click on *Self-Check Quizzes— Chapter 24* to assess your knowledge of chapter content.

18. Making Generalizations Why was the sit-in movement considered a major turning point in the civil rights movement?

19. Organizing Use a graphic organizer similar to the one below to compare examples of civil rights legislation.

Civil Rights Legislation	Provisions
Civil Rights Act 1957	
Twenty-Fourth Amendment	
Voting Rights Act	
Civil Rights Act of 1964	
Civil Rights Act of 1968	

Practicing Skills

20. Preparing a Bibliography Review the following bibliography for a report on the civil rights movement. Then answer the questions that follow.

Fairclough, Adam. <u>Martin Luther King, Jr.</u> Athens and London: University of Georgia Press, 1995.

Juan Williams. Eyes on the Prize. New York: Viking Penguin, Inc., 1987.

<u>Patterson, James T.</u> Grand Expectations, The United States, 1945–1974. New York: Oxford University Press, 1996.

Bontemps, Arna, and Jack Conroy. <u>Anyplace but Here.</u> Columbia: University of Missouri Press. (NO PUB DATE)

a. The entries presented above are not listed in the correct order. Using just the names of the authors, put them in the correct order.

b. What is incorrect in the Patterson listing?

c. Rewrite the Juan Williams listing correctly.

Geography and History

21. The map on this page shows routes of Freedom Riders. Study the map and answer the questions below.

a. Interpreting Maps Which states did the Freedom Riders travel through? What was their final destination?

b. Applying Geography Skills Why do you think the Freedom Riders faced protests during this trip?

Writing Activity

22. Writing a Script Work in small groups to write a script for a documentary on the civil rights movement in the 1950s

Route of the Freedom Riders, 1961

Dep. May 4, 1961

Arr. May 14 Dep. May 20

Greensboro N.C.

Atlanta

Birmingham

Anniston

Montgomery

Jackson

Selma

Arr. May 20 Dep. May 24

Arr. May 24 and 25

ATLANTIC OCEAN

0   200 miles

0   200 kilometers
Lambert Azimuthal Equal-Area projection

and 1960s. Your group should choose a specific topic, movement leader, or time period to write about. Use your script to produce a documentary to present to the other groups in your class.

Chapter Activity

23. Examining Interviews Work with a classmate to research interviews with Martin Luther King, Jr., and Malcolm X. Take notes on the different points of view of these civil rights leaders, and then prepare a chart illustrating similarities, differences, and any bias which shapes their beliefs.

Standardized Test Practice

Directions: Choose the phrase that best completes the following statement.

One difference between the strategies of Dr. Martin Luther King, Jr., and some later civil rights groups was that King was committed to

A ending discrimination in housing and unemployment.

B using only nonviolent forms of protest.

C demanding equal rights for African Americans.

D gaining improvements in living conditions for African Americans.

Test-Taking Tip: If you read this question carefully, you will notice that it asks for one *difference* in civil rights strategies. Three of the answer choices will represent *common goals.* Be careful to read through all the choices to find the one that represents a *different* type of strategy.

HISTORY Online

Have students visit the Web site at tarvol2.glencoe.com to review Chapter 24 and take the Self-Check Quiz.

Writing Activity

22. Documentaries should indicate a clear understanding of events and should express the emotions of the times.

Chapter Activity

23. Charts should show the similarities and differences between the two leaders.

Standardized Test Practice

Answer: B

Test-Taking Tip: Tell students to think about what some of the later civil rights groups advocated. The one issue on this list that some of the later groups did not support was nonviolence. The correct answer is B.

Bonus Question ?

Ask: What was the purpose of the March on Washington? *(to build public support for passage of the Civil Rights Act of 1964)*

Civil Rights Act of 1964: gave the federal government broad powers to prevent racial discrimination, required equal access to public facilities for citizens of all races, established the EEOC, required private employers to end workplace discrimination, gave the attorney general power to bring lawsuits to force school desegregation; Civil Rights Act of 1968: outlawed discrimination in housing

Practicing Skills

20. a. The author order should be Bontemps, Fairclough, Patterson, and Williams. **b.** The author, not the title, is underlined. **c.** Williams, Juan. *Eyes on the Prize.* New York: Viking Penguin, Inc., 1987.

Geography and History

21. a. Maryland, Virginia, North Carolina, South Carolina, Georgia, Alabama; final destination: Jackson, Mississippi; **b.** because they wanted to desegregate society

Chapter 25 Resources

Timesaving Tools

TeacherWorks™ All-In-One Planner and Resource Center

- **Interactive Teacher Edition** Access your Teacher Wraparound Edition and your classroom resources with a few easy clicks.
- **Interactive Lesson Planner** Planning has never been easier! Organize your week, month, semester, or year with all the lesson helps you need to make teaching creative, timely, and relevant.

Use Glencoe's **Presentation Plus!** multimedia teacher tool to easily present dynamic lessons that visually excite your students. Using Microsoft PowerPoint® you can customize the presentations to create your own personalized lessons.

TEACHING TRANSPARENCIES

Graphic Organizer 10 L2

Why It Matters Chapter Transparency 25 L2

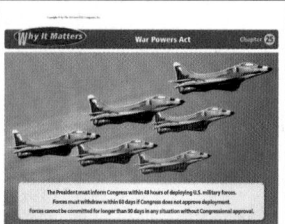

APPLICATION AND ENRICHMENT

Linking Past and Present Activity 25 L2

Enrichment Activity 25 L3

Primary Source Reading 25 L2

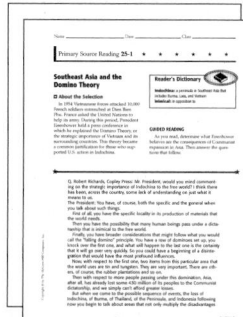

REVIEW AND REINFORCEMENT

Reteaching Activity 25 L1

Vocabulary Activity 25 L1

Time Line Activity 25 L2

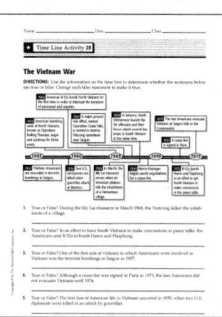

Critical Thinking Skills Activity 25 L2

Meeting NCSS Standards

The following standards are covered in Chapter 25:

Section 1	VI	Power, Authority, and Governance: B, C, F, I
Section 2	VIII	Science, Technology, and Society: A, C
Section 3	X	Civic Ideals and Practices: C, D, E, F, G, H
Section 4	VI	Power, Authority, and Governance: B, C, F

Local Standards

Chapter 25 Resources

Chapter 25 Test
Form A **L2**

Chapter 25 Test
Form B **L2**

Standardized Test Practice
Workbook Activity 25 **L2**

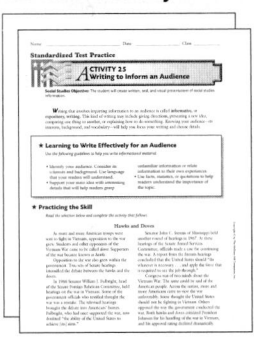

Performance Assessment
Activities and Rubrics 25
L1/ELL

ExamView® Pro
Testmaker CD-ROM

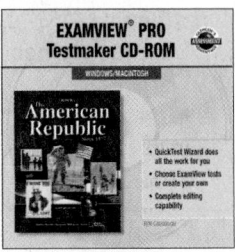

MULTIMEDIA

- Vocabulary PuzzleMaker CD-ROM
- Interactive Tutor Self-Assessment CD-ROM
- ExamView® Pro Testmaker CD-ROM
- Audio Program
- American History Primary Source Documents Library CD-ROM
- MindJogger Videoquiz
- Presentation Plus! CD-ROM
- TeacherWorks™ CD-ROM
- Interactive Student Edition CD-ROM
- Glencoe Skillbuilder Interactive Workbook CD-ROM, Level 2
- The *American Republic Since 1877* Video Program
- American Music: Hits Through History
- American Music: Cultural Traditions

SPANISH RESOURCES

The following Spanish resources are available:

- Spanish Reading Essentials and Study Guide
- Spanish Guided Reading Activities
- Spanish Reteaching Activities
- Spanish Quizzes and Tests
- Spanish Vocabulary Activities
- Spanish Summaries
- The Declaration of Independence and United States Constitution Spanish Translation

---

The following videotape programs are available
from Glencoe as supplements to Chapter 25:

- **Vietnam: A Soldier's Story** (ISBN 0-76-700772-7)
- **Richard M. Nixon: Man and President** (ISBN 1-56-501742-0)

To order, call Glencoe at 1-800-334-7344. To find classroom resources to
accompany many of these videos, check the following home pages:
A&E Television: www.aande.com
The History Channel: www.historychannel.com

Use our Web site for additional resources. All essential content is covered in the Student Edition.

You and your students can visit tarvol2.glencoe.com, the Web site
companion to the *American Republic Since 1877.* This innovative
integration of electronic and print media offers your students a wealth
of opportunities. The student text directs students to the Web site for
the following options:

- **Chapter Overviews**
- **Self-Check Quizzes**
- **Student Web Activities**
- **Textbook Updates**

Answers to the student Web activities are provided for you in the **Web
Activity Lesson Plans.** Additional Web resources and Interactive Tutor
Puzzles are also available.

Chapter 25 Resources

SECTION RESOURCES

Daily Objectives	Reproducible Resources	Multimedia Resources
SECTION 1 **The United States Focuses on Vietnam** 1. Describe the nationalist motives of Vietnamese leader Ho Chi Minh. 2. Explain the origins of American involvement in Vietnam during the 1950s.	Reproducible Lesson Plan 25–1 Daily Lecture and Discussion Notes 25–1 Guided Reading Activity 25–1* Section Quiz 25–1* Reading Essentials and Study Guide 25–1* Performance Assessment Activities and Rubrics	Daily Focus Skills Transparency 25–1 Interactive Tutor Self-Assessment CD-ROM ExamView® Pro Testmaker CD-ROM* Presentation Plus! CD-ROM TeacherWorks™ CD-ROM Audio Program
SECTION 2 **Going to War in Vietnam** 1. Describe how President Johnson deepened American involvement in Vietnam. 2. Discuss how the Vietcong and the North Vietnamese were able to frustrate the American military.	Reproducible Lesson Plan 25–2 Daily Lecture and Discussion Notes 25–2 Guided Reading Activity 25–2* Section Quiz 25–2* Reading Essentials and Study Guide 25–2* Performance Assessment Activities and Rubrics American History in Graphic Novel	Daily Focus Skills Transparency 25–2 Interactive Tutor Self-Assessment CD-ROM ExamView® Pro Testmaker CD-ROM* Presentation Plus! CD-ROM TeacherWorks™ CD-ROM Audio Program
SECTION 3 **Vietnam Divides the Nation** 1. Analyze why support for the war began to weaken. 2. Describe the motives of those in the antiwar movement.	Reproducible Lesson Plan 25–3 Daily Lecture and Discussion Notes 25–3 Guided Reading Activity 25–3* Section Quiz 25–3* Reading Essentials and Study Guide 25–3* Performance Assessment Activities and Rubrics	Daily Focus Skills Transparency 25–3 Interactive Tutor Self-Assessment CD-ROM ExamView® Pro Testmaker CD-ROM* Presentation Plus! CD-ROM TeacherWorks™ CD-ROM Audio Program American Music: Cultural Traditions
SECTION 4 **The War Winds Down** 1. Explain the events of Nixon's first administration that inspired more antiwar protests. 2. Summarize the major lessons the United States learned from the Vietnam War experience.	Reproducible Lesson Plan 25–4 Daily Lecture and Discussion Notes 25–4 Guided Reading Activity 25–4* Section Quiz 25–4* Reading Essentials and Study Guide 25–4* Performance Assessment Activities and Rubrics Supreme Court Case Studies American History in Graphic Novel	Daily Focus Skills Transparency 25–4 American Art & Architecture Interactive Tutor Self-Assessment CD-ROM ExamView® Pro Testmaker CD-ROM* Presentation Plus! CD-ROM Skillbuilder Interactive Workbook, Level 2 TeacherWorks™ CD-ROM Vocabulary PuzzleMaker CD-ROM Audio Program ABCNews Interactive™ Historic America Electronic Field Trips

0:00 OUT OF TIME?
Assign the Chapter 25 **Reading Essentials and Study Guide.**

*Also Available in Spanish

 Printed Materials   Transparency   CD-ROM   DVD

 Poster   Music Program   Audio Program   Videocassette

Chapter 25 Resources

 NATIONAL GEOGRAPHIC **Teacher's Corner**

INDEX TO
NATIONAL GEOGRAPHIC MAGAZINE

The following articles relate to this chapter.

- "Hong-Kong—Plight of the Boat People," February 1991
- "The Mekong," February 1993
- "The New Saigon," April 1995
- "Vietnam Memorial: To Heal a Nation," May 1985
- "Vietnam: The Hard Road to Peace," November 1989

NATIONAL GEOGRAPHIC SOCIETY PRODUCTS

To order the following, call National Geographic at 1-800-368-2728:

- *Historical Atlas of the United States* (Atlas)
- *Historical Atlas of the World* (Atlas)

NGS ONLINE

Access National Geographic's Web site for current events, atlas updates, activities, links, interactive features, and archives.

www.nationalgeographic.com

From the Classroom of...

Joseph Anastasio
Academy of the Holy Names
Albany, NY

The Vietnam War: A Musical History

The Vietnam War is still controversial, but few debates consider the soldiers' experiences. The following activity allows the class to analyze the experiences of the soldiers during and after the war.

To introduce the lesson, students should discuss their impressions of the war. Then, play a video of the dedication ceremony of the Vietnam Veterans Memorial. Play Billy Joel's "Goodnight Saigon" while the video is playing. Discuss and analyze the song.

Finally, ask students to write an essay that compares the soldiers' experiences in Vietnam to that of their counterparts in World War II.

MEETING SPECIAL NEEDS

In addition to the Differentiated Instruction strategies found in each section, the following resources are also suitable for your special needs students:

- *ExamView® Pro Testmaker CD-ROM* allows teachers to tailor tests by reducing answer choices.

- The *Audio Program* includes the entire narrative of the student edition so that less-proficient readers can listen to the words as they read them.

- The *Reading Essentials and Study Guide* provides the same content as the student edition but is written two grade levels below the textbook.

ADDITIONAL RESOURCES FROM GLENCOE

- American Music: Cultural Traditions
- American Art & Architecture
- Outline Map Resource Book
- U.S. Desk Map
- Building Geography Skills for Life
- Inclusion for the High School Social Studies Classroom Strategies and Activities
- Teaching Strategies for the American History Classroom (Including Block Scheduling Pacing Guides)
- Dinah Zike's High School American History Reading and Study Skills Foldables

KEY TO ABILITY LEVELS

Teaching strategies have been coded.

L1   BASIC activities for all students
L2   AVERAGE activities for average to above-average students
L3   CHALLENGING activities for above-average students
ELL ENGLISH LANGUAGE LEARNER activities

Block Schedule

Activities that are suited to use within the block scheduling framework are identified by:

Why It Matters Activity

Have students list the places where American troops have been sent since the Vietnam War and the results of those efforts. Ask students how they think the Vietnam experience has influenced these decisions. Students should evaluate their answers after they have completed the chapter.

GLENCOE TECHNOLOGY

The *American Republic Since 1877* Video Program
To learn more about the impact of the Vietnam War, have students view the Chapter 25 video, "Vietnam: A Different War," from the *American Republic Since 1877* Video Program.

MindJogger Videoquiz
Use the **MindJogger Videoquiz** to preview Chapter 25 content.

Both programs available in DVD

CHAPTER 25 The Vietnam War
1954–1975

Why It Matters

The Vietnam War created very bitter divisions within the United States. Supporters argued that patriotism demanded that communism be halted. Opponents argued that intervening in Vietnam was immoral. Many young people protested or resisted the draft. Victory was not achieved, although more than 58,000 American soldiers died. After the war, the nation had many wounds to heal.

The Impact Today

Changes brought about by the war are still evident in the United States today.
- *The nation is reluctant to commit troops overseas.*
- *The War Powers Act limits a president's power to involve the nation in war.*

The **American Republic Since 1877** *Video* The Chapter 25 video, "Vietnam: A Different War," explores the causes and the impact of this longest war in American history.

1954
- Vietminh defeat French
- Geneva Accords signed

1964
- Congress passes Gulf of Tonkin Resolution

1965
- U.S. combat troops arrive in Vietnam

United States PRESIDENTS

Eisenhower 1953–1961

Kennedy 1961–1963

L. Johnson 1963–1969

1955   *1960*   *1965*

World

1955
- Khrushchev is dominant leader in USSR

1958
- De Gaulle heads France's Fifth Republic

1964
- Japan introduces first high-speed passenger train

770

Reading Strategy ▸ PURPOSE FOR READING

K-W-L Chart Use this strategy before, during, and after a chapter or unit to engage students and tap into their knowledge. Have students create a three-column chart titled *The Vietnam War.* Explain that they will fill out the chart by writing what they **K**now about this topic in the first column, what they **W**ant or need to know in the second, and what they **L**earned in the third. Model how to fill out the chart by eliciting responses such as "the Tet Offensive" to write in the first column. Working in pairs, have students generate additional events or ideas to write in the **K** column. Then have them fill in the **W** column with what they want or need to know about the war. Finally, ask them to complete the **L** column, individually, as they read the chapter. **L1**

The dedication ceremony for the Vietnam Veterans Memorial in Washington, D.C., November 13, 1982

- **1967**
  • March on the Pentagon takes place

- **1968**
  • Tet offensive
  • Students protest at Democratic National Convention in Chicago

- **1970**
  • National Guard troops kill students at Kent State University

Nixon 1969–1974

- **1973**
  • Cease-fire signed with North Vietnam

- **1975**
  • Evacuation of last Americans from Vietnam

Ford 1974–1977

1970   *1975*

- **1967**
  • First heart transplant performed

- **1968**
  • Soviets repress Czechoslovakia's rebellion

- **1971**
  • Pakistani civil war leads to independent Bangladesh

- **1975**
  • Civil war breaks out in Angola

HISTORY
Online

Chapter Overview
Visit the *American Republic Since 1877* Web site at tarvol2.glencoe.com and click on **Chapter Overviews— Chapter 25** to preview chapter information.

771

HISTORY
Online

Introduce students to chapter content and key terms by having them access the **Chapter 25 Overview** at tarvol2.glencoe.com .

More About the Photo

The Vietnam Veterans Memorial is made of black granite panels that carry the names of the approximately 58,000 Americans who died or remain missing in action in Vietnam. Visitors often touch the names of those they knew and can make a rubbing of the soldier's name. Ask students why they think the memorial has helped the nation come to terms with the Vietnam War. *(It has brought a sense of closure and acknowledgment that those who died served their country well.)*

TIME LINE
ACTIVITY

Have students select one of the events on the time line and conduct a brief interview with someone who was a teenager or adult at the time. Encourage students to learn what the interviewee remembers about the event and what impact the event had on his or her life. Invite students to share what they learned with the class.

FOLDABLES
Study Organizer

Dinah Zike's Foldables are three-dimensional, interactive graphic organizers that help students practice basic writing skills, review key vocabulary terms, and identify main ideas. Have students complete the foldable activity in the *Dinah Zike's Reading and Study Skills Foldables* booklet.

GRAPHIC ORGANIZER ACTIVITY

Organizing Information Have students complete the following graphic organizer to make a generalization about how media coverage and student protests affected public opinion of the war. A sample generalization may be that the media coverage and protests helped force a shift in U.S. policies. Details should support the generalization made.

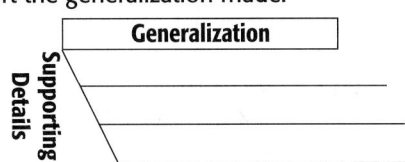

Generalization

Supporting Details

1 FOCUS

Section Overview

This section focuses on the events that led to the United States fighting the Vietnam War.

BELLRINGER
Skillbuilder Activity

Project transparency and have students answer the question.

Daily Focus Skills Transparency 25–1

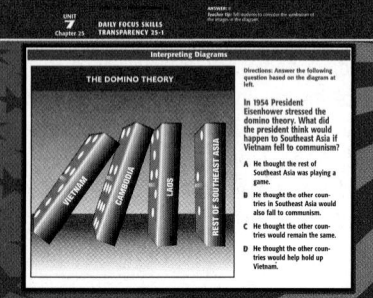

Reading Preview

Answers to Graphic: fall of China to communism and the outbreak of the Korean War

Preteaching Vocabulary
Have students use a standard dictionary or online resource to learn the correct pronunciation of the Key Terms and Names. For example, some dictionary sites have an audio feature where the user can hear words pronounced correctly.

SECTION 1 The United States Focuses on Vietnam

Main Idea
American efforts to stop the spread of communism led to U.S. involvement in the affairs of Vietnam.

Key Terms and Names
Ho Chi Minh, domino theory, guerrilla, Dien Bien Phu, Ngo Dinh Diem

Reading Strategy
Organizing As you read about the increasing involvement of the United States in Vietnam, complete a graphic organizer similar to the one below by providing reasons that the United States aided France in Vietnam.

Reasons for U.S. Support of France →

Reading Objectives
• **Describe** the nationalist motives of Vietnamese leader Ho Chi Minh.
• **Explain** the origins of American involvement in Vietnam during the 1950s.

Section Theme
Government and Democracy American involvement in Vietnam was a reflection of Cold War strategy.

Preview of Events

♦1946   ♦1950   ♦1954   ♦1958

1946
French-Vietminh War begins

1950
The United States supplies military aid to France

1954
Vietminh defeat French at Dien Bien Phu; Geneva Accords signed in Paris

1956
Ngo Dinh Diem refuses to participate in nationwide elections in Vietnam

★ An American Story ★

Lieutenant Joe Marm

In 1965 the first major battle between American and North Vietnamese soldiers took place in the Ia Drang Valley in South Vietnam. During the battle, a platoon of American soldiers was cut off and surrounded. Lieutenant Joe Marm's platoon was among those sent to rescue the trapped Americans. When his men came under heavy fire, Marm acted quickly: "I told the men to hold their fire. . . . Then I ran forward. . . . That's the principle we use in the infantry, 'Lead by your own example.'" Marm raced across open ground and hurled grenades at the enemy, and although he was shot in the jaw, he managed to kill the troops firing at his men. For his extraordinary bravery, Lieutenant Marm received the Medal of Honor:

I feel I'm the recipient of the medal for the many, many brave soldiers whose deeds go unsung. . . [T]he medal is as much theirs as it is mine. It's always tough to get men to go into battle, but we were a tight unit, and there were Americans out there that we were trying to get to. We're all in it together, and we were fighting for each other and for our guys. . . . I had the best soldiers. . . . They were fearless, and they were just great Americans and they're going to go down in history.**99**

—quoted in *The Soldiers' Story*

Early American Involvement in Vietnam

In the late 1940s and early 1950s, most Americans knew little about Vietnam. During this time, however, American officials came to view the nation as increasingly important in the campaign to halt the spread of communism.

SECTION RESOURCES

📁 Reproducible Masters
• Reproducible Lesson Plan 25–1
• Daily Lecture and Discussion Notes 25–1
• Guided Reading Activity 25–1
• Section Quiz 25–1
• Reading Essentials and Study Guide 25–1
• Performance Assessment Activities and Rubrics

📄 Transparencies
• Daily Focus Skills Transparency 25–1

Multimedia
🔘 Interactive Tutor Self-Assessment CD-ROM
🔘 ExamView® Pro Testmaker CD-ROM
🔘 Presentation Plus! CD-ROM
🔘 TeacherWorks™ CD-ROM
🔊 Audio Program

The Growth of Vietnamese Nationalism When the Japanese seized power in Vietnam during World War II, it was one more example of foreigners ruling the Vietnamese people. China had controlled the region off and on for hundreds of years. From the late 1800s until World War II, France ruled Vietnam and neighboring Laos and Cambodia—a region known collectively as French Indochina.

By the early 1900s, nationalism had become a powerful force in Vietnam. The Vietnamese formed several political parties to push for independence or reform of the French colonial government. One of the leaders of the nationalist movement was Nguyen Tat Thanh—better known by his alias, **Ho Chi Minh,** or "Bringer of Light." He was born in 1890 in central Vietnam. As a young man, Ho Chi Minh taught at a village school. At the age of 21, he sailed for Europe on a French freighter, paying his passage by working in the galley. During his travels abroad, including a stay in the Soviet Union, Ho Chi Minh became an advocate of communism. In 1930 he returned to Southeast Asia, where he helped found the Indochinese Communist Party and worked to overthrow French rule.

Ho Chi Minh's activities made him a wanted man. He fled Indochina and spent several years in exile in the Soviet Union and China. In 1941 he returned to Vietnam. By then Japan had seized control of the country. Ho Chi Minh organized a nationalist group called the **Vietminh.** The group united both Communists and non-Communists in the struggle to expel the Japanese forces. Soon afterward, the United States began sending military aid to the Vietminh.

The United States Supports the French With the Allies' victory over Japan in August 1945, the Japanese surrendered control of Indochina. Ho Chi Minh and his forces quickly announced that Vietnam was an independent nation. He even crafted a Vietnam Declaration of Independence. Archimedes Patti, an American officer stationed in Vietnam at the time, helped the rebel leader write the document. When a translator read aloud the opening—"All men are created equal; they are endowed by their Creator with certain inalienable rights; among these are liberty, life, and the pursuit of happiness"—Patti suddenly sat up, startled, recognizing the words as very similar to the American Declaration of Independence.

Picturing **History**

Rural Economy Most of Vietnam's people live in the country's low-lying fertile lands near the Red River delta in the north and the Mekong River delta in the south. What does the image below suggest about the use of human labor in the country's agricultural economy?

NATIONAL GEOGRAPHIC **Indochina, 1959**

0   200 miles
0   200 kilometers
Miller Cylindrical projection

CHINA

BURMA 1948

NORTH VIETNAM 1954   Hanoi

20°N

LAOS 1954

Gulf of Tonkin

Vientiane

17°N

Rangoon

THAILAND Never a European colony

Bangkok

CAMBODIA 1954

Phnom Penh

SOUTH VIETNAM 1954

Saigon

10°N

Gulf of Thailand

South China Sea

100°E

1954   Date of independence

Geography *Skills*

1. **Interpreting Maps** What three countries border North and South Vietnam?
2. **Applying Geography Skills** A mountain chain extends nearly 800 miles (1,290 km) from North to South Vietnam. How do you think this terrain aided the Vietnamese guerrillas who were fighting U.S. troops?

2 **TEACH**

Daily Lecture and Discussion Notes 25–1

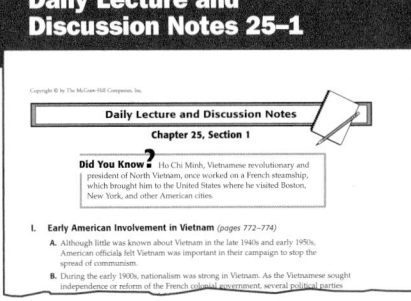

Copyright © by The McGraw-Hill Companies, Inc.

Daily Lecture and Discussion Notes

Chapter 25, Section 1

Did You Know? Ho Chi Minh, Vietnamese revolutionary and president of North Vietnam, once worked on a French steamship, which brought him to the United States where he visited Boston, New York, and other American cities.

I.   Early American Involvement in Vietnam (pages 772–774)

   A. Although little was known about Vietnam in the late 1940s and early 1950s, American officials felt Vietnam was important in their campaign to stop the spread of communism.

   B. During the early 1900s, nationalism was strong in Vietnam. As the Vietnamese sought independence or reform of the French colonial government, several political parties

Creating a Mental Map Have students draw and label a map of the Indochina peninsula. **L1** ELL

Picturing **History**

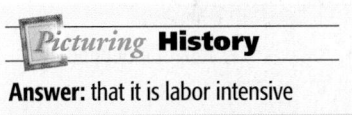

Answer: that it is labor intensive

Geography *Skills*

Answers:

1. Cambodia, China, and Laos
2. They used it to their advantage to launch hit-and-run and ambush attacks.

Geography Skills Practice

Ask: What bodies of water form the east coast of Vietnam? *(Gulf of Tonkin and the South China Sea)*

Reading Strategy ▶ **READING THE TEXT**

Monitoring Comprehension As students read the section, they may encounter text or information that they do not understand. Point out to students they should adjust their reading strategies to increase their comprehension. Model how this is done by reading the section aloud. As you read, say things such as "What do I think were the main reasons for the Vietnam War?" (predicting); "Where is Vietnam located in Asia?" (visualizing); "What have I heard about the Vietnam War, and is it correct based the information described here?" (activating prior knowledge). Modeling how you read helps students think about strategies they can use as they read independently. **L1** ELL

Guided Reading Activity 25–1

Name _____ Date _____ Class _____

★ Guided Reading Activity 25–1

DIRECTIONS: Identifying Supporting Details Read each main idea. Use your textbook to supply the details that support or explain each main idea.

☐ **Main Idea:** During the late 1940s and early 1950s, American officials came to view the nation as increasingly important in the campaign to halt the spread of communism.

1. **Detail:** One of the leaders of the nationalist movement in Vietnam was Nguyen Tat Thanh—better known by his alias, _____.
2. **Detail:** Ho Chi Minh helped organize the _____, a nationalist group that united both _____ and _____ in the struggle to expel the Japanese forces.
3. **Detail:** After World War II, the Japanese surrendered control of _____ and Ho Chi Minh quickly announced that Vietnam was an _____.
4. **Detail:** Seeking to regain their _____ _____ troops

Picturing **History**

Answer: France

Ask: What countries made up French Indochina? *(Cambodia, Laos, and Vietnam)*

✓ **Reading Check**

Answer: He sought independence for Vietnam.

---

3 ASSESS

Assign Section 1 Assessment as homework or as an in-class activity.

◉ Have students use the **Interactive Tutor Self-Assessment CD-ROM.**

Reading Essentials and Study Guide 25–1

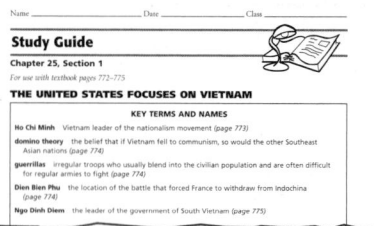

Name _____ Date _____ Class _____

Study Guide

Chapter 25, Section 1

For use with textbook pages 772–775

THE UNITED STATES FOCUSES ON VIETNAM

KEY TERMS AND NAMES

Ho Chi Minh Vietnam leader of the nationalist movement (page 773)

domino theory the belief that if Vietnam fell to communism, so would the other Southeast Asian nations (page 774)

guerrillas irregular troops who usually blend into the civilian population and are often difficult for regular armies to fight (page 774)

Dien Bien Phu the location of the battle that forced France to withdraw from Indochina (page 774)

Ngo Dinh Diem the leader of the government of South Vietnam (page 775)

❝I stopped him and turned to Ho in amazement and asked if he really intended to use it in his declaration. . . . Ho sat back in his chair, his palms together with fingertips touching his lips ever so lightly, as though meditating. Then, with a gentle smile he asked softly, 'Should I not use it?' I felt sheepish and embarrassed. Of course, I answered, why should he not?❞

—quoted in *The Perfect War*

France, however, had no intention of seeing Vietnam become independent. Seeking to regain their colonial empire in Southeast Asia, French troops returned to Vietnam in 1946 and drove the Vietminh forces into hiding in the countryside. By 1949 French officials had set up a new government in Vietnam.

The Vietminh fought back against the French-dominated regime and slowly increased their control over large areas of the countryside. As fighting between the two sides escalated, France appealed to the United States for help.

The request put American officials in a difficult position. The United States opposed colonialism. It had pressured the Dutch to give up their empire in Indonesia, and it supported the British decision to give India independence in 1947. In Vietnam, however, the independence movement had become entangled with the Communist movement. American officials did not think France should control Vietnam, but they did not want Vietnam to be Communist either.

Picturing **History**

Nationalist Leader Ho Chi Minh was already involved in fighting for Vietnam's independence when this photograph was taken in 1946. **What foreign country was he opposing at that time?**

Two events convinced the Truman administration to help France—the fall of China to communism, and the outbreak of the Korean War. Korea, in particular, convinced American officials that the Soviet Union had begun a major push to impose communism on East Asia. Shortly after the Korean War began, Truman authorized a massive program of military aid to French forces fighting in Vietnam.

On taking office in 1953, President Eisenhower continued to support the French military campaign against the Vietminh. By 1954 the United States was paying roughly three-fourths of France's war costs. During a news conference that year, Eisenhower defended United States policy in Vietnam by stressing what became known as the domino theory—the belief that if Vietnam fell to communism, so too would the other nations of Southeast Asia:

❝You have a row of dominoes set up, you knock over the first one, and what will happen to the last one is the certainty that it will go over very quickly. . . . Asia, after all, has already lost 450 million of its peoples to the Communist dictatorship, and we simply can't afford greater losses. . . .❞

—quoted in *America in Vietnam*

✓ **Reading Check** **Summarizing** Why did Ho Chi Minh lead a resistance movement against France?

The Vietminh Drive Out the French

Despite significant amounts of aid from the United States, the French struggled against the Vietminh, who consistently frustrated the French with hit-and-run and ambush tactics. These are the tactics of guerrillas, irregular troops who usually blend into the civilian population and are often difficult for regular armies to fight. The mounting casualties and the inability of the French to defeat the Vietminh made the war very unpopular in France. Finally, in 1954, the struggle reached a turning point.

TURNING POINT

Defeat at Dien Bien Phu In 1954 the French commander ordered his forces to occupy the mountain town of **Dien Bien Phu.** Seizing the town would interfere with the Vietminh's supply lines and force them into open battle.

Soon afterward, a huge Vietminh force surrounded Dien Bien Phu and began bombarding the town. "Shells rained down on us without stopping like a hailstorm on a fall evening," recalled one

---

DIFFERENTIATED INSTRUCTION

English Learners Have students examine each of the photographs in this section. Then have them write a one-sentence caption explaining what they learned about Vietnam and its people from observing the photographs. Encourage students to pay particular attention to people's activities and their facial expressions. **L1** **ELL**

📂 Refer to **Inclusion for the High School Social Studies Classroom Strategies and Activities** in the TCR.

French soldier. "Bunker after bunker, trench after trench collapsed, burying under them men and weapons." On May 7, 1954, the French force at Dien Bien Phu fell to the Vietminh. The defeat convinced the French to make peace and withdraw from Indochina.

Geneva Accords Negotiations to end the conflict were held in Geneva, Switzerland. The **Geneva Accords** temporarily divided Vietnam along the 17th parallel, with Ho Chi Minh and the Vietminh in control of North Vietnam and a pro-Western regime in control of the South. In 1956 elections were to be held to reunite the country under a single government. The Geneva Conference also recognized Cambodia's independence. (Laos had gained independence the previous year.)

Shortly after the Geneva Accords partitioned Vietnam, the French finally left. The United States almost immediately stepped in and became the principal protector of the new government in the South, led by a nationalist leader named **Ngo Dinh Diem** (NOH DIHN deh·EHM). Like Ho Chi Minh, Diem had been educated abroad, but unlike the North Vietnamese leader, Diem was pro-Western and fiercely anti-Communist. A Catholic, he welcomed the roughly one million North Vietnamese Catholics who migrated south to escape Ho Chi Minh's rule.

When the time came in 1956 to hold countrywide elections, as called for by the Geneva Accords, Diem refused. He knew that the Communist-controlled

Picturing **History**

Last Stand French troops assemble a tank near the Dien Bien Phu airfield shortly before their defeat by the Vietminh. How did this defeat influence French policy in Indochina?

north would not allow genuinely free elections, and that Ho Chi Minh would almost certainly have won as a result. Eisenhower supported Diem and increased American military and economic aid to South Vietnam. In the wake of Diem's actions, tensions between the North and South intensified. The nation seemed headed toward civil war, with the United States caught in the middle of it.

✓ **Reading Check** **Examining** What was the effect of the French defeat at Dien Bien Phu?

HISTORY Online **Study Central™** To review this section, go to tarvol2.glencoe.com and click on **Study Central™**.

SECTION 1 ASSESSMENT

Checking for Understanding
1. **Define:** domino theory, guerrilla.
2. **Identify:** Ho Chi Minh, Dien Bien Phu, Ngo Dinh Diem.
3. **Explain** the goals of the Vietminh.

Reviewing Themes
4. **Government and Democracy** Why did Ngo Dinh Diem refuse to hold countrywide elections in Vietnam in 1956?

Critical Thinking
5. **Interpreting** Why do you think the United States supported the government of Ngo Dinh Diem?
6. **Organizing** Use a graphic organizer like the one below to list provisions of the Geneva Accords.

Geneva Accords Provisions

Analyzing Visuals
7. **Analyzing Photographs** Study the Vietnam scene on page 773. How would you describe the contrast between American and Vietnamese societies? How do you think this contrast influenced American thinking toward the war?

Writing About History
8. **Descriptive Writing** Take on the role of a Vietnamese peasant in the 1940s. Write a journal entry on your feelings toward the French.

SECTION 1 ASSESSMENT ANSWERS

1. Terms are in blue.
2. Ho Chi Minh *(p. 773)*, Dien Bien Phu *(p. 774)*, Ngo Dinh Diem *(p. 775)*
3. The Vietminh fought for independence first from Japan, then from France.
4. He feared he would lose to the Vietnamese Communist party.
5. because he was pro-Western and anti-communist
6. temporarily divided Vietnam at 17th parallel; attempted to reunite nation with countrywide elections planned for 1956
7. Since Vietnam appeared to be less prosperous than the United States, it was easy to believe the United

States could defeat the Vietnamese.
8. Students' journal entries should be written from a peasant's perspective.

L2

Section Quiz 25–1

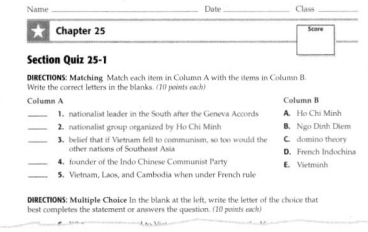

Picturing **History**

Answer: It convinced the French to make peace and withdraw from Indochina.
Ask: Where were the negotiations held to end the conflict? *(Geneva, Switzerland)*

✓ **Reading Check**

Answer: The defeat at Dien Bien Phu caused the French to withdraw and led to the Geneva Accords.

Reteach
Have students describe the nationalist motives of Vietnamese leader Ho Chi Minh.

Enrich
Invite interested students to research French rule in Indochina and its impact on the culture of Vietnam. Have them report their results in the form of a descriptive essay.

HISTORY *Online*

Study Central™ provides summaries, interactive games, and online graphic organizers to help students review section content.

4 CLOSE

Have students explain the origins of American involvement in Vietnam during the 1950s.

1 FOCUS

Section Overview

This section focuses on the commitment to send United States troops to Vietnam.

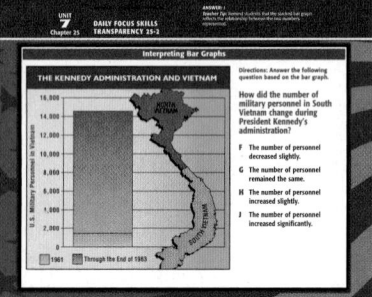

Reading Preview

Answers to Graphic:
Going to War in Vietnam
I. American Involvement Deepens
  A. Kennedy Takes Over
  B. The Overthrow of Diem
II. Johnson and Vietnam
  A. The Gulf of Tonkin Resolution
  B. The United States Sends in Troops
III. A Bloody Stalemate Emerges
  A. Frustrating Warfare
  B. A Determined Enemy

Preteaching Vocabulary
Have students look up the Key Terms and Names in the glossary. Then have them write a description or definition of each in their own words.

SECTION 2 Going to War in Vietnam

Guide to Reading

Main Idea
After providing South Vietnam with much aid and support, the United States finally sent in troops to fight as well.

Key Terms and Names
Vietcong, Gulf of Tonkin Resolution, napalm, Agent Orange, Ho Chi Minh trail

Reading Strategy
Taking Notes As you read about the beginnings of the Vietnam War, use the major headings of the section to create an outline similar to the one below.

Going to War in Vietnam
I. American Involvement Deepens
  A.
  B.
II.
  A.
  B.

Reading Objectives
• **Describe** how President Johnson deepened American involvement in Vietnam.
• **Discuss** how the Vietcong and the North Vietnamese were able to frustrate the American military.

Section Theme
Science and Technology American military procedures differed significantly from those of the Vietcong troops.

Preview of Events

♦1963	♦1964	♦1965	♦1966
1963 Number of American military advisers in South Vietnam reaches around 15,000	**1964** Congress passes Gulf of Tonkin Resolution	**1965** The United States begins bombing North Vietnam; first American combat troops arrive in Vietnam	

★ An American Story ★

Marlene Kramel

Marlene Kramel joined the Army Nurse Corps in 1965 when she was 21, and she went to Vietnam the following year. She was working in a makeshift hospital on what was a particularly quiet night. Most of the patients who filled the beds that evening were suffering from malaria.

Suddenly, a row of helicopters roared in from over the horizon, carrying wounded from a nearby battle. As the casualties came in on stretchers, the hospital turned chaotic. Doctors ran about the facility screaming orders and frantically trying to treat patients.

The only nurse on duty at the time, Kramel felt overwhelmed by the confusion. "Every one of the doctors is yelling for me," she recalled. "I didn't know what to do next. 'Start this. Do that.' Everybody's yelling at me. I couldn't do enough." Things happened so quickly that night, she insisted, that she could not remember most of it. "I can't remember blood, even. I can only remember, 'What am I going to do?' And the doctors moving at tremendous speed. And I'm there. And I'm not able to move fast enough. . . . That's all I remember."

—adapted from *The Living and the Dead*

American Involvement Deepens

The steps that led to the chaos and casualties Marlene Kramel experienced in 1966 began in the mid-1950s when American officials decided to support the government of South Vietnam in its struggle against North Vietnam. After Ngo Dinh Diem refused to

776 CHAPTER 25 The Vietnam War

SECTION RESOURCES

📁 Reproducible Masters
• Reproducible Lesson Plan 25–2
• Daily Lecture and Discussion Notes 25–2
• Guided Reading Activity 25–2
• Section Quiz 25–2
• Reading Essentials and Study Guide 25–2
• Interpreting Political Cartoons

📑 Transparencies
• Daily Focus Skills Transparency 25–2

Multimedia
🔘 Interactive Tutor Self-Assessment CD-ROM
🔘 ExamView® Pro Testmaker CD-ROM
🔘 Presentation Plus! CD-ROM
🔘 TeacherWorks™ CD-ROM
🎧 Audio Program

hold national elections, Ho Chi Minh and his followers began an armed struggle to reunify the nation. They organized a new guerrilla army, which became known as the Vietcong. As fighting began between the Vietcong and South Vietnam's forces, President Eisenhower increased American aid, and sent hundreds of military advisers to train South Vietnam's army.

Despite the American assistance, the Vietcong continued to grow more powerful, in part because many Vietnamese opposed Diem's government, and in part because of the Vietcong's use of terror. By 1961 the Vietcong had assassinated thousands of government officials and established control over much of the countryside. In response Diem looked increasingly to the United States to keep South Vietnam from collapsing.

Picturing **History**

Self-Immolation On June 11, 1963, flames erupted around a Buddhist monk as he set himself on fire to protest government religious policies. *What policies did Ngo Dinh Diem take toward Buddhism?*

Kennedy Takes Over On taking office in 1961, President Kennedy continued the nation's policy of support for South Vietnam. Like presidents Truman and Eisenhower before him, Kennedy saw the Southeast Asian country as vitally important in the battle against communism.

In political terms, Kennedy needed to appear tough on communism, since Republicans often accused Democrats of having lost China to communism during the Truman administration. Kennedy's administration sharply increased military aid and sent more advisers to Vietnam. From 1961 to late 1963, the number of American military personnel in South Vietnam jumped from about 2,000 to around 15,000.

American officials believed the Vietcong continued to grow because Diem's government was unpopular and corrupt. They urged him to create a more democratic government and to introduce reforms to help Vietnam's peasants. Diem introduced some limited reforms, but they had little effect.

One program Diem introduced, at the urging of American advisers, made the situation worse. The South Vietnamese created special fortified villages, known as **strategic hamlets.** These villages were protected by machine guns, bunkers, trenches, and barbed wire. Vietnamese officials then moved villagers to the

strategic hamlets, partly to protect them from the Vietcong, and partly to prevent them from giving aid to the Vietcong. The program proved to be extremely unpopular. Many peasants resented being uprooted from their villages, where they had worked to build farms and where many of their ancestors lay buried.

The Overthrow of Diem Diem made himself even more unpopular by discriminating against Buddhism, one of the country's most widely practiced religions. In the spring of 1963, Diem, a Catholic, banned the traditional religious flags for Buddha's birthday. When Buddhists took to the streets in protest, Diem's police killed 9 people and injured 14 others. In the demonstrations that followed, a Buddhist monk set himself on fire, the first of several to do so. The photograph of his self-destruction appeared on television and on the front pages of newspapers around the world. It was a stark symbol of the opposition to Diem.

In August 1963, American ambassador Henry Cabot Lodge arrived in Vietnam. He quickly learned that Diem's unpopularity had so alarmed several Vietnamese generals that they were plotting to overthrow him. When Lodge expressed American sympathy for their cause, the generals launched a military coup. They seized power on November 1, 1963, and executed Diem shortly afterward.

Diem's overthrow only made matters worse. Despite his unpopularity with some Vietnamese, Diem had been a respected nationalist and a capable administrator. After his death, South Vietnam's

CHAPTER 25   The Vietnam War   **777**

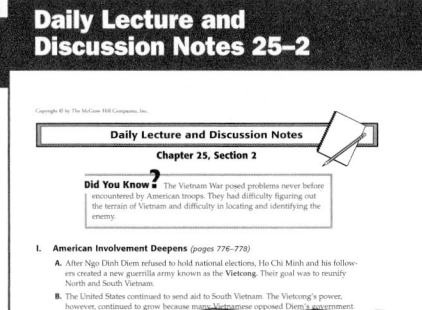

Expressing an Opinion Have students write a letter to the editor about the Diem regime and U.S. support for it. Remind students that their editorials should support or oppose the U.S. position. L1

Picturing **History**

Answer: Diem discriminated against Buddhism by doing such things as banning the traditional religious flags used to celebrate the birthday of Buddha.

Ask: What message was the monk trying to send when he set himself on fire? *(He wanted to draw attention to opposition to Diem.)*

Reading Strategy ▸ **READING THE TEXT**

Previewing Have students preview the text's structure before they begin reading. Text structures include time order, compare-contrast, description, cause and effect, and problem-solution. Noticing how ideas are organized will prepare students for the types of information they will receive. L1 ELL

☛ Refer to *Inclusion for the High School Social Studies Classroom Strategies and Activities* in the TCR.

L1/ELL
Guided Reading Activity 25–2

✓ **Reading Check**

Answer: The Vietcong wanted to reunify Vietnam.

Creating Circle Graphs Provide the data below and ask students to make a pair of circle graphs showing the results of the presidential election of 1964. **L2**

Candidate	Popular Vote	Electoral Vote
Goldwater, Rep.	27,178,188	52
Johnson, Dem.	43,129,566	486

📁 Use the rubric for creating a map, display, or chart on pages 65–66 in the *Performance Assessment Activities and Rubrics.*

Helicopters GI slang referred to helicopters as TWA—teenie-weenie airlines. They were used on a massive scale during the Vietnam War. With gas turbines replacing piston engines, the helicopters had remarkable range and maneuverability.

---

government grew increasingly weak and unstable. The United States became even more deeply involved in order to prop up the weak South Vietnamese government. Coincidentally, three weeks after Diem's death, President Kennedy was also assassinated. The presidency, as well as the growing problem of Vietnam, now belonged to Kennedy's vice president, Lyndon Johnson.

✓ **Reading Check** **Examining** What was the main goal of the Vietcong?

Johnson and Vietnam

Initially President Johnson exercised caution and restraint regarding the conflict in Vietnam. "We seek no wider war," he repeatedly promised. At the same time, Johnson was determined to prevent South Vietnam from becoming Communist. "The battle against communism," he declared shortly before becoming president, "must be joined . . . with strength and determination."

Politics also played a role in Johnson's Vietnam policy. Like Kennedy, Johnson remembered that many Republicans blamed the Truman administration for the fall of China to communism in 1949. Should the Democrats also "lose" Vietnam, Johnson feared, it might cause a "mean and destructive debate that would shatter my Presidency, kill my administration, and damage our democracy."

TURNING POINT

The Gulf of Tonkin Resolution On August 2, 1964, President Johnson announced that North Vietnamese torpedo boats had fired on two American destroyers in the Gulf of Tonkin. Two days later, the president reported that another similar attack had taken place. Johnson was campaigning for the presidency and was very sensitive to accusations of being soft on communism. He insisted that North Vietnam's attacks were unprovoked and immediately ordered American aircraft to attack North Vietnamese ships and naval facilities. Johnson

---

Different Viewpoints

The Vietnam War

As the war in Vietnam dragged on, a clear division of American opinion emerged. In January 1966, George W. Ball, undersecretary of state to President Johnson, delivered an address to indicate "how we got [to Vietnam] and why we must stay." George F. Kennan, former ambassador to Russia, testified before the Senate Foreign Relations Committee that same year, arguing that American involvement in Vietnam was "something we would not choose deliberately if the choice were ours to make all over again today."

George W. Ball:

"[T]he conflict in Vietnam is a product of the great shifts and changes triggered by the Second World War. Out of the war, two continent-wide powers emerged—the United States and the Soviet Union. The colonial systems through which the nations of Western Europe had governed more than a third of the people of the world were, one by one, dismantled.

. . . [E]ven while the new national boundaries were still being marked on the map, the Soviet Union under Stalin exploited the confusion to push out the perimeter of its power and influence in an effort to extend the outer limits of Communist domination by force or the threat of force.

The bloody encounters in [Vietnam] are thus in a real sense battles and skirmishes in a continuing war to prevent one Communist power after another from violating internationally recognized boundary lines fixing the outer limits of Communist dominion.

. . . The evidence shows clearly enough that, at the time of French withdrawal . . . the Communist regime in Hanoi never intended that South Vietnam should develop in freedom.

. . . In the long run our hopes for the people of South Vietnam reflect our hopes for people everywhere. What we seek is a world living in peace and freedom."

DIFFERENTIATED INSTRUCTION

Reading Support The increased military commitment to Vietnam touched virtually every neighborhood in the United States. As a result, almost every American was challenged to consider American actions in Vietnam. Ask students to imagine that they have just been drafted for military service in Vietnam. Have them write diary entries or letters in which they share their fears, hopes, and questions about being drafted. Invite students to share their writing with classmates. **L2**

📁 Refer to *Inclusion for the High School Social Studies Classroom Strategies and Activities* in the TCR.

did not reveal that the American warships had been helping the South Vietnamese conduct electronic spying and commando raids against North Vietnam.

Johnson then asked Congress to authorize the use of force to defend American forces. Congress agreed to Johnson's request with little debate. Most members of Congress agreed with Republican Representative Ross Adair of Indiana, who defiantly declared, "The American flag has been fired upon. We will not and cannot tolerate such things."

On August 7, 1964, the Senate and House passed the **Gulf of Tonkin Resolution,** authorizing the president to "take all necessary measures to repel any armed attack against the forces of the United States and to prevent further aggression." With only two dissenting votes, Congress had, in effect, handed its war powers over to the president. 📖 *(See page 961 for more on the Gulf of Tonkin Resolution.)*

The United States Sends in Troops Shortly after Congress passed the Gulf of Tonkin Resolution, the Vietcong began to attack bases where American

advisers were stationed in South Vietnam. The attacks began in the fall of 1964 and continued to escalate. After a Vietcong attack on a base at Pleiku in February 1965 left 7 Americans dead and more than 100 wounded, President Johnson decided to respond. Less than 14 hours after the attack, American aircraft assaulted North Vietnam.

After the airstrikes, one poll showed that Johnson's approval rating on his handling of Vietnam jumped from 41 percent to 60 percent. The president's actions also met with strong approval from his closest advisers, including Secretary of Defense **Robert McNamara** and National Security Adviser **McGeorge Bundy.**

There were some dissenters in the White House, chief among them Undersecretary of State George Ball, a long-time critic of U.S. policy in Vietnam. He warned that if the United States got too deeply involved in Vietnam, it might become difficult to get out. "Once on the tiger's back," he warned, "we cannot be sure of picking the place to dismount."

Most of the advisers who surrounded Johnson, however, firmly believed the nation had a duty to halt communism in Vietnam, both to maintain stability in Southeast Asia and to ensure the United States's continuing power and prestige in the world. In a memo to the president, Bundy argued:

> 66The stakes in Vietnam are extremely high. The American investment is very large, and American responsibility is a fact of life which is palpable in the atmosphere of Asia, and even elsewhere. The international prestige of the U.S. and a substantial part of our influence are directly at risk in Vietnam.99

—quoted in *The Best and the Brightest*

In March 1965, Johnson expanded American involvement by shifting his policy to a sustained bombing campaign against North Vietnam. The campaign was named **Operation Rolling Thunder.** That month the president also ordered the first combat troops into Vietnam. American soldiers were now fighting alongside the South Vietnamese troops against the Vietcong.

✓ Reading Check **Describing** How did politics play a role in President Johnson's Vietnam policy?

A Bloody Stalemate Emerges

By the end of 1965, more than 180,000 American combat troops were fighting in Vietnam. In 1966 that number doubled. Since the American military was

---

George F. Kennan:

"Vietnam is not a region of major military and industrial importance. It is difficult to believe that any decisive developments of the world situation would be determined in normal circumstances by what happens on that territory. . . . Even a situation in which South Vietnam was controlled exclusively by the Vietcong, while regrettable . . . would not, in my opinion, present dangers great enough to justify our direct military intervention.

. . . To attempt to crush North Vietnamese strength to a point where [it] could no longer give any support for Vietcong political activity in the South, would . . . have the effect of bringing in Chinese forces at some point.

. . . Our motives are widely misinterpreted, and the spectacle emphasized and reproduced in thousands of press photographs and stories . . . produces reactions among millions of people throughout the world profoundly detrimental to the image we would like them to hold of this country."

Learning From History

1. **Recognizing Ideologies** How do the two speakers assess the value of Vietnam and its people to the United States?
2. **Making Inferences** Why does George Kennan believe that the United States government got involved in Vietnam when it did? How does he feel about this involvement?

Different Viewpoints

Learning from History Answers:
1. Ball argues that the United States is committed to the people of Vietnam and wants to protect them from communism. Kennan argues that Vietnam has no particular significance to the United States, and while it would be unfortunate if the Vietcong took over, it would not present a danger great enough for the United States to take military action.
2. He believes that the United States was misguided in entering the war, that it has hurt the national image.

✓ Reading Check

Answer: Johnson thought his presidency would be ruined and democracy damaged if the Democrats lost Vietnam to communism.

CHAPTER 25   The Vietnam War   **779**

INTERDISCIPLINARY CONNECTIONS ACTIVITY

Art Tell students that Maya Lin's design for the Vietnam Veterans Memorial was praised as having an "extraordinary sense of dignity and nobility." It was also condemned as being "unheroic" and "a black gash of shame." Construction did not begin until it was agreed that a statue of three servicemen and a flagpole would be added. Nevertheless, many visitors to the monument are quite moved by what they see. Discuss with students what makes a monument moving and memorable. Extend the discussion by inviting interested students to submit sketches for a memorial to a person or cause that they consider noteworthy. **L2**

Lucy, Andy Griffith, and Gomer Pyle were mainstays on American television in 1968. The images of the Vietnam War were a sharp contrast.

3 ASSESS

Assign Section 2 Assessment as homework or as an in-class activity.

🌐 Have students use the **Interactive Tutor Self-Assessment CD-ROM.**

L1/ELL

Reading Essentials and Study Guide 25-2

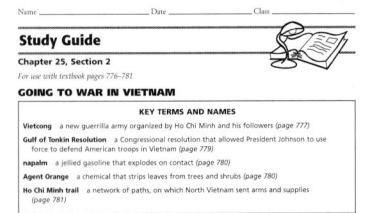

Name _____ Date _____ Class _____

Study Guide

Chapter 25, Section 2
For use with textbook pages 776–781

GOING TO WAR IN VIETNAM

KEY TERMS AND NAMES

Vietcong   a new guerrilla army organized by Ho Chi Minh and his followers *(page 777)*

Gulf of Tonkin Resolution   a Congressional resolution that allowed President Johnson to use force to defend American troops in Vietnam *(page 779)*

napalm   a jellied gasoline that explodes on contact *(page 780)*

Agent Orange   a chemical that strips leaves from trees and shrubs *(page 780)*

Ho Chi Minh trail   a network of paths, on which North Vietnam sent arms and supplies *(page 781)*

NATIONAL GEOGRAPHIC
MOMENT in HISTORY

AMERICA'S LONGEST WAR

Clinging to his M-16 rifle, a wounded American Marine is shown after being pulled to safety by a fellow soldier. In the late 1950s, American military advisers were sent to help the South Vietnamese army fight guerrillas known as the Vietcong, who were receiving weapons, supplies, and training from Communist North Vietnam. The dense jungles of Vietnam made fighting the guerrillas very difficult. By 1968 about 500,000 U.S. troops were fighting in the increasingly unpopular war. American forces finally withdrew in March 1973.

extremely strong, it marched into Vietnam with great confidence. "America seemed omnipotent then," said Philip Caputo, one of the first marines to arrive. "We saw ourselves as the champions of a 'cause that was destined to triumph.'"

Frustrating Warfare Lacking the firepower of the Americans, the Vietcong used ambushes, booby traps, and guerrilla tactics. Ronald J. Glasser, an American army doctor, described the devastating effects of one booby trap:

    ❝Three quarters of the way through the tangle, a trooper brushed against a two-inch vine, and a grenade slung at chest high went off, shattering the right side of his head and body. . . . Nearby troopers took hold of the unconscious soldier and, half carrying, half dragging him, pulled him the rest of the way through the jungle.❞

    –quoted in *Vietnam, A History*

The Vietcong also frustrated American troops by blending in with the general population in the cities and the countryside and then quickly vanishing. "It

was a sheer physical impossibility to keep the enemy from slipping away whenever he wished," one American general said. Journalist Linda Martin noted, "It's a war where nothing is ever quite certain and nowhere is ever quite safe."

To counter the Vietcong's tactics, American troops went on "search and destroy" missions. They tried to find enemy troops, bomb their positions, destroy their supply lines, and force them out into the open for combat.

American forces also sought to take away the Vietcong's ability to hide in the thick jungles by literally destroying the landscape. American planes dropped napalm, a jellied gasoline that explodes on contact. They also used **Agent Orange,** a chemical that strips leaves from trees and shrubs, turning farmland and forest into wasteland.

A Determined Enemy United States military leaders underestimated the Vietcong's strength. They also misjudged the enemy's stamina. American generals believed that continuously bombing and killing large numbers of Vietcong would destroy the enemy's morale and force them to give up. The guerrillas,

780   CHAPTER 25   The Vietnam War

CRITICAL THINKING ACTIVITY

Identifying Assumptions   In a guerrilla war, the mobility of a single soldier is as important as the mobility of an army. The United States mistakenly assumed that it could fight the Vietcong in the rice fields and jungles of Vietnam with troops trained to fight on the battlefields of Western Europe. Discuss with students other assumptions of American leaders that proved to be incorrect. **L2**

however, had no intention of surrendering, and they were willing to accept huge losses in human lives.

In the Vietcong's war effort, North Vietnamese support was a major factor. Although the Vietcong forces were made up of many South Vietnamese, North Vietnam provided arms, advisers, and significant leadership. Later in the war, as Vietcong casualties mounted, North Vietnam began sending regular North Vietnamese Army units to fight in South Vietnam.

North Vietnam sent arms and supplies south by way of a network of jungle paths known as the **Ho Chi Minh trail.** The trail wound through the countries of Cambodia and Laos, bypassing the border between North and South Vietnam. Because the trail passed through countries not directly involved in the war, President Johnson refused to allow a full-scale attack on the trail to shut it down.

North Vietnam itself received military weapons and other support from the Soviet Union and China. One of the main reasons President Johnson refused to order a full-scale invasion of North Vietnam was his fear that such an attack would bring China into the war, as had happened in Korea. By placing limits on the war, however, Johnson made it very difficult to win. Instead of conquering enemy territory, American troops were forced to fight a war of attrition—a strategy of defeating the enemy forces by slowly wearing them down. This strategy led troops to conduct grisly body counts after battles to determine how many enemy soldiers had been killed.

Bombing from American planes killed as many as 220,000 Vietnamese between 1965 and 1967. Nevertheless, the Vietcong and North Vietnamese troops showed no sign of surrendering. Meanwhile, American

casualties continued to mount. By the end of 1966, more than 6,700 American soldiers had been killed.

As the number of Americans killed and wounded continued to grow, the notion of a quick and decisive victory grew increasingly remote. As a result, many citizens back home began to question the nation's involvement in the war.

✔ **Reading Check** **Describing** What tactics did the United States adopt to fight the Vietcong?

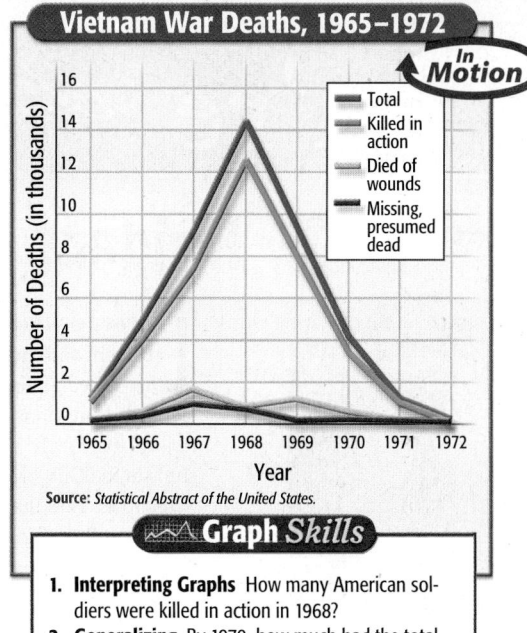

Vietnam War Deaths, 1965–1972

Number of Deaths (in thousands)

Legend:
- Total
- Killed in action
- Died of wounds
- Missing, presumed dead

Source: *Statistical Abstract of the United States.*

Graph Skills

1. **Interpreting Graphs** How many American soldiers were killed in action in 1968?
2. **Generalizing** By 1970, how much had the total number killed dropped from the peak number of deaths in 1968?

SECTION 2 ASSESSMENT

HISTORY Online **Study Central™** To review this section, go to tarvol2.glencoe.com and click on **Study Central™.**

Checking for Understanding
1. **Define:** Vietcong, napalm.
2. **Identify:** Gulf of Tonkin Resolution, Agent Orange, Ho Chi Minh trail.
3. **Explain** how the Gulf of Tonkin Resolution affected the powers of Congress and the presidency.

Reviewing Themes
4. **Science and Technology** Why did the United States use napalm and Agent Orange in its fight against the Vietcong?

Critical Thinking
5. **Analyzing** Why did fighting in Vietnam turn into a stalemate by the mid-1960s?
6. **Sequencing** Complete a time line similar to the one below to fill in events leading to American involvement in Vietnam.

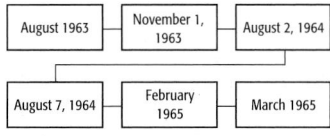

August 1963 → November 1, 1963 → August 2, 1964

August 7, 1964 → February 1965 → March 1965

Analyzing Visuals
7. **Analyzing Photographs** Look closely at the photograph on page 777 of Buddhist monk Reverend Quang Duc. What in the photograph suggests that this event was planned by Buddhists to protest their treatment in South Vietnam?

Writing About History
8. **Persuasive Writing** Imagine that you are a member of Congress in August 1964. Write a statement supporting or opposing the Gulf of Tonkin Resolution.

CHAPTER 25   The Vietnam War   **781**

SECTION 2 ASSESSMENT ANSWERS

1. Terms are in blue.
2. Gulf of Tonkin Resolution (*p. 779*), Agent Orange (*p. 780*), Ho Chi Minh Trail (*p. 781*)
3. It gave congressional war powers to the president.
4. to destroy the landscape so the Vietcong could not hide in the jungle

5. The Vietcong showed no signs of surrendering and Johnson refused to order a full-scale invasion.
6. August 1963, Henry Cabot Lodge arrives in Vietnam; November 1, 1963, Diem is overthrown; August 2, 1964, Gulf of Tonkin incident; August 7, 1964, Gulf of Tonkin

Resolution; February 1965, attack on Pleiku base; March 1965, Johnson expands bombing campaign
7. The presence of the Buddhist onlookers suggests a planned event.
8. Students' statements should express a point of view.

L2

Section Quiz 25–2

Name _____ Date _____ Class _____

⭐ Chapter 25   Score [ ]

Section Quiz 25-2

DIRECTIONS: Matching Match each item in Column A with the items in Column B. Write the correct letters in the blanks. *(10 points each)*

Column A
_____ 1. special fortified villages created by the South Vietnamese
_____ 2. chemical that strips leaves from trees and shrubs, turning farmland and forests into wasteland
_____ 3. network of jungle paths through Cambodia and Laos that bypassed the border between North and South Vietnam
_____ 4. sustained bombing campaign against North Vietnam by the United States
_____ 5. a guerrilla army organized by Ho Chi Minh to reunify the nation

Column B
A. Operation Rolling Thunder
B. Vietcong
C. Ho Chi Minh trail
D. Agent Orange
E. strategic hamlets

Graph Skills

Answers:
1. about 12,000
2. by about 10,000

Graph Skills Practice
Ask: How many American military personnel were killed in action in 1967? *(about 7,000)*

✔ **Reading Check**

Answer: search and destroy missions, bombing, the use of napalm and Agent Orange

Reteach
Have students describe President Johnson's Vietnam policy.

Enrich
Have interested students research the plight of the Vietnamese "boat people."

HISTORY Online

Study Central™ provides summaries, interactive games, and online graphic organizers to help students review section content.

4 CLOSE

Have students discuss Vietcong tactics.

1 FOCUS

Remind students that President Johnson was facing a re-election campaign in which he did not want to appear as though he was weak or soft on communism.

2 TEACH

Understanding the Gulf of Tonkin Incident To help students better understand the events, assign various students to research the following topics: foreign involvement in Indochina, rise of communism in Indochina, events that triggered the initial U.S. involvement in Vietnam, and public opinion in the United States about the events in Vietnam. Tell students that the research should extend beyond what is presented in the text. Have students make oral presentations about their topics. Then have a class discussion about the Gulf of Tonkin incident and its handling by the Johnson administration. Have students identify the points of view of Johnson, his advisers, and members of Congress. **L2**

FYI

In addition to the human cost of the Vietnam War, economists estimate that the cost to the United States of the war was at least $200 billion.

Incident in the Gulf of Tonkin

President Lyndon Johnson

In 1964 the Vietcong in South Vietnam were trying to topple the government and unite the country under communism. To prevent this, the United States had already committed money, supplies, and advisers. President Johnson asked Congress to authorize using force after reports that North Vietnam had made unprovoked attacks on U.S. warships in the Gulf of Tonkin. Congress responded with the Gulf of Tonkin Resolution. Had the warship USS *Maddox* provoked the attack? Was Johnson fully informed of events in the Gulf? You're the historian.

Read the following excerpts, then answer the questions and complete the activities that follow.

From accounts of an unprovoked attack

The sources advising President Johnson on the Gulf of Tonkin incident included the navy and the Defense Department. These excerpts suggest how difficult it was to know what had happened—and also how tension influenced the American interpretation.

U.S. Navy Commander John Herrick of the USS *Maddox*:
I am being approached by high-speed craft with apparent intention of torpedo attack. I intend to open fire in self-defense if necessary.
—from a cable of August 2, 1964

U.S. Defense Department:
While on routine patrol in international waters . . . the U.S. destroyer *Maddox* underwent an unprovoked attack by three PT-type boats in . . . the Tonkin Gulf.

The attacking boats launched three torpedoes and used 37-millimeter gunfire. The *Maddox* answered

with 5-inch gunfire. . . . The PT boats were driven off, with one seen to be badly damaged and not moving. . . .

No casualties or damage were sustained by the *Maddox* or the aircraft.
—from a press release of August 2, 1964

National Security Council Meeting:
Secretary McNamara: The North Vietnamese PT boats have continued their attacks on the two U.S. destroyers in international waters in the Gulf of Tonkin. . . .

Secretary Rusk: An immediate and direct action by us is necessary. The unprovoked attack on the high seas is an act of war for all practical purposes. . . .

CIA Director McCone: The proposed U.S. reprisals will result in sharp North Vietnamese military action, but such actions would not represent a deliberate

decision to provoke or accept a major escalation of the Vietnamese war.

President Johnson: Do they want a war by attacking our ships in the middle of the Gulf of Tonkin?

U.S. Intelligence Agency Director Rowan: Do we know for a fact that the North Vietnamese provocation took place?

Secretary McNamara: We will know definitely in the morning.
—August 2, 1964

Secretary Rusk:
We believe that present OPLAN 34-A activities are beginning to rattle Hanoi [capital of North Vietnam], and the *Maddox* incident is directly related to their effort to resist these activities. We have no intention of yielding to pressure.
—from a top secret telegram to Ambassador Maxwell Taylor (South Vietnam), August 3, 1964

782 CHAPTER 25 The Vietnam War

EXTENDING THE CONTENT

Boat People Tell students that many Vietnamese fled by boat to escape political tensions. Unfortunately, some "boat people" found themselves caught in racial tensions. For example, in 1979 Vietnamese "boat people" who were mostly ethnic Chinese arrived in Malaysia, already an ethnically diverse country. So intense was the fear that the arrival of the Vietnamese would upset the country's ethnic balance that, instead of welcoming the newcomers, the Malaysian government issued orders to shoot any "boat person" found landing on Malaysian shores.

From accounts of a possible mistake

Two days after the alleged attack, the Turner Joy *joined the* Maddox *in the Gulf. On the night of August 4, 1964, the two destroyers experienced a series of events they interpreted as a second attack. However, Commander Herrick later revised this report. President Johnson referred to the "repeated" attacks later when he asked Congress for war powers.*

Commander Herrick:
Review of action makes many contacts and torpedoes fired appear doubtful. Freak weather effects on radar and overeager sonarmen may have accounted for many reports. No actual visual sightings by *Maddox.* Suggest complete evaluation before any further action. . . .

Turner Joy also reports no actual visual sightings or wake. . . . Entire action leaves many doubts

Vietcong guerrillas

except for apparent attempt to ambush at beginning.

—**from two cables of August 4, 1964**

President Johnson:
The initial attack on the destroyer *Maddox,* on August 2, was repeated today by a number of hostile vessels attacking two U.S. destroyers with torpedoes. The destroyers and supporting aircraft acted at once on the orders I gave after the initial act of aggression. . . . Repeated acts of violence against the Armed Forces of the United States must be met not only with alert defense, but with positive reply.

—**in a television and radio address, August 4, 1964**

In 1968 Senator William Fulbright opened an investigation into the 1964 Gulf of Tonkin incident. The following exchange took place between Senator Fulbright and Secretary McNamara.

Secretary McNamara: I don't believe Commander Herrick in his cable stated that he had doubt that the attack took place. He questioned certain details of the attack. . . . Secondly, his doubts were resolved that afternoon before the retaliatory action was taken.

Senator Fulbright: I think he went further than that. He advised you not to do anything until it had been reevaluated. . . . It is a very strong statement.

Secretary McNamara

Secretary McNamara: Nothing was done until it was reevaluated.

Senator Fulbright: He says "Suggest complete reevaluation before any further action." Now that is a very strong recommendation from a man on the scene in charge of the operation. . . . Both committees, except for the Senator from Oregon [Morse], unanimously accepted your testimony then as the whole story, and I must say this raises very serious questions about how you make decisions to go to war.

Understanding the Issue

1. What statement by Rusk suggests the United States may have provoked the attack on the *Maddox?*
2. Do you think President Johnson was misled by his advisers? Explain.
3. How soon after the alleged attacks did the president address the American people? Did the United States rush to judgment in this case? Explain.

Activities

1. **Investigate** What were the conclusions of the Fulbright investigations into the Gulf of Tonkin incident? Check sources, including the Internet.
2. **Discuss** Research and review American decisions to go to war in 1898, 1917, and 1941. What were the concerns? Do you think the nation made the right decisions?

---

3 ASSESS

Have students answer the Understanding the Issue questions and complete the Activities.

Understanding the Issue
1. He named a plan of activity, the OPLAN 34-A, which implies that the United States had some type of operation underway.
2. Students' answers will vary. Students should support their points of view with facts and clear observations.
3. Two days. Students may say that the cables Commander Herrick sent on August 4 suggest more time was needed to verify the facts.

Activities
1. Answers may vary depending on the research undertaken. Students should learn that although Fulbright originally supported the administration, he came to believe that Congress had been deceived.
2. You may elect to assign this activity to be done in groups with each group member researching one of the wars. Students' conclusions will vary.

4 CLOSE

Ask students to consider how decision makers decide what information to supply to the public and how this information shapes the public's impressions.

PORTFOLIO ACTIVITY

Newspaper Story Ask students to write a newspaper editorial focusing on the effects of misinformation on Congress. Have students predict how the Gulf of Tonkin Resolution might affect the future of U.S. involvement in Vietnam. Tell them to conclude their editorial with recommendations that the president or Congress might take to prevent similar incidents. **L2**

1 FOCUS

Section Overview

This section focuses on the escalation of military action in Vietnam and the division between those who supported the war and those who did not.

BELLRINGER
Skillbuilder Activity

 Project transparency and have students answer the question.

Daily Focus Skills Transparency 25–3

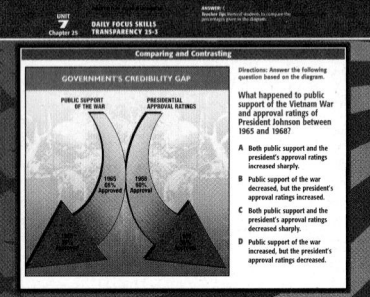

Reading Preview

Answers to Graphic: Reasons for opposition to Vietnam War: credibility gap, unfair draft system, immorality of defending a corrupt dictatorship in South Vietnam, and belief that it was a civil war in which the United States had no business

Preteaching Vocabulary
Have students scan the section to learn the meanings of the Key Terms and Names.

Guide to Reading

Main Idea
The experience of Vietnam produced sharp divisions between Americans who supported the war and those who did not.

Key Terms and Names
William Westmoreland, credibility gap, teach-in, dove, hawk, Tet offensive

Reading Strategy
Organizing As you read about Americans' reactions to the Vietnam War, complete a graphic organizer like the one below to list the reasons for opposition to the war.

Reasons for Opposition to Vietnam War

Reading Objective
• **Analyze** why support for the war began to weaken.
• **Describe** the motives of those in the antiwar movement.

Section Theme
Civic Rights and Responsibilities Many Americans protested their country's involvement in the Vietnam War.

Preview of Events

♦1965 ♦1966 ♦1967 ♦1968

1965
Teach-ins on college campuses begin

1966
Senate Foreign Relations Committee begins Vietnam hearings

1967
March on the Pentagon

January 1968
Tet offensive

★ An American Story ★

Martin Jezer, a 27-year-old copywriter living in New York City, had never considered himself a radical. "I campaigned for Lyndon Johnson in 1964," he recalled. As his opposition to the war in Vietnam grew, however, Jezer decided to stage a public protest.

On April 15, 1967, he and dozens of other young men gathered with their military draft cards in New York's Central Park. Before an audience of reporters, photographers, FBI officials, and citizens, the men pulled out matches and lighters and burned the cards.

Antiwar activists burn draft cards at the Pentagon in 1972

❝We began singing freedom songs and chanting, 'Resist! Resist!' and 'Burn Draft Cards, Not People'. . . . People in the audience were applauding us, shouting encouragement. Then some guys began to come out of the audience with draft cards in hand. They burned them. Alone, in pairs, by threes they came. Each flaming draft card brought renewed cheering and more people out of the crowd. . . . Some of the draft card burners were girls, wives, or girlfriends of male card burners. . . . It lasted this way for about half an hour.❞
—**quoted in** *The Vietnam War: Opposing Viewpoints*

A Growing Credibility Gap

Jezer's protest was just one of many, as American opposition to the Vietnam War grew in the late 1960s. When American troops first entered the Vietnam War in the spring of 1965, many Americans had supported the military effort. A Gallup poll

---

SECTION RESOURCES

📁 Reproducible Masters
• Reproducible Lesson Plan 25–3
• Daily Lecture and Discussion Notes 25–3
• Guided Reading Activity 25–3
• Section Quiz 25–3
• Reading Essentials and Study Guide 25–3

📽 Transparencies
• Daily Focus Skills Transparency 25–3

Multimedia
🔘 Interactive Tutor Self-Assessment CD-ROM
🔘 ExamView® Pro Testmaker CD-ROM
🔘 Presentation Plus! CD-ROM
🔘 TeacherWorks™ CD-ROM
🎧 Audio Program
🎵 American Music: Cultural Traditions

published around that time showed that 66 percent of Americans approved of the policy in Vietnam. As the war dragged on, however, public support began to drop. Suspicion of the government's truthfulness about the war was a significant reason. Throughout the early years of the war, the American commander in South Vietnam, General **William Westmoreland,** reported that the enemy was on the brink of defeat. In 1967 he confidently declared that the "enemy's hopes are bankrupt" and added, "we have reached an important point where the end begins to come into view."

Contradicting such reports were less optimistic media accounts, especially on television. Vietnam was the first "television war," with footage of combat appearing nightly on the evening news. Day after day, millions of people saw images of wounded and dead Americans and began to doubt government reports. In the view of many, a credibility gap had developed, meaning it was hard to believe what the Johnson administration said about the war.

Congress, which had given the president a nearly free hand in Vietnam, soon grew uncertain about the war. Beginning in February 1966, the Senate Foreign Relations Committee held "educational" hearings on Vietnam, calling in Secretary of State **Dean Rusk** and other policy makers to explain the administration's war program. The committee also listened to critics such as American diplomat George Kennan. Although Kennan had helped create the policy of containment, he argued that Vietnam was not strategically important to the United States.

✓ **Reading Check** **Explaining** Why was the Vietnam War the first "television war"?

An Antiwar Movement Emerges

As casualties mounted in Vietnam, many people began to protest publicly against the war and to demand that the United States pull out. Although many other Americans supported the war, opponents of the conflict received the most attention.

Teach-Ins Begin In March 1965, a group of faculty members and students at the University of Michigan abandoned their classes and joined together in a teach-in. Here, they informally discussed the issues surrounding the war and reaffirmed their reasons for opposing it. The gathering inspired teach-ins at many campuses. In May 1965, 122 colleges held a "National Teach-In" by radio for more than 100,000 antiwar demonstrators.

People who opposed the war did so for different reasons. Some saw the conflict as a civil war in which the United States had no business. Others viewed South Vietnam as a corrupt dictatorship and insisted that defending that country was immoral and unjust.

Anger at the Draft Young protesters especially focused on what they saw as an unfair draft system. At the beginning of the war, a college student was often able to defer military service until after graduation. By contrast, young people from low-income families were more likely to be sent to Vietnam because they were unable to afford college. This meant minorities, particularly African Americans, made up a disproportionately large number of the soldiers in Vietnam. By 1967, for example, African Americans accounted for about 20 percent of American combat deaths—about twice their proportion of the population within the United States. That number would decline to roughly match their population proportion by the war's end.

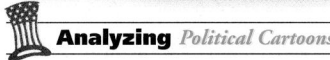
Analyzing *Political Cartoons*

Dark Passage One particular phrase came to represent the government's claims that it was on the verge of ending the Vietnam War: "the light at the end of the tunnel." Why did many people become skeptical about such government claims?

CHAPTER 25 The Vietnam War **785**

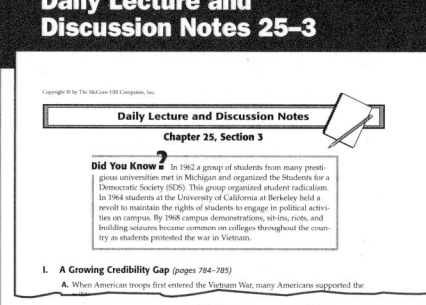

2 TEACH

Daily Lecture and Discussion Notes 25–3

Making Comparisons Have students create a chart to show a comparison between the civil rights protests and the Vietnam War protests. L1 ELL

📂 Use the rubric for creating a map, display, or chart on pages 65–66 in the *Performance Assessment Activities and Rubrics.*

✓ **Reading Check**

Answer: Combat footage appeared nightly on the evening news.

🏛 **Analyzing** *Political Cartoons*

Answer: Television news reports were different from what military leaders were reporting.
Ask: What are the people in the cartoon doing? *(They are feeling their way along a dark tunnel because there is no "light at the end of the tunnel.")*

COOPERATIVE LEARNING ACTIVITY

Symbolizing a Campaign A wide variety of hopefuls sought the presidency in 1968. To illustrate their differences, organize students into five groups, one each for Eugene McCarthy, Robert F. Kennedy, Hubert H. Humphrey, George Wallace, and Richard Nixon. Have members of each group write three words that describe their candidate and one sentence about their candidate's political views. They should then work together to create a campaign button, banner, or logo for their candidate. Have groups share and discuss their ideas. 📦

Use the rubric for a cooperative group management plan on pages 71–72 in the *Performance Assessment Activities and Rubrics.*

L1/ELL

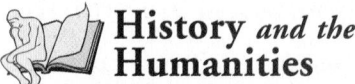

Picturing **History**

Answer: People opposed the war because of the credibility gap, the unfair draft system, the corrupt government of South Vietnam, and the belief that it was a civil war in which the United States had no business.

Ask: Why do you think the young man in the photograph is putting flowers in the barrels of the weapons? *(Students will recognize the symbolism—flowers for the peace movement.)*

Making a Poster Have students make a poster that would have been appropriate for people marching in support of or opposition to the Vietnam War. **L2**

History *and the* Humanities

🎵 American Music: Cultural Traditions: "The Big Muddy," and "Okie From Muskogee"

Picturing **History**

Flower Power Student antiwar protests ranged from violent confrontation to this peaceful but dramatic demonstration near the Pentagon in Washington, D.C. What were some reasons many people opposed the war?

The high number of African Americans and poor Americans dying in Vietnam angered African American leaders, including Dr. Martin Luther King, Jr. Early on, King had refrained from speaking out against the war for fear that it would draw attention from the civil rights movement. In April 1967, however, he broke his silence and publicly condemned the conflict:

> 66Somehow this madness must cease. I speak as a child of God and brother to the suffering poor of Vietnam and the poor of America who are paying the double price of smashed hopes at home and death and corruption in Vietnam. I speak as a citizen of the world, for the world as it stands aghast at the path we have taken. I speak as an American to the leader of my own nation. The great initiative in this war is ours. The initiative to stop must be ours.99
>
> —quoted in *A Testament of Hope*

As the war escalated, American officials increased the draft call, putting many college students at risk. An estimated 500,000 draftees refused to go. Many publicly burned their draft cards or simply did not report when called for induction. Some fled the country, moving to Canada, Sweden, or other nations. Others stayed and went to prison rather than fight in a war they opposed.

Between 1965 and 1968, officials prosecuted more than 3,300 Americans for refusing to serve. The draft became less of an issue in 1969 when the government introduced a lottery system, in which only those with low lottery numbers were subject to the draft.

Protests against the war were not confined to college campuses. Demonstrators held public rallies and marches in towns across the country. In April 1965, Students for a Democratic Society (SDS), a left-wing student organization, organized a march on Washington, D.C., that drew more than 20,000 participants. Two years later, in October 1967, a rally at Washington's Lincoln Memorial drew tens of thousands of protesters as well.

Anger over the draft also fueled discussions of voting age. Many draftees argued that if they were old enough to fight, they were old enough to vote. In 1971 the Twenty-sixth Amendment to the Constitution was ratified, giving all citizens age 18 and older the right to vote in all state and federal elections.

786 CHAPTER 25 The Vietnam War

DIFFERENTIATED INSTRUCTION

Reading Support The 1968 Democratic National Convention illustrates the divided nation of the late 1960s. Ask students with strong interpersonal skills to review the text's coverage of this event and write a paragraph explaining the divided feelings. Conclude with this comment from Robert McNamara's *In Retrospect: The Tragedy and Lesson of Vietnam:* "A nation's deepest strength lies not in its military process but rather in the unity of its people." **L2**

👉 Refer to *Inclusion for the High School Social Studies Classroom Strategies and Activities* in the TCR.

Hawks and Doves In the face of growing opposition to the war, President Johnson remained determined to continue fighting. The president was not alone in his views. Although the antiwar protesters became a vocal group, they did not represent majority opinion on Vietnam. In a poll taken in mid-1967, about 68 percent of the respondents favored continuing the war, compared to about 32 percent who wanted to end it. Of those Americans who supported the policy in Vietnam, many openly criticized the protesters for a lack of patriotism.

By 1968 the nation seemed to be divided into two camps. Those who wanted the United States to withdraw from Vietnam were known as doves. Those who insisted that the United States stay and fight came to be known as hawks. As the two groups debated, the war took a dramatic turn for the worse, and the nation endured a year of shock and crisis.

✓ **Reading Check** **Explaining** What led to the passage of the Twenty-sixth Amendment?

1968: The Pivotal Year

The most turbulent year of the chaotic 1960s was 1968. The year saw a shocking political announcement, a pair of traumatic assassinations, and a violent political convention. First, however, the nation endured a surprise attack in Vietnam.

TURNING POINT

The Tet Offensive On January 30, 1968, during Tet, the Vietnamese New Year, the Vietcong and North Vietnamese launched a massive surprise attack. In this **Tet offensive,** the guerrilla fighters attacked virtually all American airbases in South Vietnam and most of the South's major cities and provincial capitals. The bloodiest battle took place at Hué, South Vietnam's third largest city. The Communist forces seized much of the city, and it took American and South Vietnamese troops almost four weeks to drive them out. Afterward, American troops found mass graves. The Communist forces had massacred the city's political and religious leaders as well as many foreigners, intellectuals, and others associated with South Vietnam's government. Nearly 3,000 bodies were found. Thousands more remained missing.

Militarily, Tet turned out to be a disaster for the Communist forces. After about a month of fighting, the American and South Vietnamese soldiers repelled the enemy troops, inflicting heavy losses on

them. General Westmoreland boasted that the Communists' "well-laid plans went afoul," while President Johnson triumphantly added that the enemy's effort had ended in "complete failure."

In fact, the North Vietnamese had scored a major political victory. The American people were shocked that an enemy supposedly on the verge of defeat could launch such a large-scale attack. When General Westmoreland requested 206,000 troops in addition to the 500,000 already in Vietnam, it seemed to be an admission that the United States could not win the war.

To make matters worse, the mainstream media, which had tried to remain balanced in their war coverage, now openly criticized the effort. Walter Cronkite, then the nation's most respected television newscaster, announced after Tet that it seemed "more certain than ever that the bloody experience in Vietnam is to end in a stalemate."

Public opinion no longer favored the president. In the weeks following the Tet offensive, the president's approval rating plummeted to a dismal 35 percent, while support for his handling of the war fell even lower, to 26 percent.

Johnson Leaves the Presidential Race With the war growing increasingly unpopular and Johnson's credibility all but gone, some Democrats began looking for an alternative candidate to nominate for president in 1968. In November 1967, even before the Tet disaster, a little-known liberal senator from Minnesota, Eugene McCarthy, became the first dove to announce his candidacy against Johnson. In March 1968, McCarthy stunned the nation by winning more than 40 percent of the votes in the New Hampshire primary

| Fact | Fiction | Folklore |

The Peace Symbol This familiar symbol of the 1960s was originally designed to stand for the fight for nuclear disarmament. Created by British artist Gerald Holtom in 1958, the symbol was first used at a British demonstration against a research center for the development of nuclear weapons. It combined the semaphore for the letters "N" and "D," standing for nuclear disarmament. Semaphore is a system of visual signaling using two flags, one held in each hand. N is two flags held in an upside-down V, and D is one flag pointed straight up and the other pointed straight down.

✓ **Reading Check**

Answer: Protests over the draft led to discussion about the right of draft-age citizens to vote and the passage of the Twenty-sixth Amendment.

Creating a Headline Have students write a headline that might have appeared in a January 1969 newspaper summing up the mood of the country after surviving the turmoil of 1968. **L1**

FYI

The Tet offensive caught the United States military completely off guard. In the words of a West Point textbook published after the war, Tet was an "intelligence failure ranking with Pearl Harbor."

| Fact | Fiction | Folklore |

In the early 1970s another sign of the growing concern over the Vietnam War was the proliferation of POW/MIA bracelets. Each bracelet was engraved with the name and the date lost of someone who was a prisoner of war or missing in action. Most people who wore the bracelets continued to wear them until they learned the fate of the person named on their bracelet. As the war ended and service personnel came home, the bracelets were sent to the returning veterans, or, in many cases, the veteran's family.

INTERDISCIPLINARY CONNECTIONS ACTIVITY

Technology The United States used a variety of strategies in its attempt to cut off North Vietnamese supply routes and locate the ground units of the North Vietnamese and Vietcong. Ask students to research and report on some of these strategies, including saturation bombing and the use of napalm and chemical defoliants. Have students explain how each strategy worked and the kind of damage it did. As students present their information, discuss why such firepower failed to bring the Communist forces to a point of surrender. **L2**

Geography *Skills*

Answers:

1. Laos and Cambodia

2. Attacks were on almost all U.S. bases and major South Vietnam cities. It showed that the United States did not have the level of control its generals were portraying.

Geography Skills Practice

Ask: Why was the Ho Chi Minh Trail located outside of Vietnam?

(because the U.S. was not at war with Laos or Cambodia)

3 ASSESS

Assign Section 3 Assessment as homework or as an in-class activity.

💿 Have students use the **Interactive Tutor Self-Assessment CD-ROM.**

L1/ELL

Reading Essentials and Study Guide 25–3

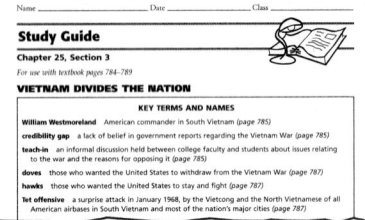

NATIONAL GEOGRAPHIC   **The Tet Offensive, 1968**   In Motion

A view of the U.S. embassy in Saigon after it was bombed during the Tet offensive.

Geography *Skills*

1. **Interpreting Maps** Most of the Ho Chi Minh Trail lies within which countries?

2. **Applying Geography Skills** How broad was the Tet offensive, and why did this shock Americans?

---

and almost defeating the president. Realizing that Johnson was vulnerable, Senator Robert Kennedy, who also opposed the war, quickly entered the race for the Democratic nomination.

With the division in the country and within his own party growing, Johnson addressed the public on television on March 31, 1968. He stunned viewers by stating, "I have concluded that I should not permit the presidency to become involved in the partisan divisions that are developing in this political year. Accordingly, I shall not seek, and I will not accept, the nomination of my party for another term as your President."

A Season of Violence Following Johnson's announcement, the nation endured even more shocking events. In April James Earl Ray was arrested for killing Dr. Martin Luther King, Jr., an event which led to riots in several major cities. Just two months later, another assassination rocked the country—that of Robert Kennedy. Kennedy, who appeared to be on his way to winning the Democratic nomination, was

gunned down on June 5 in a California hotel just after winning the state's Democratic primary. The assassin was Sirhan Sirhan, an Arab nationalist apparently angry over the candidate's pro-Israeli remarks a few nights before.

The violence that seemed to plague the country at every turn in 1968 culminated with a chaotic and well-publicized clash between protesters and police at the Democratic National Convention in Chicago. Thousands of protesters descended on the August convention, demanding that the Democrats adopt an antiwar platform.

On the third day of the convention, the delegates chose Hubert Humphrey, President Johnson's vice president, as their presidential nominee. Meanwhile, in a park not far from the convention hall, the protesters and police began fighting. A full-scale riot soon engulfed the streets of downtown Chicago. As officers tried to disperse demonstrators with tear gas and billy clubs, demonstrators taunted the authorities with the chant, "The whole world is watching!"

788 CHAPTER 25   The Vietnam War

Reading Strategy   READING THE TEXT

Analyzing Information Tell students that in 1964 the Vietnam War was not a national issue. Two factors, however, would soon bring it to national attention. The first was the controversy surrounding the Gulf of Tonkin incident. The second was campaign speeches in which Johnson pledged he would not "send American boys halfway around the world to do a job that Asian boys ought to be doing for themselves." After students have read the section, have them analyze how both events became crucial issues by 1967 and 1968. **L2**

📁 Refer to *Inclusion for the High School Social Studies Classroom Strategies and Activities* in the TCR.

Nixon Wins the Presidency The violence and chaos now associated with the Democratic Party benefited the 1968 Republican presidential candidate, Richard Nixon. Although defeated in the 1960 election, Nixon had remained active in national politics. A third candidate, Governor George Wallace of Alabama, also decided to run in 1968 as an independent. Wallace, an outspoken segregationist, sought to attract those Americans who felt threatened by the civil rights movement and urban social unrest.

Public opinion polls gave Nixon a wide lead over Humphrey and Wallace. Nixon's campaign promise to unify the nation and restore law and order appealed to Americans who feared their country was spinning out of control. Nixon also declared that he had a plan for ending the war in Vietnam, although he did not specify how the plan would work.

At first Humphrey's support of President Johnson's Vietnam policies hurt his campaign. After Humphrey broke with the president and called for a complete end to the bombing of North Vietnam, he began to move up in the polls. A week before the election, President Johnson helped Humphrey by announcing that the bombing of North Vietnam had halted and that a cease-fire would follow.

Johnson's announcement had come too late. In the end, Nixon's promises to end the war and restore order at home were enough to sway the American people. On Election Day, Nixon defeated Humphrey by more than 100 electoral votes, although he won the popular vote by a slim margin of just over 43 percent to Humphrey's 42.7. Wallace helped account for the razor-thin margin by winning 46 electoral votes and more than 13 percent of the popular vote.

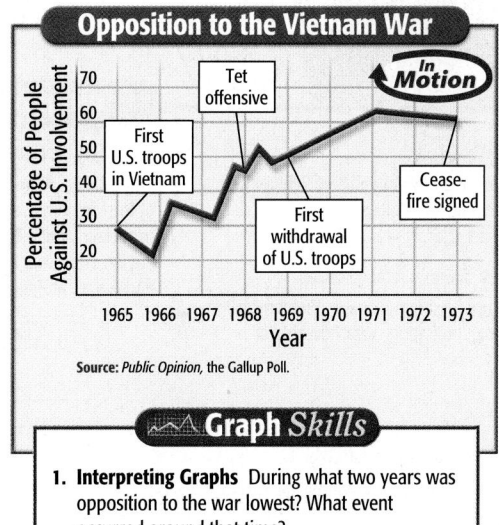

Opposition to the Vietnam War

In Motion

Source: *Public Opinion*, the Gallup Poll.

Graph Skills

1. **Interpreting Graphs** During what two years was opposition to the war lowest? What event occurred around that time?
2. **Generalizing** In what year did opposition to the Vietnam War peak? How was this sentiment logically related to the withdrawal of American troops?

Speaking to reporters after his election, Nixon recalled seeing a young girl carrying a sign at one of his rallies that said: "Bring Us Together." This, he promised, would be his chief goal as president. Nixon also vowed to implement his plan to end the Vietnam War.

Reading Check **Explaining** Why did President Johnson not run for re-election in 1968?

SECTION 3 ASSESSMENT

HISTORY Online **Study Central™** To review this section, go to tarvol2.glencoe.com and click on **Study Central™**.

Checking for Understanding

1. **Define:** credibility gap, teach-in, dove, hawk.
2. **Identify:** William Westmoreland, Tet offensive.
3. **Summarize** three important events that occurred in 1968.

Reviewing Themes

4. **Civic Rights and Responsibilities** Why did many people believe that the Vietnam War reflected racial and economic injustices in the United States?

Critical Thinking

5. **Synthesizing** Why did support of the Vietnam War begin to dwindle by the late 1960s?
6. **Organizing** Use a graphic organizer similar to the one below to list the effects of the Tet offensive.

Effects of Tet Offensive

Analyzing Visuals

7. **Analyzing Photographs** Study the photograph on page 786. The phrase "flower power" was a slogan of the hippie movement. Explain what you think the phrase meant to hippies and how the slogan was used to express opposition to the war.

Writing About History

8. **Expository Writing** Imagine that you are living in 1968. Write a paragraph for the local newspaper in which you explain your reasons for either supporting or opposing the Vietnam War.

CHAPTER 25   The Vietnam War   **789**

SECTION 3 ASSESSMENT ANSWERS

1. Terms are in blue.
2. William Westmoreland *(p. 785)*, Tet offensive *(p. 787)*
3. any three of the following: Tet offensive, Johnson's not running, Democratic National Convention, King and Kennedy assassinations
4. Low-income and minority men were more likely to be drafted.
5. mounting casualties, the draft, credibility gap, media coverage
6. war appeared unwinnable, support for war dropped, Johnson lost credibility
7. Flowers represented the growing peace movement.
8. Students' paragraph should express a clear point of view.

L2

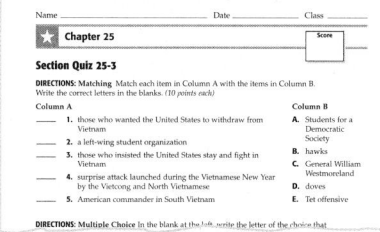

Section Quiz 25–3

Name _____ Date _____ Class _____

★ **Chapter 25**   Score ___

Section Quiz 25-3

DIRECTIONS: Matching Match each item in Column A with the items in Column B. Write the correct letters in the blanks. *(10 points each)*

Column A
___ 1. those who wanted the United States to withdraw from Vietnam
___ 2. a left-wing student organization
___ 3. those who insisted the United States stay and fight in Vietnam
___ 4. surprise attack launched during the Vietnamese New Year by the Vietcong and North Vietnamese
___ 5. American commander in South Vietnam

Column B
A. Students for a Democratic Society
B. hawks
C. General William Westmoreland
D. doves
E. Tet offensive

DIRECTIONS: Multiple Choice In the blank at the left, write the letter of the choice that

Graph Skills

Answers:
1. 1965, 1966; first U.S. troops arrive
2. 1971; Withdrawal showed government did not believe the war could be won.

Graph Skills Practice
Ask: When was the cease-fire signed? *(1973)*

Reading Check

Answer: He did not want the presidency to become involved in partisan divisions.

Reteach
Have students describe the antiwar movement.

Enrich
Have interested students write antiwar slogans for the 1968 presidential campaign.

HISTORY Online

Study Central™ provides summaries, interactive games, and online graphic organizers to help students review section content.

4 CLOSE

Have students describe the motives of those in the antiwar movement.

789

1 FOCUS

Section Overview

This section focuses on the withdrawal of United States forces and the war's impact at home.

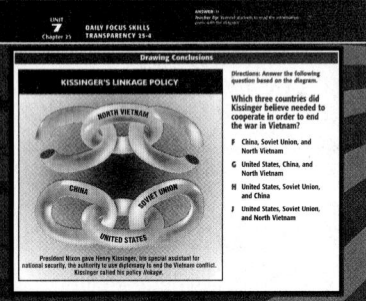
Reading Preview

Answers to Graphic: Kissinger appointment, linkage policy, Vietnamization, bombing campaign, Cambodian invasion

Preteaching Vocabulary
Have students look up the Key Terms and Names in the glossary. Then have them use two of the terms in a sentence.

SECTION 4 The War Winds Down

Guide to Reading

Main Idea
After nearly eight years of fighting in Vietnam, the United States withdrew its forces.

Key Terms and Names
Henry Kissinger, linkage, Vietnamization, Pentagon Papers, War Powers Act

Reading Strategy
Organizing As you read about the end of the Vietnam War, complete a graphic organizer similar to the one below by listing the steps that President Nixon took to end American involvement in Vietnam.

Steps Nixon Took

Reading Objectives
• **Explain** the events of Nixon's first administration that inspired more antiwar protests.
• **Summarize** the major lessons the United States learned from the Vietnam War experience.

Section Theme
Government and Democracy The Vietnam War led to changes in the way the U.S. military is deployed.

Preview of Events

♦1969	♦1971	♦1973	♦1975

1969
Secret peace negotiations between the U.S. and North Vietnam begin

1972
Nixon initiates Christmas bombings

1973
Cease-fire signed

1975
Evacuation of the last Americans from Vietnam

★ An American Story ★

Frank Snepp

On the evening of April 29, 1975, Frank Snepp, a young CIA officer, scrambled up to the American embassy rooftop to catch one of the last helicopters out of Saigon. Throughout that day, Snepp had witnessed the desperation of the South Vietnamese people as they besieged the embassy grounds in an to effort escape the approaching Communist army. Now he was leaving. Later, he recalled the scene:

❝The roof of the Embassy was a vision out of a nightmare. In the center of the dimly lit helo-pad a CH-47 was already waiting for us, its engines setting up a roar like a primeval scream. The crew and controllers all wore what looked like oversized football helmets, and in the blinking under-light of the landing signals they reminded me of grotesque insects rearing on their hindquarters. Out beyond the edge of the building a Phantom jet streaked across the horizon as tracers darted up here and there into the night sky.❞

—quoted in *Decent Interval*

Nixon Moves to End the War

Frank Snepp was one of the last Americans to leave Vietnam. Shortly after taking office, President Nixon had taken steps to end the nation's involvement in the war, but the final years of the conflict would yield much more bloodshed and turmoil.

As a first step, Nixon appointed Harvard professor **Henry Kissinger** as special assistant for national security affairs and gave him wide authority to use diplomacy to end the conflict. Kissinger embarked upon a policy he called linkage, which meant improving

790 CHAPTER 25 The Vietnam War

SECTION RESOURCES

📁 Reproducible Masters
• Reproducible Lesson Plan 25–4
• Daily Lecture and Discussion Notes 25–4
• Guided Reading Activity 25–4
• Section Quiz 25–4
• Reading Essentials and Study Guide 25–4

📖 Transparencies
• Daily Focus Skills Transparency 25–4

Multimedia
• Interactive Tutor Self-Assessment CD-ROM
• ExamView® Pro Testmaker CD-ROM
• Presentation Plus! CD-ROM
• TeacherWorks™ CD-ROM
• Audio Program
• ABCNews Interactive™

relations with the Soviet Union and China—suppliers of aid to North Vietnam—so he could persuade them to cut back on their aid.

Kissinger also rekindled peace talks with the North Vietnamese. In August 1969, Kissinger entered into secret negotiations with North Vietnam's negotiator, Le Duc Tho. In their talks, which dragged on for four years, Kissinger and Le Duc Tho argued over a possible cease-fire, the return of American prisoners of war, and the ultimate fate of South Vietnam.

Meanwhile, Nixon cut back the number of American troops in Vietnam. Known as Vietnamization, this process involved the gradual withdrawal of U.S. troops while South Vietnam assumed more of the fighting. On June 8, 1969, Nixon announced the withdrawal of 25,000 soldiers. Nixon refused to view this troop withdrawal as a form of surrender. He was determined to maintain a strong American presence in Vietnam to ensure bargaining power during peace negotiations. In support of that goal, the president increased airstrikes against North Vietnam and began bombing Vietcong sanctuaries in neighboring Cambodia.

✔ Reading Check **Identifying** When did secret negotiations with the North Vietnamese begin?

Turmoil at Home Continues

Even though the United States had begun scaling back its involvement in Vietnam, the American home front remained divided and volatile as Nixon's war policies stirred up new waves of protest.

Massacre at My Lai In November 1969, Americans learned of a horrifying event. That month, the media reported that in the spring of 1968, an American platoon under the command of Lieutenant William Calley had massacred possibly more than 200 unarmed South Vietnamese civilians in the hamlet of **My Lai.** Most of the victims were old men, women, and children. Calley eventually went to prison for his role in the killings.

Most American soldiers acted responsibly and honorably throughout the war. The actions of one soldier, however, increased the feeling among many citizens that this was a brutal and senseless conflict. Jan Barry, a founder of the Vietnam Veterans Against the War, viewed the massacre at My Lai as a symbol of the dilemma his generation faced in the conflict:

❝To kill on military orders and be a criminal, or to refuse to kill and be a criminal is the moral agony of America's Vietnam war generation. It is what has forced upward of sixty thousand young Americans, draft resisters and deserters to Canada, and created one hundred thousand military deserters a year in this country and abroad.❞

—quoted in *Who Spoke Up?*

The Invasion of Cambodia Sparks Protest

Americans heard more startling news when Nixon announced in April 1970 that American troops had invaded Cambodia. The troops wanted to destroy Vietcong military bases there.

Many viewed the Cambodian invasion as a widening of the war, and it set off many protests. At **Kent State University** on May 4, 1970, Ohio National Guard soldiers, armed with tear gas and rifles, fired on demonstrators without an order to do so. The soldiers killed four students and wounded at least nine others. Ten days later, police killed two African American students during a demonstration at Jackson State College in Mississippi.

Picturing **History**

National Trauma When members of the Ohio National Guard fired on Kent State University demonstrators, the event triggered a nationwide student strike that forced hundreds of colleges and universities to close. How does this image connect with the phrase "the war at home"?

✔ *Reading Check*

Answer: August 1969

Picturing **History**

Answer: Americans were being shot at by United States soldiers.

Designing a Memorial Have students sketch a design for a memorial to the students who died at Kent State or Jackson State. L1 ELL

ABCNEWS INTERACTIVE™

 VIDEOCASSETTE
Historic America Electronic Field Trips

View **Tape 2, Chapter 10:** "The Vietnam Veterans Memorial."

📖 **Reading Strategy** ▸ **READING THE TEXT**

Summarizing Information Organize the class into groups of five to seven students each. After students have read the section have the groups consider this fill-in-the-blank statement: The war in Vietnam was tragic because _____. Ask everyone in the group to provide at least one original answer. Have a representative of each group present the responses to the class. As a class, look for common elements in the responses. L1

📂 Refer to *Inclusion for the High School Social Studies Classroom Strategies and Activities* in the TCR.

Guided Reading Activity 25-4

Name _____ Date _____ Class _____

★ Guided Reading Activity 25-4

DIRECTIONS: Outlining Read the section and complete the outline below. Refer to your text-book to fill in the blanks.

I. Nixon Moves to End the War

A. As first step toward ending the war, Nixon appointed _____ as special assistant for _____

B. _____ was a policy designed to improve relations with the _____ and _____

C. _____ was the plan for the gradual withdrawal of American troops and for the _____ army to assume more of the fighting.

II. Turmoil at Home Continues

A. In 1968 an American platoon under the command of _____ massacred unarmed South Vietnamese in the hamlet of _____

B. In April 1969 _____

Profiles IN HISTORY

Have students make a list of the qualities essential to a hero.

📁 Use *Supreme Court Case Study 45,* New York Times v. United States.

✓ Reading Check

Answer: that the government had not been honest with them about Vietnam

3 ASSESS

Assign Section 4 Assessment as homework or as an in-class activity.

🔘 Have students use the **Interactive Tutor Self-Assessment CD-ROM.**

The Pentagon Papers In addition to sparking violence on campuses, the invasion of Cambodia cost Nixon significant congressional support. Numerous legislators expressed outrage over the president's failure to notify them of the action. In December 1970, an angry Congress repealed the Gulf of Tonkin Resolution, which had given the president near complete power in directing the war in Vietnam.

Support for the war weakened further in 1971 when Daniel Ellsberg, a disillusioned former Defense Department worker, leaked what became known as the **Pentagon Papers** to the *New York Times.* The documents revealed that many government officials during the Johnson administration privately questioned the war while publicly defending it.

The documents contained details of decisions that were made by the presidents and their advisers without the consent of Congress. They also showed how the various administrations acted to deceive Congress, the press, and the public about the situation in Vietnam. The Pentagon Papers confirmed what many Americans had long believed: The government had not been honest with them.

✓ Reading Check **Evaluating** What did the Pentagon Papers confirm for many Americans?

The United States Pulls Out of Vietnam

By 1971 polls showed that nearly two-thirds of Americans wanted to end the Vietnam War as quickly as possible. In April 1972, President Nixon dropped his longtime insistence that North Vietnamese troops had to withdraw from South Vietnam before any peace treaty could be signed. In October, less than a month before the 1972 presidential election, Henry Kissinger emerged from his secret talks with Le Duc Tho to announce that "peace is at hand."

A month later, Americans went to the polls to decide on a president. Senator George McGovern, the

Profiles IN HISTORY

Roy P. Benavidez
1935–1998

Roy P. Benavidez received the Medal of Honor, the nation's highest award for heroism, for his actions in the Vietnam War. Growing up, Benavidez worked on the streets selling empty soda bottles and cleaning a local stockyard. His father's family had been *vaqueros* (cowboys from Mexico), immigrating in the 1830s during the Texas War for Independence. His mother, a Yaqui Native American, was born in northern Mexico. Both parents died by the time Benavidez was seven, and he was raised by his uncle.

A tough life made Benavidez a fighter. In May 1968 while fighting in Vietnam, Benavidez rescued members of his Special Forces group who were surrounded by the enemy. Wounded three times while getting to the men by helicopter, he stayed with them some eight hours, preparing an evacuation. Then while carrying the men to the rescue helicopters, he was attacked from behind but managed to kill his attacker. Only after loading all the dead and wounded did Benavidez himself board a helicopter.

Democratic candidate, was an outspoken critic of the war. He did not appeal to many middle-class Americans, however, who were tired of antiwar protesters. When the votes were cast, Nixon won re-election in a landslide.

The Two Sides Reach Peace Just weeks after the presidential election, the peace negotiations broke down. South Vietnam's president, **Nguyen Van Thieu,** refused to agree to any plan that left North Vietnamese troops in the South. Kissinger tried to win additional concessions from the Communists, but talks broke off in mid-December.

The next day, to force North Vietnam to resume negotiations, the Nixon administration began the most destructive air raids of the entire war. In what became known as the "Christmas bombings," American B-52s dropped thousands of tons of bombs on North Vietnamese targets for 12 straight days, pausing only on Christmas day.

In the wake of the bombing campaign, the United States and North Vietnam returned to the bargaining table. Thieu finally gave in to American pressure and allowed North Vietnamese troops to remain in the South. On January 27, 1973, the warring sides signed an agreement "ending the war and restoring the peace in Vietnam."

DIFFERENTIATED INSTRUCTION

Reading Support Bring to class a recording of Bob Dylan's song "Blowin' in the Wind." As you play the recording, have students summarize what the lyrics are saying. Then have them write why the music helps convey the message of the lyrics. Finally, have students write a poem or song highlighting the fact that more than 58,000 Americans died or went missing in action in Vietnam. **L2**

📁 Refer to *Inclusion for the High School Social Studies Classroom Strategies and Activities* in the TCR.

The United States promised to withdraw the rest of its troops, and both sides agreed to an exchange of prisoners of war. The parties did not resolve the issue of South Vietnam's future, however. After almost eight years of war—the longest war in American history—the nation ended its direct involvement in Vietnam.

South Vietnam Falls

The United States had barely pulled out its last troops from Vietnam when the peace agreement collapsed. In March 1975, the North Vietnamese army launched a full-scale invasion of the South. Thieu desperately appealed to Washington, D.C., for help.

President Nixon had assured Thieu during the peace negotiations that the United States "[would] respond with full force should the settlement be violated by North Vietnam." Nixon, however, had resigned under pressure following the Watergate scandal. The new president, Gerald Ford, asked for funds to aid the South Vietnamese, but Congress refused.

On April 30, the North Vietnamese captured Saigon, South Vietnam's capital, and united Vietnam under Communist rule. They then renamed Saigon Ho Chi Minh City.

Reading Check **Explaining** Why did the peace talks break down in December 1972?

The Legacy of Vietnam

"The lessons of the past in Vietnam," President Ford declared in 1975, "have already been learned—learned by Presidents, learned by Congress, learned by the American people—and we should have our focus on the future." Although Americans tried to put the war behind them, Vietnam left a deep and lasting impact on American society.

The War's Human Toll The United States paid a heavy price for its involvement in Vietnam. The war had cost the nation over $170 billion in direct costs and much more in indirect economic expenses. More significantly, it had resulted in the deaths of approximately 58,000 young Americans and the injury of more than 300,000. In Vietnam, around one million North and South Vietnamese soldiers died in the conflict, as did countless civilians.

Even after they returned home from fighting, some American veterans, as in other wars, found it hard to escape the war's psychological impact. Army Specialist Doug Johnson recalled the problems he faced on returning home:

❝It took a while for me to recognize that I did suffer some psychological problems in trying to deal with my experience in Vietnam. The first recollection I have of the effect took place shortly after I arrived back in the States. One evening . . . I went to see a movie on post. I don't recall the name of the movie or what it was about, but I remember there was a sad part, and that I started crying uncontrollably. It hadn't dawned on me before this episode that I had . . . succeeded in burying my emotions.❞

—quoted in *Touched by the Dragon*

One reason it may have been harder for some Vietnam veterans to readjust to civilian life was that many considered the war a defeat. Many Americans wanted to forget the war. Thus, the sacrifices of many veterans often went unrecognized. There were relatively few welcome-home parades and celebrations after the war.

The war also lingered for the American families whose relatives and friends were classified as

Desperate Pleas When President Ford ordered all Americans to leave Vietnam immediately in April 1975, many Saigon residents stormed the U.S. embassy pleading for rescue. When did the North Vietnamese take control of Saigon?

Reading Check

Answer: Kissinger tried to win additional concessions.

Picturing **History**

Answer: April 30, 1975

FYI

Ho Chi Minh City (formerly Saigon) proclaimed 1990 its "Year of Tourism." The tunnels once used for the Vietcong guerrillas—a network of 200 miles—were one of the featured tourist attractions.

History *and the* Humanities

American Art & Architecture: Vietnam Veterans Memorial

INTERDISCIPLINARY CONNECTIONS ACTIVITY

Language Arts Have students write a newspaper or magazine article based on an interview with someone in their community who was a young adult at the time of the Vietnam War. To prepare for the interview, encourage students to use library and Internet resources to learn more about what was going on in their community at the time of the war. Have interested students combine the articles into a publication. **L2**

HISTORY Online

Objectives and answers to the student activity can be found in the **Web Activity Lesson Plan** at tarvol2.glencoe.com.

World Geography Connection

Answer: Many Americans felt responsible for the refugees' plight.

Reading Check

Answer: became more reluctant to intervene in other countries' affairs

Reteach
Have students explain the events of Nixon's first administration.

Enrich
Have students tell the story of the Vietnam War by reading articles on the war using library and Internet resources.

HISTORY Online

Study Central™ provides summaries, interactive games, and online graphic organizers to help students review section content.

4 CLOSE

Have students summarize the lessons of the Vietnam War.

---

prisoners of war (POWs) or missing in action (MIA). Despite many official investigations, these families were not convinced that the government had told the truth about POW/MIA policies in the last years of the war.

The nation finally began to come to terms with the war almost a decade later. In 1982 the nation dedicated the Vietnam Veterans Memorial in Washington, D.C., a large black stone wall inscribed with the names of those killed and missing in action in the war. "It's a first step to remind America of what we did," veteran Larry Cox of Virginia said at the dedication of the monument.

GOVERNMENT

The War's Impact on the Nation The war also left its mark on the nation as a whole. In 1973 Congress passed the **War Powers Act** as a way to reestablish some limits on executive power. The act required the president to inform Congress of any commitment of troops abroad within 48 hours and to withdraw them in 60 to 90 days unless Congress explicitly approved the troop commitment.

The legislation addresses the struggle between the executive and legislative branches over what checks and balances are proper in matters of war and foreign policy. No president has recognized this limitation, and the courts have tended to avoid the issue as a strictly political question. In general, the war shook the nation's confidence and led some to embrace a new kind of isolationism. In the years after the war, many Americans became more reluctant to intervene in the affairs of other nations.

On the domestic front, the Vietnam War increased Americans' cynicism about their government. Many felt the nation's leaders had misled them. Together with Watergate, a scandal that broke as the war was winding down, Vietnam made Americans more wary of their leaders.

HISTORY Online
Student Web Activity Visit the *American Republic Since 1877* Web site at tarvol2.glencoe.com and click on *Student Web Activities—Chapter 25* for an activity on the Vietnam War.

Reading Check **Describing** How did the Vietnam War affect Americans' attitudes toward international conflicts?

World Geography Connection

The War's Refugees
Another of the Vietnam War's enduring legacies was the wave of human migration and resettlement it prompted. From the mid-1970s through the 1980s, between 1.5 and 2 million people fled the newly installed Communist regimes in Vietnam, Cambodia, and Laos. These men, women, and children became known as "boat people" because their main route of escape was by sea. More than half of these refugees came to the United States. Between 1980 and 1990, the Vietnamese population of the United States more than doubled from about 245,000 to almost 615,000. *Why do you think the United States was willing to accept so many refugees from the Vietnam War?*

HISTORY Online **Study Central**™ To review this section, go to tarvol2.glencoe.com and click on **Study Central**™.

SECTION 4 ASSESSMENT

Checking for Understanding
1. **Define:** linkage, Vietnamization.
2. **Identify:** Henry Kissinger, Pentagon Papers, War Powers Act.
3. **Describe** what happened in Vietnam in 1975 after the United States withdrew.

Reviewing Themes
4. **Government and Democracy** Why did Congress pass the War Powers Act? How did this act reflect a struggle between the legislative and executive branches?

Critical Thinking
5. **Analyzing** Why did the invasion of Cambodia cost President Nixon congressional support?
6. **Organizing** Use a graphic organizer similar to the one below to list the effects of the Vietnam War on the nation.

Effects of Vietnam War

Analyzing Visuals
7. **Analyzing Photographs** Study the photograph on page 793 of South Vietnamese citizens attempting to enter the U.S. embassy. How do you think this image affected American attitudes toward the war? Why do you think so?

Writing About History
8. **Descriptive Writing** Imagine that you are a college student in 1970. Write a journal entry expressing your feelings about the events at Kent State University and Jackson State College.

SECTION 4 ASSESSMENT ANSWERS

1. Terms are in blue.
2. Kissinger *(p. 790)*, Pentagon Papers *(p. 792)*, War Powers Act *(p. 794)*
3. North Vietnam took control of South Vietnam, uniting the two countries under Communist rule.
4. to limit executive power; reflected the struggle over checks and balances in war and foreign policy between the executive and legislative branches
5. Nixon failed to notify Congress of this action in advance, costing him congressional support.
6. American cynicism toward government, war dead and casualties, cost, and War Powers Act
7. Answers will vary. Responses could include relief at getting out of the war or guilt for leaving allies behind.
8. Journal entries should focus on feelings.

SKILLBUILDER

Conducting an Interview

Why Learn This Skill?

Suppose that your friends went to see a concert, but you were unable to attend. How would you find out how the show was?

Learning the Skill

You probably would not normally think of asking your friends questions about a concert as conducting an interview, but that is exactly what you are doing. Interviews are an excellent way of collecting important facts and opinions from people. Interviews allow you to gather information from people who witnessed or participated in an event firsthand. For example, William Prochnau interviewed many different people and used the results to write his book *Once Upon a Distant War,* which examines the way the press covered the Vietnam War. To conduct an interview with someone, follow these steps.

- **Make an appointment.** Contact the person and explain why you want to conduct the interview, what kinds of things you hope to learn, and how you will use the information. Discuss where and when you will conduct the interview, and ask if you may use a tape recorder.

- **Gather background information.** Find out about the education, career, and other accomplishments of the person you want to interview. Research the topics you wish to discuss.

- **Prepare questions.** Group questions into subject categories. Begin each category with general questions and move toward more specific questions. Formulate each question carefully. If the answer could be simply yes or no, rephrase the question.

- **Conduct the interview.** Introduce yourself and restate the purpose of the interview. Ask questions and record responses accurately. Ask follow-up questions to fill gaps in information.

- **Transcribe the interview.** Convert your written or tape-recorded notes into a *transcript,* a written record of the interview presented in a question-and-answer format.

Practicing the Skill

Imagine you are assigned to interview someone who participated in or is old enough to remember the events that occurred during the Vietnam War.

❶ What kind of background information might you gather?

❷ What are some broad categories of questions you might ask based on what you know about the person you are interviewing and what you know about the war?

❸ What are some general questions you might want to ask within these broad categories? Consider the responses you might get to these general questions, and formulate follow-up questions for each.

Skills Assessment

Complete the Practicing Skills questions on page 797 and the Chapter 25 Skill Reinforcement Activity to assess your mastery of this skill.

> ### Applying the Skill
>
> **Conducting an Interview** The Vietnam War probably included some people you know—your parents, grandparents, aunts, uncles, or neighbors. Even if they were not directly involved with the conflict, they probably remember what the United States was like during the war. Use the questions you developed above to interview one or more of these people. Ask about their experiences regarding Vietnam, including their attitudes toward the war and its many related issues, past and present. Summarize your findings in a short report or in a comparison chart.
>
> Glencoe's **Skillbuilder Interactive Workbook CD-ROM, Level 2,** provides instruction and practice in key social studies skills.

795

Social Studies

SKILLBUILDER

TEACH

Conducting an Interview
Review the steps students will use to conduct successful interviews. Remind students that interviews become primary sources.

Encourage students to use the list of steps to create an interview checklist that they can use for each interview they conduct.

Additional Practice

L1

Reinforcing Skills Activity 25

Name _____ Date _____ Class _____

★ **Reinforcing Skills Activity 25**

Conducting an Interview

☐ **LEARNING THE SKILL**
An interview can provide firsthand and personal information you may not be able to find in a book or magazine. To begin the interview process, first contact the person you want to interview. Let them know about the purpose of the interview, and make arrangements for your meeting. Before you meet, find out as much as you can about the interviewee and about the topics you plan to discuss. Also prepare and organize your questions. As you begin your interview, introduce yourself. Listen carefully, ask additional questions for detail, and record responses. After the interview, convert your notes into a transcript.

☐ **PRACTICING THE SKILL**
DIRECTIONS: Select a person from the Vietnam War era to research. Imagine that you have the opportunity to interview this person.

GLENCOE
TECHNOLOGY

CD-ROM
Glencoe Skillbuilder Interactive Workbook CD-ROM, Level 2

This interactive CD-ROM reinforces student mastery of essential social studies skills.

ANSWERS TO PRACTICING THE SKILL

Students should review information on the war. Questions might be: for 2, what subjects did during the war, their attitude to the war; for 3, what factors influenced their attitude, if the war affected their friends or family, how they now see the war.

Applying the Skill
Students' reports will vary depending on the people interviewed and their recollections of the war. Remind students that their reports are to summarize their findings, not merely to present a transcript of the interview.

CHAPTER
25 ASSESSMENT and ACTIVITIES

GLENCOE TECHNOLOGY

MindJogger Videoquiz

Use the **MindJogger Videoquiz** to review Chapter 25 content.

Available in DVD

Reviewing Key Terms

Students' answers will vary. The pages where the words appear in the text are shown in parentheses.

1. **domino theory** (p. 774)
2. **guerrilla** (p. 774)
3. **Vietcong** (p. 777)
4. **napalm** (p. 780)
5. **credibility gap** (p. 785)
6. **teach-in** (p. 785)
7. **dove** (p. 787)
8. **hawk** (p. 787)
9. **linkage** (p. 790)
10. **Vietnamization** (p. 791)

Reviewing Key Facts

11. Ho Chi Minh (p. 773), Tet offensive (p. 787)

12. President Eisenhower defended involvement in Vietnam by stressing the domino theory and the need to stop the spread of communism.

13. The number of military personnel began to increase significantly in 1963 during the Kennedy administration.

14. The peasants resented being uprooted from their villages and family farms and resettled in strategic hamlets.

15. Ngo Dinh Diem was unpopular due to the strategic hamlet policy and his discrimination against Buddhism.

16. The Tet offensive began to turn American public opinion against the war. Mainstream media began to

---

Reviewing Key Terms

On a sheet of paper, use each of these terms in a sentence.

1. domino theory
2. guerrilla
3. Vietcong
4. napalm
5. credibility gap
6. teach-in
7. dove
8. hawk
9. linkage
10. Vietnamization

Chapter Summary

American Involvement in Vietnam

Roots of the Conflict

- Eisenhower financially supported French war against Vietnam
- Geneva Accords established North and South Vietnam
- U.S.-backed leader of South Vietnam refused national elections, fearing defeat by Communist opponent
- Kennedy sharply increased military aid and presence in South Vietnam
- Johnson escalated U.S. involvement and gained war powers after the incident in the Gulf of Tonkin

Full-Scale War

- President Johnson responded to a Vietcong attack with aggressive airstrikes; American people applauded his actions
- U.S. committed over 380,000 ground troops to fighting in Vietnam by the end of 1966

Opposition to the War

- American people questioned the government's honesty about the war, creating the so-called "credibility gap"
- Wartime economy hurt domestic spending efforts
- President Nixon was elected largely on promises to end the war and unite the divided country

The End of the War

- Nixon withdrew troops but increased airstrikes
- American troops pulled out after a 1973 peace agreement
- Congress passed the War Powers Act to limit the power of the president during times of war

---

Reviewing Key Facts

11. **Identify:** Ho Chi Minh, Tet offensive.

12. How did President Eisenhower defend American policy in Vietnam?

13. When did the number of American military personnel begin to increase in Vietnam?

14. How did Vietnamese peasants respond to the strategic hamlets program?

15. What actions made Ngo Dinh Diem an unpopular leader in South Vietnam?

16. What was the effect of the Tet offensive on Americans?

17. How did Richard Nixon benefit from the chaos in the nation in 1968?

18. What did the Pentagon Papers reveal?

Critical Thinking

19. **Analyzing Themes: Civic Rights and Responsibilities** How did Americans show their frustration with the direction the country was taking in 1968?

20. **Analyzing** How do you think the use of chemicals such as Agent Orange and napalm by the United States affected Vietnamese feelings toward Americans and the war?

21. **Organizing** Use a graphic organizer to list the reasons the United States became involved in Vietnam and the effects the war had on the nation.

22. **Interpreting Primary Sources** In the 1960s many young Americans enlisted or were drafted for military service. Some believed they had a duty to serve their country. Many had no clear idea of what they were doing or why. In the following excerpt, a young man interviewed for Mark Baker's book *Nam* presents his thoughts about going to war.

    ❝I read a lot of pacifist literature to determine whether or not I was a conscientious objector. I finally concluded that I wasn't. . . .

    The one clear decision I made in 1968 about me and the war was that if I was going to get out of it, I was going to get out in a legal way. I was not going to defraud the system in order to beat the system. I wasn't going to leave the country, because the odds of coming back looked real slim. . . .

---

criticize the war and Johnson decided not to run for another term as president.

17. Violence and chaos associated with the Democratic National Convention in the 1968 election benefited Republican candidate Richard Nixon.

18. The Pentagon Papers revealed that U.S. government officials had not been honest about the war's progress.

Critical Thinking

19. They elected Nixon, participated in violence, and protested.

20. Since the chemicals turned farmland and forest into wasteland, it made the Vietnamese more anti-American.

HISTORY Online

Self-Check Quiz

Visit the *American Republic Since 1877* Web site at tarvol2.glencoe.com and click on *Self-Check Quizzes—Chapter 25* to assess your knowledge of chapter content.

With all my terror of going into the Army . . . there was something seductive about it, too. I was seduced by World War II and John Wayne movies. . . . I had been, as we all were, victimized by a romantic, truly uninformed view of war. 99

—quoted in *Nam*

a. What options did the young man have regarding going to war?

b. Do you think World War II movies gave him a realistic view of what fighting in Vietnam would be like?

Practicing Skills

23. **Conducting an Interview** Review the material on page 795 about interviewing. Then follow these steps to prepare for an interview with President Johnson on his Vietnam policies.
   a. Study Section 2 of this chapter on the president's Vietnam policies and conduct library or Internet research on this subject.
   b. Prepare a list of 10 questions to ask the president.

Geography and History

24. The map on this page shows supply routes and troop movements during the Vietnam War. Study the map and answer the questions below.
   a. **Interpreting Maps** What nations besides North and South Vietnam were the sites of battles or invasions?
   b. **Analyzing** Why did the Ho Chi Minh Trail pass through Laos and Cambodia instead of South Vietnam?

Chapter Activity

25. **Evaluating Bias** A person's life experiences often influence his or her arguments one way or another, creating a biased opinion. Reread the speeches in Different Viewpoints on pages 778–779. What might have influenced the points of view of George Ball and George Kennan? Create a cause-and-effect chart showing possible reasons for their biases and effects their experiences have had on their political opinions.

Writing Activity

26. **Portfolio Writing** Many songs and pieces of literature have been written on the Vietnam War. Find examples of these. Then write an original poem or song lyrics in which you present antiwar or pro-war sentiments about the Vietnam War. Include your work in your portfolio.

NATIONAL GEOGRAPHIC **The Vietnam War**

Major U.S. and South Vietnamese troop movements

Major North Vietnamese supply lines

■ U.S. bases

CHINA
Dien Bien Phu
Hanoi
Haiphong
LAOS
NORTH VIETNAM
Gulf of Tonkin
20°N
Khe Sanh
THAILAND
Invasion of Laos Feb. 8–March, 1971
Demilitarized Zone
17th Parallel
Quang Tri
Hue
Da Nang
Da Nang
Tam Ky
Chu Lai
My Lai Massacre March 16, 1968
Ho Chi Minh Trail
Pleiku
Qui Nhon
CAMBODIA
SOUTH VIETNAM
Ban Me Thuot
Invasion of Cambodia May I–June 29, 1970
Nha Trang
Phnom Penh
Phoc Binh
Gulf of Thailand
Saigon
Long Binh
Can Tho
Mekong Delta
— South —10°N
China Sea
Khanh Hung
0   150 miles
0   150 kilometers
Miller Cylindrical projection
110°E
Quan Long

Standardized Test Practice

Directions: Choose the phrase that best completes the following statement.

The purpose of the War Powers Act was to ensure that the president would

A have greater authority over the military.

B consult Congress before committing troops to extended conflicts.

C have the authority to sign treaties without Senate approval.

D have a freer hand in fighting the spread of communism.

Test-Taking Tip: After Vietnam and Watergate, Congress wanted legislation to limit the president's power during wartime. Three of the answers actually do the opposite, giving the president *more* power. You can eliminate these three answers.

HISTORY Online

Have students visit the Web site at tarvol2.glencoe.com to review Chapter 25 and take the Self-Check Quiz.

Chapter Activity

25. Students' charts will vary. Students should focus on the official positions of Ball and Kennan as part of the causes for their bias.

Writing Activity

26. Students' poems or songs will vary. Encourage students to write from the perspective of a young person living during the Vietnam War era.

Standardized Test Practice

Answer: B
Test-Taking Tip: Encourage students to consider which answers would give the president more power by looking for comparative adjectives. For example, answer C mentions "greater authority" and answer D states "freer hand." The correct answer is B.

Bonus Question ?

Ask: What is the name of the university in Ohio where four students were killed by National Guard troops? *(Kent State University)*

---

21. causes: fall of China to communism and the outbreak of the Korean War; effects: cynicism toward government, casualties and war dead, cost, protests, War Powers Act

22. **a.** He could declare he was a conscientious objector, he could avoid service in a legal way, he could leave the country, or he could fight. **b.** No, he realized that the view of war presented in movies had been romanticized.

Practicing Skills

23. Students' lists of questions will vary but should focus on the president's policies.

Geography and History

24. **a.** Laos and Cambodia were also invaded. **b.** The Ho Chi Minh Trail passed through Laos and Cambodia to avoid discovery and capture of troops and supplies passing along the trail.

Chapter 26 Resources

Timesaving Tools

TeacherWorks™ All-In-One Planner and Resource Center

- **Interactive Teacher Edition** Access your Teacher Wraparound Edition and your classroom resources with a few easy clicks.
- **Interactive Lesson Planner** Planning has never been easier! Organize your week, month, semester, or year with all the lesson helps you need to make teaching creative, timely, and relevant.

Use Glencoe's **Presentation Plus!** multimedia teacher tool to easily present dynamic lessons that visually excite your students. Using Microsoft PowerPoint® you can customize the presentations to create your own personalized lessons.

TEACHING TRANSPARENCIES

Graphic Organizer 11 L2

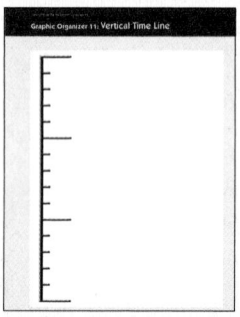

Why It Matters Chapter Transparency 26 L2

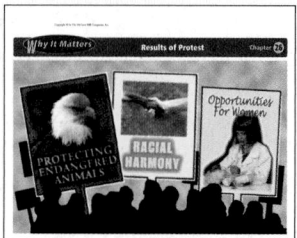

APPLICATION AND ENRICHMENT

Linking Past and Present Activity 26 L2

Enrichment Activity 26 L3

Primary Source Reading 26 L2

REVIEW AND REINFORCEMENT

Reteaching Activity 26 L1

Vocabulary Activity 26 L1

Time Line Activity 26 L2

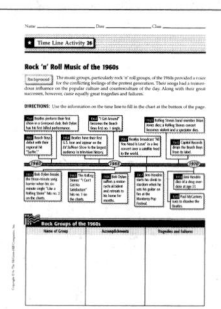

Critical Thinking Skills Activity 26 L2

Meeting NCSS Standards

The following standards are covered in Chapter 26:

Section 1	VI	Power, Authority, and Governance: A, D, F, H
Section 2	X	Civic Ideals and Practices: A, D, E, F, G, I
Section 3	X	Civic Ideals and Practices: A, D, E, F, G, I
Section 4	V	Individuals, Groups, and Institutions: B, E, F, G

Local Standards

Chapter 26 Resources

Chapter 26 Test Form A L2

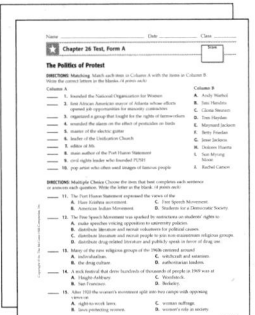

Chapter 26 Test Form B L2

Standardized Test Practice Workbook Activity 26 L2

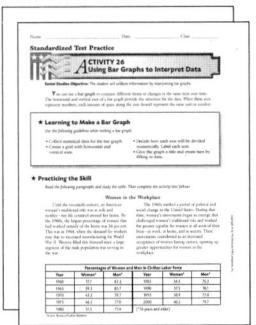

Performance Assessment Activities and Rubrics 26 L1/ELL

ExamView® Pro Testmaker CD-ROM

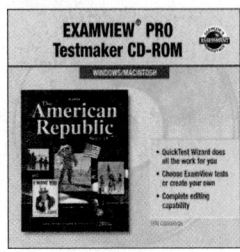

MULTIMEDIA

- Vocabulary PuzzleMaker CD-ROM
- Interactive Tutor Self-Assessment CD-ROM
- ExamView® Pro Testmaker CD-ROM
- Audio Program
- American History Primary Source Documents Library CD-ROM
- MindJogger Videoquiz
- Presentation Plus! CD-ROM
- TeacherWorks™ CD-ROM
- Interactive Student Edition CD-ROM
- Glencoe Skillbuilder Interactive Workbook CD-ROM, Level 2
- The *American Republic Since 1877* Video Program
- American Music: Hits Through History
- American Music: Cultural Traditions

SPANISH RESOURCES

The following Spanish resources are available:

- Spanish Reading Essentials and Study Guide
- Spanish Guided Reading Activities
- Spanish Reteaching Activities
- Spanish Quizzes and Tests
- Spanish Vocabulary Activities
- Spanish Summaries
- The Declaration of Independence and United States Constitution Spanish Translation

THE HISTORY CHANNEL®

The following videotape program is available from Glencoe as a supplement to Chapter 26:

- **Gloria Steinem: Ms. America** (ISBN 1-56-501518-5)

To order, call Glencoe at 1-800-334-7344. To find classroom resources to accompany many of these videos, check the following home pages:
A&E Television: www.aande.com
The History Channel: www.historychannel.com

Use our Web site for additional resources. All essential content is covered in the Student Edition.

You and your students can visit tarvol2.glencoe.com, the Web site companion to the *American Republic Since 1877.* This innovative integration of electronic and print media offers your students a wealth of opportunities. The student text directs students to the Web site for the following options:

- **Chapter Overviews**
- **Student Web Activities**
- **Self-Check Quizzes**
- **Textbook Updates**

Answers to the student Web activities are provided for you in the **Web Activity Lesson Plans.** Additional Web resources and Interactive Tutor Puzzles are also available.

Chapter 26 Resources

Daily Objectives	Reproducible Resources	Multimedia Resources
SECTION 1 **The Student Movement and the Counterculture** 1. Explain the origins of the nation's youth movement. 2. Define the goals of serious members of the counterculture.	Reproducible Lesson Plan 26–1 Daily Lecture and Discussion Notes 26–1 Guided Reading Activity 26–1* Section Quiz 26–1* Reading Essentials and Study Guide 26–1* Performance Assessment Activities and Rubrics	Daily Focus Skills Transparency 26–1 American Art & Architecture Interactive Tutor Self-Assessment CD-ROM ExamView® Pro Testmaker CD-ROM* Presentation Plus! CD-ROM TeacherWorks™ CD-ROM Audio Program American Music: Hits Through History
SECTION 2 **The Feminist Movement** 1. Describe the workplace concerns that fueled the growth of the women's movement. 2. Identify major achievements of the women's movement.	Reproducible Lesson Plan 26–2 Daily Lecture and Discussion Notes 26–2 Guided Reading Activity 26–2* Section Quiz 26–2* Reading Essentials and Study Guide 26–2* Performance Assessment Activities and Rubrics Interpreting Political Cartoons Supreme Court Case Studies	Daily Focus Skills Transparency 26–2 Interactive Tutor Self-Assessment CD-ROM ExamView® Pro Testmaker CD-ROM* Presentation Plus! CD-ROM TeacherWorks™ CD-ROM Audio Program
SECTION 3 **New Approaches to Civil Rights** 1. Describe the goal of affirmative action policies. 2. Analyze the rise of Hispanic and Native American protests.	Reproducible Lesson Plan 26–3 Daily Lecture and Discussion Notes 26–3 Guided Reading Activity 26–3* Section Quiz 26–3* Reading Essentials and Study Guide 26–3* Performance Assessment Activities and Rubrics Interpreting Political Cartoons Supreme Court Case Studies	Daily Focus Skills Transparency 26–3 Interactive Tutor Self-Assessment CD-ROM ExamView® Pro Testmaker CD-ROM* Presentation Plus! CD-ROM Skillbuilder Interactive Workbook, Level 2 TeacherWorks™ CD-ROM Audio Program
SECTION 4 **Saving the Earth** 1. Explain the origins of the environmental movement. 2. Identify the significant measures taken to combat environmental problems.	Reproducible Lesson Plan 26–4 Daily Lecture and Discussion Notes 26–4 Guided Reading Activity 26–4* Section Quiz 26–4* Reading Essentials and Study Guide 26–4* Performance Assessment Activities and Rubrics Interpreting Political Cartoons	Daily Focus Skills Transparency 26–4 American Art & Architecture Interactive Tutor Self-Assessment CD-ROM ExamView® Pro Testmaker CD-ROM* Presentation Plus! CD-ROM TeacherWorks™ CD-ROM Vocabulary PuzzleMaker CD-ROM Audio Program American Music: Hits Through History American Music: Cultural Traditions

0:00 OUT OF TIME?
Assign the Chapter 26 **Reading Essentials and Study Guide.**

*Also Available in Spanish

 Printed Materials   Transparency   CD-ROM   DVD

Poster   Music Program Audio Program

NATIONAL GEOGRAPHIC   Teacher's Corner

INDEX TO NATIONAL GEOGRAPHIC MAGAZINE

The following articles relate to this chapter.

- "Great Lakes: Troubled Water," July 1987
- "I Dream a World: America's Black Women," August 1989
- "Our Polluted Runoff," February 1996
- "Philadelphia's African Americans," August 1990

NATIONAL GEOGRAPHIC SOCIETY PRODUCTS

To order the following, call National Geographic at 1-800-368-2728:

- *Branches of Government Series* (Video)
- *Democratic Government Series: The United States* (Video)
- *Historical Atlas of the United States* (Atlas)
- *National Geographic World Atlas for Young Explorers— Classroom Library Edition* (Guide, Transparencies, Resource Masters)

NGS ONLINE

Access National Geographic's Web site for current events, atlas updates, activities, links, interactive features, and archives.

www.nationalgeographic.com

MEETING SPECIAL NEEDS

In addition to the Differentiated Instruction strategies found in each section, the following resources are also suitable for your special needs students:

- *ExamView® Pro Testmaker CD-ROM* allows teachers to tailor tests by reducing answer choices.

- The *Audio Program* includes the entire narrative of the student edition so that less-proficient readers can listen to the words as they read them.

KEY TO ABILITY LEVELS

Teaching strategies have been coded.

- **L1** BASIC activities for all students
- **L2** AVERAGE activities for average to above-average students
- **L3** CHALLENGING activities for above-average students
- **ELL** ENGLISH LANGUAGE LEARNER activities

From the Classroom of...

Daniel Levinson Wilk
District 78, New York City
Board of Education
New York, NY

Setting Goals

In preparation, have students read about social movements of the late 1960s and early 1970s. Assign each student a person from the reading and ask them to come to class in character. There should be a variety of characters: conservatives, liberals, and radicals.

In class, ask students to put on name tags and introduce themselves, each saying their name and describing their positions on major issues of the day. Then give them these directions: "Stand up, mill around, and talk to the other characters in the room. Decide whom you think you could build a political movement with. Sit down with them and build a set of goals for your movement and a strategy to achieve them." Allow at least 20 minutes for this.

Then call the students back into a larger group. Have one member of each movement present their goals and strategy, and allow other students (in character) to question the members of that movement. For the last few minutes of class, have students step out of character to discuss the exercise.

ADDITIONAL RESOURCES FROM GLENCOE

- American Music: Cultural Traditions
- American Art & Architecture
- Outline Map Resource Book
- U.S. Desk Map
- Building Geography Skills for Life
- Inclusion for the High School Social Studies Classroom Strategies and Activities
- Teaching Strategies for the American History Classroom (Including Block Scheduling Pacing Guides)
- Dinah Zike's High School American History Reading and Study Skills Foldables

Block Schedule

Activities that are suited to use within the block scheduling framework are identified by:

Performance Assessment

Refer to Activity 26 in the Performance Assessment Activities and Rubrics booklet.

Why It Matters Activity

Have students make a prediction about how the efforts of the protesters in the 1960s and 1970s continue to influence the workplace and economic opportunities of women and ethnic groups today. Students should evaluate their answers after they have completed the chapter.

GLENCOE
TECHNOLOGY

The American Republic Since 1877 Video Program
To learn more about César Chávez, have students view the Chapter 26 video, "Behind the Scenes with César," from the *American Republic Since 1877* Video Program.

MindJogger Videoquiz
Use the **MindJogger Videoquiz** to preview Chapter 26 content.

 Both programs available in DVD

CHAPTER

26 The Politics of Protest *1960–1980*

Why It Matters

Protest characterized the 1960s. Young people often led the civil rights and antiwar movements. Some of them wanted to change the entire society and urged more communal, less materialistic values. Young people were not the only protesters, however. Using the civil rights movement as a model, women, Hispanic Americans, and Native Americans also organized to gain greater recognition and equality.

The Impact Today

Changes of the 1960s still affect our lives today.
* *Women are visible in many more leadership roles in government and business.*
* *Hispanic political organizations represent a growing segment of the population.*
* *The cultural traditions of Native Americans receive greater recognition.*

 The American Republic Since 1877 Video The Chapter 26 video, "Behind the Scenes with César," profiles the role that César Chávez played in the United Farm Workers organization.

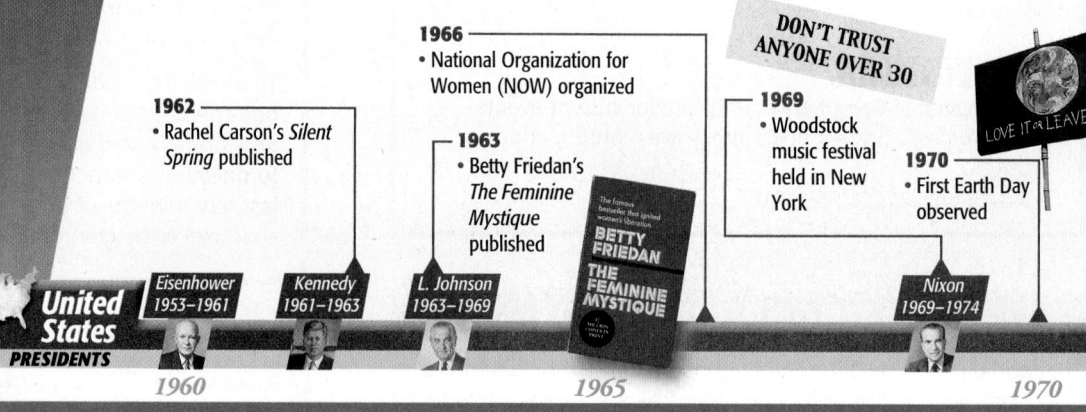

1962
* Rachel Carson's *Silent Spring* published

1963
* Betty Friedan's *The Feminine Mystique* published

1966
* National Organization for Women (NOW) organized

DON'T TRUST ANYONE OVER 30

1969
* Woodstock music festival held in New York

LOVE IT or LEAVE IT

1970
* First Earth Day observed

United States PRESIDENTS

Eisenhower 1953–1961 | Kennedy 1961–1963 | L. Johnson 1963–1969 | Nixon 1969–1974

1960 | 1965 | 1970

World

1962
* China and Soviet Union have diplomatic disagreements

1964
* China becomes world's fifth nuclear power

1966
* Indira Gandhi becomes prime minister of India

1968
* Soviet Union halts democratic uprising in Czechoslovakia

798

Reading Strategy PURPOSE FOR READING

Brainstorming and One-Sentence Summaries Students can represent many ideas in a concise manner by using this strategy. On a large sheet of flip chart paper, brainstorm with students on the qualities of a leader. After 3 to 5 minutes, ask students to write a one-sentence summary of the list, in 15 words or less, based on the following model: *A leader is a person who . . .* **L1**

Refer to *Inclusion for the High School Social Studies Classroom Strategies and Activities* in the TCR.

Labor leader César Chávez meeting with farmworkers

HISTORY
Online

Introduce students to chapter content and key terms by having them access the **Chapter 26 Overview** at tarvol2.glencoe.com.

More About the Photo

César Chávez was born in 1927, on a small farm near Yuma, Arizona. When his father lost his land during the Depression, Chávez began working as a migrant farmworker to help support the family. After serving in the navy during World War II, he returned to farm labor. Soon he became committed to improving the lives of farmworkers. For his leadership, he received the Presidential Medal of Freedom.

1972
• Use of pesticide DDT banned

1973
• Supreme Court issues *Roe* v. *Wade* ruling
• AIM and government clash at Wounded Knee, South Dakota

1979
• Nuclear accident at Three Mile Island

Ford
1974–1977

Carter
1977–1981

1975   *1980*

1972
• Britain imposes direct rule on Northern Ireland

1975
• End of the Portuguese empires in Africa

1979
• Ayatollah Khomeini leads Islamic overthrow of Iran

HISTORY
Online

Chapter Overview
Visit the *American Republic Since 1877* Web site at tarvol2.glencoe.com and click on *Chapter Overviews— Chapter 26* to preview chapter information.

799

TIME LINE
ACTIVITY

Have students classify each of the relevant events on the United States portion of the time line as connected with the efforts of one of the following groups: Hispanics, women, environmentalists, or Native Americans.

FOLDABLES
Study Organizer

Dinah Zike's Foldables are three-dimensional, interactive graphic organizers that help students practice basic writing skills, review key vocabulary terms, and identify main ideas. Have students complete the foldable activity in the *Dinah Zike's Reading and Study Skills Foldables* booklet.

GRAPHIC ORGANIZER ACTIVITY

Organizing Information Have students use graphic organizers similar to the one below to identify the causes and effects of each of the major movements discussed in the chapter.

Cause		Effect
• *threats to cultural identity* • *joblessness* • *discrimination*	**Native American Rights Movement** →	• *Indian Civil Rights Act* • *Indian Self-Determination and Educational Assistance Act* • *increased land and water rights*

799

1 FOCUS

Section Overview

This section focuses on student protests in the 1960s.

Project transparency and have students answer the question.

Daily Focus Skills Transparency 26–1

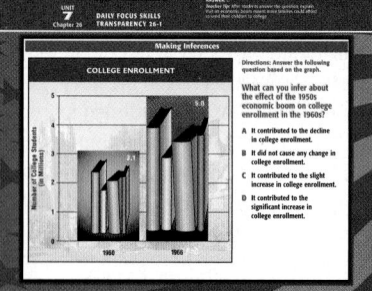

Reading Preview

Answers to Graphic:
I. The Growth of the Youth Movement
   A. The Roots of the Movement
   B. Students for a Democratic Society
   C. The Free Speech Movement
II. The Counterculture
   A. Hippie Culture
   B. New Religious Movements
   C. The Counterculture Declines
III. Impact of the Counterculture
   A. Fashion
   B. Art
   C. Music and Dance

Preteaching Vocabulary
Have students write short sentences to describe each of the Key Terms and Names.

The Student Movement and the Counterculture

Guide to Reading

Main Idea
During the 1960s, many of the country's young people raised their voices in protest against numerous aspects of American society.

Key Terms and Names
Port Huron Statement, Tom Hayden, counterculture, commune, Haight-Ashbury district, Jimi Hendrix

Reading Strategy
Taking Notes As you read about the student movement and culture of the 1960s, use the major headings of the section to create an outline similar to the one below.

The Student Movement and the Counterculture
I. The Growth of the Youth Movement
   A.
   B.
   C.
II.
   A.
   B.

Reading Objectives
• **Explain** the origins of the nation's youth movement.
• **Define** the goals of serious members of the counterculture.

Section Theme
Government and Democracy Although protest movements often challenged the opinions and values of many Americans, the courts protected the protesters' rights of self-expression under the Constitution.

Preview of Events

♦1961   ♦1964   ♦1967   ♦1970

1962
Students for a Democratic Society deliver Port Huron Statement

1964
Free Speech Movement begins; the Beatles embark on their first U.S. tour

August, 1969
400,000 young people gather at Woodstock music festival

⋆ *An American Story* ⋆

Mario Savio

On December 2, 1964, Mario Savio, a 20-year-old philosophy student at the University of California at Berkeley, stood before a supportive crowd at the school's administration building. The massive "sit-in" demonstration was the climax of a month-long battle between school officials and students over unpopular campus policies. Facing the crowd, Savio urged them to continue pressuring school officials. In his speech he called the university a cold and heartless "machine" that deserved to be shut down.

❝There's a time when the operation of the machine becomes so odious, makes you so sick at heart, that you . . . can't even tacitly take part," he declared. "And you've got to put your bodies upon the gears and upon the wheels . . . you've got to make it stop. And you've got to indicate to the people who run it, to the people who own it, that unless you're free the machine will be prevented from working at all.❞

—quoted in *Decade of Shocks*

The Growth of the Youth Movement

The 1960s was one of the most tumultuous and chaotic decades in United States history. The decade also gave birth to a conspicuous youth movement, which challenged the American political and social system and conventional middle-class values. Perhaps no other time in the nation's history witnessed such protest.

SECTION RESOURCES

📂 **Reproducible Masters**
• Reproducible Lesson Plan 26–1
• Daily Lecture and Discussion Notes 26–1
• Guided Reading Activity 26–1
• Section Quiz 26–1
• Reading Essentials and Study Guide 26–1
• Performance Assessment Activities and Rubrics

📔 **Transparencies**
• Daily Focus Skills Transparency 26–1

Multimedia
💿 Interactive Tutor Self-Assessment CD-ROM
💿 ExamView® Pro Testmaker CD-ROM
💿 Presentation Plus! CD-ROM
💿 TeacherWorks™ CD-ROM
🔊 Audio Program

The Roots of the Movement The roots of the 1960s youth movement stretched back to the 1950s. In the decade after World War II, the nation's economy boomed, and much of the country enjoyed a time of peace and prosperity. Prosperity did not extend to all, however, and some, especially the artists and writers of the "beat" movement, had openly criticized American society. They believed it valued conformity over independence and financial gain over spiritual and social advancement. Meanwhile, such events as the growing nuclear arms race between the United States and the Soviet Union made many more of the nation's youth uneasy about their future. Writer Todd Gitlin, who was a senior at the Bronx High School of Science in 1959, recalls the warning that the editors of his student yearbook delivered.

> ❝In today's atomic age . . . the flames of war would write *finis* not only to our civilization, but to our very existence. Mankind may find itself unable to rise again should it be consumed in a nuclear pyre of its own making. In the years to come, members of this class will bear an ever-increasing responsibility for the preservation of the heritage given us.❞
>
> —from *The Sixties*

Concern about the future led many young people to become more active in social causes, from the civil rights movement to President Kennedy's Peace Corps. The emergence of the youth movement grew out of the huge numbers of people of the postwar "baby boom" generation. By 1970, 58.4 percent of the American population was 34 years old or younger. (By comparison, those 34 or younger in 2000 represented an estimated 48.9 percent.)

The early 1960s saw another phenomenon that fueled the youth movement—the rapid increase in enrollment at colleges throughout the nation. The economic boom of the 1950s led to a boom in higher education, since more families could afford to send their children to college. Between 1960 and 1966, enrollment in 4-year institutions rose from 3.1 million to almost 5 million

students. College life empowered young people with a newfound sense of freedom and independence. It also allowed them to meet and bond with others who shared their feelings about society and fears about the future. It was on college campuses across the nation where the protest movements would rage the loudest.

Students for a Democratic Society Some youths were concerned most about the injustices they saw in the country's political and social system. In their view, a few wealthy elites controlled politics, and wealth itself was unfairly divided. These young people formed what came to be known as the New Left. (The "new" left differed from the "old" left of the 1930s, which had advocated socialism and communism.) A prominent organization of this group was the **Students for a Democratic Society** (SDS). It defined its views in a 1962 declaration known as the **Port Huron Statement.** Written largely by **Tom Hayden,** editor of the University of Michigan's student newspaper, the declaration called for an end to apathy and urged citizens to stop accepting a country run by big corporations and big government.

SDS groups focused on protesting the Vietnam War, but they also addressed such issues as poverty, campus regulations, nuclear power, and racism.

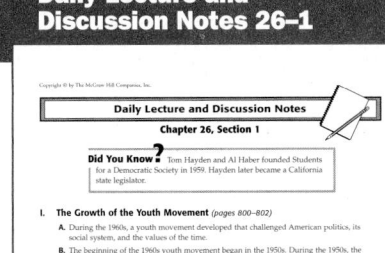

DON'T TRUST ANYONE OVER 30

Picturing **History**

Youth Movement The Students for a Democratic Society (SDS) worked to address many of the problems they saw in the 1960s. Made up primarily of college students, the group was suspicious of the motives of adults. *Where did the SDS begin its reform crusade?*

CHAPTER 26 The Politics of Protest **801**

Reading Strategy ▶ READING THE TEXT

Understanding Vocabulary Have students become familiar with different types of words. *Homophones* are words that sound the same but have different spellings and meanings. For example, *base* means a foundation whereas *bass* means a deep tone. *Homographs* are words that are spelled the same but have different meanings, origins, and/or pronunciations. Using our previous example, *bass* means a deep tone, but pronounced a different way it can mean a type of fish. Have students list the common homophones and homographs they encounter as they read the section. **L1** **ELL**

Guided Reading Activity 26–1

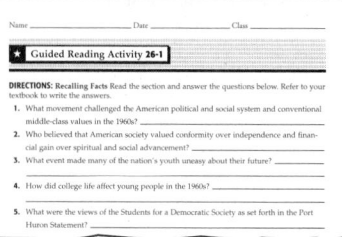

Name _____ Date _____ Class _____

★ Guided Reading Activity **26-1**

DIRECTIONS: Recalling Facts Read the section and answer the questions below. Refer to your textbook to write the answers.

1. What movement challenged the American political and social system and conventional middle-class values in the 1960s? _____
2. Who believed that American society valued conformity over independence and financial gain over spiritual and social advancement? _____
3. What event made many of the nation's youth uneasy about their future? _____
4. How did college life affect young people in the 1960s? _____
5. What were the views of the Students for a Democratic Society as set forth in the Port Huron Statement? _____

Organizing Information Have students create a chart illustrating the similarities and differences between the hippie culture of the 1960s and current countercultures. Suggest that they focus on these questions: What is the issue? What is the goal? What are the outward signs of the movement? **L2**

📁 Use the rubric for creating a map, display, or chart on pages 65–66 in the *Performance Assessment Activities and Rubrics.*

Picturing **History**

Answer: San Francisco, California
Ask: What were some of the outward signs that defined the hippie movement? *(Students' answers will vary. They might mention long hair, headbands, cowboy boots, long dresses, shabby jeans, and drug use.)*

✔ Reading Check

Answer: concern about future, increased college enrollment, injustices in the political and social system

Picturing **History**

The Counterculture Commonly known as "hippies," members of the counterculture separated themselves from society in the 1960s by trying to create their own culture of love and tolerance. *What western city was a focal point of the hippie culture?*

In 1968, for example, SDS leaders assisted in an eight-day occupation of several buildings at Columbia University in New York City to protest the administration's plan to build a new gym in an area that served as a neighborhood park near Harlem.

The Free Speech Movement Another group of protesters who captured the nation's attention were members of the Free Speech Movement, led by **Mario Savio** and others at the University of California at Berkeley. The issue that sparked the movement was the university's decision in the fall of 1964 to restrict students' rights to distribute literature and to recruit volunteers for political causes on campus. The protesters, however, quickly targeted more general campus matters and drew in more and more supporters.

Like many college students, those at Berkeley were disgruntled with the practices at their university. Officials divided huge classes into sections taught by graduate students, while many professors claimed they were too busy with research to meet with students. Faceless administrators made rules that were not always easy to obey and imposed punishments for violations. Isolated in this impersonal environment, many Berkeley students found a purpose in the Free Speech Movement.

The struggle between school administrators and students peaked on December 2, 1964, with the sit-in and Savio's famous speech at the administration

802 CHAPTER 26 The Politics of Protest

building. Early the next morning, California Governor Pat Brown sent in 600 police officers to break up the demonstration. Police arrested more than 700 protesters.

The arrests set off a new and even larger protest movement. Within a few days, thousands of Berkeley students participated in a campus-wide strike, stopping classes for two days. Much of the faculty also voiced its support for the Free Speech Movement. In the face of this growing opposition, the administration gave in to the students' demands shortly before the Christmas recess.

The following week, the Supreme Court validated the students' First Amendment rights to freedom of speech and assembly on campus. In a unanimous vote, the Court upheld the section of the Civil Rights Act assuring these rights in places offering public accommodations, which, by definition, included college campuses. The Berkeley revolt was one of the earliest outbursts in a decade of campus turmoil. The tactics the protesters used there—abandoning classes and occupying buildings—would serve as a model for college demonstrators across the country.

✔ Reading Check **Synthesizing** What were three reasons for the growth of the youth movement of the 1960s?

The Counterculture

While a number of young Americans in the 1960s sought to challenge the system, others wanted to leave it and build their own society. Throughout the decade, thousands of mostly white youths turned away from their middle- and upper-class existence and created a new lifestyle—one that promoted the virtues of flamboyant dress, rock music, drug use, and free and independent living. With their alternative ways of life, these young men and women formed what became known as the counterculture and were commonly called "hippies."

Hippie Culture Originally, hippie culture represented a rebellion against the dominant culture in the United States. This included a rejection of Western civilization, of rationality, order, and the traditional values of the middle class. At its core, the counterculture held up a utopian ideal: the ideal of a society that was freer, closer to nature, and full of love, empathy, tolerance, and cooperation. Much of this was in reaction to the 1950s American stereotype of the man in the gray flannel suit who led a constricted and colorless life.

DIFFERENTIATED INSTRUCTION

At-Risk Students Help students who are visual learners determine the main idea of the section by having them look at and think about all the visuals. They should consider the overall impression and then study the details. In pairs, students can discuss what the visuals tell them about the counterculture. Encourage students to use drawings and symbols in their notebooks to help them when they study for a quiz or test. **L1**

📁 Refer to *Inclusion for the High School Social Studies Classroom Strategies and Activities* in the TCR.

When the movement grew larger, many of the new-comers did not always understand these original ideas of the counterculture. For them, what mattered were the outward signs that defined the movement—long hair, Native American headbands, cowboy boots, long dresses, shabby jeans, and the use of drugs such as marijuana and LSD. Drug use, especially, came to be associated with the hippie culture.

Many hippies desired to literally drop out of society by leaving home and living together with other youths in communes—group living arrangements in which members shared everything and worked together. A number of hippies established communes in small and rural communities, while others lived together in parks or crowded apartments in the nation's large cities. One of the most popular hippie destinations became San Francisco's **Haight-Ashbury district.** By the mid-1960s, thousands of hippies had flocked there.

New Religious Movements In their rejection of materialism, many members of the counterculture embraced spirituality. This included a broad range of beliefs, from astrology and magic to Eastern religions and new forms of Christianity.

Many of the religious groups centered around authoritarian leaders. In these groups, the leader dominated others and controlled their lives, sometimes to the point of arranging marriages between members. Religion became the central experience in the believer's life. The authoritarian figure was a sort of parent figure, and believers formed an extended family that took the place of the family into which a member had been born. This could lead to painful conflicts. Some parents accused religious sects of using mind-control methods; some attempted to recapture and "deprogram" their children.

Two new religious groups that attracted considerable attention beginning in the 1960s were the **Unification Church** and the **Hare Krishna** movement. Both were offshoots of established religions, and both came from abroad. Members of the Unification Church were popularly known as "Moonies," after their Korean-born founder, the Reverend Sun Myung Moon. He claimed to have had a vision in which Jesus told Moon that he was the next messiah and was charged with restoring the Kingdom of God on Earth. The Hare Krishnas traced their spiritual lineage to a Hindu sect that began in India in the 1400s and worshiped the god Krishna. In dress, diet, worship, and general style of living, Hare Krishnas tried to emulate these Hindu practitioners of another time and place.

The Counterculture Declines After a few years, the counterculture movement began to deteriorate. Some hippie communities in the cities soon turned into seedy and dangerous places where muggings and other criminal activity became all too frequent. The glamour and excitement of drug use soon waned, especially as more and more young people became addicted or died from overdoses. In addition, a number of the people involved in the movement had gotten older and moved on in life. Upon witnessing the decline of Haight-Ashbury, one writer dismissed the one-time booming urban commune as "the desperate attempt of a handful of pathetically unequipped children to create a community out of a social vacuum." In the end, most of the young men and women of the counterculture, unable to establish an ideal community and unable to support themselves, gradually returned to mainstream society.

✓ **Reading Check** **Summarizing** What were the core ideals of members of the counterculture?

Impact of the Counterculture

In the long run, the counterculture did change American life in some ways. Over time, mainstream America accepted many of these changes.

Fashion The counterculture generation, as one observer of the 1960s noted, dressed in costumes rather than in occupational or class uniforms. The colorful, beaded, braided, patched, and fringed garments that both men and women wore turned the fashion industry upside down. The international fashion world took its cues from young men and

Fact	Fiction	Folklore

New 1960s Words During the 1960s, Americans coined a host of new words and phrases. The word *hippie,* used to describe members of the counterculture, probably originated from the 1930s term *hep,* for "those in the know." Other people believe *hippie* may have evolved from the 1950s word *hipster,* which referred to members of the beatnik movement.

Hippies themselves introduced a few terms to the country. They often uttered the phrase *far out* to indicate anything that was very good or very bad. Individuals who rejected the free-living counterculture lifestyle were considered *straight* or *square.*

CHAPTER 26 The Politics of Protest **803**

Responding to Music Bring recordings of music from the 1960s to class and have students listen to a few selections. Have students write down their impressions of the music. **L1**

FYI

Moonies were married in mass wedding ceremonies known as "Blessings." Rev. Moon and his wife presided over the ceremonies. Moonies believed that blessed couples would have sinless children.

✓ **Reading Check**

Answer: a society that was freer, closer to nature, and full of love, empathy, tolerance, and cooperation

Fact	Fiction	Folklore

In addition to the language of the counterculture, there was a look. Counterculture youth liked to borrow clothing styles from other cultures, especially from cultures that were less involved with mass industry than the United States. Popular styles were colorful patterned pullover shirts, or dashikis from Africa, and paisley designs from India and Persia.

History and the Humanities

🎵 American Music: Hits Through History: "Blowin' in the Wind," "Turn, Turn, Turn"

🎨 American Art & Architecture: *Map*

INTERDISCIPLINARY CONNECTIONS ACTIVITY

Performing Arts Organize the class into three or four groups and have each prepare a skit on one of the situations below. Encourage all students to participate and have each group present their skit to the rest of the class. **L2**

- A group of friends deciding whether to participate in an antiwar or a pro-war rally
- A member of the SDS speaking at a meeting of university officials
- A college student trying to explain the counterculture to his or her parents

3 ASSESS

Assign Section 1 Assessment as homework or as an in-class activity.

🖥 Have students use the **Interactive Tutor Self-Assessment CD-ROM.**

L1/ELL

Reading Essentials and Study Guide 26–1

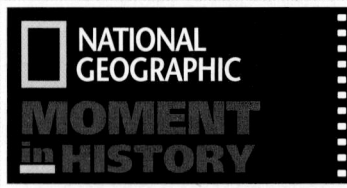

Name _____ Date _____ Class _____

Study Guide

Chapter 26, Section 1
For use with textbook pages 800–805

THE STUDENT MOVEMENT AND THE COUNTERCULTURE

KEY TERMS AND NAMES

Port Huron Statement declaration by the Students for a Democratic Society that called for citizens to stop accepting a country run by big corporations and big government (page 801)

Tom Hayden author of the Port Huron Statement (page 801)

counterculture youth who adopted alternative ways of life (page 802)

communes group living arrangements in which members shared everything and worked together (page 803)

Haight-Ashbury district a popular hippie destination in San Francisco (page 803)

Jimi Hendrix musician who was a master at the electrically amplified guitar (page 805)

L2

Section Quiz 26–1

Name _____ Date _____ Class _____

⭐ **Chapter 26** Score ____

Section Quiz 26-1

DIRECTIONS: Matching Match each item in Column A with the items in Column B. Write the correct letters in the blanks. *(10 points each)*

Column A

____ 1. one of the most famous rock 'n' roll groups

____ 2. derived its subject matter from elements of the popular culture

____ 3. defined the views of the Students for a Democratic Society

____ 4. group living arrangements in which members shared everything and worked together

____ 5. young men and women with alternative ways of life, commonly called "hippies"

Column B

A. counterculture

B. Port Huron Statement

C. pop art

D. The Beatles

E. communes

DIRECTIONS: Multiple Choice In the blank at the left, write the letter of the choice that

NATIONAL GEOGRAPHIC
MOMENT in HISTORY

Most Woodstock festival-goers were white, middle- or upper-class, and between 16 and 30 years of age.

women on the street. As a result, men's clothing became more colorful, and women's clothing became more comfortable.

Protesters often expressed themselves with their clothing. The counterculture adopted military surplus attire not only because it was inexpensive, but also because it expressed rejection of materialist values and blurred the lines of social class. For the same reasons, clothing of another age was recycled, and worn-out clothing was repaired with patches. Ethnic clothing was popular for similar reasons. Beads and fringes imitated Native American costumes, while tie-dyed shirts borrowed techniques from India and Africa.

Perhaps the most potent symbol of the era was hair. A popular 1967 musical about the period was titled, fittingly, *Hair.* Long hair on a young man was the ultimate symbol of defiance. Slogans appeared, such as "Make America beautiful—give a hippie a haircut." School officials debated the acceptable length of a student's hair—could it curl over the collar or not? Once the initial shock wore off, however,

longer hair on men and more individual clothing for both genders became generally accepted. What was once clothing of defiance was now mainstream.

Art During the 1960s, one art critic observed, the distinctions between traditional art and popular art, or **pop art,** dissolved. Pop art derived its subject matter from elements of popular culture, such as photographs, comic books, advertisements, and brand-name products. Artist **Andy Warhol,** for example, used images of famous people, such as Marilyn Monroe and Elizabeth Taylor, and repeated them over and over. Warhol also reproduced items such as cans of soup, making the pictures as realistic as possible. Roy Lichtenstein used frames from comic strips as his inspirations. He employed the bold primary colors of red, yellow, and black, and put words like *blam* and *pow* into his paintings in comic book fashion.

Pop artists expected these symbols of popular culture to carry some of the same meaning as they did in their original form. The artists sometimes referred to themselves as only the "agents" of the art and said it

NATIONAL GEOGRAPHIC
MOMENT in HISTORY

WOODSTOCK NATION

In August 1969, more than 400,000 young people descended on a 600-acre farm in upstate New York for what was billed as "three days of peace and music." Organizers of the Woodstock Music and Art Fair were overwhelmed by the turnout. Massive traffic jams, supply shortages, inadequate first aid and sanitation facilities, and torrential rainfall did not dampen the joyous spirit of the crowd. People shared their food and blankets, bathed in the rain, and listened to an amazing collection of some of the greatest musicians of the 1960s.

804 CHAPTER 26 The Politics of Protest

CRITICAL THINKING ACTIVITY

Comparing Ask students to discuss today's hairstyles, fashions, and music. **Ask: Do they reflect any of the trends of the 1960s? What messages do today's styles send?** Ask students to speculate why some members of the 1960s counterculture are now part of mainstream society. **L2**

was up to the observer to give meaning to the work and thus become part of it.

Music and Dance Counterculture musicians hoped that their music, rock 'n' roll, would be the means of toppling the establishment and reforming society. This did not happen because rock music was absorbed into the mainstream, where it brought material success worth billions of dollars to performers, promoters, and record companies.

One of the most famous rock groups, the **Beatles,** took the country by storm in 1964. "Beatlemania" swept the country, inspiring hundreds of other rock 'n' roll groups both in Great Britain and the United States.

Many of the new groups combined rock 'n' roll rhythms with lyrics that expressed the fears and hopes of the new generation and the widening rift between them and their parents. **Bob Dylan** provided these lyrics, as did the Beatles and many other musicians, while spirited performers like Janis Joplin made the songs come alive.

The use of electrically amplified instruments also drastically changed the sound and feel of the new music. One master of this new sound was **Jimi Hendrix,** a guitarist from Seattle. Hendrix lived overseas and achieved stardom only after returning to the United States with the influx of musicians from Great Britain. His innovative guitar playing continues to influence musicians today.

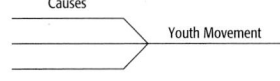

Pop Art Artists like Roy Lichtenstein mocked certain aspects of American life by using common examples of commercial art, such as comics and advertisements. *What statement is this piece of art making?*

At festivals such as **Woodstock,** in upstate New York in August 1969, and Altamont, California, later that year, hundreds of thousands of people got together to celebrate the new music. Though the fast-paced, energetic beat of rock 'n' roll was made for dancing, the style of dancing had changed dramatically. Each person danced without a partner, surrounded by others who also danced alone—a perfect metaphor for the counterculture, which stressed individuality within the group.

Headline-grabbing events such as Woodstock made it difficult for the nation to ignore the youth movement. By this time, however, other groups in society were also raising their voices in protest. For example, many women began renewing their generations-old efforts for equality, hoping to expand upon the successes gained during the early 1900s.

Reading Check **Evaluating** What lasting impact did the counterculture have on the nation?

HISTORY Online **Study Central™** To review this section, go to tarvol2.glencoe.com and click on **Study Central™**.

SECTION 1 ASSESSMENT

Checking for Understanding
1. **Define:** counterculture, commune.
2. **Identify:** Port Huron Statement, Tom Hayden, Haight-Ashbury district, Jimi Hendrix.
3. **Summarize** two legacies of the counterculture movement.

Reviewing Themes
4. **Government and Democracy** How did the U.S. Supreme Court validate the actions of the members of the Free Speech Movement?

Critical Thinking
5. **Contrasting** How were hippies different from members of the New Left?
6. **Analyzing** Why did the counterculture movement decline?
7. **Organizing** Use a graphic organizer similar to the one below to list the causes of the youth movement.

Causes → Youth Movement

Analyzing Visuals
8. **Analyzing Photographs** Look closely at the photograph of a group of hippies and their bus on page 802. How does the bus itself represent values of the counterculture?

Writing About History
9. **Descriptive Writing** Imagine you are a journalist in the 1960s. Write an article in which you visit a commune and describe the hippie culture you see.

CHAPTER 26   The Politics of Protest   **805**

SECTION 1 ASSESSMENT ANSWERS

1. Terms are in blue.
2. Port Huron Statement *(p. 801)*, Tom Hayden *(p. 801)*, Haight-Ashbury district *(p. 803)*, Jimi Hendrix *(p. 805)*
3. It contributed new styles of popular culture and encouraged greater self-expression.
4. It upheld the right to freedom of speech and assembly on campus.
5. Hippies were more interested in creating a utopian lifestyle than in political protest.
6. Many participants were unable to establish an ideal community or support themselves.
7. concern about the future; "baby boom"; social injustice
8. colorful, individualized appearance, communal transport
9. Students' articles will vary. Articles should include descriptions of what a journalist might have seen.

History *Through Art*

Answer: that war is not a game—it is destructive and dangerous
Ask: *What characterized pop art? (It used popular culture for its subject matter, and it expected the symbols of popular culture to carry the same meaning as they did in their original form. They encouraged the observer to become part of the art through their interpretation of it.)*

Reading Check

Answer: changes in fashion, music, dance, and the idea that alternatives to mainstream culture were possible

Reteach
Have students explain the origins of the nation's youth movement.

Enrich
Invite interested students to use library and Internet resources to learn more about the health food movement that began in the 1960s.

HISTORY Online
Study Central™ provides summaries, interactive games, and online graphic organizers to help students review section content.

4 CLOSE

Have students define the goals of serious members of the counterculture.

1 FOCUS

Section Overview

This section focuses on the push for greater rights and opportunities for American women.

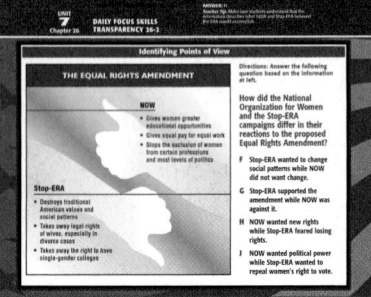
Reading Preview

Answers to Graphic: League of Women Voters: promoted laws to protect women and children; National Woman's Party: opposed protective legislation

Preteaching Vocabulary
Have students write three questions that can be answered using the Key Terms and Names.

SECTION 2 — The Feminist Movement

Guide to Reading

Main Idea
During the 1960s and 1970s, a large number of American women organized to push for greater rights and opportunities in society.

Key Terms and Names
feminism, Equal Pay Act, Equal Employment Opportunity Commission, Betty Friedan, National Organization for Women, Title IX, Phyllis Schlafly

Reading Strategy
Categorizing As you read about the women's movement, use a graphic organizer similar to the one below to compare the ideas of the two organizations that formed when the women's movement split.

Organization	Ideas

Reading Objectives
- **Describe** the workplace concerns that fueled the growth of the women's movement.
- **Identify** major achievements of the women's movement.

Section Theme
Civic Rights and Responsibilities Women organized to claim their rights and responsibilities as citizens and employees.

Preview of Events

♦1963	♦1970	♦1977	♦1984

1963 —
Betty Friedan's *The Feminine Mystique* published

1966 —
Women activists form NOW

1973 —
Roe v. *Wade* decision ensures abortion rights

1982 —
Equal Rights Amendment fails

★ An American Story ★

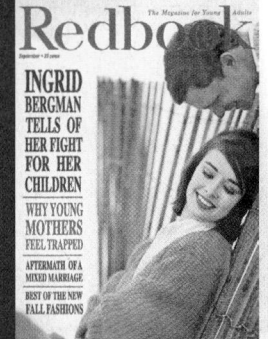

A 1960s-era women's magazine

In 1960 the housewife-oriented magazine *Redbook* asked readers to send examples of "Why Young Mothers Feel Trapped." Some 24,000 women responded. One of them was Herma Snider, a housewife and mother of three in Nevada. Snider wrote that as a high school and college student, she had dreamed of a career in journalism. After getting married and having three children, that dream died.

"Cemented to my house by three young children," she wrote, "there were days in which I saw no adult human being except the milkman as he made his deliveries and spoke to no one from the time my husband left in the morning until he returned at night." She added, "Each night as I tucked my sons into bed, I thanked God that they would grow up to be *men*, that they would able to teach, write, heal, advise, travel, or do anything else they chose."

Desperate for greater fulfillment in her life, Snider eventually took a job as a part-time hotel clerk. About this decision, she said:

❝My cashier's job is not the glamorous career I once dreamed of. And I know that it can be said that my solution is not a solution at all, merely an escape. But it seems to me that when the demands of children and household threaten to suffocate you, an escape *is* a solution.❞

—**quoted in *The Female Experience: An American Documentary***

A Weakened Women's Movement

Herma Snider was not alone. Although many women were content to be homemakers, by the early 1960s scores of them had grown dissatisfied with their roles. At the same time, those who worked outside the home were recognizing their unequal status

---

SECTION RESOURCES

📂 Reproducible Masters
- Reproducible Lesson Plan 26–2
- Daily Lecture and Discussion Notes 26–2
- Guided Reading Activity 26–2
- Section Quiz 26–2
- Reading Essentials and Study Guide 26–2
- Performance Assessment Activities and Rubrics

📄 Transparencies
- Daily Focus Skills Transparency 26–2

Multimedia
- Interactive Tutor Self-Assessment CD-ROM
- ExamView® Pro Testmaker CD-ROM
- Presentation Plus! CD-ROM
- TeacherWorks™ CD-ROM
- Audio Program

as reflected in lower pay and fewer opportunities. These developments led to the rise of a new feminist movement in the 1960s.

Feminism, the belief that men and women should be equal politically, economically, and socially, had been a weak and often embattled force since the adoption of the Nineteenth Amendment guaranteeing women's voting rights in 1920. Soon after the amendment's passage, the women's movement split into two camps. One group, the League of Women Voters, tended to promote laws to protect women and children, such as limiting the hours they could work. The National Woman's Party (NWP), on the other hand, opposed protective legislation for women. The NWP believed it reinforced workplace discrimination. In 1923 the NWP persuaded members of Congress to introduce the first Equal Rights Amendment aimed at forbidding federal, state, and local laws from discriminating on the basis of gender. Since the women's movement was divided, however, Congress could afford to ignore the amendment.

The onset of World War II provided women with greater opportunity, at least temporarily. With many men enlisted in the army, women became an integral part of the nation's workforce. When the war ended, however, many women lost their jobs to the returning men.

Despite having to return to their domestic work, many women gradually reentered the labor market. By 1960 they made up almost 40 percent of the nation's workforce. Yet many people continued to believe that women, even college-educated women, could better serve society by remaining in the home to influence the next generation of men.

 Reading Check **Examining** How did World War II affect women?

The Women's Movement Reawakens

By the early 1960s, many women were increasingly resentful of a world where newspaper ads separated jobs by gender, clubs refused them memberships, banks denied them credit, and, worst of all, they often were paid less for the same work. Generally, women found themselves shut out of higher-paying and prestigious professions such as law, medicine, and finance. Although about 40 percent of American women were in the workforce in the 1960s, three-fourths of them worked in lower paying and routine clerical, sales, or factory jobs, or

as cleaning women and hospital attendants. As more women entered the workforce, the protest against inequities grew louder.

Women had also gained a better understanding of their inequality in society from their experiences in the civil rights and antiwar movements. Often they were restricted to menial tasks and rarely had a say in any policy decisions. From the broader perspective, the women's movement was part of the 1960s quest for rights.

GOVERNMENT

Fighting for Workplace Rights Two forces helped bring the women's movement to life again. One was the mass protest of ordinary women. The second was a government initiative: the **President's Commission on the Status of Women,** established by President Kennedy and headed by Eleanor Roosevelt. The commission's report highlighted the problems of women in the workplace and helped create networks of feminist activists, who lobbied Congress for women's legislation. In 1963, with the support of labor, they won passage of the **Equal Pay Act,** which in most cases outlawed paying men more than women for the same job.

Congress gave women another boost by including them in the 1964 Civil Rights Act, a measure originally designed to fight racial bias. **Title VII** of the act outlawed job discrimination by private employers not only on the basis of race, color, religion, and

 Picturing **History**

Perfect Home, Perfect Wife This image of a proud wife in her spotless kitchen reflects some of the traditional ideas of the 1950s and 1960s. What did the women's movement criticize about these ideas?

CHAPTER 26 The Politics of Protest **807**

2 *TEACH*

Daily Lecture and Discussion Notes 26–2

Daily Lecture and Discussion Notes
Chapter 26, Section 2

Did You Know? By the early 1970s, many women refused to adopt their husbands' last names when they married. Many women used the term "Ms." in place of "Mrs." or "Miss" to show that a woman's marital status was irrelevant.

I. **A Weakened Women's Movement** *(pages 806–807)*

A. A new feminist movement began in the 1960s. Feminism, the belief that men and women should be equal politically, economically, and socially, began as early as the 1920s.

B. With the onset of World War II, women joined the nation's workforce as many men went off to fight the war. When the soldiers returned after the war, many women lost

Discussing a Topic Have students discuss women's career choices today. Ask them if parents, teachers, counselors, and others steer women toward some careers and away from others. **L1**

 Reading Check

Answer: Many took jobs outside the home.

 Picturing **History**

Answer: the idea that a woman's place was in the home

 Use *Interpreting Political Cartoons,* Cartoon 30.

FYI

In the past many people lumped women together with minority groups, using references such as "women and other minorities." In fact, since 1950, women in the United States make up a little more than half the population.

Reading Strategy **READING THE TEXT**

Using Word Parts Help students learn how suffixes can help them unlock the meaning of words. A suffix is a word part that comes after a base word or a root. It may change the meaning of the word or the way the word is used in the sentence. Provide students with these examples: *–less* means "without" (careless, powerless); *–ish* means "like" (childish, foolish); *–ful* means "full of" (playful, thoughtful). Have students find words with suffixes in the section and identify the root word's meaning. **L1** ELL

Refer to *Inclusion for the High School Social Studies Classroom Strategies and Activities* in the TCR.

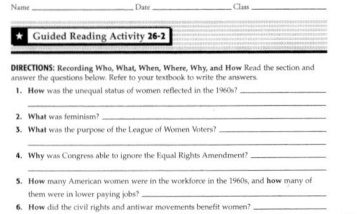

L1/ELL

Guided Reading Activity 26–2

Creating a Chart Have students learn more about the roles of women in other cultures and countries in the 1960s and 1970s. Instruct students to create a chart to compare and contrast the roles of women in the country they have chosen with American women. **L2**

📁 Use the rubric for creating a map, display, or chart on pages 65–66 in the *Performance Assessment Activities and Rubrics.*

📁 Use *Supreme Court Case Study 46, Reed v. Reed.*

✓ **Reading Check**

Answer: the mass protest of ordinary women, and the President's Commission on the Status of Women

---

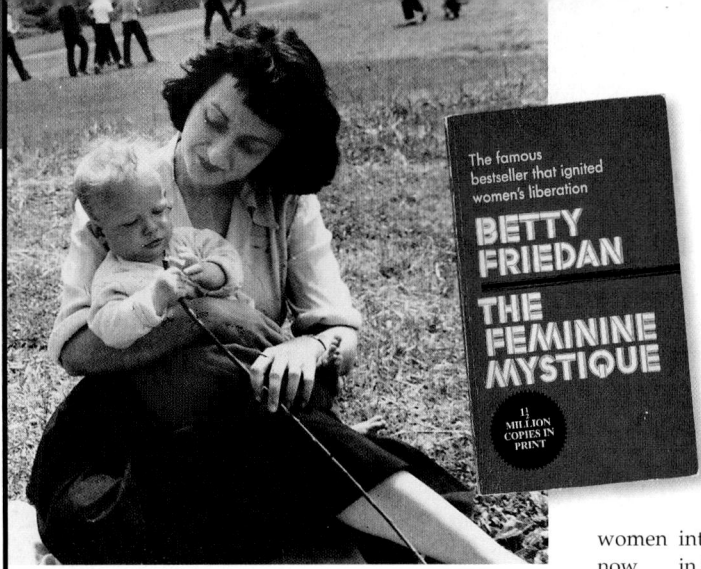

Picturing **History**

The Feminine Mystique Betty Friedan's best-selling book (right) exposed a sense of dissatisfaction that many women experienced but were reluctant to speak about openly. What political organization stemmed from women's growing sense of unfulfillment?

national origin, but also of gender. This measure became decisive legal basis for advances made by the women's movement.

The federal agency charged with administering the new law, the **Equal Employment Opportunity Commission** (EEOC), was officially operating in July 1965. Government administrators projected that in its first year, the EEOC would receive approximately 2,000 charges of unlawful employment practices. Instead, the Commission actually received almost 9,000 separate charges in its first year of operation.

The Feminine Mystique Many date the women's movement from the publication of **Betty Friedan's** *The Feminine Mystique* in 1963. Friedan had traveled around the country interviewing the women who had graduated with her from Smith College in 1942. She found that while most of these women reported having everything they could want in life, they still felt unfulfilled. Friedan described these feelings in her book:

> ❝The problem lay buried, unspoken, for many years in the minds of American women. . . . Each suburban wife struggled with it alone. As she made the beds, shopped for groceries . . . chauffeured Cub Scouts and Brownies . . . she was afraid to ask even of herself the silent question—'Is this all?'❞
> —from *The Feminine Mystique*

Friedan's book became a best-seller. Many women soon began reaching out to one another, pouring out their anger and sadness in what came to be known as consciousness-raising sessions. While they talked informally about their unhappiness, they were building the base for a nationwide movement.

The Time Is NOW In June 1966, Friedan returned to a thought that she and others had been considering, the need for women to form a national organization. On the back of a napkin, she scribbled down her intentions "to take the actions needed to bring women into the mainstream of American society, now . . . in fully equal partnership with men." Friedan and others then set out to form the **National Organization for Women** (NOW).

NOW soon leapt off the napkin and into the headlines. In October 1966, a group of about 300 women and men held the founding conference of NOW. "The time has come," its founders declared, "to confront with concrete action the conditions which now prevent women from enjoying the equality of opportunity and freedom of choice which is their right as individual Americans and as human beings."

The new organization began by demanding greater educational opportunities for women. The group also focused much of its energy on aiding women in the workplace. NOW leaders denounced the exclusion of women from certain professions and from most levels of politics. They lashed out against the practice of paying women less than men for equal work, a practice they claimed the Equal Pay Act had not eliminated.

The efforts to pass the Equal Rights Amendment pushed the organization's membership over 200,000. By July 1972, the movement even had a magazine of its own, *Ms.*, which kept readers informed on women's issues. The editor of the new magazine was **Gloria Steinem,** an author and public figure who was one of the movement's leading figures.

✓ **Reading Check** **Identifying** What two forces helped bring the women's movement to life again?

Successes and Failures

During the late 1960s and early 1970s, the women's movement fought to enforce Title VII of the Civil Rights Act, lobbied to repeal laws against abortion,

---

DIFFERENTIATED INSTRUCTION

At-Risk Students To help students with learning disabilities, pick out the most important points of this section, and then have students use the heads of the section to create a study outline. As they complete each subhead, have them write notes about the important points. Then encourage them to discuss their outlines with a partner and make any modifications that would improve the outline. **L1**

📁 Refer to *Inclusion for the High School Social Studies Classroom Strategies and Activities* in the TCR.

and worked for legislation against gender discrimination in employment, housing, and education. Along the way, it experienced success as well as failure.

Striving for Equality in Education One of the movement's notable achievements was in education. Kathy Striebel's story highlighted the discrimination female students often faced in the early 1970s. In 1971, Striebel, a high school junior in St. Paul, Minnesota, wanted to compete for her school's swim team, but the school did not allow girls to join. Kathy's mother, Charlotte, was a member of the local NOW chapter. Through it, she learned that St. Paul had recently passed an ordinance prohibiting gender discrimination in education. She filed a grievance with the city's human rights department, and officials required the school to allow Kathy to swim.

Shortly after joining the team, Kathy beat out one of the boys and earned a spot at a meet. As she stood on the block waiting to swim, the opposing coach declared that she was ineligible to compete because the meet was outside St. Paul and thus beyond the jurisdiction of its laws. "They pulled that little girl right off the block," Charlotte Striebel recalled angrily.

Recognizing the problem, leaders of the movement pushed lawmakers to enact federal legislation banning gender discrimination in education. In 1972 Congress responded by passing a law known collectively as the Educational Amendments. One section, Title IX, prohibited federally funded schools from discriminating against girls and young women in nearly all aspects of its operations, from admissions to athletics. Many schools implemented this new law slowly or not at all, but women now had federal law on their side.

Roe v. Wade One of the most important goals for many women activists was the repeal of laws against abortion. Until 1973, the right to regulate abortion was reserved to the states. This was in keeping with the original plan of the Constitution, which reserved all police power—the power to control people and property in the interest of safety, health, welfare, and morals—to the state. Early in the country's history, some abortion was permitted in the early stages of pregnancy, but after the middle of the 1800s, when states adopted statutory law, abortion was prohibited except to save the life of the mother. Women who chose to have an abortion faced criminal prosecution.

In the late 1960s, some states began adopting more liberal abortion laws. For example, several states allowed abortion if carrying a baby to term might endanger the woman's mental health or if she was a victim of rape or incest. The big change came with the 1973 Supreme Court decision in *Roe v. Wade*. The Supreme Court ruled that state governments could not regulate abortion during the first three months of pregnancy, a time that was interpreted as being within a woman's constitutional right to privacy. During the second three months of pregnancy, states could regulate abortions on the basis of the health of the mother. States could ban abortion in the final three months except in cases of a medical emergency.

Those in favor of protecting abortion rights cheered *Roe v. Wade* as a victory, but the issue was far

---

Profiles IN HISTORY

Shirley Chisholm
1924–2005

Shirley Chisholm once remarked, "Of my two 'handicaps,' being female put more obstacles in my path than being black." Her attempts to overcome these obstacles propelled the Brooklyn, New York, native into the national spotlight and provided encouragement for other women and African Americans attempting to overcome discrimination.

Chisholm first gained national prominence when she defeated two other candidates for Congress from New York's 12th District in 1968. Upon her swearing in, she became the first African American woman to serve in the United States Congress.

In Congress Chisholm became an ardent defender of several causes. An opponent of the seniority system, she protested the ways that party leaders assigned House members to committees and was instrumental in changing them. Chisholm was an early opponent of arms sales to South Africa's racist regime. She also worked on education issues and to increase day care

programs, and she cosponsored a bill to guarantee an annual income to families.

In 1972 Chisholm ran for the Democratic nomination for president. She campaigned extensively and entered primaries in 12 states, winning 28 delegates and receiving 152 first ballot votes at the convention.

She returned to Congress after the convention and continued her crusade to help women and minorities for several more terms. She declined to run for re-election in 1982, citing the difficulties of campaigning for liberal issues in an increasingly conservative political atmosphere.

INTERDISCIPLINARY CONNECTIONS ACTIVITY

Visual Arts Have students create three sketches of typical women's fashions from the 1960s and 1970s. Sketches should include clothing for several occasions. For example, students might choose to include a sketch of an outfit worn by a college student, a homemaker, and an office worker. Formal wear for special occasions such as weddings and proms could also be included. Encourage students to use library and Internet resources to locate fashion images to help them with their sketches. **L2**

📁 Use *Supreme Court Case Study 48*, *Roe v. Wade*.

During the 1960s, a new means of birth control became available to women. The Food and Drug Administration approved oral contraceptives available by prescription in 1965. The two earliest types of the "pills" were created by Frank Colton and Carl Djerassi.

3 ASSESS

Assign Section 2 Assessment as homework or as an in-class activity.

🅦 Have students use the **Interactive Tutor Self-Assessment CD-ROM.**

L1/ELL

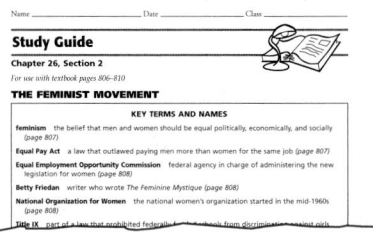

Reading Essentials and Study Guide 26–2

Profiles
IN HISTORY

Ask: What were the two handicaps Shirley Chisholm faced and which did she find more difficult to overcome? *(She thought that being a woman had put more obstacles in her way than being African American.)*

Section Quiz 26–2

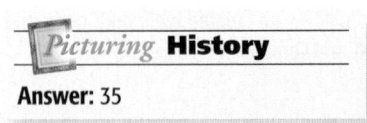

Reteach
Have students explain the work-place issues for many women.

Enrich
Have interested students research the impact of Title IX.

Reading Check

Answer: Successes: the Educational Amendments, abortion rights, and improved working conditions; Failures: not passing the ERA, lingering income gap, women still mostly in low-paying jobs

HISTORY Online

Study Central™ provides summaries, interactive games, and online graphic organizers to help students review section content.

4 CLOSE

Have students identify achievements of the women's movement.

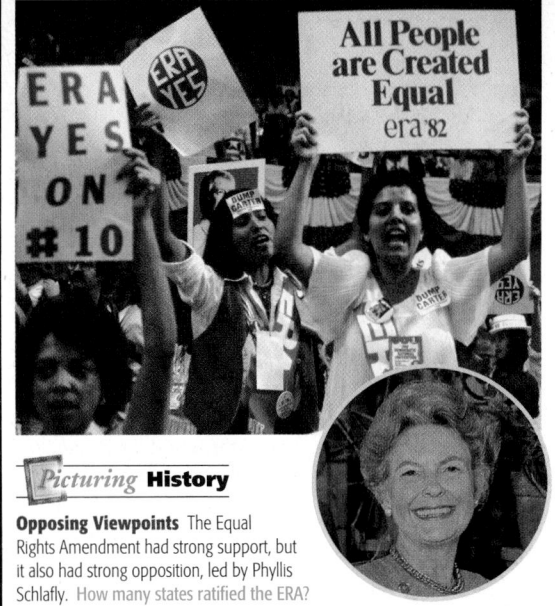

Picturing **History**

Opposing Viewpoints The Equal Rights Amendment had strong support, but it also had strong opposition, led by Phyllis Schlafly. How many states ratified the ERA?

from settled. The decision gave rise to the right-to-life movement, whose members consider abortion morally wrong and advocate its total ban. After the *Roe* v. *Wade* ruling, the two sides began an impassioned battle that continues today. *(For more information on* Roe v. Wade, *see page 964.)*

The Equal Rights Amendment In 1972 Congress passed the Equal Rights Amendment (ERA). To become part of the Constitution, this amendment to protect women against discrimination had to be ratified by 38 states. Many states did so—35 by 1979—but there was significant opposition to the amendment as well. Some people feared the ERA would take away some traditional rights, such as the right to alimony in divorce cases or the right to have single-gender colleges. Another fear was that women would be subjected to the military draft. One outspoken opponent was **Phyllis Schlafly,** who organized the Stop-ERA campaign. The ERA finally failed in 1982.

The Impact of the Women's Movement Despite the failure of the ERA, the women's movement would ultimately bring about profound changes in society. Since the 1970s, many more women have pursued college degrees and careers outside of the home than did so in previous decades. Since the women's movement began, two-career families are much more common than they were in the 1950s and 1960s, although a need for greater family income may also be a factor. Employers began to offer employees options to help make work more compatible with family life, including flexible hours, on-site child care, and job-sharing.

Even though the women's movement helped change social attitudes toward women, an income gap between men and women still exists. A major reason for the income gap is that most working women still hold lower-paying jobs such as bank tellers, administrative assistants, cashiers, schoolteachers, and nurses. Also, many women choose to leave or reduce their hours at work to bear and care for their children. It is in professional jobs that women have made the most dramatic gains since the 1970s. By the end of the 1900s, women made up roughly one-fourth of the nation's doctors and lawyers.

Reading Check
Summarizing What successes and failures did the women's movement experience during the late 1960s and early 1970s?

HISTORY Online **Study Central**™ To review this section, go to tarvol2.glencoe.com and click on **Study Central**™.

SECTION 2 ASSESSMENT

Checking for Understanding
1. **Define:** feminism, Title IX.
2. **Identify:** Equal Pay Act, Equal Employment Opportunity Commission, Betty Friedan, National Organization for Women, Phyllis Schlafly.
3. **Summarize** Shirley Chisholm's political contributions.

Reviewing Themes
4. **Civic Rights and Responsibilities** How have women's rights improved since the 1960s?

Critical Thinking
5. **Synthesizing** What two events weakened the women's movement?
6. **Organizing** Use a graphic organizer similar to the one below to list the major achievements of the women's movement.

Achievements

Analyzing Visuals
7. **Analyzing Photographs** Study the photo on page 807 of a housewife in her kitchen. Think about depictions of housewives in modern television or magazine advertisements you have seen. How would you compare the photo on page 807 with today's images?

Writing About History
8. **Persuasive Writing** Take on the role of a supporter or opponent of the ERA. Write a letter to the editor of your local newspaper to persuade people to support your position.

SECTION 2 ASSESSMENT ANSWERS

1. Terms are in blue.
2. Equal Pay Act (p. 807), Equal Employment Opportunity Commission (p. 808), Betty Friedan (p. 808), National Organization for Women (p. 808), Phyllis Schlafly (p. 810)
3. The first African American woman in Congress, she helped reform the House committee appointment system, and worked on education and day care.
4. More women have achieved equal pay for the same job, more career choices, and more political power.
5. division within the women's movement and World War II
6. Equal Pay Act; inclusion in Title VII of the 1964 Civil Rights Act; Title IX; *Roe* v. *Wade;* more career possibilities
7. Answers will vary. Answers could mention that current depictions are realistic.
8. Students' letters will vary.

American LITERATURE

Charlotte Perkins Gilman was a prominent American social critic and feminist writer in the late 1800s and early 1900s. In her most famous work, *The Yellow Wallpaper* (1899), she presents the story of a woman diagnosed with hysteria, for whom a doctor has prescribed total rest. Cut off from any intellectual activity, the woman is slowly driven mad by her "cure."

In this work, Gilman makes a statement against a common belief of the time—that women were generally unfit for scholarship. The story remained obscure for almost 50 years but was rediscovered in the 1970s. It has become a staple of many college literary courses.

Read to Discover
How does the narrator feel about her "illness"? How does her opinion differ from that of her physician and her family?

Reader's Dictionary
scoff: make fun of

phosphates: a carbonated drink, often used as medicine in the 1800s and early 1900s

congenial: agreeable; pleasant

from The Yellow Wallpaper
by Charlotte Perkins Gilman

In the following excerpt, the narrator of the story, writing in a secret journal, is describing her "illness" and how her husband John and others feel about it.

John is practical in the extreme. He has no patience with faith, an intense horror of superstition, and he scoffs openly at any talk of things not to be felt and seen and put down in figures.

John is a physician, and *perhaps*—(I would not say it to a living soul, of course, but this is dead paper and a great relief to my mind)—*perhaps* that is one reason I do not get well faster.

You see he does not believe I am sick!

And what can one do?

If a physician of high standing, and one's own husband, assures friends and relatives that there is really nothing the matter with one but temporary nervous depression—a slight hysterical tendency—what is one to do?

My brother is also a physician, and also of high standing, and he says the same thing.

So I take phosphates or phospites—whichever it is, and tonics, and journeys, and air, and exercise, and am absolutely forbidden to "work" until I am well again.

Personally, I disagree with their ideas.

Personally, I believe that congenial work, with excitement and change, would do me good.

But what is one to do?

I did write for a while in spite of them; but it *does* exhaust me a good deal—having to be so sly about it, or else meet with heavy opposition.

Analyzing Literature
1. What is the main idea in this passage? How does it support the author's point?
2. Does the narrator think this remedy will help her? Why or why not? What clues can you find about how the narrator feels about her illness?

Interdisciplinary Activity
Science Using the Internet and other resources, research some ways that diseases and illnesses were treated in the 1800s and 1900s. Do we still use these treatments today? Create a chart showing the progression of treatment for some of the illnesses you researched.

Read to Discover
Answer: The narrator feels that doing something other than resting would improve her health. Her family does not believe she is sick.

Reading Strategy

Reinforcing Vocabulary
Ask students to use each of the terms in a sentence that is not related to the reading.

Historical Connection
Charlotte Perkins Gilman drew on her own experience after the birth of her first child in writing *The Yellow Wallpaper*. The great-niece of Harriet Beecher Stowe, she wrote novels, poems, and magazine articles on a variety of subjects.

Portfolio Writing Activity
Have students write a narrative essay about a time when they were not believed. Encourage students to describe the circumstances and explore how the incident made them feel.

HISTORY Online

Refer to tarvol2.glencoe.com for additional Glencoe Literature titles, lesson plans, and study guides related to this unit.

Answers to Analyzing Literature

1. This passage contrasts what her doctors think and what she thinks. Her weak and timid disagreement emphasizes the strength and power of her male doctors' opinions.

2. No, she wants congenial work, excitement, and change. Her passivity shows in repetitions of the phrase "what is one to do?" and tentative word choices such as *relief, perhaps,* and *exhaust.*

Interdisciplinary Activity
Charts should show the progress in diagnosing and treating selected illnesses and diseases.

SECTION 3 New Approaches to Civil Rights

1 FOCUS

1 FOCUS

Section Overview

This section focuses on the efforts by minority groups to improve their status.

BELLRINGER
Skillbuilder Activity

Project transparency and have students answer the question.

Daily Focus Skills Transparency 26–3

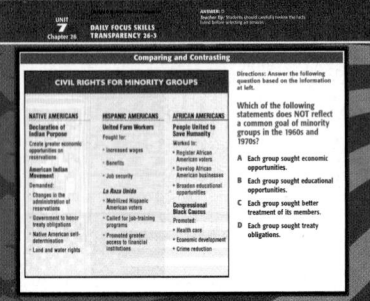

Reading Preview

Answers to Graphic: 1966: UFW pushed for better wages and working conditions; 1968: AIM protested Native American conditions; 1969: *La Raza Unida* organized Mexican Americans for job training and access to financial institutions; 1971: PUSH organized voter registration, developed African American businesses, and broadened educational opportunities; CBC focused on African American interests in Congress

Preteaching Vocabulary
Have students group the Key Terms and Names into logical categories.

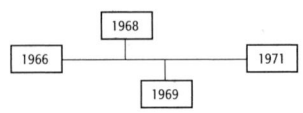

Guide to Reading

Main Idea
Throughout the 1960s and 1970s, minority groups developed new ways to improve their status in the United States.

Key Terms and Names
affirmative action, Allan Bakke, busing, Jesse Jackson, Congressional Black Caucus, César Chávez, *La Raza Unida,* bilingualism, American Indian Movement

Reading Strategy
Sequencing As you read about the civil rights movement's new approaches, complete a time line similar to the one below to record new groups and their actions.

```
           1968
1966 ───────┼─────── 1971
           1969
```

Reading Objectives
• **Describe** the goal of affirmative action policies.
• **Analyze** the rise of Hispanic and Native American protests.

Section Theme
Civic Rights and Responsibilities African Americans, Hispanics, and Native Americans organized to fight discrimination and to gain access to better education and jobs.

Preview of Events

♦1965	♦1969	♦1973
1966 Hispanic Americans form United Farm Workers of America	**1968** Kerner Commission reports on racism in the United States	**1969** Hispanic leaders form *La Raza Unida*	**1973** Native Americans and government clash in South Dakota

★ An American Story ★

Vernon Bellecourt

In 1968 Vernon and Clyde Bellecourt, along with other Native Americans in Minneapolis, were struggling to earn a living. The Bellecourts decided to take a stand against their conditions. Spurred by the 1960s protest movements and by reawakened pride in their culture, the brothers helped organize the American Indian Movement (AIM). AIM's goal was to combat discrimination and brutality by the local police. Vernon recalled how AIM worked:

❝They got a small grant from the Urban League of Minneapolis to put two-way radios in their cars and to get tape recorders and cameras. They would listen to the police calls, and when they heard . . . that police were being dispatched to a certain community or bar, they'd show up with cameras and take pictures of the police using more than normal restraint on people. . . . AIM would show up and have attorneys ready. Often they would beat the police back to the station. They would have a bondsman there, and they'd start filing lawsuits against the police department.❞

—quoted in *Native American Testimony*

Fighting for Greater Opportunity

At a time of heightened protest in the United States, Native Americans began raising their voices for reform and change. Other groups did as well. During the 1960s and early 1970s, Hispanic Americans organized to improve their status in society. In the wake of the

---

SECTION RESOURCES

📂 Reproducible Masters
• Reproducible Lesson Plan 26–3
• Daily Lecture and Discussion Notes 26–3
• Guided Reading Activity 26–3
• Section Quiz 26–3
• Reading Essentials and Study Guide 26–3
• Performance Assessment Activities and Rubrics

🗂 Transparencies
• Daily Focus Skills Transparency 26–3

Multimedia
🔘 Interactive Tutor Self-Assessment CD-ROM
🔘 ExamView® Pro Testmaker CD-ROM
🔘 Presentation Plus! CD-ROM
🔘 TeacherWorks™ CD-ROM
🔘 Audio Program

assassination of Dr. Martin Luther King, Jr., African Americans continued their fight for greater civil rights, now focusing more on access to jobs.

Affirmative Action By the end of the 1960s, many African American leaders expressed a growing sense of frustration. Although most legal forms of racial discrimination had been dismantled, many African Americans felt there had been little improvement in their daily lives. In the eyes of leading civil rights activists, the problems facing most African Americans lay in their lack of access to good jobs and adequate schooling. As a result, leaders of the civil rights movement began to focus their energies on these problems.

As part of their effort, civil rights leaders looked to an initiative known as affirmative action. Enforced through executive orders and federal policies, affirmative action called for companies and institutions doing business with the federal government to actively recruit African American employees with the hope that this would lead to improved social and economic status. Officials later expanded affirmative action to include other minority groups and women.

Supporters of the policy argued that because so few companies hired from these groups in the past, they had had little chance to develop necessary job skills. If businesses opened their doors wider to minorities, more of them could begin building better lives.

In one example of affirmative action's impact, Atlanta witnessed a significant increase in minority job opportunities shortly after **Maynard Jackson** became its first African American mayor in 1973. When Jackson took office, less than one percent of all city contracts went to African Americans, even though they made up about half of Atlanta's population. Jackson used the expansion of the city's airport to redress this imbalance by opening the bidding process for airport contracts more widely to minority firms. Through his efforts, small companies and minority firms took on 25 percent of all airport construction work, earning them some $125 million in contracts.

Challenges to Affirmative Action Affirmative action programs did not go unchallenged. Critics viewed them as a form of "reverse discrimination." They claimed that qualified white workers were kept from jobs, promotions, and a place in schools because a certain number of such positions had been set aside for minorities or women.

One of the more notable challenges to affirmative action came in 1974, after officials at the University of

Picturing **History**

Equal Opportunity Allan Bakke graduated from medical school after the Supreme Court overturned the University of California's use of specific racial quotas. *How did the Bakke case affect affirmative action?*

California Medical School at Davis turned down the admission of a white applicant named **Allan Bakke** for a second time. When Bakke learned that slots had been set aside for minorities, he sued the school. Bakke argued that by admitting minority applicants, some of whom had scored lower than Bakke on their exams, the school had discriminated against him due to his race.

In 1978, in *University of California Regents* v. *Bakke,* the Supreme Court, in a 5 to 4 ruling, declared that the university had indeed violated Bakke's rights. On the other hand, it ruled that schools could use racial criteria as part of their admissions process so long as they did not use "fixed quotas." While *Bakke* was not a strong and definitive ruling, the Court had nevertheless supported affirmative action programs as constitutional. 📖 *(See page 964 for more information on University of California Regents v. Bakke.)*

The debate over affirmative action continued through the 1980s, and by the mid-1990s, opponents had begun organizing politically to end affirmative action programs. In 1995 the University of California's Board of Regents voted to end the use of race in its admissions policy. The push to end the university's affirmative action program was led by Ward Connerly, an African American board member and business owner. Connerly strongly believed that affirmative action treated people unequally.

Connerly went on to lead the campaign for Proposition 209, an amendment to California's constitution that banned the state from giving preferential treatment on the basis of race, gender, ethnicity, or national origin. After Californians voted in favor of Proposition 209 in 1996, citizens in other states increased their efforts to ban affirmative action programs. The debate continues to the present.

CHAPTER 26 The Politics of Protest **813**

2 **TEACH**

Daily Lecture and Discussion Notes 26–3

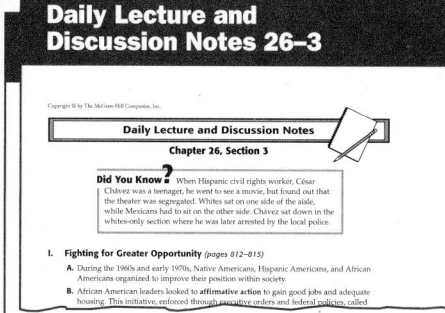

Copyright © by The McGraw-Hill Companies, Inc.

Daily Lecture and Discussion Notes

Chapter 26, Section 3

Did You Know? When Hispanic civil rights worker, César Chávez was a teenager, he went to see a movie, but found out that the theater was segregated. Whites sat on one side of the aisle, while Mexicans had to sit on the other side. Chávez sat down in the whites-only section where he was later arrested by the local police.

I. Fighting for Greater Opportunity *(pages 812–815)*

A. During the 1960s and early 1970s, Native Americans, Hispanic Americans, and African Americans organized to improve their position within society.

B. African American leaders looked to **affirmative action** to gain good jobs and adequate housing. This initiative, enforced through executive orders and federal policies, called

Discussing a Topic Have students consider how members of minority groups are portrayed in film and television today. Have them speculate on how the civil rights movement influenced these media. **L1**

Picturing **History**

Answer: supported affirmative action but ruled against fixed quotas

📂 Use *Supreme Court Case Study 51, Regents of the University of California* v. *Bakke.*

COOPERATIVE LEARNING ACTIVITY

Conducting a Debate Organize the class into two groups. Tell the groups that they are to prepare for a debate about bilingual education. Assign one group to concentrate on the pros of bilingual education; the other group should concentrate on the cons. Tell the groups to conduct research to identify facts and theories to support their assigned point of view. Conduct an informal debate in which each side presents its case and rebuts the point of view of the other side. Encourage all students to participate. 📷

Use the rubric for a cooperative group management plan on pages 71–72 in the ***Performance Assessment Activities and Rubrics.***

L1/ELL

Guided Reading Activity 26–3

Name _____ Date _____ Class _____

★ **Guided Reading Activity 26-3**

DIRECTIONS: Identifying Supporting Details Read each main idea. Use your textbook to supply the details that support or explain each main idea.

☐ Main Idea: During the 1960s and early 1970s, African Americans continued their fight for greater civil rights in the wake of the assassination of Dr. Martin Luther King, Jr.

1. **Detail:** In the eyes of leading civil rights activists, the problems facing most African Americans lay in their lack of access to _____ and _____.

2. **Detail:** _____ called for companies and institutions doing business with the federal government to actively recruit

3. **Detail:** _____ is the claim that qualified white workers are kept from jobs, promotions, and a place in schools because a certain number of such positions are set aside for minorities or women.

4. **Detail:** An activist in the civil rights movement, _____ sought the

---

Picturing **History**

Answer: Congressional Black Caucus
Ask: What organization did Jesse Jackson found? *(People United to Save Humanity—PUSH)*

📁 Use *Interpreting Political Cartoons,* Cartoon 29.

FYI

Stokely Carmichael turned down scholarships to other colleges in order to attend Howard University, a historically African American university. Following graduation from Howard, he again turned down scholarships, this time for graduate studies, and went to work for SNCC.

Analyzing Points of View

Review with students the issue of school desegregation. Have students explain why some thought that busing would be a good solution to the problem. Then have students explain why many people came to believe that busing caused more problems than it solved. **L2**

Picturing **History**

New African American Leadership Andrew Young and Jesse Jackson both worked with Dr. Martin Luther King, Jr., in the civil rights movement. Young went on to become the first African American ambassador to the United Nations, while Jackson has become a prominent member of the Democratic Party. What group of African American members of Congress became influential in the 1970s?

Equal Access to Education By the early 1970s, African American leaders also had begun to push harder for educational improvements. In the 1954 case of *Brown* v. *Board of Education of Topeka, Kansas,* the Supreme Court had ordered an end to segregated public schools. In the 1960s, however, many schools remained segregated as local communities moved slowly to comply with the Court. Since children normally went to neighborhood public schools, segregation in schooling reflected the race segregation of neighborhoods. White schools were usually far superior to African American schools, as Ruth Baston of the NAACP noted in 1965 after visiting Boston schools:

> ❝When we would go to white schools, we'd see these lovely classrooms with a small number of children in each class. The teachers were permanent. We'd see wonderful materials. When we'd go to our schools, we'd see overcrowded classrooms, children sitting out in the corridors. And so then we decided that where there were a large number of white students, that's where the care went. That's where the books went. That's where the money went.❞
>
> —quoted in *Freedom Bound*

814 CHAPTER 26 The Politics of Protest

To ensure desegregated schools, local governments resorted to a policy known as busing, transporting children to schools outside their neighborhoods to achieve greater racial balance. The Supreme Court upheld the constitutionality of busing in the 1971 case, *Swann* v. *Charlotte-Mecklenburg Board of Education.* 📖 *(See page 965 for more information on* Swann *v.* Charlotte-Mecklenburg Board of Education.*)*

Many whites responded to busing by taking their children out of public schools. Nearly 20,000 white students left Boston's public system for parochial and private schools. By late 1976, African Americans, Hispanics, and other minorities made up the majority of Boston's public school students. This "white flight" also occurred in other cities.

New Political Leaders In their struggle for equal opportunity, African Americans found new political leaders in people such as **Jesse Jackson.** In 1971 Jackson founded People United to Save Humanity, or PUSH, a group aimed at registering voters, developing African American businesses, and broadening educational opportunities. In 1984 and 1988, Jackson sought the Democratic presidential

---

DIFFERENTIATED INSTRUCTION

Reading Support To help students understand the attitudes behind passage of the Equal Pay Act and the Indian Civil Rights Act, have students analyze the following questions. **L2**

• In a company, who benefits if women are paid less than men?

• On a Native American reservation, who benefits from limited Native American government?

📁 Refer to *Inclusion for the High School Social Studies Classroom Strategies and Activities* in the TCR.

nomination. Although both attempts were unsuccessful, Jackson did win over millions of voters.

African Americans also became more influential in Congress. In 1971 African American members of Congress reorganized an existing organization into the **Congressional Black Caucus** in order to more clearly represent the concerns of African Americans.

Another leader who emerged was Louis Farrakhan of the Nation of Islam. In 1994, he helped organize the Million Man March, a gathering of African American men in Washington, D.C. to promote self-reliance and community responsibility.

✓ **Reading Check** **Examining** What were the goals of affirmative action policies?

Hispanic Americans Organize

Hispanic Americans also worked for greater rights in this period. In 1960 about 3 million Hispanics lived in the United States. This number increased rapidly after the passage of the Immigration Act of 1965.

Hispanics came to the United States from countries such as Cuba and Mexico to flee repressive political regimes or to find jobs and better lives. The largest group was Mexican Americans, many of whom arrived during and after World War II to work on huge farms in the South and West.

Many Hispanics arrived illegally, sometimes crossing the U.S.-Mexican border with the help of "coyotes," often unscrupulous guides who charged huge sums of money for their services. Because they lacked legal protection, they were often exploited by employers, working under poor conditions for little pay.

César Chávez and the UFW One notable Hispanic American campaign was the effort to win rights for farmworkers. Most Mexican American farm laborers earned little pay, received few benefits, and had no job security. In the early 1960s, **César Chávez** and **Dolores Huerta** organized two groups that fought for farmworkers. In 1965 the groups cooperated in a strike against California growers to demand union recognition, increased wages, and better benefits.

When employers resisted, Chávez enlisted college students, churches, and civil rights groups to organize a national boycott of table grapes, one of California's largest agricultural products. An estimated 17 million citizens stopped buying them, and industry profits tumbled.

Under the sponsorship of the American Federation of Labor and Congress of Industrial Organization (AFL-CIO), in 1966 Chávez and Huerta merged their two organizations into one—the **United Farm Workers**

(UFW). The union's combined strength ensured that the boycott would continue. The boycott ended in 1970, when the grape growers finally agreed to a contract to raise wages and improve working conditions.

Growing Political Activism
The League of United Latin American Citizens, or LULAC, founded in Corpus Christi, Texas, in 1929, had long worked for Mexican American rights in the court system, in hiring, and in education. In 1954 LULAC brought the landmark case of *Hernandez v. the State of Texas* to the Supreme Court, winning the right of Mexican Americans to serve on juries.

Hispanic Americans became more politically active during the 1960s and 1970s. In 1969 José Angel Gutiérrez organized a new political party in Texas called *La Raza Unida,* or "the United People." The group mobilized Mexican American voters to push for job training programs and greater access to financial institutions.

One issue both Hispanic students and political leaders promoted was bilingualism, the practice of teaching immigrant students in their own language

HISTORY Online

Student Web Activity Visit the *American Republic Since 1877* Web site at tarvol2.glencoe.com and click on *Student Web Activities—Chapter 26* for an activity on protest movements.

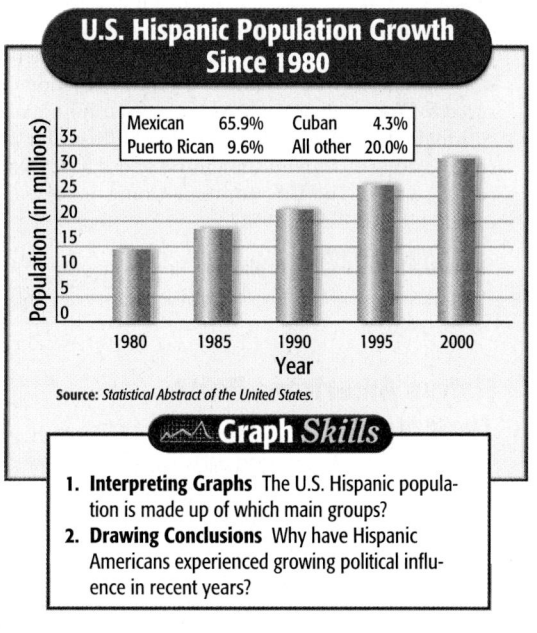

U.S. Hispanic Population Growth Since 1980

| Mexican | 65.9% | Cuban | 4.3% |
| Puerto Rican | 9.6% | All other | 20.0% |

Population (in millions) — Year: 1980, 1985, 1990, 1995, 2000

Source: *Statistical Abstract of the United States.*

〰 Graph *Skills*

1. **Interpreting Graphs** The U.S. Hispanic population is made up of which main groups?
2. **Drawing Conclusions** Why have Hispanic Americans experienced growing political influence in recent years?

✓ **Reading Check**

Answer: improve educational and social and economic opportunities for African Americans, and actively recruit minorities, including women, for jobs

HISTORY Online

Objectives and answers to the student activity can be found in the **Web Activity Lesson Plan** at tarvol2.glencoe.com.

FYI

The National Labor Relations Act of 1935 guaranteed the right to unionize and prohibited employers from interfering with union efforts to recruit members. In guaranteeing collective bargaining, the NLRA required employers to negotiate with representatives elected by workers. Agriculture was not covered by this act. Therefore, farmworkers did not benefit from its protections.

〰 Graph *Skills*

Answers:
1. Mexican, Puerto Rican, and Cuban
2. growing numbers and political and labor organizations

Graph Skills Practice
Ask: What other national origins might be represented in the Hispanic population? *(Students' answers will vary; they might mention any country in Central or South America.)*

INTERDISCIPLINARY CONNECTIONS ACTIVITY

Mathematics As the U.S. population diversifies due to immigration, the pressure to ensure equal rights for all also increases. Have students review immigration data, such as those from the U.S. Citizenship and Immigration Services Web site (http://uscis.gov/graphics/). They should create a graph showing the top three regions and the top five nations of origin of immigrants in the twenty-first century. Point out to students that during the first few years, three of the top five nations of origin were Asian—China, the Philippines, and India. **L2**

Profiles
IN HISTORY

What motivated Dolores Huerta to become an activist? *(After seeing children come to school hungry and needing shoes, she decided she could do more by organizing farmworkers than by teaching school.)*

✓ Reading Check

Answer: By forming the UFW and *La Raza Unida* and staging boycotts, they increased their wages, won contracts, improved working conditions, and lobbied successfully to achieve the Bilingual Education Act.

3 ASSESS

Assign Section 3 Assessment as homework or as an in-class activity.

🔵 Have students use the **Interactive Tutor Self-Assessment CD-ROM.**

L1/ELL

Reading Essentials and Study Guide 26–3

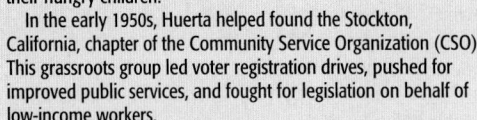

Dolores Huerta
1930–

Dolores Huerta began her career as an elementary school teacher, but she soon left, believing that she could do more good for Mexican Americans outside the classroom. "I couldn't stand seeing kids come to class hungry and needing shoes," she said. "I thought I could do more by organizing farmworkers than by trying to teach their hungry children."

In the early 1950s, Huerta helped found the Stockton, California, chapter of the Community Service Organization (CSO). This grassroots group led voter registration drives, pushed for improved public services, and fought for legislation on behalf of low-income workers.

It was through her work with the CSO that Huerta met César Chávez. Together, they organized farmworkers into a union and fought for better wages and working conditions.

José Angel Gutiérrez
1944–

As a young social activist, José Angel Gutiérrez set out to organize Mexican Americans from Crystal City, Texas, into a political force. In 1970 his newly founded political party, *La Raza Unida*, participated in local elections. Over the next few years, Mexican Americans gained control of Crystal City's school system and government.

As *La Raza Unida* gained a more national following, Gutiérrez became a prominent figure. He eventually stepped away from the political scene, serving first as a judge and then as a college professor. Gutiérrez found it difficult to stay away from politics, however, and in 1993, he ran unsuccessfully for a U.S. Senate seat. After that, he established his own legal center. Looking upon Gutiérrez's career, one historian said, "He represents the new breed of Chicano professionals produced by the colleges and universities, but he is still a Chicano with the old dream of revolution."

---

while they also learned English. Many Hispanics argued they would be at a competitive disadvantage with native English speakers unless they had schooling in their native language. Congress supported their arguments, passing the **Bilingual Education Act** in 1968. This directed school districts to set up classes for immigrants in their own language as they were learning English.

In recent years there has been some movement away from bilingualism in states with large Hispanic populations. Some educators argue that total immersion in English is the soundest road to educational success. Some American voters opposed bilingual education, believing it makes it more difficult for a child to adjust to American culture and that it was costly besides. The U.S. Supreme Court, however, upheld bilingualism in 1974.

✓ Reading Check
Explaining How did Hispanic Americans increase their economic opportunities in the 1960s?

Native Americans Raise Their Voices

Native Americans in 1970 were one of the nation's smallest minority groups, constituting less than one percent of the U.S. population. Few minority groups, however, had more justifiable grievances than the descendants of America's original inhabitants. The average annual family income of Native Americans

was $1,000 less than that of African Americans. The Native American unemployment rate was 10 times the national rate. Joblessness was particularly high on reservation lands, where nearly half of all Native Americans lived. Most urban Native Americans suffered from discrimination and from limited education and training. The bleakest statistic of all showed that life expectancy among Native Americans was almost seven years below the national average. To improve conditions, many Native Americans began organizing in the late 1960s and 1970s.

A Protest Movement Emerges In 1961 more than 400 members of 67 Native American groups gathered in Chicago to discuss ways to address their numerous problems. They issued a manifesto, known as the **Declaration of Indian Purpose,** calling for policies to create greater economic opportunities on reservations.

Unlike other groups demanding more assimilation into mainstream society, many Native Americans wanted greater independence from it. They took a step toward this goal in 1968 when Congress passed the Indian Civil Rights Act. It guaranteed reservation residents the protections of the Bill of Rights, but it also recognized the legitimacy of local reservation law.

Native Americans who viewed the government's reform efforts as too modest formed more militant groups, such as the **American Indian Movement** (AIM). Typically, such groups employed a more combative style. In 1969 AIM made a symbolic protest by

---

Reading Strategy ▸ READING THE TEXT

Evaluating Information After students have read the section, ask them to pose questions such as those below that could be used to interview someone who lived through the civil rights movement. Help students prepare open-ended questions. Then use the responses to evaluate the movement's impact on the American public. **L2**

- When were you first aware that "civil rights" was a broad movement?
- Which forms of protest most impressed you? In which, if any, did you participate?
- How did your life change as a result of the civil rights movement?
- How do you think the civil rights movement should be remembered today?

occupying the abandoned federal prison on Alcatraz Island in San Francisco Bay for 19 months, claiming ownership "by right of discovery."

A more famous and violent protest occurred later at Wounded Knee, South Dakota, where federal troops had killed around 150 Sioux in 1890. In February 1973, AIM members seized and occupied the town of Wounded Knee for 70 days. They demanded radical changes in the administration of reservations and that the government honor its long-forgotten treaty obligations to Native Americans. A brief clash between the occupiers and the FBI killed two Native Americans and wounded several on both sides. Shortly thereafter, the siege came to an end.

Native Americans Make Notable Gains
The Native American movement fell short of achieving all its goals, but it did win some notable victories. In 1975 Congress passed the Indian Self-Determination and Educational Assistance Act, which increased funds for Native American education and expanded local control in administering federal programs. More Native Americans also moved into policy-making positions at the Bureau of Indian Affairs, and the agency pushed for more Native American self-determination.

Through the federal court system, Native Americans also won a number of the land and

Native American high school student

water rights they sought. The Pueblo of Taos, New Mexico, regained property rights to Blue Lake, a place sacred to their religion. In 1980, a federal court settled a claim of the Passamaquoddy and the Penobscot groups. The government paid the groups $81.5 million to relinquish their claim on land in the state of Maine. The two groups purchased 300,000 acres with the money and invested much of the remainder. Other court decisions gave Native American groups authority to impose taxes on businesses on their reservations and to perform other sovereign functions.

Since Native Americans first began to organize, many reservations have dramatically improved their economic conditions by actively developing businesses, such as electric plants, resorts, cattle ranches, and oil and gas wells. More recently, gambling casinos have become a successful enterprise. Because of rulings on sovereignty, Native Americans in some areas are allowed to operate gaming establishments under their own laws even though state laws prevent others from doing so. In these ways, Native Americans have tried to regain control of their economic future, just as other American minorities did in the 1960s and 1970s.

☑ **Reading Check** **Analyzing** What conditions led Native Americans to organize in the 1960s?

  Study Central™ To review this section, go to **tarvol2.glencoe.com** and click on **Study Central™**.

SECTION 3 ASSESSMENT

Checking for Understanding
1. **Define:** affirmative action, busing, bilingualism.
2. **Identify:** Allan Bakke, Jesse Jackson, Congressional Black Caucus, César Chávez, *La Raza Unida,* American Indian Movement.
3. **Analyze** how the *Bakke* case, along with other cases, affected affirmative action.

Reviewing Themes
4. **Civic Rights and Responsibilities** How did the Supreme Court support civil rights during the 1970s? Cite two court cases and their decisions.

Critical Thinking
5. **Synthesizing** Why have African Americans become significantly more influential in the U.S. Congress since the early 1970s?
6. **Categorizing** Use a graphic organizer similar to the one below to identify civil rights leaders and their causes during the 1960s and 1970s.

Civil Rights Leaders	Causes

Analyzing Visuals
7. **Analyzing Graphs** Study the graph on page 815 of U.S. Hispanic population growth since 1980. The largest percentage of Hispanics is represented by Mexican Americans. What was the approximate percentage growth for Hispanic Americans from 1980 to 2000?

Writing About History
8. **Expository Writing** Write a magazine article about the conditions that gave rise to the Native American protest movement of the 1960s and 1970s. In your article, discuss the movement's goals and activities.

CHAPTER 26 The Politics of Protest **817**

SECTION 3 ASSESSMENT ANSWERS

1. Terms are in blue.
2. Allan Bakke (p. 813), Jesse Jackson (p. 814), Congressional Black Caucus (p. 815), César Chávez (p. 815), La Raza Unida (p. 815), American Indian Movement (p. 816)
3. It challenged affirmative action as reverse discrimination.

4. *Swann* v. *Charlotte-Mecklenburg Board of Education*: constitutionality of busing; *University of California Regents* v. *Bakke*: constitutionality of affirmative action
5. CBC was organized in Congress.
6. Jackson: political power for African

Americans; Chávez: right of farmworkers; Gutiérrez: Mexican American vote; Bellecourt brothers: Native American interests
7. about 100%
8. Students' articles will vary. Articles should focus on the reasons for the protest movement.

L2

Section Quiz 26–3

[Section Quiz 26–3 worksheet reproduction]

Name _____ Date _____ Class _____

★ Chapter 26   Score ____

Section Quiz 26-3

DIRECTIONS: Matching Match each item in Column A with the items in Column B. Write the correct letters in the blanks. *(10 points each)*

Column A
___ 1. organized by African American members of Congress to represent the legislative concerns of African Americans
___ 2. the practice of teaching immigrant students in their own language while they also learned English
___ 3. a militant group of Native Americans who viewed the government's reform efforts as too modest
___ 4. called for companies and institutions doing business with the government to recruit African American employees
___ 5. a manifesto calling for policies to create greater economic opportunities on reservations

Column B
A. American Indian Movement
B. affirmative action
C. bilingualism
D. Declaration of Indian Purpose
E. Congressional Black Caucus

☑ **Reading Check**

Answer: low average family income, unemployment 10 times the national rate, discrimination, limited education, and low life expectancy

FYI

The American Indian Movement (AIM) was established to protect the traditional ways of Native Americans; to engage in legal cases protecting Native Americans' treaty rights; to improve federal, state, and local social services to urban neighborhoods; and to prevent police harassment of Native Americans.

Reteach
Have students describe the goals of affirmative action policies.

Enrich
Invite students to write a biographical sketch of someone who was active in one of the causes mentioned in this section.

Study Central™ provides summaries, interactive games, and online graphic organizers to help students review section content.

4 CLOSE

Have students analyze what gave rise to Hispanic and Native American protests.

TEACH

Reading Strategy

Analyzing Primary Sources
Explain that primary sources provide a valuable source of insight into the past. Tell students that one way to gain a clear understanding of past events, especially controversial ones, is to examine several contrasting primary sources dealing with a specific event.

Ask students to select one of the *An American Story* features from this unit. Have students focus on the quoted portion of the material, which is a primary source. Have students write down two or three things that they learn about a person, place, or event as a result of the excerpt.

Additional Practice
L1

Reinforcing Skills Activity 26

Name _____ Date _____ Class _____

★ Reinforcing Skills Activity 26

Analyzing Primary Sources

◼ **LEARNING THE SKILL**
Primary sources provide firsthand accounts from our history. Letters, photographs, legal documents, diaries, and news articles are primary source documents. Because firsthand sources represent single points of view, it is important to study them in the context of their time. To do this, first identify the author of the source, as well as when and where the document was created. As you read or view your source, ask yourself questions: Who is it about? What is it about? When did it happen? Where did it happen? Why did it happen? Look for statements of fact versus opinion. Can you identify any information that might be missing from the source?

◼ **PRACTICING THE SKILL**
DIRECTIONS: Read the excerpt below from the Equal Pay Act of 1963. Then answer the questions that follow on a separate sheet of paper.

GLENCOE
TECHNOLOGY

CD-ROM
Glencoe Skillbuilder Interactive Workbook CD-ROM, Level 2

This interactive CD-ROM reinforces student mastery of essential social studies skills.

Analyzing Primary Sources

Why Learn This Skill?

To determine what happened in the past, historians do some detective work. They comb through bits of evidence from the past to reconstruct events. These bits of written and illustrated historical evidence are called *primary sources.*

Learning the Skill

Primary sources are records of events made by the people who witnessed them. They include letters, diaries, photographs, news articles, and legal documents.

Primary sources yield several important kinds of information. Often they give detailed accounts of events. However, the account reflects only one perspective. For this reason, you must examine as many perspectives as possible before drawing any conclusions. To analyze primary sources, follow these steps.

- Identify the author of the source.
- Identify when and where the document was written.
- Read the document for its content and try to answer the five "W" questions: Who is it about? What is it about? When did it happen? Where did it happen? Why did it happen?
- Determine what kind of information may be missing from the primary source.

Practicing the Skill

The primary source that follows is a small part of a United States legal document. Read the source, and then answer the questions.

> **Title IX, Education Amendments of 1972, Section 1684. Blindness or visual impairment; prohibition against discrimination**
> *No person in the United States shall, on the grounds of blindness or severely impaired vision, be denied admission in any course of study by a recipient of Federal financial assistance for any education program or activity; but nothing herein shall be construed to require any such institution to provide any special services to such person because of his blindness or visual impairment.*

❶ When was this document written?
❷ Who is affected by this legal document?
❸ What is the purpose of this legal requirement?
❹ Why do you think this document was written?

Skills Assessment

Complete the Practicing Skills questions on page 827 and the Chapter 26 Skill Reinforcement Activity to assess your mastery of this skill.

Applying the Skill

Analyzing Primary Sources Find a primary source from your past—a photo, a report card, an old newspaper clipping, or your first baseball card. Bring this source to class and explain what it shows about that time in your life.

 Glencoe's **Skillbuilder Interactive Workbook CD-ROM, Level 2,** provides instruction and practice in key social studies skills.

ANSWERS TO PRACTICING THE SKILL

❶ 1972
❷ persons who are blind or visually impaired
❸ to prevent discrimination against the blind or visually impaired in admission to an educational institution receiving federal funds
❹ to prevent discrimination

Applying the Skill
Students' answers will vary. Give students time to present primary sources and explain what they show about their lives at that time.

SECTION 4 Saving the Earth

Guide to Reading

Main Idea
During the 1960s and 1970s, environmental issues became a significant concern for many Americans.

Key Terms and Names
Rachel Carson, smog, Environmental Protection Agency, fossil fuel, Three Mile Island, Ralph Nader

Reading Strategy
Organizing As you read about the nation's environmental problems in the 1960s and 1970s, complete a graphic organizer by including actions taken to combat these problems.

Actions Taken

Reading Objectives
• **Explain** the origins of the environmental movement.
• **Identify** the significant measures taken to combat environmental problems.

Section Theme
Groups and Institutions Increased awareness of environmental issues inspired a grassroots campaign to protect nature.

Preview of Events

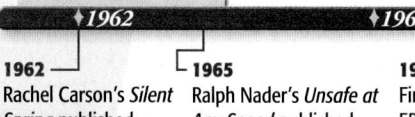

♦1962   ♦1968   ♦1974   ♦1980

1962 — Rachel Carson's *Silent Spring* published

1965 — Ralph Nader's *Unsafe at Any Speed* published

1970 — First Earth Day celebrated; EPA established

1972 — U.S. bans use of pesticide DDT

1979 — Nuclear accident at Three Mile Island

★ An American Story ★

In 1966 Carol Yannacone of Patchogue, a small community on Long Island, New York, learned that officials were using a powerful pesticide, DDT, as part of a mosquito control operation in a local lake. Alarmed that the pesticide would poison lakes and streams, Yannacone and her husband, Victor, an attorney, contacted several local scientists, who confirmed their suspicions. The Yannacones then successfully sued to halt the use of the pesticide.

The Yannacones had discovered a new strategy for addressing environmental concerns. The legal system, Victor Yannacone insisted, was the one place where facts and evidence, not politics and emotions, would decide the outcome:

❝A court . . . is the only forum in which a full inquiry into questions of environmental significance can be carried on. . . . Only on the witness stand, protected by the rules of evidence though subject to cross-examination, can a scientist be free of the harassment of legislators seeking re-election of higher political office; free from the glare of the controversy-seeking media; free from unsubstantiated attacks of self-styled experts representing vested economic interests and yet who are not subject to cross examination.❞

—quoted in *Since Silent Spring*

Spraying pesticides

The Beginnings of Environmentalism

Shortly after the Yannacones' court victory, the scientists involved in the case established the Environmental Defense Fund and used its contributions for a series of legal actions across the country to halt DDT spraying. Their efforts led to a nationwide ban on the use of the pesticide in 1972.

CHAPTER 26 The Politics of Protest **819**

1 FOCUS

Section Overview
This section focuses on the environmental issues Americans faced in the 1960s and 1970s.

Reading Preview

Answers to Graphic: Clean Air Act, Clean Water Act, Earth Day celebration, Endangered Species Act, creation of the Environmental Protection Agency (EPA)

Preteaching Vocabulary
Have students scan the section to become familiar with the Key Terms and Names.

---

2 TEACH

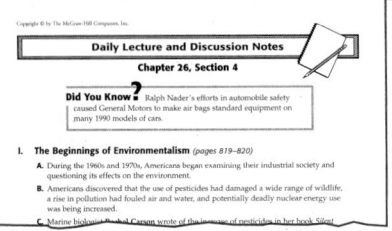
Discussing a Topic Have students discuss the ways in which they currently work to improve the environment. Ask them to explain the slogan "reduce, reuse, recycle." **L1**

Picturing **History**

Answer: DDT

Ask: What was the name of the book Carson wrote assailing the use of pesticides? *(Silent Spring)*

Reading Check

Answer: wildlife, air, and water resources

FYI

By the early 1970s, 70 percent of Americans ranked the environment as the nation's most pressing problem. That same year an estimated 20 million people participated in Earth Day—a rally to improve the environment. Across the country more than 14,000 schools and communities held events to raise awareness of environmental issues.

Picturing **History**

The Power of One Rachel Carson, a marine biologist, sounded a warning note for the environment. Her concern over how humans affect the environment helped start a new reform movement. What pesticide in particular worried Carson?

The effort to ban DDT was only one aspect of a larger environmental movement that took shape in the 1960s and 1970s. During this period, a growing number of Americans began to focus on environmental issues. They argued that pesticides had damaged wildlife and that pollution had fouled the nation's air and water.

The person who sounded the loudest alarm bell was not a political leader or prominent academic, but a soft-spoken marine biologist, **Rachel Carson.** Carson's 1962 book *Silent Spring* assailed the increasing use of pesticides, particularly DDT. She contended that while pesticides curbed insect populations, they also killed birds, fish, and other creatures that might ingest them. Carson warned Americans of a "silent spring," in which there would be few birds left to usher spring in with their songs. In her book, she imagined such a scene from a fictitious town:

66 There was a strange stillness. The birds, for example—where had they gone? Many people spoke of them, puzzled and disturbed. . . . On the mornings that had once throbbed with the dawn chorus of robins, catbirds, doves, jays, wrens, and scores of other

bird voices there was now no sound; only silence lay over the fields and woods and marsh. 99

—from *Silent Spring*

Silent Spring became one of the most controversial and powerful books of the 1960s. It sold nearly half a million copies within six months of its publication and was widely discussed. The chemical industry was outraged and began an intense campaign to discredit Carson and her arguments. Nonetheless, many Americans took Carson's warnings to heart and began to focus on environmental issues.

Reading Check **Identifying** What natural resources did environmental groups want to protect?

The Environmental Movement

During the 1960s, Americans began to feel that environmental problems plagued every region of the nation. In the Northwest, timber companies were cutting down acres of forestland. Smog, or fog made heavier and darker by smoke and chemical fumes, was smothering major cities. In 1969 a major oil spill off Santa Barbara, California, ruined miles of beach and killed scores of birds and aquatic animals. A dike project in the Florida Everglades indirectly killed millions of birds and animals. Meanwhile, pollution and garbage had caused nearly all the fish to disappear from Lake Erie. By 1970 a growing number of citizens were convinced that the time had come to do something about protecting the environment.

A Grassroots Effort Begins Many observers point to April 1970 as the unofficial beginning of the environmental movement. That month, the nation held its first **Earth Day** celebration, a day devoted to addressing the country's environmental concerns. The national response was overwhelming. In thousands of colleges and secondary schools and in hundreds of communities, millions of Americans participated in activities to show their environmental awareness, from picking up litter to demonstrating against air pollution.

Senator Gaylord Nelson of Wisconsin, who had put forth the idea of an Earth Day celebration, commented on the event: "The people cared and Earth Day became the first opportunity they ever had to join in a nationwide demonstration to send a message to the politicians—a message to tell them to wake up and do something."

After Earth Day, the grassroots effort intensified. Citizens formed local environmental groups, while nonprofit organizations such as the Sierra Club, the

Reading Strategy **READING THE TEXT**

Identifying the Main Idea Students should identify main ideas as they read. Text features, such as headings, subheadings, boldfaced terms, and graphics, are good indicators of main or key ideas. As students read, have them make a list of ideas by creating an outline or drawing a graphic organizer. **L1** ELL

Refer to *Inclusion for the High School Social Studies Classroom Strategies and Activities* in the TCR.

Audubon Society, and the Wilderness Society gained prominence. These organizations worked to protect the environment and promote the conservation of natural resources. In 1970 activists started the Natural Resources Defense Council to coordinate a nationwide network of scientists, lawyers, and activists working on environmental problems.

GOVERNMENT

The Government Steps In With the environmental movement gaining public support, the federal government took action. In 1970 President Nixon signed the National Environmental Policy Act, which created the **Environmental Protection Agency** (EPA). The EPA took on the job of setting and enforcing pollution standards, promoting research, and coordinating anti-pollution activities with state and local governments. The agency also monitored other federal agencies with respect to their impact on the environment.

The **Clean Air Act** also became law in 1970 over President Nixon's veto. This act established emissions standards for factories and automobiles. It also ordered that all industries comply with such standards within five years.

In following years, Congress passed two more pieces of significant environmental legislation. The **Clean Water Act** (1972) restricted the discharge of pollutants into the nation's lakes and rivers, and the **Endangered Species Act** (1973) established measures for saving threatened animal species. Over time these laws reduced smog and cut pollution levels in many lakes and rivers.

Love Canal Despite the flurry of federal environmental legislation, Americans continued to mobilize on the community level throughout the 1970s. One of the most powerful displays of community activism occurred in a housing development near Niagara Falls, New York, known as Love Canal.

In the 1970s, residents of Love Canal noticed a rising number of health problems in their community, including nerve damage, blood diseases, cancer, miscarriages, and birth defects. They soon learned that their community sat atop a decades-old toxic waste dump. Over time its hazardous contents had leaked into the ground.

Led by a local woman, **Lois Gibbs,** the residents joined together and demanded that the government take steps to address these health threats. Hindered at

first by local and state officials, the residents refused to back down, and by 1978 they had made their struggle known to the entire nation. That year, in the face of mounting public pressure and evidence of the dangers posed by the dump, the state permanently relocated more than 200 families.

In 1980, after hearing protests from the families who still lived near the landfill, President Carter declared Love Canal a federal disaster area and moved over 600 remaining families to new locations. In 1983 Love Canal residents sued the company that had created the dump site and settled the case for $20 million. The site was cleaned up by sealing the waste within an underground bunker and burning homes located above the dumping ground.

Concerns Over Nuclear Energy During the 1970s, a number of citizens expressed concern over the growth of nuclear power. As nuclear power plants began to dot the nation's landscape, the debate over their use intensified. Supporters of nuclear energy hailed it as a cleaner and less expensive alternative to fossil fuels, such as coal, oil, and natural gas, which are in limited supply. Opponents warned of the risks, particularly the devastating consequences of an accidental radiation release into the air.

The debate moved to the nation's forefront in shocking fashion in 1979. In the early hours of March 28, one of the reactors at the **Three Mile Island** nuclear facility outside Harrisburg, Pennsylvania, overheated after its cooling system failed. While plant

Picturing **History**

Environmental Awareness Numerous oil spills and events such as Earth Day have brought environmental concerns to the attention of Americans. *What issues does the Sierra Club address?*

L1/ELL

Guided Reading Activity 26–4

Name _____ Date _____ Class _____

★ **Guided Reading Activity 26–4**

DIRECTIONS: Using Headings and Subheadings Locate each heading below in your textbook. Then use the information under the correct subheading to help you write each answer.

I. The Beginnings of Environmentalism

    A. What was the accomplishment of the Environmental Defense Fund in 1972? _____

    B. What became one of the most controversial and powerful books of the 1960s? _____

    C. What were two reactions to Rachel Carson's arguments? _____

II. The Environmental Movement Blossoms

    A. When was the first Earth Day, and to what was it devoted? _____

Creating a Thematic Map Have students create a thematic map showing environmental issues in particular parts of the nation. **L2**

FYI

When the environmental movement began in the early 1960s, Americans generated approximately 2.7 pounds of trash per person per day. In 1999 the daily figure had risen to 4.6 pounds per person.

Picturing **History**

Answer: preservation of the environment and conservation of natural resources

History *and the* Humanities

🎵 American Music: Hits Through History: "You've Made Me So Very Happy"

🎵 American Music: Cultural Traditions: "I Heard It Through the Grapevine"

🏛 American Art & Architecture: *Day of the Fair*

DIFFERENTIATED INSTRUCTION

Kinesthetic Have interested students collect samples of all the items that can be recycled in your community. After cleaning or sanitizing the items, have them create a work of art with these items that could be used as a reminder to recycle. Have students display their creations in class and select the ones that best encourage recycling to display in a prominent place in your school. **L2**

📁 Refer to *Inclusion for the High School Social Studies Classroom Strategies and Activities* in the TCR.

TECHNOLOGY & History

Background: To help resolve recent shortages of electricity, the Department of Energy is supporting the development of solar power plants that produce electricity by converting the sun's energy into high-temperature heat using various mirror configurations. The heat is then channeled through a conventional generator. The plants consist of two parts: one that collects solar energy and converts it to heat, and another that converts heat energy to electricity.

Answer: It is renewable, easily obtained, thought to be relatively inexpensive, and can be used in many ways.

Ask: What are other renewable forms of energy in use today? *(possible answers—wind power, hydroelectric power)*

Reading Check

Answer: protecting natural resources

3 ASSESS

Assign Section 4 Assessment as homework or as an in-class activity.

⚫ Have students use the **Interactive Tutor Self-Assessment CD-ROM.**

L1/ELL

Reading Essentials and Study Guide 26–4

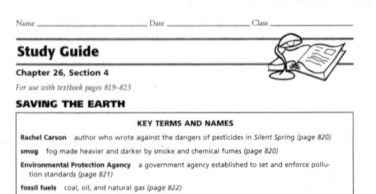

Name _____ Date _____ Class _____

Study Guide

Chapter 26, Section 4
For use with textbook pages 819–823

SAVING THE EARTH

KEY TERMS AND NAMES

Rachel Carson author who wrote against the dangers of pesticides in *Silent Spring (page 820)*
smog fog made heavier and darker by smoke and chemical fumes *(page 820)*
Environmental Protection Agency a government agency established to set and enforce pollution standards *(page 821)*
fossil fuels coal, oil, and natural gas *(page 822)*
Three Mile Island a nuclear facility outside Harrisburg, Pennsylvania *(page 822)*
Ralph Nader the leading figure in the consumer protection movement *(page 823)*

TECHNOLOGY & History

Solar Energy

Concerns in the 1970s about the environment and safe energy led to a strong interest in solar energy. Sunlight is composed of photons, particles of solar energy. The use of photovoltaic (PV) cells allows solar energy to be used for a wide range of energy needs, from powering generators to running agricultural water pumps or simple calculators. *Why was solar power seen as an environmentally friendly power source?*

1 Solar arrays or panels are made up of thousands of PV cells and capture the sun's rays.

2 This magnification shows the composition of a PV cell.

3 This schematic shows a cross-section of a cell and how its electrons respond to sunlight to create a flow of electricity.

---

officials scrambled to fix the problem, low levels of radiation escaped from the reactor.

Officials evacuated many nearby residents, while others fled on their own. Citizens and community groups expressed outrage in protest rallies. Officials closed down the reactor and sealed the leak. The Nuclear Regulatory Commission, the federal agency that regulates the nuclear power industry, eventually declared the plant safe.

The accident at Three Mile Island had a powerful impact and left much of the public in great doubt about the safety of nuclear energy. Such doubts have continued. Since Three Mile Island, 60 nuclear power plants have been shut down or abandoned, and no new facilities have been built since 1973.

The Debate Over Environmentalism The environmentalist movement that emerged in the 1970s led to a new political debate in American society. As environmentalists began proposing regulations they believed would help the environment, opponents began arguing that the regulations had hidden costs.

One controversial issue involved DDT. The World Health Organization has estimated that DDT saved 25 million lives worldwide by killing disease-spreading pests such as mosquitoes and lice. Despite DDT's

value in reducing disease, however, most nations followed the U.S. example and banned the pesticide. Soon afterward, cases of malaria and typhus began to rise again worldwide.

The debate over DDT demonstrated the difficulty in balancing the costs and benefits of environmental regulations. Supporters of nuclear power have pointed out that coal-fired power plants also put people at risk. Miners regularly develop black lung disease and die in mining accidents while mining coal for power plants. Coal-fired plants also pollute the air. Yet requiring power plants, cars, and factories to reduce their air pollution may drive up the cost of goods. This can lead to fewer jobs and more poverty, and make more products unaffordable to people of modest means. Environmental regulations can also clash with people's property rights. As a result, the environmentalist movement became increasingly controversial in the 1980s and 1990s, as interest groups, business leaders, and politicians took sides in the debate over the costs and benefits of environmentalist policies. The debate has continued to shape politics to the present day.

Reading Check **Summarizing** What is the environmental movement's main goal?

INTERDISCIPLINARY CONNECTIONS ACTIVITY

Science Invite a scientist or science teacher to address your class about an environmental issue. Ask the speaker to address how science has helped to create some of the current environmental issues, how science helps prevent other environmental problems, and how science is helping to correct existing problems. For example, the speaker might address how science and technology helped to create many of the disposable products that we use today and how science is being used to help make those products more environmentally friendly. **L2**

The Consumer Movement

During the 1960s and 1970s, a number of citizens also questioned the quality and safety of the many new "technologically advanced" products flooding the market. In an atmosphere of protest and overall distrust of authority, more and more buyers demanded product safety, accurate information, and a voice in government formulation of consumer policy.

Perhaps the most notable figure of this new consumer protection movement was **Ralph Nader,** a young lawyer from Connecticut. In the early 1960s, Nader noted what he considered an alarmingly high number of automobile fatalities. He presented his findings in a 1965 book, *Unsafe at Any Speed.* Nader charged car manufacturers with putting style, cost, and speed ahead of safety. He also challenged one of the auto industry's long-held claims that drivers were to blame for most auto accidents:

> ❝The American automobile is produced exclusively to the standards which the manufacturer decides to establish. It comes into the marketplace unchecked. When a car becomes involved in an accident, the entire investigatory, enforcement and claims apparatus that makes up the post-accident response looks almost invariably to driver failure as the cause. . . . Accommodated by superficial standards of accident investigation, the car manufacturers exude presumptions of engineering excellence and reliability, and this reputation is accepted by many unknowing motorists.❞
>
> —from *Unsafe at Any Speed*

Nader's efforts received an accidental boost from an unlikely source: the auto industry. Shortly after his book came out, a car company hired private detectives to follow Nader in an attempt to uncover information that might discredit him. The detectives found nothing, and when this corporate spying incident came to light, the publicity pushed *Unsafe at Any Speed* up the bestseller list. As a result, the public became much more aware of auto safety issues. Nader sued the car company for invasion of privacy and used the settlement money to fund several consumer organizations.

Nader's efforts helped spur Congress to pass the **National Traffic and Motor Vehicle Safety Act** in 1966. The act set mandatory safety standards and established a procedure for notifying car owners about defects. For the first time, the automobile industry was subject to federal safety regulations. Carmakers had to incorporate safety standards into their car designs so that auto crashes would be less devastating. Requirements that called for the installation of seat belts, door locks, safer fuel tanks, and other improvements have since saved hundreds of thousands of lives and prevented millions of injuries.

Nader's success led to calls for a closer examination of numerous other consumer goods during the 1960s and 1970s. Organizations lobbied Congress and state legislatures to pass laws regulating such products as dangerous toys, flammable fabrics, and potentially unsafe meat and poultry.

✓ **Reading Check** **Describing** What was the impact of the consumer protection movement?

HISTORY Online **Study Central**™ To review this section, go to **tarvol2.glencoe.com** and click on **Study Central**™.

SECTION 4 ASSESSMENT

Checking for Understanding
1. **Define:** smog, fossil fuel.
2. **Identify:** Rachel Carson, Environmental Protection Agency, Three Mile Island, Ralph Nader.
3. **List** three measures taken to combat environmental problems in the 1960s and 1970s.

Reviewing Themes
4. **Groups and Institutions** What groups lobbied for government legislation to protect the environment in the 1960s and 1970s?

Critical Thinking
5. **Evaluating** Which environmental issue do you think is the most pressing problem the environment faces today? Explain your response.
6. **Categorizing** Use a graphic organizer similar to the one below to list the environmental laws passed in the 1970s and explain their purposes.

Environmental Legislation	Purpose

Analyzing Visuals
7. **Analyzing Posters** Examine the "Love It or Leave It" poster on page 821. This phrase was first used by Vietnam War supporters, directed toward critics of the war and referring to the United States instead of the earth. How has the phrase been adapted here?

Writing About History
8. **Descriptive Writing** Take on the role of an investigative reporter and describe the environmental disaster at either Love Canal or Three Mile Island. Explain how community activism brought the issue to the nation's attention.

CHAPTER 26 The Politics of Protest **823**

SECTION 4 ASSESSMENT ANSWERS

1. Terms are in blue.
2. Rachel Carson (p. 820), Environmental Protection Agency (p. 821), Three Mile Island (p. 822), Ralph Nader (p. 823)
3. three of the following: Clean Air Act, Clean Water Act, Endangered Species Act, creation of the EPA,

Earth Day
4. the Natural Resource Defense Council, Sierra Club, Audubon Society, and Wilderness Society
5. Students' answers will vary.
6. the Clean Air Act: emission standards for cars and factories; the Clean Water Act: restricted dis-

charge of pollutants into lakes and rivers; the Endangered Species Act: measures to save animal species
7. The choices are to take care of the planet or die.
8. Students' reports will vary.

L2

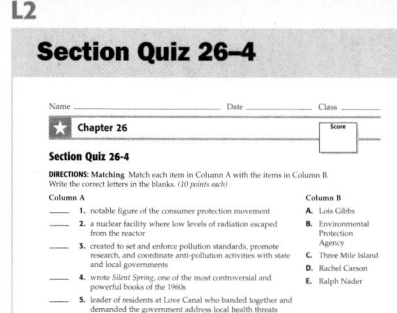

Section Quiz 26–4

Name _____ Date _____ Class _____

⭐ Chapter 26   Score ☐

Section Quiz 26-4

DIRECTIONS: Matching Match each item in Column A with the items in Column B. Write the correct letters in the blanks. *(10 points each)*

Column A
1. notable figure of the consumer protection movement
2. a nuclear facility where low levels of radiation escaped from the reactor
3. created to set and enforce pollution standards, promote research, and coordinate anti-pollution activities with state and local governments
4. wrote *Silent Spring*, one of the most controversial and powerful books of the 1960s
5. leader of residents at Love Canal who banded together and demanded the government address local health threats

Column B
A. Lois Gibbs
B. Environmental Protection Agency
C. Three Mile Island
D. Rachel Carson
E. Ralph Nader

📁 Use *Interpreting Political Cartoons,* Cartoon 33.

Reading Check

Answer: It raised awareness about the quality and safety of products.

Reteach
Have students identify significant environmental laws.

Enrich
Invite interested students to write a book review of *Silent Spring* by Rachel Carson or *Earth in the Balance: Ecology and the Human Spirit* by Al Gore.

Study Central™ provides summaries, interactive games, and online graphic organizers to help students review section content.

4 CLOSE

Have students explain the origins of the environmental movement.

NATIONAL GEOGRAPHIC

Geography&History

1 FOCUS

Have students identify the continents that contribute the parts and labor needed to assemble the Chevrolet Corvette. (*North America, South America, Europe, Asia, and Australia*)

2 TEACH

Making Generalizations Have students study the map and read the feature. Ask students to write a sentence that makes a generalization about how economic interdependence fosters communication and affects countries' willingness to resolve differences without resorting to war. **L1**

Researching the Manufacturing Process Have students work in small groups to research the source of components for a product such as computers, televisions, or appliances. Encourage students to identify products that are manufactured in your city, county, or state. Students may find it useful to interview the purchasing manager of the manufacturer to gather the needed information. If students do conduct interviews, tell them to be ready with specific questions and to be able to explain the purpose of their project. Remind students to write notes thanking the person for the information. Based on the information, have the groups prepare a world resource map similar to the one in the feature. **L2**

Engines are made in **Canada,** close to the automotive assembly centers of the United States.

Transmissions are manufactured in **Mexico,** where labor costs are relatively low.

CANADA

GERMANY

UNITED STATES
Bowling Green, KY.

MEXICO

ECUADOR

Light and durable balsa wood **floor plates** are produced in **Ecuador**, because the wood is abundant there.

The production of a GM Chevrolet Corvette in Bowling Green, Kentucky, requires the assembly of components from around the world: an engine from Canada, a transmission from Mexico, balsa wood floor plates from Ecuador, switches from Germany, circuit boards from several Asian nations, and brakes from Australia.

824   CHAPTER 26   The Politics of Protest

EXTENDING THE CONTENT

Museum Delivery Corvette owners can take delivery of their new vehicle at The National Corvette Museum in Bowling Green, Kentucky. Their cars are placed in the museum, on exhibit with the classic Corvettes displayed in the museum. New owners can take pictures of their cars in the museum display before the cars are removed from the museum and presented to them. Owners who select this option for delivery are also treated to a VIP tour of the museum, receive a specially designed Corvette Museum Delivery decal, and get a one-year membership to the museum.

A **German** factory produces very high quality **switches** that can easily be shipped to the United States.

JAPAN

Circuit boards are assembled with parts from **Japan, Thailand,** and **Singapore.**

ILAND

GAPORE

AUSTRALIA

An **Australian** company with manufacturing facilities in the United States provides the premier **brake pads** needed in high-performance vehicles.

Global Cars

The globalization of the world economy since the end of World War II has revolutionized the way in which industries and corporations operate. Tremendous advances in technology, communications, and the transport of goods have enabled corporations to turn more and more often to manufacturing facilities and resources around the world. The car industry is a good example of this trend.

For decades American automakers have operated assembly plants in foreign countries, including Brazil, Poland, India, and China. Car companies have also established plants abroad that manufacture particular components, which are then assembled in an American factory. As shown on the world map on the left, foreign manufacturers build major components of the Chevrolet Corvette and ship them to Bowling Green, Kentucky. There, workers assemble the parts—along with some 1,900 others manufactured by about 400 suppliers—into the finished car. The process of finding part suppliers outside of the company, known as "outsourcing," is one way multinational corporations try to gain a competitive advantage over their rivals. Companies contract with foreign suppliers that meet a combination of criteria, including cost, quality, and ease of delivery.

Computers and the Internet have made worldwide communication dramatically easier, faster, and cheaper.

A worker assembles a Corvette at a plant in Bowling Green, Kentucky.

Technological advances have also made manufacturing more efficient. For example, automakers can keep track of parts and suppliers so that the essential components can be delivered to factories from anywhere in the world "just in time" to assemble the finished product.

Multinational corporations now account for about two-thirds of the world's trade in products. Global corporations have become enormous, and the largest ones are wealthier than entire countries. The income of General Motors, for instance, rivals gross national products of the mid-sized economies of nations such as South Africa, Turkey, and Saudi Arabia.

The auto industry has come a long way since Henry Ford perfected assembly line production techniques that made cars affordable for the mass market. Today's automakers have adopted global assembly lines, applying Ford's innovations—standardized job tasks and division of labor—across international boundaries.

Cars are shipped all over the world. Here, Japanese cars are unloaded from a large container ship in Baltimore, Maryland.

LEARNING FROM GEOGRAPHY

1. What three criteria are considered in decisions about suppliers?

2. Why might geography no longer be as big a factor as it once was in the location of a production plant?

CHAPTER 26   The Politics of Protest   **825**

NATIONAL GEOGRAPHIC

Geography&History

FYI

The International Organization for Standards (ISO), formed in 1947, is a worldwide organization that works with standard-setting bodies in 140 countries. The ISO's mission is to encourage uniform standards across borders in order to facilitate the worldwide exchange of goods and services.

3 ASSESS

Have students answer the Learning from Geography questions.

L2

Geography and History Activity 7

4 CLOSE

Review with students the critical roles that computers, the Internet, and good transportation systems play in today's manufacturing.

NGS ONLINE

Access National Geographic's Web site for current events, atlas updates, activities, links, interactive features, and archives at www.nationalgeographic.com.

ANSWERS TO LEARNING FROM GEOGRAPHY

1. The criteria are cost, quality, and ease of delivery.

2. Answers may vary. Students should note that improved communication and transport allow parts to be delivered to the assembly line just when they are needed.

Reviewing Key Terms

Students' answers will vary. The pages where the words appear in the text are shown in parentheses.

1. **counterculture** *(p. 802)*
2. **commune** *(p. 803)*
3. **feminism** *(p. 807)*
4. **Title IX** *(p. 809)*
5. **affirmative action** *(p. 813)*
6. **busing** *(p. 814)*
7. **bilingualism** *(p. 815)*
8. **smog** *(p. 820)*
9. **fossil fuel** *(p. 822)*

Reviewing Key Facts

10. Tom Hayden *(p. 801)*, Haight-Ashbury district *(p. 803)*, Jimi Hendrix *(p. 805)*, Equal Employment Opportunity Commission *(p. 808)*, Betty Friedan *(p. 808)*, National Organization for Women *(p. 808)*, Allan Bakke *(p. 813)*, Jesse Jackson *(p. 814)*, Congressional Black Caucus *(p. 815)*, La Raza Unida *(p. 815)*, American Indian Movement *(p. 816)*, Rachel Carson *(p. 820)*, Environmental Protection Agency *(p. 821)*, Ralph Nader *(p. 823)*

11. Title VII outlawed job discrimination on the basis of gender as well as of race, color, religion, and national origin.

12. Betty Friedan wrote *The Feminine Mystique* and founded the National Organization for Women (NOW).

13. because they saw it as a threat to traditional values and social patterns

Reviewing Key Terms

On a sheet of paper, use each of these terms in a sentence.

1. counterculture
2. commune
3. feminism
4. Title IX
5. affirmative action
6. busing
7. bilingualism
8. smog
9. fossil fuel

Reviewing Key Facts

10. **Identify:** Tom Hayden, Haight-Ashbury district, Jimi Hendrix, Equal Employment Opportunity Commission, Betty Friedan, National Organization for Women, Allan Bakke, Jesse Jackson, Congressional Black Caucus, *La Raza Unida*, American Indian Movement, Rachel Carson, Environmental Protection Agency, Ralph Nader.

11. How did Title VII of the Civil Rights Act of 1964 promote women's equality?

12. How did Betty Friedan stimulate the feminist movement?

13. Why were some conservatives opposed to the Equal Rights Amendment?

14. How did Native Americans expand their political rights and economic opportunities in the 1960s and 1970s?

15. How did the environmental movement begin?

Critical Thinking

16. **Analyzing Themes: Civic Rights and Responsibilities** Choose a minority group discussed in this chapter, and explain how this group worked to gain civil rights and to improve its status in American society during the 1960s and 1970s.

17. **Organizing** Use a graphic organizer to list the protest movements of the 1960s and 1970s and their goals.

Movement		Goals
	→	
	→	
	→	
	→	
	→	

Chapter Summary

Speaking Out for Equality

Youth Movement
Protests Status Quo
- Grows out of earlier "beat" movement
- Becomes increasingly influential as "baby boom" generation matures
- Protests injustices facing African Americans, the poor, and the disadvantaged
- Free Speech Movement establishes tactics of boycotting college classes and occupying buildings
- Hippie counterculture rebels against system, visualizes utopian ideals

Women's Movement
Regains Momentum
- Fights for equal economic rights in workplace and society
- Demands equal opportunities in education
- *Roe* v. *Wade* expands access to abortion

Minority Groups
Continue the Fight
- Expand on earlier success and speed up access to previous gains
- Affirmative Action advocates equality in work environment for minority and disadvantaged groups
- Native Americans gain more power on reservations and fight discrimination, unemployment, police brutality, and poverty
- Hispanic Americans lobby for better working conditions and job training

Environmental and Consumer Groups
New Concerns Emerge
- First Earth Day sparks widespread awareness of environmental issues
- Federal government establishes pollution standards and begins monitoring environmental problems
- State and federal legislatures pass laws regulating the safety standards for a wide variety of consumer products

14. By protesting, Native Americans helped get legislation passed that provided education assistance, won land and water rights, the right to tax reservations, and other sovereign functions.

15. The environmental movement began with the Earth Day celebration.

Critical Thinking

16. Students' answers will vary. You may want to assign students to different groups.

17. Youth: improve the political and social system; Women: women's rights; Hispanics: voting and economic rights; Native Americans: economic opportunities and independence; Environment: protect the environment

18. Over time, mainstream America accepted many of the ideas of the counterculture. Individuality and self-expression became more accepted. Counterculture styles of clothing, art, music, and dance came to be considered normal.

HISTORY Online

Self-Check Quiz

Visit the *American Republic Since 1877* Web site at tarvol2.glencoe.com and click on *Self-Check Quizzes—Chapter 26* to assess your knowledge of chapter content.

18. **Evaluating** In what ways did the counterculture movement change American society?

19. **Drawing Conclusions** Why do you think so many protest movements emerged in the United States during the 1960s and 1970s?

Practicing Skills

20. **Analyzing Primary Sources** Reread "An American Story" at the beginning of Section 2 on page 806. Then answer the questions below.
   a. Whose opinion is expressed in this letter?
   b. When was this letter written? In what publication did it appear?
   c. What role in society is the writer discussing? What is her opinion of this role?

Chapter Activities

21. **American History Primary Source Document Library CD-ROM** Under *Struggle for Civil Rights,* read "Delano Grape Workers, A Proclamation." Research the opinions of other groups opposed to the grape boycott. Using the information you have gathered, work with a few of your classmates to create a two-minute television advertisement to persuade Americans to join or condemn the grape boycott. In your presentation, you should use facts you learned about the boycott.

22. **Creating a Database, Thematic Model, and Quiz** Use the Internet and other resources to research student protests in the 1960s and 1970s. Create a database of these protests that clearly depicts where, when, and why the protests took place. Then create a thematic model of this information by labeling the locations of the protests on a map of the United States. Finally, create a quiz for your classmates by writing five questions about the geographic distribution of the protests and the patterns this might suggest.

Writing Activity

23. **Persuasive Writing** Use library and Internet resources to learn about the predictions scientists are making on how future population growth and distribution will affect the physical environment. Pay special attention to the evidence that these scientists use and the types of predictions that each makes. Is there agreement or disagreement in the scientific community about population growth and its environmental effects? Present the findings of your research in a written report.

NATIONAL GEOGRAPHIC — **ERA Ratification, 1972–1982** — *In Motion*

Date Ratified:
- 1972
- 1973
- 1974
- 1975
- 1977
- Did not ratify

Albers Conic Equal-Area projection

Geography and History

24. The map above shows the states that ratified the Equal Rights Amendment between 1972 and 1982. Study the map and answer the questions below.
   a. **Interpreting Maps** How many states had ratified the Equal Rights Amendment by 1977?
   b. **Applying Geography Skills** What conclusion can you draw about the distribution of states that did not approve the ERA?

Standardized Test Practice

Directions: Choose the phrase that best completes the following sentence.

Congress did not act on the first proposed Equal Rights Amendment because

F the amendment did not do enough to protect women and children.

G the National Woman's Party opposed the amendment.

H the amendment lacked support due to a divided women's movement.

J the amendment did not address discrimination by gender.

Test-Taking Tip: Use the process of elimination to help answer this question. For example, since the intent of the Equal Rights Amendment was to reduce discrimination by gender, you can rule out answer J.

HISTORY Online

Have students visit the Web site at tarvol2.glencoe.com to review Chapter 26 and take the Self-Check Quiz.

Geography and History

24. **a.** 35 states had ratified the ERA by 1977. **b.** States that did not ratify the ERA tended to be in the more socially conservative and rural areas of the country.

Standardized Test Practice

Answer: H
Test-Taking Tip: Tell students that even if they do not remember all the details about the first Equal Rights Amendment, they may be able to eliminate some of the answers. For example, they may remember that the National Woman's Party was the group that *proposed* the amendment, and so they can rule out answer G.

Bonus Question ?

Ask: Who was the first African American woman to serve in Congress? *(Shirley Chisholm)*

---

19. Answers will vary. Students should note the relative prosperity of many Americans and the growing sense of disillusionment on the part of groups left out of social, economic, and political life.

Practicing Skills

20. **a.** Herma Snider, a young mother; **b.** 1960; *Redbook* magazine; **c.** the roles of wife, mother, and homemaker; feeling of needing more in her life beyond these roles

Chapter Activities

21. Students' projects will vary. Advertisements should be factual and persuasive.

22. Answers will vary. Encourage students to trade their quizzes and see how their classmates do.

Writing Activity

23. Answers will vary. Reports should reflect findings grounded in scientific evidence.

SUGGESTED PACING CHART

Unit 8 (1 Day)	Chapter 27 (5 Days)	Chapter 28 (5 Days)	Chapter 29 (6 Days)	Unit 8 (2 Days)
Day 1 Introduction	**Day 1** Chapter 27 Intro, Section 1	**Day 1** Chapter 28 Intro, Section 1	**Day 1** Chapter 29 Intro, Section 1	**Day 1** Wrap-Up/Project
	Day 2 Section 2	**Day 2** Section 2	**Day 2** Section 2	**Day 2** Unit 8 Assessment
	Day 3 Section 3	**Day 3** Section 3	**Day 3** Section 3	
	Day 4 Section 4	**Day 4** Section 4	**Day 4** Section 4	
	Day 5 Chapter 27 Assessment	**Day 5** Chapter 28 Assessment	**Day 5** Section 5	
			Day 6 Chapter 29 Assessment	

GLENCOE'S ASSESSMENT ADVANTAGE

Use the following tools to easily assess student learning in a variety of ways:

- Performance Assessment Activities and Rubrics
- Chapter and Unit Tests
- Section Quizzes
- Standardized Test Practice Workbook

- tarvol2.glencoe.com
- Interactive Tutor Self-Assessment CD-ROM
- MindJogger Videoquiz
- ExamView® Pro Testmaker CD-ROM
- SAT I/II Test Practice

TEACHING TRANSPARENCIES

Unit 8 Map Overlay Transparencies
L2

Cause-and-Effect Transparency 8
L2

READING SUPPORT FROM
JAMESTOWN EDUCATION

- *Timed Readings Plus in Social Studies* help students increase their reading rate and fluency while maintaining comprehension. The 400-word passages are similar to those found on state and national assessments.

- *Reading in the Content Area: Social Studies* concentrates on six essential reading skills that help students better comprehend what they read. The book includes 75 high-interest nonfiction passages written at increasing levels of difficulty.

- *Reading Fluency* helps students read smoothly, accurately, and expressively.

- *Jamestown's Reading Improvement,* by renowned reading expert Edward Fry, focuses on helping build your students' comprehension, vocabulary, and skimming and scanning skills.

- *Critical Reading Series* provides high-interest books, each written at three reading levels.

For more information about these products, see the Jamestown Education materials in the Classroom Solutions in the front of this Teacher Wraparound Edition. To order these products, call Glencoe at 1-800-334-7344.

Unit 8 Resources

ASSESSMENT

Unit 8 Pretests L2

Unit 8 Posttests L2

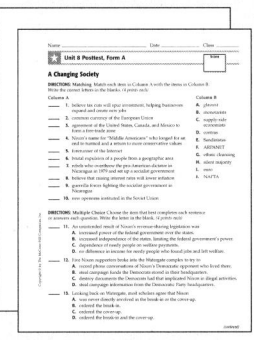

APPLICATION AND ENRICHMENT

American Biography 8 L2

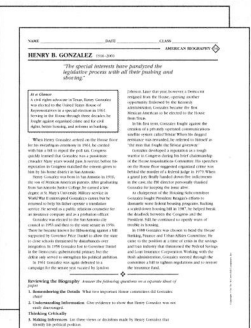

History Simulation and Problem Solving 8 L1

GEOGRAPHY

Geography and History Activity 8 L2

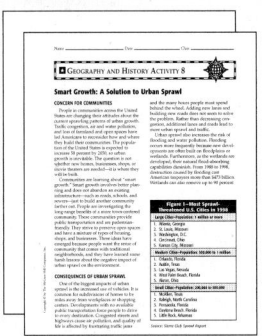

INTERDISCIPLINARY ACTIVITIES

American Literature Reading 8 L2

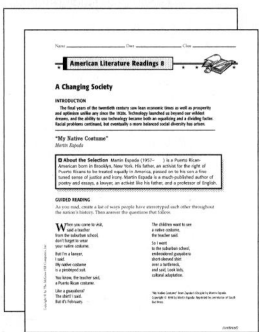

Economics and History Activity 8 L2

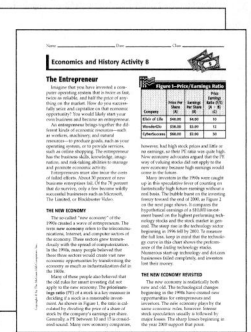

Team-Teaching Interdisciplinary Strategies and Activities 8 L2

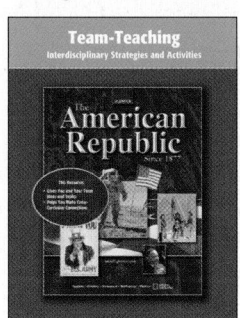

Reading List Generator CD-ROM

GLENCOE BOOKLINK

The Glencoe BookLink CD-ROM is a database that allows you to search more than 15,000 titles to create a customized reading list for your students.

- Reading lists can be organized by students' reading level, author, genre, theme, or area of interest.

- The database provides Degrees of Reading Power™ (DRP) and Lexile™ readability scores for all selections.

- A brief summary of each selection is included.

Leveled reading suggestions for this unit:

For students at a Grade 8 reading level:
- *The Haunted Land: Facing Europe's Ghosts after Communism,* by Tina Rosenberg.

For students at a Grade 9 reading level:
- *White House Years,* by Henry Kissinger.

For students at a Grade 10 reading level:
- *Living in Space,* by Giovanni Caprara.

Extending the Content

Readings for the Teacher
- *Pride and Prosperity: The 80s (Our American Century),* edited by Time-Life Books. Time Life, 1999.

Multimedia Resources
- *Watergate Hearings: Summer of Judgment.* WETA. VHS. (120 minutes)
- *Spaceship Earth: Our Global Environment.* WORLDLINK. VHS. (25 minutes)

⎓:⎓⎓ Out of Time?

If time does not permit teaching each chapter in this unit, you may want to use the **Reading Essentials and Study Guide** summaries.

Unit Overview

Unit 8 describes the changing society from 1968 to the present. **Chapter 27** explores the politics and economics of the Nixon, Ford, and Carter years. **Chapter 28** focuses on the resurgence of conservatism from 1980 to 1992. **Chapter 29** describes recent events in American history including the Clinton presidency and the terrorist attacks on the World Trade Center and the Pentagon.

Unit Objectives

After studying this unit, students will be able to:

1. Describe Nixon's foreign policy achievements.

2. Explain President Reagan's economic recovery plans.

3. Describe the ways in which technology has affected American business and communications.

Why It Matters Activity

Have students write down one fact they know or opinion they have about the following presidents: President Reagan, President George H. W. Bush, President Clinton, and President George W. Bush. Have volunteers share their statements with the class, having the class identify the statement as fact or opinion.

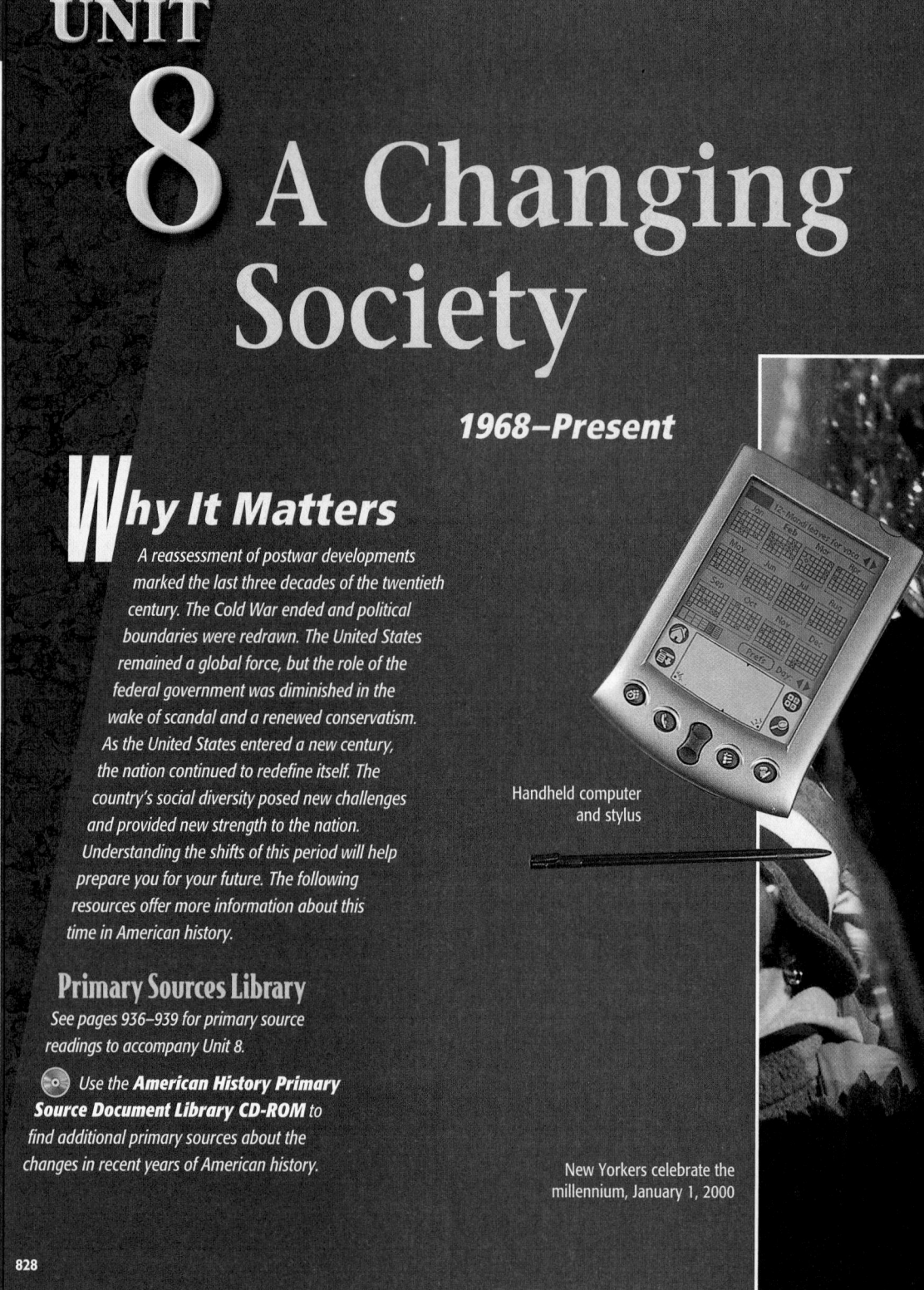

UNIT 8

A Changing Society

1968–Present

Why It Matters

A reassessment of postwar developments marked the last three decades of the twentieth century. The Cold War ended and political boundaries were redrawn. The United States remained a global force, but the role of the federal government was diminished in the wake of scandal and a renewed conservatism. As the United States entered a new century, the nation continued to redefine itself. The country's social diversity posed new challenges and provided new strength to the nation. Understanding the shifts of this period will help prepare you for your future. The following resources offer more information about this time in American history.

Primary Sources Library

See pages 936–939 for primary source readings to accompany Unit 8.

💿 *Use the **American History Primary Source Document Library CD-ROM** to find additional primary sources about the changes in recent years of American history.*

Handheld computer and stylus

New Yorkers celebrate the millennium, January 1, 2000

828

TEAM TEACHING ACTIVITY

Microchips Invite the science or technology teacher to share with students the basic makeup of a microchip and explain how we use microchips in a variety of products daily. As part of the discussion, have the class create a list of all the products they use that include microchip technology. Encourage class members to add to the list as they study this unit. 📦

"*I was not elected to serve one party, but to serve one nation.*"

—George W. Bush, 2001

GLENCOE
TECHNOLOGY

CD-ROM
American History
Primary Source
Document Library
CD-ROM
Use the **American History Primary Source Document Library CD-ROM** to access primary source documents related to this period in history.

More About the Photo

Tell students that watching the famous ball drop from One Times Square signaling the arrival of the new year has been a New York tradition since 1906. Ask students how they celebrated the millennium's arrival.

SERVICE-LEARNING PROJECT

Have students learn more about Habitat for Humanity. You may suggest that students visit www.habitat.org as a starting point for finding information. Identify a Habitat for Humanity house project that is planned for your community, or in a nearby community. Contact the Habitat affiliate nearest you to find out about opportunities for your students to participate in some phase of the program. Encourage students to record their experiences either in pictures or words.

Refer to ***Building Bridges: Connecting Classroom and Community through Service-Learning in Social Studies*** from the National Council for the Social Studies for information about service-learning.

Chapter 27 Resources

Timesaving Tools

TeacherWorks™ All-In-One Planner and Resource Center

- **Interactive Teacher Edition** Access your Teacher Wraparound Edition and your classroom resources with a few easy clicks.
- **Interactive Lesson Planner** Planning has never been easier! Organize your week, month, semester, or year with all the lesson helps you need to make teaching creative, timely, and relevant.

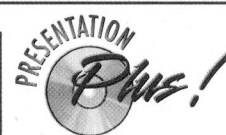

Use Glencoe's **Presentation Plus!** multimedia teacher tool to easily present dynamic lessons that visually excite your students. Using Microsoft PowerPoint® you can customize the presentations to create your own personalized lessons.

TEACHING TRANSPARENCIES

Graphic Organizer 12 L2

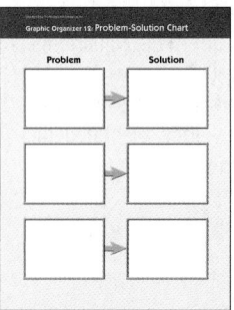

Why It Matters Chapter Transparency 27 L2

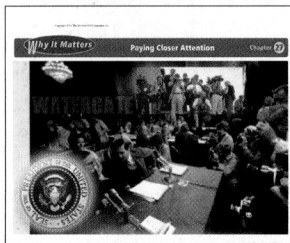

APPLICATION AND ENRICHMENT

Linking Past and Present Activity 27 L2

Enrichment Activity 27 L3

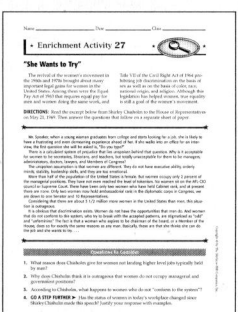

Primary Source Reading 27 L2

REVIEW AND REINFORCEMENT

Reteaching Activity 27 L1

Vocabulary Activity 27 L1

Time Line Activity 27 L2

Critical Thinking Skills Activity 27 L2

Meeting NCSS Standards

The following standards are covered in Chapter 27:

Section 1 IX Global Connections: B, D
Section 2 VI Power, Authority, and Governance: B, C, E, F
Section 3 VII Production, Distribution, and Consumption: A, B
Section 4 I Culture: A, C, E

Local Standards

ASSESSMENT AND EVALUATION

Chapter 27 Test Form A L2

Chapter 27 Test Form B L2

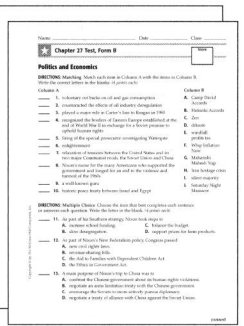

Standardized Test Practice Workbook Activity 27 L2

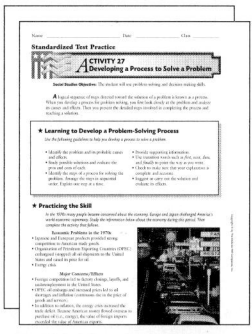

Performance Assessment Activities and Rubrics 27 L1/ELL

ExamView® Pro Testmaker CD-ROM

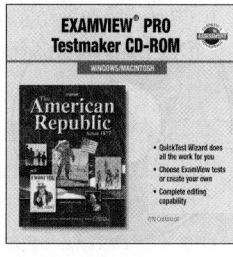

MULTIMEDIA

- Vocabulary PuzzleMaker CD-ROM
- Interactive Tutor Self-Assessment CD-ROM
- ExamView® Pro Testmaker CD-ROM
- Audio Program
- American History Primary Source Documents Library CD-ROM
- MindJogger Videoquiz
- Presentation Plus! CD-ROM
- TeacherWorks™ CD-ROM
- Interactive Student Edition CD-ROM
- Glencoe Skillbuilder Interactive Workbook CD-ROM, Level 2
- The *American Republic Since 1877* Video Program
- American Music: Hits Through History
- American Music: Cultural Traditions

SPANISH RESOURCES

The following Spanish language materials are available:

- Spanish Reading Essentials and Study Guide
- Spanish Guided Reading Activities
- Spanish Reteaching Activities
- Spanish Quizzes and Tests
- Spanish Vocabulary Activities
- Spanish Summaries
- The Declaration of Independence and United States Constitution Spanish Translation

THE HISTORY CHANNEL®

The following videotape programs are available from Glencoe as supplements to Chapter 27:

- **Richard M. Nixon: Man and President** (ISBN 1-56-501742-0)
- **The Secret Service** (Four-video Set) (ISBN 1-56-501521-5)
- **Jimmy Carter** (ISBN 1-56-501530-4)

To order, call Glencoe at 1-800-334-7344. To find classroom resources to accompany many of these videos, check the following home pages:
A&E Television: www.aande.com
The History Channel: www.historychannel.com

HISTORY Online

Use our Web site for additional resources. All essential content is covered in the Student Edition.

You and your students can visit tarvol2.glencoe.com, the Web site companion to the ***American Republic Since 1877***. This innovative integration of electronic and print media offers your students a wealth of opportunities. The student text directs students to the Web site for the following options:

- **Chapter Overviews**
- **Self-Check Quizzes**
- **Student Web Activities**
- **Textbook Updates**

Answers to the student Web activities are provided for you in the **Web Activity Lesson Plans.** Additional Web resources and Interactive Tutor Puzzles are also available.

Chapter 27 Resources

SECTION RESOURCES

Daily Objectives	Reproducible Resources	Multimedia Resources
SECTION 1 **The Nixon Administration** 1. Describe Nixon's domestic agenda. 2. Discuss Nixon's foreign policy achievements.	Reproducible Lesson Plan 27–1 Daily Lecture and Discussion Notes 27–1 Guided Reading Activity 27–1* Section Quiz 27–1* Reading Essentials and Study Guide 27–1* Performance Assessment Activities and Rubrics	Daily Focus Skills Transparency 27–1 Interactive Tutor Self-Assessment CD-ROM ExamView® Pro Testmaker CD-ROM* Presentation Plus! CD-ROM TeacherWorks™ CD-ROM Audio Program
SECTION 2 **The Watergate Scandal** 1. Describe the character of Richard Nixon and the attitude of his White House. 2. Explain the Watergate scandal and discuss its effects.	Reproducible Lesson Plan 27–2 Daily Lecture and Discussion Notes 27–2 Guided Reading Activity 27–2* Section Quiz 27–2* Reading Essentials and Study Guide 27–2* Performance Assessment Activities and Rubrics Supreme Court Case Studies	Daily Focus Skills Transparency 27–2 Interactive Tutor Self-Assessment CD-ROM ExamView® Pro Testmaker CD-ROM* Presentation Plus! CD-ROM TeacherWorks™ CD-ROM Audio Program
SECTION 3 **Ford and Carter** 1. Explain the reasons for economic troubles in the United States during the 1970s. 2. Discuss Jimmy Carter's domestic and foreign policies.	Reproducible Lesson Plan 27–3 Daily Lecture and Discussion Notes 27–3 Guided Reading Activity 27–3* Section Quiz 27–3* Reading Essentials and Study Guide 27–3* Performance Assessment Activities and Rubrics	Daily Focus Skills Transparency 27–3 Interactive Tutor Self-Assessment CD-ROM ExamView® Pro Testmaker CD-ROM* Presentation Plus! CD-ROM TeacherWorks™ CD-ROM Audio Program
SECTION 4 **The "Me" Decade: Life in the 1970s** 1. Explain the emergence of new spiritual movements and religions. 2. Discuss the disappearance of some traditional values during the 1970s.	Reproducible Lesson Plan 27–4 Daily Lecture and Discussion Notes 27–4 Guided Reading Activity 27–4* Section Quiz 27–4* Reading Essentials and Study Guide 27–4* Performance Assessment Activities and Rubrics Interpreting Political Cartoons	Daily Focus Skills Transparency 27–4 Interactive Tutor Self-Assessment CD-ROM ExamView® Pro Testmaker CD-ROM* Presentation Plus! CD-ROM Skillbuilder Interactive Workbook, Level 2 TeacherWorks™ CD-ROM Vocabulary PuzzleMaker CD-ROM* Audio Program American Music: Hits Through History American Music: Cultural Traditions

`0:00` OUT OF TIME?
Assign the Chapter 27 **Reading Essentials and Study Guide.**

*Also Available in Spanish

 Printed Materials   Transparency   CD-ROM   DVD

 Poster   Music Program   Audio Program

Chapter 27 Resources

NATIONAL GEOGRAPHIC Teacher's Corner

INDEX TO NATIONAL GEOGRAPHIC MAGAZINE

The following articles relate to this chapter.

- "Great Lakes: Troubled Water," July 1987
- "Our Polluted Runoff," February 1996
- "Tex-Mex Border," February 1996

NATIONAL GEOGRAPHIC SOCIETY PRODUCTS

To order the following, call National Geographic at 1-800-368-2728:

- *Branches of Government Series* (Video)
- *Democratic Government Series: The United States* (Video)
- *Historical Atlas of the United States* (Atlas)
- *National Geographic World Atlas for Young Explorers—Classroom Library Edition* (Guide, Transparencies, Resource Masters)

NGS ONLINE

Access National Geographic's Web site for current events, atlas updates, activities, links, interactive features, and archives.

www.nationalgeographic.com

MEETING SPECIAL NEEDS

In addition to the Differentiated Instruction strategies found in each section, the following resources are also suitable for your special needs students:

- *ExamView® Pro Testmaker CD-ROM* allows teachers to tailor tests by reducing answer choices.
- The *Audio Program* includes the entire narrative of the student edition so that less-proficient readers can listen to the words as they read them.
- The *Reading Essentials and Study Guide* provides the same content as the student edition but is written two grade levels below the textbook.
- *Guided Reading Activities* give less-proficient readers point-by-point instructions to increase comprehension as they read each textbook section.

KEY TO ABILITY LEVELS

Teaching strategies have been coded.

- **L1** BASIC activities for all students
- **L2** AVERAGE activities for average to above-average students
- **L3** CHALLENGING activities for above-average students
- **ELL** ENGLISH LANGUAGE LEARNER activities

From the Classroom of...

Mary Jo Dudek
Erie 1 Board of Cooperative Educational Services
West Seneca, NY

1776 or 1976?

Have students imagine that either George Washington, Thomas Jefferson, or James Madison had traveled from 1776 to 1976. **Ask:** *What do you think their impressions of our country's political system would be?*

After the class has discussed the topic, have students write either a journal entry or letter from the point of view of one of these former presidents as they view the United States at its bicentennial. Journal entries and letters should address whether these presidents would be proud or ashamed of what they saw. Encourage students to explain why the presidents feel the way they do.

ADDITIONAL RESOURCES FROM GLENCOE

- American Music: Cultural Traditions
- American Art & Architecture
- Outline Map Resource Book
- U.S. Desk Map
- Building Geography Skills for Life
- Inclusion for the High School Social Studies Classroom Strategies and Activities
- Teaching Strategies for the American History Classroom (Including Block Scheduling Pacing Guides)
- Dinah Zike's High School American History Reading and Study Skills Foldables

Block Schedule

Activities that are suited to use within the block scheduling framework are identified by:

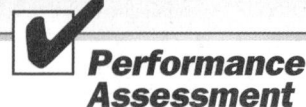

✓ *Performance Assessment*

Refer to Activity 27 in the Performance Assessment Activities and Rubrics booklet.

Why It Matters Activity

Have each student ask an adult what impact he or she thinks Watergate had on politics in America. Have students share their observations. Have students reevaluate their observations after they have completed the chapter.

GLENCOE
TECHNOLOGY

The *American Republic Since 1877* Video Program
To learn more about the circumstances surrounding the Watergate scandal, have students view the Chapter 27 video, "The Watergate Break-In," from the ***American Republic Since 1877* Video Program.**

MindJogger Videoquiz
Use the **MindJogger Videoquiz** to preview Chapter 27 content.

 Both programs available in DVD

CHAPTER
27 Politics and Economics *1971–1980*

Why It Matters

The protests of the 1960s were passionate and sometimes violent. The nation elected President Nixon on a promise to uphold the values of what Nixon called "Middle America." In foreign policy, Nixon charted a new path with a historic visit to China. At home he introduced "New Federalism." In 1974 the Watergate scandal forced Nixon to resign. Presidents Ford and Carter faced an economic downturn and a major energy crisis.

The Impact Today

Experiences of the 1970s have had an impact today.
- *The Watergate scandal has left many Americans less confident in political leaders.*
- *The Department of Energy, created by President Carter, still exists as a cabinet-level agency.*

The **American Republic Since 1877** *Video The Chapter 27 video, "The Watergate Break-In," examines the circumstances surrounding this scandal.*

1972
- Nixon visits China and the Soviet Union
- Watergate burglars arrested at Democratic National Committee headquarters

1973
- *Roe* v. *Wade* Supreme Court decision legalizes abortion
- Senate Watergate investigations begin
- OPEC price increases cause inflation

1974
- Nixon resigns
- Gerald Ford becomes president

United States PRESIDENTS

Nixon 1969–1974

Ford 1974–1977

1971

1974

World

1971
- People's Republic of China admitted to UN

1973
- Britain, Ireland, and Denmark join Common Market

1974
- India becomes world's sixth nuclear power

830

Think/Write-Pair-Share Engage your students in the subject matter through discussion by using this strategy. Have students **T**hink silently about what they know about President Nixon and the Watergate scandal. Ask them to **W**rite three to five items on their papers. Have students **P**air with another student and **S**hare their ideas. Conclude with a class discussion. **L1**

📁 Refer to *Inclusion for the High School Social Studies Classroom Strategies and Activities* in the TCR.

President Nixon with Chinese premier Zhou Enlai (on Nixon's right) during Nixon's historic visit to China in 1972

1975
• President Ford signs Helsinki Accords

1976
• Jimmy Carter elected president

Carter 1977–1981

1979
• Iranian revolutionaries seize U.S. embassy in Tehran

1977

1980

1976
• Mao Zedong dies

1977
• Human rights manifesto signed by 241 Czech activists and intellectuals

1979
• Sandinista guerrillas overthrow dictatorship of Somoza

• Margaret Thatcher becomes prime minister of Great Britain

HISTORY
Online

Chapter Overview
Visit the *American Republic Since 1877* Web site at tarvol2.glencoe.com and click on **Chapter Overviews—Chapter 27** to preview chapter information.

831

More About the Photo

Point out to students that Nixon's visit to China in 1972 was historic because the United States had refused to recognize the Communist Chinese government since 1949. Ask students to consider how the meeting shown here would help ease tensions between the two countries. *(possible answers include: the leaders appear friendly, at ease, willing to negotiate)*

TIME LINE
ACTIVITY

Have students select one of the events on the world time line and identify the continent on which the event occurred. Have students speculate on the significance of the event to events happening in the United States at the time.

FOLDABLES™
Study Organizer

Dinah Zike's Foldables are three-dimensional, interactive graphic organizers that help students practice basic writing skills, review key vocabulary terms, and identify main ideas. Have students complete the foldable activity in the *Dinah Zike's Reading and Study Skills Foldables* booklet.

GRAPHIC ORGANIZER ACTIVITY

Organizing Information Have students use a graphic organizer similar to the one below to indicate the domestic and foreign policy challenges Nixon, Ford, and Carter faced. *(Answers will vary, but domestic challenges may include the Watergate scandal for Nixon, the pardoning of Nixon for Ford, and stagflation for Carter. Foreign challenges should include détente for Nixon, problems in Southeast Asia for Ford, and the Iranian hostage crisis for Carter.)*

Challenges	Nixon	Ford	Carter
Domestic			
Foreign			

1 FOCUS

Section Overview

This section focuses on the events of the Nixon presidency.

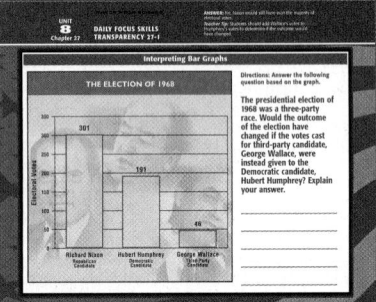
Reading Preview

Answers to Graphic:

Nixon Administration

Domestic policy	Foreign policy
New Federalism	Détente

Preteaching Vocabulary

Have students look up the meanings of the Key Terms and Names and use the words in a sentence.

SECTION 1 The Nixon Administration

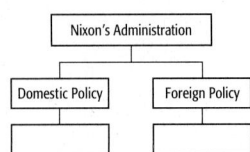

Guide to Reading

Main Idea

President Nixon sought to restore law and order and traditional values at home and to ease Cold War tensions abroad.

Key Terms and Names

Southern strategy, revenue sharing, impound, Henry Kissinger, détente, summit

Reading Strategy

Organizing As you read about President Nixon's administration, complete a graphic organizer by listing his domestic and foreign policies.

```
        Nixon's Administration
        /              \
Domestic Policy      Foreign Policy
    |                     |
[        ]            [        ]
```

Reading Objectives

- **Describe** Nixon's domestic agenda.
- **Discuss** Nixon's foreign policy achievements.

Section Theme

Global Connections One of President Nixon's most dramatic accomplishments was changing the relationship between the United States, Communist China, and the Soviet Union.

Preview of Events

♦1968	♦1970	♦1972	♦1974

1968
Nixon wins presidential election

1969
Nixon proposes Family Assistance Plan

February 1972
Nixon visits China

May 1972
Moscow hosts American-Soviet summit

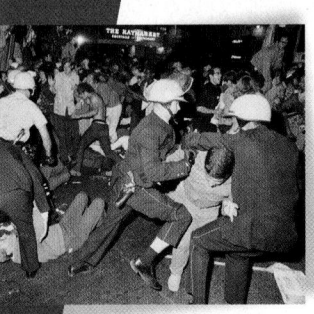

Students and police clash at the 1968 Democratic National Convention

★ *An American Story* ★

Millions of Americans saw police and demonstrators clash on the streets of Chicago at the Democratic National Convention in late August 1968. Many television viewers were outraged at the police tactics they saw. G.L. Halbert, however, was not one of them. To make his support of police efforts public, Halbert wrote a letter to *Newsweek* magazine:

❝Congratulations to Mayor Daley and the Chicago police on their tough handling of the yippies, Vietniks, and newsmen. If more mayors and police departments had the courage to crack down on those who carry only the flags of our enemies and newsmen who consistently slant their coverage of events in favor of those who would undermine and disrupt our country, there would be greater freedom for the majority of Americans rather than greater lawlessness for the few. It is a tragedy that such individuals are allowed to cringe behind our constitutional guarantees after they have wreaked destruction by their agitation.❞

—**quoted in *Newsweek*, September 16, 1968**

Appealing to Middle America

The views expressed by G.L. Halbert were not unusual. While they did not shout as loudly as the protesters, many Americans supported the government and longed for an end to the violence and turmoil that seemed to plague the nation in the 1960s. The presidential candidate in 1968 who appealed to many of these frustrated citizens was

832 CHAPTER 27 Politics and Economics

SECTION RESOURCES

📁 Reproducible Masters

- Reproducible Lesson Plan 27–1
- Daily Lecture and Discussion Notes 27–1
- Guided Reading Activity 27–1
- Section Quiz 27–1
- Reading Essentials and Study Guide 27–1
- Performance Assessment Activities and Rubrics

🖥 Transparencies

- Daily Focus Skills Transparency 27–1

Multimedia

- 💿 Interactive Tutor Self-Assessment CD-ROM
- 💿 ExamView® Pro Testmaker CD-ROM
- 💿 Presentation Plus! CD-ROM
- 💿 TeacherWorks™ CD-ROM
- 🎧 Audio Program

Richard Nixon, a Republican. Nixon aimed many of his campaign messages at these Americans, whom he referred to as "Middle America" and the "silent majority." He promised them "peace with honor" in Vietnam, law and order, a streamlined government, and a return to more traditional values at home.

The Election of 1968 Nixon's principal opponent in the 1968 presidential election was Democrat **Hubert Humphrey,** who had served as vice president under Lyndon Johnson. Nixon also had to wage his campaign against a strong third-party candidate, **George Wallace,** an experienced Southern politician and avowed supporter of segregation. In a 1964 bid for the Democratic presidential nomination, the former Alabama governor had attracted considerable support.

On Election Day, Wallace captured an impressive 13.5 percent of the popular vote, the best showing of a third-party candidate since 1924. Nixon managed a victory, however, receiving 43.4 percent of the popular vote to Humphrey's 42.7 and 301 electoral votes to Humphrey's 191.

The Southern Strategy One of the keys to Nixon's victory was his surprisingly strong showing in the South. Even though the South had long been a Democratic stronghold, Nixon had refused to concede the region. To gain Southern support, Nixon had met with powerful South Carolina senator Strom Thurmond and won his backing by promising several things: to appoint only conservatives to the federal courts, to name a Southerner to the Supreme Court, to oppose court-ordered busing, and to choose a vice presidential candidate acceptable to the South. (Nixon ultimately chose Spiro Agnew, governor of the border state of Maryland.)

Nixon's efforts paid off on Election Day. Large numbers of white Southerners deserted the Democratic Party, granting Humphrey only one victory in that region—in Lyndon Johnson's home state of Texas. While Wallace claimed most of the states in the Deep South, Nixon captured Virginia, Tennessee, Kentucky, and North Carolina. Senator Strom Thurmond's support delivered his state of South Carolina for the Republicans as well.

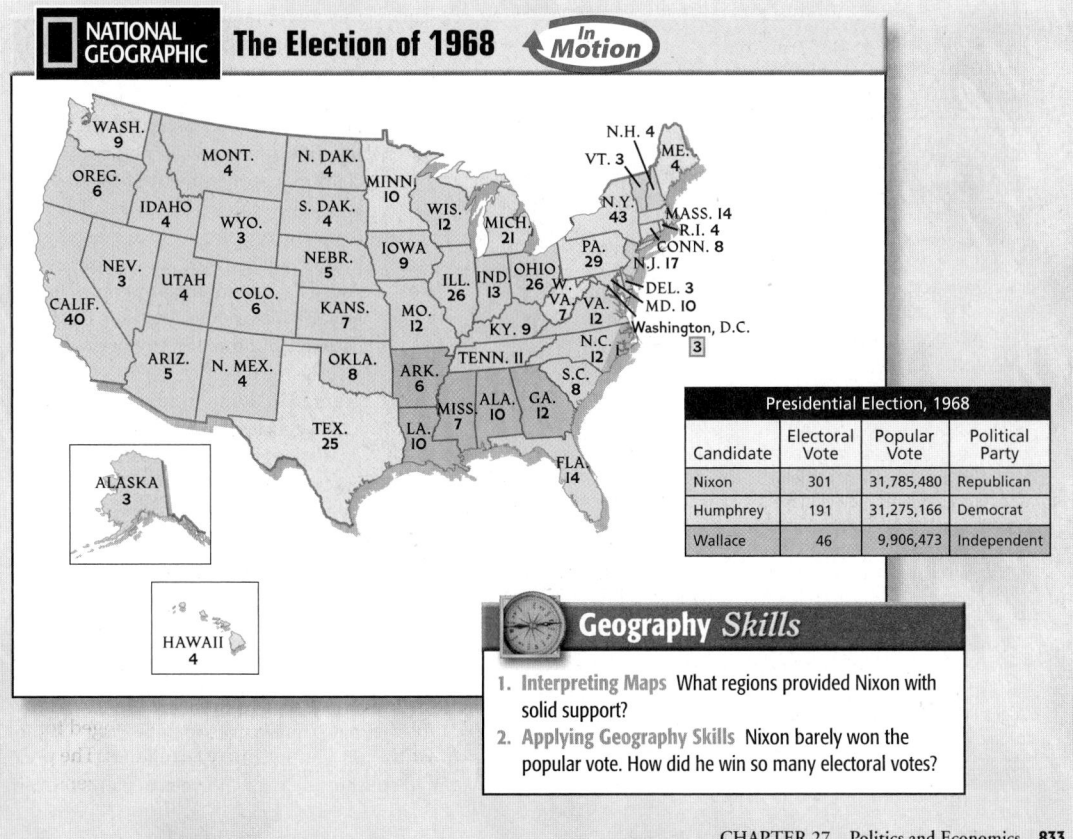

NATIONAL GEOGRAPHIC The Election of 1968 *In Motion*

Candidate	Electoral Vote	Popular Vote	Political Party
Nixon	301	31,785,480	Republican
Humphrey	191	31,275,166	Democrat
Wallace	46	9,906,473	Independent

Presidential Election, 1968

Geography *Skills*

1. **Interpreting Maps** What regions provided Nixon with solid support?
2. **Applying Geography Skills** Nixon barely won the popular vote. How did he win so many electoral votes?

2 TEACH

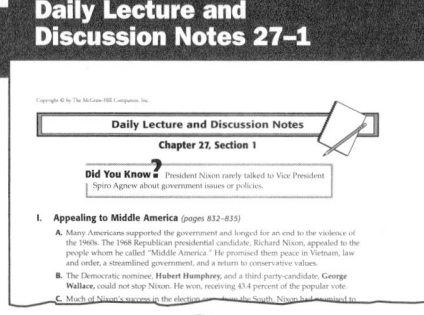

Daily Lecture and Discussion Notes 27–1

Daily Lecture and Discussion Notes
Chapter 27, Section 1

Did You Know? President Nixon rarely talked to Vice President Spiro Agnew about government issues or policies.

I. **Appealing to Middle America** *(pages 832–835)*

A. Many Americans supported the government and longed for an end to the violence of the 1960s. The 1968 Republican presidential candidate, Richard Nixon, appealed to the people whom he called "Middle America." He promised them peace in Vietnam, law and order, a streamlined government, and a return to conservative values.

B. The Democratic nominee, **Hubert Humphrey,** and a third party-candidate, **George Wallace,** could not stop Nixon. He won, receiving 43.4 percent of the popular vote.

C. Much of Nixon's success in the election came in the South. Nixon had promised to

Creating Circle Graphs Provide the data below and ask students to make a pair of circle graphs showing the results of the 1968 presidential election. **L1**

Candidate	Popular Vote	Electoral Vote
Nixon, Rep.	31,785,480	301
Humphrey, Dem.	31,275,166	191
Wallace, Ind.	9,906,473	46

 Use the rubric for creating a map, display, or chart on pages 65–66 in the *Performance Assessment Activities and Rubrics.*

Geography *Skills*

Answers:
1. Midwest and West
2. If a candidate has only a plurality in a state's popular vote, he or she still receives all of its electoral votes.

Geography Skills Practice
Which New England states voted for Nixon? *(New Hampshire and Vermont)* Which Western state voted for Humphrey? *(Washington)*

Reading Strategy   READING THE TEXT

Organizing Information Organize the class into small groups of three or four students. Have the members of each group create individual charts showing the successes and failures of the Nixon administration. Have the groups compare their charts and create a composite for the class. **L1**

Refer to *Inclusion for the High School Social Studies Classroom Strategies and Activities* in the TCR.

Guided Reading Activity 27–1

★ **Guided Reading Activity 27-1**

DIRECTIONS: Filling in the Blanks In the space provided, write the word or words that best complete the sentence. Refer to your textbook to fill in the blanks.

1. The presidential candidate in 1968 who appealed to many frustrated citizens was _____, a Republican.

2. Nixon's principal opponent was Democrat _____ who had served as vice president under Lyndon Johnson.

3. To gain Southern support, Nixon had met with powerful South Carolina senator _____.

4. Nixon's _____ dismantled a number of federal programs and gave more control to state and local governments.

5. Critics of the nation's welfare system _____ argued that the system was structured so that it was actually better for poor people to apply for benefits than to take a low-paying job.

Profiles
IN HISTORY

Ask: What were some of the accomplishments of Romana Acosta Bañuelos before being named U.S. Treasurer? *(She started her own business that grew into a multimillion-dollar enterprise, and she helped found the Pan-American National Bank.)*

Writing a Research Report

Have students write a research report describing the ways in which the Burger Court disappointed conservatives. Remind students to include bibliographic references and footnotes in proper style. **L3**

📁 Use the rubric for a book review, research report, or position paper on pages 79–80 in the *Performance Assessment Activities and Rubrics.*

Following his victory, Nixon set out to attract even more Southerners to the Republican Party, an effort that became known as the **Southern strategy.** Toward this end, the president fulfilled his agreements with Thurmond and took steps to slow desegregation. During his tenure, Nixon worked to overturn several civil rights policies. He reversed a Johnson administration policy, for example, that had cut off federal funds for racially segregated schools.

A Law-and-Order President Having also won the presidency with a promise of law and order, Nixon immediately set out to battle crime in America. His administration specifically targeted the nation's antiwar protesters. Attorney General John Mitchell declared that he stood ready to prosecute "hard-line militants" who crossed state lines to stir up riots. Mitchell's deputy, Richard Kleindienst, went even further with the boast, "We're going to enforce the law against draft evaders, against radical students, against deserters, against civil disorders, against organized crime, and against street crime."

Nixon also went on the attack against the recent Supreme Court rulings that expanded the rights of accused criminals. Nixon openly criticized the Court and its chief justice, Earl Warren. The president promised to fill vacancies on the Supreme Court with judges who would support the rights of law enforcement over the rights of suspected criminals.

When Chief Justice Warren retired shortly after Nixon took office, the president replaced him with **Warren Burger,** a respected conservative judge. He also placed three other conservative justices on the Court, including one from the South. The Burger Court did not reverse Warren Court rulings on the rights of criminal suspects. It did, however, refuse to expand those rights further. For example, in *Stone* v. *Powell* (1976), it agreed to limits on the rights of defendants to appeal state convictions to the federal judiciary. The Court also continued to uphold capital punishment as constitutional. 📖 *(See page 965 for more information on* Stone v. Powell.*)*

The New Federalism President Nixon's Republican constituency also favored dismantling a number of federal programs and giving more control to state and local governments. Nixon called this **New Federalism.** He argued that it would provide the government agencies that were closest to the citizens the opportunity to address more of their issues.

"I reject the patronizing idea that government in Washington, D.C., is inevitably more wise and more efficient than government at the state or local level," Nixon declared. "The idea that a bureaucratic elite in Washington knows what's best for people . . . is really a contention that people cannot govern themselves." Under the New Federalism program, Congress passed a series of revenue-sharing bills that granted federal funds to state and local agencies.

Although **revenue sharing** was intended to give state and local agencies more power, over time it gave the federal government new power. As states came to depend on federal funds, the federal government could impose conditions on the states. Unless they met those conditions, their funds would be cut off.

While he worked to limit federal government responsibilities, Nixon also sought to increase the power of the executive branch. Nixon did not

Profiles IN HISTORY

Romana Acosta Bañuelos *1925–*

On her first day of business in downtown Los Angeles, California, Romana Acosta Bañuelos made $36 selling tortillas. That was in 1949. She made great strides after that, becoming a successful businessperson and serving as U.S. treasurer in the 1970s.

Born in 1925 in a small town in Arizona to Mexican American immigrants, Bañuelos spent part of her childhood on a relative's small ranch in Mexico. Rising early, she tended the crops and helped her mother make empanadas (Mexican turnovers) to sell to local restaurants. "My mother was the type of woman that taught us how to live in any place and work with what we have."

That lesson inspired Bañuelos to start her own business when she returned to the United States at the age of 19. Gradually her business grew, and by the mid-1960s, it was thriving. In 1979 Romana's Mexican Food Products employed about 400 people and had sales of some $12 million annually.

Bañuelos worked at more than accumulating wealth. She contributed to scholarships for Mexican American students, especially those interested in business, which Bañuelos believes is an important path to political influence. With a number of partners, she also founded the Pan-American National Bank. It too was successful.

Bañuelos' success and community leadership led to President Nixon's appointing her as U.S. Treasurer in 1971.

DIFFERENTIATED INSTRUCTION

English Learners Have students draw a picture or icon to illustrate the Key Terms and Names for this section. Have students use at least one of their drawings in a political cartoon to illustrate an event, concept, or issue presented in this section. **L1 ELL**

📁 Refer to *Inclusion for the High School Social Studies Classroom Strategies and Activities* in the TCR.

build many strong relationships in Congress. His lack of camaraderie with lawmakers and the fact that the Republican Party controlled neither house led to struggles with the legislative branch. Nixon often responded by trying to work around Congress and use greater executive authority. For instance, when Congress appropriated money for programs he opposed, Nixon impounded, or refused to release, the funds. The Supreme Court eventually declared the practice of impoundment unconstitutional.

The Family Assistance Plan One federal program Nixon sought to reform was the nation's welfare system—**Aid to Families with Dependent Children** (AFDC). The program had many critics, Republican and Democratic alike. They argued that AFDC was structured so that it was actually better for poor people to apply for benefits than to take a low-paying job. A mother who had such a job, for example, would then have to pay for child care, sometimes leaving her with less income than she had on welfare. There was also great inequity among states since each was allowed to develop its own guidelines.

In 1969 Nixon proposed replacing the AFDC with the Family Assistance Plan. The plan called for providing needy families a guaranteed yearly grant of $1,600, which could be supplemented by outside earnings. Many liberals applauded the plan as a significant step toward expanding federal responsibility for the poor. Nixon, however, presented the program in a conservative light, arguing it would reduce federal supervision and encourage welfare recipients to become more responsible.

Although the program won approval in the House in 1970, it soon came under harsh attack. Welfare recipients complained that the federal grant was too low, while conservatives, who disapproved of guaranteed income, also criticized the plan. Such opposition led to the program's defeat in the Senate.

✓ **Reading Check** **Evaluating** What impact did third-party candidate George Wallace have on the 1968 election?

Nixon's Foreign Policy

Despite Nixon's domestic initiatives, a State Department official later recalled that the president had a "monumental disinterest in domestic policies." Nixon once expressed his hope that a "competent cabinet" of advisers could run the country. This would allow him to focus his energies on the subject that truly fascinated him, foreign affairs. Embarking on an ambitious foreign policy agenda

Fact Fiction Folklore

"Ping-Pong Diplomacy" In April 1971, nearly a year before President Nixon made his historic trip there, Communist China welcomed a different kind of U.S. delegation—the American ping-pong team. When the team received their surprise invitation, *Time* magazine called it "the ping heard round the world." The nine players, four officials, and two spouses who arrived on the Chinese mainland were the first Americans to enter China since the Communist takeover in 1949.

that included historic encounters with both China and the Soviet Union, Nixon set out to leave his mark on the world stage.

Nixon and Kissinger In a move that would greatly influence his foreign policy, Nixon chose as his national security adviser **Henry Kissinger,** a former Harvard professor. As a teenager Kissinger had fled to the United States from Germany with his family in 1938 to escape Nazi persecution of Jews. He had served as a foreign policy consultant for Presidents Kennedy and Johnson. Though Secretary of State William Rogers technically outranked him, Kissinger soon took the lead in helping shape Nixon's foreign policy.

Nixon and Kissinger shared views on many issues. Both believed simply abandoning the war in Vietnam would damage the United States's position in the world. Thus they worked toward a gradual withdrawal. Nixon and Kissinger also believed in shaping a foreign policy rooted in practical approaches rather than ideologies. They felt the nation's decades-long anticommunist crusade had created a foreign policy that was too rigid and often worked against the nation's interests. While both leaders wanted to continue to contain communism, they believed that engagement and negotiation with Communists offered a better way for the United States to achieve its international goals. As a surprised nation watched, Nixon and Kissinger put their philosophy into practice by forging friendlier relations with the Soviet Union and China.

CHAPTER 27 Politics and Economics **835**

INTERDISCIPLINARY CONNECTIONS ACTIVITY

Government Have students research the order of succession for the president and the process for replacing a vice president who leaves office during his or her term. Have students create a poster showing the steps prescribed by the Twenty-fifth Amendment to the Constitution. Then discuss as a class why it is important to have an established procedure for replacing national leaders. **L2**

Analyzing *Political Cartoons*

Answer: 1972

Ask: Why do you think the cartoonist drew the bombs perilously perched on top of one another like a shaky tower? *(Students' answers will vary. A possible answer is the cartoonist wanted to incorporate the concept of escalation and the shaky nature of the negotiations.)*

Writing a Press Release Have students write a press release detailing the strategic goals of Nixon's visit to China. Tell students that a good press release uses an inverted pyramid format with the most important information in the first sentence of the release. **L2**

3 ASSESS

Assign Section 1 Assessment as homework or as an in-class activity.

⦿ Have students use the **Interactive Tutor Self-Assessment CD-ROM.**

L1/ELL

Reading Essentials and Study Guide 27–1

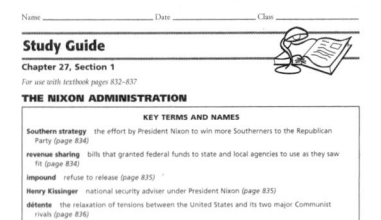

Name _____ Date _____ Class _____

Study Guide

Chapter 27, Section 1
For use with textbook pages 832–837

THE NIXON ADMINISTRATION

KEY TERMS AND NAMES

Southern strategy the effort by President Nixon to win more Southerners to the Republican Party *(page 834)*
revenue sharing bills that granted federal funds to state and local agencies to use as they saw fit *(page 834)*
impound refuse to release *(page 835)*
Henry Kissinger national security adviser under President Nixon *(page 835)*
détente the relaxation of tensions between the United States and its two major Communist rivals *(page 836)*
summit high-level diplomatic meeting *(page 837)*

Analyzing *Political Cartoons*

Arms Buildup Anxiety The urgent need to negotiate a reduction in nuclear arms is demonstrated in this 1970 cartoon. When was the SALT I agreement finally signed?

The Establishment of Détente The Soviet Union was not initially pleased when Nixon, a man with a history of outspoken anticommunist actions, became president. The Washington correspondent for the Soviet newspaper *Izvestia*, Yuri Barsukov, had called the election "unwelcome news for Moscow" and predicted that Soviet leaders "would have to deal with a very stubborn president."

Things did not turn out that way, however. Nixon was still a staunch anticommunist, but he came to reject the notion of a bipolar world in which the superpowers of the United States and the Soviet Union confronted one another. He believed the United States needed to understand the growing role that China, Japan, and Western Europe would soon

836 CHAPTER 27 Politics and Economics

play. This "multipolar" world of the future demanded a different approach to American foreign policy.

With Kissinger's help, Nixon fashioned an approach called détente, or relaxation of tensions, between the United States and its two major Communist rivals, the Soviet Union and China. In explaining détente to the American people, Nixon said that the United States had to build a better relationship with its main rivals in the interests of world peace:

❝We must understand that détente is not a love fest. It is an understanding between nations that have opposite purposes, but which share common interests, including the avoidance of a nuclear war. Such an understanding can work—that is, restrain aggression and deter war—only as long as the potential aggressor is made to recognize that neither aggression nor war will be profitable.❞

—quoted in *The Limits of Power*

Nixon Visits China Détente began with an effort to improve American-Chinese relations. Since 1949, when a Communist government came to power in China, the United States had refused to recognize the Communists as the legitimate rulers. Instead, the American government recognized the exiled regime on the island of Taiwan as the Chinese government. Having long supported this policy, Nixon now set out to reverse it. He began by lifting trade and travel restrictions and withdrawing the Seventh Fleet from defending Taiwan.

After a series of highly secret negotiations between Kissinger and Chinese leaders, Nixon announced that he would visit China in February 1972. During the historic trip, the leaders of both nations agreed to establish "more normal" relations between their countries. In a statement that epitomized the notion of détente, Nixon told his Chinese hosts during a banquet toast, "Let us start a long march together, not in lockstep, but on different roads leading to the same goal, the goal of building a world structure of peace and justice."

In taking this trip, Nixon hoped not only to strengthen ties with the Chinese, but also to encourage the Soviets to more actively pursue diplomacy. Since the 1960s, a rift had developed between the Communist governments of the Soviet Union and China. Troops of the two nations occasionally clashed along their borders. Nixon believed détente with China would encourage Soviet premier Leonid Brezhnev to be more accommodating with the United States.

CRITICAL THINKING ACTIVITY

Synthesizing Information As a class, have students identify the links between anticommunist thinking and Cold War policies. Ask students to explain how President Nixon's policy of détente represented a shift from past United States foreign policy, especially in dealing with Communist nations such as China. **L2**

U.S.-Soviet Tensions Ease Nixon's feelings about the Soviets proved correct. Shortly after the public learned of U.S. negotiations with China, the Soviets proposed an American-Soviet summit, or high-level diplomatic meeting, to be held in May 1972. On May 22, President Nixon flew to Moscow for a weeklong summit. Thus, he became the first American president since World War II to visit the Soviet Union.

Before Nixon's visit, Secretary of Commerce Maurice Stans spent 11 days in the Soviet Union. In his visits to a tractor plant, a steel mill, and an oil field, Stans recalled, "It was as friendly a meeting as if I were representing California and negotiating with the state of Arizona." Before leaving, however, Stans requested a favor from his Soviet host, Alexei Kosygin:

> 66'There is one thing I hope you will take care of: on the highway into Moscow there is a great big billboard with the United States pictured as a vicious killer, with a sword in one hand and a gun in the other, killing people all over the world. I don't think that will be a good entrance for President Nixon, and the sign ought to come down.' He said, 'It will.'99

—quoted in *Nixon: An Oral History of His Presidency*

During the historic Moscow summit, the two superpowers signed the first **Strategic Arms Limitation Treaty,** or SALT I, a plan to limit nuclear arms the two nations had been working on for years. Nixon and Brezhnev also agreed to increase trade and the exchange of scientific information.

Détente profoundly eased tensions between the Soviet Union and the United States. By the end of Nixon's presidency, one Soviet official admitted that

 Picturing **History**

Détente Discussion Soviet premier Leonid Brezhnev listens to President Nixon during Brezhnev's June 1973 visit to Washington, D.C. On June 22 the two signed an agreement on the prevention of nuclear war. *What does the word détente mean?*

"the United States and the Soviet Union had their best relationship of the whole Cold War period." President Nixon indeed had made his mark on the world stage. As he basked in the glow of his 1972 foreign policy triumphs, however, trouble was brewing on the home front. A scandal was about to engulf his presidency and plunge the nation into one of its greatest constitutional crises.

✓ **Reading Check** **Summarizing** What were the results of the 1972 American-Soviet summit?

HISTORY Online **Study Central**™ To review this section, go to tarvol2.glencoe.com and click on **Study Central**™.

SECTION 1 ASSESSMENT

Checking for Understanding

1. **Define:** impound, détente, summit.
2. **Identify:** Southern strategy, revenue sharing, Henry Kissinger.
3. **Describe** Nixon's New Federalism policy.

Reviewing Themes

4. **Global Connections** What were the results of Nixon's policy of détente?

Critical Thinking

5. **Evaluating** How did Nixon's China visit affect Soviet relations?
6. **Categorizing** Use a graphic organizer similar to the one below to describe how President Nixon established détente in the countries listed.

China	
Soviet Union	

Analyzing Visuals

7. **Analyzing Political Cartoons** Study the cartoon on page 836. What is the artist's message about the impact of the arms buildup on the average citizen in both the Soviet Union and the United States?

Writing About History

8. **Expository Writing** Take on the role of a member of President Nixon's staff. Write a press release explaining Nixon's domestic and foreign policies.

CHAPTER 27 Politics and Economics **837**

SECTION 1 ASSESSMENT ANSWERS

1. Terms are in blue.
2. Southern strategy *(p. 834)*, revenue sharing *(p. 834)*, Henry Kissinger *(p. 835)*
3. He granted federal funds to state and local agencies.
4. Détente eased tensions between the United States and the Soviet Union and led to more normal

relations between the U.S. and China.
5. The Soviet Union became more accommodating to the United States.
6. China: lifted trade and travel restrictions, withdrew Seventh Fleet from Taiwan; Soviet Union: increased trade, signed SALT I,

exchanged scientific information
7. The arms race burdened citizens.
8. Students' press releases will vary. Students should be instructed on the proper format for a news release.

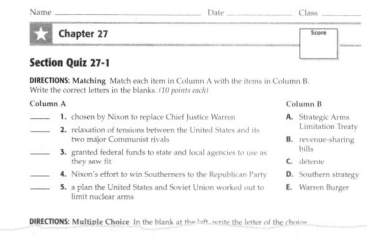

Section Quiz 27–1

Name _____ Date _____ Class _____

⭐ Chapter 27   Score ☐

Section Quiz 27-1

DIRECTIONS: Matching Match each item in Column A with the items in Column B. Write the correct letters in the blanks. *(10 points each)*

Column A
_____ 1. chosen by Nixon to replace Chief Justice Warren
_____ 2. relaxation of tensions between the United States and its two major Communist rivals
_____ 3. granted federal funds to state and local agencies to use as they saw fit
_____ 4. Nixon's effort to win Southerners to the Republican Party
_____ 5. a plan the United States and Soviet Union worked out to limit nuclear arms

Column B
A. Strategic Arms Limitation Treaty
B. revenue-sharing bills
C. détente
D. Southern strategy
E. Warren Burger

DIRECTIONS: Multiple Choice In the blank at the left, write the letter of the choice.

Picturing **History**

Answer: relaxation of tensions
Ask: Who prepared the way for Nixon's visit to the Soviet Union? *(Secretary of Commerce Maurice Stans)*

✓ **Reading Check**

Answer: signed SALT I, agreed to increase trade and exchange scientific information

Reteach

Have students describe Nixon's domestic agenda.

Enrich

Have students use library and Internet resources to research the basic provisions of the SALT I and SALT II treaties. Based on their research, have students create a chart showing the provisions of each treaty.

 HISTORY Online

Study Central™ provides summaries, interactive games, and online graphic organizers to help students review section content.

4 CLOSE

Have students discuss Nixon's foreign policy achievements.

837

1 FOCUS

Section Overview

This section focuses on Nixon's re-election, the Watergate scandal, and the president's resignation.

BELLRINGER
Skillbuilder Activity

 Project transparency and have students answer the question.

Daily Focus Skills Transparency 27–2

Reading Preview

Answers to Graphic:

I. The Roots of Watergate
   A. Nixon and His "Enemies"
   B. Mounting a Re-election Fight
   C. The Cover-Up Begins
II. The Cover-Up Unravels
   A. The First Cracks Show
   B. A Summer of Shocking Testimony
   C. The Case of the Tapes
   D. Nixon Resigns
III. The Impact of Watergate

Preteaching Vocabulary

Have students write a short summary of the Watergate scandal using all of the Key Terms and Names.

Guide to Reading

Main Idea

During his second term, President Nixon became embroiled in a scandal that ultimately forced him to resign.

Key Terms and Names

Sam J. Ervin, John Dean, executive privilege, impeach, Federal Campaign Act Amendments

Reading Strategy

Taking Notes As you read about the Watergate scandal, use the major headings of the section to create an outline similar to the one below.

The Watergate Scandal
I. The Roots of Watergate
   A.
   B.
   C.
II.
   A.
   B.

Reading Objectives

• **Describe** the character of Richard Nixon and the attitude of his White House.
• **Explain** the Watergate scandal and discuss its effects.

Section Theme

Government and Democracy The Watergate scandal intensified the lingering distrust of government that had grown in the United States during the Vietnam War.

Preview of Events

◆June 1972	◆March 1973	◆December 1973	◆September 1974

June 1972
Burglars arrested in Democratic National Committee headquarters at Watergate complex

May 1973
Senate begins Watergate investigation

October 1973
Battle over White House tapes leads to "Saturday Night Massacre"

August 1974
Nixon resigns

★ *An American Story* ★

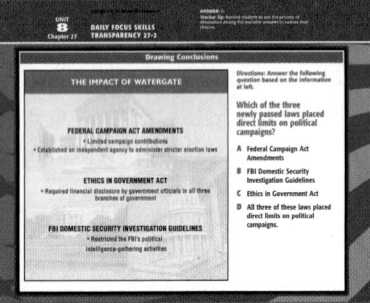

Reporters Bob Woodward and Carl Bernstein

As Bob Woodward, a young reporter for the *Washington Post,* sat in a Washington, D.C., courtroom on the morning of June 17, 1972, he was in a rather foul mood. His editor had ruined his Saturday by calling him in to cover a seemingly insignificant but bizarre incident. In the early hours of that morning, five men had broken into the Democratic National Committee (DNC) headquarters in the city's Watergate apartment-office complex.

Woodward sat toward the back of the courtroom listening to the bail proceedings for the five defendants. At one point, the judge asked each man his occupation. One of the men, James McCord, answered that he was retired from government service.

"Where in government?" asked the judge.

"CIA," McCord whispered.

Woodward sprang to attention. Why was a former member of the Central Intelligence Agency involved in what seemed to be nothing more than a burglary?

Over the next two years, Woodward and another reporter, Carl Bernstein, would investigate this question. In so doing they uncovered a scandal that helped bring about a grave constitutional crisis and eventually forced the president to resign.

—adapted from *All the President's Men*

The Roots of Watergate

The scandal known as **Watergate** originated from the Nixon administration's attempts to cover up its involvement in the break-in at the Democratic National Committee (DNC) headquarters, along with other illegal actions committed during

---

SECTION RESOURCES

📁 Reproducible Masters
• Reproducible Lesson Plan 27–2
• Daily Lecture and Discussion Notes 27–2
• Guided Reading Activity 27–2
• Section Quiz 27–2
• Reading Essentials and Study Guide 27–2
• Supreme Court Case Studies

📊 Transparencies
• Daily Focus Skills Transparency 27–2

Multimedia
🔘 Interactive Tutor Self-Assessment CD-ROM
🔘 ExamView® Pro Testmaker CD-ROM
🔘 Presentation Plus! CD-ROM
🔘 TeacherWorks™ CD-ROM
🔊 Audio Program

Nixon's re-election campaign. While the affair began with the burglary at the Watergate complex, a number of scholars attribute the scandal in large part to the character of Richard Nixon and the atmosphere that he and his advisers created in the White House.

Nixon and His "Enemies" Richard Nixon had fought hard to become president. He had battled back from numerous political defeats, including a loss to John Kennedy in the 1960 presidential election, to win the presidency in 1968. Along the way, however, Nixon had grown defensive, secretive, and often resentful of his critics.

In addition, Nixon had become president during a time when the United States was still very much at war with itself. Race riots and protests over the Vietnam War continued to consume the country. In Nixon's view, these protesters and other "radicals" were out to bring down his administration. Nixon was so consumed with his opponents that he compiled an "enemies list" filled with people—from politicians to members of the media—whom he considered a threat to his presidency.

Mounting a Re-election Fight As Nixon's re-election campaign got underway in 1972, many in his administration expressed optimism about winning a second term. The president had just finished triumphant trips to China and the Soviet Union. In May, former Alabama governor George Wallace, who had mounted a strong third-party campaign in 1968, had dropped his bid for another run at the White House after an assassin's bullet paralyzed him. Meanwhile, Nixon's Democratic

opponent, South Dakota senator George McGovern, was viewed as too liberal on many issues.

At the same time, Nixon's hold on the presidency was uncertain. Despite the high approval ratings for the president's summit meetings in Beijing and Moscow, the unpopular Vietnam War still raged. Nixon staffers also remembered how close the margin of Nixon's 1968 victory had been. Seeking to gain an edge in every way they could, Nixon's team engaged in a host of subversive tactics, from spying on opposition rallies to spreading rumors and false reports.

These tactics included an effort to steal information from the Democratic Party's headquarters. In the early hours of June 17, 1972, five Nixon supporters broke into the party's office at the Watergate complex in Washington, D.C. They had intended to obtain any sensitive campaign information and to place wiretaps on the office telephones. While the burglars were at work, a security guard making his rounds spotted a piece of tape holding a door lock. The guard ripped off the tape, but when he passed the door later, he noticed that it had been replaced. He quickly called police, who arrived shortly and arrested the men.

The Cover-Up Begins In the wake of the Watergate break-in, the media discovered that one of the burglars, James McCord, was not only an ex-CIA official but also a member of the Committee for the Re-election of the President (CRP). Reports soon surfaced that the burglars had been paid to execute the break-in from a secret CRP fund controlled by the White House.

Picturing **History**

Watergate Hotel The hotel gave its name to the scandal that brought down President Nixon. Hotel guard Frank Willis, pictured here, reported to police the evidence of a break-in at the Democratic National Committee headquarters there. What was Nixon's response to the break-in?

CHAPTER 27 Politics and Economics **839**

---

2 TEACH

Daily Lecture and Discussion Notes 27–2

Copyright © by The McGraw-Hill Companies, Inc.

Daily Lecture and Discussion Notes

Chapter 27, Section 2

Did You Know? Television covered the Senate Watergate hearings from May–November 1973. The hearings were popular among daytime television viewers.

I. **The Roots of Watergate** (pages 838–840)

  A. The **Watergate** scandal began as the Nixon administration attempted to cover up its involvement in the break-in at the Democratic National Committee (DNC) headquarters, as well as other illegal actions committed during Nixon's re-election campaign.

  B. Richard Nixon had become defensive, secretive, and resentful of his critics during his long and difficult climb to the presidency. He went as far as creating an "enemies list," naming people from politicians to members of the media.

Reading Strategy

Using Relative Chronology Have students create a graphic showing the relative chronology of the Watergate scandal starting with the break-in and ending with Nixon's resignation. Encourage students to use drawings, symbols, and colors to illustrate the events. **L1**

HISTORY Online

Objectives and answers to the student activity can be found in the **Web Activity Lesson Plan** at tarvol2.glencoe.com.

Picturing **History**

Answer: He denied any involvement and asked the CIA to intervene to stop the FBI from investigating the source for the money paid to the burglars.
Ask: What was the source of the financial support for the burglary at Watergate? *(The burglars were paid from a secret CRP fund.)*

Reading Strategy **READING THE TEXT**

Using Context Cues Show students how to use context to determine meaning. Have students examine words and phrases that come before and after an unfamiliar word for a context clue. They can also try to connect the puzzling material with what they have just read. Next, they can predict a possible meaning and see if it works in the sentence. If it does not, have them try again. **L1** **ELL**

Refer to *Inclusion for the High School Social Studies Classroom Strategies and Activities* in the TCR.

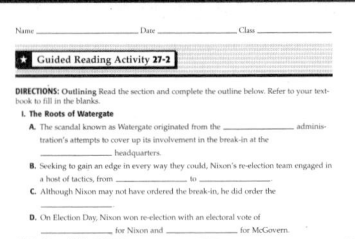

Picturing **History**

Answer: The committee voted to recommend three articles of impeachment.

Ask: What charges did the committee make? *(Nixon had obstructed justice, misused federal agencies to violate the rights of citizens, and defied the authority of Congress by refusing to deliver tapes and other evidence.)*

✓ **Reading Check**

Answer: They intended to steal sensitive campaign information and place wiretaps.

Predicting Outcomes Ask students to consider how the presidential election of 1972 might have been different had the information about the Watergate scandal been uncovered and reported the week before the election. Have students give reasons for their responses. **L2**

📁 Use *Supreme Court Case Study 49, United States* v. *Nixon.*

As questions swirled about a possible White House connection to the burglary, the cover-up began. Administration officials destroyed incriminating documents and provided false testimony to investigators. Meanwhile, President Nixon stepped in. While the president may not have ordered the break-in, he did order a cover-up. With Nixon's consent, administration officials asked the CIA to intervene and stop the FBI from inquiring into the source of the money paid to the burglars. Their justification was that such an investigation would threaten national security.

All the while, the White House strongly denied any involvement in the break-in. Nixon's press secretary dismissed the incident as a "third-rate burglary attempt," while the president himself told the American public, "The White House has had no involvement whatever in this particular incident."

The strategy worked. Most Americans believed President Nixon. Despite efforts by the media, in particular the *Washington Post,* to keep the story alive, few people paid much attention to the Watergate affair during the 1972 presidential campaign. On Election Day, Nixon won re-election by one of the largest margins in history with nearly 61 percent of the popular vote compared to 37.5 percent for George McGovern. The electoral vote was 520 votes for Nixon and 17 for McGovern.

✓ **Reading Check** **Examining** Why did members of the CRP break into the Democratic National Committee headquarters?

The Cover-Up Unravels

Shortly after his triumphant re-election, an exuberant and confident Nixon told his cabinet and staff that 1973 "can be and should be the best year ever." In a matter of months, however, the Watergate affair would erupt, and the coming year would be one of the president's worst.

The First Cracks Show In 1973 the Watergate burglars went on trial. Under relentless prodding from federal judge John J. Sirica, McCord agreed to cooperate with both a grand jury investigation and with the Senate's Select Committee on Presidential Campaign Activities, which had been recently established under Senator **Sam J. Ervin** of North Carolina. McCord's testimony opened a floodgate of confessions, and a parade of White House and campaign officials exposed one illegality after another over the next several months. Foremost among the officials was counsel to the president **John Dean,** a member of the inner circle of the White House who leveled allegations against Nixon himself.

A Summer of Shocking Testimony In June 1973, John Dean testified before Senator Ervin's committee that former Attorney General John Mitchell had ordered the Watergate break-in and that Nixon had played an active role in attempting to cover up any White House involvement. As a shocked nation absorbed Dean's testimony, the Nixon administration strongly denied the charges.

A standoff ensued for the next month, as the Senate committee attempted to determine who was telling the truth. Then, on July 16, the answer appeared unexpectedly. On that day, White House aide Alexander Butterfield testified that Nixon had ordered a taping system installed in the White House to record all conversations. The president had done so, Butterfield said, to help him write his memoirs after he left office. For members of the committee, however, the tapes would tell them exactly what the president knew and when he knew it.

Picturing **History**

Sitting in Judgment Representative Barbara Jordan from Texas was an outspoken member of the House Judiciary Committee. What was this committee's role in the impeachment process?

Picturing **History**

High Political Drama After resigning his office on August 9, 1974, President Nixon and his family say goodbye to aides and friends on the White House lawn. On the capital's streets, a reader takes in the news in the *Washington Post*, the newspaper that started the Watergate investigation. Who replaced Nixon as president?

Picturing **History**

Answer: Gerald Ford

Ask: How did Gerald Ford become vice president? What was his position before becoming vice president? *(Ford became vice president when Spiro T. Agnew was forced to resign in disgrace because he had taken bribes while governor of Maryland. Ford had been the Republican leader in the House of Representatives.)*

The Case of the Tapes All the groups investigating the scandal sought access to the tapes. Nixon refused, pleading executive privilege—the principle that White House conversations should remain confidential to protect national security. A special prosecutor appointed by the president to handle the Watergate cases, Archibald Cox, took Nixon to court in October 1973 to force him to give up the recordings. Nixon, clearly growing desperate, ordered Attorney General Elliot Richardson, and then Richardson's deputy, to fire Cox. Both men refused and resigned in protest. Solicitor General Robert Bork finally fired Cox, but the incident, nicknamed the "Saturday Night Massacre" in the press, badly damaged Nixon's reputation with the public.

The fall of 1973 proved to be a disastrous time for Nixon for other reasons as well. His vice president, Spiro Agnew, was forced to resign in disgrace. Investigators had discovered that Agnew had taken bribes from state contractors while he was governor of Maryland and that he had continued to accept bribes while serving in Washington. Gerald Ford, the Republican leader of the House of Representatives, became the new vice president. Nixon then had to defend himself against allegations about his own past financial dealings.

GOVERNMENT

Nixon Resigns In an effort to quiet the growing outrage over his actions, President Nixon appointed a new special prosecutor, Texas lawyer Leon Jaworski, who proved no less determined than Cox to obtain the president's tapes. In April 1974, Nixon released edited transcripts of the tapes, claiming that they proved his innocence. Investigators felt otherwise and went to court again to force Nixon to turn over the unedited tapes. In July the Supreme Court ruled that the president had to turn over the tapes themselves, not just the transcripts. With nowhere else to appeal, Nixon handed over the tapes.

Several days later, the House Judiciary Committee voted to impeach Nixon, or officially charge him of presidential misconduct. The committee charged that Nixon had obstructed justice in the Watergate cover-up; misused federal agencies to violate the rights of citizens; and defied the authority of Congress by refusing to deliver tapes and other materials that the committee had requested. The next step was for the entire House of Representatives to vote whether or not to impeach the president.

As the nation held its collective breath in anticipation, investigators finally found indisputable

FYI

August 8, 1974, is the date Richard Nixon announced his resignation. On the same day in 1815, Napoleon Bonaparte sailed for Saint Helena to spend the rest of his life in exile.

3 ASSESS

Assign Section 2 Assessment as homework or as an in-class activity.

⊕ Have students use the **Interactive Tutor Self-Assessment CD-ROM.**

L1/ELL

Reading Essentials and Study Guide 27-2

Name _____ Date _____ Class _____

Study Guide

Chapter 27, Section 2

For use with textbook pages 838–842

THE WATERGATE SCANDAL

KEY TERMS AND NAMES

Sam J. Ervin a senator and head of the Senate's Select Committee on Presidential Campaign Activities *(page 840)*

John Dean the counsel to President Nixon, who testified that Nixon played an active role in the Watergate cover-up *(page 840)*

executive privilege the principle that White House conversations should remain confidential to protect national security *(page 841)*

impeach official charges of presidential misconduct *(page 841)*

Federal Campaign Act Amendments A law that limited campaign contributions and set up an independent agency to administer stricter election laws *(page 842)*

INTERDISCIPLINARY CONNECTIONS ACTIVITY

Communication Have students find articles in newspapers from the Watergate era that reported on the events surrounding Watergate. Select one group of three or four students to research polling data showing Nixon's popularity from 1971 until his resignation and to create a chart reporting this data. Have volunteers provide a summary of their articles to the class and then have the group who prepared the chart show their findings. Discuss as a class the power of the press to influence public opinion. **L2**

L2

Section Quiz 27-2

Name	Date	Class

★ Chapter 27 — Score

Section Quiz 27-2

DIRECTIONS: Matching Match each item in Column A with the items in Column B.
Write the correct letters in the blanks. *(10 points each)*

Column A

_____ 1. principle that White House conversations should remain confidential to protect national security
_____ 2. member of Nixon's inner circle who leveled allegations against Nixon
_____ 3. limited campaign contributions and established an independent agency to administer stricter election laws
_____ 4. appointed by President Nixon to handle the Watergate cases and eventually fired at Nixon's request
_____ 5. senator from North Carolina and head of the Senate's Select Committee on Presidential Campaign Activities

Column B

A. John Dean
B. Federal Campaign Act Amendments
C. Sam J. Ervin
D. executive privilege
E. Archibald Cox

✓ Reading Check

Answer: Dean testified that former Attorney General John Mitchell had ordered the Watergate break-in and that Nixon had played an active role in attempting to cover up any White House involvement. This shocked the nation and led to further investigation.

Reteach

Have students describe the character of Richard Nixon and the attitude of his White House.

Enrich

Invite interested students to read and report on *All the President's Men* by Carl Bernstein and Bob Woodward.

✓ Reading Check

Answer: Congress wanted to reestablish the balance of power between the branches of government.

HISTORY
Online

Study Central™ provides summaries, interactive games, and online graphic organizers to help students review section content.

4 CLOSE

Have students explain the Watergate scandal and discuss its effects.

842

---

evidence against the president. One of the unedited tapes revealed that on June 23, 1972, just six days after the Watergate burglary, Nixon had ordered the CIA to stop the FBI's investigation of the break-in. With this news, even the president's strongest supporters conceded that impeachment and conviction in the Senate now seemed inevitable. On August 9, 1974, Nixon resigned his office in disgrace. Gerald Ford took the oath of office and became the nation's 38th president.

✓ Reading Check — **Explaining** What was the significance of John Dean's testimony before the Senate committee?

The Impact of Watergate

Upon taking office, President Ford urged Americans to put the Watergate affair behind them and move on. "Our long national nightmare is over," he declared. The effects of the scandal, however, endured long after Richard Nixon's resignation.

The Watergate crisis prompted a series of new laws intended to limit the power of the executive branch. In the 1970s Congress passed a number of laws aimed at reestablishing a greater balance of power in government. The **Federal Campaign Act Amendments** limited campaign contributions and established an independent agency to administer stricter election laws. The Ethics in Government Act required financial disclosure by high government officials in all three branches of government. The FBI Domestic Security Investigation Guidelines restricted the bureau's political intelligence-gathering activities. After Watergate, Congress also established a means for appointing an independent counsel to investigate and prosecute wrongdoing by high government officials.

Despite these efforts, Watergate left many Americans with a deep distrust of their public officials. Speaking some 20 years after the Watergate affair, Alexander Haig, a former high-level Nixon aide, said the scandal had produced, "a fundamental discrediting of respect for the presidency . . . [and] a new skepticism about politics, in general, which every American feels to this day." On the other hand, some Americans saw the Watergate affair as proof that in the United States, no person is above the law. As Bob Woodward observed:

> ❝Watergate was probably a good thing for the country; it was a good, sobering lesson. Accountability to the law applies to everyone. The problem with kings and prime ministers and presidents is that they think that they are above it, and there is no accountability, and that they have some special rights, and privileges, and status. And a process that says: No. We have our laws and believe them, and they apply to everyone, is a very good thing.❞
> —quoted in *Nixon: An Oral History of His Presidency*

After the ordeal of Watergate, most Americans attempted to put the affair behind them. In the years ahead, however, the nation encountered a host of new troubles, from a stubborn economic recession to a heart-wrenching hostage crisis overseas.

✓ Reading Check — **Evaluating** Why did Congress pass new laws after the Watergate scandal?

HISTORY Online | **Study Central™** To review this section, go to **tarvol2.glencoe.com** and click on **Study Central™**.

SECTION 2 ASSESSMENT

Checking for Understanding

1. **Define:** executive privilege, impeach.
2. **Identify:** Sam J. Ervin, John Dean, Federal Campaign Act Amendments.
3. **Evaluate** the effects of the Watergate scandal on the way American citizens viewed the federal government.

Reviewing Themes

4. **Government and Democracy** How did the Watergate scandal alter the balance of power between the executive and legislative branches of government?

Critical Thinking

5. **Evaluating** How did the discovery of the White House tapes change the Watergate cover-up investigation?
6. **Organizing** Using a graphic organizer similar to the one below, fill in the effects of the Watergate scandal.

(Effects of Watergate Scandal)

Analyzing Visuals

7. **Analyzing Photographs** Study the photograph on page 841. How would you describe the scene of Nixon's leave-taking? What in the photo suggests that this is a formal occasion? Why do you think this ceremony might be important for the nation?

Writing About History

8. **Descriptive Writing** Take on the role of a television news analyst. Write a script in which you explain the Watergate scandal and analyze the factors that led to the scandal.

842 CHAPTER 27 Politics and Economics

SECTION 2 ASSESSMENT ANSWERS

1. Terms are in blue.
2. Sam J. Ervin *(p. 840)*, John Dean *(p. 840)*, Federal Campaign Act Amendments *(p. 842)*
3. Many citizens distrusted the federal government, especially the presidency, while some saw the events as proof that no one is above the law.

4. It led to laws that limit the power of the executive branch.
5. It led to an abuse of executive privilege, but resulted in proof of Nixon's guilt.
6. Nixon's resignation, Federal Campaign Act Amendments, Ethics in Government Act, FBI Domestic Security Investigation Guidelines

7. Students' answers should thoughtfully consider the photograph.
8. Students' scripts will vary. Scripts should include suggested visuals.

SECTION 3 Ford and Carter

Guide to Reading

Main Idea
During the 1970s, Presidents Gerald Ford and Jimmy Carter attempted to lead the United States through both domestic and foreign crises.

Key Terms and Names
inflation, embargo, stagflation, Helsinki Accords, Department of Energy

Reading Strategy
Organizing As you read about the administrations of Presidents Ford and Carter, complete a graphic organizer listing the causes of economic problems in the 1970s.

Causes

$\rightarrow$ Economic Problems in the 1970s

Reading Objectives
- **Explain** the reasons for economic troubles in the United States during the 1970s.
- **Discuss** Jimmy Carter's domestic and foreign policies.

Section Theme
Economic Factors A weakening economy and growing energy crisis marred the terms of Ford and Carter.

Preview of Events

| ♦1973 | ♦1975 | ♦1977 | ♦1979 |

1973
OPEC price increases cause inflation in the United States

1974
President Ford pardons Richard Nixon

1976
Jimmy Carter wins presidential election

1979
Iranian revolutionaries seize U.S. embassy in Iran

★ An American Story ★

Lines of jobseekers at an unemployment office

On a sunny February day in 1977, Ellen Griffith and her fiancé, Roger Everson, both of Nashville, Tennessee, sat together in a place where neither of them dreamed they would be—the state unemployment office. Just a month before, Griffith, a 20-year-old salesclerk in a shopping center, and Everson, 21, had been excitedly making wedding plans. Now, with Everson laid off and Griffith on a reduced work schedule, the young couple had decided to put their future plans on hold. "It cost something to get married, you know," said Everson.

What had landed the two in this predicament was a one-two punch of a particularly bitter winter and an energy shortage that had gone on for much of the decade. The brutally cold weather in the Midwest and East had increased the demand for oil and fuel, already in short supply throughout the country. In response, the government had asked numerous companies and shops to conserve energy by cutting back on their business hours. As a result, Griffith saw her work schedule slashed from 40 hours per week to 20 hours.

As the couple sat stoically in the unemployment office waiting for their names to be called, Griffith wondered how she would pay her bills on her reduced salary and whatever she might be able to get from the state. "I just feel like we've been rained on," she said glumly.

—adapted from the *New York Times*, February 3, 1977

The Economic Crisis of the 1970s

Since the end of World War II, the American economy had been the envy of the world. During the 1950s and 1960s, many Americans enjoyed remarkable prosperity and had come to assume it was the norm. This prosperity rested in large part on easy access to

CHAPTER 27 Politics and Economics **843**

1 FOCUS

Section Overview
This section focuses on the Ford and Carter administrations and the domestic and foreign crises these presidents faced.

BELLRINGER
Skillbuilder Activity

Project transparency and have students answer the question.

Daily Focus Skills Transparency 27–3

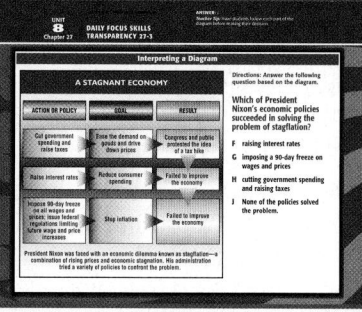

Reading Preview

Answers to Graphic: rising cost of raw materials and rising cost of fossil fuel, increased international competition, insufficient training for new jobs

Preteaching Vocabulary
Have students use a standard dictionary to look up the words *inflation*, *embargo*, and *stagflation* to gain a better understanding of the Key Terms and Names used in this section.

SECTION RESOURCES

Reproducible Masters
- Reproducible Lesson Plan 27–3
- Daily Lecture and Discussion Notes 27–3
- Guided Reading Activity 27–3
- Section Quiz 27–3
- Reading Essentials and Study Guide 27–3
- Performance Assessment Activities and Rubrics

Transparencies
- Daily Focus Skills Transparency 27–3

Multimedia
- Interactive Tutor Self-Assessment CD-ROM
- ExamView® Pro Testmaker CD-ROM
- Presentation Plus! CD-ROM
- TeacherWorks™ CD-ROM
- Audio Program

2 TEACH

Daily Lecture and Discussion Notes 27–3

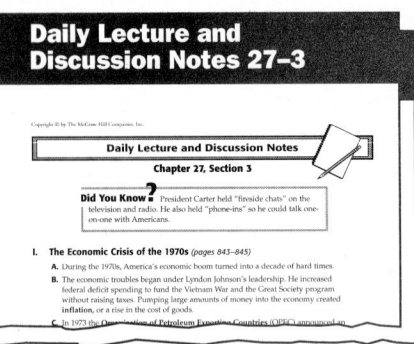

Creating a Thematic Map Have students draw a map showing the countries that currently belong to OPEC. Have them use the map to identify the regions of the world in which a large percentage of the world's oil reserves are found. **L1**

 Use the rubric for creating a map, display, or chart on pages 65–66 in the *Performance Assessment Activities and Rubrics.*

Picturing **History**

Answer: because the United States supported Israel in the Yom Kippur War

Ask: Before the 1973 OPEC embargo, what was the price of a barrel of crude oil? ($3)

FYI

OPEC is responsible for approximately 40 percent of the world's oil production and controls 75 percent of the world's proven oil reserves.

---

raw materials around the world and a strong manufacturing industry at home. By the 1970s, however, both conditions began to disappear.

A Mighty Economic Machine Slows The nation's economic troubles began in the mid-1960s, when President Johnson significantly increased federal deficit spending in an attempt to fund both the Vietnam War and his Great Society program without raising taxes. This pumped large amounts of money into the economy, which spurred inflation, or a rise in the cost of goods.

Rising costs of raw materials due to greater competition for them was another cause of inflation. In particular, the rising cost of oil dealt a strong blow to the nation's economy. More than any other nation, the United States based its economy on the easy availability of cheap and plentiful fossil fuels and had become heavily dependent on imports from the Middle East and Africa.

For years, the **Organization of Petroleum Exporting Countries** (OPEC) sold oil for its member countries. Prices remained low until the early 1970s, when OPEC decided to use oil as a political and economic weapon. In 1973 the Yom Kippur War was raging between Israel and its Arab neighbors. Tension had existed between Israel and the Arab world ever since the founding of modern Israel in 1948. Since most Arab states did not recognize Israel's right to exist, U.S. support of Israel made American relations with Arab states uneasy.

Now OPEC announced that its members would

Picturing **History**

A Scarce Commodity Americans had to schedule their lives around the availability of gasoline during the OPEC oil embargo. **Why did OPEC institute the embargo?**

embargo, or stop shipping, petroleum to countries that supported Israel, namely the United States and some Western European nations. OPEC also raised the price of crude oil by 70 percent, and then by another 130 percent a few months later.

Even before the oil embargo, President Nixon and Congress had tried to protect the American people from rising world oil prices by imposing a complex system of price controls. These controls forced oil companies to charge consumers low prices for gasoline and heating oil, even though the price of imported crude oil was rising. Oil companies could afford to do this because some of the oil they bought came from low-priced domestic sources. After OPEC raised its prices, however, the price controls created an oil shortage. There was not enough cheap oil available domestically to supply demand, and oil companies could no longer afford to pay world oil prices and still make a profit. If there had been no price controls, gasoline prices would have risen—but there would not have been an oil shortage.

Although the embargo ended a few months after it began, oil prices continued to rise. OPEC raised prices three more times in the 1970s and again in 1980. By that time, the price of a barrel of crude oil had risen from $3 in 1973 to $30 in 1980. The dramatic increase helped accelerate inflation throughout the American economy.

ECONOMICS

A Stagnant Economy Another economic problem was the decline of the manufacturing sector. In the years following World War II, the United States had dominated international trade, but by the 1970s, it faced increased international competition. Many manufacturing plants were now decades old and less efficient than the newer plants that Japan and European industrial nations built after the war.

These factors forced many factories to close, and millions of workers lost their jobs. The result was a growing pool of unemployed and underemployed workers.

Thus in the early 1970s President Nixon faced a new and puzzling economic dilemma that came to be known as "stagflation," a combination of rising prices and economic stagnation. Economists who

---

Reading Strategy   READING THE TEXT

Varying Reading Rate Students will learn that some text selections are more difficult to read than others, and they must make adjustments to their reading rate. Remind students to slow down when they encounter difficult concepts, connections to previous ideas, new vocabulary, or text that contains a great deal of information. **L1** ELL

Refer to *Inclusion for the High School Social Studies Classroom Strategies and Activities* in the TCR.

Analyzing *Political Cartoons*

Coping With Shortages Cartoonist Brant Parker reflected the public's frustration over the oil shortages of the 1970s. What message does the cartoonist convey with the statement "the figs are next"?

emphasized the demand side of economic theory, including supporters of Keynesianism, did not think that inflation and recession could occur at the same time. They believed that demand drives prices and that inflation would only occur in a booming economy when demand for goods was high. As a result, they did not know what fiscal policy the government should pursue. Increased spending might help end the recession, but it would increase inflation. Raising taxes might slow inflation but would prolong the recession.

Nixon decided to focus on controlling inflation. The government moved first to cut spending and raise taxes. The president hoped that higher taxes would prompt Americans to spend less, which would ease the demand on goods and drive down prices. Congress and much of the public, however, protested the idea of a tax hike. Nixon then tried to reduce consumer spending by getting the Federal Reserve Board to raise interest rates. When this failed, the president tried to stop inflation by imposing a 90-day freeze on wages and prices and then issuing federal regulations limiting future wage and price increases. This had little success.

✓ **Reading Check** **Explaining** How did President Nixon attempt to stop stagflation?

Ford Takes Over

When Nixon resigned in 1974, the nation's inflation rate was still high, despite many efforts to reduce prices. Meanwhile, the unemployment rate was over five percent. It would now be up to Gerald Ford to confront stagflation.

Most Americans considered Gerald Ford a decent and honest if not particularly dynamic leader. When he became vice president, Ford had readily acknowl-

edged his bland personality. "I'm a Ford, not a Lincoln," he said. Still, the new president boasted excellent credentials, including a degree from Yale Law School, naval service during World War II, and service in the House of Representatives since 1949. His fellow Republicans had elected him as minority leader in 1965. Ford would need to draw on all his experience during his time in office.

Ford Pardons Nixon On September 8, 1974, Ford announced that he would grant a "full, free, and absolute pardon" to Richard Nixon for any crimes he "committed or may have committed or taken part in" while president. "This is an American tragedy in which we all have played a part," he told the nation. "It could go on and on and on, or someone must write the end to it."

Ford insisted he was acting not out of sympathy for Nixon, but in the public interest. Ford's position was that he wanted to avoid the division that charges against Nixon and a public trial would create. Nonetheless, the pardon aroused fierce criticism. Ford's approval ratings soon plunged from 71 percent to 50 percent.

Ford Tries to "Whip" Inflation By 1975 the American economy was in its worst recession since the Great Depression, with unemployment at nearly nine percent. Rejecting the notion of mandatory wage and price controls to reduce inflation, Ford requested voluntary controls. Under a plan known as WIN—Whip Inflation Now—he urged Americans to cut back on their oil and gas consumption. The plan stirred up little enthusiasm and eventually failed. The president then turned to cutting government spending and advocating higher interest rates to curb inflation. This too failed.

CHAPTER 27 Politics and Economics **845**

 Analyzing *Political Cartoons*

Answer: Because of American dependence on foreign oil, the cartoonist implies that OPEC countries could dictate to the U.S. government.

✓ **Reading Check**

Answer: The government cut spending and raised taxes, the Federal Reserve raised interest rates, and the president imposed a 90-day freeze on wages and prices and issued regulations to limit future wage and price increases.

Creating a Graph Provide the data below and have students create a graph showing the average price of a gallon of gasoline in the United States between 1973 and 1980. **L2**

1973	$ .39	1977	$ .64
1974	.53	1978	.65
1975	.57	1979	.88
1976	.60	1980	1.22

DIFFERENTIATED INSTRUCTION

At-Risk Students Pair students with different abilities and have them work together to create a study outline for this section. Encourage students to use the section headings as a guide for structuring their outlines. They can also use the section and chapter time lines to help sequence information. **L1**

📂 Refer to *Inclusion for the High School Social Studies Classroom Strategies and Activities* in the TCR.

✓ **Reading Check**

Answer: Ford urged Americans to cut back on gas and oil consumption and undertake other energy-conserving measures; he cut government spending and advocated higher interest rates; he attempted to limit federal authority, balance the budget, and keep taxes low.

Creating a Chart Have students refer to the chapter on the Great Depression and compare the unemployment rates then with those during the years 1974–1975. Have students create a chart showing the comparison.

📁 Use the rubric for creating a map, display, or chart on pages 65–66 in the *Performance Assessment Activities and Rubrics.*

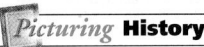 *Picturing* **History**

Reassuring Presence After the turmoil of Watergate, President Gerald Ford, shown here with First Lady Betty Ford, was a comforting leader, but he was unable to solve the problem of inflation. Through what methods did Ford try to "whip inflation now"?

As Ford attempted to revive the economy, he also attempted to limit federal authority, balance the budget, and keep taxes low. Ford vetoed more than 50 bills that the Democratic-led Congress passed during the first two years of his administration.

Ford's Foreign Policy In foreign policy, Ford continued Nixon's general strategy. Ford kept Kissinger on as secretary of state and continued to pursue détente with the Soviets and the Chinese. In August 1975 he met with leaders of NATO and the Warsaw Pact to sign the **Helsinki Accords.** Under the accords, the parties recognized the borders of Eastern Europe established at the end of World War II. The Soviets in return promised to uphold certain basic human rights, including the right to move across national borders. The subsequent Soviet failure to uphold these basic rights turned many Americans against détente.

Ford also encountered problems in Southeast Asia. In May 1975, Cambodia seized the *Mayaguez,* an American cargo ship traveling near its shores, claiming that it had been on an intelligence-gathering mission. Calling the ship's seizure an "act of piracy," Ford dispatched U.S. Marines to retrieve it. Cambodia released the crew before the marines arrived.

846 CHAPTER 27 Politics and Economics

The Election of 1976 As the 1976 presidential election approached, Americans were pessimistic and unsure of the future. With rising inflation and unemployment, many citizens were undergoing an adverse change of lifestyle. There were equally serious problems in foreign affairs. Political turmoil in developing nations threatened world stability, while the Soviet Union was pursuing an aggressive foreign policy. Americans therefore looked to elect a man who could meet these challenges.

The presidential race pitted Gerald Ford against James Earl Carter, Jr., or Jimmy Carter, as he liked to be called. Carter was somewhat of a political outsider. A former governor of Georgia, Carter had no national political experience. Nonetheless, he had won the Democratic primary with an inspiring and well-organized campaign. Carter sought to take advantage of his outsider image, promising to restore morality and honesty to the federal government. He also promised new programs for energy development, tax reform, welfare reform, and national medical care.

More than the programs he proposed, it was Carter's image as a moral and upstanding individual that attracted most supporters. Ford meanwhile characterized Carter as a liberal whose social program spending would produce higher rates of inflation and require tax increases.

In the end, Carter edged Ford with 50.1 percent of the popular vote to Ford's 47.9 percent, while capturing 297 electoral votes to Ford's 240. On Inauguration Day, to demonstrate his man-of-the-people style, Carter declined the traditional limousine ride and walked from the Capitol to the White House.

✓ **Reading Check** **Examining** What steps did President Ford take to try to control inflation?

Carter Battles the Economic Crisis

Carter devoted much of his domestic agenda to trying to fix the economy. At first he tried to end the recession and reduce unemployment by increasing government spending and cutting taxes. When inflation surged in 1978, he changed his mind. He delayed the tax cuts and vetoed the spending programs he had himself proposed to Congress. He then tried to ease inflation by reducing the money supply and raising interest rates. His main focus, however, was on the energy crisis. In the end, none of his efforts succeeded.

INTERDISCIPLINARY CONNECTIONS ACTIVITY

Economics Have the economics teacher present an explanation of cartels, including the fact that OPEC is the most long-lived cartel in history. Then have students research other cartels, either past or present. Have students determine the purpose of cartels, what holds cartels together, and what types of problems bring an end to cartels. Have students report their findings in a research report.
L2

A "War" Against Consumption Carter felt that the nation's most serious problem was its dependence on foreign oil. In one of his first national addresses, he tried to rally Americans to support what he termed a "war" against rising energy consumption. "Our decision about energy will test the character of the American people and the ability of the President and Congress to govern this nation," Carter stated.

Carter proposed a national energy program to conserve oil and to promote the use of coal and renewable energy sources such as solar power. He persuaded Congress to create a **Department of Energy** and also asked Americans to make personal sacrifices to reduce their energy consumption. Most of the public complied as best they could, although many ignored the president's suggestion.

At the same time, many business leaders and economists urged the president and Congress to deregulate the oil industry. The regulations, first imposed as part of President Nixon's price control plan, limited the ability of oil companies to pass on OPEC price increases to American consumers. As a result, oil companies found it difficult to make a profit, and they lacked the capital to invest in new domestic oil wells. These regulations, combined with OPEC price increases, helped create the energy crisis of the 1970s. Carter agreed to support deregulation but insisted on a "windfall profits tax" to prevent oil companies from overcharging consumers. The tax, however, conflicted with the basic idea of deregulation, which was to free up corporate capital for use in searching for new sources of oil. In the end, Carter's contradictory plan did not solve the country's energy crisis.

In the summer of 1979, instability in the Middle East produced a second major fuel shortage and deepened the nation's economic problems. Under increasing pressure to act, Carter made several proposals in a television address. The speech was notable for Carter's bleak assessment of the national condition. He complained about a "crisis of confidence" that had struck "at the very heart and soul of our national will." The address became known as the "malaise" speech, although Carter had not specifically used that word. Many Americans interpreted the speech not as a timely warning but as Carter blaming the people for his failures.

Carter's Leadership Problems In retrospect, President Carter's difficulties in solving the nation's economic problems lay in his inexperience and inability to work with Congress. Carter, who was proud of his outsider status, made little effort to reach out to Washington's legislative leaders. As a result, Congress blocked many of his energy proposals.

Carter also failed to translate his ideas into a concrete set of goals to inspire the nation. He offered no unifying theme for his administration, but instead followed a cautious middle course that left people confused. By 1979 public opinion polls showed that Carter's popularity had dropped lower than President Nixon's during Watergate.

 Reading Check **Summarizing** To what did President Carter devote much of his domestic agenda?

Carter's Foreign Policy

In contrast to his uncertain leadership at home, Carter's foreign policy was more clearly defined. A man of strong religious beliefs, Carter argued that the United States must try to be "right and honest and truthful and decent" in dealing with other nations. Yet it was on the international front that President Carter suffered one of his most devastating defeats.

Picturing **History**

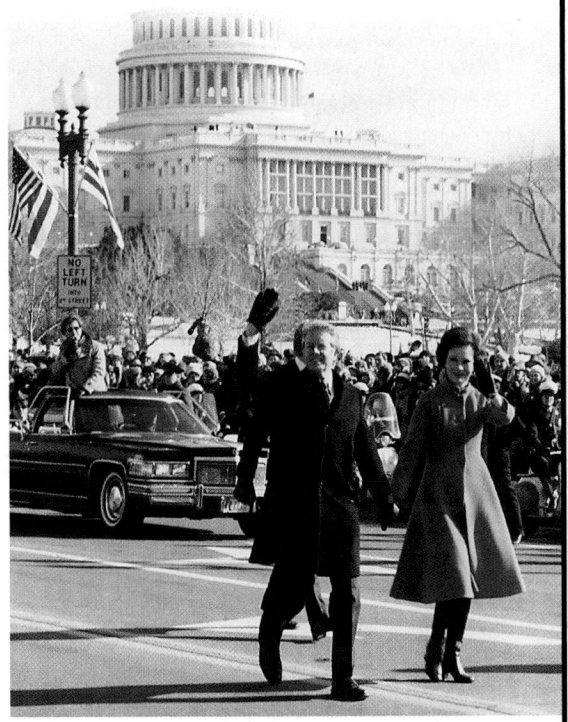

Change of Pace Jimmy Carter underscored his campaign image of being a new kind of politician by walking to the White House after his inauguration. What about Carter's image in 1976 might have been appealing to the public?

 Reading Check

Answer: His main focus was the energy crisis.

Picturing **History**

Answer: He had a down-to-earth image that appealed to people after the less accessible personalities of Nixon and Ford.
Ask: Why did Carter face leadership problems? *(He was inexperienced, he failed to work with Congress, and he did not translate his ideas into concrete goals.)*

FYI

After his inauguration, Jimmy Carter and his family chose to walk up Pennsylvania Avenue from the Capitol to the White House instead of riding in the traditional limousine. The gesture symbolized Carter's desire to lead a simple life even while in the White House.

Recognizing Ideologies Have students create a list of President Carter's foreign policy decisions that reflected his belief in human rights. Then have students select a decision and defend or reject its human rights basis. **L2**

CRITICAL THINKING ACTIVITY

Expressing an Opinion Tell students that government officials, such as state governors and the president, can grant reprieves and pardons to individuals convicted of offenses except in impeachment cases. A pardon releases the individual from any punishment due for a crime committed, but does not free the person from any implied guilt. President Ford's pardon of Richard Nixon was one of the most controversial pardons in American history. Ask students if they think President Ford did the right thing. Ask them to explain their opinions. **L2**

For over 14 months, the hostage crisis dominated the news. Some television stations opened or closed their newscasts with statements such as, "Good evening on day 334 of the Iranian hostage crisis." Thus, the crisis stayed at the forefront of public attention. Many people hung yellow ribbons around trees as a constant reminder of the hostages' plight.

3 ASSESS

Assign Section 3 Assessment as homework or as an in-class activity.

⬥ Have students use the **Interactive Tutor Self-Assessment CD-ROM.**

L1/ELL

Reading Essentials and Study Guide 27–3

HOSTAGE TO TERROR

Bound and blindfolded, American diplomat Jerry Miele is led out of the U.S. embassy in Tehran, Iran, after militants stormed the building on November 4, 1979. Ten months earlier, an Islamic fundamentalist revolution had overthrown the Shah of Iran, a staunch American ally. President Carter's decision to allow the ailing Shah to seek medical treatment in the United States led to the embassy takeover. Of the Americans taken captive, 52 were held for more than a year. The crisis contributed to Carter's defeat in the presidential election in 1980.

Morality in Foreign Policy Carter had set the tone for his foreign policy in his inaugural speech, when he announced, "Our commitment to human rights must be absolute. . . . The powerful must not persecute the weak, and human dignity must be enhanced." With the help of his foreign policy team—including **Andrew Young,** the first African American ambassador to the United Nations—Carter strove to achieve these goals.

The president put his principles into practice in Latin America. To remove a major symbol of U.S. interventionism in the region, he moved to give the Panamanians control of the Panama Canal. The United States had built and run the canal since 1903. In 1978 the president won Senate ratification of two Panama Canal treaties, which transferred control of the canal to Panama on December 31, 1999.

Most dramatically, Carter singled out the Soviet Union as a violator of human rights. He strongly condemned, for example, the Soviet practice of imprisoning people who protested against the government. Relations between the two superpowers suffered a further setback when Soviet troops invaded the Central

Asian nation of Afghanistan in December 1979. Carter responded by imposing an embargo on the sale of grain to the Soviet Union and boycotting the 1980 Summer Olympic Games in Moscow. Under the Carter administration, détente virtually collapsed.

Triumph and Failure in the Middle East It was in the volatile Middle East that President Carter met his greatest foreign policy triumph and his greatest failure. In 1978 Carter helped broker a historic peace treaty, known as the **Camp David Accords,** between Israel and Egypt, two nations that had been bitter enemies for decades. The treaty was formally signed in 1979. Most other Arab nations in the region opposed the treaty, but it marked a first step to achieving peace in the Middle East.

Just months after the Camp David Accords, Carter encountered a crisis in Iran. The United States had long supported Iran's monarch, the Shah, because Iran was a major oil supplier and a buffer against Soviet expansion in the Middle East. The Shah, however, had grown increasingly unpopular in Iran. He was a repressive ruler and had

848 CHAPTER 27 Politics and Economics

EXTENDING THE CONTENT

Habitat for Humanity The Carters have had a long-standing relationship with Habitat for Humanity, an organization promoting affordable housing in the United States and around the world. The organization builds thousands of houses for low-income families. Each house is built by volunteers, with the families themselves working alongside volunteers to build the homes. Many of the building supplies are donated or are purchased at cost. **L2**

introduced Westernizing reforms to Iranian society. The Islamic clergy fiercely opposed the Shah's reforms. Opposition to the Shah grew, and in January 1979 protesters forced him to flee. An Islamic republic was then declared.

The new regime, headed by religious leader Ayatollah Khomeini, distrusted the United States because of its ties to the Shah. In November 1979, revolutionaries stormed the American embassy in Tehran and held 52 Americans hostage. The militants threatened to kill the hostages or try them as spies.

The Carter administration tried unsuccessfully to negotiate for the hostages' release. In April 1980, as pressure mounted, Carter approved a daring rescue attempt. To the nation's dismay, the rescue mission failed when several helicopters malfunctioned and one crashed in the desert. Eight servicemen died in the accident. Hamilton Jordan, President Carter's chief of staff, described the gloomy atmosphere in the White House the day after the crash:

> ❝I arrived at the White House a few minutes before the President went on television to tell the nation about the catastrophe. He looked exhausted and careworn. . . . The mood at the senior staff meeting was somber and awkward. I sensed that we were all uncomfortable, like when a loved one dies and friends don't quite know what to say. . . . After the meeting, I wandered around the White House. . . . My thoughts kept returning to the bodies [of the servicemen] in the desert.❞
>
> —quoted in *Crisis: The Last Year of the Carter Presidency*

World Geography Connection

The Islamic State

In establishing an Islamic republic, the Ayatollah Khomeini created a state in which the codes and beliefs of Islam guide politics and thus direct nearly every aspect of life. Mullahs, or Islamic religious leaders, became political leaders as well, which allowed them to impose Islamic codes on Iranian citizens. In a religious state, religious practices are not a matter of choice but the law of the land. Politics and religion have joined forces in other parts of the Islamic world as well. In 1996 a group known as the Taliban transformed Afghanistan into an Islamic state. From insisting that men grow beards to forbidding women to work outside the home, Afghanistan's leaders enforced a social order based on an interpretation of Islam. *What long-held American principle does the creation of a religious state violate?*

The crisis continued into the fall of 1980. Every night, news programs reminded viewers how many days the hostages had been held. The president's inability to free the hostages cost him support in the 1980 presidential election. Negotiations with Iran continued right up to Carter's last day in office. Ironically, on January 20, 1981, the day Carter left office, Iran released the Americans, ending their 444 days in captivity.

✓ **Reading Check** **Summarizing** What was President Carter's main foreign policy theme?

HISTORY Online **Study Central**™ To review this section, go to tarvol2.glencoe.com and click on **Study Central**™.

SECTION 3 ASSESSMENT

Checking for Understanding

1. **Define:** inflation, embargo, stagflation.
2. **Identify:** Helsinki Accords, Department of Energy.
3. **Identify** the achievement and failure President Carter experienced in the Middle East during his administration.

Reviewing Themes

4. **Economic Factors** How did President Carter attempt to deal with the nation's energy crisis?

Critical Thinking

5. **Evaluating** Do you think President Ford should have pardoned Richard Nixon? Why or why not?
6. **Organizing** Complete a graphic organizer similar to the one below by listing the ways that President Carter applied his human rights ideas to his foreign policy.

Carter's Human Rights Foreign Policy

Analyzing Visuals

7. **Analyzing Photographs** Study the photograph on page 848. What effect do you think images such as this one had on Americans who were living or traveling in other countries?

Writing About History

8. **Expository Writing** Write an essay identifying what you believe to be President Carter's most important foreign policy achievement. Explain your choice.

CHAPTER 27 Politics and Economics **849**

SECTION 3 ASSESSMENT ANSWERS

1. Terms are in blue.
2. Helsinki Accords (p. 846), Department of Energy (p. 847)
3. the Camp David Accords and the hostage crisis in Iran
4. Carter proposed a national energy program to conserve oil and promote the use of renewable energy sources, created the Department of Energy, and deregulated the oil industry.
5. Students' answers will vary. Some students may say the pardon saved the nation from witnessing a divisive trial. Others may say that Nixon escaped punishment.
6. Answers should reflect text information, particularly about the Soviet Union and Panama on page 848.
7. They would fear attacks on themselves.
8. Students' essays will vary. Essays should include facts to support the position taken.

Section Quiz 27–3

Name	Date	Class

★ Chapter 27 | Score

Section Quiz 27-3

DIRECTIONS: Matching Match each item in Column A with the items in Column B. Write the correct letters in the blanks. *(10 points each)*

Column A
____ 1. a combination of rising prices and economic stagnation
____ 2. a historic peace treaty between Israel and Egypt that was brokered by President Carter
____ 3. religious leader and head of the new regime in Iran
____ 4. a rise in the cost of goods
____ 5. first African American ambassador to the United Nations

Column B
A. Andrew Young
B. Inflation
C. Camp David Accords
D. stagflation
E. Ayatollah Khomeini

DIRECTIONS: Multiple Choice In the blank at the left, write the letter of the choice that best completes the statement or answers the question. *(10 points each)*

World Geography Connection

Answer: Creation of a religious state violates the American principle of separation of church and state.

✓ **Reading Check**

Answer: the need to be honest, truthful, and decent in foreign relations

Reteach

Have students explain the reasons for economic trouble in the United States during the 1970s.

Enrich

Have students explain whether they agree or disagree with the 1980 Olympic boycott.

HISTORY Online

Study Central™ provides summaries, interactive games, and online graphic organizers to help students review section content.

4 CLOSE

Have students discuss Jimmy Carter's domestic and foreign policies.

849

1 FOCUS

Section Overview

This section focuses on the popular culture of the 1970s.

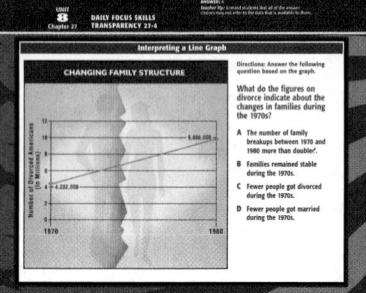
Reading Preview

Answers to Graphic: birth rate dropped, divorce rate doubled, parents and children spent less time together, and women were active outside the home

Preteaching Vocabulary
Have students write three questions that can be answered using the Key Terms and Names.

Guide to Reading

Main Idea
In the midst of widespread cynicism about their leaders and concerns about the economy, Americans sought fulfillment and escape during the 1970s.

Key Terms and Names
New Age movement, guru, transcendental meditation, *All in the Family*, disco

Reading Strategy
Categorizing As you read about life in the United States in the 1970s, complete a graphic organizer similar to the one below by listing the changes that occurred in family life during that time.

Changes in Family Life

Reading Objectives
• **Explain** the emergence of new spiritual movements and religions.
• **Discuss** social changes of the 1970s.

Section Theme
Culture and Traditions Even after the turbulent 1960s, American culture continued changing to reflect new trends and ideas.

Preview of Events

♦1970	♦1973	♦1976	♦1979

1971
All in the Family debuts

1974
Good Times debuts

1977
Disco mania peaks with release of *Saturday Night Fever; The Complete Book of Running* published

---

★ An American Story ★

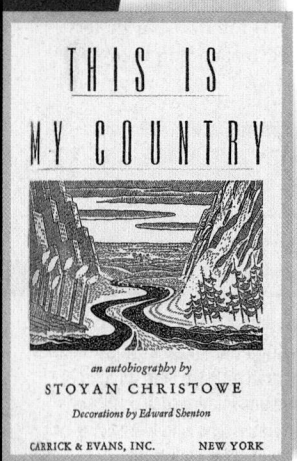

As the United States prepared to celebrate its bicentennial on July 4, 1976, a reporter asked Stoyan Christowe for his views on the state of the nation on the eve of its 200th birthday. The 77-year-old Vermont resident acknowledged that the United States was "in pretty bad shape," but added that the country would turn around—as it always had.

❝I believe in this country. I've always believed in it. There is a quotation by Benjamin Franklin, in a letter to George Washington during the Revolutionary War. Franklin talked of a cornfield during a drought, and how the cornstalks have shriveled and curled, and it was a sad sight. And then, he said a thunderstorm came along, spilling rain, and a day or two after, the sun came out, and the corn came to life, and it was a delight. . . . I know we're going through a kind of turmoil now, but the country is okay. . . . My faith in this country was never shaken. Like that cornfield—the sun will shine again, and the rains will come, and brother, those cornstalks will revive, and it will be a beautiful sight.❞

—quoted in *Newsweek,* July 4, 1976

Cover of Stoyan Christowe's book

The Search for Fulfillment

Like Stoyan Christowe, many Americans in the 1970s believed that the United States would eventually move beyond the Watergate scandal, the Vietnam War, and the country's nagging economic problems. In the meantime, some Americans sought ways to get

850 CHAPTER 27 Politics and Economics

SECTION RESOURCES

Reproducible Masters
• Reproducible Lesson Plan 27–4
• Daily Lecture and Discussion Notes 27–4
• Guided Reading Activity 27–4
• Section Quiz 27–4
• Reading Essentials and Study Guide 27–4

Transparencies
• Daily Focus Skills Transparency 27–4

Multimedia
🖭 Interactive Tutor Self-Assessment CD-ROM
🖭 ExamView® Pro Testmaker CD-ROM
🖭 Presentation Plus! CD-ROM
🖭 TeacherWorks™ CD-ROM
🎧 Audio Program
🎵 American Music: Hits Through History
🎵 American Music: Cultural Traditions

on with their daily lives. As a way of coping with anxious times, they sought escape, laughter, and fulfillment in a wide range of fads, entertainment, and spiritual movements.

Writer Tom Wolfe labeled the 1970s the "me decade," referring to the idea that many Americans grew more self-obsessed in this decade as they strove for greater individual satisfaction. Indeed, the most popular books of the period included such titles as *I'm OK, You're OK; How to Be Your Own Best Friend;* and *Looking Out for Number One.* Journalist Richard Michael Levine argued that in light of the growing feelings of despair and cynicism about American society, it was little wonder that many people turned inward. "In the damp, late autumn of 1973, it did not take a religious fanatic in a tattered overcoat to sense that the real Kingdom lay within, things being as rotten as they were without," he wrote. In their quest for self-improvement, many Americans were willing to embrace new movements.

The New Age Movement Disenchanted with the conventional religions of their parents, some young men and women sought fulfillment through the host of secular movements and activities that made up the **New Age movement.** New Age enthusiasts embraced the idea that people were responsible for and capable of everything from self-healing to creating the world. They believed spiritual enlightenment could be found in common practices, not just in traditional churchgoing. They tried activities such as yoga, martial arts, and chanting to achieve fuller spiritual awareness. Kathy Smith, a college student during the 1970s, recalled how she and others claimed to find "Zen," or enlightenment, in running and other physical activities:

> 66 They were beginning to understand how exercise affects your soul, how it affects your being. People started getting in the 'Zen' of things: the Zen of tennis, the Zen of working out, the Zen of motorcycle repair, the Zen of running. I, like many others, started connecting physical activity to the spiritual side. People also started looking at yoga and tai chi, and not only the stretching aspects of these disciplines but the mental aspects. Now they were working the body, the mind, and the spirit. 99
>
> —quoted in *The Century*

The New Age movement took many different paths to transform individuals and society. Some New Agers extolled the power of crystals and gemstones to improve life; others touted astrology. Some were inspired by the Eastern belief in reincarnation, which taught that people could be reborn many times until reaching perfection. Awareness of former lives was supposed to bring knowledge of the true inner self.

Transcendental Meditation Many Americans who were dissatisfied with established religions sought new religions. A number of these new religions originated in Asia and centered on the teachings of gurus, or mystical leaders. One of the more well-known gurus was Maharishi Mahesh Yogi. A native of India, Maharishi moved to the United States in 1959, where he led a spiritual movement known as transcendental meditation. Maharishi worked in relative obscurity until 1967, when the wildly popular rock group the Beatles began to explore his teachings. Their attention brought an American following. Transcendental meditation suggested daily meditation and the silent repetition of spiritual mantras as a way of achieving peak intelligence, harmony, and health. If all the people on Earth practiced transcendental meditation, its advocates believed, the world would enjoy peace.

Changing Families The search for fulfillment had an impact on many American families. The campaigns of the era, especially the women's movement, began to change how many women viewed their roles as wives and mothers. By 1970, 60 percent of women between the ages of 16 and 24 had joined the

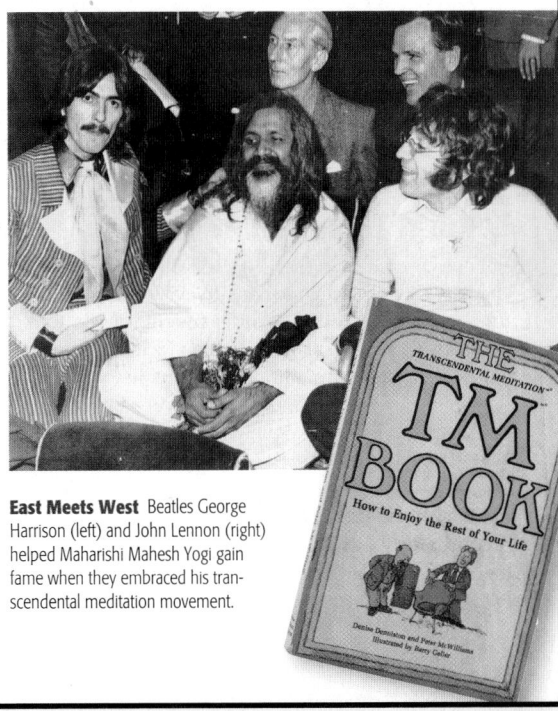

East Meets West Beatles George Harrison (left) and John Lennon (right) helped Maharishi Mahesh Yogi gain fame when they embraced his transcendental meditation movement.

2 TEACH

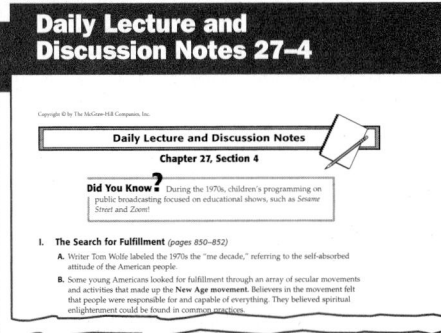

Daily Lecture and Discussion Notes 27–4

Copyright © by The McGraw-Hill Companies, Inc.

Daily Lecture and Discussion Notes

Chapter 27, Section 4

Did You Know? During the 1970s, children's programming on public broadcasting focused on educational shows, such as *Sesame Street* and *Zoom!*

I. **The Search for Fulfillment** (pages 850–852)
   A. Writer Tom Wolfe labeled the 1970s the "me decade," referring to the self-absorbed attitude of the American people.
   B. Some young Americans looked for fulfillment through an array of secular movements and activities that made up the **New Age movement.** Believers in the movement felt that people were responsible for and capable of everything. They believed spiritual enlightenment could be found in common practices.

Writing a Script Organize students into small groups to write a scene, set in the 1970s, involving conversations among an American homemaker, a manager of an automobile factory, a young unemployed worker, a college student, and a newspaper reporter. Each person should express his or her reasons why they lack confidence in the country's future. *(Reasons may include the energy crisis, foreign competition, rising inflation and unemployment rates, and social and economic inequality).* Have each group present their scripts in dramatic fashion. **L1**

📁 Use the rubric for an oral presentation, monologue, song, or skit on pages 67–68 in the *Performance Assessment Activities and Rubrics.*

you don't say...

Fads Popular fashion fads of the 1970s included platform shoes for men, leisure suits, tank tops, and Farrah Fawcett hairdos.

Reading Strategy **READING THE TEXT**

Using Possible Sentences This strategy allows students to speculate about word meanings. Choose ten vocabulary words and write them on the board. Write sentences using the words either correctly or incorrectly. Then ask students to comment on whether the sentences are "possible." As students encounter the vocabulary during the reading, have them note each term's usage in the selection's context. After reading, have students re-read the sentences and revise them as necessary. **L1** ELL

📁 Refer to *Inclusion for the High School Social Studies Classroom Strategies and Activities* in the TCR.

Guided Reading Activity 27–4

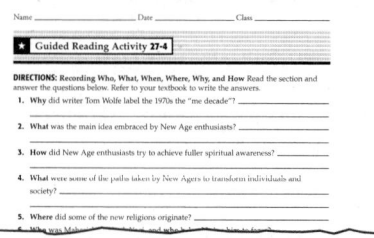

Name _____ Date _____ Class _____

★ Guided Reading Activity 27-4

DIRECTIONS: Recording Who, What, When, Where, Why, and How Read the section and answer the questions below. Refer to your textbook to write the answers.

1. Why did writer Tom Wolfe label the 1970s the "me decade"? _____
2. What was the main idea embraced by New Age enthusiasts? _____
3. How did New Age enthusiasts try to achieve fuller spiritual awareness? _____
4. What were some of the paths taken by New Agers to transform individuals and society? _____
5. Where did some of the new religions originate? _____

✔ **Reading Check**

Answer: New Age enthusiasts embraced the idea that people were responsible for and capable of almost anything. They believed spiritual enlightenment could be found in many different ways, not just traditional churchgoing.

What *Life* Was Like...

Organize students into groups to conduct research on either fashion, disco, or movies popular in the 1970s. Then hold a class discussion asking a representative of each group to report to the class what they learned.

History *and the* Humanities

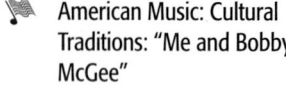

American Music: Hits Through History: "Shining Star," "Oye Como Va," "Boogie Nights," "Lean on Me"

American Music: Cultural Traditions: "Me and Bobby McGee"

📁 Use *Interpreting Political Cartoons,* Cartoon 31.

• **Bee Gees**
Disco fans around the country and the world danced to the sounds of the Australian group the Bee Gees. The movie *Saturday Night Fever* featured their music and catapulted them into the limelight.

What *Life* Was Like...

Disco

The counterculture of the 1960s provided music designed to raise people's consciousness of social issues. The disco music of the 1970s, with its simple lyrics and intense beats, was designed simply to entertain. By the end of the decade, millions of people throughout the nation and the world were dancing under flashing disco lights.

• **Fashion**
New styles of clothing, first associated with disco patrons, became common for everyone. Men wore brightly patterned synthetic shirts, bell-bottom pants, and platform shoes or boots. Women wore wildly patterned dresses or jumpsuits with high heels or boots.

---

labor force. Between 1970 and 1980, women aged 25 to 34 had the largest annual percentage growth in the workforce.

These changes in turn led to changes in family life. With women increasingly active outside the home, smaller families became the norm. The birthrate fell to an all-time low in 1976, and parents and their children began spending less time together. A greater number of families also split apart, as the divorce rate doubled from 2.5 divorces per thousand people in 1966 to 5 per thousand 10 years later.

✔ **Reading Check** **Summarizing** What were the basic beliefs of the New Age movement?

Cultural Trends in the 1970s

Popular culture in the 1970s reflected many of the changes taking place in society. Television now sometimes portrayed women in independent roles or took on formerly taboo subjects such as racism, poverty, and abortion. Meanwhile, Americans listened and danced to new forms of music and sought fun and escape in a variety of new fads.

TURNING POINT

Television in the 1970s The decade opened with a revolutionary new situation comedy on Saturday nights. Unlike earlier sitcoms, *The Mary Tyler Moore Show* featured an unmarried woman with a

meaningful career at its center. Actress Mary Tyler Moore played the main character, Mary Richards, who had left a small town for a big-city job as a television news producer. Mary sparred with her gruff but caring boss, despaired over the shallowness of the blow-dried news announcer, and had adventures with friends. Mary also went on dates but never got around to marrying.

The debut of the sitcom *All in the Family* in January 1971 marked an even bigger turning point in television programming. The show took risks by confronting potentially volatile social issues and by featuring a controversial hero, the blue-collar and bigoted Archie Bunker. Archie called his wife Edith "Dingbat" and his liberal son-in-law "Meathead." He also mocked his feminist daughter and various ethnic groups. Though Archie prided himself on being the man of the house, he never won any arguments with his liberal family or his African American neighbors.

By carefully mixing humor and sensitive issues and by not preaching to its audience, *All in the Family* provided viewers with a way to examine their own feelings about issues such as racism. Producer Norman Lear claimed that the show "holds a mirror up to our prejudices. . . . We laugh now, swallowing just the littlest bit of truth about ourselves. . . ."

Several years later, Archie Bunker's African American neighbors became the stars of another television series, *The Jeffersons.* George Jefferson, like Archie, was opinionated and prejudiced but

852 CHAPTER 27 Politics and Economics

DIFFERENTIATED INSTRUCTION

Visual/Spatial Have students videotape five minutes of a television show that originally aired in the 1970s. Have students prepare a summary of how their chosen clip demonstrates life in the 1970s. Have students show their clips and present their summaries to the class. **L1**

📁 Refer to *Inclusion for the High School Social Studies Classroom Strategies and Activities* in the TCR.

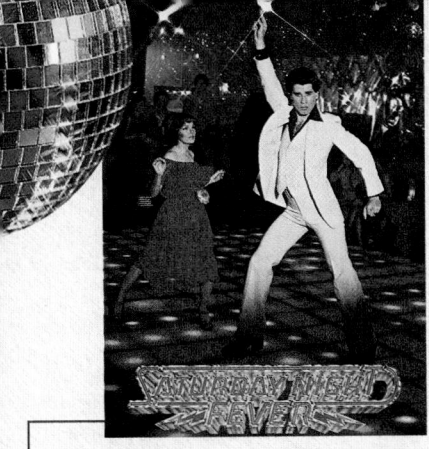

Saturday Night Fever
John Travolta played the role of Tony Manero in this 1977 film. By day Tony worked as a clerk in a Brooklyn store. At night, however, he transformed himself into a disco star. A popular success, the film showed Tony as a young working-class kid with a dream to escape his ordinary existence. Life at the disco provided a road to that escape.

ultimately likable. *The Jeffersons* portrayed African Americans in a new light: as successful and respected. *Maude,* another spin-off from *All in the Family,* featured Edith Bunker's feminist cousin, who had recently remarried after her third divorce. The strong-willed Maude did not need to depend on her new husband, Walter. This popular program drew intense controversy in 1972 when Maude made the difficult decision to have an abortion.

Maude's African American maid, Florida, generated another series in 1974. Starring Esther Rolle as Florida, *Good Times* portrayed an African American family struggling to raise three children in a low-income housing development in Chicago.

Music of the 1970s The music of this period reflected the end of the 1960s youth and protest movements. The hard-driving rock of the tumultuous 1960s gave way to softer sounds. "The fading out of ear-numbing, mind-blowing acid rock," *Time* commented in 1971, "is related to the softening of the youth revolution." The music became more reflective and less political, reflecting a desire to seek fulfillment from within. "These days, nobody wants to hear songs that have a message," said a member of the rock group Chicago. Popular entertainers in tune with the new meditative atmosphere included singers Barry Manilow and John Denver and the bands ABBA and the Eagles.

The 1970s also saw the rise of disco music. The disco craze of the later 1970s began in African

American and Latin nightclubs. There, disc jockeys played recorded dance music with a loud and persistent beat. The fast pace and easy rhythm attracted fans, but disco also seemed well suited for the "me generation." Unlike rock 'n' roll, disco allowed the people dancing to it to assume greater prominence than the music. As the co-owner of a popular discotheque in New York described the phenomena, "Everybody secretly likes to be on center stage and here we give them a huge space to do it all on."

Gus Rodriguez, who had moved with his family from Puerto Rico to Brooklyn 20 years earlier, recalled going to discos with his friends in the mid-1970s:

> ❝We would go to the discos several times a week, but the weekends were always the best. Getting ready to go out was sort of a ritual, especially on Saturdays. During the day you would go buy that shirt, or that belt, or those platform shoes, all of which seemed incredibly important at the time. You had to have a particular type of look. And we all dressed the same way. We would call each other up to coordinate what color suits everybody was wearing—who's wearing the powder-blue suit, who's wearing the white suit, who's wearing this, who's wearing that. And then we would carefully iron everything so it was just so.❞
>
> —quoted in *The Century*

Disco mania reached its peak after the 1977 movie, *Saturday Night Fever.* In the film, a middle-class

All in the Family Many Americans saw a little of themselves in the characters of this popular sitcom.

CHAPTER 27
Section 4, 850–854

In January 1977, ABC broadcast the *Roots* miniseries. Based on the 1976 novel by Alex Haley, the proram traced the history of an African family's struggle with slavery through several generations. The miniseries became a surprise hit. Media coverage of the *Roots* phenomenon indicated that restaurants and shops noticed a decline in business during the broadcast.

3 ASSESS

Assign Section 4 Assessment as homework or as an in-class activity.

🔘 Have students use the **Interactive Tutor Self-Assessment CD-ROM.**

L1/ELL

Reading Essentials and Study Guide 27–4

Name _____ Date _____ Class _____

Study Guide

Chapter 27, Section 4
For use with textbook pages 850–854

THE "ME" DECADE: LIFE IN THE 1970S

KEY TERMS AND NAMES

New Age movement secular movement of the 1970s *(page 851)*
gurus mystical leaders *(page 851)*
transcendental meditation a religious movement started by Maharishi Mahesh Yogi that suggested daily meditation and the silent repetition of spiritual mantras *(page 851)*
All in the Family a situation comedy of the 1970s that confronted uncomfortable social issues *(page 852)*
disco dance music with a loud and persistent beat that became popular in the 1970s *(page 853)*

L2

Section Quiz 27–4

Name _____ Date _____ Class _____

⭐ **Chapter 27**   Score ____

Section Quiz 27–4

DIRECTIONS: Matching Match each item in Column A with the items in Column B. Write the correct letters in the blanks. *(10 points each)*

Column A
____ 1. allowed drivers to talk to each other over a two-way frequency within a range of a few miles
____ 2. religious movement led by Maharishi Mahesh Yogi
____ 3. situation comedy that placed an unmarried woman with a meaningful career at its center
____ 4. popular singer in tune with the new meditative atmosphere
____ 5. marked the biggest turning point in television programming

Column B
A. *All in the Family*
B. CBs
C. John Denver
D. *The Mary Tyler Moore Show*
E. transcendental meditation

INTERDISCIPLINARY CONNECTIONS ACTIVITY

Science Tell students that the 1970s witnessed many scientific and technological firsts including the first CAT scan, the first test-tube baby, the first home computer, and the first portable tape players. Have students select one of these "firsts" or another invention or advance from the 1970s to research. Have students prepare a three-to-five minute oral presentation based on their research. Ask them to consider how the invention or discovery affected the development of the country, the standard of living, the nature of work, and what need it met, as well as any subsequent innovations or discoveries. **L2**

Fact	Fiction	Folklore

In the late 1990s the United States Postal Service issued a series of stamps depicting the twentieth century. The "Celebrate the Century" series featured 15 stamps for each decade. The ubiquitous smiley face was one of the images selected for the 1970s series. Two other stamps, one depicting disco and the other featuring 1970s fashion, also commemorated the 1970s.

✓ Reading Check

Answer: Millions of records were sold, and it spurred the opening of discos.

Reteach

Have students explain the emergence of new spiritual movements and religions.

Enrich

Have students create a time line of popular culture that includes the items mentioned here and other relevant events. Additional items for the time line could include popular sports of the 1970s or important movies released during the decade. Encourage students to illustrate some or all of the entires.

HISTORY Online

Study Central™ provides summaries, interactive games, and online graphic organizers to help students review section content.

4 CLOSE

Have students discuss whether some traditional values became weaker during the 1970s.

854

Fact	Fiction	Folklore

Put on a Happy Face Throughout the 1960s and 1970s, the nation experienced a "button craze" as people expressed themselves by pinning buttons with slogans to their clothing. The most popular button actually said nothing at all. In 1971 Americans began buying a yellow button with a simple smile on it. By the fall of 1971, marketers estimated that more than 20 million smile buttons had been sold, making it the most popular fad item since the hula hoop.

Italian American teenager played by John Travolta transformed himself into a white-suited disco king each Saturday night. The movie's soundtrack sold millions of copies and spurred a wave of disco openings across the country and around the world.

Fads and Fashions In addition to disco, the nation embraced many other fads during the 1970s. Americans by the millions bought T-shirts that bore personalized messages, while teenagers flew down suburban and city streets on skateboards. Obsessed with self-discovery, a number of Americans slipped mood rings on their fingers to get in touch with their innermost feelings. Supposedly, the ring's color changed to match the wearer's ever-changing mood. Blue, for example, signaled happiness and bliss, while gray denoted nervousness and anxiety.

Meanwhile, millions of drivers bought citizens band ("CB") radios for their vehicles. This radio system allowed drivers to talk to each other over a two-way frequency within a range of a few miles. Many truck drivers installed the radios in an effort to warn each other of police and speed traps. Soon, however, average drivers had purchased them, mostly for entertainment purposes. Drivers adopted their own CB name, or "handle," and talked to each other using CB jargon and code words.

Fitness was another trend during the "me decade," as many Americans turned to exercise to improve the way they felt and looked. One popular type of exercise in the 1970s was aerobics. Physician Kenneth H. Cooper popularized the exercise concept in his 1968 book *Aerobics*. It was a way to achieve cardiovascular fitness without the drudgery and isolation that often accompanies physical exercise. This new way to stay fit while having fun and interacting socially with others quickly gained popularity. By the mid-1970s, men and women were dancing in gyms across the country. Running also attracted a wide following, as scores of Americans began pounding the pavement to stay fit and trim. In a testament to the popularity of running, athlete Jim Fixx's work *The Complete Book of Running* was a bestseller following its publication in 1977.

By the end of the 1970s, a number of these fads and trends began to fade. A decade in which Americans came to recognize their country's vulnerability and its limits had ended. As the new decade dawned, Americans looked forward to regaining confidence in their country and optimism in their own futures.

✓ Reading Check
Examining What was the impact of disco music on American society?

HISTORY Online **Study Central**™ To review this section, go to tarvol2.glencoe.com and click on **Study Central**™.

SECTION 4 ASSESSMENT

Checking for Understanding

1. **Define:** guru, transcendental meditation, disco.
2. **Identify:** New Age movement, *All in the Family*.
3. **Summarize** the basic beliefs of followers of transcendental meditation.

Reviewing Themes

4. **Culture and Traditions** What new cultural trends affected American society in the 1970s?

Critical Thinking

5. **Analyzing** How did television in the 1970s reflect society at that time?
6. **Organizing** Complete a graphic organizer similar to the one below by listing the cultural trends of the 1970s.

Cultural Trends of the 1970s

Analyzing Visuals

7. **Analyzing Photographs** Study the photographs in the "What Life Was Like" feature on pages 852–853. How has popular music and fashion changed since the 1970s?

Writing About History

8. **Descriptive Writing** View a television program that was popular in the 1970s. Write a description of the program and explain how it reflected society at that time.

854 CHAPTER 27 Politics and Economics

SECTION 4 ASSESSMENT ANSWERS

1. Terms are in blue.
2. New Age movement (*p. 851*), *All in the Family* (*p. 852*)
3. daily meditation and mantras as a way of achieving peak intelligence, harmony, and health
4. television dealt with controversial issues; transcendental meditation; disco and new fashion developed; fitness became a craze
5. Television portrayed characters in situations similar to what viewers were experiencing.
6. Disco music, CBs, fitness, social issues on television, T-shirts with messages, mood rings
7. Dance music has become more varied; fashions less tailored and more casual
8. Students' descriptions will vary. Encourage students to comment on the content, music, wardrobe, language, and settings used in the television program.

Analyzing Secondary Sources

Why Learn This Skill?

This textbook, like many other history books, is a secondary source. Secondary sources draw from primary sources to explain a topic. The value of a secondary source depends on how its author uses primary sources. Learning to analyze secondary sources will help you figure out whether those sources are presenting a complete and accurate picture of a topic or event.

Learning the Skill

To determine whether an author uses primary sources effectively, ask these questions:

- Are there references to primary sources in the text, footnotes, or acknowledgments?

- Who are the authors of the primary sources? What insights or biases might these people have?

- Is the information from the primary sources interwoven effectively to support or describe an event?

- Are different kinds of primary sources considered? Do they represent varied testimony?

- Is the interpretation of the primary sources sound and logical?

Practicing the Skill

In the following excerpt from *The Cold War, 1945–1987*, author Ralph B. Levering discusses President Carter's China policy. Carter sent his national security adviser, Zbigniew Brzezinski, to China to encourage better relations and thus put pressure on the Soviets. As you read, identify the primary sources Levering uses to make his argument.

During his trip to Peking, Brzezinski did everything he could to please the Chinese leaders. . . . He stressed repeatedly the evil nature of the Soviet Union. . . . Upon his return, Brzezinski told a New York Times *reporter that the trip was intended to "underline the long-term strategic nature of the United States' relationship to China."*

. . . Soviet leaders were deeply concerned. An editorial in Pravda *on May 30, 1978, stated that Brzezinski "stands before the world as an enemy of détente."*

President Nixon and First Lady Pat Nixon visiting the Great Wall of China during their historic 1972 trip.

Pravda *also blamed China, stating on June 17 that "Soviet-American confrontation . . . is the cherished dream of Peking." On the whole, U.S. officials were not displeased by the Kremlin's anger and concern: perhaps it would make Soviet leaders more anxious to conclude the SALT negotiations and more inclined to show restraint in the Third World.*

❶ What kind of primary source does Levering use twice in this passage?

❷ Do you think this kind of primary source has any possible weaknesses?

❸ Would the use of government documents strengthen the author's argument? Why or why not?

Skills Assessment

Complete the Practicing Skills questions on page 857 and the Chapter 27 Skill Reinforcement Activity to assess your mastery of this skill.

Applying the Skill

Analyzing Secondary Sources Find and read an in-depth article in a newspaper. Then list the primary sources the article uses and analyze how reliable you think they are.

Glencoe's **Skillbuilder Interactive Workbook CD-ROM, Level 2,** provides instruction and practice in key social studies skills.

TEACH

Analyzing Secondary Sources
When researching a topic, recommend that students use several secondary sources in order to evaluate all aspects of the topic and to identify various writers' points of view.

Assign students various passages from the *An American Story* features in this book. Have students identify which portions of the information are primary sources and which are secondary sources. Have volunteers share their findings with the class.

Additional Practice

L1

Reinforcing Skills Activity 27

Name _____ Date _____ Class _____

★ Reinforcing Skills Activity **27**

Analyzing Secondary Sources

☐ **LEARNING THE SKILL**

Secondary source documents, such as your textbook, weave together a variety of primary sources. To judge the quality and reliability of a secondary source document, you need to analyze the primary sources cited by the author. As you read from a secondary source, look for references in the text such as footnotes or acknowledgments. Consider the authorship of the primary sources used. What biases might they have? Ask yourself how well the primary source material supports the information provided. Does the author use a variety of well-balanced sources? Does the author's interpretation make sense in light of the source documents used?

☐ **PRACTICING THE SKILL**

DIRECTIONS: Read the excerpt below from Kenneth E. Morris's biography of President Jimmy Carter titled *Jimmy Carter: American Moralist.* Then answer the questions that follow.

GLENCOE
TECHNOLOGY

CD-ROM
Glencoe Skillbuilder Interactive Workbook CD-ROM, Level 2

This interactive CD-ROM reinforces student mastery of essential social studies skills.

ANSWERS TO PRACTICING THE SKILL

❶ an editorial in a newspaper
❷ The reporter could be using the quote out of context. The *Pravda* editorials, as all editorials, are opinions. Since the Soviet state ran *Pravda*, articles and editorials uniformly reflected government policy.
❸ Students' answers will vary.

Applying the Skill
Students' answers will vary. Encourage students to attach the article to their analysis.

CHAPTER

27 ASSESSMENT and ACTIVITIES

Reviewing Key Terms

Students' answers will vary. The pages where the words appear in the text are shown in parentheses.

1. **impound** (p. 835)
2. **détente** (p. 836)
3. **summit** (p. 837)
4. **executive privilege** (p. 841)
5. **impeach** (p. 841)
6. **inflation** (p. 844)
7. **embargo** (p. 844)
8. **stagflation** (p. 844)
9. **guru** (p. 851)
10. **transcendental meditation** (p. 851)
11. **disco** (p. 853)

Reviewing Key Facts

12. Southern strategy (p. 834), Sam J. Ervin (p. 840), OPEC (p. 844), New Age movement (p. 851)
13. Nixon's domestic policy focused on the New Federalism and his foreign policy focused on détente.
14. Most Americans lost trust in public officials.
15. President Nixon believed wage and price freezes would stop stagflation, a combination of rising prices and economic stagnation.
16. rising oil prices, increased international competition, low job training for new jobs, and a decline in manufacturing

---

Reviewing Key Terms

On a sheet of paper, use each of these terms in a sentence.

1. impound
2. détente
3. summit
4. executive privilege
5. impeach
6. inflation
7. embargo
8. stagflation
9. guru
10. transcendental meditation
11. disco

Reviewing Key Facts

12. **Identify:** Southern strategy, Sam J. Ervin, OPEC, New Age movement.
13. What were the main aspects of President Nixon's domestic and foreign policies?
14. What was the impact of the Watergate scandal on the American people?
15. Why did President Nixon freeze wages and prices in the early 1970s?
16. What factors caused economic problems in the United States in the 1970s?
17. What changes in family life occurred in the United States in the 1970s?

Critical Thinking

18. **Analyzing Themes: Government and Democracy** How did the Watergate scandal affect the relationship among the three branches of government?

---

19. **Evaluating** What impact did cultural phenomena such as disco music, the use of CB radios, and exercise trends have on the U.S. economy?

20. **Forming an Opinion** Alexander Haig stated that the Watergate scandal led to "a fundamental discrediting of respect for the presidency . . . [and] a new skepticism about politics, in general, which every American feels to this day." Do you agree with his statement? Why or why not?

21. **Interpreting Primary Sources** When the Arab-Israeli War of 1973 developed into a stalemate, the Arab nations imposed an oil embargo on the United States, the chief supporter of Israel. Because Arab countries supplied much of the oil used in the United States, the embargo created an energy crisis. The excerpt below is taken from an article in the December 3, 1973, issue of *U.S. News & World Report.* It details the growing energy problems that the United States was facing at that time. Read the excerpt and answer the questions that follow.

66 Evidence of the full dimensions of the energy crisis in this country is becoming more clear each day.

- Electric-power brownouts, even blackouts, are predicted for many parts of the U.S. before the end of the year.
- Voltage reduction of 5 percent from 4 P.M. to 8 P.M. each day was ordered starting November 26 in all six New England States, where fuel shortages threaten homes, schools, factories. . . .
- As a first step to cut gasoline use, President Nixon was reportedly ready to order closing of service stations nationwide from 9 P.M. Saturday to midnight Sunday on weekends. . . .

Chapter Summary

Uniting a Divided Country	Scandal and Economic Turmoil	Challenging Traditional Values
• Nixon's conservative politics appeal to "Middle America." • Nixon begins pulling ground troops out of Vietnam. • Tensions with Soviet Union and China ease. • Nixon signs treaty limiting nuclear arms.	• Watergate scandal brings down Nixon. • Congress enacts new laws to limit presidential power. • Inflation, energy crisis, and foreign competition cause economic slowdown. • Ford and Carter fail to revive economy.	• New Age movement advocates self-fulfillment. • More women join the workforce. • Television shows prominently feature African Americans and independent women; address sensitive issues such as racism and abortion.

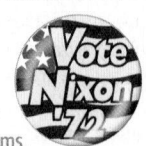

---

17. Changes in family life included smaller families, more divorces, parents and children spending less time together, and women becoming more active in the workplace and outside the home.

Critical Thinking

18. The Supreme Court forced the president to yield presidential privilege, thus decreasing the power of the executive branch. Congress passed laws establishing a greater balance of power, requiring financial disclosure from all branches of government, and establishing independent counsel to investigate wrongdoings of government officials.

19. Disco music led to the opening of dance clubs; millions of people bought CB radios; and exercise clubs opened throughout the country. Each helped the economy expand.

20. Students' answers will vary but should carefully consider current feelings toward the government.

HISTORY Online

Self-Check Quiz

Visit the *American Republic Since 1877* Web site at tarvol2.glencoe.com and click on *Self-Check Quizzes— Chapter 27* to assess your knowledge of chapter content.

• Immediate rationing of gasoline and fuel oil is being urged on the President by top oil-industry executives. . . .

One major piece of legislation . . . directs the President to take measures necessary to reduce the nation's energy demands by 25 percent within four weeks.

Speed limits would be cut nationally; lighting and heating of public and commercial buildings would be curtailed; home-owners would be given tax deductions to winterize their homes. . . .

Other pending measures would impose year-round daylight saving time and would open naval oil reserves for intensive exploration. . . .❞

a. What proposals did the U.S. government make to deal with the energy crisis?

b. What lessons do you think the United States might have learned from the crisis?

22. Categorizing Complete a chart similar to the one below by listing the attempts each president made to strengthen the nation's economy.

President	Attempts to Strengthen Economy
Nixon	
Ford	
Carter	

Practicing Skills

23. Analyzing Secondary Sources Examine the Bob Woodward quotation on Watergate's impact on page 842. Then use the steps you learned on the subject of analyzing secondary sources on page 855 to answer the following questions.

a. Who is Bob Woodward, and how was he related to the Watergate scandal?

b. How knowledgeable or reliable do you think Woodward is as a source? Why do you think so?

Chapter Activity

24. Researching Artifacts One useful way of learning about cultures of different periods is by examining artifacts from the era. Many of these artifacts can be found in museums and art galleries, while others may be found in your own home. What sorts of artifacts could you find about the 1970s? What would they tell you about the culture and lifestyle of that era? Create a chart listing possible artifacts and how they represent the 1970s.

Inflation, 1960–1992

Writing Activity

25. Persuasive Writing Imagine you are an aide to President Nixon during the early 1970s. Nixon has just returned from his historic mission to China to establish diplomatic relations with the Communist nation. Write a press release on the president's trip for reporters, explaining the reasons Nixon reversed American policy and the expected benefits from doing so.

Economics and History

26. The graph above shows inflation rates in the United States from 1960 to 1992. Study the graph and answer the questions below.

a. Interpreting Graphs How did the nation's inflation rate change between 1965 and 1980?

b. Determining Cause and Effect What factor was most important in causing this change?

Standardized Test Practice

Directions: Choose the phrase that best completes the following sentence.

As a political conservative, President Nixon wanted to

A increase federal spending on welfare programs.

B take more aggressive federal action to speed desegregation.

C return power to state governments.

D appoint activist-minded justices to the Supreme Court.

Test-Taking Tip: Think of the meaning of *political conservative:* someone who believes that the federal government's role in society should be limited. Choose the answer that best reflects this meaning.

HISTORY Online

Have students visit the Web site at tarvol2.glencoe.com to review Chapter 27 and take the Self-Check Quiz.

Chapter Activity

24. Students' charts will vary but should include analysis of 1970s artifacts.

Writing Activity

25. Students' press releases will vary but should discuss Nixon's goals.

Economics and History

26. a. The inflation rate increased from under 2 percent in 1965 to over 12 percent in 1980. **b.** The rise in the price of crude oil was the biggest factor for the ballooning rate of inflation.

Standardized Test Practice

Answer: C

Test-Taking Tip: Have students look at each answer to determine if it limits or increases the government's role. For example, students can eliminate answer A because of the phrase "increase federal spending." They can eliminate answer B because it says "more aggressive federal action."

Bonus Question ?

Ask: What did the impeachment process test? *(the system of checks and balances)*

---

21. a. Proposals included cutting speed limits, curtailing heat and lighting in public buildings, giving tax deductions for homeowners to winterize their homes, imposing year-round daylight savings time, and opening the naval oil reserves for exploration. **b.** Students' answers will vary.

22. Nixon: cut spending, raised taxes, raised interest rates, and froze wages and prices; Ford: urged Americans to cut back on gas and oil consumption and undertake other energy-conserving measures; cut government spending and advocated higher interest rates, attempted to limit federal authority, balance the budget, and keep taxes low; Carter: increased government spending, cut taxes, reduced the money supply, and raised interest rates

Practicing Skills

23. a. Woodward was a reporter for the *Washington Post* and he, along with Carl Bernstein, broke the story that uncovered the Watergate scandal. **b.** Students' answers will vary.

Chapter 28 Resources

Timesaving Tools

TeacherWorks™ All-In-One Planner and Resource Center

- **Interactive Teacher Edition** Access your Teacher Wraparound Edition and your classroom resources with a few easy clicks.
- **Interactive Lesson Planner** Planning has never been easier! Organize your week, month, semester, or year with all the lesson helps you need to make teaching creative, timely, and relevant.

Use Glencoe's **Presentation Plus!** multimedia teacher tool to easily present dynamic lessons that visually excite your students. Using Microsoft PowerPoint® you can customize the presentations to create your own personalized lessons.

TEACHING TRANSPARENCIES

Graphic Organizer 13 L2

Why It Matters Chapter Transparency 28 L2

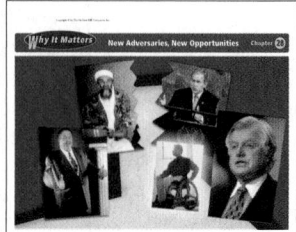

APPLICATION AND ENRICHMENT

Linking Past and Present Activity 28 L2

Enrichment Activity 28 L3

Primary Source Reading 28 L2

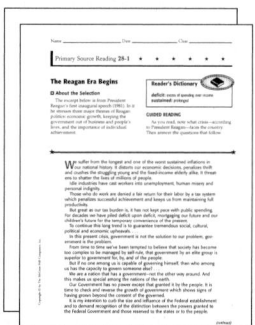

REVIEW AND REINFORCEMENT

Reteaching Activity 28 L1

Vocabulary Activity 28 L1

Time Line Activity 28 L2

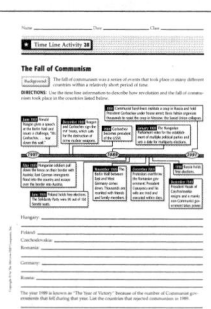

Critical Thinking Skills Activity 28 L2

Meeting NCSS Standards

Local Standards

The following standards are covered in Chapter 28:

Section 1	VII	Production, Distribution, and Consumption: F
Section 2	IX	Global Connections: B, C, D
Section 3	VIII	Science, Technology, and Society: A, B
Section 4	VII	Production, Distribution, and Consumption: F

Chapter 28 Resources

ASSESSMENT AND EVALUATION

**Chapter 28 Test
Form A** L2

**Chapter 28 Test
Form B** L2

**Standardized Test Practice
Workbook Activity 28** L2

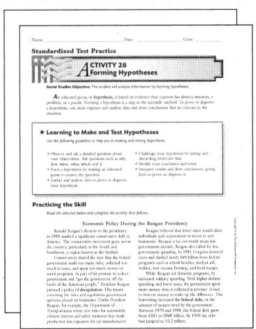

**Performance Assessment
Activities and Rubrics 28
L1/ELL**

**ExamView® Pro
Testmaker CD-ROM**

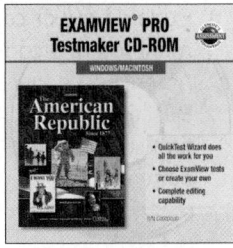

MULTIMEDIA

- Vocabulary PuzzleMaker CD-ROM
- Interactive Tutor Self-Assessment CD-ROM
- ExamView® Pro Testmaker CD-ROM
- Audio Program
- American History Primary Source Documents
  Library CD-ROM
- MindJogger Videoquiz
- Presentation Plus! CD-ROM
- TeacherWorks™ CD-ROM
- Interactive Student Edition CD-ROM
- Glencoe Skillbuilder Interactive Workbook
  CD-ROM, Level 2
- The *American Republic Since 1877* Video Program
- American Music: Hits Through History
- American Music: Cultural Traditions

SPANISH RESOURCES

**The following Spanish language materials are
available:**

- Spanish Reading Essentials and Study Guide
- Spanish Guided Reading Activities
- Spanish Reteaching Activities
- Spanish Quizzes and Tests
- Spanish Vocabulary Activities
- Spanish Summaries
- The Declaration of Independence and United States Constitution
  Spanish Translation

THE HISTORY CHANNEL®

The following videotape programs are available
from Glencoe as supplements to Chapter 28:

- **Ronald Reagan: The Many Lives** (ISBN 1-56-501099-X)
- **Ronald Reagan: The Role of a Lifetime** (ISBN 1-56-501808-7)
- **George Bush: A Sense of Duty** (ISBN 1-56-501809-5)

To order, call Glencoe at 1-800-334-7344. To find classroom resources to
accompany many of these videos, check the following home pages:
A&E Television: www.aande.com
The History Channel: www.historychannel.com

HISTORY Online

Use our Web site for additional resources. All essential content is covered in the Student Edition.

You and your students can visit tarvol2.glencoe.com, the Web site
companion to the *American Republic Since 1877.* This innovative
integration of electronic and print media offers your students a wealth
of opportunities. The student text directs students to the Web site for
the following options:

- **Chapter Overviews**
- **Self-Check Quizzes**
- **Student Web Activities**
- **Textbook Updates**

Answers to the student Web activities are provided for you in the **Web
Activity Lesson Plans.** Additional Web resources and Interactive Tutor
Puzzles are also available.

Chapter 28 Resources

SECTION RESOURCES

Daily Objectives	Reproducible Resources	Multimedia Resources
SECTION 1 **The New Conservatism** 1. Explain how discontent with government led to a conservative shift in Americans' political convictions. 2. Describe how the nation's population shifts led to a change in voting patterns.	📁 Reproducible Lesson Plan 28–1 📁 Daily Lecture and Discussion Notes 28–1 📁 Guided Reading Activity 28–1* 📁 Section Quiz 28–1* 📁 Reading Essentials and Study Guide 28–1* 📁 Performance Assessment Activities and Rubrics	📠 Daily Focus Skills Transparency 28–1 💿 Interactive Tutor Self-Assessment CD-ROM 💿 ExamView® Pro Testmaker CD-ROM* 💿 Presentation Plus! CD-ROM 💿 TeacherWorks™ CD-ROM 🎧 Audio Program
SECTION 2 **The Reagan Years** 1. Explain President Reagan's economic recovery plan. 2. Discuss Reagan's policies toward the Soviet Union.	📁 Reproducible Lesson Plan 28–2 📁 Daily Lecture and Discussion Notes 28–2 📁 Guided Reading Activity 28–2* 📁 Section Quiz 28–2* 📁 Reading Essentials and Study Guide 28–2* 📁 Performance Assessment Activities and Rubrics 📁 Interpreting Political Cartoons	📠 Daily Focus Skills Transparency 28–2 💿 Interactive Tutor Self-Assessment CD-ROM 💿 ExamView® Pro Testmaker CD-ROM* 💿 Presentation Plus! CD-ROM 💿 TeacherWorks™ CD-ROM 🎧 Audio Program
SECTION 3 **Life in the 1980s** 1. Discuss the importance of money to the culture of the 1980s. 2. Explain the growth in social activism during the decade.	📁 Reproducible Lesson Plan 28–3 📁 Daily Lecture and Discussion Notes 28–3 📁 Guided Reading Activity 28–3* 📁 Section Quiz 28–3* 📁 Reading Essentials and Study Guide 28–3* 📁 Performance Assessment Activities and Rubrics	📠 Daily Focus Skills Transparency 28–3 📠 American Art & Architecture 💿 Interactive Tutor Self-Assessment CD-ROM 💿 ExamView® Pro Testmaker CD-ROM* 💿 Presentation Plus! CD-ROM 💿 Skillbuilder Interactive Workbook, Level 2 💿 TeacherWorks™ CD-ROM 🎧 Audio Program 🎵 American Music: Hits Through History 🎵 American Music: Cultural Traditions
SECTION 4 **The End of the Cold War** 1. Identify the events that brought an end to the Cold War. 2. Explain the domestic challenges facing the Bush administration.	📁 Reproducible Lesson Plan 28–4 📁 Daily Lecture and Discussion Notes 28–4 📁 Guided Reading Activity 28–4* 📁 Section Quiz 28–4* 📁 Reading Essentials and Study Guide 28–4* 📁 Performance Assessment Activities and Rubrics 📁 Interpreting Political Cartoons	📠 Daily Focus Skills Transparency 28–4 💿 Interactive Tutor Self-Assessment CD-ROM 💿 ExamView® Pro Testmaker CD-ROM* 💿 Presentation Plus! CD-ROM 💿 TeacherWorks™ CD-ROM 💿 Vocabulary PuzzleMaker CD-ROM*

⏰ OUT OF TIME?
Assign the Chapter 28 **Reading Essentials and Study Guide.** 📁

*Also Available in Spanish

 Printed Materials   Transparency   CD-ROM   DVD

Poster   Music Program   Audio Program

Chapter 28 Resources

From the Classroom of...

Linda Kelley
Connally High School
Waco, TX

Honing Research Skills

This activity helps students understand some of the significant events at the end of the twentieth century and reviews how to find relevant information using library and Internet resources.

List 10 to 15 significant events discussed in Chapter 28. Students, working alone or in pairs, will choose one event and create either a Web page or a PowerPoint® presentation. Before beginning research, walk students through the library's reference materials. The reference librarian can help students learn how to research on the Internet and with other online resources.

The final PowerPoint® presentation or Web page is turned in as a computer file to the teacher. The teacher can then use the presentation with other classes or allow the student to make the presentation.

MEETING SPECIAL NEEDS

In addition to the Differentiated Instruction strategies found in each section, the following resources are also suitable for your special needs students:

- *ExamView® Pro Testmaker CD-ROM* allows teachers to tailor tests by reducing answer choices.

- The *Audio Program* includes the entire narrative of the student edition so that less-proficient readers can listen to the words as they read them.

- The *Reading Essentials and Study Guide* provides the same content as the student edition but is written two grade levels below the textbook.

ADDITIONAL RESOURCES FROM GLENCOE

- American Music: Cultural Traditions
- American Art & Architecture
- Outline Map Resource Book
- U.S. Desk Map
- Building Geography Skills for Life
- Inclusion for the High School Social Studies Classroom Strategies and Activities
- Teaching Strategies for the American History Classroom (Including Block Scheduling Pacing Guides)
- Dinah Zike's High School American History Reading and Study Skills Foldables

KEY TO ABILITY LEVELS

Teaching strategies have been coded.

- **L1** BASIC activities for all students
- **L2** AVERAGE activities for average to above-average students
- **L3** CHALLENGING activities for above-average students
- **ELL** ENGLISH LANGUAGE LEARNER activities

Block Schedule

Activities that are suited to use within the block scheduling framework are identified by:

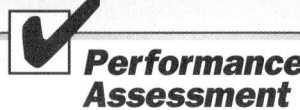

Performance Assessment

Refer to Activity 28 in the Performance Assessment Activities and Rubrics booklet.

Why It Matters Activity

Have students use recent newspapers to find an article related to one of the items listed under *The Impact Today.* Have volunteers share their articles with the class. You may want to have some students share their articles at the end of your study of this chapter, encouraging them to discuss what they have learned about the topic while studying the chapter.

GLENCOE
TECHNOLOGY

The *American Republic Since 1877* Video Program

To learn more about the history of the Berlin Wall, have students view the Chapter 28 video, "Tear Down This Wall!" from the *American Republic Since 1877* Video Program.

MindJogger Videoquiz

Use the **MindJogger Videoquiz** to preview Chapter 28 content.

 Both programs available in DVD

CHAPTER
28 Resurgence of Conservatism
1980–1992

Why It Matters

The 1980s saw the rise of a new conservatism. President Reagan, standing for traditional values and smaller government, symbolized this movement. While tax cuts and new technologies fueled an economic boom, Reagan embarked on a massive military buildup and expanded efforts to contain communism. During President George Bush's term, the United States fought the Persian Gulf War, and the Cold War came to a dramatic end with the fall of the Soviet Union.

The Impact Today

Developments of the Reagan era are still visible today.
• *The struggle between conservative and liberal ideas often defines American politics.*
• *Foreign policy has greatly changed because of the fall of the Soviet Union.*
• *The Americans with Disabilities Act has opened up doors for disabled citizens.*

The *American Republic Since 1877* **Video** *The Chapter 28 video, "Tear Down This Wall!" describes the history of the Berlin Wall, one of the Cold War's most powerful symbols.*

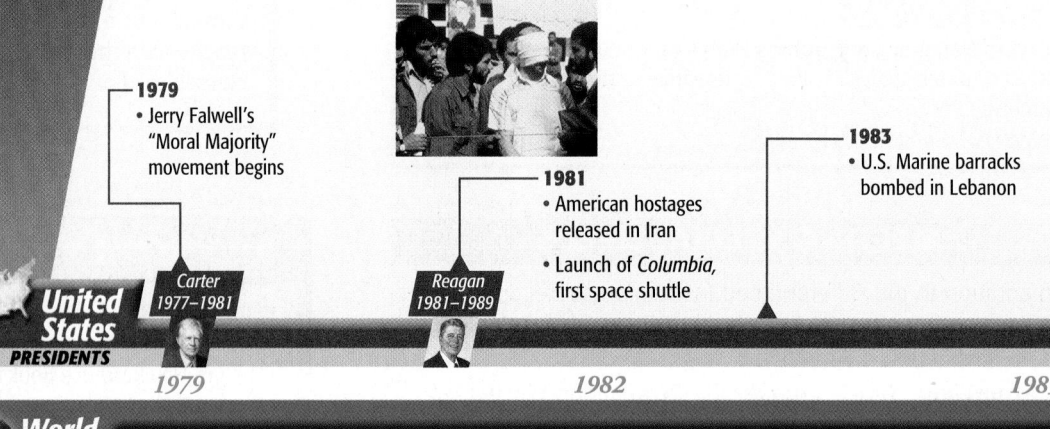

1979
• Jerry Falwell's "Moral Majority" movement begins

1981
• American hostages released in Iran
• Launch of *Columbia,* first space shuttle

1983
• U.S. Marine barracks bombed in Lebanon

United States PRESIDENTS

Carter 1977–1981

Reagan 1981–1989

1979   *1982*   *1985*

World

1979
• Iranian revolution establishes Islamic republic
• Soviets invade Afghanistan

1980
• War begins between Iran and Iraq

1985
• Mikhail Gorbachev becomes leader of Soviet Union

858

Reading Strategy   PURPOSE FOR READING

Concept Map Like web diagrams, concept maps allow students to visualize the components of a concept or key term. To begin, students should write and circle the name "Ronald Reagan" in the center of a piece of paper. Then to the left, right, and below have them write and circle each of the following three sub-categories: "Who was he? What was he like? What are some examples of what made him famous?" Students should link each of the three sub-categories to the center bubble by a line. Have students complete the concept map as they read the chapter by filling in brief answers in small bubbles around each sub-category, linking each answer to the corresponding sub-category bubble by a line. Encourage students to add additional information to the maps as they read. **L1**

HISTORY *Online*

Introduce students to chapter content and key terms by having them access the **Chapter 28 Overview** at tarvol2.glencoe.com.

More About the Photo

Remind students that the Communists erected the Berlin Wall in 1961 to prevent East Germans from fleeing to the West. Ask students to explain the symbolism of the Berlin Wall and President Reagan's challenge to Mikhail Gorbachev to tear it down.

TIME LINE ACTIVITY

Have students select one event on the United States time line and one on the world time line. For their chosen events have students write newspaper headlines that capture the emotion of the event.

President Reagan at the Berlin Wall in 1987

1986
• Iran-Contra scandal enters the news

1987
• INF Treaty between U.S. and USSR reduces land-based intermediate-range nuclear missiles

1988
• More than 35,000 cases of AIDS diagnosed for the year

G. Bush 1989–1993

1991
• Persian Gulf War occurs between Iraq and UN coalition

1988

1991

1986
• Dictatorship of Ferdinand Marcos overthrown in the Philippines

1989
• Tiananmen Square protests for democracy break out in China
• Several Communist governments in Eastern Europe collapse

1990
• Germany reunified into one nation

1991
• Soviet Union dissolves

HISTORY *Online*

Chapter Overview
Visit the *American Republic Since 1877* Web site at tarvol2.glencoe.com and click on **Chapter Overviews—Chapter 28** to preview chapter information.

859

FOLDABLES™
Study Organizer

Dinah Zike's Foldables are three-dimensional, interactive graphic organizers that help students practice basic writing skills, review key vocabulary terms, and identify main ideas. Have students complete the foldable activity in the *Dinah Zike's Reading and Study Skills Foldables* booklet.

GRAPHIC ORGANIZER ACTIVITY

Organizing Information Have students complete the following graphic organizer to analyze the issues facing world leaders and U.S. policymakers before and after the collapse of communism in the Soviet Union. *Issues before* may include military buildup and Cold War threats. *Issues after* may include economic stability, the future of various countries in the Communist bloc, and the role of the United States in world affairs.

| Issues Before | Collapse of Communism | Issues After |

859

SECTION 1 The New Conservatism

Section Overview

This section focuses on the rise of a new conservative coalition.

BELLRINGER
Skillbuilder Activity

 Project transparency and have students answer the question.

Daily Focus Skills Transparency 28–1

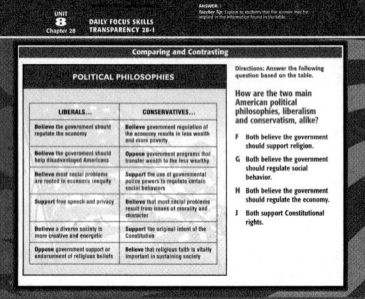

Reading Preview

Answers to Graphic:

The New Conservatism
I. Conservatism and Liberalism
  A. Liberalism
  B. Conservatism
II. Conservatism Revives
  A. Conservatism and the Cold War
  B. Conservatives Organize
III. Conservatism Gains Support
Students should complete the outline by including all heads in the section.

Preteaching Vocabulary

Have students make a list of the Key Terms and Names and add a symbol, name, or phrase to help them remember their meanings.

Guide to Reading

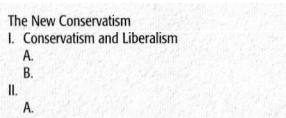

Main Idea
In the 1980s, discontent with government and changes in society resulted in the rise of a new conservative coalition.

Key Terms and Names
liberal, conservative, William F. Buckley, Sunbelt, Billy Graham, televangelist, Moral Majority

Reading Strategy
Taking Notes As you read about the rise of a new conservative coalition in the United States, use the major headings of the section to create an outline similar to the one below.

The New Conservatism
I. Conservatism and Liberalism
  A.
  B.
II.
  A.

Reading Objectives
• **Explain** how discontent with government led to a conservative shift in Americans' political convictions.
• **Describe** how the nation's population shifts led to a change in voting patterns.

Section Theme
Economic Factors High taxes as well as economic and moral concerns led the country toward a new conservatism.

Preview of Events

♦1965	♦1970	♦1975	♦1980
1964 Conservative Barry Goldwater is defeated for presidency	**1972** Nixon wins re-election	**1976** Reagan challenges Ford for nomination	**1979** Jerry Falwell's "Moral Majority" movement begins / **1980** Reagan wins presidential election

★ An American Story ★

Midge Decter

Midge Decter, a New Yorker and a writer for the conservative publication *Commentary,* was appalled at the terror that hit her city on a hot July night in 1977. On the night of July 13, the power failed in New York City. Street lights went dark. Elevators, subways, and air conditioners stopped running. The blackout left millions of people in darkness, and looting and arson rocked the city.

City officials and the media blamed the lawlessness on the anger and despair of youth in neglected areas. "They were just waiting for something like this so they could go berserk," said Lydia Rivers, a Brooklyn resident. Decter, however, had other ideas about who was to blame for the terror in her city:

66The answer is that all those young men went on their spree of looting because they had been given permission to do so. They had been given permission to do so by all the papers and magazines, movies and documentaries—all the outlets for the purveying of enlightened liberal attitude and progressive liberal policy—which had for years and years been proclaiming that race and poverty were sufficient excuses for lawlessness. . . .99

—quoted in *Commentary,* September 1977

Conservatism and Liberalism

Midge Decter's article blaming liberalism for the riots in New York during the 1977 blackout exemplifies a debate in American politics that continues to the present day. On one side of the debate are people who call themselves liberals; on the other side are those who identify themselves as conservatives. Liberal ideas generally dominated American

860 CHAPTER 28 Resurgence of Conservatism

SECTION RESOURCES

📁 Reproducible Masters
• Reproducible Lesson Plan 28–1
• Daily Lecture and Discussion Notes 28–1
• Guided Reading Activity 28–1
• Section Quiz 28–1
• Reading Essentials and Study Guide 28–1
• Performance Assessment Activities and Rubrics

📠 Transparencies
• Daily Focus Skills Transparency 28–1

Multimedia
🔘 Interactive Tutor Self-Assessment CD-ROM
🔘 ExamView® Pro Testmaker CD-ROM
🔘 Presentation Plus! CD-ROM
🔘 TeacherWorks™ CD-ROM
🔘 Audio Program

politics for much of the 1900s, but conservative ideas gained significant support among Americans in the 1970s. In 1980 Ronald Reagan, a strong conservative, was elected president.

Liberalism In American politics today, people who call themselves liberals believe several basic ideas. In general, liberals believe that the government should regulate the economy to protect people from the power of large corporations and wealthy elites. Liberals also believe that the government, particularly the federal government, should play an active role in helping disadvantaged Americans, partly through social programs and partly by putting more of society's tax burden on wealthier people.

Although liberals favor government intervention in the economy, they are suspicious of any attempt by the government to regulate social behavior. They are strong supporters of free speech and privacy, and they are opposed to the government supporting or endorsing religious beliefs, no matter how indirectly. They believe that a diverse society made up of many different races, cultures, and ethnic groups tends to be more creative and energetic.

Liberals often support high taxes on the wealthy, partly because they believe taxes weaken the power of the rich and partly because the government can transfer the wealth to other Americans to keep society more equal. They believe that most social problems have their roots in economic inequality.

Conservatism Unlike liberals, conservatives generally have a fundamental distrust of the power of government, particularly the federal government. They support the original intent of the Constitution and believe that governmental power should be divided into different branches and split between the state and federal levels to limit its ability to intrude into people's lives.

Conservatives believe that if the government regulates the economy, it makes the economy less efficient, resulting in less wealth and more poverty. They believe that the free enterprise system is the best way to organize society. They often argue that if people and businesses are free to make their own economic choices, there will be more wealth and a higher standard of living for everyone.

For this reason, conservatives generally oppose high taxes and government programs that transfer wealth from the rich to those who are less wealthy. They believe that taxes and government programs discourage investment, take away people's incentive to work hard, and reduce the amount of freedom in society.

The more the government regulates the economy, conservatives argue, the more it will have to regulate every aspect of people's behavior. Ultimately, conservatives fear, the government will so restrict people's economic freedom that Americans will no longer be able to improve their standard of living and get ahead in life.

Many conservatives believe that religious faith is vitally important in sustaining society. They believe most social problems result from issues of morality and character—issues, they argue, that are best addressed through commitment to a religious faith and through the private efforts of individuals and communities helping those in need. Despite this general belief, conservatives do support the use of the governmental police powers to regulate social behavior in some instances.

> **Reading Check** **Contrasting** How do liberal and conservative opinions about government differ?

Conservatism Revives

During the New Deal era of the 1930s, conservative ideas had lost much of their influence in national politics. In the years following World War II, however, conservatism began to revive.

Conservatism and the Cold War Support for conservative ideas began to revive for two major reasons, both related to the Cold War. First, the struggle against communism revived the debate about the role of the government in the economy. Some Americans believed that liberal economic ideas were slowly leading the United States toward communism and became determined to stop this trend. They also thought the United States had failed to stop the spread of Soviet power because liberals did not fully understand the need for a strong anticommunist foreign policy.

At the same time, many Americans viewed the Cold War in religious terms. Communism rejected religion and emphasized the material side of life. To Americans with a deep religious faith, the struggle against communism was a struggle between good and evil. Liberalism, which emphasizes economic welfare, gradually lost the support of many religious Americans, who increasingly turned to conservatism.

Conservatives Organize In 1955 a young conservative named **William F. Buckley** founded a new conservative magazine called *National Review.* Buckley's magazine helped to revive conservative ideas in the United States. Buckley debated in front

2 TEACH

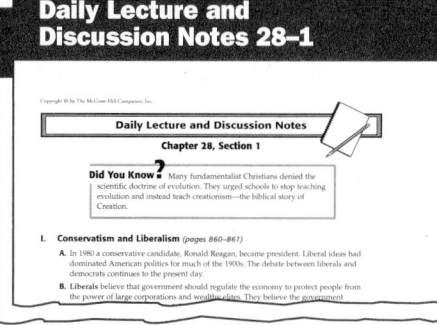

Daily Lecture and Discussion Notes 28–1

Copyright © by The McGraw-Hill Companies, Inc.

Daily Lecture and Discussion Notes

Chapter 28, Section 1

Did You Know? Many fundamentalist Christians denied the scientific doctrine of evolution. They urged schools to stop teaching evolution and instead teach creationism—the biblical story of Creation.

I. Conservatism and Liberalism (pages 860–861)

A. In 1980 a conservative candidate, Ronald Reagan, became president. Liberal ideas had dominated American politics for much of the 1900s. The debate between liberals and democrats continues to the present day.

B. Liberals believe that government should regulate the economy to protect people from the power of large corporations and wealthy elites. They believe the government

Reading Check

Answer: Liberals tend to believe in government's duty to help the poor and disadvantaged and to regulate the economy in the interests of the general public. Conservatives tend to distrust the federal government, and dislike both government regulation of the economy and government programs to transfer wealth to lower-income people.

Reading Preview

Making a List Have students use the information presented in the text to create a list of the differences between liberalism and conservatism. For each item on the list, have students provide one example. **L1**

Reading Strategy   READING THE TEXT

Summarizing Information Have students read the paragraphs under "Conservatism Gains Support" and then summarize what they have just read. Remind them that all the main ideas should be included. When the summaries are complete, have students determine whether they have included all the main ideas by asking themselves: *Can my summary be easily understood by someone who has not read the selection?* **L1**

☞ Refer to *Inclusion for the High School Social Studies Classroom Strategies and Activities* in the TCR.

Name _____ Date _____ Class _____

★ Guided Reading Activity 28-1

DIRECTIONS: Identifying Supporting Details Read each main idea. Use your textbook to supply the details that support or explain each main idea.

☐ **Main Idea:** Liberal ideas dominated American politics for much of the 1900s, but conservative ideas gained significant support among Americans in the 1970s.

1. **Detail:** Liberals believe that the federal government should play an active role in helping _____, partly through _____ and partly by putting more of the tax burden on _____.

2. **Detail:** Liberals are suspicious of any attempt to use the government to _____

3. **Detail:** Conservatives generally oppose _____ and government programs that transfer _____

4. **Detail:** Conservatives believe that taxes and government programs not only _____

✓ **Reading Check**

Answer: Because some feared that liberal ideas would lead to a Communist-style government; some also feared that any Communist influence would threaten religion.

Creating a Spreadsheet

Provide the population data for the United States and selected Sunbelt states as shown below. Explain that although you can see the population of these states increased between 1950 and 1980, the real significance can be seen when you express each state's population as a percentage of the country's total population. Have students calculate each state's population, in the selected years, as a percentage of the total U.S. population. **L2**

	1950	1960
U.S. Total	151,868,000	179,975,000
Arizona	750,000	1,302,000
California	10,586,000	15,717,000
Florida	2,771,000	4,952,000
Texas	7,711,000	9,580,000
	1970	1980
U.S. Total	203,302,000	226,546,000
Arizona	1,775,000	2,718,000
California	19,971,000	23,668,000
Florida	6,791,000	9,746,000
Texas	11,199,000	14,229,000

of college students and appeared on radio and television shows, spreading conservative ideas to an even wider audience.

Within the Republican Party, conservatives, particularly young conservatives, began to push their ideas and demand a greater role in party decision-making. In 1960 some 90 young conservative leaders met at Buckley's family estate and founded Young Americans for Freedom (YAF), an independent conservative group, to push their ideas and to support conservative candidates.

By 1964 the new conservative movement had achieved enough influence within the Republican Party to enable the conservative **Barry Goldwater** to win the nomination for president. To the dismay of the conservatives, however, President Johnson easily defeated Goldwater and won the election in a landslide.

✓ **Reading Check** **Explaining** Why did conservatism revive in the 1950s?

Conservatism Gains Support

Conservatism could not have become a mass movement if Americans had not responded to conservative ideas. The events of the late 1960s and 1970s played an important role in convincing Americans to support conservatism. After Goldwater's huge loss in 1964, American society moved decisively in a conservative direction.

GEOGRAPHY

The Rise of the Sunbelt One of the problems facing conservatives in the 1950s and early 1960s was that they generally split their votes between the Republicans and the Democrats. Two regions of the country, the South and the West, were more conservative than other areas. Southern conservatives, however, generally voted for the Democrats, while conservatives in the West voted Republican. This meant that the party that won the heavily populated Northeast would win the election. Since the Northeast strongly supported liberal ideas, both parties were pulled toward liberal policies.

This pattern began to change during World War II, when large numbers of Americans moved south and west to take jobs in the war factories. The movement to the South and West—together known as the **Sunbelt**—continued after the war. As the Sunbelt's

economy expanded, Americans living in those regions began to view the federal government differently from people living in the Northeast.

William F. Buckley

Sunbelt Conservatism Industry in the Northeast was in decline, leading to the region's nickname—the **Rust Belt.** This region had more unemployed people than any other, and its cities were often congested and polluted. These problems prompted Americans in the Northeast to look to the federal government for programs and regulations that would help them solve their problems.

In contrast, Americans in the Sunbelt opposed high taxes and federal regulations that threatened to interfere with their region's growth. Many white Southerners were also angry with the Democrats for supporting civil rights, which they interpreted as an effort by the federal government to impose its policies on the South.

When Barry Goldwater argued in 1964 that the federal government was becoming too strong, many Southerners agreed. For the first time since Reconstruction, they began voting Republican in large numbers. Although Goldwater lost the election, his candidacy showed Republicans that the best way to attract Southern votes was to support conservative policies.

Americans living in the West also responded to conservative attacks on the size and power of the federal government. Westerners were proud of their frontier heritage and spirit of "rugged individualism." They resented federal environmental regulations that limited ranching, controlled water use, and restricted the development of the region's natural resources. Western anger over such policies inspired the "Sagebrush Rebellion" of the early 1970s—a widespread protest led by conservatives against federal laws hindering the region's development.

By 1980 the population of the Sunbelt had surpassed the Northeast. This gave the conservative regions of the country more electoral votes and therefore more influence in shaping party policies. With Southerners shifting their votes to the Republican Party, conservatives could now build a coalition to elect a president.

Suburban Conservatism As riots erupted and crime soared during the 1960s and 1970s, many Americans moved to suburbs to escape the chaos of the cities. Even there, however, they found the quiet middle-class lifestyle they desired to be in danger. The rapid inflation of the 1970s had caused the

862 CHAPTER 28 Resurgence of Conservatism

DIFFERENTIATED INSTRUCTION

Reading Support Have students create a chart similar to the one below. **L1**

	Conservative	Moderate	Liberal
Social Policy			
Foreign Policy			
Economic Policy			

⬛➤ Refer to *Inclusion for the High School Social Studies Classroom Strategies and Activities* in the TCR.

NATIONAL GEOGRAPHIC **Rise of the Sunbelt, 1950–1980**

WASH.
2,378,963
4,132,000

OREG.
1,521,341
2,633,000

IDAHO
588,637
944,000

MONT.

N. DAK.

MINN.

WYO.
290,529
470,000

S. DAK.

NEV.
106,083
800,000

NEBR.

IOWA

UTAH
688,862
1,461,000

COLO.
1,325,089
2,890,000

CALIF.
10,586,223
23,668,000

KANS.

MO.

ARIZ.
749,587
2,718,000

N. MEX.
681,187
1,303,000

OKLA.

ARK.

TEX.
7,711,194
14,229,000

CANADA

ME.

VT.
N.H.
N.Y. MASS.
R.I.
CONN.
PA.
N.J.
OHIO
DEL.
ILL. IND. W. MD.
VA. VA.
KY.
TENN.
N.C.
MISS. ALA. S.C.
GA.
3,444,578
5,463,000
LA.

FLA.
2,771,305
9,746,000

PACIFIC OCEAN

MEXICO

ATLANTIC OCEAN

Gulf of Mexico

TROPIC OF CANCER

Legend
- Sunbelt states
- 749,587 Population (1950)
- 944,000 Population (1980)
- ▮ Percent growth (1 bar equals 50% growth)

Population shown only for states having 50% or more population growth between 1950 and 1980

Lambert Azimuthal Equal-area projection

0 500 miles
0 500 kilometers

Geography Skills

1. **Interpreting Maps** What Sunbelt states have more than 8 million residents?
2. **Applying Geography Skills** Nevada has the highest percentage growth in population for the time period shown. Looking at its 1950 population, how would you explain this large percentage increase?

Geography Skills

Answers:
1. California, Texas, and Florida
2. Nevada had the smallest state population in 1950. Since the percentage growth is based on the population in 1950, a state with a small population will likely have a large percentage growth.

Geography Skills Practice
Ask: Where do you think the Sunbelt got its name? *(from its sunny climate)*

3 ASSESS

Assign Section 1 Assessment as homework or as an in-class activity.

🕮 Have students use the **Interactive Tutor Self-Assessment CD-ROM.**

L1/ELL

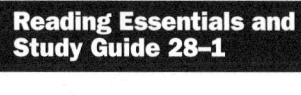
Reading Essentials and Study Guide 28-1

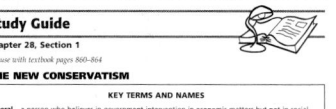
Name _____ Date _____ Class _____

Study Guide
Chapter 28, Section 1
For use with textbook pages 860–864
THE NEW CONSERVATISM

KEY TERMS AND NAMES
liberal a person who believes in government intervention in economic matters but not in social ones *(page 861)*
conservative a person who believes that government should not interfere in the nation's economy and that religious commitment could best address issues of morality *(page 861)*
William F. Buckley a conservative whose magazine helped to revive conservative ideas in the United States *(page 861)*
Sunbelt the South and West *(page 862)*
Billy Graham Protestant minister who helped build a religious revival in the United States *(page 864)*

---

buying power of the average middle-class family to shrink while taxes remained high.

Many Americans resented the taxes they had to pay for New Deal and Great Society programs when they themselves were losing ground economically. By the late 1970s, Americans had begun to rebel against these high taxes. In 1978 Howard Jarvis, a conservative activist, launched the first successful tax revolt in California with **Proposition 13,** a referendum on the state ballot that greatly reduced property taxes.

Soon afterward anti-tax movements appeared in other states, and tax cuts quickly became a national issue. For many Americans, the conservative argument that the government had become too big meant simply that taxes were too high. As conservatives began to call for tax cuts, middle-class Americans flocked to their cause.

The Religious Right While many Americans turned to conservatism for economic reasons, others were drawn to it because they feared American society had lost touch with its traditional values. For many

Americans of deep religious faith, the events of the 1960s and 1970s were shocking. The Supreme Court decision in *Roe v. Wade,* which established abortion as a constitutional right, greatly concerned them. Other Supreme Court decisions that limited prayer in public schools and expanded the rights of people accused of crimes also drew criticism from religious groups. 📖 *(See page 964 for more information on Roe v. Wade.)*

The feminist movement and the push for the Equal Rights Amendment (ERA) further alarmed religious Americans because it seemed to represent an assault on the traditional family. Many religious people were also shocked by the behavior of some university students in the 1960s, whose contempt for authority seemed to indicate a general breakdown in American values and morality. These concerns helped expand the conservative cause into a mass movement.

CHAPTER 28   Resurgence of Conservatism   **863**

INTERDISCIPLINARY CONNECTIONS ACTIVITY

Civics Have interested students examine the income, property, and sales tax rate structure in their state. Have students prepare a visual display of the rates to use during a brief oral presentation in which they either support the state's current tax policies or propose a plan to raise or lower taxes.
L3

L2

Section Quiz 28–1

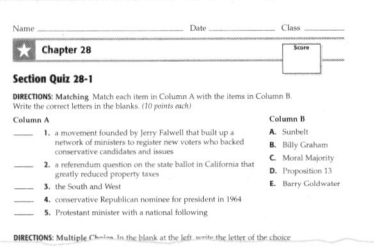

Creating a Poster Have students create a poster that expresses one of the conservative views held by a group mentioned in this section. Display their posters around the class. **L2**

Reteach
Have students explain the conservative shift in Americans' political convictions.

Enrich
Have interested students investigate how migration to the Sunbelt changed the composition of Congress.

✓ Reading Check

Answer: They thought it would improve the economy, and they wanted to return to traditional values.

HISTORY Online

Study Central™ provides summaries, interactive games, and online graphic organizers to help students review section content.

4 CLOSE

Have students describe how the nation's population shifts changed voting patterns.

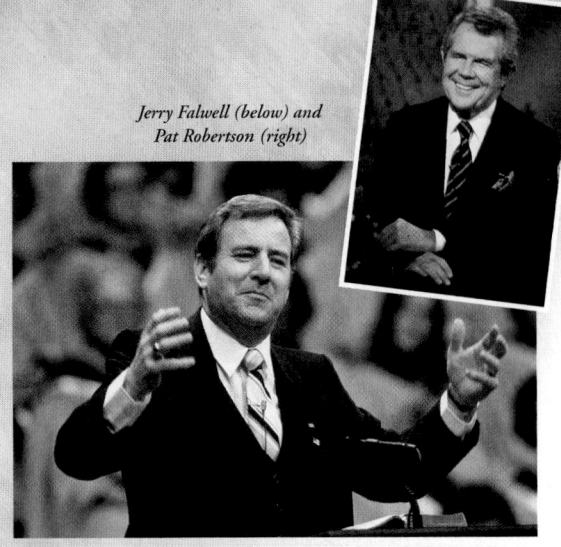

Jerry Falwell (below) and Pat Robertson (right)

Although religious conservatives included people of many different faiths, the largest group within the social conservative movement was evangelical Protestant Christians. Evangelicals believe they are saved from their sins through conversion (which they refer to as being "born again") and a personal commitment to follow Jesus Christ, whose death and resurrection reconciles them to God.

After World War II, a religious revival began in the United States. Protestant ministers such as **Billy Graham** and Oral Roberts built national followings. By the late 1970s, about 70 million Americans described themselves as "born again." Christian evangelicals owned their own newspapers, magazines, radio stations, and television networks.

Television in particular allowed evangelical ministers to reach a large nationwide audience. These "televangelists," as they were nicknamed, included Marion "Pat" Robertson, who founded the Christian Broadcasting Network, and Jerry Falwell, who used his television show *The Old-Time Gospel Hour* to found a movement that he called the **"Moral Majority."** Using television and mail campaigns, the Moral Majority built up a network of ministers to register new voters who backed conservative candidates and issues. Falwell later claimed to have brought in 2 million new voters by 1980.

A New Coalition By the end of the 1970s, the new conservative coalition of voters had begun to come together in the United States. Although the members of this coalition were concerned with many different issues, they were held together by a common belief that American society had somehow lost its way.

The Watergate scandal, high taxes, and special interest politics had undermined many Americans' faith in their government. Rising unemployment, rapid inflation, and the energy crisis had shaken their confidence in the economy. Riots, crime, and drug abuse suggested that society itself was falling apart. The retreat from Vietnam, the hostage crisis in Iran, and the Soviet invasion of Afghanistan made the nation look weak and helpless internationally. Many Americans were tired of change and upheaval. They wanted stability and a return to what they remembered as a better time. For some, the new conservatism and its most prominent spokesperson, Ronald Reagan, offered hope to a nation in distress.

✓ Reading Check **Summarizing** Why did many Americans begin to support the conservative movement?

HISTORY Online
Study Central™ To review this section, go to **tarvol2.glencoe.com** and click on **Study Central™**.

SECTION 1 ASSESSMENT

Checking for Understanding
1. **Define:** liberal, conservative, televangelist.
2. **Identify:** William F. Buckley, Sunbelt, Billy Graham, Moral Majority.
3. **Explain** why evangelical Protestant Christians began to support conservative issues.

Reviewing Themes
4. **Economic Factors** What kind of economy did conservatives want?

Critical Thinking
5. **Analyzing** How did Christian evangelicals contribute to a growing conservative national identity?
6. **Organizing** Use a graphic organizer similar to the one below to list conservative beliefs.

Conservative Beliefs

Analyzing Visuals
7. **Analyzing Maps** Study the map of the Sunbelt on page 863. What impact would the migration patterns shown have on representation in the U.S. House of Representatives?

Writing About History
8. **Persuasive Writing** Many conservatives believe that "government that governs least, governs best." Write a paragraph supporting or opposing this statement.

SECTION 1 ASSESSMENT ANSWERS

1. Terms are in blue.
2. William F. Buckley *(p. 861)*, Sunbelt *(p. 862)*, Billy Graham *(p. 864)*, Moral Majority *(p. 864)*
3. because they feared American society had lost touch with its traditional values
4. Conservatives wanted a free enterprise system.

5. Their media supported conservative candidates.
6. free enterprise, emphasis on religious values, little government regulation of the economy
7. The population increase would give the Sunbelt more seats in the House of Representatives, and

conservatives would likely be elected to fill those seats.
8. Students' paragraphs should express a clear point of view.

Guide to Reading

Main Idea
The presidency of Ronald Reagan brought a new conservative attitude to government.

Key Terms and Names
supply-side economics, Reaganomics, budget deficit, Sandra Day O'Connor, William Rehnquist, Geraldine Ferraro, contra, Iran-Contra scandal, Oliver North, Mikhail Gorbachev

Reading Strategy
Organizing As you read about the Reagan presidency, complete the graphic organizer below by filling in the major points of the supply-side theory of economics.

Supply-Side Theory

Reading Objectives
- **Explain** President Reagan's economic recovery plan.
- **Discuss** Reagan's policies toward the Soviet Union.

Section Theme
Global Connections President Reagan believed the United States should take strong action to resist Communist influence overseas.

Preview of Events

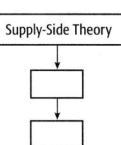

♦1980	♦1983	♦1986	♦1989

1980
Reagan elected president

1983
Terrorists bomb U.S. Marine barracks in Lebanon

1984
Reagan reelected

1986
Iran-Contra scandal breaks

1987
Reagan and Gorbachev sign INF Treaty

★ *An American Story* ★

In 1926 when he was 15 years old, Ronald Reagan earned $15 a week as a lifeguard at Lowell Park on the Rock River in Illinois. Being a lifeguard, Reagan later wrote, taught him quite a bit about human nature:

❝Lifeguarding provides one of the best vantage points in the world to learn about people. During my career at the park, I saved seventy-seven people. I guarantee you they needed saving—no lifeguard gets wet without good reason. . . . Not many thanked me, much less gave me a reward, and being a little money-hungry, I'd done a little daydreaming about this. They felt insulted. I got to recognize that people hate to be saved. . . .❞

—quoted in *Where's the Rest of Me?*

The belief that people did not really want to be saved by someone else was one of the ideas that Ronald Reagan took with him to the White House. It fit with his philosophy of self-reliance and independence.

A young Ronald Reagan

The Road to the White House

Ronald Reagan grew up in Dixon, Illinois, the son of an Irish American shoe salesman. After graduating from Eureka College in 1932, Reagan worked as a sports broadcaster at an Iowa radio station. In 1937 he took a Hollywood screen test and won a contract from a movie studio. Over the next 25 years, he made over 50 movies. As a broadcaster and actor, Reagan learned how to speak publicly and how to project an image, skills that proved invaluable when he entered politics.

CHAPTER 28 Resurgence of Conservatism **865**

---

1 FOCUS

Section Overview
This section focuses on the Reagan presidency and the new conservative attitude he brought to government.

BELLRINGER
Skillbuilder Activity

Project transparency and have students answer the question.

Daily Focus Skills Transparency 28–2

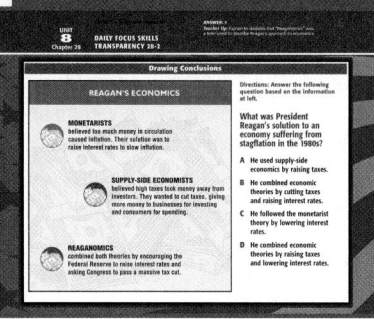

Reading Preview

Answers to Graphic: Supply-Side Theory: High taxes take away money that could be invested; Cutting taxes will generate capital to make new and larger businesses and new jobs; Larger supply of consumer goods will cause more spending.

Preteaching Vocabulary
Have students scan the section to see where the Key Terms and Names fall in relationship to the headings.

SECTION RESOURCES

📂 Reproducible Masters
- Reproducible Lesson Plan 28–2
- Daily Lecture and Discussion Notes 28–2
- Guided Reading Activity 28–2
- Section Quiz 28–2
- Reading Essentials and Study Guide 28–2
- Interpreting Political Cartoons

📽 Transparencies
- Daily Focus Skills Transparency 28–2

Multimedia
- 💿 Interactive Tutor Self-Assessment CD-ROM
- 💿 ExamView® Pro Testmaker CD-ROM
- 💿 Presentation Plus! CD-ROM
- 💿 TeacherWorks™ CD-ROM
- 🔊 Audio Program

2 TEACH

Daily Lecture and Discussion Notes 28–2

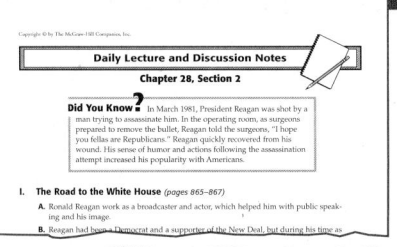

Copyright © by The McGraw-Hill Companies, Inc.

Daily Lecture and Discussion Notes
Chapter 28, Section 2

Did You Know? In March 1981, President Reagan was shot by a man trying to assassinate him. In the operating room, as surgeons prepared to remove the bullet, Reagan told the surgeons, "I hope you fellas are Republicans." Reagan quickly recovered from his wound. His sense of humor and actions following the assassination attempt increased his popularity with Americans.

I. **The Road to the White House** (pages 865–867)
  A. Ronald Reagan work as a broadcaster and actor, which helped him with public speaking and his image.
  B. Reagan had been a Democrat and a supporter of the New Deal, but during his time as

Different Viewpoints

Answers:

1. Carter felt Americans should make sacrifices so government could solve problems. Reagan felt Americans should solve problems themselves.

2. Students' answers will vary but students should support their choices with clear reasoning.

Ask: What words does Carter use to point the finger at Reagan's background as an actor? (world of tinsel and make-believe)

Discussing Public Opinion Tell students that Carter was the first incumbent president to lose a re-election bid since Herbert Hoover. As a class, discuss the events that contributed to his defeat. **L1**

Different Viewpoints

Carter and Reagan on Government

As President Carter sought re-election in 1980, he had to deal with inflation, unemployment, and an energy crisis. He urged Americans to make sacrifices so that the government could solve these problems. His opponent, Ronald Reagan, disagreed. Reagan argued that Americans should trust themselves, not the government, to solve their problems.

President Jimmy Carter:

"[A] president cannot yield to the shortsighted demands, no matter how rich or powerful the special interests might be that make those demands. And that is why the president cannot bend to the passions of the moment, however popular they might be. And that is why the president must sometimes ask for sacrifice when his listeners would rather hear the promise of comfort.

. . . The only way to build a better future is to start with realities of the present. But while we Democrats grapple with the real challenges of a real world, others talk of a world of tinsel and make-believe.

. . . A world of good guys and bad guys, where some politicians shoot first and ask questions later. No hard choices. No sacrifice. No tough decisions. It sounds too good to be true—and it is."

—from his acceptance speech at the Democratic National Convention, August 14, 1980

California governor Ronald Reagan:

"The American people, the most generous people on earth, who created the highest standard of living, are not going to accept the notion that we can only make a better world for others by moving backwards ourselves. Those who believe we *can* have no business leading the nation.

I will not stand by and watch this great country destroy itself under mediocre leadership that drifts from one crisis to the next, eroding our national will and purpose.

"Trust me" government asks that we concentrate our hopes and dreams on one man; that we trust him to do what's best for us. My view of government places trust not in one person or one party, but in those values that transcend persons and parties. The trust is where it belongs—in the people."

—from his acceptance speech at the Republican National Convention, July 17, 1980

Learning From History

1. **Recognizing Ideologies** How do the two candidates differ regarding the role of government in solving the nation's problems?
2. **Making Inferences** Ronald Reagan won the election of 1980. What part of his speech do you think may have had the most influence on voters? Why?

Moving to Conservatism In 1947 Reagan became president of the **Screen Actors Guild**—the actors' union. As head of the union, he testified about communism in Hollywood before the House Un-American Activities Committee. Reagan had been a staunch Democrat and supporter of the New Deal, but his experience in dealing with Communists in the union began shifting him toward conservative ideas.

In 1954 Reagan became the host of a television program called *General Electric Theater* and agreed to be a motivational speaker for the company. As he traveled around the country speaking to workers, secretaries, and managers, he became increasingly

conservative. Over and over again, Reagan said later, he heard stories from average Americans about how high taxes and government regulations made it impossible for them to get ahead.

By 1964 Reagan had become such a popular national speaker that Barry Goldwater asked him to make a televised speech on behalf of Goldwater's presidential campaign. Reagan's speech greatly impressed several wealthy entrepreneurs in California. They convinced Reagan to run for governor of California in 1966 and helped finance his campaign. Reagan won the election and was reelected in 1970. Ten years later, he won the Republican presidential nomination.

866 CHAPTER 28 Resurgence of Conservatism

COOPERATIVE LEARNING ACTIVITY

Evaluating Policies Have students reread the passage about supply-side economics in this section. Then organize the class into three groups and ask group members to work together to write letters to President Reagan regarding the impact of his economic polices. One group should represent business owners, another should represent workers in manufacturing industries, and the third should represent people on fixed incomes, such as senior citizens or welfare recipients. Have each group select a representative to read the group's letter to the rest of the class.

Use the rubric for a cooperative group management plan on pages 71–72 in the *Performance Assessment Activities and Rubrics*.

The Election of 1980 Reagan's campaign appealed to Americans who were frustrated with the economy and worried that the United States had become weak internationally. Reagan promised to cut taxes and increase defense spending. He won the support of social conservatives by calling for a constitutional amendment banning abortion. During one debate with Carter, Reagan asked voters, "Are you better off than you were four years ago?" On Election Day, the voters answered "No." Reagan won nearly 51 percent of the popular vote and 489 electoral votes, easily defeating Carter in the Electoral College. For the first time since 1954, Republicans also gained control of the Senate.

✓**Reading Check** **Describing** What event jump-started Ronald Reagan's political career as a conservative leader?

Reagan's Domestic Policies

Ronald Reagan believed the key to restoring the economy and overcoming problems in society was to get Americans to believe in themselves again. He expressed this idea in his Inaugural Address:

❝We have every right to dream heroic dreams. . . . You can see heroes every day going in and out of factory gates. Others, a handful in number, produce enough food to feed all of us. . . . You meet heroes across a counter. . . . There are entrepreneurs with faith in themselves and faith in an idea who create new jobs, new wealth and opportunity. . . . Their patriotism is quiet but deep. Their values sustain our national life.❞

—from Reagan's First Inaugural Address

Reagan also explained that Americans should not look to Washington for answers: "In this present crisis, government is not the solution to our problem. Government is the problem."

ECONOMICS

Reaganomics Reagan's first priority was the economy, which was suffering from stagflation—a combination of high unemployment and high inflation. According to most economists, the way to fight unemployment was to increase government spending. Increasing spending, however, made inflation worse. Stagflation puzzled many economists, who did not expect inflation and high unemployment to occur at the same time.

Conservative economists offered two competing ideas for fixing the economy. One group, known as

monetarists, argued that inflation was caused by too much money in circulation. They believed the best solution was to raise interest rates. Another group supported supply-side economics. They argued that the economy was weak because taxes were too high.

Supply-side economists believed that high taxes took too much money away from investors. If taxes were cut, businesses and investors could use their extra capital to make new investments, and businesses could expand and create new jobs. The result would be a larger supply of goods for consumers, who would now have more money to spend because of the tax cuts.

Reagan combined monetarism and supply-side economics. He encouraged the Federal Reserve to keep interest rates high, and asked Congress to pass a massive tax cut. Critics called his approach **Reaganomics** or "trickle-down economics." They believed Reagan's policy would help corporations and wealthy Americans, while only a little bit of the wealth would "trickle down" to average Americans.

Reagan made deals with conservative Democrats in the House and moderate Republicans in the Senate. Eventually Congress passed a 25 percent tax rate cut.

Cutting Programs Cutting tax rates meant the government would receive less money. This would increase the budget deficit—the amount by which expenditures exceed income. To keep the deficit under control, Reagan proposed cuts to social programs. Welfare benefits, including the food stamp program and the school lunch program, were cut back. Medicare payments, student loans, housing subsidies, and unemployment compensation were also reduced.

After a struggle, Congress passed most of these cuts. The fight convinced Reagan that he would never get Congress to cut spending enough to balance the budget. He decided that cutting taxes and building up the military were more important than balancing the budget. He accepted the high deficit as the price of getting his other programs passed.

Deregulation Reagan believed that burdensome government regulations were another cause of the economy's problems. His first act as president was to sign an executive order eliminating price controls on oil and gasoline. Critics argued that

HISTORY Online
Student Web Activity Visit the *American Republic Since 1877* Web site at tarvol2.glencoe.com and click on **Student Web Activities— Chapter 28** for an activity on the 1980s.

L1/ELL

Guided Reading Activity 28–2

Name _____ Date _____ Class _____

★ Guided Reading Activity 28-2

DIRECTIONS: Using Headings and Subheadings Locate each heading below in your textbook. Then use the information under the correct subheading to help you write each answer.
I. The Road to the White House
  A. What segment of American society supported Reagan's 1980 bid for the presidency? _____
  B. What three things did Reagan promise to do if elected president? _____
II. Reagan's Domestic Policies
  A. How did Reagan propose to keep the deficit under control? _____
  B. When was the biggest economic expansion in America's history, and what were the

✓**Reading Check**

Answer: A televised speech on behalf of Barry Goldwater's presidential campaign aided his political career as a conservative leader.

FYI

Ronald Reagan used his experience as an actor for his life in public office. Just as he had rehearsed his lines as an actor, he spent hours fine-tuning the wording and delivery of his speeches.

HISTORY *Online*

Objectives and answers to the student activity can be found in the **Web Activity Lesson Plan** at tarvol2.glencoe.com.

📂 Use *Interpreting Political Cartoons,* Cartoon 32.

DIFFERENTIATED INSTRUCTION

Reading Support Ask students to research the events that took place in El Salvador, Grenada, and Nicaragua during the Reagan administration. Have students examine the major factions in each country, their relationships with the United States, the major events, and the important leaders. Have students present their findings in chart form, accompanied by a thematic map showing all four countries. **L1**

📂 Refer to *Inclusion for the High School Social Studies Classroom Strategies and Activities* in the TCR.

you don't say...

Television In contrast to Ronald Reagan, who was at home in front of the television camera, Walter Mondale appeared awkward and uncomfortable. After losing the 1984 election, Mondale commented on the role of television. "Modern politics today requires a mastery of television," he said. "I've never really warmed up to television and, in fairness to television, it's never warmed up to me."

✓ Reading Check

Answer: Supply-side economics proposes low taxes as an incentive to generate more investment in business. In theory, this leads to new and larger businesses and more jobs. Under this theory more workers would have income with which to purchase the expanded production.

getting rid of controls would drive prices up, but in fact, they began to fall. The falling energy prices freed up money for businesses and consumers to spend elsewhere, helping the economy to recover.

Other deregulation soon followed. The National Highway Traffic and Safety Administration reduced its demand for air bags and higher fuel efficiency for cars. The Federal Communications Commission abandoned efforts to regulate the new cable television industry. Carter had already begun deregulating the airline industry, and Reagan encouraged the process, which led to price wars, cheaper fares, and the founding of new airlines.

Reagan's Secretary of the Interior, **James Watt,** increased the amount of public land corporations could use for oil drilling, mining, and logging. Watt's decisions angered environmentalists, as did the Environmental Protection Agency's decisions to ease regulations on pollution control equipment and to reduce safety checks on chemicals and pesticides.

The Economy Booms In 1983 the economy finally began to recover. By 1984 the United States had begun the biggest economic expansion in its history up to that time. The median income of American families climbed steadily, rising 15 percent by 1989. Sales of goods and services shot upward. Five million new businesses and 20 million new jobs were created. By 1988 unemployment had fallen to about 5.5 percent, the lowest since 1973.

Shifting the Judicial Balance Reagan did not apply his conservative ideas only to the economy. He also tried to bring a strict constructionist outlook to the federal judiciary. Reagan wanted judges who followed the original intent and wording of the Constitution rather than those who interpreted and expanded its meaning. He also changed the face of the Supreme

Court by nominating **Sandra Day O'Connor** to be the first woman on the Supreme Court.

In 1986 Chief Justice Warren Burger retired. Reagan chose the most conservative associate justice, **William Rehnquist,** to succeed him. He then named **Antonin Scalia,** also a conservative, to fill the vacancy left by Rehnquist. In 1987 Reagan's nomination of Robert Bork to the Court led to a bitter confirmation fight in the Senate. Liberals argued that Bork's opinions on issues were too extreme, and they managed to block his confirmation. **Anthony Kennedy,** a moderate, ultimately became the new associate justice.

Reagan Wins Re-election As the 1984 election approached, the growing economy made Reagan very popular. Democrats nominated Jimmy Carter's vice president, **Walter Mondale.** He chose as his running mate Representative **Geraldine Ferraro,** the first woman to run for vice president for a major party.

Instead of arguing issues with his opponent, Reagan emphasized the good economy. In an overwhelming landslide, he won about 59 percent of the popular vote and all the electoral votes except those from Mondale's home state of Minnesota and the District of Columbia.

✓ Reading Check **Explaining** What is supply-side economics?

Reagan Builds Up the Military

Reagan did not limit his reforms to the domestic scene. He adopted a new Cold War foreign policy that rejected both containment and détente. Reagan called the Soviet Union "the focus of evil in the modern world" and "an evil empire." In his view, the United States should not negotiate with or try to contain evil. It should try to defeat it.

The Attempt to Kill the President, March 30, 1981

Barely two months after the inauguration, on March 30, 1981, John Hinckley tried to kill President Reagan in a misguided attempt to impress actress Jodie Foster. Hinckley fired six shots as Reagan left a hotel in Washington, D.C. One bullet bounced off the president's rib and lodged near his heart. Another bullet seriously wounded press secretary Jim Brady. Reagan's recovery was long, but he stayed upbeat. His jaunty reply to his wife, "Honey, I forgot to duck," won the affection of many.

John Hinckley (center)

INTERDISCIPLINARY CONNECTIONS ACTIVITY

Peace Through Strength In Reagan's opinion, the only option open to the United States in dealing with the Soviet Union was "peace through strength"— a phrase he used during his campaign. The military buildup Reagan launched was the largest peacetime buildup in American history. It cost about $1.5 trillion over five years.

Reagan and many of his advisers believed that if the Soviets tried to match the American buildup, it might put so much pressure on their economy they would be forced to either reform their system or collapse. In 1982 Reagan told students at Eureka College that massive Soviet defense spending eventually would cause the Communist system to collapse:

66 The Soviet empire is faltering because rigid centralized control has destroyed incentives for innovation, efficiency, and individual achievement. But in the midst of social and economic problems, the Soviet dictatorship has forged the largest armed force in the world. It has done so by preempting the human needs of its people and in the end, this course will undermine the foundations of the Soviet system. 99

—quoted in *Ronald Reagan*

A Growing Deficit Reagan's military buildup drove the federal budget deficit higher and higher. At the same time, however, increased military spending helped expand the economy by providing jobs in defense industries. Originally, Reagan had hoped to offset the cost of the buildup by cutting other government programs. He also hoped, as supply-side economists had predicted, that the economic boom would lead to an increase in total tax revenue collected.

As the economy grew in the 1980s, the amount of money the government collected in taxes did rise steadily, but it was not nearly enough. With Congress unwilling to cut other programs, Reagan's defense spending pushed the annual budget deficit from $80 billion to over $200 billion.

✔ **Reading Check** **Describing** How did Reagan's Cold War military policy affect the nation's economy?

Profiles IN HISTORY

Justice Sandra Day O'Connor *1930–*

When a Supreme Court vacancy opened up in 1981, President Reagan decided to fulfill his campaign promise to name the first woman justice. He chose Sandra Day O'Connor, an Arizona appeals court judge.

When Reagan called O'Connor to ask to nominate her, she was surprised. "I was overwhelmed and, at first, speechless," O'Connor said. "After a moment I managed to tell him that I would be honored."

O'Connor grew up on the Day family's Lazy B Ranch in Arizona. Unlike most Supreme Court justices, she also had broad political experience. After earning a law degree in 1952, she found that most law firms would not hire a woman—except as a legal secretary. She went into public service, had three sons, and practiced law privately.

Appointed to a state senatorial vacancy in 1969, she successfully ran for the position and became its first woman majority leader in 1972. O'Connor won election as superior court judge in 1974 and was later appointed to the appeals court.

Her nomination to the Supreme Court had strong support from Justice William Rehnquist—a classmate at Stanford Law School—and Arizona senator Barry Goldwater. O'Connor's nomination was opposed by the Moral Majority because she had supported the Equal Rights Amendment (ERA) and refused to back an antiabortion amendment or criticize the *Roe* v. *Wade* decision. Others, however, praised her legal judgment and conservative approach to the law. As a moderate conservative, she quickly became an important swing-vote on the Court, between more liberal and more conservative justices.

The Reagan Doctrine

Building up the military was only part of Reagan's military strategy. He also believed the United States should support guerrilla groups who were fighting to overthrow Communist or pro-Soviet governments. This policy became known as the Reagan Doctrine.

Aid to the Afghan Rebels Perhaps the most visible example of the Reagan Doctrine was in Afghanistan. In late December 1979, the Soviet Union invaded Afghanistan to support a Soviet-backed government. The Soviets soon found themselves fighting Afghan guerrillas known as the *mujahadeen*.

President Carter sent about $30 million in military aid to the Afghan guerrillas, but Reagan sent $570 million more. The Soviets were soon trapped in a situation similar to the American experience in Vietnam. They could not defeat the Afghan guerrillas. As casualties mounted, the war put additional strain on the Soviet economy. In 1988 the Soviets agreed to withdraw.

Nicaragua and Grenada Reagan was also concerned about Soviet influence in Nicaragua. Rebels known as the **Sandinistas** had overthrown a

CHAPTER 28 Resurgence of Conservatism **869**

Profiles IN HISTORY

Background: It took over 190 years for a woman to sit on the Supreme Court, but only about a dozen years before a second woman was appointed to the Supreme Court. Shortly before leaving office in 1980, Jimmy Carter had appointed Ruth Bader Ginsburg to the U.S. Court of Appeals, District of Columbia Circuit. In 1993 Bill Clinton appointed her to the Supreme Court.
Ask: *What kind of discrimination did O'Connor face when she graduated from law school? (Most law firms would not hire female attorneys.)*

✔ **Reading Check**

Answer: It created more jobs in the defense industry, which generated more tax revenue; however, it caused the deficit to more than double.

3 ASSESS

Assign Section 2 Assessment as homework or as an in-class activity.

💿 Have students use the **Interactive Tutor Self-Assessment CD-ROM.**

Reading Strategy ▶ READING THE TEXT

Analyzing Information After students have studied the section, read the following quote from Donald T. Regan, who served as Ronald Reagan's chief of staff: "Like [Franklin D.] Roosevelt, Reagan changed the political landscape of the United States—and the way in which Americans saw themselves and their country—in a fundamental and probably permanent way." Ask students whether facts in the text can support this opinion. **L1**

📁 Refer to *Inclusion for the High School Social Studies Classroom Strategies and Activities* in the TCR.

Military Spending and the Deficit, 1980–1992

In Motion

Legend:
— Total Federal Expenses
— National Defense
— Federal Debt

(y-axis: In Hundreds of Billions of Dollars; x-axis: Year, 1980–1992)

Sources: Departments of Commerce and Treasury; Office of Management and Budget.

〰 Graph Skills

1. **Interpreting Graphs** How much money was spent on national defense in 1986?
2. **Analyzing** Why is the federal debt shown rising at a faster rate than that of the other two figures combined?

pro-American dictator in Nicaragua in 1979. The Sandinistas set up a socialist government. They also accepted Cuban and Soviet aid and began supporting antigovernment rebels in neighboring El Salvador.

In response, the Reagan administration began secretly arming an anti-Sandinista guerrilla force known as the contras, from the Spanish word for "counterrevolutionary." When Congress learned of this policy, it banned further aid to the contras.

Aiding the contras was not Reagan's only action in Latin America. In 1983 radical Marxists overthrew the left-wing government on the tiny Caribbean island of Grenada. In October, Reagan sent in American troops. The Cuban and Grenadian soldiers were quickly defeated and a new anticommunist government was put in place.

The Iran-Contra Scandal Although Congress had prohibited aid to the Nicaraguan contras, individuals in Reagan's administration continued to illegally support the rebels. These officials secretly sold weapons to Iran in exchange for the release of American hostages being held in the Middle East. Profits from these sales were then sent to the contras.

News of the illegal operations broke in November 1986. One of the chief figures in the **Iran-Contra scandal** was Marine Colonel **Oliver North,** an aide to

the National Security Council (NSC). He and other senior NSC and CIA officials testified before Congress and admitted to covering up their actions, including shredding documents to destroy evidence.

President Reagan had approved the sale of arms to Iran, but the congressional investigation concluded that he had not been informed about the diversion of the money to the contras. To the end, Reagan insisted he had done nothing wrong, but the scandal tainted his second term in office.

✓ **Reading Check**   **Identifying** What was the Reagan Doctrine?

New Approaches to Arms Control

As part of the military buildup, Reagan decided to place nuclear missiles in Western Europe to counter Soviet missiles in Eastern Europe. This decision triggered a new peace movement. Tens of thousands of protesters pushed for a "nuclear freeze"—a halt to the deployment of new nuclear missiles.

Reagan offered to cancel the deployment of the new missiles if the Soviets removed their missiles from Eastern Europe. He also proposed Strategic Arms Reduction Talks (START) to cut the number of missiles on both sides in half. The Soviets refused and walked out of the arms control talks.

"Star Wars" Despite his decision to deploy missiles in Europe, Reagan generally disagreed with the military strategy known as nuclear deterrence, sometimes called "mutual assured destruction." This strategy assumed that as long as the United States and Soviet Union could destroy each other with nuclear weapons, they would be afraid to use them.

Reagan believed that mutual assured destruction was immoral because it depended on the threat to kill massive numbers of people. He also felt that if nuclear war did begin, there would be no way to defend the United States. In March 1983, Reagan proposed the **Strategic Defense Initiative** (SDI). This plan, nicknamed "Star Wars," called for the development of weapons that could intercept and destroy incoming missiles.

A New Soviet Leader In 1985 **Mikhail Gorbachev** became the leader of the Soviet Union and agreed to resume arms control talks. Gorbachev believed that the Soviet Union had to reform its economic system or it would soon collapse. It could not afford a new arms race with the United States.

Reagan and Gorbachev met in a series of summit meetings. The first of these were frustrating for both,

EXTENDING THE CONTENT

Presidential Comparisons Political opponents unflatteringly compared Ronald Reagan to Calvin Coolidge, pointing out the similarity between Reaganomics and Coolidge's "trickle-down" economic policies. They also noted that Reagan, like Coolidge, seemed rather detached from the process of government. Far from being insulted, Reagan reveled in the comparison. He hung Coolidge's portrait in a prominent place in the White House and regularly quoted Coolidge's philosophy on business and government.

as they disagreed on many issues. Gorbachev promised to cut back Soviet nuclear forces if Reagan would agree to give up SDI, but Reagan refused.

Reagan then challenged Gorbachev to make reforms. In West Berlin, Reagan stood at the Brandenburg Gate of the Berlin Wall, the symbol of divided Europe, and declared: "General Secretary Gorbachev, if you seek peace, if you seek prosperity for the Soviet Union and Eastern Europe . . . tear down this wall!"

Relations Improve By 1987 Reagan was convinced that Gorbachev did want to reform the Soviet Union and end the arms race. While some politicians distrusted the Soviets, most people welcomed the Cold War thaw and the reduction in the danger of nuclear war. In December 1987 the two leaders signed the Intermediate-Range Nuclear Forces (INF) Treaty. It was the first treaty to call for the destruction of nuclear weapons.

No one realized it at the time, but the treaty marked the beginning of the end of the Cold War. With an arms control deal in place, Gorbachev felt confident that Soviet military spending could be reduced. He pushed ahead with economic and political reforms that eventually led to the collapse of communism in Eastern Europe and in the Soviet Union.

With the economy booming, the American military strong, and relations with the Soviet Union rapidly improving, Ronald Reagan's second term came to an end. As he prepared to leave office, Reagan assessed his presidency: "They called it the

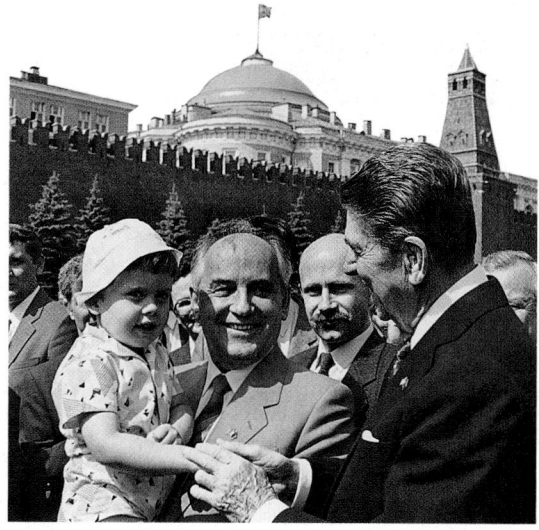

Picturing **History**

Superpower Summits During the 1980s, President Reagan and Premier Gorbachev met several times to discuss nuclear arms reductions. What Reagan defense proposal did Gorbachev want to eliminate before beginning arms reduction talks?

Reagan revolution. Well, I'll accept that, but for me it always seemed more like the great rediscovery, a rediscovery of our values and our common sense."

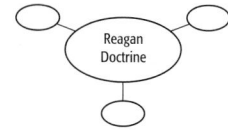 **Reading Check** **Interpreting** What was the significance of the INF Treaty?

HISTORY Online | **Study Central™** To review this section, go to tarvol2.glencoe.com and click on **Study Central™**.

SECTION 2 ASSESSMENT

Checking for Understanding
1. **Define:** supply-side economics, budget deficit, contra.
2. **Identify:** Reaganomics, Sandra Day O'Connor, William Rehnquist, Geraldine Ferraro, Iran-Contra scandal, Oliver North, Mikhail Gorbachev.
3. **List** the groups that Ronald Reagan appealed to in the 1980 presidential election.

Reviewing Themes
4. **Global Connections** What was President Reagan's stance on foreign policy?

Critical Thinking
5. **Forming an Opinion** Do you think that SDI (Star Wars) is a good idea? Why or why not?
6. **Organizing** Use a graphic organizer similar to the one below to list the ways that the Reagan doctrine was implemented.

```
        ( )
         |
  ( )— Reagan —( )
       Doctrine
         |
        ( )
```

Analyzing Visuals
7. **Analyzing Graphs** Study the graph on page 870 detailing the amount of money spent by the federal government from 1980 to 1992. What relationship do you see between military spending and the national debt?

Writing About History
8. **Expository Writing** Take on the role of a newspaper editorial writer during the Reagan administration. Write an article in which you present your opinion of Reagan's plans for a military buildup.

CHAPTER 28 Resurgence of Conservatism **871**

SECTION 2 ASSESSMENT ANSWERS

1. Terms are in blue.
2. Reaganomics (p. 867), Sandra Day O'Connor (p. 868), William Rehnquist (p. 868), Geraldine Ferraro (p. 868), Iran-Contra scandal (p. 870), Oliver North (p. 870), Mikhail Gorbachev (p. 870) **3.** social and economic conservatives,

Americans worried that the United States had become weak internationally
4. aggressive stance toward communism everywhere; military build-up to weaken Soviets
5. Students' answers will vary.
6. supported Afghan guerrillas and

anti-Sandinista guerrillas in Nicaragua, sent American troops to Grenada
7. Debt rose much faster due to interest charged on debt.
8. Students' articles will vary. Articles should express an opinion supported by fact.

Picturing **History**

Background: Mikhail Gorbachev was the leader of the Soviet Union from 1985 to 1991. He gained worldwide fame for his efforts to reform the Soviet system and to improve relations with other nations. In 1990 Gorbachev received the Nobel Peace Prize.
Answer: the Strategic Defense Initiative
Ask: What feeling does this photograph evoke? *(possible answer—friendship)*

Reteach
Have students discuss Reagan's policies toward the Soviet Union.

Enrich
Invite interested students to choose one part of the world that was influenced by the Reagan Doctrine. Ask them to research the long-term effects of the aid that was provided by the United States.

 Reading Check

Answer: It was the first treaty to call for the destruction of nuclear weapons. It marked the beginning of the end of the Cold War.

HISTORY Online

Study Central™ provides summaries, interactive games, and online graphic organizers to help students review section content.

4 CLOSE

Have students explain President Reagan's economic recovery plan and analyze its effectiveness.

1 FOCUS

Review with students the basic definitions of *urban, suburban,* and *rural.* Have students identify the type of community in which they live.

2 TEACH

Predicting Outcomes Have students study the map and the photograph. **Ask: What problems do people experience as a result of urban sprawl?** *(possible answers: traffic congestion, increased exposure to pollution)* **What benefits do people living in an urban area enjoy?** *(possible answers: access to fine dining, the arts, and entertainment; more employment options)* **Do you think the benefits outweigh the problems associated with urban sprawl? Explain your answer.** *(Answers will vary and will likely depend on the students' personal experiences.)* **L1**

Conducting a Survey Have students work in small groups to create a survey about local community development. The survey should include at least 10 questions with a range of responses. For example: Do you favor increased bus service? Responses could include Strongly Favor, Favor, Neutral, Oppose, and Strongly Oppose. **L2**

Urban America on the Move

Since the end of World War II, millions of Americans have abandoned older cities to find better lives—safer neighborhoods, bigger homes, better schools, and better jobs. Many found what they were seeking in the suburbs. Cities have grown into metropolitan areas that have continued to expand farther and farther into formerly rural regions.

The map at right shows patterns of recent population growth in the United States. The yellow and red areas represent growth since 1993, showing suburbs radiating out from the cities. A lot of growth has taken place in the Sunbelt states of the South and Southwest, helped by the spread of air-conditioning. The Atlanta region, for example, has more than doubled its population to 3.3 million in the last 30 years. It is now so big—and congested—that residents drive an average of 34 miles (55 km) per day.

Such rapid urban growth, or "sprawl," has brought a variety of cultural, social, and economic problems. In central cities and older suburbs, it has resulted in deteriorating infrastructure and a shortage of affordable housing. In the newer suburbs, growth has increased traffic and taxes and has resulted in declining air quality and a loss of open space.

Many city planners have mixed emotions about continued growth, and some—like those of Phoenix, Arizona—have tried to curb it. Such efforts have been dubbed "smart growth." Proponents of smart growth seek to improve conditions in existing communities and to limit the spread of urbanization in outlying and rural areas. Specifically, they encourage developers to build housing and businesses in city centers rather than in the suburbs. They promote the preservation of undeveloped areas and parks near metropolitan regions. Smart growth advocates endorse expanding public transportation, combining residential and commercial areas, and building pedestrian-friendly communities as ways to reduce reliance on the automobile.

With smarter growth, cities can channel development in ways that maintain quality of life and make existing communities more inviting. Faced with long commutes on congested highways, some suburban residents are now opting to return to the cities that were so readily abandoned after the Second World War.

Existing development as of 1993
Intense
Moderate
Development since 1993
Intense
Moderate

LEARNING FROM GEOGRAPHY

1. Why did many Americans move to the suburbs after World War II?

2. In what parts of the country are cities growing fastest?

872

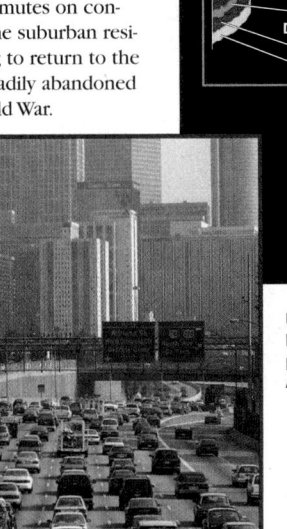

Urban sprawl, traffic congestion, high ozone levels, and skyrocketing property taxes are part of the price Atlanta has paid for rapid growth.

EXTENDING THE CONTENT

Roundabouts Traffic engineers explore various means to reduce traffic congestion by keeping the traffic flowing evenly. In England a common solution is the roundabout. This circular intersection allows traffic to pass through intersections, often without coming to a complete stop. As you enter the roundabout, you must yield to vehicles already in the roundabout. You progress around the circular intersection, exiting when you reach the street that you want to continue on. In the United States, this traffic solution can be found in Boston and Washington, D.C.

AUSTIN

Like many Sunbelt cities, Austin, Texas (right), has experienced rapid growth in recent years, much of it fueled by an influx of high-tech companies. By 2010 its population—about 465,000 in 1990—is expected to reach 800,000.

Creating an Urban Plan Tell students to imagine that they are urban planners working to design a new community that will use "smart growth" ideas. Have students research possible smart growth solutions. Then have them create rough sketches of plans for the new community. **L2**

L2

Geography and History Activity 8

Name _____ Date _____ Class _____

⬛ GEOGRAPHY AND HISTORY ACTIVITY 8 🌐

Smart Growth: A Solution to Urban Sprawl

CONCERN FOR COMMUNITIES

People in communities across the United States are changing their attitudes about the current sprawling patterns of urban growth. Traffic congestion, air and water pollution, and loss of farmland and open spaces have led Americans to reconsider how and where they build their communities. The population of the United States is expected to increase 50 percent by 2050, so urban growth is inevitable. The question is not whether new homes, businesses, shops, or movie theaters are needed—it is where the

and the many hours people must spend behind the wheel. Adding new lanes and building new roads does not seem to solve the problem. Rather than decreasing congestion, additional lanes and roads lead to more urban sprawl and traffic.

Urban sprawl also increases the risk of flooding and water pollution. Flooding occurs more frequently because new developments are often built on floodplains or wetlands. Furthermore, as the wetlands are developed, their natural flood-absorbing capabilities diminish. From 1988 to 1998,

3 ASSESS

Have students answer the Learning from Geography questions.

4 CLOSE

Have students describe the areas of their own community and the nearest large city that are fast-growing. Ask them to list the noticeable effects of these areas on regional life.

NGS ONLINE

Access National Geographic's Web site for current events, atlas updates, activities, links, interactive features, and archives at www.nationalgeographic.com.

ATLANTA

One of the fastest-growing regions in the country, metropolitan Atlanta, Georgia (right), is already larger in area than the state of Delaware. Atlanta's expansion into the surrounding counties since 1993 is shown at right in yellow and red.

CHAPTER 28   Resurgence of Conservatism   **873**

ANSWERS TO LEARNING FROM GEOGRAPHY

1. They sought safer neighborhoods, bigger homes, better schools, and better jobs.

2. Cities are growing fastest in the Sunbelt cities of the South and in the suburbs of major metropolitan areas.

1 FOCUS

Section Overview

This section focuses on the wealth of the 1980s and the resurgence of social activism.

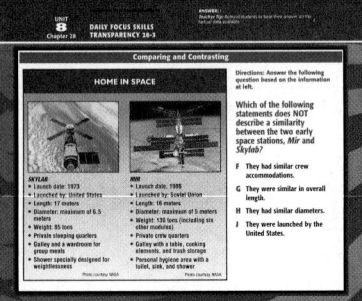

Reading Preview

Answers to Graphic: AIDS, alcohol and drug abuse, crime, homelessness, Social Security, the environment, gay and lesbian rights

Preteaching Vocabulary
Have students create a database of the Key Terms and Names that includes descriptions or definitions.

Guide to Reading

Main Idea
The 1980s was a decade characterized by wealth, but it was also a time of renewed activism.

Key Terms and Names
yuppie, AIDS, Sierra Club, American Association of Retired Persons, space shuttle, space station

Reading Strategy
Organizing As you read about life in the 1980s, complete a graphic organizer similar to the one below by listing the kinds of social issues that the United States faced in this decade.

Social Issues in the 1980s

Reading Objectives
• **Discuss** the importance of money to the culture of the 1980s.
• **Explain** the growth in social activism during the decade.

Section Theme
Science and Technology Achievements in space and technology during the 1980s symbolized the optimism many associated with the Reagan era.

Preview of Events

◆1981	◆1984	◆1987	◆1990
1981 MTV goes on the air	**1985** "Live Aid" rock concert benefit	**1986** Space shuttle *Challenger* explodes	**1988** More than 35,000 cases of AIDS diagnosed for the year

Finance traders at work

★ An American Story ★

In the 1980s many young, ambitious professionals entered the heady world of finance. Julie Katzman, in her twenties, was on the fast track:

❝I constantly spent my time at the firm. I mean, all the time. I worked probably eighty hours a week. At the end of the summer, that Labor Day weekend, I got involved in another huge acquisition. That weekend I worked two and a half days without sleeping, and from that point until early December I didn't work a single week less than a hundred hours. You spend all your time working. You're kind of wiped out, but there's a lot of fulfillment. There's an incredible adrenaline rush. This is what you live on. You live on the highs.❞

—from *Sleepwalking Through History*

A Decade of Indulgence

Cultural commentators and the media in the 1980s portrayed American society as one of wealth and success. Stories emphasized the limousines, yachts, corporate jets, and designer gowns of the wealthy. Status symbols such as expensive watches and luxury cars became important. Popular television shows such as *Dallas* and *Dynasty* glamorized the lives of the very wealthy.

By late 1983, the economy had revived after the 1981 recession. News stories described young stockbrokers, speculators, and real estate developers making multimillion-dollar deals. Hundreds of companies were bought and sold. Real estate and stock values soared. Developer Donald Trump said: "I don't do it for the money. I've got enough, much more than I'll ever need. I do it to do it. Deals are my art form. Other peo-

---

SECTION RESOURCES

📁 Reproducible Masters
• Reproducible Lesson Plan 28-3
• Daily Lecture and Discussion Notes 28-3
• Guided Reading Activity 28-3
• Section Quiz 28-3
• Reading Essentials and Study Guide 28-3

📖 Transparencies
• Daily Focus Skills Transparency 28-3

Multimedia
🔘 Interactive Tutor Self-Assessment CD-ROM
🔘 ExamView® Pro Testmaker CD-ROM
🔘 Presentation Plus! CD-ROM
🔘 TeacherWorks™ CD-ROM
🎧 Audio Program
🎵 American Music: Hits Through History
🎵 American Music: Cultural Traditions

ple paint beautifully on canvas or write wonderful poetry. I like making deals, preferably big deals."

Yuppies The new moneymakers were young, ambitious, and hardworking. Journalists called them *yuppies,* from "young urban professionals." Many worked in law or finance. They rewarded themselves with expensive stereo systems and luxury cars. They bought designer clothes and ate in upscale restaurants.

The rapid economic growth and emphasis on accumulating wealth in the 1980s was partly caused by the baby boom. By the 1980s, many baby boomers had finished college, entered the job market, and begun building their careers. Young people entering the workforce often placed an emphasis on acquiring goods and getting ahead in their jobs. Because baby boomers were so numerous, their concerns tended to shape the culture.

The strong economic growth of the 1980s benefited nearly everyone, but because much of it happened in industries that employed large numbers of middle- and upper-class professionals, it shifted the distribution of the nation's income. From 1967 to 1986, the top 5 percent of Americans earned between 15.6 and 17.5 percent of the nation's total income. In the late 1980s, their share of the nation's income began to rise. By the mid-1990s, the top 5 percent of Americans earned well over 21 percent of the nation's income.

A Retail Revolution While news commentators in the 1970s and 1980s focused on inflation, the energy crisis, corporate mergers, and yuppies, several entrepreneurs worked on pioneering a new approach to retailing—or selling products to consumers—that greatly reduced prices for Americans.

This new type of retailing, known as discount retailing, began in the 1960s. Discount retailers sell large quantities of goods at very low prices, trying to sell the goods quickly so as to turn over their entire inventory in a short period of time. By selling a lot of products at low prices, they could make more money than traditional retailers who sold fewer products at higher prices. During the 1960s, many new discount retailers were founded, including K Mart, Woolco, Target, and Wal-Mart. Annual sales by discount stores grew from about $2 billion in the mid-1960s to nearly $70 billion by 1985.

The most successful discount retailer was Sam Walton, the founder of Wal-Mart. Walton grew up in poverty in the Dust Bowl of Oklahoma during the Great Depression. He was a plainspoken man who worked 16-hour days and stressed the importance of cost cutting and good customer service. He developed a system of distribution centers to rapidly resupply his

stores, and he was one of the first retailers to use a computer database to track inventory and sales. By 1985 he was the richest person in the United States.

Others soon copied Walton's approach. By the late 1970s, retailers had begun to build huge "superstores" that enabled them to sell large quantities of goods very quickly at very low prices. One such entrepreneur was Arthur Blank, who grew up in a tiny one-bedroom apartment in Queens, New York. Blank studied accounting and worked hard as a manager. In 1978 he opened Home Depot, a chain of giant home-improvement stores. In 1983 Richard Schulze, a former air force officer, used his technical training to found Best Buy, a huge discount retailer of consumer electronics. Dozens of other entrepreneurs started discount stores in other industries. Their innovations created millions of new jobs in the 1980s and helped fuel the era's rapid economic growth.

✓ **Reading Check** **Identifying** Who were yuppies?

Technology and the Media

In the 1980s, other entrepreneurs began transforming the news and entertainment industry. Until the late 1970s, television viewers were limited to three national networks and public television. In 1970 a 32-year-old businessman named Ted Turner used money from the billboard business he had inherited from his father to buy a failing television station in Atlanta, Georgia. Turner then pioneered a new type of broadcasting by creating WTBS in 1975. WTBS was the first "superstation"—a television station that sold low-cost sports and entertainment programs via satellite to cable companies throughout the nation.

Turner's innovation changed broadcasting and helped spread cable television across the country. Dozens of networks soon appeared. Many of the new networks specialized in one type of broadcasting, such as sports, movies, or news. In 1980 Turner himself founded the Cable News Network (CNN)—the first 24-hour all-news station in the nation.

Other new stations focused on a specific audience, such as churchgoers, shoppers, or minorities. In 1980 entrepreneur Robert Johnson created Black Entertainment Television (BET). Johnson was born into a poor family in rural Mississippi, the ninth of ten children. Hard work and determination enabled him to earn a master's degree from Princeton University. Johnson believed television had tremendous power to promote African American businesses and culture. In 1978, at age 32, he developed a plan to produce television programs for African Americans. His enthusiasm

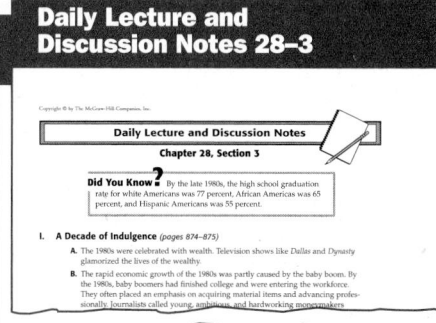

2 TEACH

Daily Lecture and Discussion Notes 28–3

Copyright © by The McGraw-Hill Companies, Inc.

Daily Lecture and Discussion Notes ✎

Chapter 28, Section 3

Did You Know? By the late 1980s, the high school graduation rate for white Americans was 77 percent, African Americas was 65 percent, and Hispanic Americans was 55 percent.

I.   A Decade of Indulgence *(pages 874–875)*

   A. The 1980s were celebrated with wealth. Television shows like *Dallas* and *Dynasty* glamorized the lives of the wealthy.

   B. The rapid economic growth of the 1980s was partly caused by the baby boom. By the 1980s, baby boomers had finished college and were entering the workforce. They often placed an emphasis on acquiring material items and advancing professionally. Journalists called young, ambitious, and hardworking moneymakers

Reading Strategy ▶

Organizing Information Have students organize the information by creating an outline of this section. Suggest that they use the headings in the text as a starting point. **L1** ELL

✓ Reading Check

Answer: young urban professionals

Reading Strategy ▶ READING THE TEXT

Monitoring Comprehension As students read the section, they may encounter text or information they do not understand. Point out to students they should adjust their reading strategies to increase their comprehension. Model how this is done by reading the section aloud. As you read, say things such as "What do I think the main focus of the 1980s was?" (predicting); "What have I heard about yuppies, and is it correct, based on the information described here?" (activating prior knowledge) Modeling how you read helps students think about strategies they can use as they read independently. **L1** ELL

Guided Reading Activity 28–3

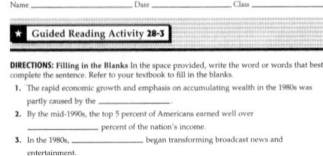

Name _____ Date _____ Class _____

★ Guided Reading Activity 28-3

DIRECTIONS: Filling in the Blanks In the space provided, write the word or words that best complete the sentence. Refer to your textbook to fill in the blanks.

1. The rapid economic growth and emphasis on accumulating wealth in the 1980s was partly caused by the _____.
2. By the mid-1990s, the top 5 percent of Americans earned well over _____ percent of the nation's income.
3. In the 1980s, _____ began transforming broadcast news and entertainment.
4. Viewers' choices were greatly expanded with the creation of _____ and _____ television channels.
5. In 1981 music and technology merged, and _____ went on the air.
6. _____, another new sound of the '80s, offered rhythmic lyrics that often focused on the _____.

✓ Reading Check

Answer: Popular entertainment included listening to music such as rap music; watching movie videos, cable or satellite TV, and music videos; and playing video games.

Picturing History

Answer: The country's general prosperity might have influenced people to believe that some solution should be found for the problems of homeless people.

Ask: Is homelessness still a problem today? *(Students should recognize that although many groups have focused on resolving this problem, it still exists.)*

History *and the* Humanities

🎵 American Music: Hits Through History: "Every Time You Go Away," "On the Road Again," "Rhythm is Gonna Get You"

🎵 American Music: Cultural Traditions: "Crossfire"

🏆 American Art & Architecture: *Still Life With Red Car* 1986

won him the support of several investors, and BET, the first and largest black-owned company on cable television, began broadcasting in 1980.

In 1981 music and technology merged, and Music Television (MTV) went on the air. MTV mixed songs and video images to create music videos. Music videos were like fast-moving short films, with costumes, makeup, and choreography. MTV was an instant hit, though its videos were often criticized for violence and sexual content. Many performers began to produce videos with their new albums. Music videos boosted the careers of artists such as Madonna and Michael Jackson.

Rap music was another new sound of the 1980s. This musical style originated in local clubs in New York City's South Bronx. Emphasizing heavy bass and very rhythmic sounds, rap artists did not usually sing but rather spoke over the music and rhythmic beats. Rap's lyrics frequently focused on the African American experience in the inner city. While rap was initially popular among East Coast African Americans, it has grown in popularity, becoming a multimillion-dollar industry.

While the music industry was changing, new forms of entertainment also developed, including video games. The first video arcade game, called Pong, was released in 1972. In the early 1980s, sales reached about

Picturing History

Homelessness During the 1980s, many people began living on the streets in makeshift shelters of boxes and rags. A lack of low-income housing and care for the mentally ill contributed to the problem. How do you think the country's general prosperity influenced people to think about this problem?

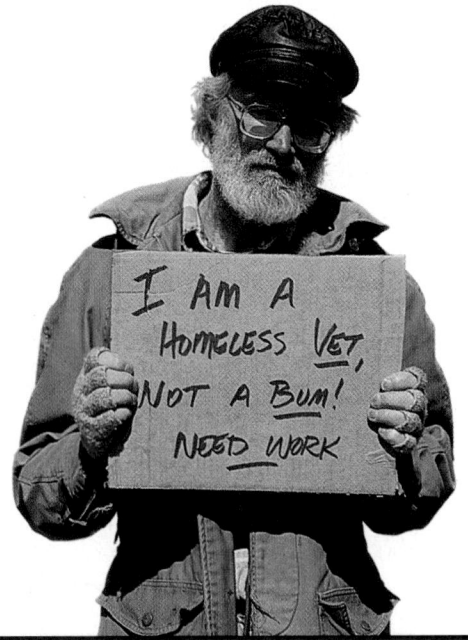

$3 billion with the release of games such as PacMan and Space Invaders. Video arcades became the new spot for young people to meet. By the mid-1980s, new technology allowed home video games to compete with arcade games in color and speed. Home video game sales rose dramatically in the 1990s.

✓ Reading Check **Describing** What forms of entertainment gained popularity in the 1980s?

A Society Under Stress

Although the 1980s were prosperous, many social problems continued to plague the nation.

Crime and Drugs Ongoing problems with drug abuse in the 1980s made many city neighborhoods dangerous. Drug users often committed crimes in order to get money for drugs, and dealers backed by street gangs fought to protect their territory. Cocaine use increased, especially a concentrated form, crack cocaine, which made users hostile and aggressive. First Lady Nancy Reagan tried to discourage teen drug use with her "Just Say No" campaign. Many young people, however, continued to use drugs, especially marijuana and amphetamines. Drug use spread from cities to small towns and rural areas.

Problems With Alcohol Abuse of alcohol was also a serious concern. Teenagers with fake identification cards could easily buy alcoholic beverages. Although teen alcohol use declined during the 1980s, thousands of alcohol-related auto accidents involved young people. In 1980 **Mothers Against Drunk Driving** (MADD), a grassroots organization, was founded to look for effective solutions to underage drinking and drunk driving. In 1984 Congress cut highway funds to any state that did not raise the legal drinking age to 21. All states quickly complied.

A Deadly Epidemic In 1981 researchers identified a disease which caused seemingly healthy young men to become sick and die. They named it "acquired immune deficiency syndrome," or **AIDS.** AIDS weakens the immune system, lowering resistance to illnesses such as pneumonia and several types of cancer. HIV, the virus that causes AIDS, is spread through bodily fluids. In the United States, AIDS was first noticed among homosexual men. Soon AIDS began to spread among heterosexual men and women as well. A few people got the disease from blood transfusions. Other victims included drug users who shared needles and, through them, infected blood. Many people were infected by sexual partners. By 1988 the

---

DIFFERENTIATED INSTRUCTION

Gifted and Talented Have interested students write a story about someone struggling with one of the social problems mentioned in the section. Encourage students to write in the first person. Remind students that this is a creative writing assignment in which they should fully develop their characters. Have volunteers read their stories to the class. **L3**

📁 Refer to *Inclusion for the High School Social Studies Classroom Strategies and Activities* in the TCR.

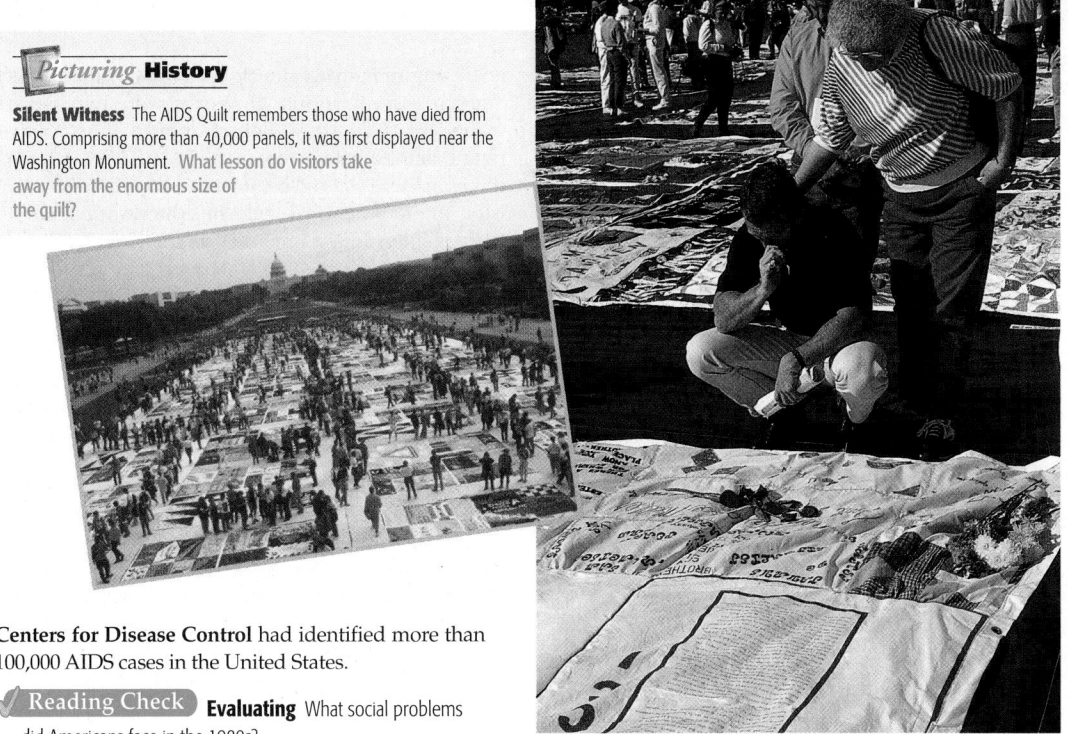

Picturing History

Silent Witness The AIDS Quilt remembers those who have died from AIDS. Comprising more than 40,000 panels, it was first displayed near the Washington Monument. What lesson do visitors take away from the enormous size of the quilt?

Picturing History

Background: Each panel of the AIDS quilt is three feet by six feet. If the panels were laid end-to-end, they would stretch for 50 miles. Portions of the quilt are constantly on display around the country.
Answer: Students' answers will vary. Students should recognize that the enormous size of the quilt is intended to reflect the enormity of the problem.
Ask: Why do you think the organizers chose to display the quilt near the Washington Monument?
(Students' answers will vary. Students might suggest that the organizers wanted to get the attention of lawmakers and the nation as a whole.)

Centers for Disease Control had identified more than 100,000 AIDS cases in the United States.

✓ Reading Check **Evaluating** What social problems did Americans face in the 1980s?

Social Activism

AIDS increased the visibility of the country's gay and lesbian community, but some homosexuals had been defending their civil rights since the 1960s. On June 27, 1969, New York City police raided a Greenwich Village nightclub called the Stonewall Inn. The police had a history of raiding the nightclub and targeting its patrons because of their sexual orientation. Frustration among the gay and lesbian onlookers led to a riot. The **Stonewall riot** marked the beginning of a gay activist movement. Soon after, organizations such as the Gay Liberation Front tried to increase tolerance of homosexuality and media coverage of gays and lesbians.

Although the 1980s witnessed the rise of a powerful conservative movement, liberal organizations and social activists continued to push their agenda as well, particularly on issues involving the environment and developing nations. In addition, elderly Americans began to organize politically for the first time.

Environmental Activism Grows Trying to promote environmental protection during the Reagan years was frustrating for environmental activists. Secretary of the Interior James Watt encouraged development on public lands, saying, "We will mine more, drill

more, cut more timber." Congress, under pressure from environmental groups, blocked many of Watt's plans. Worried about Watt's program, many new members joined groups such as the **Sierra Club.**

The environmental movement born in the 1970s continued to grow in the 1980s. Environmentalists were active in protesting nuclear power plants and protecting fragile wetlands. Communities started recycling programs. Activists became concerned about the ozone layer and rain forests.

Artists Become Activists In the 1980s, ministers, politicians, and others targeted and criticized rock musicians as promoters of drug use and other negative behavior. Still, singers, actors, and other entertainers often organized benefit concerts to help others. In hits such as "Born in the USA," Bruce Springsteen sang about working-class Americans. A social activist, he gave concerts to benefit food banks and the homeless.

To help starving people in Ethiopia, Irish rocker Bob Geldof organized musicians in England to present "Band Aid" concerts in 1984. The next year, the event grew into "Live Aid." Musicians including Paul McCartney, Madonna, The Who, and Tina Turner participated in the musical benefits. Its theme song, "We Are the World," was a best-seller. The same year, country singer Willie Nelson organized "Farm Aid" to help American farmers going through hard times.

✓ Reading Check

Answer: AIDS, alcohol abuse, crime, drug abuse, homelessness

In 1986 the surgeon general of the United States, C. Everett Koop, released a report on AIDS. The report was explicit and nonjudgmental. It was also controversial. Because Koop believed strongly that AIDS was a public health crisis, he wrote a brochure, "Understanding AIDS," and mailed it to 107 million American households.

CHAPTER 28 Resurgence of Conservatism **877**

INTERDISCIPLINARY CONNECTIONS ACTIVITY

Civics Invite someone who works in a mental health facility, free clinic, or other social agency to make a presentation to the class about ways in which students can help address an ongoing social problem such as drug abuse, AIDS, or drunk driving. Be sure to brief the speaker beforehand on any guidelines your school has about discussing sensitive issues. Allow time for the students to ask questions of the speaker. Conclude the discussion by having students make a list of several ways that they can make a real difference in their community. **L2**

Reading Check

Answer: Environmentalists were active in protesting nuclear power plants and protecting fragile wetlands, starting recycling programs, and bringing attention to global warming and the destruction of the ozone layer and rain forests.

Profiles IN HISTORY

Ask: When did Chang-Diaz's fascination with space begin? *(He became interested in 1957 when he heard about* Sputnik.*)*

3 ASSESS

Assign Section 3 Assessment as homework or as an in-class activity.

⊛ Have students use the **Interactive Tutor Self-Assessment CD-ROM.**

L1/ELL

Reading Essentials and Study Guide 28–3

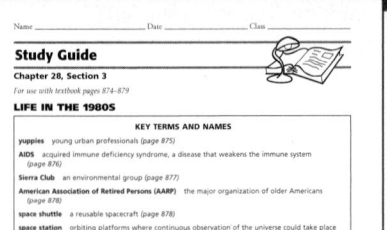

Other Groups Become Activists One noticeable political change in the 1980s was the stronger presence of senior citizens. Decades of improvements in medicine had resulted in more Americans surviving to an older age. In addition, the birthrate had declined, so younger people represented a smaller proportion of the population. The fact that more Americans were receiving Social Security payments created budget pressures for the government.

Older Americans became politically active, opposing cuts in Social Security or Medicare. Because they tended to vote in large numbers, senior citizens became an influential interest group. Their major lobbying organization was the **American Association of Retired Persons** (AARP).

✓ **Reading Check** **Summarizing** What issues did environmental activists focus on in the 1980s?

A New Era in Space

President Reagan, like many Americans, saw space as an exciting frontier. Improved technology and new exploration programs rekindled the nation's excitement for space exploration.

The Space Shuttle After Americans reached the moon, the National Aeronautics and Space Administration (NASA) began work on the space shuttle— a reusable spacecraft with wings that could rocket into space and then glide back to Earth. On April 12,

Profiles IN HISTORY

Franklin R. Chang-Diaz
1950–

Born in Costa Rica, Franklin R. Chang-Diaz dates his fascination with space to hearing about the *Sputnik* launching in 1957. His mother told him that a new star, made by humans, had been placed in the heavens. This convinced him, he said later, to become "a space explorer."

Chang-Diaz managed to save enough money—$50—to immigrate to the United States at the age of 18. He went to Hartford, Connecticut, where he had relatives. After completing high school and college, he went on to earn a doctorate in applied plasma physics and fusion technology at MIT in 1977.

His goal of becoming an astronaut came true in 1980 when NASA selected him for the space shuttle program. In the following years, Chang-Diaz worked as part of the astronaut support crew and in early space station design studies.

His first spaceflight came in January 1986 on the space shuttle *Columbia*. In the late 1980s and 1990s, Chang-Diaz flew a number of shuttle missions.

878 CHAPTER 28 Resurgence of Conservatism

1981, the first space shuttle, *Columbia*, lifted off its launch pad in Florida. On board were two astronauts: John Young and Robert Crippen. John Young was a hero to many Americans. He had flown three times in the 1960s and commanded the *Apollo 16* mission to the moon in 1972. After the shuttle landed successfully, Young remarked to the crowd: "We're really not too far, the human race isn't, from going to the stars."

Young and Crippen's flight demonstrated the shuttle's capabilities. Previously astronauts had been military pilots, but the shuttle could function as an orbiting laboratory, and civilians could now be astronauts. In 1983 **Sally Ride** became the first American woman in space, and after her flight, female astronauts became increasingly common.

In January 1986, disaster struck. The shuttle *Challenger* exploded after liftoff, killing everyone on board: Michael Smith, Dick Scobee, Judith Resnik, Ronald McNair, Ellison Onizuka, Gregory Jarvis, and Christa McAuliffe. Although Americans mourned the lost lives, President Reagan reminded everyone that the exploration of space required bravery:

❝The Challenger Seven were aware of the dangers, but overcame them and did their jobs brilliantly. . . . They had that special grace, that special spirit that says, 'Give me a challenge and I'll meet it with joy.' They had a hunger to explore the universe and discover its truths. . . . We've grown used to the idea of space, and perhaps we forget that we've only just begun. We're still pioneers. . . . [S]ometimes painful things like this happen. It's all part of the process of exploration and discovery. It's all part of taking a chance and expanding man's horizons. The future doesn't belong to the fainthearted; it belongs to the brave.❞

—from *Speaking My Mind*

In June 1986, a presidential commission reported that defective seals in the rocket boosters had caused the explosion. Engineers fixed the problem, and in September 1988, the shuttle resumed operations.

A Home in Space Between September 1988 and December 2002, the shuttle completed 87 missions. It

---

CRITICAL THINKING ACTIVITY

Supporting a Point of View Have students review the history of the space program and research its future goals. Tell students that during times of economic struggle, some have questioned the ongoing usefulness of the space program and have proposed to reduce funding for it. Others see the potential future value to Americans and all humans of continued space exploration. Have students write a persuasive essay either supporting the continued expansion of the space program or calling for reduced funding for it. **L2**

First Female Astronaut Dr. Sally Ride (below) was accepted into the astronaut program in 1978. She became the first American woman to orbit the earth when she flew aboard the space shuttle *Challenger* in June 1983. The space shuttle *Discovery* is shown on the right.

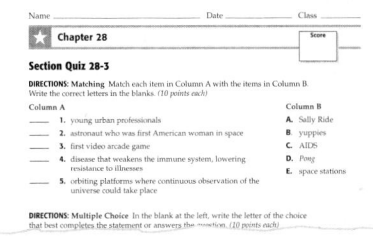

Section Quiz 28–3

placed many satellites in orbit, including the Hubble Space Telescope in 1990. This telescope gave astronomers the ability to look farther into space than ever before.

One reason NASA built the shuttle was to provide transportation to space stations—manned orbiting platforms that serve as a base of operations for space research. The United States had launched the space station *Skylab* in 1973, but it stayed in orbit only until 1979. In 1986 President Reagan announced that the United States would build a new space station.

In the years following Reagan's announcement, the space station became an international project, and 16 nations helped create the International Space Station. Shuttle astronauts began assembling the station in December 1998, and the station's first crew arrived in October 2000. By December 2002 the shuttle had completed 16 missions to the space station.

Seventeen years after the *Challenger* disaster, tragedy struck again. On February 1, 2003, the shuttle *Columbia* came apart while reentering the earth's atmosphere. All seven crew members were killed. As people around the world mourned, NASA began investigating the accident. Speaking to the nation, President George W. Bush proclaimed, "Mankind is led into the darkness beyond our world by the inspiration of discovery and the longing to understand." The president then promised that American space exploration would continue.

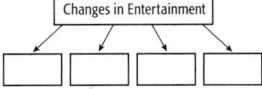 **Reading Check** **Describing** How was the space shuttle different from previous spacecraft?

Reteach
Have students explain the growth of social activism during the 1980s.

Enrich
Have students interview several people who remember significant events in the evolution of the space program. Encourage students to find people of different ages who remember such events as the first manned space flight, the landing on the moon, and the *Challenger* disaster. Based on the interviews, have students write an article about how some Americans view the space program.

Reading Check

Answer: It was reusable.

Study Central™ provides summaries, interactive games, and online graphic organizers to help students review section content.

SECTION 3 ASSESSMENT

HISTORY Online | **Study Central**™ To review this section, go to tarvol2.glencoe.com and click on **Study Central**™.

Checking for Understanding
1. **Define:** yuppie, space shuttle, space station.
2. **Identify:** AIDS, Sierra Club, American Association of Retired Persons.
3. **Summarize** the causes for which several musicians held concert benefits in the 1980s.

Reviewing Themes
4. **Science and Technology** What new innovations occurred in the nation's space program in the 1980s?

Critical Thinking
5. **Comparing** How do the social problems the United States faces today compare with those the nation faced in the 1980s?
6. **Organizing** Use a graphic organizer similar to the one below to list the changes in entertainment in the 1980s.

Changes in Entertainment

Analyzing Visuals
7. **Examining Diagrams** Study the illustration on page 875. What elements of the diagram depict the concept of materialism?

Writing About History
8. **Persuasive Writing** Choose one of the social problems of the 1980s. Write a letter to members of your favorite band asking them to perform a concert to benefit your cause. Your letter should include reasons the cause is important.

SECTION 3 ASSESSMENT ANSWERS

1. Terms are in blue.
2. AIDS (*p. 876*), Sierra Club (*p. 877*), American Association of Retired Persons (*p. 878*)
3. Band Aid and Live Aid aided famine victims in Ethiopia and elsewhere; Farm Aid helped American farmers.
4. shuttle, space probe, and civilian and female astronauts
5. Students should recognize that many problems are the same.
6. innovations included rap music; listening to music with portable cassette players; watching movie and music videos, cable or satellite TV; video games
7. Brand names shown reflect the striving for social status.
8. Students' letters will vary but should use standard grammar and be persuasive.

4 CLOSE

Have students discuss attitudes toward money in the culture of the 1980s.

TEACH

Analyzing News Media The Internet and cable television have made news more easily accessible for many people. This frequently means people are getting more news and have even more reason to analyze the content.

Ask students to compare a cable news broadcast on a given topic with its coverage on two different Web sites. Have them present their comparisons to the class.

Additional Practice

L1

Reinforcing Skills Activity 28

Name _____ Date _____ Class _____

★ **Reinforcing Skills Activity 28**

Analyzing News Media

□ **LEARNING THE SKILL**

To analyze news media in print and electronic forms, first consider the source of the story. Does the reporter cite sources? Are the sources reliable? Is the news reported from the scene of events or secondhand? Also look for evidence of unbiased reporting. Does the reporter represent both sides of the issue?

□ **PRACTICING THE SKILL**

DIRECTIONS: The excerpt below is from a June 4, 1989, *New York Times* article, "Crackdown In Beijing: Troops Attack and Crush Beijing Protest." Read the excerpt, and then answer the questions that follow on a separate sheet of paper.

The official news programs this morning reported that the People's Liberation Army had | bodies had yet to be taken to its morgue. A doctor at the Beijing Union Medical College Hospital, two

GLENCOE
TECHNOLOGY

CD-ROM
Glencoe Skillbuilder Interactive Workbook CD-ROM, Level 2

This interactive CD-ROM reinforces student mastery of essential social studies skills.

Analyzing News Media

Why Learn This Skill?

Every citizen needs to be aware of current issues and events in order to make good decisions when exercising citizenship rights. To stay informed, people use a variety of news sources, including print media, broadcast media, and electronic media.

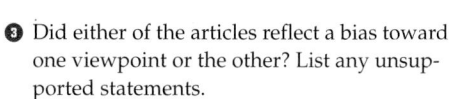

Learning the Skill

To get an accurate profile of current events, you must learn to think critically about the news. The steps below will help you think critically.

- First, think about the source of the news story. Reports that reveal sources are more reliable than those that do not. If you know the sources, you can evaluate them.

- Many news stories analyze and interpret events. Such analyses may be more detailed than other reports, but they also reflect a reporter's biases. Look for biases as you read or listen to news stories.

- Ask yourself whether the news is even-handed and thorough. Is it reported on the scene or secondhand? Does it represent both sides of the issue? How many sources are used? The more sources cited for a fact, the more reliable it usually is.

Practicing the Skill

Follow the steps below to analyze two types of print media.

❶ Find two articles, one in a current newspaper and the other in a newsmagazine, on a decision made by the president or Congress on a topic such as Social Security, education, or taxes.

❷ What points were the articles trying to make? Were the articles successful? Can the facts be verified?

❸ Did either of the articles reflect a bias toward one viewpoint or the other? List any unsupported statements.

❹ Was the news reported on the scene or secondhand? Do the articles seem to represent both sides fairly?

❺ How many sources can you identify in the articles? List them.

Skills Assessment

Complete the Practicing Skills questions on page 889 and the Chapter 28 Skill Reinforcement Activity to assess your mastery of this skill.

Applying the Skill

Analyzing News Media Think of an issue in your community or in the nation on which public opinion is divided. Read newspaper features and editorials and monitor television reports about the issue. Can you identify any biases? Which reports more fairly represent the issue? Which reports are the most reliable?

 GO Glencoe's **Skillbuilder Interactive Workbook CD-ROM, Level 2**, provides instruction and practice in key social studies skills.

ANSWERS TO PRACTICING THE SKILL

Using questions two through five, students will analyze two types of print media related to a recent decision made by the president or Congress.

Applying the Skill

Students' analyses will vary. Encourage students to recognize bias on both sides of issues and to identify sources that provide fair representations of various points of view.

SECTION 4 The End of the Cold War

Guide to Reading

Main Idea
President George Bush's foreign policy commanded broad support, but his domestic agenda did not.

Key Terms and Names
perestroika, glasnost, Boris Yeltsin, Tiananmen Square, Saddam Hussein, downsizing, capital gains tax, H. Ross Perot, grassroots movement

Reading Strategy
Categorizing As you read about the administration of President Bush, complete a chart similar to the one below by describing U.S. foreign policy in each of the places listed on the chart.

Place	Foreign Policy
Soviet Union	
China	
Panama	
Middle East	

Reading Objectives
• **Identify** the events that brought an end to the Cold War.
• **Explain** the domestic challenges facing the Bush administration.

Section Theme
Economic Factors The deficit and an economic slowdown hurt George Bush's attempt to win re-election in 1992.

Preview of Events

♦1989	♦1990	♦1991	♦1992

May, 1989
Tiananmen Square protests begin

November, 1989
Berlin Wall falls

August, 1990
Iraq invades Kuwait

January, 1991
Persian Gulf War begins

December, 1991
Soviet Union collapses

★ An American Story ★

Colin Powell

On October 31, 1990, General Colin Powell, who was the chairman of the Joint Chiefs of Staff, Secretary of Defense Dick Cheney, and other high-ranking officials met with President George Bush. In August the country of Iraq had invaded neighboring Kuwait. American troops had been rushed to the Middle East in response. Now the president had to decide whether to go to war.

General Brent Scrowcroft, a close adviser to Bush, began the meeting: "Mr. President, we are at a Y in the road. Down one branch we can continue sanctions. . . . Down the other branch we . . . go on the attack." Powell then presented the plan for attacking Iraq. Several advisers gasped at the numbers, which called for over 500,000 American troops. "Mr. President," Powell began, "I wish . . . that I could assure you that air power alone could do it but you can't take that chance. We've gotta take the initiative out of the enemy's hands if we're going to go to war." Cheney later recalled that Bush "never hesitated." He looked up from the plans and said simply, "Do it."

—adapted from *Triumph Without Victory* and *PBS Frontline Gulf War Interviews*

George Bush Takes Office

The war in the Persian Gulf was only one of many international crises that confronted President George Bush after his election in 1988. Fortunately, Bush's strength was in foreign policy. In the 1970s, he had served as ambassador to the UN and as the nation's first

CHAPTER 28 Resurgence of Conservatism **881**

1 FOCUS

Section Overview
This section focuses on the foreign policy successes and domestic problems during the presidency of George Bush.

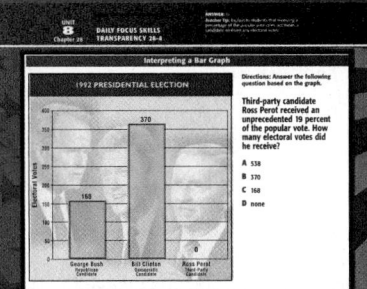

Reading Preview

Answers to Graphic: Soviet Union: cooperated with reform leader Gorbachev; China: halted arms sales and reduced diplomatic contact; Panama: invaded and seized dictator to help people hold elections and organize a new government; Middle East: imposed economic sanctions against Iraq and carried out Operation Desert Storm

Preteaching Vocabulary
For each of the Key Terms and Names, have students write a phrase or short sentence that will help them remember the significance of the term or name.

SECTION RESOURCES

📁 Reproducible Masters
• Reproducible Lesson Plan 28-4
• Daily Lecture and Discussion Notes 28-4
• Guided Reading Activity 28-4
• Section Quiz 28-4
• Reading Essentials and Study Guide 28-4
• Interpreting Political Cartoons

🖳 Transparencies
• Daily Focus Skills Transparency 28-4

Multimedia
• 🌐 Interactive Tutor Self-Assessment CD-ROM
• 🌐 ExamView® Pro Testmaker CD-ROM
• 🌐 Presentation Plus! CD-ROM
• 🌐 TeacherWorks™ CD-ROM
• 🎧 Audio Program

2 TEACH

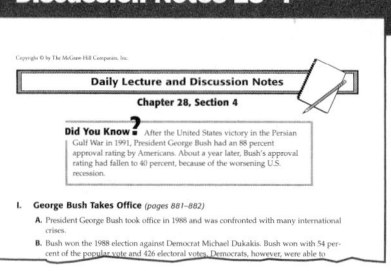

Geography *Skills*

Answers:

1. Poland, Hungary, Bulgaria, and Romania

2. It was particularly significant because it meant that Germany could be reunified.

Geography Skills Practice

Ask: What happened to Czechoslovakia? *(In 1993 it was divided into two countries: the Czech Republic and Slovakia.)*

 Reading Check

Answer: He promised no new taxes and to continue Ronald Reagan's domestic policies.

Analyzing a Point of View

Review with students what they know about the Communist government in the Soviet Union. Then ask students to defend or refute the following statement: "The collapse of the Soviet Union was inevitable." Encourage students to use reasoned arguments to support their point of view. L1

NATIONAL GEOGRAPHIC

Revolution in Eastern Europe, 1989–1993

① Democratic elections, 1989
② Non-Communist governments created, 1989
③ Berlin Wall torn down, Nov. 1989
④ Germany reunited, 1990
⑤ Baltic States became independent, 1991
⑥ Czechoslovakia separated, 1993

Lambert Azimuthal Equal-Area projection

Geography *Skills*

1. **Interpreting Maps** Which Eastern European countries abandoned communism first?
2. **Applying Geography Skills** Why was the fall of communism in East Germany significant?

diplomatic envoy to the People's Republic of China. He then headed the CIA from 1976 to 1977 before becoming vice president in 1981.

When Ronald Reagan left office, few Americans were thinking about foreign policy. They wanted a continuation of Reagan's domestic policies—low taxes and less government action. When Bush accepted the Republican nomination in 1988, he reassured Americans with this promise: "Read my lips: No new taxes."

The Democrats hoped to regain the White House in 1988 by promising to help working-class Americans, minorities, and the poor. One candidate, civil rights leader Jesse Jackson, tried to create a "rainbow coalition"—a broad group of minorities and the poor—by speaking about homelessness and unemployment. He finished second in the primaries, the first African American to make a serious run for the nomination.

The Democrats' final choice was Massachusetts governor Michael Dukakis. The Bush campaign portrayed him as too liberal, unpatriotic, and "soft on crime." The Democrats questioned Bush's leadership

abilities, but Bush had Reagan's endorsement, and with the economy still doing well, few Americans wanted to switch parties. Bush won 54 percent of the popular vote and defeated Dukakis 426 to 111 in the Electoral College. Democrats, however, kept control of Congress.

 Reading Check

Describing What kind of strategy did the Bush campaign use in the 1988 election?

The Cold War Ends

Almost immediately after taking office, President Bush had to draw on his foreign policy experience. With the help of Secretary of State James Baker, the president steered the United States through an era of sweeping change that resulted from the sudden end of the Cold War.

Gorbachev's Reforms As president, Bush continued Reagan's policy of cooperation with Soviet leader Mikhail Gorbachev. By the late 1980s, the Soviet economy was suffering from years of inefficient central planning and huge expenditures on the arms race. To save the economy, Gorbachev instituted *perestroika,* or "restructuring," and allowed some private enterprise and profit-making.

The other principle of Gorbachev's plan was *glasnost,* or "openness." It allowed more freedom of religion and speech, allowing people to discuss politics openly.

Revolution in Eastern Europe Protests in Poland had led to the first independent trade union, Solidarity, in 1980. It was suspended a year later, but with Gorbachev's support, *glasnost* spread to Eastern Europe. In 1989 peaceful revolutions replaced Communist rulers with democratic governments in Poland, Hungary, Czechoslovakia, Romania, and Bulgaria. The spreading revolution soon reached East Germany, and at midnight on November 9, 1989, guards at the Berlin Wall opened the gates. Within days, bulldozers leveled the hated symbol of Communist repression. Within a year, East and West Germany had reunited.

Reading Strategy   READING THE TEXT

Using Context Clues Students can often determine the meaning of a word they do not know by using context—the words and sentences that surround an unfamiliar word. Synonyms often appear in context when two things are compared. Antonyms may appear in context when two things are contrasted. Definitions often are surrounded by commas, dashes, or parentheses. The use of examples reveals the meaning of an unfamiliar word. As students read the section and encounter words they do not know, remind them to use these clues to identify the word's meaning. L1 ELL

Refer to *Inclusion for the High School Social Studies Classroom Strategies and Activities* in the TCR.

The Soviet Union Collapses As Eastern Europe abandoned communism, Gorbachev faced mounting criticism from opponents at home. In August 1991, a group of Communist officials and army officers staged a coup—an overthrow of the government. They arrested Gorbachev and sent troops into Moscow.

In Moscow, Russian president **Boris Yeltsin** defied the coup leaders from his offices in the Russian Parliament. About 50,000 people surrounded the Russian Parliament to protect it from troops. President Bush telephoned Yeltsin to express the support of the United States. Soon afterward, the coup collapsed, and Gorbachev returned to Moscow.

The defeat of the coup brought change swiftly. All 15 Soviet republics declared their independence from the Soviet Union. Yeltsin outlawed the Communist Party in Russia. In late December 1991, Gorbachev announced the end of the Soviet Union. Most of the former Soviet republics then joined in a federation called the Commonwealth of Independent States.

✓ **Reading Check** **Explaining** Why did Mikhail Gorbachev institute the policy of *perestroika*?

The "New World Order"

After the Cold War, the world became increasingly unpredictable. In a phrase made popular by President Bush, a "new world order" was developing. While trying to redefine American foreign policy, Bush faced crises in China, Panama, and the Middle East.

Tragedy in Tiananmen Square Despite the collapse of communism in Eastern Europe and the Soviet Union, China's Communist leaders were determined to stay in power. China's government had relaxed controls on the economy, but it continued to repress political speech and dissent. In May 1989, Chinese students and workers held demonstrations for democracy. In early June, government tanks and soldiers crushed their protests in **Tiananmen Square** in Beijing—China's capital. Many people were killed and hundreds of pro-democracy activists were arrested. Many were later sentenced to death.

These events shocked the world. The United States and several European countries halted arms sales and reduced their diplomatic contacts with China. The World Bank suspended loans. Some congressional

NATIONAL GEOGRAPHIC

MOMENT in HISTORY

A CITY REUNITED
Built in 1961, the Berlin Wall served to stem the mounting tide of immigration from Communist East Germany into the democratic western sector of the city. The wall also stood as a symbol of Cold War tensions between the world's superpowers. As reforms sparked by Mikhail Gorbachev swept through Eastern Europe, however, East German citizens began pressuring their government to open its borders. On November 9, 1989, the gates were thrown open, and East and West Berliners finally mingled freely. With great enthusiasm, they took hammers and chisels to the wall and tore down the hated symbol of division.

L1/ELL

Guided Reading Activity 28–4

Name _____ Date _____ Class _____

★ Guided Reading Activity 28-4

DIRECTIONS: Outlining Read the section and complete the outline below. Refer to your textbook to fill in the blanks.

I. **George Bush Takes Office**
  A. When Ronald Reagan left office in 1988, Americans wanted a continuation of his domestic policies—_____ and _____
  B. George Bush won _____ percent of the popular vote and defeated Michael Dukakis in the Electoral College, _____ to _____

II. **The Cold War Ends**
  A. To save his country's economy, Soviet leader Gorbachev instituted _____ or "restructuring" and allowed some _____
  B. He also instituted _____ or "openness," which allowed more freedom

✓ **Reading Check**

Answer: *Perestroika* was intended to save the Soviet economy by allowing some private enterprise and profit-making.

NATIONAL GEOGRAPHIC

MOMENT in HISTORY

The following events immediately preceded the wall's destruction: In October, East Germany celebrated its fortieth anniversary with a two-day visit by Mikhail Gorbachev. After Gorbachev left, the government arrested demonstrators who were protesting economic problems and the lack of democratic freedoms. Continued unrest forced President Erich Honecker, a hard-line Communist who had ruled East Germany since 1971, to resign. In November, the government opened its borders in an attempt to turn the tide of escaping citizens and convince them that leaving the country was unnecessary.

📁 Use *Interpreting Political Cartoons,* Cartoons 34 and 35.

DIFFERENTIATED INSTRUCTION

Reading Support To help students understand the impact of the Berlin Wall coming down, use a large map of your community and draw a line down the center of it. Ask students to look at the map closely and make a list of all the aspects of their lives that would be affected if they could not cross "the wall." Invite students to share some of the entries on their lists. **L2**

📁 Refer to *Inclusion for the High School Social Studies Classroom Strategies and Activities* in the TCR.

Creating a Circle Graph Have students use the information presented in the graph that appears at the top of this page to create a circle graph showing the proportional contribution of each region to the total oil production for these regions in 2000. **L2**

 Use the rubric for creating a map, display, or chart on pages 65–66 in the *Performance Assessment Activities and Rubrics.*

you don't say...

Saddam Iraqi leader Saddam Hussein likes to be called by his first name. When pronounced correctly, with the emphasis on the second syllable, Saddam means "leader" or "learned one." During the Persian Gulf Crisis, President Bush insisted on pronouncing the name with the emphasis on the first syllable. Pronounced this way, Saddam means "a boy who fixes or cleans shoes."

Why It Matters

Strait of Hormuz

The Strait of Hormuz is a narrow shipping lane between the Persian Gulf, the Gulf of Oman, and the Arabian Sea. Most of the crude oil produced in the Middle East passes through the Strait of Hormuz. In 1997 about 14 million barrels of crude oil passed through the Strait every day. Since the waterway is only about 40 miles (64 km) across at its widest point, it is possible that a country might block or hamper passage of ships. During the 1980s, the United States began escorting oil tankers through the Strait to protect them from Iranian attacks. If the passage were ever closed, oil would have to be shipped overland by pipeline— a much more expensive option.

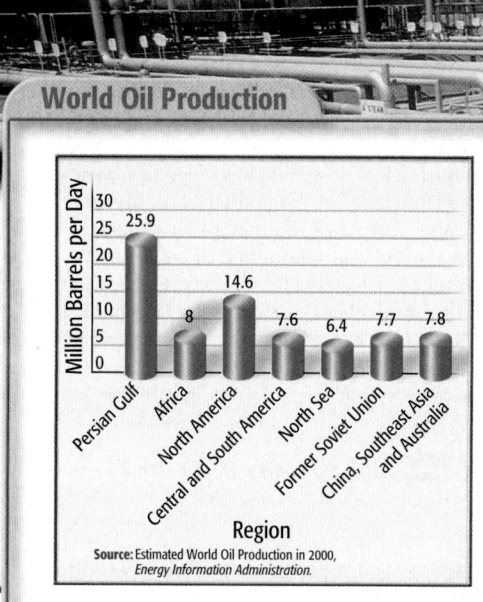

World Oil Production

Source: Estimated World Oil Production in 2000, *Energy Information Administration.*

The Persian Gulf countries consist of Saudi Arabia, Iran, Iraq, Kuwait, Qatar, and the United Arab Emirates. They may hold as much as 70 percent of the world's proven oil reserves.

leaders urged even stronger sanctions, but President Bush resisted these harsher measures, believing that trade and diplomacy would eventually moderate China's behavior.

Panama While President Bush struggled to deal with global events elsewhere, a crisis developed in Panama. In 1978 the United States had agreed to give Panama control over the Panama Canal by the year 2000. Because of the canal's importance, American officials wanted to make sure Panama's government was both stable and pro-American.

By 1989 Panama's dictator, General Manuel Noriega, had stopped cooperating with the United States. He also aided drug traffickers, cracked down on opponents, and harassed American military personnel defending the canal. In December 1989, Bush ordered American troops to invade Panama. The troops seized Noriega, who was sent to the United States to stand trial on drug charges. The troops then helped the Panamanians hold elections and organize a new government.

884 CHAPTER 28 Resurgence of Conservatism

The Persian Gulf War President Bush faced perhaps his most serious crisis in the Middle East. In August 1990, Iraq's dictator, **Saddam Hussein,** sent his army to invade oil-rich Kuwait. American officials feared the invasion was only the first step and that Iraq's ultimate goal was to capture Saudi Arabia and its vast oil reserves.

President Bush persuaded other UN member countries to join a coalition to stop Iraq. Led by the United States, the United Nations first imposed economic sanctions on Iraq and demanded the Iraqis withdraw. The coalition forces included troops from the United States, Canada, Europe, and Arab nations. The UN set a deadline for the Iraqi withdrawal, or the coalition would use force to remove them. Congress also voted to authorize the use of force if Iraq did not withdraw.

Iraq refused to comply with the UN deadline, and on January 16, 1991, the coalition forces launched **Operation Desert Storm.** Dozens of cruise

---

INTERDISCIPLINARY CONNECTIONS ACTIVITY

Economics Tell students that the 1992 defense budget of the United States was close to $300 billion. Some have suggested that instead of producing costly weapons, regardless of the need, the government should support research and put off producing weapons until a need becomes clear and cost controls are assured. Others argue that when orders to a defense plant decrease, it affects the local economy. The plant orders fewer raw materials from suppliers, the truckers who deliver goods lose business, and individual workers get laid off or work fewer hours. Discuss with students the pros and cons of decreasing or increasing defense spending for the American economy. **L2**

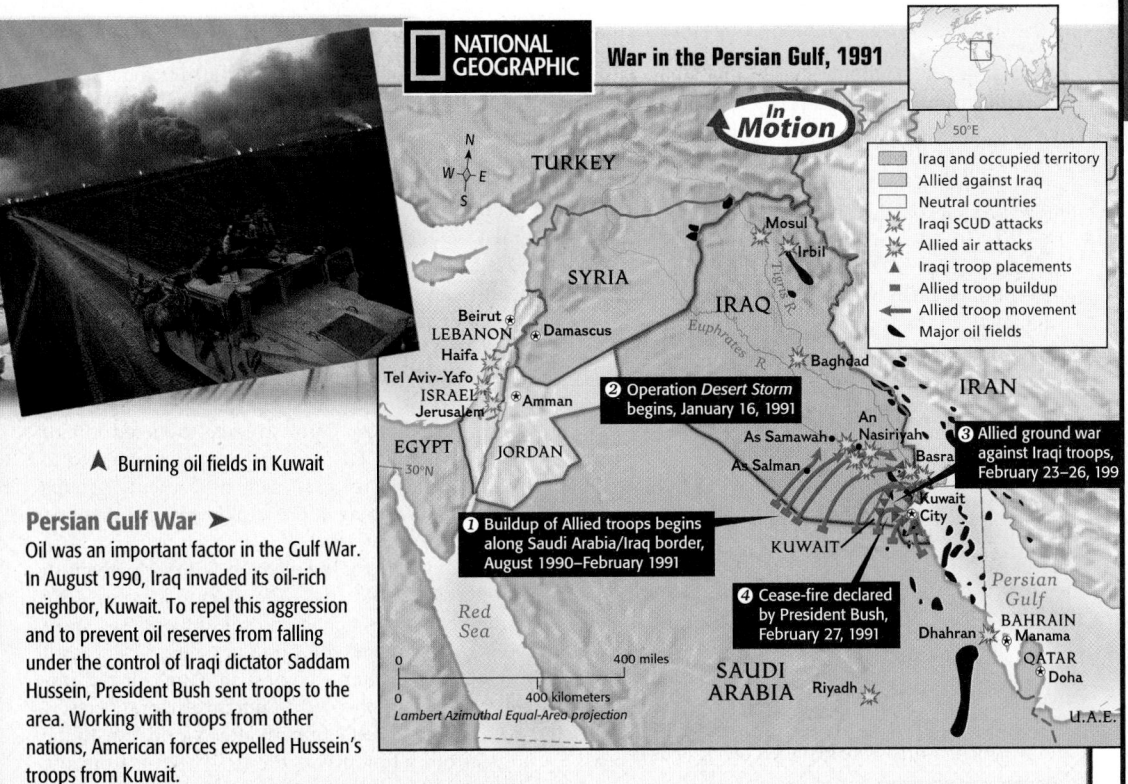

NATIONAL GEOGRAPHIC **War in the Persian Gulf, 1991**

In Motion

Legend:
- Iraq and occupied territory
- Allied against Iraq
- Neutral countries
- Iraqi SCUD attacks
- Allied air attacks
- Iraqi troop placements
- Allied troop buildup
- Allied troop movement
- Major oil fields

❷ Operation *Desert Storm* begins, January 16, 1991

❸ Allied ground war against Iraqi troops, February 23–26, 199

❶ Buildup of Allied troops begins along Saudi Arabia/Iraq border, August 1990–February 1991

❹ Cease-fire declared by President Bush, February 27, 1991

0 ——— 400 miles
0 ——— 400 kilometers
Lambert Azimuthal Equal-Area projection

▲ Burning oil fields in Kuwait

Persian Gulf War ➤

Oil was an important factor in the Gulf War. In August 1990, Iraq invaded its oil-rich neighbor, Kuwait. To repel this aggression and to prevent oil reserves from falling under the control of Iraqi dictator Saddam Hussein, President Bush sent troops to the area. Working with troops from other nations, American forces expelled Hussein's troops from Kuwait.

you don't say...

Downsizing Some companies chose to use the term *downsizing* rather than *lay-off* because *layoff* sounded too negative. After several years of downsizing, some companies started to use the term *right-sizing* to infer that cuts were being made to adjust the workforce to the correct size.

✓ **Reading Check**

Answer: American officials feared the invasion was only the first step and that Iraq's ultimate goal was to capture Saudi Arabia and its vast oil reserves.

---

missiles and thousands of laser-guided bombs fell on Iraq, destroying its air defenses, bridges, artillery, and other military targets. After about six weeks of bombardment, the coalition launched a massive ground attack. Waves of tanks and troop carriers smashed through Iraqi lines and encircled the Iraqi forces defending Kuwait.

The attack killed thousands of Iraqi soldiers. Hundreds of thousands more surrendered. Fewer than 300 coalition troops were killed. Just 100 hours after the ground war began President Bush declared victory. "Kuwait is liberated," he announced. Iraq accepted the coalition's cease-fire terms. American troops returned home to cheering crowds celebrating the U.S. victory in the first large-scale war since Vietnam.

✓ **Reading Check** **Examining** Why did President Bush take action when Iraqi troops invaded Kuwait?

Domestic Challenges

President Bush spent much of his time dealing with foreign policy, but he could not ignore domestic issues. He inherited a growing deficit and a slowing economy. As the Persian Gulf crisis began, the economy plunged into a recession and unemployment rose rapidly.

ECONOMICS

The Economy Slows The recession that began in 1990 was partly caused by the end of the Cold War. As the Soviet threat faded, the United States began reducing its armed forces and canceling orders for military equipment. Thousands of soldiers were released, and defense industry workers were laid off.

Across the nation, other companies also began downsizing—laying off workers and managers to become more efficient. The nation's high level of debt made the recession worse. Americans had borrowed heavily during the 1980s and now faced paying off large debts.

In addition, the huge federal deficit forced the government to borrow money to pay for its programs. This borrowing kept money from being available to expanding businesses. The government also had to pay interest on its debt, money that might otherwise have been used to fund programs or jump-start the economy.

CHAPTER 28 Resurgence of Conservatism **885**

3 ASSESS

Assign Section 4 Assessment as homework or as an in-class activity.

🕐 Have students use the **Interactive Tutor Self-Assessment CD-ROM.**

L1/ELL

Reading Essentials and Study Guide 28–4

Name _____ Date _____ Class _____

Study Guide

Chapter 28, Section 4
For use with textbook pages 881–886

THE END OF THE COLD WAR

KEY TERMS AND NAMES
perestroika a restructuring *(page 882)*
glasnost openness *(page 882)*
Boris Yeltsin president of Russia *(page 883)*
Tiananmen Square location of demonstrations for democracy in Beijing, China *(page 883)*
Saddam Hussein dictator of Iraq *(page 884)*
downsizing the practice by factories of laying off workers and managers in order to become more efficient *(page 885)*
capital gains tax the tax paid by businesses and investors when they sell stocks or real estate for

---

CRITICAL THINKING ACTIVITY

Synthesizing Information In the debate over whether to use force against Saddam Hussein, some who favored military action used the example of Hitler to justify their stance. Those who opposed action used the example of Vietnam. Have students explain whether each of these examples applied to the situation in Kuwait and decide whether the outcome of the war meant that one historical example was more fitting than the other. **L3**

L2

Section Quiz 28–4

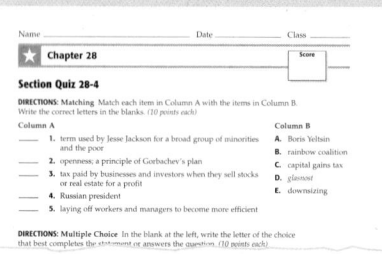

✓ Reading Check

Answer: Bush broke his promise that there would be no new taxes.

Reteach
Have students identify the events that ended the Cold War.

Enrich
Have interested students create a narrative history of America's involvement in the crises in China, the Middle East, or Panama during George H.W. Bush's presidency.

✓ Reading Check

Answer: They did not like either Bush or Clinton. Perot had the best showing of a third-party candidate since 1912.

HISTORY Online

Study Central™ provides summaries, interactive games, and online graphic organizers to help students review section content.

4 CLOSE

Have students explain the domestic challenges facing the Bush administration between 1989 and 1992.

Gridlock in Government Shortly after taking office, Bush tried to improve the economy. He called for a cut in the capital gains tax—the tax paid by businesses and investors when they sell stocks or real estate for a profit. Bush believed the tax cut would encourage businesses to expand. Calling the idea a tax break for the rich, Democrats in Congress defeated it.

Aware that the growing federal deficit was hurting the economy, Bush broke his "no new taxes" campaign pledge. After meeting with congressional leaders, he agreed to a tax increase in exchange for cuts in spending. This decision turned many voters against Bush. They blamed him both for the tax increase and for trying to cut social programs.

Extending Rights Although President Bush and Democrats in Congress disagreed on economic issues, they cooperated on other legislation. One example was the Americans with Disabilities Act (ADA), signed by Bush in 1990. The legislation forbade discrimination in workplaces and public places against people who were physically or mentally challenged. The law had widespread effect. Access ramps were added to buildings, closed-captioned television became more commonplace, and wheelchair lifts were installed on city buses.

✓ Reading Check
Summarizing Why did President Bush lose popularity as the 1992 election approached?

The 1992 Election

Although the recession had weakened his popularity, Bush won the Republican nomination. Bush promised to address voters' economic concerns, and he blamed congressional Democrats for the gridlock that seemingly paralyzed the nation's government.

The Democrats nominated Arkansas governor Bill Clinton, despite stories that questioned his character and his failure to serve in Vietnam. Calling himself a "New Democrat" to separate himself from more liberal Democrats, Clinton promised to cut middle-class taxes and spending and to reform the nation's health care and welfare programs. His campaign repeatedly blamed Bush for the recession.

Many Americans were not happy with either Bush or Clinton. This enabled an independent candidate, billionaire Texas businessman **H. Ross Perot,** to make a strong challenge. Perot stressed the need to end deficit spending. His no-nonsense style appealed to many Americans. A grassroots movement—groups of people organizing at the local level—put Perot on the ballot in all 50 states.

Bill Clinton won the election with 43 percent of the popular vote and 370 electoral votes. The Democrats also retained control of Congress. Bush won 37 percent of the popular vote, while Perot received 19 percent—the best showing for a third-party candidate since 1912—but no electoral votes.

As the first president born after World War II, the 46-year-old Clinton was the first person from the "baby boom" generation to enter the White House. It was his task to revive the economy and guide the United States in a rapidly changing and increasingly technological world.

✓ Reading Check
Evaluating Why did some people vote for H. Ross Perot in 1992? How successful was his election campaign as a third-party candidate?

HISTORY Online
Study Central™ To review this section, go to **tarvol2.glencoe.com** and click on **Study Central™.**

SECTION 4 ASSESSMENT

Checking for Understanding
1. **Define:** *perestroika, glasnost, downsizing,* capital gains tax, grassroots movement.
2. **Identify:** Boris Yeltsin, Tiananmen Square, Saddam Hussein, H. Ross Perot.
3. **Describe** how Mikhail Gorbachev tried to reform the Soviet government.

Reviewing Themes
4. **Economic Factors** How did the economy affect the 1992 election?

Critical Thinking
5. **Analyzing** How did the United States and its Western allies finally achieve victory in the Cold War?
6. **Organizing** Use a graphic organizer similar to the one below to list the causes of the recession of the early 1990s.

Budget Problems	Economic Problems	Foreign Developments

Analyzing Visuals
7. **Studying Maps** Examine the map on page 885. Which nations have significant oil resources?

Writing About History
8. **Descriptive Writing** Imagine that you are traveling in West Germany in 1989 when the Berlin Wall is being torn down. Write a letter back home to describe the event and the feelings of the German people. Also include your reaction to the situation and how you think it will affect the United States.

SECTION 4 ASSESSMENT ANSWERS

1. Terms are in blue.
2. Boris Yeltsin *(p. 883),* Tiananmen Square *(p. 883),* Saddam Hussein *(p. 884),* H. Ross Perot *(p. 886)*
3. Gorbachev wanted to allow some private enterprise and profit-making, and to allow more freedom of speech and religion.
4. The recession hurt Bush's efforts to get re-elected.
5. The West forced the Soviets to engage in an arms race they could not afford; Western powers also supported Gorbachev's reform ideas.
6. budget problems: tax increase; economic problems: recession, high consumer debt, federal deficit; foreign developments: fall of the Soviet Union, Persian Gulf War
7. Saudi Arabia, Kuwait, Iraq, and Iran
8. Students' letters will vary but should be descriptive and use standard grammar and punctuation.

Richard Rodriguez

Hispanic Americans are the fastest-growing minority in the United States. Hispanics cherish their heritage, and many speak only Spanish among their friends and family. Most of their children's teachers, however, speak only English. As a result, Hispanic students often find school confusing and humiliating. Hispanic American Richard Rodriguez describes his struggle to become educated in his autobiography, *Hunger of Memory.*

In this excerpt, Rodriguez describes the difficulties he encountered at home after he became comfortable speaking English at school.

Read to Discover

What is the reaction of Richard's relatives to his reluctance to speak Spanish to them?

Reader's Dictionary

reticent: reluctant

anglicized: made to sound English

diminutive: shorter or more affectionate version

from Hunger of Memory

by Richard Rodriguez

I grew up victim to a disabling confusion. As I grew fluent in English, I no longer could speak Spanish with confidence. I continued to understand spoken Spanish. And in high school, I learned how to read and write Spanish. But for many years I could not pronounce it. A powerful guilt blocked my spoken words; an essential glue was missing whenever I'd try to connect words to form sentences. . . .

When relatives and Spanish-speaking friends of my parents came to the house, my brother and sisters seemed reticent to use Spanish, but at least they managed to say a few necessary words before being excused. . . . I was cursed with guilt. Each time I'd hear myself addressed in Spanish, I would be unable to respond with any success. I'd know the words I wanted to say, but I couldn't manage to say them. I would try to speak, but everything I said seemed to me horribly anglicized. My mouth would not form the words right. . . .

It surprised my listeners to hear me. They'd lower their heads, better to grasp what I was trying to say. They would repeat their questions in gentle, affectionate voices. But by then I would answer in English. No, no, they would say, we want you to speak to us in

Spanish. . . . But I couldn't do it. *Pocho* then they called me. Sometimes playfully, teasingly, using the tender diminutive—*mi pochito.* Sometimes not so playfully, mockingly, *Pocho.* (A Spanish dictionary defines that word as an adjective meaning "colorless" or "bland." But I heard it as a noun, naming the Mexican-American who, in becoming an American, forgets his native society. . . .)

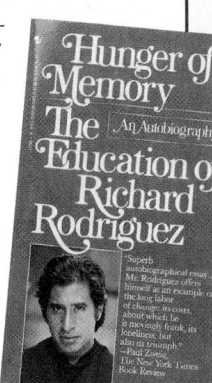

Analyzing Literature

1. **Recall and Interpret** What do you think Richard meant when he said that "an essential glue was missing" whenever he tried to speak Spanish?
2. **Evaluate and Connect** Why did Richard's relatives nickname him *Pocho?*

Interdisciplinary Activity

Journalism Interview a bilingual friend, relative, or classmate about when and where they use each of the languages they speak. Write a transcript of the interview.

Block Schedule

Team Teaching This selection from *Hunger of Memory* can be presented in conjunction with English or Language Arts.

Read to Discover

Answer: They teased him.

Reading Strategy

Reinforcing Vocabulary

Encourage students to look up the meaning of unfamiliar words such as *diminutive.*

Historical Connection

Richard Rodriguez knew only 50 words of English when he started school in Sacramento, California. He attended Stanford University and the University of California at Berkeley where he earned a doctorate in English Renaissance Literature.

Portfolio Writing Activity

Have students write a short essay about a time when they encountered a language barrier. Encourage students to describe how they overcame the difficulty of communicating with a person who spoke another language.

Refer to tarvol2.glencoe.com for additional Glencoe Literature titles, lesson plans, and study guides related to this unit.

Answers to Analyzing Literature

1. Even though he knew vocabulary, he could not connect words to have a conversation in Spanish.
2. They gave him the nickname because he would not speak to them in Spanish.

Interdisciplinary Activity
Transcripts will vary but should describe the experiences of a bilingual friend or relative, and perhaps his or her ideas of bilingual education.

CHAPTER 28 ASSESSMENT and ACTIVITIES

GLENCOE TECHNOLOGY

MindJogger Videoquiz
Use the **MindJogger Videoquiz** to review Chapter 28 content.

 Available in DVD

Reviewing Key Terms
Students' answers will vary. The pages where the words appear in the text are shown in parentheses.

1. **liberal** *(p. 861)*
2. **conservative** *(p. 861)*
3. **televangelist** *(p. 864)*
4. **supply-side economics** *(p. 867)*
5. **budget deficit** *(p. 867)*
6. **contra** *(p. 870)*
7. **yuppie** *(p. 875)*
8. **space shuttle** *(p. 878)*
9. **space station** *(p. 879)*
10. **perestroika** *(p. 882)*
11. **glasnost** *(p. 882)*
12. **downsizing** *(p. 885)*
13. **capital gains tax** *(p. 886)*
14. **grassroots movement** *(p. 886)*

Reviewing Key Facts
15. William F. Buckley *(p. 861)*, William Rehnquist *(p. 868)*, Mikhail Gorbachev *(p. 870)*, AIDS *(p. 876)*, Boris Yeltsin *(p. 883)*, Saddam Hussein *(p. 884)*, H. Ross Perot *(p. 886)*

16. Their economy was expanding and they did not want the government to interfere with their region's growth.

17. Reaganomics, cutting programs, and deregulation

18. Social issues facing the United States included AIDS, alcohol abuse, crime, drug abuse, homelessness, Social Security

19. Iraq's invasion of Kuwait and subsequent refusal to withdraw

Reviewing Key Terms
On a sheet of paper, use each of these terms in a sentence.

1. liberal
2. conservative
3. televangelist
4. supply-side economics
5. budget deficit
6. contra
7. yuppie
8. space shuttle
9. space station
10. *perestroika*
11. *glasnost*
12. downsizing
13. capital gains tax
14. grassroots movement

Reviewing Key Facts

15. **Identify:** William F. Buckley, William Rehnquist, Mikhail Gorbachev, AIDS, Boris Yeltsin, Saddam Hussein, H. Ross Perot.

16. Why did people in the Sunbelt tend to be conservative?

17. What three steps did President Reagan take to improve the economy?

18. What social issues did the United States face in the 1980s?

19. What event triggered the Persian Gulf War?

20. What economic problems did President George Bush face during his administration?

Critical Thinking

21. **Analyzing Themes: Global Connections** What event brought an end to the Cold War in the 1980s? What effect did that have on U.S. policies and on the U.S. economy?

22. **Synthesizing** How did conservatives gain political power in the 1980s?

23. **Forming an Opinion** On what part of the liberal-conservative spectrum would you place yourself? Why?

24. **Interpreting Primary Sources** President Ronald Reagan addressed the American people for the last time at the end of his presidency in 1988. The following is an excerpt from that address:

❝It's been quite a journey this decade, and we held together through some stormy seas. And at the end, together, we are reaching our destination. . . . The way I see it, there were two great triumphs, two things that I'm proudest of. One is the economic recovery, in which the people of America created—and filled—19 million new jobs. The other is the recovery of our morale. America is respected again in the world and looked to for leadership. . . .

Common sense told us that when you put a big tax on something, the people will produce less of it. So, we cut the people's tax rates, and the people produced more than ever before. The economy bloomed. . . . Common sense told us that to preserve the peace, we'd have to become strong again after years of weakness and confusion. So, we rebuilt our defenses, and this New Year we toasted the new peacefulness around the globe. . . .

Countries across the globe are turning to free markets and free speech and turning away from the ideologies of the past. . . .

Chapter Summary

Resurgence of Conservative Politics

- The Cold War promotes a strong foreign policy and an emphasis on minimal government intervention in economics.
- Cold War fears of communism encourage religious Americans to turn to conservative ideas.
- Barry Goldwater wins the 1964 Republican presidential nomination.
- The growth of the Sunbelt increases conservative support.

Reagan's Agenda

- Supply-side economics emphasizes large tax cuts.
- Reagan's administration takes a strong anti-Communist stance in Latin America, the Caribbean, and the Middle East.
- Reagan and Gorbachev begin new nuclear arms reductions.
- Military spending drives the growing budget deficit to record levels.

The Bush Years

- Communism collapses in Eastern Europe and the Soviet Union.
- The uncertainty of a "New World Order" replaces the dualism of the Cold War.
- The Persian Gulf War drives Bush's popularity to its highest level.
- A domestic economic recession weakens Bush's re-election campaign.

20. George Bush faced the economic problems of recession, high consumer debt, and the federal deficit.

Critical Thinking

21. Signing of the INF treaty in 1987 triggered a reduction in Soviet military spending and the beginning of Gorbachev's reforms; U.S. economy slowed as a result of reductions in military spending.

22. They elected two presidents who reinforced conservative values and economic policies.

23. Students' answers will vary. Answers should reflect an understanding of liberal and conservative beliefs.

24. **a.** Reagan was most proud of the economic recovery and the recovery of morale. **b.** Reagan thought attention to American history and to civic ritual would promote patriotism. Students' answers will vary.

Self-Check Quiz
Visit the *American Republic Since 1877* Web site at tarvol2.glencoe.com and click on *Self-Check Quizzes—Chapter 28* to assess your knowledge of chapter content.

[O]ne of the things I'm proudest of in the past eight years [is] the resurgence of national pride that I called the new patriotism. This national feeling is good, but it won't count for much, and it won't last unless it's grounded in thoughtfulness and knowledge. . . .

An informed patriotism is what we want. . . . Let's start with some basics: more attention to American history and greater emphasis on civic ritual. . . .
                                        —from *Speaking My Mind*

a. What did Reagan believe were his greatest accomplishments as president?

b. What did Reagan believe would promote patriotism in the nation? Do you agree with his belief? Why or why not?

25. **Organizing** Use a graphic organizer similar to the one below to list the domestic and foreign issues faced by the Reagan and Bush administrations.

Issues	Reagan Administration	Bush Administration
Domestic		
Foreign		

Practicing Skills

26. **Analyzing News Media** Choose one current issue or event and compare its coverage in two different media. Which medium supplies the most facts? Is the coverage that is provided by both media consistent? What are the advantages and disadvantages of each medium? Write a two-page analysis comparing the two media, including a conclusion about which one is better.

Writing Activity

27. **Writing a Report** Research the status today of the independent republics formed from the Soviet Union. Find out about their political, social, and economic situations. Present your findings in a written report.

Chapter Activity

28. **Creating a Thematic Graph** Using a scale of 1 to 10, evaluate how successful each president was in dealing with the issues you listed in question 25. Create a thematic graph depicting each president's success rate per issue.

The Election of 1992

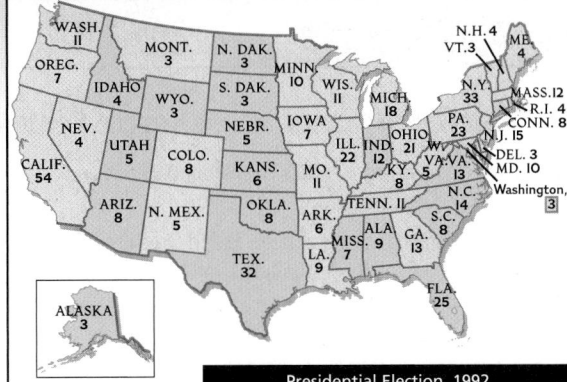

Presidential Election, 1992			
Candidate	Electoral Vote	Popular Vote	Political Party
Clinton	370	44,908,254	Democrat
Bush	168	39,102,343	Republican
Perot	0	19,741,065	Independent

Geography and History

29. The map above shows the results of the 1992 presidential election. Study the map and answer the questions below.

a. **Interpreting Maps** How far short did President Bush fall in the race for Electoral College votes?

b. **Applying Geography Skills** Bill Clinton won his strongest support in which region of the nation?

Standardized Test Practice

Directions: Choose the phrase that best completes the following sentence.

The Strategic Defense Initiative (SDI) was proposed to strengthen the military by

A preventing the expansion of Communist countries.

B reemphasizing the use of infantry troops in future wars.

C developing weapons that would intercept and destroy incoming nuclear missiles.

D severely reducing the number of American troops stationed worldwide.

Test-Taking Tip: Eliminate answers that do not make sense. Reducing the number of American troops (answer D), for example, probably would not strengthen the military.

HISTORY Online
Have students visit the Web site at tarvol2.glencoe.com to review Chapter 28 and take the Self-Check Quiz.

Chapter Activity
28. Graphs will vary. Students should be able to back up their ratings with logical reasoning.

Geography and History
29. **a.** 102 votes of the 270 needed in the Electoral College; **b.** Northeast and Pacific coast

---

Standardized Test Practice

Answer: C
Test-Taking Tip: Remind students that another name for the Strategic Defense Initiative is Star Wars. That should lead them to the fact that the initiative is probably technologically advanced. Answer C seems to be the answer that is most focused on technology. The correct answer is C.

Bonus Question ?

What industries were deregulated during the Reagan years? (*oil and gas, automobile, cable television, and airline*)

25.

Issues	Reagan Administration	Bush Administration
Domestic	stagflation growing deficit	recession unemployment growing deficit
Foreign	Soviet invasion of Afghanistan Grenada Iran-Contra scandal	Eastern Europe collapse of Soviet Union Tiananmen Square

Practicing Skills
26. Comparisons will help students analyze various media sources.

Writing Activity
27. Reports will vary but should include information about political, social, and economic conditions in the chosen country.

Chapter 29 Resources

Timesaving Tools

TeacherWorks™ All-In-One Planner and Resource Center

- **Interactive Teacher Edition** Access your Teacher Wraparound Edition and your classroom resources with a few easy clicks.
- **Interactive Lesson Planner** Planning has never been easier! Organize your week, month, semester, or year with all the lesson helps you need to make teaching creative, timely, and relevant.

Use Glencoe's **Presentation Plus!** multimedia teacher tool to easily present dynamic lessons that visually excite your students. Using Microsoft PowerPoint® you can customize the presentations to create your own personalized lessons.

TEACHING TRANSPARENCIES

Graphic Organizer 14 L2

Why It Matters Chapter Transparency 29 L2

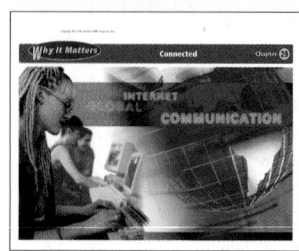

APPLICATION AND ENRICHMENT

Linking Past and Present Activity 29 L2

Enrichment Activity 29 L3

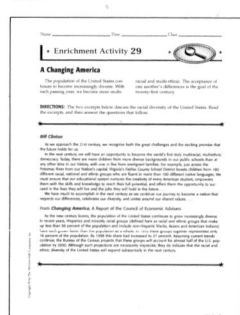

Primary Source Reading 29 L2

REVIEW AND REINFORCEMENT

Reteaching Activity 29 L1

Vocabulary Activity 29 L1

Time Line Activity 29 L2

Critical Thinking Skills Activity 29 L2

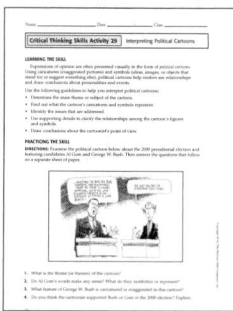

Meeting NCSS Standards

The following standards are covered in Chapter 29:

Section 1	VII	Production, Distribution, and Consumption: D, F
Section 2	VII	Production, Distribution, and Consumption: A, C, F
Section 3	IX	Global Connections: B, C, D, E
Section 4	VI	Power, Authority, and Governance: B, C, E, G
Section 5	IX	Global Connections: A, B, D, G

Local Standards

ASSESSMENT AND EVALUATION

Chapter 29 Test Form A L2

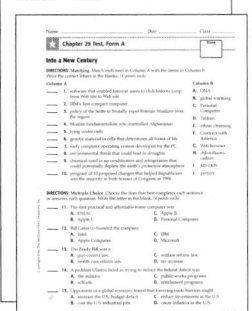

Chapter 29 Test Form B L2

Standardized Test Practice Workbook Activity 29 L2

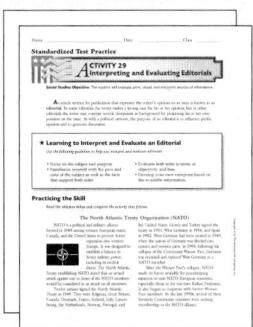

Performance Assessment Activities and Rubrics 29 L1/ELL

ExamView® Pro Testmaker CD-ROM

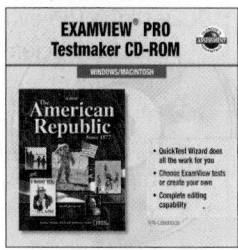

MULTIMEDIA

- Vocabulary PuzzleMaker CD-ROM
- Interactive Tutor Self-Assessment CD-ROM
- ExamView® Pro Testmaker CD-ROM
- Audio Program
- American History Primary Source Documents Library CD-ROM
- MindJogger Videoquiz
- Presentation Plus! CD-ROM
- TeacherWorks™ CD-ROM
- Interactive Student Edition CD-ROM
- Glencoe Skillbuilder Interactive Workbook CD-ROM, Level 2
- The *American Republic Since 1877* Video Program
- American Music: Hits Through History
- American Music: Cultural Traditions

SPANISH RESOURCES

The following Spanish language materials are available:

- Spanish Reading Essentials and Study Guide
- Spanish Guided Reading Activities
- Spanish Reteaching Activities
- Spanish Quizzes and Tests
- Spanish Vocabulary Activities
- Spanish Summaries
- The Declaration of Independence and United States Constitution Spanish Translation

The following videotape programs are available from Glencoe as supplements to Chapter 29:

- **Bill Clinton: In the Running** (ISBN 1-56-501824-9)
- **Hillary Rodham Clinton** (ISBN 1-56-501371-9)
- **Colin Powell: A Soldier's Campaign** (ISBN 1-56-501701-3)

To order, call Glencoe at 1-800-334-7344. To find classroom resources to accompany many of these videos, check the following home pages:
A&E Television: www.aande.com
The History Channel: www.historychannel.com

Use our Web site for additional resources. All essential content is covered in the Student Edition.

You and your students can visit tarvol2.glencoe.com, the Web site companion to the *American Republic Since 1877*. This innovative integration of electronic and print media offers your students a wealth of opportunities. The student text directs students to the Web site for the following options:

- **Chapter Overviews**
- **Self-Check Quizzes**
- **Student Web Activities**
- **Textbook Updates**

Answers to the student Web activities are provided for you in the **Web Activity Lesson Plans.** Additional Web resources and Interactive Tutor Puzzles are also available.

Chapter 29 Resources

SECTION RESOURCES

Daily Objectives	Reproducible Resources	Multimedia Resources
SECTION 1 **The Technological Revolution** 1. Describe the evolution of the computer from scientific tool to household appliance. 2. Evaluate how the computer has revolutionized science, medicine, and communications.	Reproducible Lesson Plan 29–1 Daily Lecture and Discussion Notes 29–1 Guided Reading Activity 29–1* Section Quiz 29–1* Reading Essentials and Study Guide 29–1* Performance Assessment Activities and Rubrics American History in Graphic Novel	Daily Focus Skills Transparency 29–1 Interactive Tutor Self-Assessment CD-ROM ExamView® Pro Testmaker CD-ROM* Presentation Plus! CD-ROM TeacherWorks™ CD-ROM Audio Program
SECTION 2 **The Clinton Years** 1. Describe the difficulties and successes of Bill Clinton's two terms as president. 2. Discuss the nation's involvement in world affairs during the Clinton presidency.	Reproducible Lesson Plan 29–2 Daily Lecture and Discussion Notes 29–2 Guided Reading Activity 29–2* Section Quiz 29–2* Reading Essentials and Study Guide 29–2* Performance Assessment Activities and Rubrics	Daily Focus Skills Transparency 29–2 Interactive Tutor Self-Assessment CD-ROM ExamView® Pro Testmaker CD-ROM* Presentation Plus! CD-ROM TeacherWorks™ CD-ROM Audio Program American Music: Hits Through History
SECTION 3 **An Interdependent World** 1. Explain the development of regional economic blocs around the world. 2. Assess environmental issues that have become important internationally.	Reproducible Lesson Plan 29–3 Daily Lecture and Discussion Notes 29–3 Guided Reading Activity 29–3* Section Quiz 29–3* Reading Essentials and Study Guide 29–3* Performance Assessment Activities and Rubrics	Daily Focus Skills Transparency 29–3 Interactive Tutor Self-Assessment CD-ROM ExamView® Pro Testmaker CD-ROM* Presentation Plus! CD-ROM TeacherWorks™ CD-ROM Audio Program
SECTION 4 **America Enters a New Century** 1. Describe the unusual circumstances surrounding the outcome of the 2000 presidential election. 2. Evaluate the programs President George W. Bush initiated.	Reproducible Lesson Plan 29–4 Daily Lecture and Discussion Notes 29–4 Guided Reading Activity 29–4* Section Quiz 29–4* Reading Essentials and Study Guide 29–4* Performance Assessment Activities and Rubrics American History in Graphic Novel	Daily Focus Skills Transparency 29–4 Interactive Tutor Self-Assessment CD-ROM ExamView® Pro Testmaker CD-ROM* Presentation Plus! CD-ROM Skillbuilder Interactive Workbook, Level 2 TeacherWorks™ CD-ROM Audio Program
SECTION 5 **The War on Terrorism** 1. Describe the development of Middle East terrorism. 2. Explain the response of the United States to the terrorist attacks on the World Trade Center and the Pentagon.	Reproducible Lesson Plan 29–5 Daily Lecture and Discussion Notes 29–5 Guided Reading Activity 29–5* Section Quiz 29–5* Reading Essentials and Study Guide 29–5* Performance Assessment Activities and Rubrics	Daily Focus Skills Transparency 29–5 Interactive Tutor Self-Assessment CD-ROM ExamView® Pro Testmaker CD-ROM* Presentation Plus! CD-ROM TeacherWorks™ CD-ROM Vocabulary PuzzleMaker CD-ROM* Audio Program

0:00 OUT OF TIME?
Assign the Chapter 29 **Reading Essentials and Study Guide.**

*Also Available in Spanish

 Printed Materials   Transparency   CD-ROM   DVD

Poster   Music Program   Audio Program

Chapter 29 Resources

NATIONAL GEOGRAPHIC Teacher's Corner

INDEX TO NATIONAL GEOGRAPHIC MAGAZINE

The following articles relate to this chapter.
- "Grand Staircase Escalante," July 1999
- "Rediscovering America," January 2000
- "Robot Revolution," July 1997
- "Unveiling the Universe," October 1999

NATIONAL GEOGRAPHIC SOCIETY PRODUCTS

To order the following, call National Geographic at 1-800-368-2728:
- *Branches of Government Series* (Video)
- *Democratic Government Series: The United States* (Video)
- *Historical Atlas of the United States* (Atlas)
- *National Geographic World Atlas for Young Explorers–Classroom Library Edition* (Guide, Transparencies, Resource Masters)

NGS ONLINE

Access National Geographic's Web site for current events, atlas updates, activities, links, interactive features, and archives.
www.nationalgeographic.com

MEETING SPECIAL NEEDS

In addition to the Differentiated Instruction strategies found in each section, the following resources are also suitable for your special needs students:
- *ExamView® Pro Testmaker CD-ROM* allows teachers to tailor tests by reducing answer choices.
- The *Audio Program* includes the entire narrative of the student edition so that less-proficient readers can listen to the words as they read them.
- The *Reading Essentials and Study Guide* provides the same content as the student edition but is written two grade levels below the textbook.

KEY TO ABILITY LEVELS

Teaching strategies have been coded.

L1 BASIC activities for all students
L2 AVERAGE activities for average to above-average students
L3 CHALLENGING activities for above-average students
ELL ENGLISH LANGUAGE LEARNER activities

From the Classroom of...

Philip Prale
Oak Park and River Forest
High School
Oak Park, IL

Into the Next Century–The Keeper's Project

The purpose of this project is to analyze developments of the 1900s and explain why they are worth keeping in this new century.

Construct a list of five to ten items that are Twentieth Century Keepers. Variations include:

1. Draw keepers from specific categories—Political, Economic, Social, Cultural, Religious, or Environmental.
2. Add one item that you would want to eliminate in this new century.
3. For each item write a description of the item and how it fits into the category.
4. Write an introductory paragraph explaining the general connection, besides time, of the keepers. What is the theme or central idea?
5. Make a poster with images or produce a PowerPoint® presentation of the material.

ADDITIONAL RESOURCES FROM GLENCOE

- American Music: Cultural Traditions
- American Art & Architecture
- Outline Map Resource Book
- U.S. Desk Map
- Building Geography Skills for Life
- Inclusion for the High School Social Studies Classroom Strategies and Activities
- Teaching Strategies for the American History Classroom (Including Block Scheduling Pacing Guides)
- Dinah Zike's High School American History Reading and Study Skills Foldables

 Block Schedule

Activities that are suited to use within the block scheduling framework are identified by:

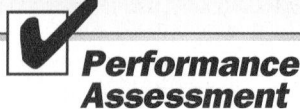

Performance Assessment

Refer to Activity 29 in the Performance Assessment Activities and Rubrics booklet.

Why It Matters Activity

As a class, have students list the ways in which businesses, schools, governments, and individuals use the Internet. **Ask: How important has the Internet become to everyday life in the United States?** Students should evaluate their answers after they have completed the chapter.

GLENCOE
TECHNOLOGY

The *American Republic Since 1877* Video Program
To learn more about how the American public dealt with the attacks of September 11, 2001, have students view the Chapter 29 video, "America's Response to Terrorism," from the *American Republic Since 1877* Video Program.

MindJogger Videoquiz
Use the **MindJogger Videoquiz** to preview Chapter 29 content.

Both programs available in DVD

CHAPTER
29 Into a New Century *1992–present*

Why It Matters

During the 1990s, a technological revolution transformed society. President Clinton pushed for budget cuts, health care and welfare reforms, and global trade. He also worked for peace in the Middle East and the Balkans. In 2000 George W. Bush won the presidency. He supported tax cuts, a new energy program, increased trade, and a missile defense system. After terrorists killed thousands of people in the United States, the new president launched a war on terrorism.

The Impact Today

Major developments of the era continue to influence modern society.
- *The use of the Internet is widespread in commerce, schools, and government.*
- *The North American Free Trade Agreement (NAFTA) continues to shape economic relations between the United States, Canada, and Mexico.*
- *The debate between conservatives and liberals continues in the United States.*

The* American Republic Since 1877 *Video The Chapter 29 video, "America's Response to Terrorism," examines how ordinary Americans responded to the terrorist attacks in New York City and Washington, D.C.

United States PRESIDENTS

G. Bush 1989–1993 · Clinton 1993–2001

1993
- Mosaic, the first popular Web browser, is released

1995
- Budget impasse shuts down federal government
- Oklahoma City bombing

1996
- Bill Clinton reelected

1998
- House of Representatives impeaches President Clinton

1990 · 1994 · 1998

World

1992
- Earth Day summit held in Rio de Janeiro, Brazil

1993
- Israeli-Palestinian peace accord signed
- European Union launched

1994
- Multiracial elections held in South Africa; Nelson Mandela elected president
- U.S., Mexico, and Canada inaugurate NAFTA

1995
- Cease-fire signed in Bosnian war

1997
- Britain returns control of Hong Kong to

890

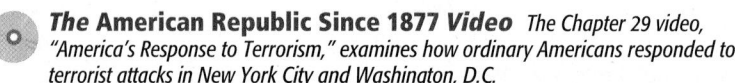

Reading Strategy — PURPOSE FOR READING

Venn Diagram These diagrams help students compare and/or contrast two or more items. Presidents Bill Clinton and George W. Bush have different personalities and faced different issues during their presidencies. Have students draw two overlapping circles on their papers. They should title one "Bill Clinton" and one "George W. Bush." As students study the chapter, have them compare and contrast the presidents by writing information for each in the appropriate circle. Information that both men share fits in the overlapping area. **L1**

Refer to ***Inclusion for the High School Social Studies Classroom Strategies and Activities*** in the TCR.

President Bush greets the soldiers of Ft. Campbell, Kentucky in March 2004.

2001
- Terrorist attacks destroy World Trade Center and damage Pentagon

2003
- Space shuttle *Columbia* explodes during reentry
- U.S. led coalition launches war on Iraq

2004
- George W. Bush reelected

2005
- Hurricane Katrina floods New Orleans

ctoral crisis
ays naming of
d president

G.W. Bush 2001–

2002

2006

o's election of
te Fox ends 71 years
gle-party rule

2003
- Serbian prime minister Zoran Djindjic assassinated

2004
- Sudan government and rebels reach agreement to end 21-year civil war
- Devastating tsunami hits southeast Asia

2005
- London subway system bombed

891

HISTORY
Online

Chapter Overview
Visit the *American Republic Since 1877* Web site at tarvol2.glencoe.com and click on **Chapter Overviews— Chapter 29** to preview chapter information.

GRAPHIC ORGANIZER ACTIVITY

Organizing Information Have students use a graphic organizer similar to the one at right to identify changes that have occurred in the United States since 1992. *(Answers may include the rise of the compact computer, the telecommunications revolution, the rise of the Internet, welfare reform, the growth of global economy, and the increase in terrorism.)*

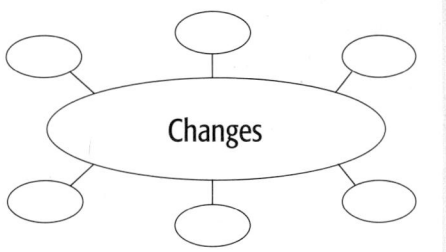

Changes

HISTORY
Online

Introduce students to chapter content and key terms by having them access the **Chapter 29 Overview** at tarvol2.glencoe.com.

More About the Photo

President George W. Bush visited Fort Campbell on the eve of the anniversary of Operation Iraqi Freedom. "Every one of you is making a difference. . . ." Bush told the thousands of troops in attendance. "Because of your service, because of your bravery, because of your dedication, the world is better off and the American people are more secure." Ask students what the significance of Ft. Campbell was. *(It was the first army base visited by the President after the attacks of September 11, 2001.)*

TIME LINE ACTIVITY

Have students review the items on the time line and classify each as something they knew about or something they did not know about. Have students select one of the items about which they know little or nothing and research it to learn at least one fact related to the event.

FOLDABLES™
Study Organizer

Dinah Zike's Foldables are three-dimensional, interactive graphic organizers that help students practice basic writing skills, review key vocabulary terms, and identify main ideas. Have students complete the foldable activity in the *Dinah Zike's Reading and Study Skills Foldables* booklet.

891

1 FOCUS

Section Overview

This section focuses on the history of the technology revolution.

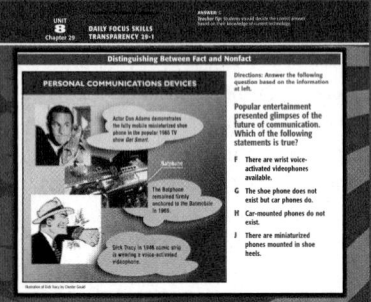
Reading Preview

Answers to Graphic:
Microprocessors: reduced computers' size, increased their speed, and expanded their function; Apple II: first practical and affordable computer; Macintosh: popularized mouse and graphic icons; Windows: made Macintosh innovations widespread

Preteaching Vocabulary
Have students choose one of the proper names from the list of Key Terms and Names. Ask students to skim the text to find the term and write a brief explanation.

SECTION 1 The Technological Revolution

Guide to Reading

Main Idea
The introduction of the first electronic digital computer in 1946 launched a technological revolution.

Key Terms and Names
ENIAC, integrated circuit, Silicon Valley, microprocessor, Bill Gates, software, telecommute, Internet, biotechnology, James Watson, Francis Crick, DNA

Reading Strategy
Categorizing As you read about the computer age, complete a chart similar to the one below to describe products that revolutionized the computer industry.

	How It Revolutionized Computer Industry
Microprocessors	
Apple II	
Macintosh	
Windows	

Reading Objectives
• **Describe** the evolution of the computer from scientific tool to household appliance.
• **Evaluate** how the computer has revolutionized science, medicine, and communications.

Section Theme
Economic Factors The computer has helped reshape the nation's economy.

Preview of Events

♦1993 ♦1999 ♦2005

1993
Mosaic, the first popular Web browser, introduced

1999
Over 86 million Americans own cell phones

2001
Human Genome Project maps the human genome

2004
New Jersey allows medical research on embryonic stem cells

★ An American Story ★

Michael Kinsley

After years as a magazine editor and television news commentator, Michael Kinsley jumped into the new technology of the Internet in 1996, by agreeing to edit an online magazine called *Slate*. "I was determined," Kinsley said, "to be on the next train to pull out of the station no matter where it was going—provided that I was the engineer."

Soon newspaper and print magazines were also developing Web resources. Television stations also used the Internet to update news stories, allowing consumers to access news when and how they wanted. As Kinsley explained:

❝Web readers *surf.* They go quickly from site to site. If they really like a particular site, they may visit it often, but they are unlikely to devote a continuous half-hour or more to any one site. . . . This appears to be in the nature of the Web and not something that is likely to change.❞

—from *"Slate* Goes Free," *Slate,* February 13, 1999

The Rise of the Compact Computer

The development of a computer capable of supporting publications such as *Slate* began at the end of World War II. The world's first electronic digital computer, called **ENIAC** (Electronic Numerical Integrator and Computer), went into operation in

---

February 1946. ENIAC weighed over 30 tons and was the size of a small house. In early 1959, Robert Noyce designed the first **integrated circuit**—a complete electronic circuit on a single chip of silicon—which made circuits much smaller and very easy to manufacture. Noyce's company was located south of San Francisco. As new companies sprang up nearby to make products using integrated circuits, the region became known as **Silicon Valley.**

In 1968 Noyce and colleague Gordon Moore formed Intel, for "Integrated Electronics," a company that revolutionized computers by combining on a single chip several integrated circuits containing both memory and computing functions. Called micro-processors, these new chips further reduced the size of computers and increased their speed.

Computers for Everyone Using microprocessor technology, Stephen Wozniak and his 20-year-old friend Steven Jobs set out to build a small computer suitable for personal use. In 1976 they founded Apple Computer and completed the Apple I. The following year they introduced the Apple II, the first practical and affordable home computer.

Apple's success sparked intense competition in the computer industry. In 1981 International Business

Picturing **History**

Apple Founders In 1984 Apple president John Sculley (center), along with Steve Jobs (left) and Steve Wozniak, show off their new briefcase-sized Apple IIc computer. On what basic technology do personal computers rely?

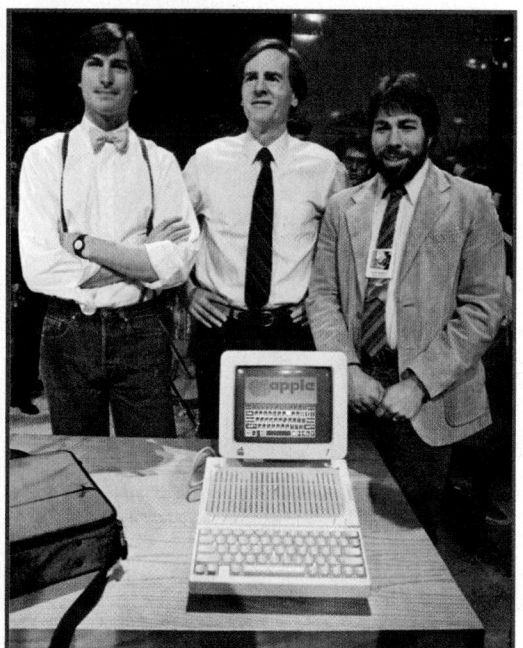

Machines (IBM) introduced its own compact machine, which it called the **"Personal Computer"** (PC). Apple responded in 1984 with the revolutionary **Macintosh,** a new model featuring a simplified operating system using on-screen graphic symbols called icons, which users could manipulate with a hand-operated device called a mouse.

Bill Gates and Microsoft

As Jobs and Wozniak were creating Apple, 19-year-old Harvard dropout **Bill Gates** co-founded Microsoft to design PC software, the instructions used to program computers to perform desired tasks. In 1980 IBM hired Microsoft to develop an operating system for its new PC. Gates quickly paid a Seattle programmer $50,000 for the rights to his software, and with some refinements, it became MS-DOS (Microsoft Disk Operating System).

In 1985 Microsoft introduced the "Windows" operating system, which enabled PCs to use the mouse-activated, on-screen graphic icons that the Macintosh had popularized. Soaring sales and rising Microsoft stock values made Gates a billionaire at the age of 31.

Compact computers became essential tools in virtually every kind of business. By the late 1990s, many workers began to "telecommute"—use computers and electronic mail to do their jobs from home via computer. The creation of wireless handheld devices and laptop computers has made computer use even more convenient. Now Internet access is available in a great deal more places and the use of the Internet is becoming much more commonplace.

✔ **Reading Check** **Describing** How was Microsoft different from other computer companies?

The Telecommunications Revolution

A parallel revolution in communications coincided with the growing impact of computers. In the 1970s, 1980s, and 1990s, the government loosened telecommunications regulations, allowing more companies to compete in the telephone and television industries. In 1996 Congress passed the Tele-communications Act. This act allowed telephone companies to compete with each other and to send

2 TEACH

Daily Lecture and Discussion Notes 29–1

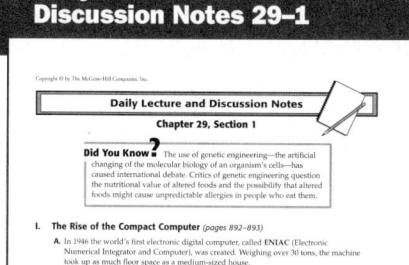

Copyright © by The McGraw-Hill Companies, Inc.

Daily Lecture and Discussion Notes

Chapter 29, Section 1

Did You Know ? The use of genetic engineering—the artificial changing of the molecular biology of an organism's cells—has caused international debate. Critics of genetic engineering question the nutritional value of altered foods and the possibility that altered foods might cause unpredictable allergies in people who eat them.

I. The Rise of the Compact Computer *(pages 892–893)*

A. In 1946 the world's first electronic digital computer, called **ENIAC** (Electronic Numerical Integrator and Computer), was created. Weighing over 30 tons, the machine took up as much floor space as a medium-sized house.

B. In 1957 Gordon Moore, Robert Noyce, and other scientists and engineers developed

HISTORY
Online

Objectives and answers to the student activity can be found in the **Web Activity Lesson Plan** at tarvol2.glencoe.com.

> **Reading Strategy**

Creating an Outline Have students create an outline for this section. Suggest that they use the headings as a starting point. **L1**
ELL

✔ **Reading Check**

Answer: The company purchased its original software rather than creating it from scratch.

Picturing **History**

Answer: microprocessor technology
Ask: How did Intel revolutionize computers? *(Intel combined several integrated circuits on a single chip containing both memory and computing functions.)*

> **Reading Strategy** **READING THE TEXT**

Using Graphic Organizers Organize students into small groups and have them create a time line illustrating the advances in technology during their lifetimes. Instruct students to start their time line with the year the first member of the group was born and try to find a significant event or milestone for each year up until the present time. Students may also add events outlined in the section that occurred before their lifetime. As a class, have students review the time lines from each group and make a composite time line. **L1**

📖 Refer to *Inclusion for the High School Social Studies Classroom Strategies and Activities* in the TCR.

✓ Reading Check

Answer: It created competition in the industry, generating innovation.

L1/ELL

Guided Reading Activity 29–1

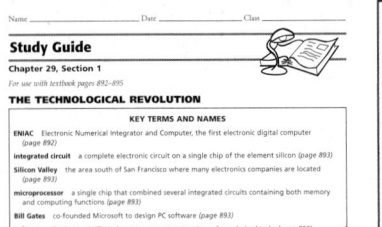

Name _____ Date _____ Class _____

★ Guided Reading Activity **29-1**

DIRECTIONS: *Recalling Facts* Read the section and answer the questions below. Refer to your textbook to write the answers.

1. When did the world's first electronic computer (ENIAC) go into operation? _____
2. What is an integrated circuit, and when was the first one developed? _____
3. What was the first practical and affordable computer for personal use? _____
4. What did Bill Gates and Microsoft design? _____
5. How did computer networks change the workplace? _____
6. How did the Telecommunications Act of 1996 change the industry? _____

✓ Reading Check

Answer: It created a global information system and encouraged the development of new software. It also spawned the "dot.com" economy.

TECHNOLOGY & History

Answer: Students might suggest that MRI is safer than x-rays or surgery and provides clearer images.

3 ASSESS

Assign Section 1 Assessment as homework or as an in-class activity.

🔲 Have students use the **Interactive Tutor Self-Assessment CD-ROM.**

L1/ELL

Reading Essentials and Study Guide 29–1

Name _____ Date _____ Class _____

Study Guide

Chapter 29, Section 1

For use with textbook pages 892–895

THE TECHNOLOGICAL REVOLUTION

KEY TERMS AND NAMES

ENIAC Electronic Numerical Integrator and Computer, the first electronic digital computer *(page 892)*

integrated circuit a complete electronic circuit on a single chip of the element silicon *(page 893)*

Silicon Valley the area south of San Francisco where many electronics companies are located *(page 893)*

microprocessor a single chip that combined several integrated circuits containing both memory and computing functions *(page 893)*

Bill Gates co-founded Microsoft to design PC software *(page 893)*

software the instructions that program computers to perform desired tasks *(page 893)*

---

television signals, but it also permitted cable television companies to offer telephone service. Such developments spurred the creation of new technologies such as Web-enabled cellular phones and other mixing of data-platforms.

✓ **Reading Check** **Explaining** How did deregulation affect the telecommunications industry?

The Rise of the Internet

Digital electronics also made possible a new worldwide communications system. The Internet let computer users post and receive information and communicate with each other. It had its roots in a computer networking system that the U.S. Defense Department's Advanced Research Project Agency established in 1969. Known as ARPANET, this system linked government agencies, defense contractors, and scientists at various universities, enabling them to communicate with each other by electronic mail. In 1985 the National Science Foundation funded several supercomputer centers across the country. This paved the way for the Internet, a global information system that operated commercially rather than through the government.

At first, Internet users employed different types of information. With the development of the hypertext transport protocol (http) and new software known as Web browsers, the Internet rapidly expanded. Users could now click on Internet links using their computer mouse and easily jump from Web site to Web site. Internet use expanded by almost 300 percent between 1997 and 2000.

The Internet also spawned a "dot-com" economy (from the common practice of using a business name as a World Wide Web address, followed by ".com"). Seemingly rich with promise, a wide variety of dot.com companies made millions of dollars for stock investors without ever earning actual profit from operations. Internet-related stocks helped fuel the prosperity of the 1990s but dropped dramatically in 2000, raising questions about the ultimate profitability of online companies.

✓ **Reading Check** **Explaining** How did the Internet expand business opportunities?

Breakthroughs in Biotechnology

Computers greatly assisted scientists engaged in **biotechnology**—the managing of biological systems to improve human life. Computers made it possible to study and manipulate genes and cells at the molecular level. Through biotechnology, researchers developed new medicines, animal growth

TECHNOLOGY & History

Magnetic Resonance Imaging

One extension of computer technology is magnetic resonance imaging (MRI). An MRI allows physicians to diagnose certain diseases, abnormalities, and injuries without resorting to x-rays or surgery. An MRI unit is made up of a large cylindrical magnet, devices for transmitting and receiving radio signals, and a computer. *Why do you think physicians prefer MRIs over x-rays and surgery?*

1 A large **cylindrical magnet** with a magnetic field 30,000 times stronger than the earth's magnetic field surrounds the patient.

2 **Radio signals** are transmitted within the machine and pass through the patient's body.

3 A **computer** converts the radio signals into precise images of the body's internal structure.

cylindrical magnet

computer

radio signals

DIFFERENTIATED INSTRUCTION

At-Risk Students Work with a computer teacher or someone from the community who works with computers to provide a hands-on demonstration of how computer technology is used in a variety of daily activities. If possible, plan a field trip to a local business or industry where students can see technology in action. Have students write a journal entry about their experience. **L1**

📁 Refer to ***Inclusion for the High School Social Studies Classroom Strategies and Activities*** in the TCR.

hormones, genetically engineered plants, and industrial chemicals.

Unraveling the Secrets of Life

The first steps toward biotechnology came in 1953, when American molecular biologist **James Watson** and his British colleague, **Francis Crick,** deciphered the structure of deoxyribonucleic acid (DNA). DNA is the genetic material in cells that determine all forms of life.

Once scientists learned how to read the message of DNA, their new knowledge improved medical research and provided law enforcement with new methods of identification. Further research has assisted genetic engineering for plants, animals, and humans.

The Human Genome Project

Super computers have also helped map the human genome, the DNA sequence for the human species. Real advances began in earnest at the National Institutes of Health (NIH) in 1990 after NIH made its data available to all scientists on the Internet. It hoped to prevent any single nation or private laboratory from limiting the use of genome findings. In February 2001, the project completed its first map of the human genome. Since this important medical advance, medical research has grown even more sophisticated. Today doctors, religious experts, and politicians debate the advisability of human cloning and the possibilities of "reprogramming"

Profiles IN HISTORY

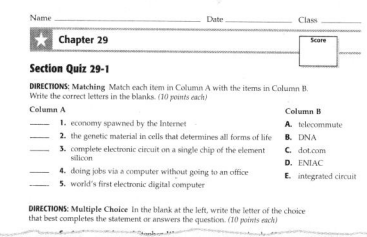

Jerry Yang
1968–

Jerry Yang was born in Taiwan in 1968 and immigrated with his family to San Jose, California, when he was 10 years old. Yang is a cofounder of Yahoo!, one of the world's best-known gateways to information and consumer goods on the Web. It is estimated that by the late 1990s, around 40 million people were visiting the Yahoo! Web site every month.

The company developed out of Yang's desire to be able to find good Web sites quickly. At Stanford University, he and cofounder David Filo were doctoral students sharing office space in a trailer. They also shared information on their favorite Web sites, and Yang began compiling a list of them. He nicknamed the list "Jerry's Guide to the World Wide Web," and he posted it on the Internet.

Inquiries to the site boomed, and Yang and Filo concluded that they had found an untapped market. With the help of a loan from an imaginative venture capitalist, Yahoo! was born. Yang says they chose the name because it suggested the sort of "Wild West" character of the Internet. The mission for Yahoo! was not just to collect Web sites but to organize them into convenient categories, such as news, sports, games, and weather. Yahoo! became a popular gateway, or "portal," to the Web.

fetal stem cells to become other tissue to help cure persistent diseases or improve organ replacement. The federal government has federal money on stem cell research, but new studies from Harvard University may indicate that similar "reprogramming" techniques can be applied to skin cells rather than fetal stem cells.

✔ Reading Check **Explaining** How did computers assist the development of biotechnology?

SECTION 1 ASSESSMENT

HISTORY Online **Study Central™** To review this section, go to **tarvol2.glencoe.com** and click on **Study Central™**.

Checking for Understanding
1. **Define:** microprocessor, software, telecommute, Internet, DNA.
2. **Identify:** ENIAC, integrated circuit, Silicon Valley, Bill Gates, biotechnology, James Watson, Francis Crick.
3. **Explain** how scientific discoveries in biotechnology have improved people's lives.

Reviewing Themes
4. **Economic Factors** How have personal computers transformed the workplace?

Critical Thinking
5. **Analyzing** How have advances in telecommunications and the rise of the Internet affected the standard of living in the United States?
6. **Organizing** Complete a graphic organizer similar to the one below by listing developments that led to the technological revolution.

Technological Revolution

Analyzing Visuals
7. **Analyzing Photographs** Study the crowd in the photograph of George W. Bush at Ft. Campbell on page 891. How would you describe the attitudes reflected in the faces of the people photographed?

Writing About History
8. **Descriptive Writing** Write two paragraphs describing the ways that you and your family use the Internet and how your way of life would be different without it.

CHAPTER 29 Into a New Century **895**

SECTION 1 ASSESSMENT ANSWERS

1. Terms are in blue.
2. ENIAC (p. 892), integrated circuit (p. 893), Silicon Valley (p. 893), Bill Gates (p. 893), biotechnology (p. 894), James Watson (p. 895), Francis Crick (p. 895)
3. led to the development of artificial genes and assisted genetic engineering of plants, animals, and humans
4. linked employees, became essential in all kinds of business, and allowed people to telecommute
5. New technology, such as Web-enabled cell phones and the Internet, made a new communications system possible and spawned the "dot.com" economy.
6. deregulation of telecommunications industry, microprocessors, Internet, personal computers, wireless technology
7. most look happy; the Bush family looks proud
8. Students' paragraphs will vary.

Profiles IN HISTORY

Ask: Before naming it Yahoo!, what did Yang call his site? *(Jerry's Guide to the World Wide Web)*

Reteach
Have students describe the evolution of the computer from scientific tool to household appliance.

Enrich
Have students prepare a demonstration of how they use the Internet for a specific purpose.

✔ Reading Check

Answer: Computers made it possible to study and manipulate genes and cells at the molecular level.

HISTORY Online

Study Central™ provides summaries, interactive games, and online graphic organizers to help students review section content.

4 CLOSE

Ask: How has the computer revolutionized daily life?

1 FOCUS

Section Overview

This section focuses on the Clinton administration.

BELLRINGER
Skillbuilder Activity

Project transparency and have students answer the question.

Daily Focus Skills Transparency 29–2

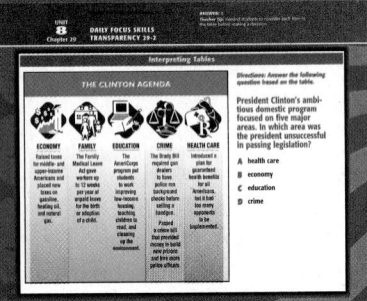

Reading Preview

Answers to Graphic:
I. Clinton's Agenda
   A. Raising Taxes, Cutting Spending
   B. Stumbling on Health Care
   C. Families and Education
   D. Crime and Gun Control
Students should complete the outline by including all heads in the section.

Preteaching Vocabulary
Have students create a two-column list with the heads Domestic Issues and Foreign Policy. Instruct students to list the Key Terms and Names under the appropriate heading.

SECTION 2 The Clinton Years

Guide to Reading

Main Idea
Although President Clinton struggled with Republicans in Congress and faced impeachment, several major economic and social reforms were achieved during his presidency.

Key Terms and Names
AmeriCorps, Contract with America, Kenneth Starr, perjury, ethnic cleansing, Dayton Accords

Reading Strategy
Taking Notes As you read about the administration of President Clinton, use the major headings of the section to create an outline similar to the one below.

The Clinton Years
I. Clinton's Agenda
   A.
   B.
   C.
   D.
II.

Reading Objectives
- **Describe** the difficulties and successes of Bill Clinton's two terms as president.
- **Discuss** the nation's involvement in world affairs during the Clinton presidency.

Section Theme
Economic Factors The United States, along with much of the industrialized world, experienced economic prosperity in the 1990s.

Preview of Events

♦1993	♦1995	♦1997	♦1999

1993 Israeli-Palestinian peace accord

1994 Republicans win both houses of Congress

1995 Federal government shuts down during budget impasse

1998 House impeaches Clinton

1999 Senate acquits Clinton; NATO aircraft bomb Serbia

★ An American Story ★

George Stephanopoulos

Bill Clinton was the third-youngest person ever to serve as president and the first of the "baby boom" generation to reach the Oval Office. Clinton brought with him a team of young energetic advisers. In the early weeks of the administration, Clinton's team spent many hours at the White House adjusting to their new life. In early 1993, they began discussing plans for Clinton's new economic strategy for paying down the deficit and reducing interest rates. George Stephanopoulos, an aide to the president, remembers their inexperienced beginnings:

66 The president presided over the rolling Roosevelt Room meetings in shirtsleeves, with glasses sliding down the end of his nose. . . . Clinton let everyone have a say, played us off against one another, asked pointed questions, and took indecipherable notes. But the reminders of who we were and what we were doing was never far away. Late one night, we ordered pizzas. When they arrived, the president grabbed a slice with the rest of us . . . [b]ut just before he took his first bite, [a secret service] agent placed a hand on his shoulder and told him to put it down. The pie hadn't been screened. . . .99

—quoted in *All Too Human*

Clinton's Agenda

Clinton's first years in office were filled with grandiose plans and the difficult realities of politics. The new president put forth an ambitious domestic program focusing on five major areas: the economy, the family, education, crime, and health care.

896 CHAPTER 29 Into a New Century

SECTION RESOURCES

📁 Reproducible Masters
- Reproducible Lesson Plan 29–2
- Daily Lecture and Discussion Notes 29–2
- Guided Reading Activity 29–2
- Section Quiz 29–2
- Reading Essentials and Study Guide 29–2

📖 Transparencies
- Daily Focus Skills Transparency 29–2

Multimedia
- 💿 Interactive Tutor Self-Assessment CD-ROM
- 💿 ExamView® Pro Testmaker CD-ROM
- 💿 Presentation Plus! CD-ROM
- 💿 TeacherWorks™ CD-ROM
- 🎧 Audio Program
- 🎵 American Music: Hits Through History

Raising Taxes, Cutting Spending As he had promised in his election campaign, Clinton focused first on the economy. The problem, in the president's view, was the federal deficit. Under Reagan and Bush, the deficit had nearly quadrupled, adding billions of dollars annually to the national debt. High deficits forced the government to borrow large sums of money to pay for its programs and helped to drive up interest rates.

Clinton believed that the key to economic growth was to lower interest rates. Low interest rates would enable businesses to borrow more money to expand and create more jobs. Low rates would also make it easier for consumers to borrow money for mortgages, car loans, and other items, which in turn would promote economic growth.

One way to bring interest rates down was to reduce the federal deficit. In early 1993, Clinton sent Congress a deficit reduction plan. In trying to cut the deficit, however, Clinton faced a serious problem. About half of all government spending went to entitlement programs, such as Social Security, Medicare, and veterans' benefits. Entitlement programs are very hard to cut because so many Americans depend on them.

Faced with these constraints, Clinton decided to raise taxes, even though he had promised to cut taxes during his campaign. Clinton's plan raised tax rates for middle- and upper-income Americans and placed new taxes on gasoline, heating oil, and natural gas. The tax increases were very unpopular, and Republicans in Congress refused to support them. Clinton pressured Democrats, and after many amendments, a modified version of Clinton's plan narrowly passed.

Stumbling on Health Care During his campaign, Clinton had promised to reform the U.S. health care system. An estimated 40 million Americans, or roughly 15 percent of the nation, did not have private health insurance. The president appointed a task force headed by his wife, **Hillary Rodham Clinton**—an unprecedented role for a first lady. The task force developed a plan that guaranteed health benefits for all Americans, but it put much of the burden of payment of these benefits on employers. Small-business owners feared they could not afford it. The insurance industry and doctors' organizations also opposed the plan.

Republicans opposed the plan as being complicated, costly, and reliant on government control. Congressional Democrats were divided. Some supported alternative plans, but no plan

had enough support to pass. Faced with public opposition, Clinton's plan died without ever coming to a vote.

Families and Education Clinton did manage to push several major pieces of legislation through Congress. During his campaign, he had stressed the need to help American families. His first success was the **Family Medical Leave Act.** This law gave workers up to 12 weeks per year of unpaid family leave for the birth or adoption of a child or for the illness of a family member.

Clinton also persuaded Congress to create the **AmeriCorps** program. This program put students to work improving low-income housing, teaching children to read, and cleaning up the environment. AmeriCorps volunteers earned a salary and were awarded a scholarship to continue their education.

Crime and Gun Control Clinton had promised to get tough on crime during his campaign. He had also strongly endorsed new gun-control laws. Despite strong opposition from many Republicans and the **National Rifle Association** (NRA), the Democrats in Congress passed a gun-control law known as the **Brady Bill.** The bill imposed a waiting period before people could buy handguns. It also required gun dealers to have police run a background check on a person's criminal record before selling them a handgun. The following year, Clinton introduced his first anticrime bill. The bill provided states with extra funds to build new prisons and put 100,000 more police officers on the streets.

✓ **Reading Check** **Explaining** Why did President Clinton's proposed health care plan fail?

Picturing **History**

High Hopes The Clintons entered the White House in 1993 determined to change the United States for the better. It took time for them to adjust to life in Washington, and many of their ambitious plans were defeated in Congress. *What legislative proposal was given to the First Lady to oversee?*

2 TEACH

Daily Lecture and Discussion Notes 29–2

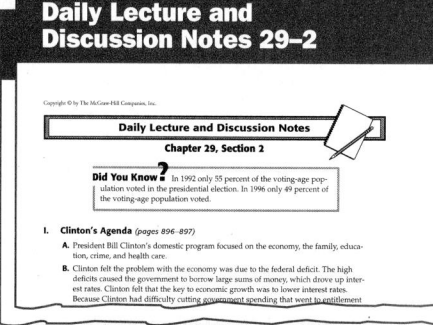

Copyright © by The McGraw-Hill Companies, Inc.

Daily Lecture and Discussion Notes

Chapter 29, Section 2

Did You Know ? In 1992 only 55 percent of the voting-age population voted in the presidential election. In 1996 only 49 percent of the voting-age population voted.

I.   Clinton's Agenda (pages 896–897)

   A. President Bill Clinton's domestic program focused on the economy, the family, education, crime, and health care.

   B. Clinton felt the problem with the economy was due to the federal deficit. The high deficits caused the government to borrow large sums of money, which drove up interest rates. Clinton felt that the key to economic growth was to lower interest rates. Because Clinton had difficulty cutting government spending that went to entitlement

Reading Strategy

Creating a Chart Have students create a chart similar to the one shown below to illustrate some of Clinton's domestic agenda. **L1**

	Issue	**Action**
Taxes		
Health Care		
Families		
Education		
Crime		
Gun Control		

📁 Use the rubric for creating a map, display, or chart on pages 65–66 in the *Performance Assessment Activities and Rubrics.*

Reading Check

Answer: Republicans said it was too costly and relied on federal control. Public opposition was also strong.

Picturing **History**

Answer: health care reform
Ask: What happened to health care reform? *(The plan died before a congressional vote.)*

Reading Strategy   READING THE TEXT

Understanding Vocabulary Remind students about the difference between *synonyms*, which are words that have similar meanings, and *antonyms*, which are words that have opposite meanings. Tell students they can easily remember this difference if they imagine that the "s" in synonyms stands for "same." As students read the text and encounter words that they are unfamiliar with, have them use a thesaurus to identify an appropriate synonym and antonym based on the words' context. **L1** **ELL**

📁 Refer to *Inclusion for the High School Social Studies Classroom Strategies and Activities* in the TCR.

Guided Reading Activity 29-2

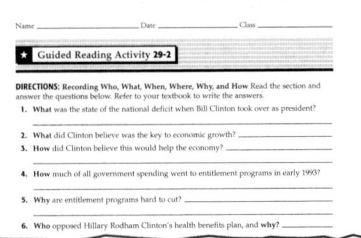

Name _____ Date _____ Class _____

★ Guided Reading Activity 29-2

DIRECTIONS: Recording Who, What, When, Where, Why, and How Read the section and answer the questions below. Refer to your textbook to write the answers.

1. What was the state of the national deficit when Bill Clinton took over as president?

2. What did Clinton believe was the key to economic growth?

3. How did Clinton believe this would help the economy?

4. How much of all government spending went to entitlement programs in early 1993?

5. Why are entitlement programs hard to cut?

6. Who opposed Hillary Rodham Clinton's health benefits plan, and why?

Picturing History

Answer: The Senate defeated several proposals, including the balanced budget amendment, while the president vetoed others.

Ask: Who was the leader of the Republicans who created the Contract with America? *(Newt Gingrich)*

✓ Reading Check

Answer: They agreed on health insurance portability and welfare reform.

FYI

William Jefferson Blythe IV was born in Hope, Arkansas, three months after his father died in a traffic accident. While in high school, Blythe took his stepfather's last name of Clinton. Bill Clinton graduated from Georgetown University and won a Rhodes Scholarship to Oxford University. At Yale University, he earned a law degree and met his future wife, law school classmate Hillary Rodham. After serving as the attorney general and governor of Arkansas, Clinton ran for president. His 1992 campaign video was titled "A Man from Hope."

Picturing History

Republicans Triumphant As a result of the 1994 midterm congressional elections, the Republican Party gained control of the House and the Senate for the first time since the 1950s. Newt Gingrich (at podium) helped lead a group of young GOP congressional representatives in passing the Contract with America legislation. How successful was the Contract with America legislation? Explain.

The Republicans Gain Control of Congress

Despite his successes, Clinton was very unpopular by late 1994. Instead of cutting taxes, he had raised them, and he had not fixed health care. Although the economy was improving, many companies were still downsizing. Several personal issues involving President Clinton further weakened public confidence in him. These factors convinced many Americans to vote Republican in 1994.

The Contract With America As the 1994 midterm elections neared, congressional Republicans, led by Newt Gingrich of Georgia, created the **Contract with America.** This program proposed 10 major changes, including lower taxes, welfare reform, tougher anti-crime laws, term limits for members of Congress, and a balanced budget amendment. Republicans won a stunning victory—for the first time in 40 years, they had a majority in both houses of Congress.

In their first 100 days in office, House Republicans passed almost the entire Contract with America, but they soon ran into trouble. The Senate defeated several proposals, including the balanced budget amendment, while the president vetoed others.

The Budget Battle In 1995 the Republicans lost more momentum when they clashed with the president over the new federal budget. Clinton vetoed several Republican budget proposals, claiming they cut into social programs too much. Gingrich believed that if Republicans stood firm, the president would back down. Otherwise, the entire federal government would shut down for lack of funds. Clinton, however, refused to budge.

By standing firm against Republican budget proposals and allowing the government to shut down, Clinton regained much of the support he had lost in 1994. The Republicans in Congress realized they needed to work with the president to pass legislation. Soon afterward, they reached an agreement with Clinton to balance the budget.

In the months before the 1996 election, the president and the Republicans worked together to pass new legislation. In August Congress passed the Health Insurance Portability Act. This act improved coverage for people who changed jobs and reduced discrimination against people with preexisting illnesses.

Later that month Congress passed the Welfare Reform Act, which limited people to no more than two consecutive years on welfare and required them to work to receive welfare benefits. Welfare reform had become a major issue by the mid-1990s because of growing evidence that welfare programs trapped people in poverty by giving them incentives to stay unemployed and to have children without getting married. Despite all the money spent on antipoverty programs, the percentage of Americans in poverty had changed very little. Both the Republican-led Congress and President Clinton agreed that the welfare system needed reforms to encourage people to go back to work.

✓ Reading Check **Identifying** What two reforms did Clinton and Congress agree to support?

The 1996 Election

As the 1996 campaign began, Clinton took credit for the economy. The economic boom of the 1990s was the longest sustained period of growth in American history. Unemployment and inflation fell to their lowest levels in 40 years. The stock market

DIFFERENTIATED INSTRUCTION

English Learners Have students with reading comprehension difficulties complete a chart similar to the one shown below. List ideas and laws from the section and each person's position. Students should fill in the resolutions column after reading the section. L1 ELL

Issues	Bill Clinton	Newt Gingrich	Bob Dole	Resolution

Refer to *Inclusion for the High School Social Studies Classroom Strategies and Activities* in the TCR.

soared, wages rose, crime rates fell, and the number of people on welfare declined. With the economy booming, Clinton's popularity climbed rapidly.

The Republican Party nominated Senator **Bob Dole** of Kansas, the Republican leader in the Senate, to run against Clinton. Dole promised a 15 percent tax cut if elected and tried to portray Clinton as a tax-and-spend liberal.

H. Ross Perot also ran again as a candidate. This time he ran as the candidate of the Reform Party, which he had created. Once again Perot made the deficit the main campaign issue.

President Clinton won re-election, winning a little more than 49 percent of the popular vote and 379 electoral votes. Dole received slightly less than 41 percent and 159 electoral votes. Perot won about 8.4 percent of the vote—less than half of what he had received in 1992. Despite Clinton's victory, Republicans retained control of Congress.

✔ **Reading Check** **Explaining** Why do you think President Clinton won re-election in 1996?

Clinton's Second Term

During Clinton's second term, the economy continued its expansion. As people's incomes rose, so too did the amount of taxes they paid. At the same time, despite their differences, the president and Congress continued to shrink the deficit. In 1997, for the first time in 24 years, the president was able to submit a balanced budget to Congress. Beginning in 1998, the government began to run a surplus—that is, it collected more money than it spent.

Putting Children First During his second term, Clinton's domestic agenda shifted toward children's issues. He began by asking Congress to pass a $500-per-child tax credit. He also signed the Adoption and Safe Families Act and asked Congress to ban cigarette advertising aimed at children. In August 1997, Clinton signed the Children's Health Insurance Program—a plan to provide health insurance for children whose parents could not afford it.

Clinton also continued his efforts to help students. "I come from a family where nobody had ever gone to college before," Clinton said. "When I became president, I was determined to do what I could to give every student that chance." To help students, he asked for a tax credit, a large increase in student grants, and an expansion of the Head Start program for preschoolers.

Clinton Is Impeached The robust economy and his high standing in the polls allowed Clinton to regain the initiative in dealing with Congress. By 1998, however,

Impeaching the President

The Constitution gives Congress the power to remove a president from office "upon impeachment for and Conviction of, Treason, Bribery, or other High Crimes and Misdemeanors." The House of Representatives has the sole power over impeachment—the formal accusation of wrongdoing in office. If the majority of the House votes to impeach the president, the Senate conducts a trial. A two-thirds vote of those present is needed for conviction. When the impeachment proceeding involves a president, the chief justice of the United States presides.

Chief Justice William Rehnquist being sworn in for the impeachment trial in the Senate

A somber President and Mrs. Clinton after the decision for impeachment was reached

Creating Circle Graphs Provide the data below and ask students to make a pair of circle graphs showing the results of the presidential election of 1996. **L1**

Candidate	Popular Vote	Electoral Vote
Clinton, Dem.	47,402,357	379
Dole, Rep.	39,198,755	159
Perot, Rfm.	8,085,402	0

📁 Use the rubric for creating a map, display, or chart on pages 65–66 in the *Performance Assessment Activities and Rubrics.*

✔ **Reading Check**

Answer: One possible answer: Clinton was reelected because the economy was booming.

History *and the* Humanities

🏳 American Music: Hits Through History: "Little Miss Can't Be Wrong"

FYI

Madeleine Albright, appointed by President Clinton, was the first woman to serve as secretary of state. This appointment made her the highest-ranking woman ever to serve in the federal government—fourth in line for presidential succession. Interestingly, she would not have been able to assume the presidency because she was not born a citizen of the United States.

INTERDISCIPLINARY CONNECTIONS ACTIVITY

Economics The government created the Earned Income Tax Credit (EITC) in 1976 to reduce the tax burden on low-income families and encourage those families to work rather than rely on welfare assistance. In 1993 President Clinton signed a bill authorizing the largest expansion of the EITC in its history. Ask students to use library and Internet resources to find the current eligibility rules to claim the EITC and then create a chart to explain the different eligibility requirements. **L2**

3 ASSESS

Assign Section 2 Assessment as homework or as an in-class activity.

🔵 Have students use the **Interactive Tutor Self-Assessment CD-ROM.**

L1/ELL

Reading Essentials and Study Guide 29–2

Name _____ Date _____ Class _____

Study Guide

Chapter 29, Section 2

For use with textbook pages 896–901

THE CLINTON YEARS

KEY TERMS AND NAMES

AmeriCorps a program that put students to work improving low-income housing, teaching children to read, and cleaning up the environment *(page 897)*

Contract with America a program proposed by congressional Republicans that called for several changes, including lowering taxes, welfare reform, and a balanced budget amendment *(page 898)*

Kenneth Starr an independent counsel appointed to investigate President Clinton in the Whitewater scandal *(page 900)*

perjury lying under oath *(page 900)*

ethnic cleansing the brutal expulsion of an ethnic group from a geographic area *(page 900)*

L2

Section Quiz 29–2

Name _____ Date _____ Class _____

⭐ **Chapter 29**   Score [   ]

Section Quiz 29-2

DIRECTIONS: Matching Match each item in Column A with the items in Column B. Write the correct letters in the blanks. *(10 points each)*

Column A	Column B
___ 1. put students to work improving low-income housing, teaching children to read, and cleaning up the environment	A. Welfare Reform Act
___ 2. lying under oath	B. Dayton Accords
___ 3. a plan for creating a Palestinian government	C. Declaration of Principles
___ 4. a peace plan regarding Bosnia	D. AmeriCorps
___ 5. limited people to no more than two consecutive years on welfare and required them to work to receive benefits	E. perjury

DIRECTIONS: Multiple Choice In the blank at the left, write the letter of the choice that best completes the statement or answers the question. *(10 points each)*

✓ Reading Check

Answer: allegations that Clinton had arranged illegal loans while he was governor of Arkansas; also allegations that he had perjured himself while testifying about his relationship with a White House intern

---

he had become entangled in a serious scandal that threatened to undermine his presidency.

The scandal began in Clinton's first term, when he was accused of arranging illegal loans for Whitewater Development—an Arkansas real estate company—while he was governor of that state. Attorney General **Janet Reno** decided that an independent counsel should investigate the president. A special three-judge panel appointed **Kenneth Starr,** a former federal judge, to this position.

In early 1998, a new scandal emerged involving a personal relationship between the president and a White House intern. Some evidence suggested that the president had committed perjury, or had lied under oath, about the relationship. The three-judge panel directed Starr to investigate this scandal as well. In September 1998, after examining the evidence, Starr sent his report to the Judiciary Committee of the House of Representatives. Starr argued that Clinton had obstructed justice, abused his power as president, and committed perjury.

After the 1998 elections, the House began impeachment hearings. Clinton's supporters charged that Starr's investigation was politically motivated. Clinton's accusers argued that the president was accountable if his actions were illegal.

On December 19, 1998, the House of Representatives passed two articles of impeachment, one for perjury and one for obstruction of justice. The vote split almost evenly along party lines, and the case moved to the Senate for trial. On February 12, 1999, the senators cast their votes. The vote was 55 to 45 that Clinton was not guilty of perjury, and 50–50 on the charge of obstruction of justice. Although both votes were well short of the two-thirds needed to remove the president from office, Clinton's reputation had suffered.

✓ **Reading Check** **Examining** What events led to the impeachment of President Clinton?

Clinton's Foreign Policy

While attracting worldwide attention, the impeachment drama did not affect world affairs. The collapse of the Soviet Union virtually ended the struggle between communism and democracy, but small bloody wars continued to erupt around the world. On several occasions President Clinton used force to bring an end to regional conflicts.

The Haitian Intervention In 1991 military leaders in Haiti overthrew Jean-Bertrand Aristide, the

country's first democratically elected president in many decades. Aristide sought refuge in the United States. The new rulers of Haiti used violence, even murder, to suppress the opposition. Seeking to restore democracy, the Clinton administration convinced the United Nations to impose a trade embargo on Haiti. The embargo created a severe economic crisis in that country. Thousands of Haitian refugees fled to the United States in small boats, and many died at sea.

Determined to put an end to the crisis, Clinton ordered an invasion of Haiti. Before the troops arrived, however, former president Jimmy Carter convinced Haiti's rulers to step aside.

Peacekeeping in Bosnia and Kosovo The United States also was concerned about mounting tensions in southeastern Europe. During the Cold War, Yugoslavia had been a single federated nation made up of many different ethnic groups under a strong Communist government. In 1991, after the collapse of communism, Yugoslavia split apart.

In Bosnia, one of the former Yugoslav republics, a vicious three-way civil war erupted between Orthodox Christian Serbs, Catholic Croatians, and Bosnian Muslims. Despite international pressure, the fighting continued until 1995. The Serbs began what they called ethnic cleansing—the brutal expulsion of an ethnic group from a geographic area. In some cases, Serbian troops slaughtered the Muslims instead of moving them.

The United States convinced its NATO allies that military action was necessary. NATO warplanes attacked the Serbs in Bosnia, forcing them to negotiate. The Clinton administration then arranged peace talks in Dayton, Ohio. The participants signed a peace plan known as the **Dayton Accords.** In 1996 some 60,000 NATO troops, including 20,000 Americans, entered Bosnia to enforce the plan.

In 1998 another war erupted, this time within the Serbian province of Kosovo. Kosovo has two major ethnic groups—Serbs and Albanians. Many of the Albanians wanted Kosovo to separate from Serbia. To keep Kosovo in Serbia, Serbian leader **Slobodan Milosevic** ordered a crackdown. The Albanians then organized their own army to fight back. Worried by reports of Serbian violence against Albanian civilians, President Clinton convinced European leaders that NATO should again use force to stop the fighting. In March 1999, NATO began bombing Serbia. The bombing convinced Serbia to pull its troops out of Kosovo.

CRITICAL THINKING ACTIVITY

Analyzing Early presidents were able to oversee all the daily activities of the executive office and still have time for leisurely pursuits. Today the president's schedule is packed with meetings, reports, decisions, and ceremonial duties. With all this activity, a president is not able to keep up with every decision of hundreds of executive agencies and offices. Ask students what part, if any, of the president's responsibilities should be delegated to another person or agency. Have students explain their responses. **L2**

Peacemaking in the Middle East Despite the overwhelming defeat Iraq suffered in the Persian Gulf War, Iraqi President Saddam Hussein remained in power and continued to make threats against Iraq's neighbors. In 1996 Iraq attacked the Kurds, an ethnic group whose homeland lies in northern Iraq. To stop the attacks, the United States fired cruise missiles at Iraqi military targets.

Relations between Israel and the Palestinians were even more volatile. In 1993 Israeli Prime Minister **Yitzhak Rabin** and Palestine Liberation Organization leader **Yasir Arafat** reached an agreement. The PLO recognized Israel's right to exist, and Israel recognized the PLO as the representative of the Palestinians. President Clinton then invited Arafat and Rabin to the White House, where they signed the Declaration of Principles—a plan for creating a Palestinian government.

Opposition to the peace plan emerged on both sides. Radical Palestinians exploded bombs in Israel and in 1995 a right-wing Israeli assassinated Prime Minister Rabin.

In 1998 Israeli and Palestinian leaders met with President Clinton at the Wye River plantation in Maryland to work out details of the withdrawal of Israeli troops from the West Bank and the Gaza Strip. This agreement, however, failed to settle the status of Jerusalem, which both sides claimed.

In July 2000, President Clinton invited Arafat and Israeli Prime Minister Ehud Barak to reach an agreement, but these talks failed. Beginning in October, violence started to break out between Palestinians and Israeli soldiers. The region was as far from peace as ever.

 Picturing **History**

Middle East Conflict The struggle over control of the Israeli/Palestinian areas intensified in the 1990s. Although President Clinton directed many negotiations to attempt to resolve the conflict, the region remained a very dangerous place. Which leaders agreed to a framework for peace in 1993?

Clinton Leaves Office As he prepared to leave office, President Clinton's legacy was uncertain. He had balanced the budget and presided over the greatest period of economic growth in American history. Clinton's presidency was marred, however, by the impeachment trial, which had divided the nation and widened the divide between liberals and conservatives. In the election of 2000, that division would lead to the closest election in American history.

✓ **Reading Check** **Identifying** In what three regions of the world did Clinton use force to support his foreign policy?

 HISTORY Online **Study Central™** To review this section, go to tarvol2.glencoe.com and click on **Study Central™**.

SECTION 2 ASSESSMENT

Checking for Understanding
1. **Define:** perjury, ethnic cleansing.
2. **Identify:** AmeriCorps, Contract with America, Kenneth Starr, Dayton Accords.
3. **Explain** why the federal government shut down in 1995.

Reviewing Themes
4. **Economic Factors** What government policies helped create the U.S. prosperity of the 1990s?

Critical Thinking
5. **Analyzing** Why was President Clinton able to win re-election in 1996?
6. **Categorizing** Complete a chart similar to the one below by explaining the foreign policy issues facing President Clinton in each of the areas listed.

Region	Issue
Latin America	
Southeastern Europe	
Middle East	

Analyzing Visuals
7. **Analyzing Photographs** Study the photographs on page 899 of Clinton's impeachment trial. What elements in the photograph reflect the seriousness of the occasion?

Writing About History
8. **Persuasive Writing** Take on the role of a member of Congress. Write a letter in which you attempt to persuade other lawmakers to vote either for or against the impeachment of President Clinton. Provide reasons for your position.

CHAPTER 29 Into a New Century **901**

SECTION 2 ASSESSMENT ANSWERS

1. Terms are in blue.
2. AmeriCorps (p. 897), Contract with America (p. 898), Kenneth Starr (p. 900), Dayton Accords (p. 900)
3. A budget impasse between Congress and Clinton led to a government shutdown.
4. a reduced federal deficit and lower interest rates
5. Americans' desire to encourage the continuation of the economic boom
6. Latin America: Haiti's democratically elected president overthrown; southeastern Europe: ethnic cleansing in Bosnia and Kosovo; Middle East: tension between Israel and the Palestinians, and Iraqi attacks on Kurds
7. Possible answers: people's somber expressions, Clinton's bowed head
8. Students' letters will vary. Letters should express a clear point of view.

Picturing **History**

Answer: Yitzhak Rabin and Yasir Arafat
Ask: What did the Declaration of Principles accomplish? (It created a plan for a Palestinian government.)

Reteach
Have students describe the difficulties and successes of American efforts toward middle East peace during the Clinton administration.

Enrich
Have interested students evaluate Clinton's foreign policy, especially his attempts to end regional conflicts in Haiti, Bosnia-Herzegovina, and Kosovo. They should also research other efforts, such as that in Somalia. Students should review and summarize appropriate magazine and newspaper articles.

✓ **Reading Check**

Answer: in southeastern Europe (Bosnia and Kosovo); in the Middle East (Iraq); was prepared to use force in Latin America (Haiti) but the crisis ended peacefully

HISTORY Online

Study Central™ provides summaries, interactive games, and online graphic organizers to help students review section content.

4 CLOSE

Have students discuss the nation's involvement in world affairs during the Clinton administration.

901

1 FOCUS

Section Overview

This section focuses on the advantages and disadvantages of economic globalization and global environmental issues.

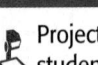

BELLRINGER
Skillbuilder Activity

Project transparency and have students answer the question.

Daily Focus Skills Transparency 29–3

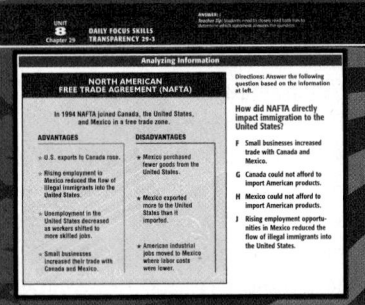

Reading Preview

Answers to Graphic: global warming, international trade, nuclear proliferation, terrorism, world economy

Preteaching Vocabulary
Have students create a database for the Key Terms and Names. Encourage them to enter additional words, terms, and names as they read this section.

SECTION 3 An Interdependent World

Guide to Reading

Main Idea
As the world adjusted to a new era, it faced the advantages and disadvantages of growing economic globalization and the end of the U.S.-Soviet rivalry.

Key Terms and Names
trade deficit, North American Free Trade Agreement, euro, nuclear proliferation, global warming, Kyoto Protocol

Reading Strategy
Organizing Complete a graphic organizer like the one below to chart the major political and economic problems facing the world at the turn of the century.

Global Concerns

Reading Objectives
• **Explain** the development of regional economic blocs around the world.
• **Assess** environmental issues that have become important internationally.

Section Theme
Global Connections Economic, health, and environmental developments in recent years have led to the world's nations becoming more interdependent.

Preview of Events

♦1993   ♦1996   ♦1999   ♦2002

1993
European Union launched

1994
United States, Mexico, and Canada inaugurate NAFTA

2000
U.S. gives permanent trade status to China

2001
China becomes member of WTO

2002
Treaty of Moscow signed

★ *An American Story* ★

Madeleine Albright

It was an important breakthrough when President Clinton appointed Madeleine Albright in 1996 to be the first woman to serve as secretary of state. Born in Czechoslovakia, Albright immigrated to the United States as a young girl. She earned a Ph.D. in Russian studies from Columbia University. Her tough-talking approach as U.S. ambassador to the United Nations earned her the nation's top foreign policy job.

As secretary of state, Albright dealt with everything from peace negotiations in the Middle East to improving trade relations with China. She also championed women's rights in developing countries. Here, she expresses her views on women's rights:

❝[Halting violence against women] is a goal of American foreign policy around the world, where abuses range from domestic violence . . . to forcing young girls into prostitution. Some say all this is cultural, and there's nothing we can do about it. I say it's criminal, and we each have a responsibility to stop it.❞

—quoted in *Madeleine Albright and the New American Diplomacy*

The New Global Economy

In the latter part of the 1900s, American leaders became more concerned with many global issues. Economies around the world had become much more interdependent. Computer technology and the Internet played a big role in forging a global economy.

SECTION RESOURCES

📂 **Reproducible Masters**
• Reproducible Lesson Plan 29–3
• Daily Lecture and Discussion Notes 29–3
• Guided Reading Activity 29–3
• Section Quiz 29–3
• Reading Essentials and Study Guide 29–3
• Performance Assessment Activities and Rubrics

📠 **Transparencies**
• Daily Focus Skills Transparency 29–3

Multimedia
🖭 Interactive Tutor Self-Assessment CD-ROM
🖭 ExamView® Pro Testmaker CD-ROM
🖭 Presentation Plus! CD-ROM
🖭 TeacherWorks™ CD-ROM
🎧 Audio Program

Selling American-made goods abroad had long been important to American prosperity. By the 1970s, however, serious trade deficits had mounted—Americans purchased more from foreign nations than American industry and agriculture sold abroad. The United States found it necessary to compete harder in the global marketplace by streamlining industry, using new technology, and opening new markets.

From World War II to the present, Republican and Democratic administrations have both tried to lower barriers to international trade. They reasoned that the U.S. economy benefited from the sale of American exports, and that the purchase of imports would keep consumer prices, inflation, and interest rates low for Americans. Opponents warned that the global economy might cost the United States industrial jobs as manufacturing shifted to lesser-developed nations with few environmental regulations and cheap labor. By the 1990s, the debate between supporters of free trade and those who wanted to limit trade to protect industries had become an important part of American politics.

Regional Blocs One means of increasing international trade was to create regional trade pacts. In 1994 the **North American Free Trade Agreement** (NAFTA) joined Canada, the United States, and Mexico in a free-trade zone. With NAFTA in operation, exports of American goods to both Canada and Mexico rose dramatically. From 1993 to 2000, it is estimated that combined exports to those two countries rose from $142 to $290 billion, an increase of 104 percent.

One concern of many Americans was that industrial jobs would go to Mexico, where labor costs were lower. Although some jobs were lost to Mexico, unemployment rates in the United States fell during this period and wages rose. Many American businesses upgraded their technology, and workers shifted to more skilled jobs or to the service industry.

NAFTA faced competing regional trade blocs in Europe and Asia. In 1993 the **European Union** (EU) was created to promote economic and political cooperation among many European nations. The EU created a common bank and the euro, a common currency for member nations. The organization also removed trade barriers between its members and set policies on imports from nations outside the community.

EU rules tended to favor imports from the European nations' former colonies in Asia, Africa, and the Pacific over competing products from the United States. The EU also banned scientifically modified food, such as hormone-treated beef from the United States. American exporters argued that hormones were a safe way to accelerate livestock growth rates and produce leaner meat. They protested that European fears lacked a scientific basis.

The **Asia Pacific Economic Cooperation** (APEC) was an attempt to create a Pacific trade community to rival the European Union. APEC represented the fastest-growing region in the world and controlled 47 percent of global trade in 2001. APEC began as a

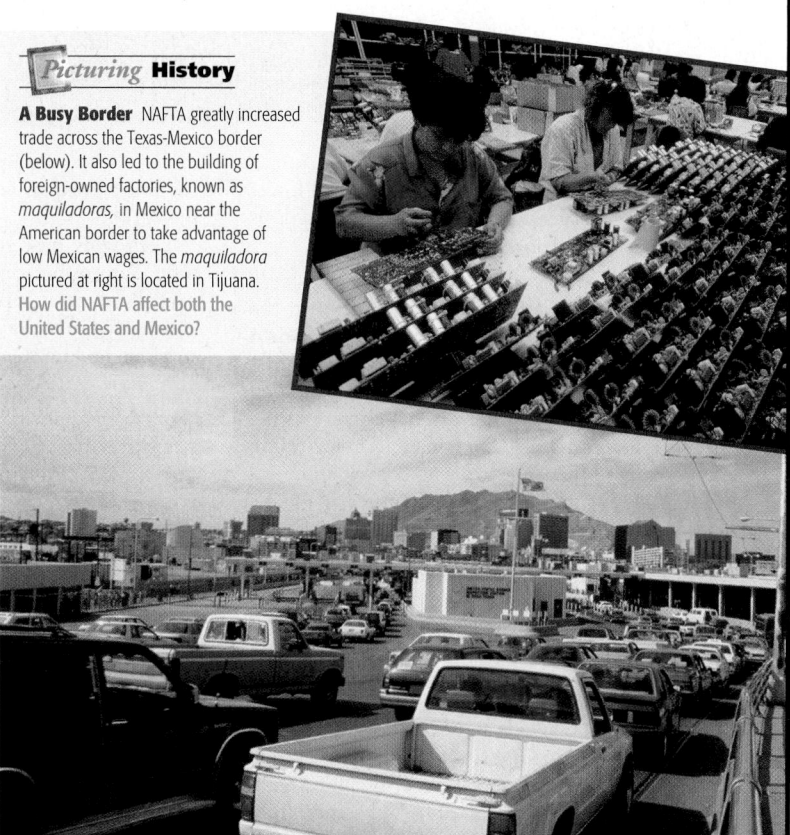

Picturing **History**

A Busy Border NAFTA greatly increased trade across the Texas-Mexico border (below). It also led to the building of foreign-owned factories, known as *maquiladoras,* in Mexico near the American border to take advantage of low Mexican wages. The *maquiladora* pictured at right is located in Tijuana. How did NAFTA affect both the United States and Mexico?

CHAPTER 29   Into a New Century   **903**

2 TEACH

Daily Lecture and Discussion Notes 29–3

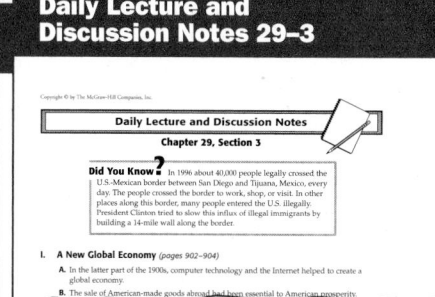

Copyright © by The McGraw-Hill Companies, Inc.

Daily Lecture and Discussion Notes

Chapter 29, Section 3

Did You Know? In 1996 about 40,000 people legally crossed the U.S.-Mexican border between San Diego and Tijuana, Mexico, every day. The people crossed the border to work, shop, or visit. In other places along this border, many people entered the U.S. illegally. President Clinton tried to slow this influx of illegal immigrants by building a 14-mile wall along the border.

I. A New Global Economy (pages 902–904)

A. In the latter part of the 1900s, computer technology and the Internet helped to create a global economy.

B. The sale of American-made goods abroad had been essential to American prosperity.

Picturing **History**

Answer: U.S. unemployment fell and wages rose as workers shifted to more skilled jobs or to the service industry. U.S. exports to Mexico rose and Mexico gained jobs.

Ask: Why did Americans fear losing jobs to Mexico rather than to Canada? (*Possible answers: wages and Mexico's standard of living were lower; workers feared that their jobs would be lost to low-wage workers in Mexico*)

Creating a Thematic Map Have students visit the European Union's official website at europa.eu.int. Have students make a map of Europe showing the EU's member countries in one color and the candidate countries in another color. **L1**

Reading Strategy   READING THE TEXT

Monitoring Comprehension One of the most important reading strategies students can learn is that they must monitor their reading comprehension. As students read, they should be aware of when they have misunderstood the information in the text. They can monitor comprehension by questioning themselves as they read. If they do not understand an important idea, they need to re-read, review, or read on to clarify what is unclear. **L1 ELL**

Refer to *Inclusion for the High School Social Studies Classroom Strategies and Activities* in the TCR.

Guided Reading Activity 29–3

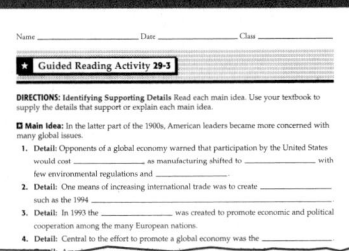

Name _____ Date _____ Class _____

★ Guided Reading Activity 29-3

DIRECTIONS: Identifying Supporting Details Read each main idea. Use your textbook to supply the details that support or explain each main idea.

☑ **Main Idea:** In the latter part of the 1900s, American leaders became more concerned with many global issues.

1. **Detail:** Opponents of a global economy warned that participation by the United States would cost _____ as manufacturing shifted to _____ with few environmental regulations and _____.
2. **Detail:** One means of increasing international trade was to create _____ such as the 1994 _____.
3. **Detail:** In 1993 the _____ was created to promote economic and political cooperation among the many European nations.
4. **Detail:** Central to the effort to promote a global economy was the _____.

The Oklahoma City National Memorial includes 168 chairs, one for each victim, in 9 rows, one for each floor of the destroyed building. Each chair is made of bronze and stone and is on a lighted glass base etched with a victim's name.

✓ Reading Check

Answer: to promote economic and political cooperation in Europe

3 ASSESS

Assign Section 3 Assessment as homework or as an in-class activity.

◉ Have students use the **Interactive Tutor Self-Assessment CD-ROM.**

Reading Essentials and Study Guide 29–3

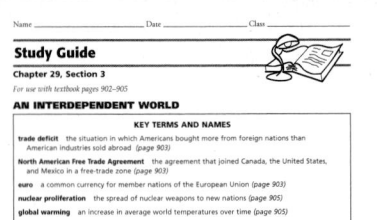

Name _____ Date _____ Class _____

Study Guide

Chapter 29, Section 3

For use with textbook pages 902–905

AN INTERDEPENDENT WORLD

KEY TERMS AND NAMES

trade deficit the situation in which Americans bought more from foreign nations than American industries sold abroad *(page 903)*

North American Free Trade Agreement the agreement that joined Canada, the United States, and Mexico in a free-trade zone *(page 903)*

euro a common currency for member nations of the European Union *(page 903)*

nuclear proliferation the spread of nuclear weapons to new nations *(page 905)*

global warming an increase in average world temperatures over time *(page 905)*

NATIONAL GEOGRAPHIC
MOMENT in HISTORY

TERRORISM IN THE HEARTLAND

A couple comforts each other after placing flowers on one of the 168 chairs that form part of the Oklahoma City National Memorial. The site was dedicated on April 19, 2000—five years to the day after Timothy McVeigh detonated a massive bomb outside the Alfred P. Murrah Federal Building in downtown Oklahoma City. Most of the 168 killed and hundreds injured were government employees, but 19 children attending a day-care facility in the building also died in the blast. A jury found McVeigh guilty, and he was executed in 2001.

forum to promote economic cooperation and lower trade barriers, but major political differences kept its members from acting together.

The World Trade Organization Central to the effort to promote a global economy was the **World Trade Organization** (WTO). The WTO administered international trade agreements and helped settle trade disputes. American supporters of the WTO cited benefits for U.S. consumers, including cheaper imports, new markets, and copyright protection for the American entertainment industry. On the other hand, the United States had no veto power in the WTO and poorer nations could outvote it.

Trade With China China's huge population offered vast potential as a market for American goods, but many Americans had strong reservations about China's record on human rights, and they worried about its threats to invade Taiwan. President Clinton pressed Congress to grant China permanent normal trade relation status, hoping to bring the nation into the world community. Despite opposition from labor unions, conservatives, and environmentalists,

the bill passed in late 2000. In 2001 China joined the WTO.

Even with these steps toward the global community, many American officials demand that China must do more to repair its history of human rights abuses and address the problem of selling pirated versions of copyrighted materials. Critics of China also argue that American manufacturers should not be threatened by low-cost goods imported from Chinese factories.

✓ Reading Check **Explaining** Why was the European Union (EU) created in 1993?

Issues of Global Concern

Although the end of the Cold War had reduced the threat of nuclear war between the United States and the Soviet Union, it also increased fears that nuclear weapons might fall into the wrong hands. Equally worrisome were efforts by several nations, including Pakistan, North Korea, and Iraq, to acquire nuclear weapons and long-range missiles. Beginning in the 1980s, nations also began to be concerned about the environment.

904 CHAPTER 29 Into a New Century

DIFFERENTIATED INSTRUCTION

Gifted and Talented Have small groups of students consider possible approaches to resolving one of the global concerns mentioned in this section. After students list their ideas, discuss them and develop a proposed solution. Prepare a letter to the United Nations explaining the issue and the group's proposed solution. **L3**

📁 Refer to *Inclusion for the High School Social Studies Classroom Strategies and Activities* in the TCR.

TECHNOLOGY

Nuclear Proliferation When Russia agreed to reduce its nuclear arsenal, fears arose that some of its weapons or radioactive material could be stolen or sold on the black market. In response, the U.S. provided funds to Russia to assist in the reduction of its nuclear stockpile.

Other efforts were made to reduce the threat of nuclear proliferation, or the spread of nuclear weapons to new nations. Congress passed legislation that cut aid and imposed sanctions on nations seeking to acquire such weapons. In 1996 President Clinton signed the Comprehensive Nuclear Test Ban Treaty, but the Senate refused to ratify it to avoid limiting American nuclear research. The 2002 Treaty of Moscow aimed at further reductions of U.S. and Russian nuclear weapons. The treaty stated that by the end of 2012 the total number of strategic nuclear warheads possessed by each country could not exceed 2,200.

Iran and North Korea caused concern in the international community by taking steps to reinvigorate their nuclear energy programs. While both countries insist that nuclear power is only used for fuel, the United States and the European Union have demanded that these nations undergo close scrutiny to ensure these programs do not lead to nuclear weapons.

Concern About Ozone In the 1980s, scientists discovered that chemicals called chlorofluorocarbons (CFCs) had the potential to deplete the earth's atmosphere of ozone. Ozone is a gas in the atmosphere that protects life on Earth from the cancer-causing ultraviolet rays of the sun. In the late 1980s, public awareness of the ozone issue increased dramatically when stories appeared documenting a large ozone "hole" over Antarctica. In 1987 the United States and 22 other nations agreed to phase out the production of CFCs and other chemicals that might be weakening the ozone layer.

Global Warming In the early 1990s, another global environmental issue developed when some scientists found evidence of global warming—an increase in average world temperatures over time. Such a rise in temperature could eventually lead to more droughts and other forms of extreme weather. A furious debate is now underway among scientists over how to measure changes in the earth's temperature and what the results mean.

Many experts believe carbon dioxide emissions from factories and power plants caused global warming, but others disagree. Some question whether global warming even exists. The issue is very controversial because the cost of controlling emissions would affect the global economy. Developing nations trying to industrialize would be hurt the most, but economic growth in wealthier nations would be hurt, too.

Concern about global warming led to an international conference in Kyoto, Japan, in 1997. Thirty-eight nations and the EU signed the **Kyoto Protocol** promising to reduce emissions, but very few put it into effect. President Clinton did not submit the Kyoto Protocol to the Senate for ratification because most senators were opposed to it. In 2001 President George W. Bush withdrew the United States from the Kyoto Protocol, citing flaws in the treaty.

 Reading Check **Identifying** What is the ozone layer, and why is it important?

 Study Central™ To review this section, go to **tarvol2.glencoe.com** and click on **Study Central™**.

SECTION 3 ASSESSMENT

Checking for Understanding

1. **Define:** trade deficit, euro, nuclear proliferation, global warming.
2. **Identify:** North American Free Trade Agreement, Kyoto Protocol.
3. **Describe** the international response to concerns about global warming.

Reviewing Themes

4. **Global Connections** Why was China an important factor in world trade?

Critical Thinking

5. **Analyzing** Do you think the new global economy has helped or hurt the United States?
6. **Organizing** Complete a graphic organizer similar to the one below by listing and describing the regional trade blocs that formed in the 1990s.

Regional Trade Blocs

Analyzing Visuals

7. **Analyzing Photographs** Study the photograph on page 904 of the Oklahoma City National Memorial. What do the empty chairs represent? How has the memorial helped relatives of the victims?

Writing About History

8. **Expository Writing** Decide which issue of global concern today is the most serious. In an essay, explain why you think it is the most serious problem, and provide some possible solutions.

CHAPTER 29 Into a New Century **905**

SECTION 3 ASSESSMENT ANSWERS

1. Terms are in blue.
2. North American Free Trade Agreement (p. 903), Kyoto Protocol (p. 905)
3. The Kyoto Protocol pledged to reduce emissions, but the United States did not sign it. Few of the 39 countries that signed it have implemented any plans.
4. China's large population provides a huge market for imported goods.
5. Students' answers will vary. Encourage students to provide reasons for their opinions.
6. NAFTA increased trade between Canada, Mexico, and the United States. EU promoted economic and political cooperation among European nations. APEC created a Pacific trade bloc.
7. bombing victims; answers should focus on the need to remember
8. Students' essays should clearly identify the issue.

CHAPTER 29
Section 3, 902–905

L2

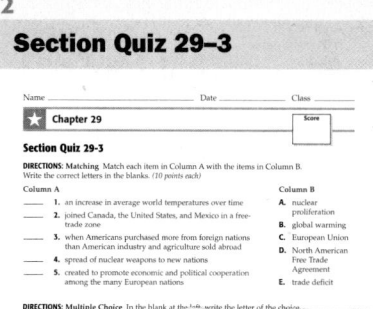

Section Quiz 29–3

Creating a Thematic Map Have students create a thematic world map showing the countries that have nuclear weapons. Have students use the maps to discuss present dangers related to nuclear weapons. **L1**

Use the rubric for creating a map, display, or chart on pages 65–66 in the *Performance Assessment Activities and Rubrics.*

Reteach

Have students explain the development of regional economic blocs around the world.

Enrich

Have students investigate the cultural diversity of their community and report their findings to the class.

Reading Check

Answer: The ozone layer is a layer of gas in the atmosphere that protects life on Earth from the cancer-causing ultraviolet rays of the sun.

Study Central™ provides summaries, interactive games, and online graphic organizers to help students review section content.

4 CLOSE

Have students list the environmental issues that have become important internationally.

905

1 FOCUS

Section Overview

This section focuses on the controversy surrounding the election of George W. Bush and the beginning of his presidency.

BELLRINGER
Skillbuilder Activity

Project transparency and have students answer the question.

Daily Focus Skills Transparency 29–4

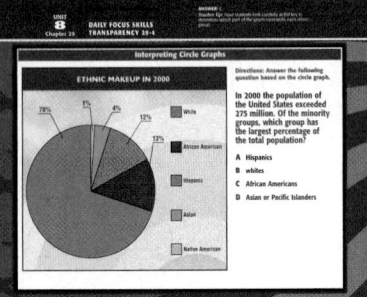

Reading Preview

Answers to Graphic: Recounts begin in Florida; Florida Supreme Court extends deadline for recount; U.S. Supreme Court rules in *Bush* v. *Gore* that recount in Florida is unconstitutional.

Preteaching Vocabulary
Have students prepare a set of study cards with each Key Term or Name on one side and significant facts or definitions on the other.

SECTION 4 America Enters
a New Century

Guide to Reading

Main Idea
The closest presidential election in American history served as the prelude to the new century. The new president initiated an ambitious program.

Key Terms and Names
Al Gore, George W. Bush, Ralph Nader, chad, strategic defense

Reading Strategy
Organizing As you read about the 2000 presidential election, complete a graphic organizer similar to the one below by charting the key post-election events culminating in George W. Bush's victory.

☐ → ☐ → ☐ → Bush's Victory

Reading Objectives
• **Describe** the unusual circumstances surrounding the outcome of the 2000 presidential election.
• **Evaluate** the programs President George W. Bush initiated.

Section Theme
Government and Democracy The 2000 presidential election was very close, and the outcome was controversial.

Preview of Events

◆Aug. 2000	◆Dec. 2000	◆Mar. 2001	◆June 2001

August 2000
Republicans nominate Bush; Democrats nominate Gore

November 2000
Election takes place; recounts begin in Florida

December 2000
Gore concedes election to Bush

January 2001
George W. Bush inaugurated as president

June 2001
Bush signs tax cut bill into law

May Akabogu-Collins

★ *An American Story* ★

The 2000 presidential election was very close. Two candidates battled over the Electoral College votes of one state—Florida. The election remained undecided for more than a month. Though this election was a spectacle of demonstrations and detailed ballot evaluations, some people tried to put it all in perspective. May Akabogu-Collins, an American citizen originally from Nigeria, contrasted the "turmoil" and "chaos" of the election with the transfer of power in other parts of the world:

❝America should be grateful that this election was as wild as it gets. Some of us originally came from places where heads would have rolled during a similar crisis. So far, not a gunshot has been heard on account of the balloting, and you call this 'wild'? An election held in Nigeria in 1993 led to the President-elect's being thrown in jail for trying to assume office and ultimately to his mysterious death. Going to court to decide who won this contest is, in my opinion, as civilized as it gets.❞

—quoted in *Time*, December 11, 2000

A New President for a New Century

The close election of 2000 was, in some ways, another legacy of Bill Clinton's years in power. Clinton's presidency had left the country deeply divided. Many people were pleased with the economy but disappointed with the president's personal behavior. As

906 CHAPTER 29 Into a New Century

SECTION RESOURCES

📁 **Reproducible Masters**
• Reproducible Lesson Plan 29–4
• Daily Lecture and Discussion Notes 29–4
• Guided Reading Activity 29–4
• Section Quiz 29–4
• Reading Essentials and Study Guide 29–4
• Interpreting Political Cartoons

🖼 **Transparencies**
• Daily Focus Skills Transparency 29–4

Multimedia
🖥 Interactive Tutor Self-Assessment CD-ROM
🖥 ExamView® Pro Testmaker CD-ROM
🖥 Presentation Plus! CD-ROM
🖥 TeacherWorks™ CD-ROM
🎧 Audio Program

the election approached, the Republicans and the Democrats both tried to find candidates who would appeal to a broad cross-section of society.

The Candidates Are Chosen The Democrats nominated Vice President **Al Gore** for president in 2000. As his running mate, Gore chose Senator Joseph Lieberman from Connecticut, the first Jewish American ever to run for vice president on a major party ticket.

The Republican contest for the presidential nomination came down to two men: Governor **George W. Bush** of Texas, son of former president George Bush, and Senator John McCain of Arizona, a former navy pilot and prisoner of war in North Vietnam. Most Republican leaders endorsed Bush, who was also popular with conservative Republicans. He easily won the nomination, despite some early McCain victories in the primaries. Bush chose former defense secretary Richard Cheney as his vice presidential running mate.

The 2000 Campaign The election campaign revolved around the question of what to do with surplus tax revenues. Both Bush and Gore agreed that Social Security needed reform, but they disagreed on the details. Both promised to cut taxes, although Bush proposed a much larger tax cut than Gore. Both men also promised to improve public education and to support plans to help seniors pay for prescription drugs.

The healthy economy helped Gore, who stressed that the Clinton-Gore administration had brought prosperity to the nation. Many voters, however, were concerned with what they perceived as a decline in moral values among the nation's leaders. Bush promised to restore dignity to the White House.

Frustrated by the similarities between Bush and Gore, well-known consumer advocate **Ralph Nader** entered the race as the nominee of the Green Party. Nader was known for his strong environmentalist views and his criticism of the power of large corporations. Nader argued that both Bush and Gore were

2 TEACH

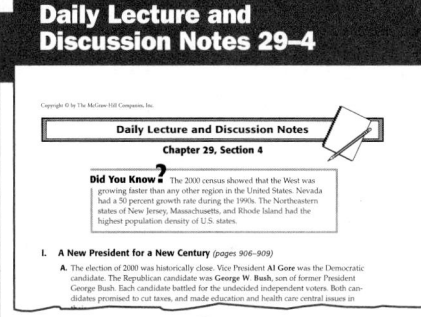

Daily Lecture and Discussion Notes 29–4

Discussing a Topic Have students discuss the ramifications of the media projecting election results. Ask students what, if any, restrictions should be put on news organizations. L1 ELL

Picturing **History**

Answer: Florida
Ask: Approximately how large was Bush's lead at midnight? *(about 130,000 votes)*

you don't say...

Name Game Traditionally former presidents retain the title of "president." George W. Bush and his father, however, are both called President Bush. Some Bush family members affectionately call the men "41" and "43," because George Bush was the forty-first president and George W. Bush is the forty-third president.

Use *Interpreting Political Cartoons*, Cartoon 36.

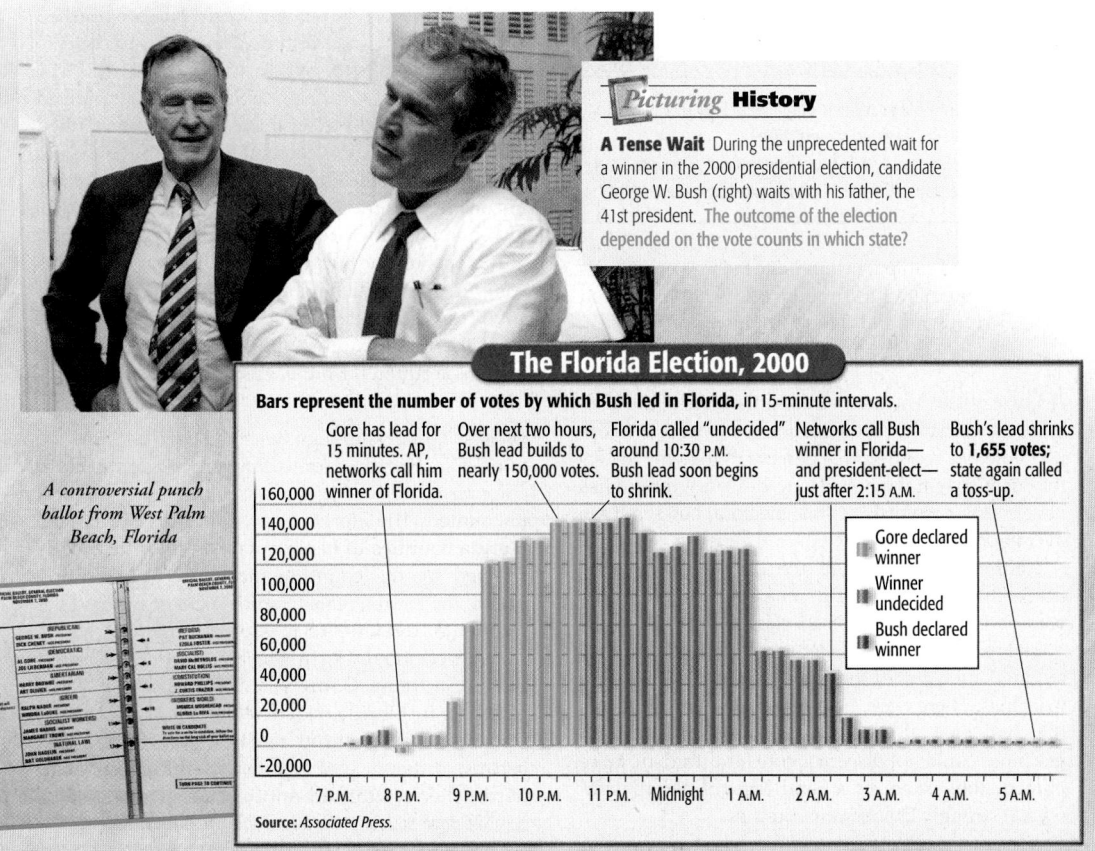

Picturing **History**

A Tense Wait During the unprecedented wait for a winner in the 2000 presidential election, candidate George W. Bush (right) waits with his father, the 41st president. The outcome of the election depended on the vote counts in which state?

A controversial punch ballot from West Palm Beach, Florida

The Florida Election, 2000

Bars represent the number of votes by which Bush led in Florida, in 15-minute intervals.

Gore has lead for 15 minutes. AP, networks call him winner of Florida.

Over next two hours, Bush lead builds to nearly 150,000 votes.

Florida called "undecided" around 10:30 P.M. Bush lead soon begins to shrink.

Networks call Bush winner in Florida—and president-elect—just after 2:15 A.M.

Bush's lead shrinks to **1,655 votes;** state again called a toss-up.

Gore declared winner
Winner undecided
Bush declared winner

Source: *Associated Press.*

Reading Strategy — READING THE TEXT

Previewing Students can quickly gain an understanding of what the text will be about by looking over features such as headings and subheadings, charted information, illustrations, captions, and graphics. Students should preview the section by looking at these elements before they begin reading so they know what they will be reading about. L1 ELL

Refer to *Inclusion for the High School Social Studies Classroom Strategies and Activities* in the TCR.

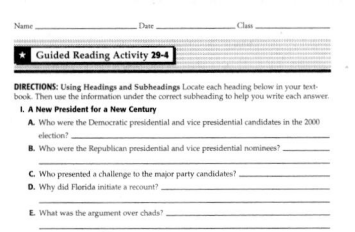
Geography *Skills*

Answers:

1. New Hampshire

2. There were a large number of electoral votes in the states Gore won.

Geography Skills Practice

Ask: Which candidate won the popular and electoral votes in Bush's home state of Texas and Gore's home state of Tennessee?
(Bush won both states.)

3 ASSESS

Assign Section 4 Assessment as homework or as an in-class activity.

☯ Have students use the **Interactive Tutor Self-Assessment CD-ROM.**

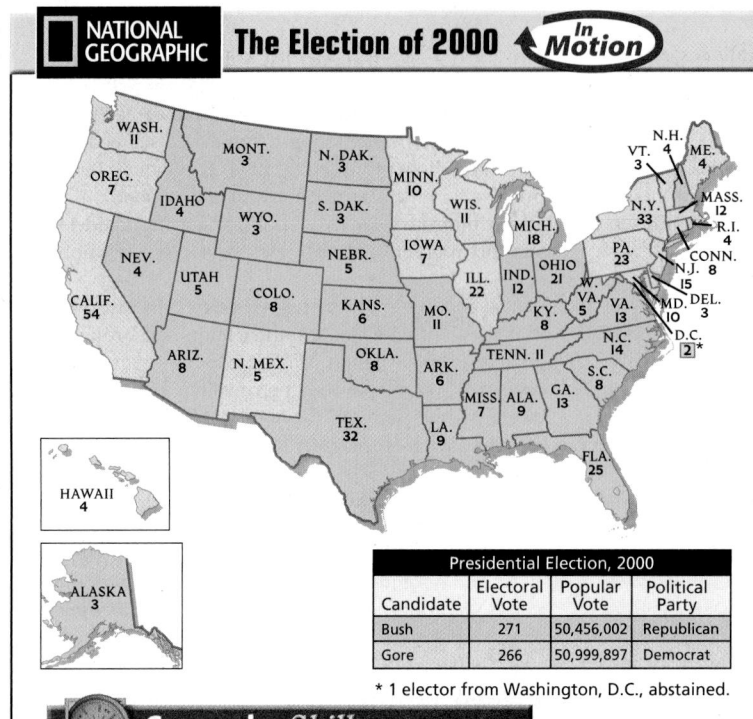

NATIONAL GEOGRAPHIC | The Election of 2000 | *In Motion*

Presidential Election, 2000			
Candidate	Electoral Vote	Popular Vote	Political Party
Bush	271	50,456,002	Republican
Gore	266	50,999,897	Democrat

* 1 elector from Washington, D.C., abstained.

Geography *Skills*

1. **Interpreting Maps** Which single New England state did George W. Bush win in the election?
2. **Applying Geography Skills** Though Gore won less than half of the states, the election was extremely close. Why?

dependent on campaign funds from large companies and were unwilling to support policies that favored American workers and the environment.

A Close Vote The 2000 election was one of the closest in American history. Gore narrowly won the popular vote. He received 48.4 percent of the vote to 47.9 for Bush. To win the presidency, however, candidates have to win a majority of state electoral votes, not the overall popular vote.

Neither candidate had the 270 electoral votes needed to win. The election came down to the Florida vote—both men needed its 25 electoral votes.

The results in Florida were so close that state law required a recount of the ballots using vote-counting machines. There were, however, thousands of ballots that had been thrown out because the counting machines could not discern a vote for president. Gore immediately asked for a hand recount of ballots in several strongly Democratic counties.

After the machine recount showed Bush still ahead, a battle began over the manual recounts. Most Florida ballots required voters to punch a hole. The little piece of cardboard punched out of the ballot is called a chad. The problem for vote counters was how to count a ballot when the chad was still partially attached. On some, the chad was still in place, and the voter had left only a dimple on the surface of the ballot. When looking at the ballots, vote counters had to determine what the voter intended—and different counties used different standards.

Under state law, Florida officials had to certify the results by a certain date. When it became clear that not all of the recounts could be finished in time, Gore went to court to overturn the deadline. The Florida Supreme Court agreed to set a new deadline. At Bush's request, the United States Supreme Court then intervened in the case to decide whether the Florida Supreme Court had acted unconstitutionally.

While lawyers for Bush and Gore prepared their arguments for the Supreme Court, the hand recounts continued. Despite having more time, not all of the counties where Gore wanted recounts were able to meet the new deadline. On November 26, Florida officials certified Bush the winner by 537 votes.

Bush v. Gore Although Bush had been declared the winner in Florida, Gore's lawyers headed back to court arguing that thousands of ballots were still uncounted. The Florida Supreme Court ordered all Florida counties to begin a hand recount of ballots rejected by the counting machines. As counting began, the United States Supreme Court ordered the recount to stop until it had issued its ruling.

On December 12, in **Bush v. Gore,** the United States Supreme Court ruled 7–2 that the hand recounts in Florida violated the equal protection clause of the Constitution. The Court argued that because different vote counters used different standards, the recount did not treat all voters equally. 📖 *(See page 962 for more information on* Bush v. Gore.*)*

DIFFERENTIATED INSTRUCTION

Reading Support Have students examine the map on page 908, identifying what each color on the map stands for. Inform students according to exit poll data urban residents voted for Gore by a large majority. Ask them to identify regions of the country where each candidate won support and to consider if the regional voting patterns agreed with or disagreed with the poll data. Then ask them to explain what these voting patterns tell us about the United States. **L2**

📁 Refer to ***Inclusion for the High School Social Studies Classroom Strategies and Activities*** in the TCR.

Both federal law and the Constitution require the electoral votes for president to be cast on a certain day. If Florida missed that deadline, its electoral votes would not count. The Court ruled 5–4 that there was not enough time left to conduct a manual recount that would pass constitutional standards. This ruling left Bush the certified winner in Florida. The next day, Gore conceded the election.

✓ **Reading Check** **Analyzing** Why did the U.S. Supreme Court stop the manual recounts in Florida?

Bush Becomes President

On January 20, 2001, George W. Bush became the 43rd president of the United States. In his inaugural address, Bush promised to improve the nation's public schools, to cut taxes, to reform Social Security and Medicare, and to build up the nation's defenses.

After taking office, the president's first priority was to cut taxes to try to boost the economy. During the election campaign, the economy had begun to slow. The stock market dropped sharply, and many new Internet-based companies went out of business. Many other businesses laid off thousands of workers. Despite opposition from some Democrats, Congress passed a large $1.35 trillion tax cut to be phased in over 10 years. In the summer of 2001, Americans began receiving tax rebate checks that put about $40 billion back into the economy in an effort to prevent a recession.

Soon after Congress passed the tax cut plan, President Bush proposed two major reforms in education. He wanted public schools to hold annual standardized tests, and he wanted to allow parents to use federal funds to pay for private schools if their public schools were doing a poor job. Although Congress refused to give federal funds to private schools, it did vote in favor of annual reading and math tests in public schools for grades 3–8.

President Bush also focused on Medicare reform. By the summer of 2002, Congress introduced a bill adding presciption drug benefits to this health care program. The bill remained mired in controversy until it was finally passed in November 2003.

Congress also reacted to a rash of corporate scandals. For example, at one large energy trading company, Enron, corporate leaders cost investors and employees billions of dollars before the company went bankrupt. The federal government tightened accounting regulations and toughened penalties for dishonest executives.

Shortly after taking office, President Bush asked Secretary of Defense Donald Rumsfeld to conduct a comprehensive review of the nation's military. The president wanted to increase military spending, but he also wanted new military programs designed to meet the needs of the post–Cold War world.

One military program Bush strongly favored was **strategic defense**—the effort to develop missiles and other devices that could shoot down nuclear missiles. Bush argued that missile defense was needed because many unfriendly nations were developing the technology to build nuclear missiles.

As the debate about the nation's military programs continued in the summer of 2001, a horrific event changed everything. On September 11, 2001, terrorists crashed passenger jets into the World Trade Center and the Pentagon. A new war had begun.

✓ **Reading Check** **Explaining** What was President George W. Bush's first priority when he took office?

HISTORY Online | **Study Central™** To review this section, go to tarvol2.glencoe.com and click on **Study Central™**.

SECTION 4 ASSESSMENT

Checking for Understanding

1. **Define:** chad, strategic defense.
2. **Identify:** Al Gore, George W. Bush, Ralph Nader.
3. **Reviewing Facts** What did the Supreme Court decide in *Bush* v. *Gore?*

Reviewing Themes

4. **Government and Democracy** What caused the vote-count controversy in Florida in the 2000 election?

Critical Thinking

5. **Forming an Opinion** Do you think the 2000 presidential election was decided fairly? Why or why not?
6. **Organizing** Complete a graphic organizer similar to the one below by listing President Bush's goals when he took office.

Bush Goals

Analyzing Visuals

7. **Interpreting Graphs** Study the graph on page 907. By how many votes was Gore leading when news networks declared him the winner in Florida? What was Bush's lead when networks declared him to be the winner?

Writing About History

8. **Persuasive Writing** Take on the role of a Supreme Court justice. Write a statement explaining how you voted in *Bush* v. *Gore.*

CHAPTER 29 Into a New Century **909**

SECTION 4 ASSESSMENT ANSWERS

1. Terms are in blue.
2. Al Gore *(p. 907)*, George W. Bush *(p. 907)*, Ralph Nader *(p. 907)*
3. There was not enough time to conduct a manual recount that passed constitutional standards, ensuring Bush's victory.
4. confusing ballot designs and unclear voting results; different standards used to manually recount ballots
5. Students' answers will vary. Students should be encouraged to present reasoned arguments for their points of view.
6. tax cuts and rebates, new energy plan, public school reform, federal funding for faith-based groups to run social service programs, medicare reform, and strategic defense
7. about 3,000 votes; about 45,000 votes
8. Students' statements will vary but should express a clear, reasoned opinion based on existing law.

L2

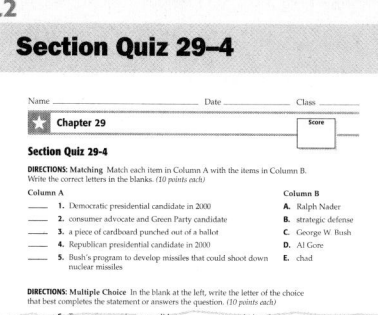

Section Quiz 29-4

Name ____ Date ____ Class ____

★ Chapter 29 | Score

Section Quiz 29-4

DIRECTIONS: Matching Match each item in Column A with the items in Column B. Write the correct letters in the blanks. *(10 points each)*

Column A

____ 1. Democratic presidential candidate in 2000
____ 2. consumer advocate and Green Party candidate
____ 3. a piece of cardboard punched out of a ballot
____ 4. Republican presidential candidate in 2000
____ 5. Bush's program to develop missiles that could shoot down nuclear missiles

Column B

A. Ralph Nader
B. strategic defense
C. George W. Bush
D. Al Gore
E. chad

DIRECTIONS: Multiple Choice In the blank at the left, write the letter of the choice that best completes the statement or answers the question. *(10 points each)*

✓ **Reading Check**

Answer: The Supreme Court ruled that it violated the equal protection clause of the Constitution.

Reteach

Have students describe the circumstances surrounding the outcome of the 2000 presidential election.

Enrich

Have interested students explore voting irregularities in other countries. Then have them compare the American election process with the process in at least two other countries.

✓ **Reading Check**

Answer: tax cuts and rebates to boost the slumping economy

HISTORY Online

Study Central™ provides summaries, interactive games, and online graphic organizers to help students review section content.

4 CLOSE

Have students evaluate the programs President George W. Bush initiated.

TEACH

Reading a Cartogram Tell students that a cartogram shows a proportional representation of land areas, population numbers, or other types of information.

Suggest that students imagine they are members of a city school board charged with the responsibility of planning where the city needs new schools. The standard city map shows the various residential areas and the borders of school districts. Ask students to consider what type of a cartogram would help them. Have students suggest other situations in which a cartogram would be helpful.

Additional Practice
L1
Reinforcing Skills Activity 29

Name _____ Date _____ Class _____

★ Reinforcing Skills Activity 29

Reading a Cartogram

□ **LEARNING THE SKILL**

Cartograms are maps that distort boundaries to show a value—other than land area—for a particular region. Because the size of a country or region is based on a specific value such as population, cartograms are excellent tools for making comparisons. To read a cartogram, begin with the title and key. These elements tell you the value used to render the cartogram. Look at the sizes of the countries or regions featured. Then compare the cartogram with a conventional map so you can see the variations in size.

□ **PRACTICING THE SKILL**

DIRECTIONS: Analyze the thematic map and cartogram below. Then answer the questions that follow on a separate sheet of paper.

GLENCOE
TECHNOLOGY

CD-ROM
Glencoe Skillbuilder Interactive Workbook CD-ROM, Level 2

This interactive CD-ROM reinforces student mastery of essential social studies skills.

910

Reading a Cartogram

Why Learn This Skill?

On most maps, land areas are drawn in proportion to their actual surface areas on the earth. On some maps, however, a small country may appear much larger than usual, and a large country may look much smaller. The shapes of the countries may also look different.

Learning the Skill

Maps that distort country size and shape are called **cartograms.** In a cartogram, country size reflects some value *other* than land area, such as population or gross national product. For example, on a conventional map, Canada appears much larger than India. In a cartogram showing world population, however, India would appear larger than Canada because it has a much larger population. The cartogram is a tool for making visual comparisons. At a glance, you can see how each country or region compares with another in a particular value.

To use a cartogram, first read the title and key to identify what value the cartogram illustrates. Then examine the cartogram to see which countries or regions appear. Find the largest and smallest countries. Compare the cartogram with a conventional land-area map to determine the degree of distortion of particular countries. Finally, draw conclusions about the topic.

Practicing the Skill

Study the cartogram shown on this page, and then answer these questions.

❶ What is the subject of the cartogram?

❷ Which region appears largest on the cartogram? Which appears smallest?

❸ Compare the cartogram to the map of the United States found in the Atlas. Which region is the most distorted in size compared to a land-area map?

❹ Provide a brief explanation for this distortion.

Population Density by Region in the U.S., 1996

Midwest
Northeast
West
South

People per square mile
- 106.9
- 317.9
- 82.6
- 33.4

Sources: *Historical Statistics of the United States: Colonial Times to 1970;* U.S. Census Bureau.

Skills Assessment

Complete the Practicing Skills questions on page 921 and the Chapter 29 Skill Reinforcement Activity to assess your mastery of this skill.

Applying the Skill

Reading a Cartogram Find statistics that compare some value for different states or countries. For example, you might compare the number of farms in each state or the annual oil consumption of countries on one continent. Be creative in your choice. Convert these statistics into a simple cartogram. Determine the relative size of each country or state according to the chosen value. For example, if the United States consumes five times more oil than Canada, then the United States should appear five times larger.

Glencoe's **Skillbuilder Interactive Workbook CD-ROM, Level 2,** provides instruction and practice in key social studies skills.

910

ANSWERS TO PRACTICING THE SKILL

❶ population density

❷ Northeast appears largest and West appears smallest.

❸ West

❹ Population density is low in much of the West.

Applying the Skill
Students' cartograms will vary depending on the statistic chosen. Encourage students to use graph paper to construct the cartogram showing correct proportions.

SECTION 5 The War on Terrorism

Guide to Reading

Main Idea
After suffering the worst terrorist attack in its history when airplanes crashed into the Pentagon and the World Trade Center, the United States launched a massive effort to end international terrorism.

Key Terms and Names
terrorism, state-sponsored terrorism, Osama bin Laden, al-Qaeda, anthrax

Reading Strategy
As you read about America's war on terrorism, complete a graphic organizer similar to the one below to show the different reasons terrorists attack Americans.

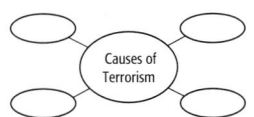
Causes of Terrorism

Reading Objectives
• **Describe** the development of Middle East terrorism.
• **Explain** the response of the United States to the terrorist attacks on the World Trade Center and the Pentagon.

Section Theme
Global Connections International terrorists targeted Americans in order to coerce the United States.

Preview of Events

```
        ♦1980              ♦1990                      ♦2000
```
1979	1988	1998	2001
Soviet Union invades Afghanistan	Al-Qaeda is organized	Bombs explode at U.S. embassies in Kenya and Tanzania	Attacks on the Pentagon and World Trade Center

---

★ An American Story ★

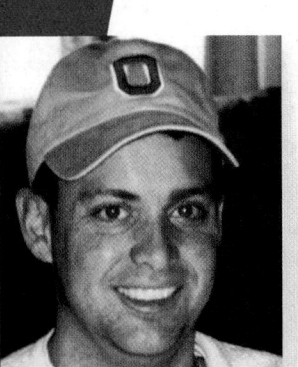
Todd Beamer

At 8:45 A.M. Eastern Daylight Time on September 11, 2001, a Boeing 767 passenger jet slammed into the North Tower of the World Trade Center in New York City. As people below gazed in horror, a second plane collided with the South Tower. Soon afterward, a third plane crashed into the Pentagon in Washington, D.C. At 9:50 A.M., the South Tower collapsed in a billowing cloud of dust and debris. The North Tower fell about 40 minutes later. The falling towers killed thousands of people, burying them beneath a vast mound of rubble.

The airplanes did not crash accidentally. Hijackers deliberately crashed them into the buildings. Hijackers also seized a fourth airplane, United Airlines Flight 93, probably hoping to crash it into the White House or the Capitol. Many passengers on Flight 93 had cell phones. After hearing about the World Trade Center, four passengers—Todd Beamer, Thomas Burnett, Jeremy Glick, and Mark Bingham—decided to do something. An operator listening over a cell phone heard Todd Beamer's voice: "Are you ready, guys? Let's roll." Soon afterward, Flight 93 crashed in a field in Pennsylvania. At that moment, Vice President Dick Cheney was in a bunker under the White House. After hearing that Flight 93 had crashed, he said, "I think an act of heroism just took place on that plane."

—adapted from *Let's Roll: Ordinary People, Extraordinary Courage*

September 11, 2001

The terrorist attacks on September 11, 2001, killed all 266 passengers and crewmembers on the four hijacked planes. Another 125 people died in the Pentagon. In New York City, nearly 3,000 people died. More Americans were killed in the attacks than died at Pearl Harbor or on D-Day in World War II.

CHAPTER 29   Into a New Century   **911**

---

1 FOCUS

Section Overview
This section focuses on the U.S. effort to end international terrorism.

BELLRINGER
Skillbuilder Activity

Project transparency and have students answer the question.

Daily Focus Skills Transparency 29–5

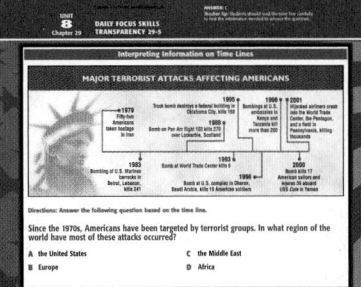

Reading Preview

Answers to Graphic: U.S. support of wealthy countries and families that control Middle Eastern oil; the belief that Western influence undermines Islamic values and beliefs; new strict fundamentalist religious movements that hope to establish a pure Islamic society; American support for Israel

Preteaching Vocabulary
Have students write a short paragraph using all of the Key Terms and Names.

SECTION RESOURCES

📁 Reproducible Masters
• Reproducible Lesson Plan 29–5
• Daily Lecture and Discussion Notes 29–5
• Guided Reading Activity 29–5
• Section Quiz 29–5
• Reading Essentials and Study Guide 29–5
• Performance Assessment Activities and Rubrics

🖋 Transparencies
• Daily Focus Skills Transparency 29–5

Multimedia
• Interactive Tutor Self-Assessment CD-ROM
• ExamView® Pro Testmaker CD-ROM
• Presentation Plus! CD-ROM
• TeacherWorks™ CD-ROM
• Audio Program

2 TEACH

Daily Lecture and Discussion Notes 29–5

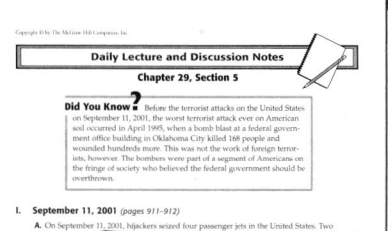

Interpreting a Photograph
Show students a picture of the flag raising at Iwo Jima and ask them how it compares to the picture of firefighters raising the flag at the site of the World Trade Center attack. **L1**

Picturing **History**

Answer: September 11, 2001

Ask: Why do you think terrorists chose the World Trade Center and the Pentagon as targets? *(Students' answers will vary. Students should recognize that the World Trade Center was a symbol of American economic power and the Pentagon is a symbol of U.S. military power.)*

FYI
Construction on the Pentagon began on September 11, 1941, exactly 60 years before terrorists attacked.

Picturing **History**
Transcending Tragedy Although the destruction of the World Trade Center (lower right) and the attack on the Pentagon (right) shocked Americans, people responded rapidly to the crisis. Across the nation, images such as that of firefighters raising a flag in the ruins of the World Trade Center (left) inspired Americans. Many lined up to donate blood. Others raised money and collected food, blankets, and other supplies for the victims and rescue workers. On what date did the attacks occur?

The attacks on the World Trade Center and the Pentagon were acts of terrorism. Terrorism is the use of violence by nongovernmental groups against civilians to achieve a political goal. Terrorist acts are intended to instill fear in people and to frighten their governments into changing their policies.

Middle East Terrorism Although there have been many acts of terrorism in American history, most terrorist attacks on Americans since World War II have been carried out by Middle Eastern groups. The reason Middle Eastern terrorists have targeted Americans can be traced back to events early in the twentieth century.

As oil became important to the American economy in the 1920s, the United States invested heavily in the Middle East oil industry. This industry brought great wealth to the ruling families in some Middle Eastern kingdoms, but most of the people remained poor. Some became angry at the United States for supporting the wealthy kingdoms and families.

The rise of the oil industry increased the Middle East's contact with Western society. As Western ideas spread through the region, many Muslims—followers of the region's dominant religion—feared that their traditional values and beliefs were being weakened. New movements arose calling for a strict interpretation of the Quran—the Muslim holy book—and a return to traditional Muslim religious laws.

These Muslim movements wanted to overthrow pro-Western governments in the Middle East and create a pure Islamic society. Muslims who support these movements are referred to as fundamentalist militants. Although the vast majority of Muslims believe terrorism is contrary to their faith, militants began using terrorism to achieve their goals.

American support of Israel also angered many in the Middle East. In 1947 the UN divided British-controlled Palestine into two territories to provide a home for Jews. One part became Israel. The other part was to become a Palestinian state, but fighting between Israel and the Arab states in 1948 left this territory under the control of Israel, Jordan, and Egypt.

The Palestinians wanted their own nation. In the 1950s, they began staging guerrilla raids and terrorist attacks against Israel. Since the United States gave military and economic aid to Israel, it became the target of Muslim hostility. In the 1970s, several Middle Eastern nations realized they could fight Israel and the United States by providing terrorist groups with money, weapons, and training. When a government secretly supports terrorism, this is called state-sponsored terrorism. The governments of Libya, Syria, Iraq, and Iran have all sponsored terrorism.

A New Terrorist Threat In 1979 the Soviet Union invaded Afghanistan. In response, Muslims from across the Middle East headed to Afghanistan to join the struggle against the Soviets. Among them was a 22-year-old Muslim named **Osama bin Laden.** Bin Laden came from one of Saudi Arabia's wealthiest

912 CHAPTER 29 Into a New Century

Reading Strategy — READING THE TEXT

Using Word Parts A *root* is the part of the word that contains its basic meaning. Unlike a base word, a root is not a word by itself. Many roots come from Greek or Latin. For example, *bio* means "life" (biology, biography); *tele* means "distant" (television, telescope); *dent* means "tooth" (dentist, trident). As they read, have students find root words in the section and find their meanings using a dictionary. **L1** ELL

Refer to *Inclusion for the High School Social Studies Classroom Strategies and Activities* in the TCR.

families. He used his wealth to support the Afghan resistance. In 1988 he founded an organization called **al-Qaeda** (al KY·duh), or "the Base." Al-Qaeda recruited Muslims and channeled money and arms to the Afghan resistance.

Bin Laden's experience in Afghanistan convinced him that superpowers could be beaten. He also believed that Western ideas had contaminated Muslim society. He was outraged when Saudi Arabia allowed American troops on Saudi soil after Iraq invaded Kuwait.

Operating first from Sudan and then from Afghanistan—then under the control of Muslim fundamentalists known as the Taliban—bin Laden dedicated himself and al-Qaeda to driving Westerners, and especially Americans, out of the Middle East. In 1998 he called on Muslims to kill Americans. Soon afterward, bin Laden's followers set off bombs at the American embassies in Kenya and Tanzania. Over 200 people died in the attacks, including 12 Americans, and more than 5,400 were injured.

Shortly after these bombings, President Clinton ordered cruise missiles launched at terrorist facilities in Afghanistan and Sudan. The attacks did not deter bin Laden. In 1999 al-Qaeda terrorists were arrested while trying to smuggle explosives into the United States in an attempt to bomb Seattle. In October 2000, al-Qaeda terrorists crashed a boat loaded with explosives into the USS *Cole*, an American warship, while it was docked in the Middle Eastern country of Yemen.

✓ **Reading Check** **Explaining** What are the three main reasons certain Muslims became angry with the United States?

America Unites

The attack on the *Cole* and the attempted bombing of Seattle were overshadowed by the close presidential election of 2000 and the policies of President George W. Bush's new administration. Then, on September 11, 2001, terrorists struck again, hijacking four American passenger planes and executing the most devastating terrorist attack in history.

Citizens Respond to the Crisis The attacks on the World Trade Center and the Pentagon shocked Americans, but they responded rapidly to the crisis. Firefighters and medical workers from other cities headed to New York to help. Across the nation, Americans donated blood, raised money, and collected food, blankets, and other supplies. Within weeks, Americans had donated over one billion dollars. From around the world came sympathy. "We are all Americans!" wrote one French journalist.

Everywhere across the nation, Americans put up flags to show their unity and resolve. They held candlelight vigils and prayer services as they searched for ways to help. If the terrorists had hoped to divide Americans, they failed. As the Reverend Billy Graham noted at a memorial service: "A tragedy like this could have torn our country apart. But instead it has united us and we have become a family."

A National Emergency The American government reacted quickly by grounding civilian airlines and alerting the armed forces. On September 14, President Bush declared a national emergency. Congress voted to authorize the use of force to fight the terrorists. Intelligence sources and the FBI quickly identified

L1/ELL

Guided Reading Activity 29-5

Name _____ Date _____ Class _____

★ Guided Reading Activity 29-5

DIRECTIONS: Recalling Facts Read the section and answer the questions below. Refer to your textbook to write the answers.

1. What did hijackers do on September 11, 2001? _____

2. What is terrorism? _____

3. What role did America's need for oil play in Middle Eastern terrorism? _____

4. What do fundamentalist militant Muslims seek? _____

5. How did some Middle Eastern _____

✓ **Reading Check**

Answer: U.S. support of wealthy countries and families, Western influence undermining traditional values and beliefs, and American support for Israel

Designing a Memorial Have students work in pairs to design a memorial to the victims and heroes of the September 11, 2001, terrorist attacks. Encourage students to use library and Internet resources to learn about the designs of other memorials. Have students note how symbolism is used in the design of many memorials. Have the pairs write a paragraph explaining the symbolism they chose for their memorial. **L2**

American Heroes

After two hijacked aircraft slammed into the twin towers of the World Trade Center on September 11, survivors in the building headed down smoky, dust-choked stairways to escape. Yet even as thousands of people streamed out of the buildings, hundreds more headed into the blazing structures, fully aware of the danger they faced.

The people climbing the staircases into the burning buildings were New York City firefighters and rescue workers. When the towers collapsed, over 300 firefighters died. The tragedy at the World Trade Center reminded everyone that these men and women who daily risk their lives to save others are true American heroes whose sacrifices must not be forgotten.

DIFFERENTIATED INSTRUCTION

At-Risk Students Have students create an illustrated time line of the terrorist attacks mentioned in this section. Instruct students to use illustrations and photographs from magazines and other sources to depict each event on the time line. Encourage students to add other related events, such as the first bombing of the World Trade Center in 1993. **L1** ELL

☞ Refer to *Inclusion for the High School Social Studies Classroom Strategies and Activities* in the TCR.

NATIONAL GEOGRAPHIC — Major Terrorist Attacks Affecting Americans, 1970–2005

1. 1970 Terrorists hijack airplanes to Jordan
2. 1979 Fifty-two Americans held hostage in Iran for more than a year
3. 1983 Bombing of U.S. Marine barracks in Beirut, Lebanon, kills 241
4. 1985 TWA flight 847 hijacked; hostages held for 17 days in Beirut, Lebanon
5. 1986 Bombing at West Berlin dance club; kills 3, injures 150
6. 1988 Bomb on Pan Am flight 103 kills 270 in Lockerbie, Scotland
7. 1993 Bomb at World Trade Center kills 6
8. 1995 Truck bomb destroys a federal building in Oklahoma City; kills 168, injures more than 500
9. 1996 Bomb at U.S. complex in Dharan, Saudi Arabia, kills 19 American soldiers
10. 1998 Bombings at U.S. embassies in Kenya and Tanzania kill more than 200
11. 2000 Bomb kills 17 American sailors and injures 39 aboard USS *Cole*
12. 2001 Hijacked airliners crash into the World Trade Center, the Pentagon, and a field in Pennsylvania, killing thousands
13. 2002 Bombs in Indonesia kill over 200
14. 2005 Attacks kill American civilians helping to rebuild Iraq

the attacks as the work of Osama bin Laden and the al-Qaeda network.

President Bush decided the time had come to end the threat of terrorism in the world. He issued an ultimatum to the Taliban regime in Afghanistan, demanding they turn over bin Laden and his supporters and close all terrorist camps. He also declared that although the war on terrorism would start by targeting al-Qaeda, it would not stop there. "It will not end," he announced, "until every terrorist group of global reach has been found, stopped, and defeated."

The president also announced that the United States would no longer tolerate states that aided terrorists. "From this day forward," he proclaimed, "any nation that continues to harbor or support terrorism will be regarded by the United States as a hostile regime." The war, President Bush warned, would not end quickly, but it was a war the nation had to fight:

> ❝Great harm has been done to us. We have suffered great loss. And in our grief and anger we have found our mission and our moment. . . . Our Nation—this generation—will lift a dark threat of violence from our people and our future. . . . ❞
>
> —President George W. Bush, Address to Joint Session of Congress, September 20, 2001

✔ Reading Check **Outlining** What steps did the president take in response to the terrorist attacks?

A New War Begins

Secretary of Defense Donald Rumsfeld warned Americans that "this will be a war like none other our nation has faced." The enemy, he explained, "is a global network of terrorist organizations and their state sponsors, committed to denying free people the opportunity to live as they choose." Military force would be used to fight terrorism, but other means would be used as well.

Fighting Terrorism At Home In an effort to protect the American people from further terrorist attacks, President Bush called on Congress to create the Department of Homeland Security to merge the

INTERDISCIPLINARY CONNECTIONS ACTIVITY

dozens of federal agencies working to prevent terrorism. Among the oranizations that the new department controls are the Coast Guard, the Border Patrol, the Immigration and Naturalization Service, the Customs Service, and the Federal Emergency Management Agency.

President Bush also asked Congress to pass legislation to help law enforcement agencies track down terrorist suspects. Congress acted with unusual speed, and the president signed the antiterrorism bill—known as the USA Patriot Act—into law in October 2001. The new law allowed secret searches to avoid tipping off suspects in terrorism cases. It also allowed authorities to obtain a single nationwide search warrant that could be used anywhere. The law also made it easier to wiretap suspects, and it allowed authorities to track e-mail and seize voice mail. Although Congress sought to balance Americans' rights with the need to increase security, civil libertarians worried that the new law eroded the Fourth Amendment's protection against unreasonable search and seizure.

Bioterrorism Strikes America

On October 5, 2001, a new terrorist attack began when a Florida newspaper editor died from anthrax. Anthrax is a type of bacteria that has been used to create biological weapons and if not treated with antibiotics it can kill quickly.

Soon, anthrax was found in news organizations and government offices, in some cases brought in through the mail. The FBI investigated the attacks, but apprehended no suspects. Government agencies responded by adopting rigorous measures to screen their mail.

War in Afghanistan

On October 7, 2001, the United States began bombing targets in Afghanistan to attack al-Qaeda's camps and the Taliban's military forces. President Bush explained that Islam and the Afghan people were not the enemy, and he pledged food, medi-

cine, and other supplies to Afghan refugees. The United States also sent aid to a coalition of Afghan groups, known as the Northern Alliance, which had been fighting the Taliban.

The American bombing campaign quickly shattered the Taliban's defenses. The Northern Alliance then launched a massive attack and by early December, the Taliban regime had collapsed. The United States and its allies then began helping Afghan leaders create a new government. In January of 2004, Afghanistan adopted a new constitution that granted equality for men and women and defined the country as an Islamic Republic. In October, Hamid Karzai became the first democratically-elected leader of Afghanistan. Parliamentary elections were set for September 2005. American and allied troops remained in Afghanistan to act as peacekeepers and continue hunting for bin Laden and other al-Qaeda terrorists.

Weapons of Mass Destruction

The United States grew concerned that groups such as al-Qaeda might acquire nuclear, chemical, or biological weapons. These weapons of mass destruction could kill tens of thousands of people at once.

In his state of the union speech in January 2002, President Bush warned that an "axis of evil," which he identified as Iraq, Iran, and North Korea, posed a grave threat to the world. Each of these countries had been known to sponsor terrorism and was suspected

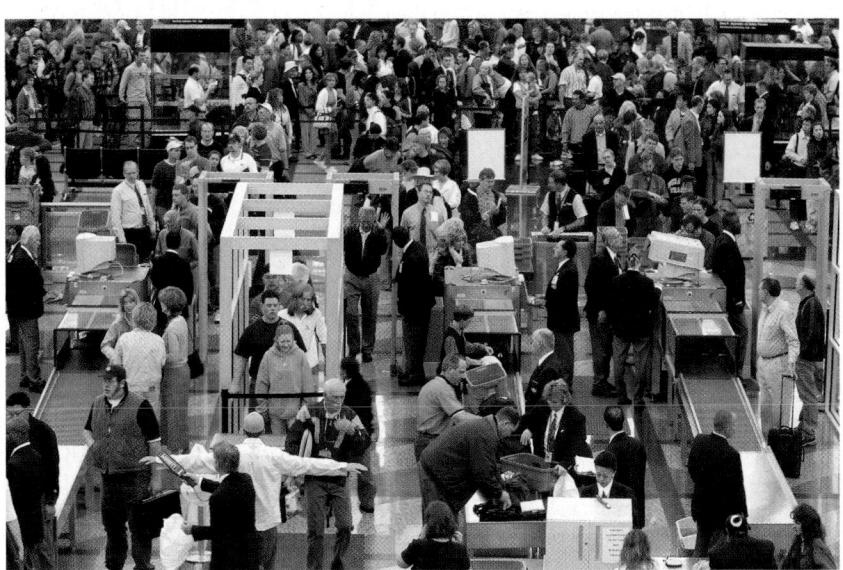

Airport Security Airline passengers, such as these at Denver International Airport, had to wait in long lines to go through checkpoints when American airports increased security measures after the terrorist attacks of 9/11.

CHAPTER 29   Into a New Century   **915**

CRITICAL THINKING ACTIVITY

Analyzing Have students find and bring to class an example of an article that uses both primary and secondary sources to tell the story of the September 11, 2001, terrorist attacks or of the massive relief effort that followed. Have students write a one-page summary of the article identifying the various points of view and explaining how the writer used a variety of source material to paint a picture of the events. As a class, discuss the importance of both types of sources in explaining historical events. **L2**

Creating a Fact Sheet Have small groups of students create fact sheets about weapons of mass destruction, including information about the types of weapons that exist, the countries that have or are developing them, and the attempts at controlling their existence and proliferation. Remind the groups that they should use good sources for their information. Have students submit a separate bibliography citing sources used. **L2**

✓ Reading Check

Answer: federal department created to protect the U.S. from terrorist attacks that combined Coast Guard, Border Patrol, Immigration and Naturalization Service, Customs Service, and the Federal Emergency Management Agency

✓ Reading Check

Answer: Iraq had developed and used weapons of mass destruction, supported terrorism, and refused to comply with U.N. resolutions

3 ASSESS

Assign Section 5 Assessment as homework or as an in-class activity.

🌑 Have students use the **Interactive Tutor Self-Assessment CD-ROM.**

L1/ELL

Reading Essentials and Study Guide 29–5

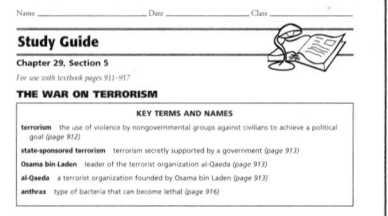

Name _____ Date _____ Class _____

Study Guide

Chapter 29, Section 5
For use with textbook pages 911–917

THE WAR ON TERRORISM

KEY TERMS AND NAMES

terrorism the use of violence by nongovernmental groups against civilians to achieve a political goal *(page 912)*
state-sponsored terrorism terrorism secretly supported by a government *(page 913)*
Osama bin Laden leader of the terrorist organization al-Qaeda *(page 913)*
al-Qaeda a terrorist organization founded by Osama bin Laden *(page 913)*
anthrax type of bacteria that can become lethal *(page 916)*

---

of trying to develop weapons of mass destruction. The president promised to take strong action: "The United States of America will not permit the world's most dangerous regimes to threaten us with the world's most destructive weapons."

Months later, North Korea announced that it had restarted its nuclear program. The Bush administration exerted diplomatic pressure to persuade the North Korean government to stop the program, but the North Koreans argued that they needed the weapons to protect themselves from a U.S. attack.

✓ Reading Check
Explaining What is the Department of Homeland Security?

Confronting Iraq

President Bush considered Iraq a more immediate threat than North Korea in developing and distributing weapons of mass destruction. Iraq's dictator, Saddam Hussein, had already used chemical weapons twice, once in Iraq's war against Iran in the 1980s and again in 1988 against the Kurds, an ethnic minority in northern Iraq who had rebelled against Hussein's regime. After the Gulf War in 1991, UN inspectors found evidence that Iraq had developed biological weapons and was working on a nuclear bomb.

Pressure on Iraq In the summer of 2002, President Bush called for a regime change in Iraq. In September he asked for a UN resolution demanding that Iraq give up its weapons of mass destruction. He made it clear, though, that the United States would act with or without UN support. He asked Congress to authorize the use of force against Iraq, and Congress granted his request.

During the congressional elections of 2002, Democrats focused on the nation's faltering economy, but President Bush made national security his chief theme. His vigorous campaigning helped Republicans add seats in the House of Representatives and regain a slim majority in the Senate.

War and Its Aftermath Soon after the elections, the United Nations approved a new resolution that set a deadline for Iraq, but the Bush administration doubted its effectiveness. The administration believed that Saddam Hussein had hidden weapons of mass destruction that were ready or nearly ready for use. Bush also believed that Hussein had ties to al-Qaeda. Many of America's traditional allies in Europe wanted to give the inspectors more time, and refused to support a resolution from the UN Security Council author-

izing the use of force. President Bush then argued that the Iraq threat justified a preemptive war—a war launched to prevent rather than to respond to an attack. The United States, Great Britain, and about 30 other countries prepared for war.

On March 20, 2003, the U.S.-led coalition attacked Iraq. Over the next six weeks, the Iraqi army dissolved as soldiers refused to risk their lives for Hussein. The coalition forces quickly seized control of the country, and on May 1, President Bush declared that the major combat was over. About 140 Americans, and several thousand Iraqis, had died. American troops captured Saddam Hussein by the end of the year.

Yet both the controversy over Iraq and the fighting continued. U.S. forces found no evidence that Iraq possessed weapons of mass destruction, and a serious link between Saddam Hussein and al-Qaeda was not discovered. The United States also lacked sufficient forces in Iraq to prevent the widespread looting that broke out after Hussein's government fell. The lawlessness that followed the war encouraged radical religious factions within Iraq and terrorits who entered the country to target American troops and consultants from coalition countries. More Americans died in Iraq after President Bush had declared the end of combat than during the war itself.

As casualties and costs mounted, President Bush sought help from the UN and other countries to stabilize and rebuild Iraq. In April 2005, Iraq's Transitional National Assembly selected Ibrahim al-Ja'afari as Iraq's prime minister.

Writing the draft of Iraq's constitution exposed the divisions within the country. The Kurds and Shiite Muslims presented a draft document in August 2005, but the Sunni Muslims disagreed with the new federal structure, which would decentralize Iraq's government and give new powers to local provincial councils. The Sunnis, who governed Iraq during Saddam Hussein's regime, believed federalism would greatly reduce their influence.

✓ Reading Check
Summarizing Why did President Bush decide to confront Iraq?

The 2004 Elections

The war on terrorism and the war in Iraq dominated the election of 2004. In the wake of the terrorist attacks, President Bush won widespread support for his firm determination to wage war on terrorism.

The Kerry Challenge President Bush and Vice President Cheney won nomination for a second term

---

EXTENDING THE CONTENT

Women's Rights On November 17, 2001, First Lady Laura Bush used the president's weekly radio address to deliver a message of support and hope for the women and children of Afghanistan. In the address she said: ". . . Fighting brutality against women and children is not the expression of a specific culture; it is the acceptance of our common humanity—a commitment shared by people of good will on every continent. . . . The fight against terrorism is also a fight for the rights and dignity of women."

without challenge. After primary campaigns that focused largely on the war in Iraq, Democrats nominated Massachusetts senator John Kerry and North Carolina senator John Edwards.

Kerry's Vietnam War service was a dominant campaign issue. He had enlisted in the Navy and fought in Vietnam, where he was decorated for valor. Kerry returned from Vietnam convinced of the war's futility and became an outspoken critic. His experiences in Vietnam made him leery of sending American troops into combat.

Making a point President Bush debates Democratic Party nominee John Kerry in the 2004 presidential election campaign.

A Choice for a Divided Nation
In policies and personalities, Bush and Kerry offered the nation a sharp choice. President Bush pledged to continue cutting taxes and building a strong national defense. He opposed abortion and endorsed a constitutional amendment to ban same-sex marriages. His supporters saw him as someone who operated on fixed moral and religious principles, trusted his instincts, and steadfastly followed a course of action once he made a decision.

Senator Kerry criticized what he considered Bush's single-mindedness, insisting that a president must be able to focus on more than one issue at a time. He pledged to address domestic economic problems while pursuing the war on terrorism. Kerry promised to strengthen Social Security and to raise taxes on the wealthiest individuals in order to fund health-care insurance for the millions of Americans who lacked health coverage. Although a Catholic, Kerry differed with church leaders on many social issues, including abortion.

While the events of September 11, 2001, had united the nation emotionally, the country remained as divided politically as it had been during the 2000 election. President Bush drew his support from the Southeast and Southwest, as well as from rural areas and outer suburbs. Senator Kerry's base was in the Northeast and on the West Coast, along with cities and inner suburbs. Both candidates devoted most of their campaigning to a few "battleground" states in the Midwest and in Florida, where voters' opinions were the most narrowly divided.

Bush Wins a Second Term Both parties saw voter turnout as the key to the victory. On Election Day the Republicans best succeeded in mobilizing their core supporters. President Bush took the lead in the popular vote and a majority in the Electoral College. His victory helped preserve the Republican majorities in Congress. "We are led, by events and common sense, to one conclusion," President Bush asserted in his second inaugural address: "The survival of liberty in our land increasingly depends on the success of liberty in other lands." The best hope for peace in our world is the expansion of freedom in all the world."

☑ **Reading Check** **Summarizing** Which issues divided the country during the 2004 presidential election?

 Study Central™ To review this section, go to **tarvol2.glencoe.com** and click on **Study Central™**.

SECTION 5 ASSESSMENT

Checking for Understanding
1. **Define:** terrorism, state-sponsored terrorism.
2. **Identify:** Osama bin Laden, al-Qaeda, anthrax.
3. **Explain** how the United States responded to the attacks on New York City and Washington, D.C.

Reviewing Themes
4. **Global Connections** Why does American foreign policy anger Islamic fundamentalists in the Middle East?

Critical Thinking
5. **Interpreting** What factors have contributed to the rise of Middle Eastern terrorist groups?
6. **Organizing** Use a graphic organizer similar to the one below to list the reasons why President Bush declared war on Iraq.

```
_____
_____
_____  ➤ War on Iraq
_____
_____
```

Analyzing Visuals
7. **Examining Maps** Study the map on page 914 of terrorist attacks. In what region of the world did most of the attacks take place?

Writing About History
8. **Persuasive Writing** The attacks on New York City and Washington, D.C., convinced many Americans that more security was needed, even if it meant giving up some freedoms. Write a letter to a newspaper explaining why you are for or against increased security.

L2

Section Quiz 29–5

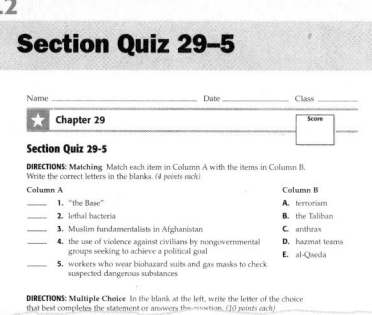

Reteach
Have students describe the development of Middle East terrorism.

Enrich
Invite interested students to report on the U.S. efforts to end international terrorism. Have students share successes, failures, and ongoing challenges.

☑ **Reading Check**

Answer: the war on terrorism, the war in Iraq, tax cuts/raises, abortion, same-sex marriages, Social Security, and health care

Study Central™ provides summaries, interactive games, and online graphic organizers to help students review section content.

4 CLOSE

Have students explain America's response to the terrorist attacks on New York and the Pentagon.

SECTION 5 ASSESSMENT ANSWERS

1. Terms are in blue.
2. Osama bin Laden (p. 913), al-Qaeda (p. 913), anthrax (p. 916)
3. citizens donated money and supplies; the government vowed to end terrorism and targeted al-Qaeda and the Taliban regime in Afghanistan
4. U.S. support for Israel and for wealthy ruling families in some Middle Eastern countries angers Islamic fundamentalists.
5. increased contact with Western society, the growth of Islamic fundamentalism, and countries that provide terrorists with money, weapons, and training
6. Iraq sponsored terrorism and had used chemical weapons; inspectors had found evidence of biological weapons and nuclear bomb making
7. the Middle East
8. Students' letters will vary.

917

Looking Back...

1 FOCUS

Remind students that we live in a representative republic. We elect the leaders of government who make decisions and perform the functions of running the government.

2 TEACH

Reading Strategy

Explaining a Quotation Tell students that on October 14, 1774, the Continental Congress issued its Declaration of Rights and Grievances intended to bring the colonists' grievances before King George III. One of the resolutions reads: "That the foundation of English liberty, and of all free government, is a right in the people to participate in their legislative council:. . ." Have students explain what the congress meant by these words. Then have them review the events of that era and determine how the king or the British Parliament had, in the colonists' view, violated these rights. **L1**

Researching a Topic Have students research changes in voting rights that occurred because of the confusion surrounding the 2000 presidential election. Have students present their findings in a bulleted list. **L2**

Representative Government

Why It Matters Bill Daley, the chairperson of Vice President Al Gore's presidential campaign, was frantically trying to reach the vice president. It was 2:00 A.M. on Wednesday morning, November 8, 2000, the day after the presidential election. The election had come down to the vote counts in one state—Florida—and the votes in Florida were showing George W. Bush as having a significant lead. Gore was preparing to publicly concede the election. Daley, however, had heard that the latest Florida counts showed Bush's lead shrinking to below one percent. There would have to be a recount. When Daley finally got Gore on the phone, Daley shouted, "Whatever you do, do not go out on the stage."

As the debate began in Florida over how to recount the ballots, Daley stressed that "technicalities should not determine the presidency of the United States; the will of the people should." The dispute over how to recount the ballots in Florida mattered deeply to both candidates and to the American people, because it involved one of the basic ideas of the American system of government—that officials are elected to represent the needs and wishes of the people.

Ballot box

Steps To . . . Representative Government

The United States has a representative government in which citizens elect representatives to speak for them on political matters. The roots of American representative government date back to the colonial era.

Virginia House of Burgesses The first representative body in colonial America was the Virginia House of Burgesses. The House was comprised of two elected representatives, or burgesses, from each of 10 of Virginia's settlements. The body had the power to pass laws for the colony. The Virginia Company, however, had the power to disallow laws passed by the Burgesses.

Despite this limitation on its authority, the House of Burgesses changed Virginia from a company-run colony into a partially self-governing colony where elected representatives made the laws. Later on, Virginia became a royal colony, ruled by a governor appointed by the king. To keep settlers' support, the king allowed the House of Burgesses to continue to meet. This established the tradition of representative government in the colonies.

> *"The right of voting for representatives is the primary right by which other rights are protected. To take away this right is to reduce a man to [the] slavery . . . of being subject to the will of another. . . ."*
>
> —*Thomas Paine, 1795*

918

EXTENDING THE CONTENT

Redistricting The Constitution requires an official census of the United States every 10 years. One of the purposes of the census is to reallocate the number of seats in the House of Representatives based on current state populations. By basing the number of House seats on a state's population, the true representative nature of the American government is maintained.

THE FIRST LEGISLATIVE ASSEMBLY IN THE NEW WORLD, JAMESTOWN, VIRGINIA, JULY, 1619

Virginia House of Burgesses

The Mayflower Compact The Mayflower Compact was an agreement signed in November 1620 by the male passengers aboard the *Mayflower* before they came ashore at Plymouth. The signers agreed to form a civil government that represented the wishes of the majority. The compact called for government leaders to "enact, constitute, and frame such just and equal laws, ordinances, acts, constitutions . . . as shall be thought most meet and convenient for the general good of the colony. . . ."

Fundamental Orders of Connecticut The notion of representative government took another step forward in 1639 when several towns along the Connecticut River joined together to create a government. They laid out the structure of this government in the Fundamental Orders of Connecticut—the first written constitution in American history. The document, which consisted of a preamble and eleven orders, gave citizens the right to elect the governor, judges, and representatives to make laws. The Orders also introduced the idea of limited government. For example, citizens could call the legislature into session if the governor refused to do so. The legislature could also remove officials from power for misbehavior.

Colonial Assemblies By the time of the American Revolution, most British colonies in America had local assemblies elected by the people. Colonial governments were not truly representative, however, because the king chose the governors and gave them the power to veto laws passed by the assemblies. Although the governors were powerful, the assemblies could control them by refusing to vote for new taxes. The American Revolution was partly caused by Britain's challenge to this system. When Britain began taxing the colonies directly, it endangered the power of the local assemblies. Americans insisted that taxation without representation violated their rights.

The U.S. Constitution These ideas of representative government and limited government would be bound together in the document that has governed the nation as a whole for more than 200 years: the U.S. Constitution. The Federalists, or those who supported the Constitution during its ratification process, strongly believed in representative government. Indeed, the authors of the *Federalist Papers,* the collection of famous essays written in support of the Constitution, preferred a government one step removed from the common people, whom they insisted "seldom judge or determine right." The fact that the Constitution placed political power "in the hands of the representatives of the people," the authors stated, "is the essential, and, after all, only efficacious security for the rights and privileges of the people."

Checking for Understanding

1. What is a representative government?
2. What was significant about the formation of the Virginia House of Burgesses?

Critical Thinking

1. Do you think a written constitution is preferrable to a constitution based on tradition? Explain.
2. Would you rather live under a representative government or in a direct democracy, where people govern themselves by voting directly on all issues? Explain.

Looking Back...

Writing a Persuasive Essay
Encourage students to write a persuasive essay that supports the position that all Americans who are eligible to vote should participate in the process of electing government representatives. Encourage volunteers to share their essays with the class. L2

3 ASSESS

Have students answer the Checking for Understanding and Critical Thinking questions.

Ask students to write a paragraph agreeing or disagreeing with the following quote from Hugh Henry Brackenridge's novel *Modern Chivalry*:
"A democracy is beyond all question the freest government: because under this, every man is equally protected by the laws, and has equally a voice in making them. But I do not say an equal voice; because some men have stronger lungs than others, and can express more forcibly their opinions of public affairs."

4 CLOSE

Review with students the reasons that the Founders chose a representative form of government over a direct democracy.

Checking for Understanding

1. A representative government is one in which citizens elect others to represent their own wishes and political opinions in government.
2. It was the first representative body in colonial America and could act on all tax laws and draft legislation.

Critical Thinking

1. Answers will vary. Some students will say a traditional constitution is more flexible and can change with the times. Others will say a written Constitution is a more reliable guide to what the Founders wanted and makes it easier to uphold the Constitution in court.
2. Answers may vary. Once students consider the large number of matters to be decided, many may support a representative democracy over a direct democracy.

CHAPTER 29 ASSESSMENT and ACTIVITIES

CHAPTER 29

GLENCOE TECHNOLOGY

MindJogger Videoquiz
Use the **MindJogger Videoquiz** to review Chapter 29 content.

 Available in DVD

Reviewing Key Terms
Students' answers will vary. The pages where the words appear in the text are shown in parentheses.

1. **microprocessor** (p. 893)
2. **software** (p. 893)
3. **telecommute** (p. 893)
4. **Internet** (p. 894)
5. **perjury** (p. 900)
6. **ethnic cleansing** (p. 900)
7. **trade deficit** (p. 903)
8. **euro** (p. 903)
9. **nuclear proliferation** (p. 905)
10. **global warming** (p. 905)
11. **chad** (p. 908)
12. **strategic defense** (p. 909)
13. **terrorism** (p. 912)
14. **state-sponsored terrorism** (p. 913)

Reviewing Key Facts

15. ENIAC (p. 892), Silicon Valley (p. 893), AmeriCorps (p. 897), Contract with America (p. 898), Kenneth Starr (p. 900), NAFTA (p. 903), Kyoto Protocol (p. 905), Al Gore (p. 907), George W. Bush (p. 907), Ralph Nader (p. 907), Osama bin Laden (p. 913), al-Qaeda (p. 913)

16. connected employees in offices together, modernized record-keeping, increased productivity, and streamlined research avenues

17. The mapping of the human genome made it possible to study and manipulate genes and cells at the molecular level. Other advances resulted in new medicines, animal growth hormones, new industrial chemicals, and genetically engineered plants.

Reviewing Key Terms
On a sheet of paper, use each of these terms in a sentence.

1. microprocessor
2. software
3. telecommute
4. Internet
5. perjury
6. ethnic cleansing
7. trade deficit
8. euro
9. nuclear proliferation
10. global warming
11. chad
12. strategic defense
13. terrorism
14. state-sponsored terrorism

Reviewing Key Facts

15. **Identify:** ENIAC, Silicon Valley, AmeriCorps, Contract with America, Kenneth Starr, NAFTA, Kyoto Protocol, Al Gore, George W. Bush, Ralph Nader, Osama bin Laden, al-Qaeda.
16. How did compact computers transform the workplace?
17. What advances in biotechnology occurred in the 1990s?
18. After his election in 1992, how did President Clinton propose to strengthen the nation's economy?
19. What regional trade blocs were formed in the 1990s to increase international trade?
20. Which state was significant in the 2000 presidential election?

Critical Thinking

21. **Analyzing Themes: Global Connections** What foreign-policy challenges did President Clinton face? Do you think he handled the situations effectively? Why or why not?

22. **Evaluating** What developments in the Middle East explain the rise of terrorist groups that want to attack Americans?

23. **Analyzing Points of View** Read the excerpt below about global warming, then answer the questions that follow.

> ❝The world is getting warmer, and by the end of the 21st century could warm by another 6 degrees Celsius (10.8 degrees Fahrenheit) . . . . And climate scientists at the heart of the research are now convinced that human action is to blame for some or most of this warming. . . .
>
> Everywhere climatologists look—at tree-ring patterns, fossil successions in rock strata, ocean-floor corings . . . they see evidence of dramatic shifts from cold to hot to cold again . . . . None of these ancient shifts can be blamed on humans . . . . There is still room for argument about the precise role of the sun or other natural cycles in the contribution to global warming. . . . Richard S. Lindzen, a leading meteorologist at the Massachusetts Institute of Technology said . . . the picture of a consensus about global warming was 'misleading to the public and even to scientists . . . .' But most climate scientists . . . now believe that the climate is being influenced by human beings.❞
>
> —from *World Press Review*, February 2001

a. According to the article, what two points of view exist about global warming?

b. Why is the debate on global warming important?

Chapter Summary

The Technological Revolution
- Personal computers grow faster and more powerful.
- Communications deregulation expands cellular phone usage.
- The Internet provides a worldwide network of information.
- Biotechnology research increases knowledge of human genetics.

The Clinton Years
- A new global economy emerges based on regional trade blocs.
- The ozone layer and global warming become major environmental issues.
- Clinton and Congress cut spending; reform welfare and health care.
- U.S. economy grows rapidly; federal budget is balanced.
- U.S. tries to end violence in Haiti, the Middle East, and the Balkans.
- Scandal and impeachment tarnish the Clinton administration.

War on Terrorism
- Terrorists destroy the World Trade Center and attack the Pentagon.
- Bush organizes a global coalition and launches a new war on terrorism.
- War in Iraq ends the regime of Saddam Hussein, but new insurgents resist the coalition's military presence.
- Afghanistan forms new government following democratic elections.
- Iraq establishes transitional government and begins drafting new constitution.

18. by lowering interest rates and reducing federal deficits
19. North American Free Trade Agreement, European Union, Asia Pacific Economic Cooperation
20. The outcome in Florida determined the winner of the election of 2000.

Critical Thinking

21. Foreign policy challenges included restoring Haiti's president, ethnic cleansing in Bosnia and Kosovo, and ongoing tensions in the Middle East. Students' evaluations of Clinton's effectiveness should be supported with examples and sound reasoning.

22. American support for Israel; American investment in the oil industry in the Middle East; belief of some Muslims that American support of wealthy

Self-Check Quiz

Visit the *American Republic Since 1877* Web site at tarvol2.glencoe.com and click on *Self-Check Quizzes—Chapter 29* to assess your knowledge of chapter content.

24. Categorizing Complete the graphic organizer below by listing changes in communications, politics, the economy, and population that occurred in the United States by the end of the 1900s.

	Change
Communications	
Politics	
Economy	
Population	

Practicing Skills

25. Reading a Cartogram Create a cartogram that reflects the importance of each state in the Electoral College. Research the number of votes held by each state, and alter the size of each state to roughly show that state's number of available votes. Create questions that refer to the information you present in your cartogram.

Chapter Activities

26. Applying Chronology Skills Absolute chronology refers to specific dates, while relative chronology looks at when something occurred with reference to when other things occurred. Practice relative chronology by listing the presidents of the twentieth century in the order they served as president. Then practice absolute chronology by giving the dates of their terms in office.

27. Researching Election Results Study the 2000 election map and chart on page 908. Then use library or Internet resources to research statistics on the 1996 presidential election. Using the 2000 election map and chart as a guide, create a similar thematic map and chart of the 1996 election. Create questions about your map and chart that would help a classmate understand the data you have compiled.

Writing Activity

28. Informative Writing Research the changing roles of the federal and state governments as a result of recent legislative reforms, including gun control and welfare reforms. Based on your research, write a short paper predicting how the role of the federal government and the state governments might change in order to implement the legislative programs. Present your predictions to the class.

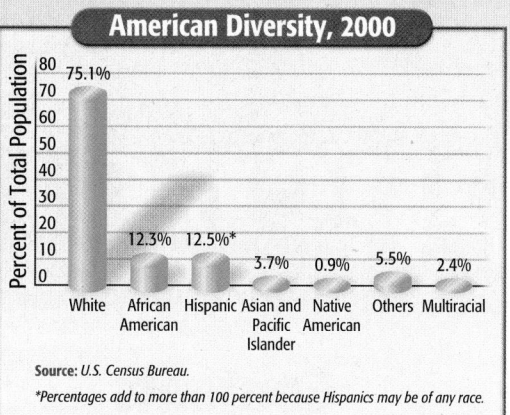

American Diversity, 2000

White 75.1% · African American 12.3% · Hispanic 12.5%* · Asian and Pacific Islander 3.7% · Native American 0.9% · Others 5.5% · Multiracial 2.4%

Source: U.S. Census Bureau.

*Percentages add to more than 100 percent because Hispanics may be of any race.

Geography and History

29. The graph above shows the diverse population of the United States at the beginning of the new century. Study the graph and answer the questions below.

a. Interpreting Graphs Why is getting accurate data on the Hispanic population difficult?

b. Making Generalizations How will population diversity affect government in the future?

Standardized Test Practice

Directions: Choose the phrase that best completes the following sentence.

The Contract with America involved

F a commitment by Russia to eliminate land-based nuclear weapons.

G a campaign promise by President Clinton to create a national health care system for all Americans.

H a legislative agenda promoted by the Republican Party in 1994.

J programs intended to increase the size and readiness of the military.

Test-Taking Tip: This question requires that you remember details of a specific program. Use the process of elimination if you are unsure. Does the Contract with America sound like a foreign policy agreement between two countries?

Have students visit the Web site at tarvol2.glencoe.com to review Chapter 29 and take the Self-Check Quiz.

27. Students' maps and questions will vary. Encourage students to work with a partner to share their maps and questions.

Writing Activity

28. Students' reports should include specific predictions about the federal and state legislative programs.

Geography and History

29. a. Students should note that some Hispanics would classify themselves in the Other or Multiracial categories. **b.** Students' answers will vary. Encourage students to give reasons for their answers.

Standardized Test Practice

Answer: H

Test-Taking Tip: Encourage students to put a face with the Contract with America. Even if they cannot remember Newt Gingrich's name they might remember that it was not a Clinton initiative and therefore they can eliminate answer G. The correct answer is H.

Bonus Question ?

Ask: Who were the Democratic and Republican presidential and vice presidential candidates in 2000? *(Democratic: Al Gore and Joseph Lieberman; Republican: George W. Bush and Richard Cheney)*

---

oil-producing countries increased Western influence and undermined traditional values and beliefs

23. a. Some scientists believe human activity causes global warming. Others think natural factors may be involved. **b.** Global warming may alter the climate. If human activity is causing global warming, we may be able to stop it.

24. communications: Internet, wireless technology; politics: government shutdowns, impeachment; economy: global economic blocs, Internet, and world economy; population: racial diversity, aging, immigration

Practicing Skills

25. Cartograms will vary but should reflect the number of electoral votes in each state.

Chapter Activities

26. Students may present their lists in the form of a chart that contains the presidents' names in order in one column and their terms in a second column.

Appendix

Contents

Presidents of the United States

In this resource you will find portraits of the individuals who served as presidents of the United States, along with their occupations, political party affiliations, and other interesting facts.

**The Republican Party during this period developed into today's Democratic Party. Today's Republican Party originated in 1854.*

1 George Washington

Presidential term: 1789–1797
Lived: 1732–1799
Born in: Virginia
Elected from: Virginia
Occupations: Soldier, Planter
Party: None
Vice President: John Adams

2 John Adams

Presidential term: 1797–1801
Lived: 1735–1826
Born in: Massachusetts
Elected from: Massachusetts
Occupations: Teacher, Lawyer
Party: Federalist
Vice President: Thomas Jefferson

3 Thomas Jefferson

Presidential term: 1801–1809
Lived: 1743–1826
Born in: Virginia
Elected from: Virginia
Occupations: Planter, Lawyer
Party: Republican**
Vice Presidents: Aaron Burr, George Clinton

4 James Madison

Presidential term: 1809–1817
Lived: 1751–1836
Born in: Virginia
Elected from: Virginia
Occupation: Planter
Party: Republican**
Vice Presidents: George Clinton, Elbridge Gerry

5 James Monroe

Presidential term: 1817–1825
Lived: 1758–1831
Born in: Virginia
Elected from: Virginia
Occupation: Lawyer
Party: Republican**
Vice President: Daniel D. Tompkins

6 John Quincy Adams

Presidential term: 1825–1829
Lived: 1767–1848
Born in: Massachusetts
Elected from: Massachusetts
Occupation: Lawyer
Party: Republican**
Vice President: John C. Calhoun

7 Andrew Jackson

Presidential term: 1829–1837
Lived: 1767–1845
Born in: South Carolina
Elected from: Tennessee
Occupations: Lawyer, Soldier
Party: Democratic
Vice Presidents: John C. Calhoun, Martin Van Buren

8 Martin Van Buren

Presidential term: 1837–1841
Lived: 1782–1862
Born in: New York
Elected from: New York
Occupation: Lawyer
Party: Democratic
Vice President: Richard M. Johnson

9 William H. Harrison

Presidential term: 1841
Lived: 1773–1841
Born in: Virginia
Elected from: Ohio
Occupations: Soldier, Planter
Party: Whig
Vice President: John Tyler

10 John Tyler

Presidential term: 1841–1845
Lived: 1790–1862
Born in: Virginia
Elected as V.P. from: Virginia
Succeeded Harrison
Occupation: Lawyer
Party: Whig
Vice President: None

11 James K. Polk

Presidential term: 1845–1849
Lived: 1795–1849
Born in: North Carolina
Elected from: Tennessee
Occupation: Lawyer
Party: Democratic
Vice President: George M. Dallas

12 Zachary Taylor

Presidential term: 1849–1850
Lived: 1784–1850
Born in: Virginia
Elected from: Louisiana
Occupation: Soldier
Party: Whig
Vice President: Millard Fillmore

13 Millard Fillmore

Presidential term: 1850–1853
Lived: 1800–1874
Born in: New York
Elected as V.P. from: New York
Succeeded Taylor
Occupation: Lawyer
Party: Whig
Vice President: None

14 Franklin Pierce

Presidential term: 1853–1857
Lived: 1804–1869
Born in: New Hampshire
Elected from: New Hampshire
Occupation: Lawyer
Party: Democratic
Vice President: William R. King

15 James Buchanan

Presidential term: 1857–1861
Lived: 1791–1868
Born in: Pennsylvania
Elected from: Pennsylvania
Occupation: Lawyer
Party: Democratic
Vice President: John C. Breckinridge

16 Abraham Lincoln

Presidential term: 1861–1865
Lived: 1809–1865
Born in: Kentucky
Elected from: Illinois
Occupation: Lawyer
Party: Republican
Vice Presidents: Hannibal Hamlin, Andrew Johnson

17 Andrew Johnson

Presidential term: 1865–1869
Lived: 1808–1875
Born in: North Carolina
Elected as V.P. from: Tennessee
Succeeded Lincoln
Occupation: Tailor
Party: Republican
Vice President: None

18 Ulysses S. Grant

Presidential term: 1869–1877
Lived: 1822–1885
Born in: Ohio
Elected from: Illinois
Occupations: Farmer, Soldier
Party: Republican
Vice Presidents: Schuyler Colfax,
Henry Wilson

19 Rutherford B. Hayes

Presidential term: 1877–1881
Lived: 1822–1893
Born in: Ohio
Elected from: Ohio
Occupation: Lawyer
Party: Republican
Vice President: William A.
Wheeler

20 James A. Garfield

Presidential term: 1881
Lived: 1831–1881
Born in: Ohio
Elected from: Ohio
Occupations: Laborer, Professor
Party: Republican
Vice President: Chester A.
Arthur

21 Chester A. Arthur

Presidential term: 1881–1885
Lived: 1830–1886
Born in: Vermont
Elected as V.P. from: New York
Succeeded Garfield
Occupations: Teacher, Lawyer
Party: Republican
Vice President: None

22 Grover Cleveland

Presidential term: 1885–1889
Lived: 1837–1908
Born in: New Jersey
Elected from: New York
Occupation: Lawyer
Party: Democratic
Vice President: Thomas A.
Hendricks

23 Benjamin Harrison

Presidential term: 1889–1893
Lived: 1833–1901
Born in: Ohio
Elected from: Indiana
Occupation: Lawyer
Party: Republican
Vice President: Levi P. Morton

24 Grover Cleveland

Presidential term: 1893–1897
Lived: 1837–1908
Born in: New Jersey
Elected from: New York
Occupation: Lawyer
Party: Democratic
Vice President: Adlai E.
Stevenson

25 William McKinley

Presidential term: 1897–1901
Lived: 1843–1901
Born in: Ohio
Elected from: Ohio
Occupations: Teacher, Lawyer
Party: Republican
Vice Presidents: Garret Hobart,
Theodore Roosevelt

26 Theodore Roosevelt

Presidential term: 1901–1909
Lived: 1858–1919
Born in: New York
Elected as V.P. from: New York
Succeeded McKinley
Occupations: Historian, Rancher
Party: Republican
Vice President: Charles W. Fairbanks

27 William H. Taft

Presidential term: 1909–1913
Lived: 1857–1930
Born in: Ohio
Elected from: Ohio
Occupation: Lawyer
Party: Republican
Vice President: James S. Sherman

28 Woodrow Wilson

Presidential term: 1913–1921
Lived: 1856–1924
Born in: Virginia
Elected from: New Jersey
Occupation: College Professor
Party: Democratic
Vice President: Thomas R. Marshall

29 Warren G. Harding

Presidential term: 1921–1923
Lived: 1865–1923
Born in: Ohio
Elected from: Ohio
Occupations: Newspaper Editor, Publisher
Party: Republican
Vice President: Calvin Coolidge

30 Calvin Coolidge

Presidential term: 1923–1929
Lived: 1872–1933
Born in: Vermont
Elected as V.P. from: Massachusetts
Succeeded Harding
Occupation: Lawyer
Party: Republican
Vice President: Charles G. Dawes

31 Herbert C. Hoover

Presidential term: 1929–1933
Lived: 1874–1964
Born in: Iowa
Elected from: California
Occupation: Engineer
Party: Republican
Vice President: Charles Curtis

32 Franklin D. Roosevelt

Presidential term: 1933–1945
Lived: 1882–1945
Born in: New York
Elected from: New York
Occupation: Lawyer
Party: Democratic
Vice Presidents: John N. Garner, Henry A. Wallace, Harry S Truman

33 Harry S Truman

Presidential term: 1945–1953
Lived: 1884–1972
Born in: Missouri
Elected as V.P. from: Missouri
Succeeded Roosevelt
Occupations: Clerk, Farmer
Party: Democratic
Vice President: Alben W. Barkley

34 Dwight D. Eisenhower

Presidential term: 1953–1961
Lived: 1890–1969
Born in: Texas
Elected from: New York
Occupation: Soldier
Party: Republican
Vice President: Richard M. Nixon

35 John F. Kennedy

Presidential term: 1961–1963
Lived: 1917–1963
Born in: Massachusetts
Elected from: Massachusetts
Occupations: Author, Reporter
Party: Democratic
Vice President: Lyndon B. Johnson

36 Lyndon B. Johnson

Presidential term: 1963–1969
Lived: 1908–1973
Born in: Texas
Elected as V.P. from: Texas
Succeeded Kennedy
Occupation: Teacher
Party: Democratic
Vice President: Hubert H. Humphrey

37 Richard M. Nixon

Presidential term: 1969–1974
Lived: 1913–1994
Born in: California
Elected from: New York
Occupation: Lawyer
Party: Republican
Vice Presidents: Spiro T. Agnew, Gerald R. Ford

38 Gerald R. Ford

Presidential term: 1974–1977
Lived: 1913–
Born in: Nebraska
Appointed as V.P. upon Agnew's resignation; succeeded Nixon
Occupation: Lawyer
Party: Republican
Vice President: Nelson A. Rockefeller

39 James E. Carter, Jr.

Presidential term: 1977–1981
Lived: 1924–
Born in: Georgia
Elected from: Georgia
Occupations: Business, Farmer
Party: Democratic
Vice President: Walter F. Mondale

40 Ronald W. Reagan

Presidential term: 1981–1989
Lived: 1911–2004
Born in: Illinois
Elected from: California
Occupations: Actor, Lecturer
Party: Republican
Vice President: George H.W. Bush

41 George H.W. Bush

Presidential term: 1989–1993
Lived: 1924–
Born in: Massachusetts
Elected from: Texas
Occupation: Business
Party: Republican
Vice President: J. Danforth Quayle

42 William J. Clinton

Presidential term: 1993–2001
Lived: 1946–
Born in: Arkansas
Elected from: Arkansas
Occupation: Lawyer
Party: Democratic
Vice President: Albert Gore, Jr.

43 George W. Bush

Presidential term: 2001–
Lived: 1946–
Born in: Connecticut
Elected from: Texas
Occupation: Business
Party: Republican
Vice President: Richard B. Cheney

Primary Sources Library

Introduction

Have students complete the activities that follow to familiarize themselves with the types of primary sources.

Printed Publications

To help students analyze printed publications, instruct students to read the first two paragraphs under "Declaration of Natural Rights" in the Declaration of Independence (page 90). Discuss this passage in class, using such questions as: Is this a primary or secondary source? What is the main idea of the passage? What do you think this passage means?

Oral Histories

Work together with an English or Language Arts teacher to help students complete the following oral history activity. Interview a relative or friend who is much older than you to see how his or her life was different from yours when he or she was a teenager. Create a list of interview questions such as: What regular chores did you have to do? What did you and your friends talk about? What were your classes like in school?

Ask students to provide a transcript, or written record, of the interview and discuss their findings with the class.

Using Primary Sources

Primary sources are written or artistic testimony to an era in history or to an important development. They can also be objects of daily life, reflecting how people lived and thought at a certain time. Perhaps a primary source represents the ideas of an industrial leader like Andrew Carnegie, who helped shape the American economy. Perhaps the source is a soldier's poem or the autobiography of a migrant worker.

Reading primary sources is important because it is an excellent way to understand how and why people believed and acted as they did in the past. While many people might have written down their stories or beliefs, the sources chosen here are from witnesses who were close to events or especially sensitive to them.

Opera glasses, late 1800s

928

Checking Your Sources

When you read primary or secondary sources, you should analyze them to figure out if they are dependable or reliable. Historians usually prefer primary sources to secondary sources, but both can be reliable or unreliable, depending on the following factors.

Time Span

With primary sources, it is important to consider how long after the event occurred the primary source was written. Generally, the longer the time span between the event and the account, the less reliable the account. As time passes, people often forget details and fill in gaps with events that never took place. Although we like to think we remember things exactly as they happened, the fact is we often remember them as we wanted them to occur.

Reliability

Another factor to consider when evaluating a primary source is the writer's background and reliability. First, try to determine how this person knows about what he or she is writing. How much does he or she know? Is the writer being truthful? Is the account convincing?

Teacher Notes

After studying the introduction to the Primary Sources Library, students should be able to meet the following objectives:

- explain how to interpret primary sources.
- explain the difference between primary sources and secondary sources.
- identify the different types of primary sources.
- understand that primary sources offer a unique view of people and events in a particular era.

Opinions

When evaluating a primary source, you should also decide whether the account has been influenced by emotion, opinion, or exaggeration. Writers can have reasons to distort the truth to suit their personal purposes. Ask yourself: Why did the person write the account? Do any key words or expressions reveal the author's emotions or opinions? You may wish to compare the account with one written by another witness to the event. If the two accounts differ, ask yourself why.

Interpreting Primary Sources

To help you analyze a primary source, use the following steps:

- **Examine the origins of the document.**
  You need to determine if it is a primary source.

- **Find the main ideas.**
  Read the document and summarize the main ideas in your own words. These ideas may be fairly easy to identify in newspapers and journals, for example, but are much more difficult to find in poetry.

- **Reread the document.**
  Difficult ideas are not always easily understood on the first reading.

- **Use a variety of resources.**
  Form the habit of using dictionaries, encyclopedias, and maps. These resources are tools to help you discover new ideas and knowledge, and they can be used to check the validity of various sources.

Log book from Lewis and Clark expedition

Classifying Primary Sources

Primary sources fall into different categories:

 Printed Publications

Printed publications include books such as biographies and autobiographies. Printed publications also include newspapers and magazines.

 Songs & Poems

Songs and poems include works that express personal thoughts and feelings or political or religious beliefs of the writer, often using rhyming and rhythmic language.

 Visual Materials

Visual materials include a wide range of forms: original paintings, drawings, and sculpture; photographs; film; and maps.

Oral Histories

Oral history collects spoken memories and personal observations through recorded interviews. In contrast, oral tradition involves stories that people have passed along by word of mouth from generation to generation.

Personal Records

Personal records are accounts of events kept by an individual who is a participant in or witness to these events. Personal records include diaries, journals, and letters.

Artifacts

Artifacts are objects such as tools or ornaments. Artifacts present information about a particular culture or a stage of technological development.

Songs & Poems

Ask students to write a poem about a happy event in their lives. Suggest that the poem be in a standard form such as a limerick, haiku, or sonnet.

Personal Records

Ask students to describe what it might be like to witness an important public event. Provide the following guidelines: Write a journal entry describing the event. Begin by giving an overview of the event, including some objective facts. Then make the event personal by focusing on your own opinions or feelings.

Visual Materials

Help students create a poster showing how your community or state changed during the 1900s. Students may use photographs or original drawings.

Artifacts

To help students analyze artifacts, provide the following instructions: Find a primary source from your past such as a photograph, a report card, or a letter. Bring this source to class and explain what it shows about the time from which it comes.

Teacher Notes

Through the study of the selections in the Primary Sources Library and their accompanying questions, students should be able to:

- find main ideas in the selections.

- analyze information in a variety of written texts in order to make inferences and generalizations.

- provide an interpretation of the material in their own words.

Block Schedule

Team Teaching These selections may be implemented in a team-teaching context, in conjunction with English/Language Arts.

Unit Link

Use the primary source selections on pages 930–931 to accompany study of Unit 1, "Foundations of Liberty," and Unit 2, "The Crisis of Union."

Reinforcing Vocabulary

Review the **Reader's Dictionary** on page 930 with students to be sure they understand any unfamiliar terms. Write *intrude* on the board. Ask students to use the term in a sentence.

Background Information

Persuasion Point out that persuasive writing attempts to sway the reader to think or act in a particular way. Ask students to identify the course of action promoted in each of the selections. Then ask: Which selection is the most persuasive? Why?

For use with Unit 1, "Foundations of Liberty," and Unit 2, "The Crisis of Union"

From the Beginnings to the Civil War

English colonists fought successfully against the English government for their rights. As the nation grew, so did feelings of nationalism—and sectionalism. A different sense of identity in the North and South contributed to the outbreak of the Civil War.

The first excerpt is from one of Patrick Henry's speeches. Known for his eloquence, Henry delivered this passionate plea at the second Virginia convention during a debate over whether to resist the English by force of arms. The second excerpt is by New York City journalist John L. O'Sullivan. In 1845, in an article on Texas annexation, O'Sullivan coined the phrase "Manifest Destiny" to sum up his feelings about territorial expansion.

The final excerpts relate to the Civil War. A Northerner wrote the "Battle Cry of Freedom," but the tune was so popular that a Confederate version was written as well. Both versions are shown against the background of an Augustus Saint-Gaudens sculpture honoring the 54th regiment of African American soldiers. The regiment's story was the subject of the movie Glory.

Reader's Dictionary

comport: to behave in a proper way

adversary: opponent or enemy

intrude: to force in or upon something without permission

Dixie: nickname for the South, popularized in Daniel Emmett's song, "Land of Dixie"; term may derive from the French *dix* for "ten," referring to Louisiana ten-dollar bank notes

"Give Me Liberty or Give Me Death" by Patrick Henry (1775)

Printed Publications

The question before the House is one of awful moment.... For my own part, I consider it as nothing less than a question of freedom or slavery.... I have but one lamp by which my feet are guided, and that is the lamp of experience.... And judging by the past, I wish to know what there has been in the conduct of the British ministry for the last ten years to justify those hopes with which gentlemen have been pleased to solace themselves.... Ask yourselves how this gracious reception of our petition comports with those warlike preparations which cover our waters and darken our land.

They tell us, sir, that we are weak; unable to cope with so formidable an adversary. But when shall we be stronger? Will it be the next week...? Will it be when we are totally disarmed...? Gentlemen may cry, Peace, Peace—but there is no peace.... I know not what course others may take; but as for me, give me liberty or give me death!

EXTENDING THE CONTENT

The Origin of "Dixie" The well-known Confederate anthem "Dixie" is attributed to Daniel Emmett, of Knox County, Ohio, a musician who first played it in New York in 1859. However, there is evidence tracing it to the African American Snowden family, also of Knox County, who made their living by farming, but were best known as the "Snowden Family Band." The Snowdens were talented musicians and composers who performed popular songs throughout rural central Ohio from the 1850s to the early 1900s. The mother, Ellen Cooper Snowden, had been born into slavery in Maryland, moved to Ohio, and married, gaining her freedom. The lyrics can be read to reflect her experiences, moving from the "land of cotton" to a difficult life in the North. On the Snowden family gravestone is inscribed "They taught 'Dixie' to Dan Emmett."

"Annexation"
by John L. O'Sullivan (1845)

Printed Publications

I t is time now for opposition to the Annexation of Texas to cease. . . . Why, were other reasoning wanting in favor of . . . the reception of Texas into the Union . . . , it surely is to be found . . . in the manner in which other nations have undertaken to intrude themselves into it . . . for the avowed object of . . . checking the fulfilment of our manifest destiny to overspread the continent. . . .

. . . Texas has been absorbed into the Union in the inevitable fulfilment of the general law which is rolling our population westward; the connexion of which with that ratio of growth in population . . . is too evident to leave us in doubt of the manifest design of Providence in regard to the occupation of this continent.

. . . Already the advance guard of the irresistible army of Anglo-Saxon emigration has begun to pour down upon (California), armed with the plough and the rifle, and marking its trail with schools and colleges, courts and representative halls, mills and meeting-houses. . . . The day is not distant when the Empires of the Atlantic and Pacific would again flow together into one. . . .

"Battle Cry of Freedom"

Songs & Poems

BATTLE CRY OF FREEDOM

Analyzing Primary Sources

1. What does Patrick Henry use to judge British intentions?
2. What is O'Sullivan's main argument in favor of annexation?
3. What is the main theme of the Union lyrics to "Battle Cry"?
4. In the Confederate lyrics to "Battle Cry," how are Northerners portrayed?

Primary Sources Library **931**

Analyzing Primary Sources

1. He judges them based on his memory of British action over the previous ten years.
2. He argues it is the destiny of the United States to control the continent from east to west.
3. Anyone loyal to the cause of freedom may fight for the Union and do so as a free person, regardless of wealth.
4. They are named as tyrants.

Primary Sources Library

Block Schedule

Team Teaching These selections may be implemented in a team-teaching context, in conjunction with English/Language Arts.

Unit Link

Use the primary source selections on pages 932–933 to accompany study of Unit 3, "The Birth of Modern America," and Unit 4, "Imperialism and Progressivism."

Reinforcing Vocabulary

Review the **Reader's Dictionary** on page 932 with students to be sure they understand any unfamiliar terms. Write *antidote* on the board. Ask students to use the term in a sentence.

Background Information

Tone Explain that *tone* in writing uses carefully chosen words to help the author express two messages—the facts, and the author's or character's feelings underneath those facts. Have students identify the tone in these selections, and support this with words in the text. (*Students' answers will vary but should compare content with word choice. For example, the flatness of the land is underscored by the flat, lifeless description of Jim's journey and arrival ["what would be would be"]. The title of Carnegie's article, "The Gospel of Wealth," and his dictatorial style emphasizes his directions on how people should spend their money.*)

932

Primary Sources Library

For use with Unit 3, "The Birth of Modern America," and Unit 4, "Imperialism and Progressivism"

From Settling the West to Becoming a World Power

In the latter part of the 19th century, immigrants flocked to the United States to settle on farms or to work in newly industrializing cities. The experience transformed both the immigrants and the still-youthful nation. Change created many political and social problems, and Progressivism tried to solve them. New challenges arose in foreign affairs as well, as the nation began to wield the influence that came with an expanding economy.

In the first excerpt, the 1918 novel My Ántonia *by Willa Cather provides us with a glimpse of the life of Easterners and immigrants who moved west. Cather drew on her own experiences to create her characters. Her fiction has a strong sense of place, as can be seen in this passage where Jim Burden gets his first sight of the Nebraska prairie.*

In the second excerpt, Andrew Carnegie presents his personal solution to the problem of a nation with both rich and poor citizens, a solution termed the "Gospel of Wealth." An immigrant himself, Carnegie became one the nation's wealthiest industrialists. His charitable donations of about $350 million supported more than 2,800 libraries and other institutions.

Reader's Dictionary

plush: a luxurious fabric

surplus wealth: in a capitalist system, the wealth remaining after labor and other costs are met

antidote: a remedy for a poison; something that prevents or relieves a problem

unostentatious: plain, not flashy or showy

932 Primary Sources Library

My Ántonia by Willa Cather

Printed Publications

I do not remember crossing the Missouri River, or anything about the long day's journey through Nebraska. Probably by that time I had crossed so many rivers that I was dull to them. The only thing very noticeable about Nebraska was that it was still, all day long, Nebraska.

I had been sleeping, curled up in a red plush seat, for a long while when we reached Black Hawk. . . . We stumbled down from the train to a wooden siding, where men were running about with lanterns. I couldn't see any town, or even distant lights; we were surrounded by utter darkness. . . .

Another lantern came along. A bantering voice called out: "Hello, are you Mr. Burden's folks? If you are, it's me you're looking for. I'm Otto Fuchs. I'm Mr.

Carnegie Library, Shelbyville, Ind.

EXTENDING THE CONTENT

Willa Cather Willa Cather was born in wooded, mountainous Virginia, and moved to the dry, flat plains of Nebraska in 1893, when she was nine. After graduating from the University of Nebraska, she moved to Pittsburgh, and then to New York, where she had a successful career as a magazine editor and journalist. Friends encouraged her to leave journalism and devote herself to fiction, suggesting she use the land in which she had lived to ground her work. Several novels, such as *My Ántonia, Song of the Lark,* and *O Pioneers!*, are set in Nebraska, in detail if not in name. Many of her books deal with the tension of not fitting in with your community, of growing up and moving away, and the pull that home will always exert.

Burden's hired man, and I'm to drive you out. Hello, Jimmy, ain't you scared to come so far west?"

. . . He told us we had a long night drive ahead of us, and had better be on the hike. He led us to a hitching-bar where two farm-wagons were tied. . . . I rode on the straw in the bottom of the wagon-box, covered up with a buffalo hide. . . .

I tried to go to sleep, but the jolting made me bite my tongue, and I soon began to ache all over. When the straw settled down, I had a hard bed. Cautiously I slipped from under the buffalo hide, got up on my knees and peered over the side of the wagon. There seemed to be nothing to see; no fences, no creeks or trees, no hills or fields. If there was a road, I could not make it out in the faint starlight. There was nothing but land: not a country at all, but the material out of which countries are made. . . . I had the feeling that the world was left behind, that we had got over the edge of it, and were outside man's jurisdiction. I had never before looked up at the sky when there was not a familiar mountain ridge against it. But this was the complete dome of heaven, all there was of it. I did not believe that my dead father and mother were watching me from up there; they would still be looking for me at the sheep-fold down by the creek, or along the white road that led to the mountain pastures. I had left even their spirits behind me. The wagon jolted on, carrying me I knew not whither. I don't think I was homesick. If we never arrived anywhere, it did not matter. Between that earth and that sky I felt erased, blotted out. I did not say my prayers that night: here, I felt, what would be would be.

"Gospel of Wealth" by Andrew Carnegie (1889)

 Printed Publications

We start, then, with a condition of affairs under which the best interests of the race are promoted, but which inevitably gives wealth to the few. . . .

There are but three modes in which surplus wealth can be disposed of. It can be left to the families of the decedents; or it can be bequeathed for public purposes; or, finally, it can be administered during their lives by its possessors. . . .

The growing disposition to tax more and more heavily large estates left at death is a cheering indication of the growth of a salutary change in public opinion. . . . Of all forms of taxation, this seems the wisest. . . .

There remains, then, only one mode of using great fortunes: but in this way we have the true antidote for the temporary unequal distribution of wealth, the reconciliation of the rich and the poor. . . . Even the poorest can be made to . . . agree that great sums . . . gathered by some of their fellow-citizens and spent for public purposes, from which the masses reap the principal benefit, are more valuable to them than if scattered among them through the course of many years in trifling amounts.

This, then, is held to be the duty of the man of Wealth: First, to set an example of modest, unostentatious living, . . . ; to provide moderately for the legitimate wants of those dependent upon him; and . . . to consider all surplus revenues which come to him simply as trust funds . . . the man of wealth thus becoming the . . . trustee for his poorer brethren, . . . doing for them better than they would or could do for themselves.

Analyzing Primary Sources

1. Is Willa Cather giving an objective description of the landscape, or do her feelings color her description? Why do you think so?
2. How does Willa Cather convey a sense of endless space?
3. What does Carnegie believe wealthy people should do with their excess money?
4. How does Carnegie think wealthy people should live? What are their other responsibilities?

Primary Sources Library **933**

Analyzing Primary Sources

1. Her feelings shape her words. Answers should recognize words such as *surrounded* and *blotted out* that convey emotional and factual meaning.
2. Burden had been crossing Nebraska all day; there was no changing scenery, only sky.
3. spend large amounts of it on public projects before their death
4. modestly, providing for the needs of those who depend on him, and spending the remainder for the good of the less fortunate

Unit Link

Use the primary source selections on pages 934–935 to accompany study of Unit 5, "Boom and Bust," and Unit 6, "Global Struggles."

Reinforcing Vocabulary

Review the **Reader's Dictionary** on page 934 with students to be sure they understand any unfamiliar terms. Write *scuttle* on the board. Ask students to use the term in a sentence.

Background Information

Imagery Point out that Steinbeck and Murphy create pictures with words, while O'Keeffe creates pictures with paint and canvas. Have students find examples of visual images in the works by Steinbeck and Murphy, and discuss other interpretations for the painting by O'Keeffe. *(Students' answers will vary but could include families' reactions to a baby's birth in Steinbeck's piece, or the dead sleeping on the field or marching on in Murphy's.)*

934

Primary Sources Library

For use with Unit 5, "Boom and Bust," and Unit 6, "Global Struggles"

From Prosperity, through the Depression, to World War

Many artists and writers blossomed in the 1920s when the freer values of modern society took hold. Artists no longer tried to copy European models so much but instead created thoroughly American works. Art flourished during the Depression as well; at that time it often focused on the sorrows and hopes of the common people. Artists of the World War II era produced many works on themes of heroism and death.

Georgia O'Keeffe (1887–1986) created some of the most original images in the history of American art. A 1929 New Mexico trip powerfully influenced her style. Known for her strong sense of color, her most famous works are of single flowers.

John Steinbeck (1902–1968) is best known for his 1940 novel, The Grapes of Wrath. *It describes the Joad family's effort to find a new life in California after they have lost their Oklahoma farm. On the trip west, the Joads and thousands of others find solace at the makeshift camps they create along the way.*

The sacrifices that come with struggle are expressed in Audie Murphy's poetry on World War II. The son of a poor Texas sharecropper, Murphy is the most decorated U.S. combat soldier of that war.

Reader's Dictionary

scuttle: to run with short, shuffling steps

biomorphic: resembling or suggesting the forms of living organisms

934 Primary Sources Library

The Grapes of Wrath by John Steinbeck (1940)

Printed Publications

The cars of the migrant people crawled out of the side roads onto the great cross-country highway, and they took the migrant way to the West. In the daylight they scuttled like bugs to the westward; and as the dark caught them, they clustered like bugs near to shelter and to water. And because they were lonely and perplexed, because they had all come from a place of sadness and worry and defeat, and because they were all going to a new mysterious place, they huddled together; they talked together; they shared their lives, their food, and the things they hoped for in the new country. Thus it might be that one family camped near a spring, and another camped for the spring and for company, and a third because two families had pioneered the place and found it good. And when the sun went down, perhaps twenty families and twenty cars were there.

In the evening a strange thing happened: the twenty families became one family, the children were the children of all. The loss of home became one loss, and the golden time in the West was one dream. And it might be that a sick child threw despair into the hearts of twenty families, of a hundred people; that a birth there in a tent kept a hundred people quiet and awestruck through the night and filled a hundred people with birth-joy in the morning. A family which the night before had been lost and fearful might search its goods to find a present for a new baby. In the evening, sitting about the fires, the twenty were one.

They grew to be units of the camps, units of the evenings and the nights. A guitar unwrapped from a blanket and tuned—and the songs, which were all of the people, were sung in the nights. Men sang the words, and women hummed the tunes.

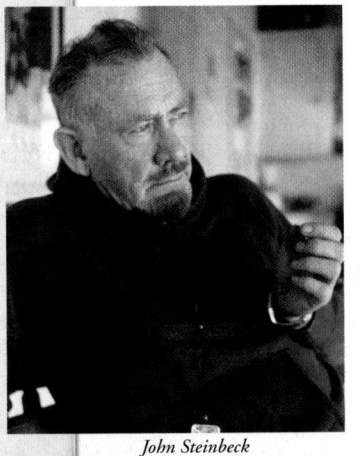
John Steinbeck

EXTENDING THE CONTENT

Audie Murphy While serving in the 3rd Infantry Division, Audie Murphy received 33 decorations, including the Medal of Honor and 5 decorations from France and Belgium. He was wounded three times. After the war, Murphy became a film star and appeared in 44 movies, many of them westerns. He also wrote poetry and became a successful songwriter. Many performers, including Dean Martin, Eddy Arnold, Charley Pride, and Roy Clark, recorded Murphy's songs. Audie Murphy also suffered from post traumatic stress disorder. He publicly called for the government to study the emotional impact of war and to extend health-care benefits to veterans suffering from war-related mental health problems. Murphy died in a plane crash in 1971. He is buried at Arlington National Cemetery. In 1996, Texas designated his birthday, June 20th, as Audie Murphy Day.

Georgia O'Keeffe's
Oriental Poppies (1927)

Visual Materials

Georgia O'Keeffe's paintings of biomorphic flowers, rocks, and skulls are *abstract* paintings, meaning that they symbolize things other than what they actually are. *Oriental Poppies*, for example, could be seen as representing a cave-like enclosure.

Georgia O'Keeffe

"Alone and Far Removed"
by Audie Murphy

Songs & Poems

Alone and far removed from earthly care
The noble ruins of men lie buried here.
You were strong men, good men
Endowed with youth and much the will to live
I hear no protest from the mute lips of the dead.
They rest; there is no more to give.

So long my comrades,
Sleep ye where you fell upon the field.
But tread softly please
March o'er my heart with ease
March on and on,
But to God alone we kneel.

Audie Murphy

Analyzing Primary Sources

1. According to Steinbeck, what binds the families of migrant people together?
2. How do you think Steinbeck feels about the migrants?
3. What is an abstract painting? How is it different from other paintings?
4. What is the main mood of Murphy's poem?

Alternative Assessment

Have students write a one-page paper describing a memorable event in their lives. Students should include descriptions about what happened, including what they heard, saw, or felt. Ask volunteers to share their work with the class.

GLENCOE
TECHNOLOGY

CD-ROM
American History Primary Source Document Library CD-ROM

Use the **American History Primary Source Document Library CD-ROM** to access other primary source documents related to art of the period between the Depression and World War II.

History *and the* Humanities

- American Music: Hits Through History: "Brother, Can You Spare a Dime?"
- American Music: Cultural Traditions: "Talking Dust Bowl," "Take Me Back to Tulsa"
- American Art & Architecture: *Migrant Mother*

Analyzing Primary Sources

1. They are bound together by fear, desperation, and loneliness.
2. Although the migrants are struggling and desperate, Steinbeck sees them as extraordinarily human, showing a full range of human emotions.
3. Abstract paintings are of items that symbolize things other than what they actually show. Many other paintings are realistic, showing people and places as they are.
4. He feels sadness for friends and comrades that were young and strong but have died, leaving him behind.

935

Unit Link

Use the primary source selections on pages 936–937 to accompany study of Unit 7, "A Time of Upheaval," and Unit 8, "A Changing Society."

Reinforcing Vocabulary

Review the **Reader's Dictionary** on page 936 with students to be sure they understand any unfamiliar terms. Write *civil disobedience* on the board with additional space between the words. Have students discuss a list of synonyms for each word and write the synonyms under the appropriate word. Ask the students what it means when two such different words are joined together.

Background Information

The Literary Letter Explain to students that what Martin Luther King, Jr., wrote in *Letter from a Birmingham Jail* was a literary letter, addressed to a specific group of clergymen but intended for a wider audience. Ask the students: **If Martin Luther King, Jr., came to your school, what might he say about the state of race relations in your town?**

936

For use with Unit 7, "A Time of Upheaval," and Unit 8, "A Changing Society"

From Divisiveness to Diversity

American society took a sharp turn in the 1960s as a new generation sought to change some American values. Change became the challenge throughout the century as many new immigrants came to the United States to make it their home. By the year 2000, the nation was much more diverse. Hispanic Americans alone made up 12.5 percent of the population, approximately the same percentage as African Americans.

The 1960s were a breakthrough time for African Americans. Martin Luther King, Jr., persuaded many white Americans to acknowledge the need for more just laws for minorities. His "Letter from a Birmingham Jail" of April 16, 1963, makes the case that nonviolent resistance is not only moral, but is as American as the Boston Tea Party.

Elva Trevino Hart, born in southern Texas to Mexican immigrants, has a story that mirrors that of many immigrants. A migrant worker as a child, Hart eventually earned a master's degree from Stanford University. In this excerpt, she describes her father and his reaction to her graduation from high school.

Reader's Dictionary

conversely: reversed in order or action

civil disobedience: peaceful refusal to obey government demands as a means of forcing government concessions or changes in the law

admonish: to warn or express disapproval

macho: a strong sense of masculine pride

Letter from a Birmingham Jail
by Martin Luther King, Jr. (1963)

Personal Records

My dear fellow clergymen: . . . Birmingham is probably the most thoroughly segregated city in the United States. On the basis of these conditions, Negro leaders sought to negotiate with the city fathers. . . . As in so many past experiences, our hopes had been blasted. . . . We had no alternative except to prepare for direct action, whereby we would present our very bodies as a means of laying our case before the conscience of the local and the national community. . . .

You may well ask: . . . Why sit-ins, marches and so forth? Isn't negotiation a better path?" . . . Indeed, this is the very purpose of direct action. Nonviolent direct action seeks to create such a crisis . . . that a community . . . is forced to confront the issue. . . .

. . . For years now I have heard the word "Wait!" It rings in the ear of every Negro with piercing familiarity. This "Wait" has almost always meant "Never." We must come to see, with one of our distinguished

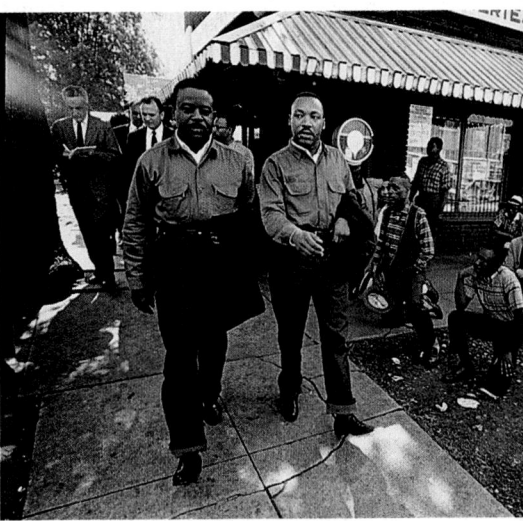
Martin Luther King, Jr., (right) and Ralph Abernathy in Birmingham, A

EXTENDING THE CONTENT

Letter from a Birmingham Jail In retrospect, it is easy to think that in a successful movement the ideas and methods were always recognized as right. This letter came early in the fight for civil rights. In it King struggles to answer his own supporters and friends who are cautioning him he is going too far too fast. At that point, even people committed to achieving equal civil rights were not sure that King's new style of mass symbolic action was the best way to achieve change. They felt it might be better to continue individual negotiations to improve conditions in specific situations. The letter's title echoes the well-known folk song, "Birmingham Jail."

Primary Sources Library

jurists, that "justice too long delayed is justice denied." . . . Perhaps it is easy for those who have never felt the stinging dark of segregation to say, "Wait." . . .

You express a great deal of anxiety over our willingness to break laws. . . . One may . . . ask: "How can you advocate breaking some laws and obeying others?" The answer lies in the fact that there are two types of laws: just and unjust. . . . One has not only a legal but a moral responsibility to obey just laws. Conversely, one has a moral responsibility to disobey unjust laws. . . .

Of course, there is nothing new about this kind of civil disobedience. . . . It was practiced superbly by the early Christians, who were willing to face hungry lions . . . rather than submit to certain unjust laws of the Roman Empire. . . . In our own nation, the Boston Tea Party represented a massive act of civil disobedience. . . .

. . . We will have to repent in this generation not merely for the hateful words and actions of the bad people but for the appalling silence of the good people. Human progress never rolls in on wheels of inevitability; it comes through the tireless efforts of men willing to be co-workers with God. . . .

I have heard numerous Southern religious leaders admonish their worshipers to comply with a desegregation decision because it is the law, but I have longed to hear white ministers declare: "Follow this decree because integration is morally right and because the Negro is your brother." . . . But even if the church does not come to the aid of justice, I have no despair about the future. . . . We will reach the goal of freedom . . . all over the nation, because the goal of America is freedom. . . . We will win our freedom because the sacred heritage of our nation and the eternal will of God are embodied in our echoing demands. . . .

Analyzing Primary Sources

1. Why does King say African Americans should not wait longer for change?

2. Who in ancient history practiced nonviolent resistance?

3. Why did Hart's father take his family so far to work in the summers?

Barefoot Heart
by Elva Trevino Hart

Printed Publications

"To get ahead, hijos (children). That's why we go a los trabajos (to work). When I first came from Mexico, I got paid dos reales al dia (two Spanish coins a day). I worked at building the railroad, . . . clearing land. . . . The only thing I would never do is strap on the contraption to burn brush with liquid fuel. Too dangerous. . . ."

I fingered the nickels in the pocket of my sun dress and tried to imagine Apa (Daddy) working for fifty cents a day. And I felt I understood why we had to go to Minnesota. Our family could make more money in the migrant fields than anywhere else. . . .

Barefoot Heart
Stories of a
Migrant Child

Elva
Trevino
Hart

* * *

(My father) had only gone as far as the fourth grade in Mexico. . . . When I was in the fourth grade, I told my father that I wanted to go to college. . . .

On (high school) graduation night I delivered the valedictory speech, entitled "He Conquers who Conquers Himself." I wish now I had said "she," but it has remained the theme of my life nevertheless. Apa came up to me afterwards with big macho tears in his eyes. I had never seen him even close to crying before.

He pressed two thousand dollars in cash into my hand. "I have been saving this for you, mija (my daughter). It's your money to go to college." . . . I knew that this money would only be enough for about one semester, but I didn't tell him. Instead I hugged him, crying violently.

Alternative Assessment

Using library and Internet resources, research one of the following organizations: SNCC, CORE, NAACP, or SCLC. Write a brief paragraph describing its leaders, actions, and contribution to the civil rights movement.

GLENCOE
TECHNOLOGY

CD-ROM
American History Primary Source Document Library CD-ROM

Use the **American History Primary Source Document Library CD-ROM** to access other primary source documents related to minorities' struggle for equality.

History *and the* Humanities

🎵 American Music: Hits Through History: "Why? (Am I Treated So Bad)"

🎵 American Music: Cultural Traditions: "We Shall Not Be Moved"

Analyzing Primary Sources

1. In the past, waiting for change often meant change never came.

2. Christian opposition to the Roman Empire was an early example of nonviolent resistance.

3. He could make more money working in the migrant fields than anywhere else.

Block Schedule

Team Teaching These selections may be implemented in a team-teaching context, in conjunction with English/Language Arts.

Unit Link

Use the primary source selections on pages 938–939 to accompany study of Chapter 29, "Into a New Century."

Reinforcing Vocabulary

Review the **Reader's Dictionary** on page 938 with students to be sure they understand any unfamiliar terms. Ask students to use each term in a sentence. Ask students why President Bush defined al-Qaeda as a *fringe* group of Muslims.

Background Information

Purpose Explain that purpose is the intent to explain, persuade, or inform. An author may have more than one purpose. Have students read President Bush's address to Congress after the attacks on New York City and Washington, D.C. **Ask:** What do you think was the purpose of President Bush's address? *(Answers will vary. Students may note that he was trying to comfort Americans in a time of loss, justify why the United States and other countries should fight terrorism, or encourage people to be brave.)*

For use with Chapter 29, "Into a New Century"

The Challenges Ahead

With the onset of the twenty-first century, Americans faced the challenge of living in a more interconnected world. World trade expanded, but so too did awareness of potential threats from abroad. For most Americans, one event changed their view of the world: the terrorist attacks on the World Trade Center in New York City and on the Pentagon in Washington, D.C., on September 11, 2001. In these horrific attacks, thousands of people were killed.

Never before had Americans felt so unsafe on their own soil. In his address on September 20, President George W. Bush attempted to calm the nation's fears by announcing a new kind of war against terrorism. He also urged the American people to remain firm and united.

Reader's Dictionary

fringe: outside border; also, a group with extremist views

haven: harbor or port; also, a place of safety

pretense: professed claim rather than a real intention or purpose

terrorism: the political use of terror, especially on civilian populations, as a means of forcing an opponent to surrender or adopt different policies

Address to Joint Session of Congress by President George W. Bush, September 20, 2001

Printed Publications

In the normal course of events, Presidents come to this chamber to report on the state of the Union. Tonight, no such report is needed. It has already been delivered by the American people.

We have seen it in the courage of passengers, who rushed terrorists to save others on the ground. . . .

We have seen the state of our Union in the endurance of rescuers, working past exhaustion. We have seen the unfurling of flags, the lighting of candles, the giving of blood, the saying of prayers. . . .

My fellow citizens, for the last nine days, the entire world has seen for itself the state of our Union—and it is strong. Tonight we are a country awakened to danger and called to defend freedom. Our grief has turned to anger, and anger to resolution. . . .

On September the eleventh, enemies of freedom committed an act of war against our country. Americans have known wars—but for the past 136 years, they have been wars on foreign soil, except for one Sunday in 1941. Americans have known the casualties of war—but not at the center of a great city on a peaceful morning. Americans have known surprise attacks—but never before on thousands of civilians. All of this was brought upon us in a single day—and night fell on a different world, a world where freedom itself is under attack.

Americans have many questions tonight. Americans are asking: Who attacked our country?

The evidence we have gathered all points to a collection of loosely affiliated terrorist organizations known as al-Qaeda. . . .

The terrorists practice a fringe form of Islamic extremism that has been rejected by Muslim scholars and the vast majority of Muslim clerics—a fringe movement that perverts the peaceful teachings of Islam. The terrorists' directive commands them to kill Christians and Jews, to kill all Americans, and make no distinctions among military and civilians, including women and children.

EXTENDING THE CONTENT

Search Dogs As rescue workers were organized to search for survivors in the aftermath of the collapse of the World Trade Center towers, search dogs and their handlers traveled to New York City to help recover victims. Over 300 dogs were a part of the rescue effort. Working 12-hour shifts, dogs and their handlers searched in teams of four after beams and large pieces of concrete were removed from the disaster area. When a dog ended its shift, it underwent a health check at a mobile veterinary clinic, which contained four operating stations and x-ray facilities. Common injuries suffered by the search dogs included eye irritations due to dust and wounded paws caused by shattered glass and concrete.

President George W. Bush, center

This group and its leader—a person named Osama bin Laden—are linked to many other organizations in different countries. . . . There are thousands of these terrorists in more than sixty countries. They are recruited from their own nations and neighborhoods, and brought to camps in places like Afghanistan where they are trained in the tactics of terror. . . .

The leadership of al-Qaeda has great influence in Afghanistan, and supports the Taliban regime in controlling most of that country. In Afghanistan, we see al-Qaeda's vision for the world. Afghanistan's people have been brutalized — many are starving and many have fled. . . .

The United States respects the people of Afghanistan—after all, we are currently its largest source of humanitarian aid—but we condemn the Taliban regime. . . . The Taliban must act and act immediately. They will hand over the terrorists, or they will share in their fate. . . .

Americans are asking: Why do they hate us?

They hate what we see right here in this chamber—a democratically elected government. Their leaders are self-appointed. They hate our freedoms. . . . These terrorists kill not merely to end lives, but to disrupt and end a way of life. . . .

We are not deceived by their pretenses to piety. We have seen their kind before. They are the heirs of all the murderous ideologies of the twentieth century. By sacrificing human life to serve their radical visions—by abandoning every value except the will to power—they follow in the path of fascism, and Nazism, and totalitarianism. And they will follow that path all the way, to where it ends: in history's unmarked grave of discarded lies.

Americans are asking: How will we fight and win this war?. . . . Americans should not expect one battle, but a lengthy campaign, unlike any other we have seen. . . . We will starve terrorists of funding, turn them one against another, drive them from place to place, until there is no refuge or rest. And we will pursue nations that provide aid or safe haven to terrorism. . . .

Our Nation has been put on notice: We are not immune from attack. We will take defensive measures against terrorism to protect Americans.

. . . So tonight I announce the creation of a Cabinet-level position reporting directly to me—the Office of Homeland Security. . . . This is not, however, just America's fight. And what is at stake is not just America's freedom. This is the world's fight. This is civilization's fight. . . .

I ask you to uphold the values of America, and remember why so many have come here. We are in a fight for our principles, and our first responsibility is to live by them. No one should be singled out for unfair treatment or unkind words because of their ethnic background or religious faith. . . .

After all that has just passed—all the lives taken, and all the possibilities and hopes that died with them—it is natural to wonder if America's future is one of fear. Some speak of an age of terror. I know there are struggles ahead, and dangers to face. But this country will define our times, not be defined by them. . . .

Great harm has been done to us. We have suffered great loss. And in our grief and anger we have found our mission and our moment. Freedom and fear are at war. The advance of human freedom—the great achievement of our time, and the great hope of every time—now depends on us. Our Nation—this generation—will lift a dark threat of violence from our people and our future. We will rally the world to this cause, by our efforts and by our courage. We will not tire, we will not falter, and we will not fail. . . .

Analyzing Primary Sources

1. Why does President Bush say that the American people themselves have already reported on the state of the nation?

2. What is so unusual about the attack that it makes Bush say that "night fell on a different world?"

3. To what "murderous ideologies" does Bush compare the terrorists?

Primary Sources Library **939**

Analyzing Primary Sources

1. He uses examples of the strong courage, compassion, and concern for others Americans have shown in the crisis as proof that the nation as a whole is strong.

2. This attack occurred within the United States and targeted civilians rather than military personnel.

3. He compares the terrorists to fascists, Nazis, and totalitarian dictators.

Documents of American History

TABLE OF CONTENTS

(above) Notes for Washington's Farewell Address

(right) Lincoln's drafts of the Gettysburg Address

Magna Carta

Why They Matter

Documents are often public statements by a president or an official body, such as a legislature, on an important issue. They have become documents because they define a particular issue so well that Americans continue to refer to them. Many documents here address fundamental American beliefs, such as the rights of the individual and the proper limits of government. Other documents, such as the Monroe Doctrine or the Truman Doctrine, address the nation's position and responsibilities in the world.

Documents matter because they are guides to American government and values. Sometimes people study them to learn how Americans came to believe in certain principles. Other times people read documents simply because these writings express certain principles passionately.

Signing the Mayflower Compact

Silver inkwell used in the signing of the Constitution

Documents That Shaped the American Republic

The first seven documents in this collection played an important role in shaping the American republic. Each contributed an essential building block for American political principles. Ultimately these principles were embodied in the Declaration of Independence, the Bill of Rights, and the Constitution.

DOCUMENT	WHY IT MATTERS
The Magna Carta In signing this charter in 1215, King John of England granted his subjects certain permanent liberties or rights, such as the right to a fair trial by a jury of their peers.	Over the centuries, English people believed that the Magna Carta gave them certain rights. They took this idea with them when they settled the American colonies. Some provisions of the Bill of Rights reflect ancient Magna Carta liberties.
The Mayflower Compact In 1620 the Pilgrims signed a compact while still aboard the *Mayflower.* This compact laid out a plan for self-government the Pilgrims would use once they landed in America.	This compact is the first plan for self-government put into effect in the English colonies. It reflected the idea that government should be based on a consensus of the entire community.
The Fundamental Orders of Connecticut Connecticut settlers agreed they would be governed according to a certain set of laws and through certain institutions. All citizens, not only those of a certain religion, could vote.	This document, the first written constitution drawn up in America, strengthened the colonists' beliefs about governing themselves.
The English Bill of Rights In 1689, after the Glorious Revolution, Parliament forced the king to accept this Bill of Rights guaranteeing basic civil rights.	This document clearly established that English subjects had certain rights and that the king could be removed from power for violating those rights.
Second Treatise of Government English philosopher John Locke wrote this document during the 1680s. One of his basic arguments was that government should be based on a contract between a ruler and those who are ruled. Rebellion is justified if a ruler violates the contract.	During the American Revolution, the colonists drew from Locke's theories of government and especially his ideas about the right to rebel.
The Virginia Statute for Religious Freedom This 1786 statute declared that the state of Virginia should not support Anglicanism or any other religious denomination.	The religious clauses of the Bill of Rights protecting the free exercise of religion and prohibiting an official religion were based on this statute.
The Federalist No. 10 In 1787 James Madison wrote this paper, one of a series arguing for stronger central government as reflected in the new Constitution.	The framework for American government today— a representative government with a strong federal government—was laid out in the Federalist Papers.

Use the **American History Primary Source Document Library CD-ROM** to find additional primary sources about American heritage.

The Magna Carta

The Magna Carta, signed by King John of England in 1215, marked a decisive step forward in the development of English constitutional government. Later it served as a model for the colonists, who carried the Magna Carta's guarantees of political rights to America.

John, by the grace of God, king of England, lord of Ireland, duke of Normandy and Aquitaine, and count of Anjou: to the archbishops, bishops, abbots, earls, barons, justiciaries, foresters, sheriffs, reeves, ministers, and all bailiffs and others his faithful subjects, greeting. . . .

1. We have, in the first place, granted to God, and by this our present charter, confirmed for us and our heirs forever that the English church shall be free. . . .

9. Neither we nor our bailiffs shall seize any land or rent for any debt so long as the debtor's chattels are sufficient to discharge the same. . . .

12. No scutage [tax] or aid shall be imposed in our kingdom unless by the common counsel thereof. . . .

14. For obtaining the common counsel of the kingdom concerning the assessment of aids. . . or of scutage, we will cause to be summoned, severally by our letters, the archbishops, bishops, abbots, earls, and great barons; we will also cause to be summoned generally, by our sheriffs and bailiffs, all those who hold lands directly of us, to meet on a fixed day . . . and at a fixed place. . . .

20. A free man shall be amerced [punished] for a small fault only according to the measure thereof, and for a great crime according to its magnitude. . . . None of these amercements shall be imposed except by the oath of honest men of the neighborhood.

21. Earls and barons shall be amerced only by their peers, and only in proportion to the measure of the offense. . . .

38. In the future no bailiff shall upon his own unsupported accusation put any man to trial without producing credible witnesses to the truth of the accusation.

39. No free man shall be taken, imprisoned, disseised [seized], outlawed, banished, or in any way destroyed, nor will we proceed against or prosecute him, except by the lawful judgment of his peers and by the law of the land.

40. To no one will we sell, to none will we deny or delay, right or justice. . . .

42. In the future it shall be lawful . . . for anyone to leave and return to our kingdom safely and securely by land and water, saving his fealty to us. Excepted are those who have been imprisoned or outlawed according to the law of the land. . . .

61. Whereas we, for the honor of God and the amendment of our realm, and in order the better to allay the discord arisen between us and our barons, have granted all these things aforesaid. . . .

63. Wherefore we will, and firmly charge . . . that all men in our kingdom shall have and hold all the aforesaid liberties, rights, and concessions . . . fully, and wholly to them and their heirs . . . in all things and places forever. . . . It is moreover sworn, as well on our part as on the part of the barons, that all these matters aforesaid will be kept in good faith and without deceit. Witness the above named and many others. Given by our hand in the meadow which is called Runnymede. . . .

The Mayflower Compact

*On November 21, 1620, 41 colonists drafted the Mayflower Compact while still aboard the **Mayflower**. It was the first self-government plan ever put into effect in the English colonies. The compact was drawn up under these circumstances, as described by Governor William Bradford:*

"This day, before we came to harbor, observing some not well affected to unity and concord, but gave some appearance of faction, it was thought good there should be an association and agreement that we should combine together in one body, and to submit to such government and governors as we should by common consent agree to make and choose, and set our hands to this that follows word for word."

In the Name of God, Amen. We, whose names are underwritten, the Loyal Subjects of our dread Sovereign Lord King James, by the Grace of God, of Great Britain, France, and Ireland, King, Defender of the Faith, etc.

Having undertaken for the Glory of God, and Advancement of the Christian Faith, and the honor of our King and Country, a Voyage to plant the first Colony in the northern Parts of Virginia, Do by these Presents, solemnly and mutually, in the Presence of God and one another, covenant and combine ourselves together into a civil Body Politick, for our better Ordering and Preservation, and Furtherance of the Ends aforesaid; And by Virtue hereof do enact, constitute, and frame, such just and equal Laws, Ordinances, Acts, Constitutions, and Offices, from time to time, as shall be thought most meet and convenient for the general Good of the Colony; unto which we promise all due Submission and Obedience. In Witness whereof we have hereunder subscribed our names at Cape Cod the eleventh of November, in the Reign of our Sovereign Lord King James of England, France, and Ireland, the eighteenth and of Scotland, the fifty-fourth. Anno Domini, 1620.

Signing of the Mayflower Compact

The Fundamental Orders of Connecticut

In January 1639, settlers in Connecticut, led by Thomas Hooker, drew up the Fundamental Orders of Connecticut—America's first written constitution. It is essentially a body of laws and a compact among the settlers.

Forasmuch as it has pleased the Almighty God by the wise disposition of His Divine Providence so to order and dispose of things that we, the inhabitants and residents of Windsor, Hartford, and Wethersfield are now cohabiting and dwelling in and upon the river of Conectecotte and the lands thereunto adjoining; and well knowing where a people are gathered together the Word of God requires that, to maintain the peace and union of such a people, there should be an orderly and decent government established according to God, . . . do therefore associate and conjoin ourselves to be as one public state or commonwealth. . . . As also in our civil affairs to be guided and governed according to such laws, rules, orders, and decrees as shall be made, ordered, and decreed, as follows:

1. It is ordered . . . that there shall be yearly two general assemblies or courts; . . . The first shall be called the Court of Election, wherein shall be yearly chosen . . . so many magistrates and other public officers as shall be found requisite. Whereof one to be chosen governor . . . and no other magistrate to be chosen for more than one year; provided aways there be six chosen besides the governor . . . by all that are admitted freemen and have taken the oath of fidelity, and do cohabit within this jurisdiction. . . .

4. It is ordered . . . that no person be chosen governor above once in two years, and that the governor be always a member of some approved congregation, and formerly of the magistracy within this jurisdiction; and all the magistrates freemen of this Commonwealth. . . .

5. It is ordered . . . that to the aforesaid Court of Election the several towns shall send their deputies. . . . Also, the other General Court . . . shall be for making of laws, and any other public occasion which concerns the good of the Commonwealth. . . .

7. It is ordered . . . that . . . the constable or constables of each town shall forthwith give notice distinctly to the inhabitants of the same . . . that . . . they meet and assemble themselves together to elect and choose certain deputies to be at the General Court then following to [manage] the affairs of the Commonwealth; . . .

10. It is ordered . . . that every General Court . . . shall consist of the governor, or someone chosen to moderate the Court, and four other magistrates, at least, with the major part of the deputies of the several towns legally chosen. . . . In which said General Courts shall consist the supreme power of the Commonwealth, and they only shall have power to make laws or repeal them, to grant levies, to admit of freemen, dispose of lands undisposed of to several towns or person, and also shall have power to call either Court or magistrate or any other person whatsoever into question for any misdemeanor. . . .

Connecticut settlers on their way to Hartford

The English Bill of Rights

In 1689 William of Orange (pictured at right) and his wife Mary became joint rulers of England after accepting a list of conditions that later became known as the English Bill of Rights. This document assured the English people of certain basic civil rights and limited the power of the English monarchy.

An act declaring the rights and liberties of the subject and settling the succession of the crown. Whereas the lords spiritual and temporal and commons assembled at Westminster lawfully fully and freely representing all the estates of the people of this realm did upon the thirteenth day of February in the year of our Seal of William and Mary Lord one thousand six hundred eighty-eight [-nine] present unto their majesties . . . William and Mary prince and princess of Orange . . . a certain declaration in writing made by the said lords and commons in the words following viz [namely]

Whereas the late king James the second, by the assistance of divers evil counsellors, judges, and ministers employed by him did endeavor to subvert and extirpate the protestant religion and the laws and liberties of this kingdom.

By assuming and exercising a power of dispensing with and suspending of laws and the execution of laws without consent of parliament. . . .

By levying money for and to the use of the crown by pretence of prerogative for other time and in other manner than the same was granted by parliament.

By raising and keeping a standing army within this kingdom in time of peace without consent of parliament and quartering soldiers contrary to law. . . .

By violating the freedom of election of members to serve in parliament. . . .

And excessive bail hath been required of persons committed in criminal cases to elude the benefit of the laws made for the liberty of the subjects.

And excessive fines have been imposed.

And illegal and cruel punishments inflicted. . . .

And thereupon the said lords spiritual and temporal and commons . . . do . . . declare that the pretended power of suspending of laws or the execution of laws by regal authority without consent of parliament is illegal. . . .

That levying money for or to the use of the crown . . . without grant of parliament for longer time or in other manner than the same is or shall be granted is illegal.

That it is the right of the subjects to petition the king and all commitments and prosecutions for such petitioning are illegal.

That the raising or keeping a standing army within the kingdom in time of peace unless it be with consent of parliament is against law. . . .

That election of members of parliament ought to be free. . . .

That excessive bail ought not to be required nor excessive fines imposed nor cruel and unusual punishments inflicted. . . .

The said lords . . . do resolve that William and Mary, prince and princess of Orange, be declared king and queen of England, France, and Ireland. . . .

Second Treatise of Government

English philosopher John Locke (above) wrote "Two Treatises of Government" in the early 1680s. Published in 1690, the "Second Treatise of Government" argues that government should be based on an agreement between the people and their ruler, and that if the ruler violates the agreement, a rebellion by the people may be justified.

Of the State of Nature

To understand Political Power right, and to derive it from its Original, we must consider what State all Men are naturally in, and that is, a State of perfect Freedom to order their Actions, and dispose of their Possessions, and Persons as they think fit, within the bounds of the Law of Nature, without asking leave, or depending upon the Will of any other Man. . . .

Of the Beginning of Political Societies

Men being, as has been said, by Nature, all free, equal and independent, no one can be put out of this Estate, and subjected to the Political Power of another, without his own Consent.

The only way whereby any one divests himself of his Natural Liberty, and puts on the bonds of Civil Society is by agreeing with other Men to joyn and unite into a Community, for their comfortable, safe, and peaceable living one amongst another, in a secure Enjoyment of their properties, and a greater Security against any that are not of it. This any number of Men may do, because it injures not the Freedom of the rest; they are left as they were in the Liberty of the State of Nature. . . .

Whosoever therefore out of a state of Nature unite into a Community, must be understood to give up all the power, necessary to the ends for which they unite into Society, to the majority of the Community. . . .

Of the Dissolution of Government

Governments are dissolved from within . . . when the Legislative is altered. . . . First, that when such a single Person or Prince sets up his own Arbitrary Will in place of the Laws, which are the Will of the Society, declared by the Legislative, then the Legislative is changed . . . . Secondly, when the Prince hinders the legislative from . . . acting freely, pursuant to those ends, for which it was Constituted, the Legislative is altered . . . . Thirdly, When by the Arbitrary Power of the Prince, the Electors, or ways of Election are altered, without the Consent, and contrary to the common Interest of the People, there also the Legislative is altered. . . .

In these and the like Cases, when the Government is dissolved, the People are at liberty to provide for themselves, by erecting a new Legislative, differing from the other, by the change of Persons, or Form, or both as they shall find it most for their safety and good. For the Society can never, by the fault of another, lose the Native and Original Right it has to preserve itself. . . .

The Virginia Statute for Religious Freedom

This statute, excerpted below, was the basis for the religion clauses in the Bill of Rights. Thomas Jefferson drafted the statute, and James Madison guided it through the Virginia legislature in 1786. The issue it addresses arose when the new state considered whether citizens should continue to support the Anglican Church, as they had in colonial times, or whether they should support any or all other denominations.

Whereas Almighty God hath created the mind free; that all attempts to influence it by temporal punishments . . . tend only to beget habits of hypocrisy and meanness, and are a departure from the plan of the Holy author of our religion; . . . that the impious presumption of legislators and rulers, civil as well as ecclesiastical, who being themselves but fallible and uninspired men, have assumed dominion over the faith of others, setting up their own opinions and modes of thinking as the only true and infallible, and as such endeavouring to impose them on others, hath established and maintained false religions over the greatest part of the world, and through all time; . . . that to compel a man to furnish contributions of money for the propagation of opinions which he disbelieves, is sinful and tyrannical; . . . that our civil rights have no dependence on our religious opinions, any more than our opinions in physics or geometry; that therefore the proscribing any citizen as unworthy the public confidence by laying upon him an incapacity of being called to offices of trust . . . unless he profess or renounce this or that religious opinion, is depriving him injuriously of those privileges and advantages to which in common with his fellow-citizens he has a natural right; that it tends only to corrupt the principles of that religion it is meant to encourage, by bribing with a monopoly of worldly honours and emoluments, those who will externally profess and conform to it. . . :

Be it enacted by the General Assembly, That no man shall be compelled to frequent or support any religious worship, place, or ministry whatsoever, nor shall be enforced, restrained, molested, or burthened in his body or goods, nor shall otherwise suffer on account of his religious opinions or belief; but that all men shall be free to profess, and by argument to maintain, their opinion in matters of religion, and that the same shall in no wise diminish enlarge, or affect their civil capacities. . . .

Thomas Jefferson

The Federalist No. 10

James Madison (pictured at right) wrote several articles for a New York newspaper supporting ratification of the Constitution . In the excerpt below, he argues for the idea of a federal republic as a guard against factions, or overzealous parties, in governing the nation.

The latent causes of faction are thus sown in the nature of man; and we see them everywhere. . . . A zeal for different opinions concerning religion, concerning government, and many other points; . . . an attachment to different leaders ambitiously contending for pre-eminence and power . . . have, in turn, divided mankind into parties . . . disposed to vex and oppress each other than to cooperate for their common good. . . . But the most common and durable source of factions has been the various and unequal distribution of property. Those who hold and those who are without property have ever formed distinct interests in society. Those who are creditors, and those who are debtors, fall under a like discrimination. A landed interest, a manufacturing interest, a mercantile interest, a moneyed interest, with many lesser interests, grow up of necessity in civilized nations, and divide them into different classes, actuated by different sentiments and views. The regulation of these various and interfering interests forms the principal task of modern legislation and involves the spirit of party and faction in the necessary and ordinary operations of government. . . .

The inference to which we are brought is that the causes of faction cannot be removed and relief is only to be sought in the means of controlling its effects. . . .

By what means is this object attainable? Evidently by one of two only. Either the existence of the same passion or interest in a majority at the same time must be prevented, or the majority, having such coexistent passion or interest, must be rendered, by their number and local situation, unable to concert and carry into effect schemes of oppression. . . .

From this . . . it may be concluded that a pure democracy, by which I mean a society consisting of a small number of citizens, who assemble and administer the government in person, can admit of no cure for the mischiefs of faction. A common passion or interest will, in almost every case, be felt by a majority of the whole; a communication and concert results from the form of government itself; and there is nothing to check the inducements to sacrifice the weaker party or an obnoxious individual. Hence it is that such democracies have ever been spectacles of turbulence and contention. . . .

A republic, by which I mean a government in which the scheme of representation takes place, opens a different prospect and promises the cure for which we are seeking. . . .

The two great points of difference between a democracy and a republic are: first, the delegation of the government in the latter to a small number of citizens elected by the rest; secondly, the greater number of citizens and great sphere of country over which the latter may be extended.

The Federalist No. 51

The author of this Federalist paper is not known. It may have been either James Madison or Alexander Hamilton. The author argues that the Constitution's federal system and separation of powers will protect the rights of the people.

In order to lay a due foundation for that separate and distinct exercise of the different powers of government, which to a certain extent is admitted on all hands to be essential to the preservation of liberty, it is evident that . . . the great security against a gradual concentration of the several powers in the same department, consists in giving to those who administer each department the necessary constitutional means and personal motives to resist encroachments of the others. . . .

Ambition must be made to counteract ambition. . . . A dependence on the people is, no doubt, the primary control on the government; but experience has taught mankind the necessity of auxiliary precautions. . . . The constant aim is to divide and arrange the several offices in such a manner as that each may be a check on the other. . . . In the compound republic of America, the power surrendered by the people is first divided between two distinct governments, and then the portion allotted to each subdivided among distinct and separate departments. . . .

In a free government the security for civil rights must be the same as that for religious rights. It consists in the one case in the multiplicity of interests, and in the other in the multiplicity of sects. . . . In the extended republic of the United States, and among the great variety of interests, parties, and sects which it embraces, a coalition of a majority of the whole society could seldom take place on any other principles than those of justice and the general good. . . . It is no less certain than it is important . . . that the larger the society, provided it lie within a practical sphere, the more duly capable it will be of self-government.

The Federalist No. 59

In this Federalist paper, Alexander Hamilton explains why Congress, and not the states, should have the final say in how federal elections are conducted.

The natural order of the subject leads us to consider . . . that provision of the Constitution which authorizes the national legislature to regulate, in the last resort, the election of its own members. . . . Its propriety rests upon the evidence of this plain proposition, that every government ought to contain in itself the means of its own preservation. . . . Nothing can be more evident, than that an exclusive power of regulating elections for the national government, in the hands of the state legislatures, would leave the existence of the union entirely at their mercy. They could at any moment annihilate it, by neglecting to provide for the choice of persons to administer its affairs. . . .

It is certainly true that the state legislatures, by forbearing the appointment of senators, may destroy the national government. But it will not follow that, because they have a power to do this in one instance, they ought to have it in every other. . . . It is an evil; but it is an evil which could not have been avoided without excluding the states . . . from a place in the organization of the national government. If this had been done, it would doubtless have been interpreted into an entire dereliction of the federal principle; and would certainly have deprived the state governments of that absolute safeguard which they will enjoy under this provision. . . .

Washington's Farewell Address

Washington never orally delivered his Farewell Address. Instead, he arranged to have it printed in a Philadelphia newspaper on September 19, 1796. Designed in part to remove him from consideration for a third presidential term, the address also warned about dangers the new nation was facing, especially the dangers of political parties and sectionalism.

Washington preparing to leave office

Friends and Fellow Citizens:

The period for a new election of a citizen to administer the executive government of the United States being not far distant . . . I should now apprise you of the resolution I have formed to decline being considered. . . .

The unity of government which constitutes you one people is . . . a main pillar in the edifice of your real independence; the support of your tranquility at home, your peace abroad; of your safety; of your prosperity in every shape; of that very liberty which you so highly prize. But as it is easy to foresee that, from different causes and from different quarters, much pains will be taken, many artifices employed to weaken in your minds the conviction of this truth. . . .

The name of American, which belongs to you, in your national capacity, must always exalt the just pride of patriotism more than any appellation derived from local discriminations. . . .

In contemplating the causes which may disturb our Union, it occurs as matter of serious concern that any ground should have been furnished for characterizing parties by geographical discriminations: Northern and Southern; Atlantic and Western; whence designing men may endeavor to excite a belief that there is a real difference of local interests and views. . . .

Let me now take a more comprehensive view and warn you in the most solemn manner against the baneful effects of the spirit of party generally. . . .

The alternate domination of one faction over another, sharpened by the spirit of revenge natural to party dissension . . . is itself a frightful despotism. . . .

Of all the dispositions and habits which lead to political prosperity, religion and morality are indispensable supports. . . . A volume could not trace all their connections with private and public felicity. Let it simply be asked where is the security for property, for reputation, for life, if the sense of religious obligation desert the oaths, which are the instruments of investigation in courts of justice? And let us with caution indulge the supposition, that morality can be maintained without religion. Whatever may be conceded to the influence of refined education on minds of peculiar structure—reason and experience both forbid us to expect that national morality can prevail in exclusion of religious principle.

The great rule of conduct for us, in regard to foreign nations, is in extending our commercial relations to have with them as little political connection as possible. . . .

In offering you, my countrymen, these counsels of an old and affectionate friend, I dare not hope that they will make the strong and lasting impression I could wish. . . . But if I may even flatter myself that they may be productive of some partial benefit. . . .

The Kentucky Resolution

The Alien and Sedition Acts of 1798 made it easier for the government to suppress criticism and to arrest political enemies. This Federalist legislation inspired fierce opposition among Republicans, who looked to the state governments to reverse the acts. Two states, Kentucky and Virginia, passed resolutions stating their right to, in effect, disregard federal legislation. The resolutions laid the groundwork for the states' rights often cited during the Civil War. Thomas Jefferson wrote the Kentucky Resolution, excerpted below, which was adopted in 1799.

RESOLVED, . . . that if those who administer the general government be permitted to transgress the limits fixed by that compact, by a total disregard to the special delegations of power therein contained, annihilation of the state governments, and the erection upon their ruins, of a general consolidated government, will be the inevitable consequence; that the principle and construction contended for by sundry of the state legislatures, that the general government is the exclusive judge of the extent of the powers delegated to it, stop nothing short of despotism; . . . that the several states who formed that instrument, being sovereign and independent, have the unquestionable right to judge of its infraction; and that a nullification, by those sovereignties, of all unauthorized acts done under colour of that instrument, is the rightful remedy; . . .

Francis Scott Key

"The Star-Spangled Banner"

During the British bombardment of Fort McHenry during the War of 1812, a young Baltimore lawyer named Francis Scott Key was inspired to write the words to "The Star-Spangled Banner." Although it became popular immediately, it was not until 1931 that Congress officially declared "The Star-Spangled Banner" as the national anthem of the United States.

O! say can you see, by the dawn's early light,

What so proudly we hail'd at the twilight's last gleaming,

Whose broad stripes and bright stars through the perilous fight,

O'er the ramparts we watch'd, were so gallantly streaming?

And the Rockets' red glare, the Bombs bursting in air,

Gave proof through the night that our Flag was still there;

O! say, does that star-spangled Banner yet wave,

O'er the Land of the free, and the home of the brave!

Fort McHenry flag

The Monroe Doctrine

When Spain's power in South America began to weaken, other European nations seemed ready to step in. The United States was developing trade and diplomatic relations with South America, and it wanted to curb European influence there. The following is a statement President Monroe made on the subject in his annual message to Congress on December 2, 1823.

The occasion has been judged proper for asserting, as a principle in which the rights and interests of the United States are involved, that the American continents, by the free and independent condition which they have assumed and maintain, are henceforth not to be considered as subjects for future colonization by any European powers. . . .

. . . We owe it, therefore, to candor and to the amicable relations existing between the United States and those [European] powers to declare that we should consider any attempt on their part to extend their system to any portion of this hemisphere as dangerous to our peace and safety. With the existing colonies or dependencies of any European power we have not interfered and shall not interfere. But with the Governments who have declared their independence and maintain it, and whose independence we have, on great consideration and on just principles, acknowledged, we could not view any interposition for the purpose of oppressing them, or controlling in any other manner their destiny, by any European power in any other light than as the manifestation of an unfriendly disposition toward the United States. . . .

Our policy in regard to Europe, which was adopted at an early stage of the wars which have so long agitated that quarter of the globe, nevertheless remains the same, which is, not to interfere in the internal concerns of any of its powers; to consider the government de facto as the legitimate government for us; to cultivate friendly relations with it, and to preserve those relations by a frank, firm, and manly policy, meeting in all instances the just claims of every power, submitting to injuries from none.

The Seneca Falls Declaration

One of the first documents to call for equal rights for women was the Declaration of Sentiments and Resolutions, issued in 1848 at the Seneca Falls Convention in Seneca Falls, New York. Led by Lucretia Mott and Elizabeth Cady Stanton, the delegates at the convention used the language of the Bill of Rights to call for women's rights.

We hold these truths to be self-evident: that all men and women are created equal; that they are endowed by their Creator with certain inalienable rights; that among these are life, liberty, and the pursuit of happiness; that to secure these rights governments are instituted, deriving their just powers from the consent of the governed. Whenever any form of government becomes destructive of these ends, it is the right of those who suffer from it to refuse allegiance to it, and to insist upon the institution of a new government. . . .

The history of mankind is a history of repeated injuries and usurpations on the part of man toward woman, having in direct object the establishment of an absolute tyranny over her.

Now, in view of this entire disfranchisement . . . we insist that they have immediate admission to all the rights and privileges which belong to them as citizens of the United States. . . .

Lucretia Mott

The Emancipation Proclamation

On January 1, 1863, President Abraham Lincoln issued the Emancipation Proclamation, which freed all enslaved persons in states under Confederate control. The Proclamation was a significant step toward the passage of the Thirteenth Amendment (1865), which ended slavery in the United States.

Whereas, on the 22nd day of September, in the year of our Lord 1862, a proclamation was issued by the President of the United States, containing, among other things, the following, to wit:

That on the 1st day of January, in the year of our Lord 1863, all persons held as slaves within any state or designated part of a state, the people whereof shall then be in rebellion against the United States, shall be then, thenceforward, and forever free; and the executive government of the United States, including the military and naval authority thereof, will recognize and maintain the freedom of such persons and will do no act or acts to repress such persons, or any of them, in any efforts they may make for their actual freedom.

That the executive will, on the 1st day January aforesaid, by proclamation, designate the states and parts of states, if any, in which the people thereof, respectively, shall then be in rebellion against the United States; and the fact that any state or the people thereof shall on that day be in good faith represented in the Congress of the United States by members chosen thereto at elections wherein a majority of the qualified voters of such states shall have participated shall, in the absence of strong countervailing testimony, be deemed conclusive evidence that such state and the people thereof are not then in rebellion against the United States.

Now, therefore, I, Abraham Lincoln, President of the United States, by virtue of the power in me vested as commander in chief of the Army and Navy of the United States, in time of actual armed rebellion against the authority and government of the United States, and as a fit and necessary war measure for suppressing said rebellion, do, on this 1st day of January, in the year of our Lord 1863, and in accordance with my purpose so to do, publicly proclaimed for the full period of 100 days from the day first above mentioned, order, and designate as the states and parts of states wherein the people thereof, respectively, are this day in rebellion against the United States. . . .

And, by virtue of the power and for the purpose aforesaid, I do order and declare that all persons held as slaves within said designated states and parts of states are, and henceforward shall be, free; and that the executive government of the United States, including the military and naval authorities thereof, will recognize and maintain the freedom of said persons. . . .

And upon this act, sincerely believed to be an act of justice, warranted by the Constitution upon military necessity, I invoke the considerate judgment of mankind and the gracious favor of Almighty God. . . .

Abraham Lincoln

The Gettysburg Address

National monument at Gettysburg

President Abraham Lincoln delivered the Gettysburg Address on November 19, 1863, during the dedication of the Gettysburg National Cemetery. The dedication was in honor of the more than 7,000 Union and Confederate soldiers who died in the Battle of Gettysburg earlier that year. Lincoln's brief speech is often recognized as one of the finest speeches in the English language. It is also one of the most moving speeches in the nation's history.

There are five known manuscript copies of the address, two of which are in the Library of Congress. Scholars debate about which, if any, of the existing manuscripts comes closest to Lincoln's actual words that day.

Four score and seven years ago our fathers brought forth on this continent a new nation, conceived in liberty and dedicated to the proposition that all men are created equal.

Now we are engaged in a great civil war, testing whether that nation or any nation so conceived and so dedicated can long endure. We are met on a great battlefield of that war. We have come to dedicate a portion of that field as a final resting-place for those who here gave their lives that that nation might live. It is altogether fitting and proper that we should do this.

But in a larger sense, we cannot dedicate, we cannot consecrate, we cannot hallow this ground. The brave men, living and dead who struggled here have consecrated it far above our poor power to add or detract. The world will little note nor long remember what we say here, but it can never forget what they did here. It is for us the living rather to be dedicated here to the unfinished work which they who fought here have thus far so nobly advanced. It is rather for us to be here dedicated to the great task remaining before us—that from these honored dead we take increased devotion to that cause for which they gave the last full measure of devotion—that we here highly resolve that these dead shall not have died in vain, that this nation under God shall have a new birth of freedom, and that government of the people, by the people, for the people shall not perish from the earth.

The Pledge of Allegiance

Students in a New York City school reciting the Pledge of Allegiance

In 1892 the nation celebrated the 400th anniversary of Columbus's landing in America. In connection with this celebration, Francis Bellamy, a magazine editor, wrote and published the Pledge of Allegiance. The words "under God" were added by Congress in 1954 at the urging of President Dwight D. Eisenhower.

I pledge allegiance to the Flag of the United States of America and to the Republic for which it stands, one Nation under God, indivisible, with liberty and justice for all.

President Harrison on Hawaiian Annexation

An early expression of American imperialism came in the annexation of Hawaii. With the support of the American government, a small number of American troops overthrew the Hawaiian monarchy in January 1893. The excerpt below is from President Benjamin Harrison's written message to Congress. He sent the message along with the treaty for annexation to Congress on February 15, 1893.

I do not deem it necessary to discuss at any length the conditions which have resulted in this decisive action. It has been the policy of the administration not only to respect but to encourage the continuance of an independent government in the Hawaiian Islands so long as it afforded suitable guarantees for the protection of life and property and maintained a stability and strength that gave adequate security against the domination of any other power. . . .

The overthrow of the monarchy was not in any way promoted by this government, but had its origin in what seems to have been a reactionary and revolutionary policy on the part of Queen Liliuokalani, which put in serious peril not only the large and preponderating interests of the United States . . . but all foreign interests. . . . It is quite evident that the monarchy had become effete and the queen's government is weak and inadequate as to be the prey of designing and unscrupulous persons. The restoration of Queen Liliuokalani . . . is undesirable . . . and unless actively supported by the United States would be accompanied by serious disaster and the disorganization of all business interests. The influence and interest of the United States in the islands must be increased and not diminished.

Only two courses are now open—one the establishment of a protectorate by the United States, and the other annexation, full and complete. I think the latter course, which has been adopted in the treaty, will be highly promotive of the best interest of the Hawaiian people and is the only one that will adequately secure the interests of the United States. These interests are not wholly selfish. It is essential that none of the other great powers shall secure these islands. Such a possession would not consist with our safety and with the peace of the world. This view of the situation is so apparent and conclusive that no protest has been heard from any government against proceedings looking to annexation.

The American's Creed

In the patriotic fervor of World War I, national leaders sponsored a contest in which writers submitted ideas for a national creed that would be a brief summary of American beliefs. Of the 3,000 entries, the judges selected that of William Tyler Page as the winner. In a 1918 ceremony in the House of Representatives, the Speaker of the House accepted the creed for the United States.

I believe in the United States of America as a Government of the people, by the people, for the people, whose just powers are derived from the consent of the governed; a democracy in a republic; a sovereign Nation of many sovereign States; a perfect union, one and inseparable; established upon those principles of freedom, equality, justice, and humanity for which American patriots sacrificed their lives and fortunes.

I therefore believe it is my duty to my Country to love it; to support its Constitution; to obey its laws; to respect its flag, and to defend it against all enemies.

The Fourteen Points

On January 8, 1918, President Woodrow Wilson went before Congress to offer a statement of war aims called the Fourteen Points. They reflected Wilson's belief that if the international community accepted certain basic principles of conduct and set up institutions to carry them out, there would be peace in the world.

We entered this war because violations of right had occurred. . . . What we demand in this war, therefore, is . . . that the world be made fit and safe to live in. . . .

The only possible programme, as we see it, is this:

I. Open covenants of peace, openly arrived at, after which there shall be no private international understandings of any kind but diplomacy shall proceed always frankly and in the public view.

II. Absolute freedom of navigation upon the seas, outside territorial waters, alike in peace and in war. . . .

III. The removal, so far as possible, of all economic barriers and the establishment of an equality of trade conditions among all the nations. . . .

IV. Adequate guarantees given and taken that national armaments will be reduced to the lowest point consistent with domestic safety.

V. A free, open-minded, and absolutely impartial adjustment of all colonial claims, based upon a strict observance of the principle that in determining all such questions of sovereignty the interests of the populations concerned must have equal weight with the equitable claims of the government whose title is to be determined.

VI. The evacuation of all Russian territory and . . . opportunity for the independent determination of her own political development and national polity. . . .

VII. Belgium . . . must be evacuated and restored. . . .

VIII. All French territory should be freed and the invaded portions restored, and the wrong done to France by Prussia in 1871 in the matter of Alsace-Lorraine should be righted. . . .

IX. A readjustment of the frontiers of Italy should be effected along clearly recognizable lines of nationality.

X. The peoples of Austria-Hungary . . . should be accorded the freest opportunity of autonomous development.

XI. Rumania, Serbia, and Montenegro should be evacuated; occupied territories restored . . . the relations of the several Balkan states to one another determined by friendly counsel along historically established lines of allegiance and nationality. . . .

XII. The Turkish portions of the present Ottoman Empire should be assured a secure sovereignty. . . .

XIII. An independent Polish state should be erected which should include the territories inhabited by indisputably Polish populations. . . .

XIV. A general association of nations must be formed under specific covenants for the purpose of affording mutual guarantees of political independence and territorial integrity. . . .

Discussion of the Fourteen Points at the Versailles peace conference

The Four Freedoms

President Franklin D. Roosevelt delivered this address on January 6, 1941, in his annual message to Congress. In it, Roosevelt called for a world founded on "four essential human freedoms": freedom of speech and expression, freedom of worship, freedom from want, and freedom from fear.

Just as our national policy in internal affairs has been based upon a decent respect for the rights and dignity of all our fellow men within our gates, so our national policy in foreign affairs has been based on a decent respect for the rights and dignity of all nations, large and small. And the justice of morality must and will win in the end.

Our national policy is this:

First, by an impressive expression of the public will and without regard to partisanship, we are committed to all-inclusive national defense.

Second, by an impressive expression of the public will and without regard to partisanship, we are committed to full support of all those resolute peoples, everywhere, who are resisting aggression and are thereby keeping war away from our Hemisphere. . . .

Third . . . we are committed to the proposition that principles of morality and considerations for our own security will never permit us to acquiesce in a peace dictated by aggressors. . . .

Let us say to the democracies, "We Americans are vitally concerned in your defense of freedom. We are putting forth our energies, our resources, and our organizing powers to give you the strength to regain and maintain a free world. We shall send you, in ever increasing numbers, ships, planes, tanks, guns. This is our purpose and our pledge." In fulfillment of this purpose we will not be intimidated by the threats of dictators that they will regard as a breach of international

Caricature of President Roosevelt

law and as an act of war our aid to the democracies which dare to resist their aggression. . . .

In the future days, which we seek to make secure, we look forward to a world founded upon four essential human freedoms.

The first is freedom of speech and expression everywhere in the world.

The second is freedom of every person to worship God in his own way everywhere in the world.

The third is freedom from want, which, translated into world terms, means economic understandings which will secure to every nation a healthy peacetime life for its inhabitants everywhere in the world.

The fourth is freedom from fear—which, translated into world terms, means a worldwide reduction of armaments to such a point and in such a thorough fashion that no nation will be in a position to commit an act of physical aggression against any neighbor—anywhere in the world. . . .

The Truman Doctrine

President Harry S Truman addressed a joint session of Congress on March 12, 1947, to request aid to fight Communist influence in Greece and Turkey. His message that communism had to be contained represents the central idea of American foreign policy during the Cold War.

The United States has received from the Greek Government an urgent appeal for financial and economic assistance. . . .

When forces of liberation entered Greece they found that the retreating Germans had destroyed virtually all the railways, roads, port facilities, communications, and merchant marine. More than a thousand villages had been burned. Eighty-five percent of the children were tubercular. Livestock, poultry, and draft animals had almost disappeared. Inflation had wiped out practically all savings. As a result of these tragic conditions, a militant minority, exploiting human want and misery, was able to create political chaos which, until now, has made economic recovery impossible.

Greece is today without funds to finance the importation of those goods which are essential to bare subsistence. Under these circumstances the people of Greece cannot make progress in solving their problems of reconstruction. Greece is in desperate need of financial and economic assistance to enable it to resume purchases of food, clothing, fuel and seeds. These are indispensable for the subsistence of its people and are obtainable only from abroad. Greece must have help to import the goods necessary to restore internal order and security, so essential for economic and political recovery. . . .

Meanwhile, the Greek Government is unable to cope with the situation. The Greek army is small and poorly equipped. It needs supplies and equipment if it is to restore the authority of the government throughout Greek territory. Greece must have assistance if it is to become a self-supporting and self-respecting democracy.

The United States must supply that assistance. We have already extended to Greece certain types of relief and economic aid but these are inadequate. There is no other country to which democratic Greece can turn. . . .

No government is perfect. One of the chief virtues of a democracy, however, is that its defects are always visible and under democratic processes can be pointed out and corrected. The Government of Greece is not perfect. Nevertheless it represents eighty-five percent of the members of the Greek Parliament who were chosen in an election last year. . . .

Greece's neighbor, Turkey, also deserves our attention. The future of Turkey as an independent and economically sound state is clearly no less important to the freedom-loving peoples of the world than the future of Greece. The circumstances in which Turkey finds itself today are considerably different from those of Greece. Turkey has been spared the disasters that have beset Greece. And during the war, the United States and Great Britain furnished Turkey with material aid. Nevertheless, Turkey now needs our support.

. . . . To ensure the peaceful development of nations, free from coercion, the United States has taken a leading part in establishing the United Nations. The United Nations is designed to make possible lasting freedom and independence for all its members. We shall not realize our objectives, however, unless we are willing to help free peoples to maintain their free institutions . . . against aggressive movements that seek to impose upon them totalitarian regimes. . . .

This is an investment in world freedom and world peace. . . . The seeds of totalitarian regimes are nurtured by misery and want. They spread and grow in the evil soil of poverty and strife. They reach their full growth when the hope of a people for a better life has died. We must keep that hope alive. . . . If we falter in our leadership, we may endanger the peace of the world—and we shall surely endanger the welfare of our own nation.

Brown v. Board of Education

On May 17, 1954, the Supreme Court ruled in **Brown v. Board of Education of Topeka, Kansas,** *that racial segregation in public schools was unconstitutional. This decision provided the legal basis for court challenges to segregation in every aspect of American life.*

These cases come to us from the States of Kansas, South Carolina, Virginia, and Delaware. They are premised on different facts and different local conditions, but a common legal question justifies their consideration together in this consolidated opinion.

In each of the cases, minors of the Negro race, through their legal representatives, seek the aid of the courts in obtaining admission to the public schools of their community on a nonsegregated basis. In each instance, they had been denied admission to schools attended by white children under laws requiring or permitting segregation according to race. This segregation was alleged to deprive the plaintiffs of the equal protection of the laws under the Fourteenth Amendment.

The plaintiffs contend that segregated public schools are not "equal" and cannot be made "equal," and that hence they are deprived of the equal protection of the laws. Because of the obvious importance of the question presented, the Court took jurisdiction. . . .

. . . Our decision . . . cannot turn on merely a comparison of these tangible factors in the Negro and white schools involved in each of the cases. We must look instead to the effect of segregation itself on public education.

In approaching this problem, we cannot turn the clock back to 1868 when the Amendment was adopted, or even to 1896 when *Plessy* v. *Ferguson* was written. We must consider public education in the light of its full development and its present place in American life throughout the nation. Only in this way can it be determined if segregation in public schools deprives these plaintiffs of the equal protection of the laws.

Today, education is perhaps the most important function of state and local governments. Compulsory school attendance laws and the great expenditures for education both demonstrate our recognition of the importance of education to our democratic society. . . . In these days, it is doubtful that any child may reasonably be expected to succeed in life if he is denied the opportunity of an education. Such an opportunity, where the state has undertaken to provide it, is a right which must be made available to all on equal terms.

We come then to the question presented: Does segregation of children in public schools solely on the basis of race, even though the physical facilities and other "tangible" factors may be equal, deprive the children of the minority group of equal educational opportunities? We believe that it does.

. . . We conclude that, in the field of public education, the doctrine of "separate but equal" has no place. Separate educational facilities are inherently unequal. Therefore, we hold that the plaintiff and others similarly situated for whom the actions have been brought are, by reason of the segregation complained of, deprived of the equal protection of the laws guaranteed by the Fourteenth Amendment. . . .

Linda Brown

"I Have a Dream"

On August 28, 1963, while Congress was debating broad civil rights legislation, Martin Luther King, Jr., led more than 200,000 people in a march on Washington, D.C. On the steps of the Lincoln Memorial, King gave a stirring speech in which he eloquently spoke of his dreams for African Americans and for the United States.

Martin Luther King, Jr., speaking at the march

Five score years ago, a great American, in whose symbolic shadow we stand, signed the Emancipation Proclamation. This momentous decree came as a great beacon light of hope to millions of Negro slaves who had been seared in the flames of withering injustice. It came as a joyous day-break to end the long night of captivity.

But one hundred years later, we must face the tragic fact that the Negro is still not free. One hundred years later, the life of the Negro is still sadly crippled by the manacles of seg-regation and the chains of discrimination. . . .

There are those who are asking the devotees of civil rights, "When will you be satisfied?"

We can never be satisfied as long as the Negro is the victim of the unspeakable horrors of police brutality.

We can never be satisfied as long as our bodies, heavy with the fatigue of travel, cannot gain lodging in the motels of the highways and the hotels of the cities.

We cannot be satisfied as long as the Negro's basic mobility is from a smaller ghetto to a larger one.

We can never be satisfied as long as a Negro in Mississippi cannot vote and a Negro in New York believes he has nothing for which to vote.

No, no, we are not satisfied, and we will not be satisfied until justice rolls down like waters and righteousness like a mighty stream. . . .

I say to you today, my friends, that in spite of the difficulties and frustrations of the moment I still have a dream. It is a dream deeply rooted in the American dream.

I have a dream that one day this nation will rise up and live out the true meaning of its creed: "We hold these truths to be self-evident; that all men are created equal. "

I have a dream that one day on the red hills of Georgia the sons of former slaves and the sons of former slaveowners will be able to sit down together at the table of brotherhood.

I have a dream that one day even the state of Mississippi, a desert state sweltering with the heat of injustice and oppression, will be transformed into an oasis of freedom and justice.

I have a dream that my four little children will one day live in a nation where they will not be judged by the color of their skin but by the content of their character. . . .

When we let freedom ring, when we let it ring from every village and every hamlet, from every state and every city, we will be able to speed up that day when all of God's children, black men and white men, Jews and Gentiles, Protestants and Catholics, will be able to join hands and sing in the words of the old Negro spiritual, "Free at last! Free at last! Thank God Almighty, we are free at last!"

President Johnson's Message to Congress

In early August 1964, President Lyndon Johnson announced that on August 5 North Vietnamese torpedo boats had attacked American destroyers in the international waters of the Gulf of Tonkin off the coast of Vietnam. Johnson appealed to the American people and to Congress for their support of his Vietnam policies.

To the Congress of the United States:

Last night I announced to the American people that the North Vietnamese regime had conducted further deliberate attacks against U.S. naval vessels operating in international waters. . . .

These latest actions of the North Vietnamese regime have given a new and grave turn to the already serious situation in southeast Asia.

Our commitments in that area are well known to the Congress. . . .

. . . The North Vietnamese regime has constantly sought to take over South Vietnam and Laos. This Communist regime has violated the Geneva accords for Vietnam. It has systematically conducted a campaign of subversion, which includes the direction, training, and supply of personnel and arms for the conduct of guerrilla warfare in South Vietnamese territory. . . .

As President of the United States I have concluded that I should now ask the Congress on its part, to join in affirming the national determination that all such attacks will be met, and that the United States will continue in its basic policy of assisting the free nations of the area to defend their freedom. . . .

The Gulf of Tonkin Resolution

On August 7, 1964, Congress passed the Gulf of Tonkin Resolution, which stood as the legal basis for the Vietnam War. Later information raised doubts about the administration's description of actions in the Gulf of Tonkin. In December 1970, after war opposition had started to grow, Congress repealed the Gulf of Tonkin Resolution.

Resolved by the Senate and House of Representatives of the United States of America in Congress assembled,

That the Congress approves and supports the determination of the President, as Commander in Chief, to take all necessary measures to repel any armed attack against the forces of the United States and to prevent further aggression.

Section 2. The United States regards as vital to its national interest and to world peace the maintenance of international peace and security in southeast Asia. Consonant with the Constitution of the United States and the Charter of the United Nations and in

accordance with its obligations under the Southeast Asia Collective Defense Treaty, the United States is, therefore, prepared, as the President determines, to take all necessary steps, including the use of armed force, to assist any member or protocol state of the Southeast Asia Collective Defense Treaty requesting assistance in defense of its freedom.

Section 3. This resolution shall expire when the President shall determine that the peace and security of the area is reasonably assured by international conditions created by action of the United States or otherwise, except that it may be terminated earlier by concurrent resolution of the Congress.

Soldiers in Vietnam

Supreme Court Case Summaries

The following case summaries explain the significance of major Supreme Court cases mentioned in the text.

Abington School District v. Schempp (1963) struck down a Pennsylvania statute requiring public schools in the state to begin each school day with Bible readings and a recitation of the Lord's Prayer. The Court held that the Constitution's establishment clause leaves religious beliefs and religious practices to each individual's choice and expressly commands that government not intrude into this decision-making process.

Abrams v. United States (1919) upheld a conviction under the Sedition Act and Espionage Act of 1917. The Court ruled that freedom of speech could be limited if there was a threat to the country.

Baker v. Carr (1962) established that federal courts can hear suits seeking to force state authorities to redraw electoral districts. In this case, the plaintiff wanted the population of each district to be roughly equal to the population in all other districts. The plaintiff claimed that the votes of voters in the least populous districts counted as much as the votes of voters in the most populous districts.

Brown v. Board of Education (1954) overruled *Plessy v. Ferguson* (1896) and abandoned the separate-but-equal doctrine in the context of public schools. In deciding this case, the Supreme Court rejected the idea that equivalent but separate schools for African Americans and white students would be constitutional. The Court stated that the Fourteenth Amendment's command that all persons be accorded the equal protection of the law (U.S. Const. amend. XIV, sec. 1) is not satisfied by ensuring that African American and white schools "have been equalized, or are being equalized, with respect to buildings, curricula, qualifications, and salaries, and other tangible factors."

The Court then held that racial segregation in public schools violates the equal protection clause because it is inherently unequal. In other words, the separation of schools by race marks the separate race as inferior. The ruling in this case has been extended beyond public education to virtually all public accommodations and activities.

Bush v. Gore (2000) found that a manual recount of disputed presidential ballots in Florida lacked a uniform standard of judging a voter's intent, thus violating the equal protection clause of the Constitution. The Court also ruled that there was not enough time to conduct a new manual recount that would meet constitutional standards. The case arose when Republican candidate George W. Bush asked the Court to stop a hand recount. This decision ensured that Bush would receive Florida's electoral votes and win the election.

Chisholm v. Georgia (1793) stripped the immunity of the states to lawsuits in federal court. The Supreme Court held that a citizen of one state could sue another state in federal court without that state consenting to the suit. The Court's decision created a furor and led to the adoption of the Eleventh Amendment, which protects states from federal court suits by citizens of other states.

Dred Scott v. Sandford (1857) was decided before the Fourteenth Amendment. The Fourteenth Amendment provides that anyone born or naturalized in the United States is a citizen of the nation and of his or her state. In this case, the Supreme Court held that a slave was property, not a citizen, and thus had no rights under the Constitution. The decision was a prime factor leading to the Civil War.

Engel v. Vitale (1962) held that the establishment clause (U.S. Const. amend. I, cl. 1) was violated by a public school district's practice of starting each school day with a prayer which began, "Almighty God, we acknowledge our dependence upon Thee." The Supreme Court ruled that religion is a personal matter and that government should not align itself with a particular religion in order to prevent religious persecution.

Escobedo v. Illinois (1964) held that Danny Escobedo's right to counsel, as provided by the Sixth Amendment, had been violated. Throughout police questioning, Escobedo asked repeatedly, but unsuccessfully, to see his attorney. The Supreme Court reversed Escobedo's murder conviction, holding that an attorney could have assisted Escobedo in invoking his Fifth Amendment right against self-incrimination. This case served as a forerunner to *Miranda v. Arizona*.

Gibbons v. Ogden (1824) made it clear that the authority of Congress to regulate interstate commerce (U.S. Const. art. I, sec. 8, cl. 3) includes the authority to regulate intrastate commercial activity that relates to interstate commerce. Before this case, it was thought that the Constitution would allow a state to close its borders to interstate commercial activity. This ruling says that a state can only regulate internal commercial activity, but Congress can regulate commercial activity that has both intrastate and interstate dimensions.

Gideon v. Wainwright (1963) ruled that poor defendants in criminal cases have the right to a state-paid attorney under the Sixth Amendment. The ruling in this case has been refined to apply only when the defendant, if convicted, can be sentenced to more than six months in jail.

Griswold v. Connecticut (1965) overturned the conviction of two Planned Parenthood employees charged with violating an 1879 state law banning the use of contraceptives. In deciding this case, the Court went beyond the actual words of the Constitution to protect a right—the right to privacy—which is not listed in the Constitution. The case also served as a forerunner to the *Roe v. Wade* decision that legalized abortion on the same basis.

Heart of Atlanta Motel, Inc. v. United States (1964) upheld the Civil Rights Act of 1964, which prohibits racial discrimination by those who provide goods, services, and facilities to the public. The Georgia motel in the case drew its business from other states but refused to rent rooms to African Americans. The Supreme Court explained that Congress had the authority to prohibit such discrimination under both the equal protection clause (U.S. Const. amend. XIV, sec. 1) and the commerce clause (art. I, sec. 8, cl. 3). With respect to the commerce clause, the Court explained that Congress had ample evidence to conclude that racial discrimination by hotels and motels impedes interstate commerce.

Korematsu v. United States (1944) allowed the federal government's authority to exclude Japanese Americans, many of whom were citizens, from designated military areas that included almost the entire West Coast. The government defended the orders as a necessary response to Japan's attack on Pearl Harbor. Yet, in upholding the orders, the Court established that government actions that discriminate on the basis of race would be subject to strict scrutiny.

Loving v. Virginia (1967) ruled that state laws that outlaw interracial marriages are unconstitutional under the Fourteenth Amendment. The Court explained that such laws violated the equal protection clause and deprived "citizens of liberty without due process of law." The Court went on to say, "Marriage is one of the basic civil rights of man, fundamental to our very existence and survival."

Mapp v. Ohio (1961) established that evidence seized in violation of the Fourth Amendment could not be used by the prosecution as evidence of a defendant's guilt at the federal, state, or local level.

Marbury v. Madison (1803) established one of the most important principles of American constitutional law. The Supreme Court held that the Court itself has the final say on what the Constitution means. It is also the Supreme Court that has the final say whether or not an act of government—legislative or executive at the federal, state, or local level—violates the Constitution.

Martin v. Hunter's Lessee (1816) affirmed that the Supreme Court has the authority to review state court decisions and is the nation's final court of appeal. The Supreme Court ruled that section 25 of the Judiciary Act of 1789 was constitutional. This section granted the Supreme Court appellate jurisdiction over state courts in certain situations, such as a state court denying the authority of federal law.

McCulloch v. Maryland (1819) established the basis for the expansive authority of Congress. The Supreme Court held that the necessary and proper clause (U.S. Const. art. I, sec. 8, cl. 18) allows Congress to do more than the Constitution specifically authorizes it to do. This case holds that Congress can enact almost any law that will help it achieve the ends established by Article I, Section 8 of the Constitution. For example, Congress has the power to regulate interstate commerce; the necessary and proper clause permits Congress to do so in ways not specified in the Constitution.

Miranda v. _Arizona_ (1966) held that a person in police custody may not be held unless reminded of his or her rights. These rights include: 1) the right to remain silent, 2) the right to an attorney (at government expense if the person is unable to pay), and 3) that anything the person says after acknowledging that he or she understands these rights can be used as evidence of guilt at a trial.

The Supreme Court explained that a person alone in police custody may not understand, even if told, that he or she can remain silent and thus might be misled into answering questions. The presence of an attorney is essential.

Morgan v. _Virginia_ (1946) challenged racial segregation in the South. Irene Morgan was convicted for refusing to give up her seat on an interstate bus bound from Virginia to Maryland. The Court ruled that the Virginia law posed an undue burden on interstate commerce and struck down the statute. However, segregation on southern buses continued on an informal basis.

National Labor Relations Board v. _Jones and Laughlin Steel Corp._ (1937) upheld President Franklin Roosevelt's New Deal legislation, the National Labor Relations Act, which allowed workers to organize unions in businesses operating or affecting interstate commerce. Employers were prohibited from discriminating against their employees because of union membership. Prior to this case, the Supreme Court had ruled much New Deal legislation unconstitutional. This ruling came less than a week after Roosevelt's proposed court-packing plan. The president intended on "packing" the Supreme Court with additional justices in order to obtain a pro-New Deal majority on the Court.

New York Times Co. v. _Sullivan_ (1964) extended the protections afforded to the press by the free press clause (U.S. Const. amend. I). In this case, the Supreme Court held that a public official or public figure suing a publisher for libel (i.e., defamation) must prove that the publisher published a story that he or she knew was false or published the story in "reckless disregard of its truth or falsity," which means that the publisher did not take professionally adequate steps to determine the story's truth or falsity.

Norris v. _Alabama_ (1935) overturned the conviction of Clarence Norris, an African American sentenced to death for a crime in Alabama. The Supreme Court held that the grand jury and trial jury had systematically eliminated African American jurors. Thus, the Court reversed the conviction because it violated the equal protection clause of the Fourteenth Amendment.

Northern Securities Company v. _United States_ (1904) dealt with the application of congressional antitrust legislation. The party involved held

three-fourths of the stock in two parallel railroad lines. By a narrow 5–4 decision, the Court upheld the application of the Sherman Antitrust Act. The Court ruled that the holding company clearly intended to eliminate competition between the two railroads, violating the constitutional right of Congress to regulate interstate commerce.

Plessy v. _Ferguson_ (1896) upheld the separate-but-equal doctrine used by Southern states to perpetuate segregation after the Civil War officially ended law-mandated segregation. The decision upheld a Louisiana law requiring passenger trains to have "equal but separated accommodations for the white and colored races." The Court held that the Fourteenth Amendment's equal protection clause required only equal public facilities for the two races, not equal access. This case was overruled by _Brown_ v. _Board of Education_ (1954).

Regents of the University of California v. _Bakke_ (1978) was the first Supreme Court decision to suggest that an affirmative action program could be justified on the basis of diversity. The Court explained that racial quotas were not permissible under the equal protection clause of the Fourteenth Amendment. However, the justices ruled that the diversity rationale was a legitimate interest that would allow a state medical school to consider an applicant's race in evaluating his or her application for admission. (Recent Supreme Court cases suggest that the diversity rationale is no longer enough to defend an affirmative action program.)

Reynolds v. _Sims_ (1964) extended the one-person, one-vote doctrine announced in _Wesberry_ v. _Sanders_ to state legislative elections. The Court held that the inequality of representation in the Alabama legislature violated the equal protection clause of the Fourteenth Amendment.

Roe v. _Wade_ (1973) held that women have the right under various provisions of the Constitution—most notably, the due process clause of the Fourteenth Amendment—to decide whether or not to terminate a pregnancy. The Court's ruling in this case was the most significant in a long line of decisions over a period of 50 years that recognized a constitutional right of privacy, even though the word _privacy_ is not found in the Constitution.

Schechter Poultry Corporation v. _United States_ (1935) overturned the conviction of the employers, who were charged with violating the wage and hour limitations of a law adopted under the authority of the

Supreme Court Cases

National Industrial Recovery Act. The Court held that because the defendants did not sell poultry in interstate commerce, they were not subject to federal regulations on wages and hours.

Schenck v. United States (1919) upheld convictions under the Federal Espionage Act. The defendants were charged under the act with distributing leaflets aimed at inciting draft resistance during World War I; their defense was that antidraft speech was protected under the First Amendment.

The Supreme Court unanimously rejected the defense, explaining that whether or not speech is protected depends on the context in which it occurs. Because the defendants' antidraft rhetoric created a "clear and present danger" to the success of the war effort, it was not protected.

Stone v. Powell (1976) reversed a Court of Appeals decision that evidence was seized illegally and should therefore be excluded. The Court ruled that the defendant was provided a fair and legal opportunity to claim a Fourth Amendment violation before a trial jury. The trial jury found that the search was constitutional and the evidence should not be excluded. The Court stated, "Where the state has provided an opportunity for full and fair litigation of a Fourth Amendment claim, a state prisoner may not be granted federal habeas corpus relief."

Swann v. Charlotte-Mecklenburg Board of Education (1971) established a new plan to ensure that public schools were not segregated. Many school systems were slow to desegregate after *Brown v. Board of Education* and used various tactics to appear to be resolving the problem. This case ordered that busing students, reorganizing school boundaries, and racial ratios all be used as methods to obtain desegregated public school systems.

Sweatt v. Painter (1950) held that it was unconstitutional for African Americans to be denied admission to the University of Texas Law School based on race. An inferior law school established for African Americans did not give the state justification to deny admission to the main school. This act was a violation of the Fourteenth Amendment.

Wabash v. Illinois (1886) held that states have no authority to regulate railroad rates for interstate commerce. The Supreme Court held that the commerce clause (U.S. Const. art. I, sec. 8, cl. 3) allowed states to enforce "indirect" but not "direct" burdens on interstate commerce. State railroad rates were ruled "direct" burdens and therefore could not be enforced by states. The decision created a precedent by establishing rate regulation of interstate commerce as an exclusive federal power.

Wickard v. Filburn (1942) indicated how far the Supreme Court had come in complying with President Franklin Roosevelt's economic philosophies. The Court upheld specific parts of the Second Agricultural Adjustment Act. In its ruling, the Supreme Court held that marketing quotas could be applied to wheat that never left the farm. Using the commerce clause (U.S. Const. art. I, sec. 8, cl. 3) as the basis for its decision, the Court ruled that wheat that never left the farm still had an effect on interstate commerce. Farmers growing their own grain depressed the overall demand and market price of wheat. The decision further extended the power of the commerce clause.

Worcester v. Georgia (1832) overturned the conviction of Samuel A. Worcester, a missionary among the Cherokee. Worcester was imprisoned under a Georgia law forbidding whites to reside in Cherokee country without taking an oath of allegiance to the state and obtaining a permit. The Supreme Court voided the state law, ruling that the Cherokee were an independent nation based on a federal treaty and free from the jurisdiction of the state. Georgia ignored the decision, and President Jackson refused to enforce it, instead supporting the removal of the Cherokee to the Indian Territory.

Flag Etiquette

> **For Americans, the flag has always had a special meaning. It is a symbol of our nation's freedom and democracy.**

Rules and Customs

Over the years, Americans have developed rules and customs concerning the use and display of the flag. One of the most important things every American should remember is to treat the flag with respect.

- The flag should be raised and lowered by hand and displayed only from sunrise to sunset. On special occasions, the flag may be displayed at night, but it should be illuminated.

- The flag may be displayed on all days, weather permitting, particularly on national and state holidays and on historic and special occasions.

- No flag may be flown above the American flag or to the right of it at the same height.

- The flag should never touch the ground or floor beneath it.

- The flag may be flown at half-staff by order of the president, usually to mourn the death of a public official.

- The flag may be flown upside down only to signal distress.

- When the flag becomes old and tattered, it should be destroyed by burning. According to an approved custom, the Union (stars on blue field) is first cut from the flag; then the two pieces, which no longer form a flag, are burned.

Continental Colors
1775–1777

First Stars and Stripes
1777–1795

Betsy Ross Flag
c. 1790

15-Star Flag
1795–1818

20-Star Flag
1818

Great Star Flag
1818

35-Star Flag
1863–1865

38-Star Flag
1877–1890

48-Star Flag
1912–1959

50-Star Flag
1960

Glossary

A
---

abolition the immediate ending of slavery (p. 199)

affirmative action an active effort to improve employment or educational opportunities for minorities (p. 813)

alien a person living in a country who is not a citizen of that country (p. 157)

allotment a plot of land assigned to an individual or family for cultivation (p. 302)

amendment a change to the Constitution (p. 112)

Americanization causing someone to acquire American traits and characteristics (p. 357)

amnesty the act of granting a pardon to a large group of people (p. 267)

amphtrac an amphibious tractor used to move troops from ships to shore (p. 636)

anarchist person who believes that there should be no government (p. 483)

annexation incorporating a territory within the domain of a country (p. 207)

annuity money paid by contract on regular intervals (p. 298)

appeasement accepting demands in order to avoid conflict (p. 590)

appropriate to allocate funds for spending (p. 124)

arbitration settling a dispute by agreeing to accept the decision of an impartial outsider (pp. 330, 429)

armistice a temporary agreement to end fighting (p. 468)

assembly line a production system with machines and workers arranged so that each person performs an assigned task again and again as the item passes before him or her (p. 515)

assimilate to absorb a group into the culture of a larger population (p. 302)

astrolabe device used to determine direction, latitude, and local time (p. 21)

attrition the act of wearing down by constant harassment or attack (p. 247)

B
---

baby boom a marked rise in birthrate, such as occurred in the United States following World War II (p. 694)

bailiff minor officer of the courts (p. 536)

benevolent society an association focusing on spreading the word of God and combating social problems (p. 195)

bilingualism the practice of teaching immigrant students in their own language (p. 815)

bill a proposed law (p. 125)

binding arbitration process whereby a neutral party hears arguments from two opposing sides and makes a decision that both must accept (p. 567)

black codes laws passed in the South just after the Civil War aimed at controlling freedmen and enabling plantation owners to exploit African American workers (p. 269)

black power the mobilization of the political and economic power of African Americans, especially to compel respect for their rights and to improve their condition (p. 764)

blitzkrieg name given to sudden violent offensive attacks the Germans used during World War II; "lightning war" (p. 591)

blockade runner ship that runs through a blockade, usually to smuggle goods through a protected area (p. 250)

blue-collar jobs in the manual labor field, particularly those requiring protective clothing (p. 693)

blues style of music evolving from African American spirituals and noted for its melancholy sound (p. 500)

Bohemian a person (as an artist or writer) leading an unconventional lifestyle (p. 493)

bonanza farm a large, highly-profitable wheat farm (p. 294)

bond a note issued by the government which promises to pay off a loan with interest (p. 153)

bounty money given as a reward, as to encourage enlistment in the army (p. 250)

brinkmanship the willingness to go to the brink of war to force an opponent to back down (p. 677)

broker state role of the government to work out conflicts among competing interest groups (p. 577)

budget deficit the amount by which expenses exceed income (p. 867)

bull market a long period of rising stock prices (p. 531)

burgesses representatives to the general assembly of the Virginia colony (p. 46)

busing a policy of transporting children to schools outside their neighborhoods to achieve greater racial balance (p. 814)

C
---

cabinet a group of advisers to the president (pp. 126, 153)

capital gains tax a federal tax paid by businesses and investors when they sell stocks or real estate (p. 886)

capitalist person who invests wealth, particularly money, in a business (p. 63)

caravel sailing ship capable of long-distance exploration (p. 21)

carpetbagger name given to many Northerners who moved to the South after the Civil War and supported the Republicans (p. 273)

cash crop a crop grown primarily for profit (p. 59)

caucus a meeting in which members of a political party choose their party's candidate for president or decide policy (p. 190)

censure to express a formal disapproval of an action (p. 673)

chad a small piece of cardboard produced by punching a data card (p. 908)

charter a constitution (p. 647)

checks and balances the system in which each branch of government has the ability to limit the power of the other branches to prevent any from becoming too powerful (p. 112)

circumnavigate to sail around (p. 27)

civilization a highly organized society marked by knowledge of trade, government, the arts, science, and, often, written language (p. 13)

closed shop an agreement in which a company agrees to hire only union members (pp. 330, 687)

cloture a motion which ends debate and calls for an immediate vote, possible in the U.S. Senate by a vote of 60 senators (p. 758)

Cold War the ideological and often confrontational conflict between the United States and the Soviet Union between 1946 and 1990 (p. 654)

Columbian Exchange series of complex societal and environmental interactions between Europe and the Americas begun with Columbus's first voyage (p. 28)

commission plan a plan in which a city's government is divided into different departments with different functions, each placed under the control of a commissioner (p. 420)

committee of correspondence committee organized in each colony to communicate with and unify the colonies (p. 83)

commune a group living arrangement in which members share everything and work together (p. 803)

concentration camp a camp where persons are detained or confined (p. 599)

concurrent powers those powers which the state and federal governments share (p. 123)

Confederacy nation declared to have been formed by the southern states that seceded from the Union in 1860–1861 (p. 235)

conference committee a special joint committee organized to help the House and Senate work on a compromise bill acceptable to both houses (p. 125)

conquistador Spanish for conqueror, the men who led the expeditions to conquer the Americas (p. 32)

conscription requiring people to enter military service (pp. 246, 457)

consensus general agreement (p. 734)

conservative a person who believes government power, particularly in the economy, should be limited in order to maximize individual freedom (p. 861)

constituent a resident of an electoral district (p. 125)

containment the policy or process of preventing the expansion of a hostile power (p. 660)

contra Spanish for counter-revolutionary, an anti-Sandinista guerrilla force in Nicaragua (p. 870)

contraband goods whose importation, exportation, or possession is illegal (pp. 164, 453)

convoy a group that travels with something, such as a ship, to protect it (p. 466)

convoy system a system in which merchant ships travel with naval vessels for protection (p. 622)

cooperative store where farmers bought products from each other; an enterprise owned and operated by those who use its services (p. 374)

cooperative individualism President Hoover's policy of encouraging manufacturers and distributors to form their own organizations and volunteer information to the federal government in an effort to stimulate the economy (p. 522)

corporation an organization that is authorized by law to carry on an activity but treated as though it were a single person (p. 320)

"corrupt bargain" an illegitimate agreement between politicians (p. 189)

cost of living the cost of purchasing goods and services essential for survival (p. 471)

cost-plus a government contract to pay a manufacturer the cost to produce an item plus a guaranteed percentage (p. 613)

cotton gin a machine that removed seeds from cotton fiber (p. 182)

counterculture a culture with values and beliefs different than the mainstream (p. 802)

covert not openly shown or engaged in (p. 679)

creationism the belief that God created the world and everything in it, usually in the way described in Genesis (p. 486)

credibility gap lack of trust or believability (p. 785)

Glossary

customs duty a tax on imports and exports (p. 77)

D

de facto segregation segregation by custom and tradition (p. 747)

debtor a person who owes a debt, usually a financial debt that cannot be paid (p. 56)

deficit spending government practice of spending borrowed money rather than raising taxes, usually an attempt to boost the economy (p. 565)

deflation a decline in the volume of available money or credit that results in lower prices, and, therefore, increases the buying power of money (pp. 327, 373)

deport to expel individuals from the country (p. 474)

détente a policy which attempts to relax or ease tensions between nations (p. 836)

developing nation a nation whose economy is primarily agricultural (p. 679)

direct primary a vote held by all members of a political party to decide their candidate for public office (p. 421)

disco popular dance music characterized by hypnotic rhythm, repetitive lyrics, and electronically produced sounds (p. 853)

disfranchise to deprive of the right to vote (p. 616)

DNA the genetic material in cells that determines all forms of life (p. 895)

dollar diplomacy a policy of joining the business interests of a country with its diplomatic interests abroad (p. 413)

domino theory the belief that if one nation in Asia fell to the Communists, neighboring countries would follow (p. 774)

dove a person in favor of the United States withdrawing from the Vietnam War (p. 787)

downsizing reducing a company in size by laying off workers and managers to become more efficient (p. 885)

dry farming a way of farming dry land in which seeds are planted deep in the ground where there is some moisture (p. 294)

due process a judicial requirement that laws may not treat individuals unfairly, arbitrarily, or unreasonably, and that courts must follow proper procedures and rules when trying cases (pp. 128, 722)

Dust Bowl name given to the area of the southern Great Plains severely damaged by droughts and dust storms during the 1930s (p. 537)

dynamic conservatism policy of balancing economic conservatism with some activism (p. 689)

E

economies of scale the reduction in the cost of a good brought about especially by increased production at a given facility (p. 320)

emancipation the act or process of freeing enslaved persons (p. 199)

embargo a government ban on trade with other countries (pp. 164, 844)

empresario a person who arranged for the settlement of Texas in the 1800s (p. 204)

enclosure movement an economic change in England in the 1500s in which landowners converted agricultural estates into sheep farms and evicted the tenant farmers (p. 44)

encomienda system of rewarding conquistadors tracts of land, including the right to tax and exact labor from Native Americans (p. 33)

Enlightenment movement during the 1700s that promoted science, knowledge, and reason (p. 68)

entrepreneur one who organizes, manages, and assumes the risks of a business or enterprise (pp. 63, 310)

enumerated powers powers listed in the Constitution as belonging to the federal government (pp. 123, 154)

espionage spying, especially to gain government secrets (p. 460)

ethnic cleansing the expulsion, imprisonment, or killing of ethnic minorities by a dominant majority group (p. 900)

eugenics a pseudo-science that deals with the improvement of hereditary qualities of a race or breed (p. 483)

euro the basic currency shared by the countries of the European Union since 1999 (p. 903)

evolution the scientific theory that humans and other forms of life have evolved over time (p. 486)

excise tax a tax paid by the manufacturer of a product and passed on to those who buy the product (p. 155)

executive privilege principle stating that communications of the executive branch should remain confidential to protect national security (p. 841)

extermination camp a camp where prisoners were sent to be executed (p. 599)

F

fallout radioactive particles dispersed by a nuclear explosion (p. 674)

fallout shelter a shelter built with the intent to house and protect people from nuclear fallout (p. 674)

Glossary

fascism a political system headed by a dictator that calls for extreme nationalism and racism and no tolerance of opposition (p. 585)

"favorite son" men who enjoyed the support of leaders from their own state and region (p. 188)

featherbedding practice of limiting work output in order to create more jobs (p. 687)

federalism political system in which power is divided between the national and state governments (pp. 111, 122)

feminism the belief that men and women should be equal politically, economically, and socially (p. 807)

feudalism political system in which powerful leaders gave land to nobles in exchange for pledges of loyalty and service (p. 19)

filibuster an attempt to kill a bill by having a group of senators take turns speaking continuously so that a vote cannot take place (p. 758)

fireside chats radio broadcasts made by FDR to the American people to explain his initiatives (p. 558)

fixed costs costs a company must pay regardless of whether or not it is operating (p. 320)

flapper a young woman of the 1920s who showed freedom from convention, especially in dress (p. 485)

flexible response the buildup of conventional troops and weapons to allow a nation to fight a limited war without using nuclear weapons (p. 725)

forage to search or raid for food (p. 258)

foreclose to take possession of a property from a mortgagor because of defaults on payments (p. 545)

fossil fuel a fuel formed in the earth from decayed plant or animal remains (p. 822)

franchise the right or license to market a company's goods or services in an area, such as a store of a chain operation (p. 693)

freedmen persons freed from slavery (p. 268)

Freedom Riders name given to a group of people who traveled to the South in 1961 to protest the South's refusal to integrate bus terminals (p. 755)

fundamentalist a Protestant evangelical Christian who believes in being saved from sins by being born again and making a personal commitment to follow Jesus Christ (p. 486)

G

general strike a strike involving all the workers in a particular geographic location (p. 472)

generation gap a cultural separation between parents and their children (p. 702)

glacier a huge ice sheet (p. 13)

glasnost a Soviet policy permitting open discussion of political and social issues and freer dissemination of news and information (p. 882)

global warming an increase in average world temperatures over time (p. 905)

gold standard a monetary standard in which one ounce of gold equaled a set number of dollars (p. 555)

goldbug a person who believes that American currency should be based on a gold standard (p. 378)

graduated income tax tax based on the net income of an individual or business and which taxes different income levels at different rates (p. 376)

graft the acquisition of money in dishonest ways, as in bribing a politician (pp. 273, 345)

grandfather clause a clause that allowed individuals who did not pass the literacy test to vote if their fathers or grandfathers had voted before Reconstruction began; an exception to a law based on preexisting circumstances (p. 382)

grassroots movement a group of people organizing at the local or community level, away from political or cultural centers (p. 886)

Great Awakening movement during the 1700s that stressed dependence on God (p. 69)

greenback a piece of U.S. paper money first issued by the North during the Civil War (pp. 245, 373)

gross national product the total value of goods and services produced by a country during a year (p. 308)

guerrilla armed band that carries out surprise attacks and sabotage rather than open warfare (pp. 449, 774)

guerrilla warfare a hit-and-run technique used in fighting a war; fighting by small bands of warriors using tactics such as sudden ambushes (p. 95)

guru a person with knowledge or expertise, especially a religious teacher and spiritual guide in Hinduism (p. 851)

H

habeas corpus a legal order for an inquiry to determine whether a person has been lawfully imprisoned (p. 246)

hacienda a huge ranch (p. 33)

hardtack a hard biscuit made of wheat flour (p. 254)

hawk someone who believed the United States should continue its military efforts in Vietnam (p. 787)

headright system in which settlers were granted land in exchange for settling in Virginia (p. 46)

hedgerow row of shrubs or trees surrounding a field, often on a dirt wall (p. 641)

hemispheric defense zone national policy during World War II that declared the Western Hemisphere to be neutral and that the United States would patrol this region against German submarines (p. 603)

heretic a dissenter from established church beliefs (p. 50)

hobo a homeless and usually penniless wanderer (p. 536)

holding company a company whose primary business is owning a controlling share of stock in other companies (p. 322)

Holocaust name given to the mass slaughter of Jews and other groups by the Nazis during World War II (p. 595)

homestead method of acquiring a piece of U.S. public land by living on and cultivating it (p. 293)

Hooverville nickname given to shantytowns in the United States during the Depression (p. 536)

horizontal integration the combining of competing firms into one corporation (p. 321)

Ice Age a period of extremely cold temperatures when part of the planet's surface was covered with massive ice sheets (p. 13)

immunity freedom from prosecution (p. 512)

impeach to formally charge a public official with misconduct in office (pp. 112, 124, 271, 841)

imperialism the actions used by one nation to exercise political or economic control over a smaller or weaker nation (p. 393)

implied powers powers not specifically listed in the Constitution but claimed by the federal government (p. 154)

impound to take possession of (p. 835)

impressment a kind of legalized kidnapping in which people are forced into military service (p. 164)

income tax a tax based on the net income of a person or business (p. 440)

indentured servant an individual who contracts to work for a colonist for a specified number of years in exchange for transportation to the colonies, food, clothing, and shelter (p. 59)

industrial union an organization of common laborers and craft workers in a particular industry (p. 327)

inflation the loss of value of money (pp. 106, 373, 844)

initiative the right of citizens to place a measure or issue before the voters or the legislature for approval (p. 421)

installment buying an item on credit with a monthly plan to pay off the value of the good (p. 534)

insubordination disobedience (p. 437)

insurrection an act of rebellion against the established government (p. 231)

interchangeable parts uniform pieces that can be made in large quantities to replace other identical pieces (p. 180)

internationalism a national policy of actively trading with foreign countries to foster peace and prosperity (p. 588)

Internet an electronic communications network that connects computer networks and organizational computer facilities around the world (p. 894)

interposition theory that a state should be able to intervene between the federal government and the people to stop an illegal action (p. 158)

iron curtain the political and military barrier that isolated Soviet-controlled countries of Eastern Europe after World War II (p. 658)

isolationism a national policy of avoiding involvement in world affairs (pp. 523, 587)

jazz American style of music that developed from ragtime and blues and which uses syncopated rhythms and melodies (p. 499)

Jim Crow laws statutes or laws created to enforce segregation (p. 382)

jingoism extreme nationalism marked by aggressive foreign policy (p. 401)

joint committee a committee organized with members from both the House and Senate to work on specific issues (p. 125)

joint-stock company form of business organization in which many investors pool funds to raise large amounts of money for large projects (p. 44)

judicial review power of the Supreme Court to determine whether laws of Congress are constitutional and to strike down those that are not (pp. 127, 162)

juvenile delinquency antisocial or criminal behavior of young people (p. 709)

kachina a good spirit that the Pueblo people believed brought messages from the gods to their town each year (p. 15)

kamikaze during World War II, a Japanese suicide pilot whose mission was to crash into his target (p. 637)

Glossary

L

labor union an organization of workers formed for the purpose of advancing its members' interests (p. 181)

laissez-faire policy that government should interfere as little as possible in the nation's economy (p. 310)

land grant a grant of land by the federal government especially for roads, railroads, or agricultural colleges (p. 317)

letters of marque licenses issued by Congress to private ship owners authorizing them to attack British merchant ships (p. 97)

liberal a person who generally believes the government should take an active role in the economy and in social programs but that the government should not dictate social behavior (p. 861)

Liberty ship basic cargo ship used by the United States during World War II (p. 614)

limited war a war fought with limited commitment of resources to achieve a limited objective, such as containing communism (p. 665)

line of demarcation north-south line of longitude through the Atlantic Ocean dividing lands in the Americas claimed by Spain and Portugal (p. 26)

linkage policy of improving relations with the Soviet Union and China in hopes of persuading them to cut back their aid to North Vietnam (p. 790)

lockout a company tool to fight union demands by refusing to allow employees to enter its facilities to work (p. 328)

long drive driving cattle long distances to a railroad depot for fast transport and great profit (p. 289)

longhouse large, rectangular building with barrel-shaped roofs covered in bark, used by some Native Americans (p. 16)

Loyalist American colonists who supported Britain and opposed the War for Independence (p. 85)

lynching an execution performed without lawful approval (p. 383)

M

mandate authorization to act given to a representative (p. 262)

Manifest Destiny idea popular in the United States during the 1800s that the country must expand its boundaries to the Pacific Ocean (p. 202)

manorialism economic system in which peasants provide services to a feudal lord in exchange for protection (p. 19)

manumission the voluntary freeing of enslaved persons (p. 102)

margin buying a stock by paying only a fraction of the stock price and borrowing the rest (p. 531)

margin call demand by a broker that investors pay back loans made for stocks purchased on margin (p. 531)

martial law the law administered by military forces that is invoked by a government in an emergency (p. 236)

Marxism theory of socialism in which a class struggle would exist until the workers were finally victorious, creating a classless society (p. 328)

mass media a medium of communication (as in television and radio) intended to reach a wide audience (p. 495)

mass production the production of large quantities of goods using machinery and often an assembly line (p. 515)

massive retaliation a policy of threatening a massive response, including the use of nuclear weapons, against a Communist state trying to seize a peaceful state by force (p. 676)

maverick a stray calf with no identifying symbol (p. 290)

mercantilism the theory that a state's power depends on its wealth (p. 65)

microprocessor a computer processor containing both memory and computing functions on a single chip (p. 893)

military-industrial complex an informal relationship that some people believe exists between the military and the defense industry to promote greater military spending and influence government policy (p. 680)

minutemen companies of civilian soldiers who boasted they were ready to fight on a minute's notice (p. 85)

missile gap belief that the Soviet Union had more nuclear weapons than the United States (p. 719)

monopoly total control of a type of industry by one person or one company (p. 321)

moratorium a suspension of activity (p. 524)

most-favored nation a policy between countries ensuring fair trading practices (p. 156)

muckraker a journalist who uncovers abuses and corruption in a society (p. 419)

mudslinging attempt to ruin an opponent's reputation with insults (p. 189)

multinational corporation large corporations with overseas investments (p. 693)

N

napalm a jellied gasoline used for bombs (pp. 644, 780)

nationalism loyalty and devotion to a nation (p. 450)

nativism a preference for native-born people and a desire to limit immigration (pp. 181, 340)

naturalism a philosophy and approach to art and literature based on the belief that nature can be understood through scientific observation and that society functions best with some governmental regulation (p. 355)

nomad a person who moves from place to place, usually in search of food or grazing land (pp. 13, 297)

nonimportation agreement a pledge by merchants not to buy imported goods from a particular source (p. 78)

normalcy the state or fact of being normal (p. 511)

Northwest Passage the mythical northern water route through North America to the Pacific Ocean (p. 34)

nuclear proliferation the spread of nuclear weapons to new nations (p. 905)

nullification theory that states have the right to declare a federal law invalid (p. 158)

Open Door policy a policy that allowed each foreign nation in China to trade freely in the other nations' spheres of influence (p. 410)

open range vast areas of grassland owned by the federal government (p. 288)

open shop a workplace where workers are not required to join a union (p. 519)

operating costs costs that occur while running a company (p. 320)

override ability of Congress to reverse a presidential veto by a two-thirds majority vote (p. 124)

pacifism opposition to war or violence as a means of settling disputes (p. 55)

party boss the person in control of a political machine (p. 345)

Patriot American colonist who supported the War for Independence (p. 85)

patronage another name for the spoils system, in which government jobs or favors are given out to political allies and friends (p. 364)

perestroika a policy of economic and government restructuring instituted by Mikhail Gorbachev in the Soviet Union in the 1980s (p. 882)

periphery the outer boundary of something (p. 621)

perjury lying when one has sworn under oath to tell the truth (pp. 670, 900)

philanthropy providing money to support humanitarian or social goals (p. 350)

Pilgrim a Separatist who journeyed to the American colonies in the 1600s for religious freedom (p. 49)

placer mining method of extracting mineral ore by hand using simple tools like picks, shovels, and pans (p. 287)

pocket veto indirectly vetoing a bill by letting a session of Congress expire without signing the bill (p. 268)

police powers a government's power to control people and property in the interest of public safety, health, welfare, and morals (p. 487)

political machine an organization linked to a political party that often controlled local government (p. 345)

poll tax a tax of a fixed amount per person that had to be paid before the person could vote (pp. 382, 759)

pool a group sharing in some activity; for example, railroad owners who made secret agreements and set rates among themselves (p. 320)

popular sovereignty government subject to the will of the people; before the Civil War, the idea that people living in a territory had the right to decide by voting if slavery would be allowed there (pp. 111, 122, 219)

populism political movement founded in the 1890s representing mainly farmers, favoring free coinage of silver and government control of railroads and other large industries (p. 372)

poverty line a level of personal or family income below which one is classified as poor by the federal government (p. 706)

presidio fort built by the Spanish in the Americas (p. 32)

prisoner of war a soldier captured by the enemy in battle (p. 254)

privateer privately owned ship licensed by the government to attack ships of other countries (p. 44)

progressivism a political movement that crossed party lines which believed that industrialism and urbanization had created many social problems and that government should take a more active role in dealing with these problems (p. 419)

prohibition laws banning the manufacture, transportation, and sale of alcoholic beverages (p. 425)

propaganda the spreading of ideas about an institution or individual for the purpose of influencing opinion (p. 453)

proprietary colony a colony owned by an individual (p. 47)

protective tariff tax on imports designed to protect American manufacturers (p. 171)

protectorate a country that is technically independent but is actually under the control of another country (p. 393)

public works projects such as highways, parks, and libraries built with public funds for public use (p. 543)

pueblo Spanish for village, term used by early Spanish explorers to denote large housing structures built by the Anasazi (p. 15)

Puritan someone who wanted to purify the Anglican Church during the 1500s and 1600s (p. 44)

Q

quartz mining method of extracting minerals involving digging beneath the surface (p. 287)

R

racism prejudice or discrimination against someone because of his or her race (p. 762)

ragtime a type of music with a strong rhythm and a lively melody with accented notes (p. 352)

ratification formal approval (p. 103)

rationing the giving out of scarce items on a limited basis (p. 629)

realism an approach to literature, art, and theater that attempts to accurately portray things as they really are and holds that society will function best if left to itself (p. 350)

reapportionment the method states use to draw up political districts based on changes in population (p. 721)

rebate a partial refund to lower the rate of a good or commodity (p. 367)

recall the right that enables voters to remove unsatisfactory elected officials from office (p. 421)

recession an economic slowdown (p. 106)

Reconstruction the reorganization and rebuilding of the former Confederate states after the Civil War (p. 266)

referendum the practice of letting voters accept or reject measures proposed by the legislature (pp. 229, 421)

relief aid for the needy, welfare (p. 544)

Renaissance French for rebirth, a period in Europe from 1350 to 1600 during which a rebirth of interest in the culture of ancient Greece and Rome occurred (p. 20)

reparations payment by the losing country in a war to the winner for the damages caused by the war. (p. 468)

republic form of government in which power resides in a body of citizens entitled to vote (p. 100)

reserved powers those powers which, according to the Constitution, are retained by the states (p. 123)

revenue tariff tax on imports for the purpose of raising money (p. 171)

revival large public meeting for preaching and prayer (p. 69)

right-to-work law a law making it illegal to require employees to join a union (p. 687)

S

safety net something that provides security against misfortune; specifically, government relief programs intended to protect against economic disaster (p. 577)

savannah a rolling grassland (p. 23)

scalawag name given to Southerners who supported Republican Reconstruction of the South (p. 273)

secede to leave or withdraw (p. 190)

secession withdrawal from the Union (p. 220)

segregation the separation or isolation of a race, class, or group (p. 382)

select committee a committee organized in the House or Senate to complete a specific task (p. 125)

self-determination belief that people in a territory should have the ability to choose their own government (p. 450)

separate-but-equal doctrine established by the 1896 Supreme Court case *Plessy* v. *Ferguson* that permitted laws segregating African Americans as long as equal facilities were provided (p. 747)

separation of powers government principle where power is divided among different branches (p. 111)

Separatist a Puritan who broke away from the Anglican Church (p. 48)

serf person bound to a manor (p. 19)

settlement house institution located in a poor neighborhood that provided numerous community services such as medical care, child care, libraries, and classes in English (p. 357)

shantytown a poor section of town consisting of crudely built dwellings usually made of wood (p. 536)

sharecropper farmer who works land for an owner who provides equipment and seed and receives a share of the crop (pp. 277, 381)

siege a military blockade of a city or fortified place to force it to surrender (p. 258)

silverite person who believes that coining silver currency in unlimited quantities will eliminate economic crisis (p. 378)

sit-down strike method of boycotting work by sitting down at work and refusing to leave the establishment (p. 568)

sit-in a form of protest involving occupying seats or sitting down on the floor of an establishment (p. 748)

Glossary

skyscraper a very tall building (p. 342)

slash-and-burn agriculture farming technique in which land is cleared and made fertile by cutting down and burning forests (p. 16)

slave code a set of laws that formally regulated slavery and defined the relationship between enslaved Africans and free people (p. 61)

smog fog made heavier and darker by smoke and chemical fumes (p. 820)

soap opera a serial drama on television or radio using melodramatic situations (p. 538)

Social Security Act a law requiring workers and employers to pay a tax; the money provides a monthly stipend for retired people (p. 569)

socialism belief that business should be publicly owned and run by the government (p. 425)

sodbuster a name given to Great Plains farmers (p. 294)

software a computer program (p. 893)

space race refers to the Cold War competition over dominance of space exploration capability (p. 725)

space shuttle a reusable spacecraft designed to transport people and cargo between Earth and space (p. 878)

space station a large satellite designed to be occupied for long periods and to serve as a base for operations in space (p. 879)

speakeasy a place where alcoholic beverages are sold illegally (p. 487)

speculation investing money at great risk with the anticipation that the price will rise (p. 531)

speculator person who risks money in hopes of a financial profit (p. 154)

sphere of influence section of a country where one foreign nation enjoys special rights and powers (p. 410)

spoils system practice of handing out government jobs to supporters; replacing government employees with the winning candidate's supporters (p. 190)

Square Deal Theodore Roosevelt's promise of fair and equal treatment for all (p. 428)

squatter someone who settles on public land under government regulation with the hopes of acquiring the title to the land (p. 203)

stagflation persistent inflation combined with stagnant consumer demand and relatively high unemployment (p. 844)

standing committee a permanent committee in the House or Senate organized for a specific area of focus (p. 125)

state-sponsored terrorism violent acts against civilians that are secretly supported by a government in order to attack other nations without going to war (p. 912)

steerage cramped quarters on a ship's lower decks for passengers paying the lowest fares (p. 337)

stock market a system for buying and selling stocks in corporations (p. 531)

strategic defense a plan to develop missiles and other devices that can shoot down nuclear missiles before they hit the United States (p. 909)

strategic materials materials needed for fighting a war (p. 605)

strike work stoppage by workers to force an employer to meet demands (p. 181)

subsistence farming farming only enough food to feed one's family (p. 59)

subversion a systematic attempt to overthrow a government by using persons working secretly from within (p. 669)

suffrage the right to vote (p. 421)

summit a meeting of heads of government (p. 837)

Sunbelt a new industrial region in southern California and the Deep South developing during World War II (p. 627)

supply-side economics economic theory that lower taxes will boost the economy as businesses and individuals invest their money, thereby creating higher tax revenue (pp. 522, 867)

syndicate a business group (p. 436)

teach-in an extended meeting or class held to discuss a social or political issue (p. 785)

Tejano Spanish-speaking inhabitants of Texas (p. 204)

telecommute to work at home by means of an electronic linkup with a central office (p. 893)

televangelist an evangelist who conducts regularly televised religious programs (p. 864)

temperance moderation in or abstinence from alcohol (pp. 196, 425)

tenant farmer farmer who works land owned by another and pays rent either in cash or crops (p. 277)

tenement multi-family apartments, usually dark, crowded, and barely meeting minimum living standards (p. 343)

termination policy a government policy to bring Native Americans into mainstream society by withdrawing recognition of Native American groups as legal entities (p. 708)

terrorism the use of violence by non-governmental groups against civilians to achieve a political goal by instilling fear and frightening governments into changing policies (p. 912)

time zone a geographical region in which the same standard time is kept (p. 316)

Title IX section of the 1972 Educational Amendments prohibiting federally funded schools from discriminating against girls and young women in nearly all aspects of their operations (p. 809)

torpedo in the 1860s, a term used for a water mine (p. 261)

trade deficit the difference between the value of a country's imports versus its exports (p. 903)

trade union an organization of workers with the same trade or skill (p. 327)

transcendental meditation a technique of meditation in which a mantra is chanted as a way of achieving peak intelligence, harmony, and health (p. 851)

transcendentalism a philosophy stressing the relationship between human beings and nature, spiritual things over material things, and the importance of the individual conscience (p. 195)

transcontinental railroad a railway system extending across the continent (p. 223)

triangular trade a three-way trade route that exchanged goods between the American colonies and two other trading partners (p. 64)

trust a combination of firms or corporations formed by a legal agreement, especially to reduce competition (p. 322)

U-boat German submarine, term means *Unterseeboot* (undersea boat) (p. 453)

unalienable nontransferable—for example, an unalienable right cannot be surrendered (p. 90)

Underground Railroad a system that helped enslaved African Americans follow a network of escape routes out of the South to freedom in the North (p. 221)

unfair trade practices trading practices which derive a gain at the expense of the competition (p. 441)

union shop a business that requires employees to join a union (p. 687)

urban renewal government programs that attempt to eliminate poverty and revitalize urban areas (p. 707)

utopia community based on a vision of a perfect society sought by reformers (p. 196)

vaquero men who herded cattle on haciendas (p. 33)

vaudeville stage entertainment made up of various acts, such as dancing, singing, comedy, and magic shows (p. 352)

vertical integration the combining of companies that supply equipment and services needed for a particular industry (p. 321)

veto power of the chief executive to reject laws passed by the legislature (p. 112)

victory garden gardens planted by American citizens during war to raise vegetables for home use, leaving more for the troops (pp. 458, 630)

Vietcong the guerrilla soldiers of the Communist faction in Vietnam, also known as the National Liberation Front (p. 777)

Vietnamization the process of making South Vietnam assume more of the war effort by slowly withdrawing American troops from Vietnam (p. 791)

War Hawks members of Congress during Madison's presidency who pressed for war with Britain (p. 165)

war on poverty antipoverty program under President Lyndon Johnson (p. 734)

welfare capitalism system in which companies enable employees to buy stock, participate in profit sharing, and receive benefits such as medical care, common in the 1920s (p. 519)

white-collar jobs in fields not requiring work clothes or protective clothing, such as sales (p. 693)

writ of assistance a search warrant enabling customs officers to enter any location to look for evidence of smuggling (p. 78)

yellow journalism type of sensational, biased, and often false reporting for the sake of attracting readers (p. 400)

yeoman farmer owner of a small farm with four or fewer enslaved persons, usually none (p. 183)

yuppie a young college-educated adult who is employed in a well-paying profession and who lives and works in or near a large city (p. 875)

Spanish Glossary

abolition/abolición el final inmediato de la esclavitud (p. 199)

affirmative action/acción afirmativa un esfuerzo activo para mejorar las oportunidades educacionales y de empleo para las minorías (p. 813)

alien/extranjero una persona que vive en un país del cual no es ciudadano (p. 157)

allotment/parcela un terreno asignado a un individuo o familia para su cultivación (p. 302)

amendment/enmienda un cambio a la Constitución (p.112)

Americanization/americanización causar que una persona adquiera características y rasgos americanos (p. 357)

amnesty/amnistía el acto de otorgar perdón a un número grande de personas (p. 267)

amphtrac/*amphtrac* un tractor anfibio utilizado para mover tropas desde barcos a la orilla del mar (p. 636)

anarchist/anarquista una persona que cree que no debe haber ningún gobierno (p. 483)

annexation/anexión incorporar un territorio dentro del dominio de un país (p. 207)

annuity/anualidad dinero pagado por contrato en intervalos regulares (p. 298)

appeasement/apaciguamiento demandas aceptadas a fin de evitar conflictos (p. 590)

appropriate/asignar apartar fondos para gastos (p. 124)

arbitration/arbitraje arreglar una disputa acordando aceptar la decisión de una persona imparcial (pp. 330, 429)

armistice/armisticio acuerdo temporal de paz para terminar con una lucha (p. 468)

assembly line/línea de montaje sistema de producción con máquinas y trabajadores arreglados para que cada persona haga su trabajo designado una y otra vez mientras el artículo pasa frente a ellos (p. 515)

assimilate/asimilar incorporar a un grupo dentro de la cultura de una población más grande (p. 302)

astrolabe/astrolabio instrumento usado para determinar la dirección, latitud y la hora de una localidad (p. 21)

attrition/atrición acto de desalentar por constantes ataques o acoso (p. 247)

baby boom/auge de nacimientos aumento marcado en la taza de natalidad, tal como ocurrió en Estados Unidos después de la Segunda Guerra Mundial (p. 694)

bailiff/alguacil oficial en rango menor de las Cortes (p. 536)

benevolent society/sociedad de beneficencia una asociación enfocada en llevar la palabra de Dios y combatir problemas sociales (p. 195)

bilingualism/bilingualismo la práctica de enseñar a estudiantes inmigrantes en su propio lenguaje (p. 815)

bill/proyecto de ley una ley propuesta (p. 125)

binding arbitration/arbitraje obligatorio proceso por el cual un partido neutral escucha argumentos de dos partidos opositores y toma una decisión que ambos deben aceptar (p. 567)

black codes/códigos negros leyes aprobadas en el Sur al terminar la Guerra Civil para controlar a los libertos y permitir a los dueños de plantaciones la explotación de los trabajadores afroamericanos (p. 269)

black power/poder negro mobilización del poder económico y político de afroamericanos especialmente para imponer respeto por sus derechos y para mejorar sus condiciones (p. 764)

blitzkrieg/guerra relámpago nombre dado a los ataques repentinos ofensivos violentos que los alemanes usaron durante la Segunda Guerra Mundial (p. 591)

blockade runner/forzador de bloqueo un barco que navega a través de un bloqueo, usualmente para pasar contrabando a través de un área protegida (p. 250)

blue-collar/collar azul trabajos de mano de obra, particularmente aquellos que requieren ropa protectora (p. 693)

blues/*blues* estilo de música que evolucionó de la música espiritual de los afroamericanos, distinguida por su sonido melancólico (p. 500)

Bohemian/bohemio una persona (como artista o escritor) que lleva un estilo de vida poco convencional (p. 493)

bonanza farm/granja en bonanza extensa granja de trigo que produce muchas ganancias (p. 294)

bond/bono una obligación emitida por el gobierno que promete pagar un préstamo con interés (p. 153)

bounty/recompensa dinero dado para animar el alistamiento en el ejército (p. 250)

brinkmanship/política arriesgada la buena voluntad para ir al borde de guerra para forzar a un oponente a que se retracte (p. 677)

broker state/estado intermediario el papel del gobierno para resolver conflictos entre grupos con intereses competitivos (p. 577)

budget deficit/déficit del presupuesto la cantidad por la cual los gastos exceden los ingresos (p. 867)

bull market/bolsa al alza largo período durante el cual los precios de acciones en la bolsa se incrementan (p. 531)

burgesses/burgueses representantes elegidos para la asamblea general de la colonia de Virginia (p. 46)

Spanish Glossary

busing/traslado obligatorio la política de transportar estudiantes a escuelas fuera de sus vecindarios para alcanzar un balance racial (p. 814)

cabinet/gabinete grupo de consejeros al presidente (pp. 126, 153)

capital gains tax/impuestos a las ganancias del capital impuesto federal pagado por inversionistas y negocios cuando ellos venden acciones y bienes raíces (p. 886)

capitalist/capitalista persona que invierte riqueza, particularmente dinero, en un negocio (p. 63)

caravel/carabela buque capaz de explorar largas distancias (p. 21)

carpetbagger/*carpetbagger* nombre dado a muchos norteños que se mudaron al Sur después de la Guerra Civil y apoyaron a los republicanos (p. 273)

cash crop/cultivo comercial cosecha cultivada para ganancia (p. 59)

caucus/junta electoral reunión llevada a cabo por un partido político para escoger su candidato a la presidencia o para decidir políticas (p. 190)

censure/censura expresar la desaprobación formal sobre una acción (p. 673)

chad/agujereado pedazo pequeño de cartón producido taladrando una tarjeta de computadora (p. 908)

charter/carta de privilegio una constitución (p. 647)

checks and balances/control y balances sistema en el cual cada ramo de gobierno tiene la habilidad para limitar el poder a los otros ramos para que ninguno vuelva a ser demasiado poderoso (p. 112)

circumnavigate/circunnavegar navegar alrededor de (p. 27)

civilization/civilización cultura sumamente desarrollada distinguida por un conocimiento de comercio, gobierno, las artes, las ciencias, y frecuentemente lenguaje escrito (p. 13)

closed shop/taller cerrado acuerdo en el que una compañía contrata solamente a miembros del sindicato (pp. 330, 687)

cloture/clausura una moción que termina con el debate y requiere un voto inmediato, posible en el Senado de EE.UU. por un voto de 60 senadores (p. 758)

Cold War/Guerra Fría conflicto ideológico caracterizado por frecuentes confrontaciones entre Estados Unidos y la Unión Soviética entre los años 1946 y 1990 (p. 654)

Columbian Exchange/Intercambio Colombiano una serie de interacciones complejas sociales y del medio ambiente entre Europa y las Américas que empezó con el primer viaje de Colón (p. 28)

commission plan/gobierno por comisión plan en el cual el gobierno municipal está dividido dentro de diferentes departamentos con diferentes funciones, cada uno bajo la dirección de un comisionado (p. 420)

committee of correspondence/comité de correspondencia comité organizado en cada colonia para comunicar entre las colonias y unificarlas (p. 83)

commune/comuna un arreglo de vivienda en el cual los miembros de un grupo trabajan juntos y comparten todo (p. 803)

concentration camp/campo de concentración un campamento donde personas están detenidas o encerradas (p. 599)

concurrent powers/poderes concurrentes poderes compartidos por los estados y el gobierno federal (p. 123)

Confederacy/Confederación nación formada por los estados sureños que se separaron de la Unión en 1860–1861 (p. 235)

conference committee/comité de conferencia una comisión paritaria especial organizada para ayudar a la Cámara y al Senado a forjar un compromiso de ley aceptable para ambas cámaras (p. 125)

conquistador/conquistador los hombres que condujeron las expediciones para conquistar las Américas (p. 32)

conscription/reclutamiento requerir que personas ingresen en el servicio militar (pp. 246, 457)

consensus/consenso acuerdo general (p. 734)

conservative/conservador una persona que cree que el poder del gobierno, particularmente en la economía, debe estar limitado para llevar al máximo la libertad individual (p. 861)

constituent/elector residente de un distrito electoral (p. 125)

containment/contención la política o proceso de prevenir la expansión de un poder hostil (p. 660)

contra/contra contrarevolucionario, la fuerza guerrilla anti-Sandinista en Nicaragua (p. 870)

contraband/contrabando artículos de los que la importación, exportación o posesión es ilegal (pp. 164, 453)

convoy/convoy un grupo que viaja junto con algo, tal como un barco, para protegerlo (p. 466)

convoy system/sistema de convoy un sistema en el cual barcos mercantes viajan con buques navales para protección (p. 622)

cooperative/cooperativa tienda donde los granjeros compraban productos el uno del otro; empresa poseída y operada por los que usan sus servicios (p. 374)

cooperative individualism/individualismo cooperativo política del Presidente Hoover para alentar a los manufactureros y distribuidores a formar sus propias organizaciones y pasar información voluntariamente al gobierno federal en un esfuerzo para estimular la economía (p. 522)

corporation/sociedad anónima organización autorizada por ley a montar una actividad, tratada como si fuera una sola persona (p. 320)

"corrupt bargain"/trato corrupto un acuerdo ilegítimo entre políticos (p. 189)

cost of living/costo de vida el costo de comprar artículos y servicios esenciales para la supervivencia (p. 471)

cost-plus/costo más beneficio contrato del gobierno para pagar el costo de fabricación para producir un artículo más un porcentaje garantizado (p. 613)

cotton gin/despepitadora de algodón máquina que sacaba las semillas de las fibras de algodón (p. 182)

counterculture/contracultura una cultura con valores y creencias diferentes de los de la cultural principal (p. 802)

covert/secreto no hecho o mostrado abiertamente (p. 679)

creationism/creacionismo la creencia que Dios creó al mundo y todo lo que hay en él, usualmente como se describe en Génesis (p. 486)

credibility gap/barrera de credibilidad falta de confianza (p. 785)

customs duties/derechos de aduana impuestos sobre importaciones y exportaciones (p. 77)

D

de facto segregation/segregación de facto segregación por costumbre y tradición (p. 747)

debtor/deudor persona que debe dinero, usualmente un préstamo financiado que no puede ser pagado (p. 56)

deficit spending/gastos déficits práctica del gobierno de gastar dinero prestado en vez de aumentar impuestos, usualmente una tentativa para levantar la economía (p. 565)

deflation/deflación un decremento de la cantidad de dinero o crédito disponible el cual resulta en precios reducidos y por lo tanto aumenta el poder adquisitivo de la moneda (pp. 327, 373)

deport/deportar expulsar del país a individuos (p. 474)

détente/détente una política que intenta relajar o borrar la tensión entre naciones (p. 836)

developing nation/nación en desarrollo nación en donde la economía es principalmente agrícola (p. 679)

direct primary/elección primaria voto tomado por todos los miembros de un partido político para elegir a su candidato para un puesto público (p. 421)

disco/música disco música popular para danza caracterizada por ritmo hipnótico, cantos repetitivos y sonidos producidos electrónicamente (p. 853)

disfranchise/privación civil privar el derecho al voto (p. 616)

DNA/ADN material genético de las células que determina toda forma de vida (p. 895)

dollar diplomacy/diplomacia del dólar política de juntar los intereses comerciales de un país con sus intereses diplomáticos en el extranjero (p. 413)

domino theory/teoría dominó la creencia que si una nación en Asia se derrumbara ante los comunistas, sus países vecinos hubieran caído en seguida (p. 774)

dove/paloma persona a favor de que Estados Unidos se retirara de la guerra en Vietnam (p. 787)

downsizing/reducción de personal reducción del tamaño de una compañia despidiendo gerentes y trabajadores para llegar a ser una empresa más eficiente (p. 885)

dry farming/cultivo seco manera de cultivar tierra seca plantando las semillas en la profundidad de la tierra donde hay algo de humedad (p. 294)

due process/proceso justo requerimiento judicial de que las leyes no deben tratar individuos injusta, arbitraria, o irracionalmente y que las cortes deben de seguir procesos y reglamentos justos al jurar casos (pp. 128, 722)

Dust Bowl/Cuenca Polvada nombre dado al área sureña de las Grandes Planicies severamente dañada por sequías y tormentas de polvo durante los años 1930 (p. 537)

dynamic conservatism/conservatismo dinámico política de alcanzar un balance entre el conservatismo económico y algún activismo (p. 689)

E

economics of scale/economía a gran escala reducción del costo de un producto a causa de la producción aumentada en una fábrica de producción (p. 320)

emancipation/emancipación el proceso de liberar a personas esclavizadas (p. 199)

embargo/embargo prohibición gubernamental contra el comercio con otros países (pp. 164, 844)

empresario/empresario persona que arreglaba el asentamiento de tierras en Texas durante los años 1800 (p. 204)

enclosure movement/movimiento encerrado un cambio económico en Inglaterra en los años 1500 en el cual los propietarios de tierras convirtieron terrenos agrícolas en granjas de ovejas y expulsaron a los granjeros arrendatarios (p. 44)

encomienda/encomienda sistema de recompensar a los conquistadores con extensiones de tierra y el derecho de recaudar impuestos y exigir mano de obra a los indígenas americanos (p. 33)

Enlightenment/Siglo Ilustrado movimiento durante los años 1700 que promovió el conocimiento, la razón, y las ciencias (p. 68)

entrepreneur/empresario persona que organiza, dirige y asume el riesgo de un negocio o empresa (pp. 63, 310)

enumerated powers/poderes enumerados poderes nombrados en la Constitución que pertenecen solamente al gobierno federal (pp. 123, 154)

espionage/espionaje espiar, especialmente para obtener secretos gubernamentales (p. 460)

ethnic cleansing/purificación étnica expulsión, encarcelamiento o asesinato de minorías étnicas por un grupo mayoritario dominante (p. 900)

eugenics/eugenesia seudociencia que trata con el perfeccionamiento de las cualidades hereditarias de una raza o especie (p. 483)

euro/eurodólar moneda básica compartida por los países de la Unión Europea desde 1999 (p. 903)

evolution/evolución teoría científica que los humanos y otras formas de vida se han evolucionado tras el tiempo (p. 486)

excise tax/arbitrios impuesto pagado por el fabricante de un producto y pasado a aquellos que lo compran (p. 155)

executive privilege/privilegio ejecutivo el principio de que las comunicaciones del ramo ejecutivo deben de permanecer confidenciales para proteger la seguridad nacional (p. 841)

extermination camp/campo de exterminación campo donde los prisioneros eran enviados para ser ejecutados (p. 599)

fallout/caída radioactiva partículas radioactivas dispersadas por una explosión nuclear (p. 674)

fallout shelter/refugio atómico un refugio construido para proteger a las personas de la caída radioactiva (p. 674)

fascism/fascismo un sistema político encabezado por un dictador que pide por nacionalismo y racismo extremo y poca tolerancia de la oposición (p. 585)

favorite son/hijo favorito hombres que disfrutaban del apoyo de los líderes de su estado y región natales (p. 188)

featherbedding/paro técnico práctica de limitar la producción con el fin de crear más trabajos (p. 687)

federalism/federalismo sistema político en el cual el poder está dividido entre los estados y el gobierno federal (pp. 111, 122)

feminism/feminismo la creencia que los hombres y las mujeres deben ser iguales política, económica y socialmente (p. 807)

feudalism/feudalismo un sistema político en el cual los líderes poderosos dieron tierra a los nobles a cambio de compromisos de lealtad y servicio (p. 19)

filibuster/filibustero un atentado para acabar con un proyecto de ley hablando continuamente a turnos un grupo de senadores para que no pueda haber un voto (p. 758)

fireside chats/pláticas hogareñas emisiones de radio transmitidas por FDR al pueblo americano para explicar sus iniciativas (p. 558)

fixed costs/costos fijos costos que una compañía debe pagar si está operando o no (p. 320)

flapper/*flapper* mujer jóven de los años 1920 que demostró libertad de las costumbres tradicionales especialmente en vestido (p. 485)

flexible response/respuesta flexible formación de tropas y armas convencionales para permitir que un país entre en una guerra limitada sin usar armas nucleares (p. 725)

forage/forrajear buscar alimento (p. 258)

foreclose/ejecutar una hipoteca tomar posesión de una propiedad por falta de pagos hipotecarios (p. 545)

fossil fuel/combustible fósil un combustible formado en la tierra de los restos descompuestos de plantas o animales (p. 822)

franchise/concesión derecho o licencia para vender los bienes o servicios de una compañía en un área tal como una cadena de tiendas (p. 693)

freedman/liberto persona liberada de la esclavitud (p. 268)

Freedom Riders/Jinetes de la Libertad nombre dado a un grupo de personas que viajaron al Sur en 1961 para protestar la negativa del Sur para integrar las terminales de autobuses (p. 755)

fundamentalist/fundamentalista un cristiano protestante evangélico que cree en ser salvado de pecados volviendo a nacer otra vez y haciendo un compromiso personal para seguir a Cristo Jesus (p. 486)

general strike/huelga general una huelga por todos los trabajadores de un lugar geográfico (p. 472)

generation gap/barrera generacional una separación cultural entre padres e hijos (p. 702)

glacier/glaciar trozo enorme de hielo (p. 13)

glasnost/*glasnost* política soviética que permitía discusión abierta de temas políticos y sociales y diseminación más libre de noticias e información (p. 882)

global warming/calentamiento global aumento en la temperatura promedio mundial tras un período (p. 905)

Spanish Glossary

gold standard/patrón oro norma monetaria en la cual una onza de oro igualaba a un número fijo de dólares (p. 555)

goldbug/*goldbug* persona que cree que la moneda americana debe de estar basada en un patrón oro (p. 378)

graduated income tax/impuesto graduado de utilidades impuesto basado en los ingresos netos de un individuo o empresa en el cual la taza del impuesto se diferencia de acuerdo a diferentes niveles de salario (p. 376)

graft/soborno adquisición de dinero de manera deshonesta tal como el sobornar a un político (pp. 273, 345)

grandfather clause/cláusula de abuelo cláusula que permitió votar a los que no aprobaron el examen de leer si sus padres o sus abuelos habían votado antes de que empezara la Reconstrucción; excepción a una ley basada en circunstancias preexistentes (p. 382)

grassroots movement/movimiento local grupo de personas que se organiza a nivel local y popular lejos de centros políticos o culturales (p. 886)

Great Awakening/Gran Despertar movimiento durante los años 1700 que enfatizó la dependencia en Dios (p. 69)

greenback/billete dorso verde billete de papel moneda de EEUU expedido por primera vez por el Norte durante la Guerra Civil (pp. 245, 373)

gross national product/producto nacional bruto valor total de bienes y servicios producidos por un país durante un año (p. 308)

guerrilla/guerrilla banda armada que usa ataques sorpresas o sabotaje en vez de la guerra organizada (pp. 449, 774)

guerrilla warfare/guerra de guerrillas técnica de tirar y darse a la huida usada en combates de guerra; peleas por pequeñas bandas de guerreros usando tácticas tales como emboscadas repentinas (p. 95)

guru/gurú persona con conocimiento y experiencia, dicho especialmente de un maestro religioso y guía espiritual en el indoísmo (p. 851)

H

habeas corpus/hábeas corpus orden legal para una encuesta para determinar si una persona ha sido encarcelada legalmente (p. 246)

hacienda/hacienda un rancho extenso (p. 33)

hardtack/*hardtack* galleta dura hecha de harina de trigo (p. 254)

hawk/halcón persona que creía que Estados Unidos debía continuar sus esfuerzos militares en Vietnam (p. 787)

headright/derecho de terreno sistema en el cual los colonizadores recibían tierra a cambio de establecerse en Virginia (p. 46)

hedgerow/seto fila de arbustos o árboles cercando un campo a menudo sobre un muro de tierra (p. 641)

hemispheric defense zone/zona de defensa hemisférica política nacional durante la Segunda Guerra Mundial que declaró que el Hemisferio Oeste fue neutral y que Estados Unidos patrullaría esta región en contra de submarinos alemanes (p. 603)

heretic/hereje disidente de creencias establecidas por la iglesia (p. 50)

hobo/vagabundo persona errante sin hogar y usualmente sin dinero (p. 536)

holding company/compañía de valores compañía de la cual el negocio principal es poseer el control de acciones en otras compañías (p. 322)

Holocaust/Holocausto nombre dado a la exterminación masiva de judíos y otros grupos hecha por los nazis durante la Segunda Guerra Mundial (p. 595)

homestead/posesionar método de adquirir una extensión de tierra pública de EEUU viviendo en ella y cultivándola (p. 293)

Hooverville/*Hooverville* apodo dado a los barrios en Estados Unidos durante la Depresión (p. 536)

horizontal integration/integración horizontal asociación de firmas competitivas en una sociedad anónima (p. 321)

I

Ice Age/Época Glacial período de temperaturas extremadamente frías cuando parte de la superficie del planeta estaba cubierta de capas masivas de hielo (p. 13)

immunity/inmunidad libertad de prosecusión (p. 512)

impeach/acusar acusar formalmente a un oficial público de mala conducta en la oficina (pp. 112, 124, 271, 841)

imperialism/imperialismo acciones usadas por una nación para ejercer el control político o económico sobre naciones más pequeñas o débiles (p. 393)

implied powers/poderes implícitos poderes no nombrados específicamente en la Constitución pero reclamados por el gobierno federal (p. 154)

impound/confiscar tomar posesión de (p. 835)

impressment/requisición un tipo de secuestro legalizado en el cual personas son forzadas a servir en el servicio militar (p. 164)

income tax/impuesto de utilidades impuesto basado en el ingreso neto de una persona o empresa (p. 440)

indentured servant/sirviente contratado individuo contratado para trabajar para un colono durante cierto número de años a cambio de transportación a las colonias, alimento, ropa y refugio (p. 59)

Spanish Glossary

industrial union/sindicato industrial organización de trabajadores comunes y obreros calificados en una industria (p. 327)

inflation/inflación pérdida del valor del dinero (pp. 106, 373, 844)

initiative/iniciativa derecho de los ciudadanos de poner una propuesta o tema ante los votantes o la legislatura para su aprobación (p. 421)

installment/pago a plazos compra de un artículo a crédito con un plan de pago mensual para pagar el valor del artículo (p. 534)

insubordination/insubordinación desobediencia (p. 437)

insurrection/insurrección un acto de rebelión en contra del gobierno establecido (p. 231)

interchangeable parts/partes intercambiables piezas uniformes que pueden ser hechas en grandes cantidades para reemplazar otras piezas idénticas (p. 180)

internationalism/internacionalismo política nacional de intercambio comercial activo con países extranjeros para promover la paz y la prosperidad (p. 588)

Internet/Internet red de comunicaciones electrónicas que conecta redes de computación y facilidades de computación de organizaciones alrededor del mundo (p. 894)

interposition/interposición teoría que un estado debiera poder intervenir entre el gobierno federal y la gente para detener una acción ilegal (p. 158)

iron curtain/cortina de hierro barrera política y militar que aisló a los países de Europa Oriental controlados por los soviéticos después de la Segunda Guerra Mundial (p. 658)

isolationism/aislacionismo política nacional de evitar el involucramiento en asuntos mundiales (pp. 523, 587)

J

jazz/jazz estilo de música americana que se desarrolló de ragtime y blues y que usa melodías y ritmos sincopados (p. 499)

Jim Crow Laws/Leyes de Jim Crow leyes creadas para reforzar la segregación (p. 382)

jingoism/patriotismo extremo nacionalismo marcado por la agresiva política extranjera (p. 401)

joint committee/comité paritaria comité organizado con miembros de la Cámara y el Senado para trabajar en temas específicos (p. 125)

joint-stock company/compañía por acciones forma de organización de negocios en la cual muchos inversionistas compran acciones para juntar grandes cantidades de dinero para grandes proyectos (p. 44)

judicial review/revisión judicial derecho de la Suprema Corte para determinar si las leyes del Congreso son constitucionales y para derribar aquellas que no lo son (pp. 127, 162)

juvenile delinquency/delincuencia juvenil comportamiento antisocial o criminal de los jóvenes (p. 709)

K

kachina/kachina espíritu bueno que la gente Pueblo creyó traía mensajes de los dioses a su pueblo cada año (p. 15)

kamikaze/kamikase durante la Segunda Guerra Mundial un piloto suicida japonés de quien la misión fue chocar en su objetivo (p. 637)

L

labor union/sindicato organización de trabajadores formada con el propósito de promover los intereses de sus miembros (p. 181)

laissez-faire/laissez-faire política que el gobierno debe interferir tan poco como sea posible en la economía del país (p. 310)

land-grant/concesión de tierras una concesión de terrenos por el gobierno federal especialmente para carreteras, vías de ferrocarril y colegios agrícolas (p. 317)

letters of marque/patente de corso cédula autorizada por el Congreso para propietarios de naves privadas autorizándoles a atacar barcos mercantes británicos (p. 97)

liberal/liberal persona que generalmente cree que el gobierno debe desempeñar un papel activo en la economía y programas sociales pero que el gobierno no debe dictar el comportamiento social (p. 861)

Liberty ship/barco de Libertad barco de carga básico utilizado por Estados Unidos durante la Segunda Guerra Mundial (p. 614)

limited war/guerra limitada guerra peleada con compromisos limitados de recursos para alcanzar un objetivo limitado, tal como la contención del comunismo (p. 665)

line of demarcation/línea de demarcación línea de longitud de norte a sur a través del Océano Atlántico que dividía las tierras en las Américas reclamadas por España y Portugal (p. 26)

linkage/enlace política de mejorar relaciones con la Unión Soviética y China con la esperanza de persuadirlas a que redujeran su ayuda a Vietnam del Norte (p. 790)

lockout/cierre patronal práctica de una empresa para rechazar las demandas sindicales negándose a permitir a los empleados a entrar al área de trabajo (p. 328)

long drive/manejo largo conducción de ganado por largas distancias a estaciones de ferrocarril para la transportación rápida y grandes ganancias (p. 289)

longhouse/casa comunal edificio grande rectangular con techo en forma de barril cubierto de corteza de árbol utilizado por unos indígenas americanos (p. 16)

Loyalist/lealista colono americano que apoyó a la Gran Bretaña y se opuso a la guerra para la independencia (p. 85)

lynching/linchamiento ejecución hecha sin aprobación legal (p. 383)

mandate/mandato autorización dado a un representante (p. 262)

Manifest Destiny/Destino Manifiesto idea popular en Estados Unidos durante los años 1800 de que el país debía extender sus fronteras hasta el Océano Pacífico (p. 202)

manorialism/señorialismo sistema económico en el cual los campesinos proporcionan sus servicios a un lord feudal a cambio de protección (p. 19)

manumission/manumisión liberación voluntaria de personas esclavizadas (p. 102)

margin/margen comprar acciones pagando solamente una fracción del precio y pidiendo prestado el resto (p. 531)

margin call/llamada de reserva demanda de un accionista a que los inversionistas paguen los préstamos hechos para la compra de acciones al margen (p. 531)

martial law/derecho marcial derecho administrado por fuerzas militares que es invocado por un gobierno en una emergencia (p. 236)

Marxism/marxismo teoría de socialismo en la cual una lucha de clases sociales existiría hasta que los trabajadores salieran finalmente victoriosos, creando una sociedad sin distinción de clases (p. 328)

mass media/medios informativos medios de comunicación (como televisión y radio) con la intención de llegar a la audiencia extensa (p. 495)

mass production/fabricación en serie producción de grandes cantidades de productos usando máquinas y a menudo una línea de montaje (p. 515)

massive retaliation/represalia masiva una política que amenaza una respuesta masiva, incluyendo el uso de armas nucleares, contra un estado comunista que trata de captar un país pacífico por la fuerza (p. 676)

maverick/*maverick* un res descarriado sin ningún símbolo de identificación (p. 290)

mercantilism/mercantilismo teoría que el poder de una estado depende de su riqueza (p. 65)

microprocessor/microprocesador procesador de computadora que contiene memoria y funciones de computación en un solo chip (p. 893)

military-industrial complex/compejo militar industrial relación informal que algunas personas creen que existe entre lo militar y la industria de defensa para promover mayores gastos militares y para influenciar la política gubernamental (p. 680)

minutemen/*minutemen* compañías de soldados civiles que se jactaban de que podrían estar listos para tomar armas en sólo un minuto (p. 85)

missile gap/diferencia de proyectiles creencia que la Unión Soviética tenía más armas nucleares que Estados Unidos (p. 719)

monopoly/monopolio control total de una industria por una persona o una compañía (p. 321)

moratorium/moratoria suspensión de actividad (p. 524)

most-favored nation/nación más favorecida política entre países asegurando prácticas de tratado de comercio justo (p. 156)

muckraker/*muckraker* periodista que revela abusos y corrupción en una sociedad (p. 419)

mudslinging/*mudslinging* intentar arruinar la reputación de un adversario con insultos (p. 189)

multinational corporation/corporación multinacional grandes corporaciones de inversión extranjera (p. 693)

napalm/*napalm* gasolina gelatinosa utilizada para bombas incendiarias (pp. 644, 780)

nationalism/nacionalismo lealtad y devoción a una nación (p. 450)

nativism/nativismo una preferencia para las personas nativas y un deseo a limitar el inmigración (pp. 181, 340)

naturalism/naturalismo filosofía y perspectiva en arte y literatura en la cual la naturaleza es tratada realísticamente, puede ser entendida a través de observación científica y que la sociedad funcionará mejor con algunas regulaciones gubernamentales (p. 355)

nomad/nómada persona que se mueve de un lugar a otro, generalmente en busca de alimentos o pastos (pp. 13, 297)

nonimportation agreement/acuerdo de no importación compromiso por mercaderes de no comprar artículos importados de una fuente indicada (p. 78)

normalcy/normalidad estado de ser normal (p. 511)

Northwest Passage/Pasaje del Noroeste ruta acuática mítica del norte a través de América del Norte al Océano Pacífico (p. 34)

nuclear proliferation/proliferación nuclear distribución de armas nucleares a nuevas naciones (p. 905)

nullification/anulación teoría que los estados tienen el derecho de declarar inválida una ley federal (p. 158)

O

Open Door policy/política de Puertas Abiertas política que permitió a cada nación extranjera en China intercambiar libremente en las esferas de influencia de otras naciones (p. 410)

open range/terreno abierto gran extensión de pastos propiedad del gobierno federal (p. 288)

open shop/taller abierto lugar de trabajo donde los trabajadores no son requeridos de ser miembros del sindicato (p. 519)

operating cost/costos de operación costos que ocurren operando una compañía (p. 320)

override/anular habilidad del Congreso de rechazar un veto presidencial por el voto de una mayoría de dos tercios (p. 124)

P

pacifism/pacifismo oposición a la guerra o violencia como un medio para arreglar disputas (p. 55)

party boss/jefe de partido persona que lleva el control de la maquinaria política (p. 345)

Patriot/Patriota colono americano que apoyó la guerra para independencia (p. 85)

patronage/patronazgo otro nombre para el sistema de despojos política en el cual puestos y favores gubernamentales son dados a aliados políticos y amigos (p. 364)

perestroika/perestroika política de reestructuración económica y gubernamental instituida por Mikhail Gorbachev en la Unión Soviética en los años 1980 (p. 882)

periphery/periferia frontera externa de algo (p. 621)

perjury/perjurio mentir cuando uno ha jurado decir la verdad (pp. 670, 900)

philanthropy/filantropía proporcionar dinero para apoyar metas humanitarias o sociales (p. 350)

Pilgrim/peregrino Separatista que viajó a las colonias americanas durante los años 1600 para libertad religiosa (p. 49)

placer mining/explotación de placeres método para extraer mineral a mano utilizando simples herramientas manuales como picos, palas y bateas (p. 287)

pocket veto/veto indirecto vetar indirectamente un proyecto de ley permitiendo que una sesión del Congreso expire sin firmar el proyecto (p. 268)

police power/fuerza policiaca poder gubernamental para controlar a personas y propiedades para la seguridad, salud, bienestar, y moral pública (p. 487)

political machine/maquinaria política organización aliada con un partido político que a menudo controlaba el gobierno local (p. 345)

poll tax/impuesto de capitación impuesto de cantidad fija por cada persona, el cual tenía que ser pagado antes de que una persona pudiera votar (pp. 382, 759)

pool/consorcio grupo compartiendo una actividad; por ejemplo, dueños de ferrocarril que tomaban acuerdos secretos y fijaban tipos entre ellos mismos (p. 320)

popular sovereignty/soberanía popular teoría política de que el gobierno está sujeto a la voluntad del pueblo; antes de la Guerra Civil, la idea de que la gente que vivía en un territorio tenía el derecho de decidir votando si ahí sería permitida la esclavitud (pp. 111, 122, 219)

populism/populismo movimiento político fundado en los años 1890 representando principalmente a los granjeros que favoreció libre acuñación de plata y el control gubernamental de ferrocarriles y otras industrias grandes (p. 372)

poverty line/línea de pobreza nivel de ingreso individual o familiar bajo del cual uno es clasificado por el gobierno federal como pobre (p. 706)

presidio/presidio fuerte construido por los españoles en las Américas (p. 32)

prisioner of war/prisionero de guerra soldado capturado por el enemigo en batalla (p. 254)

privateer/buque corsario buque de propiedad privada autorizado por el gobierno para atacar a buques de otros países (p. 44)

progressivism/progresivismo movimiento político que cruzó las líneas partidarias que creyó que la industria y la urbanización habían creados muchos problemas sociales y que el gobierno debía tomar un papel más activo para resolver estos problemas (p. 419)

prohibition/prohibición leyes que prohibían la manufactura, transportación y venta de bebidas alcohólicas (p. 425)

propaganda/propaganda diseminación de ideas sobre una institución o individuo con el propósito de influenciar la opinión (p. 453)

proprietary colony/colonia propietaria colonia propiedad de un individuo (p. 47)

protective tariff/arancel protectora impuesto en importaciones diseñado para proteger a los manufactureros americanos (p. 171)

protectorate/protectorado país que es técnicamente independiente pero que en realidad queda bajo el control de otro país (p. 393)

public works/obras públicas proyectos como carreteras, parques y bibliotecas construidos con fondos públicos para uso público (p. 543)

pueblo/pueblo término usado por los primeros exploradores españoles para denotar grandes estructuras habitacionales construidas por los Anasazi (p. 15)

Puritans/puritanos persona que quería purificar la Iglesia Anglicana en los años 1500 y 1600 (p. 44)

quartz mining/minería de cuarzo método para extraer minerales excavando debajo de la superficie (p. 287)

racism/racismo prejuicio o discriminación en contra de alguien por su raza (p. 762)

ragtime/*ragtime* tipo de música con un ritmo fuerte y una melodía animada con notas acentuadas (p. 352)

ratification/ratificación aprobación formal (p. 103)

rationing/racionamiento proporcionar escasos artículos de manera limitada (p. 629)

realism/realismo perspectiva de literatura, arte, y teatro que intenta representar las cosas tal como son y que la sociedad funcionará mejor si la dejan en paz (p. 350)

reapportionment/nueva repartición método usado por los estados para formar distritos políticos basados en los cambios de población (p. 721)

rebate/descuento devolución parcial para reducir el costo de un producto o bien (p. 367)

recall/elección de revocación derecho que permite a los votantes quitar del cargo a los oficiales elegidos que son inadecuados (p. 421)

recession/recesión retraso económico (p. 106)

Reconstruction/Reconstrucción reorganización y reconstrucción de los estados de la ex-Confederación después de la Guerra Civil (p. 266)

referendum/referéndum práctica de permitir a los votantes aceptar o rechazar medidas propuestas por la legislatura (pp. 229, 421)

relief/asistencia pública ayuda para los necesitados; beneficencia (p. 544)

Renaissance/Renacimiento período en Europa desde 1350 hasta 1600 durante el cual ocurrió el renacimiento de interés en la cultura de la antigua Grecia y Roma (p. 20)

reparations/indemnización pago hecho por el país perdedor de una guerra al país ganador por los daños causados por la guerra (p. 468)

republic/república forma de gobierno en el cual el poder reside en un cuerpo de ciudadanos con derecho al voto (p. 100)

reserved powers/poderes reservados los poderes nombrados en la Constitución que son retenidos por los estados (p. 123)

revenue tariff/arancel de ingresos impuesto en las importaciones con el propósito de recaudar dinero (p. 171)

revival/asamblea evangelista reunión pública grande para predicar y rezar (p. 69)

right-to-work law/derecho a trabajar ley que hace ilegal la demanda que los trabajadores se unan a un sindicato (p. 687)

safety net/red de seguridad algo que proporciona seguridad en contra de desgracias, específicamente, programas de beneficencia gubernamentales para proteger en contra del desastre económico (p. 577)

savannah/sabana pasto ondulante (p. 23)

scalawag/*scalawag* nombre dado a los sureños que apoyaron la Reconstrucción republicana del Sur (p. 273)

secede/separarse abandonar o retirar (p. 190)

secession/secesión retiro de la Unión (p. 220)

segregation/segregación separación o aislamiento de una raza, clase o grupo (p. 382)

select committee/comité selecto comité organizado en la Cámara o el Senado para hacer una tarea específica (p. 125)

self-determination/autodeterminación creencia que las personas en un territorio deberían tener la habilidad para escoger su propio gobierno (p. 450)

separate-but-equal/separados pero iguales doctrina establecida por la Suprema Corte en el caso *Plessy contra Ferguson* en 1896 que las leyes que segregaron a los afroamericanos fueron permitidas si facilidades iguales fueron proporcionadas (p. 747)

separation of powers/separación de poderes principio de gobierno en el cual el poder está dividido entre diferentes ramos (p. 111)

Separatist/separatista puritano que dejó la Iglesia Anglicana (p. 48)

serf/siervo persona atada a un señorío (p. 19)

settlement house/casa de beneficencia institución establecida en una vecindad pobre que proveía numerosos servicios comunitarios tal como cuidado médico, cuidado de niños, bibliotecas, e instrucción en inglés (p. 357)

Spanish Glossary

shantytown/villa miseria barrio pobre de un pueblo que consiste de viviendas mal construidas, normalmente hechas de madera (p. 536)

sharecropper/aparcero agricultor que labra la tierra para un dueño que proporciona equipo y semillas y recibe una porción de la cosecha (pp. 277, 381)

siege/sitio bloqueo militar de una ciudad o un recinto fortificado para forzarlo a rendirse (p. 258)

silverite/defensor de plata persona que cree que la acuñación de monedas de plata en cantidades sin límite eliminará la crisis económica (p. 378)

sit-down strike/huelga de brazos caídos método de boicotear el trabajo por medio de sentarse en el lugar de trabajo y de rehusar a abandonar el establecimiento (p. 568)

sit-in/plantón forma de protesta ocupando las sillas o sentándose en el piso de un establecimiento (p. 748)

skyscraper/rascacielos edificio de gran altura (p. 342)

slash-and-burn agriculture/agrícola de tala y quema técnica agrícola en la cual la tierra es preparada y fertilizada derrumbando los bosques y quemándolos (p. 16)

slave code/código de esclavos leyes aprobadas que regularon formalmente la esclavitud y definieron la relación entre los africanos esclavizados y la gente libre (p. 61)

smog/smog niebla hecha más pesada y oscura por el humo y vapores químicos (p. 820)

soap opera/novela drama en serie de radio o televisión utilizando situaciones melodramáticas (p. 538)

Social Security Act/Acta de Seguro Social ley que requiere que los trabajadores y empleados paguen un impuesto; el dinero proporciona un ingreso mensual para la gente jubilada (p. 569)

socialism/socialismo creencia que los negocios deben ser propiedad del gobierno y dirigidos por él (p. 425)

sodbuster/rompeterrón nombre dado al granjero de las Grandes Planicies (p. 294)

software/software programa de computadora (p. 893)

space race/carrera espacial se refiere a la competencia durante la Guerra Fría sobre el dominio de la exploración espacial (p. 725)

space shuttle/puente espacial nave espacial diseñada para transportar personas y carga entre la tierra y el espacio la cual puede ser usada una y otra vez (p. 878)

space station/estación espacial satélite grande diseñado para ser ocupado por largos períodos y para servir como base para operaciones en el espacio (p. 879)

speakeasy/speakeasy lugar donde son vendidas clandestinamente bebidas alcohólicas (p. 487)

speculation/especulación acciones compradas con alto riesgo con la anticipación que los precios subirán (p. 531)

speculator/especulador persona que arriesga dinero con la esperanza de obtener una ganancia financiera (p. 154)

sphere of influence/esfera de influencia sección de un país donde una nación extranjera tiene derechos y poderes especiales (p. 410)

spoils system/sistema de despojos práctica de dar puestos gubernamentales a los partidarios; reemplazando a los empleados del gobierno con los partidarios del candidato victorioso (p. 190)

Square Deal/Trato Justo promesa de Theodore Roosevelt para un trato justo e igual para todos (p. 428)

squatter/colono usurpador persona que se establece en tierras públicas bajo reglamento gubernamental con la esperanza de adquirir el título de propiedad (p. 203)

stagflation/stagflación inflación persistente combinado con la demanda estancada y una taza de desempleo alta (p. 844)

standing committee/comité permanente comité permanente en la Cámara o el Senado organizado para enfocarse en un área específica (p. 125)

state-sponsored terrorism/terrorismo patrocinado por el estado actos violentos en contra de civiles que son secretamente apoyados por un gobierno con el motivo de atacar a otras naciones sin entrar en la guerra (p. 912)

steerage/tercera clase cuarteles apretados de las cubiertas bajas de un barco para los pasajeros que pagan los pasajes más bajos (p. 337)

stock market/bolsa de valores sistema para comprar y vender acciones de corporaciones (p. 531)

strategic defense/defensa estratégica plan para desarrollar proyectiles y otras armas que pueden derribar proyectiles nucleares antes de que estos golpeen en Estados Unidos (p. 909)

strategic materials/materiales estratégicos materiales necesarios para una guerra (p. 605)

strike/huelga paro de trabajo por los trabajadores para forzar al empresario a satisfacer sus demandas (p. 181)

subsistence farming/agricultura de subsistencia labranza que sólo produce la cosecha que se necesita para alimentar a la familia de uno (p. 59)

subversion/subversión intento sistemático para derrocar un gobierno utilizando personas que trabajan secretamente desde adentro (p. 669)

suffrage/sufragio derecho al voto (p. 421)

summit/cumbre junta de jefes de gobiernos (p. 837)

Sunbelt/Región Solada nueva región industrial en el sur de California y el Bajo Sur que se desarrolló durante la Segunda Guerra Mundial (p. 627)

supply-side economics/economía de oferta teoría económica de que los impuestos bajos levantarían la economía invirtiendo su dinero los negocios y los individuos, así creando un alto ingreso del impuesto (pp. 522, 867)

syndicate/sindicato grupo de negocios (p. 436)

teach-in/plantón educacional junta o clase extendida para discutir un asunto político o social (p. 785)

Tejano/tejano habitante de Texas de habla española (p. 204)

telecommute/viajar electrónicamente trabajar en casa por medio de conexión electrónica con una oficina central (p. 893)

televangelist/televangelista evangelista que transmite regularmente programas evangélicos por televisión (p. 864)

temperance/templanza moderación o abstinencia del uso del alcohol (pp. 196, 425)

tenant farmer/granjero arrendatario granjero que labra la tierra de un terrateniente y paga la renta ya sea con dinero efectivo o cosecha (p. 277)

tenement/casa de vecindad apartamentos para varias familias, normalmente obscuros, apretados que apenas cumplen con los estándares mínimos de viviendas (p. 343)

termination policy/política de terminación política gubernamental para traer a los Nativos Americanos dentro de la sociedad principal retirando el reconocimiento de los grupos Nativos Americanos como entidades legales (p. 708)

terrorism/terrorismo el uso de violencia por grupos no del gobierno en contra de civiles para alcanzar una meta política impartiendo miedo y amenazando gobiernos para que cambien su política (p. 912)

time zone/huso horario región geográfica en la cual la misma norma horaria es mantenida (p. 316)

Title IX/Título IX sección de las Enmiendas Educacionales de 1972 prohibiendo que las escuelas que recibían fondos federales discriminaran contra niñas y mujeres jóvenes en casi todo aspecto de su operación (p. 809)

torpedo/torpedo en los años 1860 término usado para una mina acuática (p. 261)

trade deficit/déficit de intercambio diferencia entre el valor de las importaciones de un país y las exportaciones (p. 903)

trade union/gremio organización de trabajadores con el mismo oficio o destreza (p. 327)

transcendental meditation/meditación transcendental técnica de meditación en la cual una persona repite una palabra una y otra vez como manera de alcanzar la máxima inteligencia, armonía y salud (p. 851)

transcendentalism/transcendentalismo filosofía que acentúa la relación entre los seres humanos y la naturaleza, cosas espirituales sobre las materiales y la importancia de la conciencia del individuo (p. 195)

transcontinental railroad/ferrocarril transcontinental sistema de ferrocarril que se extiende a través del continente (p. 223)

triangular trade/comercio triangular una ruta comercial de tres ramas para intercambiar productos entre las colonias americanas y otros dos asociados comerciales (p. 64)

trust/cártel combinación de empresas o sociedades anónimas formada por acuerdo legal, especialmente para reducir la competición (p. 322)

U-boat/nave-U apodo inglés para submarino alemán, de Unterseeboot, término que significa barco submarino (p. 453)

unalienable/inalienable que no se puede enajenar (p. 90)

Underground Railroad/Ferrocarril Clandestino sistema que ayudó a los afroamericanos esclavizados a seguir una red de rutas de escape fuera del Sur hacia la libertad en el Norte (p. 221)

unfair trade practices/prácticas comerciales injustas prácticas comerciales que ganan el beneficio perjudicando a la competencia (p. 441)

union shop/taller sindicalizado comercio que requiere que los trabajadores se unan al sindicato (p. 687)

urban renewal/renovación urbana programas gubernamentales que intentan eliminar la pobreza y revitalizar las áreas urbanas (p. 707)

utopia/utopía comunidad basada en una visión de la sociedad perfecta buscada por los reformistas (p. 196)

vaquero/vaquero hombres que conducían el ganado en las haciendas (p. 33)

vaudeville/vodevil entretenimiento compuesto de varios actos, tal como baile, canción, comedia, y espectáculos de magia (p. 352)

vertical integration/integración vertical asociación de compañías que abastecen equipo y servicios necesarios a una industria particular (p. 321)

veto/veto poder del jefe del ejecutivo de rechazar leyes aprobadas por la legislatura (p. 112)

victory garden/huerto de victoria huertos plantados por ciudadanos americanos durante la guerra para cultivar vegetales para usar en casa así dejando más para las tropas (pp. 458, 630)

Vietcong/*Vietcong* soldados guerrilleros de la facción comunista en Vietnam, también conocidos como Frente Nacional de Liberación (p. 777)

Spanish Glossary

Vietnamization/vietnamización el proceso de hacer que el Vietnam del Sur asumiera más de los esfuerzos de la guerra sacando poco a poco a las tropas americanas de Vietnam (p. 791)

white-collar/collar blanco trabajos que no requieren ropa de protección o de trabajo, asi como los vendedores (p. 693)

writ of assistance/escrito de asistencia documento legal que permitió a los oficiales aduanales entrar cualquier lugar en busca de evidencia de contrabando (p. 78)

War Hawks/halcones de guerra miembros del Congreso durante la presidencia de Madison que insistían en la guerra contra la Gran Bretaña (p. 165)

war on poverty/guerra contra la pobreza programa anti-pobreza bajo el Presidente Lyndon Johnson (p. 734)

welfare capitalism/capitalismo de beneficencia sistema en el cual las compañías permiten a los trabajadores comprar acciones, compartir las ganancias, y recibir beneficios tal como atención médica, común en los años 1920 (p. 519)

yellow journalism/periodismo amarillista tipo de reportaje sensacional, tendencioso, y a menudo falso con el propósito de atraer a los lectores (p. 400)

yeoman farmer/terrateniente menor dueño de una granja pequeña con cuatro o menos esclavos, normalmente ninguno (p. 183)

yuppie/*yuppie* adulto joven educado en la universidad empleado en una profesión de buen salario y que vive y trabaja en o cerca de una ciudad grande (p. 875)

Spanish Glossary

Italicized page numbers refer to illustrations. The following abbreviations are used in the index:
m = map; c = chart; p = photograph or picture; g = graph; crt = cartoon; ptg = painting; q = quote

A

ABBA, 853

Abernathy, Ralph, 766

Abington School District **v.** *Schempp*, 497, *c722*, 723

abolitionists, 199–201, *m200*, 219, 221–22, *m222*, 223–24, 231; American Antislavery Society, 200, *m200*; American Colonization Society, 199; call for emancipation, 199–200; early opposition, 199; resettlement program, 199; Underground Railroad, 221–22, *m222*; William Garrison Society, 199–200

Abrams v. United States, 460

Acheson, Dean, 661, 671

Adams, Henry, *q370*

Adams, John, 77, 88, 101, 112, 157–58, 174; Declaration of Independence, 88; defense lawyer, 77; domestic problems, 157–58; political ideology, 101, 157; Quasi-War, 157; XYZ Affair, 157

Adams, John Quincy, 173, 188–89, *p189*, 192; Adams-Onis Treaty, 173

Adamson Act, 442

Adams-Onís Treaty, 173

Adams, Samuel, *p9, q9,* 78, 112, 114

Addams, Jane, 331, 347, *q347*, 357, 404

Administration of Justice Act, 84

Adoption and Safe Families Act, 899

Advanced Research Project Agency (ARPANET), 894

advertising, 323, *p518*, 519, 694, 699, 719, 899; ban on cigarette, 899; mass, 519; politics and, 719; television, 699, 719

aerobics, 854

affirmative action, 813; challenges to, 813

Afghanistan, 848, 849, 869, 912–13, Reagan Doctrine and, 869; terrorists and, 913, 914, 915–16

Africa, 18, 21–23, 61, *p61*; music of, 61, *p61*

African Americans: abolitionist movement, 199–201, 219, 221–24, 231; activism, 383–84, 442, 749–50, 753–54; affirmative action and, 813; African Colored Farmers' National Alliance, 381; after reconstruction, 381; American Antislavery Society, 200, *m200*; American Colonization Society, 199; American Revolution, impact of, 102; assassination of Martin Luther King, Jr., 765–66; black codes, 269; black nationalism, 501–02; Black Panthers, 765; black power, 764; Bloody Sunday, 760; *Brown* v. *Board of Education*, 268, 722, *c722*, 748–49, 751, 814; Chicago race riots, 473; civil rights legislation, 747, 752, 757–59; civil rights movement, 383, 688, 744–66; Colonial America, 60, 68; conditions in rural South, 381–82; constitutional amendments and, 128, 143–44, 153, 263, 268, 269–71, 382–83, 422, 722, 748; cowboys, 290; cultural assimilation, 764; culture of, 184, 498–502, 701–03, 852–53; de facto segregation, 747, 763; discrimination against, 358, 383, 626, 627, 700, 702, 707; disenfranchisement, 381–82, 616; during wartimes, 457–59, 625–27; economic disparity and, *p707*, 707–08; economic rights of, 763–65; education, 184, 268–69, 274, *p274*, 751, 756; Eisenhower and, 751–52; emancipation after independence, 102, *m103*; Emancipation Proclamation, 253, 254, 266; entrepreneurs, 185; explorers, 204; Fourteenth Amendment, 269–70; free, 184–85; freedmen, 268–69; Freedom Riders, 754–55; Great Migration of, 50, 459, 498–99, 501, 627, *m627*; Harlem Renaissance, 499–500; impact of Reconstruction, 273, 277; impact of Supreme Court rulings, 722, 747; integration, 616, 751, 756; Johnson and, 737, 752, 759–60, 763; Kennedy and, 755–56; Ku

Klux Klan, 272, *p272*, 274, *crt483*, 483–84, 755; Liberian settlement, 199; lynching, 383, 501, 688; mass migration to Kansas, 381; Montgomery bus boycott, 749–50; New England Antislavery Society, 199–200; political "firsts," 273, 809, 813, 814, 848; politics and, 271, 273, 501–02, 572–73, *p688*, 748; racial pride, 499–502; racial purity and separation, 501–02; role of religion and, 184, 750–51; segregation, 268, 380–84, 615–16, 747–49, 753–60; segregation sign, *p268*; "separate-but-equal" doctrine, 747; sharecropping, 381; sit-in movement, 753–54; unemployment and, 762; urban problems of, 761–63; violence against, 383, 483, 501, 751–52, 754, 759–60; voting rights, 501, 735; wartime contributions of, 254, *p254*, 403, 457, 472, *p472*, 616, *p616*, 785–86; workplace and, 473, 625–27, 762. *See also* slavery.

African Empires, *p18,* 18–23, *m22*; Ghana, 21–22; Mali, *p18,* 18–21, 22; Songhai, 21; West Africa, *m22*

Agent Orange, 780

Agnew, Spiro, 833, 841

Agricultural Adjustment Administration (AAA), 559, 560, *c560*, 574

agricultural revolution, 13

agriculture: backcountry farming, 59; cash crops, 59, 182; dry farming, 294; early crop cultivation, 13–14; economic crises, 182, 373–75, *g519*, 519–20, *p520*; government and, 293, 294, 559, 561, 574, 576; grape boycott, 815; political issues and, 372–76; Resettlement Act, 567; sharecropping, 277; slash-and-burn, 16; slavery and, 183–84; subsistence farming, 59; technological innovations in, 253, *p293*, 293–94; tenant farming, 59, 277; U.S. Department of, 430–31; yeoman farmers, 183

AIDS, 876–77; AIDS quilt, *p877*

Aid to Families with Dependent Children (AFDC), 835

airline industry, 517, 868; deregulation of, 868

Akabogu-Collins, May, 906, *p906, q906*

Akan people, the, 23, *p23*

Alabama, 234, 755–57, 759–60; Selma March, 759–60; vote to secede, 234

Alamo, Battle of the, 205–06

Alamogordo, New Mexico, 645

Alaska, 15

Albania, 900

Albany Conference, 75

Albany Plan of Union, 75

Albright, Madeleine, 902, *p902, q902*

alcohol, 145, 147, 196–97, 424–25, 487–88, 876

Aldrin, Buzz, 726

Alexander VI, Pope, 26

Alfred P. Murrah Federal Building, 904

Alger, Horatio, 349, *p349*

Alger, Philip R., *q406*

Alien and Sedition Acts, 157, 158, 159

aliens, 157, 158, 159

Ali, Muhammad, 731

Ali, Sonni, 22

Allen, Gracie, 538

Alliance for Progress, 725

Allied Forces, 608, 620–23

Allies, 452, 453, 465, 466, 467–68

All in the Family, 852, *p853*

allotments, 302

al-Ja'afari, Ibrahim, 1036

al-Qaeda, 913, 914, 916

amendments, 112, 126, *c126,* 128, 140–47; amendment process, *c126,* 140

America: affluence of, 692–97, 874–75; after the American Revolution, 102–03; anti-war movement, 784–86, 791–92; automobile society, 691; beginnings of modern, 282–303; civil rights movement, 382–84, 573, 616, 626, 687–89, 721, 735, 744–66, *p751, p757,* 802, 812–17; communism in, 474, 482, 585, 602, 610, 669–74; conformity in, 693; conservatism in,

Index

D

Index

Index

Index

S

Index

Index

Index

Index

Acknowledgments and Photo Credits

Acknowledgments

503 "The Negro Speaks of Rivers" and "I, Too," from *The Collected Poems of Langston Hughes* by Langston Hughes. Copyright © 1994 by the Estate of Langston Hughes. Used by permission of Alfred A. Knopf, a division of Random House, Inc.

649 From *Farewell to Manzanar* by Jeanne Wakatsuki Houston and James D. Houston. Copyright © 1973 by James D. Houston. Reprinted by permission of Houghton Mifflin Company.

887 From *Hunger of Memory* by Richard Rodriguez (Boston: David R. Godine, Publisher, 1981). Copyright © 1981 by Richard Rodriguez. Reprinted by permission of Georges Borchardt, Inc., for the author.

934 From *The Grapes of Wrath* by John Steinbeck. Copyright © 1939, renewed 1967 by John Steinbeck. Used by permission of Viking Penguin, a division of Penguin Putnam, Inc.

935 "Alone and Far Removed" by Audie Murphy. Reprinted by permission of the Estate of Audie Murphy.

936 "Letter from Birmingham Jail" reprinted by arrangement with the Estate of Martin Luther King, Jr., c/o Writers House, Inc. as agent for the proprietor. Copyright Martin Luther King 1963, copyright renewed 1991 by Coretta Scott King.

937 From *Barefoot Heart: Stories of a Migrant Child* by Elva Trevino Hart. Reprinted by permission of Bilingual Press.

960 From "I Have a Dream," reprinted by arrangement with the Estate of Martin Luther King, Jr., c/o Writers House, Inc. as agent for the proprietor. Copyright Martin Luther King 1968, copyright renewed 1996 by Coretta Scott King.

Glencoe would like to acknowledge the artists and agencies that participated in illustrating this program: Morgan Cain & Associates; Ortelius Design, Inc.; and QA Digital.

Photo Credits

Cover: (background)The Library of Congress, (flag)PhotoDisc, (tl)Brown Brothers, (tr)Digital Stock: American Perspectives, (c)PhotoDisc, (bl)National Archives, (br)NASA; **iv** (tr)Lee Boltin Picture Library; (bl)CORBIS/Bettmann, (br)J. McGrail/H. Armstrong Roberts; **v** (tr)Michael J. Howell/Stock Boston, (bl)Panhandle-Plains Historical Museum, (br)The Library of Congress; **vi** (tl)National Air and Space Museum, Smithsonian Institution, (tr)CORBIS/Bettmann, (cl)courtesy Baylor University/Wings Across America, (bl)Air Force Museum Foundation, Inc.; **vii** (tl)Collection of Janice L. and David J. Frent, (tr)Picture Research Consultants, (bl)(clockwise from top)Collection of Chester Stott/Picture Research Consultants, Bill Stormont/The Stock Market, Collection of Janice L. and David J. Frent, Collection of Janice L. and David J. Frent; **x** Bob Daemmrich; **xxii–xxiii** PhotoDisc; **xxiv** CORBIS/Bettmann; **xxv** (tl)PhotoDisc; **RA20** PhotoDisc; **1** NASA; **4** (t)PhotoDisc, (b)Mark Newman/Folio, Inc.; **5** (tl)Ron Jautz/Folio, Inc., (tr)PhotoDisc, (inset)David R. Frazier Photolibrary/Folio, Inc., (bl)Grant Heilman, (br)Picture Research Consultants, (inset)US Geological Survey; **8** CORBIS; **8–9** Lora Robins Collection of Virginia Art, Virginia Historical Society; **9** Museum of Fine Arts, Boston; **10** (l)Boltin Picture Library, (r)Richard A. Cooke III; **10–11** The City of Plainfield, NJ; **11** (l)Field Museum of Natural History, Chicago, (r)The British Museum; **12** Photo Archives, Denver Museum of Natural History; **13** (l)Lee Boltin Picture Library, (r)Lee Boltin Picture Library; **14** Richard A. Cooke III; **16** (t)Richard A. Cooke III, (b)Ohio Historical Society; **17** (l)CORBIS/Bettmann, (r)Hulton/Archive/Getty Images; **18** Giraudon/Art Resource, NY; **19** (l)The Bridgeman Art Library, NY, (r)Scala/Art Resource, NY; **21** CORBIS; **22 23** The Bridgeman Art Library, NY; **24** CORBIS/Bettmann; **25** (l)Canadian Museum of Civilization, (r)Werner Forman Archive/CORBIS; **26** (l)Runk-Schoenberger from Grant Heilman, (r)The Thomas Gilcrease Institute of American History and Art, Tulsa OK; **27** Picture Research Consultants; **30** The Library of Congress; **31** (l)Picture Research Consultants, (c)Higgins Armory Museum, (r)American Museum of Natural History; **32** The Oakland Museum; **33** Biblioteca Colombina, Sevilla, Spain; **34** (l)Bushnell-Soifer/Getty Images, (r)Historical Society of Pennsylvania; **37** George H.H. Huey; **40** The Pilgrim Society; **40–41** J.D. Bangs/Leiden American Pilgrim Museum; **41** (l)Philadelphia Museum of Art/photo by Graydon Wood, (r)National Portrait Gallery, Smithsonian Institution/Art Resource, NY; **42** State Capitol, Virginia. Library of Virginia, CA9-92; **44–45** National Maritime Museum, London; **46** (t)Association for the Preservation of Virginia Antiquities, (b)Virginia State Library, Photographic Collection; **48** Pilgrim Hall Museum, Plymouth MA; **49** (l)American Antiquarian Society, (r)private collection; **50** Courtesy The Massachusetts Historical Society; **53** The New York Historical Society; **58** Richard T. Nowitz/CORBIS; **60** The Newberry Library; **61** (l)Inko

Production, (r)Maggie Steber/SABA/CORBIS; **64** Miriam & Ira D. Wallach Division of Art, Prints and Photographs, The New York Public Library, Astor Lenox and Tilden Foundation; **65** Harvard University Art Museum; **67** Miriam & Ira D. Wallach Division of Art, Prints and Photographs, The New York Public Library, Astor Lenox and Tilden Foundation; **69** National Portrait Gallery, London; **72** (l)Colonial Williamsburg, (r)Gwynn M. Kibbe/Stock Boston; **72–73** CORBIS; **73** (l)The Library of Congress, (r)Picture Research Consultants; **74** The British Library; **75** The Library of Congress; **77** Courtesy The Earl of Halifax, Garrowby, Yorkshire, UK; **78** American Antiquarian Society; **80** The Library of Congress; **80–81** PhotoDisc; **81** (l)Kevin Fleming, (r)The Library of Congress; **82** DAR Museum on loan from Boston Tea Party Chapter; **83** North Wind Picture Archives; **87** Chicago Historical Society; **88** The Library of Congress; **88–89** Picture Research Consultants; **89** Virginia Historical Society; **91** Picture Research Consultants; **94** Henry Cabot Lodge Collection, courtesy Beverly Historical Society; **97** The Valley Forge Historical Society; **98** Archives Division, Texas State Library; **100** National Museums & Galleries on Merseyside, Liverpool, UK; **101** CORBIS/Bettmann; **104** Ian Adams; **108** Independence National Historical Park Collection, #1246; **109** The Library of Congress; **110** Fraunces Tavern Museum, New York; **111** Yale University Art Gallery. Gift of Roger Sherman White, BA 1859; **113** (l)Thomas Gilcrease Museum, Tulsa OK, (r)courtesy Independence National Historic Park Collection; **114** American Antiquarian Society; **120** PhotoDisc; **121** (t)Stock Montage, (b)file photo; **122** PhotoDisc; **128** CORBIS/Farrell Grehan; **130** Sal di Marco/TimePix **134** Dennis Brack/BlackStar/TimePix; **150** (l)Christie's Images, (r)Missouri Historical Society; **150–151** CORBIS/Bettmann; **151** Field Museum of Natural History; **152** Smithsonian Institution; **153** (t)courtesy Winterthur Museum, (b)North Wind Picture Archives; **154** Courtesy Winterthur Museum; **156** The Library of Congress; **161** White House Historical Association; **162** National Portrait Gallery, Smithsonian Institution/Art Resource, NY; **163** (t)Independence National Historical Park, (b)Doug Martin; **164** Field Museum of Natural History; **165** Smithsonian Institution; **167** Anne S.K. Brown, Brown Military Collection/Brown University Library; **169** Thomas Gilcrease Museum, Tulsa OK; **170** The National Portrait Gallery/Smithsonian Institution/Art Resource, NY; **171** Greenville County Museum of Art; **174** (tl tr br)National Portrait Gallery, Smithsonian Institution/Art Resource, NY, (bl)Yale University Art Gallery/Trumbull Collection; **176** Private collection; **176–177** Winterthur Museum; **177** (l)Texas Department of Highways and Public Transportation, (r)California State Capitol; **178** The New York Historical Society; **179** Courtesy B&O Railroad Museum; **181** Courtesy Jack Naylor; **183** Fitchburg Art Museum; **184** CORBIS/Bettmann; **185** Picture Research Consultants; **187** West Point Museum Collections, 1822. US Military Academy; **189** The Metropolitan Museum of Art. Gift of I.N. Phelps Stokes, Edward S. Hawes, Alice Mary Hawes, Marion Augusta Hawes, 1937. (37.14.34); **190** (l)private collection, (r)CORBIS; **192** The New York Historical Society; **194** Boston Athenaeum; **195** Old Dartmouth Historical Society/New Bedford Whaling Museum; **196** (l)The Connecticut Historical Society, Hartford, (r)Museum of the City of New York, Harry T. Peters Collection; **197** (t)CORBIS, (b)Antichiana, Antioch College; **198** (l)Mercer Museum/Bucks County Historical Society, (tr)Massachusetts Historical Society, (br)Picture Research Consultants; **199** (t)Ron Huntley, (b)Smithsonian Institution; **200** National Portrait Gallery, Smithsonian Institution/Art Resource, NY; **201** Collection of J. Paul Getty Museum; **202** Texas State Archives; **203** Courtesy Museum of Art, Brigham Young University; **204** Center for American History/Barker Collection/University of Texas, Austin; **205** Texas State Library & Archives Commission/photos by Eric Beggs; **207** (l)Texas State Library & Archives Commission/photo by Eric Beggs, (r)San Jacinto Museum History Association; **214** Mark Burnett; **214–215** National Park Service; **215** McLellan Lincoln Collection. Gift of John D. Rockefeller Jr., Class of 1897; **216** Courtesy Wells Fargo Bank; **216–217** Courtesy Robert M. Hicklin, Jr., Inc.; **217** Chicago Historical Society; **218** (t)courtesy Illinois Historical Society Library, (b)Chicago Historical Society; **219** American Antiquarian Society; **221** The Library of Congress; **222** Raymond Bial; **223** Kansas State Historical Society; **226** The Library of Congress; **228** (t)The Library of Congress, (b)The Supreme Court of the United States Office of the Curator, #1991.402.2; **229** Illinois State Historical Library; **230** Henry Horner Lincoln Collection; **232** Private collection/Art Resource, NY; **233** Museum of American Political Life; **234** Museum of American Political Life/photo by Steve Laschever; **235** The Library of Congress; **237** (l)CORBIS/Bettmann, (r)The Library Company of Philadelphia; **238** CORBIS; **239** George Washington at Constitutional Convention by Junius Brutus Sterns; **242** (l)Museum of the Confederacy; (c)Illinois State Historical Library; (r)Collection of Janice L. and David J. Frent; **242–243** Don Troiani, courtesy Historical Art Prints, Southbury CT; **243** The Library of Congress; **244** Cunningham Memorial Library, Indiana State University; **246** (t)American Numismatic Association; (b)CORBIS; **249** CORBIS; **250** (t)The Library of Congress, (b)Chicago Historical Society; **254** Chicago Historical Society;

Holocaust Memorial Museum, (r)National Archives, courtesy US Holocaust Memorial Museum; **597–598** Mark E. Gibson/CORBIS; **598** Yivo Institute for Jewish Research; **598–599** Yad Vashem Photo Archives, courtesy US Holocaust Memorial Museum; **599** National Archives: Suitland, courtesy US Holocaust Memorial Museum; **601** US Army Museum of Hawaii; **602** Chicago Historical Society; **603** (t)Herbert Hoover Library, (b)Thomas McAvoy/*Life*/Time Warner; **605** Picture Research Consultants; **607** CORBIS; **610** (l)private collection, (r)CORBIS/Bettmann; **610–611** Digital Stock; **611** (l c)CORBIS, (r)John Launois/Black Star; **612** CORBIS/Bettmann; **613** Courtesy Smithsonian Institution; **614–615 616** CORBIS/Bettmann; **617** (l)Air Force Museum Foundation, (r)courtesy Baylor University/Wings Across America; **618** US Naval Institute; **619** Digital Stock, (inset)Norm Avery; **622** (l)Oscar White/CORBIS, (r)CORBIS; **623** Hulton/Archive/Getty Images; **625** The Curtis Publishing Company; **626** National Archives; **628** Toyo Miyatake; **629** (l)Stock Montage, (r)CORBIS/Bettmann; **630** Dr. Seuss Collection/ Mandeville Special Collections Library/University of California, San Diego; **631** CORBIS; **632** Texas Military Forces Museum, 36th Infantry Division Gallery, Austin TX; **632–633** CORBIS/Bettmann; **634–635 637** Digital Stock; **639** (l)Robert E. Pratt, (c)Cornelius Ryan Collection of World War II Papers, Alden Library, Ohio University, Athens, (r)CORBIS; **640** AP/Wide World Photos; **641** CORBIS; **644** Digital Stock; **645** Digital Stock, (inset)Hulton/ Archive/Getty Images; **646** National Geographic Society; **646–647** National Geographic Society; **647** Kari Haavisto; **648** Alfred Eisenstaedt/TimePix; **649** (l)Robert Scheer, (r)Digital Stock; **652** National Portrait Gallery, Smithsonian Institution/Art Resource, NY. Gift of Frances O. Tames; **652–653** AP/Wide World Photos; **653** Smithsonian Institution; **654** National Portrait Gallery, Smithsonian Institution/Art Resource, NY; **655** John Florea/TimePix; **656** American Red Cross; **657** Picture Research Consultants; **659** Brown Brothers; **661** National Portrait Gallery, Smithsonian Institution. Transfer from National Gallery of Art. Gift of Ailsa Mellon Bruce, 1951; **662** CORBIS/ Bettmann; **664** National Archives; **666** CORBIS; **668** The Michael Barson Collection/Past Perfect; **669** CORBIS; **670** CORBIS/Bettmann; **671** (l)Collection of Michael Barson; **672** Robert Phillips/*Life*/Time Warner; **672–673** Getty Images; **675** (l)CORBIS, (r)Smithsonian Institution; **677** Ross Lewis Milwaukee Public Library; **679** CORBIS/Bettmann; **681** Courtesy Truman Library; **684** (l)Picture Research Consultants, (r)CORBIS/Bettmann; **684–685** SuperStock; **685** (l)Getty Images, (r)Natural Museum of American History/Smithsonian Instutution; **686** (t)Picture Research Consultants, (b)Collection of Chester Stott/Picture Research Consultants; **687** CORBIS; **689** CORBIS/Bettmann; **690** (l)CORBIS, (r)PhotoDisc; **691** (l)TimePix, (tr)courtesy Wig Wam Motel, (br)CORBIS; **692** TimePix; **693** B. Wiseman/from *Hey, Can't You Forget Business?* by Charles Preston, 1953, E.P. Dutton & Co., Inc.; **695** (t)Computer Museum History Center, (b)Christopher Thomas/Getty Images; **696** CORBIS/Bettmann; **697** CORBIS; **698** PhotoFest; **699** (l br)PhotoFest, (tr)The Kobal Collection; **700** Tom Kelley/Getty Images; **701** Globe Photos; **702** (l)Elliot Erwitt/Magnum Photos, (r)Picture Research Consultants; **703** (l)PhotoFest, (c)National Museum of American History/Smithsonian Institution, (r)Michael Ochs Archives; **706** CORBIS/Bettmann; **707** Chicago Historical Society; **709** National Archives; **710** Danny Lyon/Magnum Photos, Inc.; **711** Private collection; **714** Picture Research Consultants; **714–715** John Eastcott/Yva Momatiuk/Stock Boston; **715** CORBIS/Bettmann; **716** (l)Ohio Historical Society, (r)AP/Wide World Photos; **716–717** Paul Schultzer/*Life*/TimePix; **717** Collection of Janice L. and David J. Frent; **718** CORBIS/Bettmann; **719** Ohio Historical Society; **720** JFK Library/CORBIS/Sygma; **723** The Supreme Court of the United States Office of the Curator; **724** Lynn Historical Society; **726** (l tr)NASA, (br)Picture Research Consultants; **727** (l r)Bill Ingalls/NASA, (c)Lockheed Martin Global Communication; **728** AP/Wide World Photos; **729** John S. Boyer/National Geographic Society; **732** Chicago Historical Society; **733 734** AP/Wide World Photos; **735** (l)CORBIS/Bettmann, (t b)Collection of Janice L. and David J. Frent; **738** AP/Wide World Photos; **739** John F. Kennedy Library; **740**(l)CORBIS, (r)Bridgeman Art Library, NY; **744** CORBIS/Bettmann; **744–745** Steve Schapiro/TimePix; **745** (l)New York Public Library, (c)CORBIS, (r)Collection of Janice L. and David J. Frent; **746** United Press International; **747** The Library of Congress; **748** Carl Iwaski/TimePix; **749** Dan Weiner/courtesy Sandra Weiner; **750** CORBIS; **751** Picture Research Consultants; **753** CORBIS; **754** Vic Colley/*Nashville Banner*; **755** CORBIS; **757** Charles Moore 1963/Black Star; **758** (t)Francis Miller/TimePix, (b)Steve Schapiro/Black Star; **759** New York Public Library; **761** CORBIS; **762** Jon Kennedy/*Arkansas Democrat*; **763** AP/Wide World Photos; **764** CORBIS; **765** AP/Wide World Photos; **766** (l)AP/Wide World Photos, (r)Flip Schulke/Black Star; **768** CORBIS; **770** (l)Ordinance Museum/Aberdeen Proving Ground, (r)AP/Wide World Photos; **770–771** Diane Walker/TimePix; **771** (l)Picture Research Consultants, (r)Collection of Janice L. and David J. Frent; **772** Courtesy Medal of Honor Society; **773** Paul Miller/Black Star; **774** Archive Photos/Getty Images; **775** Everette Dixie Reese, courtesy Alan Reese; **776** from *The Living and The Dead* by Paul Hendrickson; **777** AP/Wide World Photos; **778** AP/Wide World Photos; **778–779** AP/Wide World Photos; **780** Sp4 John Olson, US Army; **782** CORBIS; **782–783** AP/Wide World Photos; **783** (t)AP/Wide World Photos, (b)COR-BIS/Bettmann; **784** Archive Photos/Getty Images; **785** Photo by DeAlba/*Washington Daily News*/Lyndon Baines Johnson Library; **786** (l)Bernie Boston, (r)Collection of Janice L. and David J. Frent; **787** Collection of Janice L. and David J. Frent; **790** CORBIS/Bettmann; **791** John Filo; **792** Picture Research Consultants; **793** Nik Wheeler/Black Star; **798** (l)Collection of Janice L. and David J. Frent, (cl)Collection of Bettye Lane/Picture Research Consultants, (cr r)Ken Regan, Camera 5; **798–799** Arthur Schatz/TimePix; **799 800** AP/Wide World Photos; **801** (t)Picture Research Consultants, (b)AP/Wide World Photos; **802** Lisa Law/The Image Works; **804** Tom Miner/The Image Works; **805** Tate Gallery, London/Art Resource, NY; **806** *Redbook*, August 30, 1960; **807** COR-BIS/ Bettmann; **808** (l)Schlesinger Library, Radcliffe College, (r)Collection of Bettye Lane/Picture Research Consultants; **809** Paul Fusco/Magnum; **810** CORBIS/ Bettmann; **811** (l)Brown Brothers, (r)Illinois State Historical Society; **812** AP/Wide World Photos; **813** (l)CORBIS/Bettmann, (r)AP/Wide World Photos; **814** Jacques M. Chenet/CORBIS; **816** (l)Arthur Schatz/TimePix, (r)Al Ransom/TimePix; **817** Bob Daemmrich/The Image Works; **818** David Brownell; **819** Nathan Benn/CORBIS; **820** Alfred Eisenstaedt/TimePix; **821** (l)Ken Regan, Camera 5, (r)Simon Fraser/Science Photo Library; **824** (tl tr)illustration by David Kimble, (c)Molded Fiber Glass Companies, (b)Chevrolet Communications; **825** (clockwise from top)(1)illustration by David Kimble, (2)General Motors Corporation, (3)Paul Conklin/PhotoEdit/ PictureQuest, (4)Used with permission. General Motors, GM, Chevrolet, Corvette and the Corvette Emblem are registered trademarks of GM Corp., (5)Jim Heafner; **828** Icon Images; **828–829** Nicole Bengiveno/NYT Pictures, The New York Times Company; **829** Charles Ommanney/CORBIS/SABA; **830** (l)Dennis Brack/Black Star, (r)CORBIS; **830–831** Magnum Photos; **831** (l)Collection of Janice L. and David J. Frent, (r)Tom Ebenhoh/Black Star; **832** CORBIS; **834** AP/Wide World Photos; **835** Matt Meadows; **836** Ranan Lurie; **837** Wally McNamee/CORBIS; **838** AP/Wide World Photos; **839** Dennis Brack/Black Star; **840** Fred Maroon/Folio; **840–841** National Archives; **841** Alex Webb/Magnum Photos; **843** CORBIS/Bettmann; **844** Owen Franken/CORBIS; **845** By permission of John Hart and Field Enterprises, Inc.; **846** (l)Wally McNamee/CORBIS, (r)Collection of Janice L. and David J. Frent; **847** CORBIS; **848** Alain Mingam/Getty Images News Services; **850** Picture Research Consultants; **851** (t)Hulton/Archive/Getty Images, (b)Picture Research Consultants; **852** (l)Picture Research Consultants, (c)Lynn Goldsmith/CORBIS; **852–853** Picture Research Consultants; **853** (l)Collection of Hershenson-Allen Archives, (r)CORBIS/Bettmann; **854** Aaron Haupt; **855** CORBIS; **858** file photo; **858–859** SIMI Valley Photo; **859** (l)file photo, (r)Dennis Brack/Black Star/PictureQuest; **860** Charles Geer Photography; **862** CORBIS/Bettmann; **864** (l)CORBIS, (r)Hoertel/Getty Images News Services; **865** Courtesy Ronald Reagan Library; **866** AP/Wide World Photos; **868** (l)CORBIS/Bettmann, (r)Halstead/Getty Images News Services; **869** Dennis Brack/Black Star; **871** Joseph C. Marquette; **872** AP/Wide World Photos; **874** CORBIS; **875** LightStream; **876** Bill Stormont/CORBIS Stock Market; **877** (l)Dennis Brack/Black Star/PictureQuest, (r)Ellen B. Neipris/Impact Visuals; **878** Joe Skipper/Reuters New Media/CORBIS; **879** (l)NASA, (r)Susan Greenwood/Getty Images; **880** Matt Meadows; **881** Leif Skoogfors/CORBIS; **883** Alexandra Avakian, Contact Press Images; **885** Bruno Barbey/Magnum Photos; **887** (l)courtesy David R. Godine Publisher, (r)Matt Meadows; **890** (bl br)CORBIS, (bc)Collection of Janice L. and David J. Frent; **890–891** AP/Wide World Photos; **891** Jason Reed/Reuters/CORBIS; **892** Diane Walker/TimePix; **893** CORBIS; **894** R. Masonneuve/ Publicphoto/Photo Researchers; **895** Reuters/Natalie Behring/Hulton Archive; **896** CORBIS; **897** Jeffrey Markowitz/Sygma; **898** Erik Freeland/ Matrix; **899** (l)Wally McNamee/CORBIS, Greg Gibson/AP/Wide World Photos; **901** Amit Shabi/ Reuters/STR/Archive Photos; **902** Bureau of Public Affairs/US Department of State; **903** (t)Annie Griffiths Belt/CORBIS, (b)Pablo San Juan/CORBIS; **904** Reuters Newmedia Inc./CORBIS; **906** Courtesy May Akabogu-Collin; **907** Reuters New Media Inc./CORBIS; **911** AP/Wide World Photos; **912** (tl)Thomas E. Franklin/Bergen Record/SABA/CORBIS, (tr)Tom Horan/AP/Wide World Photos, (br)Robert Clark/Aurora Quanta; **913** Peter Turnley/Sygma/CORBIS; **915** Steve Liss/CORBIS; **917** Shaun Heasley/CORBIS **918** CORBIS; **919** Jamestown-Yorktown Foundation; **922** (clockwise from top)CORBIS/Bettmann, Ohio Historical Society, Field Museum of Natural History, CORBIS/Bettmann, Tom Ebenhoh/BlackStar, Alfred Eisenstaedt/TimePix, CORBIS/Bettmann, Thomas E. Franklin/Bergen Record/SABA/CORBIS, J. McGrail/H. Armstrong Roberts, CORBIS; **923–927** The White House Historical Association; **927** (bc)CORBIS, (br)file photo, (others) The White House Historical Association; **928** The Oakland Museum; **930** CORBIS/Bettmann; **932** (t)CORBIS/Bettmann, (b)CORBIS; **934** CORBIS/Bettmann; **935** (l)Weisman Art Museum, (r)CORBIS/ Bettmann, (b)AP/Wide World Photos; **936** Charles Moore/Black Star; **937** The Library of Congress; **939** Getty Images; **943** Private collection; **944** The Wadsworth Atheneum; **946** Bridgeman Art Library, NY; **947 948** National Portrait Gallery, Smithsonian Institution/Art Resource, NY; **950** Chicago Historical Society; **951** (l)Maryland Historical Society, (r)Smithsonian Institution; **952** Picture Research Consultants; **953** The Library of Congress; **954** (l)Bettman/ CORBIS, (r)Andre Jenny/Focus Group/ PictureQuest; **956** National Portrait Gallery, Smithsonian Institution/Art Resource, NY; **959** Carl Iwaski/TimePix; **961** *Life*/TimePix; **962 963** PhotoDisc; **964** Supreme Court Historical Society; **965** Picture Research Consultants.

Time Line Presidential Paintings Courtesy of the White House Historical Association.

Photo Credits